# Who Was Who in America®

# Who Was Who in America®
## with world notables

## 2013-2014
## Volume XXV

MARQUIS
Who'sWho®

430 Mountain Avenue, Suite 400
New Providence, NJ 07974 U.S.A.
www.marquiswhoswho.com

# Who Was Who in America®
## Marquis Who's Who

| | |
|---|---|
| **Chairman** | James A. Finkelstein |
| **Chief Executive Officer** | Fred Marks |
| **Chief Technology Officer** | Ariel Spivakovsky |
| **Director of Sales** | Kelli MacKinnon |

**EDITORIAL**

| | |
|---|---|
| **Managing Editors** | Patricia Delli Santi |
| | Alison Perruso |
| **Content Manager** | Todd Kineavy |
| **Content Editor** | Dana Slocum |

For information, contact: Marquis Who's Who, 430 Mountain Avenue, Suite 400
New Providence, New Jersey 07974
1-800-473-7020; www.marquiswhoswho.com

WHO WAS WHO IN AMERICA® is a registered trademark of Marquis Who's Who LLC.

| | | |
|---|---|---|
| International Standard Book Number | 978-0-8379-0299-9 | (27-Volume Set) |
| | 978-0-8379-0296-8 | (Volume XXV) |
| | 978-0-8379-0297-5 | (Index Volume) |
| | 978-0-8379-0298-2 | (Volume XXV & Index Volume) |
| International Standard Serial Number | 0146-8081 | |

Manufactured in the United States of America.

# Table of Contents

# Preface

Marquis Who's Who is proud to present the 2013-2014 Edition of *Who Was Who in America*. This 25th edition features over 3,800 profiles of individuals who had previously been profiled in *Who's Who in America* and other Marquis Who's Who publications, whose deaths we are recognizing since the publication of the last edition of *Who Was Who in America*.

Of course, not every person profiled in this volume is a household name. These pages include the profiles of individuals in the fields of education, law, medicine, government, business, religion, science, broadcasting, publishing, information technology, sports, literary and cultural arts, and entertainment.

The biographical information included in the profiles that follow was gathered in a variety of manners. In most cases, those listed had submitted their personal biographical details during their lifetime. In many cases, though, the information was collected independently by our research and editorial staffs, which use a wide assortment of tools to gather complete, accurate, and up-to-date information.

All of the profiles featured in these publications are available through a subscription on www.marquiswhoswho.com. At the present time, subscribers to *Marquis Biographies Online* have access to all of the names included in all of the Marquis Who's Who publications, as well as many new biographies that will appear in upcoming publications.

The following notable individuals profiled in this volume had an enormous impact during their lifetime, and their influence is certain to live on. It has been an honor to compose this edition of *Who Was Who in America*.

**Entertainment**
Richard Attenborough
Lauren Bacall
David Brenner
Sid Caesar
Ruby Dee
Phil Everly
Joan Fontaine
James Garner
Philip Seymour Hoffman
Bob Hoskins
Peter O'Toole

Harold Ramis
Joan Rivers
Mickey Rooney
Maximilian Schell
Pete Seeger
Elaine Stritch
Shirley Temple Black
Eli Wallach
Robin Williams
Gordon Willis
Johnny Winter
Bobby Womack

**Cultural Arts**
Claudio Abbado
Licia Albanese
Gerd Albrecht

Charlie Haden
Lorin Maazel
Horace Silver

**Business**
John F. Akers
Karl Albrecht
Glenn A. Britt
S. Truett Cathy
Eileen Ford

William Clay Ford
Ace Greenberg
Charles Keating
Richard Mellon Scaife
James Schiro
Edward Ney

**Medicine, Science & Technology**
Morris Collen
Roger Easton
Gerald Edelman
Stephanie Kwolek
Dale T. Mortensen

Gerry Neugebauer
Martin Perl
Frederick Sanger
John Sperling
Jesse Steinfeld

**Sports**
Jim Fregosi
Malcolm Glazer
Tom Gola
Tony Gwynn

Chuck Noll
Jack Ramsay
Ralph Wilson
Don Zimmer

**Politics, Law, Military & Public Affairs**
Howard Baker
Thomas Hale Boggs
James Brady
Jim Jeffords
Joan Mondale

Jim Oberstar
James Schlesinger
Robert Strauss
James Traficant
Lawrence W. Walsh

**Foreign Leaders**
Jean-Luc Dehaene
Jean-Claude Duvalier
Rilwanu Lukman

Ian Paisley
Ariel Sharon
Eduard Shevardnadze
Adolfo Suárez

**Literature**
Maya Angelou
Thomas Berger
Gabriel García Márquez
Nadine Gordimer

Daniel Keyes
Carolyn Kizer
Doris Lessing
Peter Matthiessen
Walter Dean Myers

**Broadcasting/Publishing**
Al Feldstein
Casey Kasem
Don Pardo

Run Run Shaw
Win Tin
Kenneth Tomlinson

**Religion - Cardinals**
Bernard Agré
Marco Cé

Edward Bede Clancy
D. Simon Lourdusamy
Edmund C. Szoka

# Key to Information

[1] **LINDELL, JAMES ELLIOT,** [2] literature educator; [3] b. Jacksonville, Fla., Sept. 27, 1949; [4] s. Elliot Walter and Tamara Lindell; [5] m. Colleen Marie, Apr. 28, 1973; [6] children: Richard, Matthew, Lucas, Samantha. [7] BA in English, Temple U., 1971, MA in English, 1973; PhD in English Lit., U. Chgo., 1976. [8] Cert. ESL 1972. [9] Assoc. prof. English U. Chgo., 1975-80, prof. 1980-88, English dept. head 1989-2009; [10] mem. ESL Coalition, Teach for Tomorrow; bd. dir., Chgo. HS Scholarship Assn. [11] Contbr. articles to profl. jours. [12] vol. Red Cross, 1980-90. [13] Served to USMC, 1972-74. [14] Recipient Outstanding Tchr. award U. Chgo., 1990; grantee Teach for Tomorrow, 2000. [15] Fellow Assn. Tchrs. for ESL; mem. MADD, Am. Soc. ESL Tchrs. [16] Democrat. [17] Roman Catholic. [18] Achievements include the expansion of teaching English as a second language to European countries. [19] Avocations: swimming, reading, traveling. [20] Home: Chicago, Ill. [21] Died Oct. 19, 2013.

## KEY

| | |
|---|---|
| [1] | Name |
| [2] | Occupation |
| [3] | Vital statistics |
| [4] | Parents |
| [5] | Marriage |
| [6] | Children |
| [7] | Education |
| [8] | Professional certifications |
| [9] | Career |
| [10] | Career-related |
| [11] | Writings and creative works |
| [12] | Civic and political activities |
| [13] | Military |
| [14] | Awards and fellowships |
| [15] | Professional and association memberships, clubs and lodges |
| [16] | Political affiliation |
| [17] | Religion |
| [18] | Achievements |
| [19] | Avocations |
| [20] | Home address |
| [21] | Death |

# Table of Abbreviations

The following is a list of some of the most frequently used Marquis abbreviations:

## A

**A** Associate (used with academic degrees)
**AA** Associate in Arts
**AAAL** American Academy of Arts and Letters
**AAAS** American Association for the Advancement of Science
**AACD** American Association for Counseling and Development
**AACN** American Association of Critical Care Nurses
**AAHA** American Academy of Health Administrators
**AAHP** American Association of Hospital Planners
**AAHPERD** American Alliance for Health, Physical Education, Recreation, and Dance
**AAS** Associate of Applied Science
**AASL** American Association of School Librarians
**AASPA** American Association of School Personnel Administrators
**AAU** Amateur Athletic Union
**AAUP** American Association of University Professors
**AAUW** American Association of University Women
**AB** Arts, Bachelor of
**AB** Alberta
**ABA** American Bar Association
**AC** Air Corps
**acad.** academy
**acct.** accountant
**acctg.** accounting
**ACDA** Arms Control and Disarmament Agency
**ACHA** American College of Hospital Administrators
**ACLS** Advanced Cardiac Life Support
**ACLU** American Civil Liberties Union
**ACOG** American College of Ob-Gyn
**ACP** American College of Physicians
**ACS** American College of Surgeons
**ADA** American Dental Association
**adj.** adjunct, adjutant
**adm.** admiral
**adminstr.** administrator
**adminstrn.** administration
**adminstrv.** administrative

**ADN** Associate's Degree in Nursing
**ADP** Automatic Data Processing
**adv.** advocate, advisory
**advt.** advertising
**AE** Agricultural Engineer
**AEC** Atomic Energy Commission
**aero.** aeronautical, aeronautic
**aerodyn.** aerodynamic
**AFB** Air Force Base
**AFTRA** American Federation of Television and Radio Artists
**agr.** agriculture
**agrl.** agricultural
**agt.** agent
**AGVA** American Guild of Variety Artists
**agy.** agency
**A&I** Agricultural and Industrial
**AIA** American Institute of Architects
**AIAA** American Institute of Aeronautics and Astronautics
**AIChE** American Institute of Chemical Engineers
**AICPA** American Institute of Certified Public Accountants
**AID** Agency for International Development
**AIDS** Acquired Immune Deficiency Syndrome
**AIEE** American Institute of Electrical Engineers
**AIME** American Institute of Mining, Metallurgy, and Petroleum Engineers
**AK** Alaska
**AL** Alabama
**ALA** American Library Association
**Ala.** Alabama
**alt.** alternate
**Alta.** Alberta
**A&M** Agricultural and Mechanical
**AM** Arts, Master of
**Am.** American, America
**AMA** American Medical Association
**amb.** ambassador
**AME** African Methodist Episcopal
**Amtrak** National Railroad Passenger Corporation
**AMVETS** American Veterans
**ANA** American Nurses Association
**anat.** anatomical
**ANCC** American Nurses Credentialing Center

**ann.** annual
**anthrop.** anthropological
**AP** Associated Press
**APA** American Psychological Association
**APHA** American Public Health Association
**APO** Army Post Office
**apptd.** appointed
**Apr.** April
**apt.** apartment
**AR** Arkansas
**ARC** American Red Cross
**arch.** architect
**archeol.** archeological
**archtl.** architectural
**Ariz.** Arizona
**Ark.** Arkansas
**ArtsD** Arts, Doctor of
**arty.** artillery
**AS** Associate in Science, American Samoa
**ASCAP** American Society of Composers, Authors and Publishers
**ASCD** Association for Supervision and Curriculum Development
**ASCE** American Society of Civil Engineers
**ASME** American Society of Mechanical Engineers
**ASPA** American Society for Public Administration
**ASPCA** American Society for the Prevention of Cruelty to Animals
**assn.** association
**assoc.** associate
**asst.** assistant
**ASTD** American Society for Training and Development
**ASTM** American Society for Testing and Materials
**astron.** astronomical
**astrophys.** astrophysical
**ATLA** Association of Trial Lawyers of America
**ATSC** Air Technical Service Command
**atty.** attorney
**Aug.** August
**aux.** auxiliary
**Ave.** Avenue
**AVMA** American Veterinary Medical Association
**AZ** Arizona

## B

**B** Bachelor
**b.** born
**BA** Bachelor of Arts
**BAgr** Bachelor of Agriculture
**Balt.** Baltimore
**Bapt.** Baptist
**BArch** Bachelor of Architecture
**BAS** Bachelor of Agricultural Science
**BBA** Bachelor of Business Administration
**BBB** Better Business Bureau
**BC** British Columbia
**BCE** Bachelor of Civil Engineering
**BChir** Bachelor of Surgery
**BCL** Bachelor of Civil Law
**BCS** Bachelor of Commercial Science
**BD** Bachelor of Divinity
**bd.** board
**BE** Bachelor of Education
**BEE** Bachelor of Electrical Engineering
**BFA** Bachelor of Fine Arts
**bibl.** biblical
**bibliog.** bibliographical
**biog.** biographical
**biol.** biological
**BJ** Bachelor of Journalism
**Bklyn.** Brooklyn
**BL** Bachelor of Letters
**bldg.** building
**BLS** Bachelor of Library Science
**Blvd.** Boulevard
**BMI** Broadcast Music, Inc.
**bn.** battalion
**bot.** botanical
**BPE** Bachelor of Physical Education
**BPhil** Bachelor of Philosophy
**br.** branch
**BRE** Bachelor of Religious Education
**brig. gen.** brigadier general
**Brit.** British
**Bros.** Brothers
**BS** Bachelor of Science
**BSA** Bachelor of Agricultural Science
**BSBA** Bachelor of Science in Business Administration
**BSChemE** Bachelor of Science in Chemical Engineering
**BSD** Bachelor of Didactic Science
**BSEE** Bachelor of Science in Electrical Engineering
**BSN** Bachelor of Science in Nursing
**BST** Bachelor of Sacred Theology
**BTh** Bachelor of Theology
**bull.** bulletin
**bur.** bureau
**bus.** business
**BWI** British West Indies

## C

**CA** California
**CAD-CAM** Computer Aided Design–Computer Aided Model
**Calif.** California
**Can.** Canada, Canadian
**CAP** Civil Air Patrol
**capt.** captain
**cardiol.** cardiological
**cardiovasc.** cardiovascular
**Cath.** Catholic
**cav.** cavalry
**CBI** China, Burma, India Theatre of Operations
**CC** Community College
**CCC** Commodity Credit Corporation
**CCNY** City College of New York
**CCRN** Critical Care Registered Nurse
**CCU** Cardiac Care Unit
**CD** Civil Defense
**CE** Corps of Engineers, Civil Engineer
**CEN** Certified Emergency Nurse
**CENTO** Central Treaty Organization
**CEO** Chief Executive Officer
**CERN** European Organization of Nuclear Research
**cert.** certificate, certification, certified
**CETA** Comprehensive Employment Training Act
**CFA** Chartered Financial Analyst
**CFL** Canadian Football League
**CFO** Chief Financial Officer
**CFP** Certified Financial Planner
**ch.** church
**ChD** Doctor of Chemistry
**chem.** chemical
**ChemE** Chemical Engineer
**ChFC** Chartered Financial Consultant
**Chgo.** Chicago
**chirurg., der** surgeon
**chmn.** chairman
**chpt.** chapter
**CIA** Central Intelligence Agency
**Cin.** Cincinnati
**cir.** circle, circuit
**CLE** Continuing Legal Education
**Cleve.** Cleveland
**climatol.** climatological
**clin.** clinical
**clk.** clerk
**CLU** Chartered Life Underwriter
**CM** Master in Surgery
**cmty.** community

**CO** Colorado
**Co.** Company
**COF** Catholic Order of Foresters
**C. of C.** Chamber of Commerce
**col.** colonel
**coll.** college
**Colo.** Colorado
**com.** committee
**comd.** commanded
**comdg.** commanding
**comdr.** commander
**comdt.** commandant
**comm.** communications
**commd.** commissioned
**comml.** commercial
**commn.** commission
**commr.** commissioner
**compt.** comptroller
**condr.** conductor
**conf.** Conference
**Congl.** Congregational, Congressional
**Conglist.** Congregationalist
**Conn.** Connecticut
**cons.** consultant, consulting
**consol.** consolidated
**constl.** constitutional
**constn.** constitution
**constrn.** construction
**contbd.** contributed
**contbg.** contributing
**contbn.** contribution
**contbr.** contributor
**contr.** controller
**Conv.** Convention
**COO** Chief Operating Officer
**coop.** cooperative
**coord.** coordinator
**corp.** corporation, corporate
**corr.** correspondent, corresponding, correspondence
**coun.** council
**CPA** Certified Public Accountant
**CPCU** Chartered Property and Casualty Underwriter
**CPH** Certificate of Public Health
**cpl.** corporal
**CPR** Cardio-Pulmonary Resuscitation
**CS** Christian Science
**CSB** Bachelor of Christian Science
**CT** Connecticut
**ct.** court
**ctr.** center
**ctrl.** central

## D

**D** Doctor
**d.** daughter of
**DAgr** Doctor of Agriculture
**DAR** Daughters of the American Revolution
**dau.** daughter

**DAV**  Disabled American Veterans
**DC**  District of Columbia
**DCL**  Doctor of Civil Law
**DCS**  Doctor of Commercial Science
**DD**  Doctor of Divinity
**DDS**  Doctor of Dental Surgery
**DE**  Delaware
**Dec.**  December
**dec.**  deceased
**def.**  defense
**Del.**  Delaware
**del.**  delegate, delegation
**Dem.**  Democrat, Democratic
**DEng**  Doctor of Engineering
**denom.**  denomination, denominational
**dep.**  deputy
**dept.**  department
**dermatol.**  dermatological
**desc.**  descendant
**devel.**  development, developmental
**DFA**  Doctor of Fine Arts
**DHL**  Doctor of Hebrew Literature
**dir.**  director
**dist.**  district
**distbg.**  distributing
**distbn.**  distribution
**distbr.**  distributor
**disting.**  distinguished
**div.**  division, divinity, divorce
**divsn.**  division
**DLitt**  Doctor of Literature
**DMD**  Doctor of Dental Medicine
**DMS**  Doctor of Medical Science
**DO**  Doctor of Osteopathy
**docs.**  documents
**DON**  Director of Nursing
**DPH**  Diploma in Public Health
**DPhil**  Doctor of Philosophy
**DR**  Daughters of the Revolution
**Dr.**  Drive, Doctor
**DRE**  Doctor of Religious Education
**DrPH**  Doctor of Public Health
**DSc**  Doctor of Science
**DSChemE**  Doctor of Science in Chemical Engineering
**DSM**  Distinguished Service Medal
**DST**  Doctor of Sacred Theology
**DTM**  Doctor of Tropical Medicine
**DVM**  Doctor of Veterinary Medicine
**DVS**  Doctor of Veterinary Surgery

### E

**E**  East
**ea.**  eastern
**Eccles.**  Ecclesiastical
**ecol.**  ecological
**econ.**  economic
**ECOSOC**  United Nations Economic and Social Council
**ED**  Doctor of Engineering
**ed.**  educated
**EdB**  Bachelor of Education
**EdD**  Doctor of Education
**edit.**  edition
**editl.**  editorial
**EdM**  Master of Education
**edn.**  education
**ednl.**  educational
**EDP**  Electronic Data Processing
**EdS**  Specialist in Education
**EE**  Electrical Engineer
**EEC**  European Economic Community
**EEG**  Electroencephalogram
**EEO**  Equal Employment Opportunity
**EEOC**  Equal Employment Opportunity Commission
**EKG**  electrocardiogram
**elec.**  electrical
**electrochem.**  electrochemical
**electrophys.**  electrophysical
**elem.**  elementary
**EM**  Engineer of Mines
**EMT**  Emergency Medical Technician
**ency.**  encyclopedia
**Eng.**  England
**engr.**  engineer
**engring.**  engineering
**entomol.**  entomological
**environ.**  environmental
**EPA**  Environmental Protection Agency
**epidemiol.**  epidemiological
**Episc.**  Episcopalian
**ERA**  Equal Rights Amendment
**ERDA**  Energy Research and Development Administration
**ESEA**  Elementary and Secondary Education Act
**ESL**  English as Second Language
**ESSA**  Environmental Science Services Administration
**ethnol.**  ethnological
**ETO**  European Theatre of Operations
**EU**  European Union
**Evang.**  Evangelical
**exam.**  examination, examining
**Exch.**  Exchange
**exec.**  executive
**exhbn.**  exhibition
**expdn.**  expedition
**expn.**  exposition
**expt.**  experiment
**exptl.**  experimental
**Expy.**  Expressway
**Ext.**  Extension

### F

**FAA**  Federal Aviation Administration
**FAO**  UN Food and Agriculture Organization
**FBA**  Federal Bar Association
**FBI**  Federal Bureau of Investigation
**FCA**  Farm Credit Administration
**FCC**  Federal Communications Commission
**FCDA**  Federal Civil Defense Administration
**FDA**  Food and Drug Administration
**FDIA**  Federal Deposit Insurance Administration
**FDIC**  Federal Deposit Insurance Corporation
**FEA**  Federal Energy Administration
**Feb.**  February
**fed.**  federal
**fedn.**  federation
**FERC**  Federal Energy Regulatory Commission
**fgn.**  foreign
**FHA**  Federal Housing Administration
**fin.**  financial, finance
**FL**  Florida
**Fl.**  Floor
**Fla.**  Florida
**FMC**  Federal Maritime Commission
**FNP**  Family Nurse Practitioner
**FOA**  Foreign Operations Administration
**found.**  foundation
**FPC**  Federal Power Commission
**FPO**  Fleet Post Office
**frat.**  fraternity
**FRS**  Federal Reserve System
**FSA**  Federal Security Agency
**Ft.**  Fort
**FTC**  Federal Trade Commission
**Fwy.**  Freeway

### G

**GA, Ga.**  Georgia
**GAO**  General Accounting Office
**gastroent.**  gastroenterological
**GATT**  General Agreement on Tariffs and Trade
**GE**  General Electric Company
**gen.**  general
**geneal.**  genealogical
**geog.**  geographic, geographical
**geol.**  geological
**geophys.**  geophysical

geriat. geriatrics
gerontol. gerontological
GHQ General Headquarters
gov. governor
govt. government
govtl. governmental
GPO Government Printing Office
grad. graduate, graduated
GSA General Services
  Administration
Gt. Great
GU Guam
gynecol. gynecological

## H

hdqs. headquarters
HEW Department of Health,
  Education and Welfare
HHD Doctor of Humanities
HHFA Housing and Home Finance
  Agency
HHS Department of Health and
  Human Services
HI Hawaii
hist. historical, historic
HM Master of Humanities
homeo. homeopathic
hon. honorary, honorable
House of Dels. House of
  Delegates
House of Reps. House of
  Representatives
hort. horticultural
hosp. hospital
HS High School
HUD Department of Housing and
  Urban Development
Hwy. Highway
hydrog. hydrographic

## I

IA Iowa
IAEA International Atomic Energy
  Agency
IBRD International Bank for
  Reconstruction and
  Development
ICA International Cooperation
  Administration
ICC Interstate Commerce
  Commission
ICCE International Council for
  Computers in Education
ICU Intensive Care Unit
ID Idaho
IEEE Institute of Electrical and
  Electronics Engineers
IFC International Finance
  Corporation
IL, Ill. Illinois
illus. illustrated
ILO International Labor
  Organization

IMF International Monetary Fund
IN Indiana
Inc. Incorporated
Ind. Indiana
ind. independent
Indpls. Indianapolis
indsl. industrial
inf. infantry
info. information
ins. insurance
insp. inspector
inst. institute
instl. institutional
instn. institution
instr. instructor
instrn. instruction
instrnl. instructional
internat. international
intro. introduction
IRE Institute of Radio Engineers
IRS Internal Revenue Service

## J

JAG Judge Advocate General
JAGC Judge Advocate General
  Corps
Jan. January
Jaycees Junior Chamber of
  Commerce
JB Jurum Baccalaureus
JCB Juris Canoni Baccalaureus
JCD Juris Canonici Doctor, Juris
  Civilis Doctor
JCL Juris Canonici Licentiatus
JD Juris Doctor
jg. junior grade
jour. journal
jr. junior
JSD Juris Scientiae Doctor
JUD Juris Utriusque Doctor
jud. judicial

## K

Kans. Kansas
KC Knights of Columbus
KS Kansas
KY, Ky. Kentucky

## L

LA, La. Louisiana
LA Los Angeles
lab. laboratory
L.Am. Latin America
lang. language
laryngol. laryngological
LB Labrador
LDS Latter Day Saints
lectr. lecturer
legis. legislation, legislative
LHD Doctor of Humane Letters
LI Long Island
libr. librarian, library
lic. licensed, license

lit. literature
litig. litigation
LittB Bachelor of Letters
LittD Doctor of Letters
LLB Bachelor of Laws
LLD Doctor of Laws
LLM Master of Laws
Ln. Lane
LPGA Ladies Professional Golf
  Association
LPN Licensed Practical Nurse
lt. lieutenant
Ltd. Limited
Luth. Lutheran
LWV League of Women Voters

## M

M Master
m. married
MA Master of Arts
MA Massachusetts
MADD Mothers Against Drunk
  Driving
mag. magazine
MAgr Master of Agriculture
maj. major
Man. Manitoba
Mar. March
MArch Master in Architecture
Mass. Massachusetts
math. mathematics, mathematical
MB Bachelor of Medicine,
  Manitoba
MBA Master of Business
  Administration
MC Medical Corps
MCE Master of Civil Engineering
mcht. merchant
mcpl. municipal
MCS Master of Commercial
  Science
MD Doctor of Medicine
MD, Md. Maryland
MDiv Master of Divinity
MDip Master in Diplomacy
mdse. merchandise
MDV Doctor of Veterinary
  Medicine
ME Mechanical Engineer
ME Maine
M.E.Ch. Methodist Episcopal
  Church
mech. mechanical
MEd. Master of Education
med. medical
MEE Master of Electrical
  Engineering
mem. member
meml. memorial
merc. mercantile
met. metropolitan
metall. metallurgical
MetE Metallurgical Engineer

**meteorol.** meteorological
**Meth.** Methodist
**Mex.** Mexico
**MF** Master of Forestry
**MFA** Master of Fine Arts
**mfg.** manufacturing
**mfr.** manufacturer
**mgmt.** management
**mgr.** manager
**MHA** Master of Hospital Administration
**MI** Military Intelligence, Michigan
**Mich.** Michigan
**micros.** microscopic
**mid.** middle
**mil.** military
**Milw.** Milwaukee
**Min.** Minister
**mineral.** mineralogical
**Minn.** Minnesota
**MIS** Management Information Systems
**Miss.** Mississippi
**MIT** Massachusetts Institute of Technology
**mktg.** marketing
**ML** Master of Laws
**MLA** Modern Language Association
**MLitt** Master of Literature, Master of Letters
**MLS** Master of Library Science
**MME** Master of Mechanical Engineering
**MN** Minnesota
**mng.** managing
**MO, Mo.** Missouri
**moblzn.** mobilization
**Mont.** Montana
**MP** Member of Parliament
**MPA** Master of Public Administration
**MPE** Master of Physical Education
**MPH** Master of Public Health
**MPhil** Master of Philosophy
**MPL** Master of Patent Law
**Mpls.** Minneapolis
**MRE** Master of Religious Education
**MRI** Magnetic Resonance Imaging
**MS** Master of Science
**MSc** Master of Science
**MSChemE** Master of Science in Chemical Engineering
**MSEE** Master of Science in Electrical Engineering
**MSF** Master of Science of Forestry
**MSN** Master of Science in Nursing
**MST** Master of Sacred Theology
**MSW** Master of Social Work
**MT** Montana

**Mt.** Mount
**mus.** museum, musical
**MusB** Bachelor of Music
**MusD** Doctor of Music
**MusM** Master of Music
**mut.** mutual
**MVP** Most Valuable Player
**mycol.** mycological

## N

**N** North
**NAACOG** Nurses Association of the American College of Obstetricians and Gynecologists
**NAACP** National Association for the Advancement of Colored People
**NACA** National Advisory Committee for Aeronautics
**NACDL** National Association of Criminal Defense Lawyers
**NACU** National Association of Colleges and Universities
**NAD** National Academy of Design
**NAE** National Academy of Engineering, National Association of Educators
**NAESP** National Association of Elementary School Principals
**NAFE** National Association of Female Executives
**N.Am.** North America
**NAM** National Association of Manufacturers
**NAMH** National Association for Mental Health
**NAPA** National Association of Performing Artists
**NARAS** National Academy of Recording Arts and Sciences
**NAREB** National Association of Real Estate Boards
**NARS** National Archives and Record Service
**NAS** National Academy of Sciences
**NASA** National Aeronautics and Space Administration
**NASP** National Association of School Psychologists
**NASW** National Association of Social Workers
**nat.** national
**NATAS** National Academy of Television Arts and Sciences
**NATO** North Atlantic Treaty Organization
**NB** New Brunswick
**NBA** National Basketball Association
**NC** North Carolina
**NCAA** National College Athletic Association

**NCCJ** National Conference of Christians and Jews
**ND** North Dakota
**NDEA** National Defense Education Act
**NE** Nebraska
**NE** Northeast
**NEA** National Education Association
**Nebr.** Nebraska
**NEH** National Endowment for Humanities
**neurol.** neurological
**Nev.** Nevada
**NF** Newfoundland
**NFL** National Football League
**Nfld.** Newfoundland
**NG** National Guard
**NH** New Hampshire
**NHL** National Hockey League
**NIH** National Institutes of Health
**NIMH** National Institute of Mental Health
**NJ** New Jersey
**NLRB** National Labor Relations Board
**NM, N.Mex.** New Mexico
**No.** Northern
**NOAA** National Oceanographic and Atmospheric Administration
**NORAD** North America Air Defense
**Nov.** November
**NOW** National Organization for Women
**nr.** near
**NRA** National Rifle Association
**NRC** National Research Council
**NS** Nova Scotia
**NSC** National Security Council
**NSF** National Science Foundation
**NSTA** National Science Teachers Association
**NSW** New South Wales
**nuc.** nuclear
**numis.** numismatic
**NV** Nevada
**NW** Northwest
**NWT** Northwest Territories
**NY** New York
**NYC** New York City
**NYU** New York University
**NZ** New Zealand

## O

**ob-gyn** obstetrics-gynecology
**obs.** observatory
**obstet.** obstetrical
**occupl.** occupational
**oceanog.** oceanographic
**Oct.** October
**OD** Doctor of Optometry

**OECD** Organization for Economic Cooperation and Development
**OEEC** Organization of European Economic Cooperation
**OEO** Office of Economic Opportunity
**ofcl.** official
**OH** Ohio
**OK, Okla.** Oklahoma
**ON, Ont.** Ontario
**oper.** operating
**ophthal.** ophthalmological
**ops.** operations
**OR** Oregon
**orch.** orchestra
**Oreg.** Oregon
**orgn.** organization
**orgnl.** organizational
**ornithol.** ornithological
**orthop.** orthopedic
**OSHA** Occupational Safety and Health Administration
**OSRD** Office of Scientific Research and Development
**OSS** Office of Strategic Services
**osteo.** osteopathic
**otol.** otological
**otolaryn.** otolaryngological

## P

**PA, Pa.** Pennsylvania
**paleontol.** paleontological
**path.** pathological
**pediat.** pediatrics
**PEI** Prince Edward Island
**PEN** Poets, Playwrights, Editors, Essayists and Novelists
**penol.** penological
**pers.** personnel
**PGA** Professional Golfers' Association of America
**PHA** Public Housing Administration
**pharm.** pharmaceutical
**PharmD** Doctor of Pharmacy
**PharmM** Master of Pharmacy
**PhB** Bachelor of Philosophy
**PhD** Doctor of Philosophy
**PhDChemE** Doctor of Science in Chemical Engineering
**PhM** Master of Philosophy
**Phila.** Philadelphia
**philharm.** philharmonic
**philol.** philological
**philos.** philosophical
**photog.** photographic
**phys.** physical
**physiol.** physiological
**Pitts.** Pittsburgh
**Pk.** Park
**Pky.** Parkway
**Pl.** Place
**Plz.** Plaza

**PO** Post Office
**polit.** political
**poly.** polytechnic, polytechnical
**PQ** Province of Quebec
**PR** Puerto Rico
**prep.** preparatory
**pres.** president
**Presbyn.** Presbyterian
**presdl.** presidential
**prin.** principal
**procs.** proceedings
**prod.** produced
**prodn.** production
**prodr.** producer
**prof.** professor
**profl.** professional
**prog.** progressive
**propr.** proprietor
**pros.** prosecuting
**pro tem.** pro tempore
**psychiat.** psychiatric
**psychol.** psychological
**PTA** Parent-Teachers Association
**ptnr.** partner
**PTO** Pacific Theatre of Operations, Parent Teacher Organization
**pub.** publisher, publishing, published, public
**publ.** publication
**pvt.** private

## Q

**quar.** quarterly
**qm.** quartermaster
**Que.** Quebec

## R

**radiol.** radiological
**RAF** Royal Air Force
**RCA** Radio Corporation of America
**RCAF** Royal Canadian Air Force
**Rd.** Road
**R&D** Research & Development
**REA** Rural Electrification Administration
**rec.** recording
**ref.** reformed
**regt.** regiment
**regtl.** regimental
**rehab.** rehabilitation
**rels.** relations
**Rep.** Republican
**rep.** representative
**Res.** Reserve
**ret.** retired
**Rev.** Reverend
**rev.** review, revised
**RFC** Reconstruction Finance Corporation
**RI** Rhode Island
**Rlwy.** Railway

**Rm.** Room
**RN** Registered Nurse
**roentgenol.** roentgenological
**ROTC** Reserve Officers Training Corps
**RR** rural route, railroad
**rsch.** research
**rschr.** researcher
**Rt.** Route

## S

**S** South
**s.** son
**SAC** Strategic Air Command
**SAG** Screen Actors Guild
**S.Am.** South America
**san.** sanitary
**SAR** Sons of the American Revolution
**Sask.** Saskatchewan
**savs.** savings
**SB** Bachelor of Science
**SBA** Small Business Administration
**SC** South Carolina
**ScB** Bachelor of Science
**SCD** Doctor of Commercial Science
**ScD** Doctor of Science
**sch.** school
**sci.** science, scientific
**SCV** Sons of Confederate Veterans
**SD** South Dakota
**SE** Southeast
**SEC** Securities and Exchange Commission
**sec.** secretary
**sect.** section
**seismol.** seismological
**sem.** seminary
**Sept.** September
**s.g.** senior grade
**sgt.** sergeant
**SI** Staten Island
**SJ** Society of Jesus
**SJD** Scientiae Juridicae Doctor
**SK** Saskatchewan
**SM** Master of Science
**SNP** Society of Nursing Professionals
**So.** Southern
**soc.** society
**sociol.** sociological
**spkr.** speaker
**spl.** special
**splty.** specialty
**Sq.** Square
**SR** Sons of the Revolution
**sr.** senior
**SS** Steamship
**St.** Saint, Street
**sta.** station

**stats.** statistics
**statis.** statistical
**STB** Bachelor of Sacred Theology
**stblzn.** stabilization
**STD** Doctor of Sacred Theology
**std.** standard
**Ste.** Suite
**subs.** subsidiary
**SUNY** State University of New York
**supr.** supervisor
**supt.** superintendent
**surg.** surgical
**svc.** service
**SW** Southwest
**sys.** system

### T

**Tb.** tuberculosis
**tchg.** teaching
**tchr.** teacher
**tech.** technical, technology
**technol.** technological
**tel.** telephone
**telecom.** telecommunications
**temp.** temporary
**Tenn.** Tennessee
**TESOL** Teachers of English to Speakers of Other Languages
**Tex.** Texas
**ThD** Doctor of Theology
**theol.** theological
**ThM** Master of Theology
**TN** Tennessee
**tng.** training
**topog.** topographical
**trans.** transaction, transferred
**transl.** translation, translated
**transp.** transportation
**treas.** treasurer
**TV** television
**twp.** township
**TX** Texas
**typog.** typographical

### U

**U.** University
**UAW** United Auto Workers
**UCLA** University of California at Los Angeles
**UK** United Kingdom
**UN** United Nations
**UNESCO** United Nations Educational, Scientific and Cultural Organization
**UNICEF** United Nations International Children's Emergency Fund
**univ.** university
**UNRRA** United Nations Relief and Rehabilitation Administration
**UPI** United Press International
**urol.** urological
**US, USA** United States of America
**USAAF** United States Army Air Force
**USAF** United States Air Force
**USAFR** United States Air Force Reserve
**USAR** United States Army Reserve
**USCG** United States Coast Guard
**USCGR** United States Coast Guard Reserve
**USES** United States Employment Service
**USIA** United States Information Agency
**USMC** United States Marine Corps
**USMCR** United States Marine Corps Reserve
**USN** United States Navy
**USNG** United States National Guard
**USNR** United States Naval Reserve
**USO** United Service Organizations
**USPHS** United States Public Health Service
**USS** United States Ship
**USSR** Union of the Soviet Socialist Republics
**USTA** United States Tennis Association
**UT** Utah

### V

**VA** Veterans Administration
**VA, Va.** Virginia
**vet.** veteran, veterinary
**VFW** Veterans of Foreign Wars
**VI** Virgin Islands
**vis.** visiting
**VISTA** Volunteers in Service to America
**vocat.** vocational
**vol.** volunteer, volume
**v.p.** vice president
**vs.** versus
**VT, Vt.** Vermont

### W

**W** West
**WA, Wash.** Washington (state)
**WAC** Women's Army Corps
**WAVES** Women's Reserve, US Naval Reserve
**WCTU** Women's Christian Temperance Union
**we.** western
**WHO** World Health Organization
**WI** Wisconsin, West Indies
**Wis.** Wisconsin
**WV, W.Va.** West Virginia
**WY, Wyo.** Wyoming

### X, Y, Z

**YK** Yukon Territory
**YMCA** Young Men's Christian Association
**YMHA** Young Men's Hebrew Association
**YM & YWHA** Young Men's and Young Women's Hebrew Association
**yr.** year
**YT** Yukon Territory
**YWCA** Young Women's Christian Association

# Alphabetical Practices

Names are arranged alphabetically according to the surnames, and under identical surnames according to the first given name. If both surname and first given name are identical, names are arranged alphabetically according to the second given name.

Surnames beginning with De, Des, Du, however capitalized or spaced, are recorded with the prefix preceding the surname and arranged alphabetically under the letter D.

Surnames beginning with Mac and Mc are arranged alphabetically under M.

Surnames beginning with Saint or St. appear after names that begin Sains, and are arranged according to the second part of the name, e.g., St. Clair before Saint Dennis.

Surnames beginning with Van, Von, or von are arranged alphabetically under the letter V.

Compound surnames are arranged according to the first member of the compound.

Many hyphenated Arabic names begin Al-, El-, or al-. These names are alphabetized according to each biographee's designation of last name. Thus Al-Bahar, Neta may be listed either under Al- or under Bahar, depending on the preference of the listee.

Also, Arabic names have a variety of possible spellings when transposed to English. Spelling of these names is always based on the practice of the biographee. Some biographees use a Western form of word order, while others prefer the Arabic word sequence.

Similarly, Asian names may have no comma between family and given names, but some biographees have chosen to add the comma. In each case, punctuation follows the preference of the biographee.

Parentheses used in connection with a name indicate which part of the full name is usually omitted in common usage. Hence, Chambers, E(lizabeth) Anne indicates that the first name, Elizabeth, is generally recorded as an initial. In such a case, the parentheses are ignored in alphabetizing and the name would be arranged as Chambers, Elizabeth Anne.

However, if the entire first name appears in parentheses, for example, Chambers, (Elizabeth) Anne, the first name is not commonly used, and the alphabetizing is therefore arranged as though the name were Chambers, Anne.

If the entire middle name is in parentheses, it is still used in alphabetical sorting. Hence, Belamy, Katherine (Lucille) would sort as Belamy, Katherine Lucille. The same occurs if the entire last name is in parentheses, e.g., (Brandenberg), Howard Keith would sort as Brandenberg, Howard Keith.

For visual clarification:

Smith, H(enry) George: Sorts as Smith, Henry George
Smith, (Henry) George: Sorts as Smith, George
Smith, Henry (George): Sorts as Smith, Henry George
(Smith), Henry George: Sorts as Smith, Henry George

# Who Was Who in America®

**ABATE, CATHERINE M.,** retired state legislator; b. Margate, NJ, Dec. 8, 1947; d. Joseph and Carolyn (Fiore) A.; m. Ronald E. Kliegerman, Oct. 28, 1978; 1 child, Kyle. BA, Vassar Coll., 1969; JD, Boston U., 1972. Bar: N.Y. 1973, US Dist. Ct. (southern dist.) N.Y. 1976. Staff atty. Legal Aid Soc., NYC, 1972-74, 75-78, supervising atty., 1979-81, dir. tng., 1981-85, acting chairperson Gov.'s Taskforce Criminal Justice, 1983; chairperson NY State Platform Criminal Justice, 1984, NY Crime Victims Bd., 1988-90; exec. dep. commr. NY State Div. Human Rights, 1986-88; commr. NYC Dept. Probation, 1990-92, NYC Dept. Correction, 1992-94; mem. Dist. 27 NY State Senate, Albany, 1995-98; pres., CEO Cmty. Healthcare Network, 1999—2014. Dist. leader Democratic Party, 1981-86; 1st vice chmn. county com. Democratic Party, N.Y. County; bd. dirs. Village Nursing Home, 1987-99, Eleanor Roosevelt Legacy Com., 2003, Mem. Bar Assn. City N.Y. (criminal cts. com. 1982-86), Nat. Assn. Crime Victims Compensation Bd. (bd. dirs. 1989-90), Nat. Orgn. Italian-American Women (bd. dirs. 1986-2003). Democrat. Roman Catholic. Avocation: tennis. Home: New York, NY. Died May 17, 2014.

**ABBADO, CLAUDIO,** conductor; b. Milan, June 26, 1933; Degree (hon.), Aberdeen, 1986, Ferrara, 1990, Cambridge, 1994. Music dir. Teatro alle Scala Milano, 1968—86, London Symphony Orch., 1979-88, Vienna State Opera, Austria, 1986—91; fifth artistic dir., prin. condr. Berlin Philharm. Orch., 1989—2002. Founder European Commn. Youth Orch., 1978; founder, artistic dir. Gustav Mahler Jugend Orch., 1986, WIEN MODERN Festival Contemporary Art, 1988, Encounters in Berlin Chamber Music Festival, 1992, Competitions of the Salzburg Easter Festival, 1994; artistic advisor Chamber Orch. of Europe; artistic dir. Easter Festival Salzburg, 1994. Decorated with Gran Croce of the Italian Rep., 1984, French Legion D'Honneur, 1988, Bundesverdienstkreuz, Germany, 1992, Ehrenring der Stadt Wien, 1994, Goldenes Ehrenzeichen Österreich; recipient Mozart medal Mozart Gemeinde, Vienna, 1973, Golden Nicolai medal Vienna Philharm. Orch., 1980, Std. Opera award Covent Garden, London, 1989, Gold medal Internat. Mahler Soc., 1985, Internat. prizes for Recordings, Prize in the Arts Wolf Found., Israel, 2008, Conductor prize Royal Philharmonic Soc., 2012; named Gen. Music Dir. City of Vienna, 1989; named to The Gramophone Hall of Fame, 2012 Died Jan. 20, 2014.

**ABBOTT, MARY ELAINE,** photographer, lecturer, researcher; b. LaGrange, Ill., Apr. 23, 1922; d. Vergil and Goldie (Wright) Schwarzkopf; m. Harry Edward Abbott, Oct. 8, 1949; children: John Edward, Jane Ann. BA in English, Psychology, U. Iowa, 1944, student. With child welfare dept. Montgomery County Children's Home, Dayton, Ohio, 1944-47, Mich. Children's Inst., Ann Arbor, 1947-49; photographer, lectr., rschr., from 1978. Participant Taft Confs., Eagle's Nest, Oregon, Ill.; lectr. on Lorado Taft. Photographer St. Paul's Ch. history, History of Jackson County, History of Queens Cath. Ch., History of Music in Jackson County, Mich. Living, Victorian Living; photodocumentary of homes in Jackson Hist. Dist., homes and blds. of Claire Allen; commd. Taft Sculpture, Sculpture Jackson County; author: The Wondrous Works of Claire Allen, 1997; photography and artistic dir. James Agee's Knoxville, Summer 1915 in concert; commd. by Jackson Historic Dist. Commn. and State Hist. Soc., Mich. Dance Assn.; hist. dist. commn. advisor Dance for the Handicapped, Savs. and Loan "40 Doors", Amitech, Jackson Alliance of Businessmen; represented in permenant collections Ella Sharp Mus., Jackson Symphony, St. Paul's Episcopal Ch., Carnegie Libr., others; exhibited in one-woman and group shows; slides included in archives Midwest Alliance, Commn. on Art in Pub. Places, Carnegie Libr., Nat. Endowment Arts, U. Ill., Eagle's Nest. Mem. Jr. League, Jackson Chorale, Nat. Trust for Hist. Preservation; panel participant on creative process Ella Sharp Mus.; advisor Jackson Hist. Commn.; tchr. U. Chgo. Gt. Books Found.; active enrichment for advanced children, Save Outdoor Sculpture for Nat. Inst. Conservation Cultural Property, Smithsonian Instn. Recipient Photography award Ella Sharp Mus., Hist. Trinity Ch., Detroit, Cert. of Honor, Spl. Recognitions Excellence Luth. Ctr. Assn.; included in Funk and Wagnall Encyclopedia. Mem. Internat. Platform Assn. (mem. arts com., arts adv. bd., photography award, Juror's Choice in art exhibit, Inner Cir. Merit award 1993, 2d prize for photography 1994, 1st prize art show 1996), Log Cabin Soc. Mich., Internat. Platform Assn. (2d prize 1997), Nat. Mus. Women in Arts, Arts Midwest, Kappa Alpha Theta. Republican. Episcopalian. Avocations: music, history, reading, walking, frontier history. Deceased.

**ABBOTT, WILLIAM THOMAS,** private investigator; s. Benjamin Franklin and Eva Mae (Lattin) Abbott; m. Jerri Evelyn Stacy, Apr. 20, 1974. BS, Ctrl. State U., Okla., 1960; casualty claim law assoc., Am. Ednl. Inst., 1975. Cert. fraud examiner. Claim adjuster Crawford and Co., Lubbock, Tex., 1964-67, Tulsa, 1967-70; sr. claim specialist State Farm Ins. Co., Tulsa, 1970-2000; pvt. investigator Abbott Investigations, Inc., Tulsa, from 2000. Bd. dirs. Okla. Arson Adv. Coun., chmn., from 1996; mem. Tulsa Mental Health Hotline, 1971—73, Okla. Hist. Soc.; pres., bd. dirs. Vis. Nurse Assn., Tulsa, 2003—05; mem. Young Reps., 1967, Tulsa Met. Ministries, 1971—75. With USMC, 1960—64. Mem.: Okla. chpt. Internat. Assn. Spl. Investigation Units, Tulsa Claims Assn., Assn. Cert. Fraud Examiners, Okla. chpt. Internat. Assn. Arson Investigators, Adventure Cyclists, League Am. Bicyclists (life), Summit Club Tulsa, Tulsa, Elks, Am. Legion. Republican. Methodist. Avocations: bicycling, history, writing. Home: Tulsa, Okla. Deceased.

**ABDULWAHAB, AMYN,** surgeon; b. Mina, Lebanon, Aug. 11, 1937; s. Abdulghani and Khadidja Abdulwahab; m. Ingrid Hartman, Aug. 25, 1965; children: Hayyan, Reem, Haitham. MD, U. Heidelberg, Germany, 1964. Diplomate Am. Bd. Surgery. Surg. intern St. Raphael Hosp.-Yale U., New Haven, 1967-68, resident in surgery, 1968-70; asst. chief resident Boston U. Med. Ctr., 1970-71, chief resident, 1971-72, surg. rsch. fellow, 1972-73; pvt. practice Tripoli, Lebanon, from 1975; surgeon-in-chief Al Sharq Hosp., Alkhobar, Saudi Arabia, 1973-75. Chief surgery Mouasat Hosp. Damam, Saudi Arabia, 1988-89, med. dir., 1989-90; surgeon-in-chief Mishari Clinic, Riad, Saudi Arabia, 1990-91 Fellow ACS. Avocation: coin collecting/numismatics. Deceased.

**ABDUOLV, ALEKSANDR GAVRILOVICH,** actor; b. Fergana, USSR, May 29, 1953; m. Irina Alfyorova; 1 child. Student, Lunacharsky State Inst Theatre. With Theatre of Leninsky Komsomol (now Kenkom), from 1975. Debut as Lt. Pluzhnikov in Missing from the Lists; appeared in plays The Star and Death of Joaquin Murietta, Merciless Games, Yunona and Avos, Optimistic Tragedy, Enough Simplicity for Every Wise Man, Hamlet, Mourning Pray, others; films include Golden River, 1977, Never Part with the Beloved, 1980, A Woman in White, 1982, Carnival, 1982, Recipe of Her Youthfulness, 1984, To Kill the Dragon, 1988, The Barbarian and the Heretic, 1997; also numerous TV roles. Mem. Russian Union Cinematographers (sec.). Died Jan. 3, 2008.

**ABE, HITOSHI,** political science professor; b. Ohta, Tokyo, Japan, June 28, 1933; s. Seiji and Yano Abe; m. Nobuko Hayashi, 1957 (div. 1976); children: Itaru, Yukari; m. Kyo Nakata, Feb. 28, 1977. BA, U. Tokyo, 1957, MA, 1959, PhD, 1963. Assoc. prof. Seikei U., Tokyo, 1966-70, prof., 1970-77, U. Tsukuba, Ibaraki, 1977-85, U. of the Air, Chiba, 1985—2004, ret., 2004, prof. emeritus, from 2004. Author: The American Presidency, 1972, Logic of Democracy, 1973, Contemporary American Politics, 1986, Contemporary Politics and Political Science, 1989, Contemporary Political Theories, 1991, Introduction to Political Science, 1996. Fellow Am. Coun. Learned Socs., 1966-68; Fulbright scholar, 1988-89. Mem. Japanese Assn. for Am. Studies (pres. 1996-98), Japanese Polit. Sci. Assn. (dir. 1980-89), Japanese Soc. for Pub. Adminstrn. Avocations: watching a bunraku puppet show, reading a mystery novel. Home: Chiba, Japan. Died Sept. 12, 2004.

**ABERLE, DAVID FRIEND,** anthropologist, educator; b. St. Paul, Nov. 23, 1918; s. David Winfield and Lisette (Friend) A.; m. Eleanor Kathleen Gough, Sept. 5, 1955 (dec. Sept. 1990); 1 son. AB summa cum laude, Harvard U., 1940; PhD in Anthropology, Columbia U., 1950; postgrad., U. N.Mex., 1938—40, No. Ariz. U., 1971, postgrad., 1973, Harvard U., 1946—47. Instr. dept. social rels. Harvard U., Cambridge, Mass., 1947-50, rsch. assoc. Sch. Pub. Health, 1948-50; vis. assoc. prof. Page Sch., Johns Hopkins U., Balt., 1950-52; assoc. prof., then prof. dept. sociology and dept. anthropology U. Mich., Ann Arbor, 1952-60; fellow Ctr. Advanced Study in Behavioral Scis., Stanford, Calif., 1955-56; Simon vis. prof. and hon. rsch. assoc. dept. social anthropology Manchester (Eng.) U., 1960-61; prof., chmn. dept. anthropology Brandeis U., Waltham, Mass., 1961-63; prof. dept. anthropology U. Oreg., Eugene, 1963-67; prof. dept. anthropology and sociology U. B.C., Vancouver, Canada, 1967-83, prof. emeritus, 1983—2004. Cons. Inst. Devel. Anthropology, Inc., Binghamton, NY, 1978-79; cons. to attys. Navajo Tribe, 1976-77; disting. lectr. Am. Anthrop. Assn., 1986. Author: The Peyote Religion Among the Navaho, 1966, (with Isidore Dyen) Lexical Reconstruction, the Case of the Proto-Athapaskan Kinship System, 1974; contbr. articles on anthropological theory and Navajo Indians to scholarly jours.; rev. editor: Am. Anthropologist, 1952-55. With U.S. Army, 1942-46. Recipient Social Sci. Rsch. Coun. Demobilization award, 1946; Harvard U. Nat. scholar; NIMH grantee; USPHS grantee; Wenner-Gren Found. grantee, 1954-63; NSF grantee, 1965-72; Can. Coun. grantee, 1969-77; Social Scis. and Humanities Rsch. Coun. Can., 1978-80, 84-86. Fellow Royal Soc. Can., Royal Anthrop. Inst. of Gt. Britain and Ireland; mem. Am. Anthropol. Assn. (mem. panel on Navajo-Hopi land dispute 1973-95), Am. Sociol. Assn., Soc. Applied Anthropology, Am. Ethnol. Assn., Can. Anthropology Soc., Soc. Lesbian and Gay Anthropologists, Phi Beta Kappa. Jewish. Died Sept. 24, 2004.

**ABRAMS, JOAN D.,** school superintendent; b. NYC, Nov. 10, 1928; d. Leo and Rose (Levine) Scharf; m. Nathan Abrams, July 5, 1955; children: Linus Sampson, Lydia Joy. BS, CCNY, 1949; MA, Tchrs. Coll., NYC, 1953; PhD, NYU, 1971. Cert. adminstr., tchr. NY, NJ. Tchr., adminstr. NYC Pub. Schs., 1949—63; instr. tchg. methods CCNY, 1971—72; prin. Englewood Cliffs Sch., NJ, 1971—72; adj. prof. Antioch Coll., 1972; supt. schs. Montvale, NJ, 1972—74, Red Bank, NJ, from 1974. Contbr. articles to profl. jours. Fellow: Danforth Found., Edn. Professions Devel. Act, Met. Applied Rsch. Ctr.; mem.: NJ Orgn. Women as Ednl. Leaders (pres.), Red Bank C. of C., NJ Assn. Sch. Adminstrs., Assn. Supervision and Curriculum Devel., Am. Assn. Sch. Adminstrs., Am. Ednl. Rsch. Assn., Pi Lambda Theta. Died Aug. 25, 1991.

**ABRAMS, ROSALIE SILBER,** retired state agency official; b. Balt., June 2, 1916; d. Isaac and Dora (Rodbell) Silber; 1 child, Elizabeth Joan. RN, Sinai Hosp.; postgrad., Columbia U.; BS, Johns Hopkins U., 1963, MA in Polit. Sci. Pub. health nurse USNR, 1945-46; bus. mgr. Sequoia Med. Group, Calif., 1946-47; asst. bus. mgr. Silber's Bakery, Balt., 1947-53; mem. Md. Ho. of Dels., 1967-70, Md. Senate, 1970-83, majority leader, 1978-82; chmn. Dem. Party of Md., 1978-83, chmn. fin. com., 1982-83; dir. Office on Aging, State of Md., 1983-95, ret., 1995. Chair World War II Meml. Commn., 1996-2000; mem. Balt. City Commn. on Aging, 1997—2000; host Outlook TV show, 1983-90; guest lectr., witness before congl. coms. Platform com. on nat. healthcare Dem. Nat., Com., 1979—; chmn. Md. Humane Practices Commn., 1978-83, mem., 1971-74; mem. New Coalition, 1979-83, State-Fed. Assembly Com. on Human Resources, 1977-83, Md. Comprehensive Health Planning Agy., 1972-75, Md. Commn. on Status of Women, 1968—, Am. Jewish Com. Chair Med. Supplies Com. for Needy and Elderly in Odessa, Ukraine; chair dept. human resources, dept. health and mental hygiene, transp., housing and cmty. devel., econ. and employment devel., Interagy. Com., 1984-95; bd. dirs. Sinai Hosp., Balt., 1973-2000, Balt. Jewish Coun., Cross Country Improvement Assn., 1969—2000, Fifth Dist. Reform Dems., 1967—2000; chmn. legis. com. Balt. Area Coun. on Alcoholism, 1973-75; mem. adv. bd. long term care project U. Md., Balt., 1986; mem. Md. Adv. Com. for Adult and Cmty. Svcs., 1984; mem. nat. adv. bd. Pre-Retirement Edn. Planning, 1986—93; mem. State Adv. Coun. on Nutrition, 1988—; spl. trustee Sheppard-Pratt Hosp., 1992-2000. With Nurse Corps USN, 1944-46. Recipient Louise Waterman Wise Cmty. Svc. award, 1969, award Am. Acad. Comprehensive Health Planning, 1971, Balt. News Am. award, Women of Distinction in Medicine, 1971, traffic safety award, Safety First Club of Md., 1971, ann London Scott Meml. award for legis. excellence, Md. chpt. NOW, 1975, Md. Nurses Assn., 1975, svc. award Balt. Area Coun. on Alcoholism, 1975, First Citizens award Md. Senate Pres., 1999, named to Md. Women's Hall of Fame, Md. Commn. for Women and Women Legislators of Md. Gen. Assembly, 1994, numerous others; 1st ann. Rosalie S. Abrams Firsts award awarded by Women Legislators of Md., 2004, Nursing Spectrum award, 2005. Mem. AAUW, AARP, Md. Order Women Legislators (pres. 1973-75), Nat. Conf. State Legislatures (human resources and urban affairs steering com. 1977-83), Nat. Legis. Conf. (human resources task force, intergovtl. rels. com. 1975-83), Md. Gerontol. Assn. (bd. dirs. 1984—), Nat. Fedn. Dem. Women, Am. Jewish Congress, Am. Soc. on Aging, Md. Gerontol. Assn., Sigma Theta Tau Nursing Soc., Balta City Hist. Soc. (trustee 2000—). Home: Baltimore, Md. Died Feb. 7, 2009.

**ACKELL, EDMUND FERRIS,** retired academic administrator; b. Danbury, Conn., Nov. 29, 1925; s. Ferris M. and Barbara (Elias) A.; m. Judith S. Fox, Oct. 13, 1995. BS, Holy Cross Coll., Worcester, Mass., 1949; DMD, Tufts U., 1953; MD, Case Western Res. U., 1962; postgrad., U. Pa., 1955-57. Intern Bellevue Hosp., NYC, 1962-63; resident Meadowbrook Hosp., 1963-66; pvt. practice medicine, specializing in oral and maxillofacial surgery; prof. medicine and dentistry U. Fla. Med. and Dental Sch., 1966-69; dean Sch. Dentistry, 1966-69, univ. v.p. health affairs, 1969-74; v.p. health affairs U. Southern Calif., 1974-78; pres. Va. Commonwealth U., Richmond, 1978-90, pres. emeritus, 1990—2014. Served with USNR, 1943-46. Mem. AMA, ADA, Soc. Health and Human Values, American Public Health Assn., Va. Med. Assn., Va. Dental Assn. Clubs: Commonwealth, Country of Va., Keswick. Home: La Jolla, Calif. Died May 23, 2014.

**ACKERMAN, IRVING I.,** stockbroker, investment consultant; b. NYC, Sept. 20, 1921; s. Max and Celia (Schneider) A.; m. Estrella W. Wyangco, Mar. 14, 1947. BBA, CCNY, 1942, MBA, 1949; postgrad., NYU, 1951-56. Gen. mgr. Allied Investment, Manila, The Philippines,

1961-62; pres., gen. mgr., CEO I. Ackerman & Co., Inc., Makati City, The Philippines, from 1963. Founding mem. Makati Stock Exch., 1963 (became The Philippine Stock Exch., 1993)., gov., treas. Makati Stock Exch., 1965-94, gov. The Philippine Stock Exch., 1995-96; dir. Securities Investors Protection Fund, Manila, 1982—. Author: How to Invest and Win in the Philippine Stock Market, 1989, 4th edit., 2003; columnist "Stock Market", Manila Times, 1959-67. Capt., Quartermaster Corps, US Army, 1942-46, US, The Philippines. Named Outstanding Faculty Mem., Ateneo U., Makati, 1981; recipient numerous other awards and plaques, 1975—. Mem. Rotary of Makati, Makati Sports Club. Republican. Avocations: swimming, tennis, discussion groups. Home: Makati, Philippines. Died Jan. 17, 2009.

**ADACHI, MASAHISA,** mathematician, educator; b. Feb. 7, 1932; Mathematician; b. Nagoya, Aichi, Japan, Feb. 7, 1932; s. Masao and Hisako (Migamoto) A.; m. Yoshiko Tsukada, Feb. 13, 1961; children— Masamichi, Jiro. Bachelor, Nagoya U., 1953, M.S., 1955, Sc.D., 1959. Asst., Nagoya U., Japan, 1959-63, lectr., 1963-65, asst. prof., 1965-66; assoc. prof. math. Kyoto U., Japan, 1966—; vis. prof. I.H.E.S., Bures-sur-Yvett, France, 1977-78. Author: Differential Topology, 1976; Imbeddings and Immersions, 1984. Editor seminar notes: Differential Toplogy, 1982-85; coloquim: Coo-maps and singularities, 1985. Mem. Math. Soc. Japan, Am. Math. Soc., Socié té Mathematique de France. Home: Kyoto, Japan. Died Mar. 24, 1993.

**ADAMEC, LADISLAV,** former Prime Minister of Czechoslovakia; b. Frenstat pad Radhusten, Moravia, Sept. 10, 1926; m. Zdenka Adanecova; 1 child Student, Communist Party Coll. Polit. Studies, Prague, 1958-61. Dir. Mez Plant, Frenstat, Czechoslovakia; dep. chmn., chmn. regional planning commn. N Moravian Regional Nat. Com.; head dept. cen. com. Czechoslovakian Communist Party, 1963-69, head, 1989-90, mem. polit. exec. com., 1990; dep. House of Nations in Fed. Assembly, 1990-92, dep. premier, 1987-88; prime min. Govt. of Czechoslovakia, Prague, 1988—89. Mem. Communist Party of Czechoslovakia Cen. Com., 1966-92, Presidium, 1987-92, Nat. Econ. Com., 1971-92. Died Apr. 14, 2007.

**ADAMS, BUD (KENNETH STANLEY ADAMS JR.),** energy executive, professional sports team owner; b. Bartlesville, OK, Jan. 3, 1923; s. Kenneth Stanley and Blanch (Keeler) Adams; m. Nancy Neville, Oct. 26, 1946 (dec. Feb. 1, 2009); children: Susie Smith, Amy Strunk, Kenneth S.(dec.). Attended, Menlo Coll., Calif., 1941, U. Kans., 1944. Chmn. Travel House of Houston; owner Bud Adams Ranches, KSA Industries, Inc., Southwest Lincoln-Mercury, Inc.; owner, pres. Houston Oilers, 1946—97, Houston Mavericks, 1967—69, Tenn. Oilers, Nashville, 1997—99, Tennessee Titans, Nashville, 1999—2013, Nashville Kats, Arena Football League, 2005—07; chmn., CEO Adams Resources & Energy, Inc., Houston, 2001—13. Mem. exec. bd. Sam Houston Area Coun. Boy Scouts Am.; trustee Profl. Football Hall of Fame. With USNR, 1943—46. Recipient Disting. American award, Houston Chpt. of the Nat. Football Hall of Fame & Houston Athletic Comm., 1987, Golden Buckle award, Greater Houston Convention and Visitors Bur., 1988; named Houston Salesman of the Yr., Houston Sales Assn., 1960, Mr. Sportsman, Interfaith Charity Group, 1961, Significant Sig, Sigma Chi Fraternity, 1963, Westerner of the Yr., Houston Farm and Ranch Club, 1969, Disting. Alumnus, Calif. Cmty. & Jr. Coll. Assn., 1980, Outstanding CEO, Fin. World Mag., 1981, Man of the Yr., Culver Mil. Acad., 1981, King Capon, Annual Capon Charity Dinner, Inc., 1983; named one of Forbes 400: Richest Americans, Forbes, 2009—13. Mem.: Houston Geol. Soc., Houston Assn. Petroleum Landmen, Ind. Petroleum Assn. Am., Tex. Ind. Producers and Royalty Owners Assn., 100 Club of Houston (dir.), River Oaks Country Club, Petroleum Club, Houston Club, Sigma Chi (named Significant Sig 1963). Died Oct. 21, 2013.

**ADAMS, ELIZABETH HERRINGTON,** banker; b. Tulsa, May 25, 1947; d. James Dillon and Helen (Allderdice) Herrington; m. Phillip Hollis Hackney, Mar. 5, 1977 (dec. Jan. 1990); m. Keith R. Adams, Sept. 4, 1993. Student, No. Ariz. U., 1965-67, 68-69. With Coldwater (Kans.) Nat. Bank, summers 1964-67, The Ariz. Bank, Phoenix, 1969, Flagstaff, 1970-71; asst. cashier The Wilmore (Kans.) State Bank, 1972—2001, The Coldwater Nat. Bank, 1974-83, cashier, ops. officer, from 1984; v.p. The Coldwater (Kans.) Nat. Bank, 1998—2002, sr. v.p., 2002—04, exec. v.p., from 2005. Bd. dirs. The Coldwater Nat. Bank., 1972-. Bd. dirs. Pioneer Lodge Nursing Home, Coldwater, 1984-89; mem. sch. site coun., 1993-94; life mem. Girl Scouts, chmn. Neighborhood Cookie Drive, 1991-95; bd. dirs., mem. strategic planning com. Wheatbelt Area Girl Scout Coun., 1994-96—; elder 1st Presbyn. Ch., Coldwater; Kans. Lung Assn. Vol. Spkrs. Bur., 1998—; mem. Ch. Session Bd., Coldwater, 1994-2000. Mem. Fin. Women Internat., Cmty. Bankers Assn. Kans. (membership com. 1991-94, INPAC com. 1992-93), Kans. Ind. Bankers (gen. svcs. com. 1986-87), PEO, Alpha Omicron Pi, Lake Coldwater Archtl. Rev. Bd. Republican. Avocation: music (pianist). Deceased.

**ADAMS, HAROLD WILLIAM,** retired airplane designer, architect; b. Newport Beach, Calif., Oct. 8, 1910; s. William L. and Mary E. Adams; m. Nonalila Toledo, Feb. 1993; children: Mary, Nancy, Marites, Noime, Ana, Realyn. Grad. aero. engring. in aircraft design, U. So. Calif., 1930. Group leader Douglas Aircraft, Santa Monica, Calif., 1930—41, chief mech. and equipment section. El Segundo, Calif., 1941—45, asst. chief design engr. Santa Monica, 1945—60, Long Beach, Calif., 1945—60; chief designer McDonnell-Douglas, 1961—71; ret. 1st chmn. Soc. Automotive Engrs. Com. A6, 1931—45. Author: Aircraft Hydraulics, 1940, The Inside Story, The rise and Fall of Douglas Aircraft, 2000. Recipient Engr. and Maintenance award, Air Transport Assn. Am., 1968, Airplane Design award, Am. Inst. Aeronautics and Astronautics, 1969. Mem.: Commodore, So. Calif. Yachting Assn. (commodore). Avocations: yachting, surfing. Home: Batangas, Philippines. Died Aug. 14, 2007.

**ADAMS, JOHN EDMUND,** lawyer; b. Pine Apple, Ala., Dec. 26, 1896; s. David Jr. and Lucy Dell (Lee) A.; m. Nan Coleman, May 27, 1925; 1 child, John Edmund Jr. AB, U. Ala., Tuscaloosa, 1917, MA, LLB, U. Ala., Tuscaloosa, 1919. Bar: Ala. 1919, U.S. Supreme Ct. 1945. Jr. ptnr. Barnett & Adams, Florence, Ala., 1919-21, Pelham & Adams, Chatom, Ala., 1921-23, Bedsole & Adams, Grove Hill, Ala., 1923-25; pvt. practice Grove Hill, 1925-26; sr. ptnr. Adams & Gillmore, Grove Hill, 1926-52, Adams, Gillmore & Adams, Grove Hill, 1952-75, Adams, Adams & Kimbrough, Grove Hill, 1975-77, Adams & Adams, Grove Hill, 1977-81, Adams, Adams & Wilson, Grove Hill, from 1981. Mem. State Bar Commn., 1941-51; sec., bd. dirs. First Bank of Grove Hill, 1965-84. Mem. State Dem. Exec. Com. 1923-41. Served as 2nd lt. F.A., U.S. Army, 1918. Mem. Ala. State Bar (pres. 1946), Clarke County Bar Assn. (pres. 1965—), Phi Beta Kappa, Sigma Chi. Home: Grove Hill, Ala. Deceased.

**ADAMS, JOHN PHILLIPS, JR.,** economics educator, forensic economics consultant; b. Dothan, Ala., June 29, 1920; s. John Phillips Sr. and Lucile (Brown) Adams; m. Flavienne Marcelle David, Dec. 5, 1946; children: Gilles David, Sidney Michel. Student, Ga. Sch. Tech., 1939—43, U. SC, 1964—65; MA, Claremont Grad. Sch., 1968; PhD, Clarmont Grad. Sch., 1972. Commd. 2d lt. U.S. Army, 1943, advanced through grades to lt. col., 1963, ret., 1963; lectr. econs. Calif. State Poly. U., Pomona, 1968—70; prof. econs. Calif. Poly. State U., San Luis Obispo, 1970—90, prof. emeritus, from 1990. Trustee Calif. Coun. on Econ. Edn., 1972—78; forensic econs. cons., San Luis Obispo, from 1976. Pres. Calif. Ctrl. Coast chpt. Mended Hearts, Inc., Arroyo Grande, 1983—84. Mem.: Am. Acad. Econ. and Fin. Experts, Nat. Acad. Econ. Arbitrators, Nat. Assn. Forensic Economists (charter mem., West regional dir. 1986—87, v.p. 1988—92, pres. from 1995), Western Soc. Scis. Assn., Atlantic Econ. Assn., Western Econ. Assn., Am. Rehab. Econs. Assn. (exec. bd. dirs. 1992—94), Am. Econ. Assn., Nat. Assn. Uniform Svcs. (life), Aircraft Owners and Pilots Assn. (life), Ret. Officers Assn. (life), White Sands Pioneer Group (life), Alpha Tau Omega, Delta Sigma Pi, Omicron Delta Epsilon. Home: San Luis Obispo, Calif. Died May 23, 1996.

**ADAMS, NORMAN,** artist, educator; b. London, Feb. 9, 1927; s. Albert Henry Adams and Winifred Elizabeth Rose; m. Anna Teresa Butt, 1947; two children. Student, Royal Coll. Art, London, 1948-51. Tchr. St. Albans, Maidstone, Hammersmith Art Schs., 1952-61; head painting Manchester Coll. Art and Design, England, 1962-71; prof. fine art U. Newcastle Upon Tyne, 1981-86; keeper of schs. Royal Acad. Arts, London, 1986-95, prof. painting, 1986-99, prof. emeritus, 1999—2005. Public collections include Tate Gallery, London, Scottish Nat. Gallery Modern Art, Edinburgh, Ulster Mus., Belfast, No. Ireland, Nat. Gallery New Zealand, Wellington, Ctrl. Gallery, Peter Scott Gallery-Lancaster U.; commns. include St. Mary's Roman Cath. Ch., Manchester, 1995, St. Anselms Ch., Kensington, London, 1972, Our Lady of Lourdes Roman Cath. Ch., Milton Keynes, 1975; illustrator: (written by Glyn Hughes) Alibis and Convictions, 1978, (written by John Milner) A Decade of Painting, 1971-81, 1981, (written by A. Adams) Angels of Soho, 1988, Island Chapters, 1991, Life on Limestone, 1994. Avocations: art, music, literature. Home: Yorkshire, England. Died Mar. 9, 2005.

**ADAMS, VICKI PORTER,** computer publications specialist; b. Wheeling, W.Va., Apr. 10, 1939; d. Clyde Scott and Helen (McClure) Porter; m. Theodore Cecil Adams, Nov. 20, 1971. BE, Waynesburg Coll., 1961; postgrad., W.Va. U., 1962. Elem. tchr. L.A. Bd. Edn., 1961—63; tchr. jr. H.S. Thousand Oaks Unified Sch. Dist., Calif., 1963—66; computer programmer Sys. Devel. Corp., Santa Monica, Calif., 1966—70; sr. programmer NCR Corp., San Diego, 1971—75, sr. cons. publs. specialist, 1978—83; mem. staff testing Litton Mellonics, San Diego, 1975—76; mgr. tech. publs. TRW Comms., San Diego, 1976—78; feature writer Centre City News, 1983—88. Cons., writer, spkr. in field. Contbr. articles to mags. Pub. rels. mem. Crime Victims Fund, DAR. Recipient Cert. of Achievement scholarship, Nat. U., San Diego, 1982. Mem.: San Diego Rep. Businesswomen, Nat. Fedn. Press Women, Calif. Press Women. Republican. Methodist. Died Apr. 1996.

**ADAMS, WILLIAM H.,** chemist, physicist; b. Balt., Dec. 21, 1933; s. William H. and Mary Ellen Adams; m. Sandra S. Sebastian, May 17, 1986; children: Maryna N. Powell, Hans-Thomas S. Hoffmann. PhD, U. Chgo., 1960. Asst. prof. chemistry Pa. State U., University Park, 1962—66, Rutgers U., New Brunswick, NJ, 1966—69, assoc. prof. chemistry, 1969—74, prof. chemistry, 1974—99, prof. emeritus, from 1999. Home: New Orleans, La. Died Apr. 22, 2008.

**ADEGBUYI, OLATUNDE,** geologist, geochemist, educator; b. Ijebu-Igbo, Nigeria, Dec. 2, 1954; s. Solomon Mofolorunso and Racheal Asabi (Suleiman) A.; m. Omowumi Olayide Oriola, Jan. 16, 1992; children: Oluwatosin Emmanuel, Oluwatobi Rebecca, Oluwadamilola Samuel, Oluwafunmito Esther. BSc with honors, U. Ibadan, Nigeria, 1978, MSc in Mineral Exploration, 1981; diploma in geothermal energy tech., U. Auckland, New Zealand, 1989. Sr. geologist Nat. Steel Raw Materials Agy., Kaduna, Nigeria, 1979-85; lectr. II Ogun State U., Ago-Iwoye, Nigeria, 1985-91; lectr. II/I Ondo State U., Ado-Ekiti, Nigeria, from 1991. Assoc. lectr. Fed. U. Tech., Akure, Nigeria, 1990-91, 98-99. Co-author: Ancient Banded Iron Formations, 1990, Advances in Geology and Geophysics Research in Africa, 1998. Mem. Nigeria Mining and Geosci. Soc., Assn. Geoscientists for Internat. Devel., Internat. Assn. Geochemistry and Cosmochemistry. Avocations: reading, praying. Deceased.

**ADELMAN, MORRIS ALBERT,** economist, educator; b. NYC, May 31, 1917; m. Millicent Linsen Adelman, Nov. 23, 1949. BSS, CCNY, 1938; PhD in Economics, Harvard U., 1948. Economist War Prodn. Bd., Washington, 1941—42; prof. economics MIT, Cambridge, 1948—2013. Author: A&P: Cost Price Behavior and Public Policy, 1959, The Supply and Price of Natural Gas, 1962, The World Petroleum Market, 1972, The Genie Out of the. Lt. USN, 1942—46, PTO. Recipient Mineral Economics award, AIME, 1979. Mem.: Internat. Assn. Energy Economists (Energy Economics award 1981), American Econ. Assn. Home: Auburndale, Mass. Died May 8, 2014.

**ADIYODI, KENOTH GOVINDAN,** academic administrator, biologist; b. Peralam, Kerala, India, Feb. 18, 1937; s. Kavil Kambrath Govinda Poduval and Lakshmi Kenoth Pillayathiriamma; m. Rita Gomez, Dec. 15, 1966; children: Nirmal, Laxmi. BS in Zoology with honors, Madras U., India, 1958; MA in Zoology, Madras U., 1968; PhD in Reproductive Physiology, Kerala U., 1970. Lectr. Karnataka U., Mangalore, India, 1958-59, Madras U., Calicut, 1959-60, Kerala U., Calicut, 1961-64; reader Calicut U., 1970-77, prof. invertebrate reproductive physiology, 1977-94, dean Faculty of Sci., 1989-92; vice-chancellor Cochin U. of Sci. & Tech., Kerala, 1994-96; mem. union pub. svc. commn. Govt. India, New Delhi, 1996—2001. Founder, sec. Kerala Sastra Sahitya Parishad, India, 1962-65; vis. scientist U. Oxford, 1973, 77-78, U. Köln, 1973, U. Paris, 1973; founder, pres. Desiya Sastra Vedi, Nat. Sci. Forum, 1986-94; pres. Kerala Biotechnology Consortium, 1995—. Founder/editor-in-chief: Internat. Jour. of Invertebrate Reprodn., 1979-83; editor/author: Reproductive Biology of Invertebrates, Vols. I-VIII; contbr. numerous articles to profl. jours. and publs. Recipient M.P. Paul prize, 1965, ISIR Found. award, 1979, Man of Yr. award Am. Biog. Inst., 1997. Mem. Internat. Soc. Invertebrate Reprodn. (hon., sec. gen. 1975-86), Indian Soc. Invertebrate Reprodn. (pres. 1975-86), Indian Soc. Comparative Endocrinology (v.p. 1979), Indian Soc. Comparative Animal Physiology (v.p. 1994—). Hindu. Avocations: writing, music, pub. speaking, rural devel., sci./technology. Home: Chelambra, India. Died 2001.

**ADKINS, TERRY ROGER,** artist; b. Washington, May 9, 1953; BS, Fisk U., 1975; MS, Ill. State U., 1977; MFA, U. Ky., 1979. Instr. Norfolk (Va.) State U., 1981; artist-in-residence The Studio Mus. in Harlem, N.Y.C., 1982, Spl. Arts Svcs. NYSCA, N.Y.C., 1988; studio artist Nat. Program Public Sch. 1, Queens, N.Y., 1984; guest artist KOPROD Internat., Zurich, 1989, Calif. State U. at Humboldt, Arcata, Calif., 1995; vis. prof. Calif. State U., Chico, 1991; guest lectr. U. Calif., Davis, 1991, Montclair (N.J.) State Coll., 1992, U. Pa., Phila., 1993, Brown U., Providence, 1994; vis. artist Learning Through Art Program, Guggenheim Mus., N.Y.C., 1993; Falk vis. artist Weatherspoon Gallery, U. N.C., Greensboro, 1993; asst. prof. SUNY, New Paltz, N.Y., 1993-96, assoc. prof., 1996-2014 One person shows include James Wise Gallery, Norfolk State U., 1980, Arts and Humanities Ctr., Richmond, Va., 1981, Galerie Emmerich-Baumann, Zurich, 1987, Liz Harris Gallery, Boston, 1988, Galerie Andy Jllien, Zurich, 1989, Valencia C.C., Miami, 1990, Anderson Galery, Va. Commonwealth U., Richmond, 1991, LedisFlam, N.Y.C., 1992, The Chrysler Mus., Norfolk, 1993, The Hammonds House Gallery, Atlanta, 1995, Whitney Mus. Am. Art, 1995, William Benton Mus. Art, Storrs, Conn, 1997, N.J. State Mus., 1998, Sculpture Ctr., N.Y.C., 1998; represented in group exhbns. Miss. Mus. Art, Jackson, 1980, Kenkeleba Gallery, N.Y.C., 1983, 89, 92, William Patterson Coll., Wayne, N.J., 1984, The High Mus., Atlanta, 1984, The Clocktower, N.Y.C., 1984, Longwood Arts Project, N.Y.C., 1986, Salama-Caro Gallery, London, 1987, Kulturhaus Palazzo, Basel, 1987, Projekt Binz 39, Zurich, 1987, Galerie Emmerich-Baumann, Basel, 1987, S.E.C.C.A., Winston-Salem, N.C., 1989, 91, Bermans Van Eck Gallery, N.Y.C., 1989, Williams Coll. Mus. Art, 1989, The Meml. Arch, Prospect Park, Bklyn., 1990, Studio Mus. in Harlem, N.Y.C., 1990, 95, Washington Project for Arts, Washington, 1980, 90, LedisFlam, N.Y.C., 1990, 91, Carnegie Mellon Art Gallery, Pitts., 1991, The New Mus. Contemporary Art, N.Y.C., 1991, Dart Gallery, Chgo., 1991, Philippe Briet, N.Y.C., 1991, U. Wis., 1992, Hunter Mus. Art, Chattanooga, 1992, Franklin Parrasch Gallery, N.Y.C., 1992, Cin. Contemporary Arts Ctr., 1992, Orlando (Fla.) Mus. Art, 1992, Hillwood Art Mus., Brookville, N.Y., 1992, 93, Snug Harbor Cultural Ctr., S.I., N.Y., 1993, David Klein Gallery, Birmingham, Miss., 1993, Mus. for African Art, Brookville, 1994, Cleve. Ctr. for Contemporary Art, 1994, John Berggruen Gallery, San Francisco, 1994, Exit Art, N.Y.C., 1994, Mus. Arti Et Amicitiae, Amsterdam, 1995; represented in permanent collections Met. Mus. Art, N.Y.C., Hirshhorn Mus. and Sculpture Garden, Washington, High Mus. Art, Atlanta, Chrysler Mus., Norfolk, The New Sch., N.Y.C., Bank Julius Bar, Zurich, Fisk U., Nashville, Tougaloo (Miss.) Coll., Atlanta Life Ins. Co., AT&T, N.Y.C.; performances at Wash. Project of the Arts, Washington, 1981, U. Cin. Sch. Fine Arts, 1982, New Music America Festival, Washington, 1983, P.S. 1 Inst. Art and Urban Resources, N.Y.C., 1985, Kulturzentrum Rote Fabrik, Zurich, 1987, The Inst. Contemporary Art, London, 1988, Koprod Internat., Zurich, 1989, Rigiblick Theatre, Zurich, 1989, Valencia C. C. Black Box Theatre, Orlando, Fla., 1990, Hall of Sci., N.Y.C., 1991, Calif. State U., Chico, 1991; featured in numerous newspapers, mags. and catalogues. Fellow Va. Mus., 1980, Nat. Endowment for Arts, 1986, SECCA 7, 1989, Joan Mitchell Found., 1994, artist exch. fellow

Projekt Binz 39, Zurich, 1986, Jesse Howard, Jr. & Jacob H. Lazarus Metrop Mus Art Rome Prize, American Acad. in Rome, 2010 Home: Brooklyn, NY. Died Feb. 8, 2014.

**ADLER, BILL, JR.,** writer; b. NYC, Dec. 1, 1956; s. William Jay and Gloria G. A. BA, Wesleyan U., 1978; MIA, Columbia U., 1980. Congl. lobbyist Americans for Democratic Action, Washington, 1981-82; dir. Nuclear Control Inst., Washington, 1982-83, ind. political cons., 1983-86, ind. writer book packager, 1986—2014; with Adler & Robin Books, Inc., Washington. Authors: (with Arnie Kogan) What to Name Your Jewish Baby?, 1966, (with Thomas Chastain) Who Killed the Robins Family?, 1983, The Home Buyer's Guide, 1984, The Student's Memory Book, 1988, The Lottery Book, 1986, What Is A Cat: To Everyone Who Has Ever Loved a Cat, 1987, Cat's Letters to Santa, 1995; editor: The Wit and Humor of Richard Nixon, 1969, The Wit and Wisdom of Wall Street, 1985 Mem. Author's Guild, Washington Ind. Writers (pres. 1988-89). Democrat. Avocations: backpacking, cross country skiing. Home: Washington, DC. Died Feb. 28, 2014.

**ADLER, MARGOT SUSANNA,** journalist, radio producer, correspondent, writer; b. Little Rock, Apr. 16, 1946; d. Kurt Alfred and Freyda (Nacque) A. BA in Political Sci., U. Calif., Berkeley, 1968; MS, Columbia U. Graduate Sch. Journalism, 1970. Newscaster Sta. WBAI-FM, NYC, 1968-71, host talk show, 1972-90; chief Washington bur. Pacifica News Svc. Network; corr., prodr. All Things Considered, Morning Edit., Nat. Public Radio, NYC, 1978—2014, host Justice Talking, 1999—2008. Instr. radio comms. Goddard Coll., Plainfield, Vt., 1977; instr. religion and ecology Inst. for Social Ecology, Vt., 1986-93. Author: Drawing Down the Moon: Witches, Druids, Goddess-Worshippers, and Other Pagans in America Today, 1979, Heretic's Heart: A Journey Through Spirit and Revolution, 1997, Out for Blood, 2013, Vampires Are Us: Understanding Our Love Affai With the Immortal Dark Side, 2014; co-prodr., dir. (radio drama) War Day, 1985; contbr. articles to prof. jours. Nieman fellow Harvard U., 1982. Mem. Phi Beta Kappa. Avocations: swimming, bird watching, science fiction. Home: New York, NY. Died July 28, 2014.

**ADLER, RICHARD MELVIN,** architect, planner; b. NYC, Mar. 25, 1928; s. Jacob William and Betty (Uffer) A.; children: Robin Sheryl, Joy Lois; m. Marie Fusco, 1986. BArch, Pratt Inst., Bklyn., 1948. Registered architect, N.Y., others. Airport architect Port Auth. N.Y., 1952-58; ptnr. Brodsky Hoff & Adler, NYC, 1959-71; pres. BHA Architects & Engrs., NYC, 1971-75, Brodsky & Adler, NYC, 1975-80, R.M. Adler & Assocs., Peterborough, N.H., from 1993. Pres. Adler, Goodman A Kolab For Architects & Engrs., Great Neck, 1993—; chmn. bd. Geller Termotto & Adler, Teaneck, N.J., 1982—, Clendening Adler, Arlington, Tex., 1983—. Elected to budget com., Peterborough, 1998—; chmn. capital improvement com. Town of Peterborough, 1996—. Served to 1st lt., N.Y. Nat. Guard, 1948-63. Recipient Disting. Svc. award Engrs. News Record, 1974, Creative Design award ASCE, 1973. Mem. AIA (emeritus; Merit award 1977, bd. dirs. L.I. chpt. 1988), N.Y. Soc. Architects, Peterborough C. of C. Republican. Roman Catholic. Home: Peterborough, NH. Died July 9, 2012.

**ADMANI, ABDUL KARIM,** physician; b. Palitana, India, Sept. 19, 1937; s. Haji Razzak and Hajiani (Rahima) A.; children: Nadim, Nilofer. Student, Gujarat U.; BSc with honors, Karachi U.; MB BS, U. London. Tchr. Health Authority, from 1970; clin. lectr. Sheffield Med. Sch., from 1972; dir. Ranmoor Grange Nursing Home Ltd., 1975-80; chmn. Sunningdale Yorks Ltd., from 1983; county pres. BRCS, from 1982. Mem. exec. com. for racial equality in Sheffield, 1972-92, chmn., 1978—; exec. com. BMA, Sheffield, 1974—; gen. med. coun. in U.K., 1979-93; mem. Ctrl. com. of cons. and specialists in U.K., 1979-93; exec. com. Age Concern Sheffield, 1982-90, Sheffield Health Authority; chmn. ODTS of ODA, 1982—, Inst. of Transcultural Health Care in U.K., 1992—, Glen Eagle Nursing Home Ltd., 1993—; pres. Muslim Coun. of Sheffield Rotherham and Dists., 1978-94, Union of Pakistani Orgns., U.K., Europe, 1979-93. Editl. bd. Pakistan Med. Bull., 1974-94, Medi-Scene, 1981-94, ODA News Rev., 1985-96, Ethnicity & Health, 1996—; med. editor East Newspaper, London, 1996—. Active Mgmt. Com. Pakistan Muslim Ctr, Sheffield, 1986, J.P. Justice of the Peace For City of Sheffield, 1974—; chmn. Pakistan Enterprise Ctr., 1993—. Decorated Order of British Empire. Fellow Overseas Drs. Assn. (chmn. edn. and postgrad. tng. com. 1978—), British Med. Assn., Coll. of Physicians and Surgeons, Pakistan Enterprize Coun. Ltd. (chmn. 1993—), Royal Coll. Physicians (London), Edinburgh, Glasgow, Royal Soc. Medicine, Coll. Physicians & Surgeons Bangladesh, British Med. Assn.; mem. Abbeydale Rotary (pres. 1995—), Conservative Club, Medico-Chirurgical Soc. Avocations: tennis, ping pong/table tennis, snooker, chess. Died June 18, 2004.

**AGERBEK, SVEN,** mechanical engineer; b. Soerabaya, Dutch Indies, Aug. 2, 1926; came to U.S., 1958, naturalized, 1964; s. Niels Magnus and Else Heidam (Nielsen) Agerbek-Poulsen; m. Helen Hadsbjerg Gerup, May 30, 1963; 1 child, Jesper. MSME, Tech. U., Denmark, 1952; LLB, LaSalle Ext. U., 1967; postgrad., UCLA, 1969. Registered profl. engr., Calif., Ohio, Fla. With Danish Refrigeration Rsch. Inst., Copenhagen, 1952; engr. B.P. Oil Co., Copenhagen, 1952-54; refrigeration insp. J. Lauritzen, Copenhagen, 1954-56; engr. Danish-Am. Gulf Oil Co., Copenhagen, 1956-58; instr. Ohio U., Athens, 1958-60; asst. prof. Calif. State Poly. U., San Luis Obispo, 1960-62; prin. engr. dept. environ. Ralph M. Parsons Co., LA, 1962-73; engring. supr. Bechtel Power Co., Norwalk, Calif., 1973-85; pres., owner Woodcraft Cabinets, Inc., Rancho Cordova, Calif., 1985-90; owner Acrebrook Cons., Fair Oaks, Calif., from 1990; exec. v.p. U.S.E., Inc., Incline Village, Nev., from 1994. Past mem. Luth. Ch. coun., pres. Luth. Sch. bd. With Danish underground movement, WWII. Mem. ASHRAE (mem. tech. com., author Guide on Air Conditioning of Nuclear Power Plants), Danish Engring. Soc. Deceased.

**AGRÉ, BERNARD CARDINAL,** cardinal, archbishop emeritus; b. Monga, Côte d'Ivoire, Mar. 2, 1926; s. Jean Manda and Jeanne Yomin Agré. JCD summa cum laude, Pontifical Urbaniana U., Rome, 1960. Ordained priest, Abidjan, Côte d'Ivoire, 1953; headmaster, tchr., dir. of sch. Dabou, 1953—56; rector Pre-Seminary, Bingerville, Côte d'Ivoire, 1956—57; pastor Notre Dame parish, Treichville, Côte d'Ivoire, 1960—62; vicar gen. Abidjan, 1963—68; bishop of Man, Côte d'Ivoire, 1968—92, ordained, 1968; bishop of Yamoussoukro, Côte d'Ivoire, 1992—94; archbishop of Abidjan, Côte d'Ivoire, 1994—2006, archbishop emeritus, from 2006; elevated to cardinal, 2001; cardinal-priest of San Giovanni Crisostomo a Monte Sacro Alto (Saint John Chrysostom in Monte Sacro Alto), 2001—14. Chmn. Pan-African Episcopal Com. for Social Comm., 1972—96; pres. Episcopal Conferences of Francophone West Africa, 1985—91; mem. of the Com. of the Great Jubilee of the Year 2000; pres. delegate for the 10th Ordinary General Assembly of the Synod of Bishops, 2001. Roman Catholic. Died June 9, 2014.

**AGUSTIN, CARLOS L.,** transportation executive, retired military officer; b. Manila, Dec. 13, 1937; s. Carlos Gonzales and Macaria (Leong) A.; m. Imelda Dizon, June 12, 1965; children: Cecile, Carla, John Paul, Christine. BS, U.S. Naval Acad., 1960; MBA, Ateneo U., Manila, 1978. Commdg. officer various naval vessels, 1970-73; chief internat. affairs J5 AFP, Quezon City, The Philippines, 1973-75, chief plans J2, 1975-76, chief ops. J2, 1976-80; chief of staff, dep. comdt. Philippine Coast Guard, Manila, 1980-85; def. attache Philippine Embassy, Washington, 1985-88; chief pers. J1 Armed Forces of the Philippines, Quezon City, 1988-90; comdt. Philippine Coast Guard, Manila, 1990-93; gen. mgr. Philippine Ports Authority, Manila, 1993-98. Chmn. editl. bd. Maritime Rev., 1993—; editor Cavalier Mag., 1980-85. Mem. Army and Navy Club (Manila, pres. 1985, bd. dirs. 1983-85), Camp Aguinaldo Tennis Club (pres. 1989-92), Orchard Golf Club, Maritime League (pres. 1990—). Roman Catholic. Avocations: golf, tennis, swimming, diving. Home: Dasmarimas, Philippines. Deceased.

**AHLSTEN, STIG AKE GUSTAF,** dental surgeon; b. Linkoping, Sweden, Feb. 15, 1913; s. Nils and Hulda (Lundh) A.; m. Ann-Mari Helsinger, Aug. 16, 1941; children: Anders, Gustaf, Olof, Gunnar, Karin. Dental Surgeon, Dental Sch. Stockholm, 1935, Master Exam., 1939. Cert. oral surgery, oral prosthetics, Sweden. Asst. prof. Dental Sch., Stockholm, 1935-39, assoc. prof., 1939-43; cons. dental surgeon St. Gorans Hosp., Stockholm, 1936-46; dental adminstr. Pub. Dental Svc., Uppsala, 1943-79; chief dental surgeon, head oral surgery dept. Univ. Hosp., Uppsala, 1944-79; rep. dental surgeon Dental Care Ins., Uppsala, 1973-93. Master in odontology for med. students Faculty of Medicine, Uppsala U., 1949-80. Editor Jour. Odontological Soc., 1939-56; author 2 books and numerous papers in dentistry. Recipient Medal of Merit, Swedish Red Cross, 1940; decorated Cross of Liberty, Order of Finland, 1942; knight comdr. Swedish North Star Order, 1973. Mem. Swedish Dental Fedn. (exec. mem. pub. co. 1982-90), Swedish Oral Surgery Assn., Uppsala Med. Soc., Odontological Soc. Stockholm (hon.), Swedish Soc. Dental Adminstrs. (hon.). Died Mar. 9, 2002.

**AHMANN, DONALD HENRY,** technical management consultant; b. Struble, Iowa, Jan. 9, 1920; s. Henry Francis and Philomene (Wictor) A.; m. Anne Harriet Harvey, Sept. 12, 1945; children: Richard, Carol, Rebecca, Sarah, Kathryn, Elizabeth. BS, Iowa State U., 1941, PhD, 1948. Jr. chemist Manhattan Project, Iowa State U. and AEC, Ames, 1942-48; chemist GE, Schenectady, 1948-57, mgr. chemistry Vallecitos Lab., Pleasanton, Calif., 1957-67, mgr. materials and tech. nuclear systems program Cin., 1967-69, mgr. engring. neutron devices dept. Largo, Fla., 1969-85; tech. mgmt. cons., Largo, from 1985. Commr. City of Belleair Bluffs, Fla., 1985-87, mayor, 1987-91; commmitteeman Pinellas County Republican Com., 1985—; mem. Mayors Coun. Pinellas County. Mem. Am. Chem. Soc., Am. Soc. Metals, Am. Nuclear Soc., Suncoast League Municipalities (pres. 1989-90). Died Mar. 25, 2008.

**AHMED, IAJUDDIN,** former president of Bangladesh; b. Mushinganj Dist., Bangladesh, Feb. 1, 1931; s. Moulvi Muhammad Ibrahim; m. Anwara Begum; children: Sujan, Adam, Imtiayz. BS, Dhaka U., 1952, MS, 1954, Wis. U., 1958, PhD, 1962. Asst. prof. dept. soil sci. Dhaka U., Bangladesh, 1963—64, assoc. prof., 1964—73, prof., 1973—73, provost Salimullah Muslim Hall, 1975—83, chmn. dept. soil sci., 1968—69, 1976—79, dean faculty biol. sci., 1989—90, 1990—91; adv. Caretaker Govt., 1991; chmn. Pub. Svc. Commn., 1991—93, U. Grants Commn., 1995—99; vice chancellor State U. Bangladesh, 1999—2002; pres. Govt. of Bangladesh, Dhaka, Bangladesh, 2002—09, interim prime min., 2006—07. Vis. prof. Cornell U., 1983, German Tech. U., Berlin, 1984, Gatinzens U., 1984. Contbr. articles to profl. jours., newspapers. Recipient Ibrahim Meml. Gold medal, 1987—88, Sri Gjyan Atish Dipanker Gold medal, 1990, Crest award, 1991, Ekushey award Edn., 1995. Mem.: Asiatic Soc., Bangladesh Soil Sci. Assn., Indian Soil Sci. Assn., Internat. Soil Sci. Assn., Combined Tchrs. Movement (convenor 1990), Dhaka U. Tchrs. Assn. (pres.), Fedn. U. Tchrs. Assn. Died Dec. 10, 2012.

**AHREND, HERBERT G.,** advertising agency executive, consultant; b. NYC, Sept. 16, 1913; s. David H. and Martha (Herschmann) S.; 1 child, Marcia Lynn BA, Columbia U., 1935. Cert. bus. communicator. Pres. D.H. Ahrend Co., NYC, 1940-50; pres. Ahrend Assocs., Inc., NYC, 1950-87. Author: You and World Peace, 1945; contbr. articles to profl. jours. Chmn. Manhattan Block Orgn., Civilian Def. Vol. Orgn., N.Y.C., 1944-45 Recipient numerous awards from Direct Mktg. Assn. and other mktg. assns. Mem. Direct Mktg. Assn. (chmn. 1st and 2d Interdisciplinary Confs. on Interrelations of Gen. Advt. and Direct Response Techs. 1983, 85, past chmn. Bus.-to-Bus. council), Bus. and Profl. Advt. Assn. (past chmn. nat. direct mail com.), Mktg. Communications Exec. Assn., Mktg. Execs. Club N.Y. (vice chmn. 1982—), Direct Mktg. Club N.Y. (vice chmn. 1971-72) Died Nov. 1987.

**AIGNER, LUCIEN L.,** writer, photographer; b. Ersekujvar, Hungary, Sept. 14, 1901; came to U.S., 1939; s. Adolf and Carola (Stern) A.; m. Anne Lenard, Nov. 19, 1932 (div. 1953); children: John, Steven, Anne-Marie Rowan, Katherine Collins; m. Mildred A. Allen, July 2, 1955. Student, Prague U., Czechoslovakia, 1920, Friedrich-Wilhelm U., Berlin, 1921-22; LLB, U. Budapest, Hungary, 1924; postgrad., Columbia U., 1942, Winona Sch. Photography, 1957. Co-owner, editor ARAL Press, Paris; dir. art Petit Jour., Paris; writer, announcer, dir. prodn. Voice of Am., NYC, 1947-53; owner The Aigner Studios, Gt. Barrington, Mass., from 1955; pres. emeritus Lucien Aigner Mus., Inc., from 1987, chmn. adv. bd. Author: Are We to Disarm, 1931; co-author illustrator autobiography Lucien Aigner, 1979, Aigner's Paris, 1982; exhibited in one-man shows at Internat. Mus. Photography, Rochester, N.Y., 1973, Internat. Ctr. Photography, N.Y.C., 1979, Musee Carnavalet, Paris, 1981-82, Kunsthaus, Zurich, 1985, Musee de l'Elysee, Lausanne, 1986, Mus. Modern Art, Stockholm, 1982, Nagase Photo Salon, Tokyo, 1982; contbr. articles to mags., newspapers internationally. Recipient Leica award, 1936, Art Dir.'s award, 1941, Good Citizen award Freedom Inc., 1958, Nat. Endowment Arts, 1975, 77; named Chevalier French Order Arts and Letters, 1986. Mem. Profl. Photographers Am. (life, master). United Ch. Christ. Lodge: Rotary (former chmn. Internat. Student Exchange). Avocations: filmmaking, poetry, writing, drama. Home: Trumbull, Conn. Died Mar. 29, 1999.

**AISENBERG, ALAN C.,** retired physician, educator, researcher; b. NYC, Dec. 7, 1926; s. Jacob and Celia (Able) A.; m. Nadya Margulies, Oct. 2, 1952 (dec. Apr. 1999); children: James, Margaret. SB, Harvard U., 1945, MD, 1950; PhD, U. Wis., 1956. Diplomate Am. Bd. Internal Med. Internship and resident Presbyn. Hosp., NYC, 1950-53; instr. medicine Harvard Med. Sch., Boston, 1956-62, asst. prof., 1962-69, assoc. prof., 1969-84, prof., 1984—2012; asst. physician Mass. Gen. Hosp., Boston, 1959-69, assoc. physician, 1969-84, physician, 1984—2012. Mem. Clin. Trials Com. Nat. Cancer Inst., Bethesda, Md., 1977-82. Author: Glycolysis and Respiration of Tumors, 1961, Malignant Lymphoma: Biology, Natural History and Treatment, 1991; contbr. over 150 articles on rsch. in oncology to profl. jours. Recipient Guggenheim Fellowship, Guggenheim Found. Nat. Inst. for Med. Research, London, 1964-65. Mem. Am. Coll. of Physicians, Am. Soc. of Clin. Oncology, Am. Assn. Immunologists. Home: New York, NY. Died Oct. 27, 2013.

**AITMATOV, CHINGIZ TOREKULOVICH,** writer; b. Sheker Village, Kirghizia, USSR, Dec. 12, 1928; s. Aitmatov Torekul and Nahima Aitmatov; m. Keres Shamshibaev, Oct. 15, 1951 (div.); 3 children; m. Maria Urmatov, Aug. 8, 1981. Degree in Animal Husbandry, Kirghiz Agrl. Inst., Frunze, USSR, 1952; postgrad., Lit. Inst., Moscow, 1956-58. Asst. to sec. Village Soviet, Sheker Village, 1943-52; corr. Pravda, Moscow, 1958-64; first sec., chmn. Cinema Union of Kirghizia, Frunze, 1964-85; chmn. Writers' Union of Kirghizia, Frunze, 1985—2008; editor-in-chief Inostrannaya Lit. Jour., Moscow, 1988—2008. Author: A Difficult Passage, 1956, Face to Face, 1957, Jamila, 1962, Tales of Mountains and Steppes, 1963 (Lenin prize 1963), Farewell, Gulsary, 1966 (state prize 1968), The White Ship, 1966, The Ascent of Mt. Fuji, 1973, A Day Lasts More Than A Hundred Years, 1980, The Scaffold, 1988 Recipient The Gold Olive Br. The Mediterranean Culture Rsch. Ctr., 1988, The Acad. award of the Japanese Inst. of Oriental Philosophy, Tokyo, 1988, Austrian State Prize for European Lit., 1994. Mem. Acad. of Scis. of Kirghizia (full), European Acad. of Arts and Sci., World Acad. of Sci. and Arts, Club of Rome. Mem. Communist Party of the USSR. Avocations: swimming, horse riding, hist. rsch. of Middle Asia. Died June 10, 2008.

**AIZAWA, YOSHINORI OR HISASHI,** law educator; b. Matsushima-cho, Miyagi, Japan, June 25, 1915; s. Suekichi and Haruno (Kayaba) A.; m. Yoshiko Masumoto, July 16, 1937; m. Koko Takeuchi, June 21, 1945 (dec. Dec. 1993). LLB, Tokyo U., 1941; LLD, Tohoku U., Japan, 1962. Asst. prof. Fukushima (Japan) Nat. U., 1953-57, Sophia U., Tokyo, 1958-63, prof., 1964-86, prof. emeritus, from 1986, chief postgrad. law sch., 1975-76, dean law dept., 1977-78. Rschr. Cologne (Germany) U., 1964-65; vis. prof. Ateneo de Manila U., 1980, De LaSalle U., 1985-86; lectr. Bonn. U., 1988, Nat. Saitama U., 1988-2003; mem. The Coun. Religious Corp. of Japanese Govt., 1972-82; mem. rep. conf. Cause of Separation of Religion and Politics, 1984-94. Author: Religion and Politics in the Present State, 1966, A Critical Study of Current Theories on the Japanese, 1976, State and Religious Organizations, 1977, Gypies, An Introduction, 1980, Jurisprudence and Political Science, An Interdisciplinary Study, 1986, Viewpoints of the Japanese People, 1987, Gypsies, Sufferers and Wanderers, 1989, Roma, Viewed in Anthropology, 1996, Experience of a Too Straightforward Man in Wartime, 1998, A Simple and Too Honest Man, 60 Years for Peace, 2002, Speed, Deliberation and Peace, 2005, also 58 treaties, 7 transls., and 6 collaborations. Mem. rescue operation of the atom bomb victims.

Sgt. Japanese Infantry, 1942-43. Recipient spl. prize of the jury in reciting contest for Goethe poems, Tokyo, 1987, 3d Order of Merit, 1988. Mem. Peace-loving Christian Soc., Religious Law Rsch. Assn. (bd. dirs. 1980-96). Avocations: reciting poems, hiking. Home: Tokyo, Japan. Died Apr. 1, 2007.

**AIZENBERG, NAUM N.,** science researcher; b. Kiev, Ukraine, Sept. 2, 1928; s. Nison G. and Genya N. A.; n. Svetlana B. Brodetskaya, July 15, 1958; 1 child, Igor. MA, Kiev Pedagogical U., Ukraine, 1949; PhD, Belorussian State U., Minsk, Belarus, 1963; DS of Elec. Engring., St. Petersburg U., Russia, 1975. Tchr. secondary sch., Uzhgorod, Ukraine, 1949-53; asst. prof. State U. Uzhgorod, Ukraine, 1958-63, assoc. prof., 1963-75, prof., 1975-99; scientific cons. Neural Networks Techs. Ltd., Ramat-Gan, Israel, from 1999. Vis. prof. Tampere U. Tech., Finland, 1997-98. Author: Multiple-Valued Threshold Logic, 1977, Multi-valued and Universal Binary Neurons: Theory, Learning and Applications, 2000. Avocation: swimming. Home: Tel Aviv, Israel. Died June 4, 2002.

**AJAMI, FOUAD,** professor of middle eastern studies; b. Arnoun, Lebanon, Sept. 19, 1945; arrived in US, 1963, naturalized; m. Michelle Ajami. Ed., Eastern Org. Coll.; PhD in Internat. Relations and World Govt., U. Washington. Rsch. fellow The Lehrman Inst.; fellow Ctr. Internat. Studies Princeton U., prof. Dept. Politics, 1973—80; dir. Middle East Studies Program Johns Hopkins U. Paul H. Nitze Sch. Advanced Internat. Studies, Washington, 1980—2011, Majid Khadduri prof., 1980—2011; sr. fellow The Hoover Instn., 2011—14. Contbg. editor US New & World Report; contbr. on Middle Eastern issues and contemporary internat. history NY Times Book Rev., Fgn. Affairs, The New Republic, Wall Street Jour.; mem. edit. bd. Middle East Quarterly; bd. adv. Fgn. Affairs jour.; bd. dirs. Coun. Fgn. Relations. Author: The Arab Predicament: Arab Political Thought and Practice Since 1967, 1981, The Vanished Imam: Musa Al-Sadr and the Shia of Lebanon, 1986, Beirut: City of Regrets, 1988, The Dream Palace of the Arabs: A Generation's Odyssey, 1998, The Foreigner's Gift: The Americans, The Arabs and the Iraqis in Iraq, 2006. Recipient Nat. Humanities Medal, NEH, 2006; MacArthur Prize fellowship arts and sciences, 1982—87. Muslim. Died June 22, 2014.

**AKERS, JOHN FELLOWS,** retired information processing company executive; b. Boston, Dec. 28, 1934; s. Kenneth Fellows and Mary Joan (Reed) A.; m. Susan Davis, Apr. 16, 1960; children: Scott, Pamela, Anne. BS, Yale U., 1956. With IBM Corp., 1960—71, exec. asst to Frank T. Cary Armonk, NY, 1971—76, pres. data processing divsn., 1974—76, v.p., asst. group exec. plans & controls, 1976-78, v.p., group exec. data processing mktg. group, 1978—81, sr. v.p., 1982-83, group exec. Info. Systems and Communications Group, 1981-82, pres., 1983—85, pres., CEO, 1985—86, chmn., pres., CEO, 1986—89, chmn., CEO, 1989—93. Bd. dirs. N.Y. Times Co., 1985-2006, IBM Corp., 1983-93, PepsiCo., 1991-2007, Lehman Brothers Holdings, Inc., 1996-2008, W.R. Grace & Co., 1997-2014 Trustee Met. Mus. Art, Calif. Inst. Tech., United Way; Lt. USNR, 1956-60. Died Aug. 22, 2014.

**AKTAR, A.S. (ART AKTAR),** civil engineer, consultant; b. Istanbul, Turkey, Sept. 11, 1933; arrived in U.S., 1954; s. Mehmet Fuat and Zerafet Aktar; m. Muriel Steusloff, Jan. 11, 1956; children: Murat, Alev, Sinan. BSCE, Stanford U., 1958; MBA, U. Santa Clara, Calif., 1962. Registered profl. engr., Calif., N.Y. Design engr. Western Knapp Engring. Co., 1958-61; structural design engr. Utah Constrn. & Mining Co., 1961-63; job engr., project estimator, project mgr., mgr. project controls Bechtel Corp. and Bechtel Pacific Corp. Ltd., 1963-71; project mgr., v.p. engring. and procurement Nat. Bulk Carriers Inc., 1971-76; founder, pres. Techno-Econ. Cons., Inc., NYC, from 1977. Arbitrator in maritime, comml., constrn. and internat. fields; cons. on major internat. natural resource constrn. projects and mineral investment promotions; condr. seminars in field. Contbr. articles to profl. jours.; author section "Mine Evaluation" in McGraw-Hill Ency. of Sci. and Tech., 6th and 7th edits. Mem. NSPE, ASCE, AIME, Mining and Metall. Soc. Am., Am. Assn. Cost Engrs., Am. Arbitration Assn., Soc. Maritime Arbitrators, The Assembly of Turkish Am. Assns. (trustee), Galatasaray Alumni Assn. of U.S.A. (dir., pres.). Republican. Home: Ridgewood, NJ. Deceased.

**ALAM, AKHTER-UL,** editor; b. Tajnagor, Bangladesh, Feb. 22, 1939; s. Shah Abul Kasem and Ramisa Khatun; m. Rezina Begum Akhter, Aug. 22, 1962; children: Rezwan, Fahmida, Sazed. Diploma in Journalism, U. Dhaka, Bangladesh, 1963, MA in Journalism, 1970. Asst. editor, columnist Daily Azad, Dhaka, 1967-72, Daily Ittefaq, Dhaka, 1972-85, editor-in-charge, from 1985. Asst. editor Daily Paigam, Dhaka, 1965-67; editor-in-charge Monthly Mohammodi, Dhaka, 1960-62; v.p. Bangladesh Co-op. Bank, Dhaka, 1985-88; bd. dirs. Bangladesh Sangbad Sangstha, Dhaka, editorial writer Daily Azad, 1962-65; chmn. Rangpur Publs. Ltd. Author 22 books; translator 10 books; contbr. over 100 articles to periodicals. Pres. Shaujan Kalyan Samity, Dhaka, 1985—; dir. Info. Bur. Internat., 1974—; founding mem. Bangla Coll., Dhaka, Abu Dhar Gifari Coll., Dhaka. Named Hon. Citizen Gov. of Nebr., 1982; recipient Gold award Comilla Found., 1987, Islamic Found. award, 1988, Rangpur Trust award, 1988; 8 others. Mem. Bangladesh Co-op. Book Soc. (dir. 1986—), Asia Soc. N.Y. Muslim. Avocations: poetry, short stories and essays, feature writer and announcer for radio bangladesh. Home: Dhaka, Bangladesh. Deceased.

**ALAM, SULTAN SALAHUDDIN ABDUL AZIZ HISHAMUDDIN,** Sultan of Selangor; b. Istana Bandar, Kuala Langat, Malaysia, Mar. 8, 1926; s. Sultan Hisamuddin 'Alam Shah; m. Raja Saidatul Hisham, 1943; 7 children; m. 2d, Tengku Rahimah, 1956; 2 children. Student, Malay Coll., Kuala Langsar, 1936-41, Sch. Oriental and African Studies, U. London, 1947. Pres. Council of Regency, Selangor, 1952. Regent, 1960; sultan of Selangor, 1960-2001; col. Royal Malaysian Air Force, 1966; chancellor U. Agr. Malaysia, 1977; dep. paramount ruler Malaysia, 1994-99, paramount ruler, 1999-2001. Died Nov. 21, 2001.

**ALANIS, JOAN MARTÍ,** bishop; b. Nov. 29, 1929; Ordained priest, 1951; bishop Diocese of Urgell, Spain, 1971—2003, archbishop, 2001—03, bishop emeritus, 2003—09; also co-prince Urgel, Andorra. Died Oct. 11, 2009.

**ALBANESE, LICIA,** retired operatic soprano; b. Bari, Italy, July 22, 1913; d. Michele and Maria (Rugusa) Albanese; m. Joseph Gimma, Apr. 7, 1945 (dec. 1990). Studied with Giuseppina R. Baldassare Tedeschi, Milan, Italy, 1932-35; MusD cum laude, St. Peters U., Jersey City; LLD (hon.), Seton Hall U.; LHD (hon.), Manhattan Coll., Fairfield U., Conn., Caldwell Coll., NJ, Marymount Manhattan Coll., U. South Fla.; DFA (hon.), Siena Coll., Loudonville, NY; degree (hon.), Montclair State Coll. Leading artist Metropolitan Opera NY, 1940—66; singer San Francisco Opera, 1941—61. Mem. adv. council 3d St. Music Sch. Settlement; trustee Bagby Music Lovers Found., NYC; chmn. Puccini Found., NYC. Performer (made an unexpected debut): in role of Madame Butterfly, (when the leading soprano became ill), 1934; performer: (formal debut) at Royal Theater; performer: Madame Butterfly; rec. (with Beniamino Gigli) La Boheme, 1939, 1939; singer: concert in honor of Sir Neville Chamberlin and Lord Halifax, 1939, Covent Garden for the Festival of King George VI, (Operas) (debut) Met. Opera House, in Madame Butterfly and La Traviata, 1940. Bd. dirs. Rose Ponselle Found., 1987. Decorated Lady Grand Cross Order Holy Sepulchre Order of Merit of Italy; recipient Nat. Medal Arts, The White House, 1995, Handel Medallion, NYC, 2000. Achievements include singing at inauguration of Vatican City radio station and was decorated by Pope Pius XI. *As stairs are not meant for standing or resting, but for reaching a higher level, so must you see in the early steps of your education their upward thrust toward the beauties of life's future, with the challenges and opportunities which await you at the top, if only you do not rest in reflection upon the past, but, looking daringly ahead, keep climbing and, through education, reap the golden harvest of your dreams.* Died Aug. 15, 2014.

**ALBERIGO, GIUSEPPE,** religious studies educator; b. Varese, Italy, Jan. 21, 1926; s. Giovanni and Eugenia (Banfi) A.; m. Angela Nicora, Jan. 7, 1950; children: Anna, Stefano, Paola. Jurisprudence, Cath. U., Milan, Italy, 1948; Ecumenical Theology, Evang. Faculty of Theology, Munchen, Germany, 1990, Cath. Faculty Theology, Strasbourg, France, 1996, Cath. Faculty, Münster, Germany, 1999. Full prof. U. Modena, Italy, 1951-54; lectr., full prof. U. Florence, Italy, 1954-67; univ. prof. U. Bologna, Italy, 1967—2001, professor emeritus, from 2002. Sec. gen. Istituto Per Le Scienze Religiose, Bologna, 1962—, Found. per le Scienze Religiose "Giovanni XXIII", Bologna, 1990—, Cath. Hist. Rev., Wash., Rev. des Scis. Religieuses, Strasbourg, France; assoc. editor Concilium, Nijmegen, Olanda, 1980-95; editor sci. jour. Cristianesimo Nella Storia, Bologna, 1980—. Author: (book) I Vescovi Italiani al Concilio, 1959, Cardinalato e Collegialita', 1969, Chiesa Conciliare, 1981, Dalla Laguna al Tevere: Angelo Giuseppe Roncalli da San Marco a San Pietro, 2000, Breve storia del Concilio Vaticano II (1959-1965), 2005, Breve historia del Concilio Vaticano II (1959-1965), 2005; editor: (book) Conciliorum Oecumenicorum Decreta, 1962, 73, Les Concīles Oecumeniques, 1994, Concilium, 1996, Giuseppe Dossetti: Per una Chiesa Eucaristica Rilettura della Portata Dottrinale della Costituzione Liturgica del Vaticano II, 2002, L'Officina bolognese!! 1953-2003, 2004; dir. The History of Vatican II, 1959-65, 1995-01. Recipient Living Water award, Cardinal Suenens Ctr., 2005. Home: Bologna, Italy. Died June 15, 2007.

**ALBERT, GERALD,** retired clinical psychologist; b. NYC, Nov. 13, 1917; s. Andrew I. and Eleanor (Walder) A.; divorced; m. Norma Holm Haskell, 1983 (dec. 2004); children: Jay Harvey, Laurie Ellen Albert Moxham. BA, CCNY, 1938; MA, New Sch. for Social Research, 1958; EdD, Columbia U., 1964; Cert. psychoanalytic tng. program, L.I. Inst. Mental Health, Queens, NY, 1964. Editor Vulcan and Creston Pubs., NYC, 1939-45; nat. dir. advt., pub. relations Universal Pictures, div. ednl. films, NYC, 1945—50; exec. dir. Advt. Enterprises and Continental Research Inst., Queens, NY, 1951-64; asst. to full prof. LIU, 1964-85, prof. Emeritus, from 1985; dir. L.I.U. C.W. Post Counseling Ctr., 1964-70. Psychologist, supervising psychologist, clin. dir. L.I. Consultation Ctr., 1966-86, clin. cons., 1986-95; pvt. practice marriage and individual therapy, 1958-2007. Author: (cassette) How To Choose and Keep a Marriage Partner, 1980, (book)The Wonderful Magic of No-Fault Living, 1990, Japanese edit., 1996, (feature series for website) Making Your Marriage Work Better, 2001-02; editor-in-chief Jour. Contemporary Psychotherapy, 1985-87; editor: CCNY Humor Mag., 1938; contbr. 30 articles to profl. jours. Recipient 1st prize Most Effective Comms./Newsletters Cmty. Agys. Pub. Rels. Assn., 1983, named LI Marriage and Family Therapist of Yr., 1995. Fellow Am. Assn. for Marriage and Family Therapy (founder L.I. recorded telephone series "Helpful Hints for Happier Marriage" 1995, contbr. to webpage, 2001); mem. APA, Am. Soc. for Psychical Rsch., Nat. Coun. Family Rels., Soc. Clin. and Exptl. Hypnosis, Soc. Sci. Exploration, Internat. Soc. for Study of Subtle Energy and Energy Medicine, Inst. Noetic Scis. Died Dec. 2013.

**ALBERTY, ROBERT ARNOLD,** retired chemistry professor; b. Winfield, Kans., June 21, 1921; s. Luman Harvey and Mattie (Arnold) Alberty; m. Lillian Jane Wind, May 22, 1944 (dec.); children: Nancy Lou, Steven Charles, Catherine Ann. BS, U. Nebr., 1943, MS, 1944; PhD in Chemistry, U. Wis., 1947; DSc (hon.), U. Nebr., 1967, Lawrence U., 1967. Engaged in rsch. blood plasma fractionation for U.S. Govt., 1944—46; faculty mem. U. Wis., 1946—67, prof. chemistry, 1955—67, assoc. dean letters & sci., 1961—63, dean Grad. Sch., 1963—67; prof. chemistry MIT, 1967—91, dean Sch. Sci., 1967—82, prof. emeritus, 1991—2014. Cons. NSF, 1958—83, NIH, 1962—72; chmn. commn. on human resources NRC, 1974—77; dir. Colt Industries, 1978—88, Inst. for Def. Analysis, 1980—86; pres. phys. chemistry divsn. Internat. Union Pure and Applied Chemistry, 1991—93. Co-author: Experimental Physical Chemistry, 1970, Thermodynamics of Biochemical Reactions, 2003, Physical Chemistry, 2005. Recipient Eli Lilly award in Biological Chemistry, 1955; fellow Guggenheim, Calif. Inst. Tech., 1950—51. Fellow: AAAS; mem.: NAS, American Acad. Arts & Sciences (coun. 1991—94), American Chem. Soc. (chmn. com. on chemistry and pub. affairs 1978—80), Inst. Medicine, Sigma Xi, Phi Beta Kappa. Home: Cambridge, Mass. Died Jan. 18, 2014.

**ALBERY, NICHOLAS,** social inventor, editor; b. St. Albans, U.K., July 28, 1948; s. Donald and Heather (Boys) A.; m. Josefine Speyer, May 19, 1991; 1 child, Merlyn. BA, N.E.L.P., 1985; diploma, Inst. Psychotherapy and Social Studies, 1986. Dir. Natural Death Ctr., London, from 1991; gen. sec. Coun. for Posterity, from 1993; editor Global Ideas Bank (www.globalideasbank.org), from 1994; dir. ApprenticeMaster Alliance, from 1994, Poetry Challenge, U.K., from 1995; chair Inst. for Social Inventions, London, from 1985. Editor Social Inventions Jour., Poem for the Day; editor: Book of Visions-An Encyclopedia of Social Innovations, 1993, New Natural Death Handbook, 1997, Creative Speculations, 2000, Time Out Book of Country Walks, 1997, 1,001 Health tips, 1999, Social Dreams and Technological Nightmares, 1999, The Book of Inspirations, 2000; editor DoBe.org participative events website, 2000—. Recipient Award Schumacher Soc., 1994. Avocations: learning a poem for every day of the year, walking with friends. Died June 3, 2001.

**ALBINAK, MARVIN JOSEPH,** chemistry educator; b. Detroit, June 21, 1928; s. Alfred S. and Katherine (Smulson) A.; m. Gloria Ann Galamb, Aug. 26, 1961; children: Stephen, Anne, Alexandra. AB, U. Detroit, 1949, MS, 1952; PhD, Wayne State U., 1959. Rsch. chemist Ethyl Corp., Detroit, 1952-54; instr. to asst. prof. U. Detroit, 1954-58, 59-61; rsch. fellow Wayne State U., Detroit, 1958-59; sr. rsch. scientist Elec. Autolite Corp., Toledo, Ohio, 1961-62; rsch. chemist Owens-Ill., Inc., Toledo, 1962-65; asst. to assoc. prof. Wheeling (W.Va.) Coll., 1965-68; assoc. prof. to prof. chemistry and adminstr. Essex Community Coll., Balt., 1968-96, prof. emeritus, 1997. 7 U.S. patents; contbr. articles to profl. jours. Mem. Am. Chem. Soc., Sigma Xi, Phi Lambda Upsilon. Democrat. Avocations: music, theater, books, environmental activities. Deceased.

**ALBRECHT, GERD,** conductor; b. Essen, Germany, July 19, 1935; m. Friederike Sailer (div.); m. Ursula Schoffler; children: Katharina, Judith. Studied at Hamburg Music Acad., Germany, 1955—58. Korrepetitor Stuttgart State Opera, Germany, 1958—61; prin. condr. Mainz City Orch., Germany, 1961—63; music dir. Kassel Staatsoper, 1966—72; prin. condr. Berlin Deutsche Opera, 1972—77, Tonhalle-Orch. Zurich, Switzerland, 1975—80; music dir. Hamburg State Opera, Germany, 1988—97; prin. condr. Czech Philharmonic Orch., 1993—96, Yomiuri Nippon Symphony Orch., Tokyo, 1998—2007, Danish Nat. Radio Symphony Orch., 2000—04. Died Feb. 2, 2014.

**ALBRECHT, KARL HANS,** retired retail and recreational facility executive; b. Essen, Germany, Mar. 28, 1922; s. Karl and Anna Albrecht; m. Mia Tenbrink (dec.); 2 children. Prin., owner, 1948; co-founder Albrecht KG, 1961; founder Aldi Market, Dortumund, Germany, 1962; mng. ptnr. Aldi South; co-CEO Aldi Group, 1962—2001, ret., 2001. Served in Germany Army, WWII. Named one of The World's Richest People, Forbes mag., 2004—14. Catholic. Avocations: golf, orchids. Died July 16, 2014.

**ALESANA, TOFILAU ETI,** former Samoan Prime Minister; b. Vaitogi, Am. Samoa, June 4, 1924; s. James Enoka and Vaoita Aiono (Mala'itai) A.; m. Pitolua Toomata; 14 children. Grad., Maluafou H.S., Western Samoa. Br. mgr. I.H. Carruthers, Ltd., 1949-57; minister of health Govt. of Western Samoa, Apia, 1959-61, mem. pub. svc. commn., 1961-64, prime minister, minister of fin., 1982-85, prime minister, 1988—98. Minister in charge of exec. coun., cabinet, atty. gen.'s office, legislative dept., transport control bd., ombudsman's office, rural electrification com., pub. svc. assn., Western Samoa TV Corp., Alpea, 1988—. Exec. Police, Prisons and Fire Svc. Depts., Broadcasting, Fgn. Affairs, Immigration, Pub. Rels., Official Info. and Govt. Printing. Died Mar. 19, 1999.

**ALEXANDER, JANE TYLOR FIELD,** retired secondary education educator, writer; b. Whittier, Calif., May 31, 1915; d. Archibald Ray and Agnes (Withey) Tylor; m. Clifton Harold Field, Sept. 1, 1938 (dec. Oct. 1985); children: Pamela Field West, Melinda Field Bus, D. Robin Field; m. Luther Allen Alexander, July 14, 1988. BA, U. So. Calif., 1935; MA, San Diego State U., 1963. Lifetime secondary tchg. credential, Calif. Tchr. El Centro (Calif.) City Schs., 1936-41, San Diego City Schs., La Jolla, Calif., 1942-44, San Diego City Coll., 1958-61, Sweetwater Unified H.S. Dist., Chula Vista, Calif., 1961-75. Author, photographer: Naked Ladies and Other California Garden Exotica, 1994; editor classroom tips NEA Jour./Today's

Edn., 1965-80; contbr. articles to popular mags. V.p., pres. El Centro Jr. Women's Club, 1938-41; co-leader, leader Girl Scouts Am., Salt Lake City and La Mesa, Calif., 1952-56; pink lady hosps., Highland Park, Ill. and La Mesa, 1957-70; mem. Silverwood com. San Diego Audubon Soc., 1981-95; bd. dirs., pres. Buena Vista Audubon Soc., Oceanside, Calif., 1993-96; mem. Zero Population Growth. Mem. AAUW (edn. chair, pres. 1982-85, sec. 1994-95), Defenders of Wildlife, Sierra Club, Wilderness Soc., Nature Conservancy (life), Project Wildlife, Common Cause. Avocations: writing, birdwatching, piano, swimming, bridge. Deceased.

**ALEXANDER, LINCOLN MACCAULEY,** retired Canadian provincial official; b. Toronto, Ont., Can., Jan. 21, 1922; s. Lincoln MacCauley and May Rose (Royale) A.; m. Yvonne Harrison, Sept. 10, 1948 (dec. 1999); 1 son, Keith; m. Marni Beale, 2011 BA, McMaster U., 1949; grad., Osgoode Hall Law Sch., 1953; LLD, McMaster U., 1987, U. Western Ont., 1988. Bar: Ont. 1953, Queen's Counsel 1966. Ptnr. Millar Alexander Tokiwa & Isaacs, Hamilton, Ont.; elected to House of Commons, 1968, 72, 74, 79, 80; min. labour Govt. of Canada, 1979-80; chmn. Ont. Workers Compensation Bd., 1980-85; lt.-gov. Province of Ont., 1985—91. UN observer, 1976, 78. Author: Go to School, You're a Little Black Boy: The Honourable Lincoln M. Alexander: A Memoir, 2006. Past pres. Assn. Workers Compensation Bds. Can., 1980-85. Served with RCAF, 1942-45. Decorated knight Order St. John, Knight of the Mil. & Hospitaller Order St. Lazarus of Jerusalem; recipient St. Ursula award, 1969; named Man of Yr., Ethnic Press Council, 1982; recipient Cultural Achievement award Caribana Cultural Com., 1984, Cert. of Service award House of Commons, 1984, Silver Acorn Boy Scouts of Can., 1988, Outstanding Citizen award Kiwanis Found., 1989; Mel Osborne fellow Kiwanis Found., 1989. Mem. Hamilton Lawyers Club, Wentworth County Law Assn., Can. Bar Assn. Clubs: Optimists, Hamilton Cricket. Conservative. Baptist. Avocations: music, gardening. Died Oct. 19, 2012.

**ALEXANDER, UREY WOODSON,** retired military officer; b. Owensboro, Ky., Sept. 10, 1915; s. Hamilton and Elizabeth Ford (Woodson) Alexander; m. Ella Marie Cain, June 27, 1944; children: Urey Woodson, Buford C., Marie E.(dec.). BS in Engring., U.S. Mil. Acad., 1940; MA in Internat. Affairs, George Washington U., 1961; grad., U.S. Command and Gen. Staff Coll., Armed Forces Staff Coll., U.S. Army War Coll.; LLD (hon.), Dickinson Sch. Law, 1980. Commd. 2d lt. U.S. Army, 1940, advanced through grades to col, 1954, comdr. 386 F.A. Bn. Europe, 1942—45, corps and arty. adv. Greece, 1949—50; sr. Army mem. Navy Spl. Devices Ctr., LI, 1950—53; U.S. Mil. attache Warsaw, 1955—57; mem. faculty U.S. Army War Coll., Carlisle, Pa., 1958—61, 1967—70, dir. instrn., 1968—70; comdr. Heavy Arty. Group Germany, 1961—63; force planner SHAPE, Paris, 1963—64; sr. army rep. Joint Targeting Staff, Omaha, 1964—67; ret., 1970; treas., bus. mgr. Dickinson Sch. Law, 1971—80; ret., 1980. V.p. Lake Meade Property Owners Assn., Adams County, RI, 1971—78. Decorated Bronze Star, Legion of Merit. Mem.: Assn. U.S. Army, Nat. Timberwolf Assn., Rotary (pres. Carlisle 1973—74, dist. gov. S. Central Pa. 1977—78). Democrat. Bapt. Home: Richardson, Tex. Died Jan. 1, 1998.

**AL-KHAWASHKY, MOHAMMAD ISHAQ AHMAD,** health organization representative, consultant; b. Jerusalem, Mar. 1, 1931; arrived in Saudi Arabia, 1957; s. Ahmad Yehya and Bahiya Tawfik Tamini Al-H.; m. Soheila Ameen Tamimi; children: Hazem, Mazen, Samer; m. Naela Hussein Murtagi, Oct. 27, 1985; m. Salwa Rizk Ibrahim, June, 1991. MB, Cairo U., 1956, diploma in medicine, 1975, D in Anesthesiology, 1977; diploma in anesthesiology, U. Copenhagen, 1961. Resident anesthesiology Ministry of Health, Riyadh, Saudi Arabia, 1958-60, anesthesiologist, 1962-64, chief anesthesiology dept., 1965-74, chief anesthesiology and intensive care depts., 1978-82, spl. advisor, exec. dep. minister, 1982-83; dir. gen. Riyadh Ctrl. Hosp., 1977-82; mem. Kasr El-Eini faculty medicine, coun. Cairo U., 1991—98. Bd. mem., cons. Faculty of Allied Health Scis., Riyadh, 1978—82; cons. road traffic accidents Arab Health Ministers of Gulf, Saudi Arabia, 1978—82; cons. Red Crecent, Riyadh, 1975—82; cons. Ea. Mediterranean Regional Office, WHO, Alexandria, Egypt, regional advisor orgn. health care svcs., 1983—89, rep., 1989—98, spl. advisor to regional dir., Cairo, from 1999. Author: Principles of Anaesthesia, 1978; assoc. editor: Saudi Med. Jour., 1980—81; contbr. articles to profl. jours. Recipient Outstanding Achievements in Traffic Medicine award Internat. Assn. Accident and Traffic Medicine, Helsinki, 1992, Egyptian Med. Syndicate Shield, 1996, Cert. of Appreciation and Recognition of Med. and Humanity Svcs., 1996. Mem. Saudi Anaesthetic Assn. (bd. dirs. 1990—), Club of Alexandria, Gezira Sporting Club, Alexandria Sporting Club. Muslim. Avocations: reading, music, tennis, walking. Home: Nasr City Cairo, Egypt. Died Aug. 12, 2006.

**ALLAIN, WILLIAM A. (BILL ALLAIN),** former Governor of Mississippi; b. Washington, Miss., Feb. 14, 1928; m. Doris Rush, Dec. 17, 1964 (div. 1970). Grad., U. Notre Dame; JD, U. Miss. Bar: Miss. 1950. Atty. private practice, Natchez, Miss., 1975—79; asst. atty. gen. State of Miss., Jackson, 1962—75, atty. gen., 1980-84, gov., 1984—88. Infantry US Army, Korean War. Mem.: ABA, Miss. Bar Assn., Hinds County Bar Assn., Civitan Club, VFW, Am. Legion. Democrat. Roman Catholic. Home: Jackson, Miss. Died Dec. 2, 2013.

**ALLEN, KEITH WILLIAM,** retired chemist, educator; b. Reading, England, Apr. 9, 1926; s. Clifford and Dora (Harding) A.; m. Marguerite Florence Woods, July 16, 1955; children: Paul, Mary, Elizabeth, Anne, Ruth. BSc, U. Reading, 1949; MSc, U. London, 1958; DSc, City U. London, 1994. Chartered scientist, chemist, physicist. Lectr. City Univ. London, 1949-83, dir. adhesion studies, 1984-92; vis. sr. rsch. fellow Oxford Brookes Univ., England, 1990-98, vis. prof., from 1998. Editor: (book series) Adhesion 1 - Adhesion 15, 1977-91; editl. bd. Internat. Jour. Adhesion & Adhesives, Materials Sci. and Tech.; contbr. articles to profl. jours. Elder, lay preacher United Reformed Ch. Livery of Worshipful Co. of Horners and Freeman, City of London; recipient meritorious svc. award Plastics and Rubber Inst. London, 1992, Ellinger-Gardonyi medal Oil & Colour Chem. Assn., 1999, Wake Meml. medal, 1999. Fellow Royal Soc. Chemistry, Inst. Materials (adhesives sect. com. 1971—); mem. Inst. Physics., Soc. Adhesion & Adhesives (founder mem., Wake medal 1999) Avocations: walking, reading, fishing. Home: Newbury, England. Died Sept. 2, 2007.

**ALLEN, LOUISE,** writer, educator; b. Alliance, Ohio, Sept. 21, 1910; m. Benjamin Yukl Allen, June 27, 1936; children: Katherine Anne Yukl Johnston, Kenneth Allen, Richard Lee, Margaret Louise Yukl Border. Student, Cleve. Coll., Western Res. U., 1963, Lakeland C.C., 1984. Co-founder sch. writing, Cleve., 1961—62; founder, dir. Allen Writers' Agy., Wickliffe, Ohio, 1963—84; editl. assoc. criticism svc. Writer's Digest Mag., 1967—69; instr. Cuyahoga C.C., from 1965; mentor Ohio, 1973—83; writer. Author: (poems) Confetti, 1987; contbr. articles to profl. mags.; composer: (songs) The Foot of the Cross. Mem.: Women's City Club (Cleve.), Nat. League Am. Pen Women, Women Comm., Assn. Mundial de Mujures Periodistas y Escritoras, Mensa, AAUW, Euclid Three Arts Club, Shore Writers Club (founder). Republican. Congregationalist. Home: Chandler, Ariz. Died July 18, 2001.

**ALLISON, JOHN MCCOMB,** retired aeronautical engineer; b. Guthrie, Okla., Nov. 27, 1901; s. John McComb and Mary Ann (Miller) A.; m. Dorothy Louise Olson, Nov. 15, 1931; children: John, Mary Ann, David. BSME, U. Ka., 1928. Design staff Stinson Tri-Motor Airliner, 1928-29; aeronautical engr. Akron, Macon rigid airships & nonrigids U.S. Naval Air Sta., Lakehurst, N.J., 1929-33; rsch. engr. Nat. Adv. Com. for Aeronautics, Langley Field, Va., 1933—38; flight test engr. USN Test Sta., Anacostia, 1938-39; evaluator flight test performance of new Navy aircraft Anacostia, Washington, 1938-39; Bur. Aeronautics rep. various aircraft mfg. plants USNR, 1939-46; head new Navy aircraft and guided missiles test dept. U.S. Naval Air Missile Test Ctr., Pt. Mugu, Calif., 1946-50; engr. missile devel. Bur. Ordnance, Washington, 1950-57; head specifications Goodyear Aircraft Corp., Akron, 1957-59; 69proposal engr., guided missiles Rockwell Internat. (now Boeing Aircraft), Columbus, Ohio, 1959; ret., 1969. Cons. light airplane constrn. Allison Airplane Co., North Miami, Fla., 1977-85; founder Langley Fed. Credit Union, 1936. Contbr. articles to profl. jours. Del. Nat. Rep. Planning Com., Washington, 1992. Capt. USN, 1939-46. Fellow AIAA (assoc.), Ox-5 Club. Immanuel Lutheran. Achievements include patents for disclosure for a retractable hydrofoil at the normal step position of a flying boat to improve take-off; private pilot, 1931-50. Died Sept. 19, 2003.

**AL MAZROUEI, MOHAMED ABDULLA,** information systems professional; b. Abu Dhabi, United Arab Emirates, Sept. 7, 1975; s. Abdulla Mohamed Al Mazrouei and Salamah Salem Al Qubaisi; m. Mahra Rashid Al Qubaisi, Dec. 2, 1999; 1 child, Rodah. B of Mgmt. Info. Sys., Higher Coll. Tech., Abu Dhabi, 1997. Sys. analyst Abu Dhabi Nat. Oil Co., 1994-96; assistance mgr. Abu Dhabi Investment Authority, from 1997. Avocations: reading, fishing, football, travel. Home: Abu Dhabi, United Arab Emirates. Died June 2004.

**ALMOND, CARL HERMAN,** surgeon, physician, educator; b. Latour, Mo., Apr. 1, 1926; s. Hugh Herman and Sylvia (Morrison) A.; m. Nancy Ginn, June 18, 1964 (div. 1990); children: Carrie, Callie, Carl, Christopher. BS, Washington U., St. Louis, 1949, MD, 1953. Diplomate Am. Bd. Surgery, Am. Bd. Thoracic Surgery. Rotating intern Los Angeles County Gen. Hosp., 1953-54; resident surgery U. Mich., Ann Arbor, 1954-56, jr. clin. instr. surgery, 1956-57, sr. clin. instr., 1957-58; fellow surg. pathology Barnes Hosp.-Washington U., St. Louis, 1956; sr. surg. resident in urology Baylor U. Affiliated Hosps., 1958-59; resident thoracic surgery U. So. Calif., Los Angeles, 1959, fellow thoracic surgery, 1962-63; staff surgeon Univ. Hosp., Columbia, Mo., 1959-78, dir. thoracic and cardiovascular surgery, 1968-77, VA Hosp., Columbia; fellow Brompton Hosp., London, Eng., 1961; asst. prof. surgery U. Mo. Sch. Medicine, Columbia, 1959-64, asso. prof., 1964-69, prof., chief thoracic and cardiovascular surgery, from 1969; prof. and chmn. dept. surgery Sch. Medicine, U. S.C., Columbia, 1978-85, dir. gen. surgery residency program, 1979-85, assoc. dean clin. research and devel., 1986-90. Vis. prof. U. Geneva, Switzerland, 1972—73; mem. med. adv. panel FAA, 1970—75; mem. U.S. Commn. on UNESCO, 1983. Contbr. articles to profl. jours. With USNR, 1944—52. Fellow ACS; mem. AMA, Boone County Med. Soc., Columbia Med. Soc., S.C. Med. Assn., S.C. Thoracic Soc., Am. Assn. Med. Colls., Frederick H. Coller Surg. Soc., St. Louis Surg. Soc., Am. Coll. Cardiology, Am., S.C. heart assns., Am. Soc. Artificial Internal Organs, Soc. Med. Cons. to Armed Forces, Am. Coll. Chest Physicians, So. Thoracic Surg. Assn., Central Surg. Soc., Am. Assn. Thoracic Surgery, So. Surg. Assn., S.C. Surg. Soc., Chest Club, Soc. Surg. Chairmen, Marion S. DeWeese Surg. Soc., Southeastern Surg. Soc., So. Surg. Soc., Internat. Cardiovascular Soc., Soc. Thoracic Surgeons, Sigma Xi, Nu Sigma Nu, Sigma Chi. Home: Columbia, SC. Deceased.

**ALONI, SHULAMIT,** retired Israeli government official; b. Tel Aviv, Nov. 29, 1928; widow; 3 children. Diploma, David Yellin Tchrs. Tng. Coll.; LLB, Hebrew U., Jerusalem. Mem. Mapai, 1959-64, Knesset, 1965-69, 1973, 77, 81, 1984, 1988, 1992—96, chair constnl. and legal com., 1973, chair basic laws com., 1981; min. without portfolio Govt. of Israel, 1974, 1993, min. edn. & culture, 1992-93, min. comm., 1993—96, min. sci. & the arts, 1993—96. Tchr., lawyer, journalist; prodr. radio program. Author numerous books on polit. and legal subjects. Founding chairperson Israel Consumers Coun., 1966. Recipient Emil Grunzweig Human Rights award, Assn. for Civil Rights in Israel, 1998, Israel prize, 2000. Mem. Civil Rights and Peace Movement (Ratz)-Meretz. Jewish. Died Jan. 24, 2014.

**ALSTED, PETER,** lawyer; b. Copenhagen, Jan. 13, 1934; s. Gunnar Alsted and Gerda (Salomonsen) Gudme; m. Alette Arntz, 1963 (div. 1981); children: Charlotte Solovej, Gregers, Michala; m. Lissi Hansen Rosendal, Oct. 21, 1982. Candidatus Juris, U. Copenhagen, 1958. Bar: Denmark, 1962. Sole practitioner law, Copenhagen, from 1964. Chmn., bd. dir. charitable founds., corps. and profl. soc.; sec.-gen. Danish Ins. Brokers Assn., 1980-89. Contbr. to Handbook on European Comty. Co. Law (amongst others), 1997, The Holding Co. and the Zero-tax Investor, 2000, The Ltd. Partnership in Internat. Tax Planning, 2002, articles in field. Mem. Union Internationale des Avocats (corr.), SAME (nat. bd. dir.), Danish Bar Assn., Internat. Tax Planning Assn., Soc. of Trust and Estate Practitioners. Home: Charlottenlund, Denmark. Died 2004.

**ALTENBERND, A(UGUST) LYNN,** educator; b. Cleve., Feb. 3, 1918; s. Adolf Carl and Lucy M. (Cheyney) A.; m. Mary Blazekovich, Apr. 19, 1941; children: Toni (Mrs. Andrew J. Gold), Mark, Nicholas. BS in Edn, Ohio State U., 1939, MA, 1949, PhD in English, 1954. Relief visitor, Cleve., 1939-42; tchr. English John Bryan High Sch., Yellow Springs, Ohio, 1942-44; supply clk. Wright-Patterson AFB, 1944, asst. buyer spl. aircraft Procurement div., 1946-48; instr. Ohio State U., 1949-54; mem. faculty U. Ill. at Urbana, 1954-84, prof. English, from 1965, head dept., 1966-71, assoc. dean. Grad. Coll., 1980-83. Cons. English Macmillan Pub. Co., 1963-76 Editor: (with Leslie L. Lewis) Introduction to Literature: Stories, Poems, Plays, 3 vols., 2d edit, 1969, Poems, 3d edit, 1975, Stories, 3d edit, 1980, Handbooks for the Study of Fiction, Poetry, Drama, 3 vols, 1966, Exploring Literature: Fiction, Poetry, Drama and Criticism, 1970, Anthology: An Introduction to Literature, 1977. Served to 2d lt. AUS, 1944-46. Mem. MLA, Nat. Council Tchrs. English Deceased.

**ALTSCHUL, B-J,** public relations counselor; b. Norfolk, Jan. 28, 1948; d. Lemuel and Sylva (Behr) A. Student, Goucher Coll., 1965-67; BA, U. South Fla., 1970; MA, U. Md., 1995. Cert. in exec. leadership Humane Soc. U., 2009, Public Rels. Soc. America. Reporter St. Petersburg (Fla.) Times, 1973—74; dir. pub. rels. Valkyrie Press, Inc., St. Petersburg, 1974—77; founding editor Bay Life, Clearwater, Fla., 1977—79, Tampa Bay Monthly, Clearwater, 1977—79; mng. editor Fla. Tourist News, Tampa and Orlando, 1981; founder Capital Comms. of Tampa, 1981; owner, prin. b j Altschul & Assocs. (formerly Capital Comms. of Tampa), from 1985. Mgr. editl. and info. svcs. Va. Pt. Authority, Norfolk, 1985-88; dir. pub. rels. Va. Dept. Agr. and Consumer Svcs., Richmond, 1988-93; adj. faculty Old Dominion U., Norfolk, 1986-88, U. Richmond, 1990, 94, Washington Ctr. Internships, 1995-96; mgr. pub. rels. U. Md. Biotech. Inst., 1997-99; lectr. dept. comm. U. Md., 1999-01; asst. prof. Am. U., 2001-06; adj. prof. U. Md., 2006-07, Duquesne U., 2010-; dir., external rels. Montgomery County Humane Soc., 2007-. Author: Cracker Cookin' & Other Favorites, 1984; contbg. author: Virginia: A Commonwealth Comes of Age, 1988. Bd. dirs. Pinellas County Big Bros.-Big Sisters, 1980-82, Fla. Folklore Soc., 1984-85, co-captain, LUNGevity Found., 2013, co-chair Montgomery County Animal Response Team, 2010-13, humane edn. amb. reader RedRover, 2008-11, Co-chair, environ. edn. com. Sierra Club, Montgomery County, 2004-08, Recipient Excellence award, Periodicals, Am. Assn. Port Authorities, 1986. Mem. Soc. Animal Welfare Administr.; Fla. Motion Picture and TV Assn. (treas. 1976-78), Hampton Rds. C. of C. (co-chmn. pub. rels. Internat. Azalea Festival 1986, chmn. publs. 1987), Va. Conf. on World Trade (chmn. pub. rels. com.), Downtown Norfolk Devel. Corp. (chmn. urban living com.), Pub. Rels. Soc. Am. (chmn. Mid.-Atlantic Dist. 1988, chmn. govt. sect. 1989, bd. dirs., chmn. chpt. accreditation, chmn. Univ. Rels. Nat. Capital chpt. 2002-06; Assembly Delegate 2011-2013), lifetime appointment Champions of PRSSA (2013), Va. State Agy. Pub. Affairs Assn. (pres. 1990), Internat. Assn. Bus. Communicators (v.p. mem. svcs. Richmond chpt. 1996), Nat. Assn. Sci. Writers, D.C. Sci. Writers Assn. (bd. dirs. 2004-06), Forum Agr. and Consumer Topics (founder, chmn. 1992), Sierra Club (mem. Montgomery County environ. edn. com. 2004-09), Soc. Animal Welfare Adminstrs., Assn. Profl. Humane Educators. Avocations: piano, sailing, music, dance. Died May 2014.

**ALTUKHOV, YURI PETROVICH,** geneticist, researcher; b. Elan'-Koleno, USSR, Oct. 11, 1936; s. Pyotr Kornilovich and Alexandra Mikhailovna (Andreeva) A.; m. Rimma Gerasimovna Domrina, June 19, 1958 (div. Jan. 1966); 1 child, Mikhael; m. Elena Pavlovna Volkova, Nov. 2, 1966; 1 child, Dmitry. MSc, Fisheries Inst., Moscow, 1959; PhD, Moscow State U., 1964; DSc, Russian Acad. Scis., Moscow, 1972. Jr. rschr. Karadag Biol. Sta., Krimea, Ukraine, USSR, 1959-62; sr. rschr. Moscow State U., 1964-67, disting. prof., from 1999; head lab. Marine Biology Inst. Russian Acad. Sci., Vladivostok, 1967-72, head lab. Gen. Genetics Inst., from 1972, prof. Gen. Genetics Inst., from 1976, dir. Gen. Genetics Inst., from 1992. Soros prof. Open Soc. Inst., NYC, from 1994; mem. adv. bd. jour. Selection, Evolution, Paris, 1993—97, Sarsia, Bergen, from 1997, Forest Genetics, from 1995. Author: Population Genetics of Fish, 1974 (diploma 1978), Genetics Processes in Populations, 1983, 89, 2003, Population Genetics: Diversity and Stability, 1990, Population Genetics of Salmonid Fishes, 1997, Salmonid Fishes: Population Biology, Genetics and Management., 2000, Dynamics of Population Gene Pools under Anthrpogenie Pressures, 2005, Interspecific Genetic Diversity: Monitoring, Conservation, and Management, 2005; inventor method of artificial propogation of local animal populations (Gold medal 1973); dep. editor-in-chief Russian Jour. Genetics, 1993—; editor-in-chief jour. Advances in Modern Biology, 1997—. Recipient State Sci. & Tech. prize, 1996; grantee Russian Found. Basic Rsch., 1993-2005, Internat. Sci. Found., 1994-95, Open Soc. Inst., Internat. Soros Sci. Edn. Program, 1994-97. Mem. Internat. Acad. Sci., Sci. Coun. for Genetics and Selection, Marine Biology Inst.-Russian Acad. Sci. (hon.), Vavilov Soc. for Genetics and Breeding (v.p. 1994—2004), Russian Acad. Scis. (academician 1997). Avocations: music, literature, philosophy, history. Home: Moscow, Russia. Died 2006.

**AMBACHE, NACHMAN,** medical researcher; b. Ismailia, Egypt, July 8, 1917; arrived in Eng., 1929; s. Simha and Lea (Steinberg) Ambache; m. Stella Cornes, Sept. 14, 1942; children: Jonathan(dec.), Jeremy, Diana. BA in Natural Scis., Trinity Coll., Cambridge, Eng., 1939. Lectr., pathology Guy's Hosp., London, 1943—47; lectr., physiology U. Coll., London, 1947—48; med. rsch. coun. staff Inst. Ophthalmology, London, 1948—59; external staff & dir. Med. Rsch. Coun. Royal Coll. Surgeons, London, 1959—82. Contbr. chapters to books & articles to profl. jours.; editor: Jour. Physiology, 1959—66, Brit. Jour. Pharmacology, 1967—71. Fellow: Royal Soc. Medicine; mem.: Brit. Pharm. Soc., Physiol. Soc. Avocations: music, violin. Home: Chislehurst Kent, England. Died Mar. 2, 2004.

**AMBADY, NALINI,** social psychologist, educator, researcher; b. Calcutta, India, Mar. 20, 1959; came to U.S., 1983; d. Shanker and Viji Ambady; m. Raj Marphatia, June 8, 1988; children: Maya Mallika, Leena Anupama. Bachelor's degree, U. New Delhi; MS in Psychology, Coll. William & Mary; PhD in Social Psychology, Harvard U., 1991. Asst. prof. Holy Cross Coll., Worcester, Mass., 1993-94, Harvard U., Cambridge, Mass., 1994-99, Ruth & John Hazel assoc. prof. social sci., 1999—2004; prof. social psychology Tufts U., Medford, Mass., 2004—11, Stanford U., 2011—13; founder Ctr. for Social Psychological Stanford U. Answers to Real World Questions, 2011—13. Recipient, Behavioral Sci. Rsch. prize AAAS, 1993, Presdl. Early Career award, The White House, 1998, Excellence in Mentoring Award, Harvard U., 2000. Home: Palo Alto, Calif. Died Oct. 28, 2013.

**AMBELAS, ARISTIDIS,** child and adolescent psychiatrist; b. Thessaloniki, Greece, Nov. 30, 1944; arrived in UK, 1973; s. Angelos and Dimitra A.; m. Chrysanthi Kosma, Dec. 26, 1971; children: Eugenia-Dimitra, Thetis-Eirini. BS, U. Thessaloniki, 1968, MD, 1985. Cons. child psychiatrist Nat. Health Svc., Coventry, UK, 1980-86, Leicester, UK, from 1986. Clin. tchr. U. Leicester, 1986—; founder West Midlands Inst. Psychotherapy, 1979; chair Child Psychiatry Regional Adv. Group, Trent, UK, 1990-96. Lt. Greek Royal Air Forces, 1969-71. Fellow Royal Coll. Psychiatrists. First worker to show link between life events and mania; also first to describe menstruation-linked psychosis of adolescents as a distinct syndrome and propose treatment regimens; significant contribution to debate as to whether there are preclinical manifestations for schizophrenia. Home: Oadby, England. Died Apr. 2004.

**AMBROSE, MYLES JOSEPH,** lawyer; b. NYC, July 21, 1926; s Arthur P. and Ann (Campbell) A.; m. Elaine Miller, June 26, 1948 (dec. Sept. 1975); children: Myles Joseph, Kathleen Anne, Kevin Arthur, Elise Mary, Nora Jeanne, Christopher Miller; m. Lorraine Genovese, June 3, 1994. Grad., New Hampton Sch., NH, 1944; BBA, Manhattan Coll., 1948, LLD (hon.), 1972; JD, NY Law Sch., 1952. Bar: NY 1952, US Supreme Ct. 1969, DC 1973, US Ct. Appeals (Fed. cir.) 1970, US Ct. Internat. Trade 1970, DC Ct. Appeals 1973. Pers. mgr. Devenco, Inc., 1948-49, 51-54; asst. US atty. (southern dist.) NY US Dept. Justice, NY, 1954-57; instr. economics & indsl. rels. Manhattan Coll., 1955-57; asst. to sec. US Dept. Treasury, 1957-60; exec. dir. Waterfront Commn. of N.Y. Harbor, 1960-63; pvt. practice law NYC, 1963-69; chief counsel NY State Joint Legislative Com. for Study Alcoholic Beverage Control Law, 1963-65; commr. customs US Customs Bur., Washington, 1969-72; spl. cons. to Pres., spl. asst. atty. gen. The White House, Washington, 1972-73; ptnr. Spear & Hill, 1973-75, Ambrose & Casselman, P.C., 1975—78, O'Connor & Hannan, Washington, 1978—88, Ross & Hardies, Washington, 1988—98; of counsel Arter & Hadden, Washington, 1998—2002; sr. advisor Sandler Travis Trade Adv. Svc., 2002—14. US observer 13th session UN Commn. on Narcotics, Geneva, Switzerland, 1958; chmn. US del. 27th Gen. Assembly, Internat. Criminal Police Orgn., London, 1958, 28th Extraordinary Gen. Assembly, Paris, 1959; US observer 29th Gen. Assembly, Washington, 1960; mem. US del., Mexico City, 1969, Brussels, 1970, Ottawa, 1971, Frankfurt, 1972; chmn. US-Mexico Conf. on Narcotics, Washington, 1960, mem. confs., Washington and; Mexico City, 1969, 70, 71, 72; chmn. US-Canadian-Mexican Conf. on Customs Procedures, San Clemente, Calif., 1970; chmn. US del. Customs Cooperation Coun., Brussels, 1970; chmn., Vienna, 1971, US-European Customs Conf. Narcotics, Paris and; Vienna, 1971; organized Drug Enforcement Adminstrn. (DEA), 1973; hon. consul Principality of Monaco, Washington, 1973-98; mem. adv. com. on customs comml. ops. US Dept. Treasury, 1988-91; past chmn. ABA standing com. on customs law. Author: Primer on Customs Law. Bd. dirs. U. Coll. Dublin-Grad. Bus. Sch., 1996-2001; bd. mem. Daytop Village; vice-chmn. Reagan-Bush Inaugural Com., 1980; mem. advisory bd. Eisenhower Inst. of World Affairs. Decorated chevalier Order of Grimaldi (Monaco), knight comdr. Order of Merit Italian Republic, Knight of the Holy Sepulchre; recipient Presdl. Mgmt. Improvement cert. Pres. Nixon, 1970, Sec. Treasury Exceptional Svc. award, 1970, Disting. Alumnus award NY Law Sch., 1973, Alumni award for Public Svc. Manhattan Coll., 1972 Fellow American Bar Found.; mem. Friendly Sons of St. Patrick, Univ. Club (DC), Alpha Sigma Beta, Phi Alpha Delta (hon.) Republican. Roman Catholic. Home: Leesburg, Va. Died June 3, 2014.

**AMERONGEN, GERARD JOSEPH,** retired Canadian government official; b. Winnipeg, Man., Can., July 18, 1914; s. Maximilian Ernest and Maria (Waas) Taets von Amerongen; m. Elizabeth Helen Fetherstonhaugh, Dec. 6, 1943; children: Mary, Peter, Margaret, Monica, Helen, Michael, Elizabeth, John. BA, U. Alta., Can., 1943, LLB, 1944. Bar: Alta. 1946; cert. queen's counsel 1966. Chmn., legis. internship adv. and selection com. Legis. Assembly Alta. for Edmonton-Meadowlark, chmn., members svcs. com., mem., 1971—86, spkr., 1971—86. Past pres. Progressive Conservative Assn. Alta.; mem., nat. exec. Progressive Conservative Assn. Can.; founding dir. Alta. Can. Native Friendship Ctr., pers. dir.; bd. dirs. Edmonton Hosps. Mem.: Law Soc. Alta. Home: Edmonton, Canada. Died Apr. 21, 2013.

**AMMON, R. THEODORE (TED AMMON),** food products executive; b. 1950; m. Generosa Ammon (dec.); 2 adopted children. Assoc. Kohlberg Kravis Roberts & Co., 1984—92; v.p. RJR Nabisco Inc., Atlanta, 1989; founder, CEO Big Flower Press (now Vertis Inc.), NYC, 1992, chmn. bd. Founder Ammon Found., 1988; chmn. jazz Lincoln Ctr. Died Oct. 22, 2001.

**AMOS, PAUL SHELBY,** retired insurance company executive; b. Enterprise, Ala., Apr. 23, 1926; s. John Shelby and Mary Helen (Mullins) A.; m. Mary Jean Roberts, Oct. 24, 1948; 1 child, Daniel P. Co-founder, v.p. American Family Life Assurance Co. (Aflac), Columbus, Ga., 1956-64, state mgr. Ala., 1964-74, 1st v.p., dir. mktg., 1974-78, pres., 1978-83, vice chmn., 1983-90, chmn., 1990—2001, chmn. emeritus, 2001—14; pres. American Family Corp., Columbus, 1981-83, vice chmn., 1983-90. Owner Ben Franklin Stores, Milton, Fla., 1946-66; ptnr., v.p. Service Oil Co., Milton, 1958-66; pres., chmn. First Fed. Savs. & Loan, Milton, 1957-74 Trustee Asbury Theol. Sem. With USCGR, 1944-46, PTO. Named to Worksite Mktg. Hall of Fame, Workplace Benefits Assn., 2010. Mem. Columbus Chamber of Commerce Clubs: Country of Columbus; Big Eddy. Republican. Methodist. Home: Columbus, Ga. Died July 2, 2014.

**ANARFI, ISAAC KWAME,** economic educator, researcher; b. Kumasi, Ghana, June 25, 1945; came to U.S., 1986; s. James Kofi and Ama Beatrice (Pepraa) Asiamah-Anarfi; m. Serwaa Twum, Jan. 1, 1984 (div. Sept. 1992); children: Pepraa, Kwae, Oduraa; m. Afia Agyeman Duah, Dec. 15, 1993. BA in Econs., U. Cape Coast, Ghana, 1973; MA in Internat. Affairs, Ohio U., 1987, PhD in Econ. Edn., 1991. Budget rsch. officer Ministry of Fin. and Planning, Accra, Ghana, 1973-74; sr. supt. edn. Ministry of Edn., Accra, Ghana, 1974-79; lectr. social scis. Kaduna State Coll. Edn., Kafanchan, Nigeria, 1979-86; instr. Ohio U., Athens, 1989-90, adj. asst. prof. Ctr. for Econ. Edn., 1992-94; asst. prof. Rsch. in Edn. CUNY, from 1995. Cons. African issues U.S.-African Sister Cities Inc., Washington, 1994—; guest lectr. African Studies Curriculum Outreach Project, Yale U., New Haven, Conn., 1994—; guest speaker U.S.-African Sister Cities Conf., Mansfield, Ohio, 1994. Editor: The Living Classroom, 1986; contbr. articles to profl. jours. Recipient grants and fellowships Ohio U., 1987-91. Mem. ASCD, Assn. for Econ. Educators, African Studies Assn., Econ. Soc. Ghana. Avocations: lawn tennis, basketball, jogging. Home: Bronx, NY. Died 1997.

**ANAWALT, HOWARD CLARKE,** lawyer, educator, writer; b. Seattle, Mar. 11, 1938; s. Howard and Francese Caroline (Clarke) A.; m. Susan Hodgman, Aug. 6, 1960; children: Bradley David, Paul David. BA in Polit. Sci., Stanford U., 1960; JD, U. Calif., Berkeley, 1964. Bar: Calif. 1965, Wash. 1992, U.S. Ct. Appeals (9th cir.) 1965, U.S. Supreme Ct. 1989. Legis. intern Calif. State Assembly, Sacramento, 1964-65; dep. atty. gen. State of Calif., Sacramento, 1965-67; ptnr. Ferrito, Ellis, Anawalt & Hill, Los Gatos, Calif., 1973-76; prof. law Santa Clara U., Calif., 1967—2003, prof. emeritus, from 2003. Vis. scholar U. Calif., 1979-80, Stanford U., 1986, U. Wash., 1993; mem. UNESCO cons. Bucharest, Romania, 1982, Francese Clarke Anawalt Meml. Scholarship Fund (Belize and Nigeria) 1987-. Author: Ideas in the Workplace, 1988, IP Strategy Complete Intellectual Property Planning, Access and Protection, 2004-; co-author: (with Enayati) 1991 Licensing Law Handbook, 1991, 94, Idea Rights-A Guide to Intellectual Property, 2011; contbr. numerous articles to profl. jours. Organizer Sacramento Town Meeting on Vietnam War, 1966, Bay Area Draft Lawyers Com., 1965-70; spl. counsel ACLU, San Jose, Calif., 1976-81; chair mental health com. Clara Bar Assn., 1975-77, chair computer law sect., 1990-93; bd. dirs. Los Gatos Teen Ctr., 1988-99; adv. bd. mem. Ctr. for Sci., Tech. and Soc., Santa Clara U., 1999-2001; bd. mem. San Jose Chamber Music Soc., 1999-2003. Fellow Intellectual Property Inst. Japan, Order of Barristers, Internat. House of Japan. Buddhist. Avocations: languages, gardening, photography, writing, hiking, music. Home: Los Gatos, Calif. Died Aug. 6, 2013.

**ANDERSON, G. ERNEST, JR.,** retired education educator; b. Newark, July 24, 1929; s. George E. and Gladys (Pomeroy) Anderson; m. Patricia Ruth Mottram, Dec. 28, 1957; children: Russell, Carol R. BA, Amherst Coll., 1950; M.A.T., Harvard U., 1955, EdD, 1964. Tchr. & coord., data processing Newton Pub. Schs., Mass., 1957—63; rsch. assoc. & tchg. asst. Harvard U., Cambridge, Mass., 1959—64; asst. prof. & project mgr., adminstrv. data sys. U. Del., Newark, 1965—67; mem., faculty U. Mass., Amherst, 1967—97, prof., edn., 1974—97, ret., 1997. Folio reader, bd. examiners Nat. Coun. Accreditation Tchr. Examiners; cons. Gen. Learning Corp. Yale U., RI U., Japanese Ministry Edn., Chinese Computer Fedn., 1977—2000. Editor: Ednl. Data Processing Newsletter, 1963—65; editl. bd. Jour. Assn. Ednl. Data Sys., 1965—90; contbr. articles to various publs. Troop leader Boy Scouts America, com. chmn., internat. high adventure tour organizer; leader Girl Scouts USA; mem. Cmty Rels. Com., New England Nat. Scenic Trail Adv. Coun., 2010. With USN, 1951—54. Recipient Silver Beaver award, Boy Scouts America, James E. West award, Lifetime Achievement award, Conn. Educators Computer Assn., 2006; named Vol. of Yr., Branford C. of C., Conn., 2005. Mem.: Branford Elec. Rlwy. Assn. (dir. 1998—2002, v.p. 2003), Conn. Electric Rlwy. Assn. (dir. 1978—85, treas. 1979—82), Mass. Soc. Profs. (sec. 1979—88), Internet Soc., Kidlink Soc., Assn. Computing Machinery, Psychometric Soc., Am. Ednl. Rsch. Assn., Internat. Soc. Tech. Edn. (founder, pres.), Green Mountain Club, Adirondack Mountain Club. Congregationalist. Home: Madison, Conn. Died Dec. 2013.

**ANDERSON, GAIL VICTOR,** obstetrician, gynecologist; b. Pensacola, Fla., Oct. 3, 1925; s. Parke Pleasant and Sarada M. (Thompson) A.; m. Alice Harriet Midghall, Nov. 6, 1923; children: Gail V. Jr., David C., Jerrold B., Walter P., Mark S. BA, BS, Columbia Union Coll., 1949; MD, Loma Linda U., 1953. Diplomate American Bd. Ob-Gyn. Resident in ob-gyn. D.C. Gen. Hosp., Washington, 1954-55, Georgetown U. Hosp., Washington, 1955-56; chief resident in ob-gyn. D.C. Gen. Hosp., Washington, 1956-57; dir. ob-gyn. L.A. County/U. Southern Calif. Med. Ctr., 1958-70; prof. ob-gyn. U. Southern Calif. Sch. Medicine, LA, 1968—2002, chmn. dept. emergency medicine, 1971—2002. Mem. South Pasadena Sch. Bd., 1971-77; cand. city coun. South Pasadena, 1980; dir. salerni Collegium, 1958-95, pres., 1992-93. Served in1946 USN, 1943—46. Hartford Found. grantee, 1964. Fellow ACS, ACOG; mem. American Bd. Emergency Medicine (founding pres. 1987-88), American Coll. Emergency Physicians (James D. Mills award for Outstanding Contribution to Emergency Medicine, 1996). Republican. Avocations: tennis, golf, travel. Home: South Pasadena, Calif. Died Sept. 6, 2014.

**ANDERSON, GEORGE W., JR.,** real estate executive, former diplomat, former career naval officer; b. 1906; Grad., U.S. Naval Acad., Annapolis, Md., 1927. Commd. ensign USN, advanced through the grades to chief of naval ops., 1963; navigator U.S.S. Yorktown; staff mem. to Comdr. Air Force Pacific Fleet USN, staff mem. to Comdr. in Chief U.S. Fleet, mem. joint war plans com.; comdr. U.S.S. Mindoro, U.S.S. Franklin D. Roosevelt; asst. to the chmn. joint chiefs of staff USN, chief of naval ops., 1961-63; amb. to Portugal, 1963-1966; ret., 1966; chmn. bd. The Lamar Corp., Baton Rouge, from 1972, TLC Properties Inc., Baton Rouge. Named Chief of Naval Ops. Appointed by Pres. Kennedy, 1961. Died Mar. 20, 1992.

**ANDERSON, MARGARET TAYLER,** real estate broker, career consultant; b. Castle Rock, Wash., May 1, 1918; d. George Lawrence and Frances Tressie (Huntington) Tayler; m. James Kress Anderson, Dec. 31, 1940; children: Bret Douglas, Blythe Rebecca Chase, Beth Lynn Murray, Burke Stuart. AB, Willamette U., 1939, MA, 1940, Colubmia U., 1967; profl. diploma, Columbia U., 1970; DHL (hon.), Dominican Coll. Blauvelt, 1991. Cert. English, social studies tchr., N.Y. Asst. travelling libr. Oreg. State Libr., Salem, 1940; chemist Reynolds Metals, Longview, Wash., 1941; electronic technician Sperry Gyroscope, Lake Success, N.Y., 1942-43; adminstrv. asst. New Sch. Social Rsch., NYC, 1944-49; real estate broker Palisades, N.Y., 1952-99; dir. Rockland County Guidance Ctr. Women, Nyack, N.Y., 1969-91. Career counselor N.Y. State Dept. Adult and Continuing Edn., Albany, 1985-90; pres. Rockland County Bd. Realtors, 1968-69. Editor, co-author From Here to My Goal, 1979-80; co-author, co-editor N.Y. Adult Career Counseling Manual, 1988-91. Mem. com. Rockland County Dems., 1961-99; co-chair Orangetown Dems., 1962-66; fundraiser Palisades Free Libr., 1960-99; mem. alumni coun., devel., fundraising Columbia U. Tchrs. Coll., 1994-99; bd. visitors Rockland State Hosp., Orangeburg, N.Y., 1956-63. Recipient Woman of Yr. award Bus. & Profl. Women, 1977, Disting. Alumni award Columbia U. Tchrs. Coll., 1992. Mem. NOW, LWV, AAUW (v.p. 1995-2000, Woman of Achievement award Rockland County sect. 1979), Nat. Assn. Women Edn. Avocations: horticulture, husbandry, handicrafts. Died June 24, 1999.

**ANDERSON, REX ALBERT,** accountant; b. Waikari, New Zealand, Aug. 24, 1926; s. Albert George and Isabel Mary (Jarden) A.; m. Lucy Jean Munn Anderson, Mar. 3, 1951 (div. 1976); children: Grant Stewart, Gail Jeanette; m. Beverley Yvonne Shaw Anderson, Dec. 3, 1978 (widowed Jan. 12, 1992); m. Patricia Lynn Spence Anderson, Feb. 28, 1997. BCOM, Canterbury U., Christchurch, New Zealand, 1945; MCOM, 1947. Chartered accountant, New Zealand Inst. Chartered Accts. Prin. Chartered Acct. in Pub. Practice, Christchurch, New Zealand, 1954-70; sr. ptnr. RA Anderson & Knox, Christchurch, New Zealand, 1970-72; ptnr. Price Waterhouse, Christchurch, New Zealand, 1972-93. Chmn. Accting. Rsch. and Standards Bd., New Zealand Soc. Accts., 1983; pres. New Zealand Soc. Accts., 1984-85, Fedn. Asian and Pacific Accts., Manilla, 1988-89; coun. mem. Internat. Fedn. Accts., N.Y., 1985-88; commr. New Zealand Securities Commn., 1986-96. Sec. Track and Field Control Group 1974 British Commonwealth Games, Christchurch, New Zealand, 1974, New Zealand Games, Christchurch, New Zealand, 1976; mem. bd. govs. Avonside Girls H.S., Christchurch, New Zealand; chmn. Banks Ave.

Sch. Com., Christchurch; chmn. fin. com. Christchurch City Mission, New Zealand, 1997—; trustee Christchurch City Mission Found.; chair cmty. adv. bd. Pegasus Med. Group. Fellow New Zealand Inst. Chartered Accts. (past pres. 1984-85), New Zealand Order of Merit, Canterbury Univ. Alumni Assn. (pres. 1998-2000). Avocations: opera, literature, rugby union football, tennis, general fitness. Died Dec. 19, 2001.

**ANDERSON, VICTOR ELVING,** retired geneticist; b. Stromsburg, Nebr., Sept. 6, 1921; s. Edwin L. and Olga (Elving) A.; m. Carol Esther Rexion, Aug. 31, 1946; children: Catherine, Carl, Christine, Martha. AA, Bethel Jr. Coll., 1941; student, Bethel Theol. Sem., 1941-43; BA, U. Minn., 1945, MS, 1949, PhD, 1953. Faculty dept. biology Bethel Coll., 1946-60; asst. dir. Dight Inst. for Human Genetics, U. Minn., 1954-78, acting dir., 1978-84, assoc. prof. zoology and genetics, 1961-66, prof. genetics and cell biology, 1966—91. Cons. Nat. Inst. Neurol. Disease and Blindness, 1961-68; mem. devel. behavioral scis. study sect. NIH, 1972-75, chmn., 1974-75; bd. regents Bethel Coll. and Sem., 1969-74, 82-87; bd. dirs. Inst. for Advanced Christian Studies, 1971-76, 77-81, 82-86 Author: (with H.O. Goodman and S.C. Reed) Variables Related to Human Breast Cancer, 1958, (with S.C. Reed, C. Hartley, V.P. Phillips, N.A. Johnson) The Psychoses: Family Studies, 1973; (with W.A. Hauser, J.K. Penry, C.F. Sing) Genetic Basis of the Epilepsies, 1982; (with G.Beck-Mannagetta, H. Doose, D. Janz) Genetics of the Epilepsies, 1989, On Behalf of God: A Christian Ethic for Biology, 1995; contbr. articles to profl. jours. Named Alumnus of Yr., Bethel Coll. & Seminar, 1965 Mem. AAAS (pres. Acad. Conf. 1967), American Soc. Human Genetics (dir. 1967-70), Minn. Acad. Sci. (pres. 1964-65), American Sci. Affiliation (pres. 1963-65), Behavior Genetics Assn. (sec. 1972-74, pres. 1979-80), Phi Beta Kappa, Sigma Xi (exec. bd. 1972-84, pres. 1982-83) Research on genetics in human behavior, mental retardation, and epilepsy. Home: Saint Paul, Minn. Died Mar. 9, 2014.

**ANDERSON, VIRGINIA,** medical/surgical and oncological nurse; b. Homeland, Tex., Feb. 13, 1944; d. Wayne Edison and Thetis Virginia (Ware) Lee; m. S. Ray Anderson, Feb. 24, 1962; children: Michael Ray, Shirley Rachelle, Kimberly Dionne. BA, South Plains Coll., Lubbock, Tex., 1975; student, Tex. Tech U., 1975; diploma, Meth. Hosp. Sch. Nursing, Lubbock, 1977. RN, Tex. Charge nurse Hendricks Meml. Hosp., Abilene, Tex.; staff nurse Midland (Tex.) Meml. Hosp., Meth. Hosp., Lubbock, Cross Country Nurses, Boca Raton, Fla. Nat. evangelist, dist. missionary Chs. of God in Christ. Home: Lubbock, Tex. Died Nov. 9, 1995.

**ANDERSSON, BERNDT AKE SIGURD,** surgeon, pediatrician; b. Norrköping, Sweden, Oct. 4, 1918; s. B. Gustav and Elin Susanna (Larsson) A.; m. Maud B. Lindberg, Feb. 18, 1952; children: Eva, Per, Lena. PhD, Karolinska Inst., Stockholm, 1948. Registrar Dept. Gen. Surgery and Pediatric Surgery, Karlshamn, Stockholm, Sweden, 1945-52; registrar, sr. surgeon Dept. Gen. Surgery, östersund, Sweden, 1952-59; sr. surgeon U. Umeå, Sweden, 1959-72; head Dept. Gen. Surgery, Kristianstad, Sweden, 1972-83; head physician Social Ins. Svc., Kristianstad, Sweden, 1987-95; ret., 1995. Contbr. articles to profl. jours. Home: Kristianstad, Sweden. Died Feb. 16, 2008.

**ANDRE, HARVIE,** retired Canadian government official; b. Edmonton, Alta., Can., July 27, 1940; s. John and Doris (Ewasiuk) A.; m. Joan Roberta Smith, May 15, 1965; children: Coryn, Lauren, Peter Harvie. B.Sc., U. Alta., 1962; MS, Calif. Inst. Tech., 1963; PhD, U. Alta., 1966. Assoc. prof. chem. engring. U. Calgary, 1966-72; mem. House of Commons, Ottawa, 1972—93, minister of supply and services, 1984, assoc. minister nat. defense, 1985, minister consumer & corporate affairs, 1986—93. Sworn to Queen's Privy Council, 1984. Past bd. dirs. Clifford E. Lee Found.; past v.p. Social Planning Council Calgary. Mem. Chem. Inst. Can. (chmn. Calgary sect. 1970) Mem. United Church. Clubs: Calgary Petroleum, Calgary Commerce. Avocations: gardening, politics, golf. Died Oct. 21, 2012.

**ANDREWS, GEORGE R.,** U.S. ambassador to Mauritius; b. Havana, Cuba, Feb. 26, 1932; (parents Am. citizens); BA, Princeton U., 1953; MA, U. Strasbourg, France, 1954; postgrad., Fgn. Service Inst., 1978-79. Joined Fgn. Service Dept. State, 1954; consular officer Hamburg, Fed. Republic Germany, 1954-56, Paris, 1956-58; polit. officer, 1958-59; personnel officer Dept. State, 1959-62; desk officer Belgium and Luxembourg, 1962-64; polit. officer Stockholm, 1964-67; chief polit. sect. Dakar, 1967-70; charge d'affaires Conakry, 1970; consul gen. Strasbourg, 1970-71; dep. asst., sec. gen. for polit. affairs NATO, Brussels, 1971-74; dep. chief of mission Guatemala, 1974-78; chief sr. officers personnel Bur. Personnel, Dept. State, 1979-83; U.S. ambassador to Mauritius, from 1983. Died Apr. 11, 2010.

**ANDREWS, LAVONE DICKENSHEETS,** architect; b. Beaumont, Tex., Sept. 18, 1912; d. Charles and Lavone (Lowman) Dickensheets; m. Mark Edwin Andrews, July 23, 1948; 1 son, Mark Edwin III. Student, Miss Hamlin's Sch., San Francisco, Marlborough Sch., LA; AB, Rice Inst., 1933, BS in Architecture, 1934. Assoc. with outstanding architects in Southwest, 1934-37; opened own office Houston, 1937-41; architect firm Anderson, Clayton & Co. (cotton firm), 1941-51; v.p. Ancon Oil & Gas, 1957-94. V.p. Ancon Oil & Gas, Inc., 1957-92, pres., 1992-94. Also pvt. work, museum in, Washington, Naval Hist. Found. & Health Center, schs. for City of Houston. Trustee Mus. Fine Arts in Houston; mem. YWCA World Service Council. Selected as 3d of the 10 outstanding women architects in Am. Archtl. Record, 1947 Fellow AIA, Royal Inst. Architects Ireland; mem. Pallas Athene Lit. Soc. of Rice Inst., Colony Club (N.Y.C.), Houston Club, River Oaks Country Club. Episcopalian. Died June 4, 2002.

**ANDREWS, ROBERT VINCENT,** engineer, educator; b. Portland, Oreg., July 4, 1916; s. Merrill Grover and Mildred Gertrude (Snelling) Andrews; m. Marjorie Louise Kibbe, July 11, 1942. BS, Oreg. State U., 1938; MS, Tex. A&M U., 1940, PhD, 1952; postgrad., Harvard U., MIT, 1942. Registered profl. engr. Ohio, Tex. Chem. engr. Tidewater Assoc. Oil Co., Martinez, Calif., 1938—40; instr. Tex. A&M U., College Station, 1938—55, prof. chem. engring., 1938—55; rsch. and design engr. Monsanto Chem. Co., Anniston, Ala., 1948—49; design and constrn. engr. Hanford Works, Gen. Electric Co., Richland, Wash., 1951—52; dean engring., dir. Lamar Rsch. Ctr., Lamar U., Beaumont, Tex., 1955—61; engring. cons. San Antonio, from 1960; dean engring. Trinity U., San Antonio, 1961—76; trustee SW Rsch. Inst., San Antonio, from 1968. Contbr. articles to tech. jours. Served to maj. USAF, 1942—46. Mem.: Tex. Soc. Profl. Engrs. (pres. Bexar chpt. 1967—68, dir. from 1984, Engr. Yr. 1967), Am. Inst. Chem. Engrs. Democrat. Methodist. Avocations: swimming, hiking, travel. Home: San Antonio, Tex. Deceased.

**ANDRUS, ETHEL PERCY,** social service administrator; b. San Francisco, Calif., Sept. 21, 1884; d. George Wallace Andrus and Lucretia Frances Duke. PhB, U. Chgo., 1908; MA, U. So. Calif., 1928, PhD, 1930. Taught Eng. and German Lewis Inst., Chgo.; tchr. Santa Paula HS, LA, 1910—11, Manual Arts HS, Calif., 1911, East LA HS, Calif., 1916—17, prin. Calif., 1917—44; founder, pres. (support granted in 1956 for the first health insurance prog. for educators 65 or older) Nat. Ret. Tchrs. Assn., 1947; founder, pres. Am. Assn. Ret. Persons (AARP), 1958. Advocate for support to older Americans to achieve independence, purpose and dignity. Founder, editor AARP mag. Modern Maturity. Vol., Hull House, Chgo. Commons, Calif. Ret. Tchrs. Assn. Named to Nat. Women's Hall of Fame, 1993; named in honor of Ethel Percy Andrus Gerontology Center, Univ. So. Calif.; Ethel Percy Andrus Legacy award, AARP, 2008. Achievements include being the first woman appointed to lead a public secondary high school educator in the state of California. Died July 13, 1967.

**ANGELINI, CORRADO ITALO,** neurologist educator; b. Padova, Italy, Aug. 3, 1941; s. Giovanni and Marila (Gasparini) Angelini; m. Elcke Stehr, June 18, 1974 (dec. Feb. 26, 2002); children: Margherita, Giovanni, Katia. MD, U. Padova, 1965. MD, Calif. From rsch. asst. to resident Mayo Clinic, Rochester, Minn., 1970-73; asst., assoc. prof. Padova U., 1974-78, 80-93, prof. neurology, from 1994, dir. neurology residency program, from 2002. Vis. prof. UCLA, 1978—79; mem. med. commn. Union Internat. des Assn. d'Alpinisme, from 1986. Editor: MDR 1980, MDR 1990, 95, 97, Le Malattie Neuromuscolari, 1994; mem editl. bd. Neuromuscular Disorders, Jour. Clin. Neuromuscular Disease, Neurol. Scis., Basic and Applied Myology, Acta Myologica. Capt. Italian Army, 1992. Jr. fellow Muscular Dystrophy Assn., 1984. Mem. Am. Acad. Neurology (assoc.), Am. Neurol. Assn. Avocations: alpinism, skiing. Home: Noventa Padovana, Italy. Died Feb. 26, 2002.

**ANGELOU, MAYA (MARGUERITE ANNIE JOHNSON),** writer, actress; b. St. Louis, Apr. 4, 1928; d. Bailey and Vivian (Baxter) Johnson; m. Tosh Angelos, 1950, (div. 1952); m. Vusumzi Make, 1960 (div. 1963), m. Paul Du Feu, 1973 (div. 1981), 1 child Guy Johnson. Studied dance with, Pearl Primus, NYC; degrees (hon.), Smith Coll., 1975, Mills Coll., 1975, Lawrence U., 1976, Portland State U., 1973, Occidental Coll., 1979, Atlanta U., 1980, U. Ark., 1980, U. Minn., 1980, Austin Coll., 1980, Wheaton Coll., 1981, Kean Coll., 1982, Spelman Coll., 1983, Boston Coll., 1983, Winston-Salem U, 1984, U. Brunesis, 1984, Howard U., 1985, Tufts U., 1985, Va. Commonwealth U., 1985, Northeastern U., 1992, Academy of Southern Arts & Letters, 1993, Brown U., 1994, U. Durham, UK, 1995, Hope Coll., 2001, Columbia U., 2003, Eastern Conn. U., 2003. Taught modern dance The Rome Opera House and Hambina Theatre, Tel Aviv; writer-in-residence U. Kans., Lawrence, 1970; disting. vis. prof. Wake Forest U., 1974-, Wichita State U., 1974, Calif. State U., Sacramento, 1974; apptd. mem. American Revolution Bicentennial Council by Pres. Ford, 1975-76; 1st Reynolds prof. American Studies, Wake Forest U. 1981-2014, a lifetime appointment. Author: I Know Why the Caged Bird Sings, 1970, Just Give Me A Cool Drink of Water 'Fore I Die, 1971, Georgia, Georgia, 1972, Gather Together in My Name, 1974, Oh Pray My Wings are Gonna Fit Me Well, 1975, Singin' and Swingin' and Gettin' Merry Like Christmas, 1976, And Still I Rise, 1978, The Heart of a Woman, 1981, Shaker, Why Don't You Sing?, 1983, All God's Children Need Traveling Shoes, 1986, Now Sheba Sings the Song, 1987, I Shall Not Be Moved, 1990, On the Pulse of Morning: The Inaugural Poem, 1993, Lessons in Living, 1993, Wouldn't Take Nothing for My Journey Now, 1993, My Painted House, My Friendly Chicken, and Me, 1994, The Complete Collected Poems of Maya Angelou, 1994, Phenomenal Women: Four Poems for Women, 1995, A Brave and Startling Truth, 1995, From a Black Woman to a Black Man, 1996, Kofi and His Magic, 1996, Extravagant Spirits, 1997, Making Magic in the World, 1998, Even the Stars Look Lonesome, 1997, A Song Flung Up To Heaven, 2002, Angelina of Italy, 2004, Amazing Peace, 2006 (winner of The Quill award for Poetry, 2006), Celebrations: Rituals of Peace and Prayer (NAACP Image award for poetry, 2007), Mom & Me & Mom, 2013; (cookbooks) Hallelujah! The Welcome Table: A Lifetime of Memories with Recipes, 2004; (plays) Cabaret for Freedom, 1960, The Least of These, 1966, Gettin' Up Stayed On My Mind, 1967, Ajax, 1974, Moon On a Rainbow Shawl, 1988; (screenplays) Georgia, Georgia, 1972, All Day Long, 1974; author/prodr. Three Way Choice, Afro-American in the Arts (Golden Eagle award); wrote and presented Trying to Make it Home, 1988; writer for Oprah Winfrey's Harpo Prodns.; poetry writer for film Poetic Justice, 1993; appeared in plays: Porgy and Bess, 1954-55 (Europe), 1957 (U.S.), Calypso, 1957, The Blacks, 1960, Mother Courage, 1964, Medea, Look Away, 1973, Ajax, 1974, And Still I Rise, 1976, Moon on a Rainbow Shawl, 1988; (films) Porgy and Bess, 1959, Poetic Justice, 1993, How to Make an American Quilt, 1995, The Journey of August King, 1995, Madea's Family Reunion, 2006; dir. (films) Down in the Delta, 1998; (TV minseries) Roots, 1977 (Emmy Nom. best sup. actress), TV appearances include The Richard Pryor Special, Sister, Sisters, 1982, There Are No Children Here, 1993, Touched By An Angel, 1995, Moesha, 1999, Runaway, 2000; spoken word albums include The Poetry of Maya Angelou, 1969, Women in Business, 1981, Been Found, 1996; contbd. articles, short stories, poems to Black Scholar, Chgo. Daily News, Cosmopolitan, Harper's Bazaar, Life Mag., Redbook, Sunday N.Y. Times, Mademoiselle Mag., Essence, Ebony Mag., Calif. Living Mag, Ghanaian Times. Apptd. by Dr. Martin Luther King Jr. Northern Coord., Southern Christian Leadership Conf., 1959-60, apptd. by Pres. Ford to Bicentennial Commn., by Pres. Carter to Nat. Commn. on Observance of Internat. Women's Yr., ambassador, Unicef Internat., 1996. Chubb fellowship award Yale U., 1970, named Woman of Yr. in Comm., 1976; named one of Ladies Home Jour. Top 100 Most Influential Women, 1983, The Most Influential Black Americans, Ebony mag., 2006, 2007, 2008; recipient The Matrix award, 1983, Living Legacy award, Women's Internat. Ctr., 1986, The North Carolina Award in Lit., 1987, Woman of the Yr. Essence Mag., 1992, Disting. Woman of NC, 1992, Horatio Alger award, 1992, Grammy award best spoken word or non-traditional album, 1994 (for recording of "On the Pulse of the Morning"), Grammy award best spoken or non-traditional album, 1994 (for recording of "Phenomonal Woman"), NAACP Image Award for Outstanding Literary Work for "Even the Stars Look Lonesome", 1997, National Medal of Art, 2000, John Hope Franklin award, 2006, Mother Theresa award, Martha Parker Legacy award, 2007, Cornell Medallion, 2008, Gracie Allen award, 2008, Lincoln Medal, 2008, Marian Anderson award, 2008, Lifetime Achievement award, Glamour Mag., 2009, Presdl. Medal of Freedom, The White House, 2010, Literarian award for Outstanding Service to the American Literary Community, National Book Foundation, 2013; inducted into the Nat. Women's Hall of Fame, 1998, Internat. Civil Rights Walk of Fame, 2008 Mem. AFTRA, Directors Guild America, Equity, Harlem Writers Guild, American Film Inst. (trustee), Women's Prison Assn., Horatio Alger Assn. Dist. Americans, Nat. Soc. Prevention of Cruelty to Children (Maya Angelou Ctr. opened 1992), W.E.B. duBois Found., Nat. Soc. Collegiate Scholars, Nat. Soc. High School Scholars. Died May 28, 2014.

**ANSELL, BARBARA MARY,** rheumatologist; b. Warwick, Eng., Aug. 30, 1923; d. Herbert Joseph Ansell and Annie Chubb; widowed. MB BChir, Birmingham U., Eng., 1946, MD, 1969. House physician Queen Elizabeth Hosp., Birmingham, 1946-47, locum registrar in neurology, 1947; house physician Northampton Gen. Hosp., 1947-48, registrar, 1948; house physician Hammersmith Hosp., London, 1950-51; registrar spl. unit for juvenile rheumatism Can. Red Cross Meml. Hosp., Taplow, 1951-53; rsch. fellow Rsch. & Edn. Hosp., Chgo., 1953-54; registrar Hammersmith Hosp., London, 1954-57; sr. registrar London and MRC rheumatism unit Hammersmith Hosp., Can. Red Cross Meml. Hosp., Taplow, 1957-62; cons. physician in rheumatology Can. Red Cross Hosp., Taplow, 1962; head divsn. rheumatology Clin. Rsch. Ctr. Northwick Park Hosp., 1976-88; cons. rheumatologist Wexham Park Hosp., Slough, 1985-88; pvt. practice The Consulting Rms., Windsor, Berks, from 1988; consulting pediat. rheumatologist Portland Hosp. for Women and Children, London. Various short-term locum appts. in casualty, gen. practice, medicine, and pediats., 1950; locum cons. MRC rheumatism unit Can. Red. Cross Meml. Hosp, Taplow, 1960; mem. sci. adv. com. ARC, London; chmn. Brit. League Against Rheumatism, London; chmn. clin. affairs com. Brit. Soc. for Rheumatology, 1984-86. Editor, author: (book) Rheumatic Disorders in Childhood, 1980; co-editor: (books) Medicine, 3d edit., 1979, Colour Atlas of Paediatric Rheumatology, 1991. Decorated Comdr. Brit. Empire.; named Jan van Bremen lectr. Dutch Rheumatology Soc. Fellow Royal Soc. Medicine (hon.), Royal Coll. Physicians London (v.p. 1987-88), Royal Coll. Surgeons London; mem. Windsor Med. Soc., London Rheumatology Club, Royal Coll. Paediatrics and Child Health. Avocations: cooking, travel, opera. Home: Stoke Poges, England. Died Sept. 14, 2001.

**ANTHONY, MARY,** dancer, choreographer, dance theater director; b. Newport, Ky., Nov. 11, 1916; Degree in Theatre, Grinnell Coll.; studied dance with, Hanya Holm, Martha Graham. Mem. Hanya Holm Co., 1943—49; founder Mary Anthony Dance Theatre, NYC, 1956. Tchr. dance. Choreographer The Lord's Prayer for Look Up and Live, Sunday morning religious show, 1957-59, Threnody, 1956, Songs, 1957, In the Beginning, Touch and Go (musical), repertoires of Pa. Ballet, Israel's BatDor Dance Co., Dublin City Ballet, Cloud Gate Dance Theater, Taiwan. Died May 31, 2014.

**ANTONE, STEVE,** retired state legislator; b. Burley, Idaho, Nov. 17, 1921; s. Andrew and Margaret (Glover) A.; m. Helen McKevitt, June 15, 1950 (dec. May 27, 1975); 1 child, Steven K.; m. Diane Meacham, Sept. 16, 1977; 1 child, Jill. Mem. Idaho House of Reps., 1968—96. Named Statesman of Yr., Pi Sigma Alpha, 1986, Disting. Citizen, Idaho Statesman News, 1986, Friend of Agrl., Idaho Farm Bur., 1992, Friend of Idaho Cities, Outstanding Republican

Legislator, State Republican Party, 1994; recipient Boyd Martin award Assn. Idaho Cities, 1984. Republican. Methodist. Avocations: golf, boating. Home: Rupert, Idaho. Died Apr. 19, 2014.

**ANTONIONI, MICHELANGELO,** film director; b. Ferrara, Italy, Sept. 29, 1912; s. Carlo and Elisabetta Antonioni; m. Letizia Balboni, 1942 (div.); m. Enrica Fico, 1986. Cardent, Centro Sperimentale Cinematografia, Rome, 1942; diploma in econs., U. Bologna, Italy; D (hon.), U. Calif., Berkeley, 1993; LHD (hon.), La Sapienza U., Rome, 1993. Film critic, scriptwriter, 1936-40; with Italia libera, 1942; mem. editl. staff Cinema rev., 1942; film critic Corriere Padano, 1944-45, L'Italia Libera. Asst. dir.: Les visiteurs du soir; co-scriptwriter: Un pilota ritorna, I due foscari, Caccia tragica; dir.: (documentaries) Gente del Po (1943-47), 1947, N.U., Superstizione, L'amorosa menzogna, Cronaca di un amore, 1950, I vinte, 1952, La signora senza camelie, L'amore in città, 1953, Le amiche, 1955, Il grido, 1957, I am a camera, L'avventura, 1960 (Cannes Critics' award 1960), La notte, 1961 Silver Bear Berlin Film Festival 1961), L'Eclisse, 1962 (Cannes Internat. Film Festival Grand Prize), Il Deserto Rosso (The Red Desert), 1964 (Golden Lion 25th Venice Film Festival 1964), I tie volti, 1965, Blow-up, 1966 (Golden Palm Cannes Festival 1967, Best Dir. Nat. Soc. Film Critics), Zabriskie Point, 1970, Chung Kuo China, 1972, Professione: reporter (The Passenger), 1975, Il mistero di Oberwald, 1980, Identificazione di una donna, 1982 (Grand Prix Cannes 1982), Noto, mandorli, Vulcano, Stromboli, carnevale, 1992, Eros, 2004; co-dir: (with Wim Wenders) Par délà les nuages, 1994; exhbns. of pictures include Palazzo dei Diamanti, Ferrara, 1993, retrospective 25th Film Festival, Calcutta, 1994. Recipient Spl. award 35th Anniversary Cannes Film Festival, 1982, Golden Lion for entire body of work, Venice Film Festival, 1983, Maschera d'Oro for entire body of work, 1983, Prix Lumière, 1990, Cariddi d'Oro for entire body of work, Taormina, 1991, Prix Navicella, 1992, Nastro Speciale d'Argento, 1992, Felix career award, Berlin Film Festival, 1993, Nastro d'Argento career award, Rome, 1995, Acad. career award, 1995, Efebo d'Oro, 1995; named Knight Grand Cross of the Order of Merit of the Italian Republic, 1992, Comdr. Order of Arts and Letters, France, 1992, Légion d'Honneur, France, 1996. Avocations: ping-pong, tennis. Died July 31, 2007.

**ARAGONES, LUIS,** professional soccer coach; b. Madrid, July 28, 1938; Head coach Atletico Madrid, 1974—78, Real Betis, 1981, Atletico Madrid, 1982—87, Barcelona, 1987—88, Espanyol, 1990—91, Atletico Madrid, 1991—93, Sevilla, 1993—95, Valencia, 1995—97, Real Betis, 1997—98, Real Oviedo, 1999—2000, Atletico Madrid, 2001—03, Mallorca, 2000—01, 2003—04, Spain Nat. Squad, 2004—08, Fenerbahce, 2008—09. Died Feb. 1, 2014.

**ARAPASU, TEOCTIST,** patriarch of Romanian Orthodox Church; b. Tocileni, Moldowa, Romania, Feb. 7, 1915; s. Marghioala (Dumitru) A. Student, Theol. Sem., Cernica Monastery, Romania, 1932-40; Diploma in Theology, Theol. Sem., Bucharest, Romania, 1940, ThM, 1945. Ordained to ministry Romanian Orthodox Ch., 1950. Patriarchal bishop Romanian Orthodox Ch., Bucharest, 1950-62; bishop of Arad Romania, 1962-73; archbishop and met. of Oltenia Craiova, Romania, 1973-77; archbishop of Iasi, met. of Moldova, 1977-86; patriarch Romanian Orthodox Ch., Bucharest, 1986—89, 1990—2007. Author: Metropolitan Iacob Putneanul, 1978, Christian Diaconia. Decorated commodore Order of Sts. Apostles Peter and Paul, Patriarchate of Antioch, 1950, 74, gt. officer, 1958; officer Order of St. Vladimir, Alexey-The Patriarch of Moscow and All Russia, 1962; Commemorative medal Athenogoras I-Ecumenical Patriarch, 1967; officer Order of The Holy Lamb, Paavali-Archbishop of Karelia and All Finland, 1971; gt. crusader Order of Orthodox Crusaders of the Holy Tomb, Diodoros-Patriarch of Jerusalem, 1986; officer Order Sts. Methodios and Kirilos, Dorothey-Met. of Prague and All Czechoslovakia, 1986; officer The Golden Cross of the Holy Monastery of Pathmos, Dimitrios I-Ecumenical Patriarch, 1988. Died July 30, 2007.

**ARCHER, CHALMERS, JR.,** retired education educator, military service force; b. Tchula, Miss., Apr. 21, 1928; s. Chalmers Sr. and Eva Alcola (Rutherford) A. AS summa cum laude, Saints Jr. Coll., 1969; BS with honors, Tuskegee Inst., 1972, MEd with honors, 1974; post doctorate, U. Ala., 1980; cert., MIT, 1980; PhD, Auburn U., 1979. Postdoc U. Ala.; asst. to the pres. Saints Coll., Lexington, Miss., 1968-72; asst. v.p. Tuskegee Inst., Ala., 1972—82; prof. No. Va. C.C., Manassas, 1983-2001, prof. emeritus, 2001; with Army Special Forces. Author: Growing Up Black in Rural Mississippi (recipient Miss. Inst. of Arts and Letters award for Nonfiction, Best Seller award, NY Times), Green Berets in the Vanguard: Inside Special Forces, 1953-1963 (Best Seller Local award); contbg. author: The Jackson Advocate; contbr. articles to profl. jours. and newspapers; performing artist (numerous talk shows). Mem. Dem. Spkr.'s Bur. Clinton-Gore Re-election Campaign; vol. Clinton Campaign. Recipient AFRO Achivment Lifetime award; named Hon. Dr. Humanities, St. Coll., 1976, Nat. Edn. Articulation Model, Conf. on Blacks in Higher Edn., Washington, 1986. Mem.: The History Makers Chgo., Leave Rotary Club. Democrat. Baptist. Avocations: writing, motivational speaking, community service, history. Home: Manassas, Va. Died Feb. 24, 2014.

**ARDLEIGH, JOSEPH D.,** research institute executive; b. Scranton, Pa., May 24, 1914; s. Hugh Granville and Pauline (Danvers) A.; m. Susan Seward; children: Paul, Carl, Hugh, Teri. Student, NYU. Devel. mgr., operating mgr. and personnel mgr. Hoover Co., North Canton, O., 1933-37; established Sales Methods, Inc., NYC, 1937-39; membership dir. Research Inst. of Am., 1939—, v.p., 1944-53, exec. v.p., 1953-67, pres., 1967-79, pres., chief exec. offier, 1979; mng. partner Ardleigh Assos., from 1979. Past pres. Nat. Law Press; dir. Emery Air Freight Corp. Author books and articles on marketing and human relations. Trustee Manhattan Coll. Mem. Nat. Soc. Sales Tng. Execs. (hon. life), Nat. Sales Execs., C. of C., Sales Execs. Club N.Y. (past pres.) Clubs: Greenwich Country (gov.), Board Room; Union League (pres.) (N.Y.C.); Farmington Country. Home: Earlysville, Va. Died Dec. 21, 1988.

**ARÉCHIGA, HUGO,** neurobiologist, educator; b. Culiacán, Mex., Mar. 11, 1940; s. Donaciano Aréchiga and Aurora Urtuzuástegui. MD, Nat. Autonomous U. Mex., 1964; PhD in Physiology and Biophysics, Centro de Investigacion y de Estudios Avanzados del Instituto Politecnico Nacional, Mexico City, 1977. Assoc. prof. physiology Med. Sch. Nat. Autonomous U. Mex., Mexico City, 1965-69, prof. physiology, 1970-72; prof. neurobiology, dean grad. studies, from 1992; prof. physiology and biophysics CINVESTAV IPN, Mexico City, 1974-92, chmn. dept. physiology and biophysics, 1978-87, 90-92. Mem. sci. adv. coun. to Pres. of Mex., Mexico City, 1992—; dir. collaborative program Mex. Acad. Scis. and Nat. Acad. Scis. (U.S.), Mexico City, 1991-92; mem. organizing bd. Binat. Sci. Found. Mex.-U.S., Mexico City, 1991-92; dir. strategic rsch. program in health scis., Mexico City, 1995—. Contbr. articles to profl. jours. Recipient Internat. Leadership award Assn. for Policy, R & D in the 3d World, 1990, nat. award in scis. and arts Govt. Mex., 1992. Mem. Mex. Soc. Physiol. Scis. (pres. 1977-79), Mex. Acad. Sci. (pres. 1990-91, prize 1979), Nat. Acad. Medicine (pres. 1994-95), Latin Am. Acad. Scis. (pres. 1998—), Third World Acad. Scis., Am. Acad. Arts and Sciences. Achievements include identification of circadian pacemakers in the nervous system of crustacean; characterization of hormones modulating neuronal activity. Home: Mexico City, Mexico. Died Sept. 15, 2003.

**ARENDS, WENDELL LEONARD,** apartment manager; b. Lennox, SD, Aug. 18, 1922; s. Harm and Selina (Roberts) A.; children: Roger, Edith, Leonard (dec.). Grad. h.s., Hurley, SD. Cook Nichol Plate Cafe, Sioux Falls, S.D., 1942; ambulance driver, EMT Beresford, S.D., 1961-93; farmer, 1946-62; mechanic Cotton Chevrolet, Beresford, 1962-65; svc. station owner Arends Champion, Beresford, 1965-79; truck driver Fountain Implement, Beresford, 1979-81, Union County Hwy. Dept., Alcester, S.D., 1982-85; county coroner Union County, S.D., 1989-92; mgr. Evergreen Squares Apts., Beresford, from 1989. Asst. leader Lincoln County 4-H, 1950-60; pres., sec. PTA, Beresford, 1950-60; mayor City of Beresford, 1970-72; pres. Beresford C. of C., 1968-69. Sgt. U.S. Army, 1942-45, 50-51. Decorated Bronze Star with two oak leaf clusters. Republican. Mem. Evangelical Ch. Avocations: bowling, crafts. Died Nov. 21, 2002.

**ARGYLE, JOHN MICHAEL,** psychology educator, researcher; b. Nottingham, Eng., Aug. 11, 1925; s. George Edgar and Phyllis (Hawkins-Ambler) A.; m. Sonia Kemp, June 24, 1949 (dec. 1999); children: Miranda, Nicholas, Rosalind, Ophelia; m. Gillian Thompson, 2000. BA, Cambridge U., Eng., 1950, MA, 1952, Oxford U., 1952, DSc, 1979; DLitt, Adelaide U., Australia, 1982; DSc in Psychology (hon.), U. Brussels, 1982. Lectr. social psychology Oxford U., 1952-69, reader, from 1969, acting head dept. exptl. psychology, 1978-80, fellow Wolfson Coll., 1965; emeritus prof. psychology Oxford Brooker U., from 1992. Fellow Ctr. for Advanced Study in Behavioral Scis., 1958-59; vis. prof. U. Mich., U. Del., SUNY, Buffalo, U. B.C., U. Adelaide, Jerusalem U., U. Ghana, U. Leuven, U. Bologna, U. York, U. Nev., U. Kans., U. New South Wales, U. Hawaii, Flinders, Del.; lectr. in field; participant in confs. Author 16 books, including: Bodily Communication, 1975, 88; (with M. Cook) Gaze and Mutual Gaze, 1976; (with P. Trower and B. Bryant) Social Skills and Mental Health, 1978; (with P. Trower) Person-to-Person, 1979; (with A. Furnham and J.A. Graham) Social Situations, 1981; (with M. Henderson) The Anatomy of Relationships, 1985, Psychology of Happiness, 1987, 2d edit., 2001, The Psychology of Leisure, 1996, Psychology and Religion, 2000, (with A. Furnham) The Psychology of Money, 1998; editor 6 books; mem. editl. bds., cons. editor jours.; contbr. numerous articles to profl. jours. Served as flying officer RAF, 1943-47. Grantee Dept. Sci. and Indsl. Rsch., 1956-58, Med. Rsch. Coun., 1959-63, Social Sci. Rsch. Coun., 1964-67, 67-70, 70-75, 75-80, 80-85, 85-87, Oxford Regional Hosp. Bd., 1968-76. Fellow Brit. Psychol. Soc. (coun., chmn. social psychology sect. 1964-67, 72-74); mem. European Assn. for Social Psychology. Anglican. Avocations: travel, scottish country dancing. Home: Oxford, England. Died Dec. 6, 2002.

**ARIKI, SOICHIRO,** economist, researcher; b. Dalian, Liaoning, China, Mar. 24, 1929; arrived in Japan, 1947; s. Kyunosuke and Suzue (Miyaso) A.; m. Yachiyo Hiroshige, Jan. 23, 1957; children: Susumu, Hiroko. BA in Econs., Kobe U., Japan, 1954; PhD, Hitotsubashi U., Tokyo, 1972. Rsch. asst. Kobe U., 1954-56; asst. prof. Shimonoseki City Coll. Commerce, Yamaguchi Prefecture, Japan, 1956-62; prof. econ. policy Kokagakuin U., Tokyo, 1962-89; hon. sr. rsch. fellow Faculty Social Scis., Glasgow (Scotland) U., 1989-92; prof. Shimoneseki City U., 1992-96, Kyushu Sangyo U., Fukuoka, Japan, 1996—2002; ret., 2002. Author: Studies on Soviet Economy, 1972, Postwar Development of Japan's Economy, 1988, (with E. Onoye) Economic Planning (East and West), 1980. Mem. Assn. for Asian Studies, Japanese Soc. Internat. Econs. Avocations: travel, recitations. Home: Tokyo, Japan. Died 2005.

**ARISTODIMOU, CHRISTOFOROS See CHRYSOSTOMOS**

**ARMELAGOS, GEORGE JOHN,** biological anthropologist; b. Lincoln Park, Mich., May 22, 1936; s. John and Ashimo (Tsafaras) A.; m. Adina Schrager; m. Lynn Middleton Sibley, June 22, 1991; 1 child, Gabriel Sibley. BA, U. Mich., 1958; MA, U. Colo., 1963, PhD in Anthrpology, 1968. Asst. prof. anthropology U. Utah, Salt Lake City, 1965-68; asst. prof. U. Mass., Amherst, 1968-73, assoc. prof., 1973-78, prof., 1978-90; prof., chair dept. anthropology U. Fla., Gainesville, 1990-93; Goodwich C. White prof. anthropology Emory U., Atlanta, 1993—2014, chair dept. anthropology, 2003—09. Mem. adv. com. behavioral and neurol. scis. NSF, 1976-79; mem. J.T. Staley prize com. Sch. American Rsch., 1990; vis. prof. anthropology U. Colo., Boulder, summer 1983, 84, 85, 86, 87, 88. Co-author: Demographic Anthropology, 1976, Consuming Passions: Anthropology of Eating, 1980; co-editor: (with Mark Nathan Cohen) Paleopathology at the Origins of Agriculture, 1984, Diseases in Populations in Transition, 1990 (with Ron Barrett) An Unnatural History of Emerging Infections, 2013; assoc. editor biol. anthropology Current Anthropology, 1987-88; mem. editl. bd. Med. Anthropology Quar., 1986-90, Med. Anthropology, 1980-97, Human Evolution; assoc. editor Evolutionary Anthropology. Fellow AAAS (del. to coun. 1986-89), American Anthropol. Assn. (chair biol. unit 1984-87, disting. lectr. gen. anthropology divsn. 1994), American Assn. Phys. Anthropologists (pres. 1987-89); mem. Soc. Med. Anthropology (awards com. W.H. Rivers prize 1990), N.E. Anthropol. Assn. (pres. 1987-88). Democrat. Achievements include team leader of group that discovered tetracycline use in ancient Nubian populations. Home: Midway, Ga. Died May 15, 2014.

**ARMOUR, PETER JAMES,** humanities educator; b. Fleetwood, Eng., Nov. 19, 1940; s. James and Anne Mary (Monaghan) A. BA with honors, U. Manchester, 1966; PhD, U. Leicester, 1980. Lectr. Italian U. Sheffield (England), 1966-72, U. Leicester (England), 1972-79, Bedford Coll., U. London, 1979-84, U. Coll. London, 1984-89; prof. Italian Royal Holloway, U. London, 1989—99, rsch prof., 1999—2002. Vis. sr. lectr. U. Western Australia, Perth, 1973; assoc. dir. Inst. Romance Studies, London, 1991-92, 94-99; vis. prof. U. Melbourne, 1987, U. Va., 1995, 98. Author: The Door of Purgatory, 1983, Dante's Griffin and the History of the World, 1989; contbr. articles to profl. jours. Personal grantee Brit. Acad., 1983, 94. Fellow Royal Soc. Arts; mem. Soc. Italian Studies, Dante Soc. Am. (life), Soc. Dantesca Italiana, Modern Humanities Rsch. Assn., Middlesex County Cricket Club. Avocations: reading, opera, travel, cricket. Home: London, England. Died June 18, 2002.

**ARMOUR, REGINALD,** film producer and distributor; b. Chgo., Nov. 28, 1895; s. Philip and Marie (Valentine) A.; m. Joyce Armour, Nov. 25, 1957; 1 child, Andrew Philip. PhD in Econs., Edinburgh U., 1932. With RCA Victor Co., 1932-33; successively Far East gen. mgr., European gen. mgr., exec. asst. to pres., asst. gen. mgr. RKO Radio Studios, 1933-42; European rep. Walt Disney Prodns., 1942-43, with fin. field NYC, 1943-44; exec. v.p. Richard Condon, Inc., 1944-45; fgn. rep. Columbia Internat. Corp., NYC, 1945-49; appt. v.p. Republic Pictures Internat. Corp., 1950-52, supr. Europe and Near East, 1952-55, exec. v.p., mng. dir. Eng., 1955-60; pres. The Dorsey Corp., 1960-64, vice chmn., 1964-65; pres. SOS Photo-Cine-Optics, Inc., 1965-67, FB/Ceco of Calif., Inc., 1967-71, Instant Protection Systems, Inc., 1971-73; exec. v.p., treas. The Quedo Corp. and Internat. Producers Services, Inc., 1973; v.p., treas. Dyna-Sonar, Inc., 1974, Two Feathers Prodns., 1977-81; pres. Armour Enterprises, Inc., 1981-85, Group Media Prodns., Inc, 1985-90. Served to Col. AUS, 1943-45, ETO.

**ARMSTRONG, CLARA JULIA EVERSHED (MRS. ROLLIN S. ARMSTRONG),** retired academic administrator; b. Murray, Utah, Aug. 25, 1911; d. Elmer B. and Lenora K. (Tripp) Evershed; m. Rollin S. Armstrong, Sept. 29, 1956 (dec. Sept. 1974); foster children: Maxwell Rollin, Ruth Elizabeth, Robert Neil, Philip Samuel. Student, Henager Bus. Coll., 1936—37. Office mgr., credit mgr. D. N. & E. Walter & Co., Salt Lake City, 1937—48; with Latter Day Saints Bus. Coll., Salt Lake City, 1948—77, sec., 1948—52, fgn. student adviser, vet. coord., rehab. counselor, 1952—55, registrar, 1955—62, sec.-treas., 1962—76, vol. worker, 1976—80. Pres. Ward Mut. Improvement Assn., 1941—45. Mem. Lds Ch. Home: Salt Lake City, Utah. Died Apr. 12, 1999.

**ARMSTRONG, DAVID MALET,** philosopher, educator; b. Melbourne, Australia, July 8, 1926; s. J.M. and Philippa Suzanne Armstrong; m. Madeleine Annette Hayden, 1950; m. Jennifer Mary de Bohun Clark. BA First Class Honours in Philosophy, with Univ. Medal, Univ. Sydney, 1950; BPhil, Oxford Univ., 1954; PhD, Univ. Melbourne, 1960. Asst. lectr. Birkbeck Coll., London U., 1954—55; lectr., sr. lectr. U. Melbourne, 1956—63; Challis Prof. Philosophy U. Sydney, 1964—91, emeritus prof. philosophy, 1992—2014. Asst. prof. Yale Univ., 1962, vis. prof., 1998; prof. Stanford Univ., 1965, 1968, Univ. Tex., Austin, 1980, Austin, 1989, Univ. Wis., Madison, 1985; disting. vis. prof. Univ. Calif., Irvine, 1992; disting. scholar in residence Franklin and Marshall Coll., 1993, 1994, 2000; vis. prof. Univ. Graz, Austria, 1995, Univ. Norte Dame, Ind., 1997, Univ. Conn. at Storrs, 1999; Kemp Disting. prof. Davidson Coll., 2002. Author: Berkeley's Theory of Vision: A Critical Examination of Bishop Berkeley's Essay towards a New Theory of Vision, 1960, Perception and the Physical World, 1961, Bodily Sensations, 1962, A Materialist Theory of the Mind, 1968, Belief, Truth and Knowledge, 1973, Universals and Scientific Realism, 1978, The Nature of Mind, and other Essays, 1980, What is the Law of Nature?, 1983, Universals: An Opinionated Introduction, 1989, A Combinatorial Theory of Possibility, 1989, A World of States of Affairs, 1997, The Mind-Body Problem: An Opinionated Introduction, 1999, Truth and Truthmakers, 2004; co-author: Consciousness and Causality: A Debate on the Nature of Mind, 1984, Dispositions: A Debate, 1996; contbr. several articles to profl. jours. Seaman Royal Australian Navy, 1945—46. Named Officer, Order Australia, 1993. Fellow: Australian Acad. Humanities, British Acad. (corr.); mem.: American Acad. Arts & Sciences (fgn.) (hon.). Home: Sydney, Australia. Died May 13, 2014.

**ARMSTRONG, HENRY CONNER,** former Canadian government official, consultant; b. Winnipeg, Man., Can., June 16, 1925; s. William Arthur Laird and Archena May (Conner) A.; m. Barbara Fay Jackson, May 20, 1950; children: Barbara E., Nancy M., Scott J. B.Sc. in Metall. Engring., Queen's U., Kingston, Ont., 1949; MBA (Kresge fellow), U. Toronto, 1954; diploma in indsl. adminstrn. (Alcan fellow), Internat. Mgmt. Inst., Geneva, Switzerland, 1958. Various sales and marketing positions Aluminum Co. of Can., Ltd., 1954-64; commodity officer Dept. Trade and Commerce, Ottawa, Ont., 1964-66; comml. counsellor Canadian Embassy, Washington, 1966-74; chief research and planning div., resource industries and constrn. br. Dept. Industry, Trade and Commerce, Ottawa, Ont., Canada, 1974-75; dir. minerals and metals div. Dept. Energy, Mines and Resources, Ottawa, Ont., 1975-81, exec. dir. internat. minerals, 1981-82, mgr. spl. projects, 1982-83; counsellor (metals, minerals and energy) Can. High Commn., Canberra, Australia, 1983-86; counsellor (commercial) Can. Embassy, Washington, 1986-89; pvt. practice cons. Ottawa, from 1989. Served with RCAF and Royal Navy Fleet Air Arm, 1944-45. Mem. Assn. Profl. Engrs. Ont., Canadian Inst. Mining and Metallurgy, Am. Soc. for Materials. Mem. United Ch. of Can. Died Sept. 25, 2013.

**ARNAO, GIANCARLO,** dentist; b. Milano, Italy, Mar. 27, 1926; m. Christa Dirnagel, Aug. 28, 1964. Scientific cons. Forum-Droghe, Roma. Author books in field, including: Tutte Le Droghe Del Presidente, 1996. Avocation: bicycling. Home: Pancole/Grosseto, Italy. Died Nov. 14, 2000.

**ARNELL, RICHARD ANTHONY SAYER,** composer, conductor; b. London, Sept. 15, 1917; s. Richard Sayer Arnell and Helène Marie Scherf; m. Joan Heycock, 1992; 3 children from previous marriage. Student, Hall Sch., U. Coll. Sch., Royal Coll. Music. Music cons. BBC N.Am. Svc., 1943-46; lectr. Trinity Coll. Music, London, 1948-87, Royal Ballet Sch., 1958-59; music dir., bd. dirs. London Internat. Film Sch., 1975-89; music dir. Ram Filming Ltd., 1980-85; dir. A plus A Ltd., 1984-89. Fulbright vis. exch. lectr. Bowdoin Coll., Maine, 1967-68; prof. Hofstra U., N.Y., 1969-71. Editor: The Composer, 1961-64; compositions include (opera) Love in Transit, 1953, Moonflowers, 1958, (film scores) The Land, 1941, The Third Secret, 1963, The Visit, 1964, The Man Outside, 1966, Topsail Schooner, 1966, Bequest for a Village, 1969, Second Best, 1972, Stained Glass, 1973, Wires Over the Border, 1974, Black Panther, 1977, Antagonist, 1980, Dilemma, 1981, Toulouse Lautrec, 1984, Light of the World, 1988; other works include Symphonic Portrait, Lord Byron, for Sir Thomas Beecham, 1953, Landscapes and Figures, 1956, (puppet operatta) Petrified Princess, 1959, Robert Flaherty, Impression for Radio Eireann, 1960, Musica Pacifica, 1963, Festival Flourish, 1965, Overture, Food of Love, 1968, My Ladye Greene Sleeves, 1968, (ballets) Punch and the Child, 1948, Harlequin in April, 1951, The Angels, 1962, others; also 6 symphonies, 2 violin concertos, harpsichord concerto, 2 piano concertos, 6 string quartets, 2 quintets, works for string orch., wind ensembles, brass ensembles, song cycles and electronic music. Chair Friends of London Internat. Film Sch., 1982-87; chair jr. dept. Friends of Trinity Coll. of Music, 1986-87 Recipient Composer of Yr. award Music Tchrs.' Assn., 1966, Merit award Tadcaster Town Coun., 1991. Mem. Composers Guild of Great Britain (chair 1974-75, 77-79), Saxmundham Music and Arts (former pres.), Tadcaster Civic Soc. Music and Arts (chair 1988-91). Avocations: cooking, travel. Died Apr. 10, 2009.

**ARONSOHN, RICHARD FRANK,** lawyer; b. Jersey City, Aug. 8, 1938; s. Isadore William and Elizabeth (Saltzman) Aronsohn; m. Deborah Aronsohn, Dec. 19, 1965; children: William John, Elizabeth Anne. AB, Dartmouth Coll., 1960; JD, Rutgers U., 1963. Bar: NJ 1964; cert. civil trial lawyer, NJ. Law sec. Bergen County Ct., NJ, 1963—64; dep. atty. gen. State NJ, 1964—66; spl. asst. prosecutor Bergen County, 1968—70; ptnr. Aronsohn & Springstead, and predecessors, Hackensack, NJ, from 1970. Atty. Bergen Community Coll., 1967—69; chief legal counsel County Bergen, Bergen Pines County Hosp.; lectr. Inst. Continuing Legal Edn., from 1968. Contbr. articles to legal jours. Mem.: ABA, Bergen County Bar Assn. (trustee from 1978), NJ Bar Assn. (trustee from 1979). Democrat. Jewish. Home: Mahwah, NJ. Died July 12, 1996.

**ARP, HALTON CHRISTIAN (CHIP ARP),** astronomer; b. NYC, Mar. 21, 1927; s. August C. and Anita C. (Cryst) A.; m. Susanna Bixby Dakin, 1970 (div. 1982); children: Kristana, Alissa, Andrice; m. Marie-Helene DeMoulin, Jan. 19, 1984; 1 child, Delphine. AB, Harvard Coll., 1949; PhD, Calif. Inst. Tech., 1953. Astronomer Carnegie Instn. of Washington, D.C., 1957-85, Max Planck Inst. for Astrophysics, Munich, 1985—2013. Author: The Atlas of Peculiar Galaxies, 1966, Quasars, Redshifts & Controversies, 1987, Seeing Red: Redshifts, Cosmology and Academic Science, Cat Southern Pec Galaxies, 1987. Mem. Congressional Racial Equality, Pasadena, 1965; chmn. Fedn. American Scientists L.A. chpt., 1970-73. With USN, 1945-46. Recipient Newcomb-Cleveland prize AAAS, 1960, Medal Coll. de France, Paris, 1984, Alexander Humboldt Sr. Sci. award 1985. Mem. Internat. Astron. Union (working group chmn. 1988-92), American Astron. Soc. (past councilor, Helen Warner prize 1958), Astron. Soc. Pacific (pres. 1980-83). Home: Munich, Germany. Died Dec. 28, 2013.

**ARUP, SIR OVE,** architectural firm executive; b. 1895; Degrees in philosphy and math., U. Copenhagen; grad., Royal Tech. Coll., Copenhagen, 1922. With Christiani & Nielson, Hamburg, 1922, chief designer London; founder Arup & Arup Ltd., 1938; pvt. practice. Leading figure Modern Arch. Rsch. Soc. Group; tchr. Archtl. Assn. Sch. Arch., London. Prin. works include Highpoint 1, U.K., Highpoint 2, Penguin Park at Regent's Park Zoo, Finsbury Health Ctr., Sydney Opera House. Named Comdr. of Brit. Empire, 1953, Knight of Brit. Empire, 1971. Died 1988.

**ASAHINA, TAKASHI,** conductor; b. Tokyo, July 9, 1908; s. Kaichi Watanabe; m. Machiko Asahina, 1940; 2 children. LLB, Kyoto Imperial U., 1931, BA, 1937. Permanent condr., gen. dir. Osaka Philharmonic Orch., from 1947; condr. 35 overseas tours, 1953-96. Chair panel judging Tokyo Internat. Music Competition for Conducting, 1976. Condr. Berlin Philharmonic, Sinfonieorchester des Norddeutscher Rundfunks Hamburg, numerous others; recordings include complete symphonies of Beethoven, Bruckner, Brahms, Wagner's Ring des Nibelungen. Recipient Officer's Cross for sci. and art, Austria. Mem. Nippon Condrs. Assn. (pres.). Avocations: reading, sports. Home: Kobe, Japan. Died Dec. 29, 2001.

**ASDELL, SYDNEY ARTHUR,** physiologist; b. Bramhall, Cheshire, Eng., Aug. 23, 1897; arrived in US, 1930; s. John and Amy (Love) A.; m. Muriel Tregarthen Marrack, Aug. 2, 1923; children: Philip Tregarthen, Mary Kathleen. BA, Cambridge U., Eng., 1922; MA, 1923, PhD, 1926. Lectr. Massey Agr. Coll., New Zealand, 1928—30; asst. prof. physiology Cornell U., Ithaca, NY, 1930—35; prof., 1935—65; prof. emeritus, from 1965. Fulbright prof., 1952. Author: Patterns of Mammalian, 1946, Dog Breeding, 1966. With USNR, 1916—19. Recipient Marshall medal, Soc. Study Fertility, 1977. Mem.: Am. Physiol. Soc., Am. Assn. Anatomists, Japanese Soc. Reprodn. (hon.), Sigma Xi. Home: Frederick, Md. Deceased.

**ASHERSON, RONALD ANDREW,** rheumatologist; b. Cape Town, South Africa, Dec. 19, 1934; s. Asher Asherson, Milly Gelb. MB ChB, U. Cape Town, 1957; MD, Coll. Medicine South Africa, 1964; MD (hon.), U. Pleven, Bulgaria, 2002. Cert. physician N.Y., 1976. Clin. asst. prof. medicine N.Y. Hosp., Cornell Med. Ctr., 1976—82; vis. physician Rheumatology unit Hammersmith Hosp., Royal Postgrad. Med. Sch., London, 1982—86; hon. cons. St. Thomas' Hosp., London, 1987—91; hon. cons. Rheumatology U. Cape Town, Groole Schoor Hosp., Cape Town, from 1992. Sr. rsch. fellow Payne Inst., 1988—90; asst. attending physician Roosevelt Hosp., NYC, 1990—91. Co-editor: Phospholyed Binding Anhbackes, The Atiphospholipid Synuions, 1996, Vascular Nonfectations of Systems Autoimun Diseases, 2001; contbr. articles to profl. jours. Recipient Prize, Eular, 1992, ILAR, 1993. Fellow: ACP, Royal Coll. Physicians, Royal Soc. Medicine of Eng., Am. Rheumatism Assn.; mem.: South African Rheumatology Assn. Avocation: Avocation: classical music. Home: Cape Town, South Africa. Died May 6, 2008.

**ASHOONA, PITSEOLAK (PITSEOLAK),** Inuit Canadian Artist; b. Nottingham Island, Hudson Strait, Can. m. Ashoona (dec.); 12-17 children, 6-10 of which survived beyond childhood; children include Ottochie, Napatchie Pootoogook, Qaqaq Ashoona, Kiawak Ashoona, and Kumwartok Ashoona. Artistic career began with Cape Dorset printmaking project, 1950's; first prints: 1960 edit. Cape Dorset graphics; retrospective exhbn.: Can. Guild of Crafts, Montreal, 1971; drawings: Innuit Gallery, Toronto, 1971, 75; author-illustrator: (autobiography) Pitseolak, Pictures Out of My Life, 1971; numerous drawings of traditional Eskimo life and legends, Arctic animals, birds; by the end of her life she had created at least 7,000 images. Named to Order of Canada, 1977. Mem.: Royal Acad. Arts. portrait featured on Canadian stamp in commemoration of Internat. Woman's Day, 1993. Died May 28, 1983.

**ASKEW, REUBIN O'DONOVAN,** former Governor of Florida; b. Muskogee, Okla., Sept. 11, 1928; s. Leo And Alberta (O'Donovan) A.; m. Donna Lou Harper, Aug. 11, 1956; children: Angela Askew Cook, Kevin O'Donovan. BS in Public Adminstrn., Fla. State U., 1951; JD, U. Fla., 1956, D (hon.) in Public Service, 1983; postgrad., Denver U.; LLD (hon.), Fla. So. Coll., Lakeland, 1972, U. Notre Dame, 1973, U. Miami, 1975, U. West Fla., 1978, Barry U., Miami, 1979, U. Tampa, 1983, Belmont Abbey Coll., 1983; DPA (hon.), Rollins Coll., Winter Park, Fla., 1972; LHD (hon.), Eckerd Coll., St. Petersburg, Fla., 1973, Stetson U., Deland, Fla., 1973, Bethune-Cookman Coll., 1975, St. Leo Coll., Fla., 1975, Fla. State U., 1988. Bar: Fla. 1956. Asst. county solicitor Escambia County (Fla.), 1956-58; ptnr. Levin, Askew, Warfield, Graff & Mabie, Pensacola, Fla., 1958-62; mem. Fla. House of Reps., 1958-62, Fla. State Senate, 1962-70, pres. pro tem, 1968-70; gov. State of Fla., 1971-79; ptnr. Greenberg, Traurig, Askew, Hoffman, Lipoff, Quentel & Wolff, P.A., Miami, Fla., 1979; US Trade Rep. Office US Trade Rep., Exec. Office of the Pres., Washington, 1979-81; dir. Greenberg, Traurig, Askew, Hoffman, Lipoff, Rosen & Quentel, P.A., Miami and Orlando, Fla., 1981-88; of counsel Akerman, Senterfitt & Eidson, 1988—96. Chmn. jud. com. Fla. Constitution Commn., 1966-67; chmn. Edn. Commn. of States, 1973, chmn. Select Commn. Immigration and Refugee Policy, 1979; chmn. Southern Governors Conf., 1974-75; chmn. Nat. Democratic Governors Conf., 1976-77, chmn. Nat. Govs. Conf., 1977-78; chmn. Southern Growth Policies Bd., 1977-78; chmn. Fla. Comptrollers Task Force on Securities Regulation, 1985-86; pres. council of State Govts., 1977-78; chmn. Presdl. Advisory Bd. Ambassadorial Appointments, 1977-79. Contbr. articles to profl. jours. Past pres. western div. Children's Home Soc. Fla., Pensacola Oratorio Soc.; bd. dirs. City of Hope; past mem. state exec. com. Fla. Tb and Health Assn.; keynote speaker Democratic Nat. Conv., 1972; mem. The Bretton Woods com., 1986-87; bd. dirs. Orlando Regional Med. Ctr. Found., 1987-89; past bd. dirs. Pensacola YMCA, United Fund, Heart Assn., Nat. Comn. on American State and local Pub. Svc., Nat. Inst. of Former Governors; served in AUS, 1946-48; capt. USAF, 1951-53. Recipient Spirit of Life Humanitarian award City of Hope, 1969, John F. Kennedy Profiles in Courage award B'nai B'rith, 1971, Nat. Wildlife Fedn. award, 1972, Outstanding Conservationist of Yr. award Fla. Audubon Soc., 1972, Herbert H. Lehman Ethics medal Jewish Theol. Sem. America, 1973, Gen. William Booth award Salvation Army, 1973, John F. Kennedy award Nat. Council Jewish Women, 1973, Protector of Environment award Fla. Engring. Soc., 1973, Alumnus of Yr. Fla. Law Rev., 1973, Theodore Roosevelt award Internat. Platform Assn., 1975, Human Relations award NCCJ, 1976, Humanitarian of Yr. award Fla. Commn. on Human Relations, 1977, Leadership Honor award American Inst. Planners, 1978, F. Malcolm Cunningham Achievement award Nat. Bar Assn., 1978, Medal of honor Fla. Bar Found., 1979, Medal of honor Fla. Bar. Assn., 1979, Disting. Community Service award Brandeis U., 1979, Champion of Higher Ind. Edn. in Fla. award, 1979, Ethics in Govt. award Common Cause, 1980, Albert Einstein Disting. Achievement award Yeshiva U., 1982, Fla. State U. Centennial Alumnus award Nat. Assn. State Univs. and Land Grant Colls., 1987; named to The Demolay Hall of Fame, 1986; vis. Chubb fellow Yale U., 1976; res. fellow Harvard U., 1989; sr. fellow Fla. Inst. Govt., 1993 Fellow Nat. Acad. Public Adminstrn.; mem. ABA, Fla. Bar Assn., American Judicature Soc. (bd. dirs. 1979-81, Herbert Harley award 1975), Acad. Fla. Trial Lawyers, Trade Net (bd. dirs. 1981-86), Fla. Coun. of 100, Nat. Commn. American State & Local Public Services, Nat. Inst. Former Govs., Ret. Officers Assn., American Legion, Masons (33 degree), Rotary, Shriners, Order of Coif, Phi Alpha Delta, Delta Tau Delta, Alpha Phi Omega, Pi Alpha Alpha. Democrat. Presbyterian (elder). Presbyterian. Home: Tallahassee, Fla. Died Mar. 13, 2014.

**ASMUSSEN, NILS WIRENFELDT,** pharmaceutical executive; b. Copenhagen, Jan. 12, 1938; s. Robert Wirenfeldt and Grethe (Abildgaard) A.; m. Marianne Bang, July 8, 1967; 1 child, Nicolai. BA, Østersègades Gymnasium, Copenhagen, 1957; PhB, Copenhagen U., 1960; postgrad., Brunel U., Eng., 1982. Med. dir. Boehringer Ingelheim, Copenhagen, 1967-73; area med. dir. Searle, Copenhagen, 1973-79; regional med. dir. Ciba-Geigy, Copenhagen and Basel, Switzerland, 1979-83; regulatory dir. Europe Abbott, Paris, 1983-85; med. dir. Upjohn, Copenhagen, 1985-93; pres., med. dir. Wirenfeldt Asmussen, Denmark, 1993—2006. Cons. Medi-Lab, Copenhagen, 1994-2001; mem. com. Medicines Industry Assn. Denmark, 1985-93. Bd. dirs. Royal Guards Soc., Copenhagen, 1963, Gentofte Med. Lab., 1970; mem. Danish Salmon Found., Copenhagen, 1997. Guardsman Danish Royal Guards, 1962-63. Fellow Royal Soc. Medicine; mem. Am. Coll. Clin. Pharmacology, Royal Yacht Club. Avocations: hunting, skiing, sports fishing, yachting. Home: Helsingør, Denmark. Died Mar. 5, 2007.

**ASPER, ISRAEL HAROLD,** broadcasting executive; b. Minnedosa, Man., Can., Aug. 11, 1932; s. Leon and Cecilia (Zevit) A.; m. Ruth Miriam Bernstein, May 27, 1956; children: David, Gail, Leonard. BA, U. Man., Winnipeg, 1953, LLB, 1957; LLM, U. Man., 1964. Assoc. Drache, Meltzer & Co., Winnipeg, Man., 1957-59; sr. ptnr. Asper & Co., Winnipeg, 1959-70, Buchwald, Asper, Henteleff, Winnipeg, 1970-77. Chmn. bd. dirs. CanWest Capital Group, Inc., CanWest Global Comms. Corp., CanWest Pacific TV Inc., SaskWest TV Inc., CanWest Internat. Inc., TV3 Network Holdings, Ltd., TV3 Television Network, New Zealand, CanWest Trustees Ltd., Canvideo TV Sales Ltd., Global Comms. Ltd., CanWest Broadcasting Ltd. Author: The Benson Iceberg, 1970; syndicated newspaper column Taxation, 1966-77. Patron, Misericordia Hosp. Rsch. Found.; apptd. Queen's Counsel, 1975. Served as hon. lt. col. 17th Bn., Can. Militia. Recipient Alumni award U. Man., 1979; named hon. patron Misericordia Hosp., hon. fellow Hebrew U. Jerusalem. Mem. Can. Bar Assn., Can. Tax Found., Man. Bar Assn., Man. Law Soc., Internat. Inst. Communicaitons. Clubs: Canadian (Winnipeg), UniCity Racquet (Winnipeg), Manitoba. Jewish. Home: Winnipeg, Canada. Died Oct. 7, 2003.

**ASSAKUL, KRIS,** insurance executive; b. Sept. 6, 1925; Pres. Ocean Life Ins., Bangkok, from 2002, Siam Life Ins., Bangkok, from 2002. Died Jan. 25, 2002.

**ASSELIN, MARTIAL,** retired Canadian legislator; b. La Malbaie, P.Q., Feb. 3, 1924; s. Martial and Eugenie (Tremblay) A.; m. Pierrette Bouchard, Feb. 14, 1953; children: Bernard, Jean-Louis, François; m. Ginette d'Autueil, Sept. 17, 1976. BA, Sem. Chicoutimi; LLB, Laval U. Bar: Que., 1951. Mayor La Malbaie, La Malbaie, 1957-63; min. forestry Diefenbaker Cabinet, 1963; summoned to Senate of Can., 1972-90; min. state Can. Internat. Devel. Agy. & Francophonie, 1979-80; ptnr. Jolin, Fournier, Morrisset, 1980-90; lt. gov. Quebec, 1990—96. Del. of Can. to NATO Parliamentary Assembly, London, 1959; rep. of Can. Commonwealth and internat. confs., 1960-61; del. of UN to Africa, 1961. Pres. Itnernat. Assn. of French Speaking Parliamentarians, 1988-90; dir. La Laurentienne Generale, Banque Laurentienne, Sphynx et Memisca and La Laurentienne-Vie, 1976-90. Named Grand de Charlevoix Assn. des Anciens de Charlevoix, 1989. Mem. KC (3d degree), Lions Club, Clermont-La Malbaie-Pointe-au-Pic. Roman Catholic. Died Jan. 25, 2013.

**ATCHLEY, BILL LEE,** university president; b. Cape Girardeau, Mo., Feb. 16, 1932; s. William Cecil and Mary (Bicket) A.; m. Pat Limbaugh, Aug. 1954; 3 children. BS in

Civil Engring, U. Mo., Rolla, 1957, MS, 1959; PhD, Tex. A&M U., 1965. Registered profl. engr., Mo., W.Va., S.C. Baseball pitcher N.Y. Giants Orgn., 1951-52; From asst. prof. to prof. engring. mechanics U. Mo., Rolla, 1957-75; prof., dean Coll. Engring., W.Va. U., Morgantown, 1975-79; pres. Clemson (S.C.) U., 1979-85; pres., chief exec. officer Nat. Sci. Ctr. for Communication and Electronics Found. Inc., 1985-87; pres. U. of the Pacific, Stockton, Calif., 1987-95, Southeast Mo. State U., Cape Girardeau, from 1995. Cons. Systems Cons. Inc., Savannah River Lab.; chmn. Gov. W.Va. Commn. Energy, Economy and Environment, 1975, NCAA Intercollegeiate Athletics; sci. and tech. adviser to Senate and Ho. of Dels. W.Va., 1976; mem. W.Va. Bd. Registration Profl. Engrs.; sci. and tech. adviser to Gov. Mo., 1972-75, to Gov. W.Va., 1975-79; W.Va. gov.'s rep. to U.S. Govs. Commn. on Energy, 1979; energy advisor to Gov. S.C., 1980; mem. Gov.'s Council on Alcohol Fuels; mem. fed. fossil energy adv. com. Dept. Energy; mem. Nat. Coal Council 1985—; bd. dirs. Criticare Technologies Corp., Reno.; mem. Nat. Edn. Exec. Adv. Com. Author papers in field. Mem. Meth. Ch., Boy Scouts Am.; mem. habitat policy adv. com. Coun. Govts.; mem. exec. com. Calif. Campus Compact; chmn. United Way; chmn. San Joaquin chpt. Am. Cancer Soc.; bd. dirs. Bus. Coun. San Joaquin County, San Joaquin Partnership. Recipient alumni merit award Southeast Mo. State U.; Ford Found. fellow; recipient Distinguished Service award Rolla Bicentennial Com., 1975; named S.C. Engr. of Yr., 1985 Mem. ASCE, Nat. Govs. Conf., Am. Inst. Pub. Svc. (bd. nominators), Am. Soc. Engring. Edn., Nat. Soc. Profl. Engrs., Newcomen Soc. N.Am., Greater Stockton C. of C. (bd. dirs.), Future Farmers Am. (hon.), Stockton C. of C. (bd. dirs.), Stockton Bus. Coun. and San Joaquin Partnership, Sigma Nu, Phi Kappa Phi (hon.), Beta Sigma Gamma (hon.), Alpha Phi Omega (charter, adv. bd. 1992—). Methodist. Died Feb. 18, 2000.

**ATIYEH, VICTOR GEORGE,** consultant, former Governor of Oregon; b. Portland, Oreg., Feb. 20, 1923; s. George and Linda (Asley) A.; m. Dolores Hewitt, July 5, 1944; 2 children: Tom, Suzanne. Student, U. Oreg., 1941-43; D (hon.), Pacific U., 1996. With Atiyeh Bros., Inc., Portland, 1938—43, pres., 1943-78; mem. Oreg. House of Reps., 1959—65, Oreg. State Senate, 1965—78, minority leader, 1971—78; gov. State of Oreg., Salem, 1979-86; internat. trade cons. Bd. dirs. Riedel Environ. Techs., Bank Audi Calif.; chmn. bd. dirs. Atiyeh Internat., Ltd., Portland. Past regional council pres. Columbia-Pacific council Boy Scouts America; past mem. Nat. Explorer Bd.; bd. trustees, Pacific Univ.; mem. Task Force for Lebanon, bd. Japan-America Soc. of Oreg.; del. Republican Nat. Conv., 1968, 72, 76, mem. nat. platform com., 1968, 72. Served with USCGR, 1944—45. Recipient Silver Beaver and Silver Antelope awards Boy Scouts America, Disting. Public Service award, Oreg. B'nai Brith, Public Service Honor award, US Dept. Justice. Mem.: Republican Governors Assn. (former chmn.), Western Governors Conf. (former chmn.), Japan-American Soc. Oreg. (former chmn.), Phi Gamma Delta. Republican. Episcopalian. Home: Portland, Oreg. Died July 20, 2014.

**ATLEE, WILLIAM A.,** retired surgeon; b. Lancaster, Pa., Mar. 11, 1914; s. John Light and Frances (Baer) A.; m. Mary Zimmerman, Nov. 29, 1941; children: William A., Benjamin Champneys, Mary Malone, Samuel J. BA, Yale U., 1937; MD, U. Pa., 1941. Diplomate Am. Bd. Surgery. Intern Pa. Hosp., Phila., 1941-42; practice surgery Lancaster, 1945-87; pres., mem. staff St. Joseph Hosp., Lancaster, 1958-61; mem. staff Lancaster Gen. Hosp., 1958-61. Mem. bd. Edward Hand Med. Heritage Found., Lancaster. Capt. AUS, 1941-42. Fellow AMA, ACS, Am. Coll. Chest Physicians (emeritus); mem. Am. Thoracic Soc., Coll. Physicians Phila., Lancaster City and County Med. Soc., Pa. Med. Soc., Internatioanle Soc. Surgery, Pa. Assn. Thoracic Surgery, Am. Trauma Soc. (founding), Internat. Fedn. Surg. Colls., Hamilton Club, Conestoga Country Club. Republican. Episcopalian. Home: Lancaster, Pa. Died Nov. 23, 1989.

**ATTENBOROUGH, BARON RICHARD SAMUEL,** actor, film director, producer, ambassador; b. Cambridge, England, Aug. 29, 1923; s. Frederick Attenborough; m. Sheila Beryl Grant Sim, 1945; children: Jane (dec. 2004), Michael John, Charlotte. Leverhulme scholar to Royal Acad. Dramatic Art, 1941 (Bancroft Medal); DLitt (hon.), U. Leicester, 1970, U. Kent, 1981, U. Sussex, 1987; DCL (hon.), U. Newcastle, 1974; LLD (hon.), Dickinson Coll., 1983; DLit (hon.), Am. Internat. U., 1994; DLitt (hon.), Cape Town, 2000; Doctorate of Drama (hon.), RSAMD, Glasgow, 2008. Fleming Meml. lectr. R.T.S., 1989; Cameron Mackintosh vis. prof. theatre Oxford U., 1996; pro-chancellor U. Sussex, 1970-98, chancellor 1998-2008. First stage appearance as Richard Miller in Ah, Wilderness, Intimate Theatre, Palmers Green, 1941; Ralph Berger in Awake and Sing, Arts (West End debut), 1942; The Little Foxes, Piccadilly, 1942; Brighton Rock, 1947, Garrick, 1943. Joined RAF 1943; seconded to RAF Film Unit for Journey Together, 1944; demobilized, 1946. Returned to stage in The Way Back (Home of the Brave), Westminster, 1949; To Dorothy a Son, Savoy, 1950, Garrick, 1951; Sweet Madness, Vaudeville, 1952; The Mousetrap, Ambassadors, 1952-54; Double Image, Savoy, 1956-57, St. James's, 1957; The Rape of the Belt, Piccadilly, 1957-58; (films) In Which We Serve, 1942, Schweik's New Adventure, 1943, The Hundred Pound Window, 1944, A Matter of Life and Death, 1946, School for Secrets, 1946, The Man Within, 1947, Dancing With Crime, 1947, Brighton Rock, 1947, London Belongs to Me, 1948, The Guinea Pig, 1948, The Lost People, 1949, Boys in Brown, 1949, Morning Departure, 1950, Hell is Sold Out, 1951, The Magic Box, 1951, Gift Horse, 1952, Father's Doing Fine, 1952, Eight O'Clock Walk, 1952, The Ship That Died of Shame, 1955, Private's Progress, 1956, The Baby and the Battleship, 1956, Brothers in Law, 1957, The Scamp, 1957, Dunkirk, 1958, The Man Upstairs, 1958, Sea of Sand, 1958, Danger Within, 1959, I'm All Right Jack, 1959, Jet Storm, 1959, SOS Pacific, 1959, The League of Gentlemen, 1959, The Angry Silence (also co-prodr.), 1960, All Night Long, 1961, Only Two Can Play, 1962, The Dock Brief, 1962, The Great Escape, 1963, Seance On a Wet Afternoon (also prod., Best Actor, San Sebastian Film Festival and Brit. Film Acad.), 1964, The Third Secret, 1964, Guns at Batasi (Best Actor, Brit. Film Acad.), 1964, The Flight of the Phoenix, 1965, The Sand Pebbles (Hollywood Golden Globe), 1966, Dr. Dolitte (Hollywood Golden Globe), 1967, The Bliss of Mrs. Blossom, 1968; Only When I Larf, 1968, The Magic Christian, 1969, Loot, 1970, The Last Grenade, 1970, A Severed Head, 1970, 10 Rillington Place, 1971, (voice) Cup Glory, 1972, And Then There Were None, 1974, Rosebud, 1975, Brannigan, 1975, Conduct Unbecoming, 1975, The Chess Players, 1977, The Human Factor, 1979, Jurassic Park, 1993, Miracle on 34th St., 1994, E=mc2, 1996, Hamlet, 1996, The Lost World: Jurassic Park, 1997, Elizabeth, 1998, Puckoon, 2002 (also writer, dir.); (video-voice) The Trespasser, 1998; (video) Joseph and the Amazing Technicolor Dreamcoat, 1999; (TV series-voice) Tom and Vicky, 1999; (TV) David Copperfield, 1969, The Railway Children, 2000, Jack and the Beanstalk: The Real Story, 2001; producer: Whistle Down the Wind, 1961; The L-Shaped Room, 1962; prodr., dir.: Oh! What a Lovely War (16 Internat. Awards including Hollywood Golden Globe and BAFTA UN Award), 1968, Young Winston (Hollywood Golden Globe), 1972, Gandhi (8 Oscars, 5 Brit. Acad. TV and Film Artists Awards, 5 Hollywood Golden Globes, Dirs.' Guild of Am. Award for Outstanding Directorial Achievement), 1980-81, Cry Freedom (Berlinale Kamera, BFI award tech. achievement), 1987, Chaplin, 1992, Shadowlands, 1992 (Alexander Korda award for Outstanding Brit. film of Yr., BAFTA), In Love and War, 1997, Grey Owl, 1998, Closing the Ring, 2007; dir. A Bridge Too Far (Evening News Best Drama Award), 1976, Magic, 1978, A Chorus Line, 1985; publications: In Search of Gandhi, 1982, Richard Attenborough's A Chorus Line (with Diana Carter), 1986, Cry Freedom, A Pictorial Record, 1987, (with Diana Hawkins) Entirely Up to You Darling, 2008; actor: Light Keeps Me Company (Europe), 2000, The Railway Children, 2000 (TV), Joseph and the Amazing Technicolor Dreamcoat, 2000. Goodwill amb. UNICEF, 1987-2014; mem. Brit. Actors' Equity Assoc. Coun., 1949-73, Cinematograph Films Council, 1967-73, Arts Council of Great Britain, 1970-73; formed Beaver Films with Bryan Forbes, 1959, Allied Film Makers, 1960; dir. Chelsea Football Club, 1969-82, life v.p., 1993-08, life pres., 2008-14; dir. Young Vic, 1974-84; chmn. The Actor's Charitable Trust, 1956-88; chmn. European Script Fund, 1988-96, hon. pres., 1996-2014, Combined Theatrical Charities Appeals Coun., 1964-88; chmn. Brit. Acad. Film and TV Artists (v.p. from 1971-94, chmn. trustees, 1970-2014, pres. 2002-10), 1969-70, Royal Acad. Dramatic Art, mem. coun. 1963-2014, chmn., 1972-2003, Capital Radio, 1972-92, life pres., 1992-2014, Help a London Child, 1975-2014; trustee King George V Fund for Actors and Actresses; chmn. U.K. Trustees Waterford-Kamhlaba Sch., Swaziland, Duke of York's Theatre, 1979-92, Brit. Film Inst., 1981-92, Goldcrest Films & TV, 1982-87, Com. of Inquiry into the Arts and Disabled People, 1983-85, Channel Four TV (dep. chmn. 1980-86), 1987-92, Brit. Screen Adv. Coun.; Gov. Nat. Film Sch., 1970-81, 96, hon. pres. 96; pres. Muscular Dystrophy Group of Great Britain (v.p. 1962-71), 1971-96, hon. pres. 1996-2014; pres. The Gandhi Found., Brighton Festival, 1984-95, Brit. Film Yr., 1984-86; trustee Tate Gallery, 1976-82, 94-96, Tate Found., Found. Sport and Arts; pres. Arts for Health, Gardner Centre Arts, Sussex U.; gov. Motability; patron Kingsley Hall Community Ctr., 1982-2014; R.A. Centre Disability & Arts, Leicester Decorated Commander Brit. Empire, 1967, Knighted 1976; recipient Evening Std. Film award, 40 yrs. svc. to Brit. Cinema, 1983, Praemium Imperiale award, 1998, Martin Luther King Jr. Peace Prize, 1983, Padma Bhushan, India, 1983, award of merit for humanitarianism in film making, European Film awards, 1988, Shakespeare prize Outstanding Contbn. European culture, 1992, Patricia Rothermere award for lifelong service to theatre, London Evening Standard Theatre award, 2003; named Commandeur, Ordre des Arts et des Lettres, France, 1985; Chevalier, Order de la Legion d'Honneur, France, 1988; named Freeman of City of Leicester, 1990; named fellow Kings Coll. London, 1993; named Baron, Life Peer of Long Borough of Richmond upon Thames, 1993; recipient hon. fellowship U. Wales, Bangor, 1997, Manchester Poly., 1994, Kings Coll., 1993. Fellow BAFTA, Brit. Film Inst.; mem. Garrick Club, Beefsteak Club. Avocations: collecting paintings and sculpture, listening to music, watching football. Home: Richmond Green, England. Died Aug. 24, 2014.

**AUGUSTE LE BRETON, (MONTFORT),** author; b. Lesneven, Finistere, France, Feb. 18, 1913; s. Eugene and Rosalie (Gorel) Montfort; m. Marguerite Lecacheur, Aug. 29, 1964; 1 child, Maryvonne. Author: Du Rififi Chez les Hommes, 1954, Les Hauts Murs. With French Forces, 1940—44. Decorated Croix de Guerre with stars au titre de la Resistance. Mem.: Societe des Auteurs, Compositeurs, Editeurs de Musique, Societe Auteurs, Compositeurs, Dramatiques. Died May 31, 1999.

**AUGUSTYN, JAN,** civil engineer, consultant; b. Golcowa, Rzeszow, Poland, June 15, 1921; s. Franciszek and Antonina (Bober) A.; m. Władysława Sudol, July 23, 1944; children: Maria, Pawel. MS, Silesian Tech. U., Gliwice, Poland, 1949, DS, 1965. Dept. mgr. design office Biprohut, Gliwice, 1948-62; chief engr. design office Motoprojekt, Warsaw, 1962-69; dept. mgr. Inst. Bldg. Technics, Warsaw, 1969-71; prof. rsch. ctr. Mostostal, Warsaw, 1971-80, cons. rsch. ctr., 1981-86 and from 91; prof. Tech. U., Czestochowa, Poland, 1986-91. Cons. Inst. Bldg. Technics, Warsaw, 1971-80, Poland Telecommunications S.A., Warsaw, 1991—; expert Internat. Inst. Welding, 1971-91, Internat. Assn. Bridge and Structural Engring., 1974-80; del. Internat. Orgn. Standardization, 1975-85; expert Scientific Coun., Ministry of Bldg., Poland, 1981-85. Author: Failures of Steel Structures, 1976 (Ministry of Bldgs. award 1976), Technology and Design of Steel Structures, 1981 (Ministry of Bldgs. award 1982), Rational Application of Steel, 1982 (Ministry of Sci. 1983), Welded Connections, 1987 (Ministry of Bldgs. award 1988). 2nd Lt. Polish Army, 1961. Recipient State award State Awards Com. Poland, Warsaw, 1955, Best Design awards (5) Ministry of Bldgs., Warsaw, 1968-74, Scientific award Ministry of Sci. and Technics, Warsaw, 1976. Mem. Polish Assn. Bldgs. Engrs., Steel Structure sect. Polish Acad. Scis. Roman Catholic. Avocations: unprofessional cosmology, tinkering. Home: Warsaw, Poland. Deceased.

**AUTH, TONY (WILLIAM ANTHONY AUTH JR.),** artist; b. Akron, Ohio, May 7, 1942; s. William Anthony and Julia Kathleen (Donnally) A.; m. Eliza Drake; children: Katie, Emily BA in Biological Illustration, UCLA, 1965; D (hon.), U. Arts, 2012. Chief med. illustrator Rancho Los Amigos Hosp., Downey, Calif., 1964-70; cartoonist editl. page Phila. Inquirer, 1971—2012. Author/illustrator: (children's book) Sleeping Babies', 1989; anthologies of drawings; Behind the Lines, 1978, Lost in Space - The Reagan Years, 1988; Illustrator: The Tree of Here, 1993. Recipient awards Overseas Press Club, 1975, 76, 84, 86, 92, Sigma Delta Chi, 1976, Pulitzer prize for Editl. Cartooning, 1976, Herblock prize, 2005 Died Sept. 14, 2014.

**AVALOS, LUIS,** actor; b. Havana, Cuba, Sept. 2, 1946; came to U.S., 1946; s. Jose Antonio and Estrella (De Leon) A. BFA, NYU, 1969. Resident actor Lincoln Ctr. Repertory Co., N.Y.C., 1969-73. Actor: (Broadway debut) Never Jam Today, City Ctr. Theatre, N.Y.C., 1968, (stage prodns.) Camino Real, 1969, The Zoo Story, The Good Woman of Setzuan, Kool Aid, Armedians, Antigone, A Streetcar Named Desire, Twelve Angry Men, others, (feature films) Badge 373, 1970, Hot Stuff, 1979, Stir Crazy, 1980, Hollywood Homicide, 2003, $5 a Day, 2008; (TV series) The Electric Company, 1973-78, Highcliff Manor, 1979, Condo, 1983, E.R., 1984, (TV mini-series) Fresno, 1986), (TV spl.) George Burns Comedy Hour, 1985; also appeared in numerous TV episodes including Barney Miller, Simon and Simon, Benson, Kojak. Named Best Actor in Theatre, Assn. Hispanic Critics, 1974, Hispanic of Yr., Caminos mag, 1984. Mem. Actors' Equity Assn., Screen Actors Guild, AFTRA, Nat. Found. for the Arts (judge). Avocations: swimming, tennis. Died Jan. 22, 2014.

**AVE, JOOP,** former Indonesian government official; b. Yogyakarta, Indonesia, Dec. 5, 1934; Student, Fgn. Svc. Acad., 1957; Degree in Polit. Sci., U. Philippines, Manila. Dep.dir. protocol Ministry of Fgn. Affairs, 1965-67; consul N.Y., 1967-71; exec. asst. to pres. UN Gen. Assembly, 1971-72; chief of protocol Presidential Palace, 1972-78; dir. gen. protocol & consular affairs, chief state protocol Ministry Fgn. Affairs, 1978-82; dir. gen. tourism Ministry Tourism, Post and Telecomm., 1982-93; min. tourism, post & telecomm. Govt. of Indonesia, 1993—98. Died Feb. 5, 2014.

**AVERBOOK, BERYL DAVID,** retired surgeon; b. Superior, Wis., Aug. 17, 1920; s. Abraham B. and Clara (Zeichig) A.; m. Gloria Sloane, Apr. 2, 1955; children: Bruce Jeffrey, Allan Wayne. Student, Superior State Tchrs. Coll., 1938-39; BS, U. Wis., 1942, MD, 1945; postgrad., U. Colo., 1948-50. Diplomate in gen. surgery and gen. vascular surgery Am. Bd. Surgery. Intern. Akron City Hosp., Ohio, 1945-46; resident VA Hosp., Denver, 1948-50, Rochester Gen. Hosp., NY, 1950-51, VA Hosp., LA, 1951-54; chief surgery UCLA Harbor Med. Ctr., 1954—61; practice medicine specializing in gen. surgery, Torrance, Calif., 1948—2004; ret., 2004. With surgical pathology staff, Harbor UCLA Med. Ctr., 1948-9; instr. surgery UCLA-Harbor Gen. Hosp., 1954-58; practice tumor and vascular surgery, Torrance, 1961—; asst. prof. surgery UCLA Med. Ctr., 1958-61, asst. clin. prof. surgery, 1961-64; chief surg. services Los Angeles County Harbor Gen. Hosp., Torrance, 1954-61; staff Mary Med. Ctr., Torrance Mem. Med. Ctr. Contbr. articles to profl. jours. Served to capt. M.C., AUS, also res. Recipient Cert. of Recognition, Calif. State Senate, 2005, Cert. of Special Congressional Recognition for Outstanding and Invaluable Svc. to Cmty., 2005, Outstanding Svc. tribute, South Bay Med. Cmty., Torrance, Calif., 2005, Recognition of Svc. tribute, Harbor UCLA; named Physician of Yr., LA County Med. Assn., 1981. Mem.: AMA, ACS, Am. Pharm. Assn., UCLA Med. Alumni Assn., Am. Bd. Surgery, Am. Assn. Med. Colls., LA County Med. Assn., LA Acad. Medicine, Long Beach Surg. Soc., Soc. Angiology, So. Calif. Vascular Surg. Soc., Internat. Acad. Applied Thrombosis/Hemostasis, Internat. Soc. Vascular Surgery, Am. Assn. Vascular Surgery, Am. Assn. Head and Neck Surgery, Soc. Clin. Vascular Surgery, Soc. Vascular Surgery, Am. Soc. Gen. Surgeons, Phi Beta Kappa, Wis. Pharm. Alumni Assn., Wis. Med. Alumni Assn., Phi Delta Epsilon, Phi Lambda Upsalon, Rho Chi. Deceased.

**AVERY, HENRY,** business development service executive; b. Boston, Oct. 6, 1919; m. Mary Ruth Halverson. SB in Chem. Engring., MIT, 1941. Bus. devel. engr. G.L. Cabot Co., Boston, 1946-51; gen. mgr., plasticizer Coal Chems., Indsl. Chems. divs. Pitts. Coke and Chem. Co., 1951-60; exec. v.p. Pitts. Chem. Co., 1960-66, also bd. dirs.; group v.p. adminstrn. and devel. USS Chem., 1966-68, v.p. plastics, 1968-76, v.p. planning and devel., 1976-79, v.p. planning, devel. and adminstrn., 1979; v.p. Koch Devel. Co., 1979-81, Koch Venture Capital, 1979-81; pres. Avery Bus. Devel. Services, Waltham, Mass., from 1981. Lectr. seminar Strategic Planning, UN Econ. Commn., Poland, 1979, Strategy Planning, Japan, 1979; civilian aide to Sec. of Army for Western Pa., 1978-86; regional advisor SBA.

Editor ordnance sect. U.S. Army Mil. Ency. for 15th Army Group; editor sch. text book Organization and Functions of the Army Ordnance Department, Business Planning. Mem. Regional Export Expansion Council, U.S. Dept. Commerce; mem. steering com. Nat. Service Corps.; United Mental Health Services of Allegheny County; chmn. MIT Ednl. Council for Western Pa., Am. Wind Symphony (past v.p.), NCCJ; past elder and deacon Mt. Lebanon Presbyn. Ch. Mem. MIT Alumni Assn. (past regional v.p., bd. dirs.), Am. Def. Preparedness Assn. (past pres. Pitts. chpt., nat. vice chmn., exec. com.), Mil. Order of World Wars (commdr. 1976), Res. Officer Assn., Mayflower Descs., SAR, Greater Pitts. C. of C. (hon. life, past pres., chmn. bd. dirs.). Clubs: Duquesne, University, Tchrs. Coll. Press, Chemists, Sawgrass, MIT Faculty. Home: Jacksonville, Fla. Died Oct. 21, 2008.

**AXEL, GABRIEL,** film director; b. Aarhus, Denmark, Apr. 18, 1918; m. Lucie Juliette Laraignou (dec. 1996). Grad., Royal Danish Theater Actors Sch., 1945. Dir.: (films) Guld Og Gronne Skove, 1959, Tre Piger I Paris, 1963, Hagbard and Signe (The Red Mantle), 1967, Beloved Toy, 1968, Amour, 1970, Med Kaerlig Hilsen, 1971, Familien Gykdenkaal, 1975, Alt Paa et Braet, 1976, Babette's Feast, 1987 (Acad. Award for Best Fgn. Lang. Film, 1987), Christian, 1989, Lumiere and Company, 1995, Leila, 2001; (TV films): The Crime of Our Time, the Night Watch, the Vicar of Tours, The Columns of Heaven, 1986; dir., screenwriter: (films) Prince of Jutland, 1993. Recipient Lifetime Achievement award, Copenhagen Internat. Film Festival, 2003, Rungstedlund award, 2012. Died Feb. 9, 2014.

**AXFORD, ROGER WILLIAM,** adult education educator, consultant; b. Grand Island, Nebr., July 22, 1920; married; 3 children. AB in Polit. Sci., Nebr. Wesleyan U.; MA in Sociology, U. Chgo., PhD in Adult Edn. Pres. Recareering Inst., Tempe, Ariz.; assoc. prof. adult ctr. Ctr. for Higher Adult Edn. Ariz. State U., Tempe, prof. emeritus. Adult edn. educator various U.S. instns.; condr. study tours in Norway, Gt. Britain, China and Japan; vis. prof. Inter Am. Univ., Calif., P.R., U. So. Calif., Fla. State U.; lectr.-cons. in adult edn. Ill. Migrant Coun., Commonwealth of Can., U. P.R., Universidad Nacional Exptl. Simon Rodrigues in Venezuela. Author: College Community Consultation, Adult Education: The Open Door, Black American Heroes, Native Americans: 23 Indian Biographies, Spanish Speaking Heroes: 23 Biographies, Too Long Silent: Japanese Americans SPEAK OUT!, Perspectives on Adult Education Administration, Speaking About Adults, Zany Jokes for Funny Folks, Successful Recareering: How to Shift Gears, The Best Fourth of Life, Mirror for Marriage, 2001, A Peace of My Mind: An Unrepentent Peacenick, Aging Graciously!, 2003. Died Aug. 1, 2003.

**AYALA-CASTAÑARES, AGUSTÍN,** paleontologist, scientist, educator; b. Mazatlán, Mexico, Aug. 28, 1925; s. Agustin Ayala and Maria Luisa Castañares; m. Alma Irma López, 1957; children: Agustín, Alma Irma, Adriana Lilia. BS in Biology, U. Nat. Autónoma Mex., 1954, D in Biology, 1963; MS in Geology, Stanford U., 1959; D (hon.), U. Bordeaux I, France, 1988. Micropaleontologist Petroleos Mexicanos, 1950-54; prof. paleontology, hist. geology and micropale ontology Nat. Poly. Inst., Mexico City, 1955-60; rschr., head dept. micropaleontology and marine sci. U. Nat. Autñnoma Mex., 1956-67, prof. micropaleontology, from 1961, head dept. biology, 1965—67, dir. Biology Inst., 1967-73; assoc. rschr. Scripps Inst. Oceanography, U. San Diego, from 1968. Chmn. Intergovernmental Oceanographic Commn, UNESCO, 1977-82; chmn. organizing com. Joint Oceanog. Assembly, Acapulco, Mex., 1988; gen. coord. Interinat. Commn. Evaluation Higher Edn., 1991-92, Nat. Plan for creating proper infrastructure inmarine scis. and techs., Nat. Program of sci. and tech. for improvement of marine resources. Contbr. over 60 articles to profl. jours. Trustee Internat. Ctr. Living Aquatic Resources Mgmt., Manila, 1989-94. Fellow Geol. Soc. Am.; mem. Internat. Assn. Plant Taxonomy and Nomenclature, Soc. Econ. Paleontologists and Mineralogists, Soc. Paleontol. Suisse, Am. Paleontol., Paleontol. Assn. London, Acad. Sci. Investigation, Soc. Limnology and Oceanography, Am. Ecol. Soc., Soc. Systematic Zoology, Am. Assn. Petroleum Geologists, Calif. Acad. Sci. Roman Catholic. Home: Mexico, Mexico. Died Nov. 23, 2005.

**AYAYO, A.B.C. OCHOLLA,** anthropologist, educator; b. Kisumu, Kenya, May 25, 1938; s. Ayayo Silfano Kamjema and Ngalo Asenath Owiti; m. Berit Harry Ocholla (div.); 1 child, Jenny Atieno Ocholla; m. Margareta Kristina Fälkestran; children: Akinyi Magareta Ocholla, Erik Ayayo Ocholla. Tech. cert., St. Xavier Tech. Inst., Bombay, 1960; cert. in Egyptology, Cairo U., 1961; cert. in elec. engring., Czech High Tech. U., Prague, 1970; BA, Prague U., 1970; PhD, Uppsala U., Sweden, 1976. Lectr. Khartoum (Sudan) U., 1977—80; rsch. fellow Uppsala U., 1971—76; from lectr. to assoc. prof. Nairobi (Kenya) U., 1980—94, prof., from 1994, dir. Population Studies and Rsch. Inst., 1995—2003. Dean humanity Gt. Lakes U., Kisumu, Kenya, from 2003. Author: Traditional Ideologies and Ethics, 1976, The Luo Culture, 1980. Mem.: Kenya Assn. Anthropologists (chmn. 1990—99), Union African Population Studies (chmn. sci. com. 1989—2000), Pan-African Assn. Anthropology (v.p. 1989—95, pres.-elect 1994—98), Tropical Inst. Cmty. Health (life). Avocations: reading, evnironmentalist, soccer, walking, travel. Home: Nairobi, Kenya. Died Sept. 16, 2006.

**AYRES, JANICE RUTH,** social services administrator; b. Idaho Falls, Jan. 23, 1921; d. Low Ray and Frances Mae (Salem) Mason; m. Thomas Woodrow Ayres, Nov. 27, 1953 (dec. 1966); 1 child, Thomas Woodrow Jr. (dec.). MBA, U. So. Calif., 1952, M in Mass Comms., 1953. Asst. mktg. dir. Disneyland, Inc., Anaheim, Calif., 1954-59; gen. mgr. Tamasha Town & Country Club, Anaheim, Calif., 1959-65; dir. mktg. Am. Heart Assn., Santa Ana, Calif., 1966-69; state exec. dir. Nev. Assn. Mental Health, Las Vegas, 1969-71; exec. dir. Clark Co. Easter Seal Treatment Ctr., Las Vegas, 1971-73; mktg. dir., fin devel. officer So. Nev. Drug Abuse Coun., Las Vegas, 1973-74; exec. dir. Nev. Assn. Retarded Citizens, Las Vegas, 1974-75; assoc., cons. Don Luke & Assocs., Phoenix, 1976-77; program dir. Inter-Tribal Coun. Nev., Reno, 1977-79; exec. dir. Ret. Sr. Vol. Program, Carson City, Nev., from 1979. Chair sr. citizen summit State of Nev., 1996; apptd. by Gov. Guinn, Nev. Commn. Aging, 2001; presenter in field; apptd. del. by Gov. of Nev. White House Conf. on Aging, 2005; sec. to bd. dirs. Chinese Workers Mus. Am., from 2008; elected pres. Resun Corps. Assn., 2009; pres. Sr. Corps Assn., 2008; sr. advocate, elect. sec., Russia, 2010. Del. White Ho. Conf. on Aging, 2005; bd. suprs. Carson City, Nev., from 1992; obligation bond com., legis. chair; commr. Carson City Parks and Recreation, from 1993; bd. dirs. Nev. Dept. Transp., 1993; active No. Corp. for Nat. and Cmty. Svc. by Gov., 1994, V&TRR Commn., 1993, re-appointed by Gov., from 2005, chair, 1995, vice-chair, chair pub. rels. com., bd. dirs. Hist. V&TRR Bd.; chair PR Cmty./V&RR Commn. Nev. Home Health Assn.; appointed liaison Carson City Sr. Citizens Bd., 1995; chair summit Rural Nev. Sr. Citizens, Carson City; pres. No. Nev. RR Found., from 1996; chair Tri-Co-RR Commn., 1995, Gov.'s Nev. Commn. for Corp. in Nat. and Cmty. Svc., from 1997, pres., 1998, Carson City Pub. Transp. Commn., from 1998; Carson City Commn. for Clean Groundwater Act, from 1998; chairperson Celebrate Svc. Conf. Americore, 2000; apptd. by Gov. of Nev. Commn. on Aging, from 2001; apptd. by Nev. Gov. New Nev. Commn. to Restructure the Historic V&T RR, from 2002; mem. Nev. Commn. on Aging, from 2001; apptd. rep. of gov. to Nev. Commn. Recruitment V&T RR, 2002; apptd. by Nev. Treas. Brian Krolicki Women's Commn. Fin., from 2003; re-appointed to commn. by Gov. Nev. Commn. for Nat. and Cmty. Svc., from 2005; apptd. del. to White House Conf. on Aging Nev. Gov., 2005; apptd. to bd. dirs. Chinese Workers Mus. Am. Constrn. Project, 2007; elec. sec., bd. dir. Chinese Workers Mus., 2008; corp. sec. Chem. Workers Mus. Am., from 2008; elected sec. chmn. Washes Mus. Am., 2009. Recipient Gold award, Western Fairs Assn., 2000, Woman of Distinction award, Soroptimist, 2003, Carson City Optimist, 2003, Nat. Optimist Conv., Reno, Nev., 2003, Outstanding Svc. to Seniors Blue Star award, Sanford Ctr. on Aging, 2004, Outstanding Contbn. to Success of Women in Bus., Carson Valley Sorpotomists, Legand in Aging award, UNR, 2010, Leaving Legend award, U. Nev., Sanford Ctr. On Aging, 2010, Lifetime Mem. award, Nat. League Women Voters, 2012; named Woman of Distinction, Soroptimist Club, 1988, Oustanding Dir. of Excellence, Gov. State of Nev., 1989, Outstanding Nev. Women's Role Model, Nev. A.G., 1996, Woman of Distinction, Carson Valley Optimist, 2002, Nev.'s Outstanding Older Worker for Experience-Works, 2002, Oldest CEO in Nev., 2002, Outstanding Nev. Pvt. Citizen, Nev. Gov. Kenny Guinn, 2003, Outstanding Dir., Vol. Action Ctr., J.C. Penney Co., invitee to White Ho. for outstanding contbns. to Am., Living Legacy, UNR; named to White House Conf. on Aging as Gov. del., 2005; scholar, U. Reno. Mem.: AAUW (elected pres., capital br. 2009), Social Svc. Programs Sr. Advs., Nev. Sr. Corps. Assn. (elected pres. 2009), Nevada Assn. Sr. Corps Dirs. (elected pres. 2008), Chinese Mus. Am. (sec., elec. sec., bd. dirs.), Nat. Assn. Ret. and Sr. Vol. Dirs., Inc. (pres. 2003, nat. pres. from 2003), Internat. Assn. Bus. Commentators, No. Nev. Railroad Found. (pres. from 1996, 2005—08), Am. Soc. Assn. Execs., Nev. Assn. Transit Svcs. (bd. dirs., legis. chmn.), Nev. Fair and Rodeo Assn. (pres.), Nat. Soc. Fund Raising Execs., Women in Radio and TV, Pub. Rels. Soc. Am. (chpt. pres., Outstanding 25 Yr. Svc. award 2004), Internat. Platform Assn., Am. Mktg. Assn. (bd. dirs. from 1999), Am. Mgmt. Assn. (bd. dirs.), League of Women Voters (Lifetime award Status 2012), Nat. Women's Polit. Caucus. Home: Carson City, Nev. Died June 2013.

**AZCONA HOYO, JOSÉ SIMON,** former president of Honduras; b. La Ceiba, Atlantida, Honduras, Jan. 26, 1927; s. José Simón Azcona Velez and Carmen Hoyo Pérez; m. Miriam Bocock Selva; children: Miriam Elizabeth, José Simón, Javier Enrique. Degree in civil engring., Univ. Nacional Autónoma de Honduras, Tegucigalpa, 1963. Photogrammetrist, draftsman Instuto Geográfico Nacional, Tegucigalpa, head design sect., 1961-63; road bldg. supr. Dirección Central Gaminos, 1964; distbn. asst. div. del norts Empresa Nacional de Energía Eléctrica, San Pedro Sula, Cortés, 1964-66; design engr., factory bldg. engr. Industria Aceitera Honduena, San Lorenzo, Valle, 1966-67; urbanization and housing bldg. project supr. El Sauce, La Ceiba, 1967-68; head tech. dept. Federación Hondurena de Cooperativas de Vivienda Limitada, Tegucigalpa, 1969-72, gen. mgr., 1973-82; minister of communications, pub. works and transp. Republic of Honduras, Tegucigalpa, 1982-83, pres., 1986-90. Mem. Liberal Party Action Front, Tegucigalpa, 1962, 63, 64; candidate for congress, Francisco Morazán, 1963; coordinator Liberal Party Engrs. Ridista Faction, 1973-74, orgn. and publicity sec. of cen. directory, 1975-76; polit. tng. sec. Liberal Party Exec. Cen. Council, 1977-78, orgn. and publicity sec., 1979-80; pres. exec. council Liberal Party, 1983; mem. congress for Francisco Morazán, 1982-85. Died Oct. 24, 2005.

**BABA, ABDUL GHAFAR,** deputy prime minister; b. Kuala Pilah, Negri Sembilan, Feb. 18, 1925; m. Puan Asmah binti Alang Baba; 10 children. Grad., Sultan Idris Tchrs. Tng. Coll., Perak. Sec. Malacca United Malays Nat. Orgn. Divs., 1951—55, former tchr.; chmn. United Malays Nat. Orgn. Divs.; mem. Fed. Legis. Coun., Malaysia, 1955—59; chief min. Malacca, 1959—67; chmn. Majlis Amanah Rakyat, 1967—69, senator & min., 1969, min. nat. rural devel., 1969—74, min. agr. & rural devel., 1974—76, dep. prime min., from 1986; min. Nat. Rural Devel., from 1986, min. housing & local govt., from 1986. Chmn. United Malays Nat. Orgn. Econ. Bur., Majlis Amanah Rakyat Edn. Fund, MARA Shares Trust, Ayer Kroh Country Club, Fin. Complex. Died Apr. 23, 2006.

**BACALL, LAUREN (BETTY JOAN PERSKE),** actress; b. NYC, Sept. 16, 1924; m. Humphrey Bogart, May 21, 1945 (dec. Jan. 14, 1957); children: Stephen, Leslie; m. Jason Robards, July 4, 1961 (div. Sept. 10, 1969); 1 child, Sam. Student, American Acad. Dramatic Art. Actress: (Broadway plays) Franklin Street, 1942, Goodbye Charlie, 1959, Cactus Flower, 1966-68, Applause, 1969-71 (Sarah Siddons award 1975); also road co., 1971-72, London co., 1972-73 (Tony award for Best Actress in a Musical 1970), Woman of the Year, 1981 (Tony award for Best Actress in a Musical 1981, Sarah Siddons award 1983), Sweet Bird of Youth, 1983 (London, 1985, Australia, 1986, L.A., 1987; (films) To Have and Have Not, 1944, Confidential Agent, 1945, The Big Sleep, 1946, Dark Passage, 1947, Key Largo, 1948, Young Man With a Horn, 1949, Bright Leaf, 1950, How To Marry a Millionaire, 1953, Woman's World, 1954, The Cobweb, 1955, Blood Alley, 1955, Written on the Wind, 1956, Designing Woman, 1957, The Gift of Love, 1958, Flame Over India, 1959, Shock Treatment, 1964, Sex and the Single Girl, 1965, Harper, 1966, Murder on the Orient Express, 1974, The Shootist, 1976, Health, 1980, The Fan, 1981, Tree of Hands, 1987, Appointment With Death, 1987, Mr. North, 1988, Misery, 1990, A Star for Two, 1991, All I Want for Christmas, 1991, Ready to Wear (Prêt-à-Porter), 1994, My Fellow Americans, 1996, The Mirror Has Two Faces, 1996 (Golden Globe award, 1997, SAG award, 1997), The Line King: Al Hirschfield, 1996, Le Jour et la Nuit, 1997, Diamonds, 1999, Dogville, 2003, The Limit, 2003, Birth, 2004, (voice only) Howl's Moving Castle, 2004, Firedog, 2005, Manderlay, 2005, These Foolish Things, 2006, The Walker, 2007, Eve, 2008, (voice only) Scooby-Doo and the Goblin King, 2008, Wide Blue Yonder, 2010, (voice only) Firedog, 2010, The Forger, 2012, (voice only) Ernest & Celestine, 2014; (TV movies) The Paris Collections, 1968, Applause, 1973, A Commercial Break (Happy Endings), 1975, Perfect Gentlemen, 1978, Dinner at Eight, 1989, The Portrait, 1992, A Foreign Field, 1993, From the Mixed Up Files of Mrs. Basil E. Frankweiler, 1995, The Man Who Had Everything, 1998, Madeline: Lost in Paris, 1999 Too Rich: The Secret Life of Doris Duke, 1999; (TV appearances) "What's My Line?", 1953, 1965, The Rockford Files, 1979, Chicago Hope, 1998, So Graham Norton, 2000, The Sopranos, 2006, Wonder Pets, 2009, (voice only) Family Guy, 2014; Author: Lauren Bacall: By Myself, 1978, Now, 1994, By Myself and Then Some, 2005 Recipient American Acad. Dramatic Arts award for achievement, 1963, Standard award London Evening, 1973, Nat. Book award, 1980, George Eastman award, 1990, Cecil B. DeMille award Hollywood Fgn. Press Assn., 1993 Kennedy Ctr. Honors John F. Kennedy Ctr. for the Performing Arts, 1997, Women in Hollywood Tribute award, Elle Mag., 2007, Bette Davis Medal of Honor, Boston U., 2008, Hon. Acad. award, Acad. Motion Picture Arts & Sciences, 2009; decorated comdr. Order of Arts and Letters (France), 1995; named one of The 50 Most Beautiful People in the World, People, 1997. Died Aug. 12, 2014.

**BACHERT, ROBERT FREDERIC,** mathematician, systems analyst; b. Sioux City, Iowa, Sept. 26, 1932; s. Fred Harold and Gail Alvina (Bohn) B.; m. Ruth Hildegard Neubauer, Sept. 5, 1959; children: Andrew, Diana. BS in Math. and Physics cum laude, Morningside Coll., Sioux City, Iowa, 1956; MS in Math., U. Dayton, 1967. Instr. engring. graphics Princeton (N.J.) U., 1956-59; instr. math. Tri-State Coll., Angola, Ind., 1959-62; asst. engr. Systems Rsch. Lab., Inc., Dayton, Ohio, 1962-66; mathematician biophysics div. USAF/Armstrong Aerospace Med. Rsch. Lab., Dayton, 1966-70, computer systems analyst human engring. div., 1970-83, plans and programs analyst tech. integration div., 1983-85, tech. dir., 1985-89; systems study mgr./deputy for devel. planning USAF/Aeronautical Systems Div., Dayton, from 1989. Ind. cons., Dayton, 1980—. Contbr. articles to profl. jours.; developer of ideal modeling methodology. Sgt. USAF, 1951-52. Mem. Human Factors Soc., SIGART (spl. interest group on AI), Masons, Scottish Rite, Zeta Sigma. Home: Dayton, Ohio. Died Dec. 20, 1993.

**BADDILEY, SIR JAMES,** biochemist; b. Manchester, England, May 15, 1918; s. James and Ivy Logan (Cato) B.; m. Hazel Mary Townsend, Sept. 20, 1944; 1 child, Christopher James. BSc in Chemistry with 1st class honors, U. Manchester, 1941, MSc, 1942, PhD, 1944, DSc, 1954; DSc (hon.), Heriot-Watt U., 1979, Bath U., 1986; ScD, U. Cambridge, 1986. Staff dept. biochemistry Lister Inst. Preventive Medicine, London, 1949-54; Rockefeller traveling fellow Harvard U. Med. Sch., 1954; prof. organic chemistry U. Newcastle upon Tyne (formerly U. Durham), 1955-77, prof. chem. microbiology, 1977-83, emeritus prof. chem. microbiology, dir. microbiology chemistry rsch. lab., head Sch. Chemistry, 1968-78. Sci. and engring. rsch. coun. sr. fellow U. Cambridge, 1981-84; adb. bd. Brit. Nat. Com. Biochemistry, 1961-66, govt. grant bd. Royal Soc., 1962-66, coun., 1977-79, mem. coun. and coms. sci. and engring. rsch. coun., 1979-81; adv. com. CIBA and CIBA-GEIGY fellowships, 1966-88; Karl Folkers lectr., vis. prof. U. Ill., 1962. Created knight, 1977; recipient Meldola medal Royal Inst. Chemistry, 1947; Imperial Chem. Industries fellow, U. Cambridge, 1945-49, Swedish Med. Rsch. Coun. at Wenner-Grens Inst., Stockholm, 1947-49; fellow Pembroke Coll., Cambridge U. Fellow Royal Soc. (Leeuwenhoek lectr. 1967, Davy medal 1974), Royal Soc. Edinburgh, Royal Soc. Chemistry (past mem. coun., Corday-Morgan medal and prize 1952, Tilden lectr. 1959, Pedler lectr. 1978); mem. Biochem. Soc. (com. 1964), Soc. Gen. Microbiology (coun. 1973-75), Am. Soc. Biochemistry and Molecular Biology (hon.). Home: Cambridge, England. Died 2008.

**BAENDER, MARGARET WOODRUFF,** editor, freelance/self-employed writer; b. Salt Lake City, Apr. 1, 1921; d. Russell Kimball and Margaret Angeline (McIntyre) Woodruff; m. Phillip Albers Baender, Aug. 17, 1946 (dec.); children: Kristine Lynn, Charlene Anne, Michael Phillip, Russell Richard. BA, U. Utah, 1944. Clerical and pers. work, San Francisco, 1970—75; reporter and columnist Valley Pioneer, Danville, Calif., 1975—77; editor Diablo Inferno, Calif., 1971—76. Author: Shifting Sands, 1981, Tail Waggings of Maggie, 1982. Fellow: Internat. Biog. Assn.; mem.: AAUW, Internat. Women's Writers Guild, Soc. Children's Book Writers, Nat. Writers Club, Am. Biog. Inst. (Raleigh, N.C. chpt.) (life), Alpha Delta Pi. Republican. Episcopalian. Achievements include starting pen-pal svc. for children and young adults in Nyazura, Zimbawe, 1986. Died Mar. 11, 1999.

**BAER, HAROLD, JR.,** federal judge; b. NYC, Feb. 16, 1933; s. Harold and Edna (Jacobus) B.; m. Suzanne Harris, Aug. 18, 1957; children: Elizabeth Jane, Linda Gail. Grad. magna cum laude, Hobart Coll., 1954; LLB, Yale U., 1957. Bar: N.Y. 1959, US Dist. Ct. (southern dist.) N.Y. 1961, US Ct. Appeals (2d cir.) 1961, US Supreme Ct. 1964. Asst. to gen. counsel Greater NY Mutual Ins., 1958—59; asst. counsel NY State Commn. on the Govtl. Ops. NYC, 1959—60, NY State Commn. on Investigation, 1960—61; asst. US atty. (southern dist.) NY, chief organized crime unit, US Dept. Justice, NYC, 1961-66, 1st asst. US atty., chief criminal divsn., 1970-71; exec. dir. civilian complaint rev. bd. NYC Police Dept., 1966-67; ptnr. Guggenheimer & Untermyer, NYC, 1968-70, 72-82; justice NY State Supreme Ct., 1982-92; exec. jud. officer Judicial Arbitration & Mediation Services/Endispute, 1992-94; judge US Dist. Ct. (southern dist.) NY, NYC, 1994—2004, sr. judge, 2004—14. Mem. N.Y.C. mayoral com. alleged police corruption, 1993, 94. Author: Judges Under Fire: Human Rights, Independent Judges, and the Rule of Law, 2011; co-author: (with Robert C. Meade) Deposition Practice and Procedures in Federal And New York State Courts, 2011; contbr. articles to law jours. Mem. N.Y. State Bar Assn. (house of dels. 1977-89, 93-96), N.Y. County Lawyers Assn. (pres. 1979-81, bd. dirs., mem. exec. com.), Assn. Bar City N.Y. (criminal justice coun. 1980-82, judiciary com. 1993-94), Network Bar Leaders (founder, chmn. 1981-83), Assn. Justices N.Y.C. and N.Y. State (officer). Home: New York, NY. Died May 27, 2014.

**BAER, JEAN LOUISE (MRS. HERBERT FENSTERHEIM),** writer; b. Chgo., May 17, 1926; d. Fred E. and Helen (Roth) Baer; m. Herbert Fensterheim, June 20, 1968. BA, Cornell U., 1945. Writer press dept. MBC, NYC, 1945—46; publicist Air Features, Inc., NYC, 1946—49, Coll & Freedman Pub. Rels., NYC, 1949—51; program info. editor Voice America, NYC, 1953; publicity dir. Seventeen Mag., NYC, 1953—68, spl. projects dir., 1968—74, sr. editor, 1968—74. Author: Follow Me!, 1965, The Single Girl Goes to Town, 1968, The Second Wife, 1972, Don't Say Yes When You Want to Say No, 1975, How to Be An Assertive (Not Aggressive) Woman, 1976, Stop Running Scared!, 1977, The Self-Chosen, 1982, Making Life Right When It Feels All Wrong, 1988. Mem.: Newswomen's Club (NY), Overseas Press Club America (sec. bd. govs.), Woman Pays Club (NYC). Home: New York, NY. Died 1991.

**BAER, LELAND,** finance executive; b. Bedford, Eng., May 10, 1935; s. Frederick William and Annie Macmillan Baer; m. Consuelo Mateus, July 3, 1982; children: Ashley, Alexander. Cert. internat. financier, Internat. Soc. Financiers; cert. fraud examiner, Internat. Assn. Fraud Examiners. Mem. ops. staff Caltex Oil Co., London, 1950-59; gen. mgr. Am. Autos, Frankfurt, Germany, 1960-70; owner BMW NATO Sales, Germany, 1970-80, Baer Internat. Ltd., London, from 1980. Served with Brit. mil., 1953-55, Germany. Mem. Inst. of Dirs. Mem. Conservative Party. Avocations: reading, jogging, gardening, sports, driving. Home: London, England. Died Dec. 15, 2003.

**BAER, MORLEY,** photographer; b. Toledo, Apr. 5, 1916; s. Clarence Theodore and Blanche Evelyn (Schweitzer) Baer; m. Frances Manney, Oct. 14, 1946; 1 child, Joshua David. BA, U. Mich., 1936, MA, 1937. Photographer, Chgo., 1938—41, Carmel, Calif., from 1946. Instr. photography Ansel Adams Workshops, 1963—80, U. Calif., Santa Cruz, from 1975, Friends of Photography, Carmel, from 1975. Mem.: Am. Soc. Mag. Photographers, Friends of Photography (bd. dir. 1970). Died Nov. 9, 1995.

**BAERNSTEIN, ALBERT, II,** retired mathematician; b. Birmingham, Ala., Apr. 25, 1941; s. Albert and Kathryn (Wiesel) B.; m. Judith Haynes, June 14, 1962; children: P. Renée, Amy. Student, U. Ala., 1958-59; AB, Cornell U., 1962; MA, U. Wis., 1964, PhD, 1968. Instr. math. U. Wis., Whitewater, 1966-68; asst. prof. math. Syracuse U., NY, 1968-72; assoc. prof. math. Washington U., St. Louis, 1972-74, prof. math., 1974—2011, prof. emeritus, 2011—14. Fulbright sr. research scholar Imperial Coll., London, 1976-77 Mem. American Math. Soc., Math. Assn. America Home: Saint Louis, Mo. Died June 10, 2014.

**BAHNA, RALPH M.,** travel company executive; b. Grand Rapids, Mich., Aug. 23, 1942; s. Ralph and Frieda (Mushro) Bahna; m. Dorothy Ballard, 1966; children: Laura, Deborah, Adam. BA, U. Mich., 1964; MBA, U. Calif. Berkeley Haas Sch. Bus., 1965. Worked Trans World Airlines, Inc.; sr. v.p. mktg. & sales Cunard Lines, Ltd., 1973—77, pres., COO worldwide ops., 1977—81, CEO, 1981—89; chmn. Priceline.com, Inc., 2004—13. Bd. dirs. Priceline.com Inc., 1998—2013. Died Feb. 24, 2014.

**BAILE, CLIFTON A.,** biologist, researcher; b. Warrensburg, Mo., Feb. 8, 1940; s. Harold F. and Salome (Mohler) B.; m. Beth Lucile Hoover, Aug. 21, 1960; children: Christopher A., Marisa B. BS in Agr., Bus., Cen. Mo. State U., 1962; PhD in Nutrition, U. Mo., 1965; MA (hon.), U. Pa., 1979. NIH rsch. fellow Sch. Pub. Health Harvard U., Boston, 1964-66, from. instr. to asst. prof. Sch. Pub. Health, 1966-71; mgr. neurobiol. rsch. SmithKline Animal Health, Phila., 1971-75; from assoc. prof. to prof. Sch. Vet. Medicine U. Pa., Phila., 1975-82; disting. fellow, dir. R & D Monsanto Agrl. Co., St. Louis, 1982-95; adj. prof. nutrition Sch. Medicine Washington U., St. Louis, 1982-95; adj. prof. dept. animal sci. U. Mo., 1982-95; dist. prof. animal sci. & food & nutrition U. Ga., Athens, 1995—2014, D.W. Brooks Dist. Prof., 2008—14, dir. Obesity Initiative, 2012—14; Ga. Rsch. Alliance Eminent scholar Agrl. Biotech., Athens, 1996—2014; CEO ProLinia, Inc., 1999—2002, InsectiGen, Inc., 2003—14, AptoTec, Inc., 2004—14. Presenter in field. Contbr. over 350 articles to sci. publs. Rsch. fellow Ralston Purina, 1962-64, spl. postdoctoral fellow NIH, 1969; recipient Georgia Lamar Dodd award, 2002; named D.W. Brooks Dist. Prof. 2008-14 Mem. American Soc. Animal Sci. (bd. dirs. 1990-93, animal growth and devel. award 1989), American Physiol. Soc., American Inst. Nutrition, American Dairy Sci. Assn. (American Feed Mgmt. award 1979), Soc. Neurosci., Endocrine Soc. Achievements include 17 patents in field; research in control and feed intake and regulation of energy balance. Home: Athens, Ga. Died May 19, 2014.

**BAILEY, CECIL DEWITT,** aerospace engineer, educator; b. Zama, Miss., Oct. 25, 1921; s. James Dewitt and Matha Eugenia (Roberts) B.; m. Myrtis Irene Taylor, Sept. 8, 1942; children: Marilyn, Beverly. BS, Miss. State U., 1951; MS, Purdue U., 1954, PhD, 1962. Commd. 2d lt. USAF, 1944, advanced through grades to lt. col., 1965, pilot, 1944-56, sr. pilot, 1956-60, command pilot, 1960-67, asst. prof. Air Force Inst. Tech., 1954-58, assoc. prof., 1965-67, ret., 1967; assoc. prof. aero. and astronautical engring. Ohio State U., Columbus, 1967-69, prof., 1970-85, prof. emeritus, from 1985. Dir. USAF-Am. Soc. Engring. Edn. summer faculty rsch. program, Wright-Patterson AFB, Ohio, 1976—78. Contbr. articles to profl. jours., scientific papers. Mem. Soc. Exptl. Stress Analysis, Am. Soc. Engring. Edn., Am. Acad. Mechanics, Res. Officers (life), Ret. Officers Assn. (life), Ohio State U. Retirees Assn. (life), Am. Legion (life), USAF Officers Club, Sigma Xi, Sigma Gamma Tau Achievements include research in direct analytical solution to both conservative and non-conservative sys; first to successfully demonstrate algebraic equations of motion for nonstationary, time dependent sys. which bypass the differential equations of motion completely. Deceased.

**BAILEY, MARTIN JEAN,** economics educator, consultant; b. Taft, Calif., Oct. 17, 1927; s. Karl Smith and Laura (Negus) B.; m. Rosalie Grace Pattinson, Oct. 2, 1954; children: Karen, Patricia, Claire, David. BA, UCLA, 1951; MA, Johns Hopkins U., 1953, PhD, 1956. Asst. prof., assoc. prof. econs. U. Chgo., 1955-64, prof., 1965; asst. for SE Asia forces U.S. Dept. Def., Washington, 1966-68; assoc. dean mgmt. U. Rochester, N.Y., 1968-73; dep. asst. sec. for tax policy U.S. Treasury Dept., Washington, 1972-73; vis. prof. Grad. Sch. Indsl. Adminstrn. Carnegie-Mellon U., Pitts., 1973-74; prof. U. Md., College Park, 1974-84; econ. adviser U.S. Dept. State, Washington, 1983-89; prof. Emory U., Atlanta, from 1989. Bd. overseers Ctr. for Naval Analysis, Arlington, Va., 1968-82; cons. Inst. for Def. Analyses, Arlington, 1989. Author: National Income and Price Level, 1962, 2d edit., 1971, Reducing Risks to Life, 1980, Studies in Positive and Normative Economics, 1992; also numerous articles. Bd. dirs. Com. on Present Danger, Washington, 1978—. With U.S. Army, 1946-47. Mem. Am. Econ. Assn., Phi Beta Kappa. Avocations: tennis, landscaping. Home: Westminster, Md. Died 1997.

**BAILEY, ROBERT TERRY,** landscape company executive; b. Detroit, Mich., Oct. 9, 1938; s. Winfield Walter and florence Marie (Griffen) Bailey; m. Marilyn Marie Evans, Nov. 8, 1958; children: Deborah Marie, Terry Robert. Co-owner Bailey-Sperber, Inc. (DBA Century Landscape Contractors, Hydro West Landscape Contractors, Robert T. Bailey Landscape Constrn.), Agoura, Calif., from 1968. Prin. works include UCLA, U. Calif-Irvine, L.A. Internat. Airport, State of Calif. freeway sys., Hughes Aircraft Nat. Hdqrs., U.S. Olympic Com. Field and Track. Recipient state awards, Calif. Landscape Contractors Assn., 1970, 1971, L.A. Bus. and Industry award, 1973—74, 1985, 1986, Nat. Instl. Landscaping award, Mrs. Patricia Nixon, 1973. Mem.: Am. Assn. Nurserymen, Am. Landscape Contractors Assn. (nat. environ. grand award 1976, 1980, 1982, 1984, 1986, 1987). Home: Simi Valley, Calif. Died June 1987.

**BAILEY, TANIA,** retired education administrator, consultant; b. Phila., May 10, 1927; d. Henry Richardson and Dorothy (Saylor) Hallowell; m. Omar Bailey, Sept. 17, 1949; children: Bertinia H., Jeffrey, Jonathan. BA in Econs. and Sociology, Mt. Holyoke Coll., 1949; MEd, Temple U., 1969; EdD, Nova U., 1988. Cert. reading specialist, Pa.; cert. nat. counselor. Social case worker Soc. to Protect Children from Cruelty, Phila., 1949-52; reading tutor, sub. tchr. Phila. school dist., 1963-65; tchr., tutor Tredyffrin Easttown, Berwyn, Pa., 1965-67; ednl. cons. Tarleton Sch., Devon, Pa., 1968-75; reading specialist, dir. Chester County Intermediate Unit, West Chester, Pa., 1975-79; faculty field supr. Cabrini Coll., Radnor, Pa., 1977-81; dir. counseling ctr. Harcum Jr. Coll., Bryn Mawr, Pa., 1980-93, dir. ACT 101 program, 1984-87, asst. dean student affairs, 1987-90, dir. talent devel. program, 1990-93. Ednl. cons. various schs., Berwyn, West Chester, 1967—. Active Jr. League of Phila., 1945—. Mem. ACA, Counseling Assn. Greater Phila. (pres., Counseling Practitioners award 1983), Nat. Assn. Devel. of Edn., Pa. Coll. Pers. Assn., ACT 101 (bd. dirs. Ea. region). Avocations: bird watching, cross country skiing. Deceased.

**BAINUM, STEWART WILLIAM,** retired health care and lodging company executive; b. Detroit, June 10, 1919; m. Jane Goyne, 1941; children: Barbara, Stewart Jr., Roberta, Bruce Student, Columbia Union Coll. Chmn. Choice Hotels Internat. (formerly Quality Inns Internat.), Silver Spring, Md., 1968-87; vice chmn. Manor Care, Inc. (parent co.), Silver Spring, Md., 1982-87. Bd. dirs. Choice Hotels Internat. (formerly Quality Inns Internat.), 1963-87 Bd. trustees The Found. For The Nat. Capital Region, sponsor I Have A Dream Found., 1988-2014 Named Philanthropist of Yr., Montgomery County Cmty. Found., 2009. Mem. Nat. Assn. Home Builders (lifetime dir.), Met. Washington Builders Assn. (lifetime dir.), Home Builders Met. Washington (pres. 1965). Died Feb. 12, 2014.

**BAKER, ALTON FLETCHER, JR.,** retired editor; b. Cleve., Nov. 15, 1919; s. Alton Fletcher and Mildred (Moody) B.; m. Genevieve Mertzke, 1947 (div. 1975); m. Jeannette Workman Vollstedt, Feb. 14, 1976; children: Sue Baker Diamond, Alton Fletcher, III, Sarah Moody, Robin Baker O'Connor. AB, Pomona Coll., 1942. Reporter Eugene (Oreg.) Register-Guard, 1946-50, mng. editor, 1950-54, editor, 1954-88, publisher, 1954-87, chmn. bd., 1982-87. Chmn. Oreg. Press Conf., 1973 Chmn. fund drive United Way, Eugene, 1965, pres., 1966-67; bd. dirs., pres. YMCA, Eugene. Served to capt. USAAF, World War II. Mem. Oreg. Newspaper Publishers Assn. (dir. 1965-70), American Soc. Newspaper Editors, American Newspaper Publishers Assn., Eugene Country Club, deAnza Country Club (Borrego Springs, Calif.). Republican. Home: Eugene, Oreg. Died Apr. 27, 2014.

**BAKER, EDWARD GEORGE,** retired mechanical engineer; b. Freeport, NY, Oct. 20, 1908; s. Edward George and Mary (Dunham) B.; m. Mary Louise Freer, Feb. 7, 1931; children: Edward Clark, Marna Larson, Ellen Freer George W. Lewis, John Durrin, Bruce Robert. Ba, Columbia Coll., 1930; MA, 1931, EdD, 1938. Assoc. prof. math. Newark Coll. Engring., NJ, 1930—42; mem. tech. staff Am. Bur. Shipping, NYC, 1942—73. Chmn. zoning bd. adjustment Pine Knoll Shores, NC, 1979—84. Author: (book) First Course in Mathematics, 1942; contbr. articles to profl.jours. Recipient Order Long Leaf Pine award, State NC, 1982. Mem.: ASME, NY Acad. Sci., Soc. Naval Architects and Marine Engrs., Am. Math. Soc., Phi Beta Kappa. Republican. Episcopalian. Home: Morehead City, NC. Died July 8, 1997.

**BAKER, GEORGE CHISHOLM,** engineering executive, consultant; b. Dartmouth, NS, Can., Oct. 29, 1918; s. Clifford Lyall and Edith (Chisholm) B.; m. Ethel Marie Suzanne Humbert, Jan. 2, 1942; children: Alison Marie, Catherine Ann. Diploma, Royal Mil. Coll. Can., 1939, D Engring. (hon.), 1988; BA in Sci., Toronto U., 1946; D Engring. (hon.), Tech. Coll. N.S., 1987; DCL, Acadia U., 1993. Registered profl engr., Can. Pres. Kentville (N.S.) Pub. Co. Ltd., 1948-77; engr. Kentville Electric Commn., 1960-81; exec. v.p. Tidal Power Corp., Halifax, N.S., 1971-89; pres. G.C. Baker Engring. Ltd., Kentville, from 1977. Chmn. Cam Pubs. Ltd., New Glasgow, N.S., 1978-2002. Contbr. numerous articles to profl. pubs. Chmn. Acadia U. Inst., Wolfville, N.S., 1968-70; gov. Acadia U., Wolfville, 1979-92. Maj. Signal Corps Royal Can. Army, 1939-46. Decorated Order of Brit. Empire, Order of Can. Fellow Engring. Inst. Can., Can. Acad. Engring.; mem. IEEE (Centennial Gold medal). Home: Kentville, Canada. Died May 31, 2008.

**BAKER, HOWARD HENRY, JR.,** lawyer, former United States Senator from Tennessee, White House chief of staff; b. Huntsville, Tenn., Nov. 15, 1925; s. Howard Henry and Dora (Ladd) B.; m. Joy Dirksen, Dec. 22, 1951 (dec. April 25, 1993); children: Darek Dirksen, Cynthia; m. Nancy Landon Kassebaum, Dec. 7, 1996. Student, U. of South, Tulane U.; LLB, U. Tenn. Law Coll., 1949; diploma (hon.), Yale U., Dartmouth Coll., Georgetown U., Bradley U., Pepperdine U., Centre Coll., East Tenn. State U., 2007. Private law practice, 1949—67; US Senator from Tenn., 1967-85; minority leader US Senate, Washington, 1977-81, majority leader, 1981-85; ptnr. Vinson & Elkins LLP, Washington, 1985-87; chief of staff to Pres. The White House, Washington, 1987-88; ptnr. Baker, Worthington, Crossley, Stansberry & Woolf, Knoxville, Tenn., 1985-87, 88-95, Baker, Donelson, Bearman & Caldwell, Washington, 1995—2000; US amb. to Japan US Dept. State, Tokyo, 2001—05; sr. counsel Baker, Donelson, Bearman, Caldwell & Berkowitz, Washington, 2005—14; co-founder Bi-Partisan Policy Ctr. (BPC), 2007. Del. UN, 1976; vice chmn. US Senate Select Com. on Presdl. Campaign Activities (The Watergate Com.), 1973-74; mem. President's Fgn. Intelligence Bd., 1985-90 Author: (books) No Margin for Error, 1980, Howard Baker's Washington, 1982, Big South Fork Country, 1983; author: (with John Nehterton) Scott's Gulf: The Bridgestone/Firestone Centennial Wilderness, 2000. Bd. regents Smithsonian Instn.; hon. co-chair, Saving the Last Great Places of Tennessee The Nature Conservancy, Tenn. Chpt.; candidate Republican Presdl. Nomination, 1980; bd. mem. Maureen and Mike Mansfield Found., Mus. Appalachia Found. Served in USN, 1943—46. Recipient John Heinz award for Greatest Public Svc. by an Elected or Appointed Official, 1981, Presdl. Medal of Freedom, The White House, 1984, Internat. award, American Soc. Photographers, 1993, Lifetime Achievement award, The American Lawyer mag, 2008; named to The Photo Mktg. Assn. Hall of Fame, 1994. Republican. Presbyterian. Avocations: photography, tennis, golf. Died June 26, 2014.

**BAKER, JOHN ALBERT, JR.,** accountant; b. Port Angeles, Wash., July 2, 1919; s. John Albert and Rose (Anderson) Baker; m. P. Pasha Prossen, Nov. 25, 1978; children: Raymon Edward, Carlton Crawford, Cameron John, Peggy Melinda, Fred Albert. BA, Wash. State U., 1943. Sr. acct., audit supr. and sr. tax cons. Cameron & Johnstone, Honolulu, 1946—50; ptnr. Cameron, Tennent & Greaney, 1950—51, Baker & Gillette, 1951—65, Coopers & Lybrand, 1965—81; chmn. Pasha Pacific Properties, Inc., from 1981. With USMCR, 1943—46. Mem.: AICPA (bd. examiners 1964—68), Am. Acctg. Assn., Nat. Assn. State Bds. Accountancy, Hawaii Bd. of Accountancy (pres., Disting. Pub. Svc. award 1984), Nat. Tax Assn., Hawaii Estate Planning Coun., Hawaii Soc. C.P.A.s, Nat. Assn. Accountants. Deceased.

**BALABUYEV, PIOTR VASILYEVIXH,** aircraft designer; b. Valuysk, Ukraine, May 23, 1931; s. Vasiliy Ignatievich Balabuyev and Marfa Arsentievna Balabuyeva; m. Raisa Panfutievna Chmeleva, 1956; children: Irina Dovbyschuk, Maxim. Degree in mech. engring., Kharkiv Aviatin Inst., 1954; D of Tech. Scis., Kharkiv Aviation Inst., 1988. Design Antonov ASTC, Kyiv, Ukraine, 1954—56, head workshop, 1956—59, head assembly shop, 1959—60, leading designer, 1960—61; deputy chief designer Aircraft Mgt. Plant, Tashkent, Uzbekistan, 1961—65; dir. design bur. devel. plant Antonov ASTC, Kyiv, 1965—68, deputy cheif designer, 1968—71, chief designer 1st dep. gen. designer, 1971—84, gen. designer, 1984—2007. Contbr. articles to profl. jours. Achievements include being the lead designer of the world's largest aircraft, the An-225. Died May 17, 2007.

**BALASA, SABIN,** artist; b. Iancu Jianu Vilcea, Romania, June 17, 1932; s. Ion and Maria (Pirvu) Balasa; children: Matel, Tudor. Degree, Grigorescu Fine Arts Inst, 1956. Exhibitions include, Romania & abroad, from 1955, exhibitions include Easel paintings and monumental wall paintings Jassy U., from 1968, exhibitions include Bucharest Hotel, from 1983, Fresco Mil. Mus., Bucharest, from 1975. Recipient Gold medal, Internat. Parliament US, 1983, Pescara, Italy, 1965, prize, Internat. Festival Cartoons, Mamaia, 1967. Mem.: Italian & European Acads., Romanian Fine Arts Union. Home: Bucharest, Romania. Died Apr. 1, 2008.

**BALBOLOV, ENCHO,** chemistry professor; b. Bourgas, Bulgaria, Bulgaria, July 23, 1946; s. Christo Ivanov and Tonka Entsheva (Grozdeva) B.; m. KrasiMetodieva Ruseva, Apr. 20, 1975; children: Antoaneta, Methodi. MSc, Higher Inst. Chem. Tech., Bourgas, 1970, PhD, 1980; DSc, Bulgarian Acad. Scis., 2003. Sr. engr. Acrylonitrile Plant Petrochem. Works, Bourgas, 1972—73; assoc. prof. Basic Organic and Petrochem. Synthesis, from 1988; lectr., homogeneous & heterogeneous catalysis, from 1978. Head dept. organic synthesis Higher Inst. Chem. Tech., 1992-96. Co-author: Transition Metal Catalysis, 1989. Mem. Bulgarian Catalysis Soc. Democrat. Christian. Avocations: fishing, climbing. Home: Bourgas, Bulgaria. Died 2012.

**BÁLDI, TAMÁS,** retired geology educator, researcher; b. Szombathely, Vas County, Hungary, Aug. 24, 1935; s. Imre Báldi-Becht and Ilona Király Báldi-Becht; m. Mária Beke, Dec. 26, 1958; children: Éva, András, Kati. Diploma in geology, Hungary, 1958; D in Paleontology, Eötvös Loránd U. Sci., Hungary, 1961; PhD in Geoscis., Hungarian Acad. Scis., 1968. Asst. Eötvös Lóránd U., Budapest, 1958, prof., 1966—2004; museologist dept. geology paleontology Mus. Natural Sci., Budapest, 1959-66; ret. Head dept. geology Eötvös U., Budapest, 1971-94. Author: Mollusc Fauna of the Hungarian Upper Oligocene, 1973 (Miksa Hantken medal), A történeti földtan alapjai, 1978 (Niveau Prize of Editor 1978), Mid-Tertiary Stratigraphy and Paleogeographic, 1986; editor Chronostratigraphie und Neostratotypen. Home: Üröm, Hungary. Died July 1, 2014.

**BALDUCCI, MARCO,** clinical pathologist, viral epidemiologist; b. Venice, Italy, Dec. 10, 1934; s. Gilberto and Bianca (Pastorelli) B. MD, State U., Rome, 1958, DipPathology, 1960, PhD in Virology, 1971. Rsch. asst. NIH, Rome, 1963-67, rschr., 1967-73, chief rschr., 1974-76; cons. pathologist Health Dist. 1, Rome, from 1974, Health Dist. 2, Rome, from 1985. Instr. State U. Rome, 1972-76; pub. health expert WHO, Athens, Greece, 1977; rsch. dir. Epidemiol. Unit for Virus Diseases, Florence, Italy, 1978-91. Contbr. numerous articles to profl. jours. WHO fellow, Prague, 1961, WHO fellow Pasteur Inst., Paris, 1967; Regional Govt. of Tuscany grantee, 1978-91. Mem. Am. Soc. for Microbiology. Achievements include isolation and identification of new viruses Toscana Virus, Arbia Virus; demonstration of central nervous system involvement in Toscana virus infections. Deceased.

**BALDWIN, DEANNA LOUISE,** dietician; b. Oklahoma City, Jan. 14, 1946; d. Jesse Burlin and Celena Mae (Robison) Smith; m. James Stephen Baldwin, Apr. 7, 1989; 1 child, Melissa. BS, Stephen F. Austin, 1985. Dietetic tech. Pasadena (Tex.) Bayshore Hosp., 1969-70; payroll clk. Seismic Computing Corp., Houston, 1971-72; restaurant mgr., mgr. trainer H. Salt Fish n' Chips, Pasadena, 1972-75; asst. food svc. dir. E. Tex. Med. Ctr. Hosp., Tyler, 1990—92, from 1992; sales woman Mary Kay Cosmetics, 1995—2004. Avocations: singing, sewing, cooking, crafts. Home: Tyler, Tex. Deceased.

**BALDWIN, IRA LAWRENCE,** retired bacteriologist, educator; b. 1895; BS in Agrl. Chemistry, Purdue U., 1919, MS in Agrl. Chemistry, 1921, DSc (hon.), 1945; PhD in Bacteriology, U. Wis., 1926, DSc (hon.), 1972. Instr. bacteriology Purdue U., Lafayette, Ind., 1919-24, asst. prof. bacteriology, 1924-25, assoc. prof. physiology Experiment Sta., 1926; asst. prof. bacteriology U. Wis., Madison, 1927-29, assoc. prof. bacteriology, 1929-32, asst. dean Coll. Agr., prof. bacteriology, 1932-42, chmn. dept. bacteriology, 1941-44, dean Grad. Sch., 1944-45, dean Coll. Agr., dir. Agrl. Experiment Sta., 1945-48, dir. agrl. ext. svcs., 1945-48, v.p., 1948-58, spl. asst. to the pres., 1958-66, v.p. emeritus, prof. bacteriology emeritus, 1966-99; under contract svc. agy. internat. devel. U. Wis. and U.S. Dept. State, 1966-76. Contbr. articles to profl. jours. Mem. NEA (emeritus), AAAS (emeritus), Am. Soc. for Microbiology (hon., sec.-treas. 1935-42, v.p. 1943, pres. 1944), Agrl. History Soc. (emeritus), Am. Forestry Assn. (emeritus), Am. Inst. Biol. Scis. (emeritus), Am. Phytopathol. Soc. (emeritus), Am. Soc. Plant Physiology (emeritus), Ind. Acad. Sci. (emeritus), Royal Soc. Arts-Eng. (emeritus), Soc. for Exptl. Biology and Medicine (emeritus), Soc. for Internat. Devel. (emeritus), Soil Conservation Soc. Am. (emeritus), Alpha Zeta, Phi Lambda Upsilon, Sigma Xi, Phi Beta Kappa, Phi Eta Sigma, Phi Kappa Phi. Home: Tucson, Ariz. Died Aug. 9, 1999.

**BALL, ANTHONY,** materials engineer educator; b. Prescot, Eng., Sept. 5, 1939; arrived in South Africa, 1973; s. James Henry and Mary Alice (Jones) B.; m. Aune Anneli Sipowen, 1965 (div. 1989); children: Jaana, Brigitta, James; m. Jane Carol Paterson, 1990; children, William, Harry. BSc with honors, U. Birmingham, 1961, PhD, 1964, D in Engring., 1987. Registered profl. engr., South Africa; chartered engr., U.K. Rsch. fellow U. Birmingham, 1965; rsch. scientist Dept. Def., Australia, 1965-68; sr. rsch. fellow U. Witwaterstrand, Johannesburg, South Africa, 1969-71; prof. U. Capetown, South Africa, from 1972. Contbr. over 150 articles to profl. jours. Fellowship U. Cape Town, 1995; recipient Low Alberts award, 1990. Fellow Royal Soc. of South Africa, 1995, Inst. of Materials, Inst. of Mining and Metallurgy. Achievements include research on model for super plastic deformation, deformation of intermetallic compounds, modes of wear and erosion. Died June 16, 2001.

**BALLARD, J.G. (JAMES GRAHAM BALLARD),** writer; b. Shanghai, Nov. 15, 1930; s. James and Edna (Johnstone) B.; m. Helen Mary Matthews, 1953 (dec. 1964); children: James, Fay, Beatrice. Author: The Wind From Nowhere, 1962, The Drowned World, 1962, The Burning World, 1964 (rev. as The Drought, 1965), The Crystal World, 1966, Crash, 1973, Concrete Island, 1974, High-Rise, 1975, The Unlimited Dream Company, 1979, Hello America, 1981, Empire of the Sun, 1984 (Guardian Fiction Prize 1984, Booker Prize nomination 1984, James Tait Black Meml. Prize 1985), The Day of Creation, 1987, Running Wild, 1988, The Kindness of Women, 1991, Rushing to Paradise, 1994, Cocaine Nights, 1996, Super-Cannes, 2000, Millennium People, 2003, Kingdom Come, 2006; (story collections) The Voice of Time and Other Stories, 1962, Billenium and Other Stories, 1962, The Four-Dimensional Nightmare, 1963, Passport to Eternity and Other Stories, 1963, Terminal Beach, 1964, The Impossible Man and Other Stories, 1966, The Disaster Area, 1967, By Day Fantastic Birds Flew Through the Petrified Forests, 1967, The Day of Forever, 1967, The Overloaded Man, 1968, The Atrocity Exhibition, 1970, Vermilion Sands, 1971, Chronopolis and Other Stories, 1971, Low-Flying Aircraft and Other Stories, 1976, The Best of J.G. Ballard, 1977 (rev. as The Best Stories of J.G. Ballard, 1978), The Venus Hunters, 1980, Myths of the Near Future, 1982, Memories of the Space Age, 1988, War Fever, 1990, The Complete Short Stories of J.G. Ballard 2001, vol. 1 & 2, 2006, The Complete Stories of J.G. Ballard, 2009; (plays) The Assassination Weapon, 1969. Home: Shepperton, England. Died Apr. 19, 2009.

**BALLON, CHARLES,** lawyer; b. NYC, Sept. 10, 1910; s. Herman and Anna Platt Ballon; m. Harriet Milk, Aug. 19, 1954; children: Howard, Hilary, Carla. BA, Columbia U., 1930, LLB, 1932. Bar: NY 1933, US Dist. Ct. (so. dist.) NY 1935, US Ct. Appeals (2d cir.) 1935, DC 1976, US Dist. Ct. DC 1976, US Ct. Appeals DC. Ptnr. Hartman, Sheridan, Tekulsky & Pecora, NYC, 1937—41, Phillips, Nizer, Benjamin, Krim & Ballon, NYC, from 1946; bd. visitors Columbia U. Law Sch., from 1975; chmn. bd. dirs. Benjamin N. Cardozo Sch. Law; bd. dirs. Yeshiva U., NYC, 1981—86, hon. chair, from 1986. Trustee Yeshiva U., from 1980; assoc. chmn Fedn. Philanthropies NY, 1979—86; hon. chmn. United Jewish Appeal NY.; vp United Jewish Appeal NY, 1980—86. Lt. col. US Army, 1942—46. Decorated Legion of Merit US Army; recipient Learned Hand award, Am. Jewish Com., 1976, Israel Peace medal, Israel State Bonds, 1983, Disting. Svc. award, Cardozo Sch. Law, 1979. Mem.: NY State Bar Assn., Assn. Bar City NY. Jewish. Home: New York, NY. Died 1994.

**BAMBERGER, FRED HANS,** government official, lawyer, educator; b. Neustadt, Rheinpfalz, Germany, June 23, 1898; came to U.S. 1936; s. Adolf and Pauline (Goldenberg) B.; m. Mary Frances Hotchkiss, Oct. 10, 1942. LLM, JUD, U. Heidelberg, Germany, 1924; MA, Middlebury Coll., 1955. Bar: Germany, 1924, County Ct. Neustadt. Pvt. practice, Germany, 1925-33; prodn. planner Am. Optical Co., Buffalo, N.Y., 1943-46; high sch. tchr. N.Y. Cen. Sch., Eden, 1946-48; prof., dept. head Ohio No. U., Ada, 1948-51; fgn. patent analyst U.S. Patent Office, Washington, 1951-70; freelance translator Washington, 1951-82. Contbr. articles to profl. jours. With Germany Navy, 1917-19; with U.S. Army, 1942-43. Mem. Am. Translators Assn., Soc. Fed. Linguists (v.p.), Gideons Internat. Democrat. Methodist. Avocations: music, gymnastics, swimming. Home: Bethesda, Md. Deceased.

**BANANA, CANAAN SODINDO,** former president of Zimbabwe; b. Esiphezini, Essexvale dist., Zimbabwe, Mar. 5, 1936; m. Janet Mbuyazwe, Sept. 1961; children: Michael, Nathan, Martin, Nobuhle. Trained as sch. tchr., Tegwani Tng. Inst., 1958; student of theology, Epworth Theol. Coll., Zimbabwe, 1960-62; diploma, Kasai Indsl. Ctr., Japan, 1970; M.T.S., Wesley Theol. Sem., Washington, 1975; BA (hons.) in Theology, U. South Africa, 1980; LLD (hon.), Am. U., Washington, 1981, U. Zimbabwe, 1983. Ordained to ministry Meth. Ch., 1966. Mgr. Meth. Sch., Wankie and Plumtree areas, Zimbabwe, 1963-66; prin. Matjinge Boarding Sch., 1965; vis. chaplain Tegwani High Sch., 1965-75; founding mem., 1st v.p. African Nat. Coun., 1971; jailed as polit. prisoner in Zimbabwe several times, 1975-79; pres. of Zimbabwe, 1980-88; chancellor U. Zimbabwe, 1983-87. African Nat. Coun. rep. in N. Am. and the UN, 1973-75; founder mem. and pub.ity sec. People's Movement, 1976; regional coord. Zimbabwe African Nat. Union, North and South provinces, 1979-80; pres., chmn. Bulawayo Coun. of Chs., 1969-71; former mem. adv. com. World Coun. Chs.; chaplain Am. U., Washington, 1973-75; leader Emminent Ch. Persons Group on Sanctions Against South Africa, 1989, Commonwealth Observer Group on Conv. for Dem. South Africa, 1991; co-chmn. UNPanel of Experts on Sanctions Against South Africa, 1989. Author (four tracts on politics and religion) Gospel According to the Ghetto, Woman of my Imagination, Theology of Promise, Towards a Socialist Ethos, (intro. to Christian theology) Come and Share; contbr. articles to mags. and jours. Avocations: soccer, ping pong/table tennis, lawn tennis, volleyball. Died Nov. 10, 2003.

**BANCHET, JEAN,** retired chef; b. Roanne, France, Mar. 7, 1941; m. Doris Kosling. Head chef, owner Le Francais, Wheeling, Ill., 1973—89, 1999—2001. Died Nov. 24, 2013.

**BANDLER, VIVICA AINA FANNY,** theater director; b. Helsingfors, Finland, Feb. 5, 1917; d. Erik von Frenckell and Ester-Margaret Lindberg; m. Kurt Bandler, 1943 (div. 1963). BA, U. Helsinki. Artistic dir. Tampere Internat. Theatre Festival, Finland, 1989-95; pres. bd. Swedish Theatre Union/Swedish Internat. Theatre Inst., 1978-92, mem. exec. com., 1981-86, mem. drama com., 1990-92; pres. Theatre Acad. Sweden, Stockholm, 1992-99; patron Hangö Festival, Finland, 1996-97. Dir. Swedish Theatre, Helsingfors, 1948; head theatre sect. Helsinki's 400th anniversary, 1950; founded Peasants' Theatre Group, 1951; mgr., prin. dir. Lilla Teatern, Helsingfors, 1955-67; mgr., dir. Oslo Nye Teater, Norway, 1967-69; head Stockholm City Theatre, Sweden, 1969-80; artistic dir. Tampere Internat. Theatre Festival, Finland, 1989-95; dir. Eri dance theatre, Finland, 1989-2004; co-author: Addressee Unknown, 1992; author numerous dramatisations of novels, film scripts, musicals; contbr. articles to profl. publs. With armed forces, 1939-40, 41-43. Recipient Golden Boot Daily Newspaper Dagens Nyheter, Sweden, medal City of Stockholm, medal Swedish Parliament in Finland, August award Swedish Dramatists' Assn., Letterstedt Found. medal for Nordic coop., Thalia award Swedish Actor's Assn., Finland prize, Memory medal of war, 1939-40; named Comdr. Finnish Lion, Pro Finlandis, Finland, Comdr. No. Star Sweden. Mem. Swedish Author's Assn. Finland (hon.), Union Theatre Dirs. Died July 30, 2004.

**BANDY, MARY LEA,** retired museum administrator; b. Evanston, Ill., June 16, 1943; d. DeWitt Clinton and Ruth (Coale) Gibson; m. Gary Bandy, June 3, 1967. BA, Stanford U., 1965. Asst. editor Harry N. Abrams, Inc., NYC, 1966-73; assoc. editor publications Mus. Modern Art, NYC, 1973-76, assoc. coordinator exhbns., 1976-78, dir. dept. film, 1980-93, chief curator dept. film and video, asst. dep. dir. curator affairs, 1993—2006. Died Sept. 20, 2014.

**BARABINO, WILLIAM ALBERT,** science and technology researcher, inventor; b. Bay Shore, NY, Feb. 11, 1932; s. John Joseph and Anna Marie (Gates) B.; children: Susan Beth, Diane Marie, William John. Student, Fordham U., 1951; AS, SUNY, Farmingdale, 1952; student, St. Louis U., 1957; diploma, Alexander Hamilton Inst., NYC, 1963. Dist. mgr. Piper Aircraft Corp., Ctrl. Am., Mex., 1960-62; application engr. Lab. for Electronics, Boston, 1962-63; mktg. mgr. spl. equipment divsn. Itek Corp., Waltham, Mass., 1963-65; bus. cons. North Reading, Mass., 1965-68; dir. Andover Inst. Bus., Mass., 1968-70; sci. and tech. rschr. North Reading, from 1970; founder, mng. gen. ptnr. Mass Light Internat. Group, Agoura Hills, Calif., from 1992; founder, CEO In-Case Products, Inc., Agoura Hills, Calif., 1990. Cons. CTS Corp., Proctor and Gamble, Scovill Corp., Am. Enviro Products, Inc., Plessey Co., Ltd., GM, Goodyear Aerospace, Ford Motor Co. Patentee tire pressure alarm and warning systems (6), brake wear warning system, fluid level and condition detection systems, personal, feminine and infant hygiene products (7), treatment for causes of scalp diseases, based on theory then electron-microscopy capture of mitochrondia with dual set of double-walled membranes, liquid dispensing swab applicator, others; contbr. articles to profl. jours. Mem. 2000 Rep. Presdl. Task Force. Capt., rated pilot/rated navigator USAF, 1952-59. Mem. VFW, Am. Legion. Republican. Deceased.

**BARAKA, IMAMU AMIRI (EVERETT LEROI JONES),** author; b. Newark, Oct. 7, 1934; s. Coyette Leroy and Anna Lois (Russ) Jones; m. Hettie Roberta Cohen, Oct. 13, 1958 (div. Aug. 1965); children: Kellie Elisabeth, Lisa Victoria Chapman; m. Sylvia Robinson (Bibi Amina Baraka), Aug. 1966; children: Obalaji Malik Ali, Ras Jua Al Aziz, Shani Isis, Amiri Seku, Ahi Mwenge; stepchildren: Kellie, Lisa, Dominique. BA, Howard U., 1954; MA, Columbia U., New Sch. Social Rsch.; LHD (hon.), Malcolm X Coll., Chgo., 1972. Instr. New Sch. Social Research, NYC, 1961-64; founder, dir. Black Arts Repertory Theatre, NYC, 1964-66; dir. Spirit House, Newark, 1966-72; asst. prof. African Studies SUNY, Stony Brook, 1980-83, assoc. prof., 1983-85, prof. emeritus African Studies, 1985—2014. Vis. prof. U. Buffalo, 1964, Columbia U., 1964, 66-67, San Francisco State U., 1967, Yale U., 1977-78, George Washington U., 1978-79, Rutgers U., 1988; founder, editor Yugen

Mag. and Totem Press, N.Y.C., 1958; co-editor Floating Bar Mag., 1961-63; past editor Cricket mag.; publishing dir. Jihad Press, Peoples War Publications; editor The Black Nation; coordinator creativity workshops Black Power Conf., 1968; chmn. Com. for Unified Newark, 1968-75; chmn., founder Congress of African People. Author: (poetry) April 13, 1959, Spring and So Forth, 1960, Preface to a Twenty Volume Suicide Note, 1961, The Disguise, 1961, The Dead Lecturer, 1964, Black Art, 1966, Black Magic, 1967, A Poem for Black Hearts, 1967, Black Magic: Sabotage: Target Study: Black Art: Collected Poetry, 1961-1967, 1969, It's Nation Time, 1970, Spirit Reach, 1972, Afrikan Revolution, 1973, Hard Facts: Excerpts, 1975, Spring Song, 1979, AM/TRAK, 1979, Selected Poetry of Amiri Baraka/Leroi Jones, 1979, In the Tradition: For Black Arthur Blythe, 1980, Reggae or Not! Poems, 1982; (plays) A Good Girl is Hard to Find, 1958, Dante, 1961, Dutchman, 1964 (Obie award 1964), The Baptism: A Comedy in One Act, 1964, The Slave: A Fable, 1964 (second prize Internat. Art Festival Dakar 1966), The Toilet, 1964, J-E-L-L-O, 1965, Experimental Death Unit #1, 1965, The Death of Malcolm X, 1965, A Black Mass, 1966, Slave Ship, 1967, Madheart: Morality Drama, 1967, Arm Yourself, or Harm Yourself, A One-Act Play, 1967, Great Goodness of Life, 1967, Home on the Range, 1968, Police, 1968, Junkies are Full of SHHH...1968, Board of Education, 1968, Resurrection in Life, 1969, Rockgroup, 1969, The Coronation of the Black Queen, 1970, Black Dada Nihilism, 1971, Black Power Chant, 1972, A Recent Killing, 1973, Columbia the Gem of the Ocean, 1973, The New Ark's A-Moverin, 1974, The Sidnee Poet Heroical in Twenty-Nine Scenes, 1975, S-1: A Play with Music in 26 Scenes, 1976, America More or Less, 1976, The Motion of History, 1977, What Was the Relationship of The Lone Ranger to the Means of Production?: A Play in One Act, 1978, Dim Cracker Party Convention, 1980, Boy and Tarzan Appear in a Clearing, 1981, Money: Jazz Opera, 1982, Money, 1982, Song: A One Act Play about the Relationship or Art to Real Life, 1983; (essays) Cuba Libre, 1961 (Longview Best Essay of Yr. award 1961), Blues People: Negro Music in White America, 1963, Home: Social Essays, 1966, Black Music, 1968, Raise, Race, Rays, Raze: Essays Since 1965, 1971, Strategy and Tactics of a Pan-African Nationalist Party, 1971, Kawaida Studies: The New Nationalism, 1972, Crisis in Boston!, 1974, Daggers and Javelins: Essays 1974-1979, 1984, The Music: Reflections on Jazz and Blues, 1987, Jesse Jackson and Black People, 1994; (other) The System of Dante's Hell, 1965, Striptease, 1967, Tales, 1967, The Autobiography of LeRoi Jones/Amiri Baraka, 1984, Thornton Dial: Images of the Tiger, 1993, Shy's, Wise, Y's: The Griot's Tale, 1994; screenwriter: (films) Dutchman, 1967, Black Spring, 1968, A Fable, 1971, Supercoon, 1971; editor: January 1st 1959, 1959, Four Young Lady Poets, 1962, The Moderns: An Anthology of New Writing in America, 1963, In-formation, 1965, Black & White, 1965, Hands Up!, 1965, Afro-American Festival of the Arts Magazine, 1966 (pub. as Anthology of Our Black Selves, 1969), The Cricket: Black Music in Evolution, 1968, Black Fire: An Anthology of Afro-American Writing, 1968, A Black Value System, 1970, In Our Terribleness, 1970, African Congress: A Documentary of the First Modern Pan-African Congress, 1972, Confirmation: An Anthology of Afro-American Women, 1983 (American Book award 1984); editor, contbr. anthologies, mags., books. Organizer Nat. Black Pol. Conv., 1972. Served with USAF, 1954-57. Recipient poetry award Nat. Endowment for the Arts, 1981, N.J. Coun. for the Arts award, 1982; John Whitney Found. fellow, 1962, Guggenheim fellow, 1965-66, Yoruba Acad. fellow, 1965, Nat. Endowment for the Arts grantee, 1966, Rockefeller Found. fellow, 1981; named Poet Laureate of NJ, 2002-03 Mem. Black Acad. Arts & Letters, Polit. Prisoners Relief Fund, African Liberation Day Commn., All African Games, Pan African Fedn., Nat. Black Polit. Assembly (sec. gen., co-gov.), Nat. Black United Front, Cong. African People (co-founder, chmn.), Black Writers' Union, League Revolutionary Struggle, United Brothers (Newark), Newark Writers Collective. Died Jan. 9, 2014.

**BARANOV, PAVEL SERGEEVICH,** research scientist; b. Kursk, Russia, Sept. 2, 1928; s. Sergei Fedorovich and Lidia Pavlovna (Lebedeva) B.; m. Roza Hamidovna Muchamedieva, Oct. 21, 1955; 1 child, Sergei. Diploma in physics with honors, Irkutsk State U., Russia, 1951; PhD in Physics, Lebedev Phys. Inst., Moscow, 1955, Doctorate, 1974. Cert. physicist. Rsch. scientist Lebedev Phys. Inst., Moscow, 1955-61, sr. rsch. scientist, from 1961. Chief nuclear investigation High Energy Lab., Lebedev Phys. Inst., 1986-95. Contbr. articles to profl. jours. Recipient Medal for Distinction in Labor, USSR Supreme Soviet, 1970, 850th Anniversary of Moscow award, 1997; grantee Internat. Assn. for Promotion of Cooperation with Scientists of Ind. New States of Former Soviet Union-93, 1995, Russian Found. for Basic Rsch., 1995, Russian Found. for Basic Rsch.-Deutsche Forschungsgemeinschaft, 1996. Avocations: bicycling and foot trips, chess. Home: Moscow, Russia. Died Apr. 5, 2007.

**BARBAROSSA, THEODORE COTILLO,** sculptor; b. Ludlow, Vt., Dec. 26, 1906; s. Louis Henry and Maddelina (Verimonde) B.; m. Sally Ann Newhall, Nov. 20, 1962; 1 dau., Susan. Student, Mass. Coll. Art, 1927; B.F.A., Yale U., 1931; D.F.A. (hon.), Susquehanna U., Selingsgrove, Pa., 1977. Exhibited in shows at, Whitney Mus., N.Y.C., 1940, Nat. Sculpture Soc., NAD, Allied Artists, Audubon Artists, commns. include sculptures in stone, Catholic Ch. Assumption, Balt., 1957, five relief panels, Mus. Sci., Boston, two chapels and ten figures, Cath. Shrine, Washington, 1962-65, sculptures in stone for, St. Thomas Episcopal Ch., N.Y.C., 1964, Washington Cath. and Episcopal Chs., 1965-75, others, important works include, Uncle Sam Monument, Arlington, Mass., sculptures, Susquehanna U., Nat. Cathedral, Washington, Balt. Cathedral. Served with C.E. AUS, 1942-46. Recipient numerous gold medals and citations for sculpture. Fellow Nat. Sculpture Soc.; mem. Nat. Acad., Internat. Inst. Arts and Letters, Audubon Artists, Allied Artists. Clubs: Yale (Boston). Home: Arlington, Mass. Died 1992.

**BARBOUR, IAN GRAEME,** physics and religion educator; b. Peking, China, Oct. 5, 1923; s. George Brown and Dorothy (Dickinson) B.; m. Deane Kern, Nov. 29, 1947 (dec. 2011); children: John Dickinson, Blair Winn, David Freeland, Heather Deane. BA, Swarthmore Coll., 1943; MA, Duke U., 1946; PhD in Physics, U. Chgo., 1950; B.D., Yale U., 1956. Asst. prof. physics Kalamazoo Coll., 1949-51, assoc. prof., chmn. dept., 1951-53; mem. faculty Carleton Coll., Northfield, Minn., 1955-86, prof. emeritus, 1986—2013, chmn. dept. religion, 1956-71, prof. religion and physics, 1965-81, Winifred and Atherton Bean prof. sci., tech. and soc., 1981-86. Lilly vis. prof. sci., theology and human values Purdue U., 1973-74; Gifford lectr. Aberdeen, Scotland, 1989-91. Author: Christianity and the Scientist, 1960, Issues in Science and Religion, 1966, Science and Religion: New Perspectives on the Dialogue, 1968, Science and Secularity: The Ethics of Technology, 1970, Earth Might Be Fair, 1972, Western Man and Environmental Ethics, 1973, Myths, Models and Paradigms, 1974, Finite Resources and the Human Future, 1976, Technology, Environment and Human Values, 1980, Energy and American Values, 1982, Religion in an Age of Science, 1990, Ethics in an Age of Technology, 1992; mem. editorial bd. Process Studies, Zygon, Research in Philosophy and Technology; author numerous articles. Ford Faculty fellow, 1953-54; Kent fellow, 1954-55; recipient Harbison award for Disting. Teaching Danforth Found., 1963, Templeton prize, 1999; American Council Learned Socs. fellow, 1963-64; Guggenheim and Fulbright fellow, 1967-78; Nat. Endowment Humanities fellow, 1976-77; Nat. Humanities Center fellow, 1980-81 Mem. Phi Beta Kappa, Sigma Xi. Home: Northfield, Minn. Died Dec. 24, 2013.

**BARE, CLIVE WELLINGTON,** retired federal judge; b. Marion, Va., Mar. 1, 1914; s. James Gordon and Etta Virginia (Phipps) Bare; m. Esther Amanda Wade, June 28, 1940; 1 child, Clive Gordon. LLB, Cumberland U., 1933. Bar: Tenn. 1934, US Dist. Ct. (ea. dist.)/Tenn. 1945, US Ct. Appeals (6th cir.) 1954. Various positions US Dept. Justice, Washington, 1939—57; judge US Bankruptcy Ct., Knoxville, Tenn., from 1957; pres. Nat. Conf. Bankruptcyh Judges, 1970. MTO USAR, 1943—46. Decorated Combat Infantryman's Badge. Mem.: Am. Judicature Soc., Tenn. Bar Assn., ABA. Home: Knoxville, Tenn. Died July 15, 1994.

**BARELLA-MIRO, ALBERT,** retired textile engineer; b. Barcelona, Catalonia, Spain, May 3, 1918; s. Jaume and Merce (Miro) B.; m. Nuria Civit-Simon, May 27, 1946; children: Albert, Merce, Fatima, Antoni, Jaume. M.Textile Industry, Indsl. Sch., Barcelona, 1936; textile engr., Textile Engring. Sch., T3errasa, Spain, 1944; Dr. Engr., Polytech. U., T3errasa, Spain, 1959; Dr. H.c., Polytech. U., łódz, Poland, 1997. Mgr. Barella and Martí S.L., Barcelona, 1940-55; head textile sect. C.S.I.C., Barcelona, 1955-62, head of textile dept., 1962-72; dir. Instituto de Tecnologia y Textil/CSIC, Barcelona, 1972-83; dir. rsch. A.I.T.A., Barcelona, 1962-92; ret. Cons. Ingeco Gombert Esp., Barcelona, 1955-62, Unitesa, Barcelona, 1955-62, UNIDO, Vienna, 1968-82, OECD, Paris, 1967. Author 4 books on textile quality control; contbr. articles to profl. jours. Pres. Spanish Textile Standardization Com., Barcelona, 1975-92. Recipient Warner Meml. medal The Textile Inst., Manchester, Eng., 1979, Narcis Monturiol medal Catalan Govt., Barcelona, 1988, Cert. of recognition Textile Rsch. Inst., 1996. Roman Catholic. Achievements include contributions to advancement of textile research. Home: Barcelona, Spain. Died Mar. 30, 2001.

**BARKER, JOHN L.,** special education educator, writer; b. Nebraska City, Oct. 5, 1951; M in Sch. Adminstrn., Cen. Mo. State U., 1983; occupl. specialist nursing home admin., Metro Tech. Coll., Omaha, 1990. Cert. nursing home adminstr. N.Mex., R.I.; lifetime cert. tchg./adminstrn., Mo. Tchr. spl. edn. Niangua (Mo.) R-5, 2000-2001, Hickman Mills C-1, from 2001. Author, pub. Phoenix Lit. Prodns., Belton, Mo., 1996. Author: (biography) Running on Empty: The Life and Career of River Phoenix, 1998. Mem. Home Based Businesses of the Ozarks (sec. 2000-2001). Avocations: reading, rock/pop/blues music. Home: Marshalltown, Iowa. Died Feb. 2002.

**BARKER, MICHAEL DAVID,** design engineer; b. Hertford, England, Sept. 29, 1926; s. Noel Ernest and Mary (Detrolio) B.; m. Irene Mabel Marsh, Sept. 12, 1959 (dec.); m. Linda Joy Brentnall, Nov. 5, 1990. Student corr. coll., Cambridge U., Eng., 1948. Engring. apprentice D. Wickham & Co. Ltd., Ware, Hertforshire, Eng., 1943-45, 48-51, draughtsman, 1951-61, design engr., 1961—90. Patentee 5 indsl. pumps, 2 braking devices. Served to cpl. Royal Signal Corps, 1945-48, MTO. Decorated Palestine Service medal with clasp. Avocation: amateur archtl. activities. Home: Hertfordshire, England. Died Feb. 28, 2006.

**BARLOON, BLANCHE EYNON,** artist; b. Apr. 22, 1911; d. John Davies and Natalie (Eynon) Davies; m. Marvin Barloon (dec. Sept. 1, 1991); children: Anne, Peter. BS, Sweet Briar Coll., 1933; MS, Case Western Res. U., 1940; cert., Cleve. Inst. Art, 1965. Painter, 1961-94. Exhibited in group shows including Cleve. Mus. of Art, 1961, 63, 66, 67, 71, Nat. Drawing Show, Hartford, Conn., 1970, W.& J. Nat. Painting Show, Washington, Pa., Cleve., 1994 (Jury award), Lake Erie Coll., Painsville, Ohio, 1995. Home: Castro Valley, Calif. Deceased.

**BARLOW, DAVID JOHN HARDING,** psychiatrist; b. Bulawayo, Rhodesia, Feb. 26, 1928; arrived in Eng., 1955, Australia, 1966; s. Murrell Harding and Isabel Florence (Norvall) B.; m. Deidre Imogen Landless, Sept. 26, 1953; children: Jennifer Hamilton, Kenneth Barlow, Karyn Barlow, Gillian Coon. MB BCh, Witwatersrand U., Johannesburg, South Africa, 1951; DPM, Royal Colls., Eng., 1963; BA, Latrobe U., Australia, 1978. Diplomate in psychol. medicine. Psychiatrist supt. Hobson Park Hosp., Traralgon, Australia, 1966-67; dep. chmn. Mental Health Authority, Victoria, Australia, 1967-69; psychiatrist supt. Larundel Hosp., Melbourne, Australia, 1969-74, 78-87; dir. Mental Retardation Svcs., Victoria, 1975-78; mem. Mental Health Rev. Bd., Victoria, from 1987. Mem. Victorial Psychol. Coun., 1969-74; sr. assoc. dept. psychiatry U. Melbourne, 1970-74, 79-87; clin. dean Larundel Clin. Sch., Monash U., 1978-84; hon. sr. lectr. dept. psychol. medicine Monash U., 1984-87. Mem. Commn. of Inquiry into Oakley Hosp., Auckland, New Zealand, 1971. Fellow Royal Australian and New Zealand Coll. Psychiatrists, Royal Australian Coll. Med. Adminstrs.; mem. Royal Coll. Psychiatrists. Avocations: reading, music, genealogy. Died June 15, 2002.

**BARLUSCONI, GIOVANNA,** adult education educator, researcher; b. Guanzate, Como (Co), Italy, Mar. 2, 1947; d. Giuseppe Barlusconi and Rosa Camponovo. Degree in edn. (hon.), Università Cattolica del Sacro Cuore, Italy, 1971. U. rschr., lit. criticism Università Cattolica del Sacro Cuore, Milano, 1980—94, prof., theory of lit., 1994—97, prof., aesthetics Brescia, from 1997. Mem. Istituto di Italianistica - Università Cattolica del Sacro Cuore, Milano, from 1980, Centro Interuniversitario su: Simbolo, comunicazione, società, Siena, from 1997, Editl. Staff of the rev. Testo, Milano, from 1980, Editl. Staff of the rev. Symbolon, Siena, from 1996. Author: (book) La metafora del testo. Poesia come strategia del senso, Ed. di Teoria e Storia letteraria, 1986; dir.: (international critical convention) Letteratura e religione in Europa, Convegno Internazionale, tenutosi presso l'Università Cattolica Del Sacro Cuore dal 27 al 30., 1995—97; contbr. numerous critical essays in various reviews. Roman Catholic. Home: Guanzate, Italy. Deceased.

**BARNES, JOHN WADSWORTH,** director, writer; b. Belford, NJ, Mar. 25, 1920; s. Edward Crosby and Dorothy M. (Leek) B.; m. Joan Waddell, Sept. 5, 1942 (div. Jan. 1952); m. Jeanne Leah Weinstein, June 6, 1953; children: Joshua Edward, Judith Ann, Ezra David. Diploma, Monmouth Jr. Coll., Long Branch, NJ, 1939; student, U. Chgo., 1939-42. Editor Trend, a literary mag., Chgo., 1941-42; writer, dir. Columbia Broadcasting System, Chgo., 1942-46; editor Together The Urban League, Chgo., 1947; freelance writer, 1948-50; writer, dir., producer Ency. Britannica Films, Wilmette, Ill., 1951-55, London, 1955-63, Rome, 1963-65; exec. producer N.Y. Film Unit, Ency. Britannica Ednl. Corp., NYC, 1965-73; pres. John Barnes Prodns., NYC, from 1973. Bd. dirs. Nat. Shakespeare Co., N.Y.C.; Shakespeare adv. bd. Colonial Theatre, Westerly, R.I. Writer, dir., prodr.: (films) To Live Together, 1950, The Baltimore Plan (Edinburgh Film Festival) 1952, American Revolution (Boston Film Festival) 1954, The Living City (Oscar nomination 1953), Eng.: William Shakespeare, 1954, The Pilgrims, 1954, Michelangelo (Am. Film Festival award 1966); writer, co-dir.: (with Gordon Weisenborn) People of the Mississippi (Edinburgh Film Festival), 1952; prodr., co-dir. Can. Oedipus Rex, 1959, Hamlet, 1959, Eng.: Great Expectations, 1960, Greece: Athens, The Golden Age, 1961, Eng.: Magna Carta, parts I and II, 1960 (Scholastic Nat. Film award), France: Art of the Middle Ages and Chartres Cathedral, 1962, Eng: Macbeth, 1964, John Keats, His Life and Death, 1973; author: (book for musical) The Beautiful Dream of Ilya Ilich Oblomov, 1983 (TV serial) Rape of the Fair Country, BBC-TV, 1982; writer play Kidnapped, 1989, Kembles of the Garden, 1990, Huck and Jim, 1990, Alice James, 1991. Bd. of govs. St. Ann's Sch., Bklyn., 1970-75; pres. Bklyn. Heights Music Soc., Bklyn., 1985-88, pres. emeritus, 1988—. John Barnes week long showing of films Institutio Mexicano Norte Americano De Relaciones Culturales, 1966, series of weekly screenings of films Ciné 16, San Jose, Calif., 1997-98; several films named to Nat. Archives. Mem. The Dramatists Guild, Inc. Democrat. Home: Brooklyn, NY. Died June 27, 2000.

**BARNES, MELVER RAYMOND,** retired chemist; b. Salisbury, NC, Nov. 15, 1917; s. Oscar Lester and Sarah Albertine (Rowe) B. AB in Chemistry, U. N.C., 1947; D of Physics (hon.), World U., 1983; DSc in Chemistry (hon.), Assoc. Univs., 1987, PhD (hon.) of Chemistry, 1990, Albert Einstein Internat. Acad. Found. and Associated Univs., 1990. Chemist Pitts. Testing Labs., Greensboro, NC, 1948—49, N.C. State Hwy. and Pub. Works Commn., Raleigh, 1949—51, Edgewood Arsenal, Md., 1951—61, Dugway Proving Ground, Utah, 1961—70. Recipient Albert Einstein Bronze medal, 1988, Alfred Nobel Medal award Albert Einstein Internat. Acad. Found., 1991, Albert Einstein Acad. Found. Cross of Merit, 1992. Mem. AAAS, Am. Statis. Assn., Am. Chem. Soc., Am. Phys. Soc. Died 2006.

**BARNES, PETER,** retired federal official; b. Cambridge, Mass., Apr. 13, 1940; s. Tracy Barnes and Janet (White) Lawrence; m. Jan Adair; children from previous marriage: K. Tracy, John E. BA magna cum laude, Yale U., 1962; LLB cum laude, Harvard U., 1965. Bar: DC 1966, Md. 1984. Assoc. Leva, Hawes, Symington, Martin & Oppenheimer, Washington, 1965-71, ptnr., 1972—83, Venable, Baetjer & Howard, Balt., 1983—87; ptnr., shareholder Swidler & Berlin, Chtd., Washington, 1987—98; mem. Swidler Berlin Shereff Friedman, LLP, Washington, 1998-99, counsel, 1999—2001; spl. asst. to gen. counsel US Govt. Printing Office, Washington, 2004—07, project mgr., 2007—09; cons., 2008—09. Mem.: Elkridge Club, Met. Club. Home: Cockeysville, Md. Died Jan. 3, 2014.

**BARNESS, HERBERT,** land developer; b. Phila., Dec. 1, 1923; s. Joseph and Mary (Silverstein) Barness; m. Irma Suzanne Shorin, June 27, 1948; children: Lynda Anne, Nancy Ellen Stein. BS in Mech. Engring., Bucknell U., Lewisburg, Pa., 1948. Registered profl. engr. Pa.; lic. real estate and ins. broker. With Barness Orgn., Warrington, Pa., 1948—98, chmn. bd.; mem. regional bd. Contental Bank and Trust Co. Bd. dirs., treas. Pa. Soc.; chmn. bd. Pop Warner Little Scholars Inc.; bd. dirs. Washington Crossing Found. Mem. Fed. Jud. Nominating Commn., Pres. Commn. on Housing; trustee Bucknell U.; past pres., bd. dirs. Bucks County Indsl. Devel. Corp., Bucks County Planning Commn. Served to maj. USAAF, 1942—46. Recipient Ann. Teenage Achievement award, Phila., Cert. of Meritorious Svcs., Am. Legion, 1972, Outstanding Svc. to Youth award, Pop Warner Little Scholars, Technion Humanitarian award. Mem.: Bucks County Home Builders' Assn., Bucks County Bd. Realtors, Nat. Assn. Home Builders, Nat. Assn. Real Estate Bds., Soc. Am. Mil. Engrs., Nat. Soc. Profl. Engrs. Republican. Jewish. Home: Doylestown, Pa. Died Sept. 5, 1998.

**BARNETT, ERIC OLIVER,** foundation administrator; b. Feb. 13, 1929; s. Eric Everard and Maude Emily Louise (Oliver) B.; m. Louise Francesca Lindenberg, Feb. 13, 1950 (dec. Jan. 1984); m. Vivienne Goodwin, Mar. 13, 1986. Student, U. Cape Town, South Africa, 1950-52, U. South Africa, 1950-54, U. Natal, Durban, South Africa, 1955-57, Univ. Coll., London, 1957-63. Lectr. in psychology U. Natal, 1956; hon. vice chmn. Arthur Barnett Found., 1963-71, hon. chmn., from 1971. Hon. chmn. Rural Ecology and Resources Com., Southern Africa, 1978—; founder, hon. chmn. Com. for Basic Tech., 1984-96, African Epidemiology Study, 1988—; hon. chmn. Eric Barnett Found., 1997—; other philanthropic and charitable coms. Avocations: human ethology, sci. history, music, painting, salmon fishing. Deceased.

**BARNHARD, IVAN HAROLD,** education educator, investment company executive; b. Bklyn., Jan. 2, 1934; s. Daniel S. and Sydelle (Lowenthal) Barnhard; m. Vivian Blancato, June 20, 1957; children: David William, Linda Carol, Lisa Ann. BA, L.I. U., 1956; MA, Auburn U., 1962, PhD, 1969. Tchr., adminstr. pub. schs., Yonkers, NY, from 1962. Pres. Profl. Investment Group, from 1967; chmn. Hudson Holding Assos., from 1969, Marine Investor Assos., from 1969, Pine Investment Assos., from 1969; exec. v.p. Ednl. Analysis Assos., from 1971; vice chmn. bd. Peoples Nat. Bank of Rockland Co. Contbr. articles pub. to profl. jour. Dir. P.I.A. Inc., Packease-Servease Corp., Electro Motion Corp., Peoples Nat. Bank Rockland County. Recipient Jenkins Meml. award Yonkers P.T.A., 1970. Mem.: Mensa, Ga. Acad. Sci., N.Y. State Assn. Secondary Sch. Adminstrn., Nat. Assn. Secondary Sch. Prins., Am. Ednl. Research Assn., Phi Beta Mu, Tau Delta Phi, Phi Delta Kappa. Home: New City, NY. Died Aug. 18, 1998.

**BAROCCI, ROBERT LOUIS (BOB BAROCCI),** retired advertising executive; b. Milw., Feb. 8, 1942; s. Louis F. and Mary H. (Mesich) B.; m. Mary Ann Moloney; children: Robert, Candace. BS, U. Wis., 1963; MBA, Harvard U., 1965. Client svcs. rep. Leo Burnett U.S.A., Chgo., 1965-76; mng. dir. Leo Burnett, London, 1976-79; regional mng. dir. Europe, bd. dirs. Leo Burnett Co., Inc., Chgo., 1979-83; pres. Leo Burnett Internat., 1983-86; chmn., founder McConnaughy, Barocci & Brown, 1986-91; chmn. Environ. Care Mktg. Inc., 1988-93; area dir. Young and Rubicam Europe, London, 1993-95; pres., CEO Advt. Rsch Found. (ARF), 2003—13. Mem. Phi Beta Kappa, Phi Gamma Delta. Roman Catholic. Died Mar. 27, 2014.

**BARR, M.E. See BIGELOW, MARGARET**

**BARRE, RAYMOND,** former Prime Minister of France; b. Saint-Denis, Réunion, Apr. 12, 1924; s. Rene and Charlotte (Deramond) B.; m. Eva Hegedus, Nov. 19, 1954; children: Olivier, Nicolas. Student, Faculté de Droit, Paris, Inst. d'Etudes Politiques. Prof. Inst. des Hautes Etudes, Tunis, 1951-54, Faculté de Droit et de Scis. Economiques, Caen, France, 1954-63, mem., 1962; prof. Inst. d'Etudes Politiques, Paris, from 1961, U. Paris, from 1982; dir. du Cabinet to Minister of Industry, 1959-62; mem. experts com. studying financing of investments in France, 1963-64; mem. commn. Gen. Econ. and Financing of 5th Plan and other govt. coms.; v.p. Commn. of European Communities, 1967-72; mem. Gen. Council Banque de France, 1973; min. fgn. trade Govt. of France, 1976, min. econ. & fin., 1976-78, prime min., 1978-81; M.P. from Rhone dist. Nat. Assembly, 1978—2002; mayor City of Lyon, 1995—2001. Mem. internat. adv. council Inst. Internat. Studies; pres. Inst. d'études des rels. internationale, Conv. libérale europóern et sociale, Inst. internat. du Droit d'expression Francaise. Author: Economie Politique, 1956. Home: Paris, France. Died Aug. 25, 2007.

**BARRETT, GEORGE EDWARD,** lawyer; b. Nashville, Oct. 19, 1927; s. George E. and Annie (Conroy) B.; m. Eloise McBride Barrett, Sept. 14, 1957; (div. 1988); children: Anne-Louise Barrett Thompson, Mary Eloise Barrett Brewer, Kathryn Conroy Barrett Cain. BA in History, Spring Hill Coll., 1952; diploma, Oxford U., Eng., 1953; JD, Vanderbilt U., Nashville, 1957. Bar: Tenn., U.S. Ct. Appeals (6th cir.), U.S. Supreme Ct. Atty. Barrett, Johnston & Parsley, Nashville. Democrat. Roman Catholic. Home: Nashville, Tenn. Died Aug. 26, 2014.

**BARRIE, JOAN PARKER,** elementary school educator; b. LA, Aug. 25, 1932; d. Joseph Alexander and Madeline Agnes (Smith) Parker. EdB, Seattle U., 1959; MEd, Loyola Marymount, 1973. Cert. elem., secondary tchr., Calif.; cert. reading specialist, lang. devel. specialist. 6th grade tchr. Sisters of Immaculate Heart, Hollywood, Calif., 1953-56; reading specialist Lakewood (Wash.) Schs., 1959-60, Beverly Hills (Calif.) Sch. Dist., 1960-62; 2nd grade tchr., 6th grade reading specialist Inglewood (Calif.) Unified Sch. Dist., 1962-76; owner Everest Cultural Enrichments, LA, from 1975; various positions Torrance and Redondo, Calif., 1979-82; office mgr. Starbecca Records, Redondo Beach, Calif., 1982-83; 5th and 6th grades tchr. St. Anthonys, El Segundo, Calif., 1984-85; 2nd grade bilingual tchr. Hawthorne (Calif.) Sch. Dist., from 1985. Author, illustrator: Did You See It, Too?, 1982, Tiggy, Primary Academies, 1989, Reading English, 1994, Reading Spanish, 1995; composer, lyricist Valentine, 1986, (screenplay) Castles of Dreams, 1995. Active United We Stand, 1994, Concern America, Redondo Beach, 1994. Mem. NEA, Calif. Tchrs. Assn., Nat. Coun. Social Studies, S.W. Manuscripters, Dramatist Guild, Smithsonian, Ednl. Dealer. Roman Catholic. Avocations: computers, reading, beach walking, gardening. Home: Los Angeles, Calif. Died Oct. 10, 2001.

**BARTH, TOMISLAV,** biochemist, researcher, educator; b. Roztoky, Czech Republic, Aug. 22, 1938; s. Josef and Anna (Ružicková) B.; m. Jana Kaiferová, Jan. 28, 1964. BSc, Charles Univ., Prague, 1963, MSc, 1968; PhD, Acad. Scis., Prague, 1966, DSc, 1987. Tech. Rsch. Inst. of Antib., Roztoky, 1956-58; doctoral fellow Inst. Organic Chemistry Biochemistry, Prague, 1963-66, researcher, 1966-77, head of rsch., 1977-89, head of dept., 1989-95, deputy of the dir., 1990-92; head of division Prague Inst. of Advanced Studies, 1991. Researcher Inst. Animal Physiol Genetic, Prague, 1993. Contbr. articles to profl. jours. Mem.: European Aquatic Soc., Am. Peptide Soc., European Peptide Soc., Czech Biotech. Soc., Czech. Soc. Biochemistry and Molecular Biology, Sigma Xi. Achievements include patents in field. Home: Roztoky, Czech Republic. Died Oct. 2007.

**BARTHOLOMEW, ARTHUR PECK, JR.,** accountant; b. Rochester, NY, Nov. 20, 1918; s. Arthur Peck and Abbie West (Dawson) B.; m. Mary Elizabeth Meyer, Oct. 4, 1941(wid. Oct. 1992); children: Susan B. Hall, Arthur Peck III, James M., Virginia B. Keyser. AB, U. Mich., 1939, MBA, 1940. CPA. With Ernst & Whinney (name now Ernst & Young), 1940-79, successively jr. accountant, partner charge Eastern dist., Detroit office, 1940-64; nat. office, Cleve. Ernst & Whinney, 1964-65, NY office, 1965-79, also mem. mng. com. Instr. accounting U. Mich., 1940, George Washington U., 1945-46 Mem. Mich. Gov.'s Task Force for Expenditure Mgmt., 1963-64; mem. 2d Regional Plan Commn. NY; bd. dirs. Detroit League for Handicapped, 1952-64; bd. dirs., dir. & treas. Bethesda Hosp. Found., 2000-06; treas. Grosse Pointe War Meml. Assn., 1961; life trustee Greater NY Coun. Boy Scouts Am. Served from pvt. to capt. AUS, 1942-46. Recipient Silver Antelope award, Boy Scouts America, Silver Beaver award. Mem. AICPA, Inst. Mgmt. Accts. (pres. Detroit 1963-64, nat. pres. 1974-75), The Conf. Bd., Mich. Soc. CPAs, NY Soc. CPAs, Country Club Detroit, Gulf Stream Golf Club, Wall St. Club (pres. 1976-78), Ocean Club Fla. (pres. 1993-94), Little Club (pres. 1989-91), Phi Beta Kappa, Phi Kappa Phi, Beta Gamma Sigma, Phi Eta Sigma, Beta Alpha Psi, Phi Kappa Sigma. Republican. Presbyn. Home: Boynton Beach, Fla. Died Feb. 17, 2014.

**BARTOLUCCI, DOMENICO CARDINAL,** cardinal, sacred music director and composer; b. Borgo San Lorenzo, Italy, May 7, 1917; Diploma in Composition, Conservatory of Florence, Italy, 1939; attended, Pontifical Inst. Sacred Music, Accademia Nazionale di Saint Cecilia. Ordained priest of Florence, 1939; choir dir., composer Cathedral of Florence; vice-maestro of choir Basilica of Saint John Lateran, Rome; choir maestro Basilica of Saint Mary Major, Rome, 1947—52; vice maestro Sistine Chapel Choir (Capella Musicale Pontifica Sistina), Rome, 1952—56, direttore perpetuo (director for life), 1956—97; official Roman Curia, 1956—97, official emeritus, 1997—2013; elevated to cardinal, 2010; appointed cardinal-deacon of Santissimi Nomi di Gesù e Maria in via Lata (Most Holy Names of Jesus and Mary in Via Latia), 2010, cardinal-deacon, 2011—13. Guest dir. Choir of Radiotelevisione Italiana (RAI). Composer of numerous works in sacred music, including several masses. Roman Catholic. Died Nov. 11, 2013.

**BARTON, STANLEY L.,** ophthalmologist, consultant; b. Columbia Station, Ohio, May 30, 1920; 1 child, Randal L. BA, Bowling Green State U., 1943; MD, Wayne State U., 1946. Cert. Am. Bd. Ophthalmology. Capt. US Army, 1946—49, Korea. Mem.: AMA (life), Wayne County Med. Soc., Mich. State Med. Soc. Deceased.

**BARTOSEK, KAREL,** historian, writer; b. Skutec, Czech Republic, June 30, 1930; s. Karel Bartosek and Frantiska Stepankova; m. Suzanne, 1959; 3 children. Student, Charles U., Prague. Rsch. asst. Inst. History Czechoslovak Acad. Scis., 1960-69; rschr. Inst. d'Histoire du Temps Présent, CNRS, 1983-96. Author: Les Aveux des Archives, 1996; co-author: Le Livre noir du Communisme, crimes, terreur, répressions, 1997, Directeur de la revue La Nouvelle Alternative, 1986-2001. Avocations: swimming, skiing. Died July 9, 2004.

**BARZ, DIANE MACDONALD,** retired state supreme court justice; b. Bozeman, Mont., Aug. 18, 1943; d. John G. and E. Bernice (Johnson) MacDonald; m. Daniel J. Barz, Nov. 28, 1970; 1 child, Rocky Carl Student, U. Heidelberg, Fed. Republic Germany, 1964; BA magna cum laude, Whitworth Coll., 1965; JD, U. Mont. Law Sch., 1968. Bar: Mont. 1968. Law clk., rsch. asst. Mont. Supreme Ct., Mont. Criminal Commn., Helena, 1968-70; dep. atty. County of Yellowstone, Mont., 1970-75, public adminstr. Mont., 1974-78; ptnr. Poppler & Barz, Billings, Mont., 1973-79; judge US Dist. Ct. Mont., Billings, 1979—89, 1994—2003, chief judge, 1982—84, 1989, 1996; assoc. justice Mont. Supreme Ct., Helena, 1989—91; asst. US atty. Dist. Mont. US Dept. Justice, 1991—94. Account exec. United Way, Billings, 1973; sec. Yellowstone County Rep. Cen. Com., Billings, 1973-75; bd. dirs. South Cen. Mont. Regional Mental Health Ctr., Billings, Yellowstone County Civic Ctr. Commn., 1975-81, Deaconess Hosp., 4-H Mont., Salvation Army; bd. visitors U. Mont. Law Sch., 2003-09 Bur. Nat. Affairs scholar U. Mont., 1968. Mem. Mont. Bar Assn., Yellowstone County Bar Assn., Young Lawyers Assn. (v.p., sec. 1970), American Judges Assn., Mont. Judges Assn., Nat. Assn. Women Judges, Bus. and Profl. Women's Club (named Mont. Young Career Woman 1970), Jr. League Billings, Billings Jr. Chamber of Commerce, Phi Delta (named Woman of Yr. 1970). Home: Billings, Mont. Died May 14, 2014.

**BARZEL, RAINER CANDIDUS,** German legislator; b. Braunsberg, East Prussia, June 20, 1924; s. Candidus and Maria Barzel. Dr.Jurisprudence, U. Cologne, 1949. With Govt. North Rhine-Westphalia, 1949—56; mem. German Fed. Parliament, pres., 1983—84, Christian Democratic Union Party, 1971—73; fed. min. Adenauer Govt. German Affairs, 1962—63, Inter-German Affairs, 1982—83; chmn. Com. Econ. Affairs, German Fed. Parliament, 1977—79, com. fgn. affairs, 1980—82; pres. German-French Inst., 1980—83. Died Aug. 26, 2006.

**BASHAM, GARLYN ARGABRIGHT,** retired academic administrator; b. Delano, Calif., Feb. 20, 1913; s. William Everett Basham and Bessie Jane Argabright; m. Dixie Mildred Tarwater, Sept. 3, 1934 (dec. Mar. 2003); children: Roger Erryl, Laurence Anthony. BA, Santa Barbara State Coll., Calif., 1936; MA, U. So. Calif., 1940; EdD, St. John's U., Ambur, India, 1965. Tchr., counselor, dir. student activities Taft (Calif.) Union H.S. and Jr. Coll., 1936—50; dist. supt. West Kern C.C. Dist., Taft, 1950—75; pres. Taft Coll., 1950—75; ret. Author: Collected Writings, 2003. Lt. comdr. USNR, 1943—46. Mem.: Calif. Ret. Tchrs. Assn., Nat. Sojourners (pres. 1978), Kiwanis (pres. 1970), Masons (capt. 1943—2003, mem. Order of the Shrine from 1975, chair bd. dirs. Childhood Lang. Disorders Clinic 1980—90). Republican. Avocations: public speaking, reading, writing, coin collecting/numismatics. Deceased.

**BASHEER, TAHSEEN MOHAMED,** diplomat; b. Alexandria, Egypt, Apr. 5, 1925; s. Mohamed and Aziza (Ibrahim) Basheer; m. Laila Basmy. BSc, U. Alexandria, 1950; postgrad., Princeton U., 1951—53; MA, Harvard U., 1955. Chmn. Middle East Studies Soc., U. Alexandria, 1949—50; one of founding mems., former pres. Orgn. Arab Students in USA, 1950—56; spokesman, info. officer Egyptian Permanent Mission to UN, 1956—57; acting dir. League Arab States Office, London, 1965—66; sr. staff mem. Arab States Permanent Del. to UN, NYC, 1966—68; lectr. internat. affairs and Arab problems Inst. Diplomatic Affairs, Ministry Fgn. Affairs, Cairo, 1959, 1970, 1971; mem. Egyptian del. to permanent com. of info. Arab League, 1970, head of del., 1971; counsellor Egyptian Embassy to London, 1969—71; dir. Egyptian Info. Ctr., London; ofcl. spokesman Egypt, 1970, (with rank of Minister Plenipotentiary, Ministry of Fgn. Affairs), Egypt, 1971—75; dir. press, info. dept. Ministry Fgn. Affairs, spokesman Ministry Fgn. Affairs, 1972; aide to sec. gen. Arab League, Cairo, 1973, acting presdl. advisor on press affairs, 1973—74; presdl. spokesman and supr. Presdl. Press Affairs with title of ambassador, 1973—74; permanent rep. League Arab States and ambassador, 1976—80; ambassador to Can. Ottawa, from 1981. Decorated Egyptian Order of Merit (1st deg.), Egyptian Order of Republic (2d deg.), Officier de l'Ordre de Legion d'Honneur, Grande Decoration d'Honneur en Or avec plaque, King Abdulaziz Order (2d deg.), La Condecoracion del Iguila Azteca en el Grado Comendador (Mex.). Home: Ottawa, Canada. Died June 11, 2002.

**BASIL, FRANK E.,** civil engineering consultant; b. Atlanta, Sept. 20, 1912; s. E. and Helen B. (Christie) Basil; m. Sophie E. Chotas Basil, Aug. 17, 1939; children: Rodney F., Karen, Ileana. CE, Ga. Tech. Sch., 1935. Chief engr. U.S. Army Corps Engrs., 1939—51; resident mgr. Moroccan Bases, Nouasseur, Morocco, 1951—54; chief civil engr. Spanish Bases, Madrid, 1954—58; pres. Frank E. Basil, Inc., Athens, Greece, 1958—75, Wash., from 1975. Mem. Rep. Nat. Com., from 1981, Internat. Adv. Bd. Nat. Bank Wash., from 1982. With USN, 1944—45. Mem.: AAAS, Pisces (Washington), Soc. Am. Mil. Engrs., Smithsonian Instn. Club. Avocations: stamp collecting/philately, computers, reading. Home: Washington, DC. Died July 20, 1988.

**BASMAJIAN, JOHN VAROUJAN,** medical researcher, educator; b. Constantinople, Turkey, June 21, 1921; came to Can., 1923, naturalized, 1927; s. Mihran and Mary (Evelian) B.; m. Dora Belle Lucas, Oct. 4, 1947; children: Haig, Nancy, Sally. MD with honors, U. Toronto, 1945; LLD (hon.), Queen's U., 1999; DSc (hon.), McMaster U., 2001. Intern Toronto Gen. Hosp., 1945; surg. resident Sunnybrook Hosp. and Hosp. for Sick Children, Toronto, 1946-48; from lectr. to prof. U. Toronto, 1949-57; prof. anatomy, chmn. dept. anatomy Queen's U., Kingston, Ont., 1957-69; prof., dir. regional rehab. rsch. and tng. ctr. Emory U., Atlanta, 1969-77; prof. medicine McMaster U., Hamilton, Ont., 1977-86, prof. emeritus, 1986—2004; dir. rehab. ctr. Chedoke-McMaster Hosps., 1977-86; ret. Exec. sec. Banting Rsch. Found., Toronto, 1954-57; chmn. rsch. com. Fitness Coun. Can., Ottawa, Ont., 1965-69; spl. cons. med. rsch. Ga. Inst. Tech., Atlanta, 1984-90; dir. rsch. and tng. grants Ea. Seal Rsch. Inst., Toronto, 1990-95; bd. dirs. Can. Physiotherapy Found., Toronto, 1984-89; lectureships in Europe, Asia, South Am., Australia, Japan, others. Author 11 med. sci. and clin. books in multiple edits. and transls., 1953—; editor 9 med. clin. books in multiple edits., and transls., 1977—; series editor: Rehabilitation Medicine Library, 24 vols., 1977—; editl. bd. Am. Jour. Phys.

Medicine, 1968-90, Am. Jour. Anatomy, 1971-74, Electromyography and Clin. Neurophysiology, 1966-85, Electro-diagnostic-therapy, Physiotherapy Can., 1979-84, Jour. Motor Behavior, 1980—, Med Post; assoc. editor Anat. Record, 1970-73, 77—, BMA Audiotape Series, 1970-77; contbr. articles to profl. jours.; prodr. several motion pictures; inventor sci. and med. devices and techniques. Mem. and chmn. Bd. Edn., Kingston, Ont., 1960-68; founding chmn. bd. govs. St. Lawrence Coll. Applied Arts and Tech., Ont., 1964-69. Served to capt. M.C., Can. Army, 1943-46 Decorated officer Order of Ont., officer Order of Can.; recipient awards including Starr Gold medal U. Toronto, 1957, Kabakjian award Armenian Youth Fedn., 1967; NRC (Can.) vis. scientist Soviet Acad. Scis., 1963, Henry Gray Laureate, 1991,. Fellow Am. Acad. Angiology, Royal Coll. Physicians (Can.), Royal Coll. Physicians and Surgeons (Glasgow, hon.), Royal Coll. Physicians (Edinburgh, hon.), Physicians Coll. Rehabilitative Medicine (Australia, hon., Edinburgh, hon.); mem. Am. Assn. Anatomists (pres. 1985-86, Henry Gray Laureate award 1991), Can. Assn. Anatomists (founding, sec. 1965-69, J.C.B. Grant award 1985), Am. Congress Rehab. Medicine (Gold Key award 1977, Coulter lectr. 1988), Biofeedback Soc. Am. (founding, pres. 1978-79), Internat. Soc. Electromyographic Kinesiology (founding, pres. 1955-60), Order St. John of Jerusalem (hon. life mem.), Am. Orthopedic Foot Soc. (hon. life), Australian Biofeedback Soc. (hon. life), Venezuelan Biofeedback Soc. (hon. life), Mex. Soc. Anatomy (hon. life), Columbian Assn. Phys. Medicine (hon. life), Physiotherapy Assn. North Greece (hon. pres. 1995—). Avocations: travel, music, gardening, writing. Home: Burlington, Canada. Died Mar. 18, 2008.

**BASSETTI, FRED FORDE,** architect; b. Seattle, Jan. 31, 1917; s. Frederick Michael and Sophie Marie (Forde) B.; m. Mary Wilson, June 30, 1944 (div. 1969); children: Ann, Catherine, Margaret; m. Moira Feeney, June 29, 1971 (div. 1985); children: Megan, Michael; m. Gwenyth Piper Caldwell, Dec. 20, 1989; stepchildren: Megan, Ben, Piper, Sam. BArch, U. Wash., 1942; MArch, Harvard U., 1946. Registered architect, Alaska, Idaho, Mont., Oreg., Wash. Draftsman Paul Thiry, Seattle, 1944, Alvar Aalto, Cambridge, Mass., 1946; designer Naramore, Bain, Brady & Johanson, Seattle, 1946; prin. Bassetti & Morse, Seattle, 1947-62, Fred Bassetti & Co., Seattle, 1962-81, Bassetti, Norton, Metler, Seattle, 1981-85, Bassetti, Norton, Metler, Rekevics, Seattle, 1985-94, Bassetti Architects, Seattle, 1994; retired, 1994. Bd. dirs. Discuren Found., Seattle. Prin. works include Coll. Engring. Bldgs., U. Wash., 1970, Fed. Office Bldg., Seattle, 1975, U.S. Embassy, Lisbon, Portugal, 1977, PACCAR Tech Ctr., Mt. Vernon, Wash., 1985, AT&T Gateway Tower, Seattle, 1990; patentee in field. Mem. Seattle Design Com., 1976-78, Seattle Landmarks Bd., 1978-79. Named Best Local Architect, Seattle Weekly poll, 1988. Fellow AIA (pres. Seattle chpt. 1967; 57 nat. or regional awards, Seattle chpt. medal 1988); mem. Nat. Acad. N.Y.C. (academician 1997), Allied Arts of Seattle and King County (pres. 1970-72). Avocations: tennis, skiing, bicycling, windsurfing. Home: Seattle, Wash. Died Dec. 5, 2013.

**BATEMAN, CAROL VAUGHAN,** pharmacist; b. Richmond, Va., Dec. 23, 1941; d. Harold Benjamin and Verna Pearl (Vaughan) B. Student, Vanderbilt U., 1960-61; BS in Chemistry, U. Richmond, 1964; BS in Pharmacy, U. S.C., 1970. Registered pharmacist, S.C., Hawaii. Pharmacist Camden (S.C.) Walgreen Agy., 1970-74; pharmacist, IV supr. Providence Hosp., Columbia, S.C., 1974-81; asst. pharmacy dir. Hilton Head Hosp., Hilton Head Island, 1981-87, interim pharmacy dir., 1987-88; asst. pharmacy mgr. Revco, 1988-90; pharmacist Self Meml. Hosp., Greenwood, S.C., 1990-93, kinetics pharmacist, from 1993. Vice chmn. S.C. Bd. Pharmacy, 1996-97, chmn. 1997-98; clin. instr. U. S.C. Coll. Pharmacy, 1984—. Editor: Prescriptions for the Kitchen, 1987. Mem. S.C. Heart Assn. Task Force on Hypertension, 1975-81; bd. dirs. Planned Parenthood of Hilton Head, 1986-88; vol. Greenwood Free Clinic, 1997—, Vols. in Med. Missions, 1993—; bd. dirs. Abbeville County Hist. Soc., 1993-96, v.p. 1997-98, pres., 1999—; mem. Rockcreek Homeowners Assn., 1991—; co-founder S.C. Recovery and Intervention Pharmacist Team, 1988-89. Mem. S.C. Pharm. Assn. (chmn. continuing edn. com. 1974-78, v.p. 1978-79, mem. awards com. 1982-84, chmn. conv. com. 1984-85, pres. 1988-89, S.C. Pharmacist of Yr. award 1976), Am. Pharm. Assn., S.C. Soc. Health-Sys. Pharmacists (ann. award 1975), 8th Dist. Pharm. Assn. (v.p. 1991-92), Nat. Assn. Bds. of Pharmacy (mem. task force on stds. for enteral and parenteral care 1994-95, co-chmn. dist. III convention 1998), Am. Soc. Health-Sys. Pharmacists, Faculty House U. S.C., U. S.C. Alumni Assn., Phi Lambda Sigma. Republican. Methodist. Avocations: gardening, travel, collecting orientalia and pharmacy antiques, walking. Deceased.

**BATES, DONALD LLOYD,** retired civil engineer; b. Knightstown, Ind., Feb. 18, 1932; s. Edgar Richard and Lora Norinda (Miller) B.; m. Ngan Yeng, Sept. 3, 1983. BCE, U. Md., 1964; MBA, U. Ind., 1972; PhD, Columbia Pacific U., 1990. Registered profl. engr., Va., Wis., Ariz. Geologist Shell Oil Ltd., Brunei, North Borneo, 1964-66; materials engr. FHA U.S. Dept. Transp., Arlington, Va., 1966-88; quality control engr. Century Materials, Inc., Tempe, Ariz., 1988-91; civil engr. Centennial Civil Engring. Cons., Inc., Irvine, Calif., 1991-94; ret., 1994. Engring. cons. Calif. Dept. Transp., Santa Ana, 1991—. Capt. U.S. Army, 1948-52. Mem. Nat. Soc. Profl. Engrs., ASCE (vice chmn. materials com. 1991-92), ASTM, Assn. Asphalt Paving Engrs., Am. Concrete Inst. Roman Catholic. Avocation: commercial pilot. Home: Largo, Fla. Deceased.

**BATLINER, GERARD,** former Liechtenstein government official, lawyer; b. Eschen, Liechtenstein, Dec. 9, 1928; married; two children. JD, U. Fribourg, Switzerland, 1957. V.p. Fortschrittliche Burgerpartei, 1958-62; dep. mayor Commune of Eschen, 1960-62; head of govt./Minister of Justice Principality of Liechtenstein, 1962-70; lawyer Liechtenstein, 1970—2008; pres. of the parliamentary del. of Liechtenstein Coun. of Europe, 1974-77, v.p. of parliamentary del. of Liechtenstein, 1978-81, v.p. parliamentary Assembly, 1981-82; mem. European Human Rights Commn., 1983-90; chmn. sci. coun. Liechtenstein Inst., 1987-97, mem. sci. coun., 1998—2008; mem. European Commn. for Democracy Through Law, 1991—2008. Arbitrator Ct. of the OSCE, 1991. Editor: Liechtenstein Politische Schriften; author numerous publs. in field. Mem. Liechtensteinische Akademische Gesellschaft, Liechtensteinische Gesellschaft fur Umweltschutz, Historischer Verein, Liechtensteinische Kunstgesellschaft, European Commn. for Democracy Through Law. Died June 25, 2008.

**BATTERMAN, ROBERT COLEMAN,** cardiologist; b. NYC, Apr. 12, 1911; s. Rebecca (Silverman) and Max Batterman; m. June Snyder, Feb. 27, 1947 (dec. July 6, 2008); children: Christie, Mark, Hollis. BS, NYU, 1931, MD, 1935. Diplomate Am. Bd. Internal Medicine. Intern, resident Bellevue Hosp., NYU Coll. Medicine, NYC, 1936-39; fellow in therapeutics NYU U. Coll. Medicine, 1939-40, instr. in therapeutics, 1940-49, asst. prof. medicine, 1949-50; assoc. clin. prof. medicine N.Y. Med. Coll., 1951-55, assoc. prof. physiology and pharmacology, 1956-59; dir. Inst. Clin. Pharmacology and Med. Rsch., Berkeley, Calif., 1959-87. Vis. physician Highland Hosp., Oakland, Calif., Harrick Meml. Hosp., Berkeley, 1959-86, St. Francis Meml. Hosp., San Francisco, 1964-66, Calif. State Dept. Correction, Vacaville; sr. vis. physician, past asst. chief medicine Mount Zion Hosp. and Rsch. Ctr., San Francisco. Contbr. articles, abstracts to profl. pubs. Pres. Nat. Femily Coun. of Drug Addiction Inc., 1956-65, Comprehensive Health Edn. Inc., 1969-71, City of Berkeley Commn. Health Adv. Com., 1971-73; mem. Alameda County Comprehensive Health Planning Hosp. and Facility Com., 1972-76; mem. Calif. Health Facilities Authority, 1981—. Fellow N.Y. Acad. Medicine, N.Y. Acad. Scis., Internat. Acad. Law and Sci. (2d v.p. 1966-67), Internat. Angiology (pres. 1967-69), Am. Inst. Chemists, ACP; mem. Alameda-Contra Costa Med. Assn., AAAS, Am. Soc. Clin. Pharmacology and Therapeutics, Am. Rheumatism Assn., No. Calif. Rheumatism Assn., Am. Soc. Clin. Investigation, Am. Soc. Pharmacol. and Explt. Therapeutics, Am. Therapeutic Soc., Drug Info. Assn., Soc. Comprehensive Medicine, Sigma Xi, numerous other med. orgns. Home: Oakland, Calif. Died June 11, 1993.

**BAUER, ELIZABETH KELLEY (MRS. FREDERICK WILLIAM BAUER),** consulting energy economist; b. Berkeley, Calif., Aug. 7, 1920; d. Leslie Constant and Elizabeth Jeanette (Worley) Kelley; m. Frederick William Bauer, July 5, 1944; children: Elizabeth Katherine Bauer Keenan, Frederick Nicholas. AB, U. Calif., Berkeley, 1941, MA, 1943; PhD, Columbia U., 1947. Instr., US History and studies Barnard Coll., NYC, 1944—45; rsch. asst. Giannini Found., 1946—49, asst. rsch. agrl. economist, 1957—60; lectr., history U. Calif., 1949—50, exec. sec., Internat. Conf. Agrl. and Coop. Credit, 1952—53, lectr., history, 1956—57; exec. sec. South Asia Project, 1955—56; registrar Holy Names Coll., Oakland, Calif., 1971—72; rsch. assoc. Brookings Instn. and Nat. Acad. Pub. Adminstrn., Washington, 1973; fgn. affairs officer Internat. Energy Affairs, Fed. Energy Adminstrn., Washington, 1974—77, Office Current Reporting, Internat. Affairs, Dept. Energy, Washington, 1977—81; dir. policy analysis, evaluation Nat. Coal Assn., Washington, 1981—83. Author: Commentaries on the Constitution, 1790-1860, 1952; co-author (with Murray R. Benedict): Farm Surpluses: U.S Burden or World Asset?, 1960; co-author: (with Florence Noyce Wertz) The Graduate Theological Union, 1970; editor: The Role of Foreign Governments in the Energy Industries, 1977. Mem. Calif. Com. Revise Tchrs. Credential, 1961; bd. dirs. St. Paul's Towers and Episcopal Homes Found., Oakland, 1971—72; trustee Grad. Theol. Union, Berkeley, 1972—74. Recipient Superior Achievement award, Dept. Energy, 1980, Alumni citation, U. Calif., 1983, 1993. Mem.: AAAS, AAUW (Calif. chmn., higher edn. 1960—62), Mortar Bd., PEO, Prytanean Honor Soc., Pi Sigma Alpha, Phi Alpha Theta, Sigma Kappa Alpha, Pi Lambda Theta, Phi Beta Kappa. Democrat. Episcopalian. Home: Santa Rosa, Calif. Died July 18, 1999.

**BAUER, RICHARD H.,** clergyman; b. Cin., May 19, 1913; s. Samuel B. and Alice (Helck) B.; m. Eleanor Nye, July 3, 1941. Comml. Engr., U. Cin., 1936; M.Div., Garrett Theol. Sem., 1947; D.D., Ohio No. U., 1962. With Proctor & Gamble Co., 1932-44; ordained to ministry Methodist Ch., 1948; pastor in Cin., 1942-44, Ashley, Ind., 1944-47, North College Hill, Cin., 1947-53, Bellefontaine, Ohio, 1953-56; dist. supt. (Portsmouth (Ohio) dist. Meth. Ch.), 1956-60; exec. sec. interboard com. enlistment for ch. occupations United Meth. Ch., 1960-72, exec. sec. office personnel services, 1973-76; dir. devel. loans and scholarships United Meth. Ch. (Office of Personnel), 1976-78; nat. field rep. World Hunger Edn./Action Together, United Meth. Ch., from 1978. Del. World Meth. Conf., 1961, 66, 71, 81; mem. World Meth. Council, 1966-71; mem. assembly Nat. Council Chs., 1963-66, 66-69, 70-73, chmn. commn. vocation and enlistment, 1963-76, vice chmn. dept. ministry, 1966-76; sec. Meth. Council Secs., 1964-68; trustee Meth. Home Aged, 1956-60; bd. dirs., pres. Mid-South Career Devel. Center, 1974-78; chmn. Commn. on Vocation and Religion, Nat. Vocat. Guidance Assn., 1980-85; chmn. Commn. on Work and Spiritual Values, Nat. Assn. Career Devel., 1985— Contbr. articles to ch. publs. Mem. Metro/Nashville Human Rights Commn., 1983— Mem. Am. Personnel and Guidance Assn., Ch. Career Devel. Council (sec. 1974-78), UN Assn. U.S.A. (pres. Nashville chpt. 1982-87), Common Cause, Sigma Chi, Omicron Delta Kappa. Home: Nashville, Tenn. Died Oct. 17, 1988.

**BAUTISTA, REYNALDO YASAY,** civil and sanitary engineering educator; b. Espiritu, Ilocos N., The Philippines, May 24, 1961; s. Ricardo Discalzo and Aurelia (Yasay) B.; m. Genalyn Sanchez, Jan. 31, 1989; children: Joanna Marie, Reygene John, Joyce Reah, Mae Jen. BSCE, St. Louis U., Baguio City, The Philippines, 1978-83; grad. in math., U. Philippines, Baguio City, 1984; BS in San. Engring., U. Baguio, Baguio City, 1986, MA in Ednl. Mgmt. cum laude, 1996, EdD, 1998. Registered civil and san. engr., The Philippines. Project engr. Flores Constrn., Baguio City, 1983-84; prof. engring. U. Baguio, 1984-88, head dept. surveying, 1986-88; prof. civil and san. engring. Philippine Mil. Acad., Baguio City, from 1989, course dir. reinforced concrete design, from 1989, structural cons., from 1995. Rev. dir. for civil and san. engring. United Engrs. Rev. Ctr., Dagupan City, Laong City, Baguio City, 1988; structural cons. Lagman Constrn., Isabela City, 1995—, Baguio City, 1997— Author: Workbook in Reinforced Concrete DEsign, 1990 (Outstanding Author award 1990). Chapel design cons. CICM, Baguio City, 1988; mem. civil engring. works com. Pinehurst Parish, Pacdal-Baguio City, 1993; grad. sch. panelist U. Baguio, 1997—. Mem. Assn. Structural Engrs. Philippines (life), Philippine Inst. for San. Engrs. (life, Outstanding award 1989), Am. Concrete Inst., PERAA (One of 10 Outstanding Mems. award 1996). Avocations: structural designing, playing basketball, estimating, interior decorating, layout artist. Home: Baguio City, Philippines. Deceased.

**BAY, HENG-TAI,** materials engineer; b. Singapore, Sept. 17, 1942; s. Song-Leng and Gek-Ngo (Chua) Bay; m. Bridget Wai-Fong Choy, Feb. 28, 1987; 1 child, Stefanie Ruiwen. BS in Phys. Metallurgy, Wash. State U., Pullman, WA USA, 1967; MSMetE, U.of Pitts., 1969. Metallurgist Blaw-Knox Co, Wheeling, W.Va., 1967—68; staff supr. Tex. Instruments Singapore, Singapore, 1970—72; plant engr. Nat. Iron & Steel Mills, Singapore, 1973—74; gen. mgr. Sanshiba-Indonesia, Jakarta, West Java, Indonesia, 1975—78; mgr. test svcs. Chartered Industries Of Singapore, Singapore, 1979—88; cons. HT Metal Industries; BayInc-Mgmt. Consultants, Singapore, from 1990. Tech. dir. San Group Of Companies- Indonesia, Jakarta, Indonesia, 1975—78; adv. bd. mem. Singapore Mfrs. Assn., Singapore, 1985—87; assoc. cons. Nat. Productivity Bd., Singapore, 1989—92; projects cons. H T Metal Industries, Singapore, from 1993. Recipient Internat. Exch. Student Award, Wash. State U., 1963-1967. Mem.: ASM, The Metall. Soc. of AIME, Singapore Nature Soc. Achievements include Use of river reeds in Sumatra to make special long-fibre paper; accrediting test labs. for high tech. defense-related and aerospace industries; upgrading local industries in Malaysia, Thailand, China. Died Mar. 30, 2008.

**BAYER, ALAN EVERETT,** retired sociology educator; b. Webster, Mass., May 3, 1939; s. J. Otto and Doris (Carver) Bayer; children: Karen, Lisa. BS in Educational Psychology, Pa. State U., 1961; MS in Sociology, Fla. State U., 1963; PhD in Sociology, 1965. Rsch. assoc. Nat. Acad. Sciences, Washington, 1965—67; rsch. scientist American Insts. Rsch., Palo Alto, Calif., 1967—68; assoc. dir. rsch. American Coun. on Edn., Washington, 1968—73; prof., chmn. sociology Fla. State U., 1973—80; prof. sociology Va. Tech. U., 1982—2006, prof. emeritus, 2006—14; founding dir. Ctr. for Survey Rsch. Vis. fellow Boys Town Rsch. Ctr., Omaha, 1980—82. Co-author: Human Resources and Higher Education, 1970, The Power of Protest, 1975. Mem.: Assn. Study of Higher Edn., Soc. Social Studies of Sci., Nat. Coun. on Family Rels., American Ednl. Rsch. Assn., American Sociological Assn. Home: Blacksburg, Va. Died May 30, 2014.

**BAYERS, CONNIE STARR,** director, educator; b. Ottumwa, Iowa, May 17, 1950; d. James Carleton and Deloris Maxine (Ferguson) Starr; m. James Arthur Bayers, Aug. 2, 1979. BA in Sociology and Edn., Parsons Coll., 1972; MA in Mgmt. and Supervision, Ctrl. Mich. U., 1977. Ctr. dir. Chapman Coll., Norton AFB, Calif., from 1978. Ctr. adminstr. ParkColl., Wright-Patterson AFB, Ohio, 1974—78. Mem.: Am. Soc. Tng. and Devel., Phi Kappa Phi. Died Oct. 14, 1998.

**BAYLISS, SIR RICHARD IAN SAMUEL,** endocrinologist; b. Tettenhall, Eng., Jan. 2, 1917; s. Frederick William and Muryel Anne (Sanderson) B.; m. Joan Hardman Lawson, 1942 (dec.); children: Caroline (dec.), Christopher; m. Constance Frey, 1958 (div. 1979); children: Susan, Virginia; m. Marina Audrey de Borchgave D'Altena, 1979. BA, Cambridge U., 1938, MB, 1941, MD, 1946. Resident St. Thomas's Hosp., London, 1941-45; physician Royal Postgrad. Med. Sch., London, 1948-54, Westminster Hosp., London, 1954-81, Her Majesty the Queen's Household, London, 1964-70, Her Majesty the Queen, London, 1970-82. Dean Westminster Med. Sch., London, 1960-65; cons. in medicine Royal Navy, 1977-82; gov. Merck Found., Rahway, N.J., 1973-89; dir. J.S. Pathology Svcs., London, 1981-90, Pvt. Patient's Plan, London, 1978-89; cons. endocrinologist; chmn. med. adv. panel Ind. TV Commn., London. Author: Practical Procedures, 3d edit., 1960, Thyroid Disease: The Facts, 3d edit., 1998; editor: Investigations in Endocrine Disease, 1974. Decorated knight comdr. Victorian Order; fellow, Rockefeller Found., 1950—51. Fellow Royal Soc. Medicine (pres. endocrinology sect. 1966-68), Royal Coll. Physicians; mem. Assn. Physicians (pres. 1980-81), Thyroid Club (pres. 1972-78). Avocations: skiing, music. Home: London, England. Died Apr. 21, 2006.

**BAYNE, WILLIAM HENRY, JR.,** management and public relations consultant; b. Kearny, NJ, Dec. 13, 1912; s. William H. and Margaret W. (Aitken) Bayne; m. Adele Wehman, May 29, 1946; children: Edward J., William H. III. Student, Rutgers U., 1932—35, Columbia, 1935—37. Reporter N.Y. World, N.Y. Herald-Tribune, Newark Evening News, 1935—40; dir. pub. rels. Brewster Aero. Corp., Long Island City, Nebr., 1940—43; chief instrn. and edn., dept. medicine and surgery VA, Washington, 1946—48; editor, pub. Handicap Pub. Co., Washington, 1948—85, pub., 1976—85. Editor, pub. Washington Med. News Bur., 1950; chmn. Bayne Internat., 1958—80; mgmt. and pub. rels. info. svc. Grassroots/Am.: Columbus 500, 1958—80. Author: America-500 Years After Columbus, 1991. Christopher Columbus Quincentenary Jubilee Com.; mem. consumer bd. FDA; mem. Prince Georges Hist. Soc., Greater Washington Sci. Fair Assn.; mem. steering com. Pres. Truman's Nat. Health Assembl, 1948; mem. Pres.'s Com. Employment of Physically Handicapped, 1948—76, White House Conf. Handicapped Individuals, 1976—77; dir. Md. Maritime Assos., Hosp. Systems, Med. Systems Advisors, Worldwide Systems Advs., Bayne Internat., Surg. R & D Corp. With US Army, 1943—47. Recipient Md. Outstanding Sr. Citizen Jaycess, 1983—88. Mem.: AAAS, Am. Sci. Writers Assn., Prince Georges Geneology Soc., Nat. Assn. Execs., Am. Med. Writers Assn., Nat. Rehab. Assn., Am. Mgmt. Assn., Am. Inst. Mcht. Shipping, Masons. Died Apr. 24, 1993.

**BAYSHORE, CHARLES ALEXANDER,** medical consultant, retired optometrist; b. Hagerstown, Md., Aug. 30, 1919; s. Lloyd Mehring and Helen (Purdy) Basehoar; m. Margaret Cook, July 5, 1947 (dec. 1974); children: Donald, Beverly, Margo; m. Bradylee Blackwell, Feb. 23, 1975. OD, Pa. State Coll. Optometry, 1940; DOS, New Eng. Coll. Optometry, 1986. Pvt. practice, Bethesda, Md., 1940-45, Orlando, Fla., 1945-50, 53-80; ret., 1980. Adj. prof., U. Houston, 1980; cons., Control-O-Fax, Corneal Scis., Inc., Ophthalmic Products Group, Itek Corp., Syntex Ophthalmics, Inc., Frontier Contact Lenses, Vistakon, Inc. of Johnson & Johnson; consulting dir. profl. edn., Salvatori Ophthalmics, Inc., others; lectr., presenter seminars in field. Patentee, soft contact lens, bifocal soft contact lens, corneal contact lens; contbr. numerous articles to profl. publs. Rep. for pvt. aviation to CAB; mem. Orlando Aviation Planning. Bd. Capt., optometry officer USAF, 1950-53. Mem. Orange County Optometric Soc., Fla. Optometric Assn. (chmn. contact lens com. 1958-62), Am. Acad. Optometry (chmn. contact lens sect. 1966-68, pres. Fla. chpt. 1960-76), Am. Opometric Assn. (adviser contact lens com. 1970-71), Am. Optometric Found., Internat. Soc. Contact Lens Specialist (pres. 1985-88), Am. Assn. Profl. Cons. Home: Orlando, Fla. Died June 8, 2008.

**BEALE, JACK GORDON,** engineering consultant, water research foundation administrator, research scientist; b. Sydney, July 17, 1917; s. Rupert Noel and Esther Anderina (Green) B.; m. Stephania Toth-Dobrzanski, 1958 (dec. Nov. 2005); children: David John, Christopher William. Diploma in mech. engring. with honors, Sydney Tech. Coll., 1939; M of Engring., U. NSW, 1964, DS (hon.), 1997; LLD (hon.), Australian Nat. U., 1999. Chartered profl. engr., Australia. Prin. Hon. Jack G. Beale Cons. Chartered Profl. Engrs., Sydney, from 1942; chair Beale Internat. Group, from 2004, Water Rsch. Australia, from 2004. Bd. dirs. numerous pvt. and pub. cos., Australia; Min. for Conservation, Govt. NSW, Sydney, 1965-71, Min. for Environ. Control, 1971-73; mem. representing NSW, Australian Ministerial Water Resources Coun., Canberra, 1965-71, Australian Ministerial Forestry Coun., Canberra, 1965-71, Australian Ministerial Environ. Coun., Canberra, 1971-73; mem. NSW Sci. Coun., 1974; sr. adviser UN Environment Program, 1974-77, UN Devel. Program, 1975-77; chmn. Water Rsch. Found. Australia, Canberra, 1955—2004; mem. Nat. Water Rsch. Coun., 1982-83; chmn., bd. dirs. Zenith Investments, 1955—, FES (NSW) Pty. Ltd., 1987—, Energy Sys. Pty. Ltd., Sydney, 1987—, HydroCo Ltd., 1987-93, Hydro-Gen Ltd., Sydney, 1993—; mem. adv. coun. Ctr. for Resource and Environ. Studies Australia Nat. U., Canberra, 1990-2001; ptnr. HydroCo Partnership, 1993-98. Author: Environment Protection and Management, 1974, The Manager and The Environment, 1977; contbr. numerous articles to profl. publs. Mem. Legis. Assembly of NSW, Sydney, 1942-73; found. chair intradisciplinary knowledge Acad. of Letters, USA, 2004—. Decorated officer Order of Australia; recipient numerous internat. medals and awards for outstanding contbns. to mankind living in harmony with the environment, 1990—; Jack Beale Chair of Water Resources named in his honor Australian Nat. U., 1989, Ann. Jack Beale Water Resources Lecture Series named in his honor, 1990, Jack Beale Global Environ. Lecture Series named in his honor U. N.S.W., 1997; apptd. Honorable for Life by HM Queen, 1973. Fellow Instn. of Engrs. Australia (hon., life); mem. ASME (life) ASCE (life) Am. Soc. Agrl. and Biol. Sys. Engrs. (life). Achievements include first nat. water plan for Australia; devel. of an integrated soil, water and vegetation program to rejuvenate the Australian landscape, "Green Australia", integrated program to mitigate the economical and social damage of national droughts, "Droughtproofing", integrated program to mitigate the economic and social damage of national droughts, integrated network of climatically distributed hydroelectric generating facilities to ensure economically viable electricity output (patent); advanced uniformity of precipitation from overlapping distribution patterns of irrigation sprinklers; devel. of whole river valley sustainability, pioneering governmental guidelines for environ. impact statements; initiator of comprehensive Australian state and nat. environ. policy, law and mgmt., comphrensive pioneer environ. policy, law and mgmt. initiatives in developing countries. Died June 7, 2006.

**BEARDSLEY, LEAH MILDRED,** mathematics education educator, consultant; b. Ft. Foote, Md., Mar. 6, 1911; d. Cleveland and Mamie (Thompson) Kirby; m. Andrew Louis Beardsley; children: Anne Leah, Joan Ellen Berger, John Bruce. Cert. in teaching, Townson State Coll., Md., 1929; BS, Wayne State U., 1955; MS, U. Detroit, 1965. Tchr. Prince George County, Riverdale, Md., 1929-36, Detroit Pub. Schs., 1952-68, math. demonstration tchr., 1968-74, ret., 1974. Diagnostic clinic tchr. Wayne State U., 1959-60, instr., 1968; speaker numerous confs. throughout U.S. and Can. Author: The Hundred Square, 1972, Math Activities, 1976; co-author math. textbooks, 1980-85. Mem. Detroit Area Ret. Sch. Pers., Mich. Area Ret. Sch. Pers., Lansing. Mem. Nat. Coun. Tchrs. Math., Mich. Coun. Tchrs. Math. (life), Detroit Area Coun. Tchrs. Math. (life), Friends of the Libr. Episcopalian. Avocations: speaking, tutoring, painting, travel, bowling. Died Mar. 16, 1998.

**BEARMAN, JACOB E.,** statistician, educator; b. Mpls., June 28, 1915; s. Abraham Nathaniel and Etta (Zieve) B.; m. Shirley Resnick, July 9, 1942; children: Kenneth David, Deborah Anne, Diane Louise, Abby Nehama. BA magna cum laude, U. Minn., 1936, MA, 1938, PhD, 1947. Asst. prof. math. U. Minn., 1947-53; asst. prof. Pub. Health Biostats./U. Minn., 1953-56, assoc. prof., 1956-58, prof., 1958-78, prof. emeritus, from 1978; prof. epidemiology Ben-Gurion U., Beer-Sheva, Israel, from 1978, prof. emeritus, from 1995. Mem. VA Coop. Studies Evaluation Com., 1973-77; mem. policy bd. Coronary Drug Project Nat. Heart and Lung Inst., 1962-82; statis. cons. NASA Planetary Quarantine Program, 1966-75; mem. data monitoring com. Program of the Surg. Control of Hyperlipidemias, 1969—. Contbg. author: (book) Twin Research 3: Epidemiological and Clinical Studies, 1981. Capt. AUS-Ordnance Dept., 1941-46, ETO. Tng. grantee Nat. Heart Inst., 1953-68. Fellow Am. Statis. Assn. (chmn. biometric sect. 1969), AAAS; mem. Internat. Biometric Soc. Jewish. Avocations: chess, music, reading. Home: Beer Sheva, Israel. Died July 14, 2005.

**BEATTY, SAMUEL ALSTON,** retired state supreme court justice; b. Tuscaloosa, Ala., Apr. 23, 1923; s. Eugene C. and Rosabelle (Horton) B.; m. Maude Applegate, Jan. 19, 1949; children: Rosa Beatty Lord, Eugene A. BS in Commerce and Bus. Adminstrn, U. Ala., 1948, JD, 1953; LL.M., Columbia U., 1959, J.S.D., 1964. Bar: Ala. bar 1953. Pvt. practice, Tuscaloosa, 1953-56; mem. faculty U. Ala. Law Sch., 1955-70, prof. law, 1963-70, asst. dean, 1959-63; vis. prof. law U. Cin. Law Sch., 1966-67; asso. dir. Ala. Defender Project, 1967-70; dean, prof. law Mercer U. Law Sch., 1970-72, adj. prof., 1972-74; v.p., trust officer First Nat. Bank & Trust Co., Macon, Ga., 1972-74; asst. atty. gen., chief civil divsn. State of Ala., 1974; ptnr. Henley & Beatty, Tuscaloosa, Northport, Ala., 1975-76; assoc. justice Ala. Supreme Ct., 1976-89. Adj. prof. U. Ala. Grad. Sch.; speaker, lectr. in field. Contbr. legal journals Served to maj. USAAF, 1942-45, PTO. Decorated Air medal with 9 oak leaf clusters. Mem. ABA, Ala. Bar Assn., Tuscaloosa County bar assns., Nat. Orgn. Legal Problems Edn., Farrah Order Jurisprudence, Order of Coif, Phi Alpha Delta. Democrat. Methodist. Died May 21, 2014.

**BEAUDOIN, GÉRALD ARMAND,** lawyer, educator, retired Canadian legislator; b. Montreal, Qué., Can., Apr. 15, 1929; s. Armand and Aldéa (St.-Arnaud) B.; m. Renée Desmarais, Sept. 11, 1954; children: Viviane, Louise, Denise, Françoise. BA summa cum laude, U. Montreal, 1950, LLL magna cum laude, 1953, MA in Law, 1954; postgrad. in comparative law (Carnegie scholar), U. Toronto, 1954-55; DESD cum laude, U. Ottawa, Ont., 1958; LLD, U. Louvain-la-Neuve, Belgium, 1989. Bar: Called to Que. bar 1954, created queen's counsel 1969. Practiced law with Paul Gérin-Lajoie, Montreal, 1955-56; adv. counsel Dept. Justice, Ottawa, 1956-65, sr. adv. counsel, 1960-65; asst. parliamentary counsel Ho. of Commons of Can., Ottawa, 1965-69; civil law dean Faculty of Law, U. Ottawa, 1969-79, prof. constl. law, 1969-89, dir. Human Rights Ctr., 1986-88; mem. Senate of Can., 1988. Mem. Goldenberg Com. on Constn., 1967, La Commn des Svcs. Juridiques du Quebec, 1972-73, Task Force on Can. Unity, 1977-79; vis. prof. U. Sorbonne, 1985; vis. prof. faculty of law U. Ottawa, 1989-94, prof. emeritus, 1994-2008; co-chmn. spl. joint com. of Senate and Ho. of Commons. on process for amending Constn. of Can., 1991, on a renewed Can., 1991-92; mem. Senate Spl. Com. on Euthanasia and Assisted Suicide, 1994-95. Author: Essais sur la Constitution, 1979, Le partage des pouvoirs, 1980, 3d edit., 1983, La Constitution du Canada, 1990, 2004, Le fédéralisme au Canada, 2000, Les droits et libertés au Canada, 2000; (with others) Mécanismes pour une nouvelle Constitution, 1981; co-editor: La Charte Canadienne des droits et libertés, 3d edit., 1996, Perspectives Canadiennes et Européennes des droits de la personne, 1986; editor: The Supreme Court of Can.-La Cour suprême du Can., 1986, Charter Cases, 1986-87, Your Clients and the Charter, 1988, Vues Canadiennes et Européennes des droits et libertés, 1989, As the Charter Evolves, 1990, The Charter: Ten Years Later, 1992, (with G. Robertson et al) Federalism for the Future: Essential Reforms, 1998; mem. Thémis Law Rev., 1951-52; contbr. numerous articles to Can. and fgn. law revs. Mem. spl. com. to draft Can. Constn. in French, 1985-90. Decorated officer Order of Can., officer Legion of Honor; recipient The Ramon John Hnatyshyn award, 1997, Walter S. Tarnopolsky Human Rights award, 2002, French Legion of Honor, 2004 Mem. Royal Soc. Can., Acad. des Lettres du Québec, Can. Bar Assn. (nat. chmn. sect. constl. and internat. law 1971-73, 86-87), Can. Inst. Pub. Affairs, Inst. Pub. Adminstrn. (Can.), Can. Law Deans (chmn. 1972-73), Can. Inst. Inter de Droit d'Expression Française (v.p. 1973-2008), Que. Law Deans (chmn. 1975-76), Internat. Assn. Comparative Law, Internat. Commn. Jurists (v.p. for Can. 1987-90, pres. for Can. 1990-92). Roman Catholic. Home: Gatineau, Canada. Died Sept. 10, 2008.

**BEAUMONT, BRYAN ALAN,** retired judge; b. Brisbane, Australia, Dec. 29, 1938; s. Alan P. and Thora C. (Harrison) B.; m. Jeanette Alison (Wilkie) B.; m. Jan. 10, 1967; children: Justine, Madeleine, Nicholas, Eliane. LLB, U. Sydney, 1961, LLD (hon.), 2005. Solicitor, 1961-65; barrister, 1965-78; Queen's counsel, 1978-83; with Ct. Australian Capital Ter., 1983—2002; presdl. mem. Adminstrv. Appeals Tribunal, from 1983; judge Supreme Ct., Norfolk Island, 1989-93; chief justice Norkolk Island, 1993—2004; acting judge Supreme Ct., Vanuatu, Australia, 1993; judge Fed. Ct. Australia, Sydney, 1983—2005, Ct. of Appeal, Tonga, 1997—2005, Fiji Supreme Ct., 2002—05; ret., 2005. Vis. fellow Wolfson Coll., Cambridge (Eng.) U., 1990, 98, Harvard U., Boston, summer 1992. Mem. coun. Women's Coll., Sydney U., 1992-96; trustee Ensemble Theatre Found., 1996—. Decorated Order of Australia. Fellow Australian Inst. Jud. Adminstrn. (hon., chmn. 1990-92); mem. Am. Law Inst. Avocations: tennis, music, theater. Home: Lavender Bay, Australia. Died June 12, 2005.

**BECH, INGE V.,** interior design consultant; b. Aarhus, Denmark, June 29, 1912; arrived in U.S., 1939, naturalized, 1952; parents Philip Bech and Johanne (Schelde Bang) B. Student, Ecole Menagere, 1927-28, Upper Chine, 1931, Tech. Inst. Copenhagen, 1932-33. Interior decorator Bolighuset, Copenhagen, 1933-35; interior designer various archtl. and design firms, Denmark, 1935-39, 46-48; head dept. furniture and textile George Jensen, Inc., NYC, 1941-44; window display rep. Eve Bruser Studios, N.Y., 1945; interior designer Jack Lessman Interior Design, N.Y., 1948-52, Intercontinental Hotels, N.Y., 1953; dir. interior design Hilton Internat. Hotels, N.Y. and Brussels, 1954-79; pvt. cons. Brussels, from 1979. Contbr. articles to profl. jours. Died Sept. 12, 1990.

**BECK, CHARLES WESLEY, II,** lawyer; b. Ft. Worth, June 26, 1933; s. Charles Wesley and Evelyn Virginia Beck; m. Shirley Ann Trowbridge, July 21, 1978; children: Gary N. Trowbridge, Peggy A. Thomas, Julia A. Kenner. BS in Aero Engring., U. Tex., Austin, 1954, BSEE, 1961, MSEE, 1962; JD, Baylor U., Waco, Tex., 1986. Registered prof. engr., Tex., 1973; bar: Tex. 1986. Rsch. engr. defense rsch. lab. U. Tex., Austin, 1959—61; engr. LTV, Dallas, 1961—62; rsch. engr., group leader NASA Ames Rsch. Ctr., Mountain View, Calif., 1962—67; program mgr., mgr. elec. sys. Tracor, Inc., Austin, 1967—73; sub contract mgr. E-Sys., Garland, 1973—75; pres., founder Internat. Avionics, Inc., Addison, from 1970; atty. pvt.pvt. practice, from 1986. Lt. USN, 1954—58. Mem.: Tex. Bar Assn., Mensa. Republican. Achievements include invention of liquid level measurement; computer for liquid level measurement; fuel transmitter. Avocation: old cars. Home: Richardson, Tex. Died Dec. 2012.

**BECK, MARILYN MOHR,** columnist; b. Chgo., Dec. 17, 1928; d. Max and Rose (Lieberman) Mohr; m. Roger Beck, Jan. 8, 1949 (div. 1974); children: Mark Elliott, Andrea; m. Arthur Levine, Oct. 12, 1980. AA, U. So. Calif., 1950. Freelance writer nat. mag. and newspapers, Hollywood, Calif., 1959-63; Hollywood columnist Valley Times and Citizen News, Hollywood, Calif., 1963-65; West Coast editor Sterling Mag., Hollywood, Calif., 1963-74; free-lance entertainment writer LA Times, Calif., 1965-67; Hollywood columnist Bell-McClure Syndicate, 1967-72; chief Bell-McClure Syndicate (West Coast bur.), 1967-72; Hollywood columnist NANA Syndicate, 1967-72; syndicated Hollywood columnist NY Times Spl. Features, 1972-78, NY Times Spl. Features (United Feature Syndicate), 1978-80, United Press abroad, 1978-80, Internat. Editors News and Features, Chgo. Tribune/NY Daily News Syndicate, 1980-97; columnist TV Guide, 1989—92, Creators Syndicate, 1997—2014. Creator, host Marilyn Beck's Hollywood Outtakes spls. NBC, 1977, 78; host Marilyn Beck's Hollywood Hotline, Sta. KFI, LA, 1975-77; Hollywood reporter Eyewitness News, Sta. KABC-TV, LA, 1981, (TV program) PM Mag., 1983-88; on-air corr. E! TV, 1993-99, CompuServe Entertainment Authority, 1994-96, eDrive Internet Authority, 1996-97, e!online Internet Hollywood Authority, 1997-2000, Compuserve, Netscape, 2000-14, aeNTV.com, 2001-02; author: (non-fiction) Marilyn Beck's Hollywood, 1973, (novel) Only Make Believe, 1988; co-author: Unfinished Lives, What If...?, 1996. Recipient Citation of Merit LA City Coun., 1973, Press award Public Guild America, 1974, Bronze Halo award Southern Calif. Motion Picture Coun., 1982. *Being the best isn't everything; it's the only thing. "Life is too short to be little" (Disraeli).* Died May 31, 2014.

**BECK, MARTHA ANN,** curator, director; b. Cleve., June 16, 1938; d. Claude and Ellen Beck. BA in English Lit., Vassar Coll., 1960; postgrad., NYU, 1963-67. Editor, writer, rschr. The Frick Collection, 1962-64; curatorial asst. drawings dept. The Mus. Modern Art, 1968-75; founder, dir. The Drawing Ctr., 1975—91, The Ctr. for Internat. Exhibitions, 1992—2014. Served on numerous juries and panels including Nat. Endowment for the Arts, SUNY Thayer Family Fellowships, The Westchester Coun. on the Arts and the Jerome Found. Fellowships; lectr. in field. Author: (screenplays) Ashenden's Adventures as British Agent During World War I, 2005—06, Mami, 2006, Los Niños Héroes, 2008, short stories. Recipient NYU scholarship, 1964-65. Home: New York, NY. Died Jan. 6, 2014.

**BECK, MARY BERENICE,** academic administrator, nursing educator; b. 1890; D in Nursing Edn., Cath. U. Am. Dean Marquette U. Coll. Nursing; prof., dept. chmn. dept. nursing edn. Marquette Grad. Sch. Bd. dirs. Am. Jour. Nursing Co. Mem. ANA (helped to establish 1st code of ethics for nursing profession, v.p. profl. counseling and placement svc., bd. dirs.), Cath. Hosp. Assn. (com. nursing edn.), Assn. Collegiate Schs. Nursing, Nat. League Nursing Edn., Wis. League Nursing Edn. (pres.), Wis. Nurses Assn. (bd. dirs.). Died 1960.

**BECKER, GARY STANLEY,** economist, educator; b. Pottsville, Pa., Dec. 2, 1930; s. Louis William and Anna (Siskind) Becker; m. Doria Slote, Sept. 19, 1954 (dec.); children: Judith Sarah, Catherine Jean; m. Guity Nashat, Oct. 31, 1979; children: Michael Claffey, Cyrus Claffey. AB summa cum laude, Princeton U., NJ, 1951; MA, U. Chgo., 1953, PhD, 1955; PhD (hon.), Hebrew U., Jerusalem, 1985, U. Ill., Chgo., 1988, U. Palermo, Argentina, 1993, U. Economics, Prague, 1995, U. Miami, 1995, U. Athens, 2002; LLD (hon.), Knox Coll., 1985, Harvard U., 2003; DSc (hon.), SUNY, Stony Brook, 1990, Warsaw Sch. Economics, 1995, U. Rochester, 1995; LHD (hon.), Princeton U., 1991, Columbia U., 1993, Hofstra U., 1997. Asst. prof. U. Chgo., 1954—57, Ford Found. vis. prof. economics, 1969—70, Univ. prof. dept. economics, 1970—2014, chmn. dept. economics, 1984—85, prof. dept. sociology, prof. Booth Sch. Bus., 1983—2014; asst. prof. to assoc. prof. economics Columbia U., NYC, 1957—60, prof., 1960—68, Arthur Lehman prof. economics, 1968—70. Rsch. policy advisor Ctr., Econ. Analysis Human Behavior, Nat. Bur. Econ. Rsch., 1972—78; mem. domestic adv. bd. Hoover Instn., Stanford, Calif., 1973—91, sr. fellow, 1990—2014; rsch. assoc. Economics Rsch. Ctr., Chgo., 1980—2014; mem. academic advisory bd. American Enterprise Inst. Public Policy Rsch., 1987—91; bd. dirs. Unext-.com, 1999—2003. Author: The Economics of Discrimination, 1957, Human Capital, 1964, Human Capital and the Personal Distribution of Income: An Analytical Approach, 1967, Economic Theory, 1971, The Allocation of Time and Goods Over the Life Cycle, 1975, The Economic Approach to Human Behavior, 1976, A Treatise on the Family, 1981, Accounting for Tastes, 1996, The Economics of Life, 1996, Family, Society and State, 1996, Social Economics, 2000; co-author: Becker-Posner Blog, 2005; editor: Essays in Labor Economics in Honor of H. Gregg Lewis, 1976; co-editor: Essays in the Economics of Crime and Punishment, 1974; columnist: BusinessWeek, 1985—2004; contbr. articles to profl. jours. Recipient W.S. Woytinsky award, U. Mich., 1964, Profl. Achievement award, U. Chgo. Alumni Assn., 1968, Frank E. Seidman Disting. award in Polit. Economy, 1985, Merit award, NIH, 1986, Nobel Prize in Economics, Royal Swedish Acad. Sciences, 1992, Lord Found. award, 1995, Harold Lasswell award, Policy Studies Orgn., 1996, Irene Taueber award, Population Assn. America, 1997, Nat. Medal Sci., The White House, 2000, Phoenix award, U. Chgo., 2000, American Acad. Achievement award, 2001, Heartland prize, 2002, Hayek award, 2003, Italian Presidency medal, 2004, Arrow award, 2005, Provost's Tchg. award, U. Chgo., 2006, Presdl. Medal of Freedom, The White House, 2007; named to Hall of Honor, Nat. Inst. Child Health & Devel., 2003. Fellow: American Econ. Assn. (v.p. 1974, pres. 1987, Disting. fellow 1988, John Bates Clark medal 1967), American Acad. Arts & Sciences, Nat. Assn. Bus. Economists, American Statistics. Assn., Econometic Soc.; mem.: NAE, NAS, Econ. History Assn., Western Econ. Assn. (v.p. 1995—96, pres. 1996—97), Mont Pelerin Soc. (exec. bd. dirs. 1985—96, v.p. 1989—90, pres. 1990—92), Internat. Union for Sci. Study Population, American Philos. Soc., Phi Beta Kappa. Home: Chicago, Ill. Died May 3, 2014.

**BECKER, HOWARD H.,** advertising agency executive; b. NYC, May 15, 1927; s. Sam and Fannie (Green) B.; m. Harriet June, May 29, 1950; children: Susan, Mark. BBA, CCNY, 1950. Product mgr. B.T. Babbit, NYC, 1950-54; account exec. Grey Advt., NYC, 1954-57; account supr. Richard K. Manoff, NYC, 1957-58; v.p. mgmt. supr. Doyle Dane Bernbach, NYC, 1959-72, Conahay & Lyon, NYC, 1972-73; sr. v.p. mgmt. supr. SSC&B Lintas Worldwide US, NYC, 1973-84; v.p., mgmt. supr. Scali, McCabe & Sloves US, 1984, Hicks & Greist, NYC, 1985-86; pres. Becker & Assocs., Inc., from 1986. Served with U.S. Army, 1945-47. Home: New Rochelle, NY. *Since I am a reflection of my deeds, the image of which I am proudest is the good fortune, tempered by a small dose of wisdom, in marrying a good woman and raising a daughter and a son who have all reached the absolute heights of humanity and sensitivity.* Died Nov. 3, 1991.

**BECKWITH, DAN REXFORD,** insurance agent; b. Battle Creek, Mich., July 17, 1942; s. Carroll John and Alpha Ardele (Pilgrim) Beckwith; children: Anita Lynn, Diane Marie. BS in Occupl. Safety and Health, Ferris State Coll., 1976. Assoc. safety profl. Am. Bd. Cert. Safety Profls. Loss control rep. Liberty Mut. Ins., Indpls., 1976—77, Gen. Accident Ins. Co., Indpls., 1977—78, Portland, Oreg., 1978—81; special loss control rep. Aetna Ins. Co., Portland, from 1981. With US Army, 1959—65. Mem.: Am. Soc. Safety Engrs. Adventist. Home: Beaverton, Oreg. Died Dec. 13, 1998.

**BEHNKE, RICHARD FREDERICK,** investment banking executive; b. NYC, June 17, 1939; s. William Robert and Herta Adeleheid Hedwig (Reimers) B.; m. Gayle Pualani Kufferath, Aug. 28, 1971; 1 child, Christopher Arnold Keola. BA, Centre Coll. of Ky., 1961; MBA, U. Hawaii, 1969, profl. teaching cert., 1970; postgrad., Fed. Bur. Narcotics Tng. Sch., 1965. Criminal investigator, agt. U.S. Treasury Dept., NYC, 1963-68; pres., prin. Abel-Behnke Corp., Honolulu, from 1968; ptnr., appraiser Abel-Appraisers & Bus. Valuation, Inc., Honolulu, from 1990. Realtor assoc. Sand Dollar Realty, Honolulu, 1989-96. Patentee automated pub. transport system. Rsch. assoc. Ctr. for Psychosocial Rsch., Inc., Honolulu, 1991. With USN, 1962-64. Mem. Pacific and Asian Affairs Coun., Pacific Club, Hawaii Econ. Assn., Investment Soc. Hawaii, Honolulu Bd. Realtors. Avocations: hiking, jogging, charities, collecting. Died May 28, 2002.

**BEHRENDT, THOMAS RUDOLF,** lawyer; b. Halle, Fed. Republic Germany, July 14, 1951; s. Willy and Jutta (Kuska) B.; children: Halina, Carolyn. Diploma in econs., U. Munich, 1975, 1. jur. Staatsexamen, 1979; assessor jur, Bavarian Ministry Justice, Munich, 1981. Rsch. worker German Inst. for Econ. Rsch., Berlin, 1972-74, Ifo-Inst. for Econ. Rsch., Munich, 1974-75; acad. asst. U. Munich, 1976-82; pvt. practice lawyer Munich, from 1982. Mem. several bd. dirs. Contbr. articles to profl. jours. Advisor elected govt. of German Dem. Republic, 1990; advisor to Treuhand, 1990. Mem. German Econ. Soc., Peutinger Collegium, Am. Coun. on Germany, Order of St. John (Ehrenritter), Export Club. Lutheran. Avocations: books, art, golf. Home: Munich, Germany. Died June 9, 2001.

**BEIGHLEY, RUTH VIRGINIA,** college official; b. Mercer, Pa., June 18, 1934; d. Conrad Mahan and Helen Leola (Cratty) Beighley. BS, Bob Jones U., 1956; MS in Edn., Westminster Coll., 1961; EdD, Ariz. State U., 1977. Cert. tchr. Pa., Ariz. Tchr. 3d grade Slippery Rock Jointure, Portersville, Pa., 1956—57; tchr. HS Morgan County, Exel, Ky., 1957—58; tchr. Cranberry Twp., Evans City, Pa., 1958—60, Ray Sch. Dist., Kearney, Ariz., 1960—62, Yuma Dist. No. 1, Ariz., 1962—66; coord. elem. edn. Southwestern Coll., Phoenix, from 1966. Grad. asst. Ariz. State U., Phoenix, 1971—73; mem. accreditation team NATTS, Phoenix, 1983; mem. adj. faculty Ariz. Coll. of the Bible, 1986—87; mem. Assn. Supervision and Curriculum Devel., Assn. Tchr. Educators, Profl. Standards Cert. Adv. Com. Dept. Edn., Phoenix, from 1984. Mem.: Internat. Reading Assn. Republican. Baptist. Died 1995.

**BÉJART, MAURICE JEAN (MAURICE BERGER),** ballet artistic director, choreographer; b. Marseille, France, Jan. 1, 1927; s. Gaston Berger and Germaine Capellieres. Attending lycee, Marseille. Marseille Opera and Royal Opera, Stockholm, Ballet de l'Etoile, Paris, 1954—57, Ballet Theatre de Paris, 1957—59, Ballet du 20th Siecle, Brussels, 1959—87, Brussels Opera, Theatre Royal de la Monnaie, Bejart Ballet Lausanne, 1987—2007; prodr.: Symphonie pour un homme seul, 1955, Orphee, 1958, Le sacre du printemps, 1959, Bolero, 1960, Le voyage, 1962, Les noces, 1962, Tales of Hoffmann, 1962, The Merry Widow, 1963, IXe symphonie, 1964, La damanation de Faust, 1964, Romeo et Juliette, 1966, Messe pour le temps present, 1967, La tentation de St-Antoine, 1967, Baudelaire, 1968, Ni fleurs-ni couronnes, 1968, A la recherche de..., 1968, Jerait-Ce La Mort, 1970, Le Chans du Compagnon Errant, 1971, Nijinsky, Clown of God, 1971, Le marteau sans maitre, 1973, La Traviata, 1973, I Trionfi di Petrarca, 1974, Ce que l'amour me dit, 1974, Chants d'amour et de guerre, 1975, Notre Faust, 1975, Acqua Alta, 1975, Petrushka, 1977, Don Giovanni, 1980, The Magic Flute, 1981, Light, 1981, La Muette, 1981, Adagietto, 1981, History of a Soldier, 1982, Salome, 1983, Vie Et Mort Dune Marionnette Humaine, Messe pour le Temps Futur, 1983, Fragments, 1984, Dionysos, 1984, 5 Modern No Plays by Mishima, 1984, Le Concours, 1985, The Bat, 1985, Arepo, 1986, The Kabuki, 1986, Martyr of St. Sebastian, 1986, Malraux ou La Metamorphose Des Dieux, 1986, Trois Etudes pour Alexandre, Souvenir de Leningrad, Prelude A Midi D'un Faune, Fiche Signaletique, 1987, Patrice Chereau..., Dibouk, Et Valse, Piaf, Paris-Tokyo, A Force de partir, 1988; play, La Reine verte, 1963, La Reine Verte, 1963, L'Autre chant de la danse, 1974, Un Instant Dans la Vie D'autrui, 1979, Nijinsky Clown de Dieu, 1990, La mort subite, 1991, La Tour, 1991, ballets, Bugaku, 1988, 1989 Et Novs, 1989, Chaka, 1989, Eligie Pour Elle, L., Aile, 1989, Ring Um Den Ring, 1990, Pyramides, 1990, Mozart Tangos, 1990, La Mort Jubite, 1991, Tod In Wien, 1991, Maurice Bejart, 1991; author: (novels) Mathilde ou le temps perdu, 1963. Decorated Chevalier de l'Ordre des Arts et des Lettres, Grand Officer Order of the Crown Belgium; recipient Grand Prix de la Musique, 1970. Died Nov. 22, 2007.

**BEJLEGAARD, NIELS MARTIN,** retired metallurgy educator; b. Copenhagen, Feb. 23, 1939; arrived in Norway, 1982; s. Erik Bejlegaard and Gerda Solveig Mikaelsen Sund; m. Grete Lis Højegaard, Mar. 30, 1972. Student, Acad. Kursus, Copenhagen, 1959, U. Copenhagen, 1961; M in Physics, D.T.U. Copenhagen, 1977; cert. engr., U. Copenhagen. Engr. Dansk Industri Syndikat Aktieselskab, Copenhagen, 1977-79, Elektriska Svetsning Aktie Bolag, Copenhagen, 1979-80, Charles Hude Patents, Copenhagen, 1980-82; lectr. metallurgy Stavanger (Norway) Tech. Sch., 1982-2000, censor, 1984-2000; ret., 2000. Cons. Niels H. Abel Math. Competition, Stavanger, 1993—, Georg Mohr Math. Competition, Copenhagen, 1993—. Mem. London Math. Soc., Can. Math. Soc., Masons. Avocations: recreational mathematics, psychology, teaching. Home: Vanløse, Denmark. Died May 13, 2004.

**BELL, JOHN GORDON,** civil engineer; b. Leeds, Eng., Nov. 20, 1935; s. Arthur Reginald and Edith Isabel (Booth) B.; m. Evelyn Ann Rosevear, Apr. 4, 1964; children: Isabel Susan Nicola, Edith Helen. Textile engring. diploma, U. Leeds, 1953-57. Asst. to mng. dir. Wm Baines Sons Ltd., Leeds, 1957-64; contract mgr. Badger Sys. Ltd., Leeds, 1965-74; contract dir. Hobbs Badger Ltd., Bristol Avon, Eng., 1974-77; sr. project mgr. Tel. Cables Ltd., Maiduguri, Nigeria, 1978-81; contracts dir. Hamilton Green Ltd., Halesowen, 1982-85; chmn., mng. dir. Molemax Internat. Ltd., Harrogate, Eng., from 1986. Chmn., mng. dir. Euro-Cable Ploughs Ltd.; leading authority very high voltage cable installation underground by mole plow. Mem. Soc. for Trenchless Tech., Inst. Dirs. Conservative. Anglican. Avocations: piloting light aircraft, target and sport shooting, rugby union, boxing. Died June 2, 2004.

**BELL, MILDRED BAILEY,** law educator, lawyer; b. Sanford, Fla., June 28, 1928; d. William F. and Frances E. (Williford) Bailey; m. j. Thomas Bell, Jr., Sept. 18, 1948 (div.); children: Tom, Elizabeth, Ansley. AB, U. Ga., 1950, JD cum laude, 1969; LLM in Taxation, N.Y. U., 1977. Bar: Ga. 1969. Law clk. U.S. Dist. Ct. No. Dist. Ga., 1969-70; prof. law Mercer U., Macon, Ga., 1970-94, prof. emeritus, from 1994. Mem. Ga. Com. Constl. Revision, 1978-79. Bd. editors Ga. State Bar Jour., 1974-76; contbr. articles to profl. jours., chpts. in books. Mem. ABA, Ga. Bar Assn., Phi Beta Kappa, Phi Kappa Phi,. Republican. Episcopalian. Home: Fernandina, Fla. Died Jan. 30, 2002.

**BELL, ROBERT GORDON,** physician, scientist; b. St. Mary's, Ont., Can., Mar. 11, 1911; s. Robert and Elizabeth (Oliver) Bell; m. Mary Irene Ridgeway, June 18, 1938; children: Gordon Ronald, Janice Marie Bell Hambley, Mary Linda, Mary Elizabeth Bell Plouffe, Brian Joseph. Student, St. Mary's Inst.; MD, U. Toronto, Ont., Can. Pres. Glenmaple, Highland Creek, Ont., Canada, 1946—47, Shadow Brook Health Found., Willowdale, Ont., 1948—54, Willowdale Hosp., Ont., 1951—54, Bell Clinic, Willowdale, Ont., 1954—67, Donwood Inst., Willowdale, 1967—83, Bellwood Health Svcs., Inc., Willowdale, from 1983. With Royal Can.Army Med.Corps, 1942—46. Recipient Citation of Merit award, Malven Inst., Pa., 1958, Centennial medal, 1967, Queen's Silver Jubilee medal, 1977, Royal Bank award, 1985; named Officer Order of Can., 1979. Mem.: Ont. Med. Assn., Can. Med. Assn., Aesculapain Club, Civic Garden Club. Avocations: bridge, gardening, reading, travel. Deceased.

**BELLAMY, RUSSELL MILTON,** retired physician/surgeon; b. Toledo, Ohio, May 5, 1901; s. Charles Howard and Elizabeth (Morrissey) B.; m. Daisy Elizabeth Stumpf, June 15, 1926 (dec. 1967); children: Mary Elizabeth Norton, William Howard; m. Dorothy Evelyn Ethridge, Apr. 10, 1969. BS, U. Tex., 1921; MD, Baylor U., 1925. Intern Parkland Hosp., Dallas, 1926-28; sr. physician Pampa (Tex.) Clinic, 1928-83; ret., Cabot Corp., Pampa. Lt. col. USAF, 1942-46. Fellow Am. Acad. Family Physicians; mem. Tex. Med. Assn., AMA, Top O' Tex. Med. Soc., Rotary. Republican. Roman Catholic. Home: Pampa, Tex. Died 1993.

**BELLAMY, WALTER JONES,** retired professional basketball player; b. New Bern, NC, July 24, 1939; Student, Ind. U., 1957-61. Center Chgo. Packers, 1961-62, Balt. Bullets, 1963-66, NY Knicks, 1966-68, Atlanta Hawks, 1970-74; ceter New Orleans Jazz, 1974. Mem. U.S. Olympic Basketball Team, 1960. Mem. Atlanta Police Athletic League, Ga.; trustee Gate City Day Nursery Assn.; founder, 1st pres. Men of Tomorrow, Inc., Md.; bd. dirs. S.W. Youth Bus. Orgn.; membership chmn. Campbelltown/Cascade YMCA Men Internat. Club; chmn. Atlanta Labor Day Weekend Football Classic; vice chmn. College Park Bus. and Devel. Authority, Metro Atlanta Respite Svc.; bd. dirs. Gate City Day Nursery Assn., Fulton Atlanta Cmty. Action Authority. Named NBA Rookie of Yr., 1962; winner Gold medal U.S. Olympics, 1960; named to The NBA All-Star Team, 1962-65, The Naismith Meml. Basketball Hall of Fame, 1993, U.S. Olympic Hall of Fame, N.C. Sports Hall of Fame, 100% Wrong Club Atlanta Hall of Fame, Ind. U. Sports Hall of Fame Mem. NAACP (mem. exec. bd.), Ind. U. Alumni Club, Alpha Phi Alpha, Alpha Phi Omega. Achievements include mem. gold-medal-winning U.S. Olympic Team, 1960, holds single-season record for most games played-88, 1969. Died Nov. 2, 2013.

**BELLANDI, WILMA,** export packing executive; b. Wellington, Ill., Aug. 11, 1914; d. William Henry and Rella (Clinard) Boyden; m. Raymond C. Hackett, Apr. 30, 1938 (div. 1959); children: Raymond Cornell, William Boyden; m. Mario Bellandi, May 5, 1968 (dec. 1973). Student, Lewis Inst., 1934, U. Calif., Berkeley, 1954-55, John F. Kennedy U., 1975, Contra Costa Jr. Coll., 1986-87. Enrolled agt. U.S. Dept. Treasury, lic. real estate agt., Calif. Office mgr. Linen Supply Co., Oakland, Calif., 1948-50; acct. various CPA firms, Oakland, 1950-60; pvt. practice Oakland, 1960-65; real estate developer Calif., from 1965-; pres., owner Crow Industries Ltd., San Leandro, Calif., from 1983-. Pres. Oakland Real Estate Toastmistress, 1950, Bus. and Profl. Lake Merrit, Oakland, 1978; candidate for Calif. State Assembly, 1958, 60; past. pres. 7th dist. Dem. Cen. Com. Mem. Am. Soc. Accts., Navy League U.S. (pres. eb. council 1974-75), HNC Symphony Assn. (pres. 1987--), Sons of Italy, Berkeley Club (pres., fin. sec.), Oakland Lodge. Roman Catholic. Deceased.

**BELLEROCHE, DIESBACH,** genealogist, editor, bookseller; b. Paris, Apr. 10, 1956; m. Carole Rüfenacht de richigen. Diploma, Ctr. Internat. de Glion, 1984. Lectr. in field; mem. Twinning Commn. Fribourgh CH/Rueil-Malmaison F, 1990—; founder, editor Bull. de l'Institut Fribourgeois d'Heraldique et de Généalogie, 1989-93. Author: Notice généalogique sur la famille Liébert de Nitray, 1979, Descendance de Romain de Diesbach de 1716 a nos jours., Schweizer Lexikon, 1995, Les gardes-Suisses et leurs familles, 1989, La Généalogie, sous la direction de Joseph Valynseele, 1991, Les Müller, 1992, Histoire d'une ferme: Invaud, 1993; contbr. articles to profl. jours., newspapers, hist. revs.; editor web-site for genealogy: Site Généalogique du Canton de Fribourg. Mem. Commn. des preuves of Malteser Order in Switzerland, 1996—. Recipient bronze medal of order Pro Merito Melitensi, 1993, Knight of Sovereign Order of Malte, 1991. Mem. Soc. of Writers of Fribourg, Swiss Soc. Genealogy (v.p. 1989-91), Heraldic and Genealogy Inst., SAR, Union des Français de l'Etranger, 1985-95, Geneal. Soc. of Pas de Calais (founder, mem. and past sub-editor). Home: Bourguillon/Fribourg, Switzerland. Died 1999.

**BELTZNER, GAIL ANN,** music educator; b. Palmerton, Pa., July 20, 1950; d. Conon Nelson and Lorraine Ann (Carey) Beltzner. BS in Music Edn. summa cum laude, West Chester State U., 1972; postgrad., Kean State Coll., 1972, Temple U., 1972, Westminster Choir Coll., 1972, Lehigh U., 1978. Tchr. music Drexel Hill Jr. H.S., 1972-73; music specialist Allentown (Pa.) Sch. Dist., from 1973; tchr. Corps Sch. and Cmty. Devel. Lab., 1978-80, Corps Cmty. Resource Festival, 1979-81, Corps Cultural Fair, 1980, 81. Mem. bd. assocs. Lehigh Valley Hosp. and Health Network. Mem. Mus. Fine Arts, Boston, aux. Allentown Art Mus., aux. Allentown Hosp.; mem. woman's com. Allentown Symphony, The Lyric Soc. of the Allentown Orch.; mem. Allentown 2nd and 9th Civilian Police Acads.; bd. dirs. Allentown Area Ecumenical Food Bank, Allentown Arts Commn; mem. Growing with Sci. partnership—Air Products and Chems., Inc. and Allentown Sch. Dist., Good Shepherd Home Aux. Decorated Dame Comdr., Ordre Souverain et Militaire de la Milice du St. Sepulcre; recipient Cert. of Appreciation, Lehigh Valley Sertoma Club; Excellence in the Classroom grantee Rider-Pool Found., 1988, 91-92. Mem. AAUW, NAFE, ASCD, Am. String Tchrs. Assn., Am. Viola Soc., Internat. Reading Assn., Internat. Platform Assn., Allentown Edn. Assn., Music Educators Nat. Conf., Pa. Music Educators Assn., Am. Orff-Schulwerk Assn., Orgn. Am. Kodaly Educators, Am. Recorder Soc., Phila. Area Orff-Schulwerk Assn., Soc. Gen. Music, Am. Assn. Music Therapy, Internat. Soc. Music Edn., Internat. Tech. Edn. Assn., Assn. for Tech. in Music Instrn., Civil War Roundtable Ea. Pa., Choristers Guild, Lenni Lenape Hist. Soc., Lehigh Valley Arts Coun., Allentown Symphony Assn., Midi Users Group, Pa.-Del. String Tchrs. Assn., Nat. Sch. Orch. Assn., Lehigh County Hist. Soc., Confedn. Chivalry (life mem. of merit, grand coun.), Maison Internat. des Intellectuels Akademie, Order White Cross Internat. (apptd. dist. comdr. for Pa./U.S.A. dist., nobless of humanity), Airedale Terrier Club of Greater Phila., Kappa Delta Pi, Phi Delta Kappa, Alpha Lambda. Republican. Lutheran. Home: Allentown, Pa. Died Jan. 6, 2014.

**BELYTSCHKO, TED,** engineering educator; b. Proskurov, Ukraine, Jan. 13, 1943; arrived in US, 1950; s. Stephan and Maria B.; m. Gail (Eisenhart), Aug. 1967; children: Peter, Nicole, Justine. BS in Engring. Sci., Ill. Inst. Tech., 1965, PhD in Mechanics, 1968; PhD (hon.), U. Liege, 1997; Doctorate (hon.), Ecole Ctrl., Paris, 2004, U. Lyon, 2006. Asst. prof. structural mechanics U. Ill., Chgo., 1968—73, assoc. prof., 1973—76, prof., 1976—77; Walter P. Murphy prof. and McCormick Disting. prof. mech. engring. Northwestern U., Evanston, Ill., 1977—2014, chair mech. engring., 1998—2002. Editor (assoc.): (jour.) Computer Methods in Applied Mech. and Engring., 1977—2014, Jour. Applied Mechanics, 1979—85; editor: Nuc. Engring. and Design, 1980—88, Engring. with Computers, 1984—98, Internat. Jour. Numerical Methods in Engring., from 1998; hon. editor: Internat. Jour. Computational Methods, editor-in-chief:, from 2007. Chmn. U.S. Nat. Com. on Theoretical and Applied Mechanics, 2004—06. NDEA Fellow, 1965-68; recipient Thomas Jaeger prize Internat. Assn. Structural Mechanics in Reactor Tech., 1983; Japanese Soc. Mech. Engr. Computational Mechanics Award, 1993; Gold medal Internat. Conf. on Computational Engring. and Sci., 1996; Computational Mechanics Award, Internat. Assn. for Computational Mechanics, 1998; Gauss Newton medal, 2002, William Prager medal, 2011 Fellow: ASME (chmn. applied mechanics divsn. 1991, Pi Tau Sigma Gold medal 1975, Timoshenko medal 2001), American Acad. Arts & Sciences; mem.: NAS, ASCE (chmn. engring. mechanics divsn. 1982, Walter Huber Rsch. Prize 1977, Structural Dynamics and Materials Award 1990, Theodore von Karman medal 1999), NAE, American Acad. Mechanics (pres. 2004), Shock and Vibration Inst. (Baron medal 1999), U.S. Assn. Computational Mechanics (pres. 1992—94, von Neumann medal 2001, Computational Structural Mechanics Award 1997). Home: Winnetka, Ill. Died Sept. 15, 2014.

**BELZA, SVYATOSLAV,** literary and music critic; b. Chelyabinsk, Russia, Apr. 26, 1942; s. Igor Belza and Zoya Gulinskaya; divorced; 2 children. Student, Moscow State U. Rschr. Inst. World Lit. U.S.S.R. Acad. Sciences. Reviewer TV program Music on TV, man. and artistic dir.; active literary critic and TV broadcaster; author 300 literary works and reviews. Named Merited Worker of Art. Mem. Acad. Russian Art, Acad. Russian TV, Russian Union Writers. Home: Moscow, Russia. Died June 3, 2014.

**BENDER, BERND HARALD,** lawyer, educator; b. Freiburg, Germany, Apr. 6, 1919; s. Erich and Alice (Hartlaub) B.; m. Georgette Gavrilescu, Aug. 20, 1945 (div. 1973); 1 child, Michael; m. Astrid Heinze, Apr. 10, 1974 (div. 1989); 1 child, Ines; m. Jenny Gräfin von Keller, Oct. 10, 1989. JD, U. Freiburg, 1953; degree (hon.), U. Freiburg, Fed. Republic Germany. Pvt. practice, Fed. Republic Germany, 1952; prof. pub. law Freiburg U., 1970. Author: Allgemeines Verwaltungsrecht, 1952, 3d edit., 1961, Staatshaftungsrecht, 1971, 3d edit., 1981; co-author: Nachbarschutz, 1972, Umweltrecht, 1988, 4th edit., 2000. Decorated Disting. Svc. Cross 1st class (Fed. Republic Germany); recipient hon. medal Freiburg U., 1987. Mem. German Lawyers Assn. (Hans Dahs medal 1981), German Assembly Jurists (exec. bd. 1974-86), German Acad. Lawyers (chmn. adv. bd. 1981-87), Freiburg U. Sporting Club (pres. 1977-87). Home: Merzhausen, Germany. Died Oct. 5, 2002.

**BENEKE, MILDRED STONG (MILLIE BENEKE),** civic worker, city official, author; b. Prairie City, Iowa; d. Rueben Ira Beneke and Lillian (Garber) Stong Beneke; m. Arnold W. Beneke, Aug. 10, 1939; children: Bruce Arnold, Paula Rae, Bradford Kent, Cynthia Jane, Lisa Patrice. Student, Wash. U., 1942—43; off-campus student, U. Minn., Mankato State Coll., 1951—67. Exec. sec. chmn. vol. svcs. ARC, St. Paul, 1940—41; supervising vol. Minn. Correctional Inst. Women, Shakopee, from 1970, founder to bd. dirs. chmn. project interaction boutique, from 1971; v.p. Pi House, St. Paul, from 1972. Author: (plays) The Garage Sale, 1978, Politics Unusual, 1979, The Househusband and the Working Wife, 1982. Mem. Rep. Minn. Platform com., 1970, Rep. Feminist Caucus; bd. dirs. Mpls. Children's Theatre Co. Rep. chairwoman, McLeod County, 1969—73, Buffalo Creek Players, from 1975, v.p., 1980—82; alderman Glencoe City Coun., 1974—80. Named Millie Beneke Manor, Glencoe elderly housing, 1977. Mem.: Glencoe Bus. and Profl. Women (Woman of Yr. 1975), Dramatists Guild. Lutheran. Deceased.

**BENEKE, MILLIE STONG,** volunteer, writer; b. Prairie City, Iowa; d. Rueben Ira and Lillian (Garber) Stong; m. Arnold W. Beneke, Aug. 10, 1939; children: Bruce Arnold, Paula Rae, Bradford Kent, Cynthia Jane, Lisa Patrice. Student, Washington U., 1942-43, Mankato State Coll., 1951-67. Exec. sec. chmn. vol. svcs. ARC, St. Paul, 1940-41; v.p. Pi House, St. Paul, 1972-77; founder, bd. dirs., chmn. Project Interaction Boutique Minn. Correctional Instn. for Women, Shakopee, from 1971; supervising vol., from 1970. Republican chairwoman McLeod County (Minn.), 1969-73; mem. Rep. Minn. Platform com., 1970; McLeod County del. Rep. Minn. Central Com., 1969—; mem. Rep. Feminist Caucus; alderman Glencoe City Council, 1974-80. Author: (play) The Garage Sale, 1978, Politics Unusual, 1979, The Househusband and the Working Wife, 1982, also children's pays. V.p. Friends of Libr., 1975—; bd. dirs. Buffalo Creek Palyers, 1976—, v.p., 1980—; bd. dirs. Mpls. Children's Theatre Co., Housing for elderly named in her honor. Mem. Glencoe Bus. and Profl. Women (Woman of Yr. 1975), Dramatists Guild. Lutheran. Deceased.

**BENKARD, JAMES WILLARD BARTLETT,** lawyer; b. NYC, Apr. 10, 1937; s. Franklin Bartlett and Laura Derby (Dupee) B.; m. Margaret Walker Spofford, Dec. 12, 1964; children: Andrew Minturn, James Robinson, Margaret Mercer. AB, Harvard U., 1959; LLB, Columbia U., 1963. Bar: N.Y. 1963. Assoc. Davis Polk & Wardwell, NYC, 1963-73, ptnr., 1973—2005. Law clk. to Hon. Charles D. Breitel, Appellate Div. First Dept. & N.Y. Ct. Appeals, 1966—67. Trustee Vassar Coll., Poughkeepsie, N.Y., Teachers Coll., N.Y.C., Environ. Def. Fund, N.Y.C., St. Mark's Sch., Southborough, Mass, Columbia Law Sch. Alumni Assn., Scenic America Mem. American Coll. Trial Lawyers, Knickerbocker Club, River Club (N.Y.C.), Fishers Island Country Club. Home: New York, NY. Died Apr. 1, 2014.

**BENNETT, CHARLES ALFRED,** director, screenwriter; b. Shoreham, Eng., Aug. 2, 1899; came to U.S., 1937; Student pvt. schs., London. Actor, Eng. and France, 1911-26; ind. playwright Eng. and U.S., from 1927; ind. screenwriter, from 1929; ind. film dir. Hollywood, Calif., from 1948; ind. novelist Warner Books, from 1987. Author numerous plays, over 54 screenplays, 1928— including Blackmail (1st full-length European talking feature film), 39 Steps, Foreign Correspondent; dir. numerous films. Served with English Army, 1918-19, World War I. Decorated Mil. Medal for Gallantry; recipient Acad. award nomination Acad. Motion Picture Arts and Scis., 1940, Christopher award for They Will Not Die, 1955. Mem. Writers Guild Am., Screen Dirs. Guild. Clubs: Savage, Green Room (London). Avocations: horseback riding, golf. Died June 15, 1995.

**BENNETT, HARRY M.,** other: communications media, writer; b. LA, Nov. 28, 1905; s. Harry M. and Viola Ellsworth (Brown) B.; m. Lynne Waitz, May 1, 1975 (div. July 1982); 1 child: Brian. Grad., Stanford U. Vice pres. Comm. Counselors Inc.; chmn. bd. Beverage, Penney and Bennett; now prin., fin. pub. rels. cons. Harry Bennett Orgn., Newport Beach, Calif. Mem.: Pub. Rels. Soc. Am. (Silver Anvil award, 3 1st place Nat. awards), Soc. Profl. Journalists (Orange County chpt.), Dutch Treat West, Orange County Stanford Club, Sigma Delta Chi, Delta Chi. Republican. Presbyterian. Died May 23, 1988.

**BENNIS, WARREN GAMELIEL,** business administration educator; b. NYC, Mar. 8, 1925; s. Philip and Rachel (Landau) B.; m. Clurie Williams, Mar. 30, 1962 (div. 1983); children: Katharine, John Leslie, Will Martin; m. Mary Jane O'Donnell, Mar. 8, 1988 (div. 1991); m. Grace Gabe, Nov. 29, 1992. AB, Antioch Coll., 1951; D in Economics (hon.), London Sch. Econs., 1952; PhD, MIT, 1955; LLD (hon.), Xavier U., Cin., 1972, George Washington U., 1977; LHD (hon.), Hebrew Union Coll., 1974, Kans. State U., 1979; DSc (hon.), U. Louisville, 1977, Pacific Grad. Sch. Psychology, 1987, Gov.'s State U., 1991; LHD (hon.), Doan Coll., 1993; LLD (hon.), London Bus. Sch., 2004. Diplomate American Bd. Profl. Psychology. Asst. prof. psychology MIT, Cambridge, 1953-56, prof., 1959-67; asst. prof. psychology and bus. Boston U., 1956-59; prof. MIT Sloan Sch. Mgmt., 1959-67; provost SUNY-Buffalo, 1967-68, v.p. acad. devel., 1968-71; pres. U. Cin., 1971-77; U.S. prof. corps. and soc. Centre d'Etudes Industrielles, Geneva, 1978-79; exec.-in-residence Pepperdine U., 1978-79; George Miller Disting. prof.-in-residence U. Ill., Champaign-Urbana, 1978; Disting. prof. Bus. Adminstrn. U. Southern Calif. Sch. Bus., LA, 1980-88, univ. prof., disting. prof. bus. adminstrn., 1988—2014; chmn. advisory bd. Ctr. for Public Leadership Harvard U. John F. Kennedy Sch. Govt., 2010—14. Vis. lectr. Harvard U., 1958-59, Indian Mgmt. Inst., Calcutta; vis. prof. U. Lausanne (Switzerland), 1961-62, INSEAD, France, 1983; bd. dirs. The Foothill Group. Author: Planning of Change, 4th edit., 1985, Interpersonal Dynamics, 1963, 3d and 4th edits., 1975, Personal and Organizational Change, 1965, Changing Organizations, 1966, repub. in paperback as Beyond Bureaucracy, 1974, The Temporary Society, 1968, Organization Development, 1969, American Bureaucracy, 1970, Management of Change and Conflict, 1972, The Leaning Ivory Tower, 1973, The Unconscious Conspirary: Why Leaders Can't Lead, 1976, Essays in Interpersonal Dynamics, 1979, On Becoming a Leader, 1989, Why Leaders Can't Lead, 1989, Leaders on Leadership, 1992, An Invented Life: Reflections on Leadership and Change, 1993, Beyond Bureaucracy, 1993, Beyond Leadership, 1994, Herding Cats: Bennis on Leadership, 1996, Organizing Genius, 1997, The Temporary Society, 1998, Co-Leaders, 1999, Old Dogs, New Tricks, 1999, Managing the Dream, 2000; co-author (with B. Nanus): Leaders: Strategies for Taking Charge, 1985; co-author: (with I. Mitroff) The Unreality Industry, 1989; co-author: (with M. Mische) Reinventing the 21st Century, 1994; co-author: (with J. Goldsmith) Learning to Lead, 1994; co-author: (with G. Heil and D. Stephens) Douglas McGregor Re-Visited, 2000; co-author: Geeks & Geezers, 2002, On Becoming a Leader, 2003; co-author: (with Bob Townsend) Re-inventing Leadership: Strategies to Empower the Organization, 2005; co-author: (with Patricia Ward Biederman) Still Surprised: A Memoir of a Life in Leadership, 2010; cons. editor: Calif. Mgmt. Rev., Mgmt. Series Jossey-Bass Pubs. Mem. President' White House Task Force on Sci. Policy, 1960-70; mem. FAA study task force US Dept. Transp., 1975; mem. advisory com. N.Y. State Joint Legis. Com. Higher Edn., 1970-71; mem. Ohio Gov.'s Bus. and Employment Coun., 1972-74; mem. panel on alt. approaches to grad. edn. Coun. Grad. Schs. and Grad. Record-Exam Bd., 1971-73; chmn. Nat. Advisory Commn. on Higher Edn. for Police Officers, 1976-78; adv. bd. NIH, 1978-84; trustee Colo. Rocky Mountains Sch., 1978-82; bd. dirs. American Leadership Forum, 1984-89; mem. vis. com. for Humanities MIT, 1975-81; trustee Antioch Coll., Salk Inst.; chmn. adv. bd. Harvard U. Ctr. for Pub. Leadership. Capt. AUS, World War II. Decorated Bronze Star, Purple Heart; recipient Dow Jones award, 1987, McKinsey Fedn. award, 1967, 68. Mem. American Acad. Arts & Sciences (co-chmn. policy coun. 1969-71), American Mgmt. Assn. (dir. 1974-77), US Chamber of Commerce (adv. group scholars). Home: Santa Monica, Calif. Died July 31, 2014.

**BENSON, DAVID WILLIAM,** retired academic administrator; b. N. Branch, Minn., Oct. 13, 1931; s. Fredolf Ernest and Ruth (Rystrom) B.; m. Betty Juan Broders, Feb. 29, 1952; 1 child, Mary. BS, UCLA, 1954, MS, 1958; PhD, U. So. Calif., 1966. Instr. UCLA, 1958-61; asst. prof. to prof. phys. edn. Calif. State U. Northridge, 1961-67, dean acad. planning, dean acad. adminstrn., 1967-74, v.p., 1974-84; pres. Sonoma State U., Rohnert Park, Calif., 1984-92, ret., 1992. Served in USN, 1954-56. Named Disting. Tchr., San Fernando Valley State Coll., 1966. Home: Santa Rosa, Calif. Died Oct. 1, 2013.

**BERDAHL, CLARENCE ARTHUR,** educator; b. Baltic, SD, June 14, 1890; s. Anders J. and Karen (Otterness) Berdahl; m. Evelyn Tripp Berdahl, June 9, 1926. Clk. archives div. War Dept., Washington, 1914—2015; asst. periodicals div. Libr. Congress, 1916; instr. polit. sci. U. Ill., 1920—2022, asso., 1922—2025, asst. prof., 1925—2029, assoc. prof, 1929—30, prof., 1930—61, prof. emeritus dept. polit sci., 1961, chmn. div. social scis., 1935—39, chmn. dept. polit. sci., 1942—48; tchr. U. Tex., 1920, Tulane U., 1921, Ohio State U., 1923, U. Colo., 1928, Syracuse U., 1929, Columbia U., 1934, Stanford U., 1950; acting mng. editor Am. Polit. Sci. Rev., 1923; lectr. L'Institut U. Hautes Etudes Internats., Geneva, 1932; vis. prof. govt. Southern Ill. U, 1958—67; vis. prof. polit. sci. U. Del., 1965; chmn. bd. editors Ill. Studies Social Scis., 1941—52; cons. U.S. Dept. State, 1942—45; with London staff Office Strategic Svcs., 1944; mem. Internat. Secretariat, UN Conf., San Francisco, 1945; adv. com. fgn. rels. Dept. State, 1957—64, chmn., 1963—64, cons. hist. office, 1961; mem. exec. com. Commn. To Study Orgn. Peace, from 1953; mem. European Conf. Tchrs. Internat. Law and Rels., Carnegie Endowment Internat. Peace, 1926. Author (co-author): War Powers of the Executive in the United States, 1921; author: The Policy of the United States with Respect to the League of Nations, 1932, Aspects of American Government, 1950, Toward a More Responsible Two-Party System, 1950, Presidential Nominating Politics, 1952; contbr. articles to ptofl. jours. With inf. US Army, 1918. Rsch. grant, 1931—32. Mem.: Internat. Studies Assn. (adv. com. 1965—69), Conf. Tchrs. Internat. Law and Related Subjects (exec. com. 1933—42, 1947—50), Geneva Rsch. Ctr., Soc. Advancement Scandinavian Study, Fgn. Policy Assn., Am. Soc. Internat. Law (exec. coun. 1939—46, 1952—54), Midwest Polit. Sci. Assn. (pres. 1957—58), Ill. Hist. Soc., Am. Soc. Pub. Adminstrn. (coun. mem. 1944—47), Norwegian-Am. Hist. Assn., Am. Polit. Sci. Assn. (exec. coun. 1932—35, 3d v.p. 1939, 2d v.p. 1944), Cosmos (Washington), Univ., Phi Beta Kappa (Ralph Waldo Emerson award 1966—68). Home: Urbana, Ill. Deceased.

**BERG, JOSTEIN SIGURD,** retired engineering educator; b. Trondheim, Norway, May 2, 1932; s. Anders H. and Anna Bergljot (Slungaard) B.; m. Torhild Felde, Sept. 1, 1973; children: Anna S., Halldor F. Degree in Tech. Engring., Gothenburg Coll.Engring., Sweden, 1956; BSCE, S.D. State U., 1964. Registered profl. engr., Wash., Alaska. Field engr. Skanska cement A/B, Sweden, 1956-60; estimator Winston Bros., Mpls. and Pierre, S.D., 1960-62; designer Howard Needles Tammen & Bergendorf, Seattle, 1964-66; sr. engr. Sverdrup & Parcel & Assocs., Inc., Bellevue, Wash., 1967-70; asst. chief engr. Oslo City Engring. Dept., 1970-76; civil engr. I Divsn. of Aviation, State of Alaska Dept. Transp., Anchorage, 1976-83; asst. prof. Norwegian Inst. Tech., Trondheim, 1983-97; ret., 1999; asst. prof. U. Alaska, Anchorage, 1991-92, lectr. civil engring. Fairbanks, 1998; ret., 2001. Rschr. Sintef Hwy. Engring., Trondheim, 1983-91; mem. econ. concrete rd. rsch. project The Norwegian Pub. Rds. Dept., 1984-90; air route coord. Northern Forum,

Norway, 1990-96; bd. dirs. Nordic Rd. Assocs./Norwegian Sect., 1984-89. Mem. ASCE (life), Norwegian Soc. Profl. Engrs., Norwegian Rd. and Traffic Disciplinary Assn. (bd. dirs. 1993—), Sons of Norway (lodge pres. Anchorage 1979-82, Trondheim 1986-88, dist. 8 pres. 1988-90, lodge v.p. Trondheim 1999-2006). Lutheran. Avocations: skiing, jogging, orienteering. Home: Stjordal, Norway. Died June 3, 2006.

**BERGAN, TOM,** medical educator; b. Oslo, Oct. 27, 1939; m. Bodil Bergan, July 15, 1967; children: Siri, Tanja, Marit. MS, U. Rochester, 1965; MD, U. Oslo, 1966, PhD, 1972; DMS (hon.), U. Stockholm, 1993. Prof. Inst. Pharmacy U. Oslo, 1975-93; visiting prof. U. Singapore, 1985-87; prof. Inst. Med. Microbiology U. Oslo, from 1993; head dept. med. microbiology Aker Sykehus, Oslo, 1975-96. Mem. subcom. on Taxonomy of Pseudomonas and Related Organisms, 1978-97, chmn. subcom., 1986-94. Author: (textbooks) Hospital Hygiene and Vaccination, 1977, Microbiology, 1978, 88; editor Methods in Microbiology, 1974-83, Internat. Jour. Antimicrobiology Agents, Antibiotic Chemotherapy; contbr. over 500 books and sci. articles. Mem. Internat. Soc. Chemotherapy (mem. exec. com. 1985—, sec.-gen. 1989-97, pres. 1997—), European Soc. Clin. Microbiology and Infectious Diseases (mem. exec. com. 1981-92, pres. congress 1989-91, coun. 1994—), Scandinavian Soc. Antimicrobiol. Chemotherapy (sec.-gen. 1979-89), Norwegian Soc. Med. Microbiology (pres. 1991-93, exec. com. 1991-99), Internat. Soc. Infectious Diseases (councillor 1983-96), numerous Editorial Bds. for Sci. jours. Died July 19, 2001.

**BERGEN, KENNETH WILLIAM,** lawyer; b. Harlingen, NJ, Sept. 13, 1911; s. Edward Burgess and Adelia (Mertz) B.; m. Emily Fetter; children: Bruce, Carol Franklin, Nancy Flint, Roger. AB, Rutgers U., 1934; LLB, Harvard U., 1937; DHL (hon.), Colby Coll., 1983. Bar: N.Y. 1938, Mass. 1943. Atty. Tax Ct. U.S., 1942-43; ptnr. Bingham Dana LLP, Boston, 1954-83; assoc. White & Case, NYC, 1937-42; of counsel Bingham Dana LLP, Boston, from 1983; pres. Pres. Mass. Continuing Legal Edn.-New England Law Inst., Inc., 1974-77, trustee, 1969-78, pres. 1976-77; co-chmn. Conf. Reps. of ABA and trust div. Am. Bankers Assn., 1974-78; mem. adv. com. U.S. Ho. of Reps. Ways and Means Com. on Adminstrn. Fed. Tax Laws, 1956, income taxation estates and trusts, 1958; bd. dirs., co-founder, exec. dir. Tax Inst. New England, 1948—, pres., 1994—; mem. adv. com. Tax Lawyer, 1975—; mem. planning com., co-founder Colby Coll. Estate Planning and Tax Inst., 1953—; mem. Mass. Bd. Registration C.P.A.'s, 1956-60; dir., lectr. grad. tax program Northeastern U. Sch. Law, 1946-52; adv. com., lectr. Boston U. Law Sch. Grad. Tax Program; mem. adv. group Commr. of IRS, 1987. Moderator Town of Lincoln, Mass., 1966-78, 94-95; mem. Lincoln-Sudbury Regional H.S. Com., 1956-62, Lincoln Rep. Town Com., 1950-87, chmn., 1954-62; chmn. Rural Land Found. of Lincoln, 1966-92. Mem. ABA (tax sect., past sec., mem. coun.), Am. Coll. Trust and Estate Counsel (past regent), Am. Coll. Tax Counsel, Am. Law Inst., Am. Bar Found., Boston Bar Assn. (past mem. coun., chmn. sect. profl. responsibility, chmn. com. on legislation, co-chmn. peer support com.), Internat. Acad. Estate and Trust Law (exec. coun.), Mass. Soc. CPAs (hon.). Died May 11, 1999.

**BERGEN, POLLY,** actress; b. Knoxville, Tenn., July 14, 1930; d. William and Lucy (Lawhorn) Burgin; m. Freddie Fields, Feb. 13, 1956 (div. 1976); children: Kathy, Pamela, Peter. Pres. Polly Bergen Cosmetics, Polly Bergen Jewelry, Polly Bergen Shoes. Author: Fashion and Charm, 1960, Polly's Principles, 1974, I'd Love To, But What'll I Wear, 1977; author, producer for TV: Leave of Absence, 1994; Broadway plays include Champagne Complex, John Murray Andersons' Almanac, First Impression, Plaza Suite, Love Letters, Follies, The Vagina Monologues, Cabaret; (films) Cape Fear, Move Over Darling, Kisses for My President, At War with the Army, 1950, The Stooge, That's My Boy, The Caretakers, A Guide for the Married Man, Making Mr. Right, Cry-Baby, 1990, Dr. Jekyll and Ms. Hyde, When We Were Colored, 1994; performed in one woman shows in Las Vegas, Nev., and Reno; albums: Bergen Sings Morgan, The Party's Over, All Alone By the Telephone, Polly and Her Pop, The Four Seasons of Love, Annie Get Your Gun and Do Re Mi, My Heart Sings, Act One Sing Too; numerous TV appearances including star of The Polly Bergen Show; (TV appearances) The Helen Morgan Story, 1957 (Emmy award as best actress), To Tell the Truth, The Lightning Field, The Surrogate, For Hope; miniseries include The Winds of War, 79 Park Ave, War and Remembrance, 1988; writer, prodr. (TV movies) Leave of Absence, 1994. Bd. dirs. Martha Graham Dance Ctr., The Singer Co., Soc. Singers, Calif. Abortion and Reproductive Rights Action League, Show Coalition; hon. canister campaign chairperson Cancer Care, Inc., Nat. Cancer Found.; founder Nat. Bus. Coun. for ERA; mem. Planned Parenthood Fedn., American Bd. Advisors; mem. nat. advisory com. NARAL, Hollywood Women's Polit. Com. Recipient Fame award Top Ten in TV, 1957-58, Troupers award Sterling Publs., 1957, Editors and Critics award Radio & TV Daily, 1958, Outstanding Working Woman award Downtown St. Louis, Inc., Golden Plate award American Acad. Achievement, 1969, Outstanding Mother's award Nat. Mothers' Day Com., 1984, Best Achievement in New Jewelry Design award, 1986, Cancer Care award, 1989, Woman of Achievement award LWV, 1990, Extraordinary Achievement award Nat. Women's Law Ctr., 1991, Freedom of Choice award Calif. Abortion and Reproductive Rights Action League, 1992; Polly Bergen Cardio-Pulmonary Rsch. Lab., Children's Rsch. Inst. & Hosp., Denver dedicated, 1970. Mem. AFTRA, AGVA, SAG, Actors Equity. Died Sept. 20, 2014.

**BERGER, MAURICE See BÉJART, MAURICE**

**BERGER, THOMAS LOUIS,** author; b. Cin., July 20, 1924; s. Thomas Charles and Mildred (Bubbe) Berger; m. Jeanne Redpath, June 12, 1950. BA with honors, U. Cin., 1948; postgrad., Columbia U., 1950—51; LittD (hon.), L.I.U., 1986. Librarian Rand Sch. Social Sci., NYC, 1948—51; staff mem. N.Y. Times Index, 1951—52; assoc. editor Popular Sci. Monthly, 1952—53. Disting. vis. prof. Southampton Coll., 1975—76; vis. lectr. Yale U., 1981, 1982; Regent's lectr. U. Calif., Davis, 1982. Author: Crazy in Berlin, 1958, Reinhart in Love, 1962, Little Big Man, 1964, Killing Time, 1967, Vital Parts, 1970, Regiment of Women, 1973, Sneaky People, 1975, Who Is Teddy Villanova?, 1977, Arthur Rex: A Legendary Novel, 1978, Neighbors, 1980, Reinhart's Women, 1981, The Feud, 1983 (Pulitzer Prize nomination, 1984), Nowhere, 1985, Being Invisible, 1987, The Houseguest, 1988, Changing the Past, 1989, Orrie's Story, 1990, Meeting Evil, 1992, Robert Crews, 1994, Suspects, 1996, The Return of Little Big Man, 1999, Best Friends, 2003, Adventures of the Artificial Woman, 2004, (plays) Other People, 1970. With US Army, 1943—46, ETO. Recipient Rosenthal award, Nat. Inst. Arts and Letters, 1965, Western Heritage award, 1965, Ohioana Book award, 1982; Dial fellow, 1962. Home: Palisades, NY. *In my work I try to compete with that reality to which I must submit in life.* Died July 13, 2014.

**BERGIER, JEAN-FRANÇOIS,** history educator; b. Lausanne, Switzerland, Dec. 5, 1931; s. Charles and Anne Marie (Reymond) B.; m. Francesca Bergier, Jan. 9, 1974; children: Philippe, Patrick. Licence Histoire, U. Lausanne, 1954; Diplome, Ecole des Chartes, Paris, 1957; PhD, U. Geneva, 1963. Prof. Faculty Economics, Geneva, 1963-69; prof. history Swiss Inst. Tech., Zurich, 1969—99; assoc prof. history U. Paris, 1976-78. Contbr. articles to profl. jours.; author numerous books. Mem. Internat. Econ. History Assn. (gen. sec. 1965-74, hon. pres. 1986-2009), Hist. Soc. Hungary (hon.), Internat. Alpine Hist. Soc. (former pres.), Rencontres Suisses (bd. dirs., pres. 1987-96, pres. ind. commn. of experts: Switzerland Second World War, 1996-2001). Home: Zug, Switzerland. Died Oct. 29, 2009.

**BERGONZI, CARLO,** tenor, voice educator; b. Vidalenzo, Italy, July 13, 1924; m. Adele Aimi, 1950; children: Maurizio, Marco Studied at, Arrigo Boito Conservatory, Parma, Italy. Operator hotel-restaurant, Busseto, Italy.; founder, tchr. Accademia Verdiana Carlo Bergonzi, Bussetto, Italy, from 1980. Debut in opera as baritone in The Barber of Seville, as Figaro, Lecce, Italy, 1948; debut as tenor in title role of Andrea Chenier, Teatro Petruzzelli, Bari, Italy, 1951; American debut Lyric Opera, Chgo., 1955; Met. Opera debut as Radames in Aida, 1956; appeared in maj. opera cos. throughout Europe, North and South America, including La Scala, Vienna State Opera, Hamburg (Germany) Opera, Rome Opera, Phila. Grand Opera, Teatro Colon. Died July 25, 2014.

**BERKAU, GUNTHER WALTER ARTHUR,** publishing executive; b. Danzig, Germany, Sept. 22, 1924; s. Gustav Arthur and Ida Olga (Matull) B.; m. Ursula Hanna Elisabeth Salzgeber, Mar. 26, 1953; 1 child, Barbara. Student, U. Munich, U. Heidelberg, Fed. Republic Germany. Various mgmt. positions in pub., from 1965; pub., founder Aurum Verlag, Edition Ambra, Freiburg, Fed. Republic Germany, from 1974. Ind. mgmt. cons., Federal Republic of Germany, 1963-65. Lt. German Army, 1942-45. Mem. Internat. Press Club Munich Börsenerein Deutschen Buchhandels Frankfurt, Landesverband Verleger Baden, Sci Soc. for Parapsychology. Avocation: collecting old prints and books. Died July 1, 1993.

**BERLIN, EDWARD A.,** security consultant; b. Kinney, Minn., July 13, 1923; s. Franz and Ludmilla (Peterlin) Berlin; m. Lucille Katherine Clark, Dec. 26, 1945. BS, U. Minn., 1946; MA, Jackson Coll., 1953, PhD, 1955. Analyst FBI, Wash., 1942—43; rsch. analyst Naval Intelligence, Pacific Basin, 1950—77; security cons. U.S. Navy, Pearl Harbor, Hawaii, from 1957. Chmn. bd. dirs. Oceanside Properties Ltd., Honolulu, Oceanside Devel. Corp., Inc., Leisure Facilities Mich., Inc. Chmn. State Hawaii Bd. Regulatory Agys.; bd. security Pvt. Detectives and Guard Svcs., Honolulu, from 1977; ct. apptd. dir. Oceanside Properties, Fed. Bankruptcy Laws Chpt. 11; bd. dirs. Rotary Youth Found. Lt. col. US Army, 1942—46, PTO. Fellow Paul Harris Found. Mem.: Rotary Club (dist. gov. 1986—87), VFW. Republican. Roman Catholic. Home: Honolulu, Hawaii. Died Sept. 26, 1998.

**BERLINCOURT, MARJORIE ALKINS,** government official, retired; b. Toronto, Ont., Can., June 2, 1928; came to U.S., 1950, naturalized, 1956; d. Herbert John and Ellen Florence (Barker) Alkins; m. Ted Gibbs Berlincourt, Feb. 28, 1953; 1 child, Leslie Berlincourt Yale. BA, U. Toronto, 1950; MA, Yale U., 1951, PhD, 1954. Editl. dir. tech. publs. Rocketdyne, 1956-59; lectr. classics U. So. Calif., 1959-61; assoc. prof. classical history Calif. Luth. Coll., 1961-67, Calif. State U., Northridge, 1967-71; prof. Met. State Coll., Denver, 1971-72; program dir. div. fellowships for summer sems., fellowships NEH, Washington, 1972-78, dir. state programs, 1983—91, dir. divsn. fellowships, seminars, 1991-94; ret., 1995. Vis. lectr. Georgetown U., 1972 Author: De Surprise en Surprise, 1953, Entrez Petits Amis, 1954, Victory as a Coin Type, 1973; contbr. articles to profl. jours. Sterling fellow Yale U., 1950-53; recipient Calif. Faculty Rsch. award, 1970. Mem. Am. Assn. Ancient Historians. Episcopalian. Deceased.

**BERMAN, DAVID ALBERT,** pharmacologist, educator; b. Rochester, NY, Nov. 4, 1917; s. Sam Moses and Anna (Newman) B.; m. Miriam Goodman, July 13, 1945; children: Shelley, Judith. BS, U. So. Calif., 1940, MS, 1948, PhD, 1951. Instr. U. So. Calif. Med. Sch., LA, 1952-54, asst. prof., 1954-58, assoc. prof., 1958-63, prof., 1963—93, Disting. emeritus prof., 1993. Contbr. articles to profl. jours. Mem. Calif. Rsch. Adv. Panel, San Francisco, 1970-82. Recipient Elaine Stevely Hoffman Achievement award, 1971, Merit award Am. Heart Assn., 1979, Faculty Achievement award Burlington No. Found., 1988, Tchg. award Kaiser Permanente, 1993, Kaiser Permanente Tchg. award, 1971, 75, 77, 79, 81, 83, 85, 87, 89, 90-93, 96-99, 03. Mem. Am. Soc. Pharmacology and Exptl. Therapeutics, Sigma XI, Phi Kappa Phi. Home: Sherman Oaks, Calif. Died Mar. 8, 2014.

**BERMAN, HERBERT E.,** former city councilman; b. Bklyn., Oct. 8, 1933; s. Sam and Sarah Berman; m. Frances Springer, 1960; children: Shari, Russell. BA, L.I. U.; LLD cum laude, NYU, 1959, JD, 1968. City councilman Dist. 46 NYC, 1975—91, 1992—2001, chmn. edn. com., 1983—89; pres. Roosevelt Island Operating Corp., 2003—07. Spl. counsel Georgetown Civic Assn.; bd. dirs. Muscular Dystrophy Soc. Recipient Merit award Jewish War Vets. Mem. Bklyn. and Kings County Criminal Bar Assns., Futurama Civic Assn. (past pres.), Georgetown Civic Assn., Thomas Jefferson Club, Jewish War Vet., Internat. League for Repatriation Soviet Jewry (dir.). Democrat. Jewish. Died July 6, 2014.

**BERNHARD, PRINCE (LEOPOLD FREDERIK EVERHARD JULIUS COERT KAREL GODFRIED PIETER),** Prince of the Netherlands, Prince of Lippe-Biesterfeld; b. Jena, Germany, June 29, 1911; assumed Netherlands nationality, 1936; s. Prince Bernhard zur Lippe and Baroness Armgard von Sierstorpff-Cramm; m. Juliana Louise Emma Marie Wilhelmina (dec. 2004), Princess of The Netherlands, Jan. 7, 1937; children: Beatrix Wilhelmina Armgard, Irene Emma Elizabeth, Margriet Francisca, Maria Christina. Referendar juris, U. Berlin; LLD, State U. Utrecht, 1946, U. Montreal, 1958, U. B.C., 1958, U. Mich., 1965; D.Econs, Free U. Amsterdam, 1965; D.Tech. Scis., U. Advanced Tech., Delft, 1951; D. Natural Sci., U. Basel, 1971. Appted. air cdre. (hon.) R.A.F.V.R., 1941; chief Netherlands liaison British Forces; col.; major gen., chief Netherlands Mission War Office; appted. supreme commdr. lt. gen. Netherlands Armed Forces, 1944; resigned, 1945; Royal commr. bd. Netherlands Trade and Industry Fair; hon. air marshal RAF, 1964—2004; inspector gen. Armed Forces; admiral gen. Royal Netherlands Air Force; gen. Army, 1954-76; hon. cdre. R.N.Z.A.F., 1973. Ret. gen. Netherlands Army and Air Force; ret. adm. Netherlands Navy; founder, regent Prince Bernhard Fund, Praemium Erasmianum Found.; founder European Cultural Found.; founder, pres. World Wide Fund Internat.; councillor Netherlands Inst. Econs., Netherlands U. Econs., Rotterdam; hon. functions number over 200; mem. Coun. for Mil. Affairs of the Realm, Joint Def., Army, Admiralty and Air Force Couns. Mem. bd. Netherlands Trade and Industries Fair; pres., WWF, Netherlands, Rhino Rescue Trust; chair achievement bd. ICBP. Decorated knight grand cross Order of Bath, Royal Victorian Order, Order Brit. Empire; hon. commodore Royal N.Z. Air Force, 1973. Mem. Royal Aeros. Soc. (hon.), Royal Inst. Naval Architects, Aeromed. Soc., Royal Spanish Acad. Died Dec. 1, 2004.

**BERNS, DONALD SHELDON,** public health service officer; b. NYC, June 27, 1934; s. Benjamin and May (Shapiro) B.; m. Sylvia Schleicher, Feb. 5, 1956; children: Brian Keith, Neil Gary, Amy Sue. BS in Chemistry, Wilkes Coll., 1955; PhD in Phys. Chemistry, U. Pa., 1959. Postdoctoral fellow Yale U., New Haven, Conn., 1959-61; resident rsch. assoc. Argonne (Ill.) Nat. Lab., 1961-62; sr. rsch. scientist Wadsworth Ctr. N.Y. State Dept. Health, Albany, 1962-66, dir. biophysics, 1967-82; dir. clin. scis. div. N.Y. State Dept. Health, Albany, 1983-89; dir. med. rsch. orgn. Ministry of Health, Jerusalem, 1989-99; ret., 1999. Adj. prof. chemistry Rensselaer Poly. Inst., Troy, N.Y., 1971-89; prof. Sch. Pub. Health SUNY, Albany, 1984-99, Hebrew U. Hadassah Med. Sch., Jerusalem, 1989-99. Author: Directory of Medical Research in Isarel, 1st edit. 1996, 2d edit. 1998. Mem. Am. Soc. Biochemistry and Molecular Biology, Am. Chem. Soc., AAAS. Jewish. Achievements include patents in field of spectrophotometric assay determination of lipid content of biological fluids; elucidated aggregation states of biliprotein phycocyanin; supervised lab. work of extensive HIV-Sero prevalence study published in Am. Jour. Pub. Health. Home: Jerusalem, Israel. Died Mar. 11, 2008.

**BERNSTEIN, THERESA,** artist; b. Phila. d. Isidore and Anne (Ferber) B.; m. William Meyerowitz, 1919. Student, Pa. Acad., Phila. Sch. Design, Art Students League; PhD (hon.), Moore Coll. Art, 1991. Dir. Salons of Am. Ind. Artists, 1924-30; life mem. Grand Central Art Galleries, N.Y. Author: William Meyerowitz, The Artist Speaks, 1986, The Poetic Canvas, 1988, The Journal, 1991, The Israeli Journal, 1994; contbr. articles to mags., newspapers.; one-woman shows Butler Inst. Am. Art, 1973, Smith Gerard Gallery, Stamford, Conn., 1976, Summit Gallery, N.Y.C., 1979, Smithsonian Inst., Fitchburg Art Mus., Doll & Richards, Inc., Boston Publick House, Sturbridge, Mass., U. Maine, Orono, Columbus Mus., Mus. Women of Art, Washington, 1989, Mus. City of N.Y., 1990, 91; represented in permanent collections U.S. Nat. Mus., Washington, Library of Congress, Phillips Meml. Art Gallery, Chgo. Art Inst., Met. Mus. Art, N.Y. Pub. Library, Bklyn. Mus., others; also pvt. collections; represented Art U.S.A. by painting Jazz Players; exhbns. include: Carnegie Inst., NAD, Cooper Union Mus., Butler Inst. Am. Art, Boston Pub. Library, N.Y. Hist. Soc. Phila. Mus. Art, Yose Gallery, Boston, N.Y. Hist. Soc., 1983-84, Paterson Pub. Library, 1984, Grand Central Galleries, N.Y.C., 1985-86, Cape Ann Hist. Assn., Gloucester, Mass., 1986; represented in permanent collection New England Ladies, Cape Ann Hist. Assn., N.Y. Hist. Soc., N.Y. Pub. Library; dir. summer art show, Gloucester, Mass., Weston U.; chmn. Meml. Exhibit Cape Ann Festival,

1958—. Recipient Phillips prize for Progressive Painting, 1946; Green traveling fellow; John Sartain scholar; Phila. Bd. Edn. scholar; Robert Dain prize, 1964; hon. mention Soc. Am. Graphic Artists, 1954, Knickerbocker Artists, 1956, Ogunquit Art Center; Carl Matson portrait award Rockport Art Assn., 1967; figure prize for Friends, 1981; New Eng. Artists award, N. Shore Arts Assn; John A. Johnson award, 1972; Johnson Meml. prize, 1975; Clark Meml. prize, 1977; Cantorella prize Nat. Assn. Women Artists, Nat. Acad., N.Y., 1968; Watson Meml. prize 1979; World Culture prize Italian Acad. Art, 1984; North Shore (Mass.) Artist of Yr. award, 1984; Medal of Honor, Rockport Art Assn., 1986; Oscar of Art, Italian Acad. Art, 1986; Mary Mintz Koffler award Audobon Artists Annual, 1988; Medal for Artistic Achievement, Rockport Art Assn., 1986. Mem. Nat. Assn. Women Artists (jury of awards 1948-50, jury oil painting 1959, Margaret Cooper prize for oil portrait Sarah 1951, Jane Peterson prize 1955, nominating com. 1963-64, Klein Figurative award 1977), Boston Printmakers Assn., Cape Ann Soc. Artists, Nat. Assn. Women Painters and Sculptors (jury of award 1920-29), N.Y. Soc. Woman Artists (chmn. 1935-36, dir. 1959, hon. dir. 1969), North Shore Arts Assn. (hon.), Cape Ann Soc. Artists, Conn. Acad. Artists Am. (oil jury 1957-58), Allied Artists Am. (Horgan award 1975), Italian Acad. Fine Arts (hon. mem., Gold medal 1980) Achievements include being subject of book The Sketch Book 1910-1950, 1992. Died Feb. 13, 2002.

**BERRIGAN, PHILIP FRANCIS,** author; b. Two Harbors, Minn., Oct. 5, 1923; s. Thomas William and Frida (Fromhart) B.; m. Elizabeth McAlister; 2 children. AB in English, Holy Cross Coll., 1950; BS in Secondary Edn, Loyola U. of South, 1959; MA, Xavier U., New Orleans, 1961. Ordained priest Roman Catholic Ch., 1950; prof. English and religion, also student counselor St. Augustine High Sch., New Orleans; asst. pastor St. Peter Claver Ch., Balt.; worked and demonstrated with So. Christian Leadership Conf., NAACP, CORE, SNCC; co-founder, co-chmn. Cath. Peace Fellowship, Balt. Interfaith Peace Mission; lectr. on race, peace, poverty; active anti-Vietnam War movement. Author: No More Strangers, 1965, Punishment for Peace, 1969, Prison Journals of a Priest Revolutionary, 1970, Widen the Prison Gates, 1974, Of Beasts and Beastly Images, 1979. Served with inf. AUS, World War II, ETO. Convicted in two cases of destruction of draft files; acquitted of conspiracy. Died Dec. 6, 2002.

**BERRONE, LUCIO RENATO,** mathematician; b. Rosario, Argentina, July 18, 1959; s. Renato Miguel Berrone and Noemi Catalina Rosa; m. Maria Elide Lanza, Dec. 15, 1989; children: Lina Lucia, Ignacio Bruno. Diploma in math., UNR, Rosario, 1988, PhD, 1994. Prof. UNR, from 1988; investigator Conicet, Rosario, from 1997. Rev. Math. Revs., 1995—. Contbr. articles to profl. jours. Mem. Am. Math. Soc. Avocations: reading, running, writing. Home: Rosario, Argentina. Died 2002.

**BERRY, ESTER LORÉE,** vocational nurse; b. St. Joseph, La., Sept. 19, 1945; d. Sim and Ruby Jordan; (div.); children: Roderick Bryant, Pamela Elaine. A in nursing and art, Calif. State U., 1996; diploma in poetry and writing, Internat. BIB Ctr., Raleigh, NC. Lic. vocat. nurse. Ward clk. Santa Fe Hosp., Compton, Calif., 1969-72; supr. J.C. Penney's, Carson, Calif., 1973-80; asst. mgr. Std. Comm., Carson, 1981-84; lic. vocat. nurse, nurse King Drew Med., LA, 1984-94; medicine nurse Martin Luther Jr. Hosp., 1996-99; poet Nobles Theatre of the Mind, Paris, London, NYC, from 2004. Author numerous poems. Recipient Editor Choice award, 1999—2001, Laureate award, Internat. Libr. Poetry, 2006, Editor's Choice award, from 2006, Editor's Choice award best poet, 2007, Bronze Merit Medallion award, 2007, Editor's Choice award, 2007, Christal Satue Globe award, 2007, Bronze Leader award, Comdr. Club, DAV, 2001, DAV, 2010, Silver Internat. Poet of Merit, Bronze Commemorative medallion, Best Poet award, 2002—03, certificate, Profl. Women's Adv. Bd., Wall of Tolerance award, So. Poverty Law Ctr., 2004, award, Am. Biographical Inst., 2010, Continuos award, 2012, award, Am. Vets., 2013; named hon. mem., Vets. Am., 1999—2001, Best Poet of Yr., 2001, Best Poet of Yr., Internat. Libr. Poetry, 2004, Poet of Yr., 2007, Profl. Women of Yr. Adv. Bd., 2008; named to Comdrs. Club, DAV, 2002—03, Wall of Tolerance, Ala., 2004, Top 100 Profls., 2013. Mem.: Am. Biog. Inst. (founding mem. internat. women's review bd. 2010), Am. Libr. Inst. (mem. profl. women's adv. bd. 2004). Avocations: fishing, sewing, photography, crocheting, camping. Home: Cathedral City, Calif. Died Jan. 3, 2014.

**BERRY, JOSEPH JOHN,** brokerage house executive; b. NYC, Jan. 28, 1946; s. Joseph and Evelyn Berry; m. Evelyn Bonomo, Nov. 22, 1959; children: Joseph Scott, Todd Patrick, Kimberly Ann. BA in Math & Economics, Queens U.; MBA, St. John's U. V.p., exec. v.p., sr. v.p., vice chmn. Keefe, Bruyette & Woods, Inc., instl. salesperson, 1972, pres., COO, 1975, chmn., 1987—2001, co-CEO, 1999—2001. Named one of Top Fifty Irishmen on Wall Street, Irish America Mag. Died Sept. 11, 2001.

**BERRY, RICHARD ROWLAND,** retired manufacturing executive; b. Chgo., Feb. 17, 1932; s. Richard Benson and Leta Lodema (Rowl) B.; m. Joan Widicus Harrison, Aug. 8, 1954; children: Richard H., Karen L., Scott R. BS in Metall. Engring, U. Ill. Engring. trainee brass group Olin Corp., 1954, v.p. mfg., 1970, group pres. East Alton, Ill., 1980-83, exec. v.p. Stamford, Conn., 1983—92. Served in US Army, 1955-57. Mem. United Ch. of Christ. Died Feb. 4, 2012.

**BERSIN, RICHARD LEWIS,** physicist; b. NYC, July 4, 1929; s. Maxwell Hilary and Virginia (Greenfield) B.; m. Lillian Freda Braudy, Mar. 21, 1954 (div.); children: Joshua Morris, Adam Samuel; m. Ruth Ann Hargrave, July 25, 1976; children: Jacob David Antonio, Rebekah Adeline Juana. BS in Physics, MIT, 1950; MS in Math. and Physics, Northeastern U., Boston, 1962. Physicist Tracerlab, Inc., Boston, 1950-58; divsn. mgr. Lab. for Electronics Corp., Waltham, Mass., 1958-69; pres., founder Internat. Plasma Corp., Berkeley, Calif., 1969-74; exec. v.p. Dionex Gas Plasma Sys., Hayward, Calif., 1974-79; dir. dry processing Perkin Elmer Corp., Wilton, Conn., 1979-83, dir. tech. mktg., 1983-84; pres., cons. Emergent Techs. Corp., from 1985; engring. specialist Ulvac Japan, Ltd., Chigasaki, Japan, 1989-92; sr. tech. staff mem. Ulvac Techs., Inc., Methuen, Mass., 1992—2002; dir. spl. projects Refugee Immigration Ministry, Malden, Mass., from 2007. Patentee in field. Mem. Am. Vacuum Soc. Democrat. Episcopalian. Died Feb. 22, 2014.

**BERTI, ALESSANDRA,** psychiatrist, educator; b. Genoa, Italy, June 17, 1961; d. Leonello Berti and Giuseppina Bassignana; m. Sergio Mungo, Oct. 19, 1991; 1 child, Federico Giuseppe. MD, U. Genoa, 1987, degree in Psychiatry, 1991, degree in Neurophysiology, 1995, degree in Criminology, 1998. Diplomate, cert. prof. psychiatry and psychotherapy. Physician Pub. Health Svc., Genoa, 1989—93, psychiatrist, 1993; prof. U. Genoa, 1993, Master Rehab., 2000. Cons. Italian Assn., Genoa, 1988, Province, Liguria, Italy, 2000, U. Criminology, Genoa, 2000. Author: Memory, Dream and Delusion, 1994, Crime and Victim, 1999 (Nat. award, 1999), Broken Childhood, 2004. Recipient Knight's Merit, Sovereign Mil. Order Malta, 1990, Cross of Merit, Pub. Health Svc. Italy, 1992; grantee, Italian Psychiatry Assn., 1991. Mem.: Italian Assn. Psychotherapists. Avocations: diving, skiing. Home: Genoa, Italy. Died Oct. 15, 2006.

**BERTINI, GARY,** conductor, composer; b. Brichevo, Bessarabia, May 1, 1927; s. Aaron and Berthe Bertini; m. Rosette Berengole Bertini, Oct. 21, 1956; children: Orit, Michal. Diploma, Conservatorio Verdi Milano, 1948, Tel Aviv Music Edn. Coll., 1951, Conservatoire Nat. Superieur Paris, 1954, Ecole Normale de Musique, 1954, Inst. Musicologie, Sorbonne, Paris, 1955. Music dir. Rinat Chamber Chorus, 1955—72, Israel Chamber Ensemble Orch., 1965—75, Jerusalem Symphony Orch., 1978—87; prin. guest condr. Scottish Nat. Orch., 1971—81; prof. Tel Aviv U., 1976; artistic advisor Israel Festival, 1976—83; music advisor Detroit Symphony Orch., 1981—83; chief condr. Cologne Radio-Symphonie-Orch., 1983—91; orch. gen. mgr., music dir. Frankfurt Opera, 1987—91; artistic dir., gen. music dir. New Israeli Opera, Tel Aviv, 1987—97; guest condr. prin. orchs. Opera Houses, Japan. Composer (symphonic, chamber, incidental music theater, radio); contbr. articles to profl. music jours. With1949, 1948, Israeli Def. Forces. Recipient Israel State prize, 1978. Mem.: Israel League Composers. Jewish. Died Mar. 17, 2005.

**BERTON, PIERRE,** journalist, author; b. Whitehorse, Yukon, Can., July 12, 1920; s. Francis George and Laura (Thompson) Berton; m. Janet Walker, 1946; children: Penny, Pamela, Patricia, Peter, Paul, Peggy Anne, Perri, Eric. BA, U. B.C., 1941, DLitt (hon.), 1985; LLD (hon.), U. P.E.I., 1973, Dalhousie U., 1978, U. Brock, 1981, York U., 1974, U. Windsor, 1981, U. Athabasca, 1982, U. Victoria, 1983, McMaster U., 1983, U. Alaska, 1984, Royal Mil. Inst., 1985, Waterloo U., 1988; LLD (hon.), Lakehead U., Thunder Bay, Ont., Can., 2002, U. Western Ont., London, Ont., 2002. City editor Vancouver (B.C.) News Herald, 1941-42; feature writer Vancouver Sun, 1946-47; successive positions to mng. editor Maclean's Mag., Toronto, Ont., 1947-58; host The Pierre Berton Show, 1963-73; contbg. editor Maclean's Mag., 1963; asso. editor, daily columnist Toronto Daily Star, 1958-62; columnist Toronto Star, 1991-94; TV panelist Front Page Challenge, CBC, 1957-95. Chancellor Yukon Coll., 1988-93. Author: 47 books including The Royal Family, 1953, Stampede for Gold, 1955, The Mysterious North, 1956, Klondike Fever, 1958, Just Add Water and Stir, 1959, Adventures of a Columnist, 1960, The New City, 1961, The Secret World of Og, 1961, Fast, Fast, Fast Relief, 1962, Big Sell, 1963, Comfortable Pew, 1965, The Cool, Crazy, Committed World of The Sixties, 1966, Smug Minority, 1968, The National Dream, 1970, The Last Spike, 1971, The Impossible Railway, 1972, Drifting Home, 1973, Hollywood's Canada, 1974, My Country, 1976, The Dionne Years, 1977, The Wild Frontier, 1978, The Invasion of Canada, 1812-1813, 1980, Flames across the Border, 1981, Why We Act Like Canadians, 1982, The Klondike Quest, 1983, The Promised Land, 1984, Masquerade, 1985, Vimy, 1986, Starting Out, 1987, The Arctic Grail, 1988 (Periodical Marketers Can. Book of Yr. award), The Great Depression 1929-39, 1990 (Periodical Marketers Can. Authors award), Niagara, 1992, A Picture Book of Niagara Falls, 1993, Winter, 1994, My Times: Living with History 1947-1995, 1995, Farewell To The Twentieth Century, 1996, The Great Lakes, 1996, 1967-The Last Good Year, 1997, Seacoasts 1998, A Literary Resurrection, 1948-94, 1998, Worth Repeating, Pierre Berton's Canada, 1999, Welcome to the 21st Century, 1999, Marching As To War, 2001, Cats I Have Known and Loved, 2002, The Joy of Writing, 2003; screenwriter; narrator City of Gold; contbr. to numerous mags.and newspapers. Past chmn. Heritage Can. Found. Capt. Can. Army, 1942-45. Decorated Companion Order Can.; recipient Gov. Gen.'s award for creative non-fiction, 1956, 58, 72; Stephen Leacock medal for humor, 1959; J.V. McAree award for columnist of year, 1959; Nat. Newspaper awards for feature writing and staff corresponding, 1960; Grand Prix film awards.; Beefeater Club prize for lit., 1982; Can. Booksellers award, 1982, Companion Order Can., 1986, Gabriele Leger Nat. Heritage award, 1989, Coles Book award, 1989, Great Trekker award U. B.C., 1990, Graeme Gibson award, 1992, Author's Leadership award Periodical Marketers Can., 1992, Pierre Berton award, 1994, Responsibilty in Journalism award Com. for Investigation of Paranormal, 1996, Biomed. Sci. Ambs. award, 1997, John Drainie award for significant contbn. to radio or TV, 1999; named to Can. Newspaper Hall of Fame, 1982, Order of Mariposa, 1990. Mem. Authors League Am., Heritage Can., Assn. Can. Radio and TV Artists (award for integrity in broadcasting 1972, award for pub. affairs 1977), Writers Union Can. Home: Kleinburg, Canada. Died Nov. 30, 2004.

**BERUBE, PHILLIP,** state senator; b. Belcourt, ND, Apr. 6, 1905; s. Arthur and Victorine (Mongeon) Berube; m. Alma Casavant, 1929; children: Leonel, Vivian Beruve Cote, Delina Berube Grossal, Lorette Berube Leanard, Harvey, Julian Berube Lentz, Adrien, Jackie. Ed., Public Schs. Farmer, 1927—30; mem. ND State Senate, 1952—86. Mem. County Sch. Reorgn. Com., ND, 1947—69. Mem.: Farmers Union, Commercial. Roman Catholic. Home: Rolla, ND. Died May 7, 1993.

**BESENHARD, JÜRGEN OTTO,** chemistry professor; b. Regensburg, Germany, May 15, 1944; s. Josef Peter and Johanna (Becker) B.; m. Ursula Elvira Benz, Jan. 18, 1985; children: Maximilian, Sebastian, Florian, Hanna. Diploma in chemistry, Tech. U., Munich, 1970, PhD, 1973, Habilitation, 1979. Pvt. dozent Tech. U., Munich, 1980-85; prof. inorganic chemistry U. Münster, Germany, 1986-92, Tech. U. Graz, Austria, from 1993. Patentee electrochem. power sources; contbr. articles to profl. publs., 1971—; contbr. articles to profl. jours. Mem. Gesellschaft Deutscher Chemiker, Deutsche Keramische Gesellschaft, Internat. Soc. Sol. State Ionics, Internat. Soc. Electrochemistry (nat. sec. for Austria), Gesellschaft Osterreichischer Chemiker, Electrochem. Soc., Internat. Battery Materials Assn. (pres.). Home: Graz, Austria. Died Nov. 4, 2006.

**BESSMERTNOVA, NATALYA IGOREVNA,** ballerina; b. Moscow, July 19, 1941; Student, Bolshoi Theatre Ballet Sch. Dancer Bolshoi Theatre Ballet, Moscow, 1961—88, appeared as Mazurka and 7th Valsa (ballets) in Chopiniana, Pas de trois in Swan Lake, Giselle in Giselle, The Muse in Paganini, Florin in Sleeping Beauty, Leila in Leila and Madjnun, Shirin in Legend of Love, Odette-Odile in Swan Lake, Girl in Le Spectre de la Rose, Maria in The Fountain of Bakhtchisaray, Phrygia in Spartacus, Juliet (ballets) in Romeo and Juliet, Masha in The Nutcracker, Nikia in The Kingdom of Shades, Aurora in Sleeping Beauty, Kitry Queen of Driads in Don Quixote. Recipient Merit award, People's Republic of Russia RSFSR, Gold medal, Varna Competition, 1965, Lenin prize, 1986, Anna Pavlova prize, 1976, USSR State prize, 1977. Died Feb. 19, 2008.

**BETANCOR, MANUEL JULIAN,** electrical engineering educator, researcher; b. Las Palmas, Spain, Dec. 15, 1958; s. Juan Maria and Juana Catalina (Garcia-Alamo) B.; m. Mary N. Falcon, Aug. 22, 1986 (div. June 1993); m. Maria Jose Cruz, June 26, 1995. Grad. in engring., U. Poly. Madrid, 1985, PhD in Elec. Engring., 1989. Prof. colaborador U. Poly. Madrid, 195-87, assoc. prof., 1987-89; prof. elec. engring. U. Las Palmas, from 1989, dir. Oficina Transferencia de Resultados de Investigacion, from 1990, coord. internat. rels., 1990-92. European Cmty. Programme on Cooperation Between Univs. and Industry coord. Found. U. Las Palmas, 1990-95. Author: Notes of Optical Communication, 1991; contbr. articles to sci. jours., chpts. to books. Mem. IEEE, Orcl. Coll. Telecomm. Engrs., Spanish Assn. Engring. Telecomm., Orden Cachorro Canario, Agrupacion Pan y Plantos y Perras P'al Cine. Avocation: playing timple (canarian stringed instrument). Home: Las Palmas, Spain. Died 1997.

**BETHELL, JOHN,** company executive; b. Nuneaton, Warwicksh., Eng., Apr. 30, 1939; arrived in France, 1997; s. William Arthur and Elizabeth Marshall (Green) B.; m. Gillian Stewart Robertson McCartney, Aug. 22, 1964; children: Kim, John Hugh, Julie Jean, Rebecca Anne. BSc in Geology with honours, Glasgow U., Scotland, 1962. Geologist Govt. of Sierra Leone, 1962-64; mktg. asst. Texco, 1964-68; dist. mgr. Texaco Africa Ltd., Sierra Leone, 1968-72; mng. dir. Argus of Ayr Ltd., Scotland, 1972-82; chief exec. Scottish Seed Potato Devel. Coun., 1982-97; chmn. Delco Rus Ltd., Céret, France, from 1995. Chmn. Argoventure Ltd., Scotland, 1973-85; sec. S.E. Growers Ltd., Scotland, 1989-94, Clantweed, Ukraine, 1994—. Bd. dirs. Internat. Sch., Freetown, Sierra Leone, 1968-72; chmn. computer forum Scottish Conservative and Unionist Assn., 1986-90; founder chmn. River Tyne Trust, Scotland, 1990-94. Recipient Paul Harris award Rotary Internat., 1995; hon. fellow Edinburgh U., 1988-97. Mem. Rotary (hon. Kiev, Ukraine, sec. Perpignan-Agly 1990-00). Avocations: mountain climbing, classical music. Home: Céret, France. Died Mar. 29, 2000.

**BETTENCOURT, DON,** secondary school educator; b. Long Beach, Calif., Feb. 2, 1948; s. Joseph and Helena (Penning) B.; m. Sara Jean Wood, June 26, 1971; children: April Iulani, Donald Charles. BA in Speech, Calif. State U., Long Beach, 1970; MA in Edn., Pepperdine U., 1976, MA in Bus. Adminstrn., 1977, PhD in Speech Comm., 1979. Cert. tchr., Calif., Hawaii. Tchr., chair dept. U.S. history Bonita Unified Sch. Dist., San Dimas, Calif., from 1976; master tchr. of tchr. tng. Calif. Poly. U., from 1979. Corp. treas. Micocellar Tech. Corp; v.p., treas., sec. Waipouli Ranches Ltd., Kauai, Hawaii, 1976—; owner, operator Piliohana Project, 1981—. Sr. officer CAP So. Calif., 1987—; mem. Gang Task Force Cities of San Dimas, La Verne, Ontario, 1990—. Named Tchr. of Yr. Bonita Unified Sch. Dist., 1987-88. Mem. Walnut Valley Riders, UCLA Alumni Assn. (life). Republican. Roman Catholic. Deceased.

**BETZ, AUGUSTIN E. A.,** retired educator; b. Aalen, Germany, Jan. 2, 1920; s. Augustin and Elisabeth (Scheerer) B.; m. Annemarie Pape, 1956; children: Heidrun, Arnhild,

Gerlind, Volkmar, Raymund. Staatsexamen, Univ. Erlangen, 1950, Dr. phil. nat., 1952. Asst. prof. Botany Inst. Univ., Bonn, Federal Republic Germany, 1952-60; asst. prof. Tech. Univ., Braunschweig, 1961-66, assoc. prof., 1966-69; research assoc. Johnson Found. Univ. Pa., Phila., 1963-65; prof. Univ. Bonn, 1970-85 (ret.). Mem. diverse profl. orgs. Home: Koenigswinter, Germany. Died Apr. 2003.

**BEVERIDGE, TERRANCE JAMES,** microbiology professor, researcher; b. Toronto, Ont., Can., Apr. 29, 1945; s. Fredrick Charles and Doris Elizabeth (Hooks) B.; m. Janice Elizabeth Barnett, Sept. 9, 1970; children: Braden Charles, Jennifer Bree. BS, U. Toronto, 1968, Diploma in Bacteriology, 1969, MS, 1970; PhD, U. Western Ont., 1974. Sch. assoc. U. Western Ont., London, 1975-78; from asst. prof. to assoc. prof. U. Guelph, Ont., 1978-86, prof. Ont., from 1986, Killam prof. Ont., 1995-97, Can. rsch. chair Ont., from 2002. Vis. prof. Zentrum für Ultrastruckturforschung, Vienna, Austria, 1984, Biozentrum, Universtät der Basel, Switzerland, 1987; dir. Nat. Scis. and Engring. Rsch. Coun. of Can. (NSERC) Gueiph Regional STEM Facility, 1980—. Editor: Metal Ions and Bacteria, 1989, Advances in Bacterial Paracrystalline Surface Layers, 1993; editor Can. Jour. Microbiology, 1982-88, Jour. Bacteriology, 1988-97, Biorecovery, 1987—, Internat. Jour. of Resource and Environ. Biotech., 1994—, Microbiology, 1997—, Arch. Microbiology, 1998—. Recipient Steacie prize, Nat. Sci. and Engring. Rsch. Coun. of Can., 1984, Can. Soc. Microbiology award, 1994, Sigma Xi award, 1994, Culling medal, 2001. Fellow Royal Soc. Can. (dir. life scis. 1992-95), Am. Acad. Microbiology, Austrian Acad. Sci.; mem. Can. Soc. Microbiologists, Microscopical Soc. Can., Am. Soc. Microbiology (divsnl. award 1984), Electron Microscopic Soc. Am., Nat. Centre Excellence, Can. Bacterial Disease Network, Can. Inst. Advanced Rsch. (assoc. 1988—). Avocations: hiking, cross country skiing. Deceased.

**BEVERLY, LAURA ELIZABETH,** special education educator; b. Glen Jean, W.Va., Nov. 26; d. Sidney and Alma Logan. BA in Elem. Edn., W.Va. State Coll., 1960; MS in Spl. Edn., Bklyn. Coll., 1969; postgrad., Oxford U., Eng., 1974, N.Y.U., 1982. Cert. elem./spl. edn. tchr., N.Y. Tchr. Bd. Coop. Ednl. Svcs., Westbury, N.Y., from 1966. Mem. adv. bd. Am. Biographical Inst. Inc., Raliegh, N.C., 1985—. Mem. ASCD, Am. Inst. of Parliamentarians, Royal Soc. Health, Phi Delta Kappa. Avocations: reading, travel. Deceased.

**BEYER, LANDON EDWARD,** education educator, department chairman; b. Eau Claire, Wis., Aug. 30, 1949; s. Harold W. and Helen A. (Meier) B.; m. Linda K. Dybas, Feb. 22, 1986; children: Nathaniel, Leah, Emma. BS in Philosophy, U. Wis., 1972, BS in Elem. Edn., 1976, MA in Philosophy, 1974, PhD in Edn., 1981. Asst. prof. edn. Grad. Sch. Edn. and Human Devel., U. Rochester, N.Y.; vis. asst. prof. U. Wis., Madison; assoc. prof., chmn. dept. edn. Cornell Coll., Mt. Vernon, Iowa; assoc. prof. edn., chmn. dept. Knox Coll., Galesburg, Ill. Cons. and presenter in field. Author: Knowing and Acting: Inquiry, Ideology, and Educational Studies, 1988, The Curriculum: Problems, Politics, and Possibilities, 1988; (with others) Preparing Teachers as Professionals: The Role of Educations Studies and Other Liberal Disciples, 1989, Critical Reflection and the Culture of Schooling: Empowering Teachers, 1989. Fellow U. Ill., Ford Found., U. Wis., Bradish Meml. fellow. Mem. Am. Ednl. Rsch. Assn., Am. Ednl. Studies Assn. (program com. 1985, 91), Philosophy of Edn. Soc., Profs. of Curriculum. Deceased.

**BHANSALI, SHIRISH K.,** surgeon, consultant; b. Sept. 21, 1929; MBBS, Seth Gordhandas Sunderdas Med. Coll. and King Eward Memorial Hosp., Mumbai, 1953, MS in Gen. Surgery, 1957. FRCS (Eng.) 1958. Asst. surgeon, cancer and allied diseases Tata Meml. Ctr., 1960—62; hon. asst. prof. surgery Topiwala Nat. Med. Coll. and BYL Nair Charitable Hosp., Mumbai, 1963—80, hon. asst. surgeon; hon. surgeon Bhatia Gen. Hosp., Mumbai, 1962—66, Sir Hurkisondas Nurottamdas Hosp., Mumbai, 1966—96; dir. gen., g.i. surgeon, mem. governing coun. Jaslok Hosp. Res. Ctr., Mumbai, cons. surgeon, from 1986, Breach Candy Hosp., from 1993, Lilavati Hosp., 1997—2002. Vis. prof. Sahlgranska Hosp. U. Gottenberg, Sweden, 1984, Postgrad. Inst. Med. Edn. and Rsch., Chandigarh, India, 1983, Sanjay Ghandi Postgrad. Inst. Med. Scis., Lucknow, India; Ethicon vis. prof. assoc. surgeons Sayajirao Gen. Hosp. and Med. Coll., Baroda, India. Editor: (book) Management of acute pacreatitis, 2006; co-editor: Minimal access surgery: guidelines; contbr. chapters to books, scientific papers, articles to profl. conf. jours. Recipient William Rorer Best Paper award, Am. Coll. Gastroenterology, 1977, Scroll honor, Indian Assoc. Surg. Oncology Distinguished Svcs., 2000, Best Tchr. award, T.N. Med. Coll. Alumni Assoc., Mumbai, 2006, Sushrut award Excellence Surgery, 2008, Contribution award, Found. Endocrine Surgery Training and Advancement, Sixteen Gold medals, U. Mumbai, Seth G.S. Med. Coll. and K.E.M. Hosp.; Outstanding Paper fellowship, Danish Govt., 1970. Fellow: Am. Coll. Surgeons, Am. Coll. Gastroenterology; mem.: Internat. Coll. Surgeons, Internat. Hepato-Pancreo-Biliary Assoc., Internat. Coll. Digestive Surgery, Assn. Colon and Rectal Surgeons India (life), Indian Assn. Surgical Gastroenterology (life), Indian Assn. Endocrine Surgeons (life), Indian Soc. Gastroenterology (life), Indian Med. Assn. (life), Assn. Surgeons India (life), Indian Assn. Study Liver (life), Indian Assn. Gastrointestinal Endo-Surgeons (life), Indian Assn. Surg. Oncology (life), Soc. Nuclear Medicine India (life), Asian Assn. Endocrine Surgeons, Internat. Assn. Endocrine Surgeons, Internat. Soc. Surgeon, Wellington Gymkhana Club Coonoor, Willingdon Sports Club Mumbai, Bombay Presidency Radio Club, Rotary Club Bombay Ctrl. (charter pres. 1973). Home: Mumbai, India. Died Apr. 27, 2009.

**BHARGAV, GIRDHARI LAL,** Indian legislator; b. Jaipur, India, Nov. 11, 1936; s. Pandit D.L. Bhargav; m. Malti Bhargav, June 24, 1953; 4 children. BA, LLB, Rajasthan U., Jaipur. Mem. Rajasthan Legis. Assembly, 1972—89, chmn. library com., 1980, mem. govt. assurances com., estimates com., petitions com.; mem. Lok Sabha (Indian Parliament), from 1989, mem. consultative com. to min. railways, rules com., 1990—91, mem. fin. com., 1996—99, mem. consultative com. to min. fin., mem. estimates com., commerce com., rules com., 1999—2000, mem. energy com., consultative com. to min. railways, 2000—04, mem. official languages com., agr. com., 2004—09. Former dep. chmn. Pollution Control Bd. of Rajasthan; chmn. Urban Improvement Trust, Jaipur, Rajasthan, 1978—80; sec. Bharatiya Riksha Chalak Mazdoor Sangh; mem. Bharatiya Janata Party. Died Mar. 8, 2009.

**BIASIN, GIAN-PAOLO,** literature educator; b. Reggio Emilia, Italy, Nov. 7, 1933; s. Giovanni and Vittoria (Bedeschi) B.; m. Maria Rita Francia, Dec. 28, 1970; 1 child, Giovanni. Laurea Jurisprudence, Modena U., Italy, 1956; MA in Polit. Sci., Syracuse U., 1958; PhD in Romance Lit., Johns Hopkins U., 1964. Asst. prof. Cornell U., Ithaca, N.Y., 1964-67, assoc. prof., 1967-73; prof. U. Tex., Austin, 1973-81, U. Calif., Berkeley, from 1981. Chmn. comparative lit. U. Tex., Austin, 1974-75; chmn. Italian dept. U. Calif., Berkeley, 1983-88. Assoc. editor Forum Italicum, Stony Brook, N.Y., 1978—; author: The Smile of the Gods, 1968, Literary Diseases, 1975, Italian Literary Icons, 1983, Montale, Debussy, Modernism, 1989, The Flavors of Modernity, 1993. Mem. Coemit, Italian Govt. Com. on Emigration, San Francisco, 1987-90. Fulbright fellow Fulbright Commn., 1957-58, 62-63, fellow Humanities Coun., Princeton U., 1992.; Univ. Rsch. grantee U. Tex., 1979; named Knight Officer in the Order of Merit of the Italian Republic, Rome, 1987; recipient Orio Vergani prize, 1992. Mem. Internat. Assn. Study Italian Lit., MLA, Am. Assn. Italian Studies, Am. Assn. Tchrs. Italian, Dante Soc. of Am., Accademia Italiana della Cucina. Roman Catholic. Home: Berkeley, Calif. Died Aug. 24, 1998.

**BICOUVARIS, MARY VASSILICOU,** education educator, consultant; b. Tripolis, Greece, June 4, 1939; came to U.S., 1960; d. Nickolas George and Georgia (Lymberopoulos) Vassilicos; m. James Gregory Bicouvaris; children: Greg, Valerie. Elem. edn. diploma, Pedagogical Acad. Tripolis, Greece, 1958; BS in Secondary Edn., Ohio State U., 1963; LHD (hon.), Hampton U., 1989; MA in Edn., The Coll. William and Mary, 1970; PhD in Urban Svcs., Old Dominion U., 1994. History tchr. grades 7-9 Jefferson Davis Jr. High, Hampton, Va., 1963-66, 68-76; history and govt. tchr. Bethel H.S., Hampton, Va., 1976-91; govt. and internat. politics tchr. Hampton Roads Acad., Newport News, Va., 1991-95; assoc. prof. edn. Christopher Newport U., Newport News, Va., 1995—2001. Trustee Nat. Coun. for History Edn., 1990—, Christopher Newport U., 1989-95, adj. faculty; edn. advisory panel New Am. Sch. Devel. Corp., 1990—; coun. mem. Nat. Coun. for History Stds., 1991-95; adj. faculty George Washington U., bd. advisors scholar program, 1995-96; presenter in field. Contbr. articles to profl. jours. Bd. dirs., v.p., 1st v.p. UN Assn., Peninsula chpt., 1983-88; bd. dirs., 1st v.p. Peninsula Literacy Coun., 1983-86; active Greek Orthodox Ch., Newport News, PTA. Fulbright Hays scholar, Israel, Egypt, 1984, Delta Kappa Gamma Internat. scholar, 1990; recipient Disting. Educator award Am. Hellenic Ednl. and Progressive Assn., 1989, Disting. Alumni award Ohio State U. Coll. Edn., 1989, Mary Hatwood Futrell award Va. Edn. Assn., 1989; scholarships named in her honor by Hampton Lions Club, Greek Orthodox Ch. Newport News. Mem. ASCD, Nat. Coun. for History Edn. (founding mem.), Nat. Coun. for the Social Studies, coun. for Basic Edn., Am. Ednl. Rsch. Assn., Assn. Tchr. Educators, Va. Assn. Tchr. Educators, Hellenic Womans Penelope Soc. (past. pres., v.p., treas., 1st v.p. 1995-96), Phi Delta Phi. Died 2001.

**BIERINGER, WALTER H.,** retired plastic and rubber manufacturing company executive; b. Boston, Mass., Nov. 17, 1899; s. Leo and Sara (Wolfenstein) B.; m. Gertrude Marie Kessel, Aug. 5, 1922; 1 dau., Doris Marie (Mrs. Howard H. Hiatt); m. Annabelle Markson, Mar. 9, 1984. AB, Harvard U., 1921. Sr. v.p., dir. Plymouth Rubber Co., Canton, Mass., 1921—; pres. Plymouth Rubber Internat. Co., Canton. Cons., on refugee affairs State Dept., 1956; adviser on refugee affairs Pres. Truman Past pres. United Service for New Americans; past nat. chmn. United Jewish Appeal; past pres. Urban League Boston; chmn. Gov.'s Commn. on Refugees, 1946—; trustee emeritus Howard U.; former bd. overseers Brandeis U. Sch. Social Work; bd. dirs. Joint Distbn. Com., Am. ORT Fedn., HIAS Service, Inc. Served with AUS, World War I. Mem. World Trade Center Boston. Clubs: Harvard of Boston. Home: Boston, Mass. Died June 18, 1990.

**BIGELOW, DANIEL JAMES,** aerospace executive; b. Harrisville, Pa., Mar. 26, 1935; s. Raymond James and Hilda Irene (Graham) Bigelow; m. Elizabeth Jane Allison, Sept. 10, 1955; 1 child, Allison Jane. BFA in Art Advt., Kent State U., Ohio, 1957; MA in Edn., La. Tech. U., 1974; MS in Polit. Sci., Auburn U., 1986; MS, Air U., 1987; postgrad., Ohio State U., from 1989, Kent State U.; MS in Natural Resources, Indsl. Coll., 1975; MS in Strategic Intelligence, Defence Intelligence Coll., 1982. Commd. 2d lt. USAF, 1957, advanced through grades to col., 1979, ret., 1987; command pilot 167 combat missions Vietnam; air attaché to Soviet Union, 1983—85; dir. Soviet program Air War Coll. Air U., Ala., 1985—87; gen. mgr. aerospace divsn. Modern Techs. Corp., Dayton, Ohio, 1988—98, dir. programs corp. hdqrs., 1998—2001, dir. bus. svcs. corp. hdqrs., 2002—03; dir. investor rels. and corp. comm. MTC Tech., Inc., Dayton, 2003—08; dir., Comm. Aerospace Solutions BAE Sys., Dayton, 2008—09; pres. Bigelow Arrowspace Consulting, LLC, Xenia, Ohio, from 2008, Ga. Tech. Rsch. Inst., Sansara Inc., LLC. Designer artwork, writer text MTC Annual Reports, 2002—06; designer MTC Website, 2003—07. Author, editor: Soviet Studies, 1968—88; contbr. articles to profl. jours. Comdr. Army and Air Force ROTC Corps of Cadets, 1957, Kent State U. Decorated USAF Legion of Merit with one oak leaf cluster, DFC, 14 Air medals, Def. Superior medal; recipient U.S. Am. Nat. award, CIA Dir. William J. Casey, 1985; named Disting. Mil. Grad., Air Force ROTC, 1957, Disting. alumni, East Liverpool (Ohio) HS Alumni Assn., 2004. Mem.: AIAA, Arclight-Young Tiger Assn., Air Force Meml. Airman Soc. (founding mem.), Sugar Valley Ridge Homeowner's Assn. (v.p., bd. mgrs. from 2012), Air Force Meml. Found., Nat. Mus. Marine Corps. (founding mem.), Ohio Vet. United Alliance, Miami Valley Freedom Alliance (exec. team, exec. team mem.), Ohio Vets. United, Nat. Aviation Hall of Fame (patron from 2003), Fisher-Nightingale Houses, Inc. (bd. mem. from 2005), Intelligence and Nat. Security Alliance, Am. Electronics Assn., Nat. Mus. US Army (founding sponsor), Strategic Air Command Assn., 3rd Mil. Airlift Squadron Assn., Nat. Investor Rels. Inst., Nat. Mil. Intelligence Assn. (dir. programs, Ohio 2009—10, dir. Programs NMIA Ohio 2009—10), Electronic Engring. and Mfg. Group (bd. dirs. 2006—10), Internat. Test and Evaluation Assn., Inst. Navigation, Miami Valley Mil. Affairs Assn., Def. Planning and Analysis Soc., Dayton Area Def. Contractors Assn. (pres. 1999—2000, bd. dirs.), Internat. Platform Assn., Acad. Polit. Sci., Vet. Fgn. Wars (life), Red River Valley Fighter Pilot's Assn. (life), Wright "B" Flyer Assn. (life), Kent State U. Alumni Assn. (life), Nat. Def. Indsl. Assn. (life), Am. Def. Preparedness Assn. (life), Army Aviation Assn. Am., Inc., Assn. Former Intelligence Officers (Nat. & Ariz. chpt.), Air Force Assn. (life; v.p. state legis. affairs 2001—02), Airlift/Tanker Assn. (life), Air Force Mus. Found. (life), DFC Soc. (life), Mil. Officers Assn. Am. (life), Air Rescue Assn. (historian from 1998, chmn. reunion and symposium 2003, nat. bd. dirs.), F-86 Sabre Pilots' Assn., B-52 Stratofortress Assn., Ret. Officers' Assn., Armed Forces Comm. and Electronics Assn., Pararescue Assn., Pedro Helicopter Assn., Mil. Officer Assn. Am., Dayton Art Inst., Intelligence & Nat. Security Alliance, Assn. U.S. Army, Dayton Area C. of C. (vice-chmn. mil. and fed. affairs com. 2003—04, chmn. 2004—09), Air Force Assn. Cmty. Ptnrs., Waco Hist. Soc., Royal Air Force Club, Discussion Club Dayton (v.p. 1999—2000), Am. Legion, Scottish Rite, Masons, Assn. Old Crows, Order Daedalians (life; flight capt., pres. 2001—02), Order Quiet Birdmen, Anciente Order Quiet Birdmen, Shriners, Blue Key. Avocations: art, photography, jogging. Died Aug. 11, 2014.

**BIGELOW, MARGARET ELIZABETH BARR (M.E. BARR),** retired botany educator; b. Elkhorn, Man., Can., Apr. 16, 1923; d. David Hunter and Mary Irene (Parr) Barr; m. Howard Elson Bigelow, June 9, 1956 (dec.). BA with honors, U. B.C., Vancouver, Can., 1950, MA, 1952; PhD, U. Mich., 1956. Rsch. attaché U. Montreal, Que., Can., 1956-57; instr. U. Mass., Amherst, 1957-65, asst. prof., 1965-71, assoc. prof., 1971-76, prof., 1976-89, prof. emeritus, from 1989. Author: Diaporthales in N.A., 1978, Prodromus to Loculoascomycetes, 1987, Prodromus to Nonlichenized Members of Class Hymenoascomycetes, 1990; contbr. articles to profl. jours. With Can. Women's Army Corps, 1942—46. Mem. Mycol. Soc. Am. (v.p. to pres. 1980-82, editor 1975-80, Disting. Mycologist Award, 1993), Brit. Mycol. Soc., Am. Inst. Biol. Sci. (gen. chmn. ann. meeting 1986). Avocations: gardening, reading. Died Apr. 1, 2008.

**BIGGS, ELECTRA WAGGONER,** sculptor, rancher; b. Ft. Worth, Nov. 8, 1912; d. Edward Paul and Helen (Buck) Waggoner; m. John Biggs, Apr. 25, 1943; children: Electra Biggs, Helen Biggs. D in Fine Arts, Tex. Women's Christian U., 1945. Dir. W.T. Waggoner Estate, from 1975, Santa Rosa Ranch, 1976, Inter-First Bank of Ft. Worth, 1979-85. Prin. works include Harry Truman bust Truman Libr., Independence, Mo., Dwight Eisenhower, Denison, Tex., Abilene, Kans., Bob Hope, USO Bldg., Washington, John Nance Garner Tex. Tech. Mus., Louis B. Mayer, L.A., Mary Martin, N.Y.C., Will Rogers statues Ft. Worth, Claremore, Okla., Tex. Tech. U., Lubbock, Anatole Hotel Sculpture Garden, Dallas, Robert J. Kleberg Tex. A&M U., College Station, Knute Rockne U. Notre Dame, South Bend, Ind.; exhibited in numerous one-person shows. Dir. Interfirst Band, Ft. Worth, 1981-86, Ft. Worth Stock Show, 1980-86. Republican. Episcopalian. Died Apr. 23, 2001.

**BILICKI, ZBIGNIEW,** mechanical engineer, educator; b. Cracow, Poland, Apr. 1, 1944; s. Telesfor and Broniskawa (Szczepanska) B.; m. Grazyna Szubert, Jan. 6, 1968; children: Magdalena, Paula. MS, Tech. U., Gdansk, Poland, 1968, dr. habil., 1985; PhD, Inst. Fluid Flow Machinery, Gdansk, Poland, 1979, Title Prof., 1995. Engr. specialist Ship Design and Rsch. Ctr., Gdansk, 1968-78; head lab. Inst. Fluid Flow Machinery, 1978-91, dept. head, from 1991. Sr. rsch. assoc. Brown U., Providence, 1978-80, vis. asst. prof., 1985-86, 92-93; vis. prof. Tulane U., New Orleans, 1995. Author: Multiphase Science and Technology, 1994. Recipient award 4th Dept. Polish Acad. Scis., 1982, award of scientific sec., 1986. Mem. Polish Acad. Scis. (com. thermodynamics and combustion 1993—, com. energy problems 1996). Avocations: classical music, tennis. Home: Gdansk, Poland. Died June 9, 2002.

**BILLGERT, STIG NILS,** management consultant; b. Stockholm, Nov. 22, 1928; s. Nils Wilhelm and Margareta Elizabeth (Danielsson) B.; m. Marianne Gunvor Eckerberg, Mar. 15, 1958; children: Magnus, Johan, Peter, Staffan, Charlotte. MBA, Stockholm Sch. Econs., 1951. Sr. exec. v.p. ABA-Bolagen, Stockholm, 1952-60; v.p. adminstrn. Mo och Domsjo Group, Ornskoldsvik, Sweden, 1960-72; chmn., CEO Stig Billgert AB, Stockholm, from 1972.

Chmn. Stockholm Open ATP Tour Tennis Tournament, 1980-96. Mem. Royal Lawn Tennis Club (chmn. 1991-96). Avocations: tennis, sportfishing. Home: Täby, Sweden. Died Nov. 17, 2007.

**BILLINGS, FRANKLIN SWIFT, JR.,** federal judge; b. Woodstock, Vt., June 5, 1922; s. Franklin S. and Gertrude (Curtis) B.; m. Pauline Gillingham, Oct. 13, 1951; children: Franklin, III, Jireh Swift, Elizabeth, Ann. S.B., Harvard U., 1943; postgrad., Yale U. Law Sch., 1945; JD, U. Va., 1947; DL (hon.), Vt. Law Sch., 1997. Bar: Vt. 1948, U.S. Supreme Ct., 1958. With dept. electronics Gen. Electric Co., Schenectady, NY, 1943; bldg. dept. Vt. Marble Co., Proctor, 1945-46; pvt. practice law Woodstock, 1948-52; mem. firm Billings & Sherburne, Woodstock, 1952-66; asst. sec. Vt. Senate, 1949-55; sec. Vt. State Senate, 1957-59; sec. civil & mil. affairs State of Vt., 1959-61, exec. clk. to Gov., 1955-57; judge Hartford Mcpl. Ct., 1955-63; mem. Vt. House of Reps., 1961-66, chmn. judiciary com., 1961, speaker, 1963-66; judge Vt. Superior Ct., 1966-75, assoc. justice, 1975-83, chief justice, 1983-84; judge US Dist. Ct. Vt., 1984-94, chief judge, 1988-92, sr. judge, 1994—2014. Active, Town of Woodstock, 1948-. Attached Brit. Army, 1944-45. Mem. Vt. Bar Assn., Delta Theta Phi. Died Mar. 9, 2014.

**BILNEY, GORDON,** retired Australian government official; b. Renmark, South Australia, June 21, 1939; m. Sandra Calhoun, 2002; 2 children. BSc in Dental Surgery, BA in Politics, U. Adelaide. With Australian Diplomatic Svc., Jakarta, Manila, Geneva, Paris, 1966-82, adv. to min. fgn. affairs, 1973-75, high commr. to West Indies, 1980-82, head econ. divsn. Min. Fgn. Affairs, 1982-83; elected MP for Kingston, 1983—96; min. defense science and personnel, 1990-93; min. for devel. coop. and Pacific Island Affairs, 1993-96. Labor Party. Died Oct. 28, 2012.

**BINFORD, JESSE STONE, JR.,** chemistry professor; b. Freeport, Tex., Nov. 1, 1928; s. Jesse Stone and Eglan Lee (Bracewell) B.; m. Lolita Ramona Fritz, June 8, 1955; children: Lincoln Bracewell, Jason Jolly. BA in Chemistry, Rice U., 1950, MA in Chemistry, 1952; PhD in Phys. Chemistry, U. Utah, 1955. Instr. chemistry U. Tex., Austin, 1955-58; asst. prof. U. of the Pacific, Stockton, Calif., 1958-60, assoc. prof., 1960-61; Fulbright prof., chmn. dept. chemistry Univ. Nacional Autonoma de Honduras, Tegucigalpa, 1968-69; vis. rsch. prof. Thermochemistry Lab., U. Lund, Sweden, 1971, researcher, 1982-83; rsch. fellow Chelsea Coll., U. London, 1983; assoc. prof. U. South Fla., Tampa, 1961-72, prof., 1972—2003, emeritus prof., from 2004. Cons. Fla. consortium AID, Honduras, 1969, Exxon Prodn. Rsch. Co., Houston, 1974; chmn. State Univ. Faculty Senate Coun., Fla., 1975-76; dir. gen. chemistry program U. South Fla., 1978-82, 98-2003; vis. prof. dept. chem. engring. Rice U., 1993-94, rschr. Cox Lab. for Biomed. Engring., Inst. Bioscis. and Bioengring., 1993-94; mem. Inst. for Biomolecular Sci., U. South Fla., pres. faculty senate, 1999-2000. Author: (textbook) Foundations of Chemistry, 1977, 2nd edit., 1985; contbr. articles to profl. jours., 1956—2003. Active bicycle adv. com. Hillsborough County, Tampa, 1975-93, chairperson bicycle adv. com., 1990-93; faculty advisor U. South Fla. Bicycle Club, 1972-2004; coord. spl. tutoring program Danforth Found., Tampa, 1968. Grantee Petroleum Rsch. Fun, 1960-62, USPHS (NIH), 1966-68, Rsch. Corp., 1986. Mem. AAUP, AAAS, Am. Chem. Soc. (nat. and Tex. sect.), Calorimetry Conf., League of Am. Bicyclists, Golden Key, Sigma Xi, Phi Beta Kappa, Phi Lambda Upsilon, Sigma Pi Sigma, Omicron Delta Kappa, Advocate Nuc. Power. Avocations: bicycling, travel, reading. Home: Austin, Tex. Died Mar. 27, 2014.

**BINGHAM, RICHARD GEORGE,** physicist, optical designer, consultant; b. Norwich, England, July 15, 1940; s. Thomas Frederick and Emma Maud (Lusher) B.; m. Elizabeth Anne Epps, Sept. 24, 1977; children: Amanda, Rachel. BA, Cambridge U., Eng., 1962, MA, PhD, Cambridge U., Eng., 1966. Chartered engr. Optical engr. Royal Greenwich Obs., Cambridge, 1966-97; co. dir. Optical Generics Ltd., 1994-97, tech. dir., 1997-2000; co-dir. Optical Investments Ltd., 1997-2000. Editor: Metal Mirrors, 1993. Hon. rsch. fellow U. Coll. London, 1986—. Fellow Royal Astron. Soc. (past councillor); mem. Inst. Physics. Home: Cambridge, England. Died 2005.

**BINIENDA, JOHN J., SR.,** state legislator; b. Worcester, Mass., June 22, 1947; s. Thaddeus Andrew and Mary Gertrude (O'Coin) B.; m. Beverly Binienda (dec.); children: Julie Ann, John Joseph Jr., Jamie Thaddeus. BA, Worcester State Coll., 1970, postgrad., 1970-74. Mem 17th Worcester Dist. Mass. House of Reps., 1987—2014. Mem. Worcester State Coll. Alumni Assn., American Legion (Main St. chpt.), Polish Naturalization Ind. Club, Polish American Vet. Club, K.C. (3d degree), Loyal Order Moose. Democrat. Home: Worcester, Mass. Died Aug. 22, 2014.

**BINSFELD, CONNIE BERUBE,** former lieutenant governor; b. Munising, Mich., Apr. 18, 1924; d. Omer J. and Elsie (Constance) Berube; m. John E. Binsfeld, July 19, 1947; children: John T., Gregory, Susan, Paul, Michael. BS, Siena Heights Coll., 1945, DHL (hon.), 1977; LLD (hon.), No. Mich. U., 1998; DHL (hon.), Mich. State U., 1998, Thomas Cooley Sch. of Law, 1999; LLD (hon.), Saginaw Valley State U., 2000, Lake Superior State U., 2000; DHL (hon.), U. Notre Dame, 2000, Grand Valley State U., 2000, DHL (hon.). County commr. Leelanau County, Mich., 1970-74; mem. Mich. House of Reps., 1974-82, asst. Republican leader, 1979-81; del. Nav. Conv., 1980, 88, 92; mem. Mich. State Senate, 1982-90, asst. Republican leader, 1979, 81; lt. gov. State of Mich., 1990-98. Mem. adv. bd. Nat. Park Sys. Named Mich. Mother of Yr., Mich. Mothers Com., 1977; Northwestern Mich. Coll. fellow; named to Mich. Women's Hall of Fame, 1998. Mem. Nat. Coun. State Legislators, LWV, Siena Heights Coll. Alumnae Assn. Republican. Roman Catholic. Died Jan. 12, 2014.

**BIOLA BIANCO ROSMANN, JOANNA CARLA,** scientific translator; b. São Paulo, Brazil, Dec. 5, 1928; d. Luigi Biola Bianco and Alessandrina Bernasconi; m. Francesco Rosmann, May 3, 1961 (dec. Feb. 1990). Studied Mediterranean archaeology, Internat. U. Art, Florence, Italy, 1984-85, studied museology, 1984-85; studied classification arch. materials, Florence U., Italy, 1984-85. Sec. Counsulate Gen. Iceland, São Paulo, 1963-64; translator dept. anthropology Inst. Venez. Investigaciones Cientificas, Caracas, Venezuela, 1965-78; collaborator Ctr. of Studies U. Nat. Exptl. Francisco Miranda-UNEFM, Coro, Venezuela, 1983-84; exec. adminstrn. Mus. del Hombre, U. Nat. Francisco Miranda-UNEFM, Coro, Venezuela, 1979-85, adminstrn. Mus. Ceramic History & Popular Earthware, 1979-85, adminstrn. Ctr. Anthropol., Archaeolog. & Paleolog., 1979-85. Style editor Min. for Sci. & Tech., Coro, 1979-83; excavator U. Florence Lake Accesa, Italy, 1985, Villanovian Settlement; participant mem. Latin Am. Congress of Paleontology, Pt. Alegre, Brazil, 1981, 2d Internat. Congress of Etruscology, Florence, 1985, 4th Internat. Congress of Egyptology, Turin, Italy, 1991. Active Fed. European Movement Congress, Biella, 1991. Scholar Italo-Venezuelan Conv., Florence, 1984. Mem. Mediterranean Archeaolog. Soc. Avocations: epoch fashion stylings, classic ballet for children, travel. Home: Strona, Italy. Deceased.

**BIRLA, SHRI KRISHNA KUMAR,** industrialist; b. Pilani, India, Oct. 12, 1918; s. Ghanshyam Das and Maha (Devi) Birla; m. Shrimati Manorama Devi, July 3, 1941 (dec. July 29, 2008). Student, Calcutta Univ., Delhi Univ., Punjab Univ.; LittD Honoris Causa (hon.), Pondicherry Univ., 1997. Chmn. K.K. Birla Group (inc. Zuari Industries Ltd., Chambal Fertilizers Chems. Ltd., Texmaco Ltd., Sutlej Industries Ltd., India Steam Ship Co. Ltd.). Trustee Birla Edn. Trust; pres. Indian Sugar Mills Assn., 1946—47; chmn. Hindustan Times Ltd. (subs. K.K. Birla Group), 1983—2008; current chmn. Birla Inst. Tech. Sci.; former mem. Rajya Sabha (Council of States), Indian Parliament, 1984—2002. Author: Indira Gandhi--Reminiscences, Partners in Progress: Collection of Selected Speeches and Writings, Brushes With History, 2007. Pres. Indian Chambers of Commerce, Calcutta, 1963—64, Marwari Relief Soc., Calcutta, 1965—67, Fedn. Indian Chambers of Commerce and Industry, 1974—75; past pres. Bridge Fedn. of India; pres. All India Lawn Tennis Assn., 1980—85. Mem.: Gymkhana Club, Calcutta Club. Died Aug. 30, 2008.

**BIRNBAUM, JACOB,** organization and communal service executive; b. Hamburg, Germany, Dec. 10, 1926; arrived in US, 1963; s. Solomon Asher and Irene Rikl (Grunwald) Birnbaum; m. Freda Beatrice Bluestone Birnbaum, Nov. 21, 1971. BA in Modern History with honors, U. London, 1951. Tchr. Avigdor Secondary Grammar Sch., London, 1951—52; dean students Sunderland Jewish Theol. Coll., County Durham, 1952—55; dir. Hackney Jewish Cmty. Ctr., London, 1955—57, Jewish Cmty. Coun. Manchester, Salford & Prestwich, 1957—59; founder, nat. dir. Student Struggle Soviet Jewry, NYC, 1964, Ctr. Russian & East European Jewry, 1966; founder NY Youth Coun. on Soviet Jewry, 1965, Bronx Coun. Aid Soviet Jewry, 1966, NY Coordinating Com. Soviet Jewry, 1966; co-founder Queens Coun. on Soviet Jewry, 1966; founder, hon. pres. Bklyn. Coalition Soviet Jewry, 1969; co-founder, hon. chmn. Greater NY Conf. Soviet Jewry, 1971; co-founder Nat. Conf. Soviet Jewry, 1971, NY Met. Coordinating Com. Russian Jewish Immigrants, 1975. Editor: Jewish Renaissance in the USSR: The Moscow Jewish Cultural Symposium, 1976. Jewish. Achievements include established first Jewish grassroots orgn. for human rights in USSR Eastern Europe. Died Apr. 9, 2014.

**BISNAUTH, DALE ARLINGTON,** former Guyanese government official; b. Better Success, Guyana, Dec. 30, 1938; 7 children BA in History, PhD in History, U. West Indies; MDiv, U. London. Dean United Theol. Coll. West Indies; sr. lectr. U. West Indies, U. Guyana; sr. min., 1992; min. of edn. Govt. of Guyana, Georgetown, 1992—2001, min. labor, human services, & social security, 2002—04. Author: A Short History of Guyana Presbyterian Church, 1979, History of Religions in the Caribbean, 1989, The Settlement of Indians in Guyana: 1890-1930, 2000. Christian. Died Apr. 4, 2013.

**BISSBORT, SIEGBERT HEINRICH,** medical researcher; b. Pirmasens, Pfalz, Germany, June 22, 1947; s. Albrecht Bissbort, Klara Bissbort; m. Margarete Maria Dupont; children: Ulf Bissbort, Cathrin. Diploma in biology, 1973. Sci. asst. U. Tuebingen, Germany, 1974—79; rsch. scientist U. Freiburg, Germany, 1980—83; med. rschr. U. Pretoria, South Africa, from 1983. Named Alexander von Humboldt fellow, 1983. Achievements include research in enzymatic tests AChE test. Home: Pretoria, South Africa. Died Sept. 22, 2002.

**BITEO BORICÓ, MIGUEL ABIA,** former Prime Minister of Equatorial Guinea; b. 1961; Mining engr., Russia; finance min. Equatorial Guinea, 1999—2000, prime min., 2004—06. Partido Democrático De Guinea Ecuatorial. Died Dec. 6, 2012.

**BITTEL, WILLIAM HAROLD,** education educator, consultant; b. Peoria, Ill., Nov. 16, 1932; arrived in Australia, 1971; s. William Harold and Elizabeth Jenny (Clay) B.; m. Judith Margaret Quinn, May 12, 1959; children: Janet Louise, Diane Kay, John William. BA, Haverford Coll., 1954; MA, Columbia U., 1956, Oxford U., Eng., 1970; Advanced Diploma in Edn., U. Adelaide, Australia, 1975; PhD, Pacific Western U., 1991. Commd. ensign USN, 1956, advanced through grades to lt. commdr., 1959, ret., 1971; mgmt. cons. USAF, Brize Norton, Eng., 1961-64; asst. prof. Westmar Coll., Le Mars, Iowa, 1964-67; tchr. Elizabeth High Sch., Adelaide, Australia, 1971-73; lectr. U. South Australia, Adelaide, 1974-92, U. So. Queensland, Toowoomba, Australia, from 1993. Assoc. QX Enterprises, Toowoomba, 1993—. Author: I Hate to Study, 1987, 90, Make Your Own Tomorrow, 1989, Adult Learner Survival Skills, 1990. Mem. Am. Assn. for Adult and Continuing Edn., Am. Hist. Assn., United Oxford and Cambridge U. Club, Hyde Park-Bankers Lodge # 193 (Master 1990). Avocation: music. Home: Bardon, Australia. Died 2003.

**BIUNNO, VINCENT P.,** fed. judge; b. Newark, Feb. 2, 1916; s. James and Margaret (George) B.; m. Mary Ann Zocchi, June 8, 1941. Student, Columbia, 1932-33; LL.B. magna cum laude, N.J. Law Sch., 1937. Bar: N.J. bar 1937. Counselor, 1940; mem. firm Lum, Biunno & Tompkins (and predecessors), Newark, 1937-46, partner, 1946-58, 60-73; judge U.S. Dist. Ct., N.J. Dist., from 1973. Counsel to Gov. N.J., 1958-60; mem. N.J. Gov.'s Study Com. Legalized Games of Chance, 1953-54; counsel Legis. Com. to Revise Law of Evidence, 1955-57, to pres. N.J. Senate, to rules com. N.J. Supreme Ct.; bd. dirs., chmn. exec. com. Prudential Ins. Co. Am., 1960-73; mem. N.J. Gov.'s Milk Study Com., 1962-64; mem. N.J. Commn. on Def. of Indigent; N.J. pub. rate counsel, utilities, 1970-73. Mem. editorial bd. N.J. Law Jour.; author articles on legal research. Pres., trustee N.J. Law Inst., 1955—; mem. Glen Ridge Devel. Bd.; mem. adv. bd. Western Res. U. Sch. Library Sci.; trustee Hist. Soc. U.S. Dist. Ct. N.J., 1986—. Served with Signal Corps AUS, 1942-43. Fellow Am. Bar Found. (com. indexing statutory law); mem. ABA (chmn. com. on tech. in ct. systems 1982—, mem. com. electronic data retrieval 1958-73, mem. ho. of dels. 1968-73), N.J. Bar Assn. (gen. council 1962-73, chmn. jud. selection com. 1968-73), Essex County Bar Assn. (pres. 1963-64, trustee), Nat. Conf. Bar Pres.'s, Alpha Sigma Phi. Clubs: Glen Ridge Country. Home: Clifton, NJ. Died July 30, 1991.

**BIXLER, PAUL (HOWARD BIXLER),** librarian, editor; b. Union City, Mich., Oct. 27, 1899; s. Miles Fred and Lida (Gillett) B.; m. Norma Hendricks, Oct. 6, 1926; children: Giles Norman, Jon, Mark Frederick. AB, Hamilton Coll., 1922; student, U. Pa., 1922-23; MA, Harvard U., 1924; B.L.S., Western Res. U., 1933. Instr. English, Ohio Wesleyan U., 1924-26; police reporter Cleve. Press, 1926-27; instr. English, Western Res. U., 1928-35; librarian Antioch Coll., 1935-65, librarian emeritus, from 1965; mem. editorial bd. Antioch Rev., 1941—42, from 1958, chmn., 1943-58, editor, 1974-77. Library adviser Social Sci. Library, U. Rangoon, Burma, 1958-60; staff Study for Ford Found. Policy and Program, 1949; cons. program library orgn. Ford Found., 1964; vis. scholar Univ. Center, Atlanta, 1963 Author: chpts. The Administration of the College Library, 1944, Mexican Library, 1969, Southeast Asia: Bibliographic Directions, 1974; editor: Antioch Rev. Anthology, 1953, Freedom of Communication, 1954; contbr. articles to profl. jours. Judge Nonfiction Nat. Book Award, 1955; Ford Found. grantee for bibliog. research S.E. Asia, 1962-63; Ford Found. library cons. Faculty of Exact and Natural Scis., U. Buenos Aires, 1964-71 Mem. Ohio Library Assn. (pres. 1948-49, Hall of Fame 1981), ALA (council 1948-51, 56-58, exec. sec. intellectual freedom com. 1952-56), Am. Coll. and Research Libraries, ACLU, John Dewey Soc. Home: Painesville, Ohio. Died 1991.

**BJORK, KENNETH O.,** retired history professor; b. Enderlin, ND, July 19, 1909; s. Theodore S. and Martha (Arneson) Bjork; m. Thora Lie, Apr. 1, 1960; children: Kenneth T., Arnold L., Jon T.; children: Herum P., Mark P. 1 stepchild, Ellen. BA, St. Olaf Coll., 1930; MA, U. Wis., 1931, PhD, 1935; PhD (hon.), U. Oslo, 1976. Asst. prof. history U. Mont., Havre, 1935—37; asst. prof. St. Olaf Coll., Northfield, Minn., 1937—39, assoc. prof., 1939—44, prof., 1944—74, chmn. dept. history, 1960—65, prof. emeritus, from 1974. Vis. assoc. prof. U. Nebr., Lincoln, 1938, Lincoln, 1940, U. Mich., Ann Arbor, 1940—41, U. Wis., Madison, 1943—44; editor Norwegian-Am. Hist. Assn., Northfield, 1960—80, pres., 1973—75, editor emeritus, from 1980; Rockefeller Found. rep. to prof. U. East Africa, 1965—67. Author: Saga in Steel and Concrete, 1947, West of the Great Divide, 1958; contbr. articles to profl. jours. Chmn. Gov.'s Com. Refugee Relief, State Minn., 1955—58. Decorated Knight 1st Class Order St. Olav (Norway); Social Sci. Rsch. Coun. fellow, 1947—48, 1951—52, Fulbright scholar, 1959—60. Democrat. Lutheran. Died Aug. 11, 1991.

**BJÖRK, VIKING OLOV,** cardiothoracic surgeon, educator; b. Sunnansjö, Sweden, Dec. 3, 1918; s. Karl Adolf and Erika Louisa (Wikström) B.; m. Ingegerd Ebba Christina Laurell; children: Agneta, Christina, Anne (dec.), Anders. Lic. Medicine, Lund U., Sweden, 1944; MD, Karolinska Inst., Stockholm, 1948; MD (hon.), Aristoteles U., Thessaloniki, Greece, 1978, Semmelweis U., Budapest, Hungary, 1983. Intern Surg. Clinic, U. Hosp., Lund, 1944; clin. asst. Bromptons Hosp. for Diseases of Chest, London, 1945; resident surgery Sabbatsberg Hosp., Stockholm, 1946-49, resident Surg. Clinic, 1951; chief asst. thoracic surgery Sabbatsberg and Karolinska hosps., Stockholm, 1952-57; assoc. prof. thoracic surgery Karolinska Inst., Stockholm, 1949; prof. thoracic surgery U. Uppsala, Sweden, 1962, chief thoracic surgery, 1958-66; prof. thoracic & cardiovascular surgery Karolinska Inst., Stockholm, 1966-83, prof., 1983—2009; chief thoracic and cardiovascular surgery Karolinska Hosp., Stockholm, 1966-83; dir. rsch. Heart Inst. of Desert, Eisenhower Med. Ctr., Rancho Mirage, Calif., 1983-90. Physician, prof. on contract U. Siena, Italy, 1982; vis. prof. thoracic and cardiac surgery U. So. Calif., L.A., 1984-90; vis. prof. cardiac surgery U. Siena, 1984; hon. prof. surgery U. Guayaquil, Ecuador, 1981. Author: Die

Behandlung der tuberkulosen Lungenkaverne nach Monaldi, 1943, Bronchiogenic carcinoma, 1947, Brain Perfusions in Dogs With Artifically Oxygenated Blood, 1948; chief editor Scandinavian Jour. Thoracic and Cardiovascular Surgery, 1967-83; contbr. articles to profl. jours. Bd. dirs. Heineman Med. Rsch. Ctr., Charlotte, N.C., 1986. Recipient Swedish-Am. Found. Zorn scholarship, 1950, Knight of St. Charles, Monaco, 1957, Royal Order of No. Star, Sweden, 1966, Commendatore nell ordine merito della Republica Italiana, 1974, Disting. Physician award, 1979. Fellow German Surg. Assn., Soc. Thoracic and Cardiovascular Surgery of Gt. Britain and Ireland, Am. Surg. Assn. (hon.), Am. Coll. Cardiology (hon.), Corespondant etranger dans la Ileme Divsn.; mem. Am. Assn. Thoracic Surgery (hon.), European Soc. Cardiovascular Surgery (pres. 1981-82), Scandinavian Assn. Thoracic and Cardiovascular Surgery (pres. 1982), Spanish Assn. Cardiovascular Surgery, Polish Surg. Assn., Italian Surg. Assn., Assn. Thoracic and Cardiovascular Surgeons Asia, Helenic Surg. Soc., Accademico nella Accademia Romana, Soc. de Chirurgie Thoracique et Cardio-Vasculaire de Langue Francaise, Brasilian Assn. Rsch. and Devel. Heart Surgery, Royal Australasian Coll. Surgeons (hon. mem. cardiothoracic surgery divsn. 1987). Lutheran. Avocations: slalom, cross country skiing, golf. Home: Danderyd, Sweden. Died Feb. 18, 2009.

**BJÖRKMAN, ANDERS ERIK GUSTAF,** retired engineering educator; b. Stockholm, May 4, 1920; arrived in Denmark, 1961; s. Carl-Gustaf A. and Ebba M.T. (Petterson) B.; m. Kerstin C. Odqvist, May 4, 1948; children: Cecilia, Agneta, Gunilla, Birgitte. MS in Chem. Engring., Royal Inst. Tech., Stockholm, 1942, PhD, 1948; DSc, Chalmers Inst. Tech., Gothenburg, Sweden, 1957. Rsch. asst. AB Kabi, Stockholm, 1942-43; asst. prof. Royal Inst. Tech., Stockholm, 1944-48; R & D assoc. Billeruds AB, Säffle, Sweden, 1948-60; prof. chem. reaction engring., combustion, wood sci. & tech. Tech. U. Denmark, Lyngby, 1961-90, prof. emeritus, from 1990; pres. Internat. Acad. Wood Sci., Lyngby, 1993-96. Chmn. bd. Danish Paint Varnish Inst., Copenhagen, 1961-67; active Tech. Sci. Found., Copenhagen, 1967-70; treas. Internat. Union Pure Applied Chemistry, Oxford, Eng., 1984-91. Author: Hydrogenation of Sulfite Waste Liquor, 1950; contbr. articles to profl. jours. Active Swedish Ch., Copenhagen, 1961—. Recipient Albert Wallin prize Sci. Lit. Soc., Gothenburg, 1959, Gold medal Danish Industry, Copenhagen, 1991. Fellow Danish Acad. Tech. Scis., Royal Swedish Acad. Engring. Sci., Internat. Acad. Wood Sci. (Spl. Recognition award 1997). Lutheran. Achievements include extraction of lignin from milled wood, research on theories of pyrolysis/gasification of coal and pulping liquors, deactivation of catalysts, wood ultrastructure. Home: Rungsted, Denmark. Died Nov. 14, 2006.

**BLACK, MARILYN HAMMER,** non-profit organization executive; b. Sioux City, Iowa, Apr. 25, 1923; d. Franklin Wilfred and Ruth Marie (Gray) Hammer; m. Albert Scott Black; children: Barbara Black Miller, William Scott, Patricia Black Thompson. BA, U. Without Walls, 1975; MS, U. Houston-Clear Lake, 1980; PhD in Philosophy, Summit U., New Orleans, 1998. Dir. religious edn. St. Francis Episcopal Ch., Houston, 1968-72; program dir. NCCJ, Houston, 1972-80; exec. dir. Support Ctr. Houston, 1982-86; dir. C.G. Jung Edn. Ctr., Houston, 1987-91. Mem. mission coun. St. Francis Episcopal Ch., Houston, 1982. Mem. ASTD, Non-Profit Mgmt. Assn., Nat. Soc. Fund Raising Execs. (bd. dirs. 1982). Deceased.

**BLACKNER, BOYD ATKINS,** architect; b. Salt Lake City, Aug. 29, 1933; s. Lester Armond and Anna B.; m. Elizabeth Ann Castleton, June 4, 1955; children: Catherine Blackner Philpot, David, Elizabeth, Genevieve Blackner Tayler. B.Arch., B.F.A., U. Utah, 1956. Registered architect, Fla., Utah, Wyo. Asst. landscape architect Nat. Park Service, Mt. Rainier, Wash., 1956; job capt. Cannon, Smith & Gustavson, Salt Lake City, 1957, Hellmuth, Obata & Kassabaum, St. Louis, 1958-59, Caudill, Rowlett & Scott, Houston, 1959-60; project architect Victor A. Lundy, Sarasota, Fla., N.Y.C., 1960-63; pvt. practice architecture Salt Lake City, from 1963. Lectr. Salt Lake C.C., 1995; adv. coun., vis. juror, critic U. Utah Grad. Sch. Architecture, 1983-99; grad. program dept. landscape architecture and environ. planning Utah State U., 1977-92; region 8 adv. panel archtl. and engring. svcs. GSA, 1977-78; spkr. in field. Featured in (book) Sarasota School of Architecture, 1995; mem. editorial adv. bd.: Symposia mag, 1977-83; contbr. articles to mags. Vice-chmn. Utah Advanced Gift Heart Fund drive, 1964; co-chmn archtl. div. United Fund drive, 1964; mem. Salt Lake City City Walls Com., 1976-77, Salt Lake City Council for Arts, 1977-78, Utah Gov.'s Adv. Com. Low Income Housing, Utah Rev. Panel Emergency Energy Conservation Programs; adv. bd. Utah Citizens for Arts, Utah Soc. Autistic Children; dinner exec. com. Nat. Jewish Hosp., Nat. Asthma Ctr., Denver, 1983; bd. dirs. Utah State Divsn. History, Utah State Hist. Soc., 1989-97, U. Utah Med. Ctr. Found., 1998-2002; mem. Gov.'s Strategic Initiatives for History Task Force, 1991. Recipient Danforth Honor award, 1951, also numerous AIA awards including regional design awards for U. Utah Library Fountain, 1970, Westminster Coll. Fountain Plaza, 1972, Nat. award for Kearns/Daynes/Alley Annex, 1978, Western Mountain Region Hist. award of merit for Daynes/Kearns/Alley Annex, 1977, Am. Assn. Sch. Adminstrs. Exhibit award for Wilson Elementary Sch. Green River, Wyo., 1974, Award merit Producers' Council, Inc., 1978, award Nat. Lincoln Arc Welding Found., 1978, Urban Design award 3d Ann. Program, 1979, award of honor We. Mountain Region for HUD Low Income Housing Project, Salt Lake City Housing Authority, 1988, ACI award for Seven Canyon's Fountain, Liberty Park, Salt Lake City, 1994, Cmty. Svc award Salt Lake Found., 1995, Brownstone Bldg. Hist. Renovation award Salt Lake City Downtown Alliance Award Program, 1996, Honors in Arts award Salt Lake Area C. of C., 1997, Disting. Alumnus award U. Utah Founders Day Award Ceremony, 1997, people of vision award Prevent Blindness Utah, 1998, others. Fellow AIA (bd. dirs. Utah chpt. 1968, 71, sec. 1972-73, chmn. regional conf. 1974, pres. 1975-76; chmn. jury for Wyo. chpt. design awards program 1974, regional rep. to housing com., nat. honor award jury 1979, recorder nat. conv. 1982, mem. honor awards jury Western Mountain region 2000-02); mem. Salt Lake Area C. of C. (v.p. 1980-81, chmn. bd. 1982-83), U. Utah Alumni Assn. (bd. dirs. 1987-90), Salt Lake Swim and Tennis Club, Alta Club (bd. dirs. 1985-89, sec. 1991-92, pres. 1994-95), Rotary (treas. Salt Lake City club 1976-77, pres. 1979-80, v.p. 1987, pres. found. 1990-92). Died June 3, 2002.

**BLÁHA, VÁCLAV,** physician, researcher; b. Velešín, Česky Krumlov, Czech Republic, Mar. 17, 1931; s. Václav B. and Ludmila (Matušková) Bláhová; m. Alena Nápravníková Bláhová, June 14, 1958; children Adéla, Jitka Juřicová. Med. Univ. Dr., Charles U., Prague, Czech Republic, 1955; PhD, Charles U., 1968. Physician dept. internal medicine Hosp. Č. Krumlov, Czechoslovakia, 1955-60, Hosp. Č. Budějovice, Czechoslovakia, 1958-60, Inst. Railroad Health Cure, Czechoslovakia, 1960-64; researcher Inst. for Use of Radioisotopes in Medicine, Prague, 1964-68; tchr., researcher, asst. prof. dept. nuclear medicine Postgrad. Med. Sch., Prague, 1968-73; tchr., researcher Faculty of Medicine Charles U., Prague, from 1973, asst. prof. dept. nuclear medicine Faculty of Medicine, 1973-79, assoc. prof. dept. nuclear medicine Faculty of Medicine, 1979-90, prof. nuclear medicine, head dept. nuclear medicine Faculty of Medicine, 1979-90. Author: Nuclear Medicine in Health Cure, 1973, Cholescintigraphy, 1987, (with L.G. Colombetti) Adverse Reactions to Radiotracers In: Principles of Radiopharmacology Vol. II, (textbook) Nuclear Medicine, 1980, 85, 90, 96; contbr. over 100 articles to med. jours. Basic mil. duty, 1958-60. Recipient Honor prize for extraordinary merit of devel. of nuclear medicine Czechoslovak Soc. Nuclear Medicine, 1972. Mem. European Assn. Nuclear Medicine (founding mem. 1976—), Internat. Assn. Radiopharmacology (founding mem. 1978—). Avocation: classical music. Home: Prague, Czech Republic. Died Dec. 7, 2001.

**BLAIR, BETSY,** actress; b. Cliffside, NJ, Dec. 11, 1923; d. Willett Kidd and Frederica (Ammon) Boger; m. Gene Kelly, Sept. 20, 1941 (div. April 3, 1957); 1 child, Kerry Kelly Novick; m. Karel Reisz, Sept. 5, 1963 (dec. Nov. 25, 2002); stepchildren: Matthew, Toby, Barney. BA in Speech Therapy, Ctrl. School Speech & Drama, London U., 1979. Chorus dancer in Panama Hattie, 1940; N.Y.C. theatre appearances include The Beautiful People, 1941, The Glass Menagerie, 1944, My Fiddle Has Three Strings, 1945, Richard III, 1956, Face of a Hero, 1958; London appearances include The Trial of Mary Dugan, 1959, Tchin-Tchin, Paris & Spoleto, 1962 Spoon River Anthology, 1963, Danger Memory!, 1989; (films) The Guilt of Janet Ames, 1947, A Double Life, 1947, Another Part of the Forest, 1948, The Snake Pit, 1948, Mystery Street, 1950, No Way Out, 1950, Kind Lady, 1951, Marty, 1955 (Acad. award nomination 1955), Meeting in Paris, 1956, The Lovemaker, 1956, The Halliday Brand, 1957, The Cry, 1957, Lies My Father Told Me, 1960, Silver Spoon Set, 1960, All Night Long, 1962, Careless, 1962, Marry Me! Marry Me!, 1969, A Delicate Balance, 1973, Flight of the Spruce Goose, 1986, Descent Into Hell, 1986, Betrayed, 1988, The Hours, 2001; (TV movies) Othello, 1955, Marcus Welby, M.D.: A Holiday Affai, 1988; (TV appearances) The Philco Television Playhouse, 1950, Kraft Television Theatre, 1950, The Ford Theatre Hour, 1950, Goodyear Television Playhouse, 1957, ITV Television Playhouse, 1958, ITV Play of the Week, 1965, BBC Play of the Month (3 episodes), 1966-79, Shades of Greene, 1975, Tales of the Unexpected, 1980, Thirtysomething (2 episodes), 1989; (TV mini-series) Scarlett, 1994; author: The Memory of All That: Love and Politics in New York, Hollywood, and Paris, 2003 Mem. Actors Equity (Am. & British), Screen Actors Guild, Am. Film Acad., Coll. Speech Therapy. Avocations: books, bridge, swimming. Home: London NW3, England. Died Mar. 13, 2009.

**BLAIR, PHILIP JOSEPH,** lawyer; b. Dugway, Utah, Feb. 7, 1955; s. Philip T. and Mary Jo (Zurfluh) B.; m. Marilaine Sue Lister, Oct. 19, 1985. BA with Honors, U. Wis., 1976, JD, 1979. Bar: Wis.; cert. title ins. licensee, Wis., real estate broker, Wis. V.p. Shorewood Realty, Inc., Madison, 1978-81; assoc. Armstrong Law Offices, Ltd., Madison, 1981-82; atty., title officer Badger Abstract & Title Corp., Madison, from 1982. Lectr. in field. Alderman City of Madison, 1981-83, mem. plan commn., 1981-83, alcohol lic. com., 1986-89; mem. Civic Ctr. Commn., 1989—; mem. Commn. on Environment, 1991—; mem. govtl. affairs com. Greater Madison Bd. Realtors, 1986-90. Mem. Wis. Bar Assn., Dane County Bar Assn., U. Wis. Alumni Assn. (life award 1976). Lodges: KC (grand knight U. Wis. campus 1979-80). Roman Catholic. Avocations: world travel, golf. Home: Madison, Wis. Died 1994.

**BLAIR, TERRY,** state legislator; b. LaPorte, Ind., Nov. 23, 1946; m. Judy Blair; 4 children. BBA, Loyola U., 1969; MBA, U. Notre Dame, 1971. Employee Flagel, Huber & Flagel CPAs, 1978—79, T.L. Blair & Associates Inc., 1980—88; controller I Supply Co., 1988—90; pres. Buckeye Pools Inc., 1991—2014; mem. Dist. 38 Ohio House of Reps., 2009—14. Republican. Died June 26, 2014.

**BLAISE, JEAN EDMOND,** physicist; b. Raon-l'Etape, Vosges, France, June 16, 1921; s. Edmond and Alice (Kuehn) B.; m. Yvonne Marie Condé, Sept. 28, 1948; children: Véronique, François-Xavier, Cyrille. Licence ès Sciences, Nancy U., France, 1943; DSc, U. Paris, 1957. Researcher Ctr. Nat. de la Recherche Scientifique, Paris, 1946-90, Royal Holloway coll., U. London, Englefield Green, Eng., 1950-51; resident rsch. assoc. Argonne (Ill.) Nat. Lab., 1959-60, vis. scientist, 1967, 76; dir. rsch. Ctr. Nat. de la Recherche Scientifique, Paris, 1964-90, physicist lab., from 1990. Co-author: Energy Levels and Atomic Spectra of Actinides, 1992. Recipient William F. Meggers award, 1975. Fellow Optical Soc. Am. (emeritus); mem. French Phys. Soc., European Group of Atomic Spectroscopy (bd. dirs. 1972-75), European Phys. Soc. Roman Catholic. Home: Meudon, France. Died Sept. 25, 2006.

**BLAKE, HARRIS DURHAM,** state legislator; b. Jackson Springs, NC, Nov. 3, 1929; m. Barbara Blake; 1 child, Joy. Mem. Dist. 22 NC State Senate, NC, 2003—12. Mem. Appropriations on Health and Human Svcs. com., Appropriations/Base Budget com., Commerce com., Fin. com., Health Care com., State and Local Govt. com. Republican. Died June 9, 2014.

**BLANCHARD, EDMOND P.,** Canadian government official; b. Campbellton, NB, Can., May 31, 1954; s. Johne E. and Mary Rita (Hughes) B. B in Commerce, Dalhousie U., Halifax, NS, Can., 1975; LLB, Dalhousie U., Halifax, NS, 1978. Assoc. Tingley and Humphrey, Campbellton, 1979; ptnr. Tingley, Humphrey & Blanchard, Campbellton, Humphrey & Blanchard, Campbellton, 1989; min. of state for mines & energy Province of N.B., 1989-91, atty. gen., min. of justice, regional devel. corp. and intergovtl. affairs, 1991-94, min. justice, atty. gen., 1994-95, min. fin., min. state for quality, from 1995; MLA for Campbellton Riding, from 1999; judge Fed. Ct. Canada, 2000—04, Ct. Martial Appeal Ct. Canada, 2000—04, chief justice, 2004—14. Active Liberal Party-Campbellton, N.B. Mem. Law Soc. N.B., Can. Bar Assn. Roman Catholic. Home: Campbellton, Canada. Died June 27, 2014.

**BLANCHARD, FRANCIS,** former international organization official; b. Paris, July 21, 1916; s. Antoine and Marie (Seris) Blanchard; m. Marie-Claire Boue, Nov. 10, 1940; children: Philippe, Patrice, Attache, Gen. Degree, U. Paris, 1937. Residence of France, Tunis, Tunisia, 1940—41; civil adminstr. Ministry of Interior Govt. of France, 1942—47; with Internat. Labor Org., UN, from 1947, head repatriation dept., 1947—49, dir. planning and liaison, 1949—51, dep. chief manpower div., 1951—53, chief divsn., 1953—56, asst. dir. gen., 1956—68, dep. dir. gen., 1968—74, dir. gen., 1974—89. Died Dec. 9, 2009.

**BLANFORD, IRVING IVEY,** banker; b. Portsmouth, Va., Jan. 8, 1899; s. George Thomas and Claude Meredith (Sessoms) Blanford; m. Gladys Simmons Johnson, Sept. 7, 1935 (dec. 1966); children: Virginia Caroline Blanford Nicewander, Gladys Sessoms Blanford Godwin, Claudia Maria Blanford Hubbard. Student, Va. Mil. Inst., 1918. Radio operator Panama R.R., 2020; sec. Comml. Hardware Co., Norfolk, Va., 2022—25; salesman Chas. Syer & Co., Norfolk, 2026—28; food broker New Bern, NC, 2028—29; mgrs. rep. Nat. Sugar Refining Co., NJ, NYC, 1930—41; exec. dir. pub. housing City of New Bern, 1945—69; chmn. exec. com. Bank of New Bern, 1959—63, pres., 1962—72, dir., 1957—72. Dir. New Bern Morris Plan Co., 1943—57; chmn. local bd. NCNB, New Bern, from 1972. Mem. Centenary United Meth. Ch. Mem.: Dunes Club, Ea. Carolina Yacht Club (treas. 1956—57), Rotary Club (pres. 2028—29), New Bern Golf & Country Club, Shriners, Masons, Elks (exalted ruler 1938). Home: New Bern, NC. Died Sept. 8, 1989.

**BLANTON, JACK SAWTELLE,** oil industry executive; b. Shreveport, La., Dec. 7, 1927; s. William Neal and Louise (Wynn) B.; m. Laura Lee Scurlock, Aug. 20, 1949 (dec. August 6, 1999); children: Elizabeth Louise Blanton Wareing, Jack Sawtelle Jr., Eddy Scurlock; m. Lucinda B. Bailey, Oct. 14, 2000 (dec. March 2, 2002); m. Virginia Nelson, Nov. 30, 2002 BA, U. Tex., 1947, LLB, 1950. Bar: Tex. 1950. With Scurlock Oil Co., Houston, 1950-88, v.p., 1956-58, pres., 1958-83, chmn. bd., 1983-88; pres. Eddy Refining Co., Houston, 1988—2013. Chmn. bd. trustees Houston Endowment, Inc.; pres. Eddy Refining Co.; bd. dirs. Pogo Producing Co., Burlington No. Santa Fe, Inc. Past chmn. bd. trustees St. Luke's United Meth. Ch., Houston; past chmn. bd. regents U. Tex. System, 1985-89; past vice chmn., bd. dirs. Meth. Hosp., Houston. Mem. Nat. Petroleum Coun., Mid-Continent Oil and Gas Assn. (past pres.) Houston C. of C. (life), Sons Republic of Tex. (past pres. San Jacinto chpt.), Sam Houston Meml. Assn., Nat. Tennis Assn., U.S. Lawn Tennis Assn., Tex. Ind. Oil Producers and Refiners, Ex-Students Assn. U. Tex. (past pres.), Greater Houston Partnership (chmn. 1985-86), Delta Kappa Epsilon, Phi Delta Phi, Phi Alpha Delta. Clubs: Houston (Houston) (past pres.), River Oaks Country (Houston); El Dorado Country (Palm Springs, Calif.). Died Dec. 28, 2013.

**BLASER, ROBIN FRANCIS,** poet, editor, educator; b. Denver, May 18, 1925; Attended, U. Calif., Berkeley, 1944—55. Asst. catalogue libr. Widener Libr., Harvard U., 1955—59; with English dept. Simon Fraser U., 1966—86, prof. emeritus, 1986—2009; instr. summer writing program Naropa U., 1995, 2000; writer-in-residence Temple U., 2002. Author: The Moth Poem, 1964, Cups, 1968, Les Chimères: Translations of Nerval for Fran Herndon, 1969, Image Nations 1-12 & The Stadium of the Mirror, 1974, Image Nations 13 & 14, Luck Unluck Oneluck, Sky-stone, Suddenly, Gathering, 1975, Harp Trees, 1977, Image Nation 15: The Lacquerhouse, 1981, Syntax, 1983, The Faerie Queene and The Park, 1987, Pell Mel, 1988, The Holy Forest, 1993, Nomad, 1995, Wanders, with Meredith Quartermain, 2002, The Holy Forest: Collected Poems of Robin Blaser, 2007 (Griffin Poetry prize for Can. poetry, 2008), (essays) The Fire, 1974, The Metaphysics of Light, 1974, The Practice of Outside, 1975, The Violets: Charles Olson and Alfred North Whitehead, 1983, My Vocabulary Did This To Me, 1987, Poetry and Positivisms, 1989, The Elf of It, 1992, The Recovery of the Public World and Among Afterthoughts on This Occasion, 1993, Here Lies the Woodpecker Who Was Zeus, 1995, Thinking about Irreparables, a talk, 2000, The Fire: Collected Essays of Robin Blaser, 2006, (opera) The Last Supper, 2000; editor: The Collected Books of Jack Spicer, 1975, Imaginary Letters, 1979, Particular Accidents: Selected Poems, 1980, Infinite Worlds: The Poetry of Louis Dudek, 1988; co-editor (with Rob Dunham): Art and Reality: A Casebook of Concern, 1986; co-editor: (with Evan Alderson and Harold Coward) Reflections on Cultural Policy, Past, Present and Future, 1993. Mem.: Order of Can. Died May 7, 2009.

**BLASS, RONALD THEODORE,** advertising executive; b. Bklyn. m. Yvonne M. Blass; children: Kenneth L., Kathy A., Diane. Founder, exec. advertising owner & chmn. bd. dirs. Blass Communications LLC (formerly R.T. Blass, Inc.), Old Chatham, NY. Adv. bd. Indsl. Develop. Columbia County. Mem. USN, WWII. Methodist. Died Jan. 18, 2001.

**BLATT, SIDNEY JULES,** psychology professor, psychoanalyst, investigator; b. Phila., Oct. 15, 1928; s. Harry and Fannie (Feld) Blatt; m. Ethel Shames, Feb. 1, 1951; children: Susan, Judith, David. BS, Pa. State U., 1950, MS, 1952; PhD, U. Chgo., 1957; postgrad., Western New Eng. Inst. for Psychoanalysis, 1972. Postdoctoral fellow Neuropsychiat. Inst. of U. Ill. Med. Ctr., Psychiat. and Psychosomatic Inst. of Michael Reese Hosp., 1957—59; instr. Univ. Coll. U. Chgo., 1959-60; mem. faculty Yale U., New Haven, 1960—2011, prof. psychiatry & psychology, 1974—2011, prof. emeritus, 2011—14; mem. faculty Western New Eng. Inst. for Psychoanalysis, 1975—88; Sigmund Freud prof. psychoanalysis Hebrew U., 1988—89. Ayala and Sam Zacks prof. art history Hebrew U., 1988—89; Fulbright sr. rsch. fellow, 1988—89; mem. Rsch. Fellowship Rev. Panel NIMH, 1966—69, mem. Psychology Tng. Rev. Panel, 1969—74; vis. prof. Ben Gurion U., 1992, 1996, Univ. Coll., London, 1999—2003, Cath. U. Leuven, 2003, George Washington U., 2006, Bar Ilan U., 2006; Fulbright sr. specialist, from 2006. Author: Experiences of Depression: Theoretical, Research and Clinical Perspectives, 2004, Polarities of Experience: Relatedness and Self-Definition in Personality Development, Psychopathology and Therapeutic process., 2008; co-author (with J. Allison and C. Zimet): Interpretation of Psychological Tests, 1968, 2d edit., 1988; co-author: (with C.M. Wild) Schizophrenia: A Developmental Analysis, 1976; co-author: (with E.S. Blatt) Continuity and Change in Art: The Development of Modes of Representation, 1984; co-author: (with R.Q. Ford) Therapeutic Change: An Object Relations Perspective, 1994; co-editor (with D. Diamond): Attachment Research and Psychoanalysis, vols. I-III, 1999—2003; co-editor: (with Z.V. Segal) The Self in Emotional Distress, 1993; co-editor: (with J. Corveleyn, P. Luyten) The Theory and Treatment of Depression: Towards a Dynamic Interaction Model., 2005; co-editor: (with D. Diamond & J. Lichtenberg) Attachment and Sexuality. Recipient Disting. Contbns. to Rsch. award, Assn. Med. Sch. Profs. Psychology, 1995, APA Divsn. Psychoanalysis, 2000, Founders' Disting. Tchg. prize, We. New Eng. Psychoanalytic Soc., 2001, Hans H. Strupp Disting. Contbns. to Psychoanalysis award, 2000, Bruno Klopfer and Marguerite R. Hertz awards for dist. contbns. to psychol. assessment, Soc. for Personality Assessment, 1989, 1994, Disting. Sci. Contbns. award, APA Divsn. Clin. Psychology, 2004, Otto Weininger award, Can. Psychol. Assn., 2006; named Disting. Practitioner of Psychology, Nat. Acad. Practice, 1983; fellow Found. Fund Rsch. in Psychiatry, 1961—64. Mem.: AAUP, AAAS, APA, Soc. Personality Assessment (pres. 1984—86), American Psychoanalytic Assn. (Outstanding Sci. Paper prize 2005, Mary S. Sigourney award 2006). Home: Hamden, Conn. Died May 11, 2014.

**BLAZ, BEN (VICENTE TOMÁS BLAZ GARRIDO),** former United States Representative from Guam; b. Agana, Guam, Feb. 14, 1928; m. Ann Evers; children: Mike, Tom. BS, U. Notre Dame, 1951; MA, George Washington U., 1963; LLD (hon.), U. Guam, 1974. Commd. 2d lt. USMC, 1951, advanced through grades to brig. gen., chief UN & Maritime Matters Branch Internat. Negotiations Divsn., 1972—75, dep. chief of staff for reserve affairs, 1977—80, ret., 1980; prof. U. Guam, Mangilao, 1983-84; del. from Guam US House of Representatives, 1985—93. Decorated Legion of Merit, Bronze star with Combat V, Vietnamese Cross of Gallantry; recipient Freedoms Found. Medal of Freedom, 1969, Disting. Alumnus award U. Notre Dame, 1988, Asian-American award for Public Svc., 1992. Republican. Died Jan. 8, 2014.

**BLEJER, HECTOR P.,** epidemiologist; b. Caracas, Venezuela, Dec. 17, 1933; arrived in U.S., 1965; s. Luis E. and Zoraida (Prieto) Blejer. BSc, McGill U., 1956, MD, CM, 1958; DIH, U. Toronto, 1963. Diplomate Am. Bd. Preventive Medicine. Asst. med. dir. Imperial Life Co., Toronto, 1963—64; resident Denne Nicholls Clinic, Toronto, 1964—65; chief occupl. health Calif. Dept. Pub. Health, LA, 1965—74; dep. dir. field studies div. Nat. Inst. Occupl. Safety and Health, Cin., 1975—76; dir. occupl. health dept. City of Hope Med. Ctr., Duarte, Calif., 1976—78; practice medicine, specializing in occupl. medicine, toxicology and epidemiology LA, from 1979. Cons. Western Airlines, Met. Water Dist. So. Calif., Barlow Hosp.; ecologist Panam. Health Orgn., 1974—75; occupl. med. cons. U.S. Labor Dept., 1977, 1978, 1979, 1980, 1985; cons. Nat. Acad. Scis., 1972—74. Contbr. numerous articles to sci. jours., chpts. to books; author: (med. film) Asbestosis, 1983. Fellow: Am. Coll. Preventive Medicine, Am. Occupl. Med. Assn., Am. Acad. Occupl. Medicine; mem.: Western Occupl. Med. Assn., Am. Conf. Govtl. Indsl. Hygienists (hon.), N.Y. Acad. Scis., Soc. Occupl. and Environ. Health. Died Jan. 30, 1990.

**BLIN-STOYLE, ROGER JOHN,** physicist; b. Leicester, Eng., Dec. 24, 1924; s. Cuthbert Basil and Ada Mary (Nash) Bl-St.; m. Audrey Elizabeth Balmford, Aug. 30, 1949; children: Anthony Roger, Helena Anne. BA, Oxford U., Eng., 1949, MA, DPhil, 1951; DSc (hon.), U. Sussex, Eng., 1990. Rsch. fellow U. Oxford, 1951-53, sr. rsch. officer, 1954-62, fellow, lectr. physics Wadham Coll., 1956-62; lectr. in mathematical physics U. Birmingham, Eng., 1953-54; prof. theoretical physics U. Sussex, Brighton, Eng., 1962-88, founding sci. dean, 1962-68, dep. vice-chancellor, 1970-72, pro-vice-chancellor of sci., 1977-79, hon. prof. physics, 1988-90, emeritus prof. physics, from 1990. Chmn. Standing Conf of Profs. Physics, London, 1974-76, Sch. curriculum Devel. Com., London, 1983-88; pres. Inst. of Physics, 1990-92, Assoc. of Sci. Edn., 1993-94. Author: Theories of Nuclear Moments, 1957, Fundamental Interactions and the Nucleus, 1973, Nuclear and Particle Physics, 1991, Eureka! Physics of Particles, Matter and the Universe, 1997; contbr. articles to nuclear physics edn. to various publs. Lt. Royal Corps Signal, 1943-46, ETO. Hon. fellow Wadham Coll., 1987. Fellow Royal Soc., Inst. Physics (Rutherford medal and prize 1976). Avocation: music. Home: Lewes, England. Died Jan. 31, 2007.

**BLOOM, HOWARD O.,** specialty gifts wholesaler; b. Essex, Iowa, June 4, 1913; s. Chancie Paul and Lena Wilma (Hagedorn) B.; m. Charlotte J. McDiarmid, Aug. 7, 1965; stepchildren: Janet Thompson, Robert McDiarmid; children from previous marriage: Larry Howard, Dennis. Student pub. schs., Estherville, Iowa. With Estherville Creamery, 1929-33, Maytag Co., Newton, Iowa, 1933-36, Skelgas & Estate Stove Co., Mo. and Ind., 1936-40; dist. rep. George W. Helme Co., NYC, 1940-45; owner, operator The Hob-Dee Enterprises, Hawarden, Iowa, 1945-69, pres., from 1974; owner Shar-Jan, Hawarden, from 1986. Mem. Direct Selling Legion, Upper Midwest Art and Gift Assn., Nat. Assn. Fin. Cons., New Inventions Research Assn., Assn. Retarded Children, Nat. Ret. Tchrs. Assn, Hawarden C. of C. Clubs: Country, Top Notchers. Democrat. Methodist. Died Feb. 1992.

**BLOOMFIELD, LINCOLN PALMER,** political scientist; b. Boston, July 7, 1920; m. Irirangi Pamela Coates, 1948; children: Pamela, Lincoln Jr., Diana. SB, Harvard U., 1941, MPA, 1952, PhD, 1956. With US Dept. State, Washington, 1946-57, spl. asst. to asst. sec., 1952-57; sr. staff ctr. for internat. studies MIT, Cambridge, 1957—99, prof. polit. sci., 1963-91, prof. emeritus, from 1991; dir. global issues NSC, Washington, 1979-80. Mem. Presdl. Commn. 25th Anniversary UN, 1970—71; vis. prof. Grad. Inst. Advanced Internat. Studies, Geneva, 1965, 1972, 1977, 1979, Salzburg Seminar faculty, 1982, 1986, 1992, 1995; moderator State Dept. seminar fgn. policy and global issues, 1992—99. Author: Evolution or Revolution?, 1957, The UN and U.S. Foreign Policy, rev. edit., 1967, In Search of American Foreign Policy, 1974, The Foreign Policy Process: A Modern Primer, 1982, Accidental Encounters With History, 2005; editor (co-author): International Military Forces, 1964, Kruschchev and the Arms Race, 1966, Outer Space: Prospects for Man and Society, rev. edit., 1968, Controlling Small Wars, 1969, The Management of Global Disorder, 1987, Prospects for Peacemaking, 1987, Managing International Conflict, 1997; host (TV series) Monitor Channel Fifty Years Ago Today, 1989—92. Moderator First Parish Ch., Cohasset, Mass., 2000—09; bd. dirs. Unitarian-Universalist Assn., 1958—64, World Affairs Coun. Boston, 1975—2002, World Peace Found., Nat. Def. U., 1984—89, Can. Inst. Internat. Peace and Security, 1989—92. Lt. USNR, 1942—46. Recipient Chase prize, Harvard U., 1956, EDUCOM prize, Disting. Software, 1988, New Eng. Emmy award, 1992, Disting. Vis. Lectr. award, State Dept. Fgn. Svc. Inst., 1995, Leadership award, UN Assn. Greater Boston, 1997; Littauer fellow, 1952, Rockefeller fellow, 1954, 1975, Internat. Leadership Forum fellow, 2006—12. Fellow: World Acad. Art and Sci.; mem.: Coun. Fgn. Rels., Harvard Club NY, Cohasset Golf Club. Home: Cohasset, Mass. Died Oct. 30, 2013.

**BLOW, DAVID MERVYN,** biophysics educator, researcher; b. June 27, 1931; s. Edward Mervyn and Dorothy Laura Blow; m. Mavis Sears, 1955; Julian and Elizabeth PhD, Cambridge U. Med. Research Coun. Unit for Study of Molecular Biol. Systems at Cambridge U., 1959-62, Cambridge Lab. Molecular Biology, 1962-77; lectr. and fellow Trinity Coll.-Cambridge U., 1968-77; prof. biophysics Imperial Coll.-U. London, 1977—2004; dean Royal Coll. Sci. Imperial Coll., London, 1981-84; head dept. physics Imperial Coll., 1991—94. Author: The use of x-ray difraction in the study of proteins, 1980, Outline of crystallography for biologists, 2002; contbr. articles and revs. to sci. jours. Fulbright scholar NIH and MIT, 1957-59; recipient CIBA medal Biochem. Soc., 1967, Charles Léopold Meyer prize, 1979, Wolf prize in chemistry, Wolf Found., Israel, 1987. Fellow Royal Soc., Brit. Crystallographic Assn. (founding mem., pres. 1984-87); mem. Biochem. Soc., Brit. Biophys. Soc.(hon. mem.), European Molecular Biology Orgn., Associé étranger, Académie des Scis. Achievements include development of x-ray diffraction methods for determination of protein structure; first crystal structure of a proteinase enzyme; microbatch method for protein crystallization. Died June 8, 2004.

**BLUE, ROSE,** writer, educator; b. NYC, 1931; d. Irving and Frieda (Rosenberg) Bluestone. BA, Bklyn. Coll., 1953; postgrad., Bank St. Coll. Edn., 1967. Tchr. N.Y.C. Pub. Schs., from 1967. Writing cons. Bklyn. Coll. Sch. Edn., 1981-83. Author: A Quiet Place, 1969, Black, Black Beautiful Black, 1969, How Many Blocks Is The World, 1970, Bed-Stuy Beat, 1970, I Am Here (Yo Estoy Aqui), 1971, A Month of Sundays, 1972, Grandma Didn't Wave Back, 1972 (teleplay 1983), Nikki 108, 1973, We are Chicano, 1973, The Preacher's Kid, 1975, Seven Years from Home, 1976, The Yo Yo Kid, 1976, The Thirteenth Year, 1977, Cold Rain on the Water, 1979, My Mother The Witch, 1981 (teleplay 1984), Everybody's Evy, 1985, Heart to Heart, 1986, Goodbye Forever Tree, 1987, The Secret Papers of Camp Get Around, 1988, Barbara Bush First Lady, 1990, Colin Powell Straight to the Top, 1991, Barbara Jordan-Politician, 1992, defending Our Country, 1993, Working Together Against Hate Groups, 1993, People of Peace, 1994, The White House Kids, 1995, whoopi Goldberg Entertainer, 1995, Bring Me A Memory, 1996, Good Yontif, 1997, Who's That In the White House?, 1998, Staying Out of Trouble in a Troubled Family, 1998, Madeline Albright U.S. Secretary of State, 1999, You're the Boss: Positive Attitude and Work Ethic, 1999, Who Lived In The House Divided, 2000, Chris Rock, 2001, Benjamin Banneker--Mathematician and Stargazer, 2001, Monica Seles, 2002; lyricist: Drama of Love, 1964, Let's Face It, 1961, Give Me a Break, 1962, My Heartstrings Keep Me Tied To You, 1963, Homecoming Party, 1966; contbg. editor: Tchr. mag., Day Care mag. Mem. PEN, Authors Guild Am., Authors League Am., Mensa, Profl. Womens Caucus, Broadcast Music, Inc. Died 2006.

**BLUHM, BARBARA JEAN,** communications agency executive; b. Chgo., Mar. 5, 1925; d. Maurice L. and Clara (Miller) B. Student Coll. William and Mary, 1943-45; BS, U. Wis., 1947. Exec. tng. program Carson Pirie Scott & Co., Chgo., 1947-52; home economist Lever Bros. Co., Chgo., 1952-57; field rep. The Merchandising Group, Chgo., 1957-62, v.p. NYC, 1962-82, pres., 1982-87, chmn., 1987-90. Publicity chmn. James Lenox House Assn., NYC, 1980—90; active Coll. Club of Venice, Venice Art Ctr., Friends of the Venice Libr. Mem. Venice Yacht Club. Republican. Presbyterian. Home: Oakton, Va. Died Nov. 14, 2012.

**BLUMENTHAL, MICHAEL,** ophthalmologist, researcher; b. Tiberias, Israel, Nov. 11, 1935; s. Zvi Hans and Ruth (Erlich) B.; m. Naomi Gruenbaum; children: Daria, Uri, Boaz. Lectr. Hadassah Med. Sch., Jerusalem, 1966-68, sr. lectr., 1972-74; assoc. prof. faculty health scis. Ben Gurion U. Negev. Beer-Sheba, Israel, 1974-76; assoc. prof. Tel Aviv U., from 1977, head of ophthamology dept., 1984, prof. ophthalmology, 1985; head opthalmology dept. Head ein-Tal Eye Ctr., from 1985. Head of eye care Fgn. Aid to Africa Ministry Fgn. Affairs, Malawi, 1964, Dar-es-Salaam, Tanzania, 1964-65. Editor in chief The Eye: The Journal of the Israeli Ophthalmol. Soc., 1985. Cons. Ministry of Health, Jerusalem. Ophthalmology fellow Hadassah Med. Sch., 1968-70; Am. Coll. Surgeons grant, San Francisco, 1969, XXI Internat. Congress Ophthalmology, Mex., 1970, Internat. Congress Regional Ophthalmology, Can., 1970, Am. Acad. grant, 1975. Mem. European Soc. Cataract and Refractive Surgeons (pres. 1996-98), Israeli Eye Soc., Internat. Intraocular Lens Club, Am. Intraocular Implant Soc., French Ophthalmology Soc. Home: Ramat Efal, Israel. Died Apr. 28, 2007.

**BOAS, FRANK,** retired lawyer; b. Amsterdam, North Holland, The Netherlands, July 22, 1930; arrived in U.S., 1940; s. Maurits and Sophie Boas; m. Edith Louise Bruce, June 30, 1981 (dec. July 1992); m. Jean Scripps, Aug. 6, 1993 (div. Dec. 2000). AB cum laude, Harvard U., 1951, JD, 1954. Bar: US Dist. Ct. DC 1955, US Ct. Appeals (DC cir.) 1955, US Supreme Ct. 1958. Atty. Office of the Legal Adviser US State Dept., Washington, 1957-59; pvt. practice Brussels and London, 1959-79; of counsel Patton, Boggs & Blow, Washington, 1975-80; pres. Frank Boas Found., Inc., Cambridge, Mass., 1980—2005; asst. to Judge Manley O. Hudson United Nations Internat. Law Comm., 1953. Mem. US delegation UN Conf. Law of Sea, Geneva, 1958, 1960; hon. sec. Am. C. of C., Belgium, 1966—78; bd. dirs. Found. European Orgn. Rsch. and Treatment Cancer, Brussels, 1978—87, Paul-Henri Spaak Found., Brussels, from 1981, East-West Ctr. Found., Honolulu, 1990—2001, Law of Sea Inst., Honolulu, 1992—97, Pacific Forum CSIS, Honolulu, from 1996, Honolulu Acad. Arts, from 1997, U. Hawaii Found., 2000—09; vice chmn. Commn. Ednl. Exch., Brussels, 1980—87; mem. vis. com. Harvard Law Sch., 1987—91, Ctr. Internat. Affairs, 1988—2005; mem., bd. regents candidate adv. coun. U. Hawaii, 2008—09; v.p. Hawaii Army Mus. Soc., from 2011. With US Army, 1955—57. Decorated officer Order of Leopold II Belgium, comdr. Order of Merit Luxembourg, comdr. Order of Crown, comdr. Order of Leopold Belgium; recipient Tribute of Appreciation award, US State Dept., 1981, Harvard Alumni Assn. award, 1996, Resolution of Appreciation, Hawaii House Reps., 2002, Nat. Jefferson award for Outstanding Pub. Svc., 2004, Hawaii award, Am. Bd. Trial Advs., 2005, Bachman Meml. award, Pacific and Asian Affairs Coun., 2006, C. Frederick Shutte award, Hawaii State Bar Assn., 2007; fellow, Hawaii Pacific U., 2004. Mem.: ABA, Honlulu Social Sci. Assn., Honolulu Com. Fgn. Rels., Pacific and Asian Affairs Coun. (pres. 1998—2004), Fed. DC Bar Assn., Am. and Common Market Club (Brussels pres. 1981—85), Travellers Club (London), Pacific, Outrigger Canoe Clubs (Honolulu). Home: Honolulu, Hawaii. Died Mar. 16, 2013.

**BOBER, PHYLLIS PRAY,** humanities educator, art historian; b. Portland, Maine, Dec. 2, 1920; d. Melvin Francis and Lea Arlene (Royer) Pray; m. Harry Bober, Aug. 11, 1943 (div. June 1973); children: Jonathan Pray, David Hall. BA, Wellesley Coll., 1941; MA, NYU Inst. Fine Arts, 1943, PhD, 1946; LHD (hon.), U. Rome, 1993, Bowdoin Coll., 1999. From instr. to lectr., curator Wellesley (Mass.) Coll., 1947-49, 51-54; tchg. assoc. Sch. Arch. MIT, Cambridge,

Mass., 1951-53; rsch. assoc. NYU Inst. Fine Arts, NYC, 1954-73; chair, founder dept. fine arts Univ. Coll. NYU, 1967-73; prof. fine arts NYU, 1970-73; dean Grad. Sch. Arts and Scis. Bryn Mawr (Pa.) Coll., 1973-80, prof. history of art, prof. classical/Near Ea. archaeology, 1973-91, Leslie Clark prof. in humanities, 1987-91, prof. emerita, from 1991. Founder, dir. Census of Antique Works of Art Known to the Renaissance, Warburg Inst., U. London, 1947-84; staff mem. NYU Excavations in Samothrace, 1948, 49, 72; mem. Grad. Record Exam. Bd., Princeton, N.J., 1976-80; rep. to ACLS (Amer. Counc. of Learned Societies), 1982-88; Mellon vis. prof. of fine arts U. Pitts., 1986; co-dir. NEH Summer Seminar for Coll. Tchrs., Rome, 1990; vis. prof. dept. edn. Am. Acad., Rome, 1999; Ruth and Clarence Kennedy prof. in the Reniassance Smith Coll., 2000. Author: Drawings After the Antique by Amico Aspertini, 1957, Art, Culture and Cuisine, 1999; co-author: Renaissance Artists and Antique Sculpture, 1986, 90, The Rotunda of Arsinoe, vol. III, 1992; contbr. articles to profl. jours. Bd. dirs. Med. Coll. Pa., 1979-97; pres. Pa. Assn. Grad. Schs., 1977-78, Northeastern Assn. Grad. Schs., 1978-79; Dem. committeewoman, 1986-94. Sr. fellow Soc. for Humanities, Cornell U., 1984, corr. fellow German Archaeol. Inst., 1958—, fellow Accademia dei Lincei Rome, 1996—, Guggenheim fellow, 1979-80, hon. fellow Warburg Inst., U. London, 1993—; Appleton Eminent scholar in the Arts, Fla. State U., 1998. Mem. Am. Philosophical Soc., Coll. Art Assn. (bd. dirs. 1982-90, pres. 1988-90), Renaissance Soc. Am. (bd. dirs. 1982-85, pres. 1983-84), Archaeol. Inst. Am., Internat. Assn. Classical Archaeology, Dames d'Escoffier, Culinary Historians of Boston, Italian Art Soc., Culinary Soc. Phila., Amer-Italy Soc. Unitarian Universalist. Avocations: cooking, doll house miniatures, ecology. Died May 30, 2002.

**BOCCIA/STACY, JUDY ELAINE,** home health agency executive, consultant; b. San Diego, Aug. 29, 1955; d. Robert Garrett and Jerry Athalee (Carruth) Stacy; 1 child, Jennifer Lynn. BSN, Calif. State U., San Diego, 1978. RN, Calif.; lic. pub. health nurse, Calif. Staff nurse Univ. Hosp., U. Calif., San Diego, 1978-80, 81-82, Moffitt Hosp., San Francisco, 1980—81, Humana Hosp., Huntington Beach, Calif., 1982—84; intravenous and hospice vis. nurse Town & Country Nursing, Garden Grove, Calif., 1984—85; vis. nurse Vis. Nurse Assn., Orange, Calif., 1985—86; v.p. Doctors and Nurse Med. Mgmt., Newport Beach, Calif., 1986—89; dir. nursing HMSS, So. Calif., 1989—90; pres. Premier Care, Irvine, 1990—91, Homelife Nursing & Staff-builders, Lake Forest, Calif., 1991—96. Cons., Calif., 1987—1996; pres., adminstr. Homelife Nursing-Staff Builders, O.C., 1991-97; AIDS educator; presenter in field; guest radio spkr. Parish nurse. Mem. Oncology Nursing Soc., Intravenous Nurse Soc., Calif. Nurses Assn. Avocations: singing, gardening. Deceased.

**BOCOCK, MACLIN,** writer; b. Baton Rouge, Dec. 21, 1920; d. James Branch and June Lyndon Bocock; m. Albert J. Guerard, July 11, 1941 (dec. Nov. 2000); children: Collot Guerard, Nini Guerard, Lundie Guerard. BA, Radcliffe Coll., 1942. Reader Harvard U. Press, Cambridge, Mass., 1942—58; lectr. Stanford (Calif.) U., 1970-71, NEH, Washington, 1972. Author: Heaven Lies About, 1993, A Citizen of the World, 1999; co-author: The Personal Voice, 1964; contbr. short stories for periodicals. Recipient PEN syndicated Fiction award. Died Dec. 13, 2002.

**BODENSIECK, ERNEST JUSTUS,** mechanical engineer; b. Dubuque, Iowa, June 1, 1923; s. Julius Henry and Elma (Sommer) B.; m. Margery Elenore Sande, Sept. 9, 1943; children: Elizabeth Bodensieck Eley, Stephen (dec.). BSME, Iowa State U., 1943. Registered profl. engr., Ariz. Project engr. TRW Inc., Cleve., 1943-57; engr. Gen. Electric, 1957—60; supr. rocket turbomachinery Rocketdyne divsn. Rockwell Internat., Canoga Park, Calif., 1967-60, supr. nuclear turbomachinery, 1964-70; advance gear engr. Gen. Electric Co., Lynn, 1960-64; asst. mgr. engine components Aerojet Nuclear Systems Co., Sacto., 1970-71; gear and bearing cons. AIResearch divsn. Garrett Corp., Phoenix, 1971-81; transmission cons. Bodensieck Engring. Co., Scottsdale, Ariz., 1981—2001. Patentee in field. Mem. ASME, AIAA, Soc. Automotive Engrs. (various coms.), Aircraft Industries Assn. (various coms.), Am. Gear Mfrs. Assn. (mem. aerospace, gear rating and enclosed epicyclic coms.), Nat. Soc. Profl. Engrs., Pi Tau Sigma. Lutheran. Deceased.

**BOERINGER, JAMES LESLIE,** music educator; b. Pitts., Pa., Mar. 4, 1930; s. Clyde Joseph and Mildred Elizabeth Boeringer; m. Grace Nocera Boeringer, Aug. 27, 1955; children: Lisa, Margaret Jane, Daniel Wilharm. Cert. AAGO Am. Guild of Ogranist 1953. Univ. organist U. SD, Vermillion, 1959—62, Okla. Bapt. U, Shawnee, 1962—64, Susquehanna U, Selinsgrove, Pa., 1964—80; dir. Moravian Music Found., Winston-Salem, NC, 1980—84; music dir. Ch. of the Pilgrims, Washington, 1985—2001, Messiah Luth. Ch., Germantown, Md., 2000—07. Editor (music): Complete Flute Solos, 1973; author: Morning Star, 1986; author: (editor) Organa Britannica, 1988. Recipient Philips Disting. Vis. Award, Haverford Coll., 1970. Avocations: architectural restorations, gardening, acting. Home: Silver Spring, Md. Died Jan. 12, 2014.

**BOGAERT, RAYMOND LEOPOLD,** historian, educator; b. Antwerp, Belgium, July 24, 1920; s. Walter Bogaert and Elodie Deconinck; m. Jose Natalie Heremans, Dec. 30, 1946; children: Marc Roger, Christiane Marie. MA in Classics, U. Ghent, Belgium, 1942; degree in secondary edn., U. Ghent, 1943, PhD in Classics, 1961. Tchr. Athenaeum, Kapellen, Belgium, 1946—61; from asst. to prof. U. Ghent, 1961—81, ordinary prof., 1981—85. Author: Les origines antiques de la banque de dépôt, 1966, Banques et banquiers dans les cités grecques, 1968, Epigraphica III: Texts on Bankers, Banking and Credit in the Greek World, 1976, Trapezitica Aegyptiaca, 1994. Recipient 1st laureate of nat. univ. contest, Ministry of Edn., 1943, 1st laureate of nat. contest for travel, 1962, Hon. award, Internat. Colloquim on Banks, Loans and Fin. Archives in Ancient World, 2006; named Grand Officer of Order of King Leopold II, 1983. Mem.: Assn. for Encouragement of Greek Studies (Paris), Am. Soc. Papyrology, Royal Numismatic Soc. of Belgium. Roman Catholic. Avocations: travel, walking, reading. Home: Ghent, Belgium. Died Oct. 2009.

**BOGATYREV, VLADIMIR LVOVICH,** inorganic chemist; b. Perm, Russia, Feb. 20, 1935; s. Lev Ivanovich and Anna Ivanovna (Sevastyanova) B.; m. Valentina Andreevna Ivanchenko, Dec. 7, 1959; 1 child, Svetlana. Diploma in higher edn., Moscow State U., 1959; PhD in Chemistry, Inst. Inorganic Chemistry, Novosibirsk, Russia, 1964. Jr. scientist Inst. Inorganic Chemistry, Novosibirsk, 1959-61, sr. scientist, 1962-68, head rsch. lab., from 1968. Mem. sci. coun. Inst. Inorganic Chemistry, Novosibirsk, 1965—, State U., Kemerovo, Russia, 1986—; prof. Novosibirsk State U., 1972-82, Siberian U. Consumers Coop. Socs., Novosibirsk, 1997—. Author: Ion-Exchangers in Mixed Bed, 1968, Principals of Reseiving of Ultra-Pure Substances, 1981; co-author: Extraction of Inorganic Substances, 1970, X-Ray Analysis of the Ion-Exchangers, 1982, Physical and Colloidal Chemistry, 1999. Soros Found. grantee, 1993. Avocations: fishing, gardening. Home: Novosibirsk, Russia. Died May 11, 2002.

**BOGGS, THOMAS HALE, JR., (TOMMY BOGGS),** lobbyist; b. New Orleans, Sept. 18, 1940; s. Thomas Hale & Marie Corinne Morrison (Claiborne) B.; m. Mary Barbara Denechaud, Dec. 27, 1960; children: Thomas Hale III, Elizabeth, Douglas. AB, Georgetown U., 1961, LL.B., 1965. Bar: DC, 1965, US Ct. Appeals, 1966, US Supreme Ct., 1971. Economist US Congressional Joint Econ. Com. (JEC), 1961-65; spl. asst. to dir. Office Emergency Planning, 1965-66; ptnr. Squire Patton Boggs LLP (formerly Patton Boggs LLP), Washington, 1966—2014. Presdl. Commn. on Exec. Exch., 1979-81; Presdl. del. Independence of Solomon Islands, 1978, Trade Mission to People's Republic of China, 1979; bd. dirs. 1-800 CONTACTS Inc., 2002-2014 Co-author: Private Trade Barriers in the Atlantic Community, 1964, Corporate Political Activity, 1984. Mem. Charter Commn., Democratic Nat. Com., 1973; trustee Fed. City Coun., Chesapeake Bay Trust, Univ. Md. Found. Named one of The 100 Most Influential Lawyers, The Nat. Law Jour., 2006, The Most Influential Lawyers, 2011, The 50 Top Lobbyists, Washingtonian mag., 2007, The 50 Most Powerful People in DC, GQ mag., 2007, The 50 Politicos to Watch, Politico, 2010. Mem. American Judicature Soc., ABA (com. chmn.), American Maritime, Fed. Bar Assns., Delta Theta Phi. Democrat. Home: Chevy Chase, Md. Died Sept. 15, 2014.

**BOGUE, ERNEST GRADY,** retired academic administrator; b. Memphis, Dec. 9, 1935; s. Emery Grady and Ardell (Wiseman) Bogue; m. Linda Young Bogue; children: Karin, Michele, Barrett, Sara, Michael. BS, Memphis State U., 1957, MA, 1965, EdD, 1968. Asst. v.p. for acad. affairs Memphis State U., 1971—74; fellow acad. adminstrn. American Coun. Edn., Washington, 1974—75; assoc. dir. acad. affairs Tenn. Higher Edn. Com., Nashville, 1975—80; chancellor La. State U., Shreveport, 1980—91; prof. educational leadership & policy studies U. Tenn Knoxville, 1991—2012; interim chancellor U. Tenn. Chattanooga, 2012—13. Author: The Enemies of Leadership, 1985; co-author (with Stephen Trachtenberg & Gerald B. Kauvar): Presidencies Derailed: Why Universities Leaders Fail and How to Prevent It, 2013; contbr. articles to profl. jours. Bd. dirs. Norwela Coun. Boy Scouts America, Shreveport, Shreveport Opera Bd., 1981—84, United Way, Shreveport. Served to capt. USAF, 1958—61. Mem.: Southern Assn. Colleges & Schools (chmn. pers. tng. com.), American Assn. State Coll. & Universities, Shreveport Chamber of Commerce (dir. 1980—83), Omicron Delta Kappa, Phi Delta Kappa. Mem. Christ. Church. Avocations: racquetball, tennis, French horn. Died Oct. 30, 2013.

**BOKOR, PAL,** journalist; b. Budapest, Hungary, May 2, 1942; s. Mihaly and Rozsa (Steiner) B.; m. Alla Shikyaeva; children: Klara, Julia, Marton, Katalin. Student, Budapest Sch. Journalisn, 1961-62, U. Marxizm, Budapest, 1963-65, U. Lomonosov, Moscow, 1964-66. Journalist Hungarian News Agy., Budapest, 1960-64, Moscow, 1971-77, correspondent Washington, 1980-84; mng. fgn. editor Magyar Hirlap, Budapest, 1986-93; editor-in-chief Atlantic Press, from 1993. Author: Vladivostok, Kamchatka, Szahalin, 1978, A Chinese Summer, 1980, Washington, 1984, The Panda (novel), 1985, The Silver Malibu, 1988. Mem. MSZMP Communist Party, 1970. Recipient Excellence award Hungarian TV, 1982. Mem. Hungarian Assn. of Journalists. Avocations: arts, photography. Died 2006.

**BOKOR-SZEGÖ, HANNA,** international law educator; b. Budapest, Hungary, June 18, 1925; d. Ernö and Stefánia Szegö; m. Péter Bokor, Aug. 1, 1947; children: Klára, Judit. Doctor, Law Faculty, Budapest, 1949; PhD, Hungarian Acad., Budapest, 1960, DSc, 1973. Legal advisor Ministry of Fgn. Affairs, Budapest, 1950-60; rsch. fellow Inst. for Legal Scis., Budapest, 1960-96; prof. U. Econ. Scis., Budapest, 1964—2006; sci. dir. Hungarian Ctr. for Human Rights, Budapest, from 1990. Author: New States and Internat. Law, 1970, Role of International Organizations in International Legislation, 1978, Manual Internat, Law, 1997; editor-in-chief Acta Humana, Human Rights Quar., 1990—. Recipient Szentgyörgyi award Ministry of Edn., Budapest, 1995, Cross of Distinction, Pres. of Rep., Hungary, 1995, Cross of Distinction with the Stars, 2005. Home: Budapest, Hungary. Died Dec. 19, 2006.

**BOLIN, BERT RICHARD JOHANNES,** atmospheric physicist, meteorologist, researcher; b. Nyköping, Sweden, May 15, 1925; s. Richard and Karin Lovisa (Johansson) B.; m. Ulla Karin Frykstrand, June 7, 1952 (div. 1979); children: Dan, Karina, Göran. BS, U. Uppsala, 1946; MS, U. Stockholm, 1949, PhD in Meteorology, 1956. Assoc. prof. U. Stockholm, 1956-61, prof., 1961-90; sci. dir. European Space Rsch. Orgn., Paris, 1965-67; dir. Internat. Meteorol. Inst., 1961-91; scientific adv. to Swedish Prime min./vice prime min. Stockholm, 1986-91. Chmn. joint orgn. com. GARP WMO, Geneva, 1967-71; vice chmn. Swedish Natural Sci. Rsch. Coun., 1977-80; chmn. intergovtl. panel on climate change WMO/UNEP, Geneva, 1988-97. Contbr. articles to profl. jours. Recipient OMI prize World Met. Orgn., 1981, Tyler prize U. So. Calif., 1988, Grüne Rosette Köber Stiftung, 1990, Milkankovic medal European Geophys. Soc., 1993, Blue Planet prize Asahi Glass Found., 1995, Environ. prize U. Lund, 1995, Swedish Royal medal, size 12, 1997, award for sci. co-op AAAS, 1998, Climate Protection award EPA US, 1998, Global Environ. Leadership award GEF, World Bank, 1999, Zayed prize United Arab Emirates, 2004. Mem.: Indian Acad. Sci., Norwegian Acad. Sci., Academia Nazionale delle Scienze Italy, U.S. Nat. Acad. Scis., Russian Acad. Scis., Swedish Acad. Engring. Scis., Royal Swedish Acad. Scis. (Arrhenius gold medal 2000). Mem. Social Dem. Party. Avocations: choir singing, outdoor life. Home: Österskär, Sweden. Died Dec. 30, 2007.

**BOND, GEORGE CLEMENT,** anthropologist, educator; b. Knoxville, Tenn., Nov. 16, 1936; s. J. Max and Ruth Elizabeth (Clement) B.; m. Alison Murray, Sept. 21, 1940; children: Matthew, Rebecca, Jonathan, Sarah. BA, Boston U., 1959; MA, London Sch. Econs., 1962, PhD, 1968. Lectr. U. East Anglia, Norwich, Eng., 1966-68; asst. prof. Columbia U., NYC, 1968-74, assoc. prof. Teachers Coll., 1974-80, prof., 1980—2014, dir. Inst. African Studies, 1989—99, dir. Ctr. for African Edn., 2003—14. Author: Politics of Change in a Zambia Community, 1976; editor: African Christianity, 1979, Social Stratification and Education, 1981, The Social Construction of the Past, 1994, AIDS in Africa and the Caribbean, 1997, Contested Teurains and Constructed Categories, 2002, Witchcraft Dialogues, 2003; contbr. articles to scholarly publs. Home: Teaneck, NJ. Died May 4, 2014.

**BOND, WARD CHARLES,** mathematics and computer educator; b. Sidney, Nebr., June 3, 1961; s. Eugene R. and Clara Kay (Meyer) B.; m. Anna M. Angaiak, July 1993; 1 child, Baxter Wayne. BS, U. Wyo., 1985, student, from 1994. Cert. tchr., Wyo., Kans., Nebr., Alaska. Math. tchr. Laramie (Wyo.) High Sch., Decatur Commuity High Sch., Oberlin, Kans.; math. and computer tchr., coach Carbon County Sch. Dist. 2, Hanna, Wyo.; high sch. math. and sci. tchr. Lower Kuskokwim Sch. Dist., Tununak, Alaska, 1989-94 and from 94, mentor tchr. coach phys. edn., art, geography, econs. Mem. ASCD, NEA, Nat. Platform Assn., Alaska Coun. Tchrs. Math., Alaska Edn. Assn., Lower Kuskokwim Edn. Assn., Sigma Nu (Epsilon Delta chpt. Outstanding Sr. Man). Home: Tununak, Alaska. Died Oct. 21, 1997.

**BONDESON, ANDERS ERIK,** electrical engineering and fusion educator; b. Mariestad, Sweden, Dec. 12, 1953; s. Erik Matteus and Barbro Elisabeth (Leidzen) B. MS, Chalmers U. Tech., Gothenburg, Sweden, 1975, PhD, 1979. Rsch. assoc. U. Md., College Park, 1979-81, asst. prof., 1981-82; prof. Chalmers U. Tech., 1982-88; adj. scientist Ecole Polytech. Fédérale, Lausanne, Switzerland, 1988-93; prof. Uppsala (Sweden) U., 1993-95, Chalmers U. Tech., from 1995. Mem. physics com. Nat. Sci. Rsch. Coun., Sweden, 1995-00; ITER coord. EURATOM, 1993-99, mem. program com., 1996-01. Specialist editor in computational electromagnetics Computer Physics Comms., 1997; patentee various aspects of quasi-optical gyrotrons. Home: Gothenburg, Sweden. Died Mar. 20, 2004.

**BONDI, SIR HERMANN,** mathematician; b. Vienna, Nov. 1, 1919; s. Samuel and Helene (Hirsch) B.; m. Christine Mary Stockman, Nov. 1, 1947; children: Alison, Jonathan, Elizabeth, David, Deborah. BA, Trinity Coll., Cambridge U., Eng., 1940, MA, 1944; DSc (hon.), U. Bath, 1974, U. Sussex, 1974, U. Surrey, 1974, U. York, 1980, Southampton U., 1981, U. Salford, 1982, Birmingham U., Eng., 1984, U. St. Andrews, 1985, U. Vienna, 1993; D in Tech. (hon.), U. Plymouth, 1995. Lectr. math. U. Cambridge, 1948-54; prof. applied math. King's Coll., U. London, 1954-85. Vis. prof. Cornell U., Ithaca, N.Y., 1960; dir. gen. European Space Rsch. Orgn., 1967-71; chief sci. adviser Ministry of Def., 1971-77; chief scientist Dept. of Energy, 1977-80; chmn. Offshore Energy Bd., 1977-80; chmn., chief exec. Nat. Environ Rsch. Coun., 1980-84; master Churchill Coll., Cambridge, 1983-90, fellow, 1990-2005; Raman prof. Indian Acad. Scis., 1996; chmn. astronomy policy and grants com. Sci. Rsch. Coun., 1965-67; chmn. Nat. Com. for Astronomy, 1964-67; pres. Internat. Com. on Gen. Relativity and Gravitation, 1965-68; chmn. adv. coun. Sci. Policy Found.; pres. Inst. Math. and Its Applications, 1974-75 (Gold medal 1988, hon. fellowship 1993); mem. Adv. Coun. Rsch., Dept. for Fuel and Power, 1977-80; chmn. Severn Barrage Com., 1978-81. Author: Cosmology, 1960, The Universe at Large, 1961, Relativity and Common Sense, 1964, Assumption and Myth in Physical Theory, 1968, Science, Churchill & Me, 1990; also numerous articles. Decorated knight (KCB), 1973; recipient Birla Humanism prize, India, 1990, Planetary award Assn. Space Explorers, 1993, President's award for Sci. and Art, Govt. of Austria, 1997. Fellow Royal Soc., Royal Astronomy Soc. (Gold medal 2001), Cambridge Philos. Soc., Indian Acad. Scis. (hon.); mem. Brit. Humanist Assn. (pres. 1982-99), Internat. Fedn. Insts. of Advanced Studies (chmn. 1984-96). Primary areas of research in constitution of stars, structure and evolution of universe, general relativity, especially propagation of gravitational disturbances; known for steady state theory of expanding universe. Died Sept. 10, 2005.

**BONDY, PHILIP KRAMER,** retired internist; b. NYC, Dec. 15, 1917; s. Eugene Lyons and Irene (Kramer) B.; m. Sarah B. Ernst, Mar. 18, 1949; children: Jonathan L., Jessica, Steven M. AB, Columbia U., 1938; MD, Harvard U., 1942; MA (hon.), Yale U., 1961. Intern Peter Bent Brigham Hosp., Boston, 1942-43; mem. staff Grady Meml. Hosp., Atlanta, 1943, 46-48, chief resident in medicine, 1947-48; mem. faculty Emory U., 1947-48, 49-52, asst. prof. medicine, 1951-52; Alexander Browne Coxe fellow physiol. chemistry Yale U., New Haven, 1948-49, mem. faculty, 1948-49, 52-74, 77-88, prof. medicine, 1961, 77-88, prof. emeritus, from 1988, C.N.H. Long prof. medicine, 1965-74, chmn. dept. internal medicine, 1965-72, assoc. dean for vets. affairs, 1983-89, chmn. com. outpatient svcs., 1960-62; chmn. med. divsn. Royal Marsden Hosp., 1972-77; Cancer Rsch. Campaign prof. Inst. Cancer Rsch., London; cons. Ludwig Inst. Cancer Rsch., Zurich, Switzerland, 1972-77; assoc. chief of staff for rsch. West Haven VA Med. Ctr., 1977-83, chief of staff, 1983-89. Mem. med. vis. com. Brookhaven Nat. Labs., 1969-73, chmn., 1973; mem. program project com. NIH-Nat. Inst. Arthritis and Metabolic Disease, 1964-68, chmn., 1966-68; mem. exptl. biol. sect. breast cancer task force NIH-Nat. Cancer Inst., 1973-76; mem. adv. coun. NIDDK, 1990-94; mem. planning com. Med. Rsch. Svc. VA, 1985-88, chmn., 1986-88; mem. N.E. region planning com. VA. Editor-in-chief Jour. Clin. Investigation, 1957-62, Yale Jour. Biology and Medicine, 1978-92; editor: Diseases of Metabolism, 6th, 7th, 8th edits, Yearbook of Endocrinology and Metabolism, 1963-64; editorial bd. Conn. Medicine, 1959-61, Yearbook of Medicine, 1954-84, Medicine, 1963-85, Merck Manual, 1969-00, Clinics in Endocrinology and Metabolism, 1973-84, Cancer Topics, 1975-79. Sec. libr. bd. City of Woodbridge, Conn., 1960-67; sec. bd. dirs. Southbury Tng. Sch. Found.; sec., bd. trustees Southbury Tng. Sch.; mem. Coun. on Mental Retardation, Conn., 1997-03; cellist Hamden Symphony Orch., 1994-2006, prin. cellist, 1996-2004. Capt. M.C., AUS, 1943-46, chair Evergreen Woods Concert Com., 2006-10. Recipient Edward Sutliffe Brainard prize Columbia U., 1938, Sigma Xi prize Emory U., 1949, Rsch. Career award NIH, 1962, 66. Fellow AAAS (chmn. sect. N on med. sci. 1979), Royal Coll. Physicians, Royal Soc. Medicine (v.p. sect. oncology 1975-77); mem. ACP (master), Endocrine Soc. (councillor 1964-67, mem. publs. com. 1965-72, chmn. 1968-72), Assn. Am. Physicians, Assn. Physicians Gt. Britain and Ireland, Am. Soc. Clin. Investigation, Am. Fedn. Clin. Rsch., Nat. Assn. VA Chiefs of Staff (mem. exec. com. 1986-88), Soc. Exptl. Biology and Medicine, Interurban Clin. Club, Inst. Cancer Rsch. (London, hon.). Home: East Fairfield, Vt. Died Oct. 14, 2013.

**BONNER, ROBERT WILLIAM,** retired lawyer; b. Vancouver, BC, Can., Sept. 10, 1920; s. Benjamin York and Emma Louise (Weir) B.; m. Barbara Newman, June 16, 1942; children: Barbara Carolyn Massie, Robert York, Elizabeth Louise McPhee. BA in Econs. and Polit. Sci, U. B.C., 1942, LLB, 1948. Bar: B.C. 1948, created Queen's counsel 1952. With firm Clark Wilson White Clark & Maguire, Vancouver, 1948-52; atty. gen. Province of B.C., 1952-68; sr. v.p. adminstrn. MacMillan Bloedel Ltd., 1968-70, exec. v.p. adminstrn., 1970-71, vice chmn., 1971-72, pres., CEO, 1972-73, chmn. bd., 1973-74, ret., 1974; chmn. B.C. Hydro & Power Authority, 1976-85; ptnr. Bonner & Fouks, 1974-84, Robertson, Ward, Suderman, Vancouver, 1985-89. Mem. B.C. Legislature, 1952-69; mem. Energy Supplies Allocation Bd., bd. dirs. Served to maj. Royal Can. Army, 1942-45; lt. col. Res. (ret.). Mem. Can. Bar Assn., Law Soc. B.C. (life bencher), Masons, Vancouver Club, Union (Vcitoria) Club, Delta Upsilon. Social Credit Party. Home: Vancouver, Canada. Died Aug. 12, 2005.

**BONOMI, JOHN GURNEE,** retired lawyer; b. NYC, Aug. 13, 1923; s. Felix A. and Bessie (Gurnee) B.; m. Patricia Updegraff, Aug. 22, 1953; children: Kathryn, John. BA, Columbia U., 1947; JD, Cornell U., 1950; LL.M., N.Y.U., 1957. Bar: N.Y. 1952, U.S. Supreme Ct. 1966, U.S. Dist. Ct. (so. dist.) N.Y. 1975, U.S. Ct. Appeals (2d cir.) 1978. Asst. dist. atty., NY County, 1953-60; spl. counsel subcom. antitrust and monopoly, for hearings on organized crime and monopoly in profl. boxing, Kefauver Com. U.S. Senate, 1960-61; spl. asst. atty. gen. investigating 1961 N.Y.C. mayor race N.Y. State, 1961-62; chief counsel com. grievances Assn. Bar City N.Y., 1963-76; vis. scholar Harvard U. Law Sch., 1976-77; counsel firm Anderson, Russell, Kill & Olick, NYC, 1977-80; practice law NYC, 1980-96; mem. com. grievances and admissions U.S. Ct. Appeals (2d cir.), from 1983. Lectr. Fordham U. Law Sch., 1973; mem. N.Y. state judicial conf. com. on disciplinary enforcement, 1971-72. Columnist: N.Y. Law Jour. 1978-83; contbr. articles to legal jours. Trustee Village of Tarrytown, N.Y., 1965-67, 68-72; councilman, dep. supr. Town of Greenburgh, 1974; spl. counsel to Village of Irvington, N.Y., 1972. With USAAF, 1943-45, ETO. Mem. ABA (spl. com. on evaluation disciplinary enforcement Clark Com. 1967-70, cons. spl. com. on evaluation ethical stds. 1967-69), N.Y. State Bar Assn. (vice-chmn. com. grievances 1970-71, com. profl. discipline 1988-93), Am. Law Inst. (spl. com. peer rev. 1978-80), New York County Lawyers Assn. (com. profl. discipline 1993—), Assn. of Bar of City of N.Y. (cons. spl. com. on free press and fair trial, Medina com. 1966-67, com. profl. discipline 1983-88), Inst. Jud. Adminstrn., Nat. Orgn. Bar Counsel (pres. 1970-71, chmn. spl. com. on Watergate discipline 1974-76). Clubs: Harvard (N.Y.C.). Democrat. Home: Irvington, NY. Died Nov. 6, 1999.

**BOOSALIS, ELSIE,** real estate company executive; b. Cedar Rapids, Iowa, Dec. 1, 1913; adopted d. Peter and Rose (Halleck) Boosalis. Student, Phoenix Bus. Coll., 1943—44, Northwestern U., 1952—53, U. Minn. Property mgr. Peter Boosalis Bldg. Trust, Mpls., 1953—98, trustee, 1960—98. Bd. dirs. Greater Lake St. Coun.; sustaining mem. coun. Girl Scouts USA; bus. mem. Powderhorn Devel. Corp.; donor Guthrie Theater; active ARC, YMCA, WAMSO; mem. Minn. Landscapr Arboretum, Decorative Arts Coun. Inst. Arts. Fellow: Mpls. Soc. Fine Arts (life); mem.: Am. Swedish Inst., English Speaking Union, Minn. Orch. Assn. (guarantor, chmn.), Nat. Wildlife Fedn., Virtuoso Soc., Mpls. C. of C., Minn., Hennepin County Hist. Socs. Home: Minneapolis, Minn. Died Sept. 22, 1998.

**BOOTH, GEORGE D.,** marketing professional, consultant; b. Highland Pk., Mich., Jan. 4, 1927; s. George H. and Gladys L. (Rich) Booth; m. Marie Newberry Booth, July 17, 1948; children: Glenn A., Rick L. Student, Graceland Coll., 1947, Drake U., 1948. Owner, operator Booth Dept. Stores, Garden City, Mich., 1948—50, Booth Motor Sales, Monroe, Mich., 1950—56; merchandising exec. Chrysler Corp., Highland Pk., 1956—77; pres. Merchandising Bus. Svcs., Inc., Southfield, Mich., from 1978, Nat. Bus. Opportunities Ctrs. Inc., 1980—84, Nat. Print & Copy Marts, Inc., from 1980, Channel 1 Video Prodns., from 1981. Chmn. bd. dirs. MBS; editor, pub. Mini Shopper, Internat., 1969—77, Idea-Motives, 1977—78, Am. Merchandising Report, from 1983; mktg. cons., spkr. Author: Materials on Motivation, Careers. With USAF, 1945—47. Mem.: Sales Promotion Execs. Assn. (past pres. Detroit chpt., Sales Promotion Exec. of Yr. 1967), Kiwanis Club, Adcraft Advt. Club. Home: Bloomfield Hills, Mich. Died Feb. 1995.

**BOOTH, GORDON DEAN, JR.,** lawyer; b. Columbus, Ga., June 25, 1939; s. Gordon Dean and Lois Mildred (Bray) B.; m. Katherine Morris Campbell, June 17, 1961; children: Mary Katherine McCormick, Abigail Kilgore Curvino, Sarah Elizabeth, Margaret Campbell, Celecia. BA, Emory U., Atlanta, 1961, JD, 1964, LLM, 1973. Bar: Ga. 1964, D.C. 1977, U.S. Supreme Ct. 1973. Pvt. practice, Atlanta, 1964-96; ptnr. Miller & Martin, Atlanta, from 1995. Bd. dirs., v.p. Stallion Music Inc., Nashville, BAA USA, Inc.; trustee, sec. Inst. for Polit. Econ., Washington. Contbr. articles to profl. jours. Trustee Met. Atlanta Crime Commn., 1977-80, chmn., 1979-80; mem. assembly for arts and scis. Emory Coll., 1971-86, chmn., 1983. Mem. Internat. Bar Assn. (coun. sect. bus. law 1974-88, chmn. aero. law com. 1971-86), State Bar Ga., Capital City Club, Piedmont Driving Club, Univ. Club (NYC), Advocates Club, Sigma Chi. Home: Atlanta, Ga. Died Oct. 16, 2013.

**BOOTY, JOHN EVERITT,** retired theology studies educator; b. Detroit, May 2, 1925; s. George Thomas and Alma (Gamauf) B.; m. Catherine Louise Smith, June 10, 1950; children: Carol Holland, Geoffrey Rollen, Peter Thomas, Catherine Jane. BA, Wayne State U., 1952; B.D., Va. Theol. Sem., 1953, DD, 1994,. U. of the South, 1997; MA, Princeton U., 1957, PhD, 1960. Ordained to ministry Episcopal Ch., 1953. Curate Christ Episcopal Ch., Dearborn, Mich., 1953-55; asst. prof. ch. history Va. Theol. Sem., 1958-64, assoc. prof., 1964-67; prof. ch. history Episcopal Theol. Sch., Cambridge, Mass., 1967-82; acting dir. Inst. Theol. Rsch., 1974-76; dean Sch. Theology U. of South, Sewanee, Tenn., 1982-85, prof. Anglican studies, 1984-90, prof. emeritus, from 1990, historiographer Episc. Ch., 1988-99. Vis. prof., rsch. Yale Div. Sch., 1985-86; Disting. vis. prof. Episcopal Divinity Sch., 1990-91, prof. emeritus, 1991—; vis. prof. Anglican studies Gen. Theol. Seminary, 1992; Trotter vis. prof. Va. Theol. Sem., 1993, 98. Author: John Jewel as Apologist of the Church of England, 1963, Yearning to be Free, 1974, Three Anglican Divines on Prayer: Jewel, Andrewes, and Hooker, 1978, The Church in History, 1979, 2d edit., 2003, The Spirit of Anglicanism, 1979, The Godly Kingdom of Tudor England, 1981, The Servant Church, 1982, What Makes Us Episcopalians, 1982, Anglican Spirituality, 1982, Meditating on Four Quarters, 1983, 2d edit., 2003, Anglican Moral Choice, 1983, The Christ We Know, 1987, The Episcopal Church in Crisis, 1988, Mission and Ministry: A History of the Virginia Theological Seminary, 1996, An American Apostle: A Biography of Stephen F. Bayne, 1997, Reflections on the Theology of Richard Hooker: An Elizabethan Addresses Modern Anglicanism, 1999; editor: The Book of Common Prayer, 1559: The Elizabeth Prayer Book, 1976, reissued, 2005, John Jewel: The Apology of the Church of England, 1963, 74, 2002, John Donne: Divine Poems, Sermons, Meditations and Prayers, 1990, The Works of Richard Hooker, vol. 4, 1982; co-editor, contbr.: The Study of Anglicanism, 1988; contbr. articles to profl. jours. Chmn. Nat. Youth Commn., P.F. Ch., 1948-50; chmn. bd. St. Luke's Jour. Theology, 1987-91, Sewanee Theol. Rev., 1991-99. Recipient Am. Philos. Soc. award, 1964; Folger Shakespeare Libr. fellow, 1964, NEH fellow, 1978-79 Mem. Soc. for Promoting Christian Knowlege (vice chmn. 1984-87). Home: Center Sandwich, NH. Died Apr. 17, 2013.

**BORZECKI, TADEUSZ,** engineering educator; b. Busko-Zdroj, Poland, Mar. 25, 1943; s. Antoni Adam Borzecki and Leokadia Borzecka; m. Maria Teresa Kraszewska, June 25, 1966; children: Grzegorz Piotr, Przemyslaw Tadeusz. MS, Gdansk U. Tech., Poland, 1966; D in Tech. Sci., Tech. U. Gdansk, 1975. Cert. chartered engr., UK, 1985. Asst. prof. Gdansk U. Tech., 1975—2008, assoc. prof., from 2008. Mem. Practical Design Ships & other Floating Structures, Shanghai, 1998—2001, standing com. mem., Luebeck, Germany, 2001—04, Houston, 2004—07; chmn., spec. com. fabrication tech. Internat. Ship & Offshore Structures Congress, Southampton, 2003—06, standing com. mem. repr. Poland, 1994—97, 14th Internat. Ship & Offshore Structures Congress, Nagasaki, Japan, 1997—2000; chmn. tech. com. material & fabrication factors 10th Internat. Ship & Offshore Structures Congress, Lyngby, Denmark, 1985—88; vice dean rsch. Faculty Ocean Engring. & Ship Tech., Gdansk, 2005—08; editor-in-chief Polish Maritime Rsch.; sci. quarterly. Contbr. articles to profl. jours. Recipient Prize, Ministry of Higher Edn., Poland, 1973; Grant, Deutscher Akademischer Austausch Dienst, 1984, Postdoc. grant, Kummermann Found., UK, 1978—79. Mem.: Polish Soc. Naval Architects KORAB, Royal Instn. Naval Arch. Home: Gdansk, Poland. Died Nov. 2013.

**BOSWELL, EDWARD W.,** lawyer, district attorney; b. Hartford, Ala., Nov. 2, 1921; s. Edward C. and Bertha E. (Ward) Boswell; m. Sarah Gretchen McEachern, Dec. 20, 1941; children: Edward W., Gretchen Anita, Daniel C., Alice Ann. LLB, U. Ala., 1947. Bar: Ala. Dist. (atty.). With State Ala. 33d Jud. Cir., Geneva, from 1948; vice-chmn. Geneva County Dem. Exec. Com., from 1970. Capt. US Army, 1942—46. Mem.: Geneva County Bar Assn. (pres. 1970—80), Ala. State Bar Assn. (bar commr. 1960—66, 1975—81), Ala. State Child Support Enforcement Orgn., Ala. Dist. Attys. Assn., Am. Legion, Shriners Lodge, Mason Lodge, Lions Lodge (pres. 1946—84). Democrat. Methodist. Home: Atlanta, Ga. Died Dec. 4, 1987.

**BOTHA, P.W. (PIETER WILLEM BOTHA),** former President of South Africa; b. Paul Roux, Jan. 12, 1916; s. Pieter Willem and Hendriena Christina (De Wet) B.; m. Anna Elizabeth Rossouw, Mar. 13, 1943 (dec. 1997); children: Elanza, Amelia, Pieter Willem, Rozanne, Rossouw; m. Barbara Robertson, June 22, 1998 Student, U. Orange Free State, PhD (hon.), 1981; Dr. Mil. Sci. (hon.), U. Stellenbosch, 1976. M.P., 1948—84; dep. min. interior Govt. of South Africa, 1958—61; min. comml. devel. and Coloured affairs, 1961—66; min. pub. works, 1964—66; min. def., 1966—80; min. nat. security, 1978—84; leader House Assembly, 1975; prime min., 1978-84; state pres., 1984-89; chancellor U. Stellenbosch, 1984—88. Leader, Nat. Party, Cape Province, 1966-89. Decorated Grand Cross of Mil. Orders of Christ (Portugal); Decoration for Meritorious Service; Star of South Africa; Order of Propitious Clouds with Spl. Grand Cordon (Taiwan). Dutch Reformed Ch. Home: Rondebosch, South Africa. Died Oct. 31, 2006.

**BOTHWELL, JOHN CHARLES,** retired archbishop; b. Toronto, June 29, 1926; s. William Alexander and Anne (Campbell) B.; m. Joan Cowan, Dec. 29, 1951; children: Michael, Timothy, Nancy, Douglas, Ann. BA with honors in Modern History, U. Toronto, 1948; BD, Trinity Coll., Toronto, 1950, DD (hon.), 1972, Huron Coll., U. Western Ont., Wycliffe Coll. U Toronto, 1989; hon. sr. fellow, Renison Coll., U. Waterloo, 1988. Ordained priest Anglican Ch., 1952; curate St. James Cathedral, Toronto, 1951-53, Christ Ch. Cathedral, Vancouver, B.C., 1953-56; rector St. Aidan's Ch., Oakville, Ont., 1956-60, St. James' Ch., Dundas, Ont., 1960-65; canon missioner Niagara Diocese, 1965-69; nat. exec. dir. Anglican Ch. Can., 1969-71; co-adjutor bishop Niagara, 1971-73; bishop Diocese of Niagara, 1973-92, archbishop, 1985-91; Met. of Ont., 1985-91; ret., 1991; chancellor Trinity Coll., U. Toronto, 1991—2003. Hon. sr. fellow Renison Coll., U. Waterloo, 1988. Co-author: Theological Education for the 70's, 1969; author: Taking Risks and Keeping Faith, 1985, Living Faith Day By Day, 1990, Old-Time Religion or Risky Faith?, 1992; contbr. articles to various newspapers. Active numerous nat. and ecumenical coms.; Dir., com. chmn. Hamilton (Ont.) Social Planning Council, 1965-69, 71-75, v.p., 1975-77, pres., 1977-79; v.p. United Way, 1982, 83, pres., 1984-86; bd. dirs. Hamilton Found., 1982, v.p., 1983, pres., 1985 Inducted into City of Hamilton (Ont., Can.) Gallery of Distinction, 1993. Anglican. Home: Burlington, Canada. Died Jan. 28, 2014.

**BOTÍN-SANZ, EMILIO,** bank executive; b. Santander, Spain, Oct. 1, 1934; s. Emilio Botin-Sanz de Sautuola and Ana Maria García de los Rios; m. Paloma O'Shea; children: Ana Patricia, Carmen, Carolina, Paloma, Javier, Emilio. JD, U. Valladolid, Spain; Grad., U. Deusto, Bilbao, Spain. Joined Banco Santander, Madrid, 1958, vice chmn., 1971-77, CEO, 1977—86, chmn., from 1986. Bd. dirs. Banco Santander, SA, 1960—2014, Royal Bank of Scotland SA, 1988—2004, Shinsei Bank, 2000—09, Sam Investment Holdings Ltd., 2014. Named one of The 50 Most Influential People in Global Finance, Bloomberg Markets, 2012. Avocations: tennis, golf. Died Sept. 9, 2014.

**BOTTIGER, TED (RUSSELL TED BOTTIGER),** lawyer, retired state legislator; b. Tacoma, Nov. 8, 1932; s. Albert and Mabel Bottiger; m. Darlene Naughton, June 25, 1955; children: Tedene, Terri. JD with honors, U. Wash. Bar: Wash. Asst. atty. gen. State of Wash., 1960—64; asst. minority leader Wash. House of Reps., mem., 1964—71, Wash. State Senate, Tacoma, 1973—87, majority leader, 1982. Active mem. James Sales Grange, Parkland Youth Activities Coun.; past pres. Pierce County Young Democrats; past officer Wash. Young Dems. Recipient Golden Badge award, Fire Dist. Commrs. Mem.: Western Conf. Coun. State Govts. (chmn., ad hoc com. Pacific NW Energy), Nat. Conf. State Legislators (energy com.). Democrat. Lutheran. Died Jan. 23, 2014.

**BOTTINI, ERNESTO ENRIQUE,** urodynamist; b. Baires, Argentina, June 19, 1947; s. Ernesto Eugenio and Dora (Tomassini) B.; m. Margarita C. Rodriguez; children: Ernesto, Eugenia, Enriqueta, Estefania. MD, U. Buenos Aires, 1970. Diplomate Bd. Urodynamics. Resident Childrens Hosp., Buenos Aires, 1975-77, head urodynamic dept., 1978-79, chief urodynamic dept., diagnostico medico, 1980-90; chief urodynamic dept. Italian Hosp., Buenos Aires, 1979-80. Cons. pediatric dept. Italian Hosp., 1980, Nat. Children's Hosp., 1986; dir. Ceseni Enuresis and Incontinence Study and Rsch. Ctr., 1990—. Mem. Soc. Pediatric Research in Latin Am. Clubs: BAC (Buenos Aires). Roman Catholic. Avocation: lathe machinist. Home: Buenos Aires, Argentina. Died 1992.

**BOUCHER, ROBERT FRANCIS,** former academic administrator; b. London, Eng., Apr. 25, 1940; s. Robert and Johannah Boucher; m. Rosemary Ellen Maskell, Aug. 16, 1965; children: Jeremy, Timothy, Justine. PhD, Nottingham U., 1966; DHL (hon.), SUNY, NYC, 1998. Rsch. fellow Queens U., Belfast, Northern Ireland, 1966—68, lectr., 1968—70, U. Sheffield, Sheffield, England, 1970—76, sr. lectr., 1976—85, prof. mech. engring., 1985—95, pro-vice-chancellor, 1992—95, vice-chancellor, 2001—07; prin., vice-chancellor U. Manchester Inst. Sci. and Tech., Manchester, England, 1995—2000. Named a Comdr. of the Most Excellent Order of the British Empire, Queen Elizabeth II, 2000. Fellow: ASME, Instn. Mech. Engrs., Royal Acad. Engring. Home: Sheffield, England. Died Mar. 25, 2009.

**BOULAT, ALEXANDRA,** photojournalist; b. Paris, 1962; d. Pierre Boulat. Studied graphic art and art hist., Beaux Arts, Paris. Co-founder VII Photo Agy., Paris, 2001—07. Exhibitions include Wars in Former Yugoslavia, Visa Pour l'Image, Perpignan, 1995, Gallerie Debelleyme, Paris, 2002; featured in Time mag., Newsweek, Nat. Geographic Mag., Paris-Match. Recipient Harry Chapin Media award, 1994, Prix Paris-Match, 1998, Infinity award, Internat. Ctr. of Photography, NYC, 1999, World Press Photo/Art 2003 award, Overseas Press Club 2003 award; named photographer of yr., USA Photo Mag., 1998, Best Women Photographer, Bevento Oscars, Italy, 2006. Died Oct. 5, 2007.

**BOUNIAS, MICHEL,** biomathematics educator, researcher; b. Cheval-Blanc, France, Nov. 21, 1943; s. Marcel and Paula (Barroyer) B.; 1 child, Marc. Grad. in Biochemistry Engring., Nat. Inst. Applied Sci., Lyon, France, 1965; 3d degree in Biostats., U. Lyon, 1967, DSc, 1972. Doctorship rschr. Atomic Energy Com., Cadarache, France, 1965-71; rschr. Nat. Inst. Agr. Rsch., Avignon, France, 1972-92, head lab., from 1978, sr. scientist lab. biochemistry Avignon, from 1983, rsch. dir., 1985, Paris-Versailles, 1992; assoc. prof. U. Avignon, 1986-87, prof., from 1992. Sci. advisor French Normalization Agy., Agrl. Biology Commn., Ctr. for Indsl. Risk Prevention and Environ. Protection, Paris, 1990—, Coun. Sci. Info., India, 1987—, Natural Park of Luberon, France, 1970—; sci. dir. Alexandria Inst. of Medicine (I.H.S.), N.Y., 1995—. Author: 10 books, Creation of Life: Toxicology, 1991—2000; contbr. over 330 articles to profl. jours.; editor: Jour. Sc. Phys. Sci., Jour. Environ. Biology, Jour. Agrl. Biochemistry; patentee in field. Intellectual dissident Planetary. Recipient Laureate, Acad. Scis., Paris, 1985, Gold medal Protection of Nature, Australia, 1990. Fellow Indian Soc. Agrl. Chemistry, Serbian Biol. Soc.; mem. Indian Soc. Agr. Biochemists (life), Biol. Soc. (Laureate 1979). Achievements include research in enzymology biomathematics, insect metabolic control by vertebrate-like hormones and by specific enzymic systems, toxicology and clinical research; cryptotoxicology, theory of lethality; mathematical-biological theoretical physics: theorem of existence, theory of perception, foundations of further planet management and concept of science/truth. Avocation: composing symphonies. Died May 15, 2003.

**BOURDIEU, PIERRE FELIX,** sociology educator; b. Denguin, France, Aug. 1, 1930; s. Albert and Noémie (Duhau) B.; m. Marie Claire Brizard, 1962; 3 children. Student, Lycée Louis le Grand, Paris, Faculté des lettres, Ecole Normale Supérieure, 1951-54, Agrégation de Philosophie, 1956. Prof. Lycée de Moulins, 1954-55; asst. Faculté des lettres, Algeria, 1958-60, Paris, 1960-61, maitre de conférences Lille, France, 1961-64; chargé de cours Ecole Normale Supérieure, Paris, 1964-84; directeur d'études Ecole en Scis. Sociales des Hautes Etudes, Paris, from 1964; prof.-titulaire Coll. de France, Paris, from 1981. Dir. Centre de sociologie de l'edn. et de la culture, 1964-84, Centre de sociologie européenne, 1985-98, Centre European Soc. Dir. Coll. Le sens commun, 1964-92, Liber, 1997—, (revue) Actes de la recherche en sciences sociales, 1975—, Liber, 1989. Mem. Am. Acad. Arts and Scis. Died Jan. 23, 2002.

**BOURIN, JACQUES ROBERT,** marketing executive, consultant; b. Paris, Dec. 21, 1936; s. Paul Clement Bourin and Jeanne Raymonde Bracchi. Diploma in English studies, West London Coll. Commerce, 1961. Insp. Ag 1824 Life Ins. Cy, Paris, 1961—67; founder, CEO Cerp - Assurance Du Caducee, Paris, 1967—82, Fin. Mktg. Internat., Paris, 1982—90, Le Centenaire, Paris, 1982—90, Mktg. Futur, Paris, from 1993; CEO AFFIDIA, Paris, 1990—93. Cons. Société d'Etudes et de Gestion financière MEESCHAERT, Paris, 1983—88, Norwich Union Life Ins. Soc., Norwich/Paris, France (incl. Monaco), 1982—90, Groupe Mederic, Paris, 1997—2004. Contbr. articles to profl. jours. Founder, pres. L'Association Nationale pour l'Orientation des Assurés, Paris, 1973. Home: Triel sur Seine, France. Died May 10, 2013.

**BOVKUN, GALINA ALEXANDROVNA,** materials scientist, researcher; b. Minsk, Belarus, Jan. 7, 1939; d. Alexander Ignatyevich and Anastasiya Fedorovna Bovkun; 1 child, Julia. Engring degree, Kiev Poly. Inst., 1961; PhD in Materials Sci., Ukrainian Acad. Scis., 1969. Engr. Inst. Problems Materials Sci. Ukraine Nat. Acad. Scis., Kiev, 1961—64, jr. rsch. fellow Inst. Problems Materials Sci., 1969—79, sr. rsch. fellow Inst. Problems Materials Sci., from 1979. Author (with G.V. Samsonov, A.D. Verkhoturov and V.S. Sychev): Electro Spark Hardening of Metallic Surfaces, 1976; contbr. articles to sci. jours.; author: procs. internat. confs. and congresses in powder metallurgy, 1961—2006. Recipient prize, USSR Coun. Ministries Sci. and Tech., Moscow, 1986, State price for sci. and engring. in Ukraine, 1994, 1st prize, Pres. of Ukraine, Moldova and Belarus Nat. Acads. Scis., 1999. Achievements include patents in field. Home: Kiev, Ukraine. Died Sept. 28, 2009.

**BOVON, FRANÇOIS,** theology educator; b. Lausanne, Vaud, Switzerland, Mar. 13, 1938; s. André and Hélène (Mayor) B.; divorced; children: Pierre, Martin. BTh, U. Lausanne, 1961; ThD, U. Basel, Switzerland, 1965. Pastor Eglise Réformée, Canton de Vaud, Switzerland, 1965-67; prof. U. Geneva, 1967-93; Frothingham prof. History of Religion Harvard Divinity Sch., Cambridge, Mass., 1993—2013. Co-editor Revue de Théologie et de Philosophie, Lausanne, 1977-86, Studia Biblica, Leiden, The Netherlands, 1983-90. Author: (patristics and New Testament) De Vocatione Gentium, 1967, Luc le Théologien, 1988, 2nd edit., Lukas in Neurer Sicht, 1985, L'oeuvre de Luc, 1987, Das Evangelium nach Lukas, 1989, Révélations et écritures, 1993, Biblical Narratives and Apocryphal Traditions, 1995. Mem. Studiorum Novi Testamenti Societas, Assn. pour L'étude de la Littérature Apocryphe Chrétienne (pres. 1981-87), Soc. Suisse de Théologie (pres. 1973-77), Académie Internationale des Scis. Religieuses. Avocation: sports, travel,. Home: Cambridge, Mass. Died Nov. 1, 2013.

**BOWER, MARGE EMILY,** educator; b. Chgo., June 8, 1941; d. Elmore Arthur and Elsie Ruth (Sauer) Bower. BA, U. Mich., 1963; MA, Loyola U., Chgo., 1967; postgrad., Loyola U., DePaul U., Bradley U., Western Mich. U., U. Mich. Tchr. English, sch. newspaper advisor South Shore HS, Chgo., 1963—67; guidance counselor, tchr. Elmwood Pk. (Ill.) HS, 1967—84; dir. guidance Immaculate Conception HS, Elmhurst, Ill., from 1985; chmn. com. out-of-state admissions scholarships U. Mich. Nat. Alumnae Coun., 1972—75, governing bd. mem., 1972—75. Wall St. Jour. Newspaper Fund fellow, 1967. Mem.: NAWDAC Jour., Ill. Guidance & Pers. Assn. Quar (editl.bd. 1981—85), U. Mich. Alumni Assn. (dist. sec. 1986—89, dist. pres. from 1989), Ill. Sch. Counselors Assn., Ill. Assn. Counseling & Devel., North Shore U. Mich. Alumni Club (scholarship chmn. 1976—89). Home: Park Forest, Ill. Died Dec. 1990.

**BOWMAN, DEAN ORLANDO,** economist, educator; b. Chalmers, Ind., Sept. 22, 1909; s. Bruce and Aletha G. (Taylor) B.; m. Fate Thomas, June 8, 1936; 1 dau., Ann Pennington. BS, Purdue U., 1933, MS, 1934; PhD (Brookings fellow), U. Mich., 1941. Regional price exec., dep. regional adminstr. O.P.A., 1946; chief fgn. trade sect. Japan-Korea; econ. affairs div. Dept. State, 1947-48; asst. dir. Office of Industry and Commerce, Dept. Commerce, 1948-50; asst. adminstr. policy coordination N.P.A., 1951-53; coordinator long range planning Crown Zellerbach Corp., 1953-60; v.p. long range planning Autonetics div. Rockwell Internat. Corp., Anaheim, Calif., 1960-63, v.p. mgmt. systems and planning, 1963-70; dir. mgmt. programs, prof. bus. econs. U. Mich. Grad. Sch. Bus. Adminstrn., Ann Arbor, 1970-73; dean Sch. Bus., Calif. State U., Long Beach, 1973-77; asst. dean exec. edn. UCLA, 1978-79. Cons. in field. Author: Public Control of Labor Relations, 1942; Contbr. articles to publs. Served to 1st lt. OSS AUS, 1943-45. Recipient Gold medal for exceptional service Dept. Commerce, 1953; Distinguished Service award Office Emergency Planning, 1968; Brookings fellow, 1941. Deceased.

**BOYD, MARVIN G.,** electrical engineer; b. Springfield, Ill., Oct. 22, 1933; s. Eugene Boyd and Vincen Gaynell Black-Boyd; m. Thanomsri Sirikul, June 24, 1974; children: Vincinne K. Weathers-Boyd, Vivien P. Degrees in computer tech., Cen. Data Inst., LA, 1971; BSEE, LaSalle U., 1997; MSc in Gen. Engring., Kennedy-Western U., 2000. Instrument inspector Bendix Corp., Teterboro, N.J., 1959-67; aircraft and space installer McDonald-Douglas Corp., Long Beach and Huntington Beach, Calif., 1968-69; tech. rep. Lear-Spigler Corp., Oklahoma City, 1969-70, Northrop Corp., LA, 1971-74; electronic technician FAA, Springfield, Ill., 1974-96; semi-ret., from 1996. With USN, 1951-55. Mem. Am. Assn. Ret. Persons, Am. Legion (life mem.). Avocations: sports hunting and fishing, wood working, crafts. Home: Sherman, Ill. Deceased.

**BOYLE, JOANNE WOODYARD,** retired academic administrator; b. White Plains, NY, Oct. 27, 1935; d. George Gordon and Josephine (Tschinkel) Woodyard; m. Arthur J. Boyle Jr.; children: Arthur III, Elizabeth, B. Patrick, John W., Terence G., J. Teig, Morgan. BA, Seton Hill Coll., 1957; MAT, Harvard U., 1959; PhD, U. Pitts., 1983. Instr. English dept. Seton Hill Coll., Greensburg, Pa., 1958-59, asst. prof., 1960-67, assoc. prof., 1968-85, prof., 1985-87, pres., 1987—2013, pres. emeritus, 2012—13. Bd. visitors Coll. Arts & Sciences; mem. scholarship selection com. Timken Co. Ednl. Fund, Inc., Canton, Ohio; vice chair exec. com. Women's Coll. Coalition, Washington, 1993; bd. dirs. Pitts. Ballet Theatre, Integra Trust Co., Pitts. Vice chair World Affairs Coun. Pitts.; bd. dirs. Greensburg Area Cultural Coun., 1988, Westmoreland Mus. Art, Greensburg, 1988; active adv. com. Secretariat for Cath.-Jewish Rels., Washington, 1988. Named Pa. Prof. of Yr. Coun. for the Advancement and Support Higher Edn., 1985. Mem. American Assn. Higher Edn., Commn. for Ind. Colleges & Universities (exec. com. 1990), World Affairs Coun. (bd. dirs. 1990), Pa. Assn. Colleges & Universities (pers. com. 1990). Home: Laughlintown, Pa. Died Nov. 1, 2013.

**BOYLE, PATRICIA JEAN,** retired state supreme court justice; b. Detroit, Mar. 31, 1937; Student, U. Mich., 1955-57; BA, JD, Wayne State U., 1963. Bar: Mich. Law clk. Kenneth Davies, Esq., Detroit, 1963; law clk. to Hon. Thaddeus Machrowicz, US Dist. Ct. (eastern dist.) Mich., 1963-64; asst. US atty. (eastern dist.) Mich. US Dept. Justice, Detroit, 1964-68; asst. prosecuting atty. Wayne County, dir. research, tng. and appeals Detroit, 1969-74; Recorders Ct. judge City of Detroit, 1976-78; judge US Dist. Ct. (eastern dist.) Mich., Detroit, 1978-83; assoc. justice Mich. Supreme Ct., Detroit, 1983-98, ret., 1999. Active Women's Rape Crisis Task Force, Vols. of Am. Named Feminist of Year Detroit chpt. NOW, 1978; recipient Outstanding Achievement award Pros. Attys. Assn. Mich., 1978, 98, Mich. Women's Hall of Fame award, 1986, Law Day award ABA, 1998, Champion of Justice award State Bar Mich., 1998. Mem. Women Lawyers Assn. Mich., Fed. Bar Assn., Mich. Bar Assn., Detroit Bar Assn., Wayne State U. Law Alumni Assn. (Disting. Alumni award 1979) Avocation: reading. Died Jan. 13, 2014.

**BRAATHEN, OLE SIGMUND,** association executive, veterinarian; b. Ringerike, Norway, Aug. 21, 1933; s. Julius and Johanna (Ring) B.; m. Inge Gade Egedahl, Dec. 31, 1964; children: Tor Julius, Ole Christian. DVM, Veterinary Coll., Oslo, 1959. Dist. veterinarian County Notodden and Heddal, 1960; pvt. practice vet. medicine Ringerike and Romerike, Norway, 1961; veterinarian Norwegian Meat Research Lab., 1961-68, dir., 1968-80; dir. tech. devel. Norwegian Farmers Meat Mktg. Orgn., Oslo, 1980-99. Lectr., 35 countries, cons., speaker 12 nat. govts. Contbr. articles to profl. jours. Served to lt., vet. service Norwegian Army. Christian Lutheran. Avocations: meat technology, animal stress, electronics, radios and telephones. Fax: 47 67 12 19 52. Home: Bekkestua, Norway. Deceased.

**BRABOURNE, LORD,** film and television producer; b. Nov. 9, 1924; s. 5th Baron and Lady Doreen Geraldine Browne; m. Lady Patricia Edwina Victoria Mountbatten, 1946; seven children. Diploma, Eton, Oxford; DCL (hon.), U. Kent, 1999. Prodr.: Harry Black, 1958, Sink the Bismarck, 1959, HMS Defiant, 1961, Othello, 1965, The Mikado, 1966, Romeo and Juliet, Up the Junction, 1967, Dance of Death, 1968, Tales of Beatrix Potter, 1971, Murder on the Orient Express, 1974, Death on the Nile, 1978, Stories from a Flying Trunk, 1979, The Mirror Crack-d, 1980, Evil Under the Sun, 1982, A Passage to India, 1984, Little Dorrit, 1987; TV series include: National Gallery, 1974, A Much-Maligned Monarch, 1976, Leontyne, 1988; dir. Thames TV, 1975-93, chmn., 1991-95, Ch. North Downs Cable, Ltd., 1990-93; dir. Thorn EMI, 1981-86; fellow Brit. Film Inst., 1979, gov., 1979-94, Nat. Film and TV Sch., 1981-96. Mem. Brit. Screen Adv. Coun., 1985-97; trustee Brit. Acad. Film and TV Arts, 1988, Sci. Mus., 1983-94, Nat. Mus. of Photography Film and TV, 1983-94; pres. Kent Trust for Nature Conservation, 1958-98; mem. coun. Caldecott Cmty., 1969-93; chmn. bd. govs. Norton Knatchbull Sch., 1955-95, gov., 1947; bd. govs. Wye Coll., 1955-2000, chmn. govs., 1994-2000, fellow, 2000; bd. govs. Gordonstoun Sch., 1964-94, United World Coll., 1965-96; pro-chancellor U. Kent, 1993-98, mem. coun., 1968-98. Died Sept. 22, 2005.

**BRACKEN, LOUIS EVERETT,** retired sales executive, health services executive; b. Altoona, Pa., July 1, 1947; s. Everett William and Antonnette Virginia (DeFalco) B.; children: William Joseph, Jennifer Lynn. BS, U. Md., 1970. Sales trainee DeVilbiss Co., Somerset, Pa., 1970, dist. sales rep., 1970-71, dist. sales mgr., 1971-75, regional sales mgr., 1976-82; pres. Health Care Equipment Mktg. Assocs., Inc., Scituate, Mass., 1982—89; retired, 1994. Co-founder Home Strategic Planning, Inc., Boston, 1981-83, Mass. Rehab. Svcs., Inc., Randolph, Mass., 1981, Health Care Distbn. Svcs., Inc., Hanover, Mass., 1984, Associated Home Health Svcs., Inc., Everett, 1985, Health Care Billing Systems, Inc., Hanover, 1985, Continuing Med. Corp. Inc., Providence, 1987, Nat. Homecare Purchasing Network, Boca Raton, Fla., 1990, Health Care Equipment Leasing Ltd., Boca Raton, 1991. Dir. U.S. Jr. Chamber of Congress in Scituate, Scituate, Mass., 1978-81; head coach Pop Warner in Scituate, 1978. Grantee U. Md., 1965-70. Mem. Boys Club (Altoona, Pa., pres.). Republican. Roman Catholic. Avocations: golf, tennis, jogging, football, basketball, baseball. Died June 1997.

**BRAD, TRAIAN,** library director; b. Panade, Alba, Romania, Aug. 31, 1945; s. Traian and Cornelia Brad; m. Nicoleta Maria Gabor, Aug. 5, 1970; 1 child, Adriana-Cornelia. Grad., Liceum I. Muresanu, Blaj, Romania, 1967; grad. in philology with honors, U Cluj, Romania, 1972. Sec. county coun. Union Young Communists, Cluj, 1972-75; trainer Com. for Culture and Socialist Edn. Cluj County, Cluj, 1975-87; dir. Cluj County Libr. Octavian Goga, 1987-99, gen. dir., from 1999. Exec. dir. Lucian Blaga Culture Soc., Cluj, from 1990, Mihai Eminescu Found., Cluj, from 2000. Author: Panade*700 de Ani, 1999, Public Reading and Library in Cluj, 2001; editor: Library Performance Indicators and Library Management Tools, 1997; contbr. articles to profl. jours. Bd. dirs. Timotei Cipariu Found., Panade. Recipient Spl. Activity award, Romanian Pub. Libr. and Librs. Assn., 1992, Biblioteca, 1997. Mem.: Romanian Nat. Pub. Libr. Assn. (master 1998). Avocations: reading, sports. Home: Cluj, Romania. Died June 8, 2002.

**BRADFORD, BARBARA BROWN,** special education educator; b. Tampa, Fla., July 16, 1924; d. Harry Harrison and Adelia Carolyn (Fisher) Brown; m. John Powell Bradford, May 25, 1947; children: Harriet Elizabeth Bradford Roberts, John P. Jr. BA, U. S.C., 1947, MEd, 1979. Second grade tchr. Brookland Grammar Sch., West Columbia, S.C., 1947-48, Rock Hill (S.C.) City Schs., 1949-50; fifth grade tchr. Aiken (S.C.) Elem. Sch., 1948-49; child welfare worker Richland County Dept. Pub. Welfare, Columbia, S.C., 1954-61; tchr., dir. orthopaedic sch. Richland County Sch. Dist. One, Columbia, 1963-69, spl. edn. cons., 1969-71, supv., coord. spl. edn., 1971-80, coord. spl. edn., 1980, dir. programs for handicapped, 1980-87; cons. in spl. edn., from 1987. Part-time caseworker Crippled Children's Assn., Columbia, 1962-63; adj. faculty instr. U. S.C., 1978; mem. scholarships and grants com. State Dept. Edn., mem. spl. edn. resource room rules and regulations com., mem. imput com. for edn. profoundly retarded com., mem. edn. task force on related svcs. com., mem. edn. task force on least restrictive environ. com.; presenter numerous workshops and state convs. on handicapped and emotionally impaired children, 1969—. Active Happy Time Community Ctr. Bd. Mentally Retarded. Mem. NEA, Coun. Exceptional Children (past pres., sec., v.p. chpt. 165 S.C. Fedn., del. to internat. assemblies, S.C. Spl. Educator of Yr. 1979, Nat. and Local Harrie M. Selznick Disting. Svc. award 1993), S.C. Coun. Adminstrs. Spl. Edn. (pres, pres.-elect), Richland County Ret. Educators Assn., S.C. Ret. Educator's Assn., Crippled Children's Assn. (bd. dirs.). Presbyterian. Avocations: interior decorating, drawing, geneology. Died Feb. 3, 1994.

**BRADY, JIM (JAMES SCOTT BRADY),** gun control advocate, former White House press secretary; b. Centralia, Ill., Aug. 29, 1940; m. Sue Beh (div.); 1 child, Melissa; m. Sarah Jane Kemp, 1973; 1 child: Scott BS in Comm. & Polit. Sci., U. Ill., Urbana-Champaign, 1962; LHD (hon.), Drexel U., 1993. Staff mem. to to Senator Everett Dirksen US Senate, Washington, 1961—62; honor intern US Dept. Justice's Antitrust Divsn., Washington, 1962; faculty mem. Southern Ill. U., 1964—65; asst. nat. sales mgr., exec. mgr. to the pres. Lear-Seigler, Ill., 1965—66; dir. legislative & public affairs Ill. State Med. Soc., 1966—68; office mgr. Whitaker & Baxter, Chgo., 1968—69; exec. v.p. James & Thomas Advt. & Public Rels., 1969—73; comm. cons. US House of Representatives, Washington, 1973; spl. asst. to the sec. US Dept. Housing & Urban Devel. (HUD), Washington, 1973—75; spl. asst. to the dir. Office Mgmt. & Budget (OMB), Exec. Office of the Pres., Washington, 1975—76; asst. to Sec. Donald Rumsfeld US Dept. Def., Washington, 1976—77; staff mem. to Senator William V. Roth, Jr. US Senate, Washington, 1977—79; press sec. to Gov. John Connally State of Tex., Austin, 1979; spokesperson Office of Pres.-Elect, Reagan-Bus Com., 1980; asst. to Pres. Ronald Reagan, press sec. The White House, Washington, 1981—89; lobbyist, bd. dirs. Brady Campaign to Prevent Gun Violence (formerly Handgun Control, Inc.), Washington, 1988—2014. Trustee Brady Ctr. to Prevent Gun Violence (formerly Ctr. to Prevent Handgun Violence); vice-chmn. Nat. Head Injury Found., Nat. Orgn. on Disability. Recipient Disting. Eagle award, Boy Scouts of America, Robert A. Taft award for Outstanding Svc. to the Republican Party, Significant Sigma Chi award, Lincoln award, S. Roger Horchow award for Public Svc. by a Public Citizen, 1994, Presdl. Medal of Freedom, The White House, 1996; co-recipient John W. Gardner Leadership award, Independent Sector, Lenore and George W. Romney Citizen Vol. award, Jules Cohen Meml. award, Jewish Cmty. Rels. Coun. Greater Phila., Advancement of Comm. award, Annenberg Washington Program, 1990, Margaret Chase Smith award, US Dept. State, 1996. Republican. Achievements include lobbying for passage of the Brady Bill for gun control, named in his hionor, 1993; having the White House Press Briefing Room "the James S. Brady Press Briefing Room" named in his honor, 2000. Died Aug. 4, 2014.

**BRALEY, JESSIE E.,** bank executive; b. Upton, Wyo., July 23, 1927; d. Raymond Paul and Maggie Sophia (George) McAuley; m. Earl W. Braley, Oct. 14, 1956 (dec. July 1967); 1 foster child, Dwayne E. Secretarial student, U. Wyo., 1945—47; grad., Colo. Sch. of Banking, 1971. Sec. and bookkeeper Union State Bank, Upton, Colo., 1947—56; bookkeeper and teller Stockmen's Bank & Trust, Gillette, Wyo., 1958—67, asst. cashier and auditor, 1967—80, v.p. and cashier, 1980—87; v.p. and dir. Heritage Club First Interstate Bank of Gillette (merged Stockmen's Bank and Trust), from 1987. Elder 1st Presbyn. Ch., Gillette, fin. sec., from 1969; mem. Pioneer Manor Adv. Bd., from 1980, pres., 1984. Named Gillette Woman of Yr., 1980. Mem.: Bank Administrn. Inst. (Wyo. group chmn. 1980—81), Wyo. Bankers Assn. (25 Yr. plaque 1983), Nat. Assn. Bank Women (state chmn. 1968), Bus. and Profl. Women Gillette (pres. 1974—75), Order Eastern Star. Republican. Home: Gillette, Wyo. Died Mar. 3, 1999.

**BRANAND, CLAIRE DIANE,** advertising executive, writer; d. Frank X. Dostal and Clara A. Weidmann; m. David C. Branand, May 12, 1990 (dec. Sept. 29, 2001); 1 child, Wendy C. Student, Chamberlayne Jr. Coll., 1962—63; BFA, Parsons Sch. Design, 1966; student, Sch. Visual Arts, 1966—67. Layout artist R.H. Macy & Co., NYC, 1966—70; freelance art dir. and writer Washington, 1974—77; prin., owner Halpert & Assocs. Advt., Washington, 1978—90; owner Branand & Assoc., Washington, from 1990. Pres. Skye Pub., Annapolis, Md., from 1996. Author: Overboard! A Provocative History of the U.S.S. J.P. Kennedy, Jr., 2000, Here's To Your Health! Cooking With Red Wine, 2002, Getting Off By Z, 2007, The Butterfly and the Bear, 2011, Nat. Assn. Post-Polio Syndrome Newsletter. Sec. bd. dirs. Nat. Assn. Post Polio Syndrome, Washington, 1991—96. Recipient Citation, Assn. for Help of Retarded Children, 1967. Mem.: U.S. Navy League (assoc.), U.S. Naval Inst. (assoc.). Avocations: painting, writing, poetry, cooking, nutrition. Died Apr. 22, 2012.

**BRANCO, JAMES JOSEPH,** estate planner; b. Santa Maria, Azores, Portugal, Mar. 14, 1951; arrived in U.S., 1954; s. Leroy C. and Michele (Desroches) B.; m. Debra McCarren Aug. 27, 1994; children: James II, Natalie, Gabrielle. B, Brandywine Coll., 1971. CEO Profl. Financial Managers Inc., Spring Lake, NJ, 1974—2013; ptnr. Atlantic Drilling Co., Sea Girt, NJ, 1982—90. Pres. Profl. Condo Conversions, Belmar, N.J., 1977-93. Mem. Belmar Chamber of Commerce (pres. 1995-98, v.p. 1998, 99, 2000), KC (3d deg.), Pan America Club, Phi Epsilon. Republican. Roman Catholic. Avocations: racquetball, whitewater rafting, photography, tennis. Home: Manasquan, NJ. Died June 19, 2013.

**BRANCO, SAMUEL MURGEL,** retired sanitary biologist, writer, educator; b. Sao Paulo, Brazil, Sept. 5, 1930; s. Plinio and Maria (Murgel) B.; m. Wilma Cardinale, Nov. 9, 1957; children: Thais, Claudia, Marcelo, Fabio. Grad., Sao Paulo U., 1956, Docent, 1965, postgrad., 1972. Hudrobiologist Dept. Water and Sewage Lab., Sao Paulo, 1956-65; asst. prof. U. Sao Paulo, 1960-65, free-docent, 1965-66, assoc. prof., 1966-72, head prof., 1972-90. Cons. in field, 1968-90. Author: Hydrobiology Applied to Sanitary Engineering, 1969, 4th edit., 1986, Sanitary Limnology, 1984, Ecosystemics, 1989, also 24 books on environ. scis. Recipient Azevedo Neto prize Brazilian Assn. San. Engring., 1992; named Engr. of Yr., Engr. Syndicate, Sao Paolo, 1987. Mem. N.Y. Acad. Scis., Sao Paulo Acad. Sci. Home: São Paulo, Brazil. Died Dec. 28, 2003.

**BRANIGIN, ROGER D., JR.,** lawyer; b. Louisville, Mar. 1, 1931; s. Roger D. and Josephine M. Branigin; m. Marilyn Bechdolt, 1961; children: Elizabeth H. Branigin Cayton, Roger D. III, John F. AB magna cum laude, Dartmouth Coll., 1952; LLB cum laude, Harvard U., 1955. Bar: Ind. 1955. Assoc. Stuart & Branigin, 1957-62, ptnr., from 1962. Trustee Lafayette Sch. Corp., 1963-64, 65-69, pres., 1968-69, United Community Svcs., 1967-68, Capital Funds Found., 1983-84, Tippecanoe County Boys Club, 1976-77; dir. Nat. Homes Corp., 1978-90; chmn. United Way Campaign, 1984; dir. Lafayette Home Hosp., 1978-84, Westminster Village West Lafayette, West Lafayette Econ. Devel. Commn.; dir., North Cen. Health Svcs., 1984—, vice chmn. 1994-96, chmn., 1996—; former trustee Cen. Presbyn. Ch. With U.S. Army, 1955-57, USAR, 1957-59. Fellow Am. Coll. Trust and Estate Counsel, Ind. Bar Found.; mem. ABA, Ind. State Bar Assn., Tippecanoe County Bar Assn. (pres. 1974-75). Died Jan. 31, 2002.

**BRANSOME, EDWIN DAGOBERT, JR.,** internal medicine educator; b. NYC, Oct. 27, 1933; s. Edwin Dagobert and Margaretta De Witt (Homans) B.; m. Janet Grace Williams, June 27, 1959; children: Edwin D. III, April Grace. AB, Yale U., 1954; MD, Columbia U., 1958. Intern, resident, rsch. fellow Peter Bent Brigham Hosp., Harvard Med. Sch., Boston, 1958-62; rsch. assoc. Columbia U. Coll. Physicians and Surgeons, NYC, 1962-64; assoc. Scripps Clinic and Rsch. Found., LaJolla, Calif., 1964-66; from asst. prof. to assoc. prof. MIT, Cambridge, Mass., 1966-70; prof. medicine, endocrinology and physiology Med. Coll. Ga., Augusta, 1970—2000, chief sect. endocrinology and metabolism, 1970—2000, Augusta, 1999—2000, prof. emeritus, from 2000. Com. mem. US Pharmacopoeia, Rockville, Md., 1976-90, trustee, 1990-2008, pres., 1999-2000, hon. mem. US Pharmacological Convention, 2009-; cons. Accelerated Pharm., Inc., 1999—2006, med. dir., 2006-; cons. in endocrinology and metabolism, 2000—, sci. advisor., with Quality mgmt. Com., bd. dirs., 2000-06. Contbr. articles to profl. jours. Bd. dirs. TriDevel. Commn., Aiken, SC, 1987-91, treas., 1989-90; bd. dirs. Am. Diabetes Assn., Alexandria, Va., 1986-88; mem. bd. dirs. Alteon Inc., 1996-2006, Med. Quality Mgmt. Activity with Humana Mil. HS, Patient Safety Peer Review Com., 2003-12, Credentialling Com., 2005-, Aiken Opera Soc., 2009-. Postdoctoral rsch. fellow NIH, 1959-61, Am. Cancer Soc., 1962-64; recipient Pub. Policy award Ga. affiliate Am. Diabetes Assn., 1990. Fellow Am. Coll. Endocrinology; mem. Diabetes Care, Am. Cancer Soc. (faculty rsch. assoc. 1966-70), Endocrine Soc., others. Achievements include patent (with others) in method of predicting biological activity of compounds by DNA models. Died Oct. 15, 2013.

**BRASHER, CHRISTOPHER WILLIAM,** journalist, business executive; b. Georgetown, Guyana, Aug. 21, 1928; s. William Kenneth and Katie (Howe) B.; m. Shirley Juliet Bloomer, Apr. 28, 1959; children: Kate, Hugh, Amanda. MA, St. John's Coll., Cambridge U., 1951; Dr (hon.), Stirling U., Scotland, 1989, Kingston U., Surrey, Eng., 1996. Mgmt. trainee Mobil Oil Co., Eng., 1951-57; sports editor The Observer, London, 1957-61, columnist and Olympic corr., 1961-91; reporter/producer BBC TV, London, 1961-81, head gen. features, 1969-72; mng. dir. Fleetfoot Ltd., Lancaster, Eng., 1979-96; chmn. Reebok U.K. Ltd., Eng., 1990-93; founder, chief exec. London Marathon, 1980-95; chmn. Berghaus, Ltd., Washington, Eng., 1993-98, Brasher Boot Co. Ltd., Lancaster, 1993—2001. Author: Sportsmen of our Time, 1962, Tokyo, 1964, A Diary of the XVIIIth Olympiad, 1968, A Diary of the XIXth Olympia, 1972, (with Sir John Hunt) The Red Snows, 1960. Trustee John Muir Trust, 1983-92, 96—, The Kmoydart Found.; chmn. Chris Brasher Trust, 1988—, The Petersham Trust, 1999—. Decorated officer Order St. John, comdr. Brit. Empire; recipient Nat. Medal of Honour, Finland, 1975; named Sports Writer of Yr., Brit. Press Awards, 1968, 76. Mem. Racehorse Owners Assn. (coun. 1996—). Avocations: mountains, horse racing, fishing, orienteering, social running. Died Mar. 1, 2003.

**BRATAAS, NANCY OSBORN,** retired state legislator; b. Mpls., Jan. 19, 1928; d. John Draper and Flora (Warner) Osborn; m. Mark Gerard Brataas, 1948; children: Mark, Anne. Degree in Edn., U. Minn. Owner Nancy Bratass Associates; mem. Minn State Senate, 1975—92. Chairwoman Minn. Republican Party, Minn., 1963—69; state chairwoman Minn. Republican Finance Com., 1969—71. Mem.: AAUW, Zonta Internat., League Women Voters. Republican. Episcopalian. Home: Rochester, Minn. Died Apr. 17, 2014.

**BRAUN, DAVID A(DLAI),** lawyer; b. NYC, Apr. 23, 1931; s. Morris and Betty Braunstein; m. Merna Feldman, Dec. 18, 1955; children: Lloyd Jeffrey, Kenneth Franklin, Evan Albert. AB, Columbia U., NYC, 1952, LLB, 1954. Bar: N.Y. 1955, Calif. 1974. Assoc. Ellis, Ellis and Ellis, NYC, 1954—56, Davis and Gilbert, 1956—57; ptnr. Pryor, Braun, Cashman & Sherman, 1957—73, Hardee, Barovick, Konecky & Braun, NYC, 1973, LA, 1974—81; pres., CEO Polygram Records, Inc., N.Y.C., 1980—81; counsel Wyman, Bautzer, Rothman, Kuchel & Silbert, LA, 1982—85; ptnr. Braun, Margolis, Burrill & Besser, LA, 1985—87; counsel Silverberg, Rosen, Leon & Behr, 1987—89, Silverberg, Katz, Thompson & Braun, 1989—91; spl. counsel Proskauer, Rose, Goetz & Mendelsohn, 1991—93; ptnr. Monasch Plotkin & Braun, 1993—94; pvt. practice, 1994—98; sr. counsel Akin, Gump, Strauss, Hauer & Feld, LLP, LA, 1998—2006. Adj. prof. U. So. Calif. Sch. Cinema-TV; guest lectr. UCLA Ext.; adv. com. Ctr. for Law, Media and the Arts, Columbia U. Sch. Law; internet adv. bd. mem. Nat. Inst. Entertainment and Media Law, Southwestern U. Sch. Law. Co-prodr.: (off-Broadway play) A Woman of Will, 2005. Bd. visitors Columbia Coll., 1980-86, Columbia Law Sch., 1992-94; bd. dirs. Reprise! Broadway's Best in Concert, Musician's Assistance Program, 1994-98, Tu 'Um EST Cmty. Drug Rehab. Ctr., Rock and Roll Hall of Fame, 1985-93. Recipient Service award, Grammy Foundation, 2008, Columbia U. Alumni medalist. Mem. Assn. of City of NY, LA County Bar Assn., Beverly Hills Bar Assn., Nat. Acad. TV Arts and Scis. (pres. NY chpt. 1972-73), NATAS, Am. Arbitration Assn., Columbia Coll. (John Jay award, 1981), Hollywood Radio and TV Soc. (bd. dirs. 1983-86), Sigma Chi, Phi Alpha Delta. Jewish. Died Jan. 28, 2013.

**BRAYCZEWSKI, BOHDAN,** surgeon; b. Warsaw, June 19, 1932; arrived in France, 1976; Surgeon; b. Warsaw, Poland, June 19, 1932; came to France, 1976; s. Wlodzimierz and Zofia (Grzembo) B.; m. Henryka Ksiezopolska, Sept. 19, 1959; children: Monique, Wlodzimierz. MD, Acad. Medicine, Warsaw, 1957. Resident asst. Surg. Clinic, Warsaw, 1957-69; chief med. officer Polyclinique, Warsaw, 1957-69; internat. coop. physician Regional Hosp., Monastir, Tunisia, 1969-76; surgeon Polyclinique du Vaurais, LaVaur, France, 1976-77, Surg. Centre Hospitalier Regional de Rodez, France, 1977-79, Clinique Tous Vents, Bolbec, France, 1980— . Mem. French Assn. of Surgery, Rotary. Roman Catholic. Avocation: bridge. Home: Bolbec, France. Died July 15, 1999.

**BREED, HELEN ILLICK,** ichthyologist, educator; b. New Cumberland, Pa., Mar. 12, 1925; d. Joseph Simon and Della May (Brotzman) Illick; m. Henry Eltinge Breed, Jr., Nov. 23, 1957; children: Henry E., Joseph I., Brenda E. BS, Syracuse U., 1947, MS, 1949; PhD, Cornell U., 1953. Tchr. sci. Lyons (N.Y.) Cen. High Sch., 1949-50; instr. zoology and physiology Akron (Ohio) U., 1953-54; postdoctoral Ford Found. fellow, instr. physiology Vassar Coll., Poughkeepsie, N.Y., 1954-55; asst. prof. biology Russell Sage Coll., Troy, N.Y., 1955-57; asst. dir. systematic biology NSF, Washington, 1957; assoc. prof. conservation Cornell U., Ithaca, N.Y., 1957-61; rsch. assoc. biology Rensselaer Poly. Inst., Troy, 1964-68; environ. cons. Eltick Rsch. Corp., Troy, 1971-90; enivron. advisor, cons. Women's Environ. and Devel. Orgn., NYC, from 1991; internat. environ. liaison and coord. N.Y. State Summit and Agenda's 21 Program, Albany, from 1992. Ichthyology cons. Ichthyological Assocs., Lake George Project, Troy, 1969, Ithaca, 1971-80, Lima, Peru, 1972-73; internat. environ. liaison and coord. N.Y. State Summit and Agenda's 21 Program, Albany, 1992—, Cornell U. Program on Breast Cancer and Environ. Risk Factors in N.Y. State. Contbr. articles to profl. jours. Capital dist. mem. Syracuse U. campaign for excellence, Troy, 1988-90. Nat. Wildlife Fedn. fellow, 1950, Sports Fishing Inst. fellow, 1951-53, Am. Scandinavian Found. fellow, Trondheim, Norway, 1959-60, Fulbright fellow in fisheries rsch., Trondheim, Norway, 1959-60; recipient scholarship in biology Westinghouse, 1942-43, Women of Distinction in N.Y. State award, 2001. Mem. AAAS, Am. Soc. Zoologists, Soc. Systematic Zoology, Am. Soc. Ichthyologists and Herpetologists, Am. Fisheries Soc., Brunswick Hist. Soc. Lutheran. Avocations: travel, photography of ecological environments. Deceased.

**BREEDLOVE, SARAH See MADAM WALKER, C.J.**

**BREMENT, MARSHALL,** retired ambassador; b. NYC, Jan. 10, 1932; s. Isidore and Haya (Glauberman) Brement; m. Joan Bernstein, May 2, 1953; children: Diana, Mark, Gabriel; m. Pamela Sanders, June 7, 1973. BA, NY U., 1952; MA, U. Md., 1955. With US Fgn. Svc., 1956, Chinese Lang. Tng., 1958—60, Russian Lang. Tng., 1963—64; staff asst. State Dept.; asst. sec. Far East, 1956—57; cons., polit. sect. Am. Consulate Gen., Hong Kong, 1960—63; mem., polit. sect. Am. Embassy, Moscow, 1964—66, counselor, pub. affairs Djakarta, 1970—73, min. & counselor, pub. affairs Saigon, 1973—74, counselor, polit. affairs Moscow, 1974—76, Madrid, 1977—79; chief, polit. sect. US Embassy, Singapore, 1967—70; staff mem. Nat. Security Coun. White House, 1979—80; dep. permanent rep., US Mission to UN, 1981; US amb. to Iceland, 1981—85. With USAF, 1952—54. Fellow: Nat. Inst. Pub. Affairs; mem.: Am. Fgn. Svc. Assn., Phi Kappa Phi. Died Apr. 6, 2009.

**BRENNAN, EDWARD NOEL,** psychiatrist, psychoanalyst; b. NYC, Dec. 28, 1929; s. Edward L. and Margaret A. (Fenelon) Brennan; m. Alice Ann MacHardy, Oct. 20, 1956; children: Alison Marie, Elizabeth Louise, Noel Edward McKenzie. BS, Trinity Coll., 1951; MD, Yale U., 1955. Psychoanalytic tng. Psychoanalytic Clinic for Tng. and Rsch., 1964—69; rotating intern Gen. Hosp., Phila., 1955—56; resident psychiatry Boston Psychopathic Hosp., 1956—59; tchg. fellow psychiatry Harvard U., 1956—59; assoc. medicine (psychiatry) Peter Bent Brigham Hosp., Boston, psychiatry Tufts U., 1957—59; cons. Mcpl. Ct. Clinic, Cambridge, Mass., 1958—59; chief psychiat inpatient svc. Reiss Mental Health Pavillion, St. Vincents Hosp., NYC, 1961—64; asst. attending psychiatrist, 1961—64; assoc. attending psychiatrist, 1964—71; attending, 1972—91; chmn. Continuing Edn. Com., 1982—91. Supr. psychotherapy psychiat. out-patient dept., 1964—91, Collaborating Psychoanalyst Columbia U. Psychoanalytic Ctr., NYC, 1972—92; mem. faculty, from 1992; tng. and supervising analyst, from 1993; asst. Attending Psychiatrist

Presbyterian Hosp., NYC, 1976—93; assoc. attending psychiatrist, from 1993, Attending Psychiatrist Greenwich Hosp., Conn., 1979—92; hon. attending staff mem. Dept. Psychiatry, from 1993; asst. clin. prof psychiatry Columbia U., 1976—93; assoc. clin. prof psychiatry, from 1993; Diplomate Nat. Bd. Med. Examiners; with Am. Bd. Psychiatry and Neurology, qualified psychiatrist State Dept. Mental Hygiene, NY. Served to capt. USAF, 1959—61. Grantee Am. Psychiat. Assn. Mem.: continuing edn. com, continuing edn. com., Assn. Psychoanalytic Medicine., Undersea Med. Soc., Fairfield County Med. Soc., AMA, NY County Med. Soc., Am. Coll. Psychoanalysts, Am. Acad. Psychoanalysis, Soc. Liaison Psychiatry, Westchester Psychoanalytic Soc. (sec. 1978, pres. 1982), Am. Psychoanalytic Assn., Am. Assn. Gen. Hosp. Psychiatrists. Died June 25, 1998.

**BRENNAN, THOMAS JOHN,** city and state official, consultant, educator; b. Bklyn., Mar. 23, 1923; s. Thomas Joseph and Violet Emma (Jurgens) B.; m. Margaret Karen Jensen, Sept. 18, 1948; children: Debra Gail, Mark Kevin, Laurie Kathleen. AB, Wittenberg Coll., 1949; MGA, U. Pa., 1950. Cons. Pub. Adminstrn. Svc., Chgo., 1950—56; dep. sec. for adminstrn. Dept. Welfare Commonwealth Pa., Harrisburg, 1957—59; dep. sec. for state properties Pa. Dept. Property and Supplies, 1959—64; exec. officer Del. Dept. Mental Health, Dover, 1965—67; v.p. Exec. Mgmt. Svc., Arlington, Va., 1967—76; exec. dir. Gov.'s Justice Commn. Pa. Commn. on Crime and Juvenile Delinquency, 1976—79; dir. water utility City of New Brunswick, NJ, 1983—91, chief labor negotiator, 1988—91, pers. mgr., 1988—91, exec. officer police dept., 1989—91, pub. mgmt. cons., from 1991. Adj. instr. U. Del., 1965—67; adj. assoc. prof. Rider Coll., Lawrenceville, NJ, 1983—84, Lawrenceville, 1984—85; hearing officer N.J. Dept. Civic Svc., Trenton, 1976—2002; cons. exam. constrn., 1985—2000; cons. to staff com. UN, 1982—84; cons. various municipalities and agys.; presenter papers to profl. orgns. Bd. dirs. Bucks County Opera, Pa., 1975-80, Bucks County Play House, New Hope, Pa., 1970s; elected mem. alumni coun. Wittenberg U., 1989-90; mem. Merrill's Maurauders, WWII. Decorated Silver Star, Bronze Star with 2 oak leaf clusters, Combat Infantry badge; recipient various plaques; Fels scholar U. Pa., 1948. Mem. VFW (Yardley, Pa.), Internat. Personnel Mgmt. Assn., Am. Pub. Works Assn. (dist. rep. Eastern Pa. bldg. and grounds com.), Am. Water Works Assn., Internat. Chief of Police Assn., Nat. Conf. State Justice Planning Adminstrn. (regional chmn., exec. com.), Criminal Justice Tng. Inst. (chmn. planning com. 1978-79), Huntington Valley Hunt (Bucks County, bd. dirs. 1975-80), Am. Legion (New Hope, Pa.), Upper Makefield Hist. Soc. (bd. dirs.), Wharton Alumni (Phila.), U. Pa. Emeritus Soc. (steering com. 2004—), Fraternal Order of Police. Home: Wayne, Pa. Died Oct. 19, 2013.

**BRENNER, DAVID,** comedian; b. Phila., Feb. 4, 1945; s. Louis Yehuda and Estelle Anne (Rosenfeld) B. Grad., Temple U. Producer, WBBM-TV, Chgo., WRCV, Phila., KYW-TV, Phila., WNEW-TV, N.Y.C., PBL-TV, N.Y.C.; producer, writer, dir. TV documentaries, N.Y.C.; numerous nightclub appearances; TV appearances include Hollywood Squares, also as guest host Tonight Show, Nightlife, 1986-87, (TV series) Nightlife, 1986, (TV movie) Worth Winning, 1989, others; author: Soft Pretzels with Mustard, 1983, Revenge is the Best Exercise, 1985, Nobody Sees You Eat Tuna Fish, 1985, If God Wanted Us To Travel..., 1990. Served with U.S. Army. Named Las Vegas Entertainer of Year, 1978; Atlantic City Comedian of the Year, 1984, College Campus Entertainer/Comedian of the Year, 1984 Died Mar. 15, 2014.

**BRETHERICK, LESLIE,** retired research chemist; b. Wallasey, Cheshire, Eng., Sept. 3, 1924; s. Samuel and Edith (Currie) B.; m. Margaret Rosalie Smith; children; Lois, Faith, Timothy, Paul. BSc with honours, U. Liverpool, Eng., 1944. Chartered chemist, U.K. Devel. chemist May & Baker Ltd., Dagenham, Eng., 1945-60, rsch. safety advisor, 1950-60; chief chemist L. Light & Co., Colnbrook, Eng., 1960-62; sr. project leader Brit. Petroleum, Sunbury-on-Thames, Eng., 1962-82, rsch. safety chmn., 1964-82; ret., 1982. Author: Handbook of Reactive Chemical Hazards, 6 edits. (also online edits.), 1975—99; editor: Hazards in the Chemical Laboratory, 3rd edit., 1981, Hazards in the Chemical Laboratory, 4th edit., 1986; contbr. articles to chemistry jours., chapters to books. Recipient chem., health and safety divsnl. award Am. Chem. Soc., 1988. Fellow Royal Soc. Chemistry (Shell industrially sponsored safety award, 1999), nominated CHAS fellow Am. Chem. Soc., 2001; mem. Soc. Chem. Industry. Avocations: walking, photography, genealogy. Home: Dorset, England. Died Apr. 13, 2003.

**BRICKNER, PHILIP WALTER,** physician, educator; b. NYC, Aug. 10, 1928; s. Richard M. and Ruth Helen (Pilpel) B.; m. Alice Rinenberg; children: Jed Walter, Nell Cecile, Maude Lillian. BA, Swarthmore Coll., 1950; MD, Columbia U., 1954. Lic. Nat. Bd. Med. Examiners, N.Y., 1955; cert. American Bd. Internal Medicine, 1963. Intern First Med. Divsn., Bellevue Hosp., NYC, 1954-55, sr. asst. resident, 1957-58, chief resident, 1959-61, trainee N.Y. Heart Assn., 1959-61; sr. asst. resident Bronx Mcpl. Hosp., 1958-59; asst. attending physician St. Vincent's Hosp., 1963-67, assoc. attending physician, 1967-69, attending physician, 1970—2010; asst. prof. clin. medicine N.Y. U. Coll. Medicine, 1970—2014; assoc. to full prof. clin. medicine N.Y. Med. Coll., 1979—2014. Asst. physician Presbyn. Hosp., 1961-69; asst. vis. physician Bellevue Hosp., 1961-68; asst. in medicine Columbia U., 1961-73; dir. pers. health svc. Columbia U. Coll. Physicians and Surgeons, 1961-65; dir. dept. cardiology St. Francis Hosp., 1964-65, dir. dept. medicine, 1964-66; chief sec. clin. pharmacology dept. medicine St. Vincent's Hosp., 1967-69, chief sect. amb. care dept. medicine, 1968-74, chmn. dept. community medicine, 1974-2000, dir. tuberculosis studies, cmty. medicine; many others. Author: Care of the Nursing Home Patient, 1971, Home Health Care for the Aged, 1978, (with others) Health Care of Homeless People, 1985, Long Term Health Care, 1988, Under the Safety Net. The Health and Social Welfare of the Homeless in the United States, 1990; editor: Jour. Long Term Home Health Care; contbr. articles to profl. jours. Chief med. cons. East Harlem Youth Employment Svc., 1964-80; mem. nursing home adv. com. N.Y.C. Dept. Health, 1975-76; mem. adv. com. Foster Grandparent Program, N.Y.C. Office for the Aging, 1977-86; mem. Archdiocesan Task Force on the Aging, 1977-78; health adv. to the Mayor's Office, City of N.Y., 1978-89; mem. Cath. Health Assn. Task Force on Long Term Care, 1982-84; sr. program cons. Robert Wood Johnson Found., 1983-90; many others. Capt. U.S. Army Med. Corps, 1955-57. Fellow ACP, N.Y. Acad. Medicine. Died Mar. 24, 2014.

**BRIDGEWATER, NORA JANE,** medical, surgical nurse; b. Rodgers, Tex., Feb. 27, 1924; d. Wiley Levi and Phoebajane (Owens) Shelgren; m. Joe Garland Bridgewater, Aug. 7, 1940; children: Garland, Janie William Clayton, Richard, Allen, Paula, Shewanna, Russell. AA in Psychology, Bakersfield Coll., 1970, BSN, 1978. Med. nurse Kern Med. Hosp., Bakersfield, Calif., 1964-68, Mercy Hosp., Bakersfield, 1969-78, Sherrif's Dept., Laredo, Calif., 1978-87; nurse Sheriff Facility, Bakersfield, 1986-87. Sgt. U.S. Army Nurses Corps, 1938-40. Mem. Calif. Nursing Assn. Democrat. Baptist. Avocations: books, growing flowers, writing. Died 1997.

**BRIDGMAN, CHARLES FLOYD,** medical educator and illustrator; b. Loma Linda, Calif., Oct. 2, 1923; s. Turner Floyd and Elizabeth Sutton (Tillman) B.; m. Amy Roceilia Lancaster, Aug. 6, 1949; children: Sue Ellen, Paul Charles, Daniel Richard, Katy Ann, Benjamin Robert. AB in Bacteriology, U. Calif., LA, 1949, MS in Anatomy, 1951, PhD in Anatomy, Neurosciences, 1962; postgrad. cert. biomed. communications, U. Kans., 1963. Asst. prof. anatomy and art Univ. Calif., LA, 1963-70, asst. dean for learning resources, asst. prof. anatomy San Diego, 1965-70; dir., Nat. Med. Audiovisual Ctr. Nat. Libr. of Medicine, Atlanta, 1970-73, assoc. dir. for ednl. resources devel. Bethesda, Md., 1973-79; sr. scientist, Lister Hill Nat. Ctr. Biomed. Communications Nat. Libr. Medicine, 1979-86; ret., 1986. Adj. assoc. prof. anatomy Emory Univ. Med. Sch., Atlanta, 1970-74; cons. in ednl. tech. various ednl. instns. Nat. Libr. Medicine, Bethesda, 1974-86, Scripps Clinic and Rsch. Found., La Jolla, 1984-85, Sweetwater Sch. Dist., Chula Vista, Calif., 1989—. Author: Communication Media in the Health Sciences: Design, Development and Training, 1982, (textbook) Introduction to Functional Histology, 1990; contbr. over 30 articles to profl. jours. Musician UCLA Symphony, 1946-49, Univ. Ill. Med. Profs. Symphony, Chgo., 1949-51, La Jolla (Calif.) Civic Symphony, 1965-70. Cadet USAF, 1942-45. Grantee NSF, UCLA, 1963, Nat. Fund for Med. Edn., Univ. Calif. San Diego, 1970. Fellow Assn. Med. Illustrators (bd. and accreditation com.); mem. AAAS, Am. Assn. Anatomists (ednl. affairs com.), Health Scis. Communication Assn., Sigma Xi. Achievements include co-authoring and illustrating the first medical textbook to be barcoded to an optical video disc extending visual content by thousands of pictures; research on muscle spindles, Golgi tendon organs and medical education. Died 1994.

**BRIDGMAN, RICHARD DARRELL,** lawyer; b. Madison, SD, Mar. 1, 1929; s. Lloyd Alton and Fay Catherine (Turner) B.; m. Marilyn Elizabeth Smith, May 25, 1952 (div. June 1987); 1 child: Richard Darrell; m. Noreen Jan Quan, Oct. 6, 2001. AB, U. Calif., 1951; JD, Golden Gate U., 1958. Bar: Calif, 1958, U.S. Dist Ct. (no. dist.) Calif. 1958, U.S. Dist. Ct. (ea. dist.) Calif. 1982, U.S. Dist Ct. (cen. dist.) Calif. 1985, U.S. Ct. Appeals (9th cir.) 1958. Ptnr. Ericksen, Ericksen, Kincaid & Bridgman, Oakland, Calif., 1959-69, O'Neill & Bridgman, Oakland, Calif., 1969-86, San Francisco, 1986-88; pvt. practice Richard D. Bridgman, San Francisco, 1988-92, from 2001; ptnr. Bridgman & Bridgman, San Francisco, 1993—2001. Mem., bd. dirs. Lawyer's Mutual Ins. Co., Burbank, Calif., 1978-88; faculty Golden Gate U., San Francisco, 1963-69, Hastings Coll. Trial & Appellate Advocacy, San Francisco, 1978-91. Co-author: Legal Malpractice-Suing & Defending Lawyers, 1984; contbr. articles to profl. jours. Lt. U.S. Navy, 1951-54, Korea. Named Lawyer of Yr. Lawyers Club of Alameda Co., 1980. Mem. Inner Cir. Advocates, Am. Bd Trial Advocates, Am. Bd. Profl. Liability Attys. (diplomate), Calif. Trial Lawyers Assn. (bd. govs. 1976-83, sec. 1978-81), Alameda Conta Costa Trial Lawyers Assn. (pres. 1982). Died 2007.

**BRIERLEY, JOHN E. C.,** retired legal educator, former university dean; b. Montreal, Que., Can., Mar. 5, 1936; BA, Bishop's U., Lennoxville, Que., 1956; B.C.L., McGill U., 1959; Docteur de l'Universite de Paris, 1964; LL.D., Dickinson U., 1985. Teaching fellow Faculty of Law, McGill U., Montreal, 1960-61, asst. prof., 1964-68, asso. prof., 1968-73, prof., from 1973, Sir William Macdonald prof. law, 1980-94; Wainwright prof. civil law, from 1994; dean faculty law Faculty of Law, McGill U., 1974-84; retired, 1984. Vis. prof. U. Montreal, 1967-68, U. Toronto, 1971-72, U. Paris II; occasional lectr. McGill Mental Hygiene Inst., McGill Sch. Social Work, 1969-73; vis. occasional lectr. Dalhousie U., 1970-73; cons. Royal Commn. on Status of Women in Can., 1970; mem. Canadian Delegation of Experts, UNIDROIT, Rome, 1971, Conseil des affairs sociales et de la famille, Ministerial Coun. to min. Social Affairs, Que., 1971-73; pres. Sous-comite sur les Politiques et programmes familiaux, 1971-73; mem. Commn. des Biens culturels de Que., ministerial coun. to min. Cultural Affairs, Que., 1972; cons., secretaire-rapporteur various coms. Civil Code Revision Office, Que., 1967—; chmn. Com. Can. Law Deans, 1981—. Felllow Royal Soc. Can., 1995; mem. Canadian, Que., bar assns.; Assn. des professeurs de droit de Que., Assn. Canadian Law Tchrs., John Howard Soc. Que. (dir. 1965-67), Canadian Soc. for Legal History (exec. com. 1972—), Inter-Am. Comml. Arbitration Commn. (exec. com. 1972—), Internat. Acad. Comparative Law, Internat. Acad. Estate & Trust Law (exec. com.). Deceased.

**BRIGGS, HERBERT SPENCER,** lawyer; b. NYC, Feb. 9, 1910; s. Arthur Vanderbilt and Frances (Cleary) B.; m. Constance Ulmer Twiname, Dec. 30, 1973; children by previous marriage: Natasha, Thomas, Edward George. AB, Coll. City N.Y., 1929; JD, Fordham U., 1973. Bar: N.Y. 1975. Personnel research N.Y. and Queens Electric Light and Power Co., 1929-34, job and wage analyst-in-charge, 1934-42; personnel research Consol. Edison Co. N.Y., Inc., 1946-47; sr. research specialist employee remuneration The Conf. Bd., Inc., NYC, 1947-52, asst. sec., 1953, sec., 1953-73; since practiced in Carmel, N.Y. Author: Wage Payment Systems, 1948, Evaluating Managerial Positions, 1951. Served to lt. col. USAAF, 1942-46. Mem. Am., N.Y. State bar assns., Delta Sigma Phi. Republican. Episcopalian. Home: Wappingers Falls, NY. Died Mar. 18, 1994.

**BRILOFF, ABRAHAM JACOB,** accountant, educator; b. NYC, July 19, 1917; s. Benjamin and Anna (Kaplan) B.; m. Edith A. Moss, Dec. 22, 1940; children: Leonore, Alice Ebenstein. BBA, CCNY, 1937, MS in Edn., 1941; PhD, NYU, 1965; L.H.D. (hon.), SUNY-Binghamton, 1984. C.P.A., N.Y. Tchr. NYC Public Schools, 1937-44; ptnr. Apfel & Englander, C.P.A.s, NYC, 1944-51; propr. Abraham J. Briloff, C.P.A., NYC, 1951-82; ptnr. A.J. and L.A. Briloff, NYC, from 1983; mem. faculty Baruch Coll., CUNY, 1944-87, prof. accountancy, 1966-87, Emanuel Saxe Disting. prof. accountancy, 1976-87, prof. emeritus, 1987—2013. Cons. to govt. Author: Effectiveness of Accounting Communication, 1967, Unaccountable Accounting, 1972, More Debits than Credits, 1976, The Truth About Corporate Accounting, 1981, La Troisième Colonne, 1982; contbr.: articles to profl. jours. Recipient disting. service award Baruch Coll. Alumni Assn., 1982; recipient award Financial Analysts Fedn., 1969, 1970; named Disting. Alumnus CCNY, 1968, 73, 74 Mem. AICPA, American Acctg. Assn. (inducted into N.E. region Hall of Fame 1992, Acctg. Exemplar award 1995), N.Y. State Soc. CPAs. Democrat. Jewish. Home: Great Neck, NY. Died Dec. 12, 2013.

**BRINK, NILS ERIK,** ecohydrologist; b. Färila, Sweden, Nov. 27, 1921; s. Jon Olof and Anna Petréa (Hannberg) B.; m. Greta Maria Broborg, Apr. 5, 1947 (div. Aug. 31, 1994); children: Karl Johan, Anna Karin. Agronomist, Agrl. Coll. of Sweden, Uppsala, 1949, Agronomie Licentiate, 1954, DAgrl, 1962, lectr., 1963, prof., 1984. Tchr. Farm Sch., Arbrå, Sweden, 1948-49; asst., 1st asst. Agrl. Coll. of Sweden, Uppsala, 1948-62, rschr., 1962-70, asst. prof., 1970-77, Swedish U. Agrl. Scis., Uppsala, 1977-84; prof., 1984-87; emeritus prof., from 1987; rschr. on composting, 1987-99. Founder Divsn. Water Protection, Agrl. Coll., 1970; rschr. agro-hydrology, 1948-54, purification of sewage water, 1954-62, on selfpurification in soils and streams, studies on protozooan in sandfilters, 1962-72, on water pollution from agriculture and forests, leaching of nutrients and pesticides, 1972-87, composting, 1975-82, 87-99; tchr. hydrology, wat. prot. Inst. Soil Sci., Agrl. Coll., 1949-87, tchr. math., 1963-70; tchr. Inst. Tech. Stockholm, 1949-56, dept. limnology Uppsala U., 1965-69; cons. in ecohydrology, Uppsala, 1990-98; with Swedish Agr. and Forest Rsch. Coun., Nat. Swedish Environ. Protection Agy., Swedish Acad. Agr. and Forestry, Nordic Agrl. Soc., Scandinavian Coun. Applied Rsch., Swedish Soc. Conservation Nature; lectr. in field. Contbr. articles to profl. jours. and chpt. to books. Chmn. Health Care, Uppsala, 1968-72.; Officer of Res., Infantry, 1945-70, Hort.Exptl. Sta. at Swedish U. Agrl. Scis., 1987-99. Named hon. gov. Swedish Govt., Stockholm, 1984. Fellow The Masonic Order, Red Cross. Achievements include patents in Sewage Water Purification. Home: Uppsala, Sweden. Died Jan. 29, 2006.

**BRINKLEY, JOEL GRAHAM,** retired newspaper editor; b. Washington, July 22, 1952; s. David McClure and Ann (Fischer) B.; m. Sabra Chartrand, May 13, 1990; children: Veronica, Charlotte AB in Journalism & English, U. N.C., 1975. Reporter Richmond (Va.) News Leader, 1975-78, Louisville (Ky.) Courier-Jour., 1978-82, editor, 1982-83; Washington corr. The NY Times, Washington, 1983-86, White House corr., 1987, chief Jerusalem Bur., 1988-91, project editor Washington, 1991-95, political editor NYC, 1995—2006; Hearst visiting profl. in residence Dept. Comm. Stanford U., 2006—13; tactical adv. to John F. Sopko Office Spl. Insp. for Afghan Reconstruction, 2013—14. Author: The Circus Master's Mission, 1989, Defining Vision, The Battle for the Future of Television, 1997, Cambodia's Curse: The Modern History of a Troubled Land, 2011; co-author: (with Steve Lohr) U.S. vs. Microsoft: The Inside Story of the Landmark Case, 2000, Recipient Pulitzer prize for Internat. Reporting, Columbia U., 1980, George Polk award for Nat. Reporting Long Island U., 1995. Home: New York, NY. Died Mar. 11, 2014.

**BRISTOW, WALTER JAMES, JR.,** retired judge; b. Columbia, SC, Oct. 14, 1924; s. Walter James and Caroline Belser (Melton) Bristow; m. Katherine Stewart Mullins, Sept. 12, 1952; children: Walter James III, Katherine Mullins(dec.). Student, Va. Mil. Inst., 1941-43; AB, U. NC, 1947; LLB cum laude, U. SC, 1949; LLM, Harvard U., 1950. Mem. Marchant, Bristow & Bates, 1953-76, SC Ho. of Reps., 1956-58, SC Senate, 1958-76; resident judge 5th Cir. Ct. SC, 1976-88; ret., 1988. Nat. pres. Conf. Ins.

Legislators, 1974—75. Trustee Elvira Wright Fund Crippled Children, 1963—76; mem. bd. visitors ex officio The Citadel, Charleston, SC, 1967—76. With US Army, 1943—45, ETO, brig. gen. SC Army N.G. Decorated Meritorious Svc. medal; recipient Order of Palmetto, 1999, Order of Cypress, 1999. Mem.: ABA, SC Law Inst., SC Coun. Holocaust, Columbia Ball Club, Palmetto Club, Cotillion Club, Forest Lake Club, Sertoma, Wig and Robe, Alpha Tau Omega. Democrat. Home: Columbia, SC. Died Nov. 30, 2013.

**BRITT, GLENN ALAN,** corporate board member, retired broadcast executive; b. Hackensack, NJ, Mar. 6, 1949; s. Walter E. Britt and Helen Crupi; m. Barbara Jane Little, Oct. 25, 1975. AB magna cum laude, Dartmouth Coll., 1971, MBA, 1972. Controller's asst. Time, Inc., NYC, 1972-74; v.p., treas. Manhattan Cable TV, NYC, 1974-76; finance dir. Iran project, Time-Life Books Time, Inc., Alexandria, Va., 1976-78, dir. video group new bus. devel. NYC, 1980-81, sr. v.p. finance video group, 1984; v.p. network & studio ops. HBO, Inc., NYC, 1978-80, sr. v.p., CFO, 1984-86; v.p., treas. Time, Inc., NYC, 1986-88, v.p., CFO, 1988-90; sr. v.p. finance American TV & Comm. Corp., Stamford, Conn., 1981-84; sr. v.p., treas. Time Warner, Inc., NYC, 1990; exec. v.p. Time Warner Cable Group, Stamford, Conn., 1990-92; pres. Time Warner Cable Ventures, Stamford, Conn., 1992-99, Time Warner Cable Inc., 1999—2001, CEO, 2001—06, pres., CEO, 2006—09, chmn., pres., CEO, 2009—10, chmn., CEO, 2010—13. Bd. dirs. TW Telecom Inc., 1998—2005, Time Warner Cable Inc., 2003—14, Xerox Corp., 2004—14, TIAA, 2007—09, Cardinal Health, Inc., 2009—14. Bd. mem. Walter Kaitz Found., The Paley Ctr.; Pearl Harbor Meml. Fund. Recipient Joel G. Berger award, Cable Positive, Vanguard award for Disting. Leadership, Nat. Cable & Telecommunications Assn., American Horizon award, The Media Inst., Stanley B. Thompson Jr. Lifetime Achievement award, Nat. Assn. for Multi-Ethnicity in Comm. (NAMIC), Diversity Champion award, Kaitz Found., Disting. Leadership award, NY Hall of Sci., 2013; named Humanitarian of Yr., UJA-Fedn. of Yr., 2010; named to The Cable Hall of Fame, 2007, The Broadcasting & Cable's Hall of Fame, 2008. Mem. Financial Executives Inst., Woodway Country Club, Eastward Ho, Cape Cod National Golf Club & Country Club, Univ. Club. Avocations: skiing, gardening, golf. Home: Westport, Conn. Died June 11, 2014.

**BRITTON, THOMAS C.,** federal judge; b. Shanghai, Mar. 13, 1919; s. Thomas Cotton and Ruth (Yeager) Britton; m. Lois Adelaide Peterson, June 15, 1950; 1 child, Thomas Calhoun. BA, Yale U., 1942, LLD, 1948. Bar: Fla. 1948, Conn. 1948, US Ct. Appeals (5th cir.) 1948, US Supreme Ct. 1966, US Ct. Appeals (11th cir.) 1982. Pvt. practice, Miami, 1948—57; 1st asst. atty., Dade county, 1957—64; county atty., 1964—71; sr. ptnr. Shutts & Bowen, Miami, 1971—75; judge US Bankruptcy Ct. (so. dist.) Fla., Miami, 1975—82, chief judge, from 1982. Lt. USN, 1942—45. Mem.: Fla. Bar Assn. Republican. Baptist. Home: Miami, Fla. Died Feb. 2, 1990.

**BROADBENT, EDWARD GRANVILLE,** mathematics professor; b. Huddersfield, Eng., June 27, 1923; s. Joseph Charles and Lucetta (Riley) B.; m. Elizabeth Barbara Puttick, Sept. 7, 1949 (dec. July 27, 2001). BA, U. Cambridge, Eng., 1946; MA, U. Cambridge, 1947, DSc, 1975. Chartered engr. Govt. scientist Royal Aircraft Establishment, Farnborough, Eng., 1943-83; vis. prof. Imperial Coll., London, from 1983. Cons. London, 1983—. Author: Elementary Theory of Aeroelasticity, 1956; contbr. scientific papers to symposiums and profl. jours. Fellow Royal Aero. Soc. (medals 1956, 60, 91), Inst. of Math. and Applications, Royal Soc. London, Royal Acad. Engring. Anglican. Avocations: gardening, bridge, chess, theater, concerts. Home: Farnham, England. Died Mar. 2008.

**BRÖDER, ERNST-GÜNTHER,** financial executive, economist; b. Cologne, Germany, Jan. 6, 1927; D in Econs., Cologne U., Mayence U., Freiburg U., Paris U. Mem. corp. staff Bayer AG Leverkusen, Germany, 1956-61; mem. projects dept. World Bank, Washington, 1961-64; head dept. KfW-Bankengruppe (formerly Kreditanstalt für Wiederaufbau), Frankfurt, Germany, 1964-68, dep. mgr., 1968-69, mgr., 1969-75, mem. bd. mgmt., 1975-84, spokesman bd. mgmt., 1980-84; dir. European Investment Bank, Luxembourg, 1980-84, pres., chmn. bd. dirs., 1984-93, hon. pres., from 1993. Active inspection panel The World Bank, Washington, 1996-99, chmn. inspection panel, 1994-96, 98-99; adv. com. Asian Devel. Bank, 1981-82; panel of conciliators Internat. Ctr. Settlement of Investment Disputes, 1976—. Died Dec. 13, 2013.

**BRODERICK, CARLFRED BARTHOLOMEW,** retired sociology educator; b. Salt Lake City, Apr. 7, 1932; s. Frederick Anthony and Napina (Bartholomew) B.; m. Kathleen Adelle State, July 3, 1952; children: Katherine, Carlfred Bartholomew, Victor, Wendi, Jenifer, Frank, Beverly, Benjamin. AB magna cum laude, Harvard, 1953; PhD, Cornell U., 1956; postgrad., U. Minn., 1966-67. Assoc. prof. family devel. U. Ga., 1956-60; assoc. prof. family relations Pa. State U., 1960-69, prof., 1969-71; prof., dir. marriage and family therapy program U. So. Calif., LA, 1971-97, chmn. dept. sociology, 1989-91, prof. sociology emeritus, from 1997; sr. ptnr., clin. dir. Broderick, Langlois and Assocs., San Gabriel, Calif., 1981-94; ptnr. Broderick-Wood Marriage and Family Therapy, Cypress, Calif., 1984-95. Author: Sexuelle Entwickland in Kindheit und Jungend, 1970, Couples: How to Confront Problems and Maintain Loving Relationships, 1979, Marriage and the Family, 1979, 2d edit., 1983, 3d edit., 1988, 4th edit., 1992, The Therapeutic Triangle, 1983, One Flesh, One Heart, 1986, Understanding Family Process, 1993, My Parents Married On a Dare, 1996; editor: (with Jessie Bernard) The Individual, Sex and Society, 1969, A Decade of Research and Action on the Family, 1971, Jour. Marriage and the Family, 1970-75; contbr. articles to profl. jours. Pres. Cerritos (Calif.) stake Ch. Jesus Christ Latter-Day Saints, 1976-82, bishop, 1988-92, patriarch, 1992—. Fellow Am. Assn. Marriage and Family Therapists (supr., award 1997), So. Calif. Assn. Marriage and Family Therapists (pres. 1974, award 1989, 97), Nat. Coun. Family Rels. (pres. 1976, award 1989), Assn. Mormon Counselors and Psychotherapists (pres. 1982, awards 1990, 91, 97). Home: Cerritos, Calif. Died July 27, 1999.

**BRODY, ELAINE MAJORIE,** research gerontologist; b. NYC, Dec. 4, 1922; d. William J. and Frieda (Horowitz) Breslow; m. Stanley J. Brody, Feb. 21, 1943 (dec. 1997); children: Peter Robert, Laurel Ann Brody Karpman. BA, Bklyn. Coll., 1942; MSW, U. Pitts., 1945; DSc (hon.), Med. Coll. Pa., 1987. Dir. human services dept. Phila. Geriatric Ctr., 1955-87. Adj. assoc. prof. U. Penn., Phila.; clin. prof. Med. Coll. Pa., Phila.; prin. investigator 12 fed. funded studies. Author: Parent Care as a Normative Family Stress, 1986, Women in the Middle, 1990; mem. editorial bd. Jour. AM. Geriatrics Soc., 1981-84, The Gerontologist, Jour. Gerontology, 1986-87, Social Work, 1973-75. Recipient Disting. Alumni award U. Pitts. Sch. Social Work, 1982; named Woman of Yr. Ms. Mag., 1985. Fellow Gerontological Soc. America (pres. 1980, Donald P. Kent award, 1983, Brookdale award 1985)); mem. Nat. Assn. Social Workers. Home: Phoenix, Ariz. Died July 9, 2014.

**BROFSKY, HOWARD,** musician, educator; b. NYC, May 2, 1927; s. Barney L. and Frances (Reich) B.; m. Robin Westen; children: Alexander, Natasha, Gabriel. PhD, NYU, NYC, 1963. Asst. prof. U. Chgo., Chicago, IL, 60-67; prof. Queens Coll., CUNY, NYC, 1967-92, prof. emeritus, 1992—2013; pres. Vt. Jazz Ctr., 1998—2010. Prof. U. B.C., Vancouver, Can., summers 1974, 75, Boston U., summer 1978, U. Oslo, Norway, fall 1993; spl. editor music Harper & Row, Publications, N.Y.C., 1969-71. Co-author: (with J. Bamberger) The Art of Listening, 5th edit., 1988; contbr. articles to profl. jours.; several jazz recs. Mem. American Musicol. Soc., Internat. Musicol. Soc., Internat. Assn. Jazz Educators. Home: Brooklyn, NY. Died Oct. 17, 2013.

**BROGDON, BYRON GILLIAM,** radiologist, educator; b. Ft. Smith, Ark., Jan. 22, 1929; s. Paul Preston and Lela Florence (Gilliam) B.; m. Barbara Walkow Schreiber, June 23, 1978; 1 child, David Pope; stepchildren: William and Diane Schreiber. BS, U. Ark., 1951, BS in Medicine, 1951, MD, 1952. Intern Univ. Hosp., Little Rock, 1952-53, resident, 1953-55; resident in radiology N.C. Bapt. Hosp., Winston-Salem, 1955-56; asst. prof. radiology U. Fla., 1960-63; assoc. prof. radiology and radiol. scis., radiologist-in-charge diagnostic radiology div. Johns Hopkins U. and Hosp., 1963-67; prof., chmn. dept. radiology U. N.Mex., 1967-77; from prof. chmn. radiology to disting. prof. emeritus U. South Ala., Mobile, 1978—96, disting. prof. emeritus, from 1996. Sabbatical leave Univ. Coll., Galway, Ireland, 1988; cons. in forensic radiology Office Med. Exam. State Ala., 1989—; coord. internat. diagnostic course in Davos, 1984-96; trustee Forensic Sci. Found., 2001-09, vice-chair, 2003-04; mem. adv. bd. The Virtopsy Found., Bern, Switzerland, 2006-; expert cons. Ministry of Health, Singapore, 2010-. Author: Opinions, Comments and Reflections on Radiology, 1983, Forensic Radiology, 1998, a Radiologic Atlas of Abuse and Torture, Terrorism, and Inflicted Trauma (winner Highly Commended Med. Book Competition award 2003), Brogdon's Forensic Radiology, 2nd Ed., 2010, Child Abuse and Its Mimics in Skin and Bone, 2012; contbr. articles to med. jours, 65 chapters in books, 1966-. Maj. USAF, 1953—60. Finalist Ann. Telly awards, 2004; recipient Disting. Alumnus award U. Ark., 1978, Ark. Travelers Commn. award Gov. of Ark., 1985, Disting. Achievement award Wake Forest U. Med. Alumni Assn., 1990, medal U. Leuven, Belgium, 1988, from city of Brescia, Italy, 1991, medal Faculty Medicine U. Marseille, 2013, Joint Resolution of Commendation for outstanding profl. achievement Ala. Legis., 1994, Medal of Honor Leopold-Franzens U., Innsbruck, Austria, 1997, Republic of Austria Cross of Honor for Sci. and Arts 1st class, 2002, Highly Commended award, Brit. Med. Assn., 2003. Fellow Am. Coll. Radiology (pres. 1978-79, gold medal 1987), Am. Acad. Forensic Scis. (John B. Hunt award 1995, Disting. Fellow award 2001, Robert Thilault award, 2013), Internat. Assn. Forensic Radiographers Gt. Britian (patron); mem. AMA (ho. of dels. 1988-95, Physician-Spkr. award 1979), Am. Roentgen Ray Soc. (life, exec. coun. 1974-75, 77-80, 84-90, 2d v.p. 1979-80, mem. bd. sr. radiologist sect., 2005-, gold medal 1996, lectr. sr. radiology sect., 2009), Southern Radiol. Conf. (life hon., pres. 1967-68, sec. 1984-96, Eskridge lectr. 1994), Radiol. Soc. N.Am., Am. Assn. Acad. Chief Residents in Radiology (faculty advisor 1979-2002, nat. sponsor 1983-93, Malcolm Jones orator 1996), Soc. Pediat. Radiology, Assn. U. Radiologists (pres. 1973-74, gold medal 1985), Soc. Chmn. Acad. Radiol. Depts. (sec.-treas. 1969-70), Swiss Soc. Med. Radiology (hon., Schinz medal 1992), Internat. Soc. Forensic Radiology and Imaging (hon., charter mem. 2012), Internat. Skeletal Soc. (Silver medal 2001), Med. assn. State Ala. (50 yrs. med. parctices distinction award 2002), Ala. Acad. Radiology (Silver award, 2012), Country Club Mobile, Sigma Xi, Alpha Omega Alpha, Sigma Chi (Significant Sig 1999), Irish Soc. Sketetal Radiology (hon. life 2013). Home: Mobile, Ala. *For the physician-scientist-educator, the mere transference of knowledge or the acquisition of new data is not enough. He must participate fully in the affairs of the larger community and has a duty to help others to think about, or form an opinion on, issues they otherwise might not have considered.* Died Mar. 28, 2014.

**BROGGER, JAN CHRISTIAN,** social anthropology educator; b. Paris, Feb. 13, 1936; parents Norwegian citizens; PhD, U. Oslo, 1970. Sec. gen. Norwegian Fedn. Mental Health, Oslo, 1958-63; rsch. fellow U. Bergen, Norway, 1964-69; rsch. assoc. Cornell U., Ithaca, N.Y., 1964-65; sr. curator U. Oslo, 1969-74; prof. social anthropology Norwegian Univ Sci. & Tech., Oslo, from 1974, dean of the faculty of humanities, 1993-95; dir. Liberal Rsch. Inst., Oslo, 1988-2001. Cons. Mefit SpA, Rome, 1973-78; commentator Aftenposten, Oslo, 1989-99. Author 10 books in field; 2 in U.S. Recipient Dag Hammarskiold Achievement award Coll. William and Mary, Williamsburg, Va., 1993. Mem. Royal Acad. Sci. (Trondheim chpt.), European Acad. Sci. & Arts, Rotary. Roman Catholic. Avocations: music, winter sports. Deceased.

**BRONFMAN, EDGAR MILES, SR.,** philanthropist, retired liquor company executive; b. Montreal, June 20, 1929; naturalized, U.S., 1959; m. Ann Loeb, Jan. 10, 1953 (div. 1973); children: Sam, Edgar Jr., Matthew, Holly, Adam; m. Lady Caroline Townshend (annulled, Nov. 21, 1974); m. Rita Webb, 1975 (div.) remarried, 1980 (div.); children: Sara, Clare; m. Jan Aaronson, 1994 Student, Williams Coll., 1946—49; BA, McGill U., 1951; LHD (hon.), Pace U., 1982; LLD (hon.), Williams Coll., 1986. Chmn. Metro Goldwyn Mayer, 1969; chmn. adminstrv. com. Joseph E. Seagram & Sons, Inc., 1955-57, pres., 1957-71; chmn., pres., CEO Distillers Corp.-Seagram Ltd., Montreal, 1971-75; chmn. The Seagram Co. Ltd. and Joseph E. Seagram & Sons Inc., 1975—94; co-founder Scandent Group (parent company, Cambridge Integrated Services Group, Inc.), Cranbury, NJ, 1994. Pres. World Jewish Congress, 1981—2007; bd. dirs. Vivendi Universal, 2000—03. Author: (memoir) The Making of a Jew, 1996, Good Spirits: The Making of a Businessman, 1998. Mem. citizens com. for N.Y.C. U.S.-USSR Trade and Econ. Coun.; chmn. Samuel Bronfman Found.; pres. North American Consortium for Free Market Study; mem. Bus. Com. for Arts United Jewish Appeals; hon. chmn. Fedn. Jewish Philanthropies; dir. American com. Weizmann Inst. Sci.; mem. finance com. Nat. Urban League; mem. internat. adv. bd. Columbia U. Sch. Internat. & Public Affairs; chmn. Anti-Defamation League, NYC; bd. dels. Union American Hebrew Congregation; bd. dirs. American Com. Weizmann Inst. Sci., Israel. Recipient Presdl. Medal of Freedom, The White House, 1999; named Chevalier de la Légion d'Honneur, French Govt.; named one of The World's Richest People, Forbes Mag., 1999—2013, The Forbes 400: Richest Americans, 1999—2013. Mem.: Fgn. Policy Assn., Com. for Econ. Devel., Ctr. Inter-Am. Rels., B'nai B'rith (bd. overseers), Hundred Yr. Assn. N.Y., Coun. Fgn. Rels. Jewish. Died Dec. 21, 2013.

**BROOKINS, CAROL ELAINE,** purchasing administrator; b. Elsie, Mich., Dec. 17, 1933; d. Russell Allen and Vaudrey Leoma (Curtis) Barnard; m. M. Kenneth Leavitt, Dec. 30, 1950 (div. 1956); m. Myron Charles Ostrander, Mar. 24, 1964 (div. 1979); 1 child, Penny Elaine; m. Dale Alvah Brookins, July 9, 1983. Grad. high sch., White Pine, Mich. Mgr. soft lines receiving Topps Inc., Lansing, Mich., 1962-65; head bookkeeper Painters Supplies, Lansing, 1965-68, The Fig Leaf, White Pine, 1974-78; dir. purchasing Ontonagon (Mich.) Meml. Hosp., from 1978. Facility graphic artist Ontonagon Meml. Hosp. Mem. Nat. Assn. for Female Execs., Smithsonian Instn., Health Care Material Mgmt. Soc. Avocations: bow hunting, camping, needle craft, 4-wheel vehicles. Died 1999.

**BROOKS, NICHOLAS PETER,** historian, educator; b. Virginia Water, Surrey, Eng., Jan. 14, 1941; s. William Donald Wykeham and Phyllis Kathleen (Juler) B.; m. Chloë Carolyn Willis, Sept. 16, 1967; children: Carolyn Ebba, Crispin Edmund Hartley. BA, Oxford U., Eng., 1962, MA, PhD, 1969. Lectr. medieval history U. St. Andrews, Fife, Scotland, 1964-77, sr. lectr., 1977-85; prof. U. Birmingham, 1985—2014, dean faculty arts Eng., 1992-95. Adviser Toronto (Univ.) Old English Dictionary; bd. dirs. St. Andrews Univ. Excavations. Author: The Early History of the Church of Canterbury, 1984, Communities and Warfare 700-1400, 2000, Anglo-Saxon Myths, 400-1066, 2000; editor: Studies in the Early History of Britain (series), 1977-2003, Studies in Early Medieval Britain; contbr. articles to profl. jours. Trustee St. Andrews Preservation Trust, 1971-85, chmn. 1977-81; active Council for Mus. and Galleries of Scotland, Edinburgh, 1982-85. Fellow Brit. Acad., Royal Hist. Soc., Soc. Antiquaries London. Avocations: golf, gardening, walking. Home: Birmingham, England. Died Feb. 2, 2014.

**BROOMFIELD, ROBERT CAMERON,** federal judge; b. Detroit, June 18, 1933; s. David Campbell and Mabel Margaret (Van Deventer) B.; m. Cuma Lorena Cecil, Aug. 3, 1958; children: Robert Cameron Jr., Alyson Paige, Scott McKinley. BS, Pa. State U., 1955; LLB, U. Ariz., 1961. Bar: Ariz. 1961, US Dist. Ct. Ariz. 1961. Clk., bailiff for Judge Jack D. H. Hays Ariz. Superior Ct., 1961—62; assoc. Carson, Messinger, Elliot, Laughlin & Ragan, Phoenix, 1962-65, ptnr., 1966-71; judge Ariz. Superior Ct., Phoenix, 1971-85, presiding judge, 1974-85, presiding judge juvenile divsn., 1972—74; judge US Dist. Ct. Ariz., Phoenix, 1985—94, chief judge, 1994-99, sr. judge, 1999—2014; judge Fgn. Intelligence Surveillance Ct. (FISC), 2002—09. Faculty Nat. Jud. Coll., Reno, 1975-82. Contbr. articles to profl. jours. Adv. bd. Boy Scouts America, Phoenix, 1968-75; tng. com. Ariz. Acad., Phoenix, 1980-91; pres. Paradise Valley Sch. Bd., Phoenix, 1969-70; bd. dirs. Phoenix Together, 1982—87, Crisis Nursery, Phoenix, 1976-81; chmn. 9th Cir. Task Force on Ct. Reporting, 1988-91; space and facilities com. U.S. Jud. Conf., 1987-93, chmn., 1989-93, chmn. security, space and facilities com., 1993-95, budget com., 1997-2013, chmn. economy subcom., 2003-13; founding mem. Sandra Day O'Connor Inn of Ct.,

1988-94. Recipient Faculty award Nat. Jud. Coll., 1979, Disting. Jurist award Miss. State U., 1986, Disting. Citizen award U. Ariz. Alumni Assn., 2006. Mem. ABA (chmn. Nat. Conf. State Trial Judges 1983-84, pres. Nat. Conf. Met. Cts. 1978-79, chmn. bd. dirs. 1980-82, Justice Tom Clark award 1980, bd. dirs. Nat. Ctr. for State Cts. 1980-85, Disting. Svc. award 1986), Ariz. Bar Assn., Maricopa County Bar Assn. (Disting. Public Svc. award 1980), Ariz. Judges Assn. (pres. 1981-82), American Judicature Soc. (spl. citation 1985), Maricopa County Med. Soc. (Disting. Svc. medal 1979), Rotary. Home: Phoenix, Ariz. Died July 10, 2014.

**BROPHY, JERE HALL,** manufacturing executive; b. Schenectady, Mar. 11, 1934; s. Gerald Robert and Helen Dorothy (Hall) B.; m. Joyce Elaine Wright, Aug. 18, 1956; children: Jennifer, Carolyn, Jere. BS in Chem. Engring, U. Mich., 1956, BS in Metall. Engring, 1956, MS, 1957, PhD, 1958. Asst. prof. Mass. Inst. Tech., 1958-63; sect. supr. nickel alloys sect. Paul D. Merica Research Lab., Inco, Inc., Suffern, NY, 1963-67, research mgr. non-ferrous group, 1967-72, asst. mgr., 1972-73, mgr., 1973-77; dir. research and devel. and dir. Paul D. Merica Research Lab., Inco, Inc. (Inco Research and Devel. Center), 1978-80; dir. advanced tech. initiation INCO Ltd., NYC, 1980-82; v.p., dir. Materials and Mfg. Tech. Ctr. TRW Inc., Cleve., 1982-86, v.p. mfg. and materials devel. automotive sect., 1986-88; v.p. technology Brush Wellman Inc., Cleve., 1988-96; cons., from 1996. Author: (with J. Wolff) Thermodynamics of Structure; Contbr. (with J. Wolff) tech. articles to profl. jours. Fellow Am. Soc. Metals, AAAS; mem. Am. Inst. Mining and Metall. Engrs. (dir. IMD div. 1973-76), Am. Mgmt. Assn. (research and devel. council 1975-87). Clubs: Edgewater Yacht. Episcopalian. Died Aug. 23, 2013.

**BROTMAN, STANLEY SEYMOUR,** federal judge; b. Vineland, NJ, July 27, 1924; s. Herman Nathaniel and Fanny (Melletz) B.; m. Suzanne M. Simon, Sept. 9, 1951; children: Richard A., Alison B. BA, Yale U., 1947; LLB, Harvard U., 1950. Bar: NJ 1950, DC 1951. Pvt. practice, Vineland, 1952-57; ptnr. Shapiro, Brotman, Eisenstat & Capizola, Vineland, 1957-75; judge US Dist. Ct. NJ, Camden, 1975—90, sr. judge, 1990—2014; acting chief judge Dist. Ct. of V.I., 1989-92; judge US Fgn. Intelligence Surveillance Ct., 1997—2004. Mem. NJ Bd. Bar Examiners, 1970-74. Chmn. editl. bd. NJ State Bar Jour, 1969-74; contbr. articles to profl. jours. Trustee Newcomb Hosp., Vineland, 1953-68. With US Army, 1943-45, 51-52. Recipient Medal of Honor, NJ State Bar Found., 1990, Person of Yr. award, Virgin Islands Bar Assn., 1991, Herbert Harley award, American Judicature Soc., 1994, William J. Brennan Jr. award, Assn. Fed. Bar NJ, 1995. Fellow American Bar Found., Jud. Conf. US (space and facilities com. 1987-93); mem. ABA (house of dels. 1975-80, state del. 1982-93, mem. judicial immigration edn. project, chmn. adv. com. 1996-2005), Nat. Conf. Fed. Trial Judges (exec. com. 1984-87, chmn.-elect 1986-87, chmn. 1987-88, chmn. standing com. jud. selection, tenure and compensation 1988-92, chmn. steering com. of nominating com. 1992-93, standing com. Fed. Jud. Improvements 1992-2003), American Judicature Soc. (dir. 1995-2000), NJ State Bar Assn. (pres. 1974-75), Cumberland County Bar Assn. (pres. 1969-70), Assn. of Fed. Bar of State of NJ, Harvard U. Law Sch. Assn. NJ (pres. 1974-75), Fed. Judges Assn. (v.p. 1993-97), Yale U. Alumni Assn., American Legion, Jewish War Veterans, Yale Club, B'nai B'rith, Masons, Shriners. Avocations: photography, travel. Home: Voorhees, NJ. Died Feb. 21, 2014.

**BROVCHENKO, VLADIMIR GRIGORIEVICH,** nuclear engineering researcher; b. Novocoobansk, Krasnodar, Russia, Dec. 5, 1923; s. Grigori Efimovich and Anna Haritonovna (Peklo) B.; m. Zoia Petrovna Evlampieva, July 12, 1946. Grad. as engr.-physicist, Bauman Tech. U., Moscow, 1951; D Tech. Sci., Lebedev Physics Inst, Moscow, 1971. Cert. in electronic engring. Rschr. Kapitsa Inst., Moscow, 1951-55; leading rschr. Kurchatov Inst., Russian Rsch. Ctr., from 1955. Co-author: (monograph) Electronics for Electrostatic Accelerators, 1969; mem. editl. bd. Instruments and Exptl. Techniques, 1978—; contbr. articles to sci. publs., including Instruments and Exptl. Techniques. Recipient Order of the Red Star 1944, Sign of the Honour, 1984, of the Patriotic War, 1985. Mem. Italian Phys. Soc. Home: Moscow, Russia. Died May 8, 2003.

**BROWN, ADRIAN WORLEY,** manufacturing executive; b. Orlando, Fla., Feb. 4, 1928; s. James Adrian and Madoline (Worley) B.; m. Mary Lou Morris; children: Adrian W., Nancy, Betsy. AB, U. Fla., 1950, LL.B., 1955. Bar: Fla. 1955. V.p. Brown & Brown, Inc., Daytona Beach, Fla., 1955-61; chmn. Fla. Indsl. Commn., 1961-64; with Rock-Tenn Co., Norcross, Ga., from 1964, pres., 1967-78, CEO, from 1967, chmn., from 1978. Mem. Fla. Bar Assn., Ga. Bus. and Industry Assn. (chmn., mem. exec. com.), U.S. Indsl. Council (v.p., mem. exec. com.), Paperboard Packaging Council (dir., mem. exec. com., mem. sr. adv. council), Order of Coif, Phi Delta Phi, Phi Delta Theta. Methodist. Home: Atlanta, Ga. Died Oct. 12, 1997.

**BROWN, AVERT HAYDEN,** animal scientist, educator; s. A. Hayden and Imogene Wanda Brown; m. Helen Virginia Gann, Nov. 9, 1977; 1 child, Ashley. BSc, Tenn. Tech. U., 1968; MSc, U. Tenn., 1974, PhD, 1976. Cert. Am. Coll. Animal Genetics, 1995, registered Am. Registry Profl. Animal Scientist. Prof. U. Ark., Fayetteville, Ark., from 1977. Mem. editl. bd.: Jour. Animal Sci., 2001—03; contbr. articles to profl. jours. Named to American Cattle Breeders Hall Fame, 1982. Mem.: American Registry Profl. Animal Scientists (pres. 1999—2000), Sigma Xi. Home: Fayetteville, Ark. Died May 26, 2014.

**BROWN, BOB OLIVER,** retired manufacturing company executive; b. Ft. Dodge, Iowa, June 5, 1929; s. Frank Arthur and Winona (Thietje) B.; m. JoAnn Louise Brown, Sept. 7, 1963 (div. Oct. 1989); children: Scott, Douglas. BSBA, U. Omaha, 1950; MS, U. Ill., 1951. CPA, Mo. Auditor Price Waterhouse, St. Louis, 1954-58, E A Rothaus, St. Louis, 1958-62; treas. Hazell Machine, St. Louis, 1962-64, Troug Nichols, Kansas City, Mo., 1964-66; v.p. Unitog Co., Kansas City, 1966-94; ret., 1994. Capt. USMC, 1951-54, Korea. Mem. AICPA, Mo. Soc. CPA, Tax Execs. Inst., Smithsonian Assocs., VFW, Am. Legion, Kansas City C. of C. Republican. Episcopalian. Died Aug. 12, 2002.

**BROWN, HAROLD EUGENE,** retired magistrate; s. Amos Eugene and Hazel Gladys (Thomas) B.; m. Carolyn Marie Sanders, Aug. 26, 1972; children: James Daryl, Deena Leigh, Cynthia Marie. Student, U. Md. Overseas Divsn., Verdun, France, 1962-64, Germanna C.C., 1978-84. Enlisted U.S. Army, 1954, advanced through grades to sgt. maj., 1977; White House liaison Chief of Staff Army, Washington, 1969—73; dep. dir. Def. Coop. Agy., New Delhi, 1973—77; post sgt. maj., co. comdr Fort A.P. Hill, Bowling Green, Va., 1977—81; magistrate 15th dist. Supreme Ct. Va., Fredericksburg, 1982—2002, apptd. chief magistrate, 1987—2000, apptd. magistrate VI, 2000—02; ret., 2002. Marriage commr. Commonwealth Va., 1984. Bd. dirs., former dir. Rappahannock Coun. Domestic Violence; bd. dirs. Rappahannock United Way. Decorated Cross of Gallantry (Republic of Vietnam). Mem. Am. Judges Assn., Va. Magistrates Assn., Va. Cmty. Criminal Justice Assn., Ret. Sgts. Maj. Assn. Avocations: golf, photography, computer programming. Deceased.

**BROWN, JAMES FRANKLIN,** political writer, consultant; b. NYC, Mar. 8, 1928; arrived in Eng., 1932 (parents Brit. citizens); s. Josiah Brown and Tabitha Evans; m. Margaret Wood, Aug. 14, 1954; children: Alison, Julia. BA in History with honors, Manchester U., Eng., 1949, MA in History, 1951; postgrad., U. Mich., 1951-52. Dir. rsch. dept. Radio Free Europe, Munich, 1969-78, dir., 1978-83; sr. analyst Rand, Santa Monica, Calif., 1987-91, Carnegie Internat. Commn. on the Balkans, Berlin, 1995-96. Cons. Rand, Santa Monica, 1974-2009, Stiftung Wissenschaft und Politik, Ebenhausen, Germany, 1983-85; vis. prof. U. Calif., Berkeley, 1989, UCLA, 1989-91, American U., Bulgaria, 2000. Author: The New Eastern Europe: The Khruschev Era and After, 1966, Bulgaria Under Communist Rule, 1971, Eastern Europe and Communist Rule, 1988, Surge to Freedom: The End of Communist Rule in Eastern Europe, 1991, Hopes and Shadows: Eastern Europe After Communism, 1994, The Grooves of Change: Eastern Europe in the New Millennium, 2000; contbr. numerous articles to scholarly jours. Flying officer Royal Air Force, 1952-54. Rsch. scholar Columbia U., 1968-69. Mem. Nat. Liberal Club (London). Mem. Labor Party. Anglican. Avocations: america-watching, walking, cricket, watching soccer. Home: Oxford, England. Died Nov. 16, 2009.

**BROWN, JUNE IRIS,** retired librarian, artist; d. Carl M. and June (Whiting) Slaughter; m. Jim E. Brown, July 16, 1961; 1 child, Julian L. BFA, U. Ala., 1964; MS in Art Edn., U. Tenn., 1977, MLS, 1983. Tchr. art Mobile (Ala.) County Schs., 1964—65; tchr. elem. sch. Jackson County Schs., Scottsboro, Ala., 1967—81; tchr. art RoaneState Coll., Harriman, Tenn., 1977—82; libr. Harriman (Tenn.) H.S., 1985—86, Tulane U., New Orleans, 1983—84, State Libr. Ala., Montgomery, Ala., 1989—2002, ret., 2002. Organizer art shows, 2000—01. One-woman shows include L.B. Wallace Coll., 1996, Auburn at Montgomery (Ala.) Technacenter, 1997, Ala. Pub. Libr. Svc., 2001, exhibited in group shows at Ala. Landscapes, 1998—99, 33d So. Artist Show, 1999—2000, Biennials Montgomery (Ala.) Mus. Art, 1997—2005, Nightingale Biennial, 1998—2006, Ala. Artists Show, Rosa Parks Libr., 2005, honorarium, Montgomery (Ala.) Mus. Fine Arts, 2003. Mem.: Ala. Watercolor Soc., Montgomery (Ala.) Art Guild, Capri Cmty. Film Soc., Montgomery (Ala.) Mus. Fine Arts. Avocations: reading, travel, birdwatching, gardening, swimming. Home: Montgomery, Ala. Died Apr. 5, 2008.

**BROWN, LES (LESTER LOUIS BROWN),** retired journalist; b. Indiana Harbor, Ind., Dec. 20, 1928; s. Irving H. and Helen (Feigenbaum) B.; m. Jean Rosalie Slaymaker, June 12, 1959; children: Jessica, Joshua, Rebecca. BA in English, Roosevelt U., Chgo., 1950. Entertainment industry reporter, reviewer theatrical events Chgo. bur. Variety, 1953-55, Chgo. bur. mgr., 1957-65; asso. editor Downbeat mag., 1955; co-founder, operator folk music cabaret The Gate of Horn, Chgo., 1956—2004; editor radio-TV dept. NYC, 1965-73; asst. mng. editor, 1973; radio-TV corr. NY Times, 1973-80; editor in chief Channels mag., 1980-87; sr. v.p. editorial devel. C.C. Pub., NYC, 1987-91; pub. TV Bus. Internat. mag., 1988-91, editor in chief, 1990-91; columnist, 1992—2004; pub. World Guide, 1990; ret., 2004. Cons. Revson Found., 1978, Ctr. for Comm., NYC, 1991-2003, World Alliance TV for Children, 1993-2001, Golden Rose Montreux TV Festival, 1994-2001, Monte Carlo TV Festival, 1994-2001; lectr. creative writing and entertainment industries Columbia Coll., Chgo., 1959-62, scholar-in-residence, 1985; lectr. comm. Hunter Coll., NYC, 1973-75, New Sch., NYC, 1977-80, Columbia U., 1994-96; lectr. Fordham U., 1995-2002, dir. TV Pantheon Oral History Project, 1996; Poynter fellow in modern journalism Yale U., 1977, lectr., 1978-80; assoc. fellow Morse Coll., 1978-86; Presdl. fellow Aspen Inst., 1978; bd. dirs. Dore Schary Awards, World TV and Radio Coun. UNESCO; sr. fellow Freedom Forum Media Studies Ctr. Columbia U., 1992-93. Author: lyrics Abilene, 1963, Televi$ion: The Business Behind The Box, 1971, Electric Media, 1973, New York Times Encyclopedia of Television, 1977, Keeping Your Eye on Television, 1979; Les Brown's Encyclopedia of Television, 1982, Fast Forward: The New Television and American Society, 1983, Les Brown's Encyclopedia of Television, 1992 Mem. Film-TV adv. bd. N.Y. State Coun. on Arts, 1975; pres. Media Commentary Coun. Inc. With AUS, 1951-53. Aviation engr. US Army, 1951—53. Recipient Silver Cir. award N.Y. Chpt. Nat. Acad. TV Arts & Sciences, 1996. Home: Larchmont, NY. Died Nov. 4, 2013.

**BROWN, LESTER LOUIS See BROWN, LES**

**BROWN, ROBERT ORDWAY,** food products executive; b. Tyler, Minn., July 31, 1917; s. Peter J. and Ella M. (Hansen) Brown; m. Margrethe Frederiksen Brown, June 12, 1943; children: Rolf, Linnea Lauren Berg, Karla, Paul, Grete. BSChemE, U. Minn., 1939. Sect. head. Pillsbury Mills, Mpls., 1939—56; cons. engr. Robert O. Brown Co., Mpls., from 1956. Mem.: ASHRAE, AAAS., Assn. Energy Engrs., Nat. Soc. Profl. Engrs., Am. Soc. Cons. Engrs., Am. Chem. Soc., Inst. Food Technologists, NY Acad. Scis., Am. Assn. Cereal Chemists, Am. Inst. Chem. Engrs. Home: Minneapolis, Minn. Died May 4, 2008.

**BROWN, WAYNE J.,** former mayor; b. 1936; BS, Ariz. State U. Staff acct. Arthur Andersen & Co. CPA's, 1960-63; mng. ptnr. Wayne Brown & Co. CPA's, 1964-79; dir. acctg. Ariz. State Dept. Adminstrn., 1979-80; chmn. & CEO Brown Evans Distbg. Co., Mesa, Ariz., from 1980; mayor City of Mesa, 1996—2000. Died May 14, 2013.

**BROWNE, SYLVIA (SYLVIA SHOEMAKER),** spiritual medium, writer; b. Kans. City, Mo., Oct. 19, 1936; d. Celeste Coil and Bill Shoemaker; m. Gary Dufresne, 1959 (div. 1972); children: Chris Dufresne, Paul Dufresne. MS in English Lit. Tchr.; founder Nirvana Found. Psychic Rsch., 1974, Soc. Novus Spiritus, Campbell, Calif., from 1986; pres. Sylvia Browne Corp., Campbell, Calif. Co-author (with Antoinette May): (books) Adventures of a Psychic, 1990; co-author: (with Lindsay Harrison) The Other Side and Back: A Psychic's Guide to Our World and Beyond, 1999, Life on the Other Side: A Psychic's Tour of the Afterlife, 2000, Blessings from the Other Side, 2000, Past Lives, Future Healing: A Psychic Reveals the Secrets to Good Health and Great Relationships, 2001, Visits from the Afterlife, 2003, Sylvia Browne's Book of Dreams, 2003, Prophecy: What the Future Holds for You, 2004, Psychic Children: Revealing the Intuitive Gifts and Hidden Abilities of Boys and Girls, 2007, End of Days, 2008; co-author: (with Chris Dufresne) Animals on the Other Side, 2005, Christmas in Heaven, 2006, Spirit of Animals, 2007; author: Journey of the Soul, Psychic Healing: Using the Tools of a Medium to Cure Whatever Ails You, All Pets Go To Heaven: The Spiritual Lives of the Animals We Love, Journal of Love & Healing, God, Creation, and Tools for Life, 2000, Astrology Through a Psychic's Eyes, 2000, Meditations, 2000, Soul's Perfection, 2000, The Nature of Good and Evil, 2001, Prayers, 2002, Conversations with the Other Side, 2002, Sylvia Browne's Book of Angels, 2003, Mother God: The Feminine Principle to Our Creator, 2004, Sylvia Browne's Lessons for Life, 2004, Contacting Your Spirit Guide, 2005, Secrets & Mysteries of the World, 2005, Phenomenon: Everything You Need to Know About the Paranormal, 2005, If You Could See What I See, 2006, Exploring the Levels of Creation, 2006, Insight: Case Files from the Psychic World, 2006, The Mystical Life of Jesus: An Uncommon Perspective on the Life of Christc, 2006, Light a Candle, 2006, Father God: Co-Creator to Mother God, 2007, Spiritual Connections: How to Find Spirituality Throughout All the Relationships in Your Life, 2007, Secret Societies and How They Affect Our Lives Today, 2007, The Two Marys: The Hidden History of the Mother and Wife of Jesus, 2007, Temples on the Other Side: How Wisdom from "Beyond the Veil" Can Help You Right Now, 2008, Mystical Traveler: How to Advance to a Higher Level of Spirituality, 2008, All Pets Go To Heaven, 2009, Psychic Healing, 2009, Messaages From the Spirit, 2009, Accepting the Psychic Torch, 2009, The Truth About Physics, 2009, Psychic: My Life in Two Worlds, 2010, Afterlives of the Rich and Famous, 2011. Died Nov. 20, 2013.

**BRUCKMANN, DONALD JOHN,** investment banker; b. Montclair, NJ, Jan. 4, 1929; s. William A. and Elizabeth M. (Fullmer) B.; m. Mary Thudium, June 1, 1957. BA, Lafayette Coll., Easton, Pa., 1950; LL.B., Columbia U., 1955. Bar: N.Y. 1955. Assoc. Simpson, Thacher & Bartlett, NYC, to 1960; sr. v.p., dir. Smith Barney, Harris Upham & Co., investment bankers, 1963-73, Dean Witter Reynolds Inc., NYC, 1973-83; pres., chief exec. officer Dean Witter Reynolds Internat. Inc., 1974-83; dir., fin. adviser Bank Audi (USA), NYC, 1986-94, mem. adv. bd., 1995-96. Chmn. bd. Animal Med. Ctr., 1996—. Chmn. bd. mgrs. N.Y. Bot. Garden, 1976-86, trustee, 1973—; mem. coun., trustee Cooper-Hewitt Mus., N.Y.C., 1987—, chmn., 1990-93; bd. dirs. Morningside House, N.Y.C., 1960-80; bd. dirs. Pa. Ave. Devel. Corp., Washington, 1973-81, vice chmn., 1973-79; trustee Cen. Park Conservancy, N.Y.C., 1980-93; mem. internat. capital mkts. adv. com. N.Y. Stock Exch., 1980-86; trustee Animal Med. Ctr., N.Y.C., 1990—; v.p., East Hampton Beach Preservation Soc., 1982—, bd. dirs., 1988—; trustee Village Preservation Soc., founding trustee Garden Conservancy, 1989—. 1st lt. U.S. Army, 1950-52. Mem. Assn. of Bar of City of N.Y., Asia Soc. (vice chmn., bd. dirs. 1983-89), Bond Club N.Y.C., Maidstone Club, Knickerbocker Club, Devon Yacht Club. Republican. Home: New York, NY. Died Apr. 21, 1999.

**BRUEMMER, FRED,** writer, photographer; b. Riga, Latvia, June 26, 1929; emigrated to Can., 1951, naturalized, 1956; s. Arist and Dorothea (Wahl) B.; m. Maud van den Berg, Mar. 31, 1962; children: Aurel, Rene. Student Fed. Republic Germany schs.; DLitt (hon.), U. N.B., Can., 1989. Self-employed writer-photographer specializing in arctic and antarctic regions, 1961—; books include The Long Hunt, 1969, Seasons of the Eskimo, 1971, Encounters with

Arctic Animals, 1972, The Arctic, 1974, The Life of the Harp Seal, 1977, Children of the North, 1979, Summer at Bear River, 1980, The Arctic of the World, 1985, Arctic Animals, 1986, Seasons of the Seal, 1988, World of the Polar Bear, 1989, (with Eric S. Grace) Seals, 1991, The Narwhal, 1993, (with Angéle Delaunois), Les Animaux du Grand Nord, 1993, (with Karen Pandell) Land of Dark, Land of Light, 1993, Arctic Memoires: Living with the Inuit, 1993, (with Angéle Delaunois) Nanook and Naoya: The Polar Bear Cubs, 1995, Kotik: The Baby Seal, 1995, (with Thomas D. Mangelsen) Polar Dance, 1996, Seals in the Wild, 1998, Glimpses of Paradise: The Marvel of Massed Animals, 2002, Survival: A Refugee Life, 2005, Islands of Fate, 2006, Arctic Visions: Pictures from a Vanished World, 2008 Decorated Order of Can.; Recipient Queen Elizabeth II Silver Jubilee medal, 1978, Canadian Anniversary Commemorative medal, 1993, Queen Elizabeth II Diamond Jubilee medal, 2013. Fellow Arctic Inst. N.Am., Royal Can. Acad. Art, Travel Journalists Guild, N.Am. Nature Photography Assn. (Lifetime Achievement award 2003). Died Dec. 17, 2013.

**BRÜGGEN, FRANS (FRANCISCUS JOZEF BRÜGGEN),** recorder player, conductor, musicologist; b. Amsterdam, Oct. 30, 1934; s. August and Johanna (Verkley) Brüggen; m. Machtel Israels; children: Zephyr, Eos;children from previous marriage: Alicia, Laura. Studied recorder with Kees Otten, awarded recorder diploma, Muzieklyceum Amsterdam; studied musicology, U. Amsterdam. Erasmus prof. late Baroque music Harvard U., Cambridge, Mass., 1972-73; Regent's prof. U. Calif., Berkeley, 1974; prof. recorder & early 18th century music Royal Conservatory, The Hague, Netherlands; condr. symphonic music, 1981—2014; founder, condr. Orch. of the Eighteenth Century, 1981—2014. Mem. various avant-garde ensembles including SourCream; performer and condr. numerous concerts early and modern music; performer concerts with cellist Anner Bylsma and harpsichordist Gustav Leonhardt; guest condr. Minn. Orch., Concertgebouw Orch. of Amsterdam, San Francisco Symphony Chamber Orch., L.A. Chamber Orch., Tafelmusik (Toronto), St. Paul Chamber Orch., Northwest Chamber Orch. of Seattle. Recordings include Mendelssohn Symphony No. 4, Schubert Symphony No. 5, Symphonies No. 4 and 6; pub. various edits. early music. Died Aug. 13, 2014.

**BRUN, JEAN,** philosophy educator; b. Mar. 13, 1919; Philosophy educator; b. Agen, France, Mar. 13, 1919; s. Ernest and Berthe (Garnier) B.; m. Jacqueline Bessat, Jan. 10, 1940; 1 child, Jean-Pierre. Licence-es-lettres U. Sorbonne, 1939, Agregation de philosophie, 1946, Doctorat es lettres, 1961. Prof., French Inst., London, 1949-55; prof. lere super. U. Paris, 1955-57; asst. Sorbonne, Paris, 1957-61; prof. Faculte des Lettres, Dijon, France, 1961— . Author: Le retour de Dionysos, 1969, La Nudite humaine (prize, Acad. Francaise 1974), Les vagabonds de l'Occident (prize Institut 1976), Les rivages du Monde, 1979, Les masques du desir, 1981, L'Homme et le Langage, 1985, La Main et L'Esprit, 1986, La Nudité Humaine, 1987, Philosophie et Christianismé, 1988. Served to lt. French Army, 1939-42. Decorated Legion d'honneur, Ordre du Merite, Croix de Guerre, Palmes Academiques. Mem. Societe francaise de philosophie, Societe bourguignonne de philosophie, Academie des Sciences arts et Belles Lettres. Clubs: Confrerie des Chevaliers du Tastevin. Home: Fontaine les Dijon, France. Deceased.

**BRUNNER, MATHIAS JOHN,** mechanical engineer, consultant; b. Bklyn., May 28, 1922; s. John Peter and Julia Margaret (Kastner) B.; m. Lillian Alma Sholtis, Sept. 8, 1951; children: Janet L., Carol A., Douglas. B in Mech. Engring., Pratt Inst., 1943; postgrad., U. Pitts., 1946; MS in Mech. Engring., U. Pa., 1947, postgrad., 1960-63. Registered profl. engr., Pa. Jr. design engr. divsn. steam Westinghouse Elec. Corp., Lester, Pa., 1943-50, design engr., 1950-54, sr. design engr., 1954-56, fellow engr., 1956-57; specialist divsn. advanced studies reentry sys. Gen. Elec. Co., Phila., 1957-68, cons. engr., 1968-79, ssr. aerothermodynamics engr., 1979-82; pres. Brunner Assocs., Inc., Berwyn, Pa., 1982-95, Lancaster, Pa., 1995—98. Lectr. extension Pa. State U., 1948-50. Contbr. to tech. pubs.; patentee in field. Fellow AIAA (assoc., nat. aerothermodynamics tech. com.); mem. AAAS, ASME (life, chmn. 1943), Am. Rocket Soc. (vice-chmn. Valley Forge sect. 1958-60), N.Y. Acad. Scis., Nat. Soc. Profl. Engrs., Tau Beta Pi, Phi Sigma Omega. Died 1998.

**BRYANT, CHARLES GYUDE,** former President of Liberia; b. Monrovia, Liberia, Jan. 17, 1949; m. Rosie Lee-Bryant; 3 children. BSc in Econs., Cuttington U. Coll., 1972. Fleet mgr. Mesurado Group of Cos., Liberia, 1972—73; dir. Dept. Planning and Devel. Nat. Port Authority, Liberia, 1973—77; founder, pres., CEO Liberia Machinery and Supply Co., 1977—2014; interim pres. Govt. of Liberia, Monrovia, 2003—06. Co-founder Liberia Action Party, from 1984, chmn.; chmn. endowment Episc. Ch., 1984; chmn. diocesan bd. trustees Episcopalian Ch., Liberia. Died Apr. 16, 2014.

**BUBNICKI, ZDZISLAW,** computer science and engineering educator; b. Lvov, Poland, June 17, 1938; s. Franciszek and Stefania Bubnicki. MSc, Silesian Tech. U., Gliwice, Poland, 1960; PhD, Wroclaw U. Tech., Poland, 1964, DSc, 1967. Asst. prof. control and systems engring. Wroclaw U. Tech., 1960-68, assoc. prof. control and systems engring., 1968-73, full prof. control and systems engring., from 1973; dir. Inst. Info. Sci. and Engring., Wroclaw, from 1981. Pres. Wroclaw br. Polish Acad. Scis., 1991—, chmn. scientific coun. of Systems Rsch. Inst., 1989—, pres. automation com., 1988—; mem. Gen. Assembly of Internat. Fedn. for Info. Processing, 1988—, governing bd. European Union Control Assn., 2004-; chmn. Internat. Confs. on Systems Sci., Wroclaw, 1973—. Author: Convergence of Approximation Processes in Discrete Systems, 1966, Identification of Control Plants, 1980, Introduction to Expert Systems, 1990, Foundations of Management Information Systems, 1993, Uncertain Logics, Variables and Systems, 2002, Control Theory and Algorithms, 2002, Analysis and Decision Making in Uncertain Systems, from 2004, Modern Control Theory, 2005; editor-in-chief Systems Sci. internat. jour., from 1975. Recipient award for Outstanding Sci. Achievements, Ministry Rsch. and High Edn., Poland, 1992, Silver Core award, Internat. Fedn. Info. Processing, 1998, Best Paper award, Internat. Conf. in Belgium, 2000, Leadership in Sci. and Edn. award, Internat. Inst. for Advanced Studies in Sys. Rsch. and Cybernetics, 2002, Life-long Achievement award, 2003, Book of Yr. award, 2004. Mem.: AAAS, IEEE (sr.), Russian Academy Natural Sci., Internat. Inst. Gen. Systems Studies, Internat. Assn. Sci. and Tech. for Devel., IEEE Computer Soc., World Orgn. Systems and Cybernetics (hon.). Home: Wroclaw, Poland. Died Mar. 12, 2006.

**BUCHHEIM, LOTHAR-GÜNTHER,** publisher, writer; b. Weimar, Germany, Feb. 6, 1918; m. Diethild Wickboldt, 1955; children: Yves-Bruno, Nina Student, Dresden Acad., Art Acad., Munich. Owner, pub. Buchheim Verlag, Feldafing, Germany. Author: Tage und Nâchte steigen aus dem Strom, 1941, Die Künstlergemeinschaft Brücke, 1958, Graphik des deutschen Expressionismus, 1959, Max Beckmann, 1959, Otto Mueller, 1963, Das Boot, 1973, U-Boot-Krieg, 1976, Staatsgala, 1977, Mein Paris, 1977, Die Tropen von Feldafing, 1978, Staatszirkus, 1978, Der Luxusliner, 1980, U 96, 1981, Der Film-Das Boot, 1981, Das Segelschiff, 1982, Die U-Boot-Fahrer, 1985, Das Museum in den Wolken, 1986, Zu Tode gesiegt-Der Untergang der U-Boote, 1988, Malerbuch, 1988, Ehrenbürger von Chemmitz, 1992, Ernst-Hoferichter-Preis München, 1993, Die Festung, 1995, Großes Verdienstkreuz mit Stern des Verdienstordens der Bundesrepublik Deutschland, 1996, Jäger im Weltmeer, 1997, Bayer Maximiliansorden, 1998, Max-Pechstein-Ehrenpreis der Stadt Zwickau, 1999, Der Abschied, 2000, Goldener Ehreuring des Landkreises Weilheim-Schougau. With German Navy. Died Feb. 22, 2007.

**BUDREVICS, ALEXANDER,** landscape architect; b. Riga, Latvia, Jan. 3, 1925; arrived in Can., 1952; m. Milija Vite, Apr. 8, 1948; children: Valdis, Dace, Arnis. Grad. hort. sch., Latvia, 1944; grad. landscape architect, St. Albans Coll., Eng., 1949, London Coll. Art, 1951. Registered landscape architect, Ont., Can. Practice landscape architecture, 1960; staff various firms, Canada, 1960; pres. Alexander Budrevics & Assocs. Ltd., Don Mills, Ont., from 1965. Ptnr. Golf Course Devel. Assn., 1969—. Designer over 3000 projects including Nat. Home Show, CNE hort. shows, Century Sq.; contbr. articles to profl. jours. Chmn. exec. bd. Latvian Boy Scouts Assn., from 2008; pres. gen. assembly Latvian Nat. Fedn. Can., 1992—2000, hon. mem., from 2000; pres. Kristus Darz Home for the Aged, 1989—92, Ont. Swimming Pool Assn., Toronto, 1964; pres. cultural and edn. fund Latvian Nat. Fedn. Can., 2002—04. Fellow Can. Soc. Landscape Architects (life), Am. Landscape Architects Soc., Am. Inst. Landscape Architects (internat. pres. 1969-71), Ont. Assn. Landscape Architects (emeritus, pres. 1977-79, Disting. Achievement award 1987), Can. Latvian Bus. and Profl. Assn. (pres. 1971—), Latvian Nat. Fedn. Can. (pres. 2003-04), Latvian Credit Union Assn. (pres. 2007-) Lutheran. Avocations: gardening, travel. Home: Toronto, Canada. Died Apr. 11, 2014.

**BUDZIńSKI, FRANCISZEK,** economics educator; b. Żydaczó, Poland, Apr. 12, 1923; s. Józef and Rozalia (Hladec) B.; m. Janina Leszczycka, Feb. 25, 1949 (dec. Oct. 1985); m. Maria Glowińska, Mar. 17, 1990. MA in Philosophy, U. Cracow, Poland, 1949, PhD in Law, 1952; PhD in Econs., Acad. Econs., Cracow, 1965. Asst. tchr. Acad. Econs., Cracow, 1948-52; asst. prof. U. Tech., Cracow, 1952-67, prof. econs., from 1967, dir. Inst. Social and Econ. Studies, 1982-92. Author: Inventions, Patents and Economic Development, 1977, Economic Implications of International License Agreements, 1979, Science in the Development Process of Productive Force, 1983 (Ministry of Nat. Edn. award 1984), Polish Schools in Hungary during World War II, 1988 (Ministry of Nat. Edn. award 1989), Foreign Direct Investment as Instrument of International Technological Transfer, 1987, The Poles at Hungarian University Schools during World War II, 1993. Mem. Polish Acad. Scis. (econ. commn., bd. dirs. econ. commn. 1986-92), Com. Redaction Folia Oeconomica. Avocations: mountain climbing, swimming, kayaking. Home: Cracow, Poland. Deceased.

**BUDZINSKI, JAMES EDWARD,** interior designer; b. Jan. 4, 1953; s. Edward Michael and Virginia (Caliman) B. Student, U. Cin., 1971-76. Mem. design staff Perkins & Wills Archs., Inc., Chgo., 1973-75, Med. Architectonics, Inc., Chgo., 1975-76; v.p. interior design Interior Environs., Inc., Chgo., 1976-78; pres. Jim Budzinski Design, Inc., Chgo., 1978-80; dir. interior design Robinson, Mills & Williams, San Francisco, 1980-87; dir. design, interior arch. Whisler Patri, San Francisco, 1987-90; v.p. design sales and mktg. Deepa Textiles, 1990-95; v.p. Workplace Studio One Workplace L. Ferrari, San Jose, Calif., 1997-2000; strategic envisioner OneWorkplace, 2000—04; ind. design cons. Jim Budzinski Design, Residential Design and Devel., from 2004. Instr. design Harrington Inst. Design, Chgo.; cons. Chgo. Art Inst., Storwal Internat., Inc.; spkr. profl. confs. Designs include 1st Chgo. Corp. Pvt. Banking Ctr., 1st Nat. Bank Chgo. Monroe and Wabash Banking Ctr., 1978, IBM Corp., San Jose, Deutsche Bank, Frankfort, Crowley Maritime Corp., San Francisco, office for Brobeck, Phleger and Harrison, offices for chmn. bd. Fireman's Fund Ins. Cos., Nob Hill Club, Fairmont Hotel, San Francisco, offices for Cooley, Goodword, Castro, Huddleson, and Tatum, Palo Alto, Calif., offices for Pacific Bell Acctg. divsn., San Francisco, showroom for Knoll Internat., San Francisco, lobby, lounge TransAm. Corp. Hdqs., San Francisco, offices for EDAW, San Francisco, showroom for Steelcase, Inc., Bally of Switzerland, N.Am. Flagship store, San Francisco; corp. Hdqs. Next Inc., Redwood City, Calif., Schafer Furniture Design, Lobby Renovation 601 California, San Francisco, Bennedetti Furniture Inc. Furniture Design; interiors Minnis Residence, Seattle and Napa, Calif., Cortesi Residence, Cobb, Wolz/Polldine Residence, O'Brien Residence, Cobb, Calif. Pres. No. Calif. chpt. Design Industries Found. for AIDS. Home: Palm Springs, Calif. Died Feb. 7, 2014.

**BUECHNER, MARGARET,** composer, music educator; b. Hannover, Germany, May 27, 1922; came to U.S., 1951, U.S. citizenship, 1961; d. Wilhelm and Martha Voss; m. Werrner Buechner, 1948 (dvi. 1972). MusM, U. Königsberg and U. Wuerzburg and Conservatory, Germany, 1943; pvt. studies in composition and orch. with Otto Luening, Columbia U., 1954-55. Ind. composer, from 1932; choir dir., educator, 1946-87; founder, pres. Mich. Composers League, 1960-66. Host classical music ednl. radio programs, 1961-64; mem. Composers Conf., Bennington, Vt., 1954, 55. Composer, librettist numerous story ballets including The Key, Phantomgreen, The Legend of Alice, Mayerling, Elizabeth, The Erlking, stageless full-length Princess and the Pea Ballet, stageless Elf-King Ballet, stageless full-length Immensee ballet, stageless Adventures of Easter Bunny ballet; also various symphonies, tone poems, many chamber music works, concert performances; recs. with the Nürnberger Symphoniker (German Symphony Orch.), including Ballet Suite of Phantomgreen and the complete music of the evening-length ballet Elizabeth and the tone poem The Old Swedes Church, recorded with Royal Scottish Nat. Orch. Essay I and The Flight of the Am. Eagle, Symphonic Poem Erlkönig Symphonic Trilogy The Am. Civil War, Orchestral Choral Reminiscence The Liberty Bell, (ballet music of evening length) La Belle et la Bête (Beauty and the Beast) performances Grand Théatre de Bordeaux, France and in Genova, Italy; other recs. include Five Symphonic Classics, Symphonic Ballet Music, Sixteen Symphony Orch. Children's Recital Dances, The Key complete ballet music, Suites and others, also ednl. orchestral CD; many stage performances The Key, Phantomgreen; TV broadcasts The Key; collection of 71 recorded dramatic symphonic concert works on CDs. Avocation: gardening. Died June 8, 1998.

**BUESING, OLIVER R.,** surgeon; b. Grand Rapids, Mich., Jan. 19, 1910; s. William Desmond and Katherine Elizabeth (Schantz) Buesing; m. Chris O. Schott, Dec. 7, 1948 (dec. 1973); children: Mary A., Russel, Suzy Buesing Blaine; m. Inez P. Love, Aug. 7, 1981. MD, U. Mich., 1936. Diplomate Am. Bd. Surgery. Intern Butterworth Hosp., Grand Rapids, 1936—37, jr. attending surg. staff, 1938—42; commd. to lt. US Army, 1942, col., 1962; chief surg. svc. 97th Gen. Hosp., Tilton Gen. Hosp., 2d Gen. Hosp.; basic sci. course Walter Reed Rsch. & Grad. Sch., Washington, 1947. Fellow surg. pathology Emory U., Atlanta, 1948, fellow surgery, 1949—51; cons. surgeon 9th Army, 1959—60; 1st Army, 1965—66; chief dept. surgery Munson Army Hosp., 1960—65, Patterson Army Hosp., 1965—67; ret., 1967; asst. chief surg. svc. VA Ctr., Leavenworth, Kans., 1967—79; asst. clin. prof. surgery U. Kans., Leavenworth, 1967—79; emeritus, from 1979. Decorated Legion of Merit. Fellow: ACS, Southwestern Surg. Congress (sr.); mem.: AMA, Ft. Leavenworth Officers Club. Republican. Died Feb. 11, 1988.

**BUESSELER, JOHN AURE,** ophthalmologist, management consultant; b. Madison, Wis., Sept. 30, 1919; s. John Xavier and Gerda Pernille (Aure) B.; m. Cathryn Anne Hansen, Dec. 26, 1959; 1 child, John McGlone. PhB, U. Wis., 1941, MD, 1944; MBA, U. Mo., 1965; DHL (hon.), Rawls Coll. Bus., Tex. Tech. U., Lubbock, 2005. Intern Cleve. City Hosp., 1944-45; resident U. Pa. Hosp., 1948-51; practice medicine specializing in ophthalmology Madison, 1953-59; prof., founding chief ophthalmology U. Mo., Columbia, 1959-66, chmn. dept. surgery, 1960-61; exec. officer Mo. Crippled Children's Service, 1967-70; exec. dir. Kansas City Gen. Hosp. and Med. Ctr., 1969-70; founding dean Tex. Tech U. Sch. Medicine, Lubbock, 1970-73, founding v.p. health affairs Univ. Complex, 1970-75, prof. dept. ophthalmology, prof. health orgn. mgmt., 1971-98, founding chmn. dept. health orgn. mgmt., 1971—75, prof. grad. sch. faculty, 1972-80, chmn. dept. ophthalmology, 1973-75; adj. prof. bus. adminstrn. Coll. Bus. Tex. Tech., Lubbock, 1992-98. Univ. prof. (disting. and multidisciplinary) Univ. Complex, 1973-98; founding v.p., CEO Tex. Tech. Univ. Health Scis. Ctr., 1971-74; pres. Radiol. Testing Lab., Inc., Madison, 1956-59; dir. House of Vision, Inc., Chgo., 1973-82; v.p. Madison Radiation Ctr., Inc., 1956-59; cons. NASA, mem. space medicine adv. group on devel. Orbiting Space Lab., Washington, 1963-66; cons. AEC, mem. Assn. Midwestern Univs.-Argonne (Ill.) Nat. Lab. biology com., 1965-69; cons. to pres. Argonne Univs. Assn., Chgo., 1967-68; comdr. 94th Gen. Hosp., U.S. Army Res., Mesquite, Tex., 1973-75; co-founder, incorporator, bd. dirs., past pres. Joint Commn. on Allied Health Pers. in Ophthalmology, Inc.; mem. Residency Rev. Com. for Ophthalmology, 1974-80, chmn., 1978-80; sr. cons., CEO, founder Health Orgn. Mgmt. Sys. Internat., 1978—; co-founder, founding chmn., chmn. bd. dirs. Tex. Aviation Heritage Found., Inc., 1997-99; co-founder, founding chmn., chmn. bd. dirs. Silent Wings Mus. Found., Inc., 2003-06. Contbr. articles to profl. jours. Served to capt. AUS, World War II, ETO; to maj. USAF, Korea; to col. USAR, Vietnam. Decorated Air medal with cluster, Legion of Merit; recipient Gold Medallion award for disting. achievement in ophthalmology Mo. Ophthal. Soc., 1967, Tex. Tech. U. Bd. Regents Resolution of Congratulations, 1973, Cert. of Citation Tex.

Ho. of Reps., 1973, 87, Disting. Alumnus citation U. Wis. Sch. Medicine, 1987, Statesmanship award Joint Commn. on Allied Health Personnel in Ophthalmology, Inc., 2005 Fellow ACS, Am. Acad. Ophthamology (Disting. Svc. in Edn. award 1969); mem. AMA, Tex. Med. Assn., Mo. Ophthal. Soc. (founder, past sec.-treas., pres., dir.), Alpha Omega Alpha. Home: Lubbock, Tex. Died Mar. 2014.

**BUFFART, LUCAS LEONARD,** military officer; b. Voorburg, The Netherlands, Aug. 18, 1947; s. H. F. Buffart and B. M. Van Goor; m. Marjolyn Josephine Voet, Aug. 21, 1976; children: Laurien, Tineke, Harmen. Grad., Royal Netherlands Naval Acad., 1991, U.S. Naval War Coll., 1992. Staff officer Sec. of Def., 1991-94; comdr. Netherlands Destroyer Squadron, 1994-95; chief of staff admiral Netherlands Fleet, 1995; dep. chief of naval staff for plans and policy, 1996-99; dep. cinc Royal Netherlands Navy, from 1999; admiral Netherlands Fleet, Den Helder. Died Apr. 2002.

**BUITENHUIS, PETER MARTINUS,** language professional, educator; b. London, Dec. 8, 1925; s. John A. and Irene (Cotton) B. BA with honors, Jesus Coll., Oxford U., Eng., 1949, MA, 1954; PhD, Yale U., 1955. Instr. U. Okla., Norman, 1949-51; instr. Am. studies Yale U., 1954-59; assoc. prof. English Victoria Coll. U. Toronto, Ont., Canada, 1959-66; vis. prof. U. Calif., Berkeley, 1966-67; prof. McGill U., Montreal, Que., Canada, 1967-75; prof., chmn. dept. English Simon Fraser U., Burnaby, B.C., Canada, 1975-82, prof. emeritus, from 1982. Author: Hugh MacLennan, 1968, The Grasping Imagination: the American Writings of Henry James, 1970, The Great War of Words: British, American and Canadian Propaganda and Fiction, 1914-1933, 1987, The House of the Seven Gables: Severing Family and Colonial Ties, 1991; editor: Selected Poems of E. J. Pratt, 1968, (with I. Nadel) George Orwell: A Reassessment, 1988, (with D. Staines) The Canadian Imagination; contbr. articles to profl. jours., popular press. Served to sub-lt. Royal Navy, 1943-46, Eng. Can. Coun. fellow, 1962-63; Am. Coun. Learned Socs. fellow, 1972-73; Social Scis. and Humanities Rsch. Coun. fellow, 1982-83, 91-94. Mem.: Assn. Can. Studies, Can. Assn. Am. Studies (pres. 1968—70), Am. Studies Assn. Home: West Vancouver, Canada. Died Nov. 28, 2004.

**BULL, HENRIK HELKAND,** architect; b. NYC, July 13, 1929; s. Johan and Sonja (Geelmuyden) B.; m. Barbara Alpaugh, June 9, 1956; children: Peter, Nina. BArch, MIT, 1952. With Mario Corbett, San Francisco, 1954-55; pvt. practice, 1956-68; ptnr. Bull, Field, Volkmann, Stockwell, Calif., 1968-82, Bull, Volkmann, Stockwell, Calif., 1982-90, Bull Stockwell and Allen, Calif., 1990-93, Bull, Stockwell, Allen & Ripley, San Francisco, 1993-96, Bull Stockwell Allen Archs., San Francisco, 1996—2008. Vis. lectr. Syracuse U., 1963; mem. adv. com. San Francisco Urban Design Study, 1970-71. Works include Sunset mag. Discovery House, Tahoe Tavern Condominiums, Lake Tahoe, Calif., Snowmass Villas Condominiums, Aspen, Colo., Northstar Master Plan Village and Condominiums, Moraga Valley Presbyn. Ch., Calif., Spruce Saddle Restaurant and Poste-Montane Hotel, Beaver Creek, Colo., Bear Valley visitor ctr., Point Reyes, Calif., The Inn at Spanish Bay, Pebble Beach, Calif., Taluswood Cmty., Whistler, B.C., Jackson Gore Inn, Okemo, Vt. 1st lt. USAF, 1952—54. Fellow AIA (pres. N. Calif. chpt. 1968, Firm award Calif. chpt. 1989). Democrat. Home: Berkeley, Calif. Died Dec. 3, 2013.

**BULLARD, ETHEL MUNDAY,** musician, educator; b. Cranston, RI; d. Alfred James and Martha Jane (Walker) Munday; m. Henry Messenger Bullard; 1 child, Thomas Robert. MusB, Am. Conservatory Music, Chgo.; postgrad, Northwestern U.; Attended, Am. Conservatory Music & Chgo. Mus. Coll. Tchr. piano, Oak Pk., Ill. Cons. in field. Oak Pk. Musical Theatre, from 1967; dir.(mus.):, 1971—79; compiler music appreciation course: Hadley Sch. Blind, 1967. Chmn. Beye Elem. Sch. PTA, Oak Pk., 1957, v.p., 1958. Recipient Steinway award, 1967, Commemorative medal, ABI, 1986. Mem.: Sonneck Soc., MacDowell Artists Assn., Am. Music Scholarship Assn., Nat. Guild Piano Tchrs., Am. Fedn. Musicians, Nat. Fedn. Music Clubs, Ill. State Music Tchrs. Assn. (Chgo. chmn. 1961—65, piano chmn. 1968), Music Tchrs. Nat. Assn., Soc. Am. Musicians, Eastern Star, Sigma Alpha Iota (editorial bd. 1970—73, nat. editor 1973—79, bd. dir. meml. Libr. at Music Libr. at U. Mich. from 1973, Honor award 1968). Congregational. Deceased.

**BULLARD, ROGER PERRIN,** artist; b. NYC, July 2, 1913; s. Roger Harrington and Annie Adams (Sturges) B.; m. Georgie Genevieve Hosford, Nov. 15, 1944; 1 child, Virginia Anne. Student, Art Students League, NYC, 1934-37, Universal Photographers Inc., The Bullard Haven Tech. Sch., Bridgeport, Conn., 1946. Freelance artist, Fairfield, Conn., 1937-40; machinist Heime Co., Fairfield, 1947-50, Exide Battery, Fairfield, 1950-52, Dictaphone, Bridgeport, Conn., 1952-55; draftsman Aircraft Drafting, Bridgeport, 1955-57, Sikorski Aircraft and Valve Corp., Bridgeport, 1955-56; airbrush artist Poly Photo, Bridgeport, 1957; freelance photographer Fairfield, 1958-77. Contbr. pen and ink drawings to Prof. Henry Fairfield Osborn's book, Probosidea Memoirs Mus. Natural History, N.Y.C., 1933-35. With U.S. Army, 1940-45, WWII. Republican. Episcopalian. Avocations: photography, art research, tennis, writing. Deceased.

**BULLOCK, SIR ALAN LOUIS CHARLES,** English educator; b. Dec. 13, 1914; s. Frank Allen Bullock; m. Hilda Yates, 1940; 4 children. MA, Oxford U., Eng. Raleigh lectr. Brit. Acad., 1967; Stevenson meml. lectr. LSE, 1970; Leslie Stephenson lectr. Cambridge U., Eng., 1976; with St. Catherine's Coll., Oxford. Author: Hitler: A Study in Tyranny, 1952, rev. edit., 1964, The Liberal Tradition, 1956, The Schellenberg Memoirs, 1956, The Life and Times of Ernest Bevin, vol. 1, 1960, vol. 2, 1967, vol. 3, 1983; editor: (with Oliver Stallbrass) Dictionary of Modern Thought, 1977, new edit. (with S. Trombley), 1988, new edit., 1999, The Faces of Europe, 1980, (with B.R. Woodings) Fontana Dictionary of Modern Thinkers, 1983, The Humanist Tradition in the West, 1985, Hitler and Stalin: Parallel Lives, 1991, rev. edit., 1993, Building Jerusalem: A Portrait of My Father, 2000, Ernest Bevin, 2002; gen. editor: (with Sir William Deakin) The Oxford History of Modern Europe. Trustee Aspen Inst. Home: Oxford, England. Died Feb. 2, 2004.

**BUMGARNER, JAMES SCOTT See GARNER, JAMES**

**BUNTING, BEVERLY DICKERSON,** volunteer worker; b. NYC, Nov. 29, 1924; d. Walter Hudson and Eva Louise (Fiscus) Dickerson; m. Harold Dutton Bunting (dec.). Diploma in math. and sci., Cozenovia (N.Y.) Jr. Coll., 1944; BA in Psychology and Sociology, Baldwin Wallace Coll., Berea, Ohio, 1948; postgrad. in mgmt., U. Tex., Arlington, 1960. Administrv. supr. St. Paul Hosp., Dallas, 1954-72; ret., 1972. Vol. VA Vol. Svc., Marine Corps League, Meals on Wheels; tutor Kings Hwy. Sch., Coatesville, Pa., 1984—; dir. ARC Blood Drives, Olivet United Meth. Ch., Coatesville, 1984—; started pet therapy program, VA Hosp., Coatesville, 1988; rep. Am. VA; past pres. Caln Civic Club. Sgt., USMC, 1944-46. Mem. Marine Corps League (VA Vol. Svc., numerous svc. awards). Methodist. Avocations: pets, travel, gardening. Home: Yorklyn, Del. Died Apr. 13, 2008.

**BUNTING, KENNETH FREEMAN,** retired newspaper editor; b. Houston, Dec. 9, 1948; s. Willie Freeman and Sarah Lee (Peterson) B.; m. Juliana Amy Jafvert, July 13, 1989; 1 child, Maxwell Freeman. Student, U. Mo., 1966-67; AA in Journalism, Lee Coll., 1968; BA in Journalism and History, Tex. Christian U., 1970; advanced exec. program, Northwestern U., 1996. Mgmt. trainee, reporter Harte-Hanks Newspapers Inc., Corpus Christi, Tex., 1970-71; reporter, then copy editor San Antonio Express-News, 1971-73; exec. asst. to Hon. G.J. Sutton Tex. House of Reps., San Antonio, 1973-74; reporter Cin. Post, 1974-78, Sacramento Bee, 1978; reporter, asst. city editor, state capitol corr. L.A. Times, 1978-87; capitol bur. chief, city editor, dep. mng. editor, sr. editor Ft. Worth Star-Telegram, 1987-93; mng. editor Seattle Post-Intelligencer, 1993-99; assoc. publisher Seattle Post-Intelligence, 2000—09; exec. dir. Nat. Freedom Information Coalition (NFOIC), 2010—14. Journalism instr. Orange Coast Coll., Costa Mesa, Calif., 1981-82; mem. adv. bd. Maynard Inst., Oakland, Calif. Bd. dirs. Seattle Symphony, 1995-97; mem. commn. Woodland Park Zoo, Seattle, 1995-96, 98; mem. Leadership Ft. Worth; former mem. journalism adv. bd. Tex. Christian U.; former mem. minorities task force Assn. for Edn. in Journalism and Mass Comms.; past pres. Press Club, Orange County, Calif.; past bd. dirs. Covington (Ky.) Cmty. Ctr.; past 1st v.p. Young Democrats of Tex.; past treas., mem. exec. bd. Freedom of Info. Found. of Tex.; leadership coun. ARC; bd. dirs. Alfred Friendly Press Fellowships. Named to The Schieffer Sch. Hall of Excellence, 2010. Mem. Nat. Assn. Black Journalists, AP Mng. Editors Assn. (mem. ethics com. 1995-96, bd. dirs. 1996-99), American Soc. Newspaper Editors (mem. diversity, leadership coms., chair edn. com.), Soc. Profl. Journalists (bd. dirs. western Wash. chpt. 1995-96), Seattle C. of C., Alliance for Edn. (bd. dirs.), Tex. Christian U. Alumni Assn. (bd. dirs.), Freedom of Info. Found. Tex., Rainier Club, Washington Athletic Club. Unitarian Universalist. Avocations: tennis, bridge, reading. Home: Seattle, Wash. Died Apr. 20, 2014.

**BURCH, FRANCIS FLOYD,** clergyman; b. Balt., May 15, 1932; s. Thaddeus Joseph and Frances Fidelis (Greenwell) Burch. BA, Fordham U., 1956, MA, 1958; PhL, Woodstock Coll., 1957, STL, 1964; postgrad., Tronchinnes, Belgium, 1964-65; Docteur, U. Paris, Sorbonne, 1967. Joined Soc. of Jesus, 1950, ordained priest Roman Cath. Ch., 1963. Tchr. Gonzaga HS, Washington, 1957-60; from asst. prof. to assoc. prof. English St. Joseph's U., Phila., 1967—76, prof., 1976—2009, prof. emeritus, 2009, asst. acad. dean, 1972-74, bd. dirs., 1971-76, sec. bd. dirs., 1971-75. Artist-scholar-in-residence Millersville U., Pa., 1978. Author: Tristan Corbiere: l'orginalite des "Amours janues" et leur influence sur T. S. Eliot, 1970; editor (with P. O. Walzer): Tristan Corbiere: Ouevres completes, 1970, Sur Tristan Corbiere: lettres inedites adressees au poete et premieres critiques le concernant, 1975; translator: The Path to Transcendence: From Philosophy to Mysticism in Saint Augustine (Paul Henry), 1981, 3d edit., 2009, The Personalist Challenge: Intersubjectivity and Ontology (Maurice Nedoncelle), 1984, 2nd edit., 2004; contbr. articles to profl. jours. Recipient Merit award, St. Joseph's U., 1980, 1983. Mem.: MLA, Princeton Club, Sigma Tau Delta, Alpha Sigma Nu, Alpha Epsilon Delta. Died Aug. 30, 2013.

**BURCH, JOHN RUSSELL,** retired military officer; b. Lexington, Ky., Aug. 6, 1945; s. Oakley Burch and Frances Lyle Ramsey; m. Idalia Amparo Murgas (div.); children: John Russell Jr., Eustacia Frances Burch O'Malley; m. Elizabeth Allen Murphy, June 20, 1999. AA, South Puget Sound CC, Olympia, Wash., 1992; BA cum laude, St. Martin's U., Lacey, Wash., 1993; MA, Pacific Luth. U., Tacoma, Wash., 1999. From pvt. to sgt. US Army Airborne Infantry, 1964—67; commd. 2nd lt. US Army, 1967, advanced through grades to capt., 1969, with Spl. Forces (Green Berets) Vietnam, 1967—70, from sgt. to 1st sgt. Spl. Forces, 1971—90, ret., 1990. Cubmaster, scoutmaster, dist. commr., Order of the Arrow advisor Boy Scouts Am., from 1965; mem. neighborhood and coun. com. Girl Scouts USA, 1972—80. Decorated Bronze Star, Purple Heart, Meritorious Svc. medal with Oak Leaf Cluster, Air medal, Combat Infantryman Badge, Master Parachutist Badge, Spl. Forces Tab, Pathfinder Badge. Mem.: VFW, DAV, Mil. Officers Assn. Am., Sons Am. Revolution (Dept. Ky. comdr. 2008—09, chpt. pres. 2010—11), Spl. Forces Assn., Mil. Order Purple Heart (chpt. comdr. 2004—09), Mensa, Nat. Eagle Scout Assn., Sons Union Vets Civil War (camp comdr. 2006—08, Dept. Ky. comdr. from 2008), Spl. Ops. Assn., Am. Legion, Phi Theta Kappa-acad. honor soc. Roman Catholic. Avocations: history, genealogy, archaeology, Civil War reenactment, heraldry. Home: Richmond, Ky. Died Apr. 12, 2012.

**BURCHFIELD, ROBERT WILLIAM,** language professional, educator; b. Wanganui, New Zealand, Jan. 27, 1923; arrived in Eng., 1949; s. Frederick and Mary Lauder (Blair) B.; m. Ethel May Yates, July 2, 1949 (div. 1976); children: Jennifer Catherine, Jonathan Robert, Elizabeth Jane; m. Elizabeth Austen Knight, Nov. 5, 1976. Student, Wanganui Tech. Coll., New Zealand, 1934-39, Victoria U. Coll., Wellington, New Zealand, 1940-41, 46-48, MA, 1948; student, Oxford U., Eng., 1949-53, BA, 1951, MA, 1955; LittD (hon.), Liverpool, 1978, Wellington, New Zealand, 1983. Jr. lectr. English Magdalen Coll. Oxford U., Eng., 1952-53, lectr. English Christ Ch., 1953-57, lectr. St. Peter's Coll., 1955-63, tutorial fellow, 1963-79; sr. research fellow St. Peter's Coll., 1979-90; editor Oxford U. Press, Oxford, 1957—86; chief editor The Oxford English Dictionaries, Oxford, 1971-84. Author: The Spoken Word, 1981, The English Language, 1985, Unlocking the English Language, 1989; editor: A Supplement to the Oxford English Dictionary, 1972—86, The New Zealand Pocket Oxford Dictionary, 1986, Studies in Lexicography, 1987; contbr. articles to lit. mags. Served in New Zealand Army, 1941-46. Named Commdr. of the Order of the British Empire by the Queen of Eng., 1975; New Zealand Rhodes Scholar, 1949. Fellow Inst. Linguists; mem. Am. Acad. Arts and Scis., English Assn. (pres. 1978-79), Early English Text Soc. (hon. sec. 1955-68, mem. council 1968-80). Home: Oxfordshire, England. Died July 5, 2004.

**BURD, CHARLES LESLIE,** lawyer, judge; b. Huntington, W.Va., July 20, 1947; s. Leslie L. and Patricia C. (Holderby) B.; m. JoAnn Renfroe, Jan. 27, 1968 (div. Feb. 1973); 1 child, Lisa Michele; m. Tamara Lynn Wood, Dec. 21, 1979. BA, Ohio State U., 1969, JD, 1972. Bar: Ohio 1973; U.S. Dist. Ct. (so. dist.) Ohio 1975; U.S. Ct. Appeals (4th cir.) 1973; U.S. Supreme Ct. 1979. Legal aide to atty. gen. State of Ohio, Columbus, 1971-72; ptnr. Kaiser & Burd, Chesapeake, Ohio, 1973-78; sole practice Chesapeake, 1978-83; ptnr. Burd & Cooper, Chesapeake, from 1984. Acting judge Lawrence County Ct., Chesapeake, 1975-78; judge, Lawrence County Mcpl. Ct., Chesapeake, 1982—. Bd. dirs. River Cities United Way. 1st lt. U.S. Army, 1971-76. Recipient Disting. Grad. award Ohio State U., Columbus, 1983. Mem. ABA, Am. Trial Lawyers Assn., Ohio Bar Assn. (family law com. 1974-77), Ohio Acad. Trial Lawyers, Ohio Mcpl. Judges Assn., Lawrence County Bar Assn. (sec. 1974-76, v.p. 1976-77, pres. 1981-82), Lawrence County C. of C. Lodges: Elks. Republican. Avocations: travel, boating, scuba diving, horses. Deceased.

**BURGER, KÁLMÁN,** chemistry educator; b. Aszód, Hungary, Oct. 19, 1929; s. Zoltån and Judit (Biro) B.; m. Anna Gimes, Nov. 24, 1953; children: Gábor, Zsuzsanna. MS in Pharmacy, L. Eötvös U., 1954; postgrad., Hungarian Acad. Scis., 1958, DSc in Chemistry, 1966. Asst. prof. L. Eötvös U., Budapest, 1957-58, sr. asst., 1958-63, assoc. prof., 1963-68, prof., from 1968; prof., head of dept. A. József U., Szeged, 1983-96, prof. dept. inorganic and analytical chemistry, from 1996. Vis. prof. Princeton (N.J.) U., 1981; v.p. A. József U., Szeged, 1987-90. Author: Coordination Chemistry: Experimental Methods, 1973, Organic Reagents in Metal Analysis, 1973, Organicseszkie reagenti v neorganicseszkom analize, 1975, Mössbauer Spectroscopy Elsevier, 1979, Solvation, Ionic and Complex Formation in Nonaqueous Solutions, 1983, Szolvatacija, ionnie reakcii i komplexoobrazovanje v nevodnich szredach, 1984, Biocoordination Chemistry, 1990, Chemical and Instrumental Analysis, 1992; contbr. articles to profl. jours. Recipient Hon. medal Comenius U., 1984, Széchenyi award Hungarian Govt., 1995. Mem. Hungarian Acad. Scis. (mem. phys. and inorganic chemistry com. 1970—, analytical chemistry com. 1970—), Academia Peloritana dei Pericolanti. Home: Szeged, Hungary. Died June 8, 2000.

**BURGESS, MICHAEL ROY (ROBERT REGINALD),** librarian, writer editor; b. Fukuoka, Kyushu, Japan, Feb. 11, 1948; came to U.S., 1949; s. Roy Walter and Betty Jane (Kapel) B.; m. Mary Alice Wickizer, Oct. 15, 1976; stepchildren: Richard Albert Rogers, Mary Louise Reynnells AB with honors, Gonzaga U., 1969; MLS, U. So. Calif., 1970. Periodicals librarian Calif. State U., San Bernardino, 1970-81, chief cataloger, 1981-94, prof., 1984—2005, head tech. svcs. and collection devel., 1994—2005, emeritus, from 2005. Editor Newcastle Pub. Co., North Hollywood, Calif., 1971—92; pub. Borgo Press, San Bernardino, 1975—99, Brownstone Books, San Bernardino, 1991—99, Sidewinder Press, San Bernardino, 1991—99, Unicorn & Son, San Bernardino, 1991—99, Burgess & Wickizer, San Bernardino, 1991—99, Emeritus Enterprises, 1993—99, Starmont House, 1993—99; assoc. editor SFRA Rev., 1993—94, Millefleurs Info. Svcs., San Bernardino, 2000—13; editor Wildside Press/Borgo Press Imprint, 2003—13. Author 138 books under pen names Michael Burgess, R(obert) Reginald, Boden Clarke, and others, with occasional co-authors, including: Stella Nova, 1970, Cumulative Paperback Index, 1939-1959, 1973, Contemporary Science Fiction Authors, 1975, The Attempted Assassination of John F. Kennedy, 1976, Things to Come, 1977, Up Your Asteroid!, 1977, Science Fiction and Fantasy Literature, a Checklist, 1700-1974, 1979, The Paperback Price Guide, 1980, 2nd edit., 1983, Science Fiction & Fantasy Awards, 1981, If J.F.K. Had Lived, 1982, The House of Burgesses, 1983, 2nd edit., 1994, The Wickizer Annals, 1983, Tempest in a Teapot, 1983, A Guide to Science Fiction & Fantasy in the Library of Congress Classification Scheme, 1984, 2nd edit., 1988, The Work of Jeffrey M. Elliot, 1984, Futurevisions, 1985, Lords Temperal & Lords Spiritual, 1985, 2nd edit., 1995, The Work of Julian May, 1985, The Work of R. Reginald, 1985, The Work of George Zebrowski, 1986, 2nd edit., 1990, 3rd edit., 1996, Mystery and Detective Fiction in the Library of Congress Classification Scheme, 1988, The Work of William F. Nolan, 1988, 2nd edit., 1998, The Arms Control, Disarmament, and Military Security Dictionary, 1989, Hancer's Price Guide to Paperback Books, 3d edit., 1990, Reginald's Science Fiction and Fantasy Awards, 2nd edit., 1991, 3d edit., 1993, Reference Guide to Science Fiction, Fantasy, and Horror, 1992, Science Fiction and Fantasy Literature, 1975-1991, 1992, The Work of Robert Reginald, 2nd edit., 1992, The State and Province Vital Records Guide, 1993, The Work of Katherine Kurtz, 1993, St. James Guide to Science Fiction Writers, 1996, CSUSB Faculty Authors, Composers and Playwrights, 1996, 2d. edit., 2006, BP 250, 1996, Xenograffiti, 1996, 2nd edit., 2005, Codex Derynianus, 1998, Katydid and other Critters, 2001, The Dark-Haired Man, 2004, The Exiled Prince, 2004, Quaestiones, 2004, Murder in Retrospect, 2005, Codex Derynianus II, 2005, Classics of Fantastic Literature, 2005, The Eastern Orthodox Churches, 2005, Quaestiones, 2005, Trilobite Dreams, 2006, BP 300, 2007, The Phantom's Phantom, 2007, Invasion! Earth vs. the Aliens, 2007, The Nasty Gnomes, 2008, The Coyote Chronicles, 2010, The Elder of Days, 2010, Knack' Attack, 2010, Academentia: A Future Dystopia, 2011 The Judgment of The Gods and Others Verdicts of History, 2011, Cracks in The Aether, 2011, The Pachyderms Lament, 2011, The Fourth Elephant's Egg, 2011, Melanthrix the Mage, 2011, Killingford, 2012, Ware The Dark Haired Man, 2013, Invasion!, 2011, Operation Crimson Storm, 2011, The Martians Strike Back!, 2011, The Paperback Show Murders, 2011; editor: Ancestral Voices, 1975, Alistair MacLean, 1976, Ancient Hauntings, 1976, Phantasmagoria, 1976, R.I.P., 1976, The Spectre Bridegroom and Other Horrors, 1976, John D. MacDonald and the Colorful World of Travis McGee, 1977, Dreamers of Dreams, 1978, King Solomon's Children, 1978, They, 1978, Worlds of Never, 1978, Science Fiction & Fantasy Book Review, 1980, 2nd edit., 2007, Candle for Poland, 1982, The Holy Grail Revealed, 1982, The Work of Bruce McAllister, 1985, rev. edit., 1986, George Orwell's Guide Through Hell, 1986, 2nd edit., 1994, The Work of Charles Beaumont, 1986, 2nd edit., 1990, California Ranchos, 1988, 2nd edit., 2007, The Work of Chad Oliver, 1989, The Work of Colin Wilson, 1989, The Work of Ian Watson, The Work of Reginald Bretnor, 1989, The Work of Ross Rocklynne, 1989, To Kill or Not To Kill, 1990, The Work of Dean Ing, 1990, The Work of Jack Dann, 1990, The Work of Pamela Sargent, 1990, 2nd edit., 1996, The Trilemma of World Oil Politics, 1991, The Work of Louis L'Amour, 1991, The Work of Brian W. Aldiss, 1992, Geo. Alec Effinger, 1993, Polemical Pulps, 1993, Sermons in Science Fiction, 1994, The Work of Elizabeth Chater, 1994, The Work of Jack Vance, 1994, The Work of William Eastlake, 1994, The Work of William F. Temple, 1994, The Work of Gary Brandner, 1995, The Work of Stephen King, 1996, Running From The Hunter, 1996, SanQuentin, 2005, Cal State Cooks, 1965-2005, 2006, Viva California!, 2007, Across the Wide Missouri, 2007, First-century Palestinian Judaism, 2007, Choice Words, 2010, Draqualian Silk, 2010, The Youndering, 2011, To The Stars And Beyond, 2011, Once Upon A Future, 2011, Whodunit?, 2011, More Whodunits, 2011; editor: The Christians Mega Pack, 2012, The Second Christmas Megapack, 2012; author of 13,000 essays, 30 short stories; editor 2000 books for Wildside Press and others, contbr. chapter to books. Recipient MPPP award, 1987, Lifetime Collectors award for Contbn. to Bibliography, 1993, Pilgrim award, 1993; named title II fellow U. So. Calif., 1969-70. Mem. Sci. Fiction and Fantasy Writers Am., Mystery Writers Am., Internat. PEN, U.S.A. Ctr. West, Sci. Fiction Rsch. Assn., Horror Writers Assoc. Democrat. Avocations: genealogical and historical research, films. Died Nov. 20, 2013.

**BURKE, DAVID W.,** retired broadcast executive; b. June 7, 1935; m. Trixie Burke; 5 children. BA in Economics, Tufts U., 1957, LHD (hon.), 2009; MS in Economics, U. Chgo. Mem. Pres. John F. Kennedy's Labor Advisory Coun., 1960; asst. to US sec. commerce, US sec. labor, 1961-65; exec. sec. Pres. Johnson's Advisory Com. on Labor-Mgmt. Policy; legislative asst. to Senator Edward M. Kennedy, US Senate, 1965, adminstrv. asst., 1966-71; v.p. adminstrn. & devel. Dreyfus Corp., NYC, 1971-75; chief staff to Gov. State of NY, Albany, 1975-77; v.p. planning, asst. to pres. ABC News, 1977-86, exec. v.p., 1986-88; pres. CBS News, NYC, 1988-90; chair Broadcasting Bd. Govs. (BBG), 1995—2002. Died Apr. 19, 2014.

**BURKE, LILLIAN WALKER,** retired judge; b. Thomaston, Ga., Aug. 2, 1917; d. George P. and Ozella (Daviston) Walker; m. Ralph Livingston Burke, July 8, 1948 (dec.); 1 son, R. Bruce. BS, Ohio State U., 1947; LLB, Cleve. State U., 1951, postgrad., 1963-64; grad., Nat. Coll. State Judiciary, U. Nev., 1974; LLD (hon.), Cleve. State U., Cleve. Marshall Law Sch., 2011. Bar: Ohio 1951. Gen. practice law, Cleve., 1952-62; asst. atty. gen. Ohio, 1962-66; mem., vice chmn. Ohio Indsl. Commn., 1966-69; judge Cleve. Mcpl. Ct., 1969-87, chief judge, 1981, 85, vis. judge, 1988-97; ret., 1997. Guest lectr. Heidelburg Coll., Tiffin, Ohio, 1971; cons. Bur. Higher Edn., HEW, 1972. Pres. Cleve. chpt. Nat. Coun. Negro Women, 1955-57; sec. East dist. Family Service Assn., 1959-60; mem. coun. human rels. Cleve. Citizens League, 1959-79; mem. Gov.'s Com. on Status of Women, 1966-67; pres. Cleve. chpt. Jack and Jill of Am., Inc., 1960-61; v.p.-at-large Greater Cleve. Safety Coun., 1969-79; mem. Cleve. Landmarks Commn., 1990-97; woman ward leader 24th Ward Republican Club, 1957-67; mem. Cuyahoga County Ctrl. Com., 1958-68; sec. Cuyahoga County Exec. Com., 1962-63; alt. del. Rep. Nat. Conv., Chgo., 1960; bd. dirs., chmn. minority div. Nat. Fedn. Rep. Women, 1966-68; life mem., past bd. dirs. Cleve. chpt. NAACP; bd. dirs. Greater Cleve. Neighborhood Ctrs. Assn., Cath. Youth Counselling Svcs.; trustee Ohio Commn. on Status of Women, 1966-70, Consumers League Ohio, 1969-75, Cleve. Music Sch. Settlement; bd. mgmt. Glenville YWCA, 1960-70; mem. project com. Cleve. Orch.; apptd. mem. City Planning Comm. Cleve., 1997-2002. Recipient achievement award Parkwood Christian Meth. Episcopal Ch., 1968, Martin Luther King Citizen's award, 1969, outstanding achievement award Ta-Wa-Si Scholarship Club, 1969, Outstanding Svc. award Morning Star Grand chpt., Cleve., 1970, award of honor Cleve. Bus. League, 1970, svc. award St. Paul AME Ch., Lima, Ohio, 1972, Woman of Achievement award Inner Club Coun., Cleve., 1973, cert. of award Nat. Coun. Negro Women, 1969, Cleve. Found. Golf Philanthropic Leadership award, 1997; named Career Woman of Yr., Cleve. Women's Career Clubs, 1969, Jewel of Yr., Women's City Club, 2002, award for hist. preservation So. African Hist. Soc., 2002, Woman of Achievement award YWCA, 2003. Mem. ABA, Nat. Assn. Investment Clubs (pres. Dynasty Investors Club 1992-96, bd. dirs. N.E. Ohio Coun. 1993-2003), Nat. Bar Assn., Ohio Bar Assn., Cuyahoga County Bar Assn., Cleve. Bar Assn., Am. Judicature Soc., Am. Judges Assn. (bd. govs. 1982-86, chmn. conv. agenda com. 1981-83), Phillis Wheatley Assn., Women Lawyers Assn. (hon. adviser), Ohio State U. Alumni Assn. (life), Cleve. Marshall Law Sch. (life), Am. Bridge Assn. (life), Women's City Club of Cleve. (life), Altrusa, Alpha Kappa Alpha. Anglican. Home: Centreville, Va. Died Mar. 2012.

**BURNS, CHARLES FOSTER,** US magistrate, lawyer; b. Springfield, Mo, Sept. 22, 1904; s. Foster Nathaniel and Mamie Edith (Fisher) Burns; m. Viola Sophia Vogt., June 13, 1929 (dec. 1967); 1 child, Helen Loraine (Coleman). BA, U. tulsa, 1924; MA, Washington U., St. Louis, 1929; LLB, U. Tulsa, 1940. Sole practice, Miami, Fla., from 1940, Okla., from 1940; US Commr. No. Dist. Okla., 1940—71; US magistrate US Dist. Ct. (no. dist.), Miami, Fla., 1971—83, Okla., 1971—83. Mem.: Ottawa county Bar Assn., US Supreme Ct. Hist. Soc., Okla. Bar Assn., Am. Judicature Soc. Presbyterian. Home: Miami, Okla. Died May 1987.

**BURNS, JAMES MACGREGOR,** political scientist, historian; b. Melrose, Mass., Aug. 3, 1918; s. Robert Arthur and Mildred Curry (Bunce) B.; m. Janet Rose Dismorr Thompson, May 23, 1942 (div.); children: David MacGregor, Timothy Stewart, Deborah Edwards, Margaret Rebecca Antonia; m. Joan Simpson Meyers, Sept. 7, 1969 (div.). BA Williams Coll, 1939; postgrad., Nat. Inst. Public Affairs, 1939-40; PhD in Political Sci., Harvard U., 1947; postgrad., London Sch. Economics, 1949. Exec. sec. non ferrous metals commn. NWLB, 1942-43; faculty polit. sci. Williams Coll., Williamstown, Mass., 1941-88, prof., 1953-88, Woodrow Wilson prof. polit. sci. emeritus, from 1988; sr. scholar Jepson Sch. Leadership, U. Richmond, 1990-93, co-chmn., 1976-87; sr. scholar James MacGregor Burns Acad. Leadership, U. Md., College Park, from 1997. Mem. staff The Hoover Commn., 1948; faculty Salzburg Seminar in American Studies, 1954, 61; history cons. TV programs ABC, CBS; sr. scholar The Acd. of Leadership, U. Md. Author: Guam: Operations of the 77th Infantry Div, 1944, Okinawa: The Last Battle, (with others), 1947, Congress on Trial: The Legislative Process and the Administrative State, 1949, Government by the People, (with Jack W. Peltason and Thomas E. Cronin), 1981, Roosevelt: The Lion and the Fox, 1956, John Kennedy: A Political Profile, 1960, The Deadlock of Democracy: Four Party Politics in America, 1963, Presidential Government: The Crucible of Leadership, 1966, Roosevelt: The Soldier of Freedom (Pulitzer Prize in History, 1971, Nat. Book award, 1971, Francis Parkman prize, 1971), 1970, Uncommon Sense, 1972, Edward Kennedy and the Camelot Legacy, 1976, Leadership, 1978, The Vineyard of Liberty, 1982, The Power to Lead, 1984, The Workshop of Democracy, 1985, The Crosswinds of Freedom, 1989, Cobblestone Leadership, 1990, Running Alone: Presidential Leadership from JFK to Bush II--Why It Has Failed and How We Can Fix It, 2007, Packing the Court: The Rise of Judicial Power and The Coming Crisis of the Supreme Court, 2009, Fire and Light: How the Enlightenment Transformed the World, 2013; co-author: (with Stewart Burns) A People's Charter, 1991, (with George Sorenson) Dead Center: Clinton-Gore Leadership and the Perils of Moderation, 1999, (with Susan Dunn) The Three Roosevelts: Patrician Leaders Who Transformed America, 2001; co-editor: (with George Goethals & George Sorenson) Encyclopedia of Leadership, 2004 Mem. Mass. delegation Democratic Nat. Conv., 1952, 56, 60, 64, Democratic Charter Conv., 1974; mem. Mass. Democratoc Party Charter Commn., 1977-79, Mass. Democratic Charter Conv., 1979, Berkshire County delegation Mass. state conv., 1954; Democratic candidate for Congress, 1st Dist. Mass., 1958; Former trustee Stockbridge Sch., Woodrow Wilson Internat. Center for Scholars. Served with AUS, 1943-45; combat historian Guam, Saipan, Okinawa. Recipient Tamiment Inst. award for Best Biography, 1956, Woodrow Wilson prize, 1957, Christopher award, 1983, 1990, Harold D. Lasswell award, 1984, Robert F. Kennedy Book award for Cumulative Writing on Freedom, 1990, Rollo May award forHumanistic Studies, 1994. Mem. American Polit. Sci. Assn. (pres. 1975-76), New Eng. Polit. Sci. Assn. (pres. 1960-61), Internat. Soc. Polit. Psychology (pres. 1982-83), American Hist. Assn., American Philos. Soc., ACLU, American Legion, Phi Beta Kappa, Delta Sigma Rho. Democrat. Home: Williamstown, Mass. Died July 15, 2014.

**BURTON, GEORGE AUBREY, JR.,** accountant; b. Texarkana, Ark., June 21, 1926; s. George Aubrey Burton and Theo Marvis Simmons-Burton; m. Joan Cunningham, July 31, 1947 (dec. Oct. 2002); m. Gloria Brantley, June 18, 2005; children: George Aubrey Burton, III, Sandra Burton-Batten. BS, Centenary Coll., 1947—50. CPA, State Bd. Of Acctg./La., 1953. Reporter Dun & Bradstreet, Shreveport, La., 1947—49; acct. Opferkuch, Mc Guirt, Watts & West CPA's, Shreveport, La., 1949—53. Ptnr. Opferkuch, McGuirt, Watts & West CPA's, Shreveport, 1953, Burton & Penn CPA'S, Shreveport, 1964—74; CPA George A. Burton, Jr., Shreveport, 1953—64, George A. Burton, Jr. CPA, Shreveport, 1978—2014; commr. finance City Of Shreveport, 1971—78. Treas. Jaycees, Shreveport, 1953—54, exec. v.p., 1955—56, pres., 1956—57; regional v.p. La. Jaycees, 1958—59, exec. v.p., 1959—60; mem. Shreveport Airport Authority; chmn. Caddo Parish Exec. Com., La.; exec. com. La. State Fair, Shreveport, 1971—78; dir. Shreveport Chamber of Commerce, 1956—57. Seaman 1/c Navy Seabees, 1943—46, Central Pacific. Recipient JCI Life Mem., Jr. C. of C., 1973. Mem.: La. CPA Soc. (state committe), Jr. ROTC Parents Club (life). Republican. Home: Maumelle, Ark. Died June 10, 2014.

**BURTON, SANDRA JEAN,** journalist; b. Long Beach, Calif., Dec. 21, 1938; d. Charles Orrin and Helen Burton. BA, Middlebury Coll., 1963. Reporter, photographer Hunterdon County Dem., Flemington, N.J., 1963-64; sec. Time Inc., NYC, 1964-66; researcher Time Mag., NYC, 1967-70, corr. LA, 1970-73, Paris, 1977-82, bur. chief Boston, 1973-76, Hong Kong, 1982-86, Beijing, 1988-90, sr. corr. Hong Kong, 1990-97, former contbr. Mem. exec. com. Hong Kong affiliate Coun. Fgn. Rels. Author: Impossible Dream--The Marcoses, The Aquinos and The Unfinished Revolution, 1989; co-author: Massacre in Beijing, 1989. Edward R. Murrow fellow Coun. on Fgn. Rels., 1986-87. Mem. Fgn. Corrs. Club Hong Kong (v.p. 1984), Royal Hong Kong Yacht Club. Presbyterian. Avocations: writing, photography, painting, scuba diving. Died Feb. 26, 2004.

**BURTON, VIRGINIA LEE,** writer, illustrator; b. Newton Centre, Mass., Aug. 30, 1909; m. George Demetrios, 1931; 2 children. Student, Calif. Sch. Fine Arts, Boston Mus. Sketcher music, dance and theater sects. Boston Transcript. Author, illustrator: Choo Choo: The Story of a Little Engine Who Ran Away, 1937, Mike Mulligan and His Steam Shovel, 1939, Calico the Wonder Horse, 1941, The Little House, 1941 (Caldecott medal 1943). Died 1968.

**BUSH, YVONNE ROSE,** writer, counselor; b. Madelia, Minn., Jan. 29, 1935; d. Guy Pearl and Frances Louise (Traver) Burk; m. William Clarence Bush; children: Donald, Steven, Billie Jean Vogel, Thomas Lovelace, Tami li Robbins, Christopher Clark. AA Edn., Yavapai Coll., 1985; BA, Prescott Coll., 1989, MA, 1999. Cert. EMT 1987, St. Joseph's Med. Center/Newborn,Child Normal Devel. 1983, Feeding and Swallowing Disorders of Infancy; Assessment and Mgmt. 1991, Fetal Alcohol Syndrome/Instructor 1993, Parenting the Teen Years 1987, Understanding Aids 1987, Failure to Thrive, Infant Mental Health 1988, Breast Cancer Self examination/Instructor 1983. Office mgr. Allen's New Way Retail Grocery Store, Prescott, Ariz., 1980—82; head cashier K Mart, Prescott, 1982—83; case mgr. Cath. Social Services of Yavapai, Prescott, Ariz., 1987—90, Ariz. Dept. of Econ. Security, Prescott, 1990—98. Trust com. Acker Trust Bd., Prescott, 1983—85; organizer, co-leader Scholls Cmty. Orgn., Scholls, 1978—80; bd. dirs. Sierra Comm., Inc., Prescott; charter mem. Ariz. Pub. Svc. Project Voice, Phoenix; bd. dirs. Child Haven, Prescott Crisis Nursery; den mother Boy Scouts of Am., Rowland Heights, 1965—66; bd. dirs. Affordable Constrn., Inc. Prescott. Author: Bonding and Attachment, 2001, Beyond Tears, A Book To Encourage Women, 2002, Lost in the Hell Hole, 2010, Justice, from 1998. Small claims hearing officer Prescott Justice Ct., 1998—2009; bd. dirs. Willow Creek Charter Sch., Prescott, from 2004; leader women's ministries Alliance Bible Ch, Prescott, from 2002. Mem.: Prescott Pub. Library/Friends of the Libr. Conservative. Home: Prescott, Ariz. Died Sept. 29, 2013.

**BUSSE, FRED,** former mayor; b. Chgo., Mar. 3, 1866; s. Capt. Gustave and Caroline (Gross) B.; m. Josephine Lee, April 17, 1908., pub. schs. of Chgo. Town clk., Chgo.; with Cook County sheriff's office; chief clk North Town collector's office; mem. 39th, 40th Gen. Assembly State of Ill., 1894-98, mem. Sen., 1898-1902, treas., 1902-06; postmaster Chgo., 1906-07; mayor City of Chgo., 1907-11. Mem. Rep. State Com., Cook County Rep. Ctrl. Com. Mem. Masons (32d degree), Hamilton, Marquette, Chgo. Athletic, Press (life), Germania Männerchor Clubs. Home: Chicago, Ill. Died July 9, 1914.

**BUSTAMANTE VASCONCELOS, EDUARDO,** lawyer; b. Oct. 12, 1904; Lawyer; b. Oaxaca, Mexico, Oct. 12, 1904; s. Manuel Bustamante and Luz Vasconcelos; m. Cuca Davila (dec. 1971); m. Maria Luisa Bascaran, June 2, 1973. Abogado, Escuela Nacional De Jurisprudencia, Mex., Profesor Extraordirio Derecho Fiscal (hon.), Universidad Benito Juarez, Oaxaca, 1959. Lawyer Diplomate Universidad Nacional Autonoma de Mexico. Tech. officer Sria. de Hacienda, Fed. Govt., 1925-30, Under Sec., 1946-48, sec. Sria. de Patrimonio Nacional, Fed. Govt., 1958-64; dir. Banca Confia, Mexico, D.F., 1952-82; mem. bd. Bancomer, Mexico, D.F., 1964-82. Decorated Oficial de la Legiŏn de Honor; Gran Cruz de la Orden de la Corona de Bĕlgica y Gran Cruz de la Orden de Jorge Primero, Govts. of France, Belgium and Greece. Mem. Barra Mexicana. Roman Catholic. Club: Campestre de la Ciudad de Mexico. Home: Lomas de Chapultepec, Mexico. Died Nov. 28, 1991.

**BUTLER, DAVID DALRYMPLE,** screenwriter, actor; b. Larkhall, Lanarkshire, Scotland, Nov. 12, 1927; s. James and Mary (Dalrymple) B.; m. Norma Ronald; m. Kathleen Mary McPhail, May 31, 1969; children: Alexandra Katrina, Miranda Henrietta. Student, St. Andrews U., Scotland, 1946-50; Rada diploma, Royal Acad. Dramatic Art, London, 1953. Appeared for several yrs. in revues and West End prodns. including The Quare Fellow; TV shows include Emergency Ward 10; TV credits include The Strauss Family, Edward VII, Lillie, Disraeli, Within These Walls, Mount Batten the Last Viceroy, We'll Meet Again, The Further Adventures of Oliver Twist, Duchess of Duke Street, Black Beauty (Writers Guild award 1972), Countercrime, Dame of Sark; films include Voyage of the Damned (Oscar award nomination for Best Screenplay), Jesus of Nazareth, Adventures of Marco Polo, The Scarlet and the Black; plays include Person Unknown, Legend; books include Lusitania, Edward VII (2 vols.), Disraeli (2 vols.), Lillie, Mountbatten, The Last Viceroy. Mem. Am. Acad. Motion Picture Arts and Scis., Brit. Actors Equity, Writers Guild Great Britain. Home: London, England. Died May 27, 2006.

**BUTLER, KENNETH B.,** newspaper executive; b. Richland, Mich., Aug. 27, 1902; s. Ross S. and Jennie (Blain) Butler; m. Wilma Steinberg, Nov. 5, 1925; 1 child, Roger Lee; m. Doris Sibigtroth, 1969. BA, U. Wis., 1925. Reporter Madison Capital Times, 1923—25; editor Mendota Sun-Bull., Ill., 1925—27; pub. Constantine Advertiser Record, Mich., 1927—31; mgr. Conco Press, Mendota, 1931—41; pres. Kenneth B. Butler and Assoc., from 1938, Wayside Press, 1941—78. Founder Butler Typo-Design Rsch. Ctr., 1951, Time-Was Village Mus., 1967; lectr. Medill Sch. Journalism, Northwestern U., 1950—75; bus. mgr. P.E.O. Record, 1931—78; spkr. and lectr. Author: Headline Design, 1949, Effective Illustration, 1952, 101 Layouts, 1954, Double Spreads, 1955, Back of the Book Makeup, 1957, Ken Butler's Layout Scrapbook, 1958, Display Type Faces, 1959, Back of the Book Makeup, 1960, Borders, Boxes and Ornamentation, 1961, How To Stage an Oldtime Auto Event, 1961; co-author: Magnificent Whistlestop; editor: Sidelights; contbr. articles to profl. publs. Gen. chmn. Mendota Centennial Jubilee, 1953, Mendota Autorama, 1955, 1957, 1959, 1961, Constantine Centennial, Mich., 1928; mem. Sweet Corn Festival Com., 1962; chmn. Nat. Glidden Tour., 1963; bd. dirs. LaSalle County unit Am. Cancer Soc. Recipient Cmty. Svc. award, C. of C., 1976; named Kiwanis Man of Yr., 1953. Mem.: LaSalle County Hist. Soc., Mark Twain Soc., Ill. Mfrs. Assn., Farm Bur., Am. Bell Assn., Mendota C. of C. (dir. 1947—53), Ill. State, Mendota Athletic Booster Soc. (founder 1955), Men's Garden America, Elk, Horatio Alger Club (co-founder, pres. 1965—67), Antique Automobile America Club (dir. Ill. region, pres. 1960—61, treas. 1967—68, nat. bd. dirs., dir. activities Central region), Steam Car, Horseless Carriage, Model T Ford, Rolls Royce Owners, Classic Car, Pierce Arrow Soc., Mendota Antique Car, Sigma Delta Chi. Republican. Presbyterian. Home: Mendota, Ill. Died Sept. 22, 1989.

**BUTLER, MANLEY CALDWELL,** retired lawyer, former United States Representative from Virginia; b. Roanoke, Va., June 2, 1925; s. W.W.S. Butler Jr.; m. June Nolde, June 26, 1950 (dec. 2014); children: Manley, Henry, James, Marshall. AB, U. Richmond, 1948; JD, U. Va. Law Sch., 1950; LLD (hon.), Washington & Lee U., 1978. Bar: Va. 1950. Mem. Va. House of Delegates, 1962—71, chmn. Joint Republican Caucus, 1964—66, minority leader, 1966—71; mem. US Congress from 6th Va. Dist., 1972—83, Woods, Rogers & Hazlegrove, P.L.C., 1983—99. Mem. Nat. Bankruptcy Rev. Commn., 1995-97. Served in USN, 1943—46. Fellow American Bar Found., American Coll. Bankruptcy, Va. Law Found.; mem. ABA, Va. Bar Assn., Va. State Bar Assn., Roanoke Bar Assn., American Bankruptcy Inst., Raven Soc., Order of Coif, Phi Beta Kappa, Tau Kappa Alpha, Omicron Delta Kappa, Pi Delta Epsilon, Phi Gamma Delta. Republican. Episcopalian. Home: Daleville, Va. Died July 29, 2014.

**BUTLER, RAYMOND ARCHIBALD,** cartographer; b. Windsor, Va. s. J. Butler and Odie Underwood; m. Phyllis Jane Holden, June 1942; children: David Holden, Pamela Rae Butler Chryst, Keith Underwood, Melanie Butler Post. Student, Syracuse U., 1932—36. Asst. to Admiral Byrd, 1939—41; chief of Arctic Unit Aero Med. Lab., Wright Field; cartographer of Antarctic Projects Rsch. Ctr., Washington. Recipient Spl. Medal of Honor, Rear Adm. Richard E. Byrd, 1947, Mountain named in his honor at South Pole. Democrat. Baptist. Avocations: birdwatching, hiking, camping, painting oil landscapes. Deceased.

**BUTNARIU, DAN,** mathematics professor, researcher; b. Hîrlau, Iasi, Romania, Feb. 1, 1951; s. Smil and Ana (Segal) B.; m. Hadasa Schwartzenberg, Aug. 19, 1974; 1 child, Eliza. BA in Math., U. Iasi, 1974, MA in Math., 1975, PhD in Math., 1980. Asst. Polytechnic Inst., Iasi, 1975-79, lectr., 1980-83; postdoctoral Weizmann Inst., Rehovot, Israel, 1984-86; sr. lectr. U. Haifa, Israel, 1986-90, assoc. prof. math., 1991-96, prof. math., from 1997. Vis. prof. U. Tex., Arlington, 1989-90, 1996-97; chmn. dept. math. U. Haifa, Israel, 1997-99. Contbr. articles to profl. jours. Recipient prize Balkan Math. Union, 1980, prize Romanian Acad., 1999. Mem. Am. Math. Soc., Israel Math. Union, European Math. Union. Avocation: reading. Home: Haifa, Israel. Died May 7, 2008.

**BUTTERS, NELSON MARTIN,** neuropsychologist; b. Cambridge, Mass., May 7, 1937; s. Saul Rhoda and Rhoda (Kachel) B.; m. Arlene B. Goldman, Oct. 15, 1956; children: Meryl, Paul, Lisa. AB summa cum laude, Boston U., 1960; MA, Clark U., 1962, PhD, 1964. Postdoctoral rsch. fellow NIMH, Bethesda, Md., 1964—67; asst. prof. neurology Boston U., 1967—72, assoc. prof., 1972—76, prof., 1976—83; prof. psychiatry U. Calif. Sch. Medicine, San Diego, from 1983. Rsch. career scientist VA Med. Ctr., Boston, 1967—83, chief psychology svc., San Diego, from 1983; Lansdowne vis. prof. U. Victoria, B.C., Canada, 1982. Author: Alcoholic Kersakoff's Syndrome, 1960; contbr. articles to profl. jours. Fellow: APA (divsn. pres. 1982—83); mem.: Internat. Neuropsychol. Soc. (bd. govs. from 1973), Internat. Neuropsychol. Soc. (pres. 1984—85), Phi Beta Kappa. Home: Poway, Calif. Died Nov. 18, 1995.

**BUTTS, HERBERT CLELL,** retired dentist, educator; b. Dover, Tenn., Aug. 24, 1924; s. Sidney Lewis and Georgia (Sawyer) B.; m. Quay Coker; children: Marla Lyce, April Chyrese, Dawn Denise, Sidney Coker. Student, U. Tenn. Jr. Coll., 1942-43, Memphis State U., 1946-47; DDS, U. Tenn., 1950; MS, U. Iowa, 1966. Pvt. practice dentistry, Memphis, 1950-58; mem. faculty Coll. Dentistry, U. Tenn., Memphis, part-time 1950-58, 58-60, assoc. dean acad. affairs, 1978-81, spl. advisor to dean, 1986-2000; ret., 2000; fgn. svc. officer, dental edn. advisor State Dept. Fgn. Aid program, San Salvador, El Salvador, 1960-64; assoc. prof. St. Louis U. Sch. Dentistry, 1966-67; prof., chmn. dept. operative dentistry Coll. Dental Medicine, Med. U. S.C., Charleston, 1967-70, asst. dean for admissions and student affairs, 1970, 72-74, acting dean, 1971; editor-in-chief ADA, Chgo., 1974-77; dean Sch. Dental Medicine So. Ill. U., Alton, 1981-86. Editor U. Tenn. Coll. Dentistry Bull., 1990-2000. Active USNR, 1943-46. Recipient Outstanding Alumnus award U. Tenn. Coll. Dentistry, 1975. Mem. ADA, Tenn. Dental Assn. (fellowship award 1993), Memphis Dental Soc., Am. Coll. Dentists (pres. Tenn. sect. 1994, sec.-treas. Tenn. sect. 1995-98), Internat. Coll. Dentists, Am. Assn. Dental Schs., Ala. Dental Assn. (hon.), Am. Assn. Women Dentists (hon.), Omicron Kappa Upsilon. Home: Memphis, Tenn. Died Sept. 24, 2013.

**BUYSE, EMILE JULES,** film company executive; b. Brussels, Apr. 16, 1927; came to U.S., 1976; s. Omer J. and Flore G. (Copain) B.; m. Evelyne Mulpas, June 26, 1964. MA, Ecole Normale Charles Buls, Brussels, 1947. Dir. advt. and publicity for continental Europe and Middle East United Artists Corp., Paris, 1962-66; dir. advt. and publicity 20th Century-Fox Film Corp., 1966-70, v.p. internat. distbn., 1970-76; pres. 20th Century-Fox Internat. Corp., Los Angeles, 1976-81, EBE Internat., Beverly Hills, Calif., from 1981. Mem. Acad. Motion Picture Arts and Scis. Home: Santa Monica, Calif. Died Dec. 1999.

**BYERS, EUGENE BENJAMIN, SR.,** electronics executive; b. Topeka, Nov. 24, 1943; s. Fletcher Dewitt and Laura Mae (Houston) Byers; m. Barbara Jean Mulky, May 29, 1965; children: Derek, Eugene. BS, Morgan State Coll., 1965; MBA, Rutgers U., 1972. With photo products divsn. E.I. Dupont de Nemours Co., Parlin, NJ, 1965—69; prodn. mgmt. staff Ethicon Divsn. Johnson & Johnson, Somerville, 1969—71; mktg rep., data processing divsn. IBM, West Orange, 1972—82, programmer analyst Sterling Forest, NY, from 1982; pres., treas., bus. cons. EBB Enterprises, Inc., Hillside, 1969; founder, bd. dirs. Edmund L. Houston Found., 1975—78. Pub. editor EBB Found. Quar., 1980—83, Cmty. Builder, 1983—99. Exec. bd. Elizabeth Br. NAACP, 1977—81; exec. dir. EBB Found., 1969—81; chmn., bd. dirs. BHER Found.; bd. dirs. Newark/Essex Chpt. Operation PUSH, 1977—78. Engelhard Minerals and Chems. grantee, 1972. Mem.: Am. Mgmt. Assn., Rutgers U. Black MBA Assn. (Alumni award 1983), Union County Club of Nat. Assn. Negro Bus. and Profl. Women's Clubs, Inc. (Man. Yr. 1980), Am. Mktg. Assn., Hillside High School Afro-Am. Club (Man Yr. 1980), Omega Psi Phi (Chpt. Man Yr. 1980). Home: Hillside, NJ. Died Mar. 18, 1999.

**BYRNE, JOHN KEYES See LEONARD, HUGH**

**BYSTEDT, PETRUS GOSTA,** manufacturing executive; b. Haggdanger, Sweden, May 14, 1929; s. Petrus and Anna (Jonsson) B.; m. Kerstin Elmer, May 25, 1958; children: Ingrid Christina, Anna Pernilla, Per Ivar Gosta. M in Engring., Royal Inst. Tech., Stockholm, 1953; BS, Stockholm Sch. Econs., 1958. Asst. to prof. Royal Inst. Tech., Stockholm, 1953-55, asst. lectr., 1955-58; head orgn. and methods dept. Electrolux, AB, Stockholm, 1958-65, head Vacuum Cleaner div., 1965-68, dep. mng. dir., 1968-74, mng. dir., 1974-81, became chief exec. officer Electrolux group, 1981, former dep. chmn. Bd. dirs. EQT Scandinavia I, Nilörngruppen; mem. European adv. bd. N.Y. Stock Exch.; mem. adv. bd. Deloitte & Touche. Home: Lidingo, Sweden. Deceased.

**CABELA, RICHARD NEIL (DICK CABELA),** retired retail company executive; b. Chappell, Nebr., Oct. 18, 1936; s. A.C. and Marian Cabela; m. Mary Ann Kerns; 9 children. Student, Regis Coll., 1956—58; D in Bus. Adminstr. (hon.), 2010. Founder Cabela's, Inc., 1961, chmn., 1965—2013. Bd. dirs. Cabela's, Inc., 1965—2013. Regent Regis Univ., from 1994, bd. trustees. Recipient Small Businessman of the Yr. award, 1970, C.J. McElroy award, Safari Club Internat., 2001, Alumni Achievement award, Regis Univ., 2003; named one of The 25 Most Influential People in Hunting & Fishing, Outdoor Life mag., 2007; named to The Nebr. Hall of Fame award, 1994, The Direct Mktg. Hall of Fame, 2006. Roman Catholic. Died Feb. 17, 2014.

**CAESAR, SID,** actor, comedian; b. Yonkers, NY, Sept. 8, 1922; s. Max and Ida (Raphael) C.; m. Florence Levy, June 17, 1943; children: Michele, Richard, Karen. Grad., Yonkers High Sch., 1939; studied saxophone and clarinet, NYC. Played in small bands, later orchs. of Charlie Spivak, Shep Fields and Claude Thornhill following World War II; toured leading theatres and night clubs as comedian; appeared in film version Tars and Spars Revue; in Broadway musical prodns. of Make Mine Manhattan, 1948, Admiral Broadway Revue, 1948, Your Show of Shows, 1950-54; star of own show Caesar's Hour, 1954-57; star and producer own show Sid Caesar Invites You, 1958, As Caesar Sees It, 1962-63; TV guest appearances include Robert Morse Show; star of Broadway musical Little Me, 1962-63; actor: (flims) It's a Mad, Mad, Mad, Mad World, 1963, The Spirit is Willing, 1967, Ten from Your Show of Shows, 1973, Silent Movie, 1975, Fire Sale, 1977, The Cheap Detective, 1978, Grease, 1978, History of the World, Part I, 1981, Grease 2, 1982, Over the Brooklyn Bridge, 1984, Cannonball Run II, 1984, The Emperor's New Clothes, 1987, The Life and Times of Charlie Putz, 1991, Vegas Vacation, 1997, The Wonderful Ice Cream Suit, 1998; TV film appearances: Side by Side, 1988, Nothing's Impossible, 1988, Freedom Fighter, 1988, The Great Mom Swap, 1995; appeared in opera Die Fledermaus, 1987; author autobiography: Where Have I Been?, 1982. Recipient Best Comedian on TV award Look mag., 1951, 56; recipient Emmy award, best comedian, 1956, Sylvania award best comedy-variety show, 1958, Lifetime Achievement award in comedy, 1987, Career Achievement award, 2001, Star on Walk of Fame; named to U.S. Hall of Fame, 1967. Mem.: Old Falls Rod and Gun (Fallsburgh, N.Y.). Died Feb. 12, 2014.

**CAFFEY, BENJAMIN FRANKLIN,** civil and mechanical engineer; b. Jacksonville, Fla., Nov. 18, 1927; s. Eugene Mead and Catherine (Howell) C.; m. Laura Marlowe, Oct. 2, 1949 (dec. Jan. 1991); children: Benjamin, John, Lochlin; m. Suzanne Morris, Aug. 10, 1991; stepchildren: Jay, Julie, Kelly. BCE, Ga. Inst. Tech., 1949; MSCE, U. So. Calif., LA, 1964. Registered profl. engr., Calif.; cert. project mgmt. profl. Resident engr. Sch. Dist. of Glendale, Calif., 1950-51; constrn. engr. Fluor Corp., LA, 1951-56; v.p. Petroleum Combustion & Engring. Co., LA, 1956-58, Sesler & Caffey, Inc., Gardena, Calif., 1958-69, Fluor Corp., LA, 1969-76; pres. Fluor Arabia, Ltd., Saudi Arabia, 1976-81; sr. v.p. Fluor Daniel, Inc., Irvine, Calif., from 1981. Adv. bd. Ga. Tech. Sch. Civil Engring., Atlanta, 1992—. Lt. U.S. Army, 1946-48; lt. col. USAR (ret.). Fellow ASCE; mem. Project Mgmt. Inst. (trustee 1991), Soc. Am. Mil. Engrs., Chi Epsilon. Republican. Episcopalian. Home: Laguna Beach, Calif. Died 1998.

**CAHILL, JAMES FRANCIS,** retired art history educator; b. Ft. Bragg, Calif., Aug. 13, 1926; s. James Francis and Mae (Bond) C.; m. Dorothy Dunlap, July 15, 1951 (div.); children: Nicholas, Sarah; m. Tsao Hsingyuan, Mar. 28, 1988 (div.); children: Benedict and Julian (twins). BA in Oriental Languages, U. Calif., Berkeley, 1950; MA in Art History, U. Mich., 1952, PhD in Art History, 1958. Curator Chinese art Freer Gallery Art, Smithsonian Instn., Washington, 1957-65; prof. history of art, curator Oriental art U. Calif., Berkeley, 1965-94; ret., 1994. Charles Eliot Norton prof. poetry Harvard U., 1978-79. Author: Chinese Painting, 1960, Scholar Painters of Japan: The Nanga School, 1972, Hills Beyond a River: Chinese Painting of the Yuan Dynasty, 1976, The Compelling Image: Nature and Style in 17th Century Chinese Painting, 1982. Guggenheim fellow, 1972-73; recipient Charles Lang Freer medal Smithsonian Instn., 2010 Mem. American Acad. Arts & Sciences, Assn. Asian Studies, Coll. Art Assn. Home: Honolulu, Hawaii. Died Feb. 14, 2014.

**CAINE, CAROL WHITACRE,** business owner; b. Vandergrift, Pa., Mar. 14, 1925; d. Guy Alvin and Genevra Madeline (Lash) Whitacre; m. Charles Clyde Caine, Dec. 27, 1948; children: Christopher, Charles Lash. BS, Ohio State U., 1951. Part-time med. and x-ray technician Internal Medicine Lab., 1950-70; co-owner Transceiver Ctrs. of Columbus, Ohio, 1968-79, PIP Printing, Cheyenne, Wyo., 1981-94; ret., 1994. Mem. AAUW (bd. dirs. Cheyenne chpt. 1984-86), Wyo. Media Profls., Am. Soc. Radiol. Technologists, Am. Soc. Med. Tech., Nat. Fedn. Press Women, Zonta (bd. dirs. Cheyenne chpt. 1988-92), Order of Eastern Star, Alpha Phi (life). Avocations: bridge, golf, swimming. Home: Cheyenne, Wyo. Died July 15, 1999.

**CALLAGHAN, LEONARD JAMES,** Former Prime Minister of the United Kingdom; b. Portsmouth, Eng., Mar. 27, 1912; s. James and Charlotte G. (Cundy) C.; m. Audrey Elizabeth Moulton, 1938; children: Margaret Ann (Baroness Jay of Paddington), Julia Elizabeth (Mrs. Ian Hubbard), Michael James. Student elem. sch., Portsmouth; LLD (hon.), U. Wales, 1976-95; bencher (hon.), Inner Temple, 1976; LLD (hon.), Sardar Patel U., Gujarat, India, 1978, U. Birmingham, 1981; PhD (hon.), Meisei U., Tokyo, 1984; LLD (hon.), U. Sussex, 1988, U. Westminster, 1992, Open U., Milton Keynes, Eng., 1996, U. Liverpool, 1996. Tax officer Inland Revenue Dept., 1929-36; br. asst. sec. Inland Revenue Staff Fedn., 1936-47; parliamentary pvt. sec. to undersec. state dominion affairs, 1945; chmn. def. and svcs. com. Labour Pary, 1945-47; mem. youth del. to USSR, 1945, parliamentary del. to West Africa, 1947; substitute rep. Consultative Assembly Coun. Europe, 1949, rep. 2d session, 1950, Strasbourg, France, 1954; parliamentary sec. to Ministry Transport, 1947-50; parliamentary and fin. sec. to Admiralty, 1950-51; chmn. adv. com. on oil pollution of sea, 1952-63; pres. adv. com. on protection of sea, 1963—2001. Attended 6th Unofcl. Commonwealth Rels. Conf., Royal Inst. Internat. Affairs, New Zealand, 1959; dep. chmn. Parliamentary Assn. del. to Ctrl. Africa; mem. parliamentary del., Zanzibar, Mauritius, Madagascar, 1961; chief spokesman Colonial Affairs, 1956-61; attended Conf. African Socialism, Senegal, 1962-63; pres. U. Wales Swansea, 1986-95; hon. fellow U. Swansea, 1992; mem. nat. exec. com. Labour Party, 1957-80, treas., 1967-76, chmn., 1974; chief spokesman on treasury affairs, 1961-64; privy councillor, 1964; chancellor of Exchequer, 1964-67; sec. of state for home dept., 1967-70; sec. of state for fgn. and commonwealth affairs, 1974-76; prime min. and 1st lord of Treasury, 1976-79; Labour M.P. for Cardiff SS.E., 1945-87. Author: A House Divided: the Dilemma of Northern Ireland, 1973, (autobiography) Time and Chance, 1987. Lt. Royal Navy, 1942-45. Decorated Knight of Garter (Eng.); recipient Hubert H. Humphrey award for internat. statesmanship, 1978; named hon. freeman, City of Cardiff, 1975, City of Sheffield, 1979, City of Portsmouth, 1991, City of Swansea, 1993, London (Eng.) Borough of Southwark, 2001, hon. mem., Ct. Govs., Univ. Coll., Cardiff, 1978; fellow hon. life fellow, Nuffield Coll., Oxford U., hon. fellow, Univ. Coll., Cardiff, 1978, Cardiff Inst. H.E., 1991, Portsmouth U., 1981, Liverpool U., 1996, Open U., 1996. Mem. U.K. Pilots Assn. (pres. 1973-76), Internat. Maritime Pilots Assn. (hon. pres. 1971-76). Died Mar. 26, 2005.

**CALLAGY, FLORENCE MAE,** accounting executive; b. Canton, Ohio, May 6, 1920; d. Charles J. and Pearl M. (Sadler) Brown; m. Francis Henry Callagy, Sept. 14, 1940 (dec.); children: Larry Francis, Richard Michael. Student, San Diego State Coll., 1937—39, U. Calif., San Diego, 1951, student, 1966—67. Jr. acct. Kramer and Zucker CPAs, San Diego, 1951—53; office mgr., auditor Town and Country Devel. Inc., San Diego, 1953—59, sec., treas., 1953—68; sec., treas., contr. Atlas Hotels, Inc., San Diego, 1959—70, dir., from 1959, cons., from 1981; ptnr. Callagy Snyder and Assocs., San Diego, 1971—81; owner, mgr. FMC Cons., San Diego, from 1981. Sec., dir. Electa Corp., Crest Advt., Inc., Mut. Hotel Supply Co., OmniVideo, Inc., Mission Valley Inn, Inc., Mission Valley Devel., Inc., Med. Impact, Inc. Sustaining mem. capital fund com. YMCA, 1978—79; active United Comty. Svcs.; bd. dirs. San Diego Pres. Coun., 1982—83, Freedom Found., Monteverdi Chamber Orch.; mem. adv. bd. Travelor's Aid Soc., San Diego. Mem.: La Mesa C. of C., Nat. Mgmt. Assn. (past dir. San Diego chpt.), San Diego Assn. Advt. Agys., Nat. Hotel Accts. (dir. 1972—73), Calif. Staters, Toastmasters, Altrusa Internat. Inc. (holder numerous offices, dist. gov. 1983—85), San Diego Advt. Club. Deceased.

**CALLAHAN, VINCENT FRANCIS, JR., (VINCE CALLAHAN),** retired state legislator; b. Washington, Oct. 30, 1931; s. Vincent Francis and Anita (Hawkins) C.; children from previous marriage: Vincent Francis III, Elizabeth Lauren, Anita Marie, Cynthia Helen, Robert Bruce; m. Yvonne Weight, Feb. 15, 2006. BS in Fgn. Svc., Georgetown U., 1957; LHD (hon.), No. Va. C.C., 1997; PhD (hon.), Marymount U., Arlington, Va, 2008. Pres. Callahan Publications, 1957-2000; mem. Dist. 27 Va. House of Delegates, 1968—72, mem. Dist. 18, 1972—82, mem. Dist. 49, 1982—83, mem. Dist. 34, 1983—2008, minority leader, 1982-85. Author eight books including: Missile Contracts Guide, 1958, Space Guide, 1959, Underwater Defense Handbook, 1963, Military Research Handbook, 1963. Candidate for lt. gov. Va., 1965; state fin. chmn. Rep. Party of Va., 1966-68; candidate for U.S. Congress, 1976; chmn. No. Va. Cmty. Found.; chmn. Jamestown-Yorktown Found; chmn. emeritus Jamestown-Yorktown Found.; bd. visitors, George Mason U., bd. mem. 2008-2012, With USMC, 1950-53; as lt. USCGR, 1959-63. Mem. U.S. Naval Inst. (bd. mem. 2008-2012), Nat. Press Club, Kiwanis (past pres. McLean, Va.). Republican. Roman Catholic. Home: Alexandria, Va. Died Sept. 20, 2014.

**CALLAWAY, HOWARD HOLLIS (BO CALLAWAY),** resort executive, former United States Representative from Georgia; b. La Grange, Ga., Apr. 2, 1927; s. Cason Jewell and Virginia (Hand) C.; m. Elizabeth Walton, June 11, 1949, (dec. Dec. 08, 2009); children: Elizabeth Callaway Considine, Howard Hollis Jr., Edward Cason, Virginia Callaway Martin, Ralph Walton. Student, Ga. Inst. Tech., 1944-45; BS, U.S. Mil. Acad., 1949. Commd. 2d lt. AUS, 1949, advanced through grades to 1st. lt., 1952; resigned, 1952; mem. US Congress from 3d Ga. Dist., 1965—67; sec. Dept. Army, US Dept. Def., Washington, 1973-75; campaign mgr. Pres. Ford Com., 1975-76; dir. Crested Butte (Colo.) Mountain Resort, 1975—94. Republican candidate for Gov. of Ga., 1966; candidate Republican primary for U.S. Senate from Colo., 1980; chmn. Colo. Republican Com., 1981-87, chmn. GOPAC, 1987-93; mem. Def. Base Realignment & Closure Commn., 1992; com. Ga. Dept. Econ. Devel., 2001-07. 1st lt. inf. U.S. Army, 1949-52. Mem. World President's Orgn. (past pres.), Young Pres.' Orgn. (past pres.), Chief Execs. Orgn., Capital City Club (Atlanta), Piedmont Driving Club (Atlanta), Bohemian Club (San Francisco), Phi Delta Theta, Phi Kappa Phi. Republican. Episcopalian. Home: Pine Mountain, Ga. Died Mar. 15, 2014.

**CALLEJA, JOHN M.,** ship brokerage corporation executive; b. Sliema, Malta, July 29, 1931; s. Joseph Henry and Maria Assunta (Pace) C.; m. Winifred Joan Smith, Apr. 30, 1955; 1 dau., Stephanie Joan. Student, Stella Maris Coll., Gzira, Malta, 1936-45, Sundridge Park Mgmt. Ctr., Kent, Eng., 1960-61; cert., His Majesty's Dockyard Tech. Coll., Malta, 1949. Tech. estimator His Majesty's Dockyard, Cospicua, 1953-56, leading estimator, 1956-58; asst. prodn. contr. Bailey Ltd., Cospicua, 1959-60, prodn. contr., 1960-61, ship repair mgr., 1962-63; marine sales mgr. Malta Drydocks Corp., Cospicua, 1963-66, chief exec. comml. and sales div., 1966-69, gen. mgr., 1971-81, Malta Overseas Trading Co., Ltd., Valletta, 1970-71; mng. dir. Calmarine Services Ltd., Valletta, from 1981. Bd. dirs. Med. Crew, Ltd., Med. Underwater Svcs. Ltd., Cotor Svcs. Ltd., Sea Malta Co. Ltd., O.L. Shipmgmt. (Malta) Ltd. Fellow Chartered Mgmt. Inst.; mem. Assn. Cost. Engrs., Energy Inst., Malta C. of C. and Enterprise, Fedn. Industries Malta (chmn. mgmt. com. 1969-73), Assn. Ship Agts. (pres.). Clubs: Dockyard Sports and Social (life pres. 1971—), Union, Marsa Sports. Lodges: Lions. Roman Catholic. Home: Saint Julians, Malta. Deceased.

**CALVO SOTELO, LEOPOLDO,** former Prime Minister of Spain; b. Madrid, Apr. 14, 1926; s. Leopoldo Calvo-Sotelo and Mercedes Bustelo; m. Pilar IbáñezMartín, Apr. 26, 1954; children: Leopoldo, Juan, Pilar, Pedro, Victor, Jose María, Pablo y Andrés. D.C.E., U. Madrid, 1951. Dir. gen. Perlofil, S.A., Madrid, 1954, Union Española de Explosivos S.A., Madrid, 1963-70. Chmn. Spanish Rys., Madrid, 1967-68; procurador Spanish Courtes, 1972-75; dir. Urquijo Bank, Madrid, 1974-75, Hispano Americano Bank; min. commerce Spain, 1975-76, min. pub. works, 1976-77; min. for rels. with European Communities, 1978-80; v.p. for econ. affairs Spain, 1980-81, prime min., 1981-82; mem. European Parl., 1986-87; mem. bd. dirs. Banco Central Hispanoamericano, 1992; pres. Fundación José Ortega y Gasset, 1993. Served as 2d lt., C.E., Spanish Army Res., 1947-52. Mem. Unión de Centro Democrático. Roman Catholic. Died May 3, 2008.

**CAMERON, GORDON MURRAY,** chemical engineer; b. New Liskeard, Ont., Can., Apr. 9, 1932; s. Murray and Vera Alice (Strader) C.; m. Marie Therese Skutezky, Feb. 2, 1963; children: Barbara, Ian, Vera, Ewen. BSc, Royal Mil. Coll. Can., Kingston, Ont., 1953; BS with honors, Queen's U., Kingston, 1954; PhD in Chem. Engring., U. Del., 1962. Registered prof. engr. With CIL Inc., 1960-73, Chemetics Internat. Ltd., 1960-73, tech. mgr. Montreal, 1974-75, Toronto, 1975-87, dir. tech., 1987, v.p. tech., 1987-88; pres. Cecebe Technologies Inc., Burk's Falls, Ontario, Canada, 1987—2005, GEM Cameron Tech., from 2005. Mem. heat transfer com. Nat. Research Coun. of Can., Ottawa, Ont., 1966-70. Contbr. 20 tech. articles to profl. jours.; inventor, patentee in field. Mem. Can. Soc. Chem. Engring., Am. Inst. Chem. Engrs., Metall. Soc. Presbyterian. Avocations: golf, travel. Home: Burks Falls, Canada. Died May 24, 2008.

**CAMERON, RONALD BROOKS,** Former United States Representative from California; b. Kansas City, Mo., Aug. 16, 1927; Former assemblyman, Calif.; former atty. Cameron & Hoffman; del. Dem. Nat. Conv., 1960—64; state rep. Calif., 1963—67; ret. Democrat. Home: Fullerton, Calif. Died Feb. 1, 2006.

**CAMPANI, MASSIMILIANO,** surgeon, educator; b. Modena, Emilia, Italy, Oct. 7, 1916; s. Rodolfo and Giovanna (Bussoli) C.; m. Erika Von de Ferrari, June 7, 1941 (dec. June 1978); children: Rodolfo, Riccardo, Elisabetta; m. Anna Maria Fantoni. MD, U. Modena, 1941; specialist in nervous & mental diseases, U. Bologna, Italy, 1943; habilitation in gen. pathology, U. Rome, 1950, habilitation in surgery, 1954, habilitation in neurosurgery, 1958. Med. diplomate. Asst. lectr. Inst. Gen. Pathology, Modena, 1947-49; asst. prof. Inst. Surg. Pathology, Pavia, Italy, 1950-52, asst. to chair, 1953-54; prof. surg. anatomy U. Pavia, 1964-66, prof. surgery, 1969-2000. Founder 1st Emergency and Casualty Surgery Sch., U. Pavia, Italy, founder 1st Exptl. and Microsurg. Sch.; dir. Anaesthesia Sch., U. Pavia, 1960-2000. Author: Cranioplasty, 1957, Intra-and-Postoperatory Incidents, 1976, Intrarterial Transfusion, 1978. Capt. Air Sani Corp, 1942-44. Decorated War Cross, Mil. Corps, Padova, Italy, 1949; recipient Fulbright and Smith-Mund prizes, 1954. Fellow Internat. Coll. Surgery; mem. Rotary. Roman Catholic. Achievements include first isolated hyaburonic acid in inflammatory exudates, 1942, first isolated hyalauronic acid in wound healing tissue, 1953, first described degranulation of methacromatic granules of tissue mast-cells after irradiation, 1948. Home: Pavia, Italy. Died Feb. 20, 2000.

**CAMPBELL, CATHERINE CHASE,** geologist; b. NYC, July 1, 1905; d. John Hildreth and Eliza Dixon (Robbins) C.; m. Ian Campbell, Sept. 16, 1930 (dec. 1978); 1 child, Dugald Robbins. AB, AM, Oberlin Coll., 1927; AM, Radcliffe Coll., 1930, PhD, 1933. Instr. geology Mt. Holyoke Coll., South Hadley, Mass., 1927—30; tech. editor U.S. Army Air Force, Pasadena, Calif., 1943—46; head publs. br. U.S. Naval Ordnance Test Sta., Pasadena, 1946—61; geologist U.S. Geol. Survey, Menlo Park, Calif., from 1961. Author (with W.J. Kockelman): Two Examples of Earthquake Hazard Reduction in Southern California, 1983, Use of Geologic and Seismologic Information to Reduce Earthquake Hazards in California, 1984; editor (with D.R. Nichols): Environmental Planning and Geology, 1969. Fellow: Calif. Acad. Sci., Geol. Soc. Am.; mem.: No. Calif. Geol. Soc., Assn. Earth Sci. Editors, Geosci. Info. Soc., Soc. Tech. Comms., Athenaeum Club, Met. Club, Engr.'s Club, Commonwealth Club. Republican. Unitarian. Home: Whittier, Calif. Died Jan. 3, 1996.

**CAMPBELL, COLIN KYDD,** electrical and computer engineering educator, researcher; b. St. Andrews, Fife, Scotland, May 3, 1927; s. David Walker and Jean (Hutchison) C.; m. Vivian Gwyn Norval, Apr. 17, 1954; children—Barry, Gwyn, Ian BSc in Engring. with honors, St. Andrews U., 1952, PhD, 1960; MS, MIT, 1953; DSc, U. Dundee, 1984. Registered profl. engr., Ont. Comm. engr. Fgn. Office and Diplomatic Wireless Svc., London, 1946—47, Brit. Embassy, Washington, 1947—48; electronics engr. Atomic Instrument Co., Cambridge, Mass., 1954—57; asst. prof. elec. and computer engring. McMaster U., Hamilton, Ont., Canada, 1960—63, assoc. prof. elec. and computer engring., 1963—67, prof. elec. engring., 1967—89, prof. elec. and computer engring., 1989—2005, prof. emeritus, 2005. Vis. scholar Ctr. for Power Electronic Sys., Va. Poly. Inst. and State U., Blacksburg, 2000, 02. Author: Surface Acoustic Wave Devices and Their Signal Processing Applications, 1989, Surface Acoustic Wave Devices for Mobile and Wireless Communication, 1998; contbr. numerous articles to profl. jours. Served with Brit. Army, 1944-46 Recipient The Inventor insignia Can. Patents and Devel. Ltd., 1973, invitation fellow Japan Soc. for Promotion of Sci., 1995, rsch. fellow Rand Afrikaans U., South Africa, 1995. Fellow Royal Soc. Can. (Thomas Eadie medal 1983), Engring. Inst. Can., Royal Soc. Arts London, IEEE (life); mem. Sigma Xi, Royal Can. Mil. Inst. Club Toronto Avocation: fishing. Home: Ancaster, Canada. Died Sept. 9, 2008.

**CAMPOS, HAROLDO EURICO BROWNE DE,** poet, educator; b. São Paulo, Brazil, Aug. 19, 1929; s. Eurico and Elvira (Prado Browne) de C.; m. Carmen de Paula Arruda, May 8, 1954; 1 child, Ivan Persio. LLB, U. São Paulo, 1952, PhD, 1972; DLitt (hon.), U. Montreal, Can., 1996. Vis. lectr. Tech. Hochschule, Stuttgart, Germany, 1964; advanced scholar NAS, U.S., 1968; allocation DGRC, Paris, 1969; vis. prof. U. Tex., Austin, 1971, E.L. Tinker vis. prof., 1981; vis. prof. Pontifical Cath. U., São Paulo, 1971-72, asst. prof., 1973-78, assoc. prof., 1979-81, prof., 1982-89, prof. emeritus, from 1990. Vis. prof. Yale U., New Haven, 1978; founder, promoter Concrete Poetry Movement, São Paulo, 1953-56; com. mem. Cultural dell Inst. Italiano di Culture, Brazil, 2000; bd. dirs. World Poetry Acad. Author: (poetry) Auto do Possesso, 1950, Servidão de Passagem, 1962, Xadrês de Estrelas, 1976, Signantia: Quasi Coelum, 1979, Galáxias, 1984 (Roger Caillois award 1999), A Educação dos Cincos Sentidos, 1985, Finismundo: A Última Viagem, 1990, Os Melhores Poemas, 1992 (Jabuti prize 1993), Yugen, Cuaderno Japonés, 1993, Gatimanhase Felinuras, 1994, Kocrét Versek, 1997, Crisantempo, 1998 (Jabuti prize 1999), A Méquina do Mundo Repensada, 2000; (essays) O Arco-Íris Branco, 1997; (anthology) Oswald de Andrade, 1967; co-author: (with A. De Campos) Revisão de Sousândrade, 1964, Sousândrade-Poesia, 1967, Os Sertões Dos Campos, 1997, Guimarães Rosa em Três Dimensões, 1970, (with A. De Campos and D. Pignatari) Teoria da Poesia Concreta, 1965; translator: Dante: Seis Cantos do Paraíso, 1976, Qohélet (Eclesiastes), 1990 (Jabuti prize 1991), Bere'Shith, 1993, Mênis: A Ira de Aquiles, 1994, Hagoromo de Zeami, 1994 (Jabuti prize 1994), Escrito Sobre Jade, 1996, Pedra e Luz Na Poesia de Dante, 1998, Os nomes E Os navios, 1999, (with O. Paz) Transblanco, 1994; contbr. essays to books. Recipient Jabuti prize Câmara Brasileira do Livro, São Paulo, 1992, Chevalier dans L'Ordre des Palmes Academiques, Republique Francese, 1995, Octavio Paz prize Octavio Paz Found., 1999; fellow John Simon Guggenheim Found., 1972, Fulbright Hays Found., 1978. Home: São Paolo, Brazil. Died Aug. 16, 2003.

**CAMPOS, PAULO CAMPANA,** health services executive; b. Dasmarinas Cavite, Philippines, July 27, 1921; s. Jose Sayoto Campos and Luisa (Matro) Campana; m. Lourdes R. Espiritu, Dec. 9, 1951; children: Jose, Paulo, Enrique. AA, U. Philippines, 1940, MD, 1945, DSc (hon.), 1990; postgrad. various, including, Johns Hopkins Sch. of Medicine, 1951-53, 58; Nat. Scientist, 1989; MD, U. Philippines, 1990. Pres. Univ. Physicians' Svcs., Inc., 1967-98; prof. medicine Coll. Medicine/Emilio Aguinaldo Coll., 1979-86; pres. Yaman Lahi Found., Inc., 1980-93; prof. Coll. of Medicine/Univ. Philippines, 1952-82, prof. emeritus, 1989; pres. emeritus De La Salle U./Emilio Aguinaldo Coll., 1991. Fellow Third World Acad. Scis.; pres. emeritus Nat. Rsch. Coun. of Philippines, 1984—; mem. various governing couns. including Governing Coun. of Philippine Coun. for Health Rsch. and Devel., 1982-89, Governing Coun. of the Pacific Sci. Assn., 1983-89; pres. Nat. Acad. Sci. and Tech., 1978-89; mem. UNESCO Nat. Commn. of Philippine Tech. Group on Sci. and Tech., 1983-88; investigator various projects; mem. bd. of regents Univ. Philippines, 1995—; del. internat. confs. in field, other. Editorial bd.: The Medicial Jour. of Emilio Aguinaldo Coll., 1984-86, Acta Medica Philippines, 1961-73, Jour. of Philippine Med. Assn., 1963-71, The Family Physician, Asian Jour. of Medicine, others. Trustee Gota de Leche, 1963—, Joaquin P. Roces Found., Inc., 1989—; trustee Jose P. Rizal Meml. Found., Inc., 1967—, 1st v.p., 1987—. Fulbright grantee, 1952; recipient U.P. fellowship, 1958, Internat. Atomic Energy Agy. Travel grant, 1965, Rockefeller grant, 1966, IAEA fellowship, 1971, WHO travel grant, 1978, 79, NAST travel grant, 1982, ICSU travel grant, 1983, others. Fellow Am. Nuclear Soc., Philippine Assn. Advancement of Sci. (pres. 1966-68), Philippine Coll. Physicians, Philippine Heart Assn., Third World Acad. Scis.; mem. Philippine Med. Assn., N.Y. Acad. Scis., Ermita Sci. Community, WHO (expert adv. panel on health manpower 1980-83), Philippine Fulbright Assn., Philippine Music Found., Philippine Internat. Friendship Orgn., Am. Numismatic Soc., Manila Med. Soc., Philippine Diabetes Assn. (bd. dirs.), Rotary, Phi Kappa Phi, others. Home: Cavite, Philippines. Died June 2, 2007.

**CAMPS, PETRUS HENRICUS J.M. (ARNULF CAMPS),** retired religious studies educator, researcher; b. Eindhoven, The Netherlands, Feb. 1, 1925; s. Lodewijk A.L. and Catharina A. (Rutten) C. BTh, U. Nijmegen, The Netherlands, 1951; MA in Theology, U. Fribourg, Switzerland, 1952, DD, 1957. Ordained priest Roman Cath. Ch., 1950. Prof. Regional Sem., Karachi, Pakistan, 1957-61; mission sec. Franciscan Order, Weert, The Netherlands, 1961-63; prof. missiology Cath. U. Nijmegen, The Netherlands, 1963-90. Cons. Papal Coun. Dialogue, Vatican City, 1964-79; bd. dirs. Sta. WCRP, N.Y.C. Author: Jerome Xavier S.J., 1957, Partners in Dialogue, 1983, The Sanscrit Grammar of H. Roth S.J., 1988 (Book of Yr. 1988), The Third Eye, 1990, The Friars Minor in China (1294-1955), especially the years 1925-55, 1995, Studies in Asian Mission History, 1956-1998, 2000. Decorated knight Order of Dutch Lion (The Netherlands). Mem. German Assn. for Missionswissenschft, Am. Soc. Missiology, Internat. Assn. for Mission Studies, Soc. European Theologians, Internat. Assn. Cath. Missionologists. Mem. Christian Dem. Party. Died Mar. 5, 2006.

**CANNELLA, JOHN MATTHEW,** federal judge; b. NYC, Feb. 8, 1908; s. Joseph and Laura (Gullo) C.; m. Ida Rutnik, Dec. 26, 1938; children: Lauretta (Mrs. Alfred Kushay), Christine (Mrs. John J. Phelan 3d), John Matthew. BS, Fordham U., 1930, LL.B., 1933. Bar: N.Y. 1934. Gen. practice, NYC, 1934-40; asst. US atty. (so. dist.) NY US Dept. Justice, 1940-42; commnr. NY State Dept. Water

Supply Gas and Electricity, NYC, 1946-48, NY State Dept. Licenses, 1948-49; justice NY Ct. Spl. Sessions, NYC, 1949-59; mem. Ct. Gen. Sessions, NYC, 1957-58, City Ct., NYC, 1959-61, NY Criminal Ct., NYC, 1963; judge US Dist. Ct. (so. dist.) NY, 1963—77, sr. judge, 1977—96. Comdr. USCGR, 1942-45. Mem. Catholic Lawyers Guild, Columbian Lawyers Assn. Died Oct. 30, 1996.

**CANNON, HERBERT SETH,** investment banker; b. Bklyn., Dec. 3, 1931; s. Joseph and Gertrude (Kimmel) C.; m. Edith Marks, June 20, 1954; children: Naomi Sue, Nina Louise. BA, Washington and Jefferson Coll., 1953; student, Cornell U. Law Sch., 1953—54; LLB, Fordham U., 1960. Salesman Manhattan Scalloping & Embroidery Co., NYC, 1956-57; stock broker Hirsch & Co., NYC, 1956-61, Wineman, Weiss & Co., NYC, 1961-62; pres. Weis, Voisin, Cannon, Inc., NYC, 1963-70; chmn. bd. Elgin Nat. Industries, Inc., NYC, 1967-70; chmn. bd., pres. Cannon, Jerold & Co., Inc., 1970-73; chmn. bd. PUD Industries, Inc., 1971-83, CitiWide Capital Corp., 1984-88, CitiWide Securities Corp., 1984-88; pres. Cannon Enterprises Inc., real estate devel., investment bankers and fin. cons., Boca Raton, Fla., 1975-93; chmn. bd. Holistic Svcs. Corp., 1979-83; pres. HSC Consulting, Inc., from 1997. Past trustee Washington and Jefferson Coll. Served with AUS, 1954-56. Mem. Young Pres. Orgn., World Bus. Coun., Metro Pres. Orgn. *Make it happen.* Deceased.

**CANTRELL, CYRUS DUNCAN, III,** physics professor, engineering educator, director; b. Bartlesville, Okla., Oct. 4, 1940; s. Cyrus Duncan and Janet Ewing (Robinson) C.; m. Carol Louise Chandler, June 9, 1962 (div. 1971); m. Mary Lynn Marple, Nov. 18, 1972; 1 child, Katherine Anne. BA cum laude, Harvard U., 1962; MA, Princeton U., 1964, PhD, 1968. Lic. profl. engr., Tex., 2002. From asst. to assoc. prof. Swarthmore Coll., Pa., 1967-73; staff mem. Los Alamos Sci. Lab., 1973-76, assoc. group leader, 1976-78, staff mem., 1978-79, cons., 1980—89; assoc. prof. U. Paris-Nord, Villetaneuse, France, 1980; prof. elec. engring. and physics U. Tex.-Dallas, Richardson, from 1980, dir. Photonic Tech. and Engring. Ctr., from 1980, assoc. dean engring. and computer sci., 2002—08, sr. assoc. dean, from 2008. Editor: Laser Induced Fusion and X-Ray Laser Studies, 1976, Multiple-Photon Excitation and Dissociation of Polyatomic Molecules, 1986, Nonlinear Optics and Materials, 1991; author: (book) Modern Mathematical Methods for Physicists and Engineers, 2002; contbr. articles to profl. jours. Winner Nat. Westinghouse Sci. Talent Search, Washington, 1958; Nat. scholar Gen. Motors Corp., 1958-62; Woodrow Wilson Found. fellow, Princeton U., 1962-63; NSF fellow, Princeton, 1965-66 Fellow IEEE (chpt. chmn. 1978-82; Third Millenium medal 2000), Am. Phys. Soc., Optical Soc. Am. patentee infrared laser system, 1982, method and apparatus for laser isotope separation, 1987, method and apparatus for phase conjugate optical modulation, 1989. Home: Richardson, Tex. Died June 19, 2013.

**CAPEHART, HARRIET JANE HOLMES,** economics educator; b. Springfield, Ill., Sept. 29, 1917; d. Walter Creager and Mary Gladys (Copeland) Holmes; m. Homer Earl Capehart Jr., June 17, 1950; children: Craig Earl, Caroline Mary, John. AB, Vassar Coll., 1938; MA, Harvard U., 1945, PhD, 1948; LLD (hon.), U. Indpls., 1986. Instr. Wheaton Coll., Norton, Mass., 1945-46, Wellesley (Mass.) Coll., 1947-48; assoc. prof. Western Coll. for Women, Oxford, Ohio, 1948-50; assoc. prof. econs. Butler U., Indpls., 1950-53; staff adult edn. div. U. Indpls. (formerly Indiana Cen. U.), 1973-75, adj. faculty, from 1983. Lectr. summer sch. Butler U., 1948-50. Bd. trustees U. Indpls., 1969—; exec. bd. Women's Com. Indpls. Symphony Orch., 1964—; bd. dirs. Utility Women's Conf., 1986—; mem. bd. English Speaking Union, 1996—; mem. Children's Mus. Guild, aux. Indpls. Day Nursery, others. Mem. Am. Econ. Assn., Econometric Soc., AAUP, Indpls. Mus. Art, English Speaking Union (bd. mgmt. 1996—), Nat. Soc. Colonial Dames Am. (bd. mgrs. Ind.), Portfolio Club (treas. 1998—), Contemporary Club, Econ. Club, Trail Blazers, Harvard Club Ind., Radcliffe Club of Ind. (past pres.), Ind. Vassar Club (past pres.), Phi Beta Kappa, Kappa Alpha Theta. Republican. Died Oct. 20, 2002.

**CAPELO, ANTONIO-CANDIDO SIMOES,** statistics educator; b. Grandola, Alentejo, Portugal, Aug. 28, 1948; s. Arnaldo Conceicao and Germinia Simoes (Vitoria) C. Degree in electrotechnics engring., Polytechnic of Lisbon, 1972. Asst. Polytechnic of Lisbon, 1971-72, U. Padvia, 1972-80, charged prof., 1980-84; assoc. prof. U. Padua, 1984-85, prof., from 1985. Author: Variational and Quasivariational in Equalities, 1983, Modelli Matematici Inegualities, 1995, Cedam, 1995, L'Eletrodinamica di Minkowsky, 1990. Mem. Am. Math. Soc., Soc. Math. Biology, Osteria All'Anfora. Avocations: guinness, pall mall, laphroaig, history of flemish and dutch art. Home: Pavia, Italy. Died Oct. 27, 2001.

**CAPLAN, VERLA LOUISE,** elementary educator, resource consultant; b. Oskaloosa, Iowa, Nov. 1, 1914; d. Curtis Ernest and Lois Mozelle (Carr) Van Voorhis; m. Lewis Henry Caplan, Apr. 4, 1939; children: Constance, Roberta, Lewis Jr., Laurence, Gerald, Barbara. BA in History and Govt., Kans. City U., Mo., 1961; MA in Edn., U. Mo., Kansas City, 1968, postgrad., 1974, postgrad., 1968-74. Cert. nursery-primary tchr., N.Y.; cert. tchr., Iowa; life cert. elem. tchr., Mo. Elem. tchr. Kansas City Sch. Bd., 1957-60; elem. tchr. gifted children sci. 2-6th grades Independence (Mo.) Sch. Dist., 1961-85; in curricululm devel. Title III Independence Curriculum Devel. Cons. and vol. edn. in field. NSF grantee, 1974. Mem. ASCD, Internat. Reading Assn., Nat. Sci. Tchrs. Assn., Am. Childhood Educators, Mo. Tchrs. Assn., Independence Classroom Tchrs. (past pres.), Mo. Math. Tchrs. Assn., Sci. Tchrs. Mo. Deceased.

**CAPLES, LOUISE SKINNER LEIGH,** civic worker; b. Hertford, NC, Nov. 5, 1915; d. Edward Augustus and Mary Motley (Coke) Leigh; m. Delphin Delmas Caples, July 6, 1944; children: Pete L., Patricia Caples Greenwell, Richard J., Robert M. Postgrad. in Obstetrics, Margaret Hague Maternity Hosp., 1939. RN Franklin Sq. Hosp. Sch. Nursing, 1938. Bd. dirs., 1st v.p. Franklin Sq. Hosp. Aux., 1947—49; leadership chmn. Md. Coun. Hosp. Auxs., 1949—50, active recruitment nurses, 1950—60; mem. com. on careers Nat. League Nursing, 1950—54; pres. Balt. County Med. Aux., 1950—58, Med. and Surg. Faculty Md., 1959—60; organizing mem., 1st v.p. Carroll County Hosp. Aux., 1961—62; state registrar Nat. Soc. DAR, Md., 1976—79; organizing state pres. Colonial Dames XVII Century, Md., 1974—75; state rec. sec. Nat. Huguenot Soc., Md., 1980—82; pres. Nat. Soc. Daus. Am. Colonists, 1985—88; vestryman All Saints Episcopal Ch., 1965—69. Served to 1st lt. Nurse Corps US Army, 1942—45, Middle East, ETO. Mem.: Glyndon C. of C., Owings Mills C. of C., Reisterstown C. of C., Federated Women's Club Glyndon, Nat. Assn. Parliamentarians, Colonial Dames Am., Magna Charta Dames (life). Republican. Home: Easton, Md. Deceased.

**CAPOORE, HARBANS SINGH,** psychiatrist, researcher; b. Lucknow, Uttur Pradesh, India, Aug. 12, 1917; arrived in U.K., 1935. s. Gur Baksh and Jaswant Kaur Singh; m. Olive Bagshaw, Sept. 19, 1942 (dec. 1985); 1 child, Penelope Indra. BChD in Dentistry, Leeds Sch., UK, 1941, MbChB, 1943, MD, 1946; diploma in psychol. medicine, 1946. Sr. asst. med. officer W. Riding Mental Hosp., Burley, Wharfedale, U.K., 1944-46, St. Andrews Hosp., Norwich, U.K., 1947-48; cons. psychiatrist Bexley Hosp., U.K., 1949-82, Dartford Hosp., U.K., 1949-77, Queen Mary's Hosp., Sidcup, England, from 1977; hon. cons. Kent and Canterbury Hosp., Canterbury, England, from 1986. Cons. Dist. Mgmt. Team, Bexley, 1977-78, 80-82; chmn. Bexley Dist. Med. Com., Bexley, 1981-82. Reviewer, Psychosomatics Ofcl. Jour. Acad. Psychosomatic Medicine, 2000; contbr. articles to profl. jours. Fellow Royal Coll. Psychiatrists; mem. AAAS, N.Y. Acad. Scis., Med. Protection Soc. London. Avocations: reading, radio and tv, travel, gardening. Home: Loughborough Leicestershire, England. Died Aug. 23, 2003.

**CARACCIOLO, CARLO,** communications company executive; b. Firenze, Italy, Oct. 23, 1925; s. Filippo Caracciolo di Castagneto and Margareth Clarke; m. Violante Visconti di Modrone, June 20, 1996. LLD, U. Rome, 1949, Harvard U., 1950. Cert. pub. Mng. dir. Etas Kompas, Milan, 1951-75; chmn. bd. Editl. L'Espresso, S.p.A., 1957—2008, Arnoldo Mondadori Editore, Milan, 1989-90; chmn., mng. dir. Editl. Repubblica, S.p.A., 1976-97; chmn. bd. Gruppo Editl. L'Espresso, 1998—2007, hon. chmn., 2007—08. Avocation: chess. Home: Roma, Italy. Died Dec. 15, 2008.

**CARACCIOLO, FRANCIS SAMUEL,** management consultant; b. Phila., Jan. 18, 1929; s. Francis Charles and Constance (Achuff) C.; m. Clara Slater Caracciolo, Sept. 3, 1965; children: Addison L., Gloria Ann. AA, George Washington U., 1950, AB in Psychology, 1952, MA in Pyschology, 1954. Jr. exec. Gen. Motors Acceptance Corp., Washington, 1953-55; ednl. specialist Army Dept., Washington, 1955-57; dir. profl. devel., mgmt. skills Navy Dept., Washington, 1957-59, dir. adminstrn. and managerial programs, 1959-60; assoc. dir. mgmt. intern programs CSC, Washington, 1960-62, dir. mgmt. sci. programs, 1962-63, dir. Exec. Seminar Ctr. Kings Pt., N.Y., 1963-64; spl. asst. to dir. Office Career Devel., Washington, 1964-65; dir. ednl. programs Office Tech. Assistance Equal Employment Opportunity Commn., Washington, 1965-67; program specialist pub. adminstrn. Ford Found., New Delhi, 1967-70; dir. office tng. support Peace Corps, Washington, 1970; asst. adminstr Office Manpower Devel. and Tng., Social and Rehab. Svcs., HEW, Washington, 1970-73; dir. internat. exchange programs R & D, Social and Rehab. Svcs, HEW, Washington, 1973-79; team leader pub. svc. improvement UN Devel. Programs, Jamaica, W.I., 1979-80; asst. to dir. Nat. Inst. Handicapped Rsch., U.S. Dept. Edn., Washington, 1980-81; dir. spl. rehab. programs Rehab. Svcs. Adminstrn., U.S. Dept. Edn., Washington, 1981-89; prin. Ft. Myers Beach, FL, from 1989. Founder Indian Soc. for Tng. and Devel., New Delhi, 1970, spkr., 1994; pres. Three Continents Ltd., Vienna, Va., 1973-76. Mem. Nat. Italian Am. Found. (coun. of 1000). Roman Catholic. Avocations: swimming, cruising, travel. Died Aug. 15, 2001.

**CARAPANCEA, MIHAI TITUS,** ophthalmologist; b. Bucharest, Romania, Apr. 20, 1920; s. Titus Gh. and Eleonora (Zissu) C.; m. Elena Negru, Apr. 25, 1980. Dr. Medicine and Surgery, Faculty Medicine, Bucharest, 1944; DMS, U. Bucharest, 1967, Docent in Med. Scis., 1975; D of Therapeutic Philosophy (hon.), World U., 1983; D in Psychology (hon.), Parthasarathy Internat. Cultural Acad., 1993; Med. Sc. Dr. h.c. Complementary Medicines and Med. Alternativa, Open Internat. Univ., 1994. Asst. lectr. U. Bucharest, 1944-52; cons. eye specialist cons. ophthal. clinics, 1946-52; sci. rsch. worker D. Danielopolu Inst. Normal and Path. Physiology, Acad. Romania, Bucharest, 1951-53, interdisciplinary scientist, 1953-82, founder, head lab. clin. and exptl. physiology and physiopathology of eye, 1953-82, mgr. topics opthalmological rsch., 1956-82, sr. chief ophthalmologist, 1969-82, prin. sr. rsch. scientist, 1970-82, cons. adviser clin. and exptl. ophthalmology, 1983-90. Mem. Aerospace Biol. sect. Astronautic Commn. Acad. Romania, Space Medicine and Cosmic. Biol. group Radiobiology Commn., Acad. Romania. Author: Amauroses, Amblyopiae and Ocular Disorders Caused by Quininic Intoxication, 1944, Physiopathology of Hypertensive, Clinical and Experimental, Manifestations of Retinal Vessels, 1970; editor Rumania, Jour. La Porta dell'Uomo; research, over 390 publs. on corneal bio-architectonic structure; visual accommodation by topographic determinism of anatomo-functional mechanism of zonules; neurosis of hypermetropia; exophthalmia through hypertonia of striated peri-ocular musculature; non-specific action of drugs on eye; pathognomonic ERG indications in gen. fatigue phenomenon; syndrome of ciliary plexus of orbit; clinical and experimental surgery of the orbital ciliary plexus; retinal vessels theshold excitability in experimental hypertension; alternating recidivation of rickettsial and/or pararickettsial uveitis; rickettsial and/or pararickettsial retinal arterites, cataract and glaucoma; corneo-conjunctival tactile sensibility, cilio-accommodation and retinal vessels modifications at high altitude; altitude hyperophthalmotony by transfer of hydrophilic ions from blood into aqueous humour and ophthalmotonico-homeostatic reactions of calcium and of Vitamin C; hypermetropic cilio-accommodation in altitude hyperophthalmotony and augmentation of hypermetropic amplitude by Vitamin C. Count Palatine, lt. Patriarchal Venerable Noble Guard Universal Orthodox Slav-Holy Ch., Italy, 2000. Decorated Centenary Medal of King Carol I with Pro Patria bar on Ribbon, 1940, Sanitary Merit Cross 2d class, 1942, Medal of Crusade against Bolshevism, 1942, Commemorative medal, 1944, Med. Order of the Queen Mary Cross 2d class, 1945, Disting. Mark Cross of the Red Cross, 1945, Medal of Antifascist Liberation, 1954, Mil. Order of the Star 5th class, 1955, Commemorative Cross WWII, 1994; named Knight Hon. Comdr. Cross of the Chivalrous Order St. Andrew (Austria), 1992, Knight Hon. Comdr. Cross of the Internat. Order for Peoples' Concordance (Switzerland) 1992, Knight Grand Cross of the Tambauense Merit of Brazil, 1992, Knight Grand Cross of the Sovereign and Royal Order of the Crown of Susiana, Italy, 1995, Knight Grand Cross of the Sovereign and Venerable Religious Order of Ambrosini's, Italy, 1995, Ancient Royal Order of Physicians, Sri Lanka, 1995, Knight Grand Cross of the Sovereign and Religious Chivalrous Order of St. Elisabeth's, Italy, 1997, Knight Royal civalrous Order of St. Lukas, Germany, 1999, Knight Grand Cross of the Sovereign and Mil. Chivalrous Order of the Golden Sword of St. George in Locrida, England, 2000, knight grand cross Sovereign and Hereditary Order of the Black Eagle (Spain); recipient Honor medals Internat. Inst. Human Labor Problems-World Ctr. for Labor Promotion Belgium, bronze medal, 1971, silver medal, 1974, Commemorative Pennon, 1977, plaquette Labor U., Luxembourg, 1973, silver medal Soc. Encouragement Rsch. and Invention, France, 1974, Pro Mundi Beneficio medal Acad. Humanities, Brazil, 1975, gold plaquette of homage for self-devotion in social work activities and to the rich activity in behalf of labor promotion, Belgium, 1978, Silver and Gold medals Universal Acad., Switzerland, 1983, cert. of merit Universal Inst. Peace, Switzerland, 1984, Bronze medal with collar ribbon Albert Einstein Internat. Acad. Found., 1986; also numerous certs. and diplomas for disting. svcs. and outstanding achievements, 1976-99, Cert. Excellence, Sri Lanka U., 1997, Princely Gold medal and Knight Grand Officer, Chivalrous Order of St. Gereon, Germany, 1999; citation meritorious achievement Internat. Writers and Artists Assn., 2000; nobility title reconfirmed as Count of Kraina and Vraina, belonging to Ancestral House of Carapancea, Italy, 1998; nobility title conferred as Marquis of Derneck-Memmelsdorf, Germany, 1999; nobility title conferred as Count Palatine and Lt. in Patriarchal Venerable Noble Guard Universal Orthodox Slav Holy Ch., Italy, 2000. Mem. Acad. Romanian Scientists (titular mem. sci. coun.), Romanian Soc. Ophthalmology, Romanian Soc. Normal and Path. Physiology, Internat. Soc. Clin. Electrophysiology of Vision, Internat. Soc. Metabolic Eye Disease, Assn. Internat. Glaucoma Congress, French, Belgian, Italian socs. ophthalmology, Am. Soc. Ophthalmology and Optometry, Am. Soc. Contemporary Ophthalmology, Japanese Ophthal. Soc., Am. Soc. Photobiology, World U. (mem. roundtable, chmn. nat. chief del. for Rumania, internat. faculty mem.), Marquis Giuseppe Scicluna Internat. U. Found. (hon. v.p.), Diandra U. (hon. pres.), Internat. Inst. Human Labor Problems-World Ctr. for Labor Promotion (internat. v.p., mem. coun. bd., pres. Rumania sect., nat. chief del. for Rumania), Albert Einstein Internat. Acad. Found. (hon. v.p.), N.Y. Acad. Scis. (live), Universal Acad. (hon. life), Prof. Ambrosini Acad. Natural Scis. and Psychobiophysics (Academician in Med. Scis., mem. academicians' honor corps), Royal St. Lukas Gilde Antwerpen Internat. Acad. (prof. honoris causa, chief exec. counselor), Chrysalis Universal Heraldic Acad. (Academician of honor), Mediterranean's Acad. (titular academician), Giuseppe Pitrè Internat. Acad. (academician of honor), Sicilian Acad. Scis. (effective mem.), Costantiniana Acad. (academician honoris causa), Acad. Internat. House of Intellectuals, F.R.G., Internat. Acad. Scis., F.R.G. and San Marino (free mem. Internat. Sci. Coll.), Cultural Ctr. Portugal (Academician ad honorem), Tambauense Acad., Brazil (Well-Deserved mem.), World Safety Orgn. (hon. internat. cons., cert. safety exec., v.p. for Ea. Europe, exec. v.p. dir. at large, bd. dirs.), Internat. Union Physiol. Scis., European Soc. Philosophy Med. and Healthcare, Albert Schweitzer Soc. (hon. mem., sci. coun., Albert Schweitzer medal 1992), Physicians in Help of Life Orgn. (internat. v.p.), Human Factors Soc., Ergonomic Soc. French Lang., Internat. Soc. Biometeorology, Aerospace Med. Assn., French Soc. Angiology, Internat. Soc. Cybernetic Medicine, Internat. Assn. Applied Psychology, Assn. Med. Renewal, Soc. Encouragement to Progress (life, Honour Gold medal 1997), Mgmt. Profls. Assn. (program com.), Rev. Scienza 2001 (internat. acad. com. mem. hon. sci.), Rev. Internat. Surgery (editl. bd.), Internat. Parliament for Safety and Peace (chargé d'affaires at large in Rumania), Universal Alliance for Peace by Knowledge, High Sch. Rsch. (prof., attache of rsch.), World Constitution and Parliament Assn. (hon. sponsor),

European Chamber of Extra-Judiciary Arbitrators and Experts Tech. Counsellors (hon., expert of Europe for clin. and exptl. physiol. and physiopathology of the eye 1991—, dep. chargé with mission), Internat. Assn. Educators for World Peace (hon. diploma), Assn. Chivalrous Order of St. Andrews (assoc.), Phoenix Inst. (hon., life), Inst. Internat. Affairs (supreme coun.), Inst. Planetary Synthesis World Tchr. Trust (editor Rumania Jour.), World Goodwill, Internat. Assn. Eco-spiritual Movement BEAULIEU, World Fedn. Europeans, Mediterranean Species Seminum Geroplasma Found. Bank (hon.), Internat. Coll. Surgeons (Fellow in Opthalmology, founder, 1st pres. Rumanian nat. sect.), Psycho-Soc. Prophilactic Nat. Ctr. Nat. Ctr. (Italy), World Ctr. Scis. (sci. counsellor-expert in psychiatry), Sovereign and Royal Order of the Crown of Susiana (bailiff, lt. gen. Romania, Grand Master hon., Knight Grand Cross, 1995), Leonardo da Vinci (sci. expert counsellor psychiatry), Sovereign and Venerable Religious Order of Ambrosini's (Grand Master hon., Knight Grand Cross, 1995), Sovereign and Religious Chivalrous Order of St. Elisabeth's (Grand Prior for Rumania, Knight Grand Cross 1997), Royal Order of Benedictions and Holy Crusades (Grand Master hon. for Rumania 2000). Home: Bucharest, Romania. Died Aug. 2002.

**CARDOSO, ANTHONY ANTONIO,** artist, educator; b. Tampa, Fla., Sept. 13, 1930; s. Frank T. and Nancy (Mesina) C.; m. Martha Rodriguez, 1954; children: Michele Denise, Toni Lynn. BS in Art Edn., U. Tampa, 1954; BFA, Minn. Art Inst., 1965; MA, U. South Fla., Tampa, 1975; PhD in Art, Elysion Coll., Calif., 1981. Art instr., head fine arts dept. Jefferson H.S., Tampa, 1952-67, Leto H.S., Tampa, from 1967; supr. art and humanities Hillsborough County Sch., Tampa, 1985—91. Bd. dirs., supr. art Hillsboro County Schs.; rep. Tampa Art Coun.; artist, 1952-87. One-man shows include Warren's Gallery, Tampa, 1974, 75, 76, Tampa Realist Gallery, Tampa, 1975, Kotler Gallery 2005; group shows include Rotunda Gallery, London, End., 1973, Raymon Duncan Galleries, Paris, France, 1973, Brussells Internat., 1973, Tampa U. Alumni Exhibit, 2007, Tampa CC Group Exhibit, 2007; represented in permanent collections Minn. Mus., St. Paul, Tampa Sports Authority Art Collection, Tampa Arts' Coun.; executed murals Tampa Sports Authority Stadium, 1972, Suncoast Credit Union Bldg., Tampa, 1975, Kotler Gallery Exhibit, Tampa, 2004, Centro Asturiano Ball Room Gallery, 2004. Recipient Prix de Paris Art award Raymon Duncan Galleries, 1970, Salon of 50 States award Ligoa Duncan Gallery, NYC, 1970, Latham Found. Internat. Art award, 1964, XXII Bienniel Traveling award Smithsonian Instn., 1968-69, Purchaase award Minn. Mus., 1971, 1st award Fla. State Fair, 1967, Gold medal Accademia Italia, 1981-82, Medallion Merit, Internat. Parliament, Italy, 1984, Statue of Vittoria award for centro studi and richerche, Italy, 1988, Accademia D'Europa, Premio Palma D'Oro D' Europa, Italy, 1989—, El Prado Gallery, 1990—, Merit award Festival Arts Hillsborough County Tampa, 1994-2002, El Prado Gallery, Tampa, 1999-2004, Koetler Gallery Tampa, 2005, 2007, 2010, 11, Internat. Photographers award, 2007-12, Exhibit HCC Coll., 2009, 10, U. Tampa Alumnus Fine Arts Exhbn., 2010-11, (paintings exhbn.) Christ The King Cath. Ch., Tampa, Fla., 2011. Democrat. Roman Catholic. Died June 17, 2013.

**CARLES GORDO, RICARDO MARIA CARDINAL,** cardinal, archbishop emeritus; b. Valencia, Spain, Sept. 24, 1926; Attended, Corpus Christi Coll. Sem., Valencia; degree in Canon Law, Pontifical U. of Salamanca, 1953. Ordained priest of Valencia, 1951; parish priest, archpriest Ternes di Valldigna, Spain, 1953; rector San Fernando parish, Valencia, 1967—69; bishop of Tortosa, Spain, 1969—90, ordained, 1969; archbishop of Barcelona, 1990—2004, archbishop emeritus, from 2004; elevated to cardinal, 1994; cardinal-priest of Santa Maria Consolatrice al Tiburtino (Saint Mary of Consolation in Tiburtino), 1994—2013. Author: Fe y Cultura; publisher Cartas desde la vida misma, published in various journals and broadcast on the radio. Roman Catholic. Died Dec. 17, 2013.

**CARLOCK, MAHLON WALDO,** financial planner, consultant, retired school system administrator; b. Plymouth, Ind., Sept. 17, 1926; s. Thorstine Clifford and Katheryn G. (Gephart) C.; m. Betty L. Dobbs, Aug. 27, 1954; children: Mahlon W. II, Rhena M., Shawn R. BS, Ind. U., 1951, MS, 1956. Tchr. jr. high Martinsville Schs. Corp., Brooklyn, Ind., 1952-53; tchr. high sch. Indpls. Pub. Schs., 1953-63, asst. to dean of boys, 1963-73, asst. dean of boys, 1973-75, bus. mgr., 1976-87; fin. cons. Indpls., 1987-93; property builder, owner Ind. Sgt. U.S. Army, 1945-47. Mem. NEA (life), Indpls. Edn. Assn. (rep. 1958-63). Republican. Baptist. Avocation: investing in real estate. Home: Brownsburg, Ind. *Personal philosopy: You must always feel that Christ is beside you in everything you do.* Died Jan. 11, 2014.

**CARLSON, BRUCE WILLIAM,** diversified holding company executive; b. Jamestown, NY, Mar. 1, 1947; m. Angelyn Fabiano; children: Kristina, Sara, Andrew, Matthew. BS in Acctg., U. Buffalo, 1969. CPA, N.Y. Mgr. Arthur Andersen & Co., Rochester, N.Y., 1969-77; v.p. finance Andco Inc., Buffalo, 1977-86; joined Delaware North Companies, Inc., 1986, v.p., corporate contr., v.p. financial strategy, 2011—13. Mem. AICPA, Beta Gamma Sigma. Home: Grand Island, NY. Died Oct. 26, 2013.

**CARO, SIR ANTHONY ALFRED,** sculptor; b. New Malden, Surrey, Eng., Mar. 8, 1924; s. Alfred and Mary (Haldinstein) C.; m. Sheila May Girling, Dec. 17, 1949; children: Timothy Martin, Paul Gideon. MA, Christ's Coll., Cambridge U., Eng., 1944; Grad., Royal Acad. Schs., London, 1952; D.Litt. (hon.), East Anglia U., York U., Toronto, Ont., Can., Brandeis U. Asst. to Henry Moore, 1951-53; part-time tchr. sculpture St. Martin's Sch. Art, London, 1953-79; tchr. sculpture Bennington Coll., Vt., 1963, 65. Founder Triangle Artists' Workshop, U.S.A.; guest lectr. Artists' Workshop, Maastricht, The Netherlands; vis. artist workshops Barcelona, Spain, Berlin, 1987, U. Alberta, Red Deer Coll., Alberta, Can., 1989. Sculpture commd. by Nat. Gallery Art, Washington, 1977; one-man shows include, Galleria del Naviglio, Milan, Italy, 1956, Gimpel Fils Gallery, London, 1957, Whitechapel Art Gallery, London, 1963, Andre Emmerich Gallery, N.Y.C., 1964, 66, 68, 70, 72, 74, 77, 78, 79, 81, 82, 84, 86, 88, 89, 91, 94, Washington Gallery Modern Art, 1965, Kasmin Ltd., London, 1965, 67, 71, 72, David Mirvish Gallery, Toronto, Ont., Can., 1966, 71, 74, Galerie Bischofberger, Zurich, Switzerland, 1966, Kroller-Muller Mus., Netherlands, 1967, Hayward Gallery, London, 1969, Kenwood House, Hampstead, Eng., 1974, 81, 94, Galleria dell'Ariete, Milan, 1974, Richard Gray Gallery, Chgo., 1976, 78, 86, 89, 94, Watson/de Nagy Gallery, Houston, 1976, Mus. Modern Art, N.Y.C., 1975, Walker Arts Ctr., Mpls., 1975, Mus. Fine Arts, Houston, 1975, Lefevre Gallery, London, 1976, Everson Mus., Syracuse, N.Y., 1976, Mus. Fine Arts Boston, 1976, 80, Piltzer-Rheims, Paris, 1977, Waddington & Tooth, London, 1977, Brit. Coun. touring exhbn. Tel Aviv, New Zealand, Australia, Germany, 1977-79, Emmerich Gallery, Zurich, 1974, 78, 85, Harkus Krakow Gallery, Boston, 1978, 81, 83, 84, 85, 89, Knoedler, London, 1978, 82, 83, 84, 86, 89, 91, Wentzel, Hamburg, 1976, 78, Ace, Venice, Calif., 1978, Kasahara, Japan, 1979, 90, 95, Acquavella Galleries, N.Y., 1980, 84, 86, Galerie Andre, Berlin, 1980, Downstairs Gallery, Edmonton, Alta, Can., 1981, Galerie Wentzel, Cologne, Ger., 1982, 84, 85, 88, 91, Gallery One, Toronto, 1982, 85, 87-88, 90, Galerie de France, Paris, 1983, Serpendure Gallery, London, 1984, Brit. Coun. touring exhbn. Madrid, Barcelona, Bilbao, Valencia, Spain, 1986, Constantine Grimaldis Gallery, Balt., 1987, 89, 94, Galerie Renée Ziegler, Zurick, 1988, Tate Gallery, 1991, numerous others; exhibited in group shows at 1st Paris Biennale, 1959 (sculpture prize), Battersea Park Open Air Exhbn., 1960, 63, 66, Gulbenkian Exhbn., London, 1964, Documenta III Kassel, 1965, Jewish Mus., N.Y.C., 1966 (David Bright prize), Venice Biennale, 1958, 66, Pitts. Internat., 1967, 68, Met. Mus. Art, 1968, Sao Paulo, 1969 (sculpture prize), U. Pa., 1969, Everson Mus., Mus. Modern Art, N.Y.C., 1975; represented in permanent collections Walker Art Gallery, Minn., Mus. Fine Arts, Houston, Boston, Dallas, Mus. Modern Art, N.Y.C., Phila. Mus. Art, Cleve. Mus. Art, Detroit Inst. Arts, Solomon R. Guggenheim Mus., N.Y.C., Yale U. Art Gallery, New Haven, numerous others. With Fleet Air Arm of Royal Navy. Decorated comdr. Order Brit. Empire, 1969; presented key to city N.Y.C., 1976; hon. fellow Christ's Coll., Cambridge, Royal Coll. Art, London, 1986, U. Surrey, England, 1987, Knighted, 1987. Mem. American Acad. & Inst. Arts & Letters (hon.) Died Oct. 24, 2013.

**CARPENTER, DAVID LYLE,** lawyer; b. Norwalk, Ohio, 1942; BA, Coll. Wooster, 1965; MBA, U. Mich., 1969, JD cum laude, 1969. Bar: Ohio 1969. Mem. Calfee, Halter & Griswold, Cleve. Mem. ABA, Cleve. Tax Inst. (chmn.), Order Coif. Died Sept. 6, 1999.

**CARPENTER, GENE BLAKELY,** crystallography and chemistry educator; b. Evansville, Ind., Dec. 15, 1922; s. Leland A. and Juanita (Blakely) C.; m. Elizabeth E. Corkum, Apr. 15, 1949; children: Jonathan R., Anne E. BA, U. Louisville, 1944; MA, Harvard U., 1945, PhD, 1947. NRC fellow Calif. Inst. Tech., 1947-48, research fellow, 1948-49; instr. Brown U., 1949-52, asst. prof., 1952-56, asso. prof., 1956-63, prof., 1963-88, prof. emeritus, from 1988. Guggenheim fellow U. Leeds, Eng., 1956-57; vis. prof. U. Groningen, The Netherlands, 1963-64; Fulbright-Hayes lectr. U. Zagreb, Yugoslavia, 1971-72; vis. scientist Oak Ridge Nat. Lab., 1980, U. Göttingen, Fed. Republic of Germany, 1987, U. Canterbury, Christchurch, New Zealand, 1989. Author: Principles of Crystal Structure Determination, 1969; Contbr. articles to sci. jours. Mem. Am. Crystallographic Assn., Am. Chem. Soc. Home: Providence, RI. Died June 13, 2013.

**CARR, DANIEL P.,** former state legislator; married. Candidate Cheshire Dist. 04 NH House of Reps., 2004, mem. Cheshire, Dist. 04, 2008—12. Democrat. Died June 26, 2012.

**CARR, JAMES CELESTINE,** consultant radiologist; b. Dublin, June 4, 1933; s. Christopher Joseph and Margaret Mary (Groome) C.; m. Mary Imelda O'Hegarty, Sept. 22, 1962; children: Mary, Rosemarie, James, Susannah, Jonathan, Dominique. M.B.B.Ch., NUI, Dublin, 1957. Cert. F.F.R., R.C.S.I. 1968, F.R.C.R. 1990. Intern, sr. house officer Master Hosp., Dublin, 1957-59; med. dir. St. John's Hosp., Korea, 1959-61; sr. house officer St. Annes Skin & Cancer Hosp., Dublin, 1961; registrar Glasgow Royal Infirmary, 1961-64, Royal No. Hosp., London, 1964-66; asst. dir. Mass X-Ray, Dublin, 1967-70; cons. radiologist Bon Secours Hosp., Dublin, from 1966, Richmond Hosp., Dublin, 1969-87, Beaumont Hosp., Dublin, from 1987; sr. lectr. Royal Coll. Surgeons Ireland, Dublin, from 1992, dean faculty radiologists, 1985-87. Editor, author: A Century of Radiation in Ireland - an Anthology, 1995; contbr. articles to profl. jours. Mem. Med. Coun. of Ireland, 1994—; bd. dirs. Radiation Protection Inst. Ireland, 1997—. Mem. Radiol. Soc. Ireland (pres. 1979-83). Avocations: stamp collecting/philately, reading, golf, walking, history. Home: Dublin, Ireland. Died Feb. 21, 2006.

**CARRIGAN, JAMES R. (JIM CARRIGAN),** arbitrator, mediator, retired federal judge; b. Mobridge, SD, Aug. 24, 1929; s. Leo Michael and Mildred Ione (Jaycox) C.; m. Beverly Jean Halpin, June 2, 1956. PhB, JD, U. N.D., 1953; LLM in Taxation, NYU, 1956; LLD (hon.), U. Colo., 1989, Suffolk U., 1991, U. N.D., 1997. Bar: N.D. 1953, Colo. 1956. Asst. prof. law U. Denver, 1956—59; vis. assoc. prof. NYU Law Sch., 1958, U. Wash. Law Sch., 1959—60; Colo. jud. adminstr., 1960—61; prof. law U. Colo., 1961—67; ptnr. Carrigan & Bragg (and predecessors), 1967—76; bd. regents U. Colo., 1975—76; justice Colo. Supreme Ct., 1976—79; judge US Dist. Ct. Colo., 1979—95. Mem. Colo. Bd. Bar Examiners, 1969-71; lectr. Nat. Coll. Judicial, 1964-77, 95; bd. dirs. co founder Nat. Inst. Trial Advocacy, 1971-2006, chmn. bd. 1986-88, also mem. faculty, 1972-2014; adj. prof. law U. Colo, 1984, 1991-2014; bd. dirs. Denver Broncos Stadium Dist., 1996-2014; mem. steering com. new U. Colo. Law Bldg., 2005-08. Editor-in-chief: N.D. Law Rev., 1952-53, Internat. Soc. Barristers Quar., 1972-79; editor: DICTA, 1957-59; contbr. articles to profl. jours. Bd. visitors U. N.D. Coll. Law, 1983-85. Recipient Disting. Svc. award Nat. Coll. State Judiciary, 1969, Outstanding Alumnus award U. N.D., 1973, Regent Emeritus award U. Colo., 1977, B'nai Brith Civil Rights award, 1986, Thomas More Outstanding Lawyer award Cath. Lawyers Guild, 1988, Oliphant Disting. Svc. award Nat. Inst. Trial Advocacy, 1993, Constl. Rights award Nat. Assn. Blacks in Criminal Justice (Colo. chpt.), 1992, Disting. Svc. award Colo. Bar Assn., 1994, Amicus Curiae award ATLA, 1994, Colo. Trial Lawyers Assn. Lifetime Achievement award, 2000. Fellow Colo. Bar Found., Boulder County Bar Found.; mem. ABA (action com. on tort system improvement 1985-87, TIPS sect. long range planning com., 1986-97; coun. 1987-91, task force on initiatives and referenda 1990-92, size of civil juries task force 1988-90, class actions task force 1995-97), Colo. Bar Assn., Boulder County Bar Assn., Denver Bar Assn., Cath. Lawyers Guild, Inns. of Ct., Internat. Soc. Barristers, Internat. Acad. Trial Lawyers (bd. dirs. 1995-2014), Fed. Judges Assn. (bd. dirs. 1985-89), American Judicature Soc. (bd. dirs. 1985-89), Tenth Circuit Dist. Judges Assn. (sec. 1991-92, v.p. 1992-93, pres. 1994-95), Order of Coif, Phi Beta Kappa, ABA (Pursuit of Justice award 2009), Arrupe Jesuit HS (bd. trustees 2008-14). Roman Catholic. Home: Boulder, Colo. Died Aug. 15, 2014.

**CARROLL, ROBERT HENRY,** accountant; b. Cin., July 19, 1932; s. John D. and Virgeal C. (Grever) C.; m. Shirley J. Mueller, Feb. 16, 1957, children: Robert E., Deborah S., Gregory J., David K., Jennifer M. BBA, U. Cin., 1956. CPA, Ohio. With. Grant Thornton, Cin., 1955-91, ptnr., 1972-91; pvt. practice Cin., from 1991; sec., treas. Hughes-Peters Inc., Cin., from 1993. Pres. Accountacy Bd. of Ohio, 1988-89, 89-90. Trustee Ursuline Acad., Cin., 1985-92, Project Encor, Cin., 1987-92, mem. devel. com., 1992—; trustee Funds for Ind. Schs. Cin., 1988-92, St. Aloysius Orphanage, Cin., 1992-94; mem. planning com. All Saints Ch., Kenwood, 1980—; mem. devel. com. St. Xavier H.S., Cin., 1985—. Mem. AICPA, Ohio Soc. of CPAs, Bankers Club Cin., O'Bannon Creek Golf Club. Republican. Roman Catholic. Home: Cincinnati, Ohio. Died Feb. 28, 1996.

**CARROLL, STAN J.,** insurance broker; b. Avon, SD, Aug. 6, 1925; s. Raymond James and Genevieve Delores (Waggoner) Carroll; m. LaVoin B. Payne, Apr. 19, 1958; children: Christiana Moreno, Jay Bradford. BA, Cornell Coll., 1949; postgrad. in Secondary Edn., Colo. State U. Spl. agt. Am. Surety Co., San Francisco, 1950—52; sales rep. Levi Strauss & Co., San Francisco, San Jose, Calif., Phoenix, Shreveport, La., Little Rock, Denver, Corpus Christi, Tex., 1952—69; franchise owner Mr. Swiss stores, Tex., 1969—72; ins. broker and agt. Mony and Mony Securities Corp. Houston, from 1972. Bd. dirs. Harris County Water Dist. (Tex.), 1970—79. With USNR, 1943—64, PTO. Mem.: Houston C. of C., Cornell Coll. Alumni Assn., Tex. Life Underwriter, Million Dollar Round Table, Health Underwriters Assn. Am., Nat. Assn. Life Underwriters (Nat. Sales Achievement award 1976, 1980, Nat. Quality award 1976, 1980), Kiwanis Club (Houston). Republican. Methodist. Home: Katy, Tex. Died Aug. 14, 1990.

**CARROLL, THOMAS JOSEPH,** retired auditor; b. Aug. 30, 1941; s. Patrick and Mary (Jennings) Carroll; children: Thomas Joseph, Cathy. BS, U. Notre Dame. CPA. Acct. KPMG LLP, 1965; global chief auditor, mng. dir. Credit Suisse First Boston, 1991—96; gen. auditor, mng. dir., ptnr. Bankers Trust Co., 1996—99; sr. v.p., chief auditor Prudential Financial Inc. (formerly Prudential Ins. Co. of America), Newark, 1999—2014. Bd. dirs. William Holden Wildlife Found. Served in USN. Mem.: Larchmont Yacht Club, NY Yacht Club. Died Aug. 12, 2014.

**CARTER, BARRY EDWARD,** law educator; b. LA, Oct. 14, 1942; s. Byron Edward and Ethel Catherine (Turner) C.; m. Kathleen Anne Ambrose, May 17, 1987; children: Gregory Ambrose, Meghan Elisabeth. AB with great distinction, Stanford U., 1964; MPA, Princeton U., 1966; JD, Yale U., 1969. Bar: Calif. 1970, DC 1972. Program analyst Office of Sec. Def., Washington, 1969—70; mem. staff NSC, Washington, 1970—72; rsch. fellow Kennedy Sch., Harvard U., Cambridge, Mass., 1972; internat. affairs fellow Coun. on Fgn. Rels., 1972; assoc. Wilmer, Cutler & Pickering, Washington, 1973—75; sr. counsel Select Com. on Intelligence Activities, U.S. Senate, Washington, 1975; assoc. Morrison & Foerster, San Francisco, 1976—79; assoc. prof. law Georgetown U. Law Ctr., Washington, 1979—89, prof., 1989-93 and from 96; dir. internat. and transnational programs Georgetown U. Law Ctr, Washington, 2005—08; dir. Ctr. Transnational Bus. and Law, from 2008; exec. dir. Am. Soc. Internat. Law, Washington, 1992—93; acting undersec. for export adminstrn. U.S. Dept. Commerce, Washington, 1993—94, dep. undersec., 1994—96. Mem. UN Assn. Soviet-Am. Parallel Studies Project, 1976—87; vis. prof. law Stanford U., 1990; chmn. adv. bd. Def. Budget Project, 1990—93; bd. dirs. Nukem, Inc., 1998—2007; adv. coun. Zurich Credit & Political Risk, from 2001; editl. advisor Kluwer Law Internat., from 2007, Aspen Pubs., from 2007; expert cons. US Dept. Commerce, from 2012. Author: International Economic Sanctions: Improving the Haphazard U.S. Legal Regime, 1988 (Am. Soc.

Internat. Law Cert. of Merit, 1989); co-author: International Law, 6th edit., 2011; editor: International Law: Selected Documents, from 2011; contbr. articles to profl. jours. Mem. adv. com. Internat. Economic Policy, US Dept. State, from 2010; chmn. Subcom. Sanctions, from 2010. With US Army, 1969—71. Mem.: ABA, Am. Soc. Internat. Law (hon. v.p. 1993—99, counselor 1999—2000), Coun. on Fgn. Rels., DC Bar Assn., Calif. Bar Assn., Am. Law Inst., Phi Beta Kappa. Democrat. Roman Catholic. Home: Washington, DC. Died Jan. 2014.

**CARTER, FRANCIS WILLIAM,** Slavonic studies educator; b. Wednesfield, Eng., July 4, 1938; s. Frank and Gwendoline (Dunton) C.; m. Krystyna Stefania Tomaszewska, Jun. 3, 1977. BA in Geography with honors, Sheffield U., 1960; MA in Geography, London Sch. Econs., 1967; D of Nat. Sci. in Geography, Charles U., Prague, Czechoslovakia, 1975; PhD in Geography, London U., 1979; DPhil in Geography, Jagiellonian U., Cracow, Poland, 1991; PhD, U. Zagreb, 2000. Asst. lectr. geography King's Coll., London, 1965-66; joint Hayter lectr. geography UCL & SSEES, London, 1966-90; lectr., head dept. social scis. Sch. Slavonic Studies, London U., 1990-97, reader in geography of Eastern Europe, 1997-2000, prof. geography of Eastern Europe, from 2001. Author: Dubrovnik, 1972, Trade and Urban Development of Poland, 1994; editor, contbr.: Historical Geography of Balkans, 1977, Environmental Problems in Eastern Europe, 1993, The Changing Shape of the Balkans, 1996; editor/contbr.: Central Europe After the Fall of the Iron Curtain: Geopolitical Views, Spatial Patterns and Trends, The States of Eastern Europe, 2 vols., 1999. Recipient Edward Heath award Royal Geog. Soc., 1997. Mem. Inst. Brit. Geographers (environ. group com. 1990-93), Brit.-Bulgaria Soc. (pres. 1999—). Mem. Ch. of England. Avocations: travel, gardening, stamp collecting/philately. Home: New Barnet, England. Died May 4, 2001.

**CARTER, JOHN FRANCIS, II,** lawyer; b. Washington, Dec. 21, 1939; s. John F. and Majorie (Thomas) C.; children: J. F. III, Marion; m. Catherine Dulany Turner, 2000. AB, Princeton U., 1963; JD, U. Tex., 1970. Bar: Tex. 1970, US Supreme Ct. 1977. Analyst Rotan Mosle, Houston, 1967-68; ptnr. Hutcheson & Grundy, Houston, 1970-90, mng. ptnr., 1990-94; sr. counsel Akin, Gump, Strauss, Hauer & Feld, Houston, 1996-98; atty. pvt. practice, Houston, from 1998. Mem. State Bar Grievance Commn., Houston, 1976-79; internat. sr. advisor to dep. sec. U.S. Dept. Energy, 1994-96. Co-author: Incorporation in Texas, 1980. Chmn. Tex. Arts Alliance, 1981-82, Mcpl. Art Commn., Houston, 1988-90; pres. Arts Coun., Houston, 1983-84; chmn., sec. Harris County Dem. Party, Tex., 1988-90; mem. host com. Econ. Summit, Houston, 1989-90; chair Planned Parenthood of Southeastern Va., 2005-07; vice chair, bd. dirs. Va. Coll. Bldg. Authority, 2005-10; mem. exec. com. Princeton Alumni Coun., 2008-10, past pres., Va. Beach Citizens Police Acad. Alumni, 2010-; Capt. Spl. Forces, US Army, 1963-67, Panama, Vietnam. Recipient Cert. Outstanding Svc. award, US Dept. State, 1996; named a Tex. Super Lawyer, 2003—05; named one of Best Lawyers in Am., from 1996. Mem. ABA (com. chair 1987-94), Tejas Breakfast Club, Univ. Cottage Club, Princeton Club NY, Princeton Club Hampton Roads (pres.), Phi Delta Phi. Avocations: music, ballet, history. Home: Virginia Bch, Va. Died Dec. 30, 2013.

**CARTER, JOHN MACK,** publishing executive; b. Murray, Ky., Feb. 28, 1928; s. William Z. and Martha (Stevenson) C.; m. Sharlyn Emily Reaves, Aug. 30, 1948; children: Jonna Lyn, John Mack II. Student, Murray State Coll., 1944-46, LL.D., 1971; B.J., U. Mo., 1948, MA, 1949; LL.D., St. John's U., 1983. Reporter Murray Ledger & Times, 1945; asst. editor Better Homes & Gardens mag., 1949-51; mng. editor Household mag., Topeka, 1953-57, editor, 1957-58; exec. editor Together mag., 1958-59; editor American Home mag., 1959-61; editor-in-chief McCall's mag., 1961-65; v.p. McCall Corp., NYC, 1962-65; editor-in-chief Ladies Home Jour., 1965-74, publisher, 1967-70; pres., COO Downe Communications Inc., 1972-73, chmn. bd., editor-in chief, 1973-77; pres. American Home Publishing Co., 1974-75; editor-in-chief Good Housekeeping mag., NYC, 1975-95. Bd. dirs. Future Homemakers America, American Cancer Soc., Christian Ch. Found., Religion in American Life, American Bible Soc., Nat. Ctr. for Voluntary Action, Guideposts Mag. Served as lt. (j.g.) USNR, 1951-53. Recipient Walter Williams award for Writing, 1949, Honor award for disting. service in Journalism U. Mo., 1979, Faith and Freedom award Religious Heritage of America, 1980, Quality of Life award for Media American Lung Assn., 1986; named one of The 10 Outstanding Men of Yr., US Jr. Chamber of Commerce, 1963, Publisher of Yr., Brandeis U., 1977, Headliner of Yr., Women in Communications, Inc., 1978, Publisher of Yr., Mag. Publishers America, 1990; named to The Ky. Journalism Hall of Fame, 1983, The American Soc. Magazine Editors Hall of Fame, 2000 Mem. Kentuckians of N.Y. (pres.), American Soc. Mag. Editors, Sigma Delta Chi (pres. N.Y. chpt.). Home: Westbrook, Conn. Died Sept. 26, 2014.

**CARTER, KEVIN,** photographer; b. Sept. 13, 1960; Freelance photographer. Contbr. photography to NY Times. Recipient Pulitzer Prize for feature photography, 1994, Pulitzer Prize nomination for spot news photography, 1994. Died July 27, 1994.

**CARTER, RUTH B. (MRS. JOSEPH C. CARTER),** foundation administrator; b. Charlotte, Vt. d. Ira E. and Sadie M. (Congdon) Burroughs; m. Joseph C. Carter, June 28, 1935. PhB, U. Vt., 1931. Prin. Newton Acad., Shoreham, Vt., 1931-35; substitute tchr. Spaulding High Sch., Barre, Vt., 1931-35, Woodbury (Vt.) High Sch., 1935-36; tchr. Craftsbury Acad., Craftsbury Common, Vt., 1936-38; sales mgr., buyer Vt. Music Co., Barre, 1939-44; statistician Syracuse U., 1944-46; instr. English Temple U., Phila., 1946-47; records clk. sec. Phila., 1947-56; tchr. English Cen. High Sch., Phila., 1957, Springfield Twp. Sr. High Sch., Montgomery County, Pa., 1964-65; exec. dir. White-Williams Found., 1966-82, trustee, 1982-95. Author: (with Joseph C. Carter) Anchors Aweigh Around the World with Ernest Vail Burroughs, 1960, Pilgrimage to the Lovely Lands of our Ancestors, 1984. Recipient Humanitarian award Chapel of Four Chaplains, 1981, city coun. citation City of Phila., 1982, citation White-Williams Found., 1994. Mem.: DAR (regent Germantown chpt. 1983—86, pub. rels. chmn. from 1986, regent Germantown chpt. 1989—92, treas. 1992—95, registrar 1995—2001, chmn. membership from 2001, historian from 2001, treas., com. chmn., budget dir.), AAUW (admissions chmn. Phila. chpt. 1959—61, sec. 1961—64, treas. 1965—67), Vt. Hist. Soc., Women for Greater Phila., The English Speaking Union, Geneal. Soc. Vt., New Eng. Hist. Geneal. Soc., Soc. Mayflower Descs. (bd. dirs. 1983—84, sec. 1985—91), Regent's Club (Phila. chaplain 1986—88), Temple U. Women's Club, Temple U. Faculty Wives Club (rec. sec. 1983—86, sec. 1997—2000, pres. Old York group). Republican. Methodist. Deceased.

**CARTER, WILLIAM WALTON,** physicist, researcher; b. Pensacola, Fla., Nov. 7, 1921; s. Eugene Hudson and Nannie (Ledyard) C.; m. Elizabeth Jean Dedick, June 11, 1945; children— Carolyn A., Susan J., Judith J., Paul W. BS, Carnegie Inst. Tech., 1943; MS, Calif. Inst. Tech., 1948, PhD, 1949. Atomic and thermonuclear weapon R&D group leader weapons physics group, weapons div. Los Alamos Sci. Lab., 1949-59, mem. joint working com.; chief scientist Army Missile Command, Redstone Arsenal, 1959-67; asst. dir. nuclear programs, def. research and engring. Office Sec. Def., Washington, 1967-71; assoc. dir. Harry Diamond Labs. U.S. Army, 1971-74, tech. dir., 1975-84, also chmn. staff devel. council; sr. scientist Pacific-Sierra Rsch., Arlington, Va., 1984-94; scientific cons. nuclear treaty monitoring, from 1994. Designer, deployer instruments to verify nuclear treaties; chmn. steering com. Huntsville Rsch. Inst. Served to lt. USNR, 1944-46. Asso. fellow AIAA; mem. AAAS, Am. Phys. Soc., Am. Inst. Physics. Achievements include design of air samplers for worldwide network of sensors to monitor non-proliferation and nuclear test ban treaties; installation first unit in Turkmenistan; being project leader for first thermonuclear weapon to enter regular national stockpile. Home: Charlottesville, Va. Died June 7, 2013.

**CARTER, YVONNE BREAUX,** retired librarian; b. Crowley, La., Aug. 3, 1922; d. Valentin D. and Annie H. (Oertling) Breaux; m. Walter R. Carter, Apr. 23, 1943. BS in Edn. with high distinction, U. Southwestern La., 1943; BS in Libr. Sci., George Peabody Coll. Tchrs., 1950, MA, 1960, EdS, 1966. Cert. tchr. La., libr. La. . Tchr. Calcasieu Parish, Lake Charles, La., 1942—43; prin. Sardis H.S., Tenn., 1944—45; tchr. Gueydan H.S. Vermillion Parish Sch., 1945—63, Gueydan H.S. Vermillion Parish Sch. Bd., 1964; libr. U.S. Office of Edn. Dallas Region, 1967—69; adminstrv. libr. U.S. Dept. of Edn., Washington, 1969—93; ret., 1993. Asst. prof. Northwestern State U., Natchitoches, La., 1963—64, Southwestern La. U., Lafayette, 1965—67. Mem. Lafayette Pub. Libr. Found. Bd. Grantee, DAR, 2012; Kappa Kappa Iota scholar, Delta Kappa Gamma Epsilon scholar. Mem.: DAR (regent Galvez chpt. 1998, 2004), AAUW, ALA, Alpha Chpt., DC (pres.), Alpha Epsilon, Abbeville (pres.), La. Libr. Assn., Am. Assn. Sch. Librs., La. DAR (state libr. 2004—07), Attakapas Hist. Assn., Nat. Mus. Women in Arts (Washington) (charter mem.), Women's Club Lafayette (chmn. from 1996, scholarship from 1998), Nat. Soc. Daus. War 1812 (state historian 2002—03, chpt. pres. 2004—06, state historian from 2009), United Daus. Confederacy (chpt. pres. 2004—08), Beta Phi Mu, Delta Kappa Gamma, Kappa Delta Pi. Home: Lafayette, La. Died July 22, 2013.

**CARTER, YVONNE HELEN,** physician, educator; d. Percival Anthony Carter and Ellen Bore; m. Michael Joseph Bannon; 1 child, Christopher Bannon. MBBS, St Mary's Hosp. Med. School, 1983; MD, U. London, 1994; F Med. Sci. (hon.), Acad. Med. Scis. London, 1998. Hon. rsch. fellow Centre of Epidemiology, Pub. Health Medicine and Primary Health Care Keele U., England, 1990—92; gen. practitioner prin. Drs. Hollins, Morgans, Wright, Carter and Scott, Newcastle-under-Lyme, Staffordshire, England, 1990—93; clin. sr. lectr. dept. general practice U. Birmingham, England, 1992—96; gen. practitioner tutor Queen Elizabeth Postgrad. Med. Centre, Edgbaston, Birmingham, 1994—96; hon. chmn. rsch. Royal Coll. Gen. Practitioners, London, 1996—2000; hon. cons. Tower Hamlets Healthcare NHS Trust, Bancroft Road, 1996—2001; gen. practitioner prin. Drs. Boomla, Carter, Hart, Ketley, Khwaja, Parsons, Robson, Smailes and Twist, London, 1997—2003; gov. Health Found. (formerly PPP Found.), London, 1999—2007; prof. gen. practice and primary care Barts and The London, Queen Mary's Sch. Medicine and Dentistry, 1996—2003, head divsn. cmty. scis., 2001—03; vice-dean Med. Sch. Leicester Warwick Med. Schs., Coventry, 2003—04; acad. gen. practitioner, hon. cons. primary care Coventry Primary Care Trust, from 2003; dean med. sch. U. Warwick, Coventry, 2004—09, vice-dean Med. Sch., 2003—04, pro-vice chancellor, 2007—09. Hon. cons. Tower Hamlets Primary Care Trust, London, 2001—03. Editor: Research Methods in Primary Care, 1996, Master Classes in Research: Patient Participation and Ethical Considerations, 2001 (BMA Med. Book Competition non-commercial, 2001), Guide to Education and Training in Primary Care, 2001, Handbook of Sexual Health in Primary Care, 1998, Handbook of Palliative Care, 1998 (BMA Book of the Year award, 1999), 2d edit., 2005, Research Opportunities in Primary Care, 1999, Master Classes in Research: An Introduction to Qualitative Methods for Health Professionals, 1999, Master Classes in Research: The Use and Design of Questionnaires, 2000, Master Classes in Research: Statistical Concepts, 2000 (BMA 2000 Med. Book competition Primary Care Category, 2000), Master Classes in Research: Randomised Controlled Trials and Multi-Centre Research, 2000. Named to Order of the Brit. Empire, Queen's Birthday Honours List, 2000; hon. fellow, Queen Mary, U. London, 2004. Fellow: Royal Soc. of Medicine (RSM Coun. GP Section 1998—99), Royal Soc. for the Encouragement of Arts, Manufacturers and Commerce, Royal Coll. of General Practitioners (coun. mem. 1994); mem.: Inst. of Learning and Teaching, British Med. Assn. Avocations: theater, literature, current affairs. Home: Coventry, England. Died Oct. 20, 2009.

**CARY, TRISTRAM OGILVIE,** composer, writer; b. Oxford, Eng., May 14, 1925; arrived in Australia, 1974, dual citizenship; s. Arthur Joyce and Gertrude Margaret (Ogilvie) C.; m. Doris Enid Jukes, July 7, 1951 (div. 1978); children: John T.L., Robert A.J., Charlotte A. MA, Oxford U., 1948; degree (hon.), Royal Coll. Music, London, 1970. lic. music tchr. Trinity Coll. Music; cert. engr. Inst. Elec. Engring. Freelance composer, writer, tchr., 1952-74 and from 86; sr. lectr. U. Adelaide, Australia, 1974-78, assoc. prof., 1978-86, dean music, 1982-83, hon. vis. rsch. fellow, from 1986. Lectr. Royal Coll. Music, London, 1967-74; founder, dir. Electronic Music Studios, London, 1969-74; head Tristram Cary Creative Music Svcs., Adelaide, 1986—. Author: Dictionary of Musical Technology, 1992; composer: (film soundtracks) The Little Island, 1958 (Venice/Brit. Film Acad. awards, 1958); (radio score) The Ballad of Peckham Rye, 1962 (PrixItalia, 1962), scores for concert and all media. Lt. (spl.) Royal Navy, 1943-46, North Sea/Atlantic. Recipient Medal of the Order of Australia, 1991. Mem. British Acad. Composers and Songwriters. Avocations: sailing, billiards, wine, food. Died Apr. 24, 2008.

**CASE, LEE OWEN, JR.,** retired academic administrator; b. Ann Arbor, Mich., Nov. 5, 1925; s. Lee Owen and Ava (Comin) C.; m. Dolores Anne DeLoof, July 1950 (div. Feb. 1958); children: Lee Douglas, John Bradford; m. Maria Theresia Breninger, Feb. 27, 1960; 1 adopted child, Ingrid Case Dunlap. AB, U. Mich., 1949. Editor Washtenaw Post-Trib, Ann Arbor, 1949; dir. pub. rels. Edison Inst., Dearborn, Mich., 1951—54; field rep. Kersting, Brown, NYC, 1954—58; campaign dir. Cumerford Corp., Kansas City, Mo., 1958—59; v.p. devel., pub. rels. U. Santa Clara, Calif., 1956—59; v.p. planning, devel. Occidental Coll., LA, 1969—90; ret., 1990. Interim v.p. Inst. Advance Calif. State U., LA, 1994; mem. Sr. Cons. Network. Mem. Santa Clara County Planning Com. on Taxation and Legis., 1968; chmn. Santa Clara City Proposition A, 1966. 1st lt. USAAF, 1943—46. Mem.: Aviation Pioneers Assn., Santa Clara County C. of C. (founding bd. dirs. 1968), Santa Clara C. of C. (pres. 1967), Coun. for Advancement and Support Edn. (founding bd. dirs. 1974—75, 1st Tribute for Distinction in Advancement, Dist. VII 1985), Am. Coll. Pub. Rels. Assn. (bd. dirs. 1968—74), Rotary. Republican. Home: Glendale, Calif. Died Feb. 28, 1999.

**CASEY, RON,** state legislator; b. Dayton, Tex., Nov. 27, 1952; Attended, Tenn. Temple U., Chattanooga. Govt. employee Jefferson County Prosecutor's Office, Mo., Jefferson County Sheriff's Office, Mo.; assoc. commr. Jefferson County, Mo., 1986—94, Mo., 1996—2000; mem. Dist. 103 Mo. House of Reps., 2004—12. Democrat. Home: Crystal City, Mo. Died Feb. 16, 2014.

**CASHEN, FRANK,** retired professional sports team executive; b. 1922; m. Jean Cashen; children: Blaise, Stacey, Sean, Brian, Timmy, Terry, Greg. BA, Loyola Coll.; JD, U. Md. Sportswriter, columnist Balt. News-America; gen. mgr. Balt. Raceway & Bel Air Race Track; exec. asst. to pres., dir. advt. Nat. Brewing Co., Balt., 1962-65; exec. v.p. Balt. Orioles, 1965-75; sr. v.p. mktg. & sales Carling Nat. Breweries, Balt., 1975-79; adminstr. baseball Major League Baseball, NYC, 1979-80; exec. v.p., gen. mgr., COO NY Mets, 1980-92, cons., 1993. Named to The NY Mets Hall of Fame, 2010. Died June 30, 2014.

**CASSIAN, NINA,** poet, composer; b. Galati, Romania, Nov. 27, 1924; arrived in U.S., 1985; d. Joseph and Jana Cassian; m. Alexandru Iancu Stefanescu, June 26, 1948 (dec.); m. Maurice Edwards, Mar. 12, 1998. Vis. prof. NYU, NYC, 1985. Author: I'm Terrific-Adieu, 1971, Fictitious Confessions, 1974, Parlor Games, 1984; poet (in Romanian): On the Scale of One to One, 1947, The Measures of the Year, 1957, Blood, 1966, Ambitus, 1969, Requiem, 1970, Lotto Poems, 1972, Spectacle in the Open-air: Selected Love Poems, 1974, One Hundred Poems, 1975, For Mercy, 1981, Unmaking of the World, 1997, Count Down, 1983, poet (in English): Blue Apple, 1981, Lady of Miracles, 1982, Call Yourself Alive, 1988, Life Sentence, 1990, Cheerleader for a Funeral, 1992, Take My Word For It, 1998, Something Old, Something New, 2002, poet: numerous others; author (in Romanian): Memory as Dowry, 2003, 2004, 2005, translator various works; composer: Tonal Fascinations, 1980, Vivarium, 1981, Variatio Perpetua, 1984, The Magic Clarinet, 1985. Home: Roosevelt Island, NY. Died Apr. 15, 2014.

**CASTLEMAN, RIVA (ESTHER RIVA CASTLEMAN),** retired curator; b. Chgo., Aug. 15, 1930; d. William and Ann (Steinberg) C. BA, State U. Iowa, 1951; postgrad. Inst. Fine Arts, NYU, 1951. Asst. to curator dept. decorative arts Art Inst., Chgo., 1951-55; asst. editor, curator Calif. Hist. Soc., San Francisco, 1956-57; asst. John Fleming Rare Books, NYC, 1958-63; successively cataloger, curatorial asst., asst. curator, assoc. curator Mus. Modern Art, NYC, 1963-71, curator prints & illus. books, 1971-75, dir., chief curator prints & illus. books, 1975-95, dep. dir. for curatorial affairs, 1986-92. Judge San Juan Biennial of Latin American Prints, 1970, 72, Llubjana Biennial of Prints., 1971, 73, Krakow

Biennial, 1972, 74, Bradford Biennial, 1974, Tokyo Biennial, 1977; mem. advisory bd. Nat. Acad. Design. Author: Technics and Creativity: Gemini G.E.L., 1971, Modern Art in Prints, 1973, Contemporary Prints, 1973, Latin American Prints from the Museum of Modern Art, 1974, Prints of the Twentieth Century: A History, 1975, American Prints 1913-1963, 1976, Printed Art, 1980, American Impressions: Prints Since Pollock, 1985, Jasper Johns, A Print Retrospective, 1986, The Prints of Andy Warhol, 1990, Art of the Forties, 1991, Seven Master Printmakers, 1991, A Century of Artists Books, 1994, Tatyana Grosman: A Scrapbook, 2008 Bd. dirs. Cintas Found. Tamarind Lithography Workshop grantee, 1965; Corning Mus. of Glass fellow, 1954. Mem. Print Coun. American, Grolier Club, Phi Beta Kappa. Died Sept. 4, 2014.

**CASTRO, JASON ESPENILLA,** government bookkeeper, information officer; b. Masbate, Philippines, Sept. 7, 1952; s. Prisco Fernandez and Concepcion (Espenilla) Castro; m. Buenaflor Sese Castro, May 22, 1980; children: Crystal Marie, Hyacinth Marie. BSBA, U. of East, Manila, 1972; BA in Social Scis., Osmena Colls., 1985. Corp. bookkeeper Nat. Food Authority, Masbate, from 1975; dir. Masbate Credit Coop. Mem.: Assn. Masbate Govt. Communicators, Masbate Hist. Soc. (provincial sec.), Philippine Aviation Promotion Safety Consciousness Orgn., Nat. Food Authority Employees Assn. (provincial pres. from 1985), Masbate Press Club (asst.treas. from 1986), Buklod Ng Mga Kabataang Kawani (pres. 1982—84). Roman Catholic. Deceased.

**CATHY, S. TRUETT (SAMUEL TRUETT CATHY),** retired food service executive; b. Eatonton, Ga., Mar. 14, 1921; s. Joseph Benjamin and Lilla (Kimbell) Cathy; m. Jeannette McNeil; children: Dan, Don, Trudy. D (hon.), Liberty U., 2012. Owner The Dwarf House, Atlanta, 1946; founder, chmn. Chick-fil-A, Inc., College Park, Ga., 1967—2013. Founder WinShape Ctr. Found., 1984—2013, WinShape Camps, 1985—2013. Author: It's Easier to Succeed Than to Fail, 1989, Eat Mor Chikin: Inspire More People, 2002, It's Better to Build Boys Than Mend Men, 2004, How Did You Do It, Truett?: A Recipe for Success, 2007, Wealth, Is It Worth It?, 2010; co-author: The Generosity Factor, 2002. Recipient Horatio Alger award, Horatio Alger Assn., 1989, Entrepreneur of Yr. - Lifetime Achievement award, Ernst & Young, 2000, Chairman's award, Georgia Sports Hall of Fame, 2003, Catalyst Lifetime Achievement award, Injoy/John Maxwell, 2003, Norman Vincent & Ruth Stafford Peale Humanitarian award, 2003, Lifetime Achievement award, Nat. Poultry & Food Distributors Assn., 2005, President's Call to Service award, The White House, 2008, Laurel Crowned Circle award, 2009; named one of The Forbes 400: Richest Americans, 2006—14; named to The Jr. Achievement Bus. Hall of Fame, 2003, The Ind. Wesleyan U. Soc. World Changers, 2011. Southern Baptist. Died Sept. 8, 2014.

**CATTANEO, GIOVANNI,** law educator; b. Rome, Feb. 10, 1932; c. Enrico and Francesca (Pascolato) C.; m. Paola Globbio, Oct. 23, 1963; children: Annachiara, Enrico, Grazia. Degree in law, U. Milan, 1954. Law prof. U. Modena, Italy, 1959-72, U. Pavia, Italy, 1972-74, U. Milan, 1974—97. Author: La Responsabilità del Professionista, 1958, La Cooperazione del Creditore All'Adempimento, 1964, Mora del Creditore, 1974, Filiazione Legittima, 1988; editor: Diritto Di Famiglia, 1997. Mem. Centro Nat. di Prevenzione Difesa Sociale, Inst. di Diritto Agrario, Assn. Italiana di Diritto Comparato. Roman Catholic. Avocation: classical music. Died Sept. 12, 1998.

**CAUDILL, TOM HOLDEN,** military analyst; b. St. Augustine, Fla., June 21, 1945; s. Julian Terrill and Alta Jane (Holden) C.; 1 child, Mara Julia. BA in History, East Tenn. State U., 1967, MA in Internat. Rels., 1977; MA in Mgmt. Sci., Webster U., 1980. Instr. English as second lang., polit. sci., mgmt. sci. U.S. Peace Corps, Loei, Thailand, 1970-73; instr. English as second lang., polit. sci., mgmt. sci. Steed Coll., Johnson City, Tenn., 1973-76; instr. Internat. Ctr. U. Tex., Austin, 1976-77; tng. specialist Air Tng. Command USAF, Lackland AFB, Tex., 1977-80, tng. specialist Logistics Command Wright-Patterson AFB, Ohio, 1980-81, logistics mgmt. specialist, 1981-85, chief, policy and procedures Internat. Logistics Ctr., 1985-88, chief policy and analysis, from 1986, chief plans and devel., 1988; dir. Arabian programs Internat. Logistics Ctr., 1991-95; exec. fellow Woodrow Wilson Sch. Govt. Princeton U., 1995-96; dep. dir. internat. programs Air Force Security Assistance Ctr., 1996; chief prodn. policy Hdqtrs. Air Force Material Command, Wright Patterson AFB, Ohio, 1997-99; dir. ops. mgmt. Air Force Security Assistance Ctr., Wright Patterson AFB, Ohio, 1999-2000, dir. case mgmt., from 2000. Vis. instr. English as a second lang., polit. sci., mgmt. sci. Antioch Coll., Yellow Springs, Ohio, 1986—; asst. dep. plans policy mgmt. systems, 1988, dir. plans and policy, 1988, tech. lead integrated logistics support, acquisition logistics div., 1988—, instr. mgmt. sci. Author: Textbook in Logistics 1988, Policy Regulations/Procedural Instructions 1986—; contbr. articles to profl. jours., 1987—. Adminstr. Refugee Assistance Program, Greene County, Ohio, 1981-84, AFS chpt. v.p.; Scoutmaster Buckeye Trails coun. Girl Scout U.S., Yellow Springs, 1982-86; active Dayton (Ohio) Coun. on World Affairs, 1984—; pres. local chpt. Am. Field Svc., Greene County, 1988—. Mem LWV (fin. chm. Greene county chpt. 1987—). Democratic. Methodist. Avocations: travel, scouting, reading, writing. Deceased.

**CAUSSE, JEAN-BERNARD R.M.,** otologist, surgeon; b. Beziers, Hérault, France, May 13, 1944; s. Jean René and Simone (Coulombie) C.; m. Isabelle Meslin, July 19, 1968; children: Jerome, Annabelle. MD, U. Strasbourg, France, 1975. Intern, Strasbourg, 1972-75; mem. staff Causse Clinic, 1975-99, U. Hosp. Montpellier, from 1999. Corr. mem. Nat. Coun. of Noise, French Ministry of Environmen; instr. Am. Acad. Author (monograph): On Otosclerosis, 1991; contbr. over 150 articles to sci. mags. Recipient Rsch. and Tng. award Am. Acad., Pioneer award Consul Gen. Hèrault, award French Legion of Honor, 1999. Mem. Am. Otol. Soc. (corr.), Am. Acad. (corr.), Soc. Hôpitaux Paris. Avocation: photography. Died Dec. 13, 2001.

**CAYLOR, TRUMAN E.,** physician; b. Pennville, Ind., Jan. 10, 1900; s. Charles E. and Bessie (Ferree) Caylor; m. Julia Gettle Caylor, June 28, 1923 (dec. June 6, 1960); children: Carolyn Caylor Wadlington, Charles H., Constance Caylor Carney; m. Eva Abbott Caylor, May 29, 1961 (dec. 1979); m. Suzanne Black Caylor, 1980. Intern Evanston (Ill.) Gen. Hosp.; pvt. practice medicine specializing in urology Bluffton, Ind., 1924—81; co-founder, mem. staff Caylor Nickel Clinic, Bluffton; mem. staff Caylor Nickel Hosp., Bluffton, 1939—81, exec. com., 1939—75; dir.; dir. emeritus Mut. Security Life Ins. Co., Ft. Wayne, Ind. Mem. adv. com. Grace Coll., Winona Lake, Ind., from 1970, Ind. Commn. Aging, 1972—80; dir. emeritus Yorkfellow Inst., Richmond, Ind., Caylor Nickel Rsch. Found.; pres. emeritus, co-founder Caylor Nickel Rsch. Inst., 1961. Srved with US Army, 1918. Fellow: ACS; mem.: Am. Urol. Assn., Ind. State Med. Soc. (50th Yr. Cert. Distinction 1974), Ind. Coun. Sagamores, Elks Club, Scottish Rite Club, Masons Club, Shriners Club, Rotary Club (dist. gov. 1965—66), Phi Rho Sigma, Delta Upsilon. Home: Bluffton, Ind. Died July 31, 1988.

**CAZALAS, MARY REBECCA WILLIAMS,** lawyer, nurse; b. Atlanta, Nov. 11, 1927; d. George Edgar and Mary Annie (Slappey) Williams; m. Albert Joseph Cazalas (dec.). BS in Pre-medicine, Oglethorpe U., Atlanta, 1954; MS in Anatomy, Emory U., 1960; JD, Loyola U., 1967, Loyola U., New Orleans, 1967. RN, Ga.; Bar: La. 1967, US Dist. Ct. (ea. dist.) La. 1967, US Ct. Appeals (5th cir.) 1972, US Supreme Ct. 1975, US Ct. Appeals (fed. cir.) 1999. Gen. duty nurse, 1948-68; instr. maternity nursing St. Josephs Infirmary Sch. Nursing, Atlanta, 1954-59; med. rschr. in urology Tulane U. Sch. Medicine, New Orleans, 1961-65; legal rschr. for presiding judge La. Ct. Appeals (4th cir.), New Orleans, 1965-71; pvt. practice New Orleans, 1967-71; asst. US atty., 1971-79; sr. trial atty. Equal Employment Opportunity Commn., New Orleans, 1979-84; owner Cazalas Apts., New Orleans, from 1962. Lectr. in field. Contbr. articles to profl. jours. Bd. advisors Loyola U. Sch. Law, New Orleans, 1974, v.p. adv. bd., 1975; active New Orleans Drug Abuse Adv. Com., 1976-80; task force Area Agy. on Aging, 1976-80, pres. coun. Loyola U., 1978—; adv. bd. Odyssey House, Inc., New Orleans, 1973; chmn. womens com. Fed. Exec. Bd., 1974; bd. dirs. Bethlehem House of Bread, 1975-79. Named Hon. La. State Senator, 1974; recipient Superior Performance award US Dept. Justice, 1974, Cert. Appreciation Fed. Exec. Bd., 1975-78, Rev. E.A. Doyle award, 1976, Commendation for tchg. Guam Legislature, 1977, Career Achievement award Mt. de Sales Acad., 1995. Mem. Am. Judicature Soc., La. Sate Bar Assn., Fed. Bus. Assn. (v.p. 1976—, pres. 1976-78, bd. dirs. 1972-75), Fed. Bar Assn. (1st v.p. 1973, pres. New Orleans chpt. 1974-75, nat. coun. 1974-79), Assn. Women Lawyers, Nat. Health Lawyers Assn., DAR, Bus. and Profl. Womens Club, Am. Heart Assn., Emory Alumni Assn., Oglethorpe U. Alumni Assn., Loyola U. Alumni Assn. (bd. dirs. 1974-75, 77, v.p. 1976), Jefferson Parish Hist. Soc., Sierra Club, Zonta, Leconte Hon. Sci. Soc., Phi Delta Delta (merged with Phi Alpha Delta pres. 1970-72, bd. dirs., vice justice 1974-75), Alpha Epsilon Delta, Phi Sigma. Democrat. Home: New Orleans, La. Died Sept. 20, 2013.

**CÉ, MARCO CARDINAL,** cardinal; b. Izano, Italy, July 8, 1925; Theological Studies at, Pontifical Gregorian U.; Doctorate in Dogmatic Theology, Pontifical Biblical Inst., Licentiate in Sacred Scripture. Ordained priest of Crema, Italy, 1948; vice rector, tchr. sacred scripture and dogmatic theology Seminary of Crema, rector, 1957—70; appointed Titular Bishop of Vulturia; aux. bishop of Bologna, Italy, 1970—76, ordained, 1970; chaplain Catholic Action, Rome, 1976—78; patriarch of Venice, Italy, 1978—2002, patriarch emeritus, 2002—14; elevated to cardinal, 1979; cardinal-priest of San Marco (Saint Mark), 1979—2014. Roman Catholic. Died May 12, 2014.

**CELLI, ANDREW G.,** judge; b. Rochester, NY, Aug. 29, 1923; s. Romolo and Rosina (Volpe) Celli; m. Dolores Licata Celli, Apr. 11, 1959; children: Romolo, Andrea, Andrew G. Jr. Degree, U. Rochester; LLB, Bklyn. Law Sch., 1951. Bar: NY 1951, US Dist. Ct. (we. dist.) NY 1952, US Supreme Ct. 1963. Assoc. MacFarlain, Harris and Goldman, Rochester, 1951—54; ptnr. DeCesare & Celli, Rochester, 1954—67; councilman City of Rochester, 1967—70; city ct. judge, 1970—73; county judge County of Monroe, Rochester, from 1974. With USAAF, 1943—46. Decorated Star of Solidarity (Italy). Mem.: NY State Bar Assn., Monroe County Bar Assn. (trustee 1958—59). Democrat. Roman Catholic. Home: Rochester, NY. Died May 26, 1990.

**CHADWICK, HENRY,** retired theology studies educator; b. Bromley, Eng., June 23, 1920; s. John and Edith Mary (Horrocks) C.; M. Margaret Elizabeth Brownrigg, Aug. 24, 1945; children: Priscilla, Hilary Ann. Juliet. MA, Cambridge U., Eng., 1945; D. Lit. Hum. (hon.), U. Chgo., 1976; DD (hon.), Yale U., Conn., 1970. Regius prof. divinity U. Oxford, 1959-69; dean Christ Ch., Oxford, 1969-79; lectr. Cambridge (Eng.) U., 1946-58, prof., 1979—83; master Peterhouse, Cambridge, 1987—93; prof. emeritus Cambridge (Eng.) U., 1983—2008. Decorated knight of Brit. Empire Her Majesty The Queen, 1989. Fellow Brit. Acad.; mem. Am. Acad. Arts and Scis., Am. Philos. Soc., Académie des Inscriptions et des Belles Lettres Paris, Göttingen Acad. Rheinland Acad. Germany. Episcopalian. Died June 17, 2008.

**CHAHINE, YOUSSEF,** film director; b. Alexandria, Egypt, Jan. 25, 1926; Student, Alexandria U. Dir.: (films): Papa Amin, 1950, Nile Boy, 1951, The Great Clown, 1952, Lady on the Train, 1953, Men Without Women, 1953, Struggle in the Valley, 1954, The Desert Devil, 1954, Dark Waters, Struggle in the Port, 1956, Farewell to Your Love, 1957, My One and Only Love, 1957, Cairo Station, 1958, Jamilla, the Algerian, 1958, Forever Yours, 1959, In Your Hands, 1960, A Lover's Call, 1960, A Man in My LIfe, 1961, The Victorious Saladin, 1963, Dawn of a New Day, 1964, The Ring Seller (Order of Lebanon-Beyrouth), 1965, Golden Sands, 1966, The Feast of Mairun, 1967, Those People of the Nile, 1968, The Land, 1969, The Choice, 1970 (Grand Prize Carthage-Tunisia), Salwa the Little Girl Who Talks to Cows, 1972, The Sparrow, 1973, Forward We Go, 1973, Return of the Prodigal Son, 1976, Alexandria...Why (Silver Bear-Berlin Festival), 1978, An Egyptian Story, 1982, Adieu Bonaparte, 1985, The Sixth Day, 1986, Alexandria, Again and Again, 1990, Cairo...as told by Chahine, 1991, The Emigrant, 1994, Destiny, 1997 (Cannes Film Festival award), It's Only a Step, 1998, The Other, 1999, Alexandria-New York, 2004, this Is Chaos, 2007 Recipient Lifetime Achievement award, Cannes Film Festival, 1997. Died July 27, 2008.

**CHALK, EARL MILTON,** retired art director; b. Deerlodge, Mont., Sept. 14, 1927; s. Forrest A. and Jeanette Curtis (Robinson) Chalk; m. Carole Estelle Chalk, Feb. 9, 1963 (div. 1974); children: Teri, Kevin, Quinn; m. Vicki Chalk, July 1994. BFA, U. Wash., 1953. Artist Facilities Boeing, Seattle, 1954-57, writer, artist Renton, Wash., 1957-60, supr. mfg. Seattle, 1960-65, sr. supr. planning Auburn, Wash., 1965-71, art dir. mfg. engring., 1971-87; painter in oils, 1987—2001. Co-mgr., owner Art Galary, 1967-74. Puget Sound Group of North West Painters, Seattle, 1968—78, Puyallup, Washington, 1987—2001. 1st class petty officer USN, 1945-49. Recipient Rotary scholarship U. Wash., 1953. Mem. Grapha Techna. Avocations: bicycling, hiking, fishing, gardening, computers. Died May 4, 2001.

**CHAMBERLAIN, MARK MUNROE,** retired academic administrator; b. Pawtucket, RI, Dec. 10, 1931; s. Merle D. and Lois (Munroe) C.; m. Miriam C. Ewing, May 30, 1953; children: David, Douglas, Matthew; m. Barbara Goldberg, Jan. 1, 1988. BS, Franklin and Marshall Coll., 1953; PhD, U. Ill., 1956. From instr. to vice provost for student services Western Res. U., 1956-69; pres. Glassboro State Coll., 1969-84, prof. phys. sciences, 1985—2000. Commr. East Cleveland, Ohio, 1967-69. Mem. American Chemical Soc. (councilor, chmn. chem. safety), AAAS, Nat. Fire Protection Assn., Sigma Xi. Died Mar. 31, 2014.

**CHAMBERS, THOMAS JEFFERSON,** retired state supreme court justice; b. Yakima, Wash., Oct. 11, 1943; s. Thomas J. and Doris May (Ellyson) C.; m. Judy Larene Cable, June 11, 1967; children: Jolie, Jana, Tommy. BA in Polit. Sci., Wash. State U., 1966; JD, U. Wash., 1969. Bar: Wash., U.S. Dist. Ct. (we. and ea. dists.) Wash. 1969. Assoc. Lycette, Diamond & Sylvester, Seattle, 1969-71, Barokas & Martin, Seattle, 1972; sole practice Seattle, 1972—2001; justice Wash. Supreme Ct., 2001—12. Mem. Internat. Smile Power Found.; hon. bd. mem. Rise n' Shine Found. Recipient Outstanding Judge of Yr., King County Wash. Women Lawyer, 2006, Good Neighbor of Yr., Seattle Housing Authority, 1999, Disting. Alumni award, Yakima CC, 1998, U. Wash. Sch. Law, 2009. Mem. Wash. State Trial Lawyers Assn. (pres. 1985-86, Trial Lawyers of Yr., 1989), Am. Bd. Trial Advs. (pres. Wash. chpt. 1993, Trial Lawyers of Yr., 1996), Am. Trial Lawyers Assn. (past mem. bd. govs.1987-90), Wash. State Bar Assn. (pres. 1996-97). Avocations: flying, scuba diving. Died Dec. 11, 2013.

**CHAMP, STANLEY GORDON,** scientific company executive; b. Hoquiam, Wash., Feb. 15, 1919; s. Clifford Harvey and Edna Winnifred (Johnson) C.; m. Anita Knapp Wegener, Sept. 6, 1941; children: Suzanne Winnifred Whalen, Colleen Louise Szurszewski. BS, U. Puget Sound, 1941; MS, U. Wash., 1950; postgrad., MIT, 1955-57, UCLA, 1959. Cert. tchr., adminstr., Wash. Tchr. Lake Washington Sch. Dist., Kirkland, Wash., 1942-48; prof. math. U. Puget Sound, Tacoma, 1948-51; supr. mathematician Puget Sound Naval Shipyard, Bremerton, Wash., 1951-55; rsch. specialist Boeing Co., Seattle, 1955-68; v.p. R.M. Towne & Assocs., Seattle, 1968-75; founder, pres. Dynac Scis., Tacoma, from 1975. Cons. R.M. Towne Assocs., Seattle, Yantis Assocs., Bellevue, Wash. Contbr. articles to profl. jours.; patent method and apparatus determination soil dynamics insitu. Mem. N.Y. Acad. Sci., Phi Delta Kappa. Presbyterian. Avocation: model building. Deceased.

**CHAMPALIMAUD, ANTÓNIO DE SOMMER,** industrialist, banker; b. Lisbon, Portugal, Mar. 19, 1918; arrived in Brazil, 1975. s. Carlos Pinto Barreiros and Ana Maria (De Sommer) C.; m. Maria Cristina Silva de Mello, Dec. 19, 1941 (div. May 1975); children: António, Luisa, Cristina, Manuel, José, João, Luis. Student, Polytech. U., Lisbon, Portugal, 1953. Prin., pres. Cimentos Leiria, Portugal, 1942-74; prin., founder, pres. Siderurgia N., Portugal, 1961-74; pres. founder, majority shareholder Ca Cimentos Liz, Brazil, from 1976; pres., adv. bd., majority shareholder Mundial-Confianca Ins., Portugal, from 1992; Banco Pinto and Sotto Mayor, 1994; pres., adv. bd., majority shareholder Bank Totta & Acores and Crédito Predial Português, Portugal, from 1994, Banco Chem. Fin., Portugal, 1996, Bank Totta & Acores, Cuiné Bissau, Cabo Verde, Angola, Bank Standard, Mocambique. Contbr. articles to bus. mags. and jours. Decorated Grande Croix du Merite Agr. et Indsl., Portugal, 1961, Grande Croix Ordre du Mèrite de la Fèderation D'Allemagne, 1961, Grande Croix du Merite Civil, Spain, 1961; named Personality of Yr., 1994 Expresso, Portugal. Mem. Rio de Janeiro Yacht Club, Club de Regatas Vasco Da Gama, Rio de Janeiro. Avocations: art collector, cattle breeder. Died May 10, 2004.

**CHAMPLIN, MALCOLM MCGREGOR,** retired municipal judge; b. San Francisco, Apr. 13, 1911; s. Charles Chaffee and Maude (Fraser) C.; m. Betty Mee Champlin, Dec. 1953 (div.); children: Sarah, William Bradford, Mimi Lisette; m. Virginia Pearson, Dec. 2, 1955. BS, U.S. Naval Acad., 1934; JD, U. Calif., 1939; grad., U.S. Naval War Coll., 1944. Bar: Calif. 1940. Commd. ensign U.S. Navy, 1934, served in, 1934-37; practiced in Oakland, Calif., 1940, 45-67; spl. agt. FBI, 1941; ptnr. Stark & Champlin, 1947-67; mcpl. ct. judge Oakland, 1967-80. V.p., dir. Ventura Processors, Inc., 1949-53 Contbr. to Sea Power and Shipmate mags. Gen. chmn. fund drive Knowland Park Zoo, 1963, Peralta Hosp., 1982, 2d Century Children's Fund Lincoln Child Ctr. Found., 1984; bd. dirs. Lincoln Child Ctr. Found., pres., 1984-86, 94-95, trustee; chmn. spkr.'s com. Alameda County Rep. Com., 1960-64; chmn. Vets. for Eisenhower, Alameda County, 1952, 56; moderator 1st Congl. Ch., Oakland, 1978-79; bd. govs. Lake Merritt Breakfast Club, 1985-86; life mem. Rep. Presdl. Task Force, 1988—; founding mem. Ronald Reagan Presdl. Found., 1988. Comdr. USNR, 1941-45; capt. USNR ret. Decorated Navy Cross, Army Silver Star, Navy bronze star; recipient George Washington Honor Medal award Freedoms Found. at Valley Forge, 1964, James Mann award Lincoln Child Ctr., Oakland, Calif., 1987. Mem. ABA, Calif. Bar Assn., Alameda County Bar Assn., Am. Legion (past comdr. 10th dist., judge adv. dept. of Calif. 1953-54, state comdr. 1954-55, Calif. mem. nat. exec. com. 1956-58), Res. Officers Assn., Soc. Former Spl. Agts. FBI, Assn. Former Intelligence Officers, U.S. Naval Acad. Alumni Assn., Lake Merritt Breakfast Club, Commonwealth Club (San Francisco), Lions, Masons (33 degree), Phi Delta Phi. Congregationalist. Deceased.

**CHAN, FUNG-YEE,** obstetrician, gynecologist, educator; b. Hong Kong, Sept. 19, 1955; arrived in Australia, 1993; d. Nin-Pak Chan and Wai-Fan Yiu; m. Ka-Pun Fok, Oct. 1, 1980; 1 child, Elaine Fok. MB, BS, U. Hong Kong, 1979, MD, 1995. Diploma diagnostic ultrasound, Australia; cert. maternal fetal medicine, Australia. Med. officer Queen Mary Hosp., Hong Kong, 1980-89, sr. med. officer, 1989-93; cons. obstetrician Mater Mothers' Hosp., Brisbane, Australia, 1993-95, dep. dir. ob-gyn., 1995, dir. maternal fetal medicine, 1996—2002, from 2005. Clin. lectr. U. Hong Kong, 1988-92, examiner Hong Kong Midwives Bd., licentiate bd., 1987-92; cons. Univ. Health Svc., Hong Kong, 1989-92; clin. sr. lectr. U. Queensland, Australia, 1993-96, assoc. prof. 1997-2002, prof., 2002--; examiner U. Queensland, Royal Australian Coll. Ob-Gyn., Australian Med. Coun., mem. Medico legal panel, mem. Medico legal panel Hong Kong Coll. Ob-gyn. Co-author: Endosonography in Obstetrics & Gynaecology, 1996; contbr. articles to profl. jours. Li Tsoo Yiu Meml. scholar U. Hong Kong, 1974-79, British Commonwealth scholar, 1984-85; recipient Exec. Woman of Yr. award Women's Network Australia, 1998, nat. award for excellence through info. tech. Australian Fin. Rev. and Australian Info. Industry Assn., 1999. Fellow Royal Australian Coll. Obstetricians-Gynecologists, Hong Kong Acad. Medicine, Royal Coll. Obstetricians & Gynecologists; mem. Mater Mothers Staff Assn. Avocations: reading, badminton, ping pong/table tennis. Home: Brisbane, Australia. Died May 30, 2007.

**CHAN, LOIS MAI,** library and information science educator; d. Kar K. and Sau N. Mark; m. Shung Kai Chan, June 22, 1963; children: Jennifer M., Stephen Y. AB in Fgn. Langs., Nat. Taiwan U., Taipei, 1956; MA in English, Fla. State U., 1958, MLS, 1960; PhD in Comparative Lit., U. Ky., 1970. Asst. order libr. Purdue U., Lafayette, Ind., 1960-61, asst. cataloger, 1961-63; serials acquisition libr. Northwestern U., Evanston, Ill., 1963-64; asst. libr. Lake Forest Coll., Ill., 1964—66; serials cataloger U. Ky., Lexington, 1966-67; asst. prof. U. Ky. Coll. Libr. Sci., 1970-74, assoc. prof., 1974-80, prof., 1980—2011. Vis. lectr. Libr. Sch. U. Minn., Mpls., 1979; vis. prof. Grad. Sch. Libr. Studies U. Hawaii, Honolulu, 1982; project cons. Online Computer Libr. Ctr., Dublin, 1983-86, CLR U. Mich., 1988-89, Online Computer Libr. Ctr., 1999-2010; cons. Cataloging Policy and Support Office Libr. Congress, 1995-97. Author: Marlowe Criticism: A Bibliography, 1978, Library of Congress Subject Headings: Principles and Applications, 1978, Immorth's Guide to the Library of Congress Classification 3rd Edit., 1980, Theory of Subject Analysis, 1985, Library of Congress Subject Headings: Principles and Applications 2nd Edit., 1986, Mokuroku to Bunrui, 1987, Library of Congress Subject Headings: Principles of Structure and Policies for Application, 1990, Cataloging and Classification: An Introduction, 1981, Cataloging and Classification: An Introduction 2nd Edit., 1994, 3d edit., 2007, Library of Congress Subject Headings, 1981, 4th edit., 2005, A Guide to the Library of Congress Classification 5th edit., 1999; co-author: Thesauri Used in Online Databases, 1988, Dewey Decimal Classification: A Practical Guide, 1994, 2d edit., 1996, Dewey Decimal Classification: Principles and Application, 2003, FAST Faceted Applicatoin of Subject Terminology, 2010; contbr. numerous articles to profl. publs. Recipient Gt. Tchr. award U. Ky. Alumni Assn., 1980, Outstanding Profl. Achievement award, 1989, Disting. Svc. award Chinese-American Libraries Assn., 1992, Disting. Alumni award Fla. State U. Sch. Libr. & Info. Studies, 1996, Excellence Tchg. award U. Ky. Coll. Comm. & Info. Studies, 2001, Faculty Cmty. Svc. award, 2007; Rsch. grants. Mem.: ALA (Margaret Mann Citation award 1989, Beta Phi Mu award for dist. svc. edn. for librianship 2006). Mem. Christian Ch. Home: Lexington, Ky. Died Aug. 20, 2014.

**CHANDLER, KENT, JR.,** lawyer; b. Chgo., Jan. 10, 1920; s. Kent and Grace Emeret (Tuttle) C.; m. Frances Robertson, June 19, 1948; children: Gail, Robertson Kent. BA, Yale U., 1942; JD, U. Mich., 1949. Bar: Ill. 1949, U.S. Dist. Ct. (no. dist.) Ill. 1949, U.S. Ct. Appeals (7th cir.) 1955, U.S. Ct. Claims 1958. Assoc. Wilson & McIlvaine, Chgo., 1949-56, ptnr., 1957-94, spl. counsel to firm, 1994-98; of counsel Bell Jones & Quinlisk, Chgo., 1998—2007, Jones & Quinlsk LLC, Chgo., from 2007. Bd. dirs. Internat. Crane Found. Mem. zoning bd. appeals City of Lake Forest, Ill., 1953-63, chmn., 1963-67, mem. plan commn., 1955-69, chmn., 1969-70, pres. bd. local improvements, 1970-73, mayor, 1970-73, mem. bd. fire and police commn., 1975-82, chmn., 1982-84. Served to maj. USMCR, 1941-46. Mem. ABA, Ill. State Bar Assn., Chgo. Bar Assn., Lake County Bar Assn., Lawyers Club Chgo. (pres. 1985-86), Univ. Club, Onwentsia Club (Lake Forest), Old Elm Club (Highland Park, Ill.). Republican. Presbyterian. Home: Lake Forest, Ill. Died Sept. 2013.

**CHANDRACHUD, YESHWANT VISHNU,** Former Chief Justice of India; b. Poona, India, July 12, 1920; Grad. in History and Economics, Elphinstone Coll., Bombay, 1940; LLB, U. Bombay, 1942. Prof. law Govt. Law Coll., Bombay, 1949—52; advocate High Ct. Bombay, India, 1943, asst. govt. pleader, 1952, govt. pleader, 1958, judge, 1961, Supreme Ct. of India, 1972—85, chief justice, 1978—85. Chmn. bd. trustees Asiatic Soc. Mumbai, India. Died July 14, 2008.

**CHANEY, VINCENT VERLANDO,** lawyer; b. Elkins, W. Va., June 12, 1913; s. Thomas H. and Anna Gertrude (Merge) Chaney; m. Caroline O'Neale, Feb. 5, 1939; 1 child, Malcolm L.; 1 child, Michael Thomas. BA, W. Va. U., 1936; JD, 1938. Bar: W. Va. 1938, US Dist. Ct. (so. dist.) 1938, US Dist. Ct. (no. dist.)/W. Va. 1938, US Ct. Apls. (4th cir.). Assoc. Kay, Casto & Amos, 1938—50; ptnr. Kay Casto & Chaney, Charleston, W.Va., from 1950; sec., gen. counsel, dir. Ray Resources Corp., Charleston, W.Va., 1969—75, Mountaineer Gas Co., Charleston, from 1984; dir. Allegheny & western Energy Corp., Charleston, from 1981; mem. inspection teams USIA, Venezuela, 1971, Thailand, 1974, Poland, 1976, Czech Republic, 1976, US Internat. Comm. Agy., Hong Kong, China, 1978. 1st. lt. to lt. col. AUS, 1941—46. Fellow Am. Bar Found. Mem.: W. Va. Law Rev. (mem. 1936—38), Order of Coif, W. Va. U. Alumni Assn. (exec. council 1965—72, pres. 1971—72), Am. Arbitration Assn. (panel from 1972), Am. Law Inst., Am. Judicature Soc., Kanawha County Bar Assn., W. Va. State Bar (bd. gov. 1956—62, pres. 1962—63), W. Va. Bar Assn., ABA, W. Va. U. Coll. Law (vis. com. 1980—84), Kanawha Valley Dental Health Found. (mem. 1965—70), Charleston Area Med. Ctr. (trustee from 1972, chmn. bd. 1975—78), Sunrise Ctr. and Mus. (bd. dir. 1972—74), Edgewood Country, Phi Beta Kappa. Democrat. Home: Charleston, W.Va. Died 1997.

**CHANG, LEROY L.,** physicist, researcher; b. Kaifung, China, Jan. 20, 1936; came to U.S., 1959; s. Hsin-Fu and Hsien-Hen (Lee) C.; m. Helen H. Chang, 1962; children: Justin, Leslie. BS, Taiwan U., 1957; MS, U. S.C., 1961; PhD, Stanford U., 1963. Mem. rsch. staff IBM T.J. Watson Rsch. Ctr., Yorktown Heights, N.Y., 1963-68, 69-75, mgr. molecular beam epitaxy, 1975-84, tech. planning staff, 1984-85, mgr. quantum structures, 1985-92; dean of sci. Hong Kong U. of Sci. Tech., 1993-98, v.p. acad. affairs, from 1998. Fellow IEEE (David Sarnoff award 1990), Am. Phys. Soc. (Internat. prize New Materials 1985); mem. NAS, NAE, Chinese Acad. Scis., Franklin Inst. (Stuart Ballantine award 1993), Academia Sinica. Died Aug. 10, 2008.

**CHAPMAN, SAMUEL GREELEY,** political science professor, criminologist; b. Atlanta, Sept. 29, 1929; s. Calvin C. and Jane (Greeley) C.; m. Patricia Hepfer, June 19, 1949 (dec. Dec. 1978); children: Lynn Randall, Deborah Jane; m. Carolyn Hughes, June 1, 1991. AB, U. Calif.-Berkeley, 1951, MA, 1959. Officer Police Dept., Berkeley, 1951-56; police cons. Pub. Adminstrn. Service, Chgo., 1956-59; asst. prof. Sch. Police Adminstrn., Mich. State U., East Lansing, 1959-63; police chief Multnomah County, Portland, Oreg., 1963-66; asst. dir. Pres.'s Commn. on Law Enforcement and Adminstrn. of Justice, Nat. Crime Commn., Washington, 1966-67; prof. dept. polit. sci. U. Okla., Norman, 1967-91; prof. emeritus, from 1991; chmn. athletic council U. Okla., 1971-72, 79-80. Adj. prof. criminal justice U. Nev., Reno, 1995—; assoc.'s disting. lectr., 1985-86. Author: Dogs in Police Work, 1960, The Police Heritage in England and America, 1962, Police Patrol Readings, 1964, rev. edit., 1970, Perspectives on Police Assaults in the South Central United States, 1974, Short of Merger, 1976, Police Murders and Effective Countermeasures, 1976, Police Dogs in North America, 1979, 2d. edit., 1990, Cops, Killers and Staying Alive: The Murder of Police Officers in America, 1986; Murdered On Duty: The Killing of Police Officers in America, 1998; contbr. chpts. to books, articles to profl. jours. Mem. Norman City Council, 1972-83, mayor protem, 1975-76, 79-80, 81-83. Recipient Amoco Found. award, 1986. Mem. Nev. Hist. Soc. (docent, Docent of Yr, 2006), Alpha Delta Phi. Republican. Congregationalist. Died Oct. 20, 2013.

**CHAPPIE, EUGENE A.,** congressman; b. Sacramento, Calif., 1920; children: Susan Thomas, Eugene A. II, John, Tina McClendon, Linda Reilly. Supr. El Dorado County, 1950—64; mem. Calif. State Assembly, 1964—80. Chmn. com. on rules Calif. State Assembly, 1968—70, chmn. com. on social welfare, 1966—68, mem. 97th-99th Congresses from Calif. 1st Dist. With US Army, WWII, Korean conflict. Decorated Bronze Star. Republican. Died 1992.

**CHAREN, SOLOMON,** psychologist; b. Cleve. m. Thelma June Golden. BA, Western Res. U.; MA, U. Pitts.; PhD, Cath. U. Am. Pvt. practice psychology, Kensington, Md., 1950-77; dir. child guidance clinic Jewish Social Svc., Rockville, Md., 1967-77 (ret. 1977); chief psychologist Jewish Social Svc. Agy., Rockville, 1955-77. Contbr. numerous articles to profl. jours. With U.S. Army, 1943-46. Mem. APA, Ea. Psychol. Assn., Md. Psychol. Assn., D.C. Psychol. Assn. Avocation: golf. Deceased.

**CHARLAP, GUY J.,** retired scientific instrumentation consultant; b. Paris, Oct. 25, 1921; arrived in Switzerland, 1969; s. Samuel and Charlotte (Albert) C.; m. Genia Baltakse, Mar. 29, 1944; children: Jean-Paul, Elisabeth, Berthe Pascale, Franqoise, Marie Helene. Pharmacien 1 Class, U. Paris, 1946, Lic. Scis. Economist, 1954; Pharmacien Indsl., Inst. Paris, 1948; Internat. Mgmt., Nowrthwestern U., Evanston, Ill., 1979. Exec. Sifa, Paris, 1953-61; pres. Technicon Corp., Tarrytown, NY, 1961-80; pvt. cons. Greenwich, Conn., 1981-89; ret., from 1990. Councillor Rockefeller U., N.Y.C., 1974. Lt. French Mil., 1942-46. Mem. Club Des Vingt. Home: Breganzona, Switzerland. Died Jan. 24, 2009.

**CHARLTON, BETTY JO,** retired state legislator; b. Reno County, Kans., June 15, 1923; d. Joseph and Elma (Johnson) Canning; m. Robert Sansom Charlton, Feb. 24, 1946 (dec. 1984); children: John Robert, Richard Bruce. BA, U. Kans., 1970, MA, 1976. Asst. instr. polit. sci. & western civilization U. Kans., Lawrence, 1970—73; mem. Kans. House of Reps., 1980—95. Democrat. Home: Lawrence, Kans. Died July 22, 2014.

**CHASE, BETTY J.,** heath facility administrator; b. Shawnee, Okla., Feb. 12, 1934; d. Blanche Turner; m. Jay Dee Chase; children: Charles Burnham, Kaye Lynn O'Connell, Dee Ann Batten. Diploma, St. Anthony Hosp. Sch. Nursing, Oklahoma City; student, U. Okla. RN, Okla. DON Griffin Meml. Hosp., Norman, Okla.; assoc. dir. Nat. Drug Ctr. U. Okla. Health Sci. Ctr., Oklahoma City; dir. continuing edn. programs Coll. Nursing U. Okla. Health Scis. Ctr., Oklahoma City; DON, v.p. patient care svcs. Behavioral Medicine Ctr. Hillcrest Health Ctr., Oklahoma City. Trustee univ., hosps. and clinics, 1973-78, chmn. bd., 1976-78. Mem. State Health Commrs., 1973-75, feasibility study nurse practitioners role Gov.'s Task Force, Okla., 1975; v.p. Betty Chase Ctr., Oklahoma City. Mem. ANA (coun. psychiat. and mental health nursing), Nat. League for Nursing, Okla. League for Nursing, Okla. Mental Health Orgn., Okla. Nurses Assn. (pres. 1971-72, Nurse of the Yr. 1970), Okla. Orgn. Nurse Execs., Okla. Bd. Nurse Registration and Nursing Edn., Okla. Osteo. Assn. (award 1982). Home: Norman, Okla. Died Apr. 10, 1990.

**CHATAWAY, SIR CHRISTOPHER JOHN,** retired bank executive; b. Chelsea, London, Jan. 31, 1931; m. Carola Chataway. P.P.E., Magdalen Coll., Oxford, Eng. Jr. exec. Arthur Guinness Son & Co., 1953—55; staff reporter Independent TV News, 1955—56; current affairs commentator BBC TV, 1956—59, M.P. for Lewisham North, England, 1959—66, M.P. for Chichester, 1969—74; pvt. parliamentary sec. Minister or Power, 1961—62; joint party under sec. State Dept. Edn. and Sci., 1962—64, 1967—70; leader edn. com. Inner London Edn. Authority, 1967—69; minister Posts and Telecom., 1970—72, Indsl. Devel., 1972—74; pres. Commonwealth Games Coun. for England, 1990—2009; chmn. Civil Aviation Authority. Vice chmn. Orion Royal Bank Ltd.; chmn. Ind. Radio News, London Broadcasting Co., Ltd., Kitcat & Aitken, Orion Royal Bank Asset Mgmt. Ltd.; dir. Brit. Electric Traction Co., Petrofina Ltd. Representer Great Britain in Olympic Games, 1952, 1956. Recipient Gold medal, Commonwealth Games, 1954; named Knight Comdr. of the Most Excellent Order of the British Empire, Her Majesty Queen Elizabeth II, 1995. Conservative Party. Died Jan. 19, 2014.

**CHATT, JOSEPH,** chemist, educator; b. Durham, Eng., Nov. 6, 1914; s. Joseph and Margery Elsie (Parker) Chatt; m. Ethel Williams Chatt, May 31, 1947; children: Elizabeth Mary, Joseph. BA, Emmanuel Coll. Cambridge U., 1937, MA, 1941, PhD, 1940, ScD, 1956; DSc, East Anglia U., 1974, U. Sussex, 1982; D, Pierre Marie Curie U., Paris, 1981, Lund U., Sweden, 1986. Chartered chemist., dep. to chief chemist Peter Spence & Sons Ltd., Widnes, England, 1942—46; with Imperial Chem. Industries Ltd., Welwyn, 1947—62; vis. professorships and commns. & mem. Commn. Nomenclature Inorganic Chemistry, IUPAC, 1959—81, chmn., 1976—81; dir. unit nitrogen fixation Agrl. Research Coun. Eng., Brighton, 1963—80; prof. chemistry U. Sussex, Brighton, 1964—80; emeritus prof.; mem. comite de direction Laboratoire Chemie Coordination, Toulouse, 1964—69. Contbr. articles to profl. jours. Decorated Order Brit. Empire; recipient Disting. Svc. award, Am. Chem. Soc, 1971, Chugaev medal & diploma, Kurnakov Inst. Gen. and Inorganic Chemistry, Soviet Acad. Scis., 1976, Chandler medal, Columbia U., 1978, Davy medal, Royal Soc., 1979, Dwyer Meml. medal, U. NSW, Australia, 1980, Wolf prize, Wolf Found., Israel, 1981, G.W. Wheland medal, U. Chgo., 1983, Julius Steiglitz award, 1978, Royal Soc. Leverhulme, U. Rajasthan, India, 1966—67, Award, MIT, 1977, U. Lund, 1982, Japan Soc. Promotion Sci., 1979. Fellow: Emmanuel Coll. Cambridge (hon.); mem.: Civil Svc. (London), Internat. Confs. Coord. Chemistry (founder), Nat. Acad. Sci. India, Nat. Acad. Sci. Portugal, NY Acad. Scis. (life), Chem. Soc. (coun. 1952—65, 1972—76, hon. sec. 1956—62, pres. Dalton div.

1972—74), Royal Soc. (coun. 1975—77), Am. Acad. Arts and Scis. (hon.). Avocations: gardening, art. Home: Sussex, England. Died May 19, 1994.

**CHAUVET, GILBERT ANDRÉ,** physiology professor; b. Nueil, France, Oct. 2, 1942; s. Eugene Chauvet and Antonia Mainchain; m. Nadine Rocard (dec.); children: Pierre, Anne, Line. M Maths., Poitiers U., France, 1965; PhD in Molecular Physics, Nantes U., France, 1974; MD, Angers U., France, 1976. Rschr. Angers U., 1964-72, assoc. prof., 1972-76, prof. biomath. 1976-80, prof. theoretical biology, from 1980; dir. Med. Computing Dept. Angers Hosp., 1984—2002; dir., founder Inst. Theoretical Biology Angers U., 1988-2001; rsch. prof. U. So. Calif., LA, from 1994, Pitts. U., 1988-92. Rschr. Hosp. Tarnier-Cochin U. Paris V, 2001—03; rschr. Ecole Pratique de Hautes Etudes, Paris, from 2004. Author: Theoretical Physiology, 3 vols., 1987—90, La Vie Dans La Matiere, Flammarion, 1995, The Mathematical Nature of the Living World: The Power of Integration, 1995, Theoretical Systems in Biology: Hierarchical and Functional Integration, 3 vols., 1996, Comprendre l'organization du vivant et son évolution vers la Conscience, 2006; contbr. articles to profl. jours.; editor (editor-in-chief): Jour. Integrative Neuroscience. Avocation: historical monuments. Home: Paris, France. Died Dec. 6, 2007.

**CHAVIS-BUTLER, GRACE LEE,** educator; b. Charleston, SC, Aug. 26, 1916; d. Thomas and Sarah (Lafayette) Chavis; m. E. Hardy Butler, June 15, 1974 (div. Feb. 1984); remarried, Sept. 17, 1985. Diploma in Teaching, Avery Normal Inst., 1938; BA, Am. U., 1954, MA, 1955; PhD, U. Beverly Hills, 1982. Educator Washington high schs., 1955-73; chmn. history dept. Western High Sch., Washington, 1971-73; substitute tchr. Oakland (Calif.) Pub. Schs., 1973-74; substitute instr. Los Angeles Community Coll. Dist., 1974-80 and from 82. Author: Reflections on Africa, 1975; contbr. articles to newspapers, profl. jours. Mem. Friends of Vernon Br. Libr., L.A., 1978—, pres. 1980-81; vol. asst. mgr. The Mankind Ctr., L.A., 1978-79; coord. L.A.-Lusaka Sister City Annual Festival, 1980. Sgt. WAC, 1943-46. Recipient Cert. of Merit Human Relations Commn., Los Angeles, 1982, Martin Luther King award So. Christian Leadership Conf. West, 1978, Annual Fin. Support award Am. U. John Fletcher Hurst Soc., Washington, 1981-82. Mem. AAUW (life mem., 1st v.p. Los Angeles br. 1978-80, Recognition of Service award Los Angeles chpt. 1979, Significant Contbn. to Edn. Found. award State div. 1984, pres. 1988-90), Am. Inst. Parliamentarians (adminstrv. lt. gov. region 7 1984-85, pres. El Camino Real chpt., Los Angeles, 1982-84, chmn. region ann. conf. 1985), Nat. Council of Negro Women (life, chmn. ann. festival com. 1976-77), Seeds of Sequoia (v.p. 1983—), Am. U. Alumni Assn. (Recognition award 1987). Democrat. Roman Catholic. Avocations: writing poems, collecting epigrams, sewing, knitting, playing bridge. Home: Los Angeles, Calif. Died 1996.

**CHAWLA, LAL MUHAMMAD,** mathematics educator; b. Mahatpur, India, Nov. 1, 1917; s. Haji Umardin and Fatimah (Bibi) C.; m. Sakina Begum, Mar. 26, 1930 (dec. De. 1988); childen: Surriaya, Ehsan-ul-Haq, Rehana, Ikram-ul-Haq. BA in Math., U. Punjab, 1937, MA in Math., 1939; DPhil, U. Oxford, 1955. Lectr. Islamia Coll., Lahore, 1939-47; sr. lectr. Govt. Coll., Lahore, 1948-57, sr. prof., 1957-69; prin. Cen. Tng. Coll., Lahore, 1969; chmn. Bd. Edn., Sargodha, Punjab, 1970; prof. math. Kans. State U., Manhattan, 1970-82, King A Univ., Jeddah, Saudi Arabia, 1982-86. Vis. prof. U. Ill., Urbana, 1965-66, U. Fla., Gainesville, 1966-67; presenter Internat. Congress Mathematicians, Stockholm, 1962; former mem. Am. Math. Assn., London Math. Soc. Author 4 books on study of Holy Quran, 1993; author: A Quranic Exposition of the Glory of the Holy Prophet Muhammad, 1996; editor math. sect. Jour. Natural Scis. and Math., 1960-83; reviewer Am. Math. Revs., 1962-95; contbr. articles to profl. jours. Mem. Am. Math. Soc. Achievements include discovery of Chawla's Arithmatic Function, 1968; guiding research in Number Theory, Group Theory, Lattice Theory and Boolean Algebras, Isotopy Theory of Linear Systems of Algebras, Invariants of Multilinear Forms and Abstract Algebras. Home: Lahore, Pakistan. Died 2005.

**CHEIT, EARL FRANK (BUD CHEIT),** economist, educator; b. Mpls., Aug. 5, 1926; s. Morris and Etta (Warshausky) C.; m. June Doris Andrews, Aug. 28, 1950; children: Wendy, David, Ross, Julie. BS, U. Minn., 1947, LLB, 1949, PhD, 1954. Rsch. economist, prof. Sch. Bus. Adminstrn. U. Calif. Haas Sch. Bus. Adminstrn., Berkeley, 1960—2014, dean, 1976-82, 90-91, dean emeritus, 1995—2014; exec. vice chancellor U. Calif., 1965-69. Program officer in charge higher edn. and rsch. Ford Found., 1972-73; assoc. dir., sr. rsch. fellow Carnegie Coun. on Policy Studies in Higher Edn., 1973-75; sr. adv. con. Asian-Pacific econ. affairs Asia Found.; bd. dirs. Shaklee Corp., 1976-2001 Author: The Useful Arts and the Liberal Tradition, 1975, The New Depression in Higher Education, 1971, Foundations and Higher Education, 1979; editor: The Business Establishment, 1964. Trustee Richmond (Calif.) Unified Sch. Dist., 1961-65, Russell Sage Found., NYC, 1979-89; chmn. State of Calif. Wage Bd. for Agrl. Occupations, 1980-81. Home: Kensington, Calif. Died Aug. 2, 2014.

**CHEN, ANTHONY YOUNG (TONY CHEN),** illustrator; b. Kingston, Jamaica, Jan. 3, 1929; arrived in US, 1949; s. Arthur and Marie (Ho) Chen Pow; m. Pura De Castro, Mar. 2, 1957; children: Richard, David. BFA, Pratt Inst., 1955. Art dir. Newsweek Mag., NYC, 1960—71; instr. Nassau Cmty. Coll., Garden City, 1970—72; freelance illustrator, lectr., from 1971. Illustrated (book) Run, Zebra, Run, 1972 (excellence Soc. Illustrators, 1972), Doubleday Children's Bible, 1983; author: Little Koala, 1979 (outstanding Sci. book Children Book Coun., 81). Recipient Disting. Achievement award, Ednl. Press Am., 1977. Home: Lynbrook, NY. Died July 19, 1994.

**CHEN, ZHONG WEI WEI,** surgeon, researcher; b. Ningbo, Zhejiang Province, China, Oct. 1, 1929; s. Bao Zheng Chen and Yi Li Wu; m. Hui Zhu Yin, July 0, 1954; children: Lilly, Li Jian. MD, Shanghai Second Med. Sch., 1948—54. Pres. Internat. Soc. of Reconstructive Microsurgery, Louisville, Ky., 1985—88; dir. Shnanghai Sixth People's Hosp., Shanghai, China, 1973—82; chief, orthop. dept. Shanghai Sixth People's Hosp., Shanghai, China, 1970—82; head Reasearch Lab. for Replantation of Severed Limb, Shanghai, China, 1965—82. Vis. prof. NYU Med. Ctr., 1983, Harvard Med. Sch., 1988. Contbr. Chinese Journal of Medicine; author: (book) Microsurgery. Rep. Nat. People's Congress, Beijing, China, 1970, Nat. Polit. Cons. Congress, Beijing, China, 1967. Recipient QiuShi Award, State Dept. of China, 1994, Millennium Award, Internat. Soc. of Reconstructive Microsurgery, 1999. Master: Chinese Soc. for Rsch. in Rehab. of Neural Disabilities (life); mem.: Chinese Acad. Sci., Chinese Med. Assn. (life; exec. com.), Internat. Soc. of Reconstructive Microsurgery (life; exec. com.), Internat. Soc. of Surgery (life). Avocations: tennis, fishing. Home: Shanghai, China. Died Mar. 23, 2004.

**CHEUNG, MARVIN KIN-TUNG,** Hong Kong government official; b. Nov. 20, 1947; D of Bus. Adminstrn., Hong Kong Baptist U.; grad., St Paul's Co-Educational Coll., Hong Kong. Cert. Inst. of Chartered Acct. in England and Wales, Hong Kong Inst. of Certified Pub. Acct. Mem. Commodities Trading Commn., 1985—89, Deposit-Taking Companies Adv. Com., 1985—91; pres., coun. mem. Hong Kong Soc. of Acct., 1984—92; mem. Fedn of Hong Kong Industries Gen. Com., 1986—93, Urban Coun., 1985—95, Legislative Coun., 1991—95; vice-chmn. Mandatory Provident Fund Adv. Bd., 1996—98; chmn. Estate Agents Authority, 1997—2003; ind. trustee Hosp. Authority Provident Fund Scheme, 2000—04; chmn. Main Bd. Listing Com. of Hong Kong Exchanges and Clearing Ltd., 2003—05; mem. Greater Pearl River Delta Bus. Coun., 2004—06; coun. mem. Open U. of Hong Kong, from 2003; bd. mem. Airport Authority, from 2003; mem., chmn. Supervisory Com. of the Tracker Fund of Hong Kong, from 1999; non-official mem. Exec. Coun., Hong Kong Spl. Adminstrv. Region (HKSAR), from 2005. Bd. dirs. HSBC Holdings, 2009—14. Recipient Silver Bauhinia Star, Justice of the Peace. Mem.: Exchange Fund Adv. Com., Municipal Services Appeals Bd., Barristers Disciplinary Tribunal Panel, Hong Kong U. of Sci. and Tech. Educational Trust (trustee from 1990), Hong Kong U. of Sci. and Tech. (vice-chmn. from 2004), Hong Kong Internat. Film Soc. Ltd. (bd. mem.). Avocations: golf, fine wines, films, swimming. Died Sept. 13, 2014.

**CHEY, JONG HYON,** former chemical company executive; 3 children. M in Economics, U. Chgo., 1961. With Sunkyong Ltd., Seoul, 1962—98, chmn., CEO, 1973—98. Founder Korea Found. for Advanced Studies, U. Chgo. Club of Korea. Died 1998.

**CHIANG, CHIN LONG,** retired biostatistician, educator; b. Chekiang, China, Nov. 12, 1914; came to U.S., 1946, naturalized, 1963; s. Tse Shang and (Chen) C.; m. Fu Chen Shiao, Jan. 21, 1945 (dec. 2013; children: William S. (dec.), Robert S., Harriet W. BA in Econs, Tsing Hwa U., 1940; MA, U. Calif.-Berkeley, 1948; PhD in Stats, U. Calif., Berkeley, 1953. Teaching asst. U. Calif., Berkeley, 1948, research asst., 1950-51, assoc., 1951-53, instr., 1953-55, asst. prof. biostatistics, 1955-60, assoc. prof., 1960-65, prof., 1965—2014, chmn. div. measurement scis., 1970-75, chmn. faculty Sch. Public Health, 1975-76. Vis. prof. U. Mich., 1959, U. Minn., 1960, 61, Yale U., 1965-66, Emory U., 1967, U. Pitts., 1968, U. Wash., 1969, U. N.C., 1969, 70, U. Tex., 1973, Vanderbilt U., 1975, Harvard U., 1977; cons. WHO, HEW, NIH, others. Author: Introduction to Stochastic Processes in Biostatistics, 1968, Life Table and Mortality Analysis, 1978, An Introduction to Stochastic Processes and Their Applications, 1979, The Life Table and its, Applications, 1984; Assoc. editor: Biometrics, 1972-75 Nat. Heart Inst. fellow, 1959-60; Fulbright sr. lectr., 1964 Fellow American Statis. Assn., Inst. Math. Stats., American Public Health Assn., Royal Statis. Soc. London; mem. Internat. Statis. Inst., Biometric Soc. Democrat. Home: Berkeley, Calif. Died Apr. 1, 2014.

**CHIAVETTA, FRANK PETER,** chemical engineer; b. NYC, Apr. 28, 1920; s. Michael and Felicia (Marasa) Chiavetta; m. Lillian Helen Little, July 15, 1944; children: Michael, Frank, Peter. BSChemE, CCNY, 1941. Chem. engr. Am. Hard Rubber Co., Butler, NJ, 1941—42; indsl. chemist Naugatuck Chem. Div. US Rubber Co. (now Uniroyal), 1945—56; chem. engr. Aerojet Gen. Corp., Azusa, Calif., 1956—67; tech. specialist McDonnell Douglas Astronautics Corp., Santa Monica, Calif., 1967—73; engr. specialist Northrop Corp., Hawthorne, Calif., 1973—85. Contbr. articles to profl. jours.; patentee in field. Lt. comdr. USN, 1942—45, Res. ret. Mem.: Soc. Materials and Aerospace Engring. Republican. Roman Catholic. Home: Carlsbad, Calif. Died Jan. 16, 1998.

**CHILDERS, JOANNE M.,** poet; b. Sept. 5, 1926; BA, U. Cin., 1948; MA, U. Fla., 1951. Acting dir. social svc. Tacochale, Gainesville, Fla., 1958-68; rsch. and edn. asst. U. Fla., Gainesville, 1968-72. Author poetry to many revs. and mags. Nominated two times Pushcart. Died May 30, 2008.

**CHILDS, RICHARD FRANCIS,** retired scientist, educator; b. Battle Creek, MI, Sept. 20, 1918; s. Francis Marion and Mary Florence (Crilly) C.; m. Marion R. Avmitage, 1943 (div., 1953), m. Virginia Helen (Ramsdell), Aug. 2, 1958; children: Allen, Bonnie, Kathleen. BA in chem., Olivet, Olivet, MI, 1937-41; BS, MS, U. Wisconsin, Madison, WI, 1954-55; PhD in pharm., U. Arizona, Tucson, AZ, 1962. Cert. Reg. Pharmacist. Indsl. chemist Cleaver Brooks, Milwaukee, WI, 1942-43; radio instr. US Army AF, Sioux Falls, SD, 1943-46; chemist ARMOUR, Chicago, IL, 1948-50; assoc. prof. Coll. Pharm., Tucson, 1955-75; ret., 1975. Dir., Southern AZ Sci. Fair, Tucson, 1957-58. Assoc. edit. (edit. Homer B. Titton), Lightworks, Pima Community Coll. East, Tucson, AZ, 1998. Served AAF, CPL, 1943-46. Recipient Sci. Faculty, Natl. Sci. Found., U. Arizona, Purdue, Tchg. Fellowship, Natl. SCi. Found., first PhD offered by Coll. of RX, 1962. Democrat. Died Aug. 3, 2002.

**CHILVER, ELIZABETH MILLICENT,** retired academic administrator; b. Constantinople, Turkey, Aug. 3, 1914; d. Philip Perceval Graves and Leila Millicent Gilchrist; m. Richard Clementson Chilver (wid. 1985). MA, Oxford U., 1935. Freelance journalist, U.K., 1937-39; temporary civil servant HM Govt., U.K., 1939-45; journalist Daily News Ltd., U.K., 1945-47; temporary Principal Colonial Office, 1948-57; dir. Inst. Commonwealth Studies/Oxford U., U.K., 1957-61; prin. Bedford Coll./London U., 1964-71, Lady Margaret Hall/Oxford U., 1971-79, hon. fellow, 1979—2014. Mem. Royal Commn. on Med. Edn., U.K., 1966-68; trustee Brit. Mus., 1970-75, others; rsch. assoc. Queen Elizabeth House, Oxford Author: A History of Socialism, 1939; co-editor: Oxford History of East Africa II, 1965; contbr. to symposiums in field, profl. jours. Recipient Wellcome medal in Applied Anthropology, Royal Anthropol. Inst., U.K., 1961; fellowship Royal Holloway/Bedford Coll., London, 1974, Somerville Coll., Oxford, 1979. Home: Oxford, England. Died July 3, 2014.

**CHIN, MEE KOY,** science educator, researcher; b. Teluk Anson, Perak, Malaysia, May 14, 1959; s. Chee Yin Chin and Ngan Lin Chang; m. Ooi Kwen Ong; children: Jia Qi children: Yi Jin, Xiu Qi, Yi Fan. BS, MIT, 1986; PhD, U. Calif. San Diego, La Jolla, 1992. Grad. cons. AT&T Bell Labs., Holmdel, NJ, 1989—90; post-doctoral fellow U. Calif. San Diego, La Jolla, 1992—93; asst. prof. Nanyang Technol. U., Singapore, 1993—97, assoc. prof., from 2003; rsch. fellow Northwestern U., Evanston, Ill., 1997—98; dir. tech. Nanovation Technologies, Inc., Evanston, 1997—2000; chief scientist photonics Anadigics, Inc, Warren, NJ, 2000—01; v.p. engring. Phosistor Technologies, Inc, Pleasanton, Calif., 2001—02. Presenter in field. Contbr. articles to profl. jours. Scholar, MIT, 1986. Mem.: IEEE (sect. com. mem. 2003—05), Laser and Electrooptic Soc. (chair from 2006, Singapore chpt.). Achievements include patents for Design of Filters, Wavelength Demultiplexers, and Low-Voltage Modulators Based On Micro-Ring Resonators; development of world's smallest directional coupler fabricated in Gallium Arsenide and Indium Phosphide (InP) semiconductor materials; world's smallest microdisk lasers in InP; Co-founding a start-up to develop photonic integrated circuit products. Home: Singapore, Singapore. Deceased.

**CHLUPÁČ, IVO,** geologist, paleontologist, educator; b. Benešov, Czech Republic, Dec. 6, 1931; s. Karel and Marie (Kodetová) C.; m. Marta Světlíková, 1955 (div. 1967); children: Jan, Tomáš; m. Olga Hofmanová, Aug. 12, 1967; 1 child, Martin. Diploma, Charles U., Prague, Czech Republic, 1955. Geologist Geol. Survey, Prague, 1955-91; prof. faculty of scis. Charles U., Prague, 1991—2002. Sci. worker Geol. Survey, Prague, 1962-91; head dept. geology Charles U., 1991-96. Contbr. over 270 articles on paleontology and geology to profl. jours. Recipient award Czech Literary Found., Prague, 1988. Mem. Czech Geol. Soc., Acad. Leopoldina. Roman Catholic. Avocations: fossil collecting, archaeology. Home: Prague, Czech Republic. Died Nov. 7, 2002.

**CHMIELEWSKI, MARGARET ANN,** counselor, psychology educator; b. Detroit, Dec. 13, 1946; d. Joseph and Mary (Anderanin) Kakaley; m. James Andrew Chmielewski, May 19, 1973; children: Mark James, Elizabeth Ann. BA, Wayne State U., 1969, MA, 1972, PhD in Instrn. Tech., 1998. Lic. profl. counselor. English tchr. Our Lady Star of the Sea High Sch., Grosse Pointe, Mich., 1969-70, Bishop Borgess High Sch., Detroit, 1972-73; instr. in speech Wayne County Community Coll., Detroit, 1972-74; asst. prof. in psychology, counselor Madonna U., Livonia, Mich., 1977-91; coord. ednl. resources for students with disabilities Wayne State U., Detroit, from 1991. Cons. Ford Motor Co., Dearborn, 1979-81; speaker in field. Area coord. Miss Wheelchair Mich. Pageant, 1978-80; trustee Wheelchair Awareness Found., Inc., Columbus, 1979-84, pres., 1982-84; mem. Planning Coun. for Devel. Disabilities, Lansing, Mich., 1980-84; mem. various coms. Statewide Health Coordinating Coun., Lansing, 1980-87; chair Consumers Caucus, Malpractice Issue Com., exec. com., state health plan devel. com., various coms. Gov.'s Task Force on Physician Reimbursement, Lansing, 1980-82; mem. set aside com. for sheltered workshop Dept. Mgmt., 1987—; chair Task Force on Nursing Pers., Lansing, 1985; mem. parish coun. St. John Neumann Cath. Ch., Canton, 1983-88, pres., 1986-87; bd. dirs. Coun. Cath. Women Archdiocese of Detroit, 1988-90; strategic planning com. Huron Valley Girl Scouts of Am. Named Miss Wheelchair Michigan, 1976, Miss Wheelchair America, 1978-79; recipient Arkansas Travelors award Gov. Bill Clinton 1979, Gov.'s award State of Mich., 1979, Gov.'s award State of La., 1979, Gov.'s award State of Miss., 1979, Outstanding Woman of Yr. Wayne State Alumni Assn., 1980; recipient Key to the City, Montgomery, Ala., 1979, Key to the City, Mobile, Ala., 1979, Key to the City, New Orleans, 1979, Nat. Assn. of Physically Handicapped Life award. Mem.

Delta Zeta (adv., dir. Wayne State chpt. 1969-72), U.S. Trotting Assn., Mich. Harness Horseman Assn. Avocations: harness horse racing, bridge. Home: Plymouth, Mich. Died May 29, 1999.

**CHOA, JOHN RICHARD,** architect; b. Hong Kong, Feb. 20, 1932; s. James Man-Chan and Anna Tak-Yuen (Ng) Choa; m. Marina Wai-Ching Pang, Jan. 31, 1980; stepchildren: Lawrence Leong, Harold Leong. BArch, U. Hong Kong, 1957, D (hon.) of Social Sci., 2003. Registered architect. Arch. Easton & Robertson, Cusdin Preston and Smith, London, 1958—65, Cusdin, Burden & Howitt, London, 1965—69; arch., mgr. Wong & Tung & Assoc., Hong Kong, 1969—73; sr. arch. Lee, Choa and Ptnrs., Hong Kong, 1973—77; founding ptnr. Choa, Ko and Ptnrs., Hong Kong, 1977—97; proprietor Archland Co., Hong Kong, from 1997. Fellow, mgmt. com. Robert Black Coll., Hong Kong, 1999—2003; bd. dirs. Hong Kong U. Sch. Profl. and Continuing Edn., 1999—2004, mem. mgmt. bd., 1992—2004, mem. adv. bd., from 2004; ct. mem. U. Hong Kong, 1979—91, coun. mem., 1991—2003. Hon. sec. Rotary, Hong Kong, 1976—77; trustee West China Evangelistic Band Old People's Home, Inc., Hong Kong, 1982—87; pres. Hong Kong U. Alumni Assn., Hong Kong, 1985—87. Fellow: Hong Kong Inst. Architects (coun. mem. 1973—77); mem.: Hong Kong Club, Hong Kong Jockey Club, Hong Kong Golf Club. Avocations: golf, music, theater. Home: Hong Kong, Hong Kong. Died Feb. 8, 2007.

**CHOCZEWSKI, BOGDAN ADAM,** mathematics educator, researcher; b. Rdziostów, Poland, July 12, 1935; s. Stanisław and Katarzyna (Mróz) C.; m. Maria Anna Paździerko, Oct. 26, 1963 (dec. 1980); children: Jakub, Andrzej. MS, Jagiellonian U., Kraków, Poland, 1956, PhD, 1962, Dr. Hab., 1970. Cert. prof. math., 1977. Asst. Silesian Tech. U., Gliwice, Poland, 1956-62; adj. AGH U. Sci. Tech., Kraków, Poland, 1962-70, docent, 1970—77, prof., 1977-94, full prof., 1994—95, 2000—06. Prof. Pedagogical U., Kraków, 1977-93, full prof., 1995-2000. Editor Opuscula Math. Jour., 1984-93; co-author: Iterative Functional Equations, 1990; author From the History of the Institute of Mathematics & of the Faculty Applied Mathematics of the AGH, 2007; contbg. articles to profl. jour. Mem. Polish Math. Soc., Am. Math. Soc. Roman Catholic. Home: Cracow, Poland. Deceased.

**CHOE, WON IK,** judge; Pres. Ctrl. Ct., Pyongyang, Dem. People's Republic of Korea; chief Workers Party Chpt. Kangwon Province, 1998—2001. Died Sept. 9, 2001.

**CHOONHAVAN, CHATICHAI,** former Prime Minister of Thailand; b. Bangkok, Apr. 5, 1922; Student, Chulachomklao Royal Mil. Acad., Cavalry Sch., Royal Thai Army. Troop commdr. First Royal Cavalry Guards, Bangkok; asst. mil. attaché Thai Embassy, Washington; commandant Armour Sch., Bangkok; ambassador to Argentina, Austria, Turkey, Switzerland, Yugoslavia and UN Thai govt.; with Erawan Trust Co. Ltd., Erawan Internat. Co. Ltd.; dep. fgn. minister Thai govt., Bangkok, 1972, fgn. minister, 1975, industry minister, 1976; dep. leader Chat Thai Party; dep. prime minister Thai govt., Bangkok, 1986-88, minister of def., 1988-90, prime min., 1988-91. Died 1998.

**CHOU, TA-SHUE,** chemist, researcher; b. Taipei, Taiwan, Oct. 26, 1950; s. Heou-Feou and Chih (Kiang) C.; m. Jane Tsen, Mar. 7, 1981; children: Yu-Tong, Tao-An. BS in Chemistry, Nat. Taiwan U., Taipei, 1972; PhD in Chemistry, U. Tex., 1979. Food scientist Food Industry Rsch. and Devel. Inst., Hsinchu, Taiwan, 1979-80; assoc. rsch. fellow Inst. Chemistry Academia Sinica, Taipei, 1980-85, rsch. fellow Inst. Chemistry, from 1985, dir. Inst. Chemistry, 1987-96; assoc. prof. Nat. Taiwan U., Taipei, 1981—86, prof., from 1986. Project reviewer Nat. Sci. Coun., Taipei, 1982-86; mem. internat. adv. bd. MOLECULES 1996-, Invited Prof. dept. of Chemistry U. of Louis Pasteur Strasbourg France 1995 (with J.F. Biellmann), visiting scholar dept of Chemistry Princeton U. New Jersey USA 1996 (with M.F. Semmelhack), visiting prof. dept. of Chemistry Zhejiang U. 1995, hon. prof. Shanghai Inst. of Organic Chemistry 1997. Co-author: Organic Synthesis, 1994; editor-in-chief Hua-Hsueh, 1991-92; mem. editl. bd. Jour. Chinese Chem. Soc., 1988—, editor-in-chief, 1997—; mem. internat. editl. bd. Ultrasonics Sonochemsitry, 1994—; contbr. numerous sci. papers to internat. jours. 2d lt. Taiwanese Army 1972-74, Chmn. Internat. Symposium on Organic Reactions Taipei, gen. sec. Internat. Chemical Congress Taipei: Synthetic Chemistry 1991, chmn. Internat. Symposium on Organic Reactions Kyoto, vice-chmn. Internat. Symposium on Inorganic and Organic Chemistry 1992, chmn. Internat. Chemical Congress Taipei: Analytical Chemistry Kaohsiung 1993, chmn. Internat. Symposium on Asymmetric Synthesis Taichung 1994, 3rd Internat. Symposium for Chinese Organic Chemists Taipei 1994, Sino-French Symposium on Organic Chemistry Taipei 1995, 15th Internat. Congress of Heterocyclic Chemistry Taipei 1995, coordinator Franco-Chinese Symposium on Organic and Organometallic Chemistry, Strasbourg France 1996. Recipient Outstanding Rsch. award Nat. Sci. Coun., 1986-94, Rsch. award Sun Yat-Sen Meml. Found. 1986, Nat. Chung Hsing U. Honorary Lectureship 1993, Outstanding Scientist award Chinese Ednl. and Cultural Found. 1994, Specially Appointed Rsch. Fellow award Nat. Sci. Coun. 1996 Mem. American Chemical Soc. 1975, Chinese Chemical Soc. 1981, Internat. Society of Heterocyclic Chemistry, since 1994, Internat. Coun. On Main Group Chemistry 1995, exec. sec. of Chinese Chemical Soc. 1986, bd. mem. Supervisors of Chinese Chemical Soc. 1988-1990, dir. Academic Affairs of Chinese Chemical Soc.1991-1992, vice-pres. Chinese Chemical Soc. 1992, pres. Chinese Chemical Soc. 1993-1994. Achievements include development of new synthetic methodology in organic chemistry, including use of 3-sulfolenes as synthetic equivalents of substituted butadienes; use of ultrasonically dispersed potassium as a powerful reducing agent. Home: Taipei, Taiwan. Died Feb. 25, 1999.

**CHOUDHURY, HUMAYUN RASHEED,** government official Bangladesh; b. Sylhet, Bangladesh, Nov. 11, 1928; s. Abdur Rasheed and Begum A. (Rasheed) Choudhury; m. Mehjabeen Choudhury, Oct. 23, 1947; children: Nasrine Karim, Nauman Rasheed. BA with 1st class honors, Cambridge U., 1944; postgrad, Dacca U.; BS in Geology, Chemistry, Geography, Muslim U., India; diploma in Internat. Affairs, U. London; grad, Fletcher Sch. Law & Diplomacy. 3rd sec. Pakistan Embassy, Rome, 1956—59, Baghdad, Iraq, 1959—61; 2d sec. Paris; dir. pers. Ministry Fgn. Affairs, 1964—67; min. fgn. affairs, 1985—89; charge d'affaires Pakistan Embassy, Lisbon, 1967—69, dep. chief, counsellor Djakarta, 1969—71; chief Bangladesh Diplomatic Mission, New Delhi; counsellor Pakistan High Commn., 1971—72; permanent rep. Bangladesh to UN Indsl. Devel. Orgn., Internat. AEC; ambassador Bangladesh to West Germany, from 1975, Bangladesh to Saudi Arabia, 1976—81, Bangladesh to US Washington, from 1982; permanent rep. Orgn. Islamic Conf.; fgn. sec. Govt. Bangladesh, 1981—82. MP UN, NYC, from 1986, pres. gen. assembly, 1987. Died July 10, 2001.

**CHOYCE, DAVID PETER,** ophthalmologist, researcher; b. London, Mar. 1, 1919; s. Charles Coley and Gwendolen Alice (Dobbing) C.; m. Diana Graham, Sept. 3, 1949; children: Jonathan, David Gregory, Matthew Quentin. BSc, U. London, 1939, MB, BS, 1943, MS, 1962. Cons. Southend Hosp., Essex, Eng., 1954-84; ophthalmologist Hosp. for Tropical Diseases, London, 1953-88; overseas cons., ophthalmologist Henry Ford Hosp., Detroit, from 1980; pvt. practice London, from 1955. Cons. London Centre for Refractive Surgery, 1987—; mem. Brit. Acad. Experts, 1991—. Author: Intraocular Lenses and Implants, 1964; contbr. numerous articles to profl. jours. Med. Officer, Brit. Navy, 1943-46. Recipient Disting. Achievement award Am. Soc. Contemporary Ophthalmology, 1986, Mericos award Mericos Eye Inst., La Jolla, Calif., 1986, Binkhorst medal Am. Implant Soc., 1981, Internat. award of excellence in ophthalmology Hawaiian Eye Found., 1991, Innovators Lecture, ASCRS, 1993; named to Ophthalmology Hall of Fame, 2000. Fellow Royal Coll. Surgeons (Eng.; Hunterian prof.), Japanese Implant Soc.; mem. Yugoslav Implant Soc. (hon.), Kerato-Refractive Soc. (pres. 1986-89, Palaeologus medal 1984), Am. Soc. Cataract and Refractive Soc. (40th Anniversary Pioneer award 1989, nominated for induction in the Ophthalmology Hall of Fame 2000, 2001), Internat. Intraocular Implant Club (pres. 1977-80), U.K. Intraocular Implant Soc. (pres. 1980-82), So. African Implant Soc., Brit. Acad. of Experts, Expert Witness Inst., Moor Park Golf Club. Mem. Conservative Party. Achievements include research in the correction of high myopia with minus optic anterior chamber implants; medico-legal work including allegations of negligence. Home: Westcliff-on-Sea, England. Died Aug. 8, 2001.

**CHRIST, JACOB,** psychiatrist; b. Langenbruck, Basel-land, Switzerland, Feb. 10, 1926; s. Anton Leonard and Anna Alice (Kambli) C.; m. Cornelia A. van der Horst, Sept. 30, 1950 (dec. May 1952); 1 child, Frans; m. Barbara R. Fierke, Sept. 15, 1956 (dec. Nov. 1968); children: Charlotte, Martin, Catherine; m. Jane Lippincott Smith, Jan. 6, 1979; children: Heidi, Jonathan. MD, Lausanne U., Switzerland, 1951, Amsterdam U., Netherlands, 1952; MD (Thesis), U. Zürich (Switzerland), 1952. Diplomate Am. Bd. Psychiatry and Neurology; cert. Specialty Bd. Psychiatry, Switzerland. Intern U. Amsterdam Hosps., 1949-52; resident Med. Coll. Va., Richmond, 1952-53, N.Y. Hosp., Cornell Med. Ctr., 1953-54, Yale Psychiatric Inst., New Haven, Conn., 1954-55; asst. instr., clin. assoc. psychiatrist Harvard U. Med. Sch., McLean Hosp., Boston, 1956-70; assoc. prof. Emory U. Med. Sch., Atlanta, 1970-79; cons. staff Northside Community Mental Health Ctr., Atlanta, 1973-79; psychiatrist in chief External Psychiat. Svcs. of Canton Baselland, Liestal, Switzerlnad, 1979-91; pvt. practice psychiatry Basel, Switzerland, from 1991. Vis. instr. Med. U. of S.C., Charleston, 1970-77; instr. Sch. for Social Work, Basel, 1979—. Co-editor: Contemporary Marriage, 1976. Lt. USN, 1955-57. Rsch. grantee NIMH, 1967-69. Fellow Am. Psychiat. Assn., Am. Group Psychotherapy Assn. Died Mar. 17, 2008.

**CHRISTIAN, TERRY CLIFTON,** lawyer; b. Welch, W.Va., Aug. 4, 1952; s. Samuel Clifton and Mary Jane Christian; m. Wendy Lee McCoy, Feb. 14, 1991. BA, U. Del., Newark, 1984; JD, Ind. U., Indpls., 1987. Bar: Fla. 1988, US Dist. Ct. (mid. dist.) Fla. 1989, US Ct. Appeals (11th cir.) 1990 (6th cir.) 2006, US Dist. Ct. (no. and so. dists.) Fla. 1996, US Supreme Ct. 1996; cert. Bd. Legal Edn. and Specialization, Fla.; cert. Nat. Bd. Trial Advocacy. Asst. state atty. Office of State Atty., Ft. Myers, Fla., 1988-89; mng. ptnr. Christian & Assocs., P.A., Tampa, Fla., from 1989; U.S. Immigration Judge Detroit, 2003. Mem. criminal justice act panel U.S. Dist. Ct. for Mid. Dist. Fla., from 1989, for No. Dist., 1996—2000, for So. Dist., 1998—2005; spl. asst. pub. defender capital and RICO cases only, Tampa, from 1989. Author immigration and criminal law seminars. Bd. dirs. Humane Soc. Tampa Bay, 2002-03. Capt. U.S. Army Res., 1986-90. Named Best Lawyers in America, 2011; named one of Tampa's Top Atty., Tampa Bay Mag., 2010; named to Am. Leading Lawyers Bus., Chambers USA, from 2006. Mem.: FBA (exec. com. Tampa Bay chpt. 1996—2001, svc. award 1997—2001), Am. Inns of Ct. (exec. com. 2000—03, parliamentarian 2001, sec. 2002—03, svc. award 2002—03), Hillsborough County Assn. Criminal Def. Lawyers (sec. 1996—97, pres. 1997—98, bd. dirs. 1999—2002, svc. award 1998), Fla. Bar (named Fla. Super Lawyer from 2006), Am. Immigration Lawyers Assn. (sec. Ctrl. Fla. chpt. 1992—94, treas. 1994—95, v.p. 1995—97, exec. com. 2005, bd. govs. 2005, v.p. 2006—07, exec. v.p. 2007—08, pres. 2008—09, bd. govs. 2009—10, svc. award 1995—97, Outstanding Contbn. 2008, pres. from 2008, Svc. award 2009). Democrat. Roman Catholic. Avocations: reading, sports, exercise, weightlifting. Died Aug. 4, 1952.

**CHRISTOFOLETTI, ANTONIO,** geography educator; b. Rio Claro, Brazil, June 13, 1936; s. Villiariano and Olga (Rovai) C.; m. Aparecida Hebling; children: Antonio Eduardo, Anderson Luis. B in Geography, Cath. U. of Campinas, 1958; DSc, Faculty of Scis. of Rio Clan, 1968. Prof. geography Cath. U., Campinas, Brazil, 1959-71, Sao Paulo State U. (U. Estadual Paulista), Rio Claro, Brazil, 1965-94, prof. emeritus, 1994-96. Dir. Inst. Geociencias e Ciencias Exatas, Rio Claro, 1985-89; supr. Ctr. Environ. Analysis & Planning, 1993-94; titular prof. Inst. of Geoscis. and Exact Scis., Sao Paulo State U., 1979. Author: Geomorfologia, 1974, Análise de sistemas em geografia, 1979, Geomorfologia Fluvial, 1981, Perspectivas da Geografia, 1982, Geografia e Meio ambiente no Brasil, 1995, Sistemas de Informacao Geográ: Dicionário Ilustrado, 1997, Bibliografia en Sistemas de Informação Geográfica, Vol. 1, 1998, Modelugem de Sistemas Ambientais, 1999; chief editor Notícia Geomorfológica, 1966-82, Geografia, 1976-96. Home: Rio Claro, Brazil. Died Jan. 11, 1999.

**CHRYSANTHOPOULOS, THEMISTOCLES LEONIDAS,** retired ambassador; b. Canea, Crete, Greece, Aug. 9, 1915; s. Leonidas Themistocles and Jeanne (Gallenca) C.; m. Maria Botsaris, Dec. 3, 1944 (div. 1981); children: Leonidas, Daphne; m. Marie-Hermine de Magnin, Mar. 1, 1984. Degree in law, Athens U., Greece, 1938. Attache Greek Ministry Fgn. Affairs, Athens, 1945-46; mem. Paris Peace Conf., 1946; polit. advisor Greek Mil. Govt., Rhodes Dodecanese, Greece, 1947-49; vice-consul Greek Consulate Gen., Cairo, 1949-51; 2d sec. Greek Embassy, Beirut, 1951-52, press officer Washington, 1952-53, 1st sec., 1953-58, counsellor, 1958-59, charge d'affaires, 1958. Del. for Greece Founding Conf., IAEA, N.Y., 1956, UN Gen. Assembly, N.Y., 1956; consul gen. Istanbul, Turkey, 1961-65; amb. Sofia, Bulgaria, 1966-67, Tokyo, 1971-75, Ottawa, Ont., Can., 1975-78, Beijing, 1978-80. Contbr. articles to profl. jours. 2d lt. Greek mil. 1938-45. Decorated knight comdr. (Greece), Grand Cross St. Andrew (Constantinople), Grand Cross Madara (Bulgaria), Grand Cross Rising Sun (Japan), Silver Cross (Sweden). Mem. Internat. Inst. for Strategic Studies. Greek Orthodox. Avocations: citrus fruit grower in aeghion, greece. Home: Athens, Greece. Deceased.

**CHRYSOSTOMOS, (CHRISTOFOROS ARISTODIMOU),** retired archbishop of Cyprus; b. Statos, Cyprus, Sept. 27, 1927; Ordained deacon Greek Orthodox Ch., 1951, priest, 1961. Suffragan bishop, 1968-73; met. of Paphos, 1973-77; archbishop of Nova Justiniana and all Cyprus, Nicosia, 1977—2006. Died Dec. 22, 2007.

**CHRYSTIE, THOMAS LUDLOW,** investor; b. NYC, May 24, 1933; s. Thomas Witter and Helen (Duell) C.; m. Eliza S. Balis, June 9, 1955; children: Alice B., Helen S., Adden B., James McD. BA, Columbia U., 1955; MBA, NYU, 1960. With Merrill Lynch, NYC, 1955; dir. investment banking divsn. Merrill Lynch, Pierce, Fenner & Smith, Inc., NYC, 1970-75; sr. v.p. Merrill Lynch & Co., 1975-78, CFO, 1976-78; chmn. Merrill Lynch White Weld Capital Markets Group, 1978-81, Merrill Lynch Capital Resources, 1981-83; adv. on strategy Merrill Lynch & Co. Inc., 1983-88; pvt. investor Jackson, Wyo., 1988—2013. Trustee emeritus Columbia U., Nat. Mus. Wildlife Art. Capt. USAF, 1955-58. Mem. Teton Pines Tennis Club. *Whatever you are involved in, see it as part of a larger picture.* Died Dec. 24, 2013.

**CHUNDER, PRATAP CHANDRA,** lawyer; b. Calcutta, India, Sept. 1, 1919; s. Nirmal and Suhasini Chunder; m. Leena Roy Chowdhury, 1940; 4 children. MA, LLB, PhD, U. Calcutta; DLitt, DSc. Law practice, Calcutta, 1945; mem. Senate and Law Faculty of Calcutta U., 1961—68, Exec. Coun. Rabindra Bharati U., 1962—68, West Bengal Legis. Assembly, 1962—68; pres. West Bengal Provincial Congress Com., 1967—69; Min. Fin. and Judiciary in State Govt., 1968; mem. Working Com. and Ctrl. Parliament Bd. of Org. Congress, 1969—76, Janata Party, 1977—2008, Lok Sabha from Calcutta, 1977—79; Union Min. of Edn., Social Welfare, and Culture, 1977—79; mem. Calcutta Bar Assn.; pres. Internat. Edn. Conf., UNESCO, 1977—79, Indo-American Soc., 1984—92, 1997—2008, Writers' Guild of India, 1985—2008, Bengali Literary Conf., 1987—2008, All India Buddhist Mission, 1989—2008, Iran Soc., 1990—92, Indian Inst. of Social Welfare and Bus. Mgmt., 1991—2008, World Bengali Conf., 1991, Soc. for the Deaf, 1991—94, Bharatiya Vidya Bhavan Calcutta Agartala Region, 1993—2008, Inc. Law Soc., 1995—98; trustee Victoria Memorial, 1990—98, 1999—2008, Sardar V.B. Patel Mem. Trust, 1991—98; Regional Grand Master of Eastern India, 1990—93; Dep. Grand Master, 1993—94; patron Mahabodhi Soc. of India, 1995—2008; chmn. Planning Bd., Asiatic Soc., 1998—2003, West Bengal Heritage Commn., 2001—08. Former editor for several Bengali literary magazines. Author: (plays) Bubhuksa, Sahartali, Prajapati, Amlamadhor, Ajab Desh (puppet play), (TV films) Lebedeff Ki Nakiya, (films) Sankha Sindur, Job Charnocker Bibi; exhibitions include, in Calcutta, New Delhi, 1982, 1984, 1985, 1987, 1999, 2002, 2003; author: (books) Kautilya on Love and Morals, The Sons of Mystery, Job Charnock and his Lady Fair, In Captivity, Socialist Legality and Indian Law, Brother Vivekanamda, Facets of Freemasonry, Kautilya Arthasastra, Two Funny Puppet Plays, Living Education and Glimpses of Indian Culture. Recipient Best Playwright award, Calcutta U., 1965, Bhalotia Prize for Best Novel, 1991, Indira Gandhi Mem. Prize for Edn., 1992, Mother Theresa award, 1998, Medal of Sophia U., AIFACS Award for Art, 2002; named Hon. Citizen of New Orleans, USA. Fellow: Asiatic Soc. of Calcutta. Avocations: reading, writing, painting. Died Jan. 1, 2008.

**CHUNG, MONG-HUN,** company executive; b. Seoul, Korea, Sept. 14, 1948; 3 children. Grad. in Korean Lang. and Lit., Yonsei U., 1972; grad. in Bus. Adminstrn., 1979, Fairleigh Dickinson U., 1983; D in Bus. Adminstrn. (hon.), Yonsei U., 1998. Gen. mgr. Hyundai Heavy Industries Co., Ltd., 1975-77; gen. mgr., dir. Hyundai Engring. and Constrn. Co., Ltd., 1977-78, mng. dir., 1978-81; pres., CEO Hyundai Merchant Marine Co., Ltd., 1981-88, Hyundai Electronics Industries Co., Ltd., 1984-91; pres. Hyundai Magnetics Co., Ltd., 1986; chmn., CEO Hyundai Merchant Marine Co., Ltd., 1988, Hyundai Elevator Co., Ltd., 1989-92, 97-2000, Hyundai Electronics Industries Co., Ltd., 1992, Hyundai Info. Tech. Co., Ltd., 1993, Hyundai Engring. and Constrn. Co., Ltd., 1997-2000, Diamond AD Co., Ltd., 1996; vice chmn. Hyundai Group, 1996-98, mem. steering com., 1996; owner Hyundai Unicorns Pro-Baseball Club, 1996; dir. Hyundai Electronics Industries Co., Ltd., 1998-2000; chmn. Hyundai Employers Fedn., 1998-2000; dir. Hyundai Motor Co., Ltd., 1997-2000. Chmn. Ctrl. Union Saemaul Badminton, 1984, Radio Comm. Industries Korea, 1990-92, Agy. Tech. and Stds., 1991-93; vice chmn. Info. Industries Fedn., 1986; CEO Korea Elec. Testing Inst., 1994; dir. Korea Employers Fedn., 1994; chmn. in charge of overseas bus. divsn. Hyundai Group, 1998-2000; chmn. bd. dirs. Hyundai Asan Corp. Mem. Electronic Industries Assn. Korea (vice chmn. 1984-94), Assn. Korea Sports for All (vice chmn. 1984), Korea Shipowners Assn. (vice chmn. 1984), Info. and Comm. Assn. (vice chmn. 1986), Fedn. Korean Info. Industries (vice chmn. 1988-94), Korea Semiconductor Industry Assn. (vice chmn. 1991-94) Died Aug. 4, 2003.

**CHUNG, SE-YUNG,** motor company executive; b. Seoul, Republic of Korea, Aug. 6, 1923; s. Bong Sik and Seong Sil (Han) Chung; m. Young Ja Park Chung, Mar. 10, 1960; children: Sook Young, Mong Kyu, Yoo Kyoung. BS in Polit. Sci., Korea U., Seoul, 1953; MS in Polit. Sci., Miami U., Oxford, Ohio, 1957; LLD, Miami U., 1983. Mng. dir. Hyundai Engring & Constrn. Co., Ltd., Seoul, 1960—67; pres. Hyundai Motor Co., Seoul, 1967, chmn. bd.; advisor Korea Automobile Indsl. Coop., Seoul, Republic of Korea, 1970; pres. Seoul, 1977; exec. dir. Fedn. Korean Industries, Seoul, 1979—87, vice-chmn.; dep. chmn. Korea Advanced Inst. Sci. & Tech., Seoul, 1982, Korea-U.S. Bus. Coun., 1988; chmn. Hyundai Bus. Group, 1987. Decorated grand Prix Korea Mgmt. Assn.; recipient Tin Tower award, growth nat. soc. award, Dep. Prime Min., Seoul, 1980; named Hon. Comdr. British Empire, Her Majesty Queen Elizabeth II, Seoul, 1983. Mem.: Korean Invention & Patent Assn. (vice-chmn. 1982), Korea-Japan Econ. Assn. (dep. chmn. from 1981), Korea British Bus. Promotion Com. (chmn. 1977), Korea Automobile Assn. Home: Seoul, Republic of Korea. Died May 21, 2005.

**CHURCHILL, RUEL VANCE,** mathematician; b. Akron, Ind., Dec. 12, 1899; s. Abner C. and Meldora (Friend) C.; m. Ruby F. Sicks, 1922 (dec. 1969); children: Betty Churchill McMurray, Eugene S.; m. Alice B. Warren, 1972. BS, U. Chgo., 1922; MS, U. Mich., 1925, PhD, 1929. Faculty U. Mich., Ann Arbor, 1922—, prof. math., 1942-65, emeritus, from 1965. Vis. lectr. U. Wis., 1941; research U. Freiburg, Germany, 1936, Calif. Inst. Tech., 1949; research specialist USAAF, 1944; mem. NRC, 1947-50 Author: books including Complex Variables and Applications, 1948, 4th edit. (with J.W. Brown),1984, Japanese edit., 1975, Spanish edit., 1978; Operational Mathematics, 1944, Japanese edit. 1950, Fourier Series, 1941, 4th edit. (with J.W. Brown) 1987, Japanese edit., 1960, Spanish edit., 1966, Portuguese edit., 1978. Home: Ann Arbor, Mich. Deceased.

**CIFUENTES, INÈS LUCÍA,** seismologist, educator; b. London; married; 2 children. BS in Physics, Swarthmore Coll., Pa., 1976; MS in Geophysics, Stanford U., Calif., 1979; PhD in Seismology, Columbia U., NYC, 1988. Field rschr. US Geological Survey; dir. Carnegie Acad. Sci. Edn., Washington, 1994—2005; edn. and careers mgr. American Geophysical Union, 2005—14. Bd. mem. Carnegie Acad. Sci. Edn., Md., from 2002. Contbr. articles to sci. jours. Steering com. Achievement Initiative Minority Students, Md. Recipient Math. & Sci. award, Hispanic Heritage Found., 2007; named Nat. Hispanic Scientist of Yr., Mus. Sci. & Industry, Tampa, Fla., 2006. Died Dec. 16, 2014.

**CIGLAR, IVAN,** education educator, agricultural engineer, environmental scientist; b. Mala Subotica, Croatia, Dec. 20, 1933; s. Melko and Katarina Pintaric; m. Jakica Petric, Nov. 20, 1962; children: Gordan, Andrej. BA, Faculty of Agrl., Zagreb, 1961, MA, 1971, PhD, 1975. Asst. Faculty of agrl., Zageb, 1961—63; advisor for plant protection Vineyards and Orchards in Oran Algeria, 1963—65; scientist State Inst. for Plant Protection, Zagreb, 1976—81; prof. Faculty of Agrl., 1981—99; scientifically advisor Intergrated plant Protection in Orchards, from 1999. Author: Intergrated Plant Protection in Orchards and Vineyards, 1989, 1998, Safety Orchards and Vineyards, 1980, 1994; contbr. scientific papers 60 to profl. jour., 80 to profl. jour. Mem.: IOBC, Croation Soc. of Plant Protection, Croatian Soc. of Entomology. Home: Zagreb, Croatia. Died Oct. 13, 2003.

**CLABAUGH, ELMER EUGENE, JR.,** retired lawyer; b. Anaheim, Calif., Sept. 18, 1927; s. Elmer Eugene and Eleanor Margaret (Heitshusen) C.; m. Donna Marie Organ, Dec. 19, 1960 (div.); children: Christopher C., Matthew M. BBA cum laude, Woodbury U.; BA summa cum laude, Claremont McKenna Coll., 1958; JD, Stanford U., 1961. Bar: Calif. 1961, U.S. Dist. Ct. (cen. dist.) Calif., U.S. Ct. Appeals (9th cir.) 1961, U.S. Supreme Ct. 1971. With fgn. svc. U.S. Dept. State, Jerusalem, Tel Aviv, 1951-53, Pub. Adminstrn. Svcs., El Salvador, Ethiopia, U.S., 1953-57; dep. dist. atty. Ventura County, Calif., 1961-62; pvt. practice, 1962-97; mem. Hathaway, Clabaugh, Perrett and Webster and predecessors, 1962-79, Clabaugh & Perfloff, Ventura, 1979-97; state inheritance tax referee, 1968-78; ret. Bd. dirs. San Antonio Water Conservation Dist., Ventura Cmty. Meml. Hosp., 1964-80; trustee Ojai Unified Sch. Dist., 1974-79; bd. dirs. Ventura County Found. for Parks and Harbors, 1982-96, Ventura County Maritime Mus., 1982-94. With USCGR, 1944-46, USMCR, 1946-48. Mem. NRA, Calif. Bar Assn., Safari Club Internat., Mason, Shriners, Phi Alpha Delta. Republican. Deceased.

**CLABBY, WILLIAM ROBERT,** editor; b. Waterloo, Iowa, Feb. 12, 1931; s. James Francis and Pearl Marie (Bloes) C.; m. Joann Alma Carroll, Aug. 9, 1952; children—Theresa, Joseph, Dennis, Carolyn, Kathleen, Maureen, Timothy, Margaret, Brigid, Erin. Student, No. Iowa U., 1949-51; BA, U. Iowa, 1953. With Dow Jones & Co., NYC, from 1953; bur. mgr. Wall St. Jour., NYC, 1966-71; mng. editor AP-Dow Jones, 1971-77; v.p. Dow Jones News Services, 1977. Mem. Omicron Delta Kappa, Sigma Delta Chi. Roman Catholic. Died Dec. 9, 1997.

**CLAEYS, EDDY,** electrical engineer; b. Ghent, Belgium, July 21, 1964; s. Emiel Claeys and Mekeirle Georgette; m. Marisa Tondat; children: Lisa, Max. Degree, DBZ, Gent. Failure engr. Alcatel Microelectronis, Oudenaarde, Belgium, from 1983. Home:, Belgium. Deceased.

**CLANCY, EDWARD BEDE CARDINAL,** cardinal, archbishop emeritus; b. Lithgow, NSW, Australia, Dec. 13, 1923; s. John Bede and Ellen Lucy (Edwards) C. Graduate, Saint Columba's Coll., Springwood, NSW, Saint Patrick's Coll., Manly, NSW; ThD, Pontifical Urbaniana U.; Degree in Sacred Scripture, Pontifical Bibl. Inst., Rome; DD, Propaganda Fide U., Rome; HHD (hon.), Atenea Pe Manila, 2001; PhD (hon.), Cath. U., Australia, 2001. Ordained priest of Sydney, Australia, 1949, aux. bishop, 1973—78, archbishop, 1983—2001, archbishop emeritus, 2001—14; parish min. Belmore, Australia, 1950-1951, Liverpool, Australia, 1955—57; sem. staff Springwood, Australia, 1958, Manly, Australia, 1966-1973; appointed Titular Bishop of Ard Carna, 1973, ordained, 1974; archbishop of Canberra and Goulburn, Australia, 1978—83; chancellor Australian Catholic U., 1992—2001; elevated to cardinal, 1988; cardinal-priest of Santa Maria in Vallicella (Saint Mary in Vallicella), 1988—2014. Prof. sacred scripture Coll. of Saint Columbia, Springfield, 1958, Saint Patrick's Coll., Manly, 1961; chaplain U. Sydney, 1961; pres. Australian Catholic Bishops' Conference, 1986—2000; pres. delegate 9th General Assembly of the Synod of Bishops on Consecrated Life, 1994. Author: The Bible-The Church's Book, 1974, Comeback-The Church Loves You, 2002, Walk Worthy of Your Vocation, 2004, God's Trailblazers, 2005; contbr. to Australian Cath. Record. Decorated Order of Australia, 1984, Companion of Australia, 1992. Roman Catholic. Avocations: reading, golf. Died Aug. 3, 2014.

**CLARE, ANTHONY WARD,** psychiatry educator, hospital administrator; b. Dublin, Dec. 24, 1942; s. Bernard Joseph Clare and Mary Agnes Dunne; m. Jane Carmel Hogan, Oct. 4, 1966; children: Rachel, Simon, Eleanor, Peter, Sophie, Justine, Sebastian. MB BChir, Univ. Coll., Dublin, 1966; MPhil, London U., 1972; MD, Nat. U. Ireland, 1983; DSc (hon.), U. East Anglia, 1996; DPhil (hon.), Open U., Eng., 1994. Registrar St. Patrick's Hosp., Dublin, 1967-69; registrar, sr. registrar Maudsley Hosp., London, 1970-75; lectr., sr. lectr. Inst. Psychiatry, London, 1976-82; prof. psychol. medicine St. Bartholomew's Hosp., London, 1983-89; med. dir. St. Patrick's Hosp., Dublin, from 1989; clin. prof. psychiatry Trinity Coll., Dublin, from 1989. Chmn. cen. com. King's Fund, London, 1984-89, Prince of Wales Adv. Group on Disability, London, 1989-97, Agy. for Personal Svc. Overseas, Dublin, 1994-99. Author: (books) Psychiatry in Dissent, 1976, Let's Talk About Me, 1981, In the Psychiatrist's Chair, 1984, vol. II, 1995, vol. III, 1998, On Men: Crisis in Masculinity, 2000. Recipient Sony award for Best Radio Interview of Yr., Sony Corp., 1996. Fellow Royal Coll. Physicians of Ireland, Royal Coll. Psychiatrists (London; v.p. 1994-96), Royal Coll. Physicians (London); mem. Garrick Club. Avocations: broadcasting, theater, writing. Died Oct. 2007.

**CLARK, ALASTAIR TREVOR,** barrister, museum administrator; b. Glasgow, U.K., June 10, 1923; s. William George and Gladys Catherine (Harrison) C.; m. Hilary Agnes Mackenzie Anderson, May 1, 1965. BA, Magdalen Coll., 1947, MA, 1948; postgrad., Ashridge Mgmt. Coll., 1963. Called to bar: Middle Temple, Inns of Ct. 1963. Sec. to cabinet, sr. dist. officer H.M. Overseas Civil Svc., Northern Nigeria, 1948-59; prin. asst., colonial sec., acting chmn. Urban Coun., Hong Kong, 1960-72; chief sec. Western pacific high commn., acting gov. Solomon Islands, 1972-77; councillor City of Edinburgh Coun., Scotland, 1980-88; chmn. Scottish Mus. Coun., Scotland, 1981-84, 87-90; trustee Nat. Mus. of Scotland, 1985—87, Nat. Mus. of Scotland Charitable Trust, from 1987. Dir. Royal Lyceum Theatre, Edinburgh, 1982-84, Edinburgh Acad., 1979-84; gov. Edinburgh Filmhouse, 1980-81, 1987-2002; vice chmn. Almond Valley Heritage Trust, Livingston, Scotland, 1990-2003. Author: A Right Honorable Gentleman: Abubakar From the Black Rock, 1991, Was it Only Yesterday? The Last Generation of Nigeria's Turawa, 2002, Good Second Class, 2004; contbr. articles to profl. jours. Trustee Smith Art Gallery and Mus., Stirling, Scotland, 1993-2004; councillor Edinburgh Internat. Festival, 1980-86, 90-94; sec. St. John's Cathedral Coun., Hong Kong, 1963-72; assessor Scottish Sheriff Cts. Race Rels. Adv. Panel, Scotland, 1983—. Maj. Cameron Highlanders and Royal West African Frontier Force, 1942-46. Decorated Comdr. Order Brit. Empire, Lt.Royal Victorian Order; country leader fellowship U.S. State Dept., 1972; grantee Leverhulme Trust, 1979-81. Fellow Soc. of Antiquaries of Scotland, Royal Scottish Soc. of Arts (coun. mem. 1999-2002); mem. The Athenaeum, The New Club. Avocations: music, theater, collecting netsuke, reading, museums and galleries. Home: Edinburgh, Scotland. Died May 24, 2005.

**CLARK, IRA GRANVILLE,** historian, educator; b. Amarillo, Tex., Jan. 23, 1909; s. Ira Granville and Centennial Germany (Seeger) C.; m. Jennalee McFall, Aug. 8, 1937 (dec. 1994); children: Ira Granville, David McFall. BA, West Tex. State Tchrs. Coll., 1931; MA, U. Okla., 1937; PhD, U. Calif., 1947. Tchr. pub. schs., Hollister, Okla., 1931-35; instr. Cen. High Sch. and Jr. Coll., Muskogee, Okla., 1937-42; from instr. to assoc. prof. N.Mex. State U., Las Cruces, 1942-51, prof., 1951-75, prof. emeritus, from 1975. State supr. Emergency Farm Labor program Agrl. Extension Svc., Las Cruces, 1943-45; cons. N.Mex. State Engr. Office, Santa Fe, 1981-82, Rio Grande Hist. Collections, N.Mex. State U. Libr., 1984, N.Mex. State Land Office, Santa Fe, 1988-89. Author: Then Came the Railroads, 1958, Water in New Mexico, 1987 (Border Regional Libr. Assn. award 1988); author (with others): Aridity and Man, 1963. Recipient Cert. of Recognition Gov. N.Mex., Santa Fe, 1976, Paso por Aqui award Rio Grande Hist. Collections, Las Cruces, N.Mex. 1987, Hon. Mention Abel Wolman award Am. Pub. Works Assn., 1988, Heritage Preservation award State N.Mex. 1988. Fellow AAAS; mem. Am. Hist. Assn., Orgn. Am. Historians, Western Hist. Assn. (coun. 1971-73, award of honor 1976), Agrl. Hist. Soc., Hist. Soc. N.Mex. (patron, bd. dirs. award 1988), Dona Ana County Hist. Soc. (patron, Pasajero del Camino Real award 1989). Democrat. United Methodist. Avocations: walking, bridge. Home: Mesilla Park, N.Mex. Deceased.

**CLARK, MARY TWIBILL,** philosophy educator; b. Phila., Oct. 23, 1913; d. Francis S. and Regina (Twibill) Clark. BA, Manhattanville Coll., 1939, L.H.D. (hon.), 1984; MA, Fordham U., 1952, PhD, 1955; postgrad., Yale U., 1968-69; L.H.D. (hon.), Villanova U., 1977. Joined Soc. Sacred Heart, 1939. Tchr., supr. studies secondary schs. Acad. Sacred Heart, Albany, Overbrook, Rochester and NYC, 1941-51; instr. Manhattanville Coll., Purchase, N.Y., 1951-53, asst. prof., 1953-57, assoc. prof., 1957-61, prof. philosophy, 1961-84, chmn. dept., 1962-64, 66-68, 72-79, prof. emeritus, 1984—2014, Clark chair in Christian philosophy, 2005—14. Vis. prof. Villanova U., 1980, Fordham U., 1981, 90, 93, Santa Clara U., 1983, NYU, 1989, SUNY-Purchase, 1991, Fairfield U., 1992, Marquette U., 1993, U. San Francisco, 6 summers; adviser Intercollegiate Assns., Social Action Secretariat, 1956-66; mem. advisory bd. Dionysius, 1977-99, Faith and Philosophy, 1984-87 Author: Augustine, Philosopher of Freedom, 1959, Logic, 1963, Discrimination Today, 1966, Augustinian Personalism, 1970, Augustine: An Introduction, 1994; editor: An Aquinas Reader, 1972, rev. edit., 2000, The Problem of Freedom, 1973; translator: Theological Treatises of Marius Victorinus, 1981, Augustine of Hippo's Spirituality, 1984; contbr. articles to profl. jours. Trustee Country Day Sch. of the Sacred Heart, Bryn Mawr, 1993-2004. Recipient Disting. Alumna award Country Day Sch. Sacred Heart, Bryn Mawr, 1992, Disting. Alumna award Manhattanville Coll., 1999, Corunum award, Associated Alumnae of the Sacred Heart, 2005; NEH fellow, 1984-85; hon. mem. Order St. Augustine. Mem. American Cath. Philos. Assn. (pres. 1976-77, Aquinas medal 1988), American Philos. Assn. (conf. chmn. 1974-76, exec. com. 1988-91), Metaphys. Soc. (exec. com. 1985-88, v.p. 1990-91, pres. 1991-92), Internat. Patristic Assn., Soc. Medieval & Renaissance Philosophy (sec.-treas. 1977-91, v.p. 1991-92, pres. 1992-94), Internat. Neoplatonic Soc., Conf. Philos. Soc. (exec. com. 1978-86), Soc. Christian Philosophers (exec. com. 1981-84), Cath. Com. Intellectual & Cultural Affairs (exec. com. 1989-92), Kappa Gamma Pi. *Human persons are the world's richest resources - to be cherished and developed.* Died Sept. 1, 2014.

**CLARKE, CHARLES FENTON,** lawyer; b. Hillsboro, Ohio, July 25, 1916; s. Charles F. and Margaret (Patton) C.; m. Virginia Schoppenhorst, Apr. 3, 1945 (dec. July 1989); children: Elizabeth, Margaret, Jane, Charles Fenton, IV; m. Lesley Wells, Nov. 13, 1998. AB summa cum laude, Washington and Lee U., 1938; LLB, U. Mich., 1940; LLD (hon.), Cleve. State U., 1971. Bar: Mich. 1940, Ohio 1946. Pvt. practice, Detroit, 1942, Cleve., from 1946; ptnr. firm Squire, Sanders & Dempsey, from 1957, adminstr. litigation dept., 1979-85. Trustee Cleve. Legal Aid Soc., 1959-67; pres. Nat. Assn. R.R. Trial Counsel, 1966-68; life mem. 6th Circuit Jud. Conf.; chmn. legis. com. Cleve. Welfare Fedn., 1961-68; master bencher Manos Inn of Ct., 1991—; bd. dirs. Wheeling and Lake Erie R.R. Co. Pres. alumni bd. dirs. Washington and Lee U., 1970-72; pres. bd. dirs. Free Med. Clinic Greater Cleve., 1970-86; trustee Cleve. Citizens League, 1956-62, Cleve. chpt. ACLU, 1986-93; bd. dirs. citizens adv. bd. Cuyahoga County (Ohio) Juvenile Ct., 1970-73; bd. dirs. George Jr. Republic, Greenville, Pa., 1970-73, Bowman Tech. Sch., Cleve., 1970-91; vice chmn. Cleve. Crime Commn., 1973-75; exec. com. councilman Bay Village, Ohio, 1948-53; pres., trustee Cleve. Hearing and Speech Ctr., 1957-62, Laurel Sch., 1962-72, Fedn. Cmty. Progress, 1984-90; mem. planning commn. Cleveland Heights, 1994-2003. Fellow Am. Coll. Trial Lawyers; mem. Met. Bar Assn. (trustee 1983-86), Cleve. Civil War Round Table (pres. 1968), Cleve. Zool. Soc. (dir. 1970), Phi Beta Kappa. Clubs: Skating, Union (Cleve.); Tavern. Presbyterian. Home: Cleveland Heights, Ohio. Died Jan. 17, 2014.

**CLARKE, JAMES MCCLURE,** congressman; b. Manchester, Vt., June 12, 1917; m. Elspeth McClure, 1945; children: Susie, Jim, Annie, Dumont, Mark, Billy, Ambrose (dec.), Doug. Assoc. editor Asheville (N.C.) Citizen Times, 1960-69; asst. to pres. Warren Wilson Coll., 1969-81; dairy farm and apple orchard operator; mem. 98th Congress from 11th Dist. N.C., 1983-85; chmn. Buncombe County Bd. Edn., 1969-76; sec. James G.K. McClure Found., 1956-82; mem. N.C. Ho. of Reps., 1977-80, N.C. State Senate, 1981-82, 100th-101st Congresses from N.C. 11th Dist., 1987-90. Mem. Gov.'s Crime Commn.; bd. dirs. Eckerd Wilderness Ednl. Systems; trustee Thoms Rehab. Hosp., Southeastern Council Founds.; hon. trustee N.C. Symphony; former bd. dirs. Fairview Vol. Fire Dept.; former elder Warren Wilson Presbyn. Ch. Served to lt. USNR, 1942-45. Mem.: Asheville Civitan. Democrat. Died Apr. 1999.

**CLARKE, J(OHN) NEIL,** accountant; b. Aug. 7, 1934; s. George Philip and Norah Marie (Bailey) Clarke; m. Sonia Heather Beckett, 1958 (dec. 2009); 3 children. LLB, U. London. Chartered acct. Ptnr. Rowley, Pemberton, Roberts and Co., England, 1960—69; with Charter Consol., 1969—88, dep. chmn., CEO, 1982—88; chmn. Brit. Coal Corp., London, 1991—97. Chmn. Johnson Matthey, 1984—89, Anderson Strathclyde, 1987—88, Molins, 1989—91, Genchem Holdings, 1989—2006. Decorated chevalier Nat. Order of Merit (France). Mem.: Addington Golf Club, Royal West Norfolk Golf Club, Marylebone Cricket Club. Avocations: music, tennis, golf. Died Nov. 2011.

**CLAUTICE, EDWARD WELLMORE,** retired industrial engineer; b. Balt., Oct. 13, 1916; s. George Joseph and Janet Harwood (Wellmore) C.; m. Mary Madelyn Spraker, Aug. 30, 1941; children: Elizabeth F., Stephen F., Christopher G., Michael J., Edward G. BS in Engring., Johns Hopkins U., 1938; MBA, Boston U., 1964. Registered profl. engr., Pa. Commd. 1st lt. US Army, 1942-64, advanced through grades to lt. col., 1950, various tech. sci. teaching positions N.Mex, Md., Thailand, 1947-52, ret., 1964; prodn. engr. Koppers Co., Balt., 1940-41; ptnr., co-owner Lane Clautice Engr. Co., Balt., 1945-47; coord. research and devel. Ballistics Research Labs., Aberdeen Proving Ground, Md., 1952-58; research and devel. liaison officer Can. Army Devel. Establishment, Ottawa, Ont., 1958-61; chief ops. Watertown Arsenal, NY, 1961-64; chief indsl. engr. Joy Mfg. Co., Franklin, Pa., 1964-66; mgr., indsl. engr. AMF, Inc., York, Pa., 1966-79; ret., 1979. Cons. in field, York, 1979—; tchr. Pa. State U., York, 1967-1973; lectr. Soc. Mfg. Engrs., Detroit, 1967, 69, Mgmt. Engring. Trng. Agy, Rock Island, Ill., 1965. Author: A Little Nonsense, 1987, A Lotta Nonsense, 1992, Madelyn, My Wife, Our Mother, 1995, A Potpourri of Poetry, 2002; author numerous poems (2 Golds, 1 Silver, 3 honorable mention awards World of Poetry 1986-89); contbr. articles to profl. jours. Counselor, Service Corps. Ret. Execs., York, 1982-87; active Township Sewer Authority. Recipient numerous athletic awards. Mem.: Tennis (York). Republican. Roman Catholic. Avocations: theater, tennis, contract bridge, woodworking, cooking. Died Feb. 12, 2008.

**CLAY, JOHN HARRIS, JR.,** secondary school educator; b. Phila., June 7, 1961; s. John H. Sr. and Annie Louise (Jackson) C. BA, Princeton U., 1983; postgrad., Howard U., 1984-85, L.I. U., from 1994, NYU, from 1996. Lic. social studies, bilingual social studies tchr., N.Y. Tchr. Walton H.S., Bronx, N.Y., 1990, Stevenson H.S., Bronx, 1990-91, Evander Childs H.S., Bronx, 1991-92; bilingual social studies tchr. Sarah J. Hole H.S., Bklyn., from 1992. Author: City of Tranquil Light, 1998. Mem. ASCD, Woodrow Wilson Soc. (assoc.), Princeton Alumni Assn., Black Alumni of Princeton, Princeton Club of N.Y. Republican. Buddhist. Avocations: writing, research, hiking, swimming, playing piano and violin. Home: Goochland, Va. Died Nov. 20, 1999.

**CLAYMAN, DAVID,** rabbi, academic administrator; b. Cambridge, Mass., Sept. 8, 1933; s. Benjamin and Sophie (Kushner) C.; m. Rachel Kestenbaum, June 17, 1956; children: Tamar, Daniel, Jonathan. BA, Harvard Coll., 1954; B.H.L., Hebrew Coll., Brookline, Mass., 1955; M.H.L., Jewish Theol. Sem., NYC, 1959, DD (hon.), 1986. Chaplain U.S. Navy, 1959-61; assoc. rabbi Temple Har Zion, Phila., 1961-64; rabbi Congregation Ramat El, Phila., 1964-70; Israel dir. Am. Jewish Congress., Jerusalem, from 1980. Author: (jour.) The Congress Monthly, (newsletter) The Jerusalem Letter. Dir. Louise Waterman Wise Youth Hostel, Jerusalem, 1980—. Lt. USN, 1959-61. Fellow Jerusalem Ctr. for Pub. Affairs, 1976—. Mem. Rabbinical Assembly. Home: Jerusalem, Israel. Died May 21, 2003.

**CLERIDES, GLAFCOS JOHN,** former President of Cyprus, lawyer; b. Nicosia, Cyprus, Apr. 24, 1919; s. John and Elli C.; m. Lilla Erulkar, 1945 (dec. 2007); 1 child, Katherine Grad., Pancyprian Gymnasium, Nicosia, London U. Bar: Gray's Inn 1951. Practiced law, Cyprus, 1951-60; min. justice Republic of Cyprus, 1959-60; mem. Cypriot House of Reps., 1960-76, 81-93, pres., 1960-76; acting pres. Republic of Cyprus, 1974, pres., 1993—2003. Head Greek Cypriot Del. Joint Constnl. Com., 1959-60; Greek Cypriot del. London Conf., 1964; rep. negotiator Greek Cypriot Cmty. Intercommunal Talks, 1968. Author: My Deposition, vol. 1, 1988, vol. 2, 1989, vol. 3, 1990, vol. 4, 1991. Pres. Red Cross, 1961-63, hon. cert., hon. life mem., Recognition Disting. Svc.; founder Unified Party, 1969, Democratic Nat. Front; leading mem. Unified Party, Progressive Front, Dem. Nat. Front, 1976; pres. Dem. Rally, 1976-93. Served with RAF, 1939-47, POW, 1942-45. Decorated Gold Medal-Order Holy Sepulchre, Recognized Svcs. and Understanding Roman Cath. Religious Group by approval of His Holiness Pope John XXIII, Grand Cross of Saviour, Greece; mentioned in dispaches for disting. svc., 1949. Home: Nicosia, Cyprus. Died Nov. 15, 2013.

**CLINCH, JOHN HOUSTOUN MCINTOSH,** management company executive, lawyer; b. Danville, Ill., Aug. 18, 1902; s. John Houstoun McIntosh and Edna L. (Wilber) C.; m. Frances S. Bell, June 25, 1927; children: Frances Clinch Jones, J. Houstoun M. Student, U. Ill., 1920-22, John Marshall Law Sch., 1942; AB, U. Chgo., 1924. With Chgo. North Shore & Milw. Ry. (now Susquehanna Corp.), 1925-57, pres., 1948-57, Consol. Mgmt. Co., from 1957; v.p. Middle West Service Co., 1963-74; lectr., instr. Grad. Sch. Bus., U. Chgo., 1958-63; spl. asst. atty. gen. State of N.Mex., 1969-70. Spl. cons. Ill. Commerce Commn.; spl. counsel Iowa Commerce Commn., Minn. Pub. Service Commn., 1971 Mem. Winnetka Caucus Com. Mem. Chgo. Bar Assn., Sigma Alpha Epsilon. Clubs: University (Chgo.); Bird Key Yacht (Sarasota, Fla.). Episcopalian. Home: Sarasota, Fla. Died 1991.

**CLOAKE, JOHN CECIL,** retired British diplomat, historian; b. Wimbledon, Surrey, Eng., Dec. 2, 1924; s. Cecil Stedman and Maude Osborne (Newling) C.; m. Margaret Thomure Morris, Oct. 6, 1956 (dec. 2008); 1 child, John Newling. MA, Cambridge U., Eng., 1948. With Brit. Diplomatic Svc., 1948-80; assigned to London, Baghdad, Saigon, 1948-58; comml. consul Brit. Consulate Gen., NYC, 1958-62; 1st sec. Brit. Embassy, Moscow, 1962-63; with Brit. Diplomatic Svc. Adminstrn., London, 1963-68; comml. counsellor Brit. Embassy, Tehran, Iran, 1968-72; head dept. Fgn. and Commonwealth Office, London, 1973-76; amb. to Bulgaria Brit. Embassy, Sofia, 1976-80. Vis. fellow London Sch. Economics, 1972-73. Author: Templer, Tiger of Malaya, 1985, Richmond Past, 1991, Royal Bounty, 1992, Palaces and Parks of Richmond and Kew, Vol. 1, 1995, Vol. 2, 1996, Richmond Past and Present, 1999, Cottages and Common Fields of Richmond and Kew, 2001; editor, co-author: Richmond in Old Photographs, 1990; also numerous monographs and articles on local history. Chmn. Mus. of Richmond, 1986-95. With British Army 1943-46. Decorated companion Order of St. Michael and St. George, 1977. Fellow Soc. Antiquaries of London; mem. Brit. Inst. Persian Studies (coun. 1981-95, hon. treas. 1982-90), Richmond Local History Soc. (chmn. 1985-90). Avocations: local history, family history, gardening, music. Home: Richmond, England. Died July 9, 2014.

**COCKBURN, JILL,** behavioral epidemiologist, researcher; b. Newcastle, Australia, June 28, 1956; d. George Buchanon and Joy (Telfor) C.; m. Craig Douglas Wilson, Mar. 7, 1992. BS with honors, U. Newcastle, NSW, 1980, PhD, 1986; MS, London Sch. Hygiene and Tropical Medicine, 1993. Prof. rsch. acad. faculty medicine and health scis. U. Newcastle, 1986-87; rsch. acad. Sch. Pub. Health U. Sydney, NSW, 1987-88; sr. behavioural scientist Anti-Cancer Coun. Victoria, 1988-95; head discipline of behavioural sci. in relation to medicine U. Newcastle, 1996-99, head Sch. of Population Health Scis., 1999-2000; dir. rsch. Hunter Ctr. for Health Advancement, NSW, 1998-2000. Bd. dirs. NSW Cancer Coun.; mem. exec. com. Newcastle Inst. Pub. Health, 1997-98. Contbr. articles to profl. jours. Mem. psychosocial working party Nat. Breast Cancer Ctr., Sydney, 1996—; chair Cervical Screening Adv. Network, Hunter Region, 1997—; mem. adv. com. Nat. Heart Found., Newcastle, 1997—. Recipient fellowship Victorian Health Promotion Found., 1992. Died Oct. 13, 2004.

**COFFELT, JOHN J.,** retired university president; b. Neosho, Mo., Dec. 26, 1924; s. Roscoe John and Estella Matilda (Turner) C.; m. Anna Marie Nelson, Feb. 27, 1945; children: Susan Ann (Mrs. Robert Lyon), Margaret Jean (Mrs. Duane Spatar), Janet Lee (Mrs. Robert Bannon), John Byron. BS, U. Denver, 1948; MA, Northeastern State U., Greeley, Colo., 1951; EdD, U. Colo., 1962; LLD (hon.), Youngstown State U., 1984. Aircraft mechanic Boeing Aircraft Corp., Seattle, 1942-43; bookkeeper Colo. Nat. Bank, Denver, 1946-48; dir. accounts and records, registrar, instr. State Tchrs. Coll., Dickinson, N.D., 1948-52; dir. research Colo. Dept. Edn., Denver, 1952-56; dir. Colo. Legis. Com. on Edn., Colo. Sch. Bd. Assn., Boulder, 1958-62; coordinator research Okla., 1962-65; vice chancellor research and planning Okla. State Regents for Higher Edn., Oklahoma City, 1965-68; v.p. adminstrv. affairs Youngstown State U., Ohio, 1968-73, pres., 1973-84, pres. emeritus, 1984. Mem. exec. com. Mahoning Area council Boy Scouts Am.; bd. dirs. McGuffey Centre; trustee, mem. exec. com. Youngstown State Univ. Found.; trustee Butler Inst. Am. Art. Served with USAAF, 1943-45. Decorated Air medal, D.F.C.; recipient Man of Yr. award Am. Negro Police Assn., 1980-81, Man of Yr. award Youngstown C. of C., 1983 Mem. Am. Assn. State Colls. and Univs., Youngstown C. of C., Alpha Kappa Psi, Phi Delta Kappa, Phi Kappa Phi. Clubs: Mason (32 deg.), Lion. Home: Youngstown, Ohio. Died Sept. 1, 1988.

**COFFEY, DELAINE BRANDY,** counselor; b. Shreveport, La., Nov. 4, 1953; d. Howard Smith and Syrena Gray (Fuqua) Coffey; stepdau. of Bettie Coffey. AA, San Antonio Jr. Coll., 1978; BA in Psychology, U. Tex., Tyler, 1980. Lic. chem. dependency counselor; alcohol/drug counselor; internat. cert. alcohol/drug counselor. Interpreter/cons. Coffey & Assocs., Tyler, 1981-87; sr. counselor Palmer Drug Abuse Program, Longview, Tex., 1988-93; program dir. CPC Brentwood Hosp. Outreach, Longview, 1994-96, Hill Country Independence House, Kerrville, Tex., 1997-2000, Hill Country Coun. Alcohol and Drug Abuse, 2000—02. Tex. Eastern U. scholar, 1979. Fellow Tex. Cert. Bd. of Alcoholism and Drug Abuse Counselors; mem. Tex. Addiction Profls., Am. Assn. Christian Counselors. Avocations: music, dinner parties, travel, fishing, camping. Died 2002.

**COGSWELL, FREDERICK WILLIAM,** English language educator, publisher, editor, poet; b. East Centreville, NB, Can., Nov. 8, 1917; s. Walter Scott and Florence (White) C.; m. Margaret Hynes, July 3, 1944 (dec. May 1985); children: Carmen Patricia Cogswell Robinson (dec.), Kathleen Mary Cogswell Forsythe; m. Gail Fox, Nov. 6, 1985 (div. Aug. 1997); m. Adele Bartlett, Sept. 20, 1997 (dec. Jan. 2002). BA with honors, U. N.B., 1949, MA, 1950; PhD (Imperial Order Daus. Empire fellow), U. Edinburgh, Scotland, 1952; LLD (hon.), St. Francis Xavier U., 1982; DCL (hon.), King's Coll., 1985; LLD (hon.), Mt. Allison U., 1988. From asst. to assoc. prof. dept. English U. N.B., Fredericton, 1952-64, prof., 1964-83, prof. emeritus, from 1983. Exch. writer in residence Scottish Arts Coun., 1983—84. Editor: The Fiddlehead, 1952—66, Humanities Assn. Bull., 1967—72; pub.: Fiddlehead Poetry Books, 1956—82; author: Charles G.D. Roberts, 1983, Charles Mair, 1986, (poetry) The Stunted Strong, 1954, The Haloed Tree, 1957, Descent from Eden, 1959, Lost Dimension, 1960, Star People, 1968, Immortal Plowman, 1969, In Praise of Chastity, 1970, The Chains of Lilliput, 1971, The House Without a Door, 1973, Light Bird of Life, 1974, Against Perspectives, 1977, (collected poems) A Long Apprenticeship, 1980, Selected Poems, 1982, Pearls, 1983, Meditations: 50 Sestinas, 1986, An Edge to Life, 1987, The Best Notes Merge, 1988, Black and White Tapestry, 1989, Watching an Eagle, 1991, When the Right Light Shines, 1992, In Praise of Old Music, 1992, In My Own Growing, 1993, As I See It, 1994, The Trouble with Light, 1996, Folds, 1997, A Double Question, 1999, With Vision Added, 2000, Deeper Than Mind, 2001, Dry Flowers, 2002, Ghosts, 2002, Later in Chicago, 2003, The Kindness of Stars, 2004; translator: The Testament of Cresseid, 1958, One Hundred Poems of Modern Quebec, 1970, 1971, A Second Hundred Poems of Modern Quebec, 1971, The Poetry of Modern Quebec, 1976, Confrontation, 1973, The Complete Poems of Emile Nelligan, 1983; translator: (with Jo-Anne Elder) Unfinished Dreams: Contemporary Poetry of Acadie, 1991; editor: Five New Brunswick Poets, 1961; editor: (with W.S. MacNutt and Robert Tweedie) The Arts in New Brunswick, 1967; editor: (with Thelma Reid Lower) The Enchanted Land, 1968; translator: (anthologies) One Hundred Poems of Modern Quebec, A Second Hundred Poems of Modern Quebec, The Poetry of Modern Quebec, Atlantic Anthology, Vol. 1 (prose), 1983, Vol. 2 (poetry); translator: (with Jo-Anne Elder) Climates by Hermènègilde Chiasson, 1999; translator: Conversations, 2001; contbr. articles and poems to profl. jours. Mem. sr. arts fellowship awards com. Can. Council, 1972, mem. centennial poetry awards com., 1968; mem. Leave fellowship awards bd. humanities sect., 1973, 74; mem. poetry sect. Gov. Gen.'s award bd., 1973, chmn., 1974; bd. dirs. Can. Found., 1983— . Served with Canadian Army, 1940-45. Decorated mem. Order of Can., 1981; recipient Bliss Carman medal for poetry, 1945, 47, Douglas Gold medal, 1949, Gold medal for svc. to poetry as mag. editor Republic of Philippines, 1956, Gold medal as disting. poet, 1956, Coronation medal for 125 Can. anniversary, 1992, Alden Nowlan award for excellence in the arts N.B. Gov., 1995, Coronation medal, 1992; Nuffield fellow, 1959-60, Can. Coun. Sr. fellow, 1967-68. Mem. League Canadian Poets (regional exec. 1973-80, 1st v.p. 1985-86, hon. life mem.), Canadian Authors Assn., Assn. Can. Pubs. (hon. life, Honors for Contrbns. to Can. Lit. and Publs. 2000), Ind. Pubs. Assn., Atlantic Pubs. Assn. (pres. 1979-80), Assn. Can. and Que. Lits. (pres. 1978-80), N.B. Writers' Fedn. (hon. life.; pres. 1983-85) Home: Burnaby, Canada. *Anything I have accomplished has come about because it has been very easy for me to work hard at anything in which I have been interested and I have been interested in a good many things.* Deceased.

**COHEN, ARTHUR GEORGE,** real estate developer; b. Bklyn., Apr. 23, 1930; s. Louis Diamond and Frances (Kostick) C.; m. Karen D. Bassine, June 6, 1954; children: Susan, Lauren, Debra, Rochelle, Katherine. BA, U. Miami, Fla., 1951; LL.B, N.Y. Law Sch., 1954. Chmn., CEO Arlen Realty & Development Corp., NYC, 1971; chmn. API Trust, 1973-81. Trustee John Hancock Mut. Fund, 1972; bd. dirs. Citicorp, N.Y.C., 1974-80, Home Title N.Y., 1974-81; guest lectr. Harvard Bus. Sch., 1975-78, Wharton Sch., 1977; mem. real estate adv. commn. Citibank, 1978-80; founder Urban Devel. Corp., 1971 Trustee Brandeis U., Albert Einstein Coll. Medicine, N.Y. Law Sch.; bd. dirs. American Jewish World Svcs.; pres. Johnson's Pres. Club, 1963-68; chmn. fundraising for Hubert Humphrey, N.Y.C., 1968 Mem.: Glen Oaks Country, Palm Beach Country. Died Aug. 9, 2014.

**COHEN, HELEN HERZ,** small business owner, director; b. NYC, Oct. 29, 1912; d. Fred W. and Florence (Hirsch) H.; m. Albert F. Schliefer, Sept. 22, 1933 (dec. Nov. 1941); m. Edwin S. Cohen, Aug. 31, 1944: children: Edwin C., Roger, Wendy. PhB, Brown U., 1933; MA, Columbia U., 1934; postgrad., NYU, Columbia. Counselor Camp Walden, Denmark, Maine, 1930-38, owner, from 1939; tchr. social studies Alcuin Prep. Sch., 1935; office mgr. Lewis P. Weil Importer, 1935-40; pres. The Main Idea, from 1968. Founder, pres. Main Idea, Inc., 1969—. Author: Choosing a Camp for Your Child, Getting Ready for Camp; co-author: Fabulous Foods for Fifty, 1970; contbr. articles to instrnl. booklets, mags. Active alumni coun. Pembroke Coll., 1960; chmn. camp divns. Bridgton (Maine) Hosp. Fund, 1962—; trustee Fund for Advancement Camping, 1980-90. Recipient Gold Key award Columbia Scholastic Press, 1972, award Fund for Advancement of Camping Patron, 1982. Mem. Am. Camping Assn. (regional bd. dirs. 1947-50, 52-55, 56-59, 60-63, standards visitor 1957-93, chmn. pvt. camps 1961, bd. dirs. 1963—, v.p. N.Y. 1963-75, Va. sect. 1975), Pioneers of Camping, Maine Camp Dirs. Assn.

(legis. com. 1960-63, bd. dirs. 1963—, Halsey Gulick award 1991), Pembroke Coll. Club (co-founder), Cosmopolitan Club, Cornell Club, Farmington Country Club, Boar's Head Sports Club. Deceased.

**COHEN, HERBERT,** psychologist; b. Bklyn., Dec. 13, 1924; s. Abraham and Anna (Kaplowitz) Cohen; m. Carmella June Cohen, June 27, 1980; children: Robin, Roselle, Martin. BA, George Washington U., 1949, MA, 1950; PhD, Calif. Sch. Profl. Psychology, 1972. Staff psychologist East St. Louis Child Guidance Clinic, Ill., 1957—62, St. Louis State Hosp., Ill., 1952—62, Atascadero State Hosp., Calif., 1962—66, Met. State Hosp., Norwalk, Calif., 1968—74; clin. psychologist St. John's Hosp. and Health Ctr., Santa Monica, Calif., 1972—78; cmty. mental health psychologist L.A. County Dept. Mental Health, from 1980. With USAAF, 1943—46. Scholar, N.Y. War Svc., 1947—48. Mem.: APA, L.A. County Psychol. Assn., Calif. Neuropsychology Soc., Calif. Psychol. Assn. Home: Torrance, Calif. Died Jan. 12, 1995.

**COHEN, LORELEI FREDA,** psychologist; b. Detroit, Nov. 20, 1937; d. Fred M. and Anna (Margolis) Schuman; m. Norton J. Cohen, June 16, 1957; children: Debrah, Sander. BA, Wayne State U., 1960, EdS, 1978, PhD student; MA, U. Tex., 1965. Tchr., Killeen, Tex., 1960—63, Detroit Pub. Schs., 1964, Temple Israel, Detroit, 1968—82; psychologist Detroit Pub. Schs. Citywide Psychol. Svcs., from 1980; instr. child psychopathology Wayne State U., 1980. Mem. exec. bd. Detroit Assn. Retarded Citizens, 1981—84; docent Detroit Inst. Arts, 1972—78. Jesse Jones scholar, U. Tex., 1962, Wayne State U. Grad. fellow, 1974—76, from 1984. Mem.: APA, Phi Beta Kappa. Home: West Bloomfield, Mich. Died Jan. 23, 1998.

**COHEN, LYNNE GAIL,** artist, photographer; b. Racine, Wis., July 3, 1944; d. Lester N. and Sophie (Block) C.; m. Andrew M. Lugg, Mar. 23, 1968. BS in Art, U. Wis., 1967; student, University Coll., London, 1964-65; postgrad., U. Mich., 1968; MA in Art, Eastern Mich. U., Ypsilanti, 1969. Teaching fellow Eastern Mich. U., 1968, lectr., 1969-70, instr., 1970-73; lectr. U. Ottawa, Ont., 1974-81, 83, asst. prof. Ont., 1982-83; vis. artist Art Inst. Chgo., 1984. Exhibited one-man show, U. N.Mex., Albuquerque, 1975, Carpenter Ctr. for Visual Arts, Harvard U., 1978, Internat. Ctr. Photos, N.Y.C., 1978, Yarlow-Salzman Gallery, Toronto, 1979, Brown U., Providence, R.I., 1983, N.S. Coll. Art and Design, Halifax, 1984, P.P.O.W., N.Y.C., 1988, Interim Art, London, 1988; group shows, Walker Art Ctr., Mpls., 1973, Optica, Montreal, 1976, Nat. Gallery Can., 1977, 85, Light Work Gallery, Syracuse, 1981, Yarlow-Salzman Gallery, Toronto, 1983, Photographers Gallery, London, 1984, Art Gallery of Ont., Toronto, 1984, 49th Parallel, N.Y.C., 1986, P.P.O.W., 1986; represented permanent collections, Art Inst. Chgo., Nat. Gallery Can., Mus. Contemporary Art, Montreal, Bibliotheque Nationale, Paris, Internat. Mus. Photography, George Eastman House, Met. Mus. Art, N.Y.C., others. Recipient Logan award Chgo. Art Inst., 1968, Gov. General's award in Visual & Media award, 2005, Recontres d'Arles Discovery award, 2011; Can. Council grantee, 1978-79, 83, 87. Home: Ottawa, Canada. Died May 13, 2014.

**COHEN, MURRAY,** aerospace engineer, consultant; s. Benjamin and Mollie Cohen; m. Thelma Florence Fishback (div.); children: Eleanor, Gary, Robert; m. Josephine Marie Morici, Aug. 31, 1968; children: Joseph, Susan, Sandy. B Aero. Engring., Poly. U., Bklyn., 1953. Registered profl. engr., NY, 1983. Asst. to chief engr. Colonial Airlines, LaGuardia Airport, NY, 1946—48; design engr. TAAG Design, Mineola, NY, 1948—51; unit leader armament engring. Rep. Aviation Corp., Farmingdale, NY, 1951—57; group leader flight control engring. Grumman Aerospace Corp., Bethpage, NY, 1958—90; pvt. practice cons. engr. Middle Island, NY, from 1990. Condr. seminar in field. Contbr. articles to profl. jours. Organizer fundraisers Commn. Social Justice Order Sons of Italy in Am., Farmingdale, from 1972. With USAF, 1942—45. Recipient Project Sterling award, Grumman Aerospace Corp., 1978. Mem.: AIAA, NSPE (2d v.p. Suffolk County chpt.), Birchwood Computer Club (v.p.). Achievements include patents for aircraft rod end double locking device; aircraft rod end integrated locking device. Avocations: chess, photography, computers. Died Apr. 8, 2008.

**COHEN, RICHARD NORMAN,** retired insurance company executive; b. NYC, Oct. 28, 1923; s. Norman M. and Janet (Goldsmith) C.; m. Ann Robertson, Oct. 25, 1975; children: Daniel Hays, James Matthew; 1 stepchild, Mark Thompson. Grad., Phillips Exeter Acad., 1941; BA, Yale U., 1945. Salesman Cohen, Goldman & Co., NYC, 1947-50; mens fashion editor Fawcett Publications, NYC, 1951-52; life ins. broker Mass. Mut. Life Ins. Co., NYC, 1954—2000; account exec. John M. Riehle, Inc., NYC, 1961-63, v.p., 1963-83, Leonard Newman Agy. Inc., White Plains, NY, 1984-94, Arthur Gallagher & Co., White Plains, 1994-2000. Bd. dirs. The NY Times Co., 1960—72, Silver Hill Hosp., 1997—2004. Served to 2d lt. USAAF, 1943-45. Mem. Country Club of New Canaan, Yale Club (N.Y.C.), Century Country Club (White Plains, N.Y.), Beta Theta Pi. Republican. Jewish. Home: New Canaan, Conn. Died Jan. 2, 2014.

**COHEN, RONALD HOFFMAN,** lawyer; b. Caldwell, Nov. 15, 1913; s. George W. and Sylvia C. (Hoffman) Cohen; m. Estelle Sakofsky, Feb. 23, 1947 (dec. Mar. 1988); 1 child, Sally Cohen Swift; m. Roslyn Fielman, Oct. 11, 1992. BA, Amherst Coll., 1934; JD, Northwestern U., 1939. Bar: Ill. 1939, NY 1940, US Dist. Ct. (so. & ea. dists.) NY, US Ct. Appeals (2d cir.) 1960, US Supreme Ct. 1961, US Ct. Appeals (DC cir.) 1962, US Ct. Appeals (7th cir.) 1984. Assoc. firm Silver & Bernstein, NYC, 1939—42; atty. War Shipping US Maritime Commn., Washington, 1946—47, CAB, Washington, 1947—53; N.Am. counsel Sabena Belgian World Airlines, NYC, 1953—83; sole practice NYC, from 1984. Mem. Case notes Ill. Law Rev., 1937—38, Northwestern U. Law Rev., 1938—39. Served to lt. res. USCG, 1942—45, NATOUSA, PTO. Decorated officer Order of Leopold II. Mem.: ABA, Assn. Bar, NY (aero. and adminstrv. law coms.), Pine Hollow Country Club, Tau Epsilon Rho. Jewish. Home: Forest Hills, NY. Died July 27, 1997.

**COHEN, SANFORD IRWIN,** physician, educator; b. NYC, Sept. 5, 1928; s. George A. and Gertrude (Slater) C.; m. Jean Steinbruecker, Nov. 30, 1952; children— Jeffrey, Debra, John, Robert. AB magna cum laude, N.Y. U., 1948; M.B., MD, Chgo. Med. Sch., 1952. Intern Jackson Meml. Hosp., Miami, Fla., 1952-53; resident psychiatry U. Colo. Med. Center, 1953-54; resident Duke Med. Center, 1954-55, 57-58, mem. faculty, 1956-68, prof. psychiatry, 1964-68, head div. psychosomatic medicine and psychophysiol. research, 1964-68, lectr. psychology, 1960-68; instr. Washington Psychoanalytic Inst., 1964-68; cons. VA Hosp., Durham, NC, 1957-65, NIMH, 1963-66; prof. psychiatry Boston U. Med. Sch., 1970-86, chmn. dept., 1970-86; vis. research scientist health and behavior br., div. basic scis. NIMH, 1986-88; prof. psychiatry U. Miami (Fla.) Sch. Medicine, 1988-2000, vice chmn. dept., 1990-2000, prof. emeritus, from 2000. Markle scholar med. sci., 1957-62; Commonwealth fellow, Czech Republic and USSR, 1966. Contbr. articles to profl. jours., chpts. to books. Recipient Robert Morse award excellence in sci. writing, 1965 Fellow Am. Psychiat. Assn. (disting. life), Am. Coll. Clin. Pharmacology (life); mem. AAAS, Am. Psychosomatic Soc., Acad. Behavioral Medicine Rsch. Home: Hudson, Ohio. Died Sept. 2013.

**COKE, C(HAUNCEY) EUGENE,** consulting company executive, scientist, educator, author; b. Toronto, Ont., Can; s. Chauncey Eugene and Edith May (Redman) C.; m. Sally B. Tolmie, June 12, 1941. BSc with honors, U. Man., MSc magna cum laude; MA, U. Toronto; postgrad., Yale U.; PhD, U. Leeds, Eng., 1938. Dir. rsch. Courtaulds (Can.) Ltd., 1939-42; dir. R & D Guaranty Dyeing & Finishing Co., 1946-48; various exec. R & D positions Courtaulds (Can.) Ltd., Montreal, 1948-59, dir. R & D; mem. exec. com. Hart-Fibres Co., 1959-62; tech. dir. textile chem. Drew Chem. Corp., 1962-63; dir. new products fibers div. Am. Cynamid Co., 1963-68, dir. applications devel., 1968-70; pres. Coke & Assoc., Cons., Ormond Beach, Fla., 1970-78, chmn., from 1978. Pres. Aqua Vista Corp. Inc., 1971-74; vis. rsch. prof. Stetson U., 1979—; internat. authority on man-made fibers; guest lectr. Sir George Williams Coll., Montreal, 1949-59; chmn. Can. adv. com. on Internat. Standards Orgn. Tech. Com. 38, 1951-58; mem. Can. Standards Assn., 1958-59; del. Textile Tech. Fedn. Can., 1948-57, bd. dirs., 1957-59. Contbr. articles to Can., U.S., Brit., Australian profl. jours. with translations into Japanese. Vice chmn. North Peninsula adv. bd. Volusia County Coun., 1975-78; mem. Halifax Area Study Commn., 1972-74, Volusia County Elections Bd., 1974-94; bd. dirs. Coun. Assns. North Peninsula, 1972-74, 76-77; pres. Greater Daytona Beach Rep. Mens Club, 1972-75; pres. Rep. Mens Club, 1972-75; pres. Rep. President's Forum, 1976-78, v.p., 1978-81. Recipient Bronze medal Can. Assn. Textile Colourists and Chemists, 1963 Fellow AAAS, Royal Soc. Chemistry (Gt. Britain, life), Soc. Dyers and Colourists (Gt. Britain), Inst. Textile Sci. (co-founder, 3d pres.), Chem. Inst. Can. (life, coun. 1958-61), Am. Inst. Chemists, N.J. Acad. Sci.; mem. Am. Assn. Textile Tech. (life, past pres., bronze medal), Can. Assn. Textile Colourists and Chemists (hon. life, past pres., bronz medal), N.Y. Acad. Scis. (life), U.S. Metric Assn. (life), Chemists Club. Died June 20, 1999.

**COLE, JACK WESTLEY,** retired surgeon; b. Portland, Oreg., Aug. 29, 1920; MD, Washington U., St. Louis, 1944. Diplomate Am. Bd. Surgery. Intern Univ. Hosps. Cleve., 1944-46, resident in surgery, 1948-52; mem. staff Yale-New Haven Hosp., 1966-86; Ensign prof. surgery Yale U. Med. Sch., 1966-86 (ret. 1986); prof. emeritus, from 1986. Fellow ACS; mem. Am. Surg. Assn., New Eng. Surg. Soc. Deceased.

**COLEMAN, DOUGLAS LEONARD,** research scientist; b. Stratford, Ont., Can., Oct. 6, 1931; s. Leonard Coleman; m. Beverly G. Benallick; children: David, Thomas, John(dec.). BS in Chemistry, McMaster U., Hamilton, Ont., 1954; PhD in Biochemistry, U. Wis., 1958. Staff Jackson Labs., Bar Harbor, Maine, 1958—97, sr. staff scientist emeritus, 1997—2014. Recipient Claude Bernard Medal, Royal Soc., 1977, Gairdner Found. Internat. award, 2005, Albert Lasker Basic Med. Rsch. award, Lasker Found., 2010, BBVA Frontiers of Knowledge award, 2012; co-recipient Shaw prize in Life Sciences & Medicine, Hong Kong, 2009. Mem.: NAS. Achievements include research in the existence of a hormone system that contributed to controlling fat cell homeostasis. Died Apr. 16, 2014.

**COLEMAN, PETER TALI,** former Governor of American Samoa; b. Pago Pago, Am. Samoa, Dec. 8, 1919; s. William Patrick and Amata (Aumua) C.; m. Nora Stewart, May 31, 1941; children: William Patrick, Peter Talifiliga, Milton John, Amata, Burton George (dec.), Bruce Joseph, Charles Ulualofaigna, Richard James, Paul Vaelaa, Barrett Francis, Alan David, Sina Ellen, Limonmon Mary. B.BS in Econs, Georgetown U., 1949, LL.B., 1951; PhD (hon.), U. Guam, 1970. Pacific area analyst Office Ters., Dept. Interior, Washington, 1951-52; pub. defender, planning officer, customs officer Am. Samoa, 1952-55, atty. gen., 1955-56, gov., 1956-61, 78-85, 89-93; dist. adminstr. Marshall Islands dist. U.S. Trust Terr. Pacific Islands Dept. Interior, 1961-65; dist. adminstr. Dept. Interior (Mariana Islands dist.), 1965-69, dep. high commr., 1969-76, acting high commr., 1976-77; alt. U.S. commr. (S. Pacific Commn.), 1959; spl. adviser (U.S. del. from Trust Ter. Pacific Islands to South Pacific Conf. Island Leaders), 1965, 72, head of del., 1980-84; ptnr. Coleman & Faalevao, 1985-89. Chmn. Western Govs. Conf., 1980; founding mem. Pacific Basin Devel. Coun., 1980, pres., 1982-83, 89-90; mem. standing com. Pacific Islands Conf., 1982-85, 89—; founding chmn. Rep. Party of Am. Samoa, 1985-88, Rep. nat. committeeman, 1988—; mem. White House Del. to Tonga, 1988; Am. Samoa consul for Nauru Island, 1985-88. With AUS, 1940-45. Named to U.S. Army Hall of Fame Ft. Benning, Ga., 1982; John Hay Whitney Found. fellow. Home: Pago Pago, . Died Apr. 28, 1997.

**COLEMAN, WANDA,** poet, writer; b. L.A., Nov. 13, 1946; d. George and Lewana Evans; m. Austin Straus, May 1, 1981; children: Anthony, Luanda, Ian Wayne Grant. Author: (books) Imagoes, 1983, Heavy Daughter Blues, 1987, A War of Eyes & Other Stories, 1988, African Sleeping Sickness, 1990, Hand Dance, 1993, Dicksboro Hotel, 1995, Native in a Strange Land: Trials and Tremors, 1996, Bathwater Wine, 1998, Mercurochrome, 2001, The Riot Inside Me: More Trials and Tremors, 2005, Jazz and Twelve O'Clock Tales, 2008; (novel) Mambo Hips & Make Believe, 1999. NEA fellow in poetry, 1981, Guggenheim fellow in poetry, 1984, Calif. Arts Coun. fellow in fiction, 1989, in poetry, 2002, First Literary fellow L.A. Dept. Cultural Affairs; named writer's resident Djerassi Found., 1990; recipient Lenore Marshall Poetry prize, 1999. Mem. PEN Ctr. West, Writers Guild America Home: Marina Dl Rey, Calif. Died Nov. 22, 2013.

**COLGATE, STIRLING AUCHINCLOSS,** physicist; b. NYC, Nov. 14, 1925; s. Henry A. and Jeannette (Pruyn) C.; m. Rosemary B. Williamson, July 12, 1947; children; Henry A., Sarah, Arthur S. BA, Cornell U., 1948, PhD in Physics, 1952. Physicist Radiation Lab., Univ. Calif., Berkeley, 1951-52, Lawrence Livermore Lab., Calif., 1952-64; pres. N.Mex. Inst. Mining & Tech., Socorro, 1964-74; physicist Los Alamos Nat. Lab., N.Mex., 1976—2013. Contbr. over 200 articles to profl. jours. Served with Merchant Marines, 1943-46. Recipient Rossi prize, 1990, Wetherill prize, 1994. Fellow American Phys. Soc.; mem. NAS, American Astron. Soc. Home: Los Alamos, N.Mex. Died Dec. 1, 2013.

**COLL, MAX,** retired state legislator; b. Roswell, N.Mex., Feb. 26, 1932; m. Catherine Joyce Coll; children: Melanie DeTemple, Max. BA, U. Mo., 1954; JD, U. N.Mex., 1974. Landman El Paso Natural Gas Co., 1957—60; owner small bus., 1965—74; lawyer, solo practitioner, 1974—87; mem. Dist. 47 N.Mex. House of Reps., Santa Fe, 1967—74, 1981—2004. Del. N.Mex. Constnl. Conv., 1969. 1st lt. US Army, 1955—57. Democrat. Died Mar. 27, 2014.

**COLLA, OLIVIER,** engineering company executive; b. Brussels, Jan. 31, 1957; children: Quentin, Basile, Coline, Lucie. Degree in Civil Engring., U. Catholique de Louvain, 1980. Sr. engr. Brussels Capital Region, 1996—99; head Min. Mobility & Transport, 1999—2002; gen. & strategic studies mgr. STIB Brussels Pub. Transport Operator, from 2002. Deceased.

**COLLEN, MORRIS FRANK,** retired medical administrator, physician, consultant, researcher; b. St. Paul, Nov. 12, 1913; s. Frank Morris and Rose Collen; m. Frances Bobbie Diner, Sept. 24, 1937 (dec. 1996); children: Arnold Roy, Barry Joel, Roberta Joy, Randal Harry. BEE, U. Minn., 1934, MB with distinction, 1938, MD, 1939; DSc (hon.), U. Victoria, BC, Can., 2004. Diplomate American Bd. Internal Medicine. Intern Michael Reese Hosp., Chgo., 1939—40; resident LA County Hosp., 1940—42; chief med. service Kaiser Found. Hosp., Oakland, Calif., 1942—52, chief of staff, 1952—53; physician in chief San Francisco Med. Ctr.; med. dir. West Bay divsn. Permanente Med. Group, 1953—62, dir. med. methods rsch., 1962—79, dir. tech. assessment, 1979—83, cons. divsn. rsch., from 1983. Chmn. exec. com. Permanente Med. Group, Oakland, 1953—73; dir. Permanente Svcs., Inc., Oakland, 1958—73; adj. asst. prof. biomed. informatics Uniformed Svcs. U. Health Scis., 2000—05; chmn. health care sys. study sect. USPHS, 1968—72, mem. adv. com. demonstration grants, 1967, advisor VA, 1968; mem. adv. com. Automated Multiphasic Health Testing, 1971; discussant Nat. Conf. Preventive Medicine, Bethesda, Md., 1975; mem. com. on tech. in health care NAS, 1976; mem. adv. group Nat. Commn. on Digestive Diseases, U.S. Congress, 1978; mem. adv. panel to U.S. Congress Office of Tech. Assessment, 1980—85; mem. peer rev. adv. group TRIMIS program Dept. Def., 1978—90; program chmn. 3rd Internat. Conf. Med. Informatics, Tokyo, 1980; chmn. bd. sci. counselors Nat. Libr. Medicine, 1985—87, mem. lit. selection tech. rev. com., 1997—2002, chmn., 2000—02; chmn. tech. evaluation group Application of Advanced Network Infrastructure in Health and Disaster Mgmt., 2002, chmn. tech. group, 2002; program chmn. Internat. Conf. Health Promotion, Atlanta, 2003. Author: Treatment of Pneumococcic Pneumonia, 1948, Hospital Computer Systems, 1974, Multiphasic Health Testing Services, 1978, A History of Medical Informatics in the United States, 1950-90, 1995, Computer Medical Databases, 2012; editor: Permanente Med. Bull., 1943—53; mem. editl. bd.: Preventive Medicine, 1970—80, Jour. Med. Sys., Methods Info. Medicine, 1980—97, Diagnostic Medicine, 1980—84, Computers in Biomed. Rsch., 1987—94; contbr. more than 200 articles to profl. jours., chpts. to books. Fellow Ctr. Advanced Studies in Behavioral Scis., Stanford U., 1985—86; scholar Johns Hopkins Centennial scholar, 1976, scholar-in-residence, Nat. Libr. Medicine, 1987—2002. Fellow: ACP, American Coll. Med. Informatics (pres. 1987—88, Morris F. Collen medal named in his honor 1993), American Inst. Med. & Biol. Engring., American Coll. Chest Physicians, American Coll. Cardiology; mem.: NAS, AMA, Salutis Unitas (v.p. 1972), Internat.

Health Evaluation Assn. (pres. 1995—96, Lifetime Achievement award 1992, Computers in Health Care Pioneer award 1992, David E. Morgan award for achievement in health care info. 1998, Japan Shigeaki Hinohara award for preventive medicine 2001, Cummings Psyche award for behavioral medical rsch. 2001, Morris F. Collen Permanente Rsch. award named in his honor 2003, 2009), American Med. Informatics Assn. (bd. dirs. 1985—96), Nat. Acad. Practice in Medicine (chmn. 1982—88, co-chmn. 1989—91), Soc. Advisory Med. Sys. (pres. 1973), American Fedn. Clin. Rsch., Inst. Medicine (chmn. tech. subcom. for improving patient records 1990, chmn. workshop on informatics in clin. preventive medicine 1991), Internat. Med. Informatics Assn. Sr. Officers Club, Tau Beta Pi, Alpha Omega Alpha. Achievements include named a library after his name at Kaiser Permanente, Oakland, California. Home: Walnut Creek, Calif. Died Sept. 27, 2014.

**COLLEN, SHELDON ORRIN,** lawyer; b. Chgo., Ill., Feb. 7, 1922; s. Jacob Allen and Ann (Andalman) C.; m. Ann Blager, Apr. 8, 1946; 1 child, John O. BA magna cum laude, Carleton Coll., 1944; JD, U. Chgo., 1948. Bar: Ill. 1949, Minn. 1976, U.S. Dist. Ct. (no. dist.) Ill. 1949, U.S. Supreme Ct. 1965. Assoc. Adcock, Fink & Day, Chgo., 1948-51; mem. Simon & Collen, Chgo., 1951-59, Friedman & Koven, Chgo., 1959-86, Epton, Mullin & Druth, Ltd., Chgo., 1986-89; of counsel Lawrence Walner and Assocs., Ltd., 1989-90; prin. Sheldon O. Collen P.C., from 1990. Specialist fed. antitrust litigation; sec. Jupiter Industries, Inc. and subs., Chgo., 1961-86. Mem. adv. bd. Antitrust Bull. and Jour. Reprints for Antitrust Law and Econs. Curator Prince Art Gallery, Chgo.; mem. bd. edn. U. Chgo. Law Rev., 1948-49; bd. dirs. J.G. Inds. Inc., Lower Northcenter, Chgo. Youth Ctrs., Union League Found. for Boys and Girls, Contemporary Art Workshop, Edward P. Martin Soc., Ctr. for Study of Multiple Births; sec., bd. dirs. 3750 Lake Shore Dr., Inc., 1982-87; pres. Union League Civic and Arts Found., 1984-86, life trustee. With AUS, 1943-46. Fellow Norwegian Am. Mus., Decorah, Iowa. Mem. ABA, Am. Judicature Soc., Chgo. Bar Assn. (coun. corp. and securities law coms., chmn. antitrust 1976-77), Bar Assn. 7th Cir., Am. Arbitration Assn. (arbitrator), Art Inst. Chgo., Mus. Contemporary Art, Lawyers for Creative Arts, Chgo. Hist. Soc. Deceased.

**COLOMB, FERNANDO RAÚL,** astronomer, researcher; b. Córdoba, Argentina, Jan. 11, 1939; s. Fernando Enrique Colomb and Leandra Nelida Mainardi; m. Esther Delfina Beliera, Oct. 28, 1964; children: Javier Andres, Hernan Pablo, Alejandro Daniel. Lic. in physics, U. Buenos Aires, 1964; D of Physics, U. La Plata, Argentina. Cert. Minstry Edn., Argentina, 1970. Rsch. asst. U. Buenos Aires, 1959—63, Nat. Radioastronomy Obs., Charlottesville, Va., 1966—68; rschr. Radioastronomy Inst. Argentina, Villa Elisa, 1968—95, dir., 1984—95; rschr. Nat. Rsch. Coun. Argentina, Buenos Aires, 1970—96; dir. Nat. Com. Spl. Activities, Buenos Aires, from 1993. Pres. Complejo Astronómico El Leoncito, San Juan, 1984—89; pres. organizing com. XXI Gen. Assembly Internat. Astron. Union, Buenos Aires, 1990—91, v.p. Commn. 51, 1993—97; chmn. Internat. Symposium on Remote Sensing of Environment, Buenos Aires, 2000—02. Contbr. articles to profl. jours. Fellow, John Simon Guggenheim Meml. Found., 1977—78. Mem.: Astronomy Assn. Argentina (pres. 1978—81). Achievements include serving as principal investigator of satellite Mission SAC-C and SAC-D/Aquarius, jointly developed by CONAE and NASA. Home: Buenos Aires, Argentina. Deceased.

**COLTON, MATTHEW JOHN,** social sciences researcher, educator, consultant; b. Manchester, Eng., Oct. 11, 1955; s. James and Grace Patricia Colton; children: Nathan James, Emily Daisy. PhD, Oxford U., Eng., 1986. Prof. Swansea U., from 2001, Regional Ctr. Child and Adolescent Mental Health, Inst. Neurosci., Faculty Medicine, Norwegian U. Sci. and Tech., Trondheim, Norway, from 2005. Cons. St Olav's U. Hosp., Trondheim, from 2009. Author: (book) Betrayel of Trust. Leverhulme fellowship, 1995. Fellow: Acad. Social Scis. Died 2010.

**CONDE MONTERO-RIOS, FRANCISCO PEDRO,** physician, researcher; b. Vigo, Pontevedra, Spain, Oct. 10, 1945; s. Fernando Conde and Josefina Montero-RÚos; m. Gabriella Bermani, Feb. 14, 1976 (dec. 1987); 1 child, Alberto; m. Stephanie Salvarelli, Jan. 30, 1995. Grad. in medicine and surgery, U. Santiago de Compostela, Spain, 1969, MD in Medicine and Surgery, 1973, U. Genoa, Italy, 1983. Resident Hosp. Nuestra Señora del Perpetuo Socorro, Vigo, Spain, 1967-69; predoctoral fellow Centro de Investigaciones Biológicas, Madrid, 1970-72; postdoctoral fellow in immunology Agrl. Rsch. Coun., Cambridge, 1973-74; postdoctoral fellow immunology U. Cambridge, 1974-75; scientist Inst. Nat. dei Tumori, Milan, 1975-76; scientist Inst. de Bioquímica de Macromoléculas Univ. Autónoma Madrid, 1977-79; dir. immunochem. unit in rsch. dept. Hosp. Ramón y Cajal, Madrid, from 1979. Prof. microbiology U. Autónoma Madrid, 1977-78, prof. immunology, 1978-79, prof. membrane biochemistry, 1981-82; prof. del curso monográfico del doctorado U. Complutense, Madrid, 1980-81, prod. continuous tng. in medicine, 1980-81, fundamental immunochemistry, 1980-81; pres. rsch. com. Hosp. Ramón y Cajal, Madrid, 1988-89, Hosp. Ramón y Cajal Med. Assn., 1993-95; com. of workers Hosp. Ramón y Cajal, 1995; dir., founder Shift S.A. Founder Concon mag., 1984; contbr. 150 scientific, political, technical articles to jour. Dir. Labor Union Sección Sindical CSI CSIF Hosp. Ramón y Cajal, Madrid, 1995-96; mem. Nat. Health Com. Popular Party, 1993—; dir., founder trade union ASI, Madrid, 1996-98; founder, v.p. trade union ASADE Assn. Sanitaria Dem., Madrid, 1999—. Mem. nat. and internat. scientific socs. Partido Popular. Roman Catholic. Avocations: trees, photography, computers, knowledge. Home: Madrid, Spain. Died Oct. 2005.

**CONLEY, ROBERT J.,** humanities educator; b. Cushing, Okla., Dec. 29, 1940; s. Robert Parris and Peggy Marie Conley; m. Evelyn L. Snell; children: Cheryl Williams, Eddie Williams. MA, Midwestern U., Wichita Falls, Tex., 1968. Instr. Northern Ill. U., DeKalb, 1868—1971, Southwest Mo. State U., Springfield, 1971—74; coord. dept. Indian culture Eastern Mont. Coll., Billings, Mont., 1975—76; asst. programs dir. Cherokee Nation, Tahlequah, Okla., 1976—77; dir. dept. Indian studies Bacone Coll., Muskogee, Okla., 1977—78, Morningside Coll., Sioux City, Iowa, 1979—88; Sequoyah disting. prof. Cherokee studies Western Carolina U., Cullowhee, NC, 2008—14. Author: (novels) Sequoyah, The Dark Island (Spur), Cherokee Dragon, (non-fiction book) The Cherokee Nation: A History, Cherokee Thoughts: Honest and Uncensored. Recipient Lifetime Achievement award, Native Writers' Circle America, 2007; named to The Okla. Profl. Writers Hall of Fame, 1996. Home: Sylva, NC. Died Feb. 16, 2014.

**CONNOCK, ALAN JOHN,** cosmetics executive; b. Stanford-Le-Hope, Essex, Eng., Dec. 21, 1937; s. Joseph and Mary Winnie Connock; m. Elizabeth Nelson Connock, Sept. 8, 1972; 5 children. BSc, London U., 1957. Trainee Yardley London Ltd., 1961—62; sales rep. Kimberly-Clark Ltd., Kent, England, 1962—64; mech. rep. May & Baker Ltd., Essex, England, 1964—69; rep. Dragoco GB Ltd., Suffolk, England, 1969—72; dept. head Chas. Page Ltd., London, 1972—73; mng. dir. A&E Connock Ltd., Dorset, England, 1973—2004. 2d lt. Royal Signals, 1959—61. Conservative. Anglican. Avocations: gardening, music, fishing, travel. Died Jan. 6, 2004.

**CONRAD, MARCEL EDWARD,** hematologist, oncologist, educator; b. NYC, Aug. 15, 1928; s. Marcel Edward and Lulu Marie (Geraghty) C.; m. Marcia Louise Grove; children: Marcel Edward, III, Mark E., Carol J., Erin E., Julia P. BS, Georgetown U., 1949, MD cum laude, 1953. Diplomate Am. Bd. Internal Medicine, Am. Bd. Hematology. Commd. 1st lt. M.C. U.S. Army, 1953, advanced through grades to col., 1968; intern Walter Reed Gen. Hosp., Washington, 1953-54, resident, then chief resident in internal medicine, 1955-60; commdg. officer Mobile Army Surg. Hosp., Republic of Korea, 1960—61; mem. staff Walter Reed Army Inst. Rsch., 1961-74, chief dept. hematology, 1965-74; chief clin. investigation svc. Walter Reed Army Med. Ctr., 1971-74; clin. asst. prof., then clin. assoc. prof. medicine Georgetown U. Med. Sch., 1964-74; prof. medicine U. Ala. Med. Sch., Birmingham, 1974-83, also dir. div. hematology and oncology, 1974-83; prof. medicine, pathology, dir. divsn. hematology, oncology U. South Ala., Mobile, 1983-2001, dir. USA Cancer Ctr., 1985-2001, disting. prof. medicine, 2001; cons. Mobile, from 2001. Prin. investigator Minority Based Cmty. Cancer Oncology Program, 1990—2004. Contbr. numerous articles to med. publs. Advanced from 1st lt. to col. US Army, 1953—74. Decorated Legion of Merit with oak leaf cluster; recipient Skinner medal U.S. Army, 1955, Hoff medal, 1962, John Shaw Billings award, 1967, William Beaumont award, 1972, Walter Reed award, 1974, Harry Hines award Nat. Cancer Inst., 2003, Eagle Scout; named Best Dr. in America, 1981-. Fellow Internat. Soc. Hematology, ACP (Laureate award 1989, named Disting. Prof. Medicine, 2001); mem. AAAS, Assn. Am. Physicians, Internat. Soc. Hematology, Am. Soc. Clin. Investigation, Am. Physiol. Soc., Internat. Soc. Blood Transfusion, Am. Soc. Hematology, Am. Soc. Clin. Oncology, Am. Chem. Soc., Soc. Exptl. Biology and Medicine, So. Soc. Clin. Investigation, Am. Fedn. Clin. Rsch., Nate Am. Red Cross(chair Recently Com. 1968 1925), Hematology Study Section(vet. fgn. war mem. 1961-1980), Alpha Omega Alpha. Roman Catholic. Achievements include basic and clinical contributions in hematology, hepatology and oncology. Avocation: sailing. Died Sept. 26, 2013.

**CONSAGRA, PIETRO,** sculptor; b. Mazara, Italy, Oct. 4, 1920; 4 children. Student, Acad. Fine Arts, Palermo. One-man shows include Rome, 1947, 49, 51, 59, 61, Milan, 1958, 61, Venice, 1948, Brussels, 1958, Paris, 1959, Zurich, 1961, Sao Paulo Bienal, 1955, 59, Venice Biennale, 1956, 60, N.Y.C., 1962, Buenos Aires, 1962, Boston, 1962; represented in permanent collections Tate Gallery, London, Nat. Mus. and Middleheim Park, Antwerp, Mus. Modern Art, Sao Paulo, Paris, Rome, N.Y.C., Buenos Aires, Caracas, Zagreb, Helsinki, Guggenheim Mus., N.Y.C., Art Inst., Chgo., Carnegie Inst., Pitts., Inst. Fine Arts, Mpls. Recipient Grand Prize for Sculpture Venice Biennale, 1960. Home: Rome, Italy. Died July 16, 2005.

**CONSALVI, SIMON ALBERTO,** former Venezuelan government official; b. Santa Cruz de Mora, Merida State, Venezuela, July 7, 1927; m. Maria Eugenia Bigott de; 1 child. Ed., U. Ctrl. de Venezuela. Amb. to Yugoslavia Govt. of Venezuela, 1961—64; dir. Ctrl.l Office Info. Presidency, 1964—67; pres. Nat. Inst. Culture & Art, 1967—69; internat. editor El Nacional Newspaper, 1971—77; state info. min. Govt. of Venezuela, 1974, permanent rep. to UN, 1974—77, min. fgn. affairs, 1977—79, 1985—88, min. internal affairs, 1988—89, Venezuelan amb. to US Washington, 1989—94. Mem. Nat. Congress Fgn. Rel. Com.; state senator, Merida, Venezuela, 1984—89. Contbr. chapters to books, articles to profl. jours. Mem.: Nat. Acad. History. Died Mar. 11, 2013.

**CONSTANTINE, GUS,** physical education educator, coach; b. NYC, Nov. 28, 1939; s. Asomatos and Mersina (Almiros) Constantinopoulos; children: Angela, Michael, Valerie. BS, NYU, 1961, MA, 1963. Soccer and baseball coach, athletic dir. CUNY, Bronx, N.Y., 1969-98; soccer coach NYU, NYC, 1986-96, N.Y. Inst. Tech., 1996—2000. CEO Summit Soccer, Inc., Mamaroneck, N.Y.; basketball specialist U.S. Dept. State, 1965—; internat. soccer referee N.Am. Soccer League, N.Y.C., 1967-84, Internat. Futbol Fedn., Zurich, 1982-86; referee Fedn. Internat. Futbol Assn.; bd. dirs. HTC Sports Found., New Rochelle, N.Y.; N.Y. metro coll. soccer assignor Eastern Coll. Athletic Conf., 2003. Contbr. articles to sports jours. Bd. dirs. Holy Trinity Ch., New Rochelle, N.Y., St. Michael's Home, Quality Care for Elderly, Yonkers, N.Y. With U.S. Army, 1961-63. Named Hall of Fame, Bronx C.C., 2003; named to, Nat. Soccer Hall of Fame, 2002. Mem. AAHPERD, Nat. Soccer Coaches Assn. (life; nat. assessor 1993—, nat. instr. 1962—), Nat. Intercollegiate Soccer Ofcls. Assn. (charter, nat. instr., nat. assessor, Recognition award 1996, mem. Hall of Fame 2002), Nat. Collegiate Athletic Assn. (dir. nat. youth sports program 1972-86, ea. coll. athletic conf. soccer referee assigner 2003—), U.S. Soccer Fedn. (life), N.Y. Soccer Referee Assn. (life), Am. Collegiate Baseball Coaches, U.S. Soccer Fedn. (nat. instr., nat. assessor 1966—), Ea. N.Y. State Referee Adminstrn., Westchester Flames USL (dir. opers. 1998—), Am. Hellenic Ednl. Progressive Assn. Greek Orthodox. Avocations: travel, camping. Deceased.

**COOKE, SIR HOWARD,** former governor-general of Jamaica; b. Goodwill, St. James, Jamaica, Nov. 13, 1915; s. David Brown Cooke and Mary Jane Minto; m. Ivy Sylvia Lucille Tai, July 22, 1939; children: Howard Fitz-Arthur, Richard Washington McDermott, Audrey Faith. DEd (hon.), We. Carolona U., 2003; LLD (hon.), U. West Indies, 2003. Cert. teaching Mico Coll. Tchr. Mico Tng. Coll., 1936-38; headmaster Belle Castle All Age Sch., Port Antonio Upper Sch., Montego Bay Boys' Sch., 1952-58; br. mgr. Standard Life Ins. Co., 1960-71; mem. West Indies Fed. Parliament, 1958-62; unit mgr. Jamaica Mut. Life Assurance Soc., 1971-81; br. mgr. Alico Jamica, 1982-91; min. of govt. Jamaica, Kingston, 1972-80, pres. of senate, 1989-91, gov. gen. Kingston, 1991—2006. Former chmn. People's Nat. Party; sr. elder, lay pastor United Ch. Jamaica and Grand Cayman. Decorated Knight Grand Cross of the Most Disting. Order of St. Michael and St. George, Queen of Eng., 1991, Knight St. John's Ambulance (St. John's Ambulance), 1993, Knight Grand Cross of Royal Victorian Order, 1994. Mem. Masons. Mem. United Ch. Jamaica & Grand Cayman. Avocations: football, cricket, gardening, reading. Home: Montego Bay, Jamaica. Died July 11, 2014.

**COOKE, ROBERT EDMOND,** retired pediatrician; b. Attleboro, Mass., Nov. 13, 1920; s. Ronald Melbourne and Renee Jeanne (Wuillumier) C.; m. Sharon Riley, Nov. 20, 1978; children: Susan R., Anne R.; children from previous marriage: Robyn (dec. 1967), Christopher, Wendy (dec. 2005), W. Robert, Kim. BS, Yale U., 1941, MD, 1944, postgrad., 1948-50; DSc (hon.), U. Miami, 1970; D in Med. Sci. (hon.), Yale U., 1994. Intern, then asst. resident dept. pediat. New Haven Hosp., 1944-46; instr. pediat. Yale U., New Haven, 1950-51, asst. prof. pediat. & physiology, 1951-54, assoc. prof., 1954-56; from resident to assoc. pediatrician Grace-New Haven Cmty. Hosp., 1951-56; pediatrician-in-chief Johns Hopkins Hosp., 1956-73; chmn. dept. Johns Hopkins Sch. Medicine, 1956-73; Grover Powers prof. pediat. Nat. Assn. Retarded Children, 1957-59, Given Found. prof., 1962-73; vis. prof. Harvard U., 1972-73; vice chancellor health scis., prof. pediat. U. Wis., 1973-77; pres. Med. Coll. Pa., 1977-80; A. Conger Goodyear prof., med. dir. SUNY, Buffalo, 1982-88, prof. emeritus, 1989—2014, chmn. dept. pediatrics, 1985-88; pediatrician-in-chief Children's Hosp. of Buffalo, 1985-88. With Mass. Dept. Mental Health, 1980-82; chmn. med. advisory bd. Kennedy Found.; mem. adv. bd. Nat. Ctr. Rehab. Rsch., Nat. Inst. Child Health and Human Devel., 1991-2014 Editor, contbr. to pediat. textbooks, profl. jours. Trustee Children's Rehab. Inst. Capt. M.C., AUS, 1946-48. NIH postdoctoral fellow Sch. Medicine Yale U., 1948-50, John and Mary Markle scholar, 1951-55; recipient Mead Johnson award in Pediatrics, 1954, Kennedy Internat. award for Disting. Svc. in Field of Mental Retardation, 1968, Howland medal, 1992, Medallion of the Surgeon Gen., 1993. Fellow American Acad. Pediat., American Psychiat. Assn. (disting.); mem. APHA, American Pediat. Soc. (John Howland award 1991), Soc. for Pediat. Rsch. (pres. 1965-66), American Soc. for Clin. Investigation, Md. Med. Soc., American Fedn. Clin. Rsch., Inst. of Medicine, Aurelian Hon. Soc., Phi Beta Kappa, Sigma Xi, Alpha Omega Alpha. Home: Vero Beach, Fla. *My goal has been the enjoyment of socially useful achievement. To achieve that has required periods of self renewal to adapt to a rapidly changing world.* Died Feb. 2, 2014.

**COOLEY, JOHN KENT,** journalist, author; b. NYC, Nov. 25, 1927; arrived in Greece, 1999; s. John Landon and Ruth (Robinson) C.; m. Edith Stoegermayer, Mar. 21, 1951 (div. 1970; 1 child, Katherine Anne; m. Eugenia Katelani, May 22, 1970; 1 child, Alexander Anthony. BA, Dartmouth Coll., Hanover, NH, 1952; postgrad., U. Vienna, 1953, Columbia U., NYC, 1965. Editl. rschr. US High Commn., Vienna, 1950-51, 52-53; freelance reporter Paris edit. N.Y. Herald Tribune, Morocco, 1953-55; translator, press attache US Army C.E., Casablanca, Morocco, 1955-57; freelance journalist Christian Sci. Monitor, NBC News, others, Algeria, Tunisia, Libya, 1957-64; Middle East corr. Christian Sci. Monitor, Beirut, 1965-78, def. corr. Washington, 1978-80; corr., Middle East specialist ABC News, London, 1981-91, Nicosia, Cyprus, 1991-98. Occasional lecturing in US and abroad, 1967-2008 Author: Baal, Christ and Mohammed, 1965, East Wind Over Africa, 1996, Green March, Black September, 1973, Libyan Sandstorm, 1981, Payback, 1991, Unholy Wars, 1999, 2000, 2002, An Alliance Against Babylon, 2005, Currency Wars, 2008; contbr. numerous articles to mags. and jours. on Middle East. Served with Signal Corps, US Army, 1946-47, Austria. Recipient Overseas Press Club citations, 1967, 69, 74, 82, George Polk Career award LI U., 1995; Fgn. Corr. fellow Coun. on Fgn. Rels., NYC, 1964-65; Carnegie Endowment for Internat. Peace sr. assoc., 1980-81. Mem. Internat. Inst. for Strategic Studies, Royal Inst. Internat. Affairs, Am. Historical Assn., (assoc.) Phi Beta Kappa. Avocations: swimming, reading, listening to classical music, short wave radio. Died Aug. 6, 2008.

**COONS, ELDO JESS, JR.,** retired manufacturing executive; b. Corsicana, Tex., July 5, 1924; s. Eldo Jess and Ruby (Allison) Coons; m. Beverly K. Robbins, Feb. 6, 1985; children from previous marriage: Roberta Ann, Valerie, Cheryl. Student Engring., U. Calif., 1949—50. Owner C & C Constrn. Co., Pomona, Calif., 1946—48; sgt. traffic divsn. Pomona Police Dept., 1948—54; nat. field dir. Nat. Hot Rod Assn., LA, 1954—57; pres. Coons Custom Mfg., Inc., Oswego, Kans., 1957—68; chmn. bd. Borg-Warner Corp., 1968—71; pres. Coons Mfg., Inc., Oswego, 1971—84, E.B.C. Mgmt. Cons., Lake Havasu City, Ariz., 1984—2004. Mem. Kans. Gov.'s Adv. com. State Architects Assn. With Corps Engrs. US Army, 1943—46. Recipient Paul Abel award, Recreational Vehicle Industry Assn., 1978, 1st Ann. New Product award, Kans. Gov.'s Office and Kans. Engring. Soc., 1982—83; named to Exec. and Profl. Hall of Fame, Recreational Vehicle/Mobile Homes Hall of Fame, Hot Rod Hall of Fame, 1961, Internat. Drag Racing Hall of Fame, 1991. Mem.: KT, Mcpl. Motor Officers Assn., Am. Inst. Mgmt. (fellow pres.'s coun.), Nat. Juvenile Officers Assn., Oswego C. of C. (dir.), Rotary (pres. Oswego club 1962—63), Shriners, Young Pres. Orgn., Am. Legion, Masons. Achievements include originator first city sponsored police supervised drag strip. Home: Las Cruces, N.Mex. Deceased.

**COOPER, HARRY EZEKIEL,** music educator; b. Kansas City, Mo., Dec. 10, 1897; s. Ezekiel and Helen (Moore) Cooper; m. Agnes Bickford, Nov. 18, 1926; children: Robert Ezekiel, Alice Caroline. MusB, Horner Inst. Fine Arts, 1920; MusD, Bush Conservatory, 1923; AB, Ottawa U., 1937. Supt. music Liberty Schs., Mo., 1917—19; prof. music, chmn. dept. William Jewell Coll., 1919—28; dean music Ottawa U., 1928—37; chmn. dept. music, prof. music Meredith Coll., from 1937. Organist, choirmaster Kansas City Chs., Mo., 1911—37, Christ Ch., Raleigh, NC, 1937—47, 1st Bapt. Ch., from 1948; organist NC Symphony Orch., 1949; condr. Raleigh Oratorio Soc., 1940—48. Contbr. musical articles, various songs, others. Fellow: Am. Guild Organists; mem.: Raleigh Chamber Music Guild (pres. 1942—43), NC Music Tchrs. Assn. (pres. 1943—44). Home: Chapel Hill, NC. Deceased.

**COPLEY, ALFRED L.,** biomedical scientist, physician; b. Germany, June 19, 1910; came to U.S., 1937; m. Nina Trygavadottir, Apr. 1949 (dec. June 1968); 1 child, Una Dora. MD, U. Heidelberg, Germany, 1935, Basel U., Switzerland, 1936; Dr. med. h.c., U. Heidelberg, 1972. Physiologist, biorheologist; rsch. prof. life sci., bioengring. Poly. U., Bklyn., from 1974. Founder, editor-in-chief Biorheology, 1962—, Thrombosis Rsch.; founder, coeditor-in-chief Clin. Hemorheology. Fellow N.Y. Acad. Scis., AAAS, World Acad. Art and Sci. Died Jan. 1992.

**CORBY, SIR BRIAN,** insurance company executive; b. Raunds, Northants, Eng., May 10, 1929; s. Charles Walter and Millicent Corby; m. Elizabeth Mairi McInnes, 1952; children: Fiona, Jane, Nicholas. MA, St. John's Coll., Cambridge, Eng., 1952; DSc (hon.), City U., London, 1989; D.Litt. (hon.), Coun. for Nat. Acad. Awards, 1991; DSc (hon.), U. Hertfordshire, 1996. Mgr. O'seas Life Prudential Assurance Co. Ltd., London, 1966-68, asst. gen. mgr., 1968-73, dep. gen. mgr., 1974-75, gen. mgr., 1976-79; chief actuary Prudential Corp. Plc., London, 1980-81, group chief exec., 1982-90; chmn. Prudential Corp. Plc, London, 1990-95, Montanaro Smaller Cos., Investment Trust Plc, London, 1995-99, Moorfield Estates Plc, London, 1996-2000, The Brockbank Group, London, 1997-2000. Chmn. South Bank Bd., U.K., 1990-98; bd. dirs. NASD, Inc. Pres. Geneva Assn., 1990-93, Nat. Inst. Econ. & Social Rsch., 1994-2003; chancellor U. Hertfordshire, 1993-96 Created knight bachelor Order of Brit. Empire. Fellow Inst. Actuaries; mem. Confedn. Brit. Industry (pres. 1990-92). Home: Herts, England. Died Apr. 23, 2009.

**CORDONI, BARBARA KEENE,** special education educator; b. Peoria, Ill., Dec. 21, 1933; d. Edward Leland Keene and Grace (Wolpert) Werner; m. Gregory Walter Kupiec, June 9, 1984; children: Mark, Heather, Lance, Tara. BA, Southwestern U., 1955; MEd, Duke U., 1974, EdD, 1976; D in Ednl. Psychology. Certified Sch. Psychologist Specialization in Learning Disabilities. Tchr. Catskills (N.Y.) Pub. Sch., 1955-56, Oneonta (N.Y.) Pub. Sch., 1956-57; dir. Nursery Sch., Woodstock, N.Y., 1959-62; dir. pvt. sch. Merritt Island, Fla., 1967-72; resource tchr. Brevard County Schs., Merritt Island, 1972-73; clin. instr. Duke U., Durham, N.C., 1973-75; asst. prof. Greensboro (N.C.) Coll., 1975-77, So. Ill. U., Carbondale, Ill., 1977-81, assoc. prof., 1981-87, prof., from 1987. Coordinator So. Ill. U. Clin. Ctr. Achieve Program, Carbondale, 1977—; cons. in field. Author: Living with a Learning Disability, 1987, 2d rev. edit., 1990; contbr. numerous articles to profl. jours. Mem. Ill. Gov.'s Adv. Council, Springfield, Ill., 1982-90; participant Pres.'s Commn. for Employment of the Handicapped, Washington. Named Outstanding Woman of the Year, 1970, Brevard County Tchr. of the Year, 1972, Fla. Dist. Tchr. of the Year, 1973; recipient Disting. Teaching award, 1977, Wallace Phillips Meml. Award for Outstanding Svc. in the Field of Learning Disabilities, 1977. Mem. Coun. for Exceptional Children, Learning Disabilities Assn. Am. (Lifetime Achievement award 1997), N.C. Assn. for Rsch. in Edn., Am. Ednl. Rsch. Assn., Internat. Dyslexia Assn., Internat. Acad. for Rsch. in Learning Disabilities, Golden Key, Kappa Delta Pi, Phi Delta Kappa. Democrat. Methodist. Avocations: bird watching, travel abroad. Deceased.

**CORDOVEZ, DIEGO,** retired ambassador, former Ecuadorean government official; b. Quito, Ecuador, Nov. 3, 1935; s. Luis Cordovez-Borja and Isidora Zegers de Cordovez; m. Maria Teresa Somavia, 1960 (dec. 2003); 1 child, Diego Law grad., U. Chile, 1962. Bar: Chile 1962. Fgn. svc. officer Govt. of Ecuador, 1962-63; econ. affairs officer UN, NYC, 1963; polit. officer on spl. missions to Dominican Republic, 1965, Pakistan, 1971; dir. ECOSOC, 1973-78; asst. sec.-gen. for econ. and social matters UN, NYC, 1978-81, under sec.-gen. for spl. polit. affairs, 1981-88, rep. for implementation Geneva Accords, from 1988; min. fgn. affairs Govt. of Ecuador, Quito, 1988—92, amb. to UN NYC, 2005—07. Spl. rep. of UN sec.-gen. on Libya-Malta dispute, 1980-82; sec.-gen.'s rep. on UN Commn. of Inquiry on histage crisis in Teheran, 1980; sr. officer responsible for efforts to resolve Iran-Iraq war, 1980-88; UN mediator, Afghanistan, 1982-88; UN spl. envoy to Grenada, 1983. Author: UNCTAD and Development Diplomacy, 1971. Decorated Order of Merit (Ecuador). Mem. American Soc. Internat. Law. Avocations: reading, carpentry. Died May 24, 2014.

**COREY, JIM,** protective services official; b. Scotland, Feb. 24, 1922; arrived in US, 1922; s. James William and Margaret (Stewart) Corey; m. Sunny Lee, May 1, 1964; children: Garth, Shanon Nanilei, Heather Leinani. BA, Mich. State U., 1948; MA, U. Hawaii, 1954; MS, U. Wis., 1959. Cert. in guidence counselor. Property mgr., broker, Hawaii; advanced through grades to col. US Army, 11th Airborne Div., 82d Airborne Div. and STRAC 18th Airborne Corps; World War II, Korea and Vietnam, comdr. Green Berets, Indo China, 1942—71; ret, 1971; supervising mgr. Housing Authority, Hawaii, 1976—81; vice dir. Civil Def., Hawaii, Honolulu, from 1982. Exec. bd. mem, Aloha Coun. Boy Scouts America, Honolulu; course dir. Woodbadge, 1975. Recipient Silver Beaver award, Boy Scouts America, 1961. Mem.: VFW (post comdr., Honolulu), Green Beret Assn. (past pres.), Honolulu Bd. Realtors, Inst. Real Estate Mgmt. (property mgr.), Outrigger Canoe Club (Honolulu). Home: Kaneohe, Hawaii. Died Nov. 27, 1995.

**CORLEY, RALPH RANDALL,** electrical engineer; b. Eldorado, Ark., July 22, 1941; s. Leander Gene and Vallie (Patterson) C.; m. Sharron Jeane Denney, Sept. 16, 1961; children: Ralph Randall Jr., Richard Clinton, Chad Justin. BSEE, So. Meth. U., 1964. Registered profl. engr., Tex. Elec. engr. Alcoa, Point Comfort, Tex., 1964-68; chief elec. engr. Cavalier Constrn. Co., Kwinana, West Australia, 1968-72; project elec. engr. Alcoa, Pitts., 1972-74, corp. safety engr., 1978-80, chief elec. engr. Mobile, Ala., 1974-78, elec. maintenance supt. Warrick County, Ind., 1980-87, reliability and systems supt., 1987-96, cons., from 1996. Contbr. articles to profl. mags. Mem. IEEE, Aircraft Owners and Pilots Assn. Methodist. Avocations: pvt. pilot, golf. Home: Venice, Fla. Died Jan. 9, 2008.

**CORNELIUS, ALETA,** artist, painter; b. Pittsburgh, PA, Mar. 21, 1922; d. James Alvin and Ethel Aleta (Lewis) Cornelius; children: Ethel Aleta, James Alvin; m. Walter S. Eastman, Oct. 1992. Student in painting & design, Carnegie Mellon Univ., Pittsburgh, PA. Sec., dir. PIttsburgh Associated Artists, Pittsburgh, PA, 1948-53; tchr. (painting) YWCA, Pittsburgh, PA, Providence, RI; art tchr. Rocky Hill Country Day, East Greenwich, RI; owner Pvt. Art Gall., Providence; curator Hyannis Art Assn., Cape Cod, MA; art dir. Dahl, Orresman, Morgan, Mousey, RI, 1963-72; freelance painter & restorer Aleta Cornelius Studio, Flagler beach, Fla., from 1972. Chartered pres., hon. mem. Flagler County Counc. for the Arts, 1989; logo designer, catalog designer, Fla. Artists Grp., judge, art shows, restoration and appraisals, Grps. in South and North East, 1954-90, 1970—, appointed grant panel, Fla. Arts Counc., Tallahassee, 1991-92, served as judge and juror for many art exhbns. Designer, (book cover) Little Brown, Kind Hearted Tiger, 1955, (catalog and layout) Fla. Artists Grp., 1979, (logo) numerous grps., 1985, 93; one man shows: Attleboro Mus., MA, Providence Art Club, Cape Cod Art Assn. Gall., Gal. Internat., NY; exhibitions: Am. Acad. of Arts and Letters, NY, Whitney Annual, NY, Metropolitan Mus., NY, Carnegie Inst., Pittsburgh, PA, Carnegie Inst. summer show, Pitsburgh, PA, Attleboro Mus., Attleboro, MA; juried shows: Corcoran, Wash., D.C., Pepsi-Cola, Nat. Acad. of Design, NY, (Achievement award), Butler Art Mus., OH, Boston Arts Festival, Rhode Island Arts Festival (1st prize), Nat. Acad. of Design, New England Artists - Jordan Marsh, Fla, Artists Grp.; contbr. articles to profl. publications. Mem. Presdl. Task Force, Republican Party, Wash., 2000, Nat. Com., Republican Party, Wash., 2000, Senatorial Com., Republican Party, Wash., 2000, Fla. and Flagler County, Republican Party, Wash., 2000; apptd. grant arts coun. Sec. of State of Fla., 1991-92. Recipient Kappa Kappa Gamma Pi Timne Achievement Awd., Hot Spgs., VA, 1952, Childe Hassam Purchase Awd., Am. Acad. of Arts & Letters, NY, 1960, First Prize R.I. Art Festival, Providence Jour. and City, R.I., 1960, Life Mag. 19 Am. Artists, Life Mag., 1951-52, many awards Pitts. Assn. Artists shows, Purchase award 100 Friends of Pitts. Art, many others; named Hon. Alumnus Carnegie Mellon U., 2000. Mem. (hon.), charter pres., Flagler County Coun. for the Arts (life), 1989-2000, Kappa Kappa Gamma. Republican. Baptist. Deceased.

**CORNELIUS, WILLIAM EDWARD (BILL CORNELIUS),** retired utilities executive; b. Salt Lake City, Sept. 6, 1931; s. Edward Vernon and Gladys (Bray) C.; m. Mary Virginia Bunker, June 13, 1953; children: Mary Jean, Linda Anne. BS, U. Mo., 1953; M. Liberal Arts, Washington U., St. Louis, 1983. C.P.A., Mo. Mgr. Price Waterhouse & Co., St. Louis, 1955-62; asst. comptroller Union Electric Co., St. Louis, 1962-64, dir. corporate planning, 1964-67, exec. v.p., 1968-80, pres., 1980-88, chmn., CEO, 1988—93. Bd. dirs. Union Electric Co., 1988-93, Ameren Corp., 1997-2004 Served to 1st lt., AUS, 1953-55. Named St. Louis Man of Yr., 1991. Mem. Mcpl. Theater Assn. (bd. dirs.), Beta Theta Pi. Home: Saint Louis, Mo. Died Aug. 6, 2014.

**CORNFORTH, SIR JOHN WARCUP (KAPPA CORNFORTH),** chemist; b. Sydney, Sept. 7, 1917; s. John William and Hilda (Eipper) Cornforth; m. Rita H. Harradence, Sept. 27, 1941; children: Brenda Osborne, John, Philippa Horder. BSc, U. Sydney, 1937, MSc, 1938; PhD, Oxford U., 1941, DSc (hon.), 1976, Swiss Fed. Inst. Tech. (ETH), Zurich, 1975, Trinity Coll., Dublin, U. Liverpool, U. Warwick, U. Aberdeen, U. Hull, U. Sussex, U. Kent. Mem. sci. staff Med. Rsch. Coun., London, 1946—62; dir. Milstead Lab. Chem. Enzymology, Shell Rsch. Ltd., Sittingbourne, Kent, England, 1962—75; Royal Soc. rsch. prof. U. Sussex Sch. Chemistry & Molecular Sciences, Brighton, Kent, England, 1975—82, prof. emeritus, 1982—2013. Co-author: The Chemistry of Penicillin, 1949; contbr. articles to profl. jours. Decorated Comdr., Order of Brit. Empire (CBE) Her Majesty Queen Elizabeth II, Companion, Order of Australia; recipient Stouffer prize, 1967, Prix Roussel, 1972, Centenary medal, Australia, 2003; corecipient Nobel Prize in Chemistry, Royal Swedish Acad. Sciences, 1975; named Australian of Yr., 1975. Fellow: American Chem. Soc. (Ernest Guenther award 1969), Royal Soc. Chemistry (Corday-Morgan medal 1953, Flintoff medal 1966), Royal Soc. (Davy medal 1968, Royal medal 1976, Copley medal 1982); mem.: NAS (assoc.), Netherlands Acad. Sci., Biochem. Soc. (CIBA medal 1966), Australian Acad. Sci. (corr.), American Soc. Biol. Chemists (hon.). Achievements include research in chemistry of penicillin, synthesis of steroids and other biologically active natural products, chemistry of heterocyclic compounds, biosynthesis of steroids, enzyme chemistry. Home: Lewes, England. Died Dec. 14, 2013.

**CORONEL, RAUL ANGULO,** sculptor; b. Mexicali, Mex., Feb. 26, 1926; s. Jose Agapito and Emilia Angulo Coronel; m. Leanore Burden Cobb, Nov. 17, 1951 (dec. Nov. 18, 1999). BS, U. Calif., Berkeley, 1951; BA, La. State Coll., 1954; cert. gemologist, GIA Santa Monica, Calif., 1984. Pres. Stoneware Design Inc., LA, 1966—70; cons. designer Winbrook China, Santa Monica, 1970—80, Arch Pottery, LA, 1970—80, Westwood Ind., NJ, 1980; treasure craft designer Calif., 1980—81. One-man shows include Paul Rivas Gallery, 1962, Represented in permanent collections U.S. Info. Ctr., Montevideo, Uruguay, Lytton Savs. & Loan, Palo Alto, Calif., Bank of Commerce, Ft. Worth, mural, Summa Corp. (Howard Hughs), Malibu, Calif. With USMCR, 1943—46. Recipient awards, Cal. State Fair, 1955—61, Young Ams., N.Y., 1955. Republican. Baptist. Avocations: painting, writing, gemology, music. Home: Tustin, Calif. Died Aug. 18, 1999.

**CORPANY, B. W.,** fund raising executive; b. Wichita Falls, Tex., June 8, 1934; s. Herbert L. and Sarah Ellen (Sisk) C.; m. Carol Lorraine Seaberg, Feb. 24, 1956; 1 child, John Frederic. BS, Baylor U., 1961; MEd, U. Houston, 1970. Tchr./coach Galvestonn (Tex.) pub. schs., 1961-63; bus. adminstr. Div. Fgn. Missions, Assemblies of God, various locations, 1963-77; mktg. mgr. Singer Sewing Machine Co., Beirut, Lebanon, 1977-78; asst. Wayne Shabaz & Assocs., Houston, 1978-80; exec. dir. Mission of Mercy, Tacoma, Wash., from 1980. Bd. dirs. Goodwill Industries, Tacoma, 1986—, Tacoma YMCA, 1986—, div. capt. fund-raising dr., 1986—. Mem. Rotary. Republican. Assemblies of God. Avocations: racquetball, jogger, reading. Home: Colorado Springs, Colo. Died Oct. 15, 1991.

**CORPUZ, TERESA AGRIFINA,** school principal; b. San Francisco, Apr. 4, 1951; d. Faustino Ceria and Virginia (Baltazar) C. BA in English, San Francisco State U., 1972; MS in Counseling, Calif State U., Hayward, 1981. Cert. secondary tchr., Calif. Tchr. Mendota (Calif.) Sch. Dist., 1973-75, Tracy (Calif.) Sch. Dist., 1975-82; counselor Livermore (Calif.) Sch. Dist., 1982-83; vice-prin. Albany (Calif.) Unified Sch. Dist., 1983-85, prin., from 1987, Sunnyvale (Calif.) Elem. Sch. Dist., 1985-87. Cons. sch. edn. U. Calif., Berkeley, 1987-88. Bd. dirs. Albany-Berkeley YMCA, 1987-89. Recipient Calif. Educator award Calif. State Dept. Edn. and Milken Family Found., 1987. Mem. Assn. Calif. Sch. Adminstrs., Assn. Supervision and Curriculum Devel., Phi Delta Kappa, Delta Kappa Gamma. Democrat. Roman Catholic. Avocations: travel, cross country skiing, reading, photography. Home: San Francisco, Calif. Died 1998.

**COTHREN, EVANGELINE (MRS. J.C.),** retail store owner; b. Light, Ark., May 16, 1925; d. Vance and Laura May (Newberry) Cupp; m. J.C. Cothren; 1 child, Jackson David. BS, Ark. State U., 1944; MA in Bus. Edn., Peabody Coll., 1952. Bookkeeper Vance Cupp & Sons, Light, from 1935, Union Auto Sales, Memphis, 1945-46; tchr. bus. edn. Greene County Tech. High Sch., Paragould, Ark., 1947-74; propr. Evangeline's Footwear, Paragould, from 1974. Sec. Chaffin-Cothren Auto Sales, Paragould, 1983—; co-chair Greene County Courthouse Preservation Soc. Inc., 1991-; chmn. Greene County Scholarship Fund, 1988-, Beaark Endowment Found. Greene County, 2001-; bd. mem. Ark. Cmty Found., 1996-2002. Mem. Paragould Centennial Celebration, 1986, Greene County Sesquicentennial, Paragould, 1986, Ark. Sesquicentennial, Little Rock, 1986; v.p. Northeast Ark. Devel. Council, Jonesboro, 1987— Named Ark. Tchr. Yr., Ark. Edn. Com., 1971, Disting. Educator, Peabody Coll.; 1971. Mem. Paragould C. of C. (pres. 1986—), Delta Kappa Gamma (scholarship com. 1985—, various nat. offices held 1948—). Baptist. Home: Light, Ark. Died Jan. 18, 2008.

**COTTERILL, RODNEY MICHAEL,** biophysics researcher; b. Bodmin, Cornwall, Eng., Sept. 27, 1933; arrived in Denmark, 1967; s. Herbert Harold and Aline Ivy (Le Cerf) C.; m. Vibeke Ejler Nielsen, Feb. 7, 1959; children: Marianne, Jennifer. BSc, U. Coll., London, 1957; MS, Yale U., 1958; PhD, Cambridge U., Eng., 1962; DSc, London U., 1973. Assoc. physicist Argonne (Ill.) Nat. Lab., 1962-67; prof. Danish Tech. U., Lyngby, 1967—2003. Vis. prof. U. Tokyo, 1978, 1985; lectr. Am. Mus. Natural History, NYC, 2003. Author: The Material World, 1985, No Ghost in the Machine, 1989, Enchanted Looms, 1998, Biophysics: An Introduction, 2002. Cpl. RAF, 1952—54. Recipient Hermer Meml. prize, Copenhagen U., Denmark, 1978; named Knight of the Danebrog, Denmark, 1979; James Arthur letr. Am. Mus. Natural History, N.Y., 2003. Fellow Royal Danish Acad. Scis. and Letters, Inst. Physics U.K. (chartered physicist). Avocations: sailing, choral singing, chess, writing. Home: Farum, Denmark. Died June 24, 2007.

**COUCHMAN, ROBERT GEORGE JAMES,** retired foundation executive; b. Toronto, Ont., Can., Feb. 21, 1937; s. Robert George and Mary (Bigelow) C.; m. Jane Barker (div. 1985); children: Barbara, Stephen, Michael. BA, Queen's U., Kingston, Ont., 1965; MEd, U. Toronto, 1969. Tchr. Scarborough (Ont.) Bd. Edn., 1957-63; dir. student svcs. Etobicoke (Ont.) Bd. Edn., 1963-74; exec. dir. Family Svc. Assn. Met. Toronto, 1974-89; pres. Donner Can. Found., Toronto, 1989-93; assoc. Re Think Group, 1993; dir. Terra Nova, 1995-97; chmn. Outward Bound Can., 1990—94. Co-chmn. UN Can. Com. Internat. Yr. of Family, 1993-94; patron Outward Bound Can., 1995-99; mem. nat. adv. com. Fed. Minister of Health on Rural Health. Author: Reflections on Canadian Character, 2003; contbr. 40 articles to profl. jours Chmn. Outward Bound Wilderness Sch., 1987-88, Outward Bound Can., 1990-94; pres. Can. Mental Health Assn., Ont., 1971-73; dir. White Ribbon Found. of Can.; bd. dirs. Addiction Rsch. Found., Ont., 1980-86, Metro Toronto Housing Co., 1982-88, United Way Metro Toronto, 1994-96; vice chmn. Vanier Inst. of the Family, 1988-90; chmn. Atlin Big Water Soc.; gov., Grey Owl Nature Trust, 1997-2000, advisor Can. Arctic Resources Com.; exec. dir. PQR Found., 1993— Mem.: Yukon Family Svcs. Assn. (exec. dir. 1999—2001), Ont. Assn. Profl. Social Workers (hon.), Rotary (com. chmn.). United Church. Home: Whitehorse Yukon, Canada. Died May 3, 2008.

**COURTENAY, WALTER ROWE, JR.,** biology professor, researcher; b. Neenah, Wis., Nov. 6, 1933; m. Francine Marie Saporito, June 11, 1960 (div.); children: Walter Rowe Courtenay, III, Catherine Simpson Kantner. BA, Vanderbilt U., Nashville, 1956; MS, U. Miami, Coral Gables, Fla., 1960; PhD, 1965. Vis. asst. prof. zoology Duke U., Durham, 1964—65; asst. prof. zoology Boston U., 1965—67; assoc. ichthyology Harvard U., Cambridge, Mass., 1965—70; prof. zoology Fla. Atlantic U., Boca Raton, 1967—99; rsch. fishery biologist, vol. US Geol. Survey, Gainesville, Fla., from 2001. Contractor Office Tech. Assessment, US Congress, Washington, 1991—92. Editor: (book) Distribution, Biology, and Management of Exotic Fishes. Recipient U. Rsch. award, Fla. Atlantic U., 1992, Disting. Tchr. award, 1972—73. Mem.: Am. Soc. Ichthyologists and Herpetologists, Am. Fisheries Soc. (William E. Ricker Resource Conservation Award 2007). Avocation: photography. Home: Gainesville, Fla. Died Jan. 30, 2014.

**COURTNEY, JAMES WHITFIELD,** optometrist; b. Paducah, Ky., Jan. 8, 1951; s. James Elvis and Mary Ruth (Carlin) C.; m. Lana Jill Hatcher, Aug. 2, 1986; children: Jacob, Carlin, Addie, Jamie, Anne. BS in Optometry, U. Houston, 1974, OD, 1976. Pvt. practice, Murray, Ky., from 1976. Mem. Am. Optometric Assn. (contact lens sect.), Ky. Optometric Assn., Murray Rotary (pres. 1994-95). Republican. Baptist. Avocations: hunting, running, genealogy. Home: Murray, Ky. Died May 21, 2008.

**COWAN, HENRY JACOB,** architectural engineer, educator; b. Aug. 21, 1919; s. Arthur and Erna (Salisch) C.; m. Renate Proskauer, June 22, 1952; children: Judith Anne, Esther Katherine. BS with honors, U. Manchester, Eng., 1939, MS, 1940; PhD, U. Sheffield, Eng., 1952; DEng, U. Sheffield, 1963; MArch, U. Sydney, Australia, 1984, DArch (hon.), 1987. Mem. faculty of architecture U. Sydney, from 1953, prof., from 1953, head dept., 1953-84, dean arch., 1966-67, pro-dean, 1968-84. Vis. prof. Cornell U., 1962, Kumasi (Ghana) U., 1973, Trabzon (Turkey) U., 1976; pres. Bldg. Sci. Forum of Australia, 1969-71. Author 27 books, including: The Master Builders, Science and Building, Architectural Structures, Dictionary of Architectural and Building Technology, 4th edit., Environmental Systems, The Science and Technology of Building Materials, Handbook of Architectural Technology, Structural Systems; editor Archtl. Sci. Rev., 1958—2006, Vestes, 1966—78; book rev. editor:. With Royal Engrs., 1941-45. Decorated officer Order of Australia. Fellow ASCE, Coun. for Tall Bldgs., Royal Australian Inst. Archs. (hon. 1979), Royal Soc. Arts (Hartnett medal 1998), Inst. Structural Engrs. (Spl. Svc. award 1988), Instn. Engrs. Australia (R. W. Chapman medal 1956, J. Monash medal 1994). Home: Mosman, Australia. Died July 15, 2007.

**COWLES, FLEUR (MRS. TOM M. MEYER),** author, artist; b. Montclair, NJ, Jan. 20, 1908; s. m. Bertram Clapper (div.); m. Atherton Pettingell (div.); m. Gardner Cowles, Dec. 27, 1946 (div. 1955); m. Tom Montague Meyer, Nov. 18, 1955. LLD, Elmira Coll., NY, 1954. Spl. cons. Famine Emergency Com., White House, Washington, 1946; assoc. editor, dir. spl. editorial depts. Look mag., 1947, fgn. corr., 1955-58; assoc. editor Quick mag., 1949; editor Flair mag., 1950-51, Flair Annual, 1952; fgn. dir. Cowles Mags., Inc. Cons. to chief of staff Hdqrs. USAF, 1950; mem. nat. adv. com. on women's participation Fed. Civil Def. Adminstrn., 1953-55; Spl. rep. Pres. Eisenhower (with rank of spl. ambassador) at coronation of Queen Elizabeth II of Eng.; founder Inst. Am. Studies Oxford (Eng.) Coll. Author: Bloody Precedent, 1952, The Case of Salvator Dali, 1959, The Hidden World of Hadhramoutt, 1963, Tiger Flower, 1968, Treasures of the British Museum, 1970, Lion and Blue, 1974, Friends and Memories, 1975, All Too True, 1981, The Flower Game, 1983, Flower Decorations, 1985, People as Animals, 1986, 87, An Artist's Journey, 1988, The Life and Times of the Rose, 1992, She Made Friends and Kept Them, 1995, The Best of Flair, 1996; exhibited paintings, London, 1959, 63, 66, 75, N.Y.C., 1960, 62, 64, 67, 73, Rome, 1961, Paris, 1962, Athens, 1966, Los Angeles, 1967, Madrid, 1967, Rio de Janeiro, 1966, 68, Dallas, 1969, 71, São Paulo, 1965, 66, 72, Seattle, 1970, San Francisco, 1973, Detroit, 1974, Kans., 1975, Dusseldorf, 1976, El Paso, 1985, Bermuda, 1986, Singer Mus., Holland, 1977, Cheekwood Mus., Nashville, 1978, Hammer Galleries, 1978, Partridge Gallery, London, 1978, 83, Gregg Juarez Gallery, 1980, Roelant Gallery, Amsterdam, 1980, S. L. Gallery, Dallas, El Paso Mus., 1985, Wako Galleries, Tokyo, 1988, Galeria de Arte Grife y Escoda, Barcelona, Spain, 1990, Chris Beetles Gallery, London, 1991, Portal Gallery, Chgo., 1991, Tiller Gallery, Dallas, 1992, Nat. Mus. Women in Arts, Washington, 1993, Red Fox Fine Art Gallery, Middleburg, 1993, The Alisan gallery, Hong Kong, 1995—, Galeria Montevideo, Swan Coach House Gallery, Atlanta, 1999. Pres. Leakey Trust, Europe; trustee LSB Leaky Found., Soc. Rehab. Facially Disfigured, SatelLife, Boston, Am. Mus. in Britain; chmn. Friends of Royal Geog. Soc. Decorated chevalier Legion of Honor (France), Queen's Coronation medal (U.K.), Order So. Cross (Brazil); comdr. Order So. Cross (Brazil), Order of Bienfaisence (Greece); La dama de Isabel Catolica (Spain); established Fleur Cowles Fellowships at U. Tex. at Austin. Fellow Royal Coll. Art (hon., founder), Inst. for Am. Studies Oxford U. Home: London, England. Died June 5, 2009.

**COX, PAT,** artist; b. Pasadena, Calif., Mar. 6, 1921; d. Walter Melville and Mary Elizabeth (Frost) Boadway; m. Dale William Cox Jr., Feb. 19, 1946; children: Brian Philip, Dale William III, Gary Walter. BA, Mills Coll., 1943, MA, 1944. Graphic artist Pacific Manifolding Book Co., Emeryville, Calif., 1944-45; tchr. art to adults China Lake, Calif., 1957-63; tchr. art to children Peninsula Enrichment Program, Rancho Palos Verdes, Calif., 1965-67; graphic artist Western Magnum Corp., Hermosa Beach, Calif., 1970-80; tchr. art workshop Art at Your Fingertips, Rancho Palos Verdes, 1994-95. One-woman shows include Palos Verdes Art Ctr., Rancho Palos Verdes, Calif., 1977, 79, 83, 92, Thinking Eye Gallery, LA, 1988, Ventura Coll. Art Galleries, Calif., 1994, Mendenhall Gallery, Whittier Coll., Calif., 1995, The Gallery at Stevenson Union, So. Oreg. U., Ashland, 1996, Fresno Art Museum, Fresno, Calif., 1999; two person exhibits Laguna Art Mus., Laguna Beach, Calif., 1971, Creative Arts Gallery, Burbank, Calif., 1993; group exhibits include Long Beach Mus. Art, Art Rental Gallery, 1979, LA County Mus. Art, Art Rental Gallery, 1979, Palm Springs Mus. Art, 1980, Laguna Art Mus., 1981, N.Mex. Fine Arts Gallery, 1981, Pacific Grove Art Ctr., 1983, Phoenix Art Mus., 1983, Riverside Art Mus., 1985, Laguna Art Mus., 1986, Zanesville Art Ctr., Ohio, 1987, The Thinking Eye Gallery, LA, 1987, 89, Hippodrome Gallery, Long Beach, 1988, N.Mex. State Fine Arts Gallery, 1988, Newport Harbor Art Mus., 1988, Downey Mus. Art, 1990, 92, Internat. Contemporary Art Fair LA, 1986, 87, 88, 92, U. Tex. Health Sci. Ctr., 1992, Long Beach Arts, 1991, 92, 93, Young Aggressive Art Mus., Santa Ana, 1993, U. Ark. Fine Arts Gallery, Fayetteville, 1994, Laura Knott Art Gallery, Bradford Coll., Mass., 1994, Bridge Street Gallery, Big Fork, Mont., 1994, St. John's Coll. Art Gallery, Santa Fe, 1995, LA Harbor Coll., Calif., 1995, Walker Art Collection, Garnett, Kans., 1995, San Francisco State U., 1996, Coleman Gallery, Albuquerque, 1996, Loyola Law Sch., LA, 1996, San Bernardino County Mus., 1996, Prieto Gallery, Mills Coll., Oakland, Calif., 1996, U. So. Calif. Hillel Gallery, LA, 1997, The Stage Gall. Merrick, NY, 1999, Nabisco Gall., E. Hanover, NJ, 2000, California State U., LA, 2001, Pasadena Historical Mus. Gallery, Calif., 2002, Schneider Mus. Art So. Oreg. U., Ashland, Oreg., 2003, Biola U., La Mirada, Calif., 2006, Albuquerque Mus Art., 2007, Sidney and Berne Davis Art Ctr., Ft. Myers, Fla., 2008, 57 Underground Pomona Calif., 2009, Zask gallery, Rancho Palos Verdes Calif., 2010. Trustee LA Art Assn., 1972-79, Somarts Bay Gallery, San Francisco, 2004, LA World Airports Exhbm., 2005; bd. dirs. Palos Verdes Art Ctr., 1966-70, 87-89, chair exhbn. com., 1982-85, co-chair Art for Fun(d)s Sake, 1966; judge Tournament of Roses Assn., Pasadena, 1975; mem. strategic planning Palos Verdes Art Ctr., 1988; mem. Pacific Pl. Planning Commn. Percent for Art, San Pedro, Calif., 1989; juror Pasadena Soc. Artists, 1973, 81, Women Painters West, 1984-85; office term R.E. Holding Co., 2005-. Recipient Silver Pin award Palos Verdes Art Ctr., 1988, Calif. Gold Discovery award V.I.P. Jury Panel, LA, 1994. Mem. Nat. Watercolor Soc. (juror 1981, 1st v.p. 1980, 4th v.p. 1984), Nat. Mus. Women in the Arts, Oakland Mus. Art, Mus. Contemporary Art, LA County Mus. Art, Palos Verdes Cmty. Art Assn. (cert. appreciation 1981). Avocations: gardening, reading. Home: Palos Verdes Estates, Calif. Died Feb. 15, 2014.

**COYNE, WILLIAM JOSEPH,** former United States Representative from Pennsylvania; b. Pitts, Aug. 24, 1936; s. Phillip and Mary (Ridge) C. BS in Acctg., Robert Morris Coll., 1965. Mem. Dist. 22 Pa. House of Reps., 1970-72; mem. Pitts. City Council, 1973-80, US Congress from 14th Pa. Dist., Washington, 1981—2003. With AUS, 1955-57. Democrat. Roman Catholic. Died Nov. 3, 2013.

**CRAFT, ROBERT HOMAN,** banker, corporate executive; b. L.I., NY, Feb. 9, 1906; s. George Wallace and Nellie A. (Homan) C.; m. Janet M. Sullivan, Feb. 5, 1938; children: Robert Homan, Carol Ann (Mrs. C. Barry Schaefer), George Sullivan. BS, U. Pa., 1929. Asst. treas. Guaranty Trust Co. of N.Y., 1937-40, 2nd v.p., 1940-43, v.p., treas., 1943-52; exec. v.p. Am. Securities Corp., NYC, 1953-56; pres., vice chmn. Chase Internat. Investment Corp., 1956-60; pres., chmn. exec. com. Paribas Corp., 1960-64; chmn. fin. com. Miss. River Corp., 1965-78, fin. v.p., 1965-70, also bd. dirs., past chmn. bd. dirs.; chmn. fin. com., mem. exec. com. Mo. Pacific R.R. Co., 1965-76; chmn. fin. com. Miss. River Transmission Corp., also bd. dirs. Trustee, mem. exec. com., chmn. investment policy com. N.Y. Bank Savs., 1944-64; chmn. fin. com. Tex. and Pacific Ry. Co., 1965-76; chmn. fin. com., mem. exec. com. Mo. Improvement Co., Chgo. & Ea. Ill. R.R., 1965-76, Mo.-Ill. R.R. Co., 1965-76; bd. dirs., mem. exec. com. Mass. Mut. Corp. Investors, Mass. Mortgage Income Investors; mem. exec. com. Merc. Trust Co., St. Louis, 1965-71, now advisor, bd. dirs.; mem. Lower Manhattan adv. bd. Chem. Bank N.Y. Trust Co.; bd. dirs. Sentinal Funds, Mich. Chem. Corp., Modern Am. Mortgage Co., 1st. Beehive Co., Intertel Corp.; chmn. A.B.S. Industries; bd. dirs., mem. exec. com., investment policy com. Mass. Mut. Life Ins. Co.; bd. dirs., chmn. fin. com. Combined Commn. Corp.; cons. Fed Res. Bd. 1952. Bd. dirs., treas. N.Y. Heart Assn., 1941-66; vice chmn. Youth Consultation Svc., 1967, gen. chmn., 1968-96; mem. emeritus bd. advisors Ariz. State U. Mem. Investment Bankers Assn. Am. (pres. 1956-57), Pilgrims of U.S., Univ. Club, Bond Club, Wall St. Club (past pres., gov.), Fox Meadow Tennis Club, Scarsdale (N.Y.) Golf Club, Blind Brook Club, Shenorock Shore Club, Rockefeller Ctr. Luncheon Club, Augusta Nat. Golf Club, Colony Club (Springfield, Mass.), Desert Forest Golf Club, Ponte Vedra Club (Fla.), Desert Mountain Golf Club (Scottsdale, Ariz.). Died Dec. 26, 1999.

**CRAIG, JOHN CHARLES,** educational consultant; b. Belvidere, Ill., Dec. 28, 1946; s. John George and Ruth Effie (Coan) C.; m. Mary Louise Loftus, Feb. 16, 1974; children: David Thomas, Jesse Lindsey. BS, No. Ill. U., 1969; PhD, Northwestern U., 1984. Cert. edn. adminstr., tchr. Tchr. Rockford (Ill.) Pub. Sch., 1969-71; rschr., cons. Ill. State Bd. Edn., Springfield, 1971—2007, Am. Insts. Rsch., from 2007. Bd. dirs., v.p. Ill. Fedn. Tchrs., 1987-93, pres. Ctrl. Ill. Area Coun., 1983-91, Ill. Fedn. State Office Educators, Springfield, 1992-96; cons. nat. ednl. std. setting activities, nat. geographic std. and assessment, history steering com., nat. assessment edn. progress 2003; mem. design team Ill. Goal Assessment Program; designer Ill. Prairie State Achievement Test, 1996-99. Editor: Alternate Assessment, Social Sciences, Alternate Assessment, Geography; contbr. articles to profl. jours. Prodr., broadcaster Sta. WSSR Radio, Springfield, 1976-87; leader Boy Scouts Am., Springfield, 1987-03. Mem. Nat. Coun. Social Studies, Ill. Coun. Social Studies (bd. dirs. 2001—07), Ill. State Hist. Soc. (bd. dirs. 2005-2012). Avocations: model railroads, woodworking. Died May 23, 2013.

**CRANDALL, STEPHEN HARRY,** engineering educator; b. Cebu, Philippines, Dec. 2, 1920; s. William Harry and Julia Josephine (Kuenemann) C.; m. Patricia Estelle Stickel, Jan. 21, 1949; children: Jane S., William S. M.E., Stevens Inst. Tech., 1942; PhD, MIT, 1946. Registered profl. engr. Mem. staff radiation lab MIT, Cambridge, 1942-43, instr. math, 1944-46, asst. prof. mech. engring., 1947-51, assoc. prof., 1951-58, prof., from 1958, Ford prof. engring., 1975-91, prof. emeritus, from 1991, head div. applied mechanics, 1957-59, 61-67, head. div. mechanics and materials, 1968-71. Vis. prof. Marseille, France, 1960, U. Nat. Autonoma Mex., Mexico City, 1967, Ecole Nat. Superieure de Mecanique, Nantes, France, 1978, Fla. Atlantic U., 1993, Korean Advanced Inst. Sci. and Tech., 1996; exch. prof. Imperial Coll., London, 1949; NSF sci. faculty fellow, vis. scholar U. Calif., Berkeley, 1964-65; hon. rsch. assoc. Harvard U., 1971-72; Lady Davis vis. prof. Technion, Israel, 1987. Author: Engineering Analysis, 1956, Random Vibration in Mechanical Systems, 1963, (with others) Dynamics of Mechanical and Electromechanical Systems, 1968; editor: Random Vibration vol. 1, 1958, Random Vibration vol. 2, 1963, (with others) Mechanics of Solids, 1959, author (with others), 3d edit., 1978; contbr. artcles to profl. jours. Recipient ASCE Von Karman medal, 1984, Freudenthal medal, 1996, Alexander von Humboldt sr. U.S. scientist award, 1989; Fulbright fellow, London, 1949. Fellow AAAS, ASME (Worcester Reed Warner medal 1971, v.p. 1978-80, hon. mem. 1988, Timoshenko medal 1990, Den Hartog award 1991, Caughey Dynamics award, 2009), Am. Acad. Arts and Scis., Am. Acoustical Soc. (Trent-Crede medal 1978), Am. Acad. Mechanics (pres. 1997, Disting. Svc. medal 1993); mem. NAS, NAE, NSPE, Soc. Indsl. and Applied Math., Am. Math. Soc., Am. Soc. for Engring. Edn., Internat. Union Theoretical and Applied Mechanics (chmn. U.S. del. 1974), Russian Acad. Engring. (fgn. mem.). Home: Concord, Mass. Died Oct. 29, 2013.

**CRANDELL, CHESTER J.,** state legislator; b. Holbrook, Ariz., June 19, 1946; m. Alice Crandell; 9 children. BS in Agr. Edn., U. Ariz.; MEdn, Northern Ariz. U. Mem. Govs. P20 Com. on Stds. & Assessments; employee Southwest Forest Industries; mem. CTE Adv. Com. to State Bd. of Edn.; designated pub. lobbyist NAVIT Sch. Dist.; asst. supt. Joint Technol. Edn. Dist.; mem. Dist. 5 Ariz. House of Reps., 2011—13; mem. Dist. 6 Ariz. State Senate, 2013—14. Republican. Lds Church. Died Aug. 4, 2014.

**CRANE, WILLIAM HARRY,** accounting educator; b. Mar. 21, 1925; Home: Montgomery, Ala. Died Oct. 21, 1994.

**CRAWFORD, HELEN MARIETTA,** teacher, artist, writer, retired; b. Lincoln, Mo., Jan. 22, 1907; d. Robert Finley and Margaret Eliza (Moore) Wilson; m. Hugh Byron Hudelson, Nov. 30, 1933 (dec. Apr. 1959); children: Robert Lee, Donna May, David Martin, Ralph Allen, James Arthur; m. John Hindman Crawford, Aug. 26, 1962 (dec. Sept. 1974); stepchildren: John William, George Wesley. BS, Sterling Coll., 1927, BA, 1930; postgrad., Wyo. U., 1932-59, Portland State U., 1964-65. Tchr. Torrington (Wyo.) Pub. Sch., 1930-33, 1959-64, West Hills Christian Sch., Portland, Oreg., 1964-67; pres. Woman's Christian Temperance Union, Portland, 1973-80. Editor, lectr. Oreg. Woman's Christian Temperance Union, Portland, 1973-80; art tchr. pvt. classes, Wyo., Oreg., Kans., 1930-83. Author: Discovering Young Life, 1986, Poems of Praise, 1991, Our Wonderful World, 1992; also illustrator. County coordinator I Love Kans., Topeka, 1986—. Mem. AARP, Ret. Tchrs., Garden Club (Sterling, Kans.). Republican. Presbyterian. Avocations: gardening, flower arranging, painting, quilting, ceramics. Deceased.

**CRAWFORD, KENNETH CHARLES,** retired academic administrator; b. Nokomis, Ill., Oct. 31, 1918; s. Charles Bryant and Blanche Dora (Gates) C.; m. Madge Marie Douglas, Aug. 23, 1942; 1 son, James Douglas. BA, Ill. Coll., 1946, S.JD (hon.), 1970; JD, U. Va., 1951; grad., Command and Gen. Staff Coll., 1957, Army War Coll., 1962; MA, George Washington U., 1962. Bar: Va. 1951, Ga. 1967, Korean 1965, U.S. Supreme Ct. 1970, D.C. 1977. Commd. 2d lt. U.S. Army, 1942, advanced through grades to col., 1962; served in (F.A. and JAG Corps); tchr. legal subjects U. Md., U. Ga., Ga. State U., Nat. U., Washington, 1957-67; comdr. JAG Sch., 1967-70; ret., 1970; pres., CEO Ken Crawford Ednl. Inst., Inc., 1986-89. Editor: Laws of the Republic of Korea, 1964. Assoc. dir. edn. Southwestern Legal Found., Dallas, 1970-71, Atty. at Law, 1990-92; dir. edn. and tng. Fed. Jud. Ctr., Washington, 1971-86; cons. Fed. Jud. Ctr., 1986-87. Decorated Legion of Merit with 2 oak leaf clusters, Soldiers medal, Bronze Star, Belgian Fourragere, Disting. Citizen citation Ill. Coll., 1993. Mem. State Bar Va., Korean Bar, Order of Coif. Home: Birmingham, Ala. Died Nov. 18, 2012.

**CRAWFORD, PURDY,** lawyer, retired consumer products and services company executive; b. Five Islands, Nova Scotia, Nov. 7, 1931; m. Bea Crawford; 6 children. BA, Mount Allison U., 1952; Bachelors in Law, Dalhousie Law Sch., 1955; LLM, Harvard Law Sch., 1956; D (hon.), U. New Brunswick, 2010. Assoc. Osler, Hoskin & Harcourt LLP, 1958—62, ptnr., 1962—70, sr. ptnr., 1970—85, counsel, 2000—14; spl. lectr. York U. Osgoode Hall Law Sch., 1964—68; lectr. U. Toronto Law Sch., 1969—71; CEO Imasco Ltd., Montreal, 1985—95, non-exec. chmn., 1995—2000, Maple Leaf Foods, Inc., 2011—12. Bd. dirs. Dominion Textile Inc., Montreal, Inco Ltd., Toronto, Trinova Corp., Ohio.Imasco Ltd., 1985-2000, FootLocker Inc., 1995-2007, Emera Inc., 1995-2004, Clearwater Seafoods Inc., 2002-06, Manitoba Telecom Services, Inc., 2004-06 Recipient Yee Hong Golden Achievement award, 2007; named a Companion of the Order of Canada, 2007, Champion of Public Edn., The Learning Partnership, 2007; named an Officer of the Order of Canada, 1996; named to The Nova Scotia Bus. Hall of Fame, 1997, The Canadian Bus. Hall of Fame, 2000. Died Aug. 12, 2014.

**CREECH, HERBERT,** lawyer, educator; b. Harlan, Ky., Mar. 17, 1947; s. Herbert and Delphia (Caudill) C.; m. Jill S. Hobbs, Dec. 21, 1969 (div. Mar. 1979); children: Michelle, Briana, Charlotte, Ransley. BA, U. Ky., 1968, JD, 1973. Bar: Ohio 1973, U.S. Dist. Ct. (so. dist.) Ohio 1974, U.S. Ct. Appeals (6th cir.) 1974, U.S. Supreme Ct. 1982. Law clk. Dayton Fed. Cts., Ohio, 1973-75; asst. prosecutor Montgomery County Prosecutor's Office, Dayton, 1976-78; sole practice Dayton, from 1978. Instr. Antioch Coll., Yellow Springs, Ohio, 1977-81; Sinclair Coll., Dayton, 1976-81. Mem. Dayton Dem. Club. Served with U.S. Army, 1969-71, Vietnam. Named to Hon. Order Ky. Col. Mem. ABA, Ohio State Bar Assn., Fed. Bar Assn., Dayton Bar Assn., Assn. Trial Lawyers Am. Democrat. Avocations: sports, politics, writing, travel. Deceased.

**CRICK, RONALD PITTS,** ophthalmologist, consultant; b. Toronto, Ont., Can., Feb. 5, 1917; arrived in U.K., 1919; s. Owen Pitts and Margaret (Daw) C.; m. Jocelyn Grenfell Robins, Mar. 22, 1941; children: Martin, Gillian, Jonathan, Adrian, Humphrey. MRCS LRCP, King's Coll. Hosp. Med. Sch., 1939. DOMS, FRCS (Eng.), FRCOPhth. Registrar ophthalmic, cons. ophthalmic surgeon King's Coll. Hosp., London, 1946-82, hon. cons. ophthalmic surgeon, from 1982. Cons. ophthalmic Royal Eye Hosp., London, 1950-69, Belgrave Hosp. for Children, London, 1950-66; tchr. ophthalmology U. London, 1960-82; chmn. ophthalmic tng. com. South East Thames Regional Hosp. Bd., London, 1973-82. Co-author: (with R.B. Trimble) A Textbook of Clinical Ophthalmology, 1987, (with P.T. Khaw), 3rd edit., 2002; contbr. chpts. in books. Hon. chmn. Internat. Glaucoma Assn., London, 1974-2000, pres., 2000—. Surgeon lt. Royal Naval Vol. Res., 1939-46. Recipient Duke-Elder Glaucoma award Internat. Glaucoma Congress, 1985, Alim Meml. lectr. Ophthalmol. Soc. Bangladesh, 1992. Fellow Royal Coll. Surgeons (examiner ophthalmology), Royal Soc. Medicine (v.p. ophthamology); mem. Am. Soc. Contemporary Ophthalmology (charter, medal of Achievement 1985), European Glaucoma Soc., Royal Motor Yacht Club, Royal Automobile Club Pall Mall. Avocations: swimming, sailing, reading, motoring. Died 2009.

**CRIPPEN, FRED MERRIL,** principal, educator, farmer; b. Gove, Kans., Sept. 27, 1905; s. Charles Gerald and Emma Jane (Rhodes) C.; m. Arlene Rose Hefner, May 1, 1927; 1 child, Donald Eugene. BE, Fort Hayes State U., Kans., 1957. Tchr. Gove County, Kans., 1924-29, supt. Kans., 1929-33, prin., tchr. Kans., 1933-45, 48-65, supt. county Kans., 1965-66; prin. St. Francis (Kans.) Grade Sch., 1945-48; tchr. Grinnell (Kans.) Grade Sch., 1966-69; prin., tchr. Missouri Flats Sch., Gove County, 1969-71, ret., 1971. Former mayor, mem. city coun. City of Gove. Mem. Kans. Tchrs. Assn., Internat. Orgn. Odd Fellows. Republican. Methodist. Avocation: woodworking. Deceased.

**CRIQUI, FERNAND,** scientific writer; b. Strasbourg, France, May 14, 1921; s. Fernand and Alice (Sigle) C.; m. Margot Westermann, Sept. 1, 1949. Grad., U. Strasbourg, 1945. Prof. Univ. Centre for Teaching of Journalism, Strasbourg, 1959-83. Contbr. to many French and fgn. sci., med. & cultural periodicals, 1946—; author numerous monographs & books, over 2000 articles. Laureat de l'Acad. Française, 1970. Mem. AAAS, N.Y. Acad. Scis., Mouvement Universel de la Responsabilité Scientifique, Soc. des Ecrivains d'Alsace et de Lorraine. Avocations: chess, tennis, music. Deceased.

**CROCKER, FRANKIE,** radio broadcast executive; b. 1937; Student, U. Buffalo, U. So. Calif. With WUFO, Buffalo, news dir., jazz show host; with WZUM, Pitts., WGCI, Chgo., KUTE Calif., WWRL N.Y.; host WMCA-FM, NYC, WLIB-FM, 1972. Video jockey MTV Video Hits 1 Music Channel. Recipient DJ of the Yr. award (15), Program Dir. of Yr. award (3) Billboard Mag., Celo award. Died Oct. 22, 2000.

**CROCKER, GEORGE WESLEY,** investment executive, geologist; b. Pleasanton, Tex., Feb. 22, 1930; s. John Wesley and Katy Mae (Daughtrey) Crocker. BS in Geology, Tex. A&M U., 1951; postgrad. Audited Investments, U. Houston, 1961. Gen. ptnr. Crocker European Investments, London, from 1977; chmn. Perchem, Ltd., Harlow, England, from 1977; pres. Energeco Spa, Rome, from 1978, Perchem Spa, Milan, from 1979, Dudigen, Switzerland, from 1981. Asst. mgr. Baritina de Venezuela, Caracas, 1955—60; acquistion diversification Baroid-NL Industries, Houston, 1960—63, mgr., Rome, London, 1963—73; dir. European ops. ICD-NL Industries, London, 1973—77. Recipient Queens award, London, 1983. Mem.: AIME, Soc. Petroleum Engr., Am. Club (London, Rome). Republican. Methodist. Home:, England. Died May 28, 2009.

**CROCKER, JOY LAKSMI,** retired musician, composer; b. San Antonio, June 12, 1928; d. Hugo Peoples and Anna Kathryn (Ball) Rush; m. Richard Lincoln Crocker, July 24, 1948 (div. July 1977); children: Nathaniel Homer, Martha Wells Sandino, David Laramie. MusB, Yale U., 1950; MS, Yale U., Berkeley, Calif., 1956; postgrad., Grad. Theol. Sem., 1978-81. Min. music First Congl. Ch., Branford, Conn., 1949-62; dir. music therapy West Haven (Conn.) Hosp.; min. music St. Stephen's Episcopal Ch./Sch., Orinda, Calif., 1963, First Bapt. Ch., Oakland, Calif., 1964-66, Greek Orthodox Cathedral, Oakland, 1969, San Quentin (Calif.) Protestant Chapel, 1976-78, Plymouth United Ch. of Christ, Oakland, 1977-84; pianist, assoc. dir. First Bapt. Ch., Managua, Nicaragua, 1984-94; organist, pianist Mills Grove Christian Ch., 1995—96; organist St. Andrews Presbyn. Ch., Pleasant Hill, Calif., 1996—2001; dir. music ministries Trinity Meth. Ch., Berkeley, 2001—05; ret., 2005. Prof. organ San Francisco Conservatory Music, 1962-69; chmn. piano dept. Nicaraguan Nat. Conservatory Music, 1984-93; founder-dir., prof. Bapt. Conservatory of Music U. Poly., Managua, 1989—; instr. Yogalayam Yoga Ashram; creator, dir. diverse low-budget innovative music edn. programs, 1969—; mem. adjudicator Nat. Guild Piano Tchrs., Music Tchrs. Assn. Calif.; invited lectr. 3d Encuentro Iberoamericano de Prof. y Estudiantes de Musica, Cuba, 1999; piano concert and master class tours, Cen. and South Am., 1995. Pianist, Internat. Symposium of Universal Articulate Understanding of Sci., 1999; concert/presentation World Parliament of Religions South Africa, 1999; pianist Balboa Park Pause for Peace Millennial Concert, 1999-2000, World Bank Counter Summit, Prague, UN 55th Anniversary Global Peace Walk Vigil, 2000. Civic and legislation coord. Ch. Women United, Oakland unit and state unit, 1996—, chair for global concerns; bd. dirs. Quantum Leap 2000, 1999—; pianist, organist Ch. Women United State Unit; San Francisco Bay area coord. for Hague Appeal for Peace; commr. World Summit on Peace and Time, Costa Rica, 1999, del./concert pianist World Social Forum, Brazil, 2001; pianist World Coun. Ch. Ann. Conv., Oakland, Calif., 2002, Forgiveness First Internat. Conv., Kamloops B.C., 2002. Recipient award, San Francisco Concerto Orch., 1997, Music Tchrs. Assn. Calif., 1998, 2000—02, 2004; named Woman of Yr., Bus. and Profl. Women's Club, Inc., 1995. Mem. Am. Guild Organists, Am. Coll. Musicians, Music Tchrs. Assn. Mem. United Ch. of Christ. Avocations: travel, political activism. Deceased.

**CROFTON, SIR JOHN WENMAN,** physician; b. Dublin, Mar. 27, 1912; arrived in UK, 1933; s. William Mervyn Crofton and Mary Josephine Abbott; m. Eileen Chris Mercer, Dec. 14, 1945; children: Richard, Patricia, Pamela, Alison, Ian. BA, Cambridge U., Eng., 1933, MA, 1937, B Medicine B Surgery, 1937, MD, 1946; DHC, U. Bordeaux, France, 1996; DSc h.c., U. London, 2001. House physician St. Thomas' Hosp., London, England, 1937-38; mem. staff tuberculosis unit Brit. Med. Rsch. Coun., 1947-48; lectr., sr. lectr. Royal Postgrad. Med. Sch., London, England, 1947-51; sr. med. asst. inst. Diseases of the Chest, London U., 1949-50; prof. respiratory diseases and tuberculosis Edinburgh (Scotland) U., 1952-77, dean faculty medicine, 1963-66, vice prin., 1969—70. Cons. WHO, Geneva, 1968-98, 2001-09 Co-author: (non-fiction) Respiratory Diseases (3 English, 1 Russian, 1 Italian and 1 Spanish edit.), 1969, Tobacco: A Global Threat (in 8 langs.), 2002; co-author: (editor) Clinical Tuberculosis (in 23 langs.), 1992, 1999; contbr. articles to profl. jours. Lt. maj., lt. col. Royal Army Med. Corps, 1939—46, Eng. Recipient Weber-Parkes prize, Royal Coll. Physicians London, 1966, WHO medal tobacco activities, 1988, Edinburgh medal Sci. and Soc., 1995, Galen medal Therapeutics, Soc. Apothecaries (London), 2001, Union medal Tuberculosis and Tobacco, Internat. Union Tuberculosis and Lung Diseases, 2005; named Knight Comdr. of the Most Excellent Order of the British Empire (KBE), Her Majesty Queen Elizabeth II, 1977. Fellow: Royal Coll. Physicians Edinburgh (pres. 1973—76). Avocations: mountain climbing, music, reading. Home: Edinburgh, Scotland. Died Nov. 3, 2009.

**CROMARTY, ARTHUR MARTIN,** retired judge; b. Bklyn., July 3, 1919; s. Alexander and Ellen (Fallon) C.; m. Ellin A. Hirsch, Feb. 15, 1947 (dec. 2013); children: Alice Cromarty Herrick, Ross, Peter. BS, U. Ala., Tuscaloosa, 1942; JD, St. John's U., 1948; postgrad., Nat. Jud. Coll., Reno, 1971. Bar: N.Y. 1949, US Dist Ct. (eastern dist.) N.Y. 1952, US Supreme Ct. 1954. Assoc. Eugene J. Blumberg, Amityville, N.Y., 1948-50; jr. ptnr. Blumberg & Cromarty, Amityville, 1950-54; ptnr. Blumberg, Cromarty & Fitz Gibbons, Amityville, 1954-66; justice NY State Supreme Ct., Babylon, 1966—93; adminstrv. judge Suffolk County, Babylon, 1974-91; of counsel Long, Tuminello, LLP, 1993—2014. Atty. Village of Lindenhurst, 1951-56. Elected councilman Town of Babylon, 1956-57, elected supr., 1958-63; chmn. bd. suprs. County of Suffolk, Riverhead, 1962-63; vice chmn. N.Y. State Thruway Authority, Albany, 1963-66; chmn. Suffolk County Republcan Com., Blue Point, 1959-66, mem. 1960-63; mem. exec. com. N.Y. State Republican Com., 1960-66. Capt. USAAF, 1943-45, ETO. Mem. ABA, Nat. Assn. Trial Ct. Adminstrs., Cath. Lawyers Guild (Judge of Yr. 1986, bd. dirs.), N.Y. State Bar Assn., N.Y. State Trail Lawyers Assn., N.Y. State Assn. Justices Supreme Ct., Suffolk County Bar Assn., Kiwanis. Avocations: golf, reading. Home: Lindenhurst, NY. Died May 1, 2014.

**CRONIN, PAUL WILLIAM,** consultant, former congressman, entrepreneur; b. Boston, Mar. 14, 1938; s. William Joseph and Anna (Murphy) C.; m. Kathleen Sears, 1957 (div. 1987); children: Kevin P., Kimberley A. Student, Merrimack Coll., Andover, Mass., 1957-58; BA in Govt. and Econs, Boston U., 1962; MPA, Harvard U., 1969. Chief asst. to Congressman F. Bradford Morse, 1963-67; mem. 93d Congress from Mass.; mem. com. sci. and astronautics, interior and insular affairs subcoms. on energy, sci. and tech., mines, nat. parks; founder, pres., chief exec. offic Highline Industries Inc.; founding mem. Solar Rating and Cert. Corp., 1980; chmn. Highline Products Corp., Old Saybrook, Conn.; owner PWC & Assocs., Andover, Mass. Mem. adv. bd. Solar Energy Rsch. Inst. and Western Sun; nat. pres. Solar Energy Industries Assn.; trustee Solar Energy Rsch. Found.; mem. Internat. Energy Conf., Paris, France, 1976; del. UN Conf. on New and Renewable Sources of Energy, Nairobi, Kenya, 1981; bd. dirs. Mass. Port Authority. Pres., mem. exec. com., precinct capt. Andover Rep. Town Com., 1960; del. Rep. State Convs., 1962, 64, 66, 70, 74, 78, 82-90, Rep. Nat. Conv., 1968, 72, 76, 88;N.E. regional dir. Rep. Congl. Campaign Com., 1969-70; selectman Town of Andover, 1963-66; mem. Mass. Ho. of Reps., 1967-69; chmn. Mass. Multiple Sclerosis Soc., Bon Secours Hosp. Guild, Men of Merrimack Coll.; mem. Haus Rissen Seminar for Am. Opinion Leaders, Hamburg and Berlin, 1983; presdl. advisor Merrimack Coll.; exec. com. Boston U.; candidate for Gov. Mass., 1990; co-chair Corp. Rels. Com., Merrimack Coll. Recipient Outstanding Young Man award Jr. C. of C., 1964, Future Leader award Fgn. Policy Assn., Paul Revere Leadership medal, Young Rep. Outstanding Citizen award, DAV disting. svc. award, VFW silver star for involvement with a rescue; named Coll. Rep. Man of Yr., 1990; named to Hall of Fame Lawrence Boys' Club, 1982. Mem. Mass. Selectmans Assn. (life), Mass. Legis. Assn. (life), Nat. Assn. State Legislators, Solar Energy Industries Assn. (pres.), Former Mems. Congress (life), C.L.A. Grad. Sch. Alumni Assn. Boston U. (pres. 1988-89), Lawrence Boys Club (pres. 1990-91), Hibernians, Lanam, Capitol Hill-Harvard Club, KC, Elks. Home: Needham, Mass. Died Apr. 5, 1997.

**CROUCH, PAUL FRANKLIN,** minister, religious organization administrator; b. St. Joseph, Mo., Mar. 30, 1934; s. Andrew Franklin and Sarah Matilda (Swingle) C.; m. Janice Wendell Bethany, Aug. 25, 1957; children: Paul F., Matthew W. BTh, Central Bible Coll. and Sem., Springfield, Mo., 1955. Ordained to ministry, 1955; dir. fgn. missions film and audio visual dept. Assemblies of God, 1955-58; assoc. pastor 1st Assembly of God, Rapid City, S.D., 1958-60, Central Assembly of God, Muskegon, Mich., 1960-62; gen. mgr. TV & film prodn. center Assemblies of God, Burbank, Calif., 1962-65; gen. mgr. Sta. KREL, Cornona, Calif., 1965-71, Sta. KHOF, KHOF-TV, Glendale, Calif., 1971-73; founder, pres. Sta. KTBN-TV, Trinity Broadcasting Network, Los Angeles, 1973—2013. Recipient Best Religious film award Winona Lake Film Festival, 1956 Mem. Nat. Assn. Religious Broadcasters, Western Religious Broadcasters Assn., Assn. Christian TV Stas. (founder) Died Nov. 30, 2013.

**CROWLEY, JOSEPH B.,** lawyer; b. Chgo., July 15, 1905; Student, Crane Jr. Coll., Northwestern U.; JD, Chgo.-Kent Coll. Law, 1926. Bar: Ill. 1926. Former master in chancery Superior Ct., Cook County, Ill.; now mem. firm Tews, Theisent & Crowley, Chgo. Mem. ABA, Ill. Bar Assn., Chgo. Bar Assn. Home: Chicago, Ill. Died Mar. 31, 1990.

**CRUM, HENRY HAYNE,** lawyer; b. Denmark, SC, Oct. 1, 1914; s. J. Wesley Jr. and Priscilla (Hart) C.; m. Mary Bass, July 27, 1946; children: Elizabeth, J. Wesley III, H. Hayne III. AB, Wofford Coll., 1935; LLB, U. S.C., 1939. Bar: S.C. 1939, U.S. Ct. Appeals (4th cir.) 1953, U.S. Dist. Ct. S.C. 1959, U.S. Tax Ct. 1963, U.S. Supreme Ct. 1953. Ptnr. Crum & Crum Attys., Denmark, 1939-40 and from 45.

Mem. S.C. Supreme Ct. Grievance and Discipline Com., 1978-81, S.C. Supreme Ct. Specialization Adv. Bd. for Taxation, 1982-84, S.C. Bar Resolution of Fee Disputation Bd., 1983-84; city atty. City of Denmark, 1946-76. With AUS, 1940-45, ETO, Col. USAR ret. Decorated Bronze Star, ETO Ribbon with 5 Campaign Stars, Bronze Arrowhead. Democrat. Methodist. Avocations: golf, tennis, reading. Home: Denmark, SC. Deceased.

**CRUMBAUGH, JAMES CHARLES,** retired psychologist; b. Terrell, Tex., Dec. 11, 1912; s. Charles Miller and Hallie Virginia (Dansby) C.; m. Edna Mae Bailey, 1938 (dec. 1946); 1 child, Charles; m. Teresa Amanda Croteau, June 14, 1975 (dec. Feb. 1989); m. Lois Dickson Hicks, Nov. 10, 1992. AB, Baylor U., Waco, Tex., 1935; AM, So. Meth. U., Dallas, 1938; PhD, U. Tex., 1953. Lic. psychologist, Miss.; cert. logotherapist. Psychologist, tchr. Memphis State U., 1947-56; chmn. Dept. Psychology MacMurray Coll., Jacksonville, Ill., 1957-59; rsch. dir. Bradley Ctr., Inc., Columbus, Ga., 1959-64; staff psychologist VA Med. Ctr., Augusta, Ga., 1964-65, Gulfport, Miss., 1965-80; so. regional dir. Inst. Logotheraphy, Berkeley, Calif., from 1980. Rsch. cons. Internat. Graphoanalysis Soc., Chgo., 1968—. Author: Counseling for Graphoanalysts, 1970, Everything to Gain, 1973; co-author: Logotherapy, 1980; sr. author (with M.T. Manolick) The Purpose-in-Life Test, 1965; co-editor: Primer of Projective Techniques, 1990. With U.S. Army air Corps, 1941-45. Rsch. fellow Duke U., 1954-55. Mem. APA, Miss. Psychol. Assn. (Kinlock Gill award 1989), Southeastern Psychol. Assn., So. Soc. Philosophy and Psychology, Psi Chi. Roman Catholic. Avocation: writing. Deceased.

**CRUMP, MICHAEL JOHN,** tax specialist; b. LA, Oct. 11, 1946; s. Eugene L. and Elizabeth M. (Finn) Crump; m. Susan Jane Pendergast, Apr. 5, 1975; 1 child, Catherine. BA, U. San Francisco, 1968; JD, U. San Diego, 1972. Rsch. asst. US Dist. Ct., San Diego, 1974—75; tax analyst Marshall Acctg., Long Beach, Calif., 1975, Tymshare Unitax, Anaheim, Calif., 1975—78, tax mgr., from 1978. Mem. IRS Task Force, 1982—86; apptd. v.p. Unitax-McDonnell Douglas Corp., 1986; lectr. in field. Author manuals in field. Mem.: Nat. Assn. Computerized Tax Processors (treas. 1978—81, v.p. 1981—82, pres. 1982—84), Nat. Soc. Pub. Accts., Xplor (v.p. 1980—81). Democrat. Roman Catholic. Home: Laguna Beach, Calif. Died Sept. 1986.

**CUBA, IVAN,** artist; b. Notts, Eng., 1920; Student, U. Auckland, New Zealand; DLitt, Editorial Poets Acad. India. Editor: International Poets India. Hon. rep., pres. Temple of Arts Mus., U.S.A., Centro Studi E Scambi Internat., Italy. Served in WWII, POW. Recipient Poet Laureate gold Medal Rome, 1979, Greek gold medal, 1941; named poet laureate Internat. Acad., 1995, M. Madhusudan award India, 2000, silver medal Internat. Man of Yr., 1996. Fellow Acad. Leonardo da Vinci Rome (life). Achievements include development of Cuba-Lox theory on Stars and Tannin theory on Arteriosclerosis. Home: Auckland, New Zealand. Died Feb. 9, 2007.

**CUCKNEY, SIR JOHN GRAHAM,** banker; b. India, July 12, 1925; s. E. J. Cuckney; m. Muriel Boyd Cuckney, 1960 (dec. 2004). MA, U. St. Andrews. Civil asst., gen. staff War Off, 1949—57; dir. various indsl. & fin. cos., 1957—72; dir. Lazard Bros. & Co., 1964—70, J. Bibby & Sons, 1970—72; chmn. Standard Indsl. Trust, 1966—70, Mersey Docks & Harbour Bd., 1970—72, Bldg. Econ. Devel. Com., 1976—79; ind. mem. Ry. Policy Rev. Com., 1966—67; spl. mem. Hops Mktg. Bd., 1971—72; chief exec., 2d permanent sec. Property Svcs. Agy., 1972—74; sr. crown agt., chmn. Crown Agts. Oversea Govts. & Adminstrns., 1974—78; chmn. Port London Authority, 1977—79, Thomas Cook Group Ltd., 1978—87, Internat. Mil Svcs. Ltd., 1974—85; dir. Midland Bank PLC, 1978—88, Brooke Bond Group PLC, 1978—84, chmn., 1981—84; dir. John Brown PLC, 1981—86, chmn., 1983—86; dir. Royal Ins. Holdings PLC, from 1979, dep. chmn., 1982—85, chmn., from 1985, Internat. Maritime Bur., 1981—85, Westland Group PLC, 1985—89; dep. chmn. T.I. Group PLC, from 1985; dir. Brixton Estate PLC, from 1985, Lazard Bros. & Co., from 1988; chmn. 3i Group PLC, from 1987, Investors Industry Group PLC, from 1987. Elder brother Trinity House, from 1980. Died Oct. 30, 2008.

**CUGINI, ANTHONY,** federal agency administrator; BS in Chem. Engring., MS in Chem. Engring., PhD in Chem. Engring., U. Pitts. With Procter and Gamble, Gulf Rsch., Nat. Energy Tech. Lab, from 1987, focus area lead computational and basic scienecs focuse area, dir. office rsch. and devel. (ORD), dir. Died Jan. 8, 2014.

**CULBERTSON-GEORGE, DANETTE MARIE,** medical/surgical nurse; b. Burlington, Wis., Sept. 2, 1957; d. Roger Gene and Mary Agnus (Landa). Student, Waubonsee Community Coll., 1988, Parkland Jr. Coll., 1977, U. Ill., 1979. Staff nurse RN Copley Hosp., Aurora, Ill.; nurse Copley Home Health Care, Aurora, Ill. Mem. Ill. Assn. for Advancement of Assoc. Degree Nursing, Phi Theta Kappa. Deceased.

**CULLEN, PETER WRAY,** water resource educator; b. Melbourne, Victoria, Australia, May 28, 1943; children: Michelle, Belinda. B.Agr.Sci., U. Melbourne, 1965, M.Agr.Sci., Dip.Ed., U. Melbourne, 1968. Lectr. U. Melbourne, Victoria, 1966-70; rsch officer Port Phillip Authority, Melbourne, 1971-72; lectr. Canberra Coll. Adv. Edn., 1973-88; prof. resource sci. U. Canberra, 1989—2002. Chair ACT Parks and Conservation Ctr., Canberra Recipient Jolly award, Australian Soc. Limnology, 1989; named Environmentalist of Yr., Govt. of Australia, 2001 Fellow Australian Acad. Tech. Sci. and Engring.; mem. Royal Australian Inst. Pks. and Recreation, Environ. Inst. of Australia. Home: Holt, Australia. Died Mar. 14, 2008.

**CULLER-PENNEY, ANNETTE LORENA,** writer, public relations executive; b. Cordele, Ga., July 1, 1916; d. Jake Phillip Haynes Culler Sr. and Maude Burke; m. Robert A. Penney, 1963 (dec. 1996). BBA, Southern Ga. Coll., 1942, George Wash. U., 1956; postgrad., American U., 1961-62; diploma, Lewis Hotel Sch., 1978. News reporter Washington bur. Fairchild Publishing, 1946-61; pres. Internat. Mktg. Communications, Inc., Upperville, Va. Author: Dirksen, The Golden Voice of the Senate, 1968 Mem. Nat. Press Club, Internat. Home Fashions League (pres. 1952-53, v.p. 1961-62), Piedmont Rep. Women (v.p. 1984-85, pres. 1986-87), Women's Nat. Press Club (3d v.p. 1954), Am. Newswomen's Club (v.p. 1970). Baptist. Avocations: tennis, ice and roller skating, skiing, fund raising, history. Died Jan. 2, 2014.

**CUMMINS, KENNETH BURDETTE,** retired science and mathematics educator; b. New Washington, Ohio, July 27, 1911; s. Royal Clinton and Pearl (Rittenour) C. AB, Ohio Wesleyan U., 1933; MA, Bowling Green State U., 1939; PhD, Ohio State U., 1958. Tchr. sci. and math. Sulphur Springs (Ohio) High Sch., 1933-40; tchr. sci. and math. New Washington High Sch., 1941-57; asst. prof. math. Kent State U., 1957-59, assoc. prof., 1959-64, prof., 1964-81, emeritus prof., from 1981. Chmn. dept., 1964-65; Dir. Math. Inst., NSF, 1959-73. Author: Teaching of Mathematics, 1970; Contbr. articles to profl. jours. Recipient alumni award for distinguished teaching Kent State U., 1968, 76, President's medal, 1981; Christofferson-Fawcett Math. Edn. award Ohio, 1981 Mem. Math. Assn. Am., Nat. Coun. Tchrs. Math., Cen. Assn. Sci. and Math. Tchrs., Ohio Acad. Sci., Mortar Board, Phi Beta Kappa, Sigma Xi, Sigma Pi Sigma, Pi Mu Epsilon, Kappa Delta Pi. Died May 13, 1998.

**CUMMINS, NEIL JOSEPH, JR.,** land surveyor, lawyer; b. Oxnard, Calif., Sept. 14, 1945; s. Neil Joseph and Helen Louise (Porter) Cummins; m. Lynn D. Mealer, Sept. 16, 1967. Student, Claremont Men's Coll., 1962—64, Calif. State Poly. Coll., 1965—67; JD, Mid Valley Coll. Law, 1978. Registered profl. engr., Ariz., Calif., Nev., land surveyor, Calif., Nev., Ariz.; bar: Calif. 1978. Designer Ludwig Engring., San Bernardino, Calif., 1967—69; field supr. Sikand Engring., Van Nuys, Calif., 1969—77; land surveyor Reseda, Calif., 1977—88. Lectr. civil engring. Calif. Poly. Coll., Pomona, 1979—80. Fellow: ASCE; mem.: ABA, Calif. Land Surveyors Assn. (chmn. So. Calif. sect. 1984), Los Angeles County Bar Assn., Am. Water Works Assn., Am. Congress Surveying and Mapping. Died Nov. 26, 1988.

**CUNNINGHAM, PATRICK COLM,** research scientist, science administrator; b. Kilmacthomas, County Waterford, Ireland, May 24, 1933; s. Edmond and Marcella Mary (Power) C.; m. Anastasia Dolores Quigley, June 28, 1961; children: Eamon, Donal, Colm, Niamh, Niall, Orla, Dara, Ciara. B. Agr. Sci., U. Coll. Dublin, 1956; M. Agr. Sci., 1958, PhD, 1967; MS, Cornell U., 1964. Scientific officer Dept. Agr. and Food, Dublin, 1958-59; rsch. officer An Foras Taluntais, Dublin, 1959-64; sr. rsch. officer Carlow, Ireland, 1964-70; prin. rsch. officer, 1970-79; sr. prin. rsch. officer, 1979-87; head plant pathology dept., 1980-88; sr. prin. rsch. officer TEAGASC, Carlow, 1987-88; cons. fungicide efficacy, from 1988. Contbr. articles to profl. rsch. jours., chpts. to books. Bd. mgmt. Christian Bros. Sch., Carlow, 1988-91. Recipient Sir Edwin J. Butler award for plant pathology rsch., 1994. Mem. Am. Phytopathol. Soc., Soc. Irish Plant Pathologists (founder, pres. 1991-94), Brit. Soc. Plant Pathology (founder), Brit. Mycological Soc., Assn. Applied Biology, Carlow Golf Club (pres. 1994-95). Roman Catholic. Avocations: reading, golf, walking, ecology. Home: Carlow, Ireland. Died Oct. 16, 2003.

**CURIS, CARLO,** retired bishop; b. La Maddalena, Sardinia, Italy, Nov. 2, 1923; D of Canon Law, Pontifical Lateran U., Rome. Ordained priest Roman Cath. Ch., 1947. Mem. Diplomatic Corps of Holy See, Uruguay, Chile, India, U.S., Italy, from 1956; apptd. apostolic del. Sri Lanka; raised to archepiscopal titular see of Medeli, 1971; consecrated bishop, 1971; apostolic pro-nuncio to Sri Lanka, 1976; apostolic pro-nuncio in Nigeria, 1978-84; apptd. apostolic del. for Israel and Jordan, apostolic pro-nuncio in Cyprus Jerusalem, 1984-90; apostolic pro-nuncio in Can., 1990—99. Died Sept. 29, 2014.

**CURRAN, LOUIS JEROME, JR.,** choral master; b. Meriden, Conn., June 13, 1934; s. Louis Jerome and Gertrude Marie (Frederick) C. Mus.B. (H.B. Jepson scholar), Yale U., 1956, postgrad., 1959-62, New Eng. Conservatory Music, 1956-57, Oxford U., 1963-65; Mus.M., U. Tulsa, 1963. Organist, master of choristers Cathedral Ch. St. Mary, Fall River, Mass., 1956-57; dir. music 1st Congl. Ch., Wallingford, Conn., 1960-62; asso. prof. music N.E. Mo. State U., Kirksville, 1965-66; dir. music Central Congl. Ch., Worcester, Mass., 1966-67, Grace Episcopal Ch., Amherst, Mass., 1967-68; dir. music, master of choristers Ch. of St. Peter, Worcester, 1970-82, Ch. of Notre Dame, Worcester, 1982-85; founding full prof. dept. music Worcester Poly. Inst., 1966—2005. Also European and Am. concert tours including Cathedrals of Canterbury, Worcester, Chichester, Wells, Westminster Abbey, Notre Dame, Paris, Basilica, Madrid, St. Peter's Basilica, Rome, St. Francis Basilica, Assisi, Italy, Nat. Radio TV, Brussels. Mem. Worcester Cultural Commn., 1978-80. Served with AUS, 1957-59. Recipient Beacon prize Universalist Unitarian Ch., 1993; Fulbright scholar Oxford U. Mem. Orgn. Hist. Soc., Intercollegiate Mus. Council (nat. bd. 1977-80), Am. Guild Organists, Am. Musical Soc., Coll. Music Soc., Am. Choral Dirs. Assn. Democrat. Episcopalian. Home: Meriden, Conn. Died Dec. 30, 2013.

**CURTIS, DOLORES ROGERS,** writer; b. Columbus, Ohio, Apr. 16, 1929; d. Charles William and Lillian Beatrice Rogers. Student, Ctrl. State U., Xenia, Ohio, 1956—57; B.Elem.Edn., Ohio State U., 1963; attended, John Carroll U., 1980. Bookkeeper Spiegel's, Chgo., Kronfeld's, Manhattan, NY; libr. U.S. Govt. Facility, Columbus; sec. to traveling entertainer, 1949—54; tchr. Columbus Pub. Schs., 1963—68, Cleve. Bd. Edn., 1968—93. Author: Rhyming Pretzels, 2002. Avocations: reading, art, playing piano and organ, writing. Deceased.

**CURTIS, HUGH AUSTIN,** retired Canadian legislator; b. Victoria, Can., Oct. 3, 1932; s. Austin Ivor and Helen (Shepherd) Curtis; m. Sheila Diane Halford, Mar. 16, 1957; children: Gary Hugh, David Charles, Susan Diane Helen. Grad., HS. Sales mgr. broadcasting co.; alderman Dist. Saanich, BC, Canada, 1962—64, mayor, 1964—73; mem. BC Legislature, 1972—86, min. mcpl. affairs & housing, 1975—78, provincial sec., min. govt. services, 1978—79. Pres. Union BC Municipalities; chmn. Mcpl. Fin. Authority. Co-recipient John Gillin Jr. Meml. award, 1954. Mem.: Social Credit Party BC, Union Club BC. Anglican. Home: Victoria, Canada. Died May 27, 2014.

**CURTIS, JAMES THEODORE,** lawyer; b. Lowell, Mass., July 8, 1923; s. Theodore D. and Maria (Souliotis) Koutras; m. Kleanthe D. Dusopol, June 25, 1950; children: Madelon Mary, Theodore James, Stephanie Diane, Gregory Theodosius, James Theodore Jr. BA, U. Mich., 1948; JD, Harvard U., 1951; ScD (hon.), U. Mass., 1972. Bar: Mass. 1951. Assoc. Adams & Blinn, Boston, 1951-52; legal asst., asst. atty. gen. Mass., 1952-53; pvt. practice law Lowell, 1953-57; sr. ptnr. firm Goldman & Curtis, and predecessors, Lowell and Boston, from 1957. Elected mem. Lowell Charter Commn., 1969—71; del. Dem. Party State Convs., 1956—60; chmn. Greater Lowell Heart Fund, 1967—68; mem. adv. bd. Salvation Army, sec., 1956—58; mem. Bd. Higher Edn. Msss., 1967—72; bd. dirs. U. Mass. Rsch. Found., Lowell, 1965—72, Merrimack Valley Health Planning Coun., 1969—72; trustee U. Mass., Lowell, 1963—72, chmn. bd., 1968—72. With 10th mt. divsn. US Army, 1943—45, spl. agent counter intelligence corps. US Army, 1945—46. Decorated Knight Order Orthodox Crusade Holy Sepulcher. Mem.: ATLA, ABA, U. Mich. Alumni Assn., Harvard Law Sch. Alumni Assn., Am. Judicature Soc., Mass. Acad. Trial Lawyers, Middlesex Conty Bar Assn., Mass. Bar Assn., DAV, Lowell Hist. Soc., Harvard Club (Lowell, pres. 1969—71, bd. dirs.), Masons, Delta Epsilon Pi. Home: Lowell, Mass. Deceased.

**CUTLER, MORENE PARTEN,** civic worker; b. Waxahachie, Tex., July 27, 1911; d. Bedford Taylor and Lofie Mae (Stockton) Parten; m. Robert Ward Cutler, Apr. 27, 1954 (dec. Dec. 1993). Student, Trinity U., 1929, U. Okla., 1931, U. Tex., 1933. Asst. to dir. N.Y. Sch. for Interior Decoration, NYC, 1938; chief cons. Hilton Hotels Corp., Chgo., 1946-48; free-lance interior designer, 1948-54. Author: Stagecoach Inn--Iron Skillet and Velvet Potholder, 1981. 1st. pres., chmn. bd. dirs. Salado (Tex.) Bicentennial Com., 1974—, chmn. Salado Sesquitennial Com., 1984—; bd. dirs. Cen. Tex. Bicentennial Com., 1974; mem. Internat. Debutante Ball, N.Y.C., 1956—, Beautify Tex. Coun., 1976—; chmn. Beutify Salado Com., 1979-80; founder Tex. Bluebonnet Com., 1961; trustee Cen. Tex. Area Mus., Salado, 1968-75; hon. mem. Ellis County Mus., Waxahachie, 1967—. Recipient Tex Good Will awards, 1960—, Outstanding Dist. Gov. award Beautify Tex. Coun., 1984. Mem. AIA (founder N.Y. aux. chpt. 1958, citation 1966), Chautauqua Preservation Soc. (bd. dirs. Waxahachie chpt. 1975), Preservation Soc. Newport County, Salado C. of C. (bd. dirs. aux. chpt. 1974-75), Tex. Soc. Washington. Clubs: Met. (N.Y.C.). Episcopalian. Deceased.

**DAGUM, CAMILO,** economist, educator; b. Argentina, Aug. 11, 1925; arrived in Can., 1972, naturalized, 1978; s. Alexander and Nazira (Hakim) D.; m. Estela Bee, Dec. 22, 1958; children: Alexander, Paul, Leonardo. PhD (gold medal summa cum laude), Nat. U. Cordoba, 1949, degree (hon.), 1988, U. Bologna, 1988, U. Montpelier, France, 1995; D (hon.), U. Naples, 2004. Mem. faculty Nat. U. Cordoba, 1950-66, prof. econs., 1956-66, dean Faculty Econ. Scis., 1962-66; sr. rsch. economist Princeton U., 1966-68; prof. Nat. U. Mex., 1968-70; vis. prof. Inst. d'Etudes du Devel. Econ. and Social U. Paris, 1967-69, U. Iowa, 1970-72; prof. econs. U. Ottawa, Ont., Can., 1972-91, chmn. dept., 1973-75, mem. acad. senate, 1981-84, bd. govs., 1983-84, prof. emeritus, from 1992. Prof. stats. and econs. U. Milan, 1990-94, chmn. Inst. Quantitative Methods, 1993-94; prof. econs. and stats. U. Bologna, Italy, 1994-02; pres. Cordoba Inst. Social Security, 1962-63; cons. to govt. and industry, 1956—; rsch. prof. U. Rome, 1956-57, London Sch. Econs., 1960-62, Inst. Sci. Econmique Appliquèe, Coll. France, 1965; vis. fellow Birkbeck Coll., U. London, 1960-61, Australian Nat. U., 1985; guest scholar Brookings Instn., 1978-79; vis. prof. U. Siena, Italy, 1987, 88, U. Rome, 1989; spkr. in field. Author books on eocn. theory; editor econ. and statis. jours.; contbr. articles to profl. jours. Mem. Acad. Coun. Rsch. Ctr. on Income Distbn., U. Siena, 1986—, Sci. Com. on Econ. Rsch. and Analysis Program, U. Montreal, 1992-96, Sci. Adv. Com. U. Bologna, Buenos Aires. Res. officer Argentina Army, 1948. Decorated Pro-Patria Gold medal, 1948; hon. prof. Inst. Advanced Studies, Salta, Argentina, 1972; extraordinary prof. Cath. U. Salta, 1981; elected mem. Accademia di Scienze e Lettere, Istituto Lombardo, 1992—. Fellow Acad. Sci. of Bologna; mem. Internat. Inst. Sociology, Internat. Statis. Inst., Statis. Soc., Econ. Soc., Econ. History Soc., Argentina, U.S. Eastern Econ. Assn., Econometric Soc.,

Am. Statis. Assn., Am. Econ. Assn., Can. Econ. Assn., Can. Statis. Soc., Assn. Social Econs., N.Y. Acad. Scis. Roman Catholic. Home: Ottawa, Canada. Died Nov. 5, 2005.

**DAHL, DONALD L.,** former state legislator; b. Hillsboro, Kans., Mar. 19, 1945; BA, Tabor Coll. Mem. Dist. 70 Kans. House of Reps., 1997—2008, spkr. pro tem, 2006—08. Mem. Kans. Supreme Ct. Nominating Commn., 2013—14. Served in USN. Republican. Christian. Died Apr. 18, 2014.

**DAHL, ROBERT ALAN,** political science professor; b. Inwood, Iowa, Dec. 17, 1915; s. Peter Ivor and Vera (Lewis) D.; m. Mary Louise Bartlett, 1940 (dec. 1970); children: Ellen Kirsten, Peter Bartlett (dec.), Eric Lewis, Christopher Robert; m. Ann Goodridge Sale, 1973. AB, U. Wash., 1936; PhD, Yale U., 1940; LLD (hon.), U. Mich., 1985, U. Alaska, 1987; D of Philosophy (hon.), U. Oslo, 1994; LLD (hon.), Law Sch. for Social Rsch., 1996, Harvard U., 1998; D honoris causa (hon.), U. Madrid Complutense, 2001; LLD (hon.), Grinnell Coll., 2001; LittD (hon.), Columbia U., 2005. Mgmt. analyst USDA, 1940; economist Office Prodn. Mgmt., Office Price Adminstrn. & Civilian Supply, War Prodn. Bd., 1940-42; faculty mem. Yale U., 1946—55, Eugene Meyer prof. polit. sci., 1955-64, Sterling prof. polit sci., 1964—86, Sterling prof. polit sci. emeritus, sr. rsch scientist sociology, 1986—2014, Ford Rsch. prof., 1957-58, chmn. dept. polit. sci., 1957-62. Lectr. polit. sci., Flacso, Santiago, Chile, 1967; pres. American Polit. Sci. Assn., 1967. Author: Congress and Foreign Policy, 1950, (with E. Browne) Domestic Control of Atomic Energy, 1951, (with C.E. Lindblom) Politics, Economics and Welfare, 1952, A Preface to Democratic Theory, 1956, (with Haire and Lazarsfeld) Social Science Research on Business, 1959, Who Governs?, 1961, Modern Political Analysis, 1963, Political Oppositions in Western Democracies, 1966, After the Revolution?, 1970, Polyarchy: Participation and Opposition, 1971, Regimes and Oppositions, 1972, Democracy in the United States, 1972, (with E.R. Tufte) Size and Democracy, 1973, Dilemmas of Pluralist Democracy, 1982, A Preface to Economic Democracy, 1985, Controlling Nuclear Weapons, 1985, Democracy, Liberty and Equality, 1986, Democracy and the Critics, 1989, The New American Political (Dis) Order, 1994, Toward Democracy: A Journey Reflections: 1940-1997, 1997, On Democracy, 1999, Politica e virtu, 2001, How Democratic Is the American Constitution?, 2002, Intervista sul Pluralismo, 2002, On Political Equality, 2006. Served in US Army, 1943-45. Decorated Bronze Star with cluster; Cavaliere of Republic of Italy, 1988; recipient Woodrow Wilson prize, 1963, 90, Talcott Parsons prize, 1977, Wilbur Lucius Cross medal, 1986, Elaine and David Spitz award, 1991; Guggenheim fellow, 1950, 78, fellow Ctr. for Advanced Study in Behavioral Sciences, 1955-56, 67. Fellow American Acad. Arts & Sciences (Talcott Parsons prize 1977); mem. NAS, American Philos. Soc., American Polit. Sci. Assn. (pres. 1966-67, Woodrow Wilson prize 1963, James Madison prize 1978, Gladys Kammerer award 1983, Benjamin Lippincott award 1989, Johan Skytte prize 1995), New Eng. Polit. Assn. (pres. 1951), ACLU, Brit. Acad., Phi Beta Kappa. Home: Hamden, Conn. Died Feb. 5, 2014.

**DAICHES, DAVID,** retired English literature educator, author; b. Sunderland, Eng., Sept. 2, 1912; s. Salis and Flora (Levin) Daiches; m. Isobel Mackay, July 27, 1937 (dec. Aug. 1977); children: Alan Harry, Jennifer Rachel, Elizabeth Mackay; m. Hazel Margaret Newman, Dec. 22, 1978 (dec. Sept. 1986). MA, U. Edinburgh, Scotland, 1934; DLitt (hon.), U. Edinburgh, 1976; DPhil, U. Oxford, Eng., 1937; LHD (hon.), Brown U., 1964; Docteur de l'Universitè (hon.), Sorbonne, U. Paris, 1973; DLitt (hon.), U. Sussex, Brighton, Eng., 1978, U. Glasgow, Scotland, 1987, U. Guelph, Ont., Can., 1990; DUniv (hon.), U. Stirling, Scotland, 1980; Dottore 'ad honorem', U. Bologna, Italy, 1989. Bradley fellow Balliol Coll., Oxford U., 1936-37; asst. prof. English U. Chgo., 1940-43; 2d sec. Brit. Embassy, Washington, 1944-46; prof. English Cornell U., 1946-51; univ. lectr. English Cambridge U., 1957-61; fellow Jesus Coll., 1957-62; dean Sch. English Studies U. Sussex, 1961-67, prof. english, 1961-77, prof. emeritus, 1977—2005. Dir. Inst. for Advanced Study in Humanities, Edinburgh U., 1980-86, Gifford lectr., 1983. Author over 40 books including The Novel and the Modern World, 1939, A Study of Literature, 1948, Robert Burns, 1950, Two Worlds, 1956, Critical Approaches to Literature, 1956, Literary Essays, 1956, Milton, 1957, A Critical History of English Literature, 1960, More Literary Essays, 1968, Scotch Whisky, 1969, Sir Walter Scott and His World, 1971, A Third World, 1971, Robert Burns and His World, 1971, Prince Charles Edward Stuart, 1973, Robert Louis Stevenson and His World, 1973, Moses, 1975, James Boswell and His World, 1976, Scotland and the Union, 1977, Glasgow, 1977, Edinburgh, 1978, Literature and Gentility in Scotland, 1982, Robert Fergusson, 1983, God and the Poets, 1984, A Weekly Scotsman and Other Poems, 1994; editor: Literature and Western Civilization, 6 vols., 1972-76, Fletcher of Saltoun: Selected Political Writings and Speeches, 1979, Edinburgh: A Traveller's Companion, 1986. Decorated Comdr. Brit. Empire. Fellow Royal Soc. Lit., Royal Soc. Edinburgh; mem. MLA (hon.), Assn. for Scottish Lit. Studies (hon. pres.), Saltire Soc. (hon. pres.), Scottish Arts Club (Edinburgh). Home: Edinburgh, Scotland. Died July 15, 2005.

**DAILEY, JANET,** writer; b. Storm Lake, Iowa, May 21, 1944; d. Boyd and Louise Haradon; m. William Dailey (dec. Aug. 5, 2005); 2 stepchildren. Sec., Nebr., Iowa, 1963-74. Author (Cord & Stacy series): No Quarter Asked, 1974, Fiesta San Antonio, 1977, For Bitter or Worse, 1978; author: (Calder series) This Calder Range, 1982, Stands a Calder Man, 1983, This Calder Sky, 1981, Calder Born, Calder Bred, 1983, Calder Pride, 1999, Green Calder Grass, 2002, Shifting Calder Wind, 2003, Calder Promise, 2004, Lone Calder Star, 2005, Calder Storm, 2006, Santa in Montana, 2010; author: (Aspen series) Aspen Gold, 1991, Illusions, 1997; author: (Americana series) After the Storm, 1975, Dangerous Masquerade, 1976, Valley Of the Vapours, 1976, Night Of The Cotillion, 1976, Show Me, 1976, Bluegrass King, 1977, Six White Horses, 1977, Northern Magic, 1982, Giant Of Mesabi, 1983, Dakota Dreamin', 1984, Difficult Decision, 1986, Southern Nights, 1986, The Travelling Kind, 1986, The Mating Season, 1986, Kona Winds, 1986, The Matchmakers, 1986, A Lyon's Share, 1986, The Indy Man, 1986, Heart Of Stone, 1986, The Homeplace, 1987, The Bride Of The Delta Queen, 1987, Summer Mahogany, 1987, Bed Of Grass, 1987, That Boston Man, 1987, Enemy In Camp, 1987, A Tradition Of Pride, 1987, Big Sky Country, 1987, Boss Man From Ogalala, 1987, Reily's Woman, 1987, One Of The Boys, 1987, Land Of Enchantment, 1987, Beware Of The Stranger, 1987, That Carolina Summer, 1987, Lord Of the High Lonesome, 1987, The Widow And The Wastrel, 1987, The Thawing Of Mara, 1987, Low Country Liar, 1987, To Tell The Truth, 1988, Strange Bedfellow, 1988, Sentimental Journey, 1988, Savage Land, 1988, A Land Called Deseret, 1988, Green Mountain Man, 1988, Tidewater Lover, 1988, For Mike's Sake, 1988, Wild And Wonderful, 1988, With A Little Luck, 1988, Darling Jenny, 1988, Fire And Ice, 1988, Sonora Sundown, 1988; author: (novels) Something Extra, 1975, Sweet Promise, 1976, Master Fiddler, 1977, Ivory Cane, 1977, The Rogue, 1979, Touch the Wind, 1979 (NY Times bestseller), Nightway, 1980, Ride Thunder, 1980, Hostage Bride, 1981, The Lancaster Men, 1981, For the Love of God, 1982, Foxfire Light, 1982, Terms of Surrender, 1982, Wildcatter's Woman, 1982, The Best Way to Lose, 1983, Mistletoe and Holly, 1983, The Second Time, 1983, Separate Cabins, 1983, Western Man, 1983, Leftover Love, 1984, Silver Wings Santiago Blue, 1984, The Pride of Hannah Wade, 1985, Glory Game, 1985, The Great Alone, 1986, Heiress, 1987, Rivals, 1988, Masquerade, 1990, Tangled Vines, 1992, Riding High, 1994, The Proud and the Free, 1994, Legacies, 1995, The Healing Touch, 1996, Notorious, 1996, Castles in the Sand, 1996, A Capital Holiday, 2001, Scrooge Wore Spurs, 2002, The Not Forgotten War, 2003, Maybe This Christmas, 2003, Because of You, 2004, Can't Say Goodbye, 2004, Dance with Me, 2004, Everything, 2004, Eve's Christmas, 2006, Man of Mine, 2007, Something More, 2007, Wearing White, 2007, With This Kiss, 2007. Recipient Golden Heart award, Romance Writers America, 1981, Contemporary award, Romantic Times, 1983. Died Dec. 14, 2013.

**DAKIN, ARTHUR HAZARD,** writer; b. Boston, Jan. 25, 1905; s. Arthur Hazard and Emma Frances (Sahler) Dakin. AB, Princeton U., 1928, MA, 1929, PhD, 1933; D. Phil., Oxford U., 1938. Author: Von Hügel and the Supernatural, Man the Measure, (chapters) Audiovisual Aids to Instruction (edited by W. Exton), The Heritage of Kant (edited by G.T. Whitney and D.F. Bowers), A Paul Elmer More Miscellany, Paul Elmer More. Exec. officer U.S. Naval Tng. Sch., Hampton, Va.; officer-in-charge Advance Base Reshipment Depot Battalion, Iroquois Point, Oahu, T.H., World War II. Ret. comdr. USNR. Mem.: Metaphys. Soc. Am., Am. Philos. Assn., Saint Nicholas Soc. City N.Y., Huguenot Soc., Soc. Colonial Wars, University Club (N.Y.C.)., Century Club, Princeton Club, Phi Beta Kappa. Home: Amherst, Mass. Died Nov. 25, 2001.

**DALE, JUDY RIES,** religious organization administrator, consultant; b. Memphis, Dec. 13, 1944; d. James Lorigan and Julia Marie (Schwinn) Ries; m. Eddie Melvin Ashmore, July 12, 1969 (div. Dec. 1983). BA, Rhodes Coll., 1966; M in Religious Edn., So. Bapt. Theol. Sem., 1969, grad. specialist in religious edn., 1969. Cert. tchr. educable mentally handicapped, secondary English, adminstrn. and supervision spl. edn. EMH tchr., curriculum writer, tchr. trainer Jefferson County Bd. Edn., Louisville, 1969-88, ednl. cons., 1988-90; dist. coord. Gt. Lakes dist. Universal Fellowship Met. Cmty. Chs., Louisville, 1990—2002, spl. asst. comm. and lay resources, 2006—09. Lectr. U. Louisville, 1976—77, 1987—90, Jefferson CC, Louisville, 1987—93; mem. program adv. com. Internat. Conf. Spl. Edn., Beijing, 1987—88; mem. faculty Samaritan Inst. Religious Studies, 1992—98. Editor, writer: A Manual of Instructional Strategies, 1985, Handbook for Begining Teachers, 1989; editor: Around the Fellowship, 2006—07, The MCC Impact, from 2008. Bd. sec. Com. Ten, Inc., Louisville, 1987—91; v.p. GLUE, 1988—92, pres., 1992—94; mem. steering com. Ky. Fairness Alliance, 2005—06, treas., 2005—06; mem. membership com. Cmty. Health Trust, 1991—94; chair acad. affairs com. Samaritan Inst. Religious Studies, 1996—97, trustee, 1992—98; mem. programs and budget divsn. Universal Fellowship Met. Cmty. Chs., 1990—97, mem. gen. coun., 1990—2002, active women's secretariat steering com., 1991—95, mem. core team, 1993—2000, chair, 1997—2000, fin. team, 1997—2005, bd. adminstrn., 2003—05, chmn. risk mgmt. team, 2003—05, sec., 2004—05, chair, 2005. Recipient Hon. Order of Ky. Cols., 1976, MCC Disting. Lay Leadership award, 1999; named Outstanding Elem. Tchr. Am., 1975. Mem.: ACLU, NOW, AAUW, Ky. Coun. Exceptional Children (bd. dirs. 1978—90, Mem. of the Yr. 1987), Coun. Exceptional Children (keynote spkr., mem. exec. com. 1984—88, internat. pres. 1986—87, bd. govs. 1981—88), Women's Alliance, Parents, Family and Friends Lesbians and Gays, Nat. Gay & Lesbian Task Force, Nat. Ctr. Lesbian Rights, Internat. Platform Assn., Gay and Lesbian Assn. Anti-Defamation, Lambda Legal Def. and Edn. Fund, Phi Kappa Phi. Democrat. Avocations: reading, handwork. Home: Louisville, Ky. Died Feb. 27, 2014.

**DALLE, FRANÇOIS LEON MARIE-JOSEPH,** manufacturing executive; b. Hesdin, France, Mar. 18, 1918; s. Joseph and Jeanne (Dumont) Dalle; m. Genevieve Clement, Dec. 8, 1982. degree, Laureate, Faculty Law, U. Paris. Bar:. With Adv. Ct. Appeal Paris, 1941—42; plant mgr. Monsavon, Clichy, France, 1945—2005, asst. gen. mgr., 1945—48, L'Oreal, 1950—57, mgr. mktg. Paris, 1948—50, pres., dir. gen., 1957—2005. Dir. Philips France, Banque Nat. de Paris, Union des Annonceurs, Nestle, South Africa, Ctr. Europeen d'Edn. Permanente; pres. Saipo, Mennen France, Nat. Indsl. Com. Paris, 1984; mem. coun. Ctr. d'Etudes Litteraires Sci. Appliquees. Author (with Jean Bounine-Cabale): L'entreprise du Futur, 1971; author: Quand l'entreprise s'eveille a la conscience sociale, 1975; author: (with Nicolas Thiery) Dynamique de l'auto-reforme de l'entreprise, 1976. Decorated comdr. Legion d'honneur, Ordre Nat. du Merite, Palmes Academiques, medaille de la Resistance France. Mem.: Inst. de Liaison des Entreprises de Grande Consommation (dir.), Inst. de l'Entreprise (founder, v.p. 1975), INSEAD, Futuribles Internat. Assn., Entreprise et Progres Assn. (founder. pres. 1969, mem. exec. com. 1971), Conseil Nat. du Patronat Francais (mem. staff 1968, exec. coun. mem. 1972—75), Humanisme et Entreprise (pres. exec. com. 1968), Inst. Pasteur (v.p. 1970—78, hon. dir. 1978), Revue des Deux Mondes Club (Paris). Home: 75007 Paris, France. Died Aug. 9, 2005.

**DAMGOV, VLADIMIR NIKOLOV,** physicist; b. Sofia, Bulgaria, Nov. 22, 1947; s. Nicola Markov and Velka Tzenova (Vlatchkova) D.; m. Tatyana Nikolova, Feb. 11, 1973; children: Nicolai, Jordan, Nadejda. MD, Moscow Tech. U., 1971; PhD, Moscow State U., 1977; DSc, Bulgaria Acad. Scis., Sofia, 1992. Rsch. scientist Bulgarian Acad. Sci., Inst. Electronics, Sofia, 1971-73, 1978-87; sr. rsch. scientist Bulgarian Acad. Sci., Space Rsch. Inst., Sofia, 1988-96, prof., from 1997. Sect. chmn. Internat. Conf. Nonlinear Oscillations, Kiev, Ukraine, 1979; scientific sec., Varna, Bulgaria, 1984; reviewer European Microwave Conf., Budapest, Hungary, 1987; mem. internat. scientific com. IMACS Symposium, Montreal, Que., Can., 1993; mem. internat. scientific com. Internat. Conf. Nonlinear Dynamics, Zakopane, Poland, 1995; mem. internat. scientific coun. Internat. Rsch. Ctr., Warsaw, Poland, 1995—. Author: Nonlinear and Parametric Phenomena: Theory and Applications in Radiophysics and Mechanics, 1996; contbr. articles to profl. jours.; patentee in field of radiophysics, mechanics, and nonlinear dynamics. Rsch. grantee European Union, United Kingdom, 1993. Mem. N.Y. Acad. Scis., Union of Scientists in Bulgaria (chmn. sect. mechanics 1994—, bd. dirs. 1994—). Avocations: painting, travel. Home: Sofia, Bulgaria. Died June 20, 2007.

**DANIELS, DORAL LEE,** education educator; b. Clinton, Ind., Nov. 2, 1925; s. Oather and Orva Rosetta (Stinson) D.; m. Frances Elizabeth Hyslop, Nov. 8, 1945; children: Mark, Kirk, Brett. BS, Ind. State, 1949; MA, Ball State U., 1954. Tchr. Parksley (Va.) High Sch., Accomack County Sch. Corp., 1946-47; 6th grade tchr. Cicero (Ind.) Twp. Sch. Corp., 1950-51, Tipton (Ind.) Sch. Corp., 1951-55; mid. sch. tchr. Kokomo (Ind.)-Center Twp. Sch. Corp., 1955-92; assoc. instr. Ind.'s Tech. Coll., Kokomo, from 1992. Sec. Assn. for Childhood Edn., 1955-78, Kokomo Tchr.'s Assn., 1950-88, Nat. Edn. Assn., 1950-88; pres. Schoolmasters, Kokomo, 1955-90, Ind. State Tchrs. Assn., 1950-88; commr. Boy Scouts Am., 1955-87; surrogate parent Kennedy Ctr., The Acad., 1992-2002. With USN, 1943-46, ETO, PTO. Fellow Kokomo Wood Carvers Assn. (sec.-treas. 1980); mem. Ea. Woodland Woodcarvers Convers Ind., VFW, Nat. L.S.J.T. Assn., Landing Ship Tank Assn. Ind. (plank owner 1994), Ind. Dist. Past Lt. Govs. Assn., Elks, Kiwanis (pres. 1971, lt. gov. 1993-94, 98-99, Col. J.L. McCulloch award 1994, Legion of Honor 1995). Methodist. Avocations: wood carving, photography. Died Oct. 20, 2002.

**DANIELS, JESSE L.,** retired counselor; b. Carrollton, Ga., Sept. 14, 1936; s. Will and Emma (Boykin) D.; m. Mary M. Keith (dec. Oct. 1973); children: Darrell, Ronald, Teresa, Lisa; m. Ruby Watts. AAS, Atlanta Jr. Coll., 1981, AS, 1982; student, Ga. State U., 1982-84. Lic. counselor, Va., Ga. Enlisted man USAF, 1955, advanced through grades to tech. sgt., ret., 1971; ins. counselor N.C. Mut. Life Ins. Co., Atlanta and Newport News, Va., 1971-73; officer mgr., real estate assoc. T.M. Alexander Assocs. Realty, Atlanta, 1973-76; owner, mgr. Food Gallery Grocers, East Point, Ga., 1985-87; ret., 1987. Counselor in field. Mem. VFW, Am. Legion, Masons (worshipful master 1986-87, nat. dep. 1988—), Shriners. Home: Atlanta, Ga. Died Jan. 25, 1990.

**DANIELSON, WALTER GEORGE,** lawyer; b. Anaconda, Mont., July 3, 1903; s. John and Tekla Christina (Jonsson) Danielson; m. Beryl Marie Pearce, Aug. 17, 1935; children: Karin Lynn Godfrey, John Howard. LLB, U. Mont., 1929, JD (hon.), 1970; diploma of honor, Pepperdine U., 1980. Bar: Calif. 1929. Pvt. practice, LA; vice consul for Sweden, LA, 1937—55, consul, 1955—69, consl gen., 1969—76, emeritus, 1976; sec. L.A. Consular Corps, from 1976. Trustee Luth. Hosp. Soc. So. Calif., LA; bd. dirs. Calif. Hosp. Decorated Knight Royal Order Vasa, comdr., Royal Order North Star, Sweden, officers cross Hungar7, Knight Royal Order St. Olav, Norway, Knight's cross 1st class Royal Order Dannebrog, Denmark. Mem.: L.A. Bar Assn., Calif. State Bar, Swedish Club, Vasa Order Am., Calif. Club. Home: Los Angeles, Calif. Died Aug. 30, 1999.

**DANTO, ARTHUR COLEMAN,** writer, philosopher, critic; b. Ann Arbor, Mich., Jan. 1, 1924; s. Samuel Budd and Sylvia (Gittleman) D.; m. Shirley Rovetch, Aug. 9, 1946 (dec. July 1978); children: Elizabeth, Jane; m. Barbara Westman, Feb. 15, 1980. BA, Wayne State U., 1948; MA, Columbia U., 1949, PhD, 1952; postgrad., U. Paris, 1949-50; D (hon.), Parsons Sch. Design, 1990, Sch. Visual Arts, 1995, Pa. Acad. Fine Arts, 1996, Conn. Coll., 1997, Wayne State U., 1999, Coll. Art & Design, Detroit, 2001, Mass. Coll. Art, 2002; DLitt, Columbia U., 2004; PhD in History, U. Turane, Italy, 2007. Instr. U. Colo., Colo., 1950-51; mem. faculty Columbia U., 1952—75, Johnsonian prof. philosophy, 1975-92, chmn. Dept. Philosophy, 1979-87, co-dir. Ctr.

for Study of Human Rights, 1978-92, prof. emeritus, 1992—2013. Andrew W. Mellon Fine Arts lectr., 1995; Albertus Magnum prof. U. Cologne, 2005. Author: Analytical Philosophy of Knowledge, 1968, What Philosophy Is, 1968, Analytical Philosophy of Hist., 1965, Nietzsche as Philosopher, 1965, Analytical Philosophy of Action, 1973, Mysticism and Morality, 1972, Jean-Paul Sartre, 1975, The Transfiguration of the Commonplace, 1981 (Lionel Trilling Book prize 1982), Narration and Knowledge, 1985, The Philosophical Disenfranchisement of Art, 1986, The State of the Art, 1987, Connections to the World, 1989, Encounters and Reflections: Art in the Hist. Present, 1990 (Nat. Book Critics Circle Prize for Criticism, 1990), Beyond the Brillo Box: Art in the Post Hist. Period, 1992, Mark Tansey: Visions and Revisions, 1992, Robert Mapplethorpe, 1992, Embodied Meanings: Critical Essays and Aesthetic Meditations, 1994, Playing with the Edge: The Photographic Achievement of Robert Mapplethorpe, After the End of Art: Contemporary Art and the Pale of Hist., 1997 (Eugene Kayden prize 1997), The Body/Body Problem, 1999, Philosophizing Art, 1999, The Madonna of the Future, 2000, The Abuse of Beauty: Aesthetics and the Concept of Art, 2003, Unnatural Wonders: Essays in the Gap Between Art and Life, 2004, Andy Warhal, 2009; editor Jour. Philosophy; art critic The Nation, 1984-2009; contbg. editor ARTFORUM; cons. editor for various other publlications Bd. dirs. Amnesty Internat., 1970-75, gen. sec., 1973. Served with AUS, 1942-45. With US Army, 1942—45, N. Africa, Italy. Recipient prize for Disting. Criticism Mfr.-Hanover/Art World, 1985, George S. Polk award for Criticism, 1985, Nat. Book Critics Circle prize for criticism, 1990, ICP Infinity prize for writing in photography, 1993, Prix Philosophie, 2003, Icelandic Lit. prize, 2005; fellow Fulbright Found., 1949, Guggenheim Found., 1969, 82, American Coun. Learned Socs., 1961, 70; Fulbright disting. prof. Yugoslavia, 1976; Phi Beta Kappa prof. Arts & Sciences Fellow AAAS; mem. American Philos. Assn. (v.p. 1969, pres. 1983), American Soc. Aesthetics (v.p. 1987, pres. 1989), Coll. Art Assn. (Frank Jewett Mather prize for Criticism). Home: Brookhaven, NY. Died Oct. 25, 2013.

**DARGER, STANFORD PARLEY,** retired bank executive, former state legislator; b. Salt Lake City, Oct. 15, 1920; s. Perry Stanford and Eva (Williams) Darger; m. Arlene Barlow, June 17, 1946; children: Stanford Parley, Janet Darger Denali, Ann Darger Hatch, Jane Darger Thomas, John Barlow. BS in Bus. & Mktg., U. Utah, 1944. Pres. Darger Co., Salt Lake City, 1947—53, Darger Ford, Magna, Utah, 1953—55; exec. v.p. Retail Mchts. Assn., Salt Lake City; divsn. mgr. Salt Lake City Area Chamber of Commerce, 1955—73; sr. v.p., mktg. mgr. Valley Bank & Trust Co., 1973—85. Dir., mem. exec. com. Utah Resources Internat.; pres., chmn. Sport Pix, Inc., Salt Lake City, 1984—87. Mem. exec. com., treas. Salt Lake City Conv. and Visitors Bur., 1985—88; mem. Utah House of Reps., 1962—72, chmn. appropriations com., 1967—68, majority whip, 1978; del. Utah State Republican Conf., 1962, 1964, 1968; finance sec., bus. mgr. Mormon Tabernacle Choir, 1958—75. Named Exec. of Yr., Nat. Retail Assn., 1970. Mem.: Utah Chamber of Commerce (pres. 1971), Bank Mktg. Assn., American Inst. Banking, Ft. Douglas Country Club. Republican. Avocation: collecting antique and classical automobiles. Home: Salt Lake City, Utah. Died May 7, 2014.

**DARRAS, DENNIS CONSTANTINE,** power engineer; b. Athens, Greece, Oct. 26, 1922; s. Constantine Dennis and Hellen George (Mihopoulou) D.; m. Stella Rallou, June 17, 1953; children: Hellen, Constantine. Grad., Coryalenios and Anargyrios Coll., Greece, 1939; MS in Mech. and Elec. Engring., Nat. Metsovion Polytech., Greece, 1949. With Socony-Vacuum Oil Co., 1949-50, Pub. Power Corp., Athens, 1950, head power generating stations, operating dept., 1954-58, head prodn. and transmission sys., 1958-66, gen. mgr. prodn.-transmission, 1967-70, dir. gen. prodn.-tramsmission and distbn., 1970-74; design and constrn. engr. PROMAFFAIRS AG. Tech.-econ. cons., advisor to various enterprises and cos. worldwide, 1975—; designer/constructor energy networks, including 29 power generating stas., coal-oil-gas, hdyro and nuclear, high and super-high voltage transmission lines, switchyards and the assoc. equipment, 1950-96. Former pres. Hellenic Electromech. Soc. Served with Royal Hellenic Navy, World War II. Decorated chevalier Légion d'Honneur, officer Légion d'Honneur France; decorated Gallant Disting. Action Order, Navy War Cross, Convoy Escort medal with 7 stars, Nat. Resistance medal; recipient Pro Mundi Beneficio award Acad. Brasileira de Ciencias Humanas, 1975. Mem. IEEE, Tech. Chamber Greece (editor-in-chief Cronicles), Athenian Club, Glyfada Golf Club. Avocations: swimming, boating, photography, golf. Home: Paris, France. Deceased.

**DARWIN, FRED ARRANTS,** management consultant; b. Chattanooga, May 28, 1913; s. Fred Perry and Alexandra Allen (Arrants) Darwin; m. Hope Genung Sparks, Sept. 30, 1939 (dec. 1987); children: Fred Arrants, Hope Darwin Beisinger. Student, U. Chattanooga, 1929—31; BS, U.S. Naval Acad., 1935; MS, Harvard U., 1936. Registered profl. engr. Sr. supr. traffic dept. We. Union Telegraph Corp, Chgo., 1936—41; asst. dir. engring. Hazeltine Electronics Corp., NYC, 1946—49; exec. dir. com. guided missiles R&D bd. Dept. Def., Washington, 1949—54; mgr. guided missiles Crosley divsn. Avco Mfg. Corp., Cin., 1954—56; mgr. missile electronics McDonnell Aircraft Corp., St. Louis, 1956—61, gen. mgr. electronics equipment divsn., 1961—63; asst. to pres. Librascope group Gen. Precision, Inc., 1963—65; bus. counselor, owner Gen. Bus. Svcs., Dallas, from 1966. Mem. spl. com. radio tech. commn. for aeros. Dept. State, Dept. Navy, 1946; cons. del. UN Provisional Internat. Civil Aviation Orgn., 1946; mem. Stewart spl. com. Nat. Guided Missiles Program, 1950, Gardner spl. com., 1953. Contbr. articles to profl. jours. Comdr. USNR, 1941—46. Mem.: IEEE, Aero. Weights Engrs., Naval Acad. Alumni Assn., East Dallas C. of C., Harvard Grad. Soc., Harvard Club, Alpha Lambda Tau. Democrat. Presbyterian. Achievements include invention of multiple-coincidence mixer used in pulse-train coding; development of originator word transponder. Home: Arlington, Tex. Died Oct. 6, 1996.

**DARWISH, MAHMOUD,** poet; b. al-Birwa, Palestine, 1942; refugee in Lebanon, 1948-49; m. Rana Qabbani (div.). Journalist, Haifa, Israel, until 1971; editor Al-Ittihad, Shu'un Filastiniyya, Beirut, Al Jadid; now editor Al-Karmal mag., Paris. Writings include: (verse) Sparrows Without Wings, 1960, Olive Branches, 1965, A Lover from Palestine, 1966, The End of Night, 1967, Sparrows Die in Galilee, 1970, A Letter from Exile, 1970, My Beloved Wakes Up, 1971, Love You, Love You Not, 1972, The Palestinian Chalk Circle, 1972, Selected Poems, 1973, The Seventh Attempt, 1973, Splinters and Bones, 1974, That Is Her Picture and This Is Her Lover's Suicide, 1975, Weddings, 1977, Collected Poems, 1977, The Music of Human Flesh, 1980, Madāh al-dhillal-'āli, 1983, Victims of a Map, 1984, Ban on Panegyrics to the Sea, 1984, Farewell War, Farewell Peace, 1985, Lesser Roses, 1986, Sand and Other Poems, 1986, It Is a Song, It Is a Song, 1986, The Tragedy of Narcissus and the Comedy of Silver, 1989, I See What I Want, 1990, 11 Planets, 1992; (other writings) Something About Home, 1971, Diaries of Ordinary Grief, 1973, A Memory of Oblivion, 1987. Recipient Lotus prize, 1969, Mediterranean prize, 1980, Lenin Peace prize, 1983. Died Aug. 9, 2008.

**DAUENHAUER, RICHARD LEONARD,** writer; b. Syracuse, NY, Apr. 10, 1942; s. Leonard George and Jane Grier D.; m. Nora Marks, Nov. 1973. BA in Russian, Syracuse U., 1964; MA in German, U. Tex., 1966; PhD in Comparative Lit., U. Wis., 1975. Asst. prof. comparative lit. Alaska Meth. U., Anchorage, 1969-75; staff assoc. Alaska Native Found., Anchorage, 1976-78; assoc. prof. humanities Alaska Pacific U., Anchorage, 1979-83; program dir. Sealaska Heritage Found., Juneau, 1983-97; freelance writer, cons., 1997—2005; pres.'s prof. native languages & culture U. Alaska, Juneau, 2005—14. Author: Glacier Bay Concerto, 1980, Frames of Reference, 1987; author, editor For Healing Our Spirit: Tlingit Oratory, 1990, Russians in Tlingit America: The Battles of Sitka, 1802 And 1804, 2008, Benchmarks: New and Selected Poems, 1963-2013, 2013; contbr. articles to profl. jours. Recipient Govs. award Arts, State Alaska, 1989, American Book award Before Columbus Found., 1991, Edith R. Bullock prize for Excellence U. Alaska Found., 2013; named Poet Laureate of Alaska, 1981-88; Fulbright fellow, 1966. Home: Juneau, Alaska. Died Aug. 19, 2014.

**DAUGHDRILL, JAMES HAROLD, JR.,** retired academic administrator; b. LaGrange, Ga., Apr. 25, 1934; s. James Harold and Louisa Coffee (Dozier) D.; m. Elizabeth Anne Gay, June 26, 1954; children: James Harold III, Louisa Rish Daughdrill Hoover, Elizabeth Gay Daughdrill Boyd. Student, Davidson Coll., 1952-54, DD, 1974; AB, Emory U., 1956; BD, Columbia Theol. Sem., 1967, M.Div., 1969. Ordained to ministry Presbyn. Ch., 1967. Pres. Kingston Mills, Inc., Cartersville, Ga., 1956-64; minister St. Andrews Presbyn. Ch., Little Rock, 1967-70; sec. of stewardship Presbyn. Ch. in U.S., Atlanta, 1970-73; pres. Rhodes Coll., 1973-99. Past chmn. Nat. Advisory Com. on Instl. Quality and Interity, US Dept. Edn.; past chair Assn. American Colleges; past dir. American Coun. on Edn.; mem. Blue Ribbon adv. com. Memphis Public Schools; dir. Southern Univ. Conf.; bd. dirs. Bulab Holdings, Inc., Union Planters Nat. Bank, Buckman Labs. Author: Man Talk, 1972; co-author: New Directions for Higher Education Source Book. Past chmn. Tenn. Coun. Pvt. Colls.; past pres. Coll. Athletic Conf.; past chmn. bd. So. Coll. Univ. Union; past trustee Memphis-Brooks Art Gallery, Hutchinson Sch.; past bd. dirs. Tenn. Ind. Colls., Liberty Bowl, Chickasaw coun. Boy Scouts Am., Memphis U. Sch., Memphis Ptnrs.; mem. exec. bd. Dixon Gallery and Gardens; trustee The Frank E. Seidman Award in Polit. Economy; mem. blue ribbon adv. com. to the supt. Memphis Public Schools Named Educator of Yr. Greater Memphis State, Memphis Planner of Yr., Pillar of Memphis Jewish Nat. Fund; recipient Spirit of Life award City of Hope, Svc. award Rotary Club Memphis Community, 1987, McCallie Sch. Alumnus of Yr. award 1978, Disting. Nat. Eagle Scout award, 1991; honored by Tenn. Legislature for disting. svc. to higher edn. and to State of Tenn., 1998. Mem. NCJJ (nat. trustee), Assn. Presbyn. Colleges & Universities (bd. dirs.), World Bus. Coun. (young pres.' orgn., Young Man of Yr. 1961), Chief Executives Orgn. (past), Memphis Chamber of Commerce (past bd. dir.), Univ. Club (N.Y.C.), Phi Delta Theta, Omicron Delta Kappa, Kappa Delta Epsilon (nat. hon.). Home: Memphis, Tenn. Died May 3, 2014.

**DAUGHERTY, CONNIE RUTH,** early childhood educator; b. Litchfield, Minn., Aug. 23, 1939; d. Edmund Robert and Ruth Helen (Bengtson) Swanson; m. John Charles Daugherty; children: Mary Beth, Stephanie Ann, John Michael. Student, North Pk. Coll., Chgo., 1957—59; BS in Primary Edn., U. Minn., 1964; postgrad., Mankato State U. Cert. tchr. Minn. Head tchr. St. Peter Play Group, Minn., 1967—68; owner, dir., head tchr. Jack and Jill Nursery Sch., St. Peter, from 1970. V.p. Jacon Inc.; cons., mem. Gustavus Adolphus Coll. Early Childhood Program Cert. Com.; cons. Minn. State Dept. Edn., 1978. Contbr. articles to profl. jours. Sec. bd. dirs. Cmty. Hosp. Aux., 1965—75; v.p. bd. dirs. St. Peter Play Group, 1965—66; mem. Right to Read Com., 1974—76; active Girl Scouts US; mem. coun. 1st Lutheran Ch., St. Peter, 1977—81, v.p., 1980, chmn. youth com., mem. mut. ministry com., 1981—83, mem. call. com. sr. pastor, 1976—77; del. Minn. Synod Luth. Ch. America, 1978—79; bd. dirs. St. Peter Dollars Scholars, 1979—81, v.p., 1980—81; bd. dirs. Gustavus Libr. Assocs., from 1980, vol. chmn., 1980—83; bd. dirs. Early Childhood Family Edn., from 1987, chmn., 1989—90; mem. staff support com. 1st Luth. Ch., 1990, mem. nomination com. for ch. coun., 1990; chmn. auction com. Cmty. Hosp. Aux. Hospice Benefit. Mem.: Gustavus Adolphus Coll. Libr. Assocs. (exec. bd. 1989—90), 1006 Soc. St. Peter C. of C., Minn. Valley Assn. Edn. Young Child (treas. 1974—75), Minn. Assn. Edn. Young Child, Nat. Assn. Edn. Young Child, Shoreland Country Club, Minnetonka Country Club. Republican. Died 1992.

**DAVENPORT, ALAN GARNETT,** civil engineer, educator; b. Madras, India, Sept. 19, 1932; naturalized, Can. s. Tom and May Davenport; m. Sheila Rand Smith, Apr. 13, 1957; children: Thomas Sidney, Anna Margaret, Andrew Hope, Clare Rand. BA, Cambridge U., Eng., 1954, MA, 1958; MASc, U. Toronto, Ont., Can., 1957, DEng (hon.), 1989; PhD, U. Bristol, Eng., 1960; D. in Applied Sci. (hon.), U. Louvain, Belgium, 1979; D. in Tech. (hon.), Tech. U. Denmark, 1982; DSc (hon.), McGill U., Montreal, Que., Can., 1983, U. Toronto, Ont., 1989; DEng (hon.), Waterloo U., Ont., Can., 1986; DSc (hon.), U. Guelph, Ont., 1993, U. La Plata, Argentina, 1993; DEng, Carlton U., 1996, U. Bristol, 1998; DSc (hon.), U. Western Ontario, London, Canada, 2002. Lectr. U. Toronto, Ont., Canada, 1955-57; research officer Nat. Research Council, Ottawa, Ont., Canada, 1957-58; asst. prof., then prof. U. Western Ont., London, Canada, 1960—2009, founding dir. boundary layer wind tunnel lab., 1965—2009, rsch. dir. Inst. for Catastrophic Loss Reduction, 1999; dir. Ctr. for Studies in Constrn., 1990—2009. Cons. World Trade Ctr., NYC, CN Tower, Toronto, Sears Bldg., Chgo., Sunshine Skyway Bridge, Fla., Hong Kong and Shanghai Bank Bldg., Bank China Bldg., Hong Kong, Gt. Belt Bridge, Denmark, Normandy Bridge, France, Millau Viaduct, France, others. Editor: Can. Jour. Civil Engring., 1974—79; mem. editl. bd. Can. Jour. Civil Engring., 1979—81. Chmn. Can. nat. com. UN-Internat. Decade Natural Disaster Reduction, from 1993. Decorated Order of Can. (CM); recipient Nobel prize, 1963, Cancam medal, Cancam 83, Saskatoon, Can., 1983, Queen Elizabeth medal, 1952—77, Gold medal, Inst. Structural Engrs., 1987, Oleg A. Kerensky medal, 1988, Ernest C. Manning award of distinction, Can. Confedn. medal, 1967—92, Killam prize, 1993, Can. Gold medal for sci. and engring., Natural Sci. and Engring. Rsch. Coun. Can., 1994, Gold ribbon d'Or award, French Autoroute Authority, Hellmuth prize for rsch., U. Western Ont., Otto H.G Flaschbart medal, Wind Engring. Soc. Germany, Austria and Switzerland, 2000, John F. Kennedy medal, Engring. Inst. Can., 2000, Albert Caquot prize, French Assn. Civil Engrs., 2001, Spl. Achievement award, Am. Inst. Steel Constrn., 2005, Lynn S. Beedle award, Coun. Tall Bldgs and Urban Habitat, 2005, Davenport medal, Internat. Com. Wind Engring., 2007; named to Engring. Hall of Distinction, U. Toronto, 1999. Fellow: Royal Soc. Can. (Rutherford lectr. 1988), Engring. Inst. Can. (Duggan medal 1960, Gzowski medal 1963, 1978, Julian C. Smith medal), Can. Soc. Civil Engring. (A. B. Sanderson award 1985); mem.: ASCE (State of Art Civil Engring. award 1973, Can.-Am. Civil Engring. award 1977, Jack Cermak medal 2003), Coun. Tall Bldgs. and Urban Habitat (Lynn S. Beedle Achievement award), Am. Inst. Steel Constrn. (Spl. Achievement award 2005), Royal Acad. Engring. (fgn. mem.), Can. Acad. Engring. (pres.), Nat. Acad. Engring. (assoc.), Internat. Assn. Shell Structures (Tsubai prize 1997), Internat. Assn. Bridge and Structural Engring. (award of Merit), Assn. Profl. Engrs. Ont. (Silver medal 1977, Bell Can. Forum award 1992), Can. Meteorol. Soc. (prize in Applied Meteorology 1965), Am. Meteorol. Soc. Avocations: sailing, squash, tennis. Home: London, Canada. Died July 19, 2009.

**DAVERTJANIS, PANAGIOTIS ANASTASIOS,** civil engineer, consultant; b. Amfissa, Greece, Oct. 9, 1958; s. Anastasios Nikolaos and Mimitra Athanasios Karampetsou D. Diploma, Sch. Ednl. Engring. Techs., Selete, Greece, 1981. Official Orgn. Constrn. Working Bldgs. Greece, Itea Fokidas, 1989-93; civil engr. Itea Fokidas, from 1983. With Greek Mil., 1981-82. Home: Itea Fokidas, Greece. Died 2002.

**DAVEY, THOMAS RONALD ALBERT,** metallurgical engineer, educator, consultant; b. Melbourne, Victoria, Australia, Mar. 27, 1925; s. Thomas Raymond and Lillie Rose (Harris) D.; m. Kathleen Ann Bonython, July 24, 1954; children: David John, Lucy Ann, Julia Dianne. BSc, U. Melbourne, 1947, BMetE, 1948, MMetE, 1954, DAppSci, 1967. Rsch. metallurgist Broken Hill Assoc. Smelters, Port Pirie, South Australia, 1949-54; chief rsch. officer B.H.A.S., Port Pirie, 1958-59; works engr. Norddeutsche Affinerie, Hamburg, Germany, 1954-57; rsch. metallurgist Imperial Smelting Corp., Avonmouth, Eng., 1957-58, sect. leader, cons., 1959-63; sr. prin. rsch. scientist div. chem. engring. CSIRO, Melbourne, 1963-69, rsch. planner minerals rsch. labs., 1972-79; prof. metall. Colo. Sch. Mines, Golden, 1969-72; prof. metall. engring. U. Melbourne, 1979-81; cons., mng. dir. Metacon, Melbourne, from 1981. Cons. UN, Bolivia, 1970-72, numerous corps., N.Am., Europe, 1970-91; coun. mem. U. Melbourne, 1981-85, grad. coun. mem., 1975-87, chmn., 1981-82, v.p., 1984-87, 96-99, hon. life mem., 2001-. Contbr. some 68 articles to profl. jours.; holder 26 patents in field. Recipient Wilhelm Hofmann medal W. Hofmann Internat. Consortium, 1977, 87. Fellow Instn. Mining and Metall., Australian Inst. Mining and Metallurgy (Pres.'s medal 1987); mem. AIME (The Metals Soc. Honor recipient 2000, Extractive Metallurgy Lectr. Award recipient 1988, best paper gold medal 1955), Australian Mineral Industry Cons. Assn. Home: Berwick, Australia. Deceased.

**DAVIS, DOROTHY SALISBURY,** writer; b. Chgo., Apr. 26, 1916; d. Alfred Joseph and Margaret Jane (Greer) Salisbury; m. Harry Davis, Apr. 25, 1946 (dec. 1993). AB,

Barat Coll., Lake Forest, Ill., 1938. Mystery and hist. novelist, short story writer. Author: A Gentle Murderer, 1951, A Town of Masks, 1952, Men of No Property, 1956, Death of an Old Sinner, 1957, A Gentleman Called, 1958, The Evening of the Good Samaritan, 1961, Black Sheep, White Lamb, 1963, The Pale Betrayer, 1965, Enemy and Brother, 1967, God Speed The Night, 1968, Where the Dark Streets Go, 1969, Shock Wave, 1972, The Little Brothers, 1973, A Death in the Life, 1976, Scarlet Night, 1980, A Lullaby of Murder, 1984, Tales for a Stormy Night, 1985, The Habit of Fear, 1987, In the Still of the Night, 2001. Recipient Life Achievement award Bouchereon, 1989. Mem. Authors Guild, Mystery Writers of America (former pres., recipient Grand Master award 1985), Adams Roundtable. Home: Palisades, NY. Died Aug. 3, 2014.

**DAVIS, DOUGLAS MATTHEW, JR.,** artist, educator, author; b. Washington, Apr. 11, 1933; s. Douglas Matthew and Pauline Elizabeth (Burton) D.; m. Mary Virginia Miller (div.); children: Laura, Mary Elizabeth; m. Jane Bell (dec. 2005); 1 child, Victoria BA, Am. U., 1956; MA, Rutgers U., 1958. Art critic Newsweek mag., 1969-77, gen. editor, 1977-80, sr. writer architecture, photography, contemporary ideas, 1980-88; artist-in-residence TV Lab. Sta. WNET-TV, NYC, 1972; lectr. Cooper Union, UCLA, Osaka (Japan) U. of Arts. Fulbright lectr., Russia, Chgo. Art Inst., 1994; dir. Internat. Network for Arts; dir. ind. project Solomon R. Guggenheim Mus., Russian-American Co.; advisor architecture & design US Dept. State Art in Embassies Program; vis. prof. Art Ctr. Coll., Pasadena, 1989-90, UCLA, 1990-91; adj. prof. Columbia U., N.Y.C., 1990, adj. prof. Fine Art U. Southern Calif., L.A., 1992-93; cons. in media Rockefeller Found., N.Y.C., 1990-91; cons. in Web site design P.S.I. Inst. for Art & Urban Resources; fulbright scholar Moscow State U., 1995; Disting. vis. artist Ramapo Coll., 1996; lectr. Parsons Sch. of Design, 1998; cons. in digital media The Cornell Theory Ctr., N.Y.C., 1997 Exhibited videotapes, films, drawings, prints, objects in one-man shows, including, San Francisco Mus. Modern Art, 1975, Everson Mus., Syracuse, N.Y., Whitney Museum American Art, N.Y.C., 1977, 81, Neue Galerie, Aachen, W. Ger., 1978, Neuer Berliner Kunstverein, Berlin, 1978, Folkwang Mus., Essen, W. Ger., 1979, Galerie Stampa, Basel, Switzerland, 1979, P.S.I. Gallery, N.Y.C., 1980, Mus. Sztuki, Lodz, Poland, 1982, 95, Wadsworth Atheneum, Hartford, Conn., 1983, Guggenheim Mus., 1988, Lehman Coll. Art Gallery, 1994-95; exhibited in group shows, including, Whitney Mus. American Art, 1971, 75, 85, Mus. Contemporary Art, Chgo., 1975, Cracow (Poland) Bienale, 1976, Venice (Italy) Biennale, 1976, 78, Kassel (W. Ger.) Documenta 6, 1977, Met. Mus., N.Y.C., 1982, Mus. Modern Art, 1984, Kolnischer Kunstverein, 1989, Kwangiu Biennale, 1995, Gov.'s Conf. on Art & Tech., N.Y.C., 1998, Ruebling Hall, Williamsburg, N.Y.C., 1999, Whitney Mus. American Art, N.Y.C., 1999, Nene Galerie, Graz, Austria, 1999, Zentrum fuer Kunstund Media, Karlsruhe, Germany, 1999; represented in permanent collections, Hirschorn Mus., Washington, Ludwig Mus., Cologne, Victoria and Albert Mus., London, Met. Mus. Art, N.Y.C., Wadsworth Atheneum, Hartford, Conn., Dahlem Mus., W. Berlin, Guggenheim Mus., N.Y.C., Los Angeles; appeared in various telecasts and radio performances, U.S. and Europe, 1969—2014; author: Art and the Future, 1973, Artculture: Essays on the Post-Modern, 1977, Photography as a Fine Art, 1983, The Museum Transformed, 1990, The Five Myths of Television Power: Or, Why the Medium Is Not the Message, 1993. Nat. Endowment for Arts fellow, 1971, 75, 80; Deutscher Akademischer Austauschdients artists fellow Berlin, 1977; fellow Graham Found., 1988, Trust for Mut. Understanding, 1989, 91. Mem. Artist's Equity, Coll. Art Assn. Died Jan. 16, 2014.

**DAVIS, EARL PRICHARD (PAT DAVIS),** lawyer; b. Blytheville, Ark., Sept. 10, 1918; s. Thomas Wils and Nellie Pearl (Tanner) D.; widower; children: Ruth Mitchell Davis Smith, Thomas Earl. BA, S.We. Coll. (now Rhodes Coll.), Memphis, 1941; LLB, U. Va., 1947, JD, 1970. Bar: Tenn. 1947. Ptnr. Davis and Davis, Memphis, 1948-87; pvt. practice, Memphis, 1987—2002. Lt. col. USAF, 1941-45, ETO. Home: Memphis, Tenn. Died July 29, 2002.

**DAVIS, EDGAR GLENN,** healthcare executive, educator; b. Indpls., May 12, 1931; s. Thomas Carroll and Florence Isabelle (Watson) Davis; m. Margaret Louise Alandt, June 20, 1953 (dec. Sept. 2008); children: Anne-Elizabeth, Amy Alandt, Edgar Glenn Davis Jr.; m. Joanne Warvel Davis, Apr. 4, 2009. AB, Kenyon Coll., 1953; MBA, Harvard U., 1955. With Eli Lilly & Co., Indpls., 1958—63, mgr. budgeting and profit planning, 1963—66, mgr. econ. studies, 1966—67, mgr. Atlanta sales dist., 1967—68, dir. market rsch. and sales manpower planning, 1968—69, dir. mktg. plans, 1969—74, exec. dir. pharm. mktg. planning, 1974—75, exec. dir. corp. affairs, 1975—76, v.p. corp. affairs, 1976—90, v.p. health care policy, 1990; pres., chmn. bd. dirs. Centre for Health Sci. Info., Boston, from 1990; fellow Ctr. for Bus. and Govt. Kennedy Sch. of Govt. Harvard U., 1991—95; adj. prof. Butler U., Indpls., from 1995. Exec. in residence Butler U. Coll. Bus., 1995—2009; mem. Inst. Ednl. Mgmt., Harvard U. Grad. Sch. Edn., 1987; chmn. staff Bus. Roundtable Task Force on Health, 1981—85; U.S. rep. UN Indsl. Devel. Orgn. Conf., Lisbon, 1980, Casablanca, 1981, Budapest, 1983, Madrid, 1987; participant meeting of experts on pharms UNIDO, 1981; rep. to UN Commn. on Narcotic Drugs, Vienna, 1981, UN Econ. and Social Coun., NYC, 1981, UN Indsl. Devel. Orgn. Conf.; Ctr. for Bus. and Govt. fellow Kennedy Sch. Govt., Harvard U.; co-chmn. Harvard Conf. on Govt. Role in Civilian Tech., 1992, Harvard Conf. Pharmaceutical Rsch., Innovation and Pub. Policy, 1993, Harvard Biotech. Roundtable, 1991—96; vis. scholar, advisor Health and Welfare Unit, Inst. for Econ. Affairs, London; vis. scholar Green Coll. Oxford (Eng.) U., from 1994; chmn. Nat. Fund for Med. Edn., from 1994; dir. English Speaking Union, Indpls.; gov. Soc. Indiana Pioneers; lectr. in field; mem. bd. visitor Jordon Coll. Fine Arts Buttee U., from 2012. Contbr. articles to profl. jours. Pres. Eli Lilly and Co. Found., 1976—88; trustee Indpls. Symphony Orch., from 2010, life trustee; bd. trustees Indpls. Symphony Ochestra, from 2013; mem., bd. dirs. Ivy Tech. CC Found., from 2014, bd. trustees; pres., chmn. bd. Indpls. Health Inst., 1988—91; trustee Kenyon Coll., Gambier, Ohio, Ind. Hist. Soc., 2000—10; pres. bd. trustees Boston Biomed. Rsch. Inst., 1991—95, trustee emeritus; chmn. Nat. Fund for Med. Edn., from 1996; bd. dirs. Carnegie Coun. on Ethics and Internat. Affairs, 1985—92; accredited nongovtl. observer rep. to UN Goodwill Found. Ind. Inc., 1987—95; bd. dirs. Sta. WFYI Pub. TV, Indpls., 1983—91, Am. Symphony Orch. League, 1987—92, mem. dirs. coun., from 1987; bd. dirs. Nat. Health Coun., 1984—91, Pub. Affairs Coun., Washington, 1984—92, Nat. Fund for Med. Edn.; bd. advisors Christian Theol. Sem., Bishops Sch., LaJolla, Calif.; chmn. bd. dirs. Ind. Repertory Theatre, 1979—85; mem., bd. dir. The Nature Conservancy, Ind. Chpt., bd. trustees; vice chmn., exec. com., bd. dirs. Indpls. Symphony Orch. and Ind. State Symphony Soc., 1977—91; chmn. task force on fine arts Commn. for Future of Butler U.; chmn. exec. com. Pan Am. Econ. Leadership Conf. 10th Pan Am. Games, Indpls.; bd. govs. Soc. Ind. Pioneers; mem. bd. visitors Coll. Fine Arts, Butler U., from 2012. Mem.: NAM (vice-chmn. health policy com. 1987—91, bd. dirs.), Am. Symphony Orch. League N.Y. (mem. dir. coun.), Inst. Medicine NAS, Ind. Soc. Pioneers (bd. govs.), Indian Lake Yacht Club (Mich.), Svc. Club Indpls., Dramatic Club of Indpls., Univ. Club (Indpls.) (bd. dirs.), Literary Club Indpls., Reform Club London, Edgartown Golf Club, Contemporary Club, Woodstock Club, Naples Yacht Club, Edgartown Yacht Club (Martha's Vineyard). Home: Naples, Fla. Died Aug. 25, 2014.

**DAVIS, ERNEST,** manufacturing executive; b. Hot Springs, Ark., May 21, 1917; s. Willis Albert and Julia Anna (Pearcy) Davis; m. Charlotte Jane Kickhaefer, June 27, 1942; children: Robert Edward, Judith Ann Davis McNeish. BMus in Edn., Northwestern U., 1942, BBA, 1947. Tchr. spl. edn. Hot Springs Pub. Schs., 1937—38; acct. Hummel & Downing, Milw., 1947; sec. Kickhaefer Mfg. Co., Milw., 1949—54, v.p., 1954—61, pres. Port Washington, Wis., 1961—85, chmn., from 1985. Dir. Akerlow Industries, Inc., Grafton, Wis., 1978—80; dir., founder Ozaukee Bank, Cedarburg, Wis., 1975—87. Pres. Shorewood Sch. Bd., Wis., 1965; mem. Dean's Coun. Sch. Bus. Northwestern U., Evanston, Ill., 1978; mem. Grafton Water and Wastewater Commn., 1976—86. Mem.: Am. Metal Stamping Assn. (bd. dirs. 1965—66), Rotary Cedarburg (pres. 1971—72). Republican. Home: Grafton, Wis. Died Dec. 27, 1996.

**DAVIS, JOHN ANDERSON,** economics educator; b. Springfield, Ill., June 8, 1924; s. Emerson and Mae (Denney) D.; m. Lois Colvin, Sept. 16, 1947 (dec. 1977); 1 son, Stephen Colvin; m. Barbara Robson, May 8, 1986; stepchildren: Kimberly, Todd, John. Student, Trinity U., San Antonio, 1942-43; BA, So. Meth. U., 1949, MA, 1950; PhD, U. Ala., 1957. Asst. state mgr. Inter-Ocean Ins. Co., Tex., 1945-50; asst. prof. econs. Lincoln Meml. U., Harrogate, Tenn., 1950-51; instr. social scis. Memphis State U., 1951-54; research asso. Ala. Bus. Research Council, U. Ala., 1955-56, univ. instr. econs., 1956-57; assoc. prof. econs Miss. State U., 1957-59, prof. econs., from 1959, chmn. dept., 1959-83, prof. econs. emeritus, dept. head emeritus, 1987. Sec.-treas. Dallas Assn. Accident and Health Underwriters, 1945-50; mem. Ala. Bus. Research Council, 1955-56, Com. Miss. Economy, 1957-58; chmn. Miss. Council on Econ. Edn., 1968, now mem. exec. bd.; adj. prof. philosophy (part time) Miss. State U., 1989—. Editor: Jour. So. Culture, 1965—, Midsouth Jour. Econs. Chmn. bd. advisers YMCA Miss. State U., 1963-64. Recipient Golden Triangle award YMCA, 1964, Outstanding Prof. award Grad. Coll. Bus. Students' Assn., Miss. State U., 1983 Mem. Miss. Econ. Assn. (sec. 1964-65), So. Econ. Assn., Miss. Mfrs. Assn., Am. Econ. Assn., AAUP, Southwestern Social Sci. Assn., Southwest Econs. Assn. (Disting. Service award 1987), Mid-South Acad. Economists (editor-in-chief jour., pres. 1966-67, exec. bd., Disting. Service award 1978, J. Anderson Davis lectureship established 1985), Beta Gamma Sigma, Alpha Kappa Psi, Delta Sigma Phi. Home: Starkville, Miss. Died Mar. 26, 1991.

**DAVIS, JOHN ROWLAND (JACK DAVIS),** retired academic administrator; b. Mpls., Dec. 19, 1927; s. Roland Owen and Dorothy (Norman) D.; m. Lois Marie Falk, Sept. 4, 1947; children: Joel C., Jacque L., Michele M., Robin E. BS, U. Minn., 1949, MS, 1951; postgrad., Purdue U., 1955-57; PhD, Mich. State U., 1959. Hydraulic engr. U.S. Geol. Survey, Lincoln, Nebr., 1950-51; instr. Mich. State U., 1951-55; asst. prof. Purdue U., 1955-57; lectr. U. Calif., Davis, 1957-62; hydraulic engr. Stanford Rsch. Inst., South Pasadena, Calif., 1962-64; prof. U. Nebr., Lincoln, 1964-65, dean coll. engring. and architecture, 1965-71, faculty rep. intercollegiate athletics; prof., head dept. agrl. engring. Oreg. State U., Corvallis, 1971-75, instl. athletic rep., 1972-87, dir. Agrl. Expt. Sta., assoc. dean Sch. Agr., 1975-85, dir. spl. programs Office of Academic Affairs, assoc. dir. athletics, 1987-89, prof. emeritus, assoc. dir. athletics, 1989—2014. Governing bd. Water Resources Research Inst., 1975-85; dir. Western Rural Devel. Center, 1975-85, Agrl. Research Found., Jackman Inst.; cons. Stanford Research Inst., Dept. Agrl., Consortium for Internat. Devel.; dir. Engrs. Council Profl. Devel., 1966-72; pres. Pacific-10 Conf., 1978-79. Contbr. articles to profl. jours. Mem. budget commn. City of Corvallis, 2003-14. With USNR, 1945-46. Fellow American Soc. Agrl. Engrs. (dir. 1971-73, Agrl. Engr. Yr. award Pacific N.W. region 1974), NCAA (v.p. 1979-83, sec.-treas. 1983-85, pres. 1985-87), Heartland Humane Soc. (pres. bd. dirs. 2002). Home: Corvallis, Oreg. Died Apr. 25, 2014.

**DAVIS, LOWELL LIVINGSTON,** cardiovascular surgeon; b. Urbanna, Va. BS in Biology, Morehouse Coll., 1949; MS in Biology, Atlanta U., 1950; MD, Howard U., 1955; postgrad., U. Pa., 1959-60. Diplomate Am. Bd. Surgery, Am. Bd. Thoracic Surgery. Intern Jersey City (N.J.) Med. Ctr., 1955-56; resident Margaret Hague Maternity Hosp., Jersey City, 1956-57; resident ob-gyn. Elmhurst (N.Y.) Gen. Hosp., 1957-58, chief resident ob-gyn., 1958-59; resident in gen. surgery U.S. VA Hosp., Tuskegee, Ala., 1960-61; resident to chief resident in gen. surgery Nassau County Med. Ctr., Hempstead, NY, 1961-64; resident in cardiothoracic surgery Cook County Hosp., Chgo., 1967-68, sr. resident, 1968-69; pvt. practice NYC, 1964-65; pvt. practice thoracic and cardiovascular surgery, from 1975; clin. assoc. prof. surgery L.A. County Gen. Hosp., U. So. Calif. Med. Sch., from 1988. Fellow U. Oreg., Portland, 1972, St. Vincent Hosp., Portland, 1972, Med. Coll. Wis., Milw., 1973, Pacific Med. Ctr. Inst. of Med. Scis., San Francisco, 1974, Allen-Bradley Med. Scis. Rsch. Lab. Med. Coll. Wis., 1975, Hosp. for Sick Children, London, 1977-78, Tex. Heart Inst., Houston, 1983, Cardiac Surgery Rsch. Lab.; fellow, vis. prof. Hadassah Med. Sch. and U. Hosp., Jerusalem, 1987; vis. surgeon NYU Med. Sch., 1991, Mayo Clinic, Rochester, Minn., 1991, U. Dusseldorf, Germany, 1991, Deutsches Herzzentrum, Berlin, 1991, Deutsches Herzzentrum, Munich, 1991, Klinik für Thorat-Herz-Und Gefab Chirurgie, Hanover, Germany, 1991, U. Vienna, Austria, 1992; vis. student N.Y. Hosp., Cornell U, 1991; vis. surgeon U. Ala. Med. Ctr., Birmingham, 1991. Contbr. articles to profl. jours. With USN, 1943-46, USNR, 1965-71, comdr., 1965-67, capt. USNR, 1970. Recipient Asiatic Pacific Campaign medal with one Gold Star, Presdl. Unit citation. Fellow ACS, Internat. Coll. Angiology, Am. Coll. Angiology, Internat. Coll. Surgeons, N.Y. Acad. Medicine, Am. Coll. Chest Physicians, Am. Coll. Cardiology; mem. AAAS, Assn. Mil. Surgeons U.S., Am. Assn. for Thoracic Surgery, Soc. Thoracic Surgeons, Albert Starr Cardiac Surg. Soc. (founding), Am. Coll. Emergency Physicians, Lyman Brewer III Internat. Surg. Soc., Royal Soc. Medicine, Denton A. Cooley Cardiovasc. Surgery Soc., L.A. Surg. Soc. Deceased.

**DAVIS, MARILYN WEISS,** retired realtor; d. Arthur and Amelia L. Weiss; children: Pamela, Leonard, Alan. BA, Tulane U., 1953. With Latter & Blum, New Orleans, 1988—2003. Mem.: La. State Real Estate Assn. (dir., edn. found. course com., bus. and industry com. 1995), New Orleans Met. Assn. Realtors (chair edn. com., forms com., grievance com., state dir. 1993, edn. com., grievance com., state dir. 1994—95), New Orleans Coun. Realtors (pres. 1995—96), Nat. Coun. Jewish Women, East Jefferson Wellness Ctr. Home: Metairie, La. Died Feb. 7, 2008.

**DAVIS, RUBY DEE** See DEE, RUBY

**DAVIS, THOMAS HENRY,** airline executive; b. Winston-Salem, NC, Mar. 15, 1918; s. Egbert L. and Annie (Shore) D.; m. Nancy Carolyn Teague, Oct. 28, 1944; children: Thomas Henry, Winifred (Mrs. Blackwell Bennett Pierce), George Franklin, Nancy (Mrs. Nancy McGloughlin), Juliana Davis (Mrs. Steven West). Student, U. Ariz., 1935-39; LLD (hon.), Wake Forest U., 1984. Aircraft salesman Piedmont Aviation, Inc., Winston-Salem, 1940, v.p., treas., 1941-43, pres., treas., 1943-81, chmn. bd., chief exec. officer, treas., 1981-83, chmn. exec. com., 1983-88. Bd. dirs. Brendles, Inc.; dir. emeritus Wachovia Corp., Duke Power Co., ALLTEL Corp., USAir, Inc.;mem. Winston-Salem Redevel. Commn., Utilities Commn., 1955-75. Trustee Wake Forest U. Recipient Winston-Salem-Forsyth County. of C. Disting. Service award, 1954, Frank Dawson trophy for outstanding service to aviation in N.C., 1949; U. Ariz. Alumni Achievement award, 1976; Tony Jannus award for service to air transp. industry, 1980; William R. Ong Meml. award for meritorious svc. to gen. aviation industry Nat. Air Transportation Assn., 1993; named to Va. Aviation Hall of Fame, 1980; Disting. Service award N.C. Citizens Assn., 1983; Daniel Guggenheim medal, 1984, Achievement award Aero Club Washington, 1983, Aviation Trail Blazer award Dayton, Ohio C. of C., 1983; Thomas H. Davis fellowship in pulmonary medicine established by Am. Lung Assn., 1985; named to N.C. Bus. Hall of Fame, 1988; named Citizen of the Carolinas Mem. Soaring Soc. Am., Newcomen Soc., Winston-Salem C. of C. (past pres., Disting. Community Service award 1986), Pi Kappa Alpha (Order of West Range). Clubs: Rotary, Forsyth Country, Old Town (Winston-Salem); Wings (N.Y.C., Disting. Achievement award 1989); Skyline Country (Tucson). Democrat. Baptist. Home: Winston Salem, NC. *Never depend on someone else to do for you what you can and should do for yourself.* Died Apr. 22, 1999.

**DAVISON, AUDREY M.,** lawyer, consultant; b. Flasher, ND, Dec. 30, 1919; d. Frank and Laura Wyman Colegrove; m. John Roats, June 5, 1938 (div. June 1949); 1 child, Gary Charles Roats; m. Kenneth Bradley Davison (dec.); 1 child, Nelson Bradley. BA in Music, U. Wash., 1950; MA, Stanford U., 1963; JD, San Francisco Law Sch., 1992. Rsch. assoc. Vets. Hosp. and Stanford U., Palo Alto, Calif., 1965—67; sr. clin. lab. scientist Cmty. Hosp. of Los Gatos/Saratoga, Calif., 1973—85, San Jose Med. Group, 1986—94; cons. in environ. law Seattle, from 1994. Rsch. scientist VA, Palo Alto, 1967—73; instr. DeAnza C.C., Cupertino, Calif., 1974—79. Organizer citizen participation for preservation of foothills, Santa Clara County, Calif., 1970—75. Mem.: Assn. Women in Sci. (bd. dirs. Seattle chpt. 1997—99, co-chair outreach com.), Toastmasters Internat. (Dist. 2 officer from 1997, Area 3 Gov. from 1997, com. chair Success/Leadership Program 1998—99, Outstanding Mem. cert. and pin 1998). Achievements include development of 2.5% agarose column separation of antihemophilic globulin separation from frozen human plasma. Deceased.

**DAVISON, SIDNEY IVAN See DIAMOND, DAVE**

**DAY, FRANK E.,** lawyer; b. Omaha, May 21, 1918; s. L.B. and Neva (Grimwood) D.; m. Geraldine Binning, Mar. 6, 1943; children: L.B., Chrisann Deurwarder, Linda Jean. BA, U. Nebr., 1940, JD, 1942; LLD, Western States Coll., Portland, Oreg., 1965. Bar: Oreg. 1942, U.S. Dist. Ct. Oreg., U.S. Ct. Appeals (9th cir.) 1947, U.S. Supreme Ct. 1964. Sole practice, Portland, 1945-47; judge Oreg. Dist. Ct., Portland, 1947-51; ptnr. Reiter, Day, Wall & Bricker, Portland, 1951-72; pres. Day, Prohaska & Gregores, Portland, 1972-85; v.p. Burt & Day PC, Portland, 1985-86; pres., ptnr. Day & Gregores P.C., Portland, from 1986. Past bd. dirs. Portland Area Council Boy Scouts Am., Portland, bd. dirs. Vol. lawyers, Portland, 1985. Served to capt. U.S. Army 1942-45. Mem. ABA, Am. Law Inst. (life) Def. Research Inst. Fed. Communications Bar Assn., Oreg. Bar Assn., Oreg. Assn. Def. Counsel, Multnomah County Bar Assn., Washington County Bar Assn., Fedn. Ins. and Corp. Counsel. Clubs: Multnomah Athletic (Portland). Lodges: Elks, Masons, Shriners. Home: Portland, Oreg. Died Nov. 26, 1991.

**DAY, GALE EDWARD,** surveyor; b. Lorimer, Iowa, Feb. 25, 1924; s. Ralph and Anna Gertrude (Walters) Day; m. Maybelle Anna Herbert, Dec. 14, 1959; adopted children: Loretta Mae Archibald, Hazel Louella McNutt, Carolyn Lea Williams. Student, Iowa State Coll., 1946—49. Lic. land surveyor Utah, Nev., Ariz., Mont. Land surveyor Bush & Gudgell, Inc., Salt Lake City, 1951—68, land surveyor, officer mgr. St. George, Utah, 1968—99, v.p., 1970—99. With USMC, 1944—46. Mem.: Utah Home Builders Assn., Utah Coun. Land Surveyors (past pres., sec.-treas.), Elks. Methodist. Home: Saint George, Utah. Died Apr. 12, 1999.

**DAY, KENNETH ARTHUR,** psychiatrist, educator; b. London, July 18, 1935; s. Arthur and Irene Laura (Pope) Day; m. Sheila Mary Torrance, June 27, 1959 (div. 1993); children: Caroline, Paul Vincent, Matthew Charles; m. Diana Ruth Robinson, Nov. 6, 1993. MB, ChB, Bristol U., Eng., 1961; DPM, Royal Coll. Surgeons, London, 1965. House physician/surgeon Bristol Hosps., 1961-62; registrar Bristol Mental Hosps., 1962-66; sr. registrar dept. psychiatry U. Newcastle-Upon-Tyne, Eng., 1966-69; sr. lectr. dept. psychiatry U. Newcastle-upon-Tyne, Eng., 1986-97; cons. psychiatrist Northgate and Prudhoe Nat. Health Svc. Trust, Morpeth, England, 1969-92, med. dir., 1992-96, hon. cons., from 1996. Sci. adviser Dept. Health, London, 1981—87; Mental Health Act commr., England, 1987—95; mem. Mental Health Rev. Tribunal, England, from 1989. Author: books on mental retardation; contbr. articles to profl. jours. Recipient Burden Rsch. prize and gold medal, 1985; named hosp. unit in his honor, Northgate Hosp., 1996; Winston Churchill Trust fellow, 1972, WHO fellow, 1990. Fellow: Royal Geog. Soc., Internat. Assn. Sci. Study of Intellectual Disability (v.p. 1992—96, hon. officer), Royal Soc. Arts, Royal Soc. Medicine, Royal Coll. Psychiatrists (chair sect. for psychiatry of mental handicap 1983—87, Blake Marsh lectr. 1989); mem.: Worshipful Soc. Apothecaries (liveryman), European Assn. Mental Health and Mental Retardation (founder, v.p. 1992—98), City Livery Club, Royal Photog. Soc. (assoc.). Avocations: sports, art, photography, painting, natural history. Home: Tyne and Wear, England. Died June 2, 2008.

**DAY, MAURICE JEROME,** automobile parts distributing company executive; b. Saginaw, Mich., Jan. 3, 1913; s. Thomas and Margaret (Cavanaugh) D.; m. Mary Fitzgerald, Aug. 12, 1944 (dec. 1989); children: Mary Joann, Jeanne Ellen, Paul Maurice, Barbara Claire. BS, Mich. State U., 1934, MS, 1935, PhD, 1937. Metallurgist Carnegie-Ill. Steel Corp., Gary, Ind., 1937-38, tech. trade rep. Chgo., 1941-45, mgr. alloy div., 1945-47; phys. chemist U.S. Steel Research Lab., Kearny, N.J., 1938-41; metall. engr. U.S. Steel Corp., Pitts., 1947-52; mgr. materials and processes div. Armour Research Found., Chgo., 1952-53, asst. dir., 1953-54; v.p. research and devel. Crucible Steel Co. Am., Pitts., 1955-57, v.p. tech., 1957-59, v.p. comml., 1959-63, sr. v.p., 1963-65; indsl. cons., 1965-68; pres., dir. Hawley Mfg. Co., San Francisco, 1966-76; chmn. bd. Argus, Inc., 1969-75; pres. Argus, Inc, 1970-75; chmn. bd., chief exec. officer, dir. Seaport Corp., Sacramento, from 1975; pres., chief exec. officer, dir. Noma Worldwide, Inc., 1979-84. Dir. Brown Co. N.Y.C., Crucible Steel Co. Can., Oxford Electric Corp., Argus, Inc., Interphoto Corp., Crucible Steel Internat. (S.A.), Trent Tube Co.; Chmn. manganese panel, minerals and metals adv. bd., mem. panel guided missiles Nat. Acad. Scis.; Trustee Packaging Found., chmn. bd., 1963-65 Mem. Am. Ordnance Assn., Navy League U.S., Am. Soc. Metals, Def. Orientation Conf. Assn., A.I.S.I., Pa. Soc. Clubs: Duquesne (Pitts.). Died Oct. 14, 2002.

**DEAL, WILLIAM BROWN,** medical school dean, physician, educator; b. Durham, NC, Oct. 4, 1936; s. Harold Albert and Louise (Brown) D.; m. April Autrey, May 2, 1998; children: Kimberly Deal Wolpert, Kathleen Louise. AA, Mars Hill Coll., 1956; AB, U. N.C., 1958, MD, 1963. Intern in medicine U. Fla. Hosp., Gainesville, 1963-64, asst. resident, 1966-68, fellow in infectious diseases, 1968—69, chief resident, instr. dept. medicine, 1969-70; asst. prof. dept. medicine U. Fla., 1970-73, assoc. dean Coll. of Medicine, 1973-77, assoc. prof. dept. cmty. health and family medicine, 1973-75, assoc. prof. dept. medicine, 1973-75, prof., 1975-88, acting dean Coll. of Medicine, 1977-78, dean Coll. of Medicine, v.p. clin. affairs, 1978-88, clin. prof. medicine, from 1988; assoc. dean, prof. medicine U. Ala. Sch. of Medicine, 1991-96, sr. assoc. dean, prof. medicine, 1996-97, dean, 1997—2004, prof. medicine Birmingham; interim CEO UAB Health Sys., 1998-99; v.p. medicine U. Ala., Birmingham, from 2000, sr. v.p., dean emeritus, from 2004. Pres. Maine Med. Ctr. Found., Portland, Maine, 1988—90; asst. to sr. v.p. AMA, 1980; lectr. Northwestern U., 1980; vis. clin. tutor City Hosp. U. Edinburgh, Scotland, 1967; chair nat. adv. com. Summer Med. Dental Edn. Program; bd. dirs. PNP Pharm., Inc., from 2004. Contbr. articles to numerous profl. jours. Fellow: ACP, Royal Soc. Medicine; mem.: AMA (liaison com. on med. edn. 1982—87, chmn. governing coun. sect. on med. schs. 1986—87, exec. com. AAMC 1986—88, disting. svc. mem. AAMC from 2005), Noble Order of the Flea, Alpha Omega Alpha (bd. dirs. 1986—95, pres. 1993—95), Beta Theta Pi, Phi Chi. Home: Vestavia Hills, Ala. Died Mar. 15, 2013.

**DEAN, ERIC,** philosophy and religion educator; b. London, Oct. 30, 1924; arrived in US, 1947, naturalized, 1971; s. Francis Ernest and Mabel Johanna (Ritchie) D.; m. Betty Jane Garret, July 30, 1948; children: Daphne, Eric Jr., Jonathan. Student, North Park Coll., Chgo., 1947—58; AB, U. Chgo., 1950; BD, 1953, PhD, 1959; DD (hon.), Hanover Coll., 1978; DD, Christian Theol. Sem., 1979. Ordained to ministry Presbyterian Ch., 1955; instr. philosophy, asst. prof. No. Central Coll., Naperville, Ill., 1956—57; prof. philosophy, religion Wabash Coll., Crawfordsville, Ind., from 1957; overseer St. Meinrad Archabbey, Ind., from 1968; dir. Wabash Exec. Program, from 1983. Author: (book) The Good News about Sin, 1982; contbr. articles to profl. jours. With USAF, 1942—47. Mem.: N. Am. Acad. Ecumenists, Am. Soc. Ch. History, Ind. Acad. Religion (pres. 1966—67), Am. Theol. Soc. (pres. 1968—69). Democrat. Presbyterian. Avocations: bicycling, backpacking. Home: Crawfordsvlle, Ind. Died 1989.

**DEAN, JOE,** retired athletic director; b. Brazil, Ind., Apr. 26, 1930; m. Doris Kernan Hall, 1952; children: Joe Jr., Mardi, Mark. Grad., La. State U. Color analyst Southeaster Conf. Basketball Games, 1969—87; dir. athletics La. State U., 1987—2000. Named to The Nat. Collegiate Basketball Hall of Fame, 2012, The Ind. Basketball Hall of Fame, The NABC Hall of Fame, The La. Hall of Fame, The La. State U. Hall of Fame. Died Nov. 17, 2013.

**DEAN, PAUL CLEMENT,** oil industry executive; b. Detroit, Tex., July 23, 1898; s. William A. and Minnie Lee Dean; m. Lola Mae Guyer, Mar. 20, 1934 (div. 1958); children: Jane Dean Travis(dec.), Nancy Dean McClane; m. Irene Morgan Popplewell, July 28, 1966; 1 stepchild, Catherine Morgan Holly. Student, Austin Coll., Sherman, Tex., 1915—16, U. Tulsa, 1916; BA, U. Okla., 1920. Geologist Roxanna Petroleum, Tulsa, 1917—19, Sun Oil Co., Dallas, 1921—23, Waite & Phillips Co., Tulsa, 1923—25; ptnr. Dean & Adkisson, Ft. Worth, 1925—34, Dean Bros. & Great Expectations Oil Corp., Ft. Worth, 1934—68; pres. Woodlawn Corp., Ft. Worth, from 1968. With US Army, 1918. Mem.: Soc. Petroleum Engrs., Am. Inst. Mining Engrs., Am. Assn. Petroleum Geologists, Chaparral Club (Dallas), Petroleum Club, Shady Oaks Country Club, Ft. Worth Geol. Club, Sigma Gamma Epsilon. Died Aug. 23, 1993.

**DE ARMOND, ANNA JANNEY,** English educator; b. Phila., Feb. 10, 1910; d. James Keyser and Emily (Janney) De A. AB with highest honors, Swarthmore Coll., 1932; postgrad., Bryn Mawr Coll., 1932-33, 34-35; MA, Columbia U., 1934; PhD, U. Pa., 1947; DHL, U. Del., 1993. From instr. English to prof. English U. Del., Newark, 1935-75, prof. emeritus English, from 1975. Vis. prof. Sheffield (Eng.) U., 1967, New Eng. U., Armidale, NSW, Australia, 1974, Ocean U. Qingdao, People's Republic China, 1988; Fulbright prof. U. Munich, 1956-57; mem. coms. Del. Humanities Forum; mem. commn. on English, Harvard U., 1965; dir. NDEA English Inst., 1966; adviser Am. sudies conf. Bd. Associated Rsch. Couns., Washington, 1957-58; cons. office edn. HEW, 1967, Del. Coun. Tchr. Edn., 1965-74; cons. English, Salem County, N.J., 1960-61; lectr. in field; presenter radio, TV. Author: Andrew Bradford, 1949, reprint, 1969; contbr. articles and book revs. to profl. jours. Mem. Phila. Zoo, Pa. Hist. Soc. Mem. AAUW, ACLU, UN Assn., Modern Lang. Assn., Women's Internat. League, Phi Beta Kappa (founder U. Del. chpt.). Avocations: travel, music, theater. Died Mar. 26, 2008.

**DEBARTOLO, HANSEL MARION, JR.,** otolaryngologist, plastic surgeon; b. Aurora, Ill., May 13, 1947; s. Hansel Marion and Rosemary (Boetto) Debartolo; m. Susan Elizabeth Debartolo, June 26, 1977; children: Doré, Hansel III, Merrit, Janae, Raquel. BA cum laude, U. Minn., 1969; MD, Loyola U., Chgo., 1972; JD, William Howard Taft U. Diplomate Am. Bd. Otolaryngology, Nat. Bd. Med. Examiners, Am. Acad. Anti-Aging (bd. examiner). Intern, resident Mayo Clinic and Mayo Found., Rochester, Minn.; fellow in surgery Mayo Clinic, Rochester; fellow in otorhinolaryngology Geisinger Clinic, Danville, Pa.; former chief staff AmSurg, Joliet, Ill. Ptnr. Chgo. White Sox, H.M.D., Racing Stables, Chgo. Metro TV, Sportsvision, CETUS Internat., Granada Cosmisky Parks Assocs., Hard Master Recording; CEO H.M.D. Devel.; attending surgeon Mendota (Ill.) Hosp. Contbr. articles to profl. jours. Bd. dirs. Debartolo Rsch. Found. Fellow: Am. Acad. Cosmetic Surgery, Drs. Mayo Soc. Life, Am. Acad. Anti-Aging Medicine, Am. Rhinologic Soc., Priestly Surg. Soc., Chgo. Larynigol. and Otological Soc., Deafness Rsch. Assn. (life), Am. Acad. Otorhinolaryngology (legis. key physician Ill., mem. bd. govs.); mem.: AAAS, Am. Soc. Cosmetic Dermatology, Pa. Acad. Ophthalmology and Otolaryngology, Ill. Soc. Opthalmology and Otolaryngology (mem. exec. coun., sec.-treas., chief editor proceedings), Am. Acad. Advancement Medicine, Hunter Boat Owners Assn., Sailboat Harbor Prairie Harbor Yacht Club, Aurora Country Club. Roman Catholic. Avocations: tennis, skiing, golf, bicycling, amateur radio. Home: Aurora, Ill. Died May 2, 2014.

**DE BEAUGRANDE, ROBERT,** language educator; b. Mar. 4, 1946; MA in German and English Lang. and Lit., Free U. Berlin, 1971; PhD in Comparative Lit. and Linguistics, U. Calif., Irvine, 1976. Asst. prof. English U. Fla., Gainesville, 1978—80, assoc. prof. English, 1980—83, prof. English, 1983—91, U. Vienna, Austria, 1991—97, U. Botswana, Gaborone, 1997—99, United Arab Emirates U., 1999—2001, U. Federal Paraiba, Paraiba, Brazil, from 2001. Vis. prof. Fed. U. Minas Gerais, Belo Horizonte; guest prof. U. Bielefeld, Germany, 1979, U. Minn., Mpls., 1984, U. Alexandria, Egypt, 1993, U. Cape Town, 1999; vis. prof. numerous other univs.; lectr. in field. Mem. editl. bd. Discourse Processes, Discourse Studies, Discurso y Sociedad, Empirical Studies of the Arts, English for Special Purposes, Functions of Language, Poetics, Revista Española de Linguistica Aplicada, Revista Brasileira de Linguistica Aplicada; author: Factors in a Theory of Poetic Translating, 1978, Text, Discourse and Process: Toward a Multidisciplinary Science of Texts, 1980; co-author (with Wolfgang Dressler): Introduction to Text Linguistics, 1981; author: Text Production, 1984, Writing Step by Step: A Textbook for College Writers, 1985, Critical Discourse: A Survey of Contemporary Literary Theorists, 1988, Linguistic Theory: The Discourse of Fundamental Works, 1991, New Foundations for a Science of Text and Discourse, 1997; editor: European Approaches to the Study of Text and Discourse, 1980; editor: (translator) Empirical Foundations for the Study of Literature, 1982; editor: (with Abdulla Shunnaq and Mohammed Heliel) Language, Discourse and Translation in the West and the Middle East, 1994; exec. prodr.(with Meta Grosman and Barbara Seidhofer): Language Policy and Language Education in Emerging Nations: Focus on Slovenia and Croatia, 1998; contbr. numerous articles to profl. jours., chpts. to books. Grantee Office of Instructional Resources grantee, 1982—83, Travel grantee, Am. Coun. Learned Socs., 1985, Internat. Rsch. Exchange, 1987, Fulbright Hayes grantee, Coun. for Internat. Exchange of Scholars, Nat. U. Singapore, 1988—89, Vis. Acad. Specialist grantee, USIS, 1992; fellow John Simon Guggenheim Meml. fellow, 1984—85. Died June 6, 2008.

**DE BELLIS, PASQUALE,** medical educator; b. Gioia del Colle, Bari, Italy, July 10, 1942; s. Vincenzo De Bellis and Maria Cristina Galli; m. Gianfranca Nervo, July 1, 1972; children: Claudio, Paolo, Andrea. Medicine and surgery, U. Genoa, 1970. Specialization in anesthesiology and intensive care U. Siena, 1973, specialization in medical toxicology U. Pavia, 1976, specialization in clinical pharmacology U. Pavia, 1986, specialization in applied pharmacology U. Modena, 1978, specialization in legal medicine and assurance U. Genoa, 1982, specialization in pediatrics U. Genoa, 1991. Physician Galliera Hosp., Genoa, Italy, 1970—78, physician, dept. anesthesia and intensive care med. vice-dir., 1978—84, physician, dept. anesthesia and intensive care med. dir., 1984—2001; pediatric cons., dept. ophthalmology S.Martino U. Hosp., Genoa, 1990—97, physician, dept. anesthesia and intensive care med. dir., from 2002, physician, dept. of cardionephrology med. dir., from 2005. Prof. ophthalmology sch. U. Genoa, 1994—96, prof. anesthesiology and critical care sch., from 1996, prof. gen. surgery and cardiac surgery schs., from 2003. Recipient Golden Esculapio, 1992, Cittadino Gioiese, 2003. Mem.: Am. Soc. Anesthesiologists, Soc. Critical Care Medicine, European Soc. Anesthesia, European Soc. Intensive Care Medicine, European Soc. Pediatric and Neonatal Intensive Care, Soc. Italiana Anestesia Rianimazione Emergenza Dolore, Soc. Italiana Terapia Intensiva (component mem. nat. coun. 2000), Soc. Italiana Anestesia Analgesia Terapia Intensiva, Am. Soc. Regional Anesthesia, Assoc. Anestesisti Rianimatori Ospedalieri Italiani (regional pres. liguria and nat. adviser 1992). Home: Genova, Italy. Died Aug. 26, 2009.

**DE BURGOS, RAFAEL FRUHBECK,** retired conductor; b. 1933; Grad. in Conducting summa cum laude, Munich's Hochschule für Musik. Mem. Royal Acad. of Fine Arts of San Fernando, 1975; chief condr. Spanish Nat. Orch.; gen. music dir. Deutsche Oper Berlin; prin. condr. Vienna Symphony Orch.; music dir. Rundfunk-Sinfonieorchester Berlin; artistic dir. and prin. condr. Dresden Philharmonic, chief condr., 2004—11; hon. condr. Spain National Orch.; with Yomiuri Nippon Symphony Orch., Japan, 1974, prin. dir., 1980, prin. guest condr., 1983—90, hon. condr., 1990—2014. Recipient Gold Medal, Vienna, Gustav Mahler Internat. Soc., Jacinto Guerrero prize, 1997; named Conductor of the Year, Musical America, 2011. Died June 11, 2014.

**DE CAIRES, CECIL FRANCIS,** life insurance company executive; b. Georgetown, Guyana, Nov. 25, 1917; arrived in Barbados, 1962; s. Francis and Josephine (Gonsalves) de C.; m. Thelma Rosalind Elias, Jan. 28, 1942; children: Geoffrey Francis, Ian Francis. Grad. parochial sch., Georgetown. Founder, pres., CEO, Life of Barbados Ltd., Wildey, 1971-98, exec. chmn., 1998—2002. Bd. dirs. Roybar Investment Corp. subs. Royal Bank Can., Sunbury Gt. House Inc., CGT Ins. Co. Ltd., Can. Pres. Barbados Assn. for Mentally Retarded Children, 1969-73, Caribbean Assn. for Mental Retardation, 1981-83; 1st chmn. Thelma Vaughan Meml. Home for Physically Handicapped Children in Barbados, 1973; chmn. fin., devel. and planning com. Nat. Children's Home, 1983-87; chmn. Richmond Fellowship of Caribbean, 1987-89; hon. consul of Portugal for Barbados, 1996—. Decorated Companion of Honour (Barbados); named Master Entrepreneur, Ernst & Young and CIBC Entrepreneur of Yr., 1997; recipient award for 50 years outstanding contbn. to life ins. industry Life Underwriters assn. Barbados, 1997. Mem. Life Assurance Cos. Assn. Barbados (pres. 1963-65), Ins. Assn. Caribbean (hon.

life, pres. 1976-78), Barbados Yacht Club, Lions (charter pres. Georgetown 1960-62, founder Barbados 1961, dist. gov. dist 60 W.I. and Guyanas 1963-64). Roman Catholic. Avocations: golf, community service. Home: Saint Michael, Barbados. Died Oct. 9, 2003.

**DECKER, FRANZ PAUL,** symphony conductor, opera conductor; b. Cologne, Germany, June 22, 1928; s. Caspar and Elisabeth (Scholz) D.; m. Christa Terka, May 26, 1969; children: Arabella, Ariadne. Grad. high sch.; student, State Inst. for Mus. Edn., Cologne; M.Conducting, U. Cologne; Doctorate (hon.), Concordia U., Montreal, Que., Can., McGill U. Choir dir., asst. condr., Municipal Theater, Giessen, 1945, condr. opera, Cologne, 1945, municipal dir. music, Krefeld, 1946-50, prin condr., State Opera house, Wiesbaden, 1950-53, permanent dir., Municipal Symphony Orch., Wiesbaden, 1953-56, general music director, Bochum, 1956-64, chief condr., artistical dir., Rotterdam Philharmonic Orch., 1962-68, permanent condr., mus. dir., Montreal Symphony Orch., 1967-76; artistic adv. Calgary Philharmonic Orchestra, 1975-77, Winnipeg Symphony Orchestra, 1980-82, prin. guest condr. New Zealand Symphony, 1981-89, music dir., 1990-94; chief condr. and artistical dir. Orquestra Sinfonica de Barcelona, 1986-91; prin. guest condr. Nat. Arts Ctr. Orch., Ottawa, 1991-99, Edmonton Symphony Orch., 2003-04 Decorated Edgar Roquette Pinto medal Brazil, 1963, Herscheppend Schep Ik medal Netherlands, 1968; Order of Merit 1st class Fed. Republic of Germany; received Jubilee medal Queen Elizabeth II, Highest Spanish Decoration, Creus de Sant Jordi Catalunya, 2006. Died May 19, 2014.

**DECKER, MARY DURYEA,** volunteer, educator, retired social worker; b. Portland, Oreg., Mar. 17, 1928; d. Oliver Martin Nisbet, MD and Lois Marguerite (Mangus) Nisbet; m. Richard Adrian Duryea, Aug. 23, 1950 (dec. Apr.1958); 1 child, Maria Duryea; m. Edward Albert Decker, Jan. 28, 1967. BS in Speech and Sociology, Northwestern U., 1950; MA in Speech and Edn., Stanford U., 1961. Cert. adminstr., counselor, instr., Calif. cmty. colls. Social worker, supr. City of Austin, Tex., 1950-54; med. social worker Monterey (Calif.) County Hosp., 1955-57; instr. speech, counseling San Jose (Calif.) City Coll., 1961-62; residence hall dir. Stanford (Calif.) U., 1962-65; dean students Scripps Coll., Claremont, Calif., 1965-69; asst. vice chancellor U. Calif., San Diego, 1969-75; chief student svcs. officer 3 campuses San Diego C.C. Dist., 1976-88; project mgr. Combined Case Mgmt., Lincoln County, Oreg., 1991-93. Mem., chair chief student svc. offices Region X, Calif. C.C. Chancellor's Office, 1976-88; mem. Gov.'s Coun. on Nutrition and Volunteerism, 1978-80. Mem., pres. Vol. Bur. San Diego, 1970-72; mem., v.p. United Way, San Diego, 1971-78; bd. dir., v.p. Girl Scouts San Diego, 1976-88; trustee North Lincoln Health Dist., Lincoln City, Oreg., 1990—, chair bd., 1995-97; vice chair Gov.'s Coun. Alcohol and Drug Programs, Salem, Oreg., 1994-99; bd. dir. Oreg. Pacific Area health Ed. Ctr., Newport, 1992-99; mem. statewide adv. com. Area Health Edn. Ctr. Program, 1999—; apptd. by gov. to bd. trustees Oreg. Health and Sci. U., 2001—. Recipient grant Ford Found., 1985-88. Mem. Univ. Club Portland. Republican. Presbyterian. Deceased.

**DE COU-LANDBERG, MICHELLE V.,** retired language educator; b. France, Sept. 16, 1934; arrived in US, 1963, naturalized; d. Lucien-Louis and Suzanne (Fourneret) Vuillermet; m. James Herbert De Cou (div.); children: Claire De Cou, Michel-David De Cou, Jacques-Frédéric De Cou; m. Erik W. Landberg. Licence d'anglais, U. Dijon, France, 1957; postgrad., Claremont Grad. Sch., Calif., 1960; MA in English Lit., George Mason U., Fairfax, Va., 1976. Cert. English and French tchr. Va., 1967, elem. edn. Va., 1987. French asst. Diss Grammar Sch., Suffolk, England, 1957—58; English tchr. French govt., Chambéry Savoie, 1958—59, St. Jean de Maurienne, 1960—61, Luang-Prabang, Laos, 1961—62; French tchr. Arlington County Pub. Schs., Va., 1967—68, Fairfax County Pub. Schs., Fairfax, Va., 1972—73, ESL tchr., 1975—96; ret., 1996. Del. to Vietnam Citizen Ambs. Program, 1994. Author: The Global Classroom, vol. 1, 1994, vol. 2, 1995; contbr. articles to profl. jours. Pres. Common Ground Found., Reston, Va., 1977—79, Herndon-Reston F.I.S.H., Herndon, Va., 1982—85; chmn. coll. and career bound program Kids R First, Reston, 2000—10. Recipient Golden Eagle award, Fairfax County Pub. Schs., 1994; named Reston Citizen of Yr., Reston Cmty. Assn., 1981; Fulbright travel scholar, 1959—60. Mem.: TESOL (chmn. elem. edn. sect. 2003), AAUW. Democrat. Buddhist. Avocations: travel, hiking, genealogy, human rights issues. Home: Reston, Va. Died July 26, 2013.

**DECROW, KAREN,** lawyer, educator, writer; b. Chgo., Dec. 18, 1937; d. Samuel Meyer and Juliette (Abt) Lipschultz; m. Alexander Allen Kolben, 1960 (div. 1965); m. Roger DeCrow, 1965 (div. 1972, dec. 1989). BS, Northwestern U., Evanston, Ill., 1959; JD, Syracuse U., NY, 1972; DHL (hon.), SUNY, Oswego, 1994. Bar: NY, US Dist. Ct. (northern dist.) NY. Resorts editor Golf Digest mag., Evanston, Ill., 1959-60; editor American Soc. Planning Officials, Chgo., 1960-61; writer Ctr. for Study Liberal Edn. for Adults., Chgo., 1961-64; editor Holt, Rinehart, Winston, Inc., NYC, 1965; textbook editor L.W. Singer, Syracuse, NY, 1965-66; writer Eastern Regional Inst. for Edn., Syracuse, 1967-69, Public Broadcasting System, 1977; tchr. women and law, 1972-74; nat. bd. mem. NOW, 1968-77, nat. pres., 1974-77, also nat. politics task force chair; cons. affirmative action; pvt. practice Jamesville, NY, 1974—2014. Lectr. topics including law, gender, internat. feminism to corps., polit. groups, colls. and univs., US, Can., Mex., Finland, China, Greece, former USSR; nat. coord. Women's Strike for Equality, 1970; moot ct. judge; NY State del. Internat. Women's Yr., 1977; originator Schs. for Candidates; participant DeCrow-Schlafly ERA Debates, from 1975; founder (with Robert Seidenberg, MD) World Woman Watch, 1988; gender issues advisor Nat. Congress for Men; mem. Task Force on Gender Bias. Author: (with Roger DeCrow) University Adult Education: A Selected Bibliography, 1967, American Council on Education, 1967, The Young Woman's Guide to Liberation: Alternatives to a Half-Life While the Choice Is Still Yours, 1971, Sexist Justice, 1974, First Women's State of the Union Message, 1977, (with Robert Seidenberg, MD) Women Who Marry Houses: Panic and Protest in Agoraphobia, 1983, Turkish edit., 1988, 2d Turkish edit., 1989, United States of America vs. Sex: How the Meese Commission Lied About Pornography, 1988, (with Jack Kammer) Good Will Toward Men: Women Talk Candidly About the Balance of Power Between the Sexes, 1994; editor: The Pregnant Teenager (Howard Osofsky), 1968, Corporate Wives, Corporate Casualties (Robert Seidenberg, MD), 1973; contbr. articles to USA Today, NY Times, NY Times Bus. Sect., LA Times, Chgo. Tribune, Nat. Law Jour., Women Boston Globe, Vogue, Mademoiselle, Ingenue, Newsday, Chgo. Sun Times, Penthouse, Washington Post, LA Times Mag., Policy Review, Miami Herald, Internat. Herald Tribune, Social Problems, Houston Chronicle, Pitts. Press, Nat. NOW Times, Syracuse U. Mag., San Francisco Chronicle, Civil Rights Quar., Women Lawyers Jour., other newspapers, mags.; regular columnist: Syracuse New Times, 1985-2007; columnist NY Times Spl. Features; recording: Opening Up Marriage, 1980. Hon. trustee Elizabeth Cady Stanton Found.; active Hon. Com. to Save Alice Paul's Birthplace; Liberal party candidate for Mayor of Syracuse, 1969. Recipient Profl. Recognition award for best newspaper column Syracuse Press Club, 1990, 94, 95, 96, 2000, Best Column award, 1994-95, 99, 2001, 02, Best Column award NY Press Assn., 1991-92, 95, award Barnard Coll., Vet. Feminists of America and the Barnard Ctr. for Rsch. on Women, Woman of Achievement/Distinction award Gov. George E. Pataki, 1998; Svc. to Soc. award Northwestern U. Alumni Assn., 2002, Achievement award The Post-Standard, Syracuse, 2003; named to Hall of Achievement Medill Sch. Journalism Northwestern U., 2007, Disting. Lawyer award, Onondaga County BAr Assn., 2008, Ruth Schapiro award, NY State Bar Assn., 2009; named to Nat. Women's Hall of Fame, Seneca Falls, NY, George Arents Pioneer medal, 2009, Female Lawyers & Judges, US Dept. State Womens History Month. Mem. NOW (pres. 1974-77, bd. dirs. 1968-74, v.p.), ACLU (Ralph E. Kharas Disting. Svc. in Civil Liberties award 1985), NY Women's Bar Assn. (ctrl. NY chpt. pres. 1989-90, jud. screening com., Joan L. Ellenbogen Founder's award 2003, Doris Hoffman medal 2005), Women's Bar Assn. State NY (founder, Ctrl. NY chapt., 1977, judicial screening com., ctrl. NY chapt. pres., 1989-90, nom. com., 1996, 2001, Doris Hoffman medal 2005), NY Bar Assn., Onondaga County Bar Assn. (profl. ethics com., fed. cts. com., grievance com., co-chair membership com. 2006, governance com. 2006, nominating com. 2006, bd. dirs. 2005-2007; Disting. Lawyer award 2008), NY State Bar Assn.(mem. com. women in law 2009, Women Law com. mem., 2009, Ruth Schapiro award 2009), Elizabeth Cady Stanton Found. (trustee), Feminists for Free Expression (adv. com.), Abortion Rights Mobilization (bd. dir.), Nat. Coalition Against Censorship, Working Women's Inst. (bd. advisors), Syracuse Friends Chamber Music, Atlantic States Legal Found., Yale Polit. Union (hon. life), Nat. Congress Men (gender issues advisor), Mariposa Edn. and Rsch. Found., Nat. Coun. Children's Rights (adv. panel), Wilderness Soc., Northwestern U. Alumni Assn., Women's Inst. Freedom Press, Art Inst. Chgo., Nat. Women's Polit. Caucus, Theta Sigma Phi; co-chair, Women on Move Prog., NY state Bar Assn. Achievements include pioneer feminist lawyer by veteran feminists of America, June 2008. *I feel especially lucky to be able to participate, as Holmes said, in the passion of our times. The movement to create equality between women and men is the most interesting and exciting during this period in history. My goal is a world where the gender of a baby will have little or no relevance to future pursuits or pleasures - personal, political, economic, social, or professional. It is exhilarating to watch society change in that direction.* Died June 6, 2014.

**DEE, RUBY (RUBY DEE DAVIS),** actress, writer, film director; b. Cleve., Oct. 27, 1924; d. Marshall Edward and Emma (Benson) Wallace; m. Ossie Davis, Dec. 9, 1948 (dec. Feb. 4, 2005); children: Nora, Guy, Hasna. BA, Hunter Coll., 1945; ArtsD (hon.), Fairfield U.; D (hon.), Iona Coll., Va. State U.; apprentice, Am. Negro Theatre, 1941-44; LHD (hon.), SUNY, Old Westbury, 1990; DFA (hon.), Spelman Coll., 1991. Ind. actress, writer, dir., v.p. Emmslyn II Prodns., from 1945. Author: (poetry) Glowchild, 1972, (musical) Take It from the Top, (collected poetry, humor, short stories) My One Good Nerve, co-author (with Ossie Davis): With Ossie & Ruby: In This Life Together, 1998 (Grammy award for Best Spoken Word Album, 2007), Life Lit by Some Large Vision: Selected Speeches & Writings, 2006; adaptor: (African folk tales) Two Ways to Count to Ten, The Tower to Heaven, (play) Books With Legs, 1993; contbr. column NY Amsterdam News; co-writer (film) Uptight; dir., adaptor (stage prodn.) Zora is my Name!, 1983; stage appearances include Jeb, 1946, Raisin in the Sun, 1959, Purlie Victorious, 1961, The Imaginary Invalid, 1971, Wedding Band, 1972 (Drama Desk award 1972), Boesman and Lena, 1970 (Obie award 1971), Anna Lucasta, Taming of the Shrew, Checkmates, 1988, The Glass Menagerie, 1989, Flyin West, 1994, Two Hah-Hahs and a Homeboy, 1995; actress: (films) Gone are the Days, The Jackie Robinson Story, 1950, Take a Giant Step, St. Louis Blues, A Raisin in the Sun, Purlie Victorious, To Be Young, Gifted and Black, Buck and the Preacher, Countdown at Kusini, Cat People, 1982, Do the Right Thing, 1989 (NAACP Image award as best actress 1989), Jungle Fever, 1991, Cop & 1/2, 1993, Whitewash, 1994, Just Cause, 1995, Simple Wish, A, 1997, Baby Geniuses, 1999, Little Bill, 2001, Feast of All Saints, 2001, Unchained Memories, 2002, Baby of the Family, 2002, Dream Street, 2005, No. 2, 2006, The Way Back Home, 2006, American Gangster, 2007 (Best Supporting Actress, African Am. Film Critics Assn., 2007, Outstanding Performance by a Female Actor in a Supporting Role, SAG, 2008), All About Us, 2007; narrator: Time to Dance: The Life and Work of Norma Canner, A, 1998, Unfinished Journey, 1999; numerous TV appearances including It's Good to be Alive, 1974, Today Is Ours, 1974, The Defenders, Police Woman, Peyton Place, (TV films) To Be Young, Gifted and Black, All God's Children, The Nurses, Roots: The Next Generation, I Know Why the Caged Bird Sings, Wedding Band, It's Good to Be Alive, Decoration Day (Emmy award for Supporting Actress in a Miniseries or Special 1991), The Atlanta Child Murders, (TV spl. with Ossie Davis) Martin Luther King: The Dream and the Drum, The Winds of Change, Windmill of the Gods, TV miniseries Stephen King's The Stand, 1994, Tuesday Morning Ride, 1995, Mr. & Mrs. Loving, 1996, Captive Heart: The James Mink Story, 1996, Porgy and Bess: An American Voice, 1998, Passing Glory, 1999, Having Our Say: The Delany Sisters' First 100 Years, 1999, Finding Buck McHenry, 2000, A Storm in Summer, 2000, Taking Back Our Town, 2001, Their Eyes Were Watching God, 2005; co-producer: (TV spl.) Today is Ours, The Ernest Green Story, 1993, (radio show) Ossie Davis and Ruby Dee Story Hour, 1974-78, (TV series) With Ossie and Ruby, 1981, (home videotape) Hands Upon The Heart, 1991, Middle Ages, 1992, Hands Upon The Heart II, 1993; rec. artist poems and stories; host (with Ossie Davis) African Heritage Movie Network. Recipient Martin Luther King Jr. award Operation PUSH, 1972, Drama Desk award, 1974, (with Ossie Davis) Frederick Douglass award NY Urban League, 1970, (with Ossie Davis) NAACP Image award Hall of Fame, Master Innovator For Film award Sony, 1991, Nat. Medal of Arts, 1990, Chmn.'s award, NAACP, 2008, Beacon of Change award Maj. League Baseball, 2008; Kennedy Ctr. Honors (with Ossie Davis), 2004. Mem. NAACP, CORE, Student Non-Violent Coordinating Com., SCLC. Died June 12, 2014.

**DEECKEN, GEORGE CHRISTIAN,** retired financial executive; b. Jersey City, Apr. 12, 1922; s. George R. and Florence C. (Foley) D.; m. Josephine J. Hennequin, Nov. 17, 1955 (dec. 1991); children: George W., John R., James R. BS, N.Y. U., 1948. C.P.A., N.Y. Mgr. Price, Waterhouse & Co., NYC, 1941-55; controller, treas. Christian Herald Assn., NYC, 1955-59; v.p. finance & adminstrn. Remington Rand (divsn. Sperry Rand Corp.), NYC, 1959-66; pres. lamp divsn. Internat. Tel. & Tel. Co., NYC, 1966-68; sr. v.p., CFO Wickes Corp., Saginaw, Mich., 1968-71; sr. v.p., controller Chemical Bank, NYC, 1971-81; exec. v.p., CFO Young & Rubicam, Inc., NYC, 1981-84. Served to capt. USAAF, World War II. Mem. AICPA, N.Y. State Soc. CPAs, Financial Executives Inst. Clubs: Union League (N.Y.C.). Home: Westport, Conn. Died Feb. 2, 2013.

**DEEMS, FRANKLIN E.,** wire and cable manufacturing executive; CFO Southwire Co., Carrolton, Ga. Died 1993.

**DEGENER, OTTO,** botanist, writer; b. East Orange, NJ, May 13, 1899; s. William and Marie Ludovica Keampf (von Baldenstein) Degener; m. Isa Irmgard Margarete Elisabeth Hansen, Jan. 10, 1953. BS, Mass. Agr. Coll., 1922; MS, U. Hawaii, 1923; postgrad., U. Mass., 1924—25, ScD (hon.), 1952; postgrad., Marine Biol. Lab., Columbia U. and NY Bot. Garden, 1951—52. Asst. botanist Mass. State Coll., 1924; instr. botany U. Hawaii, 1925—27; naturalist Hawaii Nat. Pk., Islands Maui and Hawaii, 1929; collaborator Hawaiian Botany Resident in Hawaiian Islands, NY Bot. Garden, NYC, from 1933. Bot. explorer Anne Archbold Expedition, Melanesia, 1940—41; cons. Revegetating Canton Atoll Equator, FAA, 1950—51, 1957—58. Author: Plants of Hawaii National Park, with Descriptions of Ancient Hawaiian Customs and an Introduction to the Geologic History of the Islands, 1930, Flora Hawaiiensis or New Illustrated Flora of the Hawaiian Islands, vol. I, 1933, vol. II, 1935, vol. III, 1938, vol. IV, 1940, vol. V, 1957, vol. VI, 1963, Naturalists' South Pacific Expedition: Fiji, 1949; contbr. articles to profl. jours. Recipient Linne medal, Royal Swedish Acad. Sci., Stockholm, 1962, Willdenow medal, Bot. Garden and Mus., Berlin, 1979, Commendation, Hawaii Senate, 1979; grantee, NSF. Mem.: AAAS, Hawaiian Bot. Soc., Am. Mus. Natural History, Nat. Pks. Assn. Republican. Home: Waialua, Hawaii. Died Jan. 5, 1987.

**DEGIACINTO, VICKIE HALE,** gifted and talented educator, elementary school educator; b. Eldorado, Ill., Feb. 26, 1947; d. Charles Walter and Marion Hise Hale; m. Charles Ray DeGiacinto, June 21, 1968; children: Clayton Hale, Caren Pauline Schaecher, Catherine Rachel. BSc, So. Ill. U., Carbondale, 1971; MSc, So. Ill. U., Edwardsville, 1973. Cert. regular edn., spl. edn., reading specialist, gifted edn. tchr. Ill. State Bd. Edn. Head tchr. spl. edn. Madison County Assn. Retarded Citizens, Edwardsville, Ill., 1971—72; learning disabilities tchr. Evansville, Vanderburgh Schs., Evansville, Ind., 1972—73; tchr. Edwardsville Schs., from 1975. Sec. West Point Parents' Club, 1993—95. Recipient Outstanding Young Educator, Edwardsville Jaycees, 1979. Mem.: NEA, Edwardsville Edn. Assn., Ill. Edn. Assn., St. Louis Assn. Gifted Edn. Roman Catholic. Avocations: reading, cooking. Home: Edwardsville, Ill. Died Mar. 13, 2008.

**DE GIORGI, ENNIO,** mathematics educator; b. Lecce, Italy, Feb. 8, 1928; Prof. math. analysis Scuola Normale Superiore, Pisa, Italy. Recipient Wolf Found. Math. prize, 1990. Mem. Acad. Nat. Lincei. Died Oct. 25, 1996.

**DEGNBOL-MARTINUSSEN, JOHN (EMIL),** political science educator, academic administrator, consultant; b. Nykobing, Mors, Denmark, June 22, 1947; s. Erik Emil and

Eva (Knudsen) M.; divorced; children: Sandra, Nanna; m. Vibeke Degnbol, 1994. BA in Polit. Sci., Aarhus U., Denmark, 1969, MSc in Polit. Sci., 1974, Dr.scient.pol., 1980. Sr. lectr. Aarhus U., 1971-72; asst. prof. Inst. of Polit. Sci., Aarhus U., 1972-78, assoc. prof., 1978-81; prof., chmn. study coun. internat. devel. studies Roskilde (Denmark) U., 1981-97, dean Grad. Sch. Internat. Devel. Studies, from 1998. Cons. Danida, Asian Devel. Bank, ILO, UNDP, others; mem. Rsch. Coun. for Developing Countries, 1986-98; chmn. Nordic Inst. Asian Studies, Copenhagen, 1991-93; pres. Danish Social Sci. Rsch. Coun., 1992-95; mem. standing com. for social scis., com. for advanced Asian studies European Sci. Found., 1993-95, mem. exec. coun., 1995-99; chmn. Danish Coun. for Internat. Devel. Coop., 1996—. Author: Transnational Corporations in a Developing Country: The Indian Experience, 1988, Democracy, Competition and Choice, 1994, Society, State and Markets, 1997, Politics, Institutions and Industrial Development, 2001, several other books. Mem. exec. bd. Danish Devel. Coop., Copenhagen, 1982-91; mem. Danish Commn. on Security and Devel., Copenhagen, 1987-93; pres. Danish Assn. Internat. Coop., Copenhagen, 1982-91. Recipient several grants. Mem. Danish Assn. Devel. Rschrs. (founder, exec. com. 1983-86). Home: Fredericksberg, Denmark. Died Sept. 23, 2002.

**DEGONIA, MARY ELISE,** government community relations executive, publisher; b. St. Louis, Sept. 23, 1954; d. Joseph Milton and Janice Doris (Walls) DeG. Student, Riverside Community Coll., 1971-73, Calif. State U., 1973-76. Dir., youth svcs. Los Padrinos, San Bernardino, Calif., 1975-78; chief, planning and evaluation Mayor's Office of Employment and Tng., San Bernardino, 1978-79; program mgr., v.p. Mondale Task Force on Youth, Washington, 1979-80; sr. policy analyst Nat. Youth Work Alliance, Washington, 1979-81; v.p. govt. rels. Youth Employment, Washington, 1981-88; pres. Capitol Perspectives, Washington, from 1988. Pub. Capitol Perspectives Update; dir. pub. policy and legislation Nat. Youth Employment Ctr., N.Y.C., 1979-89; founding mem. Nat. Assn. for Community Base Orgn., Washington, 1979-83. Co-author: State Coordination Guide, 1987, Food for Thought, 1988, Stalking the Large Green Grant, 1979, Fund Diversification Guide, 1988. Founding chmn. Calif. Child, Youth and Family Coalition, Sacramento, 1976-78; nat. bd. dirs. Wider Opportunities for Women; sr. adv. Nat. Coun. La Raza Jobs for Youth, 1998—. Recipient Outstanding Performance award, U.S. Dept. Labor, Washington, 1980, Disting. Achievement award, U.S. Basics, Alexandria, Va., 1988. Mem. Nat. Youth Employment Coalition, State Issues Forum (exec. mem., bd. dirs.), Nat. Job. Tng. Partnership. Avocations: scuba diving, surfing, saxaphone playing, desert hiking. Deceased.

**DE GRAZIA, ALFRED,** philosopher, behavioral scientist; b. Chgo., Dec. 29, 1919; s. Alfred J. and Katherine (Lupo) de G.; m. Jill B.L. Oppenheim, May 11, 1942 (dec.); children: Catherine de Grazia Vanderpool, Victoria F. de Grazia Paggi, Jessica M. de Grazia Jeans, Paul R., John S., Carl M. (dec. 2000), Christopher; m. Nina Mavridis, Dec. 21, 1972 (div.); m. Anne-Marie Hueber, Apr. 23, 1982. AB, U. Chgo., 1939, PhD, 1948; student, Columbia Law Sch., 1940-41. Mem. faculty Northwestern U., 1948, U. Minn., 1948-50, Brown U., 1950-52, Stanford U., 1952-57; research prof. social theory NYU, 1959-83. Vis. lectr. U. Istanbul, Turkey, U. Rome, U. Gothenburg, Sweden, U. Bombay, India; rector (pro tem) U. New World, Switzerland, 1971; cons. in field, 1948—2014; chmn. bd. Princeton Info. Tech., Inc., 1967-70; adv. bd. Simulmatics Corp., 1967 Author: Public and Republic, 1949, Elements of Political Science, 1952, World Politics, 1949, The Western Public, 1954, The American Way of Government, 1957, Grass Roots Private Welfare, 1958, American Welfare, 1960, Science and Values in Administration, 1961, Political Behavior and Organization, 2 vols, 1962, Apportionment and Representative Government, 1963, Republic in Crisis, Congress Against the Executive Force, 1965, The Velikovsky Affair, 1966, Congress and the Presidency, 1965; (poetry) Passage of the Year, 1967; Kalos: What Is to be Done with Our World, 1973, Politics for Better or Worse, 1973, 8 Bads-8 Goods: The American Contradictions, 1975, Art and Culture: 1001 Questions on Policy, 1979, Chaos and Creation: Quantavolution in Human and Natural History, 1981, Homo Schizo II: Human Nature and Behavior, 1983; Home Schizo I: Human and Cultural Hologensis, 1984, God's Fire: Moses and the Management of Exodus, 1984, The Disastrous Love Affair of Moon and Mars, 1984, The Lately Tortured Earth, 1984, The Burning of Troy, 1984, The Divine Succession: A Science of Gods Old and New, 1984, Cosmic Heretics, 1984, (with Earl R. Milton) Solaria Binaria, 1985, The Student, 1991, The Taste of War, 1992, The Babe, 1992, The End of Spydom, 1992, Strengthening the UN, 1997, A Cloud over Bhopal: Causes, Cosequences and Constructive Solutions, 1985, Twentieth Century Fire-Sale, 1996, The American State of Canaan-The Peaceful Prosperous Juncture of Israel and Palestine as the 51st State of the United States of America, 2009; poems; editor: Congress: First Branch of Government, 1966; founder, editor jour.: American Behavioral Scientist, 1957-66; author, prodr. (CD-ROM) Quantavolution and Catastrophes', 1997, (CD-ROM) Recontructing American History, 1400-2000, 1998, (CD ROMS) Love Letters of World War II, 2000. Mem. U.S. del. to UNESCO, 1960; first pres. Found. Vol. Welfare, 1957-59; chmn. research com. N.Y.C. Republican party, 1961; cons. Rep. Nat. Com., 1964; organizer Ind. Voters, Ill., 1946-48, Calif., 1953-56. Served to capt. AUS, 1942-46, ETO; adv., Korea, 1951-52, Vietnam, 1967-68. Decorated Bronze Star; recipient Chevalier Legion of Honor, 2013 Mem. Phi Beta Kappa. Achievements include designing computerized reference retrieval system in social scis., Universal Reference System, 1962-67; co-founder Inst. of Quantavolation Studies, U. Bergamo, Italy, 2002. Home: Villaines-La-Gonais, France. Died July 12, 2014.

**DEHAENE, JEAN-LUC,** bank executive, former Prime Minister of Belgium; b. Montpellier, Belgium, Aug. 7, 1940; married; 4 children. Student, U. Namur. Commr. Flemish Assn. Cath. Scouts, 1963-67; attache study svcs. ACW, 1965-72; counselor Ministry Pub. Works, Brussels, 1972-73, Ministry Health, Brussels, 1973-74; counselor, than chief cabinet Ministry Econ. Affairs, Brussels, 1974-77; cabinet chief Office Flemish Affairs, Brussels, 1977-78; cabinet chief to prime min. Brussels, 1979-81; min. Instnl. Reforms and Social Affairs, Brussels, 1981-88; vice prime min. Govt. of Belgium, Brussels, 1988-92, min. comm. & instnl. reform, 1988-92, prime min., 1992—99; mayor City of Vilvoorde, Belgium, 2001—07; chmn. Dexia SA, Brussels, 2008—14. Chmn. Club Financial Control Panel UEFA (Union European Football Associations), from 2009. Recipient Vlerick award, Vlerick Leuven Gent Mgmt. Sch., 2003. Died May 15, 2014.

**DEHAINAUT, RAYMOND KIRK,** international studies educator; b. South Charleston, W.Va., May 19, 1930; s. Oscar DeHainaut and Edith (Kirk) Cochrum; m. Claudiene Delaine Munday, June 7, 1953; 1 child, Raymond Marc. BS cum laude, W.Va. U., 1952; MDiv, Vanderbilt U. Divinity Sch., 1954; PhD, Drew U., 1970. Campus minister La. State U., Baton Rouge, 1954-58, Rutgers U., New Brunswick, N.J., 1959-62; ednl. missionary Student Christian Movement, Cordoba, Argentina, 1964-68; campus minister U. South Fla., Tampa, 1969-72; ednl. missionary, dir. NCC Com. Intercultural Dialogue, Bogota, Colombia, 1972-76; campus minister U. South Fla., 1976-85; ednl. missionary United Meth. Gen. Bd. Global Missions, NYC, 1985-95; adj. prof. internat. studies U. South Fla., from 1995. Exchange dir. student work Soochow U., China, 1979-80. Author: Faith and Ideology in Latin American Perspective, 1972; contbr. articles to profl. publs. Pres. Meth. Fedn. Social Action, 1977-78; dist. supt., dir. Sch. Barahona, Dominican Republic, 1990-93. Recipient MSM Ball award for peace with jusctice work in El Salvador, 1980, Lee and Mae Ball award Meth. Fedn. Social Action, 1982. Mem. Amnesty Internat., Phi Beta Kappa. Died July 5, 1998.

**DEHOUSSE, MARTIN EUGENE,** mathematics professor; b. Herstal, Liége, Belgium, Jan. 18, 1920; s. Pierre Lambert and Juliette (Francotte) D.; m. Genevieve Mathot, Feb. 25, 1946 (dec. Dec. 1988); children: Martine (dec. Nov. 1999), Marie-France. Licentiate sci. math., Free U. Brussels, 1946; PhD summa cum laude, Free U., Brussels, 1958. Tchr. Inst. du Arts et Metiers, Brussel City, Belgium, 1946-58; rational mechanic electronics theory Inst. Meurice-Çhimie, Brussels, Belgium, 1950-58; CC math. stats. Offcl. U. Congo, Belgium, 1958-62; prof. U. Burundi, 1960-76; prof. of analytical and celestial mechs. Nat. U. Congo, Congo, 1962-91. Mgr. Belgian acad. projects overseas brachistochrone for electron, 1960, vibration and gravity, 1964, 68, meteorite crater in Rwanda, 1973, effect earth's rotation on g and Eötvös's balance, 1958, 75, 80, colour photo Moon and comp. of surf, 1968, new function sagittal cross-section of human skull, 1970, 94, rocket's launching to east, 1973, 84, astron. determined time of Hesiode, 1973, 84, telescope collection cosmic rays, 1981, orbit determined minor planet, 1997, supernova 1054 and Constantin IX, 1999, comet of Julius Caesar 43 B.C., 2000. Contbr. chpts. to books and articles to scientific publs. Pres. Fedn. Internat. Deportes et Internes of Resistance, 1954. Decorated Grand Officier de l'Ordre la Couronne Cmmdr. O.C. glaives vermeil Croix de Guerre (Belgium), Medal of Merit Arts, Scis. and Letters (Zaire). Mem. The Biometric Soc., Soc. Stats. France, Soc. Math. Belgium, Club U. Found., C.A. Royal African Club, European Acad., Rotary. Avocations: piano, bridge. Deceased.

**DEJONG, PETER,** retired minister; b. Grand Rapids, Mich., July 10, 1915; s. John and Jennie (Elenbaas) DeJ.; m. Thelma Marie Klooster, Oct. 19, 1939; children: Jeanne Louise, Arthur Allen, Douglas Jay, Dennis Ray, David Lee, Daniel Warren, Mark William, Kenneth John. Student, Modesto Jr. Coll., Calif., 1932-33; AB, Calvin Coll., Grand Rapids, 1936; ThB, Calvin Theol. Sem., Grand Rapids, 1939; AM, U. Wash., 1963. Ordained to ministry, Christian Reformed Ch. Pastor Christian Reformed Ch., Hamshire, Tex., 1939-42, Oak Harbor, Wash., 1942-44, East Saugatuck, Mich., 1949-52, Seattle, 1952-62, Smithers, B.C., Can., 1962-66; Telkwa, B.C., Can., 1962-64; pastor Christian Reformed Ch., Sarnia, Ont., Can., 1966-70, Dutton, Mich., 1970-80; editor The Outlook, Grand Rapids, 1977-89. Contbr. articles to profl. publs. Lt. (j.g.) USNR, 1944-46. Home: Grand Rapids, Mich. Died July 11, 1999.

**DE JONGH, WILHELMUS KAREL (WILLY K. DE JONGH),** physicist; b. Eindhoven, The Netherlands, Jan. 25, 1931; s. Joseph and Maria Cornelia (Theelen) de J.; m. Gerda Johanna Lotte Herrmann, July 5, 1957; children: Linda, Wilhelmus Joseph, Heinz. BSc, H.T.S., Eindhoven, 1951. Asst. sales Willem Smit Transformers, Nijmegen, The Netherlands, 1953-54; R&D nuclear physics N.V. Philips, Eindhoven, 1954-55, project engr., 1955-65, X-ray lab. mgr., 1966-76, prin. sr. scientist, 1977-88; pres. R&D Omega Data Systems, Veldhoven, The Netherlands, from 1989. Cons., lectr. N.V. Philips, 1966-88, Omega Data Systems, 1989—. Contbr. articles to profl. jours.; patentee in field; inventor in field. Achievements include invention of UniQuant method for standardless x-ray fluorescence analysis of elements, used world wide in science and industry. Home: Veldhoven, Netherlands. Died Mar. 31, 2004.

**DELAHAY, PAUL,** retired chemistry professor; b. Sas Van Gent, The Netherlands, Apr. 6, 1921; came to the U. S., 1946, naturalized, 1955; s. Jules and Helene (Flahou) D.; m. Yvonne Courroye, 1962. BS in Gen. Engring, U. Brussels, 1941, MS in Chemistry, 1945; MS in Elec. Engring, U. Liege, 1944; PhD in Chemistry, U. Ore., 1948. Instr. chemistry U. Brussels, 1945-46; research assoc. U. Oreg., 1948-49; faculty La. State U., 1949-65, prof. chemistry, 1955-56, Boyd prof. chemistry, 1956-65; prof. chemistry NYU, NYC, 1965-87, Frank J. Gould prof. sci., 1974-87. Author: New Instrumental Methods in Electrochemistry, 1954, Instrumental Analysis, 1957, Double Layer and Electrode Kinetics, 1965; Editor: Advances in Electrochemistry, 1961-74. Guggenheim fellow Cambridge (Eng.) U., 1955-56; Guggenheim fellow N.Y. U., 1971-72; Fulbright prof. Sorbonne, Paris, France, 1962-63; Recipient medal U. Brussels, 1963, Heyrovsky medal Czechoslovak Acad. Sci., 1965, Alumni Achievement Award in Chemistry., U. Oreg., 2001. Mem. Internat. Soc. Electrochemistry (hon.), American Chem. Soc. (award pure chem. 1955, Southwest award 1959), Electrochem. Soc. (Turner prize 1951, Palladium award 1967, chmn. theoretical div. 1957-59), AAAS, American Phys. Soc., Internat. Union Pure and Applied Chemistry (chmn. commn. electrochem. data 1959-63, titular mem. analytical sect. 1961-65), Internat. Soc. Electrochemistry (hon. mem., 2000), Sigma Xi. Died June 21, 2012.

**DELAMURAZ, JEAN-PASCAL,** Swiss government official; b. Longirod, Vaud, Switzerland, Apr. 1, 1936; m. Catherine Reymond, Nov. 22, 1962; 2 children. B. of Polit. Sci., U. Lausanne, Switzerland, 1960. Mem. Lausanne Parliament, 1966-69, Lausanne local govt., 1970-73; mayor City of Lausanne, 1974-81; mem. Nat. Council, Swiss Parliament, 1975-83, Cantonal Govt., Canton of Vaud, 1981-83; fed. councillor, head Dept. of Def., 1984-87; head Dept. Econ. Affairs, 1988-98; v.p. Fed. Council, 1988, 95; pres. Govt. of Switzerland, 1989, 96. Served to capt. Swiss Army, 1956. Mem. Radical Democratic Party. Avocations: sailing, travel, music. Died 1998.

**DELEECK, HERMAN,** economics educator; b. Borgerhout, Antwerpen, Belgium, Aug. 29, 1928; m. Marie-Louise Swaelen, Oct. 12, 1959; children: Stefaan, Elisabeth, Antoon. JD, U. Louvain, Belgium, 1952, D Econs., 1966. Senator Parliament, Brussels, 1977-87; prof. socio-econs. U. Antwerp, 1965-93; prof. extra-ordinary U. Louvain, 1968-94; prof. extra-ordinary State U. of Leyden, The Netherlands, 1988-96. Pres. Nat. Commn. on Poverty, Belgium, 1986-91, Nat. Found. Persons with Handicaps, Belgium, 1990-96; mem. Royal Commn. Reform Social Security, Belgium, 1982-85. Author books on social security, income distribution and poverty. Dir. Ctr. for Social Policy, Belgium, 1973-90. Recipient Price A.A. Janssen award Belgian Assn. Banks, Brussels, 1966, Price Camille Huysmans award, Antwerp, 1974, chair Cleveringa, State U. Leyden, The Netherlands, 1985. Mem. Royal Acad. Belgium, European Inst. Social Security. Home: Hove, Belgium. Died Oct. 21, 2002.

**DEL GUERCIO, LOUIS RICHARD MAURICE,** surgeon, educator; b. NYC, Jan. 15, 1929; s. Louis and Hortense (Ardengo) Del G.; m. Paula Marie Helene de Vautibault, May 18, 1957; children: Louis, Francsca, Paul, Catherine, Maria, Michelle, Christopher, Anthony. BS cum laude, Fordham U., 1949; MD, Yale U., 1953. Diplomate Am. Bd. Surgery, Am. Bd. Thoracic Surgery. Intern Columbia-Presbyn. Med. Ctr., NYC, 1953—54; resident St Vincent's Hosp., NYC, 1954—58, Cleve. City Hosp., 1958—60; practice medicine specializing in thoracic surgery, from 1960; assoc. prof. Albert Einstein Coll. Medicine, NYC, 1966—70, prof. surgery, 1970—71, dir. Clin. Rsch. Ctr.-Acute, 1967—71; clin. prof. surgery NJ Coll. Medicine, Newark, 1971—76; prof. surgery NY Med. Coll., NYC, from 1976, chmn. dept., 1976—2001, emeritus prof. surgery, from 2001; chief surgery Westchester County Med. Ctr., 1976—2001; instr. Yale Sch. Nursing, 1953. Mem. surg. study sect. NIH, 1970-74; mem. com. on shock NRC-NAS, 1969-71; merit rev. bd. VA, 1971-74; mem. health care tech. study sect. Dept. HHS, 1980-84; cons. Nat. Ctr. Health Svcs. Rsch., 1980-84, NY State Office Profl. Med. Conduct, 2004—; chmn. bd. dirs. Daltex Med. Scis., Inc.; cons. in field. Author: (with B.G. Clarke) Urology, 1956, The Multilingual Manual for Medical History Taking, 1972, (with S.G. Hershey, R. McConn) Septic Shock in Man, 1971; editor-in-chief Critical Care Monitor, 1980-85, Complications in Surgery, 1990—; contbr. articles to med. jours.; patentee in field. Bd. trustees Maria Fareri Children's Hosp., Westchester Med. Ctr., 2006—. With Mcht. Marine, 1946-47; with AUS, 1949-51; col. med. dept. USAR, 1990—. Recipient award in medicine Fordham U. Alumni Assn., 1974, Gold award Am. Acad. Pediat., 1973, Humanitarian award Boys' Towns of Italy, 1994; grantee Health Rsch. Coun. NY, 1965-71, NIH, 1962-71. Fellow ACS, Coll. of Critical Care Medicine, Am. Thoracic Soc.; mem. Am. Trauma Soc. (founder), Soc. Critical Care Medicine (founder, pres. 1976), Am. Surg. Assn., Am. Physiol. Soc., Soc. Univ. Surgeons, French Nat. Acad. Surgery, Equestrian Order of Holy Sepulchre Jerusalem, Yale U. Sch. Medicine Alumni Assn. (exec. com. 2001—); hon. police surgeon City of N.Y. *Adaptability and the determination of what is possible are the keys to personal success and contentment.* Died Mar. 2013.

**DEL RUSSO, ALESSANDRA LUINI,** retired law educator; b. Milan, Jan. 2, 1916; d. Avvocato Umberto and Candita (Recio) Luini; m. Carl R. del Russo, Apr. 12, 1947; children: Carl Luini, Alexander David. PhD in History with honors, Royal U., Milan, 1939; SJD summa cum laude, Royal U., Pavia, Italy, 1943; LLM in Comparative Law, George Washington U., Washington, 1949. Bar: Md. 1956, Md. Ct. Appeals, Ct. of Appeals (Milano) 1947, U.S. Ct. Appeals (D.C. cir.) 1950, U.S. Supreme Ct. 1955. Legal adviser Allied Mil. Govt. and Ct., Milan, 1945-46, U.S. Consulate Gen., Milan, 1946-47; pvt. practice Washington, Bethesda, Md., 1950-58; atty. adviser Legis. Ref. Libr. of Congress, Washington, 1958-59; atty. U.S. Commn. on Civil Rights, Washington, 1959-61; prof. Howard U. Sch. Law, Washington, 1961-81, dir. grad. program, 1972-74, prof. emerita, from 1981; adj. prof. Stetson U. Coll. Law, St. Petersburg, Fla., 1980-95, adj. prof. emerita, from 1995. Professorial lectr. George Washington U. Law Ctr., 1970-80; mem. legal cons. com. U.S. Commn. on Status of P.R., Washington, 1965-66; lectr. in field. Author: International Protection of Human Rights, 1971; editor and chmn. of symposium on International Law of Human Rights, Howard U. Sch. of Law, Washington, 1965; contbr. numerous articles to internat. and Am. profl. jours. Rsch. grant Howard U., 1963. Mem. ABA, Brit. Inst. Internat. and Comparative Law, Am. Soc. Internat. Law. Republican. Roman Catholic. Achievements include 1st woman to receive LLM in Comparative Law from George Washington U. Deceased.

**DELVAUX, PAUL E.,** artist; b. Antheit, Liege, Belgium, Sept. 23, 1897; s. Jean and Laure (Jamotte) D.; m. Anne-Marie DeMartelaere. Student pub. schs. Prof. Ecole Nationale Superieure d'Architecture et des Arts, Brussels; pres., bd. dirs. Academe Royale des Beaux Art. Recipient Rembrandt prize, 1972. Mem. Academie Francaise section Beaux-Arts. Deceased.

**DELVOYE, PIERRE CHARLES,** preventive medicine physician, educator; b. Ath, Belgium, Aug. 12, 1945; s. Jean Delvoye and Odette Jorion; m. Paulette Delvoye-Jonart, Sept. 26, 1977; children: Pierre Jean, Sébastien. MD, Free U., Brussel, 1970. Cert. physician Belgium, 1970, gynaecologist Free U., 1974, epidemiologist Pub. Health Sch., ULB, 1973; ethicist ULB Faculty Philosophy, 1999. Head, dept. ob-gyn. Gen. Hosp., Ath, 1976—2004; head, dept. preventive medicine RHMS, Ath, from 2004. Cons. UNFPA, NYC, 1979—2008; sr. lectr. Free U. Brussels, ULB, from 1987; cons. Worldbank, Washington, 1995—2005; med. adviser Office of Birth and Childhood, Brussels, from 2003. Contbr. scientific papers to med. jours. Mem. WWF, Amnesty internat., Handicap Internat., Brussels, 1978—2010. Master: Perinatal Ctr. Gen. Hosp. Ath, Family Plannng Ctr., Sci. Com. ONE Hainaut Belgium. Achievements include research in endocrine mechanisms of breastfeeding; epidemiology of reproductive health preconception care. Home: Ath, Belgium. Deceased.

**DE MAEYER, EDWARD,** virologist; b. Mechelen, Belgium, June 4, 1932; s. Pieter Jan and Maria Louisa (Van Aken) De Maeyer; m. Jacqueline Guignard, June 3, 1961. MD, U. Louvain, 1957; Agrege, de l'Enseignement Superieur, 1964. Rsch. fellow Children's Hosp. and Harvard U., Boston, 1958—60; rsch. asst. Rockefeller Inst., 1960—61; lectr. virology U. Louvain, Belgium, 1961—65; maitre de recherche CNRS, France, 1966—74, dir., 1997, dir. rsch., from 1998. Chief Laboratoire Institut Curie; tchr. microbiology Pasteur Inst. Fulbright Fellow, 1958—61; mem. Nat. Com. Sci. Rsch., France, 1986—91, Prix Antoine Lacassagne de la Ligue Nationale Francaise Contre le Cancer, 1988; adv. bd. Internat. Soc. for Interferon and Cytokine Rsch., from 1988; expert viral diseases WHO, 1981—2002. Contbr. articles to profl. jours. Recipient Jean-Louis Camus prize, Paris, 1971, Prix Gaston Rousseau de l'Academie des Sciences, 1976; fellow Lederle Internat. fellow, 1959—60. Mem.: Internat. Soc. for Interferon Rsch. (pres. 1984—85, adv. bd. from 1988), Am. Soc. Microbiology, AAAS, French Microbiology Soc. (prize), Sigma Xi. Home: Orsay, France. Died June 22, 2003.

**DEMET, FRANCIS JOSEPH,** lawyer; b. Sept. 11, 1923; s. Thomas John and Margarete (Vogt) Demet; m. Margadette Moffatt, Nov. 27, 1954; children: Donal, Maura, Kerry, Michael, Barry, Kevin, Brigid, Deirdre. AB, Loras Coll., 1948; LLB, Georgetown U., 1951. Bar: Wis. 1952, U.S. Dist. Ct. (we. and ea. dists.) Wis. 1952, U.S. Dist. Ct. (no. dist.) Ill. 1956, U.S. Ct. Appeals (7th cir.) 1953, U.S. Supreme Ct. 1978. Ptnr., pres. Demet & Demet, Milw., from 1952. Author (and editor) legal publs. Mem.: Internat. Assn. Fin. Planners (v.p. 1981—83), Book Fellows Milw., Am. Judicature Soc., Milw. Bar Assn., Wis. Bar Assn., Internat. Inst. Milw., Lincoln Fellowship of Wis., Bar Assn. 7th Fed. Cir. (bd. govs. from 1972), Milw. Athletic Club, Milw. Hist. Soc., Milw. Art Mus., Civil War Round Table. Home: Milwaukee, Wis. Died June 4, 1993.

**DE MITRI, TOMMASO DOMENICO,** retired physician; b. Nardo, Italy, Mar. 7, 1926; s. Andrea and Maria Rosaria (Zuccaro) de M.; m. Maria Stucchi, Sept. 25, 1957; children: Andrea Ambrogio, Alberto Paolo, Marina B. MD in Surgery, U. Milan, 1950, specialists degree in otolaryngology, 1953. Asst. Hosp. Polyclinic, Milan, 1956-61, Univ. Clinic, Sassari, Italy, 1961-63; 1st asst. City Hosp., Legnano (Milan), 1963-70, head physician Sondrio, Italy, 1970-77, Jesi, Ancona, Italy, 1977-91. Cons. univ. prof. U. Ferrara, Italy, 1969. Contbr. articles to profl. jours. Mem. N.Y. Acad. Scis. Avocations: photography, history, coin collecting/numismatics. Home: Busto Arsizio, Italy. Died Oct. 24, 2008.

**DEMMLER, JOHN N.,** retired manufacturing executive; b. Kewanee, Ill., Oct. 31, 1904; s. Henry Louis and Ella Blanche (Nowry) D.; m. Jeannette Smith, June 20, 1929; children: Alice Barth, Martha, Jean Kane. BSME, U. Ill., 1926. Ptnr. William Demmler & Bros., Kewanee, Ill., 1926-50; pres. Demmler Mfg. Co., Kewanee, 1950-68, retired, 1968. Mem. Tau Beta Pi. Clubs: Union League (Chgo.); Midland Country (Kewanee). Lodges: Masons, Elks. Republican. Presbyterian. Home: Denver, Colo. Died June 1993.

**DEMOLA, JAMES, SR.,** church administrator; Asst. gen. overseer, dist. overseer Christian Ch. of N. Am., from 1986; sr. pastor Springs of LIfe Christian Ctr., Mullica Hill, NJ, from 1963. Appears, prodr. cable TV program The Word is Alive. Mem. Christian Ch. Deceased.

**DE MORAES, ANTÔNIO ERMÍRIO,** import/export company executive, investor; b. São Paulo, Brazil, June 4, 1928; Student, Colo. Sch. Mines. Chmn., CEO Grupo Votorantim. Contbr. weekly newspaper column, Folha de Sao Paulo. Named one of The World's Richest People, Forbes Mag., 2008—14. Died Aug. 24, 2014.

**DENBO, ALEXANDER,** retired bank executive; JD-LLB, Dickinson Sch. Law, 1932. Bar: N.J., 1934, U.S. Supreme Ct., 1952. Judge Mcpl. Ct., Burlington City, N.J., 1943-52, Burlington County Dist. Ct., 1952-55; exec. v.p. Mechanics Nat. Bank, 1954-55; pres. First Nat. State Bank West Jersey (formerly Mechanics Nat. Bank), 1955-77. Cons. trust dept. Fidelity Bank & Trust Co. N.J.; commr. Supreme Ct., 1938; former solicitor Willingboro Twp., Florence Twp., Pemberton Twp., Bordentown Twp., Edgewater Park Twp., Beverly Housing Authority, Burlington Twp., Fieldsboro Borough; bd. dirs. Beverly Bldg. Loan Assn., MacAndrews & Forbes Co. Treas. County of Burlington, N.J., 1944-52; solicitor bd. edn. Twp. Pemberton Edgewater Park Sewerage Authority; v.p. N.J. Divsn. Am. Cancer Soc., 1945; pres. Burlington County Cancer Soc., 1945; past chmn. bond drives ARC, United Jewish Appeal; past trustee Rancocas Valley Hosp., Zurbrugg Hosp. N.J., Dickinson Sch. Law, Carlisle, Pa.; mem. citizens adv. com. City of Burlington, 1967; dir. Burlington County Coll. Found.; pres. Temple B'Nai Israel, Burlington, 1967; mem. Burlington City Indsl. Com.; chmn. Am. Jewish Com., Burlington County; bd. govs. Greater Trenton Symphony Assn.; Burlington County cmty. coun. McGuire Air Force Base; past mem. Com. Labor Mgmt. Rels., Burlington City; past mem. adv. com. N.J. League Municipalities; past mem. Legis. Com. Revision Election Laws, 1944; past mem. law enforcement com. Gov.'s Fire Safety Conf., 1948; treas. bldg. fund. com. St. Mary's Hall Doane Acad. Recipient Citizenship award Jewish War Vets. U.S., 1953, Citation, Borough of Fieldsboro, 1960, Mayor and Coun. Burlington Twp., 1973, Borough Fieldsboro, Edgewater Park Twp., Bd. Edn. Borough Fieldsboro. Mem. ABA, Burlington County Bar Assn. (pres. 1956), N.J. State Bar Assn., Am. Judicature Soc., Am. Arbitration Assn. (nat. panel), Burlington Trade Assn. (sec. 1937), Assn. U.S. Army (pres. Fort Dix chpt. 1976), Burlington County Hist. Soc., Jr. Order Mechanics, B'nai B'rith, Kiwanis (pres. 1945), Burlington Lodge, Moose, Tall Cedars Lebanon, Elks. Achievements include naming of sch. the Alexander Denbo Sch. Died Oct. 12, 2001.

**DENNIS, FELIX,** publishing executive; b. Kingston-Upon-Thames, Middlesex, Eng., May 27, 1947; s. Reginald Dennis and Dorothy Grace (Coller) Sawyer. Grave digger Harrow County Coun., London, 1963-64; window dresser Liberty Dept. Store, London, 1963-64; blues musician Eng., 1967-68; st. seller mags. London, 1967-68; editor Oz Mag., 1969-73; mng. dir. Dennis Pub., London, 1973-83; chmn. Dennis Publishing Group, London and NY, 1983—2007. Dir., founder Microwarehouse, Inc., Macuser Mag., N.Y.C., 1985-87, others. Co-author: Muhammad Ali: The Holy Warrior, 1975, Bruce Lee: King of Kung Fu, 1974; author: How To Get Rich: One of the World's Greatest Entrepreneurs Shares His Secrets, 2008 Active numerous charity and sponsorships worldwide. Named Young Designer of Yr., U.K. mags., 1971, Publisher of Yr., U.K. mags., 1993; recipient Marcus Morris award Periodcal Publishing Assn., 1991. Avocations: planting trees, reading poetry, collecting wine, playing blues and jazz, admiring beautiful women. Home: Stratford-upon-Avon, England. Died June 22, 2014.

**DENOMME, J. MAURICE,** real estate broker, insurance agent; b. Providence, Sept. 4, 1938; s. Gaspard and Celia (Audette) Denomme; m. Winifred M. Carmody, Oct. 12, 1962; children: Mary Beth, Paula J. Student, Johnson and Wales Bus. Coll., 1967. Real estate broker, ins. agt. Century 21 Denomme Realty Inc., Port Charlotte, Fla., from 1971. Pres. Charlotte County Young Reps., Fla., 1975—77. Mem.: Punta Gordo Port Charlotte Bd. Realtors (pres. 1982—83), Kiwanis (pres. 1983—84), Elks, KC. Roman Catholic. Home: Pt Charlotte, Fla. Died Jan. 1, 1998.

**DENT, ERNEST DUBOSE, JR.,** pathologist; b. Columbia, SC, May 3, 1927; s. E. Dubose and Grace (Lee) D.; m. Dorothy McCalman, June 16, 1949; children: Christopher, Pamela; m. 2d, Karin Frehse, Sept. 6, 1970. Student, Presbyn. Coll., 1944-45; MD, Med. Coll. S.C., 1949. Diplomate clin. pathology and pathology anatomy Am. Bd. Pathology. Intern U.S. Naval Hosp., Phila., 1949-50; resident pathology USPHS Hosp., Balt., 1950-54, chief pathology Norfolk, Va., 1954-56; assoc. pathology Columbia (S.C.) Hosp., 1956-59; pathologist, dir. labs. Columbia Hosp., S.C. Baptist Hosp., 1958-69; with Straus Clin. Labs., LA, 1969-72; staff pathologist Hollywood (Calif.) Community Hosp, St. Joseph Hosp., Burbank, Calif., 1969-72; dir. labs. Glendale Meml. Hosp. and Health Ctr., 1972-94; ret. Bd. dirs. Glendale Meml. Hosp. and Health Ctr. Author papers nat. med. jours. Mem. Am. Cancer Soc., AMA, L.A. County Med. Assn. (pres. Glendale dist. 1980-81), Calif. Med. Assn. (councillor 1984-90), Am. Soc. Clin. Pathology, Coll. Am. Pathologists (assemblyman S.C. 1965-67; mem. publs. com. bull. 1968-70), L.A. Soc. Pathologists (trustee 1984-87), L.A. Acad. Medicine, S.C. Soc. Pathologists (pres. 1967-69). Lutheran. Home: San Marcos, Calif. Died Dec. 3, 2002.

**DENTON, ESTELLE ROSEMARY,** retired federal agency administrator; d. Daniel Poncy and Alice Gardiner; m. Benjamin E. Denton, Jr., May 15, 1948 (dec.); children: David Alan, Benjamin E., Kathleen Ann. AA, Bus. Inst. Pa., Sharon, 1943; Associate in Bus. Adminstrn., U. Va., 1965. Asst. clk. Selective Svc., Sharon, 1943—46; adminstrv. exec. sec. Navy Dept., Washington, 1946—57; def. dept. exec. asst. Chief Human Resources, Richmond, Va., 1958—62; chief naval ops. admiral Chester W. Nimitz and Naval Aviation Vice Admiral Apollo Soucek; human resources asst. SBA, Richmond, 1963, loan officer asst., 1964, exec. asst. to dir. fin. assistance, 1964—66, exec. asst. to dist. dir., 1966—73; exec. asst. to exec. dir. Va. Redevel. Housing Authority, 1974—76; exec. asst. pres. Nat. Realty Com., Washington, 1976—78; spl. programs officer Va. Dept. Emergency Svcs., Richmond, 1978—87; ret., 1987. Author: (novels) Once Upon A Scandall, Once Upon A Whistleblower!!!. Adv. coun. Congressman Eric Cantor, Richmond, 1998—2004. Recipient Pub. Rels. award, SBA, 1968—71, Cert. of Appreciation, Dept. Emergency Svcs. and Fed. Emergency Mgmt. Agy., 1986—87. Mem.: Pinehurst Assn. Writers Group, Profl. and Bus. Woman's Club. Republican. Roman Catholic. Home: Pinehurst, NC. Died Feb. 24, 2014.

**DENTON, JEREMIAH ANDREW, JR.,** former United States Senator from Alabama, retired military officer; b. Mobile, Ala., July 15, 1924; s. Jeremiah Andrew and Irene Claudia (Steele) D.; m. Kathryn Jane Maury, June 6, 1946 (dec. Nov. 22, 2007); children: Jeremiah Andrew III, Donald, James, William, Madeleine, Michael, Mary Elizabeth. Student, Spring Hill Coll., Mobile, 1942-43, LHD, 1974; BS in Engring., U.S. Naval Acad., 1946; student, Armed Forces Staff Coll., 1958-59, Naval War Coll., 1963; MA in Internat. Affairs, George Washington U., 1964; HHD (hon.), St. Leo's Coll.; LLD (hon.), Troy State U. Commd. ensign U.S. Navy, 1946, advanced through grades to rear adm., 1973; aviator, flight instr., staff officer, 1946-65; combat pilot in USS Independence, 1965; comdt. Armed Forces Staff Coll., Norfolk, Va., 1974-77; ret., 1977; exec. asst. to pres. Spring Hill Coll., 1977-80; cons. to pres. Christian Broadcasting Network, 1978-80; Sol Feinstone lectr. US Mil. Acad., West Point, NY, 1975; US Senator from Ala., 1981-89. Author: When Hell Was In Session, 1976. Bd. regents Spring Hill Coll.; founder Coalition for Decency. Decorated Navy Cross, D.S.M. (Def. Dept. and Navy), Silver Star with two oak leaf clusters, Bronze Star with five oak leaf clusters, D.F.C., Purple Heart with oak leaf cluster, Air medal with oak leaf cluster, Navy Commendation medal; recipient John Paul Jones award Navy League, 1973, Ct. of Honor award Ala. Nat. Exchange Club, Ala. Legislature resolution, 1973, awards Valley Forge Freedoms Found., 1974, 76, For God and Country award Capitol Hill First Friday Club, 1974, Cross of Mil. Service UDC, 1975, Douglas MacArthur Meritorious Service award Norfolk chpt. Assn. U.S. Army, 1977 Mem. Ends of Earth Soc. (working com.), American Legion, VFW (Armed Forces award 1974), Catholic War Vets. (Celtic Cross award 1974), Res. Officers Assn. (hon. life) Clubs: K.C. (Patriot of Year award Princeton, N.J. 1975, Lantern award 1981), Knights of Malta. Republican. Roman Catholic. Research on prisoner of war behavior, attitudes and performance, 1973-74. Home: Theodore, Ala. Died Mar. 28, 2014.

**DEPEW, HARRY LUTHER,** lawyer; b. Neodesha, Kans., Nov. 18, 1923; s. Clarence William and Dorothy J. (Bushaway) Depew; m. Frances Allene Crisp, Mar. 27, 1951; children: Douglas D., Dennis D. BS in Bus., Kans. U., 1948, LLB, 1951. Bar: Kans. 1951. County atty. County of Wilson, Kans., 1955—58; ptnr. Depew Law Firm, Neodesha, 1952—2003; ret., 2003. With US Army, 1942—45, with US Army, 1951—52, Korea. Mem.: Kans. Bar Assn. (various coms.), Wilson County Bar Assn. (past pres.), SE Kans. Bar Assn. (past pres.), C. of C., Lions. Republican. Died Aug. 31, 2005.

**DE QUADROS, CIRO ARAUJO,** epidemiologist, educator; b. Rio Pardo, Brazil, Jan. 30, 1940; MD, Cath. Sch. Medicine, Brazil; MPH, Nat. Sch. Pub. Health, Rio de Janeiro, 1968. Chief epidemiologist Smallpox Eradication Prog., WHO, Ethiopia, 1970; Expanded Prog. on Immunization Pan American Health Orgn., 1991, dir. Div. Vaccines and Immunization Washington; interim pres., CEO Sabin Vaccine Inst. (SVI), Washington, 2006. Assoc. adj. prof. Johns Hopkins Sch. Hygiene & Public Health; assoc. prof. Case Western Reserve U. Sch. Medicine; adj. prof. Dept. Tropical Medicine George Washington U. Sch. Medicine. Author: Vaccines: Preventing Disease Protecting Health; presented papers in over 100 confs. Mem. bd. Internat. AIDS Vaccine Initiative; chmn. ind. rev. com. Global Alliance for Vaccines & Immunization; chmn. tech. adv. group on vaccines & immunizations Pan. Am. Health Orgn. Recipient Order of the Bifurcated Needle, WHO, Internat. Child Survival Award, UNICEF and the Carter Ctr., Prince Mahidol Award, Thailand, 1993, Order of Rio Branco, Govt. of Brazil, 1999, Albert B. Sabin Gold Medal, 2000, Order of Public Health, Govt. of Bolivia, 2003, Internat. Public Health Hero award, U. Calif., Berkeley. Mem.: AAAS, Inst. Medicine, NY Acad. Sciences, American Soc. Tropical Medicine & Hygiene, Nat. Coun. Internat. Health, American Public Health Assn. Achievements include participating in the organization of the first national epidemiology center in Brazil. Died May 28, 2014.

**DERLACKI, EUGENE L(UBIN),** retired otolaryngologist; b. Chgo., Mar. 16, 1913; s. Walter and Jadwiga (Pamulowna) D. BS, Northwestern U., 1936, MD, 1939; postgrad. otolaryngology, Rush Med. Coll., 1940, U. Ill., 1941-42. Diplomate: Am. Bd. Otolaryngology. Intern Cook County Hosp., Chgo., 1939-40, jr. resident, 1941, sr. resident, 1942-43; sr. attending staff Northwestern Meml. Hosp., 1946—2002; prof. otolaryngology Northwestern U. Med. Sch., 1957—2002, now prof. emeritus, from 2002. Contbr. articles to profl. jours. Past pres. Am. Hearing Research Found. Served with M.C. AUS, 1943-46. Mem. AMA, Am. Acad. Otolaryngology (past pres.), Coll. Allergists, Am. Otol. Soc. (past pres.), Am. Laryngol., Rhinol. and Otol. Soc. Deceased.

**DE ROTHSCHILD, BARON ELIE ROBERT,** banker; b. Paris, May 29, 1917; s. Baron Robert and Nelly (Beer) de Rothschild; m. Liliane Fould-Springer, 1942 (dec. 2003);

children: Nathaniel, Elizabeth, Nelly. Lycee Louis le Grand, Faculty of Law, Universite de Paris. Past pres. Rothschild Bank, Zürich, Switzerland, Assicurazioni Generali, Trieste & Venice, Italy. Recipient Croix de guerre, Ufficiale Ordine al Merito della Repubblica Italiana; named Officier, Legion d'honneur; named one of Top 200 Collectors, ARTnews Mag., 2004—08, 2005, 2006. Avocation: collector of Old Masters, Impressionism & Modern Art. Died Aug. 6, 2007.

**DERRICK, BUTLER CARSON, JR.,** lawyer, former United States Representative from South Carolina; b. Springfield, Mass., Sept. 30, 1936; s. Butler Carson and Mary English (Scott) D.; m. Beverly Davis; children: Lydia Gile, Butler Carson III, Charlotte Grantham, George Grantham. Student, U. SC, 1954-58; LLB (hon.), U. Ga., 1965; D (hon.), Lander Coll., 1978, Erskine Coll., 1978; LLD (hon.), U. SC, 1986; LHD (hon.), Med. U. SC, 1988. Bar: S.C. 1965, D.C. 1988. Ptnr. Derrick & Byrd, Edgefield, SC, 1970-75; mem. Edgefield County S.C. House of Reps., 1969—75; mem. US Congress from 3rd S.C. Dist., Washington, 1975-95; ptnr. Williams & Jensen, PC, Washington, 1995—98, Powell, Goldstein, Frazer & Murphy, Washington, 1998—2004, Nelson, Mullins, Riley & Scarborough, LLP, Washington, 2004—14. Named Conservationist of Yr. S.C. Wildlife Fedn., 1977; Conservationist of Yr. Nat. Wildlife Fedn., 1977; one of Our Ten Best Friends in Congress Outdoor life mag.; recipient Disting. River Conservation award American Rivers Conservation Council, 1977 Mem. S.C. Bar Assn., ABA, D.C. Bar Assn., Edgefield County Bar Assn. (past pres.), Spl. Forces Assn. (hon., mem. Green Berets), Phi Beta Kappa Democrat. Episcopalian. Home: Washington, DC. Died May 5, 2014.

**DERRIDA, JACQUES,** philosopher, writer; b. El Biar, Algeria, July 15, 1930; s. Aime and Georgette (Safar) D.; m. Marguerite Aucoutuner; children: Pierre, Jean. Attended, Ecole Normale Supérieure, France, 1952-56; Licence es Lettres, U. Paris, Sorbonne, 1953; Licence de Philosophie, U. Paris, Sorbonne, 1953; Diplome d'Etudes Superieures, 1954, cert. d'Ethnologie, 1954, agregation de Philosophie, 1956; postgrad., Harvard U., 1956-57; Doctorat en Philosophie, 1967, Doctorat d'Etat es Lettres, 1980. Professeur de lettres superieures Lycee du Mans, 1959-60; prof. philosophy U. Paris, 1960-64, Ecole Normale Superieure, Paris, 1965—84; dir. Ecole des Hautes Etudes en Scis. Sociales, Paris, 1984—2004; prof. philosphy, french and comparative lit. U. Calif., Irvine, 1986—2003. Mem. planning bd. Coll. Internat. de Philosophie, 1982-83, dir., 1983-84, mem. adminstrv. coun., 1986. Author: La voix et le phénomène: Introduction au probleme du signe dans la phenomenologie de Husserl, 1967, De la grammatologie, 1967, L'écriture et la différence, 1967, La dissémination, 1972, Marges de la philosophie, 1972, Positions: Entretiens avec Henri Ronse, Julia Kristeva, Jean-Louis Houdebine, Guy Scarpetta, 1972, Glas, 1974, L'Archeologie du frivole, 1976, Eperons: Les Styles de Nietzsche, 1976, Limited Inc., 1977, La vérité en peinture, 1978, La carte postale: De Socrate a Freud et au-dela, 1980, L'Oreille de l'autre: Otobiographies, transferts, traductions, 1982, D'un ton apocalyptique adopte naguere en philosophie, 1983, Feu la cendre/Cio'che resta del fuoco, 1984, Signeponge/Signsponge, 1984, Otobiographies: L'Enseignement de Nietzsche et la politique du nom propre, 1984, Memoires: Lectures for Paul de Man, 1986, Parages, 1986, Psyché: Inventions de l'autre, 1987, De l'esprit: Heidegger et la question, 1987, Mémoires: Pour Paul de Man, 1988, Acts of Literature, 1991, The Other Heading: Reflections on Today's Europe, 1992, Memoirs of the Blind: The Self-Portrait and Other Ruins, 1993, Aporias, 1994; translator, author of intro.: Edmund Husserl's L'Origine de la geometrie, 1962 (Prix Cavailles Societe des Amis de Jean Cavailles 1964). Decorated officier des Palmes Academiques, 1980, chevalier, 1968, commandeur des Arts et des Lettres, 1983; recipient Prix Nietzsche Assn. Internat. de Philosophie, 1988; named to Liste d'Aptitude a l'Enseignement superieur, 1968. Died Oct. 8, 2004.

**DERZAI, MATTHEW,** retired telecommunications company executive; b. Heerlerheide, Limburg, The Netherlands, Sept. 2, 1928; s. Matt Derzai and Angela Ocepek; m. Karen Adele Stokes, June 14, 1958 (div. 1988); children: Melinda Anne, Cynthia Kim, Wendy Cheryl; m. Yolande M. Derzai, Apr. 1989. B of Applied Sci., U. Toronto, Can., 1955. Registered profl. engr. Engr. Bell Can., Montreal, 1954-64, staff engr., 1967-75; engr. AT&T, NYC, 1964-67; head dept. tech. services Internat. Telecommunications Union, Geneva, 1975-79; computer services engr. Canadian Telecommunications Carriers Assn., Ottawa, Ont., Can., 1979-83; gen. mgr., sec.-treas. Frequency Coordination System Assn., Ottawa, 1983-94. Contbr. articles to profl. jours. Mem. IEEE, Assn. Profl. Engrs. Ontario. Avocations: skiing, boating. Home: Manotick, Canada. Died 2004.

**DESAI, H. K.,** electrical engineer; BSEE, Maharaja Sayajirao U., India; MSEE, U. Calif., Berkeley. Mem., OC50 group Orange County Bus. Jour.; v.p., engring. sys. products Western Digital Corp., 1995; v.p., engring. QLogic Corp., dir., engring., 1990—95, pres., chief tech. officer, interim CEO, 1995—96, CEO Aliso Viejo, Calif., 1996—99, chmn., CEO, 1999—2010, exec. chmn., 2010—14; chmn. Lantronix, Inc., 2002—07. Former bd. dirs. Microsemi Corp. Mem. Tech. Network; charter mem. The Indus Entrepreneurs (TiE). Recipient Exec. of the Yr. award, American Electronics Assn., 1999, Entrepreneur of the Yr. award, Ernst & Young, 2000, Dir. of the Yr. award, Forum for Corporate Directors, 2002. Died June 8, 2014.

**DESBARATS, PETER HULLETT,** journalist, educator, academic administrator; b. Montreal, Que., Can., July 2, 1933; s. Hullett John and Margaret Ogston (Rettie) D. Student, Loyola Coll., Montreal, 1951. Feature writer The Gazette, Montreal, 1953-55; local reporter Reuters, London, 1955; feature writer The Winnipeg (Can.) Tribune, 1956, legis. reporter, 1957-60; polit. reporter, feature writer The Montreal Star, 1960-65; editor Parallel Mag., Montreal, 1965; host nightly news and pub. affairs show Sta. CBC-TV, Montreal, 1966-70; Ottawa editor Toronto Star, 1970-72; Ottawa bur. chief Global TV, 1973-80; sr. cons. Royal Commn. on Newspapers, Ottawa, 1980-81; dean Sch. Journalism U. Western Ont., London, Canada, 1981-96, assoc. prof. journalism, 1981-86, prof., 1986-96, adj. prof., 2005—06. Fellow Can West Global, 2007; faculty, Info. and Media Studies U. Western Ont.; mem. comm. adv. com. Can. commn. UNESCO; cons. Task Force on Broadcasting Policy, 1985, Royal Commn. Electoral Reform, 1991, House of Commons Broadcasting com., Ottawa, 2002, others; dir. Univ. Club U. Western Ont., 1987, also chair numerous coms.; mem. Ont. Task Force Cardiovasc. Scis., 1991, Can. Observers' Mission to Romania, 1992; commr. Commn. on Inquiry into Deployment of Can. Forces to Somalia, 1995—96; columnist The Globe and Mail, Toronto, 1997—2002, The Free Press, London, 1998—2002; former Can. corr. The Nat. Observer, Washington; MacLean Hunter chair comm. ethics Ryerson U., Toronto, 2000—01; mem. social scis. and humanities rsch. coun. Can. adjudication com. Std. Rsch. Grants Program, 2005—06; spkr. on journalism and the role of the media numerous sites throughout the U.S., Can., overseas. Author: The State of Quebec, 1965, Gabrielle and Selena, 1966, René: A Canadian in Search of a Country, 1976; author: (book of poetry) The Night the City Sang, 1977; author: The Hecklers, 1979, Canada Lost/Canada Found: The Search for a New Nation, 1981, Colin and the Computer, 1985, Guide to Canadian News Media, 1990, rev. edit., 1996, Somalia Cover-up: A Commissioner's Journal, 1997, (plays) The Great White Computer, 1966, Her Worship, 2002, Lucretia, 2003, The Practical Joke, 2005; editor: What They Used to Tell About Indian Legends from Labrador, 1969, Freedom of Expression and New Communication Technologies, 1998; mem. editl. bd. Can. Jour. Comm., 1987—90, co-host PBS series The Editors, 1987—91. Mem. Ont. Task Force on Cardiovascular Svcs., 1991, Ont. Citizens Panel on Increasing Organ Donations, 2006—07; bd. dirs. Performing Arts Ctr. for Today, London, 1993—95, Orch. London, 1993—99, London Mus. Archaeology, 1993—2003, v.p., 2001—03, pres., 2003—05. Recipient Best News Broadcaster award Assn. Can. TV and Radio Artists, 1977, Best TV Interviewer award Assn. Can. TV and Radio Artists, 1980, 125th Anniversary Confedn. Can. medal, 1992; named officer Order of Can., 2007. Mem.: Soc. Environ. Journalists (adv. bd. from 1995), Can. Journalism Found. (bd. dirs. 1997—2005, adv. bd. 2005—06, Excellence award 2007), Can. Civil Liberties Assn. (bd. dirs. 1998—2008), Can. Assn. Journalists. Home: London, Canada. Died Feb. 11, 2014.

**DE SÉGUIN DES HONS, LUC DONALD,** physician, medical biologist; b. Paris, Nov. 4, 1919; s. Gabriel and Florence Louisa (Payne) de S. des H.; m. Macha Plaoutine, Dec. 12, 1952; children: Michel, Andre, Cyril. MD, Algiers U., Algeria, 1943; biologist, Ordre Nat. Medecins, Paris, 1952. Master rsch. C.S.F. and Pasteur Inst., Paris, 1946-53; pres. Labs. Seguin, Drancy, France, from 1948. Researcher biol. properties of microwaves French Acad. Scis., 1945-52. Patentee automatic analyzers. Served with Free French Forces, 1943-45. Mem. Union Syndicats Medicaux Region Parisienne (founder, pres. 1966-70), Union 93 (founder, pres. 1967-92). Avocation: political philosophy. Deceased.

**DESHPANDE, GOVIND PURUSHOTTAM,** humanities educator; b. Nasik, India, Dec. 8, 1938; s. Purushottam Narhar Deshpande and Asha Desphande; m. Kalandi Govind Ainapure, June 6, 1963; children: Ashwini, Sudhanva. BA, M.S. U. Baroda, India, 1954; MA, U. Poona, India, 1960; PhD, Jawaharlal Nehru U., New Delhi, 1975. Asst. editor China Report, New Delhi, 1966—68; asst. prof. ISIS, New Delhi, 1968—75; assoc. prof. Sch. Internat. Studies Jawaharlal Nehru U., 1975—84, prof., 1985—2013, dean Sch. Internat. Studies, 1997—99. Hon. fellow, hon. dir. Inst. Chinese Studies, Delhi, India, 2000—01; editor Internat. Studies, New Delhi, 1997—99. Founding editor: Jour. Arts and Ideas; author: (plays) A Man for Dark Times, 1974 (Maharashtra State Govt. award, 76), A Passage to Darkness, 1997 (Maharashtra State Govt. award, 97, Best Playwright award for overall contbn., 98). Hindu. Home: New Delhi, India. Died Oct. 16, 2013.

**DE SILVA, SUNIL RADHAKANTHA,** chemical engineer; b. Colombo, Sri Lanka, Jan. 13, 1943; arrived in Norway, 1982; s. Edgar Reginald and Shirley Iris (Rodrigo) D.S.; m. Ann Elaine Gibson, May 3, 1969; children: Snezana Tanya, Eksath Rohan. B in Tech., Loughborough U., England, 1967, PhD, 1972. Scientist Tech. U. Karlsruhe, Germany, 1970-72, Tech. U. Clausthal, Germany, 1972-76; engring. mgr. Donaldson Europe, Belgium, 1976—82; sr. scientist Chr. Michelsen Inst., Norway, 1982-88; mng. dir. POSTEC-Rsch., Norway, 1988-93; prof. Telemark Coll., Norway, 1995—2002. Postdoctoral fellow Norwegian Rsch. Coun., 1982-83; adj. prof. Telemark Coll., 1988-95; dept. head Tel-Tek, Norway, 1994; hon. prof. Xi'an U. Architecture and Tech., China, 1995. Mem. editl. bd. Bulk Solids Handling, Powder Handling and Processing; mem. editl. adv. bd. Particle and Particulate Systems Characterization; contbr. articles to profl. jours. Mem. Inst. Chem. Engrs. Home: Porsgrunn, Norway. Died Apr. 29, 2002.

**DE SIMONE, DANIEL V.,** retired engineering association executive, engineer; b. Chgo., May 4, 1930; s. James L. and Helen Catherine (Lattanzio) De S.; children: Jane Ellen Dittmar, James, Daniel. BS in Elec. Engring., U. Ill., 1956; JD, NYU, 1960. Bar: N.Y. 1960, U.S. Supreme Ct. 1964, Va. 1981. Teaching asst. U. Ill., 1954-56; engr. Bell Telephone Labs., 1956-62; cons. to asst. sec. for sci. & tech. US Dept. Commerce, Washington, 1962-64, dir. Office Invention and Innovation, Nat. Bur. Standards, 1964-69; exec. dir. Study of Nat. Conversion to Metric System for U.S. Congress, 1969-71; sci. policy asst. The White House, Washington, 1971-73; exec. dir. Fed. Council for Sci. and Tech., Exec. Office of Pres., Washington, 1972-73; dep. dir. Congl. Office Tech. Assessment, Washington, 1973-80; pres. The Innovation Group, Inc., Arlington, Va., 1980-84; exec. dir. Am. Assn. Engring. Socs., Washington, 1984-89; exec. v.p. World Fedn. Engring. Socs., 1985-89. Author: Technological Innovation— Its Environment and Management, 1967, Education for Innovation, 1968, A Metric America, 1971, To Preserve the Sense of Earth from Space, 1984 Served with USAF, 1948-52 Recipient Outstanding Achievement award IEEE, 1956, Gold Medal award for disting. achievement in fed. svc., 1969, Career Svc. award Nat. Civil Svc. League, 1972; Ford Found. fellow, 1963, Disting. Alumni award U. Ill., 1989. Home: San José, Costa Rica. Died Sept. 15, 2009.

**DESMOND, LEIF,** writer; b. Inglewood, Calif., Mar. 2, 1920; s. Guy Marion and Elma Agusta (Miller) Smith; m. Soledad Saenz, July 9, 1945 (div. Apr. 1982); children: Judith, Virginia, Marilyn Susan, Theresa, Loretta, Lawrence, Glenn; m. Yolanda Elkins Rambo, June 21, 1982. Student, Iowa State Coll., 1939-40, 42, San Fernando State Coll., 1959-65, U. Calif. Ext., 1961; AA in Bus. Adminstrn., Ventura Coll., Calif., 1959. Author: In the June of Summer, 1986, The Sparrow Safari, 1995, In Old October, 1996. Avocations: creative landscaping, agriculture, animals, philosophy, nature. Deceased.

**DESSER, MAXWELL MILTON,** artist, art director, film-strip producer; b. NYC; s. Solomon and Sadie (Franklin) Desser; m. Mary Alice Natkin, Mar. 7, 1953. Student, Pratt Inst., 1930-32; grad., Cooper Union U., 1940; student, Am. U., 1941-42, NYU, 1945-46, Am. U. Free lance art dir., film-strip producer, NYC, 1935—; owner Desser Prodns., NYC; producer filmstrips Crawl (Internat. TV and Film Festival N.Y. Silver medal 1967), Dun's Market Identifiers (Internat. TV and Film Festival N.Y. gold medal 1968). Author: Using the Library, 1957; painting represented in International Waters Tour, Gt. Britain, Scotland, Can., U.S. Served to lt. USNR, 1942-45. Recipient Nat. Art League Gold medal, 1962, 64, 68, Spl. Tribute Gold medal honor Knickerbocker Artists, 1973, 87. Mem. Am. Watercolor Soc. (v.p. 1983—, Silver medal 1975, sec., dir. 1973-93, Dolphin fellow, ten awards 1975-89, rep. U.S., Gt. Britain and Can. Traveling Show 1991-93, U.S. in Internat. Waters exhbn. 1991-93, High Winds medal 1998), Allied Artists Am. (Silver medal 1978), Nat. Soc. Painters (Grumbacher Gold medal 1974, 91, Dr. Soloway award 1995), Audubon Artists (Silver medal 1981, bd. dirs. 1979-82), Allied Artists (Gold Medal honor 1989), Nat. Acad. Academician (cert. merit 1976, 90, 93, The Nat. Acad. Adolph and Clara Obrig prize 1997), Salmagundi Club (Emanuel Krueger award 1991, first prize 1994, Napoli award 1995, others). Died 1999.

**DEVENS, JOHN SEARLE,** natural resources administrator, former mayor; b. Shickshinny, Pa., Mar. 31, 1940; s. John Ezra and Laura (Bulkley) D.; m. Sharon I. Snyder (div. 1979); children: John, Jerilyn, James, Janis. BS, Belmont Coll., 1964; MEd, Emory U., 1966; PhD, Wichita State U., 1975. Dir. speech and hearing Columbia Coll., Columbia, SC, 1967—70; head dept. audiology Inst. Logopedics, Wichita, Kans., 1970—71; supr. audiology State of Alaska, Fairbanks, 1971—73; asst. prof. U. Houston, Victoria, Tex., 1975—77; pres. Prince William Sound C.C., Valdez, Alaska, 1977—92, Sterling Coll., Craftsbury Common, Vt., 1993—96; dir. Valdez Hearing and Speech Ctr.; exec. dir. Prince William Sound Regional Citizens' Adv. Coun., 1997—2014; prin., owner The Lake House a Country Inn, Valdez, 2000—14. Owner, operator Valdez Hearing and Speech Ctr., 1977—92, Lake House Country Inn, from 2000. Prodr. films on hearing problems; contbr. articles to profl. jours. Mayor City of Valdez, 1985-89, mem. city coun., 1980-89; nat. chmn. adv. com. Horsemanship for Handicapped, 1964-67; mem. Alaska Governor's Coun. for Handicapped, 1980-82; pres. Valdez chpt. Alaska Visitors Assn., 1980; mem. small cities adv. coun. Nat. League Cities, 1983-87, mem. internat. econ. devel. task force; mem. Nat. Export Coun.; bd. dirs. Resource Devel. Coun.; Democratic nominee US House of Reps., 1990, 92; hosted internat. conf. on oil spills for mayors Mem. American Speech-Lang. Hearing Assn. (cert. clin. competence in audiology and speech and lang. pathology), American Chamber of Commerce in Korea, Valdez Chamber of Commerce, Alaska Mcpl. League (bd. dirs. 1984-89). Democrat. Methodist. Avocation: charter boat operator. Home: Copper Center, Alaska. Died June 13, 2014.

**DE VETTA-VAN REENEN, HELENA MARIA,** psychologist; b. Gouda, Zuid, Netherlands, May 20, 1928; d. Hubertus Nicolaas van Reenen and Helena Maria van Reenen-Teekens; m. William De Vetta, Jan. 12, 1957 (dec. Apr. 1998); children: Helena Maria Shackleton-de Vetta, David Anthony de Vetta. BA, U. South Africa, Pretoria, 1967; BA with honors, U. South Africa, 1969, MA in Psychology, 1971, DLitt and Phil., 1977, Diplomate in Datametrics, 1998; MPhil in Theology, St. Augustine's U., Johannesburg, 2001. Lic. clin./counseling, rsch. psychologist. Counseling psychologist Family Adv. Ctr., Bulawayo, Zimbabwe, 1967—69; clin. psychologist St. Giles Med. Rehab. Ctr., Harare, Zimbabwe, 1970—74; lectr. in abnormal psychology U. Zimbabwe, Harare, 1975—77; head dept. psychology U. Zululand, Kwa-Dlangezwa, South Africa, 1979—82; head student counseling and rsch. Med. U. South Africa, Ga-Rankuwa, 1983—93; pvt. practice psychology Pretoria, 1993—2003. Author: A Clinical Study of Some Alcohol Addicts, 1971 (Distinction, 1972), Factors Associated With Alcohol and Drug Abuse, 1976, Spiritual Intelligence, 2001; contbr. articles to profl. jours. Vol. counselor, lectr. ch. and charitable orgns. Mem.: APA (assoc.), South African Psychol. Assn., Internat. Assn. Cross-Cultural Psychology. Roman Catholic. Avocations: reading, travel, needlecrafts. Home: Kruiningen, Netherlands. Died Dec. 11, 2006.

**DEWAR, JAMES MCEWEN,** marketing, aerospace and defense executive, developing nations consultant; b. Williamsport, Pa., Aug. 4, 1943; s. James Livingston and Margaret Ann (McEwen) D.; m. Margaret Cawley, Feb. 27, 1982; children: Alec, Porter, Leah. BS in Internat. Affairs, Trinity U., 1965, postgrad., 1965-66. Mgr. Dash brand Procter & Gamble Corp., Cin., 1969-71; CEO, DeLair & Dewar, Inc., Tucson and Washington, 1972—2001; chmn. bd. Cabot South Asia Inc. subs. Cabot Corp., 1982-87; pres., dir.-gen. ASI, Inc. subs. Boeing Co., 1987-97; CEO, J. Dewar Indochine, Ltd., Hanoi, Vietnam, 1993—2005; CEO J. Dewar N.Am., Inc., Washington, from 2005, J. Dewar Internat. Ltd., Washington, from 2006. Pres., interim cons. CEO, N.Am. Automotive Project, Southfield, Mich., 1993-98; bd. dirs. Metz Constrn. Co., Marine Environ. Rsch. Corp., Computational Analysis Corp.; mem. Aerospace, Def. and Automotive Industry Devel. Commn., Detroit, 1994. Contbr. numerous articles to profl. publs. Bd. dirs. Casa de Los Ninos, Tucson, 1974-2007, Safari Club Internat., Tucson, 1974-2000, Internat. Marine Fisheries Corp.; founding mem. Dist. Atty.'s Victim/Witness Adv. Program; mem. White House Talent Pool, 1975-76, White House Nat. Cambodia Crisis Com., 1979-80, U.S. Aerospace Indsl. Reps. in Europe 1987-97; adj. Mil. Order World Wars, Tucson, 1977-80, perpetual mem.; chmn. internat. bd. advs. Ariz.-Sonora Desert Mus., 1979-80, 2006-; bd. advs. guardian ad litem program Superior Ct. Ariz., 1976-82. Capt. USAF, 1966-70, Vietnam. Recipient Key to City of Seoul, 1973, citation Pres. of Korea, 1973, award for work with Mother Teresa, Cabot Found., 1982-87. Mem. Am. Soc. Agrl. Cons., Dirs. Guild Am., Assn. Old Crows, Australian/Asian Order Old Bastards (Sydney), Army Navy Club, Mountain Oyster Club, Automobile Club France, Maxim's Bus. Club (Paris), St. James Club (Paris), Chambers Club (New Delhi), Hanoi Club. Home: Mc Lean, Va. Died July 25, 2013.

**DEWEY, DONALD WILLIAM,** magazine publisher, editor, writer; b. Honolulu, Sept. 30, 1933; s. Donald William and Theckla Jean (Engeborg) D.; m. Sally Rae Ryan, Aug. 7, 1961; children: Michael Kevin, Wendy Ann. Student, Pomona Coll., 1953-55. With Pascoe Steel Corp., Pomona, Calif., 1955-56, div. Reynolds Aluminum Co., Los Angeles, 1956-58, Switzer Panel Corp., Pasadena, Calif., 1958-60; sales and gen. mgr. Western Pre-Cast Concrete Corp., Ontario, Calif., 1960-62; editor, pub. R/C Modeler Mag., Sierra Madre, Calif., from 1963, Freshwater and Marine Aquarium Mag., Sierra Madre, from 1978. Pres., chmn. bd. R/C Modeler Corp., Sierra Madre, 1963— Author: Radio Control From the Ground Up, 1970, Flight Training Course, 1973, For What It's Worth, Vol. 1, 1973, Vol. 2, 1975; contbr. articles to profl. jours. Sustaining mem. Rep. Nat. Com., 1981—; charter mem. Nat. Congl. Club, 1981—; mem. Rep. Presdl. Task Force, 1981—, U.S. Senatorial Club, 1983—, 1984 Presdl. Trust, Conservative Caucus, Nat. Tax Limitation Com., Nat. Conservative Polit. Action Com., Ronald Reagan Presdl. Libr. Served with Hosp. Corps, USN, 1951-55. Mem. Acad. Model Aeronautics, Nat. Aeronautic Assn., Republican. Lutheran. Home: Sierra Madre, Calif. Deceased.

**DEY, MANNA (PROBODH CHANDRIA DEY),** singer; b. May 1, 1919; s. Purna Chandra and Mahamaya Dey; m. Sulochana Kumaran, Dec. 18, 1953 (dec. 2012); children: Ajit, Abhijit. Grad., Scottish Church Coll., India, Vidyasagar Coll. Asst. music dir. Krishna Chandra Dey, India, S.D Burman, India, 1942. Singer TV films, Upar gagan Vishal, 1950, (songs) Ketaki Gulab Juhi, Yeh Dosti (Sholay), Ek Chatur Naar (Padosan), Ke Prothom Kachhe Esechi. Recipient Nat. Singer of India, Govt. India, Padma Shri, 1971, Padma Bhushan, 2005, Padmabhusan award, 2005, Dadasaheb Phalke award, 2009, Life Time Achievement award, Govt. of Maharastra, 2005. Died Oct. 24, 2013.

**DEYL, ZDENEK,** chemistry educator; b. Prague, Czechoslovakia, Jan. 7, 1934; s. Zdenek and Marie (Dohnalova) D.; m. Vera Fikerova, Aug. 5, 1955; 1 child, Robert. Grad., Inst. Chem. Tech., Prague, 1957, PhD, 1960; DSc, Inst. Chem. Tech., 1974; D in Natural Scis., Charles U. Prague, 1968. Rsch. engr. Skoda Engring., Dysina, 1957-60; jr. rsch. assoc. Rsch. Inst. Food Industry, Prague, 1960-64; rsch. assoc. Inst. Physiology Czech Acad. Scis., Prague, 1964-89, sr. rsch. assoc., from 1992; dir. internat. affairs Min. Edn., Prague, 1989-92; prof. analytical chemistry Inst. Chem. Tech., Prague, from 1995. From assoc. prof. to prof. U. Pardubice, 1988—; vis. scientist, prof. MIT, Cambridge, MAss., 1964-66, Boston U. Med. Sch., 1968, 86, 88, U. Oulu, Finland, 1972, 74, 76; cons. Glaxo R&D, Verona, Italy. Co-editor Jour. Chromatography, 1968—; editor 6 monographs on chromatography and electrophoresis; contbr. more than 200 articles to profl. jours. 1st lt. Czechoslovak Army Res., 1968. Recipient Sci. State award Czech Govt., 1978, State medal, 1988. Mem. Czech Chem. Soc. (chmn. sect. chromatography and electrophoresis 1985-93). Avocations: driving, dogs. Home: Prague, Czech Republic. Died 2005.

**DIAMOND, DAVE (SIDNEY IVAN DAVISON JR.),** journalism educator; b. Howard, SD, Aug. 7, 1936; s. Imogene (Reeve) Davison. BS in Journalism, U. So. Miss., 1958; MA in Profl. Writing, U. So. Calif., 1982; MA in English, N.W. Mo. State U., 1986; PhD in English, Columbia Pacific U., 1992. With programming dept. RKO-Gen. Broadcasting, LA, 1965-66, Westinghouse Broadcasting, LA, 1967-68, RKO-Gen. Broadcasting KFRC, San Francisco, 1968-71, CBS, San Francisco, 1971, KIIS Radio, LA, 1972-76, KFI Radio, LA, 1976-82; prof. journalism Black Hills State U. Author: (as Link Pennington) Slade Western series; author: (novels) Cool Hand in a Hot Fire, 2004 With U. S. Army, 1953-54. Recipient Midwest Fiction award Mich. State U., 1997, Mark Twain award for Disting. Contributrion to Midwestern Literature, 2006 Died May 5, 2014.

**DICKINSON, PHILIP JOHN,** dietician, researcher; b. Manchester, Eng., Sept. 29, 1972; s. John Charles and Patricia Dickinson. BSc with honors, U. of Wales Inst. Cardiff, 1998. Cert. Brit. Dietetic Assn., 1998. Dietitian Hammersmith Hospitals NHS Trust, London, 1998—99; diabetes specialist dietitian Manchester Diabetes Ctr., from 1999; hon. rsch. fellow U. of Manchester, from 2000. Mem. of jour. rev. bd. The Jour. of Diabetes Rsch. and Clin. Practice, from 2002, The Jour. of Pharmacol. Rsch., Milan, from 2003. Contbr. articles to profl. jours. Mem.: N. Am. Assn. for the Study of Obesity, Am. Diabetes Assn., Brit. Dietetic Assn. Home: Urmston, England. Died 2006.

**DICKSON, CONSTANCE PIERCE,** retired law librarian; b. Boston; d. Lorin Edward and Kathryn (Josephs) Pierce; m. William Simmonds Dickson (dec. July 2013); children: Mark Pierce, Carol Anne. AB, Tufts U., Medford, Mass., 1956; MLS, U. Md., 1973. Law libr. Dow, Lohnes & Albertson, Washington, 1973-74, Dewey Ballantine Bushby Palmer & Wood, Paris, 1974-78, Y.B. Kim & Assocs., Seoul, Republic of Korea, 1978—81, Brownstein Zeidman & Schomer, Washington, 1982-84, Gibson, Dunn & Crutcher, Washington, 1984—2005, Duane Morris LLP, Washington, 2005—07; ret., 2007. Mem. American Assn. Law Libraries (membership com. 1987-88, stats. com. 1988-89, PLL survey 1989-91, CRIV 1993-95, gov. rels. com. 1996-98, AMPS com. 1999-2001, AMPS spl. com. 2001-03, salary survey rev. 2002-03), PLL program com. 1996-99), Law Librarians Soc. Washington (PLL sec. 1984-85, v.p. 1989-90, pres. 1990-91, chair bylaws com. 1992-93), Phi Kappa Phi, Beta Phi Mu. Home: Bethesda, Md. Died Oct. 17, 2013.

**DIERICKX, PAUL JOSEPH,** toxicologist, researcher; b. Leuven, Belgium, Sept. 16, 1946; s. Henri and Lea (Abts) D.; children: Hadewig, Lobkt, Gerwin. MSc, Cath. U. Leuven, 1971, PhD, 1974. Asst. in endocrinology Cath. U. Leuven, 1975-77; aggregated rsch. leader Inst. Pub. Health, Brussels, from 1978; asst. in botany Cath. U. Leuven, 1971-74. Invited referee for numerous jours.; participant numerous European collaborative studies EEC, from 1987, Interuniv. Poles of Attraction, 1991—95, Multictr. Evaluation of In Vitro Cytoxicity, 1989—95, evaluation-guided devel. of new in-vitro tests on systemic toxicity and kinetics, from 1998, EU A-CUTE-TOX Sci. Program, from 2004. Contbr. articles to profl. jours. Mem. Belgian Soc. Biochemistry, Belgian Soc. Toxicology, In Vitro Toxicol. Soc., Scandinavian Soc. Cell Toxicology, Belgian Soc. for the Promotion of Alternative Methods to Animal Experiments (co-founder 1993), Belgian Coun. for Lab. Animal Sci., European Soc. Toxicology In Vitro. (mem. editl. bd.), Soc. Pharmaco-Toxicologie Cellulaire (mem. sci. com. EDIT programme). Achievements include research in role of glutathione and glutathione transferases in xenobiotic detoxification; correlation between in vivo and in vitro toxicology, in vitro methods for human, chronic, nephrohepatic and ecotoxicity. Died 2006.

**DIETZ, DOROTHY BRILL,** artist, designer; Student, San Bernardino Jr. Coll., U. So. Calif., Oreg. State U., Mills Coll., Coll. of Desert, Rudolph Schaefer's Sch. Design, Academie Julian, France, 1959, U. Hawaii, L'Ecole du Cordon Bleu, France; grad., Japanses Art Ctr., San Francisco, 1957, Wash. Sch. Art, 1964, Unity Sch. Christianity, 1969; U.S. student, Instituio San Miguel de Allende, Mex., 1960, Sorbonne, France, 1959. Ct. reporter San Bernardino Justice Ct., San Bernardino Superior Cts.; practice as interior designer, from 1947. One-woman shows include Dietz Galleria, 1959-69, Bank of Am., Palm Desert, Calif., 1962, Ferrall's Playhouse, Palm Springs, 1961, The Villages, San Jose, Calif., Del Mesa Carmel, Calif., 1980; one-woman and group shows in Calif., Paris, Mexico City, Honolulu Mem. Honolulu Acad. Arts. Recipient Taka Mizu Dietz award Japanese Govt., 3 1st Place awards, 1 5th Place award nat. art contests. Mem. Assn. of Unity Chs., Alpha Chi Omega. Clubs: President's (Oreg. State U.). Republican. Deceased.

**DIGGINS, RUTH LOIS,** music educator; b. Rhodes, Iowa, Nov. 10, 1900; d. Charles and Bertha Roberts; m. Mace Edson Diggins, Aug. 12, 1920; 1 child, Dean R. Student, Drake U., 1918—19; grad., Palmer Sch. Chiropractic, Davenport, Iowa, 1922. Owner & mgr. Diggins Dance Sch., Mason City, Iowa, Hampton Dance Sch.; music tchr., piano, vocal, violin & guitar, from 1915, Hampton, Iowa, from 1924; gen. practice, chiropractic medicine Iowa, 1924—73. Dir., ch. choirs Congl. Ch., Hampton, 1948—72, Ch. of Christ, Hampton, 1952—60. Mem.: Treble Clef Music Club (Hampton) (pres.), E.C.D. Club, Women's Club, Bus. & Profl. Women's Club. Deceased.

**DIGOUTTE, JEAN-PIERRE,** microbiologist; b. Damas, Syria, Nov. 21, 1927; s. Louis and Fernande (Lelong) D.; m. Janine Boucheron, Dec. 20, 1951; children: Philippe, Thierry, Véronique. MD, U. Lyon, France, 1953; grad., Inst. Pasteur, Paris, 1965. Head Hosp. of Atar, Mauritania, 1957-60; dir. pub. health lab. Niamey, Niger, 1961-64; dir. Inst. Pasteur, Bangui, Central African Republic, 1966-72, Cayenne, French Guiana, 1972-78; del. gen. Insts. Pasteur Outre-Mer, Paris, 1977-79; sci. del. for Africa, 1979; dir. Inst. Pasteur, Dakar, 1979-95; retired, 1995. Author papers new arthropod born virus and arbovirus pathogens for man. Decorated chevalier Ordre Nat. du Mérite, officer ORdre National de la Lé gion D'Honneur, chevalier, palmes academiques. Mem. Am. Soc. Tropical Medicine and Hygiene (emeritus), Soc. Pathologie Exotique. Home: Paris, France. Died Feb. 15, 2005.

**DI JESO, DUKE DON FERNANDO,** biochemistry educator; b. Cosenza, Italy, Oct. 29, 1931; s. Pasquale and Adelaide (Scopa) di J. BA, Vittorio Emanuele II, Naples, Italy, 1949; MD, Univ. Med. Sch., Naples, 1955; PhD, Perugia U., Italy, 1959; DSc, U. Paris, 1965. Rschr. Biochem. Inst., U. Med. Sch., Naples, 1952-54; rschr. biochem. dept. Cancer Inst., Naples, 1954-56; assoc. prof. phys. chemistry dept. U. Padua (Italy), 1956-57; rschr. biochem. dept. Cancer Inst., Naples, 1957-60; prof. libero docente Biochemistry Inst., U. Med. Sch., Naples, 1961; assoc. prof. biochemistry dept. Coll. de France, Paris, 1961-63; assoc. prof. Biochemistry Inst., U. Med. Sch., Pavia, Italy, 1963-67; assoc. prof. biochemistry and molecular biology dept. Cornell U., Ithaca, N.Y., 1967-69; prof. biochemistry Biochemistry Inst., U. Med. Sch., Pavia, from 1969. Bd. dirs. Postdoctoral Med. Sch. Neurophysiopathology, U. Pavia, 1990-93; dir. Cardiovasc. Biochemistry Ctr., 1990-96; pres. ethics com. Interuniv. Ctr. for Adaptative Disorder and Headache, 1993-99; sci. and artistic advisor Internet Uniform Resources Locator Kronosnet.com, 1995—. Editor, author: Membrane-Bound Enzymes, 1971, Advances in Experiemental Medicine and Biology, vol. 14; editor, pub. Medicina Democratica, 1976—, Glenans, 1985—, Aggiornamenti of the Italian Study Group on Radioimmunological Surgery and Immuno-Scintigraphy, 1993—, Sud-Mag., 1994-1996; internet editor, author. Pres. Cooperativa Editoriale Pavese, Pavia, 1969-75, Laureati Cattolici, Pavia, 1970, CISL-Universita, Pavia, 1975-79, Medicina Democratica, Italy, 1976-90, Lega Navale Italiana, Pavia, 1990—. Decorated ufficiale della Repubblica (Italy); Abroad Rsch. grantee NATO, Tr. An Italian Com. of Nat. Rsch. Coun., 1961-63, Italian Nat. Rsch. Coun., 1967-69; recipient Concorso Nazionale di Poesia Amisani, Mede Municipality and Amisani Assn., Mede, Italy, 1988, Premio Letterario Casentino, Casentino Prize Com., Stia, Italy, 1981, 88-93, Internat. D'Arte Moderna, Rome, 1992, Ungaretti, Sorrento, 1992, Naples, 1995, Luci di Poesia, Milan, 1993, Coppa Eduardo at Il Delfino d'Argento, 1993, Omaggio a Pirandello, Rome, 1994, Golfo di Napoli, Naples, 1994, Cascate di Stelle, Milan, 1995; Delfino d'Argento, Anzio, 1997; Duke of St. John of Acre; Count Palatine by Emperor Leopold edict. Mem. Italian Soc. Biochemistry, Am. Chem. Soc., French Soc. Biology, Internat. Brain Rsch. Orgn., Italian Fulbright Assn. (mem. exec. bd., award 1967), Assn. Professionale Univ., Italian Soc. Cardioneurology, Italian Soc. Pharmacology, Italian Soc. Neurosci., Royal Soc. Medicine, Nobilis Academia Sanctae Theodorae Imperatricis, Senator Micenei Internat. Acad., Mr. Multi-Hulls of Glénans Internat. Assn., The Hist. file. Avocation: sailing. Home: Pavia, Italy. Deceased.

**DILLE, ROLAND PAUL,** retired academic administrator; b. Dassel, Minn., Sept. 16, 1924; s. Oliver Valentine and Eleanor (Johnson) D.; m. Beth Hopeman, Sept. 4, 1948; children: Deborah, Martha, Sarah, Benjamin. BA summa cum laude, U. Minn., 1949, PhD, 1962, LHD (hon.), 1995. Instr. English U. Minn., 1953-56; asst. prof. St. Olaf Coll., Northfield, Minn., 1956-61; asst. prof. English Calif. Lutheran Coll., Thousand Oaks, Calif., 1961-63; prof. English Moorhead (Minn.) State U., 1964-94, pres., 1968-94, pres. emeritus, 1994—2014; co-founder Tri-College U., 1967; ret., 1994. Author: Four Romantic Poets, 1969; contbr. numerous articles and revs. to profl. jours. Treas. American Assn. State Colls. & Universities, 1977-78, bd. dirs., 1978-80, chmn., 1980-81; mem. Nat. Coun. for Humanities, 1980-86; vice-chair Commn. on Higher Edn., North Cen. Assn., 1989-91, chair, 1991-93. With inf. AUS, 1944-46. Disting. Svc. to Humanities award given by Minn. Humanities Commn. named in his honor; named one of The 100 Most Effective American Coll. Presidents, 1987, Heritage award, Clay County Hist. Soc., 2011-14. Mem. Phi Beta Kappa., Fargo-Moorhead Chamber of Commerce, (Annual Leadership award, 2009) Home: Moorhead, Minn. Died May 26, 2014.

**DILLING, KIRKPATRICK WALLWICK,** lawyer; b. Evanston, Ill., Apr. 11, 1920; s. Albert W. and Elizabeth (Kirkpatrick) D.; m. Betty Ellen Bronson, June, 1942 (div. July 1944); m. Elizabeth Ely Tilden, Dec. 11, 1948; children: Diana Jean, Eloise Tilden, Victoria Walgreen, Albert Kirkpatrick (dec.). Student, Cornell U., 1939-40; BS in Law, Northwestern U., 1942; postgrad., DePaul U., 1946-47, L'Ecole Vaubier, Montreux, Switzerland; Degré Normal, Sorbonne U., Paris. Bar: Ill. 1947, U.S. Dist. Ct. (no. dist.) Ill., Ind., Mich., Md., La., Tex., Okla., Wis., Idaho, U.S. Ct. Appeals (2nd, 3rd, 5th, 7th, 8th, 9th, 10th, 11th, fed. and D.C. cirs.), U.S. Supreme Ct. Ptnr. Dilling and Dilling, from 1948. Counsel Cancer Control Soc., Nat. Coun. for Improved Health; bd. dirs. Nutradelle Labs., Ltd., V.E. Irons, Inc.; v.p. Midwest Medic-Aide, Inc.; spl. counsel Herbalife (U.K.) Ltd., Herbalife Australasia Pty., Ltd.; lectr. on pub. health law. Contbr. articles to pub. health publs. Bd. dirs. Adelle Davis Found., Liberty Lobby. 1st lt. AUS, 1943-46. Recipient Humanitarian award Nat. Health Fedn. Mem. ABA, Ill. Bar Assn., Chgo. Bar Assn., Assn. Trial Lawyers Am., Stalwart Cornell Soc. Engrs., Am. Legion, Air Force Assn., Pharm. Advt. Club, Rolls Royce Owners' Club, Tower Club, Cornell U., Chicago Club, Delta Upsilon. Republican. Episcopalian. Deceased.

**DILLON, LEO (LIONEL JOHN DILLON JR.),** illustrator; b. Bklyn., Mar. 2, 1933; m. Diane Clare Sorber, 1957; 1 child, Lee Illustrator: (with Diane Dillon): Ashanti to Zulu, African Traditions, 1977 (Caldecott medal), Two Pairs of Shoes, 1980, Why Mosquitoes Buzz in People's Ears: A West African Tale, 1984 (Caldecott medal), Honey, I Love, and Other Love Poems, 1986, The People Could Fly, American Black Folktales, 1987, paperback, 1993, Tale of the Mandarin Ducks, 1990, Who's in Rabit's House?: A Masai Tale, 1990, paperback, 1992, Pish, Posh, Said Hieronymus Boach, 1991, Race of the Golden Apples, 1991, The Sorcer's Apprentice, 1993, The African Cookbook, 1993, Many Thousand Gone: African Americans from Slavery to

Freedom, 1993, Switch on the Night, 1994, The Color Wizard (Bank Street Ready-to-Read Leval 1), 1989, Aida, 1990, paperback, 1997, Race of the Golden Apples, 1991, Her Stories: African American Folktales, Fairy Tales and True Tales, 1995, The Hundred Penny Box, 1995, The Girl Who Dreamed Only Geese: And Other Tales of the Far North, 1997, Wild Child, 1998, To Everything There Is A Season, 1998, Rap a Tap Tap: Here's Bojangles-Think of That!, 2002, Jazz on a Saturday Night, 2007 numerous others; illustrator numerous book covers. Recipient Hamilton King award, Gold Medal for Children's Book Illustration, Soc. Illustrators, Hugo award, 1971. Died May 26, 2012.

**DIMITROVA, GHENA,** opera singer; b. Beglej, Bulgaria, May 6, 1941; Début Sofia (Bulgaria) Opera; singer laureate Internat. Competition, Treviso, Italy, 1972; appearances in France, Italy, Spain, S. America and Moscow; in opera houses of Paris, Vienna, Munich, Hamburg, Milan, Berlin, Madrid, Barcelona, Rome, Naples, London's Convent Gardens, New York's Met. and Zurich; recordings include Nabucco and Oberto, Conte de San Bonafacio. Recipient Gold medal and First prize Fourth Internat. Competition for Young Singers, Sofia, 1970, Golden Archer and Giovanni Zenatello prizes, 1981. Died May 11, 2005.

**DIMOPOULOU-VOSNIADOU, MARIA,** research scientist; d. Aliki Vosniadou; m. Antonis Dimopoulos, Dec. 27, 1975; children: Aris Dimopoulos, Eleftheria Dimopoulou. BSc, Athens U., 1973; MSc, London Sch. Econs. & Polit. Sci., 1974; PhD, Athens U. Econs. & Bus., 1992. Asst. prof. Athens U. Econs. & Bus., Athens, Greece, from 1977. Dir. com. Info. Soc., 2003—04. Contbr. numerous jour. articles in field. Mem.: Hellenic Operational Rsch. Soc. (corr.). Orthodox Christian. Avocations: reading, travel. Home: Athens, Greece. Died Oct. 29, 2005.

**DINI, JOSEPH EDWARD, JR., (JOE DINI),** state legislator; b. Yerington, Nev., Mar. 28, 1929; s. Giuseppe and Elvira (Castellani) D.; m. Mouryne Landing; children: Joseph, George, David, Michael. BSBA, U. Nev., Reno, 1951. Mem. Nev. State Assembly, Carson City, 1967—2001, majority leader, 1975, speaker, 1977, 87, 89, 91, 93, 97, 99, minority leader, 1985, interim fin. com. mem., 1985-01, speaker pro tem, 1973, co-spkr., 1995, chmn. water policy com. Western Legis. Conf., 1993-94, 96-00, speaker emeritus, 2001; pres. Dini's Lucky Club Casino, Yerington, Nev., 1972—2014. Mem. legislative com. Nev. State Assembly, 1971-77, 91, 93, 95, 97, vice chmn., 1981-82, 96-97, chmn., 1982-83, 93-94. Mem. Yeringion Vol. Fire Dept.; mem. Lyon County Dem. Ctrl. Com., Nev. American Revolution Bicentennial Commn.; past dist. gov., active mem. 20-30 Club. Recipient Outstanding Citizen award Nev. Edn. Assn., 1973, Friend of Edn. award Nev. State Edn. Assn., 1986, Citizen of Yr. award Nev. Judges Assn., 1987, Dedicated and Valued Leadership award Nat. Conf. State Legislatures, 1989, Excellence in Public Svc. award Nev. Trial Lawyers Assn., 1990, Silver Plow award Nev. Farm Bur., 1991, Skill, Integrith, Responsibility award Assoc. Gen. Contractors, 1994, Guardian of Small Bus. award Nat. Fedn. Ind. Bus., 1996, Spl. Recognition award Nev. State Firefighters Assn., 1998, Appreciation award Nev. Emergency Preparedness Assn., 1998, Friendship Medal of Diplomacy, Taiwan, 2000; named Conservation Legislator of Yr. Nev. Wildlife Fedn., 1991, Alumni of Yr., U. Nev. Alumni Assn., 1997, Legislator of Yr., Nev. Rural Water Assn., 1999, Italian American of Yr. Augustus Soc. Las Vegas, 2001, Arts Advocate Nev. Arts Advocates, 2002. Mem. Mason Valley Chamber of Commerce (pres.), Rotary (pres. Yerington 1989), Lions (pres. Yerington chpt. 1975), Masons, Shriners, York Rite, Scottish Rite, Order Eastern Star, Gamma Sigma Delta, Phi Sigma Kappa (Disting. Alumna award 1993). Home: Yerington, Nev. Died Apr. 10, 2014.

**DISALVO, LOUIS HENRY,** marine biologist, consultant; b. Sellersvile, Pa., Dec. 21, 1940; arrived in Chile, 1978; s. Rosario Antonino and Beulah Carol (Chalfant) DiS. AB, Rutgers U., 1962; MS in Zoology, Ariz. State U., 1965; PhD in Zoology, U. N.C., 1970. Lectr. Cath. U. Am., Washington, 1970-71; assoc. rsch. microbiologist U. Calif., Berkeley, 1971-77; internat. trade rep. Chile Aledo Transnat. Trading Corp., Alameda, Calif., 1977-79; prof. U. Catolica Norte, Coquimbo, Chile, 1979-88; owner Louis H. DiSalvo Marine Sci. Cons. and Aquaculture Lab., Coquimbo, 1988—2000; scientific tech. translator/editor, from 2000. Vis. prof. U. Catolica Norte, Coquimbo, 1988—; UN-FAO expert; aquanaut NOAA. Contbr. articles to profl. and popular periodicals. Mem. AAAS, Am. Assn. Limnology and Oceanography, Comite Ciencias Mar: Chile, World Aquaculture Soc., Sigma Xi. Avocations: photography, tennis, archery. Died May 19, 2008.

**DISCEPOLA, NUNZIO (NICK DISCEPOLA),** retired Canadian government official; b. Italy, Nov. 27, 1949; m. Michele Discepola; children: Lisa, Laura, Michele, Marco. BS, McGill U., 1972, MBA, 1977. Mayor City of Kirland, Quebec, 1989—92; mem. Canadian Parliament, Ottawa, 1993—97, 1997—2004, parliamentary sec. to solicitor gen., 1996—98. Liberal Party Of Can. Died Nov. 21, 2012.

**DISHONG, DIANE ELIZABETH,** medical/surgical nurse, rehabilitation nurse; b. Massillon, Ohio, Aug. 8, 1958; d. Theodore William and Judith Anne (Hoisington) Weiand; m. Morris William Dishong, Sept. 11, 1984; 1 child, Jeffrey William. Lic. practical nurse summa cum laude, Canton Practical Nursing Sch., 1984. Cert. in CPR, first aid. LPN, office nurse, Canton, Ohio; LPN Timken Mercy Med. Ctr.; staff LPN Akron (Ohio) Gen. Med. Ctr.; LPN in chem. rehab. Massillon Cmty. Hosp.; staff nurse Stark County Eye Care Clinic. Owner, CEO Bill's Beer Barn Beverage Drive Thru, Inc., Canton. Recipient hwy. safety award Nat. Hwy. Council. Mem. MADD, LPN Assn. Ohio. Home: Canton, Ohio. Died Jan. 2001.

**DIXON, ALAN JOHN,** lawyer, former United States Senator from Illinois; b. Belleville, Ill., July 7, 1927; s. William G. and Elsa (Tebbenhoff) D.; m. Joan Louise Fox, Jan. 17, 1954; children: Stephanie Jo, Jeffrey Alan, Elizabeth Jane. BS, U. Ill., 1949; LL.B., Washington U., St. Louis, 1949. Bar: Ill. 1950. Practiced in, Belleville, 1950-76; police magistrate City of Belleville, 1949; asst. atty. St. Clair County, Ill., 1950; mem. Ill. House of Reps., Springfield, 1951-63, Ill. State Senate, 1963—71, minority whip, 1964—70; treas. State of Ill., 1971-77, sec. of state, 1977-81; US Senator from Ill. Washington, 1981—93; sr. counsel Bryan Cave LLP, St. Louis, 1993—2014. Del. Democratic Nat. Conv., 1968, 1976; chmn. Def. Base Closure & Realignment Commn., 1994—95. Author: (autobiography) The Gentleman from Illinois: Stories from Forty Years of Elective Public Service, 2013. Mem. American Legion, Belleville Chamber of Commerce, ABA, Ill. Bar Assn., St Clair Country Club, Nat. Assn. Secretaries of State (pres 1979-80). Democrat. Died July 6, 2014.

**DIXON, CHARLES HARWOOD,** retired secondary education educator, clergyman; b. Crieff, Perthshire, Scotland, Jan. 15, 1926; arrived in South Africa, 1953; s. Frank Metcalfe and Annie Mackie (Anderson) D.; m. Ann Rosemary Murton Chinn, July 8, 1957; children: Mary Louise, Susan Janet Brits, Kathleen Laura Seegers, Isobel Margaret Van Niekerk, Lucy Frances. BSc with honors, U. St. Andrews, Scotland, 1947, BD, 1953; BEd, Rhodes U., South Africa, 1981, MEd, 1990; DipEd, Edinburgh U., 1959; MA in Ancient Studies, U. Stellenbosch, 2000. Ordained to ministry Ch. of Eng., 1949. Chaplain St. Paul's Cathedral, Dundee, Scotland, 1949-53; missionary priest Diocese of St. John's, South Africa, 1953-67; dean St. John's Cathedral, Umtata, South Africa, 1967-72; tchr. Union H.S., Graaff-Reinet, South Africa, 1973-84; headmaster Nqweba H.S., Graaff-Reinet, 1985-88; sr. lectr. Transkei Tchrs. In-Svc. Coll., Umtata, 1989-93; tchr. Butterworth (South Africa) H.S., 1994-97; ret., 1997. Rsch. officer Diocese of St. Johns, 1966-67; acting warden St. John's Coll., Umtata, 1954, 56, 59; chief examiner Transkei Edn. Dept., Republic of Transkei, 1980-86, moderator physics, 1990-95; curate-in-charge St. John's Ch., Maclear, 1989-99; vis. curate St.Matthew's Fellowship, East London, 1995-99; min. Graaff-Reinet Ch. England Fellowship. Author series of newspaper articles, series of mag. articles, rsch. reports. Mayor's chaplain Municipality of Graaff-Reinet, 1980. With Royal Observer Corps, Dundee, 1943-53. Recipient Dux medal Morrison's Acad., Crieff, 1942. Mem. South African Tchrs. Assn., South African Inst. Physics, N.Y. Acad. Scis., South African Assn. Tchrs. Phys. Sci. Avocations: music (piano, organ, choral singing), chess, astronomy. Deceased.

**DIXON, JOHN WAYNE,** accountant; b. Brownwood, Tex., Jan. 6, 1944; s. Lee Dixon and E. Pauline (Parkman) Sanborn; m. Carolyn Sicklesteel, Dec. 1, 1974; 1 child, Brian L. BBA, Washburn U., 1973; MBA, U. Kans., 1982. Gen. mgr. Jefferson Devel. Co., Inc., Ozawkie, Kans., 1973-77; dir. mcpl. info. systems State of Kans., Topeka, 1977-82; dir. purchasing and acctg. Douglas County, Lawrence, Kans., from 1982. With USAF, 1961-70, Vietnam. Mem. Kans. Assn. Pub. Purchasing (bd. dirs. 1988-89, chmn. com. 1989-90), Nat. Inst. Govtl. Purchasing, Govtl. Fin. Officers Assn., Am. Legion (comdr. 1988-90, Legionnaire of Yr. 1986), VFW, La Societe des 40 Hommes et 8 Chevaux, Sons of Am. Legion. Avocations: golf, bowling. Deceased.

**DIXON, WILLIAM CORNELIUS,** lawyer; b. Dexter, NY, July 1, 1904; s. Frank and Celia (Potter) D.; m. Arvilla Pratt, Nov. 20, 1934; children— Anne Arvilla, Nancy Cornelia. AB, U. Mich., 1926, JD, 1928. Bar: Ohio 1928, Calif. 1948, Supreme Ct. U.S 1948. Asso. Holliday-Grossman-McAfee, Cleve., 1928-32; asst. dir. law Cleve., 1932-33; practiced law, 1933-38; justice Supreme Ct. Ohio, 1938; spl. asst. in anti-trust div. to atty. gen. U.S. Dept. Justice, 1944-54, chief asst. trial sect. anti-trust div., 1945, apptd. chief West Coast offices Anti-trust div., 1946, chief trial counsel for Govt. U.S. versus Standard Oil Co. Calif. et al, 1948, chief Los Angeles Office, 1948-54; pvt. law practice Los Angeles, 1954-59; asst. atty. gen. in charge state anti-trust enforcement Calif., 1959-63. Legal adviser and mem. Joint War and State Depts., Zaibatsu Mission to Japan, 1946 Dir. relief for Ohio under Emergency Relief Act, 1938-39; moderator Los Angeles Assn. Congl. Chs., 1957; moderator Congl. Conf. So. Calif. and S.W., 1960; mem. constn. commn. United Ch. of Christ; mem. United Ch. Bd. for Homeland Ministries, 1962-65. Papers included in Truman Library, Library of Contemporary History, U. Wyo., Ohio State U. and UCLA libraries. Mem. Calif., Los Angeles bar assns., Delta Sigma Rho, Pi Kappa Alpha. Democrat. Home: San Marcos, Calif. *The past and unachieved goals in life soon pass into history. The goals of today become the achievements and successes of tomorrow.* Died Jan. 1996.

**DLUGOSZEWSKI, LUCIA,** artistic director; b. Detroit, June 16, 1934; Student, Wayne State U.; studied with, Carl Beutel, Edward Bredshall, Ktja Andy, Grete Sultan, Felix Salzer, Edgard Varese. Composer: (structure for the Poetry) Everyday Sound, 1949, Archaic Timbre Piano Music, 1958, Space Is a Diamond, 1970, Tender Theatre Flight Nageire, Densities, Nova, Corona, Clear Core, Amos Elusive Empty August, Strange Tenderness of naked Leaping, (commd. by Mikhail Baryshnikov), Disparate Stairway Radical other Quartet, 1994, Radical Quidditas Dew Tear Duende; artist dir. Erik Hawkins Dance Co., from 1998; recording artists: various labels. Recipient Recipient Koussevitzky Internat. Recording award, 1979, Phoebe Kechum Thorne award, others; named Musician of Yr. Musical Am., Village Voice, 1975; Guggenheim fellow. Died Apr. 2000.

**DOANE, HAROLD EVERETT,** recording executive; b. NYC, Oct. 17, 1904; s. Thomas J. and Mary S. (Blaisdell) D.; m. Mary G. Gardner, Dec. 20, 1936 (div. 1941); m. Faith S. Tracy, Oct. 17, 1943 (div. 1966); children: Priscilla Clare Tello, Richard Henry Tracy; m. Vivian Dillon Dunn, May 3, 1966. Asst. cameraman D.W. Griffith Orienta Point Studios, Mamaroneck, N.Y., 1921-22; radio announcer Sta. WGBU, Fulford, Fla., 1925-26, Sta. WBNY, NYC, 1926-27, Sta. WMCA, NYC, 1927, Sta. WKBQ, NYC, 1927-28; owner Sta. WCOH, Mt. Vernon, N.Y., 1928-29; rsch. engr. NYC, 1929-35; dir. Gramercy Pictures Corp., NYC, 1935-37; prodr. Spotlight Prodns., Inc., 1940-41; tech. ops. dir. war fin. com. N.Y. State divsn. U.S. Treasury Dept., 1941-44; gen. mgr. Art Records, Miami, Fla., 1945-59, pres., from 1959, Artrec Pubs., Miami, Fla., from 1950. Mem. nat. adv. bd. Am. Security Coun.; rep. Pres. Task Force. Mem. Nat. Acad. Rec. Arts and Scis., Fla. Motion Picture and TV Assn., N.Y. Advt. Club. Republican. Died May 6, 1999.

**DOENGES, RUDOLPH CONRAD,** finance educator; b. Tonkawa, Okla., Dec. 7, 1930; s. Rudolph Soland and Helen Elizabeth (Lower) D.; m. Ellen Ione Gummere, Oct. 5, 1963; children: Rudolph Conrad, John Soland, William Gummere. AB magna cum laude (scholar 1948-54), Harvard U., 1952, MBA, 1954; D.BA (Ford Found. fellow 1963-64), U. Colo., Boulder, 1965. Mktg. analyst Ford Motor Co., Dearborn, Mich., 1954; gen. mgr. Doenges-Long Motors and Western Auto Rentals, Colorado Springs, 1958-61; mem. faculty U. Tex., Austin, 1964-2000, prof. fin., 1974-2000, Arthur Andersen & Co. prof. fin., 1983-2000, assoc. dean Grad. Sch. Bus., 1972-76, chmn. dept. fin., 1976-80, assoc. dean Coll. Bus. Adminstrn., 1987-97. Author: (with E. W. Walker) Case Problems in Financial Management, 1968, Consumer Credit in Texas, 1970; editor: Readings in Money and Banking, 1968, (with H. A. Wolf) Corporate Planning Models, 1971; contbr. articles in field to profl. jours. Gen. Bd. Pensions United Meth. Ch., 1988-96; trustee Iliff Sch. Theology, 1992-96. Served with USN, 1955-58. Mem. Austin C. of C., Fin. Mgmt. Assn. (dir. 1980-82), Southwestern Fin. Assn. (pres. 1973-74), Southwestern Fedn. Adminstrv. Disciplines (pres. 1975-76), Austin Soc. Fin. Analysts, El Paso Club (Colorado Springs), Austin Club, Garden of the Gods Club. Republican. Methodist. Died Sept. 14, 2001.

**DOHERTY, WILLIAM THOMAS, JR.,** historian, retired educator; b. Cape Girardeau, Mo., Mar. 30, 1923; s. William Thomas and Kittie (Baird) D.; m. Dorothy Ashley Huff Zienowicz, Aug. 13, 1947 (dec. 2002); children: Victor Sargent, Dorothy Ashley, Catherine Baird, Julia Holbrook, William Thomas III. AB, BS, S.E. Mo. State U., 1943; MA, Am. U., 1950; PhD, U. Mo., 1951. Instr. history Westminster Coll., Fulton, Mo., 1947-48, Christian Coll., 1949-50, U. Mo., 1948-49, 50-51; asst. prof. history U. Miss., 1951-53, assoc. prof. history, 1956-58, prof., chmn. dept. history, 1958-61; asst. prof., then assoc. prof. history U. Ark., 1953-56; prof. history, dir. Ford Found. 3 yr. Master's program Kan. State U., Manhattan, 1961-63; prof. history, chmn. dept. W.Va. U., Morgantown, 1963-79, univ. historian, 1979-88, prof. emeritus, 1988—2013. Author: Louis Houck: Missouri Historian and Entrepreneur, 1960, Berkeley, U.S.A.: A Bicentennial History of a Virginia and West Virginia County 1772-1972, 1972, West Virginia History, 1974, West Virginia University: Symbol of Unity in a Sectionalized State, 1982, West Virginia Studies, 1984, West Virginia: Our Land, Our People, 1990; editor: Minerals, Vol. IV in Conservation History of the United States, 1971; editor in chief West Virginia History Jour., 1979-88; contbr. numerous articles to profl. jours. Served with AUS, 1943-46. Decorated Bronze star medal, 1946. Mem. American Hist. Assn., Southern Hist. Assn., Orgn. American Historians, AAUP, Kappa Delta Pi, Sigma Tau Delta, Phi Alpha Theta. Democrat. Home: Silver Spring, Md. Died Sept. 25, 2013.

**DOHR, DONALD R.,** metallurgical engineer, researcher; b. Rio de Janeiro, Niteroi, Apr. 12, 1924; came to U.S., 1944; s. Nicholas and Candida (Caramuru) D.; m. Virginia Marion O'Donnell, Mar. 30, 1960 (dec. Feb. 1987). ME, Stevens Inst. Tech., 1952, MS in Metallurgy, 1968. Jr. metallurgist Crucible Steel Co., Harrison, N.J., 1952-54; metallurgist Engelhard Industries, Newark, 1954-56, Foster Wheeler Corp., Carterei, N.J., 1956-60, Weston Instruments, Inc., Newark, 1960-66; sr. metallurgist Singer Co., Denville, N.J., 1966-71; unit head materials and processes lab. Kearfott Guidance & Navigation Corp. (formerly Singer Co.), Little Falls, N.J., 1971-91. Author: Liquid Phases Sintering Mechanisms, Magnetic Properties of Metals & Alloys. Staff sgt. U.S. Army, 1944-46, PTO. Mem. Am. Soc. Metals-Internat., Nat. Soc. Profl. Engrs., Soc. Mfg. Engrs. Republican. Roman Catholic. Achievements include patents in Magnetic Field Force Application and Threat Tensioner. Home: West Orange, NJ. Died Oct. 2, 1999.

**DOIRON, CRAIG A.,** electronics executive; b. 1961; MBA, Wash. U., St. Louis, 1994. Procurement positions, Micro Motion Emerson Electric Co., 1996—2000, v.p., materials, 2008, v.p., product mgmt., 2008—11. Died Aug. 16, 2011.

**DOKUCHAEV, VLADIMIR PLATONOVICH,** physicist, researcher; b. Semenov, Russia, Aug. 19, 1932; s. Platon Ivanovich and Eugenia Ivanovna (Volskaya) D.; m. Ariadna Victorovna Tolmacheva, oct. 4, 1966; children: Juri, Lionid. Student, U. Gorkii, 1951-56, DSc, 1959. Rschr. Radio Inst., Gorkii, Russia, 1959-80; prof. U. Gorkii, 1980; chmn., head dept. Gorkii State U., 1983-88; prof. Internat. Soros Sci. Edn. Program, 1998, 2000. Author: Generation and Radiation of Variously Physical Character Waves, 2005; contbr. articles to profl. jours. Dep. dist. coun., City of Gorkii, 1968-72. Mem. Radio Soc. Russia. Avocations: swimming, gardening. Home: Nizhny Novgorod, Russia. Died Oct. 9, 2002.

**DOLE, CHARLES EDWARD,** aeronautical engineering educator; b. Pitts., Oct. 6, 1916; s. Arthur Lucian and Esther Cook (Mohr) D.; m. Emily Mitchell Wiseman, Aprl 6, 1957; 1 child, Susan Dole De Bicki. BS in Mech. Engring., Drexel Inst. of Tech., Phila., 1941; BS in Aero. Engring., USN Post Grad Sch., Annapolis, Md., 1949; MS in Aero. Engring., U. Minn., 1950; EdD, U. So. Calif., 1971. Engr. Glenn L. Martin Co., Middle River, Md., 1937-42, 1945-46; Lt. to maj. USMC, 1942-63; prof. U. So. Calif., Los Angeles, from 1963. Mem. Faculty Senate, U. So. Calif., Los Angeles, 1971-73, fuel consul bd., 1974-75. Author: book: Math & Phys. for Aviation Personnel, 1973, Flight Theory & Aerodynamics, 1981, Fundamentals of Aircraft Material Factors, 1985, Flight Theory For Pilots 1988, Flight Safety Technology Workbook, 1996. Mem. Eagle Scout Assn., USMC Aviation Assn. Republican. Protestant. Died May 9, 1999.

**DOLIBOIS, JOHN ERNEST,** retired ambassador; b. Luxembourg, Dec. 4, 1918; arrived in US, 1931, naturalized, 1941; s. Charles Nicholas and Maria M. (Winter) Dolibois; m. Winifred Helen Englehart Dolibois, Jan. 17, 1942; children: John Michael, Robert Joseph, Brian Charles. AB, Miami U., Oxford, Ohio, 1942, D (hon.) in Pub. Svc., 1984. Indsl. engr. Procter & Gamble Co., Cin., 1942, 1946—47; alumni dir. Miami U., 1947—66, v.p. devel. & alumni affairs, 1966—81; hon. consul Luxembourg, Ohio, 1977—81; US amb. to Luxembourg US Dept. State, Luxembourg, 1981—85. Contbr. articles to profl. jours. Mem. Cmty. Improvement Corp., Oxford, 1966—69, US Bd. Fgn. Scholarships-Fulbright Program, 1968—76; bd. dirs. American Alumni Coun., 1970—74; chmn. Coun. Advancement & Support Edn., 1972—76; mem. Bd. Econ. Devel. Luxembourg, 1977—81. Served to capt. US Army, 1942—46. Decorated Grand Cross Grand Ducal Order Crown of Oak, Comdr. Grand Ducal Order Merit, Luxembourg; recipient A.K. Morris award, 1966, Benjamin Harrison medal, 1977. Mem.: Oxford Country (Cercle Munster, Luxembourg), Hamilton City, Psi Chi, Omicron Delta Kappa, Phi Eta Sigma, Phi Kappa Phi, Beta Theta Pi, Phi Beta Kappa. Presbyterian. Home: Oxford, Ohio. Died May 2, 2014.

**DOLLARD, ELIZABETH K.,** lawyer; b. Bklyn., Mar. 16, 1913; d. Hans C. and Lydia (Warner) Klintrup; m. Charles Dollard, Oct. 8, 1949. Student, Conn. Coll., 1932-34; AB, U. Wis., 1936; LL.B., Yale U., 1939. Bar: N.Y. 1941, Vt. 1956. Practiced in, NYC, 1941-56, Bennington, Vt., 1956-71. Mem. exec. com. Bennington County Indsl. Corp. Founder Bennington Mental Health Clinic, 1956, Red Brick Sch., Bennington, Bennington Mus.; mem. exec. com., fellow Inst. Soc. Ethics and Life Scis., Hastings Center; mem. exec. com., v.p. St. Joseph's Coll., Paran Recreations, Yale Law Sch. Fund. Mem. Am. Bar Assn., Vt. Bar Assn. (treas.), N.Y. State Bar Assn., Internat. Bar Assn., Assn. Bar City N.Y., World Assn. Lawyers for World Peace Through Law, ACLU, Common Cause, Children's Def. Fund, Phi Beta Kappa. Died Mar. 1988.

**DOMASH, ALVIN E.,** lawyer; b. Chgo., Mar. 21, 1932; s. Norman and Bessie (Gilman) D.; m. Helen A. Mendelson; children: David, Larry, Mark. LLB with honors, U. Ill., 1955. Asst. gen. atty. N.Y. Cen. R.R., Chgo., 1958-68; ptnr. Lord, Bissell & Brook, Chgo., from 1968. Lectr. trial practice John Marshall Law Sch., Chgo. Contbg. editor U. Ill. Law Forum. Served to lt. (j.g.) JAGC, USN, 1955-57. Mem. Ill. Bar Assn. (chmn. continuing legal edn. sect.), Chgo. Bar Assn., Soc. Trial Lawyers, Nat. Assn. R.R. Trial Counsel, Internat. Soc. Barristers, N.Y. Cen. Hist. Soc., Ill. Cen. Hist. Soc., Cen. Electric Rail Soc., Order of Coif. Avocations: miniature trains, ships, doll houses. Home: Northbrook, Ill. Died Feb. 22, 1991.

**DOMJAN, JOSEPH,** artist; b. Budapest, Hungary, Mar. 15, 1907; s. Paul and Maria (Lika) D.; m. Evelyn A. Domjan, Mar. 13, 1944; children— Alma Domjan Melbourne, Michael P., Daniel G. BA, Hungarian Royal Acad. Fine Arts, 1940, MA, 1942. Founder Domjan Mus., Sarospatek, Hungary, 1977. Exhibited in over 550 one-man shows including Ernst Mus., Budapest, 1955, Mus. Art and History, Geneva, 1975, Cin. Art Mus., 1958, 74, N.J. State Mus., Trenton, 1966, 73, Dallas Pub. Libr., 1964, 77, Mueso della Bellas Artes, Mexico City, 1966, Cuyuga Mus., Auburn, N.Y., 1975, Tate GAllery, London, 2005; represented in numerous permanent collections including Met. Mus., Victoria and Albert Mus., Tate Gallery, London, Mus. Modern Art, Paris, Albertina Graphische Sammlung, Vienna, Nat. Gallery Fine Arts, Libr. of Congress, Washington, Nat. Mus., Stockholm, Mus. Modern Art, Tokyo; author, illustrator 24 books; author: The Proud Peacock, 1966, The Little Cock, 1966, The Artist and the Legend, 1975, Bellringer, 1975, Wing Beat, 1976, Edge of Paradise, 1979. Rockefeller Found. grantee, 1958; Recipient numerous prizes Soc. Illustrators, numerous prizes Am. Inst. Graphic Arts, numerous prizes Print Club of Albany, numerous prizes Am. Color Print Soc. Mem. Nat. Acad. Design, Soc. Am. Graphic Artists, Soc. Illustrators, Print Council Am., Silvermine Guild, Internat. Platform Assn. Died Nov. 28, 1992.

**DOMROESE, CAROL IRENE,** gifted education specialist; b. St. Louis, Nov. 25, 1933; d. Louis Edward and Margaret Emily (Brauer) Litfin; m. Kenneth Arthur Domroese, Dec. 28, 1957; children: Michael, Mark, Margret. BS in Edn., Concordia Coll., River Forest, Ill., 1955; MA in Edn., Concordia Coll., 1962; cert. of advanced studies, Nat. Coll. of Edn., 1989; MS in Spl. Edn., Rosary Coll, 1990. Cert. elem. tchr., social/emotional disorders, learning disabilities. Tchr. Christ Luth. Sch., Chgo., 1955-61; physical edn. tchr. Walther High Sch., Melrose Park, Ill., 1961-62; elem. tchr. Grace Luth. Sch., River Forest, Ill., 1965-66; learning disabilities diagnostician Ill., 1970-71; learning disabilities resource cons. Oak Park (Ill.) Elem. Sch. Dist. 97, Holmes Sch., 1972-86, gifted tchr., 1986-88, gifted tchr., cons., from 1988. Contbr. articles to profl. jours. Elder Grace Luth. Ch., River Forest, 1989-93, chmn., 1989-93; vol. at local pub. librs., 1975—. Grantee Ill. State Bd. Edn., 1989, curriculum improvement sect., 1992, Coun. for Exceptional children, 1975, planning grant Ill. State Bd. of Edn., 1993, rsch. grant Gender and Math Oak Park Elem. Dist. 97, 1995. Mem. NEA, ASCD, Ill. Edn. Assn., Coun. for Exceptional children (pres. chpt 557 1974-75), Ill. Coun. for Exceptional Children (com. chmn. 1981-84), Assn. for Citizens with Learning Disabilities (officer 1979-83, 85-89), Learning Games Librs. Assn. (dir. 1981—), Ill. Coun. for the Gifted, Nat. Assn. for Gifted Children, Nat. Coun. Tchrs. of Math. Lutheran. Avocations: bicycling, travel, art appreciation, camping, music. Home: Oak Park, Ill. Died Feb. 1997.

**DONDERS, JOSEPH GERARD,** priest; b. Tilburg, N. Brabant, The Netherlands, Mar. 11, 1929; arrived in U.S., 1984; s. Jan P. J. and Riet L. (Panhuijsen) Donders. BA, Gregorian U., Rome, 1958, MA, 1960, PhD, 1962. Ordained priest Roman Cath. Ch., 1957. Lectr. Tilburg U., Holland, 1962-68; vis. reader Nairobi (Kenya) U., 1968-74, prof., chmn. dept. philosophy and religious studies, 1974-84; exec. dir. Africa Faith and Justice Network, Washington, 1984-87; prof. Mission and Cross-cultural Studies Washington Theol. Union, Washington, 1987, prof. emeritus, from 2003. Author: Jesus the Stranger, 1971 (Nat. Religious Book award, 1979), Non Bourgeois Theology, 1986, Praying and Preaching the Sunday Gospel, 1990 (Cath. Book Club selection, 1991), numerous others. Mem.: Teilhard de Chardin Assn., Thomistische Vereniging, Philos. Assn. Kenya (founder 1972), U.S. Cath. Mission Assn. (bd. dirs. from 1990). Roman Catholic. Avocations: writing, lecture tours, travel. Died Mar. 7, 2013.

**DONEA, JEAN MICHEL,** engineering educator; b. Clermont-sur-Berwinne, Belgium, June 9, 1937; s. Julia Meurens; m. Marie Paule Forthomme, Apr. 21, 1965. Civil engr., U. Liege, 1961, doctorate in applied scis., 1973. Asst. U. Liege, Belgium, 1961-65, prof., 1965-76 and from 96; rsch. officer European Commn., Ispra, Italy, 1976-89, prin. rsch. officer, 1989-96, head of applied mechanics divsn. Organizer postgrad. courses, Ispra, 1976-85; vis. prof. Politechico Milan, 1986-89; divsn. coord. SMIRT Confs., 1975. Editor 2 books; mem. editl. bd. Computer Methods in Applied Mechanics and Engring., Engring. Computations, Nuclear Engring. and Design, Internat. Jour. for Numerical Methods in Fluids, Jour. European des Eliments Finis, Computers & Structures, Internat. Jour. for Numerical Methods in Engring. Lt. Belgium Army, 1963-64. Mem. Internat. Assn. for Computational Mechanics. Home: Liège, Belgium. Died June 19, 2004.

**DONNELLY, ROBERT WILLIAM,** bishop emeritus; b. Toledo, Ohio, Mar. 22, 1931; Attended, St. Meinard Sem. Coll., Ind., Mt. St. Mary's West Sem., Norwood, Ohio. Ordained priest Diocese of Toledo, Ohio, 1957; ordained bishop, 1984; aux. bishop Diocese of Toledo, Ohio, 1984—2006, aux. bishop emeritus Ohio, 2006—14. Roman Catholic. Died July 21, 2014.

**DONNER, WILLIAM TROUTMAN,** psychiatrist; b. Sharon, Pa., Jan. 8, 1921; s. Raymond H. and Edna (Troutman) D.; m. Alice Easby Wilkinson, Apr. 12, 1946; children: William W., Marda Elisa, Mary Alice, Margot Ramona. Student, U. Pa., 1939-42, MD, 1945. Intern Allegheny Gen. Hosp., Pitts., 1945-46; resident Friends Hosp., Phila., 1948-50, Hosp. of U. Pa., 1950-51; practice medicine specializing in psychiatry Abington, Pa., 1951-95. Psychiatrist Neuropsychiat. Assocs. of Old York Rd., Abington, 1962-64; dir. mental health clinic Abington Meml. Hosp., 1958-64, interim chmn. dept. psychiatry, 1983-85; instr. U. Pa., 1951-58, assoc. psychiatry, 1958-78; clin. asst. prof. Hahnemann Med. Coll., 1978-96; acting chmn. Dept. Psychiatry, Abington (Pa.) Meml. Hosp., 1988-95, chmn. dept. Psychiatry Abington (Pa.) Meml. Hosp., 1994-95, emeritus chair, 1995. Contbr. articles to tech. jours. Pres. bd. dirs. Family Svc. Montgomery County, 1966-67. Served with AUS, 1946-48. Mem. Am. Geriatric Soc., Am. Psychiat. Assn., Am. Assn. Geriatric Psychiatry, Pa. State Med. Soc., Montgomery County Med. Soc. Home: Jenkintown, Pa. Deceased.

**DONOHOE, JAMES ALOYSIUS, III,** real estate developer; b. Washington, Oct. 6, 1945; s. James Aloysius Jr. and Virginia (Barry) D.; m. Mary Jo Grimm, Dec. 26, 1970; children: James A. IV, Maurian C. BS in Real Estate, American U., 1969. Asst. estimator The Donohoe Companies Inc., Washington, 1968-70, supt. constrn. divsn., 1970-72, project mgr. constrn. divsn., 1972-76, dir. real estate devel. divsn., 1976-81, pres. real estate devel. divsn., 1981-88, pres. CEO, 1988—2013; pres., CEO Fed. Ctr. Planning Corp., Washington, 1988—2013. Mem. bd. regents Cath. U., Washington, DCBA Jubilee Housing, Washington, Washington Hosp. Ctr. Sgt. D.C. NG, 1975. Mem. Washington Bd. Trade, Washington Bd. Realtors, D.C. Builders, Congl. Country Club, City Club. Republican. Roman Catholic. Avocations: boating, racquet ball, tennis. Died Nov. 4, 2013.

**DONOHUE, CARROLL JOHN,** lawyer; b. St. Louis, June 24, 1917; s. Thomas M. and Florence (Klefisch) D.; m. Juanita Maire, Jan. 4, 1943 (div. July 1973); children: Patricia Carol, Christine Ann Donohue Smith, Deborah Lee Donohue Wilucki; m. Barbara Lounsbury, Dec., 1978. AB, Washington U., St. Louis, 1939, LLB/JD magna cum laude, 1939. Bar: Mo. 1939. Ptnr. Husch, Eppenberger, Donohue, Cornfeld & Jenkins, St. Louis, from 1949. Contbr. articles to profl. jours. Campaign chmn. ARC, St. Louis County, 1950; mem. ad. com. Child Welfare, St. Louis, 1952-55; mem. exec. com. Slum Clearance, 1949, bond issues coms., 1995; mem. bond issue com. St. Louis County Bond Issue, screening and supervisory coms., 1955-61, county citizen's com. for better law enforcement, 1953-56, chmn. com. on immigration policy, 1954-56; mayor City of Olivette, Mo., 1953-56; chmn. St. Louis County Bd. Election Commrs., 1960-65; chmn. com. Non-Partisan Ct. Plan; vice chmn. bd. Regional Commerce and Growth Assn. (lifetime recognition award 1996); pres. St. Louis C.C. Found.; bd. dirs. Downtown St. Louis, Inc. (leadership award 1996), Civil Entrepreneurs Orgn., Caring Found., Gateway Mayors Emeritus Inc., Anti-Drug Abuse Edn. Fund, P.T. Boat. Comdr. USN, WWII. Decorated Bronze Star medal, Navy and Marine Corps medal; recipient Disting. Alumni award Washington U., 1991, Good Guys award NOW, 1995. Mem. ABA, Mo. Bar Assn. (past bd. govs., chmn. ann. meeting, editor jour. 1940-41), St. Louis Bar Assn. (past pres., v.p., treas., Disting. Lawyer award 1992), Order of Coif, Mo. Athletic Club, Univ. Club, Omicron Delta Kappa, Sigma Phi Epsilon, Delta Theta Phi. Died Oct. 12, 2002.

**DOOLITTLE, WARREN T.,** retired federal official; b. Webster City, Iowa, July 24, 1921; s. Edward and Rhoda Leone (McGuire) D.; m. Jane Anne Beddow, Dec. 29, 1942; children: Linda Jane, Randolph James, Steven Eric. BS in Forestry, Iowa State U., 1946; MS in Forestry, Duke U., 1950; PhD in Forestery, Yale U., 1955. Enlisted USAF, 1943, advanced through grades to lt. col., 1969, navigator Europe, 1943-45, South Korea, 1951-52; rsch. scientist USDA Forest Svc., Asheville, NC, 1946-57, Washington, 1957-59, from asst. dir. to dir. Upper Darby, Pa., 1959-74, assoc. dep. chief Washington, 1974-80, ret., 1980. Contbr. articles to profl. jours. Moderator Congrl. Ch., Asheville, N.C., 1956-57. Lt. col. USAF, 1943-69. Decorated DFC; recipient Disting. Alumni award Yale U., 2005, Dude U., 1999 Fellow Soc. Am. Foresters (pres. 1986, John Beale Meml. award 1983); mem. Am. Forests (B.E. Fernow award 1993), Internat. Soc. Tropical Foresters (pres. 1984-01), Res. Officers Assn. Republican. Avocations: golf, skiing. Home: Asheville, NC. Died Mar. 20, 2013.

**DORNETTE, RALPH MEREDITH,** religious organization administrator, educator, minister; b. Cin., Aug. 31, 1927; s. Paul A. and Lillian (Bauer) D.; m. Betty Jean Pierce, May 11, 1948; 1 child, Cynthia Anne Dornette Orndorff. AB, Cin. Bible Coll. (now Cin. Christian U.), 1948; DD (hon.), Pacific Christian Coll. (now New Hope Internat. U.), Fullerton, Calif., 1994, D.D., 1974. Ordained to ministry Christian Ch., 1947. Min. Indian Creek Christian Ch., Cynthiana, Ky., 1946-51; assoc. prof. Cin. Bible Coll. (now Cin. Christian U.), 1948—51; sr. min. First Christian Ch., Muskogee, Okla., 1951-57; founding min. Bellaire Christian Ch., Tulsa, 1957-59; exec. dir. So. Calif. Evangelistic Assn., Torrance, Calif., 1959-62, 68-77; sr. min. Eastside Christian Ch., Fullerton, Calif., 1962-68; dir. devel., prof. ministries Cin. Bible Coll. & Sem., 1977-79; exec. dir. Ch. Devel. Fund, Inc., Fullerton, 1968-77, CEO, 1979—97; sr. preaching min. 1st Christian Ch., Downey, Calif., 1971, 91, Lahabra, 1982—87; preaching min. Hemet Valley Christian Ch., Calif., 1992-98; ret., 1998. Pres. So. Calif. Christian Mins. Assn., Fullerton, 1975. Author: Bible Answers to Popular Questions, 1954, Walking With Our Wonderful Lord, 1955, Bible Answers to Popular Questions II, 1964. Pres. Homeowners Assn., Anaheim, Calif., 1980-81. Named Churchman of Yr. Pacific Christian Coll., Fullerton, 1973; recipient Disting. Alumni award Cin. Bible Coll. and Seminary, 1994. Mem. N.Am. Christian Conv. (conv. com. Cin. chpt. 1963, chair nat. registration 1963, v.p. 1972, exec. com. 1963, 70-72, 80-82). Died 2007.

**DORSEY, RHODA MARY,** retired academic administrator; b. Boston, Sept. 9, 1927; d. Thomas Francis and Hedwig (Hoge) D. BA magna cum laude, Smith Coll., 1949, LLD, 1979; BA, Cambridge U., Eng., 1951, MA, 1954; PhD, U. Minn., 1956; LLD, Nazareth Coll. Rochester, 1970, Goucher Coll., 1994; DHL (hon.), Mount St. Mary's Coll., 1976, Mount Vernon Coll., 1979, Coll. St. Catherine, 1983, Johns Hopkins U., 1986, Towson State U., 1987, Coll. Notre Dame of Md., 1995, Coll. of Notre Dame Md., 1995. Mem. faculty Goucher Coll., Balt., 1954-94, prof. history, 1965-68, dean, v.p., 1968-73, acting pres., 1973-74, pres. Balt., 1974-94, pres. emeritus, 1994—2014. Lectr. history Loyola Coll., Balt., 1958-62, Johns Hopkins U., Balt., 1960-61; bd. trustee Roland Park County Sch. Bd. dirs. Friends of Cambridge U., sec., 1989-93; bd. dirs. Gen. German Aged Peoples Home, Balt., Greater Balt. Med. Ctr., Md. Humanities Coun., Baltimore County Landmarks Preservation Commn.; bd. dirs., chair Hist. Hampton, Inc.; trustee Loyola, Notre Dame Libr., Balt., Roland Park Country Sch.; chair Governor's Commn. Svc. Named Outstanding Woman Mgr. of 1984 U. Balt. Women's Program in Mgmt. and WMAR-TV, Woman of Yr. Balt. County Commn. for Women, 1993; recipient Outstanding Achievement award U. Minn. Alumni Assn., 1984, Andrew White medal Loyola Coll., Balt., 1985; named in peer survey as one of The 100 Most Effective Coll. and Univ. Pres. in U.S., Chronicle of Higher Edn., 1986. Mem. Internat. Women's forum, Smith Club, Hamilton St. Club (Balt.), Cosmopolitan Club (N.Y.C.). Home: Cockeysville, Md. Died May 10, 2014.

**DOUGHERTY, JOHN CHRYSOSTOM, III,** retired lawyer; b. Beeville, Tex., May 3, 1915; s. John Chrysostom and Mary V. (Henderson) D.; m. Mary Ireland Graves, Apr. 18, 1942 (dec. July 1977); children: Molly Ireland, John Chrysostom IV; m. Bea Ann Smith, June 1978 (div. 1981); m. Sarah B. Randle, 1981 (dec. June 1997). BA, U. Tex., 1937; LLB, Harvard U., 1940; diploma, Inter-Am. Acad. Internat. and Comparative Law, Havana, Cuba, 1948. Bar: Tex. 1940. Atty. Hewit & Dougherty, Beeville, 1940-41; ptnr. Graves

& Dougherty, Austin, Tex., 1946-50, Graves, Dougherty & Greenhill, Austin, 1950-57, Graves, Dougherty & Gee, Austin, 1957-60, Graves, Dougherty, Gee & Hearon, Austin, 1961-66, Graves, Dougherty, Gee, Hearon, Moody & Garwood, Austin, 1966-73, Graves, Dougherty, Hearon, Moody & Garwood, Austin, 1973-79, Graves, Dougherty, Hearon & Moody, Austin, 1979-93, sr. counsel, 1993—97; ret., 1997. Spl. asst. atty. gen., 1949-50; Hon. French Consul, Austin, 1971-86; lectr. on tax, estate planning, probate code, cmty. property problems; mem. Tex. Submerged Lands Adv. Com., 1963-72, Tex. Bus. and Commerce Code Adv. Com., 1964-66, Gov.'s Com. on Marine Resources, 1970-71, Gov.'s Planning Com. on Colorado River Basin Water Quality Mgmt. Study, 1972-73, Tex. Legis. Property Tax Com., 1973-75; adv. com. Mex. Ctr. Inst. of Latin-Am. Studies U. Tex., 1997—1999. Co-editor: Texas Appellate Practice, 1964, 2d edit., 1977; contbr. Bowe, Estate Planning and Taxation, 1957, 65; Texas Lawyers Practice Guide, 1967, 71, How to Live and Die with Texas Probate, 1968, 7th edit., 1995, Texas Estate Administration, 1975, 78; mem. bd. editors: Appellate Procedure in Tex., 1964, 2d edit., 1982; contbr. articles to profl. jours. Bd. dirs. Tex. Beta Students Aid Fund, 1949-84, Grenville Clark Fund at Dartmouth Coll., 1976-90, Umlauf Sculpture Garden, Inc., 1990-91, New Life Inst., 1993-2001; past bd. dirs. Advanced Religious Study Found., Holy Cross Hosp., Sea Arama, Inc., Nat. Pollution Control Found., Austin Nat. Bank; trustee St. Stephen's Episcopal Sch., Austin, 1969-83, Tex. Equal Access to Justice Found., 1986-90, U. Tex. Law Sch. Found., 1974-2002; mem. adv. com. Legal Assts. Tng. Inst., U. Tex., 1990-98; mem. vis. com. Harvard Law Sch., 1983-87. Capt. C.I.C., AUS, 1941-44, JAGC, 1944-46, maj. USAR. Decorated Medaille Française, France, Medaille d'honneur en Argent des Affairs Etrangeres, France, chevalier l'Ordre Nat. du Merite; recipient Wm. Reece Smith Spl. Svcs. to Pro Bono award Nat. Assn. of Pro Bono Coords., 2000. Fellow: Am. Bar Found., Tex. Bar Found., Am. Coll. Trust and Estate Counsel, Am. Coll. Tax Counsel; mem.: ABA (ho. of dels. 1982-88, standing com. on lawyers pub. responsibility 1983-85, spl. com. on delivery legal svcs. 1987-91, com. legal problems of the elderly 1997-2000, Sr. Lawyers divsn. Pro Bono Lawyer of 1999), Am. Arbitration Assn. (nat. panel arbitrators 1958-90), Travis County Bar Assn. (bd. dirs. 1974-76, pres. 1976-77), Internat. Acad. Estate and Trust Law (exec. coun. 1988-90), State Bar Tex. (chmn. sect. taxation 1965-66, pres. 1979-80, com. legal svcs. to the poor 1986-94), Am. Judicature Soc. (bd. dirs. 1985-87), Am. Law Inst. (adv. com. project law governing lawyers 1990-97), Tex. Supreme Ct. Hist. Soc. (trustee 1997—2012, chmn. 1999-2002), Philos. Soc. Tex. (pres. 1989, bd. dirs. 1989—2004), Harvard Law Sch. Assn. (com. on pub. svc. law 1990-95, chmn. 1990-95, coun. 1991-95, exec. com. 1992-95), Tex. Appleseed, Inc. (bd. dirs. 1996-2010), The Austin Project (bd. dirs. 1999-2012), Rotary. Presbyterian. Died Feb. 20, 2014.

**DOUGLAS, DAME MARY TEW,** anthropology and humanities educator; b. San Remo, Italy, Mar. 25, 1921; came to U.S., 1977; m. James Douglas, 1951; children: Janet, James, Philip. BA, U. Oxford, Eng., 1943, MA, 1947, BSc, 1948, PhD, 1951, Doctorate (hon.); doctorate (hon.), U. Uppsala, U. Notre Dame, Jewish Theol. Sem., U. East Anglia, U. Essex, U. Warwick, U. Pa., U. Surrey, Sigilo Doro U. Palermo, U. Brunel, U. London. Rsch. fellow Internat. African Inst. for Fieldwork, Belgian Congo, 1949-50, 53, 87; lectr. anthropology Univ. Coll., London, 1951-62, prof. social anthropology, 1971—77; dir. rsch. on culture Russell Sage Found., NYC, 1977-81; Avalon Found. prof. in humanities Northwestern U., Evanston, Ill., 1981-85; vis. prof. depts. religion and anthropology Princeton U., 1985-88. Author: Lele of the Kasai, 1963, Purity and Danger, 1966, Natural Symbols, 1970, Implicit Meanings, 1975, The World of Goods, 1979, Risk and Culture, 1982; In the Active Voice, 1982, How Institutions Think, 1986, Risk Acceptability, 1987, Risk and Blame, 1992, In the Wilderness, 1993, Thought Styles, 1996, Missing Persons, 1998, Leviticus as Literature, 1999, Jacob's Tears, 2004; editor: Essays in the Sociology of Perception, 1982. Hon. fellow U. Coll. London, 1994; decorated Comdr. British Empire, 1992. Fellow Royal Swedish Acad.; mem. AAAS, Am. Acad. Arts and Scis., Academia Europaea, Brit. Acad. Died May 16, 2007.

**DOWNING, WILLIAM H.,** life insurance agency executive; b. Kenosha, Wis., Nov. 13, 1919; s. Virgil Leonard and Charlotte Olivia Downing; m. Lois Elizabeth Downing, June 9, 1950 (dec. May 1997); children: Scott William, Mark Bradley. Student, Marquette U., 1937-38; BA, U. Ky., 1942; LLB, Mpls. Coll. Law, 1952. Owner, mgr. Bill Downing, advt., Bakersfield, Calif., 1951-57, Bill Downing & Assocs., Bakersfield, from 1957. Died Dec. 6, 2002.

**DOWNS, DIARMUID,** engineer; b. Kilburn, Middlesex, Eng., Apr. 23, 1922; s. John and Ellen (McMahon) D.; m. Mary Carmel Chillman, Dec. 29, 1951; children: Ann, Lucy, Clare, Martin. BS, London U., 1942; DSc, City U., 1978, Cranfield Inst. Tech., 1981. Engr. Ricardo Cons. Engrs., Shoreham-by-Sea, 1942—84, dir., 1957—67, mng. dir., 1967-84, chmn., 1976-87; dir. Gabriel Communications, London, 1986-93. Coun. chmn. U. Surrey, Guildford, Eng., 1985-91, pro-chancellor 1992-94; mem. Adv. Coun. for Applied R & D, London, 1976-80, Sci. Engring. Rsch. Coun., London, 1981-85, Design Coun., London, 1981-89, Brit. Coun., London, 1987-93. Fellow Instn. Mech. Engring. (pres. 1978-79), Soc. Automotive Engrs. (dir. 1983-86), Royal Soc., Royal Acad. Engineers, Hove Club. Roman Catholic. Home: Hove, England. Died Feb. 12, 2014.

**DOWNS, JAMES FRANCIS,** anthropologist, journalist, educator; b. Pasadena, Calif., Dec. 20, 1926; s. James Griffith and Martha (Switzer) D.; m. Gay Sterling, 1961 (div. 1970); children: Christian James, Martha Joy Wedgeworth, Mark C.; m. Shizuko Watabe, Nov. 25, 1992; stepchildren: Maki Watabe, Ai Watabe. BA, U. Calif., Berkeley, 1958, MA, 1960, PhD, 1961. Asst. prof. U. Rochester, N.Y., 1961-63; assoc. prof. Calif. State U., LA, 1962-63, U. Ariz., Tucson, 1963-69; prof. U. Hawaii, Hilo, 1969-80; sr. instructional technologist, program mgr. Univ. Rsch. Corp., Md., 1986-90; dir. Thunderbird Japan Ctr. Thunderbird Am. Grad. Sch. Internat. Mgmt., Ariz., 1992-99. Chmn. Ctr. for Cross-Cultural Edn. Tng. Rsch., U. Hawaii, 1970-74; co-prin. investigator Tibetan Rsch., NSF, 1966-68; prin. investigator Navajo Rsch., NIMH, 1961-62; cons. cross-cultural bus. orgns., 1982—; vis. scholar Tokyo U. Fgn. Studies, 1986-87. Author: Two Worlds of the Washo, 1963, The Navajo, 1974, Human Variation, 1965, Human Nature, 1967, Tibetan Pilgrimage, 1987. Warrant officer USN/USNR, 1944-47, 50-51, 74-75, 78-81. Decorated Navy Commendation medal; named Ky. Col. Mem. Am. Anthropol. Assn. (bd. dirs. 1978), Soc. Internat. Cultural Tng. and Rsch. (bd. dirs. 1977), Nat. Assn. for Practice Anthropology (pres. 1978), Nat. Turfwriters Assn. (assoc.), Fgn. Corrs. Club. Japan. Democrat. Buddhist. Avocation: horseback riding. Died June 10, 1999.

**DOWNS, JON FRANKLIN,** drama educator, director, writer; b. Bartow, Fla., Sept. 15, 1938; s. Clarence Curtis and Frankie (Morgan) D. Student, Ga. State Coll., 1956-58; BFA, U. Ga., 1960, MFA, 1969. Drama dir. Ga. Perimeter Coll. (formerly DeKalb Coll.), Clarkston, 1969-99. Dir., author The Beastly Purple Forest (marionettes) U. Ga., 1968, Dracula: A Horrible Musical, DeKalb Coll., 1971; dir. A Streetcar Named Desire, DeKalb, 1974, Brigadoon, DeKalb, 1981, West Side Story, 1983, Amadeus, 1984, Noises Off, 1986, The Three Musketeers, 1988, A Midsummer Night's Dream, 1990, A Little Night Music, 1991, Hamlet, 1993, over 200 others; actor Wedding in Japan, N.Y.C., 1960, Dark at the Top of the Stairs, N.Y.C. and on tour, 1961, A Life in the Theatre, DeKalb Coll., 1981, A Funny Thing Happened on the Way to the Forum, 1998, numerous others; designer Sweeney Todd, DeKalb Coll., 1970, Romulus, 1971, Grass Harp, 1972, many others; writer, dir. plays Tokalitta, Gold!, The Vigil; on tour of Ga. summers 1973-76; author: The Illusionist, 1979, Rapunzel, 1997; film reviewer Southernflair mag., 1994-2005, arts editor, 2000-2005. Grantee arts sect. Ga Dept. Planning and Budget, 1973, 74, State Bicentennial Commn., 1975, Nat. Bicentennial Commn., 1975. Mem. Southeastern Theater Conf. (state rep. 1971-73), Ga. Theater Conf. (exec. bd. 1970-73, 79-82). Home: West Columbia, SC. Died Nov. 3, 2013.

**DOYEN, ROSS ORVILLE,** retired state legislator; b. Rice, Kans., Oct. 1, 1926; s. Orville Girard and Millie Elda (Derby) D.; m. Judith Kay Elniff, Oct. 10, 1964; children: Cynthia, Angela. BS, Kans. State U., 1950. Engaged in farming and ranching, Concordia, Kans.; mem. Kans. House of Reps., 1958-68, Kans. State Senate, 1969—92; pres. Nat. Conf. State Legislatures, 1981-82. Bd. dirs. Kans. Advocacy and Protective Services Devel. Disabled; dir. 1st Bank and Trust Co., Concordia. Mem. Presdl. Adv. Com. Federalism, 1981; Adv. Commn. Intergovtl. Relations, 1981. Served with USNR, 1944-46. Recipient numerous public service awards. Mem. Council State Govts. Lodges: Rotary. Republican. Methodist. Home: Concordia, Kans. Died July 3, 2014.

**DOYLE, JOSEPH ANTHONY,** retired lawyer; b. NYC, June 13, 1920; s. Joseph A. and Jane (Donahue) D.; m. Eugenie A. Fleri, Aug. 19, 1944; children: Christopher, Stephen, Eugenie, Jane, Richard. BS, Georgetown U., 1941; LLB, Columbia U., 1947. Bar: N.Y. 1948. Assoc. Shearman & Sterling, NYC, 1947-57, ptnr., 1957-79, 81-97; asst. sec. for manpower, reserve affairs & logistics Dept. Navy, US Dept. Def., Washington, 1979-81. Bd. dirs. The Fuji Bank and Trust Co. Bd. dirs. USO of Met. N.Y., 1982-90. Lt. USNR, 1941-45. Decorated Navy Cross, D.F.C. with 3 gold stars, Air medal with 7 gold stars; recipient Disting. Public Service award Sec. of Navy, 1980. Mem. Met. Club (Washington). Democrat. Roman Catholic. Home: New York, NY. Died Apr. 4, 2014.

**DOYLE, PATRICK JOHN,** otolaryngologist, department chairman; b. Moose Jaw, Sask., Can., Nov. 17, 1926; s. William E. and Bertha L. (Fisher) D.; m. Irene Strilchuk, May 21, 1949; children: Sharon, Patrick, Robert, Barbara, Joseph, Kathleen. BSc, U. Alta., 1947, MD, 1949. Diplomate Am. Bd. Otolaryngology (bd. dirs., v.p. 1986-88, pres. 1988-90). Intern U. B.C. Hosp., 1949-50; resident in medicine and pediatrics, 1950-51; resident in otolaryngology U. Oreg. Hosp., 1958-61; asst. prof., then asso. prof. U. Oreg. Med. Sch., 1965-70; mem. faculty U. B.C. Med. Sch., from 1963, prof. otolaryngology, 1972-91, prof. otolaryngology emeritus, from 1992, head dept., 1972-91, program dir. residency tng. program, 1972-91. Head div. otolaryngology St. Paul's Hosp., mem. numerous nat. med. coms. Author numerous articles in field; mem. editorial bds. profl. jours. Fellow Royal Coll. Surgeons Can., Am. Laryngol., Rhinol. and Otol. Soc. (v.p. western sect. 1988, pres. 1994), Am. Laryngol. Soc., Am. Acad. Otolaryngology-Head and Neck Surgery (v.p. 1984, bd. dirs. 1985-87), Am. Otol. Soc.; mem. Can. Soc. Otolaryngology-Head and Neck Surgery (pres. 1987), Pacific Coast Oto-Ophthal. Soc. (pres. 1977), Soc. Univ. Otolaryngologists, U. Oreg. Otolaryngology Alumni Assn. (pres. 1968-70), Am. Otological Soc., Centurion Club, Tinnitus Rsch. Found. Roman Catholic. Home: Vancouver, Canada. Died 2008.

**DRAINVILLE, GERARD,** retired bishop; b. L'Ile-Dupas, Que., Can., May 20, 1930; Ordained priest Roman Catholic Ch., 1953; bishop Diocese of Amos, 1978—2004. Roman Catholic. Died May 11, 2014.

**DRAN, ROBERT JOSEPH,** lawyer; b. Abington, Pa., Apr. 12, 1947; s. Joseph A. and Claire B. (Kowalski) D.; m. Sandra Ann Hyatt, Aug. 16, 1969; children: Arjay, Stacey, Elizabeth. AB, Stanford U., 1969; JD, MBA, Harvard U., 1973. Bar: Calif. 1973, U.S. Dist. Ct. (cen. dist.) Calif. 1973. Assoc. Adams, Duque & Hazeltine, LA, 1973-75; assoc. gen. counsel Envirotech Corp., Menlo Park, Calif., 1975-79; mgr. legal dept. Cooper Labs. Inc., Palo Alto, Calif., 1979-82, assoc. gen. counsel, 1982-85, v.p., 1983-85; v.p., gen. counsel The Cooper Cos., Inc., Palo Alto, 1985-88, v.p., sec., gen. counsel and chief adminstrv. officer, 1988-89; of counsel Pillsbury, Madison & Sutro, San Francisco, San Jose, Calif., from 1990. Commr. Am. Youth Soccer Orgn., Redwood City, Calif., 1982-83; bd. dirs., team mgr. Little League, Babe Ruth League and Colt League Baseball, Redwood City and San Carlos, Calif., 1983—; pres. San Carlos Babe Ruth League, 1989-90, treas., 1991—. Mem. Am. Corp. Counsel Assn. Republican. Roman Catholic. Home: San Carlos, Calif. Died July 5, 1996.

**DRAPER, J(OSIAH) EVERETT,** artist, author, educator; b. East Orange, NJ, Oct. 17, 1915; s. Harold Walcott and Anna Frederika (Petersen) D.; m. Evelyn Ruth Wehlau, Sept. 25, 1943; children: Pamela Ruth Draper Whyte, Richard Everett. Grad. in Advt. Design, Pratt Inst., Bklyn.; student Illustration (Harvey Dunn), Grand Ctrl. Sch. of Art, NYC. Art dir. Prudential Ins. Co., Newark and Jacksonville, N.J., Fla., 1935-72; pres. J.E. Draper AWS, Inc., Ponte Vedra, Fla., 1972. Adj. instr. art and design Newark Sch. Fine and Indsl. Att, 1947-51; instr. water color workshotps internationally, 1972—. Author: Putting People in Your Painting, 1986, People Painting Scrapbook, 1989; artist: paintings in many one man shows, over 400 corp., govt. and privat collections, permanent collections of several museums and univs.; twice seclected for Am. Watercolor Soc. travelling exhbns. Pres. St. Augustine (Fla.) Art Assn., 1973-76. Master sgt. U.S. Army Intelligence, 1941-45. Mem. Am. Watercolor Soc. (Carolyn Stern award 1967), Fla. Watercolor Soc. (past pres.), Salmagundi Club, Ponte Vedra Club, Whiskey Painters of Am. Episcopalian. Avocations: art, photography. Died 2006.

**DRAY, WILLIAM HERBERT,** philosophy educator; b. Montreal, June 23, 1921; s. William John and Florence Edith (Jones) D.; m. Doris Kathleen Best, Sept. 18, 1943; children: Christopher Reid, Jane Elizabeth. BA in History, U. Toronto, 1949; BA in Philosophy, Politics and Econs., Oxford U., 1951, MA, 1955, DPhil, 1956; LLD (hon.), Trent U., 1987. Lectr. U. Toronto, 1953-55, asst. prof., asso. prof., 1956-63, prof., 1963-68, Trent U., 1968-76, chmn. dept. philosophy, 1968-73; prof. philosophy U. Ottawa, Ont., 1976—85, prof. emeritus, from 1986. Author: Laws and Explanation in History, 1957, Philosophy of History, 1964, 2d edit., 1993, Perspectives on History, 1980, On History and Philosophers of History, 1989, History as Re-enactment, 1995; editor: Philosophical Analysis and History, 1966; co-editor: Substance and Form in History, 1981, Philosophie de l'histoire et la Pratique historienne d'aujourd'hui, 1982, The Principles of History, 1999. Served with RCAF, 1941-46, Active Res., 1956-66, wing comdr. ret. Am. Council Learned Socs. fellow, 1960-61; Can. Council fellow, 1971-72, 78-79; Killam research fellow, 1980-81; Nat. Humanities Ctr. fellow, 1983-84; recipient Can. Council Molson prize, 1986, Lifetime Achievement award Collingwood Soc., 2005. Fellow: Royal Soc. Can. Home: Richmond Hill, Canada. Died Aug. 6, 2009.

**DREYFUS, GRACE HAWES,** volunteer; b. Victory, NY, Dec. 26, 1892; d. John Bently and Pearl (Van Hoosen) Hawes; m. Louis G. Dreyfus, Jr., June 14, 1917. Grad., U. N.Y., 1913. Founder Grace Dreyfus Clinic and Orphanage, Teheran, Iran, 1941. Decorated Elmi 1st class Iran. Mem. Channel City Women's Forum (charter mem.), Nat. Inst. Arts and Letters (v.p. Santa Barbara), Affiliates U. Calif. (hon. life dir. Santa Barbara br.), Red Lion and Sun (life mem., Iran), Internat. Platform Assn., Nat. Contract Bridge League, English Speaking Union, Channel City Women's Forum, Little Town Club, Valley Club, Coral Casino Club, Valley Montecito Club (Santa Barbara). Died June 1985.

**DRIJVERS, HENDRIK WILLEM,** Semitic languages/cultures of Near East educator; b. Winschoten, Groningen, Netherlands, Sept. 25, 1934; s. Jan and Sara Hendrika (Poppen) D.; m. Antonia Johanna Schutte, Mar. 23, 1953; children: Jan Willem, Nelleke, Gerhart, Hendrik Jan, Margreet. D in Semitic Langs., U. Groningen, 1965, PhD in Semitic Langs., 1966, DDiv, 1969. Ordained to ministry Dutch Reformed Ch., 1957. Assoc. prof. Semitic langs. U. Groningen, 1970-76, ordinary prof., from 1976, dean faculty of arts, 1981-84. Vis. prof. Inst. for Advanced Studies, Princeton, 1977-78; chmn. sect. arts Dutch Acad. Coun., 1981-87; mem. governing bd. U. Groningen, 1972-74. Author: The Book of the Law of Countries, 1965, Bardaisan of Edessa, 1966, Baal Shamin, Lord of Heaven, 1971, Old Syriac Inscriptions, 1972, The Religion of Palmyra, 1976, Cults and Beliefs at Edessa, 1980, East of Antioch, 1984, History and Religion in Late Antique Syria, 1994, The Finding of the True Cross, 1997, The Old Syriac Insciptions of Edessa, 1999; editor: Religion, Culture and Methodology, 1973, IV Symposium Syriacum, 1987. Mem. Dutch Acad. Avocation: collecting art and studio glass. Home: Groningen, Netherlands. Died Feb. 11, 2002.

**DROBINSKI, GÉRARD,** medical educator, researcher; b. Paris, Sept. 15, 1945; s. Benjamin and Esther Bieder Drobinski; m. Nicole Madeleine Fihman, July 3, 1970; children: Philippe, Agnes. MD, Pitié Salpetriere Med. Sch., Paris, 1971; PhD in Biomechanics, Pierre and Marie Curie U., Paris, 1998. Asst. physician Pitié Salpétriere Univ. Hosp., Paris, 1975, assoc. physician, 1978, dir. catheterization lab. and interventional cardiology, 1984; prof. medicine

Paris Hosp. and Med. Coll., 1999; coord. French Nat. Univs. coordinated tchgs. of interventional cardiology U. Pierre and Marie Curie, Paris, from 2001. Cons. French Ministry of Health, Paris, Paris Hosps. Adminstrn. 2d lt. French Air Force Med. Svc., 1972—73. Fellow: European Cardiol. Soc.; mem.: French Cardiol. Soc. Achievements include patents for ultrasound percussion system. Home: Fontenay Aux Roses, France. Died July 24, 2005.

**DRYBURG, ANN,** secondary school educator; b. Roscoe, Pa., Nov. 8, 1913; d. Walter and Jane V. (Cairns) D. BS in Elem. Edn., BS in Secondary Edn., Waynesburg Coll., 1947. Cert. elem. tchr., secondary history tchr., elem. and secondary religious edn. tchr. Prin., tchr., grades 1-8 Centerville Dist., West Brownsville, Pa.; jr. high sch. math. tchr. Bethlehem-Ctr. Sch. Dist., Fredericktown, Pa. Recipient Am. Nat. Red Cross award, 1942-43, Pres. Harry Truman award, 1948, Am. Legion award, 1983. Mem. NEA, ASCD, Pa. State Edn. Assn., Beth Center Edn. Assn., Centreville Edn. Assn. (teas.), Nat. Coun. and State Coun. Tchrs. Math. Home: Brownsville, Pa. Died Nov. 20, 1997.

**DUBIEF, JEAN,** climatologist; b. Rennes, France, Oct. 28, 1903; s. Henry Georges Adolphe and Berthe (Biver) D.; m. Marguerite Tenthorey, Feb. 19, 1954 (dec. Aug. 1996); 1 child, Yves. Ingenieur, Ecole Nat. Sup. Agronomique, Algeria, 1920; ScD, U. Alger, 1953. Mem. Faculty of Scis., mem. staff Inst. Meteorology and Earth Physics Algeria, 1924-62; chief Obs. Phys. de Globe, Tamanrasset, Algeria, 1931-42; adj. physician Inst. Earth Physics, Paris, 1962-68; rschr. climatology Cameroon, 1965-70; chmn., CEO Tenthorey, 1969-83. Author: Essai sur L'Hydrologie Superficielle du Sahara, 1953, Le Climat du Sahara, Vol. 1, 1959, Vol. 2, 1963, Daie Sahara, eine Klima-Wuste, 1971, L'Ajjer. Sahara central, 1999; contbr. articles to profl. jours. Served with French Army, 1939-40, 42-54. Decorated chevalier Legion of Honor, chevalier du Merite Saharien, chevalier du Merite Agricole, officer Palmes Academiques. Mem. Union Geodesic et Geophysique Internat., Geographie Soc. Paris, Assn. French Geographers, La Rahla Club, Explorers Club (N.Y.C.). Roman Catholic. Died 2003.

**DUBIN, CHARLES LEONARD,** lawyer; s. Harry and Ethel D.; m. Anne Ruth, 1951. BA, U. Toronto, Ont., 1941; LL.B., Osgoode Hall Law Sch., 1944. Bar: Ont. 1944, appointed Queen's Counsel 1952. Practiced in, Toronto, 1945-73; judge Ont. Ct. Appeals, Toronto, 1973—96, chief justice, 1990-96; counsel Torys LLP (formerly Tory Tory Des Lauriers & Binnington Barristers), Toronto, 1996—2008; dir. Can. Steamship Lines, 2003—05. Royal Commr. to inquire into air safety in Can., 1979; Head of Inquiry into the practices and procedures of Hosp.for Sick Children, 1983; Royal Commr. to inquire into use of drugs and banned practices in athletics, 1988; apptd. to Bd. of Canadian Centre for Ethics in Sport, 2000-03, hon. counsel, 2003; lectr. Osgoode Hall Law Sch., 1945-48. Recipient Order of Can., 1997. Mem. York Club, Toronto Hunt Club, Toronto Club. Home: Toronto, Canada. Died Oct. 27, 2008.

**DUBININ, YURIY VLADIMIROVICH,** retired ambassador; b. Nalchik, USSR, Oct. 7, 1930; m. Liana Dubinin; children: Natalia, Irina Tatyana. Grad., Moscow State Inst. Internat. Relations, 1954, PhD in History, 1978. Mem. Diplomatc Service, from 1955, USSR Ministry of Fgn. Affairs, 1959-63, 68-78; 1st sec., embassy councellor USSR Embassy in France, 1963-68; ambassador to Spain USSR, 1978-87, permanent rep. to UN, 1987—90, ambassador to USA Washington, NYC, 1986—90, amb. to France Paris, 1990—91; dep. prime min. Russian Fedn., 1994—96. Author: USSR-France: Experience of Cooperation, 1978; contbr., translator articles in field. Recipient several govt. awards. Died Dec. 20, 2013.

**DUBOIS, JACQUES-EMILE,** chemistry and information science educator, researcher; b. Lille, France, Apr. 13, 1920; s. Paul and Marie Emilienne (Chevrier) D.; m. Bernice Claire Shaaker, May 24, 1952; children: Rhoda Nicole, Alain. PhD in Phys. Sci., U. Grenoble, 1947; Dr. hon. causa, U. Regensburg. Dir. chem. inst., dean sci. faculty Univ. Saar, 1949-57; prof. chem. informatics U. Paris VII, 1957—89; adv. sci., higher edn. Minister of Edn., Paris, 1962-63, dep. dir. higher edn., 1963-65; dir. R&D Ministry Def., Paris, 1965-77; founder, pres. Ardic, Paris, from 1971; co-dir. inst. Curie, Paris, 1977-80; sci. dir. Gen. Electric Co., Paris, 1979-83. Mem. liberation com. ISERE, 1944—45; v.p. Codata Internat., Paris, 1980—88, pres., 1994—98; v.p. then pres. Codata France, from 2001; v.p. Ctr. for Sci. Def. Studies, U. Marne-la-Vallée, from 1994, chmn. Iupac Interdiv. Com. on Machine Documentation, 1969—77. Co-editor: (4 books) Data and Knowledge in a Changing World, 1996; bd. consulting editors Tetrahedron, 1983-90; author numerous chpts. in books and encys.; inventor DARC Topological Sys. for on-line info. sys. and for computer assisted design in chemistry; patentee in field; contbr. numerous articles to profl. jours. Decorated comdr. Legion of Honor, comdr. Acad. Palms, comdr. Order of Merit (France), comdr. Order of Merit (Germany), Order of Merit Ivory Coast, Order of Merit Senegal; recipient Jecker prize, Berthelot medal French Acad. Sci., 1965, Stas medal Belgian Chem. Soc., 1950, Grand Prix de la Technique City of Paris, 1975, Resistance medal French Govt., 1946, CAOC medal, 1991; Fulbright Smith-Mund grantee U. Columbia, 1956; Ramsey fellow, 1949; recorded by Chem. Heritage Found., 2001. Mem. French Phys. Chmistry Soc. (pres. 1974-76), French Chem. Soc. (coun. 1965-68), Faraday Soc., Am. Chem. Soc. (Skolnik award 1992). Home: Paris, France. Died Apr. 2, 2005.

**DUBOSE, DOROTHY,** educator, publishing consultant; b. Nicholls, Ga., Sept. 10, 1931; d. Charlie Norman and Lelia Mae (Solomon) DuB. BA in English and Edn. summa cum laude, Berry Coll., 1952; MA, Tchrs. Coll. Columbia U., 1969; postgrad., Vanderbilt U., Emory U. Editorial dir., product devel. Macmillian Pub. Co., 1970-86; dir. Scholars Pub., 1990—94; English instr. Clayton State Coll., Morrow, Ga., 1987-96; on-site degree program coord., instr. The Union Inst., Atlanta, 1990-93; coord. Ctr. for Acad. Devel., Nat-Louis U., 1990—2004; editor Learning Power, 1996—2004; online instr. Nat. Louis U., 2004—09. Lang. arts cons. Appleton Century Pub. Co. Author: Gulliver's Travels Booknotes, What Is It?; editor Theshold Early Learning Libr., Learning Abilities, Scholastic Elem. Tchr., N.J. Edn. Assn. Rev., The Tenn. Tchr. Vol. tutor N.Y.C. Literacy Vols., 1986, mem. publs. planning com. New Readers Press, 1986, leader Literacy Vols. tutor tng. workshops, 1987-91, 2009-; pres. Macmillan Women's Group, 1974-75, 76-77, Women's Nat. Book Assn. (NYC) (bd. dirs. 1980-86); docent Jimmy Carter Presdl. Libr., 2005-, vol., Global Village Project, 2012. Named Outstanding Vol. Clayton County, United Way, 1991. Avocations: gardening, languages. Home: Atlanta, Ga. Died Jan. 2010.

**DUDLEY, CHRISTOPHER (CHARLES CHRISTOPHER DUDLEY),** federal agency administrator; b. 1966; married. BS in Mktg. and Bus. Mgmt., Clemson U., 1988. Dep. US marshal (northern dist.) Ga. US Marshals Svc., US Dept. Justice, Atlanta, 1990—98, supervisory dep. US marshal Washington, 1998, sr. inspector then chief Internat. Investigations Br., 1999—2004, chief Domestic Investigations Br., 2004—06, chief of staff to dir., 2006, assoc. dir. adminstrn., dep. dir., 2009—12. Mem.: Internat. Liaison Officer's Assn. (former chair), Nat. Sheriffs' Assn., Internat. Assn. of Chiefs of Police, Fed. Law Enforcement Officers Assn. Died Nov. 23, 2012.

**DUDLEY, THORA LOUISE,** rehabilitation services professional; b. Ansley, Ala., June 12, 1927; d. Willie Gussie and Henry Dudley. BA, Talladega Coll., 1958; MA in Rehab. Tchg., Hunter Coll., 1959. Cert. Am. Braille Assn. Rehab. tchr. N.Y. Assn. for Blind, NYC, 1959—92; ret. Task force hiv/aids N.Y. Assn. for Blind, NYC, 1992. Singer: (record) My Heavenly Father Watches Over Me. Mem. Lighthouse Choral Group, NYC, 1965—89; performer Tuskegee U., Ala.; pres. chancel choir Butler Meml. United Meth. Ch., Bronx, NY, 1981, lay spkr., 2003, pres. united meth. women, 1986. Recipient Resident of Honor Ho., Talledega Coll., 1954—58, 1st pl., Legendary Apollo Theater, 1970; scholar, Vocat. Rehab. Group, 1958. Mem.: NAACP (life), Little Theater Group (assoc. Key Award 1958), Alpha Kappa Alpha (parliamentarian 1980, charter mem. Eta Omega Omega chpt.). Methodist. Achievements include first black, blind woman to graduate college and graduate school in the state of Alabama; One of the first blind members of Alpha Kappa Alpa. Avocations: singing, reading. Died May 26, 2008.

**DUE, OLE,** judge, educator; b. Korsör, Sealand, Denmark, Feb. 10, 1931; s. Henrik Peter and Jenny Christine (Jensen) D.; m. Alice Maud Halkier Nielsen; children: Poul Henrik, Pernille, Peter, Torben. LLB, Copenhagen U., 1955; JD (hon.), Stockholm U., 1991. Civil servant Ministry of Justice, Copenhagen, 1955, head divsn., 1970, head dept., 1975, appeal ct. judge a.i., 1978; judge Ct. of Justice of the European Communities, Luxembourg, 1979, pres., 1988-94; hon. prof. Copenhagen U., from 1994. Mem. Danish del. Hague Conf. on Pvt. Internat. Law, Netherlands, 1964-76. Contbr. articles to profl. jours., chapters to books. Decorated grand cross Order of Dannebrog (Denmark), Ordre de la Couronne (Belgium), Ordre de la Couronne de Chene (Luxembourg); named hon. bencher Gray's Inn, London, 1988, King's Inns, Dublin, 1989. Mem.: Danish Inst. Internat. Affairs (chmn. bd. dirs. 1995—2002). Home: Espergärde, Denmark. Died Jan. 2005.

**DUEKER, MIKE (MICHAEL J. DUEKER),** economist, researcher; s. Kenneth and Donna Dueker; m. Alicia Dueker; 1 child, Markus. BS in Mathematics, U. Oreg., 1986; MS in Economics, Northwestern U., 1987; PhD in Economics, U. Wash., Seattle, 1991. Asst. v.p., rsch. economist Fed. Res. Bank St. Louis, 1991—2008; chief economist Russell Investments, 2008—14. Achievements include development of dynamic time-series models of qualitative variables. Died Jan. 29, 2014.

**DUFRESNE, ARMAND ALPHEE, JR.,** state justice; b. Auburn, Maine, Jan. 17, 1909; s. Armand and Emelina (Couture) D.; m. Colette M. Thibault, Oct. 5, 1939; children: Louise M., Pauline J., Carmen D. AB, U. Montreal, 1930; LL.B., Boston Coll., 1935; LL.D. (hon.), U. Maine-Orono, 1973. Bar: Maine 1936. Since practiced in Lewiston; corp. counsel Lewiston, 1937-38; asst. county atty. Androscoggin County, 1939-40; county atty., 1941-44; judge of probate, 1945-56; justice Superior Ct. Maine, 1956-65, Supreme Jud. Ct. Maine, 1965-70, chief justice, 1970-77, active ret. justice, 1977-85. Mem. Jud. Council Maine, 1954-65, 70-77 Named Laureatus Alumnus, Association des Anciens, Séminaire de Sherbrooke (Que., Can.), 1975 Mem. Am., Maine, Androscoggin County bar assns. Home: Lewiston, Maine. Died Apr. 19, 1994.

**DUKE, ANTHONY DREXEL (TONY DUKE),** retired sociologist, educator, philanthropist; b. NYC, July 28, 1918; s. Angier Buchanan and Cordelia (Biddle) D.; children by previous marriage: Anthony D. Jr., Nicholas R., Cordelia Duke Jung, Josephine Duke Brown, December Duke McSherry, John O., Douglas D.; m. Maria Luly de Lourdes Alcebo, Sept. 27, 1975; children: Lulita C., Washington A., James B. Student, Princeton U., 1941; DHL (hon.), Adelphi Coll., 1957, L.I. U., 1988, Drexel U., 1991. With Import Export Co., 1946-50; prin. A.D. Duke Realty, Inc., 1955-65. Chmn. bd. dirs., pres., founder Boys Harbor Inc., 1937-2014 Trustee Big Brother Movement, 1951-63; past trustee Henry St. Settlement, N.Y.C.; del. Internat. Conf. Pvt. Sector Initiatives, 1986; hon. commr. Manhattan Borough Projects, 1954-57, Civic Affairs and Pub. Events, N.Y.C.; mem. N.Y.C. Youth Bd., 1955-58; rep. Internat. Rescue Com., Vietnam War, Meriel refugee crisis Cuba, 1983; active Save the Children, Pomfret Sch., Duke U. Lt. comdr. USNR, 1941-46, PTO, ATO, ETO. Decorated Bronze Star. Recipient Town and Country Most Generous Am. award 1988, Save the Children award, 1977; Presdl. citation for pvt. sector commendation, 1986, Citation for Promotion of Human Welfare Commonwealth of Mass., 1987. Mem. Bodman & Achelis Found., Nat. Com. on American Fgn. Policy, Maidstone Club (former gov.), Piping Rock (former gov.), River Club, Racquet & Tennis Club, Beaver Dam Club. Home: Brookhaven, NY. Died Apr. 30, 2014.

**DUKE, ROBERT DOMINICK,** lawyer; b. Goshen, NY, Oct. 14, 1928; s. Robert DeWitt and Elma Christina (Dominick) D.; m. Jeannette Parham, Apr. 24, 1954; children: Katherine Campbell, Robert Dominick, Peter Benjamin DeWitt, Lois Christina. BA, Va. Mil. Inst., 1947; LL.B., Yale U., 1950; MBA, U. Pa., 1952. Bar: N.Y. 1950, Conn. 1989. With Cravath, Swaine & Moore, NYC, 1951-52, 54-64, Freeport-McMoRan Inc. and predecessors, NYC, 1964—84, gen. counsel, 1970—84, sr. v.p., 1973—80; sr. v.p., gen. counsel The Brink's Co. (formerly The Pittston Co.), Richmond, Va., 1984—93, sr. counsel, 1993—2002, also bd. dirs., 1991—93. Served as 1st lt. JAGC, U.S. Army, 1952-54. Mem.: ABA, Assn. Bar City NY, Silver Spring Golf Club. Presbyterian. Home: Redding, Conn. Died 2014.

**DUNCOMBE, RAYNOR LOCKWOOD,** astronomer; b. Bronxville, NY, Mar. 3, 1917; s. Frederic Howe and Mabel Louise (Taylor) D.; m. Julena Theodora Steinheider, Jan. 29, 1948; 1 son, Raynor B. BA, Wesleyan U., Middletown, Conn., 1940; MA, U. Iowa, 1941; PhD, Yale U., 1956. Astronomer U.S. Naval Obs., Washington, 1942-62; dir. Nautical Almanac Office, 1963-75; prof. aerospace sci. U. Tex., Austin, from 1976; emeritus prof., 2007. Research assoc. Yale U. Obs., 1948-49; lectr. dynamical astronomy U. Md., 1963, Yale Summer Inst., 1959-70, Office Naval Research Summer Inst. in Orbital Mechanics, 1971, NATO Advanced Study Inst., 1972; cons. orbital mechanics Projects Vanguard, Mercury, Gemini, Apollo, USN Space Surveillance System; mem. NASA space scis. steering com., NASA research adv. panel in applied math., 1967; adviser Internat. Com. on Weights and Measures, Internat. Radio Consultative Com., Internat. Telecommunications Union; mem. NAS-NRC astronomy survey com., 1970-72, Hubble Space Telescope Astrometry Team, 1976—. Author: Motion of Venus, 1958, Coordinates of Ceres, Pallas, Juno and Vesta, 1969; editor: (with V.G. Szebehely) Methods in Celestial Mechanics, 1966, Dynamics of the Solar System, 1979; (with D. Dvorak and P.J. Message) The Stability of Planetary Systems, 1984; assoc. editor: Fundamentals of Cosmic Physics, 1971; exec. editor: Celestial Mechanics, 1977-85; contbr. articles to profl. jours. Fellow Royal Astron. Soc., AAAS (sect. chmn.); assoc. fellow AIAA; mem. Internat. Astron. Union (pres. com. on ephemerides), Minor Planet 3368 named Duncombe, 1988), Am. Astron. Soc. (chmn. div. dynamical astronomy 1970), Inst. Navigation (councillor 1960-64, v.p. 1964-66, pres. 1966-67, Superior Achievement award 1967, Hays award 1975, fellowship 2010), ASME (sponsor applied mechanics div. 1968-70), Internat. Assn. Insts. Nav. (v.p.), Assn. Computing Machinery, Sigma Xi. Home: Middleburgh, NY. Died July 12, 2013.

**DUNKEL, ARTHUR,** international organization executive; b. Switzerland, Aug. 28, 1932; married; 2 children. Degree in Econ. and Comml. Scis., U. Lausanne, Switzerland, 1956; Doctor of Polit. Scis., U. Fribourg, Switzerland, 1980. With dept. pub. economy Fed. Office for Fgn. Econ. Affairs, Bern, Switzerland, 1956-60, head sect. for OECD affairs, 1960-64, head sect. for cooperation with developing countries, 1964-71, head sect. for world trade policy, permanent rep. with rankmin. plenipotentiary to Gen Agreement on Tariffs & Trade, 1971-76; del. Swiss govt. for trade agreements, amb. plenipotentiary, head delegation trade negotiations Gen. Agreement on Tariffs and Trade (GATT), Switzerland, 1976-80; dir. gen. GATT, Geneva, 1980—93. Sr. lectr. U. Geneva, U. Fribourg; vice chmn., rapporteur UNCTAD Intergovernmental Group on Supplementary Financing, 1968; rapporteur UNCTAD Bd., 1969; chmn. GATT Com. on Balance of Payments Restrictions, 1972-75; chmn. UN Conf. on Wheat Agreement, 1978. Contbr. numerous articles to economic jours. Recipient Freedom prize Max Schmidheiny Found., 1989, Consumers for World Trade award, 1990. Died June 8, 2005.

**DUNKEL, PETER CARL,** university administrator; b. New Britain, Conn., Aug. 12, 1962; s. William Carl and Dorothy Signe (Peterson) D.; m. Kristina, Dec. 14, 1985; children: Peter Wesley, Stephen Christopher, Elizabeth Samantha. BA, Wesleyan U., Middletown, Conn., 1984; MA, Fuller Theol. Sem., Pasadena, Calif., 1988; postgrad., UCLA. Corp. fin. analyst Merrill Lynch Capital Markets, NYC, 1984-86; dir. capital programs Biola U., La Mirada, Calif., 1989-91, Calif. Luth. U., Thousand Oaks, 1992-93, dir. devel., from 1994. Sec.-treas. bd dirs. China Ministry Internat., Pasadena, 1993—. Vol. L.A. Mission, 1991—. Mem. Nat. Soc. Fundraising Execs., Coun. for Advancement and Support of Edn. Republican. Evangelical. Avocations: golf, jazz. Home: Scotch Plains, NJ. Died 1996.

**DUNLOP, THOMAS P.H.,** English language educator, counselor; b. Washington, June 12, 1934; m. Betty J. Pieston, June 7, 1969; children: Preston H., Alexander P., Angela K. AB, Yale U., 1956; postgrad., U. N.C., George Mason U. Various positions Dept. State, Washington, 1960-93; TESOL tchr. Ladd Inst., Arlington, Va., from 1993. 1st lt. USAF, 1957-60. Fulbright scholar. Avocations: history, classical music. Home: Alexandria, Va. Died Feb. 1, 2008.

**DUNN, MARGIE P.,** principal; b. Amarillo, Tex., Nov. 7, 1949; d. Charles Breedlove and Earnestine Park Powell; m. Michael Larry Dunn, June 27, 1992; 1 child, Virginia Nicole

Clinkenbeard. BA, U. Tex., 1971, MA, 1988; EdD, Tex. A&M U., 1998. Tchr. Austin Independent Sch. Dist., 1972-73; program dir. Cedar Valley Coll., Dallas, 1979-84; tchr. Red Oak (Tex.) Independent Sch. Dist., 1984-86; asst. supt. Venus (Tex.) Independent Sch. Dist., 1988-97; prin. Dallas Bapt. U. Lab. Sch., from 1996. Adj. prof. Dallas Bapt. U., 1996—, Cedar Valley Coll., 1979-88. Spkr. in field. Mem. Assn. Sch. Curriculum Dirs., Tex. Elem. Prins. and Supervisors Assn., Assn. Tex. Bapt. Schs. Baptist. Home: Green Valley, Ariz. Died Nov. 2, 2000.

**DUNN, ROBERT LAWRENCE,** lawyer; b. Westerly, RI, Jan. 2, 1938; m. Sammie Louise Sanford (dec. Sept. 1999); children: Christopher Jon, Geoffrey Robert; m. Linda Elizabeth Barry, 2003. BA, Cornell U., 1958; JD magna cum laude, Harvard U., 1962. Bar: N.Y. 1962, Calif. 1966, U.S. Dist. Ct. (no. dist.) Calif. 1966, U.S. Ct. Appeals (9th cir.) 1966, U.S. Dist. Ct. (ea. dist.) Calif. 1970, U.S. Supreme Ct. 1984, U.S. Dist. Ct. (cen. dist.) Calif. 1987. Law clk. to cir. judge U.S. Cir. Ct., Hartford, Conn., 1962-63; assoc. Paul, Weiss, Rifkind, Wharton & Garrison, NYC, 1963-65, Bancroft, Avery & McAlister, San Francisco, 1965-71; ptnr. Bancroft & McAlister, San Francisco, 1971-93, Cooper, White & Cooper, San Francisco, 1993-99; corp. counsel Real Restaurants, Sausalito, Calif., 1999—2008; lectr. in fields. Author: Recovery of Damages for Lost Profits, 1978, rev. edit., 2005, Recovery of Damages for Fraud, rev. edit., 2004, Expert Witnesses: Law and Practice, 1996, Winning with Expert Witnesses in Commercial Litigation, 2003; editor-in-chief Dunn on Damages, 2010-; contbr. articles to profl. jours. Planning commn. Town of Corte Madera, Calif. 1974-78, town coun., 1978-84, mayor, 1979, 82; bd. dirs. Merola Opera Program, 1995—, Philharmonia Baroque Orch., San Francisco, 1991-94. 1st lt. U.S. Army, 1958-59. Mem.: Ferrari Club Am. Avocations: travel, opera, literature. Home: Corte Madera, Calif. Died 2013.

**DUNNING, JOHN HARRY,** economics educator; b. Eng., June 26, 1927; s. John Murray and Anne Florence (Baker) D.; m. Christine Mary Brown, Aug. 4, 1975; 1 son by previous marriage, Philip. BSc in Economics, U. London, 1952; PhD, Southampton U., 1957; PhD (hon.), U. Uppsala, Sweden, 1975, U. Autonomous Madrid, 1991; PhD, U. Antwerp, 1997; PhD (hon.), Chinese Culture U., Taiwan, 2007, U. Lund, Sweden, 2007; PhD, U. Reading, 2008. Lectr. U. Southampton, 1952-64; mem. faculty U. Reading, Eng., 1964-92, found. prof. econs., 1964-74, Esmee Fairbairn prof. internat. investment and bus. studies, 1975-87, chmn. dept. econs., 1964-87, ICI rsch. prof. internat. bus., 1987—92. Vis. prof. U. Western Ont., London, Can., 1968-69, U. Calif. Berkeley, 1976; vis. prof. internat. mgmt. U. Boston, 1976; prof. internat. bus. Rutgers U., N.J., 1989-2002; chmn. Economists Adv. Group Ltd., 1985-2000; mem. chems. econ. devel. com. Royal Econ. Soc., 1970-77; mem. S.E. Econ. Planning Coun., 1965-69; mem. coms. econ. and social rsch. coun. OECD, European Commn., UN; hon. prof. U. Beijing, 1995; lectr. in field. Author: Explaining International Production, 1988, Multinational Enterprises, Technology and Competitiveness, 1988, Multinational Enterprises and the Global Economy, 1993, rev. edit. (with S. Lundar), 2008, The Globalization of Business, 1993, Alliance Capitalism and Global Business, 1997, Globalization at Bay, 2000, (with R. Narula) Multinationals and Industrial Comptetitiveness, 2004, Seasons of Scholar, 2008; editor: The Multinational Enterprise, 1971, International Investment, 1972, Economic Analysis and Multinational Enterprise, 1974, Structural Change in the World Economy, 1990, The Theory of Transnational Corporations, 1992, The New Globalism and Developing Countries, 1997, Governments, Globalization and International Business, 1997, Regions, Globalization and the Knowledge Based Economy, 2001, Making Globalization Good, 2003, Seasons of a scholar: some personal reflections of an international business economist, 2008, New Challenges for International Business: Back to the future, 2009; contbr. articles to acad. and profl. jours. Recipient Third Decade of Yr. award, OBE award, Her Magisty the Queen, 2008, Hon. award, U. Reading, 2008. Home: Henley-on-Thames, England. Died Jan. 29, 2009.

**DUNWOODIE, MARALYN SCHROEDER,** nurse; b. Stillwater, Okla., May 19, 1942; d. Victor Angus Schroeder and Alice Elizabeth (Elston) Gregg; m. L. Edward Sizemore, July 26, 1964 (div. Apr. 1972); 1 child, Nona Camille Sizemore; m. Ralph H. Dunwoodie, May 17, 1975 (div. May 1990). BS in Nursing, Tex. Christian U., 1964; grad., U. N.C., 1969—70. DON, Gainesville, Tex., 1967, RN Nev. Claims rep. Aetna Medicare, Reno, 1978—79; Medicaid svcs. examiner Nev. Medicaid, Carson City, 1979—81; med. rev. specialist Blue Shield Nev., Reno, 1981—82; patient care coord. CNA Ins., Reno, 1982—83; head nurse ICU, head nurse emergency dept., utilization rev. supr. St. Mary's Hosp., Reno, 1983—95. Pres. Reno chpt. Parents Without Ptnrs., 1973; mem. emergency sys. adv. bd. City of Reno, 1974; mem. citizens adv. bd. City of Sun Valley, Nev., 1980. Lt. (j.g.) USN, 1963—66, lt. USNR. Mem.: Assn. Operating Room Nurses (workshop chmn. Reno 1976). Democrat. Unitarian. Home: Sparks, Nev. Died July 11, 1995.

**DUPLESSIS, AUDREY JOSEPH,** school system administrator; b. New Orleans, June 23, 1920; d. Louis Joseph and Sidonie Josephine (DeLaRose) Boyer; m. Norwood Jerome Duplessis, Sr., June 27, 1984. B in Vocat. Edn., So. U., Baton Rouge, 1942; BA, Calif. State U., 1959, MA, 1966. Tchr., dir. Tri State Coll., New Orleans, 1948-50; from elem. tchr. to dir. Magnet Sch. L.A. Unified Schs., 1954—2002, dir. Magnet Sch., from 2002. Playground L.A. Unified Schs., 1956-59, reading resource tchr., 1965-70, curriculum coord., 1972-78, dir. L.A. Unified Magnet Sch., 1978-02; reading tchr. Calif. Lutheran Coll., Thousand Oaks, 1968-70. Mem. United Tchrs. PAC, L.A., 1980-88. Recipient svc. award Congress of Parents, L.A., 1988, spl. recognition U.S. Congress, 1988. Mem. Internat. Assn. Childhood Edn. (state pres. 1987-89, appreciation award 1989), St. Brigid Edn. Com., Delta Sigma Theta. Democrat. Roman Catholic. Avocations: reading, sewing, travel, opera, music. Home: Carson, Calif. Deceased.

**DURAND-REVILLE, LUC,** business executive; b. Apr. 12, 1904; Business executive; b. Cairo, Apr. 12, 1904 (parents French citizens); s. Maurice and Jeanne (Reville) Durand;; m. Françoise Warnod, Mar. 28, 1926; children: Eveline Durand-Reville Lobry, Eric, Blaise. Lic. en Droit diplôme H.E.C. Pres. various colonial cos. in Africa, 1934—; mem. French Senate, 1945-58; mem. Econ. and Social Council France, 1958-74; v.p. Cie Optorg, Puteaux, 1970-89; hon. chmn. Acad. Comml. Scis., Acad. Overseas Scis., Soc. Polit. Econs.; corr. Inst. of France; hon. v.p. Internat. C. of C.; hon. bd. dirs. European League Econ. Community. Served to capt. French Army, 1939-45. Decorated officer Legion of Honor, comdr. Nat. Order Merit; knight comdr. Order Brit. Empire; comdr. Palmes Acadé miques (hon.). Mem. Mt. Pelerin Soc. Mem. Radical Party. Mem. Evangelical Ch. Club: Cercle Republicain. Author numerous books and articles on developing countries. Home: Paris, France. Died Aug. 26, 1998.

**DURING, EBBA MARIA,** educator; b. Stockholm, Aug. 21, 1937; d. Ragnar Knut and Inga Majlis (Smith) Sandstrom; m. Gustav During, Nov. 9, 1957; children: Carl Gustav, Cecilia Erica Maria. PhD, U. Stockholm, 1986. Asst. scientist Univ. Stockholm, 1978-85, lectr., 1985-86, 91-94, researcher scientist, 1986-91, 94-96, lectr., rschr. scientist, 1997—2001, prof., 2001. Cons. in field. Author: The Fauna of Alvastra, 1986, Osteology - The Testing of Bones, 1992, 1994, They Died on Board the Vasa, 1995, 1998. Grantee The Hildebrand Found., Stockholm, 1986, King Gustav VI Adolf's Found., Stockholm, 1991, 95, The Swedish Soc. Physicians, Stockholm, 1994, The Langman Culture Found., 1995, 98, Berit Wallenberg Found., 1997, The Vasa Mus. Found., 1997. Mem. Am. Assn. Phys. Anthropologists, European Anthrop. Assn., Dental Anthropolgy Assn., N.Y. Acad. Scis., Soc. Swedish Archaeology, Paleopathology Assn. Avocations: music, gardening, outdoor activities, reading. Died 2007.

**DÛRR, HANS-PETER EMIL,** physicist; b. Stuttgart, Germany, Oct. 7, 1929; s. Rupert and Eva (Kraepelin) D.; m. Carol Sue Durham, Oct. 27, 1956; children: Rosemarie, Michael, Caroly, Peter. Diploma in physics, Tech. U. Stuttgart, 1953; PhD, U. Calif., Berkeley, 1956. Rsch. assoc. Werner Heisenberg, 1958-76; sci. mem. Max-Planck Inst. Physic & Astrophysics, Munich, 1963—92; vice-chmn. Werner-Hesenberg-Inst. Physic, Munich, 1972-77, 81-86, chmn., 1978-80, 87-92, chmn. emertitus, 1997—2014. Chmn. adv. bd. Sci. Ctr. Munich; mem. Global Commn. Fund UN; mem. internat. adv. group UN Conf. Human Settlements, 1996; mem. adv. coun. Found. Rights Future Generations, 1999. Recipient Right Livelihood award, 1987, Waldemar-von-Knoeringen award, 1989, Ecology prize Goldene Schwalbe, 1990, Natura Obligat medal 1991, Elise and Walter A. Haas Internat. award, 1993. Mem. Fedn. German Scientists (bd. dirs. 1980-86), Internat. Found. Survival and Devel. Humanity, Inst. Social-Ecol. Rsch., Club Rome. Home: Munich, Germany. Died May 18, 2014.

**DUSSAULT, JEAN H.,** endocrinologist, medical educator; b. Que., Apr. 6, 1941; BA, U. Montreal, 1960; MD, Laval U., 1965; MSc, U. Toronto, 1969. Intern Hosp. Enfant-Jesus, 1964-65, chief resident, 1965-67; Med. Rsch. Coun. Can. sr. rschr. in endocrinology U. Toronto/Wellesley Hosp., 1967-69, UCLA Sch. Medicine/Harbor Gen. Hosp., 1969-71; from asst. prof. to assoc. prof. Laval U. Sch. Medicine, Quebec City, 1971-81, prof. medicine, 1981—2004; dir. rsch. unit ontogenesis and molecular genetics Ctrl. Hosp./Laval U., 1986-96. Recipient Ross award Am. Acad. Pediatrics, 1976, Manning award Can. Assn. Endocrinology and Metabolism/Can. Diabetes Assn., 1987, 88, Spl. Rhône-Poulenc Sante Pediat. award, 1987, Wallae Robert Guthrie prize ISNS, 1999; named to Ordre du Can., 1988, Ordre Nat. du Que., 2000. Fellow Royal Coll. Physicians (Can.); mem. Am. Thyroid Assn. (Van Meter-Armour award 1980), Can. Med. Assn., Am. Fedn. Clin. Rsch., Endocrine Soc., Can. Soc. Clin. Rsch., Can. Soc. Endocrinology and Metabolism, Soc. Pediatric Rsch., N.Y. Acad. Sci. Died Mar. 23, 2003.

**DUTCHER, FLORA MAE,** retired education educator; b. McCook, Nebr., Jan. 26, 1908; d. Austin Wilson and Minnie Magnolia (Tucker) D. AA, McCook Jr. Coll., 1936; BA, U. Nebr., 1943, MA in Edn. and Adminstrn., 1951. Tchr. rural elem. Hitchcock and Red Willow County Schs., Nebr., 1926-35; elem. tchr. McCook Pub. Schs., 1936-39; tchr. social studies McCook Jr. High Sch., 1939-50; prin. North Ward Elem. Sch., McCook, 1950-55; tchr. of edn. courses McCook Jr. Coll., 1955-73, dean women, 1960-65. Pres. dist. 5 Nebr. Edn. Assn., 1949-50; sponsor Phi Theta Kappa, McCook, 1956-73. Author: Then and Now, 1992; contbr. articles to profl. jours. Vol. High Plains Mus., McCook, 1988—; hunger enabler Am. Bapt. Chs., McCook; tchr. high sch. Sunday sch. First Bapt. Ch., McCook, 1946-73, historian, 1989—; historian for Chatauqua, McCook Area coun. Arts and Humanities, 1975, 90. Recipient scholarship Sweetbrier Shop, McCook, 1947. Mem. AAUW (pres. 1945-47), Bus. and Profl. Women (pres. 1961-62, 73-74), State Staff Ret. Tchrs. (program chmn. 1974-78), McCook Area Ret. Tchrs. Assn. (pres. 1982-86, historian 1988, 95), Delta Kappa Gamma. Democrat. Avocations: reading, genealogy, scrapbooker, cooking, ch. work. Home: Mc Cook, Nebr. Died Apr. 22, 2008.

**DUTT, JAMES L.,** food company executive; BA, Washburn U., 1950; MBA, U. Dayton, 1966. With Beatrice Foods Co., Kans., from 1947, mgr. dairy plant Dayton, from 1961, various mktg. and mgmt. positions, then exec. v.p. dairy and soft drink divs., 1974, dir. internat. dairy ops., 1974, pres. internat. food ops. Chgo., from 1975, exec. v.p., 1975-77, pres., from 1977, chief operating officer, from 1977, chief exec. officer, from 1979, also dir. Dir. various corps. including GATX Corp., McDermott Internat. Bd. dirs. Art Inst. Chgo., Lyric Opera Chgo., Chgo. Council on Fgn. Relations. Mem. Grocery Mfrs. Am. (dir.), Nat. 4-H Council. Died Oct. 28, 2002.

**DUTTON, SHARON GAIL,** retired elementary school educator; b. Greenville, SC, Jan. 5, 1947; d. Melvin Thornton and Bessie Mae (Whitmire) B. BS in Elem. Edn., E. Tenn. State U., 1969; MA in Early Childhood Edn., Western Carolina U., 1976, EdS in Early Childhood Edn., 1983. Cert. tchr. N.C. elem, secondary, sch. adminstrn., early childhood. Tchr. grade 4 Brevard (N.C.) Elem. Sch., 1970; tchr. grade 3 Rosman (N.C.) Elem. Sch., 1970, tchr. grade 2, 1970-72, tchr. reading, 1972-73, tchr. grades 2, 3, 1973-87, tchr. grade 4, 1987-89; ret. Transylvania Sch. System, 1998. Tchr. Headstart Rosman Elem. Sch. 1971, summer sch., 1972; lead tchr. Teacher Corps Grade 2 Western Carolina U., Cullowhee, N.C., Rosman, 1974-76; clin. practicum and reading conf. Western Carolina U., VA Ctr., Oteen, N.C., summer 1976. Organist, pianist, East Fork Bapt. Ch., Brevard, N.C. Mem. NEA, ASCD, Am. Fedn. Tchrs., N.C. Assn. Edn., Transylvania County Assn. Edn. Democrat. Avocations: art, crafts, reading, piano and organ playing, listening to classical and pipe organ music. Home: Rosman, NC. Deceased.

**DUVALIER, JEAN-CLAUDE (BABY DOC DUVALIER),** former president of Haiti; b. Port-au-Prince, Haiti, July 3, 1952; s. Francois and Simone (Ovide) Duvalier; m. Michelle Bennett, May 1980 (div. 1990); 2 children. Degree in Law, Port-au-Prince U., 1970; degree, U. Haiti, 1970. Pres. Govt. of Haiti, Port-au-Prince, 1971—85. Decorated grand collier de l'Ordre Jean-Jacques Dessalines le Grand, grand croix plaque or de l'Ordre Honneur et Merite, grand croix plaque or de l'Ordre Petion et Bolivar, grand cordon special de l'Ordre des Nuages Propices China, grand collier de l'Ordre de Saint-Denis de Zante, grand croix del'Ordre Internat. du Bien Public France, grand cordon avec l'Etoile du Liberia du Tres Venere Ordre de Chevalerie des Pionniers du Liberia. Home: Grasse, France. Died Oct. 4, 2014.

**DWORKIN, MARTIN,** retired microbiologist; b. NYC, Dec. 3, 1927; s. Hyman Bernard and Pauline (Herstein) D.; m. Nomi Rees Buda, Feb. 2, 1957; children: Jessica Sarah, Hanna Beth. BA, Ind. U., 1951; PhD (NSF predoctoral fellow), U. Tex., Austin, 1955. NIH research fellow U. Calif., Berkeley, 1955-57, vis. prof., summers 1958-60; asst. prof. microbiology Ind. U. Med. Sch., 1957-61, assoc. prof., 1961-62; from assoc. prof. to prof. U. Minn., 1962—2004, prof. emeritus, 2004—14. Vis. prof. U. Wash., 1965, Stanford U., 1978-79, co-dir. Microbial Diversity Course Marine Biol. Lab., Woods Hole, 1990-94; vis. scholar Oxford (Eng.) U., 1970-71; Found. for Microbiology lectr., 1973-74, 76-77, 81-82; Sackler scholar Tel Aviv U., 1992. Author: Developmental Biology of the Bacteria, 1985, Microbial Cell-Cell Interactions, 1991; contbr. numerous articles, revs. to profl. publs.; mem. editorial bd. Jour. Bacteriology, 1967-74, 86-88, Ann. Revs. Microbiology, 1975-79, The Prokaryotes, 2d edit., editor-in-chief 3d edit. Alt. del. Democratic Nat. Conv., 1968; mem. Minn. Dem. Farm Labor Central Com., 1969-70. Served with U.S. Army, 1946-48. Recipient Career Devel. award NIH, 1963-73; John Simon Guggenheim fellow, 1978-79 Fellow American Acad. Arts & Sciences (chmn. Midwest ctr., v.p., 2002), American Soc. Microbiology (vice chmn. div. gen. microbiology 1977-78, chmn. 1978-79, div. councillor 1980-82, Roger Porter award 2006); mem. Soc. Gen. Microbiology (Eng.). Home: Saint Paul, Minn. Died Feb. 6, 2014.

**DYADKIN, YURIY DMITRIEVICH,** earth sciences educator; b. Urzum, Kirov, Russia, Nov. 26, 1929; s. Dmitriy Ivanovich and Alexandra Nikolaevna (Lopatina) D.; m. Irina YakovlevnaGamsulova, Oct. 26, 1954; 1 child, Tatiana. Mining engr., Leningrad Inst., Russia, 1952, candidate tech. scis., 1955, D of Tech. Scis., 1965. Asst., prof. Leningrad Mining Inst., from 1956, prorector on rsch., 1968-72, head dept. ore mining and mining thermophysics, 1968-91; head dept. ore mining St. Petersburg (Russia) Mining Inst., Tech. U., 1991-97. Author: Principles of Mining Thermophysics for the North, 1968, Mining of Geothermal Deposits, 1989; author (with others) Comprehensive Rock Engring., 1993; editor Jour. Phys. Processes in Mining, 1973—; mem. editl. bd. Internat. Jour. Rock Mechanics and Mining Scis., 1978—. Recipient The Badge of Honour, Supreme Coun. USSR, Moscow, 1963, grants of scholarship Fulbrights Program of Internat. Exchange, U. Minn., 1979, Stanford U., 1987; named Honored Scientist of Russia, Fedn., Moscow, 1980. Mem. Russian Geothermal Assn. (pres. 1991), Internat. Geothermal Assn. (bd. dirs. 1995), Internat. Bur. Mining Thermophysics (presidium mem. 1976), Acad. Natural Scis. of Russia (academician 1992), Internat. Acad. Ecology and Protective Sci. (academician 1996), Acad. of Discovery (academician 1997). Home: Saint Petersburg, Russia. Died Jan. 21, 2002.

**DYK, ROBERT PEDER,** journalist; b. Oakland, Calif., Mar. 6, 1937; s. Robert and Marirose (Donahue) D.; m. Susan Francesca Scott, Aug. 1976 (dec. 1983); children: Thomas Karl, Mary Eloise Gabrielle. Student, Colo. Coll., Colorado Springs. News dir. Sta. KAPP, Redondo Beach, Calif., 1962-64; producer-editor-writer stas. KMPC-KTLA, Los Angeles, 1964-65, sta. KABC-TV, Los Angeles, 1965-72; reporter CBS Radio News, London, 1972-78, ABC Radio News, London, 1978-79, staff TV fgn. corr., from 1979. Served with U.S. Army, 1960-62. Recipient award

Acad. TV Arts and Scis., 1971; K.P. Nat. scholar, 1955 Mem. Am. Corrs. Assn. London, Sigma Delta Chi (Disting. Service award 1979), Soc. Calif. Pioneers. Died Mar. 22, 2008.

**DYSTEL, OSCAR,** retired publishing executive; b. NYC, Oct. 31, 1912; s. Jacob and Rose (Pintoff) D.; m. Marion Deitler, Oct. 2, 1938 (dec. 2003); children: Jane Dee, John Jay (dec. 2003) BA in Advertising, NYU, 1935; MBA, Harvard Bus. Sch., 1937. Circulation mgr. Sports Illus. & American Golfer, 1937; circulation, promotion mgr. Esquire & Coronet mags., Chgo., 1938-40; circulation mgr. Coronet mag., 1940, editor, 1940-42, 44-48; mng. editor Collier's, 1948-49; exec. staff Cowles Mags., Inc., 1949-51; editorial adviser Parents Inst., Inc., 1951-54; pres., CEO Bantam Books, Inc., NYC, 1954-78, chmn., CEO, 1978-80. Editor of: U.S.A. Mag; pub.: OWI, 1942-43; Author: Analysis of Paid and Controlled Circulation Among Business Papers, 1938. Bd. dirs. Nat. Multiple Sclerosis Soc. Engaged in psychol. warfare ops. Allied Force Hdqrs., 1943-44, MTO. Decorated Medal of Freedom; recipient Curtis Benjamin award Assn. Am. Pubs., 1990; Brandeis U. fellow. Mem. Dutch Treat Club, Fairview Country Club, Tamarisk Country Club. Home: Purchase, NY. Died May 28, 2014.

**EASTON, DAVID,** political science educator; b. Toronto, Can., June 24, 1917; m. Sylvia Johnstone, Jan. 1, 1942 (dec. 1990); 1 child, Stephen Talbot. BA, U. Toronto, 1939, MA, 1943; PhD, Harvard U., 1947; LLD (hon.), McMaster U., Can., 1970, Kalamazoo Coll., 1972. Andrew MacLeish Disting. Svc. prof. dept. polit. sci. U. Chgo., 1947-82, prof. emeritus, 1982—2014; Sir Edward Peacock prof. Queen's U., Can., 1971-80; Disting. prof. U. Calif., Irvine, 1981—2014. Cons. Brookings Inst., 1953, Mental Rsch. Health Inst., U. Mich., Ann Arbor, 1955-56, Royal Commn. Biculturalism/Bilingualism, Can., 1965-67; commn. examiners, grad. rec. exam. polit. sci. Ednl. Testing Svc., Princeton, N.J., 1966-68; Ford prof. govt. affairs Ford Found., N.Y., 1960-61; pres. Internat. Com. Social Sci. Documentation, 1969-71; chair bd. trustees Acad. Ind. Scholars, 1979-81; co-chair Internat. Com. Devel. Polit. Sci. Author: The Political System: An Inquiry into the State of Political Science, 1953, A Framework for Political Analysis, 1965, A Systems Analysis of Political Life, 1965, The Analysis of Political Structure, 1990; co-author: Children in the Political System: Origins of Political Legitimacy, 1969; editor: Varieties of Political Theory, 1966; co-editor: Divided Knowledge: Across Disciplines, Across Cultures, 1991, The Development of Political Science, 1991. Fellow ctr. advanced study behavioral scis. Stanford U., 1957-58. Fellow American Acad. Arts & Sci. (v.p. 1984-89, co-chair Western Ctr. 1984-89), Royal Soc. Can.; mem. American Polit. Sci. Assn. (pres. 1968-69). Died July 19, 2014.

**EASTON, ROGER LEE,** physicist, consultant; b. Craftsbury, Vt., Apr. 30, 1921; m. Barbara Easton. Grad., Middlebury Coll., Vt., 1943. Rsch. physicist US Naval Rsch. Lab., Washington, 1943—80; founder, cons. RoBarCo, Canaan, NH. Mem. Dist. 11 NH House of Reps., Grafton County, 1982—86; gubernatorial candidate NH, 1986. Recipient Disting. Civilian Svc. award, USN, 1960, Nat. Medal Tech., The White House, 2004; named to The Nat. Inventors Hall of Fame, 2010. Mem.: IEEE, Am. Philos. Soc. (Magellanic Premium award 1998), Nat. Aeronautic Assn. Achievements include recognition as the pioneer of satellite-based global positioning systems (GPS); design of a time navigation geopositioning system (TIMATION) for the US Navy, which used multiple satellites carrying stable and ultra-precise clocks to send signals allowing earth-based receiving devices to calculate their exact locations; development of the Vanguard, Minitrack, and Navy Space Surveillance Systems for spacecraft tracking, navigation and timing technology; patents in field. Home: Canaan, NH. Died May 8, 2014.

**EATON, WILLIAM JAMES,** newspaperman; b. Chgo., Dec. 9, 1930; s. Wlliam Millar and Rose (Ellenbast) E.; m. Marilynn Myers, Sept. 6, 1952 (div. Sept. 24, 1980); children: Susan, Sally Ann. BS, Northwestern U., 1951, MS, 1952. With City News Bur., Chgo., 1952-53; with U.P.I., Washington, 1955-66; corr. Washington Bur. Chgo. Daily News, 1966-76, Knight-Ridder Newspapers, 1977-78, Los Angeles Times, 1978—2005. Chmn. standing com. corrs. U.S. Capitol Press Gallery, 1973 Author: (with Frank Cormier) Reuther, 1970. Served with AUS, 1953-55. Recipient Sidney Hillman award, 1970, Pulitzer prize for nat. reporting, 1970; Nieman fellow Harvard, 1962-63 Mem.: Washington Press (pres. 1976-77). Died Aug. 23, 2005.

**EBASHI, SETSURO,** scientist, educator; b. Tokyo, Aug. 31, 1922; s. Haruyoshi and Hisaji (Watanabe) E.; m. Fumiko Takeda, May 20, 1956. MD, U. Tokyo, 1944, PhD, 1954. Prof. pharmacology U. Tokyo, 1959-83, prof. biophysics, 1971-83, prof. emeritus, from 1983; prof. Nat. Inst. Physiol. Sci. (NIPS), Okazaki, Japan, 1983—86, dir.-gen., 1985—91, prof. Grad. U. Advanced Studies, 1988—91, prof. emeritus, from 1993; pres. Okazaki Nat. Rsch. Inst., 1991-93; prof. emeritus Nat. Institute for Physiological Scis., Okazaki, Aichi, Japan. Guest Investigator of Rockfeller Inst. 1959, vis. prof. U. Calif., San Francisco, 1963, Harvard U., Cambridge, Mass., 1974; pres. Internat. Union for Pure and Applied Biophysics, 1978-81, Internat. Union Pharmacology, 1990-94, Prof. and chmn. Grad. Course of Physiological Scis. Grad. U.1988-1991. Contbr. articles to sci. journals. Decorated grand cordon Order of the Sacred Treasure, Order Cultural Merit (Japan); recipient Asahi prize Asahi Newspaper Pub. Co., Tokyo, 1968, Imperial prize Japan Acad., 1972, Peter Harris award Internat. Soc. Heart Rsch., 1986, Internat. prize for Biology, 1999. Mem.: Japan Acad. (Sec.-Gen. 2000), Acad. Europaea, Acad. Nat. dei Lincei, Acad. Royal Medicine de Belgique, German Acad. Leopoldina, Royal Soc. (London), Am. Acad. Arts and Scis., Am. Soc. Biochemistry and Molecular Biology, NAS, Am. Physiol. Soc. (hon.). Home: Okazaki, Japan. Died July 17, 2006.

**EBEID, ATEF MOHAMMED (ATEF OBEID),** former Egyptian government official; b. Tanta, Egypt, Apr. 14, 1932; married; 2 children. BA in Commerce, Cairo U., 1952; MA, U. Ill., 1956, PhD in Bus. Admin., 1962. Mgmt. cons. Ministry of Industry, Egypt, 1955-63, 67-84; gen. mgr. Arab Rsch. & Admin. Ctr. Mgmt. Consulting Firm, 1963—73; min. cabinet affairs, min. state for adminstrv. devel. Govt. of Egypt, Cairo, 1984-93, min. state for public sector, adminstrv. devel. and environ., 1993—99, prime min., 1999—2004. Mgmt. cons. Ministry of Electricity, Egypt, 1965, Ministry of Housing, 1966, Ministry of Higher Edn., 1967, Ministry of Info., 1968; mgmt. cons. to UNDP, 1971, ILO, 1981; mgmt. cons., then pres. Internat. Mgmt. Ctr., 1973-84; prof. mgmt. Cairo U., 1982-84. Contbr. articles to profl. jours. Nat. Democratic Party. Islam. Died Sept. 12, 2014.

**EBERHART, CATHY FRANCES,** retired academic administrator; b. Brooklyn, NY, Dec. 9, 1945; d. Noah Krall and Rosalind (Mirsky); m. Stefan Eberhart, 1968 (dec. 2005). BA in Sociology, Antioch Coll., Yellow Springs, Ohio, 1968; MA, U. Heidelberg, Germany, 1981, PhD in Philosophy of Edn., 1993. Counselor disturbed adolescents Bodelschwingh Kinderheim, Manneheim, Germany, 1971-77; rsch. asst., counselor U. Heidelberg, 1980-82; acad. dean Schiller Internat. U., Heidelberg and Dunedin, Fla., 1986-91, v.p. acad. affairs, 1991—2009, Potomac Coll., Washington, 2009—11. Home: Largo, Fla. Died Oct. 9, 2013.

**ECCLES, PETER WILSON,** lawyer; b. Lawrence, NY, Jan. 31, 1936; s. Wilson and Mable Smith Eccles; m. Achla Chib Eccles; children: Peter Rahul, Radika Elizabeth. BA magna cum laude, Dartmouth Coll., 1958; JD cum laude, Harvard Law Sch., 1963. Atty. World Bank, 1963—65; assoc. Cleary Gottlieb Steen & Hamilton Law Firm, 1965—69; v.p. Goldman Sachs & Co., 1969—74; v.p., mgr. corp. fin. Ultrafin Internat., 1974—77; v.p., mng. dir. Citibank, 1977—86; dir., investment banking Prudential Bache Capital Funding, 1987—90; pres. Eccles Assocs., 1990—96; sr. advisor UN Devel. Program, 1990—91. Mem. exec. com., trustees Found. for Child Devel., 1973—77; charter mem. Exec. Leadership Coun., 1986—90; mem. bd. visitors Rockefeller Ctr. Social Sci., 1986—93; mem. Coun. on Fgn. Relations, from 1993; bd. dirs. Citizens Com. for Children, 1967—74. Mem.: Phi Beta Kappa. Died Dec. 13, 1996.

**ECKER, SIDNEY WOLF,** urologist, consultant; s. Morris and Rose Ecker; m. Karen Garber, Mar. 1, 1964; children: Felice Ecker-Ramaikas, Erica. BS, U. Scranton, 1962; MD, Albert Einstein Coll. Medicine, Bronx, NY, 1966. Diplomate Am. Bd. Urology, Diplomate Nat. Bd. Med. Examiners. Surg. intern Georgetown U. Med. Sch., Washington, 1966—67, urology resident, 1967—71; pvt. practice Am. Urol. Assn., 1973—96; chmn. surgery sect. Shady Grove Adventist Hosp., Rockville, Md., 1996—97, chmn. surg. rev., 1991—95; mem. regular affilitate staff Walter Reed Army Med. Ctr., Washington, from 1998; chief of urology Wash. VA Med. Ctr., Washington, 2001—03, surg. cons., from 2005; clin. prof. of urology Georgetown U. Med. Sch., Washington, from 2004; symposium chair Am. Psychiatric Assn., San Fransisco, 2009, Internat. Found. Gender Edn., Alexandria, Va., 2010. Guest worker surgery br. NIH, Bethesda, Md., 1968—69; urol. surgeon to Belize Found. for Global Health, Washington, 1975; vis. urologist to China People to People Med. Ambs., Spokane, 2002; spkr. in fields. Contbr. scientific papers to profl. publs. Maj. USAF, 1971—73. Recipient Residents Sci. Presentation 1st prize, Wash. Urol. Soc., 1969. Fellow: ACS (life); mem.: Wash. Urological Soc. (pres. 1991—92), Med-chi Md. (life), Am. Urol. Assn. (life), Cosmos Club Wash. Avocations: Apple and Mac computers, photography, travel and travel lecturing, international cooking. Home: New Hope, Pa. Died Aug. 24, 2014.

**ECKERT, WILLIAM ALTHEN, JR.,** lawyer; b. New Orleans, Sept. 1, 1919; s. William Althen and Elvina Henrietta Eckert; m. Lillian Virginia Crumpler, Dec. 31, 1942; children: Julie Claire Eckert Moyers, William Althen III. BA, La. State U., 1939; LLB with honors, U. Ark., 1948. Bar: Ark. 1948, US Dist. Ct. (we. dist.) Ark. 1948, US Supreme Ct. 1967. Ptnr. Crumpler & Eckert, Magnolia, Ark., 1949—54, Keith, Clegg & Eckert, Magnolia, from 1955; mcpl. judge Magnolia, 1955—82; dir. First Nat. Bank, Magnolia, First United Bancshares, El Dorado, Ark. Editor: Ark. Law Rev., 1948. Served to capt. USAAF, 1941—46. Mem.: ABA, Ark. Bar Assn., Masons lodge, Omicron Delta Kappa. Democrat. Methodist. Home: Magnolia, Ark. Died 1999.

**ECROYD, LAWRENCE GERALD,** trade association administrator; b. Montreal, Que., Can., Sept. 14, 1918; s. George Smith and Marie (Guibord) E.; m. Dorothy Gertrude Howson, Dec. 26, 1949; children: Lynn (Mrs. Thomas Egan), Claire (Mrs. Lawrence Northway), Beverly, Bruce. Intermediate cert., U. London, 1960; MBA, Fla. Atlantic U., 1972. B.C. mgr. Can. C. of C., Vancouver, 1946-53; exec. dir. Mitchell Press Ltd., Vancouver, 1953-61; exec. v.p. Travel Industry Assn. Can., Ottawa, Ont., 1961-73; pres. Can. Inst. Plumbing and Heating, Toronto, 1973-84, cons., from 1984. Served to lt. comdr. Royal Can. Navy, 1941-45. Recipient Bota award tourism, 1973. Mem. Am. Soc. Assn. Execs. (Merit award 1971, Cert. Assn. Exec. 1974), Inst. Assn. Execs. (Can.). Home: Ottawa, Canada. Died Mar. 30, 2003.

**EDELIN, KENNETH CARLTON,** physician; b. Washington, Mar. 31, 1939; s. Benedict and Ruby (Goodwin) Edelin; m. Barbara Evans Edelin, Aug. 5, 1978; children: Kenneth Carlton, Kimberly Cybele, Joseph Evans, Corrine Ruby-Elizabeth. BA, Columbia Coll., 1961; MD, Meharry Med. Coll., 1967. Intern Wright-Patterson AFB Hosp., Ohio, 1967—68; resident Boston City Hosp., 1971—74; instr. ob-gyn sch. Medicine Boston U., 1974—76, asst. prof., 1976, assoc. prof., 1977—78, prof. ob-gyn, dept. chmn., 1978—89. Asst. dir. ob-gyn Boston City Hosp., 1974—76, assoc. dir., 1977—78, dir., 1978—89; gynecologist-in-chief U. Hosp., 1978—89; med. dir. Boston Family Planning Project; pres. Roxbury Comprehensive Cmty. Health Ctr., Inc. Author: Broken Justice: A True Story of Race, Sex, and Revenge in a Boston Courtroom, 2007. Pres. New Eng. com. NAACP-Legal Def. Fund, Inc. Capt. USAF, 1968—71. Fellow: Obstetrical Soc. Boston, American Coll. Obstetricians & Gynecologists; mem.: Assn. Gynecologist Laparoscopists, Assn. Profs. Ob-Gyn, American Fertility Soc., New Eng. Med. Soc., Nat. Med. Assn., Planned Parenthood Fedn. America (chmn. 1989—92), Sigma Pi Phi. Died Dec. 30, 2013.

**EDELMAN, ALVIN,** lawyer; b. Chgo., Dec. 12, 1916; m. Rose Marie Slossy, Sept. 22, 1940; children: Marilyn Frances Edelman Snyder, Stephen D., Leon F. BS in Law, Northwestern U., 1938, JD, 1940. Bar: Ill. 1940. Practiced in Chgo., from 1940; pres. Edelman & Edelman, Chartered and predecessors, from 1973; gen. counsel Internat. Coll. Surgeons. Lectr. Internat. Mus. Surg. Sci. and Hall of Fame; chmn. wills and gifts com. Medinah Temple of Masonic Shrine, Chgo., 1975-79; pres. Lawyers Shrine Club of Medinah Temple, 1971-73. Contbr. articles to profl. jours. Fellow Am. Coll. Trust and Estate Counsel; mem. ABA, Ill. Bar Assn., Chgo. Bar Assn. (chmn. grievance com. 1971-72), Phi Beta Kappa (pres. Chgo. area assn. 1975-85), Phi Beta Kappa Fellows (bd. dirs. 1985—, nat. v.p. 1986-95, nat. pres. 1996-2001), Elks (past exalted ruler). Died Dec. 7, 2006.

**EDELMAN, GERALD MAURICE,** biochemist, neuroscientist, educator; b. Queens, NY, July 1, 1929; s. Edward and Anna (Freedman) Edelman; m. Maxine Morrison, June 11, 1950; children: Eric, David, Judith. BS, Ursinus Coll., Collegeville, Pa., 1950, DSc, 1974; MD, U. Pa., 1954, DSc, 1973; PhD, Rockefeller Inst., NYC, 1960; DSc (hon.), Gustavus Adolphus Coll., 1975, Williams Coll., 1976, U. Paris, 1989; LSc (hon.), U. Cagliari, 1989; DSc (hon.), Georgetown U., 1989, U. degli Studi di Napoli, 1990, Tulane U., 1991, U. Miami, 1995, Adelphi U., 1995, U. Bologna, 1998, U. Minn., 2000, Moscow State U., 2008, Rockefeller U., 2008, U. Louvain, 2009; MD (hon.), U. Siena, Italy, 1974, U de A Coruña, Spain, 2000. Med. house officer Mass. Gen. Hosp., Boston, 1954—55; asst. physician Rockefeller Inst. Hosp., 1957—60; asst. prof., asst. dean grad. studies Rockefeller Inst., 1960—63, assoc. prof., assoc. dean, 1963—66; prof. Rockefeller U., 1966—74, Vincent Astor disting. prof., 1974—92; prof., chmn. dept. neurobiology Scripps Rsch. Inst., La Jolla, Calif., 1992—2014. Mem. biophysics and biophys. chemistry study sect. NIH, 1964—67; mem. adv. bd. Basel Inst. Immunology, Switzerland, 1970—77, chmn., 1975—77; non-resident fellow, trustee Salk Inst. Biol. Studies, La Jolla, 1973—85, bd. trustees, 1975—85; founder, dir. Neurosciences Inst., NYC, 1981—93, La Jolla, 1993—95, San Diego, from 1995. Author: The Mindful Brain, 1978, Neural Darwinism, 1987, Topobiology, 1988, The Remembered Present, 1989, Bright Air, Brilliant Fire: On the Matter of the Mind, 1992, A Universe of Consciousness: How Matter Becomes Imagination, 2000, Wider than the Sky: The Phenomenal Gift of Consciousness, 2004, Second Nature: Brain Science and Human Knowledge, 2006. Bd. governors Weizmann Inst. Sci., Israel, 1971—87; trustee Rockefeller Bros. Found., 1972—82; bd. trustees Carnegie Instn., Washington, 1980—87. Capt. US Army Med. Corps, 1955—57. Recipient Spencer Morris award, U. Pa., 1954, Ann. Alumni award, Ursinus Coll., 1969, Albert Einstein Commemorative award, Yeshiva U., 1974, Buchman Meml. award, Calif. Inst. Tech., 1975, Rabbi Shai Shacknai Meml. prize, Hebrew U.-Hadassah Med. Sch., Jerusalem, 1977, Regents medal of excellence, NY State, 1984, Hans Neurath prize, U. Wash., 1986, Sesquicentennial Commemorative award, Nat. Libr. Medicine, 1986, Cécile and Oskar Vogt award, U. Dusseldorf, 1988, Disting. Grad. award, U. Pa., 1990, Warren Triennial Prize award, Mass. Gen. Hosp., 1992, C.V. Ariens-Kappers medal, Netherlands Inst. Brain Rsch., 1999, Jiménez Díaz Meml. prize, Jiménez Díaz Found., Madrid, 1999, Medal of Presidency of Italian Republic, 1999, Medal of City of Paris, 2002, Cátedra Santiago Grisolia prize, Spain, 2003, Caianiello Meml. Internat. award, Italy, 2003; co-recipient Nobel Prize for Physiology/Medicine, Karolinska Inst., 1972. Fellow: AAAS, Jewish Acad. Arts & Sciences (Albert Einstein Commemorative medal 1986), NY Acad. Medicine, NY Acad. Sciences; mem.: NAS, American Chem. Soc. (Eli Lilly award 1965), Coun. Fgn. Rels., Soc. Devel. Biology, Acad. Sciences Inst. France (fgn.), American Psychoanalytic Assn. (hon.), Japanese Biochem. Soc. (hon.), Pharm. Soc. Japan (hon.), American Soc. Cell Biology, American Acad. Arts & Sciences, Genetics Soc. America, American Assn. Immunologists, American Soc. Biol. Chemists, American Philos. Soc., Century Assn., Harvey Soc. (pres. 1976—77), Cosmos Club, Alpha Omega Alpha, Sigma Xi, Phi Beta Kappa. Home: La Jolla, Calif. Died May 18, 2014.

**EDGE, DAVID OWEN,** science educator; b. High Wycombe, Eng., Sept. 4, 1932; s. Stephen Rathbone Holden and Kathleen Edith (Haines) E.; m. Barbara Corsie, Feb. 21, 1959; children: Aran Kathleen, Alastair Clouston, Gordon. BA in Physics, Cambridge U., 1955, MA, 1959, PhD in Radio Astronomy, 1959. Producer Sci. Talks BBC, London, 1959-66; dir. Sci. Studies Unit Edinburgh (Scotland) U., 1966-89, reader Sci. Studies, reader emeritus, from 1979, mem. Univ. Ct., 1983-86; quality assurance auditor Higher Edn. Quality Coun./Quality Assurange Agy., from 1992. Chair Sci. Policy Support Group, 1989-93. Co-author: Astronomy Transformed, 1976; co-editor: Science in Context, 1982; joint editor Social Studies Sci. 1971-82, editor, 1982—. Hdqrs. adviser Scout Assn., Scotland, 1967-85; cir. steward Meth. Ch., Edinburgh and Forth Cir., 1984-86. Soc. for Humanities fellow Cornell U., 1973. Fellow AAAS, Royal Astron. Soc., Royal Soc. Arts, Royal Soc. Edinburgh; mem. Soc. for Social Studies Sci. (council 1980-81, pres. 1985-87, Bernal prize 1993), N.Y. Acad. Scis., History of Sci. Soc., Brit. Soc. for History of Sci., Brit. Assn. for Advancement Sci., Scout and Guide Grad. Assn. (pres., former chmn.), European Assn. for Study of Sci. and Tech. Mem. Liberal Democrats. Avocations: music, travel, sports, editing footnotes. Home: Edinburgh, Scotland. Died Jan. 28, 2003.

**EDMONDS, JAMES TILDEN (JIM EDWARDS),** former city official; b. Wichita, Kans., June 10, 1944; s. James Alanson and Patricia Bess (Strohl) E.; m. Kay Nell Birdwell, June 17, 1967 (div.); m. Annette Edmonds BA, Abilene Christian U., 1966. Adminstrv. asst. to mayor City of Houston, 1967; adminstrv. asst. to gov. State of Tex., 1968-69; exec. asst. to mayor City of Houston, 1969-73; exec. asst. to pres. Houston Chamber of Commerce, 1974-76; ptnr. Peat, Marwick & Mitchell, Houston, 1976-82, Masterson Co. and WE Investors, Houston, from 1982; commr. Port of Houston Authority, 1966—2013, chmn., 2000—13. Bd. dirs. Masterson Co., Houston, Meml. Hosp. System, Houston, TOS Industries, Houston, Gen. Homes Corp., Houston; mem. adv. bd. Abilene Christian U. Pres. Greater Houston Assn.; mem. San Jacinto River Authority. Mem. Houston Chamber of Commerce Mem. Church of Christ. Club: Houston. Avocation: bird hunting and farming. Home: Houston, Tex. Died May 11, 2014.

**EDMONDSON, MARY ELLEN,** artist; b. McLean, Va., Nov. 8, 1919; d. William Grant and Mary Pauline (Neff) E. Student, George Washington Jr. Coll., Washington, 1938—39; degree in art, Abbott Art Sch., 1943. Artist, illustrator Fed. Govt. Petroleum Adminstrn. for War, 1942-46, Bur. Reclamation, 1946-49. Exhibited in group shows Art League, Alexandria, Va., 1972-87, Miniature Soc. Washington, 1974-96 (awards 1978, 89, 91), Royal Miniature Soc., London, 1995. Mem. Ga. Miniature Soc. (1st place graphics 1996), Miniature Soc. N.J. (2d place in fine prints, 1977, 3d place, 1994). Democrat. Avocations: reading, walking, art with children. Home: Mc Lean, Va. Died Nov. 8, 2013.

**EDMONDSON, WILLIAM BROCKWAY,** retired foreign service officer; b. St. Joseph, Mo., Feb. 6, 1927; s. Harold and Anna Laura (Sherman) E.; m. Donna Elizabeth Kiechel, Oct. 6, 1951; children: Barbara Elizabeth Edmondson Schneider, Paul William. AB with high distinction, U. Nebr., 1950; MA, Fletcher Sch. Law and Diplomacy, 1951; student African area studies, Northwestern U., 1957-58. Joined U.S. Fgn. Service, 1952; fgn. affairs officer Bur. UN Affairs, State Dept., 1951-52; adviser U.S. delegation 11th session UN Trusteeship Council, 1952; vice consul Dar es Salaam, Tanganyika, 1952-55; 3d sec., then 2d sec. embassy Bern, Switzerland, 1955-57; research analyst, then acting chief W. Africa div. Office Research and Analysis for Africa, State Dept., 1958-61; 2d sec., then 1st sec. and consul, polit. sect. chief Am. embassy, Accra, Ghana, 1961-64; officer charge Ghanaian affairs Bur. African Affairs, State Dept., 1964-65; counselor of embassy, dep. chief of mission Lusaka, Zambia, 1965-68; chargé d'affaires ad interim, 1968-69; assigned Nat. War Coll., 1969-70; dep. dir. African programs Bur. Ednl. and Cultural Affairs, Dept. State, 1970, dir. Office African Programs, 1971-74; minister-counselor, dep. chief mission Am. embassy, Pretoria, South Africa, 1974-76; dep. asst. sec. for African affairs State Dept., 1976-78; ambassador to South Africa Pretoria, 1978-81; sr. fgn. service insp., 1981-82; dep. insp. gen., 1982-86. Served to 1st lt. AUS, 1944-48. Mem. Am. Fgn. Svc. Assn. Diplomatic and Consular Officers Ret. (past pres., hon. life gov.), DACOR Bacon House Found. (past pres., trustee), Phi Beta Kappa. Home: Prescott, Ariz. *Persistent hard work, sincerity, broad intellectual curiosity and a strong touch of idealism in striving for a better world are qualities I admire and try to emulate.* Died Dec. 5, 2013.

**EDSTROM, JOHN OLOF,** industrial engineer, educator; b. Stockholm, May 11, 1926; s. Johan and Martha Torborg (Andersson) E.; m. Gunnel Kling, Nov. 24, 1950; 1 child, Ingeborg. Dipl.ing., Royal Inst. Tech., 1950, tech. lic., 1953, dr.sci., 1958. Rsch. asst. Royal Inst. Tech., Stockholm, 1950-53, prof. ferrous metallurgy, 1960, prof. prodn. tech., 1977-93, prof. emeritus, from 1993. Rsch. assoc. U. Minn., Mpls., 1954; research metallurgist Jernkontoret, Stockholm, 1955-57; head metall. rsch. dept. Sandvik Co., Sandviken, Sweden, 1958-60, v.p. R&D, 1960-65, exec. v.p., 1965-70; pres. Norrbotten Steelworks, Luleå, Sweden, 1970-76; chmn. Swedish Welding Commn., 1986-97; chmn. U. Luleå, 1970-77, MINPRO, 1989-96; hon. profl. E. China Inst. Metallurgy, 1987—. Contbr. articles to profl. jours. Decorated comdr. Order of Vasa; recipient Bergs medal Royal Inst. Tech., 1973, Rinman medal, 1992, Brinell medal, 1998. Mem. Royal Swedish Acad. Engring. (dir. 1979-82), Inst. Metal Rsch. (dir. 1970-92), MEFOS (dir. 1970-2003), Swedish Inst. Prodn. Engring. Rsch. (dir. 1977-80), AIME, Metal Soc., Iron and Steel Inst. Japan (hon.), Svenska Metallografforbundet, Verein Deutsche Eisenhuttenleute, Svenska Bergsmannaforeningen, Sankt Orjans Gille. Achievements include patents in field. Home: Stocksund, Sweden. Deceased.

**EDWARDS, CLIFFORD HENRY COAD,** law educator; b. Jamalpur, Bihar, India, Nov. 8, 1924; s. George Henry Probyn and Constance Ivy (Coad) E.; m. Kathleen Mary Faber, Jan. 6, 1951; children: Jeanette Marie, John Philip, Michael Hugh, Margaret Susan. LLB with 1st class honors, U. London, 1945. Sr. lectr. Kumasi Coll., Chana, 1956-58; assoc. prof. law U. Man., Winnipeg, 1958-64, prof., dean Sch. Law, 1964-79; pres. Man. Law Reform Commn., 1979—2006; dean emeritus U. Man., Winnipeg, from 1986. Queen's coun., 1980. Recipient Stanton Tchg. Award for Excellence, U. Man., 1994. Mem. Soc. Internat. Ministries (chmn. 1984-90), Man. Bar Assn. (Disting. Svc. award 1995), Order of Can, Order of Manitoba. Mem. Anglican Ch. Home: Winnipeg, Canada. Died July 5, 2008.

**EDWARDS, H. B., JR.,** lawyer; b. Hahira, Ga., Jan. 28, 1921; s. H. B. and Lovelle (Hodges) Edwards; m. Marie Howell; children: H. B. III, John Kent, William D. LLB, U. Ga., 1944, JD, 1969. Bar: Ga. 1944, US Ct. Appeals 1952, US Supreme Ct. Ga. 1952, US Dist. Ct. (so. dist.) Ga. 1947. Pvt. practice law, Valdosta, Ga. With USAAF, 1943—45. Mem.: DAV (comdr. 1960), 40 and 8 La Soc. (chef de Gare 1956), Amvets (comdr. 1958), Am. Legion (comdr. 1952), Eagles Lodge (pres. 1968—69), Lions Lodge (dir. 1952—55). Baptist. Deceased.

**EDWARDS, KENNETH NEIL,** chemical engineering executive; b. Hollywood, Calif., June 8, 1932; s. Arthur Carl and Ann Vera (Gomez) E.; children: Neil James, Peter Graham, John Evan. BA in Chemistry, Occidental Coll., 1954; MS in Chem. and Metall. Engring., U. Mich., 1955. Prin. chemist Battelle Meml. Inst., Columbus, Ohio, 1955-58; dir. new products rsch. and devel. Dunn-Edwards Corp., LA, 1958-72; sr. lectr. organic coatings and pigments dept. chem. engring. U. So. Calif., LA, 1976-80; CEO Dunn-Edwards Corp., from 2001. Bd. dirs. Dunn-Edwards Corp., LA; co-chair indsl. adv. coun., mem. pres.'s cir. Calif. Poly. U., San Luis Obispo. Contbr. articles to sci. jours. Recipient Judo Masters belt (6th dan), Korean Judo Assn., 2000, 38th Western Regional Indsl. Innovations award, 2003. Mem. Am. Chem. Soc. (chmn. divisional activities 1988-89, exec. com. divsn. polymeric materials sci. and engring. 1963—, chair divsn. 1970, mem. devel. adv. com. 1996-99, Disting. Svc. award 1996, chair Disting. Svc. award selection 1997—, chair So. Calif. local sect. 1999), Alpha Chi Sigma (chmn. L.A. profl. chpt. 1962, counselor Pacific dist. 1967-70, grand profl. alchemist nat. v.p. 1970-76, grand master alchemist nat. pres. 1976-78, nat. adv. com. 1978—). Achievements include patents for air-dried polyester coatings and application, for process and apparatus for dispensing liquid colorants into a paint can, fluidic fillers, and for mechanical mixers. Home: Sagle, Idaho. Died Feb. 20, 2013.

**EDWARDS, SAMUEL ROGER,** retired internist; b. Santa Barbara, Calif., Aug. 11, 1937; s. Harold S. and Margaret (Spaulding) E.; m. Marcia Elizabeth Dutton, June 17, 1961; children: Harold S. II, Charles Dutton. BA, Harvard U., 1960; MD, U. So. Calif., 1964. Intern Presbyn. Hosp., Phila., 1964-65; resident in internal medicine U Calif., San Francisco, 1968-70; fellow in cardiology Pacific Presbyn. Med. Ctr., San Francisco, 1970; pvt. practice specializing in internal medicine Santa Paula, Calif., 1971-94; med. dir. Santa Paula Convalescent, Twin Pines Convalescent Hosps., 1974-95; pres. med. staff Ventura (Calif.) County Med. Ctr., 1979-80, med. dir., 1983-95, hosp. adminstr., 1995—2002; ret., 2002. Chief dept. medicine Ventura County Gen. Hosp., 1975; chief med. staff Santa Paula Meml. Hosp., 1977; mem. clin. faculty sch. medicine UCLA, 1980—95; chmn. Citizens State Bank of Santa Paula, 1994—97; bd. dirs. Santa Barbara Bank and Trust, 1998—2006; chmn. Limoneira Co., 2003—04, bd. dirs. Lt. comdr. USNR, 1966-68. Recipient Disting. Svc. award Ventura County Heart Assn., 1974. Fellow: ACP; mem.: AMA, Am. Coll. Hosp. Execs. Episcopalian. Home: Santa Paula, Calif. Died Jan. 25, 2014.

**EGAN, DANIEL FRANCIS,** priest; b. NYC, June 18, 1915; s. Thomas J. and Mary (Bierne) E. AB in Philosophy, Cath. U. Am., 1941, MA in Edn., 1945; LHD (hon.), Marist Coll., 1980, Dominican Coll., 1988. Joined Soc. of Atonement, Roman Cath. Ch., 1936, ordained priest, 1945; cert. alcohol/drug abuse counselor. Assigned Negro mission So. U.S., 1947-49; assigned preaching missions Ea. U.S., 1949-59; founder half-way house for female drug addicts Village Haven, NYC, 1963; founder live-in therapeutic community for female addicts New Hope Manor, Barryville, N.Y., 1970-78; program dir. St. Joseph's Rehab. Ctr. for Male Alcoholics, Saranac Lake, N.Y., 1978-79; assigned W.I. missions, Jamaica, 1979-81; dir. Drug Prevention Programs for Children, Youth, Adults, Graymoor, Garrison, N.Y., from 1981, Drug Rehab. and Prevention, Calcutta, India, 1989-92; drug, alcohol counselor St. Christopher's Inn, Graymoor, N.Y., from 1992. Mem. White House Conf. on Youth, 1960, White House Conf. on Drugs, 1960; lectr. on drug abuse to various orgns., 1960—; mem. drug task force N.Y. State, 1978-79; pastoral min. Woodycrest AIDS Hosp., N.Y.C., 1994. Contbr. articles to profl. jours.; appearances on nat. and internat. tv on drug issues; subject of: The Junkie Priest (John D. Harris). Recipient Nat. Cath. Good Samaritan award, 1974, Aquinas Humanitarian award Mt. St. Mary Coll., N.Y., 1986, Alumni award Cath. U. Am., 1991, awards from U.S. Army, USN, USMC for pioneering drug programs in armed forces, svc. award Am. Coun. Drug Edn., 1995. Mem. New Eng. Police Women's Assn. (hon., award 1965). *If we had the vision of faith, we would see beneath every behavior - no matter how repulsive - beneath every bodily appearance - no matter how dirty or deformed - a priceless dignity and value that makes all material facts and scientific technologies fade into insignificance!.* Deceased.

**EGERTON, JOHN WALDEN,** author; b. Atlanta, June 14, 1935; s. William Graham and Rebecca Crenshaw (White) E.; m. Ann Elizabeth Bleidt, June 6, 1957; children: Brooks Bleidt, March White. Student, Western Ky. State Coll., 1953-54; BA, U. Ky., 1958, MA, 1960. With public relations dept. U. Ky., 1958-60; dir. public info. U. South Fla., 1960-65; staff writer Southern Edn. Report mag., 1965-69, Race Relations Reporter mag., 1969-71; founder Southern Foodways Alliance (SFA), 1999—2013. Contbg. editor, 1973-74, free lance writer, Nashville, 1971—2013, journalist in residence, Va. Poly. Inst. & State U., Blacksburg, 1977-78; contbg. editor: Saturday Rev. of Edn, 1972-73, Southern Voices, 1974-75; syndicated food columnist, Atlanta Journal Constitution, 1988-89; sr. corr. The Tennessean, 1996; sr. lectr. Amerucan Studies, U. Tex., 1997; author: A Mind to Stay Here, 1970, The Americanization of Dixie, 1974, Visions of Utopia, 1977, Nashville: The Faces of Two Centuries, 1979, Generations: An American Family, 1983, Southern Food: At Home, On the Road, In History, 1987, Side Orders, 1990, Shades of Gray, 1991, Speak Now Against the Day: The Generation Before the Civil Rights Movement in the South, 1994, Ali Dubyiah and the Forty Thieves, 2006; contbr. articles to mags. Served with AUS, 1954-56. Died Nov. 21, 2013.

**EGESTAD, BÖRJE,** chemical engineer, researcher; b. Edebo, Sweden, Dec. 25, 1950; arrived in Denmark, 1991; s. Olle and Margareta (Andersson) E.; m. Sinikka Marjatta Taurio, Sept. 9, 1978; children: Magnus, Felix, Enid. M Chem. Engring., Royal Inst. Tech., Stockholm, 1973, PhD, 1985. Tchg. asst. Royal Inst. Tech., 1972-79; postdoctoral fellow U. Waterloo, Ont., Can., 1979-80; rsch. asst. Karolinska Inst., Stockholm, 1980-85, rsch. assoc., 1986-91, asst. prof., 1990—2006; head dept. bioanalysis NeuroSearch A/S, Ballerup, Denmark, 1991-98, dir. analytical chemistry, 1998—2005, mem. mgmt. group, 2000—06, dir. CRO coord., from 2006. Vis. sci. worker Clin. Rsch. Ctr., Harrow, Eng., 1988. Contbg. author: The Chemistry of the Human Body, 1989; contbr. articles to Jour. Chromatography, Rapid Comm. Mass Spectrometry, Jour. Lipid Rsch. Scholar Royal Inst. Tech., 1974. Mem. Swedish Chem. Soc., Am. Soc. Mass Spectrometry. Avocations: photography, skiing, gardening. Home: Herlev, Denmark. Died Apr. 10, 2006.

**EHLERS, ELEANOR MAY COLLIER (MRS. FREDERICK BURTON EHLERS),** civic worker; b. Klamath Falls, Oreg., Apr. 23, 1920; d. Alfred Douglas and Ethel (Foster) Collier; m. Frederick Burton Ehlers, June 26, 1943; children: Frederick Douglas, Charles Collier. BA, U. Oreg., 1941; degree, Stanford, 1942. Cert. master gardener Oreg. State U., 1993. Tchr. Salinas Union HS, 1942—43; pres. Cmty. Concert Assn., 1966—74, bd. dirs., from 1950, Favell Mus. Western Art & Artifacts, 1971—80; mem. Child Guidance Adv. Coun., 1956—60, Govs. Adv. Com. Arts & Humanities, 1966—67, Govs. Com. Governance of CC, 1967, Established Women's Guild Merle West Med. Ctr., 1965, sec., bd. dirs., 1962—65, 1976—90, bd. dirs., from 1962, mem., bldg. com., 1962—67, mem., planning com., chmn., edn. & rsch. com. hosp. bd., from 1967; piano tchr. Klamath Falls, from 1958; chpt. pres. Am. Field Svc., 1962—63; mem., adv. com. Boys & Girls Aid Soc., 1965—67; bd. mem. Friends of Mus. U. Oreg., 1966—69, Arts in Oreg., 1966—68, Klamath County Colls. for Oreg.'s Future, from 1968, PBS TV Sta. KSYS, 1988—92; co-chmn. Friends Collier Pk. Collier Pk. Logging Mus., 1986—88, sec., from 1988; pres., bd. dirs. Merle West Med. Ctr., 1990—92, vice chmn., from 1992. Recipient Greatest Svc. award, Oreg. Tech. Inst., 1970—71, Internat. Woman of Achievement award, Quota Club, 1981, U. Oreg. Pioneer award, 1981; named Woman of Month Klamath Herald News, 1965. Mem.: AAUW (local pres. 1955—56, Oreg. Endowed fellowship), P.E.O. (Oreg. dir. 1968—75, state pres. 1974—75, trustee, Internat. Continuing Edn. Fund 1977—83, chmn. 1981—83), Oreg. Music Tchrs. Assn. (pres. Klamath Basin dist. 1979—81), Pi Lambda Theta, Mu Phi Epsilon, Pi Beta Phi. Presbyterian. Deceased.

**EHR, ROBERT THOMAS,** engineering executive; b. Muskegon, Mich., Mar. 12, 1944; s. Gerald William and Eleanor Catherine (Adamczyk) Ehr; m. Mary Evelyn Craven, Mar. 7, 1970; children: Craig, Christine, Jessica. Attended, U. Detroit, 1964—67; BEE, Marquette U., 1968. Engr. TRW Vidar, Mountain View, Calif., 1972—76, engring. supr., 1976—80, engring. mgr., 1980—82, Fairchild Test Sys., San Jose, 1982—83; mfg. engring. mgr. Telenova, Inc., Los Gatos, Calif., 1983—87, dir. engring., 1987—99. Mem.: No. Calif. Contest Club (sec. treas. 1983—84). Republican. Home: San Jose, Calif. Died Mar. 28, 1999.

**EHRLICH, EUGENE,** communications executive; b. NYC, Jan. 10, 1930; s. Max Ehrlich and Rose Krauthamer; children: Karen, Jeffrey. BS, NYU, 1951. Program mgr. NASA, Washington, 1962-79; communications engr. Aerospace Corp., El Segundo, Calif., 1979-81, Spacecom, Gaithersburg, Md., 1981-82; sr. communications engr. TRW Inc., Redondo Beach, Calif., from 1982. Avocations: tennis, hiking. Home: Playa Del Rey, Calif. Died Mar. 13, 1995.

**EHRLICH, GEORGE EDWARD,** rheumatologist, consultant; b. Vienna, July 18, 1928; came to US, 1938, naturalized, 1944; s. Edward and Irene (Elling) E.; m. Gail S. Abrams, Mar. 30, 1968; children: Charles Edward, Steven L. Abrams, Rebecca Sayles. AB cum laude, Harvard U., Cambridge, Mass., 1948; MB, MD, Chgo. Med. Sch., 1952. Intern Michael Reese Hosp., Chgo., 1952; resident Francis Delafield Hosp., NYC, 1955, Beth Israel Hosp., Boston, 1956, New Eng. Center Hosp., Boston, 1957; fellow rheumatology NIH, Bethesda, Md., 1958, Hosp. for Spl. Surgery, NYC, 1959-61, asst. attending physician, 1960-64; spl. fellow Sloan Kettering Inst., 1960-61; instr. medicine Cornell U., 1960-64; dir. Arthritis Center, chief rheumatology Albert Einstein Med. Center and Moss Rehab. Hosp., Phila., 1964-80; asst. prof. medicine Temple U., 1964-67, asso. prof. medicine, 1967-72, prof. medicine, 1972-80, asso. prof. rehab. medicine, 1964-74, prof., 1974-80; vis. lectr. U. Pa., 1964-80; prof. medicine, dir. div. rheumatology Hahnemann U., Phila., 1980-83; v.p. Anti-Inflammatory/Endocrine CIBA-Geigy Pharmaceuticals, Summit, NJ, 1983-86; head med. affairs CIBA-Geigy Ltd.,

Switzerland, 1987-88; pres. George E. Ehrlich Assocs., pharmaceutical cons. Adj. prof. clin. medicine NYU Med. Ctr., 1984—; lectr. medicine U. Pa., 1989-91, adj. prof. medicine, 1992—; expert advisor, cons. Diabetes and Other Noncommunicable Diseases unit WHO, 1990-98, Chronic Disease Mgmt., 1998—; chmn. Internat. Low Back Pain Initiative; rep. of pres. Internat. League Assns. Rheumatology for Soft Tissue Rheumatisms, 1993-97, exec. com.; liaison to WHO, 1997—; mem. arthritis adv. com. FDA, 1993-96, chmn., 1993-96; expert, FDA, 1997-99; mem. coun. Chairs, FDA, 1996—; chmn. sci. adv. bd. Hochrheininstitut (Rheumatic Disease and Rehab. Rsch. Inst. of Upper Rhine in Germany, France and Switzerland for Treatment, Tchg., and Rsch.), 1993—; bd. dirs. Greenwich Inst. Am. Edn.; chmn., U.S. mem. Expert Adv. Panel on Chronic Degenerative Diseases, WHO, 1996—. Author: Differential Diagnosis of Rheumatoid Arthritis, 1972, Oculocutaneous Manifestations of Rheumatic Diseases, 1973; editor: Total Management of the Arthritic Patient, 1973, Rehabilitation Management of Rheumatic Conditions, 1980, 2d edit., 1986; editor: (with J. Fries) Prognosis, 1981; editor: (with H.E. Paulus) Controversies in the Clinical Evaluation of Analgesic-Anti-Inflammatory-Antirheumatic Drugs, 1981; editor: (with P. Utsinger, N. Zvaifler) Rheumatoid Arthritis, 1985; editor: (with W. Simon) Medicolegal Consequences of Trauma, 1992; editor: (with N. Khaltaev) Low Back Pain, 2000; editor: (with W. Simon A. Sadwin) Conquering Chronic Pain After Injury, 2002; editor: Jour. Albert Einstein Med. Ctr., 1966—71, Arthritis and Rheumatic Diseases Abstracts, 1968—71; mem. editl. bd.: Inflammation, 1974—88, Psychosomatics, 1977—83, Sexual Medicine Today, 1977—84, Jour. Rheumatology, from 1982, Internat. Jour. Immunotherapy, from 1984, Immunopharmacology, from 1985, Med. Problems Performing Artists, 1985—92, Brazilian Jour. Rheumatology, 1992, 1996—99, Italian Jour. Rheumatic Diseases, from 1999; contbr. articles to profl. jours. Pres. Ea. Pa. chpt. Arthritis Found., 1970-72; mem. Phila. Mayor's Sci. and Tech. Adv. Coun., 1972-81; chmn. ad hoc adv. com. Bur. Drugs, FDA, 1971; subcom. on redefinition of disability Social Security Adminstrn., 1982-86. Served to comdr. MC USNR, 1953—55, with USNR, 1975, comdg. officer med. co. 4-3 USNR, 1978—81. Decorated Cavaliere Order of Star of Italian Solidarity; recipient citations, City Phila., 1969, 1974, Distinguished Alumnus award, Chgo. Med. Sch., 1969, Dr. Joseph Lee Hollander award, Ea. Pa. chpt., Arthritis Found., 2004. Fellow ACP, Royal Coll. Physicians Edinburgh, Phila. Coll. Physicians, Am. Coll. Rheumatology (elected master, 1994, com. for publ. Arthritis and Rheumatism, 1977-79, mem. editl. bd. 1980-83), Rheumatism Socs. Ecuador, India (hon.); mem. AMA (editl. bd. Jour. 1972-82), Am. Soc. Clin. Pharmacology and Therapeutics, Assn. Mil. Surgeons (Philip Hench award 1971), Brit. Assn. Rheumatology and Rehab. (overseas mem., editl. bd. 1979-82), Internat. Soc. for Behcet's Disease (hon. life pres.), Harvard Club (Boston, NYC), Alpha Omega Alpha. Home: Philadelphia, Pa. *Respect for the ideas of others, but ultimately responsible for my own ideas, thus, a liberal philosophy in a conservative setting. Like Brecht's Galileo, I should like to be remembered as a lover of old wines and new ideas.* Died Feb. 28, 2014.

**EIJCK, MICHIEL VAN,** science educator; b. Amsterdam, July 29, 1968; MSc in Biology, U. Amsterdam, 1993, PhD, 2006. Cert. Sci., Tech., Soc., Free U. Amsterdam, 1997. Sci. tchr. Ignatius Gymnasium, Amsterdam, 1994—2000; rsch. asst. Amstel Inst., Amsterdam, 2000—06; nserc-crystal fellow U. Victoria, Canada, 2006—07; asst. prof. sci. edn. Eindhoven U. Tech., Netherlands, from 2007. Author: (book) Authentic Science Revisited. Rsch. grant, Nat. Sci. Engring. Rsch. Coun. Can., 2006—07. Mem.: Equity & Ethics Com. Nat. Assn. Rsch. Sci. Tchg., European Sci. Edn. Rsch. Assn., Nat. Assn. Rsch. Sci. Tchg. Achievements include design of teaching quantitative concepts with ICT in biology education. Deceased.

**EISENBERG, THEODORE,** law educator; b. Bklyn., Oct. 26, 1947; s. Abraham Louis and Esther (Waldman) E.; m. Lisa Wright, Nov. 27, 1971; children: Katherine Wright, Ann Marie, Thomas Peter. BA, Swarthmore Coll., 1969; JD, U. Pa., 1972. Bar: Pa. 1972, N.Y. 1974, U.S. Ct. Appeals (2d cir.) 1974, Calif. 1977. Law clk. US Ct. Appeals (DC cir.), 1972-73; law clk. to Justice Earl Warren US Supreme Ct., 1973; assoc. Debevoise & Plimpton, NYC, 1974-77; prof. law UCLA Law Sch., 1977-81, Cornell U. Law Sch., Ithaca, NY, 1981-96, Henry Allen Mark prof. law, 1996—2014. Vis. prof. law Harvard U. Law Sch., 1984-85, 2004; vis. prof. law, Stanford U. Law Sch., 1987, adj. prof. statistical sciences, Cornell U., 2008- Author: Civil Rights Legislation, 1981, 5th edit., 2004, Bankruptcy and Debtor-Creditor Law, 1984, 3d edit., 2004; editor Jour. Empirical Legal Studies; mem. adv. bd. Law and Soc. Rev., American Law & Econ. Rev.; contbr. articles to profl. jours. Am. Bar Found grantee, NSF grantee. Fellow Royal Statis. Soc., American Acad. Arts & Sciences; mem. ABA, Assn. Bar City N.Y., Law & Soc. Assn., American Law & Econ. Assn., American Bankruptcy Inst. Home: Ithaca, NY. Died Feb. 23, 2014.

**EISENHART, EDNA JANE,** retired secondary education educator; b. Sidman, Pa., Apr. 25, 1922; d. John Conrad and Edna Marie (Hill) Peffer; m. Jacob Henry Eisenhart Jr., May 29, 1943 (dec. 1987); children: Craig Alan, Lynne Ellen Eisenhart Emig, Jane Constance Eisenhart Wolansky. BS, Juniata Coll., Huntingdon, Pa., 1944. Cert. home economist, Pa. Asst. dietitian Lewistown (Pa.) Hosp., 1944; asst. chemist Thiokol Corp., Trenton, N.J., 1945-48; tchr. home econs. Bristol Borough (Pa.) Sch. Dist., 1960-81, ret., 1981. Nat. trainer Coop. Disaster Child Care Program, New Windsor, Md., 1983—; co-chair alumni support fund Juniata Coll., 1984-85; mem. edn. com. Am. Cancer Soc., Huntingdon, 1986—; vol. trainer Huntingdon County Spouse Abuse Program, 1987—; nutrition cons. Head Start, Huntingdon, 1987—. Fellow Am. Home Econs. Assn., Pa. Edn. Assn., Pa. Ret. Pub. Sch. Employees Assn.; mem. AAUW (pres. 1990—). Mem. Soc. Of Friends. Avocations: reading, writing, quilting, needle work, travel. Home: Huntingdon, Pa. Died Mar. 2, 2008.

**EISENHOWER, JOHN SHELDON DOUD,** writer, former ambassador; b. Denver, Aug. 3, 1922; s. Dwight David (34th Pres. of U.S.) and Mamie (Doud) E.; m. Barbara Jean Thompson, June 10, 1947 (div. 1986); children: Dwight David II, Barbara Anne, Susan Elaine, Mary Jean; m. Joanne Thompson, Apr. 9, 1990. BS, U.S. Mil. Acad., 1944; MA in English Lit., Columbia, 1950; LHD (hon.), Northwood Inst., 1970. Commd. 2d lt. U.S. Army, 1944, advanced through grades to lt. col., 1963; assigned 1st Army, Europe, 1945, Army of Occupation, Europe, 1945-47, Korean War, 1952-53, Army Gen. Staff, 1957-58, White House Staff, 1958-61; resigned, 1963; brig. gen. USAR, 1974; engaged in writing, 1965-69; US amb. to Belgium US Dept. State, Brussels, 1969-71. Cons. to the Pres.; also chmn. Interagency Classification Review Com., 1972-73; chmn. bd. Acad. Life Ins. Co., Atlanta; mem. adv. council Nat. Archives, 1974-77; chmn. President's Advisory Com. on Refugees, 1975; mil. editor Algonguin Books of Chapel Hill. Author: The Bitter Woods, 1969, Strictly Personal, 1974, Allies: Pearl Harbor to D-Day, 1982, So Far From God: The U.S. War with Mexico, 1846-48, 1989, Intervention!: The United States Involvement in the Mexican Revolution, 1913-17, 1993, Agent of Destiny: The Life and Times of General Winfield Scott, 1997, Yanks: The Epic Story of the American Army in World War I, 2001, General Ike: Apersonal Reminiscence, 2003, They Fought at Anzio, 2007, Zachary Taylor, 2008, A Morning in June: Defending Outpost Harry, 2010, Soldiers and Statesmen: Reflection on Leadership, 2012; editor: Letters to Mamie, 1978 Mem. diplomatic coun., bd. govs. USO, 1983-85; trustee Alumni Fedn. Columbia U., 1976-80. Decorated Legion of Merit, Bronze Star, Combat Inf. badge, Grand Cross Order of Crown Belgium, Chungmu Disting. Service medal (Korea); recipient Grad. Faculties Alumni award for Excellence Columbia U., 1970. Mem. Diplomatic and Consular Officers Ret., Capitol Hill Club. Republican. Died Dec. 21, 2013.

**EISNER, ELLIOT WAYNE,** art educator; b. Chgo., Mar. 10, 1933; s. Louis Eisner. MA in Art & Edn., Roosevelt U., 1954; MS in Art Edn., Ill. Inst. Tech., 1955; MA in Edn., U. Chgo., 1958, PhD in Edn., 1962. High school art tchr., Chgo., 1956—58; art tchr. U. Chgo., 1958—60, instr. edn., 1961—62, asst. prof. edn., 1962—65; instr., art edn. Ohio State U., 1960—61; assoc. prof. edn. & art Stanford U. Graduate Sch. Edn., 1965—70, prof., 1970—2000, Lee Jacks prof. edn., prof. art, 2000—14. Mem. editl. bd. Kappan, 1995—2000; mem. editl. advisory bd. Just & Caring Edn., 1995—2000. Contbr. articles various profl. jours.; co-author (with David W. Ecker): Readings in Art Education, 1966; co-author: (with Alan Peshkin) Qualitative Inquiry in Education: The Continuing Debate, 1990; co-author: (with Elizabeth Vallance) Conflicting Conceptions of Curriculum series on Contemporary Educational Issues, 1974; author: Confronting Curriculum Reform, 1971, Educating Artistic Vision, 1972, The Arts, Human Development, and Education, 1976, The Education Imagination: On the Design and Evaluation of School Programs, 1979, The Art of Educational Evaluation: A Personal View, 1985, The Role of Discipline-Based Art Education in America's Schools, 1988, The Enlightened Eye: Qualitative Inquiry and the Enhancement of Educational Practice, 1991, Cognition and Curriculum Reconsidered, 1994, Evaluating and Assessing the Visual Arts in Education: International Perspectives, 1996, The Kind of Schools We Need: Personal Essays, 1998, The Arts and the Creation of the Mind, 2002 (The Grawemeyer award for Edn., U. Louisville, 2005). Recipient Sir Hubert Read award, Internat. Soc. Edn. through Art (INSEAD), 1997, Jose Vasoncelos World award of Edn., 1992, Harold McGraw Jr. prize in Edn., Nat. Art Edn. Assn., 1998, Brock Internat. prize, 2004, Grawemeyer award, U. Louisville, 2005, Palmer O. Johnson Memorial award, American Educational Rsch. Assn. Mem.: Nat. Acad. Edn., Royal Norwegian Soc. Sciences & Letters, Royal Soc. Arts UK, Nat. Acad. of Edn., John Dewey Soc. (pres. 1998—2000), J. Paul Getty Ctr. for Edn. in the Arts. Achievements include research in the rold of artistic thinking in the conduct of social sci. rsch., programs to further arts edn. in American schools, the role of artistry in ednl. theory and practice. Died Jan. 10, 2014.

**EITAN, RAFAEL,** Israeli government official; b. Moshav Tel Adashim, Jezre'el Valley, Israel, 1929; married; 3 children. Grad., Nat. Def. Coll. Founder Tzomet party, 1983; mem. state control and fgn. affairs and def. coms. Israeli Knesset, 1984, mem. fgn. affairs and def. com., 1988-90, former chmn. anti-drug abuse com., min. agriculture, 1990-91, min. agriculture and environ., dep. prime min., 1996—99. Former chmn. Israel-Russian Fedn. Parliamentary Friendship League. Author: (autobiography) A Soldier's Story. Mem. Israel Def. Forces, 1948-83, chief of staff, 1978-83. Avocations: carpentry, farming. Died Nov. 23, 2004.

**ELETA A. FERNANDO,** ambassador; b. Panama City, Republic of Panama, Aug. 10, 1921; m. Graciela Quelquejeu de Eleta. AB in Social Scis., Stanford U., 1942; BS in Structural Engring., MIT, 1947; LLD (honoris causa), Yankton Coll., 1961. Sec. of treasury Republic of Panama, 1958-60, sec. of state, 1964-68, ambassador at large, from 1968; founding gov. Interam. Devel. Bank, from 1960. Pres. bd. Panama Broadcasting Corp., S.A., Haras Cerro Punta, S.A., Nature Conservancy of Panama, Caribbean Thoroughbred Racing Confedn., Nutricion Animal, S.A., Aseguradora Mundial de Panama; bd. mem. Desarrollo Industrial, Banco Exterior, S.A. Decorated Grand Cross of leading orders of Panama, 1958, Italy, 1959, Peru, 1960, Panama, 1960, Argentina, 1964, El Salvador, 1965, Mexico, 1966, Guatemala, 1966, Spain, 1966, Ecuador, 1968, Taiwan, 1968, Chile, 1968, Italy, 1968, Malta, 1979. Mem. Camara de Comercio de Panama, Sindicato de Industriales de Panama, Asociacion Panameña de Ejecutivos de Empresa, Sociedad Panameña de Ingenieros y Arquitectos, Consejo Interamericano de Comercio y Produccion. Deceased.

**ELIOT, CHARLES WILLIAM, II,** landscape architect, planning consultant; b. Cambridge, Mass., Nov. 5, 1899; s. Samuel Atkins and Frances Stone (Hopkinson) E.; m. Regina Phelps Dodge, Oct. 11, 1928 (dec. Jan. 12, 1979); children: Charles W. III, Carolyn Eliot Hitchcock, John, Lawrence Gray. BA, Harvard U., 1920, M of Landscape Architecture, 1923. Registered landscape architect, Mass. Sheldon traveling fellow Harvard U., Europe, 1923-24; pvt. practice landscape architect and planning cons. Boston, 1924-26; city planner, dir. planning Nat. Capital Park and Planning Commn., Washington, 1926-33; exec. officer Nat. Planning Bd., Washington, 1933-34, Nat. Resources Bd., Washington, 1934-35, Nat. Resources Com., Washington, 1935-39; dir. Nat. Resources Planning Bd., Washington, 1939-43, Haynes Found., Los Angeles, 1944-45; pvt. practice planning cons. Pasadena, Calif., 1946-54, Cambridge, Mass., 1954-93. Pvt. practice landscape architect and cons., Md. and Va., 1926-33; lectr. U. Calif., Pasadena, 1944, Insts. Community Devel., UCLA, 1945, Stanford U., 1946, U. Pa., 1951, MIT, 1951, 65-68, U. Mich., 1954, numerous other schools; prof. landscape architecture Grad. Sch. Design Harvard U., 1955-59, prof. city and regional planning, 1959-66. Author: Shipstead Act, 1928; dir. radio program Destination Tomorrow, 1944-45. Sec. Mass. Trustees of Pub. Reservations, 1924-26; organizer, sec. Mass. Govs. Com. on Open Spaces, 1924-26; chmn. Los Angeles County Citizens Com. Parks, Beaches and Recreation, 1945; mem. Los Angeles Dem. Com., 1948; cons., dir. resources program Ford Found., 1952-53; petitioner Bay Cir. and Hist. Dist. Acts, 1956-65; chmn. comprehensive plan com.; mem. Boston Met. Area Planning Coun., 1964-93, Back Bay Hist. Dist. Study Com., 1965-66, Cambridge Hist. Com., 1967-93, Cambridge Bicentennial Corp., 1974-77, Mass. Conservation Coun., 1975, Calif. Revision of Planning Laws, numerous other coms. and couns. Served ARC Ambulance Svc., 1918, Italy. Decorated Croce di Guerra; recipient Hon. Mention award Boston Contest, 1944, Loring award Boston Met. Area Planning Council, 1977, 15 Yr. Service award, 1981, Citizen of Yr. award Cambridge 350th Anniversary Com., 1981, Rexford Tugwell award U. So. Calif., 1986, Founders award, 1989; Chubb fellow Yale U., 1951. Fellow Am. Acad. Arts and Scis., Am. Soc. Landscape Architects (Medal 1982); mem. Am. Inst. Planners (bd. govs. 1929-32, 42-45, Disting. Service award 1961, 67), Boston Soc. Landscape Architects (pres. 1957-60), Am. Soc. Planning Officials (bd. dirs. 1934-36, Disting. Service medal 1972), Mass. Assn. Olmsted Parks (Award 1985), Nat. Assn. Olmsted Parks, Mass. Fedn. Planning Bds. (Hon. Mem. award 1980), Nature Conservancy, Soc. Preservation of New Eng. Antiquities, Ipswich Hist. Soc. (pres. 1976-78, Longfellow medal 1989), Cambridge Hist. Soc., Soc. Propagation of Gospel Amoung Indians and Others, Nat. Parks and Conservation Assn. (bd. dirs. 1929-33), Sierra Club, Wildnerness Soc., Bunker Hill Monument Soc. (emeritus, pres. 1959-71), Mass. Trustees Reservations (life, sec. 1925-26, standing com. 1926-29, 57-64, adv. council 1964-93, Conservation award 1969), Am. Unitarian Universalist Assn., numerous other assns. and orgns. Clubs: Cosmos (Washington). Unitarian Universalist. Home: Cambridge, Mass. Died Mar. 16, 1993.

**ELKHADEM, SAAD ELDIN AMIN,** foreign language and literature educator, writer, editor, publisher; b. Cairo, May 12, 1932; emigrated to Can., 1968, naturalized, 1974; s. Amin Saad and Zahra Amin (Tharwat) E.; m. Madiha Mahmoud, July 16, 1962; 1 child, Sherifa. PhD, U. Graz, 1961. Press attache Egyptian Govt., Berne, 1962-65; dir. Office for Cultural Relations, Cairo, 1965-67; asst. prof. U. N.D., Grand Forks, 1967-68; assoc. prof. German U. N.B., Fredericton, Can., 1968-74, prof. dept. German and Russian, 1974-95, prof. emeritus, from 1995. Author: Sechs Essays ueber den deutschen Roman, 1969, Ajniha Min Rasas, 1972, Zur Geschichte des deutschen Romans, 1974, Tajarib Laylah Wahidah, 1975, Dictionary of Literary Terms, 1976, The York Press Style manual, From Travels of the Egyptian Odysseus, 1979, The York Companion to Themes and Motifs of World Literature, 1981, History of the Egyptian Novel, 1985, Ulysses' Hallucinations or the Like, 1985, The Ulysses Trilogy, 1988, The Plague, 1988, Canadian Adventures of the Flying Egyptian, 1990, Chronicle of the Flying Egyptian in Canada, 1991, The Concise Dictionary of Greek, Roman, Norse and Egyptian Mythology, 1991, Crash Landing of the Flying Egyptian, 1992, Wings of a Lead: A Modern Egyptian Novella, 1994, Five Innovative Egyptian Short Stories, 1994, An Egyptian Satire about a Condemned Building, 1996, The Blessed Movement: An Egyptian Micronovel, 1997, The Great Egyptian Novel, 1998, Creative Writing, 1999, Brief Definitions of All Essential Literary Terms, 2000, One Night in Cairo, 2001, On Egyptian Fiction: Five Essays, 2001; editor Internat. Fiction Rev., 1974-96; editor, gen. mgr. York Press, (also transl.) Life is Like a Cucumber: Colloquial Egyptian Proverbs, 1993, The Sayings of the Prophet Muhammad, 1994; gen. editor Authoritative Studies in World Literature; contbr. articles to profl. jours. Can. Council grantee, 1974-75; recipient Min. of State multiculturalism awards, 1989, 90. Mem. MLA. Home: Halifax, Canada. Died Feb. 25, 2003.

**ELKINS, WILSON HOMER,** former academic administrator; b. Medina, Tex., July 9, 1908; s. Willie and May (Stevens) E.; m. Dorothy Blackburn, June, 1938 (dec. 1971); children: Carole, Margaret; m. Vivian Helen Noh, Aug. 4, 1972. BA, MA, U. Tex., 1932; BLitt, Oxford U., Eng., 1936; DPhil., Oxford U., 1936. Instr. U. Tex., Austin, 1936-38; pres. San Angelo Jr. Coll., Tex., 1938-48, U. Tex., El Paso, 1949-54, U. Md., College Park, 1954-78, pres.

emeritus, 1978—94. Cons. in field. Author: Forty Years as a College President, Memoirs of Wilson Elkins, 1981. Vice chmn. So. Reg. Edn. Bd., 1959-61; bd. visitors U.S. Naval Acad., 1967-70, Air U. of Maxwell AFB, 1958-61, others. Rhodes scholar, 1933-36; named Disting. Alumnus, Schreiner Coll., 1979, U. Tex., 1972. Mem. Nat. Assn. Land Grant Colls. and State U. (pres. 1970-71), Middle States Assn. of Schs. and Colls. (pres. 1966-67), So. Univ. Conf. (pres. 1971). Democrat. Episcopalian. Avocations: golf, travel, politics. Home: Hyattsville, Md. Died Mar. 17, 1994.

**ELLINGER, RORY,** state legislator; b. St. Louis, June 13, 1941; m. Linda Locke; children: Margaret Ellinger-Locke, Martin Ellinger-Locke. BA in History, U. Mo., Kansas City, 1963; MA in History, U. Mo., Columbia; JD, U. Mo., Kansas City. Atty., pres. Ellinger & Associates, PC, Mo.; press sec. to Lt. Gov. Thomas Eagleton State of Mo., Mo.; legal counsel NAACP of St. Charles County, Mo.; exec. dir. Legal Services of Northeast Mo.; asst. gen. counsel Mo. Public Svc. Commn.; mem. Dist. 72 Mo. House of Reps., 2011—14. Democrat. Died Apr. 9, 2014.

**ELLIOT, RALPH GREGORY,** lawyer; b. Hartford, Conn., Oct. 20, 1936; s. K. Gregory and Zarou (Manoukian) E. BA, Yale U., 1958, LLB, 1961. Bar: Conn. 1961, U.S. Dist. Ct. Conn. 1963, U.S. Ct. Appeals (2d cir.) 1966, U.S. Supreme Ct. 1967, U.S. Ct. Appeals (fed. cir.) 1993, U.S. Ct. Appeals (1st cir.) 1997. Law clk. to assoc. justice Conn. Supreme Ct., Hartford, 1961-62; assoc. Alcorn, Bakewell & Smith, Hartford, 1962-67, ptnr., 1967-83, Tyler, Cooper & Alcorn, Hartford, from 1983. Adj. prof. law U. Conn., Hartford, 1973—; sec. Superior Ct. Legal Internship Com., Conn., 1971—; chmn. Superior Ct. Legal Specialization Screening Com., Conn., 1981—, U.S. Dist. Ct. Panel Spl. Masters, Hartford, 1983-88. Chmn. bd. editors Conn. Law Tribune, 1986-87. Chmn. Constn. Bicentennial Commn., Conn., 1986-91; mem. Criminal Justice Commn. Conn., 1991-95. Recipient Fenton P. Futtner award Conn. Reps., 1993, Pub.'s award Conn. Law Tribune, 2003, E. Bartlett Barnes Meml. award Conn. Freedom of Info. Commn., 2004, Award of Excellence, U. Conn. Law Sch. Alumni Assn., 2004. Fellow Am. Bar Found.; mem. ABA (standing com. on ethics and profl. responsibility 1989-95, standing com. on profl. discipline 1998-2001, ho. of dels. 1983-87), Conn. Bar Assn. (officer, bd. govs. 1971-79, 83-87, pres. 1985-86, John Eldred Shields Disting. Profl. Svc. award 1993), Am. Law Inst., Yale Law Sch. Assn. (pres. 1988-90, chmn. exec. com. 1990-92), Yale Club (pres. 1977-79, Nathan Hale award 1984, Betty McCallip Meml. award 1991), Hartford Club, Grad. Club (New Haven), Phi Beta Kappa. Republican. Episcopalian. Deceased.

**ELLIOTT, DICK F.,** former state legislator; b. Cassatt, SC, Sept. 26, 1937; m. Martin Oppenheimer; children: Marcy, Evan, Josh, Ali. Owner Elliott Realty Corp., from 1959; major owner Beachwood Golf Club, from 1967; developer, owner Eagle Nest Golf Club, from 1970; mem. Dist 36 SC House of Reps., 1982—92; mem. Dist. 28 SC State Senate, 1993—2012. Recipient Woman of Year, Westchester ORT, 1990, Women's Press Club, NY, 1991, Govt award, Westchester Cmty. Opportunity Prog., 1994, honoree, Open Door Med. Ctr., 1995, Careers for the Disabled award, 1996, Svc. award, NY.Jewish War Vet., 1997. Mem.: Mental Health Assn. (bd. mem.), Anti-Defamation League (bd. mem.), America Jewish Com. (vice pres.), Westchester League Women Voters (pres. mamaroneck), Westchester Munic Planning Fedn., Westchester Co. Village Off Assn. (former pres.). Democrat. Presbyterian. Died June 7, 2014.

**ELLIOTT, JACK,** folk musician; Albums Bull Durham Sacks and Railroad Tracks, Young Brigham, Me & Bobby McGee, South Coast, 1995 (Grammy award, 1995), Ramblin' Jack, 1996, Kerouac's Last Dream, 1997, Friends of mine, 1989, Long Ride, 1999. Recipient Bill Graham Lifetime Achievement award Bay Area Music Awards, 1996, Nat. Medal of Arts award, Pres. Clinton, 1998. Died Aug. 18, 2001.

**ELLIOTT, MYRTLE EVELYN KEENER,** remedial education educator; b. Annawan, Ill., Apr. 11, 1898; d. John William and Mary (Baldwin) Keener; m. Leo Louis Elliott, Aug. 19, 1935 (dec. 1948); children: Mary Ellen Agan, Winona Sample, James, Joan. AB, Cornell U., 1921; MA, Columbia U., 1926; postgrad. summer, U. Iowa, 1928, Ohio State U., 1931, U. Chgo., 1933, San Francisco State Coll., 1949, Fresno State Coll., 1958, postgrad. summer, 1959, postgrad. summer, 1961. Tchr. pub. high schs., Panora, Iowa, 1921—23, Dewitt, Iowa, 1923—25; head English dept., dean girls Kemmerer, Wyo., 1926—29; dean girls and English Pendleton, Oreg., 1929—30; tchr. Ely, Nev., 1930—31; girls' adviser boarding schs. U.S. Indian Svc., 1931—35; tchr. Latin and English Cut Bank, Mont., 1944—46; tchr. older educable retarded children Kern County Supt. Schs., Bakersfield, Calif., 1949—68; pvt. remedial work with children and adults. Recipient Alumni Merit award, Cornell Coll., 1977. Fellow Am. Assn. Mental Deficiency; mem. Coun. Exceptional Children, Internat. Reading Assn., NEA, Calif. Tchrs. Asn., Calif. Ret. Tchrs. Assn., Nat. Congress Parents and Tchrs. (hon. life mem.), Calif. Congress Parents and Tchrs. (hon. life mem.), Catholic Daus. Am., Columbia Tchrs. Coll. Alumni Assn. (past local chmn.), Cornell Coll. Alumni Assn. (sec. Ctrl. Valley group 1958-), AAUW, Phi Beta Kappa. Home: Bakersfield, Calif. Died Dec. 12, 1986.

**ELLIOTT, ROY FRASER,** lawyer; b. Ottawa, Ont., Can., Nov. 25, 1921; B in Comm., Queen's U., Kingston, Ont., Can., 1943; LLB, Osgoode Hall Law Sch., 1946; grad., Harvard U. Sch. Bus. Adminstrn., 1947. Bar: Ont. 1946, Que. 1948; created queen's counsel. Ptnr. Stikeman, Elliott, Toronto, Ont., Canada, 1952—2005. Bd. dir. CAE Inc., Toronto; lectr. co. law McGill U., Montreal, 1951. Contbg. author, editor: Que. Corp. Manual, 1948-53; co-editor: Doing Business in Canada. Named to Order of Can., 1980. Mem. Montreal Bar Assn., Can. Bar Assn., Law Soc. Upper Can. Home: Toronto, Canada. Died Jan. 26, 2005.

**ELLISON, ROSEMARY,** curator; Chief curator Indian Arts and Crafts Bd. U.S. Dept. Interior, So. Plains Indian Mus. and Crafts Ctr., Anadarko, Okla. Died July 2002.

**ELSON, JOHN ALBERT,** geology educator; b. Kiating, China, Mar. 2, 1923; s. Albert Joseph and Evelyn Amelia (Hockey) E.; m. Jeanne Bridgman Hickey, Jan. 4, 1957; children— Sarah Bridgman, Rebecca Anne Wood. B.Sc., U. Western Ont., 1945; M.Sc., McMaster U., 1947; PhD, Yale, 1956. Lectr. McMaster U., Hamilton, Ont., Can., 1945-46; geologist Geol. Survey Can., Ottawa, Ont., 1946-56; faculty McGill U., Montreal, Que., Can., 1956—, prof., from 1968, chmn. dept. geol. scis., 1974-75. Cons. geologist, 1956-67 Fellow Geol. Soc. Am., Geol. Assn. Can.; mem. AAAS, Am. Soc. Photogrammetry, Glaciological Soc., Am. Quaternary Assn., NRC Can. (asso. com. for quaternary research 1971-74), Can. Quaternary Assn., Sigma Xi. Died June 11, 2010.

**ELVANDER, NILS AXEL,** political scientist, educator; b. Linköping, Sweden, Apr. 16, 1928; s. Ivar Anderson and Marta (Elferson) Elvander; m. Synnöve Hedenberg Elvander (div. 1985); children: Ragnhild, Cecilia, Liv, Jan; m. Anita Seim Elvander, Oct. 11, 1996. BA, Uppsala U., Sweden, 1951, MA, 1955, PhD, 1961. Lectr. polit. sci. Uppsala U., 1956—60, asst. prof. polit. sci., 1961—67, prof. polit. sci., 1967—90, prof. indsl. rels., 1990—93; ret., 1993. Rsch. leader Swedish Coun. for Mgmt., Stockholm, 1982—88. Author: Interest Organizations in Sweden, 1969, Swedish Tax Policy 1945-1970, 1972, articles in field. Avocation: collecting butterflies. Home: Uppsala, Sweden. Deceased.

**EMERSON, WALTER CARUTH,** artist, educator, retired; b. Dallas, Jan. 24, 1912; s. Walter Caruth and Dale (Chisholm) E.; m. Mary Elizabeth Hicks, July 15, 1961; children: Mary Jane, William Ross. Student, Aunspaugh Sch. Art, Dallas, 1923-24; student, Olin Travis Sch. Art, Dallas, 1926-27, John Knott Art Classes, 1932-33, Southwestern Sch. Theatre, 1934-35; BA, So. Meth. U., 1941. Founder, dir. art dept. Pollock Paper Corp., Dallas, 1937—52; course designer, instr. art and art history So. Meth. U., 1940—63; organizer, dir. art dept. USN, Washington, 1941—45; producer Pencil Personalities, Sta. WFAA-TV, Dallas, 1958; art dir. food and drug divsn. Hunt Oil Co., 1963—69; course designer, instr. Christian Coll. S.W., 1969—70; creator, instr. credit courses Dallas County C.C. Dist., 1972—74; founder, dir. Art Acad. Dallas, 1974—2001, ret., 2001. Editorial cartoonist Dallas Morning News, 1941, N.Y. Mirror, 1956-58; lectr. throughout U.S., Kim Dawson Agy., Dallas, 1977—; initiated instrn. leading to coll. degrees in art for inmates of Dallas County Jail, 1973. Author: The Truth About Santa Anna, 1973, 75, 85; author syndicated column Art Alive, 1979—; contbr. articles to profl. jours.; paintings in Tex. State Mus. and in various other museums and pvt. collections. Founder Americans Unified, Dallas, 1979. Served to lt. USN, 1941-45. Mem. Better Bus. Bur., Mus. N.Mex. Found., Kimbell Art Mus., Dallas Mus. Art, Dallas Zool. Soc., Dallas Arboretum and Bot. Soc., Dallas Symphony Assn., Rotary (pres. pres.'s club Dallas 1970-71), Dallas Knife and Fork Club (pres. 1973-74). Home: Dallas, Tex. *Let go and let God (Anon.).* Died June 7, 2002.

**EMMERICK, RONALD ERIC,** Iranian philology educator; b. Sydney, NSW, Australia, Mar. 9, 1937; s. Eric Steward and Myrtle Caroline (Smith) E.; m. Margaret Ann Frohnsdorff, July 4, 1962; children: Paul Ronald, Catherine Ann, Veronica Jane. BA with honors, U. Sydney, 1959; BA, U. Cambridge, Eng., 1961, PhD, 1965. Tchg. fellow U. Sydney, 1959; rsch. fellow St. John's Coll., Cambridge, 1964-67; lectr. Sch. Oriental and African Studies, U. London, 1964-71; prof. Iranian philology U. Hamburg, Germany, from 1971. Vis. assoc. prof. Oriental Inst., U. Chgo., 1967-68. Author: Tibetan Texts Concerning Khotan, 1967, Saka Grammatical Studies, 1968, The Book of Zambasta, A Khotanese Poem on Buddhism, 1968, The Sutra of Golden Light, 1970, 5th edit., 1996, The Khotanese Surangamasamadhisutra, 1970, Saka Documents V, 1971, Saka Documents VI, 1973, A Guide to the Literature of Khotan, 1979, 2d edit., 1992, The Siddhasara of Rivigupta, Vol. 1: The Sanskrit Text, 1980, The Siddhasara of Ravigupta, Vol. 2: The Tibetan Version, 1982; (with P.O. Skjaervo) Studies in the Vocabulary of Khotanese, vol. I, 1982, vol. II, 1985, The Tumshquese Karmavacana Text, 1985, vol. III, 1997; (with E.G. Pulleyblank) A Chinese Text in Central Asian Brahmi Script, 1993; (with R.P. Das) Vagbhata's Astangahrdayasamhita, 1998; contbr. articles to profl. jours. Fellow Australian Acad. Humanities (hon.); mem. Royal Asiatic Soc., Soc. Asiatique, German Oriental Soc., Am. Oriental Soc., Soc. Linguistica Europaea, Inst. L'Africa e L'Oriente (corr.), British Acad. (corr.), Österreichische Acad. der Wissenschaften (corr.). Home: Quickborn, Germany. Died Aug. 31, 2001.

**ENDRUSICK, ROSE MARIE,** secondary school educator; b. Creighton, Pa., Feb. 11, 1929; d. Paul Anthony and Ann Catherine Fricioni; m. Stanley Endrusick, June 19, 1950; children: Anne, Scott. BS, Drexel Inst. Tech., 1950; MA, Calif. State U.-L.A., 1970. Cert. Culinary Inst. Am., 1973. Tchr. home econs., Springdale, Pa., 1950—53, Glendale, Calif., 1953—55, Arcadia Unifed Sch. Dist., Calif., 1955—83. Designer antique doll clothes. Hon. life mem. Arcadia/San Gabriel PTA. Named Outstanding Tchr. in Arcadia, So. Calif. Industry Edn. Coun., 1968. Mem.: NEA, Doll Collectors Gallery Calif. (v.p. 1981—83). Republican. Roman Catholic. Died Jan. 1996.

**ENGEL, CHARLES ROBERT,** chemist, educator; b. Vienna, Jan. 28, 1922; s. Jean and Lucie (Fuchs) E.; m. Edith H. Braillard, Aug. 6, 1951; children: Lucie Tatiana Berthoud, Christiane Simonne, Francis Pierre, Marc Robert. BA, U. Grenoble, 1941; MSc, Swiss Fed. Inst. Tech., Zurich, 1947, DSc, 1951; State-DSc, U. Paris, 1970. Research fellow, asst. Swiss Fed. Inst. Tech., Zurich, 1948-51; asst. prof. med. research Collip Med. Research Lab. U. Western Ont., London, 1951-55, asso. prof. med. research, 1955-58, hon. spl. lectr. chemistry, dept. chemistry, 1951-58; prof. chemistry Laval U., Quebec, Que., 1958-90, prof. emeritus, from 1995. Vis. prof. Inst. de Chimie des Substances Naturelles CNRS, Gif-sur-Yvette, France, 1966-67 Mem. editorial bd. Steroids, 1964-91; hon. editorial bd. Current Abstracts of Chemistry, 1971-72, Index Chemicus, 1971-72; mem. editorial adv. bd. Can. Jour. Chemistry, 1974; editor Can. Jour. Chemistry, 1986-91.; mem. French govtl. commn. chem. terminology, 1992-2001. Lt. for Can.-Que., Equestrian Order of Holy Sepulchre of Jerusalem, 1970-89, mem. Grand Magisterium, Vatican, 1989-93; bd. dirs. Cath. Culture Ctr., London, Ont. Decorated comdr. Equestrian Order of Holy Sepulchre of Jerusalem, comdr. with star, knight grand cross; knight Legion of Honour (France); recipient medal Austrian Ministry Edn., Commemorative medal for 125th Anniversary of Confedn. of Can., 1992. Fellow Chem. Inst. Can. (chmn. organic divsn. 1965-66, exec. med. divsn. 1968-79), Royal Soc. Chemistry (London); mem. Am. Chem. Soc., French Chem. Soc., Swiss Chem. Soc., New Swiss Chem. Soc., Can. Soc. Biochem., Molecular and Cellular Biology, French-Can. Assn. for the Advancement of Scis., N.Y. Acad. Scis., Order Chemists Que., Sigma Xi. Home: Quebec, Canada. Died Dec. 26, 2002.

**ENGLISH, CHARLES BRAND,** lawyer; b. Urbana, Ohio, June 10, 1924; s. Edwin L. and Margaret (Br) E.; m. Constance Coulter, 1946 (dec. 1953); 1 child, Thomas C.; m. Eva Uber, Oct. 3, 1954; children: Gwendolyn, Carolyn (dec.). Student, Dartmouth, 1941-42, Denison U., 1942-43; AB, U. Mich., 1944, LLB., 1947; LHD (hon.), Urbana U., 1978. Bar: Ohio 1947. Pvt. practice law, Urbana, 1947-87; ret., 1987; farm mgr. severy dairy units, 1950-60; bd. dirs. Milk Producers Union, Cin., 1957-62, Nat. Milk Producers Fedn., 1966-69; v.p. Cin. Milk Sales Assn., 1966-72, dir., 1962-72. Contbr. articles to jours. Founder, first pres. Urbana Jaycees, Jr. C. of C., 1948; mem. bd. edn. Triad Sch. Dist., 1951-59, Glen Helen Adv. Bd. Antioch Coll., 1959-76; open space legal adviser Com. for Country Common, 1963-76; mem. Ohio Land Use Rev. Adv. Council, 1976-77; trustee Urbana Coll., 1966-77, vice chmn., 1969-73, sec., 1973-76; bd. dirs. Assn. Ind. Colls. and Univs. Ohio, 1969-77, Ohio Citizens' Council for Health and Welfare, 1973-77; mem. Champaign County Bd. Mental Retardation, 1967-75. Recipient Outstanding Performance award Freedom Support Radio Free Europe, 1954; named One of Hon. 100 alumni Ohio State U. Sch. Natural Resources, 1970; co-honoree The Eva and Charles B. English Fine Arts Scholarship Champaign County Arts Coun., 1988. Mem. ABA, Ohio State Bar Assn. (com. internat. comparative law 1959), Champaign County Bar Assn. (pres. 1958), Ohio Conservation Found. (trustee 1969-85, sec.-treas. 1969-73), Am. Humanist Assn. (bd. dirs. 1957-66, sec. 1959-66), Fellowship of Religious Humanists (bd. dirs., sec. 1967-72), Community Water Resources Com. Champaign County (co-chmn. 1970-71), S.W. Ohio Water Devel. Study (adv. bd. 1969-72), The Legacy Club, Nature Conservancy. Unitarian Universalist. Home: Kronberg, Germany. Deceased.

**ENGLISH, EVA UBER,** volunteer arts council executive; b. Neumarkt, Silesia, Germany, Apr. 20, 1925; came to U.S., 1954, naturalized, 1957; d. Konrad and Margarete (Reimann) Uber; m. Charles B. English, Oct. 3, 1954; children: Gwendolyn, Carolyn (dec.). Lab. asst. diploma, Fachschule Chemistry & Physics, 1943. Lab. asst. Bosch GmbH., Reichenbach, Silesia, 1944; with U.S. Mil. Govt., Wiesbaden, 1946-49; cons. edn. br. Am. Consulate, Frankfurt, West Germany, 1949-54; pres. Champaign County Mental Health Assn., Urbana, Ohio, 1967-69; mem. Logan-Champaign County Bd. Mental Health and Retardation, 1970-77, v.p., 1970-72. Bd. dirs. Springfield (Ohio) Symphony Orch. Assn., 1968-80; founder, pres., vol. exec. dir. Champaign County Arts Coun., 1974-79, chmn. arts-in-schs. program, 1974-82, trustee, 1974-88. Co-honoree The Eva and Charles B. English Fine Arts Scholarship Endowment, Champaign County (Ohio) Arts Coun., 1988—. Home: Kronberg, Germany. Died May 25, 2004.

**ENOCH, HERBERT ZVI,** agrometeorologist, sculptor; b. Bad-Nauheim, Germany, Mar. 20, 1933; s. Daniel and Hanna Johanna (Zwas) E.; m. Yael Juliane Blum, Dec. 23, 1956; children: Simon, Yonat. BSc in Agronomy, Agrl. U., Copenhagen, 1959, PhD, 1963. Research asst. Agrl. U., Copenhagen, 1959-63; scientist Agrl. Rsch. Orgn., Bet-Dagan, Israel, 1963-79, sr. scientist, from 1980. Vis. scientist Glasshouse Crops Rsch. Sta., Littlehampton, Eng., 1970-71, U. Tokyo, 1978; lectr. sch. forestry Yale U., New Haven, 1980-81; vis. rsch. fellow Conn. Agrl. Rsch. Sta., New Haven, 1981, U. Paris, Orsay, 1986, Lancaster (Eng.) U., 1991, 92. Sr. editor: Carbon Dioxide Enrichment of Greenhouse Crops, 1986; prin. art works include various sculptures in stone, concrete, mixed media. Danish Rsch. Coun. fellow, 1959-63, Japanese Soc. Promotion of Sci., Tokyo, fellow, 1978, Tansley Found. fellow, Eng., 1990; rsch. grantee Rsch. Inst. of Innovative Tech. for the Earth, Kyoto, Japan, 1994-95. Mem. European Agrl. Soc., Internat. Hort. Soc., Sigma Xi. Jewish. Home: Savyon, Israel. Died 2000.

**ENSMINGER, LUTHER GLENN,** retired chemist; b. Mt. Perry, Ohio, Oct. 17, 1919; s. Charles Henry and Mary Elfa (Koehler) E.; m. Emma Jean Couch, May 12, 1951 (div. Apr. 1973); children: Luther, Douglas, Phillip, Deborah; m. How Leng Cheng, Nov. 11, 1983 (div. Dec. 1988); m. Lee

Rose Olson, Oct. 19, 1992. BSc, Ohio State U., 1942, BSc with honors, 1948. Chemist FDA, Cin., 1948-56, chemist, lab. supr. LA, 1956-59, sci. adminstr. Washington, 1959-79, ret., 1979; sci. cons. Arlington, Va., from 1979. Vol., tutor for immigrant high sch. and coll. students (YMCA awards for outstanding tutoring work 1992, 93). Contbr. articles to profl. jours. Sec. Lee-Ballston Citizens Assn., 1965-75; coach Little League Softball, Arlington, Va. With US Army, 1942—45, WW II, North Africa, Italy. Decorated 2 Bronze Battle Stars US Army; recipient Seven Who Care award, 1990, Letter of Commendation award, Commonwealth Va. Bd Edn., 1990, Outstanding Svc. to Cmty. award, YMCA Met. Washington, 1996. Fellow Assn. Ofcl. Analytical Chemists (exec. sec. 1967-79, mem. exec. com. 1960-79); mem. Beta Gamma Sigma, Consumer Opinion Inst., Am. Legion. Republican. Presbyterian. Achievements include supervising development and validation of analytical methods for government regulatory purposes in 60 subject areas world-wide; organizing annual scientific meetings for adoption of methods. Avocations: gardening, coin collecting/numismatics, clarinet, ballroom dancing. Home: Washington, DC. Died July 11, 2013.

**EPPERT, LUANA KYLE,** retired secondary school educator, sculptor, writer; b. Shreveport, La., June 24, 1918; d. Lewis Francis and Silver Enola (Hatten) Kyle; m. Leo Clinton Eppert. BA, L.A. U., 1960; MA, U. So. Calif., 1962, U. Utah, 1965, U. Nev., Las Vegas, 1972. Cert. secondary tchr. Calif., Nev. Housewife, sculptress, 1948—59; tchr. LA, 1961—71, Las Vegas, Nev., 1972—84; ret., 1984. Author: The Greek Women, 1989; one-woman shows include, Maui, Hawaii, 1963, Las Vegas, 1973, Island of Paros, Greece, 1973. Hostess U.S. State Dept., LA, 1958—60. Recipient Best of Show award, Las Vegas Art Coun., 1974. Mem. Soc. Of Friends. Avocation: needlecrafts. Deceased.

**ERBURU, ROBERT FRANCIS,** retired publishing executive; b. Ventura, Calif., Sept. 27, 1930; BA in Journalism, U. Southern Calif., 1952; JD, Harvard Law Sch., 1955. Atty. Gibson, Dunn & Crutcher LLP, LA; pres. Times Mirror Co., LA, 1974—80, CEO, 1980—86, chmn., CEO, 1986—96. Chmn. Fed. Reserve Bank San Francisco, 1989—91. Mem. trustees coun. Nat. Gallery Art, Washington, DC, 1985—93; chmn. bd. Huntington Libr., Art Collections, and Botanical Gardens; trustee William and Flora Hewlett Found., Ahmanson Found. Mem. Newspaper Assn. America (bd. govs., exec. bd., exec. com., bd. dirs. 1980-92, officer 1988-92, chmn. 1991-92), Coun. Fgn. Rels. (bd. dirs.), Calif. Bus. Roundtable, Bus. Coun., Home: Los Angeles, Calif. Died May 11, 2014.

**ERICKSON, ARTHUR CHARLES,** architect; b. Vancouver, BC, Can., June 14, 1924; s. Oscar and Myrtle (Chatterson) Erickson. Student, U. BC, Vancouver, 1942-44, LittD (hon.), 1985; BArch, McGill U., Montreal, Que., Can., 1950, DEng (hon.), 1971; LLD (hon.), Simon Fraser U., Vancouver, 1973, U. Man., Winnipeg, Can., 1978, Lethbridge U., 1981; LittD (hon.), Frank Lloyd Wright Sch. Arch., 2001, MArch (hon.), 2001. Asst. prof. U. Oreg., Eugene, 1955-56; assoc. prof. U. B.C., 1956-63; ptnr. Erickson-Massey Architects, Vancouver, 1963-72; prin. Arthur Erickson Architects, Vancouver, 1972-91, Toronto, Ont., Can., 1981-91, Los Angeles, 1981-91, Arthur Erickson Archtl. Corp., Vancouver, 1991—2009. Prin. works include, Simon Fraser U., Lethbridge U. Alta., Bloedel Bldg., Can. Pavilion Expo '70, Osaka (1st prize nat. competition, Archtl. Inst. Japan award for best pavillion), Robson Sq./Law Cts. (honor award), Mus. Anthropology (honor award), Eppich Residence (honor award), Habitat Pavillion (honor award), Sikh Temple (award of merit), Champlain Heights Cmty. Sch. (award of merit), San Diego Conv. Ctr., Calif. Plz., LA, Fresno City Hall, Can. Embassy, Washington, Roy Thompson Hall, Toronto, Bank of Can., Ottawa, Koerner Libr., Liu Internat. Conf. Ctr., U. BC, Scotibank Dance Ctr., Internat. Glass Mus., Tacoma, 2003. Mem. com. urban devel. Coun. of Can., 1971; bd. dirs. Can. Conf. Arts, 1972; mem. design adv. coun. Portland Devel. Commn., Can. Coun. Urban Rsch.; trustee Inst. Rsch. Pub. Policy; mem. internat. coun. Mus. Modern Art, NYC, 1982—86. Capt. Can. Intelligence Corps., 1945—46. Decorated officer Order of Can., companion; recipient Molson prize, Can. Coun. Arts, 1967, Triangle award, Nat. Soc. Interior Design, Royal Bank Can. award, 1971, Gold medal, Tau Sigma Delta, 1973, Residential Design award, Can. Housing Coun., 1975, August Perret award, Internat. Union Archs. Congress, 1975, Pres. award Excellence, Am. Soc. Landscape Archs., 1979, Chgo. Architecture award, 1984, Gold medal, French Acad. Archtitecture, 1984. Fellow: AIA (Pan Pacific citation Hawaiian chpt. 1963, Gold medal 1986), Royal Archtl. Inst. Can. (award 1980, Gold medal 1984), Royal Inst. Scottish Archs. (hon.), Royal Inst. Brit. Archs. (hon.), Frank Lloyd Wright Found. (hon.); mem.: Royal Can. Acad. Arts (academician), ARCAB Wash. State Archtl. Assn., Coll. d'arquitectos de España (hon.), Coll. d'architectos de Mex. (hon.), Archtl. Inst. BC, S.F.U. Faculty Club. Home: Vancouver, Canada. Died May 20, 2009.

**ERKKILA-RICKER, BARBARA H.,** writer, photographer; b. Boston, July 11, 1918; d. John William and Adelia Parsons (Jones) Howell; m. Onni R. Erkkila, Apr. 27, 1941 (dec. 1981); children: John W., Kathleen L., Marjorie A.; m. G. Ashton Ricker, Feb. 5, 2000.(dec. 2008) Student, Boston U. Evening Coll., 1959—62. Corr. Gloucester (Mas.) Daily Times, 1936-53, feature writer, from 1953, women's editor, 1967-72, cmty. news editor, 1972-74. Editor weekly mag. Essex County Newspapers, Gloucester, 1973, editl. asst., 1974-85, writer, photographer, 1970—; tchr. Russian, Ipswich (Mass.) Pub. Schs., evenings, 1962-63, Boston U. Study Tour, Soviet Union, 1960; jewelry designer; quarry historian. Author: History of Sacred Heart Church, 1972, Hammers on Stone, 1981, Village at Lane's Cove, 1989, 2008; editor Lane's Cove Cook Book, 1954; contbr. articles to profl. jours. Asst. traffic mgr. Lepage's, Inc., 1936-40; price panel OPA, 1944-46; ARC nurse's aide class Addison Gilbert Hosp., 1942-43; active Gloucester Hist. Commn., 1967-69, 93-2000; formerly active Girl Scouts U.S.A.; sec. Lanesville CC, 1957-94; apptd. granite industry cons. Cape Ann Hist. Assn. Mus., Mass., 1997; cons. Ann. Mus., 1997 Recipient 2d prize for feature writing UPI, 1970, historian award Town of Rockport, 1978, First Walker Hancock award City of Gloucester, 1999, Gloucester Hist. Commn. Cultural award, 2009. Mem. Sandy Bay Hist. Soc., Ohio Geneal. Soc., Westford Hist. Soc., Cape Ann Hist. Assn., North Shore Rock and Mineral (charter), North Shore Button Club. Congregationalist. Home: Gloucester, Mass. Died Dec. 14, 2013.

**ERSKINE, HAROLD LESTER,** engineer, researcher; b. Rockland, Mass., July 24, 1924; s. Harold L. Sr. and Flora Abbie (Preble) E.; m. Eleanor S. Rude, Oct., 1990. BS in Chem. Engring., Northeastern U., 1949; MS, Kans. State U., 1950. Registered profl. engr., Pa., Can. Rsch. engr. Mellon Inst./U.S. Steel, Pitts., 1950-53; applications engr. Pitts. Corning, 1953-56; project engr. engring. and cons. div. Koppers Co., 1956-59; prin. chem. engr. Sun Co., Phila., 1959-83; pvt. practice cons. engr. Berwyn, Pa., from 1983. With U.S. Army, 1943-46. Mem. Am. Inst. Chem. Engrs., ACS, Nat. Soc. Profl. Engrs. Home: Devon, Pa. Deceased.

**ERSKINE, RALPH,** architect, town planner; b. London, Feb. 24, 1914; arrived in Sweden, 1939; s. George and Mildred (Gough) Erskine; m. Ruth Monica Francis, Aug. 29, 1939; children: Jane Kristina, Karin Elizabeth, Patrick Jon. RIBA, Regent St. Poly, London, 1937, MRIPI, 1938; Dr.Tech., U. Lund, 1975; DLitt (hon.), Heriot-Watt U., Edinburg, 1982; postgrad., Royal Acad. Arts, Stockholm. Cert. arch., town planner. Pvt. practice architecture, Drottningholm, Scotland, from 1940. Decorated comdr. Brit. Empire; recipient Kasper Salin prize, 1970, 1981, Swedish Ytong prize, 1974, Litteris et Artibus medal, Sweden, 1980, Gold medal, Royal Architecture Inst. Can., 1982, Guld Kanga award, Stockholm, 1983, Wolf Found. Internat. prize, 1984, Royal Gold medal, Royal Inst. Brit. Architects, 1987. Home: Drottningholm, Sweden. Died Mar. 16, 2005.

**ESENWEIN-ROTHE, INGEBORG,** economist, statistician; b. Chemnitz, Germany, June 24, 1911; d. Hermann A. and Auguste (Kühl) Rothe; m. Hermann O. Esenwein, Mar. 1, 1948 (dec. May 1973). Dr.rer.pol., U. Leipzig, Germany, 1937; habilitation, U. Münster, Germany, 1954; Dr.rer.pol. h.c., U. Trier, 1986. Apprentice to a banking house, 1928-30; with Civil Svc., Leipzig, 1938-41, Salzburg, Austria, 1941-45; lectr. polit. econs. and stats. Chemnitz Coll., 1947-50; lectr. Coll. Whilhelmshaven, Germany, 1950-61, prof., 1961-62, U. Göttingen, Germany, 1962, U. Erlangen/Nürnberg, 1962-76, emeritus prof., from 1976. Author books including: Die Verkehrs-Effizienz, 1956, Die Struktur des Bankwesens als Gegenstand Wirtschaftsstatisticher Analyse, 1959, Die Wirtschaftsverbände von 1933 bis 1945, 1965, Allgemeine Wit Schaftsstatistik, 1969, Die Methoden der Wirtschaftsstatistik, vols. 1 and 2, 1976, Einführung in die Demographie/Bevölkerungsstruktur und Bevölkerhgsp rozess aus der Sicht der Statistik, 1982, Wilhelmlexis Demographic Nationalokonom 2, edit., 1993; contbr. art publs.; editor: Kompendium der Volwirtschaftslehre, 2 vols., 5th edit., 1972, Statistische Studien 10 vols., 1968, Verdienst-Orden d Freistaats Bayern, 1984. Mem. Gesellschaft fur Wirtschafts-und Sozialwissenschaften, Deutsche Statistiche Gesellschaft, Deutsche Gesellschaft für Bevölkerungswissenschaft e. V., 1964, Internat. Union for Sci. Study of Population, Internat. Stat. Inst., 1972, Akademie fur Raumforschung und Landesplanung. Evangelical Lutheran. Died July 12, 2002.

**ETO, SHINKICHI,** education educator; b. Mukden, China, Nov. 16, 1923; s. Toshio and Nui (Yamashita) E.; m. Kazuko Ohno, July 16, 1949; children: Hikaru, Mari, Izumi. LLB, U. Tokyo, 1948. Assoc. prof. internat. rels. U. Tokyo, 1956—67, prof. internat. rels., 1967—84; pres. Asia U., Tokyo, 1987-95; chancellor Toyo Eiwa Ednl. Instn., Tokyo, 1998—2002; vis. prof. Peking U., from 1997. Author: East Asian Political History, 1979, A Biography of Satow Eisaku, 1987, International Relations, 2000, Selected Works of Shinkichi Eto, 2003-2006, 2006; co-translator: My Thirty-Three Years' Dream, 1982. Recipient Purple Ribbon Order Japanese Govt., 1991, Fukuoka Asian Culture Prize Fukuoka Prefectural Govt., 1996, The 2d Order of the Sacred Treasure, Gold and Silver Star, 2001. Mem. Japan Fedn. Unesco Assns. (adviser 1978—), Japanese Soc. Asian Studies (dir. emeritus 1986—), Japan Assn. Internat. Rels. (dir. emeritus 1992—), Japan Assn. Internat. Law (dir. emeritus 1994—) Home: Tokyo, Japan. Died Dec. 12, 2007.

**ETRA, BLANCHE GOLDMAN,** lawyer; b. NYC, Mar. 8, 1915; d. Jack and Anna (Simon) Goldman; m. Harry Etra, Apr. 19, 1939; children: Aaron, Marshall, Donald, Jonathan. BA, Barnard Coll., 1937; LLB, Columbia U., 1939; DHL (hon.), Yeshiva U., 1988. Bar: NY 1939, US Supreme Ct. 1960. Assoc. Hautman, Sheridan & Tekulsky, NYC, 1938—39, Etra & Etra, NYC, 1939—77, ptnr., from 1977. Bd. dirs. Cardozo Sch. Law, NYC, from 1978; bd. overseers Albert Einstein Coll. Medicine, NYC. Recipient Louise Waterman Wise award, Am. Jewish Congress, NYC, 1975, Disting. Svc. award, Albert Einstein Coll. Medicine, 1978. Mem.: NY Women's Bar Assn., Assn. of Bar of City NY. Jewish. Died Jan. 3, 1995.

**ETROG, SOREL,** artist; b. Jassy, Romania, Aug. 29, 1933; Student, Tel Aviv Art Inst., 1953-55, Bklyn. Mus. Art Sch., 1958. Canadian rep. Venice Biennale, 1966. Commissions: Los Angeles County Mus., 1966, Can. Pavilion-Expo 67, 1967, Olympia York Ctr., Toronto, 1972, Bow Valley Sq., Calgary 1975, SunLife Can., Toronto, 1984; designed and illustrated books: The Bird That Does Not Exist by Claude Aveline, 1967, Chocs by Eugene Ionesco, 1969, Imagination Dead Imagination by Samuel Beckett, 1972; designed Can. Film Award, 1968, Toronto Symphony Anniversary Coin, 1973; writer, dir. film Spiral, 1975; designer sets and costumes for W.B. Yeats's Celtic Hero, 1978; author: Dream Chamber, 1982, Hinges (play), The Kite/Le Cerf Volant, 1984, L'Aquilone/The Kite, 1984, others; The Kite performed Toronto 1984; curator sculpture exhbn., Montreal Olympic Games, 1967, contemporary outdoor sculpture, Guildwood hall, Toronto, 1982; pub. collections include Nat. Gallery Can., Art. Gallery Ont., Montreal Fine Arts Mus., Tate Gallery, London, St. Peter's Coll. Oxford, Kunst Mus., Basel, Musée d'Art Moderne, Paris, Mus. Modern Art, N.Y.C., Guggenheim Mus. N.Y., Kroeller-Mueller Mus., Holland, Hirshhorn Mus., Washington, Jerusalem Mus., Birla Acad., Calcutta, UCLA, Hart House, U. Toronto, Bank of Can., Ottawa; solo exhbns. in Montreal, Toronto, N.Y.C., Paris, London, Chgo., Los Angeles, Geneva, Amsterdam, Tel Aviv, Venice, Milan, Rome, other cities; subject several monographs. Bd. dirs. Toronto French Sch., Celtic Arts. Mem. Royal Can. Acad., Arts and Letters Club. Died Feb. 26, 2014.

**EUSDEN, JOHN DYKSTRA,** theology studies educator, minister; b. Holland, Mich., July 20, 1922; s. Ray Anderson and Marie (Dykstra) E.; m. Joanne Reiman, June 14, 1950; children: Andrea Bonner, Alan Tolles, John Dykstra Jr., Sarah Jewell. AB, Harvard U., 1943; postgrad., Harvard Law Sch., 1946; BD cum laude, Yale U., 1949, PhD in Religion, 1954. Ordained to ministry United Ch. of Christ, 1949. Instr. in religion Yale U., 1953-55, asst. prof., 1955-60; assoc. prof. religion, chaplain Williams Coll., Williamstown, Mass., 1960-70, Nathan Jackson prof. Christian theology, 1970-90, vis. prof. environ. studies, 1990-92; vis. prof. religion and Asian studies Mt. Holyoke Coll., Mass., 1992—93; min. 1st Congl. Ch., Bennington, Vt., from 1991; cons. Asian programs and environ. studies Williams Coll., Williamstown, Mass., from 1992. Lectr., research fellow Kyoto U., 1963-64, 76, 81-82; theologian-in-residence Am. Ch. in Paris, 1972; lectr. Doshisha U., Kyoto, Japan, 1976, 82; bd. dir. Associated Kyoto Program, Japan. Author: Puritans, Lawyers and Politics in Early 17th Century England, 1958, 68, Zen and Christian: The Journey Between, 1981, (with John H. Westerhoff III) The Spiritual Life: Learning East and West, 1982, (with Westerhoff) Sensing Beauty: Aesthetics, the Human Spirit, and the Church, 1998, Fullness of Life, Thirsting for Healing and Wholeness, 2009; contbr. articles to profl. jours.; translator, editor, author introduction: The Marrow of Theology (William Ames), 1975, 86; author introduction: Zen Buddhism and Christianity in Y. Takeuchi Festschrift (Japanese edition), 1993, Christology: The Dialogue of East and West in Christology in Dialogue, 1993, Chinese Healing: A Practical Mysticism in John Sahadat Festschrift, 2002. Adv. coun., campus ministry program Danforth Found., 1966-70; bd. dirs. Wellesley Coll. Parents Assn., 1972-75, pres., 1974-75; rsch. fellow Ctr. for Study of Japanese Religion, Kyoto, 1976-94; trustee Lingnan Found., NYC, 1964—, Buxton Sch., Williamstown, Mass., 1970-83, Chewonki Found., Wiscasset, Maine, 2002—; leader trips, People's Republic of China, 1978, 81, 86, 88, 90, 94. 1st lt. USMCR, 1943-45. Scholar Harvard U.; faculty fellow Am. Assn. Theol. Schs., 1958-59, Sterling fellow Yale U., 1950-53, fellow Folger Shakespeare Libr., 1958-59, 71-72; Lilly postdoctoral grantee, 1963-64, Danforth campus ministry grantee, 1963-64; fellow Am. Council Learned Socs., 1967-68; Fulbright rsch. travel grantee, 1967-68; research fellow U. Utrecht, Netherlands, 1968; rsch. grantee Williams Coll., 1976. Mem. AAUP, Am. Acad. Religion, Am. Soc. Ch. History, Am. Soc. Christian Ethics, Nat. Assn. Coll. and Univ. Chaplains, Soc. Values in Higher Edn., Appalachian Mountain Club, Randolph Mountain Club (pres. 1973-75). Home: Brunswick, Maine. Died Apr. 27, 2013.

**EVANGELOU, GRIGORIOS NIKOLAOS,** surgeon; b. Thessaloniki, Macedonia, Greece, Aug. 4, 1930; s. Nikolaos and Efrosini (Kalisperi) E.; m. Evgenia Daroglou, July 12, 1969; children: Efrosini, Nikolaos. MD, U. Thessaloniki, 1954. Med. diplomate. Dir. pers. NATO, Izmir, Turkey, 1957-59; chief Surg. Dept., Ioannina, Greece, 1964-66; chief surg. dept. Mil. Hosp., Alexandroupolis, Greece, 1967-71, 401 Gen. Mil. Hosp., Athens, 1971-75, 424 Gen. Mil. Hosp., Thessaloniki, 1976-78, NIMTS Hosp., Athens, 1979-85, 91-97; ret., 1998. Assoc. prof. U. Athens, 1977-97. Contbr. articles to profl. jours. Brig. M.C., Greek mil., 1981. Fellow ACS; mem. Hellenic Surg. Soc. (v.p.), Hellenic Surg. Soc. (pres.). Home: Athens, Greece. Died June 14, 2002.

**EVANS, ARTHUR RICHARD,** school system administrator, visual arts educator; s. Arthur and Tena (Rollinson) E. BS, Pa. State U., 1971, MEd in Art Edn., 1972. Cert. art educator, supr., N.J. Grad. teaching asst. Pa. State U., University Park, 1971-72; art educator Fairchance-Georges Jr. Sr. High Sch., Uniontown, Pa., 1972-74; art instr. Pa. State U., Fayette County, Pa., 1973-74; adj. prof. Ocean County Coll., Toms River, NJ, 1974-80, Kean Coll., Union, N.J., from 1991; art educator Lakewood (N.J.) High Sch., 1974-84; counselor Stockton State Coll., Pomona, NJ, 1984-86; supr. student tchrs. Monmouth Coll., West Long Br., NJ, from 1991; visual arts chairperson Grover Cleve. Mid. Sch., Elizabeth, NJ, from 1988, supt. art dept., 1996—98. Coun. mem., commr. edn. adv. coun. for arts edn., Trenton, N.J., 1990—, standards panel mem. Fine and Performing Arts, N.J., 1992—; panel mem. Core Course Proficiency Panel for Fine and Performing Arts, Trenton, 1992-93; chairperson Middle States Assn. Colls. and Schs., Trenton, 1980, 81. Profl. solo art exhibits incl.: J and M Madison Art Gallery, Middletown, N.J., 1977, Georgian Ct. Coll., Lakewood, N.J., 1978, C.C. Phila., 1981, Lakehurst (N.J.) Naval Air Engring. Ctr., 1984, Monmouth County Libr., Shrewsbury, N.J., 1984, Ocean County Coll., Toms River, 1986, St. John's Ch., Passaic, N.J., 1988, Univ. of the

Arts Phila., Felician Coll., Lodi, N.J., 1988, C.C. of Phila., Consolidated Bank and Trust Co., Richmond, Va.; exhibited in group shows at Atlantic City Boardwalk, 1976 (2d place award), The Painted Bride Arts Ctr., Phila., 1982, The Gallery of the Art Inst., Phila., 1983, C.C. Phila., 1987, Glassboro State Coll. Westby Gallery, 1990; subject of several articles in local newspapers. Grantee Elizabeth Bd. Edn., 1989, 91; recipient First Pl. Art award for Painting, Millburn-Short Hills C. of C., 1987, Third Pl. Art award for Paintings, Hazlet Art Festival, 1988, Dr. Martin Luther King Scholarship Grant award Pa. State U., 1970. Mem. Alliance for Arts Edn. N.J., Art Educators N.J., Polit. Sci. Adv. Coun. of Brookdale, Assn. for Supervision and Curriculum Devel., Pa. State U. Alumni Assn., Phi Delta Kappa. Avocations: piano (classical, ragtime, modern), reading, languages. Home: Philadelphia, Pa. Died May 19, 1998.

**EVANS, BILL See LATEEF, YUSEF**

**EVANS, JOHN VICTOR,** former Governor of Idaho; b. Malad City, Idaho, Jan. 18, 1925; s. David Lloyd and Margaret (Thomas) E.; m. Lola Daniels, 1945; children: David L., John Victor, Martha Anne, Susan Dee, Thomas Daniels. BA in Bus. and Econs, Stanford U., 1951; LLD (hon.), U. Idaho, 2007. Mem. Idaho State Senate, 1953-59, 67-74, majority leader, 1957-59, minority leader, 1969-74; mayor City of Malad, Idaho, 1960-66; former farmer, rancher, businessman; lt. gov. Idaho, 1975-76; lt. gov. State of Idaho, Boise, 1975—77, gov., 1977—87. V.p., dir. J.N. Ireland & Co., Bankers, Malad, 1955-75; v.p. Bear River Water Users, 1963-65; pres. Deep Creek Irrigation Co., 1965-73, Oneida R.C. & D., 1968-74; former pres. D.L. Evans Bank; former sec. ICBA. Del. Democratic Nat. Conv., 1960, 80, 84, 88; chmn. Subcon. State Land Bd. Lease Rates & Policies, 1975-76; chmn. Law Enforcement Planning Com., 1975-76. Served with inf. US Army, 1944—46. Decorated Asiatic Pacific ribbon, Good Conduct medal; named to The Idaho Hall of Fame, 1996; recipient Distinguished Svc. award, Assn. Idaho Cities, 1974, Idaho Conservationist of Yr. award, 1978, Mini/Cassia Businessman of Yr. award, 1995. Mem. Nat. Governors Assn. (chmn. subcom. on nuclear energy 1979), Western Governors Assn. (chmn. 1978-79), Farm Bur., American Legion, VFW, Masons, Kiwanis, Eagles, Rotary. Democrat. Ch. Of Jesus Christ Of Latter-Day Saints. Died July 8, 2014.

**EVERLY, PHIL (PHILIP EVERLY),** composer, musician; b. Chgo., Jan. 19, 1939; s. Ike and Margaret Everly; m. Jackie Ertel (div.); children: Jordan, Patricia, Mickey;, Christopher. Composer, singer: (albums with The Everly Brothers) The Everly Brothers, 1958, Songs Our Daddy Taught Us, 1958, It's Everly Time, 1960, A Date With the Everly Brothers, 1960, Both Sides of an Evening, 1961, Instant Party, 1962, Golden Hits, 1962, Rock n' Soul, 1965, Beat and Soul, 1965, In Our Image, 1965, Two Yanks in England, 1965, Roots, 1968, Stories We Could Tell, 1972, Pass the Chicken, 1973, EB'84, 1984, Born Yesterday, 1986; (solo albums) Star Spangled Springer, 1973, Phil's Diner, 1974, Mystic Line, 1975, Phil Everly, 1979; appeared with parents as The Everlys on country music radio programs, 1940. Inducted into The Rock & Roll Hall of Fame, 1986. Died Jan. 3, 2014.

**EWAN, JOSEPH (ANDORFER),** botanist, biohistorian, research bibliographer; b. Phila., Oct. 24, 1909; s. Horace Gilbert and Emma (Magill) E.; m. Ada Nesta Dunn, Aug. 20, 1935; children: Kathleen Kilburn, Dorothy Saranne, Marjorie Magill. AB, U. Calif., Berkeley, 1934; ScD (hon.), William and Mary Coll., 1972, Tulane U., 1980. Asst. phanerogamic botany U. Calif., Berkeley, 1933-37; instr. biology U. Colo., Boulder, 1937-44; botanist Fgn. Econ. Adminstrn., Bogota, Colombia, 1944-45; asst. curator, div. plants Smithsonian Instn., Washington, 1945-46; assoc. botanist, Bur. Plant Industry USDA, Beltsville, Md., 1946-47; asst. prof. botany to Ida A Richardson prof. Tulane U., New Orleans, 1947-77; rsch. assoc. Mo. Bot. Garden, St. Louis, 1986-97. Vis. prof. U. Hawaii, Honolulu, 1967, 74, U. Oreg., Eugene, 1978, 81, Ohio State U., Columbus, 1982; ofcl. del. Internat. Conf. Centre Nat. Rsch., Paris, 1956; found. bd. mem. Longue Vue Gardens, New Orleans, 1971-79. Author: Rocky Mountain Naturalists, 1950, William Bartram Botanical and Zoological Drawings, 1968 (Grolier award 1968); co-author: (with Nesta) John Banister, Natural History of Virginia, 1970, Biographical Dictionary of Rocky Mountain Naturalists, 1981 Recipient Eloise Payne Luquer medal Garden Clubs Am., 1978, Henry Shaw medal Mo. Bot. Garden, 1994; cert. Bot. Soc. Am., 1989; Guggenheim Found. fellow, 1954, Regent's fellow Smithsonian Inst., 1984-85. Fellow Linnean Soc. (London); mem. Am. Fern Soc. (v.p. 1941-47, pres. 48-49), Torrey Bot. Club, Calif. Bot. Soc., Internat. Soc. Plant Taxonomists, Am. Soc. Plant Taxonomists, Cooper Ornithol. Soc., Am. Antiquarian Soc., Soc. History of Natural History (Founder's medal 1986), History of Sci. Soc. Avocation: naturalists' bookplates. Died Dec. 5, 1999.

**EWANCHUK, MICHAEL,** retired school system administrator; b. Gimli, Man., Can., Mar. 14, 1908; s. Wasyl and Paraskeva Ewanchuk; m. J. Muriel Smith, Aug. 2, 1941 (dec. 1997). Student, Detroit City Coll., 1928—30; BA, U. Man., 1939, BEd, 1941, MEd, 1950; LLD (hon.), U. Winnipeg, 1979; D in Canon Law (hon.), St. John's Coll., U. Man., 1989. H.s. prin.; apptd. sch. inspector, 1946—73; ret., 1973. Chmn. Ukrainian Curriculum com. U. Man., lectr. stats. and testing; statistician Man. H.S. exams. and std. tests; chmn. editl. com. Secondary Edn. in Can., 1968. Author: Pioneer Settlers: Ukrainians in the Dauphin Area 1896-1926 (Shevchenko meda., Ukrainian Can. Congress), Sisler and His Times, Vita: A Ukrainian Community, Spruce, Swamp and Stone, Pioneer Profiles: Ukrainian Settlers in Manitoba, Hawaiian Ordeal: Ukrainian Contract Workers 1897-1910, Reflections and Reminiscences: Ukrainians in Canada, Young Cossack, a novella, Pioneer Ukrainian Settlers, William Kurelek: The Suffering Genius, East of the Red: Early Ukrainian Settlements, East of the Red: Early Ukrainian Settlements North of the Dawson Trail vol. 2, Vertical Development: A New Generation of Ukrainian Canadians vols. 1 & 2; contbr. articles to profl. jours. Flight lt., navigation and pers. counseling RCAF, World War II. Recipient Queen's Jubilee medal, Lt. Gov. Hon. Peter Liba, 2002. Fellow: Can. Coll. Tchrs.; mem.: Ukrainian Acad. Arts and Sci., Can. Assn. Sch. Supts. (pres.), Man. Inspectors' Assn. (pres.), U. Man. Alumni Assn. (pres.). Home: Winnipeg, Canada. Died Aug. 26, 2004.

**EWING, FRANK MARION,** lumber company executive, real estate developer; b. Albany, Ga., Apr. 24, 1915; s. Frank Marion and Alpharetta (Tucker) E.; m. Hanna Anderson, June 15, 1935; children: Grace Marit (Mrs. Paul Atherton), Linda Tucker (Mrs. Richard R. Mace), Frances Marion (Mrs. Brian Tennery); m. Jo Anne Bacon Hilley, Mar. 12, 1964; children: Andrew L.; (adopted) Kathleen Melinda, Wayne Edgar; m. Marilyn Hassett Petrie, Mar. 2, 1973; m. Judith H. Viets, July 24, 1999. BA (Sereno Gaylord scholar), Yale U., 1936. Pres., chmn. bd. Frank M. Ewing Co., Inc., Washington, from 1937, Lumber Distbn. Co., Petersburg, Va., 1942-57; Pres., chmn. bd. Ewing Lumber & Millwork Corp., Beltsville, Md., 1958-71; chmn. bd. Kettler Bros. Inc., Gaithersburg, Md., 1965-88; developer Beltsville Indsl. Center, 1950-89. Bd. dirs. Washington Mut. Investors Fund.; industry adv. com. WPB, 1942-46; industry adv. com. to sec. commerce, 1947-50, dep. and later acting asst. sec. def., 1955-56. Gen. campaign chmn. Prince Georges Community Chest, 1955; bd. dirs. Childrens Hosp., Washington. Mem. Prince Georges C. of C. (pres. 1956-57), Kiwanis (bd. dirs. Prince Georges 1948-52), Masons, Chevy Chase Club, Met. Club, Burning Tree Club (Washington), St. Andrew's Royal and Ancient Golf Club (Scotland), Tryall Club (Jamaica). Home: Naples, Fla. Died Sept. 16, 2013.

**EYNON, THOMAS GRANT,** sociology educator; b. Evanston, Ill., Aug. 10, 1926; s. John and Ruth (Deal) E.; m. Janet Arstingstall, Nov. 24, 1956; children: James Walter, John Robert, Sarah Carolyn. BS in Psychology, Ohio State U., 1953, MA in Anthrology, 1955. Asst. prof. to assoc. prof. Ohio State U., 1959-68; prof. sociology So. Ill. U., from 1968, dir. grad. studies, 1986-93, dir. undergrad. studies, 1993-96. Vis. prof. St. Lawrence U., 1962-70, U. Minn., 1970-75, U. Stockholm, 1972, Nat. U. Ireland, Galway and Dublin, Queens U. Belfast, Oxford U., London Sch. Econs., U. Leeds, 1973, Ill. Inst. Tech. Rsch. Inst., 1974, Niigata Japan, 1991, 92, 93, 96, 97, 98; dir. Social Sci. Rsch. Bur., 1977-79; commr. Ill. Juvenile Justice Commn., 1983-95; mem. Gov.'s Task Force on Prison Crowding, 1983-84, Task Force Released Prisoners, 1988-89. Author: Offender Classification in the United States, 1976, editor Sociol. Quar., 1981-84; contbr. numerous articles and revs. to profl. jours., chpts. in books. Mem. adv. bd. Ill. Dept. Corrections, 1970-79, chmn., 1979—; chmn. REading is Fundamental Program, 1978-87; mem. Gov.'s Task Force Mental Health, 1970-72. Naval Aviator USNR, 1944-51, PTO, Korea. Decorated Silver Star, Purple Heart, DFC; recipient Sturges Pub. Svc. award, 1998; Scott fellow 1955. Mem. Midwest Sociol. Soc. (treas. 1987—). Methodist. Home: Carbondale, Ill. *If no one misses me I wasn't there, and if I am remembered let it be for my faith, hope, and charity.* Died Apr. 13, 1998.

**FADER, SEYMOUR JEREMIAH,** management and engineering consulting company executive; b. NYC, Feb. 9, 1923; s. Louis and Bertha (Stachel) F.; m. Shirley Ruth Sloan, June 26, 1951; children: Susan Deborah, Steven Micah. Student, CCNY, 1938-42; BSEE, U. Pa., 1949, MBA in Indsl. Mgmt., 1950. Mgr. prodn. Bogue Elec. Mfg. Co., Paterson, N.J., 1950-56; mgr. planning and control Rowe Mfg. Co., Whippany, N.J., 1956-58; cons., engr. Koor Crafts & Industries, Ltd., Tel Aviv, 1958-59; dir. mfg. ops. ESC Electronics Corp., Palisades Park, N.J., 1959-62; mgr. mfg. Artistic Mfg., Sun Chem. Corp., Carlstadt, N.J., 1962-66; mgr. ops. Fairchild Instrumentation Fairchild Camera & Instrument Corp., Clifton, N.J., 1966-67; v.p. Graphic Products, Inc., Hackensack, N.J., 1967-69; gen. mgr., v.p. Berkey Tech., Berkey Photo, Inc., Woodside, N.Y., 1969-72; pres. Suste Assocs., Paramus, N.J., from 1972. Asst. prof. mgmt. Ramapo Coll., Mahwah, N.J., 1972-75, assoc. prof., 1975-80, prof. mgmt. and indsl. rels., 1980-83, prof. emerigus, 1993—, bd. dirs., creator Ramapo Coll. USA-Eng. Study Abroad programs, 1983-93; program coord., exec. dir. Overseas Program, Southside Va. C.C., 1994-95; adj. prof. mgmt. Grad. Sch. Bus., Fordham U., 1982—; arbitration panelist Better Bus. Bur. of Bergen, Passaic and Rockland Counties, 1983—; creator, exec. program dir. overseas program Coll. Consortium for Study Abroad, 1995—. Author: Fundamentals of Management for First0Line Supervisors, 1974, The Manufacturing Manager, 1975; co-author: Jobmanship, 1979; contbr. articles to profl. jours.; patentee coreless reeler, desk-tip copier, photocopier. Mem. pub. health study N.J. State Assembly Commn. on Conservation, Natural Resources, Air and Water Pollution, 1972-73; commr. Paramus Environ. Commn., 1973-78, vice chmn., 1977-78, chmn. inventory and land use com., 974-78. With U.S. Army, 1942-45. Mem. Am. Mgmt. Assn. (cert. of achievement 1974), Am. Arbitration Assn. (panelist), Am. Inst. Indsl. Engrs., Soc. Advancement of Mgmt., Nat. Panel Consumer Arbitrators, Am. Prodn. and Inventory Control Soc., Delta Mu Delta. Died July 24, 1999.

**FAGER, CHARLES ANTHONY,** neurosurgeon; b. Nassau, The Bahamas, Jan. 16, 1924; came to U.S., 1924; s. Charles Anthony and Mary Frances (Amoury) F.; m. Margaret Bulkley, May 30, 1947; children: Christopher, Gregory (dec. 2014), Mary Louise, Jeffrey. Student, Wagner Coll., 1943; MD, SUNY, 1946. Diplomate American Bd. Neurol. Surgery (bd. dirs. 1976-82). Intern Syracuse (N.Y.) U., 1946-47, resident, 1947-48, Cushing Gen. Hosp./Lahey Clinic, Burlington, Mass., 1950-53; neurosurgeon Lahey Clinic Med. Ctr., Burlington, 1953—84, chmn. dept. neurosurgery, 1963-84, chmn. emeritus, 1984—2014. Chmn. coun. dept. chmns., 1965-67, 73-79; exec. com. New Eng. Bapt. Hosp., Boston, 1966-67, 73-78, pres. staff, 1973; vice chmn. med. adminstrv. bd. New Eng. Deaconess Hosp., 1973; Balado Meml. lectr. Argentine Neurosurg. Soc., Buenos Aires, 1972, Teachenor Meml. lectr. Kans. Neurosurg. Soc., Kansas City, 1972, Gardner lectr. Cleve. Clinic, 1986. Author: Atlas of Spinal Surgery, 1989; contbr. numerous articles to profl. jours., chpts. to surg. texts. Capt. USAF, 1948-50. Recipient Dudley award SUNY, 1946, Alumni Achievement award Wagner Coll., 1972. Mem. ACS (chmn. adv. coun. neurosurgery 1980-82), American Assn. Neurol. Surgeons (Lifetime Achievement award AANS/Congress Neurol. Surgeons 1992), Neurosurg. Soc. America (pres. 1976-77, Gold medal 2000), New Eng. Neurosurg. Soc. (pres. 1967-68), Boston Soc. Neurology & Psychiatry (pres. 1967-68). Roman Catholic. Avocations: gardening, tennis. Home: Wellesley, Mass. Died Apr. 8, 2014.

**FAGERSTRÖM, RITVA KYLLIKKI,** psychiatrist, psychotherapist, psychologist, researcher; b. Korpilahti, Finland, Mar. 28, 1943; m. Raimo Eino Uolevi Lehto, July 11, 1991. BA, U. Helsinki, 1971, MA, 1972, lic. in philosophy, 1977, MD, 1983; PhD, U. Tartu, 1996. Asst. psychiatrist Psychiat. Clinic/The Hosp. of U. of Helsinki, 1979-85; psychiatrist The Mehiläinen Clinic, Helsinki, from 1985. Spl. reader Psychol. Reports and Perceptual and Motor Skills, 1993-95. Contbr. more than 55 articles to profl. jours. Mem. N.Y. Acad. Scis. Avocations: reading, travel. Home: Helsinki, Finland. Died Oct. 26, 2002.

**FAIRCLOUGH, ELLEN LOUKS,** former Canadian government official, member privy council; b. Hamilton, Ont., Can., Jan. 28, 1905; d. Norman Ellsworth and Nellie Bell (Louks) Cook; m. David Henry Gordon Fairclough, Jan. 28, 1931 (dec.); 1 child, Howard Gordon (dec.). Student, Hamilton; LLD, McMaster U., 1975. Founder, prin. acctg. practice, 1935—57; adv. mem. Can. Del. to UN, 1950; mem. House of Commons Can., 1950—63; del. Conf. of Parliamentarians from NATO Countries, Paris, 1955; state sec. Canada, 1957—58; amb. extraordinary, Argentina presdl. inauguration, 1958; min., citizenship & immigration, 1958—62; former mem. Privy Coun. Postmaster Gen., 1962—63; apptd. sec. Hamilton Trust & Savs. Corp., 1963—77. Past v.p. Young Conservatives Ont.; bd. dirs. Can. Coun. Christians & Jews; patron Huguenot Soc., United Empire Loyalists Assn. Hamilton Br. Can; alderman Hamilton City Coun., 1946—50, controller, 1950; past chmn. Hamilton Hydro Electric Commn., 1974—86; hon. treas. dir. Chedoke-McMaster Hosps. Found., 1977—89, exec. dir., 1983—86. Decorated Order of Can. Fellow: Chartered Accts.; mem.: Hamilton C. of C., Imperial Order Daus. Empire (officer, provincial & nat. chpts. 1935—48), Gen. Accts. Assn. Can. (life), United Empire Loyalist Assn. (dominion sec. 1935—40), Faculty Club, Albany Club (Toronto), Hamilton Club, Zonta Lodge (pres., Hamilton 1940—42). Anglican. Home: Hamilton, Canada. Died Nov. 13, 2004.

**FAITH, RUTH L.,** retired mathematician; b. Blairsville, Pa., Mar. 13, 1929; d. Harry S. and Ruth H. Faith. BS, Indiana U. of Pa., 1950; MBA, U. South Fla., Tampa, 1983. E.A. (inactive), IRS, 1975. Math. U.S. Geol. Survey, Washington, 1950, Douglas Aircraft, El Segundo, Calif., 1955—56; aerodynamist Singer Corp., White Oak, Md., 1956—70; tax acct. self employed, Cape Coral, Fla., 1970—77; sec. treas. Source, Inc., Cape Coral, Fla., 1978—91, ret. N. Ft. Myers, Fla., 1991. Dir. Source Inc., Cape Coral, Fla., from 1980. Contbr. articles pub. to profl. jour. Ruth Faith Endowed scholarship fund Fla. Gulf Coast Univ., 2001. Mem.: Am. Bus. Women's Assn. (pres. 1971). Achievements include patent for bar code reader, 1968-69. Deceased.

**FANG, ZHAOLING,** artist; b. Wuxi, Jiangsu, China, Jan. 14, 1914; d. Shouyi and Shuying (Wang) Fang; m. Xingao Fang, 1938 (dec. 1950); 8 children. Attended, U. Manchester, Eng., U. Hong Kong, DLitt (hon.), 1996. Exhibitions include Beijing Internat. Ink and Wash Exhbn., 1988 (Zhongshan Cup, grand prize, 1988), Art '81, U. Hong Kong, 1981, one-woman shows include Mickelson Gallery, Washington, DC, 1973, 1975, Raya Gallery, Melbourne, Australia, 1977, Hugh Moss Gallery, London, 1972, 1978, Ji Gu Zhai Art Gallery, Hong Kong, 1971, Shanghai Gallery Art, 1997, Beijing Mus. Art, 1997, An Ode to Earth and Life, Tokyo Fuji Art Mus., 2000, A Life in Painting, Asian Art Mus. San Francisco, 2005. Named Painter of Yr., Hong Kong Artists Guild, 1991. Died Feb. 20, 2006.

**FANGER, POVL OLE,** civil engineer, researcher; DSc, Tech. U. Denmark, Copenhagen, 1970, MSc in Civil Engring., 1957; DSc (hon.), U. Coimbra, Portugal, 2001, Slovak U. Tech., Bratislava, 2002, Moscow State U. Civil Engring., 2002, Silesian U., Poland, 2003, Tech. U. Civil Engring., China, 2003, Hokkaido U., Japan, Cathol U. Leuven, Belgium, Tech. U. Sofia, 2004. Prof. Tech. U. Denmark, Copenhagen, from 1977; dir. Internat. Ctr. for Indoor Environment and Energy, Copenhagen, 1998—2003; hon. prof. Tianjin U., Bucharest, Tsinghua U., Beijing, 2004; univ. prof. Syracuse U., from 2006. Author: (book) Thermal Comfort; contbr. articles to profl. jours. Recipient prize, Larsen & Nielsen Found., Copenhagen, 1970, SCANVAC prize, 1982, Stockholm Bldg. award, 1988, Hall-Thermotank Gold medal, Brit. Refrigeration Inst., 1990, Hon. medal, Finnish Engring. Soc., 1994, prize, Villum Kann Rasmussen Fund, Copenhagen, 1996, Hermann Rietschel Hon. Plaque, German Industry Soc., 1996, Hon. Gold medal, Polish Engring. Soc., 1996, Hermann Rietschel Hon. Gold medal, German Engring. Soc. VDI, 1997, Carl von Linde Meml. Gold medal, German Soc.

Refrigeration and Air-Conditioning, 2001, KGH Hon. medallion, Yugoslavian Engring. Soc. KGH, 2001, REHVA Gold medal, Fedn. European Heating and Air-Conditioning Assns., 2001, Hon. medal, Brazilian Soc. Indoor Environment, 2001; named Civil Engr. Yr., Odense Engring. Sch., 2001. Fellow: CIBSE, Royal Soc. Health (John Edward Worth Silver medal 1997), Am. Soc. Heating, Refrigerating and Air-Conditioning Engrs. Inc. (Louise & Bill Holladay Disting. Fellow medal 1982, F. Paul Anderson medal 1992), Brit. Engring. Soc. (hon. Napier Shaw Medal of Rsch. 1989); mem.: NAE (assoc.; assoc. 2001), Russian Acad. Arch. and Bldg. Sci., Internat. Acad. Refrigeration, Engring. Soc. (hon.), Danish Acad. Tech. Scis., Internat. Acad. Indoor Air Scis. (founding mem. 1990, pres. 1996—2002), Royal Acad. Engring. (fgn. mem. 1994), Rumford Club for Bldg. Svcs. Engring. (hon.). Achievements include research in effect of the indoor environment on human comfort, health and productivity; energy applications in buildings. Home: Copenhagen, Denmark. Died Sept. 18, 2006.

**FARBER, VIOLA ANNA,** dancer, choreographer, educator; b. Heidelberg, Germany, Feb. 25, 1931; came to U.S., 1938, naturalized, 1944; d. Eduard and Dora (Schmidt) F.; m. Jeffrey Clarke Slayton, June 14, 1971. Student, Am. U., 1949-51, Black Mountain Coll., 1951-52. Dancer Merce Cunningham Dance Co., NYC, 1952-65; instr. dance Adelphi U., NYC, 1959-67, Bennington (Vt.) Coll., 1967-68, NYU, 1971-73; dir., tchr. Viola Farber Dance Studio, NYC, 1969-84; also artistic dir., choreographer, dancer Viola Farber Dance Co., NYC, 1969-86; chair dance dept. Sarah Lawrence Coll., from 1988; artistic dir. Centre National de Danse Contemporaine, Angers, France, 1981-83. Guest performer as vampire in Katherine Litz' Dracula; bd. dirs. Found. for the Contemporary Performance Arts; tchr. Am. Dance Festival, Durham, N.C., 1987, ADF, Seoul, Korea, 1990; guest tchr. throughout U.S., Asia and Europe including Holland, Germany, Denmark, others. Choreographer Viola Farber Dance Co., Ballet Theatre Contemparain, Angers, France, Ballet Thèâtre Français, Repertory Dance Theatre, Utah, Manhattan Festival Ballet, Nancy Hauser Dance Co., Dance depts. Adelphi, NYU, Ohio State U. and U. Utah, Janet Gillespie and Present Co.; commd. by Heinz Found.; collaborated with Robert Rauschenberg and David Tudor on video tape Brazos River, 1976; choreographed Jeux Chorégraphique for Ballet Thèâtre Français de Nancy, 1980, Extemporary Dance co., London, Plymouth, Eng., 1984, London, 1986; performed Centre Poompidou, Paris, 1979; choreographer for Emlyn Claid, London, 1986, Pauline Daniels, London, 1986, Nat. Youth Dance Co., Eng., 1986, New Dance Ensemble, Mpls., 1988; chroeographer Duet for Emmy and Karen, 1989; choregographed and performed Au Fil du Temps, Lyon, France, 1989, with Mathilde Monnier Ainsi de Suite, Paris, 1992, Montpellier, 1994, Shipwreck, 1995, choreographed and performed at Joyce Theater, N.Y.C. with Ralph Lemon, 1995; guest tchr. London Contemporary Dance Sch., Richard Alston Dance Company, Centre Nat. de Danse Contemporaraine, Angers, France, 1996; tchr. Am. Dance Festival, 1996; choregrapher, performer with Jeff Slayton It's Been a While; guest choreographer USIA auspices with Ce De Ce Dance Co., Setubal, Portugal; choregrapher Dreams of Wind and Dust. Recipient Gold medal with Jeff Slayton, Paris Dance Festival, 1971, awd. French Republic-Ofc. of the Order of Arts and Letters, 1998; Guggenheim fellow, 1983-84; grantee NEA, 1975, 79, NEA, 1976, 81, N.Y. State Coun. on Arts, 1974-79, CAPS, 1974, 78, N.Y. Dept. Cultural Affairs, 1977. Died Dec. 24, 1998.

**FARKAS, LESLIE GABRIEL,** plastic surgeon; b. Ruzomberok, Hungary, Apr. 18, 1915; Can., 1968; s. Charles Samuel and Olga (Kustra) F.; m. Susanna Gál, Oct. 23, 1971; 1 child, Julia. MD, U. Istropolitana, Bratislava, 1941; PhD, Charles U., Prague, 1959; DSc, Charles U., 1968. Resident surgeon Mil. Hosp. and Field Svc., Czechoslovakia, 1941-45; resident in plastic surgery Charles U., Prague, 1945-48, asst. prof., 1948-65, assoc. prof., 1965-68; dep. dir. plastic surgery rsch. lab. Czechoslovak Acad. Scis., 1963-68; dir. divsn. cong. anomalies Hosp. Sick Children, Toronto, Ont., Canada, 1968-69, rsch. fellow divsn. exptl. surgery, 1969-70, asst. scientist Rsch. Inst., 1970-77, sr. scientist, 1977-81, dir. plastic surgery lab. Rsch. Inst., 1970-81, asst. prof., 1970-78, rschr. Ctr. Craniofacial Care and Rsch., from 1982; assoc. prof. U. Toronto, 1978-81, spl. rsch. lectr., 1981-82, assoc. rsch. prof., from 1982. Dir. craniofacial measur. lab., Hosp. for Sick Children, Toronto, 1986—; cons. cleft palate program U. Iowa, 1975-78, dept. neurology Shriver Ctr., Waltham, Mass., 1984-95; with divsn. plastic surgery Royal Victoria Hosp., Montreal, Que.; mem. panel 5th Internat. Congl. Plastic Reconstructive Surgery, Melbourne, Australia, 1971; mem. panel cleft-lip nose Am. Cleft Palate-Craniofacial Assn., Hilton Head, SC, 1991; invited vis. expert med. anthropometry Min. Health Govt. of Singapore, 1987; invited tchr. course med. anthropometry orthodontics Orthodontic and Human Scis. Congress U. Med. Sch., Szeged, Hungary, 1996; session chmn. 8th Internat. Congress on Cleft Palate and Related Craniofacial Abnormalities, Documentation, Anthropometry, Database, Singapore, 1997; cons. in field Author: Hypospadias, 1967, Constructive, Reconstructive and Esthetic Surgery of the Male Urogenital Tract, 1973, Anthropometry of the Head and Face in Medicine, 1981, Anthropometric Facial Proportions in Medicine, 1987, Anthropometry of the Head and Face, 2d edit., 1994; contbr. numerous articles to sci. jours. Recipient Cert. Excellence for rsch. in attractive face Am. Soc. Aesthetic Plastic Surgery, Boston, 1985, Aleš Hrdlička Commemorative medal Czechoslovakia Acad. Scis., Prague, 1992, Vis. Scholar award dept. pediats. faculty medicine U. Calgary, Can., 1992, Salamon Frigyes Commemorative medal Orthodontic Soc. Hungary, 1996, Best Paper of the Yr. award for Surface Anatomy of the Face in Down's Syndrome: Anthropometric Proportion Indices in the Craniofacial Regions in Jour. Craniofacial Surgery, 2002; Med. Rsch. Coun. grantee, 1970-72, Atkinson Charitable Found. grantee, 1973-76, Smythe Found. Can. grantee, 1976-81, Physicians Svcs., Inc. grantee, 1991-99. Fellow Royal Coll. Surgeons; mem. Acad. Medicine Toronto, Am. Soc. Plastic and Reconstructive Surgeons (mem. faculty symposium reconstructive auricle 1972), Can. Soc. Plastic Surgeons, Plastic Surgery Rsch. Coun., Can. Assn. Anatomists, Biomat. Soc. Can., Can. Craniofacial Soc., Internat. Soc. Craniomaxillofacial Surgery, Japanese Soc. Aesthetic Plastic Surgery (hon.). Roman Catholic. Home: Willowdale, Canada. Died 2008.

**FARKAS, MIKLÓS,** mathematician, educator; b. Budapest, Hungary, June 15, 1932; m. Katalin Kéri, Aug. 29, 1978. MSc, U. Budapest, 1955; PhD, Hungarian Acad. Sci., Budapest, 1959, DSc, 1974. Rsch. fellow U. Budapest, 1954-57; asst. prof., then assoc. prof. math. Budapest U. Tech., 1957-67, prof., 1967—2002, head dept., 1968-87, prof. emeritus, from 2002. Head dept. math. U. Lagos, Nigeria, 1964—67; vis. prof. U. Caracas, Venezuela, 1980—81, U. Alta., Edmonton, Canada, 1984—85, U. Antioquia, Medellin, Colombia, 1999—2002. Author: Special Functions, 1964; author: (monograph) Periodic Motions, 1994; author: Dynamical Models in Biology, 2001; editor: Mathematical Dictionary, 1974; contbr. articles. Recipient A. Szentörgyi prize, Hungarian Ministry Edn., 2001; named Honored Educator, 1964. Mem. János Bolyai Math. Soc., Am. Math. Soc., Soc. for Math. Biology. Avocation: tennis. Home: Budapest, Hungary. Died Aug. 28, 2007.

**FARMER, ROBERT LINDSAY,** lawyer; b. Portland, Oreg., Sept. 29, 1922; s. Paul C. and Irma (Lindsay) F.; m. Carmen E. Engebretson, Sept. 8, 1943; children: Cort W., Scott L., Eric C. BS, UCLA, 1946; LLB, U. So. Calif., 1949. Bar: Calif. 1949. Since practiced in, LA; mem. Farmer & Ridley, LA, from 1949. Trustee Edward James Found., West Dean Estate, Chichester, Eng. Served with AUS, 1943-46. Mem. ABA, Los Angeles County Bar Assn., Order of Coif, Beta Gamma Sigma, Kappa Sigma, Phi Delta Phi, Annandale Golf Club (Pasadena, Calif.). Home: Pasadena, Calif. Died Nov. 28, 2013.

**FARMER, VICTOR COLIN,** research scientist; b. Woodlawn, Ireland, Dec. 31, 1920; s. Charles Thompson Farmer and Sarah Frances McFadden; m. Jane Wyllie Donald, Apr. 7, 1947; children: Francis, Joan, George. BSc first class honours, Glasgow U., Glasgow, 1943; PhD, Aberdeen U., 1947. Sci. officer (ret. as sr. prin. sci. officer) Macaulay Inst. for Soil Rsch., Aberdeen, Scotland, 1944—83; vis. rsch. worker CSIRO Divsn. Soils, Adelaide, 1984—85; Hannaford rsch. fellow U. Adelaide, Adelaide, Australia, 1984; vis. rsch. worker Inst. di Chimica Agarica, Portici, Italy, 1989; vis. prof. Dept. Soil Sci., U. Saskatchwwan, Canada, 1990, Dept. di Chimica Agraria, Portici, Italy, 1991; vis. scientist Inst. Nat. de Rsch. Agronomique, Versailles, France, 1991; hon. fellow Macaulay Inst., Aberdeen, Scotland, from 1990. Contbr. articles 164 to profl. jour., scientific papers. Fellow: Royal Soc. Chemistry, Royal Soc. Edinburgh; mem.: Clay Minerals Group (Disting. Mem. 2003), Clay Minerals Soc. (Pioneer in Clay Sci. 1999). Achievements include patents for Synthesis of imogolite. Home: Aberdeen, Scotland. Died Aug. 20, 2006.

**FARNON, ROBERT JOSEPH,** music, composer; b. Toronto, Ontario, Canada, July 24, 1917; s. Robert Joseph and Elsie Emily (Menzies) F.; m. Patricia Mary Smith, Aug. 13, 1963; children: David, Robert, Brian, Peter, Deborah. Student, Broadus Farmer Sch. Music, 1930-32, Humberside Coll., 1932-34, Toronto Tech. Coll., 1934-35. Prin. trumpet CBC Concert Orch., 1936-38; musical dir. CBC, 1939-42; condr. BBC TV and radio. Mem. BBC Music Adv. Com.; guest condr. internat. orchs. Compositions include: Symphony No. 1, 1939, Symphony No. 2, 1941, Rhapsody for Violin and Orch., 1956, Saxophone Triparte, 1974, Prelude and Dance for Harmonica and Orch., 1969, Canadian Impressions Suite, 1952; composer film music Gt. Brit., Can., U.S.; arranger, condr. recs. for Frank Sinatra, Lena Horne, Tony Bennett, Sarah Vaughan, The Singers Unltd., George Shearing, Pia Zadora, several European vocal and instrumental soloists. Pres. Guernsey Softball Assn.; pastron Guernsey Youth Band; hon. pres. Robert Farnon Soc., London. Served with Can. Army, 1943-46. Recipient Ivor Novello awards, 1956, 60, 72, Nordring Festival prize for music arranging, 1975, Grammy award for best instrumental arrangement, 1996; nominated for Grammy award for arranging, 1976. Mem. Can. Authors, Composers and Pub. Assn., Brit. Performing Rights Soc., Brit. Acad. Song Writers, Composers and Authors, Light Music Soc. (London, hon.), Variety Club of Gt. Brit., Palm Beach Club (London). Mem. Church of England. Home: Guernsey, Channel Islands. Died Apr. 23, 2005.

**FARRELL, JOHN STANISLAUS,** manufacturing executive, director; b. County Down, No. Ireland, May 19, 1931; arrived in Can., 1931, naturalized, 1931; s. George Stanislaus and Agnes Anna (McCartney) F.; m. Vyra June white, Aug. 7, 1959; children— John McCartney, Lizanne Jennifer BASc in Elec. Engring., U. Toronto, 1956. Registered profl. engr., Can. With ITT Can., Ltd., Montreal, Que., Can., 1962-69, dir. avionics and transmission, 1968-69; mktg. dir. Leigh Instruments, Ltd., Carleton Place, Ont., 1969-70, gen. mgr., 1970-73; pres., chief exec. officer Gestalt Internat. Ltd., Vancouver, B.C., Can., 1973-76; v.p. Cornat Industries, Ltd., Vancouver, 1976-78; sr. v.p. Versatile Corp., Vancouver, 1978-86; exec. dir. Rimquest Internat., Vancouver, 1986-88; pres. Versatech Trading and Devel. Corp., Vancouver, from 1988, also bd. dirs. Chmn., dir. Auspulp Pty. Ltd., Australia, Jara Mgmt. Inc., U.S.; bd. dirs. Versatech Trading and Devel. Corp., Vancouver, Tikal Resources Corp., Calgary, Alta., Can. Chmn. Resource Svcs. Australia, Sydney. With RCAF, 1950-59. Mem. Profl. Engrs. of Ont. Clubs: Vancouver Lawn Tennis and Badminton. Home: West Vancouver, Canada. Died Nov. 14, 2001.

**FARRELLY, ALEXANDER ANTHONY,** former governor; b. St. Croix, V.I., Dec. 29, 1923; s. Patrick and Mary (Hardcastle) F.; children: Velma, Allyson, Richard, Steve (dec.); m. Joan Harrigan, Aug. 3, 1991. BA, St. John's Coll., 1951, LLB, 1954; LLM, Yale U., 1961. Former mem. Dem. Nat. Com., V.I.; past chmn. V.I. Dem. Party; gov. U.S. V.I., 1987—95. Participant, adminstr. Boy Scouts of Am. and Girl Scouts of Am. Roman Catholic. Died Sept. 10, 2002.

**FARRIS, ROBERT GENE,** transportation company executive; b. Bartlesville, Okla., June 21, 1930; s. Carlton Kittrell and Ruby Lee (Richeson) F.; m. Betty C. Raimond, Dec. 28, 1951; children: Robert Raimond, William Carlton, Jonathan Bradley. BBA, U. Tex., 1952. Safety dir. Valley Transit Co., Inc., Harlingen, Tex., 1955-56, pers. dir., 1956-57, v.p., 1957-62, pres., 1963-99, chmn. bd., also bd. dirs., from 1963. Bd. dirs. Tex. State Bank, Harlingen, Tex. Regional Bancshares, McAllen, Tex., Millennium Fuels Corp., Dallas. Pres. Harlingen Indsl. Found., 1968-69; v.p. Rio Grande coun. Boy Scouts Am., 1971-72; trustee Marine Mil. Acad., Harlingen, 1977—; bd. dirs. Tex. Tourist Coun., Austin, 1980-84; past crusade chmn. Am. Cancer Soc.; past mem. bd. 1st United Meth. Ch., Harlingen. lst lt. U.S. Army, 1952-54, Korea. Named Friend of Tex. Transit, Tex. Dept. Hwys. and Pub. Transp., 1978. Mem. Nat. Bus Traffic Assn. (bd. dirs. 1980-85), Tex. Motor Transp. Assn. (bd. dirs. 1976-80), Harlingen C. of C. (pres. 1967-68), Rio Grande Valley C. of C. (pres. 1975-76), Algodon Club (past pres.), Phi Gamma Delta. Methodist. Home: Harlingen, Tex. Died Sept. 24, 2013.

**FARTHING, CHARLES FRANK,** medical educator, AIDS researcher; b. Christchurch, New Zealand, Apr. 22, 1953; came to U.S., 1989; s. Jack Raymond and Ngaire Emily (Green) F. MB, ChB, Otago Med. Sch., Dunedin, New Zealand, 1976; MD in Infestious Disease, SUNY, 1993. Diplomate Am. Bd. Internal Medicine. Intern, resident Christchurch Hosp., 1977-81; fellow in renal medicine Riyadh (Saudi Arabia) Mil. Hosp., 1981-82; registrar in genitourinary medicine St. Thomas' Hosp., London, 1982-83; resident in dermatology, AIDS rsch. fellow St. Stephen's Hosp., Westminster Hosp., London, 1983-89; acting investigator div. infectious disease NYU Med. Ctr., NYC; chief of medicine AIDS Healthcare Found., 1994—2007; Asia Pacific dir. medical affairs for infectious diseases Merck Sharp & Dohme, Hong Kong. Bd. dirs. Found. for AIDS Counseling and Treatment, London, Elton John AIDS Found. Author: Colour Atlas of AIDS, 1986, AIDS Treatment, 1988; also articles. Mem. All Party Parliamentary Com. on AIDS, London, 1986-89; patron London Lighthouse Recipient award for svcs. to AIDS, Terence Higgins Trust, London, 1986; fellow Winston Churchill Meml. Trust, 1988. Fellow Royal Australasian Coll. Physicians, Royal Soc. Medicine; mem. ACP, AMA, Royal Coll. Physicians, Brit. Med. Assn. Episcopalian. Avocations: theater, skiing, travel, ballet, opera. Home: Los Angeles, Calif. Died Apr. 5, 2014.

**FARWELL, BYRON EDGAR,** writer; b. Manchester, Iowa, June 20, 1921; m. Ruth Saxby; children: Joyce, Byron John, Lesley. Student, Ohio State U., 1939-40; A.M., U. Chgo., 1968. Dir. adminstrn. Chrysler Internat., Geneva, 1959-70; archeologist. Delivered Anne S.K. Brown Meml. lectr. on mil. history, Brown U., Providence, R.I., 1996. Author: The Man Who Presumed, 1953, 4th edit., paperback, 1989, U.K. edit., 1958, Books on Tape, 1995, Burton: A Biography of Sir Richard Francis Burton, 1964, 75, U.K. edit., 63, 88, 95, Books on Tape, 1994, Prisoners of the Mahdi, 1967, paperback 1971, 89, UK edit., 1967, Books on Tape, 1994, Queen Victoria's Little Wars, 1972, U.S. paperback edit., 1985, 2d edit., 1989, U.K. edit., 1973, Books on Tape, 1994, The Great Anglo-Boer War, 1976, U.K. edit., 1977, paperback edit., 1990, Books on Tape, 1994, Mr. Kipling's Army, 1981, U.K. edit., 1987, Books on Tape, 1994, For Queen and Country, 1981, paperback edit., 1987, Books on Tape, 1994, The Gurkhas, 1984, U.K. paperback edit., 1985, U.S. paperback edit., 1990, Books on Tape, 1994, Eminent Victorian Soldiers, 1985, paperback edit., 1986, U.K. edit., 1988, Books on Tape, 1993, The Great War in Africa, 1914-1918, 1986, UK edit., 1987, U.S. paperback edit., 1989, Books on Tape, 1994, Armies of the Raj, 1989, U.K. edit., 1990, U.S. paperback edit., 1991, Books on Tape, 1994, Ball's Bluff: A Small Battle and its Long Shadow, 1990, Books on Tape, 1994, Stonewall: A Biography of General Thomas Jackson, 1992, paperback edit., 1993, Books on Tape, 1993; Over There: The United States in the Great War, 1916-18, 1999; The Encyclopedia of Nineteenth Century Land Warfare, 1999; contbg. editor: Military History, World War II; contbr. The Reader's Companion to Military History, Oxford Companion to American Military History, 1996; contbr. numerous articles to Colliers Ency., newspapers, revs., mags.; mem. edit. bd. Small Towns Inst.; lectr. in field. Former councilman and mayor, Hillsboro, Va.; hon. mem., bd. dirs. Oatlands of Nat. Trust; former trustee Am. Mil. Inst.; mem. adv. bd. Nat. History Soc. Capt. C.E., U.S. Army, 1940-45, ordnance corps, 1950-53. Fellow Royal Soc. Lit. (U.K.), fell. Royal Geog. Soc. (U.K.). Died 2000.

**FAUBION, JERRY TOLBERT,** fiber and chemical company executive, management consultant; b. Pidcoke, Tex., June 9, 1917; s. Roy Arthur and Lillie (Pendleton) F.; m. Irene F. Stierli; 1 child: Roy Michael. BS in Engring. Adminstrn., Tex. A&M U., 1940. Registered profl. engr., Tex. Salesman McEvoy Corp., Houston, 1940—42; mech. engr., chem. engr., prodn. engr. Dow Chem. Co. Tex. div., Freeport, 1942—43, supt. prodn. control, 1943—55, mgr. prodn. coordination, 1955—57, mgr. planning and distbn., 1957—63; mgr. organic chems. product adminstrn. Dow Chem. Co., Midland, Mich., 1963—64, mgr. packaging dept., 1964—66; pres., dir. Dow Badische Co., Williamsburg, Va., 1966—75, Faubion Enterprises, Inc., Williamsburg, from 1976. Bd. dirs. Virchem S.A./N.V., Brussels,

1978—82, United Va. Bankshares, Inc. (now Crestar Fin. Corp.), Richmond, 1973—88, Chesapeake Corp., Richmond, 1976—88, Crestar Bank, 1973—88, Am. Filtrona Corp., Richmond, 1983—88; lectr. Coll. William and Mary. Mem. Freeport City Coun., 1950—51, Brazosport (Tex.) Ind. Sch. Bd., 1952—57, pres., 1955—57; trustee Freeport Cmty. Hosp., 1960—61; chmn. Williamsburg Cmty. Hosp., 1988—90; elder Presbyn. Ch.; bd. dirs. Williamsburg Cmty. Hosp., 1970—81, 1984—90. Republican. Home: Williamsburg, Va. Died Dec. 14, 1995.

**FAULCONER, THOMAS PLEASANT,** aircraft and small ships consultant, retired engineering executive; b. San Diego, Apr. 7, 1912; s. Thomas Nichols and Margaret (Adams) F.; m. Lillian Mathis, Feb. 14, 1965; children: Marion Dauchy, Katharine, Ann. BS in Mech. Engring., U. Calif., 1940. Engr. Consol. Aircraft Corp., San Diego, 1936—38, engr. charge landing gear design, 1940—41, dir. edn., 1941—43, asst. dir. indsl. rels., 1943—46, asst. chief engr. flying automobile, 1946—49; mgr. indsl. rels. Solar Aircraft Corp., San Diego, 1949—53; pres. Jet Air Engring. Corp., San Diego, 1953—55; mil. rels. rep. Convair div. Gen. Dynamics Corp., 1958—59; pres. Rick-Faulconer Engring. Corp., 1957—59, Thomas Faulconer Co., Inc., 1959—71, Geo. E. Barney Co., Inc., San Diego, 1959—62, Faulconer Bros., Inc., 1962—69. Cons. aircraft and small ships, from 1984. Author: Introduction to Aircraft Design, How to Make Money in California Real Estate, 1962, A New Concept of the Theory of Virtual Mass, High Altitude, High Speed Interceptor Study, FLAUNT-Fleet Air Ultra Naval Transport Harrier Carrier, 1984; editor, illustrator: Preparing for Aviation; prodr.: (various videotapes); contbr. tech. mags., profl. jours.; patentee (sliderule, caliper, traffic folding barrier system, sailing yacht leeway reducing keel). Mem. engring. adv. coun. U. Calif., 1946—70; mem. edn. and aviation com. San Diego C. of C., 1946—47. Lt. USCGR, 1943—45. Fellow: AIAA (assoc.); mem.: Mensa, U.S. Naval Inst., San Diego Maritime Mus., San Diego County Industries Assn. (dir. 1946—48), Rotary Point Loma (dir. 1946—56, pres. 1954), San Diego Yacht Club. Died Sept. 8, 1999.

**FAULISO, JOSEPH JOHN,** former lieutenant governor; b. Stonington, Conn., Feb. 23, 1916; s. Anthony and Rose M. (Grills) F.; m. Ann Marie Schwerdtfeger; 1 son, Richard J. (dec. 1993) Student, Providence Coll.; LL.B., Boston U., 1939. Bar: Conn. Assoc. Bailey & Wechsler; ptnr. Fauliso Katz & Hansen, Hartford, Conn.; mem. Conn. State Senate, Hartford, Conn., 1966—80; lt. gov. State of Conn., Hartford, Conn., 1981-90. Judge City and Police Ct. of Hartford, Conn. Circuit Ct. Mem. ABA, Conn. Bar Assn., Hartford County Bar Assn. Democrat. Roman Catholic. Home: Hartford, Conn. Died Aug. 20, 2014.

**FAULKNER, HERBERT WILLIAM,** tourism management educator; b. Bowral, Australia, Apr. 19, 1945; s. Arthur and Gweneth (Wilkinson) F.; m. Shirley Anne Alexander, May 11, 1968; children: Joanne, Benjamin, Katharine. BA in Geography, U. New England, Armdale, Australia, 1972, BA with honors, 1974; PhD, Australian Nat. U., 1979. Tchr. NSW Dept. Edn., Armidale, 1965, 68-73; nat. svcman. Australian Army, 1966-67; rsch. scholar Australian Nat. U., Canberra, 1974, 77-78; lectr. Warnambool Inst. Advanced Edn., Australia, 1975-76, U. Wollongong, Australia, 1979-81; prin. rsch. officer Bur. Transport Econs., Canberra, 1981-83; dir. Commonwealth Dept. Sport Recreation and Tourism, Canberra, 1983-87; inaugural dir. Commonwealth Bur. Tourism Rsch., Canberra, 1987-93; prof. Griffith U., Gold Coast, Australia, from 1993. Dir. Ctr. for Tourism and Hotel Mgmt. Rsch., Griffith U., 1993—; dep. CEO Coop. Rsch. Ctr. Sustainable Tourism, 1993—. Avocations: weightlifting, gardening, surfing. Home: Oxenford, Australia. Died Jan. 28, 2002.

**FAULKNER, WALTER THOMAS,** lawyer, director; b. New Haven, Sept. 17, 1928; s. Walter Thomas and Alice Marion (McGushin) F.; m. Joan Lee Hills, Mar. 17, 1956; children: John, Andrew, George, Susan. AB, Providence Coll., 1952; LL.B., Columbia U., 1955. Bar: N.Y. State 1956. Assoc. Rogers, Hoge & Hills, 1959-65, ptnr., 1965-86, Kelley Drye & Warren, 1987—2011. Sec. Sterling Drug Inc., 1973-78, Bacardi Corp., 1975-96. Bd. govs. Sound Shore Med. Ctr. Westchester. Served with AUS, 1946-48. Mem. Assn. of Bar of City of N.Y., ABA, N.Y. State Bar Assn., Am. Soc. Corp. Secs. Home: Larchmont, NY. Died Nov. 4, 2011.

**FAURRE, PIERRE LUCIEN,** business executive; b. Paris, Jan. 15, 1942; s. Lucien Marie and Anne Jeanne (Dame) F.; m. Pierrette Claudine Mome, July 24, 1962; children: Pierre, Sylvie. Degree in engring., Ecole Polytechnique, Paris, 1962; PhD, Stanford U., 1967; doctorate, U. Paris, 1972. Asst. mgr. Centre D'Automatique Ecoles des Mines, Paris, 1967-71; sci. dir. IRIA, Rocquencourt, France, 1971-72; exec. sec. gen. SAGEM, Paris, 1972-83, exec. v.p., CEO, 1983-87, chmn. bd., CEO, from 1987. Chmn. bd., chief exec. officer SAT, 1988-98; prof. math. Ecole Polytechnique, Paris, 1982-93, chmn. bd. 1993—. Author: Navigation inertielle optimale, 1971, Elements d'Automatique, 1974, 2d edit., 1984, Elements of System Theory, 1977, Operateurs rationnels positifs, 1979; also articles. Decorated officer Ordre Nat. du Merite, Officer Legion of Honor; recipient prix Laplace, 1962, prix Constantin de Magny, 1979, Académie de Sciences, prix Science et Défense, 1984. Mem. French Nat. Acad. Scis., Acad. Europaea, Internat. Acad. Astronautics, Soc. Math. de France. Died Feb. 2001.

**FEATHER, WILLIAM, JR.,** printing company executive; b. Cleve., Apr. 4, 1915; s. William and Ruth (Presley) F.; m. Sara Heedy, Oct. 22, 1938 (div. Nov. 1957); children: Megan, Deborah, Sara; m. Margaret R. Feather, June 4, 1959; children: Tyler, William. BA, Princeton U., 1938. Reporter Cleve. News, 1938—40; pres. William Feathers Printers, Inc., Oberlin, Ohio, from 1940. Trustee NSIDSF Co., Balt., from 1978. Lt. USN, 1942—46. Mem.: Elyria Country Club, Union Club. Republican. Home: Gulf Stream, Fla. Died May 1, 1996.

**FEAVER, GEORGE ARTHUR,** political science professor; b. Hamilton, Ont., Canada, May 12, 1937; arrived in U.S., 1967; s. Harold Lorne and Doris Davies (Senior) F.; m. Nancy Alice Poynter, June 12, 1963 (div. 1978); m. Ruth Helene Tubbesing, Mar. 8, 1986 (div. 1991); children: Catherine Fergusson, Noah George, Anthea Jane, Elysia Beatta. BA with honors, U. B.C., 1959; PhD, London Sch. Econs., 1962. Asst. prof. Mt. Holyoke Coll., South Hadley, Mass., 1962-65; lectr., rsch. assoc. London Sch. Econs. and Univ. Coll., London, 1965-67; assoc. prof. Georgetown U., Washington, 1967-68, Emory U., Atlanta, 1968-71, U. B.C., Vancouver, Canada, 1971-74, prof., 1974—2002, prof. emeritus, from 2002. Vis. fellow Australian Nat. U., Canberra, 1987, London Sch. Econs., 1991-92. Author: From Status to Contract, 1969; editor: Beatrice Webb's Our Partnership, 1975; editor: The Webbs in Asia: The 1911-12 Travel Diary, 1992; co-editor: Lives, Liberties and the Public Good, 1987; contbr. articles to profl. and gen. jours., chpts. to books. Fellow Can. Coun., 1970-71, 74-75, Am. Coun. Learned Socs., 1974-75, Social Scis. and Humanities Rsch. Coun. of Can., 1981-82, 86-91, Andrew Mellon fellow Harry Ransom Humanities Rsch. Ctr., U. Tex., Austin, 2006-07. Mem. Can. Polit. Sci. Assn., Am. Polit. Sci. Assn., Am. Soc. Polit. and Legal Philosophy, Conf. Study Polit. Thought, Inst. Internat. Philosophie Politique, The Traveller's Club (London). Avocations: rambling, wine appreciation. Home: Vancouver, Canada. Died May 12, 2008.

**FEDERICI, BILL (WILLIAM VITO FEDERICI),** retired newspaper reporter; b. Bklyn., June 22, 1931; s. Theodore and Margaret (DeMaio) F.; m. Arlene Ann McAuliffe, Oct. 1, 1955 (dec.); children: William Theodore, Robert Gerard. Student, Hofstra Coll., 1949-50, St. John's U., 1954-56. With N.Y. Daily News, 1947—51, with, 1955—81, spl. reporter, 1965-72, asst. city editor in charge investigations, 1975-79, Bklyn. editor, 1979—81. Dir. spl. projects Office Spl. State Prosecutor, N.Y.C., 1972-75; exec. dir. corporate affairs Bklyn. Union Gas Co., 1987-96 Author series on child abuse which initiated N.Y. laws to protect children, 1969. Served with USN, 1950-54, Korea. Recipient several journalism awards, including George Polk award Long Island U., 1970, Sigma Delta Chi award for met. reporting, 1975 Home: Longboat Key, Fla. Died Apr. 22, 2014.

**FEDORCHUK, VITALY VASILEVICH,** former Russian government official, former intelligence official; b. Zhitomir, Ukraine, 1918; Grad., KGB Acad. With KGB, 1939—82; chmn., state security com. Ukraine, 1970—82; nat. chmn., 1982; min., internal affairs., head, M.V.O. militia, 1982—86. Mem. Politburo Ctrl. Com. Ukrainian Communist Party, 1973—76, Ctrl. Com., 1979—89; dep. mem. USSR Supreme Soviet. With Soviet Armed Forces, World War II. Died Feb. 29, 2008.

**FEHRENBACH, T.R. (THEODORE REED FEHRENBACH),** writer; b. San Benito, Tex., Jan. 12, 1925; s. T.R. and Rose Mardel (Wentz) F.; m. Lillian Breetz, Aug. 22, 1951. BA magna cum laude, Princeton U., 1947. Field supr. Travelers Ins. Co., San Antonio, 1954-56; owner ind. ins. agy. San Antonio, 1956-69; mng. trustee Fehrenbach Trusts, 1970—2013; pres. Royal Poinciana Corp., San Antonio, 1971-92. Author: This Kind of War, 1963, This Kind of Peace, 1966, Lone Star (PBS TV Series 1985-86), 1968, Fire and Blood, 1973, Comanches, 1974, Seven Keys to Texas, 1983, Texas: A Salute From Above, 1985, others; contbr. numerous articles, stories to mags., U.S. fgn. periodicals. Mem. Tex. 2000 Commn., 1981-82; chmn. Tex. Hist. Commn., 1987-91; mem. design adv. com. Tex. Quarter Dollar, 2001-03. 1st lt. AUS, 1943-46, lt. col., 1950-53, Korea. Recipient Disting. Civilian Svc. medal, Freedoms Found. award, 1965, Evelyn Oppenheimer award, 1968, Lon Tinkle award from Tex. Inst. Letters for excellence sustained throughout a career, 2005, citations Tex. House of Reps., 1969, 73, Tex. Legislature, 1977, 2003 Bookend award Tex. Book Festival, 2005; T.R. Fehrenbach Book awards created in his honor Tex. Hist. Commn., 1986; named Disting. Citizen, San Antonio, 1973, Knight of San Jacinto, Primicerius Order of St. Maurice; Ann. T.R. Fehrenbach award named in honor and given for promotion of the history of Tex., 2007, Tex. medal of Arts, 2009, Katchi Kapshida award, Republic of Korea. Fellow Am. Numismatic Soc., Tex. State Hist. Assn.; mem. Philos. Soc. Tex., Authors Guild, Sci. Fiction Writers Am., Conopus Club, Argyle Club, Torch Club, Princeton Club of N.Y.C., Phi Beta Kappa. Republican. Episcopalian. Home: San Antonio, Tex. Died Dec. 1, 2013.

**FEIN, LEONARD J.,** contemporary Jewish studies educator, author; b. Bklyn., July 1, 1934; s. Isaac M. and Clara (Wertheim) F.; m. Zelda Kleiman, 1955 (div.); children: Rachel, Naomi (dec. 1996), Jessica. AB, U. Chgo., 1953, BA, 1955, MA, 1957; PhD, Mich. State U., 1962; LHD (hon.), Hebrew Union Coll., 1991; D Hebrew Letters (hon.), Balt. Hebrew U., 1991. Asst. prof. MIT, 1962-66, assoc. prof., 1966-70; dep. dir., dir. research MIT-Harvard Joint Center for Urban Studies, 1968-70; prof. polit. and social policy Brandeis U., 1970-73, Klutznick prof. contemporary Jewish studies, 1973-80; editor-in-chief Moment mag., 1975-87. Cons. Upward Bound, Grad. Sch. Edn., Harvard U., Sch. Edn., NYU, Union American Hebrew Congregations, Inst. Jewish Life; vis. scholar Religion Action Ctr. Author: Politics in Israel, 1967, Israel: Politics and People, 1968, The Ecology of the Public Schools: An Inquiry Into Community Control, 1971, Where Are We? The Inner Life of American Jews, 1988, Against the Dying of the Light: A Parent's Story of Love, Loss and Hope, 2001; editor: American Democracy: Essays on Image and Realities, 1965, Jewish Possibilities: The Best of Moment mag., 1987. Chmn. research adv. council Mass. Commn. Against Discrimination, 1963-66; chmn. commn. on urban affairs Am. Jewish Congress, 1968-70; mem. exec. com. Am.-Israel Pub. Affairs Com., 1969-74; founder, exec. com. Mazon: A Jewish Response to Hunger; trustee, mem. exec. com. Combined Jewish Philanthropies, Boston, 1969-75, life trustee, 1982—2014; bd. dirs. New Israel Fund. Social Sci. Research Council fellow, 1961-63, 66; recipient Smolar award, 1979, 83 Jewish. Home: Boston, Mass. Died Aug. 13, 2014.

**FEIN, RASHI,** health sciences educator; b. NYC, Feb. 6, 1926; s. Isaac M. and Clara(Wertheim) F.; m. Ruth Judith Breslau, June 19, 1949; children: Alan, Michael, Karen, Bena (dec. 1995) Student, Bridgeport Jr. Coll., 1942—43; BA in Economics, Johns Hopkins U., 1948; MA, Harvard U., 1976; PhD in Political Economy, Johns Hopkins U., 1956; LittD (hon.), SUNY, 1996. Mem. staff Pres.'s Commn. on Health Needs, 1952; from lectr. to assoc. prof. U. N.C., 1952-61; statistician Bur. of Census, 1958-59; sr. staff Pres.'s Coun. Econ. Advisers, 1961-63; sr. fellow Brookings Inst., 1963-68; prof. Harvard U., 1968-99, prof. emeritus, 1999—2014; Heath Clark lectr. London Sch. Hygiene and Tropical Medicine, 1980; chmn. med. assistance adv. coun. to sec. US Dept. Health, Edn. & Welfare (HEW), 1967-69; mem. adv. com. research and devel. Social Security Adminstrn. (SSA), 1968-71; mem. Nat. Manpower Policy Task Force, 1967-79, Office Tech. Assessment, Health Adv. Panel, 1981-86. Mem. spl. med. adv. group VA, 1987-91; mem. nat. advisory rsch. resources coun. NIH, 1995-99 Author: Economics of Mental Illness, 1958, The Doctor Shortage: An Economic Diagnosis, 1967, (with Gerald Weber) Financing Medical Education: An Analysis of Alternative Policies and Mechanisms, 1971, (with Charles Lewis and David Mechanic) A Right to Health: The Problem of Access to Primary Medical Care, 1976, Alcohol in America: The Price We Pay, 1984, Medical Care, Medical Costs: The Search for a Health Insurance Policy, 1986, 89, (with Julius Richmond) The Health Care Mess: How We Got Into It and What It Will Take To Get Out, 2005, Lessons Learned: Medicine, Economics, and Public Policy, 2010 Mem. bd. overseers Beth Israel Deaconess Med. Ctr., Boston; trustee Hebrew Sr. Life, Boston; mem. com. of visitors Goucher Coll.; bd. dirs. Harvard Cmty. Health Plan Found., 1980—87; mem. tech. bd. Millbank Meml. Fund, 1975—78, 1986—90, bd. dirs., 1987—90. Recipient John M. Russell award for Advancement Knowledge in Medicine, 1971; fellow Inst. History Medicine Johns Hopkins U., 1951-52; traveling fellow WHO, 1971. Mem. APHA, AAUP, Inst. Medicine of NAS (Adam Yarmolinsky medal for contbns.), Nat. Acad. Social Ins., American Econ. Assn., American Advisory Coun. World Orgn. for Ednl. Resources and Tech. Tng. Union. Jewish. Died Sept. 8, 2014.

**FEINBERG, WILFRED,** federal judge; b. NYC, June 22, 1920; s. Jac and Eva (Wolin) Feinberg; m. Shirley Marcus, June 23, 1946; children: Susan Stelk, Jack, Jessica Twedt. BA, Columbia U., 1940, LLB, 1946, LLD (hon.), 1985, Syracuse U., 1985; LLD (hon.), Bklyn. Law Sch., 1998. Bar: N.Y. 1947. Law clk. Hon. James P. McGranery US Dist. Ct. (eastern dist.) Pa., 1947—49; assoc. Kaye, Scholer, Fierman & Hays, NYC, 1949—53; ptnr. McGoldrick, Dannett, Horowitz & Golub, NYC, 1953—61; dep. supt. NY State Banking Dept., NYC, 1958; judge US Dist. Ct. (southern dist.) NY, NYC, 1961—66, US Ct. Appeals (2nd cir.), NYC, 1966—91, chief judge, 1980—88, sr. judge, 1991—2014. Mem. US Jud. Conf. US, 1980—88, chmn. exec. com., 1987—88, mem. Devitt award com., 1989, 1990, mem. long-range planning com., 1991—96; Madison lectr. NYU Law Sch., 1983; Sonnett lectr. Fordham U. Law Sch., 1984; Inaugural Howard Kaplan Meml. lectr. Hofstra U. Law Sch., 1986; The Future of Justice lectr. Inst. of Comparative Law, Chuo U., Japan, 1991. Editor-in-chief: Columbia Law Rev., 1946; contbr. to profl. jours. and mags. With US Army, 1942—45. Recipient Learned Hand medal for Excellence in Fed. Jurisprudence, 1982, Gold medal, award for disting. svc. in the law, NY State Bar Assn., 1990, Medal for Excellence, Columbia Law Alumni Assn., 1990, Pursuit of Justice award, Internat. Assn. Jewish Lawyers and Jurists, 1993, Disting. Public Svc. award, NY County Lawyers Assn., 1994, Edward Weinfeld award, 1995, Ann. Wilfred Feinberg prize named in his honor for best student work at Columbia Law Sch. related to fed. courts, 1998, Edward J. Devitt Disting. Svc. to Justice award, 2003. Mem.: ABA, Am. Law Inst., Am. Judicature Soc., N.Y. County Lawyers Assn., Assn. of Bar of City of N.Y., Phi Beta Kappa. Died July 31, 2014.

**FEINDEL, WILLIAM HOWARD,** neurosurgeon, consultant; b. Bridgewater, NS, Can., July 12, 1918; s. Robert Ronald Feindel and Annie Swansburg; m. Dorothy Faith Roswell Lyman, July 28, 1945; children: Christopher, Alexander, Patricia, Janet, Michael, Anna. BA, Acadia U., Can., 1939, DSc (hon.), 1963; MSc, Dalhousie U., Can., 1942; MD, CM, McGill U., Can., 1945, DSc (hon.), 1984; DPhil in Neuroanatomy, Oxford U., Eng., 1949; LLD (hon.), Mt. Allison U., 1983, U. Sask., Can., 1986. Diplomate American Bd. Neurol. Surgery; licentiate Med. Coun. Can. Rsch. asst. Montreal (Can.) Neurol. Inst., 1942-44, fellow in neuropathology, 1944-45, dir. neuro-isotope lab., 1959-88, dir. inst., 1972-84; dir. gen., dir. profl. svcs. Montreal Neurol. Hosp., 1972-84; rsch. asst., demonstrator in anatomy Oxford U., Eng., 1946-49; demonstrator in neurosurgery McGill U., 1951-52, lectr. neurosurgery, 1952-55, William Cone prof. neurosurgery, 1959-88, chmn. dept. neurology and neurosurgery, 1972-77, dir. Cone lab. neurosurg. rsch., 1959-88; assoc. prof. surgery U. Sask., 1955-56, prof. surgery, 1956-59; coord. rsch. in positron emission tomography Montreal Neurol. Inst. and Hosp.,

1975-84, dir. brain imaging ctr., 1984-87, dir. neuro history project, 1987—2014; chancellor Acadia U., 1991-96, chancellor emeritus, hon. gov., 1996—2014. Prin. investigator brain tumor project NIH, Bethesda, Md., 1986-89, mem.-reviewer neurol. disorders program project rev., 1983-88, external reviewer spl. programs, 1989-95; lectr. dept. history medicine and sci. U. B.C., 1976-78; neurol. cons. St. Paul's and City Hosps., Saskatoon, sask., 1955-59; cons. neurosurgeon Royal Victoria Hosp. and Catherine Booth Hos., Montreal, 1959-79, Sherbrooke (Que.) Gen. Hosp., 1964-85, Montreal Gen. Hosp., 1978-2014; cons. Champlain Valley Physicians Hosp., Plattsburgh, NY, 1973-85; neurosurgeon-in-chief Montreal Neurol. Hosp., 1961-72, sr. neurosurgeon, 1985-2014; neurologist and neurosurgeon-in-chief Royal Victoria Hosp., 1971-85, cons. neurosurgeon, 1985-2014; mem. sci. com. Found. for Study Ctrl. and Peripheral Nervous Sys., Geneva, 1983-2014; mem. expert panel on neurology WHO and Pan-American Health Orgn., 1976-94, cons. in neuroscis., 1996-2014; med. advisor to bd. Internat. Children's Inst., 1999-2014 Author more than 500 articles on epilepsy, neurosurgery, brain imaging and history of medicine; editor: Memory, Learning and Language—The Physical Basis of Mind, 1960, The Anatomy of the Brain and Nerves by Doctor Thomas Willis, tercentenary edit., 1965; co-editor: Dynamics of Brain Edema, 1976, Brain Imaging and Metabolism, 1985. Mem. bd. curators Osler Libr., McGill U., 1963-2014, curator Penfield Archive, 1976-2014, hon. assoc. libr. Osler Libr., 1964-65, hon. libr., 1996-2014, chmn. publications com.; bd. govs. Acadia U., 1981-89, mem. exec. com., 1984-86. Decorated officer Order of Can.; grand Officer de l'Ordre National du Québec; Rhodes scholar Merton Coll. Oxford U., 1939; recipient Neilson award Hannah Inst. History Medicine, 1997, Golden Jubilee medal Queen Elizabeth II, 2003, Laureate Can. Med. Hall of Fame, 2003, Lifetime Achievement award Montreal Neurol. Inst. and McGill U., 2005; William Feindel lectureship named in his honor, Montreal Neurol. Inst., 1994, William Feindel chair neuro-oncology endowed at Montreal Neurol. Inst. and McGill U., 2001; William Feindel Lectureship in Neuro-Imagery established Quebec Brain Imaging Rsch. Group, 2005. Fellow ACS, Royal Coll. Physicians and Surgeons Can., Royal Soc. Can.; mem. American Assn. Neurol. Surgeons, American Acad. Neurol. Surgeons (pres. 1976), American Neurol. Assn. (v.p. 1976), American Epilepsy Soc. (J. Kiffin Penry award 1998), American Soc. Neurol. Surgeons (v.p. 1978), Can. Neurosurg. Soc. (pres. 1968), Montreal Medico-Chirurg. Soc. (pres. 1974), Osler Soc. McGill U. (pres. 1945, hon. pres. 1985-88, 90-97), James McGill Soc. (pres. 1997), Acad. Mexicana Cirugia (hon.), American Osler Soc., Osler Club London (hon.), Univ. Club Montreal, Faculty Club McGill U., Montreal Indoor Tennis Club, Alpha Omega Alpha. Anglican. Avocations: medical history, music, book-binding, maya culture. Home: Montreal, Canada. Died Jan. 12, 2014.

**FEIST, GENE,** theater director; b. NYC, Jan. 16, 1923; s. Henry and Hattie (Fishbein) F.; m. Kathe Snyder (Elizabeth Owens), Feb. 10, 1957 (dec. 2005); children: Nicole, Gena. B.F.A., Carnegie Mellon U., 1951; MA, N.Y. U., 1952. Founding dir. Roundabout Theater Co., Inc., NYC, 1965, artistic dir., 1965—89, Roundabout Conservatory and Ensemble, NYC, 1980-95; founder Fourth Street Theatre, NYC. Lectr., cons. Staged prodns. John Houseman Theatre, Cherry Lane Theatre, East End Theatre, Actors' Studio; author: (plays) James Joyce's Dublin, 1975, Jocasta and Oedipus, 1970, also others; adapted plays for stage, including Ibsen's The Master Builder, Chekhov's Uncle Vanya, Pirandello's Naked, also others. Lucille Lortel Found. Lifetime Achievement Award, 1996 Mem. Dramatists Guild America, Soc. Stage Dirs. and Choreographers, League American Theaters & Producers, Internat. Theatre Inst., League Resident Theatres. Died Mar. 17, 2014.

**FEJFAR, ZDENĚK MIROSLAV,** cardiologist; b. Libáň, Bohemia, Czechoslovakia, Oct. 14, 1916; s. Václav Fejfar and Rzena (Appeltová) Fejfarová; m. Marie Hana Hanková, Mar. 20, 1943. D of Gen. Medicine, Charles U., Prague, Czechoslovakia, 1945; DSc, Czechoslovakian Acad. Scis., Prague, 1959. House physician Charles U., 1945-46, registrar, 1947-51, lectr. med. faculty, 1950-59, prof. internal medicine, from 1965; Brit. Coun. scholar London, 1946-47; sr. rsch. worker Inst. for Cardiovascular Rsch., Prague, 1951-59; chief med. officer in charge cardiovascular diseases unit WHO, Geneva, 1959-73; sr. rsch. worker Inst. for Clin. and Exptl. Medicine, Prague, 1973-95. Author, editor: 25 books and more than 600 sci articles. Recipient J. E. Purkyne medal, Pres. Czech Republic, 1966, Citation Internat. Achievement, Am. Heart Assn., 1977, Gold Medal, Slovak Med. Soc., 1981. Fellow: Royal Soc Med; mem.: Brit Soc Cardiology (corr.), French Soc Cardiology (corr.), Czech Soc. Angiology (hon.), Am Col Cardiology (hon. Disting Serv Award 1974), Swiss Soc Cardiolgoy (hon.), Peruvian Soc Cardiology (hon.), Czechoslovakian Soc Cardiology (hon.), Slavia (Prague). Avocations: hiking, music. Home: Prague, Czech Republic. Died July 20, 2003.

**FELDSTEIN, AL (ALBERT BERNARD FELDSTEIN),** retired editor, artist, writer; b. Bklyn., Oct. 24, 1925; s. Max and Beatrice (Segal) F.; m. Claire Szép, Sept. 2, 1944 (div. Jan. 1967); children: Leslie, Susan (dec.), Jamie; m. Natalie Lee Sigler, Jan. 27, 1967 (dec. Sept. 1986); children: Alan Weiss, Mark; m. Michelle Key Faribault, Aug. 10, 1989; 1 child, Katrina Pryor. Student, Bklyn. Coll., 1942-43; League scholar, Art Students League, 1942-43; D in Arts (hon.), Rocky Mountain Coll, 1999. Freelance artist and writer comic book industry, NYC, 1945-47; freelance artist, writer and editor E.C. Publs. Inc., NYC, 1947-55; editor Mad mag., 1955-85; supr. Mad TV spl., 1974; author TV scripts; illustrator children's record album covers; landscape and wildlife painter, from 1986. Invited consignor Sotheby auctions, 1991-95. One-man show Rusty Parrot Lodge, Jackson, Wyo., 1991-92, Visions West Gallery, Livingston, Mont., 1992-93, Mont. Trails Gallery, Bozeman, 1993-96, Von Eschen Gallery, Boulder, Colo., 1993-94, Sheep Mountain Gallery, Livingston, 1994, Silverthorne Gallery, Jackson, 1994-96, Corbett Gallery, Bigfork, Mont., 1995—, B & R Gallery, Canyon Country, Calif., 1995-97, Ribbons and Bows Gallery, Great Falls, Mont., 1995, Golden Spirit/Johnson Gallery, Pasadena, Calif., 1996-97, Gia's Gallery, Butte Mont., 1995-96, Rocky Mountain Legends Gallery, Livingston, Mon., 1995-96, The Frame Gallery, Agoura Hills, Calif., 1997-1998, Planet Bronze Gallery, Bozeman, 1998—, Mont. Wild Gallery, Livingston, 1998.; also exhibited Gallatin Valley Land Trust Juried Show, Bozeman, 1993, Southeastern Wildlife Exposition, Charleston, S.C., 1994, Round-Up Art Show, Pendleton, Oreg., 1995, 97, Nat. Mus. Wildlife Art Miniature Show, Jackson, Wyo., 1996, 97, 98, Custer County Art Ctr., Miles City, Mont., 1997. With USAAF, 1943-45. Recipient 1st pl. award for wildlife and landscape acrylics, Grand Champion award for acrylic Teton County Fair, 1990, finalist (top 100) Art for Parks, 1991, 1st pl. award for landscape and portrait grand champion Park County Fair, 1992, 1st pl. award for landscape Mont. Winter Fair, 1993, 1st pl. award for landscape and wildlife grand champion Park County Fair, 1994, Ink Pot award for outstanding lifetime achievement in comic art San Diego Comic Conv., 1994, finalist (top 200) Arts for the Parks, 1995, 1st pl. profl. award grand champion, res. grand champion, Park County Fair, 1995, 97, Gold medal Best of Show, Pendleton Round-Up Art Show, 1995. Home: Livingston, Mont. Died Apr. 29, 2014.

**FELIX-DAVIES, DERRICK DAVID,** physician; b. High Wycombe, Eng., June 30, 1925; s. John Llewelyn Felix-Davies and Mary Elizabeth Felix; m. Joan Kellett Felix-Davies, Dec. 29, 1949 (div. 1963); children: David, Paul; m. Joan Anne Sly, Mar. 14, 1970; children: Rachel, Claire, Kate. Med. tutor Royal Postgrad. Med. Sch., London, 1953—56; sr. registrar Medicine Queen Elizabeth Hosp., Birmingham, England, 1956—60; rsch. fellow Gen. Hosp. of Harvard U., Boston, 1960—61; clin. rsch. fellow, cons. physician U. Birmingham, from 1961; assoc. prof. SUNY-Buffalo, 1975—76; med. adviser Nat. Exhbn. Ctr., Birmingham, from 1976; chmn. European Congress of Rheumatology Symposium on Auranofin, Moscow, 1983. Contbr. articles internal medicine. Grantee Royal Coll. Physicians, London. Avocations: sailing, collecting paintings. Home: West Midlands B93 8JJ, England. Died May 1, 1988.

**FELS, CATHARINE PHILLIPS,** artist, writer; b. Kirksville, Mo., Aug. 29, 1912; d. Addison Leroy and Myrtle Helen (Randall) Phillips; m. Leonard A. Fels, July 11, 1936 (dec. 1974); 1 child, Margery Palmer. Attended, U. Calif.-Berkeley, 1932—33, attended, 1941—43; BFA, U. So. Calif., 1949, MFA, 1950. Asst. prof. UCLA, 1950—54; assoc. prof. U. So. Calif., LA, 1954—67, Calif. State U., LA, 1968—78, prof. emeritus, from 1978. Author (artist): End Time, 1983; editor: Graphic Work of Louis Monza, 1974; exhibitions include Istanbul Tech. U., Turkey, 1983, one-woman shows include No. Ariz. Mus., Flagstaff, 1986. Bd. dirs. South Bay Cmty. Art Assn., 1954—65, Downey Mus. Art, 1974—78. Recipient 1st prize in printmaking, Nat. Art Edn. Assn., 1978, 1st prize in watercolor, Hawthorne Arts Festival, 1977, purchase prizes prints, NW Printmakers, 1950, San Francisco Mus. Art, 1948, paper, Seljuk Arch., Internat. Aesthetics Congress, Dubrovnik, Yugoslavia, 1980; fellow Helene Wurlitzer Found. N.Mex., 1970. Mem. Am. Soc. for Asethetics and Art Criticism, Far West Soc. for Philosophy of Edn., Artists Equity Assn. Inc. (pres. L.A. chpt. 1976-78, chmn. nat. ethics com. 1978-83, bd. dirs. 1973-78), Taos Art Assn. (bd. dirs. 1981-83), Taos Seven, Soc. of Friends. Deceased.

**FENIMORE, GEORGE WILEY,** management consultant; b. Bertrand, Mo., 1921; BBA in Fin., Northwestern U., 1941; JD, Harvard U., 1947; postgrad., UCLA, 1955; LLD (hon.), Southwestern U., 1992. Bar: Mich. 1948. Asst. to dir. planning Ford Motor Co., Dearborn, Mich., 1947-48; exec. to v.p. and gen. mgr. Hughes Aircraft Co., Culver City, Calif., 1948-53; adminstrv. mgr. tech. products Packard Bell Electronics Co., 1954-55; with TRW, Inc., LA, 1955-64; v.p., gen. mgr. TRW Internat., LA, 1959-64; v.p. internat. ops. Bunker Ramo Corp., LA, 1964-65; dir. pub. rels., then corp. sec. Litton Industries, Inc., Beverly Hills, Calif., 1965-73, v.p., corp. sec., 1973-81, sr. v.p., corp. sec., 1981-86, mgmt. cons., from 1986. Past chmn. bd. Southwestern U. Sch. Law; mem. Calif. Tchrs. Retirement Bd.; cons. JCM Group. Bd. dirs. Children's Bur. L.A., Child Shelter Homes a Rescue Effort; sec. French Found. for Alzheimer's Rsch.; past mem. Calif. Fair Polit. Practices Commn., 1986-91; mem. United Way Emergency Food Sys. Study Task Force; elder, chmn. fin. com. Westwood Presbyn. Ch.; past trustee Sheldon Jackson Coll., Sitka, Alaska; mem. Beverly Hills Mayor's Econ. Adv. Com. and MOVE com., Calif. Fraud Assessment Commn. Maj. USAAF, WW II. Recipient Citizen of Yr. award, Beverly Hills Lions Club, 1976, Spirit Honoree, Beverly Hills Edn. Found., 1986, Beverly Hills YMCA, 1988, Brentwood/San Vicente C. of C., 1987, Hon. Citizen award, Beverly Hills City Coun., 1986, Guardian Angel award, Child S.H.A.R.E., 1989, Lifetime Achievement award, 2001, Highest award for Lifetime Svc. to Cmty., Key to City of Beverly Hills, 1990, State Gold award, Calif. Tchrs. Assn., 1993. Mem. Am. Soc. Corp. Secs. (dir., past nat. dir., past pres. L.A. Group), Beverly Hills C. of C. (past pres., Citizen of Yr. award 1979, chmn. edn. com., bd. dirs., David Orgell Meml. award 1990), Mandeville Canyon Assn. (past pres.), Bar Assn. Mich., L.A. Country Club, Rotary (past pres. Beverly Hills, Paul Harris fellow, William C. Ackerman trophy 1986), Shriners. Presbyterian. Home: Long Beach, Calif. Died July 21, 2013.

**FERGUSON, KINGSLEY GEORGE,** retired psychologist; b. Newcastle-on-Tyne, Eng., Apr. 13, 1921; emigrated to Can., 1927; s. William George and Isobel (Finnegan) F. BA in English and French, U. Western Ont., 1943; MA in Psychology, U. Toronto, 1951, PhD, 1956. Diplomate Am. Bd. Profl. Psychology. Staff psychologist Sunnybrook Vets. Hosp., Toronto, Ont., Canada, 1949-50; chief psychologist Westminster Vets. Hosp., London, Ont., Canada, 1950-61, Montreal Gen. Hosp., Ont., Canada, 1961-68; psychologist-in-chief Clarke Inst. Psychiatry, Toronto, 1968-86. Chmn. Ont. Bd. Examiners in Psychology, Toronto, 1972-77. Served to lt. Can. Navy, 1942-45 Fellow Can. Psychol. Assn.; mem. Am. Psychol. Assn., Ont. Psychol. Assn. (pres. 1959-60; Lifetime Achievement award 1994-97). Died June 13, 2009.

**FERGUSON, ROBERT S.,** film consulting executive; b. NYC, May 8, 1915; s. Samuel I. and Augusta H. Ferguson; m. Helene B., Aug. 1, 1940; children: Carole Jane, Sandra Joan. BS, NYU, 1936. With Scripps-Howard Newspapers, 1936—38, Warner Bros. Pictures, 1938—40; v.p. world-wide mktg. Columbia Pictures, Inc., 1940—73; v.p. corp. relations Columbia Pictures Industries, Inc., 1973—74; v.p. world mktg. Am. Film Theatre, 1974—75; v.p. div. entertainment Rosenfeld, Sirowitz & Lawson Advt., 1975—76; v.p. world mktg. Horizon Pictures, 1976—77; pres. Cinema Think Tank, from 1977. Dir. Natco Industries, Inc.; instr. in film Adelphi U.; cons. to chmn. Columbia Pictures Industries, Inc., 1979—83; cons. to chmn. bd., from 1983. Mem.: Motion Picture Assn. Am., Variety Clubs Internat., Screen Publicists Guild, Sci., Motion Picture Pioneers, Motion Picture Acad. Arts. Home: Atlantic Beach, NY. Died Sept. 16, 1988.

**FERNANDES, ANGELO INNOCENT,** retired religious organization administrator; b. Karachi, British India, July 28, 1913; Grad., Papal U., Kandy, Sri Lanka, 1937. Ordained priest to Roman Cath. ch., 1937. Archbishop City of New Delhi, 1959-90, archbishop emeritus, from 1990; pres. Cath. Internat. Edn. Office, 1990-94. Exec. pres. World Conf. on Religion and Peace, 1970-84; chmn. office ecumenical and inter-religious affairs Fedn. Asian Bishops Conf., 1985-89; chmn. justice devel. and peace commn. Cath. Bishops Conf. India, 1968-76, 86-90. Author: As You Pray So You Live, 1992, 2d large edit., 1996, Building Bridges: The Missing Dimension in Education, 1993, Vatican Two Revisited, 1997. Mem. Vatican Justice and Peace Acad. Died Jan. 30, 2000.

**FERNANDEZ, HAPPY CRAVEN (GLADYS),** academic administrator; b. Scranton, Pa., Mar. 3, 1939; d. Orvin William and Florence (Waite) Craven; m. Richard Ritter Fernandez, June 10, 1961; children: John Ritter, David Craven, Richard William. BA, Wellesley Coll., 1961; MA in Teaching, Harvard U., 1962; MA, U. Pa., Phila., 1970; EdD, Temple U., 1984. Social studies tchr. various pub. schs., 1961-64; from vis. asst. prof. to prof. Sch. Social Adminstrn. Temple U., Phila., 1974—92; exec. dir. Parents Union for Pub. Sch., Phila., 1980-82; dir. The Child Care and Family Policy Inst., Phila., 1988-92; city councilwoman Phila., 1992-98; candidate for mayor City Phila., 1998-99; pres. Moore Coll. of Art and Design, Phila., 1979—2012. Cons. Nat. Com. for Citizens in Edn., Columbia, Md., 1982—87, Phila. Youth Study Ctr., 1988—90; commr. Phila. Gas Commn, 1992—97; trustee Edn. Law Ctr., Phila., 1983—2005; bd. dirs. Cultural Fund, 1996—98; chair Select Com. on Bus. Taxes, 1992—98, Select com. on Land Reuse, 1997—98; pres. Delaware Valley Child Care Coun., 1988—90. Author: Parents Organizing to Improve Schools, 1976, The Child Advocacy Handbook, 1980, Elder Care and Child Care Policies of Philadelphia Area Businesses, 1991. Chair bd. dirs. Am. for Dem. Action, Phila., 1984—86; chair Children's Coalition, 1982—86, Parents Union for Pub. Schs., Phila., 1972—75, founder, from 1972, chair, 1978—80; bd. dirs. Phila. Citizens for Children and Youth, 1986—93, bd. mem., pres., 2007—09; pres. bd. Parkway Coun. Found., Phila., 2006—12; del. Dem. Nat. Conv., 1988, 1992, 1996; bd. dirs. Greater Phila. Cultural Alliance, 2006—08, chmn. bd., 2004—06, Pa. Women's Forum, from 2000; trustee The Phila. Award, 2004—10, chair, 2007—08. Recipient Women in Edn. award Women's Way, 1989, Pub. Citizen of Yr. award NASW, 1991, Local Elected Ofcl. award Pa. Citizens for Better Libr., 1993, Pub. Svc. award Homeowners Assn. Phila., 1994 Phila. Op. Smile award, 1999, Woman of Yr.-Ivy Willis award, 2000, Fleisher Art Meml. Founders award 2001, Woman of Achievement award AAUW, 2005; named Outstanding Advisor, Health Promotions Coun., 1994, 2002-, Disting. Dau. of Pa., 2002—; Wellesley Coll. scholar, 1961. Mem.: Mayors Coun. Arts (vice chair from 2010), Pa. Assn. Indepedent Colls. & Univs. (bd. mem. 2010—12), Nat. Assn. Ind. Colls. and Univs. (bd. dirs. 2003—06), Assn. Ind. Schs. of Art and Design (nat. sec. 2001—04, bd. mem. 2001—12, vice chmn. nat. bd. dirs. 2004—09, bd. mem. Philagratike 2008—12). Mem. United Church Of Christ. Avocation: tennis. Home: Philadelphia, Pa. Died Jan. 19, 2013.

**FERNANDO, CECIL T.,** engineering executive; b. Mt. Lavinia, Sri Lanka, Nov. 10, 1924; s. Condegamage Theodore and Cornelia Henrietta (Fonseka) F.; m. Delicia Mary Senaratne, June 9, 1947; children: Ramya Surangani, Shreeni Damitha. BS of Engring. with honors, Coll. Engring., Poona, India, 1950. Irrigation engr. Dept. Irrigation, Sri Lanka, 1950-65; gen. mgr. River Valleys Devel. Bd., Sri Lanka, 1966-67; cons. Bank of Ceylon, Sri Lanka, 1968; mng. ptnr. Enging. Cons., Colombo, 1968-77, mng. dir., chmn., 1977-89; mng. ptnr. Engring. Cons. Internat., Colombo, from 1990; chmn. Samitar Ltd., Colombo, 1978-89, Engring. Cons. Ltd., Colombo, from 1990. Fellow Inst. Engrs. India, Inst. Engrs. Sri Lanka, ASCE, Assn. Cons. Engrs. Sri Lanka, Sri Lanka Assn. Advancement Sci. Buddhist. Avocations: stamp collecting/philately, sports, classical music, nature. Home: Colombo, Sri Lanka. Died Dec. 2004.

**FERRÉ, GIANFRANCO,** fashion designer, artistic director; b. Legnano, Lombardy, Italy, Aug. 15, 1944; s. Luigi and Andreina (Morosi) F. Degree in architecture, Politecnico, Milan, 1969. Fashion designer, Milan, 1978—96; designer Oaks by Ferré, Milan, 1978-94, Studio 0.001 by Ferré, Milan, 1987—89, Ferréjeans, Milan, 1989-95, Forma O by Ferré, 1989—96, Gieffeffe, Milan, 1995—96; artistic dir. Christian Dior, Paris, 1989—96. Sr. adv. Chinese Govt., 1993. Decorated Commendatore dell'Ordine (Italy), 1986; recipient award Asahi Shimbun newspaper and WWD Japan fashion mag., 1983, Best Designer of Yr. award Modepreis, Munich, 1985, Cutty Sark Men's Fashion award, N.Y., 1985, Gold Medal of Civic Merit, City of Milan, 1985; Dé d'Or prize Internat. Fashion Critics, 1989, L'Occhio d' Oro award, 1983, 83-84, 85, 86-87, 87-88, 89, Gold Medal of Civic Merit, Town of Legnano, 1989, Milanese of Yr. award Famiglia Meneghina, 1989, Lorenzo il Magnifico award, 1990, Il Fiorino d'Oro, 1991, Diva-Wollsiegel, 1992, Pitti Immagine Uomo, 1993, Crystal Apple award, 1995. Died June 17, 2007.

**FERTEL, RUTH U.,** restaurant owner; b. 1927; Pres. Ruth's Chris Steak House, New Orleans, 1965-97, chmn., founder, from 1997. Died Apr. 16, 2002.

**FETNER, ROBERT HENRY,** radiobiologist; b. Savannah, Ga., Feb. 22, 1922; s. William Westcott and Lucille Fedora (Goodrich) F.; m. Mary Carolyn Guiney, July 8, 1972; 1 dau., Amber. BS, U. Miami, Fla., 1950, MS, 1952; PhD, Emory U., 1955. Mem. faculty Ga. Inst. Tech., Atlanta, from 1955, prof. radiation biology, from 1963, dir. Sch. Biology, 1964-70. Cons. in field. Contbr. articles in field to profl. jours.; patentee computer digitizer. Served with AUS, 1942-45. Decorated Combat Inf. badge. Mem. Ga. Acad. Sci. (editor bull. 1960-64), Sigma Xi, Phi Kappa Phi. Presbyterian. *My most rewarding career experience has been as a participant in the search for knowledge in science.* Died Oct. 14, 2013.

**FEUILLE, RICHARD HARLAN,** lawyer, director; b. Mexico City, June 10, 1920; s. Frank and Margaret (Levy) F.; m. Louann Johnston Hoover, Oct. 20, 1948; children: Louann H., Richard H., Robert R., Joseph L. (dec.), James M., Patrick F. (dec.), Margaret J. BA, U. Va., 1947, LLB, 1948; JD, 1970. Bar: Tex. 1948. Assoc. Jones, Hardie, Grambling & Howell, El Paso, Tex., 1948-53; ptnr. Hardie, Grambling, Sims & Feuille, El Paso, 1953-57; sr. ptnr. Scott, Hulse, Marshall & Feuille, El Paso, from 1957. Bd. dirs. El Paso Nat. Bank (now known as JPMorgan Chase Bank), 1964—93. Active United Fund El Paso, 1963—, pres., 1968, 75—, bd. dirs., 1966-72, founder, v.p. trust fund, 1969—; pres. El Paso Cmty. Concert Assn., 1961-67; mem. adv. coun. U. Tex. at El Paso, 1968—, mem. exec. com., 1968-70; bd. dirs. Providence Meml. Hosp., 1986-92; bd. dirs. St. Clement's Episcopal Parish Sch., El Paso, pres., 1993-95; trustee YWCA, El Paso; bd. dirs. El Paso Cmty. Found., 1980—, pres., 1983-84, chmn. bd., 2004-05. Maj. USAAF, 1942-46, PTO, Iwo Jima. Decorated bronze star; recipient Disting. Svc. award City of El Paso and Rotary Club, 2002. Mem. ABA (estate and gift tax com.), El Paso County Bar Assn. (pres. 1972-73), Tex. Bar Assn., Am. Bar Assn., Greater El Paso Tennis Assn. (bd. dirs.), Rotary Club of El Paso, Order Coif, Phi Beta Kappa, Omicron Delta Kappa. Episcopalian (vestryman, sr. warden). Clubs: Coronado Country (El Paso), El Paso Tennis (El Paso) (pres. 1973). Home: El Paso, Tex. Died Oct. 22, 2013.

**FEUVREL, SIDNEY LEO, JR.,** lawyer, educator; b. Birmingham, Ala., June 7, 1948; s. Sidney Leo and Tommie Eula (Nolan) F.; m. Glenda Kay Erwin, May 8, 1970 (div. 1979); 1 child, William Michael; m. Lillian Torrence, Apr. 22, 1989. BA, Mercer U., 1978, JD, 1981; student comparative criminal law, Moscow U., Russia, 1979; student East-West trade law, Warsaw U., Poland, 1979; student U.S. govt. law studies, U. Utah, 1980. Bar: Fla. 1981, Ga. 1981, U.S. Dist. Ct. (no. dist.) Ga. 1981, U.S. Dist. Ct. (mid. dist.) Fla. 1983, U.S. Ct. Appeals (11th cir.) 1983, U.S. Supreme Ct. 1989; cert. mediator and arbitrator, Federal Dist. Ct., U.S. Bankruptcy Ct. (mid. dist.), Fla. Air traffic controller FAA, Memphis, 1970-74, Atlanta, 1974-76; pvt. practice law Atlanta, 1981, Orlando, Fla., from 1981. Adj. prof. Fla. Inst. Tech., Melbourne, 1983-91, Velenica C.C., Orlando, 1990—, Webster U., Orlando, 1990—; cert. family mediator, ins. mediator, county ct. mediator Fla. Supreme Ct. Bd. dirs. Griffin Prep. Sch., Ga., 1977. With USN, 1966-69, Vietnam 1967-68. Mem. ATLA, Rotary (treas. 1985), 3d Degree Mason, 32 Degree Scottish Rite Mason, Noble of Shrine (Atlanta), Orange County Bar Assn. (pro bono panel), Am. Arbitration Assn. (apptd. panel of arbitrators), Am. Trial Lawyers Assn., Acad. of Fla. Trial Lawyers. Avocations: travel, skiing, scuba diving, private piloting. Home: Orlando, Fla. Died Sept. 22, 1998.

**FIBICH, FELIX,** choreographer, actor, dancer; b. Warsaw, Aug. 5, 1917; came to U.S., 1950; s. Symcha and Sara (Fibich) Goidblat; m. Judith Berg, Aug. 1942 (dec. 1992) Student, Judith Berg Sch. Dance, Warsaw, 1937, State Theatre, Ashkhabad, U.S.S.R., 1941-43, Juilliard Sch., 1952. Lectr., demonstrator, asst. dir. Broadway shows including Cafe Crown, Brooks Atlanson Theatre, 1989. Toured extensively with Felix Fibich Dance Co.; performer on concert stage, theatre, TV, off-Broadway, film, Yiddish Theater; on tour (play) Lulu, 1996 Home: New York, NY. Died Mar. 20, 2014.

**FICHTEL, RUDOLPH ROBERT,** retired association executive; b. NYC, Dec. 12, 1915; s. Paul Gotthard and Helen (Szapka) F.; m. Elsie E. Terebesy, Dec. 24, 1942; children: Nancy Lynn, Robert Paul, Richard John. BBA cum laude, Coll. City N.Y., 1938; cert., Am. Inst. Banking, 1941; diploma fin. pub. relations, Northwestern U., 1950; MBA, NYU, 1951; diploma banking, Rutgers U., 1954. Tchr. N.Y.C. Pub. Schs., 1938-39; adminstr. East River Savs. Bank, 1939-42; dir. pub. relations, editor, asst. sec. Savs. Banks Assn. N.Y. State, 1945-53; dir. pub. relations council, savs. and mortgage div. Am. Bankers Assn., NYC and Washington, 1953-64; nat. dir. Am. Inst. Banking, 1964-78; regional v.p. United Student Aid Funds, Inc., NYC, 1978-87; ret. Mem. lender relations com. Higher Edn. Loan Programs; mem. faculty Am. Inst. Banking, Stonier Grad. Sch. Banking; contbg. editor Am. Inst. Banking textbooks; speaker. Contbr. articles to profl. jours. Vol. tutor Literacy Program, N.Y.C.; income tax counsellor Am. Assn. Retired Persons. Served to capt. AUS, 1942-45, ETO. Recipient highest award citation Internat. Council Indsl. Editors, 1948, Dr. Marcus Nadler award for excellence in finance; N.Y. U., 1951 Mem. Beta Gamma Sigma. Home: Flushing, NY. *Success in my life has been the result of hard work, continuing search for knowledge, constant effort to understand and relate to people, and total dedication to excellence in full partnership with a loving family.* Died Mar. 2013.

**FICHTER, JOHN W.,** retired state legislator; b. West Conshocken, Pa., Jan. 2, 1935; s. John J. and Ella N. (Lukens) F.;m. Mary Ann Brunner, 1955; children: Barbara Fichter Metz, Dorothy Fichter Cross, Lancy L. BBA, Ursinus Coll., 1975. Mktg. rep. Eagle Sys.; benefits mgr. Alan Wood Steel Co.; mem. Dist. 70 Pa. House of Reps., Harrisburg, 1993—2006. Chmn. East Norriton Planning Commn., 1965-70, East Norriton Bd. Auditors, 1970-84; mem. Pa. Republican State Com., 1980-92; leader area 8 Montgomery County; former mem. bd. dirs. Montgomery County Pub. Libr., Montgomery County Sr. Ctr. Mem. Pa. Assn. Twp. Ofcls. (past chmn.), Montgomery County Assn. Twp. Ofcls. (past chmn.), Greater Norristown Jr. Chamber of Commerce (past pres.), Triangle Club (past pres.). Republican. Home: Norristown, Pa. Died Feb. 11, 2014.

**FIDANQUE, STANLEY BRANDON,** heavy equipment distribution company executive; b. Panama City, Panama, Feb. 3, 1918; s. Constance Cardoze, Nov. 28, 1942; children: Gay, Marjorie, Lynn, Stanley B. BA, Stanford U., 1939; MA, Columbia U., 1942. Sales and mgmt. exec. Fidanque Bros. & Sons, Panama City, 1942-64, Cardoze & Lindo, S.A., Panama City, from 1964. Bd. dirs. 6 cos. in Panama. Bd. dirs. 15 civic orgns. in Panama, pres. of 5. Named Exec. of Yr. in Pvt. Enterprise, Panama, 1989. Mem. Nature Conservancy (sec.), Human Rights Orgn. (pres.). Avocations: swimming, horseback riding, golf. Home: Panama City, Panama. Died Oct. 18, 2001.

**FIDOS, HENRYK,** mechanical engineer; b. Sulistrowice, Radom, Poland, Aug. 18, 1919; arrived in South Africa, 1973; s. Józef Fidos and Anna Pejas; m. Krystyna Galicz, July 7, 1956; 1 child, Michael Henryk. MS in engring., Tech. U., Warsaw, Poland, 1951; D in Engring., Tech. U., Munich, 1969. Cert. profl. engr., South Africa. Sr. lectr. Tech. U., Warsaw, 1951—63; rsch. engr. Siemens AG, Erlangen, Germany, 1964—71, Noranda Rsch. Ctr., Point Clair, Canada, 1971—72; postdoctoral fellow U. Waterloo, Canada, 1972—73; sr. chief rsch. officer Coun. Sci. and Indsl. Rsch., Pretoria, South Africa, 1973—84; ret., 1999. External examiner Tech. U., Durban, South Africa, 1978—82; dir. Metall. Consulting, Pretoria, South Africa, 1985—92. Author: (book) Modern Methods of Casting, 1959; translator: Pressure Die-Casting Process, 1963; contbr. articles to profl. jours. Mem.: N.Y. Acad. Sci., South African Inst. Foundrymen (Morganite medal 1978, Alexander medal 1980), Polish Assn. Foundrymen (Silver medal 1961). Roman Catholic. Achievements include patents in field. Avocations: classical music, reading, theater, violin, woodworking. Home: Pretoria, South Africa. Died Jan. 31, 2003.

**FIELD, FRANCIS EDWARD,** electrical engineer, educator; b. Casper, Wyo., Nov. 20, 1923; s. Jesse Harold and Persis (St. John) F.; m. Margaret Jane O'Bryan, Oct. 13, 1945; children: Gregory A., Christopher B., Sheridan Diane. BSEE, U.S. Naval Acad., 1945; MA in Internat. Affairs, George Washington U., 1965; AMP, Harvard U., 1970. Master cert. graphoanalyst, 1984; comml. pilot. Owner Field Lumber Co., Lander, Wyo., 1948—50; commd. ensign U.S. Navy, 1945, advanced through grades to capt., 1966, ret., 1975; rsch. engr., adj. faculty George Washington U., Washington, 1975—90. Pres. EXTANT, cons. firm, McLean, Va., 1981—; program dir. NSF, Washington, 1982-90. Author: Chronicle of a Workshop, 1977. Trustee Fremont County Mus. Bd., 1998—2003. Mem. Mayflower Soc., Masons, Sigma Xi, Am. Legion, VFW. Republican. Home: Mc Lean, Va. Died Oct. 28, 2013.

**FIELD, JULES B.,** theatre executive; b. New Castle, Ind., Feb. 13, 1919; s. Michael and Ida (Seeman) Blumenfeld; m. Muriel Joan Wolf, Sept. 10, 1961; stepchildren: Mark, Jimmy, Peggy. Grad. high sch., Toledo, Ohio. Owner Sullivan St. Playhouse, NYC. Producer off-broadway plays including Waltz of the Toreadors, 1958, Hedda Gabler, 1959, John Gabreil Borkman, 1959; assoc. producer off-broadway play The Fantasticks, 1960 Bd. dirs., benefit chmn. Riverdale Mental Health Assn., N.Y.C., 1985. With USN, 1943-46. Mem. Friars Club, Internat. Gaslight Club (co-founder). Democrat. Jewish. Avocations: travel, singing, tap dancing. Died Apr. 1994.

**FIELD, NORMAN J.,** physicist; b. NYC, Dec. 5, 1922; s. Morris S. and Clara (Edinburg) Field; m. Gladys Katz Field, Nov. 23, 1946; children: Joan, Kenneth, Richard, Elaine. BS cum laude, City U. NY, 1942; MS in Physics, Poly. Inst. Bklyn., 1959; LHD (hon.), Monmouth Coll., West Long Branch, NJ, 1979. Electronic engr. radar lab. Signal Corps, Ft. Monmouth, NJ, 1942—44, physicist, chief, optical microscopy engring. labs., 1946—54, asst. dir. rsch., 1954—58; asst. dir. Inst. Exploratory Rsch., US Army Rsch. and Devel. Lab., Ft. Monmouth, 1958—62; dep. dir. rsch. US Army Electronics Lab., 1962—64; chief applied physics div. US Army Electronics Command, 1964—68, chief office sci. and tech., 1968—70, dir. program mgmt., army area comm. sys., 1970—74, dir. internat. logistics, 1975—79; adj. prof., lectr. physics Monmouth Coll., from 1956; pres. Monmouth Regional HS Bd. Edn., from 1957, Friends Monmouth County Libr. Assn., from 1981. Contbr. articles to profl. jours. With US Army, 1944—46. Decorated Bronze Star with oak leaf cluster, Purple Heart. Mem.: Monmouth County Sch. Bds. Assn. (pres. 1972—73), NY Acad. Scis., Assn. US Army (pres. from 1978), Nat. Sch. Bds. Assn., Am. Ordnance Assn., NJ Fedn. Dist. Bds. Edn. (v.p. 1966), Am. Assn. Physics Tchrs., Optical Soc. America, Am. Phys. Soc. Home: Cliffside Park, NJ. Died Oct. 25, 1991.

**FIETSAM, ROBERT CHARLES,** retired accountant; b. Oct. 18, 1927; s. Celsus J. and Viola (Ehret) F.; m. Miriam Runkwitz, Apr. 12, 1952; children: Robert C., Guy P., Nancy A., Lisa R. BS, U. Ill., 1955. CPA, Mo., Ill. Claims adjuster Ely & Walker Dry Goods, St. Louis, 1947-48; acct. Price Waterhouse & Co., St. Louis, 1949-54; staff acct. J.W. Boyle & Co., East St. Louis, 1955-59; owner R.C. Fietsam, CPA's, Belleville, Ill., 1959-68, mng. ptnr., 1969—2010. Mem. Belle-Scott Com., 1979—; bd. dirs, pres. Belleville Ctr., Inc., 1980-81; mem. Ill. Pub. Accts. Registration Com., 1985-87. Bd. dirs. Meml. Hosp., 1982-85, Meml. Found., Inc., 1986-91, Bellville Hosp. Golf Classic, mem., 1983-91, chmn. 1986-91, Ill. Bd. Examiners, 1994-2002, vice chair, 1997-98, chair 1998-99, coun. v.p., pres. St. Paul United Ch. of Christ, 1969-73; mem. accountancy com. U. Ill., St. Louis. With USAF, 1951-53. Recipient honor for completing equivalent of 4 trips around the world on a bicycle, Schwinn Fitness, Nautilus Inspiration award, Active Aging Week award, Nautilus, 2004, Outstanding Cmty. Svc. Citizen cert. recognition, Turkey Hill Grange, 2003, Lifetime Svc. award, Greater Belleville C. of C., Inc., 2007. Mem. AICPAs (coun. 1981-84, 85-90), Ill. CPA Soc. (Lifetime Achievement award, pres. so. chpt. 1972-73, Mr. Southern Chpt. award 1976, Chgo. state bd. dirs. 1979-81, sr. v.p. 1987-88, pres. 1988-89, bd. dirs. 1989-90, ICPAC PAC 1979-92, chmn. PAC 1989-92, coun. 1981-84, 85-90, 92, Pub. Svc. award 1982-83), Nat. Assn. State Bds. Accountancy (del. 1994-2002), Ill. State Bd. Accountancy, Mo. Soc. CPA's, U. Ill. Greater Belleville Illini Club (past pres.), Belleville C. of C. (pres. 1973-74, Lifetime Svc. award, 2007), Belleville Jr. C. of C. (life, key Man award 1959-60, Outstanding Citizen award 1976), Greater Belleville C. of C. Inc. (Ambassadors 1973—), U. Ill. Alumni Assn. (life), Lambda Chi Alpha Alumnae Assn., St. Clair Country Club (treas. 1969, 71), Optimists (life, Belleville Chpt. pres. 1979-80, Disting. Pres. award 1979-80, Optimist of Yr. Belleville, 1977, Ill. Dist. 1980), Elks. Home: Belleville, Ill. Died Mar. 29, 2013.

**FINCH, JUNE JOHNSON,** secondary school educator; b. Chgo., Ill., June 6, 1927; d. Willard Thomas and Lucile Sarah (Adams) Finch; m. William Hayes Finch, July 3, 1948; children: Lisa Lynnette, Tina Stephanie. Student, Northwestern U., 1944; BE, Chgo. State U., 1948; postgrad., DePaul U., 1953; MA, Governors State U., 1977. Tchr. Hayes Sch., Chgo., 1948—53, Lewis Champlain Sch., Chgo., 1957—59, Dixon Sch., Chgo., 1959—70, Powell Sch., Chgo., 1973—76, math. lab. resource tchr.; elem. math. tchr. tng. ctrs. Chgo. Public Schs., 1970—73, coordinator living metric environ. program, 1976—77, coord. intensive math. improvement program, 1977—84, coord. bur. math., 1984—87; instrnl. coordinator, dist. 14, 1987—89. Instr. Loyola U., Chgo., 1972; cons. in field.; mem. Chatham-Avalon CC, Chgo.; vestryperson, Social Svc. Guild, St. Monica's Guild Episc. Diocese Chgo. Recipient Outstanding Tchr., Powell Sch., 1978; named Tchr. Yr., Dixon Sch., 1965. Mem.: Met. Math., Math. Assn. Am., Ill. Assn. Supervision and Curriculum Devel., Assn. Supervision and Curriculum Devel., Chgo. Elem. Tchrs. Math., Nat. Council Suprs. Math., Ill. Council Tchrs. Math., Nat. Council Tchrs. Math., Paragons, Les Plus Belles, Delta Sigma Theta, Phi Delta Kappa. Episcopalian. Home: Chicago, Ill. Died June 7, 1999.

**FINCH, NATHAN C.,** lawyer; b. LA, Aug. 14, 1909; s. Nathan Swain and Jeannette Cochrane Finch; m. Janet Snedden Finch, Feb. 21, 1935; children: Douglas S., James C., Barbara Finch Lawson. AB, Stanford U., 1931, LLB, 1934. Bar: Calif. 1934. Assoc. Howe & Finch, Palo Alto, Calif.; ptnr. Finch, Montgomery & Wright, Palo Alto, 1961—79, of counsel, from 1979. Bd. dirs. David & Lucille Packard Found., Monterey Bay Aquarium Found., Watkins-Johnson Co.; mem. Palo Alto Bd. Edn., 1951—61. Recipient Gold Spike award, Stanford U., 1980. Mem.: ABA, Santa Clara County Bar Assn., Calif. Bar Assn., Palo Alto Club. Republican. Died Nov. 13, 1990.

**FINKELSTEIN, EDWARD SYDNEY,** retired retail executive; b. New Rochelle, NY, Mar. 30, 1925; s. Maurice and Eva (Levine) F.; m. Myra Schuss, Aug. 13, 1950; children: Mitchell, Daniel, Robert (dec.) BA, Harvard U., 1946, MBA, 1948; DCS (hon.), N.Y.U., 1988. Successively trainee, buyer mdse. adminstr. Macy's, NYC, 1948-62, sr. v.p., dir. merchandising N.J., 1962-67, exec. v.p., merchandising & sales promotion, 1967-69, pres. Calif., 1969-74, chmn., pres., CEO New York, 1974-80; chmn., CEO R.H. Macy & Co. Inc., 1980-92; chmn. Finkelstein Associates, NYC, 1992-97; chmn., CEO CWT Specialty Stores, Inc. d/b/a/ Cherry & Webb, NYC, 1997-99. Mem. adv. bd. Yale Sch. Mgmt., 1984-89; bd. dirs. R.H. Macy & Co. Inc., 1971-92 Mem. nat. advisory coun. Cystic Fibrosis Found., 1975-80, trustee, 1977-80, hon. trustee, 1980-2014; mem. advisory bd. Harvard Bus. Sch., 1983-91. With USN, 1943-46. Mem. Harvard Club. Jewish. Died May 31, 2014.

**FINKELSTEIN, NISSON A.,** motor company executive; b. Milton, Mass., June 11, 1925; s. Benjamin H. and Tena Finkelstein; m. Rona G. Glassman, Sept. 3, 1950; children: Jesse Adam, Loren Andrew. AB, Harvard U., 1945; PhD,

MIT, 1950. Chmn., pres. Inertial Motors Corp., Doylestown, Pa. Pvt. practice cons., Wilmington, Del. Home: Wilmington, Del. Died Oct. 24, 1989.

**FINN, CHARLOTTE KAYE,** interior designer; b. NYC, May 11; d. Edward and Florence (Karp) Kaye; m. Allen Charles Finn (dec. Oct. 2000); children: Andrew, Richard, Gregg. BA cum laude, Hunter Coll. Cert. Braille transcriber, Libr. of Congress. Apprentice designer J.H. Harvey, 1958-64; pvt. practice interior design White Plains, NY, 1965. Design cons. R.H. Macy's, 1977-78; product designer H.J. Stotter, George Kovacs, Grindley-of-Stoke, Sigma Marketing, Smith & Weigler. Work featured in publs. including House Beautiful, Interior Design, Residential Interiors, N.Y. Times, Palm Beach Life, Palm Beach Daily News, Home Furnishings Daily, The Designer, Home Environment, Sensuous Interiors, Prentice Hall; author Planning, Designing and Decorating a Room-Step by Step A How to Manual for Anyone, 2005. Recipient S.H. Hexter award, Burlington House award. Mem.: NOW, LVW, Phi Beta Kappa. Deceased.

**FINN, LILA EVERETT,** actress; b. Los Angeles, Nov. 28, 1909; d. Elmore Edward and Lila Georgia (Baugh) E.; 1 child, Barry Everett Shanley. Treas. Stunt Women Assn. of Motion Pictures. Mem.: Screen Actors Guild, Pacific Palisades Club, Rivera Tennis Club. Home: Pacific Palisades, Calif. Died Nov. 15, 1996.

**FINNEGAN, CYRIL VINCENT,** retired dean, zoology educator; b. Dover, NH, July 17, 1922; emigrated to Can., 1958; s. Cyril Vincent and Hilda A. (McClintock) F.; children: Maureen A., Patrick S., Cathaleen C., Kevin S., Eileen D., Gormlaith R., Michaeleen S., Mairead B., Conal E. BS, Bates Coll., Lewiston, Maine, 1946; MS, U. Notre Dame, 1948, PhD, 1951. From instr. to asst. prof. St. Louis U., 1952-56; asst. prof. U. Notre Dame, South Bend, Ind., 1956-58; from asst. prof. to prof. zoology U. B.C., Vancouver, 1958-88, emeritus, from 1988, assoc. dean sci., 1972-79, dean sci., 1979-85, dean emeritus, from 1988, assoc. acad. v.p., 1986-88. Contbr. articles to profl. jours. Served to sgt F.A. and C.E. AUS, 1942-45, NATOUSA, CBI. Postdoctoral research fellow NIH, 1952-53; Killum sr. fellow, 1968-69. Mem. Soc. Devel. Biology, Can. Soc. Cell Biology, Tissue Culture Assn., Internat. Soc. Develop. Biology, Sigma Xi Roman Catholic. Home: Vancouver, Canada. Deceased.

**FISCHBARG, ZULEMA F.,** pediatrician; b. Buenos Aires, Mar. 22, 1937; arrived in U.S., 1962; d. Naun and Esther (Pollner) Fridman; m. Jorge Fischbarg; children: Gabriel Julian, Victor Ernesto. MD, U. Buenos Aires, 1960. Pediatric intern Children's Hosp., Louisville, 1962-63, resident in pediatrics, 1963, chief resident in pediatrics, 1964; fellow hematology Michael Reese Med. Ctr., Chgo., 1964-66, Presbyn. St. Lukes Hosp., Chgo., 1966-67; fellow pediatric hematology Children's Meml. Hosp., Chgo., 1967-68; asst. clin. pediatrician U. Chgo., 1968-69; instr. in pediatrics Cornell U. Med. Sch., NYC, 1970-72, asst. prof. in pediatrics, 1972-76; assoc. prof. clin. pediatrics Weil Med. Coll., Cornell U., NYC, from 1978; emeritus assoc. attending pediatrician N.Y. Hosp., Queens; med. specialist, sch. health Dept. Health, NYC, from 1994. Assoc. in pediat. Lenox Hill Hosp., NYC; instr. in medicine Ill. U., Chgo., 1967—68; assoc. attending physician N.Y. Hosp., NYC, from 1972. Fellow: Am. Acad. Pediat. Democrat. Jewish. Deceased.

**FISCHER, HANS CHRISTIAN PETER,** retired engineering educator; b. Stockholm, Sept. 29, 1920; s. Otto Fabricius and Karen Beate (Wulff) F.; m. Mimmi Mary Lise Catherine Ehrnrooth, Sept. 12, 1952; children: Catherina Fischer-Dillenbeck, Helene Fischer-Guste. MSc, Royal Inst. Tech., Stockholm, 1944, DSc, 1960. Rsch. engr. Bofors (Sweden) Nobelkrut, 1941-45; head rsch. lab. Atlas Copco, Nacka, Sweden, 1945-62; prof. mechanics of materials Sch. Engring. Uppsala (Sweden) U., 1962-85, prof. emeritus, from 1985. Contbr. papers to profl. jours. Mem. Royal Swedish Acad. Engring. Scis. (pres. commn. pile driving 1966-70). Home: Nacka, Sweden. Died Dec. 2, 2001.

**FISCHER, ROBERT BLANCHARD,** academic administrator, researcher; b. Hartford, Conn., Oct. 24, 1920; s. Charles Albert and Matilda (Nylen) F.; m. Mary Ellen Mitchell, June 29, 1946; children: Lois, Marcia, Philip, Vivian, Valerie. BS, Wheaton Coll., 1942; PhD, U. Ill., 1946. Rsch. chemist U.S. Army Atomic Bomb Project, Chgo., 1944-46; instr. chemistry U. Ill., Urbana, 1946-48; prof. chemistry Indiana U., Bloomington, 1948-63; dean sch. of sci. Calif. State U.-Dominguez Hills, Carson, 1963-79, dean emeritus, from 1979; provost, sr. v.p. Biola U., La Mirada, Calif., 1979-88, disting. prof., 1988-89, provost, disting. prof. emeritus, from 1989. Research assoc. Calif. Inst. Tech., Pasadena, 1959-60; cons. in field. Contbr. articles to profl. jours. Fellow AAAS, Am. Sci. Affiliation (nat. pres. 1965-66); mem. Am. Chem. Soc. (sect. and region chmn.). Republican. Avocations: theology, amateur radio, sports. Home: La Mirada, Calif. Died Mar. 20, 2013.

**FISHER, FREDERICK HENDRICK,** oceanographer emeritus; b. Aberdeen, Wash., Dec. 30, 1926; s. Sam (Sverre) and Astrid K. Fisher; m. Julie Gay Saund, June 17, 1955 (dec. 1993); children: Bruce Allen, Mark Edward, Keith Russell, Glen Michael; m. Shirley Mercedes Lippert, Oct. 10, 1994 (div. 2003). BS, U. Wash., Seattle, 1949, PhD, 1957. Tchg. asst. U. Wash., 1949-53; rsch. asst. UCLA, 1954-55; grad. rsch. physicist Marine Phys. Lab., Scripps Inst. Oceanography, 1955-57, rsch. physicist, rsch. oceanographer, 1958-91, assoc. dir., 1975-87, dep. dir., 1987-93, acting assoc. dir., 1993-94, rsch. oceanographer emeritus, from 1997; rsch. fellow acoustics Harvard U., 1957-58. Dir. rsch. in reverse osmosis and desalination Havens Industries, San Diego, 1963-64; prof., chmn. dept. physics U. R.I., Kingston, 1970-71; mem. governing bd. Am. Inst. Physics, 1984-90. Assoc. editor: Jour. Oceanic Engring., 2001—. Mem. San Diego County Dem. Ctrl. Com., 1956-57, 60-62. Midshipman U.S. Naval Acad., 1945-47, with USNR, 1945. NCAA nat. tennis doubles champion, 1949; named to U. Wash. Athletic Hall of Fame, 1989; recipient Disting. Svc. award IEEE Oceanic Engring. Soc., 1991, Disting. Tech. Achievement award IEEE/OES, 1996, 3d Millenium Medal IEEE, 2000. Fellow: Acoustical Soc. Am. (assoc. editor jour. 1969—76, v.p. 1980—81, pres. 1983—84, emeritus); mem.: IEEE (life; sr. editor Jour. Oceanic Engring. 1988—91, emeritus editor from 2001), Am. Geophys. Union, The Oceanographic Soc., Marine Tech. Soc., Seattle Tennis Club. Achievements include co-designer and project scientist ocean research platform FLIP, 355' long manned spar buoy with 300' draft in vertical position, 1960-62; co-discoverer of boric acid as cause of low frequency sound absorption in the ocean; measured effect of pressure on sound absorption and electrical conductivity of magnesium and calcium sulfate and other salts related to high frequency sound absorption in the ocean; conducted sound propagation measurements at long range 30-800 miles in the ocean. Deceased.

**FISHER, NEAL FOSTER,** artist, writer; b. Indpls., Oct. 20, 1929; s. Willard Farmer and Ann Mae Mabbitt. Author: (book) Before the Dawn, 2003. Pvt. US Army, 1951. Avocations: painting, photography. Deceased.

**FISHMAN, JACK,** biochemistry educator; b. Cracow, Poland, Sept. 27, 1930; s. Naftali and Rachel F.; m. Barbara White, Nov. 29, 1963; children: Howard, Neil, Leslie, Daniel. BA in Chemistry, Yeshiva U., 1950; MA, Columbia U., 1952; PhD in Chemistry, Wayne U., Detroit, 1955. Research assoc. Sloan Kettering Inst., NYC, 1956-59, asst., 1959-60, assoc., 1960-63; investigator Inst. Steroid Research, Montefiore Hosp., Bronx, N.Y., 1963-70, sr. investigator, 1970-74, dir., 1974-77; asso. prof. Albert Einstein Coll. Medicine, NYC, 1967-70, prof., 1971-80; adj. prof. Rockefeller U., NYC, 1977-80, prof. biochem. endocrinology, 1980-88; pres. Ivax Corp., Miami, Fla., 1988—2013; prof. Cornell Med. Sch., 1993—2013. Cons. FDA, WHO, Nat. Inst. Aging, NSF, Contraceptive Devel. Br. NIH, Endocrinology Study Sect. NIH, NRC Can. Recipient John Scott medal for Invention of Naloxone, 1983; USPHS fellow Oxford U., 1955-56 Mem. American Chem. Soc., Endocrine Soc., American Soc. Biol. Chemists, AAAS, N.Y. Acad. Sciences Jewish. Home: Miami, Fla. Died Dec. 7, 2013.

**FISHMAN, SYLVIA C.,** editor, publisher; b. NYC, Oct. 19, 1920; d. Benjamin and Blanch (Kosmensky) Krauss; m. Bernard Fishman, Sept. 24, 1918; children: Carol Fertig, John Fishman. AAS., Fashion Inst. Tech., NYC, 1971; cert., William Paterson Coll., 1973, Jersey State Coll., 1973, Rutgers U., 1982. Lectr., author, designer Sylvia C. Fishman, Bogota, N.J., from 1973; founder, pres. Stumpwork Soc., Bogota, from 1979; editor, pub. Stumpwork Soc. Chronicle, Bogota, from 1979; cons. Statue of Liberty Clothing & Textile Exhibit, NYC, from 1986; with documentation Ellis Island Clothing & Textile Collection, NYC, from 1986. Lectr. "Threads of Nostalgia, the Ellis Island Connection," throughout U.S., 1986—; bd. advisors cooperative extension svc. Rutgers U., N.J., 1959—. Author: STS Stumpwork Tech. Sug., 1985, (booklet) The Art of Stumpwork, 1978; contbr. articles to profl. jours. Mem. Friends of Ft. Lee (N.J.) Libr., 1970—. Mem. NETWORK, Textile Conservation Group (N.Y.C.), Embroiderers' Guild Am. Democrat. Jewish. Avocations: photography, opera, ballet. Died May 1996.

**FITAK, BOHDAN ANDRZEJ,** chemist, educator; b. Warsaw, Feb. 21, 1934; s. Walenty and Janina F.; m. Danuta Lubian, July 19, 1959; 1 child, Ewa. MS in Pharmacy, Med. U., Warsaw, 1955, PhD, 1968, Dr. Habil., 1973. Cert. 2d degree specialist Med. Ctr. for Postgrad. Edn., Warsaw, 1975. Rschr. Mil. Food Rsch. Ctr., Warsaw, 1959-60; from asst. to sr. lectr. Med. U., Warsaw, 1960-80, assoc. prof., 1980-90, prof., 1990—2002. Postdoctoral fellow U. Tex., Houston, 1968-69; cons. WHO, Asia, 1986-89; head Commn. on Drug Analysis, Polish Acad. Scis., Warsaw, 1996-2003; regional editor Chemia Analityczna, Warsaw, 1996-2003; founding mem. U. Tex. M.D. Anderson Assocs., Houston, 1983-2003. Co-author: Dictionary of Practical Chemistry, 1992; patentee in field. Recipient Golden Cross of Merit State Coun. of Poland, 1981, Polonia Restituta Bachelor Cross Pres. of Poland, 1990, Medal of the Commn. of Nat. Edn. Min. Nat. Edn., 2000. Mem. Polish Pharm. Soc., Internat. Assn. Bioinorganic Scientists. Roman Catholic. Home: Warsaw, Poland. Died Feb. 7, 2002.

**FITCH, RACHEL FARR,** health policy analyst; b. July 27, 1933; d. Allen Edward and Rosie Leola (Jones) Farr; m. Coy Dean Fitch, Mar. 31, 1956; children: Julia Anne, Jaquelyn Kay. Student, Little Rock U., 1965-67; BS, St. Louis U., 1974, MS, 1976, PhD, 1983. RN, Mo. Psychiat. staff nurse VA Ft. Root Hosp., North Little Rock, Ark., 1954-57; surg.-med. staff nurse St. Vincent Infirmary, Little Rock, Ark., 1957-65; acute care nurse Georgetown U. Hosp., Washington, 1968-69; pub. health nurse to adminstr. South office Vis. Nurse Assn. Greater St. Louis, 1970-73; cons. in edn. St. Louis City Health Dept., 1977-80; rsch. specialist Sen. John C. Danforth, St. Louis, 1980; owner RFF Assocs., 1983-86. Project dir. study of infant mortality in city of St. Louis, 1978. Mem. community health edn. com. Am. Heart Assn., 1977-87; bd. dirs. LWV of Mo., 1984-2001, 2003—, dir. health issues, 1987-99, 1st v.p. 1999-2001, 2003-07, bd. dirs. 2007-; chmn. Mo. Consumer Health Care WATCH, 1996-2002; mem. adv. com. Mo. Medicaid Consumer, 1996-97; mem. Mo. Welfare Coord. Com., 1997-99; mem. healthcare mgmt. and policy adv. com. Maryville U., 2002-04; mem. Mo. Found. for Health Advocates steering com., 2003-04; sec. St. Louis U. Hosp. Aux. Mem. APHA, Acad. Polit. Sci., Grand Jury Assn. St. Louis (bd. dirs.), Woman's Club St. Louis U. Sch. Medicine (past pres., bd. dirs. 2004—), St. Louis Vol. Assn., Jr. League St. Louis, Sigma Theta Tau. Died July 26, 2013.

**FITZHENRY, ROBERT IRVINE,** publisher; b. NYC, Apr. 10, 1918; s. Irvine and Margaret (Lane) F.; m. Hilda Anderson, Jan. 22, 1949; children: Sharon, Bridget (dec.), Hollister. BA, U. Mich., 1939. Overnight mgr. United Press, 1939-41; dir. gen. sales Harper & Row Pubs., NYC, 1946-66; co-founder, pres. Fitzhenry & Whiteside Ltd., pubs., Markham, Ont., Can., 1966. Editor: Fitzhenry-Whiteside Book of Quotations, 1981, 2d edit., 1993, Harper Book of Quotations, 1983, 3d edit., 1993. Chmn. Pound Ridge Dem. party, 1960-64. With USAAF, 1941-45. Mem. Am. Book Pubs. Council (chmn. book distbn. com. 1946-48, Canadian Book Pubs. Council, exec. com. 1972-73) Clubs: Metropolitan (N.Y.C.). Home: Uxbridge, Canada. Died Jan. 4, 2008.

**FITZPATRICK, JANE PRATT,** entrepreneur; b. Cuttingsville, Vt., Nov. 18, 1923; m. John H. Fitzpatrick, Sept. 7, 1944 (dec. 2011); children: Nancy Jane, JoAnn Fitzpatrick Brown. HHD (hon.), N. Adams State Coll., Mass., 1978; LHD (hon.), U. Mass., 1987, Am. Internat. Coll., Springfield, Mass., 1994. Co-founder, chmn. bd. Country Curtains, Stockbridge, Mass., 1956—2013. Life trustee Boston Symphony Orch., trustee, 1982—96; trustee emerita The Norman Rockwell Mus., Stockbridge, Mass. Chmn. Berkshire Theatre Festival, Stockbridge, Mass, (bd. pres. 1977-98). Died Nov. 9, 2013.

**FLACK, HARLEY E.,** academic administrator; b. Feb. 12, 1943; m. Mignon Flack; children: Harley Jr., Christopher, Oliver, Michael. Founding dean, prof. Coll. Allied Health Sciences, Howard U., 1974—87; provost, exec. v.p. Rowan U., NJ, 1989—94; pres. Wright State U., Dayton, Ohio, 1994—98. Mem. Miami Rsch. Found., Ohio Aerospace Inst., chair. Composer: (8 pieces for voice aand African instruments) The Goree Suite, (numerous works for piano and voice including) A Nation: All Families. Bd. dirs. Miami Valley Econ. Devel. Coalition, Nat. City Bank, Dayton Philharm. Orch. Assn., Greene Progress Coun.; hon. adv. bd. A Special Wish Found., Inc.; mem. nat. adv. com. Acad. Leadership Acad. Am. Assn. State Colls. and Univs.; bd. trustees Robert K. Greenleaf Servant-Leadership Ctr. Died Mar. 29, 1998.

**FLAHERTY, JIM (JAMES MICHAEL FLAHERTY),** former Canadian government official; b. Lachine, Quebec, Canada, Dec. 30, 1949; s. Edwin Benedict and Mary (Harquail) Flaherty; m. Christine Elliott Flaherty; children: John, Galen, Quinn. BA, Princeton U.; JD, York U. Osgoode Law Sch. Atty., 1975—95; mem. from Whitby-Ajax Provincial Legis. Ontario, 1995—2005; mem. Whitby-Oshawa, House of Commons, Canada, 2006—14; min. finance Govt. of Canada, Canada, 2006—14. Mem.: Head Injury Assn. (former pres. Durham region). Conservative. Roman Catholic. Died Apr. 10, 2014.

**FLAVIN, DAN,** artist; b. NYC, Apr. 1, 1933; Student, Cathedral Coll. Immaculate Conception, 1947-52, U. Md., Korea, 1954-55, New Sch. Social Research, 1956, Columbia U., 1957-59. Lectr. U. N.C., 1967; Albert Dorne vis. prof. U. Bridgeport, 1973. Works represented in, Met. Mus. Art, N.Y.C., Mus. Modern Art, N.Y.C., Whitney Mus., N.Y.C., Guggenheim Mus., N.Y.C., Phila. Art Mus. Commn., installations of work include, Kunstmus, Basel, Switzerland, 1975, platforms, Grand Cen. Sta., N.Y.C., 1976, Kröller Müller Mus., Eindhoven, Netherlands, 1977, U.S. Courthouse, Anchorage, Alaska, 1980, numerous exhbns. including Mus. Contemporary Art, Chgo., 1967-68, Nat. Gallery Can., Jewish Mus., N.Y.C., 1969-70, Scottish Nat. Gallery Modern Art, 1976, Contemporary Arts Ctr., Cin., 1977, Art Inst. Chgo., 1977, Univ. Art Mus., Berkeley, Calif., 1978, Ottawa Nat. Mus., 1979, Guggenheim Mus., N.Y.C., 1982, 1992, Margo Leavin Gallery, LA, 1984, Städtische Galerie im Städel (auth, catalog), Franfurt am Main, Ger, 1993, Tex Gallery, Houston, 1993, Pace Gallery, NY, 1993-94, Galerie Annemarie Verna, Zurich, Switz, 1994, (auth, catalog), KunstbauLenbachhaus München, Ger, 1994 & John Good Gallery, NY, 1994. Recipient William and Norma Copley Found. award, 1968; Nat. Found. Art and Humanities award, 1966; Skowhegan medal for sculpture, 1965 Died Nov. 29, 1996.

**FLEENOR, ANN,** lawyer; b. San Francisco, Dec. 31, 1941; BA, Dominican Coll., San Rafael, Calif., 1963; JD with great distinction, McGeorge Sch. of Law, Sacramento, 1998. Bar: Calif. 1998. Staff atty. Sr. Legal Hotline, Legal Svcs. of No. Calif., Sacramento, from 1999. Mem. sch. bd. Twin Ridges Elem. Sch. Dist., North San Juan, Calif., 1981—90. Mem.: Traynor Honor Soc., Order of the Coif. Died Jan. 18, 2008.

**FLEISCH, HERBERT ANDRÉ,** pathophysiologist; b. Lausanne, Switzerland, July 22, 1933; s. Alfred and Ilse (Ullmann) F.; m. Mariapia Ronchetti, May 18, 1959; children: Marie-Gabrielle, Isabelle, Marie-Laure. MD, U. Lausanne, 1959. Asst. dept. physiology U. Lausanne, 1958—59, asst. dept. surgery, 1961—62; postdoctoral fellow dept. radiation biology U. Rochester, NY, 1959—60; dir. Lab. Exptl. Surgery, Davos, Switzerland, 1963—67; prof., chmn. dept. pathophysiology U. Berne Med. Sch., Switzerland, 1967—97; dean Med. Sch. U. Berne, 1981—83, prof. emeritus, from 1997. Author: Bisphosphonates in Bone Disease—From the Laboratory to the Patient, 1993, 4th edit., 2000 (transl. into Italian, Japanese, German and Spanish). Recipient William F. Neuman award Am. Soc. Bone and Mineral Rsch., 1992, Erwin-Uehlinger medal Deutsch Gesellschaft für Osteologie, 1997, Quality of Life award Internat. Myeloma Found., 2000, Pieter Gaillard award Internat. Bone Mineral Soc., 2001, Third Internat. LIFE award Aging Soc. Italy, 2001. Mem. Union Swiss

Socs. Exptl. Biology (pres. 1987-90). Achievements include research in physiology, pathophysiology and pharmacology of bone and calcium metabolism, especially the development of a new class of drugs for bone disease (the bisphosphonates). Home: Pully, Switzerland. Died May 15, 2007.

**FLEISCHER, HUGH WILLIAM,** retired lawyer; b. Riverside, Calif., Aug. 14, 1938; s. Frederick John and Helen Marie (Bendorf) F.; m. Lanie Lacey, May 31, 1960; children: Robin, Erin, Ian. BA, Washington U., St. Louis, 1961; JD, U. Denver, 1964; LLD (hon.), U. Alaska, Anchorage, 2008; D in Law, U. Alaska, 2008. Bar: Colo. 1964, U.S. Supreme Ct. 1970, Alaska, 1971, Mo. 1972. Atty. U.S. Dept. Justice, Washington, 1964-70, Alaska Legal Svcs. Corp., Anchorage, 1971-72; atty., adviser St. Louis Legal Aid Soc., 1972; ptnr. Hedland, Fleischer, Friedman, Brennan & Cooke, Anchorage, 1972-96; sole practitioner, 1996—2013. Co-dir., McGovern for Pres. campaign, Anchorage, 1972; pres. Bartlett Dem. Club, Anchorage, 1987; bd. dirs. Alaska Pub. Interest Group, 1974—, Out North Theater, 1988-94; pres. Anchorage Friends of Libr., 1989-92; bd. dirs. Alaskans Against the Dealth Penalty, 1993—, pres., 2003—. Recipient Charlie Parr Lifetime Achievement award, AKA-CLU, 2009. Avocation: reading. Home: Anchorage, Alaska. Died Oct. 9, 2013.

**FLEISCHHAUER, CARL-AUGUST,** former judge of international court of justice; b. Düsseldorf, Dec. 9, 1930; s. Kurt and Leonie (Schneider-Neuenburg) F.; m. Liliane Sarolea, 1957; 2 children. Student, U. Heidelberg, U. Grenoble, U. Paris, U. Chgo. Rsch. fellow Max-Planck Inst. Comparative Fgn. Pub. Law and Internat. Law, Heidelberg, 1960-62; with Fgn. Svc. of Germany, 1962-83, legal adviser fed. fgn. office, 1975, dir.-gen. legal dept., 1976; under-sec.-gen. legal affairs, legal counsel UN, 1983-94; judge Internat. Ct. Justice, 1994—2003. Contbr. articles to profl. jours. Recipient various decorations. Avocations: modern history, literature. Deceased.

**FLEMING, IAN (IAN LANCASTER FLEMING),** journalist, writer; b. Mayfair, Eng., May 28, 1908; s. Valentine and Evelyn (St. Croix) Fleming; m. Ann Rothermere, Mar. 24, 1952 (dec. 1981); 1 child, Casper Robert (dec.). Attended Eton; studied at Kitzbuhel, Austria; studied in Munich and Geneva, attended Royal Military Acad. at Sandhurst. With Reuters; stockbroker Rowe & Pitman; journalist Moscow, 1929; writer for the Atticus column Sunday Times. Author: (novels) Casino Royale, 1953, Live and Let Die, 1954, Moonraker, 1955, Diamonds Are Forever, 1956, From Russia, With Love, 1957, Dr. No, 1958, Goldfinger, 1959, For Your Eyes Only, 1960, Thunderball, 1961, The Spy Who Loved Me, 1962, On Her Majesty's Secret Service, 1963, You Only Live Twice, 1964, The Man with the Golden Gun, 1965, Octopussy and the Living Daylights, 1966, (non-fiction) The Diamond Smugglers, 1957, Thrilling Cities, 1963, (children's story) Chitty Chitty Bang Bang, 1964; contbr. Herbert Yardley's The Education of a Poker Player; actor: River Rivals, 1967. Personal asst. to lt. then comdr. for the dir. of Naval Intelligence, Adm. John Godfrey, 1939. Best known for the popular series of James Bond spy novels, which were made into hit movies; The Lilly Library, Indiana University Bloomington owns Ian Fleming's original manuscripts for all of the James Bond novels (except Thunderball, The Man With the Golden Gun, and Octopussy and The Living Daylights). Home: Canterbury, Kent, England. Died Aug. 12, 1964.

**FLERKÓ, BÉLA,** anatomist, educator; b. Pécs, Hungary, June 14, 1924; s. Béla and Etelka (Teimel) F.; m. Vera Bárdos, July 23, 1951. MD, Univ. Med. Sch., Pécs, 1948; PhD, Hungarian Acad. Sci., Budapest, 1956, DSc, 1967; PhD (hon.), U. Kuopio, Finland, 1982. Instr. dept. anatomy Univ. Med. Sch., Pécs, 1948-51, asst. prof., 1951-61, assoc. prof., 1961-64, prof., 1964-94, prof. emeritus, from 1994, dir. dept. anatomy, 1964-92, rector med. sch., 1979-85. Contbr. articles to profl. jours.; co-author: Hypothalamic Control of the Anterior Pituitary, 1962, 3d edit., 1972. Med. lt. Hungarian Army Res., 1953. Recipient Nat. award Hungarian Govt., 1978, Albert Szent-Györgyi award, 1992, Mid Cross of Order of Hungarian Rep., 1995, György Szabo award Hemmingway Found. Mem. Hungarian Soc. Endocrinology (pres. 1973-81), Internat. Soc. Neuroendocrinology (pres. 1988-92, G. Harris Meml. Lecture 1979), Hungarian Acad. Scis. (hon. mem. 1999, Gold medal 2001), Academia Europaea. Avocations: classical music, photography. Home: Pécs, Hungary. Died Apr. 2003.

**FLERSHEM, ROBERT GARRETT,** history professor; b. Chgo., Ill/, May 22, 1914; s. Rudolph Byford Flerstem and Lucy May Garrett; m. Elizabeth Flershem, Sept. 1940 (div.); children: Meredith T., Gerald B.; m. Yoshiko Flershem, Jan. 7, 1965. BA, Williams Coll., Williamstown, Mass., 1936; MA, U. Pa., Phila., 1940. Sales corr. Nat. Gypson Co., Buffalo, 1937—38; investigator adjuster Indeminty Ins. Co. NA, Phila., 1938—41; tchg. asst. Am. Conyers, 1946—47; invesitgator adjuster Am. Casualty, Phila., 1948—51; dir. USIA Foreign Svc. Ctr., 1951—60, 1969—70, USIA Washington Rsch., 1961—68. Asst. curator Phila. Comm. Mus., 1946—48. Contbr. articles to profl. jour. Lt. Can. Army, 1942—46. Named hon. Kanazawa citizen, 2002; grantee, Am. Philos. Soc., ACLS, others. Mem.: Assn. for Asian Studies, Am. Hist. Soc. Home: Kanazawa, Japan. Died Oct. 23, 2006.

**FLETCHER, ALAN GORDON,** retired university dean; b. Gibson's Landing, BC, Can., Jan. 2, 1925; s. William G. and Florence (Smith) F.; m. A. Irene Flynn, Aug. 6, 1949; children: Christopher Lee, Lynn Patricia, Elizabeth Joan, Anne Marie. B.Applied Sci., U. B.C., 1948; MS, Calif. Inst. Tech., 1952; PhD (Walter P. Murphy fellow), Northwestern U., 1965. Registered profl. engr., B.C. Engr.-in-tng. B.C. Electric Co., Ltd., Vancouver, 1948-52, hydraulic designer, 1952-56; supr. hydro planning B.C. Engring. Co., Vancouver, 1956-59; asst. prof., asso. prof. civil engring. U. Idaho, 1959-62; asso. prof. civil engring. U. Utah, 1964-69; dean U. N.D. Sch. Engring., Grand Forks, 1969-89, dir. Engring. Expt. Sta., 1969-77, ret., 1989; dir. N.D. Mining and Mineral Resources Research Inst., 1979-82. Pres. bd. Vancouver-Central YMCA; bd. govs. Vancouver Met. YMCA; mem. com. on higher edn. Synod of Lakes and Prairies, United Presbyn. Ch., 1978-82; pres. N.D. Commn. for United Ministries in Higher Edn., 1980-84. Danforth asso., 1965— Mem. ASCE, Am. Soc. Engring. Edn., B.C. Assn. Profl. Engrs., Sigma Xi, Chi Epsilon, Sigma Tau, Tau Beta Pi (Elwyn F. Chandler award). Presbyterian (elder). Home: Bella Vista, Ark. Died Dec. 1999.

**FLETCHER, DOROTHY JEAN,** hospital administrator, educator; b. Cleve., May 14, 1932; d. Melvin Albert Heidloff and Dorothy Florence Geiger; m. Archibald Eaton Fletcher, Jr., Oct. 9, 1932; children: David Jeffrey, Sally, Thomas Eaton. Degree in Nursing, St. Luke's Hosp., Cleve., 1953; BS in Health Studies, Barat Coll., Lake Forest, Ill., 1981; MA in Human Resource Devel., Webster U., St. Louis, 1986. RN Ill., cert. addictions counselor, Ill., addictions nurse, Ill.; ordained Presbyn. Ch., 1999. From staff nurse to discharge planning RN Ctrl. DuPage Hosp., Winfield, Ill., 1972—75, discharge planning RN, 1975—76; dir. nursing Nursing Home, Waukegan, Ill., 1981—82; from staff nurse to case mgr. behavioral svcs. Highland Pk. Hosp., Ill., 1982—94, case mgr. behavioral svcs., 1992—94. Mem. long range planning com. Sch. Dist. 65, Lake Bluff, from 2003. Vol. Lake County Forest Preserves, Ill., 1994—97; elder Presbyn. Ch., Lake Forest, 1999, chmn. program, 1995—2003; bd. dirs. Lake Bluff Libr., Ill., 1985—90. Recipient Outstanding Alumni award, Barat Coll., 2003, Mother Burke award, 2003. Mem.: LWV (chmn. voting com. 2004—05), Shields Township Dems. (observer sch. dist. voting from 2002), Lake Forest Lake Bluff Arts (assoc.), Botanic Gardens (docent from 1995). Democrat. Presbyn. Avocations: history, genealogy, reading, baseball, gardening. Home: Lake Bluff, Ill. Died June 5, 2008.

**FLETCHER, MARTHA ANN MESSERSMITH,** retired counselor, educator; b. Indpls., June 9, 1935; d. Lloyd Lowell and Fae Elizabeth (Houston) Messersmith; m. Lindsay Bruce Smith, Dec. 28, 1957 (div. 1974); children: Montgomery Bruce, Jean Elizabeth; m. Robert Rolph Fletcher, May 16, 1976; 1 child, Nancy Roberta. BA, DePauw U., 1956; MEd, U. Houston, 1967. Cert. tchr. Tex., Ind., profl. counselor Tex., mediator, lic. family mediator. Coord. elem. phys. edn. programs Cities Clarendon Hills and Hinsdale, Ill., 1957—61; tchr., speech therapist Tex. Sch. Cerebral Palsied, Galveston, 1961—64; developer, dir. social svcs. Moody House, Galveston, 1962—67; missionary Global Missions Meth. Ch., LaPaz, Bolivia, 1968—74; coord., instr., trainer ednl. paraprofls. program Mountain View Coll., Dallas, 1974—82, counselor, 1982—2006; marriage enrichment workshops South Africa, Nepal, Tonga, Philippines, Canada, from 2000. Contbr. articles to profl. jours. Mem. adv. bd. Dallas C.C., Ministry; tchr., advisor Highland Pk. United Meth. Ch. Recipient Student Devel. award, 1995; named Innovator of Yr., 1982. Mem.: Reconciliation Acad. Dallas (charter bd. mem. 2007), Tex. Educators Ednl. Paraprofls. (state dir. 1982—83). Home: Dallas, Tex. Died June 1, 2012.

**FLICKER, TED (THEODORE JONAS FLICKER),** scriptwriter, director, actor; b. Freehold, NJ, June 6, 1930; s. Sidney K. and Ray (Lopatin) F.; m. Barbara Perkins, Sept. 30, 1966. Student, Bard Coll., 1948-50; diploma, Royal Acad. Dramatic Art, 1952. A founder of improvisational theatre in, U.S., 1955. Producer, dir., actor, Compass Theatre, Chgo., 1955, Compass Players, St. Louis, 1956; writer dir.: Broadway musical The Nervous Set, 1959; producer, dir., actor: improvisational theatre The Premise, 1960-64; writer, dir.: (films) The Troublemaker, 1963, The President's Analyst, 1968, Up in The Cellar, 1970, Jacob Two Meets The Hooded Fang, 1974, Just a Little Inconvenience, 1977, Last of the Good Guys, 1978; dir.: (films) Playmates, 1970, Where The Ladies Go, 1979; creator, writer, dir.: TV series Barney Miller, 1974. Served with AUS, 1952-54. Recipient Obie award, 1960; Vernon Rice award, 1960 Mem. Directors Guild America (council 1970-73), Writers Guild America (dir. 1973-75), Screen Actors Guild, Actors Equity. Died Sept. 12, 2014.

**FLORES, CIRILO,** bishop; b. Corona, Calif., June 20, 1948; BA, Loyola Marymount Univ., 1970; JD, Stanford Univ.; MDiv, St. John's Sem., Camarillo, Calif., 1991. Atty., private practice in civil litigation; ordained priest Diocese of Orange, Calif., 1991; parochial vicar St. Barbara parish, Santa Ana, Calif., St. Joachim parish, Costa Mesa, Calif., Our Lady of Guadalupe parish, La Habra, Calif., 1997—2000; pastor St. Anne parish, Santa Ana, Calif., 2000—08, St. Norbert parish, Orange, Calif., 2008—09; ordained bishop, 2009; aux. bishop Diocese of Orange, 2009—13; coadjutor bishop Diocese of San Diego, 2013, bishop, 2013—14. Mem. editl. bd. Orange County Catholic. Past. bd. mem. Pub. Law Ctr.; past bd. mem. Catholic Charities Orange County. Roman Catholic. Died Sept. 6, 2014.

**FLORESCU, RADU NICOLAE,** retired historian; b. Bucharest, Romania, Oct. 23, 1925; s. Radu Alexander and Vera Marie Florescu; m. Nicole Elizabeth Michel, Dec. 2, 1951; children: Nicholas, John, Radu, Alexandra. BA in Politics, Philosophy & Economics, MA in Politics, Philosophy & Economics, Oxford U., Eng., 1951, BLitt, 1951; PhD, Ind. U., 1962. Instr. history Boston Coll., Chestnut Hill, Mass., 1953-56, asst. prof., 1956-62, assoc. prof., 1962-89, prof., 1989-97, prof. emeritus, 1997—2014. Cons. US Embassy, Bucharest, 1969, Senator Edward Kennedy, Boston, 1989, mem. consul of Romania, Boston, 1996. Co-author: In Search of Dracula, 1975, Dracula Prince of Many Faces: His Life and His Times, 1989, In Search of Dracula, 1994, In Search of Frankenstein: Exploring the Myths Behind Mary Shelly's Monster, 1998, (award Dracula Soc. 1997) (with Matei Cazacu) Dracula's Bloodlines, 2013; author: Frankenstein, 1975, The Struggle Against Russia in the Romanian Principalities: A Problem in Anglo-Turkish Diplomacy, 1821-1854, 1989, In Search of Dr. Jekyll and Mr. Hyde, 1998, 1998, Essays on Romanian History, 1999. Hon. sec. Oxford Soc., New Eng., 1968-88. Recipient Gladstone Meml. prize, 1948; Fulbright fellow, 1967, 68; sr. fellow St. Antony Coll., 1973-74. Fellow Romanian Acad. Soc. (sr.); mem. Soc. Romanian Studies (pres., bd. dirs. 1989). Democrat. Avocations: bicycling, tennis, ping pong/table tennis, skiing. Died May 18, 2014.

**FLOWER, DAVID, JR.,** retired lawyer, retired tax specialist; b. Boston, May 24, 1916; s. David Flower Sr. and Sadie Esther Flower; m. Mary Jane Hindlian. BA, Harvard Coll., 1939; grad., Harvard Law Sch., 1942. Dir. tax affairs Raytheon Co., Waltham, Mass., 1946—86, cons., 1986—91; ret. Died Feb. 28, 2008.

**FLYGAARD, OLE,** economics educator; b. Ringkøbing, Jylland, Denmark, Apr. 25, 1929; s. Marius Thøger and Anna Elisabeth (Johansen) F.; m. Bodil Marie Christensen, Aug. 13, 1955; children: Hans Jørgen, Elisabeth, Niels Peter. Degree in polit. sci., U. Copenhagen, 1955. Asst. Nordish Brand Ins., Copenhagen, 1956-57; ofcl. Statens Lignings Direktorat, Copenhagen, 1957-63; lectr. Merchant Sch., Hillerod, Denmark, 1963-65, Aalborg (Denmark) H.S., 1969-93; dir. Nakskov (Denmark) H.S., 1965-69; instr. econs. U. Aalborg, 1973-95, ret., 1995. Chmn. Handelskolernes Liererforening, Copenhagen, 1977-79. Mem. Folketinget, Copenhegen, 1973-75, 78-81; judge Lands Skatte-Retten, Copenhagen, 1974-75, 80-86; Danish justice Georgisme Party, Danmarks Rets Forbund. Avocations: economics, gardening, stamps, classical music. Home: Aalborg, Denmark. Died Nov. 25, 2002.

**FOGLE, RICHARD HARTER,** emeritus language educator; b. Canton, Ohio, Mar. 8, 1911; s. James Underhill and Amanda (Harter) F.; m. Catherine Pace Cox, Sept. 6, 1939; children— Catherine Harter, Faith Underhill. BA, Hamilton Coll., 1933, Litt.D., 1967; MA, Columbia, 1936; PhD, U. Mich., 1944. English-Latin master Brent Sch., Baguio, The Philippines, 1936-38; Instr. English U. Rochester, 1939-40; instr. English U. Mich., 1943-46; asst. prof., then prof. Tulane U., 1946-54, head dept. English, 1954-63, chmn., 1957-60, 63-66; prof. English U. N.C., Chapel Hill, 1966-68, Univ. Distinguished prof. English, 1968-81, prof. emeritus, from 1981. Vis. prof. Mich. State U., 1960, U. Ill., 1962, Harvard U., 1964, U. Hawaii, 1966. Author: The Imagery of Keats and Shelley, 1949, John Keats, Selected Poetry and Letters, 1951, Hawthorne's Fiction, 1952, rev. edit., 1964, Melville's Shorter Tales, 1960, The Idea of Coleridge's Criticism, 1962, The Romantic Movement in American Writing, 1966, Romantic Poets and Prose Writers, 1967, Hawthorne's Imagery, 1969, The Permanent Pleasure, 1974; mem. editorial bd. Keats-Shelley Jour., Am. Lit., 1964-70. Bd. govs. U. N.C. Press, 1974-80. Fellow Carnegie, 1949-50, Guggenheim, 1950-51. Fellow Melville Soc. (pres. 1961); mem. MLA (exec. com. 19th century Am. lit. group 1977—), Keats-Shelley Assn. (disting. scholar 1985). Deceased.

**FOGLEMAN, JULIAN BARTON,** lawyer; b. Memphis, Apr. 17, 1920; s. John Franklin and Marie Julia (McAdams) F.; m. Melba Margaret Henderson, Aug. 11, 1950; children: Margaret Elisabeth Heath, Julian Barton, John Nelson, Jennifer Leigh Vaughan, Frances Lorie Irwin. BS, U. Ark., 1941, LL.B., 1943, JD, 1969. Bar: Ark. 1943. Practiced in Marion, 1946-54, West Memphis, 1954—; pvt. practice, 1946-52; assoc. Hale & Fogleman, 1952-66, ptnr., 1967-73, Hale, Fogleman & Rogers, 1974—2001, Fogleman & Rogers, from 2002. City atty., Marion, 1951-81, dep. pros. atty., 1957-64 Chmn. fin. dir. Crittenden dist. Chickasaw coun. Boy Scouts Am., 1969, mem. exec. bd. coun., 1970-71, 75-80; bd. dirs. Crittenden County Charities, 1994-97, v.p., 1995; bd. dirs. Ark. Good Rds. Transp. Coun., 1976-96; mem. Ark. Cmty. Based Rehab. Commn., 1978-86, Crittenden County Bd. Edn., 1987-92. With inf. AUS, 1943-45, ETO. Fellow Am. Bar Found., Ark. Bar. Found. (bd. dirs. 1989-92); mem. ABA, Ark. Bar Assn. (ho. of dels. 1972-75, 81-84, exec. council 1972-75, 81-84, outstanding lawyer citizen award 1995-96), N.E. Ark. Bar Assn. (past pres.), Crittenden County Bar Assn. (past pres.), Phi Alpha Delta, Sigma Chi. Methodist. Home: Marion, Ark. Died Sept. 17, 2012.

**FOLEY, TOM (THOMAS STEPHEN FOLEY),** former ambassador, former United States Representative from Washington; b. Spokane, Wash., Mar. 6, 1929; s. Ralph E. and Helen Marie (Higgins) F.; m. Heather Strachan, Dec. 1968. BA, U. Wash., 1951, LL.B., 1957. Bar: Wash. Ptnr. Higgins & Foley, 1957-58; dep. prosecuting atty. Spokane County, Spokane, 1958-60; asst. atty. gen. State of Wash., Olympia, 1960-61; asst. chief clerk, spl. counsel US Senate Interior & Insular Affairs Com., Washington, 1961-64; mem. US Congress from 5th Wash. Dist., Washington, 1965—95, majority whip, 1981-86, majority leader, 1987-89, speaker of the House, 1989—95; chmn. US House Agrl. Com., Washington, 1975—81; ptnr. Akin, Gump, Strauss, Hauer & Feld LLP, Washington, 1995-97, 2001—08; US amb. to Japan US Dept. State, Tokyo, 1997—2001. Instr. law Gonzaga U., 1958-60; mem. bd. advisors Ctr. Strategic and Internat. Studies; mem. advisory council American Ditchley Found., mem. Def. Policy Bd., Homeland Security Advisory Coun., 2006-13; chmn., Pres. Fgn. Intelligence Advisory Bd., 1995-97, North American Trilateral Commn. Co-author: (with Jeffrey R. Biggs) Honor in the House: Speaker Tom Foley, 1999 Bd. overseers Whitman Coll.; bd. advisors Yale U. council; bd. dirs. Council on Fgn. Relations. Recipient Washington Medal of Merit, 2003; named

Knight Comdr. of the Most Excellent Order of the British Empire, Her Majesty Queen Elizabeth II, 1995. Mem. Phi Delta Phi. Democrat. Home: Washington, DC. Died Oct. 18, 2013.

**FOLKENS, ALAN THEODORE,** clinical and pharmaceutical microbiologist; b. Graceville, Minn., Oct. 26, 1936; s. Martin and Catherine (Laman) F.; m. Pearl June Putnam, July 29, 1961; children: Lee Alan, Kimberly Mae Folkens Anderson, Shannon Lee Folkens Tobin, Eric Martin. BA, Omaha U., 1962; PhD, U. S.D., 1971. Acting dir., dir. allied health professions Ill. State U., Normal, 1971-73; chief clin. microbiologist Peoria (Ill.) Tazewell Pathology Group, 1973-84; lab. dir. Delta Med. Ctr., Greenville, Miss., 1984-85; R&D clin. and pharm. microbiologist Alcon Labs., Inc., Ft. Worth, from 1985, assoc. dir., from 1995. Vis. faculty E. Tenn. State U., Johnson City, 1978-86; adj. faculty U. Ill. Peoria Sch. Medicine, 1980-84, Ill. State U., Normal, 1973-84, U. N. Tex., Denton, 1992-94; presenter symposium in field. Contbr. chpt. to book and articles to profl. jours. Bd. edn., past pres. Blessed Sacrament Sch., Morton, Ill., 1978-81; chmn. sickle cell anemia screening Ill. State U., Normal, 1972; chmn. Tootsie Roll drive for retarded children, K.C., Morton, 1975. Trainee NIH, 1967. Mem. Am. Soc. Microbiology, Am. Soc. Clin. Pathology, Am. Acad. Microbiology (diplomate), Assn. Rsch. in Vision and Ophthalmology, Assn. Rsch. to Prevent Blindness, N.Y. Acad. Scis., Phi Sigma, Sigma Xi. Independent. Roman Catholic. Achievements include work in FDA approval of Ciloxan for topical ophthalmic therapy. Died Sept. 9, 1996.

**FONG, BOBBY,** academic administrator; b. 1950; m. Suzanne Dunham; children: Jonathan, Colin. BA in English magna cum laude, Harvard U., 1973; PhD in English Lit., UCLA, 1978. Prof. Berea Coll., Ky., 1978—89; nat. fellow, asst. program dir. Assn. Am. Colls., Washington; prof. English, dean arts and humanities Hope Coll., Holland, Mich., 1989—95; dean faculty, prof. English Hamilton Coll., Clinton, NY, 1995—2001; pres. Butler U., Indpls., 2001—11, Ursinus Coll., Collegeville, Pa., 2011—14. Recipient Man of Yr. Award, Minority Bus. & Profl. Achievers of Indpls., Ctr. for Leadership Devel., 2008, President's award, Nat. Assn. Student Pers. Administrators, 2011. Mem.: Assn. American Colleges & Universities (chair 2012). Died Sept. 8, 2014.

**FONTAINE, JOAN (JOAN DE BEAUVOIR DE HAVILLAND),** actress; b. Tokyo, Oct. 22, 1917; m. Brian Aherne, Aug. 19, 1939 (div. June 5, 1945), m. William Dozier, May 2, 1946 (div. Jan. 25, 1951), 1 child, Deborah Leslie; m. Collier Young, Nov. 12, 1952 (div. Jan. 3, 1961); m. Alfred Wright, Jr., Jan. 27, 1964 (div. June 1969). Actress: (films) No More Ladies, 1935, A Million to One, 1938, You Can't Beat Love, 1937, The Man Who Found Himself, 1937, Quality Street, 1937, Music for Madame, 1937, A Damsel in Distress, 1937, Maid's Night Out, 1938, Blond Cheat, 1938, Sky Giant, 1938, The Duke of West Point, 1938, Gunga Din, 1939, Man on Conquest, 1939, The Women, 1939, Rebecca, 1940, Suspicion, 1941 (Acad. Award for Best Actress, 1941), This Above All, 1942, The Constant Nymph, 1943, Jane Eyre, 1944, Frenchmen's Creek, 1944, The Affairs of Susan, 1945, From This Day Forward, 1946, Ivy, 1947, Letter from an Unknown Woman, 1948, The Emperor Waltz, 1948, You Gotta Stay Happy, 1948, Kiss the Blood Off My Hands, 1948, September Affair, 1950, Born to Be Bad, 1950, Darling, How Could You!, 1951, Something to Live For, 1952, Ivanhoe, 1952, Decameron Nights, 1953, Flight to Tangier, 1953, The Bigamist, 1953, Casanova's Big Night, 1954, Serenade, 1956, Beyond a Reasonable Doubt, 1956, Island in the Sun, 1957, Until They Smile, 1957, A Certain Smile, 1958, Voyage to the Bottom of the Sea, 1961, Tender Is The Night, 1962, The Witches (The Devil's Own), 1966; (TV films) The Light That Failed, 1961, The Users, 1978, Dark Mansions, 1986, Good King Wenceslas, 1994; (TV appearances) Four Star Playhouse, 1953, 55, Letter to Loretta, 1955, General Electric Theatre, 1956, 57, 58, 60, 61, The Ford Television Theatre, 1956, The 20th Century-Fox Hour, 1956, On Trial, 1956, 57, Westinghouse Desilu Playhouse, 1959, Startime, 1960, Alcoa Presents: One Step Beyond, 1960, Checkmate, 1961, The Dick Powell Show, 1962, Wagon Train, 1963, The Alfred Hitchcock Hour, 1963, The Bing Crosby Show, 1965, Cannon, 1975, Ryan's Hope, 1980, Aloha Paradise, 1981, The Love Boat, 1981, Hotel, 1986; (TV mini-series) Crossings, 1986; (plays) A Certain Smile, 1958, Tea and Sympathy, 1979, Lion in Winter, 1982; author: (autobiography) No Bed of Roses, 1979. Died Dec. 15, 2013.

**FOOTE, PERRY ALBERT,** pharmacy educator; b. Erie, Pa., July 25, 1899; s. Perry Albert and Lucetta (McDill) F.; m. Lydia Ann Tachon, Aug. 1928 (dec. May 1963); children: Mrs. Alfred M. Miller Jr., Perry Albert Jr., Roger W.; m. Virginia Shewey Flanigan, May 31, 1969. BS in Chem. Engring., U. Wis., 1922, MS in Pharmacy, 1926, PhD in Pharm. Chemistry, 1928. Instr. pharmacy U. Wis., Madison, 1926-28; assoc. prof. U. Fla., Gainesville, 1928-29, prof. pharm. chemistry, 1929-68, dir. Sch. Pharmacy, 1939-49, dean Coll. Pharmacy, 1949-67, dean, prof. emeritus Coll. Pharmacy, 1967-95. Author: Tablets, 1928; co-author: American Pharmacy, 1945-66; contbr. articles to profl. jours. Pvt. Student Army Tng. Corps., 1918. Recipient Lascoff award Am. Coll. Apothecaries, 1946, Beal award Fla. Pharmacy Assn., Tallahassee, 1947, Rexall trophy Rexall Drug Co., 1957, Proclamation of Svc. award Gov. Fla., Tallahassee, 1966. Mem. Am. Pharm. Assn., Am. Assn. Colls. Pharmacy (pres. 1962-63), Am. Chem. Soc. (chmn. Fla. sect. 1932), Rotary Club (bd. dirs. 1943-45). Democrat. Home: 1717 NW 23rd Ave # Phb Gainesville FL 32605-3082

**FORD, EILEEN OTTE,** retired modeling agency executive; b. NYC, Mar. 25, 1922; d. Nathaniel and Loretta Marie (Laine) Otte; m. Gerard William Ford, Nov. 20, 1944 (dec. Aug. 24, 2008); children: Margaret, Gerard William, M. Katie, A. Lacey. BS, Barnard Coll., 1943. Stylist Elliot Clarke Studio, NYC, 1943-44, William Becker Studio, 1945; copywriter Arnold Constable, NYC, 1945-46; reporter Tobe Coburn, 1946; co-founder Ford Model Agy., NYC, 1946, CEO, 1946—95. Author: Eileen Ford's Model Beauty, 1968, Secrets of the Model's World, A More Beautiful You in 21 Days, 1972, Beauty Now and Forever, 1977. Bd. dirs. London Philharmonic Recipient Harpers Bazaar award for promotion internat. understanding., Woman of Yr. in Advt. award, 1983. Died July 9, 2014.

**FORD, MALCOLM SPENCER,** electromechanical and electronic engineer; b. Aldershot, England, Feb. 15, 1943; s. Wilfred Cedric Ford and Sylvia Irene Jeffrey; m. Luzmila Natalia Deza Ramirez, Oct. 8, 1970; children: Malcolm, Wilfred, Cynthia, Elaine. Lic. pvt. pilot, yacht master, scuba diver. Supr. Pervuian Ship-Yard, Callao, 1970—72; chief engr. Sugarmill Cap Tuman, Chiclayo, 1972—75; maintenance mgr. P&A Donofrio, Lima, 1975—78; founder, mgr. Britecnica, 1978—97; founder, dir. Corp. Refrigeration, 1997—2002, tech. dir., from 2002; founder, dir. Disenos Originales Fabricaciónes SAC, 2003—07. With Royal Navy, 1958—70, chief petty officer weapons radio elec. mechanician Royal Navy, 1969—70. Mem.: ASHRAE, Eng. Inst. Elec. Engrs. Achievements include design of the first ice skating rink in Peru. Avocations: flying, sailing, scuba diving, Karate, history. Home: Lima, Peru. Died 2007.

**FORD, MORGAN,** federal judge; b. nr. Wheatland, ND, Sept. 8, 1911; s. Morgan J. and Mary (Langer) F.; m. Margaret Duffy, July 30, 1955; children: William, Patrick and Michael (twins), Mary Ellen. BA, U. North Dakota, 1935; LL.B., Georgetown U., 1938. Tchr. Dist. 102, Everest Twp., Cass Co., N.D., 1933-34; state mgr. Royal Union Fund, Des Moines, 1938-39; pvt. practice Fargo, ND, 1939-49; pres. Surety Mut. Health & Accident Ins. Co., Fargo, 1939-49; v.p. 1st State Bank of Casselton, N.D., 1941-49; judge U.S. Customs Ct., NYC, 1949—80, US Ct. Internat. Trade, 1980—85, sr. judge, 1985—92. City atty., Casselton, 1942-48, mem. adv. bd. for registrants in selective service, 1942. Died Jan. 2, 1992.

**FORD, PHYLLIS M.,** retired park and recreation resources educator; b. Ludlow, Mass., Mar. 18, 1928; d. Wendell Bradford and Phyllis Grey (Symonds) F. BS, U. Mass., 1949; MA, Ariz. State U., 1954; D of Recreation, Ind. U., 1962. Rsch. asst. dept. zoology U. Mass., Amherst, 1949-50; prog. dir. YWCA, East Orange, N.J., 1950-51; tchr. Florence (Ariz.) High Sch., 1951-54; tchr., supr. City of Hammond (Ind.) Pub. Schs.; assoc. prof. Recreational and Park Mgmt. U. Oreg., Eugene, Oreg., 1961-69; assoc. prof., chmn. Leisure Edn. Prog. U. Iowa, 1969-71; prof. head Leisure Studies and Svcs. U. Oreg., Eugene, 1971-85; prof., chmn. dept. physical edn. and leisure studies Wash. State U., Pullman, 1985-87; prof. and chmn. Park and Recreation Resources Mich. State U., 1987-90; ret., 1990. Cons. in outdoor edn. various schs., 1962-84. Author: Principles and Practices of Outdoor/Environmental Education, 1981, Take A New Bearing, 1991; co-author: Camp Administration, 1971, Administration and Leadership of Outdoor Pursuits, 2d edit., 1992, Leadership in Recreation and Leisure Services, 1985. Mem. AAHPERD (chmn. outdoor edn. 1985), Am. Camping Assn., Nat. Recreation Pk. Assn. Deceased.

**FORD, RICHARD EDWIN,** volunteer; b. Wabash, Ind., Feb. 27, 1939; s. Wilbur Edwin and Florence Gertrude (Jeup) Ford. BS, Ind. U., Bloomington, 1961; LHD (hon.), Manchester U., North Manchester, Ind., 2005; AS (hon.), Ivy Tech CC, Ind. Sales rep. Ford Meter Box Co., Wabash, Ind., 1961—69; liaison officer US EPA, Washington, 1971—75; vol. various charitable orgns., from 1976. Bd. dirs. Ind. U. Found., Bloomington. Founder Charley Creek Found., Wabash, from 2002; trustee Am. Mus. Britain, bd. dirs.; mem. Dr. James Ford Hist. Home, Wabash; emeritus chmn. Nat. Trust for Historic Preservation Council; owner Charley Creek Inn, Wabash. Mem.: Univ. Club (Washington), Knickerbocker Club (NY), Mark's & Annabel's Clubs (London), Univ. Club Winter Pk. (Fla.), Arts Club (Washington), Propylaeum Club (Ind.), Woodstock Club, U. Club, Skyline Club, Columbia Club (Indpls.), Elks. Republican. Methodist. Avocation: travel. Died Apr. 16, 2014.

**FORD, WILLIAM CLAY,** retired automotive executive; b. Detroit, Mar. 14, 1925; s. Edsel Bryant and Eleanor Lowthisn (Clay) F.; m. Martha Firestone, June 21, 1947; children: Martha, Sheila, William Clay, Elizabeth. BS in Economics, Yale U., 1949. Mem. sales & advt. staff Ford Motor Co., 1949, vice chmn., 1980-89, chmn. finance com., 1987—95; quality control mgr. gas turbine engines Lincoln-Mercury Divsn., Dearborn, Mich., 1951, mgr. spl. product ops., 1952, v.p., 1953, gen. mgr. Continental divsn., 1954, group v.p. Lincoln and Continental divisions, 1955, v.p. product design, 1956-80; owner, chmn. Detroit Lions, Inc., 1964—2014. Bd. dirs. Ford Motor Co., 1948—2005; indsl. rels., labor negotiations with UAW, 1949. Mem. advisory coun. Tex. Heart Inst.; chmn. emeritus Edison Inst.; hon. life trustee Eisenhower Med. Ctr. Mem. Soc. Automotive Engineers (assoc.), Automobile Old Timers, Econ. Club Detroit, Masons, K.T., Phelps Assn., Psi Upsilon. Died Mar. 9, 2014.

**FORESTER, KARL SPILLMAN,** federal judge; b. Harlan, Ky., 1940; BA, U. Ky., 1962, JD, 1966. With Eugene Goss Esp., 1966—68; mem. firm Goss & Forester, 1968—75, Forester, Forester, Buttermore & Turner, P.S.C., 1975—88; judge US Dist. Ct. (eastern dist.) Ky., Lexington, 1988—2001, chief judge, 2001—05, sr. judge, 2005—14. Mem. Ky. Bar Assn., Harlan County Bar Assn., Fayette County Bar Assn. Died Mar. 29, 2014.

**FORMAN, ROBERT EDGAR,** retired sociology professor; b. Mpls., July 17, 1924; s. Phillip Erwin and Lotta Louise (Holmgren) Forman; m. Ruth Anne Linsley (dec.); children: Lucy Jeanne, Mark Richard, Dan Robert. BA cum laude, U. Minn., Mpls., 1948, MA in Sociology, 1949, PhD in Sociology, 1959. Instr. sociology U. Minn., Duluth, 1949—50, St. Olaf Coll., Northfield, Minn., 1951—53; counselor Dean of Students Office U. Minn., Mpls., 1954—59; asst. prof. sociology Rockford Coll., Ill., 1959—61; from asst. prof. to prof. and dept. chair Wis. State U., Oshkosh, 1961—69; prof. sociology U. Toledo, 1969—86, prof. emeritus, from 1986. Author: Black Ghettos, White Ghettos and Slums, 1971, How to Control Your Allergies, 1979; co-author: The University & It's Foreign Alumni, 1964; contbr. chapters to books, articles to profl. jours. Cpl. US Army, 1944—46. Avocations: music, home workshop. Home: Deer Park, Wash. Died July 14, 2014.

**FORREST, VIRGINIA OGDEN RANSON,** civic leader; b. Balt., June 24, 1896; d. Henry Warfield and Nannie Deaver (Cooper) Ranson; m. Frederick Beasley Williamson, Jr., July 4, 1917 (dec. July 1957); children: Virginia Williamson Hutton, Beverley Williamson Magill, Frederick Beasley Williamson III; m. Wilbur Studley Forrest, Apr. 20, 1960 (dec. Mar. 1977). Student, Calvert Sch., Arundell Sch. Chmn. New Hope Chpt. ARC, Pa., 1939—43, chmn. home svc., 1943—45, head flood disaster chpt., 1955; hon. v.p. New Hope Art Assocs., 1940; organizer adviser Bucks County Conservation Alliance, Martin County Conservation Alliance, 1966—74; bd. dirs. Honey Hollow Watershed Assn., 1969—; mem. adv. com. Jonathan Dickinson State Pk., Martin County, Fla., 1970—; dir. Goodall Rubber Co., hon. dir., 1973—. Pres. Jr. League, Elizabeth, NJ, 1924—26, hon. mem., 1944; with Soc. Prevention Cruelty Children Family Welfare Bd., Elizabeth, 1928, YWCA, Elizabeth, 1928, Abington Meml. Hosp. Women's Bd., Pa., 1941, Vis. Nurse Assn., New Hope, 1941—49; mem. NJ Recreation Soc., Elizabeth, 1934—35; rep., NJ to nat. conv., Chgo., 1935; mem. hostess com. Franklin Inst., Phila., 1941; bd. dirs., 2nd v.p. Garden Club, Stuart, Fla., 1951—60. Trustee Egnolf Day Nursery, Elizabeth, 1923—26, Holmquist Sch. Girls, New Hope, Martin County Pub. Libr., Stuart, 1958—61; bd. dirs. Keep Fla. Beautiful Com., Free Pub. Libr., Elizabeth, 1926—39, sec., 1927—36; mem. founders bd. Transylvania U., Lexington, Ky., 1979. Recipient award, Fla. Fedn. Garden Clubs, 1961, Gov.'s gold medal, Conservation award, 1961, US Dept. Interior, 1979, Gov. Kirk's Conservation award, 1970, Honoree award, Martin County Audubon Soc., 1976, Hon. mem., Ky. Coll., 1978; named Women of Achievement, Del. Valley Girl Scouts, 1987. Mem.: LI (Eastport, NY), Martin County Anglers (dir. 1966—), Woman Fly Fishers America, Colonial Dames NJ, New Hope Hist. Soc. (dir. 1959—60, 1967—), Audubon Socs., Bucks County (dir., Citation Conservation 1972), Bald Eagle Project (Fla.) (chmn. 1959—, mem. wild life com. 1959—, v.p. 1962—69, hon. v.p. 1970—, adviser, award 1960), Martin County (dir. 1957—58, dir. emeritus 1978—, chmn. exec. com. 1973—74), Hartwood Club (Monticello, NY), Mt. Vernon Club (Balt.), Fla. Fedn. Garden Clubs (hon. mem.). Home: Pennswood Village # D105 Newtown PA 18940-2401

**FORST, DONALD H.,** newspaper editor; b. July 3, 1932; m. Gael Greene, 1961 (div.); m. Starr Ockenga. BA, U. Vt.; MA, Columbia U. Graduate Sch. Journalism. Mng. editor Newsday, 1971—77; editor The Herald Examiner, 1977—85; founding editor NY Newsday, 1985—95; editor The Village Voice, 1995—2005; instr. journalism U. Albany. Died Jan. 4, 2014.

**FORTE, LORD CHARLES (BARON FORTE),** catering company executive; b. Nov. 26, 1908; m. Irene Mary Chierico, 1943; 6 children. Student, Alloa Acad., Dumfries Coll., Mamiani, Rome. Dep. chmn. Trust House Forte PLC, 1970—78; chief exec., 1971—78; exec. chmn., 1978—81; chmn., 1982—92; pres., 1992—96; mem. Consultative Adv. Com. to Ministry Food, 1946, London Tourist Bd.; pres. Italian C. of C., Gt. Britain, 1952—78, Westminster C. of C., 1983—86. Contbr. articles catering trade. Decorated Grand officier Ordine al Merito dell Repubblica Italiana cavaliere di Gran Croce della Repubblica Italiana, knight; grantee Catering Inst., Exec. Com., Brit. Inst. Mgmt., Royal Soc. Arts. Mem.: Caledonian, Carlton. Died Feb. 28, 2007.

**FORTEZA, BARTOMEU,** philosophy educator; b. Felanitx, Baleares, Spain, June 17, 1939; s. Bartomeu Forteza and Elisa Pujol; m. Ma Dolores González, Jan. 22, 1977; children: Ricardo, Maria, B. Israel. Licentiate philosophy, Gregorian U., Rome, 1977, U. Barcelona, Spain, 1978; PhD, U. Barcelona, 1993. Tchr. H.S. Boscan, Barcelona, 1978-81, H.S., Cardedeu, Spain, 1981-82, H.S. CanTunis, Barcelona, 1982-86, H.S. Les Marine, Castelldefels, Spain, 1986-95; mem. rsch. group U. Barcelona, from 1995; prof. Ramon Llull U., Barcelona, 1999-2000. Mem. Inst. Sci. Edn., U. Autónoma, Barcelona, 1982-88; head master H.S. Les Marines, Castelldefels, 1992-94; prof. philosophy and enterprise U. Barcelona, 1997-98; course mgr. Fund Bosch Gimpena, Barcelona, 1998-99. Author: Objectivity in the Linguistic Philosophy of Thomas Hobbes, 1999; translator, editor: Thomas Hobbes: Liberty and Necessity, 1991, The Hobbes: El Cuerpo, 2000; contbr. articles to profl. jours. Mem. Catalan Soc. Philosophy, N.Y. Acad. Scis. Home: Barcelona, Spain. Died Dec. 5, 2000.

**FORTIER, JEAN-MARIE,** retired archbishop; b. Que., Can., July 1, 1920; s. Joseph and Alberta (Jobin) F. Student, Grand Sem. Que., 1940-45; L.Th., Laval U., Que., 1945; postgrad., U. Louvain, Belgium, 1946-48; Licentiate in Ch. History, Gregorian U., Rome, 1950. Ordained priest Roman Catholic Ch., 1944; sec. to bishop of Hearst, Ont., Can., 1945-46; tchr. ch. history Grand Sem. Que., 1950-60; consecrated bishop Ste. Anne de la Pocatiere, Que., 1961-65, Gaspe, Que., 1965-68; archbishop Sherbrooke, Que.,

1968-96; archbishop emeritus, 1986—2002; mem. Congregation for Sacraments and Divine Cult, 1975-84; v.p. Can. Cath. Conf., 1971-73, pres., 1973-75, Comité Episcopal des Communications Sociales, 1976-84; v.p. l'Assemblee des Evêques du Quebec, 1981-85, pres., 1985-89. Mem. Knights Holy Sepulchre of Jerusalem, Assn. Eveques de Que. (pres. 1985-89), Assn. des Chevaliers de Colomb de Que., Filles d'Isabelle. Died Oct. 31, 2002.

**FOSSEEN, NEAL RANDOLPH,** business executive, former banker, former mayor; b. Yakima, Wash., Nov. 27, 1908; s. Arthur Benjamin and Florence (Neal) F.; m. Helen Witherspoon, Sept. 26, 1936; children: Neal Randolph Jr., William Roger. BA, U. Wash., 1930; LD (hon.), Whitworth Coll., 1967. With Wash. Brick, Lime & Sewer Pipe Co., 1923-32, v.p., 1932-38; pres. Wash. Brick & Lime Co., 1938-58; dir. Securities Intermountain Co., 1954-71; v.p., dir. Old Nat. Bank Wash., 1958-68, Wash. Bancshares, 1968-71, vice chmn., 1971-72, chmn. bd., pres., 1972-73; dir. Utah-Idaho Sugar Co., 1968-79, 1st Nat. Bank Spokane, 1972-79. Dir. Spokane Indsl. Park, 1959-72, treas., 1959-66; dir. North Coast Life Ins. Co., 1965-76, Quarry Tile Co., 1965-68, Day Mines, Inc., 1968-81; chmn. emeritus, dir. Old Nat. Bancorp., 1973-77; pres. 420 Investment Co., 1982-84; hon. dir. Met. Mortgage Co., 1995-2001. Mem. exec. com. Expo '74; mem. adv. bd. Mus. Native Am. Culture, 1957-81; mayor City of Spokane, 1960-67, mayor emeritus, 1967—; mem. adv. bd. emeritus Spokane Intercollegiate Rsch. and Tech. Inst., 1993-96; past chmn. adv. bd. Wash. State Inst. Tech.; bd. dirs., past pres. coun. Boy Scouts Am.; bd. dirs. Wash. Rsch. Coun., sec., 1968-74; bd. dirs. YMCA, 1969-80, Pacific Sci. Found., 1970-73, Mountain States Legal Found., 1979-85; mem. adv. bd. Grad. Sch. Bus., U. Wash., 1974-81, emeritus, 1981—, mem. adv. bd. dept. history, 1981—; chmn. Regent Gonzaga U., 1948-61, emeritus, 1961—, benefactor, (hon.) LD, 1999; mem. adv. bd. Coll. Engring., Wash. State U., 1949-79; hon. trustee Found. N.W.; trustee Rockwood Cmty. Found., 1993-97, Gonzaga Dussault Found., Fosseen-Kusaka Disting. Professorship, Jackson Found. Scholarship, U. Wash., 1998; mem. adv. bd. Advanced Tech. Ctr., 1989-94, Mukogawa Fort Wright Inst., Whitworth Coll. Internat. Mgmt., City Innovation; founding. dir. Athetic Round Table. Col. USMCR, ret. Recipient Shrine award El Katif Temple, 1974, Non Sibi, Sed Patriae award Marine Corps. Res. Officers Assn., Outstanding Svc. award Fairchild AFB, Spokan Mcpl. League, Forward Spokane award Spokane County Hotel and Restaurant Coun., Liberty Bell award Spokane County Bar Assn., Book of Golden Deeds, Exchange Club, Sister City Outstanding Svc. award Town Affiliation Assn., Disting. Citizen award Ea. Wash. U., 1982, Founders Day award, 1994, Disting. Citizen award Air Force Air Mobility Command, 1995, Citizen League Lifetime Svc. award, 1997, Inland N.W. Philanthropy award Found. N.W., 1999; named hon. citizen Nishinomiya, Japan; inducted to Inland N.W. Hall of Fame. Mem. VFW, Ret. Officers Assn., Assn. Wash. Bus. (past pres.), Spokane C. of C. (v.0. 1946-51), Spokane-Nishinoniya Sister City Soc. (pres.), Srs. N.W. Golf Assn. (gov.), Mil. Order World Wars (Perpetual), Order of the Rising Sun (Japan), Balboa de Mazatlan Club (Mex.), Spokane Club (life), Spokane Country Club (life), Prosperity Club, Travellers Century Club, Spokane Ski Club, Rotary (Paul Harris fellow, benefactor), Beta Theta Pi (Oxford Cup award), Alpha Kappa Psi. Home: Spokane, Wash. Died July 31, 2004.

**FOSTER, ELIZABETH READ,** historian, emeritus educator; b. Chgo., June 26, 1912; d. Conyers and Edith (Kirk) Read; m. Richard Wingate Foster, Dec. 31, 1938; children—Richard Coulson, Timothy, Benjamin Read, Daniel Wingate. AB, Vassar Coll., 1933; A.M., Columbia, 1934; PhD, Yale, 1938. Instr., then asso. prof. history Ursinus Coll., Collegeville, Pa., 1953-65; asso. prof. U. Del., 1962-63; acting dir. Yale Parliamentary Diaries project Yale, 1965-66; prof. history Bryn Mawr Coll., 1966-81, prof. emeritus, from 1981, acting dir. of libraries, 1984, dean Grad. Sch. Arts and Scis., 1966-73. Author: The Painful Labour of Mr. Elsyng, 1972; The House of Lords, 1603-1649, 1983; editor: Proc. in Parliament 1610, 2 vols, 1966; Judicature in Parlement by Henry Elsyng Clark of the Parliaments, 1991; editorial bd. Am. Hist. Rev., 1979-81, Yale Ctr. Parliamentary History, 1966—. Mem. Royal Hist. Soc., Conf. Brit. Studies (council 1968-73, 79-84), Soc. of Antiquaries of London, Middle Atlantic Conf. on Brit. Studies (exec. com. 1979-82), Am. Hist. Assn. Died Nov. 1999.

**FOSTER, LAWRENCE GILMORE,** retired public relations executive; b. Jersey City, July 27, 1925; s. Lawrence Gilmore Sr. and Lillian (Tyrrell) F.; m. Ellen Louise Miller, Sept. 10, 1949; children: Cindi Foster Falck, David, Nanci Foster Carlson, Gregg Foster, Lawrence G. III. BS in Journalism, Pa. State U., 1948. Reporter Newark News, 1948-52, bur. chief, 1952-54, night editor, 1954-57; public rels. asst. Johnson & Johnson, New Brunswick, NJ, 1957-62, asst. dir. public rels., 1962-66, dir. public rels., 1966-73, corporate v.p. public rels., corporate officer New Brunswick, 1973-91; cons., 1991—2013. Author: A Company That Cares, 1987. Founding trustee Robert Wood Johnson Univ. Hosp., New Brunswick, 1981-2013, Global Public Affairs Inst.; bd. trustees Robert Wood Johnson Found., 1987-2013, Pa. State U., University Park, 1980-89; pres. Pa. State Fund Council, 1980-83. Recipient Silver Anvil award Public Relations Soc. America, 1983, Gold Anvil award, 1989; named Public Relations Profl. of Yr. PR News, 1984, Disting. Alumnus Pa. State U., 1979. Mem. Bus. Roundtable (mem. pub. info. com.), Public Rels. Workshop, European Pub. Rels. Roundtable, Arthur Page Soc. (v.p.), Overseas Press Club, Bay Head Yacht Club. Roman Catholic. Avocations: writing, boating. Home: State College, Pa. Died Oct. 17, 2013.

**FOWLKES, NANCY LANETTA PINKARD,** social worker; d. Amos Malone and Nettie (Barnett) Pinkard; m. Vester Guy Fowlkes, June 4, 1955 (dec. 1965); 1 child, Wendy Denise. BA, Bennett Coll., 1946; MA, Syracuse U., 1952; MSW, Smith Coll., 1963; MPA, Pace U., 1982. Dir. publicity Bennett Coll., Greensboro, NC, 1946-47, 49-50; asst. editor Va. Edn. Bull. ofcl. organ Va. State Tchrs. Assn., Richmond, 1950-52; asst. office mgr. Cmty. Svc. Soc., NYC, 1952-55; social caseworker, asst. supr. Dept. Social Svcs. Westchester County, White Plains, NY, 1959-67, supr. adoption svcs., 1967-77, supr. adoption and foster care, 1977-89. Mem. adv. bd. White Plains Adult Edn. Sch. First v.p. Eastview Jr. HS, 1970-71; area chmn. White Plains Cmty. Chest, 1964; sec. Mt. Vernon Concert Group, 1952-54; fund raising co-chmn. Urban League Guild of Westchester, 1967; pres. White Plains Interfaith Coun., 1972-74; pres. northeastern jurisdiction United Meth. Ch., 1988-92; chmn. adminstrv. bd. Meth. Ch., 1970-72, 82-83, vice chmn., 1978-80, vice chmn. trustees, 1973-77, treas., 1978-83; lay spkr., v.p. Met. dist. United Meth. Women, 1977-79, exec. bd. NY conf.; NY conf. rep. Upper Atlantic Regional Sch., 1981-83, mem. nominating com., 1982-83, trustee NY conf., 1982-88, pres. NY conf., 1983-87; bd. dirs. Global Ministries United Meth. Ch., 1988-96, women's divsn., 1988-96, v.p., chair sect. finance women's divsn., 1992-96, supt., 1997—, chair program divsn. NY conf., 1989-93; v.p. superintendency commn. Met. North Dist., 1997—; chair Episcopal residence NY Conf. Episcopacy Com., 1997-2002; mem. NY Conf. Bd. Ordained Ministry, 2000—, Bishop's Ptnrs. in Mission Leadership Coun., 2005—, mem. nominating com. N.Y. conf., 2006—, mem. bd. laity N.Y. conf., 2006—; chmn. Dist. Coun. on Ministry, 2002-05, lay leader 2005—; bd. dirs. Family Svc. Westchester, Bethel Meth. Home, Ossining, NY, White Plains YWCA, 1985-93, Scarritt Bennett Ctr., Nashville, 1990-2000, Gum Moon Women's Residence, San Francisco, 1992-96, White Plains-Greenburg NAACP, 1993-98. Mem. NASW, Acad. Cert. Social Workers, Jack and Jill of Am. Inc. (chpt. pres. 1954-56, regional sec.-treas. 1967-71), Nat. Bus. and Profl. Women's Club (chpt. sec. 1954-56), Internat. Platform Assn., Theta Sigma Phi (sec.-treas.), Zeta Nu Omega, Alpha Kappa Alpha (pres. 1960-64, treas. 1975-78), Regency Bridge Club (pres. 1963-65). Home: White Plains, NY. Died Nov. 23, 2013.

**FOX, JEFFREY,** bank executive; b. Bklyn., Feb. 1, 1950; s. Milton and Evelyn (Strasser) Fox; m. Jill Diane Gibson, Sept. 4, 1971; 1 child, Eric Lance. Diploma, Am. Inst. Banking, NYC, 1976, Nat. Comml. Lending Sch. Trainee Household Fin., NYC, 1970—72, asst. mgr., 1970—72; loan officer ops. Bank Commerce, NYC, 1972—77; mgr. Dial Fin., Albuquerque, 1977—80; adminstr. First State Bank, Albuquerque, 1980—82, br. mgr., 1980—82, 1st Interstate Bank, Albuquerque, from 1982. Ptnr. VAL Fox Enterprises, Rio Rancho, N.Mex., from 1981. Editor: Manual: Teller Tng., 1980; author: In-House Audit Guide, 1980. Bd. dirs. Easter Seal Soc. N.Mex., Albuquerque, 1984—86. Mem.: Optimist (v.p. 1981—84, dir. 1981—84), Albuquerque Consumer Credit Assn. Democrat. Jewish. Died Sept. 3, 1997.

**FRANCA, CELIA,** ballet director, choreographer, dancer, narrator; b. London, Eng., June 25, 1921; m. Leo Kersley (div.); m. James Morton, Dec. 7, 1960 (dec.); m. Bert Anderson (dec.). Student, Guildhall Sch. Music, Royal Acad. Dancing; LLD (hon.), Assumption U. of Windsor, 1959, Mt. Allison U., 1966, U. Toronto, 1974, Dalhousie U., 1976, York U., 1976, Trent U., Peterborough, Ont., Can., 1977, McGill U., 1986; DCL (hon.), Bishop's U., 1967; DLitt (hon.), Guelph U., 1976; DFA, Carleton U., Ottawa, 1995. Founder, artistic dir. Nat. Ballet Can., Toronto, 1951-74; co-founder Nat. Ballet Sch., Toronto, 1959—2007; co-artistic dir. The Sch. OF Dance. Mem. jury 5th Internat. Ballet Competition, Varna, Bulgaria, 1970, 2d Internat. Ballet Competition, Moscow, 1973 Debut: corps de ballet Mars, The Planets (Tudor), Mercury Theatre, London, 1936; soloist, Ballet Rambert, London, 1936-38, leading dramatic dancer, Ballet Rambert, 1938-39, guest artist, Ballet Rambert, 1950, dancer, Ballet des Trois Arts, London, 1939, Arts Theatre Ballet, London, 1940, Internat. Ballet, London, 1941, leading dramatic dancer, Sadler's Wells Ballet, 1941-46, guest artist, choreographer, Sadler's Wells Theatre Ballet, London, 1946-47, dancer, tchr., Ballets Jooss, Eng., 1947, ballet mistress, leading dancer, Met. Ballet, London, 1947-49, dancer, Ballet Workshop, London, 1949-51, prin. dancer, Nat. Ballet Can., 1951-59; prin. roles include Black Queen in Swan Lake; title roles in Lady from the Sea; choreographer: ballets, including Midas, London, 1939, Cancion, London, 1942, Khadra, London, 1946, Dance of Salome, BBC-TV, 1949, The Eve of St. Agnes, BBC-TV, 1950, Afternoon of a Faun, Toronto, 1952, Le Pommier, Toronto, 1952, Casse-Noisette, 1955, Princess Aurora, 1960, The Nutcracker, 1964, Cinderella, 1968, numerous others for CBC, Can. Opera Co.; author: The National Ballet of Canada: A Celebration, 1978. Hon. patron Osteoporosis Soc. Can. Decorated Order of Can.; recipient Key to City of Washington, 1955, Woman of Yr. award B'nai B'rith, 1958, award for outstanding contbn. to arts Toronto Telegram, 1965, Centennial medal, 1967, Hadassah award of merit, 1967, Molson award, 1974, award Internat. Soc. Performing Arts Adminstrs., 1979, Can. Dance award, 1984, Gold Card IATSE local 58, 1984, diplôme d'honneur Can. Conf. Arts, 1986, Woman Yr. award St. George's Soc. Toronto, 1987, Order of Ont., 1987, Gov. Gen. award, 1994, Children's Charity award Variety Club of Ont., 1995; twice visited China at invitation of Chinese govt. to teach; in Beijing mounted full-length Coppelia, 1980; honored as one of founders of Can.'s maj. ballet cos. at Alta. Ballet Co.'s 15th anniversary, 1981. Home: Ottawa, Canada. Died Feb. 19, 2007.

**FRANCE, PETER NIGEL,** consulting engineer; b. Irby, Eng., July 6, 1950; s. John Mervyn and Muriel (Woods) F.; m. Heather Buchan Cookson, Apr. 8, 1972. BS with honors in Elec. Engring., Trinity Coll., Eng., 1984. Profl. engr., Europe. Tech. apprentice Marconi Co., Chelmsford, Eng., 1966-67; tech. engr. apprentice Plessey Telecoms, Liverpool, Eng., 1967-72; sr. engr. Plessey South Africa, Johannesburg, 1972-75, prodn. supt. Cape Town, 1975-78; patrol supr. Nippon Telecom Consulting, Tehran, Iran, 1978-79; site engr. ITT U.K. Ltd., Nigeria, 1979-81; resident engr. Merz & McLellan, Java, 1981-87; project mgr. Kennedy & Donkin, Strathclyde, Scotland, 1987-91; mng. dir. Dataspeed Control Sys., Wirral, Eng., from 1987, cons. on sys. to oil and gas industry, from 1994. Mem. IEEE, Inst. Diagnostic Engrs., Inst. Dirs. (mem. com. 1994-95), British Computer Soc. (assoc.). Mem. Tory Party. Mem. Ch. of Eng. Avocations: skiing, golf, sailing, shooting, classic cars. Home: Wirral, England. Died Aug. 3, 2002.

**FRANCES, KATRINA See VAN ALLEN, KATRINA**

**FRANCIS, EULALIE MARIE,** psychologist; b. Holmdel, NJ; d. Richard Erickson and Cora Mina (Patterson) F. BS, Newark State, NJ, 1945; EDM, Rutgers U., New Brunswick, 1957, MA, 1961; PhD, Rutgers U, Harvard U., NJ, Mass., 1971, 1973. Cert. Edn. Psychology. Tchr. Elem. Edn. Pub. Schs., Middletown, N.J., 1945-51, Elem. supr. Red Bank, N.J., 1951-63, dir. learning disability and psychologist East Brunswick, N.J., 1984. Cons. Nat. Assn. Mental Health N.Y.C., Family and childrens Sorriccs Natigna, N.Y.C., Lincoln Sch. Tchrs. Coll., Columbia U. 1981-89; Dir. Rsch. Div. NEA Assn. Trenton N.J. 1988-89. Author, editor: Kinesthetic Method of Reading, Theory and Techniques of Auditory Perception in Reading 1964-68. Adv. State Hist. Site Coun. Trenton N.J. 1986, Cultural and Heritage Com. Holmdel N.J. 1987-89. Mem. Arts Counc. of Princeton, Monmouth Mus. Lincroft, N.J., AAUW, Adv. Com. on Status of Women, Dir. Youth and Family Svcs., Princeton Child Devel. Inst., Rumson Country Club, Springlake Golf. Republican. Presbyterian. Avocations: flying private plane, swimming, photography, painting. Deceased.

**FRANCIS, FREDDIE,** film director, cinematographer; b. London, Dec. 22, 1917; m. Gladys Dorrell, 1940 (div. 1961); 1 child, Kevin Francis; m. Pamela Mann, 1963; children: Gareth, Suzanna. Apprentice to stills photographer Gaumont Brit. Studios; clapper boy B.I.P. Studios, Elstree, Eng.; camera asst. Brit. Dominion; cameraman Shepperton Studios, after World War II. Dir. (films) The Day of the Triffids, 1962, Two and Two Make Six, 1962, The Brain, 1962, Paranoiac, 1963, Nightmare, 1964, The Evil of Frankenstein, 1964, Traitor's Gate, 1964, Dr. Terror's House of Horrors, 1964, Hysteria, The Skull, 1965, The Psychopath, 1966, Torture Garden, 1967, The Deadly Bees, 1967, They Came From Beyond Space, 1967, The Intrepid Mr. Twigg, 1968, Dracula Has Risen From the Grave, 1968, Mumsy, Nanny, Sonny and Girly, 1969, Trog, 1970, The Vampire Happening, 1971, Tales From the Crypt, 1972, The Creeping Flesh, 1973, Tales That Witness Madness, 1973, Son of Dracula, 1974, Craze, 1974, Legend of the Werewolf, 1975, The Ghoul, 1976, Golden Rendezvous, 1977, The Doctor and the Devils, 1985, Dark Tower, 1987; (TV episodes) Man in a Suitcase, 1967-68, The Saint, 1967-68, The Champions, 1969, The Adventures of Black Beauty, 1972, Star Maidens, 1976, Sherlock Homes and Doctor Watson, 1980, Tales From the Crypt, 1996; cinematographer (films) A Hill in Korea, 1957, Time Without Pity, 1957, Virgin Island, 1958, Room at the Top, 1959, The Battle of the Sexes, 1959, Never Take Sweets From A Stranger, 1969, Sons and Lovers, 1960, Saturday Night and Sunday Morning, 1960, The Innocents, 1961, Night Must Fall, 1964, The Elephant Man, 1980, The French Lieutenant's Woman, 1981, The Jigsaw Man, 1983, Dune, 1984, Memed My Hawk, 1984, Return to Oz, 1985, Code Name: Emerald, 1985, Clara's Heart, 1988, Her Alibi, 1989, Brenda Starr, 1989, Glory, 1989 (Acad. Award for Best Cinematography, 1990), The Man in the Moon, 1991, Cape Fear, 1991, School Ties, 1992, Calliope, 1994, Princess Caraboo, 1994, Rainbow, 1996, The Straight Story, 1999; (TV movies) The Executioner's Song, 1982, The Plot to Kill Hitler, 1990, A Life in the Theatre, 1993; (TV episodes) Disneyland, 1961 Died Mar. 17, 2007.

**FRANCO, ALEXANDER,** construction company executive; b. Havana, Cuba, Sept. 5, 1963; came to the U.S., 1963; s. Sotero and Maria Franco. BA, Columbia U., 1983; MBA, Pace U., 1987. CPA. Sr. auditor Price Waterhouse, NYC, 1987-92; legis. asst. Fla. Ho. of Reps., Tallahassee, 1993-94; exec. dir. Interamerican Businessmen's Assn., Miami, Fla., from 1995; mgr. Coastal Constrn. Products, Miami, from 1996. V.p. Cuba Consulting Group, Miami, 1995—. Author: Business Opportunities in a Free Cuba, 1995, The Cuban Business and Legal Environment in the 1950s, 1996. Founder, pres. Ronald Reagan Rep. Alliance, Miami, 1989&; active Hispanic leadership tng. program Cuban Am. Nat. Coun., Miami, 1992; active Leadership Miami, Greater Miami C. of C., 1993. Named Outstanding Young Man of Am., 1989; recipient Outstanding Achievement award Cuba Bus. Roundtable, Miami, 1995. Republican. Deceased.

**FRASER, JASON LEE,** biologist, consultant; b. Hamilton, North Island, New Zealand, Nov. 10, 1974; s. Lindsay Fraser and Denice Donovan; life ptnr. Sarai Lewis; 1 child, Eli Fraser-Lewis. Grad. in Environ. Mgmt. (hon.), Natural Sciences, Joondalup, Western Australia, 2001. Project mgr. Dept. Conservation and Land Mgmt., Perth, Western Australia, Australia, 1999—2000; prin. biologist Ecosystematica Environ. Consulting, 2001—05; sr. regional biologist ENV Environ., Perth, Western Australia, Australia, from 2006. Bus. mgr. Ecosystematica, Perth, Western Australia, Australia. Author: (book) Mammals of the Great Sandy

Desert; contbr. scientific papers; presenter: (DVD Series) Best Practice Capture Handling & Restraint, 2005. Mem.: Environ. Inst. of Australia, Golden Key Nat. Honor Soc. (life). Achievements include Portableresearch design and commercial development of the 'ecosystematica' portable reptile funnel trap. Avocations: nature activities, reading, sports, motorcycling. Home: Mandurah, Australia. Deceased.

**FRAZER, CLOYCE CLEMON,** retired educator; b. Warren, Ark., Jan. 2, 1919; s. Charles Columbus and Maude Mae (Jones) Frazer; m. Beverly Jane Mundorff, Apr. 10, 1942. BA, Calif. State U., San Jose, 1952; MA, Calif. State U., Sacramento, 1961. Cert. spl. seconddary life diploma in indsl. arts Calif., 1959, gen. sec. life diploma Calif., 1960, std. teaching credentials life Calif., 1971, lic. comml. pilot lic. with flight instr. cert. FAA, 1949, cert. aircraft adn polwer plant lic. 1948. Aircraft mechanic, flight instr., Oakland, Calif., 1946—50; tchr. Folsom Calif. Unifed Sch. Dist., Sacramento City Unifed Sch. Dist., 1954—63, San Mateo Calif. Union High Sch. Dist., 1963—83, dept. head, 1963—73, program evaluator, 1976—77. Pres. Cresmoor H.S. Faculty Assn., 1965—66; treas. Calif. Aerospace Edn. Assn., from 1983; pres. Calif. Aerospace Edn. Assn. No. Sect., 1978—79. Contbr. articles to profl. jours.;, co-author curriculum materials. Mem. advocacy com. San Mateo County Commn. on Aging, 1985—90. Served to major USAF, 1941—79. Recipient honorable mention for sculputre San Mateo County Fair and Floral Festival, 1967, Earl Sams Aerospace Educator Yr. award, 1990. Mem.: NEA, Res. Officers Assn. US, Ret. Officers Assn., Exptl. Aircraft Assn. (Individual Achievement award 1982), Aircraft Owner and Pilots Assn., Am. Craft. Coun., Vocat. Edn. Assn., Calif. Indsl. Edn. Assn., Western Aerospace Mus., Fourteenth Air Force Assn., Air Force Assn., Calif. Ret. Tchrs. Assn. (pres. San Mateo County divsn. 1986—90), Calif. Tchrs. Assn., Ret. Officers Club, Caterpillar Club, Epsilon Pi Tau. Democrat. Deceased.

**FRECHETTE, ERNEST ALBERT,** foreign language educator emeritus; b. Rutland, Vt., July 7, 1918; s. Albert E. and Edna (Galarneau) F.; children: John, Andrew, Inez. AB, Assumption Coll., 1950; EdM, Worcester State Coll., 1954; EdD, Boston U., 1967. Foreign lang. tchr. Provincetown (Mass.) High Sch., 1952-54, Wachusett Regional High Sch., Holden, Mass., 1954-57, Provincetown High Sch., 1957-59; head foreign lang. dept. Apponequet Regional High Sch., Lakeville, Mass., 1959-62; foreign lang. supr. Mass. Dept. Edn., Boston, 1962-69; lectr., prof. Bridgewater State Coll., Tufts U., Boston U., S.E. Mass. U., 1962-73; prof. Fla. State U., Tallahassee, 1969-91, prof. emeritus, from 1991. Editorial cons. So. Conf. on Lang. Tchng., 1987-90; dir. Fgn. Lang. in Elem. Sch. Inst., Tallahassee, 1989; cons. multilingual, multicultural edn. Editor Fla. Fgn. Lang. Assn. Newsletter, 1969-90; co-author: Research Within Reach, 1985; test rev. editor Modern Lang. Jour., 1973-79; assoc. editor Am. Coun. on Tchg. of Fgn. Langs., 1970-78. Maj. U.S. Army, 1940-46. Grantee in field, 1975-88. Mem. Fla. Fgn. Lang. Assn. (pres. 1977-78). Roman Catholic. Avocations: dance, study of wines and fragrances, golf. Died Apr. 11, 1999.

**FREDERICKS, CLAUDE,** playwright, educator; b. Springfield, Mo., Oct. 14, 1923; s. Claude Matthew and Vira Beatrice (Toothman) F. Student, Harvard U., 1941-43. Founder, dir. The Banyan Press, Pawlet, Vt., from 1947; prof. literature Bennington (Vt.) Coll., 1961-93. Playwright: The Idiot King (produced by Living Theatre, N.Y.C. 1954), Translation of Pirandello's Tonight We Improvise (produced by Living Theatre 1959), On Circe's Island and A Summer Ghost (produced by Artists Theatre, N.Y.C. 1962, pub. by Bennington Rev., 1965, by Hill and Wang, 1965). Died Jan. 11, 2013.

**FREDERICKS, DAVID MICHAEL,** merchant banker, venture capitalist; b. Balt., Sept. 17, 1950; s. John Leonard and Emily F.; children: Marcy Lee, Ian Michael. BS in Mgmt., Indiana U. of Pa., 1972. CPA, N.Y. Owner, ptnr. K&F Constrn., LI, N.Y., 1967-69, ICW Ltd., LI, N.Y., 1969-71; staff acct. Price Waterhouse & Co., LI, N.Y., 1972-75; ptnr. Touche Ross & Co., NYC, 1975-84; mng. dir. Fredericks Michael & Co. Inc., NYC, from 1985; non-exec. chmn. bd. dirs. Fredericks Michael & Co. Ltd., London, from 2001. Chmn. FM Ventures, Inc., 1989—. Contbr. in field. Mem. Concerned Citizens of Montauk (N.Y.), 1976—, bus. adv. coun. Ind. U. of Pa., 1996—; bd. dirs. N.Y. Gilbert & Sullivan Players, N.Y.C., 1982-86. Named Eberly Entrepreneur of Yr. Achievements in Finance, 1997. Mem. AICPA, N.Y. State Soc. CPAs, N.Y. Athletic (N.Y.C.) Club, Union (N.Y.C.) Club. Roman Catholic. Deceased.

**FREEDMAN, AARON DAVID,** retired medicine and biochemistry educator, dean; b. Albany, NY, Jan. 4, 1922; s. Jacob Abraham and Pauline Rebecca (Hoffman) F.; m. Alice Maurer, Sept. 10, 1948, dec. 2001; children: Abigail, Jonathan, Jeremy; m. Virginia Weliky, Apr. 14, 2005. AB, Cornell U., 1942; MD, Albany Med. Coll., 1945; PhD, Columbia U., 1958; MA, U. Pa., 1972. Diplomate Am. Bd. Internal Medicine. Asst. prof. medicine and biochemistry Columbia U., NYC, 1958-65; clin. prof. U. Kans., Kansas City, 1965-69, chmn. dept. medicine Menorah Med. Ctr., 1965-69; prof., assoc. dean U. Pa., Phila., 1969-75, exec. dir. Grad. Hosp., 1972-75; prof. medicine Med. Sch. CUNY, 1975—2006, acting dean, 1978-79, dep. dean acad. affairs, 1990-92, emeritus prof., from 2006. Examiner N.Y. State Bd. Med. Examiners, Albany, 1962-65; cons. Touro Coll., N.Y.C., 1980; career investigator N.Y. Pub. Health Rsch. Coun., 1963-65; dir. Danciger Med. Inst., Kansas City, Mo., 1966-69. Mem. Ardsley (N.Y.) Bd. of Edn., 1962-65. Libman Fund fellow, 1951-54, USPHS fellow, 1958-60. Mem. Am. Soc. for Cell Biology, Am. Soc. Biochemistry and Molecular Biology. Jewish. Home: Estes Park, Colo. Died Apr. 20, 2013.

**FREEDMAN, ALBERT,** oncologist; b. Tel Aviv, Apr. 22, 1925; arrived in Australia, 1928; s. Nachum Zvi and Dina (Kroin) F.; m. Ruth Robeeno, Mar. 14, 1956; children: Harry, Danny, Tyrell. MB, BS, U. Sydney, Australia, 1947. Pathology registrar St. Vincent's Hosp., Sydney, 1949-50; registrar Children's Hosp., Birmingham, 1950-51; physician Spl. Unit Cancer Rsch., Sydney, 1959-90; dir. State Cancer Coun., NSW, Australia, 1970-79; dir. med. oncology Prince of Wales Hosp., 1980-90; cons. physician, Sydney, 1990-2001. Vis. oncologist Royal Hosp. for Women, Sydney, 1960-89; mem. med. bd. Wolper Jewish Hosp., Sydney, 1985-95; external cons. Nat. Health and Med. Rsch. Coun., Canberra, Australia, 1970-92. Co-author: The Epidimiology of Cancer in Papua New Guinea, 1974, Hypothalamus, Pituitary and Cancer, 1976; contbr. articles to profl. jours. Mem. bd. Moriah Coll., Sydney, 1985-89. Mem. Australian Soc. for Study of Obesity, Haematology Assn. Australia and New Zealand (Blood club 1990—), Fellowship Jewish Drs. (pres. 1975-78, med. ethics com. 1985-95), Royal Australian Coll. Physicians, Am. Soc. Clin. Oncology, Am. Diabetes Assn. (profl. sect.). Avocations: baroque music, ancient history. Home: Sydney, Australia. Died Oct. 28, 2008.

**FREEDMAN, HARRY,** composer; b. Lodz, Poland, Apr. 5, 1922; arrived in Can., 1925; s. Max and Rose (Nelken) F.; m. Mary Louise Morrison, Sept. 15, 1951; children: Karen Liese, Cynthia Jane, Lori Ann. Student, Winnipeg Sch. Art, 1936—40, Royal Conservatory Music, 1945—50. Musician Toronto Symphony, 1946—70; dir. Can. Music Centre. Composer: Tableau, 1952, Images, 1958, Tokaido: chorus and wind quintet, 1964, (orch.) Tangents, 1967, Tapestry, 1973, A Dance on the Earth, 1988, Town, 1981, Concerto for Orch., 1982, Third Symphony, 1983, Manipulating Mario, 2003, (ballets) Rose Latulippe, 1966, Romeo and Juliet, 1973, Oiseaux Exotiques, 1984, (soprano and flute) Toccata, 1968, Debussy orchestration Piano Preludes, 1971, (childrens choir) Keewaydin, 1971, Rhymes from the Nursery, 1986, Aqsaqniq, 2001, (violin and piano) Encounter, 1974, (clarinet) Lines, 1974, (narrator and chamber ensemble) The Explainer, 1976, (saxophone and orch.) Celebration, 1977, (choir) Green...Blue...White, 1978, Voices, 1999, Valleys, 2002, (Operas) Abracadabra, 1979, (chorus and orch.) Nocturne 3, 1980, (brass quintet and orch.) Royal Flush, 1980, (clarinet and string quartet) Chalumeau, 1981, (narrator and orch.) A Garland for Terry, 1985, (string orch.) Contrasts, The Web and the Wind, 1986, (music theater) Fragments of Alice, 1987, (concerto for percussion ensemble and orch.) Touchings, 1989, (marimba solo) Bones, 1989, (piano and choir) Songs from Shakespeare, 1990, (soprano and string quartet) Spirit Song, 1990, (22 solo strings) Indigo, 1994, (flute, viola and harp) Touchpoints, 1994, (soprano and lute) Bright Angels, 1995, (saxophone quartet) Saxtet, 1995, (bass clarinet and cello) Higher, 1996, (orchestra and 4 choirs) Borealis, 1997, (harp solo) Dances, 1997, (viola and orch.) Marigold, 1999, (16 solo strings) Graphic 9: for Harry Somers, 2000, (string quartet) Graphic 8, 2000, Phoenix, 2003, (symphonic) Duke, 2001, (flute) Romp and Reverie, 2002, (scores) Stratford Shakespeare Festival, films, stage, TV, (violin, cello and piano) A Gift for King Freddy, 2004, (flute, clarinet, violin, cello and piano) Graphic 10 (Matisse: Jazz), 2004; host: Music on a Sunday Afternoon, 1987. Served with RCAF, 1942-45. Decorated officer Order of Can.; Can. Coun. sr. arts grantee, 1960, 63, 73-74, 81, 97-98; recipient Can. film awards, 1970, Composer of Yr. award Can. Music Coun., 1979, Lynch-Staunton award Can. Coun., 1998; Tanglewood scholar, 1949, Royal Conservatory scholar, 1950. Mem. Can. League Composers (founding mem., pres. 1975-78). Died Sept. 16, 2005.

**FREEMAN, GLENN RICHARD,** retired state legislator; b. Cumberland, Ky., July 17, 1933; Student, Cumberland Coll., Western Ky. U.; BA, U. Ky. Mem. Ky. House of Reps., 1970—71, 1974—77, Ky. State Senate, Frankfort, 1996—2000. Mem. Harlan County Airport Bd. With U.S. Army. Named VFW Citizen of Yr., 1974. Mem. Masons, Shriners. Democrat. Died June 7, 2014.

**FREEMAN, JOHN MARK,** pediatric neurologist; b. Bklyn., Jan. 11, 1933; s. Leon Lucas and Florence (Kann) F.; m. Elaine Kaplan, Aug. 26, 1956; children: Andrew David, Jennifer Beth, Joshua Leon. BA, Amherst Coll., 1954; MD, Johns Hopkins U., 1958. Internship Harriet Lane Home, Johns Hopkins U., Balt., 1958-59, residency in pediat., 1959-61; fellow in neurology Columbia Presbyn. Hosp., NYC, 1961-64; rsch. physician Walter Reed Army Inst. Rsch., Washington, 1964—66; asst. prof. pediat. and neurology Stanford U., Calif., 1966-69; assoc. prof. neurology and pediat. Johns Hopkins U., 1969-82, prof. neurology & pediat., 1982—2007, prof. emeritus, 2007—14, Lederer prof. pediatric epilepsy, 1991—2003, dir. pediatric neurology, 1969-90, dir. pediatric epilepsy ctr., 1973—2002, dir. birth defects treatment center, 1969-90; active staff Johns Hopkins Hosp. Pres. Epilepsy Assn. Md., 1977-82; mem. profl. adv. bd. Epilepsy Found. America, 1975-82, sec., 1977, v.p., 1982-2014, hon. life dir., 1991-2014 Author: The Practical Management of Meningomyelocele, 1974; editor: Prenatal and Perinatal Factors Associated with Brain Disorders, 1985; co-author: Tough Decisions: A Casebook in Medical Ethics, 1987, 2nd edit., 2000, The Epilepsy Diet Treatment: An Introduction to the Ketogenic Diet, 1994, 3rd. edit, 2000, Seizures and Epilepsy in Childhood: A Guide for Parents, 1990 (Nat. Book award, 1991), 3rd edit., 2002; contbr. articles to profl. jours. Served with AUS, 1964-66. Recipient Lucy Moses prize, Columbia Presbyn. Med. Ctr., 1966, Frank Ford Tchg. award, Johns Hopkins U., 1983, Disting. Alumni award, 2007, Cmty. Leadership award, Epilepsy Assn. Md., 1991, Spl. Friend award, Upton Sch., Balt. City Sch. Sys., 1992; named Physician of Yr., Gov.'s Com. on Employment Handicapped, 1979, Health Care Profl. of Yr., Gov.'s Com. on Employment of Persons with Disabilities, 1990. Fellow: American Acad. Pediatrics (chmn. neurology sect. 1978—80), American Acad. Neurology; mem.: American Neurol. Assn., American Epilepsy Soc. (Lennox award 1993, Penry award 2001), American Fedn. Clin. Rsch., American Pediat. Soc., Child Neurology Soc. (exec. com. 1979—81, Hower award 2004), Professors of Child Neurology (pres. 1980—82). Home: Baltimore, Md. Died Jan. 3, 2014.

**FREEMAN, JONATHAN,** epidemiologist; b. Chgo., Aug. 18, 1939; s. Gustave and Elizabeth Gignoux (Hulse) F.; m. Elsie Joan Lachenmayer, June 23, 1964; children: Noah, Esther. AB, Harvard Coll., 1963; MD, Duke U., 1968; DSc, Harvard U., 1982. Diplomate Am. Bd. Internal Medicine, Am. Coll. Epidemiology. Asst. prof. Harvard Med. Sch., Boston, 1983-90; asst. prof. epidemiology Harvard Sch. Pub. Health, Boston, from 1990. Fellow Infectious Diseases Soc. Am.; mem. Am. Epidemiol. Soc. Deceased.

**FREGOSI, JIM (JAMES LOUIS FREGOSI),** professional baseball team manager, retired professional baseball player; b. San Francisco, Apr. 4, 1942; m. Joni Fregosi; children: Jim Jr., Jennifer, Nicole, Robbie. Student, Menlo Coll. Shortstop LA Angels, Calif., 1961-71, NY Mets, 1972-73, Tex. Rangers, 1973-77, Pitts. Pirates, 1977-78; mgr. Calif. Angels, 1978-81, Louisville Redbirds, 1983-86, Chgo. White Sox, 1986-88; spl. assignment scout, coach Phila. Phillies, 1989-90, minor league pitching instr., spl. assignment scout, 1990, mgr., 1991-97; spl. asst. to gen. mgr. San Francisco Giants, 1997-98; mgr. Toronto Blue Jays, 1999—2000. Named to The American League All-Star team, 1964, 66-70; recipient American League Gold Glove award, 1967. Died Feb. 14, 2014.

**FRELICH, PHYLLIS ANNETTE,** actress; b. Devils Lake, ND, Feb. 29, 1944; d. Phillip and Esther (Dockter) F.; m. Robert Steinberg, May 17, 1968; children: Reuben, Joshua. BS in L.S, Gallaudet Coll., 1967. Acting tchr. Nat. Theater of the Deaf, Waterford, Conn., 1977-79, 83, R.I. Sch. for Deaf, Providence, 1977-78, U. R.I., North Kingston, 1978. Actress: (plays) When You Coming Back, Red Ryder?, 1973, Songs from Milkwood, Broadway, Children of a Lesser God (Tony award for Best Actress), 1980, Poets from the Inside, N.Y.C., Public Theater, 1980, Night of 100 Stars, 1982, The Debutante Ball, 1984, Big River, 2003, Prymate, 2004; (films) Judgement, 1992, Santa Few, 1997, Children on Their Birthdays, 2002; (TV movies) Love Is Never Silent, 1985, Bridge to Silence, 1989, Sweet Nothing in My Ear, 2008;(TV series) Santa Barbara, 1988; (TV appearances) Barney Miller, 1981, Gimme a Break!, 1985, New Love, American Style, 1985, Spenser: For Hire, 1986, Hunter, 1991, L.A. Law, 1992, Pacific Blue, 1998, ER (2 episodes), 1998-99, Diagnosis Murder, 1999, Sue Thomas: FBI, 2004, CSI: Crime Scene Investigation, 2011 Recipient Humanitarian award Gallaudet Coll., 1980; Rough Rider award State of N.D., 1981; California's Year of Handicapped award, 1980; Critic's Circle award, 1980 Mem. Actors Equity Assn., Nat. Assn. Deaf Home: New York, NY. Died Apr. 10, 2014.

**FRENCH, ROBERT WARREN,** economics educator emeritus, writer, consultant; b. South Bend, Ind., May 8, 1911; s. Robert Warren and Lura (Keller) F.; m. Dorothy Louise Smith, July 8, 1934 (dec. June 1990); children: Nancy Alice French McWhorter, Judith Kay French Tronsrue; m. Nadene Shaner, Jan. 2, 1993. AB, U. Mich., 1932, MA, 1933, PhD, 1937. Fellow Brookings Instn., 1934-35; Teaching fellow econs. U. Mich., 1935-37; ptnr. Johnson-Smith Co., 1937-41; assoc. prof. internat. trade dir. bur. bus. research Coll. Commerce, La. State U., 1941-46; prof. internat. trade, dir. bur. bus. research, coll. bus. adminstrn. U. Tex., 1946-49; prof. econs., dean sch. bus adminstrn. Tulane U., 1949-55, v.p., 1953-56; dir. Port of New Orleans, 1956-60; pres. Tax Found., Inc., 1960-63; dir. exec. programs, prof. mgmt. Grad. Sch. Bus. Adminstrn., U. So. Calif., 1963-65; staff assoc. office of pres. U. Ill., Chgo., 1965-68; prof. econs. and mgmt. U. Ill. (Coll. Bus. Adminstrn.), 1965-70; acting dean U. Ill. (Coll. of Bus. Adminstrn.), 1966-68; asst. to pres. U. Ala., Birmingham, 1970-81; prof. econs. and bus. adminstrn. U. Ala. (Sch. Bus.), 1970-81, prof. emeritus, from 1981; interim dir. Center for Internat. Programs U. Ala., 1980-81. Lectr. bus. Miles Coll., 1973-76; vis. lectr. 1982-83; exec. dir. Pub. Affairs Research Council La., 1950-54; cons. Nat. Indsl. Conf. Bd., 1963, Assn. Western Rys., 1966-67, U.S. GAO, 1968-78, So. Regional Edn. Bd., 1973-75, Ala.-Miss. Dist. Export Council, 1978-81, Tenn. Higher Edn. Commn., 1974. Editor: La. Bus. Rev, 1941-46, Tex. Bus. Rev, 1946-49; Contbr.: Am. Peoples Ency, 1952-57, The Tax Exec., Vol. VIII, Tulane Tax Inst, 1951, Basics for Business, 1968, Living Together: Buchanan and Clark, 1904-1975, others. Trustee Dillard U., 1960-94, Hist. Soc. Mich., 1984-90, Western Mich. Meth. Conf. Commn. Archives and History, 1983-89, 93-96; bd. dirs. Amistad Research Ctr., 1969-80; bd. mgmt. Flint Goodridge Hosp., 1959-60; bd. councilors Grad. Sch. Bus. Adminstrn. U. So. Calif., 1961-63. Mem. Am. Soc. Pub. Adminstrn. (editorial bd. 1959-65), Hist. Soc. Mich., Chgo. Hist. Soc., Berrien County Hist. Assn., Chgo. Archtl. Found., Art Inst. Chgo., Berrien Community Found., Mich. Gateway Cmty. Found., Phi Kappa Phi, Pi Gamma Mu, Omicron Delta Kappa, Beta Gamma Sigma, Alpha Lambda Delta. Home: Buchanan, Mich. Died Mar. 1999.

**FRENCH, STANLEY GEORGE,** university dean, philosophy educator; b. Hamilton, Ont., Can., Sept. 24, 1933; s. Reginald George and Marie (Larson) F.; children: Shona, Sean, Lina, Ewan. BA, Carleton U., 1955; MA, U. Rochester, 1957; PhD, U. Va., 1959; spl. student, Oxford U., 1961, U. Nice, France, 1975-76, Royal Victoria Hosp., McGill U., Montreal, 1987-88. Assoc. prof. philosophy U. Western Ont., London, 1965-68; prof. philosophy Sir George Williams U., Montreal, Que., 1968, chmn. dept. philosophy, 1969-71; prof. philosophy, dean grad. studies Concordia U., Montreal, 1971-86, dir. humanities interdisciplinary doctoral program, 1992—97. Mem. joint com. on programs Council of Univs., 1972-75; chmn. Westmount Sch. Commn., 1972; pres. London Council for Adult Edn., 1965-66; chmn. Bd. Edn. City of London, 1968; bd. govs. Sir George Williams U., 1969-71; internat. vis. scholar The Hastings Ctr., 1992; vis. scholar U. B.C. Ctr. Rsch. Women's Studies and Gender Relations. Author: The North West Staging Route, 1957, Philosophers Look at Canadian Confederation, 1979, Interpersonal Violence, Health and Gender Politics, 1993, Violence Against Women: Philosophical Perspectives, 1998, also monographs; cons. editor: Humanities Research Coun. Can., 1970-2003; editorial adv.: Gnosis, 1977-2003; contbr. articles to profl. jours., chpts. to books. Served as officer RCAF, 1951-56. Can. Council grantee, 1962; Internat. vis. scholar The Hastings Ctr., 1992. Mem. Soc. for Philosophy and Pub. Affairs (exec. bd. dirs.), Montreal Conf. Polit. and Social Thought, Sociètè de Philosophie du Montreal, Sociètè de Philosophie du Quebec, Can. Philos. Assn., Am. Philos. Assn., Am. Soc. Polit. and Legal Philosophy, Mind Assn., Can. Assn. Grad. Schs. (sec.-treas. 1980-81), Can. Bioethics Soc. Home: Wentworth North, Canada. Died Sept. 15, 2003.

**FRERE, PAUL,** journalist; b. LeHavre, Principality of Monaco, Jan. 30, 1917; s. Maurice Paul and Germaine Ernestine (Schimp) F.; m. Suzanne Juliette Millo; children: Marianne, Martine, Nicole. Ingenieur comml., U. Libre, Brussels, Belgium, 1940. Sec. Ucobelwag & Ucobelloc, Brussels, 1941-45; freelance auto journalist Vence, France, 1946—2008; service mgr. Auto Import Co., 1948-52; auto racing driver, 1952-60; European editor Road & Track Mag., 1970—75; pres. European "Car of the Year" award, 1970-85; v.p. tech. commn. FISA, 1972-84; European editor Road & Track Mag., 1980—2008; hon. pres. European "Car of the Year" award, 1985—2008. Author several books on driving technique and auto. devel., 1956-2008. Recipient Prix Charles Faroux Soc. of Automobile Engrs., 1963, Pemberton Trophy Guild Motoring Writers, 1974; winner Le Mans 24 hour race and South African Grand Prix, 1960. Mem. Brit. Racing Drivers Club (hon.), Club Internat. Anciens Pilotes de Grand Prix, Soc. Belgian Automobile Engrs. Avocations: music, sports. Died Feb. 23, 2008.

**FRETER, MARK ALLEN,** marketing executive, public relations executive, consultant; b. Chgo., Oct. 31, 1947; s. John Maher and Christopher Patricia (Allen) F. BA, U. Calif., Santa Barbara, 1969; MBA, U. Calif., Berkeley, 1971. Regional dir. HBO Svcs., Inc., L.A. and Denver, 1979-84; v.p. affiliate rels. X-Press Info. Svcs., Denver, 1984-85; v.p. mktg. Telecrafter Corp., Denver, 1985-86; mktg. dir. Computer Svcs. Corp., Boulder, Colo., 1986-87; prin., v.p. pub. rels. svcs. MultiMedia, Inc., Denver, 1987-88; dir. documentation and corp. comm., product specialist, op. cons. Data Select Systems Inc., Woodland Hills, Calif., 1988-91; pres., CEO The Aspen Group Ltd., Valencia, Calif., from 1988; mgr. mktg. comm. WorldCom, San Antonio, 1991-96; sr. mgr. product devel. GCI, Inc., Anchorage, 1996-97; sr. product mgr. Qwest Comms., San Antonio, 1997-98; sr. product mgr. mgmt. Earthlink Network, Inc., Pasadena, Calif., 1998-99; sr. product mgr. value added internet svcs., e-commerce Broadwing Comms., Austin, Tex., 1999-2000; group mktg. mgr. e-bus. svcs. Verizon Comms., Irving, Tex., from 2000. Lectr. Internat. Coun. Shopping Ctrs., N.Y.C., 1977; conf. planner ICSC-West, San Francisco, 1978-79; tng. program devel. HBO, N.Y.C., 1982. Youth coach South Suburban YMCA, Littleton, Colo., 1984-86. Recipient First Pl. cert. for Retail Ad Campaign San Diego Advt. Assn., 1980. Mem. Calif. Cable TV Assn., No. Calif. Promotion Mgrs. Assn. (v.p. 1977-78), So. Calif. Promotion Mgrs. Assn. (sec., treas. 1976-77). Democrat. Mem. Soc. Friends. Avocations: skiing, ice hockey, reading, coaching youth sports. Deceased.

**FREUND, ECKHARD,** electrical engineering educator; b. Düsseldorf, Germany, Feb. 28, 1940; s. Karl and Margret (Meya) F.; m. Brigitte Keudel; children: Viviane, Ariane. Diploma in engring., Tech. Sch. Darmstadt, Fed. Republic Germany, 1965; D Engring., Tech. U. Berlin, 1968. Scientist U. Raumfahrt, Oberpfaffenhofen, Fed. Republic Germany, 1965-70; guest prof. aero. engring. U. So. Calif., LA, 1972-76, 83; guest scientist European Space Ops. Ctr., Darmstadt, Fed. Republic Germany, 1970-71; sci. coord. Fraunhofer Inst., Karlsruhe, Fed. Republic Germany, 1976-78; prof. dept. elec. engring. Fernuniversität, Hagen, Fed. Republic Germany, 1978-84; prof. dept. elec. engring., dir. Inst. Robotics Rsch. U. Dortmund, Fed. Republic Germany, from 1985. Sci. adviser Jet Propulsion Lab., NASA, Pasadena, Calif., 1983. Author: Time Variable Multivariable Systems, 1971, Sgtate Space Control, I/II, 1986, 87, Mobile Robots and Multi-Robot Systems, 1993; contbr. some 350 articles on robotics and automation to tech. publs. Home: Schwerte, Germany. Died Jan. 15, 2005.

**FRIBERG, BARBRO EVA ELISABETH,** retired nursing educator; b. Jörn, Vasterbotten, Sweden, Oct. 17, 1937; d. Karl Gottfrid and Hildur Kristina Eriksson; m. Sven Friberg, Sept. 2, 1966; children: Ronny, Ann, Petter, Klas. RN, Red Cross, Boden, 1963; MS, Umeå U., Sweden, 1994, Licentiate in Med. Sci., 1997, MD, 1999. Head RN Hosp., Arvidsjaur, Sweden, 1963—64; oper. rm. nurse No. U. Hosp., Umeå, 1964—68; nursing tchr. Coll. Health and Caring Scis., Umeå, 1968—99; asst. prof. dept. nursing Umeå U., 1999—2003. Cons. ABB Airtech AB, Stockholm, from 1990, various oper. depts., Sweden, from 1990, Norway, from 1990, Finland, from 1990, Toul Hosp., Västerås, Sweden, from 1999; cons. in field. Contbr. articles to profl. jours.; author: Assistant in the Operating Room, 1970, Medical Surgical A&B, 1981, Somatic Illness, 1981, Oncology, 1988, Orthopaedic Asepsis in the Operating Theatre, 1999. Mem.: Assn. Operating Rm. Nurses, Swedish Assn. Operating Rm. Nurses (hon.). Democrat. Avocations: skiing, walking, reading, singing. Home: Umeå, Sweden. Died Aug. 2007.

**FRIBOURGH, JAMES H.,** retired university administrator; b. Sioux City, Iowa, June 10, 1926; s. Johan Gunder and Edith Katherine (James) F.; m. Cairdenia Minge, Jan. 29, 1955; children: Cynthia Kaye, Rebecca Jo, Abbie Lynn. Student, Morningside Coll., 1944-47; BA, MA, U. Iowa, 1949, PhD, 1957; LHD (hon.), DHL (hon.), Morningside Coll., 1989. Instr. Little Rock Jr. Coll., 1949—56; assoc. prof. biology Little Rock U., 1957—60, prof., chmn. life scis. divsn., 1960—69; vice chancellor U. Ark., Little Rock, 1969—72, interim chancellor, 1972—73, exec. vice chancellor acad. affairs, 1973—82, interim chancellor, exec. vice chancellor acad. affairs, 1982, provost, exec. vice chancellor, from 1983, disting. prof., 1984—94, disting. prof. emeritus, 1994—2011; ret. Cons. in field; assoc. Marine Biol. Lab., Woods Hole, Mass. Contbr. articles to profl. jours. Mem. Ark. Gov.'s Com. on Sci. and Tech., 1969-71; bd. dirs., mem. nat. adv. bd. Nat. Back Found., 1979; vice chmn. NCCJ, 1981-82; div. rep. United Way of Pulaski County, 1980-82; bd. dirs. Ark. Dance Theatre, Little Rock, 1980-82; vestryman Good Shepherd Episcopal Ch.; del. Episcopal Diocese of Ark.; fellow Ark. Mus. Sci. and History, 1987. Fribourgh Hall named in his honor, U. Ark., Little Rock, 1994, Inaugural Science Leadership award U., 2011; NSF fellow History of Sci. Inst., 1959-60. Fellow AAAS, Coll. Preceptors (London), Am. Inst. Fishery Rsch. Biologists, Ark. Mus. Sci. and History; mem. Am. Fisheries Soc. (chmn. com. on internationalism cert. fisheries scientist), AAUP (pres. Ark. conf.), Electron Microscopy Soc. Am., Am. Soc. Swedish Engrs. (corr. mem.), Ark. Acad. Sci. (pres. 1966), Ark. Dean's Assn. (pres. 1982), Am. Assn. State Colls. and Univs., Am. Swedish Inst., Swedish Club (Chgo.), Rotary (Paul Harris fellow), Vasa Order Am. Lodge, Sigma Xi, Phi Kappa Phi. Clubs: Swedish, Vasa Order Am. Lodges: Rotary (Paul Harris fellow). Democrat. Home: Little Rock, Ark. Died Mar. 6, 2014.

**FRIEDMAN, ALAN JACOB,** museum consultant, former museum director; b. Bklyn., Nov. 15, 1942; s. George and Eleanor (Goldberger) F.; m. Mickey Thompson, Dec. 26, 1966. BS in Physics, Ga. Inst. Tech., 1964; PhD in Physics, Fla. State U., 1970. Research asst. Ga. Inst. Tech., Atlanta, 1960-64, Fla. State U., Tallahassee, 1964-69; asst. prof. Hiram (Ohio) Coll., 1969-74; dir. astronomy & physics Lawrence Hall of Sci. U. Calif., Berkeley, 1973-84; conseiller scientifique Cite des Scis. et de l'Industrie, Paris, 1982-84; CEO NY Hall of Sci., Corona, 1984—2006; mem. Nat. Assessment Governing Bd., from 2006. Vis. asst. prof. American studies and English Temple U., Phila, 1975; research fellow English dept. U. Calif., Berkeley, 1972-73; vis. lectr. English dept. San Franicsco State U., 1974-75. Co-author: Planetarium Educator's Workshop Guide, 1980, Einstein as Myth and Muse, 1985, Planetarium Activities for Student Success, 12 vols., 1993. Younger Humanist fellow NEH, 1972-73; recipient Disting. Service award Mid-Atlantic Planetarium Soc., 1982, Merit award Astron. Assn. Northern Calif., 1983, AAAS award for Public Understanding of Sci. & Tech., 1996; named to The Centennial Honor Roll, American Assn. Museums, 2006. Fellow AAAS, Internat. Planetarium Soc. (Svc. award 1990); mem. American Assn. Physics Tchrs., Internat. Planetarium Soc. (pres. 1985-86), Assn. Sci.-Tech. Ctrs. (bd. dirs. 1989-97), Phi Beta Kappa. Died May 4, 2014.

**FRIEDMAN, MILDRED,** architecture educator, design educator, curator; b. LA, July 25, 1929; d. Nathaniel and Hortense (Weinsveig) Shenberg; m. Martin L. Friedman; children: Lise, Ceil, Zoe. BA, UCLA, 1951, MA, 1952; DFA (hon.), Mpls. Coll. Art, 1984; DFA, Hamlin U., 1987. Instr. design L.A. City Coll., 1952-54; archtl. designer Cerny Associates, Mpls., 1957-69; design curator Walker Art Ctr., Mpls., 1970-90; freelance cons. NYC, 1990—2014. Mem. arch. and design panel Nat. Endowment Arts, 1975—78, mem. policy panel design arts, 1979—82, mem. presdl. design awards jury, 1991; mem. vis. com. Sch. Arch. and Planning MIT, 1985—88; mem. vis. com. Grad. Sch. Design Harvard U., from 1994; bd. dirs. Internat. Design Conf., Aspen, 1989—91, Chgo. Inst. Arch. and Urbanism, 1990—93, Nat. Inst. Archtl. Edn., from 1993; mem. deisgn jury Am. Acad. Rome, 1991; gueest instr. UCLA, 1992; mem. jury to select architect for Whitehall Ferry Terminal, NYC, 1992; vis. instr. Harvard U., 1993; cons. Battery Park City Authority, NYC; guest curator Bklyn. Mus., 1992—2002; guest curator for Frank Gehry retrospective exhbn. Solomon R. Guggenheim Mus., NYC, 2001; guest curator for Vital Forms exhbn. Bklyn. Mus. Art, 2001—02. Author, editor: Gehry Talks, 1999; editor Design Quar., 1970-91, numerous catalogues; participating author for catalogue on the work of Jack Lenor Larson, Mus. Arts & Design, 2004. Recipient Outstanding Achievement award YWCA, 1984, Outstanding Svc. award U. Minn., 1991; fellow Intellectual Interchange program Japan Soc., 1982, Chrysler Design award, 2002; grantee Nat. Endowment Arts, 1992-93, Graham Found. for Advanced Studies in Fine Arts, 1997; recipient Graham Found grant for Design Quar. Anthology. Mem. AIA (hon., nat. awards jury 1981, 87, bd. dirs. Minn. chpt. 1984-86, Inst. Honors 1994). Died Sept. 3, 2014.

**FRISCH, BERTRAM,** materials science educator; b. Dudweiler, Saarland, Germany, Apr. 23, 1931; s. Alfons and Melanie (Karst) F.; m. Gisela Schwarz, Dec. 22, 1956; children: Barbara, Arnulf. Diploma in Engring., Tech. Hochschule Aachen, Fed. Republic Germany, 1956; D in Natural Scis., U. Saarlandes, Fed. Republic Germany, 1958. Asst. U. Saarlandes, 1956-64, lectr., 1964-69, prof., from 1969. Author: Frisch, Dransfeld, Thiele; Kamidelloz: Die Werkstätten der Spätbronzezeitlichen Paläste Hebelt, 1985; contbr. articles to profl. jours. Recipient Order of Merit, 2002. Mem. Verein Deutscher Eisenhüttenleute, Deutsche Keramische Gesellschaft. Avocations: history, tennis. Home: Dudweiler, Germany. Died Nov. 23, 2006.

**FRITZ, BARBARA HUGHES,** lawyer; b. Rusk County, Tex., Feb. 11, 1928; d. Charles Allen and O'Dell (Harris) Hughes; m. Richard J. Fritz, June 14, 1952; children: Catherine, Maranda. BBA, U. Houston, 1974, JD, 1977. Bar: Tex. 1977; cert. in family law Tex. Bd. Legal Specialization. Product mgr. Johns-Manville Sales Corp., Houston, 1956—66; creative dir. copy Madison Advt. Inc., Louisville, 1968—71; store mgr. Spalding Svc. Inc., Louisville, 1971—73; ptnr. Fritz & Fritz, Victoria, Tex., 1977—87; ct. master 4th Administrv. Jud. Dist. Tex., from 1987. Mem.: Phi Kappa Phi, Order Barons, Assn. Trial Lawyers America, Tex. Bar Assn. Died 1998.

**FRÖMAN, PER OLOF,** theoretical physics scientist; b. Högsby, Sweden, Apr. 27, 1926; s. Hugo and Judith (Kratz) F.; m. Nanny Johansson, Mar. 26, 1959; 1 child, Gunnar. D Theoretical Physics, Uppsala U., 1957. Asst. prof. theoretical physics Uppsala U., 1957—60, prof. theoretical physics, 1964—92; prof. mechanics Royal Inst. Tech., Stockholm, 1960—64. Author: (with Nanny Fröman) JWKB Approximation, Contributions to the Theory, 1965, Russian translation, 1967, Phase-Integral Method Allowing Nearlying Transition Points, 1996, Physical Problems Solved by the Phase-Integral Method, 2002, paperback, 2005, Stark Effect in a Hydrogenic Atom, 2008; contbr. articles to profl. jours. Mem. Austrian Acad. Scis., Royal Soc. Scis. Uppsala (sec. 1974-82). Avocation: sailing. Home: Uppsala, Sweden. Died Sept. 14, 2007.

**FROWNER, BYRON,** retired electrical engineer, researcher; b. Washington, May 12, 1937; s. Benjamin Franklin and Mary Magdalene Frowner; children: Blair, Ian, Sydny, Emanuel. BSEE, CUNY, 1959. Gen. engr. US Navy, Bklyn., 1959—69; asst. elec. engr. NYC Transit Authority, Bklyn., 1970—78, Dept. Environ. Protection, NYC, 1980—84; sr. project mgr. Health & Hosps. Corp., NYC, 1985—91; sr. constrn. engr. NY Power Authority, White Plains, 1994—2002; ret. Author: Special Relativity: Einstein's Error, 1994. Mem.: AAAS, NY Acad. Scis. Avocations: history, sports. Home: Bronx, NY. Died Jan. 8, 2014.

**FRÜHBECK DE BURGOS, RAFAEL,** conductor; b. Burgos, Spain, Sept. 15, 1933; s. Guillermo and Estefania (Ochs) Frühbeck de Burgos; m. Maria Carmen Martinez, Dec. 21, 1959; children: Rafael, Gema. Attended, Bilbao Conservatory, Madrid Conservatory, HS for Music, Munich; student, U. Munich, Richard Strauss Price, 1958, U. Madrid; D (hon.), U. Navarra, Pamplona, Spain, 1994, U. Burgos, 1998. Chief condr. Mcpl. Orch., Bilbao, Spain, 1958—62, Nat. Orch., Madrid, 1962—78, gen. music dir. Dusseldorf Symphony, Germany, 1966—71, music dir. Montreal Symphony, Can., 1974—76, Vienna Symphony, Austria, 1991—96, Deutsche Oper, Berlin, 1992—97, Rundfunk Symphony Orch. Berlin, 1994—2000, RAI Nat. Symphony Orch., Turin, Italy, 2001—07, chief condr. Dresden Philharm. Orch., Germany, 2004—11, Danish Nat. Symphony Orch., Copenhagen, from 2012, prin. guest condr. Nat. Symphony, Washington, 1980—90, Yomiuri Nippon Symphony Orch., Tokyo, 1980—90, Dresden Philharm. Orch., 2003—04, hon. condr. Yomiuri Nippon Symphony Orch., Tokyo, 1991, Nat. Orch., Madrid, 1998, creative dir. Cin. Symphony Orch. Masterworks Series, 2011—13. Decorated Encomienda Orden de Alfonso X El Sabio (Spain), Gran Cruz Orden del Merito Civil (Spain); recipient Prize of Musical Interpretation, Larios CEOE, Madrid, 1992, Ehrenmedaille in Gold, Burgermeister, Vienna, 1995, State of Vienna, Austria, 2000, Gold medal to the Civil Merit of Austria, 1996, Gold medal, Internat. Gustav Mahler Soc., Vienna, 1996, Fundacion Guerrero prize of Spanish Music, Madrid, 1996, Big Cross to the Civil Merit, Republic of Germany, Berlin, 2001, Gold medal to the Labour Merit, Madrid, 2004, Gold medal to the Beautiful Arts, Ministry Culture Spain, 2008; named one of Condr. of Yr., Musical America, 2011. Mem.: Real Acad. de Bellas Artes de San Fernando (Madrid). Home: Madrid, Spain. Died June 11, 2014.

**FRYE, RICHARD NELSON,** retired historian, educator; b. Birmingham, Ala., Jan. 10, 1920; AB, U. Ill., 1939; AM, Harvard U., Cambridge, 1940, PhD, 1946; postgrad., Princeton U., NJ, 1941, Sch. Oriental Studies, London, 1946-47; doctorate (hon.), U. Tajikistan, USSR, 1991. Exec. sec. Near East com. American Council Learned Societies, 1948-50; asst. prof. Middle East studies Harvard U., Cambridge, Mass., 1949-53, assoc. prof., 1953-57, prof. Iranian studies, 1957-90, prof. emeritus, 1990—2014. Vis. prof. Franfurt U., 1958-59, Hamburg U., 1968-69; vis. lectr. Iranian archaeology Hermitage Mus., 1966-67, Tajikistan U., 1990-91; cons. and lectr. in field. Author: Iran, 1953, History of Bukhara, 1954, Heritage of Persia, 1963, The Histories of Nishapur, 1965, Excavations of Qasr-i Abu Nasr, 1973, Bukhara, the Medieval Achievement, 1965, Persia, 1968, Middle Iranian Inscriptions from Dura Europas, 1968, The Golden Age of Persia, 1975, The Ancient History of Iran, 1983, The Heritage of Central Asia: From Antiquity to the Turkish Expansion, 1996, Greater Iran, 2005, Ibn Fadlan's Journey to Russia, 2005; asst. editor Speculum, 1950-60; mem. editl. bd. Central Asian Jour., 1960-72, Indo-Iranica, 1965-74; editor: Vol. 4, Cambridge History of Iran, 1975, Bulletin and Monograph series Asia Inst., 1969-74, 1986-99; contbr. articles to profl. jours. Dir., Asia Inst., Pahlavi U., Iran, 1969-75. Fellow Acad. Sciences Tajikistan Republic; mem. American Orient Soc. (v.p. 1966), Nat. Assn. Armenian Studies and Research (founder), Iranian Studies. Avocations: iranian studies, archaeology. Died Mar. 27, 2014.

**FU, SHOUCHENG JOSEPH,** biomedicine educator; b. Beijing, Mar. 19, 1924; s. W.C. Joseph and W.C. (Tsai) F.; m. Susan B. Guthrie, June 21, 1951; children: Robert W.G., Joseph H.G., James B.G. BS, MS, Cath. U., Beijing, 1944; PhD, Johns Hopkins U., 1949. Postdoctoral fellow Nat. Insts. Health, Bethesda, Md., 1949—51, scientist,

1951—55; Gustav Bissing fellow Johns Hopkins U. at Univ. Coll. London, 1955—56; chief enzyme and bioorganic chemistry lab. Children's Cancer Rsch Found (now Dana Farber Cancer Inst.), 1956—65; rsch. assoc. Harvard U. Med. Sch., Boston, 1956—65; prof., chmn. bd. chemistry Chinese U., Hong Kong, 1966—70, dean sci. faculty, 1967—69; vis. prof. Coll. Physicians and Surgeons Columbia U., NYC, 1970—71; prof. biochemistry and molecular biology U. Medicine and Dentistry of N.J., Newark, 1971—2003, prof. emeritus, from 2003, asst. dean, 1974—77; acting dean Grad. Sch. Biomed. Scis., 1977—78, prof. ophthalmology, 1989—2003, prof. emeritus, from 2003. Founder, pres. CMDNJ Credit Union (now North Jersey Fed. Credit Union), 1974-75. Contbr. articles to profl. jours. Capt. USPHS, 1959—. Named Hon. Disting. Prof. and Acad. Advisor Inner Mongolia Med. U., Huthot, Peoples Republic of China, 1988—. Fellow AAAS, Royal Soc. Chemistry (U.K.); mem. Royal Hong Kong Jockey Club, Am. Club Hong Kong, Sigma Xi (Newark chpt. pres. 1976-80, sec. 1974-76, 81-82). Home: Maplewood, NJ. Deceased.

**FUCHS, LILLIAN,** classical musician, educator, composer; b. Nov. 18, 1901; d. Philip and Kate (Weiss) F.; m. Stein Ludwig; children: Barbara Stein Mallow, Carol Stein Amado (twins). Grad. in Violinwith highest honors, Juilliard Sch. Music. Mem. Perole String Quartet; tchr. viola and chamber music Juilliard Sch. Music; composer viola and violin solos. Instr. Aspen Music Sch. Festival; recorded Mozart duos for violin, viola and symphony concertante with Joseph Fuchs. Composer, published studies, sonatas for viola solo; arranger violin and viola concerts. Recipient Artist Tchr. award, 1979, award Am. Viola Soc., 1981, award Music Edn. Assn. of N.J., 1960, Morris Loed prize, Isaac Newton Seligman prize; one of 1st viola artists to perform and record 6 cello suites by J.S. Bach on the viola. Home: New York, NY. Died Oct. 5, 1995.

**FUNK, CYRIL REED, JR.,** agronomist, educator; b. Richmond, Utah, Sept. 20, 1928; s. Cyril Reed and Hazel Marie (Jensen) F.; m. Donna Gwen Buttars, Feb. 2, 1951; children: Bonnie Arlene, David Christopher, Carol Jean. BS (Scholarship A 1955), Utah State U., 1952, MS, 1955; PhD, Rutgers U., 1961; DAgr (hon.), Utah State U., 1994. Mem. faculty Rutgers U., New Brunswick, NJ, from 1956, rsch. prof. turfgrass breeding plant biology and pathology dept., from 1969, also instr. grad. faculty. Author, patentee in field. Served to 1st lt. AUS, 1952-54. Recipient Green Sect. award U.S. Golf Assn., 1980, Achievement award Lawn Inst., 1977; named to Hall of Disting. Alumni, Rutgers U. Fellow Crop Sci. Soc. Am., Am. Soc. Agronomy (research award N.E. sect. 1979); mem. AAAS (fellow 1992), Am. Sod Producers Assn. (hon.), Golf Course Supts. Assn. (hon. mem.; Disting. Service award 1979), Internat. Turfgrass Soc., N.J. Turfgrass Assn. (Achievement award 1976, Hall of Fame award 1984), N.J. Golf Course Supts. Assn. (hon.), N.J. Acad. Scis., Sigma Xi, Phi Kappa Phi, Acad. Scis. Uzbekistan (hon.), Acad. Agrl. Scis. Kyrgyzstan (hon.). Mem. Lds Ch. Achievements include developing numerous turfgrasses. Died Oct. 4, 2012.

**FÜR, LAJOS,** retired Hungarian government official; b. Egyhaázasdatóc, Hungary, Dec. 21, 1930; s. Lajos and Ulianna (Csuti) F.; m. Friderika Biró, 1976; children: Sarolta, Lajos. BS, U. Scis., Debrecen, 1954, MA, 1971; DPhil., Acad. Scis., Budapest, 1983. Asst. Lajos Kossuth U., Debrecen, 1954-56; asst. libr. Agrl. Mus., Budapest, 1958-64, fellow, 1964-87; asst. prof. Lorand Eötroös U., Budapest, 1987-90, prof., 1990; min. def. Govt. of Hungary, Budapest, 1990—94. Author: (books) Too Many Graves, 1987, Where are the Soldiers?, 1988, Minority and Science, 1989, Fate and History, 1991. Founder Hungarian Democratic Forum, Budapest, vice chmn., 1989, acting chmn., 1991; mem. Presidium; nat. chmn. MDF, 1991; mem. Parliament, 1990, chmn. Parliamentary Com. on Humanitarian Law and Minority and Religious Issues; sec. Revolutionary Com. Hajdö-Bihar Dist., 1956. Recipient Niveau prize Periodical Alföld. Mem. Acad. Sciences (com. history of agrl. sci.). Avocations: reading, historical essays. Died Oct. 22, 2013.

**FURBUSH, MARY CHAPMAN,** volunteer; b. Danville, Va., Feb. 16, 1913; d. Fred L. and Martha L. (Hubbard) Furbush; m. Spencer Sanderson Furbush, Aug. 24, 1940. Grad., Chatham Hall, 1929; student, Goucher Coll., 1929—32. NH state chmn. Flag of the USA com. DAR, 1959—62; chpt. regent, 1960—62; state rec. sec. Flag of the USA com. DAR, NH, 1962—65; nat. vice chmn. motion picture com., 1968—71; state chmn. sch. com., 1974—77; nat. vice chmn. motion picture com. Constn. Week com., 1977—80, vice chmn., 1986—87. Mem. Sch. Bd. Somersworth, NH, 1946—49; trustee Forest Glade Cemetery, 1946—65, Trust Funds City of Somersworth, 1954—56; gov. NH Gen. Soc. Mayflower Descs., 1965—67, asst. gen., 1969—78, dep. gov. gen., from 1978; v.p. NH soc. Nat. Soc. Daus. Colonial Wars, 1968—71; pres. NH soc., 1971—74, nat. chaplain, 1974—77, nat. 1st. v.p., 1977—80; mem. Orders of Distinction com. Nat. Soc. Daus. of Barons of Runnymede, surety, 1974—79, from 1987. Recipient Valuable Service award, Pres. US, 1948. Mem.: Nat. Soc. Daus. Colonial Wars, Nat. Soc. Colonial Dames XVII Century (nat. chaplain 1974—77, 1st v.p. 1977—80, nat. chmn. awards com. from 1983), Nat. Soc. Dames Ct. Honor, Piscataqua Pioneers (v.p. 1970—75), Huguenot Soc. NH (v.p.), Nat. Soc. Daus. Am. Colonists (N.H. v.p. 1975—79, from 1982), Strawbery, Mass. Huguenot Soc., NH Soc. DAR (state program chmn. com. 1985—86), NH Huguenot Soc. (state pres. from 1984), Smithsonian Assos., Somersworth Hist. Soc., NH Hist. Soc., Nat. Hist. Soc., Order of Americans of Armorial Ancestry, Banke, Jamestowne Soc. Democrat. Episcopalian. Deceased.

**FURGLER, KURT,** former Swiss government official, lawyer; b. St. Gall, Switzerland, June 24, 1924; m. Ursula Stauffenegger; 6 children. Student, U. Fribourg, U. Zurich, U. Geneva, Grad. Inst. Internat. Studies; LLD, Boston U., 1985. Lawyer, St.-Gall, 1950—71; mem. Nat. Coun., Swaziland, 1955—71, Fed. Coun., 1972—86, v.p., 1976, 1980, 1984, pres., 1977, 1981, 1985; head Fed. Dept. Justice and Police, 1972—83, Dept. Pub. Economy, 1983—86. Leader Christian Dem. Party Group Fed. Coun. Died July 23, 2008.

**FUSTERO, ROBERT RAYMOND (BOB FUSTERO),** retired political organization worker; b. Atlantic City, June 29, 1951; s. Jose M. and Genevieve (Solanas) Fustero. BA, American U., 1976. Clk. Giant Food Inc, Landover, Md., 1973—2001; dir. Jose&Genevieve Fustero Instn., Silver Spring, Md., 2001—03. Gubernatorial candidate Dem. Party, Md., 2002. Mem.: Americana Finnmark Assn. (treas. 2003, v.p. 1998—2000, pres. 2000—02), Montgomery Citizens Safer Md. (assoc.). Conservative. Avocations: writing, lectures, consultations. Home: Silver Spring, Md. Died Oct. 22, 2013.

**FUTRELL, ROBERT FRANK,** military historian, consultant; b. Waterford, Miss., Dec. 15, 1917; s. James Chester and Sarah Olivia (Brooks) F.; m. Marie Elizabeth Grimes, Oct. 8, 1944 (dec. 1978); m. JoAnn McGowan Ellis, Dec. 15, 1980 BA with distinction, U. Miss., 1938, MA, 1939; PhD in History, Vanderbilt U., 1950. Spl. cons. U.S. War Dept., Washington, 1946; historian USAF Hist. Office, Washington, 1946-49; assoc. prof. mil. history Air U., Maxwell AFB, Ala., 1950-51, prof., 1951-71, sr. historian, 1971-74, prof. emeritus mil. history, from 1974. Professorial lectr. George Washington U., 1963-68; guest lectr. Air U. Squadron Officer Sch., Air Command and Staff Coll., Air War Coll., Air Force Acad., Army War Coll., Militärgeschichtliches Forschungsamt, German Fed. Republic, 1951—, Sch. Advanced Airpower Studies; participant Air Force Acad. Mil. History Symposia, 1968—, Militärgeschictliches Forschungsamt, Freiburg, German Fed. Republic, 1988; vis. prof. mil. history Airpower Rsch. Inst., Ctr. for Aerospace Doctrine Rsch. and Edn., Air U., 1982-85, hist. advisor to USAF project Corona Harvest, 1969-74; cons. East Aviation Svcs. & Tech., Inc., Chantilly, Va.; hist. advisor Lafayette Mus. Found., Air Force Acad., 1990. Author: Ideas, Concepts, Doctrine: A History of Basic Thinking in the United States Air Force, 1907-1964, 1971, rev. edit., 1907-84, 2 vols., 1989, The United States Air Force in Korea, 1950-1953, 1961, rev. edit., 1983, The United States Air Force in Southeast Asia: The Advisory Years to 1965, 1981, (with Wesley Frank Craven, James L. Cate) The Army Air Force in World War II, 1948-1958; contbr. chpts. to hist. books, articles to scholarly publs. Served to capt. USAAF, 1941-45, lt. col. USAF Res., ret. Recipient Meritorious Civilian Svc. award USAF, 1970, Exceptional Civilian Svc. decoration Sec. of USAF, 1973. Mem. Ala. Hist. Assn., The Ret. Officers Assn., SAR (pres. Montgomery County chpt. 1971-74), So. Hist. Assn., Air Force Hist. Found. (mem. editorial advisors 1969-81, trustee 1985—), Inst. Mil. Affairs, Montgomery Capital City Club, Kiwanis Club of Montgomery, Phi Eta Sigma, Pi Kappa Pi. Methodist. Died Mar. 17, 1999.

**GABEL, RICHARD H.,** manufacturing executive; b. Phila., May 7, 1911; s. Samuel Landis Gabel and Edna Virgilia Bowman; m. Mary Virginia Derr, July 20, 1940 (dec. Jan. 1985); children: Caroline D., H. Landis, Eloise Gabel Smyrl, Marianne. BS MechE (valedictorian), U. Pa., 1932, MechE, 1946. V.p. Pacific Tube Co., Los Angeles, 1942; sec. Johnson & Hoffman Mfg. Corp., Carle Place, N.Y., 1952; v.p. Superior Tube Co., Norristown, Pa., 1934-67, exec. v.p., 1967-82, pres., from 1982, also bd. dirs. Mem. adv. com. Norristown Area Office, Phil. Nat. Bank, 1954-76; mem. adv. com. metallurgy and material scis., U. Pa., 1958-64, dir. engr. alumni soc., 1940-42; mem. adv. com. fabricated metals study, Southeastern Pa. Econ. Devel. Corp.; chmn. mfg. and ops. com. Welded Steel Tube Inst., Cleve., 1972-73. Several patents in field. Mem. adv. com. Montgomery County Emergency Disaster Council, 1950-69; bd. dirs., mem. exec. com. Inter-County Hospitalization Plan, 1975-85; bd. dirs., mem. distbn. com. Cen. Montgomery County Found., Norristown, 1975—; chmn. bd. Montgomery Hosp., Norristown, 1980-81, pres., 1982-83, chmn bd., 1982—; chmn. bd. trustees Cen. Presbyn. Ch., Norristown, 1952-55, chmn. bldg. com.; bd. dirs. Montgomery Nat. Bank, Norristown, Pa., 1951-54, Inter-County Hospitalization Plan, Horsham, Pa., 1974-85. Named to Gallery of Disting. Engring. Alumni, U. Pa., 1976, Norristown Area High Sch. Hall of Fame, 1987. Mem. Am. Tube Assn. (bd. dirs. 1980—), Am. Soc. Metals (fin. com.), Sigma Tau. Clubs: Union League, Mask and Wig (Phila.); Bay Head (N.J.) Yacht; Merion Golf (Ardmore, Pa.). Home: Gladwyne, Pa. Died Jan. 22, 1990.

**GABLE, JAMES G.,** retired engineering executive; b. Phila., Mar. 26, 1918; s. James F. and Stella (Gingrich) Gable; m. Ruth Ann Goetz, Oct. 14, 1940 (dec. 1977); children: Suzanne R. Tognazzini, Mary C. Price, James E. BSEE, Carnegie-Mellon U., 1940. Registered profl. engr. Calif. design engring. mgr. Westinghouse Electric Corp., Buffalo, 1951—54, divsn. gen. mgr., 1954—62; orgn. devel. mgr. Lockheed Missiles & Space Co., Sunnyvale, Calif., 1962—70; pvt. cons., 1970—74; v.p. Micro Power Sys., Inc., Santa Clara, Calif., 1974—85; ret., 1985. Chmn. Town Long Range Fiscal Planning Commn.; engr. mem. Town Drainage Com., Los Altos Hills, Calif. Served to 1st lt. US Army, 1943—45, ETO. Mem.: Calif. Soc. Profl. Engrs., Nat. Soc. Profl. Engrs., Jesters, Shriners, KT (past comdr.), Masons (32 degree). Achievements include patents in field. Home: Sunnyvale, Calif. Died Mar. 12, 1991.

**GADAMER, HANS GEORG,** philosopher, educator; b. Marburg, Germany, Feb. 11, 1900; 2 children. PhD in Philosophy, U. Marburg, Germany, 1922, habilitation, 1929; PhD honorus causa, U. Bamberg, Germany, Boston U., McMaster U., Ottawa, Can., U. Tübingen, Germany, U. Prahce, Czeschien, U. Tuipsig, Germany, U. Wroclaw, Poland. Cert. tchr., Germany. Lectr. in philosophy U. Marburg, 1929-33, asst. prof. philosophy, 1933-37, assoc. prof. philosophy, 1937-39, prof. philosophy, 1939, U. Leipzig, Germany, 1939, dean philosophy faculty, 1945-46, chancellor, 1946-47; endowed chair philosophy U. Frankfurt, Germany, 1947-49, U. Heidelberg, Germany, 1949-68, emeritus prof. philosophy, from 1968. Pres. Heidelberg Acad., 1968-72. Author: Wahrheit und Methode, 1960, Platos dialektische Ethik, 1968, Zur Begriffswelt der Vorsokratiker, 1968, Werner Scholz, 1968, Hegels Dialektik. Füfn hermeneutische Studien, 1971, Wer bin ich und wer bist du? Kommentar zu Paul Celans' Atemkristall, 1973, Wahrheit und Methode. Grundzüge einer philosophischen Hermeneutik, 1975, Vernunft im Zeitalter der Wissenschaft, 1976, Philosophische Lehrjahre, 1977, Poetica. Ausgewählte Essays, 1977, Die Aktualität des Schönen. Kunst als Spiel, Symbol und Fest, 1977, Beitrag in Philosophie in Selbstdarstellungen, 1977, Die Idee des Guten, 1978, Kleine Schriften, I-IV, 1967-77, Heideggers Wege, 1983, Lob der Theorie, 1983, Das Erbe Europas, 1989, Gedicht und Gespräch, 1990, Über die Verbogenheit der Gesundheit, 1993; editor Neuen Anthropologie, Bd. 1-3, 1972, 4 and 45, 1973, 6 and 7, 1975, Fortigshellung der Gesamnelten Werke in 10 Bänden, 1995; editor, founder Philosophischen Rundschau. Pres. German Philos. Soc., 1962, Internat. Union for Advancement of Study of Hegelian Philosophy, 1963; dir. Cusanus Commn., Heidelberg, 1951-77. Decorated Fed. Svc. Cross with Star, German Dem. Republic, 1972, Shoulder Sash, 1990, Cross of Order of Merit, 1993; recipient Reuchlin prize City of Pforzheim, 1971, Order of Merit, 1971, Hegel prize City of Stuttgart, 1979, Martin-Schleyer prize, 1987; named Hon. citizen City of Naples, 1990. Mem. Acad. Scis. Leipzig, Acad. Scis. Heidelberg, Acad. Scis. Athens, Acad. Scis. Budapest, Acad. Scis. Brussels, Acad. Scis. Rome, Acad. Scis. Turin, Acad. Scis. London, German Acad. for Lang. and Poetry, Am. Acad. Arts and Scis. (hon.). Home: Heidelberg, Germany. Died Mar. 14, 2002.

**GADIENT, WALTER G.,** financial executive; b. New Albany, Ind., June 2, 1923; s. Walter A. and Elsa M. (Goodbub) Gadient; m. Emilie L. Richards, Oct. 23, 1949; 1 child, James. BS, Ind. U., 1946, MBA, 1947. 2d v.p. Lincoln Nat. Life Ins. Co., 1947—60; v.p. Robert F. Maine Co., 1960—65; 1st v.p. Dean Witter & Co., Inc., 1965—70; exec. v.p. Lincoln Nat. Corp., Chgo., 1970—83; pres., dir. Lincoln Nat. Direct Placement Fund, from 1972. Bd. dirs. Lincoln Nat. Convertible Securities Fund, Efficient Health Sys. Inc.; adv. bd. Frontenac Venture Group. Trustee Roosevelt U., Chgo., from 1973. With AUS, 1943—46. Mem.: Investment Analysts Soc. Chgo., Bond Club Chgo., Chgo. Club. Died Feb. 1992.

**GAGLIARDI, LEE PARSONS,** federal judge; b. Larchmont, NY, July 17, 1918; s. Frank M. and Mary F. (DeCicco) G.; m. Marian Hope Selden, Aug. 5, 1943; children: Elizabeth G. (Mrs. Charles J. Tobin III) Marian S. (dec.). Grad., Phillips Exeter Acad.; BA, Williams Coll., 1941; JD, Columbia U., 1947. Bar: N.Y. 1948. Asst. to gen. atty. N.Y. Central R.R. Co., NYC, 1948-55; partner Clark, Gagliardi, Gallagher & Smyth, NYC, 1955-72; judge U.S. Dist. Ct. (so. dist.) N.Y., from 1972, now sr. judge. Chmn. Bd. Police Commrs., Mamaroneck, N.Y., 1970-72; sec. Westchester County Caddie Scholarship Com., 1964-72; bd. govs. New Rochelle Hosp. Med. Ctr., N.Y., 1975-85; bd. dirs. Sherman Fairchild Found., Inc., 1979-93. Mem. Dorset (Vt.) Field Club, Wilderness Country Club (Naples, Fla.). Deceased.

**GALLAGHER, JAMES JOHN,** retired child development educator; b. Pitts., June 11, 1926; s. Martin and Anna Mae (Walsh) G.; m. Gertrude Cunningham, Sept. 10, 1949; children: Kevin, Sean, Shelagh, Brian. BA, U. Pitts., 1948, MS, 1949; PhD, Pa. State U., 1951. Chief psychologist Dayton Hosp. Children, Ohio, 1951-52; asst. prof. Mich. State Coll., East Lansing, 1952-54; from assoc. prof. to prof. Inst. Rsch. on Exceptional Children, Urbana, Ill., 1954-66; assoc. commr. edn. US Office Edn., Washington, 1967-69; asst. sec. US Dept. Health, Edn., & Welfare (HEW0, Washington, 1969-70; dir. U. NC Frank Porter Graham Child Devel. Ctr., Chapel Hill, NC, 1970-87, sr. scientist emeritus, 1987—2014. Vis. prof. Duke U., Durham, N.C., 1966-67; pres. World Coun. Gifted Children, 1982-86. Author: Teaching the Gifted Child, 1964, 4th edit., 1993; co-author: Educating Exceptional Children, 1986, 3d edit., 1993. Served in USN, 1943-45. Recipient Wallin Award Coun. Gifted Children, Washington, 1966, Old North State award Gov. of NC, 2013; named Contbr. to Edn., Assn. Children with Learning Disabilities, Washington, 1972. Mem. Nat. Assn. Gifted Children (disting. scholar 1988, pres. elect. 1992). Avocations: golf, tennis, chess. Home: Chapel Hill, NC. Died Jan. 17, 2014.

**GALLAGHER, RORY,** musician, vocalist, composer; b. Ballyshannon, County Donegal, Ireland, Mar. 2, 1948; Guitarist, vocalist Taste band, 1969-72, Rory Gallagher Band, from 1972. Solo albums include Deuce, 1971, Blueprint, 1973, In the Beginning, 1974, Against the Grain, 1975, Calling Card, 1976, Photo Finish, 1978, Top Priority, 1979, Jinx, 1982, (with Taste) Taste, 1969, On the Boards, 1970. Died June 14, 1995.

**GALLANT, MAVIS,** author; b. Montreal, Que., Can., Aug. 11, 1922; Doctoral (hon.), U. St. Anne, NS, Can., 1984, York U., Toronto, 1984, U. Western Ont., 1990, Queen's U., 1992, U. Montreal, 1995, Bishop's U., 1995. Writer-in-residence U. Toronto, 1983-84 Author: Green Water, Green Sky, 1959, 60, A Fairly Good Time, 1970; short stories The Other Paris, My Heart Is Broken: 8 Stories and a Short Novel (Brit. title An Unmarried Man's Summer), 1964, The Affair of Gabrielle Russier; introductory essay, 1971; The

Pegnitz Junction, a Novella and Five Short Stories, 1973, The End of the World and Other Stories, 1974; short stories From the Fifteenth District, 1979, Home Truths, 1981, Overhead in a Balloon, 1985; play What Is To Be Done? (produced Toronto 1982), 1984, Paris Notebooks: Essays and Reviews, 1986, (short stories) In Transit, 1989, (short stories) Across the Bridge, 1993; The Moslem Wife and other stories, 1994, Collected Stories, 1996, Paris Stories, 2002, Varieties of Exile, 2003, Montreal Stories, 2004, The Cost of Living: Early and Uncollected STories, 2009; contbr. to New Yorker, 1951-2014 Decorated Order of Can.; recipient Gov.-General's Lit. award, 1982, Molson award, 1997, Medaille de la Ville de Paris, 1999, Penn/Nabokov award, 2004 Fellow Royal Soc. Lit.; fgn. hon. mem. American Acad. & Inst. Arts & Letters. Home: Paris, France. Died Feb. 18, 2014.

**GALLMAN, MARIA DE NORONHA,** artist, retired art educator; b. Cascais, Portugal, Sept. 17, 1922; arrived in US, 1949; d. Manuel Jose and Maria de Noronha Madruga; m. David C. Gallman, Jan. 6, 1973. BA in Art and Design, Hunter Coll., 1953; M, Montclair Coll., 1957; student, Ctr. for Arts and Artists, Paris. Cert. iconographer St. Augustine Art Assn., 1995. Instrnl. chmn. Lyndhurst H.S., Paterson, NJ, 1958—60; instr. art Oglethorpe U., Atlanta, 1964—67; asst. prof. art Atlanta U., 1968—71, lectr. grad. sch., 1968—71; lectr. Alice Lloyd Coll., 1972. Lectr., art judge Internat. Platform Assn., 1968—72; chmn. arts and culture Ptnrs. of Ams., Ga. and Pernambuco, Brazil, 1978—87; advisor St. Augustine (Fla.) Art Assn., 1987—95. Represented in permanent collections Met. Gallery, Recife, Brazil, Oglethorpe U., Atlanta, pvt. gallery, St. Augustine, exhibitions include Met. Mus. Art, NYC, Fla. So. Coll., Seton Hall U., NJ, Fordham U., NYC, Columbia U., Nat. Arts Gallery. Past pres. Altrusa Club, Atlanta. Recipient S.E. Art Exhbn. award for Seas, 1965; named Painter of Yr., Grumbacher Gallery, NYC, 1962; grantee, Oglethorpe U., Atlanta. Fellow: Royal Arts Soc. London (life); mem.: Kappa Pi (hon.; life), Nat. Soc. Arts and Letters (life; NY chpt.). Methodist. Deceased.

**GALVÃO, ROBERTO DIÉGUEZ,** engineering educator, consultant; b. Recife, Brazil, Feb. 26, 1943; s. José Galvão and Edith Diéguez Gal. BSc in Mech. and Indsl. Engring., Cath. U. Rio de Janeiro, 1965; MSc in Indsl. Engring., U. Ala., Tuscaloosa, 1967; PhD in Mgmt. Sci., Imperial Coll. London, 1977. Trainee GE, Rio de Janeiro, 1964—65; plants and terminals asst. mgr. Esso Brazil, Rio de Janeiro, 1968—70, operation rsch. sect. head, 1970—73; full prof. Fed. U. Rio de Janeiro, from 1977. Cons. Ministry Sci. and Tech., Brasília, Brazil, from 1992, Ministry Edn., Brasília, Brazil, from 2000; head postgrad. dept. indsl. engring. Fed. U. Rio de Janeiro, 1980—82. Contbr. articles to profl. jours. Recipient Intellectual Achievements award, Fed. U. Rio de Janeiro, 2004; grantee, NRC, from 2000; scholar, Fulbright Commn., 1966—67, Capes Ministry Edn., 1973—77. Mem.: Fedn. Ops. Rsch. Soc. (v.p. L.Am. 1990—92), L.Am. Ops. Rsch. Soc. (pres. 1982—84), Brazilian Operational Rsch. Soc. (Outstanding Contbn. award, Sci. Contbns. award 2003), Brazilian Ops. Rsch. Soc. (pres. 1979—82). Roman Catholic. Avocations: chess, photography, reading, classical music. Home: Rio de Janeiro, Brazil. Died 2010.

**GAMBLE, ALVAN (GEORGE ALVAN GAMBLE),** retired marketing consultant, former Canadian government official; b. Guelph, Ont., Can., Jan. 10, 1916; s. Hugh Miskelly and Margaret (Quarrell) G.; m. Jean Christeen Melrose, Aug. 3, 1940; children: Stephen John, Timothy Clifford (dec.), Lois Rebekah. Mgr., cons., co./union negotiations conciliator, Toronto, Ont., 1945-52; dir. merit employment project Am. Friends Svc. Com., Indpls., 1952-55; exec. asst. to gen. dir., dir. info. Can. Mental Health Assn., Toronto, 1955-62; dir. health svcs. Smith Kline & French (Can.), 1962-68; mktg. analyst Paul Maney Labs. (Can.) Ltd., Toronto, 1968-71; chief market rsch. and immigration fgn. svc. info. adviser Govt. of Can. Employment and Immigration Commn., Ottawa, Ont., 1971-81, cons. mktg. and pub. rels., 1981-90, ret., 1990. Mem. Markham Twp. (Ont.) Planning Bd., 1959; provincial health minister's rep. Bd. of Health Regional Municipality of York, 1965-71; bd. dirs. Union Villa Sr. Citizens Residence, Markham, 1965-71; vol. feature writer columnist Can. evang. chs. periodicals. Served with RCAF, 1940-45. Decorated Order of Can.; recipient Silver Jubilee medal, 1977, Assoc. Ch. Press award Atlantic Bapt., Canadian Ch. Press awards (2). Fellow Am. Pub. Health Assn.; mem. Profl. Mktg. Rsch. Soc. (life). Clubs: Nat. Press (Ottawa). Baptist. Home: Ottawa, Canada. Died Aug. 12, 2002.

**GAMBLE, HARRY T.,** retired professional sports team executive, former college football coach; b. Pitman, NJ, Dec. 26, 1930; m. Joan Gamble; children: Harry Jr., Tom. BA, Rider Coll., 1952; MS, Temple U., PhD in Bus. Edn. Head coach Audobon High Sch., Clayton High Sch., Lafayette Coll. Leopards, Pa., 1967—70, U. Pa. Quakers, Phila., 1971—80; vol. asst. coach Phila. Eagles, 1981, spl. teams/tight ends coach, 1982, coach/personnel asst., 1983, dir. football ops., 1984, gen. mgr., 1985, pres., gen. mgr., 1985—94, gen. mgr., 1995. Recipient Bert Bell Man of the Yr. award, Bakers Club of Phila.; named South Jersey Coach of Yr., Brooks-Irvine Meml. Football Club, 1960, Man of Yr., Archdiocese of Phila. Catholic Youth Org., 1994; named to The Gloucester County Sports Hall of Fame, 1985, The South Jersey Coaches Hall of Fame, 1985. Died Jan. 28, 2014.

**GAMBLE, JARVIS L.,** lawyer; b. June 21, 1917; s. Garriott L. and Emma E. (Collins) Gamble; m. June L. Newman, June 8, 1940; children: Charles, James. LLB, Ind. U., 1938. Bar: Ind. 1938, N.Y. 1970, U.S. Dist. Ct. (no. dist.) Ind. 1938, U.S. Dist. Ct. (no. dist.) N.Y. 1976. Ins. adjuster to regional claims mgr. Employers Liability Assurance Corp., South Bend, Ind., 1937—58, Cleve., 1937—58; claims supr. to corp. sec. Agrl. Ins. Co., Watertown, NY, 1958—76; ptnr. Larmonth, Ratcliff & Gamble, Watertown, 1976—92. Served with F.A. USAR, 1943—46, 1st lt. JAGC USAR, 1950—52. Republican. Methodist. Died June 2, 1992.

**GANEV, STOYAN,** former Bulgarian government official, educator; b. Pazardjik, Bulgaria, July 23, 1955; m. Marina Ganev, 1 daughter, Maria. Grad. with honors, Sch. of Math.; grad. law sch., Kliment Ohridsky U., Sofia; PhD in Constl. Law, Moscow U., 1985. Former tchr. constl. law Kliment Ohridsky U., Sofia; chmn. United Dem. Ctr. of Union of Dem. Forces, co-chmn. parliamentary group; elected mem. 7th Grand Nat. Assembly, 1990; elected to parliament, 1991; dep. chmn. coun. of ministers Govt. of Bulgaria, 1991-92, min. fgn. affairs, 1991-93; pres. 47th session of Gen. Assembly UN, 1992. Chmn. United Christian Democratic Ctr.(formerly United Democratic Ctr), 1992—; adj. prof. NYU. Regent Cathedial of St. John. the Divine, N.Y., 1993—. Recipient United Nations Peace medal, 1992. Home: Greenwich, Conn. Died July 2, 2013.

**GANGWARE, EDGAR BRAND, JR.,** retired music educator; b. Sandusky, Ohio, May 17, 1922; s. Edgar B. and Wilhelmina (Schoeneman) G.; m. Dorcas Euana Biniores, Sept. 3, 1949 (dec. 1991); children: E. Brand III, Frank Roy, Robert William. BS in Edn./Mus. Supervision, Wittenberg U., 1943, BMus in Piano, 1947; MMus in Composition, Northwestern U., 1948, PhD in Music Theory, 1959. Asst. band dir. Wittenberg U., Springfield, Ohio, 1940-43; dir. bands St. Paris (Ohio) High Sch., 1942-43; instr. piano Wittenberg U., 1946-47; asst. band dir. Northwestern U., Evanston, Ill., 1947-49; dir. instrumental music Bemidji (Minn.) State U., 1952-66, dir. summer music clinic, 1952-66; dir. instrumental music Northeastern Ill. U., Chgo., 1966-91; pres. G&M Internat. Music Dealers, Northbrook, Ill., from 1984. Adjudicator-clinician, 1952-92; cons. educator Dept. of Music, State of Ill., 1966-85, North Ctrl. Accrediting Agy., 1966-86; founder, dir. Northeastern Ill. U. Alumni and Friends Band, 1978-94. Editor-in-chief Sch. Musician Dir. Tchr. Mag., Chgo., 1979-88; composer Concerto Miniature for Timpani, 1948, others. Mem. Original Youth Coun. in Northbrook, 1968-70; pres. Civic Music Assn., Bemidji, 1965-66. 1st lt. U.S. Army, 1942-46. Named to Hall of Fame for Ill. Band Dirs., Phi Beta Mu, Northwestern U., 1992. Mem. Am. Bandmasters Assn. (pres. 1985-86), In-and-About Chgo. Music Educators Club (pres. 1987-88), Music Educators Nat. Conf., Coll. Band Dirs. Nat. Assn., Nat. Band Assn. (AWAPA award 1992), Ill. Music Educators Assn., Northeastern Ill. U. Alumni Assn. (Outstanding Contbn. 1978), Phi Beta Mu. Methodist. Avocations: travel, swimming. Home: Riverside, Ill. Deceased.

**GANT, HORACE ZED,** lawyer; b. Van Buren, Ark., Apr. 1, 1914; s. George Washington and Ida Elizabeth (Stephenson) Gant; m. Edith Imogene Farabough, Oct. 10, 1937; children: Alice Margaret, Linda Beth, Zed George, Paul David. LLB, U. Ark., 1936, JD, 1969. Bar: Ark. 1936, US Dist. Ct. (we. dist.) 1937, US Supreme Ct. 1943. Asst. pros. atty., Van Buren, 1936—41; pvt. practice, 1941—43; atty. War Relocation Authority, Washington, 1943, US Dept. Interior, Washington, 1947, field atty. Little Rock, Va., 1947—73; chancery judge Ark. 15th Jud. Dist., Van Buren, 1973—75; ptnr. Gant & Gant, Van Buren, from 1975. Bd. dirs. Harbor House and Gateway House, Ft. Smith, Ark., 1974—84; chmn. Western Ark. Adv. Coun., Ft. Smith, 1976—81; chancery ct. master Ark. 12th Jud. Dist., Ft. Smith, 1976—91; chmn. bd. dirs. Western Ark. Legal Svcs., Ft. Smith, 1991, pres. bd. dirs., 1991—92. Pres. Mental Health Assn., Ft. Smith, 1978; chmn. Boggan Edn. Scholarship Trust Fund; deacon 1st Baptist Ch., Van Buren; trustee Boggan Edn. Scholarship Trust Fund. Lt. comdr. USN, 1943—46. Mem.: Ark. Bar Assn., Masons (master 1942—43). Democrat. Home: Van Buren, Ark. Deceased.

**GAON, BENJAMIN D.,** retired manufacturing executive; b. Jerusalem, Feb. 11, 1935; m. Rachel Gaon; children: Moshe, Boav, Yoav, Michal. Mgr. Koortrade Europe, Amsterdam, 1978-82; pres., CEO Co-Op, 1982-88; CEO Koor Industries Ltd., Tel Aviv, 1988—98; founder B. Gaon Holdings, 1998—2008. Chmn. Tadiran, Mashav, Shemen, Koortrade and Koor Tourist Enterprises; bd. dirs. Makhteshim, Agan, Elrov, Lanoptics, Bateman Engring.; cofounder Palestine Internat. Bus. Forum, 1995-2008 Bd. trustees Hebrew U., Israeli Cancer Inst., Indsl. Edn. Bd.; mem. Rabin-Peres Nobel Prize Com., Alliance Capital Middle East Fund. Recipeint Romanisiano award Tel Aviv U., Internat. Partnership award Calif. Israel C. of C. Mem. Industrialists Assn. (pres., Pres.'s award 1995). Died May 10, 2008.

**GARCÍA MÁRQUEZ, GABRIEL (GABRIEL JOSÉ DE LA CONCORDIA GARCÍA MÁRQUEZ),** writer; b. Aracataca, Magdalena, Colombia, Mar. 6, 1928; s. Gabriel Eligio García and Luisa Santiaga Márquez; m. Mercedes Barcha, 1958; children: Rodrigo, Gonzalo. Attended, U. Bogotá; LLD (hon.), Colombia U., 1971. Journalist, corr. El Universal, Cartagena, Colombia, El Espectador, Rome, Paris, El Heraldo, Barranquilla, Colombia. Founder, former exec. dir. Film Inst., Havana, Cuba. Author: (novels/short stories in English translation) Leaf Storm, and Other Stories, 1955, No One Writes to the Colonel, 1961, In Evil Hour, 1961 (Esso Lit. prize, Colombia, 1961), One Hundred Years of Solitude, 1967 (Chianciano award, Italy, 1969, Prix de Meilleur Livre, France, 1969, Romulo Gallegos prize, Venezuela, 1972, Books Abroad/ Neustadt Internat. prize for lit., 1972), Innocent Eréndira, and Other Storis, 1972, The Autumn of the Patriarch, 1975, Chronicle of a Death Foretold, 1981, Collected Stories, 1984, Love in the Time of Cholera, 1988 (LA Time Book Prize for fiction, 1988), Collected Novellas, 1990, The General in his Labyrinth, 1990, Strange Pilgrims, 1994, Love and Other Demons, 1994, Memories of My Melancholy Whores, 2004 (LA Times Book prize, 2006), (nonfiction) The Story of a Shipwrecked Sailor, 1970, Clandestine in Chile: The Adventures of Miguel Littín, 1986, News of a Kidnapping, 1996, For the Sake of a Country within Reach of the Children, 1998, Living to Tell the Tale, 2002, numerous other works pub. in Spanish. Co-founder Ibero-Am. New Journalism Found., 1994; founder, pres. Fundación Habeas; former dir. L.Am. Film Found.; founder Cuban Press Agy. Recipient Colombian Assn. Writers & Artists award, 1954, Nobel Prize for Literature, Swedish Acad., 1982, Serfin prize, 1989, Prince of Asturias Found. award, 1999. Fellow: AAAL (hon.). Home: Mexico City, Mexico. Died Apr. 17, 2014.

**GARDINER, WILLIAM CECIL, JR.,** chemistry professor; b. Niagara Falls, NY, Jan. 14, 1933; s. William Cecil and Annie Charlotte (Hicks) G.; children— Grace, Charlotte, Amy Louise; m. Regina R. Monaco, July 15, 1991. AB, Princeton U., 1954; postgrad., U. Heidelberg, 1954-55, U. Göttingen, 1955-56; PhD, Harvard U., 1960. Instr. chemistry U. Tex., Austin, 1960-62, asst. prof., 1962-66, assoc. prof., 1966-72, prof., 1972—2000. Cons. on chemistry of combustion reactions to govtl. agencies. Contbr. articles on rates of chem. reactions to tech. jours. Fulbright fellow, 1954-55, 75-76; Guggenheim fellow, 1975-76; Humboldt fellow, 1979, 82; Thyssen fellow, 1983; Lady Davis prof., 1985. Fellow Japan Soc. for Promotion Sci; mem. Am. Chem. Soc., Am. Phys. Soc., AAAS, Combustion Inst., Phi Beta Kappa, Sigma Xi. Died Nov. 17, 2000.

**GARDNER, DALE ALLAN,** retired astronaut; b. Fairmont, Minn., Nov. 8, 1948; s. William Rex and Alic Bertha (Boehne) G.; m. Sue Grace Ticusan, Feb. 19, 1977 (div. 1992); children: Lisa Amanda, Todd Allan. BS in Engring. Physics, U. Ill., 1970. Commd. naval flight officer U.S. Navy, 1970, advanced through grades to comdr., 1984; naval flight officer Pensacola, Fla., 1970-71, Patuxent River, Md., 1971-73, Miramar, Calif., 1973-76, Point Mugu, Calif., 1976-78; astronaut NASA, Houston, from 1978; support crew astronaut for STS-4, 1982; mission specialist on STS-8, launched from Kennedy Space Ctr., Fla., Aug. 30, 1983, 3d flight for Orbiter Challenger, Aug. 30, 1983, completed 98 orbits of Earth in 145 hours, Aug. 30, 1983; mission specialist for Space Shuttle mission launch, Oct. 1984; dep. chief space control ops. divsn. US Space Command, Colo. Springs, 1986—88, dep. dir. for space control Peterson AFB, 1989—90; with TRW, Inc., Colo. Springs, Colo., 1990—2003; mgr. applied rsch & renewable activities Nat. Renewable Energy Laboratory, 2003—13. Decorated Merit Unit Commendation, 1976, Def. Superior Svc. medal, 1984, 1989, 1990, Disting. Flying Cross, 1989; recipient Humanitarian Svc. medal, 1979, Sea Svc. Deployment Ribbon, Space Flight medal NASA, 1983, Lloyd's of London Meritorious Svc. medal, 1984 Mem. Phi Eta Sigma, Tau Beta Pi, Sigma Tau Republican. Episcopalian. Died Feb. 19, 2014.

**GARDOM, GARDE BASIL,** former lieutenant governor of British Columbia; b. Banff, Alta., Can., July 17, 1924; s. Basil and Gabrielle Gwladys (Bell) G.; m. Theresa Helen Eileen Mackenzie, Feb. 11, 1956; children: Kim Gardom Allen, Karen Gardom MacDonald, Edward, Brione Gardom, Brita Gardom McLaughlin. BA, LLB, U. BC, Vancouver, Can., 1949; LLD (hon.), U. B.C., 2003, U. Victoria, 2004. Called to bar 1949. With Campbell, Brazier & Co., 1949; sr. ptnr. Gardom & Co., Vancouver, 1960-75; apptd. Queen's Counsel, 1975; mem. BC Legis. Assembly for Vancouver-Point Grey, 1966-87; atty. gen. BC, 1975-79; min. intergovtl. rels., 1979-86; policy cons. Office of Premier, 1986-87; agt. gen. BC, 1987-92, Europe; mem. Premier's Econ. Adv. Coun., 1988-91; lt.-gov. BC, 1995—2001; dir. Brouwer Claims Can., 2002—11. Dir. Justitute Inst. BC. Hon. dir. Boys and Girls Club Vancouver; hon. chmn. Bibl. Mus. Can.; hon. patron Pacific Alzheimer Rsch. Found.; former mem. adv. coun. BC Cmty. Achievement awards. Decorated Order of BC; named to BC Sports Hall of Fame, 1995; named Freeman of City of London, 1992; hon. col. BC Regiment. Mem. Can. Bar Assn., BC Law Soc., Heraldry Soc. Can., Royal United Svcs. Inst. Vancouver, Govt. House Garden Soc., Brock House Soc., Royal Commonwealth Soc., Vancouver Lawn Tennis and Badminton Club (hon. life), Union Club BC, Can. Club Vancouver (life), Knight of Justice, Order St. John, Royal Overseas Club, Phi Delta Theta. Anglican. Home: Vancouver, Canada. Died June 18, 2013.

**GARNER, JAMES (JAMES SCOTT BUMGARNER),** actor; b. Norman, Okla., Apr. 7, 1928; m. Lois Clarke, Aug. 17, 1956; children: Kimberly, Gretta, Scott. Student, N.Y. Berghof Sch., U. Okla. Actor: (films) Sayonara, 1957, Shoot-out at Medicine Bend, 1957, Darby's Rangers, 1958, Up Periscope, 1959, Cash McCall, 1960, The Children's Hour, 1962, The Great Escape, 1963, The Americanization of Emily, 1964, 36 Hours, 1964, The Thrill of It All, Move Over Darling, The Art of Love, 1965, A Man Could Get Killed, 1966, Duel at Diablo, 1966, Mister Buddwing, 1966, Hour of the Gun, 1967, How Sweet It Is, 1968, Marlowe, 1969, Support Your Local Sheriff, 1971, Support Your Local Gunfighter, 1971, Skin Game, 1971, They Only Kill Their Masters, 1972, One Little Indian, 1973, HEALTH, 1979, The Fan, 1980, Victor/Victoria, 1982, Tank, 1984, Murphy's Romance, 1985, Sunset, 1987, Fire in the Sky, 1993, Maverick, 1994, My Fellow Americans, 1996, Twilight, 1998, Space Cowboys, 2000, Atlantis: The Last Empire (voice), 2001, Divine Secrets of the YaYa Sisterhood, 2002, The Notebook, 2004; actor, exec. prodr.: (films) Grand Prix, 1066; actor: (TV series) Maverick, 1957-60, Nichols, 1971-72, The Rockford Files (Emmy award for oustanding lead actor in a drama series, 1977), 1974-80, Man of the People, 1991-92, God, the Devil and Bob, 2000-01, First Monday, 2002, 8 Simple Rules...for Dating My Teenage Daughter,

2003-05; (TV mini-series) Space, 1985, Streets of Laredo, 1995, Century of Country, 1999; (TV movies) The Long Summer of George Adams, 1982, Heartsounds, 1984, Promise (also exec. prodr. Emmy for outstanding comedy/drama spl., 1987), 1986, My Name Is Bill W. (also exec. prodr.), 1989, Decoration Day, 1990 (Golden Globe Award for Best Performance by an Actor in a Mini-Series or Motion Picture Made for TV, 1991), Barbarians at the Gate, 1993 (Golden Globe Award for Best Performance by an Actor in a Mini-Series or Motion Picture Made for TV), Breathing Lessons, 1994, The Rockford Files: I Still Love LA, 1994, The Rockford Files: A Blessing in Disguise, 1995, The Rockford Files: Punishment and Crime, 1996, The Rockford Files: Friends and Foul Play, 1996, The Rockford Files: If the Frame Fits, 1996, The Rockford Files: Godfather Knows Best, 1996, Dead Silence, 1997, The Rockford Files: Murder and Misdemeanor, 1997, Legalese, 1998, The Rockford Files: If It Bleeds.It Leads, 1999, Shake, Rattle and Roll: An American Love Story, 1999, One Special Night, 1999, The Last Debate, 2000, Roughing It, 2002; (TV guest appearances) Chicago Hope (4 episodes), 2000; co-author: (with Jon Winokur): The Garner Files, 2011 Joined U.S. Mcht. Marine; served with U.S. Army, Korea. Decorated Purple Heart; recipient Clio award for Polaroid commls., 1978, SAG 41st Annual Lifetime Achievement award, 2005. Democrat. Died July 19, 2014.

**GASPAR, JUAN DE LOS REYES,** urban planner; b. Zamboanga City, The Philippines, Feb. 13, 1938; s. Jose Sumang and Josefina (de los Reyes) G.; m. Ofelia Ledesma, June 26, 1971; children: Francis, Joceline. BSc in Acctg., U. of the East, Manila, The Philippines, 1959; AB in Philosophy, St. Francis Xavier Sem., Davao, The Philippines, 1964; BSE in English, Ateneo de Zamboanga, The Philippines, 1968; MA in Urban and Regional Planning, U. of the Philippines, Quezon City, 1989; M. Ednl. Adminstrn., Western Mindaneo State U., Zamboanga City, 1979, M.P.A. in Program Devel., 1994. Faculty mem./instr. Notre Dame Sem., Cotabato City, The Philippines, 1964-65, Ateneo de Zamboanga, 1966-78; asst. prof. Western Mindanao State U., Zamboanga City, 1979-80; city planning and devel. coord. City Govt. of Zamboanga, from 1980. Pres. faculty Ateneo Zamboanya U. Grad. Sch., 1998-, Integrated Social Svcs. Found., Inc., Zamboanga City, 1987-90, 94-95; founder, pres. Citizens League for Good Govt. of Zomboanga City, 1970—; coord. youth Nat. Movement for Free Elections, Zamboanga City, 1986—. Recipient Cath. Action award Gold Medal of Merit, Cath. Action of The Philippines, 1970, Gold Medal for Campus Leadership, Arellano U., 1955. Mem. Nat. League of Local Planning and Devel. Coords. (pres. 1993-94), Asian Inst. Mgmt. Alumni Assn. of Western Mindanao State U. (treas. 1992—), Alumni Assn. of Ateneo de Zamboanga, Alumni Assn. Western Mindanao, Alumni Assn. of U. of the Philippines, Rotary (pres. 1997-98). Roman Catholic. Avocations: reading, writing, singing. Home: Zamboanga City, Philippines. Deceased.

**GAUCHER, DONALD HOLMAN,** public opinion research company executive; b. Port Arthur, Tex., Aug. 2, 1931; s. Leon Phillip and Hattie Lu (Holman) G.; m. Jane Peel Heyck, June 15, 1957; children: Susan Heyck, Beverly Jane. BA, The Rice Inst., Houston, 1953, BSChemE, 1954; grad., Sch. of Reactor Tech., Oak Ridge, Tenn., 1955; JD cum laude, U. Houston, 1962. With Humble Oil and Refining Co., Houston, 1957-64, Std. Oil (N.J.), NYC, 1964-68, Exxon Co. USA, Houston, 1968-91; pres. Gaucher Rsch. Assoc., Houston, from 1991. Mem. pub. opinion task force Am. Petroleum Inst., Washington, 1986-91, Chem. Mfrs. Assn., Washington, 1991-96; cons. Exxon Chem. Co., Houston, 1991-97, 2001. Pres. Mus. So. History, Sugar Land, Tex., 1997-99. Mem. Am. Nuc. Soc., Am. Inst. Mining, Metall. and Petroleum Engrs., Am. Assn. Pub. Opinion Rsch., Tex. Bar Assn., Kiwanis, Sons of Confederate Vets. (past comdr. Albert Sidney Johnston Camp), Mil. Order of Stars and Bars (past comdr.), Sons of the Republic of Tex., Terry's Tex. Rangers Assn., Knights of Momus, Galveston Artillery Club, Order of Barons, Phi Delta Phi. Avocations: tennis, bird photography, golf. Died June 15, 2002.

**GAUDAUR, JACOB GILL, JR.,** former professional sports team executive, retired professional football player; b. Orillia, Ont., Can., Oct. 5, 1920; s. Jacob Gill and Alice Grace (Hemming) G.; m. Isabel Grace Scott, Apr. 16, 1943; children: Jacqueline, Diane, Janice. Grad., Orillia, Collegiate Inst., 1940. Mem. Hamilton Tigers Football Team, Ont., 1940, 48-49; mem. Toronto Argonauts Football Team, Ont., 1941, Toronto Indians, 1945-46, capt., 1945-47; mem., co-capt. Montreal Alouettes, Que., Can., 1947; mem., capt. Hamilton Tiger-Cats Football Team, 1950-51, dir., 1952, mem. team, 1953, pres., gen. mgr., 1954-68; pres. Ea. Football Conf., Can. Football League, 1959, pres. league, 1962; commr. Can. Football League, 1968-84; pres., owner Gaudaur Motor Co., Burlington, Ont., 1956-62; pres. JayGil Ltd., Burlington and Toronto, 1963—2007. Chmn. bd. govs. Can. Sports Hall of Fame. Served with RCAF, 1942-45. Served in Royal Canadian Air Force, 1942—45. Decorated officer Order of Canada, 1985; recipient Queen's Golden Jubilee medal, 2002; named to Can. Football Hall of Fame, 1984, Toronto Argonauts Hall of Fame, 1984, Can. Sports Hall of Fame, 1990 Mem.: Albany (Toronto); Burlington (Ont.) Golf and Country, Variety Internat, Masons. Anglican. Can. Sr. One-Mile Rowing Champion, 1941. Home: Burlington, Canada. Died Dec. 4, 2007.

**GAUVENET, ANDRÉ JEAN,** engineering educator; b. Nuits-St.-Georges, Côte d'Or, France, Mar. 31, 1920; s. Emile Félix and Louise Adrienne (Tixier) G.; m. Hélene Frédérique Gras-Gauvenet, May 15, 1948; children: Christian, Françoise, Anne. Cert., Ecole Normale Supérieure, Saint-Cloud, 1942; Diplôme d'Etudes Supérieures, U. Sorbonne, Paris, 1944. Prof. Coll. Turgot, Paris, 1942-43; engr. Lab. Cen. d'Electricité, Paris, 1943-45; researcher Soc. Alsacienne Constrns. Mech., Paris, 1945-48; prof. Ecole Normale Supérieure, Saint-Cloud, 1948-54; sci. attache French Embassy, NYC, 1954-56; engr. nuclear safety and radiation protection Commissariat ã l'Energie Atomique, Paris, 1956-82; inspector gen. nuclear safety and security Electricité France, Paris, 1982-85; prof. safety engr. Ecole Nationale Superieure des Techniques Avancées, Paris, 1988-95, Ecole Poly. Féminine, Sceaux, 1990-95. Author: (with others) Space Techniques, 1965, Images de la science, 1984, The Atomic Adventure, 1993; contbr. articles to profl. jours. Decorated Légion d'honneur French govt., 1972, Mérite Commandeur, Palm Academiques. Fellow Am. Nuclear Soc.; mem. Soc. Française Nucléaire, Am. Phys. Soc., European Phys. Soc., Soc. Française Physique, Cercle d'Union Interalliée, N.Y. Acad. Scis. Home: Paris, France. Died Feb. 21, 2002.

**GAVA, ANTONIO,** former Italian government official; b. Castellamare di Stabia, Italy, July 30, 1930; Chair Union Provinices Italy, 1968, provincial sec. Naples, 1969; chair 1st Regional Assn. Campania, Christian Dem. Group, Campania; M.P. Govt. of Italy, Rome, 1972—90, min. posts & telecommunications, 1986—88, min. interior, 1988—90. Died Aug. 8, 2008.

**GAY, PAUL EDWARD,** real estate company executive; b. Charleston, W.Va., July 18, 1938; s. Nathan Ray and Nadia (Young) Gay. At, U. So. Calif., 1961. V.p. L. B. Kaye Assoc., Ltd., NYC, 1967—70, William B. May Co., Inc., 1970—71; pres. Paul Gay & Co., Inc., 1971—77; pres. and chmn. James N. Wells' Sons, Inc., from 1977. Pres. Twenty-Third St. Assn., NYC, 1979—81, chmn., 1981—83; mem. planning task force William Sloan House YMCA, 1985—86; mem. Chelsea Planning and Preservation Com. of Community Bd. 4, from 1984; bd. deacons First Presbyn. Ch., 1969—72; mem. Housing Task Force Presbytery of N.Y., 1970—73; founder and trustee Chelsea Cmty. Ch., from 1975; bd. dir. McBurney YMCA, 1978—84; property mgmt. com. bd. dir. YMCA of Greater N.Y., from 1979; bd. dir. Washington Sq. Music Festival; trustee Hudson Guild, 1981—84. Mem.: Nat. Assn. Realtors, N.Y. State Assn. Realtors, Young Men's Real Estate Assn. N.Y., Real Estate Bd. N.Y.C., South Street Seaport Mus., Hundred Yr. Assn., N.Y. Landmarks Conservancy, Mcpl. Art Soc. N.Y.C., Cooper-Hewitt Mus., N.Y. Archival Soc., W.Va. Soc. of N.Y., Nat. Arts Club, Phi Mu Alpha Sinfonia, Chi Psi. Republican. Home: New York, NY. Died Apr. 8, 1987.

**GAYMON, WILLIAM EDWARD,** psychology educator; b. Bryn Mawr, Pa., Nov. 11, 1929; s. Frederick and Victoria (Brown) G.; m. Estelle Smith (dec. 1985); children: William Victor, Nicole Gabrielle; m. Violeta Nedkova, Aug. 6, 1988. BS in Psychology, Howard U., 1951, MS in Psychology, 1956; PhD in Psychology, Temple U., 1964. Dir. Peace Corps, Liberia, 1967-69, Niger, 1969-71; assoc. dir. Office of Naval Rsch., Arlington, Va., 1971-74; sr. rsch. fellow Am. Insts. for Rsch., Washington, 1974-77; sr. rsch. assoc. Richard A. Gibboney Assocs. Inc., Washington, 1977; dir. Africa Region U.S. Peace Corps, Washington, 1977-79; dep. chief UN Sudano Sahelian Regional Office, Ouagadougou, 1979-84; dep. resident rep. UN Devel. Programme, Cotonou, Benin, 1984-88; resident rep., resident coord. operational activities UN System, Sao Tome & Principe, 1988-89; rsch. prof. of Internat. Affairs, dir. Ctr. Pub. Policy & Diplomacy Lincoln University (Pa.), from 1990. Mem. adv. bd. Fgn. Policy Assn., N.Y.C., 1991—. Contbr. articles to profl. jours. 1st lt. USAF, 1953-55. Mem. APA. Home: Gambrills, Md. Died June 3, 1997.

**GAYNER, ESTHER K.,** artist; b. Trenton, NJ, Feb. 3, 1914; d. Leon and Ida Gootl (Morris) Kasman; m. Irving C. Gayner, Mar. 17, 1946; children: Stephen Hersh, Jay David. Student, Trenton Sch. for Indsl. Arts, 1929-31; BS, N.J. State Tchrs. Coll., 1935; postgrad., Ednl. Alliance Art Sch., 1938-39, New Sch. for Social Research, 1958-73, Mus. of Modern Art Sch., 1966-67. One-woman show New Sch. Assos. Gallery, N.Y.C., 1964; two-woman show Jewish Community Center Gallery, Wilmington, Del., 1974; group shows include Audubon Artists Nat. Exhbn., Lever House, N.Y.C., N.Y.C. Pks. and Recreation, 1988 (award in exhbn. "Discoveries IV"), Albany (N.Y.) Inst. History and Art, Cayuga Inst. History and Art, Auburn, N.Y., Jesse Besser Mus., Alpena, Mich., Bergen County (N.J.) Mus., Mus. of S.W., Midland, Tex., Oshkosh (Wis.) Pub. Mus., Okla. Art Center, Oklahoma City, Pallazzo Vecchio, Florence, Salvator Rose Pub. Gardens, Naples, Italy, many others; traveling exhbn. in 5 cities in Israel, also Cairo; represented in permanent collections Jesse Besser Mus., Butler Inst. Am. Art, Youngstown, Ohio, Slater Meml. Mus., Norwich, Conn., numerous pvt. collections in, U.S., Eng., and Israel. Mem. Nat. Assn. Women Artists (pres. 1974-76, Nat. Medal of Honor award 1972, Paula Kapp award 1969, Georgi Meml. award 1975, Gehner prize 1979, 87, Levitt award for collage 1989), Artists Equity N.Y., Am. Soc. Contemporary Artists (exec. bd., Graphics award 1981, Winsor and Newton award for collage painting 1982), Alliance Queens Artists of N.Y.C.(Merit award 1986, Merit award for collage 1989). Died Aug. 1992.

**GEBHARDT, CHRISTOPH HEINRICH,** physician, surgeon, educator, researcher; b. Hamm, Westfalen, Germany, Mar. 25, 1943; s. Erich Waldemar and Anneliese Martha (Hegemann) G.; m. Gisela Erika Segeth, Feb. 26, 1948; children: Michael, Claudia. MD, U. Düsseldorf, Germany, 1969; PhD, U. Erlangen, Germany, 1979. Bd. cert. surgery. Intern U. Düsseldorf, 1969-70, resident, 1970-73, St. Josef Hosp., Wuppertal, Germany, 1973-76, asst. chief surgery, 1976; attending surgeon U. Erlangen, 1977-79, asst. chief surgery, 1979-84; chief of surgery Klinikum Nürnberg, from 1984. Author: Chirurgie des exokrinen Pankreas, 1984; contbr. articles to profl. jours. Recipient award for best sci. exposition German Soc. Surgery, 1995, Film award German Soc. Surgery, 1997. Fellow ACS; mem. Rotary Club Nürnberg-Erlangen. Home: Nürnberg, Germany. Died May 30, 2003.

**GEERLINGS, GERALD KENNETH,** architect, etcher; b. Milw., Apr. 18, 1897; s. Jacob and Cattalina (Geerlings); m. Elizabeth Filby Edmunds, Sept. 2, 1924, (dec. Dec. 1986); children: Barbara Filby (Mrs. Merrill Soldier), Gillian (Mrs. David D. Brown III). BA in Architecture, U. Pa., 1921, MA in Architecture, 1922; student, St. John's Coll., Eng., Royal Coll. Art, London. Employed as a newspaper reporter, Milw.; 2 yrs. a head designer York & Sawyer, also Starrett & Van Vleck (architects), NYC; own archtl. practice in NYC, 1926-68; rep. by Associated Am. Artists, NYC. Author several books.; contbr. articles to mags. and Ency. Brit; etchings exhibited in Europe, also in Am.; collection entitled Contemporary Etching, frequently, 1929—; and in Fine Prints of the Year, London; retrospective exhbn. Associated Am. Artists Gallery, N.Y.C., 1989; etchings in permanent collections including Victoria and Albert Mus., London, Congl. Library, Met. Mus., N.Y.C., Nat. Collection Fine Arts, Washington, Bklyn. Mus., Chgo. Art Inst., Boston Pub. Library, Phila. Mus. Art. (Awards include 1st prize for best etching Chgo. Century of Progress 1933), others.; contbr. etching to Graphic Excursions: American Prints in Black-and-White, 1900-'50, 1991. Served from pvt. to 2d lt. F.A. AEF, World War I; Served from capt. to col. USAAF, World War II; spl. civilian cons. USAF, 1949-55. Decorated Legion of Merit with oak leaf cluster, Army Commendation medal.; recipient Gold medal Phila. Acad. Fine Arts, La Médaille de la Ville de Paris (Silver medal) City of Paris, 1988. Mem. AIA, Archtl. League N.Y., Am. Soc. Graphic Artists, Pastel Soc. Am., Theta Xi, Tau Sigma Delta. Home: New Canaan, Conn. *In retrospect it seems to me it was important to disregard the possibility of not surviving both wars and the dismal effects of the Depression, and to have faith in the future.* Deceased.

**GÉHER, KÁROLY,** electrical engineering educator; b. Derecske, Hungary, Aug. 13, 1929; s. Lajos and Vilma (Vajsz) G.; m. Judit Glücklich, July 19, 1958. Diploma, Tech. U., Budapest, Hungary, 1952, D Engring., 1963; DSc, Acad. Scis., Budapest, 1973. Asst. lectr. Tech. U., Budapest, 1952-59, asst. prof., 1959-64, assoc. prof., 1964-74, prof. elec. engring., 1974-99, prof. emeritus, from 2000. Rsch. fellow Telecomm. Rsch. Inst., Budapest, 1958-67. Author: (in Hungarian) Linear Networks, 1968, 4th edit., 1979, Theory of Network Tolerances, 1971, (with others) Design of Linear Circuits, 1992; editor-in-chief: (in Hungarian) Telecommunications, 1993, 2d edit., 2000. Recipient Best Tech. Book award Tech. Pub. Co., 1969, award Acad. Scis. Hungarian Acad. Scis., 1985, Szent-Györgyi award, 1998, Széchenyi award 1998. Mem. IEEE, Sci. Soc. Telecomm. (Best Paper award), N.Y. Acad. Scis. Avocations: collecting postcards, classical music. Home: Budapest, Hungary. Died Aug. 14, 2006.

**GEHRING, WALTER JAKOB,** retired biology professor, geneticist; b. Zurich, Switzerland, Mar. 20, 1939; s. Jakob and Marcelle (Rebmann) G.; m. Elisabeth Lott, Jan. 31, 1964; children: Stephan, Thomas. Diploma in Zoology, U. Zurich, 1963, PhD, 1965; PhD (hon.), U. Torino, Italy, 2003, U. Nuevo Léon, Mex., 2003, U. Pierre et Marie Curie, France, 2007, U. Barcelona, 2009, U. Salento, Italy, 2008, Bundesverdienstkreuz, Germany, 2010. Rsch. assoc. U. Zurich, 1963-67; postdoctoral fellow Yale U., New Haven, 1967-69, assoc. prof., 1969-72; prof. U. Basel, Switzerland, 1972—2011. Recipient Otto Nägeli prize Zurich, 1982, Warren Triennial prize Harvard Med. Sch., Cambridge, Mass., 1986, Dr. Albert Wander prize, Bern, Switzerland, 1986, Charles Léopold Mayer prize Inst. of France, Paris, 1986, Louis Jeantet prize for medicine City of Geneva, 1987, Prix d'Honneur, Moet Hennessy Louis Vuitton, 1993, Newcomb Cleve. prize AAAS, 1994-1995, Otto Warburg-medaille, 1996, Paul Wintrebert prize U. Pierre and Marie Curie, 1996, March of Dimes prize Devel. Biology, 1997, Karl von Frisch prize German Zool. Soc., 2000, Kyoto prize Inamori Found., 2000, Preis der Alfred Vogt Stiftung zur Förderung der Augenheilkunde, Zürich, 2001, Premio Balzan, Fondazione Internat. Premio E. Balzan, 2003. Mem. AAAS, NAS, European Molecular Biology Orgn., European Devel. Biology Orgn., Deutsche Akademie der Naturforscher Leopoldina, Academia Europaea, Genetics Soc. Am., Internat. Soc. for Developmental Biology, Swiss Soc. for Cell Biology, Molecular Biology and Genetics, Am. Soc. for Developmental Biology, Human Genome Orgn., Royal Soc. London (fgn.), Acad. Scis. Paris (fgn. mem.), Sigma Xi. Avocations: birdwatching, photography. Home: Therwil, Switzerland. Died May 29, 2014.

**GEIGER, GEORGE RAYMOND,** philosophy educator; b. NYC, May 8, 1903; s. Oscar Harold and Nina Cecelia (Daly) G.; m. Julia Louise Jarratt, Dec. 25, 1934. AB, Columbia U., 1924, B.Lit., 1925, MS, 1926, PhD, 1931. Asst. prof. philosophy Bradley Poly. Inst., Peoria, Ill., 1928-30, 35-37; assoc. prof. philosophy U. N.D., 1930-34, U. Ill., 1934-35; prof. philosophy Antioch Coll., Yellow Springs, Ohio, 1937-68, John Dewey prof. humanities, from 1968. Vis. prof. philosophy U. Wis., 1947-48, U. Calif.-Santa Barbara, 1963 Author several books, from 1933; including Philosophy and the Social Order, 1947; John Dewey in Perspective, 1958, Science, Folklore and Philosophy, 1966, The Philosophy of Henry George, new edit, 1976; contbr.: The Philosophy of John Dewey, 1939, Value: A Cooperative Inquiry, 1949, The Cleavage in Our Culture, 1952, Modern Philosophies and Education, 1955; bd. editors: Am. Jour. Econ. and Sociology; founding editor Antioch Review, 1941. Mem. Am. Philos. Assn. (sec.-treas. Western div. 1944-47, nat. sec.-treas. 1947-53), Phi Beta Kappa. Home: Yellow Springs, Ohio. Died 1998.

**GEISE, HARRY FREMONT,** retired meteorologist; b. Oak Park, Ill., Jan. 8, 1920; m. Juanita Calmer, 1974; children: Barry, Gary, Harry;children from previous marriage: Marian Frances, Gloria Tara. At, U. Chgo., 1938—39, Meteorol. Svc. Sch., Lakehurst, NJ, 1943—44. Meteorologist WLS-AM and Prairie Farmer newspaper, Chgo., 1941—42, 1946; chief meteorologist Kingsbury Ordnance, 1943; assoc. Dr. Irving P. Krick Meteorol. Cons., 1947—49; rschr. Army Air Corps, 1948—49; host weather and travel shows WBKB-TV (now WBBM-TV) and WOPA-AM, Chgo. and Oak Park, 1950—51; devel. radio and TV shows San Francisco and San Jose, 1954—55; dir. media divsn, Irving P. Krick Assoc., 1955—59; broadcast meteorologist Columbia Pacific Radio and TV networks, 1957—58; weatherman KNXT-TV (now KCBS-TV), Hollywood, Calif., 1957—58; comml. weather svc., 1962—80; instr. meteorology Santa Rosa Coll., 1964—66, Sonoma State Coll., 1967—68; weather dir. WCBS-TV, NYC, 1966—67. Meteorologist Nat. Def. Exec. Res., 1968—74. Contbr. articles in field, to periodicals. With USMC, 1944—45. Recipient first Calif. Tchg. Credential for Eminence in Meteorology, 1964. Mem.: Royal Meteorol. Soc. (life). Achievements include first to pvt. weather svcs. in Chgo; development of new temperature forecasting technique; research in relationship between specified solar emission and major change in earth's weather patterns; tornado forecasting; long-range forecasting up to 4 years in advance. Home: Carmichael, Calif. Died Mar. 2, 1995.

**GELB, ARTHUR NEAL,** retired newspaper editor; b. NYC, Feb. 3, 1924; s. Daniel and Fanny G.; m. Barbara Stone, June 2, 1946; children: Michael, Peter. BA, NYU, 1946; DHL (hon.), CCNY, 1997. Joined as copyboy N.Y. Times, 1944; reporter, 1947-58; asst. drama critic N.Y. Times, 1958-61, chief cultural corr., 1961-63, culture and met. editor, 1967-76, dep. mng. editor, 1976-86, mng. editor, 1986-89; pres. The N.Y. Times Co. Found., 1990-00. Author: (with Barbara Gelb) O'Neill, 1962, (with Dr. Salvatore Cutolo) Bellevue Is My Home, 1956, (with A.M. Rosenthal) One More Victim, 1967, (autobiography) City Room, 2003; editor: The Pope's Journey to the United States, 1965, The Night the Lights Went Out, 1965, Sophisticated Traveler series, 1986-88, Great Lives of the Twentieth Century, 1989. Mem. bd. NYU Ireland House, Nat. Arts Journalism Fellowship Program Adv. Bd., Columbia Journalism Rev., Earth Times; chmn. adv. bd. 2d Century Project, N.Y. City 100; co-chmn. bd. J. Anthony Lukas Prize. Decorated comdr. Order Arts and Letters (France); recipient Pipe Night award Players Club, 1989, Eugene O'Neill Soc. medal, 1995, Eugene O'Neill Found. award, 1996, Leadership award Arthur Ashe Athletic Assn., 1996, Award Cath. Interracial Coun., 1996, NYU Alumni Achievement award, 1997. Mem. Century Club. Died May 20, 2014.

**GELZER, JUSTUS,** secretary general; b. Basel, Switzerland, Nov. 8, 1929; s. Heinrich and Charlotte (Ludecke) G.; m. Antoinette Miescher, Sept. 29, 1960; children: Adel, Samuel, Anna. MD, Basel Med. Sch., 1954. Bd. Cert. Pediat. MD, biologist, Biol. Rsch. Labs. CIBA Ltd., Basel, 1964-67; dir. Microbiology Subdivsn., dept. dir. Biology Rsch. CIBA Pharm. Ltd., Summit, N.J., 1967-70; rsch. head biology Pharm. divsn. CIBA-GEIGY Ltd., Basel, 1970-80, head strategic rsch. planning med. dept. Pharm. Divsn., from 1985. Mem. Ciba Pharma Mgmt. Com., 1993. Contbr. articles to profl. jours. Exec. com. mem., sec.-gen., and senate Swiss Acad. Med. Scis.; exec. com. mem. Swiss chpt. Mother + Child Internat. Assn. for Maternal and Neonatal Health. Maj. Swiss Med. Corps., ret. Mem. AMA, Swiss Med. Assn., Swiss Pediat. Soc., Swiss Soc. Microbiology. Home: Basel, Switzerland. Died Jan. 18, 1998.

**GENRICH, WILLARD ADOLPH,** lawyer; b. Buffalo, Feb. 19, 1915; s. John E. and Emma P. (Luescher) G.; m. Eleanor M. Merrill, Mar. 15, 1941; children: Willa Genrich Long, Ellen Genrich Rusling, Willard A., Jeffrey M. LLB, U. Buffalo, 1938; LHD, Medaille Coll., 1973, N.Y. Med. Coll., 1981, Hofstra U., 1985, SUNY, 1986; LLD, Canisius Coll., 1975, L.I. U., 1979, Hobart Coll., 1981, Fordham U., 1984, N.Y. Inst. Tech., 1979; D in Comml. Sci., Niagara U., 1980; D in Civil Law, Mercy Coll., 1981; D in Chiropractic Sci., N.Y. Chiropractic Coll., 1983; LLD, D'Youville Coll., 1987. Bar: N.Y. 1939. Spl. agt. FBI, 1942-46; pvt. practice Amherst, N.Y., from 1946; pres. Genrich Builders, Inc., Buffalo, from 1966. Owner, operator 2 hotels; dir. real estate corps.; bd. dirs. N.Y. State Higher Edn. Assistance Corp., 1962-73; bd. regents U. State N.Y., 1973-95, vice chancellor bd. regents, 1977-79, chancellor, 1980-85, chancellor emeritus, 1986—; del. N.Y. State Constl. Conv., 1967. Past trustee N.E. br. YMCA; trustee First Presbyn. Ch.; hon. mem. bd. visitors Batavia Sch. Blind. Recipient Pres.'s award Daemen Coll., 1975, Disting. Citizen's award De-Veaux Sch., 1975, Disting. Alumni award U. Buffalo Law Sch., 1978, Disting. Alumni award Alumni Assn. SUNY-Buffalo, 1980, Disting. Citizen's Achievement award Canisius Coll. Bd. Regents, 1980, Citation of Appreciation, Commn. of Ind. Colls. and U. Western N.Y. Consortium of Higher Edn., 1978, Pres.'s award Hilbert Coll., 1983, John Jay award Commn. Ind. Colls. and Univs., 1984, Svc. award Daemen Coll., 1984, Bernard E. Hughes Recognition award N.Y. State Assn. Health, Phys. Edn. Recreation and Dance, 1986, Disting. Svc. award N.Y. State 4201 Schs. Assn., 1986, Merit award N.Y. State Assn. of Two Yr. Colls., 1986, 1st Disting. Alumnus award Benett High Sch., 1990, Friend of Children award N.Y. Assn. Sch. Psychologists, 1991, Community Svc. award Amherst GOP, 1991, hon. life membership award, N.Y. State, Parent Tchr. Assn., 1993, Daemen Coll. Pres. award, 1994, Park Sch. award, Disting. Edn. Svc., award 1995, Home Economic Tchr. Assn. Corning award. Mem. ABA, N.Y. State Bar Assn., Erie County Bar Assn., Am. Judicature Soc., N.Y. Hon. State PTA (life), Rotary, Amherst South Rotary Club (hon.). Home: Buffalo, NY. Died 1999.

**GENTRY, BERN LEON, SR.,** management consultant; b. Goldsboro, NC, Sept. 9, 1941; s. Theodore Alfonso and Ruth Ester (Taylor) G.; m. Jane A. Price, Nov. 11, 1965; children: Michelle Lorraine, Bern Leon. Student, Rutgers U., 1959-61, Temple U., 1961-63, Cornell U., 1966-67, U. Okla., 1971. Tax acct. IRS, Phila., 1965-66; collection mgr., credit mgr., appliance store mgr., soft goods mdse. mgr. Sears, Roebuck & Co., Phila., 1966-71; program mgr., dir. nat. urban affairs U.S. Jr. C. of C., 1971-73, cons., from 1973; pres. Together, Inc., Tulsa, from 1973. Contbr. articles to profl. jours. Mem. nat. adv. bd. Boys Clubs Am., 1971—; mem. nat. Black alliance for grad. level edn. U. Mich.; past pres., bd. dirs. Tulsa Econ. Opportunity Task Force; pres. Community Service Agy.; bd. dirs. Jr. Achievement. Recipient award of accomplishment Sears Staff Sch., 1967; award of appreciation Black Peoples Unity Movement Econ. Devel. Corp., 1971; George Washington Honor medal Freedoms Found., 1974, 76; Keys to cities of Roanoke, Va.; Keys to cities of Baton Rouge, La.; Keys to cities of New Orleans; named Outstanding Young Man Camden, 1970; Outstanding Chpt. Pres. N.J. Jaycees; Outstanding Jaycee. Mem. Nat. Urban League, NAACP, Am. Mgmt. Assn., Nat. Assn. Human Rights Workers, Assn. Black Found. Execs., Nat. Assn. Pub. Relations Execs., Nat. Civil Service League, Nat. Assn. Community Devel., Nat. Assn. Vol. Services Coordinator, Camden Jaycees (pres. 1970-71), Tulsa Met. C. of C. Home: Tulsa, Okla. Died July 11, 2012.

**GENTRY, CURT (CURTIS MARSENA GENTRY),** author; b. Lamar, Colo., June 13, 1931; s. Curtis Herman and Coral Eloise (McMillin) G.; m. Laura Wilson Spence, Oct. 30, 1954 (dec. 1975); m. Gail Stevens, June 13, 1976 (div. 1982). Student, U. Colo., 1949-50; BA, San Francisco State U., 1957. Sports writer Lamar (Colo.) Daily News, 1947-49; Boulder corr. Denver Post, 1949-50; salesman Paul Elder, Books, San Francisco, 1954-57; mgr. Tro Harper, Books, San Francisco, 1957-62; book reviewer San Francisco Chronicle, 1957-65. Author: The Madams of San Francisco, 1964, The Vulnerable Americans, 1966, Frame-Up: The Incredible Case of Tom Mooney and Warren Billings, 1967 (Mystery Writer's award 1968), The Last Days of the Late, Great State of California, 1968, The Killer Mountains, 1968, J. Edgar Hoover: The Man and the Secrets, 1991 (PEN Nonfiction award 1992); co-author: Jade: Stone of Heaven, 1962, John M. Browning: American Gunmaker, 1964, A Kind of Loving, 1970, Operation Overflight, 1970, Second in Command, 1971, (with Vincent Bugliosi) Helter Skelter: The True Story of the Manson Murders, 1974 (Edgar Allen Poe award Mystery Writers America 1975). Served in USAF, 1950-54, Korea. Mem. Authors Guild America, ACLU, E Clampus Vitus (Jackson, Calif.). Democrat. Avocations: U.S. and western history, fiction, cooking, motion pictures. Home: San Francisco, Calif. Died July 10, 2014.

**GERAS, NORMAN MYRON,** political scientist, educator; b. Bulawayo, Zimbabwe, Aug. 25, 1943; arrived in U.K., 1962; s. Jack Geras, Beryl Kate Salis; m. Adèle Daphne Weston, Aug. 7, 1967; children: Sophie, Jenny. BA in Philosophy, Politics and Econs., Oxford U., Eng., 1965. Asst. lectr. govt. U. Manchester, England, 1967—70, lectr. in govt., 1970—84, sr. lectr. in govt., 1984—90, reader in govt., 1990—94, prof. govt., 1995—2003. Mem. editl. bd. New Left Review, 1976—92, Socialist Register, 1995—2003. Author: The Legacy of Rosa Luxemburg, 1976, Marx and Human Nature: Refutation of a Legend, 1983, Literature of Revolution: Essays on Marism, 1986, Solidarity in the Conversation of Humankind: Ungroundable Liberalism of Richard Rorty, 1995; co-author: The Ashes '97: The View from the Boundary, 1997; author: The Contract of Mutual Indifference: Political Philosophy After the Holocaust, 1998, Enlightenment and Modernity, 2000, Men of Waugh: Ashes 2001, 2002, Crimes Against Humanity: Birth of a Concept, 2011. Avocations: walking, playing piano, movies, jazz, cricket. Home: Manchester, England. Died Oct. 18, 2013.

**GERBER, MICHAEL ALBERT,** pathologist, research scientist; b. Kassel, Germany, Oct. 18, 1939; came to U.S., 1966; s. Bruno and Luise (Kramer) G.; m. Luviminda Gerber; 1 child, Elisa. MS, Gutenberg Gymnasium, Wiesbaden, Fed. Republic Germany, 1960; MD, Gutenberg U., Mainz, Fed. Republic Germany, 1966. Resident in pathology Mt. Sinai Sch. Medicine, NYC, 1969-72, fellow in exptl. pathology, 1972-73; chief electron microscopy VA Hosp., Bronx, N.Y., 1973-74; from asst. prof. to assoc. prof. pathology Mt. Sinai Sch. Medicine, NYC, 1973-79, prof. pathology, 1980-87; co-dir. cellular molecular pathology City Hosp. Ctr. at Elmhurst, N.Y., 1982-87; prof., chmn. pathology Tulane U. Sch. Medicine, New Orleans, from 1987, dir. grad. program in molecular & cellular biology, 1991. Assoc. editor Hepatology. Author book; contbr. more than 200 articles to profl. jours. Mem. adv. com. FDA, Washington, 1985. Recipient Rsch. Career Devel. award NIH, 1980. Mem. AAAS, Coll. Am. Pathologists, Fedn. Am. Socs. for Exptl. Pathology, Am. Assn. Pathologists, Am. Assn. Study Liver Diseases, U.S. and Can. Acad. Pathology, Am. Coll. Gastroenterology, Hans Popper Hepatopathology Soc. (pres.), Deutsche Gesellschaft for Pathology. Died 1999.

**GERGOV, GEORGE IVANOV,** civil engineer; b. Sofia, Bulgaria, Mar. 30, 1938; s. Ivan Gergov Petkov and Ivanka Georgieva Gergova; m. Anka Atanasova Michailova; children: Irina Gergova, Antoaneta Gergova. MSCE, U. Architecture, Civil Engring. and Geodesy, 1962, DSc, 1995; postgrad. in Hydrology, Padova U., 1970; postgrad. Engring. Rsch. Ctr., Colo. State U., 1980; postgrad. Hydraulics Rsch. Inst., Iowa State U., 1980; PhD, State Hydrol. Inst. St. Petersburg, 1974. Hydro engr. Vodproject, Sofia, Bulgaria, 1962—64; rsch. hydrologist, sr. rschr., sci. sec., dep. dir. Nat. Inst. Meteorology and Hydrology, Sofia, 1964—90, head Sediment and Morphology of Rivers divsn., from 1992. Prof. Hydrology Sofia U., from 1990. Author: Hydrological Studies, 2001; co-author: Applied Ecology of the Black Sea, 1998, Schwebsteff und geschieberegime der Donau, 1993, River Sediments Grain Size Distribution in Bulgaria, 1991, Applied Ecology of Sea Regions. The Black Sea, 1990; co-editor: British-Bulgarian Collaboration in Hydrology, 2000; mem. editl. bd. Bulgarian Jour. Meteorology and Hydrology, Internat. Jour. Sediment Rsch.; contbr. articles to profl. jours. Recipient St. Ciril and Metodious medal, Bulgaria, 1986. Mem.: Mid. East World Assn. Soil and Water, N.Y. Acad. Scis., World Assn. Soil and Water (v.p. Mid. East sect. from 1996), Bulgarian Nat. Water Assn. (v.p. from 1999), Bulgarian Ecol. Soc. (v.p. from 1999), Global Water Partnership for Bulgaria, Brit. Hydrol. Soc., Internat. Assn. Hydrol. Sci., Nat. Water Tech. Union Bulgaria, Union Bulgarian Scientists, Internat. Hydrology Program (nat. com. 1976—84), Nat. Inst. Meteorology and Hydrology (sci. coun. 1980—94). Avocation: photography. Home: Sofia, Bulgaria. Died Dec. 7, 2006.

**GERSOVITZ, SARAH VALERIE,** painter, printmaker, playwright; d. Solomon and Eva Gamer; m. Benjamin Gersovitz, June 22, 1944; children: Mark, Julia, Jeremy. Grad., MacDonald Coll., Montreal Mus. Fine Arts; postgrad., Concordia U. Tchr. painting and drawing Bronfman Centre, Montreal, from 1972. One-woman shows include Montreal Mus. Fine Arts, 1962, 65, Art Gallery Greater Victoria, 1966, U. Alta, 1968, Burnaby Art Gallery, 1969, Art Gallery Hamilton, 1969, Mt. St. Vincent U., 1971, Coll. St. Louis, 1972, Inst. Cultural Peruano, Lima, 1973, Confedn. Art Gallery, 1976, St. Mary's U., 1976, U. Sherbrooke, 1979, 83, 95, Peter Whyte Gallery, 1982, London Regional Art Gallery, 1982, Holland Coll., 1982, Stewart Hall Art Gallery, 1984, U. Kaiserslautern (W. Ger.), 1984, Bibliothèque Nat. Québec, 1997, Galérie de la ville, D.D.O., Québec, 1999, Retrospective, Stewart Hall, Print Claire, Québec, 2000, Galérie Auguste-Chénier, Ville Marie, Québec, 2003, others; represented in permanent collections Libr. of Congress, N.Y. Pub. Libr., Nat. Gallery South Australia, Inst. Cultural Peruano, Lima, Am. Embassy, Ottawa, House of Humour and Satire, Gabrovo, Bulgaria, Israel Mus., Jerusalem, numerous Can. mus., univs. and embassies including Nat. Gallery Can., Montreal Mus. Fine Arts, Le Musèe du Quèbec, Le Musèe d'Art Contemporain; group exhbns. include most recently 3d Internat. Art Biennial Ville Marie, Que., 1996, 2000, 02, III Trienale, Harirov, Czech Republic, 2002, Sichuan Exlibris Assn., China, 2002, 2d Internat. Biennale d'art miniature, Ostow, Poland, 2002, numerous others U.S. and Abroad; author: A Prtrait of Portia, 1989. Recipient numerous art awards including 1st prize 9th Internat. Biennale Gabrovo, Bulgaria, 1989, 1st prize Seagram Fine Arts Expn., 1968, Travel award, 1991; Graphic Art prize Winnipeg Art Gallery Bienial, 1962; Anaconda award Can. Soc. Painters-Etchers, 1963, 67; 1st prize Concours Graphique, U. Sherbrooke, 1977; purchase award Mus. de Que., 1966, Nat. Gallery South Australia, 1967, Dawson Coll., 1974, Thomas More Inst., 1977, Law Faculty U. Sherbrooke, 1979, 1st prize and 2 gold medals Nat. Playwriting Competition, Ottawa, 1982, 1st prize prize Country Playhouse, 1985, Jacksonville U., 1988. Mem. Royal Can. Acad. Arts (coun. 1981-82, 92-94), Dramatists Guild. Died 2007.

**GERST, PAUL HOWARD,** physician; b. Sept. 24, 1927; s. David and Hilde (Werbel) G.; m. Elizabeth Carlsen, Aug. 3, 1957; children— Steven R., Jeffrey C., Andrew L. AB, Columbia U., 1948, MD, 1952. Diplomate: Am. Bd. Surgery, Am. Bd. Thoracic Surgery. Intern Columbia Presbyn. Med. Center, NYC, 1952-53, resident, 1956-62, mem. staff, from 1962; instr. physiology U. Pa., 1955-56; practice medicine specializing in surgery NYC, from 1962; asst. clin. prof. surgery Columbia U., 1964-72; prof. surgery Albert Einstein Coll. Medicine, 1972—2003. Dir. surgery Bronx-Lebanon Hosp. Ctr., NYC, 1964—2003 Contbr. articles to profl. jours. Served 1st lt. U.S. Army, 1953-55. USPHS postdoctoral fellow, 1955-56; recipient Rsch. Career Devel. award, 1964-65. Fellow ACS; mem. Am. Physiol. Soc., N.Y. Soc. for Thoracic Surgery, N.Y. Surg. Soc., N.Y. Soc. for Cardiovasc. Surgery, Am. Heart Assn. Home: Hackensack, NJ. Died Sept. 29, 2013.

**GESKE, NORMAN ALBERT,** retired museum director; b. Sioux City, Iowa, Oct. 31, 1915; s. Albert Geske and Delossa Stone; m. Jane Pope Geske, Sept. 18, 1968. BA, U. Minn., 1938; MA, NYU Inst. Fine Arts, 1953; DFA (hon.), Doane Coll., 1969. Dir. Hennepin County Historical Soc., Mpls., 1940—41; curator Walker Art Ctr., Mpls., 1947—50; asst. dir. U. Nebr. Art Galleries, 1950—53, acting dir., 1953—56; dir. Sheldon Meml Arts Gallery, U. Nebr., Lincoln, 1956—83, dir. emeritus, 1983—2014. Am. commr. XXXIV Biennale, Venice, Italy, 1968. Author: The Figurative Tradition in Recent American Art, 1968, The Graphic Art of Rudy Pozzatti, 1970, American Sculpture, 1970, Ralph Albert Blakelock, 1847-1919, 1975, Light and Color-Images from New Mexico, 1981, Art and Artists in Nebraska, 1983, Rudy Pozzatti: A Printmaker's Odyssey, 2002; co-author (with Karen Janovy): The American Painting Collection of the Sheldon Memorial Art Gallery, 1988. Bd. dirs. Mus. Nebr. Art, Kearney. Sgt. US Army, 1940—44. Recipient Gov.'s Art award, Nebr. Arts Coun., 1979, Leonard Thiessen award, 2004, Disting. Svc. award, Kearney State Coll., 1980, Mayor's Arts award, City of Lincoln, 1987, Sowers award, Lincoln Found., 1990, Pioneer award, Nebraskaland Found., 2004. Mem.: Nebr. Art Assn., Assn. Art Museum Dirs. (hon.). Democrat. Home: Lincoln, Nebr. Died Sept. 6, 2014.

**GETTIS, HAZEL GILMORE,** religious studies educator; b. Prescott, Ark., May 16, 1920; d. Lee Burton and Frances (Nelson) Williams; m. Earl Gettis, Sr., Jan. 7, 1965 (dec. April 3, 2002); 1 child, Earl Jr. AB, Philander Coll., 1965; MA, Webster Coll., 1976; PhD, Kans. U., 1985; D in Christian Counseling, 1998. Tchr. Nat. Congress Christian

Edn., from 1980; lectr. Hegg Workshops, 1990; pres. Hegg Reocrding Co., Inc., St. Louis, 1985. Founder Hegg Christian U., 1990; tchr., gospel singer, 1965—. Author: Mission of Gospel Music, 1985, Suggestive Passivity, 1991; recording artist, presenter gospel music concerts. With Thomas A. Dorsey Choral Union, 1970—. Deceased.

**GETZELS, JACOB WARREN,** psychologist, educator; b. Bialystok, Poland, Feb. 7, 1912; came to U.S., 1921, naturalized, 1933; s. Hirsch and Frieda (Solon) G.; m. Judith Nelson, Dec. 24, 1949; children: Katharine, Peter, Julia. BA, Bklyn. Coll., 1936; MA, Columbia U., 1939; PhD, Harvard U., 1951; L.H.D. (hon.), Hofstra U., 1984. Instr. ednl. psychology U. Chgo., 1951, asst. prof. ednl. psychology, 1952-54, assoc. prof., 1955-57, prof., 1957-84, now R. Wendell Harrison Disting. Service prof. edn. and behavioral scis. emeritus. Vis. prof. psychology U. P.R., summer, 1962, Stanford U., summer, 1963; mem. U.S. Office Edn. Mission to Soviet Russia, 1960, mem. research adv. council, 1964-70; mem. council of scholars Library of Congress, 1980-84 Author: (with A. Coladarci) The Use of Theory in Educational Administration, 1955, (with P.W. Jackson) Creativity and Intelligence: Explorations with Gifted Students, 1962, (with J.M. Lipham and R.F. Campbell) Educational Administration as a Social Process, 1968, (with I. Taylor) Perspectives in Creativity, 1975, (with M. Csikszentmihalyi) The Creative Vision: A Longitudinal Study of Problem Finding in Art, 1976; contbr. articles to profl. jours. Mem. bd. visitors Learning R & D Center, U. Pitts., 1973-79; bd. dirs. Spencer Found., 1971-91. Recipient Research award Am. Personnel and Guidance Assn., 1959; Tchrs. Coll. medal, 1977; Nicholas Murray Butler medal for theory or philosophy of edn. Columbia U., 1980; Disting. Alumnus award Bklyn. Coll., 1984; Center for Advanced Study in Behavioral Scis. fellow, 1960-61; Center for Policy Study (U. Chgo.) fellow, 1967-75 Fellow AAAS; mem. Am. Psychol. Assn., Nat. Acad. Edn. (1st. v.p. 1972-76), Nat. Soc. for Study Edn. (dir. 1975-77), Am. Ednl. Research Assn. Died Apr. 2001.

**GEX, EMILE JOSEPH, JR.,** lawyer; b. Bay St. Louis, Miss., Oct. 11, 1922; s. Emile Jospeh and Laurin Alda (Plunkett) Gex; m. Juanita Loveless, Jan. 29, 1949; children: Guy Stephen, Kerry Glenn. BA, U. Miss., 1943, JD, 1945, M in Urban and Regional Planning, 1971. Bar: Miss. 1943. Sole practice, Bay St. Louis, 1945—53; traffic mgr. Crosby Chems., Inc., Picayune, Miss., 1954—69; sr. planner Regional Planning Commn., New Orleans, from 1971. Cons., Picayune, from 1971; v.p. Lacoste & Assocs., Oxford, Jackson, Miss., from 1972. Author: Real Evidence in Mississippi, 1945, Zoning in Mississippi, 1970, Goods Movement, 1978; co-author: New Orleans Regional Transportation Energy Contingency Plan, 1980. Cubmaster Boy Scouts Am., Picayune, 1960—64. Study fellow, U. Miss., 1970. Mem.: Rotary Club (Bay St. Louis), Jaycees, Kappa Sigma (chpt. pres. 1943—45), Phi Delta Phi (chpt. pres. 1945). Died Mar. 14, 1993.

**GHYOOT, VALMOND GEORGE,** real estate consultant, educator; b. Okiep, Western Cape, South Africa, Nov. 28, 1951; s. George Stephens Julius Ghyoot and Annie Maria Elizabeth Scholtz; m. Carina Elizabeth Homan; 3 children. B of Building, U. Port Elizabeth, South Africa, 1974; B of Commerce with honors, U. South Africa, 1978, M of Commerce, 1981, D of Commerce, 1992. Property valuer South African Coun. for the Profl. Valuers, 1998, Appraiser Dept. of Justice, Republic of South Africa, 1995. Prof. of real estate U. of South Africa, Pretoria, Gauteng, South Africa, 1978—2008. Real property cons. Real Solutions, Krugersdorp, Gauteng, South Africa, from 1979. Author: The property finance business; editor: Multicultural sensitivity for managers; contbr. newspaper, magazine; author: (training video) Discovering the World of Property, (book) Property Marketing Research, The Estate Agency Business; contbr. book,; author: An Introduction to Commercial Property Finance Development and Investment. Recipient Svc. award, Internat. Real Estate Soc., 2004. Mem.: Pacific Rim Real Estate Soc., Am. Real Estate Soc., African Real Estate Soc. (dir. 1997—2008). Home: Rant en Dal, South Africa. Died 2012.

**GIACOMELLI, GIORGIO MARIA,** emeritus physics professor; b. Cagli, Italy, May 30, 1931; s. Giuseppe and Elda (Marinelli) G.; m. Maltoni Giuseppina, Aug. 8, 1958; children: Paolo, Roberto. Laurea in Fisica, U. Bologna, Italy, 1954; PhD in Physics, U. Rochester, 1958. Prof. incaricato U. Bologna, Italy, 1958-63, asst. ordinario, 1964-71, prof., from 1974, dir. Inst. physics, 1975—82; rsch. assoc. CERN, Geneva, 1959-61; vis. assoc. physicist Brookhaven Nat. Lab., Upton, NY, 1964-66; vis. physicist Fermilab, Batavia, Ill., 1973-75, 87; prof. U. Padua, Italy, 1971-74; vis. prof. U. Calif., Riverside, 1971; dir. Inst. Physics, Bologna, 1982—88. Coord. sci. popularization site Scienzagiovane. Contbr. more than 750 articles in profl. jours. Recipient Premio Operosità Scientifica, U. Bologna, 1967, Premio A della Riccia, 1970. Fellow Am. Phys. Soc.; mem. NY Acad. Scis., Acad. Sci. Bologna, Acad. Teatina Sci., Socio Benemerito, Italian Phys. Soc. (Premio Citta di Bari award 1963), European Phys. Soc., Marchigiano dell'anno (Gold medal 2013). Home: Bologna, Italy. Died Jan. 30, 2014.

**GIA-RUSSO, A(NTHONY) PAUL,** retired minister, lawyer; b. Petrella Tifernina, Italy, Jan. 25, 1910; s. Vincenzo and Anita (Amorosa) G-R.; m. Eleanor L Bauer, Feb. 12, 1938; children: Don Paul, Mark Henry. AB in Citizenship and Pub. Affairs, Syracuse U., 1932, JD, 1936; MA, U. Chgo., 1939; MDiv, Chgo. Theol. Sem., 1940. Ordained to ministry United Ch. of Christ, 1940. Min. Congl. Ch., Oak Lawn, Ill., 1938-42, Pilgrim Congl. Ch., Milw., 1942-56; tchr. comparative religion, philosophy of religion U. Wis., Milw., 1958-65; min. Congl.-United Ch. of Christ, Brown Deer, Wis., 1969-80, ret., 1980. Speaker in field. Lilly Endowment grantee. Mem. Delta Sigma Rho. Home: Milwaukee, Wis. *The fundamental forces of history are rarely comprehended or controlled. We can never return to Eden and we will never reach Utopia. There are great prices to be paid for being civilized.* Died Dec. 10, 2001.

**GIBBONS, BARBARA,** author, columnist, cooking educator; b. Newark, 1934; m. Walter I. Gibbons (dec.); 1 child, Susan. Writer nat. syndicated column The Slim Gourmet, United Features Syndicate, 1971—2014; organizer, instr. low-calories cooking classes, 1968—2014. Author: The Slim Gourmet Cookbook, 1976 (Tastemaster award), The International Slim Gourmet Cookbook, 1978 (Tastemaster award), Family Circle Creative Low Calorie Cooking; The Consumer Guide Diet Cookbook, The Diet Watchers Cookbook, The Year-Round Turkey Cookbook, 1979, Lean Cuisine, 1979, The Light and Easy Cookbook, 1980, Calories Don't Count, 1980, Salads for All Seasons, 1982, Slim Gourmet Sweets and Treats, 1982, The Thirty-Five Plus Diet for Women, 1987 (New York Times Bestseller List), Light & Spicy, 1989. Mem.: Travel Journalists Guild, Nat. Fedn. Press Women, Authors Guild, American Soc. Journalists and Authors, Newswomen's (NYC). Died Mar. 26, 2014.

**GIBBS, JORDAN SMITH,** music educator, artist; b. Kinston, NC, Sept. 11, 1936; d. Ernest Simpson Smith and Nell Brown (Johnson) Griffin; m. Gerald Goodwin Gibbs Jr., July 7, 1956; children: Anne, Stephen. Student, Duke U., 1954-56, George Washington U., 1974-77; Cert. in Piano, Conservatoire Royal de Musique, Mons, Belgium, 1980; BA in Music, Old Dominion U., 1984. Pvt. piano tchr., Cornwall-on-Hudson, N.Y., 1960-61; ch. organist TUSLOG Interdenominational Chapel, Ankara, Turkey, 1962-63; pvt. piano tchr. Mons, Belgium, 1978-79; piano tchr. Friends Sch., Virginia Beach, Va., 1984-86; pvt. piano tchr. Virginia Beach, from 1993; & Duke U. Libr. Assocs., 1989-92. Sec. bd. ARC, West Point, N.Y., 1959-60, hosp. vol., Ft. Sill, Okla., 1961, Ft. hood, Tex., 1969-70, Carlisle, Pa., 1970-71, vol. controller office, Norfolk, Va., 1987-88; asst. leader Girl Scout Mt. Vernon Scout Dist., Alexandria, Va., 1972-73; vol. Meals on Wheels Mt. Vernon Presbyn. Ch., Alexandria, 1972-73, Art League of Alexandria, 1972-73; vol. radiology clinic Internat. Red Cross, Mons, Belgium, 1978-80; sec.-treas. Shape Cycling Club, 1978-79; active docent Chrysler Mus., Norfolk, Va., 1992-99, bd. dirs. glass assocs., 1997-99; mem. worship com., fellowship com., flower guild First Presbyn. Ch., Virginia Beach, Va.; mem. Colonial Williamsburg (Va.) Found. Assocs., Libr. Assocs. Flower Guild, 1997-99; publicity chmn. SHAPE Art Assn., Mons, Belgium, 1978-79, Popular Choice Art Exhibit, SHAPE Hdqs., 1979; piano soloist Rachmaninoff Anniversary Celebration, Georgetown, Washington, 1974. Recipient Radiology Svc. award Red Cross, 1978-80. Mem. Met. Mus. Art, Va. Mus. FineArts, Phillips Collection, The Walters Art Gallery, Ctr. Contemporary Art, Muscarelle Mus. Art, Va. Hist. Soc., Nat. Trust, Nat. Mus. Women in the Arts, Am. Liszt Soc., Inc., Hermitage Found. Aux., Norfolk Soc. of Arts, Linkhorn Park Garden Club (editor yearbook 1992-94, sec. 1994-96, 1st v.p. 1996-98, rec. sec. 1998—, Ann. Flower Arrangements award 1999), Southwood Garden Club (rec. sec. 1971-72, 1st v.p. 1972-73), SACLANT Officers Wives Club (bd. dirs. 1982), Zeta Tau Alpha Alumnae (v.p. 1984-86, Sigma Alpha Iota (bd. dirs. 1980-84, Sword of Honor 1982, Grad. SAI Scholastic award 1984, SAI alumnae treas. 1990-99, treas. 1990-98, Stephen ministry program 1999—). Avocations: golf, tennis, skiing, needlepoint. Died Dec. 2002.

**GIBSON, ELIZABETH HARRIS,** retired counselor and educational administrator; b. Buhl Tuscaloosa County, Ala. d. Levi and Carrie (Craig) Harris; m. Alvernis Rochelle, Aug. 9, 1944 (div. 1966); children: Cyntheia, Karen D.; m. John Gibson Jr., Mar. 9, 1974. BA, Stillman Coll., Tuscaloosa, 1952; MEd, Wayne State U., 1960; Edn. Specialist Degree, U. Ala., 1971. Cert. tchr., counselor, Ala. Tchr. Tuscaloosa City Schs., 1953-71; tchr., counselor City Pub. Schs., Tuscaloosa, 1965-71; dir., coordinator career counseling and placement Saginaw Valley State U., University Center, Mich., 1971-78; ret., 1978. Summer freshman counselor U. Ala., 1968-70. Chmn. bd. dirs. Child Day Care Learning Ctr., Bethel A.M.E. Ch., Saginaw, 1979—, organizer, chmn., adviser quality of life outreach, 1982-83; sec., mem. exec. bd. Mitten Bay (Mich.) coun. Girl Scouts U.S., 1978—; mem., organizer, convenor, chmn. Saginaw Nat. Issues Forum, 1982. Recipient Educator of Yr. award United Sisterhood-Wolverine State Bapt. Assn., 1981, Outstanding Svc. award Nat. Issues Forum, Washington, 1986. Mem. AAUW, LWV (sec.), Top Ladies of Distinction, Zeta Phi Beta (Woman of Yr. 1985, named to Zeta Hall of Fame 1988). Methodist. Avocations: civic and church activities, human betterment. Deceased.

**GILBERT, JAMES FREEMAN,** geophysics educator; b. Vincennes, Ind., Aug. 9, 1931; s. James Freeman and Gladys (Paugh) G.; m. Sally Bonney, June 19, 1959; children: Cynthia, Sarah, James. BS, MIT, 1953, PhD, 1956; D honoris causa, Utrecht U., 1994; D in Engring. (hon.), Colo. Sch. Mines, 2004. Research assoc. MIT, Cambridge, 1956-57; asst. research geophysicist Inst. Geophysics & Planetary Physics, UCLA, 1957, asst. prof. geophysics, 1958-59; sr. research geophysicist Tex. Instruments, Dallas, 1960-61; prof. Inst. Geophysics & Planetary Physics, U. Calif. San Diego, La Jolla, 1961—2001, assoc. dir., 1976-88, prof. emeritus, 2001—14; chmn. grad. dept. Scripps Inst. Oceanography, La Jolla, 1988-91. Chmn. steering com. San Diego Supercomputer, 1984-86. Contbr. numerous articles to profl. jours. Recipient Arthur L. Day medal Geol. Soc. America, 1985, Internat. Balzan prize, 1990; Fairchild scholar Calif. Inst. Tech., Pasadena, 1987; fellow NSF, 1956, Guggenheim, 1964-65, 72-73, Overseas fellow Churchill Coll. U. Cambridge, Eng., 1972-73. Fellow AAAS, American Geophys. Union (William Bowie med. 1999); Nat. Acad. Sciences, European Union Geoscis. (hon.); mem. Seismology Soc. America (Reid medal 2004), American Math. Soc., Royal Astron. Soc. (recipient Gold medal 1981), Acad. Nat. dei Lincei (fgn.), Sigma Xi. Home: Del Mar, Calif. Died Aug. 15, 2014.

**GILBRETH, LILLIAN EVELYN MOLLER,** consulting engineer, educator; b. Oakland, Calif., May 24, 1878; d. William and Annie (Delger) Moller; m. Frank Bunker Gilbreth, Oct. 19, 1904 (dec. June 14, 1924); children: Anne Moller (Mrs. Robert E. Barney), Mary Elizabeth (dec.), Ernestine Moller (Mrs. Charles E. Carey), Martha Bunker (Mrs. Richard E. Tallman) (dec.), Frank Bunker, William Moller, Lillian Moller (Mrs. Donald D. Johnson), Frederick Moller, Daniel Bunker, John Moller, Robert Moller, Jane Moller (Mrs. Donald D. Johnson). B in Lit., U. Calif., 1900, M in Lit., 1902; PhD, Brown U., 1915; M in Engring., U. Mich., 1928; D in Engring., Rutgers U., 1929; ScD, Brown U., 1931, Russell Sage Coll., 1931; LLD, U. Calif., 1933; ScD, LLD, Smith Coll., 1945; DHL (hon.), Alfred U., 1948; doctorate in Indsl. Psychology, Purdue U., 1948; DHL (hon.), Temple U., 1949; doctorate in Engring. (hon.), Stevens Inst. Tech., 1950; ScD (hon.), Colby Coll., 1951, Syracuse U., 1952; LLD (hon.), Mills Coll., 1952; ScD (hon.), Lafayette Coll., 1952; LLD (hon.), Ariz. State U., 1964; degree (hon.), Pratt Inst. Pres. cons. engrs. in mgmt. Gilbreth, Inc., Montclair, N.J., from 1924; dir. courses in motion study Purdue U., 1925-32, prof. mgmt., 1935-48; chmn. dept. personnel rels. Newark Coll. Engring., 1941-43; tchr. P.I. Formosa, 1953-54; prof. mgmt. U. Wis., 1955; lectr. on tech. and human rels. problems in mgmt. Europe, Mex., U.S., Asia, Australia, Can., from 1955. Mem. coms. on civil def. U.S. Govt., Presdl. Emergency Com. for Unemployment Relief, 1930; ednl. advisor, Office of War Info. during World War II; cons. Inst. Rehabilitation Medicine. Author (with Frank B. Gilbreth) Motion Study, 1911, Fatigue Study, 1917, Applied Motion Study, 1917, Motion Study for the Handicapped, 1919, The Psychology of Management, 1921, Living with Our Children, 1928, Normal Lives for the Disabled (with Edna Yost), 1945, The Foreman and Manpower Management (with Alice Rice Cook), 1947, Management in the Home (with O.M. Thomas, Eleanor C. Clymer), 1954, 59; contbr. to Indsl Engring. handbook. Mem. housing com. 20th Century Fund; mem. N.J. State Bd. Regents, 1929-33; mem. Essex Co. Vocat. Bd.; trustee Russell Sage Coll., 1943-45, Montclair Libr., 1944-54; vol. Girl Scouts. Recipient Henry Lawrence Gantt medal (with Frank Gilbreth), Nat. Inst. Social Scis., Wallace Clark Internat. award, gold medal Comite Internat. de l'Orgn. Sci., Washington award, Allan R. Cullimore medal, 1959, Hoover medal ASCE, 1966; US Postal Svc. issued stamp in her honor, 1984; named to Nat. Women's Hall of Fame, 1995. Fellow Brit. Inst. Mgmt. (hon.); mem. AAUW, Am. Mgmt. Assn. (hon.), Inst. Mgmt., Soc. Advancement of Mgmt. (hon.), Acad. Masaryk, Am. Psychol. Assn., ASME (hon.)(first woman mem.), Engring. Inst. Can. (hon.), Am. Home Econs. Assn. (hon.), Soc. Indsl. Engrs. (hon.), Inst. Sci. Mgmt. Poland, Women's Engring. Soc. London, NAE (first woman elected), Internat. Acad. Mgmt., Phi Beta Kappa. Achievements include first female professor in the engineering school at Purdue University; patents in field. Died Jan. 2, 1972.

**GIN, SUE LING,** food service executive; b. Aurora, Ill., Sept. 23, 1941; m. William G. McGowan, July 5, 1984 (dec. June 8, 1992). Chmn., CEO Flying Food Group, LLC, Chicago, 1983—2014; founder, pres. New Mgmt. Ltd., Chgo. Bd. dirs. Exelon Corp., 2000—14, Centerplate, Inc., 2004—14. Mem. Womens Leadership Forum (bd. dirs.). Died Sept. 23, 2014.

**GINS, MADELINE,** poet, artist, architect; b. NYC, Nov. 7, 1941; d. Milton and Evelyn (Friedman) G.; m. Arakawa, July 19 (dec. 2010) BA, Barnard Coll., 1962. Pvt. practice architecture, NYC. Pres. Containers of Mind Found., N.Y.C., 1988—. Exhbns. include Kunsthalle, Hamburg, 1972, Nat. Gallery, Berlin, 1972, Stadtische in Lenbachhaus, Munich, 1972, Frankfurt Kunstverein, Frankfurt, 1972, Kunsthalle Bern, 1972, Ronald Feldman Gallery, N.Y., 1990, Guggenheim Mus., N.Y.C., 1997; group exhbns. include Contemporary Art and Urbanism in France, Musee des Arts de Tsukuba, Ibaraki, 1990, Musee Nat. d'Art, Osaka, 1990; author: Word Rain, 1969, What the President Will Say and Do!!, 1979, Helen Keller o Arakawa, 1994, Architecture, Sites of Reversible Destiny, 1994; co-author: For Example-A Critique of Never, 1974, The Mechanism of Meaning, 1971, 3d edit. 1989, others; essays and poetry. Home: New York, NY. Died Jan. 8, 2014.

**GITLER HAMMER, SAMUEL CARLOS,** retired mathematician; b. Mexico City, July 14, 1933; came to U.S., 1987; s. Moises Gitler and Maria Hammer; m. Raquel Goldwain de Gitler, Sept. 2, 1956; children: Isidoro, Miriam, Susana. BS in Engring., U. Mex., Mexico City, 1955, BS in Math., 1955; MS, Princeton U., 1958, PhD, 1960. Rsch. assoc. Brandeis U., Waltham, Mass., 1960-61; prof. Centro de Investigacion IPN Mexico, Mexico City, 1961-87, head dept., 1976-84; prof. U. Rochester, NY, 1987—2000, chmn. dept., 1987-91. Contbr. papers in algebraic topology to profl. publications Mem. El Colegio Nacional, Mexico City, 1985. Recipient Premio Nacional de Ciencias prize Gov. of Mexico, 1976. Mem. American Math. Soc., Mexican Math. Soc. (pres. 1972-74). Home: Rochester, NY. Died Sept. 9, 2014.

**GIULINI, CARLO MARIA,** orchestra conductor; b. May 9, 1914; married; 3 children. Grad., Accademia Santa Cecilia, Rome; DHL (hon.), DePaul U., 1979. Played viola Santa Cecilia Orch.; debut as condr. Rome, 1944; organized Orch. of Milano Radio, 1951; prin. condr. La Scala, Milan, 1953—55; condr. Philharmonia Orch., London; prin. guest condr. Chgo. Symphony Orch., 1969—78; music dir. Vienna (Austria) Symphony Orch., 1973—76, LA Philharmonic Orch., 1978—84. Debut in Gt. Britain, Edinburgh Festival; conducting Verdi's Falstaff, 1955; appeared at Edinburgh, Lucerne, Vienna festivals; condr. revivals of Don Carlos and Il Berbier di Siviglia, Covent Garden, Israel, Holland. Recipient Gold medal, Buickner Soc., 1978. Died June 14, 2005.

**GJERDE, BJARTMAR ALV,** former Norweigan government official; b. Sunnmo re, Norway, Nov. 6, 1931; s. Hjalmar and Astrid (O vrelid) Gjerde; m. Anna Karin Hoel, 1954; children: Bjartmar Arve, Espen, Hans Petter. Grad., Harvard U., 1964. Journalist Sunnmo re Arbeideravis, 1948—53; editor Fritt Slag, Oslo, 1953—58; sec. Parliamentary Group Labour Party of Norway, Oslo, 1961—62; head Workers Edn. Orgn., Oslo, 1962—81; dir. gen. Norwegian Broadcasting Corp., Oslo, 1981—89. Mem. Adv. Broadcasting Coun., 1963—74, Cultural Coun., 1963—85; dep. mem. Norwegian Parliament, Oslo, 1969—73; min. Norwegian Dept. Ch. and Edn., Oslo, 1971—76, Norwegian Dept. Industry, Oslo, 1976—78, Norwegian Dept. Oil and Energy, Oslo, 1978—81; bd. dirs. Aetat, 1989—95. Mem. Nat. Coun. Young People, 1958—61, Coun. Adult Edn., 1966—71; chmn. Young Workers Orgn., 1958—61, Oslo Labour Party, 1969—73; mem., ctrl. bd. Labour Party, 1958—61. Died Nov. 28, 2009.

**GLADSTONE, ERNEST,** educator, inventor; b. Bklyn., July 8, 1931; s. Jacob and Anna G.; m. Renee Rahlens, Aug. 13, 1955; children: Karen Sue, Alisa Ruth, Steven Craig, Jessica Lee. BA in English, Bklyn. Coll., 1958. Inventor, Bklyn., from 1949; contractor, 1955-57; tchr. N.Y.C. Bd. Edn., Bklyn., 1957-68, 74-86; developer Bklyn., 1968-73. Author: Complete Guide to Select Living, 1969, The Photodissociation Hypothesis of Photosynthesis, 1990, also articles in field; inventor of method and arrangement for generating hydrogen, arrangement and method for supplying hydrogen gas, high definition TV system, Le Process Vierge Champagnes; patentee in field. Cpl. U.S. Army, 1953-55. Mem. Internat. Assn. for Hydrogen Energy. Republican. Jewish. Died Aug. 16, 2008.

**GLASER, PETER EDWARD,** retired mechanical engineer, consultant, educator; b. Zatec, Bohemia, Czechoslovakia, Sept. 5, 1923; came to U.S., 1948, naturalized July, 1954; s. Hugo and Helen (Weiss) G.; m. Eva F. Graf, Oct. 16, 1955; children: David, Steven, Susan. Diploma, Leeds Coll. Tech., Eng., 1943; 1st state exam, Czech Tech U., Prague, Czechoslovakia, 1948; MS, Columbia U., NYC, 1951, PhD, 1955. Head design dept. Werner Mgmt. Co., NYC, 1948-53; from mem. profl. staff to cons. Arthur D. Little, Inc., Cambridge, Mass., 1955—94, v.p., 1985, cons., 1994—99; pres. Power from Space Cons., Inc., Lexington, Mass., 1995—2005; ret., 2005. Cons. NASA, Washington, 1963-67, mem. adv. coun., 1986; mem. case study task force Lunar Energy Enterpise, 1988-89; mgmt. adv. bd. Ctr. for Space Power, Tex. A&M U. System, 1990-94; sr. adv. bd. mem. Space Studies Inst., 1990-2014; mem. bd. assessment NIST program NRC, 1993-96; cons. NRC, Washington, 1960-62, panel mem., 1994-95, Heritage Found., Washington, 1982-83; adv. panelist Office Tech. Assessment, Washington, 1980-81; mem. Awards Adv. Coun. of Space Found., 1988-96. Editor: The Lunar Surface Layer, 1964, Thermal Imaging Techniques, 1964, Solar Power Satellites-The Emerging Energy Option, 1993, Solar Power Satellites-A Space Energy System for Earth, 2d edit., 1998, Solar Power Systems in Space; contbr. Standard Handbook of Powerplant Engineering, 1998; assoc. editor Space Power Jour., 1980-86; editor-in-chief Jour. Solar Energy, 1972-85, mem. editl. bd., 1985-93; mem. editl. bd. Space Policy, Space Power, Jour. Practical Applications in Space, Solar Energy; patentee solar power satellite, 1973; guest editor spl. issue of "Space Policy" on Space Solar Power, 1999-2000. Mem. bd. overseers Combined Jewish Philanthropies, Boston, 1984-88; voting mem. engring. coun. Columbia U., N.Y.C., 1984; advisor Space Solar Power Rsch. Soc., Japan, 1998-2014 Recipient Carl F. Kayan medal Columbia U., 1974, Farrington Daniels award Internat. Solar Energy Soc., Australia, 1983; named to The U.S. Space Found. Space Tech. Hall of Fame, 1996. Fellow AAAS, AIAA; mem. ASME, Internat. Astron. Fedn. (chmn. space power com. 1984-89), Internat. Acad. Astronautics, Internat. Solar Energy Soc. (pres. 1967-72), American Astron. Soc. (bd. dirs. 1977-84), Sunsat Energy Coun. (pres. 1978-94, chmn. 1994-2000), Nat. Space Soc. (bd. advisors 1990-94, dir. 1994-97, bd. govs. 1997-2014), United Socs. in Space (regent 1997-2014), American Soc. for Macro-Engring. Avocation: archaeology. Home: Lexington, Mass. Died May 29, 2014.

**GLAZE, MICHAEL (JAMES),** former ambassador; b. Rochford, Essex, Eng., Jan. 15, 1935; s. Derek Newey and Shirley Winifred (Ramsay) G.; m. Rosemary Duff, May 21, 1965; children: Fiona, Deirdre. MA in Modern and Medieval Langs., Cambridge U., Eng., 1958; postgrad., Oxford U., Eng., 1958. Dist. officer Brit. Overseas Civil Svc., Lesotho, 1959-65; dep. permanent sec. Fin. Ministry, Lesotho, 1965-70; prin. Dept. of Trade, U.K., 1971-73; 1st sec. Brit. Diplomatic Svc., London, Abu Dhabi and Morocco, 1973-80, consul gen. Bordeaux, France, 1980-83; Brit. amb. to Cameroon, 1983-87; Brit. amb. to Angola, 1987-90; Brit. amb. to Ethiopia, 1990-94; dep. sec. gen. Most Venerable Order St. John, 1994-2001. Lt. Brit. Army, 1953—55. Decorated companion Order St. Michael and St. George (Eng.), officer Order of St. John. Anglican. Avocations: golf, music, gardening. Deceased.

**GLAZER, LAURENCE CHARLES,** real estate developer; b. Mt. Vernon, NY, Oct. 12, 1945; s. Irwyn and Leona (Hyman) G.; m. Jane Lovenheim, Aug. 6, 1967 (dec. Sept. 5, 2014); children: Melinda Beth, Richard Harris, Kenneth Jacob. BS in Acctg. cum laude, U. Buffalo, 1967; MBA in Finance & Acctg., Columbia U., 1969. V.p. Falcon Fund, NYC, 1967-69; CEO Great Lakes Press, Rochester, NY, 1969-84; exec. v.p. Case-Hoyt Corp., Rochester, 1984-87; mng. ptnr. Buckingham Properties, Rochester, 1970—2014. Mem. Kidney Found. Upstate N.Y., Rochester, Pittsford Environ. Rev. & Planning Bd., 1988-92; bd. dirs. Temple B'Rith Kodesh, Rochester, 1980-87, Norman Howard Sch., Rochester Inst. Tech. Sch. of Bus., 1992, Jewish Home of Rochester, Family Planning and Relocation Svcs., Rochester Recipient Lifetime Achievement award, NY State Comml. Assn. Realtors (Rochester chapter), 2008. Mem.: Tennis of Rochester, Midtown Tennis. Democrat. Jewish. Avocations: squash, bonsai, flying. Home: Rochester, NY. Died Sept. 5, 2014.

**GLAZER, MALCOLM IRVING,** professional sports team owner; b. Rochester, NY, Aug. 25, 1928; m. Linda Glazer, 1961; children: Avram, Kevin, Bryan, Joel, Ed, Darcie. Pres., CEO First Allied Corp.; chmn. Zapata Corp., Houston, 1994—2002; owner, pres. Tampa Bay Buccaneers, Fla., 1995—2014; shareholder Manchester United, 2003—14, owner, 2005—14. Bd. dirs. Splty. Equipment Cos. Active American Cancer Soc., Sloan-Kettering Cancer Ctr., United Jewish Appeal, Jewish Guild for the Blind. Named one of Forbes 400: Richest Americans, from 2006, Most Influential People in the World of Sports, Bus. Week, 2008. Died May 28, 2014.

**GLEDHILL, JAMES EDWIN,** retired elementary and secondary school educator; Student in Psychology, Edn., French, English, U. Pa., Phila., 1946—49; BA in Psychology, French, Carleton Coll., Northfield, Minn., 1951; EdM in Guidance and Counseling, Rutgers U., New Brunswick, NJ, 1966. Cert. tchr. secondary sch. NJ, student personnel svcs. NJ, supr. NJ, dir. student personnel svcs. NJ. Guidance counselor Audubon H.S., NJ, 1964—67, Mid. Township H.S., Cape May Courthouse, NJ, 1969—72; guidance counselor elem. sch. Camden Bd. Edn., NJ, 1990—2004, ret., 2004. Tchr. adult sch. German Cheltenham H.S., from 2006. Named Disting. Toastmaster, Ea. Pa. and So. NJ Toastmasters, 1977, Oustanding Counselor, Broadway Sch., Camden, 1998. Mem.: NEA, ASCD, Am. Assn. Tchrs. German, Am. Assn. Tchrs. French, Pa. Sch. Counselors Assn., Camden County Counselors Assn., NJ Sch. Counselors Assn., Nat. Career Devel. Assn., Am. Sch. Counselors Assn., Am. Counseling Assn. Home: Jenkintown, Pa. Died Aug. 1, 2008.

**GLEZOS, MATTHEWS,** retired consumer products and services company executive; b. Montreal, Aug. 27, 1927; s. George and Katerina (Bakalos) G.; m. Sophia Protonotarios, Sept. 23, 1953; children: George, Mary. B in Commerce, McGill U., 1952. Tax assessor taxation divsn. Govt. of Can., Montreal, 1953-55; tax mgr., treas. Imasco Ltd., Montreal, 1955-78, v.p., treas., 1978-84; pres. Imasco B.V., Amsterdam, 1984-89, ret., 1989. Mem. Royal Montreal Golf Club. Home: Mount Royal, Canada. Died Oct. 20, 2003.

**GLIMCHER, MELVIN JACOB,** orthopedic surgeon; b. Brookline, Mass., June 2, 1925; s. Aaron and Clara (Fink) Glimcher; m. Karin Wetmore, Mar. 8, 2000; children from previous marriage: Susan Deborah, Laurie Hollis, Nancy Blair. Student, Duke U., 1943-44; BS in Mech. Engring. with highest distinction; BS in Physics with highest distinction, Purdue U., 1946; MD magna cum laude, Harvard Medical Sch., 1950; postgrad., Mass. Inst. Tech., 1956-59; PhD in Engring. (hon.), Purdue U., 2004. Intern surgery Strong Meml. Hosp., Rochester, NY, 1950-51; 3d asst. resident surgery Mass. Gen. Hosp., Boston, 1951-52, 2d asst. resident, 1952-53, asst. resident orthopedic surgery, 1954-55, chief resident, 1956, chief orthopedic service, 1965-71, chmn. dept. orthopedic surgery, 1968-71; asst. resident orthopedic surgery Children's Med. Center, Boston, 1953-54, jr. resident, 1955-56; mem. faculty Harvard Med. Sch., 1956—2009, Edith M. Ashley prof. orphopedic surgery, 1965-71, Harriet M. Peabody prof., 1971—2009, Peabody disting. prof., 2009—14; also chmn. dept.; orthopedic surgeon-in-chief Children's Hosp. Med. Center, Boston, 1971-81, dir. Lab. for Study of Skeletal Disorders and Rehab., 1980—2009. Trustee Forsyth Dental Inst., Hosp. Spl. Surgery, NYC, New Eng. Sinai Hosp. With USMCR, World War II. Recipient Soma Weiss award Harvard Med. Sch., 1950, Borden Research award, 1950; Kappa Delta award, 1959; Internat. Assn. Dental Research award, 1964; Ralph Pemberton award American Rheumatism Soc., 1969; Bristol-Meyers/Zimmer instl. grant for excellence; Disting. Achievement in Orthopaedic Research award Orthopaedic Research Edn. Found.; William Neuman award American Soc. Bone and Mineral Rsch., 1996; Physician Achievement award Arthritis Found., 1996. Fellow American Acad. Arts and Scis., American Acad. Orthopaedic Surgeons (Silver anniversary Kappa Delta prize 1974, Alfred Shands award jointly awarded with Orthop. Rsch. Soc 1997), American Orthopedic Assn.; mem. Orthopedic Research Soc. (past pres.), Assn. Bone and Joint Surgeons (Nicholas Andry award 1978), Internat. Soc. for Study Lumbar Spine (Volvo award 1983), Societe Internationale de Chirurgie Orthopedique et de Traumatologie. Home: Coral Gables, Fla. Died May 12, 2014.

**GLYNN, ROBERT,** lawyer, foundation chairman; b. NJ, Oct. 30, 1929; 1 child, Katherine F.J. Glynn. BA, Harvard U., 1951, LLB, 1956. Staff atty. Internat. Fin. Corp., Washington, D.C., 1961-65; ptnr. Fox, Glynn & Melamed, NYC, 1968-87, Becker, Glynn, Melamed & Muffly LLP, NYC, from 1987; chmn. bd. dirs. and dir. gen. Lampadia Found., from 1993. Home: New York, NY. Died 2001.

**GOBRECHT, HEINRICH FRIEDRICH,** physicist, researcher; b. Bremen, Germany, July 20, 1909; s. Heinrich Ludwig and Caroline Friederike (Oesterhelweg) G.; m. Christa Johanna Schubbe, Aug. 25, 1938; children: Klaus, Juergen, Jens. Student, U. Hanover, 1929-32, U. Göttingen, 1932-33, U. Marburg, 1933-34, U. Dresden, 1934-36; diploma in engring., Tech. High Sch., Dresden, 1936, D in Engring., 1937, D Engring. Habilitation, 1939. Chief engr. TV dept. Loewe-Radio, Berlin, 1938-45, Siemens-Radio, Arnstadt, 1946-47; prof. physics and dir. Phys. Inst. U. Berlin, 1948-77, prof. emeritus, from 1977. Dir. Phys. Inst. U. Berlin, 1952-77. Author, editor: Bergmann-Schaefer, Experimentalphysics, (5 vols.); contbr. over 200 articles to spl. periodicals. Burgomaster City of Oberlungwitz, Saxonia, Germany, 1945. Mem. German Phys. Soc., Gesellschaft Deutscher Naturforscher und Arzte. Home: Berlin, Germany. Died May 25, 2002.

**GODETTE, STANLEY RICKFORD,** microbiologist; b. Berbice, Guyana, Nov. 27, 1940; s. Wilfred Arnold and Dorothy Charles (Jordan) G.; m. Desiree Carole Hazlewood, Sept. 9, 1967; 1 child, Dionne Carole. BS, Howard U., 1965, MS, 1972. Microbiologist Children's Nat. Med. Ctr., Washington, 1965-69, lab. mgr., 1969-79; health care cons. DIMPEX Assocs., Washington, 1979-85; dir. Met. Health Svcs. Lab., Washington, 1985-90; asst. adminstr. Al-Amal Hosp., Jeddah, Saudi Arabia, 1990-92; pres. Fredol Assocs., Ft. Washington, Md., from 1992. Mem. Am. Soc. for Med. Tech. (bd. dirs. 1980—), N.Y. Acad. Scis., Clin. Lab. Mgmt. Assn., Gyana Berbice Assn. (treas. 1985-90, pres. 1990—, award of merit 1990). Home: Fort Washington, Md. Died Sept. 1999.

**GOFFIN, GERRY,** recording artist, producer, songwriter; b. NYC, Feb. 11, 1939; m. Carole King, 1958 (div. 1968); m. Michelle Goffin; 5 children Songwriter: (with Carole King) Will You Love Me Tomorrow (by Shirelles), Take Good Care of My Baby (by Bobby Vee), 1961, The Loco-Motion (by Little Eva), 1962, Go Away Little Girl (by Steve Lawrence), 1963, Up on the Roof, You Make Me Feel Like a Natural Woman, (with Michael Masser) Do You Know Where You Are Going To?,1976, Saving All My Love for You (by Whitney Houston); ablums include It Ain't Exactly Entertainment, 1973, Back Room Blood, 1996; prodr. rec. (by the Monkees) More of the Monkees, 1967, Head, 1968, More Greatest Hits, 1982, Then & Now...The Best of the Monkees, 1986, Listen to the Band, 1991; vocals Songs (by B.J. Thomas), 1973. Named to The Songwriters Hall of Fame, 1987, The Rock & Roll Hall of Fame, 1990. Died June 19, 2014.

**GOGGIN, JOSEPH ROBERT,** retired financial consultant; b. Chgo., Apr. 24, 1926; s. William Nobel and Loretta Ann (Davis) G.; m. Barbara Jean Laibach, Sept. 21, 1957; children: Tracy Jean Goggin Layton, Sandra Lynn Goggin Adams. With Mut. Trust Life Ins. Co., Chgo., 1947-88, asst. treas., treas., CFO, exec. v.p., chmn. financial com., dir., 1968-88; dir. Enterprise Savs. Bank, Chgo., 1986-89; pres. Focus Financial Group, Inc., 1988-89. Served with USMCR, 1942-46. Mem. Investment Analysts Soc. Chgo. Clubs: Chgo. (Chgo.). Home: La Grange Park, Ill. Died Aug. 9, 2012.

**GOLA, TOM (THOMAS JOSEPH GOLA),** retired professional basketball player, former state legislator; b. Phila., Jan. 13, 1933; m. Caroline Gola; 1 child, Thomas. Forward Phila. Warriors, 1955—61, San Francisco Warriors, 1962, NY Knicks, 1962—66; head basketball coach La Salle U., Phila., 1968—70; mem. Dist. 170 Pa. House of Reps., 1969—70; contr. City of Phila., 1970—74. Named Helms Found. Player of Yr., 1954, UPI Player of Yr, 1955, All Time All-American Team Sport Mag., 1960; Named to The NBA All-Star Team, 1960-64, The Naismith Meml. Basketball Hall of Fame, 1975, Nat. Polish-American Sports Hall of Fame, 1977; selected MVP La Salle U., Phila., 1955; mem. NBA Champions, 1955. Died Jan. 26, 2014.

**GOLD, ALAN B.,** former Canadian chief justice; b. Montreal, July 21, 1917; m. Lynn Lubin; children: Marc, Nora, Daniel. BA, Queen's U., Kingston, Ont., Can., 1938; LLD (hon.), Queen's U., 1982; LLL cum laude, U. Montreal, 1941, LLD (hon.), 1978, McGill U., 1984, Yeshiva U., 1987. Bar: Que. 1941; Queen's counsel. Lectr. Faculty of Law McGill U., Montreal, 1957-71; dist. judge, vice chmn. Labour Rels. Bd., Que., 1961-65; assoc. chief judge Provincial Ct., P.Q., 1965-70, chief judge P.Q., 1970-83, pres. Jud. Coun. P.Q., 1978-83, chmn. Conseil du Referendum P.Q., 1980; chief justice Superior Ct., P.Q., 1983-92; chancellor Concordia U., 1987-92; chancellor emeritus Corcordia U., 1992—2005; sr. counsel, chmn. dept. alternative dispute resolution Davies Ward Phillips & Vineberg LLP, Montreal, 1992—2005, chair alternative dispute resolution dept. Chief arbitrator under collective labour agreements between Govt. P.Q. and Employees, 1966-83, between Shipping Fedn. Can. Inc. and Maritime Employers Assn. and Internat. Longshoremen's Assn., 1967-75; mem. multinat. panel Arbitration and Mediation Ctr. Ams.; spl. mediator and arbitrator in disputes concerning Fgn. Svc., Rys., Airlines, Royal Mint, Can. P.O., constrn. industry, other areas of pub., para-pub., pvt. sectors; scholar in residence McGill U. Faculty of Law, 1982; pres. Jr. Bar Assn., Montreal, 1951-52; mem. coun. Bar of Montreal, 1952-53, various other coms.; mem. bd. examiners Bar of P.Q., 1952-61, various other coms.; founder, dir., officer Legal Aid Bur., Montreal, 1956-60; mem. multinat. panel arbitrators and mediators concerning N.Am. Free Trade Agreement, Comml. Arbitration Mediation Ctr. Ams. Bd. dirs., exec. coun. Regie de la Place des Arts, 1973-82; mem., vice-chmn. Societe de la Place des Arts de Montreal, 1982—; pres. Jewish Pub. Establishments Commn., Fedn. CJA, 1993-97, bd. dirs. Fedn. CJA 1993-97; pres. bd. dirs. Jerusalem Found. Can. Inc., 1980-83; bd. govs. McGill U., 1974-83, chmn. 1978-82, gov. emeritus, 1984-2005; gov. Soc. Pro Musica, 1970-2005, I Musici de Montreal, 1988-2005; bd. dirs., chmn. Conseil d'adminstrn. de l'orchestre, 1997-2005. Decorated officer Order of Can., Ordre Nat. du Qué.; recipient Human Rels. award Can. Coun. Christians and Jews, 1985, Disting. Bora Laskin award Yeshiva U., 1987, Médaille du Premier Ministre du Qué., 1987, Montreal medal Queen's U., 1985, Bar of Québec medal,

1990-91, Nat. Assembly of Québec medal, 1992, Université de Montréal medal, 1992, Samuel Bronfman Can. Jewish Contress, 1992, Commemorative medal for 125th anniversary of Can., Case District I, Disting. Friend of Edn. award, 1993, Pres.'s award Tel Aviv U., 1998. Mem. Bar Province Quebec, Montreal Bar (various offices) Nat. Acad. Arbitrators (hon., life, U.S.), Soc. Profls. in Dispute Resolution (charter, U.S., Spl. award for excellence 1981), Corp. Professionnelle des Conseillers en Rels. Industrielles de law Province de Quebec, Conseil de l'Order (pres. 1989-91), Acad. Grands Montréalais, Clin. Rsch. Inst. Montreal (chmn. ethics com. 1990-94), Phi Delta Phi. Home: Montreal, Canada. Died May 15, 2005.

**GOLDANSKII, VITALII IOSIFOVICH,** chemist, physicist; b. Vitebsk, USSR, June 18, 1923; s. Iosif Efimovich and Yudif' Iosifovna (Melamed) G.; m. Lyudmila Nikolaevna Semenova; children: Dmitrii, Andrei. Grad. in Chemistry, Moscow U., 1944, M of Chemistry, 1947, DSc in Physics, 1954. Scientist Inst. Chem. Physics-USSR Acad. Scis., Moscow, 1942-52 and from 1961, from div. head to dir., from 1988; sr. scientist P.N. Lebedev Phys. Inst.-USSR Acad. Scis., Moscow, 1952-61; asst. prof. Phys.-Tech. Inst., Moscow, 1947-51; asst. prof., then prof. Inst. Phys. Engring., Moscow, from 1951. Author: Kinematics of Nuclear Reactions, 1959, Mössbauer Effect and its Applications in Chemistry, 1963, Physical Chemistry of Positron and Positronium, 1968, Tunneling Phenomena in Chemical Physics, 1986, many others; contbr. numerous articles and revs. to profl. jours.; patentee (numerous) in field. Chmn. Russian Pugwash Com., Moscow, 1987—; people's dep. of USSR; mem. com. fgn. affairs Supreme Soviet of USSR, 1989-92. Decorated Lenin Order, Order of October Revolution, numerous other orders and medals; recipient Lenin prize, 1980; Golden Mendeleev medal USSR Acad. Scis., 1975, Karpinsky prize Friedrich von Schiller Found., Hamburg, Germany, 1983, Boris Pregel award N.Y. Acad. Scis., 1990, Alexander von Humboldt award, Germany, 1991, Golden Semenov medal Russian Acad. Scis., 1996. Fellow Am. Chem. Soc. (hon.), Am. Phys. Soc., Am. Acad. Arts and Scis., Am. Philos Soc., Acad. Scis. German Dem. Republic, Royal Swedish Acad. Scis., Royal Danish Acad. Scis. and Lettrs, Deutsche Akademie der Naturforscher Leopoldina, World Acad. Arts and Sci., Hungarian Eotvos Lorand Phys. Soc.; mem. NAS USA (fgn., assoc.), N.Y. Acad. Scis. (life.), Russian Acad. Scis., Finnish Acad. Scis. (fgn.), Acad. Europaea, Acad. Georgia. Avocations: writing humor and aphorisms, record collecting, movies, cds, videos. Home: Moscow, Russia. Deceased.

**GOLDBERG, SIR ABRAHAM,** medical educator; b. Edinburgh, Dec. 7, 1923; s. Julius and Rachel (Varinofsky) G.; m. Clarice Cussin, Sept. 3, 1957; children: David, Jennifer, Richard. MB, BChir, U. Edinburgh, 1946, MD with Gold Medal, 1956; DSc, U. Glasgow, Scotland, 1966. Nurrfield rsch. fellow UCH Med. Sch., London, 1952-54; Eli Lilly travelling fellow U. Utah, 1954-56; sr. lectr. medicine U. Glasgow, 1956-57, titular prof. medicine, 1967-70, regius prof. practice medicine, 1978-89, prof. emeritus, from 1990. Founder, pres. faculty phar. medicine Royal Colls. Physicians U.K., 1989-91; chmn. U.K. Com. on Safety of Medicines, 1980-86; editor Scottish Med. Jour., 1962-63; chmn. grants com. Med. Rsch. Coun., London, 1973-77; chmn. biomed. rsch. com. Scottish Home and Health Dept., Edinburgh, 1977-83. Co-author: Diseases of Porphyrin Metabolism, 1962, Clinics in Haematology-The Porphyrias, 1980; co-editor: Recent Advances in Haematology, 1971, Disorders of Porphyrin Metabolism, 1987, Pharmaceutical Medicine and the Law, 1991. Served to hon. maj. Royal Army Med. Corps, 1947-49. Decorated knight bachelor, 1983; hon. sr. rsch. fellow dept. modern history U. Glasgow, 1990. Fellow Royal Soc. Edinburgh, Royal Coll. Physicians London (Fitzpatrick lectr. 1988), Royal Coll. Physicians Edinburgh, Royal Coll. Physicians and Surgeons Glasgow; mem. Assn. Physicians Gt. Britain. Jewish. Avocations: medical history, literature, writing, walking, swimming. Home: Glasgow, Scotland. Died Sept. 1, 2007.

**GOLDBERG, MILTON D.,** investment company executive; b. Chgo., Nov. 27, 1914; s. Isadore J. and Mollie A. (Feinberg) G.; m. Madeline E. Levine, Nov. 26, 1936; children: Lee Goldberg Cone, Kay E. PhB, U. Chgo., 1935. V.p. Isgo Corp, Chgo., 1935-54, pres., 1954-76, chmn., from 1976. Fellow Brandeis U., Waltham, Mass., 1963. Mem.: Lomas Santa Fe Country (Solana Beach, Calif.). Home: La Jolla, Calif. Died Mar. 28, 1990.

**GOLDMAN, JOHN MICHAEL,** physician, consultant hematologist, educator; b. London, United Kingdom, Nov. 30, 1938; s. Carl Heinz and Bertha (Brandt) G. BM BCh, Oxford U., 1963, DM, 1981. Medicine Gen. Med. Coun., 1963. Dir. LRF Ctr. Adult Leukaemia Imperial Coll. London Hammersmith Hosp., London, 1989—2004; chmn. dept. haematology Imperial Coll. London Sch. Medicine Hammersmith Hosp., 1994—2004; med. dir. Anthony Nolan Bone Marrow Trust, London, 1989—2010; chair Internat. Chronic Myeloid Leukemia Found., from 2009. Editor Bone Marrow Transplantation, 1985—. Recipient Hon MD Poitiers, U. of Poitiers; Fogarty scholar, Hematology Br., Nat. Inst. Health, 2005—06. Fellow Royal Coll. Physicians, Acad. Med. Scis., European Group for Bone Marrow Transplantation (pres. 1990-94); European Hematology Assn. (pres. 1996-98). Achievements include research in Scientific papers on haematology, leukaemia, bone marrow transplantation, molecular biology. Home: London, England. Died Dec. 24, 2014.

**GOLDMAN, LEON,** dermatologist, laser surgeon; b. Cin., Dec. 7, 1905; s. Abraham and Fanny (Friedman) G.; m. Belle Hurwitz, Aug. 23, 1936; children: John, Steve, Carol. MD, U. Cin., 1929. Prof. dermatology U. Cin., 1951-76, dir. laser lab., 1961-76, dir. laser treatment ctr., 1961-76; dir. laser lab. Children's Hosp., Cin., 1971-76, Jewish Hosp., Cin., 1979-83; laser cons. U.S. Naval Hosp., San Diego, from 1983. Author 7 books on laser medicine and laser surgery; contbr. numerous articles to profl. jours. Chmn. Cancer Coun., Cin., Ohio, 1978; pres. and co-founder Am. Soc. for Laser Medicine and Surgery, 1980-81; bd. dirs. Am. Soc. for Investigative Dermatology. Named Father of Laser Medicine, Opto-Electronik Congress, Munich, 1977; recipient W.D. Mark medal, Am. Soc. for Medicine and Surgery, 1981, Fineraud award, Am. Acad. Dermatology, 1984, Polaky medal Polaky U., Czechoslovakia, 1985, Schawlow medal Laser Industry Am., 1985, Pioneer award Internat. Soc. for Optical Engring, 1992, Epstein Photomedicine award, 1992. Mem. Laser Inst. Am. (life), Am. Soc. for Laser Medicine and Surgery (dir. laser art 1993). Jewish. Achievements include 3 patents in laser medicine and laser surgery. Home: San Diego, Calif. Died Dec. 2, 1997.

**GOLDMAN, MYRON A.,** financial analyst; b. Chgo., May 27, 1926; s. Nicholas N. and Anna (Cohen) G.; m. Hermine Prosk, July 11, 1948; children: Susan M., Wendy G. BS in Commerce, De Paul Univ., 1947, JD, 1949. Pres. Polynesian Sales Corp., Chgo., 1948-61, Galamo Sales Corp., Chgo., 1956-61; account exec. First Hanover Corp. (and predecessor firms), Chgo., 1961-70, Weis Securities Inc., Chgo.; floor trader Mid-Am. Commodity Exch., Chgo., 1974-75; tech. mkt. analyst FGL, West Des Moines, Iowa, 1975-78; account exec. Commodity Cons. Inc., West Des Moines, Iowa, 1978-80; pres. Mag Fin. Svcs. Ltd., West Des Moines, Iowa, from 1980-. Contbr. articles to profl. jours. Mem. Nat. Futures Assn. Brotherhood (treas. 1986--), B'Nai Jeshurun. Jewish. Died July 28, 1991.

**GOLDSCHMIDT, DIETRICH HANS ALFRED,** sociology educator; b. Freiburg, Germany, Nov. 4, 1914; s. Hans Julius and Sophie Clara (Bickel) G.; m. Ursula Liesel Theune, June 16, 1945; children: Johannes, Christopher, Martina, Susanne, Dorothea. Dipl.Ing., Tech. U. Berlin, 1939; Dr. rer. pol., U. Goettingen, Fed. Republic Germany, 1953. Engr. DEMAG Motoren, Berlin, 1939-44; asst. U. Goettingen, 1945-46, 51-56; editor Goettingen Universitaets Zeitung, 1946-49; fellow U. Birmingham, Eng., 1949-50; prof. Tchg. Tng. Coll., Berlin, 1956-63; dir. Max Planck Inst. for Human Devel. and Edn., Berlin, 1963-82; prof. adj. in sociology Free U. Berlin, from 1963. Mem., chmn. various ednl. rsch. orgns., 1956—. Author, editor numerous publs. in religion, edn., antisemitism, Third World, politics, 1945—. Mem., chmn. various social orgns., 1956—; mem. Synod of Evangelische Kirche in Deutschland, 1958-84; mem. various nat. ch. commns., 1958-96. Home: Berlin, Germany. Died May 20, 1998.

**GOLDSMITH, MARVIN L.,** civil engineer; b. Bklyn., May 24, 1925; s. Abe and Dora (Wolovelsy) G.; m. Helen Pashin, Dec. 22, 1945; children: Susan B., Douglas, Matthew C. BCE, CCNY, 1945; MCE, Bklyn. Poly. Inst., 1951. Registered profl. engr., N.Y. Weight engr. Otis Elevator Co., NYC, 1945-46; design draftsman F.H. McGraw Co., NYC, 1946; sgt. U.S. Army, 1946-47; design engr. H.A. Brassert & Co., NYC, 1947-48, Ammann & Whitney, Inc., NYC, 1949-50, Walter Kidde, Co., NYC, 1950-52; engr. Ramseyer & Miller, Inc., NYC, 1952-60; cons. Ramseyer & Miller, Inc., T.M.C., India, 1954-58; v.p., cons. Kenrich Corp., NYC, 1961-71 and from 72. Ptnr., cons. Miller Goldsmith Assocs., N.Y.C., 1972—; pres. Jazz Archives, Inc. Mem. Ame Concrete Inst., Sigma Kappa Tau, Internat. Assn. Jazz, Record Rsch. Assn. (collectors). Democrat. Jewish. Avocation: jazz record producer & collector. Died Mar. 29, 1990.

**GOLDSTEIN, IRWIN STUART,** philosophy educator; b. Windsor, Ont., Can., July 12, 1947; arrived in U.S., 1951; s. Allen and Idelle (Wasserman) G.; children: Rebecca, Rachel Louise, Sheena Miriam. BA, Carleton U., 1970; MLitt, U. Bristol, Eng., 1974; PhD, U. Edinburgh, Eng., 1979. Vis. positions U. Tex., Dallas, 1982-83; asst. prof. philosophy Loyola U., Chgo., 1980-81; asst. prof. Davidson (N.C.) Coll., 1983-87, assoc. prof., 1987-98, prof., 1998—2014. Lectr. Soc. for Classical Realism, Berkeley, Calif., Rochester (N.Y.) Inst. Tech., American Philos. Assn., British Soc. for Ethical Theory, others. Contbr. articles to numerous profl. jours. Carleton U. grantee, 1969-70; U. Edinburgh scholar, 1977-79, 84; Davidson Coll. rsch. grantee, 1984-85. Mem. American Philos. Assn. (lectr.), Internat. Soc. for Value Inquiry, Southern Soc. Philosophy & Psychology, N.C. Philos. Soc. Avocations: art, swimming, travel, reading. Died Aug. 30, 2014.

**GOLDSTEIN, LOUIS,** theoretical physicist; b. Dombrad, Szabolcs, Hungary, Mar. 25, 1904; arrived in US, 1939; s. Morris Goldstein and Josephine (Stern) Goldsten; 1 child, John C. Licence es Sciences, Sorbonne, Paris, 1926, Doctorat es Sciences, 1932. Rsch. worker Institut Henri Poincare U. Paris, 1932—39; dept. physics NYU, 1939—40; instr. dept. physics CCNY, 1941—43; staff mem. Radiation Lab, Columbia U., NYC, 1943—45; staff mem., cons. Los Alamos Nat. Lab, from 1946. Contbr. articles to profl. jours. Fellow: Am. Phys. Soc.; mem.: Bnai Brith. Democrat. Jewish. Achievements include Achievements include forecasting a number of new theoretical concepts of a series of new physical properties of matter prior to their experimental observation; including their behavior at and production of low temperatures. Home: Stoddard, Wis. Died Aug. 26, 1999.

**GOLDWATER, BERT M.,** federal judge; Apptd. bankruptcy judge U.S. Dist. Ct. Nev., 1995. Died 2006.

**GOLINO, FRANK R.,** retired diplomat; b. Erie, Pa., Oct. 26, 1936; s. Dominic F. and Mary (Dober) G.; m. Christine J. Harrison, Jan. 31, 1981 (div.); children by previous marriage: Fabrizio R., Louis R. AB cum laude, Gfannon U., 1957; MA, Fordham U., 1960; Cert., Bologna Center, Sch. for Advanced Internat. Studies, Italy, 1959. Chmn. Middle East and North Africa area studies, Fgn. Service Inst. US Dept. State, Washington, 1968-70, internat. relations officer, 1970-72; 2d sec. Am. Embassy, Valletta, Malta, 1972-74, Rome, 1974-76; consul Am. Consulate, Johannesburg, Africa, 1976-81, prin. officer Trieste, Italy, labor attache Madrid; dir. Office Agrl Devel., Bur. Internat. Orgn. Affairs US Dept. State. Lectr. Loyola U., Rome, 1975-76, St. Mary's-Notre Dame, rome, 1976 Editor Middle East sect. Colliers Ency., 1960-61; contbr. articles to profl. jours. Recipient Superior Honor award US Dept. State, 1980; Italian Fgn. Ministry fellow, 1958 Mem. Am. Fgn. Service Assn., Am. Polit. Sci. Assn., Internat. Polit. Sci. Assn., Middle East Inst., Middle East Studies Assn. Lodges: Rotary. Roman Catholic. Home: Trieste, Italy. Died Feb. 13, 2008.

**GOMEZ, ANA LYDIA MAS,** retired government official, educator; b. San Juan, Sept. 30, 1913; d. Jose and Concepcion (Marti) Mas Nadal; m. Edmundo Gomez, Dec. 24, 1934. BA, U. PR, 1937; MA, Columbia, 1948. Jr. econ. analyst US Dept. State, 1945—48, agrl. econ. asst., econ. officer, 1948—52, asst. agrl. attache, 1952—54, econ. officer, attache, 1965—73; asst. agrl. attache US Dept. Agr., 1954—65; lectr. economics U. Ams., Mex. City, from 1975. Recipient Superior Svc. award, US Dept. Agr., 1956. Mem.: Am. Econ. Assn. Home: Mexico City, Mexico. Died Apr. 1, 2008.

**GONTHIER, CHARLES DOHERTY,** retired judge; b. Montreal, Que., Can., Aug. 1, 1928; m. Mariette Morin; children: Georges, François, Pierre, Jean-Charles, Yves. BA, Paris Coll. Stanislas, Montreal, 1947; BCL, McGill U., Montreal, 1951, LLD (hon.), 1990; DHC (hon.), U. Montreal, 2002; DU (hon.), U. Ottawa, 2003. Queen's counsel, 1971. Atty. Hackett, Mulvena and Laverty, Montreal, 1952-57, Laing, Weldon, Courtois, Clarkson, Parsons, Gonthier & Tetrault (now McCarthy & Tetrault), Montreal, 1957-74; judge Superior Ct. Que., Montreal, 1974-88, Que. Ct. Appeal, Montreal, 1988-89, Supreme Ct. Can., Ottawa, 1989—2003; ret., 2003; of counsel McCarthy Tetrault LLP, 2004; wainwright sr. rsch. fellow Mcgill U. Lang. Faculty Commr. Comm. Security Establishment, Ottowa, 2004; adj. prof Mcgill U. Sec. Montreal br. Can. Inst. Internat. Affairs, 1957-58; pres. Jr. Bar Montreal, 1960-61; mem. Com. on Bldg. Contracts Que. Civil Code Rev., 1969-72; com. on discipline Bar Que., 1973-74; chmn. Commn. for Nat. Judges, 1st World Conf. on Independence of Justice, Montreal, 1983; pres. Can. Judges Conf., 1988-89; commr. Comm. Security Establishment, Ottawa, 2006. Chmn. Assn. Anciens Coll. Stanislas, Montreal, 1954-55; hon. sec. Montreal Mus. Fine Arts, 1961-76; bd. dirs. McCord Mus. Can. History, Montreal, 1976-89; chmn. bd. Coll. Stanislas, Montreal, 1984-90; mem. Internat. Commn. Jurists; chmn. bd. govs. Ctr. for Internat. Sustainable Devel. Law. Decorated knight L'Ordre des Palmes Académiques (France); Wainwright Sr. Rsch. fellow McGill U. Law Faculty, 2004. Fellow Am. Coll. Trial Lawyers (hon.); mem. Univ. Club (Montreal), Can. Bar Assn. (hon., pres. jr. bar sect. 1961-62, sec. Que. divsn. 1963-64), Can. Inst. Adminstrn. Justice (pres. 1986-87), Assn. Henri Capitant, Que. Assn. Comparative Law, Internat Acad. Comparative Law. Roman Catholic. Died July 16, 2009.

**GOODLAND, ROBERT JAMES APPLEBY,** environmental scientist; b. Brigg, North Lincolnshire, Eng. m. Jonmin Wooh Goodland, 1985; 1 child, Arthur. PhD, McGill U., Montreal, 1969. Cons. The World Bank Group, 1975—78, ecologist, group environ. adviser Washington, 1978—2001; tech. dir. Extractive Industry Review World Bank's Oil, Gas and Mining Portfolio, 2001—04. Author 39 books and monographs. Environ. bd. mem. Trucost Plc., London. Recipient World Bank Group's Excellence award, Harold Jefferson Coolidge medal, Internat. Union for the Conservation of Nature (IUCN), 2009. Fellow: World Resources Inst. (sr.); mem.: Internat. Soc. Conservation Biology (prize, Millennial Conservationist 2000), Internat. Soc. Ecol. Economics (founding bd. mem. 1988—2001, Boulding prize 1994), World Commn. Dams (founder & adviser 1998—2001), Ecol. Soc. America (met. chair 1989—90), Internat. Assn. Impact Assessment (pres. 1993—96, Rose-Hulman prize 1996). Home: Mc Lean, Va. Died Dec. 28, 2013.

**GOODMAN, GEORGE JEROME WALDO (ADAM SMITH),** writer, television journalist, consultant; b. St. Louis, Aug. 10, 1930; s. Alexander Mark and Viola (Cremer) G.; m. Sallie Cullen Brophy, Oct. 6, 1961 (dec. Sept. 18, 2007); children: Alexander Mark, Susannah Blake. AB magna cum laude, Harvard U., 1952; AB Rhodes scholar, Oxford U., Eng., 1952-54. Reporter Barron's, 1957; contbg. editor, assoc. editor Time and Fortune mags., 1958—60; portfolio mgr., v.p. Lincoln Fund, 1960—62; co-founder New York mag., 1967, contbg. editor, v.p., 1967—77; exec. editor, then cons. Esquire, 1978—81; 1st editor, exec. v.p., bd. dirs. Instl. Investor, 1967—72; chmn. Continental Fidelity Group, 1980—98, also dir. Exec. v.p., dir. Instl. Investor Systems, 1969-72; dir. USAIR, Inc., 1978-99, Hyatt Hotels, 1977-81, Cambrex, Inc., 1981-2003, Providentia Ltd., Sweden, 1984-86; mem. dirs. adv. bd. MetLife, 2003—; lectr. Harvard Bus. Sch., Princeton; commentator NBC News, 1974, PBS, 1981-2014; creator, host, editor-in-chief Adam Smith's Money World, PBS, 1984-97; 1st U.S. pub. affairs TV broadcast in Russia, 1990-2014; host, editor-in-chief Adam Smith's Money Game, PBS, 1998-99; editl. chmn. N.J. Monthly, 1976-79; adv. com. publs. U.S. Tennis Assn., 1978-83; chmn. Adam Smith Global TV, 1997-2014; lectr. media and global affairs Princeton U., 2003-14. Screenwriter, L.A., 1962-65, screenplay The Wheeler Dealers; author: The Bubble Makers, 1955, A Time for Paris, 1957, Bascombe, The Fastest Hound Alive, 1958, A Killing in the Market, 1958, The Wheeler Dealers, 1959; under pseudonym Adam Smith: The Money Game, 1968 (#1 bestseller), Supermoney, 1971 (#1 bestseller), Powers of

Mind, 1975, Paper Money, 1981, The Roaring 80's, 1988; mem. editl. bd. N.Y. Times, 1977; contbr. articles to profl. jours. Trustee Glassboro (N.J.) State Coll., 1967-71, co-chmn. presdl. selection com., 1968; trustee C.G. Jung Found., 1981-88; mem. adv. council econs. dept. Princeton U., 1970-89, chmn., 1975-77; rep. com. on shareholder responsibility Harvard U., 1971-74, mem. vis. com. psychology and social relations dept., 1974-80—, mem. vis. com. Middle East Inst.; mem. adv. council Sloan Fellowships, Princeton U., 1976-79, Ctr. for Internat. Studies, Princeton U., 1990-2014; trustee The Urban Inst., 1986-96, Found. for Child Devel., 1986-88. Served with AUS, 1954-56. Recipient G.M. Loeb award for Disting. Achievement for Bus. & Financial Writing U. Conn., 1969, Media award for Econ. Understanding with TV documentary Amos Tuck Sch., Dartmouth Coll., 1978, Overseas Press award, 1996; Ind. award Brown U., 1993; nominee 8 Emmy awards, 1985-97, winner Best Interview 1995, winner 3 Emmys, graphics, 1985-94, Adam Smith Internat. PBS Documentaries gold medal Houston Internat. Film Festival, 2001, 02. Mem.: Assn. Harvard Alumni (bd. dirs. 1972—75), Authors Guild (bd. dirs. 1975—2006), Authors League Fund (v.p.), Coun. Fgn. Rels., Knickerbocker Club, Century Assn., Harvard Club. Home: Princeton, NJ. Died Jan. 3, 2014.

**GOODMAN, MADELEINE JOYCE,** dean, human geneticist, educator; b. NYC, Sept. 11, 1945; d. Joseph and Pauline Ida (Applebaum) Schwarzbach; m. Lenn Evan Goodman, Aug. 29, 1965; children: Allegra, Paula. BA, Barnard Coll., 1967; diploma in Human Biology, Oxford U., 1968; PhD, U. Hawaii, 1973. Asst. prof. U. Hawaii, Honolulu, 1974—79, assoc. prof., 1979—85, prof., 1985—94, dir. women's studies, 1978—85; asst. v.p. Acad. Affairs, 1986—94, interim sr. v.p., 1992—93; dean Coll. Arts & Scis., Vanderbilt U., Nashville, 1994—96, prof. biology, 1994—96; pres. Pacific Health Rsch Inst., Honolulu, 1982—86. Author: Sex Differences in the Life Cycle, 1983; contbr. articles to profl. jours. Officer Disciplinary Coun. Hawaii State Supreme Ct., Honolulu, 1983—94. Grantee, NSF, 1981—84, Am. Cancer Soc., 1982—83, Pub. Health Svc., 1987—94. Mem.: AAAS, Human Biology Coun., Hawaii Assn. Women in Sci. (pres. 1981—83), Sigma Xi (nat. lectr. 1987—89, pres. Hawaii chpt. mem. nat. bd. dirs., chair nat. nominating com.). Died Oct. 2, 1996.

**GOODMAN, ROY MATZ,** corporate financial executive, former state senator; b. NYC, Mar. 5, 1930; s. Bernard A. and Alice (Matz) G.; m. Barbara Christine Furrer, June 28, 1955; children: Claire Goodman Pellegrini Cloud, Leslie Alice, Randolph Bernard. BA cum laude, Harvard U., 1951, MBA with distinction, 1953; DHL (hon.), Pratt Inst., 1994; LLD (hon.), Baruch Coll. CUNY, 2002. Assoc. buying and new bus. dept. Kuhn, Loeb & Co., 1955-60; pres. Drug Devel. Corp., Ex-Lax, Inc., Roycemore, Inc., 1962-71; mem. Dist. 26 NY State Senate, 1969—2002; pres., CEO UN Devel. Corp., NYC, 2002—14. Chmn. legis. com. on public pvt., coop., 1985-88; chmn. housing and urban devel. com., 1968-76; pres. Goodman Family Found.; bd. dirs. 1st Empire State Corp., 1984-2000; mem. adv. bd. Chem. Bank, 1963-65, commr. finance, fin. adminstr. City of NY, 1966-68; mem. NYC. Banking Commn., 1966-68; past trustee NYC Police Pension Fund, NYC Fire Dept. Pension Fund, 1966-68; mem. Mayor's Cabinet and Supercabinet, 1966-68, NYC Treas., 1966-68; chmn. State Charter Revision Commn. for NYC, 1972-76; adj. prof. public admin. Baruch Coll. CUNY, 1975; mem. Mayor Guiliani Transition Team, 1993; mem. Gov. Pataki Transition Team, 1994. Bd. dirs. Citizens Com. NYC.; past mem. bd. Brotherhood-In-Action; trustee Heart Rsch. Found.; exec. asst. to chmn. NY State Assembly Jud. Com., 1963-64; asst. to atty. gen. State NY, 1960; pres. 9th A.D. Republican Club, 1963-64; del. NY State Rep. Convs., 1966-2000, del. Republican Nat. Conv., 1968, 72, 76, 80, 84, 88, 92, 96, 2000, 2004, Presdl. Elector, 1984; chmn. NY County Republican Com., 1981-2002, treas., 1965; NY State co-chmn. Bush-for-Pres. campaigns, 1988, 92, Bush-Quayle Nat. Finance Com., 1988, 92; candidate for Mayor of NYC., 1977; trustee Carnegie Hall Soc., Inc., Carnegie Hall Corp., past trustee Columbia Coll. Pharm. Scis., LI Coll. Hosp., NY Com. Young Audiences, United Jewish Appeal, Tel Aviv U., Freedom House, Dalton Schs. Brotherhood-In-Action, Heart Rsch. Found.; presdl. appointee to Nat. Commn. Fine Arts, 1985-89, Nat. Endowment Arts Coun., 1989-96, trustee John F. Kennedy Ctr. for Performing Arts, 2002-14; amb. arts NEA, 2000; fellow Met. Mus. Art; patron Met. Opera; sponsor NY Philharm. Soc.; mem. Regents vis. com. NY State Mus.; trustee Temple Emanu-El; mem. NY Com. for Young Audiences, Harvard Com. on Univ. Resources,; mem. bd. overseers John F. Kennedy Sch. Govt./Harvard U. Lt. USNR, 1953-56. Decorated Adm.'s Meritorious Svc. citation; recipient Disting. Service award Jaycees, 1966, Mt. Scopus citation Hebrew U., Jerusalem, 1968, Scroll of Honor United Jewish Appeal, 1970, Kennedy Ctr. award for Disting. Leadership in Arts-in Edn., Nat. Arts Club Citation of Merit, City U., Medal of Merit, 1972, Man of Yr. award Brotherhood-in-Action, 1972, Humanitarian award Soc. for Prevention Cruelty to Children, 1976, citation for cmty. service Odyssey House, 1976, Our Town newspaper award for leadership in City Charter revision, 1976, Fiorello H. LaGuardia Meml. award, 1979-80, citation for outstanding service NY Young Rep. Club, 1982, Disting. Alumni award Hunter Coll. Elem. Sch. Parents Assn., 1985, Service awards NY Police Found. and NY Fire Safety Found., 1986, Patriotic Service award US Treasury Dept., NY Gov.'s Arts medal, 2002, Sutton Area Cmty. Svc. award, 2002, WNYC Radio Arts Award, 2002, UN Delegations' Citizen of the World award, 2002, Alliance of NY Arts Org. Arts Advocate award, 2002, City Club of NY Disting. New Yorker award, 2002, Internat. Coun. for Caring Communities Caring Citizen of the Humanities Award, 2003; named to honor scroll Columbia Assn. of NYC Police Dept., 1979, NY State Rep. of Yr. Ripon Soc., 1972, Cmty. Activist award Lenox Hill Neighorhood Assn., Inc., 1995, Artists fellowship award, John LaFarge Meml. award for interracial justice, Local Hero award Stanley Isaacs Assn., Playwrights Horizon award, 1995, Gari Melchers Meml. medal, 1995, South Street Seaport Mus. award, 1995, Friend of the Arts award Town Hall Found., 1995, Legacy of Hope award NY Foundling Home, Carnegie Hall, 1996, Margaret Sanger award Family Advs. NY, 1997; Statesman Father of Yr. award, 1984, named to Econ. Hon. Soc. St. John's U., 1991. Mem. Anti-Defamation League (bd. govs. NY), American Young Pres.'s Orgn., Fin. Analysts Fedn., NY Soc. Security Analysts, Council Fgn. Rels., Woodrow Wilson Internat. Ctr. Scholars (mem. adv. group), Assn. Harvard Alumni (past dir.), Harvard Club (gov.), Century Assn., Century Country Club, Dutch Treat Club, Senate Club (pres.), Harvard Bus. Sch., City Club, Omicron Delta Epsilon (hon.). Republican. Jewish. Home: New York, NY. Died June 3, 2014.

**GOODWIN, FELIX LEE,** retired educational administrator, retired army officer; b. Lawrence, Kans., Nov. 24, 1919; s. Felix and Lucille Marie (Lee) G.; m. Esther Brown, Nov. 1, 1941 (dec.); children: Cheryl Washington, Sylvia, Judith Barnes; m. Barbara Gilpin, Aug. 15, 1988. BS, U. Md., 1958; M of Pub. Adminstrn., U. Ariz., 1965, EdS, 1974, EdD, 1979. Enlisted U.S. Army, 1939, advanced through grades to lt. col., 1963; ret., 1969; asst. prof. army mil. sci. dept. U. Ariz., Tucson, 1968-69, asst. to pres., 1969-83. Chmn. Pima County Merit Sys. Commn., 1975-77, 79-82, Pima County Law Enforcement Merit Coun., 1973-82; mem. Ariz. Bicentennial Commn., 1974-77, chmn., 1976-77. Decorated Legion of Merit, Army Commendation medal with 2 oak leaf cluster, Meritorious Svc. medal; recipient Cert. of Appreciation, City of Tucson, 1967, 83, Man of Yr. award Una Noche Plateada, Tucson, 1976, Leadership award Tucson Urban League, 1975, IRS award, 1981; named Hon. Citizen, Sierra Vista, Ariz. Mem. NEA, NAACP (life), DAV (life), NRA, Nat. Alliance Black Sch. Educators (life), Soc. Ethnic and Spl. Studies Assn. U.S. Army, Am. Legion, Amvets, Ret. Officers Assn., Kiwanis (life), K.C., VFW, Phi Delta Kappa, Alpha Phi Alpha (life), Pi Lambda Theta, Alpha Delta Delta, Beta Gamma Sigma. Roman Catholic. Home: Tucson, Ariz. Deceased.

**GOODWIN, RONALD ALFRED,** composer; b. Plymouth, Devon, Eng., Feb. 17, 1925; s. James and Bessie Violet (Godsland) G.; m. Ellen Gertrud Drew, July 3, 1947 (div. Feb. 1986); 1 child, Christopher-Russell; m. Heather Elizabeth Mary Dunsden, Sept. 22, 1986. Cert. film composer, conductor. Composer (commls.) Drake 400 Suite, 1980, New Zealand Suite, 1984, Aramada 400 Suite, (film scores), Lancelot and Guinevere (The Sword of Sir Lancelot), 1963, 633 Squadron, 1963, Those Magnificent Men in Their Flying Machines, 1965, The Great Spy Mission, 1966, Where Eagles Dare, 1969, Battle of Britain, 1970, Frenzy, 1972, Force Ten from Navarone, 1978, Valhalla, 1988, Summer Breeze, 1991, City of Lincoln, 1991, The Tall Ships, 1995, Freefall, 1998. Hon. pres. City of Leeds (Eng.) Coll. of Music Friends Orgn., 1989; trustee PRS Mems. Fund, 1994—. Recipient Ivor Novello award Brit. Acad. Songwriters, Composers and Authors, 1958, 71, 94, nomination Golden Globe, Hollywood Fgn. Press Assn., 1972; fellow City of Leeds Coll. Music, 1993. Mem. Brit. Acad. Songwriters, Composers and Authors, Worshipfull Co. Musicians (liveryman 1971—). Avocations: walking, reading, chess. Home: Reading, England. Died Jan. 8, 2003.

**GOOTZEIT, JACK MICHAEL,** rehabilitation institute executive; b. NYC, Sept. 27, 1924; s. Morris and Pauline (Genn) G.; m. Rose Weiss, Mar. 21, 1948; children: Sholom Martin, Elias Steven. BS in Phys. Therapy, NYU, 1955, MA in Psychology, 1956, Ed.D., 1963. Rsch. asst. NYU Sch. Edn., NYC, 1954; phys. therapy adviser Vis. Nurse Svc. N.Y., 1957-58; assoc. dir. sheltered workshop and tng. ctr. Westchester Assn. Retarded Children, White Plains, N.Y., 1958-65; dir. habilitation svcs. N.Y.C. Assn. for Help Retarded Children, 1959-67; exec. dir. Insts. Applied Human Dynamics, Bronx, N.Y., 1957-95; exec./founder, from 1995; exec. dir. Insts. Applied Human Dynamics St. Jude Habilitation Inst., from 1966. Cons. Chapman & Garber, architects state schs. for retarded, 1965-66; cons. N.Y. State Dept. Mental Hygiene; Bronx chpt. Assn. Brain Injured Children, 1965-66; cons. psychologist Operation Headstart, Ringwood, N.J., 1967; adj. assoc. prof. Hunter Coll., 1968-76, Pace U., 1979. Author: Situational Diagnosis and Therapy, 1960; Handbook on Personal Adjustment Training, 1965; Effecting Communication and Interaction in the Mentally Retarded; The Development of Behavior and Its Modification, 1975; Foundations for Serving the Severe and Multihandicapped; The Multihandicapped: Serving the Severely Disabled, 1981; media presentation series in neuro and sensory psychology. contbr. articles to mags. Instr. water safety ARC, 1941—, staff instr. rehab. swimming, 1950—. Served with AUS, 1942-45; MTO. Decorated Bronze Star, Purple Heart; recipient Disting. Svc. award N.Y. chpt. Nat. Rehab. Assn., 1965, Exceptional Svc. award N.E. region, 1978, Profl. of Yr. award Met. N.Y. chpt., 1977. Fellow Am. Assn. Mental Deficiency, Am. Soc. Group Psychotherapy and Psychoanalysis; mem. Am. Psychol. Assn., Rehab. Counseling Assn., Am. Phys. Therapy Assn., Am. Acad. Psychotherapy, AAAS, N.Y. Acad. Scis. Home: Bronx, NY. Deceased.

**GOPAL, SARVEPALLI,** history educator; b. Madras, India, Apr. 23, 1923; s. Sarvepalli Radhakrishnan. Degree, U. Madras, Oxford U.; MA, PhD; DLitt (hon.), Andhra U., 1975, Sri Venkateswara U., Tirupati, 1979, Banaras U., 1984, Hyderebad U., 1993. Lectr. & reader, history Andhra U., Waltair, India, 1948—52; asst. dir. Nat. Archives, New Delhi, 1952—54; dir., hist. divsn. Ministry External Affairs, New Delhi, 1954—66; reader, South Asian history Oxford U., England, 1966—71; fellow St. Anthony's Coll., 1966—95, hon. fellow, from 1966; prof., contemporary history Jawaharlal Nehru U., New Delhi, 1971—83, prof. emeritus, from 1983. Author: The Viceroyalty of Lord Ripon, The Viceroyalty of Lord Irwin, British Policy in India, Jawaharlal Nehru, 3 vols. Radharishnan; editor: Selected Works of Jawaharlal Nehru, 1969—98; gen. editor, from 1998. Chmn. Nat. Book Trust of India, 1973—76, Indian Inst. Advanced Study, 1993—98, Inst. Social Scis., 1995—98, Madras Inst. Devel. Studies, 1995—97; mem. exec. bd. UNESCO, 1976—80. Died Apr. 20, 2002.

**GORDIMER, NADINE,** writer; b. Springs, South Africa, Nov. 20, 1923; d. Isidore and Nan (Myers) Gordimer; m. Reinhold Cassirer, Jan. 29, 1954; children: Oriane, Hugo. Attended, U. Witwatersrand, Johannesburg; degree (hon.), Yale U., Harvard U., Columbia U., New Sch. Social Rsch., NYC, U. Leuven, Belgium, U. York, Eng., U. Cape Town, South Africa, Cambridge U., Eng. Author: (novels) The Lying Days, 1953, A World of Strangers, 1958, Occasion for Loving, 1963, The Late Bourgeois World, 1966, A Guest of Honour, 1970 (James Tait Black Meml. prize, Scotland, 1971), The Conservationist, 1974 (Man Booker prize for fiction, 1974), Burger's Daughter, 1979, July's People, 1981, A Sport of Nature, 1987 (Anisfield-Wolf Book award, 1988), My Son's Story, 1990, None to Accompany Me, 1994, The House Gun, The Pickup, 2001 (Commonwealth Writers' prize, 2002), Get a Life, 2005, (fiction collections) Face to Face, 1949, The Soft Voice of the Serpent, 1952, Six Feet of the Country, 1956, Friday's Footprint, 1960 (W. H. Smith Commonwealth Li. award, Eng., 1961), Not for Publication, 1965, Livingstone's Companions, 1970, Selected Stories, 1975, No Place Like: Selected Stories, 1978, A Soldier's Embrace, 1980, Something Out There, 1984, Correspondence Course and other Stories, 1984, The Moment Before the Gun Went Off, 1988, Once Upon a Time, 1989, Jump: And Other Stories, 1991, Why Haven't You Written: Selected Stories 1950-1972, 1992, Loot: And Other Stories, 2003, Beethoven Was One-Sixteenth Black, 2007, (essay collections) The Black Interpreters, 1973, The Essential Gesture: Writing, Politics and Places, 1988, Writing and Being: The Charles Eliot Norton Lectures, 1995, Living in Hope and History: Notes from Our Century, 1999, (nonfiction) On the Mines, 1973, Lifetimes Under Apartheid, 1986. Goodwill amb. UN Devel. Programme. Decorated Comdr., Order of Arts & Letters, France; recipient Ctrl. News Agy. Lit. ward, South Africa, 1975, 1975, 1991, 1980, Modern Lang. Assn. award, 1982, Malaparte prize, Italy, 1985, Nelly Sachs prize, Germany, 1986, Nobel Prize for Literature, Swedish Acad., 1991, Internat. Botev prize, 1996, Presdl. Medal of Honour, Republic of Chile; grantee Neil M. Gunn Fellowship, Scottish Arts Coun., 1981. Fellow: Royal Soc. Lit.; mem.: AAAL (hon.), Am. Acad. Arts & Scis. (hon.). Home: Johannesburg, South Africa. Died July 13, 2014.

**GORDON, EUGENE IRVING,** electrical and computer engineering educator; b. NYC, Sept. 14, 1930; s. Sol and Gertrude (Lassen) G.; m. Barbara Young, Aug. 19, 1956 (div. 1990); children: Laurence Mark, Peter Eliot; m. Renate Albrecht-Gordon, Dec. 31, 1991. BS, CCNY, 1952; PhD in Physics, MIT, 1957. Rsch. assoc. MIT, Cambridge, 1957; mem. tech. staff Bell Labs., Murray Hill, N.J., 1957-59, supr., 1959-64, dept. head, 1964-68, dir., 1968-83; cons., 1983-84; chmn., pres. Lytel Inc., Somerville, N.J., 1984-87; v.p., dir. rsch. Hughes Aircraft Co., Malibu, Calif., 1987-88; pres. Photon Imaging Corp., Edison, N.J., 1988-90. Patentee in field; editor EDS Trans, 1963-65, Jour. Quantum Electronics, 1965-76; contbr. articles to profl. jours. Fellow IEEE (Zworykin award 1975, Edison medal 1984, Centennial medal 1984); mem. NAE. Democrat. Jewish. *The philosophy underlying my approach to life has been "Better light a candle than curse the dark." As a physicist I know that it is virtually impossible to produce light without some heat, but it always has come as a surprise to me how little heat human beings will tolerate even in the presence of abundant illumination.* Died Sept. 15, 2014.

**GORDON, NATHAN (LEE),** violist; b. NYC, Feb. 8, 1915; s. Louis and Dora (Lipshitz) G.; m. Marjorie Fishberg; children: Maxine, Peter Jon. Cert., The Juilliard Sch. Music, 1936. Violist Met. Opera Orch., NYC; solo violist NBC Symphony under Toscanini, NBC String Quartet, Chautauqua (N.Y.) Symphony Orch., Pitts. Symphony Orch., Kroll String Quartet, Detroit Symphony Orch.; faculty Dalcroze Music Sch., NYC; prof. viola, condr. Duquesne U., Pitts.; faculty Carnegie Tech. U., Pitts., Chatham Coll., Pitts., U. Mich., Wayne State U., Detroit, Bowling Green (Ohio) State U., Interlochen (Mich.) Acad. of the Arts, Ind. U., Bloomington. Mem. faculty Congress of Strings; condr. Dearborn (Mich.) Orch.; lectr. and cons. in field; founder Gateway to Music, Pitts., Excursions in Music, Detroit. Soloist recital tours to Greece, Israel; contbr. articles to various mags. Recipient awards Mich. Senate and Ho. of Reps.; established Nathan Gordon Viola Scholarship, Am. String Tchrs. Assn.; named Artist-Tchr. of Yr. Am. String Tchrs. Assn. Mem. Am. Fedn. Musicians, Detroit Musicians League, Mich. Music Tchrs. Assn., Detroit Fedn. Musicians, Am. Viola Soc., Chamber Music Am., Palm Beach Cultural Coun., Boca Raton Music Study Club. Avocations: sports, travel. Home: Boca Raton, Fla. Deceased.

**GORDONCILLO, ONESIMO CADIZ,** retired archbishop; b. Jimalalud, Phillipines, Feb. 16, 1935; Ordained priest of Dumaguete Diocese, Philippines, 1961—74; auxiliary bishop of Dumaguette, titular bishop of Gunugus, 1974—76; appointed bishop of Tagbilaran, 1976—86; archbishop of Capiz, 1986—2011. Roman Catholic. Died Nov. 13, 2013.

**GORSKI, ROBERT ALEXANDER,** chemist, consultant; b. Passaic, NJ, Nov. 24, 1922; s. Stephen T. and Wanda P. (Amlicke) G.; m. Helen Marie Thompson, Aug. 19, 1944; children: Robert J., Mary Ann B., Mark G., Stephen J., Paul

F. BA in Sci., La Salle U., 1947; MS in Chemistry, U. Pa., 1948, PhD in Phys. Chemistry, 1951. Chemist DuPont, Wilmington, Del., 1951-53; rsch. chemist DuPont Freon Products Lab., Wilmington, Del., 1953-60, sr. rsch. chemist, 1960-70, rsch. assoc., 1970-78, tech. assoc., 1978-85; cons. DuPont Fluorochemicals Lab., Wilmington, Del., 1985-91; ret., 1991. Author book chpt.; contbr. articles to profl. jours. With U.S. Army, 1943-46, ETO. Mem. Am. Chem. Soc., Nat. Geog. Soc., KC, Sigma Xi Republican. Roman Catholic. Achievements include patents for solvents, refrigeration, blowing agents for plastic foams and fire extinguishing. Avocations: sports, reading. Deceased.

**GORUP, GREGORY JAMES,** marketing executive; b. Kansas City, Kans., Mar. 27, 1948; s. Mike and Helen F. Gorup; m. Kathleen Susan Grogan, Apr. 12, 1986 (div.); children: Michael Thomas, Ryan Nicholas. BA in Econs., St. Benedict Coll., 1970; MBA, U. Pa., 1972. Market analyst product planning and devel. dept. Citibank, NYC, 1972-73, market planning officer corp. product mgmt. divsn., 1973-74, product mgr. securities svcs., 1974-75; v.p., dir. product devel. Irving Trust Co., NYC, 1975-80, mgr. product mgmt. dept., 1980-81; v.p. mktg. U.S. area Credit Suisse, 1981-84; sr. cons. Wesley, Brown and Bartle, NYC, 1985-86; bank mktg. mgr. Digital Equipment Corp., NYC, 1986-87; money mktg. mgr. Reuters N.Am., 1987-88; pres. Gorup Assocs., 1989-91; dist. v.p. Nat. Computer Sys., N.Y., 1991-94; regional mgr. Soc. Worldwide InterBank Fin. Telecomm., 1994-96, sr. regional mgr., 1996-98, mgr., 1998-2000, sr. mgr., 2000—01; dir. Rogue Wave Software, LSOS Div., Mamaroneck, NY, from 2001. Mem. Rep. Nat. Com., Nat. Rep. Senatorial Com., U.S. Shooting Team. Mem. NRA (life), West Point Soc. N.Y., Wharton Bus. Sch. Club, Princeton Club N.Y., Orienta Beach Club, Willow Wood Gun Club, Army "A" Club, U.S. Naval Inst., Naval League of the U.S., Air Force Assn. Roman Catholic. Deceased.

**GOTLIEB, PHYLLIS FAY BLOOM,** author; b. Toronto, Ont., Can., May 25, 1926; d. Leo and Mary (Kates) Bloom; m. Calvin Gotlieb, June 12, 1949; children: Leo, Margaret, Jane. BA, U. Toronto, 1948, MA, 1950. Author: Poetry Within The Zodiac, 1964, Ordinary, Moving, 1969, Doctor Umlaut's Earthly Kingdom, 1974, The Works, 1978, Red Blood Black Inck White Parer: New and Selected Poems 1961-2001, 2002; (novels) Sunburst, 1964, Why Should I Have All the Grief?, 1969, O Master Caliban!, 1976, A Judgement of Dragons, 1980, Emperor, Swords, Pentacles, 1982, The Kingdom of the Cats, 1985, Heart of Red Iron, 1989, Flesh and Gold, 1998, Violent Stars, 1999, Mind World, 2002, Birthstones, 2007; (story collection) Blue Apes, 1995; story collections Son of the Morning and other stories, 1983; co-editor: Anthology Tesseracts 2. Mem. Sci. Fiction Writers Am. Home: Toronto, Canada. Died July 14, 2009.

**GOURLEY, JAMES LELAND,** editor, publishing executive; b. Mounds, Okla., Jan. 29, 1919; s. Samuel O. and Lodema (Scott) G.; m. Vicki Graham Clark, Nov. 24, 1976; children: James Leland II, Janna Lynn Rousey, Kelly Clark, Brandon Clark. BA in Liberal Studies, U. Okla., 1963. Editor, pub., pres. Daily Free-Lance, Henryetta, Okla., 1946-73; editor, pub. Oklahoma City Friday, from 1974; CEO Nichols Hills Pub. Co., from 1974; pres. Suburban Graphics, Inc., 1991-93. Pres. Central Okla. Newspaper Group, 1987, 90, 93, 96, 98, 99, 2000—; pres. Sta. KHEN, KHEN-FM, Henryetta, 1955-63; pres. Hugo Daily News, Okla., 1953-63; chief of staff gov. Okla., 1959-63; chmn., pres. State Capitol Bank, 1962-69; v.p. sta. KXOJ Sapulpa, 1972-75; treas. Sta. KJEM-FM, Oklahoma City, 1962-67. Mem. Pres. Nat. Pub. Advisory Com. to U.S. Sec. Commerce, 1963-66; exec. dir. Gov's Comm. Higher Edn., 1960-61; Dem. candidate for gov. Okla., 1966. Dist. chmn. Boy Scouts Am., 1963-65; bd. dirs. So. Regional Edn. Bd., 1959-67, Okla. Symphony Soc., 1976-88, Oklahoma City Crimestoppers, 1982—, Salvation Army, Oklahoma City, 1985-87, Okla. Goodwill Industries, 1989-91; mem. Gov.'s Reform Com., 1984; bd. trustees Okla. City Univ., 1993—; bd. dirs. Okla. City Edn. Round Table, 1992—; mem. steering com. Ofcl. Maps for Kids, 2000-2003. Maj. AUS, 1942-46, ETO. Recipient Best Okla. Small Daily newspaper awards, 1949-58, 69-72, Best Large City Weekly newspaper awards, 1977-80, 83-85, 87-91, 94-95, 97, 98, 2004, 05, Rotary Lifetime Achievement award, 2006, Disting. Alumni award, U. Okla., 2007; inducted into Okla. Journalism Hall of Fame, 1980. Mem. UP Internat. Editors Okla. (pres. 1958-59), Okla. Disciples of Christ Laymen (pres. 1964-65), Suburban Newspapers Am. (dir. 1980-89), Nat. Newspaper Assn., Okla. Press Assn. (pres. 1988-89, treas. 1991-93; Milt Phillips award 2010), Oklahoma City C. of C. (dir. 1975—), Henryetta C. of C. (pres. 1955), Oklahoma City Golf and Country Club (bd. dirs. 1991-95), Oklahoma City Com. of 100, Rotary (pres. Oklahoma City club 1992-93), Okla. Econ. Club, Fortune Club, Mil. Order of World Wars, Mil. Officers Assn., Pi Kappa Alpha. Republican. Died Oct. 19, 2013.

**GOVINDA, TARAJYOTI,** psychologist; b. Melbourne, Australia, Sept. 6, 1958; d. Frank Victor and Laurel Elizabeth (Higgins) B.; m. Gregory Bray, Oct. 22, 1989. BA, Swinburne U., Hawthorn, Australia, 1978; diploma in edn., Hawthorn Coll. Advanced Edn., 1979; diploma in counselling psychology, Royal Melbourne Inst. Tech., 1994. Tchr. Edn. Dept. Victoria, 1979-84, guidance officer, 1984; pvt. practice cons. psychology various cities, Australia, from 1986. Co-founder, bd. dirs. The Theosophical Sch. Healing, Daylesford, Australia, 1994—, Theosophical Ednl. Svcs., 1994—; founder, dir. Transformational Coll. Edn., 1998. Author: The Language of the Heart is Spoken Allover the World, 1991, The Healing Hands of Love: A Guide to Spiritual Healing, 1997, The Archangels and the Angels, 1998, Becoming Whole: The Psychology of Light, 1998, The Joy of Enlightenment, 1999; spkr. in field. Mem. Australian Psychol. Soc. Ltd., The Theosophical Fellowship. Avocations: playing music, singing, painting, jungian philosophy. Died Apr. 5, 1999.

**GRACE, JOHN WILLIAM,** retired Canadian government official; b. Ottawa, Ont., Can., Jan. 6, 1927; s. Archibald William and Mary Beatrice (O'Connor) G.; m. Ruth Ellen Herbert, Sept. 8, 1954; children— James E., Ruth E. Grace Ridgely, John W., Allen C., Anne B. Margaret E. BA, St. Patrick's Coll., Ottawa, 1949; MA, Cath. U. Am., 1952; PhD, U. Mich., 1958. Instr. English lang. and lit. U. Mich., Ann Arbor, 1956-59; journalist Ottawa Jour., 1959-62, assoc. editor, 1962-78, v.p., editor in chief, 1978-80; commr. Can. Radio and Telecommunications Commn., Ottawa, 1980-83; privacy commr. Govt. of Can., 1983-90, info. commr., 1990—98. Mem. Collegiate Inst. Bd. Can., 1963-69, chmn., 1967; bd. govs. U. Ottawa, 1968-81, chmn. exec. com., 1970; mem. Can. Council, 1971-77; bd. dirs. Welfare Council Can. Rackham fellow U. Mich., 1957; winner Nat. Newspaper Awards, 1975, 77; recipient Citation for Merit, Nat. Newspaper Awards, 1974 Mem.: Gatineau Fish & Game. Roman Catholic. Avocations: gardening; skiing; boating. Home: Ottawa, Canada. Died Feb. 5, 2009.

**GRAHAM, WILLIAM HOWARD,** theatre producer, consultant, lecturer; b. Phila., Mar. 23, 1926; s. William Howard Sr. and Kathleen Mary (O'Gorman) G.; m. Mary Caroline Alexander, June 13, 1953; children: Mary Catherine, William, Michael, Robert, Carole, Laura, Elizabeth. BA, LaSalle U., 1950; MA, Cath. U. America, 1954. Instr. Cath. U. America, Washington, 1952-57, asst. prof., 1958-69, assoc. prof., 1970-93, chmn. drama dept., 1977-93; comm. cons. (bus., media, ministry), 1951—2013. Exec. prodr. Nat. Players Classical Tour Co., Olney, Md.; v.p. Olney Theatre Corp., 1968-85, pres., 1986-94; chmn. Olney Theatre Ctr. for the Arts Mem. Nat. Inst. for the Word of God (assoc. bd. dirs., co-founder 1972), Actors Equity Assn., SAG, AFTRA. Roman Catholic. Avocation: family. Home: Silver Spring, Md. Died Oct. 15, 2013.

**GRAM, NIELS FREDERIK,** retired chemical engineer, writer; b. Frederiksberg, Denmark, Dec. 9, 1927; s. Kai and Elly Ida (Christophersen) Gram; m. Anne-Mette Poulsen Gram, Nov. 10, 1956; 4 children. MSc in Chem. Engring., Tech. U. Denmark, 1951. Rsch. asst. Tech. U., Copenhagen, Denmark, 1951; from chem. engr. to dep. dir. Paul Bergsoe & Son, Glostrup, Denmark, 1952-85; sect. chief Industriradet, Copenhagen, 1985-92; sr. adviser Dansk Industri, Copenhagen, 1992-94. Author: The Bergsoe Solder Book, 1977; editor, author: Metalstobegods, 1969; author, co-author (metallurgy) Danish Ency., 1994-2001. Served in Danish armed svcs., 1951-52. Mem. Danish Acad. Tech. Scis. (pres. 1977-83). Home: Naerum, Denmark. Died Sept. 29, 2001.

**GRAMSTORFF, JEANNE B.,** retired farmer; b. Floydada, Tex., June 23, 1930; d. David Stephen Battey and Ruth Asbury Pitts; m. John C. Gramstorff, Feb. 14, 1951 (dec. Feb. 1993); children: Susan G. Gramstorff Fetzer, John C. BA, Tex. Tech U., 1951. Cert. tchr. Tex. Tchr. Perryton (Tex.) Mid. and HS's, 1951-66; farmer Gramstorff & Son, Farnsworth, Tex., 1951-2000; ret., 2000. Bd. dirs. Perryton Nat. Bank. Trustee, officer Perry Meml. Libr., Perryton, from 1956, pres., 2000—03; officer Tex. Panhandle Libr. Sys. Coun., Amarillo, from 1978, chmn., 2001—02; bd. dirs. Lydia Patterson Inst., 1993—2000; sec. Accord Agr., Inc., Farnsworth, from 1995; historian, v.p., pres. N.W. Tex. United Meth. Women; chmn. religion and race com., chmn. dist. mission N.W. Tex. Conf. United Meth. Ch., 2004—06, chmn. comm. religion and race, 2004—05, mem. ann. conf., 1976—2004, mem. conf. ministry team, 2004—06. Avocations: reading, needlepoint. Deceased.

**GRAÑENA, ALBERT,** hematologist, educator; b. Barcelona, Sept. 26, 1947; s. Pedro and Antonia (Batista) Grañena; m. Asuncion Aracil (div. Nov. 1988); children: Albert, Marc, Ariadna; m. Olga Millon Grañena, 2008. MD, U. Barcelona, 1969, PhD summa cum laude, 1979, Specialist Internal Medicine, 1981, Specialist Hematology, 1981, PhD Summa Cum Laude. Asst. physician Hosp. Clinic, Barcelona, 1970—72, specialist in hematology, 1972—79, sr. cons. in Hematology, head Marrow Transplant Program, 1979—93; prof. medicine U. Barcelona, from 1993; head hematology svc. Inst. Catala Oncologia, Barcelona, from 1993, Hosp. Bellvitge, Barcelona, from 2004; sr. advisor clin. rsch. Inst. Recerca Hosp. Sant Pau, OIBER-BBN Group Oncogenesis & Antitumoral R & D. Assoc. prof. Escuela Farreras Valenti, Barcelona, from 1974; prof. U. Barcelona, from 1985; cons. Inst. I/ Dexeus, Barcelona, from 1998; lectr. to nat. and internat. med. congresses. Contbr. articles to internat. jours., to nat. jours. Bd, dirs. Fundacio Josep Carreras. Recipient IX DuPont prize, Oviedo, Spain, 1999, award, Chief Hematology Hosp. Vall D Hebron, 2012; named Main investigator Joint Com. Spanish EEUU for sci. coop.; nominee Best Scientist of The Yr. award, U. Cambridge, 2002; Presidential grant, Fundacio Josep Carreras, Barcelona, 1995—2001. Mem.: European Bone Marrow Tranplantation Soc., Internat. Soc. Hematology, Am. Soc. Hematology. Home: Barcelona, Spain. Died Oct. 18, 2013.

**GRANGAARD, DONALD R.,** retired banker; b. 1918; m. Irene Grangaard; children: Cheryl, Janet, John, Blake, Paul. BS in Commerce, U. N.D., 1939; JD, William Mitchell Coll. Law, 1948. With 1st Bank System, Inc., Mpls., 1939-83; v.p., liaison officer Eastern div. parent co. 1st Nat. Bank of Austin, 1959-68, sr. v.p. adminstrn., 1968-69, pres., CEO, 1969-77, chmn., CEO, 1977-81, chmn., 1981—83. Served with AUS, 1942-46. Died Mar. 4, 1999.

**GRANGER, SHELTON B.,** human service and civil rights consultant, social agency executive; b. Harrisburg, Pa., Feb. 21, 1921; s. Augustus T. and Katherine (Harris) Granger; m. Dorothy Steele Granger, June 18, 1943; children: Carol, Katherine, Diane, Shelton, Richelle. BA, Howard U., 1942; MS, Columbia U., 1947. Cert. social worker. Dir. indsl. rels. Cleve. Urban League, 1947—51, exec. dir., 1958—62, Mpls. Urban League, 1951—58. Cons. Pres.'s Com. on Juvenile Delinquency Dept. Justice, 1962; dir. human resources devel. Latin Am. div. Bus. Agy. Internat. Devel., 1963—65; deputy asst. sec. Dept. HEW, 1965—66; deputy asst. sec. for internat. affairs, 1966—69; assoc. prof. political sci., cons. urban affairs Macalester Coll., St. Paul, 1969—71; exec. dir. Health and Welfare Coun., Inc., Phila., 1972—78; cons. govt. agys., private industry in human svcs. and civil rights programs, from 1979; field worker Urban League Greater NY; recruitment specialist Peace Corps, Cleve.; cons. Ford Found.; guest lectr. U. Minn. Sch. Social Work, U. Md. Sch. Social Work; field instr. Sch. Applied Social Scis. Case-Western Reserve U., Atlanta U. Sch. Social Work, U. Minn. Sch. Social Work; assoc. prof. Lincoln U., Pa. Author: The Urban Crisis-Challenge for the Century, 1970; contbr. articles to profl. jours. 1st lt. US Army, 1942—46. Democrat. Unitarian Universalist. Died Sept. 25, 1991.

**GRANNIS, VANCE BURNS,** lawyer; b. South St. Paul, Sept. 3, 1908; s. David L. and Macha Lucinda (Vance) Grannis; m. Margrete Louise, June 7, 1934; children: Vance B., Macha Joy, Linda. BA, Carleton Coll., 1929; LLD, U. Minn., 1932. Bar: Minn. 1932, US Supreme Ct. 1965, US Dist. Ct. Minn., US Ct. Appeals. Ptnr. Grannis and Grannis, South St. Paul, 1932—75, pres. Pa., 1975—80, Grannis, Grannis, Farrell and Knutson, 1980—89, Grannis & Halage, Pa., 1990—95; dir. Twin City Testing and Engring. Lab. Inc., St. Paul. Bd. dirs. Dakota County Referral and Transp. Srs., 1978—82, Dakota County Ctr. Arts, 1981—82. Mem.: South St. Paul C. of C. (pres. 1948), U. Minn. Alumni Assn. (pres. 1960—61), Minn. Bar Assn. (sr. counselor 1982), Pool and Yacht (St. Paul) Club, Southview Country (South St. Paul) Club, Silver Bay Country Club, St. Paul Athletic Club. Died May 3, 1999.

**GRANT, MICHAEL,** retired university president, author; b. London, Nov. 21, 1914; arrived in Italy, 1966; s. Maurice Harold and Muriel Ethel (Jörgensen) G.; m. Rut Anne-Sophie Beskow, Aug. 2, 1994; children: Jan Patrick Michael, Antony Harold. Litt.D, Trinity Coll., Cambridge, Eng., 1936; LLD (hon.), D. Litt. (hon.). Fellow Trinity Coll., Cambridge, 1938-49; rep. Brit. Coun., Turkey, 1948-45, dep. dir. European divsn., 1945-48; prof. humanity Edinburgh (Scotland) U., 1938-49; vice chancellor U. Khartoum, 1946-48; pres., vice chancellor Queen's U., Belfast, No. Ireland, 1948-59. Author numerous books including Ancient History, 1952, Roman Imperial Money, 1954, Roman Literature, 1954, Greeks (with Don Pottinger), 1958, Romans (with Don Pottinger), 1960, The World of Rome, 1960, Myths of the Greeks and the romans, 1962, The Birth of Western Civilization: Greece and Rome, 1964, The Civilization of Europe, 1966, Cambridge, 1966, Gladiators, 1967, The Climax of Rome: The Final Achievements of the Ancient World, AD 161-337, 1968, The Ancient Mediterranean, 1969, Julius Caesar, 1969, The Ancient Historians, 1970, The Rome Forum, 1970, Nero: Emperor in Revolt, 1970, Cities of Vesuvius: Pompeii and Herculaneum, 1971, Herod the Great, 1971, Roman Myths, 1971, Cleopatra, 1972, The Jews in the Roman World, 1973, Gods and Mortals in Classical Mythology (with John Hazel), 1973, Caesar, 1974, The Army of the Caesars, 1974, The Twelve Caesars, 1975, Eros in pompeii: The Secret Rooms of the National Museum of Naples, 1975, The Fall of the Roman Empire: A Reappraisal, 1976, Saint Paul, 1976, Jesus: An Historian's Review of the Gospels, 1976, The History of Rome, 1978, Art and Life of Pompeii and Herculaneum, 1979, The Etruscans, 1980, Greek and Latin Authors, 800 BC-AD 1000, 1980, From Alexander to Cleopatra: The Hellenistic World, 1980, History of Ancient Israel, 1984, The Roman Emperors: A Biographical Guide to the Rulers of Ancient Rome, 31 BC-AD 476, 1985, The Classical Greeks, 1988, A Social History of Greece and Rome, 1992, Constantine the Great, 1993, Saint Peter, 1994, My First Eighty Years (autobiography), 1994, The Antonines, 1994, Art in the Roman Empire, 1995, Greek and Roman Historians: Information and Misinformation, 1995, The Severans, 1996, From Rome to Byzantium, 1998, The Collapse and Recovery of the Roman Empire, 1999, Sick Caesars, 2000. Capt. Brit. Army, 1939-40. Decorated Order of Brit. Empire, comdr. Brit. Empire, Premio del Mediverraneo, Florence, Premio, Mazara del Vallo, Italy, 1983, Pres.'s Gold Medal for Edn., Sudan, 1977. Mem. Am. Numismatic Soc. (corr.), Royal Numismatic Soc. (past pres.), Virgil Soc. (pres., 1963-66), pres., Classical Assn., 1978-79. Home: Gattaiola Lucca, Italy. Died Oct. 4, 2004.

**GRANT, ROBERT MCQUEEN,** humanities educator; b. Evanston, Ill., Nov. 25, 1917; s. Frederick Clifton and Helen McQueen (Hardie) G.; m. Margaret Huntington Horton, Dec. 21, 1940; children: Douglas McQueen, Peter Williams, Susan Hardie, James Frederick. AB, Northwestern U., 1938; postgrad., Episcopal Theol. Sch., 1938-39, Columbia U., 1939-40; BD, Union Theol. Sem., 1941; STM, Harvard U., 1942, ThD, 1944; DD, Seabury-Western Theol. Sem., 1969, U. Glasgow, 1979; LHD, Kalamazoo Coll., 1979; DD, Ch. Div. Sch. Pacific, 1992. Ordained to ministry Episcopal Ch., 1942. Minister St. James Ch., South Groveland, Mass., 1942-44; instr. to prof. N.T. U. of South, 1944-53, acting dean, 1947; vis. lectr. U. Chgo., 1945, research assoc., 1952-53, assoc. prof., 1953-58, prof., 1958-87, prof. emeritus, 1988—2014, Carl Darling Buck prof. humanities, 1973-87, Carl Darling Buck prof. emeritus, 1988—2014. Vis. lectr. Vanderbilt U., 1945-47, Seabury-Western Theol. Sem., 1954-55, 89, Augustinianum (Rome), 1990; lectr. American Council Learned Socs., 1957-58; vis. prof. Yale U., 1964-65, Fla. State U., 1989. Author: Second-Century Christianity, 1946, 2d edit., 2003, The Bible in the Church, 1948, rev. edit. (with David Tracy), 1984, Miracle and

Natural Law, 1952, The Sword and the Cross, 1955, The Letter and the Spirit, 1957, Gnosticism and Early Christianity, 1959, 63, Gnosticism: An Anthology, 1961, The Earliest Lives of Jesus, 1961, Historical Introduction to the New Testament, 1963, The Apostolic Fathers, vol. I, 1964, vol. II (with H. H. Graham), 1965, vol. IV, 1966, U-Boats Destroyed 1914-1918, 1964, 2002, The Formation of the New Testament, 1965, History of Early Christian Literature (revision from E. J. Goodspeed), 1966, The Early Christian Doctrine of God, 1966, After the New Testament, 1967, U-Boat Intelligence 1914-1918, 1969, 2002, Augustus to Constantine, 1970, new edit., 2004, Theophilus of Antioch Ad Autolycum, 1970, Early Christianity and Society, 1977, Eusebius as Church Historian, 1980, Christian Beginnings: Apocalypse to History, 1983, Gods and the One God, 1986, Greek Apologists of the Second Century, 1988, Jesus after the Gospels, 1989, Heresy and Criticism, 1993, Irenaeus of Lyons, 1997, Early Christians and Animals, 1999, Paul in the Roman World, 2001, U-Boat Hunters, 2003; (with D. N. Freedman) The Secret Sayings of Jesus, 1960, (with G. Menzies) Joseph's Bible Notes, Hypomnestikon, 1996. Fulbright research prof. U. Leiden, 1950-51; Guggenheim fellow, 1950, 54, 59. Fellow American Acad. Arts and Scis.; mem. Soc. Bibl. Lit. (pres. 1959), American Soc. Ch. History (pres. 1970, co-editor 1962-87), Chgo. Soc. Bibl. Research (pres. 1963-64, editor 1956-61), Phi Beta Kappa. Home: Chicago, Ill. Died June 10, 2014.

**GRAS, PIM WILLEM,** radio producer, journalist, jazz historian; b. Amsterdam, The Netherlands, Dec. 16, 1933; s. Simon Petrus and Jozina Wilhelmina (Jongeneel) G.; m. Christina Petronella Rappange, Mar. 14, 1959; children: Thijs, Caroline. Grad. in tchg., Kweekschool, Amsterdam, 1954. Tchr., Amsterdam, 1954-61; newsreader, editor ANP/NOS, Hilversum, The Netherlands, 1961-91; jazz producer NOS Radio, Hilversum, 1968-93; japp producer Concertzender, Amsterdam/Hilversum, from 1993; bd. dirs. Dutch Jazz Archive, Amsterdam, from 1980. Clarinet, saxophone player in traditional jazz bands. Author: Jazz uit het historisch archief, 1974; chief editor NJA Bull., 1991—; contbr. articles to Dutch jazz periodicals; recorded with The New Orleans Seven, 1956-58, Charley's novelty orch. The Crwths, 1967-68, Spiegle Willcox, 1992, 94. Home: Amsterdam, Netherlands. Died Dec. 25, 2000.

**GRASHIN, ANATOLIY FEODOROVICH,** physicist, researcher; b. Moscow, May 6, 1932; s. Feodor Georgievich Grashin and Antonina Ivanovna Aleeva; m. Nataly Pavlovna Andrusenko, Nov. 4, 1972 (div.); children: Sergey, Olga, Varvara; m. Maria Pavlovna Andrusenko, May 8, 1992; 1 child, Peter. MS, Moscow Engring. Physics Inst., 1956, DSc, 1960; D in Physics and Math., Higher Attestation Commn. USSR, 1970. Cert. prof. theoretical physics Higher Attestation Commn. USSR, 1972. Asst. prof. Moscow Engring. Physics Inst., 1956, lectr., 1956-59, head of rsch., from 1977; sci. worker Inst. for Theoretical and Exptl. Physics, Moscow, 1959-66; prof. Moscow Regional Pedagogical Inst., 1966-77. Mem. methodol. coun. Ministry of Edn., USSR, 1969-78, tech. coun., 1983-88; mem. expert coun. Univ. People's Friendship of Russia, 1978—. Author: Quantum Mechanics, 1974; contbr. articles to profl. jours. Mem. Soc. ZNANIE (methodol. coun. 1970-80), N.Y. Acad. Scis. Avocations: sports, classical music. Home: Moscow, Russia. Deceased.

**GRASSO, RENATO,** physiologist; b. Turin, Italy, Oct. 3, 1962; s. Vincenzo and Ornella (Sardo) G. MD, U. Turin, 1989; PhD, U. Verona, 1995. Hon. rsch. fellow U. Leeds, U.K., 1992-93; rschr. U. Verona, Italy, 1995-96; sr. rschr. Coll. de France, Paris, 1995-96; assoc. rschr., head Gait Lab. Neuromotor Psysiology divsn. IRCCS-S. Lucia Rehab. Hosp., Rome, from 1997. Cons. IRST, Trento, Italy, 1989, FIDIA Spa, Abanoterme, Italy, 1992. Contbr. articles to profl. jours. Med. lt. Sanitary Corp., 1989-91. Mem. SIF, Soc. for Neurosci. Home: Rome, Italy. Deceased.

**GRAY, CHARLES HENRY,** actor, theater director; b. Omaha, Nov. 27, 1921; s. Charles Henry and Celia (Stangl) Gray; m. Kiki Rice; 1 child, David Moulton. BA, U. Minn., 1948; MA, Tulane U., 1950, U. Without Walls, 1961. Instr. Tulane U., New Orleans; staff dir., instr. U. Houston, Houston; prodr., dir. Houston Music Theatre, Houston; dir., narrator KTRK-TV, Houston; actor, writer CBS-TV, Hollywood, Calif. Actor: Rawhide, Gunslinger, Young and the Restless. Mem.: SAG. Democrat. Buddhist. Home: Joshua Tree, Calif. Died Aug. 2, 2008.

**GRAY, HERBERT ESER (THE RIGHT HONOURABLE HERBERT GRAY),** former Canadian government official; b. Windsor, Ont., Can., May 25, 1931; s. Harry and Fannie Gray; m. Sharon Sholzberg, July 23, 1967; children: Jonathan, Elizabeth Anne. Student, Kennedy Coll. Inst., Windsor; postgrad., McGill U. Grad. Sch. Commerce, Que., Osgoode Hall Law Sch., Toronto. Mem. House of Commons, Ottawa, Ont., Canada, 1962—2002; dep. prime min. Govt. of Canada, 1997—2002. Chmn. standing com. on finance, trade & econ. affairs House of Commons, Ottawa, 1966—68, served as parliamentary sec. to Min. of Finance, 1968—69, min. without portfolio, 1969, min. of nat. revenue, 1970—72, min. consumer & corporate affairs, 1972—74, min. industry, trade & commerce, 1980—82, min. regional econ. expansion, 1982—84, pres. of Treasury Bd., 1982—84, opposition leader, 1984—90, dep. leader opposition, 1989—90, leader opposition, 1990; financial critic off. opposition Ho. of Commons, Ottawa, 1991—93; leader, solicitor gen. of Can. House of Commons, Ottawa, 1993—97; min. Millennium Bur. Can., Ottawa, 1998—2002. Del. IMF and World Bank, 1967, 1969, 1970; co-chmn. Can. del. OECD Ministerial, 1970; leader Can. del. Commonwealth Fin. Mins., 1970. Mem.: Jaycees (pres. Windsor sect. 1961—62), Richelieu Club, Rotary (hon.), B'nai B'rith Lodge. Died Apr. 21, 2014.

**GRAY, KENNETH JAMES,** former United States Representative from Illinois; b. West Frankfort, Ill., Nov. 14, 1924; s. Thomas W. Grat and Anna (Reed) Gray; m. Gwendolyn June Croslin (dec.); children: Diann, Rebecca, Jimmy. Student, Army Advanced Sch. Owner Gray Motors, West Frankfort, Ill., 1942—54; operated air svc. Benton, Ill.; mem. US Congress from 25th Ill. Dist., 1955—63, US Congress from 21st Ill. Dist., 1963—73, US Congress from 24th Ill. Dist., 1973—74, US Congress from 22nd Ill. Dist., 1985—89; pres. Ken Gray & Associates; owner Ken Gray's Antique Car Mus. Founder Walking Dog Found. for Blind, 1950; bd. dirs. Nat. Coal Mus. Served with USAAF, 1943—45. Decorated Bronze star (3). Mem.: VFW, Forty and Eight, American Legion, Kiwanis, Elks. Democrat. Baptist. Home: West Frankfort, Ill. Died July 12, 2014.

**GRAY, ROBERT KEITH (BOB GRAY),** retired public relations company executive; b. Hastings, Nebr., Sept. 2, 1923; s. Garold C.J. and Marie (Burchess) G. BA in Political Sci., Carleton Coll., 1943; MBA, Harvard Bus. Sch., 1949; DBus (hon.), Marymount Coll., 1981; LLD (hon.), Hastings Coll., 1982; HHD (hon.), Creighton U., 1989. Assoc. prof. finance Hastings Coll., Nebr., 1950-51; prof. U. Southern Calif., Los Angeles, 1952; spl. asst. sec. Dept. Navy, US Dept. Def., 1954; spl. asst. to Pres. The White House, Washington, 1955-57, appointments sec., 1958, sec., 1959-60; v.p. Hill & Knowlton, Inc., Washington, 1961-64, sr. v.p., 1965-70, exec. v.p., 1971-76, vice chmn., 1977-81, chmn., CEO, from 1991; founder, chmn. Gray & Co. Public Communications Internat. (merger Hill and Knowlton, Inc.), Washington, 1981-86; chmn., CEO Hill & Knowlton Public Affairs Worldwide, Washington, 1986-91, Hill & Knowlton USA, Washington, 1986-91; chmn., pres. Gray & Co. II, Washington, 1988—92; chmn. Gray Investment Properties, Inc., Washington, 1988—92; pres., CEO Member Services Co., Washington, 1988—92; chmn, CEO Powerhouse Leasing Corp., Washington, 1988—92. Author: Casebook on Organization and Operation of a Small Business Enterprise, 1950, Eighteen Acres Under Glass, 1962, Presidential Perks Gone Royal: Your Taxes Are Being Used for Obama's Re-election, 2012 Mem. public info. adv. coun. World Wildlife Fund; bd. dirs. Freedoms Found., Valley Forge, Pa.; trustee Fed. City Coun., Washington; mem. nat. adv. bd. Am. U.; dir. emeritus Wolf Trap Found.; bd. dirs. Eisenhower World Affairs Inst.; mem. internat. adv. bd. Internat. Inst. for Peace through Tourism; bd. councilors Sch. Bus. Adminstrn., U. Southern Calif.; mem. pvt. sector public rels. com. and internat. coun., USIA; dir. communications Reagan-Bush Campaign, Washington, 1980; co-chmn. Presdl. Inaugural, Washington, 1981; hon. chmn. for 1989 Bush-Quayle Inaugural, 1985; adv. bd. Ctr. Strategic and Internat. Studies, Commn. on Bicentennial of U.S. Constn., 1988; mem. bd. Alliance to Save Energy; adv. com. Presdl. Debates, 1988, Public Edn. Task Force of Pub./Pvt. Careers Project at the Kennedy Sch. Govt. Harvard U.; mem. steering com. Nat. Air and Space Mus. joint project with the Ctr. for Democracy; mem. Com. for Single Six-Yr. Presdl. Term; prin. benefactor Gray Ctr. Communications Arts, Hastings Coll., Neb; Comdr. USN, 1944-46 Decorated knight comdr. Order of Merit, Grande Officiale (Italy); recipient Medaille de Vermeil, Mayor of Paris, 1982, Disting. Nebraskalander award, 1985; named Marketeer of Yr., Adweek mag. Mem.: 1925 F St., George Town (chmn.) (Washington), Masons. Republican. Episcopalian. Avocations: writing; beaching; sky diving; tennis. Home: Miami Beach, Fla. Died Apr. 18, 2014.

**GRAY, SANDRA RAE,** retired education educator; b. East Palestine, Ohio, Nov. 8, 1932; d. Kenneth Ray Morris and Nina Olivia (Jamsen) Rex; m. Donald Noel Gray Jr., Nov. 9, 1951; children: Pamela, Donald, Douglas. BA in speech communications, Calif. State U., 1967, MA in speech communications, 1974. Tchr. Tustin (Calif.) Unif. Sch. Dist., 1971-95, ret., 1995; tchr. Riverside (Calif.) Sch. Dist., 1968-71; teaching asst. U. Souther Calif., LA, 1974-77; tchr. Saddleback Coll., Mission Viejo, Calif., 1982-84, Calif. State U., LA, 1976. Pres. adv. coun. annual fund Calif. State U., 1992-95; pres. Calif. State Speech Coun., 1976-78; chmn. Nat. Forensic League (Big Orange Chpt.), Ripon, Wis., 1992-93. Recipient Calif. State Speech Coun. Hall of Fame Calif. H.S. Speech Assn., 1982. Mem. AAUW. Republican. Protestant. Avocations: writing, travel, reading. Died 2004.

**GRAY, SIMON JAMES HOLLIDAY,** writer, educator; b. Oct. 21, 1936; s. James Davidson Gray and Barbara Cecelia Mary (Holliday) Davidson; m. Beryl Mary Kevern, 1965 (div. 1997); 2 children; m. Victoria Rothschild, 1997. Student, Westminister Sch., Dalhousie U., Halifax, N.S.; MA, U. Cambridge. Supr. English U. B.C., 1960-63. Sr. instr., 1963-64; lectr. Queen Mary Coll., U. London, 1965-84. Author: (novels) Colmain, 1963, Simple People, 1965, Little Portia, 1967, A Comeback for Stark, 1968, Breaking Hearts, 1997, (non-fiction) An Unnatural Pursuit and Other Pieces, 1985, How's That For Telling 'Em Fat Lady, 1988, Fat Chance, 1995, Enter a Fox, 2001, The Smoking Diaries, 2005, The Year of the Jouncer, 2006, The Last Cigarette: Smoking Diaries Volume 3, 2008, (plays) Wise Child, 1968, Sleeping Dog, 1968, Dutch Uncle, 1969, The Idiot, 1971, Spoiled, 1971, Butley, 1971 (Evening Std. award), Otherwise Engaged, 1975 (Best Play, N.Y. Drama Critics Cir., Evening Std. award), Plaintiffs and Defendants, 1975, Two Sundays, 1975, Dog Days, 1976, Molly, 1977, The Rear Column, 1978, Close of Play, 1979, Quartermaine's Terms, 1981, Tartuffe, 1982, Chapter 17, 1982, The Common Pursuit, 1984, Plays One, 1986, Melon, 1987, Hidden Laughter, 1991, The Holy Terror, 1992, Cell Mates, 1995, Simply Disconnected, 1996, Life Support, 1997, Just the Three of Us, 1997, The Late Middle Classes, 1999, Japes, 2000, Old Masters, 2004, Little Nell, 2007, Missing Dates, 2008, (TV movies) After Pilkington, 1987, Quartermaine's Terms, 1987, Old Flames, 1990, They Never Slept, 1991, The Common Pursuit, 1992, Running Late, 1992, Unnatural Pursuits, 1993, Femme Fatale, 1993, (film) A Month in the Country, (radio plays) The Holy Terror (rev.), 1989, The Rector's Daughter, 1992, With a Nod and a Bow, 1993, Suffer the Little Children, 1993, Little Nell, 2006. Mem. Dramatists Guild. Died Aug. 6, 2008.

**GRAYSON, DAVID S.,** retired paper company executive; b. Binghamton, NY, Oct. 16, 1943; s. Milton M. and Helen A. (Oretskin) G.; m. Wendy W. Grayson (div. June 1986); children: Natalie, Marc, Dayna. BS, Coll. Forestry, Syracuse, NY, 1965; MS, Rensselaer Poly., 1967. Various positions Riegel Paper div. James River Co., Milford, N.J., 1967-80; sales mgr. Kerwin Paper, Appleton, Wis., 1980-81; pres., founder Am. Fine Paper, Appleton, 1981—2008, gen. mgr., 2007—11. Jewish. Home: Neenah, Wis. Deceased.

**GRAZIANO, MARGARET A.,** chaplain, recreational therapist, educational consultant, volunteer; b. Ore., Nov. 25, 1916; d. Agostino Graziano and Madeline Rinella; children: Vincent, Margaret, Salvatore, Anne, Agatha, Prudence, Rosemary, Joseph. BA, Holy Names Coll., 1946; BM, Maryhurst Coll., 1951; MEd, U. Portland, 1961. Cert. correctional chaplain Am. Correctional Cath. Chaplains Assn., Am. Correctional Chaplains Assn., 2000, alcohol counselor Oreg., in adminstrn. and supervision U. Portland. Tchr. Sister of the Holy Names, Oreg., 1937—75; music tchr. Montessori, Eugene, Oreg., 1974—76; young musicians artist camp Maryhurst Coll., 1972—82; specialized counselor Triple H. Ranch, Jasper, Oreg., 1972—74; chem. dependancy counselor Treatment Ctr. Youth, Eugene, Oreg., 1975—79; asst. vol. coord. Lane County Adult Corrections, Eugene, Oreg., 1976—2011, chaplain, 1995—2006; recreational therapist Johnson Unit, 2004—05. Chem. dependency facilitator Intensive Treatment Program, Eugene, Oreg., Serbu Detention Ctr., 2008. Co-editor (with Susan Clayton): Best in the Business-Corrections Today, 1999. Vol. St. Vincent de Paul Soc. Lane County, 2008, Lane County Jail; bd. dirs. Committed Ptnrs. for Youth, from 2000, Don Bosce House, 2000—11; rep. Lane County Human Potential Workshop, Eugene, Oreg., 1970; chmn. Governors Task force on Vol., 1965; cmty. svc. Inner City Burnside Area, Portland, Oreg., 1972; mem. planning com. Seattle Diocese against Death Penalty, 1968. Recipient Alumni award, St. Mary's Acad., 2005, E.R. Cass award, ACA, 2003, Murname Soc. Justice award, Cath. Cmty. Svc., 2004, Pro Ecclesia et Pontifice award, Received From Pope, 2008; named one of four honorees, Newman Ctr./ U. Ore., 2005. Mem.: Willamette Bus. Leaders, Sisters of the Holy Names (superior 1958), Sons of Italy (trustee/chaplain 1998—2011). Avocations: travel, art, music, drama, films. Home: Lake Oswego, Oreg. Died May 11, 2014.

**GREASER, MAYLIN H.,** retired dredging company executive; b. North Wales, Pa., Jan. 15, 1909; s. John B. and Katie B. G.; m. Ruth N. Philipp, Mar. 13, 1943. BS in Civil Engring., Pa. State U., 1930. Engaged in constrn. and dredging bus., 1930-79; with Am. Dredging Co., Ft. Washington, Pa., 1949-79, successively gen. supt., dir., 1951-79, v.p., 1953, pres., 1954-79; ret., 1979. Mem. Delaware River Ports' Council for Emergency Ops. Lt. col. C.E., AUS, 1942-45. Fellow Soc. Am. Mil. Engrs. (past pres., dir. Phila. post.); mem. Port of Phila. Maritime Soc. (past pres.), ASCE (life), Delaware Valley Council (past pres.), Mil. Order World Wars, Franklin Inst., Am. Legion, Cricket Club, Skytop Club (Pa.). Presbyterian. Home: Philadelphia, Pa. Died Jan. 25, 1991.

**GREAVES, WILLIAM GARFIELD,** film director, producer; b. Harlem, Oct. 8, 1926; s. Garfield G. and Emily (Muir) G.; m. Louise Ann Archambault, Aug. 23, 1959; children: David, Taiyi, Maiya. Cert., New Inst. for Film and TV, Bklyn., 1951, Film Inst., CCNY, 1952; LHD (hon.), King Meml. Coll., 1977, Tougaloo Coll., 1991. Freelance songwriter, NYC, 1944-52; dancer Pearl Primus and Asadata Dafora Dance Cos., NYC, 1944-45; featured actor Am. Negro Theater, various Broadway, film and TV prodns., NYC, 1945-52; mem. N.Y. Actors Studio, from 1948; filmmaker Nat. Film Bd. of Can., Ottawa, Canada, 1952-60, Montreal, Canada; public info. officer UN Internat. Civil Aviation Orgn., Montreal, 1961-63; film producer, director UN-TV, NYC, 1963-64; film producer, writer, dir. William Greaves Prodns., NYC, 1964—2014. Founder, dir., tchr. acting Can. Drama Studio, Montreal, Ottawa, and Toronto, Ont., Can., 1953-63; tchr. Strasberg Inst., N.Y.C., 1969-82; freelance lectr. film, US and abroad; substitute moderator Actors Studio, N.Y.C., 1970-82; panelist various arts agys.; guest lectr. numerous colls., univs. Appeared in: (plays) Finian's Rainbow, 1947, The Fight Never Ends, 1948, Lost in the Stars, 1949, Lost Boundaries, 1949; Exec. producer, co-host (TV series) Black Journal, 1968-70 (Emmy award 1970); host (TV series) Blackstream; producer, dir., writer: (films) Symbiopsychotaxiplasm: Take One, 1968, Ali: The Fighter, 1971, The Marijuana Affair, 1974; exec. producer (films) Bustin' Loose, 1981; co-creator, dir. (multi-media prodn.) 2 Tributes to Paul Robeson Carnegie Hall and The Shubert Theatre (N.Y.C.); producer, dir., writer (documentaries) Black Power in America: Myth or Reality?, 1986, That's Black Entertainment, 1989, Ida B. Wells: A Passion for Justice (featuring on camera reading by Toni Morrison 1989), 1991 (First Place Documentary award Black Filmmakers Hall of Fame), Ralph Bunche: An American Odyssey, 2001 Trustee Schomburg Ctr. for Research in Black Culture, N.Y.C.; mem. arts adv. bd., chmn. film panel The Princess Grace Found.; bd. dirs. N.Y. Actors Studio; mem. film panel Dore Schary Awards. Recipient over 80 internat. film festival awards, 1969-92, Dusa award N.Y. Actors Studio, 1980, Russwurm award Nat. Urban League, 1970, Indy award Assn. Ind. Video and Film Producers, 1986, Emmy award, 1970; named to The Black Filmmakers Hall of Fame, 1980; spl. hommage and retrospective Black American Filmmakers, Paris, 1980 Mem. AFTRA, Dirs. Guild America, Writers Guild America, Screen Actors Guild, Actors Equity Assn., Assn. Ind. Video and Filmmakers (v.p. 1980-83), American Guild Authors and Composers. Avocation: jogging. *Success is largely dependent on an individual's capacity to convert the most adverse and negative experience or circumstance into something constructive and productive.* Died Aug. 25, 2014.

**GREEN, ADELINE MANDEL,** social worker; b. St. Paul; d. Meyer and Eva Ulanove; m. Nathan G. Mandel (div.); children: Meta Susan Mandel, Myra Halpern; m. Maurice L. Green. BS, MSW, U. Minn. LCSW. Past investigator Ramsey County Mothers Aid and Aid to Dependent Children Ramsey County Welfare Bd., St. Paul; psychiat. social worker Wilder Child Guidance Clinic, St. Paul; psychiat. social worker, supr. outpatient psychiatry clinic U. Minn. Hosps., Mpls., supr., clin. instr. psychiatry-social svc., outpatient psychiatry clinic; pvt. practice family and marriage counseling South Bay Clinic, Los Gatos, Calif. Past chmn. Diagnostic Clinic for Rheumatic Fever-Wilder Clinic, St. Paul; assoc. Family and Child Psychiat. Med. Clinic. Past pres. St. Paul sect. Coun. Jewish Women. Mem.: NASW, Am. Assn. Marriage and Family Counselors, Minn. Welfare Conf., Acad. Cert. Social Workers, Brandeis U. Women. Democrat. Home: Costa Mesa, Calif. Died Mar. 12, 1999.

**GREEN, DAVID L.,** former state legislator; b. Rosetta, Miss., Oct. 14, 1951; widowed. Student, S.W. Miss. Jr. Coll. Dep. sheriff; police officer; mem. Miss. House of Reps., 1980—2005. Active Voters League. Mem. NAACP, Heroine of Jericho, Masons, Ea. Star, Shriners. Democrat. Baptist. Home: Gloster, Miss. Died July 25, 2014.

**GREENBERG, ACE (ALAN COURTNEY GREENBERG),** retired diversified financial services company executive; b. Wichita, Kans., Sept. 3, 1927; s. Theodore H. and Esther (Zeligson) G.; m. Ann Greenberg (div.); children: Lynn, Theodore; m. Kathryn Olson, June 27, 1987 BS, U. Mo., 1949. Trader The Bear Stearns Companies Inc., NYC, 1949—58, gen. ptnr., 1958—78, chmn. bd., CEO, 1978-93, chmn. bd., 1993—2001, chmn. exec. com., sr. mng. dir., 2001—08; vice chmn. emeritus J.P. Morgan & Chase Co., NYC, 2008—14. Bd. dirs. The Bear Stearns Companies, Inc., 1985—2008, Viacom Inc., 2003—14. Author: Memos from the Chairman, 1996; co-author (with Mark Singer): The Rise and Fall of Bear Stearns, 2010. Winner Nat. Bridge Championship, 1977; recipient Horatio Alger award, 1997. Mem. Soc. American Magicians, Harmonie Club, Bond Club, Deep Dale Club. Jewish. Avocation: bridge. Home: New York, NY. Died July 25, 2014.

**GREEN CLAIR, CAROLYN,** civic worker; b. Boston, Sept. 18, 1907; d. James Maddocks and Marietta Cecelia (Foeley) Green; m. Miles Nelson Clair, June 16, 2028 (div. Jan. 1981); children: Cynthia York Clair Norkin, Valerie DeLuce Clair Stelling, Ardith Monroe Clair Houghton. BS, Boston U., 1930, postgrad, 1933. Clk. corp., dir. Thompson & Lichtner Co., Inc., 1951—77; assoc. Assn. Country Women World, from 1968; pres. New Eng. Farm & Garden Assn., 1968—71; lectr., from 1972; alt. UN, 1974—80; del. Conf. U.S. Norway, Kenya, Australia and U.N, 1974—80; treas. MNCC, Inc., from 1977; chmn. fellowship Woods Hole Oceanographic Instn.; mem. Women's Rep. Club NYC, English-Speaking Union, Friend Librs. Boston U.; bd. dirs. Boston Morning Musicales, Tufts U., 1966—80; pres. Women's Nat. Farm Assn., 1972—74; chmn. adv. bd., 1974—76; mem. adv. bd. Nat. Arboretum, Washington, 1974—78; v.p. Mass. Hort. Soc., 1970—79. Lectr. environ. concerns. Recipient award, Brit. War Relief, 1945, Internat. award, Woman's Nat. Farm and Garden Assn. Inc., Appreciation cert., Brigham and Women's Hosp./Mass. Gen. Hosp., 1994. Mem.: Arnold Arboretum, Bostonian Soc., Nat. Trust Historic Preservation, Nat. Wildlife Fedn., Audubon Soc., Assn. Country Women World, Internat. Platform Assn., Pan Am. Soc., Mass. Hist. Soc., New Eng. Hist. Soc. (life), Buzzards Yacht Club. Republican. Episcopalian. Died 1998.

**GREENE, CHARLES CASSIUS,** advertising agency executive; b. Sullivan, Ill., June 6, 1897; s. Cassius Wilbur and Katherine (Mouser) B.; m. Ursula Lally, 1927. Ph.B., U. Chgo., 1919, JD, 1921; postgrad., Sch. Commerce Northwestern U., 1932-33. Bar: Ill. Account exec. Albert Frank (advt.), Chgo., 1926-31; v.p. Carroll Dean Murphy (advt.), Chgo., 1931-36, Critchfield & Co. (advt.), Chgo., 1936-40, Buchanan & Co. (advt.), Chgo., 1940-44; v.p., resident mgr., dir. Doremus & Co. subs. Omincom, Inc., Chgo., 1944-70, cons., 1970-77. 2d lt. inf. U.S. Army, World War I. Mem. Pub. Rels. Soc. Am. (past pres. Chgo., nat. v.p.), Am. Legion (past comdr. advt. men's post #38), Execs. Club, Chgo. Athletic Assn., Rotary, Phi Beta Kappa, Phi Kappa Psi, Phi Delta Phi. Republican. Home: 55 E Monroe St Ste 3230 Chicago IL 60603-5798 Office: 10 S Riverside Plz Ste 19 Chicago IL 60606-3708

**GREENE, RALEIGH WILLIAM, JR.,** lawyer; b. St. Petersburg, Fla., 1927; married BS, U. Fla., 1950, JD, 1951. With Fla. Fed. Savs. and Loan Assn., St. Petersburg, 1952, pres., 1968, former chief exec. officer, now chmn. emeritus, also bd. dirs.; founding mem. Greene & Mastry P.A. Bd. dirs. Gen. Telephone Co. Fla. Died May 15, 1994.

**GREENE, WALLACE MARTIN, JR.,** military officer; b. Waterbury, Vt., Dec. 27, 1907; s. Wallace Martin and Belle (Cooley) G.; m. Vaughan Hemsley Emory, June 30, 1930; children: Vaughan, Emory, Wallace Martin III. BS, U.S. Naval Acad., 1930; student, Marine Corps Schs., 1931, 39, 50, Brit. Sch. Combined Ops., 1941, Royal Engring. Sch., 1941; grad., Nat. War Coll., 1953; LLD (hon.), U. Vt. Commd. 2d lt. USMC, 1930, advanced through grades to gen., 1964. Marine detachment U.S.S. Tenn., 1932-34; assigned Marine Barracks, Guam, 1936-37; with 4th U.S. Marines, Shanghai, China, 1937-39, 1st Marine Brigade, Cuba, 1940-41, 1st Marine Divsn., 1942, 3rd Marine Brigade, Samoa, 1942-43, 22d Marines, Marshall's campaign, 1944, 2d Marine Divsn., Marianas campaign, 1944, staff Fleet Marine Force, Pacific, 1948-50; joint staff Joint Chiefs of Staff, 1953-55; asst. divsn. comdr. 2d Marine Divsn., 1955-56; commdg. gen. Recruit Tng. Command, Parris Island, S.C., 1955-56, Marine Corps Base, Camp Lejeune, N.C., 1956-57; asst. chief of staff Hdqs. USMC, 1958; dep. chief-of-staff, 1959, chief of staff, 1960-63; comdt. USMC, 1964—. Decorated Legion of Merit with gold star, D.S.M., Grand Cordon Order of Cloud and Banner (Rep. of China), Order of Svc. Merit (Korea), Grand Official Order of Naval Merit (Brazil), Nat. Order Vietnam. Mem. U.S. Naval Inst., Marine Corps Assn. Home: Washington, DC. Died Mar. 8, 2003.

**GREENWOOD, FRANK,** information scientist, educator; b. Rio de Janeiro, Mar. 6, 1924; came to U.S., 1935; s. Heman Charles and Evelyn (Heyns) G.; m. Mary Mallas, Oct. 24, 1972; children: Margaret, Ernest, Nicholas. BA, Bucknell U., Lewisburg, Pa., 1950; MBA, U. Southern Calif., LA, 1959; PhD, UCLA, 1963; D (hon.), Commonwealth Open U., 1999. Cert. systems profl., project mgmt. profl. Various positions The Tex. Co., US, Africa and Can., 1950-60; assoc. prof. U. Ga., Athens, 1961-65; chmn. dept. computer sys. Ohio U., Athens, 1966-76; dir. computer ctr. U. Mont., Missoula, 1977-84; prof. mgmt. info. sys. Southea. Mass. U. (now U. Mass.), North Dartmouth, 1985-89, Ctrl. Mich. U., Mt. Pleasant, 1990-93; pres. Greenwood & Assocs., Ltd., Bloomfield Hills, Mich., 1993. Instr. on-line clases Jones Internat. U., Englewood, Colo., Gatlin Ednl. Svcs., Ft. Worth, Tex. Author: Casebook for Management and Business Policy: A Systems Approach, 1968, Managing the Systems Analysis Function, 1968; (with Nicolai Siemens and C.H. Marting Jr.) Operations Research: Planning, Operating and Information Systems, 1973; (with Mary Greenwood) Information Resources in the Office Tomorrow, 1980, Profitable Small Business Computing, 1982, Office Technology: Principles of Automation, 1984, Business Telecommuncations: Data Communications in the Information Age, 1988, Introduction to Computer-Integrated Manufacturing, 1990, How to Raise Office Productivity, 1991, Meeting the Challenges of Project Management: A Primer, 1998; columnist: Computerworld mag., 1972-73, The Daily Record, 1982-83, (with Mary Greenwood) Herald News, 1986, The Beacon, 1986, Morning Sun, 1990-93; contbr. monographs, articles to profl. jours. and chpts. to books. Sgt. AUS, 1943-45. UCLA Alumni scholar, 1961; Ford Found. fellow, 1962-63. Mem. Wamsutta Club (New Bedford, Mass.). Greek Orthodox. Avocation: exercise. Home: Waterford, Mich. *Do what you believe you should (and not what others do). Put your trust in your own capacity to provide products/services others need (and don't seek security as a "corporate slave"). Mental and physical health are the key to all else.* Died Dec. 29, 2010.

**GREENWOOD, GORDON EDWARD,** retired education educator; b. Jasonville, Ind., Aug. 21, 1935; s. Arthur Lee and Annette Rose (Goodman) G.; m. Priscilla Normandy, Aug. 20, 1935; children: Joseph Arthur, Richard Roy, Donald Edward. BS in Secondary Edn., Ind. State U., 1958, MA in Secondary Adminstrn, 1962; EdD in Ednl. Psychology, Ind. Univ., 1967. English tchr. Cen. High Sch., Dowagiac, Mich., 1958-60; social studies tchr. Wiley High Sch., Terre Haute, Ind., 1960-65; rsch. and teaching asst. Ind. U., Bloomington, 1965-67; from asst. prof. to prof. U. Fla., Gainesville, 1967—76, prof. emeritus, 2001. Sect. head ednl. psychology sect. Coll. Edn., U. Fla., Gainesville, 1976-79, 87-93; prof. Ednl. Psychology, Gainesville, 1976-2001; dir. seven rsch. grants for fed., state and local govts., U. Fla., 1971-79. Author: Problem Situations in Teaching, 1971, Case Studies for Teacher Decision Making, 1989, Professional Core Cases for Teacher Decision-Making, 1997, Educational Psychology Cases for Teacher Decision-Making, 1999, Educational Psychology Cases, 2002; contbr. articles to profl. jours. Mem. Citizens Against a Radioactive Environ., Gainesville. Recipient spl. merit award Alachua County Fla. Sch. Bd., Gainesville, 1979. Mem. SAR (pres. Gainesville chpt, 2005-06, 10-11, regional v.p. north-ctrl. region, 2007-2009, Am. Ednl. Research Assn., Fla. Ednl. Research Assn., Am. Soc. Clin. Hypnosis, Order of Crown of Charlemagne, Baronial Order of Magna Charta, Descendents of Knights of Bath. Democrat. Avocation: genealogy. Home: Gainesville, Fla. Died Sept. 14, 2013.

**GREGOR, ANN,** literature and language educator, reporter, application developer; b. Bklyn., Apr. 17, 1925; d. Antonio and Maria Violeta Gimigliano. BA in English, Rutgers U., Newark, 1962; MA in English, NYU, 1968. File, payroll clerk NY Jour. Am. Gen. Elec, 1942—56; booth agt. NYC Transit Authority, 1956—65; HS instr. Riverhead HS; instr. asst. prof. Orange County C.C., Middletown, 1967—70; instr. Reading Area CC, Pa.; ESL instr. L.A. Unified Sch. Dist., Calif., 1972—82; bus. programmer Farmers Ins., L.A., Mercer Island, Washington, 1983—88. Avocations: crossword puzzles, classical music, reading, poetry. Died 2007.

**GREHL, MICHAEL T.,** newspaper editor; b. Evanston, Ill., Dec. 6, 1928; s. Paul Michael and Jean (Tree) G.; m. Audrey Ann Ewert, Sept. 13, 1957 AA, North Park Jr. Coll. and Sem., Chgo., 1949; BA, U. Ill., 1952. Reporter, city editor, mng. editor So. Illinoisan, Carbondale, 1952-56; reporter Anchorage Times, 1956-57; reporter, night city editor, mng. editor Comml. Appeal, Memphis, 1957-68, editor, from 1975, Evansville Press, Ind., 1968-75. Served with U.S. Army, 1946-47, PTO Mem. Am. Soc. Newspaper Editors Home: Memphis, Tenn. Died Mar. 1990.

**GREINER, ROBERT PHILIP,** lawyer, real estate broker; b. Herkimer, NY, July 3, 1930; s. Max Henry and Margaret Mary (O'Hara) G. BA, U. Rochester, 1951; MBA, Syracuse U., 1957; LLB, UCLA, 1964. Bar: Calif. 1965; CPA, Calif.; lic. real estate broker, Calif.; notary pub. Calif., 2006. Pvt. practice acct., CPA, 1962-64; lawyer L.A. Pub. Defenders Office, 1965-87; pvt. practice lawyer and real estate broker Calif., from 1987. Pres. Guide Dog Boosters, Los Alamitos, Calif., 1984. Staff sgt. USAF, 1951-55. Mem.: World Affairs Coun. Sonoma County. Home: Sebastopol, Calif. Died Oct. 16, 2013.

**GREVILLE, ANTHONY EDEN,** mining executive; b. Pretoria, South Africa, Dec. 21, 1921; s. Stanley Eden and Doreen Ellen (Sands) G.; m. Patricia Mary Hamlyn, Mar. 28, 1947 (div. 1978); children: Roderick, Morley, Damon, Justin, Virginia; m. Hendrina Jacoba Kidson, Dec. 21, 1978; children: Derick, Christoff, Barend. BSc, U. South Africa, Pietermaritzburg, 1947; BSc with honors, Natal U., Durban, South Africa, 1952; MSc, Natal U., 1954. Chartered engr. Rsch. scientist South African Govt., Pretoria, 1948-49; lectr. Natal U., 1950-52; cons. Asbestos Mines, Pietersburg, South Africa, 1952-53; field mgr. Rio Tinto Corp., Namibia, South Africa, 1953-55; mgr. R & D G & W Base Minerals/Zimco Group, Johannesburg, South Africa, 1956-76; chmn. Kimony (Pty) Ltd., Johannesburg, from 1976. Vis. scientist Ill. U., Urbana, 1965; cons. Transvaal Graphite, Ltd., Germiston, South Africa, 1977, Cullinan Minerals, Ltd., Olifantsfontein, South Africa, 1981. Editor (sci. and tech. jour.) Gemini, 1972-75; patentee in field. Mem. com. Progressive Movement, Johannesburg, 1987; chmn. Prince Albert (South Africa) Ratepayers Assn., 1995. Served with South African mil., 1940-45. Fellow Geol. Soc. London; mem. Geol. Soc. South Africa, Insn. Mining and Metallurgy. Mem. Dem. Party. Episcopalian. Avocation: musicology. Home: Sea Point Cape Town, South Africa. Died July 18, 2002.

**GREVILLE, THOMAS N(ALL) E(DEN),** educator; b. NYC, Dec. 27, 1910; s. Algernon Palgrave Eden and Hermione Rockwell (Nall) G.; m. Esther Christine Bagnall, Sept. 3, 1934 (div. 1950); children: Alice Eden, Edgar Murdock Eden; m. Florence Nusim, July 23, 1951. BA, U. of South, 1930; MA, U. Mich., 1932, PhD, 1933. Actuarial asst. Acacia Mut. Life Ins. Co., Washington, 1933-37; instr. U. Mich., 1937-40, vis. prof., 1962-63; actuarial mathematician U.S. Bur. Census, 1940-46, USPHS, 1946-52; statis. cons. U.S. Ops. Mission to Brazil, 1952-54; asst. chief actuary U.S. Social Security Adminstrn., 1954-57; chief mathematician U.S. Army Q.M.C., 1957-61; v.p. S.A. Miller Co., Washington, 1961-62; prof. Math. Research Center and Sch. Bus. U. Wis., Madison, 1963-81, prof. emeritus, from 1981. Actuarial adviser Nat. Center for Health Statistics, 1973-76; pres. Psychical Research Found., Chapel Hill, N.C., 1980-85; Fulbright lectr., Brazil, 1971 Author: United States Life Tables and Actuarial Tables 1939-41, 1946, (with A. Ben-Israel) Generalized Inverses: Theory and Applications, 1974; editor: Theory and Applications of Spline Functions, 1969. Fellow Soc. Actuaries, Am. Statis. Assn.; mem. Inter-Am. Statis. Inst., Parapsychol. Assn. Home: Charlottesville, Va. Died Feb. 18, 1998.

**GRIFFIN, THOMAS AQUINAS, JR.,** utilities executive; b. NYC, Mar. 16, 1927; s. Thomas Aquinas and Nobila Evelyn (Duca) Griffin; m. Gloria Dahmer, June 24, 1950; 1 child, Keith. BEE, CCNY, 1951. Successively tester elec. engring. dept., cadet engr., prodn. engr., inside plant engr., asst. v.p. sales dept., asst. v.p. distbn. ops., v.p. Consol. Edison, NYC, 1970—72; v.p. Orange & Rockland Utilities, Inc., NYC, 1972—73, exec. v.p., 1973—78, pres., COO, from 1978. Vice chmn. N.Y. Gas Group, NYC, 1984; dir. Rockland Electric Co., Pearl River, NY, from 1974, Pike County Light & Power Co., Pearl River, NY. Trustee Good Samaritan Hosp., Suffern, NY, from 1984, Hist. Soc. Rockland County, New City, NY, from 1984; bd. dirs. Better Bus. Bur. of Bergen, Passaic and Rockland Counties, Paramus, NJ, 1984. Mem.: Soc. Gas Lighting (pres. 1975—76), IEEE, Seaview Country (Absecom, N.J.), Rockland Country (Sparkill, N.Y.) (pres. 1981—82), Engrs. Club (gov. 1969—73). Republican. Roman Catholic. Home: Honolulu, Hawaii. Died Nov. 14, 1998.

**GRIFFITHS, SIR ELDON WYLIE,** former British government official; b. Wigan, Lancashire, Eng., May 25, 1925; came to U.S. 1992; s. Thomas Herbert Wylie and Edith May (Jones) G.; m. Marie Elizabeth Beatrix den Engelse, 1985. BA, Emmanuel Coll., Cambridge, Eng., 1948, MA, 1957, Yale U., 1949. Corres. Time-Life mags., Denver, L.A., 1949-51; writer Time, NYC, 1951-55; chief European corres. Newsweek, London, 1955-59, fgn. editor NYC, 1959-63; speech writer to prime min. Govt. of United Kingdom, London, 1963-64, under sec. of state for environment & sport, 1970—74; mem. Parliament Bury St. Edmunds Constituency/Ho. of Commons, Suffolk, 1964-92. Dir. Ctr. for Internat. Bus., Chapman U.; dir. Stratham/Intervest; cons. numerous cos. in field. Contbr. numerous articles on polit., diplomatic and econ. issues; author 2 books; Columnist Orange County Register. Pres. Spl. Olympics, U.K.; active in numerous other charitable and trade orgns. Mem. Carlton Club (London), Pilgrims Club (London), Royal Overseas League (London), Korea-Am. Friendship Soc. Republican. Anglican Ch. Home: Mission Viejo, Calif. Died June 3, 2014.

**GRILLEY, BERYL H.,** retired speech educator; b. Pendleton, Oreg., Feb. 9, 1909; d. Wesley W. Harrah and Rose Olcott; m. Donald Grilley, Oct. 18, 1930 (dec.); children: Wesley, Gayle. BA, U. Oreg., MS, 1954. Cert. tchr. Oreg. Speech & hearing pathologist Sch. Dist. 16, Pendleton, 1954—74; tour guide, tchr. World Travel Tours, 1974—94; ret., 1994. Mem. sch. bd., Pendleton. Columnist: East Oregonian, 1974—94. Chmn. Boy Scouts Am., PTA, Girls Scouts U.S., numerous others, 1940—2005. Named 1st Citizen, Pendleton C. of C., 1963; named to Hall of Fame,

Pendleton Round-Up, 1999. Mem.: PEO (pres. 1942—2005), Umatila County Hist. Soc., Delphian Club. Republican. Presbyterian. Avocations: horseback riding, bridge. Died 2007.

**GRIMM, ANN CHRISTINE,** librarian, researcher; b. Kent, Ohio, Apr. 8, 1947; d. William L. and Gladys W. (Meussner) Wannemacher; m. Marshall J. Grimm, May 20, 1972; 1 child, Karen R. BS, Kent State U., 1969; AMLS, U. Mich., 1971. Asst. coordinator, research, info. and publs., research assoc. U. Mich. Transp. Research Inst., Ann Arbor, 1972-79, coordinator, research, info. and publs., from 1979. Co-editor: Public Information Programs on Alcohol and Highway Safety, 1972; contbr. articles to profl. jours. Bd. dirs. Friends of Hands-On-Mus., Ann Arbor, 1988-90. Mem. Spl. Libraries Assn., Assn. Advancement Automotive Medicine, Nat. Child Passenger Safety Assn. (v.p. for media 1983-85). Home: Ann Arbor, Mich. Died Feb. 20, 1997.

**GROCE, JAMES FREELAN,** retired financial adviser; b. Lubbock, Tex., Nov. 24, 1948; s. Wayne Dee and Betty Jo (Rice) G.; m. Patricia Kay Rogers; 1 child, Jason Eric. BS cum laude, Tex. Tech U., 1971; MS in Personal Fin. Planning, Coll. Fin. Planning, 2005. Registered profl. engr., Tex. Petroleum engr. Texaco, Inc., Sweetwater, Tex., 1971-74, drilling and prodn. engr. Wichita Falls, Tex., 1974-77, asst. dist. engr. Midland, Tex., 1977-78; sr. prodn. engr. Bass Enterprises Prodn., Midland, 1978-81; petroleum engr. Murphy H. Baxter Co., Midland, 1981-82, Henry Engring., Midland, 1982-87, Fasken Oil and Ranch Interests, Midland, 1987, mgr. engring./ops., 1987-95; 2d v.p. wealth mgmt., fin. planning specialist Morgan Stanley Smith Barney, Midland, 1996—2012. Scoutmaster Boy Scouts Am., Midland, 1980-83, merit badge counselor, 1987; mem. Community Bible Study, Midland, 1987-93. Mem. Soc. Petroleum Engr. (local sect. chmn. 1987, 25 Yr. Mem.), Am. Assn. Individual Investors (charter mem.), Mensa, Tex. Tech. Ex-Student Assn., Century Club, Tau Beta Pi, Rotary Club Midland, Exch. Club Midland. Avocations: individual investments, real estate, gardening. Home: Midland, Tex. Died Sept. 3, 2013.

**GROEBLI, WERNER FRITZ,** professional ice skater, realtor; b. Basel, Switzerland, Apr. 21, 1915; s. Fritz and Gertrud (Landerer) G.; m. Yvonne Baumgartner, Dec. 30, 1954 (dec. 2002) Student architecture, Swiss Fed. Inst. Tech., 1934—35. Lic. realtor, Calif. Chmn. pub. rels. com. Profl. Skaters Guild Am., 1972-2008. Performed in ice shows, Patria, Brighton, Eng., 1937; command performance in, Marina, London, 1937, Symphony on Ice, Royal Opera House, 1937; mem. Ice Follies, 1939-81, ptnr. (with Hans Mauch) in comedy team Frick & Frack, 1939-53; solo act as Mr. Frick (assisted by comedy team), 1955-81; numerous TV appearances including Snoopy on Ice, 1973, Snoopy's Musical on Ice, 1978, Sportsworld, NBC-TV, 1978, Donnie and Marie Osmond Show, 1978, Mike Douglas Show, 1978, Dinah Shore Show, 1978; films include Silver Skates, 1942, Lady Let's Dance, 1943, Jinxed, 1981; interviewed by Barbara Walters NBC Today, 1974; appeared in Christmas Classics on Ice at Blue Jay Ice Castle, 1991. Served with Swiss Army, 1934-37. Named Swiss jr. skating champion, 1934; named to Madison Sq. Garden Hall of Fame for 10,000 performances in Ice Follies, 1967, U.S. Figure Skating Assn. World Hall of Fame, 1984; recipient Hall of Fame Ann. award Ice Skating Inst. Am.; his skates exhibited at Smithsonian Inst. Lasted 15,000 performances in Ice Follies; originator of "Frick" cantilever spread-eagle skating movement; comedic choreography cons. Died Apr. 14, 2008.

**GRONBECK, BRUCE ELLIOT,** communications educator; b. Bertha, Minn., Mar. 9, 1941; s. Edward Leslie and Bernice Cecilia Gronbeck; m. Wendy Lee Gilbert, 1968; children: Christopher E., Jakob A.L.S., Ingrid C. Julyk. BA, Concordia Coll., Moorhead, Minn., 1963, LHD (hon.), 1991; MA, U. Iowa, Iowa City, 1966, PhD, 1970; D in Comms. (hon.), Uppsala U., Sweden, 1997, U. Jyvaskyla, Finland, 2000. Asst. prof. comm. studies U. Mich., Ann Arbor, Mich., 1967—73; assoc. prof. U. Iowa, Iowa City, 1973—78, prof., 1978—94, A. Craig Baird Disting. prof., 1994—2014. Fulbright sr. specialist U. Jyvaskyla, 2005; lectr. in field. Author: The Articulate Person, 1983, Writing Television Criticism, 1984; editor: Spheres of Argument, 1989, Media, Consciousness, and Culture, 1991, Presidential Campaigns and American Self Images, 1994; author: Communication Criticism: Rhetoric, Social Codes, Cultural Studies, 2001, Persuasion in Society, 2001; editor: Critical Approaches to Television, 2004; author: Principles of Public Speaking, 2007, Principles and Types of Public Speaking, 2007. Dir. public rels. United Way Johnson Country, Iowa City, 1980—86; mem. ctrl. com. Johnson County Democratic Party, Iowa City, 1976—81, Iowa County Democratic Party, Williamsburg, Iowa, 1996—2014; commr. youth soccer Iowa City Kickers, Iowa City, 1978—84. Recipient Rsch. award, Maharishi U., 1981, Koch prize, Magic Lantern Soc., 2006, Lifetime Achievement award, Public Address Conf., 2006; named Outstanding Prof. in Comm., Comm. & Theatre Assn. Minn., 1999, Golden Anniversary Disting. Scholar in Argumentation, American Forensic Assn., 1999; fellow, Ctr. Comm. & Culture, 1978, Fulbright Found., 1992, 2004—14, Ctr. Comm. & Culture, 1989; First fellow, U. Colo., Boulder, 2004. Master: Golden Key Internat. Honor Soc. (hon.); fellow: Nat. Comm. Assn. (Mentor award 2002, Disting. Svc. award 1999, Disting. scholar 1998); mem.: Internat. Soc. Study of Argumentation, Ctrl. States Comm. Assn. (life; pres. 1975—76, named Outstanding Young Tchr. 1978), Nat. Comm. Assn. (life; pres. 1993—94), USTA. Democrat. Avocations: tennis, fishing, travel. Home: Longmont, Colo. Died Sept. 10, 2014.

**GRONDONA, JULIO HUMBERTO,** sports association executive; b. Avellaneda, Argentina, Sept. 18, 1931; m. Nelída Paríani. Attended, U. Salvador, La Plata Engring. Faculty. Founder, pres. Arsenal Futbol Club, Argentina, 1957—76; pres. Atlético Independiente, Argentina, 1976—81, Argentine Football Assn., 1979—2014; exec. mem. Fédération Internationale de Football Assn. (FIFA), 1988—2014. Died July 30, 2014.

**GROOME, SALLY LUCYNTHIA,** former army officer; b. Pelham, NC, Oct. 9, 1936; d. John Whitlock and Addie Estelle (Vass) Groome. BA, Furman U., 1959; MPA, Shippensburg U., 1983; Diploma, Naval Coll. of Command and Staff, 1975, US Army War Coll., 1981; PhD, Old Dominion U. Commd. 2nd lt. US Army, 1960, col., 1982; mil. asst. to sec. army Dept. of Army, Washington, 1977—78; exec. officer personnel info. systems dir. US Mil. Personnel Ctr., Alexandria, Va., 1978—79, exec. officer personnel info. sys. dir., 1979—80; dep. chief of staff US Army War Coll., Carlisle, Pa., 1981—83, dir. nat. security studies dept. corr. studies, 1983—84; dir. tng. Hdqrs. USA ROTC Cadet Command., Ft. Monroe, Va., 1984—86. Bd. dirs., chmn. fundraising com. Peninsula Shelter for Abused Children. Mem.: The Ret. Officers Assn., Old Point Comfort Exch. Club, DAV. Methodist. Avocations: travel, reading, music. Home: Hampton, Va. Died Sept. 6, 2002.

**GROSCH, K. A.,** retired physicist; b. Trannroda, Germany, Feb. 16, 1923; s. Paul and Elisabeth Grosch; m. Kathleen Ann Ilsley (dec.); children: Paul Arthur, Nicolas John; m. Marita Maria Brandenburg, Dec. 18, 1992 (dec.). BSc in special physics, U. London, England, 1958; PhD, U. London, 1963. Lab. asst. Malaysian Rubber Producers Rsch. Assn., Welwyn Garden City, Herts, England, 1955—58, sr. scientific officer, 1958—63, prin. scientific officer, 1963—69; tire evaluation mgr. The European Tire Devel. Ctr., Uniroyal Tire Co., Aachen, Germany, 1969—75, tire devel. mgr., 1975—79, Continental Tire Co., Aachen, 1979—88; ret., cons., 1988. Contbr. articles various profl. jours. Recipient Plastics and Rubber Inst. Colwyn medal, Inst. of Materials, England. Home: Roetgen, Germany. Deceased.

**GROSS, EDWARD,** retired sociologist; b. Nagy Genez, Romania; s. Samuel and Dora (Levi) G.; m. Florence Rebecca Goldman, Feb. 18, 1943; children— David P., Deborah L., Teagardin. BA, U. B.C., Can., 1942; MA, U. Toronto, Ont., Can., 1945; PhD, U. Chgo., 1949; JD, U. Wash., 1991. Prof. Wash. State U., Pullman, Wash., 1947-51, 53-60; prof. U. Wash., Seattle, 1951-53, 65-89, prof. emeritus, from 1990; prof. sociology U. Minn., Mpls., 1960-65. Vis. prof. Australian Nat. U., Canberra, 1971, U. Queensland, U. New South Wales, Griffith U., Australia, 1977; invited lectr. Cen. China Poly. Inst., 1987; lectr. arts and sci. honor program U. Wash., 1998—; pres. resident coun. Ida Culver Broadview Ret. Facility, 2005-06, lectr. Legal Films Ida Culver Broadview, 2009-. Author: Work and Society, 1958, Univ. Goals and Academic Power, 1968, Changes in Univ. Orgn., 1964-71, The End of a Golden Age: Higher Ed. in a Steady State, 1981, Embarrassment in Everyday Life, 1994; co-author (with A. Etzioni) Orgn. in Soc., 1985; contbg. author: Handbook of Sociology and Encyclopedia of Sociology, 2d edit.; former assoc. editor Social Problems, Symbolic Interaction, Can. Jour. Sociology; contbr. articles to profl. jour. Trustee Temple Beth Am, Seattle, 1993-97. Fulbright scholar Australia, 1977, 87. Mem.: Wash. State Bar Assn., Am. Sociol. Assn. (emeritus), Pacific Sociol. Assn. (pres. 1971, coun. 1983—85). Home: Vashon, Wash. Died July 21, 2013.

**GROSS, EITAN MOSHE,** surgeon, educator; b. Tel Aviv, Apr. 30, 1954; s. Chaim and Aliza Gross; m. Shalvit Landau, Feb. 5, 1978; children: Matan Akiva, Naama, Yair. MD, Hadassah Hebrew U., Israel, 1986. Cert. in Gen. Surgery Israel, 1992, in Pediatric Surgery Israel, 1997, diplomate Gen. Surgeon Israel, Pediatric Surgeon Israel. Intern Hadassah U. Hosp., Jerusalem, 1985—86, resident in gen. surgery, 1986—92, fellow, pediatric surgery, 1992—97; resident in gen. surgery Mount-Sinai Med. Ctr., NYC, 1988—89; fellow, gen. and oncological pediatric surgery U. Tenn., Le Bonheur Children's Med. Ctr., St. Jude Children's Rsch. Hosp., 1994—96; attending in pediatric surgery Hadassah Med. Ctr., Jerusalem, 1997; sr. lectr. pediatric surgery Hadassah Hebrew U., Jerusalem, from 2000, head pediat. surg. oncology unit, from 2007. Mem. Nat. Coun. for Pediat., Israel, 1998. Lt. col. Navy, 1972, Israel. SOUDAVAR Meml. scholarship, Meml. Sloan-Kettering Cancer Ctr., 2005. Mem.: Internat. Soc. Pediatric Surg. Oncology (assoc.), Israel Surg. Assn. (assoc.), Israel Med. Assn. (assoc.), Pediatric Surgery Soc. (assoc.). Jewish. Avocations: swimming, hiking, diving. Home: Jerusalem, Israel. Died May 2012.

**GROSS, JOHANNES,** journalist; b. Neunkhausen, Germany, May 6, 1932; m. Elisabeth Gotthardt, 1961; 1 child, Julia. LLB, Marburg U., Germany, 1954; LLD (hon.), U. Fla., 1980. Corr. Deutsche Zeitung, Germany, 1959-61, polit. editor, 1961; head polit. dept. Deutschlandfunk, Germany, 1962-68; dir. programs, dep. dir. gen. Deutsche Welle, Germany, 1968-74; editor Capital, Germany, 1974-80; editl. dir. Capital, Impulse, Koeln, Germany, 1980-94. Author: Über die Deutschen, 1992, Für und Gegenwitz, 1993, Die Begründung der Berliner Republik, 1995, Tacheles gesprochen, 1996. Mem. Internat. Press Inst. (bd. dirs. 1992), Deutscher Autorenrat (mem. presiding com. 1995), Zukunftskommission Bayern u. Sachsen. Died Sept. 29, 1999.

**GROSS, LILLIAN,** psychiatrist, educator; b. NYC, Aug. 18, 1932; m. Harold Ratner, Feb. 4, 1961; children: Sanford Miles, Marcia Ellen. BA, Barnard Coll., 1953; postgrad., U. Lausanne, Switzerland, 1954-56; MD, Duke U., 1959. Diplomate Bd. Pediatrics, Am. Bd. Psychiatry and Neurology, Am. Bd. Child Psychiatry. Intern Kings County Hosp., Bklyn., 1959-60, resident, 1967-70, psychiatrist devel. evaluation clinic, 1970-72; resident Jewish Hosp., Bklyn., 1960-62; physician in charge pediatric psychiat. clinic Greenpoint (N.Y.) Hosp., 1964-67; pvt. practice pvt. practice, Great Neck, N.Y., from 1970. Clin. instr. psychiatry Downstate Med. Ctr., Bklyn., 1970-74, clin. asst. prof., 1974-99; lectr. in psychiatry Columbia U., 1974-99; psychiat. cons. N.Y.C. Bd. Edn., 1972-75, Queens Children's Hosp., 1975-96; mem. med. bd. Saras Ctr., Great Neck, N.Y., 1977—. Child psychiatry fellow Kings County Hosp., 1969-70, pediatric psychiatry fellow, 1962-63. Fellow Am. Acad. Pediatrics, Am. Acad. Child Psychiatry, Am. Psychiat. Assn. (life), N.Y. Soc. Clin. Hypnosis (pres.); mem. AMA, Nassau Pediatric Socs., Soc. Adolscent Psychiatry, N.Y. Coun. Child Psychiatry, Am. Med. Women's Assn. (Nassau, pres. 1985-86, 95-96), N.Y. Med. Socs., Internat. Soc. Study of Multiple Personality and Dissociation (founder, pres. L.I. component study group), Greater Long Island Psychiat. Soc. Deceased.

**GROSS, MAURICE CHARLES,** chemistry educator, consultant; b. Schirmeck, France, Dec. 25, 1941; s. Henri and Marie Jeanne (Banzet) G.; m. Elisabeth Hatt, Aug. 17, 1964; children: Carole, Laurent. DSc in Chemistry, U. Louis Pasteur, Strasbourg, France, 1970. Maitre de confs. U. Strasbourg, 1970-75, prof., 1976, dir. Inst. Univ. Tech., 1975-83; v.p. Université III, Strasbourg, 1976-90; dir. lab. d'electrochimie U. Louis Pasteur, from 1973; dir. rels. with univs. Nat. Ctr. Sci. Rsch. (CNRS), Paris, from 1994. Advisor Ministry of Rsch., Paris, 1986-88; cons. for exporting tng. several cos., Paris, 1982—. Author 7 books; contbr. more than 200 articles to profl. jours. Named Palmes Academiques officer Min. Nat. Edn., Paris, 1994, Chevalier Ordre Nat. du Merite, 1994, Chevalier Legion D'Hommeur, 1999. Mem. Rotary. Roman Catholic. Achievements include identification of significant structure-redox reactivity relationships in macrocyclic and supramolecular complexes. Home: Oberschaeffolsheim, France. Died Dec. 8, 2001.

**GROSSI, FILIPPO,** industrial engineer; b. San Remo, Imperia, Italy, Aug. 21, 1921; s. Francesco Paolo and Giulia (Scribani Rossi) G.; m. Silvana Peterlongo, Mar. 16, 1972; 1 child, Francesca. Dr. Engring., Politechnique Lausanne, 1945, Politecnico Torino, 1946. Gen. mgr., mng. dir., pres. Techint SpA, Milan, 1948-88; pres. Techint Finanziaria SRL, Milan, from 1988. Pres. Iniziative Industrial Spa, Santa Luce, 1997, Techint Engring. Co., Lugano, Switzerland, 1978-92, Pomimi Farrel SpA, Castellanza, Varese, Italy, 1987-92; v.p., pres. Snia Techint SpA, Rome, 1977-91; v.p. Camer di Commercio Milan, Moscow, 1989-2001; mem. panel 121 Congrès Nat. des Sociétés Historiques Scientifiques, Nice, 1996. Author: Généalogie and History of the astronomes Cassini and Maraldi. Col. Italian Air Force, 1941-43. Recipient In-Arch Inst. Naz. Architettura, 1967, Interpetrol D'Oro Mostra Internat. Petrolio Ambiente, 1973, Cittadino Benemerito City of San Remo, 1990. Mem. AIM, Assn. Dimore Storiche Italiane, Monticello (Italy) Golf Club. Avocations: golf, sailing, skiing, astronomy. Home: Lugano, Switzerland. Died June 12, 2003.

**GROSSMAN, ALLEN RICHARD,** poet, educator; b. Mpls., Jan. 7, 1932; s. Louis S. and Beatrice (Berman) Grossman; m. Meryl Mann (div.); children: Jonathan, Adam; m. Judith Spink, June 9, 1964; children: Bathsheba, Austin, Lev. BA, Harvard U., 1955, MA, 1956, Brandeis U., Waltham, Mass., 1957, PhD, 1960. Asst. prof. Brandeis U., 1961-70, assoc. prof., 1970-75, prof., 1975-83, Paul A. Prosswimmer prof. poetry and gen. edn., 1984-91; Andrew W. Mellon prof. humanities Johns Hopkins U., Balt., 1991—2005, prof. emeritus, 2005—14. Vis. prof. U. Negev, Israel, 1972. Author: (poetry) A Harlot's Hire, 1959, The Recluse, 1965, And The Dew Lay All Night Upon My Branch, 1974, The Woman on the Bridge over the Chicago River, 1979, Of The Great House, 1982, The Bright Nails Scattered on the Ground, 1986, The Ether Dome and Other Poems New and Selected (1979-1990), 1991, The Song of the Lord, 1991, How to Do Things with Tears, 2001, Sweet Youth, 2002, Descartes' Loneliness, 2007, True-Love: Essays on Poetry and Valuing, 2009, (prose) Poetic Knowledge in the Early Yeats, a study of The Wind Among the Reeds, 1969, The Sighted Singer Two Works on Poetry, 1992, The Long Schoolroom: Lessons in the Bitter Logic of the Poetic Principle, 1997, The Passion of Laocoon: Warfare of the Religious Against the Poetic Institution, 2002; inclusion in various edit.'s Scribner's Best Poems, 1988, 1991—93; contbr. numerous works of poetry and prose to periodicals and anthologies. Recipient A.B. Cohen award for Tchg., 1965, Pushcart prize, 1975, 1987, 1990, Disting. Svc. award, Brandeis U., 1982, Sara Teasdale Meml. prize in Poetry, Wellesley Coll., 1987, Sheaffer-PEN/New Eng. award for Lit. Distinction, 1988, Bassine Citation, Acad. Am. Poets, 1990, Bollingen prize in American Poetry, Yale U. Beinecke Libr., 2009, Garrison award for Poetry, American Acad. Poetry prize, Witter Bynner Prize for Poetry, AAAL; named Mass. State Prof. of Yr., Coun. Advancement & Support of Edn., 1987; grantee Nat. Endowment Arts, 1985; fellow John Simon Guggenheim Meml. Found., 1983, John D. and Catherine T. MacArthur Found., 1989—94. Fellow: American Acad. Arts & Sciences. Died June 27, 2014.

**GROSSMAN, BURTON E.,** investment company executive; b. Corpus Christi, Tex., Feb. 15, 1918; s. Edward and Bessie Grossman; m. Miriam Siegel, Apr. 23, 1980; children: Bruce Edward, Cynthia Helene. BS in Bus. Adminstrn., U. Tex., 1940; DBA (hon.), John Dewey U., NYC, 1981; LlD, U. Far East, 1983; LLD (hon.), Mexican Acad. Internat. Law, 1985; D (hon.), U. of the Ams., Mexico City, 1988. Chmn. bd. Grossman y Asociados, Tampico, Mexico, from 1964, Sociedad Indsl., from 1972; chmn. bd., CEO Grupo Continental S.A., Tampico, 1977—. Chmn. bd., CEO Asesores de Pensiones S.A., Grabados Fernando Fernandes,

Mexico, chmn. bd., CEO Intercontinental Bankshares Corp., San Antonio. Sr. mem. exec. com. Chancellor's Coun. U. Tex. Sys.; mem. investment com. Rotary Internat. Served to capt. U.S. Army, 1942-46. Mem. Inst. Advanced Studies (Tamaulipas, chmn. bd. trustees), U. Tex. Cancer Found. (bd. visitors), Pres.'s Club U. Tex., Pres.'s Club So. Meth. U., Am. Mgmt. Assn., Conf. Bd., Nat. Advt. Assn. Mex., Rotary Internat. (past internat. treas.). Avocations: golf, tennis, big game hunting, collection of cigar bands. Home: San Antonio, Tex. Died 1999.

**GROSSMAN, EDWARD JEROME,** music educator, composer; b. Denver, Feb. 8, 1947; s. Sydney Harold and Adeline Elizabeth (Davis) Grossman. BA with distinction, U. Colo., Boulder, 1969; JD, U. Denver, 1979. Pvt. piano tchr., from 1989. San Fernando east valley area chair Calif. Fedn. Music Clubs Jr. Festival, 2003—12; chair Classical-Romantic Festival San Fernando East Valley Br. MTAC, from 2012. Author: (piano solo) Bangkok Market (selection of Nat. Fedn. Music Clubs Festivals Bull., 2004), 7 other piano solos. Recipient Am. Jurisprudence award, 1978. Mem.: Music Tchrs. Assn. of Calif. (pres. San Fernando East Valley br. 2000—03, info. publicity chair, composers today coun. 2006—11), Calif. Bar Assn., Colo. Bar Assn, Phi Beta Kappa. Home: Denver, Colo. Died June 2013.

**GRUA, FRANÇOIS,** law educator; b. Lagny, France, July 5, 1949; s. Jacques Grua and Huguette Carrier; m. Laure-Aimée Siban, June 30, 1988; children: Charles, Louis. LLD, U. Francois Rabelais, 2001. Prof. U. Pointe-à-Pitre, France, 1983-85, U. Tours, France, 1985—2005. Author: Les Contrats de Base de la Pratique Bancaire, 2001; contbr. articles to profl. jours. Named Officier des Palmes Académiques. Home: Vouvray, France. Died Jan. 14, 2005.

**GRUBAUGH, VIRGINIA JANE,** retired educator; b. Cadillac, Mich., June 10, 1923; d. Donald Jerome and Irene (Jenkins) Bittel; m. Dean James Grubaugh, Apr. 7, 1947 (dec. July 1963); children: Kay Irene Grubaugh Gugala, Thomas Joseph. BA, Nazareth Coll., 1943; MA in Edn., Cen. Mich. U., 1970. Cert. secondary tchr., Mich. Tchr. phys. edn., English Algonac (Mich.) Pub. Schs., 1944, Shepherd (Mich.) Pub. Schs., 1944-46; tchr. English, history Saints Peter & Paul High Sch., Saginaw, Mich., 1946-47; mid. sch. tchr. phys. edn. and English, Sacred Heart Acad. High Sch., Mt. Pleasant, Mich., 1955-59; tchr. Am. history, English, Spanish and phys. edn. Farwell (Mich.) Area Schs., 1962-63; tchr. Spanish, French, English Mt. Pleasant Pub. Schs., 1963-86. Author: Parish History (50th Year) Jubilee Journal, 1948. Local/state pres. People to People Internat., Mt. Pleasant, 1970, 74-76; state pres. Mich. chpt. Am. Assn. Tchrs. of Spanish and Portuguese, 1982-84; precinct del. Republican Party, Mt. Pleasant, 1973-74; mem. recycling Solid Waste Adv. Com., Mt. Pleasant, 1989-91. U.S. Office Edn. scholar U. Mex., 1945. Mem. NEA, Mich. Edn. Assn. (life, Elizabeth Siddall Internat. Understanding award 1973), Mt. Pleasant Edn. Assn. (sec. 1970-72), Mich. Edn. Assn. (life), Mich. Assn. Ret. Sch. Pers. (life), Isabella County Ret. Sch. Pers. (pres. 1991-1993, 2001-2003), AAUW (pres. Mt. Pleasant br. 1969-71, 84-86, 90-92), Regent Ct. Sacred Heart (rec. sec.), Cath. Daus. Ams., Phi Delta Kappa (sec. Cen. Mich. U. chpt. 1990-91). Republican. Roman Catholic. Avocation: travel. Home: Mount Pleasant, Mich. Died May 31, 2008.

**GRUEL, LOUIS,** sociologist; b. Rennes, France, Oct. 18, 1947; s. Louis Paul and Madeleine Eleonore Gruel; m. Danielle Marie Fiche, Apr. 12, 1969 (dec. Dec. 30, 2009); 1 child, Marianne Rozenn Le Chenadec-Gruel. PhD in Sociology, U. Paris X, 1982. Cert. sociologist Ministry of Nat. Edn., 1972. Sociologist Sauvegarde de l'Enfance, Rennes, 1974—81; contract engr. U. Rennes 2, 1982—89, sr. lectr., 1989—92, accreditation to supr. rsch., 2005; project leader Obs. Nat. de la Vie Etudiante, Paris, 1992—2007; pvt. practitioner, from 2008. Mem. sci. com. EPSE-LMDE, Paris. Author: (book) Pardons et Chatiments Les Jures Francais, La Rebellion de 68, Pierre Bourdieu Illusionniste; co-author: Le Financement de La Vie Etudiante, La Vie Etudiante; contbr.; co-author (with O Galland & G Houzel): Les Etudiants en Franla. Mem. ADMD, Paris, from 2006. Mem.: Assn. France de Sociology. Home: Vieux-Vy sur Couesnon, France. Died Dec. 25, 2009.

**GRUNBERG-MANAGO, MARIANNE,** biochemist; b. Petrograd, USSR, Jan. 6, 1921; d. Vladimir Grunberg and Catherine Riasanoff; m. Armand Manago, 1948 (dec.); two children. Grad., U. Paris; Hon. Doctorate, Ind. U., 1999. From rsch. asst. to head biochemistry divsn. Nat. Ctr. Scientific Rsch., Paris, 1946-61. Assoc. prof. Harvard U., 1958-61, v.p. Comm. for Sciences and Tech. UNESCO, 1985. Editor-in-chief Biochemie. Mem. AAAS (fgn.), Internat. Union Biochemistry (pres. 1985-88), Soc. Biol. Chemistry, American Soc. Biol. Chemists, Internat. Coun. Sci. Unions, N.Y. Acad. Scis., Acad. Sciences (France). Died Jan. 3, 2013.

**GUAN, DINGHUA,** researcher, educational association administrator; b. Beijing, Peoples Republic China, Oct. 25, 1927; s. Zhuguang Guan and Gongwei Ye; m. Huiqun Huang, Jan. 06, 1956; children: Youfei Guan, Yougeng Guan. BA, Qinghua U., Beijing, 1950, Inst. Russian Lang., 1953; PhD, USSR Acad. Scis., Moscow, 1960. Engr. Radio Beijing, 1953-57; lab. head Inst. Radiobroadcasting, Beijing, 1960-61; rschr. Inst. Electronics Academia Sinica, Beijing, 1961-64, Inst. Acoustics Academia Sinica, Beijing, 1964, dep. dir., 1981-84, dir., 1984-93. Chmn. Beijing Assn. Sensor Tech., 1986, West Pacific Regional Comm. on Acoustics, 1994-97, WG96 Sci. Com. on Ocean Rsch. (SCOR), 1991-94. Author: Sound and Ocean, 1982; contbr. to profl. jours. Recipient Advanced Sci. Worker award Academia Sinica, 1964, Academia Sinica prize, 1980, Nat. Natural Sci. award Beijing State Com. Sci. and Tech., 1982, Sci. Worker with Outstanding Contribution award State Com. Sci. and Tech., 1984, Nat. Outstanding Sci. and Tech. Worker award, 1997. Mem. Acoustical Soc. China (v.p., sec. gen. 1982, pres. 1989-94), Chinese Soc. Oceanography (sec. gen. 1984, v.p. 1990-94, cons. 1999), Soc. Lab. Instrument (pres. 1984), Soc. Transducers Tech. (v.p. 1984, pres. 1990), Am. Soc. Acoustics, Soc. Sci. Instruments (mem. standing com. 1991). Avocations: music, swimming, chinese opera, chinese history. Home: Beijing, China. Died Mar. 19, 2003.

**GUFFI, MICHELE EMILIO ALFREDO,** cardiothoracic surgeon, consultant; b. Roveredo, Switzerland, Oct. 26, 1961; s. Giancarlo and Myriam Ida (Pattani) G.; m. Eliete Araujo Fernandes, Jan. 24, 1995; 1 child, Sofia. MD, U. Lausanne, Switzerland, 1986. Clinic res. Surgery Clinic, Lucerne, Switzerland, 1987, Fribourg, Switzerland, 1988-89, Clinic of Gen. and Orthopaedic Surgery, Lugano, Switzerland, 1990-91; cardiovasc. surg. resident Beneficencia Portuguesa, São Paulo, Brazil, 1991-93; fellow in cardiothoracic surgery U. Ala., Birmingham, 1993; vis. physician Nat. Heart Lung Inst., London, 1994; staff surgeon Univ. Hosp. Lausanne, 1994-95; cons. surgeon Columbia Hosp. de la Tour, Geneva, from 1996. Contbr. articles to profl. jours.; inventor in field. With Swiss Army, 1980-90, Fribourg. Mem. N.Y. Acad. Scis., Iternat. Soc. for Artificial Organs, Swiss Med. Fedn. Roman Catholic. Avocations: piano, old motorbikes, swimming. Home: Lugano, Switzerland. Died July 12, 2005.

**GUGGENHEIM, HANS GEORG,** journalist, writer; b. St. Gallen, Switzerland, Mar. 30, 1927; s. Karl Benno Guggenheim and Nelly Berta Zollikofer; m. Anne-Grete Schonneman-Jensen, March 2, 1974; 1 child, Maria-Helena. Maturitat, Kantons Schule, St. Gallen, 1946; postgrad., U. Zurich, U. Hamburg, U. Geneva, Sorbonne, Paris. Tour mgr. Globus Gateway, Switzerland, 1963-70, Am. Express, USA, 1970-95; pvt. practice Ardeche, France, from 1946. Author: Around the World in 80 Ways, 1979, (play) The Last Days, 1963. Designated Chgo. Ambassador City of Chgo., 1979; named hon. citizen Atlanta, disting. vis. Dade County. Avocations: theater, literature, music, painting. Died June 7, 2003.

**GUIMARAES, RUI MANUEL,** cardiologist; b. Braga, Portugal, Jan. 3, 1951; s. Manuel C. and Julia G. Guimaraes; m. Paula G. Goncalves; 1 child, Pedro; m. Zelia Costa-e-Silva, Feb. 3, 1992. MD, Faculdade Medicina Lisboa, Lisbon, Portugal, 1979. Intern Civil Hosps. Lisbon, 1979-86, asst. ICU, from 1986. Cons. Hosp. St. Louis, Lisbon, 1987—, Hosp. Inst. Urologia, 1997. Contbr. articles to sci. jours. Fellow Portuguese Soc. Cardiology (Young Investigator's award 1984), Soc. Internat. Medicine; mem. Order of Physicians. Home: Lisbon, Portugal. Died Feb. 7, 2002.

**GÜLER, ERDEN,** pharmacy educator, consultant; b. Eskisehir, Turkey, July 24, 1943; s. Turgut Mehmet and Suzan (Koçak) G.; m. Rana Karpat, July 7, 1969; children: Ihsan, Zeynep. Degree in pharmacy, Ankara U., Turkey, 1967; PhD, Istanbul U., Turkey, 1976. Asst. in pharmacy Anadolu U., Eskisehir, 1970-71, Istanbul U., 1971-79, postdoctoral asst., 1979, asst. prpof. pharmacy, 1983-89; prof. pharmacy Anadolu U., 1989—2003. Head pharmacist in Eskisehir region, 1970-72; head dept. pharm. tech., Eskisehir, 1984-2003, emeritus prof., 2003—; mem. pharm. scis. com., Ankara, 1986-90. Editor Acta Pharmaceutica Turcica, mem. editl. bd., 2003-; editor: Interaction Between Drugs, Foods, Alcohol and Contact Lenses, Drug Index, 1996-97, Examples of Naturapic Extemporaneous Drugs According to their Pharmacological Effects, 2003, OTC Drug Consumption in Eshisehir Region and Its Statistical Evaluation, 2003. 1st lt., Mil. Depo., Ankara, 1967-69. Mem. Turkish Pharmacists Assn. Ankara, Turkish Pharmacists Assn. Eskisehir, N.Y. Acad. Scis., Nat. Geographic Soc. Home: Eskisehir, Turkey. Died Mar. 6, 2004.

**GULLEY, JIM,** former state legislator; b. Charlotte, NC, May 10, 1939; s. Creighton Alexander and Naomi Reid Gulley; m. Suzanne Hargett; children: James M. Jr., Janet Elissa Biggs. BS in Electrical Engring., Charlotte Coll. With The Nat. Cash Register Co.; owner Carolina Computer Systems; mem. Dist. 103 NC House of Reps., NC, 1997—2010. Mem.: Matthews Vol. Fire Dept. (bd. dirs.). Republican. Baptist. Died May 20, 2014.

**GUNTHEROTH, WARREN GADEN,** pediatrician, cardiologist, educator; b. Hominy, Okla., July 27, 1927; s. Harry William and Callie (Cornett) G.; m. Ethel Haglund, July 3, 1954(dec. 2007); children: Kurt, Karl, Sten; m. Sally Comish, Nov. 28, 2009. Attended, Harvard Coll., 1948; MD, Harvard U., 1952. Diplomate: Am. Bd. Pediatrics, Am. Bd. Pediatric Cardiology, Nat. Bd. Med. Examiners. Intern Peter Bent Brigham Hosp., Boston, 1952-53; fellow in cardiology Children's Hosp., Boston, 1953-55, resident in pediatrics, 1955-56; rsch. fellow physiology and biophysics U. Wash. Med. Sch., Seattle, 1957-58, mem. faculty, from 1958, prof. pediatrics, from 1969, head divsn. pediatric cardiology, 1964-91. Author: Pediatric Electrocardiography, 1965, How to Read Pediatric ECGs, 1981, 4th edit., 2006, Crib Death (Sudden Infant Death Syndrome), 1982, 3d edit., 1995, Climbing With Sasha, a Washington Husky, 1995, Paradise Found and Lost, 2009, My Life Loves and Battles, 2010; also more than 330 articles; mem. editl. bd. Am. Heart Jour., 1977-80, Circulation, 1980-83, Am. Jour. Noninvasive Cardiology, 1985-94, Jour. Am. Coll. Cardiology, 1988-94 Jour. Noninvasive Cardiology, 1988-, Am. Jour. Cardiology, 1977-; sect. editor Practice of Pediatrics, 1979-87, Pediatric Cardiology, 2004-07. Served with USPHS, 1950-51. Spl. research fellow NIH, 1967. Mem. Soc. Pediatric Rsch., Biomed. Engring. Soc. (charter), Am. Heart Assn. (chmn. N.W. regional med. rsch. adv. com. 1978-80), Cardiovascular System Dynamics Soc. (charter), Am. Coll. Cardiology. Democrat. Avocation: music. Home: Seattle, Wash. *My career includes medical practice, teaching and research; my hobby is music and writing.* Died 2012.

**GUO, SHENG MING,** retired history professor; b. Zhengjiang, Jiangsu, China, Dec. 25, 1915; came to U.S., 1989, naturalized, 1996; s. Dun Xue Guo and Xiao Chun Wu; m. Hong Yi Wang, Jan. 24, 1945; children: Victor Kuo, John Kuo, Meide Guo. BA in History, Nat. Ctrl. U., Chongching, China, 1938; MA, Ctrl. Inst. Polit. Sci., Chongching, 1941; postgrad., Tulane U., 1949. Vice consul Chinese Consulate, New Orleans, 1945-47, acting consul, 1948-50; prof. history Kuangsi (China) U., 1951-53, Hunan (China) U., 1953-56, East China Normal U., Shanghai, 1957-89. Advisor Chinese Assn. Medieval History, Beijing, 1976—, Shanghai Assn. Social Sci., 1983—; U.S. State Dept. vis. prof., Georgetown U., Harvard U., U. Chgo., Stanford U., also others, 1983. Author: A Survey of Western Historiography, 1983 (State prize 1985), An Outline of World Civilization, 1989 (State prize 1991); editor-in-chief: Dictionary of World History, 1986; editor History of Foreign Countries in Ency. Sinica, 1987. Presbyterian. Avocation: gardening. Deceased.

**GURLEY, FRANKLIN LOUIS,** lawyer, military historian; b. Syracuse, NY, Nov. 26, 1925; Swiss national, 1994 (dual nationality); s. George Bernard and Catherine Veronica (Moran) G.; m. Elizabeth Anne Ryan, June 17, 1950. AB, Harvard U., 1949, JD, 1952. Bar: Mass. 1952, N.Y. 1956, Ill. 1956, Mich. 1956, D.C. 1956. Fgn. service staff officer Dept. State, Washington and Germany, 1953-55; atty. N.Y. Central R.R. Co., 1955-56; asst. dist. atty. New York County, 1956-57; atty. firm Dewey, Ballantine, Bushby, Palmer & Wood, NYC, 1957-63; gen. counsel, sec. IBM Europe Corp., Paris; also mng. atty. IBM Corp., Armonk, N.Y., 1963-68; sr. v.p., gen. counsel Nestle S.A., Vevey, Switzerland, 1968-83, spl. legal adv., 1984-85; internat. legal cons., from 1985. Author: 399th in Action in World War II, 1946, Into the Mountains Dark, 2000, (play) King Philip's War, 1952; chief editor Beachhead News (Germany), 1945-46; contbr. articles to profl. and mil. jours. Pres. Tappan Landing Assn. Tarrytown N.Y. 1958-60. Served with inf. AUS, 1944-46, ETO. Decorated Bronze Star, Combat Inf. Badge; 7th Army mile run champion, 1945; set West Point and Heptagonal 1000-yard records in track, 1948. Mem. SAR (sec., bd. mgrs. N.Y. chpt. 1957-63, founding mem. Swiss chpt. 1970), 100th Inf. Divsn. Assn. (historian 1984—). Deceased.

**GURUGE, ANANDA WEIHENA PALLIYA,** diplomat, linguist educator; b. Galle, Sri Lanka, Dec. 28, 1928; s. Seodoris Weihena Palliya and Rupawathie Lekamvasam (Gamage) G.; m. Sujata Nalini Jayasinghe, Aug. 27, 1952 (dec.); 1 child, Anura; m. Chandrakanthi Darshanika Gunasekera, Nov. 14, 1994. BA with honors, U. Ceylon, Sri Lanka, 1950, PhD, 1953; LittD (hon.), Sri Jayawardenepura U., Sri Lanka, 1987. Provincial adminstr. home affairs and edn. to acting permanent sec. ministry of edn. and cultural affairs Govt. Sri Lanka, Sri Lanka, 1952-67; adminstrv. asst. to vice chancellor and prof. Sanskrit and linguistics Vidyodaya U., Sri Lanka, 1959-64; vis. prof. Asian studies SUNY, Buffalo, N.Y., 1967-68; staff mem. UNESCO, Paris, New Delhi, Bangkok, 1968-85; amb. to UNESCO, France, Spain, and Algeria Govt. Sri Lanka, Paris, 1985-92, amb. to USA and Mexico Washington, D.C., 1992-1994. Edn. planning and mgmt. cons. to Asian and African Nations, UNESCO, 1969-85; mem. exec. bd. UNESCO, Paris, 1987-91; chmn. adminstrv. fin. commn. UNESCO, Paris, 1989-91; sr. spl. advisor to dir. gen. UNESCO, U.S., 1995. Author: (book) Return to Righteousness, 1965, Buddhism: The Religion and Its Culture, 1975, Mahavamsa, 1989, Asoka: A Definitive Biography, 1993, Educationally Speaking, 1994, Under the Roof of UNESCO, 1995. Active mem. predsl. restructuring com. Govt. Sri Lanka, Colombo, 1989. Recipient Kalakirti Eminence in Literary Works award Govt. Sri Lanka, 1987, Desamanya Disting. Pub. Svc. award, Govt. Sri Lanka, 1992, Silver medal UNESCO, 1991, Human Rights medal UNESCO, 1992. Fellow Royal Asiatic Soc. Britain and Northern Ireland; mem. Royal Asiatic Soc. Sri Lanka, Cosmos Club (Washington D.C.), City Club (Washington D.C.). Buddhist. Avocations: reading, writing, archaeology, nature. Home: Nugegoda, Sri Lanka. Died Aug. 6, 2014.

**GURZADYAN, GRIGOR,** astronomer; b. Baghdad, Oct. 15, 1922; Grad., State Engring. U. of Armenia, 1944; postgrad., Academician Victor Ambartsumian, 1944. Cofounder Space Astronomy; head stars and nebulae physics dept. Byurakan Obs., 1950—66, head extra-atmospheric astronomy lab., 1978—92; head Garni Astronomy Lab., 1973—78, Garni Space Astronomy Inst., 1992—2004; head of chair space instrument-making State Engring. Univ. of Armenia, 1979—2014. Author: various publs. Recipient professorship, 1962, Sign of Honor, Armenian Soviet Socialist Republic, 1975. Mem.: Internat. Astron. Union. Achievements include development of theory of common chromospheres (roundchromes) of close binary stars and of evolution of binary globular clusters; design of space orbital observatories; first to directed the UV and X-ray observations of sun via rocket astrophysy. observatories K-2, K-3 and K-4 by means of ballistic rockets R-5; one of the founders of space astronomy; one of the main scientists of the founding team of the byurakan astrophysy. obs; research in authored the most significant theoretical papers devoted to planetary nebulae, interstellar matter and flare stars. Died Feb. 22, 2014.

**GUSTAFSON, DWIGHT LEONARD,** retired dean; b. Seattle, Apr. 20, 1930; s. Carl Leonard and Rachel Doris (Johnson) G.; m. Gwendolyn Anne Adams, May 28, 1952; children: Dianne, David, Donna, Gale. BA, Bob Jones U., 1952, MA, 1954; LLD, Tenn. Temple U., 1960; MusD, Fla. State U., 1967. Grad. asst., div. music Bob Jones U., Greenville, S.C., 1952-54, acting dean Sch. Fine Arts, 1954-56, 2004, dean, 1956-97, dean emeritus, 1997—2014. Condr. Bob Jones U. Orch., U. Opera, 1954-2007. Composer: two one-act operas The Hunted and Simeon; also choral and orchestral works. Fla. State U. fellow, 1966-67. Mem. Pi Kappa Lambda. Avocation: travel. Home: Greenville, SC. Died Jan. 28, 2014.

**GUTHRIE, M. FRANCES,** elementary educator, department supervisor; b. Kansas City, Mo., July 9, 1937; d. Francis Mathias and Mary Ethel (Thompson) Heinen; m. James William Guthrie, June 12, 1965; children: James William II, John Robinson. MusB, Okla. City U., 1959; M in Teaching, U. Cen. Okla., 1962. Cert. elem. tchr., Okla. Second grade tchr. Putnam City Schs., Oklahoma City, 1961-70; first grade and kindergarten tchr. Holy Trinity Cath. Sch., Okarche, Okla., 1976-85; second grade tchr. Christ the King Cath. Sch., Oklahoma City, 1985-86, Corpus Christi Cath. Sch., Oklahoma City, from 1986. Pres. Putnam City Classroom Tchrs. Assn., Oklahoma City, 1967-68; parent rep. Okarche (Okla.) Sch. Bd., 1990-91. Scholarship recipient Kappa Kappa Iota, Oklahoma City, 1977, 78; Ten Yr. Svc. award Cath. Schs. of Okla., Oklahoma City, 1991. Mem. NEA, Nat. Cath. Edn. Assn., Okla. Edn. Assn. (rights and responsibilities commn. mem. 1966-67), Kappa Kappa Iota (vice pres. 1969), Delta Kappa Gamma. Democrat. Roman Catholic. Avocations: reading, sewing, walking, fishing. Deceased.

**GUTNER, LYNETTE N.,** social worker; b. St. Louis, Mar. 28, 1931; d. Isadore and Fannie (Gordon) Nelson; m. Kenneth Howard Gutner, Apr. 26, 1952; children: Kim Allison Gutner-Davis, Lisa Beth, Toddi Louise. MusB, Northwestern U., 1952; MSW, Loyola U., Chgo., 1980. Lic. clin. social worker, Ill., Colo. Therapist Salvation Army Community Counseling Ctr., Arlington Heights, Ill., 1980-86; pvt. practice Northbrook, Ill., 1987—2003, Aspen, Colo., 1987—2003. Field instr. Jane Addams Sch. Social Work, Chgo., 1984-86; group facilitator Highland Park (Ill.) Hosp., 1980-82; relapse prevention specialist Ctr. for Applied Scis., Hazelcrest, Ill., 1990. Mem. NASW, Ill. Soc. Clin. Social Workers, Acad. Cert. Social Workers. Avocations: skiing, tennis, bridge, reading, music. Deceased.

**GUZY, PETER MICHAEL,** cardiologist, educator; b. Monongahela, Pa., Oct. 30, 1940; BS in Chemistry, U. Notre Dame, 1962; PhD in Biochemistry, U. Ky., 1970; MD, Med. Coll. of Ohio, 1973. Resident McMaster U., Hamilton, Ont., Can., 1973-75, U. Toronto, Ont., Can., 1975-76; fellow in cardiology UCLA Sch. Medicine, 1976-79; asst. prof. medicine UCLA div. Cardiology, 1979-83, assoc. prof. medicine, 1984-90, clin. prof. medicine, from 1990. Dir. UCLA Pacemaker Clinic, 1980-95. Bd. dirs. Am. Heart Assn., 1984-87. Named Tchr. of Yr., UCLA Dept. Medicine, 1981—82. Fellow Am. Coll. Cardiology, Royal Coll. Physicians, Surgeons of Can. Died Dec. 25, 2012.

**GWYNN, TONY (ANTHONY KEITH GWYNN),** college baseball coach, sportscaster, retired professional baseball player; b. LA, May 9, 1960; s. Charles and Vendella Gwynn; m. Alicia Gwynn; children: Anthony, Anisha Nicole. BA, San Diego State U., 1981. Outfielder San Diego Padres, 1982—2001; vol. asst. coach San Diego State U. Aztecs, 2001—02, head baseball coach, 2002—14. Baseball analyst TBS Network, 2007—14. Founder Tony Gwynn Found. Recipient Silver Slugger award, 1984, 1986, 1987, 1989, 1994, 1995, 1997, Gold Glove award, 1986, 1987, 1989—91, Branch Rickey award, 1995, Chairman's award, San Diego Padres, 1995, Lou Gehrig Meml. award, Phi Delta Theta, 1999, Roberto Clemente Man of the Yr. award, 1999; named MVP, Rookie Northwest League, 1981, Coach of Yr., Mountain West Conf., 2004; named to Nat. League All-Star Team, Maj. League Baseball, 1984—87, 1989—99, World Sports Humanitarian Hall of Fame, 1999, MLB All Century Team, 2000, Nat. Baseball Hall of Fame, 2007. Achievements include leading the National League in: batting average, 1984, 1987-89, 1994-97; hits, singles, 1984, 86, 87, 89, 94, 95, 97; at-bats, runs, 1986; on-base percentage, 1994. Died June 16, 2014.

**HAAVIKKO, PAAVO JUHANI,** author, publisher; b. Helsinki, Finland, Jan. 25, 1931; s. Heikki Adrian Haavikko and Rauha Pyykonen; m. Marja-Liisa Vartio Sairanen, 1955 (dec. 1966); 2 children; m. Ritva Rainio Hanhineva, 1971. PhD, U. Helsinki. Real estate salesman, writer, 1951-67. Mem. bd. of Yhtyneet Kuvalehdet mag. co. and Suuri Suomalainen Kirjakerho (Gt. Finnish Book Club), 1969; lit. dir. Otava Pub. Co., 1967-83; dir. Arthouse Pub. Group, 1983-2008; mem. bd. Finnish Writers' Assn., 1962-66; mem. State Com. for Lit., 1966-67. Author: (poetry) Tiet etäisyyksiin, 1951, Tuuliöinä, 1953, Synnyinmaa, 1955, Lehdet lehtiä, 1958, Talvipalatsi, 1959, Runot, 1962, Puut, kaikki heidän vihreytensä, 1966, Neljätoista hallitsijaa, 1970, Runoja matkalta salmen ylitse, 1973, Kaksikymmenta ja yksi, 1974, Runot 1949-1974, 1975, Runoelmat, 1975, Toukokuu, Ikuinen, 1975, Kullervon tarina, 1975, Viiniä Kirjoitusta, 1976, Sillat: valitut runot, 1984, Viisi Sarjaa nopeasti virtaavasta elämästä, 1987, Rakkaudesta ja Kuolemasta, 1989, Talvirunoja, 1990, Runot! runo, 1992, Puiden yhvertaisundesta, 1993, Kirjainmerkit mustat, 1993, Tyrannin yhistys, 1994; (fiction) Yksityisiä asioita, 1960, Toinen taivas ja maa, 1961, Vuodet, 1962, Lasi Claudius Civiliksen salaliittolaisten pöydällä, 1964, Barr-niminen mies, 1976, Anastasia ja mina, 1992, Romaanit ja novellit, Fleurin konlusyksy, 1993, Pahin ja paras, 1996, Nuijasota, 1996; (plays) Münchhausen, 1958, Nuket, 1960, Agricola ja kettu, 1968, Ylilääkäri, 1968, Audun ja jaakarhu, 1969, Brotteruksen perhe, 1969, Kilpikonna, 1970, Sulka, 1973, Ratsumies, 1974, Kuningas lähtee Ranskaan, 1974, Harald Pitkäikäinen, 1974, Nevahvimmat miehet ei ehjiksi jää, 1976, Kaisa ja Otto, 1977, Kuningas Harald, jaahyvaiset, 1978, Soitannollinen ilta Viipurissa 1918, 1978, Näytelmät, 1978, Viisi pientä draamallista tekstiä, 1981, Rauta-aika, 1982; (other) Puhua, vastata, opetta, 1972, Kansakunnan linja, 1977, Ihmisen ääni, 1977, Ikuisen rauhan aika, 1981, Kullervon tarina, 1982, Vuosisadan merikirja, 1983, Wärtsilä 1843-1984, 1984, Pimeys, 1984, Näkyväistä maailmaa, 1985, Vaella Helsingissä, 1986, Yritys omaksikuvaksi, 1987, Kansakunnan synty, 1988, Erään opportunistin iltapäivä, 1988; (memoir I), Vuosien aurinkoiset varjot, 1994, (memoir II) Prospero, 1995, Suomen kansan uusia runoja, 1984. Decorated Knight 1st Class of White Rose of Finland, 1978; recipient 8 state lit. prizes, Aleksis Kivi Found. prize, 1966, Pro Finlandia medal, 1967, State Drama prize, 1969, Neustadt Internat. prize for lit. Finnish Lit. Soc., 1984, Academician, 1994, Rauta-aika, Prix Italia, 1984, Nordic Literature prize Acad. Sweden, 1994, Nordic Drama prize 1996. Died Oct. 6, 2008.

**HADDAD, LOUIS NICHOLAS,** paralegal; b. Beggs, Okla., Sept. 3, 1923; s. Abraham and Tammam (Lelo) H.; m. Jacqueline Marie Pratali, Sept. 22, 1945 (div. 1952); children: Carole, Shirley, Charles; m. Martha Maria Laengst, Dec. 31, 1954; children: Sheila, Stephanie. Co-owner Haddad Bros. Wholesalers, Lancaster, Calif., 1955-57; regional v.p. Nulite Corp., No. Calif., 1957-60; owner, mgr. Shamrock Motors, Seaside, Calif., 1960-68, Gateway Liquors, Seaside, 1968-70, Wagontown Auto Sales, Seaside, 1971-73, Camptown West Motor Homes, Seaside, 1973-79; co-owner, mgr. Monterey (Calif.) Bay Tribune, 1983-89. Councilman City of Seaside, 1964-66, 78-80, mayor, 1966-72; charter bd. dirs. Monterey Peninsula Boys Club; bd. dirs. Alliance on Aging, Assn. Monterey Bay Area Govts., Monterey Peninsula Water Mgmt. Dist., 1993-97; chmn. Laguna Grande Agy., Seaside County Sanitation Dist., Monterey Overall Econ. Devel. Com.; chmn. adv. com. Project Aquarius; mem. Seaside Planning Comn.; vice chmn. So. Monterey Bay Water Pollution Control Agy.; chmn. tri-county bd. Calif. Coun. on Criminal Justice; former vice chmn. Monterey County Local Agys. Formation Com. Capt. U.S. Army, 1940-46, 50-55. Mem. VFW, NCO Assn. Am. (hon.), Am. Legion, Seaside C. of C. (bd. dirs.), K.C., Lions (past pres. Seaside chpt.), Rotary (past pres. Seaside chpt.). Republican. Roman Catholic. Deceased.

**HADEN, CHARLIE,** jazz bassist, composer; b. Shenandoah, Iowa, Aug. 6, 1937; Formed group with Ornette Coleman, Biley Higgins and Don Cherry; performing debut NYC, 1959. Performed throughout, U.S., Europe, played with: Archie Shepp, Keith Jarrett, Alice Coltrane, Pee Wee Russell, Liberation Music Orch., others; recs. include Escalator Over the Hill, (with Carla Bley) Relativity Suite, (with Don Cherry) Expectations, (with Keith Jarrett) Tribute, Ballet of the Fallen, Dream-Keeper, (with Don Cherry, Ed Blackwell) The Montreal Tapes I, 1994, Liberation Music Orchestra, 1996, Now is the Hour, 1996; appeared at, Newport Jazz Festival, 1966-67, 70-72, Monterey Jazz Festival, 1966-67. Recipient Downbeat Critic's New Star award, 1961, acoustic base award, 1989; Guggenheim Found. grantee, 1970; Nat. Endowment Arts grantee, 1973 Died July 11, 2014.

**HADEN, CLOVIS ROLAND,** retired academic administrator, engineering educator; b. Houston, Apr. 10, 1940; s. Clovis Newton and Mary Aline (Baker) H.; m. Joyce Elaine Weathers, Aug. 8, 1956; children: Cathy, Kimberly, Clay. Student, Navarro Coll., Corsicana, Tex., 1958—59; BSEE, U. Tex., Arlington, 1961; MSEE, Calif. Inst. Tech., Pasadena, 1962; PhD, U. Tex., 1965. Lic. profl. engr., Tex., Okla. Asst. prof. U. Okla., 1965—68; dir. Sch. Elec. Engring. and Computing Scis., 1972—78; assoc. prof. Tex. A&M U., College Station, 1968—71, prof., 1971—72, dir. Inst. Solid State Electronics, 1969—72; dean Coll. Engring and Applied Scis. Ariz. State U., Tempe, 1978—87, dean Coll. Engring. and Applied Scis., 1989—91, v.p. for acad. affairs, 1987—88, provost west campus Phoenix, 1988—89, mem., pres. Rsch. Park bd. Tempe, 1983—91; bd. dirs. Ariz. Transp. Rsch. Ctr., 1980—91; vice chancellor for acad. affairs La. State U., Baton Rouge, 1991—93; vice chancellor/dean engring., dir. engring. experiment sta. Tex. A&M U., 1993—2002. Mem. Ariz. Gov.'s Comm. on Sci. and Tech., 1980-82, chmn. transp. subcom., 1981-83, mem. adv. coun. for engring., 1979-91; mem. Ariz. Gov.'s High Tech. Coun., 1990-91; mem. Tex. Gov.'s Coun. Sci. & Tech., 1997-2002; chair strategic planning La. Ednl. Quality Support Fund, 1991-93; mem. Nat. Engring. Dean's Exec. Bd., 1984-87, 95-2000; mem. adv. group Coun. on Competitiveness, 1994-95; chmn. bd. Ariz. R&D Co., 1983-90; mem. adv. bd. A.T. Kearney, 1986-90; mem. Tex. Bd. Profl. Engrs., 2002-06. Exec. editor: Electric Power Sys. Rsch. Jour., 1978—. Bd. mgrs. Tempe YMCA, 1982-84; mem. Ariz. Econ. Devel. Bd., 1982-85; bds. dirs. Harrington Arthritis Rsch. Ctr., 1983-87, Inter-tel, Inc., 1983-05, Square D. Co., 1985-91, E-Sys., 1994-95, WAVO Corp., 1990-99, Crosstex Energy, 2002-06, Res. Valley Partnership, 2004—12, Star Rotor Inc., 2008-12. Adm. Tex. Navy, 2011. Recipient George Washington Honor medal, Freedoms Found., 1989, Disting. Alumnus award U. Tex., Arlington, 1995, Econ. Devel. award Phoenix area, 1985; Bur. Engring. rsch. fellow, 1964. Fellow IEEE (Oklahoma City Engr. of Yr. award 1977), Am. Soc. Engring. Edn. (chair pub. policy com. 1997-99, Lamme award 2007, Lamme award com. mem. 2008-11, Marlowe award 1998); mem. NSPE, Ariz. Soc. Profl. Engrs. (Engr. of Yr. award 1983), Ariz. Assn. Indsl. Devel., Coun. Tex. Engring. Deans (chmn. 1995-98), Tex. Soc. Profl. Engrs. (bd. dirs. 1995-98), Soc. Mfg. Engrs., Sons Am. Revolution, Sons of Republic of Tex., Golden Key, Wingfield Family Soc. (v.p., 2010-12, pres. 2012-), Sigma Xi, Phi Kappa Phi, Eta Kappa Nu, Tau Beta Pi, Tex. Navy. Republican. Mem. Ch. of Christ. Home: College Station, Tex. Died Aug. 24, 2013.

**HADFIELD, JAMES IRVINE HAVELOCK,** surgeon; b. Rickmansworth, Herts, England, Dec. 7, 1930; s. Geoffrey and Sarah Victoria Eileen (Irvine) H.; m. Ann Pickernell Milner, May 1, 1957; children: Esme Victoria, Helen Sarah, Geoffrey Irvine. Student, Brasenose Coll., Oxford, England, 1948-52; student, St. Thomas' Hosp. Med. Sch., 1952-55; MA BM BCH, Oxford U., 1955. Intern St. Thomas's Hosp.; resident St. Thomas's & Leicester Royal Infirmany; house surgeon St. Thomas' Hosp., London, 1955; lectr. dept. anatomy St. Thomas' Hosp. Med. Sch., London, 1957; RSO sr. registrar Leicester Royal Infirmary, Leicester, England, 1960-62; surg. tutor Oxford U., Oxford, England, 1962-66; hon. cons. surgeon Radcliffe Infirmary, Oxford. Bd. dirs., vice chmn. Seltzer PLC; chmn. med. exec. com. Bedford Gen. Hosp., 1980-85; hon. cons. surgeon Radcliffe Infirmary, 1963-66. Contbr. articles to profl. jours. Trustee Bedford Charity, Bedford, England, 1970; gov. Harpur Trust, 1985. Hon. fellow Assn. Surgeons Pakistan, 1985, Assn. Surgeons India, 1989. Fellow Royal Coll. Surgeons England (cert.), Royal Coll. Surgeons Edinburgh (cert.), Internat. Coll. Surgeons, Assn. Surgeons Gt. Britain, Brit. Assn. Urological Surgeons, Anatomical Soc. Gt. Britain-Ireland, Leander Club (Heney on Thames), Vincents Club (Oxford). Mem. Ch. of England. Avocations: fishing for trout and salmon, shooting game. Home: Bedford, England. Died May 17, 2006.

**HADLEY, JOHN BART,** financial analyst; b. Oil City, Pa., Feb. 17, 1942; s. James Edward and Genevieve A. (Rowley) Hadley. BA, Hiram Coll., 1964; MBA, U. Pa., 1967. Fin. analyst Westinghouse Electric Corp., Bloomington, Ind., 1967—69, mgr. fin. planning Pitts., Tucson, Richmond, 1969—71, staff asst. corp. fin. planning Pitts., 1971—74; bus. analyst Farah Mfg. Co., El Paso, 1974—75, fin. analyst treasury, 1975—76, divsn. contr. young men's and boys' divsn., 1976—77; chief agy. and fin. rev. U.S. Ry. Assn., Washington, 1977—79, chief fin. analysis, 1979—80, spl. asst. to dir. fin. analysis, 1980—82; mgr. ops. budget NJTRO, 1982—85, mgr. capital budgets, from 1986. Samuel S. Fels Scholar, U. Pa., 1967. Mem.: Transp. Rsch. Forum, Inst. Mgmt. Accts., Wharton Sch., Cir. K (sec. 1963), Propeller (publicity coord. 1966—67), Chi Sigma Phi. Episopalian. Home: Collingdale, Pa. Died Dec. 1999.

**HAEBERLE, ROSAMOND PAULINE,** retired music educator; b. Clearwater, Kans., Oct. 23, 1914; d. Albert Paul and Ella (Lough) H. BS in Music Edn., Kans. State U., 1936; MusM, Northwestern U., 1948; postgrad., Wayne State U., 1965-66. Profl. registered parliamentarian. Tchr. sch. dist., Plevna, Kans., 1936-37, Esbon, Kans., 1937-41, Frankfort, Kans., 1941-43, Garden City, Kans., 1943-44, music supr. Waterford Twp., Mich., 1944-47, tchr. Pontiac, Mich., 1947-80, ret., 1980. Pres. Pontiac Fedn. Tchrs., 1961-63. Bd. dir. Pontiac Oakland Town Hall; adv. coun. Waterford Sr. Citizens, chmn., 1990-93; pres. Oakland County Pioneer and Hist. Soc., 1992-94. Recipient Tchrs. Day award, Mich. State Fair, 1963. Mem.: Mich. DAR (parliamentarian state, Excellence in Cmty. Svc. award 1995), DAR (regent 1983—85, Gen. Richardson chpt., libr. and parliamentarian), AAUW (pres. Pontiac br. 1970—72, founds. chair Pontiac br.), Mich. Assn. Retired Sch. Persons, Pontiac Area Ret. Sch. Pers. (pres. 1981—84, parliamentarian), Louise Saks Parliamentary Unit, Mich. Registered Parliamentarians (pres. Louise Saks unit 1990—92), Pontiac Area Fedn. Women's Club (pres. 1976—78, 1981—84), Detroit Women's Club, Waterford-Clarkston Bus. and Profl. Women's Club (bylaws and parliamentarian), Bloomfield Rep. Women's Club (parliamentarian 1999—2003), Mich. Bus. and Profl. Women's Club (dir. dist. 10 1965—67, Honored Recognition award 2000, Citations award 2000), Mich. Fedn. Music Clubs (pres. Tuesday musicale of Pontiac 1984—86, pres. S.E. dist. 1986—90, state pres. 1993—95, chair Northeastern Region Nat. Music Week 1996—99, chmn. Music for the Blind Northeastern region from 2000, parliamentarian from 2001, chmn. state bylaws and citations com.), Mich. Fedn. Bus. And Profl. Women's Club (Woman of Achievement award dist. IX 1994), Pontiac Bus. and Profl. Women (pres. 1959—61, Woman of Yr. award 1974), Ea. Star (60 yr. award 2004), Zeta Tau Alpha, Mu Phi Epsilon (70 yr. award), Beta Sigma Phi (life). Republican. Methodist. Avocations: travel, playing piano, reading, bell ringing, dance. Died 2006.

**HAGER, BROR OLOF,** engineer; b. Soderhamn, Sweden, Dec. 19, 1907; s. Olaf and Britta (Vestberg) H.; m. Irma Maria Ekstrom, July 15, 1939; children: Britt, Eva, Ulla. Grad., Royal Inst. Tech., Stockholm, 1933. Chem. rsch. engr. Boliden Co., Stockholm, 1934-46; owner, mgr. Hager Aktiebolag, Djursholm, Sweden, from 1946. Contbr. articles to profl. jours.; patentee in field (300). Recipient Gold medal Royal Swedish Acad. Engring., 1961, Invention award Nat. Swedish Bd. Tech. Devel., 1982. Mem. Swedish Inventors Assn. (dir. 1961-65, award 1973), Am. Wood Preservers Assn. Home: Djursholm, Sweden. Died Oct. 13, 2001.

**HAGGARD, JOEL EDWARD,** lawyer; b. Portland, Oreg., Oct. 10, 1939; s. Henry Edward and Kathryn Shirley (O'Leary) H.; m. Mary Katherine Daley, June 8, 1968; children: Kevin E., Maureen E., Cristin E. BSME, U. Notre Dame, 1961; M in Nuclear Engring., U. Okla., 1963; JD, U. Wash., 1971. Bar: Wash. 1971, U.S. Dist. Ct. (we. dist.) Wash. 1971, U.S. Ct. Appeals (9th cir.) 1971, U.S. Supreme Ct. 1971. Nuclear engr. Westinghouse Corp. Bettis Atomic Power Lab., Pitts., 1963-67; research engr. aerospace div. The Boeing Co., Seattle, 1968; engr., mgmt. cons. King County Dept. Pub. Works, Seattle, 1969-71; assoc. Houghton, Cluck, Coughlin & Riley, Seattle, 1971-74, ptnr., 1975-76; pvt. practice law Seattle, 1977 and from 85; ptnr. Haggard, Tousley & Brain, Seattle, 1978-84. Judge marriage tribunal, Archdiocese of Seattle, 1975-90; chmn. Columbia River Interstate Compact Commn., 1975—; arbitrator King County Superior Ct., 1986—. Contbr. articles to profl. jours. Past trustee, mem. exec. com., past sec. Seattle Symphony. Mem. ABA, Wash. Bar Assn. (past chmn. environ. law sect., fee arbitration com., past mem. rules of profl. conduct com.), Seattle-King County Bar Assn., Rainier Club, Wash. Athletic Club, Astoria Golf and Country Club, Magnolia Cmty. Club (past pres., bd. dirs.). Deceased.

**HAINSWORTH, DAVID JAMES,** electronics executive; b. St. Louis, Nov. 29, 1941; s. Joseph C. and Anna M. Hainsworth; m. Beverly Ann Berner, Oct. 25, 1969 (div. 1985); children: Lorry Ann, Jessica Nicole. Student, Coll. Sch. Ozarks, 1960—63, Forest Park CC, 1967—68, U. Mo., 1968—69. Purchasing agt. Anheuser-Busch, Inc., St. Louis, 1967—70; asst. to v.p. mktg. D & D Bean Co., Greeley, Colo., 1970—77; asst. mgr. Outwest Bean, Inc., Littleton, Colo., 1977—78, gen. mgr., treas., 1978—81, pres., 1981—85, Glenn L. Cogil and Assocs., 1984—86; v.p. ops. Internat. Power Techs., Inc., Littleton, from 1986. Sec. adv. bd. Wichita (Kans.) Bank Coops., 1980—82; participant Mktg. and Internat. Trade Conf., 1980; mem. nat. adv. bd. Farm Credit Adminstrn., Washington, 1983—85. Mem. citizen's budget rev. com. Arapahoe County Dist. 6 Sch. Dist., 1980—81; area leader Rep. Com. Arapahoe County; active choirs, youth orgns. Oak Hill Presbyn. Ch., St. Louis, 1958—69, First United Meth. Ch., Greeley, 1969—78; supply pastor Hollister (Mo.) Presbyn. Ch., 1961—63. With USAF, 1963—67, Vietnam. Mem.: Rocky Mountain Bean Dealers Assn. (bd. dirs. 1979—83, v.p. 1981—83), Hispanic C. of C. (corp. rep. from 1986), Englewood C. of C., Traffic Club Denver, Rotary. Died May 16, 1998.

**HAIR, JAY DEE,** association executive; b. Miami, Fla., Nov. 30, 1945; s. Wilbur B. and Ruth A. Johnson; m. Rebecca McDaniel, May 17, 1970 (div. Aug. 1993); children: Whitney, Lindsay; m. Keota Knapp, Oct. 4, 1993; stepchildren: Colin, Benjamin. BS, Clemson U., 1967, MS, 1969; PhD, U. Alta., 1975; postgrad., Govt. Execs. Inst., Sch. Bus. Adminstrn., U. N.C., 1980. Asst. prof. wildlife biology Clemson (S.C.) U., 1968-69; assoc. prof. zoology/forestry, adminstr. fisheries and wildlife scis. N.C. State U., Raleigh, 1977-81, adj. prof. zoology and forestry, 1982-95; pres. Nat. Wildlife Fedn., Washington, 1981-95, IUCN-The World Conservation Union, Gland, Switzerland, 1994-96. Spl. asst. to asst. sec. for fish, wildlife and parks Dept. Interior, 1978-80; mem. Nat. Petroleum Coun., Dept. Energy, 1981-84; rep. Natural Resources Coun. Am., 1981; bd. dirs. Sol Feinstone Environ. Awards Program, 1982—; mem. USTR Investment Policy Adv. Com., 1994—, Pres.'s Coun. on Sustainable Devel., 1993-95, U. Wyo. Inst. for Environment and Natural Resources Rsch. Policy, 1994—, Rails to Trails, 1986-93, Global Tomorrow Coalition, 1987-94, Riggs Nat. Bank, 1989-93, Globescope adv. Coun., 1984—, Nat. Pub. Lands Adv. Coun., 1984-86; mem. Nat. Wetland Policy Forum, 1987-88; vice chmn. Nat. Groundwater Forum, 1984-86, Nat. Nonpoint Source Inst., 1985—, Keystone Ctr., 1985-93, Clean Sites, 1986—; mem. biotech. sci. adv. com. EPA, 1987-89; mem. Acad. Mgmt., 1988—; mem. nat. adv. bd. Sci. Journalism Ctr., U. Mo.-Columbia, 1987-88, bd. cons., 1987-88; bd. govs. Nat. Safety Coun. Environ. Health and Safety Inst., 1986—; U.S. bd. dirs. Internat. Union for Conservation of Nature and Natural Resources, 1989-94. Editor: Ecological Perspectives of Wildlife Management, 1977; contbr. articles to profl. jours. Bd. govs. Nat. Shooting Sports Found., 1981—; mem. conservation com. Boy Scouts Am., 1981; pres. N.C. Cued Speech Assn., 1978-81; chmn. bd. dirs. Cued Speech Ctr., Inc., 1979-81; bd. dirs. Parents and Profls. for Handicapped Children, N.C., 1979-81; mem. Wake County Hearing-Impaired Assn., (N.C.), 1978—; pres. Alexander Graham Bell Nat. Assn. Deaf, 1979. Served to 1st lt. U.S. Army, 1970-71. Named S.C. Wildlife Conservationist of Yr. Gov.'s Ann. Conservation Awards Program, 1977, N.C. Conservationist of Yr., 1980; recipient N.C. Gov.'s award for pub. svc.; Alumni Disting. Svc. award Clemson U., 1986, Centennial Disting. Alumni award, 1989; 4-H Alumni award Purdue U., 1988; Edward J. Cleary award Nat. Acad. Environ. Engrs., 1989, U. Edmonton Alumni Recognition award "Wall of Fame," 1995. Mem. Wildlife Soc. (Disting. Service award Southeastern sect. 1980), Soc. Am. Foresters, AAAS, Internat. Assn. Fish and Wildlife Agys., Ducks Unltd., Wildlife Soc., N.C. Acad. Scis., N.C. Wildlife Fedn., S.C. Wildlife Fedn. (F. Bartow Culp disting. svc. to conservation award 1978, Disting. Svc. award Southeast sect. 1980, Nat. Wildlife Fedn. Outstanding Affiliate award 1978), Am. Fisheries Soc., Am. Forestry Assn., Scabbard and Blade, Tiger Brotherhood, Blue Key, Phi Kappa Delta. Died Nov. 15, 2002.

**HAIRFIELD, HARRELL D.,** electrical engineer; b. Oklahoma City, Jan. 19, 1930; s. Harrell D. and Bula L. (Crawford) Hairfield; m. Johnnie Karr, Mar. 8, 1952; children: Harrell D. III, GeeGee Ann, John Charles. BSEE, Okla. State U., 1957. Field engr. Western Electric, Winston-Salem, NC, 1957—65; site mgr. Radiation Inc., Point Mugu, Calif., 1965—66; mem. tech. staff Rockwell Internat., Anaheim, Calif., 1966—79; project engr. Brunswick Corp., Costa Mesa, Calif., 1979—80; engr. specialist Litton Guidance & Control Sys., Woodland Hills, Calif., 1982—86. With US Army, 1951—54. Home: Finley, Okla. Died Dec. 1991.

**HALEVY, ABRAHAM HAYIM,** horticulturist, plant physiologist; b. Tel-Aviv, July 18, 1927; s. Naftali and Henria (Ginzburg) H.; m. Zilla Horngrad, Aug. 20, 1952 (dec. 1981); children: Avishag, Noa, Itali; m. Esther Passal, Apr. 15, 1991 (dec. Dec. 2000). MSc, Hebrew U., Jerusalem, 1955, PhD, 1958; DSc (hon.), U. Waterloo, Can., 2003. Rsch. assoc. Plant Ind. Sta., USDA, Beltsville, Md., 1958-59; lectr. in horticulture and plant physiology Hebrew U., Rehovot, Israel, 1960-64, sr. lectr., 1964-67, assoc. prof., 1967-71, prof., from 1971, head dept. ornamental horticulture Jerusalem, 1967-83, 86-90. Vis. prof. Mich. State U., 1964-65, U. Calif.-Davis, 1970-71, 75-76, 82-84, 86, 87, 89, 91; sci. advisor to Israeli Min. of Edn. Editor Scientia Horticolturae, Plant Growth Regulators, Jour. Crop Prodn.; editor-in-chief Israel Jour. Botany, 1985-93; editor: Handbook of Flowering, vols. 1-6, 1985-89, Flowering Newsletter, 1986-89; contbr. over 350 sci. papers in field to publs. Served with Israeli Def. Forces, 1948-50. Recipient Israel prize, 2002. Fellow Am. Soc. Hort. Sci. (A. Laurie award 1960-63), Internat. Soc. Hort. Sci.; mem. Internat. Soc. Horticulture (coun.), Norwegian Acad. Sci. and Letters, Internat. Bulb Soc. (Herbert medal 2006, Hall Fame 2006). Jewish. Home: Tel Aviv, Israel. Died Oct. 27, 2006.

**HALL, BEVERLY BARTON,** librarian; b. Cin., July 15, 1918; d. Clarence Earl Barton and Maude Ethel Wedmore; m. Randolph Van Lew Hall, Apr. 26, 1947; children: Barton M., Martha H. Kern, Patricia H. Pellerin. BA, Middlebury Coll., 1940; BS, Columbia U., 1941; MS, So. Conn. State Coll., 1975. Cert. tchr./libr. grades K-12, Conn. Libr. Wellesley (Mass.) Coll., 1941-42, Great Neck (N.Y.) Pub. Libr., 1942-44, Yale U. Sch. Law, New Haven, 1944-50, Amity Regional H.S., Woodbridge, Conn., 1967-80. Author: Secret of the Lion's Head, 1995 Founder, bd. dirs. Orange (Conn.) Pub. Libr., 1956-63; founder, St. John's Ch. Libr., Naples, Fla., 1993—2011. Republican. Episcopalian. Avocations: reading, counted cross-stitch, music. Home: Salem, Conn. Died Sept. 18, 2013.

**HALL, SIR PETER GEOFFREY,** urban and regional planning educator; b. London, Mar. 19, 1932; came to U.S., 1980; s. Arthur Vickers and Bertha (Keefe) H.; m. Carla Maria Wartenberg, Sept. 7, 1962 (div. 1967); m. Magda Mroz, Feb. 13, 1967. BA in Geography, Cambridge U., Eng., 1953, PhD, 1959; DDS (hon.), Birmingham U., Eng., 1991; PhD (hon.), Lund U., Sweden, 1992; DLitt (hon.), Sheffield U., 1995, Newcastle U., 1995; DEng (hon.), Tech. U. Nova Scotia, Can., 1996; ArtsD (hon.), Oxford Brookes U., 1997; LLD (hon.), Reading U., 1999; DSc (hon.), U. West Eng., 2000; DSc, U. Loughborough, 2005; D Laws, U. Manchester, 2001; DLitt (hon.), Herriot Watt U., 2002, Guildhall U., London, 2002; DSS (hon.), Queen Mary, U. London, 2004; DTech (hon.), U. Greenwich, 2004; DSc (hon.), Loughborough U., 2005. Lectr. Birkbeck Coll., U. London, 1957-65; reader London Sch. Econs., 1966-67; prof. U. Reading, Eng., 1968-89, chmn., 1971-77, dean faculty urban and regional studies, 1975-78, bd. mgmt., 1983-86, prof. emeritus, 1989—2014; prof. dept. city and regional planning U. Calif., Berkeley, 1980-92, assoc. dir. Inst. Urban and Regional Devel., 1980-88, dir., 1989-92, prof. emeritus, 1993—2014. Prof. planning and regeneration Bartlett Sch. Planning U. Coll. London, London, from 1992; dir. sch. pub. policy Bartlett Sch. Planning Univ. Coll. London, 1996—97; spl. advisor Dept. of Environment, London, 1991—94; mem. Urban Task Force, 1998—99; dir. Inst. of Cmty. Studies, 2001—04; chair Reblackpool, 2004—08. Author: The World Cities, 1966, 3d edit., 1984, Europe 2000, 1977 (Bentinck prize 1979), Great Planning Disasters, 1980, The Inner City in Context, 1981, Silicon Landscapes, 1985, Can Rail Save the City?, 1985, High-Tech America, 1986, 3rd edit., 2014, Western Sunrise, 1987, Cities of Tomorrow (Balzan prize 2005), 1988, London 2001, 1989, Cities and Civilization, 1998, London Voices London Lives, 2007, Good Cities Better Lives, 2013; co-author: The Rise of the Gunbelt, 1991, Technopoles of the World, 1994, Sociable Cities, 1998, 2nd edit., 2014, Urban Future 21, 2000, Working Capital, 2002, The Polycentric Metropolis, 2006. Advisor Social Democratic Party, 1983-85; active S.E. Econ. Planning Coun., 1966-79, London Voices London Lives, 2007, Social Sci. Rsch. Coun., 1974-79. Recipient Balzan Internat. prize, 2005. Fellow Brit. Acad., Royal Geog. Soc. (Gill Meml. prize 1968, Founder's medal 1991), St. Catharine's Coll. (hon.); mem. Royal Town Planning Inst. (hon., Gold medal 2003), American Planning Assn., Athenaeum Club, Brit. Acad. Avocations: reading, travel. Home: London, England. Died July 30, 2014.

**HALLETT, ARCHIBALD CAMERON HOLLIS,** physics educator; b. Bermuda, Feb. 5, 1927; s. Rupert Carlyle Hollis and Jessie (Cameron) H.; m. Clara Frances Edith Gilbert, Sept. 5, 1950; children: William Langton Hollis, Mary Francis Hollis, James Archibald Hollis. Student, St. Andrew's Coll., Aurora, Ont., Can., 1943-44; BA, Trinity Coll., U. Toronto, 1948; PhD, Kings Coll., Cambridge U., Eng., 1951. Mem. faculty dept. physics U. Toronto, 1951-77, prof., 1963-77; asso. dean faculty U. Toronto (Arts and Sci.), 1966-70; prin. University Coll., U. Toronto, 1970-77; pres. Bermuda Coll., 1977-92; sec. Bermuda Maritime Mus. Assn., from 1992. Mem. bd. editors: Jour. Low Temperature Physics, 1969-79, Bermuda Jour. Archaeology & Maritime History, 1989—. Mem. Am. Phys. Soc. Home: Pembroke, Bermuda. Died Oct. 6, 2003.

**HALLINAN, MAUREEN THERESA,** sociologist, educator; b. Flushing, NY, June 11, 1940; d. Joseph and Beatrice (O'Reilly) Hallinan; m. Art Grubert, Sept. 11, 1976 (div. May 4, 2010); children: Renee, Christopher. BA, Marymount Coll., 1961; MS, U. Notre Dame, 1968; PhD, U. Chgo., 1972. Prof. sociology U. Wis., Madison, 1980-84, U. Notre Dame, Ind., 1984—2012, prof. emeritus, 2012—14. Author: The Structure of Positive Sentiment, 1974; editor: Sociology of Edn., 1981—86, The Social Context of Instruction: Group Organization and Group Processes, 1983, The Social Organization of Schools: New Conceptualizations of the Learning Process, 1987, Change in Societal Institutions, 1990, Restructuring Schools: Promising Practices and Policies, 1995, Handbook of the Sociology of Education, 2000, Chinese edit., 2004, paperback edit., 2006; co-editor: Stability and Change in American Education: Structure, Process and Outcomes, 2003, School Sector and Student Outcomes, 2006; assoc. editor: Social Forces, 1977—80, 1998—2001, Sociology of Edn., 1979—81, 1991—2001; contbr. articles to profl. jours. Recipient U. Notre Dame Rsch. Achievement award, 2003. Fellow: American Ednl. Rsch. Assn.; mem.: Nat. Acad. Edn. (v.p. fellows 2001—05), Sociol. Rsch. Assn. (sec.-treas. 1999—2000, pres. 2000—01), American Sociol. Assn. (session organizer 1980, 1984, 1989, sec.-treas. 1988—90, chmn. sociology edn. sect. 1991—92, session organizer 1992, pres. 1995—96, session organizer 1996—2001, Willard Waller award 2004), Kappa Delta Phi (laureate chpt. 2007), Phi Beta Kappa. Died Jan. 28, 2014.

**HALVER, JOHN EMIL,** nutritional biochemist; b. Woodinville, Wash., Apr. 21, 1922; s. John Emil and Helen Henrietta (Hansen) Halver; m. Jane Loren, July 21, 1944; children: John Emil IV, Nancylee Halver Hadley, Janet Ann Halver Fix, Peter Loren, Deborah Kay Halver Hanson. BS, Wash. State U., 1944, MS in Organic Chemistry, 1948; PhD in Med. Biochemistry, U. Wash., 1953. Plant chemist Assoc. Frozen Foods, Kent, Wash., 1946-47; asst. chemist Purdue U., 1948—49; instr. U. Wash., Seattle, 1949—50, affiliate prof., 1960—75; prof. U. Wash. Sch. Fisheries, 1978—92; prof. emeritus U. Wash., 1992—2012. Condr. research on vitamin and amino acid requirements for fish; identified aflatoxin B1 as specific carcinogen for rainbow trout hematoma; identified vitamin C2 for fish; dir. Western Fish Nutrition Lab. U.S. Fish and Wildlife Service, Dept. Interior, Cook, Wash., 1950—75, sr. scientist, nutrition, Seattle, 1975—78; cons. FAO, UNDP, Internat. Union Nutrition Scientists, Nat. Fish Research Inst., Hungary, World Bank, Euroconsult, UNDP, IDRC; affiliate prof. prof. U. Oreg. Med. Sch., 1965—69; vis. prof. Marine Sci. Inst. U. Tex., Port Aransas; pres. Fisheries Devel. Technology, Inc., 1980—90, Halver Corp., 1978—2012. Lay leader Meth. Ch., 1965—70. Capt. US Army, World War II, col. USAR. Decorated WWII, Purple Heart, Bronze Star with oak leaf cluster, Meritorious Service Conduct medal. Fellow: Am. Inst. Nutrition, Am. Inst. Fishery Research Biologists; mem.: NAS, Hungarian Acad. Sci., World Aquaculture Soc., Am. Fishery Soc., Am. Chem. Soc., Am. Sci. Affiliation, Soc. Exptl. Biol. Medicine, Rotary, Alpha Chi Sigma, Pi Mu Epsilon, Phi Lambda Upsilon. Methodist. Achievements include founder JE Halver Fellowship at University of Washington; founder JE Halver Lecture at Washington State University. Home: Seattle, Wash. Died Oct. 24, 2012.

**HAMILTON, CHICO (FORESTSTORN HAMILTON),** jazz drummer; b. L.A., Sept. 20, 1921; s. Jesse and Pearl Lee (Gonzales Cooley) Hamilton; m. Helen Hamilton (dec. 2008). Mem. Lena Horne's backup band, 1948—55; ind. drummer, band leader, 1954—2013. Jazz drummer performed with Lionel Hampton, Lester Young, Gerry Mulligan's Quartet, Count Basie, Lena Horne, Lester Young, Billie Holliday; led bands including Buddy Collette, Jim Hall, Eric Dolphy, Charles Lloyd, Gabor Szabo, Larry Coryell, Eric Gayle, John Abercrombie, Arthur Blythe, Steve Turre, Rodney Jones; appeared in: (films): Sweet Smell of Success, 1957, Jazz on a Summer's Day, 1959; dubbed music onto various movie film soundtracks including Hope/Crosby film Road to Bali; albums include Gerry Mulligan/Chet Baker, Chico Hamilton, Passin' Thru, Man From Two Worlds, Chic Chic Chico, The Dealer, Nomad, Gongs East, Reaching for the Top; lp's include Euphoria, Transfusion, Reunion, Arroyo. Recipient Jazz Masters award, NEA, 2004, Living Jazz Legend award, John F. Kennedy Ctr. for the Performing Arts, 2007. Died Nov. 25, 2013.

**HAMILTON, JOHN ALFRED,** retired television host, producer, writer, director; b. Richmond, Va., Aug. 24, 1929; s. Charles Henry and Viola Belle (Morrisette) H.; m. Nancy Marina Bradsher, Sept. 17, 1955 (dec. 2007); children: John Alfred Jr., Barbara Anne. BA, U. Richmond, 1951; postgrad. in law, NYU, 1951-53; MS, Columbia U., 1956; postgrad., Harvard U., 1961-62. Editor Northern Va. Daily, Strasburg, 1956-58; assoc. editor Richmond News Leader, 1958-63, Detroit Free Press, 1963-68; mem. editorial bd. The NY Times, NYC, 1968-74; anchor Sta. WNET-TV, NYC, 1974-75; host, producer, commentator Sta. WNEW-TV, NYC, 1975-76, Sta. WPIX-TV, NYC, 1976-81; exec. producer, host TV series Watch on Washington, from 1981; founder, owner Hamilton Productions Inc., Washington, from 1980. Cons. Financial News Network, N.Y.C., 1987-91, Independent News Network, N.Y.C. and Washington, 1983-91. Co-author: N.Y. Times Guide for Voters, 1972, The Media and the Cities, 1972; contbr. articles to N.Y. Times Mag., Saturday Rev., exec. producer PBS film Worth Fighting For (Emmy award 1989). Founding dir. N.J. Shakespeare Theater Festival, Drew Univ., Madison, N.J.; trustee Emmanuel Cancer Found., Bloomfield, N.J.; bd. dirs. Citizens Union, N.Y.C.; trustee Bd. Assocs., U. Richmond. With U.S. Army, 1953-55. Korea. Nieman fellow, Harvard U., 1961-62; recipient Ernie Pyle Meml. award, Nat. Headliners Club medal, ABA Gavel award, American Soc. TV Cameramen Pub. Service award, N.Y. Publications Assn. award, Excellence award Internat. TV Assn., Excellence in Communication award Internat. Assn. Bus. Cos., Emmy award for TV series Watch on Washington, 1990; shared in Pulitzer prize as Detroit Free Press assoc. editor, 1968. Fellow Soc. Nieman Fellows; mem. Radio TV News Dirs. Assn., Nat. Acad. TV Arts & Sciences, American Fedn. TV and Radio Artists, US Senate & US House of Reps. News Galleries, Phi Beta Kappa. Clubs: Harvard U. of N.Y.C. (admissions com.), City of N.Y. (trustee); Rector's Club, U. Richmond; Canoe Brook Country (Summit, N.J.); Nat. Press of Washington; Hidden Creek Country (Reston, Va.). Episcopalian. Avocations: golf, gardening. Home: Mc Lean, Va. Died June 7, 2014.

**HAMILTON, MARY ANN,** medical, surgical nurse; b. Chgo., Apr. 20, 1942; d. Thomas E. and Eileen M. (Ryan) Murray; m. Clayton B. Hamilton, Aug. 12, 1967; children: Tanya Michelle, Kimberly Anne, Kirsten Leigh. RN, St. Anne's Hosp. Sch. Nursing, Chgo., 1964. Staff nurse St. Anne's Hosp., Chgo., 1964-66, Good Samaritan Hosp., Phoenix, 1966-67; charge nurse Landmark Med. Ctr., El Paso, 1967-71, asst. nurse mgr., 1985-87; staff nurse Vista Hills Med. Ctr., El Paso, 1987-89, charge nurse, asst. nurse dir. med. and oncology, 1989-93; interim nurse dir. med. and oncology Columbia Med. Ctr. East, 1991-93, nurse dir., 1992-93. Home: El Paso, Tex. Died 1998.

**HAMMADI, SADOON,** former Iraqi government official, economist; b. Karbala, Iraq, June 22, 1930; m. Lamia Hammadi, 1961; 5 children. Educated in, Beirut, U.S. Prof. econs. U. Baghdad, 1957; dep. head econ. rsch. Nat. Bank Libya, Tripoli, 1961-62; min. agrarian reform Govt. of Iraq, 1963; econ. advisor to presl. coun. Govt. of Syria, 1964; econ. expert UN Planning Inst., Syria, 1965-68; pres. Iraq Nat. Oil Co., 1968; min. oil & minerals Govt. of Iraq, Baghdad, 1969-74, min. fgn. affairs, 1974-83, prime min., 1991, parliament spkr., 1996—2003. Author: Towards a Socialistic Agrarian Reform in Iraq, 1964, Views about Arab Revolution, 1969, Memoirs and Views on Oil Issues, 1980. Avocations: swimming, walking, coin collecting/numismatics, reading novels. Died Mar. 14, 2007.

**HANAMEY, ROSEMARY T.,** nursing educator; b. Detroit, May 16, 1937; d. Albert Edward and Catherine Margaret (Shaheen) Hanamey. BSN, Mercy Coll., Detroit, 1959; MS, Boston Coll., 1963; postgrad., U. Mich., 1982; PhD student, U. Mich., Sch. Edn. RN Mich., 1959. Staff nurse Mt. Carmel Mercy Hosp., Detroit, 1959—60, Mass. Gen. Hosp., Boston, 1960—63; instr. nursing Mercy Coll., Detroit, 1963—65, asst. prof., 1967—69; asst. exec. sec. Mich. Nurses Assn., Lansing, 1965—67; exec. sec. Mich. Conf. AAUP, Detroit, 1969—70; instr. nursing Madonna Coll., Livonia, Mich., 1972—76; asst. prof. nursing Ea. Mich. U., Ypsilanti, 1976—80; vol. parish nurse St. Joseph Cath. Ch., Dexter, Mich., from 1997. Mem. careers com. Mich. League Nursing, Detroit, 1977—97; cons. Detroit Practical Nurse Ctr., 1980—85; mem. parish nurse partnership St. Joseph Mercy Health Sys., Ann Arbor, Mich., from 1997. Author: (videotape) Intravenous Therapy: Monitoring and Problem Solving, 1977 (2nd place, 1978), Intravenous Therapy: Basic Concepts, 1977 (3rd place, 1978). Precinct del. Dem. Party, Detroit, 1966—69. Grantee, USPHS, 1961—62; scholar, Marygrove Coll., Detroit, 1955—56. Mem.: Dexter Kiwanis Club. Avocations: swimming, walking. Home: Dexter, Mich. Died Oct. 27, 2013.

**HANDLEY, VERNON GEORGE,** conductor; b. Enfield, Eng., Nov. 11, 1930; s. Vernon Douglas and Claudia Lillian Handley; m. Barbara Black, 1954 (div.); 2 children; m. Victoria Parry-Jones (div.); 2 children; m. Catherine Newby, 1987; 1 child. Student, Oxford U., Guildhall Sch. of Music; doctorate (hon.), U. Surrey, 1980; Mus D (hon.), Liverpool U., 1992. Condr. Oxford U. Mus. Club and Union, 1953-54, Oxford U. Dramatic Soc., 1953-54, Tonbridge Philharm. Soc., 1958-61, Guildford Philharm. Orch. and Choir, 1962-83; assoc. condr. London Philharm. Orch., 1983-86, guest condr., 1966-72; prof. orch. and conducting Royal Coll. Music, 1966-72; prin. condr. Ulster Orch., 1985-89, Malmö Symphony Orch., 1985-89; prin. guest condr. Liverpool Philharm. Orch., 1989-94, condr. emeritus, 1994-2008; prin. guest condr. Melbourne Symphony Orch., 1993-95; chief condr. W. Australian Symphony Orch., 1994-96; assoc. condr. Royal Philharm. Orch., 1994-2008, guest condr., 1961-94, prin. conductor, English Symphony Orch., 2007-08; toured Germany, 1966, 80, South Africa, 1974, Holland, 1980, Sweden, 1980, 81, Australia, 1986; numerous recs. Recipient Arnold Bax Meml. medal for conducting, 1962, Hi-Fi News Audio award, 1982, Gramophone Record of Yr., 1986, 89, Brit. Phonographic Industry award, 1988, Lifetime Achievement award Classical Brit awards, 2007; named Condr. of Yr., Brit. Composer's Guild, 1974; fellow Goldsmith's Coll., London, 1987; named an named an Honorary Comdr. of the Most Excellent Order of the British Empire, Her Majesty Queen Elizabeth II, 2004 Mem. Royal Philharm. Soc. (hon.). Avocations: bird photography, building furniture. Died Sept. 10, 2008.

**HANDLEY, WILLIAM ROBERT CHARLES,** electrical engineer; b. London, May 11, 1938; s. William and Dorothy Adelaide (Spon) Handley; m. Gwendoline Wright, Dec. 1, 1993; stepchildren: Robert, Terry; m. Mhairia Christina Bruce, June 24, 1967 (div. Aug. 1992); children: Faith, Rebeccah, James. BA with honors, Open U., England, 1977; MPh, U Bath, England, 1999. Electrical journeyman Ionic Electric, London, 1959—65; lab. engr. Morganite Carbon, London, 1965—66; 4th asst. engr. CEGB, England, 1967—74; 2nd engr. London Electricity, 1974—78, 1st engr., 1978—2000; EHV sys. protection engr. 24 Seven, Bexley Heath, England, from 2000. Church warden St. John C. of Eng., Chelsea, England, 1966—67, St. Barnabas Bow Ch. of Eng., from 2000. Mem.: Instn. Elec. Engrs., IEEE (assoc.). Avocation: choral singing. Home: London, England. Deceased.

**HANDMAN, BOBBIE (BARBARA HANDMAN),** retired foundation administrator; b. Phila, Mar. 11, 1928; d. Benjamin and Sophie Handman; m. Wynn Handman; 1 child, Laura. BA in Philosophy, Barnard Coll. Sr. v.p., N.Y. regional dir. People for the American Way Found., Washington, 1981—2003. Organizer A Quiet Walk for the First Amendment. Recipient Nat. Medal of Arts for Advocacy, The White House, 1998. Democrat. Died Nov. 14, 2013.

**HANDY, NIXEON CIVILLE,** poet, educator; b. Ocean Park, Calif., Mar. 5, 1909; BEd, UCLA, 1930; MEd, Cen. Wash. State Coll., 1958. Dean of women Wenatchee (Wash.) Valley Coll., 1961-66; dir. adult edn. United Meth. Ch. at Sandpoint, Seattle, 1967-69; dir. religious edn. First Meth. Ch., Des Moines, Wash., 1970-71. Author: (poetry books) Do Not Disturb the Dance: Enter It, 1973, Earth House, 1978, Grandma Casey, 1981, A Little Leaven, 1987, River as Metaphor, 1992. Deceased.

**HANIGAN, LAWRENCE,** retired rail transportation executive; b. Notre-Dame-de, Stanbridge, Can., Apr. 3, 1925; s. John Henry and Alice (Lareau) H.; m. Anita Martin, July 20, 1946; children: Carmen, Doris, Guy, Patricia, Michael. Sales mgr. Boisse Lumber Co., Montreal, 1950-52; regional mgr. Cooper-Widman Ltd., Montreal, 1952-70; mem. City of Montreal Exec. Com., 1970-78; chmn. Montreal Urban Community Exec. Com., 1972-78; chmn., gen. mgr. Montreal Urban Community Transit Commn., 1974-85; chmn. VIA Rail Canada Inc., 1985-93. Home: Quebec, Canada. Died Oct. 31, 2009.

**HANNA, CHERYL,** law educator; b. Detroit, July 22, 1966; m. Paul Henninge; 2 children. BA magna cum laude, Kalamazoo Coll., 1988; JD cum laude, Harvard Law Sch., 1992. Md. 1992, Mass. 1993. Adminstrv. dir. Md. Democratic Campaign for Clinton/Gore, Balt., 1992; asst. state's atty. Balt. City State's Atty. Office, 1993-94; prof. Vt. Law Sch., South Royalton, 1994—2014. Vis. prof. Hastings Coll. Law, 2000—01; chair Richard & Barbara Snelling Ctr. for Govt., 2010. Mem. Vt. Gender Bias Task Force; advisor Albert Schweitzer Fellowship, Vt., 1997. Irving Kaufman fellow Harvard Law Sch., 1993; recipient Margaret R. Williams Emerging Profl. award Vt. Women in Higher Edn., 1998, Sister Elizabeth Candon Disting. Svc. award Mem. American Assn. of Law Schools (sect. law and social sci). Democrat. Died July 27, 2014.

**HANNIGAN, FRANK,** sportswriter, television writer and commentator, golf course design consultant; b. NYC, Mar. 29, 1931; s. Frank A. and Harriet (Pratnicki) H.; children: Keith, Susan BA, Wagner Coll., 1951. With US Golf Assn., Far Hills, NJ, 1961-89, sr. exec. dir., 1983-89. Author: The Rules of Golf Illustrated and Explained, 1981 Served with U.S. Army, 1952-54 Recipient 1st place award Golf Writers Assn. America, 1964, 81 Mem.: Somerset Hills Country (Bernardsville, N.J.). Democrat. Avocation: gardening. Home: Saugerties, NY. Died Mar. 22, 2014.

**HANRAHAN, EDWARD BRACKETT,** physical science educator; b. NYC, Sept. 27, 1933; s. Edward Brackett and Margaret Hahrahan; m. Dorothy Hanrahan, Oct. 30, 1954; children: Edward Brackett III, Kathleen Susan, Sheila Jane. AB, Columbia U., 1956; AM, U. Ill., 1966, PhD in Geography, 1971. Commd. 2d lt. USAF, 1956, advanced through grades to maj., 1966; assoc. prof. geography USAF Acad., 1968-73; asst. dir. USAF Project CHECO, 1973-74; chief climatological svcs. br. USAF Environ. Tech. Applications Ctr., 1974-76; ret. USAF, 1976; univ. registrar Hampton U., 1977-91, assoc. prof. environ. sci., 1991-2000; ret., 2000. Adj. prof. geography Old Dominion U., 1985. Mem. Assn. Am. Geographers, Am. Meteorology Soc. (pres. chpt.), Am. Geographic Soc. Died Dec. 30, 2002.

**HANSEN, GEORGE VERNON,** former United States Representative from Idaho; b. Tetonia, Idaho, Sept. 14, 1930; s. Dean Erlease and Elmoyne Bendicta (Brewer) H.; m. Constance Sue Camp, Dec. 19, 1952 (dec. April 9, 2013); children: Steven, James, Patricia, William, Joanne. AB in History & Russian with honors, Ricks Coll., Rexburg, Idaho, 1956; Grad., Grimms Bus. Coll., 1958; postgraduate studies in Edn., Idaho State U., 1956—57, postgraduate studies in Edn., 1962—63. Grain elevator mgr., 1950—51, 1954; Tchr. math. secondary public sch., 1956-58; guest lectr. ins. & estate planning colleges & high schools; spl. agt. NY Life Ins. Co., 1958—65; mayor City of Alameda, Idaho, 1961-62; city commr. City of Pocatello, Idaho, 1962-65; mem. US Congress from 2nd Idaho Dist., Washington, 1965—69, 1975—85; dep. under sec. congressional liaison, dep. adminstr. for agrl. stabilization & conservation svc. USDA, 1969—71, v.p. Commodity Credit Corp., 1969—71. Author: To Harass Our People: The IRS and Government Abuse of Power, 1981. Chmn. Bannock County Heart Assn., 1962-64. Served with USAF, 1951-54, USNR, 1964-70. Recipient Distinguished Service award Pocatello Jaycees, 1961 Mem. Idaho Municipal League (bd. dirs. 1961-63), Pocatello Chamber of Commerce, American Legion, Idaho Farm Bur., Life Ins. Underwriter Assn. Republican. Mem. Clubs: Kiwanian (bd. dirs.), Pocatello 20-30 (past pres.). Lds Church. Home: Arlington, Va. Died Aug. 14, 2014.

**HANSEN, WAYNE RICHARD,** radioecologist; b. Rice Lake, Wis., Aug. 6, 1939; s. Richard Lyman and Helen Ann (Nethig) H.; m. Nancy Jane Rohde, Sept. 10, 1960; children: Richard W., William R. BS, U. Wis., Eau Claire, 1961; MS, U. Kans., 1963; PhD, Colo. State U., 1970. Diplomate Am. Bd. Health Physics (bd. dirs. 1990-94). Health physicist U. Colo., Boulder, 1963-67, Bur. Radiol. Health, Rockville, Md., 1970-71, EPA, Washington, 1971-75; sr. radiobiologist NRC, Washington, 1975-77; group leader enrivon. surveillance Los Alamos Nat. Lab., 1977-84, dep. div. leader health, safety and environ., 1984-87, chief scientist environ. rsch., 1987-90, group leader environ. scis., from 1990. Sr. scientist accident response group Dept. Energy, Albuquerque, 1986-94. Contbr. articles to profl. jours., chpt. to book. Vice chmn. N.Mex. Gov.'s Radiation Tech. Adv. Coun., Sante Fe, 1983-93. Fellow AAAS; mem. Health Physics Soc. (coun. Rio Grande chpt. 1988-90), N.Mex. Acad. Sci. Lutheran. Died Jan. 27, 2008.

**HANSON, FRED B.,** lawyer; b. Alexandria, Va. s. August Theodore and Flora Alice (Kays) H.; m. Jane Roberts, Oct. 24, 1934 (dec. Jan. 1971); m. Lucy Merrick, Dec. 10, 1971 (dec. Nov. 1987); children: Linscott, Per, Marta; m. Marilynn S. Lane, Aug. 12, 1989. Student, DePauw U., 1924-26, Northwestern U., 1927-28; LLB, Ill. Inst. Tech., 1932. Bar: Ind. 1925, Ill. 1932, U.S. Dist. Ct. (no. dist.) Ill. 1932. Ptnr. Ross, Berchem & Hanson, Chgo., 1932-34; sole practice Chgo., 1934-37 and from 52; atty. Standard Oil Co., Chgo., 1937-46; ptnr. Hanson & Doyle, Chgo., 1946-52, The Firm of Fred B. Hanson Assocs., Chgo., 1952-86; sole practice Chgo., from 1986. Gen. counsel., bd. dirs. various banks and cos. Author: Claim Handling, 1956; contbr. articles to profl. jours. Atty. Village of Glenview, 1950-54, judge, 1946-50; trustee Maryhaven, Glenview, 1946-72. Lt. sgt. USNR, 1943-46; PTO. Mem. ABA, Ill. Bar Assn., Chgo. Bar Assn., Chgo. Yacht Club. Democrat. Avocations: bridge, travel. Home: Sun Lakes, Ariz. Died Dec. 17, 2001.

**HANSON, JAMES EDWARD,** industrialist; b. Jan. 20, 1922; s. Robert and Louisa Ann Hanson; m. Geraldine Kaelin, 1959 (dec. 2004); children: Robert William, John Brook 1 stepchild, Karyn. Exec. chmn. Hanson PLC, London, 1965—97. Died Nov. 1, 2004.

**HANUS, BORIVOJ,** mechanical engineer, educator; b. Praha, Czech Republic, July 30, 1921; s. Ladislav Hanuš and Marie Vacková Hanušová; m. Blažena Beranová, June 26, 1958. Degree in Mech. Engring., České Vysoké Učení Technické, Praha, 1947; PhD, Czech Acad. Scis., Praha, 1959, DSc, 1980; automation prof., Tech. U., Liberec, Czech Republic, 1966. Steam turbine designer Českomoravská Kolben Daněk Factory, Praha, 1942—56; automation rschr. Závody Prumyslové Automatizace Enterprise, Praha, 1956—67; automation prof. Tech. U. Liberec, from 1967, inst. leader, 1968—70, dept. leader, 1970—75, 1984—86, vice dean, 1976—85, chmn. edn. coun., from 1995. Digital control cons. ČEZ Power Engring. Inst., Praha, 1968—70. Author: Technical Cybernetics Principles, 1986, Digital Control of Technological Processes, 2000, numerous textbooks; mem. editl. coun. Automatizace, from 1960. Recipient Trudovogo Krasnogo Znameni, State Order USSR, 1958; named Outstanding Worker, State Order Czech Republic, 1985, Deserving Tchr., Min. Edn. Czech Republic, 1981, Deserving Worker, Min. Machine Industry, 1983. Mem.: Czechoslovak Assn. Sci. and Tech. Socs., Czech Tech. Found., Nat. Com. Internat. Fedn. Automation Control. Avocations: reading, travel, history. Home: Prague, Czech Republic. Died Oct. 23, 2008.

**HARBIN, JOHN PICKENS (JACK HARBIN),** retired oil industry executive; b. Waxahachie, Tex., July 17, 1917; s. Elijah Pickens and Mary Joy (Beale) H.; m. Dorothy Lee Middleton, Dec. 13, 1940 (dec. 2002); children: Linda Ann Harbin Robuck. Student, Trinity U., San Antonio, 1935-37; BBA, U. Tex., 1939. Acct. Carter Oil Co., Tulsa, 1939-40, Creole Petroleum, Venezuela, 1940-42, 45-48; contr. Halliburton Co., Duncan, Okla., 1948-59, v.p. finance Duncan and Dallas, 1959-62, Dallas, 1962-67, sr. v.p. finance, 1967-72, chmn., CEO, 1972-83. Pres., trustee Boy Scout Cir. Ten Coun. Found., Dallas, 1967-96; elder Highland Park Presbyn. Ch. Named to The Coll. Bus. Hall of Fame, 1985, Tex. Bus. Hall of Fame, 1994; recipient Silver Beaver award Boy Scouts Circle Ten Coun., Disting. Eagle Scout award Mem. American Petroleum Inst. (hon. dir. 1983-2014), Petroleum Equip. Suppliers Assn. (pres. 1974), Tex. Rsch. League (bd. dirs., past chmn. 1978-79), Southwestern Med. Found., Navy League of U.S., Dallas Petroleum Club (past pres. and dir.), Brook Hollow Golf Club, Dallas Country Club (past dir.), The Brook Club, Beta Alpha Psi. Avocation: tennis. Home: Dallas, Tex. Died July 27, 2014.

**HARDER, ROBERT CLARENCE,** retired state official; b. Horton, Kans., June 4, 1929; s. Clarence L. and Olympia E. (Kubik) H.; m. Dorothy Lou Welty, July 31, 1953; children: Anne, James David. AB, Baker U., Baldwin, Kans., 1951; MTh, So. Meth. U., 1954; ThD in Social Ethics, Boston U., 1958; LHD (hon.), Baker U., 1983, Ottawa U., 1991. Ordained to ministry Meth. Ch., 1959; pastor East Topeka Meth. Ch., 1958-64; mem. Kans. House of Reps., 1961-67; rsch. assoc. Menninger Found., Topeka, 1964-65; instr. Washburn U., Topeka, 1964, 68, 69; dir. Topeka Office of Econ. Opportunity, 1965-67; tech. asst. coordinator to Gov. State of Kans., 1967-68; dir. community resources devel. League of Kans. Municipalities, 1968-69; dir. Kans. Dept. Social Welfare, Topeka, 1969-73, sec., 1973-87, Kans. Dept. Health and Environment, 1992—95; projects adminstr. Topeka State Hosp., 1987-89. Adj. prof. public adminstrn. Kans. U., 1987-95, instr. Sch. Social Welfare, 1971-87; cons. Menninger Topeka, 1991-92 Contbr. articles to profl. jours. Recipient Disting. Svc. award East Topeka Civic Assn., 1963, Romana Hood award, 1965, Cert. of Recognition, State of Kans., 1979, 87, Spl. Commendation award Kans. Senate, 1987, Spl. Commendation, Kans. Ho. of Reps., 1987, Outstanding Alumnus award Perkins Sch. Theology, So. Meth. U., 1994, M. L. King Jr. Living the Dream Humanitarian award, 1997, Disting. Svc. award Kans. Children's Svc. League, 1998, Grant award for Exceptional Volunteerism, 1999, Advocacy award Disability Caucus, 2003, cert. appreciation Scott Sch., 2003, Award of Excellence Friends Edn. Award, 2004, Cmty. Leader award Topeka Pub. Schs., 2004, others; named Outstanding Pub. Ofcl. of the Yr., 1987, Servant Leader award United Meth. Ch., East Kans. Conf., 2009. Mem. American Soc. Public Adminstrs. (Public Adminstr. of Yr. Kans. chpt. 1980), American Public Welfare Assn., Kans. Health Care Commn., Kans. Conf. Social Welfare (Outstanding Person of Yr. 1987). Democrat. Home: Topeka, Kans. Died Apr. 12, 2014.

**HARDY, SANDRA E.,** theater educator, director; b. Norwalk, Conn., Nov. 12, 1937; d. Edward and Vera (Spong) Hardy; life ptnr. Joanne S. Baumrind; 1 child, Jade Baumrind-Hardy. BA in English, Ctrl. Conn. U., 1958; MA in American Studies, Fairfield U., Conn., 1971; PhD in Theatre, NYU, 1981. Cert. standard tchr. Conn., 1971. Tchr. Ctrl. HS, Bridgeport, Conn., 1965—77; asst. prof. theatre Augustana Coll., Rock Island, Ill., 1982—85; assoc. prof. U. Maine, Orono, 1988—2014. Tchg. assistantship NYU, 1978—81. Musician (comedian) theatre, nightclubs, radio, TV; dir.: (theatre, nightclubs, radio, TV); contbr. articles to profl. jours. Mem.: SAG, AGVA, 802 Musician's Union NYC, American Guild of Variety Artist, Dramatist Guild, Assn. Teachers Higher Edn., American Coll. Theatre Festival (Hedcla Gayler Festival's Best Classic Translation award). Home: Bangor, Maine. Died June 19, 2014.

**HARGRAVE, RUDOLPH,** retired state supreme court justice; b. Shawnee, Okla., Feb. 15, 1923; s. John Hubert and Daisy (Holmes) Hargrave; m. Madeline Hargrave, May 29, 1949; children: Cindy Lu, John Robert, Jana Sue. LLB, U. Okla., 1949. Bar: Okla. 1949. Pvt. practice, Wewoka,

Okla., 1949—64; asst. county atty. Seminole County, 1951-55; judge Seminole County Ct., 1964-67, Seminole County Superior Ct., 1967-69; dist. judge Okla. Dist. Ct. (22nd dist.), 1969—78; justice Okla. Supreme Ct., Oklahoma City, 1978—2010, chief justice, 1989—90. Former v.p. Nat. Conf.Chief Justices; mem. Okla. Jud. Conf. Mem.: ABA, Okla. Bar Assn., Seminole County Bar Assn., Masons, Lions. Democrat. Methodist. Died Apr. 1, 2014.

**HARIMI, MOHAMED,** engineering educator; b. Algiers, Hussain-Dey, Algeria, Dec. 30, 1966; m. Amel Ouadah; 1 child, Ahlam. MSc in Mech. Engring., U. Putra Malaysia, 2000, PhD in Mech. Engring., 2006; M. Eng. in Gas Engring., Algerian Petroleum Inst., Boumerdes, Algeria, 1991. Rschr. U. Putra Malaysia, Selangor, 1997—2006; lectr. U. Malaysia Sabah (SKTM), Kota Kinabalu, from 2002. Cons. CIDB Malaysia, Selangor, 2003—05. Recipient Internat. Educator of Yr., IBC, Eng., 2007; named one of Outstanding Scientists of 21st Century, 2007. Mem.: Malaysian Palm Oil Bd. Islam. Achievements include Optimisation of fibre and shell from palm oil waste used in the incineration process; Guideline for Thermal Comfort, Roof Drainage and Supply Chain for Metal Roofs in Sabah. Avocations: travel, stamp collecting/philately. Home: Kota, Malaysia. Died Apr. 2009.

**HARITOS-FATOUROS, MIKA MARIA,** psychologist, psychotherapist; BA in Psychology, U. Coll., London, 1954; MA in Ednl. Psychology, London U., 1963. Assoc. prof. Aristotle U., Thessaloniki, Greece, 1975, prof., 1978, emeritus prof., 1999, rschr., 1999—2008. Vis. prof. psychology Panteion U., Athens, from 1999. Author: Violence Workers: Police Torturers and Murderers Reconstruct Brazilian Atrocities, 2003 (award New Eng. Coun. Latin Am. Studies, 2003, award Am. Soc. Criminology's Divsn. Internat. Criminology, 2003), Psychological Origins of Institutional Torture. Pres. com. for licence in psychology and psychotherapy Greek Ministry of Health, Athens, 1993—2001. Mem.: Greek Assn. Behavioral Rsch. & Therapy (pres.), European Assn. Counselling (v.p. from 2007). Achievements include research in street children, counselors without frontiers. Home: Athens, Greece. Deceased.

**HARLAND, PETER WINSTON,** retired publishing executive; b. Shipley, Eng., Oct. 19, 1934; s. Lawrence Winston and Rita Doreen (Harrison) H.; m. Jennifer Sutcliffe, May 6, 1961; children: Deborah Joy Margaret, David Winston. BA in History with honors, Sidney Sussex Coll., Cambridge, Eng., 1956. Dep. editor Chatham News, U.K., 1952-58; sub-editor No. Echo, Darlington, U.K., 1958-60, The Daily Telegraph, Manchester, 1960, Oxford (Eng.) Mail, 1961-65; editor Yorkshire Evening Press, York, Eng., 1965-66, Telegraph & Argus, Bradford, Eng., 1967-73; mng. editor Times Newspapers Ltd., London, 1973-81; mng. dir. Bookwatch Ltd., Amersham, 1982—2003. Judge Nat. Press Awards, 1970-73; nat. pres. Guild of Editors, U.K., 1970-71. Co-author: Race and the Press, 1970. Former chmn. Amersham & Chesham Bois Choral Soc.; mem. Thame (Eng.) Urban Dist. Coun., 1962-65; sec. Chiltern Christian Trust. Named Campaigning Journalist of the Yr., Nat. Press Awards, 1968. Anglican. Avocation: singing. Home: Eynsham, Witney, Oxford, England. Died June 7, 2005.

**HARPER, ELIZABETH A.,** retired occupational therapist; b. Rochester, Minn., Feb. 15, 1935; d. Ephraim John Koeneman and Margaret Richman; m. Gordon E. Harper, Dec. 28, 1957; children: William Jacque, James Walter. BS, Ohio State U., 1957. Staff occupl. therapist VA Hosp., Long Beach, Calif., 1957—59; dir. occupl. therapy Palo Alto (Calif.) Stanford Hosp. Ctr., 1959—63; basic motor skills specialist Portola Valley Sch. Dist., 1974—76; occupl. therapist sensory integration specialist Children's Hosp. Stanford, Palo Alto, 1976—78, Children's Health Coun., Palo Alto, 1978—89; occupl. therapist Santa Clara County Dept. Edn., 1989—91; occupl. therapy cons. pvt. practice Santa Clara, San Mateo, Calif., 1991—96; ret., from 1996. Sensory integration faculty mem. Sensory Integration Internat., Torrance, Calif., from 1976, sensory integration faculty mem. emeritus, from 1986. Mem.: Calif. Occupl. Therapy Assn., Am. Occupl. Therapy Assn. (registered occupl. therapist, alt. del.). Libertarian. Avocations: hiking, walking, swimming, gardening. Home: Portola Valley, Calif. Died 2003.

**HARRELL, CAROLYN LAWTON** See KILGORE, CAROLYN HARRELL

**HARRIS, CHARLES UPCHURCH,** seminary president, clergyman; b. Raleigh, NC, May 2, 1914; s. Charles Upchurch and Saidee (Robbins) H.; m. Janet Jeffrey Carlile, June 17, 1940; children: John C., Diana Jeffrey (Mrs. Melvin). BA, Wake Forest Coll., 1935, DHL (hon.), 1979; BD, Va. Theol. Sem., 1938, DD (hon.), 1958; postgrad., Union Theol. Sem., 1939-40; DCL (hon.), Seabury-Western Sem., 1972. Ordained deacon P.E. Ch., 1938, priest, 1939; rector All Saints Ch., Roanoke Rapids, N.C., 1938-39; asst. rector St. Bartholomew's Ch., NYC, 1939-40; rector Trinity Ch., Roslyn, L.I., 1940-46, Highland Park, Ill., 1946-57; pres., dean Seabury-Western Theol. Sem., Evanston, Ill., 1957-72, pres., dean emeritus, from 1972; dean Lake Shore Deanery; vicar St. John's Ch., Harbor Springs, Mich., 1969-85, vicar emeritus, from 1985; founder St. Gregory's Ch., Deerfield, Ill.; hon. canon St. James Cathedral, Chgo., 1975-82; pres. Episc. Theol. Sch., Claremont, Calif., 1977-82. Trustee Sch. of Theology, Claremont, 1979-82; chmn. exam. chaplains 5th and 6th provinces Episcopal Ch.; cons. nat. dept. Christian edn.; pres. Chgo. Inst. Advanced Theol. Studies, 1968-70; sec. Drafting Com. on Holy Eucharist, 1970-79; pres. Chgo. Inter-Sem. Faculties Union, 1971-72; vice chmn. N. Am. com. St. George's Coll., Jerusalem, 1981-83, pres, 1985-91; pres. Cyprus-Am. Archaeol. Inst., 1985-91, chmn., 1991, 98—; mem. exec. com. Nat. Cathedral, Washington, 1978-84, 95; v.p. Chgo. Inst. Advanced Theol. Studies, 1967-72; mem. Anglican Theol. Rev. Bd., 1959—, editor, 1971-72, pres., 1968-85, v.p., 1985—, pres. emeritus, 1991; mem. Am. Schs. Oriental Rsch., 1959—, trustee, 1969-72, 76-78, treas., 1984-87, chmn., CEO, 1992-94; hon. chmn. Inst. Christianity & Antiquities, Calif., 1996—; hon. pres. Cyprus Am. Archaeol. Rsch. Inst., 1997-98, chmn., 1998—. Author: (with A. LeCroy) Harris-Lecroy Report, 1975; contbr.: Sermons on Death and Dying, 1975; asst. editor Anglican Theol. Rev., 1958-71, editor, 1971-72. Trustee Little Traverse Conservancy, 1986; mem. bd. visitors Wake Forest U., 1979-94, Div. Sch. U. Chgo.; mem. bd. coun. Am. Rsch. Ctrs. Overseas, 1989-94, treas., 1991-95; mem. adv. com. Inst. for Antiquity and Christianity, 1987-94; mem. Com. of 40, Va. Theol. Sem., 1988-92. Mem. Am. Theol. Soc., Am. Acad. Religion, Soc. Bibl. Lit., Soc. Colonial Warriors, SAR, Conf. of Anglican Theologians. Clubs: University, Wequetonsing Golf (Harbor Springs); Little Sturgeon Trout; Desert Forest (Carefree, Ariz.). Home: Chicago, Ill. Died Sept. 16, 2001.

**HARRIS, EARL DOUGLAS,** state agency administrator; b. Athens, Ga., Apr. 9, 1947; s. Roland Russell and Martha Sue (Davis) H.; m. Jean Wright, Dec. 26, 1975; cchildren: Jeannette, Stephanie. BSAE, U. Ga., 1970, MBA, JD, 1973. Bar: Ga. 1973, U.S. Dist. Ct. (mid. dist.) Ga. 1973, U.S. Ct. Appeals (5th cir.) 1973, U.S. Ct. Claims 1977, U.S. Tax Ct. 1977, U.S. Patent Office 1977, U.S. Customs Ct. 1977, U.S. Supreme Ct. 1977, U.S. Ct. Customs and Patent Appeals 1980, U.S. Ct. Internat. Trade 1981, U.S. Ct. Appeals (5th, 11th and federal cir.) 1981. Sole practice of law and patent law, Watkinsville, Ga., 1973-76, 86-92; city atty. Town of Bogart, 1974-75, 85-90; sr. ptnr. Harris & Rice, Watkinsville, 1977-79; mem. Harris, Rice & Alford, P.A., Watkinsville, 1978-80; ptnr., pres. Harris & Alford, P.A., 1980-85; Ga. asst. commr. agr., from 1992. Mem. Ga. State Olympic Law Enforcement Commd., 1996; pres. Fed. Title Corp., 1978—90; county atty. Oconee County, Ga., 1978—80; atty. Town of Bishop, 1980—89; corp. sec. Lawlog Corp., 1980—90. Contbr. over 230 articles to profl. publs. Bd. dirs. The Oconee Enterprise, Inc., 1987-93, Clarke County unit Am. Cancer Soc., 1970-72, Ga. Fed. State Shipping Point Inspection Svc., Inc., 1995—; mem. Oconee County Dem. Exec. Com., 1976-94, treas., 1976-82; pres., trustee N.E. Ga. Presbytery, 1987-91; trustee Masonic Children's Home Ga., 1985-89; trustee, gen. counsel Ga. Scottish Rite Found., Inc., 1989-2000, chmn. bd., 2000—; pres., chmn. bd. dirs. Ga. Masonic Charities Found., Inc., 1996-98; active Boy Scouts Am. Served with USMC, 1965-68; with USAF, 1968. Mem. State Bar Ga., Alcovy Cir. Bar Assn., Western Cir. Bar Assn., Sphinx Soc., Gridiron Secret Soc., AGHON Soc. (past pres.), U. Ga. Agrl. Alumni Assn. (pres. young alumni div. 1975-76, dir. at Large, 1996-97, sec.-treas., 1997-99), Oconee County C. of C. (dir., sec. 1976-78), Masons (Past Grand Master of Masons in Ga., Wollstein award, Ga. Lodge of Rsch. Calloway award), Scottish Rite (33 degree, sovereign grand insp. den. Ga., mem. supreme coun. USA So. Jurisdiction), Order of Eastern Star (past patron), Societas Rosicruciana in Civitatibus Foederatis (IX grade, Chief Adept for Ga.), Shriners, KT (grand comdr. Ga., knight comdr. of the Templar nat. award), Tall Cedars of Lebanon, Royal Order of Scotland (Ga. screener), Red Cross of Constantine (Pussiant sovereign), Knights of York Grand Cross of Honor (past prior), York Rite Coll. (past gov.), Knight Templar Priests (past preceptor), Philathes Soc., Blue Key (past pres.), Omicron Delta Kappa, Sigma Iota Epsilon, Alpha Zeta, Phi Alpha Delta. Presbyterian (ruling elder). Died July 23, 2002.

**HARRIS, EARL EDWARD,** business educator; b. West Burlington, Iowa, Nov. 15, 1931; s. Earl and Anne M. (Mollen) H.; m. Evonne L. Meier, May 29, 1954; children: Julie Ann, James Edward. BA, U. No. Iowa, 1953; MA, U. Minn., 1949; Ed.D., No. Ill. U., 1965. Tchr. Davenport (Iowa) Community Schs., 1955-63; head bus. edn. dept. West High Sch., 1960-63; asst. prof. edn. No. Ill. U., DeKalb, 1963-64, assoc. prof., 1965-67, prof., 1968-89, prof. emeritus, from 1989, chmn. bus. edn. and adminstrv. services dept., 1973-81, dir. office of research Coll. of Bus., 1981-83. Exec. dir. Ill. Inst. for Entrepreneurship Edn., 1988-91, exec. dir. emeritus, 1991—; cons. in field; chmn. region V planning com. distributive end. U.S. Office Edn., 1966-69; moderator Ill. Ho. Small Bus. Conf., 1985;chmn. evaluation and publ. com. Nat. Council for Mktg. Edn., 1986-87; mem. State of Ill.'s Gov.'s Small Bus. Adv. Council, 1985-88, chmn. task force on regional econ. devel., 1985-87; mem. State of Ill. Entrepreneurship task force, chmn. strategic planning com., 1984-88; founder, dir. Ill. Inst. for Entrepreneurship Edn., 1988-91; co-chmn. State of Ill. Mktg. Edn. action team, 1984-87; chmn., trustee Nat. Distributive Edn. Profl. Devel. award, 1985-87. Author: An Articulated Guide for Cooperative Occupational Education, 1971, 78, Marketing Research, 1971, 78, Employer Preferences and Teacher Coordinator Practices, 1971, Methods of Teaching Business and Distributive Education, 3d edit, 1974, Retailing Principles and Practices, 7th edit, 1981, Handbook for Cooperative Vocational Education in Illinois, 1977, Annotated Bibliography of Instructional Materials in Cooperative Vocational Education, 1977, State of Illinois Marketing and Distributive Education curriculum Planning Guide, 1978, Curriculum Guide in Food Marketing, 1978, Curriculum Guide in Wholesaling, 1978, Curriculum Guide in General Retail Merchandising, 1978, Curriculum Guide in Finance and Credit, 1979 in Transportation and Warehousing, 1980, in Automotive and Petroleum, 1981, State of Illinois Management Model for Economic Development, 1984, Strategies for Maximizing the Contributions of Small Business and Economic Development, 1985, Marketing Ventas Al Pan Menor, 1991, others; editor: Nat. Bus. Edn. Yearbook, 1976, Retail Store Planning and Design Manual, 1986, Ill. Devel. Council News vol. 6, nos. 1 and 2, 1986, Retail Marketing for Employers, Managers and Entrepreneurs, 1988, internat. edit., 1989, Inservice Guide for Entrepreneurship Education in Illinois, 1988; editor mktg. and distbn. sect.: Nat. Bus. Forum, 1976-77; mng. editor: Mktg. and Distributive Educators' Digest, 1981-84; contbr. articles to profl. jours., chpts. to books. Mem. DeKalb County Devel. Corp., 1974-88; bd. dirs. Ill. Found. Mktg. Edn., 1965—; bd. dirs. Ill. Devel. Coun., 1983-89, also life mem.; bd. govs. Yavapai Coll., Prescott, Ariz., 1994—; mem. steering and exec. coms. 20/20 Forum, Prescott, 1993—; bd. dirs. Yavapai Coll. Found., 1995—. Recipient Outstanding Svc. award Distributive Clubs Am., 1963, Outstanding Svc. award Ill. chpt., 1967, Teaching Excellence award No. Ill. U., 1969, Man of Yr. award Distributive Edn. Clubs Ill., 1972, Svc. award Distributive Edn. Clubs Ill., Disting. Svc. award State of Ill. Bus. Edn., 1983, Disting. Svc. award Nat. Mktg. Edn. Assn., 1986, Leavey award Freedom Found., 1988, Nat. award Freedom Found., 1987, Mktg. Educator of Yr. award Sales and Mktg. Execs., 1988, Disting. Alumni award No. Ill. U., 1988, Golden Medallion award SBA, 1988, Entrepreneur of Yr. award Ernest and Young Inc. Mag., 1989, Disting. Svc. award Vocat. Edn. and Pers. Devel. Assn., 1989, Disting. Svc. award Ill. Devel, Coun.; named to nat. entrepreneuship Hall of Fame Inst. Am. Entrepreneurs, 1989. Fellow U.S. Assn. Small Bus. and Entrepreneurship (bd. dirs., v.p 1988); mem. Am. Vocat. Assn. (life chmn. distributive edn. publs. com. 1966-74, evaluation com. 1981-82), Ill. Bus. Tchr. Edn. Assn. (sec., pres. 1976-79, outstanding svc. award 1983), Nat. Bus. Edn. Assn., Mktg. and Distributive Edn. Assn. (life mem., chmn. coms.), Nat. Assn. Distributive Edn. Tchrs. (life), Council Distributive Tchr. Educators, Ill. Co-op. Vocat. Edn. Coordinators Assn. (dir.), Ill., Ill. Found. for MKtg. Edn. (bd. dirs. 1968—), Nat. Mktg. Edn. Found. (bd. dirs. 1987—), Secondary Mktg. and Distributive Edn. Coordinators Assn. (dir.), Delta Pi Epsilon (life), Pi Omega Pi, Beta Gamma Sigma. Presbyterian (ruling elder). Deceased.

**HARRIS, EWING JACKSON,** lawyer; b. Sylvia, Tenn., Mar. 17, 1901; s. John Chastain and Sarah Frances (Walker) H.; m. Lena Sue Hartman, Mar. 28, 1931; children: Frances Ann Scott, Marjorie Sue Lucht, Ewlene. LLB, Cumberland U., 1928. Bar: Tenn. 1928. Pvt. practiced, Bolivar, from 1932; city atty., 1942—85; county atty. Hardeman County, 1942—70; dir. Bank Bolivar; pres. State Bd. Elections, 1949—53. Mem. Tenn. State Senate, 1937—39; del. Tenn. Constl. Conv., 1965. Fellow: Am. Coll. Probate Counsel; mem.: C. of C., Am. Judicature Soc., Hardeman County Bar Assns., Spl. Joint Com., Tenn., America, Rotary, Masons, Phi Beta Gamma. Methodist. Home: Bolivar, Tenn. Died Sept. 26, 1994.

**HARRIS, GUY HENDRICKSON,** chemical research engineer; b. San Bernardino, Calif., Oct. 2, 1914; s. Edwin James and Nellie Mae (Hendrickson) H.; m. Elsie Mary Dietsch, Mar. 15, 1940; children: Alice, Robert, Mary, Sara. AA, San Bernardino Valley Coll., 1934; BS, U. Calif., Berkeley, 1937; AM, Stanford U., 1939, PhD, 1941. Analytical chemist Shell Devel. Co., Emeryville, Calif., 1937-38; organic chemist William S. Merrell Co., Cin., 1941-45; rsch. chemist Fiber Bd., Emeryville, 1945-46; from organic chemist to assoc. scientist The Dow Chem. Co., Pittsburg, Calif., 1946-62, assoc. scientist Walnut Creek, Calif., 1964-82; sr. lectr. U. Ghana, Legon Accra, 1962-64; chmn. dept. chemistry John F. Kennedy U., Orinda, Calif., 1964-69; pvt. practice cons. Concord, Calif., 1982-88; rsch. engr. U. Calif., Berkeley, from 1988; prof. (hon.) Huainan Inst. Tech., China, 2000. Contbr. K & O Encyclopedia Chem. Tech., 1959, 70, 84, 97, Reagents in Mineral Tech., 1990. Fellow AAAS, Royal Soc. Chemistry; mem. AIME, Soc. Mining Engrs. (disting. mem.), Bus. Men's Fellowship USA, The Commonwealth Club, Sigma Xi. Roman Catholic. Achievements include 51 patents in field of mineral processing reagents in particular Z200 (R) agricultural chemicals and process for manufacture. Deceased.

**HARRIS, HENRY WILLIAM,** physician; b. Catawba, NC, Jan. 6, 1919; s. Henry William and Katie (Coulter) H.; m. Margaret Ann Roberts, Nov. 29, 1950; children: Henry William, John R., James P. BA, U.N.C., 1940; MD cum laude, Harvard U., 1943. Diplomate: in pulmonary disease Am. Bd. Internal Medicine. Intern Harvard Med. Service, Boston City Hosp., 1944-45, asst. resident medicine, 1945-46; resident fellow Thorndike Meml. Lab., 1944, 46; resident chest service Bellevue Hosp., NYC, 1947; staff physician Gundersen Clinic, LaCrosse, Wis., 1948-53; asst. prof. medicine U. Utah Coll. Medicine, 1955-59, asso. prof., 1959-60; chief pulmonary disease service VA Hosp., Salt Lake City, 1955-60; prof. chmn. dept. medicine Woman's Med. Coll. of Pa., 1960-67; chmn. dept. medicine Catholic Med. Center Bklyn. and Queens, 1967-70; asso. prof. clin. medicine N.Y.U. Sch. Medicine, 1969-70, prof., from 1970. Adj. staff chest svc. Bellevue Hosp., N.Y.C.; hon. staff Tisch Hosp., N.Y.C.; sr. coms. Bur. Tb, Dept. of Health, N.Y.C., 1989-2004. Mem. editorial bd.: Annals of Internal Medicine, 1976-80; Contbr. articles to profl. publs. Bd. dirs. Am. Lung Assn., 1961-79, v.p., 1972-73; bd. dirs. N.Y. Lung Assn., 1974-95, v.p., 1983—, pres. 1987-90; bd. dirs. Am. Bur. Med. Advancement in China, 1978-2005, v.p., 1983-87, pres. 1987-92, chmn. H. Wm. Harris vis. prof. com., 1986-96. Served to capt., M.C. AUS, 1953-55. Fellow ACP; mem. Am. Thoracic Soc. (pres. 1962-63). Died Dec. 19, 2011.

**HARRIS, J. OLLIE,** state legislator; b. Anderson, SC, Sept. 2, 1913; s. J. Frank and Jessie (Hambright) H.; m. Abbie Jane Wall; children: J. Ollie Jr., Jane Wall. Grad., Cupton-Jones Coll. of Embalming, Nashville, 1934. Lic. enbalmer, Tenn., 1935. With Lutz-Jackson Funeral Home (later Lutz-Austell Funeral Home), Shelby, 1928-47; owner Harris Funeral Home, Kings Mountain, Tenn., from 1947; mem. N.C. State Senate, 1971-72, 75-82. Chmn. human resources com. N.C. State Senate, 1977, 79, 81, vice-chmn. ways and means and sr. citizens coms.; mem. senate rules com., banking com., judiciary #1 com., appropriation com.,

Univ. Bd. Govs. com., Govtl. Ops. com. Mem. Mental Health Study Commn., Mental Health, Mental Retardation, Alcohol, and Drug Abuse Commn; pres. Kings Mountain chpt. ARC; former pres. Kings Mountain C. of C., trustee Gardner-Webb Coll.; active Shelby Vol. Fire Dept., 1934, Kings Mountain Fire Dept., 1969; coroner Cleveland County, Tenn., 1946-70. Former chmn. Bd. Deacons Kings Mountain Bapt. Ch. Served with U.S. Army, 1943-45, ETO. Recipient Veland award, 1979, Outstanding Legislator in Pub. Health award N.C. Assn. Health Depts., 1979, award N.C. Council of Mental Health, Mental Retardation and Substance Abuse, 1987; named Outstanding Legislator N.C. Health Care Assn., 1979. Mem. N.C. Funeral Dirs.' Assn. (pres. 1960), N.C. State Bd. Enbalmers (pres. 1958), Am. Legion (past commdr. Kings Mountain chpt.), VFW (past commdr. Kings Mountain, Shelby chpts.). Clubs: Kings Mountain Country (past pres.). Lodges: Lions (past pres. Kings Mountain club). Deceased.

**HARRIS, MARVIN DEWITT,** special education educator; b. Baton Rouge, Sept. 19, 1964; s. Willie Harris and Cherrie (Woodlief) Seales. BA in Spl. Edn., So. U., Baton Rouge, 1988. Cert. tchr., La. Spl. edn. tchr. East Baton Rouge Parish Sch. Bd., 1989-96, dean students, from 1996. Grant writer in field. Mem. com. Boy Scouts Am., Baton Rouge, 1991-92; vol. coach Spl. Olympics, Park Elem. Sch., chmn. "I Care", 1995; coord. edn. Park Clinic/Park Elem. Connection, 1995. Acad. Distinction Fund grantee, 1994-95. Mem. La. Fedn. Tchr.-AFT. Democrat. Seventh Day Adventist. Avocations: photography, music, computers, reading, art. Home: Baton Rouge, La. Died Oct. 12, 1997.

**HARRIS, T. GEORGE,** editor; b. Hillsdale, Ky., Oct. 4, 1924; s. Garland and Luna (Byrum) Harris; m. Sheila Hawkins, Oct. 31, 1952 (dec. Jan. 1977); children: Amos, Anne, Crane, Gardiner; m. Ann Rockefeller Roberts, Mar. 3, 1979 (div. Apr. 1993); children: Clare, Joseph, Mary Louise, Rachel Pierson; m. Jeannie Pinkerton, Sept. 12, 1998; 1 child, Arthur Joseph Clancy (dec.). Student, U. Ky., 1946, Oxford U., 1948, Yale U., PBK, 1949. Reporter Clarksville (Tenn.) Leaf-Chronicle, 1942; corr. Time-Life, Dallas, Atlanta and Washington, 1949—55; Chgo. bur. chief Time-Life-Fortune, 1955-58, San Francisco bur. chief, 1960-62; sr. editor Look mag., 1962-68; editor in chief Psychology Today mag., 1969-76, 88-90, US, 1977; founding editor Am. Health mag., Behavior Today, AH Fitness Monthly, Spirituality & Health, 1980-90; exec. editor Harvard Bus. Rev., Boston, 1992-93; cons. Beliefnet.com, from 1993, Procter & Gamble Creative Svcs. Group, from 1993; editor UCSD-Connect Hi-tech. Weekly, 2000—08. Sci. adv. ABC's 20/20 Program, Inst. Advancement of Health. Editor: WGBH TV Bodywatch on PBS Weekly; cons. editor Sci. & Spirit, Next, Runner, Somatics, Aware, Industry Week, Psychologia Contemporanea, Japanese Man the Mystery, Modern Maturity, Psychologie Heute, Science & Spirit Mags., Addison-Wesley Pub. Co., Abby Press of Benedictine Order, Age Wave, columnist Beliefnet.com. Bd. dirs. Am. Health Found., Church Soc. for Coll. Work, Nat. Vol. Ctrs., Rockefeller Bros. Fund, Go Code Corp.; med. adv. US YMCA; regent Cathedral of St. John the Divine, NYC. Staff sgt. US Army, WWII. Recipient Bronze Star for Heroism, Battlefield Commn. for leadership under fire at Bastogne, Belgium; named Ky. Col., 2001; named to U. Ky. Hall of Fame, 2008. Mem.: Time-Life Alumni, Century Assn., Yale Club NYC, UCSD Faculty Club, La Jolla Beach and Tennis Club, Phi Beta Kappa. Episcopalian. Died Oct. 23, 2012.

**HARRIS, WILLIAM JOHN,** retired management holding company executive, consultant; b. Hamilton, Ont., Can., Feb. 6, 1928; s. William Frederick and Leila Matilda (Rodway) H.; m. Grace Edna Paddock, Oct. 12, 1957; children: Jeffrey Louis, Susan Marie, Laura Ann. Student, Wash. U., St. Louis, 1949-51. Sales and advt. mgr. Tuckett Ltd. (subs. Imperial Tobacco), Hamilton, 1951-64; mktg. mgr. Imperial Tobacco divsn. Imasco Ltd., Montreal, Que., Can., 1965-75, corp. sec., 1976-79; sr. v.p. Imasco Ltd., Montreal, 1980-89, ret., 1989. Cons. in field, 1990—. Recipient Gold Medal award Assn. Can. Advertisers Inc., 1979. Roman Catholic. Avocations: music, gardening, carpentry, golf. Died Aug. 22, 2003.

**HARRISON, BETTINA HALL,** retired biology professor; b. Foxboro, Mass. d. Malcolm Bridges and Rita Louise (Busiere) Hall; m. John W. Harrison, July 12, 1941 (dec.); children: John W., Deborah, Christine. BS, U. Mass., 1939; AM, Radcliffe Coll., 1940; PhD, Boston U., 1968. Faculty Lasell Jr. Coll., Auburndale, Mass., 1940-41, 52-56, Maine Mills Lab., 1941-43, 49-51; with Cen. Main Hosp., 1943-45; faculty biology U. Mass., Boston, 1965—96; ret., 1996. Contbr. articles to profl. jours. Life corporator Boston Mus. Sci. Mem.: AAAS, N.Y. Acad. Sci., New Eng. Soc. Electron Microscopy (pres. 1963—64). Deceased.

**HARRISON, EARL GRANT, JR.,** educational administrator; b. Media, Pa., Oct. 10, 1932; s. Earl Grant and Carol Rogers (Sensenig) H.; m. Jean Spencer Young, July 6, 1957; children: Colin Young, Dana How. BA, Haverford Coll., 1954, LLD (hon.), 1991; BDiv, Yale U., 1959; MA in Social and Philos. Founds. Edn., Columbia U., 1965. Instr. Religion and Philosophy Antioch Coll., 1956-58; dir. Coun. Religion Ind. Schs., NYC, 1959-64; tchr. Bklyn. Friends Sch., 1964-65; dir. religious edn. William Penn Charter Sch., Phila., 1965-68; headmaster Westtown (Pa.) Sch., 1968-78; head of sch. Sidwell Friends Sch., Washington, 1978-98. Interim exec. dir. Friends Coun. on Edn., Phila., 2000-01; bd. mgrs. Haverford Coll., 1973-85; mem. instl. rev. bd. Nat. Eye Inst., 1987-2003; trustee The Kendal Corp., 1999-2003. Trustee Good Hope Sch., St. Croix, 1974-80, 82-88. Mem. The Headmasters Assn. (v.p. 1986-87), Country Day Headmasters Assn. (pres. 1992-93), Assn. Ind. Schs. Greater Washington (pres. 1989-90). Democrat. Avocations: tennis, travel. Died 2003.

**HARRISON, WILLIAM NEAL,** author, educator; b. Dallas, Oct. 29, 1933; m. Merlee Portman, Feb. 1, 1959; children: Laurie, Sean, Quentin. BA, Tex. Christian U., 1955; MA, Vanderbilt U., 1960; postgrad., U. Iowa, 1961-62. Prof. English U. Ark., 1968—2013. Bd. dirs. Associated Writing Programs, 1970—75; bd. advisors Ark. Natural & Cultural Heritage Commn., 1976—81. Author: (novels) The Theologian, 1965, In a Wild Sanctuary, 1969, Lessons in Paradise, 1971, Roller Ball Murder and Other Stories, 1975, Africana, 1976, Savannah Blue, 1981, Burton and Speke, 1982, Three Hunters, 1989, The Buddha in Malibu: Stories, 1998, The Blood Latitudes, 2000, Texas Heat and Other Stories, 2005, Black August, 2011; (screenplays) Rollerball, 1975, Mountains of the Moon, 1990. Guggenheim Meml. fellow, 1973-74 Home: Fayetteville, Ark. Died Oct. 22, 2013.

**HART, CHARLES ANTHONY,** microbiology educator, researcher, physician; b. Stockton-on-Tees, Durham, Eng., Feb. 25, 1948; s. Edmund and Alice Edna (Griffin) H.; m. Jennifer Ann Bonnett, June 25, 1971 (dec. Sept. 21, 2007); children: Caroline Joanne, Rachel Louise, Laura Jane. BSc, London U., 1969, B in Medicine and Surgery, 1972, PhD, 1978. Wellcome rsch. scholar Royal Free Hosp. Sch. of Medicine, London, 1974-76; registrar Liverpool (Eng.) Health Authority, 1977-78; MRC rsch. fellow U. Liverpool, 1978, lectr., 1979-82, sr. lectr., 1983-86, prof., from 1986. Hon. cons. med. microbiology Royal Liverpool Children's Hosp., 1983—; vis. prof. U. Santo Tomas, Manila, 1987; co-dir. Nat. Ctr. for Zoonosis Rsch., 2006—. Author: Colour Atlas of Pediatric Infectious Diseases, Handbook of Childhood Infections, Color Atlas of Medical Microbiology, Microterrors, Sexually Transmitted Infections and AIDS in the Tropics; editor: Annals of Tropical Medicine, Jour. Infection, Transactions Royal Soc. Tropical Medicine. Fellow Royal Coll. Pathologists, Royal Coll. Paediatrics and Child Health, Royal Soc. Tropical Medicine; mem. Liverpool Paediatric Club (pres. 1991-93), Liverpool Med. Instn. (pres. 2002-03). Avocations: music, squash, gardening, sailing. Home: Thingwall/Wirral, England. Died Sept. 21, 2007.

**HARTGEN, VINCENT ANDREW,** museum director, educator, artist; b. Reading, Pa., Jan. 10, 1914; s. William J. and Jane (Hadfield) H.; m. Frances Caroline Lubanda, July 6, 1940; children: David Thomas, Stephen Anthony. BFA, U. Pa., 1940, MFA, 1941; DFA (hon.), U. Maine, 1987. Traveling curator Anna Hyatt Huntington Exhbn. of Sculptures, 1937-39; dir. U. Maine Art Gallery; prof., head art dept. U. Maine, 1946-75, John H. Huddilston prof. art, 1962-82, John H. Huddilston prof. emeritus, 1983—2002, curator art collections, 1975-82. Art adviser Cultural Olympics, U. Pa., 1939-41; mem. Gov.'s Commn. Arts and Humanities, 1966-70 Works in collections including, Boston Mus. Fine Arts, Brooks Meml. Mus., Memphis, Howard U. Collection, John and Norma Marin Collection, Mus. Contemporary Arts, Houston, Wichita (Kans.) Art Mus., Butler Inst. ARts, Youngstown, Ohio, Everhart Mus., Scranton, Pa., U. Maine, Art Collection, Wadsworth Atheneum, Hartford, Smith, Colby colls., Reading (Pa.) Mus., Phoenix Art Mus., ITT Collection, Brandeis U., Elvejhem (Wis.) Mus., Kalamazoo Inst. Coll., Walker Art Inst., Mpls., Sheldon Swope Gallery, Terre Haute, Ind., one-man exhibits include Binet Gallery, N.Y.C., Md. Inst., Howard U., Everhart Mus., Claflin U., Coll. of Pacific, U. Idaho, Bermuda Art Assn., Chase Gallery N.Y., Farnsworth Mus., Rockland, Maine, State Dept. Art in the Embassies, Fifty Drawings Cen. Place Gallery, Bangor, Maine Art Gallery, 1992, U. Maine, 1994; also more than 150 throughout mus. and galleries in U.S. Trustee Haystack Mountain Sch. Crafts, Liberty, Maine, 1953-55. Served with U.S. Army, 1942-45. U. Pa. fellow; recipient BAID award, 1935, Soldier Art award, 1945; Audubon Artists award, 1950, Audubon Artists medal for creative aquarelle, 1965, Silver medal Audubon Artists, 1974, Distinguished Faculty award, 1965, Gov.'s Art award State of Maine, 1967, Franklin Mint Bicentiennial Medal Design award, 1972, U. Maine Alumni Black Bear award, 1974; named A Maine State Treasure State of Maine Dept. Edn., 1994. Mem. AAUP, Audubon Artists, Am. Watercolor Soc., Phi Kappa Phi. Home: Orono, Maine. *To have lived, and to have seen such an incredible and beautiful world as this is to easily understand my consummate joy in having been an artist and teacher for such a long life.* Died Nov. 27, 2002.

**HARTMAN-IRWIN, MARY FRANCES,** retired language professional; b. Portland, Oreg., Oct. 18, 1925; d. Curtiss Henry Sabisch and Gladys Frances (Giles) Strand; m. Harry Elmer Hartman, Sept. 6, 1946 (div. June 1970); children: Evelyn Frances, Laura Elyce, Andrea Candace; m. Thomas Floyd Irwin, Apr. 11, 1971. BA, U. Wash., 1964-68; postgrad., Seattle Pacific, 1977-79, Antioch U., Seattle, Wash., 1987, Heritage Inst., 1987. Lang. educator Kennewick (Wash.) Dist. # 17, 1970-88. Guide Summer Study Tours of Europe, 1971-88. Sec. Bahai Faith, 1971-99, libr., 2000, Pasco, Washington, 1985-88; trustee Mid. Columbia coun. Girl Scouts U.S. Fulbright scholar, 1968. Mem. NEA, Wash. Edn. Assn., Kennewick Edn. Assn., Nat. Fgn. Lang. Assn., Wash. Fgn. Lang. Assn., Literacy Coun. (literacy tutor Tillamook Bay C.C.). Avocations: painting, sewing, writing essays and short stories. Deceased.

**HARTMANN, ULRICH,** retired diversified financial services company executive; b. Berlin, Aug. 7, 1938; s. Alfred Hartmann; m. Inge Hartmann; 2 children. Law student, Munich, Berlin and Bonn, 1958-67. Auditor Tereuarbeit AG, Düsseldorf, 1967-71; asst. to bd. mgmt. Deutsche Leasing AG, Frankfurt, 1971-72; corporate counsel VEBA Kraftwerke Ruhr AG, Gelsenkirchen, 1973-75; head bd. office and pub. rels. VEBA AG, Düsseldorf, 1975-80; mem. bd. mgmt. Nordwestdeutsche Kraftwerke AG, Hamburg, 1980-85, Preussenelektra AG, Hannover, 1985-89; CFO, mem. bd. mgmt. VEBA AG, 1990—93, CEO, chmn. bd. mgmt., 1993—2007. Died Jan. 13, 2014.

**HARTSFIELD, HENRY WARREN, JR., (HANK HARTSFIELD),** retired astronaut; b. Birmingham, Ala., Nov. 21, 1933; s. Henry Warren and Alice Norma (Sorrell) H.; m. Judy Frances Massey, June 30, 1957; children: Judy Lynn, Keely Warren (dec. March 10, 2014) BS, Auburn U., 1954; postgrad., Duke U., 1954-55, Air Force Inst. Tech., 1960-61; MS, U. Tenn., 1970; DSc (hon.), Auburn U., 2006. Commd. 2d lt. USAF, 1955, advanced through grades to col., 1974, assigned to tour with 53d Tactical Fighter Squadron Bitburg, Fed. Republic Germany, 1961-64; instr. USAF Test Pilot Sch., Edwards AFB, Calif., 1965-66; assigned to Manned Orbiting Lab. USAF, 1966-69; astronaut, NASA Lyndon B. Johnson Space Ctr., 1969-97, mem. support crew Apollo 16, Skylabs 2, 3, 4 missions, pilot STS-4; comdr. STS-41D, STS-61A; ret., 1977; civilian astronaut NASA; dep. dir. Flight Crew Ops. Directorate, 1987-89; dir. tech. integration and analysis Office Space Flight, NASA Hqrs., 1989-90; dep. dir. ops. space sta. projects Marshall Space Flight Ctr. NASA, 1990-91; mgr. man-tended capability phase Space Sta. Freedom Program, 1991-94; mgr. Internat. Space Sta. Ind. Assessment at Johnson Space Ctr., 1994-97; ret., 1998; dir. Houston ops. Raytheon Sys. Co., 1998-99; v.p. aerospace engrng. svcs. Raytheon Tech. Svcs. Co., 1999—2005. In space: 483 hours. Decorated Meritorious Service medal, D.S.M. NASA, 1982, 88, Space Flight medal NASA, 1982, 84, 85; recipient Nat. Geog. White Space Trophy, 1973; named to The US Astronaut Hall of Fame, 2006 Mem. Soc. Exptl. Test Pilots, Air Force Assn., Sigma Pi Sigma Home: Seabrook, Tex. Died July 17, 2014.

**HARTSHORN, ROLAND DEWITT,** lawyer; b. Cordele, Ga., May 27, 1921; s. George DuBois and Nola Nancy (Redwine) Hartshorn; m. Mildred Stromick, Aug. 15, 1953; children: Marie Anne Hartshorn Kuhn, Elizabeth Lee, Roland David. JD, Emory U., 1948. Bar: Ga. 1948, Va. 1956, DC 1956. Pvt. practice, Atlanta, 1948—50, 1956—70; ptnr. Thomas, Thomas & Hartshorn, Springfield, Va., 1970—75, Holst & Hartshorn, Arlington, Va., Falls Church, Va., from 1975. Served to capt. US Army, 1950—56. Mem.: Fairfax County Bar Assn., Moose, Lions. Republican. Presbyterian. Home: Falls Church, Va. Died Feb. 19, 1994.

**HARTWELL, PATRICIA LOCHRIDGE,** educator, editor; b. Austin, Tex., Sept. 22, 1916; d. Lloyd Pampel and Franklyn Ware (Blocker) Lochridge; m. Henry Nelson Bull, Dec. 17, 1945 (div.); children: Stephen Medaris, Jefferson Lochridge; m. Dickson Jay Hartwell, Aug. 6, 1953 (dec.); children: Jay Craig, Ware Blocker. BA, Wellesley Coll., Mass., 1937; MS, Columbia U., NYC, 1938. Dir. info. Children's Fund, UNICEF, NYC; edtor The Arizonian, Scottsdale; exec. dir. Fine Arts Commn., Scottsdale, 1976, Arts Coun. Hawaii, Honolulu, 1976—80; adj. lectr. dept. journalism U. Hawaii, Honolulu, 1983—93. Editor: Artreach, 1985—90; contbr. articles to mags. Bd. dirs. Arts Coun. Hawaii, 1981—88. Mem.: Kaneohe Yacht Club. Democrat. Presbyterian. Home: Honolulu, Hawaii. Died Dec. 28, 1998.

**HARVAN, SEAN C.,** marketing executive; b. Monsey, NY, Nov. 25, 1970; BS in Polit. Sci., Ariz. State U., 1993. Devel. officer, dir. prospect rsch. The Rockefeller U., NYC, 1994-96; project dir. Interpub. Group of Cos., Inc., NYC, 1997-98, McCann Erickson, Tokyo, from 1999. Cons. Asahi Breweries Ltd., Tokyo, 1999—. Republican. E-mail: sean. Home: Tokyo, Japan. Died May 12, 2008.

**HARVEY, WALTER H(AYDEN),** hematologist, medical oncologist; b. Shreveport, La., Feb. 12, 1949; s. Max Richard and Marion Lee (Polk) Campbell; 1 child, Erica Dawn. BS, Ea. Tenn. State U., Johnson City, 1971; DO, Kirksville Coll. Osteo, Medicine, Kirksville, Mo., 1976. Diplomate Am. Osteo. Bd. Internal Medicine, Med. Oncology, Hematology. Rsch. chemist Beecham Pharms. Rsch. Divsn., Bristol, Tenn., 1971-72; intern Riverside Hosp. of Wichita (Kans.), 1976-77, resident in internal medicine, 1977-79; fellow jr. faculty Am. Cancer Soc.-M.D. Anderson Cancer Ctr., Houston, 1979-80; fellow in hematology and med. oncology Brooke Army Med. Ctr., San Antonio, 1980-82, dir. bone marrow transplant program, 1983-87; chief divsn. hematology and oncology Darnall Army Hosp., Ft. Hood, Tex., 1982-83; dir. bone marrow transplant lab., clin. rsch. U. Tex. Med. Br., Galveston, 1987-91; pvt. practice clin. rsch. Ft. Myers, Fla., 1991-93; clin. rschr. Hematology/Oncology Assocs. S.W. Fla., Naples, from 1993. Maj. M.C., U.S. Army, 1980-87. Recipient Army Svc. Ribbon, 1982, Army Commendation Medal, 1983, Meritorious Svc. medal, 1987, Def. Svc. Medal Desert Shield, 1990. Fellow Am. Coll. Osteo. Internists (achievement award 1997); mem. AMA, AAAS, Internat. Soc. for Hematotherapy and Graft Engring., Am. Osteo. Assn., Assn. Mil. Osteo. Physicians and Surgeons, Assn. Mil. Surgeons U.S., S.W. Oncology Group, Am. Soc. Clin. Oncology, Pediat. Oncology Group, Am. Soc. Hematology, Am. Soc. for Blood and Marrow Transplantation, So. Med. Assn., So. Assn. for Oncology (founder), Fla. Soc. Clin. Oncology, Multinat. Assn. Supportive Care in Cancer, Lee County Med. Soc., Collier County Med. Soc., Am. Cancer Soc. (chmn. lung cancer task force 1991-94), Leukemia Soc. Am. (exec. com. 1993-94, adv. com. 1994—). Avocations: tag and release billfishing, gardening, hiking, snorkeling. Deceased.

**HARVEY-JONES, JOHN HENRY,** retired chemical company executive; b. London, Apr. 16, 1924; s. Mervyn and Eileen Harvey-Jones; m. Mary Evelyn Bignell, 1947; 1 child. Grad. student, Royal Naval Coll., Dartmouth, Devon, Eng.; LLD, LLD, U. Manchester, 1985; LLD, U. Liverpool,

1986, U. London, 1987, Cambridge U., 1987; DSc (hon.), U. Bradford, 1986; DSc, U. Leicester, 1986, U. Keele, 1989, Exeter Coll., 1989. Commd. officer Royal Navy, 1937—56, advanced grades to lt. comdr.; ret., 1956; with Imperial Chem. Industries Plc, London, 1956—87, techno-commercial dir., 1967, dep. chmn. HOC div., chmn. petrochem. divsn., 1970—73, dep. chmn., 1978—82, chmn., 1982—87; chancellor U. Bradford, 1986—91; non-exec. chmn. Burns Anderson Bus. Internat. Bd. Com.; non-exec. dep. chmn. Grand Met. Ltd.; non-exec. dir. Guinness Peat Aviation Ltd., 1987—2008; chmn. Economist Newspaper Ltd., 1989—94, Parallax Enterprises Ltd., 1987—96; v.p. Consel Europeen des Federations de L'Industrie Chimique, 1982—84, pres., 1984—86; vice-chair Policy Studies Inst., 1980—85; chmn. coun. St. James' and Abbey Sch., Malvern, 1987, Woldfowl Trust, 1987—94; pres. Wider Share Owner Ship Coun., 1988—2008; mem. Book Trust Appeal Fund, 1987—2008; v.p. Hearing and Speech Trust, 1985—2008, Heaton Woods Trust, 1986—2008. Mem. coun. Youth Enterprise Scheme, 1984—86; vice chmn. Gt. Ormond St. Redevel. Appeal; v.p. Newnham Coll. Appeal, 1987; mem. ct. govs. Kidney Rsch. Unit Wales Found., 1989—90; mem. Manpower Svcs. Commn. Author: Making it Happen, Reflections on Leadership, 1987, Troubleshooter, 1990, Getting it Together, 1991, TV series include Troubleshooter, Troubleshooter Spls. Trustee The Sci. Mus., 1983—87, The Police Found., 1983—2008. Decorated Comdr. Order Brit. Empire, Comdr.'s Cross Order Merit Germany; recipient Nat. Tng. awards, 1987, City ad Guilds Insignia award, 1987, award excellence, Internat. Assn. Bus. Communicators, 1991; named Radar Man of Yr., 1987, Pipesmaker of Yr., 1991; sr. ind. fellow Leicester Poly., 1990. Mem.: English Speaking Union (gov. 1987—2008), Confedn. Brit. Industry (mem. pres. com.), Indsl. Participation Assn. (v.p. 1983—2008), Inst. Mktg. (hon. v.p.), Policy Studies Inst. (vice chmn. 1980—2008), Soc. Chem. Industry (Centenary medal 1986), Ct. Brit. Shippers Coun., European Coun. Chem. Mfrs. Fedns. (v.p. 1982—84), Brit. Inst. Mgmt. (vice chmn. 1980—2008, Gold medal 1985), Groucho's Club, Athenaeum Club. Avocations: sailing, swimming, cooking, literature. Died Jan. 10, 2008.

**HASELTINE, MAURY WILSON,** artist, art consultant; b. Portland, Oreg., May 7, 1925; d. Milton Earl and Bernadean Helen (Grebel) Wilson Capps; m. Philip Dean Janney, Mar. 15, 1944 (div. 1954); m. James Lewis Haseltine, Aug. 15, 1955; children: Thomas, Jean, Suzanne Haseltine McDonald, Angela Haseltine Pozzi. Student, Reed Coll., Portland, 1942—44, student, 1946, NW Coll. Art., 1945—47, Eastern N.Mex. U., 1950. Free-lance artist, painter Lake Oswego, Oreg., 1955—61, Salt Lake City, 1961—68, Olympia, Wash., from 1968, art cons., from 1974. Dir. classes creative activities State Capitol Mus., Olympia, 1968—71, tchr., 1969—78. Exhibited in group shows at Expo 74 Invitational, Tacoma Art Mus., 1973 (Hon. mention), Anacortes Arts Festival, 1975 (1st prize), Govs. Invitational, 1979, 1981, one-woman shows include Evergreen State Coll., 1980, U. Puget Sound, 1984, Reed Coll., 1986. Active, founding mem. Friends Evergreen Gallery, Portland Art Mus., from 1950, Assocs. State Capitol Mus., Olympia, 1969, Seattle Art Mus., from 1970, Evergreen State Coll., Wash., 1982. Unitarian Universalist. Home: Olympia, Wash. Died June 6, 1998.

**HASIK, JAN MARIAN,** medical educator; b. Rawicz, Poland, Mar. 15, 1922; s. Jan and Teodozja (Papmel) H.; m. Władysława Piątkowska, Mar. 19, 1950; children: Mariola, Jan Tadeusz, Piotr. MD, Med. Acad., Poznań, Poland, 1951, Dr Habilitation, 1964; Dr Honoris Causa, Martin-Luther U., Halle, Germany, 1987. From asst. to sr. asst. to asst. prof. Med. Acad., Poznań, 1951-64, docent, 1964-72, prof., from 1972, dean med. faculty, 1975-81. Dir. Inst. Internal Diseases, Poznań, 1985; chief Gastroenterology Clinic, Poznań, 1971. Author 80 books in field; editor-in-chief Med. News; contbr. numerous papers to med. jours. Avocations: travel, history of medicine. Home: Poznań, Poland. Deceased.

**HASSIM, ABU MUSTAPHA,** obstetrician, gynecologist, educator; b. Johannesburg, Transvaal, South Africa, Apr. 29, 1931; arrived in Eng., 1958; s. Mustapha and Zainab Suberdar (Khan) H.; m. Cynthia Lucas, May 4, 1963; children: Conan, Siobhan and Anthea (twins), Oona. BSc, Witwatersand U., Johannesburg, South Africa, 1951, MB, ChB, 1955; DRCOG, Royal Coll. Ob-Gyn., London, 1958, MRCOG, 1961. Bd. examiners Royal Colls. London. Jr. resident Baragwanath Hosp., Johannesburg, South Africa, 1956-59; sr. resident Bargawanath Hosp., Johanensburg, South Africa, 1962, 63; rotating resident Lond Hosp. (Mile End), 1959-62; chief Ob.-Gyn. Univ. Hosp., Lusaka, Zambia, 1964-65; WHO prof. in ob.-gyn. U. Zambia, Lusaka, 1966-73; sr. cons., chmn. Barnet (Eng.) Hosp., from 1974. Hon. lectr. Royal Free Hosp., London, 1976—. Contbr. over 35 articles to profl. jours. including: Jour. Ob.-Gyn., Brit. Commonwealth, Am. Jour. Ob.-Gyn., Internat. Surgery, Brit. Jour. of Surgery and others; co-author: Maternity Care in Developing Countries, 2001. Recipient fellowship Ford Found., Johns Hopkins Med.Sch. Balt., 1969, Harvard Sch. of Medicine, Hosp. de La Mujer, Mexico, 1969, Anglo Am. Zambia del. to Internat. Ob.-Gyn. Congresses in Malaysia, Australia, Japan, Brazil, 1967-88. Fellow ACS, Royal Coll. Ob-Gyn. London (examiner), Internat. Coll. Surgeons, Royal Soc. Medicine; mem. Brit. Med. Assn. Avocations: horticulture, landscape gardening, dry-stone walling. Home: London, England. Died Sept. 14, 2003.

**HASSO, SIGNE ELEONORA CECILIA,** actress; b. Stockholm, Aug. 15, 1915; came to U.S., 1940, naturalized, 1948; d. Kefas Johannes and Helfrid Elisabet (Lindstrom) Larsson; divorced; 1 child, Henry (dec.). Student, Royal Acad. Dramatic Arts. Actress, Royal Dramatic Theatre of Sweden, 1927-55, adj. prof. drama dept., U. Miami; appeared in plays in Scandinavia, Eng., Scotland, U.S., Can., films, Europe and U.S.; films including House on 92nd Street, Double Life, Crisis, I Never Promised You a Rose Garden, 1977; (TV movies) Evita Peron, 1981, Mirrors, 1985; appeared on television, Europe and U.S.; writer, corr., lyricist, composer; performed in Cabaret, Broadway and nat. tour, 1967-69, A Little Night Music, Folkan Theatre, Stockholm, 1978-79; recorded Where the Sun Meets the Moon, songs of own lyrics; author: Momo (prize), 1977, Kom Slott, 1978, The Seventh Day, 1986; poetry Verbal Lace, co-author: (with Helena Davis) Discover Yourself, 1985; Not Yet, 1988, Again, 1989, Friend of Time, 1990. Decorated knight 1st class Royal Order of Vasa, Dama Spanish Imperial Order of Charles V; recipient Swedish Oscar, 1937, Gosta Ekman Scandinavian theatrical award, 1939, Le Grand Prix Edison for English lyrics of album Scandinavian Folksongs with Alice and Svend, 1965, diploma for disting. achievement, 1973, Star on Hollywood Walk of Fame, 1994; named Swedish Am. of Yr., Order of Vasa, 1989. *Success (in anything) is not a Destination— it is a Journey.* Died June 7, 2002.

**HASTINGS, CYNTHIA LAMPROS,** graphic artist, photographer; b. Lawrence, Mass., Mar. 21, 1942; d. Theodore and Imelda (Daigle) Lampros; m. Joseph MacAlphine Hastings, Aug. 8, 1963 (div. Oct. 1987); children: Lauren Smith, Erik Smith, Sharon Castellanos, Joseph David. AAS, Westbrook Coll., Portland, Maine, 1962; BFA with Photo Concentration, Montserrat Coll. of Art, Beverly, Mass., 1998. Freelance designer CLH Graphics, Andover, Mass., from 1989. Computer illustrator: The Surface Plane, 1992. Home: Andover, Mass. Died Feb. 1999.

**HASTINGS, JOHN WOODLAND,** biologist, educator; b. Salisbury, Md., Mar. 24, 1927; s. Vaughan Archelaus and Kathrine (Stevens) H.; m. Hanna Machlup, June 6, 1953 (dec. 2009); children: Jennifer, David, Laura, Karen. BA, Swarthmore Coll., 1947; MA, Princeton U., 1950, PhD, 1951; MA, Harvard U., 1966. AEC postdoctoral fellow Johns Hopkins, 1951-53; instr. to asst. prof. biol. scis. Northwestern U., 1953-57; from asst. prof. to prof. biochemistry U. Ill., Urbana, 1957-66; prof. biology Harvard U., Cambridge, 1966-87, Paul C. Mangelsdorf prof. natural sciences, 1987—2011; master Pforzheimer House, 1976-96. Summer rsch. participant Oak Ridge Nat. Lab., 1958; vis. lectr. biochemistry Sheffield (Eng.) U., 1961-62; instr. physiology Marine Biol. Lab., Woods Hole, Mass., 1961-66, dir., 1962-66, dir. marine ecology, 1989-91, mem. corp., 1961, trustee, 1966-74, exec. com., 1968-74; guest prof. Rockefeller U., 1965-66, Inst. Biol. Phys. Chemistry Paris, 1972-73, U. Konstanz, Ger., 1979-80, Nat. Biology Inst., Okazaki, Japan, 1986, U. Munich, 1993; Disting. vis. scientist Calif. Inst. Tech., 2000, Jet Propulsion Lab., 2000-04; mem. panel molecular biology NSF, 1963-66, mem. adv. com. biology and medicine, 1968-71; com. postdoctoral fellowships chemistry Nat. Acad. Sciences, 1965-67, com. photobiology, 1965-71, com. on phototherapy, 1971-73, com. on low frequency radiation, 1975-77; mem. Commn. Undergrad. Edn. in Biol. Scis., 1965-66; space biology com. NASA, 1966-71; biochemistry tng. com. Nat. Inst. Gen. Med. Sciences, 1968-72; mem. internat. adv. bd. Marine Biol. Lab., Eilat, Israel, 1968-2014; faculty assoc. Calif. Inst. Tech., 2000. Co-author: (with Therese Wilson) Bioluminescence: Living Lights, Lights for Living, 2013; Contbr. profl. jours. With USN, 1944—45. Guggenheim fellow, 1965-66, NIH fellow, 1972-73, Yamada Found. fellow, Osaka, Japan, 1986, Humboldt fellow, 1993, recipient Alexander von Humboldt prize, 1979, Lifetime Achievement award, American Soc. Photobiology, 2003, Peter C. Farrell Sleep Medicine prize, Harvard Med. Sch., 2006. Fellow AAAS, American Soc. Biol. Chemists, Biophys. Soc., Soc. American Microbiologists, American Soc. Photobiology (pres. 1999-2001), Soc. Gen. Physiology (pres. 1963-65), Soc. Chemi- and Bio-luminescence (founding pres. 1994-98), Pierian Sodality (pres. 1999-2001), Johns Hopkins Soc. Scholars, mem. Nat. Acad. Scis., American Acad. Arts & Sciences, Phi Beta Kappa (hon.) (Alpha Iota chpt.). Home: Lexington, Mass. Died Aug. 6, 2014.

**HASTY, RICHARD SPENCER,** retired minister; b. Dover, NH, Sept. 12, 1928; s. Harold Clyde and Jennie Odelle (Sanborn) H.; m. Margaret Lawrence Howlett, June 16, 1956 (div. 1988); children: Margaret Lawrence, Christopher Spencer, Victoria Merritt. AB, U. N.H., 1950; STB, Harvard U., 1956; D of Ministry, Andover Newton Theol. Sch., 1989. Ordained to ministry Unitarian Soc., Fall River, Mass., 1956. Min. The Unitarian Soc., Fall River, Mass., 1956-63, The First Parish, Duxbury, Mass., 1963-72, Portland, Maine, 1972-87; interim min. St. Johns Unitarian Ch., Cin., 1987-88, First Unitarian Universalist Ch., Detroit, 1988-90, Universalist Unitarian Ch., Peoria, Ill., 1990-91; interim sr. min. First Unitarian Ch. Cleve., Shaker Heights, 1991-92; min. Unitarian Universalist Soc. Greater Springfield, Mass., 1992-98, min. emeritus Mass., from 1998; vis. min. Brisbane (Australia) Unitarian Universalist Fellowship, 1999, Capital Unitarian Universalist Congregation, Victoria, B.C., Can., 2000. Mem. Interfaith Coun. Western Mass., 1992-98; mem. ecumenical and interfaith divsn. Coun. Chs. of Greater Springfield, 1992-98; vis. min. Capital Unitarian Universalent Congregation, Victoria, B.C., Can., 2000. Mem. site com. Washington Sch., Springfield, 1993-98; mem. Mich. Orgn. for Human Rights, 1988-90, Maine Citizens Against Govt. Censorship, 1985-87; clk. Portland Ministry-At-Large, 1972-85. 1st lt. U.S. Army, 1951-53. Mem. Conn. Valley Dist. Unitarian Universalist Mins. Assn. (v.p. 1995-97, pres. 1997-98, Good Officers person 1993-97), Conn. Valley Dist. (bd. dirs. 1997-98). Democrat. Avocations: mountain climbing, swimming, sculpture, music, reading. Deceased.

**HATAKEYAMA, SEIJI,** machinery company executive; b. Tokyo, Mar. 28, 1922; s. Issey and Sotomi Hatakeyama; m. Hisako Naruse Hatakeyama, Oct. 18, 1957. BME, Yamanashi U., 1942. Dir. Ebara Corp., Tokyo, from 1958, pres., from 1976; v.p. World Wildlife Funds-Japan, Tokyo, Japan Inst. Invention & Innovation, Tokyo. Mem.: Sewage Treatment Plant Constructors Assn. (pres. Tokyo), Agrl. Engrng. Assn. (pres. Tokyo), Rotary. Avocations: tennis, art, painting, Noh. Home: Minato-ku Tokyo, Japan. Died 1988.

**HATFIELD, WILLIAM RUKARD HURD,** actor; b. NYC, Dec. 7, 1920; s. William Henry Jr. and Adele Steele (McGuire) H. Student, Bard Coll.; grad., Chekhov Theatre Studio, Dartington Hall Devon, Eng. Tchr., lectr. Michael Chekhov Theatre Sch., N.Y.C., 1986, 87, Chekhov symposium London, 1988, 4 master classes Trinity Coll., Dublin, Ireland, 1988, Bridgeport (Conn.) U., UCLA, Fairfield (Conn.) U. Co-author (with Michael Chekhov): To the Actor; stage appearances include Twelfth Night, King Lear, The Cricket on the Hearth, The Possessed, 1942, The Skin of Our Teeth, The Ivy Green, Venus Observed, Love's Labour's Lost, 1953, Camino Real, 1953, Anastasia, 1954, Julius Caesar, 1955, The Tempest, 1955, The Duchess of Malfi, 1957, Marat/Sade, 1970, Victory, 1974, A Doll's House, 1975, Son of Whistler's Mother, 1997, The Respectful Prostitute, Dark of the Moon, l'Histoire D'un Soldat; film appearances include Dragon Seed, 1944, The Picture of Dorian Gray, 1945, Diary of a Chambermaid, 1946, The Unsuspected, 1947, Joan of Arc, 1948, The Checkered Coat, 1948, Tarzan and the Slave Girl, 1950, Bullfight, 1954 (named 1 of 10 Best Performances Herald Tribune), The Beginning of the End, 1957, The Left-Handed Gun, 1958, King of Kings, 1961 (Blue Ribbon award), El Cid, 1961, Mickey One, 1965, Harlow, 1965, The Double-Barrelled Detective Story, 1965, The Boston Strangler, 1968, Von Richtofen and Brown, 1971, Chinatown at Midnight, Destination Murder, King David, Crimes of the Heart, Her Alibi; TV appearances include The Rivals, 1950, The Importance of Being Earnest, 1950, The Nativity Play, 1952, Greed, 1953, Seventh Heaven, 1953, The King's Bounty, 1955, The Prince and the Pauper, 1957, The Last Man, 1958, Don Juan in Hell, 1960, One Day in the Life of Ivan Denisovich, 1963, The Invincible Mr. Disraeli, 1963 (Emmy nomination), A Cry of Angel, 1963, Lamp at Midnight, 1965, Ten Blocks on the Camino Real, 1966, The FBI, 1972; audio recordings include Hearing Poetry I and II, The Picture of Dorian Gray, The Tempest, Romeo and Juliet, Rip Van Winkle and The Legend of Sleepy Hollow Poetry of Poe; lectr. Met. Mus. Art Festival, 1997; contbr. articles to profl. jours. Hon. com. mem. People for the Ethical Treatment of Animals. Named Hon. Citizen of Md. by Gov. Shafer, 1988, Hon. Citizen of Va.; recipient Life Achievement award Acad. Sci.-Fiction and Fantasy, 1984, Humanitarian award People for Ethical Treatment of Animals, 1988. Fellow Players Club; mem. AFTRA, SAG, Actor's Equity Assn, United Arts Club. Avocations: restoring old houses, animal liberation, writing, painting. Home: Rathcormack Co, Ireland. Deceased.

**HATZE, HERBERT,** science educator, consultant; b. Vienna, July 29, 1937; s. Franz and Margarethe (Marinoni) H.; m. Roswitha Margaretha Tahedl, Dec. 3, 1966; children: Gunter, Roland, Sandra. Diploma in kinesiology, Bafl, I.F.S., Vienna, 1960; BSc, U. South Africa, Pretoria, South Africa, 1970, BSc (hons.), 1972, PhD, 1974. Lectr. in tech. mat. Tech. Coll., Steyr, Austria, 1961-67; rsch. assoc. Human Scis. Lab., Johannesburg, 1967-71; head of biomechanics lab. U. Stellenbosch, Stellenbosch, South Africa, 1971-75; vis. prof. U. Watterloo, Can., 1976; sr. chief scientist Nat. Rsch. Inst. Math. Scis., Pretoria, South Africa, 1976-81; prof. biomechanics U. Vienna, 1981—2002. Cons. Prince, Inc., Wilson, Dunlop, 1990—; reviewer scientific jours., 1971—. Author: Myocybernetic Control Models of Skeletal Muscle, 1981, Methoden Biomechanischer Bewegungsanalyse, 1986; contbr. articles to profl. jours. Referee Swiss Nat. R.F. ANFF, Switzerland, Austria, 1988—; apptd. sci. expert at the European Commn., 1995-99. Mem. Internat. Soc. Biomechanics (founding), Fachbereich Stiftung Warentest, N.Y. Acad. Scis. (active), Internat. Standard Comm. (Geoffrey Dyson award 1998). Avocations: classical music, literature, sports. Home: Vienna, Austria. Died Aug. 26, 2002.

**HAUGSTVEDT, ASBJORN,** former government official; b. Bergen, Norway, Nov. 20, 1926; Social welfare insp. City of Bergen, 1961—69, head social welfare adminstrn.; mem. Bergen city Coun., 1967; mem. central coun. Christian Democratic Party, 1969—75, 2d vice-chmn., 1971—75; chmn. parliamentary group Christian Dem. Party, 1972—73; pres. Odelsting, 1977—81; min. trade & shipping, 1983—86; mem. com. for arms control and disarmament, 1975; del. to gen. assembly UN, 1969, 1974; UN Law of the Sea Conf., 1976; mem. Nordic Coun. Died June 26, 2008.

**HAUSER, HANS,** electrical engineer, consultant; b. Vienna, Mar. 1, 1958; s. Johann and Elisabeth Hauser; m. Michaela Cizek, June 22, 1960; children: Anna-Katharina, Lukas Johannes. MSc, Vienna U. Tech., 1983, PhD, 1988. With Telecom Austria, Vienna, 1978; univ. asst. Vienna U. Tech., 1983-94, univ. docent, 1994-98, vice head faculty elec. engrng. and info. tech., 1998—99; head Inst. Material Sci. and Elec. Engrng., Vienna, 1999-2000, Inst. Indsl. Electronics and Material Sci., Vienna, 2000—02; head materials sci. dept. Inst. Sensor and Actuator Sys., Vienna, 2002—04. Cons. Schiebel Elektronische Geräte GmbH, Vienna, 1994—, Electrovac GmbH, Klosternenburg, Austria, DaimlerChrysler AG, Stuttgart, Germany, 2001-, Bombardier Transp GmbH Wiener Neudorf, Austria, 1998—; chmn. Internat. Workshop Simulation Magnetization Process, Vienna, 1995, Sensors and Packaging, Vienna, 1998-2003; vis. prof. Siemens AG, Erlangen, Germany, Ames Lab. Iowa State U., 2003-2004. Contbr. articles to profl. jours. and books. Grantee Austrian Sci. Found., 1991-95, 2000-06, Austrian Nat. Bank Found., 1993-95, 98-2000; Fulbright scholar, 2003-04. Mem. IEEE (sr.), Österreichischer Verband Elektrotechnik. Achievements include patents for Inclination Measurement System for Trench Wall Construction; for Signal Transmission for Underground Engineering; for Magnetoresistive Sensors; for Giant Magnetiompedance Sensors; in Magneto-Optical Sensors and Components; for Regeneration of Lead Acid Accumulators; research in magnetic materials, dielectrics, superconductors. Home: Vienna, Austria. Died Aug. 2007.

**HAWORTH, JAMES CHILTON,** pediatrics educator; b. Gosforth, Eng., May 29, 1923; emigrated to Can., 1957, naturalized, 1972; s. Walter Norman and Violet Chilton H.; m. Eleanor Marian Bowser, Oct. 18, 1951; children—Elizabeth Marian, Peter Norman James, Margaret Jean, Anne Ruth. M.B., Ch.B, U. Birmingham, Eng., 1945, MD, 1960. House physician Birmingham Gen. and Children's Hosps., 1946-47; fellow Cin. Children's Hosp., 1949-50; house physician Hosp. for Sick Children, London, 1951; pediatric registrar Alder Hey Children's Hosp., Liverpool, Eng., 1951-52; sr. registrar Sheffield Children's Hosp., 1953-57; pediatrician Winnipeg (Man., Can.) Clinic, 1957-65; asst. prof. dept. pediat. U. Man., Winnipeg, 1965-67, assoc. prof., 1967-70, prof., 1970-94, head dept. pediat., 1979-85, senate mem., 1985-90, prof. human genetics, 1987-94, prof. emeritus, from 1994, sr. scholar dept. biochemistry and med. genetics, 1999—2005. Mem. active staff Health Scis. Centre-Children's, 1957-93; cons. staff St. Boniface Hosp., 1974-93; hon. staff Health Sci. Ctr., 1993—. Contbr. articles to profl. jours. Bd. dirs. Man. Med. Svc. found., 1988—2008, exec. dir., 1995-2004. Served with Royal Naval Vol. Res., 1947-49. Fellow Royal Coll. Physicians (Can., London), Can. Coll. Med. Geneticists (hon.); mem. Can. Soc. Clin. Investigation, Am. Pediatric Soc., Soc. Pediatric Rsch., Can. Pediatric Soc. Home: Winnipeg, Canada. Died July 20, 2014.

**HAWTHORNE, JOHN WILLIAM,** engineering executive; b. NYC, Sept. 15, 1941; s. William John and Beatrice (Johnson) H.; m. Francis Louise Jones, Nov. 26, 1994; children: A. Martha, Jessica J., William J. II. BSCE, Tufts U., 1965; MS, U. Cin., 1968; MBA, Va. Poly. Inst., 1977. Project engr. Colgate-Palmolive Co., Jeffersonville, Ind., 1967-69; v.p. Betz, Converse & Murdock, Plymouth, Pa., 1969-78; sr. v.p. regional mgr. Camp Dresser & McKee, Chgo., from 1978. Mem. Am. Acad. Environ. Engrs., Am. Arbitration Assn., Am. Water Works Assn., Water Environ. Fedn. Home: Gates Mills, Ohio. Deceased.

**HAY, JOHN WOODS, JR.,** retired banker; b. Rock Springs, Wyo., Apr. 23, 1905; s. John Woods and Mary Ann (Blair) Hay; m. Frances B. Smith, Dec. 28, 1948; children: Helen Mary, John Woods III, Keith Norbert, Joseph Garrett. AB, U. Mich., 1927. Pres., dir. Rock Springs Nat. Bank, 1947—95, Rock Springs Grazing Assn., 1939—95, Blair & Hay Land & Livestock Co., Rock Springs, 1949—97. Former trustee, v.p. William H. and Carrie Gottsche Found. Mem.: Rotary, Jesters, Shriners, Masons, Sigma Alpha Epsilon. Republican. Epsic. Home: Rock Springs, Wyo. Died Nov. 8, 1997.

**HAYASHI, CHIKIO,** statistics researcher; b. Tokyo, July 6, 1918; s. Ryuichi and Chise (Harada) H.; m. Ohashi Reiko, Apr. 24, 1955; children: Sachio, Yukikazu. BA in Sci., U. Tokyo, 1942, DSc, 1954. Rsch. fellow Tokyo U., 1945-46; rsch. mem. Inst. Statis. Math., Tokyo, 1947-56, chief 2d divsn., 1956-73, dir. gen., 1974-86, prof. emeritus; prof. U. Air, Chiba, Japan, 1986-94. Part-time prof. Hokkaido U., Tokyo U., Hitotsubashi U., Keio U., Tokyo Inst. Tech., Nogoya U., Osaka U., Kyoto U., Hiroshima U., Kyushu, Japan, 1954-86. Author: Mathematical Statistics, 1954 (Ouchi prize), Quantification of Qualitative Data, 1965 (NHK Hoso Cultural prize), Statistics, 1982 (Purple Ribbon medal), Data Science, 1997 (Japanese Statis. Soc. prize). Author: Mathematical Statistics, 1954 (Ouchi prize), Quantification of Qualitative Data, 1965 (NHK Hoso Cultural prize), Statistics, 1982 (Purple Ribbon medal). Mem. Royal Statis. Soc. (hon.), Japanese Soc. for Logic, Methodology and Philos. Sci. (hon.), Japanese Statistical Soc. (hon.), Japanese Forestry Soc. (hon.). Home: Mitaka, Tokyo, Japan. Deceased.

**HAYASHI, TERUO TERRY,** physician, educator; b. Sacramento, July 23, 1921; s. Jinnosuke and Koto (Watanabe) H.; m. Ursula M. Promann, Nov. 29, 1953; children: William Promann, Peter John, James Douglas, Ann Koto, Robert Terry. Student, U. Calif.-Berkeley, 1939-42, Temple U., 1943-44, MD, 1948. Diplomate Am. Bd. Ob-Gyn (bd. dirs. 1976-88, chmn. 1984-88). Intern Temple U. Hosp., 1949, resident, 1951-54; instr. Temple U. Med. Sch., 1954-59, asst. prof., 1960-62, assoc. prof., 1963-65; prof. ob-gyn U. Pitts., 1965-95, chmn. ob-gyn, 1974-89. Study sect. human embryology and devel. NIH, 1964-68, mem. com. perinatal biology and infant mortality br., 1970-73; chmn. maternal and child health research com. Nat. Inst. Child Health and Human Devel., 1979-83; chmn. Am. Bd. Ob./Gyn., 1985-88. Served with AUS, 1949-51. Mem. Am. Coll. Ob-Gyn, Soc. Gynecol. Investigation, Am. Soc. Biol. Chemists, Am. Gynecol. and Obstet. Soc. (sec. 1981-84, pres. 1985-86), Sigma Xi, Alpha Omega Alpha. Home: Pittsburgh, Pa. Died Feb. 7, 1997.

**HAYES, ANN CARSON,** retired computer company executive; b. Hamlin, Tex., Apr. 25, 1941; d. Fred Elbert and Nona Faye (Riddle) Carson; m. James Russell Brown, May 7, 1959 (div. July 1973); children: James Allen Brown, Daniel Russell Brown, Robert Anthony Brown, Debra Faye Brown; m. Robert Lee Hayes, Nov. 15, 1975. AAS, Howard Coll., Tex., 1972; student, Regents Coll., NYC, 1986. Lic. ins. agt. Nat. Assn. Self-Employed. Freelance artist, Big Spring, Tex., 1956-76; real estate agt. Century 21, Littleton, Colo., 1976-78, Huntsville, Ala., 1978-79; art dir. Hayes and Co., Splendora, Tex., from 1979; CEO Hayes Enterprises, New Caney, Tex., 2000—11. Executor Hayes Tax Svc., New Caney. Democrat. Episcopalian. Avocations: sculpting, glass etching. Home: Big Spring, Tex. Died Apr. 12, 2014.

**HAYES, JANET GRAY,** retired management consultant, former mayor; b. Rushville, Ind., July 12, 1926; d. John Paul and Lucile (Gray) Frazee; m. Kenneth Hayes, Mar. 20, 1950 (dec. 2013); children: Lindy, John, Katherine, Megan. AB, Ind. U., 1948; MA magna cum laude, U. Chgo., 1950. Psychiat. caseworker Jewish Family Svc. Agy., Chgo., 1950-52; vol. Denver Crippled Children's Service, 1954-55, Adult and Child Guidance Clinic, San Jose, Calif., 1958-59; mem. San Jose City Coun., 1971-75, vice mayor, 1973-75, mayor San Jose, 1975—82; co-chmn. com. urban econs. U.S. Conf. Mayors, 1976-78, co-chmn. task force on aging, mem. sci. and teck task force, 1976-80, bd. trustees, 1977-82; bd. dirs. League Calif. Cities, 1976-82, mem. property tax reform task force, 1976-82; chmn. State of Calif. Urban Devel. Adv. Com., 1976-77; mem. Calif. Commn. Fair Jud. Practices, 1976-82; client-community relations dir. Q. Tech., Santa Clara, Calif., 1983-85; bus. mgr. Kenneth Hayes MD, Inc., 1985-88; CEO Hayes House, Book Distbr., from 1998. Mem. Democratic Nat. Campaign Com., 1976; mem. Calif. Democratic Commn. Nat. Platform and Policy, 1976; del. Democratic Nat. Conv., 1980; bd. dirs. South San Francisco Bay Dischargers Authority; chmn. Santa Clara County Sanitation Dist.; mem. San Jose/Santa Clara Treatment Plant Adv. Bd.; chmn. Santa Clara Valley Employment and Tng. Bd. (CETA), League to Save Lake Tahoe adv. bd., 2000—05; bd.past mem. EPA Aircraft/Airport Noise Task Group; bd. dirs. Calif. Center Rsch. and Edn. in Govt, Alexian Bros. Hosp., 1983-92; bd. dirs., chmn. adv. council Public Tech. Inc.; mem. bd. League to Save Lake Tahoe, 1984-2000; pres. bd. trustees San Jose Mus. Art, 1987-89; founder, adv. bd. Calif. Bus. Bank, 1982-85; polit. advisor Citizens Against Airport Pollution, 2003-14 AAUW Edn. Found. grantee. Mem. Assn. Bay Area Govts. (exec. com. 1971-74, regional housing subcom. 1973-74), LWC (pres. San Francisco Bay Area chpt. 1968-70, pres. local chpt. 1966-67), Mortar Bd., Phi Beta Kappa, Kappa Alpha Theta. Democrat. Died Apr. 21, 2014.

**HAYES, JOHN THOMPSON,** biology professor, academic administrator; b. Newton, Mass., Sept. 10, 1940; s. William Danforth Jr. and Charlotte Matilda (Thompson) H.; m. Nancy Jean VanDyke, Jan. 30, 1965 (div. Aug. 1978); children: Jonathan VanDyke, Dianne Jellesma; m. Patricia Anne Lynch, Aug. 23, 1980; 1 child, Robert Brennan. BA cum laude, Amherst Coll., 1962; MS, Cornell U., 1966, PhD, 1968. Postdoctoral fellow U. Ga. Savannah River Ecology Lab., Aiken, SC, 1967-69; mem. faculty Paine Coll., Augusta, Ga., from 1969, prof. biology, from 1976; mgr. for computer-based edn. Med. Coll. Ga., Augusta, 1984-85. Contbr. articles to profl. jours. Mem. Assn. for Ednl. Communications and Tech., Extramural Assocs. NIH, Ga. Acad. Sci., Ga. Assn. for Instructional Tech., Ecol. Soc. Am., S.C. Entomol. Soc., Sigma Xi, Phi Kappa Phi. Unitarian-Universalist. Avocations: photography, travel, distance running, singing, hiking. Deceased.

**HAYMAN, RICHARD WARREN JOSEPH,** conductor; b. Cambridge, Mass., Mar. 27, 1920; s. Fred Albert and Gladys Marie (Learned) Hayman; m. Maryellen Daly, June 25, 1960; children: Suzanne Marie, Olivia Kathryn. D Hum. (hon.), Detroit Coll. Bus., 1980. Freelance composer, arranger 20th Century Fox, Warner Bros., MGM, Universal Film Studios; music arranger, dir. Vaughn Monroe Orch. records and TV show, NYC, 1945-50; chief arranger Arthur Fiedler and Boston Pops Orchestra, 1950-95; mus. dir. Mercury Record Corp., NYC, 1950-65, Time-Mainstream Records, NYC, 1960-70; prin. pops condr. Detroit Symphony Orchs.; prin. pops condr., McDonnell Douglas chair St. Louis, 1976—2002; prin. pops condr. Birmingham (Ala.), Hartford (Conn.), Calgary (Can.), Grand Rapids (Mich.) Symphony Orch., London (Ont., Can.) Orch. Composer: No Strings Attached, Dansero, Skipping Along, Carriage Trade, Serenade to a Lost Love, Olivia, Suzanne, Freddie the Football, Grand Prix March, How in the World, Ritual Dance and numerous others; rec. artist Naxos Internat. Records, from 1991; Fla. Sunshine Pops Orchestra, Symphony Orchestra. Recipient Best Instrumental Record award, Sta. WERE, Cleve., 1963, McDonnell Douglas award, 2000, Star dedicated, Hollywood Blvd. Walk of Fame. Mem.: ASCAP, NARAS (Best TV Comml. Jingle award 1960), American Fedn. Musicians. Roman Catholic. Died Feb. 5, 2014.

**HAYNES, THOMAS MORRIS,** philosophy educator; b. Waukesha, Wis., Oct. 24, 1918; s. George Albert and Lois (Morris) H.; m. Jane Louise Riggs, Sept. 12, 1942; children: Christopher Thomas, Jonathan Marshall, Carolyn Martha. AB, Butler U., 1941; PhD, U. Ill., 1949. Indsl. engr. RCA, Indpls., 1942-44; research and devel. engr. P.R. Mallory, Indpls., 1944-46; U. Ill. postdoctoral fellow Faculty Law U. Paris, 1949-50; instr. philosophy U. Ill., 1950-51; research asst. U. Ill. (Coll. of Law), 1950-51; instr. philosophy Lehigh U., 1952-54, asst. prof., 1954-61, asso. prof., 1961-69, prof., 1969-83, prof. emeritus, adj. prof., 1983-91. Founder, pres. World-Sense, Inc.; dir. World-Sense Dialogue. Mem. AAUP, Am. Philos. Assn., N.Y. Acad. Scis., Environ. Def. Fund, World Wildlife Fund, Natural Resources Def. Coun., The Wilderness Soc., Nat. Wildlife Fedn. (assoc.), The Nature Conservancy, Worldwatch Libr., Union Concerned Scientists (sponsor), Amnesty Internat., Woodrow Wilson Internat. Ctr. for Scholars (assoc.), Phi Beta Kappa, Phi Kappa Phi. Deceased.

**HAYS, JAMES S.,** lawyer; b. NYC, Jan. 1, 1901; s. Herman Joseph and Arline (Denzer) Hays; m. Florence Meyer, Apr. 19, 1931; children: Helen Gordon, Judith Eiseman. LLB, Cornell U., 1922. Bar: N.Y. 1922. Mem. firm Kaye, Scholer, Fierman Hays & Handler, NYC, from 1925, sr. ptnr, 1950—70, of counsel, 1970—80, founding ptnr., from 1980. Dir. Norfolk So. R.R., 1945—50. Pres. Jewish Home & Hosp. for Aged, NYC, 1950—55, bd. chmn., 1955—63, hon. chmn., from 1970; trustee Fedn. Jewish Philanthropies, NYC, 1950—65; dir. Welfare Council Greater N.Y., 1962. Mem.: ABA, N.Y. County Bar Assn., Bar Assn. City N.Y., Quaker Ridge Golf., Harmonie. Democrat. Jewish. Died Mar. 9, 1989.

**HAYWARD, MARY MAVIS,** retired chemist; b. Johannesburg, June 23, 1928; d. George Atherstone and Alma Beatrice (Laschinger) Webb; m. Ian Norrie Hayward, Oct. 4, 1952; children: Keith, Martin, Patrick. BSc, Witwatersrand U., Johannesburg, 1948. Factory chemist IXL Co., Johannesburg, 1949; indsl. chemist Johannesburg Municipality, 1949-51, Coun. Indsl. and Sci. Rsch., 1951-52. Author: Anglican Women's Fellowship Handbook, 1965, Anglican Women's Fellowship Vestments, 1967, Anglican Women's Fellowship Funeral Booklet, 1967; editor Nat. Coun. Women Newsletter, 2000-04. Mem. nat. exec. com., past pres. Johannesburg Br., past sec. Nat. Coun. Women South Africa, 1955—70; mem. nat. exec. com, past pres. Johannesburg Diocese, treas., past sec. Anglican Women's Fellowship, 1966-99; exec. com. Nat. Com. Women World Day & Prayer, 1985-2001. Mem. South African Assn. Women Grads., Rand Women Pioneers. Avocations: amateur philately, bridge playing. Home: Bedfordview, South Africa. Deceased.

**HAYWARD, TERESA CALCAGNO,** foreign language educator; b. NYC, Jan. 28, 1907; d. Vito and Rosalie (Amato) Calcagno; m. Peter Hayward, Feb. 6, 1932; children: Nancy, Peter. BA, Hunter Coll., 1929; MA, Columbia U., 1931. Tchr. romance langs. Jr. High Sch. 164, NYC, 1936—57, High Sch. 141, Riverdale, NY, 1957—71; tchr. English to Japanese women Nichibei Fujinkai, Riverdale, from 1972; chmn. Riverdale chpt., 1976—92, Manhattan, from 1992. Bd. dirs. Riverdale chpt. UN Assn., from 1973. Mem.: Hunger and Social Outreach com. Christ Ch.(Riverdale). Democrat. Episcopalian. Avocations: piano, art, travel. Home: Salem, SC. Died 1997.

**HAZELBAKER, EILEEN GENEVA,** retired medical technologist; b. Decatur County, Kans., Dec. 2, 1928; d. clint Leonard and Edith Helen (Vermilion) Huff. m. Fred R. Hazelbaker, Oct. 5, 1974; 1 son by previous marriage, Wayne Leroy Wohler. Degree in gen. sci., Ft. Hays State Coll., Kans., 1953. Intern Stormont-Vail Hosp., Topeka, 1953; med. technologist hosp. in Kans. and Wash., 1954-67, Syringa Gen. Hosp., Grangeville, Idaho, 1967-90; ret. Mem.: Extension, Rebekahs, Sr. Citizens Area Agy. on Aging. Mem. Christian Ch. (Disciples Of Christ). Home: Grangeville, Idaho. Died 1999.

**HEAD, BEN THOMAS,** lawyer; b. Oklahoma City, Nov. 1, 1920; s. Ben Thomas Head and Virginia (Broados) Pine; m. Mary C. Johnston, June 17, 1949 (div. June 1983); children: Marcy, Paul, Eric; m. June Leftwich, Mar. 22, 1986. BBA, U. Okla., 1942, LLB, 1948, JD, 1970. Bar: Okla., Tex. Pres., chmn., chief exec. officer RepublicBank, Austin, Tex., 1978-84; sr. lectr. banking U. Tex., Austin, 1984-88; U.S. trustee U.S. Dist. Ct. (so. and we. dists.) Tex., Houston, 1988-93. Pres., CEO United Va. Bank (now SunTrust), Newport News, Va., 1975-78; chmn. City Savs., San Angelo, Tex., 1986-87. V.p. Oklahoma City C. of C., 1973, chmn. Austin C. of C., 1983; pres. progress com. Newport News., Va., 1978; bd. dirs., chmn. fin. com. Austin Presbyn. Sem., 1982-90; bd. dirs. fin. com. Tex. Presbyn. Found., 1988—; trustee, vice chmn. bd., Hampton U., 1980-2001. Col. U.S. Army, 1942-46, India. Named Exec. of Yr. Austin C. of C., 1983. Mem. Rotary. Avocations: golf, walking. Deceased.

**HEAD, IVAN LEIGH,** law educator; b. Calgary, Alta., Can., July 28, 1930; s. Arthur Cecil and Birdie Hazel (Crockett) H.; m. Barbara Spence Eagle, June 23, 1952; children: Laurence Allan, Bryan Cameron, Catherine Spence, Cynthia Leigh; m. Ann Marie Price, Dec. 1, 1979. BA, U. Alta., 1951, LLB, 1952; LLM, Harvard U., 1960; LLD (hon.), U. Alta., 1987, U. West Indies, 1987, U. Western Ont., 1988, U. Ottawa, 1988, U. Calgary, 1989, Beijing U., 1990, St. Francis Xavier U., 1990, U. Man., 1991, U. Notre Dame, 1991, Carleton U., 1996. Bar: Alta. 1953; Queen's Counsel, Can. Practiced in, Calgary, 1953-59; partner Helman, Barron & Head, 1955-59; fgn. service officer Dept. External Affairs, Ottawa, Kuala Lumpur, 1960-63; prof. law U. Alta., 1963-67; assoc. counsel to Minister of Justice, Govt. of Can., 1967-68, spl. asst. to prime minister of Can., 1968-78; pres. Internat. Devel. Rsch. Centre, Ottawa, 1978-91; prof. law, dir. Liu Centre for the study of global issues U. B.C., Vancouver, Canada, 1991—99, prof. emeritus, 2000—04. Sr. fellow Salzburg Seminar; bd. dirs. Acad. Ednl. Devel., Can. World Youth. Author: International Law, National Tribunals and the Rights of Aliens, 1971, On a Hinge of History, 1991, The Canadian Way, 1995; editor: This Fire Proof House, 1967, Conversation with Canadians, 1972; contbr. articles to profl. jours. Trustee Internat. Food Policy Rsch. Inst., 1979-88; mem. Ind. Commn. on Internat. Humanitarian Issues, 1983-87. Decorated officer Order of Can.; officer Grand Cross, Order of The Sun (Peru); Chief Justice's medallist U. Alta. Law Sch.; Frank Knox Meml. fellow Harvard Law Sch., 1959-60; named to Sports Wall of Fame U. Alta. Mem. Internat. Law Assn., Can. Council Internat. Law, Can. Inst. Internat. Affairs, Am. Soc. Internat. Law, Law Soc. Alta., Inter-Am. Dialogue. Anglican. Home: West Vancouver, Canada. Died Nov. 1, 2004.

**HEARD, WILLIAM ROBERT,** retired insurance company executive; b. Inpls., Apr. 25, 1925; s. French and Estelle (Austin) Heard; m. Virginia Ann Patrick, Feb. 6, 1951; children: Cynthia Ann, William Robert II. Student, Ind. U., 1948—49. With Grain Dealers Mut. Ins. Co., 1948, exec. v.p. Indpls., 1978—79, pres., CEO, dir., 1979—90, also chmn. bd. dirs.; pres., CEO, dir. Companion Ins. Co., 1979—90, also chmn. bd. dirs.; ret., 1994. Past chmn. Alliance Am. Insurers; chmn., mem. exec. com. IRM. With USNR, 1942—46. Mem.: VFW, Sales and Mktg. Execs. Internat. (past bd. dirs.), Mill and Elevator Fire Prevention Bur. (bd. dirs.), Mill and Elevator Rating Bur. (bd. dirs.), Property Loss Rsch. Bur. (bd. dirs., chmn.), Ins. Claims Svc. (bd. dirs.), Ind. Mill and Elevator Rating Bur. (bd. dirs.), Hoosierland Rating Bur. (bd. dirs.), Ind. Insurors Assn. (bd. dirs.), Property and Casualty Ins. Coun., Sales and Mktg. Execs. Indpls. (past pres.), Excess Loss Assn. (vice chmn., bd. dirs.), Ind. BBB (bd. dirs., mem. exec. com., vice chmn.), Ins. Inst. Ind. (bd. dirs., mem. exec. com.), Assn. Mill and Elevator Ins. Cos. (chmn., bd. dirs.), Pearl Harbor Survivors Assn. (hon.), Indpls. Skyline Club, Econ. Club Indpls., Fla. 1752 Club (past pres.), Hon. Order Ky. Cols., Am. Legion, Pi Sigma Epsilon. Deceased.

**HEARST, GLADYS WHITLEY HENDERSON,** writer; b. Wolfe City, Tex. d. William Henry and Helen Butler Whitley; m. Ernest Koester Hearst, Aug. 3, 1991 (dec. 1992); m. Robert David Henderson, May 17, 1933 (dec. 1941); m. Charles Joseph Hearst, Oct. 30, 1943 (dec.). Student, Trinity U., 1924—26; BA, U. Tex., 1928, M in Journalism, 1928, postgraxd, 1938—40. Editor Future Farmer News, Austin, Tex., 1930—33; dir. Svc. Bur., Tex., Congress Parents & Tchrs., Austin, Tex., 1933—36, Student Union, U. Tex., 1939—42; freelance writer, from 1945; instr. U. Northern Iowa, 1946—47, Writing Waterloo YWCA, 1966—69; vice chmn. Black Hawk County Dem. Party, 1945—57; mem. County Ext. Program Planning Com., 1965—68. Editor: (book) Cedar Falls Naval Station, 1942—45; contbr. poems to anthology (Iowa Arts Coun. grant). Past deaconess United Ch. Christ, chmn. long-range planning com., 1975—79; sec. Westminster Manor Residents Assn., 1983—85. Served to lt. USN, 1942—45, WAVES. Mem.: AAUW (life; Iowa chmn. status women 1954—56, pres.Cedar Falls br.), Ret. Faculty-Staff Assn., Readers Guild, PEO, Women in Comms. (nat. citation 1969, nat. chmn. laws 1969—74, task force long-range planning com. mem. 1973—74, charter mem., v.p. NE Iowa chpt. 1978, nat. pres., Disting. Svc. award 1962, grant Austin Chpt. 1986—87), U. Ladies. A writer Cedar Falls Centennial Pageant, U. Tex. Faculty Woman's Capital Gains Investment (pres. 1970—73, treas. 1970—73), Sigma Delta Chi, Kappa Tau Delta, Zeta Tau Alpha. Presbyterian. Deceased.

**HEATH, EDWARD RICHARD GEORGE,** former Prime Minister of the United Kingdom; b. Broadstairs, Kent, Eng., July 9, 1916; s. William and Edith Heath Grad. (Organ scholar), Balliol Coll. Oxford U., 1939; DCL (hon.), Oxford U., U. Kent; D Tech. (hon.), Bradford Tech. Inst., Westminster Coll., Salt Lake City, U. Sorbonne. With Civil Svc., 1946-47. Mem. Parliament, 1950-74; lord commr. of Treasury, 1951-53; dep. chief whip, 1953-55; parliamentary sec. to Treasury, and govt. chief whip, 1955-59; Minister of Labor, 1959-60; Lord Privy Seal, 1960-63; sec. state for industry, trade and devel., and pres. Bd. of Trade, 1963-64; leader Conservative party, 1965-75; Prime Minister, 1970-74; mem. Ind. Commn. Internat. Devel. Issues, 1977-79; lectr. Harvard U., Yale U., Princeton U., Cornell U., Dartmouth Coll., Calif. Pomona U., U. Ga., Gothenburg (Sweden) U., also others; DeRoy prof. U. Mich. Rec. artist EMI, RCA, albums include Elgar's 'Cockaigne Overture, Beethoven's Triple Concerto, European Brass by The Black Dyke Mills Band. Author: One Nation: A Tory Approach to Social Problems, 1950; Old World, New Horizons, 1970; Sailing: A Course of My Life, 1975; Music: A Joy for Life, 1976; Travels: Peoples and Places in My Life, 1977; Carols: The Joy of Christmas, 1977, also others. Chmn., London Symphony Orch. Trust, 1963-70, also guest condr.; guest condr. nat. and internat. symphonies including Berlin Philarm., Chgo. Symphony, Zurich Chamber Orch.; Shanghai Philarm. and Beijing Cen. Symphony Orch.; founding com. European Cmty. Youth Orch., also pres., 1977-80. Decorated mem. Brit. Empire privy councillor, 1955; Godkin lectr., Harvard U., 1967; recipient various awards for efforts in EEC, including Charlemagne prize City Aachen, 1963, Freiherr Von Stein Found., award, 1971, Estes J. Kefauver prize, 1971; gold medal City of Paris, 1978, World Humanity Award, 1980, Gold Medal, European Parliament, 1981; named Parliamentarian of Yr., The Spectator and Highland Spring, 1988; winner Classic Sydney Hobart yacht race, 1969; capt. Brit. Admiral Cup Team, 1971, 79, Brit.-Sardinia Cup Team, 1980; vis. Chubb fellow, Yale U., 1975; Montgomery fellow, Dartmouth Coll., 1980. Hon. fellow Royal Coll. Organists, Royal Can. Coll., Bailliol Coll. and Nuffield Coll., Oxford, Organists. Mem.: Carlton, Royal Yacht Squadron, N.Y. Yacht, Brit. Sportsman (chmn.). Home: Vienna, Austria. Died July 17, 2005.

**HEATH-STUBBS, JOHN (FRANCIS ALEXANDER),** poet; b. London, July 9, 1918; s. Francis and Edith (Marr) H-S. BA with first class honors, Oxford U., Eng., 1943, MA, 1972. English master Hall Sch., Hampstead, Eng., 1945; editl. asst. Hutchinson's Illus. Encyclopedia, 1945-46; Gregory fellow in poetry Leeds (Eng.) U., 1953-55. Vis. prof. English U. Alexandria, Egypt, 1955-58, U. Mich., Ann Arbor, 1960-61; part-time lectr. in English Coll. St. Mark and St. John, London, until 1973. Author: (poetry) Wounded Thammuz, 1942, Beauty and the Beast, 1943, The Divided Ways, 1946, The Swarming of the Bees, 1950, The Triumph of the Muse, 1958, The Blue Fly in His Head, 1962, Selected Poems, 1965 (Arts Coun. Gt. Britain award, 1965), Satires & Epigrams, 1968, Artorius, Book One, 1970; author: (with S. Spender, F.T. Prince) Penguin Modern Poets No. 20, 1972; author: Four Poems in Measure, 1973, Twelve Labours of Hercules, 1974, Parliament of Birds, 1975, The Watchman's Flute, 1978, The Mouse, The Bird, The Sausage, 1978, Birds Reconvened, 1980, Buzz Buzz, 1981, This Is Your Poem, 1981, Naming the Beats, 1982, The Immolation of Alepi, 1985, Cats Parnassus, 1987, Time Pieces, 1988, Collected Poems, 1988, A Partridge in a Pear Tree, 1988, A Ninefold of Charms, 1989, The Game of Love & Death, 1990, Parson Cat, 1991, Chimeras, 1992, Sweet Apple Earth, 1993, Galileo's Salad, 1996, Torriano Sequences, 1997, The Sound of Light, 1999, The Return of the Cranes, 2002, (translations) Poems from Giacomo Leopardi, 1947, Aphrodite's Garland, 1952; author: (with P. Avery) Hafiz of Shiraz, Thirty Poems, 1955; author: (poetry) Selected Prose & Poetry of Giacomo Leopardi, 1966, The Horn (A. V. Vigny), 1969; author: (with P. Avery) The Ruba'iyat of Omar Khayyam, 1979; author: Eight Poems of Sulpicia, 2000, (criticism) The Darkling Plain, 1950, Charles Williams, 1955, The Ode, 1969, The Verse Satire, 1969;: The Pastoral, 1969;; editor: Selected Poems of Shelley, 1947, Selected Poems of Tennyson, 1947, Selected Poems of Swift, 1947; editor: (with D. Wright) The Forsaken Garden, 1950; editor: Images of Tomorrow, 1953; editor: (with Wright) The Faber Book of 20th Century Verse, 1954, The Faber Book of 20th Century Verse, rev. edit., 1965; editor: Selected Poems of Alexander Pope, 1965, Poems of Science (P. Salman), 1984; author: Hindsights, 1993. Recipient Queen's Gold medal for poetry, 1973, Cross of St. Augustine, 1999, Order of Brit. Empire. Fellow Royal Soc. Lit., Charles Williams Soc. (pres. 1999-2006). Mem. Ch. Eng. Home: London, England. Died Dec. 26, 2006.

**HECKMAN, WILLIAM JOSEPH,** oil and chemical company executive, negotiator; b. NYC, Aug. 29, 1909; s. John Herman and Margaret Lauretta (Ferguson) H.; m. Mildred Berta Rogers, Sept. 3, 1938; children: William Rogers, Laura Graham Nokes. Student, CCNY, 1927-29. Office mgr. Scandia Mfg., NYC, 1927-29; asst. sec. Gerry Estates, Inc., NYC, 1929-38; asst. gen. purchasing agt. Texaco, NYC, 1938-45; prodn. mgr., various other positions Warner-Hudnut, NYC, 1945-50; v.p. purchasing and transp. Aramco Overseas Corp., The Hague, Holland, 1950-53; dir. purchasing Olin Mathieson Chems., Balt. and NYC, 1953-60; v.p. spl. projects Olin Corp., NYC and Stamford, Conn., 1960-74; dir. Ormet Corp. and subs., 1961-74; bus. cons. Sun City, Ariz., from 1974. Dir. purchasing and transp. Arabian-Am. Oil Co., N.Y.C., 1950-53. Dir., v.p. Sun City Recreation Ctrs., Inc., 1984-86; trustee Ohio Valley Improvement Assn. Mem. Lake Club, N.Y. Athletic Club. Republican. Roman Catholic. Died Oct. 1990.

**HEE, THOMAS WAH SUNG,** accountant; b. Honolulu, Feb. 9, 1955; s. Clifford S.C. and Blanche K.Q. (Ching) H. BBA, U. Hawaii, 1978; grad. with high honors, Sch. of Bank Adminstrn., 1988. CPA Hawaii. Programmer First Hawaiian Bank, Honolulu, 1979-80, sr. fin. analyst, 1980-83, officer acctg., 1983-88, asst. v.p., from 1988. Chair fin. com. Hemophilia Found. Hawaii, 1981-85, also bd. trustees 1985—. Mem. Nat. Assn. Accts., Honolulu Marathon Assn. (chair data processing 1980), Ala Moana Jaycees (pres. 1985). Home: Honolulu, Hawaii. Deceased.

**HEEBE, FREDERICK JACOB REAGAN,** federal judge; b. Gretna, La., Aug. 25, 1922; s. Bernhardt and Marguerite (Reagan) H.; m. Doris Stewart, Oct. 6, 1984; children by previous marriage: Frederick Riley, Adrea Dee. BA, Tulane U., 1943, LLB, 1949. Bar: La. 1949. Practice in, Gretna, 1949-60; judge divsn. B 24th Jud. Dist. Ct., Jefferson Parish, La., 1961—66; judge US Dist. Ct. (eastern dist.) La., New Orleans, 1966—72, chief judge, 1972—92, sr. judge, 1992—2014. Mem. Community Welfare Council Jefferson Parish; chmn. Jefferson Parish Bd. Public Welfare, 1953-55; Mem. Jefferson Parish Council, 1958-60, vice chmn., 1958-60; Bd. dirs. Social Welfare Planning Council New Orleans, New Orleans Regional Mental Center and Clinic, W. Bank Assn. for Retarded. Served to capt., inf. AUS, World War II. Decorated Purple Heart, Bronze Star. Mem. ABA, La., New Orleans, Fed. Bar Assns., American Judicature Soc., Phi Beta Kappa. Died Aug. 10, 2014.

**HEFFNER, RICHARD DOUGLAS,** historian, educator, communications consultant, television producer; b. NYC, Aug. 5, 1925; s. Albert Simon and Cely (Bender) H.; m. Anne de la Vergne, Dec. 14, 1946; m. Elaine Segal, July 30, 1950; children: Daniel Jason, Charles Andrew. AB, Columbia U., 1946, MA (Mitchell fellow), 1947. Tchg. asst. history U. Calif., Berkeley, 1947-48; instr. American history Rutgers U., 1948-50, univ. prof. comm., pub. policy, from 1964; lectr. history Columbia, 1950-52; prof. history Sarah Lawrence Coll., 1952-53; dir. public affairs WNBC-TV, NYC, 1955-57; dir. programs Met. Ednl. TV Assn., NYC, 1957-59; editl.l cons. CBS, Inc.; mem. editl. bd., dir. spl. projects CBS-TV Network, 1959-61; v.p., gen. mgr. ednl. TV Channel 13 WNET, NYC, 1961-63; pres. Richard Heffner Associates., Inc., NYC, 1964—2013. Mem. program adv. bd. Teleprompter Corp.; dir. commn. campaign costs 20th Century Fund, 1968-69; dir. study TV's environ. messages Ford Found., 1970-72; chmn. bd. classification rating adminstrn. Motion Picture Assn. America, 1974-94. Producer-moderator Richard Heffner's Open Mind, NBC-TV, 1956—59, Channel 13, NYC, from 1973, moderator-host National Educational TV series People and Politics, 1964, exec. editor-host WPIX-TV From the Editor's Desk, 1981—86; author: A Documentary History of the United States, 1952; author: (with Alexander Heffner) 8th Edit., 2009; author: Conversations with Elie Wiesel, 2001, As They Saw It, A Conversational History of Modern America, 2003; editor: Alexis de Tocqueville's Democracy in America, 1956, 2010. Mem. exec. com., vice chmn. bd. NYC Police Found.; chmn. judiciary com. cameras cts. NY State, 1987-89. Sr. fellow Freedom Forum Media Studies Ctr., NYC, 1994-95. Mem. AAAS, Acad. Motion Picture Arts & Scis., American Hist. Assn., Nat. Assn. Ednl. Broadcasters, Phi Beta Kappa. Clubs: Century. Home: New York, NY. Died Dec. 17, 2013.

**HEFNER, ARCHIE,** lawyer; b. Gridley, Calif., Dec. 4, 1922; s. Robert Emmet and Caroline Vida (Sheppard) Hefner; m. Barbara Bowler, June 2, 1945; children: William R., Madeline, Mark D. Student, Calif. State U., Chico, 1940—43, U. of Pacific, 1943; JD, U. Calif.-Hastings Coll. Law, 1949. Bar: Calif. 1950. Assoc. Hoberg & Finger, San Francisco, 1950—51; ptnr. Hefner, Stark & Marois and predecessor, Sacramento, from 1951; sr. ptnr., pres. Archie Hefner, Inc., Sacramento, from 1981. Trustee Sacramento Pioneer Found., 1972, Sacramento Regional Found., from 1986, Sacramento Symphony Found., 1984—87; chmn. Sacramento Host Commn., 1983—84, Sacramento Opera Assn. Adv. Bd., from 1985; pres. Sacramento Symphony Assn., 1974—76; bd. dirs. Sacramento Tree Found., from 1982; dir. Sacramento Symphony Assn., 1968—80. Served to lt. (j.g.) USNR, 1942—46, PTO. Mem.: ABA, Order of Coif., Sacramento Execs. Assn. (pres. 1957), Sacramento Met. C. of C. (pres. 1966), Sacramento Jr. C. of C. (pres. 1955), Am. Judicature Soc., Rotary, Shriners, Masons, Scottish Rite. Republican. Home: Sacramento, Calif. Died Nov. 1998.

**HEILIGMAN, HAROLD A.,** chemical engineer; b. Reading, Pa., Jan. 8, 1900; s. Max and Bertha (Fidler) Heiligman; m. Marion E. Bailey, Mar. 15, 1933. Degree in Chem. Engring., Lehigh U., 1921. Rsch. engr. E.J. Lavino & Co., Phila., 2022—26, asst. tech. dir., 1926—43, gen. mgr. tech. dept., 1943—61, v.p. R & D, 1961—64; dir. Nobilium Products, Phila., 1938—43, Colonial Abrasive Products, Conshohocken, Pa., 1940—80; cons. Internat. Mineral & Chem. Co., Libertyville, Ill., 1965—72. Cons. in field. Contbr. articles to profl. jours. Fellow: ASTM (Award of Merit 1971), Am. Ceramic Soc. (Disting. Svc. award, St. Louis sect. 1971), Am. Inst. Chemists. Republican. Jewish. Achievements include research in chemistry. Home: Norristown, Pa. Died June 1989.

**HEILMEIER, GEORGE HARRY,** electrical engineer, researcher; b. Phila., May 22, 1936; s. George C. and Anna I. (Heineman) Heilmeier; m. Janet Faunce, June 24, 1961; 1 child, Elizabeth. BSEE, U. Pa., Phila., 1958; MS in Engring., Princeton U., NJ, 1960, MA in Solid State Electronics & Engring., 1961, PhD in Solid State Electronics & Engring., 1962; Deng (hon.), Stevens Inst. Tech., Hoboken, NJ, 1995, Technion-Israel Inst. Tech., 1997. With RCA Labs., Princeton, 1958—66, dir. solid state device rsch., 1966—69, dir. device concepts, 1969—70; White House fellow, spl. asst. to sec. US Dept. Def., Washington, 1970—71, asst. dir. def. rsch. & engring., electronic & phys. sciences, 1971—74; dir. Def. Advanced Projects Agy. (DARPA), 1975—77; v.p. corp. rsch., devel., engring. and strategic planning Tex. Instruments Inc., 1977—83, sr. v.p., chief tech. officer, 1983—91; pres., CEO Bell Comm. Rsch., Inc., Livingston, NJ, 1991—96; chmn., CEO Telcordia Technologies, Inc. (formerly Bell Comm. Rsch., Inc.), 1996—97, chmn. emeritus, 1997—2014. Mem. adv. group on electron devices US Dept. Def., 1979—91; mem. bd. overseers. U. Pa. Sch. Engring. & Applied Sci., from 1989; mem. def. sci. bd. Pres.'s Nat. Security Telecom. Adv. Com., 1991—97; mem. Pres.'s Com. on Nat. Medal of Sci., 1992—94, US Adv. Coun. Nat. Info. Infrastructure, Nat. Security Agy. Adv. bd., Def. Adv. Bd.; bd. dirs. TRW Inc., 1992—2002, Compaq Computer Corp., 1994—2002, Automatic Data Processing Inc., 1995—2003, Teletech Holdings, 1998—2005, INET Technologies, Inc., 2001—14; chmn. General Motors Technology Adv. Bd. Contbr. articles to profl. jours. Recipient IR-100 New Product award, Indsl. Rsch. Assn., 1968—69, Arthur Fleming award, US Jaycees, 1974, Disting. Civilian Svc. award, US Dept. Def., 1975, 1977, Nat. Medal Sci., The White House, 1991, Computers & Commn. prize, NEC Found., Japan, 1992, Indsl. Rsch. Inst. medal, 1993, John Scott award, City of Phila., 1996, John Fritz medal, American Assn. Engring. Societies, 1999, Pioneer of Stealthaward for Visionary Leadership and Trailblazing Contributions of Enduring Nat. Significance in the Devel. of Low Observable Aircraft, 2002, Kyoto prize, Inamori Found., Japan, 2005, Edwin Land medal, Optical Soc. America, 2006; named Tech. Leader of Yr., Industry Week, 1994; named to The Consumer Electronics Hall of Fame, 2006, The Nat. Inventors Hall of Fame, 2009. Fellow: IEEE (life David Sarnoff award 1976, Outstanding Achievement award 1984, Philips award 1985, Founder's award 1986, Medal of Honor 1997); mem.: NAE (Founder's award 1992, Charles Stark Draper prize 2012), American Acad. Arts & Sciences, U. Pa. Alumni Assn., Eta Kappa Nu (Outstanding Young US Engr. award 1969, Vladimir Karapetoff Eminent Meml. award 1993), Tau Beta Pi, Sigma Xi. Conservative. Methodist. Achievements include discovery of new electro-optic effects in liquid crystals, which led to the first working liquid crystal displays based on what he called the dynamic scattering mode (DSM) making possible for the first time the electronic control of the reflection of light; development of the first liquid crystal displays for calculators, watches, and instrumentation; patents in field. Avocations: reading, sports. Died Apr. 21, 2014.

**HEINRICH, JOHN WILLIAM, SR.,** manufacturing executive; b. Alameda, Calif., Aug. 10, 1916; adopted s. Ida Heinrich; m. Ernestine Loehwing, Nov. 11, 1940; 1 child: John William. Attended, Healds Bus. Coll., 1935. Retail salesman Tex. Co., wholesale Firestone Tire & Rubber, 1938—42; truck bus. rep. B.F. Goodrich Co., San Francisco, 1945—49; mfg. agt. John Heinrich & Assocs., Sacramento, 1949—66; pres. John Heinrich Co., Sparks, Nev., from 1966. Dir. Hesik Co.; advisor U.S. Army Ordnance Dept. With US Army, 1942—46. Mem.: NAM, Mfrs. Agts. Assn., Nat. Fedn. Ind. Bus., El Macero Country Club, Nat. 20-30 Club. Republican. Home: El Macero, Calif. Died Oct. 8, 1987.

**HEINZ, ELISE BROOKFIELD,** lawyer, former state legislator; b. Plainfield, NJ, Jan. 14, 1935; d. Winfield Bernard and Rachel Edwards (Clarke) H.; m. James Edwin

Clayton, 1961; children: Jonathan Brown Clayton, David Lake Clayton. BA, Wellesley Coll., 1955; LL.B. cum laude, Harvard U., 1961. Bar: D.C. 1961, Va. 1969. Atty. Fowler, Leva, Hawes & Symington, Washington, 1961-64; individual practice law Washington, 1964-68, Arlington, Va., 1968—90; mem. Va. House of Delegates, 1978-82. Adj. prof. Georgetown U. Law Center, 1971-72 Mem. Chesapeake & Ohio Canal Nat. Hist. Park Commn. Mem. ABA, American Law Inst., Nat. Women's Polit. Caucus. Democrat. Died Jan. 19, 2014.

**HEISLEY, MICHAEL E.,** retired manufacturing executive, professional sports team executive; b. Washington, Mar. 13, 1937; m. Agnes Heisley; 5 children. BA, Georgetown U., 1960. With Robertson-Ceco Corp., Toms Foods, Inc., WorldPort Comm. Inc., Pettibone Corp.; founder The Heico Companies. LLC, St. Charles, Ill., 1979; owner Memphis Grizzlies (formerly Vancouver Grizzlies), 2000—12. Chmn. Davis Wire Corp., Toms Foods, Inc. Mem. St. Patrick's Cath. Ch. Named one of The Forbes 400: Richest Americans, Forbes mag., 2006—13. Mem. Turnaround Mgmt. Assn., Union League Club, Chgo. Club. Home: Saint Charles, Ill. Died Apr. 27, 2014.

**HELD, PHILIP,** artist; b. NYC, June 2, 1920; s. Conrad Christopher and Charlotte (Ditchett) H.; m. Ann Caine, Sept. 12, 1950 (dec. Dec. 1991); 1 child, Andrew Christopher; m. Millie Johnson Berkowitz, Oct. 31, 1992 (dec. June 1995); stepchildren: Brent, Amy. Student, Art Students League, NY, 1938—42, Sch. Art Student League, 1946, Sch. Art Studies, NYC, 1947-48, Tchrs. Coll., Columbia U., 1949. Tchr. Scarborough Sch., NY, 1947-52, Fieldston Sch., NY, 1952-71, chmn. art dept. NY, 1962-71; art edn. coordinator Booker-Bay Haven Sch., Sarasota, 1971-79; instr. painting, photography, calligraphy Visual, Performing Arts Center, Sarasota County, 1980-83; chief photographer Sarasota County Sch. Bd. Pub. Info. Office, 1984-90, Gruber-Peters Prodns., Hollywood, Calif., from 1991. Photographer Fla. Film Commn., Sarasota C. of C.; contbr. photographer Radcliffe Quar., Inform, Nat. State Leadership Tng. Inst. on Gifted and Talented, Ebony mag.; staff photographer Venice Symphony Orch., Sarasota-Manatee Cmty. Orch., 1990-94, Sarasota Pops Orchestra, 1995—, Tuscan Ways (Tours), Italy, 1996—; bass trombone West Coast Big Band, 1996—. One-man shows: Eggleston Gallery, NYC, 1948, Berkshire Mus., Mass., 1949, 67, Camino Gallery, NYC, 1960, 62, Phoenix Gallery, NYC, 1965, 67, Fontana Gallery, Phila., 1965, 67, 72, Gladstone Gallery, Woodstock, N.Y., 1965, Polari Gallery, Woodstock, 1970, Brevard Coll., Fla., 1973, Lighthouse Gallery, Tequesta, Fla., 1980; exhibited in group shows: Mus. Modern Art, NYC, 1958, Pa. Acad. Fine Arts, 1962, U. Mass., 1966, Albany Inst. Arts and History, 1960, 63, LIU, 1960, Brown U., 1963, Phila. Mus., 1968, St. Johns U., 1970, Winthrop Coll., SC, 1963, St. Paul Art Center, 1963, Drew U., 1966, Ringling Mus., Sarasota, Fla., 1973, Riverside Mus., NYC, 1959, 60, Gallery Contemporary Art, Winston Salem, NC, 1972, Fontana Gallery, Phila., 1975-76, Regional Shows, Fa. Gulf Coast, 1975—, Gallery of Sarasota, 1976, Hilton Leech Gallery, 1977, Pleiades Gallery, NYC, 1977, Fla. Artists Group XXIX Ann., 1978, Harmon Gallery, Naples and Sarasota, Fla., 1978, 80, 83, NY State Council on Arts Exhbn., 1977-80, Fla. Artists Group XXXI Ann., Sarasota, 1980, St. Petersburg Pub. Library, 1982, Lighthouse Gallery, Tequestar, Fla., 1982, Fla. Artists Group XXXIII Ann., 1983, S.W.Fla. Artscape, 1989, Parkshore Gallery, Naples, Fla., 1989, Fla. Artists Group 41st Ann. Naples Art Gallery, 1990, Fla. Artists Group 42d Ann., 1991, Fl. So. Coll., Lakeland, 1991, Lee County Alliance of the Arts, Ft. Myers, Fla., 1991, Parkside Gallery, Naples, 1991, Fla. Artists Group 43d Ann., Longboat Key Art Ctr., Fla., 1992, Ann. Lee County Alliance of the Arts, Ft. Myers, Fla., 1992; 2-artist exhbn. Lee County Alliance of the Arts, 1992, Orlando Mus. of Art Biennial Juried exhbn., 1995, Fla. Competitive Exhbn. Vero Beach Art Club, 1995, Art and Design Soc. Fort Walton Beach, Fla., 1995, Ctr. Emerging Art Competitive Exhbn., Boca Raton, Capitol Gallery, Tallahassee, Fla., 1996, Fla. Artist Group Ann., 1997, Art Ctr., St. Petersburg, 1998; represented in permanent collections: Smithsonian Inst., Washington, U. Mass., Berkshire Mus., Pittsfield, Mass., Art Students League of NY, Ringling Mus., Winterthur (Del.) Mus., Barnett Bank of Fla.; photographer motion picture film com. Sarasota (Fla.) C. of C.; contbg. photographer Alive! Mem. Sarasota Brass Quintet, Joyful Noise Brass Quartet, The Jazz Ambs., Venice Symphony (personnel mgr. 1995-96), Charlotte Symphony; bass trombonist West Coast Big Band, Skyliners Big Band, Sarasota Pops Orch., Venice Symphony Orch., Charlotte Symphony Orch.; 1st trombone Sarasota Suncoast Concert Band; chmn. Woodstock Artists Assn., 1959-60, bd. dirs., 1957-61. With US Army, 1942-46. Kleinert Found. grantee, 1966 Mem. Art Students League of New York (life), Sarasota Art Assn., Fla. Artists Group, Art League Manatee County, Am. Fedn. Musicians, Sarasota Art Assn. (past bd. dirs.). *It is merely a commonplace to observe that all ages have had their problems and difficulties; but I am glad to be a part of my time and place ... and to have the chance in a quiet way to contribute to its arts, and hence its life.* Died June 1999.

**HELGASON, SIGURDUR,** retired airline executive; b. Reykjavik, Iceland, July 20, 1921; s. Helgi and Olof (Sigurjonsdottir) Hallgrimsson; m. Unnur Einarsdottir, Dec. 20, 1952; children: Olof, Edda, Helgi, Sigurdur. BBA, Columbia U., 1947. Vice chmn. Icelandic Airlines/Loftleidir, Reykjavik, 1953—74; pres. Icelandic Airlines Inc., NYC, 1961—74; CEO Internat. Air Bahama, 1969—74; mng. dir. Flugleidir hf (Icelandair), Reykjavik, 1974—79; pres., CEO, 1979—84; chmn. bd., 1984—91; trustee Internat. House, NYC, St. Joseph Hosp., Reykjavik, 1979. Decorated knight Order Falcon, comdr. Cross of Order of Falcon, (Iceland), grand officer Order Oak Crown Luxembourg; recipient Al Merito Civil, Spain, 1990, Order of Merit award, Iceland Sports Fedn., 1983, Gold medal, Icelandic Aero. Soc., 1986; named Hon. Citizen, Winnipeg, Man., Can., 1965. Mem.: Lutheran, Wings Club, Rotary, Internat. Air Transport Assn., Internat. C. of C., Icelandic-Am. Soc. Home: Reykjavik, Iceland. Died Feb. 8, 2009.

**HELLWIG, GÜNTER,** mathematician, educator; b. Oberschöna, Germany, Feb. 9, 1926; s. Martin and Frida (Sohr) H.; m. Birgitta Öman, Mar. 25, 1961; children: Annette, Armin, Veronika, Angelika. Diploma in math., U. Göttingen, Germany, 1949; Dr.rer.nat., Tech. U., Berlin, 1951, habilitation, 1952. Pvt. docent Tech. U., 1952-58, ordinary prof., dir. Inst. Math., 1958-66; ordinary prof. Rheinisch-Westfälische Technische Hochschule, Aachen, Germany, 1966—91, dir. Inst. Math., 1966-91. Author: Partial Differential Equations, 1960, English translation, 1964, Differential Operators of Mathematical Physics, 1964, English translation, 1967, Höhere Mathematik I, 1971; contbr. numerous articles to sci. jours. With German Air Force, 1943-45. Fulbright Found. grantee, 1954-55. Mem. Deutsche Mathematiker Vereinigung. Lutheran. Home: Aachen, Germany. Died June 17, 2004.

**HELMS, FRED BRYAN,** retired lawyer; b. Union County, NC, Apr. 12, 1896; s. Emanuel M. and Frances P. (Austin) H.; m. Margaret V. Harrelson, July 14, 1927 (dec.); children: Margaret Harrelson (Mrs. Joseph B. Tyson), Frances (Mrs. Frances H. Abernathy); m. Susan Erwin Williamson, Mar. 3, 1978 (div. Jan. 1994). Student, U. Ga., 1919-20; JD, Wake Forest Coll., 1922; postgrad., Columbia U., 1922. Bar: N.C. 1922. Tchr. pub. schs., Union County, 1914-15; mgr. chain clothing stores Athens, Ga., East Moline, Ill., Muscatine, Iowa, 1919-22; since practiced in Charlotte; pros. atty. City of Charlotte, 1925-27; county judge Mecklenburg County, N.C., 1927-31; pvt. practice, specializing in civil law, from 1931; ptnr. firm Smith Helms Mulliss & Moore and predecessors, ret. Organizer, 1st pres. Charlotte Community Chest (now United Way), 1932-33; chmn. Citizens Com., 1941-45; mem. Commn. to Study and Revise Ins. Laws N.C., 1945-47, Commn. for Improvement Adminstrn. of Justice in N.C., 1947-49, N.C. Jud. Council, N.C. Gov.'s adv. commn. on segregation, Nat. Commn. Reform Fed. Criminal Laws.; Past trustee Wingate Coll. Presdl. elector N.C., 1956; Organizer, atty., commr. Charlotte Meml. Hosp. Authority. Served as 2d lt., F.A. U.S. Army, 1918-19. Recipient Silver medallion NCCJ, 1958; Disting. Svc. Citation in law Wake Forest U., 1971, Disting. Alumnus award, Wingate Coll., 1989. Fellow Am. Coll. Trial Lawyers; mem. Am. Soc. Internat. Law, ABA, N.C. State Bar (v.p. 1944-46, pres. 1946-47), N.C. Bar Assn. (inducted into Gen. Practice Hall of Fame 1991), Mecklenburg County Bar Assn., Am. Judicature Soc., Am. Law Inst., Am. Legion, City Club, Charlotte Country Club, Kiwanis. Democrat. Home: 2909 Barrington Ln Charleston SC 29414-7305 Office: 227 N Tryon St Charlotte NC 28202-2136 *My ambition from childhood, has been and is, to be a qualified, worthy, loyal and active member of and leader in the profession of the law (one of the three great professions), my church, my city, my state and my country; and at all times to be devoted to my family, my home and my God.*

**HELMUTH, JOHN WILLIAM,** agricultural economist, director university facility; b. Harrisonville, Mo., Feb. 21, 1944; s. Floyd E. and Martha M. (Hershey) H.; m. Kerry O'Brien, Aug. 10, 1968 (dec. Oct. 1984); children: Erika F., Evan H.; m. Paula Forrest, Dec. 26, 1987. BA in Math., U. Mo., 1966, PhD in Argl. Econs., 1970; MS in Argl. Econs., U. Conn., 1969. Commodity account exec. Hornblower & Weeks-Hemphill, Noyes, Inc., LA, 1973-74; agrl. economist Econ. Rsch. Svc., USDA, Washington, 1974-76; staff economist Agrl. Mktg. Svc., USDA, Washington, 1978-79, Office of Chief Economist, Commodity Futures Trading Commn., Washington, 1976-78; chief economist com. on small bus. US House of Representatives, Washington, 1979-87; exec. coord. 1988 World Food Conf., Des Moines, 1987-88; asst. dir. econs. Ctr. for Agrl. and Rural Devel. Ctr. for Argl. and Rural Devel., Iowa State U., Ames, from 1987, dir. natural resources and conservation policy div., 1988-90. Invited presenter various orgns. including Indsl. Biotech. Assn., Chgo., 1989, Dakota Resource Coun., Mandan, N.D., 1989, 35th Ann. Nat. Farmers Orgn. Conv., San Antonio, 1989, 1990 Farm Aid TV Concert, Indpls., Nat. Assn. Attys. Gen., 1990, others; provider expert testimony state and fed. govtl. and pvt. party proceedings. Co-editor, contbr. chpt.: 1988 World Food Conference Proceedings, Vol. I: Policy Addresses, 1989; co-editor: 1988 World Food Conference Proceedings, Vol. II: Issue Papers, 1989; co-contbr. chpt.: Federal Marketing Programs in Agriculture: Issues and Options, 1983, Future Frontiers in Agricultural Marketing Research, 1983; contbr. articles to profl. publs.; author Perspective on Prices column The Beverly Hills Ind., 1974; mem. editorial bd. Jour. Futures Markets. Mem. zoning bd. of adjustments City of Ames, Iowa, 1990—; treas., bd. dirs. Reston (Va.) Children's Ctr., 1985-87; vol. speakers bur. Hospice of No. Va., 1985-87; chmn. bd. elders Good Shepherd Luth. Ch., Reston, 1980-81, pres., 1986-87. Capt. USAF, 1970-73. Decorated Joint Svc. Commendation medal with oak leaf cluster; recipient George Washington Honor medal Freedoms Found. at Valley Forge. Mem. Am. Econ. Assn., Agrl. Econs. Assn. Home: Cheyenne, Wyo. Died Nov. 26, 1999.

**HEMBERG, ESKIL,** music director, composer; b. Stockholm, Jan. 19, 1938; s. Bengt E. E. and Ingeborg R. (Thelander) H.; m. Birgit S. Ohlsson, July 8, 1962; children: Anna Maria, Johan, Love. Degree in music teaching, Royal Coll. Music, Stockholm, 1961, higher cantor's degree, 1961, higher organist's degree, 1964. Exec. producer Swedish Radio, Stockholm, 1963-70; planning mgr., dir. fgn. rels. Nat. Inst. Concerts, Stockholm, 1970-83; managing and artistic dir. Gothenburg (Sweden) Opera and Symphony, 1984-87; gen. dir. Royal Opera, Stockholm, 1987-96; prof. Swedish studies, artist in residence Bethany Coll., Lindsborg, Kans., 2000—04. Condr. Stockholm U. Chorus, 1959-84, Grammophone Records. Composer operas, choral works, chamber music. Sweden state grantee, 1972, 73, 75, 81; recipient Johannes Norrby medal Royal Acad. Music, 1978, Zoltan Kodaly medal Hungary, 1982, Pro Arte et Scientia medal U. Gothenburg, 1987, His Majesty the King's Own medal, 1993, Gold medal Royal Opera, Stockholm, 1996, Kurt Atterberg prize, 1997; decorated comdr. Order of Merit (Portugal) 1991, Grosses Bundes-Verdienstkreuz (Germany), 1995. Mem. Royal Swedish Acad. Music, Assn. Internat. Dirs. de l'Opera, Swedish Composers Assn. (pres. 1971-83), Internat. Fedn. for Choral Music (advisor, bd. dirs. 1984-90, pres. 1999-2004), Swedish Choral Dirs. Assn., Swedish Composers Rights Assn. (v.p. 1972-83), Internat. Music Coun. UNESCO (pres. 1991-93). Home: Nacka, Sweden. Died June 26, 2004.

**HENDERSON, ANGELO B.,** journalist; b. Louisville, 1962; m. Felecia Henderson; 1 child, Grant. BA in Journalism, U. Ky., 1985. Journalist The Detroit News, 1989—95; joined The Wall Street Jour., Detroit, 1995—2003; host Your Voice with Angelo Henderson WCBH-AM 1200, Detroit. Deacon Hartford Meml. Bapt. Ch., Detroit. Recipient Journalism award Detroit Press Club Found., 1993, Unity award for Excellence in Minority Reporting for Public Affairs/Social Issues, 1993, Best of Gannett award for Bus. & Consumer Affairs Reporting, 1996, Pulitzer prize for Feature Writing, 1999; named to The U. Ky. Disting. Alumni Hall of Fame, 2005 Mem. Nat. Assn. Black Journalists (former pres. Detroit chpt., award for outstanding coverage of the black condition 1992). Died Feb. 15, 2014.

**HENDERSON, DORLAND JOHN,** retired electrical engineer; b. Salisbury, NC, Feb. 4, 1898; s. William Everett and Sally Bettie (Lord) H.; m. Elizabeth Cleotta Van Cleave, Aug. 8, 1924 (dec. Nov. 1931); 1 child, Joel Dorland; m. Elizabeth Hoyt Baker, Dec. 28, 1955. BSEE, Purdue U., 1918. Lic. profl. engr., N.J. Elec. test engr. Ill. Steel Co., Gary, Ind., 1920-21; chief electrician Maintenance of Way Pa. R.R., NYC, 1922-31; supt. drawbridges N.J. State Hwy. Dept., 1932-42, chief engr. elec. div., 1942-64, dir. traffic engring., 1964-70; ret., 1970. Author: Comments on Goverment of the City of Newark 1972-1985, 1986; designed low-level fluorescent lighting on Barnegat Bay's Rte. 72 bridge, N.J., 1959. Mem. Urban Transp. Task Force, Newark, 1987, North Newark Partnership, Friends of Br. Brook Park, Friends of Newark Pub. Library, Newark Mus., N.J. Hist. Soc., Nat. Trust for Hist. Preservation; trustee Newark Preservation and Landmarks Com. Served with S.C. U.S. Army, 1918-19. Named Man of Yr., North Ward Property Owners, Newark, 1984; recipient Disting. Citizen award Newark Mcpl. Council, 1983; cited with wife for numerous honors on restoration and gardens of 18th century farmhouse, 1964-76. Democrat. Avocation: woodworking. Home: Lillian, Ala. Deceased.

**HENDERSON, GEORGE POLAND,** publisher; b. London, Apr. 24, 1920; s. George James and Emma Rouse (Wilson) H.; m. Shirley Prudence Cotton, Apr. 27, 1953; children: Crispin Alastair Poland, Antony James Willis. Student, U. London, 1938-40. Comml. ref. libr. Guildhall Libr., London, 1938-63; dir. Kellys' Directories Ltd., Kingston-upon-Thames, 1963-66; dir., chmn. bd. CBD Rsch., Ltd., Beckenham, from 1966. Compiler, editor: Current British Directories, 6 edits., 1953-71, European Companies: Guide to Sources of Information, 3 edit., 1961-72, Directory of British Associations, 11 edit., 1965-92. Capt. Royal Artillery, Eng., 1940-46. Fellow Inst. of Dirs., Royal Philatelic Soc.; mem. Royal Instn. of Gt. Britain, European Assn. Directory Pubs. (pres. 1976-78), Assn. Brit. Directory Pubs. (pres. 1974-75). Avocations: travel, gardening, postal history. Home: Beckenham, England. Died Jan. 7, 2008.

**HENDERSON, SARAH COTHRAN,** civic worker, former educator; b. Greenwood, SC, Feb. 2, 1915; d. Thomas White and Willie Maude (Boswell) Cothran; m. William Edward Henderson (dec. Jan. 1980); 1 child, William Edward. AB, Lander Coll., 1937; MEd, Furman U., 1963; postgrad, Clemson U., 1971—73; degree, LaVerne Coll., 1971, Furman U., 1976. Jr. tchr. Greenville County Schs., SC, 1950—78, SC Retired Educators Assn., 1978—86; regent Nathaneal Greene Chpt. DAR, 1974—76; state chmn. pub. relations SC Soc., 1976—79, state conf. chmn., 1982, dist. 1 dir., 1979—82; historian Palmetto State Officers Club, SC, 1982—85, recording sec., 1985—88, treas., from 1988; rec. sec. Cornelius Keith Chpt. Nat. Soc. Daus. Am. Colonists. Recipient Outstanding Ednl. Achievement award, Friends Edn. Greenville County & Pleasantburg Rotary Club, 1974. Mem.: Friends Greenville Libr., Friends SC State Mus., Nat. Archives, Nat. Trust Hist. Preservation, Furman U. Alumni Assn., Lander Coll. Alumni Assn., Huguenot Soc. SC, Ligon Family Assn., Greenville Hist. Soc., SC Geneal. Soc., Order Washington, Colonial Order Crown, Plantagenet Soc., Nat. Soc. Magna Charta Dames, Greenville Geneal. Soc. (charter, archivist 1980—83), Greenville Art Assn., Greenville Woman's. Presbyterian. Home: Greenwood, SC. Deceased.

**HENDRICKSE, RALPH GEORGE,** medical educator; b. Cape Town, South Africa, Nov. 5, 1926; s. William George and Johanna Theresa (Dennis) H.; m. Begum Abdurahman; 5 children. MB, BChir, U. Cape Town, South Africa, 1948, MD, 1957, DSc in Medicine (hon.), 1998. Staff mem. McCord Zulu Hosp., Durban, South Africa, 1949-54; sr. registrar Univ. Coll. Hosp., Ibadan, Nigeria, 1955-57; lectr., sr. lectr. U. Ibadan, 1957-62, prof., head dept. pediat., 1962-69, dir. Inst. Child Health, 1964-69; prof. tropical pediat. internat. child health U. Liverpool, England, 1969-91, dean Sch. Tropical Medicine, 1988-91, ret., prof. emeritus, from 1991. Cons. Fed. Ministry Health, Nigeria, 1965-69; founder, life mem., former v.p. Paediatric Assn. Nigeria, 1969—; mem. Tropical Medicine Bd. MRC UK, 1977-81. Founder, editor-in-chief Annals of Tropical Pediat., 1981-

2003; editor-in-chief, author: (textbook) Pediatrics in the Tropics, 1991; prodr. (film) Sickle Cell Anemia in Nigerian Children, 1964. Rockefeller fellow, 1961-62, Heinz (sr.) fellow Brit. Ped. Assn., 1961. Fellow Royal Soc. Tropical Medicine Hygiene (mem. coun. 1978-80, 85-87), Royal Coll. Physicians (Edinburgh, London, Frederick Murgatroyd Meml. prize 1970), Royal Coll. Pediat. Child Health (hon. founder 1996); mem. Brit. Pediat. Assn. (mem. acad. bd. 1983-86, Heinz fellow 1961, hon. membership Recognition Outstanding Contbns. Pediat. Child Health award 1995), Internat. Pediat. Assn. (adv. expert tropical pediat. 1986—). Avocations: photography, sketching, swimming, theater. Home: Liverpool, England. Died Dec. 2009.

**HENGEL, MARTIN,** theology educator; b. Reutlingen, Germany, Dec. 14, 1926; s. Gottlob and Berta (Kistenmacher) H.; m. Marianne Kistler, Aug. 3, 1957. ThD, U. Tübingen, Fed. Republic Germany, 1959, Habilitation, 1967; DDH (hon.), St. Andrews U., Scotland, 1981; DD (hon.), Durham U., 1985; DDH (hon.), Cambridge U., 1989; DTheol. (hon.), U. Uppsala, Sweden, 1979, U. Strasbourg, 1988; LittD (hon.), U. Dublin, 2000. Mng. dir. Hengella GmbH, Aalen, Fed. Republic Germany, 1953-54, 57-64; prof. theology U. Erlangen (Fed. Republic Germany), 1968-72, U. Tübingen, 1972-92, prof. emeritus, 1992—2009. Author: Die Zeloten, 1961, 2d edit., 1989, Judentum und Hellenismus, 1969,3d edit., 1988, Nachfolge und Charisma, 1968, Der Soken Gottes, 1985, Studies in the Gospel of Mark, 1983, Between Jesus and Paul, 1983, The Cross of the Son of God, 1986, Earliest Christianity, 1986, The Johannine Question, 1989, The Hellenization of Judaea in the First Century after Christ, 1989, The Prechristian Paul, 1991, Studies in Early Christology, 1995, Judaica et Helenistica, Kleine Schriften I, 1996, (with Anna Maria Schoemer) Paul between Damascus and Antioch, 1997, Judaica, Helenistica et Christiana, Kleine Schriften II, 1999, The Four Gospels and the One Gospel of Jesus Christ, 2000. Fellow Brit. Acad. (corr.); mem. Heidelberger Akademie der Wissenschaften, Roal Netherlands Acad. Arts and Scis. (fgn. mgm.). Home: Tübingen, Germany. Died July 2, 2009.

**HENKEL, ZANE GREY,** retired investor; b. Denison, Iowa, Jan. 19, 1937; s. Franz Henry and Ennice Pearl (Hoskinson) H.; m. Beverly Grace Joy, June 18, 1960; children: Daniel Greyson, Stephen Christopher, Nathan Zachary, Philip Alexander. BA, Drake U., 1970; MEd, Auburn U., 1973. Cert. secondary tchr., Fla., Ga., Ala., Miss., La., Iowa. Freelance musician, Des Moines, 1954-62; owner, mgr. Henkel Music Studio, Des Moines, 1960-62; instr. music, co-dir. Elmer Conservatory, Milw., 1962-65; rehab. supr. State of Iowa, Des Moines, 1974-81; disability investigator and vocat. specialist Social Security Adminstrn., Des Moines, 1981-87. Spl. asst. to U.S. Senator Henry Jackson, 1975; real estate developer, Polk City, Iowa, 1977-85. Mem. Nat. Rehab. Assn. (pres. Iowa vocat. evaluation div. 1977), Cen. Iowa United Profls. (pres. 1984-85), Phi Beta Kappa, Phi Kappa Phi. Avocation: foreign and domestic travel. Home: Lynchburg, Va. Died Apr. 9, 1991.

**HENNESSY, ELLEN ANNE,** lawyer, pension consultant, educator; b. Auburn, NY, Mar. 3, 1949; d. Charles Francis and Mary Anne (Roan) H.; m. Frank Daspit, Aug. 27, 1974. BA, Mich. State U., 1971; JD, Cath. U., 1978; LLM in Taxation, Georgetown U., 1984. Bar: D.C. 1978, U.S. Ct. Appeals (D.C. cir.) 1978, U.S. Supreme Ct. 1984. Various positions NEH, Washington, 1971-74; atty. office chief counsel IRS, Washington, 1978-80; atty.-advisor Pension Benefit Guaranty Corp., Washington, 1980-82; assoc. Stroock & Stroock & Lavan, Washington, 1982-85, Willkie Farr & Gallager, 1985-86, ptnr. Washington, 1987-93; dep. exec. dir. and chief negotiator Pension Benefit Guaranty Corp., Washington, 1993—98; sr. v.p. and dir. Actuarial Sci. Assoc. Holdings Inc., 1998—2000; sr. v.p. Aon Cons. Inc., Washington, 2000—03; pres. & CEO Fiduciary Counselors, Inc., from 1999. Adj. prof. law Georgetown U., Washington, from 1985; mem. com. on continuing profl. edn. Am. Law Inst./ABA, 1994—97; dir. Women's Inst. for a Secure Retirement, Nat. Women's Law Ctr., Goodyear Retiree VEBA. Mem. ABA (supervising editor taxation sect. newsletter 1984-87, mem. standing com. on continuing edn. 1990-94, chair joint com. on employee benefits 1991-92, mem. standing com. on tech. and info. sys. 2002—06, mem. task force on corp. responsiblity, 2002-03), Worldwide Employee Benefits Network (pres. 1987-88), DC Bar Assn. (mem. steering com. tax sect. 1988-93, chair continuing legal edn. com. 1993-95), Am. Coll. Employee Benefits Counsel (bd. govs. 2000-03). Democrat. Avocation: whitewater canoeing. Home: Washington, DC. Died Feb. 4, 2011.

**HENRION, ROSEMARY PROVENZA,** psychotherapist, educator; b. Greenville, Miss., Oct. 2, 1929; d. Vincent and Camille (Portera) Provenza; m. Albert Joseph Henrion, Sept. 8, 1956 (dec.); 1 child, Albert Joseph Jr. BSN, U. Tex., Galveston, 1963; MSN in Psychiat./Mental Health Nursing, Vanderbilt U., 1972; MEd in Secondary Edn., U. So. Miss., 1974. RN Tex.; cert. logotherapist, profl. psychotherapist. Psychotherapist St. Mary's Hosp., Galveston, Tex., 1951—52, office and pvt. duty surg. nurse, 1952—53; supr. ob-gyn. nursing Greenville Gen. Hosp., 1954—56, head nurse, ob-gyn. and med.-surg. nursing, 1953—54; instr. nursing Providence Hosp. Sch. Nursing, Waco, Tex., 1957—59; dir. inservice edn., asst. dir. nursing svc. Meml. Hosp., Gulfport, Miss., 1966—67, dir. nursing svc., 1967—68; psychiat. clin. nurse specialist Biloxi VA Med. Ctr., Miss., 1972—89, in-house cons., 1975—92, assoc. chief nursing svc., 1989—92; clin. nurse specialist VA Outpatient Ctr., Pensacola, Fla., 1992—98; adj. clin. prof., psychiat.-mental health nursing La. State U., New Orleans, 1975—76; adj. clin. prof. grad. nursing program U. So. Miss., Hattiesburg, 1983—92, liaison prof., logotherapy course Vienna, 1985; faculty V.F. Inst. Logotherapy, Berkeley and San Jose, Calif., 1983—92, Abilene, Tex., 1993—2011; clin. instr. grad. nursing program U. So. Ala., 1998—99. Mem. Internat. Acad. Behavioral Medicine, COunseling & Psychotherapy Inc., from 1990; internat. bd. dirs. V. F. Inst. of Logotherapy, from 1992; instr. advanced clin. logotherapy course World Congress Logotherapy, Dallas, from 1993; first guest lectr. internat. program on logotherapy U. South Africa, Pretoria, 2005; co-founder Inst. Meaningful Living, from 2003; educator, cons. St. Joseph Homes, Mobile, Ala., 2004—07, St. Mary's Homes, Mobile, from 2007, quality assurance specialist. Co-author: The Power of Meaningful Intimacy: Key to Successful Relationships, 2004; contbg. author: International Forum for Logotherapy, 1983—2010, Favorite Counseling and Therapy Techniques, 1997, Favorite Counseling and Therapy-Homework Assignments, 2000, Existential Psychotherapy of Meaning, 2009, Meaningful Living Continued Despite Lymphedema Diagnosis, 2010, Logotherapy Revisited, 2012. Mem. Pope John Paul II Cultural Ctr. Mem.: AAUW, Nat. Mus. Women Arts, Women's Mus.: Inst. for the Future (charter mem. 2000—08), Am. Assn. Med. Psychotherapists and Psychodiagnosticians, Nat. Women's History Mus. (charter mem. from 2000), Women's Mus. (Smithsonian affiliate mem. from 2009), Miss. Bd. Nursing (pres. 1977—79), Vanderbilt Alumni Assn., Sigma Theta Tau Internat. (Iota chpt. from 1972). Died Apr. 2, 2014.

**HENRY, JOSEPH,** retired conductor; b. Toledo, Ohio, Oct. 10, 1930; s. Thomas and Kathleen (Whyte) H.; m. Evelyn H. (Hipona), Jan. 1, 1995. MusB, Eastman Sch. of Music, 1952, MusM, 1953, D Musical Arts, 1965. Condr. Hillel Little Symphony, Rochester, NY, 1948-53; instr. in music U. Wis., Stevens Point, 1955-57; condr., music dir. Utica (N.Y.) Symphony, 1962-66; condr., prof. SUNY, Oswego, 1967-79; condr., prof., dir. orchs. Ohio U., Athens, 1979-83; music dir. Bay View Festival Chamber Orch., summers 1981, 82, 83; condr., prof. East N.Mex. U., Portales, 1983-85; music dir. Southwest Symphony, 1984-94; music. Missoula (Mont.) Symphony Orch., 1985—2006. Music theory clinician American Symphony Orch. League, Mpls., 1990. Composer orchestral work Chromophon, 1970. Sgt. U.S. Army, 1953-55. Fulbright grantee U.S. Inst. Edn., Vienna, Austria, 1957-59. Mem. Conductors Guild Avocation: gardening. Home: Missoula, Mont. Died June 1, 2014.

**HENRY, MARGUERITE,** author; b. Milw., Apr. 13, 1902; d. Louis and Anna (Kaurup) Breithaupt; m. Sidney Crocker Henry. Author: Auno and Tauno: A Story of Finland, 1940, Dilly Dally Sally, 1940, Birds at Home, 1942, Geraldine Belinda, 1942, (with Barbara True) Their First Igloo on Baffin Island, 1943, A Boy and a Dog, 1944, Little Fellow, 1945, Justin Morgan Had a Horse, 1945 (Newbery Honor award 1948, Jr. Scholastic Gold Seal award 1948, Friends of Lit. award 1948), Robert Fulton: Boy Craftsman, 1945, Misty of Chincoteague, 1947 (Boys' Club of Am. award, Lewis Carroll Shelf award, Newbery Honor award), Benjamin West and His Cat, Grimalkin, 1947, Always Reddy, 1947, King of the Wind, 1948 (John Newbery medal 1949), Sea Star: Orphan of Chintoteague, 1949, Little-or-Nothing from Nottingham, 1949, Born to Trot, 1950, Album of Horses, 1951, Portfolio of Horses, 1952, Brighty of the Grand Canyon, 1953 (William Allen White award 1956), Wagging Tails: An Album of Dogs, 1955, Cinnabar: The One O'Clock Fox, 1956, Black Gold, 1957 (Sequoyah Children's Book award 1959), Muley-Ears, Nobody's Dog, 1959, Gaudenzia: Pride of the Palio, 1960 (Clara Ingram Judson award Soc. Midland Authors 1961), Misty, the Wonder Pony, by Misty, Herself, 1961, All About Horses, 1962, Five O'Clock Charlie, 1962, Stormy, Misty's Foal, 1963, White Stallion of Lipizza, 1964, Portfolio of Horse Paintings, 1964, Mustang, Wild Spirit of the West, 1966 (Western Heritage award Nat. Cowboy Hall of Fame 1967, Sequoyah Children's Book award 1969), Dear Readers and Riders, 1969, Album of Dogs, 1970, San Domingo: The Medicine Hat Stallion, 1972 (Clara Ingram Judson award Soc. Midland Authors 1973), Stories From Around the World, 1974, Pictorial Life Story of Misty, 1976, One Man's Horse, 1977, The Illustrated Marguerite Henry, 1980, Marguerite Henry's Misty Treasury, 1982, Our First Pony, 1984, Misty's Twilight, 1992, (pop-up book) Marguerite Henry's Album of Horses, 1993, Brown Sunshine of Sawdust Valley, 1996, Our First Pony, 1997; "pictured geographies" series Alaska, 1941, Argentina, 1941, Brazil, 1941, Canada, 1941, Chile, 1941, Mexico, 1941, Panama, 1941, West Indies, 1941, Australia, 1946, Bahamas, 1946, Bermuda, 1946, British Honduras, 1946, Dominican Republic, 1946, Hawaii, 1946, New Zealand, 1946, Virgin Islands, 1946; films: Brighty, 1967, Justin Morgan Had a Horse, 1971, Peter Lundy and the Medicine Hat Stallion, 1977, King ofthe Wind, 1990; documentary: The Story of a Book, 1979. Recipient Lit. for Children award So. Calif. Coun., 1973, Kerlan award Univ. of Minn., 1975; named Author of Diamond Jubilee Yr. Ill. Assn. of Tchrs. of English, 1982. Died Nov. 26, 1997.

**HERBERT, JAMES ALAN,** writer; b. Burlington, Vt., July 29, 1945; s. Alan Wells and R. Marion Moren; m. Margaret Beyer, 1992; 1 child: Alicia Ayn. Student, Wittenberg U., Springfield, Ohio, 1963—65; BS in Econs., SUNY, Buffalo, 2000, MA in Econs., 2002. With McLean Trucking Co., 1969-86. Author: The Tenth Millennium, 1988, Rock and Roll Politics, 1992, Economics 2000, 1996, Redesigning Social Security, 2004, Rethinking Vietnam, 2012 Committeeman Conservative Party, N.Y., 1971. Served to cpl. USMC, 1966-69, Vietnam Recipient Conspicuous Svc. award State of N.Y., 1991. Mem. US Masters Swimming Avocations: boating, golf, gardening. Died July 27, 2014.

**HERMANCE, RONALD EDMUND, JR.,** bank executive; b. 1947; m. Kris Hermance; children: Emily, Christopher, Alexander. BS, St. John Fisher Coll. CFO Southold Savings Bank, NY; sr. exec. v.p., COO Hudson City Savings Bank, 1988—97, pres., COO, 1997—2002, Hudson City Bancorp, Inc., 1999—2002; pres., CEO Hudson City Bancorp, Inc. and Hudson City Savings Bank, 2002—05, chmn., pres., CEO, 2005—14. Bd. dirs. Fed. Home Loan Bank NY, 2005—14. Died Sept. 11, 2014.

**HERNANDEZ-ILLESCAS, JUAN HOMERO,** internist, infectologist, educator; b. Papantla, Veracruz, Mexico, Jan. 4, 1935; s. Juan Bartolo Hernandez-Garcia and Emma Illescas; m. Gloria Tena, Sept. 12, 1964; children: Gloria Andrea, Juan Homero, Emma Juliana., UNAM, Mexico City, 1958; diploma tropical medicine, Sorbonne, Paris, 1961; diploma hosp. adminstrn., Mexico City, 1972. Dir. Nat. Med. Edn., Mexico City, 1972-79; med. dir. October Hosp. Issste, Mexico City, 1979-80; dir. hosp. normus Ministry Health, Mexico City, 1984-98; head infectology unit Clinica Londres, Mexico City, from 1998. Prof. medicine UNAM, Mexico City, 1965—93, LaSalle U., Mexico City, 1981; prof. infectory Nursery Sch., Panamerican U., Mexico City, 1998—2000; med. dir. Durango Hosp., Mexico City, 1990—92; head Atlantic Bank Med. Svcs., Mexico City, 1993—96. Contbr. more than 90 articles to profl. jours. Recipient Knight of French Palmes Academiques medal, 1980; named emmerit infectologist of 20 de Noviembre Hosp., Mexico City. Mem. APHA, Med. Assn. Physicians with Scholarships in France (founder, sec., treas., v.p., pres.), Internal Medicine Mexico Assn. (founder, sec. 1982-83), Soc. Mexican de Salud Publica, Assn. Fronteriza Mexicana Estadounidense de Salud Publica, Soc. Mexicana de Infectologia, Assn. Mexican de Hosps., Inst. Mexicano de Cultura Academia de Ciencias Medicas, Found. UNAM (founder), Assn. des Members des Palmes Academiques, Assn. Mex. Med. Quality (founder), Alianza Francesa de Mexico, N.Y. Acad. Scis. Roman Catholic. Avocations: astronomy, collecting art and antiques, books, music, writing monographs on virgin of guadalupe. Home: Mexico City, Mexico. Died May 4, 2003.

**HERNON, RICHARD FRANCIS,** civil engineer; b. NYC, July 14, 1940; s. Francis Augusta and Mary Columba (Francis) H.; m. Susan Teresa Hartnett (dec. Jan. 1975); m. Jane Margaret Murphy, June 12, 1977; children: Robert Elizabeth, Richard Jr., Patrick. BCE, Rutgers U., 1962; MCE, NJ Inst. Tech. (formerly Newark Coll. Engring.), 1969. Registered profl. engr., N.J. Constrn. engr. N.J. Dept. Transp., Trenton, 1964-74, fleet mgr., 1974-76; county engr. Hudson County, Jersey City, 1976-80; dir. N.J. Transit Waterfront Transp., Jersey City, 1980-2000; mgr. transp. engring. T&M Assocs., Middleton, N.J., from 2000, sr. v.p., 2000—11. Pres. Rutgers Engring. Soc., New Brunswick, 1977, Island Heights (N.J.) Voters and Taxpayers, 1973-75; chmn. Island Heights Planning Bd., 1973-75. Served to 1st Lt. U.S. Army, 1962-64. Mem. ASCE. Roman Catholic. Home: Toms River, NJ. Died Mar. 20, 2013.

**HERR, STANLEY,** veterinarian; b. Potgietersrus, South Africa, May 8, 1934; s. Max and Sylvia (Lowenstein) H.; m. Colleen Joyce Cooper; children: Susan Ann Herr Nel, Wendy Herr Court, Dale Colin, Adrian. B in Vet. Sci., U. Pretoria, South Africa, 1966, B in Vet. Sci. with honors, 1979, postgrad. honors course, 1980, M in Med. Vet., 1986. Cert. vet. specialist. State veterinarian Agrl. Tech. Sci., South Africa, 1966-67; pvt. veterinarian South Africa, 1967-75; sr. lectr. U. Pretoria, 1976-78; state veterinarian Onderstepoort (South Africa) Vet. Rsch. Inst., 1979-82, asst. dir., 1982-92, Onderstepoort Vet. Inst., from 1992. Contbr. chpts. to books and articles to profl. jours. Pvt. Israeli Army, 1955-56. Mem. South Africa Vet. Assn. Jewish. Avocation: chess. Home: Pretoria North, South Africa. Died June 15, 2000.

**HERR, STANLEY SHOLOM,** law educator; b. Newark, Aug. 7, 1945; s. Louis J. and Ruth G. (Greenberg) H.; m. Raquel Schuster, June 17, 1979; children: David Louis, Deborah Ann, Ilana Ruth. BA cum laude, Yale U., 1967, JD, 1970; DPhil, Oxford U., 1979. Bar: D.C. 1971, U.S. Dist Ct. D.C. 1971, U.S. Ct. Appeals (5th cir.) 1972, Md. 1984, U.S. Supreme Ct. 1984. Staff atty. Stern Community Law Office, Washington, 1970-71; sr. staff atty. Nat. Law Office of Nat. Legal Aid Defender Assn., Washington, 1971-73; Joseph P. Kennedy Jr. fellow Balliol Coll. Oxford (Eng.) U., 1973-76; vis. scholar, instr. Law Sch. Harvard U., Cambridge, Mass., 1976-80; Rockefeller Found. fellow, vis. scholar Law Sch. Columbia U., NYC, 1980-82; project dir. mental patients' rights guidebook NIMH, Northampton, Mass. and Bethesda, Md., 1982-83; vis. assoc. prof. law U. Md., Balt., 1983-84, assoc. prof. law, 1984-95, prof. law, from 1995. Sr. rsch. fellow Schell Ctr. for Internat. Human Rights, Yale Law Sch., 1995—; cons. U.S. Dist. Ct. Mass., Boston, 1979-81; co-founder, v.p. & bd. dir. Homeless Persons Representation Project, Balt., 1987—; vis. prof. Tel Aviv U., 1990-91; vis. scholar Law Sch., Hebrew U., Jerusalem, 1990-91, 1999-2000; Kennedy Pub. Policy fellow, The White House, 1993-95; cons. NAS; Switzer disting. rsch. fellow Nat. Inst. on Disability and Rehab. Rsch., 1999-2000; vis. Crossman prof. Haifa U., 1999-2000. Author: The New Clients: Legal Services for Mentally Retarded Persons, 1979, Rights and Advocacy for Retarded People, 1983, Legal Rights and Mental Health Care, 1983, A Guide to Consent, 1999, Aging, Rights and Quality of Life, 1999; contbr. articles to legal jours., chpts. to books. Bd. dirs. Am. Jewish Soc. for Svc., N.Y.C., 1972—, Am. Assn. Mental Retardation, Internat. Acad. Law & Mental Health; cons. U.S. Pres.'s Com. on Mental Retardation, 1978-80; mem. Md. Gov.'s Commn. to Revise Mental Retardation and Devel. Disability Laws, 1985-86; pres. Greater Balt. Shelter Network, 1987. Recipient Rosemary F. Dybwad Internat. award Nat. Assn. Retarded Citizens, 1973, Leadership award Region IX Am. Assn. Mental Deficiency, 1984, Thomas Ferciot Disting. Profl. Svc. award Balt. Assn. Retarded Citizens, 1987, Swartz medallion for Humanitarian Svc., Swartz found., 1990, Burton Blatt award Young Adult Inst., Rights of the Disadvantage award Md. Bar Found., 1999, Regent's faculty award for excellence in pub.

svc., 1999; named Fulbright scholar 1990-91, fellow World Inst. on Disability, 1993, Paul Hearne Disability Rights award, 2001. Mem. Am. Assn. Mental Retardation (pres. legal process divsn. 1978-80, 82-84, bd. dirs. 1993-95, v.p. 1996, pres.-elect 1997, pres. 1998-99, Humanitarian award 1996, Sandra Jensen Humanitarian award Region II 1997), ABA (commn. on mental and phys. disability law 1997-2000, chair editl. adv. bd., mental and phys. disability law reporter, 1997-2000), Assn. Retarded Citizens U.S. (chmn. legal advocacy com. 1984-90). Avocation: foreign travel. Died Sept. 24, 2001.

**HERRIDGE, ALISTAIR FREDERICK,** retired engineer; b. Rangiora, Canterbury, New Zealand, Nov. 10, 1937; s. Frederick George and Rita Irene (Claridge) H.; m. Julianne Lois Jaine, Dec. 31, 1960; children: Shirley Jean Herridge, Iain George. Diploma in tractor equipment, Engring. Tech. Tng. Internat., Australia, 1968; DSc in Engring., Albert Einstein Internat. Acad. Found., 1991. Trade cert. New Zealand Cert. Bd. Carpentry apprentice Hanrahan & Watson Builders, Ashburton, New Zealand, 1954-59; carpentry foreman Lynn's Hardware & Joinery, Ashburton, 1959-61; carpentry foreman and engr. Burnetts' Motors, New Zealand, 1961-70; builder, operator, owner Ashburton, 1971-73; pvt. practice engring., 1973-96; ret. Chmn. Lynn Hist. Woodworking Trust and Mus. Ornamental Turning, Ashburton. Contbr.: Turning and Woodwork, 1991. Bd. dirs. Ashburton Enterprise Agy., 1996-2003. Recipient Acad. Found. cross of merit award Albert Einstein Internat. Acad. Found., 1992. Mem. NRA, Soc. Mfg. Engrs. (com. mem. South Island chpt. 1986-93, Pres. award 1992), New Zealand Crippled Childrens Soc., Disabled Persons Assn., New Zealand Spinal Trust. National Party New Zealand. Presbyterian. Avocations: collecting fine porcelain, shooting firearms, cars, reading. Home: Ashburton, New Zealand. Died July 27, 2005; Ashburton New Lawn Cemetery.

**HERRINGTON, DALE ELIZABETH,** lay worker; b. Logansport, La., Feb. 1, 1913; d. Charles Ross and Ola Delnorte (Tillery) Currie; m. Cecil Doyle Herrington, June 25, 1939; 1 child, Jo Earle Herrington Hartt. BS, Stephen F. Austin Univ., 1932, MA, MEd, Stephen F. Austin Univ., 1948. Cert. tchr., Tex. Min. edn. First Bapt. Ch., Garrison, Tex., 1947-81, organist, from 1947, lay worker, from 1947, tchr. Sunday sch. Bible, from 1947, woman's missionary union dir., 1990-92. Tchr. Garrison Pub. Schs., 1940-76; dir./asst. dir. Vacation Bible Sch., Garrison, 1950-92; vol. local newspaper, nursing home and sch., city libr., ch. libr. Chmn. Greater Garrison City Libr. Named Mother of Yr., First Bapt. ch., Garrison, 1988, Citizen of Yr., Garrison, 1992. Mem. Nat. Ret. Tchrs. Assn., Tex. Ret. Tchrs. Assn. (life), Stephen F. Austin Alumni Assn. (life), Lions (Sweetheart), Heritage Soc., Genealogy Soc., United Dau. Confederacy, Order Eastern Star (past Matron, organist), Delta Kappa Gamma. Home: Garrison, Tex. *If I should consider rewards in this life, my second blessing would be in seeing young people whose lives I have touched and helped them to mold, taking active roles in the church and community and service to our fellowman.* Deceased.

**HERTZBERG, RONALD,** cosmetics executive; b. Paterson, NJ, June 6, 1932; s. Harry and Frances (Grabowsky) H.; children: Beverly, Pearce, Taryn. BS, Sch. Commerce, NYU, 1955. Asst. to v.p. Wella Corp., Englewood, N.J., 1957—60; dir. sales adminstrn. Helene Curtis, Chgo., 1960—63; asst. sales mgr. Zotos Internat., NYC, 1963—68; v.p. mktg., dir. Cleopatra Wigs, NYC, 1969; nat. sales mgr., dir. mktg. Faberge, NYC, 1969—72; nat. sales mgr., mktg. mgr. Revlon, NYC, 1972—73; v.p. mktg., exec. v.p. Turner Hall Corp., Great Neck, NY, 1973—78; pres. Pearce Properties, Inc.; exec. dir. United Beauty and Barber Assn. Author: articles and guide books in field; innovator, cosmetics products. 1st lt. USMC, 1955—57. Mem.: Nat. Beauty Barber Mfrs. Assn., Am. Film Inst. Died Aug. 20, 1998.

**HERZENBERG, LEONARD ARTHUR,** medical educator, immunologist; b. Bklyn., Nov. 5, 1931; s. William & Ann (Seidlitz) H.; m. Leonore Alderstein, 1953; children: Janna, Berri, Michael, Eric BA in Biology and Chemistry, Bklyn. Coll., 1952; PhD in Biochemistry and Immunology, Calif. Inst. Tech., 1955. Am. Cancer Soc., postdoctoral fellow Pasteur Inst., Paris, 1955—57; officer, USPHS NIH, Bethesda, Md., 1957—59; asst. prof. genetics Stanford U. Sch. Medicine, Calif., 1959—64, assoc. prof. genetics Calif., 1959—64, prof. dept. genetics Calif., 1969—2003, prof. emeritus, genetics Calif., 2003—13. Mem. genetics study sect. NIH.; disting. prof. immunology, U. Calif. Irvine, Coll. Medicine, 1998; mem. adv. bd. Max-Planck Inst., Freiberg, 1987-2013, Munic, 1990-, Radiation Effects Res. Found., Nagasaki/Hiroshima, Japan, 1990-96, Fox Chase Cancer Inst., Phila., Pa., 1990-96, AIDS Cmty. Res. Consortium, 1992-2013, Res. Inst. for Biol. Sci., Noda City, Japan, 1996-2013, Chiba U., Chiba, Japan, 1997-2013; reviewer, OIG prog., Nat. Cancer Inst.; mem. scietific review bd., Medinox, 1995-2013. Founding editor and editl. bd. mem., International Immunology, 1988-2000; co-editor, Handbook of Experimental Immunology, 4th-5th edit., 1988-2013; mem. editl. adv. bd., Encyclopedia of Life Sciences, 1997; contbr. articles to sci. publs. Recipient Internat. Soc. Analytic Cytology Hon. award, 1998, Edwin F. Ullman award, American Assn. Clin. Chemistry, 2002, Novartis prize in Immunology, Internat. Union Immunological Societies, 2004, Abbott Lab. award in Clin. and Diagnostic Immunology, American Soc. for Microbiology, 2005, Kyoto prize in Advanced Tech., Inamori Found, 2006; co-recipient Ceppellini award, Internat. Found. for Rsch. in Experimental Medicine, 2007; Guggenheim Fellow, 1976, 1986. Fellow AAAS, Internat. Soc. Analytical Cytology (Hon. award for Sci. & Technol. Achievements 1998); mem. NAS, NY Acad. Sciences, American Acad. Microbiology, American Assn. Microbiology, Genetics Soc. America, American Assn. Immunologists (Lifetime Achievement award 1998, mem. com. public affairs, 1993-96), Soc. Devel. Biology., Phi Beta Kappa, Sigma Xi. Achievements include invention of fluorescence-activated cell sorter; research in redox regulation of gene expression and diseases, regulation of lymphocyte development, in apoptosis in the immune system and in disease processes, in cell biology of AIDS in model systems and patients; development of multi-parameter flow cytometry and scanning cytometry. Died Oct. 27, 2013.

**HESLIN, CATHLEEN JANE,** artist, designer, entrepreneur; b. Bklyn., Feb. 24, 1929; d. Charles Jenkins and Katherine (Bauer) Hunter; m. John Thomas Heslin, June 24, 1950. AA, Packer Collegiate Inst., Bklyn., 1950; postgrad., Duke U., 1952, Pratt Inst., 1952. Sr. artist, designer Klopman Mills, Rockleigh, N.J., 1966-72; free-lance designer, 1972-90; propr. Quilters Corner, Tappan, N.Y., 1978-90. Author: History of Rockleigh, N.J., 1648-1973, 1973, Old Order Amish-The People and Their Quilts, 1988; inventor Quilters Quarter measuring device. Councilwoman Borough of Rockleigh, 1973-85, 90-92, pres. coun., 1983-85, historian, 1973-90, chmn. anniversary dedication com., 1973, environ. com., 1974, action com., 1974-75, borough hall com., 1975, acquisition com., 1975, chmn. bicentennial com., 1974-76, chmn. fin. com., 1977-78, chmn. hist. adv. com., 1977-86, liaison to Bergen County hist. programs, 1978, pub. safety com., 1979-84, chmn. bldg. com., 1983-85, housing commn., 1984, Hist. Preservation Commn., 1987-90, ins. com., 1990, liaison to planning bd., 1990, designs for Rockleigh Commons; mem. Rockleigh Planning Bd., 1973, 87-89; Rep. mayoral nominee Borough of Rockleigh, 1988; founder Cathleen Heslin Found., 1990; trustee Abram Demaree Homestead, 1982-84; established Rockleigh Wildlife Sanctuary and Land Preserve. Recipient various certs. of appreciation. Mem. Tappantown Hist. Soc. (dir.), Soc. Archtl. Historians, Am. Soc. Planning Ofcls., Bergen County Hist. Soc. (trustee 1984-90), Historic Homes Assn. N.J. Achievements include being obtained State and Nat. Historic Dist. status for Borough of Rockleigh, 1976. Deceased.

**HESLOT, HENRI,** molecular and cell biologist; b. Paris, Apr. 27, 1921; s. François and Henriette (Guérin) H.; m. Jeanne chambon, Sept. 11, 1950; children: André, Sylvie, François, Jean. Ingenieur Agronome, Inst. Nat. Agronomique, Paris, 1945; Lic. en Scis., U. Paris, 1948; PhD, Inst. Nat. Agronomique, 1957. Rschr. CNRS, Paris, 1946-48; fellow Brit. Coun., Cambridge, Eng., 1948-49; dir. lab. INRA, Paris, from 1961; maitre de conf. de génétique Inst. Nat. Agronomique, Paris, from 1961, prof. genetic and molecular biology, from 1970. Cons. to beverage industries. Author: Molecular Biology and Genetic Engineering of Yeast, 1992,; contbr. numberous articles to profl. jours.; patentee in field. Recipient Mérite Agricole Min. of Agr., 1976, Palmes Académiques Min. of Edn., 1976. Mem. Acad. Agr. of France, Soc. of Microbiology, Soc. Biochemistry, Conseil des Applications de L'Academie des Scis. Avocations: islamic and far eastern art, travel, photography. Home: Paris, France. Deceased.

**HESS, BERND ARTUR,** chemistry professor; b. Selters, Germany, Apr. 17, 1954; s. Paul and Dina H.; m. Angela Voss; children: Esther, Dina, Paul. Diploma in chemistry, U. Bonn, 1977, PhD, 1980. Rsch. fellow U. Wuppertal, Germany, 1980-86; from vis. prof. to prof. U. Bonn, Germany, 1986-97; chair theoretical chemistry U. Erlangen, Germany, 1998—2002, U. Bonn, from 2003. Avocations: stringed instruments, singing. Home: Alfter, Germany. Died 2005.

**HESS, DONALD K.,** retired academic administrator; b. Lititz, Pa., Nov. 18, 1930; s. Charles & Anna Hess; m. Nancy Gordon, June 9, 1951; 1 child, Jennifer Lynn Hess Zannetos. BA, Franklin & Marshall Coll., 1952; MPA, Syracuse U., 1953; LHD (hon.), Franklin & Marshall Coll., 2011. With AEC, Washington, 1953-58; assoc. dir. Advanced Research Projects Agy., Dept. Def., Washington, 1958-66, Office Econ. Opportunity (OEO), Washington, 1966-70; dir. Peace Corps, Korea, 1970-72, Washington, 1972-74; v.p. campus affairs U. Rochester (N.Y.), 1974-83, v.p. adminstrn., 1983-96, emeritus v.p. adminstrn., 1997—2013. Bd. dirs. PSCInc. Trustee, bd. visitors Franklin & Marshall Coll. Home: Williamsburg, Va. Died Sept. 15, 2013.

**HESS, PETER,** mathematics educator; b. Zurich, Switzerland, Sept. 1, 1941; s. Oskar and Luise (Vonwiller) H; m. Annalea Pult, Apr. 2, 1966; 3 children. Diploma in math, Fed Inst Tech, Zurich, 1965—65; PhD in Math, 1968—68. Instr. U. Chgo., 1969—70, rsch. assoc., 1970—71, U. Calif., Berkeley, 1971—72; assoc. prof. math. U. Zurich, 1972—78, prof., from 1978. Contbr. articles to profl jours, to profl. jours.; co-editor: Commentarli Math. Helvetici, from 1982, Zeitschift fur Analysis and Anwedg., from 1982, Jour. Nigerian Math. Soc., from 1986, Differentuial and Integral Equations, from 1987. Recipient Silver medal Fed Inst Tech, Zurich, 1968—68, Silver medal, Fed. Inst. Tech., Zurich, 1968. Mem.: Am. Math. Soc., Swiss Math. Soc., Am Math Soc, Swiss Math Soc. Avocations: music, cello, biking, music, cello, bicycling. Home: Gossau 8625, Switzerland. Died Nov. 1992.

**HESS, WALTER OTTO,** surgeon, educator; b. Zurich, Switzerland, July 26, 1918; s. Walter and Hermine (Schäublin) H.; m. Charlotte Schmidlin, May 17, 1947 (dec. Feb. 1974); children: Gerhard Walter, Claudia Renate. MD, U. Zurich, 1944. Lic. MD, Switzerland. Resident pathology Swiss Rsch. Inst., Davos, Switzerland, 1945-46; resident Surgical Clinic U. Basle, Switzerland, 1946-49, first resident, 1950-57; resident Surgical Clinic U. Heidelberg, Fed. Republic of Germany, 1949-50; prof. surgery Alexandria (Egypt) U., 1957-59; pvt. practice Zurich, Switzerland, 1960-81. Prof. Surgery U. Basle, Switzerland, 1964-85; leading physician Inst. Med. Experts, Zurich, 1988-93. Author: Chirurgie des Pankreas, 1950, Operative Cholangiographie, 1954, Erkrankungen der Gallenwege und des Pankreas, 1959, 1986-93 (prize 1960), 2d edit. in English, French and Spanish, 1996, Textbook of Bilio-pancreatic Diseases, 4 vols., 1997; co-author: A History of the Pancreas, 2002. Dep. Cantonal Parliament, Zurich, 1968-81; del. Internat. Red Cross, Geneva, 1969-72; Counsellor Community Coun., Kilchberg, Switzerland, 1975-79. Capt. Swiss Army, 1951-54. Named Hon. Mem. Italian Soc. Surgery, Rome, 1972, Acad. Lancisiana, Rome, 1973, Surgical Assn. Cuba, Havana, 1974, Acad. Peruana de Cirugua, 1975, Colegio Brasiliero de Cirugioes, 1975, Acad. de Ciencias Medicas de Cordoba, 1977, Hon. Prof. U. Ica, Peru, 1978. Mem. Swiss Med. Assn., Swiss Soc. Surgery, Swiss Soc. Gastroenterology, Internat. Hepato-Pancreato-Biliary Assn. (hon.), Masons (W. master 1984-90 In Labore Virtus, Grand Officer Swiss Grand Lodge). Mem. Liberal Party. Avocation: history. Died Dec. 17, 2002.

**HEUMANN, KLEMENS RICHARD,** electrical engineering educator, researcher; b. Lünen, Germany, May 15, 1931; s. Aloys and Anna Maria (Frank) H.; m. Renati Heumann. Diploma in engring., Rheinisch-Westfälische Technische Hochschule, Aachen, Fed. Republic Germany, 1956; DEng, Tech. U. Berlin, 1961. Rsch. engr. AEG Rsch. Inst., Berlin, 1956-68, gen. mgr., 1969-78; prof. power electronics U. Hannover, Fed. Republic Germany, 1978-83, Tech. U. Berlin, from 1983. Cons. in field. Co-author: Characteristics and Applications, 1968; author: Fundamentals of Power Electronics, 1974, Converter Techniques, 1978; contbr. numerous articles to profl. jours. Recipient William E. Newell award IEEE Power Electronics Soc., 1985. Mem. Verband Deutscher Elektrotechniker, IEEE. Roman Catholic. Avocations: history, bicycling, gardening. Home: Berlin, Germany. Died 2004.

**HEYCK, BILL (THOMAS WILLIAM HEYCK),** historian, educator; Recipient Tempo All-Professor Team, 1993, Chicago Tribune. Died Sept. 7, 2014.

**HEYER, ROBERTA CALVERT,** artist, educator; b. Medina, Ohio, Jan. 7, 1919; d. Howard R. Calvert and Ethel H. (Acklin) Nippell; m. Robert E. Grice, Aug. 16, 1941 (div. 1948); m. Warren C. Heyer, June 26, 1952; children: Andrew D., Kathryn R., Robin L. BA in Edn., San Diego State Coll., 1940; MA in Art, San Diego State U., 1976. Cert. coll. instr., elem. tchr. Tchr. San Diego Unified Schs., 1949—52; instr. art history Mesa Coll., San Diego, from 1976, Grossmont C.C., El Cajon, Calif., 1979—83. Exhibitions include San Diego State U., 1974—83, San Diego Art Inst., 1974—84, San Diego Mus. Art, 1978, 1981, Jewish Cmty. Ctr., 1979, Brea Civic Cultural Gallery, 1984, Danforth Gallery, Livingston, Mont., 1985. Old San Diego Planned Dist. Rev. Bd., 1977—84; chair edn. com. San Diego County Human Rels. Com., 1975—76; mem. art adv. com. Congressman Bates; mem. San Diego County Human Rels. Com., 1973—77. Recipient Outstanding Svc. award, Morse HS, 1972. Mem.: Coll. Art Assn. Am. Home: San Diego, Calif. Died Jan. 14, 1996.

**HIBBERT, CHRISTOPHER,** writer; b. Enderby, Eng., Mar. 5, 1924; s. Harold Victor and Catherine Maud (Doar) H.; m. Susan Piggford; children: James, Tom, Kate. MA, Oxford U., Eng., 1948; DLitt (hon.), Leicester U., Eng. Author: The Destruction of Lord Raglan, 1961, Corunna, 1961, Il Duce: The Life of Benito Mussolini, 1962, The Battle of Arnhem, 1962, The Court at Windsor, 1964, The Roots of Evil, 1964, Agincourt, 1965, Garibaldi and his Enemies, 1966, The Making of Charles Dickens, 1967, London: Biography of a City, 1969, The Dragon Wakes: China and the West, 1970, The Personal History of Samuel Johnson, 1971, George IV (2 vols.), 1972, 73, The Rise and Fall of the House of Medici, 1974, Edward VII, 1976, The Great Mutiny: India 1857, 1978, The French Revolution, 1980, Rome: The Biography of a City, 1985, The English: A Social History, 1986, The Grand Tour, 1987, Venice: The Biography of a City, 1988, The Virgin Queen: The Personal History of Elizabeth I, 1990, Redcoats and Rebels: The War for America, 1770-1781, 1990, The Story of England, 1992, Cavaliers and Roundheads: The Civil War in England 1642-1649, 1993, Florence: The Biography of a City, 1993, Nelson: A Personal History, 1994, Wellington: A Personal History, 1997, George III: A Personal History, 1998, Queen Victoria: A Personal History, 2000, Redcoats and Rebels: The American Revolution through British Eyes, 2002, Napoleon: His Wives and Women, 2002, Disraeli: A Personal History, 2004; editor: The Encyclopaedia of Oxford, 1988, Capt. British Army, 1942-45, ETO. Decorated Military Cross, 1945. Mem. Army and Navy Club, Garrick Club. Avocations: travel, cooking, gardening. Home: Henley-On-Thames, England. Died Dec. 21, 2008.

**HICKS, BILLY FERRELL,** minister, educator; b. El Dorado, Ark., Aug. 12, 1930; s. Ferrell Farris and Olivia Marvell (Lookadoo) H.; m. Anna Bee Gillaspie, Jan. 25, 1952. BA, Ouachita Bapt. Coll., Arkadelphia, Ark., 1956; BS, Henderson State Coll., Arkadelphia, Ark., 1960. Ordained to ministry Bapt. Ch., 1956. Assist. hwy. engr., Ark., 1954-55; coach, tchr. Laura Connor High Sch., Augusta, Ark., 1956-57; tchr. Newport (Ark.) High Sch., 1957-59; coach, tchr. Magnolia (Ark.) Jr. High Sch., 1959-63; tchr. Dollarway High Sch., Pine Bluff, Ark., 1963-65, coach. tchr., 1967-71; head sci. dept. Smackover (Ark.) High Sch., 1965-66; tchr. L.M. Goza Jr. High, Arkadelphia, 1966-67; coach, tchr. Pine Bluff Sch. Dist., 1971-85, Tex. Refinery Corp., 1971-74; radiol. def. officer Office Emergency Svc., Clark County and State Ark., 1986-92. Minister First Bapt. Mission, Augusta, Ark., 1956-57; cons in field. Author: A Beautiful Dream and Other Poems, 1994, numerous other poems (Golden Poet award 1985-90, 91, Poet of Merit award 1990). Served to 1st lt. U.S. Army, 1952-54, Korea. Recipient Leaders in Am. Sci. award, 1962-63. Mem. Am. Assn. Ret. Persons, Ark. Ret. Tchrs. Assn., Audubon Soc.,

NRA, Jackson County Tchrs. Asns. (pres. 1958), Am. Legion, Kiwanis (sec. 1970), Bass Masters, N.Am. Hunting Club, Ducks Unltd. Avocations: singing, writing, gardening, hunting, fishing. Deceased.

**HICKS, J. ROBERT,** industrial packaging executive, retired; b. Chicago, July 7, 1930; s. Robert David and Ada Medora (Yoder) H.; m. Gloria D. (Brown), Feb. 14, 1956 (divorced); 1 child, Michael Patrick; m. Jeannine E.G. (Weyns), Dec. 23, 1972; 1 child, Stefanie Maria. BA in Bus. Adminstrn., Knox Coll., Galesburg, Ill., 1952; student, Am. Inst. Banking, 1955. Mgr. tech. svcs. ITW Signode, Glenview, Ill., 1956-68, mgr. sales engring. Europe Dinslaken, Germany, 1968-76, mng. dir. Zaventem, Belgium, 1976-81, mgr. application rev. Europe Newbury, Eng., 1981-87; European sales mgr. ITW Shippers, Carnières, Belgium, 1987-95; ret. Ill. Tool Works, Glenview, Ill., 1995; pres. Hicks Cons., Hever, Belgium, from 1995. Sgt. US Army, 1952—54, Korea. Mem. Am. Belgian Assn., (1st Am. pres. 1992-97). Home: Hever, Belgium. Died Jan. 24, 2003.

**HIELM, BORJE GUSTAV,** retired airline captain, historian, journalist; b. Helsinki, Finland, June 24, 1927; s. Ejnar Olof and Alfa Maria Viola (Ahrenberg) H.; m. Sirkka Anna Liisa Peltola Hielm, Jan, 1950 (div. Sept. 1, 1954); m. Christina Margareta Laxen Hielm, Feb. 26, 1955; children: Maria Christina, Anna Katrina, Margit Charlotta, Finn Gustav Sebastian. Navigator's lic., Air Svc. Tng., Hamble Hants, Eng., 1949; airline transport pilot's lic., 1949. Glider pilot Finnish Aeronautical Assn., Jamjarvi, Finland, 1945, 47; pilot tng. Finnish Air Force Air Acad., Kauhava, Finland, 1946; fighter pilot Finnish Airforce, Utti, Finland, 1947-48; first officer Finnair, Helsinki, Finland, 1951-55, capt., 1955-82; dir. Finnish Aviation Mus., Vantaa, Finland, 1983-92; ret., 1992. Chmn. Finnish DX Club, Helsinki, Finland, 1954-58; commentator YLE Finnish Broadcasting and TV on Space and Aviation, 1958—; founder, chmn, IPMS Finland, Helsinki, 1968-72. Prodr., author: Series of 7 1/2 hour programs on history on the Space Age, Finnish TV; Space News, 1963-78; editor-in-chief Feeniks Mag., 1983-2001; contbr. articles to profl. jours. Pres. Nylands Constitutionals, Espoo, Finland, 1976-88, South Espoo Constnl. Soc., Finland, 1977-88; v.p. Constnl. Party, Helsinki, Finland, 1982-86; mem. Espoo City Coun., 1977-84, Electoral mem. in Presdl. Elections, 1978. Named Flight Capt., Pres. Finland, 2003. Mem. Sydkustens Soldatgossar (sec.), Finnish Aviation Mus. Soc., Aviation Mus. Support Fund. Lutheran. Avocations: aviation history, clippings, model building, painting, photography. Home: Helsinki, Finland. Died Dec. 17, 2004.

**HIERING, JAMES G.,** lawyer; b. Seaside Park, NJ, Apr. 16, 1931; s. Albert C. and Phoebe M. (McGann) Hiering; m. Nancy Lee Newman, June 10, 1955 (div.); children: Lisa, Susan, Leslie; m. Cynthia C. Common, Apr. 17, 1970 (div.); children: Julie, Tricia; m. Mary C. Morrison, Dec. 13, 1986. AB, Princeton U., 1953; LLB, Harvard U., 1956. Bar: Ill. 1956. Ptnr. Keck, Mahin & Cate, Chgo., from 1956. Dir. Schawk Inc., Barnegat Power & Cold Storage Co. Mem.: ABA, Bar Assn. 7th Fed. Cir., Ill. Bar Assn., Chgo., Am. Judicature Soc., Execs. Chgo. Club, Economic Club, Chgo. Yacht Club, Met. Club, University Club. Republican. Presbyterian. Died Mar. 12, 1992.

**HIGHT, HAROLD PHILIP,** retired security company executive; b. Crescent City, Calif., Apr. 17, 1924; s. Vernon Austin and Mary Jane (Gontau) H.; m. Margaret Rose Edelman, Nov. 19, 1945 (div. 1949); children: Linda Marie, Beverly Sue; m. Doris Louise Dunn, June 20, 1982 (dec. 1998). Student police sci., Coll. of Redwoods, 1969. With Pan Am. World Airways, South San Francisco, Calif., 1945-51, 52; officer Richmond (Calif.) Police Dept., 1952-54; aircraft electrician Internat. Atlas Svc., Oakland, Calif., 1954-56; security officer radiation lab. AEC, Livermore, Calif., 1956-58; chief police Port Orford (Oreg.) Police Dept., 1958-61; dep. sheriff, sgt., evidence technician Del Notre County Sheriff's Dept., Crescent City, 1961-85; ret., 1985; security officer, sgt. Del Notre Security Svc., Crescent City, 1985. With USN, 1941-45, 51-52. Mem. Internat. Footprint Assn. (sec., treas. bd. dirs. Crescent City 1985—), Navy League U.S. (2d v.p. Crescent City 1984—), Tin Can Sailors, Masons, Scottish Rite (32d degree), Elks, Grange. Republican. Roman Catholic. Avocations: model railroads, walking. Home: Palo Cedro, Calif. Died Feb. 15, 2008.

**HILL, JOHN HOWARD,** retired lawyer; b. Pitts., Aug. 12, 1940; s. David Garrett and Eleanor Campbell (Musser) H. BA, Yale U., 1962, JD, 1965. Bar: Pa. 1965, US Dist. Ct. (we dist.) Pa. 1965, US Ct. Appeals (3d cir.) 1965, US Supreme Ct. 1982. Assoc. Reed, Smith, Shaw & McClay, Pitts., 1965-75, ptnr., 1975-90; of counsel Jackson Lewis LLP, Pitts., 1991—2004, ret., 2004. Bd. dirs. Travelers Aid Soc., Pitts., 1972-99, treas., 1982-87, pres., 1987-90; bd. dirs. Pitts. Opera, Pitts. Symphony Soc. Mem.: ABA, Allegheny County Bar Assn., Pa. Bar Assn., Pa. Soc., Fox Chapel Golf Club, Duquesne Club, Phi Gamma Delta. Republican. Presbyterian. Home: Pittsburgh, Pa. Died Aug. 10, 2013.

**HILL, LUTHER LYONS, JR.,** lawyer; b. Des Moines, Aug. 21, 1922; s. Luther Lyons and Mary (Hippee) H.; m. Sara S. Carpenter, Aug. 12, 1950; children— Luther Lyons III, Mark Lyons. BA, Williams Coll., 1947; LLB, Harvard U., 1950; LLD (hon.), Simpson Coll., 1979. Bar: Iowa 1951. Law clk. to Justice Hugo L. Black U.S. Supreme Ct., 1950-51; assoc., ptnr. Henry & Henry, Des Moines, 1951-69; mem. legal staff Equitable Life Ins. Co. of Iowa, 1952-87, exec. v.p., 1969-87, gen. counsel, 1970-87; of counsel Nyemaster, Goode, McLaughlin, Voigts, Wiest, Hansell O'Brien, Des Moines, from 1992. Past counsel, adminstr. Iowa Life and Health Ins. Guaranty Assn. Bd. dirs., past pres. United Comty. Svcs. Greater Des Moines; past trustee, past chmn. Simpson Coll., Indianola, Iowa. Capt. M.I., AUS, WWII, ETO. Mem. ABA, Iowa Bar Assn., Polk County Bar Assn., Assn. Life Ins. Counsel, Des Moines Club, Wakonda Club. Avocation: mountain climbing. Home: Des Moines, Iowa. Died Apr. 23, 2013.

**HILLARY, SIR EDMUND PERCIVAL,** diplomat, explorer, mountaineer, bee farmer; b. Auckland, New Zealand, July 20, 1919; s. Percival Augustus and Gertrude Clark Hillary; m. Louise Mary Rose, 1953 (dec. March 31, 1975); children: Peter, Sarah, Belinda (dec. March 31, 1975); m. June Mulgrew, 1990 Student, U. Auckland; LLD (hon.), Victoria U., B.C., Can., U. Victoria, New Zealand. Bee farmer; dir. Field Ednl. Enterprises of Australasia Pty. Ltd.; participant New Zealand Garwhal expdn. to Himalayas, 1951; with Brit. expdn. to Cho Oyu, 1952; with Brit. Mt. Everest expdn. under Sir John Hunst, 1953; leader New Zealand Alpine Club expdn. to Barun Valley, 1954, New Zealand Trans-Antarctic expdn., 1955—58; reached South Pole as part of Commonwealth Trans-Antarctic Expdn., led New Zealand sect., 1958; leader Himalayan expdns., 1961, 63, 64, climbing expdn. on Mt. Herschel, Antarctica, 1967; leader of jetboat expdn. River Ganges expdn., 1977; accompanied Neil Armstrong in small, twin engine plane over Arctic Ocean and landed at North Pole, 1985. Built hosp. for Sherpa tribesmen, Nepal, 1966; high commr. to India, also accredited to Bangladesh, Bhutan and Nepal, 1985-89. Author: High Adventure, 1955, East of Everest, 1956, (with Sir vivian Fuchs) The Crossing of Antarctica, 1958, The New Zealand Antartic Expedition, 1959, No Latitude for Error, 1961, (with Desmond Doig) High in the Thin Cold Air, 1963, Schoolhouse in the Clouds, 1965, Nothing Venture, Nothing Win, 1975, From the Ocean to the Sky: Jet Boating Up the Ganges, 1978 (with Peter Hillary) Two Generations, 1983, View From the Summit, 1999. Served with Royal New Zealand Air Force, 1944-45, PTO. Decorated Knight Comdr. Order of the British Empire, 1953, Knight of the Garter, 1995; named to Order of New Zealand, 1987, Gurkha Right Hand 1st Class, Star of Nepal 1st Class; recipient Cullum Geog. medal, 1954, Hubbard medal, 1954, Polar medal, 1958, James Wattle Book of Yr. award, New Zealand, 1975, Centennial award Nat. Geographic soc., 1988. Mem.: Am. Himalayan Found. (hon. pres.). Achievements include with Tenzing Norgay, first people on May 29, 1953 to climb Mount Everest, the world's tallest peak; helped lead a team to South Pole in 1955; first person to drive to the pole, using a modified farm tractor; first man to stand at both poles as well as the summit of Everest; made return to Antarctica on the 50th anniversary the Scott Base in 2007 at the age of 87. Home: Auckland, New Zealand. Died Jan. 11, 2008.

**HILLER-KETTERER, INGEBORG,** science educator, researcher; b. Schwenningen, Germany, Sept. 26, 1938; d. Hermann and Emma Ketterer; m. Gotthilp Gerhard Hiller, July 29, 1970; children: Jaime-Ramon, Konstantin. State cert. for tchrs., Univ. Edn., Reutlingen, Germany, 1967; PhD, U. Tuebingen, Germany, 1971. Asst. prof. U. Edn., Esslingen, Germany, 1970—74, prof., 1974—83, Reutlingen, Germany, 1983—87, Ludwigsburg, Germany, 1987—2003. Author: (book) Child, Society and Gospel, 1971, Performance and Justice, 1972, Cancerous Children in School, 1996. Fellow, Friedrich-Ebert Found., 1968—71. Home: Reutlingen, Germany. Died Nov. 13, 2004.

**HILLS, PETER JOHN,** engineering educator; b. Ewell, Surrey, Eng., Aug. 17, 1938; s. Neville Morris and Geraldine Yvonne (Cazalet) H.; m. Lesley Edna Slater, July 27, 1968; children: Karin Elizabeth, Fiona Suzanne. BSc in Engring., Imperial Coll., London, 1961; MSc, Birmingham U., Eng., 1962. Chartered engr., U.K. Engr. Ministry of Transport, U.K., 1962-63; lectr. Imperial Coll., London, 1964-72; asst. dir. rsch. U. Leeds, Eng., 1972-77; prof. U. Newcastle Upon Tyne, Eng., from 1977, dean of the faculty of engring., from 1996; cons. Scott Wilson Kirkpatrick Ltd., Eng., from 1990. Cons. Colin Buchanan and Ptnrs., London, 1964-72, Max Lock Group, Nigeria, 1964-76, Dept. Transport, London, 1985—. Co-author: Traffic in Towns, 1963; co-author: Roads and Traffic in Urban Areas, 1987; assoc. editor Internat. Jour. Transp., 1971-80, (Europe) IVHS Jour., 1993—. Decorated Order of British Empire, 1995; named Fellow of City and Guilds (London) Inst., 1993. Fellow Instn. of Hwys and Transp. (pres. 1992-93), Chartered Inst. Transport; mem. Instn. Civil Engrs. Avocations: jazz, motor racing, twentieth-century history. Home: Newcastle Upon Tyne, England. Died Dec. 16, 2002.

**HILSMAN, ROGER,** political scientist, educator; b. Waco, Tex., Nov. 23, 1919; s. Roger and Emma (Prendergast) H.; m. Eleanor Willis Hoyt, June 22, 1946; children: Hoyt R., Amy, Ashby, Sarah. BS, U.S. Mil. Acad., 1943; MA, Yale U., 1950, PhD in Internat. Rels., 1951. Commd. 2d lt. U.S. Army, 1943, advanced through grades to maj., 1951; with (Merrill's Marauders), Burma, 1944; comdg. officer (OSS guerrilla group in), Burma, 1944-45; asst. chief Far East intelligence operations, Hdqrs. OSS, Washington, 1945-46; spl. asst. to exec. officer CIA, 1946-47; planning officer NATO affairs, Joint American Mil. Advisory Group, London, 1950-52; internat. politics br. US European Command, 1952-53; research fellow Center Internat. Studies, Princeton, 1953-54, research asst., 1954-55; research assoc., lectr. Woodrow Wilson Sch.; lectr. internat. relations Columbia U., 1958; research assoc. Washington Center Fgn. Policy Research, lectr. internat. affairs Johns Hopkins U. Sch. Advanced Internat. Studies, 1957-61. Chief fgn. affairs divsn., legislative reference service Library Congress, 1956-58, dep. dir. for research, 1958-61; dir. bur. intelligence & research State Dept., 1961-63; asst. sec. forFar Eastern affairs, 1963-64; prof. govt. Columbia U., 1964-89, prof. emeritus, 1990-2014; lectr. Nat. War Coll., Air U., Army War Coll., Indsl. Coll. Armed Forces.; Fulbright Disting. lectr., India, 1985; USMC Found. chair mil. affairs, 1991. Author: Strategic Intelligence and National Decisions, 1956, To Move a Nation: The Politics of Foreign Policy in the Administration of John F. Kennedy, 1967, The Politics of Policy Making in Defense and Foreign Affairs: Conceptual Models and Bureaucratic Politics, 1971, The Crouching Future: International Politics and U.S. Foreign Policy— A Forecast, 1975, To Govern America, 1979, The Politics of Governing America, 1985, The Politics of Policy Making: Conceptual Models and Bureaucratic Politics, 1987, 90, 92, American Guerrilla: My War Behind Japanese Lines, 1990, George Bush vs Saddam Hussein: Military Success! Political Failure?, 1992, The Cuban Missle Crisis, The Struggle Over Policy, 1996, From Nuclear Military Strategy to a World Without War, A History and Proposal, 1999; co-author: Military Policy and National Security, 1956, Alliance Policy in the Cold War, 1959, NATO and American Security, 1959, Foreign Policy in the Sixties, 1965, The Superpowers and Revolution, 1986, Nuclear Strategy and Arms Control, 1986, A Layman's Guide to the Universe: The Earth, Life on Earth, and the Migrations of Mankind, 2003, Classical Chinese Cooking: For the Occasional and Amateur Chef, 2005 Rockefeller fellow, 1958. Democrat. Home: Chester, Conn. Died Feb. 23, 2014.

**HINDIN, MAURICE J.,** judge; b. LA, Oct. 10, 1910; s. Theodore J. and Ida (Fisch) Hindin; m. Dorothy Sweet, Aug. 11, 1938; children: Arthur, Carol. BS in Bus. Adminstrn., U. Southern Calif., 1938, JD, 1935. Bar: Calif. 1935, (US Supreme Ct.) 1942. Sr. ptnr. Hindin, McKittrick & Marsh, LA, 1972; judge LA Jud. Dist. Ct., from 1972. Mem.: ABA, LA County Bar Assn., Calif. State Bar Assn. Home: Los Angeles, Calif. Died July 1990.

**HINKELMAN, KENNETH WILLIAM,** dentist, educator; b. Braddock, Pa., Aug. 10, 1940; s. Bernard William and Elsie Elizabeth (Sonnenberg) H.; m. Elizabeth Jean Kolcun, June 10, 1961; children: Amy L., Kimberley S., Rachel B. BS, U. Pitts., 1962, DDS, 1965, MEd, 1973, PhD, 1976. Coordinator of dental auxs. Kellog Community Coll., Battle Creek, Mich., 1970-71; instr. U. Pa. Sch. Dental Medicine, Pitts., 1971-74, asst. prof., 1974-77, assoc. prof., 1977-81; prof., chmn. dept. restorative dentistry, U. Alta., Edmonton, Can., from 1981, also bd. dirs. Contbr. articles to profl. jours. Bd. dirs. Learning Resources U. Alta. Faculty of Dentistry, Edmonton, 1981—. Served to capt. U.S. Army, 1965-67. Fellow Acad. Dental Materials; mem. Can. Dental Assn., Alta. Dental Assn., Am. Assn. Dental Schs., Sigma Xi, Omicron Kappa Upsilon. Lodges: Masons. Home: Edmonton, Canada. Died Aug. 7, 2008.

**HINMAN, SUKI,** psychologist; b. Balt., Mar. 5, 1948; d. Charlton Joseph and Jane Cunningham (van Meter) H. BA with honors, U. Ark., 1972, MA, 1975, PhD, 1983. Lic. psychologist, Ark. Grad. rsch. asst. Dept. Agrl. Econs. and Rural Sociology, U. Ark., Fayetteville, 1974-75; program devel. and evaluation specialist Father Flanagan's Boys Home, Kansas City, Kans., 1975-76; rsch. assoc. Ark. Rehab. Rsch. & Tng. Ctr., Fayetteville, Hot Springs, 1976-86; cons. and trainer Region VI Rehab. Continuing Edn., Hot Springs, 1984-86; adj. grad. faculty rehab. edn. U. Ark., Fayetteville, from 1986; clin. dir. Community Re-Entry Svcs. of Ark., Benton, 1986-87; psychologist Hot Springs Rehab. Ctr., 1988; clin. dir. Community Re-Entry Ctr. of South Fla., Ft. Lauderdale, 1988-89; adult in-patient coord. Profl. Counseling Assocs., Inc., Little Rock, 1989-93; psychologist Birch Tree Cmtys., Inc., Benton, Ark., from 1993. Cons., trainer Tenn. Rehab. Ctr., Smyrna, 1982-83, Program for Early & Spl. Edn., Bentonville, Ark., 1978, Teaching Family Workshop/BIABH, Texarkana, Ark., 1981-82, Benton Svcs. Ctr./Div. Mental Health, 1984; lectr. in field; conductor workshops in field. Contbr. articles to profl. jours. Mem. APA, Nat. Head Injury Found., N.Y. Acad. Scis., Nat. Rehab. Assn. (Ark. ann. conf. chair 1977-87), Assn. for Behavior Analysis, Assn. for Advancement of Behavior Therapy, Ark. Bd. Examiners in Psychology (sec., credentials rev. chmn. 1986-90). Avocations: remodeling, gardening, art, reading. Deceased.

**HINZE, JUERGEN ANDREAS MICHAEL,** chemistry professor; b. Berlin, June 28, 1937; s. Robert Franz and Eva Alwine (Braun) H.; m. Christine Werk-Hinze Schmidtmeier, Nov. 24, 1988; children: Friedrich, Henrich Werk. Vordiplom, Tech. U., Stuttgart, 1959; PhD, U. Cin., 1962. Postdoctoral fellow Rice U., Houston, 1962-64, Tech. U., Stuttgart, 1964-66, U. Chgo., 1966-67, prof. chemistry, 1967-75, U. Bielefeld, Germany, from 1975. Guest prof. MPI Astrophysics, Munich, 1973, Harvard Smithsonian Ctr. for Astrophysics, Cambridge, Mass., 2000; mem. senate U. Bielefeld, 1976—92, chmn., 1978—80, 1989—90. Editor: Energy Storage and Red. in Molecules, Plenum, 1983, El. Atom and El.-Mol. Collisions, 1982, Large Lin. Systems, 1980, Unitary Groups, 1981. Mem. Am. Chem. Soc., Am. Phys. Soc., Bunsen Ges., European Phys. Soc., Deutsche Phys. Ges., Ges. Deutscher Chemiker (regional chmn. 1975-98). Avocations: skiing, tennis, sailing. Home: Bielefeld, Germany. Died Oct. 10, 2008.

**HIPSCHER, JEROME JAY,** educator, writer, actor; b. Bklyn., May 9, 1932; s. Charles and Helen (Blumberg) H.; m. Joan Miller, Nov. 6, 1960; children: Hara, Phillip, Marla. AA, Queensboro C.C., 1978; BA, Fla. Internat. U., 1984, Masters, 1986; cert., Inst. Children's Lit., 1996, Writers Digest Sch., 1995. Spl. delivery technician U.S. Postal Svc., Jamaica, N.Y., 1959-89; tchr. Broward County, Fla., 1990-92, Dade County, Fla., 1989-92; writer Orlando, Fla., from 1992; attraction host Walt Disney World, Orlando, Fla., from 1995, Universal Studios, Orlando, Fla., from 1991. Exec. officer Am. Postal Workers Union, Jamaica, 1959-76; exec. dir. Jamaica Bay Coun., Queens, N.Y., 1974-78; actor Screen Actor Guild, Miami, Fla., 1984-92; student senator Fla. Internat. U., Miami, 1984-86. Author: Stickywick, 1994, Abuse Trilogy, 1994, (poems) Daddy, 1995 (Pres. award 1995). Lobbyist Crime in the St. bill; adv. cmty. coun., founder, lobbyist Gateway East Nat. Park. With U.S. Army, 1950-52, Korea. Recipient N.Y.C. Mayor's Youth award, 1976, Comprehensive Ednl. Tng. Act grant U.S. EPA, 1977-78, Pres.'s EPA award White House, 1978, U.S. EPA Spl. award, 1976. Mem. K of Pythians, AARP (founding pres. Southwest Orlando chpt. 1996). Avocation: public speaking. Home: Orlando, Fla. Died Apr. 3, 2008.

**HIRSHAN, LEONARD,** retired agent; b. NYC, Dec. 27, 1927; s. Samuel and Dorothy (Kaufman) H.; children: Karen, Sarah. BA, NYU, 1950. With William Morris Agy., 1951—2001; founder Leonard Hirshan Mgmt., 2001—14. Bd. dirs. William Morris Agy., L.A., N.Y.C., Center Theater Group, L.A.; bd. govs. Cedars-Sinai Hosp., L.A., 1987. Recipient Seymour Heller award, Talent Managers Assn., 2012. Home: Beverly Hills, Calif. Died Jan. 31, 2014.

**HISLOP, JOHN THOMPSON, II,** accountant, financial services executive; b. Milw., Jan. 27, 1941; s. Reginald Mainwaring and Anna H. (Thompson) H.; m. Kim Susan Hallquist, Feb. 5, 1972; children: John, Jennifer, Anna. BBA, U. Wis.-Milw., 1965. CPA. Tax acct. Arthur Andersen & Co., Milw., 1965—68; asst. controller Medalist Industries, Milw., 1968—71; sec., treas. Amerotex, Brownwood, Tex., 1971—73; v.p., controller Datapoint Corp., San Antonio, 1973—85; v.p., CFO Intelogic Trace, Inc., San Antonio, 1985—98. Dep. sheriff Kendall County, Boerne, Tex.; sr. warden, vestryman St. Helenas Episc. Ch., Boerne. Republican. Home: Boerne, Tex. Died Dec. 9, 1998.

**HITCHING, HARRY JAMES,** retired lawyer; b. NYC, Nov. 20, 1909; s. Harry and Sara (James) H.; m. Virginia Wyber, June 1933 (dec. Feb. 12, 1972); children: Virginia B. (Mrs. Daniel Andrews), James F.; m. Jeanne Austin Buckner, Aug. 25, 1972. AB, Columbia, 1929, LL.B. (Kent scholar), 1931, JD, 1969. Bar: N.Y. 1932, Tenn. 1938, Ga. 1969. Pvt. practice, NYC, 1931-37; prin. atty. TVA, 1937-40, asst., gen. counsel, 1940-44; mem. firm Miller and Martin, Chattanooga, 1944-46; partner Miller & Martin and predecessor firm Miller, Martin and Hitching, 1946-92. Gen. counsel Skyland Internat. Corp., Benwood Found., Chattanooga Area Regional Transp. Authority; div. counsel Vulcan Materials Co.; dir. Krystal Co. Mem. Miller Park Bd.; Chmn. bd. Tonya Meml. Found., Estate Planning Council Chattanooga; chmn. advisory bd. Chattanooga Salvation Army; bd. dirs. Chattanooga Opthalmol. Found., Community Found. Greater Chattanooga. Served to ensign USCGR, 1943-45. Mem. ABA, Tenn. Bar Assn., Ga. Bar Assn., Chattanooga Bar Assn. (v.p.), Chattanooga Bar Found., Chattanooga C. of C. (treas., dir., Newcomen Soc. N.Am. Clubs: Lookout Mountain Fairyland, Mountain City (Chattanooga), Lookout Mountain Golf (Chattanooga), Geology (Chattanooga), Torch (Chattanooga) (pres.). Episcopalian. Died Nov. 5, 2000.

**HJÄLMÅS, KELM SUNE,** urologist, educator; b. Göteborg, Sweden, May 31, 1933; s. Henrik Salomon and Margit Hjälmås; m. Inger Britt-Marie Bergström, May 28, 1955; children: Mimmi Hultengren, Ann, Åse Rinman, Bitte, Emma. MD, Göteborg U., 1963, D in Med. Sci., 1963. Registrar, then cons. in pediat. urology U. Children's Hosp., Göteborg, 1963—98; prof. pediat. urology Göteborg U., from 1980; head dept pediat. urology U. Children's Hosp., Göteborg, 1986—94. Cons. U. Children's Hosp., Göteborg, from 1998. Author: Micturition in Infants and Children with Normal Lower Urinary Tract, 1076; co-author: Indian Textbook of Paediatric Surgery, 1998, Pediaatric Urology, 2001, Neurogenic Bladder: Children and Adults, 2004; contbr. articles to profl. publs. Master: Internat. Children's Continence Soc. (pres. 1995—2001), European Soc. Paediat. Urology (pres. 1999—2003), German Med. Info. Ctr. (hon.; pres. 1989—2002), Club Italiano Enuresis Notturna (hon.). Achievements include first to among the first to describe urinary bladder function in infants and children, in health and disease. Avocations: sailing, music. Home: Göteborg, Sweden. Died May 4, 2004.

**HOARE-TEMPLE, PIERS HOWARD,** building maintenance executive; b. London, Mar. 5, 1946; s. Euan Temple and Margot Carol Blaut Temple Hoare; m. Jane Evelyn Montague Browne, Aug. 19, 1978; 1 child, Guy Arthur Anthony. Salesman Va. Oak Tannery, Luray, 1965-67; barrister The English Bar, London, 1972-87; chmn. bd., majority shareholder Blaut Verwaltung & Grundstücks GmbH & Co., Neu Isenburg, Germany, from 1987, Heritage Restoration Ltd., Jersey, Channel Islands, from 1991, Heritage Restoration GmbH, Dusseldorf, Germany, 1992—2003; owner Reisebüro Engels, Friedberg, Germany, 1987—94. Cons. Riverside (Great Stour Ltd.), Canterbury, Eng., 1994, dir. Canterbury Leisure Devel. Ltd., 1993—2006. Mem. mgmt. com., trustee Hearing Rsch. Trust, London, 1988—; chmn. Richmond Legal Advice Svc., London, 1973—. Lt. comdr. Naval Res. Decorated Reserve Decoration, Her Majesty the Queen, 1985. Mem. Criminal Bar Assn., Conservative Lawyers Assn., Pres.'s Res. Officers' Assn. (com. mem.), Royal Naval Res. Officer Dining Club (v.p.), Naval Club London (counselor bd. & chmn. mgmt. coun.), Old Pauline Club (com. mem.). Ch. of Eng. Avocations: travel, wining and dining, swimming. Home: London, England. Deceased.

**HOBBS, JOHN RAYMOND,** immunology educator; b. Aldershot, Eng., Apr. 17, 1929; s. Frederick Walter Haydn and Anna Helena (Froseler) Hobbs; m. Patricia Lilian Arnott, Aug. 7, 1954; children: Wendy, Lucy, Trudy. B.Sc. with spl. honors, Middlesex Hosp. Med. Sch., 1953; MBBS, 1956, MD, 1963. Tutor in chem. pathology Westminster Med. Sch. (Eng.), 1959—62, chmn. bone marrow team, from 1971; lectr. in chem. pathology Royal Free Hosp. Med. Sch., London, 1963—63; sr. lectr. in chem. pathology Postgrad. Med. Sch., 1963—70; prof. chem. pathology U. London, 1970—84, prof. chem. immunology, from 1984, chmn. numerous sci. coms., from 1959; mem. council Royal Coll. Pathologists, 1971—74; pres. sect. pathology Royal Soc. Medicine, London, 1972—73; vis. prof. numerous univs, from 1969; rep. Overseas Devel. Ministry, India, 1968—70. Contbr. numerous articles to profl. jours. Served with Royal Army Med. Corps, 1947—49. Recipient Vicker's award, Assn. Clin. Biochemists, 1981, Silver medal, City of Bruges (Belgium), 1972, Paul Martini prize, 1973; named Disting. Clin. Chemist, Can. Soc. Clin. Chemists, 1977. Mem.: Internat. Fedn. Clin. Chemists (chmn. expert panel on proteins 1970—79), Bd. of European Bone Marrow Transplantation, Internat. Coop. Group for Bone Marrow Transplant, Athenaeum (London). Mem. Ch. Of Eng. Home: Ruislip, Middlesex, England. Died July 2008.

**HOBBS, KENNETH GORDON, JR.,** retired obstetrician-gynecologist; b. Chgo., Oct. 16, 1924; MD, St. Louis U., 1954. Diplomate Am. Bd. Ob-Gyn., 1961. Intern Queen Angels Hosp., LA, 1954-55, resident in ob-gyn, 1955-58; mem. staff St. Joseph Hosp., Orange, Calif.; pvt. practice ob-gyn; now ret. Clin. prof. ob-gyn. U. Calif.-Irvine Coll. Medicine, 1965. Fellow Am. Coll. Ob-Gyn., Calif. Med. Assn., Orange County Med. Assoc., Orange County Ob-Gyn Soc., Univ. Calif., Irvine, S.W. Ob-Gyn. Soc. Home: Santa Ana, Calif. Deceased.

**HOBSBAUM, PHILIP DENNIS,** English educator; b. London, June 29, 1932; s. Joseph and Rachel Shapira Hobsbaum; m. Hannah Kelly, Aug. 7, 1957 (div. 1968); m. Rosemary Phillips, July 20, 1976; 2 stepchildren. MA, Cambridge U.; PhD, Sheffield U.; lic., Royal Acad. Music, Guildhall Sch. Music. Lectr. in English Queen's U., Belfast, Ireland, 1962-66; lectr. in English lit. U. Glasgow, Scotland, 1966-72, sr. lectr. English lit., 1972-79, reader English lit., 1979-85, prof. Eng. Lit., 1985—2005. Author: A Theory of Communication, 1970, A Reader's Guide to Charles Dickens, 1972, Tradition and Experiment, 1979, A Reader's Guide to D.H. Lawrence, 1981, Essentials of Literary Criticism, 1983, A Reader's Guide to Robert Lowell, 1988, Metre, Rhythm and Verse Form, 1996; editor: Wordsworth: Selected Poetry and Prose, 1989; co-editor: Channels of Communication, 1992. Mem. Labour party. Clubs: College, BBC. (Glasgow) Avocations: dogwalking, piano playing. Home: Glasgow, Scotland. Died June 28, 2005.

**HOBSON, ANNE GLEN,** pharmacist; b. Lawrence, Mass., Apr. 11, 1925; d. William Harvey and Alexanderina (Brown) Sparks; m. William C. Hobson, Jan. 9, 1960; children: Floyd, Bruce, Scott, William. Student, Radcliffe Coll., 1942—43; BA, Stanford U., 1946, MA, 1947; postgrad., U. Houston, 1970; PhD, U. Tex., 1972, BS in Pharmacy, 1974. Registered pharmacist Tex. Rsch. asst., preventive medicine U. Calif., San Francisco, 1947; rsch. assoc., pharmacology Stanford Med. Sch., San Francisco, 1948; tchr. US Army Dependents Sch., Manila, 1949—51, Miss Harker's Sch., Palo Alto, Calif., 1951—53; med. lab. technician Palo Alto Clinic, 1953—54; tchr. Anglo-Am. Sch., Kifissia, Athens, Greece, 1954—56, Bloomfield HS, NJ, 1957—58, Clark HS, NJ, 1958—59, Molesworth AFB, England, 1960—61, Hartshead Sec. Sch., Ashton-under-Lyne, 1962—63, Droylsden Secondary Sch. Girls, England, 1963—64, Trenton HS, 1965—66, Sam Rayburn HS, Pasadena, Tex., 1967—70; chief lab. technician Dale County Hosp., Ozark, Ala., 1956—57; asst. prof. Hellenika Anglaise Collegion, Athens, Greece, 1959—60, Ashton CC, Ashton-under-Lyne, England, 1961—62; asst. coord. Trenton Jr. 5 Exptl. Sch. Program, 1964—65; rsch. assoc. Princeton U., NJ, 1966—67; chief adult councilor Juvenile Drug Addiction, Pasadena, 1970—72; pharmacist, asst. mgr., mgr. Sommers Drug Stores, Austin, 1974—76; owner, pharmacist Hobson Pharmacy, Pflugerville, Tex., 1976—87. Contbr. articles to profl. jours. Recipient Outstanding Alumna award, U. Tex., 1977; NSF grant, 1970—74. Fellow: Am. Coll. Apothecaries; mem.: AAUW, Greater Pflugerville C. of C. (treas. 1985—86), Better Bus. Bur., Bus. and Profl. Women, Tex. Tchrs. Assn., Am. Tchrs. Assn., Am. Inst. History Pharmacy (Recognition award 1973), Capital Area Pharm. Assn., Tex. Pharm. Assn., Am. Pharm. Assn., Am. Soc. Hosp. Pharmacists, Am. Luth. Ch. Women's Assn. Club, Rainbow Girls Club, Kappa Epsilon. Republican. Episcopalian. Achievements include research in RH blood factor and leukemia, mongolism, possible causal relationship between jaundice and hepatitis. Home: Derbyshire, England. Died Apr. 13, 2010.

**HOCHACHKA, PETER WILLIAM,** biology educator; b. Therien, Alta., Can., Mar. 9, 1937; s. William and Pearl (Krainek) H.; m. Brenda Clayton, Dec. 12, 1970; children: Claire, Gail, Gareth William. BSc with honors, U. Alta., Edmonton, 1959; MSc, Dalhousie U., Halifax, NS, Can., 1961; PhD, Duke U., 1965; DSc, St. Francis Xavier, 1998. Rsch. asst. U. Alta., 1958-69; vis. investigator Woods Hole (Mass.) Oceanog. Inst., 1962; asst. prof. biology U. Toronto, Ont., Canada, 1964-65; postdoctoral fellow Duke U., Durham, NC, 1964-66; asst. prof. U. B.C., Vancouver, Canada, 1966-70, assoc. prof., 1970-75, prof., 1975—2002. Rsch. scientist R-V Alpha Helix of NSF (U.S.) Amazon Expdn. and Bering Sea Expdn., 1967-68, R-V Alpha Helix Guade Lupe Expdn., 1970, Eklund Biol. Sta., McMurdo, Antarctica, 1976-77, 82-83, 93, Palmer Peninsula, 1986; sr. scientist Oceanic Inst., Hawaii, 1970-71, R-V Alpha Helix, Galapagos Expdn., 1970-71, Amazon Expdn., 1976; vis. investigator Inst. Arctic Biology, U. Alaska, 1971, Pacific Biomed. Rsch. Ctr., U. Hawaii, 1975, Nat. Marine Fisheries, Honolulu, 1976, 81, 82, 84, 89, Plymouth Marine Lab., Eng., 1978, Concord Field Sta., Harvard U., 1984; sr. rsch. scientist R-V Alpha Helix Hawaii (Kona Coast) Expdn., 1973; vis. investigator dept. physiology U. Hawaii, 1973, vis. investigator dept. biochemistry, 1976; vis. prof. Friday Harbor Marine Lab., U. Wash., 1975, Harvard U. Med. Sch., 1976-77; mem. R-V Alpha Helix Expdn. to Philippines, 1979; mem. Kenya lungfish program, dept. physiology and biochemistry U. Nairobi, 1979-80; vis. sr. scientist Heron Island Biol. Rsch. Sta., 1983; vis. Q.E. sr. fellow at 27 Australian sci. instns., 1983; mem. U.S. Antarctic Rsch. Program, 1982-83, R/V Polar Duke rsch. expdn., Palmer Peninsula, Antarctica, 1986, high-altitude biochem. adaptaion program, La Raya, Peru, 1982, 87. Author: Strategies of Biochemical Adaptation, 1973, Living Without Oxygen, 1980, Biochemical Adaptation, 1984, Metabolic Arrest and the Control of Biological Time, 1987; editor: The Mollusca, Vol. 1: Metabolic Biochemistry and Molecular Biomechanics, Vol. 2: Environmental Biochemistry and Physiology, 1983; mem. editl. bd. Molecular Physiology, Am. Jour. Physiology, Biochem. Systematics & Ecology, Functional Ecology; co-editor Comp. Biochem. Physiol.; contbr. more than 200 articles to profl. jours. Decorated officer Order of Can., 1999; recipient Gold medal for natural scis. Sci. Coun. B.C., 1987, Killam Rsch. prize U. B.C., 1988, 89, Killiam Meml. Sci. award, 1993, Gold medal Natural Scis. and Rsch. Coun., 1995, Acad. of Yr. award Can. U. Faculty Assns., 1995, Queen Elizabeth II Jubilee medal, 2002; Queen Elizabeth II sr. fellow, Australia, 1983; grantee NRC, 1976. Fellow AAAS, Royal Soc. Can. (v.p. Acad. Scis. 2000, Flavelle medal 1990); mem. Soc. Exptl. Biology, Can. Soc. Zoologists, Am. Soc. Biochem. and Molecular Biology, NY Acad. Scis., Am. Physiol. Soc.,Soc. Integrative & Comparative Biology, Sigma Xi. Home: Vancouver, Canada. Died Sept. 16, 2002.

**HOCHENEGG, LEONHARD,** psychiatrist; b. Innsbruck, Austria, Jan. 24, 1942; s. Hans and Annemarie (Grass) Hochenegg; m. Fatima Rendon, Nov. 4, 1976; children: Fatima, Anni, Hans, Franz, Dominick, Clara, Theres, Eugen. Grad., U. Innsbruck, 1967, MD, 1972. Intern U. Hosp., Innsbruck, 1967-75; asst. Pharmacological Inst. U. Innsbruck, 1967-69, psychiatristin clin., 1972; pvt. practice medicine mental hosp. U. Hosp., Hall, Austria, 1969-72; pvt. practice psychiatric clinic St. Gallen, Switzerland, 1972; pvt. practice neurology and psychiatry Hall, from 1980. Editor: (book) Heiltees, 1987, Die Kunst Nicht Krank zu Werden, 1988, Das Wunder der Heilung, 1994; contbr. articles to profl. jours. Died Feb. 2009.

**HOEBER, PAUL B.,** publisher; b. NYC, Oct. 11, 1914; s. Paul B. and Catherine (Putzel) H.; m. Elizabeth Price, June 20, 1940; children— Paul Richard, Thomas Edward. Student, Antioch Coll., 1931-34, Am. U. Sch. Pub. Affairs, 1934-37. With Paul B. Hoeber, Inc. (med. book dept. Harper & Bros.), 1937-69, pres., 1945-69; exec. v.p. Am. Elsevier Pub. Co., 1970-72, pres., 1972-75; chmn. bd. Agathon Press, Inc., from 1975; pres. APS Publs., Inc., from 1975. Served with USNR, 1942-45, South Atlantic Fleet; Served with USNR, 1942-43, South Atlantic Fleet; inactive Res. Mem.: Players (N.Y.C), Overseas Press (N.Y.C). Democrat. Home: New York, NY. Died Apr. 15, 1991.

**HOEFFEL, MARTIN EDWARD,** lawyer; b. Emerald Twp., Ohio, Oct. 2, 1903; s. John Albert and Magdalena (Rusch) Hoeffel; m. Catherine Maria Hahn, Nov. 6, 1937; children: Anthony, John, Susan Hoeffel Ladd. LLD, Ohio State U. Bar: Ohio. Pvt. practice, Napoleon, Ohio, from 1934; ptnr. Hoeffel, Funkhouser, Hanna & Fisher; pros. atty. Henry County, Ohio, 1935—41. Solicitor Cities of Napoleon, Liberty Ctr. and Hamler, Ohio; mem. bd. grievances, discipline Supreme Ct. Ohio, 1968—74. Fellow: Ohio Bar Assn. (bd. govs. probate and trust sect. 1973—77); mem.: ABA, Henry County Bar Assn., No. Ohio Bar Assn., Elks, KC Club, Kiwanis Club (lt. gov. internat. 1958). Democrat. Roman Catholic. Deceased.

**HOFFBERGER, JEROLD CHARLES,** corporation executive; b. Balt., Apr. 7, 1919; s. Samuel H. and Gertrude (Miller) H.; m. Alice Berney, June 10, 1946; children: David B., Richard J., Carol S., Charles P. Grad., Tome Sch., 1937, U. Va., 1940. Pres., dir. Nat. Brewing Co., Balt., 1947-75; pres., chmn. bd., chief exec. officer Carling Nat. Breweries, Inc., Balt., 1975-78; bd. dir. Real Estate Holding Co., 1987; chmn., pres. Balt. Orioles, 1965-79, pres., 1979-83; owner Sunset Hill Farm, 1980-92. Chmn. bd. dirs. Diversified Resource Mgmt. Ltd., 1978-90, Phoenix Health Corp., 1993—, Phoenix Bar Code Health Sys.; bd. dirs. Mchts. Terminal Corp. Past trustee United Jewish Appeal; vice chmn. bd. dirs. Hoffberger Found.; pres. Coun. Jewish Fedns. and Welfare Funds, 1975-78; chmn. United Israel Appeal, 1978-83; trustee Johns Hopkins Hosp., Balt., 1960-91; mem. adv. bd. Johns Hopkins Sch. Health and Pub. Hygiene, Balt.; bd. dirs. Ctr. for Pub. Policy in Israel; chmn. adv. coun. Wilmer Ophthalmol. Inst., 1990-93; hon. chmn. UIA, 1983—; chmn. bd. dirs. Jewish Agy., 1983-87, gov., 1975-92. Mem. U. Va. Alumni Assn., Nat. Steeplechase and Hunt Assn. (past steward), Suburban Country Club, Ctr. Club, Phi Epsilon Pi. Jewish. Died Apr. 9, 1999.

**HOFFMAN, CHARLES LOUIS,** physician; b. Dayton, Ohio, May 10, 1925; s. Hugh Holland and Ruth Louise (Thiele) H.; m. Nancy Adele Fahrendorf, June 14, 1947; children: Thomas C., Mary Lynne Hoffman Lamb, Lori Hoffman Brustkern, William Edward. Student, U. Dayton, 1943; AB, Oberlin Coll., Ohio, 1945; MD, St. Louis U., 1949. Med. intern US Marine Hosp., Balt., 1949-50, chief op. dept. Kirkwood, Mo., 1950-51; chief med. officer 2nd Coast Guard Dist., St. Louis, 1951; resident internal medicine US Marine Hosp., San Francisco, 1951-53, chief resident internal medicine, 1953-54, asst. chief internal medicine, 1954-55; pvt. practice internal medicine Marin County, Calif., 1955-92; cons. internal medicine and pulmonology Neumiller Hosp., Tamal, Calif., 1957-83; active staff Marin Gen. Hosp., 1955—92; chief of med. staff Ross Gen. Hosp., Calif., 1969. Exec. com. Ross Gen. Hosp., 1968-71, 82-88; med. dir. Rafael Convalescent Hosp., 1987—; med. coord. Regional Cancer Found., San Francisco, 1992-2004; co-founder Med. Ins. Exch. Calif., 1975. Knighted, Sovereign Mil. Order of St. John of Jerusalem, 1992. Fellow AMA, Calif. Med. Assn.; mem. Calif. Soc. Internal Medicine (bd. dirs. 1976-79), Marin Med. Soc. (pres. 1975-76, bd. dirs. 1966-69, 74-77, 88—), Calif. Acad. Medicine, Serra Club of Marin (pres. 1961), Gen. Soc. Mayflower Descendants, Calif. Soc. Mayflower Descendants, Internat. Med. Assn. Lourdes, Elks (Man of Yr. in the Healing Arts 1976). Republican. Roman Catholic. Avocations: swimming, scuba diving, bridge, backgammon. Died Aug. 11, 2012.

**HOFFMAN, PHILIP SEYMOUR,** actor; b. Fairport, NY, July 23, 1967; s. Gordon Stowell and Marilyn Loucks (O'Connor) Hoffman; children: Cooper Alexander, Tallulah, Willa. BFA in Drama, NYU Tisch Sch. Drama, 1989. Co-artistic dir. LAByrinth Theater Co.; co-founder Cooper's Town Productions. Actor: (TV films) The Yearling, 1994, A Child's Garden of Poetry, 2011; (TV miniseries) Empire Falls, 2005; (films) Triple Bogey on a Par Five Hole, 1991, My New Gun, 1992, Leap of Faith, 1992, Scent of a Woman, 1992, Szuler, 1992, My Boyfriend's Back, 1993, Money for Nothing, 1993, Joey Breaker, 1993, The Getaway, 1994, When a Man Loves a Woman, 1994, Nobody's Fool, 1994, The Fifteen Minute Hamlet, 1995, Hard Eight, 1997, Twister, 1996, Boogie Nights, 1997, Montana, 1998, Next Stop Wonderland, 1998, The Big Lebowski, 1998, Happiness, 1998, Patch Adams, 1998, Culture, 1998, Flawless, 1999, Magnolia, 1999, The Talented Mr. Ripley, 1999, State and Main, 2000, Almost Famous, 2000, Forest Hills Bob, 2001, Love Liza, 2002, Punch-Drunk Love, 2002, Red Dragon, 2002, 25th Hour, 2002, Owning Mahowny, 2003, Cold Mountain, 2003, Along Came Polly, 2004, Mission: Impossible III, 2006, Before the Devil Knows You're Dead, 2007, The Savages, 2007, Charlie Wilson's War, 2007, Synecdoche, New York, 2008, Doubt, 2008, Pirate Radio, 2009, Moneyball, 2011, The Ides of March, 2011, The Master, 2012 (Best Supporting Actor, Critics Choice Awards, 2013), A Late Quartet, 2012, The Hunger Games: Catching Fire, 2013, God's Pocket, 2014, A Most Wanted Man, 2014; actor, exec. prodr. (films) Capote, 2005 (Best Actor, Nat. Bd. Review, 2005, Best Actor, Broadcast Film Critics Assn., 2005, Best Actor, Critics Choice Awards, 2005, Best Actor, Boston Soc. Film Critics, 2005, Best Performance by an Actor in a Motion Picture-Drama, Hollywood Fgn. Press Assn. (Golden Globe award), 2006, Best Actor, Nat. Soc. Film Critics, 2006, Outstanding Performance by a Male Actor in a Leading Role, Screen Actors Guild, 2006, Best Actor in a Leading Role, British Acad. Film and TV Arts, 2006, Best Performance by an Actor in a Leading Role, Acad. Motion Picture Arts & Sciences, 2006), actor, writer, dir. Jack Goes Boating, 2010, actor, exec. prodr. (TV films) Trending Down, 2014; dir.: (plays) The Last Days of Judas Iscariot, 2005, The Little Flower of East Orange, 2008; actor: True West, 2000 (Theatre World award, 2000), The Seagull, 2001, Long Day's Journey Into Night, 2003, Jack Goes Boating, 2007, Death of a Salesman, 2012; appeared in (documentaries) I Knew It Was You: Rediscovering John Cazale, 2010, Salinger, 2013. Named one of The 100 Most Influential People in the World, TIME mag., 2006. Died Feb. 2, 2014.

**HOFFMAN, WILLIAM SAMUEL,** biochemist, physician; b. Balt., July 5, 1899; s. Louis Benjamin Hoffman and Lena Miller; m. Miriam Berliner, July 26, 1928; children: Paul Arthur (dec.), Nancy. AB, Johns Hopkins U., 1918, PhD in Chemistry, 1922; MD, U. Chgo., 1929. Diplomate Bd. Internal Medicine; lic. physician, Ill. Asst. in physiol. chemistry Johns Hopkins Med. Sch., 1922-25, instr., 1925-27; intern Cook County Hosp., 1929-30; NRC fellow in medicine Rush Med. Coll., 1931-32; prof. biochemistry Chgo. Med. Sch., 1932-44; acting dir. Hektoen Inst. for Med. Rsch., Chgo., 1944-46; acting dir. of labs. Cook County Hosp., Chgo., 1944-46, dir. biochemistry, 1946-53, professorial lectr. in medicine, 1953-67, professorial lectr. emeritus, 1967—; physician Sidney Hillman Health Ctr. Chgo., 1953-68; cons. VA Hosp., Hines, Ill., 1954-74. Contbr. articles to profl. jours. Mem. Phi Beta Kappa, Alpha Omega Alpha, Sigma Xi. Democrat. Achievements include research on biochemical analytic methods, protein metabolism, water and electrolyte metabolism, penicillin, salicylates, renal disease, diabetes, gout, and pesticides. Home: 1600 East Ave Rochester NY 14610-1617

**HOFFMANN, MARTIN RICHARD,** lawyer; b. Stockbridge, Mass., Apr. 20, 1932; m. Margaret Ann McCabe; children: Heidi H. Slye, William, Bern. AB, Princeton U., NJ, 1954; LLB, U. Va. Sch. Law, Charlottesville, 1961. Bar: DC 1961. Law clk. to Hon. Albert V. Bryan US Ct. Appeals (4th cir.), 1961-62; asst. US atty. US Dept. Justice, Washington, 1962-65; minority counsel US House of Reps., Washington, 1965-67; legal counsel to Senator Charles H. Percy US Senate, Washington, 1967-69; asst. gen. counsel Univ. Computing Co., Dallas, 1969-71; gen. counsel AEC, Washington, 1971-73; spl. asst. to sec. & dep. sec. US Dept. Defense, Washington, 1973-74, gen. counsel, 1974-75, sec. Dept. Army, 1975-77; mng. ptnr. Gardner, Carton & Douglas, Washington, 1977—89; v.p., gen. counsel, sec. Digital Equipment Corp., Maynard, Mass., 1989-93; sr. vis. fellow MIT Ctr. for Policy, Tech. & Indsl. Devel., Cambridge, 1993—95; of counsel Skadden, Arps, Slate, Meagher & Flom, Washington, 1996-2000. Bd. dirs. Castle Energy, Phila., Sea Change Corp., Maynard, Mass. Maj. USAR, 1954-73. Mem. Met. Club. Home: Washington, DC. Died July 14, 2014.

**HOFMANN, HANS J.,** paleontology educator; MS, McGill U., 1959, PhD in Stratigraphy and Palaeontology, 1962. Prof. U. Cin., McMaster U.; precambrian palaeontologist Geological Survey of Canada, 1966; prof. paleontology dept. geology U. Montréal, 1969; adj. prof. McGill Univ, Montreal, Quebec, Canada. Recipient Willet G. Miller medal Royal Soc. Can., 1995. Deceased.

**HÖGMAN, CLAES F.,** transfusion medicine specialist, researcher; b. Halmstad, Sweden, Apr. 1, 1926; s. Folke G.W. and A.Signe B. (Torpson) Högman; m. Anna-Brita Öhman, Feb. 17, 1952; children: John, Christina, Patrik, Nils, Magareta. MD, Karolinska Inst. Med. Sch., Stockholm, 1951; PhD, Uppsala U., Sweden, 1962; habil., Uppsala U., 1988. Mem. staff Karolinska U. Hosp., Stockholm, 1950—56; asst. prof. State Inst. Blood Group Serology, Stockholm, 1956—60; asst. prof. dept. clin. chemistry Uppsala (Sweden) U. Hosp., 1960—65; dir. U. Hosp. Blood Ctr., Uppsala, 1965—89, prof., chief physician, 1988—91, prof., sci. cons., from 1991. Sec. gen. 12th Cong. Internat. Soc. Blood Transfusion, Stockholm, 1964. Contbr. articles to internat. profl. jours. Recipient Karl Landsteiner Meml. award, Am. Assn. Blood Banks, 1986, James Blundell award, Brit. Blood Transfusion Soc., Lancaster, Eng., 1993; named Deutsch Gesellschaft Transfusion Landsteiner hon. lectr., Wurzburg, 1991. Fellow: Internat. Soc. Blood Transfusion (v.p., pres. 1969—78, Presdl. award 2006), Royal Soc. Scis. Uppsala; mem.: Swedish Med. Soc., Swedish Med. Assn. Home: Uppsala, Sweden. Died Nov. 7, 2006.

**HØGSNES, GEIR,** social studies educator, consultant; b. Trondheim, Norway, Dec. 2, 1950; s. Brynjar Høgsnes; life ptnr. Luciane Silva Corrente; children: Jenny Golden, Anders. Dr. polit, U. Oslo, 2003. Research fellow Inst. Social Rsch., Oslo, 1981—98; assoc. prof. Norweigan Inst. Sci. & Tech., 1996—98, U. Oslo, 1999—2000, prof., 2000—09, head dept. sociology & human geography, 2002—07. Home: Oslo, Norway. Died June 3, 2009.

**HOGWOOD, CHRISTOPHER JARVIS HALEY,** music educator; b. Nottingham, Eng., Sept. 10, 1941; s. Haley Evelyn and Marion Constance (Higgott) Hogwood. BA, Cambridge U., Eng., 1964, MA, 1969; postgrad., Charles U., Prague, Czechoslovakia, 1964-65; DMus (hon.), Keele U., Eng., 1991; PhD (hon.), Zurich U., Switzerland, 2007; MusD (hon.), Cambridge U., Eng., 2008, Royal Coll. Music, 2013. Founding mem. Early Music Consort London, 1965—76; music faculty Cambridge U., from 1975, hon. prof. music, from 2002, founding. dir., 1973—2006, emeritus dir., 2006—14, Acad. Ancient Music, London, 2006—14; prof. music Gresham Coll., 2010—14; prof.-at-large Cornell U., 2012—14. Artistic dir. Handel & Haydn Soc., Boston, 1986—2001, condr. laureate, 2001—14; hon. prof. music Keele U., 1986—90; dir. music St. Paul Chamber Orch., 1987—92, prin. guest condr., 1992—98; internat. prof. early music performance Royal Acad. Music, London, 1992—2014; vis. prof. dept. music King's Coll., London, 1992—96; artistic dir. Summer Mozart Festival Nat. Symphony Orch. USA, 1993—2001; assoc. dir. Beethoven Academie, Antwerp, 1998—2002; prin. guest condr. Kammerorchester Basel, 2000—06, Orquesta Ciudad de Granada, 2001—04, Orch. Sinfonica di Milano Giuseppe Verdi, 2003—06. Author: (book) Music at Court, 1977, The Trio Sonata, 1979, Haydn's Visits to England, 1980; editor: Music in Eighteenth Century England, 1983; author: Handel, 1984; editor: Holmes' Life of Mozart, 1991, The Keyboard in Baroque Europe, 2003, Handel: Water Music and Music for the Royal Fireworks, 2005. Decorated Comdr. of the Brit. Empire Her Majesty Queen Elizabeth II; recipient Wilson Cobbett medal, Worshipful Co. Musicians, London, 1986, Disting. Musician award, Inc. Soc. Musicians, 1997, Martinu medal, Bohuslav Martinu Found., Prague, 1999, Handel prize, Halle, Germany, 2008; named Freeman, Worshipful Co. Musicians, London, 1989, Christopher Hogwood Historically Informed Performance Fellowship in his honor, Handel & Hadyn Soc., 2001; Hon. fellow, Jesus Coll., Cambridge, 1989—2014, Pembroke Coll., Cambridge, from 1992. Died Sept. 24, 2014.

**HOIE, HELEN HUNT,** artist; b. Leetsdale, Pa. d. Ludwig and Katherine (Hunt) Bencker; m. Claus Hoie, Nov. 17, 1956 BA, Carnegie Mellon U., 1933. One person shows Southampton Coll., N.Y., 1971, Benson Gallery, Bridgehampton, N.Y., 1972, 77, 84, Babcock Galleries, N.Y.C., 1974, 77, 81, Vered Gallery, East Hampton, 1982, 84, 85, 86, 87, Stavanger Mus., Norway, 1983, Forum Gallery, N.Y.C., 1984; exhibited in group shows: Am. Inst. Arts and Letters, N.Y.C., Hassam Fund Exhbn., 1971, 78, Bklyn. Mus., 1975, Guild Hall Mus., East Hampton, N.Y., 1982, 85, Bernice Steinbaum Gallery, N.Y.C., 1983, Bergen Mus. Sci. and Art, Paramus, N.J., 1985, Harmon-Meek Gallery, Naples, Fla., 1987, Nat. Acad. of Design Ann., 1986, Provincetown Ma. Mus. of Art, 1986; represented in permanent collection: Guild Hall Mus., East Hampton, Centre Coll. Ky., Danville, Parish Art Mus., Southampton, N.Y. Trustee Guild hall Mus., East Hampton, 1970-84, 85—, chairperson mus. com.; chmn. bd. dirs. St. Bartholomew's Community Club, N.Y.C., 1945-48. Recipient Alumni Achievement award Carnegie Mellon U., 1976, 1st prize Nat. Soc. Painters in Casein and Acrylic, 1978. Mem. Women in Arts. Episcopalian. Died Dec. 2000.

**HOLDEN, TONY,** science administrator; b. Northampton, Northamptonshire, Eng., Nov. 20, 1958; s. Desmond Allan and Muriel Anne Holden. BSc in Engring., U. of London, 1981; PhD, U. London, 1984. Chartered engr., Inst. of Elec. Engineers, U.K., European engr., European Fedn. Nat. Engring. Assns., European Cmty. Advanced rsch. fellow U. of Cambridge, 1989—94, asst. dir. of rsch., from 1994. Cons. to various bus., engring. and govt. orgns. Author: (book) Knowledge-based CAD and Microelectronics; contbr. articles and papers to profl. publs. Mem.: Inst. of Dirs. Deceased.

**HOLDER, GEOFFREY LAMONT,** dancer, actor, choreographer, director; b. Port-of-Spain, Trinidad, Aug. 1, 1930; s. Arthur and Louise (De Frense) H.; m. Carmen de Lavallade, June 26, 1955; 1 son, Leo. Student, Queens Royal Coll., Port-of-Spain; student in native dances, W.Indies. Stage debut as mem. Roscoe Holder's Dance Co., Trinidad, 1942; formed own dance co., 1950; toured P.R. and the Caribbean, 1953, U.S. debut, 1953; Broadway debut: House of Flowers, 1954; solo dancer with Met. Opera, N.Y.C., 19S6-57; dramatic debut Waiting for Godot, 1957; concerts with Geoffrey Holder Dance Co., N.Y.C., 1956-60; appeared at Festival of Two Worlds, Spoleto, Italy, 1958, Festividadi Ballet Hispanico, N.Y., 1979; dir., costume designer: The Wiz, Broadway, 1975-78, 78-84, 84 (Drama Desk award best costume design 1975, Tony award best costume design 1975, Tony award best director of musical 1975); dir., costume designer, choreographer: Timbuktu, 1978; stage appearances as dancer include House of Flowers, 1954, Aida, 1956, La Perichole, 1956, Show Boat, 1957, Josephine Baker's Revue, 1964; stage appearances as actor Waiting for Godot, 1957, Twelfth Night, 1960, The Masque of St. George and the Dragon, 1973, From the Memoirs of Pontius Pilate, 1976, Night of One Hundred Stars Two, 1985, The Players Club Centennial Salute, 1989, Night of One Hundred Stars Three, 1990, Give My Regards to Broadway, 1991; choreographer Brouhaha, 1960, Mhil Daiim, 1964, Three Songs for One, 1964, I Got a Song, 1974, Fifty Golden Years of Showstoppers, 1982; costume designer The Twelve Gates, 1964, Three Songs for One, 1964; actor: (films) All Night Long, 1961, Doctor Dolittle, 1967, Krakatoa, East of Java, 1969, Everything You've Always Wanted to Know About Sex, 1972, Live and Let Die, 1973, Swashbuckler, 1976, Annie, 1982, Dance Black America (voice only), 1985, Boomerang, 1992; (TV movies) The Man Without a Country, 1973, John Grin's Christmas, 1986, Ghost of a Chance, 1987, (series) Chef du Jour, 1995; paintings exhibited, Barbados Mus., San Juan, P.R., Barone Gallery, N.Y.C., Gallery of Brooks Atkinson Theatre, N.Y.C., Gropper Gallery, Cambridge, Mass., Griffin Gallery, N.Y.C., Grinnel Galleries, Detroit; recorded albums of W. Indian songs and album of song stories; author: Black Gods, Green Islands, 1957, Geoffrey Holder's Caribbean Cookbook, 1974; contbr. articles to Playbill Recipient United Caribbean Youth award, 1957, Monarch award Nat. Council Culture and Art, 1982, Ellis Island Medal of Honor, Nat. Ethnic Coalition of Organizations, 1986, Liberty award, N.Y.C., 1986; Guggenheim fellow, 1957. Mem. AFTRA, Screen Actors Guild, Actors Equity Assn., AGVA. Died Oct. 5, 2014.

**HOLLANDER, ANNE,** writer; b. Cleve., Oct. 16, 1930; d. Arthur and Jean Hill (Bassett) Loesser; m. John Hollander, June 15, 1953 (div. 1977); children: Martha, Elizabeth; m. Thomas Nagel, June 26, 1979. BA in Art History, Barnard Coll., 1952. Author: Seeing Through Clothes, 1978, Moving Pictures, 1989, Sex and Suits, 1994, Feeding the Eye, 1999, Fabric of Vision, 2002. Guggenheim fellow, 1975. Fellow N.Y. Inst. for the Humanities (interim dir. 1995-96); mem. Costume Soc. America, College Art Assn., PEN American Ctr. (pres. 1995-96), Century Assn. Home: New York, NY. Died July 6, 2014.

**HOLLANDER, ZANDER,** editor, writer; b. NYC, Mar. 24, 1923; s. Herman and Tobye (Karesh) H.; m. Phyllis Isabelle Rosen, Dec. 13, 1951; children: Susan, Peter (dec. 2009) Student, Queens Coll., 1941-43, 45-47. Rewrite man United Press, NYC, 1945-47; sports writer N.Y. World Telegram and Sun, NYC, 1947-65; pres., publisher Associated Features, NYC, 1966—2014. With AAF, 1943-45 PTO. Avocations: tennis, skiing. Died Apr. 11, 2014.

**HOLLEIN, HANS,** architect, artist; b. Vienna, Mar. 30, 1934; s. Leo H. Hollein; m. Helene Jennewein (dec. 1999) Student, Acad. Fine Arts, Vienna, Ill. Inst. Tech.; MArch, U. Calif., Berkeley, 1960. Prof. architecture State Acad. Fine Arts, Düsseldorf, Germany, 1967—2014. Works exhibited Mus. Modern Art, N.Y.C., 1967, Venice, 1972, 78, 80, 82, 84, Stadt Mus., Albertina Mus., Vienna; editor archtl. mag. Bau, 1964-71. Recipient R.S. Reynolds Meml. award, 1966, 84, Bards award for Excellence in Architecture & Urban Design, 1970, Nat. Com. prize Brno Biennial, Czechoslovakia, 1968, Austrian State prize for Environ. Design, City of Vienna prize, 1974, Rosenthal award, 1974, Grand Austrian State Prize for Architecture, 1983, Pritzker Architecture prize Hyatt Found., 1985. Mem. Architektenkammer Nordrheinwestfalen, Ingenieurkammer, Inst. für Formgebung. Home: Düsseldorf, Germany. Died Apr. 24, 2014.

**HOLLENBERG, CHARLES HERBERT,** medical foundation executive; b. Winnipeg, Man., Can., Sept. 15, 1930; s. Abraham and Minnie (Pitt) H.; m. Mimi Hollenberg, 1956; 1 child, Anthony. BSc, U. Man., Winnipeg, 1950, MD, 1955, DSc (hon.), 1983, McGill U., Montreal, Que., Can., 1985. Prof. medicine McGill U., 1969-70; prof., chmn. dept. U. Toronto, Ont., Can., 1970-81, Charles H. Best prof. med. rsch., 1981-83, vice provost health scis., 1983-89; chmn. dept. medicine Toronto Gen. Hosp., 1981-83, dir. Banting and Best Diabetes Ctr., from 1981; pres. Ont. Cancer Treatment and Rsch. Found., Toronto, from 1991. Bd. dirs. Gt. West Life, Winnipeg; pres. Gairdner Found., Toronto, 1972—. Decorated officer Order of Can. Master ACP; fellow Royal Soc. Can., Royal Coll. Physicians; mem. N.Am. Soc. for Study Obesity (councillor, fin. com. 1991—), Can. Inst. in Acad. Medicine (pres.-elect 1992—), Endocrine Soc., Univ. Club, Sigma Xi. Died 2003.

**HOLLIDAY, ROBERT KELVIN (BOB HOLLIDAY),** state legislator, publishing executive, editor; b. Logan, W.Va., Feb. 11, 1933; s. James Kelvin and Helen Kathleen (Harris) Holliday; m. Deborah Ann Holliday; children: Kelvin, Kathleen Eddy, Stephen, Robert L., Jeffrey, Tracey, Brandon. BA, W.Va. U. Tech., 1954; MA, Marshall U., 1955. Co-owner, editor Montgomery (W.Va.) Herald, 1955—85; co-owner, editor The Fayette Tribune, 1955—85, Fayette Tribune, 1955—85, Meadow River Post, Rainelle, W.Va., 1966—85; with W.Va. Divsn. Corrections, 2001—03. Mem. W.Va. House of Delegates, 1963-68, W.Va. State Senate, 1968-72, 80-94; adj. polit. sci. instr. W.Va. U. Inst. Tech., 1994, 99, 2000, 02-05, W.Va. State Coll., 1997-98, Bluefield State Coll., 1996, Greenbrier County College, 1995, Glenville State Coll., 1997. Author: Tests of Faith, 1966, About Montgomery, 1956, Our Chat, 1956, A Portrait of Fayette, 1960, Politics in Fayette County, 1958. Mem. W.Va. State Democratic Exec. Com., 1978-80; pres. Fayette Needy Assn., 1960-68; elder Presbyn. Church;

sgt. U.S. Army. Recipient Governor's Living Dream award Martin Luther King Jr., 1988, Outstanding Leadership award W.Va. NAACP, 1988, award Kanawha-Fayette Cmty. Svc., Inc., 1985-2005, Disting. award Gov. Manchin's West Va., 2010, Pax Reunion award Fayette Vols.; named Outstanding Legislator, W.Va. Trial Lawyers Assn., 1988, 92. Mem.: Southern Poverty Law Ctr. (AARP from 1996), American Fed. of State County & Municipal Employees Union, W.Va.Rehab Assn. (Structural Barriers award 1988), W. Va. Edn. Assn. (Pearl S. Buck award 1982), W. Va. Mental Health Assn. (past dir.), New Rivers Nat. River (founder), Shriners, Masons (32d degree). Home: Fayetteville, W.Va. Died Feb. 28, 2014.

**HOLLIDAY, ROBIN,** geneticist, cell biologist, sculptor; b. Jaffa, Palestine, Nov. 6, 1932; s. Albert Clifford and Eunice Dora (Blackwell) H.; m. Diana Collet Parsons (div. 1983); children: David, Caroline, Rebecca, Emma; m. Lily Irene Huschtscha, Sept. 9, 1986; 1 child, Mira. BA, U. Cambridge, Eng., 1955, PhD, 1959. Rsch. scientist John Innes Inst., Hertford, Eng., 1958-65; rsch. assoc. dept. genetics U. Wash., Seattle, 1962-63; rsch. scientist Nat. Inst. Med. Rsch., Mill Hill, London, 1965-70, head divsn. genetics, 1970-88; chief rsch. scientist CSIRO, North Ryde, Australia, 1988-97; ret., 1997. Author: The Science of Human Progress, 1981, Genes, Proteins and Cellular Aging, 1986, Understanding Aging, 1995, Slaves and Saviours, 2000, Aging: the Paradox of Life, 2007, Origins and Outcomes: an Autobiography, 2008; contbr. rsch. articles to sci. jours; edited books. Recipient Lord Cohen medal Brit. Soc. Aging Rsch., 1987; Fulbright scholar, 1962. Fellow Royal Soc. London (Royal Medal, 2011), Indian Nat. Sci. Acad. (fgn.), Australian Acad. of Sci.; mem. European Molecular Biology Orgn. Achievements include research in mechanism of recombination (Holliday structure), epigenetic control of gene expression, understanding aging. Home: West Pennant Hills, Australia. Died Apr. 9, 2014.

**HOLLOWAY, JOSEPH,** theatrical producer, director; b. Wheeling, W. Va., Oct. 25, 1951; s. Walker Peterson and Barbara (Bruning) H. BFA, NC Sch. Arts, 1974; MA, U. Ill., 1976; grad., Fountain Valley Sch., Colo. Springs, 1970. Freelance dir., choreographer, NY, 1978—84; theatrical cons. Leigh Infield Assocs., NYC, 1982—84; dir., choreographer Berkshire Ctr. Performing Arts, Lenox, Mass., 1981; exec. dir. New Directions Theater, NYC, from 1983. Nat. Assn. Regional Ballet choreographic fellow, 1980. Mem.: Players. Avocations: tennis, sailing. Died May 27, 1999.

**HOLLOWAY, WILLIAM JUDSON, JR.,** federal judge; b. June 23, 1923; AB, U. Okla., 1947; LLB, Harvard U., 1950; LLD (hon.), Oklahoma City U., 1991. Ptnr. Holloway & Holloway, Oklahoma City, 1950—51; atty. gen. litigation section, claims divsn. US Dept. Justice, Washington, 1951—52; assoc., ptnr. Crowe & Dunlevy, Oklahoma City, 1952—68; judge US Ct. Appeals (10th Cir.), Oklahoma City, 1968—84, chief judge, 1984—91, sr. judge, 1992—2014. Mem.: FBA, ABA, Oklahoma County Bar Assn., Okla. Bar Assn. Died Apr. 25, 2014.

**HOLOUBEK, GUSTAW,** actor; b. Cracow, Poland, Apr. 21, 1923; s. Gustaw and Eugenia Holoubek; m. Danuta Kwiatkowska; m. Maria Wachowiak; m. Magdalena Zawadzka; 2 children. Assoc. prof. State Higher Theatrical Sch.; vice chmn. SPATiF (Assn. Polish Theatre & Film Actors), 1963—70, chmn., 1970—81, dep. to Seym, 1976—82. Actor: Wyspianski Theatre, Katowice, (artistic mgr.):, 1954—56,: Polish Theatre, Warsaw, 1958—59, Dramatic Theatre, Warsaw, Poland, 1959—82; dir.(artistic mgr.):, 1972—82; actor: Warsaw theatres; (plays) Leprosy at the Palace of Justice, Le diable et le bon Dieu, Rzeznia, Electra, The Iceman Cometh, King Lear, Oedipus, Richard II & Hadrian VII, November Night, Operetka; (TV films); dir.: (films) Mazepa. Decorated State prize 1st class, Order Banner of Labor 2d class, Knight's Cross of Polonia Restituta; recipient Meritorious Activist Culture award, 1972, Warsaw City prize, 1975, Com. Polish Radio & TV award, 1980. Home: Warsaw, Poland. Died Mar. 6, 2008.

**HOLT, NANCY LOUISE,** artist; b. Worcester, Mass., Apr. 5, 1938; d. Ernest Milton and E. Louise (Jellicoe) H.; m. Robert I. Smithson, June 8, 1963 (dec. 1973). BS in Biology, Tufts U., 1960; DFA (hon.), U. South Fla., 1996. Vis. artist U. R.I., U. Mont.; lectr., Princeton U., N.J. Author: Ransacked, 1980, Time Outs, 1985; one-woman shows include Art Gallery, U. Mont., 1972, Art Center, U. R.I., Kingston, 1972, LoGiudice Gallery, N.Y.C., 1973, Bykert Gallery, N.Y.C., 1974, Walter Kelly Gallery, Chgo., 1974, Franklin Furnace, N.Y., 1977, Whitney Mus. Young American Filmmakers Series, N.Y.C., 1977, John Weber Gallery, N.Y.C., 1979, 82, 84, 86, 93, Flow Ace Gallery, L.A., 1985; sculpture commns. include Views through a Sand Dune, Narragansett Beach, R.I., 1972, Hydra's Head, Artpark, Lewiston, N.Y., 1974, Sun Tunnels, Great Basin Desert, Utah, 1976, Rock Rings, Western Wash. U., Bellingham, 1978, Inside Out, Washington, 1980, Star-Crossed, Miami U., Oxford, Ohio, 1979-81, Wild Spot, Wellesley Coll., Mass., 1979-80, Annual Ring, Saginaw, Mich., 1981, Catch Basin, Toronto, Ont., Can., 1982, Sole Source, Dublin, Ireland, 1983, Time Span, Laguna Gloria Art Mus., Austin, Tex., 1981, Dark Star Park, Arlington, Va., 1979-84, Waterwork, Gallaudet Coll., Washington, 1984, Pipeline and Starfire Anchorage, 1986, End of the Line/West Rock, Southern Conn. State U., New Haven, 1985, Astral Grating, N.Y.C., 1987, Spinwinder, Southeastern Mass. U., 1991, Ventilation III: Finn Air, Tampere Mus., Finland, 1992, Ventilation IV: Hampton Air, Guild Hall Mus., Easthampton, N.Y., 1992, Solar Rotary, U. South Fla., 1995, Up and Under, Nokia, Finland, 1998; films include Swamp, 1971, Pine Barrens, 1975, Sun Tunnels, 1978; videotapes include Underscan, 1974, Revolve, 1977, Art in the Public Eye, 1988. CAPS grantee, 1975, 78; Guggenheim fellow, 1978; Nat. Endowment for Arts grantee, 1975, 78, 83, 85, 88; WNET Artist in Residence grantee, 1977; Beard's Fund Inc., grantee, 1977 Home: Galisteo, N.Mex. Died Feb. 8, 2014.

**HOLTHUIS, LIPKE BIJDELEY,** emeritus curator; b. Probolinggo, Indonesia, Apr. 21, 1921; s. Bernard Jan and Neeltje (bij de Ley) H. PhD, Nat. U., Leiden, The Netherlands, 1946; PhD (hon.), U. Trondheim, Norway, 1972. Asst. curator Nat. Mus. Natural History, Leiden, 1941-47, curator, 1947-59, sr. curator, 1959-86, emeritus curator, from 1986. Mem. Internat. Commn. Zool. Nomenclature, 1953-96, v.p., 1964-77, acting pres., 1965-72, sec. gen., 1977-89. Contbr. over 500 articles to profl. jours. Recipient Spl. Recognition award U.S. Nat. Mus. Natural History, 1986; named Officer Order of Orange-Nassau, Queen of the Netherlands, 1986. Mem. Zool. Soc. London (corr. mem. 1951—), Carcinological Soc. Japan (hon.), Sociedade Brasileira de Carcinologia (hon.), Soc. Bibliography Natural History (hon.), Zool. Soc. Israel (hon.). Avocations: study of Crustacea, history of biology, bibliophyly. Home: Leiden, Netherlands. Died Mar. 7, 2008.

**HOLTZ, ALAN STEFFEN, SR.,** surgeon; b. Moline, Ill., Feb. 5, 1922; s. Gustav and Clara Helena (Steffen) H.; m. Janet Ellen Wright, Dec. 27, 1950 (dec. 1995); children: Alan S. Jr., Janet Ann. BA in Biology, U. Mo., 1947, BS in Medicine, 1949; D in Medicine, Washington U., St. Louis, 1951. Diplomate Am. Bd. Surgery. Intern, surg. resident St. Louis City Hosp., 1951-56, dir. emergency dept., 1957-66, fellow in surgery, 1962; chief resident surgeon U. N.C. Meml. Hosp., Chapel Hill, 1956-57; pvt. practice, staff surgeon St. Joseph Hosp., Kirkwood, Mo., 1957-84, v.p. med. affairs, 1984-87; field staff surveyor Am. Coll. Surgeons Commn. on Cancer, Chgo., from 1988. Bd. dirs. Grace Hill Neighborhood Health Ctr., St. Louis, 1988—. Staff sgt. U.S. Army, 1942-46, ETO; col. USAR, 1979-82. Fellow ACS; mem. St. Louis Med. Soc., St. Louis Surg. Soc., Nathan A. Womack Surg. Soc. Democrat. Episcopalian. Avocations: reading, history, trout fishing. Died 2007.

**HOLTZMANN, HOWARD MARSHALL,** lawyer, judge; b. NYC, Dec. 10, 1921; s. Jacob L. and Lillian (Plotz) Holtzmann; m. Anne Fisher, Jan. 14, 1945 (dec. Aug. 1967); children: Susan Holtzmann Richardson, Betsey Holtzmann; m. Carol Ebenstein Van Berg, Dec. 23, 1972. AB, Yale Coll., 1942, JD, 1947; LittD (hon.), St. Bonaventure U., 1952; LLD (hon.), Jewish Theol. Sem., NYC, 1990. Bar: NY 1947. Atty. Colorado Fuel & Iron Corp., Buffalo, 1947-49; ptnr. Holtzmann, Wise & Shepard, NYC, 1949-95; judge Iran-US Claims Tribunal, The Hague, Netherlands, 1981-94; sr. claims judge Claims Resolution Tribunals for Dormant Accounts, Zurich, Switzerland, 1998—2002. US del. UN Commn. on Internat. Trade Law, 1975—, Hague Conf. on Pvt. Internat. Law, 1985; advisor U.S.A. Arbitration agreements with USSR, Russian Fedn., China, Hungary, Bulgaria, Czechoslovakia, Poland and German Dem. Republic. Author, editor: A New Look at Legal Aspects of Doing Business with China, 1979; co-author: (with J.E. Neuhaus) A Guide to the UNCITRAL Model Law on International Commercial Arbitration-Legislative History and Commentary, 1988 (cert. of merit Am. Soc. Internat. Law 1991); co-author, co-editor (with E. Kristjansdottir) International Mass Claims Processes - Legal and Practical Perspectives, 2007; contbr. chpts. to books and articles to law jours. Mem. governing coun. Downstate Med. Sch. SUNY, Bklyn., 1961-78, NY Weill Cornell Coun., 2003-; trustee St. Bonaventure U., Olean, NY, 1968-90, trustee emeritus, 1990—; chmn. bd. Jewish Theol. Sem., NYC, 1983-85, hon. chmn., 1985—; trustee Inst. Internat. Law, Pace U. Sch. Law, 1992—; mem. bd. advisors Lighthouse Internat. Decorated comdr. Swedish Royal Order of Polar Star; recipient Yale medal, 2006, Medal of Honor, Vienna, Austria; Assoc. fellow, Pierson Coll., Yale, from 2005, Sterling fellow, Yale U. Mem. ABA (chmn. com. code ethics comml. arbitrators 1973-77), Permanent Ct. of Arbitration (chmn. steering com. on internat. mass claims), Internat. Coun. for Comml. Arbitration (hon. vice chmn.), Am. Arbitration Assn. (hon. chmn., Gotshal Internat. Arbitration award 1980, Peacemaker award 2006), Internat. C. of C. (vice chmn. arbitration commn. 1979-2001), Stockholm Arbitration Inst. (adv. bd.), Am. Bar Found., NY County Lawyers Assn., Internat. Law Assn., Am. Fgn. Law Assn. (v.p. 1995-2003, Disting. Svc. award 1999), Internat. Bar Assn., NY State Bar Assn., Assn. Bar City of NY, Am. Soc. Internat. Law (cert. merit 1991), Soc. Profls. in Dispute Resolution, Indsl. Rels. Rsch. Assn., Am. Judicature Soc., Am. Assn. for Internat. Commn. of Jurists. Home: New York, NY. Died 2013.

**HOLYER, ERNA MARIA,** retired adult education educator, writer, artist; b. Weilheim, Bavaria, Germany, Mar. 15, 1925; d. Mathias and Anna Maria (Goldhofer) Schretter; m. Gene Wallace Holyer, Aug. 24, 1957 (dec. 1999). AA, San Jose Evening Coll., 1964; student, San Mateo Coll., 1965—67, San Jose State U., 1968—69, San Jose City Coll., 1980—81; DLitt, World U., 1984; DFA (hon.), The London Inst. Applied Rsch, 1992. Freelance writer under pseudonym Ernie Holyer, from 1960; tchr. creative writing San Jose Met. Adult Edn., Calif., 1968—2006; ret., 2006. Exhibited in group shows at Crown Zellerbach Gallery, San Francisco, 1973-4, 76-77; I.B.C. Gallery, San Francisco, 1978 (medal of Congress, 1988, 89, 92, 94, Congress Challenge trophy, 1991), L.A., 1981, Cambridge, Eng., 1992, Cambridge, Mass., 1993, San Jose, Calif., 1993, Edinburgh, 1994, San Francisco, 1996; author: Rescue at Sunrise, 1965, Steve's Night of Silence, 1966, A Cow for Hansel, 1967, At the Forest's Edge, 1969, Song of Courage, 1970, Lone Brown Gull, 1971, Shoes for Daniel, 1974, The Southern Sea Otter, 1975, Sigi's Fire Helmet, 1975, Reservoir Road Adventure, 1982, Wilderness Journey, Golden Journey, California Journey, 1997, Self-Help for Writers: Winners Show You How, 2002, Dangerous Secrets: A Young Girl's Travails Under the Nazis, 2003, Survival: An Electrifying Tale, 2004; contbr. articles to mags. and newspapers Recipient Woman of Achievement Honor cert. San Jose Mercury-News, 1973, 74, 75, Lefoli award for excellence in adult edn. instr. Adult Edn. Senate, 1972, Women of Achievement awards League of Friends of Santa Clara County Commn., San Jose Mercury News, 1987, various art awards. Mem. N.L.A.P.W. Inc., World Univ Roundtable (doctoral). Deceased.

**HOLZBACH, JAMES FRANCIS,** civil engineer; b. Elizabeth, NJ, July 26, 1936; s. Norman Bernard and Mary Elizabeth (Devine) H.; m. Juliette Horwitz, May 21, 1977. BSCE, U. Notre Dame, 1960. Registered profl. engr., N.Y. Commd. ensign C.E. Corps USN, 1960, advanced through grades to lt. comdr., 1967, resigned, 1970; contract adminstr. Teetor-Dobbins Cons. Engrs., Rochester, N.Y., 1970-72; assoc. engr. Monroe County Dept. Engring., Rochester, 1972-90, acting chief constrn., 1990-92, mng. engr., from 1993. Contbr. articles to profl. jours. Active Dispute Rev. Bd. Found. Mem. ASCE, Am. Underground Constrn. Assn., Dispute Rev. Bd. found. Home: Rochester, NY. Died Nov. 18, 2001.

**HONAN, WILLIAM HOLMES,** retired journalist; b. NYC, May 11, 1930; s. William Francis and Annette (Neudecker) H.; m. Nancy Burton, June 22, 1975; children: Bradley, Daniel, Edith. BA, Oberlin Coll., Ohio, 1952; MA, U. Va., 1955. Editor The Villager (weekly newspaper), NYC, 1957-60; asst. editor New Yorker mag., 1960-64; freelance writer nat. mags., 1964-68; asso. editor Newsweek, 1969; asst. editor New York Times Mag., 1969-70, travel editor, 1970-72, 73-74, arts and leisure editor, 1974-82, culture editor, 1982-88, chief cultural corr., 1988-93, nat. higher edn. corr., 1993—2000; mng. editor Saturday Rev., 1972-73. Author: Greenwich Village Guide, 1959, Ted Kennedy: Profile of a Survivor, 1972, Bywater: The Man Who Invented the Pacific War, Brit. edit., 1990, Visions of Infamy: The Untold Story of How Journalist Hector C. Bywater Devised the Plans That Led to Pearl Harbor, 1991, Remember, Japanese edit., 1991, Treasure Hunt: A New York Times Reporter Tracks the Quedlinburg Hoard, 1997, (Play) Zingers, 2001, (pamphlet) Another La Guardia, 1960; compiler, editor: Fire When Ready, Gridley: Great Naval Stories From Manila Bay to Vietnam, 1993; contbr. articles to nat. mags. and profl. jours. Served with AUS, 1956-57. Died Apr. 28, 2014.

**HOOKSTRATTEN, EDWARD GREGORY,** lawyer; b. Whittier, Calif., June 12, 1932; s. E.G. and Winona (Hewitt) H.; m. Pat Crowley (div.) children: Jon Crowley, Ann; m. Aimee Richelieu BS, U. Southern Calif., 1953; JD, Southwestern U. Sch. Law, L.A., 1957; LLD, Southwestern U. Sch. Law, 1984. Bar: Calif. 1958, U.S. Supreme Ct. 1974. Pvt. practice law, Beverly Hills, Calif., 1960—2014. Commr. bd. adminstrn. L.A. Retirement System, 1970-71; commr. L.A. Dept. Public Utilities and Transp., 1971-73, v.p., 1973; commr. L.A. Dept. Recreation & Parks, 1973-75, v.p., 1974; bd. dirs., life mem. U. Southern Calif. Associates; bd. dirs. L.A. Police Meml. Found.; trustee Southwestern U., 1984-2014 Mem. L.A. County Bar Assn., Beverly Hills Bar Assn., Bel Air Country Club, Beverly Hills Tennis Club, Friars Club (N.Y.C.). Died Jan. 22, 2014.

**HOPE, THEODORE SHERWOOD, JR.,** retired lawyer; b. NYC, Oct. 7, 1903; s. Theodore Sherwood and Winifred (Ayres) Hope; m. Emily Louise Blanchard, June 28, 1934; 1 child, Peter Blanchard. AB, Harvard U., 1925; LLB, Columbia U., 1928. Bar: NY 1931, US Supreme Ct. 1936. Instr. Columbia U. Law Sch., NYC, 1928—29; assoc. instr. Johns Hopkins U. Inst. Law, Balt., 1929—32; pvt. practice NYC, 1932—33; with Paramount Bankruptcy Trustees, NYC, 1933—34; assoc. Donovan Leisure Newton & Irvine (Formerly Donovan Leisure Newton & Lumbard), NYC, 1934—40, 1941—49, ptnr., 1949—86, counsel, from 1986; assoc. prof. law Cornell U. Law Sch., 1940—41. Contbr. articles to legal jours. Mem. Fellows Coun., 1983—87. Fellow: Pierpont Morgan Libr.; mem.: Am. Soc. Internat. Law, NY State Bar Assn., Browning Inst., Inc. (life), Assn. Bar City NY, Harvard Club NYC, Lotos Club. Home: Danbury, NH. Died Oct. 9, 1998.

**HOPPER, ARTHUR FREDERICK,** biological science educator; b. Plainfield, NJ, Sept. 7, 1917; s. Arthur Frederick and Catherine (Hoenig) H.; m. Amy Patricia Hull, Dec. 28, 1940 (dec. Nov. 1982); children: Arthur Frederick, Geoffrey Victor, Christopher James, Gregory Lorton; m. Patricia Ann Vennett, Sept. 6, 1986. AB, Princeton U., 1938; MS, Yale U., 1942; PhD, Northwestern U., 1948. Instr. Northwestern U., Evanston, Ill., summer 1948; asst. prof. Wayne U., Detroit, 1948-49; asst. prof. to prof. Rutgers U., New Brunswick, N.J., 1949-80, dir. biol. scis. grad. program, 1973-75; rsch. assoc. Brookhaven (N.Y.) Nat. Lab., 1961-68; visiting prof. U. Liège Med. Sch., Belgium, 1967-68; prof. emeritus Rutgers U., New Brunswick, from 1980. Rsch. assoc. Detroit Cancer Inst., 1948-49; scientist aboard Columbia U. R/V "Vema", summer, 1955, 58; vis. investigator Battelle N.W., Richland, Wash., summer 1970, Jackson Meml. Lab., Bar Harbor, Maine, summers, 1971, 73. Author: Foundations of Animal Development, 1st ed. 1979, 2d ed. 1985; contbr. articles to profl. jours. Chmn. troop 53 Boy Scouts Am., Bedminster, N.J., 1953-58; v.p., pres. Bedminster Bd. Edn., 1957-63; coach, mgr. Far Hills Little League Baseball, 1954-56; pres. Somerset County Bd. Edn., Somerville, N.J., 1960-63; coord. radiology def. Somerset County, 1959-63; bd. dirs. Palm Beach County Kidney Assn., Lake Worth, Fla., 1988-90, mem. med. adv. bd., 1993—. 1st lt. USAAF, 1943-46; lt. col. USAFR, 1946-68. Rsch. grantee NSF, USPHS, Am. Cancer Soc., Lalor Found, Rutgers U. Rsch. Coun., 1950-80. Mem. AAAS, Soc. Integrative and Comparative Biology, Soc. Devel. Biologists, Sigma Xi. Home: Monroe, NC. Died Feb. 13, 2008.

**HORN, HARTMUT GERHARD,** sociologist, psychologist; b. Oldenburg, Germany, Mar. 1, 1930; s. Johannes H. and Gertrud (Mueller) H.; m. Brigitte Haemmerling; children: Friedemann L., Peter A. Diploma in Psychology, U.Marburg, Fed. Republic of Germany, 1956; Cert. primary and secondary tchr., Paedag. Inst., Weilburg, Fed. Republic of Germany, 1959; PhD in Sociology, U. Marburg, 1963; cert. spl. tchr., Paedag.Hochschule Ruhr, Dortmund, Fed. Republic of Germany, 1965. Indsl. Psychologist Dortmund-Hoerder-Huetten-Union, 1956; tchr. various High Schs., Spl. Schs., 1959-63; lectr. in psychology, sociology and social psychology various colls. and univs., Marburg, Giessen and Bochum, 1960-70; head of test dept. Deutsches Inst. fuer Intern. Paed. Forschung, Frankfurt, Fed. Republic of Germany, 1963-66; assoc. prof. psychology Paedagogische Hochschule Ruhr, Dortmund, Fed. Republic of Germany, 1966-70, prof. sociology, 1970-80, U. Dortmund, Fed. Republic of Germany, 1980-95, prof. emeritus, 1995—2002. Cons. editor Jour. of Learning Disabilities; author, editor numerous articles and books. Mem. Deutsche Gesellschaft für Soziologie. Home: Berlin, Germany. Died Mar. 1, 2002.

**HORN, PAUL JOSEPH,** musician; b. NYC, Mar. 17, 1930; s. Jack L. and Frances (Sper) H.; m. Ann Mortifee; children from previous marriage: Marlen L., Robin F. Mus.B., Oberlin Conservatory Music, 1952; Mus.M. (fellow), Manhattan Sch. Music, 1953; student, Acad. Meditation, Himalayas, India, 1967-68; PhD (hon.), U. Victoria, Canada, 1999. Tchr. system transcendental meditation UCLA (also at Berkeley and centers throughout U.S. and Can.); Mem. Sauter-Finegan Band, 1956-57, Chico Hamilton Quintet, 1957-58, NBC Staff Orch., Hollywood, Calif., 1960; free-lance studio work, 1960-70; formed Paul Horn Quintet, 1959, Golden Flute Records, 1982. Rec. artist for, Dot, World Pacific, HiFi, Columbia, RCA Victor records, producer, artist, Epic Records, Kuckuck Records, concerts throughout U.S. and Europe, 1957—, tours to People's Republic China, 1978, 81, concert tour of USSR, 1983, 86, 88, Nepal and Tibet, 1998; producer: TV documentary Paul Horn in China; (Recipient Grammy nomination 1966, 87, 99, 2 Grammy awards 1966), motion picture appearances; guest TV performer; star: TV series The Paul Horn Show; made solo flute recs. in Taj Mahal, (Inside), 1968, 89; in Gizeh pyramids, (Inside the Great Pyramid), in Lithuania (Inside the Cathedral, Inside Canyon de Chelly), in Lhasa, Tibet (Inside the Potala), Mushroom Records, 1976, Golden Flute Records, 1984, Kuckuck Records, 1986, Canyon Records, 1997; author: (autobiography) Inside Paul Horn, 1990. Bd. dirs. Victoria Symphony Orch., Performing Rights Orgn. Can., Pro Can. Served with AUS, 1953-56. Also awards from Jazz Polls; also awards from Downbeat mag., awards from Playboy mag. Died June 29, 2014.

**HORN, RUSSELL EUGENE,** engineering executive, consultant; b. York, Pa., May 4, 1912; s. Eugene M. and Charlotte (Snyder) H.; m. Eleanor B. Baird, Jan. 12, 1934; children: Russell Eugene, Ralph Elliot, Rosalind Emily (Mrs. Lee Kunkel), Robert Errol. BS, Pa. State U., 1933. Foreman Pa. Dept. Hwys. dist. office, York, Pa., 1933-35; draftsman, supr., designer C.S. Buchart, architect, 1935-41; exec. v.p., chief engr. Buchart Engring., 1945-59, pres., chief engr., 1959-61, Buchart-Horn, Inc., 1961-72, chmn. bd. dirs., 1972-2000. Pres. PACE Resources, inc., 1970-87, chmn. bd. dirs. 1970-2001, bd. dirs.; chmn. AAA White Rose Motor Club, 1975-78. Bd. dirs. Auto Club So. Pa.; bd. dirs. emeritus Retirement Homes of Meth. Ch., 1978—. Col. AUS, 1940-45. Mem. NSPE, Soc. Am. Mil. Engrs., Pa. Soc. Profl. Engrs. (pres. Lincoln chpt. 1961), Pa. Assn. Cons. Engrs. (pres. 1965, bd. dirs. 1966), Pa. Hwy Info. Assn. (bd. dirs.), Am. Soc. Hwy. Engrs. (nat. pres. 1962), Tech. Socs. Coun. Southeastern Pa. (chmn. 1963), Engring. Soc. York, Profl. Engrs. Pvt. Practice, Am. Concrete Inst., Assn. Pa. Constructors Assn. Hwy Ofcls. N. Atlantic States, Assn. U.S. Army Res. Officers Assn., ASCE, VFW, Cons. Engrs. Coun., Am. Legion, Pa. State U. Alumni Club (York County), Univ. Club, Lake Club, Exch. Club (Golden Deeds award 1979), Mt. Nittany Soc. Pa. State U., Masons (32 deg., Order of the Double Eagle award 1983, Legion of Freedom award 1986, outstanding engring. alumnus 1987), York County Agrl. Soc. (life), Moose Home: York, Pa. Died Dec. 4, 2013.

**HORNADAY, KENNETH C.,** utilities executive; b. Mooresville, Ind., June 9, 1933; s. Albert T. and Mary (Lewis) Hornaday; m. Maxine Loree Montgomery, May 26, 1967; children: Gary Lee, Ken, William T.; m. Patricia Dankey. AA, San Diego Cmty. Coll., 1972; BBA, Nat. U., 1978, MBA, 1981. Utilities mgr. Naval Air Sta., Miramar, San Diego, 1976—79, North Island, San Diego, 1979—80; utilities and hazardous waste mgr. Naval Regional Med. Ctr., San Diego, 1980—82, comml. activities program analyst, 1982—83; pub. utilities specialist Pub. Works Ctr., San Diego, from 1983. With USN, 1951—65. Recipient Fed. Exec. Com. Disting Svc. award, 1980, Sustained Performance award, 1982, 1984. Mem.: Nat. Mgmt. Assn., Nat. Univ. Alumni Assn., Scottish Rite, Masons. Republican. Died Dec. 18, 1985.

**HORNE, DONALD RICHMOND,** writer, educator; b. Sydney, NSW, Australia, Dec. 26, 1921; s. David and Florence (Carpenter) H.; m. Myfanwy Gollan, Mar. 22, 1960; children: Julia, Nicholas. Student, U. Sydney, 1939-41, Canberra U., 1944-45; LittD (hon.), U. New S. Wales, 1986; D. Univ., Griffith U., Brisbane, 1988-91; D.Univ. (hon.), U. Canberra, 1996. Editor The Observer, Sydney, 1958-61, The Bulletin, Sydney, 1961-62, 67-72; creative dir. Jackson Wain, Sydney, 1962-66; co-editor Quadrant, Sydney, 1963-66; prof. U. NSW, Sydney, 1973-86; contbg. editor Newsweek Internat., Sydney, 1973-76; chmn. Australia Coun., Sydney, 1985-90, Ideas for Australia, Sydney, 1991-94; emeritus prof. U. NSW, Sydney, Australia, from 1987. Chmn., adv. bd., Copyright Agy. Ltd., Sydney, 1983-84, The Australian Ency., Sydney, 1986-88; chancellor U. of Canberra, 1992-95, U. New S. Wales, 1973-86; mem. univ. coun. U. New S. Wales, 1983-86, chmn. Faculty Arts, 1982-86; fellow Australian Acad. Humanities, 1995—; exec. com. Australian Assn. Cultural Freedom, 1962-66; adv. com. NSW Cultural Grants, 1976-79. Author: (social critique) The Lucky Country, 1964, Southern Exposure, 1967, God is an Englishman, 1969, The Next Australia, 1970, Death of the Lucky Country, 1976, Winner Take All, 1981, The Trouble With Economic Rationalism, 1992, The Coming Republic, 1992, The Avenue of the Fair Go, 1997, Looking for Leadership, 2001, (history), Ten Steps to a More Tolerant Australia, 2003, In Search of Billy Hughes, 1979, Time of Hope, 1980, The Story of the Australian People, 1985, The Lucky Country Revisited, 1987, (cultural critique) Money Made Us, 1976, Right Way Don't Go Back, 1978, The Great Museum, 1984, The Public Culture, 1986, 94, Ideas for a Nation, 1989, The Intelligent Tourist, 1993, (autobiography) The Education of Young Donald, 1967, Confessions of a New Boy, 1985, Portrait of an Optimist, 1988, An Interrupted Life, 1998, Into the Open: Memoirs 1958-99, 2000, (fiction) The Permit, 1965, But What if There are No Pelicans?, 1971, His Excellency's Pleasure, 1977, (pamphlet) Power From the People, 1977, Occational Paper/Think or Perish, 1988; editor: Change the Rules!, 1977; contbr. profl. jours, newspapers; appearance on radio and TV. Mem. Australian Imperial Force, 1942-44, Australian Citizenship Coun., 1998-2000, NSW Century Fedn. Com., 1999-2001, Australian Republican Movement (founder 1991), Exec. Govt. Com., 1985-87, Australian Constl. Commn., 1985-87; consultative com. NSW Law Found. Constl. Change project; founder Arts Action Australia, 1989; Ideas for Australia Program, 1991-94, The Australia Coun., 1985-90; co-covenor Changing the Sys. Forum, 1980, Nat. Conf. Dem. Constn., 1977; convenor Forum for Constl. Change, 1979, Citizens for Democracy, 1976-77, Nat. Ideas Summit, 1990. Decorated officer Order of Australia, 1982. Mem. Australian Soc. Authors (pres. 1984-85, councillor 1982—). Home: Sydney, Australia. Died Sept. 8, 2005.

**HORNER, ALTHEA JANE,** psychologist; b. Hartford, Conn., Jan. 13, 1926; d. Louis and Celia (Newmark) Greenwald; children: Martha Horner Hartley, Anne Horner Benck, David, Kenneth. BS in Psychology, U. Chgo., 1952; PhD in Clin. Psychology, U. So. Calif., U. Park, 1965. Lic. psychologist NY, Calif. Tchr. Pasadena (Calif.) City Coll., 1965-67; from asst. to assoc. prof. LA Coll. Optometry, 1967-70; supr. Psychology interns Pasadena Child Guidance Clinic, 1969-70; pvt. practice specializing in psychoanalysis and psychoanalytic psychotherapy NYC, 1970-83; supervising psychologist dept. psychiatry Beth Israel Med. Ctr., NYC, 1972-83, coord. group therapy tng., 1976-82, clinician in charge Brief Adaptation-Oriented Psychotherapy Rsch. Group, 1982-83; assoc. clin. prof. Mt. Sinai Sch. Medicine, NYC, 1977-91, adj. assoc. prof., from 1991; mem. faculty Nat. Psychol. Assn. for Psychoanalysis, NYC, 1982-83; sr. mem. faculty Wright Inst. LA Postgrad. Inst., 1983-85; pvt. practice LA, 1983—2004; clin. prof. dept. psychology UCLA, 1985-95; ret., 2004. Author: (with others) Treating the Neurotic Patient in Brief Psychotherapy, 1985, Object Relations and the Developing Ego in Therapy, 1979, rev. edit., 1984, Little Big Girl, 1982, Being and Loving, 1978, 3rd edit., 2005, Psychology for Living (with G. Forehand), 4th edit., 1977, The Wish for Power and the Fear of Having It, 1989, The Primacy of Structure, 1990, Psychoanalytic Object Relations Therapy, 1991, Working With the Core Relationship Problem in Psychotherapy, 1998, Chrysalis, 1999, Get Over It! Untie Your Relationship Knots and Move On, 2000, Dealing with Resistance in Psychotherapy, 2005; mem. editl. bd. Jour. Humanistic Psychology, 1986—, Am. Jour. Psychoanalysis; assoc. editor Jour. Am. Acad. of Psychoanalysis; contbr. articles to profl. jours Mem. APA, Am. Acad. Psychoanalysis (sci. assoc.), So. Calif. Psychoanalytic Soc. and Inst. (hon.). Home: Sierra Madre, Calif. Died Dec. 24, 2013.

**HORNER, JOHN EDWARD,** retired academic administrator; b. Passaic, NJ, Dec. 12, 1921; s. William Joseph and Cardera Estelle (Bissell) H.; m. Anne Catherine Evans, Aug. 16, 1952; children: Joanne Horner Woerner, Jefrey John, heather Horner Hohlt, Scott Edward. AB cum laude, Drew U., 1943; AM, Columbia U., 1947; PhD, Ohio State U., 1955; LLD (hon.), Ind. U., 1978, Drew U., 1971, Ind. State U., 1979, Wabash Coll., 1978, Hanover Coll., 1986; LittD (hon.), Morehead State U., 1975, Heidelberg Coll., 1990. Tchr. English, coach baseball, football Morristown (N.J.) H.S., 1945-49; instr. Latin and English Drew U., Madison, N.J., 1950-52; asst. prof., dir. athletics Kans. Wesleyan U., Salina, 1952-53; adminstrv. asst. Ohio State U., Columbus, 1954-56; asst. to pres., dean grad. sch. U. Omaha, Nebr., 1956-58; pres. Hanover (Ind.) Coll., 1958-87, pres. emeritus, 1987—2014. Cons./examiner North Ctrl. Assn., Chgo., 1956-87. Contbr. articles to profl. jours., chpts. to books. Chmn. Ind. State Scholarship Commn., Indpls., 1977-79; pres. Presbyn. Coll. Union, Phila., 1963-64; ruling elder Presbyn. Ch., Hanover; chmn. bd. dirs. Historic Madison, Inc., 1981-87; pres. Ind. State Libr. and Historic Bd., Indpls., 1974-87; chmn. Ind. State Student Assistance Commn., 1977-79. With USAAF, 1943-44. Named Sagamore of the Wabash, Gov. of Ind., 1964, 79, 83, Ky. Col., 1967; Phi Beta Kappa fellow, 1943; Fulbright scholar, 1949-50. Mem. American Assn. Pres. of Pvt. Colleges & Universities (pres. 1978-80). Republican. Presbyterian. Avocations: reading, travel, golf, drama, music, athletics. Home: Durham, NC. Died Feb. 12, 2014.

**HORNUNG, GERTRUDE SEYMOUR,** art educator; b. Boston, Oct. 31, 1908; d. Samuel Parker and Rose Anne Seymour; m. Robert M. Hornung, Oct. 31, 1932; 1 child, Elizabeth Smith. AB, Wellesley Coll., 1929; MA, Western Res. U., 1939; PhD, 1949. Lectr., instr., supr. adult programs Cleve. Mus. Art, 1937—60; lectr. Am. U., Rome, 1974—75, Tehran, 1975, Bangkok, 1978, Dublin, 1970, Cleve., from 1960, Honolulu Acad. Arts, 1973—85; pres. Decorative Arts Trust Cleve Cir., 1987. Trustee Kent (Ohio) U. Mus., from 1987. Mem.: Am. Assn. Mus., Internat. Com. Mus. Edn., Internat. Coun. Mus., Nat. Art Educators Assn. Home: Saratoga Springs, NY. Died Apr. 28, 2000.

**HORTON, STANLEY MONROE,** retired religious studies educator; b. Huntington Park, Calif., May 6, 1916; s. Harry Samuel and Myrle May (Fisher) H.; m. Evelyn Gertrude Parsons, Sept. 11, 1945; children: Stanley Jr., Edward, Faith. BS, U. Calif., Berkeley, 1937; MDiv, Gordon Div. Sch., 1944; MST, Harvard U., 1945; ThD, Cen. Bapt. Sem., 1959. Ordained to ministry Assemblies of God, 1946. Instr. Met. Bible Inst., North Bergen, Mo., 1945-48; prof. Central Bible Coll., Springfield, Mo., 1948-78; disting. prof. Assemblies of God Theol. Sem., Springfield, 1978—91; gen. editor Pentecostal Textbook Series/Logion Press, 1991—2000. Author: What the Bible Says About the Holy Spirit, 1976, Acts Commentary, 1991, The Ultimate Triumph, 1991. Mem. American Sci. Affiliation, Nat. Assn. Professionals Hebrew, Nat. Assn. Evangs., Near East Archeol. Soc., Soc. Pentecostal Studies (pres. 1979-80), Evang. Theol. Soc. Republican. Home: Springfield, Mo. Died July 12, 2014.

**HOSHINO, SADAO,** physicist; b. Tokyo, Sept. 7, 1926; s. Shuichi and Eiko (Godai) Hoshino; m. Toki Kusaka, Nov. 14, 1954; children: Moriyuki, Hiroshi, Takashi. Rsch. asst. Osaka (Japan) U., 1948, Tokyo Inst. Tech., 1948-49, rsch. assoc., 1949-59, assoc. prof., 1959-60; rsch. assoc. Pa. State U., State College, 1956-59; asst. physicist Brookhaven Nat. Lab., Upton, NY, 1958-59; assoc. prof. U. Tokyo, 1960-66, prof., 1967-87, prof. emeritus, 1987; prof. Tsukuba (Japan) U., 1987-90. Author: Neutron Diffraction, 1961; editor, author:, 1976; contbr. scientific papers to profl. jours. Mem.: Crystallog. Soc. Japan (pres. 1986), Phys. Soc. Japan (pres. 1984—85), N.Y. Acad. Scis., Am. Phys. Soc. Avocations: japanese fencing, music, reading, gardening. Home: Yokohama, Japan. Died Feb. 17, 2004.

**HOSKINS, BOB (ROBERT WILLIAM HOSKINS),** actor; b. Bury St. Edmunds, Suffolk, Eng., Oct. 26, 1942; s. Robert and Elsie Lillian Hoskins; m. Jane Livesey, 1967 (div. 1978); children: Alex, Sarah; m. Linda Banwell, 1982; children: Jack, Rosa. Student, Stroud Green Sch. Stage debut in Romeo and Juliet, Victoria Theatre, Stoke-on-Trent, 1968; joined Royal Shakespeare Co., 1976; stage appearances include Pygmalion, Albery, Eng., 1974, Aldwych, 1976, The World Has Turned Upside Down, 1978, Has Washington Legs?, 1978, True West, 1989, Guys and Dolls, 1981 (Critics Circle award for Best Actor, 1982), Old Wicked Songs, 1996-97, Stage, 1996-97, As You Desire Me, 2005; actor: (TV appearances) The Main Chance, 1972, Villains (4 episodes), 1972, Kate, 1972, Play for Today (3 episodes), 1972-74, Crown Court (3 episodes), 1973, New Scotland Yard, 1973, Sir Yellow, 1973, Softly Softly: Task Force, 1973, Thick as Thieves, (3 episodes), 1974, On The Move, 1975, Thriller, 1976, The Crezz, 1976, Three Piece Suit, 1977, Van der Valk, 1977, Rock Follies of '77 (3 episodes), 1977, Pennies From Heaven (6 episodes), 1978, Big Jim and the Figaro Club (6 episodes), 1979-81, Weekend Playhouse, 1984, Performance, 1993, Tales from the Crypt, 1996, The Forgotten Toys (voice only), 1997, Frasier, 2003, The Street (2 episodes), 2009; (TV movies) And All Who Sail in Her, 1973, If There Weren't Any Blacks You'd Have to Invent Them, 1974, Brecht & Co., 1979, Othello, 1981, The Beggar's Opera, 1983, Mussolini and I, 1985, The Dunera Boys, 1985, World War II: When The Lions Roared, 1994, David Copperfield, 1999, Noriega: God's Favorite, 2000, Don Quixote, 2000, The Lost World, 2001, The Good Pope: Pope John XXIII, 2003, The Wind in the Willows, 2006, Pinocchio, 2008; (miniseries) Shoulder to Shoulder, 1974, Flickers, 1980, The Changeling, 1993, The Englishman's Boy, 2008, Neverland, 2012; actor: (films) Up the Front, 1972, National Health, 1973, Inserts, 1974, Royal Flush, 1975, Zulu Dawn, 1980, The Long Good Friday, 1981, Pink Floyd's The Wall, 1982, Beyond the Limit, 1983, Lassiter, 1984, The Cotton Club, 1984, Brazil, 1985, Sweet Liberty, 1986, Mona Lisa, 1986 (Best Actor award Cannes Festival, Nat. Soc. Film Critics, 1987), A Prayer for the Dying, The Lonely Passion of Judith Hearne, 1987, Who Framed Roger Rabbit?, 1988, Mermaids, 1990, Heart Condition, 1990, Shattered, 1990, The Favor the Watch and the Very Big Fish, 1990, The Projectionist, 1990, Hook, 1991, The Inner Circle, 1991, Passed Away, 1991, Blue Ice, 1992, Super Mario Bros., 1993, The Big Freeze, 1993, Nixon, 1995, Michael, 1996, Cousin Bette, 1996, Twenty-Four/Seven, 1997, 1 Inch Over the Horizon, 1997, Spice World, 1997, Cousin Bette, 1998, Parting Shots, 1998, Felicias Journey, 1999, Captain Jack, 1999, Live Virgin, 1999, A Room for Romeo Brass, 1999, The White River Kid, 1999 Let the Good Times Roll, 1999, Enemy at the Gates, 2001, Last Orders, 2001, Where Eskimos Live, 2002, Maid in Manhattan, 2002, The Sleeping Dictionary, 2003, Den of Lions, 2003, Vanity Fair, 2004, Beyond the Sea, 2004, Unleashed, 2005, Son of the Mask, 2005, Truth, Divorce and the American Way, 2005, Stay, 2005, Garfield: A Tail of Two Kitties, 2006, Hollywoodland, 2006, Paris, je t' aime, 2006, Sparkle, 2007, Outlaw, 2007, Go Go Tales, 2007, Ruby Blue, 2007, A Christmas Carol, 2009, Made in Dagenham, 2010, Outside Bet, 2012, Snow White and the Huntsman, 2012; actor, writer, dir. The Raggedy Rawney, 1988; actor, dir. The Rainbow, 1994; actor, exec. prodr. The Secret Agent, 1996, Mrs. Henderson Presents, 2005. Avocations: photography, gardening, playgoing. Died Apr. 29, 2014.

**HOUBOLT, JOHN CORNELIUS,** physicist; b. Altoona, Iowa, Apr. 10, 1919; s. John H. and Hendreika (Van Ingen) H.; m. Mary Morris, June 14, 1949; children: Mary Cornelia, Joanna, Julie. BS in Civil Engring., U. Ill., 1940, MS in Civil Engring., 1942; PhD in Technical Sciencs, Swiss Fed.

Inst. Tech., Zurich, 1958, D (hon.), 1975, Clarkson U., 1990, U. Ill. Urbana-Champaign, 2005. Bridge engr. I.C. R.R., 1940; city engr. Waukegan, Ill., 1941; aero. research scientist NASA, Hampton, Va., 1942-49; assoc. chief dynamic loads div. NACA-NASA, 1949-62; chief theoretical mechanics div. NASA, 1962-63; sr. v.p., dir. Aero Research Asso. Princeton Inc., N.J., 1963-76; chief scientist Langley Research Center, Hampton, Va., 1976-85. Exchange scientist Royal Aircraft Establishment, Eng., 1949; dir. Doweave, Inc., Walker-Gordon Labs.; Mem. Air Force Scientific Adv. Bd. Assoc. editor: Jour. Spacecraft and Rockets. Recipient Rockefeller Public Svc. award, 1956, Exceptional Sci. Achievement award NASA, 1963, Structures, Structural Dynamics and Materials award AIAA, 1967, Disting. Civil Engring. Alumni award U. Ill., 1969, Illini Achievement award U. Ill., 1970, Dryden Rsch. lectr. award, 1972, Space Act award NASA, 1983, Pa. Engr. of Yr. award, 1989, U. Ill. Alumni award, 1997, Spirit of St. Louis medal, 2000. Fellow AIAA (hon. v.p. tech.); mem. Nat. Acad. Engineers, Tau Beta Pi, Chi Epsilon, Phi Kappa Chi, Sigma Xi. Achievements include rsch., numerous reports in aeros., aeroelasticity, structures, atmosphere turbulence, space flight and moon landing. Home: Scarborough, Maine. Died Apr. 15, 2014.

**HOUGEN, EVERETT DOUGLAS,** tool manufacturing company executive; b. Sceptre, SK, Can., July 7, 1916; arrived in U.S., 1936; s. Louis Oscar and Corinna (Brillon) Hougen; m. Therese Yvonne Perrault, July 5, 1941; children: Douglas, Victor, Randall, Bradley. Student, Dominion Bus. Coll., Winnipeg, Can. Apprenticeship GE Inst., Flint, Mich.; quality control bd. Curtis Wright, Clifton, NJ, 1942—45; mgr. body ship Kaiser-Frazier, Patterson, 1946—48; instr. GE Inst., 1948—58, also pres.'s coun.; pres. Hougen Mfg. Flint, 1959—83, Blair Equipment Co., 1953—78; dir. Hougen Mfg. Fla., Largo. Lectr. in field. Mem.: Presdl. Task Force, Nat. C. of C., Motor and Equipment Mfg. Assn., Nat. Soc. Mfg. and Engring. Republican. Achievements include patents for holecutter; magnetic drill; rotabroach. Home: Flint, Mich. Died Feb. 17, 1999.

**HOWARD, GEORGE TURNER, JR.,** retired surgeon; b. Harlan, Ky., May 31, 1913; MD, Harvard U., 1937; LLD, Lincoln Meml. U., 1996. Diplomate Am. Bd. Surgery. Intern, then resident in surgery Boston City Hosp., 1937-41; resident in surgery Meml. Hosp. Cancer and Allied Disease, NYC, 1941-42; mem. staff St. Mary's Hosp., Ft. Sanders Hosp., U. Tenn. Meml. Hosp., Children's Hosp., East Tenn. Bapt. Hosp.; ret., 1982. Fellow ACS, Royal Soc. Health, Acad. Internat. Medicine, Southeastern Surg. Congress. Deceased.

**HOWARD, LOUISE A.,** mental health nurse; b. Sumter, SC, May 30, 1952; d. Hartwell and Lucille (McBride) Jones; m. Alex C. Howard, June 27, 1971; children: Tywanda, Alexis. Lic. in practical nursing, Columbia, SC, 1979; diploma in nursing, U. S.C., Columbia, 1982. Staff/charge nurse med./surg. dept. and CCU Providence Hosp., Columbia; head nurse Dept. Mental Health, State of S.C., Columbia, supr. Pub. speaker on AIDS. Vol. Lupus Found., ARC, local high sch. Mem. ANA (cert. psychiat./mental health nurse). Home: Columbia, SC. Died May 1996.

**HOWE, RICHARD RAY,** lawyer; b. Decatur, Ill., Dec. 23, 1932; s. Elbert Davis and Marie (Harris) Howe; m. Elaine Bondurant, Apr. 17, 1954; children: Richard R., Scott W., Dale A., Tracy. AB, U. Mo., 1954, JD, 1959. Bar: Mo. 1959. Mem. Canton Bd. Edn., 1962—68, sec., 1962—67, v.p., 1967—68; pros. atty. Lewis County, Mo., 1969—72; commr. to chmn. Commn. Reapportion Mo. Legislature, 1971. Trustee Canton Pub. Libr., 1961—70; chmn. Rep. Central Com., Lewis County, 1971—76, 1979—86, 9th Congl. Dist. Rep. Com., 1974—76; mem. to vice chmn. Mo. Commn. Human Rights, 1974—76. Served with USAF, 1955—57. Mem.: Kiwanis, Masons, Am. Judicature Soc., Assn. Trial Lawyers Am., Am. Bar Assn., Phi Alpha Delta, Alpha Tau Omega. Deceased.

**HOWELL, JOHN BERNARD LLOYD,** physician, medical educator; b. Swansea, Wales, Aug. 1, 1926; s. David John and Hilda Mary (Hill) H.; m. Heather Joan Rolfe, July 12, 1952; children: Susan Gillian, David Nicholas Lloyd, Peter Jonathan Lloyd. BSc in Physiology, Middlesex Hosp. Med. Sch., London, 1947, MB BS, 1950, PhD, 1957; DSc (hon.), U. Southampton, Eng., 1994. Lectr. physiological medicine Middlesex Hosp. Med. Sch., London, 1954-56; Eli Lilly travelling fellow Johns Hopkins Hosp., Balt., 1957-58; sr. lectr., cons. physician Manchester (Eng.) Royal Infirmary, 1960-69; Found. prof. medicine U. Southampton Med. Sch., 1969-91, dean of medicine, 1978-83, emeritus prof. medicine, from 1991. Contbg. author: (textbook) Cecil & Loeb's Textbook of Medicine, 1971, 75, Respiratory Medicine, 1991, 95; editor: (monograph) Breathlessness, 1966; contbr. articles to profl. jours. Chmn. Southampton and S.W. Hampshire Health Authority, Southampton, 1983-98. Fellow Royal Coll. Physicians (London), ACP (hon.); mem. British Med. Assn. (pres. 1989-90, chmn. bd. sci. and edn. 1991-98), British Thoracic Soc. (pres. 1988-89), Med. Rsch. Soc., Can. Thoracic Soc. (hon. life), Gen. Med. Coun., Soc. of Scholars Johns Hopkins U. Avocations: france, wines. Home: Southampton, England. Died Apr. 19, 2008.

**HOWELLS, MURIEL GURDON SEABURY (MRS. WILLIAM WHITE HOWELLS),** volunteer; b. White Plains, NY, May 3, 1910; d. William Marston and Katharine Emerson (Hovey) Seabury; m. William White Howells, June 15, 1929; children: Muriel Gurdon Howells Metz, William Dean. Founder Brit. War Relief Soc., Madison, Wis., 1941, pres., 1941-43; apptd. visitor dept. decorative arts and sculpture Boston Mus. Fine Arts, 1955-72, dept. Am. decorative arts, 1972-97. Mem. ladies com. Inst. Contemporary Art, Boston, 1955-68; co-founder, trustee Strawbery Banke Mus., Inc., Portsmouth, N.H., 1958-75, overseer, 1975-81, hon. overseer, 1981—; co-founder, steering com. Guild, 1959-91. Bd. dirs. Garden Club Am., 1959-62, nat. chmn. medal award com., 1962-65, judge flower arrangements; pres. Piscataqua Garden Club, 1952-54; mem. Harvard Solomon Islands Expdn., Malaita, 1968; 1st chmn. Boston chpt. Venice Com., Internat. Fund for Monuments (now Save Venice Inc.), 1970-71, vice chmn. Boston chmn., 1971-77, mem. exec. com., 1971-89, hon. chmn., 1989—; mem. ARC Motor Corps, 1941-43. Recipient King's medal for Svc. in the Cause of Freedom, 1946, Hist. Preservation award zone 1 Garden Club Am., 1976. Mem. Nat. Soc. Colonial Dames N.H., Soc. Preservation of New England Antiquities, Mayflower Soc., Women's Travel Club (pres. 1967-69), Chilton Club, Colony Club. Died July 1, 2002.

**HOYT, MARY FINCH,** writer, media consultant, retired federal official; b. Visalia, Calif., Dec. 17, 1923; m. Robert Swanson (dec.); m. James M. Hoyt (div.); m.George K. Tanham (div.); 2 children. Free-lance mag. writer, speechwriter, formerly with Ladies' Home Jour. mag.; info. officer Peace Corps; pres. sec. to Mrs. Edmund Muskie US Senate, 1968, pres. sec. to Mrs. George McGovern, 1972; ptnr. McClure, Schultz & Hoyt; press sec. to Mrs. Rosalynn Carter and East Wing coord. The White House, Washington, 1977-81; dir. communications Nat. Trust for Hist. Preservation, Washington, 1989-93; author, editor, media cons., 1993—2013. Author: American Women of the Space Age, 1966, East Wing: Politics, the Press and a First Lady, 2001; co-author (with Eleanor McGovern): Uphill: A Personal Story, 1974. Mem. Presdl. Commn., 1977. Democrat. Home: Washington, DC. Died Oct. 17, 2013.

**HOYTE, HUGH DESMOND,** president of Republic of Guyana; b. Georgetown, Guyana, Mar. 9, 1929; s. George Alphonso and Gladys Marietta Hoyte; married. BA, U. London, 1950, LL.B., 1959. Bar: Hon. Soc. Middle Temple 1959, Queen's counsel, 1970, sr. counsel, 1970. Pvt. practice law, Guyana, from 1960. Mem. gen. council People's Nat. Congress, 1962—, mem. cen. exec. com., 1972—, legal adviser to gen. sec., from 1973—, chmn. prodn. sub-com. of cen. exec. com. from 1984, leader, 1985—; chmn. Customs Tariff Tribunal, 1966-68; elected to Parliament, People's Nat. Congress, 1968; minister of home affairs Republic of Guyana, 1969-70, minister of fin., 1970-72, minister works and communication, 1972-74, minister econ. devel., 1974-80, v.p. econ. planning and fin., 1980, v.p. prodn., 1983, prime minister and 1st v.p., 1984-85, pres. of Guyana, 1985—; mem. Nat. Elections Commn., from 1966; chmn. Timber Grants Wages Council, 1967; legal adviser Guyana Trades Union Congress, several other trade unions. Mem. Guyana Bar Assn. (chmn. legal practitioners com. 1964). Died Dec. 22, 2002.

**HUANG, KIM,** physicist; b. Beijing, Sept. 1919; B in physics, Yanying U., 1941; PhD in physics, U. Bristol, 1948; postdoctoral rsch., U. Liverpool, 1949—51. Prof. physics U. Beijing, 1951—77; dir. Inst. Semiconductors Chinese Acad. Sci., 1977—83, hon. dir. Inst. Semiconductors, from 1983. Co-author (with Max Born): Dynamic Theory of Crystal Lattices; contbr. articles to profl. jour. on semiconductors and solid state physics. Recipient State Preeminent Sci. and Tech. award, Pres. of China, 2001. Mem.: Royal Swedish Acad. Sci., Chinese Acad. Sci. Died July 6, 2005.

**HUANG, PAN MING,** soil science educator; b. Pu-tse, Taiwan, Sept. 2, 1934; arrived in Can., 1965; s. Rong Yi and Koh (Chiu) H.; m. Yun Yin Lin, Dec. 26, 1964; children: Daniel Chian Yuan, Crystal Ling Hui. BSA, Nat. Chung Hsing U., Taichung, Taiwan, 1957; MSc, U. Man., Winnipeg, Can., 1962; PhD, U. Wis., Madison, 1966. Cert. prof. agrologist. Asst. prof. soil sci. U. Sask., Saskatoon, Canada, 1965-71, assoc. prof., 1971-78, prof., from 1978. Invited rsch. chair Nat. Taiwan U., 1996, 2003, 04; nat. vis. prof., head dept. soil sci. Nat. Chung Hsing U., 1975-76, chair. prof. soil chemistry, 2007-, Y.C. Tang chair prof., Zhejiang U., 2007-; mem. agr. adv. bd. Lewis Pubs., 1991—; hon. prof. Huazhong Agr. U., 1992—, Guanxi Agrl U., 1993—, Henan Agrl. U., 1996—, Langzhou U., 1999—; acad. advisor Chinese Acad. Scis., 1996—; hon. scientist Rural Adminstrn., Republic of Korea, 2004—06. Author: Soil Chemistry, 1991, Environmental Soil Chemistry and Its Impact on Agriculture and the Ecosystem, 2000; editor: 18 books; mem. editl. bd.: Chemosphere, 1987—97, Pedosphere, from 1990, Trends in Agr. Sci., 1991—95, Advances in Environ. Sci., 1993, Geodema, 1994—2007, Soil Sci. Plant Nutrition, 1998—2005, Water, Air, and Soil Pollution, 1998—2001, Humic Substances in the Environment, from 1998, spl. editor, mem. editl. bd.: Water Pollution Rsch. Jour. Can., 1983—89, 1991—93, Agro's Ann. Rev. Crop Ecology, from 1995, mem. editl. adv. bd.: Trends in Soil Sci., from 1995, lead series editor: Wiley-IUPAC, Biophysico-Chemical Processes in Environmental Systems, from 2006; contbr. over 300 articles to profl. jours., chapters to books. Bd. dirs. Saskatoon Chinese Mandarin Sch., 1977-79, Saskatoon Soc. for Study Chinese Culture, 1983—. 2d lt. Taiwan Mil. Tng. Corps, 1957-59. Recipient Soil Sci. Rsch. award, Soil Sci. Soc. Am., 2000; grantee, numerous agys., from 1965, UN Environment Program, Nat. Scis. & Engring. Rsch. Coun., Can. Fellow: AAAS, World Innovation Found., Am. Soc. Agronomy, Soil Sci. Soc. Am. (rep. Clay Minerals Soc. 1979—83, chmn. divsn. S-9 1983—84, bd. dirs. 1983—84, editor spl. pub. 1986, Internat. Soil Sci. award com. 1986—87, assoc. editor 1987—92, Marion L. and Christie M. Jackson Soil Sci. award com. 1990—92, rep. to Internat. Union Pure and Applied Chemistry 1990—2000, fellow com. 1992—94, chmn.-elect divsn. S-2 1993—94, chmn. 1994—95, past chmn. 1995—96, spl. awards com. 1995—96, chair nominations com. divsn. S-2 1995—96, bd. dirs. 1995—96, editor spl. pub. 1998, Soil Sci. Rsch. award 2000), Can. Soc. Soil Sci.; mem.: Can. Network Toxicology (team on metal speciation 1993—96), Internat. Humic Substances Soc. (leader Can. nat. chpt. 1992—2005), Internat. Union Pure & Applied Chemistry (assoc.; commn. environ. analytical chemistry 1993—95, titular mem. com. fundamental environ. chemistry 1995—97, 1999—2001, divsn. chemistry & environment 2001—05, titular mem. divsn. chemistry and environment from 2006), Internat. Assn. Study Clays (treas. 1993—2001), NY Acad. Scis., Am. Chem. Soc., Internat. Union Soil Sci. (chmn. working grp. MO 1990—2004, chmn. commn. 2.5 soil phys., chem., biol. interfacial reactions 2004—06), Sigma Xi. Avocations: music, reading. Home: Saskatoon, Canada. Died Sept. 13, 2009.

**HUBER, RICHARD MILLER,** American studies consultant; b. Ardmore, Pa., July 27, 1922; s. John Y. Jr. and Caroline (Miller) H.; divorced; children: Cintra Hutchinson Huber McGauley, Richard Miller Jr., Casilda Carter Huber. BA, Princeton U., 1945; PhD, Yale U., 1953. Mem. faculty Princeton (N.J.) U., 1950-54; pres. Princeton Manor Constrn. Co., 1958-62; producer, moderator Sta. WHWH-AM-FM, Princeton, 1965-67; corr. Sta. WNET-TV, NYC, 1967-68; dean Sch. Gen. Studies Hunter Coll., NYC, 1971-77, exec. dir. div. continuing edn., 1977-82; asst. dir. TV and radio Nat. Endowment for the Humanities, Washington, 1983-84, spl. asst. to chmn., 1984-85; pres. Huber Assocs., Washington, from 1985. Pres. Prodn.-in-Progress, Inc., Washington, 1986-89; cons. Am. studies Dept. State and U.S. Info. Agy., 1989—. Author: Big All The Way Through: The Life of Van Sandvoord Merle-Smith, 1952, The American Idea of Success, 1971, rev. edn., 1987, How Professors Play the Cat Guarding the Cream: Why We're Paying More and Getting Less in Higher Education, 1992; editor: (with Wheaton J. Lane) New Jersey Historical Series, 31 vols., 1965. Mem. Coun. of Friends, Princeton U. Libr. 2nd lt. USAAF, 1942-45, Italy. Decorated Air medal; recipient N.J. Hist. Soc. award, 1965, award of merit Am. Assn. State and Local History, 1965, Author's award N.J. Assn. Tchrs. of English, 1965, award of recognition N.J. Hist. Commn., Trenton, 1983; Woodrow Wilson fellow, 1946, Yale Univ. fellow, 1948, Danforth tchg. fellow, 1953 Mem. Soc. Am. Historians, Am. Studies Assn. Republican. Episcopalian. Avocations: tennis, jogging, swimming. Home: Washington, DC. Died May 19, 2013.

**HUCK, JOHN LLOYD,** pharmaceutical executive; b. Bklyn., July 17, 1922; s. John Lloyd and Adrienne (Warner) H.; m. Dorothy Bertha Foehr, Nov. 20, 1943; children: Lloyd E., Jeanne Huck Leslie-Hughes, Virginia Huck Stalcup. BS in Chemistry, Pa. State U., 1946. Research chemist Hoffmann-LaRoche, Nutley, NJ, 1946, sales rep., 1948, dir. sales tng., 1951, asst. gen. sales mgr., 1955, dir. product devel., 1958; dir. mktg. Merck Sharp & Dohme Div., West Point, Pa., 1958; v.p. mktg. planning MSD div., 1966, v.p. sales and mktg., 1968, exec. v.p., 1969, exec. v.p., gen. mgr., 1972, pres., 1973; sr. v.p. Merck & Co., Rahway, NJ, 1975, exec. v.p., 1977, dir., 1977-86, pres., chief operating officer, 1978-85, chmn. bd., 1985-86; chmn. bd., chief exec. officer Nova Pharm. Corp., Morristown, NJ, 1986-88, chmn. bd., 1988-91; dir. Found. Mt. Nittany Med. Ctr., from 2008. Patentee in field. Trustee Pa. State U., 1977-92, v.p., 1985-88, pres. bd., 1988-91; trustee Morristown Meml. Health Found., Inc., N.J., 1979-96, chmn. bd., 1986-88; trustee Geraldine R. Dodge Found., 1987-2003. 1st lt. USAAF, 1942-46. Alumni fellow Coll. Medicine Pa. State U., 1980, Coll. of Sci., 1983; named to Nutley Hall of Fame, 2003. Mem. Centre Hills Country Club. Home: State College, Pa. Died Dec. 4, 2012.

**HUDDLESON, SCOTT ALDEN,** military officer; b. LA, Oct. 5, 1952; s. Homer Alden and June (Hetzel) H.; m. Joanne Elizabeth Darrow, June 11, 1977; children: Stephanie, Joshua, Nathanael. BS in Behavioral Sci., USAF Acad., 1974; MA in Communications, U. No. Colo., 1977; MS in Space Ops., USAF Inst. Tech., 1984. Commd. 2d lt. USAF, 1974; advanced through grades to lt. col.; missile crew comdr. 90th Strategic Missile Wing, Cheyenne, Wyo., 1974-78; chief acad. instr. 4315th Combat Crew Tng. Squadron, Lompoc, Calif., 1979-82; systems dir. 13th Missile Warning Squadron, Clear AFB, Alaska, 1984-85; mission controller, dep. dir. mission transfer Consol. Space Ops. Ctr. Cadre Air Force Satellite Network, Sunnyvale, Calif., 1985-87; chief strategic planning U.S. Space Command/Plans, Colorado Springs, Colo., 1988-90; comdr. 6th missile Warning Squadron Cape Cod Air Force Sta., Sagamore, Mass., from 1990. Died Mar. 24, 2008.

**HUDSON, EDWARD VOYLE,** retired apparel executive; b. Seymour, Mo., Apr. 3, 1915; s. Marion A. and Alma (Von Gonten) H.; m. Margaret Carolyn Greely, Dec. 24, 1939; children: Edward G., Carolyn K. Student, Bellingham Normal Coll., 1933-36, U. Wash., 1938. Asst. to mgr. Natural Hard Metal Co., Bellingham, 1935—37; ptnr. Met. Laundry Co., Tacoma, 1938—39; propr., mgr. Peerless Laundry & Linen Supply Co., Tacoma, 1939—2005; ret., 2005. Propr. Ind. Laundry & Everett Linen Supply Co., 1946-74, 99 Cleaners and Launderers Co., Tacoma, 1957-59; chmn. Tacoma Pub. Utilities, 1959-60; trustee United Mut. Savs. Bank; bd. dirs. Tacoma Better Bus. Bur., 1977—; mem. regional bd., SBA, 1965. Pres. Wash. Conf. on Unemployment Compensation, 1975-76; pres. Tacoma Boys' Club, 1970; v.p. Puget Sound USO, 1972-91; elder Emmanuel Presbyn. Ch., 1974—; past campaign mgr., pres. Tacoma-Pierce County United Good Neighbors. Recipient Disting. Citizen's cert. USAF Mil. Airlift Com., 1977; U.S. Dept. Def. medal for outstanding pub. svc., 1978. Mem. Tacoma Sales and Mktg. Execs. (pres. 1957-58), Pacific NW Laundry, Dry Clearning and Linen Supply Assn. (pres. 1959, treas. 1965-75), Internat. Fabricare Inst. (dir. dist. 7, treas. 1979, pres. 1982), Am. Security Coun. Bd., Tacoma C. of C. (pres. 1965), Air Force Assn. (pres. Tacoma chpt.

1976-77, v.p. Wash. state 1983-84, pres. 1985-86), Navy League, Puget Sound Indsl. Devel. Coun. (chmn. 1967), Tacoma-Ft. Lewis Olympia Army Assn. (past pres.), Def. Orientation Civilian Assn., Elks Club (vice chmn. bd. trustees 1984, chmn. 1985-86), Shriners (potentate 1979), Masons, Scottish Rite, Jesters Club, Rotary (pres. Tacoma chpt. 1967-68), Tacoma Knife and Fork Club (pres. 1964). Republican. Home: Tacoma, Wash. Died June 7, 2008.

**HUDSON, NEWT (WILLIAM NEWTON HUDSON),** retired state legislator; b. Ocilla, Ga., Dec. 12, 1926; m. Eddie Grace Dix (dec.); children: Randy, Dixie, Suzanne; m. Gayle David Hudson BS in Agrl., U. Ga., 1950. Tchr., Irwinville; asst. county agent Colquitt County; extension agent Wilcox County, 1955—83; mem. Ga. House of Reps., Atlanta, 1982—2002. Served in USN, 1944-45 Mem. VFW, Elks, Masons, Lions. Democrat. Methodist. Avocations: hunting, fishing. Home: Rochelle, Ga. Died Aug. 12, 2014.

**HUEBNER, ROBERT JOSEPH,** medical research scientist; b. Cin., Feb. 23, 1914; s. Joseph Frederick and Philomena (Brickner) H.; m. Harriet Lee, Feb. 5, 1975; children by previous marriage— Elizabeth, Frances, Geraldine, James, Virginia, Roberta, Edward, Louise, Daniel. Student, Xavier U., 1932-35, U. Cin., 1937-38; MD, St. Louis U., 1942; LL.D., U. Cin., 1965; D.Sc. (hon.), Edgecliff Coll., 1970, U. Parma, Italy, 1970; D.Sc. hon. degree, U. Leuven, 1973. Commd. jr. asst. surgeon USPHS, 1942, advanced through grades to med. dir., 1953; mil. duty Alaskan area USCG, 1943- 44; virus and rickettsial disease research NIH, 1944-56, chief virus sect., 1949-56; chief lab. infectious disease Nat. Inst. Allergy and Infectious Diseases, 1956-68; chief viral carcinogenesis br. Nat. Cancer Inst., Bethesda, Md., from 1968. Gehrman lectr. U. Ill., 1955, Eli Lilly lectr., 1957; Gudakunst lectr. U. Mich., 1958, Harvey lectr., 1960, Puckett lectr., 1960 Contbr. numerous articles to profl. jours. Recipient Bailey K. Ashford award, 1949; certificate merit St. Louis U., 1949; James D. Bruce Meml. award, 1964; Pasteur medal, 1965; Distinguished Service medal USPHS, 1966; Howard Taylor Ricketts award, 1968; Nat. medal Sci., 1969; Kimble award, 1970; Rockefeller award, 1970; Guido Lenghi award, 1971 Fellow Am. Pub. Health Assn., N.Y. Acad. Scis.; mem. Nat. Acad. Scis., AAAS, Am. Assn. Immunologists, Am. Epidemiol. Soc., Fedn. Am. Socs. Exptl. Biology and Medicine, Wash. Acad. Sci. (award biol. scis. 1949), Internat. Union Against Cancer, Am. Acad. Microbiology, Am. Assn. Cancer Research, AMA, Md. Angus Assn. (pres. 1959-60), Sigma Xi, Alpha Omega Alpha. Home: Rockville, Md. Died Aug. 26, 1998.

**HUGHES, DOROTHY TODD,** retired music educator; b. Bedford, Ind., Sept. 5, 1898; d. John Richard and Addie May (Todd) H. Diploma, U. Cin., 1922; BS in Music Edn., NYU, 1928, MA in Music, 1932; postgrad., Stanford U., 1931, Ind. U., 1956-57. Life cert. music educator, Pa., Ohio. Supr. of music Johnson City Pub. Schs., Tenn., 1921-24, Ashtabula Pub. Schs., Ohio, 1924-26; asst. prof. music Ohio U., Athens, 1928-29; supr. of music Ohio Pub. Schs., Lakewood, 1929-30; assoc. prof. music Millersville U., Pa., 1931-63. Author: Piano Fun with Family and Friends, 1936, Creative Rhythms, 1941, Rhythmic Games and Dances, 1942. Mem. AAUW, Pa. Assn. Sch. Retirees, Women's Welsh Clubs Am., Cambrian Soc. Delaware Valley, Sigma Alpha Iota (chaplain 1974-75, chpt. photographer 1977-79, Rose of Honor award 1977). Republican. Avocations: gardening, travel, reading, cooking, sewing. Home: Levittown, Pa. Deceased.

**HUGHES, SUE EVANS,** social worker; b. Waterbury, Conn., Oct. 2, 1942; d. George T. and Mary Evans; m. William F. Hughes, Jan. 1, 1979; children: Christopher, Eric. BA, U. Pitts., 1964, MSW, 1967. Lic. social worker, Pa. Clin. social worker Children's Hosp. of Pitts., 1967-72, supr. dept. social work, 1972-76, assoc. dir. dept. social work, 1976-84, dir. dept. social work, 1984-92; pvt. practice social work cons. Pitts., from 1992. Instr./adj. prof. Sch. Social Work, U. Pitts., 1977-92; cons. Pitts. Regional Hosps., 1972-76. Co-author: Fragile Families Troubled Children, 1977; contbr. articles to profl. jours. Bd. dirs. Parental Stress Ctr., Pitts., 1981-90, United Mental Health, Pitts., 1977-82, Pitts. Psychoanalytic Ctr., Pitts., 1978-83, Regional Health Ctr., Rangeley, Maine, 1995—. Fellow Pa. Soc. for Clin. Social Work; mem. NASW, Rangeley Libr. Assn., Phi Beta Kappa. Avocations: travel, skiing. Died Dec. 31, 2002.

**HUGHES, THOMAS PARKE,** history professor; b. Richmond, Va., Sept. 13, 1923; s. Hunter Russell and Mary Bronaugh (Quisenberry) H.; m. Agatha Chipley, Aug. 7, 1948; children: Thomas P. (dec.), Agatha H., Lucian P. BME, U. Va., Charlottesville, 1947, PhD, 1953; D (hon.), Royal Inst. Tech., Stockholm, 2000, Northwestern U., Evanston, Ill., 2001. Instr. U. Va., Charlottesville, 1951-54; asst. prof. history Sweet Briar (Va.) Coll., 1954-56; assoc. prof. history Washington and Lee U., Lexington, Va., 1956-63, MIT, Cambridge, 1963-66; prof. history Inst. Tech., So. Meth. U., Dallas, 1969-73; mem. faculty U. Pa., Phila., 1973-94, prof. history & sociology of sci., 1973-94, Andrew W. Mellon prof., 1987-94, prof. emeritus, 1994—2014. Vis. assoc. prof. history Johns Hopkins U., Balt., 1966-69; Torsten Althin prof. Royal Inst. Tech., Stockholm, 1985-90; founding rsch. prof. Tech. Univ., Darmstadt, Germany, 1986-87; vis. rsch. prof. Wissenschaftszentrum Berlin, 1988-94; vis. prof. MIT, 1991, 93, 94-2014, E.T.H. Zürich, 1997, Stanford U., 1999—2001. Author: Elmer Sperry: Inventor and Engineer, 1971 (Dexter prize), Networks of Power: Electrification in Western Society 1880-1930, 1983 (Dexter prize), American Genesis: A Century of Invention and Technological Enthusiasm 1870-1970, 1989 (Pulitzer Prize finalist); editor: (with Agatha C. Hughes) Lewis Mumford: Public Intellectual, 1990, Rescuing Prometheus, 1998, Systems, Experts, and Computers, 2000, Human-Built World: How to Think About Technology and Culture, 2004. Chmn. NRC com., 1996—99; mem. adv. coun. Smithsonian Inst., 1984—90. Served to lt. (j.g.) USN, 1943—46. Fulbright postdoctoral fellow, Germany, 1958—59, NSF fellow, 1975, Inst. Advanced Study fellow, Berlin, 1983, Guggenheim fellow, 1986. Mem. NAE, Soc. History of Tech. (pres. 1978-80, Leonardo da Vinci medal 1984), Soc. Social Studies Sci. (Bernal prize 1990), History of Sci. Soc. (coun. 1976-79), American Acad. Arts & Sciences, Johns Hopkins U. Soc. Scholars, Swedish Royal Acad. Engring. Scis., American Philos. Soc., Phi Beta Kappa. Home: Philadelphia, Pa. Died Feb. 3, 2014.

**HUIZENGA, JOHN ROBERT,** nuclear chemist, educator; b. Fulton, Ill., Apr. 21, 1921; s. Harry M. and Josie B. (Brands) H.; m. Dorothy J. Koeze, Feb. 1, 1946 (dec. 1999); children: Linda J., Jann H., Robert J., Joel T. AB, Calvin Coll., 1944; PhD, U. Ill., 1949. Lab. supr. Manhattan Wartime Project, Oak Ridge, 1944-46; instr. Calvin Coll., Grand Rapids, Mich., 1946-47; assoc. scientist Argonne Nat. Lab., Chgo., 1949-57, sr. scientist, 1958-67; professorial lectr. chemistry U. Chgo., 1963-67; prof. chemistry & physics U. Rochester, 1967-78, Tracy H. Harris prof. chemistry & physics, 1978-91, Tracy H. Harris prof. emeritus chemistry and physics, 1991—2014, chmn. dept. chemistry, 1983-88. Vis. prof. Joliot-Curie Lab., U. Paris, 1964-65, Japan Soc. for Promotion of Sci., 1968; chmn. Nat. Acad. Sci.-NRC Com. on Nuclear Sci., 1974-77; mem. energy rsch. adv. bd. US Dept. Energy, 1984-90; numerous adv., vis. coms. to univs., govt. and nat. labs. Author: (with R. Vandenbosch) Nuclear Fission, 1973; (with W.U. Schröder) Damped Nuclear Reactions, 1984; Cold Fusion: The Scientific Fiasco of the Century, 1992, Five Decades of Research in Nuclear Science, 2009; contbr. articles to profl. jours. Fulbright fellow Netherlands, 1954-55; Guggenheim fellow Paris, 1964-65; Guggenheim fellow Berkeley, Calif., 1973; Guggenheim fellow Munich, W.Ger., 1974; Guggenheim fellow Copenhagen, 1974; recipient E.O. Lawrence award AEC, 1966, Leroy Rundle Grumman medal, 1991; named Disting. Alumnus Calvin Coll., 1975 Fellow AAAS, American Phys. Soc., American Acad. Arts & Sciences; mem. NAS (chmn. NAS-NRC com. on nuclear and radiochemistry 1988-91), American Chem. Soc. (award for nuclear applications in chemistry 1975), Phi Beta Kappa, Sigma Xi, Phi Kappa Phi. Home: La Jolla, Calif. Died Jan. 26, 2014.

**HULTEN, PONTUS,** museum director, consultant; b. Stockholm, June 21, 1924; s. Eric and Elsei (Vougt) H.; children: Felix, Klara. Doctor Art History, U. Stockholm, 1951. Founding dir. Nat. Mus. Modern Art, Stockholm, 1958-73; dir. Musee Nat. d'Art Moderne, 1973-81; founding dir. Mus. Contemporary Art, LA, 1981-84; art dir. Palazzo Grassi Spa, Venice, Italy; dir. New Art Sch., Paris; founding dir. Jean Tinguely Mus., Basel, Switzerland, Kunsthalle, Bonn, Germany. Cons. New Sci. Mus., Paris; adv. cons. to pres. Centre Georges Pompidou, Paris. Died Oct. 25, 2006.

**HUMPHREY, ALBERT S.,** research and development company executive; b. Kansas City, Mo., June 2, 1926; s. Albert Swartzendruver and Margaret Elizabeth (Benton) H.; m. Virginia Potter, Oct. 6, 1957 (div. Feb. 1970); children: Albert S. III, Virginia Potter, Jonathan Benton Cantwell, Heidi; m. Myrian Alice Octaaf de Baere, Oct. 20, 1983; children: Roosje Willems, Jonas Willems, Stephania Humphrey. BSc in Chem. Engring., U. Ill., 1946; MSc in Chem. Engring., MIT, 1948; MBA in Fin., Harvard U., 1955. Staff engr. East Coast Tech. Svc. Esso Standard Oil Co., Elizabeth, NJ, 1948-50; chief chem. and protective group Office of Chief Chem. Officer, U.S. Army Chem. Corp., Washington, 1952-54; asst. to pres. Penberthy Instrument Co., Seattle, 1955-56; chief product planning Boeing Airplane Co., Seattle, 1956-60; mgr. value analysis Small Aircraft Engine Divsn. G.E., Boston, 1960-61; mgr. rsch. and devel. planning P.R. Mallory & Co. Inc., Indpls., 1961-63; cons., presenter exec. seminars in bus. planning Stanford Rsch. Inst. and NASA Office Advance Rsch. & Tech., Menlo Park, Calif., 1965-70; chmn., CEO Bus. Planning & Devel. Inc., Kansas City, from 1970. Mem. faculty Sch. Adult Edn. U. Wash., Seattle, 1955-58; vis. prof. Newcastle upon Tyne Poly. Sch. Bus. and Mgmt., Eng., 1982—; bd. dirs. Friborg Instruments, London, Hidden Valley Ltd., Birmingham, Eng., Randolph Crescent Mgmt. Co., London, Parkwood Films Ltd., Bedford, England, Intl. Strategic Mgmt. Ltd., London, England; mem. exec. adv. bd. Nat. Bur. Cert. Cons., San Diego, dir. European ops.; bus. gov. John Kelly Tech. Colls., London. Contbr. articles to profl. jours. Lt. comdr. USN, 1944-46. Mem. British Inst. Dirs., British Inst. Mktg., Am. Inst. Chem. Engrs. (cert.), Harvard U. Alumni Assn., MIT Alumni Assn., U. Ill. Alumni Assn., Sigma Xi, Tau Beta Phi, Phi Delta Theta. Republican. Episcopalian. Avocations: assisting under-priviledged to start new bus. enterprises, skiing. Died Oct. 31, 2005.

**HUMPHREY, FRED A.,** retired physician; b. Broken Bow, Nebr., Mar. 16, 1896; s. A.R. and Nellie (Nightengale) H.; m. Violet Osborne, June 20, 1921; 1 child, Betty Clee Humphrey Snow (dec. Apr. 1985). B.Sc., U. Nebr., 1919, MD, 1921. Practice medicine, Ft. Collins, Colo., 1922-77; former mem. staff Poudre Valley Meml. Hosp., Ft. Collins. Past dir. Poudre Valley Nat. Bank Trustee Colo. Blue Shield, 1952-67. Mem. Am. Acad. Gen. Practice (v.p., exec. com. 1951), AMA (chmn. council on rural health 1959-63), Colo. Med. Soc. (pres. 1949-50), Larimer County Med. Soc. (pres. 1935), Woodward Gov.'s Co. (emeritus dir. 1971—), Am. Legion (past post comdr.) Clubs: Masons (32 deg.), Shriners, Elk (past exalted ruler). Home: Fort Collins, Colo. Died Dec. 13, 1989.

**HUMPHREY, PAUL,** commercial writer; b. NYC, Jan. 4, 1915; s. Joseph Lee and Winifred (Bell) H.; m. Eleanor Nicholson, June 22, 1945; children: Paula, Paul, Joel. BA, MA, U. Rochester, 1940. Vice prin. Penfield (N.Y.) High Sch., 1946-47; instr. U. Rochester (N.Y.), 1947-48; dir. FE Compton & Co., Chgo., 1949-61; ind. writer Spencerport, N.Y., from 1962. Author: School Policy Code Manual, 1970, How To Run Your Own Employment Agency, 1990, Suburban Briefs, 1992, Ballad Bar, 1994, Ladies First, 1997, Maud Humphrey, Imprint on Illustration, 1997; writer humorous verse Weekly News, biographies, assigned news features; contbr. articles to profl. jours. Mem. Rochester Poets Soc. (pres. 1957), Poets & Writers N.Y.C., Authors Guild N.Y.C., Writers and Books. Avocations: antique automobiles, opera, travel. Died Sept. 28, 2001.

**HUNKIN, GEOFFREY GILBERT,** consulting engineer; b. Cornwall, Eng., Aug. 2, 1923; arrived in U.S., 1968, naturalized, 1975; s. Edwin Gilbert and Florence Adelaide (Bunt) Hunkin; m. Margot A.E. Drinkwater, Nov. 30, 1945; children: Philip Bingham, Elinor Patricia, Geoffrey Bingham. BS, Sch. of Mines, Cornwall, 1949. With Mysore Gold Mining, India, 1949—52, Macalder Mines, Kenya, 1952—57, Rio Algom Mines, Canada, 1957, Stanrock Mines, Canada, 1958, Silvermines, Ireland, 1965—68, Anaconda Co., Utah, N.Mex., 1968—71; mgr. mining and engring. Westinghouse Electric Corp., Denver, 1971—74; cons. engr. in pvt. practice Canada, Australia, U.S., 1974; pres. Hunkins Engrs., Inc., Ground Water Sampling, Inc., Englewood, Colo., from 1976. Lectr. in field. Lt. Royal Navy, 1940—45. Recipient Robert Earll McConnell award, AIME, 1977; named Disting. mem., Soc. Mining Engrs., 1977. Fellow: Inst. Mining and Metallurgy; mem.: Metall. and Petroleum Engrs., Can. Inst. Mining, Soc. Petroleum Engrs. of AIME, Soc. Mining Engrs. of AIME, Cons. Engrs. Coun. Am., Nat. Soc. Profl. Engrs., ASTM, Petroleum Club Denver, Columbine Country Club, Shriners, Masons. Republican. Episcopalian. Achievements include patentee in field. Home: Littleton, Colo. Died Jan. 23, 1988.

**HUNT, PATRICIA,** real estate broker; b. Tyler, Tex., July 23, 1946; d. Alton Carter and Louise Ayers (Murphy); 1 child, Christina. BBA, Tex. Tech U., 1965; MA, U. Dallas, 1976. Lic. real estate broker. With Model, Neiman-Marcus Co., Dallas, 1965—66, Kim Dawson Agy., Dallas, 1966—68; ind. real estate broker Dallas, from 1976. Founder, chmn. Cattle Barons' Ball Benefit Am. Cancer Soc., Dallas, 1974; active Young Republicans, Dallas, from 1976, Republican Assembly, Dallas, from 1980. Recipient 10th Anniversary award, Cattle Barons' Ball, 1984. Mem.: DAR, Daus. Republic Tex., Ballet & Symphony League, Dallas Opera, Dallas Bd. Realtors, Tex. Bd. Realtors, The 500 (Dallas). Home: Dallas, Tex. Died 1999.

**HUNT, VALERIE VIRGINIA,** electrophysiologist, educator; b. Larwill, Ind., July 22, 1916; d. Homer Henry Hunt and Iva Velzora Ames. BS in Biology, Fla. State Coll., 1936; MA in Physiol. Psychology, Columbia U., 1941, EdD in Sci. Edn., 1946; DD, Phoenix Inst., San Diego, 1984. Sci. tchr. Anniston (Ala.) H.S., 1936-38; asst. anatomy nursing dept. Columbia U., NYC, 1939-40; chmn. health edn. Boston YWCA, 1942-43; instr. Columbia U. Teachers Coll. & Coll. Physicians & Surgeons, NYC, 1943-46; asst. prof. U. Iowa, Iowa City, 1946-47; assoc. prof., dir. divsn. phys. therapy UCLA, 1947-64, prof. physiology, dir. electromyographic lab., 1964-80, prof. emeritus, 1980—2014; dir. BioEnergy Fields Lab. BioEnergy Fields Found., Malibu, Calif., 1980—2014; CEO Malibu Pubublishing Co., 1995—2014. Cons. Nat. Bd. YWCA, 1943-46, Nat. Early Childhood Edn., 1948-50, UCLA Sch. Engring. Prosthetics Inst., 1949-51, Calif. Dept. Edn., 1950-60, Chrysler Motor Co. Space Divsn. Rsch., 1952, NASA Space Biology, 1958, Grand Kamalani Wellness Ctr., Maui, Hawaii; field reader US Dept. Health, Edn. & Welfare (HEW), 1958-65; reviewer sci. textbooks McMillan Pub., Prentice-Hall, McGraw-Hill, W.B. Saunders & Co., 1959-67; cons. Fetzer Found. Energy Field Rsch., 1989, Heart Math Found., 1992. Author: Recreation for the Handicapped, 1955, Corrective Physical Education, 1967, Movement Education for Preschool, 1972, Guidelines for Movement Behavior: Curricula for Early Childhood Education, 1974, Infinite Mind: Science of the Human Vibrations of Consciousness, 1996, Mind Mastery Meditations, 1997, Naibhu, 1998, Uncork Your Consciousness, 2008; contbr. articles to profl. jours. Pres. United Cerebral Palsy, L.A., 1947-51; mem. adv. com. Harlan Shoemaker Clinic for Neurol. Disabilities, 1948-53; bd. dirs. Found. for Jr. Blind, 1949-52, Crippled Children Soc., 1953-58, YWCA, L.A., 1955-65; adv. com., Internat. Congress for Exceptional Children, 1964-72, Rory Found., L.A.; vestry bd. mem. St. Matthew Episcopal Ch., L.A., 1965-69. Rsch. grantee USPHS, 1957-61, Adelphi Found., 1960-63, Rolf Found., 1965-71; recipient Heritage award Calif. Dance Educator Assn., 1987, N.B. Rudman award Found. Exceptional Leadership, 1995; Dame Order of St. John of the Americas, 1996. Mem. NSF, N.Y. Acad. Sciences, Pi Lambda Theta, Kappa Delta Pi (colloquium Energy Field Medicine, 2008). Avocations: travel, gardening, music, art, lecturing. Home: Malibu, Calif. Died Feb. 15, 2014.

**HUNTER, BERNICE THURMAN,** writer; b. Toronto, Nov. 3, 1922; d. William Henry and Francelina (Coe) Thurman; m. Lloyd Hunter, Nov. 16, 1942; children: Anita Louise, Heather Anne. Comml. diploma, Runnymede Coll., 1939. Bookkeeper T. Eaton Co., Toronto, 1940-45, office worker, 1967-72. Speaker Toronto Sch. Bd., 1982—. Author: (children's books) That Scatterbrain Booky, 1981 (IODE award 1982), The Railroader, 1988 (Vicky Metcalf award 1990), A Place for Margaret, 1989 (Can. Authors award 1990), The Firefighter, 1992 (Silver Birch award 1993, Red Cedar Book award 1997-98). Mem. Writers Union of Can., Canscaip. Died May 29, 2002.

**HUNTER, DONALD H.,** justice Indiana Supreme Court; b. Anderson, Ind., Oct. 21, 1911; s. Carl Edward and Mary (Samuels) H.; m. Violet K. Oemler, Oct. 11, 1941;

children— Jean Ellen (Mrs. John E. Stillions), Samuel E. LL.B., Lincoln U., 1937. Bar: Ind. bar 1941. Dep. atty. gen., Indpls., 1943, 46-47; hearing examiner Ind. Pub. Service Commn., 1948; asso. practice law Mr. Carl S. Willard, LaGrange, Ind.; judge LaGrange Circuit Ct., 1948-62; jud. mem. Statewide Com. for Revision of Adoption Laws, 1950-52, Adv. Com. on Probation and Parole for Ind. Citizens Council, 1953-55; judge Appellate Ct. Ind., 1963-66; then presiding justice, mem. Constnl. Revision Commn., from 1967; chief justice Ind. Supreme Ct., 1967-74, asso. justice, from 1974. Mem. Ind. Council of Freedoms Found. at Valley Forge; advancement chmn. Boy Scouts Am. Served with AUS, 1943-46. Decorated Bronze Star medal, Purple Heart medal; named a Sagamore of the Wabash Gov. Ind., 1976 Mem. Am., Ind. State, Indpls., Madison County bar assns., Am. Legion, V.F.W., Phi Delta Phi, Phi Alpha Delta, Tau Kappa Epsilon. Clubs: Mason. Republican. Methodist. Died Oct. 27, 1991.

**HUNTER, SAM,** art historian, educator; b. Springfield, Mass., Jan. 5, 1923; s. Morris and Lottie (Levine) H.; m. Maïa Spiegelman, Dec. 14, 1986; 1 child, Harrison Morris; children by previous marriage: Emily C., Alexa J. AB, Williams Coll., Williamstown, Mass., 1943; student, U. Florence, Italy, 1949-51; hon. degree Academico, Brera Acad. Fine Arts, Milan, 1993. Art critic N.Y. Times, 1947-49; editor Harry N. Abrams, Inc., art books publisher NYC, 1952-53; lectr. Barnard Coll.; asst. prof. UCLA, 1955-57; curator Mus. Modern Art, 1956-58; chief curator, acting dir. Mpls. Inst. Arts, 1958-60; dir. Rose Art Mus., Poses Inst. Art, Brandeis U., Waltham, Mass., 1960-65, assoc. prof. art history dept., 1963-65; dir. Jewish Museum, NYC, 1965-68; vis. prof. Cornell U., 1967-69; lectr. New Sch. Social Research, NYC, 1967-68; Regent's prof., vis. critic U. Calif. at Riverside, 1968; vis. critic SUNY, 1968-69; prof. art and archeology Princeton U., 1969-91, prof. emeritus, 1991—2014, faculty curator modern art Univ. Art Mus., 1969-91; dir. Princeton U. (The Corp. and Visual Arts Conf.), 1978. Robert Sterling Clark vis. prof. Clark Art Inst. and Williams Coll., Williamstown, Mass., 1976; art cons. N.J. Nightly News, PBS-TV, 1978-79, M. Knoedler, Inc., N.Y.C., Commodities Corp., Princeton; dir. Am. Art, since 1950; cons. to bd. trustees Mus. of Art, Ft. Lauderdale, Fla., 1985-87; chmn. NEA adv. com. for GSA Art Commn., Newark Fed. Courthouse, 1987; (exhbn.) Seattle World's Fair, 1962; juror Internat. Art Jury 32d Venice Biennale, Italy, 1964; exec. dir. study visual arts in pub. higher edn. Bd. Higher Edn., Mass., 1968-69; dir. critic's choice program N.Y. State Council on Arts, 1968-69; v.p., editor-in-chief, v.p. Harry N. Abrams, Inc. (art pubs.), 1971-72; dir. Monumenta outdoor sculpture exhbn., Newport, R.I., An American Renaissance: Painting and Sculpture since 1940, Mus. of Art, Ft. Lauderdale, 1986; mem. adv. bd. Modarco (S.A.), art investment group, London; lectr. contemporary Am. art USIA tour Japan, 1975; mem. spl. commn. art in state bldgs., State of Mich., 1976; cons. guest curator Mus. Art, Fort Lauderdale, Fla., 1985-87; mem. bd. overseers Rose Art Mus., Brandeis U.; cons. Marisa del Re Gallery, N.Y.C., Fujisankei Mus. Japan, Very Spl. Arts, Washington. Author: Jackson Pollock, 1956, Modern French Painting, 1956, Picasso: Cubism to the Present, 1957, David Smith, 1957, Piet Mondrian, 1958, Joan Miro: His Graphic Work, 1958, Modern American Painting and Sculpture, 1959, Hans Hofmann, 1963, Larry Rivers, 1969, New Art Around the World, 1966, American Art Since 1960, 1970, Josef Albers, 1971, American Art of the Twentieth Century, 1973, (with John Jacobus) rev. edit., 1974, Chryssa, 1974, Modern Art, from Post-Impressionism to the Present, 1976, Larry Rivers, 1990, Alex Katz, 1992, Marino Marini, 1992, Modern Art: Painting, Sculpture, Architecture, 3d rev. edition, 1992; catalogue The Dada Surrealist Heritage, 1977, Kunst der Gegenwart, 1978, Isamu Noguchi, 1978, American Art, 1979, Art in Business, 1979, Twentieth Century Art, 1980, Tony Smith, 1979, Seymour Lipton Sculpture, 1982, Aspects of Postmodernism, 1982, George Segal, 1984, (introduction) The Museum of Modern Art: The History of the Collection, 1984, (with John Jacobus) Modern Art, Painting, Sculpture, Architecture, rev. edit., 1985, 3d edit., 1992 An American Renaissance: Painting and Sculpture Since 1940, 1986, Picasso at War, 1987, Michael Hafftka: Recent Paintings, Di Laurenti Gallery, N.Y.C., 1987, In the Mountains of Japan: The Open-Air Museums of Hakone and Utsukushi-Gahara, 1988; catalogs: Roberto Barni: Myths for Our Time, Di Laurenti Gallery, N.Y.C., 1987, Pub. Sculpture in Monaco, Printemps des Arts, Monte Carlo, 1986, also catalogs for various exhbns. Ft. Lauderdale (Fla.) Mus. Art, 1987, Visions/Revisions: Contemporary Representation, Marlborough Gallery, N.Y.C., 1988, Theodoros Stamos, Kouros Gallery, N.Y.C., 1988, The Linear Image: American Master Works on Paper, Marisa del Re Gallery, N.Y.C., 1989, Francis Bacon, Joseph H. Hirschhorn Mus. and Sculpture Garden, Washington, 1989, Marino Marini: The Sculpture, 1993, Gaston Lachaise, 1993; gallery catalogues, American Masters of the Sixties: Early and Late Works, 1990; combined catalogues, exbhns.: Very Special Arts, Against All Odds: Healing Power of Art, An American Master: Jackson Pollock: 1930-51, The Royal Veno Mus., Tokyo, 1994; Am contbr.: sect. on Am. painting to Art Since 1945, 1958, James Brooks, 1963, New Directions in American Painting, 1964; curator exhbns.; contbr. articles to mags. Mem. arts and humanities task force Carter-Mondale campaign, 1976. Served as lt. (j.g.) USNR, 1944-46. J.S. Guggenheim Meml. fellow, 1971-72 Mem. Coll. Art. Assn., Phi Beta Kappa. Home: Skillman, NJ. Died July 27, 2014.

**HUNTER, THOMAS HARRISON,** physician, educator; b. Chgo., Oct. 12, 1913; s. Edwin Llewellyn and Argyra (Harrison) H.; m. Anne E. Fulcher, Mar. 6, 1943; children: Charles, Elizabeth, William, Thomas, Peter. AB cum laude, Harvard U., 1935, MD cum laude, 1940; Henry fellow, Cambridge U., Eng., 1935-38; L.H.D., Rush U., 1981. Intern, resident Presbyn. Hosp., NYC, 1942-45, asst. physician, 1945-47; instr. medicine Columbia, 1945-47; asst. and asso. prof. medicine Washington U. Sch. Medicine, 1947-53, asst. dean, 1947-52, asso. dean, 1952-53; dean Sch. Medicine, U. Va., 1953-64, prof., from 1953, chancellor for med. affairs, 1965-70, v.p. med. affairs, 1970-71, Owen R. Cheatham prof. sci., dir. human biology and society program, from 1971. Cons. USPHS; temporary staff mem. Rockefeller Found., 1962-63; fellow Center Advanced Studies in Behavioral Scis., Stanford, 1977-78; bd. overseers Harvard, 1956-62; mem. com. on med. edn. Brown U.; bd. overseers Sch. Medicine, Morehouse Coll.; mem. corp. vis. com. Sch. Medicine, Tufts U. Recipient Thomas Jefferson award, 1970; named Va. Cultural Laureat, 1981 Mem. Assn. Am. Physicians, Am. Clin. and Climatol. Soc., Am. Soc. Clin. Investigation, AAAS, AMA, Am. Acad. Arts and Scis., Assn. Am. Med. Colls. (pres. 1960, chmn. com. on internat. relations in med. edn., Abraham Flexner award 1988), Raven Soc., Phi Beta Kappa, Sigma Xi, Alpha Omega Alpha. Home: Keswick, Va. Died 1997.

**HUNTOON, ROBERT BRIAN,** chemist, food industry consultant; b. Braintree, Mass., Mar. 1, 1927; s. Benjamin Harrison and Helen Edna (Worden) H.; m. Joan Fairman Graham, Mar. 1, 1952; children: Brian Graham, Benjamin Robert, Elisabeth Ellen, Janet Lynne, Joelle. BS in Chemistry, Northeastern U., 1949, MS, 1961. Analytical chemist Mass. Dept. Public Health, microbiologist Met. Dist. Commn. Boston, 1950-53; rsch. and devel. chemist Heveatex Corp., Melrose, Mass., 1953-56; with Gen. Foods Corp., 1956-70, acting quality control mgr. Woburn, Mass., 1965-67, head group rsch. and devel. Tarrytown, NY, 1967-70; dir. quality control U.S. Flavor div. Internat. Flavors & Fragrances, Teterboro, NJ, 1970-83, mgr. tech. svcs., 1983-87, mgr. product devel., 1987-89, cons., 1989-92; ind. cons. product devel., from 1989. Contbr. articles to profl. jours. Served with USCG, 1945—46. Mem. Essential Oils Assn. (com. mem.), Flavor and Extracts Mfg. Assn. (com. mem.), Am. Chem. Soc., Inst. Food Technologists, Internat. Platform Assn., Indsl. Mgmt. Club (v.p. 1967) (Woburn), Croton Yacht Club, Saugus River Yacht Club (treas. 1967-68). Republican. Presbyterian. Achievements include patents for gelatin compositions and mfg. processes; research in flavor and food quality control. Died Dec. 5, 2013.

**HURWITZ, SAUNDRA HARRIET (SANDI HURWITZ),** analyst, educator; b. Orange, NJ, May 19, 1937; d. Julius Meyer and Laura (Mann) H. BA, Calif. State U., 1958, MPA, 1972. Mgmt. specialist II City of L.A. Cmty. Devel. Dept., 1976-95; prin. devel. specialist County of L.A. Cmty. Devel. Commn., LA, 1991-95; contract specialist L.A. Homeless Svcs. Authority, 1995-96; prof. Calif. State U., LA, from 1978. Cons. SH & Assocs., 1997—. Chair Cmty. Devel. Commn., Monterey Park, Calif., 1985-94; bd. dirs. Plz. Cmty. Ctr., L.A., 1997—. Recipient Youth Achievement award Downtown Businessmen Assn., L.A., 1977, Outstanding Achievement Alumni appreciation Calif. State U. Alumni Assn., 1977. Mem. Am. Soc. Pub. Adminstrn. (bd. dirs.). Avocations: dance, painting, gardening, cooking, crafts, needlecrafts. Died 2003.

**HUSE, RICHARD A.,** tourism educator; b. Niagara Falls, NY, Apr. 21, 1929; s. Arthur Miles and Bessie (Rose) H.; m. Marion M. McArthur, Nov. 4, 1950; children: Miles David, Caroline Rose. BS in Journalism, Advt. and Communications, U. Fla., 1955; MS in Econs. and Advt., MA in Edn. Founds., Niagara U., 1970. Mgr. small bus. Greater Tampa (Fla.) C. of C., 1956-58; asst. dir. Contractor's and Bus. Assn., St. Petersburg, Fla., 1958-61; dir. Conv. and Visitors Bur., Savannah, Ga., 1961-66, Niagara Falls, N.Y., 1966-68; sr. instr., founding faculty mem. Travel and Tourism Inst. Niagara U., Niagara Falls, 1968-72; prof. of Tourism Sch. Hospitality Mgmt. Fla. Internat. U., Miami, from 1972. Cons. various island nations including The Bahamas, Netherlands Antilles, P.R., Peru, Colombia, Dominican Republic, also pvt. cos., 1973—. Editor: Savannah mag., 1962-66. Chmn. Easter Seals campaign, Savannah, 1964; div. chmn. United Fund, Niagara Falls, 1969. Served as sgt. USAF, 1946-49. Named to Tourism Hall of Fame H.F.T. Assn., 1973, 74, 75. Mem. Meeting Planning Inst., Travel Industry Assn. Am., Travel and Tourism Research Assn., Am. Soc. Travel Agts., So. Fla. Travel Industry Assn. Democrat. Methodist. Avocation: fishing. Died Apr. 1, 1991.

**HUSKETH, ALMA ORMOND,** retired language educator; b. Dover, NC, Aug. 17, 1918; d. William Henry and Ella Carrie (White) Ormond; m. Edward Thomas Husketh Jr., June 12, 1943 (dec. May 8, 1986); children: Edward Thomas III, William Ormond, Craig Moss. BA in English, U. N.C., Greensboro, 1939; MS in Libr. Sci., U.N.C., Chapel Hill, 1966. Tchr. Eng. Granville County Bd. Edn., Creedmoor, NC, 1939—44, 1946—60; libr. S. Granville High Sch., Oxford, NC, 1962—80; tchr. Eng. Lenoir Bd. Edn., Kinston, NC, 1944—46; instr. Eng. Vance-Granville C.C., Henderson, NC, 1988—94; ret., 2004. Columnist Butner-Creedmoor News, NC, 1988—2004. Author: (poem) Values, 1999. Tchr., Sunday sch. supt. Banks United Meth. Ch., Franklinton, NC, 1939—2004. Mem.: DAR, N.C. Ret. Sch. Personnel, Frankinton Woman's Club, Saturday Book Club, Alpha Delta Kappa. Democrat. Methodist. Avocations: walking, reading, creative writing. Deceased.

**HUSS, GLENN I.,** meteoriticist; b. Haswell, Colo., May 10, 1921; s. Ernest Abram and Martha Marie (Armbruster) H.; m. Margaret Ann Nininger, June 21, 1952; children: Gary Robert, Peggy Ann, Susan Marie. BA, U. Denver, 1951, MA, 1952. Mgr., preparator Am. Meteorite Mus., Sedona, Ariz., 1955-60; dir. Am. Meteorite Lab., Denver, from 1960. Served with U.S. Army, 1942-45, ETO. Mem. AAAS, Internat. Assn. Geochem. and Cosmochem., Am. Astron. Soc., Geochem. Soc., Meteoritical Soc., Ariz. Acad. Sci. Home: Westminster, Colo. Died Sept. 28, 1991.

**HUSSEY, BARON MARMADUKE JAMES (LORD HUSSEY),** broadcasting company executive; b. Woking, Surrey, Eng., Aug. 29, 1923; s. Eric Hussey; m. Susan Katharine Waldegrave; children: James Arthur, Katharine Elizabeth. MA with honors in History, Oxford U., Eng., 1949; DLitt (hon.), Coun. for Nat. Acad. Awards, London, 1991. Various positions Associated Newspapers, London, 1949-64, dir., 1964-67; mng. dir. Harmsworth Pubs., London, 1967-70; mng. dir., CEO Times Newspapers, London, 1970-81, dir., 1981-86; chmn. BBC, London, 1986-96; ret., 1996. Lt. Brit. Army, 1942-46. Home: London, England. Died Dec. 27, 2006.

**HUSZAR, LASZLO ISTVAN,** urban and regional development specialist; b. Budapest, Hungary, Nov. 15, 1932; arrived in U.K., 1956; s. Antal and Margit (Enten) H.; m. Esther Pasint Magyar, June 21, 1969 (div. May 1979); children: David Magyar, Peter Magyar, Catherine; m. Chularat Jeetniyom, June 21, 1979; 1 child, Anthony. Dip Ing Arch, Tech. U., Budapest, 1956; BSc in Econs., London Sch. Econs., 1961. Rsch. fellow in planning Univ. of Sci. and Tech., Kumasi, Ghana, 1961-65; sr. lectr. in planning Archt. Assn. Sch., London, 1965-70; lectr. in regional planning Nottingham (Eng.) U., 1967-71; founding ptnr. Huszar Brammah and Assocs., London, from 1971; deputy project mgr. Kuala Lumpur Met. Area Devel. Study, Malaysia, 1972. Project mgr. South Thailand Regional Planning Study, Songkhla, 1973-74, Resettlement Studies in Sumatra and Sulawesi, Indonesia, 1975-77; project dir. Bandung Urban Devel. Study, Indonesia, 1977-78, Sabah Regional Planning Study, Malaysia, 1979-80, Ea. Seabord Regional Planning Study, Thailand, 1981-82, Nat. Planning Study, Bandar Seri Begawan, Brunei, 1985-87; sr. urban policy advisor Indonesian Govt. and Internat. Bank for Reconstruction and Devel., Jakarta, 1987-90; project dir. Medan Urban Devel. project, Indonesia, 1994-96, seconded to Volta River Authority to locate and plan 16 resettlement township, 1963-65. Co-author: The Towns of Ghana, 1964; contbg. author: The Volta Resettlement Experience, 1970; author reports. Sec. Hungarian Revolutionary Student Com., Budapest, 1956, London, 1956-61; participant in round-table discussions on current affairs BBC Hungarian Programmes, London, 1991-93; gen. sec. Nat. Fedn. of Hungarians in England, 2006-. Mem. Highgate Soc. (coun. mem. 1998-2002), Reform Club, Pall Mall. Avocation: bridge. Home: London, England. Died May 26, 2007.

**HUTCHEON, FORBES CLIFFORD ROBERT,** engineer, company executive; b. NYC, June 10, 1913; s. Forbes Gerard and Bertha Johanna (Von Biela) H. m. Mary D. Kearny, June 1, 1939; children: Pamela M., David F. BME, Polytechnic Inst. Bklyn., 1948. Asst. regional mgr. Latin Am. Carrier Corp., Internat. Div., NYC, 1947-49, product mgr. San Juan, P.R., 1950-51, Havana, Cuba, 1952-53; asst. gen. mgr. Stewart Mfg. Co., Cedar Grove, N.J., 1953-54; owner, chmn. C.R. Hutcheon, Inc., Bloomfield, N.J., from 1954. Mem. ASHRAE (life), Rotary (dist. com. chmn. 1979-85). Republican. Episcopalian. Died May 27, 1997.

**HUTCHISON, RAY (ELTON RAY HUTCHISON),** lawyer; b. Rockwall, Tex., Sept. 16, 1932; children: Brenda, Julie. BBA with honors, Southern Meth. U., 1957, JD cum laude, 1959. Bar: Tex. 1959. Mem. Tex. House of Reps., Dallas County, 1972-76; mng. ptnr. Hutchison Boyle Brooks & Fisher, Dallas and Austin, Tex., 1969—95; of counsel Vinson & Elkins LLP, Dallas, 1996—2012; sr. counsel Bracewell & Guiliani LLP, 2012—14. Assoc. editor Southwestern Law Jour. Del. Tex. Constitutional Conv., 1974; chmn. Tex. Republicans, 1975-78; mem. Republican Nat. Com., 1975-78, exec. com., 1976-78. Served with USN, 1950-54. Mem. Order of Woolsack, Barristers Fraternity, Delta Theta Phi, Phi Eta Sigma. Home: Dallas, Tex. Died Mar. 30, 2014.

**HUTT, WILLIAM IAN DEWITT,** actor, theater producer; b. Toronto, Ont., Can., May 2, 1920; s. Edward Dewitt and Caroline Francis (Wood) H. BA, Trinity Coll. U. Toronto, 1949; D.Litt. (hon.), U. Guelph; PhD (hon.); D.F.A. (hon.), U. Ottawa; LL.D. (hon.), U. Western Ont., 1981. Debut as actor with Bracebridge Summer Stock Co., Ont., Can., 1949; mem. Canadian Players Co.; appearing as: Macbeth in Macbeth; mem. Stratford (Ont.) Shakespeare Festival Co., 1953—, appearing in numerous roles including: Froth in Measure for Measure, 1954; Ford in The Merry Wives of Windsor, 1956, Polonius in Hamlet, 1957, Worcester in Henry IV, part 1, 1958, Jacques in As You Like It, 1959, Prospero in The Tempest, 1962, 76, Banquo in Macbeth, 1962, Pandarus in Troilus and Cressida, 1963, Richard II in Richard II, 1964, Dorante in The Bourgeois Gentleman, 1964, Shallow in Falstaff, 1965, chorus in Henry V, 1966; title role in: Tartuffe, 1968, Trigorin in The Seagull, 1968, Sir Epicure Mammon in The Alchemist, 1969, Volpone, 1971, King Lear, 1972, the king in All's Well That Ends Well, 1977, the fool in King Lear; James Tyrone in Long Day's Journey into Night, Dr. Dorn in The Visit; appeared in Mary Stuart at Phoenix Theatre, N.Y.C., 1957, The Makropoulos Secret, 1957; Broadway play Tiny Alice, 1965, Saint Joan at Lincoln Theatre, N.Y.C., 1967, The Sly Fox, Alliance Theatre Co., Atlanta; numerous Canadian TV programs including Beckett, 1970; documentary-drama series The National Dream, 1974, The First Night of Pygmalion, 1975; Canadian tour as Klestakov in The Government Inspector, 1967, Sir Epicure Mammon in The Alchemist, 1969; appeared as Caesar in Canadian tour of Caesar and Cleopatra; appeared in film The Fixer, Budapest, Hungary; starred in film The Wars, 1981; dir. plays at Stratford (Can.) Festival, most recent being, As You Like It, 1972, A Month in the Country, 1973, Oscar Remembered, 1975, The Tempest, 1976, Man for All Seasons, 1986, Henry VIII, 1986, Sheridan's School for Scandal, 1987; G. B. Shaw's St. Joan, Stratford, 1975; artistic dir., Theatre of London; most recent stage appearance at Vancouver Playhouse, 1984-85, Stratford Festival,

Can., 1986-88, Shaw Festival, Can., 1989-90. Served to lt. World War II, ETO. Decorated companion of Order of Can., 1969; recipient Priz Anik; Tyrone Guthrie award, 1954 Died June 27, 2007.

**HUTTERMANN, ALOYS P.,** science educator, researcher; b. Gelsenkirchen, Germany, Sept. 3, 1938; s. Aloysius and Elisabeth Huettermann; m. Ute Theresia Hummler, Nov. 15, 1969; children: Aloys Hugo, Wolfram Juergen. D of Natural Scis., chemistry diploma, U. Karlsruhe, Germany, 1968. Lectr. U. Karlsruhe, 1964—68; postdoctoral fellow McArdle Lab. for Cancer Rsch., U of Wis., Madison, 1968—69; acad. rat U. Goettingen, Germany, 1970—80, prof., 1980—82, prof., head dept., from 1982. Cons. Govt. of Fed. Republic of Germany, Bonn, 1983-90; mem. adv. bd. Otto Warburg Ctr. for Agrl. Biotech., Rehovot, Israel, 1984-2002; bd. dirs. Cath. Acad. Exch. Svc., Bonn, 1996—; mem. several COST actions European Cmty., Brussels, 1987-98; coord. rsch. project European Union, Brussels, 1997—; hon. fellow Hebrew U. Jerusalem, 2002. Author: The Ecological Message of the Torah—Knowledge, concepts and laws which made survival in a land of "milk and honey" possible, 1999; editor 8 books on cell biology, forest pathology and biotechnology. Mem. adv. bd. Cath. Diocese of Hildesheim, Germany, 1994-2000; mem. internat. coun. Root and Br. Orgn., Jerusalem, 1994-2000. Named Hon. Fellow, Hebrew U. of Jerusalem, 2002. Mem. numerous sci. orgns. Achievements include over 50 patents in biotechnology field in Germany and worldwide. Home: Göttingen, Germany. Died 2009.

**IBERALL, ARTHUR SAUL,** physicist, publisher; b. NYC, June 12, 1918; s. Benjamin and Anna (Katz) I.; m. Helene Rubenstein, Jan. 28, 1940; children: Eleanora Iberall Robbins, Pamela Iberall Rubin, Althea, Valerie Iberall O'Connor. BS, CCNY, 1940, postgrad., 1940-41, George Washington U., 1942-45; degree (hon.), Ohio State U., 1976. Gen. physicist Nat. Bur. Standards, Washington, 1941-53; research dir. ARO Equipment Corp., Cleve., 1953-54; chief physicist Rand Devel. Corp., Cleve., 1954-65; chief scientist, pres. Gen. Tech. Services, Inc., Upper Darby, Pa., 1965-81; editor, pub. CP2: Commentaries-Physical and Philosophical, from 1990. Vis. scholar UCLA, 1981-92; grad. teaching U. Calif., Irvine, 1993; leader interdisciplinary group for devel. of homeokinetics as a phys. unified social sci. Author: Toward a General Science of Viable Systems, 1972, On Pulsatile and Steady Arterial Flow, 1973, Physics of Membrane Transport, 1973, Bridges in Science: From Physics to Social Science, 1974, On Nature, Life, Mind and Society, 1976, What's Wrong with Evolution, 1989, How to Run a Society, 1991, Foundations for Social and Biological Evolution, 1993, (with H. Soodak) Primer for HomeoKinetics: A Physical Foundation for Complex Systems, 1998; editor: (with J. Reswick) Technical and Biological Problems of Control; A Cybernetic View, 1970, (with A. Guyton) Regulation and Control in Physiological Systems, 1973; assoc. editor: Am. Jour. Physiology, Integrative and Comparative Physiology, 1976-90; contbr. tech. articles to profl. jours. Festschift in his honor U. Conn., Storrs, 1998. Fellow ASME (chmn. auto. control div. 1973); mem. Am. Phys. Soc., N.Y. Acad. Scis., Biomed. Engring. Soc. (Alza Disting. lectr. 1975), Am. Cybernetic Soc., Microcirculation Soc., Instrument Soc. Am., Biophys. Soc., Sigma Xi. Clubs: Cosmos. Democrat. Jewish. Achievements include 35 yrs. of continuing rsch. in study of phys. complexity; integration of interdisciplinary study based on phys. principles as unique new discipline. *Three things stand out— developing the integrity of self as a human being, learning how to participate in a good family life, and integrating, in a singular fashion, the thrust of a general physical science with all aspects of reality both personal and societal. The first two themes require no special note here. Many have mastered the rules. The third is worth an added comment. Consider the Enlightenment's claim of a unified science capable of dealing with nature, life, humankind, mind, and society. Would it not be worthy of a man's life pursuit? It is.* Died Dec. 6, 2002.

**IIDA, YOTARO,** heavy manufacturing executive; b. Feb. 25, 1920; Student, U. Tokyo, 1943. Joined Mitsubishi Heavy Industries Ltd., 1943, gen. mgr. utility power sys., 1973-76, 77, gen. mgr. utility and indsl. power sys., 1976-77, dir., dep. gen. power sys., 1977-81, mng. dir., gen. mgr. power sys., 1981-83, exec. v.p., gen. mgr. power sys., 1983-85, pres., 1985-86, 88-91, chair, 1991-95. Mem. Soc. Japanese Aerospace Cos. (chair). Died Sept. 9, 2002.

**IKEYA, MOTOJI,** physics educator; b. Suita, Osaka, Japan, May 17, 1940; s. Tokuji and Masa (Nakayasu) I.; m. Yoshiko Okada, May 5, 1969; children: Jun, Yuri. B Engring., Osaka U., 1963, M Engring., 1965, PhD, 1970. Rsch. assoc. dept. nuclear engring Nagoya (Japan) U., 1967-69, lectr., 1969-73; rsch. assoc. dept. physics U. N.C., Chapel Hill, 1970-73; prof. Tech. Coll., Yamaguchi U., Ube, 1973-87; prof. physics dept. Osaka U., Toyonaka, 1987-91, prof. dept. earth and space sci., from 1991. Pres. Applied Electron Spin Resonance Workshop, Osaka, 1985-2001; co-pres. Internat. Symposium on Electron Spin Resonance Dosimetry, München, 1988, Why Do Animals Behave Unusually Before Earthquakes, 1998, Precursor Phenomena Before Big Earthquakes, 2000. Editor: ESR Dating and Dosimetry, 1985; author: ESR Dating, 1987, ESR Microscopy, 1992, New Applications of ESR, 1993. Recipient Osaka Sci. Prize Osaka City Prefecture, 1986. Mem. Phys. Soc. Japan, Geochem. Soc. Japan. Avocations: taiji, swimming, gardening. Home: Ikeda, Japan. Died Mar. 2006.

**IMHOFF, WALTER FRANCIS,** retired investment banker; b. Denver, Aug. 7, 1931; s. Walter Peter and Frances Marie (Barkhausen) I.; m. Georgia Ruth Stewart, June 16, 1973; children: Stacy, Randy, Theresa, Michael, Robert. BSBA, Regis U., Denver, 1955; D Pub. Svc. (hon.), Regis U., 1991. Asst. v.p. Coughlin & Co., Denver, 1955-60; pres., chief exec. officer Hanifen, Imhoff Inc., Denver, 1960-2000; mng. dir. Stifel, Nicolaus & Co., 2000—10. Guest lectr. U. Colo., 1976 Trustee Regis Coll., 1975—95, treas., 1976—79, vice chmn., 1981, chmn., 1982—89, life trustee, from 1998; bd. dirs. NCCJ, 1980—89, chmn., 1986—89, life trustee, from 1998; bd. dirs. Arapahoe Libr. Found., 1990—94, Channel 6 Ednl. TV, treas., 1996—97, vice chmn., 1997—98, chmn., 1998—99; bd. dirs. Highland Hills Found., from 1993, Denver Area coun. Boy Scouts Am., from 1986, v.p., 1989—2003, trustee, from 2003, life trustee, from 2013; bd. dirs. St. Joseph's Hosp., mem. exec. com., 1991, vice chmn., 1994, chmn., from 1995; bd. dirs. Kempe Children's Found., 1992—2012, chmn., 1994—97; bd. dirs. 9 Who Care, 1998—2006, Caring for Colo., from 2001; chmn. Colo. Concern, 1988—2007, emeritus trustee, from 2007; chmn. St. Joseph Hosp. Found., 2004—07; chmn. exec. com. 2% Club, from 2000; trustee Irish Cmty. Ctr., 2001. Named Outstanding Alumnus Regis Coll., 1970, 2011, named to Colo. Bus. Hall of Fame Denver C. of C. & Jr. Achievement, 2011. Mem. Bond Club Denver (pres. 1965), Colo. Mcpl. Bond Dealers Assn. (pres. 1973), Mid-Continent Securities Industry Assn. (dir. 1972-75), Securities Industry Assn. (chmn. S.W. region 1991-95, dir. 1993-96), Nat. Assn. Security Dealers, Pub. Securities Assn. (dir. 1972-75), Denver C. of C. (bd. dirs. 1986-91, treas. 1989-91), Rose Hosp. Found., Centennial C. of C. (vice chmn.), NCCJ, Alpha Kappa Psi, Alpha Sigma Nu. (Daniel Ritchie Ethics Bus. award 2008) Clubs: Denver (pres. 1981-82). Republican. Roman Catholic. Home: Greenwood Village, Colo. Died Feb. 11, 2014.

**IMPARATO, EDWARD THOMAS,** writer; b. Flushing, NY, Jan. 6, 1917; s. Charles and Romilda (Delli Bovi) I.; m. Jean Catherine De Garmo, Aug. 1, 1947. BS, U. Tampa, 1963. V.p. Merrill Lynch, Clearwater, Fla., 1963-74; fin. cons. J.C.I., Inc., Belleair, Fla., 1974-92; free-lance author Belleair, Fla., from 1992. CEO, chmn. (INSAT) Internat. Systems, Clearwater, 1987-92. Author: How to Manage Your Money, 1964, Into Darkness, 1994, MacArthur-Melbourne to Tokyo, 1996, Rescue from Shangri-La, 1997, History of the 374th Troop Carrier, 1997, General Douglas MacArthur Speeches and Reports 1908-1964, 2000, The Wisdom and Vision of Douglas MacArthur-General USA, 2000, Gen. MacArthur "Acclaimed", 2000. Col. USAF, 1938-61. Decorated Legion of Merit, D.F.C., Air medal with oak leaf cluster, Am. Def. Svc. medal; recipient WWII Victory medal, 1945, Natl. Def. Svc. medal, 1945, Am. Campaign award, 1945, Medal for Humane Action, 1945; named to Sr. Hall of Fame for vol. svc., 1998; honored as Father of Morton F. Plant Hosp. Found., 1978. Mem. Order Daedalians, Retired Officers Assn. Independent. Deceased.

**IMRIE, CHRISTOPHER,** organic chemistry educator; b. Newcastle-upon-Tyne, United Kingdom, Aug. 23, 1963; s. Robert Carswell and Kathleen Mary Imrie; m. Kim Michele Hudson, July 31, 1998; children: Katherine Alexis, Alexandra Isolde, Alastair Robert Ekhara. BSc in chemistry, with honors, U. Leeds, England, 1984; PhD in chemistry, U. Strathclyde, Scotland, 1989. Postdoctoral rsch. fellow U. Aberdeen, Scotland, 1990—92; temp. lectr. in organic chemistry U. Pretoria, Pretoria, South Africa, 1992—94; lectr., sr. lectr. in organic chemistry U. Port Elizabeth, Eastern Cape Province, South Africa, from 1994. Contbr. articles various profl. jours. Recipient Crabtree prize, U. Leeds, 1982, Leblanc medallion, 1984. Mem.: Royal Soc. of Chemistry (normal mem.). Home: Port Elizabeth, South Africa. Died Nov. 27, 2007.

**INDENBAUM, DOROTHY,** musician, researcher; b. NYC, Nov. 24; d. Abraham and Celia (Pine) Shapiro; m. Eli Indenbaum; children: Arthur, Esther. BA, Bklyn. Coll., 1942; MS, Queens Coll., 1962; PhD, NYU, 1993. Prof. Dalcroze Sch. Music, NYC, 1957-93, chmn., from 1995; prof. Hunter Coll., NYC, 1970-77. Assoc. dir. Aviva Players, N.Y.C., 1977—. Performed piano with chamber music ensembles; co-author: (Sandra H. Shichtman) Gifted Sister: The Story of Fanny Mendelssohn, 2007. Chmn. Am. Jewish Congress, 1958-60, YIVO, 1980—, Bohemian Club, 1980—, 92nd St YMHA, 1985—. Mem. Am. Women Composers (bd. dirs. 1988-93), Internat. Alliance for Women in Music (bd. dirs. 1993—), Sonneck Soc., League for Yiddish, Musicians Club (bd. dirs. 1983—), Sigma Alpha Iota (program chmn.). Home: New York, NY. Died June 2014.

**INGER, GÖRAN JAN AXEL,** law educator; b. Kungsör, Sweden, Nov. 27, 1917; s. Axel Karl Johan and Esther Sandra Maria (Berselius) I.; m. Margret Yvonne Magnusson, May 24, 1976. BA, Uppsala U., 1941, BD, 1945, DD, 1961, MA, 1962, LLM, 1970; LLD, Lunds U., 1972. Clergyman Swedish Ch., Diocese of Strangnas, 1945; sr. master Södra Latin Sch., Stockholm, 1963-65; assoc. prof. Uppsala (Sweden) U., 1965-70, prof., 1976-83, Lunds U., Lund, Sweden, 1970-76. Expert cons. Swedish Nat. Ency., Hoganas, 1987—. Author: Ecclesiastical Visitations in Medieval Sweden, 1961, The Confession in the Swedish Legal Procedure I, until 1614, 1976, In Custody for Confession in the Swedish Legal History of Procedure, 1976, The Confession in the Swedish Legal Procedure II, 1614-1948, 1994, Swedish Legal History, 1997, Uppsala 14 II, 1997, Infamy: From Infamia to Deprivation of Civil Rights, 2001. Decorated knight Order of North Star, knight comdr. Finnish Order of Lion; recipient medal for merit State of Sweden, 1982. Home: Uppsala, Sweden. Died Oct. 10, 2006.

**INMAN, WILLIAM HOWARD WALLACE,** pharmacoepidemiology educator; b. London, Aug. 1, 1929; s. Wallace Mills and Maude Mary (Andrews) I.; m. June Evelyn Maggs, July 21, 1962; children: Stella Evelyn Downey, Rosemary June Bullough, Charlotte Elizabeth Culina. MA, Cambridge U., Eng., 1950, MB, BChir, 1956. Med. advisor I.C.I. Ltd., Manchester, Eng., 1959-64; prin. med. officer Com. on Safety in Medicine, London, 1964-80; prof. pharmacoepidemiology U. Southampton, Eng., from 1980, dir. drug safety rsch. unit, 1980-94; v.p. Rehab. Engring. Movement Adv. Panels, from 1995. Author: Monitoring for Drug Safety, 1984, Don't Tell the Patient, 1999. Fellow Royal Coll. Physicians (London). Died Oct. 20, 2005.

**INSALATA, S. JOHN,** arbitrator; b. Chgo., Nov. 2, 1933; s. Sabato Chistopher and Marie Olivia (Gomes) I.; m. Bernadine Borst, 1968 (div. 1969). JD, Loyola U., Chgo., 1957, M in Social and Indsl. Rels., 1965; cert., Hague Acad., World Court, Holland, 1962. Bar: Ill. 1958, U.S. Dist. Ct. Ill. 1958, U.S. Ct. Appeals 1958, U.S. Supreme Ct. 1960. Clk. Taylor, MIller, Bush, Magnor, Chgo., 1957-58; legis. counsel N.A.M.A. Trade Assn., Chgo., 1958-65; gen. counsel Ill. Bar Assn., Springfield, 1966; asst. prof. adminstrv. law and legis. DePaul U., Chgo., 1967-70; pvt. practice Chgo. Contbr. articles to profl. jours. Named Atty. of Yr., DePaul U., Chgo., 1964. Mem. Scottish Rite Masons, Medinah Shriners, Pi Kappa Delta. Avocations: writing, speaking, photography, philetaly, travel. Deceased.

**INSKEEP, RICHARD GLENN,** retired publishing executive; b. Bluffton, Ind., Aug. 25, 1924; m. Harriett Simmmons, 1949. BS in Bus., Ind. U., 1950. Pub. Jour. Gazette, Fort Wayne, 1973-97; pres. Jour. Gazette Co., Fort Wayne, 1973—80, chmn. Pres. Jour. Gazette Found., 1987—. Served in US Army, 1944—46. Recipient Sagamore of Wabash award, 1962, 69, Ind. U. Disting. Alumni award, 1992, Hoosier Press Freedom Found. award 1996; inducted into Ind. Journalism Hall of Fame, 1991, Greater Fort Wayne Bus. Hall of Fame, 1998. Home: Fort Wayne, Ind. Died Jan. 8, 2014.

**INTORRE, BENJAMIN JOSEPH, SR.,** chemist; b. Bklyn., Nov. 10, 1929; s. Angelo and Pietra (Cammileri) I.; children: Benjamin, Angelo, Louis Leonard; stepchildren: Donna, Christopher. BS, St. Francis Coll., Bklyn., 1950; MA, Clark U., 1957, PhD, 1960. Chemist Interchemical, N.Y., N.J., 1960-67, Arde, N.J., 1967-68; chem. engr. Burns and Roe, N.J., 1968-76; chemist Stone and Webster, N.Y., 1976-77, Consol. Edison, N.Y., 1978-87, instr., cons. N.Y., from 1987. Contbr. articles to profl. jours. Pres. Good Neighbor Fund, Dumont, N.J., 1975. With U.S. Army, 1951-53. Mem. Am. Chem. Soc., Clowns of Am., World Clown Assn., Soc. Am. Magicians, Am. Musicians Union (pres./treas. 1975—, editor newsletter 1976—). Republican. Roman Catholic. Avocations: music, magic, balloon sculpture, lecturing, consulting. Died May 2, 2008.

**IRVING, THOMAS BALLANTINE,** retired Spanish language educator, consultant; b. Preston, Ont., Can., July 20, 1914; s. William John and Jessie Christina (MacIntyre) I.; m. Amanda Antillón, Aug. 17, 1950 (div. 1955); children: Diana, Lillian, Nicholas; m. Evelyn Esther Uhrhan, June 30, 1961. BA, Toronto U., 1937; Maîtrise ès Lettres, Montreal U., 1938; PhD, Princeton U., 1940. Instr. Spanish U. Calif., Berkeley, 1940-42, Carleton U., Ottawa, Can., 1942-44; dir. Colegio Nueva Granada, Bogotá, Colombia, 1944-45; asst. prof. Wells Coll., Aurora, N.Y., 1945-46; catedrático U. de San Carlos, Guatemala, 1946-48; from assoc. prof. to prof. U. Minn., Mpls., 1948-65; prof. North Ctrl. Coll., Naperville, Ill., 1965-67, U. Guelph, Ont., Can., 1967-69, U. Tenn., Knoxville, 1969-80, ret., 1980. Dir. summer sch. U. San Carlos, Guatemala City, 1946-48; trustee, dean Am. Islamic Coll., Chgo., 1981-86; vis. prof. U. Americas, Puebla, Mex., 1984. Author: Darío y la patria, 1958, Falcon of Spain, 1954, Islam Resurgent, 1979, Kalilah and Dimnah, 1980, The Maya's Own Words, 1986, The Qur'an: First American Version, 1985, Selections from the Noble Reading, 1968, rev. edit., 1980. Lt. Royal Can. Naval Svc., 1942-44. Fulbright fellow, Iraq, 1956-57; recipient Star Imtiaz, Govt. Pakistan, 1983. Mem. Lions Club. Muslim. Died 2006.

**IRWIN, ARMON WORTH,** construction executive; b. Sparta, Mo., Oct. 20, 1917; s. James Corbett and Ora (Wall) Irwin; m. Betty Jane Brielmaier, Feb. 11, 1944; children: James, John, Mary, Deborah, Thomas, Charles, Susan, Margaret. BSCE, Mo. Sch. Mines, 1948. Engr. R.E. McKee Gen. Contractor, Inc., Santa Fe, 1948—54, supt., 1954—66, project mgr. San Francisco, 1966—71, M.M. Sundt Constrn. Co., Inc., Tucson, 1971—77, field ops. mgr., 1977—82, Sundt Indsl. Contractors, Inc., Tucson, from 1982. With US Army, 1942—45, PTO. Mem.: Am. Soc. Mining Engrs., ASME, Mining Club of Southwest. Republican. Roman Catholic. Home: Tuscon, Ariz. Died Mar. 9, 1998.

**ISAACS, MARY JO,** principal; b. Winston-Salem, NC, June 27, 1931; d. James Spurgeon and Era Isaacs (Brookshire). Student, Mars Hill Jr. Coll., 1951; AB cum laude, Meredith Coll., 1953; MEd, U. NC Greensboro, 1958. Tchr. Sedge Garden Elem. Sch., Winston-Salem Forsyth County Schs., 1953—59, supr. elem. edn., 1959—71; prin. Diggs Intermediate Sch., 1971—76, Brunson Elem. Sch., from 1976; tchr. Western Carolina U., Cullowhee, NC, with, 1964—65. Pres. Winston-Salem Maids Melody, 1957; v.p. Winston-Salem Altrusa Club, 1967—68, pres., 1968—69; bd. dirs. Forsyth Singers' Guild, 1959—60, Group Homes Forsyth County, 1976—87, Children's Theatre, 1977—81. Mem.: Assn. Supervision & Curriculum Devel., NC Assn. Childhood Edn. (sec. 1965—67), NC Assn. Sch. Adminstrs., NC Prins.Asst. Prins. Assn., NC Assn. Educators (dir. div. prins. from 1984), Forsyth County Prins. Assn. (pres. 1986—87), Forsyth County Elem. Prins. Assn. (sec.-treas. 1973—74, 1984—85), Winston-Salem Forsyth County Edn. Assn. (pres. 1959—61), Assn. Childhood Edn., NC (pres. div. suprs. and dirs. instrn. NC 1970—71), Delta Kappa Gamma, Phi Delta Kappa. Democrat. Baptist. Home: Pfafftown, NC. Died Sept. 1989.

**ISAACS, ROBERT CHARLES,** retired lawyer; b. July 16, 1919; s. David and Elsie (Weiss) I.; m. Doris Frances Shapiro, Nov. 20, 1943 (dec. 1982); 1 child, Leigh Richard; m. Mary Lou Anderson, Dec. 12, 1986. BA cum laude, NYU, 1941, JD, 1943. Bar: N.Y. 1943. Dep. asst. atty. gen. N.Y. State Dept. Law, Albany, 1943, spl. asst. atty. gen., 1946; ptnr. Nordlinger Riegelman Benetar, NYC, 1946-71, Aranow Brodsky Bohlinger Benetar & Einhorn, NYC, 1972-79, Benetar Isaacs Bernstein & Schair, NYC, 1979-88. Mem. Lebanon (N.H.) Zoning Bd. Adjustment, 1988-2004; adj. prof. law St. John's U. Sch. Law, N.Y.C., 1961-72; mem. panel mediators and fact finders N.Y. State Pub. Employment Rels. Bd., 1968-88. Contbr. articles to profl. publs. Capt. U.S. Army, 1943-45, 51. Mem. ABA, ASCAP, Am. Arbitration Assn. (mem. panel arbitrators 1988), N.Y.C. Bar Assn., NYU Law Review Alumni Assn. Home: Hanover, NH. Died Aug. 28, 2011.

**ISAACS, STEPHEN DAVID,** journalism educator, writer; b. Indpls., Dec. 8, 1937; s. Norman Ellis and Dorothy (Ritz) I.; m. Diane Morgan Scharfeld, June 8, 1963; children: Deborah Alice, David Arthur, Sharon Diane. BA, Harvard U., 1959. Editor Louisville Times, 1959-60; reporter The Economist, Guardian, London, 1960-61; editor, reporter Washington Post, 1961-76; dir. L.A. Times-Washington Post News Svc., Washington, 1976-78; sr. v.p., editor Mpls. Star, 1978-82; prodr. CBS News, NYC, 1982-86, Rodman-Downs Productions, NYC, 1986-88; prof. journalism, assoc. dean Columbia U. Grad. Sch. Journalism, NYC, 1988—2012, prof. emeritus, 2012—14. Chmn., CEO Pvt. Network Productions, Dobbs Ferry, N.Y. Author: Jews and American Politics, 1974. Home: New York, NY. Died Aug. 28, 2014.

**ISDALE, CHARLES EDWIN,** chemical engineer; b. De-Quincy, La., Mar. 10, 1942; s. Vester Edwin and Katherine Gwendolyn (Wincey) I.; m. Lucille Brown, Aug. 26, 1962; children: Charles Edwin Jr., Jennifer Denise Hunt, Amberly Lauren. BSChemE, La. State U., 1965; MBA, So. Ill. U., 1978. Registered profl. engr., Ill., La. Chem. engr. Firestone Synthetic Rubber, Lake Charles, La., 1965-69, A.E. Staley Mfg. Co., Decatur, Ill., 1969-72; dir. engring. and maintenance VIOBIN Corp., Monticello, Ill., 1972-80; pres. Control Enterprises, Inc., Savoy, Ill., 1980-95, College Station, Tex., 1995-97; sr. lectr. dept. chem. engring. Tex. A&M U., College Station, from 1998. Cons. Nabisco Brands, East Hanover, N.J., 1984—, Clorox, Jackson, Miss., 1987—, Alpharma, Chicago Heights, Ill., 1987—, Chinook Group, Sombra, Ont., Can., 1987—. Active Cornerstone Ch., College Station, Tex. Mem. AIChE (sect. chmn. 1972-73), Instrument Soc. of Am. (Man of Yr. 1986). Achievements include design of a configurable multivariate control method, a method for removal of solvent to low ppm levels from enzymes, design of a batch wheat germ oil extraction plant, design of an animal gland extraction plant; patents on processing beef lung for production of heparin. Deceased.

**ISENBERG, EUGENE M.,** retired oil industry executive; b. 1929; m. Ronnie Isenberg; children: Diane, Lynda. BA, U. Mass; MA, Princeton U. Various mgmt. positions Exxon Corp., 1955—68; chmn. Genimar Inc., 1969—82; CEO Nabors Corporate Services Inc.; chmn., CEO Nabors Industries Ltd., 1987—2011. Bd. dirs. Nabors Industries Ltd., 1987—2011, Covanta Holding Corp. (formerly Danielson Holding Corp.), 1990—2004. Gov. American Stock Exch. LLC, 1996-05, Nat. Assn. Securities Dealers; pres. U. Mass. Amherst Found.; mem. Nat. Petroleum Coun. Died Mar. 16, 2014.

**ISHIKAWA, TADAO,** government agency administrator, educator; b. Tokyo, Jan. 21, 1922; s. Chukichi and Yoshi Ishikawa; m. Yoshiko Ishikawa (dec.); 4 children. BA in Econs., Keio U., Tokyo, 1946; LLD, Keio U., 1960; D Pub. Adminstrn. (hon.), Western Mich. U., 1989; LLD (hon.), York U., Toronto, Ont., Can., 1990. Mem. law faculty Keio U., 1946-87, prof., 1955-87, v.p., 1965-69, dean, 1971-77, pres., 1977-93. Vis. scholar Harvard U., Cambridge, Mass., 1956—57, U. Calif., Berkeley, 1970—71; vice chmn. Provisional Coun. Ednl. Reform, 1984—87; chmn. Japan-China Friendship Com. for 21st Century, 1984—97, U. Coun., Ministry Edn., 1987—99, Tokyo Met. Bd. Edn., 1988—96, Juvenile Problem Coun., 1989—99, Lower House Election Redistricting Coun., 1994—2004. Author: The History of the Chinese Constitution, 1953, A Study of the History of the Chinese Communist Party, 1959 (Keio U. prize 1960), People's Republic of China-Its Reality and Analysis, 1964, International Politics and Red China, 1968, Contemporary Issues of Present-Day China, 1970, My Dreams and My Choice, 1993; contbr. articles to profl. jours. Recipient Award for Cultural Merit Japanese Govt., 1991, Grand Cordon award Order of the Rising Sun, 1995, Order of Cultural Merit, 2000. Mem. Japan Assn. Pvt. Colls. and Univs. (pres. 1983-88), Japan Polit. Sci. Assn., Japan Assn. for Asian Polit. and Econ. Studies, Japan Assn. Internat. Rels. Home: Tokyo, Japan. Died Sept. 25, 2007.

**ISHIMARU, HAJIME,** physics and engineering educator; b. Sapporo, Hokkaido, Japan, Feb. 21, 1940; s. Osamu and Sumiko (Matsumoto) I.; m. Masako Kodera, Feb. 23, 1969; chldren: Dan, Goh. BS in Physics, Hokkaido U., Sapporo, Japan, 1963; MS in Physics, Tohoku U., Sendai, Japan, 1965; DS in Physics, Nagoya U., Japan, 1968, DSc, 1970; D in Engring., Tokyo U., 1980. Cert. vacuum sci. and Tech. Rsch. assoc. Tokyo U., Tokyo, 1969-72, Nat. Lab. High Energy Physics, Tsukuba, Ibaraki, Japan, 1972-75, assoc. prof., 1975-84, prof., from 1984, The Grad. U., Tsukuba, Ibaraki, Japan, from 1988. Cons. Superconductive Super Collider Lab., Dallas, 1991—, Synchrotron Radiation Rsch. Ctr., Hsinchu, Taiwan, 1986—; founder ALVALAB Found., 1989. Author: Aluminum Vacuum Technol., 1988; mem. editl. bd. Vacuum Journal, 1974. Steering com. Sakusa Village, Sakura 1982, ACCS cable TV svc. Tsukuba 1985—, active PTA, Sakura 1984, Namiki Football Club Sakura 1984. Recipient Vacuum Tech. award Vacuum Soc. Japan Tokyo 1979, 82, Best Shop Note award Am. Vacuum Soc. N.Y.C. 1978, Albert Nerken award, 1994, Remarkable Patent award Ministry of Sci. and Tech., Tokyo, 1983, 85, Short Note award Brit. Vacuum Coun. London 1985, Takagi award Precision Measurements Tech. Found. 991, Taiwan hon. for tech. contbn. to vacuum tech. to Synchrotron Radiation Rsch. Ctr. project 1993, The Order of the Sacred Treasure Gold Rays with Neck Ribbon by Japanese govt. Fellow Am. Vacuum Soc. Died Oct. 6, 1997.

**ISOMURA, IWAO,** automotive executive; b. Yamaguchi, Japan, 1932; m. Chieko Isomura; 2 children. Degree in Econs., Kyoto U., 1956. Joined Toyota Motor Corp., from 1956, gen. mgr. human resources divsn., 1978, gen. mgr. tng. and edn. divsn., gen. mgr. domestic planning divsn., gen. mgr. domestic mktg. divsn., dir., 1984—88, mng. dir., 1988—90, sr. mng. dir., 1990—92, exec. v.p., 1992—96, vice chmn., from 1996. Avocation: golf. Died Jan. 2004.

**ITÔ, KIYOSI,** retired mathematician, educator; b. Kuwana, Mie, Japan, Sept. 7, 1915; s. Seitaro and Tsuyo (Mizutani) I.; m. Shizue Oizumi, Sept. 23, 1938; children: Keiko, Kazuko, Junko. MS, U. Tokyo, 1938, PhD, 1945; Doctorate (hon.), U. Paris VI, 1981, E.T.H. Zürich, 1987, U. Warwick, UK, 1992. Statistician Statis. Bur. Govt. Tokyo, 1939—43; assoc. prof. Nagoya Imperial U., Japan, 1943—52; prof. Kyoto U., Japan, 1952—79, prof. emeritus, 1979—2008. Dir. Rsch. Inst. Math. Scis., Kyoto U.; with Inst. Advanced Study, Princeton U., 1954—56; prof. U. Aarhus, 1966—69, Cornell U., 1969—75, Gakushuin U.; guest lectr. Tata Inst., Bombay. Author: (books) Probability Theory, 1953, Stochastic Processes, 1957. Recipient Asahi prize Asahi Newpaper Co., Tokyo, 1978, Imperial prize Japan Acad. Sci., Tokyo, 1978, Fujiwara Found. prize, Tokyo, 1985, Wolf prize in Math. Wolf Found., Israel, 1987, Carl Friederich Gauss prize for Applications Math., Internat. Math. Union, 2006. Mem. Japan Acad. Home: Kyoto, Japan. Died Nov. 17, 2008.

**IURZOLLA, EZIO,** mechanical engineering educator; b. Trieste, Italy, Nov. 3, 1912; s. Giovanni and Irene (Lupetina) I.; m. Maria Luisa Zetto; children: Maria Viviana, Maria Federica, Fabio. Degree in Mech. Engring., Politechnic U., Brûnn, 1933; postgrad., U. Padua, Italy, 1936; Qualification for Univ. Teaching, U. Rome, 1950. Instr. U. Padua, 1945-50, asst. prof., 1950-60, prof., from 1960. Contbr. over 100 articles to profl. jours.; author books. Decorated War Cross (Gold Medal) Commendatore della Repubblica Italiana. Deceased.

**IYENGAR, B. K. S. (BELLUR KRISNAMACHAR SUNDARARAJA IYENGAR),** physical education educator, writer; b. Bellur, India, Dec. 14, 1918; m. Ramamani Iyengar, 1943; children: Prashant, Geeta, Vinita, Suchita, Sunita, Suvitha. Yoga tchr. Ramamani Iyengar Meml. Yoga Inst., 1975—2014. Author: Light on Yoga, 1966, The Art of Yoga, 1985, The Tree of Yoga, 1988, Light on Pranayama: The Yogic Art of Breathing, 1989, Light on the Yoga Sutras of Patanjali, 1996, Light on Life: The Yoga Journey to Wholeness, Inner Peace, and Ultimate Freedom, 2005, Yoga: The Path to Holistic Health, 2007, Yoga, Wisdom, and Practice, 2009, Yaugika Manas: Know and Realize the Yogic Mind, 2010, Core of the Yoga Sutras: The Definitive Guide to the Philosophy of Yoga, 2012; appeared in (documentaries) Breath of the Gods: A Journey to the Origins of Modern Yoga, 2012. Recipient Padma Shri, 1991, Padma Bhushan, 2014; named one of The 100 Most Influential People in the World, TIME mag., 2004. Died Aug. 20, 2014.

**JABERG, EUGENE CARL,** theology educator, administrator; b. Linton, Ind., Mar. 27, 1927; s. Elmer Charles and Hilda Carolyn (Stuckmann) J.; m. Miriam Marie Priebe; children: Scott Christian, Beth Amy, David Edward. BA, Lakeland Coll., 1948; BD, Mission House Theol. Sem., 1954; MA, U. Wis., 1959, PhD, 1968. Ordained to ministry, United Ch. of Christ, 1959. U.S. army corr., 1949—50; staff announcer WKOW-TV, Madison, Wis., 1955-58, 67-68, WHBL, Sheboygan, 1943—55, WHA, Wis. U. Sta., 1967—68, KTCA-TV, Mpls., 1968—80, freelance host; minister Pilgrim Congl. Ch., Madison, 1956-57; assoc. prof. speech Mission House Theol. Sem., Plymouth, Wis., 1958-62; asst. prof. communications United Theol. Sem., New Brighton, Minn., 1962-76, prof. communication, 1976-91, dir. admissions, 1984-87, dir. MDiv program, 1988-90, prof. emeritus, from 1991, acting dir. Masters programs, 1997-99. Bus. ptnr. Dimension 3 Media Svcs., Mpls., 1988-90; coord. spl. projects CTV North Suburbs Cable Access, 1991-2002; vis. scholar Cambridge U., Eng. Author, editor: A History of Lakeland-Mission House, 1962; author: The Video Pencil, 1980; contbr. articles, revs. to various publs.; producer films, videotapes. Artistic dir. Interfaith Players, Mpls., 1965-73; TV prodr., moderator Town Meeting of Twin Cities, Mpls., 1967-70; prodr., writer, host various radio and TV series, Mpls., 1970-89; mem. Ctr. Urban Encounter, Mpls., 1972-74, New Brighton Human Rights Commn., 1975-77; bd. mem. office comm. United Ch. Christ, N.Y.C., 1975-81; mem. North Suburban Sys. Cable Access Commn., 1986-91. Kaltenborn Radio scholar, 1957; grantee Assn. Theol. Sems., 1983; recipient Minn. Community TV award, 1993, Judges Choice award Alliance of Cmty. Media, 1999; named into Gallery of Distinction Lakeland Coll., 1996; named to Sta. CTV-15 Hall of Fame, Roseville, Minn., 1998. Mem. Religious Speech Communication Assn. (co-chmn. 1972-74), World Assn. Christian Communication. Democrat. Avocations: travel, hiking, spectator sports, films. Home: Saint Paul, Minn. Died Oct. 2013.

**JACKSON, DONALD LEE,** lawyer; b. Lafayette, Ind., Feb. 2, 1939; s. Morris M. and Melva M. (Bechdolt) Jackson; m. Lucinda Grant, Nov. 10, 1962; children: Jeffrey Grant, Eric Lee. BS, Ind. U., 1960; JD, Ind. U.-Indpls., 1966. Bar: Ind. 1966, US Dist. Ct. (so. dist.) Ind. 1966, US Ct. Appeals (7th cir.) 1968, US Supreme Ct. 1973. Ptnr. Bingham Summers Welsh & Spilman, Indpls., from 1966. Contbr. articles to profl. jours. Served to 1st lt. US Army, 1962—64. Fellow: Ind. Bar Found., Indpls. Bar Found. (pres. from 1982), Am. Bar Found.; mem.: ABA (del. house of dels. from 1983, profl. discipline, com. from 1983), Ind. U.-Indpls. Law Sch. Alumni Assn. (bd. dirs.), Ind. Alpha Alumni Scholarship Found. (pres.), Am. Judicature Soc. (bd. dirs.), Ind. State Bar Assn. (chmn. house of dels. 1984—85, treas. 1985—86), Indpls. Bar Assn. (pres. 1981), Phi Delta Phi, Phi Delta Theta. Home: Bettendorf, Iowa. Deceased.

**JACKSON, LAMBERT BLUNT,** academic administrator; b. Wilmington, Del., July 27, 1940; s. Wendell Ford and Margaret (Blunt) J.; m. Doris Vidal Jackson; children: L. Blunt, Margaret Julia Chantal, Etienne Vidal. BA, U. Del., 1964, MA in Am. Studies, 1965, PhD in History of Am. Civilization, 1976. Master The Marvelwood Sch., Cornwall, Conn., 1965-67; tchg. asst. dept. English U. Del., 1970-72, instr. dept. history, 1973-76, interim dir. Am. Studies Program, 1974; rsch. assoc. acad. founds. dept. Rutgers U., Camden, N.J., 1976-77, 78-79, acting dir., 1977-78, 80-81, adj. faculty dept. English, 1980-88, asst. dir. acad. founds. dept., 1984-87, acting dir., 1987, dir. Edn. Opportunity Fund Program, from 1988, assoc. dept. urban studies, from 1989, mem. grad. English faculty, from 1995. Mgmt. cons. Hispanic Health and Mental Health Assn. of So. N.J., Inc., 1981; supr. student tchr. English Rutgers-Camden Dept. Edn., 1983-85; project dir. City of Camden Youth Commn., 1986; devel. cons. Casa PRAC, Vineland, N.J., 1987; workshop leader Episcopal Diocese of N.J., 1989; cons. Hispanic Family Ctr., Camden, 1988. Author: They Serve: A History of And Salute to Service Clubs in Delaware, 1976, The American Poet, The Prairie Poet. Mem. Urban Coun. of Camden City Episcopal Parishes, 1983—; mem., v.p. Hispanic Task Force of Camden County, 1985-94; mem. Bishop's Hunger Task Force Episcopal Diocese of N.J., 1985, chair, 1986; del. rep. from diocese of N.J. to Nat. Impact Conf., Washington, 1986; mem. bd. trustees William Alexander Procter Found., 1986-92; warden, mem. vestry, clk. Grace Episcopal Ch., Haddonfield, N.J., 1986-90; commn. on ministry Diocese of N.J., Trenton, 1988—, anti-racism commn., 1997—, Hispanic commn., 1997—; trustee, treas. Shepherd's Gate, 1989—; curriculum com. Camden Bd. Edn., 1997-2000; officer Freinds of the Camden Libr., 1998—; pres. N.J. Minority Edn. Devel. Program. Grantee N.J. Dept. Higher Edn., 1979-80, 1990—, Pew Charitable Trust, 1987-90, Divsn. of Women, State of N.J., 1988-89, HUD, 1992-94, NSF, 1994-97, Bell Atlantic, 1997-98; recipient Andelot fellowship, 1964-65, 68-69, Univ. fellowship, 1968-69, 69-70, Tchg. assistantship, 1970-71, 71-72, Disting. Svc. award Rutgers Adminstrv. Assembly, 1990. Episcopalian. Avocations: collector of Am. and Chinese antiques, hist. restoration, garden design. Home: Haddonfield, NJ. Deceased.

**JACKSON, RONALD SHANNON,** drummer, composer; b. Ft. Worth, Jan. 12, 1940; s. William Jackson and Ella Mae (Shannon) Walton, June 18, 1978; m. Natalie Francis; children: Sunday Kyoanlie, Talkeye. Musician various artists including Charles Mingus, Betty Carter, Albert Ayler, 1966-68, Ornette Coleman, Cecil Taylor, 1975-79; musician R.S.J. Decoding Soc., from 1979, Bill Laswell, Bill Frisell, from 1980. Rec. artist 12 LPs (with R.S.J. and The Decoders), over 40 LPs with other artists. Buddhist. Home: New York, NY. Died Oct. 19, 2013.

**JACOBS, ANDREW, JR., (ANDY JACOBS),** former United States Representative from Indiana; b. Indpls., Feb. 24, 1932; s. Andrew and Joyce Taylor (Wellborn) J.; m. Kimberly Hood; children: H.B. James Andrew, B.N. Steven Michael. BS, Ind. U., 1955, LL.B., 1958. Bar: Ind. Practiced in Indpls., 1958-65, 73-74; mem. Ind. House of Reps., 1958-60, US Congress from 11th Ind. Dist., 1965-73, 1975-83, US Congress from 10th Ind. Dist., 1983-96. Adj. prof. Ind. U., 1996—. Author: The 1600 Killers: A Wake-Up Call for Congress, 1999, Slander and Sweet Judgment: The Memoir of an Indiana Congressman, 2000 Served with USMC, 1950-52. Mem. Indpls. Bar Assn., American Legion. Democrat. Roman Catholic. Died Dec. 28, 2013.

**JACOBS, ELEANOR ALICE,** retired clinical psychologist, educator; b. Royal Oak, Mich., Dec. 25, 1923; d. Roy Dana and Alice Ann (Keaton) J. BA, U. Buffalo, 1949, MA, 1952, PhD, 1955. Clin. psychologist VA Hosp., Buffalo, 1954-83, EEO counelor, 1962-79, chief psychology service, 1979-83; clin. prof. SUNY, Buffalo, 1950-83. Speaker on psychology to community orgns. and clubs, 1952-2002; Mem. adult devel. and aging com. NICHD, HEW, 1971-75 Researcher for publs. on hyperbaric medicine, hyperoxygenation effect on cognitive functions in aged. Recipient Outstanding Superior Performance award Buffalo VA Hosp., 1958, Spl. Recognition award SUNY, Buffalo, Spl. Recognition award SUNY, 1971; W.L. McKnight award Miami Heart Inst., 1972; Adminstrs. commendation VA, 1974; Dirs. commendation VA Med. Center, Buffalo, 1978; Disting. Alumni award SUNY, Buffalo, 1983; named Woman of Yr. Bus. and Profl. Women's Clubs, Buffalo, 1973 Mem. Am. Psychol. Assn., Eastern Psychol. Assn., N.Y. State Psychol. Assn., Am. Group Psychotherapy Assn., Am. Soc. Group Psychotherapy and Psychodrama, Psychol. Assn. Western N.Y. (Disting. Achievement award 1976), Group Psychotherapy Assn. Western N.Y., Undersea Med. Soc., Sigma Xi. Died Sept. 22, 2002.

**JACOBS, KLAUS JOHANN,** employment agency executive; b. Dec. 3, 1936; Grad., Stanford U. Dir. purchases and mktg Jacobs AG, 1962—73, gen. mgr., 1973—82; owner Jacobs Suchard, 1982—90, Adia Personnel Svcs., 1992; chmn. Adecco S/A, 1996—2002; co-chair Adecco SA, 2004—05, CEO, 2005—06, honorary pres., 2006—08.

Founder, hon. chmn. The Jacobs Found.; founder, mem. Nat. Park Hohe Tauern; mem. World Scout Found., 1986—2008; vice chmn., treas. Carnegie Hall, acting exec. dir., 2004—08; bd. dirs. Zurich Opera. Died Sept. 11, 2008.

**JACOBS, RICHARD DEARBORN,** consulting engineering company executive; b. Detroit, July 6, 1920; s. Richard Dearborn and Mattie Phoebe (Cobleigh) J.; divorced; children: Richard, Margaret, Paul, Linden. BS, U. Mich., 1944. Registered profl. engr., Ill., Mich., Wis., Miss. Engr. Detroit Diesel Engine divsn. Gen. Motors, 1946-51; mgr. indsl. and marine engine divsn. Reo Motors, Inc., Lansing, Mich., 1951-54; chief engr. Kennedy Marine Engine Co., Biloxi, Miss., 1955-59; marine sales mgr. Nordberg Mfg. Co., Milw., 1959-69, Fairbanks Morse Engine divsn. Colt Industries, Beloit, Wis., 1969-81; pres. R.D. Jacobs & Assocs., cons. engrs., naval arch. & marine engrs., Roscoe, Ill., from 1981. With AUS, 1944-46. Mem. ASTM, Soc. Naval Archs. and Marine Engrs. (chmn. sect. 1979-80), Soc. Automotive Engrs., Am. Soc. Naval Engrs., Soc. Am. Mil. Engrs., Navy League U.S., Propeller Club U.S., Masons. Unitarian Universalist. Deceased.

**JACOBSON, DONALD THOMAS,** management consultant; b. Powers Lake, ND, June 5, 1932; s. Martin I. and Gladys E. (Thronson) Jacobson; m. Andrea Marie Moore, Aug. 14, 1954 (dec.); 1 child, Kathryn E. BA, Whitman Coll., 1954; MBA, Stanford U., 1956. Sales and mktg. mgmt. Guy F. Atkinson Co., Portland, Oreg., 1959—63; sales control mgr. Boise Cascade Corp., Portland, 1964—66; v.p. and dir. rsch. Lund, McCutcheon, Jacobson, Inc., Portland, 1966—74; pres. Mgmt./Mktg. Assocs., Inc., Portland, 1974—96. Contbr. articles on mgmt. and mktg. to profl. jours. Mem. Oreg. Rep. Club, 1960-64, mem. bd. dirs., v.p. 1960, pres. 1961; mem. County Rep. Ctrl. Com., 1962-64; chmn. Oreg. Bus. Workshops, 1974-76; exec. com., dir. Full-Circle, Inc., 1971-77; mem. Portland Metro. C. of C., bd. dirs., 1987-90. Lt. US Army, 1956—59. Decorated commendation ribbon; recipient Oreg. Econ. Devel. award, 1973, chmn.'s award Outstanding Svc., Portland Metro. C. of C., 1987. Mem. Am. Mktg. Assn. (pres. Oreg. chpt. 1972-73, bd. dirs. 1967-74, 89-93, Oreg. Marketer of Yr. award 1991, chair Internat. Outreach Com. 1992-93), Mktg. Rsch. Assn., Nat. Assn. Bus. Economists, Met. Chambers Econ. Devel. Coun. Portland Area (chmn. mktg. task force 1983-85, emerging issues com. 1987-89, labor policy com. 1988-91, chmn. Oreg. chpt. 1986-87, bd. dirs. 1986-90), U.S. Dept. Commerce (nat. def. exec. res. 1966-96, chmn. Oreg.-Idaho assn. 1969-70), Oregonians for Cost-Effective Govt. (bd. dirs. 1986-90, bd. advisor 1991-92), Econ. Roundtable (coord. 1982-96), Whitman Coll. Alumni Assn. (bd. dirs. 1971-75, pres. 1975-77), Stanford U. Bus. Sch. Assn. (founding pres. Portland chpt. 1971-72), Phi Beta Kappa. Republican. Lutheran. Died Sept. 14, 1996.

**JACOBSON, EDWARD,** retired secondary school educator, principal; b. NYC, Apr. 12, 1914; s. Joseph and Kitty Jacobson; children: Mark, Betsy. PhB, U. Vt., 1939, MA, 1940; profl. degree in edn., Columbia U., 1962. Owner, dir. Camp Dunmore for Boys, Salisbury, Vt., 1946—60; tchr., prin. Drum Hill Jr. HS, Peekskill, NY, 1948—74; tchr. Fulbright, Scotland, 1960—61, 1974—75. Mem. regional planning commn., Middlebury, Vt.; mem., chmn. planning commn. Whiting, Vt.; vol. Porter Hosp., Middlebury. Lt. sr. grade USN, 1942—45, ATO, PTO. Mem.: Phi Beta Kappa. Democrat. Jewish. Home: Whiting, Vt. Died Aug. 23, 2008.

**JACOBY, BENJAMIN,** plant physiologist educator; b. Insterburg, Germany, June 2, 1927; came to Israel, 1935; s. Julius and Kaete Else Jacoby; m. Mina Weiss, Mar. 31, 1955; children: Uri, Michal. MSc, Hebrew U. Jerusalem, Rehovot, Israel, 1955, PhD, 1960. Mem. faculty Hebrew U. Jerusalem, Rehovot, from 1957, prof. agrl. botany, from 1978, head dept., 1990-96, prof. emeritus, from 1996; rsch. fellow King's Coll., London U., 1961-62; rsch. plant physiologist UCLA, 1967-68. Vis. prof. U. Calif., Davis, 1976-77, U. Ill., Urbana-Champaign, 1983-84. Contbr. over 90 articles to profl. jours. Mem. Am. Soc. Plant Physiology, European Soc. Plant Physiology, Israel Bot. Soc., Scandinavian Soc. Plant Physiology. Home: Rehovot, Israel. Died Nov. 27, 2002.

**JAEGER, ARNO,** operations research educator; b. Berlin, July 10, 1922; s. Gustav and Amalie (Beau) J.; m. Charlotte Streichan, Oct. 29, 1998. Diploma in math., U. Goettingen, 1948, D in Natural Scis., 1949. Brit. coun. fellow Manchester (Eng.) U., 1949-50; lectr. U. Coll. Ibadan, Nigeria, 1950-52; rsch. assoc. U. Ill., Urbana, 1952-53; assoc. prof. U. Cin., 1953-59, prof., 1959-68, Charles Phelps Taft prof., 1968-70, dir. grad. studies, 1961-70; prof. Ruhr U., Bochum, Germany, from 1970, dir. Inst. Mgmt. Sci. and Ops. Rsch., from 1971. Vis. prof. U. Wuerzburg, 1956, Free U., Berlin, 1957, U. Goettingen, 1957, Miami U., Oxford, Ohio, 1958, U. Munich, 1958, 62, U. Mannheim, 1965, U. Karlsruhe, 1966-68, Tongji U., Shanghai, 1982, Fachhochschule Bingen, 1991-92, U. Potsdam, 1992-93. Author: Introduction to Analytic Geometry and Linear Algebra, 1967, Mathematik und Leben—Eine seltene Gleichung, 1997; co-author: Lineare Wirtschaftsalgebra, 1969, Lineare Algebra und Lineare Programmierung, 1987; editor Econometrics and Ops. Rsch., 1965—; translator: Lineare Programmierung und Erweiterungen, 1966. Home: Bochum, Germany. Died Feb. 24, 2004.

**JALLINGS, ELIZABETH ANN FRANKLIN,** advocate, educator; b. Madison, Wis., June 9, 1916; d. Newton Lucuis and Bertha Sophia (England) Franklin; m. Jack K. Jallings, Aug. 17, 1940; children: Susan, Nancy, Rebecca, Jonathan. BA, U. Wis., 1940, MA, 1966. Ordinance inspector U.S. Govt., Chgo., 1941-42; nursery sch. tchr. Madison, 1952; cottage parent Wis. Sch. for Girls, Oregon, Wis., 1955-64; tchr. Madison Area Tech. Coll., 1966-86; ret. Cmty. vol. Girl Scouts Am., 4-H, Madison, 1950—; political activist Women's Internat., Madison, 1986—, League for Peace & Freedom, Madison, 1986—. Independent. Avocations: sculpture, reading. Home: Oregon, Wis. Died Apr. 6, 2008.

**JAMES, CHARLES THOMAS,** metallurgical engineer, safety engineer; b. Poughkeepsie, NY, July 3, 1928; s. Charles Coulter and Ann Katherine (Mackenhaupt) J.; m. Rosario Lopez Noel; children: Ann Margarita, Caroline Ramona. B in Metall. Engring., M in Metall. Engring., Rensselaer Polytechnic Inst. Registered profl. engr., Pa., N.J. Sr. scientist E.W. Bliss Co., Swarthmore, Pa., 1967-70; safety engr. Am. Mut. Ins. Co., Bryn Mawr, Pa., 1972-75; mfg. devel. engr. King Fifth Wheel, Mountainton, Pa., 1976-79; chief metallurgist Roebling Steel Co., Roeb King, Pa., 1979-80; prodn. engr. Phila. Naval Base, 1980-88; cons. engr. Sanders & Thomas, Pottstown, Pa., 1988-90. Cons. Charles T. James, P.E., Newtown, Pa., 1995—; rsch. engr. Bethlehem Steel Co., 1962-67; product metallurgist Allegheny Ludlum Steel Co., Watervliet, N.Y., 1956-62. Mem. Am. Heart Assn., Newtown, 1996, 97, Am. Cancer Soc., 1997. With U.S. Army, 1950-52. Mem. Am. Soc. for Safety Engrs., ASTD, Am. Soc. Materials (life). Achievements include production cycles for titanium and zirconium mill product; discovered factors governing hydrogen embrittlement of steel; discovered factors governing east of cold extrusion of steel; set up mill testing lab for steel company. Deceased.

**JAMES, DON (DONALD EARL JAMES),** retired college football coach; b. Massillon, Ohio, Dec. 31, 1932; m. Carol Hoobler; children: Jeff, Jill, Jeni. BA, U. Miami, 1954; M.Ed., U. Kans., 1957. Grad. asst. U. Kans., 1956-57; tchr., coach Southwest Miami (Fla.) High Sch., 1957-59; defensive backs coach Fla. State U., Tallahassee, 1959—61, defensive coord., 1961—66, U. Mich., Ann Arbor, 1966-68, U. Colo., Boulder, 1968-70; head football coach Kent State U., 1971-74, U. Wash. Huskies, 1974-92; ret., 1993. Coach North-South Shrine Game, Miami, 1973, Ohio Shrine Game, 1973, 74, America Bowl, 1976, East-West Shrine Game, San Francisco, 1979, Japan Bowl, 1979 Served with Transp. Corps U.S. Army, 1954-56. Recipient Munger award, Maxwell Football Club, 1991, Eddie Robinson award, Football Coaches Assn. America, 1991, Paul "Bear" Bryant award Nat. Sportscasters & Sportswriters Assn., 1991; named Coach of Yr. Mid American Conf., 1972, Ohio Coach of Yr. Coll. Football Coaches Assn., 1972, Nat. Coach of Yr. American Football Coaches Assn., 1978, Pac-10 Coach of Yr, 1980, 1990-91, Nat. Coach of Yr. Athlon Publications, 1981, Pre-Season Coach of Yr. Playboy Mag., 1982, Coach of Yr., The Sporting News, 1991; named to The Miami Sports Hall of Fame, 1992, The Husky Hall of Fame, 1994, Coll. Football Hall of Fame, 1997. Mem. Omega Delta Kappa Lodges: Rotary. Achievements include head coach of Rose Bowl Champions, 1978, 82, Sun Bowl Champions, 1979, Pac-10 Champions, 1980, 81, 90-92, Aloha Bowl Champions, 1982, Orange Bowl Champions, 1985, Freedom Bowl Champions, 1985; head coach of NCAA Division 1A football national championship winning University of Washington Huskies, 1991. Died Oct. 20, 2013.

**JAMES, WILLIAM HALL,** retired former state official, educator; b. North Providence, RI, July 20, 1910; s. John William and May J.; m. Virginia Stowell, June 24, 1950, 1 child, Hillery Stowell. Student, U. Lausanne, 1928-29; BPhil, Brown U., 1933; MA, Yale U., 1946, PhD, 1955; LLD, U. New Haven, 1976. Tchr. New Canaan (Conn.) Bd. Edn., 1933-36; teaching prin. Easton (Conn.) Bd. Edn., 1936-42, 46-47, supervising prin., 1947-53, supt. schs., 1953-58, Branford (Conn.) Bd. Edn., 1958-66; staff Commn. Higher Edn., Hartford, Conn., 1966-77, dir. accreditation and scholarships, 1966-77; ret., 1977. Cons. Greater New Haven State Tech. Coll., 1977-78, Conn. Commn. Higher Edn., 1980-81; adj. prof. history So. Conn. State Coll., New Haven, 1947-49, adj. prof. econs. and labor-mgmt. rels., 1981-92, adj. prof. labor-mgmt. rels.; adj. prof. internat. rels., Eurasian affairs and history Western Conn. State Coll., Danbury, 1949-58; adj. prof. ednl. adminstrn. U. Bridgeport, Conn., 1958; adj. prof. econs. and indsl. rels. U. New Haven, West Haven, Conn., 1979-90, adj. prof. indls. rels.; adj. prof. labor-mgmt. rels., mgmt. Teikyo Post U., Waterbury, Conn., 1988-93; lectr. in field. Author: The Monetarists and the Current Crisis, 1975, The Monetarists and the Conyinuing Crisis, 1997, The Monetarists and the Evolving Crisis: Wake Up, Americans; We are Losing our Great Nation, 2011 Mem. North Branford (Conn.) Commn. Econ. Devel., 1980-95, chmn., 1981-95; mem. PTA. Maj. USAAF, 1942-46. Recipient Disting. Friend of Greater New Haven State Tech. Coll. award, 1984; Paul Harris fellow Rotary Found; named to Branford's Edn. Hall of Fame. Mem. SAR, NEA, Conn. Edn. Assn., Conn. Assn. Pub. Sch. Supts., Conn. Assn. Advancement Sch. Adminstrn., Am. Assn. Sch. Adminstrs., Yale Post-Doctoral Seminar Group (pres. 1968-69), Conn. State Employees Assn., Conn. Coun. Higher Edn. (treas. 1971-77), Am. Assn. Higher Edn., Royal Can. Geog. Soc., Numerical Control Soc., Rotary, Schoolmasters Rotary U.S. (sec.-treas. 1965-69), Am. Legion (post comdr. Easton 1948-49), China-Burma-India Vets. Assn., Exchange Club. Home: Northford, Conn. Died Aug. 19, 2014.

**JAMES, WILL(IAM)(RODERICK),** writer, artist; b. Great Falls, Mont., June 6, 1892; s. William J. Left an orphan, adopted by fur trapper, and taught by him to write. Went to work with cow and horse outfits at 13; continued on western and Can. ranges; engaged in capture of wild horses in Nev. and took part in rodeos. Owner of 12,000 acre ranch. Author: Cowboys, North and South, 1924, The Drifting Cowboy, 1925, Smoky, 1926 (Newberry medal, adopted by Tex. State Textbook Commn. 1935), Cow Country, 1927, Sand, 1929, Lone Cowboy, 1930 (adopted by Book-of-the-Mth. Club 1930), (short stories) Sun-up, 1931, Big-Enough, 1931, (short stories) All in The Day's Riding, 1932, The Three Mustangeers, 1933, In the Saddle with Uncle Bill, 1935, Scorpion, 1936, Cowboy in the Making, 1937, Look-See, with Uncle Bill, 1938, Flint-Spears, 1938, The Dark Horse, 1939, Horses I've Known, 1939, My First Horse, 1939; contbr. short stories and articles to leading periodicals since 1934; films: Lone Cowboy, 1933, Smokey, 1934; illustrated his own books. Mem. Mounted Scouts, U.S. Army, CAmp Kearney, Calif., WWI. Home: Billings, Mo. Died Sept. 3, 1942.

**JANDA, VLADIMIR,** physiatrist, neurologist, educator; b. Prague, Czechoslovakia, Apr. 19, 1928; s. Válav and Božena (Rohlíčková) J.; m. Jana Kotrbová, June 6, 1972; children: Vladimír, Jan. MD, Charles U., Prague, 1952; PhD, Charles U., 1965, DSc, 1980. Dir. rehab. medicine dept. Charles U. Hosp., from 1967, Postgrad. Med. Sch., Prague, from 1967; dir. Physiotherapy Sch. Charles U. 3d Med. Sch., from 1992. Cons. WHO, Geneva, 1965; vis. prof. U. Queensland, Brisbane, Australia, 1982, hon. assoc., 1995; hon. prof. U. Novokuzneck, Russia, 1993. Author 16 books on muscle testing function (transl. into Czech, Swedish, English, German, and Bulgarian); contbr. over 160 articles to med. jours. Named Hon. Alumni, U. Queensland, 1993. Hon. mem. med. socs. in Sweden, Germany, Russia, U.S., Czech Republic, and Slovakia. Roman Catholic. Home: Prague, Czech Republic. Died Nov. 25, 2002.

**JANEWAY, MICHAEL CHARLES,** journalism educator, retired editor; b. NYC, May 31, 1940; s. Eliot and Elizabeth Ames (Hall) J.; m. Mary Struthers Pinkham, Dec. 18, 1965 (div.); children: Samuel Struthers, Mary Warwick; m. Barbara Sudler Maltby, June 25, 1994. BA, Harvard U., 1962. Reporter Newsday, Garden City, N.Y., 1963; writer, editor Newsweek, NYC, 1964; assoc. editor The New Leader, 1965; editor The Atlantic Monthly, Boston, 1966-70, mng. editor, 1970-76, exec. editor, 1976-77; spl. asst. to Sec. Cyrus Vance US Dept. State, Washington, 1977-78; editor Sunday mag. Boston Globe, 1978-81, asst. mng. editor, 1981-82, mng. editor, 1982-85, editor, 1985-86; fellow Harvard U. Inst. of Politics, 1986-87; exec. editor trade and reference div. Houghton Mifflin, 1987-89; prof., dean Medill Sch. Journalism Northwestern U., Evanston, Ill., 1989—96; dir. Nat. Arts Journalism prog. Columbia U., 1996—2011, prof. journalism, 1996—2011, prof. emeritus, 2011—14. Co-editor: Who We Are: An Atlantic Chronicle of the United States and Vietnam, 1969, A Story of Our Time: American Politics and the Press in an Era of Loss, 1999; author: Republic of Denial: Press, Politics and Public Life, 1999, Fall of the House of Roosevelt: Brokers of Ideas & Power from FDR to LBJ, 2004. Trustee Sta. WTTW-TV, 1991—. Served with AUS, 1963-64. Shaw Travelling fellow Harvard, 1962-63 Mem. American Antiquarian Soc., Phi Beta Kappa. Home: New York, NY. Died Apr. 17, 2014.

**JANG, JU-SEOG,** electrical engineering educator; b. Pusan, Korea, June 12, 1961; s. Moonduk and Myosun (Kim) J.; m. Hyun-Ju Ha, Oct. 19, 1989; children: Jin-Young, Ji-Young. BS, Pusan Nat. U., Republic of, 1984; MS, Korea Advanced Inst. Sci./Tech, Seoul, Korea, 1986, PhD, 1989. Rsch. assoc. U. Colo., Boulder, 1989-91; sr. rschr. Electronics and Telecom. Rsch. Inst., Taejon, Korea, 1991-93; lectr. Nat. Fisheries U. Pusan, 1993-95; asst. prof. Pukyong Nat. U., from 1995. Vis. assoc. Calif. Inst. Tech., Pasadena, 1994-95. Contbr. articles to profl. jours. Recipient Acad. award Korean Inst. Elec. Engrs., 1989, Paper award Optical Soc. Korea, 2001. Home: Haeundae-Gu Pusan, Republic of Korea. Died June 10, 2004.

**JANISCHEWSKYJ, WASYL,** electrical engineering educator; b. Prague, Czechoslovakia, Jan. 21, 1925; arrived in Can., 1950; s. Ivan and Hanna (Ravych) J.; m. Emilia Miszczuk; children: Roxolana, Marko. Student, Tech. U. Hannover, Fed. Republic of Germany, 1948-50; B of Applied Sci., U. Toronto, 1952, M of Applied Sci., 1954; Hon. Doctor, Natl. Tech. U. of Ukraine Polytechnical Inst., Kyiv, 1998. Registered profl. engr., Ont. Testing engr. Moloney Electric Co., Toronto, Can., summer 1952; demonstrator/instr. U. Toronto, 1952-55, lectr. to prof., 1959-90, prof. emertius, from 1990, asst. dept. head elec. engring., 1964-70, assoc. dean faculty of applied sci. and engring., 1978-82; elec. engr. Aluminium Labs., Kingston, Ont., 1955-59; elect. engr. NRC, Ottawa, Ont., Can., summer 1961, Ont. Hydro, Toronto, Can., summers 1962-65. Contbr. over 100 articles to profl. jours. Fellow IEEE; mem. Internat. Elec. Commn., Internat. Conf. on Large High Vol. Elec. Systems, Can. Elec. Assn., Assn. Profl. Engrs. Ont., Taras Shevchenko Sci. Soc., Ukrainian Free Acad. Scis. Mem. Ukranian Orthodox Ch. Home: Toronto, Canada. Deceased.

**JANKE, KENNETH,** investment consultant; b. Ft. William, Ont., Can., May 13, 1934; s. Adolf Earthman and Julianna (Dika) J.; m. Sally Mildred Roach, June 29, 1957; children: Kenneth Stuart, Laura Lynn, Julie Ann. Student, Mich. State U., East Lansing, 1952-56. Asst. mgr. Household Fin. Co., Detroit, 1958—60; gen. mgr. Nat. Assn. Investors, Royal Oak, Mich., 1960—76, pres., CEO, 1976—2002, chmn., CEO, from 2002. Bd. dirs. Investment Edn. Inst., Royal Oak, pres. 1995-2002, chmn., 2002—; bd. dirs. World Fedn. Investors, Brussels, pres., 1995—. Author: Ask Mr. Naic, 1982, Golf Is A Funny Game (But It Wasn't Meant To Be), 1992, Starting and Running a Profitable Investment Club, 1996, Firsts, Facts, Feats and Failures in the World of Golf, 2006; co-author: Wit and Wisdom of Golf, 1997, The Love of Golf, 2007; columnist mag. Better Investing. Chmn. Mich. Golf Hall of Fame, Lake Orion; pres. Am. Cancer Soc.-Oakland Country, Southfield, Mich., 1974-75; pres., bd. dirs. NAIC Growth Fund, Royal Oak; bd. dirs. AFLAC, Inc., Columbus, Ga.; bd. advisors Mich. PGA, West Bloomfield. With U.S. Army, 1956-58, ETO. Recipient Disting. Svc. award Investment Edn. Inst., 1972, Founder award Am. Cancer Soc., 1970; inductee Dearborn Sports Hall of Fame, Mich., 2002.

Fellow Fin. Analysts Soc. Detroit (pres. 1984—), Fin. Analysts Fedn.; mem. Nat. Investor Rels. Inst. (pres. Detroit 1985—), We. Golf Assn. (bd. dirs., pres.), Indianwood Golf and Country Club (Lake Orion, Inductee Mich. Golf Hall of Fame, 2008), NFL Alumni (Lauderdale, Fla.), Scalawag's Country Club (Mt. Clemens, Mich.), Masons. Republican. Episcopalian. Avocation: golf. Home: Bloomfield Hills, Mich. Died July 23, 2011.

**JARUZELSKI, WOJCIECH,** former President of Poland; b. Kurow, Lublin, July 6, 1923; m. Barbara Jaruzelski; 1 child, Monika Grad., Gen. Karol Swierczewski Acad. Gen. Staff. Served with Polish Armed Forces in USSR and Poland, 1943-45; various Sr. Army posts, 1945-65; chief of Central Polit. Dept. of Armed Forces, 1960-65, chief gen. staff, 1965-68; dep. minister of Nat. Def., 1962-68, minister, 1968-83; chmn. Nat. Def. Com., 1983-90, premier, 1981-85, brig. gen. 1956, div. gen., 1960, gen. arms, 1968, gen. of army, 1973; mem. Polish United Workers' Party Central Com., 1964-90, mem. Polit. Bur., 1971-89; 1st sec., 1981-89; dep. to Seym, 1961, 85; v.p. Chief Council of Union of Fighters for Freedom and Democracy, 1972-89; chmn. Mil. Council Nat. Salvation, 1981-83; mem. presidium All-Poland Com. Nat. Unity Front, 1981-83; provisional mem. Nat. Council Patriotic Movement for Nat. Rebirth, 1982-83, mem., 1983-89; pres. Republic of Poland, 1989-90. Decorations include Order of Builders of People's Poland, Order of Banner of Labour (1st class), Knight's Cross of Order of Polonia Restituta, Silver Cross of Virtuti Militari and Cross of Valour, Medal of 30th Anniversary of People's Poland, Order of Red Banner (USSR), Order of Lenin, others. United Workers' Party. Died May 25, 2014.

**JASRAI, PUNTSAGIIN,** former Prime Minister of Mongolia; b. Gobi-Altai Province, Mongolia, Nov. 26, 1933; s. Puntsag Jaltsav and Dulmaa Manlai; m. Dulamsuren Luvsan, Apr. 1, 1959; children: Delgermaa, Jamsran, Jantsan. Diploma in Econs., Inst. of Econs., Moscow, 1961; candidate of scis., Acad. of Scis., Ulaanbaatar, Mongolia, 1971. Tchr. Local Primary Sch., Gobi-Altai, Mongolia, 1950-54, State Econs. Coll., Ulaanbaatar, Mongolia, 1961-65; adminstrv. officer Local Govt., Gobi-Altai, 1954-56; dep. dir. Nat. Stats. Bur., Ulaanbaatar, 1966-70; dir. Nat. Com. of Prices and Stds., Ulaanbaatar, 1970-76; dep. Peoples Great Hural, Ulaanbaatar, 1974-92; mgr. of dept. Mongolian People's Revolutionary Party, Ulaanbaatar, 1976-78; 1st dep. dir. State Planning Com., Ulaanbaatar, 1978-84, dir., 1984-89; dep. chmn. Coun. of Ministers, Ulaanbaatar, 1984-89; chmn. Assn. Indsl. and Svc. Cooperatives, Ulaanbaatar, 1989-92; prime min. Govt. of Mongolia, Ulaanbaatar, 1992—96; M.P. State Great Hural, Ulaanbaatar, from 1992. Dir. Assn. Mongolian Consumers Co-operatives, 1990. Author: Methodology of Statistics, 1967, Calculations of Costs of Agricultural Products, 1974. Active Ctrl. Com. Mongolian Revolutionary Youth Union, Ulaanbaatar, 1970-74. Decorated Order of Red Banner, Order of Polar Star; recipient Honor medal Peoples Great Hural, 1971, 81. Avocations: music, poetry, ice skating, hiking. Died Oct. 25, 2007.

**J.C., Mrs. See COTHREN, EVANGELINE**

**JEBSEN, ATLE,** ship owner; b. Bergen, Norway, Nov. 10, 1935; s. Kristian Stange and Sigfrid (Kjerland) Jebsen; m. Arnhild Hoivik Jebsen; children: Arne Lange, Sissi, Bjorn. BA in Economics, Queens Coll., Cambridge, Eng., 1959, MA, 1961. Chartering clk. broker A/S Kristian Jebsens Rederi, Dreggen, Bergen, 1962—65; mng. dir., chmn., CEO A/S AJ Marine Svcs. (formerly Jebsen-Group's); chmn. bd. dirs. Den Norske Krigsforsikringen for Skib, Oslo, Bedriftsforsamling Elkem A/S; chmn. Jebsens Drilling; bd. dirs. Norwegian Export Coun., BP Norway, Ltd. U.A.; chmn. Norges Skipshypotek, Ltd., 1978—86; bd. dirs. The Baltic & Internat. Maritime Coun., pres., 1985—87. Mem.: Norwegian Shipowner's Mut. War Risk Ins. Assn. (chmn.), Norwegian Shipping & Offshore Fedn. (bd. dirs., pres. 1982—83, chmn. fin. com.), Norwegian Shipowners Assn. (pres. 1982—83). Avocations: tennis, fishing, mountain climbing. Home: Store Milde, Norway. Died Oct. 13, 2009.

**JEFFARES, ALEXANDER NORMAN,** academic advisor; b. Dublin, Aug. 11, 1920; s. Cecil Norman and Agnes (Fraser) J.; m. Jeanne Agnes Calembert; 1 child, Felicity Anne Jeffares Sekine. MA, U. Oxford, Eng., 1946, D Philosophy, 1948; MA, PhD, U. Dublin, Ireland; PhD (hon.), U. Lille, France, 1975. Prof. English lit. U. Edinburgh, S. Australia, 1951-56; dept. chmn., prof. English lit. U. Leeds, Eng., 1957-74; prof. English lit. U. Stirling, Scotland, 1974-86; mng. dir. Academic Adv. Svcs., Ltd., Crail, Scotland, from 1977. Bd. dirs. Colin Smythe, Ltd., Eng. Author: History of Anglo-Irish Literature, 1982, A New Commentary on Yeats's Poems, 1986; (with A. Kamm) An Irish Childhood, W.B. Yeats, A New Biography, 1988, A Jewish Childhood, 1988, Yeats's Poems, 1989, Yeats's Vision, 1990, (poems) Brought Up in Dublin, 1987, Brought Up to Leave, 1987. Vice-chmn. Muckhart Community Coun., Scottish Arts Coun. Fellow Royal Soc. Lit., Royal Soc. Edinburgh (v.p.), Australian Acad. Humanities, Trinity Coll. (hon.); mem. Arts Coun. London, Royal Commonwealth Soc., Scottish Pen (chmn.), Book Trust Scotland (pres.), Athenaeum Club. Anglican. Home: Crail, Scotland. Died June 1, 2005.

**JEFFERIES, WILLIAM MCKENDREE,** internist, educator; b. Richmond, Va., Oct. 1, 1915; s. Richard Henry and Mary Adeline (Harris) J.; m. Jeanne Telfair Mercer, Dec. 28, 1946 (dec. Dec., 1991); children: Richard Mercer, Scott McKendree, Colin Tucker, Leslie McLaurin. BA summa cum laude, Hampden Sydney Coll., 1935; MD, U. Va., 1940. Diplomate Am. Bd. Internal Medicine. Instr. in Math., Physics, Chemistry McGuires Univ. Sch., Richmond, Va., 1936; resident Mass. Gen. Hosp., Boston, 1940-42; flight surgeon San Antonio Aviation Cadet Ctr., 1942; post surgeon India China Div. Air Transport Command, 1943-45, divsn. med. inspector, 1945; rsch. fellow Am. Cancer Soc. Com. on Growth NRC Harvard Med. Sch., Boston, 1946-49; from instr. to asst. prof. medicine Case Western Reserve Med. Sch., Cleve., 1949-92; clin. prof. medicine U. Va. Sch. of Medicine, Charlottesville, from 1993. Mem. internship com. Univ. Hosps., Cleve., 1955-65; bd. dirs. Brush Found., 1966-67; mem. com. for human investigation Luth. Med. Ctr., Cleve., 1977-92; chmn. diabetes adv. com. Euclid Gen. Hosp., Cleve., 1979-82. Author: (med. books) Safe Uses of Cortisone, 1981, Safe Uses of Cortisol, 1996; contbr. articles to profl. jours., chpts. to books. Com. mem. Boy Scouts Am., Shaker Heights, Ohio, 1957-68; past chmn. coun. of deacons, bd. of ministry and fellowship Plymouth Ch. of Shaker Heights. Lt. col. med. corps U.S. Army (attached to air force) India Burma Theatre. Fellow ACP; mem. AAAS, SAR, AMA, N.Y. Acad. Scis., Albemarle County Med. Soc., Am. Thyroid Assn. (Van Meter award 1949), Clin. Immunology Soc., Endocrine Soc., Am. Fertility Soc., Am. Fedn. for Clin. Rsch., Ctrl. Soc. for Clin. Rsch., Friends of Nat. Libr. of Medicine, Am. Legion, Cheshire Cheese Club, Raven Soc., Phi Beta Kappa, Omicron Delta Kappa, Alpha Omega Alpha, Kappa Alpha, Phi Beta Pi. Avocations: golf, fly fishing, skiing. *Anything worth doing is worth doing to the best of your ability.* Deceased.

**JEFFERS, JOHN WILLIAM,** lawyer; b. NYC, May 11, 1936; s. William Hicks and Thelma Leone (Seeger); m. Theresa Kathleen Jeffers; children: Michael D., Thomas W., James B., John P. AB cum laude, Harvard U., Cambridge, Mass., 1958; JD, U. Pa., Phila., 1964. Bar: Ohio, 1964, U.S. Dist. Ct. (no. dist.) Ohio 1965. Assoc. Rosenthal,Roesch, Buckman & McLandrich, Cleve., 1964-67, Weston, Hurd, Fallon, Paisley & Howley, Cleve., 1967-71, ptnr., from 1971. Capt. USMC. Mem. Ohio Assn. Civil Trial Attys. (chmn. med. malpractice com. 1987-94, 2006, exec. com. 1990-97), Cleve. Bar Assn. (past chmn. Cuyahoga County Common Pleas and Ct. Appeals com.). Avocations: travel, tennis, golf, bicycling. Died 2014.

**JEFFORDS, JIM (JAMES MERRILL JEFFORDS),** former United States Senator from Vermont; b. Rutland, Vt., May 11, 1934; s. Olin Merrill and Marion (Hausman) J.; m. Elizabeth Daley, 1961 (div. 1978); remarried Aug. 26, 1986 (dec. April 13, 2007); children: Leonard Olin, Laura Louise. BS, Yale U., 1956; LLB, Harvard U., 1962. Bar: Vt. 1962. Law clk. to Hon. Ernest Gibson US Dist. Ct. Vt., 1962—63; ptnr. Bishop, Crowley & Jeffords LLP, Rutland, 1963-66, Kenney, Carbine & Jeffords LLP, Rutland, 1966-69; atty. gen. State of Vt., Montpelier, 1969—73; ptnr. George E. Rice, Jr. & James M. Jeffords, 1973-74; mem. US Congress from Vt. at-large Dist., 1975—89, US House Agrl. Com., 1978-79; US Senator from Vt., 1989—2007; chmn. US Senate Health, Edn., Labor, & Pensions Com., 1997—2001, US Senate Health, Edn., Labor & Pensions Com., 2001, US Senate Environment & Pub. Works Com., 2001—03. Town agt. Shrewsbury, 1964-68, zoning adminstr., 1966-68; mem. Jud. Selection Bd., 1967-68; chmn. Hwy. Dept. Investigating Com., 1968; mem. Vt. State Senate, 1967-68; mem. Nat. Commn. on Employment and Unemployment Stats., 1978-89, Congl. Tourism Caucus, 1979-89 Author: My Declaration of Independence, 2001, An Independent Man: Adventures of a Public Servant, 2003. Served in USNR, 1956-59; capt. Res. (ret.). Mem. ABA, Vt. Bar Assn., Rutland County Bar Assn., American Judicature Soc. (dir. 1973-76), VFW, Lions, Elks. Independent. Home: Wilmington, NC. Died Aug. 18, 2014.

**JEJEEBHOY, JAMSETJEE,** social worker; b. Bombay, Apr. 19, 1913; s. Rustamjee and Soonabai Rustamjee Jamsetjee; m. Shirin Jehangir Cama, Oct. 3, 1943; children: Ayesha Jamsetjee, Rustom Jamsetjee. BA, St. Xavier's Coll., Bombay, 1935. Bd. dirs. Beaulieu Investment Pvt. Ltd., Bombay. Chmn. emeritus M.F. Cama Athorman Inst., M.M. Cama Edn. Fund, Bombay; chmn. Sir Jamsetjee Jejeebhoy Charity Funds, Bombay, Sir Jamsetjee Jejeebhoy Parsee Benevolent Instn., Bombay, Seth Rustamjee Jamsetjee Jejeebhoy Gujarat Schs. Fund, Bombay, Iran League, Bombay, Bombay Panjrapole, Framjee Cowasjee Inst., Bombay; trustee Byramjee Jeejeebhoy Parsee Charitable Instn., Bombay, A H Wadia Charity Trust, Bombay, Parsee Surat Charity Fund, Bombay, Destitute Eranee's Charity Fund and Dharamshala, Bombay, Cowasji Behramji Divecha Charity Trust, Bombay, Ashburner Fire Temple, Bombay, Zoroastrian Bldg. found., Bombay; mem. exec. com. B D Petit Parsee Gen. Hosp., Bombay. Named Hon. Freeman and Liveryman, Worshipful Co. of Clockmakers, Eng., 1995. Mem. Malabar Hill Club, Willingdon Sports Club (Bombay), Royal Western India Turf Club (Bombay), Ripon Club (Bombay). Avocations: coin collecting/numismatics, collecting curios and objets d'art. Home: Bombay, India. Died Aug. 10, 2006.

**JELJASZEWICZ, JANUSZ,** microbiologist, researcher; b. Wilno, Poland, Aug. 8, 1930; s. Aleksander and Helena (Talkowska) Jeljaszewicz Budna; m. Antonina Kraucka, Jan. 15, 1963 (div. Oct. 1969); m. Anna Szczesna Dabrowska, Feb. 11, 1995; children: Malgorzata, Anna. MD, Univ. Med. Sch., Poznan, Poland, 1954, PhD, 1959. Cert. in med. microbiology. Asst. dept. microbiology Univ. Med. Sch., Poznan, 1954-60, sr. asst. Warsaw, Poland, 1960-65; head rsch. project CDC, USPHS, Atlanta, 1963-80; chmn. Coordinating Commn. for U.S.-Poland Sci. Collaboration, Warsaw, 1963-90; head Lab. Bacteriology Nat. Inst. Hygiene, Warsaw, 1963-80, prof., chmn. dept. bacteriology, 1977-80, head Lab. Bacteriol. Metabolites, 1980-96, dir., from 1996. Chmn. sci. adv. coun. to Min. of Health Poland, Warsaw, 1978-88; vis. prof. Med. Faculty, U. Cologne, Germany, 1973—; expert on acute bacterial infections WHO, 1973—. Editor 28 books; contbr. more than 400 articles to profl. jours. Fellow Infectious Diseases Soc. Am.; mem. AAAS, Am. Soc. for Microbiology, N.Y. Acad. Scis., Deutsche Gesellschaft für Mikrobiologie, others. Avocations: collecting books, understanding human motivation, history. Home: Warsaw, Poland. Died May 7, 2001.

**JELLISON, RICHARD MARION,** retired history professor; b. Muncie, Ind., Dec. 26, 1924; s. Carl R. and Leora Melvina (Folkner) J.; m. Kathleen Elizabeth Frick, May 5, 1945; children: Richard G., Stephanie L., Leslie N. BS, Ball State U., 1948; MA, Ind. U., 1949, PhD in American Colonial & Econ. History, 1953. Instr. history Ind. U., Bloomington, 1952-56; instr. Mich. State U., East Lansing, 1956-58; assoc. prof. Eastern Ill. U., Charleston, 1958-62; prof. Miami U., Oxford, Ohio, 1962—91, chmn. dept. history, 1971—88, prof. emeritus, 1991—2013. Lectr. U. Berlin, 1966, Siena, Italy, 1968, Budapest, Hungary, 1974 Author: Society, Freedom and Conscience: The American Revolution in Virginia, Massachusetts and New York, 1976; contbr. articles to profl. jours. Served with U.S. Navy, 1942-44, PTO. Colonial Williamsburg summer research fellow, 1958-62; recipient Effective Educator award Miami U. Alumni Assn., 1985 Mem. American Hist. Assn., Inst. Early American Culture, American Assn. History Medicine, Orgn. American Historians, Internat. Soc. History Medicine, Ohio Hist. Soc., Ind. Hist. Soc., S.C. Hist. Soc., AAUP (pres. Miami U. chpt. 1967) Home: Bluffton, SC. Died Nov. 5, 2013.

**JEMISON, T.J. (THEODORE JUDSON JEMISON),** retired religious organization administrator; b. Selma, Ala., Aug. 1, 1918; m. Celestine C. Catlett, 1945; childrne: Bettye Jane, Dianne Frances, Theodore Judson Jr. BS, Ala. State Coll., 1940; MA in Div., Union U., 1945; DD, Natchez Coll., 1953, Union U., 1971. Ordained to ministry Bapt. Church, 1945. Pastor, minister Mt. Zion Bapt. Ch., Staunton, 1945-49, Mt. Zion 1st Bapt. Ch., Baton Rouge, 1949—53; gen. sec. Nat. Bapt. Conv. U.S.A., Inc., 1953-87, pres., 1987—94. Mem. bd. cen. Nat. Council Churches in U.S. Named Minister of Yr. Nat. Beta Club, 1973, Citizen of Yr. for Outstanding Contbns. in Civics, Recreation, Edn. City of Baton Rouge; recipient Disting. Service award East Baton Rouge Edn. Assn., 1973. Mem. Alpha Phi Alpha. Lodges: Shriners, Masons. Died Nov. 15, 2013.

**JENKINS, CLARA BARNES,** psychology educator; b. Franklinton, NC, 1943; d. Walter and Steffa (Griffin) Barnes; m. Hugh Jenkins, Dec. 24, 1949 (div. Feb. 1955). BS, Winston-Salem State U., 1939; MA, N.C. Ctrl. U., 1947; EdD, U. Pitts., 1964; postgrad., NYU, 1947—48, U. N.C., 1963, N.C. Agrl. and Tech. State U., 1971. Cert. notary pub. N.C. Tchr. pub. schs., Wendell, NC, 1939—43, Wise, NC, 1943—45; mem. faculty Fayetteville State U., 1945—53, Rust Coll., Holly Spring, Miss., 1953—58; asst. prof. Shaw U., 1958—64; prof. edn. and psychology St. Paul's Coll., Lawrenceville, Va., 1964—91. Vis. prof. edn. Friendship Jr. Coll., Rock Hill, SC, 1947, N.C. Agrl. and Tech. State U., 1966—83. Former mem. bd. dirs. Winston-Salem State U.; bd. dirs. annual giving fund U. Pitts. Named United Negro Coll. Fund Faculty fellow, 1963—64; grantee, Am. Bapt. Conv., 1963—64. Mem.: APA, AAAS, AAUW, NEA, AAUP, So. Poverty Law Ctr., Leadership Coun., Soc. Profls. Edn., Philosophy Edn. Soc., Jean Piaget Soc., Soc. Rsch. in Child Devel., Acad. Polit. Sci., Am. Soc. Notaries, Am. Assn. Higher Edn., Doctoral Assn. Educators, History Edn. Soc., Assn. Tchr. Educators, Internat. Platform Assn., Am. Acad. Polit. and Social Sci., Va. Edn. Assn., Am. Hist. Assn., Nat. Soc. for Study Edn., Kappa Delta Pi, Phi Delta Kappa, Zeta Phi Beta, Phi Eta Kappa. Episcopalian. *Indeed, it is helpful to mankind to have worthwhile experiences in life. Individuals who are fortunate enough to have had mountain top experiences should share them with others in the valley below.* Died Apr. 2, 1999.

**JENKINS, DAVID ALAN,** association executive; b. Corning, Iowa, Dec. 16, 1952; s. Roy Bennett and Patricia Sue (Burton) Jenkins; m. Kim Renee Hooten, Mar. 17, 1979; 2 children. BME, U. Idaho, 1974; MM, Ohio U., 1977. Gen. mgr. trainee Affiliated Home Ctrs., 1976—77; adminstrv. resident Meth. Hosps. Dallas, 1978—79, dir. comm., 1979—80, project coord., mktg. analyst, 1979—80; v.p. Oak Cliff C. of C., Dallas, 1980, acting gen. mgr., 1980—81, exec. v.p., 1981—82, pres., 1982—83; exec. v.p. Odessa C. of C., 1983—85; pres. Met. Evansville C. of C., from 1985. Mem. adminstrv. bd. chmn. com. Altersgate United Meth. Ch., 1989; mem. regional mgmt. bd. Ind. Corp. for Sci. and Tech., from 1989; bd. dirs. region V Small Bus. Adminstrn., from 1988. Named one of Outstanding Young Men of Am., 1981, 1982. Mem.: Ind. C. of C. (pres.-elect), SBA of Indpls., Ind. Commerce Execs. Assn. (bd. dirs. from 1987, pres. 1990—91), Am. C. of C. Execs. (emerging cities task force, info. cen. com. 1989). Republican. Meth. Avocations: golf, fishing, family activities, entertaining, travel. Died Nov. 15, 2009.

**JENKINS, JON C.,** writer, educator; b. Salt Lake City, Mar. 5, 1943; arrived in The Netherlands, 1992; s. Oscar Walker and H. Donnell Jenkins; m. Maureen A. Raphael, Oct. 16, 1946; children: Jean-Paul M., Michael-James M. Dir. Imaginal Tng., Groningen, The Netherlands, from 1992, e-maginal Works, Groningen, The Netherlands, from 2000. Editor: The Encyclopedia of World Problems and Human Potential, 1991; author: (book) The Other World in the Midst of This World, 1997, The Social Process Triangles, 1997; (CD ROM) The International Facilitator's Companion, 1999. With USN, 1960-64. Mem. ASTD, Internat. Assn. Facilitators. Home: Groningen, Netherlands. Died Apr. 6, 2010.

**JENSEN, MARY ANN,** retired curator; b. Milw., Nov. 24, 1936; d. Marinus Christian and Anna Marie (Christensen) Jensen. Student, Lawrence Coll., 1957; BA, Downer Coll., 1958; postgrad, U. Wis., 1963. Asst. dir., acting dir. Wis. Ctr. Theatre Rsch., Madison, 1963—66; curator of theatre collection Princeton U., NJ, 1966—2000; cons. Shubert Archives, NYC, 1976—78. Compiler exhbn. catalogue, Let Joy Be Unconfined, 1981. Contbr. articles to profl. jours. Mem.: ALA, U.S. Inst. Theatre Tech., American Soc. Theatre Rsch. (editor newsletter 1968—72), Theatre Library Assn. (v.p. 1983—85), Coun. on Nat. Library & Info. Assn., Princeton (N.Y.C.). Episcopalian. Home: Princeton, NJ. Died Mar. 4, 2014.

**JIN, BA (LI YAOTANG),** writer; b. Chengdu, Sichuan, China, Nov. 25, 1904; m. Xiao Shan, 1944 (dec. 1972). Student, Fgn. Lang. Sch., Chengdu, 1925, Paris, France, 1927-28. Editor Ban Yue, 1928; editor-in-chief Wenhua shenghuo, Shanghai, 1935-38, 46; mem. editorial bd. Fenghuo, 1937-38, Na han, 1937; chief editor People's Lit. Pub. Ho., Beijing, 1957-58, Shanghai Lit., 1961; vice chmn. 5th Mcpl. Chinese People's Polit. Consultative Conf., 1977-83; mem. presidium 6th Nat. Congress, Chinese Communist Party, 1983-88; vice chmn. 7th Nat. Congress, Chinese Communist Party, from 1988. Branded as a counterrevolutionary and purged, 1968-77; vice chmn. China Fedn. Literary and Art Circles. Author: (fiction) Mie wang, 1929, Sichu de taiyang, 1930, Aiging de san buchu (Wu, Yu, Dian), 1931-33, Fuzhou, 1931, Guangming, 1931, Jiliu (Jia, Chun, Qiu), 1931-40, Hai de meng, 1932, Chuntian li de qiutian, 1932, Sha ding, 1932, Dian yi, 1932, Mobu, 1932, Yue ye, 1933, Xin sheng, 1933, Jiangjun, 1933, Mengya, 1933 (pub. as Xue, 1946), Chenmo, 1934, Lina, 1934, Shen, gui, ren, 1935, Chen luo, 1935, Fa de gushi, 1936, Lun luo, 1936, Chuang xia, 1936, Chang sheng ta, 1937, Hei tu, 1939, Ba Jin duanpian xiaoshuo xuanji, 1940, Short Stories of Ba Jin, 1941, Long, hu, gou, 1941, Huo (3 vols.), 1941-45, Feiyuan wai, 1942, Qi yuan, 1944, Huanhun Cao, 1945, Yaliannuo, 1945, Di-si bingshi, 1946, Xiao ren xiao shi, 1947, Han ye, 1947 (pub. as Cold Nights, 1978), Bai niao zhi ge, 1947, Qingye de bei ju, 1948, Ba Jin Xuanji, 1951, Piao bo, 1952, Women huishen liao Peng Dehuai si ling Yuan, 1953, Fu yu zi, 1953, Ba Jin duanpian xiaoshuo xuan, 1955, Baowei heping de renmen, 1955, Mingzhu he Yuji, 1957, Luoche shang, 1959, Li Dahai, 1961, Short Stories, 1978, Autumn in Spring and Other Stories, 1981, Sanwen suibi xuan, 1982, Duanpian xiaoshuo xuan, 1982, Bing zhong ji, 1984; (other) Zhiqiaogeko de canju, 1926, Wuzhengfuzhuyi yu shiji wenti, 1927, Duantoutai shang, 1929, Cong zibenzhuyi dao annaqizhuyi, 1930, Hai xing zaji, 1932, Lutu suibi, 1934, Ba Jin zizhuan, 1936, Diandi, 1935, Menjianir, 1935, Ba Jin xuanji, 1936, Sheng zhi chanhui, 1936, Eguo xuwuzhuyi yundong shihua, 1936, Ziyou xue: wuyi xundaozhe de wu shu zhounian, 1937, Zhanzheng yu jingji, 1937, Duan jian (2 vols.), 1937, Meng yu zui, 1938, Xibanya de shuguang, 1939, Lutu tongxun (2 vols.), 1940, Wu ti, 1941, Kong su, 1941, Lutu zaji, 1946, Huainian, 1947, Huashacheng de jieji, 1951, Ba Jin xuanji, 1951, Ba Jin daibiao zuoxuan, 1951, Shenghuo de hui L, 1953, Yingxiong de gushi, 1953 (pub. as Living Amongst Heroes, 1954), Tan Jiehefu, 1955, Ba Jin sanwen xuan, 1955, Da huanle de rizi, 1957, Ba Jin wenji (14 vols.), 1958-62, Xin sheng ji, 1959, Youyi ji, 1959, Zan ge ji, 1960, Qingtu bu jin de ganqing, 1963, Xianliang qiao pan, 1964, Sui xiang lu, 1979 (pub. as Random Thoughts, 1984), Tan zi ji, 1982, Ba Jin lun chuangzuo, 1983, Xiezuo shenghuo de huigu, 1984, Tong nian de huiyi, 1984, Bing zhong ji, 1984, Bei chuang ji shi, 1985, Ba Jin quan ji (8 vols.), 1986-90, Dangdai zawen xuancui, 1986, Ren sheng de taiyang: Zuojia yishujia zhi qingshao nian, 1988, Selected Works of Ba Jin (2 vols.), 1988, Chang he bu jin lui: huainian Shen Congwen xiansheng, 1989, Kangzhan jishi, 1989; editor: Tao huang, 1942. Mem. Cultural and Ednl. Commn., 1949-54. Recipient Internat. Friendship medal (USSR), 1990. Mem. Chinese Writers Anti-Aggression Assn. (founder), China Assn. Lit. Workers, All-China Fedn. Lit. and Art Circles (vice-chmn. 1953), China People's Union Chinese Writers (vice chmn. 1953, chmn. 1958-68), Afro-Asian Writers' Congress (dep. chief 1958), Sino-Soviet Friendship Assn. (v.p. 1959-68), China Welfare Inst., China Fedn. Lit. and Art Circles (vice-chmn.), China PEN (pres.), Nat. Lit. Found. (pres. 1986-89). Died Oct. 17, 2005.

**JMOR, SALAH ABDULRAHMAN,** import/export company executive, educator; b. Qoratou, Iraq, June 27, 1956; s. Adulrahman-Aga Jihanbakhsh-Aga and Bedria Majid-Khan Jmor; m. Taban Ahmad Ali-Agha, May 30, 1990; children: Alan, Saman, Ary. BSc, U. Sulaimaniya, Iraq, 1978; BA, Geneva U., 1984, MA, 1987, MA, 1988, PhD, 1992. BSC, Engineering, U. of Sulaimaniya/ Iraq, 1978. Rep. Kurdish Nat. Liberation Movements UN, Geneva, 1982—92; dir., ptnr. Jmor Bus. & Consulting, Geneva, 1992—2003; dir. Global Trade Inst., Geneva, 2001—05. Vis. assoc. prof. European U., Geneva, 1994—96, City U., Zurich, 1995—96, Bus. Sch. Lausanne, Switzerland, 1996—97, Thunderbird, Phoenix, 1996—99, Internat. U., Geneva, 1998—2002; assoc. prof. Kent (Ohio) State U., 1998—2003. Author: The Origin of Kurdish Question, Practice of International Trade; contbr. articles to profl. jours. Founder, leader Kurdistan Nat. Congress, London, 1988—92, dep. Brussels, 2000—03; exec. dir. Jmor Found., Geneva, 2002—03. Mem.: Forum Suisse Politique Internat., State of World Forum, Inst. U. d'Etudes Dével. Allumni's Club, Inst. U. Hautes Etudes Internat. Alumni's. Home: Petit - Lancy, Switzerland. Died June 28, 2005.

**JOBE, FRANK WILSON,** orthopedic surgeon; b. Greensboro, NC, July 16, 1925; MD, Loma Linda U., Calif., 1956; PhD (hon.), U. Tokushima, Japan. Diplomate American Bd. Orthop. Surgery. Intern LA County Gen. Hosp., 1956-57, resident, orthop. surgery, 1960-64; staff Centinela Hosp. Med. Ctr., Inglewood, Calif., med. dir., bio mechanics; staff U. Southern Calif. Med. Ctr., L.A.; clin. prof. dept. orthopedics U. Southern Calif. Sch. Medicine; spl. adv. to chmn. L.A. Dodgers, 2008—14, team physician, 1968—2008. Authored several med. publications, books and chapters to books. Served in 101st Airborne Divsn. US Army, 1943—46. Decorated Bronze star, Combat Medical Badge; recipient Glider Badge, Dave Winfield Humanitarian award, Profl. Baseball Scouts Found., 2012; named to The American Orthopedic Soc. Sports Medicine Hall of Fame, The Profl. Baseball Athletic Trainers Hall of Fame. Fellow ACS, American Acad. Orthop. Surgeons (past mem., com. on sports medicine, chmn., com. on shoulder, 1982-87); mem. Western Orthop. Assn., LA Chpt. (program chmn., 1978-79), Internat. Soc. of the Knee (founding mem.), American Orthop. Assn., Major League Baseball Physicians Assn. (pres. 1976-77, sec. 1977-79), American Shoulder & Elbow Surgeons (founding mem., pres. 1985-86, Charles S. Near award, 1987, 1997), American Orthop. Soc. for Sports Medicine (founding mem., chmn. membership com., 1978-79, O'Donohue award, 1984). Achievements include being responsible for the procedure known as Tommy John surgery (LA Dodgers pitcher Tommy John, diagnosed with a career-threatening torn ulnar collateral ligament was repaired by this procedure). Died Mar. 6, 2014.

**JOHANSEN, ROBERT HENNY,** horticulturist, geneticist; b. Grafton, ND, July 26, 1922; m. Donna Joan Mootz, Jan. 17, 1948; children: Robert, Ann, Gail, Brian. BS agr., North Dakota AC, Fargo, ND, 1949, MS, 1954, PhD horticulture, 1964. Prof. emeritus North Dakota State U, 1993. Asst. (horticulture) North Dakota State U, Fargo, ND, 1950, asst. prof., 1957, assoc. prof., 1960, prof., 1993. Cons. Calbee Co., Japan, 1984. Author: (articles) Valley Potato Grower, 1992, (article) Nat. Potato Breeding Report, 1982—83, ND State Seed Jour., 1962—85, Am. Potato Jour., 1957—65; contbr. ICSV6 USN, 1944—96, USS Anteom. Recipient 25 yr. of svc. to ND, Quarter Century Club, 1974, Canner Packer, 1975, Meritorious, Red River Valley Potato Growers, 1978, Harvest Bowl, 1979, Outstanding Svc, Potato Chip/Snack Food Assoc., 1984, Excellence in Rsch., Grower Mag., 1984, Meml., SD Hort. Soc., 1985, Agr. of the Yr., Alpha Zeta, 1985, Outstanding Svc, US Seed Potato Industry, 1986, Appreciation Day, Walhalla Potato Growers, 1987, Appreciation, High Plains Vegetable Growers, 1989—90, Pioneer of the Yr., NW Farm Mgr. Assoc., 1990, Appreciation, CA Potato Growers, 1991, Excellence in Horticulture, R.L. Wodarz, 1981, Disting. Svc., Prairie Potato Coun., 1992; grantee funding, Frito-Lay, Red River Valley Potato Growers Assoc., Simplot, Snack Food Assoc., U of CA, USDA-ARS. Mem.: Faculty Senate, NDSU Harvest Bowl Comm. (V chmn. 1985, chmn. 1974—79, V chmn. 1980—81), Red River Valley Potato Ext. Adv. Comm., Potato Crop Adv. Comm., NCR 150 Potato Processing Comm. (sec. 1984), Potato Assoc. of Am. (pres. 1970—71), Potato Assoc. of Am. (life), Univ. Athletic Comm. (sec. 1978—79), Elks, VFW, Am. Legion. Lutheran. Achievements include featured in 1980 issue of Binford's Guide; first to finding new potato varieties; research in potato breeding; reducing sugar accumulation in potato clones; virus resistance. Avocation: gardening. Home: Centralia, Wash. Died July 18, 1996.

**JOHNELL, OLOF G.,** medical educator; s. Herbert Johnell; m. Inga Redlund-Johnell, Apr. 20, 1972; children: Anna, Kristina. Degree, U. Lund, 1991; MD, PhD. Vice chmn. sci. adv. bd. IOF, Nyon, Switzerland, from 2000; prof. U. Lund, Malmo, Sweden, from 1991. Assoc. editor: Jour. of Bone and Mineral Rsch., from 2003. Achievements include medical clinical research. Home: Malmo, Sweden. Died Apr. 2006.

**JOHNS, MARGY GOVER,** dean, educator; b. Somerset, Ky., Sept. 7, 1931; d. Milton E. and Margaret Ellen (Beattie) Gover; m. Jerry Johns, Dec. 15, 1951; 1 child, Joni Lynn Johns Gibson. BS, Ea. Ky. U., 1955, MA, 1965; postgrad., Purdue U., 1965-72. Tchr. Harlan County Sch. Bd., Somerset, 1955-59, Somerset Schs., 1959-65; with counseling and admissions dept. Somerset Community Coll., 1965-66, assoc. prof. polit. sci., community svcs. coord., 1979-84, community svc. coord., 1979-84, dir. extended programs, 1986-92, asst. acad. dean, from 1992, prof., 1992; bicentennial coord. State of Ky., Frankfort, 1975-76. Mem. State of Ky. Gov.'s Com. on Literacy; planner Ky. energy conservation program Murray State U.; presenter Nat. Conf. Adult Learning, 1990, 91, 92; mem. Nat. Quality in Off-Campus, 1991. Sec., v.p. Ky. Dem. Women, 1972-82, 5th dist. dir., 1978-80; del. Nat. Dem. Conv., 1976, 80, state del., 1992, 93, 94, 95, mem. exec. com., 1992; vice chmn. County Dem. Exec. Com., Somerset, 1980-83, 92—; pres. Pulaski County Dem. Women, 1993—, treas., 1995—. Mem. Somerset and Pulaski C. of C. (chmn. cert. cities 1988). Avocation: video tapes. Deceased.

**JOHNSEN, KJELL,** physicist, educator; b. Meland, Norway, June 11, 1921; s. Georg Martin and Borghild (Hagen) J.; m. Aase Birgitte Jordal, Dec. 29, 1945; children: Arnlaug, Georg Kjetil, Ottar. Elec. Engr., Tech. U. Norway, Trondheim, 1948, Dr. Techn., 1954. Asst. Tech. Univ. Norway, Trondheim, 1947-48; rsch. asst. Chr. Michelsen Inst., Bergen, Norway, 1948-52; physicist CERN, Geneva, Switzerland, 1952-57; prof. elec. engring. Tech. Univ. Norway, Trondheim, 1957-59; sr. scientist CERN, Geneva, 1959-86, project dir. ISR, 1966-74; part-time prof. physics U. Bergen, Norway, 1972-86; tech. dir. ISA project Brookhaven (N.Y.) Nat. Lab., 1979-82; ret., 1986. Mem. adv. bd. AT divsn. Los Alamos (N.Mex.) Nat. Lab., 1987-91; chmn. HERA machine evaluation com. Deutsches Elekronen-Synchrotron, Hamburg, Germany, 1984-91; chmn. evaluation com. Norwegian CERN activities Norway Dept. Edn., Oslo, 1991-92. Author numerous publs. in field; co-author: Circular Accelerators and Storage Rings, 1993. Recipient Norsk Data Physics prize Norwegian Phys. Soc., 1981, Robert R. Wilson prize Am. Phys. Soc., 1990. Hon. mem. Norwegian Acad. Tech. Scis. Home: La Rippe, Switzerland. Died July 18, 2007.

**JOHNSON, BARRY EDWARD,** retired mathematician; b. Woolwich, London, England, Aug. 1, 1937; s. Edward and Evelyn Mary Johnson; m. Jennifer Pat Munday (div. 1979); children: Martin, Susan, Adrian; m. Margaret Blyth Jones, Sept. 15, 1991. BSc, U. Tasmania, Australia, 1956; BSc with honors, U. Tasmania, 1957; PhD, U. Cambridge, Eng., 1961. Instr. U. Calif., Berkeley, 1962; vis. lectr. Yale U., New Haven, Conn.; lectr. U. Exeter, England, 1963—65, U. New Castle upon Tyne, England, 1965—68, reader, 1968—69; prof., 1969—2001. Vis. prof. U. Calif., Berkeley, 1990—91, vis. prof., 1999. Author: (Book) Cohomology of Banach Algebras, 1972. Named Fellow of the Royal Soc., 1978. Mem.: Am. Math. Soc., London Math. Soc. (pres. 1980—82). Home: Newcastle upon Tyne, England. Died May 5, 2002.

**JOHNSON, BRUCE CANNON,** lawyer; b. Conway, NC, Dec. 22, 1934; s. Russell Hagood and Mary Sue (Cannon) Johnson; m. Rosalyn Worell Railey, Dec. 24, 1961; children: Lynne, Amy, Jenny, Polly. AB, U. NC, 1957, LLB, 1960. Bar: NC 1960, US Ct. Mil. Appeals 1960, US Supreme Ct. 1963. Ptnr. Johnson, Johnson & Johnson, Conway, 1963—83, Johnson & Jones, Conway, 1984. Solicitor Recorders Ct., Jackson, NC, 1967—68; asst. solicitor Superior Ct., Jackson, 1967—68; dir. 1st Citizens Bank of Conway. Served to capt. US Army, 1960—63. Mem.: ABA, 6th Jud. Bar Assn. (pres. 1978), Northampton Bar Assn. (pres. 1978—80, 1984—86), NC.Acad. Trial Lawyers, Assn. Trial Lawyers Am., NC Bar Assn., Ruritan club, Masons lodge, Phi Beta Kappa. Democrat. Methodist. Home: Conway, NC. Died Oct. 15, 1995.

**JOHNSON, CURTISS SHERMAN,** writer, former publishing executive; b. Meriden, Conn., Apr. 7, 1899; s. Sherman Foster and Adele (Curtiss) Johnson; m. Mary Lawton Johnson, Sept. 12, 1922 (dec. 1968); children: Curtiss Sherman, Dorothy L.(dec.); m. Barbara Burleigh Johnson, Nov. 1968. BS, Wesleyan U., 1921. Advt. mgr. Manning Bowman & Co., Meriden, 1921—26; v.p. The Silex Co., Hartford, Conn., 1927—28; rep. Curtis Pub. Co., Phila., 1928—32; mem. staff Gov. Conn., 1940—46; pres. Curtiss Johnson Publs., Conn., 1946—60; v.p. Deep River Nat. Bank; dir. Deep River Savs. Bank; mem. Conn. Flood Control and Water Policy Commn., Hartford, 1954, Conn. Safety Commn.; dir. emeritus Middlesex Hosp. Author: Three Quarters of a Century, 1949, Politics and a Belly-Full, 1962, America's First Lady Boss, 1965, Deadline, 1969, History of Pratt-Read Corporation, 1976; co-author (with R. H. Macy): The Indomitable, 1964; co-author: (with Raymond E. Baldwin) Connecticut Statesman, 1972. Trustee Henry Whitfield State Mus.; chmn. emeritus Conn. River Mus. Lt., inf. US Army, maj. Conn. State Guard. Mem.: Conn. Editl. Assn. (pres. 1941—43). Home: 30 Bokum Rd Essex CT 06426-1532

**JOHNSON, DEWEY E(DWARD), JR.,** dentist; b. Charleston, SC, Mar. 19, 1935; s. Dewey Edward and Mabel (Momeier) Johnson. AB in Geology, U. N.C., 1957, DDS, 1961. Pvt. practice dentistry, Charleston, 1964-92; assoc. to Stanley H. Karesh, DDS Charleston, 1970-77; tech. market rschr., designer, 1970-90. Indsl. designer, various orgns., 1965, 75, 77, 88, 91, 92, 01. Served to lt. USNR, 1961-63. Mem. ADA, Royal Soc. Health, Charleston C. of C. (cruise ship com. 1969), Charleston Dental Soc., Hibernian Soc., Charleston Mus., Internat. Platform Assn., Charleston Libr. Soc., S.C. Hist. Soc., Gibbes Art Gallery, Preservation Soc. of Charleston, Navy League U.S., Optimist Club, Phi Kappa Sigma, Sigma Gamma Epsilon, Psi Omega. Achievements include various scientific and engineering designs; patentee in dental matrix device. Deceased.

**JOHNSON, EVANS COMBS,** historian; b. Valley, Ala., Nov. 14, 1922; s. John Will and Cordelia Combs (Harrell) J.; m. Betty Drees, Jan. 28, 1959. AB, U. Ala., 1943; MA, 1947; PhD, U. NC, 1953. Assoc. prof. history Huntingdon Coll., Montgomery, Ala., 1947—48; asst. prof. history Stetson U., DeLand, Fla., 1953—57; assoc. prof., 1957—69; prof., from 1969; chmn. dept., 1971—89. Author: (book) Oscar W. Underwood: A Political Biography, 1982 (James Sulzby award, 1982). With USAAF, 1943—44. Mem.: Phi Alpha Theta (chmn. manuscripts com. from 1983). Democrat. Episcopalian. Avocations: stock market, antiques. Home: De Land, Fla. Died 1998.

**JOHNSON, MARGUERITE ANNIE See ANGELOU, MAYA**

**JOHNSON, MARTIN CLIFTON, SR.,** retired physician; b. Santa Fe, Nov. 16, 1933; s. Henry J. and Dorothy (Clifton) J.; m. Priscilla Bollam, June 13, 1959; children: Martin Clifton II, Kurt B., Kirsten L. Ustach, Katharine E. AB, Stanford U., 1955, MD, 1959. Diplomate Am. Bd. Neurol. Surgery, Am. Bd. Pediat. Neurosurgery, Am. Bd. Forensic Examiners, Am. Bd. Forensic Medicine; cert. Homeland Security Level III. Intern in surgery Palo Alto (Calif.) Stanford U. Hosp., 1959-60; fellow in neurosurgery Mayo Found., Rochester, Minn., 1960-61; asst. resident gen. surgery Presbyn. Med. Ctr., San Francisco, 1963-64; asst. resident, sr. resident, chief resident in neurosurgery U. Cin., 1964-68; pvt. practice neurosurgery/pediat. neurosurgery Portland, Oreg., 1968-99. Lt. comdr. M.C. USNR, 1960-69; col. M.C. AUS, 1988-99, ret. Fellow ACS, Am. Acad. Pediats.; mem. AMA, Portland Met. Med. Soc.,Oreg. Neurosurg. Soc., Oreg. Med. Soc., Congress Neurol. Surgeons, Am. Assn. Neurol. Surgeons, Am. Assn. Pediatric Neurosurgery, Internat. Pediat. Soc. Neurological Surgery, Multnomah Athletic Club, Columbia Aviation Club. Home: Wilsonville, Oreg. Died Feb. 18, 2012.

**JOHNSON, RICHARD WALTER,** entrepreneur; b. Mpls., Oct. 2, 1928; s. Walter Benjamin and Evelyn (Peterson) J.; m. Marlys Jean Tiller, Feb. 21, 1988; children: Richard Walter, William Charles, Nancy Ann, Thomas Gregory, Michael Richard. BBA with distinction, U. Minn., 1949. C.P.A., Nebr., Ill. With Arthur Andersen & Co. (C.P.A.'s), 1949-74, mng. partner Omaha, 1960-74; chmn. bd., chief exec. officer Western Securities Co. of Del.,

Omaha, from 1975; pres., CEO Modern Equipment Co., Omaha, from 1975. Bd. dirs., exec. com. Jr. Achievement Omaha, 1962—, pres., 1966-67; gen. campaign chmn. Heart of the Midlands United Way, 1972, chmn. pacemaker sect. fund raising campaign, 1964, chmn. corporate standards com., 1966, assoc. gen. chmn., 1968, treas., mem. exec. com., 1969; bd. dirs. Fontenelle Forest Nature Ctr. Assn. Mid-Am. council Boy Scouts of Am., Omaha Symphony Assn., Omaha Big Bros. Assn., Omaha Playhouse Assn.; Trustee Creighton U. Pres.'s Council. Recipient One of Outstanding Young Men in Am. award, 1965, Gifford award Fontenelle Forest Assn., 1997. Mem. AICPA, Nebr. Soc. CPAs, Newcomen Soc. N.Am., Omaha C. of C. (chmn. membership rels. com. 1962—, bd. dirs. 1965-76, mem. exec. com., v.p. 1968-72), Omaha Club, Omaha Country Club, Garden of the Gods Club (Colorado Springs), Masons, Shriners, Rotary Internat., Beta Gamma Sigma, Beta Alpha Psi. Home: Omaha, Nebr. Deceased.

**JOHNSON, SAMUEL BRITTON,** ophthalmologist, educator; b. Canyon, Tex., Apr. 25, 1926; s. Lee Livingston and Clementine (Smith) J.; m. Peggy Ruth Boswell, June 25, 1949 (div. May 8, 1980); children: Margaret Neal, Lee Sayers, Alice Boswell; m. Barbara Jean Herfurth, Dec. 20, 1982. BS, West Tex. A&M, 1946; MD, Tulane U., 1948. Diplomate Am. Bd. Ophthalmology. Intern Knoxville (Tenn.) Gen. Hosp., 1948-49; resident New Orleans Eye, Ear, Nose and Throat Hosp., 1949-50; chief resident New Orleans EENT Hosp., 1952-53; staff mem. ophthalmology Army Hosp., Ft. Sill, 1950-51, Navy, Quantico, Va., 1951-52; pvt. practice Jackson, Miss., 1953-55; prof., chmn. dept. ophthalmology med. sch. U. Miss., Jackson, from 1955; chief ophthalmology svc. Univ. Hosp., Jackson, from 1955. Chmn. exec. com. State Comprehensive Plan Blind, Jackson, 1984-85, State Plan Svc. Blind, 1988-89; cons. in field. Author: (with others) Rhoades Textbook of Surgery, 1977, Textbook of Rehabilitation Counseling, 1993. Mem., pres., chmn. bd. dirs. Miss. Opera, Jackson, 1953-77, hon. bd. dirs. chmn. in perpituity, 1977—; mem. exec. com., trustee Miss. Sch. Blind, Deaf & Rehab.-Blind, 1979-89. Lt. USNR. Fellow ACS, Am. Acad. Ophthalmology, Law-Sci. Acad. Am.; mem. AMA, Miss. Eye, Ear, Nose and Throat Soc. (pres. 1969-70), La.-Miss. Ophthalmology and Otorhinolaryngology (pres. 1970), Ctrl. Med. Soc. of Miss. (pres. 1972-73), Miss. State Med. Soc., Signature/Royal Maid Blind Industries, Inc. (bd. dirs. 1985—). Avocation: aviation. Home: Jackson, Miss. Deceased.

**JOLLY, ALISON BISHOP,** zoologist, author; b. Ithaca, NY, May 9, 1937; d. Morris Gilbert and Alison Mason (Kingsbury) Bishop; m. Richard Jolly, Oct. 12, 1963; children: Margaretta, Susan Alison, Arthur Morris, Richard Brabazon. BA, Cornell U., 1958; PhD, Yale U., 1962. Rsch. assoc. NY Zool. Soc., Bronx, NY, 1962—64; part-time tchr. Cambridge U., 1967—69, Sussex U., Brighton, 1971—74, 1978—81, vis. scientist, 2000—14; guest investigator Rockefeller U., NYC, 1982—87; vis. lectr. Princeton U., 1987—2000. Author: Lemur Behavior, 1966, The Evolution of Primate Behavior, 1972, 2nd edit., 1985, A World Like Our Own: Man and Nature in Madagascar, 1980, Luna's Legacy: Sex and Intelligence in Human Intelligence, 1999, Lords and Lemurs: Mad Scientists, Kings with Spears, and the Survival of Diversity in Madagascar, 2004; editor: Madagascar, 1981, (BBC-TV) Tropical Time Machine, 1983, Monkey in the Mirror, 1995; co-editor: Play, 1976. Fellow: AAAS; mem.: Duke U. Primate Ctr. (bd. visitors from 1982), Wildlife Preservation Trust Internat. (coun. mem. from 1978, bd. dirs.), Internat. Soc. Primatologists (pres.). Home: New York, NY. Died Feb. 6, 2014.

**JONES, BEN,** former Grenadian Prime Minister, government official, lawyer; b. St. Andrews, Aug. 5, 1924; Student, Chiswick Poly., London, Gray's Inn, U. London. With solicitors firm, London, 1962-64; pvt. practice Grenada, 1964-65; magistrate St. George's, Grenada, 1965-66; sr. asst. sec. Grenada Ministry External Affairs, St. George's, 1966-67; opposition senator St. George's, 1967-79; dep. prime min., 1984—89; min. legal affairs, 1985-88; atty.-gen., 1987-88; min. external affairs, 1985-90; min. agr., forestry, lands, from 1987; min. of tourism, 1987-90; min. of fisheries, 1990—91; prime min., 1989—90; pvt. practice lawyer, 1991—2001. Avocations: tennis, gardening, reading. Died Feb. 10, 2005.

**JONES, BILLIE MCCLEARY,** retired music educator; b. Seattle, July 10, 1913; d. William Smith and Eva Emaline (Anderson) McCleary; m. Willis Marion Jones, Sept. 17, 1938 (div.); 1 child, Robert William. BA, U. Wash., 1935. Music supr. Waterville (Wash.) Pub. Schs., 1936-38; piano instr. Olympic Jr. Coll., Bremerton, Wash., 1945-48; music specialist Seattle Pub. Schs., 1959-70; ret., 1970. Mem. AAUW (pres. Casas Adobes br., Tucson, 1988-89, recipient Svc. award 1989, rec. sec. Ariz. area 1990—), PEO Club (treas. Tucson chpt. 1984-85), Tucson Musical Arts Soc. (sec. 1987-88), Questors Club (sec. Tucson chpt. 1989-90), Ladies Mus. Club (treas. Seattle chpt. 1965-67), Pi Lambda Theta, Mu Phi Epsilon (named Alumnus of Yr. 1979). Avocation: antique collecting. Home: Tucson, Ariz. Died July 14, 2008.

**JONES, ED,** congressman; b. Yorkville, Tenn., Apr. 20, 1912; s. William Frank and Hortense (Pipkin) J.; m. Mary Llewellyn Wyatt, June 9, 1938; children: Mary Llew Jones McGuire (dec.), Jennifer Wilson Kinnard. BS, U. Tenn., 1934; student, U. Wis., 1944, U. Mo., 1945. With Tenn. Dept. Agr., 1934-41, Tenn. Dairy Products Assn., 1941-43; agrl. agt. I.C. R.R., 1943-49, 52-69; Tenn. commr. agr., 1949-52; mem. 91st-100th congresses from 8th dist. Tenn., 1969-89; mem. com. on adminstrn., mem. com. on agr. Chmn. Tenn. Agrl. Stablzn. Conservation Commn., 1962-69. Chmn. subcom. on conservation credit and rural devel., on procurement and printing; mem. joint com. on libraries. Trustee Bethel Coll., McKenzie, Tenn. Named Man of Year Progressive Farmer mag., 1951, Man of Year Memphis Agrl. Club, 1957, Man of Year Nat. Limestone Inst., 1979, Legislator of Yr. Tenn. Conservation League, 1986; recipient Distinguished Dairy Service award U. Tenn. Dairy Club, 1966; Distinguished Pub. Service award Am. R.R. Assn., 1970; Distinguished Nat. Leadership award Future Farmers Am., 1970; award U. Tenn. Block and Bridle Club, 1972; Disting. Service to Agr. award Gamma Sigma Delta, 1980; award for Disting. Service to So. Agr. Progressive Farmer mag., 1980; Disting. Service award Nat. Assn. Conservation Dists., 1984, Nat. Rural Electric Cooperative, 1985, Nat. Cooperative Bus. Assn., 1986, Martin Disting. Alumnus award U. Tenn., 1986. Mem. Alpha Gamma Rho. Lodges: Masons, Shriners, Elks. Democrat. Presbyterian. Died 1999.

**JONES, EVERETT LEROI See BARAKA, IMAMU**

**JONES, JANICE LOUISE,** researcher, writer; b. Selma, Calif., Dec. 17, 1956; d. Howard Edward Jones and Betty Irene (Fulbright) Thornbury. BA in Journalism, Calif. State U., Fresno, 1980; postgrad., Claremont Grad. Sch., 1988-89. Researcher, freelance contbr. L.A. Times, from 1980. Mem. AAUW (co-dir. L.A. chpt. 1988-89, fellowship 1988-89). Avocations: travel, floral design, reading. Home: Lake Forest, Calif. Died July 25, 2008.

**JONES, LEON HERBERT, JR., (HERB JONES),** artist; b. Norfolk, Va., Mar. 25, 1923; s. Leon J.; m. Barbara Dean, Sept. 14, 1947; children: Robert Clair, Louis Herbert. Student, William and Mary Coll., 1942—44. Marine structural draftsman and designer Norfolk (Va.) Shipbuilding & Dry Dock Co., 1944—46; free-lance comml. artist, 1946—49; prin. Herb Jones Realty, Norfolk, 1949—58; owner, mgr. Herb Jones Art Studio, Norfolk, from 1958. One-man shows include Norfolk Mus., 1968, Potomac Gallery, Alexandria, Va., 1979, Virginia Beach Maritime Mus., 1983, Village Gallery, Virginia Beach, Va., 1984, The Best of Herb Jones, 1998, exhibited in group shows at Chrysler Mus., Norfolk, 1973—74, traveling show, 1983, exhibited in group shows at Chesapeake Jubilee, 1984 (Va., Excellence award), Peninsula Fine Arts Festival, Newport News, 1984, one-man shows include Currituck Wildlife Show, NC, 1984. Recipient Gold Centaur award, 1983, three Awards Excellence Printing Industries of Virginias, 1987, Oscar d'Italia award, Acad. Italia Calvatore, 1985, award Mid-Atlantic Waterfowl Festival, 1986, 1st and 3d Place awards, 1993, Great Citizen of Hampton Roads award, Cox Cable TV, 1991, Best Art Print Show award, Printing Industries Va., 1995, Granby Hall of Fame, 1997. Mem.: Lion's Internat., Nat. Am. Film Inst., Tidewater Artists Assn., Nat. Soc. Arts and Lit. Methodist. Died July 10, 1998.

**JONES, PHYLLIS EDITH,** nursing educator; b. Barrie, Ont., Can., Sept. 16, 1924; d. Colston Graham and Edith Luella (Shand) J. BScN, U. Toronto, 1950, MSc, 1969; DNSc (hon.), U. Turku, Finland, 1993. With Victorian Order Nurses, Toronto, 1950-53, asst. dir., 1959-63; supr. Vancouver Dept. Health, 1953-58; prof. nursing U. Toronto, 1963-89, dean Faculty Nursing, 1979-88, prof. emeritus, from 1989. Cons. WHO, 1985—86. Contbr. articles to profl. jours. Can. Nurses Found. fellow, 1967-69; grantee Nat. Health R&D, Ont. Ministry Health. Fellow APHA; mem. Coll. Nurses Ont., Registered Nurses Assn. Ont., Can. Pub. Health Assn., Can. Soc. Study Higher Edn., N.Am. Nursing Diagnosis Assn. (charter), ProNursing Finland (hon.). Home: Owen Sound, Canada. Died May 7, 2007.

**JONES, THOMAS VITCORY,** retired aerospace transportation executive; b. Pomona, Calif., July 21, 1920; s. Victor March and Elizabeth (Brettelle) J.; m. Ruth Nagel, Aug. 10, 1946; children: Ruth Marilyn, Peter Thomas. Student, Pomona Jr. Coll., 1938-40; BA with distinction, Stanford U., 1942; LLD (hon.), George Washington U., 1967. Engr. El Segundo div. Douglas Aircraft Co., 1941-47; tech. adviser Brazilian Air Ministry, 1947-51; prof., head dept. Brazilian Inst. Tech., 1947-51; staff cons. Air Staff of USAF, Rand Corp., 1951-53; asst. to chief engr. Northrop Corp., Los Angeles, 1953, dep. chief engr., 1954-56, dir. devel. planning, 1956-57, corporate v.p., 1957, sr. v.p., 1958-59, chmn., pres., CEO, 1960—76, chmn., CEO, 1976—89. Author: Capabilities and Operating Costs of Possible Future Transport Airplanes, 1953. Bd. dirs. Los Angeles World Affairs Council, Calif. Nature Conservancy; trustee Inst. for Strategic Studies, London. Fellow AIAA (hon.); mem. Los Angeles Chamber of Commerce, Navy League U.S. (life), Aerospace Industries Assn., U. Southern Calif. Assocs., Town Hall, Nat. Acad. Engring. Clubs: California; The Beach (Santa Monica); Georgetown, California Yacht, Bohemian. Home: Los Angeles, Calif. Died Jan. 7, 2014.

**JONES DAVIES, MARIE-THÉRÈSE LOUISE,** literature educator; b. Lyon, France, June 16, 1920; d. Louis and Louise (Chaput) Robelin; 1 child, Margaret. Doctorat d'Etat, U. Sorbonne, 1957. Prof. agrégée Lycees and Univ., Nancy and Lyon, France, 1943-46; English tchr. Llandovery Grammar Sch., U. Cardiff, 1947-48; prof. agrégée U. Lyon, 1948-52; prof. agrégé, rsch. worker CNRS, King's Coll., London, 1953-54; prof. U. Rennes, France, 1957-66, U. Sorbonne, Paris, 1966-87, prof. emeritus, 1987-92. Lectr. U. Exeter, Keele, Poznan (Poland), Valencia, Stratford on Avon, Lisbon and Coimbra, Madrid, Rome; invited lectr. Merton Coll., Oxford, 1981, Barnard Coll., Columbia U., N.Y., 1987, Tokyo; examiner for competitive entrance exam. Ecole Normale Superieure, Paris, 1966-75. Author: Un Peintre de la vie londonienne, Thomas Dekker, 1958 (Prix A. Rocheron, Acad. Française Bronze Medal CNRS), Beaumont et Fletcher, Le Chevalier de l'Ardent Pilon, 1958, Inigo Jones, Ben Jonson et le Masque, 1967, Ben Jonson, collection SEGHERS, 1973, 2d edit., 1980, Victimes et Rebelles, L'ecrivain dans la Societe élisabéthaine, 1980, Shakespeare le theatre du Monde, 1987, Prix Biguet Acad. Française, 1988 (Silver medal); editor 25 vols. Studies on the Renaissance. Named Officier dans l'Ordre des Palmes Académiques. Mem. Etudes Anglaises (exec. com.), Internat. Shakespeare Assn. (hon. v.p.), N.Y. Acad. of Scis., Soc. Française Shakespeare (pres. 1978-84, 87-93, hon. pres.), Soc. Internat. Recherches sur la Renaissance (pres.). Avocations: travel, theatre going. Died 2006.

**JOPLIN, SCOTT,** musician, composer; b. Linden, Texas, Nov. 24, 1868; Studied under Julius Weiss. Musician Colombian Expo., Chgo., 1893-94; mem. Tex. Medley Quartette, 1894-98. Composer: The Great Crush Collision, Maple Leaf Rag, 1899, The Entertainer, Treemonisha (Pulitzer Prize 1976), soundtrack to movie Sting (Acad. award, 1973). Died Apr. 1, 1917.

**JORDAN, RAMONA PIERCE,** home economics educator, art education educator, elementary education educator; b. Orlando, Fla., Jan. 24, 1954; d. Arthur Lloyd and Mildred (Duke) Pierce; m. William Winford Jordan, 1986. BS in Home Econs., U. Montevallo, 1974, cert. elem. edn., art, 1977; recert. in reading, Auburn U., 1984. Tchr. reading Elmore County Bd. Edn., Millbrook, Ala., 1977-78; learning disabilities tchr. Minor High Sch., Birmingham, Ala., 1978-79; tchr. reading Wetumpka (Ala.) Elem. Sch., 1982-90; tchr. home econs. Elmore County High Sch., Eclectic, Ala., from 1990. County contact Elmore County Home Econ. Assn., Eclectic, 1992—; judge Eclectic Beautiful Contest, 1992—; cookoff judge Elmore County Cattlemen Assn., 1991-92. Mem. Ala. Vocat. Assn., Nat. Vocat. Assn., Eastern Elmore County Assn. of Retarded Citizens (bd. dirs. 1992—), Alpha Delta Kappa (historian 1991-93). Baptist. Avocations: travel, sewing, cooking, gardening, crafts. Home: Montgomery, Ala. Died Jan. 7, 1996.

**JORÉDIÉ, LÉOPOLD,** former New Caledonian government official; b. 1947; Pres. province of the north Govt. of New Caledonia. Mem. Front de Libération Nationale Kanak Socialiste. Died Sept. 8, 2013.

**JORGENSEN, RALPH GUBLER,** lawyer, accountant; b. NYC, Mar. 12, 1937; s. Thorvald W. and Florence (Gubler) J.; m. Patricia June Spivey, June 21, 1971 (dec. Oct. 1997); 1 child, Misty AB, George Washington U., 1960, LLB, 1962. Bar: Md. 1963, NC 1972, US Dist. Ct. DC 1963, US Ct. Appeals (DC cir.) 1963, US Dist. Ct. Md. 1964, US Dist. Ct. (ea. dist.) NC 1972, US Dist. Ct. (mid. dist.) NC 1977, US Ct. Appeals (4th cir.) 1974, US Tax Ct. 1976, US Ct. Claims 1979, US Supreme Ct. 1971; CPA, Md., Nev., NC. Sole practice, Washington, Silver Spring, Md., 1963-71, Tabor City, NC, from 1971. Bd. dirs. Columbus County ARC, NC, 1974 Mem. Alpha Kappa Psi Democrat. Baptist. Home: Tabor City, NC. Died Dec. 12, 2013.

**JOY, LA VERNE GOUGH,** club woman; b. Campbell, Va., Jan. 27, 1908; d. Glover Lafayette and Nancy Catharine (Bowling) Gough; m. Russell Samuel Joy, Oct. 27, 1929 (dec. Feb. 1971); 1 child, Betty Ann Cajigas. Student, U. Va., 1928, Strayer Bus. Coll., 1941. Cert. tchr. Lynchburg Coll., 1929. Prin., tchr. Campbell County Pub. Schs., 1929—31, substitute tchr., 1931—41; with CIA, Washington, 1941—69. Recipient Outstanding Svc. award, CIA, 1969, Pioneer Club plaque Lynchburg Coll., 1981, Bible Lands & Jerusalem Study & Tour awards, Mayor Jerusalem & W.F. Wagner, Bapt. Min., 1978—79. Mem.: DAR (chpt. regent 1973—77, state treas. Va. 1979—82, Outstanding Achievement award 1983), Daus. Colonial Dames XVII Centruy (chpt. treas. 1983—85), Daus. Am. Colonists (state treas. DC 1982—85), Daus. Colonial Wars (state treas. Va. from 1980). Republican. Episcopalian. Home: Fairfax, Va. Died Nov. 20, 1999.

**JOYCE, EDWARD MATTHEW,** retired broadcast executive; b. Phoenix, Dec. 13, 1932; m. Maureen Jarry; children: Brenda, Randall. Student, U. Wyo. With Sta. WBBM, CBS, Chgo., 1954-59, Sta. WCBS, CBS, NYC, 1959-69, dir. news and pub. affairs, 1966-69; exec. producer spl. events for radio CBS News, NYC, 1969-71; dir. news Sta. WCBS-TV, 1970-77, v.p. news CBS TV Stas. div., 1977-78; v.p., gen. mgr. Sta.-WBBM-TV, 1978-80, Sta. KNXT-TV, Los Angeles, 1980, WCBS-TV, 1981; exec. v.p. CBS News, 1981-83, pres., 1983-86. Author: Prime Times, Bad Times, 1988. Recipient award for reporting of Chappaquiddick Soc. Silurians, 1969; recipient award N.Y. State AP Broadcasters Assn., 1969 Mem.: Metropolitan (N.Y.C.). Home: Georgetown, Conn. Died Aug. 2, 2014.

**JUDD, LAURENCE CECIL,** sociology and Asian studies educator, consultant; b. Houston, Aug. 27, 1920; s. Nathan Banks and Laura Cecilia (Lehmann) J.; m. Virginia Agnes (Moffat); children: Jonathan Bruce, Patrick Arthur, Kathryn Ann, David Alan, Steven Moffat. BA, Rice U., 1942; BD, Yale U., 1946; MS, Cornell U., 1954, PhD, 1961. Sec. youth work New Haven (Conn.) Conf. Chs., 1942-44; pastor Foxon Congl. Ch., East Haven, Conn., 1944-46; asst. min. Chinese Presbyn. Ch., San Francisco, 1946-47; missionary United Presbyn. Ch., China and Thailand, 1948-70; tchr. Bangkok Christian Coll., Thailand, 1948-51; acting mgr. Padung Rashdr Sch., Pitsanuloke, Thailand, 1951-53; dir. Nan Rural Project, Thailand, 1954-59; assoc. dir. rural life dept. Ch. Christ in Thailand, Thailand, 1961-70; prof. sociology, dir. Asian studies program Ill. Coll., 1970-86. Exec. sec. Christian Rural Fellowship Thailand, 1966-70, pres. Coun. Thai Studies, 1974-76; dir. Ill. Coll. S.E. Asia Study Tours, 1976, 80, 83, 86, rsch. assoc. Payap U., Chiang Mai, Thailand, 1986—. Author: Chao Rai Thai: Dry Rice Farmers in North Thailand, 1977, A Vision to Some, 1987, Chao Rai Thai 1987 Update, In Perspective: Trends in Rural Development Policy and Programs in Thailand 1947-87, 1989; editor: Rural Leaders Handbook (in Thai), 1968, JAX PAX News, 1986—; contbr. articles to jours. in field. Bd. dirs. Morgan County Inter Agy. Coun., 1971-79, chmn., 1973-74; bd. dirs. Jacksonville Symphony Soc., 1971-81, Gt. Rivers Presbytery, 1970—; chmn. adv. coun. Health

Edn. Ctr. West Cen. Ill., 1979-80, Prairie Coun. on Aging, 1991-97, Project Life Area Agy. on Aging, 1992-97; program chair Jacksonville Peace Coalition, 1986—. Comparative Edn. fellow Ford Found., 1960-61, Med. Humanities fellow So. Ill. U. Sch. Medicine, 1978; summer rsch. grantee U. Chgo., 1979. Mem. NAACP, Jacksonville Rotary, Rotary in Thailand, LWV, Assn. Asian Studies, Union Concerned Scientists, Physicians for Soc. Responsibility, West Ctrl. Ill. Coun. on World Affairs, World Federalist Assn., Ill. Environ. Coun., Am. Assn. Ret. Persons, Phi Kappa Phi. Democrat. Avocations: reading, writing, peace studies, tutoring, gardening. Died Jan. 28, 2008.

**JUDGE, JOHN PATRICK,** political activist; b. Washington, Dec. 14, 1947; s. John Joseph and Marjorie Alice (Cooley) J. BA, U. Dayton, 1969. Counselor Draft Info. Ctr., Dayton, 1965-72, Vietnam Vets. Against the War/Nat. GI Project, Dayton, 1972-76; field worker Ctrl. Com. Conscientious Objectors, Phila., 1976-80; fundraiser Com. Solidarity with People of El Salvador, Washington, 1984-88, 90-92; archivist, dir. Mae Brussell Rsch. Ctr., Santa Cruz, Calif., 1989-90; co-founder Draft & Mil. Project, Washington, from 1990; exec. sec. Coalition on Polit. Assassinations, Washington, 1994—2014. Mem. governing bd. Nat. Coun. Universal Amnesty, N.Y., 1969-72, Nat. Agent Orange Coalition, St. Louis, 1973-75, Nat. Com. Against Registration & Draft, Washington, 1980-85; mem. Covert Ops. Working Group, Washington Author: Judge for Yourself, 1990; co-editor Prologue, 1989-94 Lobbyist, organizer Com. for Open Archives, Washington, 1989-94; spkr./lectr. Prevailing Winds Rsch.; organizer D.C. Cmty. Action Network, 1994-95. Avocations: reading, lecturing, writing, travel. Home: Washington, DC. Died Apr. 15, 2014.

**JUDSON, JEANNETTE ALEXANDER,** artist; b. NYC, Feb. 23, 1912; d. Philip George and Gertrude (Leichter) Alexander; m. Henry Judson, Sept. 23, 1945; children: S. Robert Weltz Jr., Pauline Raiff; 1 stepson, E. William Judson. Student, Columbia U., 1930-31, N.A.D., 1956-59, Art Student League, NYC, 1959-61. One-man shows Fairleigh Dickinson U., 1965, Bodley Gallery, N.Y.C., 1967, 69, 71, 73, NYU, 1969, Pa. State U., 1969, Laura Musser Mus. Art, Muscatine, Iowa, 1969, Syracuse U. House, N.Y.C., 1975, Ludlaw-Hyland Gallery, 1980, Key Gallery, N.Y.C., 1982, Graphic Arts Coun., White Plains, N.Y., 1993, Broome St. Gallery, N.Y.C., 1994, 96, award, 1994; 2 person show, Am. Standard Gallery, 1980; exhibited in group shows including anns. Nat. Assn. Women Artists, N.Y.C., France, Italy, 1965—, Audubon Artists, N.Y.C., 1962, 64, 65-67, Allied Artists, N.Y.C., 1966-67, Graphic Arts Coun. exhibit of collages, 1973, Key Gallery, N.Y.C., 1981; small works exhibits Key Gallery, 1983, NYU, N.Y.C., 1982, Marbella Gallery, N.Y.C., 1989, Graphic Arts Coun., N.Y.; represented in permanent collections Joseph H. Hirshhorn Mus., NYU, Norfolk (Va.) Mus. Arts and Scis., Brandeis U., Peabody Art Mus., Mus. N.Mex., Sheldon Swope Art Mus., Syracuse U., Evansville Mus. Arts and Scis., Rutgers U., Colby Coll., Butler Inst. Am. Art, Laura Musser Mus., Fordham U., Lehigh U., Ga. Mus. Art, U. Ga., Fairleigh Dickinson U., Lowe Mus., U. Miami, Washington County (Md.) Mus. Fine Arts, Miami Mus. Modern Art, Bruce Mus., Greenwich, Conn., Bklyn. Mus., Hudson River Mus., Dartmouth Coll. Mus., Columbia U., Art In Embassies program Dept. State, Am. Embassy, Stockholm, Sweden and Sofia, Bulgaria, also numerous pvt. collections; exhbns. of Nat. Assn. Women Artists, Am. Soc. Contemporary Artists, 1990, 91. Mem. Nat. Assn. Women Artists (Grumbacher award 1967, Lillian Cottan award 1979, Eve Holman award 1997, oil nominating com. 1977-79), Artists Equity N.Y., Art Students League (life), Am. Soc. Contemporary Artists (Dorothy Feigin award 1976, House of Heydenriek award 1977, Ralph Mayer Meml. award 1985, Doris Kreindler award 1994). Died Jan. 2002.

**JUDY, FREDERICK A.,** lawyer; b. NYC, June 4, 1933; s. Robert P. and Constance (Clark) Judy; 1 child, Meredith H. BS, Denison U., 1955; LLB, Cornell U., 1958. Bar: NY 58, Fla. 84. Assoc. Neale & Wilson, Scarsdale, NY, 1958—61, Smith, Ranscht, Pollock & Barne, White Plains, NY, 1961—67; ptnr. Judy & Miller, Scarsdale, 1967; atty. Scarsdale, 1969—72. Bd. dirs. Scarsdale Family Counseling Svc., from 1983, Scarsdale Art Ctr., from 1983; mem. White Plains YMCA, 1969—75, Am. Baptist Chs., 1972—76. Mem.: Am. Judicature Soc., Fla. Bar, Westchester County Bar Assn., NY State Bar Assn. Home: Yorktown Heights, NY. Died May 17, 1989.

**JUHÁSZ, ZOLTÁN ANDOR,** chemistry educator; b. Kispest, Hungary, June 4, 1929; s. Jozef J. and Katalin (Berán) J.; m. Zoltanne Eva Hollos, Nov. 4, 1953; 1 child, Zoltan. MSc in Chemistry, U. Sci. Elte, Budapest, Hungary, 1951; D in Tech., U. Tech. of Vesprém, Hungary, 1959; PhD, Hungarian Acad. Scis., Budapest, 1971, DSc, 1982. Rschr. Rsch. Inst. of Mining, Budapest, 1951-56; head rsch. lab. Ore Mining Co., Eger, Hungary, 1956-70; cons. Tech. U. Budapest, 1970-82; head professorship U. Veszprém, 1982-95, prof. emeritus, from 1995. Author: (with L. Opoczhy) Mechanical Activation of Minerals By Grinding, 1990, Szilikátok Mechanikai Aktiválása, 1982. Mem. Hungarian Acad. Scis. (mem. or chmn. various coms., 1960—, award 1995, Acad. prize winner, 1996). Home: Budapest, Hungary. Died May 24, 2003.

**JULIANA, JAMES NICHOLAS,** manufacturing executive; b. Camden, NJ, Apr. 1, 1922; s. Nicholas and Rosa (de Noti) J.; m. Elizabeth D. Sutton, Nov. 8, 1947 (dec. 2006); children: James S., Patrick C., Mary E., Thomas E., David J., Richard S., Robert Francis, Ronald Joseph (dec. 1960). BS, Washington Coll., Md., 1944. Spl. agt. FBI, 1947-53; asst. exec. dir., exec. dir., chief counsel to minority US Senate Permanent Sub-com. on Investigations, 1953-58; exec. dir. Civil Aeronautics Bd., 1958-61; pres., dir. Internat. Fact Finding Inst., 1961-62; pres. James N. Juliana Associates, Washington, 1962-81, 84—; sec., dir. Alaska North American Corp., Washington, 1970-77; v.p. fed. affairs Braniff Internat., 1977-81; prin. dep. asst. sec. for manpower, reserve affairs & logistics US Dept. Def., Washington, 1981-84; dir. Tround Internat., 1984-97, chmn., pres., CEO, 1993-97; dir. IX Sys., 1985-98; pres. Coalition Mil. Distributors, 1991—2013. Mem. Presidet's Com. on Mental Retardation, 1971-77; exec. v.p. Armed Forces Mktg. Council, Washington, 1974-81; bd. visitors, bd. govs. Washington Coll., Chestertown, Md., 1978-84. Served with USNR, 1944-46. Mem. Soc. Former Spl. Agts. of FBI, Coalition of Mil. Distbrs., Kappa Alpha, Omicron Delta Kappa. Home: Ocean City, NJ. Died Nov. 18, 2013.

**JULIANA (LOUISE EMMA MARIE WILHELMINA), PRINCESS,** former Queen of the Netherlands, Princess of the Netherlands, Princess of Orange-Nassau, Duchess of Mecklenburg, Princess of Lippe-Biesterfeld; b. Apr. 30, 1909; d. Prince Henry of Mecklenburg-Schwerin and Queen Wilhelmina; m. Prince Bernhard of Lippe-Biesterfeld, 1937; children: Beatrix Wilhelmina Armgard, Irene Emma Elisabeth, Margriet Francisca, Maria Christina. Princess regent, 1947, 48; Queen of Netherlands, 1948-80; abdicated throne, 1980. Died Mar. 20, 2004.

**JUNJI, NARIOKA,** ophthalmologist; b. Matsuyama, Japan, Apr. 24, 1968; s. Narioka Chikara and Narioka Hisako. MD, Tokushima U., Sch. Medicine, 1987—93. Asst. prof. Ehime U., Toon, Japan, from 2006. Contbr. articles to med. jours. Home: Ehime, Japan. Deceased.

**JURITH, EDWARD HOWARD,** lawyer; b. Bklyn., Sept. 11, 1951; s. William Martin and Eileen (Huber) Jurith; m. Kathleen M. Healy, May 26, 1984; children: Theodore Edward, William Callahan. BA in Polit. Sci., cum laude, American U., Washington, 1973; JD, Bklyn. Law Sch., 1976. Bar: NY 1977, DC 1983, US Dist. Ct. DC 1983, US Ct. Appeals 1983, US Supreme Ct 2001. Legis. aide to Rep. Frank J. Brasco US House of Representatives, 1971-74; rsch. asst. Bklyn. Law Sch., 1975-76; assoc. Lyon & Erlbaum, Kew Gardens, NY, 1976-81; counsel US House Narcotics Abuse & Control Com., Washington, 1981-87, staff dir., 1987-93; dir. legis. affairs Office Nat. Drug Control Policy (ONDCP), Washington, 1993-94, gen. counsel, 1994—2011, acting dir., 2001, 2009, sr. counsel. Atlantic fellow in pub. policy U. Manchester, England, 1997—98; adj. assoc. prof. law Wash. Coll. Law, Am. U., from 2011. Mem.: ABA, Criminal Cts. Bar Assn., NY State Bar Assn., DC Bar Assn., Pi Sigma Alpha, Omicron Delta Kappa, Phi Kappa Phi. Roman Catholic. Died Nov. 9, 2013.

**JURJI, EDWARD J.,** educator, writer, lecturer; b. Latakia, Syria, Mar. 27, 1907; came to the U.S., 1933, naturalized, 1947; s. Jabra and Mary (Jureidini) J.; m. Nahia K. Khuri, Aug. 20, 1932 (dec. April 1957); children: Layla (dec.), Edward David; m. Ruth Guinter, Nov. 27, 1958. BA, Am. U., Beirut, Lebanon, 1928, MA, 1934; PhD, Princeton U., 1936; B.D., Princeton Theol. Sem., 1942. Tchr. dept. edn., Iraq, 1928-30, Am. Sch. for Boys, Baghdad, 1930-33; ordained to ministry Presbyterian Ch., 1942; mem. Inst. Advanced Study, Princeton, N.J., 1936-38; faculty Princeton Theol. Sem., 1939-77; lectr. univ. Theol. Sem., Princeton U., 1942-52; book rev. editor Theol. Sem., Princeton U. (Princeton Sem. Bull.), 1945-77, asso. prof. Islamics, comparative religion, 1946-54, prof., 1954-63, prof. history religions, 1963-77, prof. emeritus, from 1977. Interim minister Christ Presbyn. Ch., Trenton, N.J., 1939-41, Hopewell, N.J., 1943-45; interim minister 4th Ave. Presbyn. Ch., Bay Ridge, N.Y., 1977-81; vis. prof. numerous colls., univs., sems.; lectr. Middle East internat. and intercultural affairs; lectr. advanced program world religions Union Theol. Sem., N.Y.C., 1958, 60; Haskell lectr. Oberlin, 1959; Fulbright research prof. U. Madras, India, 1960; Mem. Presbytery of N.Y.C.; chmn. Sesquicentennial Comparative Religion Conf., 1963; dir. World Religious Conf., 1964, 66 Author: Illumination in Islamic Mysticism, 1938, Christian Interpretation of Religion, 1952, The Middle East, Its Religion and Culture, 1957, 2d edit., 1973, The Phenomenology of Religion, 1963; Editor: Great Religions of the Modern World, 1947, most recent edit., 1981, Portuguese transl., 1956, The Ecumenical Era in Church and Society: Symposium in Honor of John A. Mackay, 1959, Religious Pluralism and World Community, 1969; Co-editor: Proc. of First Gallahue Conf. on World Religions, 1966; editorial bd.: Muslim World Jour. Collaborator: Tarikh el Arab (3 vols.); Saudi Arabia; Contbr.: articles on religion, Eastern religions to Colliers Ency., 1957; book revs. to Jour. Ch. and State; also articles and essays on Arabic philosophy, Islamic law, religious pluralism fgn. affairs, intercultural dialogue, world religions to profl. publs.; Cons. staff: Random House Dictionary of the English Language, 1966, coll. edit., 1968, Great Religions of World, Nat. Geog. Soc., 1971, rev. edit., 1978, Funk and Wagnalls New Ency, 1972; editorial cons.: Berlitz Sch. Langs. of Am., Inc., 1981. Bd. dirs. St. Nicholas Cathedral Home, 1980-82; mem. acad. and mus. adv. com. Islam Centennial, 1980—. Recipient Author award N.J. Assn. Tchrs. English, 1964; Edward F. Gallahue grantee. Mem. Soc. Sci. Study Religion, Internat. Assn. History Religions, AAUP. Home: Princeton, NJ. Died July 9, 1990.

**JUVILER, PETER HENRY,** political scientist, educator; b. London, Mar. 26, 1926; s. Adolphe Adam and Katie (Henry) J.; m. Anne C. Stephens, June 20, 1982; children: Gregory, Geoffry. BE, Yale U., 1948, ME, 1949; PhD, Columbia U., 1960. Project engr. Sperry Gyroscope Co., 1949-52; tchr. polit. sci. Princeton U., 1957-58, Columbia U., 1959-60, Hunter Coll., CUNY, 1960-64; prof. Barnard Coll., from 1974, prof. emeritus, spl. lectr., from 2001. Bd. mem. Columbia U. Ctr. for Study Human Rights, 1986—2008; chair, co-chair Columbia U. Seminar on Human Rights, 1988—2010; dir. human rights studies Barnard Coll., 2001—05. Author: Revolutionary Law and Order, 1976, Freedom's Ordeal: The Struggle for Human Rights and Democracy in Post-Soviet States, 1998; co-editor, contbr. Gorbachev's Reforms: U.S. and Japanese Assessments, 1988, Human Rights for the 21st Century, 1993, Religion and Human Rights: Competing Claims?, 1999, Non State Actors in the Human Rights Universe, 2006; contbr. numerous articles to profl. jours. With USN, 1944-46. Recipient Alumnus of Yr., Harriman Inst. Columbia U., 2011. Home: New York, NY. Died May 20, 2013.

**KABBAH, AHMED TEJAN,** former President of Sierra Leone; b. Pendembu, Kailahun, Sierra Leone, Feb. 19, 1932; m. Patricia Tucker (dec. 1998); children: Mariama, Abu, Michael, Tejan. BA, U. College Aberyswyth, Wales, 1959; LLD (hon.), U. Sierra Leone, Freetown, Southern Conn. State U., 2001. Bar: Hon. Soc. Gray's Inn, London 1969. Dist. commr. Bombali & Kambia, Kono, Moyamba & Bo; permanent sec. Ministry Trade & Industry, Ministry Soc. Welfare, Ministry Edn.; with UN Devel. Program, NYC, 1972—92, dep. chief West Africa Divsn., head of Eastern & Southern Africa Divsn., dep. dir. & dir. personnel, dir. adminstrn. & mgmt. divsn., resident rep. Lesotho, 1973; chmn. Nat. Advisory Coun., Sierra Leone, 1992; pres. Republic of Sierra Leone, 1996—97, 1998—2007, min. def., comdr. in chief of armed forces, 2002—07. Leader Sierra Leone's People's Party (SLPP), 1996—2005. Recipient Grand Comdr., Order of the Republic of Sierra Leone. Muslim. Died Mar. 13, 2014.

**KAEGBEIN, PAUL F.,** library and information educator; b. Dorpat, Estonia, June 26, 1925; s. Paul Heinrich and Elfriede Helene (Meyer) K.; m. Irene Borkowski, July 15, 1950 (dec. 2002); children: Irene, Christine. PhD in History, Humboldt U., Berlin, 1948. Libr. Humboldt U. Libr., Berlin, 1951-52, Technol. U. Libr., Berlin, 1952-61, dir., 1962-75, Sch. Librarianship, Cologne, Germany, 1975-81; prof. U. Cologne, from 1975. Mem. exec. bd. Baltic Hist. Com., Goettingen, 1979-99; mem. com. Wolfenbuettel Round Table on Libr. History, 1985-94; mem. profl. com. Herder Inst., 1994-97. Author: Deutsche Ratsbuechereien, 1950, Baltische Bibliographie, from 1994; co-author: Vier Jahrzehnte baltische Geschichtsforschung, 1987, 2d edit., 1992, Fuenfzig Jahre baltische Geschichtsforschung, 1997; editor: Roerig, Fritz: Wirtschaftskraefte im Mittelalter, 1952, 2d edit., 1971, Blumfeldt, Evald, Nigolas Loone: Bibliotheca Estoniae historica 1877-1917, 1987, Bibliothekswissenschaft als spezielle Informationswissenschaft, 1986, 2d edit, 1989, Deutsche Bibliothekskataloge im 19. Jahrhundert, 1992, Technische und naturwissenschaftliche Bibliotheken in ihrer historischen Entwicklung und Bedeutung fuer die Forschung, 1997; co-editor: Libr. History Rsch. in the Internat. Context, 1990, Studies on Rsch. in Reading and Librs., 1991, The History of Reading and Librs. in the Nordic Countries, 1993, Population Shifts and Social Change in Russia's Baltic Provinces, 1850-1914, 1995, Baltic Biographical Archive, 1995—98, series 2, from 2003, Baltic Biographical Index, 1999, Das Baltikum in Geschichte und Gegenwart, Vol. 1, 2001, Fernhandel und Handelspolitik der baltischen Staedte in der Hansezeit, 2001; contbr. articles to profl. jours. Mem. Internat. Assn. Technol. U. Librs. (hon., treas., v.p. 1968-74), German Rsch. Soc. (libr. com. 1970-75), German Spl. Librs. Assn. (hon., chmn. 1971-79), Found. Prussian Cultural Heritage (chmn. libr. com. 1972-82), Internat. Fedn. Libr. Assn. (chmn. profl. bd. 1983-85), Baltic Hist. Com. (hon.), Beta Phi Mu. Lutheran. Home: North Rhine Westphalia, Germany. Died 2002.

**KAFI, ALI,** former Algerian government official; b. Al Harroch, Oct. 7, 1928; Amb. to Egypt, Tunisia Govt. of Algeria, pres. Algiers, Algeria, 1992-94; chmn. High Coun. of State, 1992—94. Col. Algerian Army. Mem. Nat. Liberation Front, Nat. Assn. War Vets. (sec. gen.). Islam. Died Apr. 16, 2013.

**KAGEL, MAURICIO,** composer; b. Buenos Aires, Dec. 24, 1931; married. Studied with, Juan Carlos Paz, Alfredo Schiuma, Buenos Aires; student philosophy and lit., U. Buenos Aires. Assoc. Agrupación Nueva Musica, Argentina, 1949; co-founder Cinémathèque Argentina, 1950; choral dir. Teatro Colón, Cologne, Fed. Republic Germany, 1949-56; film and photography critic Gente de Cine and Nueva Vision, Buenos Aires, 1952-56; condr. Colón Chamber Opera and Teatro Colón, 1955; condr. contemporary concert music Rhineland Chamber Orch., late 1950; prof. composition SUNY, Buffalo, 1965; dir. Inst. for New Music, Rheinische Musikschule, Cologne, 1969; prof. new music theater Musikhocheschule, Cologne, 1974. Lectr., demonstrator modern music, U.S.A, 1961, 63; guest lectr. Internat. Festival Courses for New Music, Darmstadt, Fed. Republic Germany, 1960-66, Berlin Film and TV Acad., 1967; founder, Kölner Ensemble für Neue Musik, 1961; others. Works include Palimpsestos for chorus a cappella, 1950, String Sextet, 1953, Traummusick for instruments and musique concrete, 1954, Anagrama for speaking chorus, 4 vocalist and chamber ensemble, 1958, Transición I for electronic sounds, 1958, Transición II for piano, percussion and 2 magnetic tapes, 1959, Pandora's Box for magnetic tape, 1961, Sonant for electric guitar, harp, double bass and 20 instruments, 1961, Sur scène for 6 participants in mixed media, with musicians instructed to interfere with actors and singers, 1962, Heterophonie for optional ensemble, 1962, Phonophonie 4 melodramas for 2 voices and sound sources, 1963, Composition and Decomposition, 1963, Diaphonie for chorus, orch. and slide projections, 1964, Music for Renaissance Instruments for 23 performers, 1966, String Quartet, 1967, Montage for different sound sources, 1967, Ornithologica multiplicata for exotic birds, 1968, surrealistic film score Ludwig van, 1969, Staatstheater, 1971, Variations ohne Fuge for orch., 1972, Con voce for 3 mute actors, 1972, scenic play Mare nostrum, 1975, Kantrimiusik, 1975, Varieté, 1977, opera Die Erschöpfung der Welt, 1980, also Pas de Cinq, Sankt-Bach-Passion, opera without words Ensemble, Oral Treason, Acustica for large variety percussive mechanisms, opera TantzSchul, 1988, Quodlibet; scriptwriter, music composer, dir. film Midnight Music; composer, producer other films, radio plays, live theater, gallery exhbns.; composer sound tracks classic silent films Nosferatu, Un Chien Andalou (retitled MM 51), Hallelujah (Scotoni prize City of Zurich 1969); works performed throughout Europe including Vienna State Opera, Austria, ann. Elektron Music Festival, Sweden, Pro Musica Nova, Bremen, Fed. Republic Germany, 8th Almeida Internat. Festival Contemporary Music and Performance, London, also at Avery Fisher Hall, N.Y.C.; author numerous articles Recipient Koussevitzky Prize, 1966; Karl Sczuka Prize for play Ein Aufnahmezustand, 1969; Scotoni Prizeof the City of Zurich for film Hallelujah, 1969; Mozart Medal, City of Frankfurt, 1983; Commandeur de L'Ordre des Arts et des Lettres, France, 1985. Died Sept. 18, 2008.

**KAHN, GUINTER,** dermatologist; b. Trier, Germany, May 11, 1934; came to U.S., 1938; s. Joseph and Sophie Kahn; divorced; children: Bruce, Michelle. BA cum laude, U. Omaha, 1954; MD, U. Nebr., 1958; Hon. degree (hon.), 2001. Diplomate American Bd. Dermatology, American Bd. Dermapathology. Intern Phila. Gen., 1958-59; resident in surgery Offenbach City Hosp., Germany, 1959-60; resident dermatology U. Miami Sch. Medicine, 1965-68; pvt. practice Miami, 1974—2014. Dir. residency tng. Skin and Cancer Unit Mount Sinai Hosp., Miami Beach, 1973-74. Capt. U.S. Army, 1960-65. Recipient First Prize in Hollis Gerrard Meml. Essay Contest North American Dermatologic Soc., 1970, First Prize Nelson Paul Anderson Meml. Essay Contest Pacific Dermatological Assn., 1972, Disting. Inventor of Yr. award, 1988. Mem. Rotary, Alpha Omega Alpha. Achievements include discovery of Minoxidil for hair growth. Died Sept. 17, 2014.

**KAISER, MARY AGNES,** chemist, chemical company executive; b. Pittston, Pa., June 11, 1948; d. Fredolin Anthony and Agnes Regina (Searfoss) K.; m. Cecil Dybowski, May 11, 1979; 1 child, Marta. BS, Wilkes Coll., 1970; MS, St. Joseph's U., Phila., 1972; PhD in Chemistry, Villanova U., Pa., 1976. Postdoctorate U. Ga., Athens, 1976-77; research chemist E.I Du Pont De Nemours & Co., Wilmington, Del., 1977-79, supr. research, 1979-86, sr. supr., 1986—2002, rsch. fellow, 2002—06, sr. rsch. fellow, from 2006. Co-Author: Environmental Problem Solving Using Gas and Liquid Chromatography, 1982; contbr. articles to profl. jours. Recipient Alumni award, Villanova U., 1997. Mem. Am. Chem. Soc. (chmn. div. analytical chemistry, Analytic Divsn. Disting. Svc. award 2004, Del. Sect. award 2009), Fedn. Analytical Chemistry and Spectros Copy Soc. (chmn. governing bd.), Ea. Analytical Symposium (pres.), Chromatography Forum (chmn.), Sigma Xi (research recognition award 1970), Phi Kappa Phi. Avocations: swimming, walking, travel. Home: Newark, Del. Died July 10, 2011.

**KAJIYAMA, SEIROKU,** government official; b. Hitachi Ota, Ibaraki, Japan, Mar. 27, 1926; m. Harue Kajiyama; 2 children. Engring. Degree, Nihon U., 1949. Mem. Ibaraki Prefectural Assembly, 1955-69, spkr., 1967-69; mem. Ho. of Reps., Tokyo, from 1969, dep. chief cabinet sec., 1974-76, parliamentary vice-min. constrn., 1976-79, parliamentary vice-min. internat. trade and industry, 1979-80; dir. commerce and industry divsn. Liberal Dem. Party, Tokyo, 1980-83; chmn. com. on commerce and industry Ho. of Reps., Tokyo, 1983-87, min. of home affairs chmn. Nat. Pub. Safety Commn., 1987-89, min. internat. trade and industry, 1989-90, min. of justice, chmn. diet affairs com., 1990-92; sec.-gen. Liberal Dem. Party, Tokyo, 1992-96; chief cabinet sec., govt. spokesman Govt. Japan, Tokyo, 1996-97. Avocations: golf, reading. Died June 2000.

**KALOW, WERNER,** pharmacologist, toxicologist; b. Cottbus, Germany, Feb. 15, 1917; emigrated to Can., 1951, naturalized, 1957; s. Johannes Bernhard and Maria Elisabeth (Heyde) K.; m. Patricia M. Arnold, May 3, 1991; children from earlier marriage: Peter Bernard, Barbara Irene. Student in medicine, U. Greifswald, Ger., 1935-36, U. Graz, Austria, 1936-37, U. Gottingen, Ger., 1939-40; MD, U. Konigsberg, Ger., 1941. Research asst. Berlin U., 1947-49; research fellow, instr. U. Pa., 1949-51; lectr. U. Toronto, Ont., Can., 1951-53, asst. prof. pharmacology, 1953-55, assoc. prof., 1955-62, prof., from 1962, chmn. dept. pharmacology, 1966-77. Dir. biol. research C.H. Boehringer Sohn, Ingelheim, Ger., 1965-66 Author: Pharmacogenetics, Heredity and the Response to Drugs, 1962; editor: (with B.N. La Du) Pharmacogenetics, 1968, (with R.A. Gordon and B.A. Britt) International Symposium on Malignant Hyperthermia, 1973, (with H.W. Goedde and D.P. Agarwal) Ethnic Differences in Reactions to Drugs and Xenobiotics, 1986, Pharmacogenetics of Drug Metabolism, 1992, (with U.A. Meyer and R. Tyndale) Pharmacogenomics, 2001, 05. Recipient Drug Info. Assn. Disting. Career award, 1997. Fellow Royal Soc. Can.; mem. Pharm. Soc. Can. (pres. 1963-64, Upjohn award 1982), Can. Physiol. Soc., Am. Soc. Pharmacology and Exptl. Therapeutics (Oscar B. Hunter Meml. award 1993), Can. Anaesthetist Soc. (hon., Rsch. Recognition award 1993), Canadian Coun. Arts (Killam award 2001), Deutsche Pharmakologische Gesellschaft. Achievements include discovering pharmacogenetic variants of cholinesterase, 1956, thereby initiating the science of pharmacogenetics, 1962; devel. pharmaco-diagnosis of malignant hyperthermia, 1970; promoted studies of pharmacoanthropology (interethnic drug comparisons), 1983-84; used caffein metabolism as a tool of biochemical epidemiology, 1986. Home: Toronto, Canada. *It is good to be curious. It is better if being curious is one's work.* Died 2009.

**KALSEM, MILLIE E.,** investment company executive; b. Huxley, Iowa, Dec. 12, 1896; d. Ole J. and Anna Nelson Kalsem. BS, Iowa State Coll., 2021; student, Michael Reese Hosp., Chgo., 2022—23; postgrad., U. Ill. Med. Sch., 1936. Tchr. home economics. & physiology Monticello HS, Iowa, 2021—22; hosp. dietitian Beaver Valley Gen. Hosp., New Brighton, Pa., 2023, Iowa Meth. Hosp., Des Moines, 2023—27, Ill. Tng. Sch. Nurses and Cook County Sch. Nursing, 1927—38; chief exec. dietitian Cook County Hosp., 1938—62; v.p., dir., registered rep. Lorraine L. Blair, Inc.; investment broker Chgo. Bd. govs. Iowa State U. Found, 1977. Recipient merit award, Iowa State Coll., 1946, Alumni medal, 1956; named one of 100 Women, Women's Centennial Congress, Carrie Chapman Catt, 1940. Mem.: Order of Knoll, Women's Fin. Forum Am. (rsch. chmn. 1954—57, regional dir. from 1960), Chgo. Dietetic Assn., Ill. Dietetic Assn. (organizer and 1st pres.), Am. Dietetic Assn. (v.p. 1946—47), Art Inst. Chgo. (life), Chi Omega, Phi Kappa Phi, Omicron Nu. Home: Ames, Iowa. Died Feb. 20, 1989.

**KALTENBACH, MARTIN HANS,** cardiologist, medical educator; b. Lörrach, Baden, Germany, Sept. 23, 1928; s. Hans Berthold and Lise Agnes (Maurer) K.; m. Dorothee Elisabeth Edelmann, Feb. 20, 1960. MD, U. Marburg, Germany, 1955; priv. dozent, U. Frankfurt, Germany, 1966, prof. medicine, 1972. Physician Hosp. Lörrach, Germany, 1955-58, Hosp. Frankfurt, Germany, 1958-62; MD U. Hosp., Frankfurt, 1958-66; med. rschr. Frankfurt, Cleve., Zürich, 1966-72; prof. medicine, head dept. cardiology U. Frankfurt, 1972-93; cons. Heart Ctr., Frankfurt, from 1993. Author: Research Medicine, 1978 (Morawitz prize German Cardiology Soc., 1978), Medical Research Cardiology (Albert Knoll prize 1981), Research Interventional Cardiology (A Grünzig award European Soc. Cardiology 1988). Founding mem. German Heart Found., 1970, Rockenberg-Verein for Juvenile Convicts, 1977. Decorated Bundesverdienst Kreuz 1st class (Germany); recipient Ethica award, 2005. Fellow Am. Heart Assn., European Heart Assn.; mem. German Cardiac Soc. (pres. 1990, Carl Ludwig medal 2004). Mem. Free Dems. Germany. Home: Dreieich, Germany. Died Mar. 24, 2006.

**KAMENS, HAROLD,** lawyer; b. Passaic, NJ, Apr. 28, 1917; s. Isadore and Esther (Reingold) Kamens; m. Bernice F. Kamens, Jan. 11, 1949; children: Roberta Kamens Rabin, Edward A., Elizabeth. JD, Rutgers U., 1940, BS in Acctg., 1945. Bar: US Dist. Ct. 1941, NJ 1941, NY 1981, US Ct. Appeals (3rd cir.), US Supreme Ct. 1970. Sole practice, Newark, from 1946. Lectr. Seton Hall U., Fairleigh Dickinson U., Inst. Continuing Legal Edn., numerous other profl., bus. groups; chmn. estate planning com. probate sect. NJ State Bar. Contbr. articles to legal jours.; editor: Tax Notes NJ Law Jour., from 1947. Mem.: Assn. Fed. Bar NJ (v.p. taxation from 1977), Passaic County Bar Assn. (chmn. fed. taxation 1965—75), Essex County Bar Assn. (chmn. 1965—74), NJ Bar Assn. (chmn. com. fed. taxation 1967), Fed. Bar Assn. (chmn. taxation com. 1976—77). Died 2001.

**KAMINSKY, ARTHUR CHARLES,** lawyer; b. Bronx, NY, Dec. 29, 1946; s. Daniel and Claire (Sternberg) Kaminsky; m. Andrea Lynn Polin, Dec. 28, 1969; children: Alexis Kate, Thomas Suradet, Eric Vorapong. BA cum laude with distinction, Cornell U., 1968; JD, Yale Law Sch., 1971. Bar: NY 1974, US Dist. Ct. (so. dist.) NY 1975, US Tax Ct. 1977, US Supreme Ct. 1984. Assoc. Paul Weiss Rikfind Wharton & Garrison, 1973—74; ptnr. Taft & Kaminsky, NYC, 1974—81; pres. A.C.K. Sports Inc., NYC, 1977—95, Profl. Sports Investors Inc., NYC, 1982—89; exec. v.p. Marquee Group Inc., 1995—2000; pres. Athletes & Artists, 2002—13. Mem., selection com. US Olympic Hockey Team, Mpls., 1980. Co-author: One Goal, A Chronicle of the 1980 US Olympic Hockey Team, 1984; columnist NY Times, 1973—77. Intern 3rd Congressional Dist. NY Adlai E. Stevenson Meml., 1967; dep. campaign mgr., Lindsay for Pres. NYC, 1972; del., credentials com. Democratic Nat. Conv., Miami, 1972; adminstrv. asst. Rep. Michael Harrington, Washington, 1972—73; pres. Plandome Civic Assn., 1981—82; trustee African-American Athletic Assn., 1992—99; analyst HS and Coll. Sports Broadcasts Telecare TV, from 2001. Recipient Outstanding Sr. award, Cornell U., 1968, Friends of Edn. award, NY State Teachers Union, 1988; named one of The 100 Most Powerful People in Sports, Sporting News, 1991—92; finalist Thurman Arnold Moot Ct. Competition, 1970; nominee Charter mem., Jericho HS Hall of Fame, 1991. Mem.: ABA, Assn. Bar of City NY, NY State Bar Assn., Quill and Dagger, Sports Lawyers Assn. (lectr.), Com. Entertainment and Sports, New Sch. Soc. Rsch. (lectr.), Plandome Country Club, Friars Club (bd. govs. 2000—05), Phi Beta Kappa (hon.). Democrat. Jewish. Home: Manhasset, NY. Died Dec. 5, 2013.

**KAMINSKY, GLADYS,** retired bookkeeper; b. Bronx, NY, Nov. 29, 1918; d. Benjamin E. and Julia (Weiss) Schwartz; m. Irving Isidore Kaminsky, Aug. 9, 1941 (dec. May 1992); children: Mark Edward, Julia Helen Richter. Student, Franklin Sch. Bus., 1935-36. Sec., asst. bookkeeper Empire Notion Co., 1936-37; sec. Mogul Camera Co., 1937-39; legal sec. Assoc. Fur Coat & Trimming Mfrs. Inc., 1939-45; bookkeeper, sec., registrar, office mgr. Marble Hill Nursery Sch., 1962-75. Mem. Ind. Jewish Hist. Soc., treas. 1980-94; treas. Jewish War Vets. Ladies Aux., N.Y.C., 1948-49; sec. Condo Bldg. in Fla., 1992-97; sec.-treas. New Horizons Club Indpls., Hebrew Congregation, 1999—; founding mother, dir., bd. sec. constitution and bylaws com. Marble Hill Nursery Sch., N.Y.C., 1953-56; sec. PTA, Pub. Sch. 122, Bronx, 1957-59; del. to United Parents Assn., N.Y.C., 1959-62; exec. com. mem. PTA J.H.S. 143, Bronx, 1962-65; campaign worker Dem. Party, N.Y., 1950-75, Columbus, Ind., 1976-78' sec. Columbus Hebrew Congregation, 1976-78, treas., 1978-81. Mem. LWV, Nat. Assn. Ret. Federal Employees, Am. Assn. Ret. Persons (organizer Columbus chpt., v.p. 1980-81), Nat. Mus. Women in Arts, Ctr. for Sci. in Pub. Interest, People for Am. Way, Emily's List, Gray Panthers, Jacques Cousteau Soc. (charter). Democrat. Jewish. Avocations: photography, crossword puzzles, bridge, spending time with children and grandchildren. Home: Indianapolis, Ind. Died June 15, 2001.

**KAMMEN, MICHAEL,** historian, educator; b. Rochester, NY, Oct. 25, 1936; s. Jacob M. and Blanche (Lazerow) K.; m. Carol Koyen, Feb. 26, 1961; children: Daniel Merson, Douglas Anton. AB, George Washington U., 1958, LHD (hon.), 1991; PhD, Harvard U., 1964. Mem. faculty Cornell U., 1965—2008, Newton C. Farr prof. American history & culture, 1973—2008, chmn. dept. history, 1974—76, dir. ctr. for humanities, 1977—80. Vis. prof. history Yale U., 2005-06; 1st holder chair in American history Ecole des Hautes Etudes en Sciences Sociales, Paris, France, 1980-81; Commonwealth Fund lectr. in American history U. London, 1976. Author: A Rope of Sand: The Colonial Agents, British Politics and the American Revolution, 1968, Deputyes and Libertyes: The Origins of Representative Government in Colonial America, 1969, People of Paradox: An Inquiry Concerning the Origins of American Civilization, 1972 (Pulitzer Prize for history, 73), Colonial New York: A History, 1975, A Season of Youth: The American Revolution and the Historical Imagination, 1978, Spheres of Liberty: Changing Perceptions of Liberty in American Culture, 1986, A Machine That Would Go of Itself: The Constitution in American Culture, 1986 (Francis Parkman and Henry Adams prizes, 87), Selvages & Biases: The Fabric of History in American Culture, 1987, Sovereignty and Liberty: Constitutional Discourse in American Culture, 1988, Mystic Chords of Memory: The Transformation of Tradition in American Culture, 1991, Meadows of Memory: Images of Time and Tradition in American Art and Culture, 1992, The Lively Arts: Gilbert Seldes and the Transformation of Cultural Criticism in the United States, 1996, In the Past Lane: Historical Perspectives on American Culture, 1997, American Culture, American Tastes: Social Change and the 20th Century, 1999, Robert Gwathmey: The Life and Art of a Passionate Observer, 1999, A Time to Every Purpose: The Four Seasons in Am. Culture, 2004, Visual Shock: A History of Art Controversies in American Culture, 2006, Digging Up the Dead: A History of Notable American Reburials, 2010; editor: What is the Good of History?: Selected Letters of Carl L. Becker, 1900-1945, 1973, The Origins of the American Constitution: A Documentary History, 1986, Contested Values: Democracy and Diversity in American Culture, 1994, Alexis de Tocqueville, Democracy in America, 2009; editor-in-chief: The Past Before Us: Contemporary Historical Writing in the United States, 1980. Bd. dirs. Social Sci. Rsch. Coun., 1980-83. Fellow NEH, 1967, 72-73, 84-85, 97-98, Humanities Ctr. Johns Hopkins U., 1968-69, Ctr. for Advanced Study in Behavioral Sciences, Stanford, 1976-77; Guggenheim fellow 1980-81, Regents fellow Smithsonian Instn. 1990, Times-Mirror Found. Rsch. Prof. American Studies, The Huntington Libr., San Marino, Calif., 1993-94; guest scholar Woodrow Wilson Ctr., Washington, 1997-98, award, American Hist. Assn., 2009. Mem.: AAAS, Soc. American Historians, Mass. Hist. Soc., American Antiquarian Soc., Orgn. American Historians (exec. bd. 1989—92, pres. 1995—96), American Hist. Assn. (coun. 1976—79), Phi Beta Kappa. Home: Ithaca, NY. Died Nov. 29, 2013.

**KAMNIK, CAROL LEE,** geriatrics services professional, social worker; b. Phila., Apr. 20, 1945; d. Lewis Norman and Ruth Edna (Speier) Eppihimer; m. John Joseph Kamnik, Aug. 5, 1972; 1 child, Michael Patrick. Assoc. Gen. Studies summa cum laude, Montgomery County C.C., Blue Bell, Pa., 1989; BA in Sociology summa cum laude, Gwynedd-Mercy Coll., Gwynedd Valley, Pa., 1993; MS in Health Edn., Beaver Coll., Glenside, Pa., 1997. Care mgr. Montgomery County Aging and Adult Svcs., Willow Grove, Pa., from 1993. Cir. leader, mem. exec. bd. Lehman United Meth. Ch., Hatboro, Pa., 1980—, 1982-86, 89-91, lay ministry tng., 1986-88, facilitator caring and sharing group, 1986; adult reading tutor Vols. in Teaching Alternatives, 1989-91; mentor, budget counseling and resource referral Women in Cmty. Svc., 1991-95; alumni diplomat Gwynedd-Mercy Coll., 1993-94, 97—. Mem. AAUW, Nat. Assn. Case Mgrs., Sigma Phi Sigma, Phi Theta Kappa. Democrat. Methodist. Avocations: pin collecting, reading. Home: Hatboro, Pa. Died Apr. 1, 2008.

**KANE, WILLIAM EVERETT,** lawyer, banker; b. Albany, Ga., Aug. 12, 1943; s. Allen R. and Coty Everett Kane; children: William Everett, Katherine Elizabeth. BA, Princeton U., 1966; JD, Yale U., 1970. Bar: Calif. 1971. Gen. mgr. Continental Ill. Ltd., London, Hong Kong and Tokyo, 1971—73; chief overseas div. First Nat. Fin. Corp., London, 1973—75; sr. ptnr. Kane & Keilly, LA, 1975—79; chmn. bd., pres. K & K Properties, Inc., L.A. and Monterey, Calif., from 1976; pres. Kane & Kelly Assocs., Inc., L.A., Monterey and NYC, from 1975. Cons. in field. Author: Civil Strife in Latin America, 1972, also monographs; bd. editor Yale Law Jour., 1968—70. Gen. Motors Corp. scholar, 1961—62, Fulbright fellow, 1966—67. Mem.: State Bar Calif., Am. Bar Assn., Internat. Bar Assn., Pacheco, Princeton, Colonial. Republican. Died Oct. 30, 1991.

**KANG, YOUNG WOO,** special education educator; b. Kyonggi, Republic of Korea, Jan. 16, 1944; arrived in U.S., 1972, naturalized, 1984; s. Myung Ki Kang and Lin Hee Lim; m. Kyoung Sook Suk, Feb. 26, 1972; children: Paul, Christopher. BA, Yonsei U., Seoul, Republic of Korea, 1972; PhD in Lit. (hon.), Yonsei U., 2003; MEd, U. Pitts., 1973, PhD, 1976. Cert. rehab. counselor; tchr. ESL, spl. edn. Spl. edn. cons. Gary (Ind.) Sch. Corp., 1976—2004. Prof., dean Taegu U., 1978—2000, chair prof., 2008—12; adj. prof. Northeastern Ill. U., Chgo., 1979—2000; vice-chmn. World Com. Disability, 1995—2012; sr. advisor Roosevelt Inst., 1996; presenter in field; policy adv. Nat. Coun. Disability, 2001—09; spkr in field. Author: (book) A Light in My Heart, 1987, Love, Light, Liberty, 1989, Secrets to

Success through Education, 1995, Dreams of a Father and His Sons, 1998, There is No Mountain That We Can Not Climb, 2000, Success is Inside Me: From Bad Luck to a Presidential Appointee, 2002; author: (with Kyoung Sook Kang) Two Candles Shining in the Darkness of the World, 1990; author: My disability-God's Ability= Seven Principles of Triumphant Life, 2004, Where There is a Dream There is a Future, 2006, Todays Challenges - Tomorrows Glories, 2009. Pres. Edn. Rehab. Exch. Found. Internat., from 1993; presdl. apptd. mem. Nat. Coun. Disability, from 2002; bd. dirs. Nat. Orgn. Disability, 1995—2003, Goodwill Industries Internat., from 1998. Recipient Outstanding Contribution Award, Asian American Alliance, 2003, Global Korea Award, Coun. Korean Studies, Mich. State U., 2004, Ann. Human Rights Award, Fairfax County, Va., 2006, Commemorative Chair award, Henry Wallace Visitors Ctr. Hyde Park NY, Franklin and Eleanor Roosevelt Inst., 2006, Disting. Alumnus of the Yr., Yonsei University, Seoul, Republic of Korea, 2007, Global Service to Humanity award, Rotary Found. Rotary Internat., 2007—08, Disting. Alumni Fellow Award, U. Pitts., 2008. Mem.: Internat. Coun. Exceptional Children, Korean Ctrl. Presbyn. Ch. Washington, Rotary Club (Washington), Rotary (chmn. internat. svc. and youth svc. coms. dist. 6540 1983—85, one of 75 candles in 75th anniversary celebration 1992, Meritorious Svc. citation 1982, Pual Harris fellow 1987, scholar 1973). Presbyterian. Avocations: public speaking, writing, reading, travel, advocating rights of disabled. Home: Springfield, Va. Died Feb. 24, 2012.

**KANSAS, HELENE VIVIAN,** retired secondary education educator; b. NYC, Mar. 25, 1926; d. Louis and Birdie (Kleinberg) Felner; m. Robert Kansas, May 28, 1949; children: Susan, Geoffrey, Tina. BA, Hunter Coll., 1947; postgrad., Columbia U., 1979. Tchr. fgn. langs. N.Y.C. Bd. Edn., 1947-49, Brevard County (Fla.) Bd. Edn., 1968-88; ret., 1988. Project dir. Fla. Latin Forum, 1966—2004. Mem. Dem. Exec. Com. Brevard County, Satellite Beach, Fla., 1965—, treas., 1992—; chmn. Charter Commn., Satellite Beach City Coun., 1985-86. White Rose honoree March of Dimes, 1995. Mem. Classical Assn. Fla. (exec. sec. 1993—), Fla. Fgn. Lang. Assn. (Latin Tchr. of Yr. award 1986), Classical Assn. Midwest and South, ACLU, Sierra Club, Environ. Def. Fund. Home: Satellite Bch, Fla. Died Feb. 6, 2008.

**KANUTH, MICHELLE SUSAN,** science educator; d. Robert Dale and Evelyn Lavonne Cronk; m. James Gordan Kanuth, Nov. 10, 2000; 1 child, Robert Gordon. BS, Ohio State U., Columbus, 1974; MS, U. Cin., Ohio, 1978; PhD, U. Ky., Lexington, 1992. Cert. med. technologist Am. Soc. Clin. Pathologists, 1974, specialist in blood banking Am. Soc. Clin. Pathologists, 1978, clin. lab. scientist Nat. Credentialing Agy. Lab. Pers., 1982. Blood bank specialist reference lab. Mass. Gen. Hosp., Boston, 1978—80; dir. med. tech. program Miriam Hosp., Providence, 1980—82; asst. prof. U. Ky., Lexington, 1983—86; assoc. prof. U. Louisville, 1987—2000, U. Tex. Med. Br., Galveston, Tex., 2000—09, prof., disting. tchg. prof., from 2009, emeritus prof., from 2011, disting. tchg. prof. life. Chmn. immunology and immunohematology exam. com. Nat. Credentialing Agy. for Lab. Pers., 1993—97; pres. Ky. Soc. for Med. Tech., 1987—88. Recipient Utmb Health award, Jael B. Alperin Outstanding Support Specialist award, 2013; named Med. Technologist of Yr., Ky. Soc. for Med. Tech., 1988. Mem.: Am. Assn. Blood Banks, Am. Soc. Clin. Pathologists, Am. Soc. Clin. Lab. Sci. (cons. editor jour. from 1995, chmn. rsch. and edn. fund 1997—2001, chair com. on ednl. programs and initiatives 2009—11, mem. consumer response team, chmn. rsch. and edn. fund from 2011, Profl. Achievement Immunology award 1992, named Educator of Yr. Ky. chpt. 2001, Robin H. Mendelson award 2002, Joseph J. Kleiner award 2002), U. Tex. Med. Branch Academy Master Tchrs., Phi Kappa Phi, Lambda Tau, Alpha Mu Tau, Omicron Sigma. Presbyterian. Avocations: reading, travel. Home: Nassau Bay, Tex. Died Aug. 5, 2013.

**KAPLAN, ALEX H.,** psychiatrist; b. Hull, Eng., Sept. 25, 1912; came to U.S., 1914; s. Nathan and Dora (Bogdanoff) K.; m. Ada Marie Leibson, June 7, 1936; children: Dale H. Carriero, Lawrence Paul, Robert Alan. BS, CCNY, 1932; MD, St. Louis U., 1936. Diplomate Am. Bd. Psychiatry, Am. bd. Psychonalysis. Resident in psychiatry Grasslands Hosp., Valhalla, N.Y., 1937-39, Rockland State Hosp., Orangeburg, N.Y., 1939-43; asst. prof. psychiatry Washington U. Sch. Med., St. Louis, 1955-70, assoc. prof., 1970-77, prof., from 1977. Acting dir. St. Louis Child Guidance Clinic, 1955-58; psychiatrist-in-chief St. Louis Jewish Hosp., 1959-66; med. dir. St. Louis Psychoanalytic Found., 1965-72, assoc. med. dir., 1972-82; psychiatric cons. Family, Children, and Vets. Out-Patient Clinics., 1946-58. Contbr. articles to profl. jours. Lt. M.C. USNR, 1943-46. Fellow Am. Psychiat. Assn., Am. Psychoanalytic Assn. (treas. 1971-77, pres. 1977-79); St. Louis Psychoanalytic Soc. (pres. 1966-68, 82-84), Am. Coll. Psychoanalysts (pres. 1987), Eastern Mo. Psychiatric Soc. (pres. 1958-59), Am. Orthopsychiatric Assn., Chgo. Psycholanalytic Soc. Democrat. Avocation: tennis. Home: Saint Louis, Mo. Died Feb. 19, 1996.

**KAPLAN, JUSTIN,** writer; b. NYC, Sept. 5, 1925; s. Tobias D. and Anna (Rudman) K.; m. Anne F. Bernays, July 29, 1954; children: Susanna Bernays, Hester Margaret, Polly Anne. BS, Harvard U., 1944, postgrad., 1944-46; LHD (hon.), Marlboro Coll., 1984. Free-lance editing, writing, NYC, 1946-54; sr. editor Simon & Schuster, Inc., NYC, 1954-59; lectr. English Harvard U., 1969, 73, 76, 78; prose writer in residence Emerson Coll., Boston, 1977-78. Vis. lectr. Griffith U., Brisbane, Australia, 1983; lectr. in field; judge Nat. Book Awards, 1968, 73, 78, 87, 93, Pulitzer prizes, 1989, 94, 97, 2003; resident Bellagio Study and Conf. Ctr., Italy, spring, 1990; Jenks prof. contemporary letters Coll. of Holy Cross, Worcester, Mass., 1992-95. Author: Mr. Clemens and Mark Twain, 1966, Lincoln Steffens, A Biography, 1974, Mark Twain and His World, 1974, Walt Whitman: A Life, 1980, (with Anne Bernays) The Language of Names, 1997, (with Bernays) Back Then: Two Lives in 1950's New York, 2002, When the Astors Owned New York: Blue Bloods and Grand Hotels in a Guilded Age, 2006; editor: Dialogues of Plato, 1948, With Malice Toward Women, 1949, The Pocket Aristotle, 1956, The Gilded Age, 1964, Great Short Works of Mark Twain, 1967, Mark Twain, A Profile, 1967, Walt Whitman: Complete Poetry and Collected Prose, 1982, The Harper American Literature, 1987, 94, Best American Essays, 1990; gen. editor: Bartlett's Familiar Quotations, 17th edit., 2002; contbr. to NY Times, New Republic, American Scholar, Newsweek, Ploughshares, Yale Rev., others. Participant cultural programs USIA, Israel, Dominican Republic, Mex., 1985. Recipient Pulitzer prize for Biography, 1967, Nat. Book award for Arts & Letters, 1967, Nat. Book award for Biography, 1981, Guggenheim fellowship, 1975—76. Fellow: Mass. Hist. Soc., Soc. American Historians, American Acad. Arts & Sciences; mem.: American Acad. Arts & Letters, Harvard Club (NY), Phi Beta Kappa. Home: Cambridge, Mass. Died Mar. 2, 2014.

**KAPLAN, MARTIN MARK,** microbiologist; b. Phila., June 23, 1915; s. Wolf and Minnie (Swedlow) K.; m. Lenna Bouchal, Dec. 15, 1944; children: Alexa, Peter, Jeffrey. VMD, U. Pa., 1940, MPH, 1942; DSc (hon.), U. Wis., 1987. Assoc. prof. Middlesex U., Waltham, Mass., 1942-44; vet. officer Relief and Rehab. Orghn. UN, Athens, Greece, 1945-47; vet. officer FAO, Warsaw, Poland, 1947-49; chief vet. pub. health WHO, Geneva, 1949-76, now cons.; sec.-gen. Pugwash Confs. on Sci. and World Affairs, Geneva, 1976-88. Author, editor: Laboratory Techniques in Rabies, 1992; editor: Health Aspects of Chemical and Biological Weapons, 1970, Health Hazards of the Human Environment, 1972. Recipient K.F. Meyer Gold Headed Cane, Am. Vet. Epidemiology Soc., 1967, Schofield Meml. medal, U. Guelph Vet. Coll., 1974, Centenary Medal award, U. Pa., 1984, M.G. Candau Lectr. medal, WHO, 1983. Mem. AAAS. Avocations: music, tennis. Home: Collonge, Switzerland. Died Oct. 16, 2004.

**KAPLAN, ROBERT PHILLIP (BOB KAPLAN),** retired Canadian government official; b. Toronto, Ont., Can., Dec. 27, 1936; s. Solomon Charles and Pearl (Grafstein) K.; m. Estherelke Tanenbaum Kaplan, Oct. 10, 1961; children: Jennifer Mia, John David, Raquel Katherine. BA, U. Toronto, 1958, LLB, 1961. Bar: Called to Ont. bar 1963. Pvt. practice, Toronto; mem. Canadian House of Commons, Don Valley and York Centre, 1968-74; mem. standing com. on finance, trade & economic affairs M.P. for York Centre, 1974—83; solicitor gen. Govt. of Canada, 1980-84; liberal justice critic, 1984-90. Co-author: Bicycling in Toronto, 1971. Mem. Can. Bar Assn., Law Soc. Upper Can., Canadian Civil Liberties Assn. Liberal. Jewish. Home: Toronto, Canada. Died Nov. 5, 2012.

**KAPLICKY, JAN,** architect; b. Prague, Apr. 18, 1937; m. Amanda Levete (div.); 1 child, Josef; m. Eliska Kaplicky Fuchsova; 1 child, Johana. Attended, Coll. of Applied Arts & Architecture, Prague. With Denys Lasdun & Ptnrs., 1969—71, Renzo Piano & Richard Rogers, 1971—73; assoc. Spencer & Webster, 1974—75; with Lois de Soissons, 1977—83, Foster Assocs., 1979—83; co-founder, ptnr. Future Systems design studio, 1979—2009. Projects include, Mobile Zelt, London, 1992, Hauer-King House, 1994, Media Ctr. at Lord's Cricket Ground, bridge linking West India Quay and Canary Wharf, designs for, Comme des Garcons, NYC, Tokyo (Archtl. Record Houses and Interiors award 2003), Paris, Selfridges Bldg., Birmingham (Retail Destination of Yr., 2004, Civic Trust award, 2004, Structural Steel Design awards (Structural Frame), RIBA award for Architecture (Midlands), 2004, ICE Project Award Winner, 2004), others; author: More for Inspiration Only, 1999, Confessions - Principles Architecture Process Life, 2002, Czech Inspiration, 2005, others. Recipient Outstanding Retail Experience award, Selfridges Kids, 2002, Contravision Internat. Wrap award, New Look, 2003, Designer of Yr., FX Internat. Interior Design awards, 2003, Retail Week awards, 2004. Died Jan. 14, 2009.

**KAPUSCINSKI, RYSZARD,** journalist; b. Pinsk, Poland, Mar. 4, 1932; s. Jozef and Maria (Bobka) K.; m. Alicja Mielczarek; 1 child. MA Faculty History, Warsaw U.; D honoris causa, U. Silesia, Katowice, 1997. With Sztandar Mlodych, 1951, Polityka, 1957-61; corr. Polish Press Agy., Africa, Latin Am., 1962-72; with Kultura, 1974-81. Vis. prof. Temple U., Phila.; vice chmn. com. rsch. and prognosis Polish Acad. Scis. Author: Busz po polsku, Czarne gwiazdy, Kirgiz schodzi z konia, Gdyby cala Afryka..., Dlaczego zginal Karl von Spreti, Chrystus z karabinem na ramieniu, Jeszcze dzien zycia, Cesarz, Wojna futbolowa, Szachinszach, Notes, Lapidarium, Laidarium II, Lapidarium III, Lapidaria, Imperium Heban, Lapidarium IV, Z Afryki. Decorated Golden Cross of Merit, Knight's Cross, Order Polonia Restituta; recipient B Prus, 1975, Internat. prize Internat. Journalists Orgn., 1976, State prize (2d class), 1976, German prize for European Understanding, 1994, Lit. award Alfred Jurzykowski Found., 1994, Prix d'Astrolab, 1995, Jan. Parandowski PEN Club prize, 1996, Lit. award Turzanski Found., 1996, Joseph Conrad Lit. award J. Pilsudski Inst. Am., 1997, Hansische Goethee-Preis, 1999, S.B. Linde lit. award Twin Cities Toruń-Götingen, 1999, Viareggio award, 2000, Omegna award, 2000, Calabria award, 2000, Creola award, 2000. Mem. Nat. Coun. Culture, European Acad. Sci. and Art, Polish Acad. Sci. and Art. Died Jan. 23, 2007.

**KARANTOKIS, NICOLAS GEORGIOU,** contractor, developer; b. Nicosia, Cyprus, Jan. 13, 1917; s. Georgios Nicola and Panayiota Georgiou Karantokis; m. Lella Phisentzides, Apr. 27, 1947; 3 children. Student, Pancyprian Gymnasium Nicosia, 1935, Athens U., 1939. Interpreter Recruiting Office, 1941—42; contractor Brit. Army, 1943—60; chmn. Medcon Constrn. Ltd., Nicosia, from 1956; chmn., mng. dir. Medcon Group. Chmn., com. Tripiotis Ch., Nicosia. Home: Nicosia, Cyprus. Died Jan. 2006.

**KARAOSMANOGLU, ATTILA,** retired bank executive; b. Manisa, Turkey, Sept. 20, 1932; s. Ibrahim Ethem and Fatma Eda Karaosmanoglu; m. Sukriye Ozyet, Mar. 11, 1960; 1 child, Ozgur. BA in Economics, U. Ankara, Turkey, 1954; PhD in Economics, U. Istanbul, Turkey, 1958. Faculty mem. U. Ankara, 1955-60; head econ. planning dept. State Planning Orgn., Turkey, 1960-62; cons. Orgn. Econ. Cooperation & Devel. (OECD), Paris, 1965-66; dep. prime min. Govt. of Turkey, Ankara, 1971-72; economist, sr. economist World Bank, Washington, 1966-71, chief economist, 1973-75, dir., 1975-82, v.p. East Asia and Pacific region, 1982-87, v.p. Asia region, 1987—91. Vis. scholar Harvard U., 1956-57; exch. faculty NYU, 1957-58. Died Nov. 10, 2013.

**KARKI, BENI BAHADUR,** councilman; b. Dolakha, Nepal, Sept. 4, 1929; s. Bahadur Khadaga and Lalita K.; m. Ishowri Devi; 1 child: Bahadur Rajendra. Mem. parliament Gorkha Parishad, Nepal, 1959-61; mem., treas. Nepali Congress, 1964-80; chmn. Nat. Coun., Nepal, from 1990. Founder Gorkha Parishad, Nepal, 1950; life mem. Tuberculosis Cancer Soc., Red Cross; pres. Nepal Japan Friendship Coun. Mem. Lions Club (hon.). Home: Lalitpur, Nepal. Died Jan. 2005.

**KARLSSON, PER WENNERBERG,** mathematics educator; b. Copenhagen, Dec. 26, 1936; s. Hans August Gunnar and Eva (Kohrtz) K.; m. Karen Margrethe Mortensen, Feb. 11, 1961; children: Henrik Michael, Helle Birgitte. MSc in Electrophysics, Tech. U. Denmark, 1961; MSc in Math., U. Copenhagen, 1965. Asst. prof. Tech. U. Denmark, Lyngby, 1961-63, assoc. prof., 1963—2003, emeritus prof., from 2004. Co-author: Multiple Gaussian Hypergeometric Series, 1985; reviewer Zentralblatt für Math., 1970—, Math. reviews, 2000-; referee various profl. math. jours., 1973—; contbr. articles on hypergeometric functions to profl. jours. Mem. Soc. Indsl. and Applied Math., Dansk Math. Forening, Nat. Acad. Scis. India. Home: Virum, Denmark. Died Nov. 2012.

**KARMEL, PETER HENRY,** economist; b. Melbourne, Australia, May 9, 1922; s. Simeon Karmel and Ethel Rose Holtz; m. Lena Garrett, Oct. 30, 1946; children: Prudence, Thomas, Joanna, Rosemary, Philippa, Samantha. BA, U. Melbourne, 1942; PhD, U. Cambridge, 1948; LLD (hon.), U. Papua, 1970; DLitt (hon.), Flinders U., 1971; LLD (hon.), U. Melbourne, 1975; DLitt (hon.), Murdoch U., 1975; D (hon.), U. Newcastle, 1978; LLD (hon.), Queensland U., 1985; DLitt (hon.), Macquarie U., 1992; LLD (hon.), Australian Nat. U., 1996. Prof. econs. U. Adelaide, Adelaide, 1950—62; vice chancellor Flinders U., 1963—71; chair Australian U. Commn., Canberra, 1971—77, Tertiary Edn. Commn., 1977—82; vice chancellor Australian Nat. U., 1982—87; chair Nat. Inst. Arts, 1988—2003. Chair chancellor U. Papua New Guinea, Port Moresby, 1965—71; chair Australia Coun., 1974—77, Australian Coun. Ednl. Rsch., 1979—99, Australian Inst. Health, 1987—92, Australian Coun. AIDS, 1988—92. Contbr. articles to profl. jours. Recipient Centenary medal, 2001; named a Comdr. of the Order of the British Empire, Her Majesty Queen Elizabeth II, 1967, Companion of the Order of Australia, 1976. Fellow: Australian Coll. Educators, Acad. Social Scis. Australia (pres.). Home: Yarralumla, Australia. Died Dec. 30, 2008.

**KARPATI, GEORGE,** neurologist; b. Hungary, May 17, 1934; m. Shira Tannor, July 31, 1966; children: Adam, Joshua. MD, Dalhousie U., Halifax, NS, 1960; Doctorate (hon.), U. Marseille, 1995. Postdoctoral tng. Mont. Neurol. Inst., Can., 1960-64, neuroscientist; rsch. tng. NIH, Bethesda, Md., 1965-67; asst. prof. neurology & neurosurgery McGill U., 1967—78, prof. neurology & neurosurgery Mont., 1978—2009, Isaac Walton Killam chair neurology, 1984—2009; assoc. dir. Mont. Neurol. Inst., 1984-92. Co-author: Pathology of Skeletal Muscle, 1984; contbr. over 280 articles to sci. jours. Recipient 125th Commemorative medal of Can., Gov. Gen. of Can., 1993; recipient Disting. Scientist award Can. Soc. Clin. Investigation, 1997, Queen's Jubilee Medal, 2002; named an Officer of the Order of Can., 2001, Chevalier de l'ordre nationale du Québec, 2005 Fellow Royal Coll. Physicians and Surgeons Can., Am. Acad. Neurology, Royal Soc. Can.; mem. Am. Neurol. Assn., Can. Acad. Medicine (elected 1992). Achievements include research in neuromuscular diseases, nerve-muscle biology, and gene therapy. Died Feb. 6, 2009.

**KASEM, CASEY (KEMAL AMIN KASEM),** retired radio and television personality; b. Detroit, Apr. 27, 1933; m. Linda Kasem (div.); children: Julie, Mike, Kerri; m. Jean Kasem, 1 child. Student, Wayne State U. Radio announcer Stas. WJLB, WJBK, Detroit; disc jockey Cleve., Buffalo and Oakland Calif., 1961; host nat. weekly radio show American Top 40, 1970—88; host nat. TV shows America's Top Ten, 1980-90. Actor: (feature films) The Girls From Thunder Strip, 1966, Doomsday Machine, 1967, Cycle Savages, 1969, Two Thousand Years Later, 1969, Free Grass, 1969, Wild Wheels, 1969, The Incredible Two-Headed Transplant, 1971, The Day the Lord Got Busted, 1976, New York, New York, 1977, Disco Fever, 1978, The Dark, 1979, Ghostbusters, 1984, (voice) Transformers: The Movie, 1986; (TV epsiodes) Charlie's Angels, Hawaii Five-0, Fantasy Island, (radio show) War of the Worlds; voice-over artist over 2,000 cartoons including Batman, Scooby Doo, Cattanooga Cats. Served with U.S. Army, 1952, Korea. Died June 15, 2014.

**KASHIWAGI, YUSUKE,** bank executive; b. Dalian, China, 1917; s. Hideshige and Kiyo (Yamada) K.; married; 4 children. LLB, Tokyo Imperial U., 1941. Dir. gen. internat. fin. bur. Japan Ministry Fin., Tokyo, 1966-68, vice minister fin., 1968-71, spl. advisor to the minister, 1971-72; dep. pres. Bank Tokyo, 1973-77, pres., 1977-82, chmn. bd., 1982-92, sr. advisor, 1992-96, Bank of Tokyo-Mitsubishi, Ltd., 1996—2004. Author: Gekidohki no Tsuuka Gaikon (Monetary Diplomacy in Turbulent Times), (1972, Watashi no Rirekisho (My Hometown-Dalian-New York-Tokyo), 1987. Named to Grand Cordon of the Order of the Sacred Treasure, Emperor of Japan, 1989. Mem. Rotary (Tokyo), Tokyo Club. Avocations: travel, golf. Home: Tokyo, Japan. Died 2004.

**KATZ, BARBARA STEIN,** special education educator; b. Springfield, Mass., July 22, 1933; d. Harry and Pearl (Black) Stein; m. Charles Murry Katz, July 14, 1957; children: Helen L., Robert A. BS, Am. Internat. Coll., Springfield, 1956, MA in Ednl. Psychology in Learning Disabilities, 1979. Cert. in elem. edn., moderate spl. needs, Mass. Elem. tchr. Springfield Pub. Schs., 1956-60; Jr. Great Books discussion leader, 1968-69; Gillingham remedial tchr. Pub. Schs., Longmeadow, Mass., 1975-78, spl. edn. tchr. Chicopee, Mass., 1978-98. Proprietor Lynn Katz Photography. Pres. Kodimoh Synagogue Women's Group, Springfield, 1972-74; troop leader Girl Scouts U.S., Longmeadow, 1967-70; reader Lower Pioneer Valley Collaborative, 1998-2002. Horace Mann grantee, 1988. Mem.: NEA, Nat. Trust Hist. Preservation, Trustees Reservations, Mass. Tchrs. Assn., Jewish Geriatric Svcs. (life), Mizrachi (life), Hadassah (life). Avocations: painting, reading, walking, swimming. Home: Longmeadow, Mass. Died Nov. 28, 2013.

**KATZ, LEWIS,** former professional sports team executive; b. Camden, NJ, Jan. 11, 1942; s. Milton and Betty Katz; m. Marjorie Nemarow, 1966 (dec. 2013); children: Drew, Melissa Marjorie. BS in Biology, Temple U., 1963; JD, Dickinson U., 1966; D (hon.), Temple U., 2014. Law clk. to Chief Justice John C. Bell Jr. Pa. Supreme Ct.; ptnr. Katz, Ettin, Levine & Weber, P.A., Cherry Hill, NJ; chmn., CEO Kinney Sys. Holding Corp., 1990—98; owner, gen. ptnr. N.J. Nets, East Rutherford, 1998—2004. Bd. dirs. NBA. Hon. chair Campus Capital Fund Dr.; established Boys and Girls Club, Camden County, NJ; bd. dirs. Temple U., Phila. Recipient Bridge Builders award, Ptnrs. Livable Cmtys. Died May 31, 2014.

**KATZ, MICHAEL BARRY,** humanities educator; b. Wilmington, Del., Apr. 13, 1939; s. George Joseph and Beatrice Katz; m. Edda Britt Katz; children: Paul, Rebecca, Sarah. BA, Harvard U., 1961, MAT, 1962, EdD, 1966. Prof. history OISE & U. Toronto, 1966—73, York U., Toronto, 1973—78, U. Pa., Phila., 1978—2014, Walter H. Annenberg prof. history, 2001—14. Archivist Social Sci. Rsch. Coun. Com. for Rsch. on the Urban Underclass, NYC, 1989—95; chair Dept. History U. Pa., 1991—95, 2011—12; mem. Social Sci. Rsch. Coun. Com. on Philanthropy and Non-Profits, NYC, 2000—14. Author: The Irony of Early School Reform: Educational Innovation in Mid-Nineteenth Century Massachusetts, 1968, Class, Bureaucracy, and Schools: The Illusion of Educational Change in America, 1971, The People of Hamilton, Canada West: Family and Class in a Mid-Nineteenth Century City, 1975 (Albert C. Corey award, 1976), Poverty and Policy in American History, 1983, In the Shadow of the Poorhouse: A Social History of Welfare in America, 1986, Reconstructing American Education, 1987, The Undeserving Poor: From the War on Poverty to the War on Welfare, 1990, Improving Poor People: The Welfare State, the Underclass, and Urban Schools as History, 1995, One Nation Divisible: What America Was and What It Is Becoming, 2006, The Price of Citizenship: Redefining the American Welfare State, 2001, Why Don't American Cities Burn?, 2012; co-author (with Mark J. Stern): The Social Organization of Early Industrial Capitalism, 1981; editor: The Underclass Debate: Views from History, 1993; co-editor (with Thomas Sugrue): W.E.B. DuBois, Race, and the City: The Philadelphia Negro and its Legacy, 1998; co-editor: (with Christoph Sachsse) The Mixed Economy of Social Welfare: England, Germany, and the United States from the 1870's to the 1930's, 1996. Mem. Rsch. for Action, Phila., 1996—2002; v.p. Haines Landing Cottage Assn., Oquossoc, Maine, 2001—02. Recipient Sr. Scholar award, Spencer Found., 1999, Provost award for Disting. Graduate Student Teaching & Mentoring, 2007; fellow, Inst. for Advanced Study, 1973—74, Guggenheim Found., 1975—76, Shelby Cullom Davis Ctr., 1984—85, Russell Sage Found., 1988—89, Open Soc. Inst., 1998—99. Fellow: Soc. American Historians, Nat. Acad. Edn.; mem.: American Philosophical Soc., Nat. Acad. Social Ins., Pa. Hist. Soc., Urban History Assn., Social Sci. History Assn., Organ. of American Historians, History of Edn. Assn. (pres. 1975—76), American Hist. Assn., U. City Hist. Soc., Appalaichan Mountain Club, American Canoe Assn. Avocations: kayaking, hiking, bicycling. Died Aug. 23, 2014.

**KAUFMAN, BEL,** author, educator; b. Berlin, May 10, 1911; d. Michael J. and Lala (Rabinowitz) K.; m. Sydney Goldstine (div.); children: Jonathan Goldstine, Thea Goldstine. BA magna cum laude, Hunter Coll., 1934; DHL, Hunter Coll, 2001; MA with highest honors, Columbia U., 1936; LLD honors, Nasson Coll., Maine, 1965. Adj. prof. English CUNY; lectr. throughout country, also appearances on TV and radio. Mem. Commn. Performing Arts. Editorial bd., Phi Delta Kappan.; Author: Up the Down Staircase, 1965, Love, etc, 1979 Bd. dirs. Shalom Aleichem Found.; mem. advisory council Town Hall Found. Recipient plaque Anti-Defamation League, award and plaque United Jewish Appeal, Paperback of Year award, Ky. Col. award, Bell Movie award, Nat. Treasure awrd Seasoned Citizens Theatre, 2001, Flame Keepers award Perpetuity; also ednl. journalism awards; named to Hall of Fame Hunter Coll., winner short story contest sponsored by NEA and PEN, 1983. Mem. Author's Guild, Dramatists Guild, P.E.N., English Grad. Union, Phi Beta Kappa. Died July 25, 2014.

**KAUL, HANS-PETER,** judge; b. Glashütte, Germany, July 25, 1943; married; 4 children. JD, U. Heidelberg and Lausanne, 1971; postgrad., Cambridge U., Eng., 1972, Ecole Nationale d'Adminstrn., Paris, 1972—73, Acad. Internat. Law, The Hague, 1974, Max Planck Inst. for Comparative Internat. and Pub. Internat. Law, 1973—75; LLD (hon.), U. Cologne, 2008. Asst. UN Conf. on Succession of States with Respect to Treaties, Vienna, 1977; consul, press attaché Germany Embassy to Norway, Oslo, 1977—80; with Office of UN Affairs, Fedn. Fgn. Office, Bonn, Germany, 1980—84; counsellor, spokesman German Embassy to Israel, Tel Aviv, 1984—86; polit. counsellor Germany Embassy to U.S., Washington, 1986—90; dep. dir. Office of Near Ea. Affairs Fed. Fgn. Office, Bonn, 1990—93; first counsellor Permanent Mission of Germany to UN, NYC, 1993—96; dir. Office for Pub. Internat. Law Fed. Fgn. Office, Bonn/Berlin, 1996—2002; amb., commr. Fed. Fgn. Office for Internat. Criminal Ct., 2002—03; judge Internat. Criminal Ct., The Hague, 2003—14, v.p., 2009—12, pres. pre-trial divsn., 2009—12. Mem. Nat. Expert Commn. on Code of Crimes Against Internat. Law, 1999—2001. Contbr. articles to profl. jours. Mem. nat. adv. com. on internat. humanitarian law German Red Cross Soc., from 1996. Capt. German Army, 1963—67. Recipient Integration prize, Found. Apfelbaum, 2008. Mem.: American Soc. Internat. Law, Internat. Criminal Law Network, German Soc. for Mil. Law and Internat. Humanitarian Law, German Soc. for Fgn. Policy, German Soc. for UN, German Soc. Internat. Law. Died July 21, 2014.

**KAVLI, FRED,** retired manufacturing and engineering executive, physicist; b. Eresfjord, Norway, Aug. 20, 1927; came to U.S., 1956; 2 children. Degree in Applied Physics, Norwegian Inst. Tech., 1955. Founder, CEO, sole shareholder automotive and aerospace sensor engring.-mfg. Kavlico Corp., Moorpark, Calif., 1958—2000; ret. Bd. dirs. The Found. for Santa Barbara City Coll.; trustee Found. for U. Calif., Santa Barbara; founder, chmn. The Kavli Found./The Kavli Operating Inst.; benefactor The Kavli Insts. (in neuroscience) at Columbia U., Yale U., UC San Diego, Norwegian U. Sci. & Tech; (in astrosci.) Stanford U. Chgo., MIT, Peking U., U. Cambridge; (in nanosci.) Harvard U., Caltech, Cornell U., Delft U. Tech.; (in theoretical physics) UC Santa Barbara, Chinese Acad. Sci; 2000 - mem. Pres. Bd. sci. and innovation, U. Calif.; endowed several chairs, one in engring. at the U. Calif., Santa Barbara, another chair in Optoelectronics and Sensors, U. Calif., Irvine, in Nanosystems Sciences at UCLA, and Cosmology, Calif. Inst. Tech. Recipient Royal Norwegian Order of Merit for Outstanding Svc., 2005, Bower award for Business Leadership, Franklin Inst., 2011; named Disting. Grand Patron, Alliance of the Arts, 1998, in honor of the Fred Kavli Theatre for Performing Arts at the Thousand Oak Civic Arts Plaza; named to The Scientific American 50: Policy Leader Yr., 2005. Fellow: Am. Acad. Arts & Sciences; mem.: Norwegian Acad. Technological Scis., US President's Coun. Advisors on Sci. and Tech. (PCAST). Achievements include patents in field. Died Nov. 21, 2013.

**KAWARA, ON,** artist; b. Kariya, Aichi Prefect, Japan, Jan. 2, 1933; One Million Years (Past and Future), 2000, and made over 2000 paintings since 1960's, exhibitions include Nippon Exhibition, Tokyo Met. Art Mus., 1953, Takemiya Gallery, 1954, Hibiya Gallery, 1954, Dwan Gallery, NY, 1967, One Million Years, Düsseldorf, Paris, and Milan, 1971, Mus. of Modern Art, NY, 1970, Mus. of Contemporary Art, LA, Serralves Found. Mus. of Contemporary Art, Portugal, and numerous other exhibitions.; author: (artist books) One Million Years, 1999, I Met, 2004, I Went, 2007, I Got Up, 2008. Died July 10, 2014.

**KAY, DENNIS MATTHEW,** retired publishing company official; b. Chgo., Sept. 20, 1936; s. Edward Francis and Rose Anne (Koziel) Kolodzinski; m. Judy R. Kalinsky, Jan. 9, 1965; 1 child, Alan Edward. BBA, Loyola U., 1976. Customer svc. agt. Am. Airlines, Chgo., 1959-69; expeditor Time Inc., Chgo., 1969-73, traffic mgr. People mag., 1973-75, Time mag. traffic mgr., 1975-78, ops. mgr., 1978-81, electronic data mgr., 1981-83, plant mgr. Waterloo, Wis., 1983-88, field ops. mgr., 1988-95, nat. prodn. analyst, 1995-96, field ops. mgr., 1996-99; ret., 2000; owner, pres. Luvitgifts Online Gift and Collectible Stores, from 2000. With 31st Arty. Detachment, 1959—61, Vicenza, Italy. Recipient MM&D Excellence award Time Inc., 1989, Prodn. Excellence awards, 1993, 94, Pres. award, 1993. Mem.: Moose Lodge River Grove 378 (gov. 1982-83), Am. Legion. Roman Catholic. Avocations: stamp collecting/philately, piano, model building. Home: Lake In The Hills, Ill. Died Dec. 12, 2013.

**KAYLOR, OMER THOMAS, JR.,** lawyer; b. Hagerstown, Md., July 14, 1923; s. Omer Thomas and Mabel E. (Slagen) K.; m. Jean Jaskin Johnston, Aug. 23, 1947; children: Omer Thomas, Laura, Gwen, Mark, John. B, Washington and Lee U., 1945, JD, 1949. Bar: Md. Sec., dir. Farmer & Mchts. Bank, Hagerstown, 1960-93. Pres. Hagerstown United Fund, Hagerstown UMCA; v.p. Washington County Mus., 1984-97; mem. Md. State Legis., 1950-54; chair Washington County Ethics Commn. Mem. Washington County Bar Assn. (past pres.), Assembly Club (Hagerstown), Fountain Head Country Club. Republican. Mem. United Ch. of Christ. Home: Hagerstown, Md. Died Apr. 19, 1999.

**KAZAMA, TOSHIO,** retired humanities educator; b. Tokyo, Jan. 2, 1924; s. Kiichi and Mume (Yamana) K.; m. Kazuyo (Shimomura), May 10, 1955; children: Keiichi, Shinjiro, Naoto. Attended, Tokyo U., 1947—52. Instr., asst. prof. liberal arts Hosei U., Tokyo, 1969-74, prof. liberal arts, 1974-94; mem. emeritus Japanese Assn. Indian and Buddhist Studies. Author: A New Interpretation of Bi Yan Ji, 1978. Cadet, Japanese Shipping Engr., 1945. Avocation: seal engraving. Home: Mitaka, Japan. Died Dec. 2014.

**KEARNS, MERLE GRACE,** retired state legislator; b. Bellefonte, Pa., May 19, 1938; d. Robert John and Mary Katharine (Fitzgerald) Grace; m. Thomas Raymond Kearns, June 27, 1959; children: Thomas, Michael, Timothy, Matthew. BS, Ohio State U., 1960. Tchr. St. Raphael Elem. Sch., Springfield, Ohio, 1960-62; substitute tchr. Mad River Green Dist., Springfield, 1972-78; instr. Clark Tech. Coll., Springfield, 1978-80; commr. Clark County, Ohio, 1981-91; mem. Ohio State Senate, Columbus, 1991-2000, majority whip, 1998—2000; mem. Ohio House of Reps., Columbus, 2001—05, majority leader, 2005; dir. Ohio Dept. Aging, 2005—07; ret., 2007. Pres. Bd. County Commrs., 1982—83, 1987, 1990. Sec. County Commrs. Assn. Ohio, 1988, 2d v.p., 1989—90, 1st v.p., 1990; mem. exec. com. Springfield Reps., 1984—2001; chair Ohio Children's Trust Fund, 1995—2000; past chair Legis. Office of Edn. Oversight; active NCSL Welfare Reform Task Force, 2001—05; vice-chair Policy Consensus Initiative Bd., from 2002; chair Head Start Plus Study Coun.; hon. chair Srs. 4 Kids, Ohio, 2007; senate pres. public position Ohio Commn. on Conflict Mgmt. and Dispute Resolution, 2007; bd. dirs. Springfield Symphony, 1980—86, Arts Coun., 1980—85; bd. dirs., mem. exec. bd. Nat. Conf. State Legislatures, 2000—03. Recipient Public Policy Leadership award, 1997, Disting. Svc. Public Officials award, Assn. Ohio Philanthropic Homes, 1999, 1st Ann. Jane Swart Disting. Services to Nursing, 2000, Citizenship award, Ohio State U. Coll. Human Ecology, 2000, Legislator of Yr., Behavioral Health Authorities Assn., 2003, Ohio Better World award, Ohio Mediation Assn., 2004; named Woman of the Yr., Springfield Pilot Club, 1981, Wittenburg Woman of Accomplishment, 1991, Watchdog of Treasury, 1991, 1996, 2000, Legislator of the Yr., Assn. Mental Health and Drug Addiction Svcs. Bds., 1996, Public Children's Services Agencies Ohio, 1999, Ohio Cmty. Colleges, 1997, Ohio Disting. Nurses, 2000, Advance Practice Nurse Assn., 2002, Legis. Co-Person of the Yr., Assn. Joint Vocat. Sch. Superintendants, 1996, Mental Health Adv. of the Yr., 2002, Outstanding Head Start Legislator of the Yr., Miami Valley, 2002, Legislator of Yr., Ohio Fedn. Teachers, 2003, Advocate of Yr., Ohio County Alzheimer Assn., 2004, Alzheimer Legis. Advocate of Yr., 2004, Outstanding Citizen, Clark County Leadership Forum, 2006, The One of Top Ten Women, Miami Valley, Dayton Daily News, 2007;, Ohio State U. scholar, 1957—59. Mem.: LWV (bd. dirs. 1964—78, pres. 1975—78), Ohio Nurses Assn. (Legislator of the Yr. 1995, 1999), Rotary, Omicron Nu. Republican. Roman Catholic. Avocation: reading. Home: Port Clinton, Ohio. Died Aug. 9, 2014.

**KEATING, BERN,** writer, journalist; b. Fassett, Can., May 14, 1915; came to U.S., 1920; s. John Julian Keating and Laure Lalonde; m. Marian West, June 10, 1939; 1 child, John G. BA magna cum laude, U. Ark., 1938. Reporter, relief editor Palm Beach (Fla.) Post Times, 1938-41; news editor Utica N.Y. Radio, 1941; freelance journalist, writer Greenville, Miss., from 1945. Author over 25 books, 800 mag. articles, 1 documentary movie. With U.S. Navy, 1942-45. Recipient Lifetime Achievement award Miss. Inst. Arts Letters, 1995. Mem. Travel Journalists Guild (founder, pres.), Authors Guild, Am. Soc. Journalists Authors. Deceased.

**KEATING, CHARLES,** actor; b. London, Oct. 22, 1941; m. Mary Keating; children: Sean, Jamie. Actor: (films) Funny Money, 1982, The Rocking Horse Winner, 1983, Awakenings, 1990, The Bodyguard, 1992, The Thomas Crown Affair, 1999, Harlem Aria, 1999, Deuce Bigelow: European Gigolo, 2005; (TV series) As the World Turns, 1989-90, Another World, 1983-85, 91-98, 99, All My Children, 1987-88, Going to Extremes, 1992-93, Port Charles, 1997-2003, (TV miniseries) Brideshead Revisited, 1982, Fresno, 1986, (TV fims) Richard II, 1978, A Deadly Game, 1979, A Talent for Murder, 1984; (theatre) Loot!, The Doctor's Dilemma, A Man for All Seasons, Light Up the Sky, Pygmalion. Recipient Best Lead Actor in Drama Series Daytime Emmy, 1995 Avocations: gardening, painting. Died Aug. 8, 2014.

**KEATING, CHARLES HUMPHREY, JR.,** former bank executive; b. Cin., Dec. 4, 1923; s. Charles Humphrey & Adelle Keating; m. Mary Elaine (Fette) Keating; children: Kathleen, Mary, Maureen, Elaine, Elizabeth, Charles III. Student, U. Cin., 1941, JD, 1948. Sole practice, to 1948-1955; ptnr. Keating Muething & Klekamp, 1955-72; exec. v.p. American Financial Corp., 1972-76; chmn., CEO American Continental Corp.(formerly known as American Continental Homes), Phoenix, 1976—89. Served in USN, 1942-46 Mem. Presidential Committee on Obscenity and Pornography, 1969-70. Democrat. Roman Catholic. Died Mar. 31, 2014.

**KEEFER, DON HOOD,** actor; b. High Spire, Pa., Aug. 18, 1916; s. John E. and Edna E. (Hood) K.; m. Catherine F. McLeod, May 7, 1950 (dec. 1997); children: Don, John, Thomas. Student, Am. Acad. Dramatic Art, 1937-39. Actor, NYC, from 1941. Founder, mem. Actors Studio, N.Y.C., 1947-2014 Appeared in Broadway Prodns. including Junior Miss, 1941-42, Harriet, 1942-43, Othello, 1945, Death of a Salesman, 1949-50, Flight Into Egypt, 1951, (films) Death of a Salesman, Caine Mutiny, 1959, The Russians are Coming, The Russians Are Coming, 1966, Butch Cassidy and the Sundance Kid, 1969, Away All Boats, Sleeper, 1973 The Way We Were, 1973, Creepshow, 1982; performer and arranger (one man show) Anton Chekhov, 1964 (Edinburgh Internat. Festival 1980). Mem.: The Players. Avocation: art collector. Home: Sherman Oaks, Calif. Died Sept. 7, 2014.

**KEEN, HELEN BOYD,** artist; b. Tacoma, Wash., Aug. 12, 1894; d. James Munro and Margaret (Delprat) Keen. One-man shows include Tacoma Art League, 1945, Seattle Art Mus., 1945, Zoe Dusanne Gallery, Seattle, 1952, Artists Gallery, NYC, 1956, 1960, Art Gallery Greater Victoria, B.C., Can., 1966, exhibited in group shows at Seattle Art Mus., 1939—45, Tacoma Art League, 1938—45, US State Dept. Show, Paris, 1956—57, Pa. Acad. Fine Arts, 1957, Bklyn. Mus., 1957, Blue Hill Gallery, Maine, Seligman Gallery, Seattle, 1962—66, Norfolk Mus. Arts and Sci., Va., 1963, Weye Gallery, NYC, 1968, Avanti Gallery, 1972, Smithsonian Archives, Washington, 1980, Represented in permanent collections Seattle Art Mus., Addison Gallery Am. Art, Mass., Tacoma Art Mus., Art Gallery Greater Victoria, B.C., Can., pvt. collections; dir.:. Recipient First award, Tacoma Art League, 1945; named Premio Oscar de Italia Accademia Italia, 1985. Mem.: Nat. Geographic Assn. Republican. Episcopalian. Died Jan. 20, 1992.

**KEEN, MARIA ELIZABETH,** retired educator; b. Chgo., Aug. 19, 1918; d. Harold Fremont and Mary Eileen Honore (Dillon) K. AB, U. Chgo., 1941; postgrad., U. Wyo., summer 1943; MA, U. Ill., 1949; postgrad., U. Mich., 1957. Tchr. high sch., Wyo., 1942-43, Mich., 1943-44; tchr. Am. Coll. for Women, Istanbul, Turkey, 1944-47; mem. faculty U. Ill., Urbana, 1947-88, prof. emerita, from 1988. Mem. Champaign Community Devel. Com. Mem. AAUW, AAUP (past treas.), AAAS, LWV, Animal Protection Inst., Defenders of Wildlife, Am. Inst. Biol. Scis., Nat. Coun. Tchr. Educators, U. Ill. Athletic Assn. (sec., bd. dirs.), Ont. Geneal. Soc., Orton Dyslexia Soc., Art Inst. Chgo., Women's Philharm. (charter), Women in Arts (charter), Women's Humane Soc., Illini Union (faculty staff social com.), Nat. Humane Soc., Phi Kappa Epsilon (hon.). Baptist. Deceased.

**KEENER, HARRY ALLAN,** academic administrator; b. Greensboro, Pa., Dec. 22, 1913; s. Franklin Hodson and Mary Ann (Kelley) K.; m. Elizabeth Margaret Hartley, July 26, 1941; children: Allan Wayne, William Franklin. BS, Pa. State U., 1936, PhD, 1941; MS, W.Va. U., 1938. Grad. asst. W.Va. U., Morgantown, 1936-38, Pa. State U., University Park, 1938-41; instr. to prof. U. N.H., Durham, 1941-78, dir. agrl. experiment sta., 1958-78, dean Coll. of Life Sci. and Agr., 1961-78, prof. and dean emeritus, from 1978. Bd. collaborators U.S. Plant, Soil and Nutrition Lab., Ithaca, N.Y., 1956-59, U.S. Pasture Rsch. Lab., University Park, 1952-62; mem. N.H. Soil Conservation Com., 1958-78. Co-author: (textbook) Milk Production and Processing, 1960 (Spanish edit. 1962); contbr. articles to profl. jours. Recipient Granite State award U. N.H., 1980. Mem. N.Y. Acad. Sci., Alpha Gamma Rho, Sigma Xi, Gamma Sigma Delta, Phi Kappa Phi. Deceased.

**KEFALIDES, NICHOLAS ALEXANDER,** physician, educator; b. Alexandroupolis, Greece, Jan. 17, 1927; came to U.S., 1947, naturalized; s. Athanasios and Alexandra (Aematidou) K.; m. Eugenia Georgia Kutsunis, Nov. 24, 1949; children: Alexandra Jane (dec.), Patricia Ann, Paul Thomas. BA, Augustana Coll., Rock Island, Ill., 1951; BS, U. Ill., Chgo., 1953, MS in Biochemisry, 1956, MD, 1956, PhD in Biochemistry, 1965; MS (hon.), U. Pa., 1971; doctorate (hon.), U. Reims, France, 1987. Resident in internal medicine U. Ill. Coll. Medicine, Chgo., 1960-62, NIH fellow in infectious disease, 1962-64, asst. prof. medicine, 1964-65, U. Chgo., 1965-69, assoc. prof. medicine, 1969-70; assoc. prof. medicine and biochemistry U. Pa., Phila., 1970-74, prof. medicine, 1974—96, prof. medicine emeritus, from 1996, prof. biochemistry and biophysics, from 1975; assoc. dean rsch. U. Pa. Sch. Medicine, 1994-95; pres. Assn. Sr. and Emeritus, Sch. Medicine, U. Penn., 2010—12. Vis. prof. Oxford (England) U., 1977—78, 1984—85; mem., chmn. pathobiochemistry study sect. NIH, 1982—86, dir. project on burns, Peru, 1957—60; dir. Connective Tissue Rsch. Inst., Phila., 1977—2002; chmn. Instn. Rev. Bd. U. Pa., 1995—98, exec. chmn., 1998—2003; initiator, chair Gordon Rsch. Confs. on Basement Membranes, 1982; sci. mentor biotech. cos. Sci. Ctr., Phila., 2002—10; chair Penn. Assoc. Sr. & Emeritus Faculty Program Com., 2008—11; pres. sr. emeritus faculty Assn. U. Pa. Sch. Med., from 2010. Author: (with J. P. Borel) Basement Membranes: Cell and Molecular Biology, 2005, Echoes from the CobbleStones-A Memoir, 2009(translated to greek), Finding Aesculapius Across the Atlantic Amemoir, 2012; creator lecture series Lunch for Hungry Minds, Phila., 1998—; contbr. chpts. to books, articles to profl. jours. Lt. comdr., surgeon US Public Health Svc., 1957—60. Recipient Borden Rsch. Found. award, 1956, award for pioneering rsch. on connective tissue Collagen Gordon Confs. and Collagen Corp., 1997; Guggenheim fellow, 1977. Fellow AAAS; mem. Am. Assn. Pathologists, Am. Soc. Clin. Investigation, Am. Soc. Biochemistry and Molecular Biology, Am. Soc. Cell Biology. Achievements include discovery of Collagen type IV in basement membranes and its role in suppressing tumor cell growth and angiogenesis. Home: Merion Station, Pa. Died Dec. 6, 2013.

**KEHOE, JAMES W.,** federal judge; b. 1925; AA, U. Fla., 1947, LL.B., 1950. Bar: Fla. Assoc. firm Worley, Kehoe & Willard, 1952-55; asst. county solicitor Dade County, Fla., 1955-57; assoc. firm Miltor R. Wasman, 1957-61; judge Civil Record Ct., Miami, 1961-63, 11th Jud. Cir. Ct., Fla., 1963-77, U.S. Ct. Appeals (3d cir.), 1977-79, U.S. Dist. Ct. (so. dist.) Fla., from 1979, sr. judge, from 1993. Mem. ABA, Fla. Bar Assn. Died Dec. 13, 1999.

**KEHOE, THOMAS FRANCIS,** curator; b. Janesville, Wis., Nov. 29, 1926; s. Robert Bartholomew Kehoe and Ada Stevens; m. Alice Eve Beck, Sept. 18, 1956 (div. Nov. 1993); children: Daniel Miles, Thomas David, Cormac Joel; life ptnr. Mary Anne Siderits. BA in Anthropology, Beloit Coll., 1950; MA in Anthropology, U. Wash., 1957; postgrad., Harvard U., 1957-62. Dir., curator U.S. Dept. Interior, Mus. Plains Indian, Browning, Mont., 1952-59; curator, provincial archaeologist Mus. Nat. History, Regina, Can., 1959-65; dir. Nebr. State Hist. Soc. Mus., Lincoln, 1965-66; asst. clin. prof. anthropology U. Wis., Milw., 1968-82; curator anthropology Milw. Pub. Mus., 1968-90, curator emeritus, from 1991; coord. ethnology working groups Internat. Coun. Mus., Paris, 1974-83; Fulbright prof., rschr. U. Tubingen, Germany, 1978-83. Lectr. Groningen (The Netherlands) Inst. Archeology, 1979, U. Leicester (Eng.), 1981; U.S. corr. ArchaeoZoologia, Internat. Coun. Archaeozoology, Bordeaux, France, 1986-90; rschr., spkr. in field. Author: Stone Tipi Rings in North-Central Montana and the Adjacent Portion of Alberta, Canada, 1960, The Boarding School Bison Drive, 1967, The Gull Lake Site, 1973, Solstice-Aligned Boulder Configurations in Saskatchewan, 1979; contbr. articles and revs. to profl. jours., chpts. to books. Mem. Boy Scouts Am., 1944 (Eagle Scout). With U.S. Army, 1945-46. Rsch. Travel grantee NEA, 1972, Nat. Mus. Can., 1972-73, 75, 77, Am. Coun. Learned Socs., 1974-75, 77-78, NSF, 1982. Fellow Am. Anthrop. Assn. (mus. tng. and profl. standards com. 1975, bd. dirs. 1987, exec. bd. gen. anthropology divsn. 1987-89, mus. symposium organizer and chair 1988); mem. Am. Mus. Assn., Soc. Am. Archaeology, Am. Ethnological Soc., Coun. Mus. Anthropology, Wis. Archeol. Survey, Sask. Archeol. Soc. (charter), Sask. Assn. Profl. Archaeologists. Avocation: cross country skiing. Deceased.

**KEILIS-BOROK, VLADIMIR ISAACKOVICH,** geophysicist; b. Moscow, July 31, 1921; s. Isaack and Kseniya (Ruvimova) Keilis-Borok; m. Ludmila Malinovskaya, Oct. 6, 1956; 1 child from previous marriage, Irina. PhD in Mathematical Geophysics, Acad. Sci. USSR, Moscow, 1948; DSc (hon.), Institute du Physique du Globe, Paris, 1998. Rsch. fellow Earth Physics Inst., Acad. Scis. USSR, 1943—49, sr. rsch. fellow, 1949—60, chair dept. computational geophysics, 1970—89; founder, co-dir. Abdus Salam Internat. Ctr. Theoretical Physics, 1985—2013; founder, dir. Internat. Inst. Earthquake Prediction Theory & Math. Geophysics, Russian Acad. Sciences, 1989—98, rsch.group leader, 1998—2013, prof. earth & planetary sciences, 1999—2002; prof-in-residence UCLA, 2002—13. Expert on technological meetings Nuclear Test Ban Treaty, 1960—90; founding chmn. Internat. Com. for Geophysical Theory & Computers, 1964—79; v.p. Internat. Assn. Seismology & Physics of the Earth's Interior, 1983—87; pres. Internat. Union of Geodesy & Geophysics, 1987—91; bd. mem., chair mathematics & natural sciences section Internat. Coun. of Scientific Unions, 1988—91; mem. Union's Scientific Com. for the UN Decade for Natural Disasters Reduction, 1990—99, Internat. Working Group on the Geological Safety of Nuclear Waste Depositories, 1994—97. Contbr. articles to profl. jours. Recipient 21st Century Collaborative Activity award for Studying Complex Systems, McDonnell Found., First Lewis Fry Richardson medal for Exceptional Contributions to Non-Linear Geophysics, 1998. Mem.: AAAS (fgn. hon. 1969), Royal Astronomical Soc., Acadeia Eurpaea, Pontifical Acad. Scis, Austrian Acad. Scis., Russaian Acad. Scis. (mem. Com. for Internat. Security & Disarmament 1998—2000), US Nat. Acad. Scis. (fgn. assoc. 1971). Died Oct. 19, 2013.

**KELEMEN, ENDRE,** hematologist, researcher; b. Szekszard, Hungary, Jan. 17, 1921; s. József and Klára (Kardoss) K. MD, Pazmany Peter U., Budapest, Hungary, 1945; degree in Hematology, Min. Health, Budapest, Hungary, 1960; DSc, Hungarian Acad. Sci., 1966. Resident to assoc. prof. Med. U. Szeged, Hungary, 1945-58; assoc. prof. Postgrad. Sch. Medicine, Budapest, Hungary, 1958-67; scientific leader Semmelweis U. Budapest, Hungary, 1967-92; head Bone Marrow Transplantation unit Nat. Inst. Hematology, Budapest, Hungary, 1992-95. Pres. Nat. Coll. Hematology, 1991-95, mem. com. for degree hematologist, 1992—. Author: Inflammatory Oedema: Salicylates, 1960, Physiopathology and Therapy of Human Blood Diseases, 1969, Atlas of Human Hemopoietic Development, 1979; contbr. 300 articles to profl. jours. Pres. Bone Marrow Transplantation Found., Budapest, Hungary, 1991; mem. Pub. Welfare Found. Hungarian Nat. Bank, Budapest, Hungary, 1991—; freeman of Szekszard, 1989. Recipient Exptl. Haematology fellow Paterson Labs., Manchester, U.K., 1966, 67, Marshalko Grand prize Hungarian Haematological Soc., 1989; fellow Internat. Union Contra Cancer, Lyon, France, 1974, 75. Mem. European Soc. Haematology, Hungarian Soc. Hematology (pres. 1976-82, hon. life pres. 1997—), German Soc. Hematology and Oncology (hon.), Internat. Soc. Exptl. Haematology (Szècheny prize 1992, Laureatus Academiae 1995, Szent-Györgyi prize 1996), Hungarian Acad. Sci. (rep. gen. assembly 1998). Achievements include discovery of thrombopoietin. Died 2001.

**KELL, LEONE BOWER,** retired nutritionist; b. Dighton, Kans., Nov. 27, 1898; d. Carroll and Nettie Maxon (Cheever) Bower; m. William Edgar Kell, June 23, 1924 (dec. 1955); children: George(dec.), Eugene R.(dec.) 1 stepchild, Ruth Kell Noble. BS, Kans. State U., 1923; MS, 1928; postgrad., Cornell U., 1937—38, Stanford U., 1946. Tchr. elem. schs. Lane County, Kans., 1917—19; tchr. Manhattan HS, Kans., 1923—24; grad. asst. child devel. Kans. State U., Manhattan, 1927—28; instr., 1929—37; asst. prof., 1938—40; assoc. prof. family and child devel., 1940—46; prof., 1947—65; prof. emeritus, 1965—. Prof. home econs. Kobe Coll., Nishinomiya, Japan, 1967—70. Contbr. articles to profl. jours. Missionary United Ch. Bd. World Ministries, United Ch. Christ, Japan, 1967—70. Mem.: Soc. Rsch. Child Devel., Nat. Coun. Family Relations, Am. Home Econs. Assn., Phi Kappa Phi. Democrat. Congregationalist. Home: Brewster Pl 1205 SE 29th St Apt 525 Topeka KS 66605-1417

**KELLAND, LLOYD ROYSTON,** pharmacist, researcher; b. Barnstable, Devon, UK, Aug. 29, 1958; s. Bobbie Royston and Sylvia Mabel Anne Kelland; children: Robert William, Claire Louise. BPharm (hon.), U. Bath, 1979, PhD, 1984, DSc, 2000. MRPharmS Torbay Hosp., Devon, 1980. Basic grade pharmacicst NHS, Torquay, 1980; postdoctoral scientist Inst. Cancer Rsch., London, 1984—88, team leader, 1988—2001; head rsch. Antisoma, London, from 2001. Author: (book) Platinum-based Drugs in Cancer Therapy, 170 sci. articles. Parent gov. Sandcross Sch., Reigate, United Kingdom, 1994—2001. Mem.: Royal Soc. Medicine, Am. Soc. Clin. Oncology, Am. Assn. Cancer Rsch. Achievements include patents for therapeutic acridone and acridine compounds; quino acridinium salts as therapeutic agents. Died Aug. 2008.

**KELLEHER, JAMES FRANCIS,** retired Canadian government official, lawyer; b. Sault Ste. Marie, Ont., Can., Oct. 2, 1930; m. Helen; 2 children BA, Queen's U., 1952; grad., Osgoode Hall, 1956. Sr. ptnr. Kelleher, Laidlaw and MacDonald, Sault Ste. Marie; mem. Canadian Parliament, Ottawa, 1984—90, minister for internat. trade, 1984-86, solictor gen. of Can., 1986—88; mem. Canadian Senate, 1990—2005. Past dir. Great Lakes Power Ltd., Ont. Housing Corp.; past Canadian rep. Sault Ste. Marie Internat. Bridge Authority Past pres. Plummer Meml. Pub. Hosp., Sault Ste Marie; chmn. United Way Campaign, Sault Ste. Marie; past bd. dirs. Art Gallery of Algoma Mem. Sault and Dist. Law Assn. (past pres.), Sault Ste. Marie C. of C. (past dir.), Assn. Profl. Engrs. Ont. (mem. council). Mem. Progressive Conservative Party. Club: Nat. Retriever of Can. (past pres.) Died June 1, 2013.

**KELLER, JAMES E.,** retired state supreme court justice; b. Harlan, Ky., 1942; m. Elizabeth Keller; 2 children. Student, Ea. Ky. U.; JD, U. Ky. Pvt. practice, 1966—76; master commr. Fayette Cir. Ct., 1969-76, judge, 1976-99; justice Ky. Supreme Ct., 1999—2005; spl. counsel Gess Mattingly & Atchison, PSC, Lexington, Ky., 2005—14. Former chair Lexington-Fayette Urban County Criminal Justice Commn.; mem. Judicial Advisory Com. to Governor's Office of Child Abuse & Domestice Violence Services; chair Child Support Guidelines Review Commn.; mem. Special Legislative Task Force on Parenting & Child Custody; chair Ky. Civil Filing Fees Com.; mem. Gubernatorial Task Force on Delivery, Funding Quality Public Defendant Services. Co-founder Kid's Time Clinic, Ky., Parents Education Clinic, Ky., Mediation Ctr. of Ky. Recipient 5th Annual Kentuckians Involved in Dependents' Support award, 1990, Mediation Ctr. award, Mediation Ctr. of Ky., 1992, Henry V. Pennington Outstanding Trial Judge award, Ky. Acad. Trial Attorneys, 1994, Bowling Green Bar Assn. award, 1995, Law Day award, 1998; named to The U. Ky. Coll. Law Hall of Fame, 2005. Mem. Ky. Bar Assn., Fayette County Bar Assn. (Henry T. Duncan Memorial award 1987) Died June 2, 2014.

**KELLEY, MICHAEL ROBERT,** English language educator, communications executive; b. Washington, Aug. 20, 1940; s. Robert Jenkins and Mary Josephine (Marsden) K.; m. Janet Maryann Curtis, Jan. 28, 1967 (div. 1978); 1 child Owen Michael; m. Robin Jane Blackwelder, June 9, 1994. AB, Cath. U. America, 1962, MFA in Speech & Drama, 1965, PhD in English Literature & Linguistics, 1970. Lectr. English Cath. U. America, Washington, 1967-70; asst. prof. George Mason U., Fairfax, Va., 1970-75, assoc. prof., 1975-79, prof. English, 1979—2013, asst. to pres., 1982—86; exec. dir. George Mason U. TV, Fairfax, 1981—2013; owner Shannondale Wireless, Fairfax, 1985—2013. Dir. Corp. for Public Broadcasting, Washington, 1979-83; pres. Alleghany Highlands Broadcasting, Fairfax, 1979-85. Author: Flamboyant Drama: A Study of The Castle of Perseverance, Mankind and Wisdom, 1979, Parents Guide to Television, 1983; contbr. articles to profl. jours. Pres. George Mason U. Instructional Found., Fairfax, 1982-2013; pres. St. Gertrude Found.; dir. St. Gertrude's Sch., Washington, 1985-93; CEO Capitol Connection Teleport, Fairfax; mem. advisory bd. George Mason Fund for the Arts, Fairfax Mem. MLA, Medieval Acad. America, Wireless Cable Assn. Avocations: piano, guitar, mandolin. Home: Fairfax, Va. Died Nov. 11, 2013.

**KELLS, LYMAN F.,** astrophysicist, researcher; b. Seattle, May 19, 1917; s. Lucas Carlisle and Edith Rosetta (Stefani) Kells; divorced; children: Leila S. Newcomb, Christina V. Cohen. PhD, U. Wash., 1944. Rsch. scientist Manhattan project Kellex Corp., Carbide Carbon, NYC, 1944-46; rsch. chemist Std. Oil Devel., N.J., 1946-48; mem. faculty Hunter Coll., NYC, 1948-49; asst. prof. Iona Coll., New Rochelle, N.Y., 1949-51; rsch. chemist Gen. Chem. Divsn., Allied Chem., Morristown, N.J., 1951-61; spl. lectr. Newark Coll. Engring., 1961; assoc. prof. chemistry East Tenn. State U., Johnson City, 1962-64; prof. chemistry Westmar Coll., LeMars, Iowa, 1964-74; ind. theoretical rschr. Seattle, from 1974. Author: (Collected Works) Physical Chemistry, Physics and Astronomy, 1972, Reaction Mechanisms, Kinetics, Molecular Bonding, 1973, Supplement Number Two: Variable Stars, Velocity of Light, Nature of Theories, 1978, Binary Theory of Variable Stars and the Velocity of Light, 1984, Astrometry, Binary Theory and Observations, 1990, Variable Stars, Relativity, Nature of Sciences, 1992. Fellow: AAAS; mem.: N.Y. Acad. Scis., Astron. Soc. Pacific, Am. Chem. Soc., Am. Astron. Soc. Democrat. Unitarian Universalist. Deceased.

**KELLY, DAVID CHRISTOPHER,** British government official; b. Llwynypia, Wales, U.K., May 14, 1944; s. Thomas John and Margaret (Williams) K.; m. Janice Vawdrey, July 15, 1967; children: Sian Elizabeth, Rachel Angharad, Ellen Rhiannon. BS, Leeds U., Eng., 1967; MS, Birmingham U., Eng., 1968; DPhil, U. Oxford, Eng., 1972. Sr. sci. officer Nat. Environ. Rsch. Coun., Oxford, Eng., 1973-78, prin. sci. officer, 1978-82, sr. prin. sci. officer, 1982-84, Min. Def., Salisbury, Eng., 1984-92, dep. chief sci. officer, 1992-96, dep. chief sci. officer Proliferation/Arms Control Secretar London, from 1996. Spl. advisor UN Spl.

Commn. on Iraq, 1994-99. Editor Jour. Gen. Virology, 1977-82, Jour. Virology, 1978-83, Jour. Invertebrate Pathology, 1979-84. Named Companion of Order of St. Michael and St. George, 1996. Home: Abingdon, England. Died July 18, 2003.

**KELLY, WILLIAM MCDONOUGH,** retired Canadian senator; b. Georgetown, Ont., Can., July 21, 1925; s. John Doyle and Margaret Shirley (Carpenter) K.; m. Elizabeth Anne Paul, 1944; children: Ann Walsh, Patricia Parr. BS, U. Toronto, 1950; postgrad., U. Ill., Harvard U. From engr. to sr. v.p. Consumers' Gas Co., 1951-71; pres. Can.-Arctic Constrn. Co., 1972-80; Senator from Port Severn, 1982—2000. Pres. Kelco Mgmt. Ltd., Severn Boat Haven Ltd.; bd. dirs. Contrans Inc., Rothmans Internat. PLC (U.K.), Rothmans Internat. NV (The Netherlands). Gov. Can. Sports Hall of Fame, Coun. on Drug Abuse; life mem. World Wildlife Fund Can.; bd. govs. Ryerson Polytech. Inst., also past chmn. Lt. Can. Army, 1944-46. Decorated comdr. Order of St. Lazarus of Jerusalem. Fellow Engr. Inst. Can., Inst. Gas Engrs.; mem. Assn. Profl. Engrs., U.K., Masons, Toronto Club, Rideau Club, Albany Club. Progressive Conservative. Mem. Ch. of Eng. Avocations: sailing, hunting, tennis. Home: Mississauga, Canada. Died Nov. 16, 2013.

**KEMILÄINEN, AIRA TELLERVO,** historian, educator, researcher; b. Kuopio, Finland, Aug. 4, 1919; d. Juho Arvi and Aino Tyyne (Hyvärinen) K. MA, U. Helsinki., Finland, 1943; PhD, U. Helsinki, Finland, 1956. H.S. tchr., Helsinki, 1945-50, 57-62; asst. Nat. Archives of Finland, Helsinki, 1950, archivist, 1952-57; sr. lectr. U. Helsinki, 1961-86; sr. lectr., assoc. prof. U. Jyväskylä, Finland, 1962-70, prof. world history, 1971-86, prof. emerita, from 1986. Author: Nationalism. Problems Concerning the Word, the Concept and Classification, 1964, Die Historische Sendung der Deutschen in Leopold von Rankes Geschichtsdenken, 1968, L'Affaire d'Avignon (1789-91) from the Viewpoint of Nationalism, 1971, Finns in the Shadow of the Aryans. Race Theories and Racism, 1998, Under the Pressure of WWII, Diary and Letters, 2001; contbr. articles to profl. jours. Mem. vol. female orgn. def. Lotta Svärd, 1938-44. Johann Gottfried Herder scholar, 1954-55, ASLA-Fulbright rsch. scholar, 1958-59, Finnish State scholar, 1974; decorated Chevalier Order White Rose Finland 1st class. Mem. Finnish Hist. Soc., Finnish Acad. Sci. and Letters (award 2003), Swedish History of Sci. Soc., Internat. Soc. for Study of European Ideas, Assn. for Study of Ethnicity and Nationalism, Finnish Fedn. Univ. Women (br. pres. 1970-82). Avocation: summer cottage. Home: Vantaa, Finland. Died July 10, 2006.

**KEMPER, RUFUS CROSBY, JR.,** retired bank executive; b. Kansas City, Mo., Feb. 22, 1927; s. Rufus Crosby and Enid (Jackson) Kemper; m. Mary Barton Stripp; children: Rufus Crosby III, Pamela Warrick Gabrovsky, Sheila Kemper Dietrich, John Mariner, Mary Barton Wolf, Alexander Charles, Heather Christian. Grad., Phillips Acad., Andover, Mass., 1942; student, U. Mo.; LL.D. (hon.), William Jewel Coll., 1976; DFA (hon.), Westminster Coll., 1983. Joined City Nat. Bank & Trust Co. (now UMB Fin. Corp.), Kansas City, 1950; exec v.p. UMB Financial Corp., 1957—59, pres., 1959—71, chmn., CEO, 1971—2000; sr. chmn. UMB Financial Corp. & UMB Bank, 2000—04; ret., 2004. Hon. trustee Thomas Jefferson Found.; mem. nat. com. Whitney Mus. American Art, NYC.; commr. Nat. Mus. American Art., Washington; founder, chmn. bd. trustees The Kemper Mus. Contemporary Art, Kansas City; trustee Kemper family foundations; founder, bd. dirs. The Agriculture Future of America Served USNR, WWII. Recipient Key Man Kansas City Jr. Chamber of Commerce, 1952, Disting. Svc., 1964, Man of Yr. Award Kansas City Press Club, 1974, Outstanding Kansas Citian Award Native Sons Kansas City, 1975, 82, 1st Advocacy Award Mid-Continent Small Bus. Assn., 1980, Banker Adv. of Yr. Award Small Bus. Adminstrn., 1981, Lester Milgram Humanitarian Award, 1982, Man of Yr. Award Downtown, Inc., 1982, Pirouette Award Kansas City Ballet Guild and Kansas City Tomorrow Alumni Assn., 1983, Faculty Alumni Award U. Mo. Columbia Alumni Assn., 1982, Mo. Arts Coun. Award, 1984, Kansas City Chancellor's Medal U. Mo., 1984, Disting. Svc. Award St. Paul Sch. Theology, 1987, Advocacy Award Mo. Citizens for the Arts, 1987, Outstanding Patron of Excellence in the Arts and Architecture American Inst. Architects - Kansas City, 1994, VIP Leadership Award Centurions Leadership Program Greater Kansas City Chamber of Commerce, 1995; named Man of Yr. Kansas City Press Club, 1974, Kansas Citian of Yr., 1997; named one of The Top 200 Collectors ARTnews mag., 2004. Mem. American Royal Assn. (v.p., bd. dirs.), Man of the Month Fraternity, Beta Theta Pi (Man of Yr. 1974) Clubs: River, Carriage, Kansas City Country, Kansas City, 1021, Mo, Chathan, Mass., Garden of the Gods, Cheyenne Mountain Country (Colorado Springs, Colo.). Republican. Episcopalian. Avocations: Collector Old Masters, modern and contemporary art, farming, tennis, sailing, horseback riding, raising cattle. Home: Lawrence, Kans. Died Jan. 2, 2014.

**KENDRICK, JOSEPH TROTWOOD,** former foreign service officer, writer, consultant; b. Pryor, Okla., Feb. 5, 1920; s. Joseph Trotwood and Anne (Williams) K.; m. Loreine York, July 18, 1942 (div. 1954); m. Elise Fleager Simpkins, Aug. 20, 1955 (div. 1977); children: Pamela York, Drew Trotwood (dec. 1970), Juliette Simpkins, Katherine Mary. Student, U. Okla., 1938-40; BS, Georgetown U., 1948; MA, Columbia, 1951; PhD, George Washington U., 1979. Joined Fgn. Svc., U.S. Dept. State, 1941; assigned Nicaragua, Poland, USSR, Germany, 1941-54; spl. asst. to dir. Office Ea. European Affairs, U.S. Dept. State, Washington, 1954-57, pub. affairs adviser, 1958; 2d sec., consul Am. Embassy, Kabul, Afghanistan, 1959-61; dep. polit. adviser SHAPE, Paris, 1962-64; polit. counselor Am. Embassy, Oslo, 1964-68; dep. dir. Office Atomic Energy and Aerospace, U.S. Dept. State, 1968-70, dir., 1970-71, spl. asst. to dir. Bur. Pol. Mil. Affairs, 1971-72; detailed to Dept. Def., 1972-73; dean, Center for Area and Country Studies, Fgn. Svc. Inst., U.S. Dept. State, 1974-75; writer, cons., 1975—2003. Vis. fellow Cambridge (Eng.) U., 2000-01. Author: Executive-Legislative Consultation on Foreign Policy: Strengthening Executive Branch Procedures; co-author: Into the Mystery of Afghan Nuristan: The Journey of Three Young Diplomats Into the Unknown. Served to lt. (jg.) USNR, 1944-46. Recipient Outstanding Civilian Service medal Dept. Army, 1974. Mem. Am. Assn. Advancement Slavic Studies, Am. Fgn. Service Assn., Am. Polit. Sci. Assn., Inst. Strategic Studies (London), Delta Chi. Died Jan. 2, 2003.

**KENDRICKS, GEORGE THOMAS,** lawyer; b. Manistique, Mich., May 18, 1918; s. Ralph L. and Harriett E. (Durocher) Kendricks; m. E. Jane Jory, Mar. 18, 1943; children: Linda L. Kendricks Peterson, Janet, Thomas J. BA, Nothern Mich. U., 1938; LLB, U. Wis., 1947. Bar: Wis. 1947, Mich. 1948. Ptnr. Kendricks, Bordeau, Adamini, Keefe, Smith & Girard, PC and predecessor firm Marquette and Gwinn, Mich., 1948. Lt. USNR, 1942—45. Mem.: ABA, Marquette County Bar Assn., Mich. Bar Assn., Mason Club, Kiwanis Club. Home: Leesburg, Va. Died 1991.

**KENNEDY, B(YRL) J(AMES),** medicine and oncology educator; b. Plainview, Minn., June 24, 1921; s. Arthur Sylvester and Anna Margaret (Fassbender) K.; m. Margaret Bradford Hood, Oct. 21, 1950; children: Sharon Lynn, James Bradford, Scott Douglas, Grant Preston. BA, BS, U. Minn., 1943, MB, 1945, MD, 1946; MS in Exptl. Medicine, McGill U., Montreal, Que., Can., 1951. Diplomate Am. Bd. Internal Medicine, Am. Bd. Med. Oncology. Intern in medicine Mass. Gen. Hosp., Boston, 1945-46, resident in medicine, 1946, 51-52; fellow in medicine Harvard Med. Sch.-Mass. Gen. Hosp., 1947-49; rsch. fellow in medicine McGill U. Med. Sch., 1949-50; fellow in medicine Cornell U. Med. Sch., NYC, 1950-51; asst. prof. medicine U. Minn. Med. Sch., Mpls., 1952-57, assoc. prof., 1957-67, prof., 1967-91, Masonic prof. oncology, 1970-91, prof. emeritus, from 1991, Regents prof. medicine, 1988-91, Regents prof. emeritus, from 1991, B.J. Kennedy chair in clin. med. oncology, 2000. Contbr. articles to profl. jours. Past chmn. bd. Presbyn. Homes of Minn., St. Paul, bd. dirs., 1964-93. Recipient Nat. Divsn. award Am. Cancer Soc., 1975, Recognition award Assn. Comty. Cancer Ctrs., 1985, Spl. Recognition award Am. Soc. Internal Medicine, 1989, Charles Bolles Bolles-Roger award Hennepin Med. Soc., 1996; B.J. Kennedy Lectureship in Oncology named in his honor Minn. Med. Found., 1990, B.J. Kennedy Oncology Scholarship named in his honor Minn. Med. Found., 1998, B.J. Kennedy Chair in Med. Oncology named in his honor Minn. Med. Found., 1999. Fellow ACP (master 1996, Laureate award Minn. 1992); mem. AMA (Sci. Achievement award 1992), Am. Cancer Soc. (Disting. Svc. award 1991, Medal of Honor-Clin. Rsch. award 1996), Am. Soc. Clin. Oncology (pres. 1987-88), Am. Assn. Cancer Rsch., Am. Assn. Cancer Edn. (pres. 1982-83, Margaret Hay Edwards Achievement medal 1990), Minn. Med. Alumni (Harold S. Diehl award 1999), Town and Country Club (St. Paul). Avocation: photography. Deceased.

**KENNEDY, CORNELIA GROEFSEMA,** federal judge; b. Detroit, Aug. 4, 1923; d. Elmer H. and Mary Blanche (Gibbons) Groefsema; m. Charles S. Kennedy, Jr. (dec.); 1 son, Charles S. III. BA, U. Mich., 1945, JD with distinction, 1947; LL.D. (hon.), No. Mich. U., 1971, Eastern Mich. U., 1971, Western Mich. U., 1973, Detroit Coll. Law, 1980, U. Detroit, 1987. Bar: Mich. bar 1947. Law clk. to Chief Judge Harold M. Stephens US Ct. Appeals (DC Cir.), Washington, 1947-48; assoc. Elmer H. Groefsema, Detroit, 1948-52; partner Markle & Markle, Detroit, 1952-66; judge 3d Judicial Circuit Mich., 1967-70, US Dist. Ct. (eastern dist.) Mich., Detroit, 1970-79, chief judge, 1977-79; judge US Ct. Appeals (6th Cir.), 1979-99, sr. judge, 1999—2014. Mem. Commn. on the Bicentennial of the U.S. Constitution (presdl. appointment). Recipient Sesquicentennial award U. Mich. Fellow American Bar Found.; mem. ABA, Mich. Bar Assn. (past chmn. negligence law sect.), Detroit Bar Assn. (past dir.), Fed. Bar Assn., American Judicature Soc., Nat. Assn. Women Lawyers, Am. Trial Lawyers Assn., Nat. Conf. Fed. Trial Judges (past chmn.), Fed. Jud. Fellows Commn. (bd. dirs.), Fed. Jud. Ctr. (bd. dirs.), Phi Beta Kappa. Died May 12, 2014.

**KENNEDY, CORNELIUS BRYANT,** retired lawyer; b. Evanston, Ill., Apr. 13, 1921; s. Millard Bryant and Myrna Estelle (Anderson) K.; m. Anne Martha Reynolds, June 20, 1959; children: Anne Talbot, Lauren K. Mayle. AB, Yale U., 1943; JD, Harvard U., 1948. Bar: Ill. 1949, D.C. 1965. Assoc. Mayer Meyer Austrian & Platt, Chgo., 1949-54, 55-59; asst. to U.S. atty. Dept. Justice, Chgo., 1954-55; counsel to minority leader U.S. Senate, 1959-65; sr. ptnr. Kennedy & Webster, Washington, 1965-82; of counsel Armstrong, Teasdale, Schlafly & Davis, Washington, 1983-88; public mem. Adminstrv. Conf. U.S., 1972-82, sr. conf. fellow, 1982-90, chmn. rulemaking com., 1973-82; ret., 1988. Contbr. articles to profl. jours. Fin. chmn. Lyric Opera Co., Chgo., 1954; chmn. young adults group Chgo. Coun. Fgn. Rels., 1958-59; pres. English Speaking Union Jrs., Chgo., 1957-59; trustee St. John's Child Devel. Ctr., Washington, 1965-67, 75-87, pres., 1983-85; exec. dir. Supreme Ct. Hist. Soc., 1984-87, commodore Sailing Club Chesapeake, 1966. 1st lt., AC U.S. Army, 1942-46. Fellow Am. Bar Found.; mem. Am. Law Inst., ABA (coun. sect. adminstrv. law 1967-70, chmn. sect. 1976-77), Fed. Bar Assn. (chmn. com. adminstrv. law 1963-64), Legal Club Chgo., Explorers Club, Capitol Hill Club, Chevy Chase Club, Sailing Club of Chesapeake, Adventurer's Club, Hillsboro Club. Home: Charlottesville, Va. Died June 7, 2014.

**KENNEDY, JOSEPH WINSTON,** lawyer; b. Marshalltown, Iowa, June 5, 1932; s. Roy Wesley and Julia Harriet (Plum) K.; m. Barbara B. Bowman, July 11, 1954 (div. June 1982); children: Kimberle Ann, Kamella Lucille; m. Paula Terry Smith, Nov. 24, 1984. BS cum laude, McPherson Coll., Kans., 1954; JD with honors, George Washington U., 1958. Bar: Kans. 1958, U.S. Dist Ct. Kans. 1958, U.S. Ct. Appeals (10th cir.) 1976, U.S. Supreme Ct. 1970. Spl. agt. Office of Naval Intelligence, Washington, 1954-58; assoc. Morris, Laing, Evans & Brock, Wichita, Kans., 1958-62; ptnr. Morris, Laing, Evans, Brock & Kennedy, Wichita, 1962—2006. Chmn. profl. divsn., atty. United Way of the Plains, Wichita, 1990-93. Recipient Best Lawyers in Am. award, 1987, 89-90, 91-92, 93-94, 95-96. Mem. ABA, Kans. Bar Assn. (bd. law examiners 1993-2002), Wichita Bar Assn. (bd. govs. 1964-66). Deceased.

**KENNEDY, MARIGOLD ANN See SEMPLE, GOLDIE**

**KENNEDY, RAYMOND MCCORMICK, JR.,** interior designer, educator; b. Glendale, Calif., Sept. 19, 1930; s. Raymond McCormick and June (Sparks) Kennedy, adopted s. Myrtle Abrahamson Kennedy. BA in architecture, U. Calif.-Berkeley, 1956. Draftsman Bechtel Corp., San Francisco, 1956—58, Maher & Martens, Architects, San Francisco, 1956, free lance designer, 1966—67, designer, 1956, Bernard J. Block, Architect, San Francisco, 1967—69; v.p. Rodgers Assocs., San Francisco, 1969—77; pres. RMK Design, Inc., San Francisco, 1977—83, Kennedy-Bowen Assocs., San Francisco, from 1983. Mem. faculty Acad. Art Coll., San Francisco, 1982—86, mem. adv. coun., 1991—95. Bd. dirs. San Francisco Easter Seals Soc., 1974—79, adv. coun., 1991—95; bd. dirs. Design Found., Inc., 1986—87, pres., 1986—87. Served with US Army, 1952—54. Fellow: Am. Soc. Interior Designers (dir. Northern Calif. chpt. 1983, v.p. Northern Calif. chpt. 1983, sec. bd. 1984, pres. 1987—88, nat. bd. dirs. 1989, nat. pres. 1991—92); mem.: Assocs. San Francisco's Archtl. Heritage, Internat. Furnishings and Design Assn., Am. Inst. Archs., Golden Gate U. Assn., Nat. Trust Hist. Preservation, Press Club, Commonwealth Club. Deceased.

**KENNER, RONALD W.,** writer, editor; b. Chgo., Apr. 21, 1935; s. Jack Morris and Sandra Cohan Kenner; m. Mary Abbott, Feb. 29, 1964. BA in English Lit., Calif. State U., LA, 1975, postgrad., 1975-76. World news editor, deskman, staff writer Daily Pilot, Costa Mesa, Calif., 1960-61; editor Humboldt Star, Winnemucca, Nev., 1961-62; corr. No. Nev. United Press, 1961-62; deskman, staff writer The Register, Santa Ana, Calif., 1962-64; corr. Orange County (Calif.) Assoc. Press, 1962-64; writing cons. book editing Mexico City, 1964-65; reporter, staff writer L.A. Times, Metro, LA, 1965-66; editor ctrl. desk Call-Enterprise Newspapers, Bellflower, Calif., 1966-67; mng. editor Norwalk Call, 1966-67; co-editor press & pub. rels. bur. News Features, Internat. & Kenner Press Features, Copenhagen, 1967-69; metro reporter, staff writer L.A. Times, 1969-70; v.p. pub. rels., press dir. CompuTransit Corp., LA, 1970-73; supr. publs. Santa Fe Internat. Corp., Orange, Calif., 1977-78; author, book editor, freelance, publs. rels. publicity dir. Kenner Press Features, LA, 1978-89, News Features Internat., Copenhagen, 1978-89; author, book editor, editorial cons. LA, 1990-95. Guest lectr. writing classes UCLA, Calif. State U., Northridge, Northbridge H.S. Author: (biography) Max the Butcher, 1982; co-author: The Garbage People, 1971, 1995; editor numerous biographies; editl. cons.: Those Who Dared and Rescued, 1995, Anne Frank in Historical Perspective: A Teaching Guide for Secondary Schools, 1995; contbr. articles to profl. jours. Recipient John Swett award Calif. State Tchrs. Assn., 1967, Spl. Recognition award Nat. Assn. Adult Educators; co-recipient Pulitzer prize with 35-man L.A. Times metro staff for Watts Riot coverage, 1965. Mem. Pen Ctr. USA West. Avocation: travel. Home: Los Angeles, Calif. Deceased.

**KENNET, LORD (WAYLAND HILTON YOUNG),** politician, writer; b. Eng., Aug. 2, 1923; s. 1st Baron Kennet and Kathleen (Bruce); m. Elizabeth Ann Adams, 1948; 6 children. Student, U. Cambridge, Eng. With fgn. office Brit. Govt., London, 1946-47, 49-51; del. parliamentary assemblies WEU and Council of Europe, London, 1962-65; parliamentary sec. Ministry of Housing and Local Govt. House of Lords, London, 1966-70; opposition spokesman Fgn. Affairs and Sci. Policy, London, 1971-74; chief whip Social Democrat Party London, 1981-83. Chmn. Adv. Com. on Oil Pollution of the Sea, 1970-74, CPRE, 1971-72, Internat. Parliamentary Confs. on the Environment, 1972-78; dir. Europe Plus Thirty, 1974-75; mem. European Parliament, 1977-79. Author: (as Wayland Young) The Italian Left, 1949, The Deadweight, 1952, Now or Never, 1953, The Montesi Scandal, 1957, Still Alive Tomorrow, 1958, Strategy for Survival, 1959, The Profumo Affair, 1963, Eros Denied, 1965, Thirty-Four Articles, 1965, Existing Mechanisms of Arms Control, 1965; (with Elizabeth Young) London's Churches, 1986; (as Wayland Kennet) Preservation, 1972, The Futures of Europe, 1976, The Rebirth of Britain, 1982; polit. pamphlets and articles on defence, disarmament, environment, multinational companies. Home: London, England. Died May 7, 2009.

**KENT, ALLEN,** library and information sciences professor; b. NYC, Oct. 24, 1921; s. Samuel and Anna (Begun) K.; m. Rosalind Kossoff, Jan. 24, 1943; children: Merryl Frances Kent Samuels, Emily Beth Kent Yeager, Jacqueline Diane Kent Maryak, Carolyn May Kent Hall. BS in Chemistry, CCNY, 1942. Sci. editor Intersci. Publications, 1946-51; research assoc. Ctr. Internat. Studies, MIT, 1951-53; prin. documentation engr. Battelle Meml. Inst., Columbus, Ohio, 1953-55; assoc. dir. Ctr. for Documentation and Communication Research; prof. library sci. Western Res. U., Cleve., 1955-63; dir. office communications programs, chmn. interdisciplinary doctoral program info. sci., prof. info. sci., edn. and computer sci. U. Pitts., 1963-76; dir.

Knowledge Availability Sys. Ctr., 1963—91; Univ. Disting. Service prof. library and info. sci. and assoc. dean U. Pitts. Sch. Library and Info. Sci., 1976-91, interim dean, 1985-86, prof. emeritus, 1992—2014. Mem. mgmt. info. com. Health and Welfare Assn. Allegheny County, Pa., 1972-80; dir. Marcel Dekker, Inc., N.Y., 1978-93. Author (with others): Machine Literature Searching, 1956; author: (with J.W. Perry) Documentation and Information Retrieval, 1957; author: Tools for Machine Literature Searching, 1958, Centralized Information Services, 1958, Mechanized Information Retrieval, 1962, 2d edit., 1966, also fgn. transls. Specialized Information Centers, 1965, Information Analysis and Retrieval, 1971, Resource Sharing in Libraries, 1977, On-Line Revolution in Libraries, 1978, Structure and Governance of Library Networks, 1979, Use of Library Materials, 1979, Information Technology, 1982; editor, co-editor numerous books in field, exec. editor Ency. Libr. and Info. Sci., 1968—2003, Ency. Computer Sci. and Tech., 1972—2002, Ency. Microcomputers, 1984—2001, Ency. of Telecomm., 1988—98. Chmn. bd. Interuniv. Comms. Coun. Inc., 1971-74. Served with USAAF, 1942-46. Recipient Info. Tech. Merit award Eastman Kodak Co., 1968. Fellow AAAS; mem. ALA, Assn. Computing Machinery, American Soc. Info. Sci. (award of merit 1977, award for Best Info. Sci. Book of Yr. 1980, Pioneer in Info. Sci. 1987), Acad. Sr. Profls. Eckerd Coll. Home: Pittsburgh, Pa. *My goal has been to be useful. This entails service, dedication to my profession and to the institution which supports my work, and absolute standards of honesty.* Died May 1, 2014.

**KERMAN, JOSEPH WILFRED,** musicologist, critic; b. London, Apr. 3, 1924; U.S. citizen; married, 1946; 3 children. PhD in Music, Princeton U., 1951. Instr. music Princeton U., 1948-49; dir. grad. studies Westminster Choir Coll., 1949-51, from asst. prof. to assoc. prof., 1951-60, chmn. dept., 1961-64, 91-93; prof. music U. Calif., Berkeley, 1960-94, Jerry & Evelyn Hemmings Chambers prof. music, 1985-87, prof. emeritus, 1994—2014; C.E. Norton prof. poetry Harvard U., 1997. Heather prof. music Oxford U., 1972-74. Author: Opera as Drama, 1956, rev. edit., 1989, The Elizabethan Madrigal, 1962, The Beethoven, Quartets, 1967, The Masses and Motets of William Byrd, 1981, Contemplating Music, 1985, Write All These Down, 1994, Concerto Conversations, 1999, The Art of Fugue, 2005; (with others) History of Art and Music, 1968, Listen, 1972, 8th edit., 2003, The New Grove Beethoven, 1983; editor: Beethoven: Autograph Miscellany, 1970, Music at the Turn of the Century, 1970; co-editor Jour. 19th Century Music U. Calif., 1977-88; contbr. essays and revs. to Hudson Rev., N.Y. Rev. Recipient Nat. Inst. Arts & Letters award, 1956, Kinkeldey award American Musicol. Soc., 1970, 81, Deems Taylor award ASCAP, 1981, 95; Guggenheim fellow, 1960, Fulbright fellow, 1967, NEH fellow, 1982. Fellow American Philosophical Soc., American Acad. Arts & Sciences, Brit. Acad. (corr.), Royal Musical Assn. (hon. fgn.), American Musicol. Soc. (hon.). Died Mar. 17, 2014.

**KERWIN, LARKIN,** retired physics educator; b. June 22, 1924; m. Maria Guadalupe Turcot, 1950; 8 children. Cert. engring. studies, St. Francis Xavier U., 1943, BSc summa cum laude, 1944; MSc magna cum laude, MIT, 1946; DSc magna cum laude, U. Laval, 1949; LLD (hon.), St. Francis Xavier U., 1970, U. Toronto, 1973, Concordia U., Montreal, 1976, U. Alta., 1983, U. Dalhousie, 1983, U. Moncton, 1985; DSc (hon.), U. B.C., 1973, McGill U., 1974, Meml. U. Newfoundland, 1978, U. Ottawa, 1981, Royal Mil. Coll. Can., 1982, U. Winnipeg, 1983, U. Windsor, 1984, U. Montreal, 1991; DCivil Law (hon.), Bishop's U., 1978. Tchg. asst. St. Francis Xavier U., 1944; lab. demonstrator U. Toronto, 1945; rsch. physicist Geotech. Corp., Cambridge, Mass., 1945; lab. asst. physics dept. U. Laval, Que., 1946-48, from asst. prof. to assoc. prof., 1948-56, prof., chair atomic physics, 1956, dir. Mass Spectrometry Lab., 1955-66, chmn. dept. physics, 1961-67; dir. Van de Graaf Accelerator Lab., 1961-72, vice-dean faculty of scis., 1967-68, acad. vice-rector, 1969-72, rector, 1972-77, prof. emeritus, 1991. Pres. Assn. Univ. and Coll. Can., 1975-75, Nat. Rsch. Coun. Can., 1980-89, Can. Space Agy., 1989-92, Can. Acad. Engring., 1989-90. Author: Atomic Physics, An Introduction, 1963; mem. editl. bd. Interdisciplinary Sci. Revs. Mag., 1981—; contbr. numerous articles to profl. jours. Trustee Nat. Museums of Can., 1980-89; adv. coun. Ottawa chpt. Can. Soc. Weizmann Inst. Sci., 1981; Can. rep. Versailles conf. on tech. and employment, 1982; bd. govs. Carleton U., 1983-86. Recipient Centenary medal, 1967, Jubilee medal, 1977, Centenary medal of Roumania, 1977, medal of Laval Alumni, 1978, Gold medal, Can. Coun. Profl. Engrs., 1982, Outstanding Achievement award, Govt. Can., 1987, Centenary medal, 2002, Jubilee medal, 2002; named knight, Equestrian Order of Holy Sepulchre of Jerusalem, 1970, knight comdr., 1972, comdr. with star, 1974, officer, Order of Can., 1978, knight grand cross, Equestrian Order of Holy Sepulchre of Jerusalem, 1980, companion, Order of Can., 1980, Officer, Order of Que., 1987, officier, Legion Honor, France, 1989; named to Ordre du Merite, Soc. Saint-Jean Baptiste de Que., 1979. Fellow AAAS, Royal Soc. Can. (pres. 1977-78), Royal Soc. Arts, Am. Inst. Physics; mem. Internat. Union Pure and Applied Physics (pres. 1987-91), Assn. Canadienne Française pour l'Avancement des Sci. (Pariseau medal 1965, Jacques Rousseau medal 1983), Am. Phys. Soc., Corp. Profl. Engr. Que., Sociedad Mexicana Fisica, Can. Assn. Physicists (pres. 1954, Gold medal 1969), Académie des Grands Québecois. Home: Sillery, Canada. Died May 1, 2004.

**KESTER, CHARLES MELVIN,** lawyer; b. Batesville, Ark., Jan. 19, 1968; s. Monty Charles and Phyllis Smith Kester; m. Cheryl Goodwin, June 1, 1991. BA in Philosophy summa cum laude, Liberty U., 1991; JD magna cum laude, Georgetown U., 1994. Bar: Ark. 1994, US Dist. Ct. (ea. and we. dists.) Ark. 1995, US Ct. Appeals (8th cir.) 1995, US Ct. Fed. Claims, 2002, US Supreme Ct. 1998, US Ct. Appeals (9th cir.) 2007, US Ct. Appeals (5th cir.), 2008, US Ct. Appeals (6th Cir.), 2011, US Ct. Appeals 1st Cir., 2012, US Ct. Appeals (10th cir.), 2013. Law clk. U.S. Ct. Appeals 8th Cir., Fargo, ND, 1994-95; atty. Lingle Law Firm, Rogers, Ark., 1995—96; pvt. practice law Fayetteville, Ark., from 1996. Assoc. editor Georgetown Law Jour., 1993-94; contbr. articles to profl. jours. Mem.: Ark. Bar Assn. (appellate practice com. 1997—2000, young lawyers sect. adv. coun. 1998—99, sec. labor and employment law sect. 2002, chair 2004), Ark. Trial Lawyers Assn. (amicus curiae com. 1997—2006), Phi Alpha Delta. Avocations: camping, rock climbing, spelunking. Home: Fayetteville, Ark. Died Mar. 3, 2014.

**KEY, OTTA BISCHOF,** retired educator; b. Englewood, Colo., May 19, 1907; d. Herbert and Lulu Bonita (Kitterman) Bischof; m. Elra Richard Key, Aug. 21, 1938 (dec. June 1993); children: Paul, Kathryn. BFA, Kans. U., 1933; MA, Ctrl. Mich. U., 1967. Cert. Christian educator. Tchr., Luray, Kans., 1923; elem. tchr., 1924-26; tchr. jr. h.s. Russell, Kans., 1926-29; tchr. art Meml. H.S., Lawrence, Kans., 1934-38; instr. art edn. Maryville (Mo.) U., 1937-38, Saginaw (Mich.) Valley Coll., 1957-70; ednl. asst. Meml. Presbyn. Ch., Midland, Mich., 1958-73; ednl. asst. religion dept. Millikin U., Decatur, Ill., 1976-84. Student adviser Meml. H.S., Lawrence, 1934-38, dir. art exhibits, 1934-38; tchr. synod schs. Presbyn. Ch., 1955-58; mem. edn. City Ch. Coun., Decatur, Ill., 1978-84. Author: Teaching Volunteers Teachers, 1984. Cooperator Decatur Ch. coun., 1976-84, Ch. Women United, Decautur, 1974-93; supporter Am. United, Washington, 1970-97, Presbyn. Ch., 1973-93. Scholarships established McCormick Presbyn. Sem., Louisville Presbyn. Sem.; recipient award Presbyn. Ch., 1958-93. Mem. Assn. of Presbyn. Ch. Educators, Assn. of Great Lakes Ch. Educators. Democrat. Ecumenical. Avocations: reading current events, ecumenical activities, visual arts, family education. Deceased.

**KEYES, DANIEL,** author; m. Aurea Georgina Vazquez; children: Leslie, Hillary. BA in Psychology, Bklyn. Coll., 1950, MA in English, 1961. Assoc. fiction editor Magazine Mgmt. Co., NYC, 1950-52; v.p. Fenko and Keyes Photography, Inc., 1952-53; tchr. English N.Y.C. Bd. Edn., 1955-62; instr. English Wayne State U., Detroit, 1962-66; mem. faculty Ohio U., Athens, 1966—72, prof. English and creative writing, 1972-97, prof. emeritus, 2000—14. Author: (novels) Flowers for Algernon (Hugo award 1959, Nebula award 1966, movie version: Charly, 1968 (Acad. award), The Touch, 1968, The Fifth Sally, 1980, (nonfiction) The Minds of Billy Milligan, 1981 (Spl. award Mystery Writers Am., Kurd Lasswitz award, 1st prize Best Fgn. Book award 1986), Unveiling Claudia, 1986, Daniel Keyes Collected Stories, 1993 (Japan), The Milligan Wars, 1994 (Japan), Daniel Keyes Reader, 1995 (Japan), Until Death Do Us Part: The Sleeping Princess, 1998 (Japan), The Asylum Prophecies, 2009; (TV movie) Flowers for Algernon, 2000, (non-fiction) Algernon, Charlie and I: A Writer's Journey, 2000; (13 episode TV series) flowers for Algernon (Japan), 2002, The Touch, revised 2003; supervising prodr. (TV movie) The Mad Housers, 1990. With U.S. Maritime Svc., 1945—47. Ohio Arts Council Individual Artist fellow, 1986-87; recipient Baker Fund award 1986-87, Disting. Alumnus Honor award Bklyn. Coll. CUNY, 1988, Kurd Lasswitz award, 1986 Mem.: PEN, Sci. Fiction Writers America (Author Emeritus award 2000), Mystery Writers America, Dramatists' Guild. Home: Boca Raton, Fla. Died June 15, 2014.

**KEYES, JOAN ROSS RAFTER,** education educator, writer; b. Bklyn., Aug. 12, 1924; d. Joseph W. and Hermia (Ross) Rafter; m. William Ambrose, Apr. 26, 1947 (dec.); children: William, Peter, Dion, Kenzie. BA, Adelphi U., Garden City, NY, 1945; MS, Long Island U., Greenvale, NY, 1973. Prodn. asst. CBS Radio, NYC, 1943-44; cub news reporter Bklyn. Daily Eagle, 1945-46; advt. copywriter Gimbel's Dept. Store, NYC, 1946-47; adj. prof. L.I. U., Greenvale, NY, from 1984; tchr. Port Wash. Pub. Schs., NY, 1970-94. Lectr., cons. pub. sch. dists. nationwide, 1978—; workshop leader Tchrs. English to Speakers Other Langs. convs., 1981—; cons. Kids' Readers, 2005. Author: Beats! Conversations in Rhythm, 1983, (video program) Now You're Talking, 1987, (computer program) Quick Talk, 1990, Oxford Picture Dictionary for Kids Program, 1998; contbr. articles to ednl. mags. Lectr., catechist Our Lady of Fatima Ch., Port Washington, 1987—; vol. Earthwatch, Mallorca, 1988. Australia/New Zealand ednl. grantee Port Washington Pub. Schs., 1992. Mem. Tchrs. of English to Speakers of Other Languages, Am. Fedn. of Tchrs., N.Y. State United Tchrs., Port Wash. Tchrs. Assn. Republican. Roman Catholic. Avocations: music, painting, travel, tennis, piano, guitar, song writing, golf. Home: Port Washington, NY. Died Aug. 23, 2013.

**KEYS, DONALD FRASER,** educational organization administrator; b. LA, June 9, 1924; s. Gilbert Schurman and Margaret (Snell) K.; m. Betty Jane Pedersen, Aug. 29, 1950 (div. 1966); children: Fraser Thuesen, Christopher Webster. Student, Pasadena Jr. Coll., 1939-42, U. So. Calif., 1950. Engr., announcer Sta. KWSD, Mt. Shasta, Calif., 1948-53; communiations technician U.S. Forest Svc., Santa Barbara, Calif., 1953-55; field rep. Calif. United World Federalists, LA, 1955-56; UN observer Lucis Trust, NYC, 1957; exec. dir. Nat. Com. For a Sane Nuclear Policy, NYC, 1958-67, Internat. League for Human Rights, NYC, 1968-69; UN rep. World Assn. World Federalists, NYC, 1969-82; pres., exec. dir., founder Planetary Citizens, NYC, 1974-84, Mt. Shasta, from 1984. Cons., writer UN Delegations, 1969-86; bd. dirs. Alcyone Light Ctr., Hilt, Calif., 1986-90, The Baconian Found., Ashland, Oreg., 1987-90, Josephine Taylor Found., Mt. Shasta, 1990-91; adv. bd. mem. The Club Budapest, 1994. Author: (books) Earth at Omega: The Passage to Planetization, 1982; co-editor Disarmament: The Human Factor, 1981. Sgt. USAF, 1943-45. Died Apr. 10, 2008.

**KHADILKAR, BHUSHAN MADHUKAR,** chemistry educator; b. Satara, Maharashtra, India, Dec. 19, 1957; s. Madhukar Pandurang and Padma Madhukar (Dixit) K.; m. Sujata Vidyasagar Menon, Feb. 17, 1984; 1 child, Aditi Bhushan. BSc, Ruia Coll., Mumbai, India, 1979, MSc, 1981; PhD, U. Mumbai, 1986. Rsch. chemist Alembic Chem. Works Co., Ltd., Baroda, India, 1981-82; lectr. dept. chem. tech. Mumbai Univ., 1987-92, sr. lectr. dept. chem. tech., from 1992. Contbr. articles to profl. jours. Fellow Indian Chem. Soc.; mem. Indian Pharm. Assn., Indian Soc. Surface Sci. and Tech. Avocations: hypnotherapy, ednl. psychology, Indian classical music, Yoga. Died Dec. 2001.

**KHAN, AKBAR,** import/export company executive; b. Datia, India, Jan. 25, 1947; arrived in Japan, 1970; s. Babar Khan and Kaniz Fatima; m. Eri Tahira Kishibe, Jan. 13, 1974; 1 child, Aftab. BA, Karachi U., Pakistan, 1969. Cert. acct. Chmn. Daishin Boeki Shokai, Osaka, Japan, from 1980; dir. Welcome Internat., Karachi, from 1980; mng. dir. Glory Internat., Karachi, from 1986; chmn. Daishin Used Heavy Spare Parts Trading Co., Sharjah, United Arab Emirates, from 1995. Mem. Pakistan Assn. Kansai (v.p. 1997). Home: Izumiotsu City, Japan. Died Nov. 21, 2004.

**KHAN, BROTIN,** engineer; b. Calcutta, India, Sept. 8, 1941; s. Bhupendra Nath and Bina (Chaudhury) Khan; m. Agnes Clara Szabo Khan, Sept. 30, 1972; children: Monica, Andrash. BS, Bihar Inst. Tech., Sindri, 1962; DTech in Engring., Tech. U., Budapest, 1970. Asst. design engr. Heavy Engring. Corp. Ltd. Ranchi, Bihar, 1962—65; sr. devel. engr. Engring. Rsch. Ctr., Telco Ltd., Poona, Maharastra, India, 1970—72; chief engr. design WMI Cranes Ltd., Mumbai, 1972—76; mng. ptnr. Ardec Internat., Kolkata, India, 1976—79; founder, dir. Ardec India Pvt. Ltd., Kolkata, from 1949; dir. Petron Mech. Industry Pvt. Ltd., Mumbai. Tchr. Ramakrishna Mission, Ranchi, 1962. Mem.: Indian Inst. Standards (charter engr.), Inst. Engrs. India, Inst. Self Defence & Nat. Character (Gold medal Transworld Tradefare Selection 1984—85), Saturday Ltd-.(Kolkata). Avocations: yoga, meditation. Home: Calcutta, West Bengal 700 071, India. Died Dec. 20, 2006.

**KHAN, GHULAM ISHAQ,** former President of Pakistan; b. Bannu district, Pakistan, Jan. 20, 1915; m. 1950; 6 children Student, Islamia Coll., Peshawar, Pakistan, Punjab U. Sub-divisional and treas. officer, magistrate first class North-West Frontier Province Civil Svc., India, 1940-44, with, 1940-47, sec. to chief min., 1947, sec. home food, dir. civil supplies to Govt., 1948, devt. commr., sec. Devt. Dept., 1953-56; devt. and adminstrn. sec. for agr., animal husbandry, forests and industries Coops. and Village Aids, 1949-52; sec. for devt. and irrigation Govt. of Western Pakistan, 1956-58; mem. Western Pakistan Water and Power Devt. Authority, 1958-61, chair, 1961-66; sec. fin. Govt. of Pakistan, 1966-70, cabinet sec., 1970; with Govt. State Bank of Pakistan, 1971-75; sec. gen. Ministry Def., Islamabad, 1975-77; sec. gen.-in-chief, advisor for planning and co-ordination Govt. of Pakistan, Islamabad, 1977-78, adv. to chief martial law adminstr., 1978—79, min. fin. & coordination, 1978-79, min. fin., commerce & coordination, 1979-85, chmn. Senate, 1985-88, pres., 1988—93; mem. Land Reforms Commn., 1958-59, chair, from 1978; chair exec. com. Nat. Econ. Coun., 1978; dep. chair Planning Commn., 1979-82, chair, 1982, Econ. Coordination Com. of the Cabinet, 1978-85. Chair joint ministerial com. of bd. of govs. World Bank, IMF. Died Oct. 27, 2006.

**KHAN, NASIR ALI,** psychiatrist, educator; b. London, June 14, 1939; came to U.S., 1965; s. Ahmad A. and Bilquis B. (Khan) K.; m. Kay S. Kraus, May 21, 1967; children: Tahira, Zafar, Alexander. MD, U. London, 1962; Owners & Presidents Mgmt. Program cert., Harvard U., Boston, 1995. Diplomate American Bd. Psychiatry & Neurology. Resident in psychiatry Harvard U. Med. Sch., 1965-68, fellow in psychiatry, 1968-69; chief geriatric svcs. Mass. Dept. Mental Health, Boston, 1969-73; supt. Danvers (Mass.) State U., 1974-79; dir. Bournewood Hosp., Brookline, Mass., 1979—2014. Asst. clin. prof. psychiatry Tufts U. Med. Sch., Boston; bd. dirs., chmn., pres. 1st Psychiat. Planners Inc., Brookline; bd. dirs., treas. Newton Psychiat. Group; chmn. exec. com. Newton-Wellesley Hosp., 1990, pres. med. staff, 1995. Author: Handbook of Psychiatry, 1972. Coach Newton Youth Soccer, 1982-84. Recipient "Heroes in the Fight" award, Nat. Alliance on Mental Illness (Mass. Chapter), 2008; named Cmty. Clinician of Yr., Charles River Dist. Medical Soc., 2014. Fellow American Psychiat. Assn.; mem. Nat. Assn. Psychiat. Health Sys., Assn. Gen. Psychiatrists (bd. dirs., pres. Brookline 1990-92), Mass. Med. Soc. Mass. Assn. Pvt. Psychiat. Hosps. (bd. dirs., pres. 1990-91), Waquoit Bay Yacht Club (Falmouth, Mass., chmn. race com. 1986-88). Democrat. Avocations: skiing, squash, cars. Home: Newton, Mass. Died Apr. 9, 2014.

**KHRENNIKOV, TIKHON NIKOLAYEVICH,** composer; b. Eletsk, Lipetsk, Russia, June 10, 1913; s. Nikolay and Varvara (Kharlamova) Khrennikov; m. Klara Arnoldovna Vax, 1936; 1 child. Student, Moscow Conservatorie, 1932—36. Dir., music Ctrl. Theatre Soviet Army, 1941—54; gen. sec. Soviet Composers' Union, 1948—57, 1st sec., 1957—2007. Com. mem. USSR Parliamentary Group; mem. CPSU, 1947—2007, Ctrl. Auditing Com., 1961—76, Santa Cecilia, 1983; dep. USSR Supreme Soviet, 1962—2007. Composer: Three Piano Concertos, 1933, 1971, 1983, Five Pieces for Piano, 1933, First Symphony, 1935, Three Pieces for Piano, 1935, Suite for Orchestra from Music for Much Ado About Nothing, 1936, (incidental music) Don Quixote, 1941, Second Symphony, 1942, (plays) (incidental music) Long Ago, 1942, (Operas) In the Storm, 1939, Frol Skobeyev, 1950, Mother, 1956, A Hundred Devils and One Girl, 1963, Kithless Son-in-Law, 1966, White Night, 1967, Boy Giant, 1969, Much Ado About Hearts, 1974, Dorothea, 1983, Golden Calf, 1985, concert for violin & orch., concert for cello & orch., (ballets) Our

Courtyard, 1970, Love for Love, 1976, The Hussars' Ballad, 1978, Third Symphony, 1973, concert 2 for violin & orch. Chmn., Tchaikovsky contest organizing com. Internat. Music Festival in USSR. Decorated Order of Lenin,, Red Banner of Labour; recipient State prize, 1942, 1946, 1951, 1967, 1979, prize, UNESCO Internat. Music Coun., 1977, Lenin prize, 1974, Glinka prize, 1979; named People's Artist of R.S.F.S.R., 1954, People's Artist of USSR, 1963. Mem.: Internat. Assn. Composers Unions (chair 1991—92), German Acad. Arts, Tiberia Acad., Santa Cecilia Acad. Died Aug. 14, 2007.

**KIENER, FRANZ XAVER,** psychologist, educator; b. Krandorf, Bavaria, Fed. Republic of Germany, Apr. 17, 1910; s. Josef and Barbara (Stangl) K.; m. Berta Maria Ponnath; children: Ulrike, Elisabeth, Mechthild, Franz. PhD, U. Munich, 1937, habilitation, 1964. Pvt. practice, Passau, Fed. Republic of Germany, 1937-38; psychologist Enlisted Forces, Vienna, Hanover, Berlin, Breslau, Fed. Republic of Germany, 1938-43; counselor Econ. Coll., Passau, 1947-63; prof. psychology Technical U. Berlin, 1964-78. Author: Clothing, Fashion and People, 1956, Hand, Gesture and Character, 1962,The Word as Weapon: Towards a Psychology of Verbal Aggression, 1983. Home: Tegernheim, Germany. Died Nov. 9, 1996.

**KIESZKOWSKI, MAREK,** environmental engineer, researcher; b. Warsaw, Sept. 3, 1935; s. Maria Kieszkowska and Witold Kieszkowski; m. Anna Zdrojewska, Dec. 3, 1960; 1 child, Monika Kieszkowska. PhD, Tech. U. Warsaw, 1959. Assistant to Professor Inst. of Precision Mechanics, 1990. Asst. to prof. Inst. of Precision Mechanics, Warsaw, 1990; head environ. protection dept. Erubel, from 1965. Contbr. over 120 articles to profl. jours. Home: Warsaw, Poland. Died Feb. 2007.

**KIKONYOGO, CHARLES NYONYINTONO,** bank executive; Gov. Bank of Uganda, Kampala. Died June 30, 2001.

**KILBANE, THOMAS JAMES,** lawyer; b. Cleve., Aug. 19, 1937; s. Thomas Bryan and Nora (Coyle) K.; m. Lucy Clay Ryan, July 31, 1965; children: Nora, Sarah, Thomas, Clare, Brendan, Terrence, Grace, Egan. BA, Holy Cross Coll., 1959; MS, Western Res. U., 1960; JD, Capital U., 1967. Bar: Ohio 1968, US Dist. Ct. (so. dist.) Ohio 1960. Dist. mgr. Williams & Co., Inc., Charleston, W.Va., 1960—69; gen. referee Franklin County Probate Ct., Columbus, Ohio, 1970—73; assoc. Bessey & Kilbane, Columbus, 1973—75; pvt. practise 19Columbus, from 1975. Mem. faculty Ohio Legal Ctr. Inst.; lectr. Capital U. Continuing Edn. Faculty; trustee Birthright Columbus, 1974—77; mem. adv. bd. Salvation Army, Columbus, from 1981. Mem.: Columbus Bar Assn. (fee arbitration panel, chmn. probate law com.), Ohio State Bar Assn., Columbus Lawyers Club (pres.). Died Jan. 23, 1998.

**KILGORE, CAROLYN HARRELL (CAROLYN LAWTON HARRELL),** writer; b. Macon, Ga., Apr. 10, 1911; d. Furman Dargon and Mary Elliott (Nottingham) Lawton; m. Glover Futch Harrell, June 17, 1933 (dec. Oct. 1983); children: Mary Elliott Harrell Reeves, Carolyn Harrell Foley; m. Morris Ward Kilgore, Jan. 13, 1991 (dec. Jan. 1995). BA, Wesleyan Coll., 1933; cert. tech. writing, Rensselaer Poly. Inst., 1962. Newswriter Marine Corps Supply Ctr., Albany, Ga., 1957-59; tech. writer Thiokol Chem. Corp., Huntsville, Ala., 1960-63; publs. engr. Lockheed Aerospace Rsch. and Engring. Ctr., Huntsville, 1964-72. Author: (history) Kith and Kin: A Portrait of a Southern Family (1630-1934), 1984, When the Bells Tolled for Lincoln: Southern Reaction to the Assassination, 1997; contbr. numerous articles to mags. and newspapers. Recipient citation for outstanding performance in writing, editing and prodn. of four book-length volumes of classified documents pertaining to R & D of space vehicles, Lockheed-Huntsville Rsch. and Engring. Ctr., 1965. Mem. DAR, Nat. Soc. Colonial Dames, XVIII Century Huguenot Soc. S.C., Soc. 1st Families of S.C., Macon, Ga., Writers' Club (pres. 1957). Avocations: classical music, family history. Home: Round Top, Tex. Died Oct. 11, 2001.

**KILGORE, JOE MADISON,** former congressman, lawyer; b. Brown County, Texas, Dec. 10, 1918; s. William Henry and Myrtle (Armstrong) K.; m. Jane Redman, July 28, 1945; children: Mark, Dean, Bill, Shannon. Student, Trinity U., 1935-36, U. Tex., 1936-41. Bar: Tex. 1946. Practiced, Edinburg, Tex., 1946-54; mem. Tex. Ho. of Reps., 1946-55, 84th to 88th Congresses, 15th Dist. Tex.; now mem. firm McGinnis, Lochridge & Kilgore, L.L.P., Austin, Tex. Former sr. chmn. bd. Tex. Regional Bancshares; bd. dirs. Tex. State Bank, Photo Control Corp., Reno Air Tex.; regent U. Tex., 1967-73; coun. Adminstrv. Conf. U.S., 1968-72; active U. Tex. Centennial Commn., 1981—. Chmn. adv. coun. Coll. Medicine Tex. A&M; bd. visitors M.D. Anderson Hosp. and Tumor Inst., 1975-78; chmn. adv. com. Tex. Legis. Conf., 1975-80; mem. investment com. Meth. Home; bd. dirs. Southwestern Legal Found., 1981-85, Scott and White Hosp., 1983—, Scott, Sherwood and Brindley Found., 1983—; bd. dirs. Tex. Research League, 1981—; former trustee Southwestern U., 1989-92; mem., former pres. Austin Area Rsch. Orgn., active numerous other civic orgns. Served as lt. col. USAAF, World War II; maj. gen. ret. Decorated Silver Star, Legion of Merit, D.F.C., Air medal with 2 oak leaf clusters, 4 personal citations; named to Tex. Aviation Hall of Fame, 1997. Fellow Am. Bar Found., Tex. Bar Found.; mem. ABA, Travis County Bar Assn., State Bar Tex., U. Tex. Ex-Students' Assn. (pres. 1994-95, chmn. 1995-96), Delta Theta Phi. Methodist. Home: Austin, Tex. Died Feb. 10, 1999.

**KILLEDAR, ABID MOHAMMED,** oil company executive; b. Bombay, Sept. 20, 1941; s. Mohammed Moosa and Ayesha (Mohammed) K.; m. Saeeda Killedar, Feb. 24, 1969; children: Samreen Rizwan Naqvi, Ahmer. BSc in Geology with honors, U. Karachi, Pakistan, 1962, MSc in Geology, 1963. Geologist, field/well site and office geologist Oil and Gas Devel. Corp., Karachi, 1964-74, Sonatrach, Algiers, Algiera, 1974-81; from sr. geologist to sr. mgr. joint ops. Pakistan Petroleum Ltd., Karachi, from 1981, in-charge wellsite, 1981-89. Gen. sec., pres. Student's Union, U. Karachi. Recipient numerous awards. Mem. Soc. Petroleum Engrs., Pakistan Assn. Petrol Geoscientists, Petroleum Inst. Pakistan. Avocations: reading, driving, sports, gardening, household chores. Home: Karachi, Pakistan. Died Aug. 1, 2010.

**KIM, SI-WOOK,** economist, educator; b. Chongyang, Korea, Oct. 23, 1950; s. Byong-Shik and Il-Rye (Park) K.; m. Sun-Hee Hyun, Apr. 12, 1979; children: Soyon, Hayon, Jaeson. BA in Econs., Yonsei U., Seoul, Korea, 1973; MPA, Seoul Nat. U., 1977; PhD in Econs., U. Calif., Santa Barbara, 1986. Asst. prof. dept. econs. Hanyang U., Seoul, from 1988. Deceased.

**KIMBALL, PENN TOWNSEND, II,** retired educator, journalist; b. New Britain, Conn., Oct. 12, 1915; s. Arthur G. and Effie (Smallen) K.; m. Janet Evelyn Fraser, Apr. 8, 1947 (dec. 1982); 1 child, Elisabeth Kimball; m. Julie M. Ellis, July 27, 1985; 1 adopted child, Laura BA, Princeton U., 1937, Balliol Coll., Oxford U., Eng., 1939, MA, 1946; postgrad., Yale U., 1950-51, Columbia U., 1951-58, MPhil, 1987, PhD, 1988. Reporter US News & World Report, 1939-40, PM Newspaper, 1940-41; contbg. editor TIME mag., 1945-46; sr. editor New Republic, 1947; adminstrv. asst. to Gov. Chester Bowles State of Conn., Hartford, 1948-49; exec. sec. to Senator William Benton US Senate, 1949-50; asst. to Sunday editor The NY Times, 1951-54; with TV Radio Workshop, Ford Found., 1954-55; sr. editor Colliers, 1955-56; partner Louis Harris & Associates, NYC, 1957-58; adminstrv. asst. to Gov. Averell Harriman State of NY, 1958; prof. Columbia Grad. Sch. Journalism, 1959-85, prof. emeritus, 1986—2013; mem. adminstrv. bd. Bur. Applied Social Research, 1963-67; cons. editor Harris Survey, 1963-74; faculty Salzburg (Austria) Seminar in American Studies, 1967. Vis. lectr. Dartmouth, U. Calif. at Berkeley, U. Conn., New Sch. for Social Research, U. Wash.; Haas lectr. in broadcast journalism U. Wash., 1987; vis. scholar Joint Ctr. for Polit. Studies, 1988-89; guest scholar Woodrow Wilson Internat. Ctr. for scholars, 1991-92 Author: Bobby Kennedy and The New Politics, 1968, The Disconnected, 1972, The File, 1983, Keep Hope Alive!: Super Tuesday and Jesse Jackson's 1988 Campaign for the Presidency, 1991, Downsizing the News: Network Cutbacks in the Nation's Capitol, 1994; mem. editorial bd. Columbia Journalism Rev., 1963-85; contbr. articles to nat. mags. Sec. Conn. House Appropriations Com., 1949, mem. citizens commn., 1968-69, mem. bd. finance, Westport, Conn., 1953-55, mem. charter commn., 1957, justice of peace, 1959-60, rep. town meeting, 1959-63; mem. Conn. Constl. Conv., 1965; faculty Nat. Urban Fellows summer program Yale, 1969-70; dir. public affairs Urban Devel. Corp., State N.Y., 1971-72; mem. nat. adv. com. election systems project Nat. Municipal League-League Women Voters, 1971-73; asst. dir. S. Bronx Devel. Orgn., 1979-80. Served to capt. USMCR, 1941-45, PTO; maj. Res. (ret.). Rhodes Scholar, 1937-39 Mem. PEN, Author's League, American Assn. Pub. Opinion Research, Phi Beta Kappa. Clubs: National Press (Washington). Democrat. Congregationalist. Home: Chilmark, Mass. Died Nov. 8, 2013.

**KIMBROUGH, EDWARD ERNEST,** academic orthopaedic surgeon; b. Sept. 29, 1929; BA, Vanderbilt U., 1950, MD, 1953. Surg. intern U. Minn. Hosps., 1953-54, resident in surgery, 1954-55; resident in orthopedic surgery Brooke Army Hosp., San Antonio, 1957-59; pres. Moore Clinic, Columbia, S.C., 1963-83; chmn. dept. orthopedics U. S.C., Columbia, 1983-95; ret. Home: Columbia, SC. Died Jan. 24, 2008.

**KIMURA, MUTSUO,** legislator; b. Niimi, Okayama, Japan, July 29, 1913; s. Seima and Suma Mikami; m. Mieko Kimura, Jan. 20, 1940; children: Shunsuke, Taisuke; 1 child, Yusuke. B in Laws, Tokyo U., 1938. Dir. road transport bur. Ministry Transport, 1961—64, dir. tourism bur., 1964; minister, 1974—76; pres. House Councillors, 1983—86. Recipient Aart Appreciation. Buddhist. Avocations: golf, reading. Home: Tokyo, Japan. Died Dec. 2001.

**KINER, RALPH MCPHERRAN,** sportscaster, retired professional baseball player; b. Santa Rita, N.Mex., Oct. 27, 1922; m.Nancy Chaffee, 1951 (div. 1968); children: Michael, Scott, Kathryn; m. Barbara George (div.); m. DiAnn Shugart, Dec. 1982 (dec. 2004); adopted children: Tracee, Kim; 1 stepdaughter, Candice Beck. Attended Pasadena City Coll. Left fielder Pitts. Pirates, 1946-53, Chgo. Cubs, 1953-54, Cleve. Indians, 1955; gen. mgr. San Diego Padres (Pacific Coast League), 1955—60; announcer Chgo. White Sox, 1961, N.Y. Mets., WWOR-TV, 1962—2013. Served in USN, 1943-45 Named to The Nat. League All-Star Team, 1948-53; Recipient By Saam award, 1985; elected to The Nat. Baseball Hall of Fame, 1975, Pa. Hall of Fame, N.Y. Mets Hall of Fame, 1984 Home: Palm Beach, Fla. Died Feb. 6, 2014.

**KING, CHARLES THOMAS,** retired school superintendent, educator; b. Coatsville, Pa., July 19, 1911; s. John Henry and Estella (Orr) K.; m. Dorothy Eckman, Nov. 30, 1933; children: Marilyn Mae, Kenneth Alan, Donald Edwin. BS, West Chester State Coll., 1932; EdM, Temple U., 1944; EdD, Rutgers U., 1957. Tchr. West Pottsgrove Twp. Sch., Stowe, Pa., 1933-35, Haverford Twp. Sch., Havertown, Pa., 1935-38, dir. elem. health and phys. edn., 1938-42; prin. Llanerch Sch., Havertown, Pa., 1942-45; supervising prin.

West Pottsgrove Twp. Sch., Stowe, Pa., 1945-47; prin. Glenwood and Short Hills Schs., Millburn, N.J., 1947-51, asst. to supt., 1951-59, asst. supt., 1959-62, supt., 1962-74. Mem. state adv. council on Handicapped 1968-72; mem. state cert. appeals com., 1972-74 Pres. Millburn Cmty. Coun., 1954-56; bd. dirs. Millburn Pub. Libr., 1962-74 Millburn Twp. Com.; chmn. N.J. Coun. Econ. Edn., 1972-74; deacon Congl. Ch., 1963-66; chmn. Pilgrim Congl. Ch., 1993-97. Recipient Cmty. Svc. award Millburn Twp. Com., 1995. Mem. Essex County Supts. Roundtable (chmn. 1965-66), West Chester State Coll. Alumni Assn. (chpt. pres. 1981-83, Disting. Alumni award 1982), Millburn Coaches Assn. (Man of Yr. award 1989), Rotary (pres. 1957-58, bd. dirs. 1996-97, Paul Harris fellow 1986, Svc. Above Self plaque 1989), Millburn Old Guard (pres. 1997), Phi Delta Kappa (chpt. pres. 1959-60, emeritus 1974). Home: Reno, Nev. Deceased.

**KING, HENRY EDWARD ST. LEGER,** solicitor; b. Oct. 11, 1936; s. Robert James and Dorothy Louisa Marie (Wickert) K.; m. Kathleen Bridget Wilcock, 1964 (dissolved 1989); 2 children (1 dec.); m. Margaret Empson Cox, 1996. MA, LLB, Cambridge U., Eng. Solicitor, Eng. 1964, Hong Kong 1977. Solicitor Denton Wilde Sapte, 1964-67, ptnr., 1967-96, chmn., 1993-96. Chmn. bd. dirs. Rentokil Initial PLC; bd. dirs. Brambles Investments PLC, TotalFinaElf Exploration U.K. PLC. Mem. Riverside Racquet Club. Avocations: travel, theater, music. Died Mar. 16, 2002.

**KING, HUESTON CLARK,** retired otolaryngologist, educator; b. Bklyn., Feb. 3, 1929; s. William Clark and Alice Packard (Hueston) K.; m. Wilma Marguerite Grove, June 13, 1953; children: Brian G., Melinda K. AB in Biology, Princeton U., 1950; MD, Columbia U., 1954. Diplomate Am. Bd. Otolaryngology; lic. physician, Fla., NC; cert. Nat. Bd. Med. Examiners. Intern Jackson Meml. Hosp., U. Miami (Fla.) Sch. Medicine, 1954-55; resident in otolaryngology Walter Reed Army Med. Ctr., Washington, 1956-58; staff Coral Gables (Fla.) Hosp., 1962-82, Bapt. Hosp., 1962-82, Mercy Hosp., 1962-82, South Miami Hosp., Fla., 1962-82, Cedars of Lebanon Hosp., 1962-82, Jackson Meml. Hosp., 1962-82; with Venice (Fla.) Hosp., 1983-94. From clin. faculty to assoc. prof. dept. otolaryngology U. Miami Med. Sch., 1962-82; clin. prof. dept. otolaryngology U. Tex. Southwestern Med. Ctr., Dallas, 1998-2006, U. Fla.; lectr. in field. Author: (textbook) An Otolaryngologist's Guide to Allergy, 1991; sr. author: (textbook) A Practical Guide to Management of Nasal and Sinus Disorders, 1993, Allergy in ENT Practice: A Basic Guide, 1998, 2d edit. 2004; editor: Otolaryngologic Allergy, 1981; editor Allergy Digest, food allergy sect. Current Sci., allergy sect. Current Opinion, 1999-01; contbr. chpts. to books, articles to profl. jours. Bd. dirs. Woodmere at Jacaranda, Venice, 1997—99; committeeman Venice Found., 1995—97. Fellow ACS (emeritus), Am. Acad. Facial Plastic and Reconstructive Surgery (emeritus), Am. Acad. Otolaryngic Allergy (past pres. 1979-80, dir. med. edn. 1983-88), Am. Coll. Allergy, Asthma and Immunology; mem. Fla. Med. Assn., Sarasota Couty Med. Assn., Venice Yacht Club. Home: Tampa, Fla. Died Nov. 29, 2013.

**KING, ROBERT AUGUSTIN,** engineering executive; b. Marion, Ind., Sept. 3, 1910; s. Roy Melvin and Estella Bernice (Sheron) K.; m. Johanna A. Akkerman, July 19, 1975; children: Robert Alexander, Sharon Johanna, Estella Regina; children by previous marriage: Hugh Melbourne, Mary Elizabeth. BSChemE, U. Okla., 1935. Chief chemist Phillips Petroleum Co., Borger, Tex., 1935-43; sr. process engr. E. B. Badger & Sons, NYC and London, 1944-53; dist. mgr. Stone & Webster, NYC, 1954-56; mng. dir. Badger Co., The Hague, Netherlands, 1957-64; pres. King-Wilkinson, Inc., Houston, 1965-84, also dir.; pres. Robert A. King Inc., from 1985. Mem. Am. Inst. Chem. Engrs., Am. Chem. Soc., Inst. Petroleum (London). Clubs: Petroleum, Braeburn Country (Houston); Chemists (N.Y.C.). Democrat. Episcopalian. Home: Houston, Tex. Died 1998.

**KING, ROBERT THOMAS,** editor, writer; b. Hillside, NJ, Oct. 29, 1930; s. Philip Arthur and Lucy (Davis) K.; m. Fredericka Bredow, 1978 Student, Emmanuel Coll., Cambridge, Eng., 1948-50; BA, Birmingham U., Eng., 1955; postgrad., Shakespeare Inst., Stratford-Upon-Avon, Eng., 1955-56. Trainee Oxford U. Press, NYC, 1957-59; chief copy editor NYU Press, 1959-61, editor, 1961-63, mng. editor, 1963-66; dir. U. SC Press, Columbia, 1966-84. Contbr. articles to profl. jours., mags., newspapers. Recipient Lucy Hampton Bostick award, 1978. Mem. Am. Assn. Univ. Presses (bd. dirs. 1972-74, chmn. goals and long-range problems com.), Andiron Club, Grolier Club, Torch Club (Columbia). Episcopalian (dir. The Episcopalian, vestry, lic. lay reader). Home: Greenville, SC. Died June 2013.

**KING, ROLLIN WHITE,** retired airline executive; b. Cleve., Apr. 10, 1931; s. Warren Griffin and Elizabeth (White) King; m. Mary Ella Ownby Dewar King, July 5, 1976; children: Rollin White, Edward Prescott. Student, Cornell U., Ithaca, NY, 1954; BA, Western Res. U., 1955; MBA, Harvard Bus. Sch., 1962. Mem. mgmt. staff NSA, Washington, 1955—60; v.p. King, Pitman Co. Investment Counsel, San Antonio, 1962—63; founder, pres. Southwest Airlines Co., Dallas, 1967; ptnr. King Investments Co., Dallas, 1978—79; mng. dir. Russell Reynolds Associates, Inc., Dallas, 1984—89; prin. Rollin King Assocs., 1989—2014. With AUS, 1956—58, with USNR, 1958—64. Mem.: Wings (NYC), River, Dallas Crescent, Brook Hollow Golf. Died June 26, 2014.

**KINGET, G. MARIAN,** educator, psychologist; b. Belgium, June 2, 1910; came to U.S., 1948, naturalized, 1957; d. Rene Jules Henri and Elisa (Declercq) K. PhD summa cum laude, U. Louvain, Belgium, 1948; postdoctoral, N.Y. U., 1948-49, Columbia U., 1949-50. With U. Chgo., 1950-52; asst. prof. psychology Mich. State U., East Lansing,

1952-55, asso. prof., 1955-66, prof., 1966-81, emeritus prof., 1981. Author: On Being Human, 1975, 2d edition, 1987, Psychotherapie et Relations Humaines (transl. Spanish, Italian, and Portuguese), Vol. II, 1962, The Drawing-Completion Test, 1952, (with Carl R. Rogers) Psychotherapie et Relations Humaines (transl. Spanish, Italian and Portuguese), Vol. I, 1962, Psychotherapie en Menselifjke Verhoudingen, 1959; contbr. (with Carl R. Rogers) chpts. to books. Mem. Am., Midwestern, Mich. psychol. assns., AAUP. Died 1997.

**KINGSDOWN, LORD (ROBIN LEIGH-PEMBERTON),** retired banker, non-executive director; b. Lenham, Kent, Eng., Jan. 5, 1927; Gov. Bank of Eng., London, 1983-93. Decorated Knight Order of Garter, Baron, Life Peer, 1993; Lord Lt. County of Kent, Eng., 1982-2002; honorary col. Kent & Sharpshooters Yeomanry, 1979-92; pro chancellor U. Kent, 1977-84 Home: Sittingbourne, England. Died Nov. 24, 2013.

**KIRCHNER, JAMES WILLIAM,** retired electrical engineer; b. Cleve., Oct. 17, 1920; s. William Sebastian and Marcella Louise (Stuart) K.; m. Eda Christene Landfear, June 11, 1950 (dec. May 1977); children: Kathleen Ann Kirchner Duda, Susan Lynn Kirchner Buonpane; m. Mary Jane Freebairn, Sept. 17, 2004; children: Lisa Ann Freebairn, Robert V. Freebairn III, Joseph G. Bounpane. BSEE, Ohio U., 1950, MS, 1951. Registered profl. engr., Ohio. Instr. elec. engring. Ohio U., Athens, 1950—52; mgr. liaison engring. Lear Siegler Inc., Maple Heights, Ohio, 1952—64; coord. engring. svcs. Case We. Res. U., Cleve., 1964—72, gen. mgr. Med. Ctr. Co., 1972—91; ret., 1991; sec. corp. Thermagon, Inc., Cleve., 1992. Mem. Portage County Republican Exec. Com., 1961-62; treas. PTA, Aurora, Ohio, 1963-65, v.p., 1965-66; mem. The Ch. in Aurora, 1956—. Served with USAAF, 1942-45, PTO Mem. NSPE (life), IEEE (life), VFW (life), Ohio Soc. Profl. Engrs. (life), Cleve. Engring. Soc. (chmn. environ. com. 1976), Am. Soc. Engring. Edn. (life). Home: Aurora, Ohio. Died Feb. 1, 2013.

**KIRIMA, NICODEMUS,** archbishop; b. Karatina, Nyeri, Kenya, Mar. 3, 1938; s. Zebedee and Bilhah (Wanjira) Kariithi. BA in Sociology, St. John Fisher Coll., 1968; MA in Edn., U. Rochester, 1970. Ordained priest Roman Cath. Ch. Asst. parish priest Archdiocese of Nairobi, Kenya, 1962-64, headmaster secondary sch., 1964-66, parish priest, 1970, theology faculty lectr., asst. prin., 1971-74; prin. St. Thomas Aquinas Sem., Nairobi, 1974-78; bishop Diocese of Mombasa, Kenya, 1978-88; archbishop of Nyeri Kenya, 1988—2007. Chmn. Kenya Bishops Conf., 1988-90, Ea. Africa Bishops Conf., 1989—. Author: African Religious Heritage, 1974. Gov.'s bd. mem. Kenya Inst. Edn., Nairobi, 1980-88; mem. Cath. U. Coun., 1989, Kenyatta U. Coun., 1993. Mem. United Nairobi Club. Died Nov. 27, 2007.

**KIRK, RONALD J.,** protective services official; b. Chgo., May 30, 1936; s. Arthur G. and Rita B. (Voigt) K.; m. Jean J. Farley, Sept. 1, 1962; children: Lisa T., John F. Student, DePaul U., 1972-76, Lewis U., 1987-88. Lic. pvt. investigator, Ill. Lt. Chgo. Police Dept., 1961-87; v.p. Apollo Detective Agy., Inc., Harvey, Ill., from 1987. Bd. dirs. Nat. Council of Investigators and Security Services, Washington. With USAR, 1976-80. Mem. Spl. Agts. Assn. (pres. 1988), Rotary (bd. dirs. 1988, Blue Island, Ill., Paul Harris fellow). Republican. Roman Catholic. Avocation: civil war history. Home: Chicago, Ill. Died June 9, 1989.

**KIRKEBY, OLIVER MURLE,** counselor, religion educator, sociologist; b. Henning, Minn., Sept. 14, 1930; s. Ole B. and Wilhelmena Kirkeby; children from previous marriage: Paul, Beth, Jayne; m. Judith Dixon Hillestad, June 9, 1987. BA, Concordia Coll., 1953; MA, U. Windsor, Can., 1972; D of Ministry, Trinity Sem., 1980; PhD, Wayne State U., 1982. Ordained to ministry Am. Evang. Luth. Ch. Assoc. pastor First Luth. Ch., Stoughton, Wis., 1958-60; pastor Trinity Luth. Ch., Chgo., 1960-63; dir. Metro-Luth. Campus Ministry, Detroit, 1963-74; pastor Salem Luth. Ch., Detroit, 1974-80; lay assoc. Zion Luth. Ch., Ferndale, Mich., 1980-90; internat. counselor Wayne State U., Detroit, 1985-90. Researcher various Luth. Chs., Mich., 1963—; with Global Mission Com. S.E. Mich. Synod, Detroit, 1989—. Contbr. articles to profl. jours. Trustee Scandinavian Symphony Soc. Mich., 1980—; sec., v.p. Highland Park (Mich.) Libr. Commn., 1972-87; pres. Rotary Internat., Highland Park, 1979-80. Recipient Paul Harris award Rotary, 1980. Mem. Soc. Bibl. Lit., Nat. Assn. of Fgn. Student Advisors, Mich. Coun. Social Studies, World Futurist, Am. Coll. Nursing Home Adminstrs., People to People, Sons of Norway. *The greatest treasure is a life that is shared and passed on to grandchildren who in turn can share with their parents when they are not too busy.* Deceased.

**KIRSH, HERB,** retired state legislator; b. NYC, May 17, 1929; s. Isadore and Yetta Kirsh; m. Suzanne Selikowitz, 1950 (dec. 2009); children: Mike, Bruce, Kevin, Larry. BA, Duke U., 1949. Operator Kirsh Dept. Store; mayor pro-tem City of Clover, SC, 1971—75, mayor, 1975—78; mem. Dist 47 SC House of Reps., 1978—2010. Recipient Disting. Svc. award, SC Mcpl. Assn., 1985; named Clover Man of Yr., 1976. Mem.: Clover County Chamber of Commerce (former pres.), Clover Jaycees (charter mem.), Shriner, Mason. Democrat. Jewish. Home: Clover, SC. Died Jan. 28, 2014.

**KISEKKA, SAMSON,** former Prime Minister of Uganda; b. 1913; Physician; prime min. of Uganda, 1986-91; v.p., min. internal affairs Uganda, 1991—94; presdl. advisor, 1994—99. Chief spokesman for Nat. Resistance Army. Died Oct. 25, 1999.

**KISTNER, KLAUS-PETER,** retired management educator; b. Frankfurt, Germany, July 14, 1940; s. Karl and Doris (Johann) K.; m. Ilse Fellmann, Aug. 18, 1967. Diploma in econ., U. Bonn, Fed. Republic Germany, 1965, D Econ., 1969. Rsch. asst., then lectr. econ. U. Bonn, 1965-74; prof. mgmt. sci. U. Bielefeld, Germany, 1974—2006, prof. emeritus. Lectr. German MBA program, Moscow. Author: Queueing with Breakdowns, 1974, Theory of Prod. and Cost, 1981, Optimization Methods, 3d edit., 2003, Production Planning, 3d edit., 2006, Theory of Prod. and Cost, 2d edit., 1993, Business Administration for Undergraduates II, 1997, Business Administration for Undergraduates I, 4th edit., 2002, Exercises to Bus. Admin. for Undergraduates, 2000; contbr. articles to profl. jours. Mem.: German Ops. Rsch. Soc. Home: Steinhagen, Germany. Died Jan. 9, 2014.

**KITCHEN, LAWRENCE OSCAR,** retired aerospace transportation executive; b. Ft. Mill, SC, June 8, 1923; s. Samuel Sumpter and Ruby Azalee (Grigg) K.; m. Brenda Lenhart, Nov. 25, 1978; children by previous marriage: Brenda, Alan, Janet. Student, Foothill Coll. Aero. engr. U.S. Navy Bur. Aeronautics, Washington, 1946-58, staff asst. to asst. chief bur., 1958; with Lockheed Missiles & Space Co., Sunnyvale, Calif., 1958-70, mgr. product support logistics, 1964-68, dir. fin. controls, 1968-70; v.p.-fin. Lockheed-Ga. Co., Marietta, 1970-71, pres., 1971-75, Lockheed Corp., Burbank, Calif., 1975-76, pres., COO, 1976-85, chmn., CEO, 1986-88. Mem. nominating com. Aviation Hall of Fame; served in USMC, 1942-46. Mem. AIAA, Nat. Def. Transp. Assn., Navy League, Soc. Logistics Engrs., Air Force Assn., Assn. U.S. Army. Died Dec. 15, 2013.

**KIYOTA, YUKIHIRO,** electrical engineer; b. Suginami, Tokyo, Japan, Dec. 17, 1963; s. Masakazu and Yukiko Kiyota; m. Junko Kiyota, Mar. 27, 1967; 1 child, Tomokazu. B in Sci and Engring., Waseda U., Tokyo, 1986, M, 1988, D, 1996. Sr. engr. Hitachi, Kokubunji, Tokyo, 2000—03; engring. mgr. Hitachi Global Storage Techs., Odawara, Kanagawa, 2003; disting. engr. SONY, Atsugi, Kanagawa, from 2003. Mem. conf. program com. Internat. Workshop on Junction Tech., from 2000, Internat. SiGe Tech. and Device Meeting, from 2002, Internat. Electron Device Meeting, 2005—06; editor Japanese Jour. Applied Physics, 2004—11. Contbr. articles to profl. jours. Recipient Editl. Contbn. award, Japanese Jour. Applied Physics, 2011. Achievements include research in semiconductor process and device; bipolar and CMOS for RF applications and CMOS image sensors; epitaxial growth and shallow junction (Rapid Vapor-phase doping), and devices like bipolar and CMOS for RF applications and image sensors. Home: Tokyo, Japan. Deceased.

**KIZER, CAROLYN ASHLEY,** poet, educator; b. Spokane, Wash., Dec. 10, 1925; d. Benjamin Hamilton and M. (Ashley) K.; m. Stimson Bullitt, Jan., 1948 (div. 1954); children: Ashley Ann, Scott, Jill Hamilton; m. John Marshall Woodbridge, Apr. 11, 1975 (dec. June 2, 2014) BA, Sarah Lawrence Coll., 1945; postgrad. (Chinese govt. fellow in comparative lit.), Columbia U., 1946-47; studied poetry with Theodore Roethke, U. Wash., 1953-54; LittD (hon.), Whitman Coll., 1986, St. Andrew's Coll., 1989, Mills Coll., 1990, Wash. State U., 1991. Specialist in lit. U.S. Dept. State, Pakistan, 1964-65; first dir. lit. programs Nat. Endowment for Arts, 1966-70; poet-in-residence U. N.C. at Chapel Hill, 1970-74; Hurst Prof. Lit. Washington U., St. Louis, 1971; lectr. Spring Lecture Series Barnard Coll., 1972; acting dir. grad. writing program Columbia U., 1972; poet-in-residence Ohio U., 1974; vis. poet Iowa Writer's Workshop, 1975; prof. U. Md., 1976-77; poet-in-residence, disting. vis. lectr. Centre Coll., Ky., 1979; disting. vis. poet East Wash. U., 1980; Elliston prof. poetry U. Cin., 1981; Bingham disting. prof. U. Louisville, Ky., 1982; disting. vis. poet Bucknell U., Pa., 1982; vis. poet SUNY, Albany, 1982; prof. Columbia U. Sch. Arts, 1982; prof. poetry Stanford U., 1986; sr. fellow in humanities Princeton U., 1986; vis. prof. writing U. Ariz., 1989, 90, U. Calif., Davis, 1991; Coal Royalty chair U. Ala., 1995. Participant Internat. Poetry Festivals, London, 1960, 70, Yugoslavia, 1969, 70, Pakistan, 1969, Rotterdam, Netherlands, 1970, Knokke-le-Zut, Belgium, 1970, Bordeaux, 1992, Dublin, 1993, Glasgow, 1994; sr. fellow humanities council Princeton U., 1986. Author: Poems, 1959, The Ungrateful Garden, 1961, Knock Upon Silence, 1965, Midnight Was My Cry, 1971, Mermaids in the Basement: Poems for Women, 1984 (San Francisco Arts Commn. award 1986), Yin: New Poems, 1984 (Pulitzer Prize in Poetry 1985), The Nearness of You, 1987 (Theodore Roethke prize, 1988); Proses: On Poems & Poets, 1994, Picking & Choosing: Prose on Prose, 1995, Harping On: Poems 1985-1995, 1996, The Complete Pro Femina, 2000, Cool, Calm and Collected Poems, 1960-2000; editor: Woman Poet: The West, 1980, Leaving Taos, 1981, The Essential Clare, 1993, 100 Great Poems by Women, 1995; translator Carrying Over, 1988; founder, editor: Poetry N.W., 1959-65; contbr. poems, articles to American and British jours. Recipient award American Acad. & Inst. Arts & Letters, 1985, President's medal Eastern Wash. U., 1988, 5 Gov.'s awards State of Wash., 1965, 85, 95, 98, 2001, Silver medal Commonwealth Club, 1997, 2002, Aiken Taylor prize Sewanee Rev., 1998, Patterson prize, 2002, Western State Lifetime Achievement award, 2002, 1st prize Ind. Public Book award, 2002, L.A. Times Top Ten Books award, 2002, Acad. prize, 2003, Poets' prize, 2003. Mem. PEN, Amnesty Internat., Poetry Soc. America (Masefield prize 1983, Frost medal 1988). Episcopalian. Died Oct. 9, 2014.

**KIZUKA, TAKASHI,** mathematician; b. Karatsu, Saga Prefecture, Japan, Feb. 14, 1952; s. Sunao and Michiyo Kizuka; m. Michiko Naitou, Feb. 4, 1950; 1 child, Moe. B, Kyoto U., Japan, 1975; M, Tohoku U., Sendai, Japan, 1977, DSc, 1983; PhD, Tohoku U., 1985. Lectr. faculty math. Kyushu U., Fukuoka, Fukuoka Prefecture, Japan, 1994—2008. Mem.: Am. Math. Soc. Home: Fukuoka Prefecture, Japan. Died Feb. 6, 2008.

**KLEBE, GISELHER,** composer; b. Mannheim, Fed. Republic of Germany, June 28, 1925; s. Franz and Gertrud (Michaelis) K.; m. Lore Schiller, Sept. 10, 1946; children: Sonja, Annette. Student, Konservatorium, Berlin, 1940-43; studied composition with Baris Blacher, 1946-1951. Lectr. composition and theory Detmold Music Acad., 1957, prof. composition, 1962. Pres. Acad. Arts, Berlin, 1986-89, Dramatists Union Div. Music, 1986. Compositions include 13 operas, including Die Tödlichen Wünsche, 1959, Jakobowsky und der Oberst, 1965, Die Fastnachsbeichte, 1983; 5 ballets; orchestral works include Die Zwitschermaschine, 6 symphonies, Concerto for Pipe Organ and Orchestra, Begrüssung Salutations, Concerto for Clarinet and Orchestra, Song for Orchestra, Nocturne for Orchestra, Concerto for Harpe and Orchestra, Soirée for Trombone and Chamber Ensemble, Concerto for Violoncello and Orchestra in One Movement; chamber music includes 3 string quartets, works for speaker, piano, cembalo and contrabass, Roman Elegies for speaker, piano and contrabass, Elegia Appassionata for piano trio, Berlioz Variations for pipe organ and percussion, Al Rovescio for flute, harp, piano and metallidiophone, Alborada for harp solo, Der Dunkle Gedanke for clarinet and piano, Il Ritorno—Variations on the Moudscheinsonae of Beethoven, for horn and piano; sacred music includes Stabat Mater, Mass for choir and pipe organ, Chorale and Tedeum, Weihnachtsoratorium; organ works; vocal works include (song) Warum hat die Sonne einen Aschenrand, oratorium composed for Amnesty International, Play up for Big Band. Recipient Berliner Kunstpreis, 1952, Kompositionspreis der Unesco, 1954, GroBer Kuntspreis des Landes Nordrhein-Westfalen, 1959, Premio Marzotto für die Vereinigung Europas, 1964, Bundesverdienstkreuz 1. Klasse, 1975. Mem. Free Acad. Arts Hamburg, Acad. Arts Berlin, Acad. Fine Arts Munich, Internat. Harp Ctr. (hon. dir.). Died Oct. 5, 2009.

**KLEIN, DANIEL EUGENE, JR.,** federal judge; b. 1934; BA, Union Coll., 1956; LLB, U. Md., 1964, JD, 1969. Bar: Md. 1964. Law clk. to Judge Prendergast Supreme Bench Balt., 1963-64; law clk. to Hon. Edward S. Northrop, U.S. Dist. Ct. for Dist. Md., 1964-65; ptnr. Klein & Harlan and predecessors, Balt., 1965-78; U.S. magistrate juge for Md., U.S. Dist. Ct., Balt., 1978-99, chief U.S. magistrate judge, 1997-99. With USAF, 1956-60; mem. Md. Air N.G., 1962-82. Died Feb. 2002.

**KLEIN, LAWRENCE ROBERT,** economist, educator; b. Omaha, Sept. 14, 1920; s. Leo Byron and Blanche (Monheit) Klein; m. Sonia Adelson, Feb. 15, 1947; children: Hannah, Rebecca, Rachel, Jonathan. BA in Economics, U. Calif., Berkeley, 1942; PhD in Economics, MIT, 1944; MA, Lincoln Coll., Oxford U., 1957; LLD (hon.), U. Mich., 1977, Dickinson Coll., 1981, U. Pa., 2006; DSc (hon.), Widener Coll., 1977, Elizabethtown Coll., 1981, Ball State U., 1982, Technion, 1981, U. Nebr., 1983, Nat. Ctrl. U. Taiwan, 1985, Rutgers U., 1992; LHD (hon.), Bard Coll., 1986, Bilkent U., 1989, St. Norbert Coll., 1989; EdD (hon.), Villanova U., 1978; PhD (hon.), Bar Ilan U., 1994; DLitt (hon.), U. Glasgow, 1991; D (hon.), U. Vienna, 1977, Bonn U., 1974, Free U. Brussels, 1979, U. Paris, 1979, U. Madrid, 1980, Southern Helsinki Sch. Economics, 1986, U. Lodz, 1990, Carleton Univ., 1997, U. Piraeus, 1999, Acad. Economic Studies, Romania, 1999, U. Toronto, 2002, Konan U., 2002, Keio U., 2002, U. Costa Rica, 2005, U. Slovenia, 2005. Faculty Cowles Commn. Rsch. in Economics, U. Chgo., 1944—47; rsch. assoc. Nat. Bur. Econ. Rsch., Cambridge, Mass., 1948—50; faculty U. Mich., 1949—54; rsch. assoc. Oxford Inst. Statistics, 1954—58; faculty mem. Dept. Economics U. Pa. Wharton Sch. Bus., Phila., 1958—91, Benjamin Franklin prof. economics & finance, 1968—91, Benjamin Franklin prof. emeritus economics, 1991—2013. Cons. McMillan Co., 1965—74, E.I. du Pont de Nemours, 1966—68, UN Conf. Trade Devel., 1966—80, AT&T, 1969, Fed. Res. Bd., 1973, UN Indsl. Devel. Orgn., 1973—75, Coun. Econ. Advisers, 1977—80; prin. investigator econometric model project Brookings Instn., Washington, 1963—72; mem. com. on prices Fed. Res. Bd., 1968—70; chmn. bd. trustees Wharton Econometric Forecasting Assocs., Inc., 1969—80; chmn. profl. bd. Wharton Econometric Forecasting Associates, Inc., 1980—2013; mem. advisory bd. Strategic Studies Ctr., Stanford Rsch. Inst., 1974—76; mem. advisory coun. Inst. Advanced Studies, Vienna, Inst. Internat. Economics, Washington. Author: The Keynesian Revolution, 1947, Textbook of Econometrics, 1953, An Econometric Model of the United States, 1929-1952, 1955, Wharton Econometric Forecasting Model, 1967, Essay on the Theory of Economic Prediction, 1968, An Introduction to Econometric Forecasting and Forecasting Models, 1980; author, editor: Brookings Quar. Econometric Model of U.S., Ecometric Model Performance, 1976, Lectures in Econmetrics, 1983; editor: Internat. Econ. Rev., 1959—65; mem. editl. bd.: Empirical Economics; contbr. articles to profl. jours. Founding trustee Economists for Peace & Security; trustee Maurice Falk Inst. Econ. Rsch., Israel, 1969—75; chmn. econ. advisory com. for Gov. of Pa., 1976—78; hon. chmn. adv. bd. Pa. Inst. Econ. Rsch. Recipient William F. Butler award, NY Assn. Bus. Economists, 1975, President's Medal, U. Pa., 1980, Nobel Prize in Economics, Royal Swedish Acad. Sciences, 1980. Fellow: Nat. Assn. Bus. Economists, American Acad. Arts & Sciences, Econometric Soc. (past pres.), Brit. Acad. (corr.); mem.: NAS, Russian Acad. Sci. (fgn.), Eastern Econ. Assn. (pres. 1974—76), American Econ. Assn. (exec. com. 1966—68, pres. 1977, John Bates Clark Medal 1959), Social Sci. Rsch. Coun. (fellow 1945—46, 1947—48), American Philos. Soc. Achievements include creation of econometric models and the application to the analysis of economic fluctuations and economic policies. Home: Gladwyne, Pa. Died Oct. 20, 2013.

**KLEIN, RALPH PHILLIP,** former Canadian government official; b. Calgary, Alta., Can., Nov. 1, 1942; m. Hilda Hepner (div.); 2 children; Colleen Klein, 1972; 1 child, 2 step children LLD (hon.), U. Calgary, 2011. Dir. pub. rels. Alta. div. Red Cross; dir. pub. rels. Calgary United Way Fund, 1966-69; with CFCN, 1969-80; newsreader radio div., later television reporter, 1969-80; mayor City of Calgary, 1980-89; legislator Calgary-Elbow constituency Alta. Legislature, Edmonton, 1989—2007, min. environment, 1989—92, min. fed. & intergovernmental affairs, 1993—94, premier, 1992—2006; sr. adv. Borden Ladner Gervais, 2007—13. Leader Progressive Conservative Assn. Alberta, 1992—2006. Recipient Golden Jubilee medal, Her Majesty Queen Elizabeth II, 2002, Alberta Centennial medal, 2005; named an Officer of the Legion of Honour, Govt. of France, 2008; named to The Alberta Order of Excellence, 2010. Died Mar. 29, 2013.

**KLEINLOGEL, ALEXANDER LUDWIG WILHELM,** educator; b. Mannheim, Fed. Republic Germany, July 15, 1929; s. Ludwig and Stanislawa (Krystalska) K.; m. Karin Hackler, Oct. 12, 1957; children: Cornelia, Verena, Achim. Staatsexamen, Dr.phil, U. Heidelberg, 1953; Habilitation, Ruhr-U., Bochum, 1980. Studienassessor secondary sch., Wertheim, Fed. Republic of Germany, 1955-60, researcher, 1960-64; studienrat Secondary Sch., Mannheim, 1964-65; akad. rat/oserrat Ruhr-U., Bochum, 1965-71, studienprof., 1971-81, Univ. prof., from 1981; jr. fellow Ctr. for Hellenic Studies, Washington, 1968-69. Author: Geschichte d. Thukydides-Textes im Mittelalter, 1965; contbr. articles to profl. jours. Mem. Mommsen-Gesellschaft, Deutsche Altphil. Verband. Roman Catholic. Home: Bochum, Germany. Died Aug. 13, 2002.

**KLETZ, TREVOR ASHER,** chemical engineer, educator, writer; b. Darlington, Durham, UK, Oct. 23, 1922; s. William and Frances (Amshewitz) Kletz; m. Denise Valerie Winroope, Oct. 28, 1958 (dec. 1980); children: Anthony Michael, Nigel Howard. BSc in Chemistry, Liverpool U., 1944; DSc in Chem. Engring., Loughborough U., 1986, D (hon.) in Tech., 2006. Chartered chemist, chartered engr. Rsch. chemist Imperial Chem. Industries, Billingham, England, 1946—51, various prodn. positions, 1952—67, safety advisor Wilton, England, 1968—82; adj. prof. Loughborough U., 1978—82, rsch. fellow, 1982—86, sr. vis. rsch. fellow, 1986—2000, adj. prof., 2000—13; cons. process safety Cheadle, England, 1986—2002. Adj. prof. Tex. A&M U., 2003—13. Author: Critical Aspects of Safety and Loss Prevention, 1990, An Engineer's View of Human Error, 3d edit., 2001, Hazop and Hazan - Identifying and Assessing Chemical Industry Hazards, 4th edit., 1999, Lessons from Disaster - How Organizations have no Memory and Accidents Recur, 1993, What Went Wrong? - Case Histories of Process Plant Disasters, 4th edit., 1998, Learning from Accidents, 3d edit., 2001, Computer Control and Human Error (with others), 1995, Dispelling Chemical Engineering Myths, 3d edit., 1996, Process Plants: A Handbook for Inherently Safer Design, 2d edit., 1998, By Accident, 2000, Still Going Wrong--Case Histories of Process Plant Disasters, 2003; contbr. numerous articles to profl. jours. Decorated officer Order Brit. Empire; recipient Award for Personal Achievement in Chem. Engring., Chem. Engring. mag., 1990, Lifetime Achievement award Instn. Occupl. Safety & Health, 2006. Fellow AIChE (Bill Doyle award 1985), Instn. of Chem. Engineers (Coun. medal 1986, Ned Franklin medal 1993, Brennan medal 1995, 2001), Royal Acad. Engring., Royal Soc. Chemistry. Jewish. Avocations: reading, walking, railways. Home: Cheadle, England. Died Oct. 31, 2013.

**KLIMA, JIRI,** electrical engineer, educator; b. Prague, Czech Republic, June 6, 1944; s. Jiri Klima and Marie Klimova; m. Vera Nesvadbova, June 1994; children: Jolana Morley, Karolina Bartosova, Eva Klimova, Jiri. MSEE, Tech. U., Prague, 1968. Prof. Dept. Elec. Engring. Czech U. Agr. in Prague, 1970—2003, dean tech. faculty, from 2003; design engr. Chemoprojekt, Prague, 2000—06. Cons. Consult Prague, from 1990. Author over 200 tech. papers. Recipient Czech outstanding award, Grant Agy. of Czech Republic, 2004; grantee Excellent Work award, 2003. Achievements include research in new mathematical models. Home: Prague, Czech Republic. Died Dec. 19, 2008.

**KLING, WILLIAM,** economist, consultant, retired diplomat; b. NYC, May 8, 1915; s. Irving and Sophie (Kling) K.; m. Suzanne Kaufman (M.D.), June 28, 1940; children: Robert Irving, Michael Paul, Virginia Airini Susan. BS, CCNY, 1937; MS, Mass. State Coll., 1938; PhD, Clark U., 1943. Grad. asst. Mass. State Coll., 1937-38, Clark U., 1938-39; instr. CCNY, 1939-40; agrl. economist Dept. Agr., also War Food Adminstrn., 1940-45; agrl. attache Bucharest, Rumania, Budapest, Hungary, Belgrade, Yugoslavia, Sofia, Bu, Albania, 1945-47; first sec., consul Am. embassy, London, 1948-54, 1st sec., consul Wellington, New Zealand, 1954-60; assigned Dept. of State, Washington, 1960-68, chief div. of functional intelligence, 1961-63, dep. dir. and acting dir. Office of Functional and External Research, 1962-63, econ. adviser to asst sec. for African Affairs, 1963-66, dep. dir. econ. affairs Office Inter African Affairs, 1966-68; dir. govt. affairs Uniroyal, Inc., Washington, 1968-73; Washington rep. Am. Soybean Assn., 1973-79; prin. William Kling Assos. (consultants), Falls Church, Va., from 1979; cons. Japanese Fedn. Agrl. Coop. Assns., 1979; dir. econs. and stats. div. Distilled Spirits Council U.S., Inc., Washington, 1979-86, dir. industry stats. div., 1986-97; ret. Mem. Nat. Def. Exec. Rsc., 1970; cons. Fed. Emergency Mgmt. Agy., 1970; mem. export policy task force U.S. C. of C., 1978-79, mem. multilateral trade negotiation task force and chmn. agr. subgroup, 1978-79. Editor: DISCUS UPC News, Annual Statis, Rev. Distilled Spirits Industry, Pub. Revenues from Alcohol Beverages, Tax Briefs, 1980-85, Retail Outlets for the Sale of Distilled Spirits, 1992, 97, Distilled Spirits Brand Directory, 1993, 95, 97; contbr. articles to profl. jours. Recipient Meritorious Honor award State Dept., 1968 Mem. Am. Fgn. Service Assn., Soc. Govt. Economists., Diplomatic and Consular Officers Ret. Clubs: Nat. Economists, Internat. Economists. Deceased.

**KLOCKE, JOHN D.,** lawyer; b. Buffalo, Nov. 6, 1924; s. Eugene L. and Geraldine A. (Haberer) Klocke. BBA, Canisius Coll., 1948; JD, U. Buffalo, 1951. Bar: NY 51. Mng. ptnr. Condon, Klocke, Ange, Geruase & Sedita, Buffalo, 1958—76, Klocke & Ange, Buffalo, 1976—79; pvt. practice Buffalo, from 1979. Trustee, asst. treas. Catholic Charities, Buffalo, from 1972. Served with US Army, 1943—45, PTO. Died Oct. 2, 1990.

**KNAPPENBERGER, T. GAILLARD, JR.,** lawyer; b. Chgo., June 18, 1911; s. T. G. and Grace M. (Gallion) Knappenberger; m. Jill Pitts, Jan. 3, 1953. BS, U. Ill., 1933, JD, 1936. Bar: Ill. 1936, Fla. 1957. With Travelers Ins., Peoria, Ill., 1936—39; br. office claims mgr. Akron and Columbus; spl. asst. to v.p. Kemper Ins. Group, Chgo., 1939—46; pub. adminstr. Champaign, Ill., 1953—61; pub. guardian, conservator, 1953—61. Served to 1st sgt. USAF, 1942—46, PTO. Mem.: Champaign County Bar Assn., Colony Cabana Club (Delray Beach, Fla.), Champaign Country Club, Elks. Home: Champaign, Ill. Died Aug. 17, 1988.

**KNODT, DIETMAR OTTO WILHELM,** architect; b. Marburg, West Germany, June 23, 1936; came to U.S., 1958; s. Wilhelm K.F.P. and Gertrud L. (Hofmann) K.; m. Ann Armstrong, Feb. 18, 1967; children: Michael Christian, Kirsten Ann. Student, Grinnell Coll., 1959; BArch, Ohio State U., 1963. Lic. architect Ohio, Fla., Ky., Vt., N.Y. Draftsman Ted H. Prindle & Assocs., Columbus, 1963-67; project mgr. Brubaker/Brandt, Inc., Columbus, 1967-70; prin. Knodt/Maddox, Inc., Dublin, Ohio, from 1970. Recipient Boss of Yr. award Archtl. Secs. Assn., 1979. Mem. AIA (pres. local chpt. 1994), Builders Exchange of Ohio (mem. jury, Craftsmanship award 1980), Nat. Trust of Hist. Preservation (officer 1986—), Ohio State U. Alumni Assn. (life), Columbus C. of C., Maennerchor Club, Sawmill Athletic Club. Home: Columbus, Ohio. Deceased.

**KNOTT, DOUGLAS RONALD,** dean, agricultural sciences educator, researcher; b. Fraser Mills, BC, Can., Nov. 10, 1927; s. Ronald David and Florence Emily (Keeping) K.; m. Joan Madeline Hollinshead, Sept. 2, 1950 (dec.); children: Holly Ann, Heather Lynn, Ronald Kenneth, Douglas James (dec.); m. Pat Decker, June 1, 2002 (dec.); m. Irene Sosulski, July 8, 2005. BSA, U. B.C., 1948; MS, U. Wis., 1949, PhD, 1952. Asst. prof. U. Sask., Saskatoon, 1952-56, assoc. prof., 1956-65, prof., 1965-93, head dept. crop sci., 1965-75, assoc. dean rsch. Coll. Agr., 1988-93; prof. emeritus, from 1993. Author: The Wheat Rusts—Breeding for Resistance, 1989; also numerous papers. Named to Saskatchewan Agr. Hall of Fame. Fellow Am. Soc. Agronomy, Agrl. Inst. Can.; mem. Can. Soc. Agronomy, Genetics Soc. Can., Order of Can. Mem. United Ch. of Can. Avocation: tennis. Home: Saskatoon, Canada. Deceased.

**KNOWLER, FAITH MARION,** civic worker; b. Muscatine, Iowa, Jan. 22, 1911; d. Will and Mary M. (Dankert) Stamler; m. Lloyd A. Knowler, June 30, 1935; children: Mary Louise, William Clayton. BA, U. Iowa, 1933; postgrad., Washington U., St. Louis, 1933-34; MA, U. Iowa, 1937. Caseworker Citizens Com. for Relief & Employment, St. Louis, 1934-35, U. Hosp. Social Svc. Dept., Iowa City, 1935, 61-63. Co-founder Youth Homes, Inc., Iowa City, 1972, bd. dirs., 1972—, pres. bd., 1978, mem. pers. com., 1985—; mem. Coun. for Internat. Visitors to Iowa City, 1986—; v.p. for planning United Way Johnson County, Iowa City, 1976, bd. dirs., 1976-79, 87-90. Mem. Alumni Assn. U. Iowa, AAUW (pres. 1943-44, bd. dirs. 1944-45), League Women Voters of Johnson County (pres. 1975-77), League Women Voters of Iowa (com. chmn. 1977-79), U. Iowa Alumni Assn., 19th Century Club, Univ. Club (pres. 1966-67), P.E.O. Democrat. Unitarian Universalist. Home: Iowa City, Iowa. Died Oct. 30, 2002.

**KNOWLTON, CLARK S.,** sociology educator, consultant; b. Salt Lake City, Dec. 31, 1919; s. Ezra Clark and Mary Albrea (Shumway) K.; m. Ruth Marion DeYount, Aug. 30, 1948; children: David, Daniel, Keith, Ann. BA in Sociology, Brigham Young U., 1947, MA in Sociology, 1948; PhD, Vanderbilt U., 1955, Escola Livre Sociologia, Paulo, Brazil, 1950-51. Grad. asst. Vanderbilt U., 1948-49; assoc. prof. Ga. So. Coll., 1952-58, N.Mex. Highlands U., 1958-62; prof. Tex. Western Coll., 1962-68; prof. sociology U. Utah, Salt Lake City, from 1968, dir. Ctr. for Study of Social Problems, 1968-72, dir. social rsch. and devel. div., 1972-78. Lectr. in field; program organizer Ctr. Land Grant Studies.; chmn. numerous univ. coms. and depts. Mem. editorial bd. Am. Biog. Inst.; Author: Sirios e Libanese, 1961; mem. editorial adv. bd. Southwestern Rev. Mgmt. and Econs., 1980—; contbr. numerous articles and reports to profl. jours., chpts. to books. Bd. dirs. Our Lady's Youth Ctr., 1963-68, El Paso Boys' Club, 1964-68, Project BRAVO, 1966-68, Cen. City Community Ctr., Salt Lake City, 1970-75, Granite Mental Health Assn., 1982-88, Cath. Community Svcs., 1982-88; bd. dirs. Cen. City Community Ctr., 1978-80, chmn., 1980—; vice chmn., bd. dirs. Utah Immigration Project, 1982-88; mem. evaluation panel United Way, 1986-87. Pvt. U.S. Army, 1942-46. Named Honorable Col. and Aide de Camp, State of Mex.; rsch. grantee U. Tex.-El Paso, 1962, 63, 65, Office Juvenile Delinquency and Youth Devel., Dept. Health, Edn. and Welfare, 1965-67, U. Utah Rsch. Com., 1969, 72, Russell Sage Found., 1972; recipient award Socio, 1975, Cath. Community Svcs., Salt Lake City, 1988. Mem. Am. Sociol. Soc., Rural Sociol. Soc., Univ. Archaeol. Soc., Western Social Sci. Assn., Assn. Arid Land Studies (founder), Soc. Land Grant Rsch., Assn. Borderland Scholars, Soc. for Early Hist. Archaeology (pres. 1972-74, bd. dirs. 1974—, trustee, chmn. publs. com.). Mem. Lds Ch. Avocations: writring, mexican american history research, bird and wildlife observation. Died Jan. 1991.

**KNOX-DAVIES, PETER SIDNEY,** plant pathologist, educator; b. Elandsputte, Transvaal, South Africa, Dec. 7, 1929; s. Edwin Probart and Maud Frances (Thorpe) Knox-Davies; m. Laetitia Potgieter, Dec. 20, 1972; children: John, Evan, Ula. BSc, U. Natal, 1951; MS, U. Wis., PhD, 1959. Lectr. U. Natal, 1951—59, sr. lectr., 1959, U. Stellenbosch, South Africa, 1962—70, prof., 1970, head, dept. plant pathology, from 1970. Mem., editl. com. Phtophylactica Jour., from 1976; contbr. articles to profl. jours. Fellow: South African Soc. Plant Pathology (pres. 1968—69, 1978—80); mem.: Bot. Soc. South Africa, Fedn. Brit. Plant Pathologists, Brit. Mycol. Soc., Bot. Soc. America, Internat. Protea Assn. (hon.), Am. Phytopath. Soc., South African Soc. Plant Pathology and Microbiology, Internat. Soc. Plant Pathology (coun. mem. 1968—83). Home: Stellenbosch, South Africa. Died Mar. 25, 1999.

**KOBAYASHI, MANJI,** literature educator; b. Tokyo, Mar. 29, 1931; s. Kinuji and Sakae (Takahashi) Kobayashi; m. Fumiko Uchiyama, Mar. 11, 1967; children: Hitoshi, Yukari. BA, Doshisha U., Kyoto, Japan, 1954, MA, 1957, Columbia U., 1966. Lectr. English Doshisha U., Kyoto, 1961-64, asst. prof. English lit., 1964-68; assoc. prof. faculty letters Kobe U., Japan, 1968—79, prof., 1979—94, prof. emeritus, from 1994; prof. English Baika Women's Coll., Osaka, Japan, 1994-2001. Author: (book) The Climate of Modern Poetry, 1975. Fulbright Found. grantee, 1963—65. Mem.: Yeats Soc. Japan (com. 1989—99), English Lit. Soc. Japan (bd. dirs. 1989—91). Home: Osaka, Japan. Died Feb. 3, 2007.

**KOCH, STEVEN A.,** bank executive; b. Dec. 24, 1952; BSBA, Valparaiso U., 1974. Died Jan. 12, 2008.

**KODAMA, JUNZO,** physician, researcher; b. Kobe-shi, Hyogo-ken, Japan, Aug. 10, 1927; s. Kanjiro and Fumie Kodama; m. Akiko Takagi, Oct. 14, 1956; children: Hiroko, Mineo, Takayuki. Degree, Med. Sch. Osaka, Japan, Osaka U., 1960; MD, Julius Maximilians U., Würzburg, Germany, 1963. Asst. Julius Maximilians U., 1963-67; head physician Kokuritsu-Osaka Byoin, 1967-83; head of dept. clin. lab. Nat. Ctr. Cardiovascular Disease, Suita, Japan, 1983-90; med. dir. Inst. Med. Care and Health Maintenance Sanyo Electronics Group, Moriguchi, Japan, 1990-96. Inventor in field. Recipient award Seijinbyo Kenkyu Shinko Zaidan, Osaka, 1972; grantee Ministry Edn. and Culture, Tokyo, 1973, Ministry of Welfare, Tokyo, 1975. Mem. Japanese Soc. Internal Medicine, Internat. Soc. Hematology. Buddhist. Avocations: carpentry, model railways. Home: Kobe, Japan. Died May 26, 2004.

**KOEGEL, WILLIAM FISHER,** lawyer; b. Washington, Aug. 18, 1923; s. Otto Erwin and Rae (Fisher) K.; m. Barbara Bixler, Feb. 2, 1946 (dec. 1968); children: John Bixler, Robert Bartlett; m. Ruth Swan Boynton, June 21, 1969 (dec. 1983); m. Irene Lawrence, Aug. 4, 1984. BA, Williams Coll., 1944; LL.B., U. Va., 1949. Bar: N.Y. 1950. From assoc. to ptnr. Clifford Chance US LLP (formerly Rogers & Wells), NYC, 1949—88, head litigation dept., 1977-88, sr. counsel, from 1989. Chmn. Scarsdale (N.Y.) Republican Town Com., 1965-71; pres. trustees Hitchcock Presbyn. Ch., Scarsdale, 1970-73, 78-79, 82-83. Served with AUS, 1943-45, ETO. Fellow ACTL; mem. ABA, N.Y. State Bar Assn., Bar Assn. City N.Y., Order of Coif. Clubs: Town (Scarsdale) (pres. 1976-77); Shenorock Shore, Fox Meadow Tennis, The Moorings. Home: Somers, NY. Died Feb. 2014.

**KOGAN, IAN I.,** theoretical physicist, educator; b. Glazov, Russia, Sept. 14, 1958; s. Ilya Kogan and Nadezhda Yakybova; m. Bella Ladyzhenskaya, Nov. 14, 1987; children: Pavel, Mark David. M.Sc., MFTI, Moscow, 1981; Ph.D, Inst. Theoretical and Exptl. Physics, Moscow. Reader in physics Oxford U., England, from 1988. Mem.: Inst. Physics. Avocation: acting. Deceased.

**KOHN, MISCH HARRIS,** artist, retired art educator; b. Kokomo, Ind., Mar. 26, 1916; s. Jacob and Anna (Kaplan) K.; m. Lore Lisa Traugott, May 19, 1945; children: Jessica, Tamara. BFA, John Herron Art Inst., Indpls., 1939; DFA (hon.), Ind. U., 1991. Assoc. prof. art Ill. Inst. Tech., Chgo., 1953-65, prof., 1965-72, Calif. State U., Hayward, 1972-86, prof. emeritus, from 1986. Head dept. visual design Inst. Design, Chgo., 1951; instr. U. Wis., summer 1957; mem. artists adv. com. John Simon Guggenheim Meml. Found., 1962-74; instr. exptl. printmaking U. Chgo., 1969; mem. Pennell Fund com. Libr. Congress, 1972-79. One-man shows, 1942—, including Art Inst. Chgo., 1951, 61, 70, L.A. County Mus. Art, 1957, Cin. Art Mus., 1961, John Herron Mus., 1961, Bklyn. Mus., 1981, numerous colls. and univs.; retrospective exhbn. Mary Porter Sesnon Art Gallery, U. Calif., Santa Cruz, 1985, KALA Inst. Gallery, Berkeley, Calif., 1988; represented in permanent collections Mus. Modern Art, Bklyn. Mus., Met. Mus. Art, Nat. Gallery, Libr. Congress, Smithsonian Instn., Art Inst. Chgo., Bibliotheque Nat., among others. Recipient Alice McFadden Eyre gold medal Pa. Acad., Pennell medal, 1952, Burr Meml. gold medal Phila. Free Libr., 1960, prize Bklyn. Mus. Nat. Print Exhibit, 1968; fellow Ford Found., 1959, grantee, 1960; Guggenheim fellow, 1952, 55, Tamarind fellow, 1960; grantee Nat. Endowment for Arts, 1980. Fellow Acad. Fine Arts of Design (hon., Florence, Italy); mem. Nat. Acad. Design, Am. Graphic Arts Soc., Print Coun. Am., Phila. Print Club (Internat. Graphic Arts Soc. prize 1969). Died Feb. 12, 2002.

**KOKTVEDGAARD, MOGENS,** education educator; b. Vejle, Denmark, Nov. 18, 1933; s. Olaf and Ida (Holst) K.; m. Hanne Tolboll, June 26, 1965; children: Olaf, Kristian. Cand.jur., Univ. Copenhagen, 1957, Dr. jur., 1965; Dr.jur. (hon.), Univ. Stockholm, 1993. Lectr. Univ. Copenhagen, 1961-66, prof., 1966, dean of law sch., 1971, vice-rector, 1972-81; chmn. Danish Radio and TV Bd., from 2000. Chmn. Monopolies Commn., Denmark, 1980-89; editor: Weekly Law Report, Denmark, 1976—. Author: Immaterialretspositioner, 1965, Danish Patent Law, 1979, Intellectual Property, 2001, Danish Trademark Law, 1998, Law of Competition, 2002. Decorated knight 1st Order, Queen of Denmark; recipient Gold medal Univ. Copenhagen, 1959. Mem. Danish Copyright Soc. (chmn. 1968), Royal Acad. Fine Arts, Acad. Tech. Scis., Academia Europaea. Died June 2003.

**KOLESNICHENKO, YAROSLAV IVANOVYCH,** physicist, researcher; b. Pyatigorsk, Russia, Feb. 2, 1943; s. Ivan Vasyljovych and Maria Andriivna (Balko) K.; m. Lidia Semenivna Ponomarenko, July 24, 1968; children: Bohdan, Oleh. Student, Dnipropetrovsk State U., Ukraine, 1959—64; M of Physics and Math., Ukrainian Acad. Scis., Kiev, 1969; D of Physics and Math., I.V. Kurchatov Inst. Atomic Energy, Moscow, 1978. Engr., jr. rschr. Inst. Physics Ukrainian Acad. Scis., Kiev, 1965-70, sci. rschr. Inst. Nuc. Rsch., 1970-82, head divsn. fusion theory, from 1982; prof., 1989. Mem. editl. bd. Nuc. Fusion-IAEA, 1976-84, 2006—. Grantee Internat. Sci. Found., 1994-95, CRDF-Ukrainian Govt., 1997-99, 2000-04, 06-07. Mem. Ukrainian Phys. Soc. (co-head Inst. br. 1991-96). Home: Kiev, Ukraine. Died Mar. 7, 2008.

**KOLKO, GABRIEL,** historian, educator; b. Paterson, NJ, Aug. 17, 1932; s. Philip and Lillian Kolko; m. Joyce Manning, June 11, 1955 (dec. 2012) BA, Kent State U., 1954; MS, U. Wis., 1955; PhD, Harvard U., 1962. Assoc. prof. U. Pa., 1964-68; prof. history SUNY-Buffalo, 1968-70, York U., Toronto, Ont., Canada, 1970-92, Disting. research prof., 1986-92, prof. emeritus, 1992—2014. Author: Wealth and Power in America: An Analysis of Social Class and Income Distribution, 1962, The Triumph of Conservatism: A Reinterpretation of American History, 1900-1916, 1963, Railroads and Regulations, 1877-1916, 1965, The Politics of War: The World and United States Foreign Policy, 1943-45, 1968, The Roots of American Foreign Policy: An Analysis of Power and Purpose, 1969, The Limits of Power: The World and United States Foreign Policy, 1945-1954, 1972, Main Currents in Modern American History, 1976, Anatomy of a War: Vietnam, the United States, and the Modern Historical Experience, 1985, Confronting the Third World: United States Foreign Policy, 1945-1980, 1988, Century of War: Politics, Conflicts and Society Since 1914, 1994, Vietnam, Anatomy of a Peace, 1997, Another Century of War?, 2002, The Age of War: The United States Confronts the World, 2006, After Socialism: Reconstructing Critical Social Thought, 2006, World in Crisis: The End of the American Century, 2009. Fellow Social Sci. Research Council, 1963-64; Guggenheim fellow, 1966-67; fellow American Council Learned Societies, 1971-72; Killam fellow, 1974-75, 82-84 Fellow Royal Soc. Can. Home: Amsterdam, Netherlands. Died May 19, 2014.

**KOLLEK, TEDDY (THEODOR HERZL KOLLEK),** former mayor; b. near Vienna, Hungary, May 27, 1911; s. Alfred and Margaret (Fleischer) K.; m. Tamar Anna Schwartz, 1937; children: Amos, Osnat. Tchr. He-Halutz, 1931-35, rep., 1938-40; various positions Ein Gev, Haifa, Palestine, 1935-38; with polit. dept. Jewish Agy., Eng., 1940-50; head U.S. divsn. Israeli Fgn. Ministry, 1950-51, min. plenipotentiary to U.S. Washington, 1951-52; dir. gen. Office of Prime Min., Jerusalem, 1952-65; mayor City of Jerusalem, 1965-93. Author: (with M. Pearlman) Jerusalem: A History of Forty Centuries, 1968, Pilgrims of the Holy Land, 1970, (with Amos Kollek) For Jerusalem: A Life, 1978. Chmn. bd. Israel Mus., 1964-2007; founder Jerusalem, Found., 1966. Recipient Peace prize Assn. German Pubs., 1985. Home: Jerusalem, Israel. Died Jan. 2, 2007.

**KOMAREK, VALTR,** former Czechoslovakian government official, economist; b. Hodonin, Aug. 30, 1930; 1 child, Martin. 1st dep. premier Govt. of Czechoslovakia, Prague, 1989—90. Honorary chmn. Czech Social Democratic Party, 2011—13. Czech Social Democratic Party. Died May 16, 2013.

**KONDOYANNIS, PANOS N(IKOLAS),** medical educator, orthopedic surgeon; s. Nikolas and Helen Kondoyannis; married; 1 child. DSc, U. Athens, 1969. Cert. of specialty in orthopaedic surgery, laser surgery, athletic injuries. Sr. house officer Princess Margaret Rose Hosp., Edinburgh, Scotland, 1968-69; staff U.S. Army Gen. Hosp., Frankfurt, Germany, 1969-70; dir. Gen. Mil. Hosp., Athens, 1971-87; commd. capt. Hellenic Army Med. Corps, 1969, advanced through grades to major gen., 1987; assoc. Med. Ctr. of Athens, from 1984; dir. The Nimits Gen. Hosp., Athens, from 1990; assoc. prof. orthop. and laser surgery Teufen Fr. U., Switzerland, from 1992. Vis. prof. Harvard Med. Sch./Mass. Gen. Hosp., Boston, 1983; cons. Laser Ctr. of Athens, 1989—. Co-author: Lasers in Medicine, 1994; contbr. articles to profl. jours. Cons. Nat. Ctr. for Emergencies, Athens, 1986-88. Fellow ACS, Brit. Orthopaedic Assn., Hellenic Instl. Osteoporosis; mem. Hellenic Orthopaedic Assn. (v.p. 1988-89, pres. 1990), Hellas-Israel League of Friendship, NY Acad. Scis., Laser Med. Assn. (v.p. 1994—, pres. 1996—), Swedish Orthopedic Assn. (hon. mem.), Soc. Med. Innovation and Tech. Achievements include first to laser medicine and surgery. Died Dec. 2008.

**KOPIT, JONATHAN THRONE,** lawyer; b. NYC, May 23, 1946; s. Alexander and Charlotte Louise (Throne) K.; m. Ina Cheryl Cohen, June 28, 1978. AB, Columbia Coll., 1968; JD, Columbia U., 1972. Bar: N.Y. 1972, Mich. 1974, U.S. Supreme Ct. 1981. Research atty. Mich. Ct. Appeals, Lansing, 1972-76; from assoc. to ptnr. Plunkett & Cooney, PC, Detroit, from 1976. Contbr. articles to profl. jours. Mem. Nat. and Mich. Chpt. Multiple Sclerosis Soc., 1974. Harlan Fiske Stone scholar Columbia U. Sch. Law, 1972. Mem. ABA (tort ins. and litigation sects., appellate com. 1984—), Mich. Bar Assn. (workers compensation sect.), Assn. Trial Lawyers Am., Mich. Trial Lawyers Assn., Columbia Law Alumni Assn. Avocations: swimming, reading history and finance. Home: Huntington Wd, Mich. Died Sept. 18, 1993.

**KOPLIK, PERRY H.,** durable goods company executive; Exec. v.p. Castle & Overton Inc., NYC, 1932-1960; prin. Perry H. Koplik & Sons Inc., NYC, from 1960, chmn. Died Sept. 2001.

**KORFMANN, MANFRED OSMAN,** archeologist, educator; b. Cologne, Germany, Apr. 26, 1942; married; 2 children. PhD, U. Frankfurt, Germany, 1970. Rschr. U. Frankfurt, 1971-72, privat-dozent, 1980-82; prof. prehistoric, protohistoric archeology, Tübingen U., 1982—2005; referent prehistoric, near ea. archeology German Archeological Inst., Istanbul, Turkey, 1972-77, Berlin, 1977-82. Dir. archeologic excavations, Troy, Turkey, 1988-2005. Author: Sling and Bow in Southwestern Asia, 1972, Tilkitepe, The First Attempts Towards Prehistoric Research in Eastern Turkey, 1982; editor Studia Troica; contbr. over 120 articles to profl. jours. Recipient Max Planck Rsch. award, 1994. Mem. German Archeological Inst., Acad. Sci. Georgia, Inst. Archeologists Am. (hon.), Austrian Archeology Inst. Home: Ofterdingen, Germany. Died Aug. 11, 2005.

**KORHONEN, ERKKI AULIS,** financial services company executive, consultant; b. Helsinki, Finland, Mar. 28, 1941; s. Arvo Aulis amd Sumi Dagmar (Jarvinen) K.; m. Marja Sinikka Saramies, June 20, 1965; children: Jorma, Katri. ML, Univ. Helsinki, 1966; MCR, Imede Lausanne, Switzerland, 1987. Br. mgr. Bank of Helsinki, 1968-80; dist. court judge Dist. Ct. Ulvila, Finland, 1969-70; civil servant Supreme Adminstrv. Ct., Helsinki, 1973-77; gen. mgr. Tekseks, Helsinki, 1980-90, Foodteks, Helsinki, 1980-90, Teksinvest, Helsinki, 1986-90, Citic NV, Holland, 1990-92; v.p. Puolimatka Internat., Finland, 1991-92; gen. mgr. Melanopa Oy, Helsinki, from 1989. Supervisory bd. dirs. Sponsor, Finland, 1989-91; bd. dirs. Fidelity, Finland, 1989-91. Ensign Finnish Navy, 1960-61. Avocation: sailing. Home: Espoo, Finland. Died Jan. 1, 2002.

**KORNHUBER, HANS HELMUT,** neurologist, researcher; b. Metgethen, Germany, Feb. 24, 1928; s. Arnold E. and Gertrud (Wieberneit) Kornhuber; children: Karl, Anselm, Johannes, Malte. MD, U. Heidelberg, 1955; Dr. med. (hon.), U. Brussels. Hon. prof. U. Rosario; docent neurology and neurophysiology U. Freiburg, 1963—65; rsch. fellow dept. physiology Johns Hopkins U., Balt.; prof. neurology Ulm U., Germany, from 1967; head Ctr. Head and Nerve Diseases; senator, head gen. studies program. advisor German Rsch. Coun. Author numerous books in field; contbr. articles to profl. jours. Organizer Decentralized Rehab. and Home Patient Care. Recipient Hans Berger prize, German Soc. Neurophysiology, Sci. prize, U. Ulm, Hallpike Nylen prize, Barany Soc., Kurt Schneider prize, Ger Psychiat., Lazarus medal, Cross of Merit, Fed. Republic Germany. Mem.: Barany Soc., German Zool. Soc., German Neurol. Soc., German Physiol. Soc., Humboldt Soc. (hon.), Chilean Soc. oto-neurology/Ophthalmo-neurology (hon.), German Soc. Biomed. Engring. (hon.), Belgian Soc. Neurophysiology (hon.). Home: Blaubeuren, Germany. Deceased.

**KORRY, EDWARD MALCOLM,** journalist, diplomat, consultant; b. NYC, Jan. 7, 1922; m. Patricia McCarthy, 1950; 1 son, 3 daughters. BA, Washington & Lee U., 1942; postgrad., Advanced Mgmt. Program, Harvard U. Bus. Sch., 1960. Sucessively radio news editor London Cable Desk, chief U.N. bur., chief corr. Balkans, chief corr., gen. mgr. Germany United Press, Berlin, 1942-51, chief European corr., gen. mgr. French Empire Paris, 1951-58; European editor Look Mag., Paris & London, 1958-60; asst. to pres. Cowles Publs. Co., N.Y., 1960-63; U.S. Ambassador to Ethiopia, 1963-67; U.S. Ambassador to Chile, 1967-71; pres. Assn. Am. Pubs., N.Y., 1972-73, U.N. Assns., 1973-75; cons. U.S. State Dept. and various public service orgns., N.Y., 1975-76; writer, lectr., 1976-78; vis. prof. govt. Conn. Coll., Stonington, Conn., 1979-81; vis. scholar Ctr. for Internat. Affairs, Harvard U., Cambridge, Mass., 1981-85; writer, cons., from 1985. Mem. Council on Fgn. Relations. Died Jan. 30, 2003.

**KOSOWICZ, FRANCIS JOHN,** concert organist; b. Lowell, Mass., July 20, 1946; s. Stanley Marion and Mildred Helen (Lavigne) K.; m. Augusta Benning Blundon, Sept. 15, 1985. Student, Harvard U., 1960-64, Manhattanville Coll., 1963-66, Iona Coll., 1964-66, U. Mass., 1971-73, U. Salamanca, Spain, 1983; MusM, Lancashire Sch. of Music, Blackpool, Eng., 1988; studies with numerous master tchrs. including Charles A. MacGrail, Edgar Hilliar, E. Power Biggs, William Harms, Richard Casper, Walter Ehret, Montserrat Torrent, Guy Bovet. Dir. music St. Catherine's Ch., Graniteville, Mass., Chapel of Peace, Kings Point, Bermuda, Holy Trinity Chapel, Gia Le, Socialist Republic of Vietnam; artist-in-residence St. Joseph's Abbey, Spencer, Mass., Holy Ghost Monastery, Conyers, Ga., Christian A. Herter Ctr., Boston. Cons. U.S. Dept. Def., Washington, 1970, Cabin Creek (W.Va.) Quilts. Author, editor: Book of Worship for United States Forces, 1974; contbr. articles to profl. jours.; solo organist La Sonora Tecolutla, Veracruz, Mex., 1975-76, Cathedral of Most Holy Trinity, Hamilton, Bermuda, Cathedral of Redemption, Hue, Socialist Republic of Vietnam, Cathedrale Met., Guadalajara, Mex., Catedrale Nueva, Salamanca, Cathedral, Ciudad Rodrigo, Spain, other recitals in U.S., Can., Mex., Europe, Australia, Oceania; composer: Wedding for Organ, 1967, Imperial Suit, 1975, Carillon Snow Piece, 1975; performer All-Bach Organ Concert commemorating Bach's 303d Birthday, Christ Ch. Cathedral, Nassau, The Bahamas, Mar. 21, 1988. Advisor to Pres. of U.S., Washington, 1968; founder Roane Arts and Humanities Council, Inc., Spencer, W.Va., 1977, The Jehan Alain Found., Romainmotier and Geneva, Switzerland; co-founder, treas. The Roane County Humane Authority/Soc., 1990-93. With USN, 1966-72, Vietnam. Decorated 3 Bronze Stars; recipient Gold Medal Ministry of Culture, People's Republic of China, 1993. Mem. Am. Musicological Soc., Organ Hist. Soc., Consociatio Internationalis Musicae Sacrae, Universa Laus, Am. Guild Organists (state chmn. W.Va. 1980-85), Royal Coll. Organists, Royal Can. Coll. Organists, Southeastern Hist. Keyboard Soc. (life). Home: Charleston, W.Va. Died 2001.

**KOSTRZEWSKI, JAN KAROL,** epidemiologist, researcher; b. Cracow, Poland, Dec. 2, 1915; s. Jan Michal and Maria (Sulikowska) Kostrzewski; m. Ewa Maria Sobolewska, Sept. 3, 1948; children: Anna, Magdalena, Piotr, Maria. Diploma, Warsaw U., 1945; MD, Jagiellonian U. Med. Faculty, Cracow, 1948; MPH, Harvard, 1958; MD (hon.), Mil. Med. Acad., Poland, 1979; MD, Med. Acad., Lublin, Poland, 1985. Diplomate. Asst., vaccine prodn. Nat. Inst. Hygiene, Warsaw, 1942—51, head, dept. epidemiology, 1951—61; prof., epidemiology Warsaw Med. Acad., 1954—58; mem., panel experts WHO, Geneva, from 1960, vice chmn., internat. commn. global eradication smallpox, 1978—79, chmn., expanded programme immunization, global adv. group, 1978—85; vice-minister, chief sanitary insp. Ministry Health, Warsaw, 1962—67, min., health, social welfare, 1968—72; v.p. World Health Assembly, Boston, 1969—70, mem. exec. bd. Geneva, 1973—76, chmn., 1975—76; chmn., internat. comm. eradication smallpox India, Nepal, Bhutan, 1977, Ethiopia, 1979; v.p. Polish Acad. Scis., 1980—83, sec., med. sect., 1972—79, pres., 1984—89; chmn., rsch. strengthening group Spl. Programme Rsch. and Tng. Tropical Diseases, 1982—86; chmn., tech. adv. group Diarrhoeal Disease Control Programme, 1985—88; heath clk. lectr. London Sch. Hygiene and Tropical Med., 1986—87. Author: Health of Polish People Morbidity and Mortality, 1977; editor: Communicable Diseases and Their Control on Polish Territories in the 20th Century; co-author, 2001, Epidemiology: A Guide to Teaching Methods; co-editor, 1973; chief editor Jour. Epidemiological Rev., 1953—88, Polish Sci., 1986—89; contbr. scientific papers. Mem., vice chmn. Patriotic Movement Nat. Rebirth, Warsaw, 1983—89; with MP, 1985—89. Lt. Polish Resistance Army, 1944—45 Polish Army, 1948—49. Fellow: Indian Nat. Sci. Acad.; mem.: Internat. Ctr. Diarrhoeal Diseases Rsch. (trustee Bangladesh 1979—85, chmn. 1983—84), Internat. Epidemiol. Assn. (coun. mem. 1977—84, pres. 1977—81), Acad. Nat. Medecine Paris (corr.), Assn. Microbiologists Epidemiologists Russia (hon.), Societas Medica Polonorum (hon.), Polish Epidemiol. Assn. (hon.), Acad. Med. Scis. (Russia), Polish Epidemiol. Assn. (mem. exec. com. 1957—88, pres. 1988—91). Roman Catholic. Avocations: sports, photography. Home: Warsaw, Poland. Died May 27, 2005.

**KOTHARI, HEMRAJ,** mechanical engineer, management consultant; b. Sujangarh, Rajasthan, India, Nov. 10, 1933; s. Khoobchand and Gulab (Singhee) Kothari. BSc, Calcutta U., 1953; DWP, Woolwich (Eng.) Poly., 1959; advance cert. in planning and estimating, City & Guilds, London, 1959; PhD (hon.), World U., Ariz., 1991. Registered and chartered profl. engr., London, U.S., India, Europe; cert. mgmt. cons. Prin. Kothari Cons., Calcutta, from 1961, Kothari Orgn., Calcutta, from 1961. Owner, editor Kothari Pubs., Calcutta, from 1961; dir., editor India Internat. News Svc., Calcutta, from 1961; founder, organizer 1st All India Engr.'s Conf., 1st and 2d All India Dirs. Conf., 1st All India Specialized Pubs. Conf. and Exhbn.; Indian del. to various internat. confs. Editor, dir.: The Dir., Profl. Engr., Compact Weekly, What's On in Calcutta, Films and Femme, Sci. and Engring., other jours. and mags., founder, editor: Who's Who Indian series, other reference works; contbr. articles to profl. jours. Apptd. assessor municipalities Gov. of West Bengal. Fellow: Inst. Dirs., Royal Soc. Health, Royal Soc. Arts, Commerce and Mfg., Inst. Mech. Engrs. (life), Indian Coun. Arbitration (life; past mem. governing coun.), Inst. Valuers (life), Assn. Engrs. (life), Instn. Stds. Engrs. (life), Royal Asiatic Soc. London (life), Brit. Interplanetary Soc. (life), Inst. Commerce (life), Inst. Engrs. (life), Geol., Mining and Metallurgical Soc. (life), Inst. Plant Engrs. (life); mem.: AAEI (life), ASME (life), NAS (life), IASLIC (life), Am. Arbitration Assn. (panelist), Assn. Indian Engrs. UK (founder), Asian Media Info. and Communication Centre (Singapore), Nat. Geographic Soc. U.S.A., Assn. Food Scientists and Technologists (life), Bhartiya Vidhya Bhawan (life), Indian Coun. World Affairs (life), Indian Inst. Pub. Adminstrn. (life), Indian Libr. Assn. (life), Bombay Nat. History Soc. (life), Indian Nat. Trust Art and Cultural Heritage (life), Asiatic Soc. Bengal (life), Indian Soc. Tng. and Devel. (life), Indian Soc. Tech. Edn. (life), Computer Soc. India (life), NY Acad. Scis. (life), Agr.-Hort. Soc. India (life), Indian Inst. Metals (life), Geo Met. Inst. India (life), Indian Sci. Congress Assn. (life), Indian Soc. Soil Sci. (life), Computer Soc. India (life), Fedn. Karnataka Chambers Commerce and Industry (patron), Assn. Engrs. (former v.p.), Engring. Coun. U.K., Nat. Forensic Coun. (special panelist), Inst. Mgmt. Cons. India (former com. mem.), Internat. C. of C. Mem. Jain Ch. Avocations: films, reading, journalism. Deceased.

**KOUTROUVELIS, PANOS GEORGE,** radiologist; b. Feneos, Corinth, Greece, May 12, 1928; came to U.S., 1956; s. George Spiros and Dimitra (Revis) K.; m. Maria Chaconas, Sept. 25, 1960; children: Aristides, Alexander, Harris, Dimitri. MD, Med. Sch., Athens, 1956. Intern Trinity Luth. Hosp., Kansas City, 1956-57; resident St. Lukes Hosp., Kansas City, 1957-58; attending radiologist VA Hosp.,

Washington, 1961-63; chmn. dept. radiology Potomac Hosp., Woodbridge, Va., 1973-83; founder, pres. Northern Va. Radiology & Nuclear Medicine, Falls Church, 1961—2013. Editor-in-chief, founder: (mag.) Imager Med. Imaging Technique and Achievements. Recipient Achievement in Medicine award American Hellenic Ednl. Progressive Assn. Fellow American Coll. Nuclear Medicine (Disting. Nuclear Medicine award 1991); mem. American Coll. Radiology, N.Y. Acad. Sci., Radiol. Soc. North America, Soc. Nuclear Medicine, Fairfax County Med. Soc., Hellenic American Soc. for the Health Sciences (pres. 1992-93). Achievements include patent for a 3-D sterotactic device for needle guidance; development of sterotactic technique for percutaneous lumbar discectomy, technique for needle biopsies, cyst aspirations and laser procedures; a new method for localised prostate cancer with interstitial radiation therapy by transgluteal stereotaxis and CT guidance, 1994. Home: McLean, Va. Died Nov. 6, 2013.

**KOZMA, ADAM,** electrical engineer; b. Cleve., Feb. 2, 1928; s. Desire and Vera (Nagy) K.; m. Eileen Marie Somogyi, Oct. 24, 1956 (dec. Jan. 1978); children: Paul A. (dec.), Peter A.; m. Rebecca Chelius, Feb. 6, 1993. BSME, U. Mich., 1952, MS in Engring.-Instrumentation Engring., 1964; MS in Engring. Mechanics, Wayne State U., 1961; PhD in Elec. Engring., U. London, 1968; diploma of membership, Imperial Coll., 1969. Design engr. US Broach Co., Detroit, 1951-57; rsch. engr. Inst. Sci. & Tech., Willow Run Labs. U. Mich., Ann Arbor, 1958-69; gen. mgr. Electro Optics Ctr. Harris, Inc., Ann Arbor, 1969-73; sr. rsch. engr. radar div. Environ. Rsch. Inst. Mich., Ann Arbor, 1973-75, mgr. elec. and electromagnetics dept., 1975-76, mgr. tech. staff, 1976-77, v.p., dir. radar div., 1977-85, v.p., corp. devel., 1985-86; v.p., dir. def. electronics engring. div. Syracuse (N.Y.) Rsch. Corp., 1986-88; head intelligence systems dept. MITRE Corp., Bedford, Mass., 1988-89, head advanced systems dept., 1990-93; adj. prof. Coll. Engring. U. Mich., Ann Arbor, 1993—2002, vis. scholar, 2003—06. Cons. Conductron Corp., Ann Arbor, 1966, IBM, Endicott, N.Y., 1967-68, U.S. Army Missile Command, Huntsville, Ala., 1974-76, MITRE Corp., 1993-2001, Veridian-ERIM-Internat., Inc., 1998-2001; lectr. various univs.; engring. cons., 1993-2005. Co-author: Hologram Visual Displays (Motion Picture TV Engrs. honorable mention 1977); patentee in field. With US Army, 1946—47, with USAR, 1947—51, with reserve USAF, 1953—61. Fellow IEEE (life), Optical Soc. Am.; mem. Aero. and Electronics Systems Soc. of IEEE (radar sys. panel 1984-2006, emeritus, 2006- bd. govs. 91-93), Geosci. and Remote Sensing Soc. of IEEE, Am. Def. Preparedness Assn. (chmn. various coms. avionics sect. 1975-88, Ordnance medal 1984), Soc. Photo-Optical Instrumentation Engrs., Sigma Xi (50 yr. active mem.). Lutheran. Avocations: tennis, skiing, bicycling. Died Jan. 31, 2014.

**KRAEMER, DIETER MANFRED,** chemist; b. Bielsko-Biala, Poland, Nov. 17, 1936; s. Julius Kraemer and Elfriede Alma Keipper; m. Julia Elsa von Rospatt, Aug. 25, 1961 (div. July 1971); children: Christian Jakob (dec.), Henrich Julius. Diploma in chemistry, U. Mainz, 1963; DPhil, U. Frankfurt, 1967. Fellow Harvard U. and rsch. assoc. Mass. Gen. Hosp., Boston, 1968-69; cons. Harvard U., Cambridge, Mass., 1970; head biochem. rsch. & devel. Roehm Co., Darmstadt, Germany, 1970-96, ret., 1997. Vis. scientist Weizmann Inst. Sci., Rehovot, Israel, 1998—2002. Co-author numerous scientific books; contbr. articles to profl. jours. Fellow, Max Planck Inst. Muelheim, 1965—68, Harvard U. Mem. Am. Chem. Soc., Gesellschaft Lichtforschung, Initiative Roemisches Mainz. Achievements include development of an improved test for colorectal cancer; invention of various solid phase systems for covalent immobilization of biomolecules for biocatalysis, separation/purification, diagnostics and depletion therapy; elucidated the effects of ultraviolet light on the DNA of mammalian skin. Avocations: Roman literature, history, poetry, music, languages. Home: Mainz, Germany. Died Sept. 29, 2005.

**KRAKEL, DEAN,** historian; b. Ault, Colo., July 3, 1923; s. Eldon A. and Gretta (Cross) Krakel; m. Iris Lesh, June 1947 (div. 1994); children: Ira Dean, Jennie L., Jack R. BA, No. Colo. U., 1950; MA in History, U. Denver, 1952; DHL (hon.), U. Colo., 1976. Asst. curator Colo. State Hist. Soc., Denver, 1950—52; dir., archivist U. Wyo. Library, Laramie, 1952—56; dep. dir. Mus. and Fine Arts Program, US Air Force Acad., Colo., 1956—61; exec. dir. Thomas Gilcrage Inst., Tulsa, 1961—64; dir., exec. v.p. Nat. Cowboy Hall of Fame, Oklahoma City, 1964—85; dir. Anti Metric Soc., from 1976. Author: (book) South Platte Country, 1952, Saga of Tom Horn, 1952, James Boren: A Study in Discipline, 1968, Tom Ryan, 1971, End of The Trail: The Odyessey of a Statue, 1973, Adventures In Western Art, 1977, Mitch: On the Tail End of the Old West, 1981, Schwering: Painting On the Square, 1981, Dear Mr. Remington, 1991. Served USN, 1943—46. Recipient Am. Heritage award, No. Colo. U., 1978, Gari Melcher Medal Arts, NY Art Soc., 1985. Mem.: Nat. Cowboy Hall of Fame (Gold Buckle Rodeo award 1974, trustees' gold medal award 1975). Avocation: art. Home: Tucson, Ariz. Died July 2, 1998.

**KRANITZ, THEODORE MITCHELL,** lawyer; b. St. Joseph, Mo., May 27, 1922; s. Louis and Miriam (Saferstein) K.; m. Elaine Shirley Kaufman, June 11, 1944 (dec. Mar. 10, 2012); children: Hugh David, Karen Gail and Kathy Jane (twins). Student, St. Joseph Jr. Coll., 1940-41; BS in Fgn. Svc., Georgetown U., 1948, JD, 1950. Bar: Mo. 1950, U.S. Supreme Ct. 1955. Pres., sr. ptnr. Kranitz & Kranitz, PC, St. Joseph, from 1979. Author: articles in field. Pres. St. Joseph Comty. Theatre, Inc., 1958-60; bd. dirs. United Jewish Fund St. Joseph, 1957—61, pres., 1958-63; sec. Boys' Baseball St. Joseph, 1964-68; trustee Temple Adath Joseph, 1970-74, 77-80; bd. dirs. Temple B'nai Sholem, 1976—, Lyric Opera Guild Kansas City, 1980-91; founder, pres. St. Joseph Light Opera Co., Inc., 1989-90; mem. St. Joseph Postal Customers Adv. Coun., 1993-2005, chmn., 1993-95; mem., sec. St. Joseph Downtown Assn., 1995-97 Mem. Mo. Bar, St. Joseph Bar Assn. (pres. 1977-78), Am. Legion, Air Force Assn., B'nai B'rith (dist. bd. govs. 1958-61). Home: Saint Joseph, Mo. Died Sept. 26, 2013.

**KRAPP, FRANZJOSEPH,** lawyer; b. Mainz, Germany, Apr. 27, 1931; D Pub. and Canon Law, U. Mainz, Speyer, and Inssbruck, Austria, 1956, D Polit. Sci., 1965. Barrister; specialized solicitor in tax law; dep. head Mainz (Germany) Police Dept., 1959-61; adminstrv. advisor, 1961-66; pvt. practice, Mainz, 1967-71; adj. prof., from 1976. Hon. mem. U.S. Ct. Mil. Appeals, Washington, 1986—. Died Feb. 2005.

**KRASIKOV, YURII VLADIMIROVITCH,** psychologist, educator; b. Ordzonikidze, Russia, Nov. 16, 1946; s. Dick-Vladimir Vladimirovitch Krasikov and Irina Pavlovna Sokolova; m. Polina Aleksandrovna Reshetnikova, Feb. 5, 1967; 1 child, Nicholas. PhD, USSR Acad. Sci., Moscow, 1980; DSc, Moscow State U., 1991. Redactor Ir Pub. House, Ordzonikidze, 1968-70; engr. Labor Control Quality Prodn., Ordzonikidze, 1970; redactor TV Studio, Ordzonikidze, 1971-76, 83-85, corr., 1979-80; asst. North-Ossetian State U., Ordzonikidze, 1980-83, 85-86, 1988-94, rschr., 1986-88, prof., 1994-99; head, psych. chair, from 1999. Mem. APA, Internat. Coun. Psychologist (area chair for Russian Fedn.). Avocations: mountain climbing, travel. Home: Vladikavkaz, Russia. Died 2007.

**KREISBERG, STEVEN E.,** lawyer; b. NYC, Apr. 10, 1942; s. Leo and Lucille (Levy) Kreisberg; m. Betsy Fuges, Dec. 7, 1969; children: Jonathan Evan, Daniel Emerson, Juliet Eva. BA, Dickinson Coll., 1962; JD, Columbia U., 1967; diploma in criminology, Cambridge U., 1968. Bar: NY 1968, Fla. 1973, US Dist. Ct. (So. Dist.), Fla. 1980, US Ct. Appeals (4th, 5th and 11th Cirs.) 1981, US Supreme Ct. 1997. Criminal def. atty. Legal Aid Soc., NYC, 1968—70; asst. dir. NJ Office Juvenile Justice, Trenton, 1970—71; law asst. Civil Ct., NYC, 1972—76; asst. fed. pub. defender Miami, Fla., 1976—80; pvt. practice, from 1980. Adj. prof. criminal justice Fla. Internat. U., Miami, 1976. Editor: Columbia Jour. Law and Social Problems, 1967. 1st lt. US Army, 1962—64. Democrat. Jewish. Home: Miami, Fla. Deceased.

**KRIPALANI, LAKSHMI ASSUDOMAL,** educator; b. Hydersbad Sindh, Pakistan, Aug. 24, 1920; arrived in US, 1962, naturalized, 1972; d. Assudomal Shewakram and Hari Assudomal (Advani) Kripalani. Diploma, Montessori Internat., 1946; BA with honors, U. Bombay, 1962; MA, Iowa U. and Seton Hall U., 1966. Cert. supr. and prin. 1976. Founder, headmistress New India Sch., 1943—47; founder Pawai Refugee Camp Sch. Refugees, Bombay, 1947; head mistress Garrison Sch., Bombay, 1948—62; dir. Montessori Sch., Iowa City, 1962—64; founder Montessori Sch., Newark, 1964—65, Montessori Ctr. NJ, 1966, gen. dir.; internat. examiner Montessori Tchr. Tng. Ctrs., from 2005; cons. in field; mem. Expert Review Panel AMS Rsch.; main advisor Mammolina Children Home, Beijing. Columnist Montessorian. Contbr. in field; author: Montessori in Practice, 2010 (AMS Proiring award, 2010). Recipient Lifetime Achievement award, Am. Montessori Soc., 2010, Hon. Cert. Montessorian Edn. award, Montessorian World Internat., 2010. Mem.: Am. Order of Merit, Nat. Council Montessori Tchr. Trainers, Assn. Montessori Internat., Nat. Assn. North Am. Montessori Tchr. Assn., NJ Edn. Assn., Assn. Supervision and Curriculum Devel., Mensa (life). Democrat. Unitarian. Home: Montclair, NJ. Died Nov. 12, 2013.

**KRIPKE, MYER SAMUEL,** rabbi; b. Toledo, Ohio, Jan. 21, 1914; s. Jacob Michael and Nettie (Goldman) K.; m. Dorothy E. Karp, June 13, 1937; children: Saul A., Madeline F., Netta E. (dec. 2011) BA, NYU, 1933; MA, Columbia U., 1937; MHL, Jewish Theol. Sem. of America, NYC, 1937, DD (hon.), 1970. Ordained rabbi 1937. Rabbi Beth El-Sinai Congregation, Racine, Wis., 1937-39, Patchogue (N.Y.) Jewish Ctr., 1939-41, Congregation Beth El, New London, Conn., 1941-46, Beth El Synagogue, Omaha, 1946-75, rabbi emeritus, 1975—2014. Adj. assoc. prof. theology Creighton U., Omaha, Author: Insight and Interpretation, 1988; co-author: Let's Talk About Loving, 1980; religious columnist Omaha Jewish Press; contbr. articles to profl. jours. Mem. Citizen's Assembly, United Way, 1982-2014 Mem. Nebr. Rabbinical Assn. (pres. 1972-73), Rabbinical Assy., B'nai B'rith, Zionist Orgn. America, Rotary. Home: Omaha, Nebr. *The pressing question of life's meaning is relieved by giving love and service to family, friends, and mankind, and by clinging to values and causes greater than ourselves.* Died Apr. 11, 2014.

**KROEGER, ARTHUR,** retired academic administrator, retired federal official; b. Naco, Alta., Can., Sept. 7, 1932; s. Heinrich and Helena (Rempel) K.; m. Gabrielle Jane Sellers, May 7, 1966 (dec.); children: Alexandra, Kate. BA with honors, U. Alta., 1955; MA, Oxford U., Eng., 1958; LLD (hon.), U. Western Ontario, Can., 1991, U. Calgary, 1995, Carleton U., 2003, U. Alta., 2004. Fgn. service officer Can. Dept. External Affairs, 1958-71, treasury bd. secretariat, 1971-75, dep. min. Indian and No. affairs, 1975-79; dep. min. transp. Can., Ottawa, Ont., 1979-83; sec. Ministry of State for Econ. Devel., Ottawa, Ont., 1983-84; spl. adv. to clk. Privy Council; dep. min. Regional Indsl. Expansion; dep. min. Energy, Mines & Resources; dep. min. employment & immigration, 1988-92; chancellor Carleton U., Ottawa, Canada, 1993—2002. Vis. fellow Queen's U., Kingston, Ont., 1994-99; vis. prof. U. Toronto, 1993-94; chmn. Pub. Policy Forum, Ottawa, 1992-94. Program chmn. Gov. Gen.'s Study Conf., 1995; chmn. Can. Policy Rsch. Networks, 1999-2006; bd. dirs. The Parliamentary Ctr., 1993-2006; chmn. Nat. Stats. Coun., chmn., 2005-08, Nat Police Svcs. Adv. Bd., 2006; mem. Panel on Voluntary Sector Governance, 1997-99. Decorated companion Order of Can.; recipient Pub. Svc. Outstanding Achievement award, 1989, Disting. Alumnus award U. Alta.; Rhodes scholar, 1955; hon. fellow Pembroke Coll., Oxford. Mem. Can. Assn. Rhodes Scholars (exec. mem., pres. 1995-97). Clubs: Five Lakes Fishing. Home: Ottawa, Canada. Died May 9, 2008.

**KROGH, THOMAS EDVARD,** curator, geochronologist; s. Johan Edvard and Marjorie Ruth; m. Kathleen Myers, Sept. 9, 1961; children: Erik, Kari, Sara, Jason. BSc, Queen's U., 1959, MSc, 1961, DSc (hon.), 1991; PhD, MIT, 1964. Staff scientist Carnegie Instn., Washington, 1964-75; curator Royal Ont. Mus., Toronto, 1975—2001. Prof. geology U. Toronto, 1976; emeritus, 2001. Recipient Past Pres. medal Mineral. Assn. Can., 1994, J.T. Wilson medal Can. Geophys. Union, 1991. Fellow Am. Geophys. Union, Geochem. Soc., Geol. Assn. Can. (Logan medal), Norwegian Acad. Sci., Royal Soc. Can. Avocations: gardening, cooking. Home: Tottenham, Canada. Died Apr. 2008.

**KROGH, TORBEN,** journalist; b. Copenhagen, Aug. 26, 1943; s. Erik and Lilli (Hasle) K.; m. Leila Moller, Aug. 19, 1966; two children. MA, Danish Sch. Journalism, Aarhus, 1965. Editor-in-chief Information, Copenhagen, 1969-72, 84-87, Socialistish Dagblad, Copenhagen, 1974-81, Udenrigs, Copenhagen, from 1993. Cons. in field; chair Danish Sch. Journalism, 1990—, Danish Inst. Journalism Tng., 1990—; exec. bd. UNESCO, 1991-95, pres. gen. conf., 1995-97; chmn. Danish Nat. Commn. for UNESCO. Author: Viggo Horup, 1984, History of the Danish Labour Movement, 1982, Gert Petersen, 1987; author, editor: Danish Media Policy, 1996, Farewell to the Parties, 1998. Mem. Danish Fgn. Policy Assn. Home: Copenhagen, Denmark. Died June 26, 2007.

**KRUMMACHER, JOHANN-HENRICH KARL,** minister, writer; b. Heidelberg, Badenia, Germany, Dec. 27, 1946; s. Daniel Moritz Adolf and Margarete Hedwig Emma (Gabbert) K.; m. Ingrid Elisabeth Weng, July 16, 1986; children: Marcus, Florian, Benjamin, Daniel, Jakob, Lukas. Abitur gymnasium, Heidelberg, 1966; student, U. Heidelberg, U. Tübingen, 1966-72. Ordained to ministry Luth. Ch., 1972. Curate Luth. Ch., Sigmaringen, 1972-75, Luth. St. John's Ch., Kornwestheim, 1975-85; pastor, master philosophy Hegel Gymnasium, Stuttgart, 1986-92; pastor Luth. St. Georg's Ch., Zavelstein, 1992-96; exec. dir. Protestant Acad., Bad Boll, 1996—2005; mem. Parliament (Deutscher Bundestag), from 2005. Chief editor Das Plateau, Stuttgart, 1990—2005; companion Radius Pub. Co. Author numerous books and radio essays on ethics and culture. Pres. Soc. for Ch. and Art, Stuttgart, 1993; trustee Fachhochschule Calw-Univ. of Applied Scis., from 2003; mem. adminstrv. coun. German Nat. Pub. TV, from 2002; mem. admisntrv. bd. German Found. Peace Rsch., from 2005; mem. adminstrv. bd. German Nat. Libr., from 2006; mem. jury German Film Award, from 2006; mem. adminstrv. bd. Theodor-Heuss-Found., from 2006. Mem. Lions. Home: Bad Teinach, Germany. Died Feb. 25, 2008.

**KRUPP, JUDY-ARIN,** national and international consultant; b. New London, Conn., Feb. 4, 1937; d. Harold and Minnie (Watchinsky) Peck; m. Alan Frederick Krupp, June 15, 1958; children: Peter, Larry, Susan, Karen. BA, Conn. Coll., 1958; MS in Edn., Queens Coll., 1960; 6th yr. cert., U. Conn., 1979, PhD, 1980. Tchr. gen. sci. Westbury (N.Y.) Pub. Schs., 1958-60; tchr. biology Roslyn (N.Y.) Pub. Schs., 1960-61. Cons. edn. Europe, Near East, Far East, Can. and U.S., 1980—. Author: Adult Development: Implications for Staff Development, 1980, The Adult Learner, A Unique Entity, 1982, When Parents Face the Schools, 1984; contbr. over 50 articles to profl. jours. and chpts. to books. Trustee Home Care/Lutz Jr. Ms., Manchester, Conn., 1970-76; pres. Hosp. Aux., Manchester, 1976; vol. Conn. Arthritis Assn., Newington, 1980—, Ohio Arthritis Assn., Columbus, 1980. Recipient appreciation award Conn. Arthritis Assn., 1985; NSF grantee, 1959. Mem. Am. Psychol. Assn., Assn. for Supervision and Curriculum Devel., Nat. Staff Devel. Council (trustee 1987-88), Conn. Orgn. for Profl. Devel. (pres. 1984-85, Outstanding Leadership award 1984, Outstanding Ct. Staff Developer award 1989), Am. Counseling Assn. (rep. adult devel. and aging com. 1985-87), Am. Assn. for Adult and Continuing Edn. Avocations: downhill and cross-country skiing, jogging, mountain climbing, bicycling, plants. Died Nov. 5, 1994.

**KRUTTER, FORREST NATHAN,** lawyer; b. Boston, Dec. 17, 1954; s. Irving and Shirley Krutter; married Lisa Stewart-Krutter BS in Econs., MS in Civil Engring., MIT, 1976; JD cum laude, Harvard U., 1978. Bar: Nebr. 1978, U.S. Supreme Ct. 1986, NY 1991. Antitrust counsel Union Pacific R.R., Omaha, 1978-86; sr. v.p. law, sec. Berkshire Hathaway Group, Omaha, 1986—2013, pres. Pres. Friedel Jewish Acad. Co-author: Impact of Railroad Abandonments, 1976, Railroad Development in the Third World, 1978; author: Judicial Enforcement of Competition in Regulated Industries, 1979; contbr. articles Creighton Law Rev. Mem. ABA, Jewish Federation of Omaha (pres. 1999-2002), Phi Beta Kappa, Sigma Xi. Home: Greenwich, Conn. Died Sept. 26, 2013.

**KRYUCHKOV, VLADIMIR ALEKSANDROVICH,** former Russian government official; b. Volgograd, USSR, Feb. 29, 1924; Grad., Nat. Corr. Inst. Law, 1949; grad. Higher Diplomatic Sch., USSR Fgn. Ministry, 1954. Lawyer; mem. Communist Party Soviet Union, from 1944; dept. expert Cen. Com., 1959-63; sect. head, 1963-65; asst. sec. Cen. Com., asst. chmn. state security com. USSR Coun. Ministers, 1965-67; head Secretariat of State Security Com., 1967-71, 1st dep. head, acting head, head com.'s bd., 1971-78, dep. chmn. com., head its bd., 1978-88; chmn. USSR State Security Com., 1988—91. Died Nov. 23, 2007.

**KUBASOV, VALERI NIKOLAYEVICH,** retired cosmonaut; b. Vyazniki, Russia, July 1, 1935; m. Lyudmila Kubasov; children: Ekaterina, Dmitry. MS in Engring., Moscow Aviation Inst., 1958. Flight engr. Soyuz-8, 1969; crew Salyut 1, 1971; flight engr. Apollo-Soyuz Test Project, 1975; comdr. Soyuz 36, 0198; dep. dir. RKK Energia, 1993. Author various studies. Recipient Hero of the Soviet Union, 1969, 1975, Order of Lenin, 1969, 1975, 1980, Medal for Merit in Space Exploration, 2011. Died Feb. 19, 2014.

**KUCHEL, THOMAS HENRY,** former U.S. senator, lawyer; b. Anaheim, Calif., Aug. 15, 1910; s. Henry and Lutetia (Bailey) K.; m. Betty Mellenthin, June 2, 1942; 1 child, Karen C. Bianchi. AB cum laude, U. So. Calif., 1932, JD, 1935, LLB. Bar: Calif. 1935, D.C. 1968. Pvt. practice, Anaheim, 1935-46; mem. Calif. State Assembly, 1937-40, Calif. State Senate, 1940-46; controller State of Calif., 1946-53; U.S. senator, 1953-69; ptnr. Wyman, Bautzer, Rothman, Kuchel & Silbert, L.A., Washington, from 1969. Asst. Rep. leader U.S. Senate, 1959-69; mem. appropriations, interior and insular affairs coms. Del. Conf. of 9th Jud. Cir., 1973, 74, 75, 76, 77; U.S. rep. 29th session UN Gen. Assemly; bd. dirs. John F. Kennedy Ctr. for Performing Arts; bd. councilors U.So. Calif.; bd. govs. Town Hall Calif. Served to lt. USNR, 1942-45. Mem. U. So. Calif. Gen. Alumni Assn. (gov.), Am. Legion, Phi Delta Phi, Phi Kappa Psi, Phi Kappa Phi., Masons (33rd degree), Elks, Burning Tree C.C., Univ. Club (Washington), L.A. C.C. Died Nov. 21, 1994.

**KUDO, EMIKO IWASHITA,** former state official; b. Kona, Hawaii, June 5, 1923; d. Tetsuzo and Kuma (Koga) Iwashita; m. Thomas Mitsugi Kudo, Aug. 21, 1951; children: Guy J.T., Scott K., Candace F. BS, U. Hawaii, 1944; MS in Vocat. Edn., Pa. State U., 1950; postgrad., U. Hawaii, U. Oreg. Tchr. jr. & sr. h.s., Hawaii, 1945-51; instr. home econs. edn. U. Hawaii Tchrs. Coll., Honolulu, 1948-51, Pa. State U., State College, 1949-50; with Hawaii Dept. Edn., Honolulu, 1951-82, supr. sch. lunch svc., 1951-64, home econs. edn., 1964-68, adminstr. vocat.-tecy. edn., 1968-78; dep. supt. State Dept. Edn., Honolulu, 1978-82, cons. Am. Samoa vocat. edn. state plan devel., 1970-71; vocat. edn. U. Hawaii, 1986. Internat. secondary program devel. Ashiya Ednl. Sys., Japan, 1986-91; cons. to atty. gen. mental health svcs. for children and adolscents State of Hawaii, 1994; chief planner devel. State of Hawaii Children & Adolscents Mental Health Svcs. Implementation Plan, 1994-95; state coord. industry-labor-edn., 1972-76; mem. nat. task force edn. and tng. for minority bus. enterprise, 1972-73; mem. steering com. Career Info. Ctr. Project, 1973-78; co-dir. Hawaii Career Devel. Continuum project, 1971-74; mem. Nat. Accreditation and Instl. Eligibility Adv. Coun., 1974-77, cons., 1977-78; mem. panel Internat. Conf. Vocat. Guidance, 1978, 80, 82, 86, 88; state commr. edn. commn. of the states, 1982-90; mem. Hawaii edn. coun., 1982-90. Author handbooks and pamphlets in field. Dir. Dept. Parks and Recreation, City and County of Honolulu, 1982-84; bd. dirs. Honolulu Neighborhood Housing Svcs., 1991—; exec. bd. Aloha coun. Boy Scouts Am., 1978-88; bd. trustees St. Louis H.S., 1988-95; mem. Gov.'s Commn. on Sesquicentennial Observance of Pub. Edn. in Hawaii, 1990-91; mem. Commn. State Rental Housing Trust Fund, 1992-98; mem. steering com. Hawaii Long Term Care Coalition, 1992—. Japan Found. Cultural grantee, 1977; Pa. State U. Alumni fellow, 1982; named to Konawaea H.S. Hall of Fame, 1997. Mem. ASCD, NEA, Am. Assn. Retired Persons (mem. state legis. com. 1990-92), Pa. State U. Disting. Alumni, Western Assn. Schs. and Colls. (accreditation team mem. Ch. Coll. of Hawaii 1972-73), Am. Vocat. Assn., Hawaii Vocat. Assn., Hawaii Edn. Assn. (trustee 1992—), Hawaii State Ednl. Officers Assn., Am. Family Consumer Sci. Assn., Hawaii Assn. Curriculum & Devel., Am. Tech. Edn. Assn., Hawaii Recreation and Park Assn., Omicron Nu, Pi Lambda Theta, Phi Delta Kappa, Delta Kappa Gamma. Deceased.

**KUEHN, JAMES MARSHALL,** newspaper editor; b. Mobridge, SD, May 23, 1926; s. Christ A. and Selma (Brandon) K.; m. Phyllis Yvonne Larson, Apr. 3, 1950; children— Douglas James(dec.), Deborah Kay, Diana Lisa. BA, U.S.D., 1949. State editor Rapid City (S.D.) Jour., 1949-54, wire editor, 1954-58, mng. editor, 1958-66, exec. editor, 1966-73, v.p.-editor, 1973-86. Vice pres. Rapid City Library Bd., 1969-73; dir. emeritus Mt. Rushmore Nat. Meml. Soc.; dir. Mt. Rushmore Inst, 2006—. Served with C.E. AUS, 1945-46. Named to South Dakota Hall of Fame, 2010. Mem. Rapid City C. of C. (v.p. 1970-73), S.D. C. of C. (dir. 1978-81), Lambda Chi Alpha. Lodges: Kiwanis (pres. 1973-74), South Dakota Hall of Fame. Republican. Lutheran. Home: Rapid City, SD. Died June 10, 2013.

**KULIMOETOKE, TOMASI,** government official of Wallis and Futuna Islands; King of Wallis Mata-Utu on Uvea, 1959—2007; mem. Conseil du Territoire. Died May 7, 2007.

**KULLANDER, KLAS OLOF,** research scientist, educator; b. Vaksala, Sweden, Oct. 5, 1966; s. Sven Gunnar and Eva Elisabeth Kullander; m. Maria Katarina Jansson, June 21, 2003. PhD in Med. sci., Uppsala U., Sweden, 1997. Postdoctoral European Molecular Biology Lab., Heidelberg, Germany, 1998—2001; assoc. dir. AstraZeneca, Gothenburg, Sweden, 2002—03. Adj. faculty Gothenburg U., Sweden, 2003—04, assoc. prof., from 2004. Recipient Lifetime Contbn. award, UCLA Engring. Alumni Assn., 2004. Mem.: Marie Curie Fellowship Assn. (fellowship 1998—2001). Home: Uppsala, Sweden. Died June 23, 2004.

**KULLANDER, SVEN GUNNAR,** physicist, researcher; b. Karlstad, Sweden, Mar. 9, 1936; s. Carl Fredrik and Anna Maria (Svensson) K.; m. Eva Elisabeth Westrom, Dec. 23, 1961; children: Anna, Fredrik, Klas, Elisabeth. MSc, Stockholm Royal Inst. Tech., Sweden, 1961; PhD in Physics, Uppsala U., 1964, D Philosophy, 1971. Rsch. asst. Enrico Fermi Inst. Nuclear Studies, U. Chgo., 1961-63; rsch. engr. Gustaf Werner Inst. for Nuclear Chemistry, Uppsala U., 1964-65; vis. scientist machine synchrocyclotron divsn. CERN, Geneva, 1966, staff exptl. physics divsn., 1967-72; assoc. prof. high energy physics divsn. Uppsala U., 1973-78, prof. high energy physics divsn., dir., 1979—2001; dir. Gustaf Werner Inst., 1979-86. Guest prof. Max Planck Inst. Nuclear Physics, Heidelberg, 1987, Rsch. Ctr. Nuclear Physics, Osaka U., 1986-92; coord. CERN SC, Geneva, 1968-69; rsch. program adv. com. Kernforschungsanlage, Julich, Germany; bd. dirs. Swedish Space Physics Inst., Kiruna, Sweden, 1993-99, Natural Sci. Rsch. Coun., 1980-83; chmn. Math. Physics Comm., 1980-83; coun. mem. CERN, 1980-83, rsch. bd., 1982-84; head dept. radiation scis. Uppsala U., 1986-89, dean faculty math. & natural sciences, 1989-93. Author: Mikrokosmos, 1984, Tjernobyl in Perspective, 1986, Out of Sight, 1994, Varmarnasland, 2005. Sgt. Infantry, Karlstad, 1956-57. Mem. Finnish Soc. Science & Letters, The Royal Swedish Acad. Scis. (bd. dirs., v.p. 2004-06), The Royal Acad. Arts & Scis. of Uppsala, The Royal Science Soc. Uppsala, Rotary Uppsala. Avocations: tennis, gardening, travel. Home: Uppsala, Sweden. Died Jan. 28, 2014.

**KULSKI, JERZY YUREK KAZIMIERZ,** molecular biologist, researcher; b. Flensberg, Germany, Apr. 19, 1947; arrived in Australia, 1949; s. Wladyslaw Waclaw and Valerie (Mokrous) K.; m. Martijntje Marijke de Groot, Apr. 30, 1976; children: Ruslan, Jan. BSc with hons., U. Western Australia, Nedlands, Australia, 1971, PhD, 1979. Med. lab. technologist Fremantle (Australia) Hosp., 1971—77; tutor in biochemistry U. Western Australia, Nedlands, 1978—79, sr. rsch. officer microbiology, 1984—90, with Ctr. Immunology and Instrumentation, 1998—2000, with Ctr. Forensic Sci., from 2007; postdoctoral fellow U. Calif., Berkeley, 1980—81, NIH, Bethesda, Md., 1981—83; med. scientist in charge Royal Perth (Australia) Hosp., 1991—98; with divsn. molecular life sci. Tokai U. Sch. Medicine, Bohseidai, Isehara, Japan, Ctr. for Bio-informatics and Biol. Computing, Murdoch (Australia) U., 2000—07. Cons. Geno Dive Pharma, Inc., Tokyo, 2002—. Contbr. over 140 sci. articles to profl. jours. chpts. to books, 1974—. Recipient Commonwealth Univ. award Australian Govt., 1967, Damon Runyon-Walter Winchell award, U.S.A., 1980, award Japan Soc. for Promotion of Sci. Mem.: Am. Soc. for Microbiology. Avocations: travel, reading, photography. Home: Shenton Park, Australia. Deceased.

**KUMAR, LAL,** plastic surgeon; b. Johone Bahru, Johone, Malaysia, Jan. 31, 1940; s. Govind and Malathi (Padmanthan) K.; m. Celine Elizabeth Gonzago, Nov. 18, 1969; children: Natasha, Shaun, Dev, Dinesh. MD, U. Singapore, 1967. Cons. and chief plastic surgery Nat. Hosp., Kuala Lumpur, Malaysia, 1978-80; cons. plastic surgeon Kumar Plastic and Aesthetic Surgery, Kuala Lumpur, from 1980. Vis. cons. Tawakal Hosp., Assunta Hosp., Subank Med. Ctr., Kuala Lumpur, 1980—. Mem. Malaysian Assn. Plastic Surgeons (founder, pres. 1988), ASEAN Fedn. Plastic Surgeons (founder, pres. 1996-98), Oriental Soc. Aesthetic Plastic Surgery (founder, pres. 1991-97). Hinduism. Avocations: freemasonry, gardening, writing. Home: Petalingjaya, Malaysia. Died Apr. 18, 2006.

**KUMIN, MAXINE WINOKUR,** poet, writer; b. Phila., June 6, 1925; d. Peter and Doll (Simon) Winokur; m. Victor Montwid Kumin, June 29, 1946; children: Jane Simon, Judith Montwid, Daniel David. AB in History & Literature, Radcliffe Coll., Cambridge, Mass., 1946, MA in Comparative Literature, 1948; LHD (hon.), Centre Coll., 1976, Davis & Elkins Coll., 1977, Regis Coll., 1979, New England Coll., 1982, Claremont Grad. Sch., 1983, U. NH, 1984, Bowdoin Coll., 2002. Instr. Tufts U., Medford, Mass., 1958-61, lectr. English, 1965-68. Vis. lectr. U. Mass., Amherst, 1973, Princeton U., NJ, 1977, 1979, 1981—82; adj. prof. Columbia U., NYC, 1975; Fannie Hurst prof. lit. Brandeis U., 1975; poetry cons. Libr. of Congress, 1981—82; staff mem. Bread Loaf Writers' Conf., 1969-1971, 1973, 1975, 1977, Sewanee Writer's Conf., 1993—94; vis. prof. MIT, 1984, U. Miami, 1995, Pitzer Coll., 1996; McGee prof. writing Davidson Coll., 1997; writer in residence Fla. Internat. U., 1998—2000; master artist Atlantic Ctr. Arts, New Smyrna Beach, Fla., 1984—2002; poet laureate State of NH, 1989—94. Author: (poetry) Halfway, 1961, The Privilege, 1965, The Nightmare Factory, 1970, Up Country, 1972 (Pulitzer Prize for poetry, 1973), House, Bridge, Fountain, Gate, 1975, The Retrieval System, 1978, Our Ground Time Here Will Be Brief, New and Selected Poems, 1982, The Long Approach, 1985, Nurture, 1989, Looking for Luck, 1992 (Poets' Prize, 1994), Connecting the Dots, 1996, Selected Poems 1960-1990, 1997, The Long Marriage, 2001, Bringing Together: Uncollected Early Poems 1958-1988, 2003, Jack and Other New Poems, 2005, Still To Mow, 2007, (novels) Through Dooms of Love, 1965, The Passions of Uxport, 1968, The Abduction, 1971, The Designated Heir, 1974, Quit Monks or Die, 1999, (short stories) Why Can't We Live Together Like Civilized Human Beings?, 1982, (children's books) Follow the Fall, 1961, Spring Things, 1961, Summer Story, 1961, A Winter Friend, 1961, Mittens in May, 1962, Sebastian and the Dragon, 1964, Speedy Digs Downside Up, 1964, Faraway Farm, 1967, When Grandmother Was Young, 1969, When Great-Grandmother Was Young, 1971, The Microscope, 1984, Mites to Mastodons, 2006; co-author (with Anne Sexton): Eggs of Things, 1963, More Eggs of Things, 1964, Joey and the Birthday Present, 1974, The Wizard's Tears, 1975; author (essays): To Make a Prairie: Essays on Poets, Poetry and Country Living, 1980, In Deep: Country Essays, 1987, Women, Animals, and Vegetables: Essays and Stories, 1994, Inside the Halo and the Journey Beyond, 1999, Always Beginning: Essays on a Life in Poetry, 2000; contbr. poems to mags. Recipient Lowell Mason Palmer award, 1960, William Marion Reedy award, 1968, Eunice Tietjens Meml. Prize for poetry, 1972, Borestone Mountain award, 1976, Alumnae Recognition award, Radcliffe Coll., 1978, Excellence in Lit. award, American Acad. & Inst. Arts & Letters, 1980, Levinson award, 1987, Aiken Taylor prize, 1995, Centennial award, Harvard Grad. Sch. Arts & Sciences, 1996, Lifetime Achievement award, NH Writers Project, 1998, Ruth Lilly Poetry prize, 1999, Charity Randall award, 2000, Robert Frost award, Plymouth Coll., 2001, Arts medal, Harvard U., 2005. Mem.: Writers Union, Authors Guild, PEN America, Poetry Soc. America, Acad. American Poets (chancellor, fellow 1986-2002). Died Feb. 6, 2014.

**KUNG, LING-YANG,** electronics engineer, educator; b. Kaoyaw, Canton, Peoples Republic of China, Oct. 31, 1944; s. Cheung-Kote and May-Siu (Lee) K. PhD/Electronic Engring., summa cum laude, Poly. di Torino, Italy, 1971. Researcher Istituto Nazionale Eletrotecnico Galileo Ferraris, Turin, Italy, 1970-71; assoc. prof. Nat. Cheng Kung U., Tainan, Taiwan, 1972-79, prof., 1981-90, prof. elect. engring. dept., from 1990; computer system analyst DB Data Processing, New Rochelle, N.Y., 1979-80. Vis. expert Nat. Sci. Coun., Taipei, 1981—; founder dir. Inst. Info. Engring., Tainan, 1987—; cons. Teco Electric, Taipei, 1977-78, Digital Equipment Corp., Taoyuan, Taiwan, 1988-92, China Steel Cooperation, Kaoshiung, Taiwan, 1989-90. Patentee in field; contbr. articles to profl. jours. Grantee Nat. Sci. Coun., 1981—; named one of top ten talent in info. technology of Taiwan, 1990. Mem. IEEE, Assn. for Computing Machinery, Digital Equipment Cooperation User Group, Don Bosco Alumni Club (advisor 1985—). Avocations: hiking, biking. Home: Tainan, Taiwan. Died Sept. 1, 1998.

**KUNHARDT, ERICH ENRIQUE,** physicist, researcher; b. Montecristy, Dominican Republic, May 31, 1949; came to U.S., 1961; s. Juan Enrique and Irma Mercedes (Grullon) K.; m. Christine Ann Koza, Oct. 23, 1976. BS, NYU, 1969; PhD, Poly. U., Bklyn., 1976. Asst. prof. Tex. Tech U., Lubbock, 1976-80, assoc. prof., 1980-83, prof., 1983-85, Poly. U., 1985-91; George Mead Bond prof. physics Stevens Inst. Tech., Hoboken, 1991—2006, Inst. prof., 1999—2006, dean Sch. Sci. & Humanities, 2000—06, dean Sch. Sci. and Liberal Arts, 2001—06; provost NY Polytechnic U., 2006—09. Dir. Weber Rsch. Inst., Poly, U., 1986-91. Editor: Breakdown and Discharges in Gases, 1983, The Liquid State and its Electrical Properties, 1985; mem. advisory bd. Jour. Transport Theory and Statis. Physics; contbr. articles to profl. jours. Recipient Citation for Excellence in Rsch. Nassau County, 1988. Mem. IEEE, American Phys. Soc. Achievements include observation of plasma wavepacket bifurcation; research on kinetic behavior of a streamer, and on method for closure of fluid equations; patents for atmospheric pressure plasma sources. Died Aug. 5, 2014.

**KUPERMAN, MICHAEL ARON,** language educator, writer; b. Chgo., June 22, 1971; s. Bonnie and Mike Walker (Stepfather); m. Mandy Chien Kuperman, July 21, 2002. BA, U. Fla., 1993. Lectr. Kao Yuan Inst. Tech., Lu Chu, Kaoshiung, Taiwan, from 1987. Contbr. articles to profl. jours.;, author poems. Deceased.

**KUPISZ, KAZIMIERZ ANTONI,** literature educator; b. Dabie, Poland, Mar. 2, 1921; s. Antoni and Stefania (Kalinska) K. MA in Polish Philology, U. Łódź, Poland, 1948, MA in French, 1950, PhD, 1962. Vice dir., tchr. secondary sch., Łódź, Poland, 1947-60; asst. Roman philology dept. U. Łódź, 1956-62, tutor, 1963-68, asst. prof., 1969-83, prof., from 1983, vice dean philology, 1969-91, head Roman philology chair, 1969-91. Author: Studies of XVI Century Feminist Literature in France, 3 vols., 1980-95; contbr. articles to profl. jours. Recipient Gold Cross Merit, Poland, 1970, Bachelor's Cross Poland's Revival, 1985, Honor prize, Acad. Fine Lit. and Arts of Lyon, France, 1994. Fellow Łódź Scientific Soc.; mem. Soc. Montaigne Friends, Soc. Francaise Seiziemistes. Roman Catholic. Home: Lodz, Poland. Died May 20, 2003.

**KUROKAWA, KISHO,** architect; b. Aichi Prefecture, Japan, Apr. 8, 1934; s. Miki and Ineko K.; m. Akayo Wakao; 2 children. B.Arch., Kyoto U., Japan, 1957; M.Arch., Tokyo U., 1964. Pres. Kisho Kurokawa Architect & Assocs.; chmn. Urban Design Cons., Inc.; prin. Inst. Social Engring., Inc.; analyst Japan Broadcasting Corp., 1974—2007. Hon. prof. U. Buenos Aires, 1985-2007, S.E. U., China, 1999-2007; vis. prof. Tsinghua U., Beijing, 1986-2007; advisor Internat. Design Conf., Aspen, Colo., 1974-2007; chmn. Japan Com. on Bicentennial of French Revolution, 1988-2007; commr. World Architecture Triennale, Nara, Japan, 1991-2007; advisor Mcpl. Govt. Shenzhen, China, 1999-2007, Prime Min., Rep. of Kazakhstan, 2000-2007, Mcpl. Govt. Guangzhou, China, 2000-07. Author: Prefabricated House, Metabolism, 1960, Urbab Design, 1965, Action Architecture, 1967, Homo-Movens, 1969, Architectural Creation, 1969, The Work of Kisho Kurokawa, 1970, Creating Contemporary Architecture, 1971, Conception of Metabolism, In the Realm of the Future, 1972, The Archipelago of Information: The Future Japan, 1972, Introduction to Urbanism, 1973, Metabolism in Architecture, 1977, A Culture of Grays, 1977, Concept of Space, 1977, Concept of Cities, 1977, Architecture et Design, 1982, Towards Japanese Space, 1982, Thesis on Architecture, 1982, A Cross Section of Japan, 1983, Architecture of the Street, 1983, Under the Road: Landscape under Roads, 1984, Drawing Collection of World Architecture, 1984, Kisho Kurokawa: Il Futuro Nella Tradizione, 1984, Prospective Dialogues for the 21st Century, 1985, Philosophy of Symbiosis, 1987, New Tokyo Plan, 2025, 1987, Kisho KUROKAWA Architecture of Symbiosis, 1988, Rediscovering Japanese Space, 1989, Era of Nomad, 1989, Thesis on Architecture II, 1990, Hanasuki, 1991, Intercultural Architecture-The Philosophy of Symbiosis, 1991, Kisho Kurosawa-From Metabolism to Symbiosis, 1992, Poem of Architecture, 1992, New Wave Japanese Architecture, 1993; exhbns. include Heinz Gallery, Royal

Inst. British Architects, 1981, Inst. Français d'Architecture, 1982, Construma by Ministry of Bldg. and Urban Devel., Budapest, Hungary, 1984, Central House for Architects, Moscow, 1984, Mus. Finnish Architecture, Helsinki, 1985, Buenos Aires Biennale of Architecture, 1985, Mus. Architecture in Wroclaw and Warsaw, 1986, Calif. Mus. Sci. and Industry, 1987, U. Calif., Columbia, 1992, Sackler Galleries Royal Acad. Arts, 1993. Dir. Rsch. Forum on Liberal Soc., 1977-2007; rep. Japan Forum of Design and Culture, 1990-2007; gen. prodr. World Architecture Exposition, Nara, 1988, 90-2007; adv. Japanese Nat. Railways, 1970-81; mem. Japan Found. Steering Com., Ministry Fgn. Affairs, 1972-80, Ctrl. Coun. Edn. Ministry Edn., 1977-81, Adv. Com. to the Prime Min., Policy-making Study Group for Concept of Garden City State, 1978-80, Security, 1979-80, Culture, 1979-80; commentator Japan Broadcasting Corp., 1974-91; v.p. Japan Fedn. Profl. Archtitects Assn., 1978-80; mem. Japanese-Chinese Friendship for the 21st Century Com., 1985; chmn. Japan Com. Bicentennial of French Revolution, 1988-89. Decorated Comdr., Order of Lion, Finland, Chevalier de l'Ordre des Arts et des Letteres, Ministry of Culture, France, 1989; recipient Takamura Kotaro Design award, 1965, Hiroba prize, 1977, Japan S.D.A. award silver prize Sony Tower, 1977, Chubu Archtl. award Ishikawa Cultural Ctr., 1978, Store Front Competition Silver prize for head Offices Chubu Gas Group, 1978; hon. citizenship, Sofia, Bulgaria, 1979, B.C.S. award Nat. Ethnological Mus., 1979, Gold medal Acad. Architecture, France, Richard Neutra award State Poly. U., Calif., 1988, Grand prix with Gold medal Hiroshima Mus., Sofia Biennale, 1989, prize Japan Art Acad., 1992, Chgo. Athenaeum Mus. Internat. Architecture award, 2006 Fellow AIAA (hon., award of Excellence for book Intercultural Architecture), Royal Inst. Brit. Architects (hon.), Union Architects Bulgaria (hon.), Royal Soc. Arts U.K. (life); mem. Japan Inst. Architects, Archtl. Inst. Japan, City Planning Inst. Japan, Japan Sopc. Futurology, Japan Soc. Ethnology, Japan Soc. Landscape Design (pres. 2000-07), Union Architects Kazakhstan (hon.). Avocation: photography. Died Oct. 12, 2007.

**KURSUNCU, AHMET RASIM,** representation and business development executive; b. Konya, Turkey, May 17, 1920; s. Ahmet Tahir and Lutfiye Kursuncu; m. Fatma Zehra Oray, Oct. 5, 1946; 1 child, Cigdem Demet Dervisoglu. BS, MIT, 1943, MS, 1944. Constrn. control engr. Etibank-Catalagzi Thermal Power Plant, 1947—50, constrn. chief engr., Istanbul H.V. Transmission Line, 1951—53, various positions to gen. mgr., 1954—68; gen. mgr. Fenni Gama ic ve Isve Dis Ticaret A.S., Ankara, from 1968. Lt. Turkish Army, 1953—54. Mem.: Ankara Tennis Club, Cankaya Lions Club (charter). Home: Ankara, Turkey. Died May 18, 2008.

**KUYKENDALL, DAN HEFLIN,** Former United States Representative, Tennessee; State rep., Tenn., 1966—75; pres. Kuykendall Co.; trestee US Capital Hist. Soc. Republican. Died June 12, 2008.

**KUZYUKOV, ANATOLIY NIKOLAYEVICH,** research scientist, educator; b. Odessa, Ukraine, Jan. 6, 1937; s. Hikolay Alexandrovich Kuzyukov and Anna Parfiryevna Rachinskaya; m. Alla Nikolayevna Girko, Feb. 7, 1957; children: Olga, Andrey. Degree in metall. engring., Mining Metall. Inst., Irkutsk, Russia, 1959; Candidate Tech. Scis., NIKKHIMMASH, Moscow, 1971; D in Tech. Scis., Inst. Physics and Chemistry, Moscow, 1991. Operator Oil-Chem. Plant, Angarsk, Russia, 1959, engr., 1959-62; key engr. Sci. Rsch. Inst. of Chem. Machine Bldg., Severodonetsk, Ukraine, 1962-68, maj. sci. officer, 1968-77, mgr. lab., 1977—2004; prof. Severodonetsk Tech. Inst., Eastern Ukrainian State U., from 1992. Author: Inspection of Defence of Chemical Machinery from Corrosion, 1982, Theory and Practice of Corrosion and Protection of Metals and Equipment of Chemical and Petrochemical Industries, 2005, Intergranular Corrosion-Mechanical Destruction of Metals, 2006; contbr. over 185 articles to profl. jours.; inventor in field. Maj. lt. Ukraine armed forces. Recipient Orden Mark of Honor, 1971. Mem. All-Union Assn Corrosionists, Assn. Ukrainian Corrosionists, NY Acad. Scis. Avocations: mountain skiing, volleyball, chess, literature, collecting stamps and postcards. Home: Severodonetsk, Ukraine. Died Mar. 9, 2007.

**KWIK, KING HAN,** naval architect, researcher; b. Purworejo, Indonesia, May 30, 1935; m. Ilse Tulaar, Sept. 20, 1960; children: Harry, Anne. M of Engring., Tech. U. Aachen, Germany, 1960; D of Engring., Tech. U. Hannover, Germany, 1969. Sci. ofcl. U. Hamburg, Germany, 1960-69, lectr., 1969-2000. Expert marine traffic engring. German Ministry of Transport, Hamburg, 1983-87. Contbr. chpts. to books, articles to profl. jours. Home: Hamburg, Germany. Died 2007.

**KWOLEK, STEPHANIE LOUISE,** chemist, researcher; b. New Kensington, Pa., July 31, 1923; d. John and Nellie (Zajdel) Kwolek. BS, Carnegie-Mellon U., 1946; DSc (hon.), Worcester Poly. Inst., 1981, Clarkson U., 1997, Carnegie Mellon U., 2001. Chemist E.I. duPont de Nemours & Co., Inc., Wilmington, Del., 1946—59, rsch. chemist, 1959—67, sr. rsch. chemist, 1967—74, rsch. assoc., 1974—86. Contbr. articles to profl. jours.; prodr.:. Recipient Award for contbns. to Kevlar, American Soc. Metals, 1978, Engring./Tech. award, Soc. Plastics Engineers, 1985, Harold deWitt Smith award, ASTM, 1988, George Lubin Meml. award, SAMPE, 1991, Medal of Excellence in composite materials, U. Del., 1992, Jack Kilby award, Kilby Awards Found., 1994, American Innovation award, Patent & Trademark Office, 1995, Achievement award, Indsl. Rsch. Inst., Inc., 1996, Nat. Medal Tech., US Dept. Commerce Tech. Adminstrn., 1996, Perkin medal, Soc. Chem. Industry, 1997, Commonwealth award, Commonwealth Trust and PNC Bank, 1998, Lemelson-MIT Lifetime Achievement award, 1999, Henry E. Millson award, AATCC, 2001; named a Women in Tech. Internat., 1996; named to U. Akron Polymer Processing Hall of Fame, 1985, Dayton, Ohio Engring. and Sci. Hall of Fame, 1992, Nat. Inventors Hall of Fame, 1995, The Nat. Women's Hall of Fame, 2003. Mem.: Phi Kappa Phi, Franklin Inst. Phila. (Howard N. Potts medal 1976), Nat. Acad. Engring., American Inst. Chemists (Chem. Pioneer award 1980), American Chem. Soc. (award for creative invention 1980), Carnegie Mellon U. Alumni Assn. (Merit award 1983, Disting. Achievement award 1998), DuPont Country Club, Phi Beta Kappa, Sigma Xi. discovery of the technology that led the development of Kevlar fiber, a bulletproof material five times stronger than steel; patents in field. Died June 18, 2014.

**KYLLONEN, FRANCES THOMPSON,** retired art educator; b. Omaha, Oct. 24, 1915; d. Jacob S. and Effie Anna (Robinson) Thompson; m. Toimi E. Kyllonen, Dec. 31, 1940 (dec.); children: Roger L. (dec.), Julie F. Rose. AA, Stephens Coll., 1936; BA, U. Mo., 1941, MA, 1946, MEd, 1968. Cert. tchr. social studies and art, Mo. Secondary art instr., art coord. kindergarten-12th grades Columbia (Mo.) Pub. Schs. Recipient award for outstanding contbns. to the profession of art edn. Mo. Art Edn. Assn., 1982. Mem. Nat. Art Edn. Assn. (chair retired art educator affiliate 1991-93), Pi Lambda Theta, Delta Kappa Gamma. Deceased.

**LABARGE, MARGARET WADE,** medieval history professor, historian, writer; b. NYC, July 18, 1916; arrived in Can., 1940; d. Alfred Byers and Helena (Mein) Wade; m. Raymond C. Labarge, June 20, 1940 (dec. May 1972); children: Claire Labarge Morris, Suzanne, Charles, Paul. BA, Radcliffe Coll., 1937; LittB, Oxford U., Eng., 1939; LittD (hon.), Carleton U., Ottawa, Ont., Can., 1976; LLD (hon.), U. Waterloo, Ont., Can., 1993; HHD (hon.), Mount St Vincent U., Halifax, NS, 2003. Lectr. history U. Ottawa, Carleton U., 1950-62; adj. prof. history Carleton U., Ottawa, 1983—2005. Author: Simon de Montfort, 1962, A Baronial Household, 1965, Gascony, 1980, A Small Sound of the Trumpet, 1987, A Medieval Miscellany, 1997, others; contbr. articles to profl. jours. Bd. dirs. St. Vincent's Hosp., Ottawa, 1969-81; chmn. 1977-79; pub. rep. bd. dirs. Can. Nurses Assn., 1980-83; bd. dirs. Carleton U., 1984-93, Coun. on Aging, 1986-93 (pres., 1989-91). Recipient Alumnae Recognition award Radcliffe Coll., 1987, Founders award, Carleton U., 2001 Fellow Royal Soc. Can.; mem. Medieval Acad., Soc. of Can. Medievalists (pres. 1993-94), Order of Can., Phi Beta Kappa. Roman Catholic. Avocations: travel, reading, walking. Died Aug. 31, 2009.

**LACH, ALMA ELIZABETH,** food and cooking writer, consultant; b. Petersburg, Ill. d. John H. and Clara E. Satorius; m. Donald F. Lach; 1 child, Sandra Judith. Diplome de Cordon Bleu, Paris, 1956. Feature writer Children's Activities mag., 1954-55; creator, performer childrens cooking TV show Let's Cook, 1955; food editor Chgo. Daily Sun-Times, 1957-65; hostess weekly food program on CBS, 1962-66; pres. Alma Lach Kitchens, Inc., Chgo., from 1966; performer TV show Over Easy, PBS, 1977-78. Dir. Alma Lach Cooking Sch., Chgo.; lectr. U. Chgo. Downtown Coll., Gourmet Inst., U. Md., 1963, Modesto (Calif.) Coll., 1978, U. Chgo., 1981; resident master Shoreland Hall, U. Chgo., 1978-81; food cons. Food Bus. Mag., 1964-66, Chgo.'s New Pump Room, Lettuce Entertain You, Bitter End Resort, Brit. V.I., Midway Airlines, Flying Food Fare, Inc., Berghoff Restaurant, Hans' Bavarian Lodge, Unocal '76, Univ. Club Chgo. Author: A Child's First Cookbook, 1950, The Campbell Kids at Home, 1953, Let's Cook, 1956, Candlelight Cookbook, 1959, Cooking a la Cordon Bleu, 1970, Alma's Almanac, 1972, Hows and Whys of French Cooking, 1974, reprint, 1998; contbr. to World Book Yearbook, 1961-75, Grolier Soc. Yearbook, 1962; columnist Modern Packaging, 1967-68, Travel & Camera, 1969, Venture, 1970, Chicago mag., 1978, Bon Appetit, 1980, Tribune Syndicate, 1982; inventor: Curly-Dog Cutting Bd., 1995, Alma's Walker Tray, 1996; one woman show: 50 pixellist art pictures, 1999, Tavern Club, Chgo., 2002-2004, Ann Arbor Pub. Lib., 2008. Recipient Pillsbury award, 1958, Grocery Mfrs. Am. Trophy award, 1959, certificate of Honor, 1961, Chevalier du Tastevin, 1962, Commanderie de l'Ordre des Anysetiers du Roy, 1963, Confrerie de la Chaine des Rotisseurs, 1964, Les Dames D'Escoffier, 1982, Culinary Historians of Chgo., 1993, Lifetime Achievement award Les Dames D'Escoffier, 2007. Mem. Am. Assn. Food Editors (chmn. 1959), Ann Arbor Women Arts, Ann Arbor City Club. Home: Ann Arbor, Mich. *The art of cooking rests upon one's ability to taste, to reproduce taste, and to create taste. To achieve distinction the cook must taste everything, study cookbooks of all kinds, and experiment constantly in the kitchen. I stress in my writing and teaching the logic of food preparation, for the cook who possesses logic, knows how to create dishes rather than being content merely to duplicate the recipes of others.* Died 2013.

**LADD, DONALD MCKINLEY, JR.,** retired lawyer; b. Huntington Pk, Calif., Oct. 24, 1923; s. Donald McKinley and Rose (Roberts) Ladd; m. Eleanor June Martin, June 29, 1951; children: Donald, Richard, Cameron. BA, Denison U., 1945; JD, Stanford U., 1950. Bar: Calif. 1950, cert.: Calif. (criminal law specialist). Assoc. Anderson McPharlin & Conners Firm, LA, 1951; legal staff Union Pacific RR, LA, 1953—56; sr. dep. prosecutor Pasadena, Calif., 1956—58; with Office Dist. Atty., Santa Clara, Calif., 1958—88; asst. dist. atty., 1971—88. Served to capt. reserve USMC, 1943—46, served to capt. reserve USMC, 1951—52. Mem.: Stanford Law Alumni Assn., Calif. Dist. Attys. Assn., Bay Area Prosecutors Assn., Brit. Am. Club, English-Speaking Union Club, Marines Meml. Club, Am. Commons Club, Phi Alpha Delta, Blue Key, Omicron Delta Kappa. Home: Los Altos, Calif. Deceased.

**LAFOLLETTE, ROBERT MARION, JR.,** senator; b. Maidon, Wis., Feb. 6, 1895; s. Robert Marion and Belle (Case) LaF.; m. Rachel Wilson Young, Sept. 17, 1930; children: Joseph Oden, Bronson Cutting. LLD, U. Wis., 1938. Sec. to Sen. Robert M. LaFollette, Washington, 1923-29; elected to fill unexpired term of father as mem. U.S. Senate, 1925; re-elected to U.S. Senate, 1929-47. Author, econ. cons. Recipient Colliers Mag. award, 1946. Mem. Cosmos, Met. Clubs, Congl. C.C., Maple Bluff C.C. Home: Madison, Wis. Died Feb. 24, 1953.

**LALONDE, FRANCINE,** retired Canadian legislator; b. Ste.-Hyacinthe, Que., Aug. 24, 1940; children: Dominique, Philippe, Julien. Degree in edn. psychology, École normale Cardinal-Lé; lic. in history, U. Montreal. Instr. occupl. health and safety, history and adminstrn. U. Montreal, U. Que., Montreal, Chicoutimi, école Hautes Études Commls.; mem. Can. Parliament for Bloc Québécois for Mercier, 1993—2004; mem. Can. Parliament for Bloc Québécois for La Pointe-de-l'Ile, 2004—11. Ofcl. opposition critic on human resources and lit., v.p. standing com. on human resources devel., 1993-97; critic on industry, employment and econ. devel. Bloc Québécois, 1997-99, critic on fgn. affairs, mem. standing com. fgn. affairs and internat. trade, 1999-2014 Dir. info. and prs. CEGEP sect. CSN, 1969-83, 1st woman v.p., pres. Nat. Tchrs.' Fedn., chair coordinating com. pvt. sector fedns.; coord. Soc. Coop. Produits Électriques et Moteurs, 1984; minister responsible for status of women Govt. Que., 1985; cand. for presidency Parti Québécois, 1985, mem. nat. exec. coun., 1988, program advisor, 1991. Died Jan. 17, 2014.

**LAMBERT, ANGELA MARIA,** writer, journalist; b. Beckenham, Kent, Eng., Apr. 14, 1940; d. John Donald and Edith Paula Alice (Schroeder) Helps; m. Martin John Lambert (div. 1966); children: Carolyn Ruth, Jonathan Martin; ptnr. Stephen Vizinczey; 1 child, Marianne Jane Vizinczey-Lambert; ptnr. Antony John Price, 1986. Grad. in Philosophy, Politics and Econs., St. Hilda's Coll., Oxford, Eng., 1961. Editor Cassell & Co., London, 1961-62; rsch. asst. Labour Cabinet Min., House of Lords, London, 1964-68; journalist SUN Newspaper, London, 1969-71; reporter Ind. TV News ITN), London, 1972-76, London Weekend TV, 1976-78, Thames TV, London, 1978-89; columnist, interviewer The Independent, London, 1989-96; interviewer The Daily Mail, 1996-2000; feature writer, interviewer The Sunday Telegraph, 2000—03. Author: Unquiet Souls: 1880-1918, 1984 (Runner-up Whitbread Biog. prize 1984), 1939: The Last Season of Peace, 1989, Love Among the Single Classes, 1989, No Talking After Lights, 1991, A Rather English Marriage, 1993, The Constant Mistress, 1995, Kiss & Kin, 1997, Golden Lads and Girls, 1999, The Property of Rain, 2001, The Lost Life of Eva Braun, 2006. Mem. English P.E.N. (exec. com. 1991-95), Friends of Classics. Labour Party. Anglican. Avocations: reading, writing, travel. Home: London, England. Died Sept. 2007.

**LAMBERT, BENJAMIN JOSEPH, III,** former state legislator; b. Richmond, Va., Jan. 29, 1937; m. Carolyn Morris. Optometrist; mem. Dist. 71 Va. House of Delegates, Va., 1978—85; mem. Dist. 9 Va. State Senate, Va., 1986—2008. Named Most Outstanding Young Man for City Richmond, 1972, Optometrist of Yr., Nat. Optometric Assn., 1979, Va. Optometric Assn., 1980. Mem.: NAACP, Nat. & Va. Optometric Assn., Richmond Med. Soc., Va. Optometric Soc., Richmond Optometric Soc. (former pres.), Crusade for Voters. Democrat. Baptist. Died Mar. 2, 2014.

**LAMBIRD, PERRY ALBERT,** pathologist; b. Reno, Nev., Feb. 7, 1939; s. C. David and Florence (Knowlton) Lambird; m. Mona Sue Salyer, July 30, 1960; children: Allison Thayer Watson, Jennifer Salyer, Elizabeth Gard, Susannah Johnson. BA, Stanford U., 1958; MD, Johns Hopkins U., 1962; MBA, Okla. City U., 1973. Diplomate Am. Bd. Pathology. Postdoc. fellow, internal medicine Johns Hopkins Hosp., Balt., 1962—63, resident pathologist, 1965—68, chief resident, 1968—69; med. cons. USPHS, Washington, 1963—65; pathologist Med. Arts Lab., Okla. City, 1969—96, chmn., from 1998, Okla. Meml. Hosp., SW Med. Ctr., from 1974, Nat. Cancer Inst., 1974—81, PATH-COR Inc., from 1995; propr. Lambird Mgmt. Cons. Svc., Okla. City, from 1974; assoc. prof., pathology and orthop. surgery U. Okla. Coll. Medicine, 1980—90, prof., from 1990; pres. Ind. Pathology Inst. Inc., 1984—88, chmn. bd. dirs., from 1988. Cons. in field.; reviewer Jour. Am. Med. Assn., from 1983. Contbr. articles to profl. jours. Pres. Okla. Symphony Orch., 1974—75, Ballet Okla., 1978—79; del. Rep. Nat. Conv., 1976, alt. del., 1984; bd. regents Uniformed Svcs. U. Health Scis., 1983—88; mem., task force entitlements and human assistance programs US House of Reps., 1983—88; bd. dirs. Commn. Office Lab. Assessment, from 1988, chmn., 1992—94. Recipient Exec. Leadership award, Okla. City U., 1976, Outstanding Pathologist award, Am. Pathology Found., 1984; named Disting. Practitioner, Nat. Acad. Practice, 1990. Fellow: Coll. Am. Pathologists (gov. 1984—92), Am. Soc. Clin. Pathologists; mem.: AMA (house dels., coun. mem., med. svc., Recognition award 1969—98), Johns Hopkins Med. and Surg. Assn., Okla. City Clin. Soc., Osler Soc., Okla. Soc. Cytopaths (pres.), Am. Soc. Cytology, NY Acad. Sci., Southern Med. Assn., Okla. Assn. Pathologists (pres.), Am. Assn. Pathologists, Arthur Purdy Stout Soc. Surg. Pathologists, Okla. Found. Peer Rev. (dir.), Am. Pathology Found. (pres.), Okla. Soc. Cytopathology (pres.), Okla. County Med. Soc. (pres.), Okla. Med. Assn. (house dels., trustee, pres.), Alpha Omega Alpha, Phi Beta Kappa (Phi Beta Kappa of Yr. 1996). Republican. Methodist. Died Aug. 26, 1999.

**LAMBRAKIS, CHRISTOS,** publisher; b. Feb. 24, 1934; Ed., LSE. Pub., editor weekly Tachydromos (Courier), from 1955; owner, pub., editor daily Ta Nea (News), 1957—2009; owner daily To Vima (Tribune), Weeklies Economicos Tachydromos (Econ. Courier), 1957, Omada

(The Team), 1958, Pub. Monthly Epoches, 1963; pres. Greek sect. Internat. With Press Inst. Imprisoned, SyrosPrison Island, 1967. Recipient FIEJ Golden Pen of Freedom award, 1968. Died Dec. 21, 2009.

**LAMBSDORFF, OTTO GRAF,** former German government official; b. Aachen, Germany, Dec. 20, 1926; Student, U. Bonn, U. Cologne; LLD, 1952. With Free Dem. Party, Aachen, 1951—93, chmn. Aachen Dist. Br., 1951-53, elected to German Bundestag, 1972, econ. policy spokesman, 1983-88, chmn., 1988—93; fed. minister economics Govt. of West Germany, Aachen, 1977-83. Died Dec. 5, 2009.

**LAMPE, AGNES LAURA,** musician, fine arts association administrator; b. St. Paul, Iowa, July 12, 1899; d. Henry Stephen and Thersia (Steffensmeier) L. MusB, DePaul U., 1939, MA, 1941. Joined Sch. Sisters of St. Francis, Roman Cath. Ch., 1915. Choral dir. Alverno Coll., Milw., 1941-70, conductor, founder Madrigal Singers, 1957-70; dir. children's chorus Florentine Opera Co., Milw.; founder, coord. Soc. of Fine Arts, Alverno Coll., Milw., from 1960. Named Milwaukeean of the Month, 1980; recipient Nat. Merit award Nat. Cath. Music Educators Assn., 1972. Home: Milwaukee, Wis. Deceased.

**LAMPERT, LEONARD FRANKLIN,** mechanical engineer; b. Mpls., Nov. 13, 1919; s. Arthur John Lampert and Irma (Potter) Smith. BME, U. Minn., 1943, B in Chem. Engring., 1959, MS in Biochemistry, 1964, PhD in Biochemistry, 1969. Registered profl. engr., Minn. With flight measurement rsch. dept. Douglas Aircraft Corp., El Segundo, Calif., 1943-47; researcher, tchr. U. Minn., Mpls., 1947-83; with rsch. engring. dept. Mpls. Honeywell Corp., 1950-55; info. scientist Control Data Corp., Mpls., 1982-88; mech. engr. Leonard Lampert Co., White Bear Lake, Minn., from 1988. Scientist Eurasion Watermilfoil Control, White Bear Lake, 1989—; stockholder rep. Lampert Lumber Co., St. Paul, 1988—. Contbr. articles to profl. jours. Mem. Am. Inst. Chem. Engrs. (award 1959), Am. Chem. Soc., U. Minn. Alumni Assn. (advisor) MIT Alumni Assn. (advisor), Phi Gamma Delta (advisor), Gamma Alpha, Phi Lambda Upsilon. Republican. Avocations: ballroom dancing, waterskiing, bicycling, geography, travel. Home: Minneapolis, Minn. Died Jan. 9, 2011.

**LANCASTER, EDITH EARLE,** librarian; b. Fulton, Aug. 8, 1927; d. Leslie Gurnie and Bertha Florence (Burgess) Lancaster. BA, Trevecca Nazarene Coll., 1952; MA, George Peabody Coll. Tchrs., 1953. Asst. libr. Trevecca Nazarene Coll., Nashville, 1953—56, NW Nazarene Coll., Nampa, Idaho, 1956—57; head libr., from 1957; vis. libr. Australian Nazarene Bible Coll., Thornsland, Queensland, 1978, cons., 1982. Mem.: ALA, Idaho Libr. Assn., NW Assn. Pvt. Colls. & Univs. (libr. divsn.), Christian Librs. Assn., Pacific NW Libr. Assn., Soroptimists Internat. (Nampa) (bd dirs., editor newsletter). Republican. Nazarene. Died Oct. 25, 1998.

**LANDIS, LEONARD ROBERT,** finance company executive; b. NYC, Oct. 10, 1923; s. Aaron and Lucille (Neuman) Landis; m. Elayne Shapiro, July 18, 1960; children: Carolyn, Dean, Andrew. BS in Mech. Engring., Cornell U., 1947. Indsl. engr. Maidenform Brassaire Co., Bayonne, NJ, 1947—49; plant mgr. Stone Mfg. Co., Elizabeth, NJ, 1949—51, Nat. Mfg. Co., Hillside, NJ, 1951—53; CEO, pres. United Credit Corp., NYC, 1954—98. Mem. Local Draft Bd., NYC, 1971—98. Capt. US Army, 1942—45. Recipient The New Life award, Bonds for Israel, 1980. Mem.: Financemens Club, Comml. Fin. League, Nat. Comml. Fin. Assn. (dir. 1970—98), One Hundred Club (N.Y.C.), Harmonie Club, B'nai B'rith (trustee 1970—98). Home: New York, NY. Died Nov. 10, 1998.

**LANDSBERG, HANS HERMAN,** economist; b. Posen, Poland, Sept. 9, 1913; came to U.S., 1936; s. Max and Clara (Kantorowicz) L.; m. Gianna Giannetti; 1 child, Ann. BS in Econs., London Sch. Econs., 1936; MA, Columbia U., 1941. Economist Nat. Bur. Econ. Rsch., NYC, 1939-42; economist UNNRRA UN, Rome, 1945-46, economist FAO Washington, 1946-48; economist U.S. Dept. Commerce, Washington, 1948-51, Gass, Bell & Assoc., Washington, 1951-60; sr. fellow Resources for Future, Washington, 1960-83, sr. fellow emeritus, from 1983. Mem. adv. bd., asst. sec. state for Oceans and Interant. Environ. and Sci. Affairs, Washington, 1980—; mem. vis. com. dept. mineral econs. Colo. Sch. Mines, Golden, 1987—; mem. sci. and industry adv. bd. Nat. Renewable Energy Lab., Golden, 1989—. Co-author: High Energy Costs: Uneven, Unfair, Unavoidable?, 1981, Resources in America's Future, 1962; editor: Energy: The Next 20 Years, 1976; co-editor: World Mineral Exploration, 1988, Competitiveness in Metals-The Impact of Public Policy, 1992. 1st lt. U.S. Army, 1944-46, ETO. Recipient Econs. award AIME, 1980, ann. prize for outstanding contbn. to profession of energy econs. Internat. Assn. Energy Economists, 1984. Fellow AAAS, AAAS; mem. Am. Econ. Assn., Internat. Assn. Energy Econs. Democrat. Jewish. Died Oct. 14, 2001.

**LANDSBURG, ALAN WILLIAM,** film producer; b. NYC, May 10, 1933; s. Harry and Fannie (Koslowe) L.; m. Sally Breit, Feb. 12, 1957 (div.); children: Valerie, Michael; m. Linda Otto, Mar. 7, 1976 (dec. 2004) BA, NYU, 1953. Producer NBC, NYC, 1956-59, CBS, NYC, 1959-60; writer-producer Wolper Productions, 1960-68; exec. producer Metromedia Producers Corp., LA, 1968-70; chmn. bd. Alan Landsburg Productions, LA, 1970-85, The Landsburg Co., LA, from 1985. Author: In Search of Ancient Mysteries, 1977, In Search of Myths and Monsters, 1977, In Search of Extraterrestrials, 1977, (with Sally Landsburg) Outer Space Connection, 1977; exec. producer: (TV movies) Bill, 1981, Adam, 1983, The Ryan White Story, 1989, A Mother's Right: The Elizabeth Morgan Story, 1992; writer, exec. producer Unspeakable Acts Served in U.S. Army, 1953-55; chmn. Calif. Horseracing Bd., 2002 Recipient Emmy award TV Arts & Sciences Acad., 1970, 73, Peabody award, 1964. Mem. Writers Guild America, Dirs. Guild, Acad. TV Arts & Sciences, Acad. Motion Picture Arts & Sciences Home: Beverly Hills, Calif. Died Aug. 14, 2014.

**LANDWEHR, GOTTFRIED,** physicist, researcher; b. Osnabrück, Germany, Aug. 22, 1929; s. Hans and Margarete (Strackeljahn) L.; m. Angela Vieweg, 1959; children: Uta, Harald. Diploma in physics, TH Karlsruhe, Germany, 1952; Dr. rer. nat., TH Braunschweig, Germany, 1956; Dr. rer. nat. honoris causa, U. Giessen, Germany, 1998; Dr honoris causa, U. J. Fourier Grenoble, France, 1998. Rsch. scientist Phys.-Techn. Bundesanstalt, Braunschweig, 1953-59, 61-68; rsch. assoc. U. Ill., 1959—61; prof. exptl. physics U. Würzburg, Germany, 1968-78, 83-97, prof. emeritus, 1997—2013; dir. Hochfeldmagnet Labor Grenoble (France) Max Planck Inst., 1978-83. Curator Volkswagenstiftung, Hannover, Germany, 1986-96. Editor: High Magnetic Fields in Semiconductor Physics, 1987, 89, 91, (with others) Landau Level Spectroscopy, 1990; editor numerous articles for profl. jours. Decorated Bavarian Order of Merit; recipient Bundesverdienstkreuz award Pres. Germany, 1987. Mem. Russian Acad. Scis., Bavarian Acad. Sciences Home: Wuerzburg, Germany. Died Jan. 24, 2013.

**LANE, ELISABETH ANN,** interior designer; b. Orange, NJ, Mar. 5, 1942; d. William Spurrier and Ruth (Hoehle) L. BFA, Ohio Wesleyan U., 1963; grad., Brera Acad., Milan, Italy, 1964. Dir. interior design, buyer O'Neill & Bishop Inc., Haverford, Pa., 1969-99; tchr. Interior Design Schs., 1996—2002; owner, design bus. Villanova, Pa., 1999—2002. Mem. Am. Soc. Interior Design (regional dir.), Nat. Home Fashions League, Kappa Kappa Gamma. Republican. Mem. Soc. Of Friends. Deceased.

**LANGDON, ROBERT ADRIAN,** historian; b. Adelaide, Australia, Sept. 3, 1924; s. Arthur Louis and Doris Dodd (McFarling) L.; m. Iva Louise Layton, Dec. 6, 1958 (dec. 1984); children: Iva Treasure Langdon Carmody, Louise Vivienne. MA (hon.), Australian Nat. U., 1987. Journalist Advertiser Newspapers Ltd., Adelaide, 1953-61, Pacific Publs. Pty. Ltd., Sydney, Australia, 1962-68; exec. officer Pacific Manuscripts Bur. Australian Nat. U., Canberra, 1968-86, vis. fellow Pacific and Asian history, from 1986. Bd. dirs. Jour. Pacific History, Canberra; mem. adv. com. Australian South Pacific Cultures Fund, 1974-96. Author: Tahiti: Island of Love, 1959, 5th edition, 1979, The Lost Caravel, 1975, The Lost Caravel Re-explored, 1988, Every Goose A Swan: An Australian Autobiography, 1995, The Language of Easter Island (with D. Tryon), 1983; contbr. to encycs. and learned publs. Awarded Cruz de Caballero, Orden de Isabela la Catolica, King of Spain, 1980. Mem. Pacific History Assn. (sec.-treas. 1981-83, pres. 1987-90), Hakluyt Soc., Polynesian Soc., Soc. Oceanistes, Societe des Etudes Oceaniennes. Avocations: walking, swimming, photography. Home: Aranda, Australia. Died Sept. 2003.

**LANGE, DAVID RUSSELL,** former Prime Minister of New Zealand; b. Otahuhu, New Zealand, Aug. 4, 1942; s. Eric Roy and Phoee (Fysh) L.; m. Naomi Joy Crampton, 1968 (div. 1991); children: Roy, Bryon, Emily. LLB, U. Auckland, 1966, LLM with honors, 1966. Bar: N.Z. 1966. Barrister, solicitor, Kaikohe, N.Z., 1968, Auckland, N.Z., 1970-77; M.P. for Mangere N.Z., from 1977; opposition spokesperson on justice, 1978; opposition spokesperson on social welfare, shadow minister of justice, 1979; dep. leader of opposition, 1979-83; leader, 1983-84; shadow minister overseas trade, fgn. affairs, regional devel. and Pacific Island affairs, 1983-84; privy councillor, 1984; prime min. New Zealand, Wellington, 1984-89, min. in charge security intelligence service, from 1984, min. fgn. affairs, 1984-87, min. edn., 1987-89, atty.-gen., min. state, 1989-91. Named Privy Councillor, 1984, Companion of Honor, 1990. Mem. Labour Party. Home: Mangere Bridge, New Zealand. Died Aug. 13, 2005.

**LANGGUTH, ARTHUR JOHN,** journalist, educator, writer; b. Mpls, July 11, 1933; s. Arthur John and Doris Elizabeth (Turnquist) Langguth. BA cum laude, Harvard U., 1955. Corr. Cowles Newsletter, 1959; mem. bur. Look Mag. Bur., Washington, 1959; polit. corr. for Presdl. election Valley Times Cowles Publ., San Fernando Valley, Calif., 1960, corr. Calif. gubernatorial election, 1962; reporter NY Times, Dallas, 1963, NC, 1963, corr. S.E. Asia, 1964, bur. chief Saigon (Vietnam), 1965; spl. assignment NY Times Mag., 1968, 70; reporter NY Times, Miss., 1963, Ala., 1963; prof. U. Southern Calif. Annenberg Sch. Journalism, 1976—2003, prof. emeritus, 2003—14. Author: Macumba: White and Black Magic in Brazil, 1975, Hidden Terrors, 1978, Saki: A Life of Hector Hugh Munro, 1981, Patriots, The Men Who Started the American Revolution, 1988, A Noise of War: Caesar, Pompey, Octavian and the Struggle for Rome, 1994, Our Vietnam: The War 1954-1975, 2000, Union 1812: The American Who Fought the Second War of Independence, 2006, Driven West: Andrew Jackson and the Trail of Tears to the Civil War, 2010, After Lincoln: How the North Won the Civil War and Lost the Peace, 2014, (fiction) Jesus Christs, 1968, Wedlock, 1973, Marksman, 1974. Fellow Shaw Traveling Fellow, Harvard Coll., 1955—56, John Simon Guggenheim Meml. Found., 1976—77. Mem.: Author's Guild. Home: Los Angeles, Calif. Died Sept. 1, 2014.

**LANGHAM, NORMA E.,** playwright, educator, poet, composer, inventor; b. California, Pa. d. Alfred Scrivener and Mary Edith (Carter) L. BS, Ohio State U., 1942; B in Theatre Arts, Pasadena Playhouse Coll. Theatre Arts, 1944; MA, Stanford U., 1956; postgrad., Summer Radio-TV Inst., 1960, Pasadena Inst. Radio, 1944-45. Tchr. sci. California High Sch., 1942-43; asst. office pub. info. Denison U., Granville, Ohio, 1955; instr. speech dept. Westminster Coll., New Wilmington, Pa., 1957-58; instr. theatre. California U., Pa., 1959, asst. prof. Pa., 1960-62, assoc. prof. Pa., 1962-79, prof. emeritus Pa., from 1979, co-founder, sponsor, dir. Children's Theatre Pa., 1962-79. Founder, producer, dir. Food Bank Players, 1985, Patriot Players, 1986, Noel Prodns., 1993. Writer: (plays) Magic in the Sky, 1963, Founding Daughters (Pa., Nat. DAR awards 1991), Women Whisky Rebels (Pa. Nat. DAR awards 1992), John Dough (Freedoms Found. award 1968), Who Am I?, Hippocrates Oath, Gandhi, Clementine of '49, Soul Force, Dutch Painting, Purim, Music in Freedom, The Moon Is Falling, Norma Langham's Job Johnson; composer, lyricist: (plays) Why Me, Lord?, (text) Public Speaking; co-inventor (computer game) Highway Champion. Recipient Exceptional Acad. Svc. award Pa. Dept. Edn., 1975, Appreciation award Bicentennial Commn. Pa., 1976, Gregg award Calif. U. of Pa. Alumni Assn., 1992, Emeriti Faculty award California U. Pa., 2000. Mem. AAUW (co-founder Calif. br., 1st v.p. 1971-72, pres. 1972-73, Outstanding Woman of Yr. 1986, 97), DAR, Internat. Platform Assn. (poetry award 1993, 94, monologue award 1997), California U. Pa. Assn. Women Faculty (founder, pres. 1972-73), California 150, California Hist. Soc., Pa. Assn. Safety Edn., Washington County Hist. Soc., Dramatists Guild, Ctr. in Woods, Mensa, Alpha Psi Omega, Omicron Nu. Presbyterian (elder). Deceased.

**LANGMAN, RODNEY E.,** immunologist; b. Barmera, Australia, Feb. 2, 1944; s. Frank J. and Veronica M. (Ford) L.; m. Laura A., Oct. 8, 1979 (div. Dec. 1992); 1 child, Deborah A. BS, U. Adelaide, 1967, BS with honors, 1968; PhD, Australian Nat. U., 1972. Postdoctoral student U. Alberta, Edmonton, 1972-73, rsch. assoc., 1973-74; rsch. scientist Salk Inst., LaJolla, Calif., 1975-76, staff scientist, 1977-80, sr. staff scientist, from 1980; lectr. U. Victoria, B.C., Can., 1976-77; sr. lectr. biology U. Calif., San Diego, from 1998. Cons. Baxter Travenol, Duarte, Calif., 1982-83. Author: (monograph) The Immune System, 1989. Deceased.

**LANITIS, NICHOLAS CONSTANTINE,** investments and business executive, writer; b. Limassol, Cyprus, Sept. 15, 1917; s. Constantine Panayi and Thereza (Nicolaides) L.; m. Vanda E.M. Lainas, Aug. 21, 1947; children: Hebe, Vladimir, Thereza, Julia. BA, Cambridge U., Eng., 1939; MA, Trinity Coll., 1957. Founder, chmn. Lanitis Bros. Ltd., Nicosia, Cyprus, from 1943, Food Products Co., Ltd., Channel Islands, from 1986, Gen. Fin. Corp. Ltd., Bahamas, from 1964, Lanitis Bros. Trading Ltd., Turks and Caicos Islands, from 1965. Co-mng. dir. Cyprus Wines and Spirits Co. Ltd., Limassol, 1944-47; dep. contr. supplies Govt. of Cyprus, 1940-42. Author: Rural Indebtedness and Agricultural Co-operation in Cyprus, 1944, rev. edit. 1992, Our Destiny, 1963, also booklets. Founder, 1st chmn. The Cyprus Employers Fedn., 1960-63, Cyprus Productivity Ctr., 1961-63; founder, 1st sec. Social Progress Soc., 1944-47. Trinity Coll. scholar, 1957. Home: Andorra la Vella, Andorra. Died Jan. 9, 2005.

**LANSDOWNE, JAMES FENWICK,** artist; b. Hong Kong, Aug. 8, 1937; s. Ernest and Edith (Ford) L. LHD (hon.), U. Victoria, 1980. Exhibited one-man shows including: Royal Ont. Mus., Toronto, Ont., 1956, Audubon House, N.Y.C., 1958, Tryon Galleries, London, Eng., 1961, 63, Kennedy Galleries, N.Y.C., 1962, Smithsonian Instn., Washington, 1969, 77, Oakland, Calif., 1977, Vancouver, B.C., 1981, Toronto, Ont., 1977; represented permanent collections: Montreal Mus. Fine Arts, Art Gallery Victoria, Audubon House, Ulster Mus., Belfast, Ireland, pvt. collection, Brit. royal family; co-author: (with John A. Livingston) Birds of the Northern Forest, 1966, Birds of the Eastern Forest, 1968, Vol. II, 1970; author: Birds of the West Coast, Part I, 1976, Vol. II, 1980; illustrator: Rails of the World (S. Dillon Ripley), 1977, A Guide to the Behavior of Common Birds (Donald Stokes), 1979. Decorated officer Order of Canada. Fellow Explorers Club; mem. Royal Can. Acad. Arts, Fedn. Can. Artists, Can. Nature Fedn., Order BC. Died July 27, 2008.

**LAPOLT, MARGARET,** librarian; b. Austin, Pa., June 9, 1931; d. Thomas Wilbur and Frances Leona (Smith) Bennett; m. Sanford Howard LaPolt, Apr. 14, 1957 (dec. Nov. 1996); children: Cheryl Lynn LaPolt Remson, Mark Alan LaPolt. BSEd, Mansfield U., Pa., 1953; MSEd, Western Conn. State U., Danbury, 1963; MSLS, So. Conn. State U., New Haven, 1973. Tchr. 5th grade Bd. Edn., Clearfield, Pa., 1953-54; tchr. 6th grade Emporium (Pa.) Bd. Edn., 1954-58; tchr. 5th grade Darien (Conn.) Bd. Edn., 1958-64; tchr. 3d grade Stratford (Conn.) Bd. Edn., 1965-69, libr., 1969-70, Norwalk (Conn.) Bd. Edn., 1973-92, part-time libr., 1993—2005, ret., 2002. Singer, Norwalk Cmty. Chorus, 1961-73; singer Cmty. Bapt. Ch., Norwalk, 1958—, bd. deacons, 1993-99, trustee, 1981-87. Computer grantee, Norwalk Bd. Edn., 1985. Mem. ALA, Kappa Delta Phi, Kappa Pi. Avocations: knitting, embroidery, travel, walking. Died July 19, 2008.

**LAPPERT, MICHAEL FRANZ,** chemistry educator; b. Brno, Moravia, Czechoslovakia, Dec. 31, 1928; s. Julius and Kornelie (Beran) L.; m. Lorna McKenzie, Feb. 14, 1980. BSc, No. Polytechnic, London, 1949, PhD, 1951; DSc, U. London, 1960; D Natural Scis. (hon.), U. Munich, 1989. Asst. lectr. Northern Polytechnic, London, 1952-53, lectr., 1953-55, sr. lectr., 1955-59; lectr. U. Manchester (Eng.) Inst. Sci. and Tech., 1959-61, sr. lectr., 1961-64; reader U. Sussex, Brighton, Eng., 1964-69, prof., 1969-97, rsch. prof., 1997—2014. Joint editor Inorganic Polymer Chemistry, 1961; co-author: Metal and Metalloid Amides, 1980, Organo-Zirconium and Hafnium Chemistry, 1986; vol. editor Vol. 4 Comprehensive Organometallic Chemistry II, 1995. Fellow Royal Soc. Chemistry (pres. Dalton div. 1989-91, main group element award 1970, Tilden lectr.

1972, organometallic award 1978, Nyholm lectr. 1994, Frankland lectr. 1999), Royal Soc.(FRS, 1979); mem. Am. Chem. Soc. (Kipping award 1976). Home: Brighton, England. Died Mar. 28, 2014.

**LAROCHE, GÉRARD LAURENT,** adult education educator, writer; b. Cambridge, Mass., June 20, 1920; s. J. Arthur and Juliette Anne (Lajeunesse) LaRoche; m. Joyce Iris Cynthia Latchem, Oct. 18, 1947; children: Marianne Aimée, Jérôme Augustin, David Gerard. BA, Boston Coll., 1942, MA, 1943; MA in Romance Philology, Harvard U., 1947, postgrad, 1950. Instr. French Tufts U., Medford, Mass., 1948—51; rsch. analytic specialist, translator, br. chief, lectr. linquistics Nat. Security Agy., Ft. Meade, Md., 1952—79; ret., 1979. Asst. professorial lectr. George Washington U., Washington, 1962—65; rsch. assoc. Cath. U. Am., Washington, 1966—74, lectr. linguistics Grad. Sch., Dept. Agr., 1974—76; guest lectr. music history U. Md., College Park, 1967; lectr. calligraphy Montpelier Cultural Arts Ctr., Laurel, Md., 1997—2000; lectr. music/arch. various high schs., 1967—75. Author: (book) The Memoirs of Gérard LaRoche, 1995; exhibitions include Drawings from the War Years 1943-1951, Sharon Arts Ctr., NH, 1989. Choir dir. St. Ambrose Ch., Cheverly, Md., 1964—89. Sgt. US Army, 1943—45. Named Hon. Citizen, Ohey and Hasselt, Belgium, 1985; grantee O'Malley Tchg. fellow, Boston Coll., 1942—43. Republican. Roman Catholic. Avocations: violin, photography, historical restoration, cabinet and model making, sound recording. Home: Cheverly, Md. Died Oct. 6, 2013.

**LAROSE, ROGER,** retired pharmaceutical executive, retired dean; b. Montreal, Que., Can., July 28, 1910; s. Alfred Fervac and Anna (Contant) L.; m. Rita Dagenais, Aug. 10, 1936 (dec. Oct. 1960); 1 child, Louise Larose Cuddihy; m. Julienne Begin, Aug. 3, 1961. BA, U. Montreal, 1929, BSc in Pharmacy, 1932. Asst. prof. pharmacy U. Montreal, 1934, dean faculty pharmacy, 1960—65, vice rector adminstrn., 1969—79; from med. rep. to mgr. pharm. divsn. Ciba Co. Ltd., Montreal, 1936—57, v.p., 1958—68, pres., 1968—73, dir., 1967; chmn. Ciba-Geigy Can. Ltd., 1978—82. Vice-chmn., exec. com. Bank Canadian Nat., 1969-80; gov. Can. Bankers Inst., 1973-80. Pres. Can. Pharm. Mfrs. Assn., 1961-62, Montreal Symphony Orch., 1978, pres., mng. dir., 1979-81 Decorated officer Order Can., 1973. Mem. St. Denis Club (Montreal). Roman Catholic. Home: Outremont, Canada. Died Nov. 6, 2005.

**LARSEN, ETHEL PAULSON,** retired secondary school educator; b. Superior, Wis., Jan. 24, 1918; d. Ole Peter Paulson and Petra Marie (Boardsen) Gilbertson; m. James Eugene Larsen, June 13, 1943; children: Robert, Karen Larsen DePalermo, Deborah Larsen Farmer, Candice Larsen Herrera. AA, Kendall Coll., 1940; student, U. Wis., 1940-44; BS, SW Tex. U., 1960; postgrad., U. Tex., 1961-67. Tchr. Lakefield (Minn.) Pub. Schs., 1944-46; credit mgr. Sagebiel's Automotive Parts, Seguin, Tex., 1948-49; supervisory clk. supply Edward Gary AFB, San Marcos, Tex., 1951-56; property/acctg. chief Gary Army Air Field, San Marcos, 1956-59; tchr. Seguin High Sch., 1960-80; substitute tchr. Seguin Pub. Schs., 1981-83; reporter, photographer Seguin Citizen newspaper, 1981; now ret. Developer speech-journalism curriculum, Minn. State Bd. Edn., 1945; pres. AAUW, Seguin, 1965-66, Seguin Classroom Tchrs., 1971-72; del. to Tex. State Tchrs. Assn., Austin, 1970. Founding mem. York Creek Flood Prevention Dist. for Hays, Comal and Guadalupe counties, 1953-54; Voice of Democracy chair VFW Aux., Geronimo, Tex., 1970-78; writer radio scripts for improved farm-city rels., 1956; vol. tax aide, Seguin, 1987-90; Circle leader 1st United Meth. Ch., Seguin, 1989—; mem. T.B. Bd. Guadalupe County, 1954-57. Mem. Nat. Writers Club, Seguin Garden Club, Seguin-Guadalupe County Ret. Tchrs. (pres. 1990—), Nat. Coun. State Garden Clubs, Inc. (life), Tex. Garden Clubs, Inc. (life, horticulture chmn. Dist. VII 1997-98), Inc. (life), Tex. State Garden Clubs (life, Tex. dist. VII), Tex. Agrl. Ext. Svc. (master gardener), Order Ea. Star, Oakwood Art Group, Delta Kappa Gamma (Theta Kappa chpt. pres. 1978-80). Avocations: writing, art, photography, farm management. Home: Seguin, Tex. Deceased.

**LARSEN, LOREN JOSEPH,** retired pediatric orthopedic surgeon; b. Idaho Falls, Idaho, Oct. 10, 1914; s. Charles Wilford and Marie (Jacobsen) L.; m. June Elmer, Mar. 20, 1943; children: Mary Ann, Loren J. Jr. BA, U. Utah, 1939; MD, U. Chgo., 1941. Intern Alameda County Hosp., 1942; resident orthopedic surgery Samuel Merit Hosp., Oakland, Calif., 1943-44; postgrad. tng. U. Calif., 1944-46, San Francisco Gen. Hosp., 1946-47; clin. prof. orthopedic surgery U. Calif., San Francisco, 1957-60; chmn. emeritus dept. orthopedic surgery Children's Hosp., San Francisco, 1957-88; chief of staff emeritus Shriner's Hosp. Crippled Children, San Francisco, 1968-80; pvt. practice San Francisco. Cons. orthopedics U.S. Army Letterman Gen. Hosp., San Francisco, 1959—, U.S. Naval Hosp., Oakland, Calif., 1960-75, King Faisal Hosp., Ridyaah, Saudi Arabia, 1968. Contbr. 37 articles to profl. jours. Mem. Scoliosis Rsch. Soc. (founding), Am. Orthopedic Foot and Ankle Soc. (founding). Republican. Achievements include discovery of reporting syndrome, later named Larsen Syndrome; genetic research to determine the location of the chromosome and genes responsible for inheritance characteristics. Home: Petaluma, Calif. Died Dec. 2002.

**LARSEN, ROLF,** former state supreme court justice; b. Pitts., Aug. 26, 1934; s. Thorbjorn Ruud and Mildred (Young) L. Student, Pa. State U., U. Pitts., Duquesne U. Sch. Philosophy, U. Santa Clara; LL.B., Dickinson Sch. Law, 1960. Bar: Pa. 1960. Pvt. practice law, 1960-73; judge Allegheny County Ct. Common Pleas, 1974-77; justice Pa. Supreme Ct., 1978—94. Lectr. Duquesne U. Sch. Law. Served in US Army, 1954-56. Recipient Humanitarian award, Outstanding Jurist award Pa. Dist. Attorneys Assn., 1985, Judicial Excellence award Pa. State AFL-CIO, 1986, Ann. award Pa. Trial Lawyers Assn., 1986, Justice Michael A. Musmanno award Phila. Trial Lawyers Assn., 1986. Mem.: Masons. Democrat. Died Aug. 11, 2014.

**LARSON, CHARLES ROBERT,** retired military officer; b. Sioux Falls, SD, Nov. 20, 1936; s. Eldred Charles and Gertrude Edythe (Jensen) L.; m. Sarah Elizabeth Craig, Aug. 19, 1961; children: Sigrid Anne, Erica Lynn, Kirsten Elizabeth. BS in Marine Engring., U.S. Naval Acad., 1958. Commd. ensign USN, 1958, advanced through grades to adm., 1990; naval aviator, attack pilot, 1958-63; nuclear power, submarine tng., 1963-64; assigned nuclear subs., 1964-76; naval aide to Pres. Richard Nixon The White House, 1969-71; comdg. officer USS Halibut, 1973-76; comdr. submarine devel. group one, head operational deep submergence program, 1976-78; chief naval ops. staff Strategic Submarine Programs, 1978-79; dir. long range planning group Washington, 1978-82; comdr. submarines, Mediterranean, 1982-83; supt. U.S. Naval Acad. Annapolis, Md., 1983-86; comdr. 2d Fleet, 1986-88; dir. plans, policies & ops. USN, 1988-90; comdr. US Pacific Fleet (USPACFLT), 1990-91, US Pacific Command (USPACOM), Hawaii, 1991-94; supt. US Naval Acad., 1994-98; v.p. US Naval Inst., 1994-98; sr. fellow The CNA Corp., Alexandria, Va., 1998—2004; cons. Via Finance, LLC, 2004—14; nat. security adv. Howard Dean's Presdl. Campaign, 2004. Bd. dirs. Northrop Grumman Corp., 2002—09, Esterline Technologies Corp., 2004—09. Mem. USO Coun., Honolulu, 1990-92; mem. Honolulu area coun. Boy Scouts America, 1990-94. Decorated Def. D.S.M., Navy D.S.M. (7), Legion of Merit (3), Bronze Star, others; White House fellow, 1968-69. Mem. NAS (com. on internat. security and arms control), Coun. on Fgn. Rels. Democrat. Home: Annapolis, Md. Died July 26, 2014.

**LARSON, RICHARD EVERETT,** lab administrator; b. New London, Conn. s. Everett Richard and Rachel (Amendola) L. BS, U. Conn., Storrs, 1977, MS, 1981; student, U. R.I., Kingston, 1982-83. With USCG, from 1990. Episcopalian. Avocations: golf, fishing. Deceased.

**LARSSON, CARL ERIK,** artist, educator; b. Malmú, Sweden, Mar. 11, 1920; s. Sven and Gerda Carolina (Dahlin) L.; m. Anna Theresia Thomasson, July 7, 1945; 1 child, Paul Robert. Diploma, Acad. Fernande Leger Paris, 1950. Sport instr. Cycklisten, Malmö, 1955-57; art tchr. Malmö Schs., 1963-85; art and design tchr., owner art sch. Malmö, 1966-90; art curator Gallery Hipp, Malmö, 1972-82; theater instr. Musafällan, Malmö, from 1991. Exhibited in over 50 art shows including Galerie Denise Rene, Paris, 1949, Galleri Tokanten, Copenhagen, 1950, Galeri Gramunken, Stockholm, 1953, Malmö Mus., 1969, Galerie Mouffe, Paris, 1971, Galerie Vallombreuse, Biarritz, 1972, NEA Bicentennial, Washington, 1976, Galerie PLAC Zamkowy, Warsaw, 1981, Galeri Nove Miasto, Warsaw, 1981, Landskrona Mus., 1982, Bulows Galleri, Malmö, 1991, Tingshuset Trelleborg, 1995, Svenska Konstnärsgalleriet, Kristianstad, 1997, Galleri Valvet, Malmö, 1997; movie artist Dagboken, 1953, Blitz Blatz, 1953. Mem. Art Com. Malmö City, 1989-91. Cpl. Swedish Army, 1943-55. Illums Bolighus scholar, 1950. Mem. Culture Assn. Old Town Malmö (chmn. 1991—), Revysmakarna (chmn. 1990—). Avocation: collecting books. Home: Malmö, Sweden. Died Nov. 22, 2003.

**LASHMAN, L. EDWARD,** arbitrator, mediator, consultant; b. New Orleans, June 6, 1924; s. L. Edward and Edith Ruth (Deutsch) L.; m. Elizabeth Gitt Fichman, June 6, 1948 (dec. Aug. 1984); children: Deborah, Rebekah, David W. (dec. Feb. 1993), Judith; m. Joyce Blicher Schwartz, July 25, 1987. Student, U. N.C., 1940-42, Tulane U., New Orleans, 1951—52. Ptnr. Caire Assocs., New Orleans, 1946-51; with CIO and AFL-CIO, 1951-67; asst. to sec., dir. cong. liason HUD, Washington, 1967-69; mng. ptnr. Urban Housing Assocs., Denver, 1969-70; v.p. U. Mass., 1970-75; dir. external affairs, sr. planning counselor Harvard U., Cambridge, Mass., 1975-89; sec. adminstrn. and fin. Commonwealth of Mass., Boston, 1989-91, chmn. Mass. bd. regents pub. higher edn., 1986-88; chmn. Commonwealth Land Bank, Boston, 1975-77, Mass. Housing Fin. Agy., Boston, 1977-79; ret., 1991. Acting exec. dir. (pro bono) Mass. State Lottery, 1999; contract mediator U.S. Equal Employment Opportunity Commn.; contract arbitrator U.S. Postal Svc. Exec. com. Denver County Dem. Party, 1952-64; chmn. Colo. Urban League, Denver, 1961-63; acting COO (pro bono) Judge Baker Children's Ctr., Boston, 1993-94; dir. Nat. Housing Conf., Washington, 1969-75; v.p. Handel & Haydn Soc., Boston, 1982-84; chmn. Housing Needs Com., Town of Weston, Mass., 2001-06. With U.S. Army, 1943-46, ETO. Mem. Am. Arbitration Assn., Mass. Assn. Mediation Programs, Norfolk and Suffolk County Superior Ct. Mediation Panels, Joint Labor Mgmt. Com. Mediation Panel. Avocations: fly fishing, cooking, photography. Died Aug. 2012.

**LATEEF, YUSEF (BILL EVANS),** composer, educator; b. Chattanooga, Oct. 9, 1920; BA, Manhattan Sch. Music, MA in Music Edn., 1975; EdD, U. Mass., 1975. Tchr. saxophone Stan Kenton Summer Jazz Clinics, 1963. Past. assoc. prof. music Manhattan C.C.; lectr. colls.; vis. prof. music Mass. and Hampshire Coll., Amherst. Leader quartet, N.Y.C., 1960; featured with Charles Mingus, 1960-61, Babatundi Olatunji, 1961-62, with Cannonball Adderley Combo, European Tour, 2 years; now combo leader; musician various instruments including tenor saxophone, flute, oboe, Middle Eastern and Asian instruments; recs. on Impulse, Prestige, Landmark labels, others; records include Part of the Search; albums include The Boeue Yusef Lateef, The Diverse Yusef Lateef, The Gentle Giant, Hush 'n Thunder, Blues for Orient, Cry-Tender, Eastern Sounds, Expression!, Gentle Giant with W.K. Barron, Imagination with Doug Watkins, Into Something with Elvin Jones, Live Session, The Many Faces of Yusef Lateef, Plays for Lovers, Sounds of Yusef, Live at Pep's, Club Date, Little Symphony, Yusef Lateef's Flute Book of the Blues, Lateef in Nigeria, 1985, Gong, 1957, Jazz for the Thinker, 1985, Morning with Curtis Fuller, Nocturnes with Schick, C. Salvo, P. Tucker, 1989, Other Sounds with W. Harding, H. Lawson, E. Farrow, D. Jackson, 1957, 89; composer symphany Do I (Tahira) recorded with the Hamburg Germany Radio Orch. Recipient Grammy award for best new-age performance, 1987 Home: Amherst, Mass. Died Dec. 23, 2013.

**LATORRACA, JOSEPH PAUL,** writer; b. Montclair, NJ, May 3, 1942; s. Joseph N. and Isabelle E. Latorraca; m. Sharon Hutter, July 3, 1971 (div. June 1976). BA, Rutgers U., 1964, MEd, 1975. Tchr. French East Brunswick H.S., NJ, 1964—79; prin. St. Malachy Cath. Sch., Tamarac, Fla., 1984—88; aquatics dir. Woodmont Country Club, Tamarac, 1979—84, 1989—96; profl. writer, from 1996. Contbr. short stories and chpts. to books. Usher St. Bernard's Cath. Ch., Sunrise, Fla., from 1997. Recipient 1st Place for Children's Fiction, Foster City Arts and Cultural Coun., Calif., 1999. Roman Catholic. Deceased.

**LAUGHLIN, NAOMI MYERS,** realtor; b. Oliver, Ill., Mar. 11, 1913; d. Jesse and Mary Grace (Macke) Myers; m. Otis Alton Worthington, July 24, 1936 (dec. Apr. 1948); m. Cyril James Laughlin, Feb. 19, 1955. BA, George Washington U., 1934. Cert. assn. exec. Realtor, Silver Spring, Md., 1943-50 and from 70. Recipient 1st A.V. Pisani Lifetime Achievement award, Capital Area Realtors Assn. Mem. AAUW (hon., past pres.), Realtors Land Inst. (hon., pres. 1976-77, ind. land specialist), Montgomery County (Md.) Bd. Realtors (exec. v.p. 1950-70, pres. fed. credit union 1981-84, Lifetime Achievement award, 2003), Manor Country Club (hon.). Democrat. Roman Catholic. Deceased.

**LAUGHLIN, TOM (THOMAS ROBERT LAUGHLIN),** actor, producer, director, writer; b. Mpls., Wis., Aug. 10, 1931; m. Delores Taylor. Student, Ind. U., U. Minn.; studies with Dr. Maria Montessori, Italy, 1960-65. Dir., actor film Born Losers, 1967; producer, actor, co-screenwriter: Billy Jack, 1973, The Trial of Billy Jack; dir.: (films) The Proper Time, The Young Sinner, 1965, Billy Jack Goes to Washington, 1978, The Return of Billy Jack, 1986. Mem. Dirs. Guild Am. Died Dec. 12, 2013.

**LAUREL, STAN (ARTHUR STANLEY JEFFERSON),** actor, comedian; b. Ulverston, North Lancanshire, Eng., June 16, 1890; came to U.S., 1910; s. Arthur and Margaret (Metcalfe) J.; m. Lois Nielson, Aug. 13, 1926; children: Lois, Stanley Robert (dec.) Student, Bishop Auckland. Various adminstrv. jobs Metropole Theater; mem. The Karno Troupe, 1910. Actor in vaudeville and in films; appeared in films including: Nuts in May, 1917, The Lucky Dog, (with Oliver Hardy) Forty Five Minutes From Hollywood, 1926, Duck Soup, 1927, Big Business, 1929, Pardon Us, 1931, Do Detectives Thnk?, The Second Hundred Years, A Perfect Day, Be Big, The Music Box, Pack Up Your Troubles, 1932, The Devil's Brother, 1933, Bogus Bandits, 1933, Sons of the Desert, 1933, Babes in Toyland, 1934, Hollywood Party, 1934, The Bohemian Girl, 1936, Our Relations, 1936, Way Out West, 1937, Swiss Miss, 1938, Blockheads, 1938, The Flying Deuces, 1939, Saps at Sea, 1940, Nothing But Trouble, 1944, The Bullfighters, 1945; dir. film, Yes, Yes Nanette, 1926. Died Feb. 23, 1965.

**LAURENT, BRUNO FRANCOIS CLAUDE,** chemical engineer, researcher; b. Nancy, France, July 19, 1970; s. Jean Jules Henri Laurent and Colette Louise Lucie Mary. Diplome d'Ingenieur, ENSIC-INPL, 1990—92; Diplomarbeit, Technische Hochschule Karlsruhe, 1992—93; PhD, U. of Cambridge, 1994—98. Rschr. Dept. of Chem. Engring., Cambridge, 1993—94, from 1998. Fellow: Philos. Soc., Isaac Newton Inst.; mem.: Cambridge U. Soft Matter Group, Particle Tech. Subject Group. Catholic. Achievements include research in characterisation of granular flow. Home: Cambridge, England. Deceased.

**LAVELLE, BRIAN FRANCIS DAVID,** lawyer; b. Cleve., Aug. 16, 1941; s. Gerald John and Mary Josephine (O'Callagahan) L.; m. Sara Hill, Sept. 10, 1966; children: S. Elizabeth, B. Francis D. Jr., Catherine H. BA, U. Va., 1963; JD, Vanderbilt U., 1966; LLM in Taxation, NYU, 1969. Bar: NC 1966, Ohio 1968, US Tax Ct. 1969, US Ct. Appeals (4th cir.) 1998. Assoc. VanWinkle Buck, Wall, Starnes & Davis, Asheville, N.C., 1968-74, ptnr., from 1974. Lectr. continuing edn. NC Bar Found., Wake Forest U. Estate Planning Inst., Am. Coll. Trust and Estate Counsel, San Diego, Hartford Tax Inst., Duke U. Estate Planning Inst. Contbr. articles on law to profl. jours. Trustee Carolina Day Sch., 1981-92, sec., 1982-85; bd. dirs. The Salvation Army, 1986—, Western NC Cmty. Found., 1986-2001, sec., 1987-90; bd. advs. U. NC Ann. Tax Inst., 1981—. Capt. JAG USAF, 1966-67. Mem. ABA, Am. Coll. Trust and Estate Counsel (state chmn. 1982-85, regent 1984-90, lectr. continuing edn.), NC Bar Assn. (bd. govs. 1979-82, v.p. 1997-2000, councillor tax sect. 1979-83, councillor estate planning law sect. 1982-85, 2002-05), NC State Bar (splty. exam. com. on estate planning and probate law 1984-90, chmn. 1990-91, cert. 1987), Rotary, Biltmore Forest Country, Royal Brigade of Guards. Anglican. Home: Asheville, NC. Died Nov. 18, 2012.

**LAVRENOV, IGOR VIKTOROVICH,** physicist, oceanographer, mathematician, educator; b. Tomsk, Russia, Feb. 16, 1954; s. Viktor Georgievich Lavrenov and Valeria Ilyinichna Lavrenova; m. Svetlana Ivanovna Lavrenova; children: Ekatherine, Ilya, Tatyana. PhD, Inst. Oceanography, Moscow, 1981; D in Phys. and Math. Scis., Arctic and Antarctic Inst., St. Petersburg, Russia, 1992. Jr. sci. worker Oceanog. Inst., Leningrad, 1981—84, sr. sci. worker, 1984—88, leading sci. worker, 1988—94; head lab. Arctic and Antarctic Rsch. Inst., St. Petersburg, 1994—2001, head dept., 2001—07. Cons. Meteorol. Inst., Debilt, Netherlands, 1992, Oceanography Ctr., Ensenada, Mexico, 1996, Ensenada, 1998, Ensenada, 2000; cons., prof. Korea Meteorol. Adminstrn., Seoul, 2002. Author: Wind Waves in Non-Uniform Ocean, 1998 (award, 2000), Wind Waves in Ocean, 2003; contbr. articles to profl. jours. Grantee, Russian Found. Fund, Moscow, 1996, 1998, 2001, 2004, INTAS, Belgium, 1999, 2001. Achievements include being a co-developer of Russia's first global wind wave model in 2000. Avocations: travel, swimming, languages. Home: St. Petersburg, Reunion Island. Died June 6, 2007.

**LAVRNJA, ILIJA,** education educator; b. Hrvatsko Polje, Croatia, Aug. 1, 1952; s. Milos and Kata Lavrnja; m. Lidija Arbutina, Apr. 28, 1982; children: Milos, Dusan. Tchr., Ljubljana U. Edn., Slovenia, 1975; M in Pedagogy, Belgrade U., Yugoslavia, 1981; PhD in Pedagogy, Rijeka U., Croatia, 1983. H.s. tchr. H.S. Tech., Kranj, Slovenia, 1975—77, Backa Palanka, Yugoslavia, 1977—78, Grammar Sch., Rijeka, Croatia, 1978—79; prof. edn. U. Rijeka, from 1979. Head of dept. U. Rijeka, 1988—92, chief of staff for didactics, from 1994; editl. staff Horizons of Tech., Ljubljana, from 1990. Author: Polozaj Ucenika u Odcojno-Obrazounoh Process, 1985, Adult Education in Croatian Society, Poglavlja Iz Didaktike, 1998; contbr. articles to profl. jours. Recipient Recognition award, Rectory of U. Lugano, Switzerland, 1991. Mem.: Internat. Soc. for Comparative Adult Edn., Hrvatski Pedagosko-Knoizevni Zbor (subdir. 1991—93), Strasbourg Human Rights Orgn. Home: Rijeka, Croatia. Died Dec. 22, 2002.

**LAWRENCE, ALICE LAUFFER,** artist, educator; b. Cleve., Mar. 2, 1916; d. Erwin Otis and Florence Mary (Menough) Lauffer; m. Walter Ernest Lawrence, Sept. 27, 1941 (dec. Dec. 2001); 1 child, Phillip Lauffer. Diploma in art, Cleve. Inst. Art, 1938; BS in Art Edn., Case Western Res. U., 1938. Grad. asst. in art edn. Kent (Ohio) State U., 1939-40; art tchr. Akron (Ohio) and Cleve. Pub. Schs.; comml. artist B.F. Goodrich Co., Akron, 1942-44; sub. art tchr. Akron Pub. Schs.; sketch artist numerous events Akron, 1945-91. Portrait sketch artist for various cos., including Estée Lauder, O'Neil's Dept. Store, Polsky's, Summit, Rolling Acres, Chapel Hill, Walden Books, K-Mart. Contbr. poetry to anthologies; exhibited prints and drawings at Akron Art Inst. (winner). Mem. Cuyahoga Valley Art Ctr., Women's Art Mus., Akron Art Mus., 1963-94, Rep. Nat. Com., 1998, New Rep. Nat. Fund. Recipient 2d pl. in drawing, Butler Mus. Am. Arts, 1940-41, recipient 1st pl. drawings and prints, Cleve. Mus. Art, 1944, Purchase award Massillon Mus. Mem. Woman's Art League Akron (sec. 1962), Ohio Watercolor Soc., Internat. Soc. Poets (life, Outstanding Achievement in Poetry Silver award 2003). Republican. Avocation: poetry. Home: Massillon, Ohio. Died May 27, 2008.

**LAWSON, THOMAS VINCENT,** retired wind engineer; b. Soissons, France, Jan. 22, 1925; s. John Boyd and Mary Alexandra (Chambers) L.; m. Pauline Elizabeth Gaunt, Aug. 6, 1948; children: Alexandra Barbara, Theodore Thomas, Charity Jenny, Oscar Charles, Pandora Pauline, Darcie Tabitha. BSc, U. Leeds, Eng.; diploma, Imperial Coll., London. Lectr. aero. engring. U. Bristol, England, 1949-62, sr. lectr., 1962-72, reader in indsl. aerodynamics, 1972-83, sr. rsch. fellow, 1983—2001. Chmn. wind engring. group Engring. Scis. Data Unit Internat., U.K., 1972-2002, mem. structural vibration group, 1980-90; mem. wind loading com. Brit. Standards Inst.; ret. Author: Wind Effect on Buildings, 2 vols., 1980, Wind Loading Handbook: Guide to the Use of BS6399, Part 2, 1996, Building Aerodynamics, 2001; mem. editl. bd. Jour. Atmospheric Environment, 1965-90, Jour. Aerodynamics and Wind Engring., 1975—. Fellow Royal Acad. Engring., Royal Aero. Soc. Home: Bristol, England. Died Mar. 9, 2009.

**LAWTON, DAVID L.,** linguist, educator; b. NYC, Mar. 20, 1924; s. Charles E. and Gladys E. (Cooke) Lawton; m. Jean Margaret Hahn, 1949; children: Robin, Martin. BA, Hiram Coll., 1949; MA, Western Res. U., 1950; PhD, Mich. State U., 1963. Instr. Alpena CC, Mich., 1954—57; chmn. Lansing CC, 1957—64; assoc. prof. Inter Am. U., San German, PR, 1964—65, prof., dean Hato Rey, 1965—68; prof. linguistics Ctrl. Mich. U., Mount Pleasant, from 1968. Smith-Mundt prof. U. Guadalajara, Mex., 1960—62; Fulbright prof. U. Quito, Ecuador, 1971. Precinct del. Mount Prospect Dem. Com., 1980. Recipient Premier Performance award, Ctrl. Mich. U., 1971, 1975—76; fellowship, NSF, 1977, Am. Coun. Learned Socs., 1977. Mem.: Am. Dialect Soc., Internat. Soc. Caribbean Linguists, Linguistic Soc. Am., Mich. Linguistic Soc. (sec.-treas. from 1971, editor 1973—76). Democrat. Episcopalian. Avocations: sailing, camping. Home: Orlando, Fla. Died July 6, 1989.

**LAYNE, JOHN FRANCIS,** accountant; b. Milw., Mar. 25, 1928; s. Lawrence E. and Blanche E. (Tetzlaff) Layne; m. Esther A. Ornberg, Mar. 10, 1951; children: Loretta E., John W., Mark L. BS in Bus. Adminstrn., U. Ctrl. Fla., 1972. Enlisted USAF, 1948, advanced through grades to chief warrant officer-4, 1964, test contr., systems devel. Air Proving Ground Ctr. Eglin AFB, 1962—65, standardization/evaluation contr. Far East, Okinawa and Vietnam, 1966—70; ret., 1970; acct. Electric Specialty, Orlando, Fla., 1971—74, contr., 1975—77; fin. field rep. Tupperware divsn. Dart, Orlando, Fla., 1978—90, credit analyst, from 1991. Asst. bus. chmn. 46th Nat. Sq. Dance Conv.; v.p. Ctrl. Fla. Assn. Sq. Dancers, 1977—78, pres., 1978—79; chmn. 1978 Fla. Sq. Dance Conf.; active Fla. Fedn. Sq. Dancers, 1978—82, pres., 1982—83. Decorated Bronze Star, Medal of Honor Republic of Vietnam; recipient Excellence award, Far East coun. Boy Scouts Am., 1968, Am. Sq. Dance Soc., 1983, Couple of Yr. award, Ctrl. Fla. Assn. Sq. Dancers, 1984. Mem.: Nat. Assn. Enrolled Agts., Nat. Soc. Pub. Accts. (emeritus). Home: Deltona, Fla. Died Apr. 6, 1997.

**LAYTON, IRVING PETER,** poet, teacher; b. Neamtz, Romania, Mar. 12, 1912; arrived in Can., 1913; s. Moses Lazarovitch and Klara (Moscovitch) Layton; m. Faye Lynch, Sept. 13, 1939 (div.); m. Betty Frances Sutherland, Sept. 13, 1946 (div.); children: Max Rubin, Naomi Parker; m. Aviva Cantor, Sept. 13, 1961 (div.); 1 child, David Herschel; m. Harriet Bernstein, Nov. 23, 1978 (div. Mar. 1984); 1 child, Samantha Clara; m. Anna Pottier, Nov. 8, 1984. BS in Agr., Macdonald Coll., Can., 1939; MA, McGill U., Can., 1946; DCL, Bishop's U., Can., 1970; DCL (hon.), Concordia U., 1976; DLitt, York U., Can. Prof. York U.; lectr. Sir George Williams U., Montreal, 1950—68; poet-in-residence U. Guelph, 1969—70, U. Ottawa, 1978—79; vis. prof. Concordia U., 1978—79; writer-in-residence U. Toronto, 1981—82. Author: Here and Now, 1945, Now Is the Place, 1948, The Black Huntsmen, 1951; co-author: Cerberus, 1952, Love the Conqueror Worm, 1953, In the Midst of My Fever, 1954, The Long Pea-Shooter, 1954, The Cold Green Element, 1955, The Blue Propeller, 1955, The Bull Calf and Other Poems, 1956, Music On A Kazoo, 1956, A Laughter in the Mind, 1958, Red Carpet for the Sun, 1959 (English Poetry award, 1960), The Swinging Flesh, 1961, Balls For a One-Armed Juggler, 1963, Ed. Love Where the Nights Are Long, 1963, The Laughing Rooster, 1964, Prix Litteraire de Quebec (1st prize, 1963), (poems) Periods of the Moon, 1967, The Shattered Plinths, 1968, (prose & poetry) The Whole Bloody Bird, 1969, Nail Polish, 1971, Engagements: Selected Prose, 1972, Lovers and Lesser Men, 1973, The Pole Vaulter, 1974, Seventy-Five Greek Poems, 1974, The Darkening Fire (Selected Poems, 1945-68), 1975, Il freddo Verde Elemento (Giulio Einaudi, Torino), 1974, The Unwavering Eye (Selected Poems 1969-75), 1979, For My Brother Jesus, 1976, The Covenant, 1977, (prose) Taking Sides, 1977, New Directions (Selected Poems), 1977, The Uncollected Poems of I.L., 1977, The Tightrope Dancer, 1978, The Love Poems of Irving Layton (deluxe edition), 1978, Irving Layton-Aligi Sassu Portfolio, 1978, Droppings from Heaven, 1979, An Unlikely Affair: Layton-Rath Correspondence, 1980, For My Neighbours in Hell, 1980, The Love Poems of I.L., 1980, In an Ice Age-Bilingual Selected Poems, 1981, Europe and Other Bad News, 1981, A Wild Peculiar Joy, 1982, Shadows On The Ground, 1982, The Gucci Bag, 1983; co-editor (with L. Dudek): Canadian Poems 1850-1952, 1953, Las Poemas de Amor, 1983, With Reverence and Delight: The Love Poems of Irving Layton, 1984; co-editor: Where Burning Sappho Loved, 1985; co-editor: (with Salvatore Fiume) A Tall Man Executes a Jig, 1986; co-editor: Waiting for the Messiah, 1985, Dance with Desire, 1986, Final Reckoning: Poems, 1982-1986, 1987, Fortunate Exile, 1987, A Wild Peculiar Joy: Selected Poems, 1989, Tutto Sommato, 1989, Italian Critics on Irving Layton, 1989, Wild Gooseberries: Selected Letters of Irving Layton, 1989, I. Layton-Robert Creeley Correspondence, 1989, others. Served to lt. RCA, 1942—43. Recipient Can. Coun. award, 1959, Can. Coun. Spl. Arts award, 1967, Can. Coun. Arts award, 1979—81, Long Term award, Achievement in Life award, Ency. Britannica, 1979; nominee Nobel prize, Italy & Republic of Korea, 1982; Can. Found. fellowship, 1957. Mem.: 22nd Ann. Internat. Poetry Forum. Avocations: handball, swimming, chess, freethinking. Died Jan. 4, 2006.

**LAZORCHAK, JOSEPH MICHAEL,** economist; b. Paterson, NJ, June 7, 1957; s. Michael and Lena Madeline (Nejmeh) L. BS, Montclair State U., 1979; MA, Fordham U., 1980. Asst. staff mgr. AT&T, Basking Ridge, N.J., 1980-84; mem. tech. staff Bellcore, Morristown, N.J., 1984-94, sr. cons. customer solutions Livingston, N.J., 1994-95; pres. Joseph M. Lazorchak Econ. Cons., Inc., Mine Hill, NJ, 1996—99. Mem. Am. Econ. Assn., Nat. Assn. Bus. Econs., Inst. Mgmt. Cons. Republican. Roman Catholic. Avocations: photography, electronics, boating. Died Nov. 30, 1999.

**LEBLOND, CHARLES PHILIPPE,** anatomy educator, researcher; b. Lille, France, Feb. 5, 1910; s. Oscar and Jeanne (Desmarchelier) L.; m. Gertrude Sternschuss, Oct. 22, 1936 (dec.); children— Philippe L., Paul N., Pierre F., Marie Pascale; m. Odette Lengrand, July 12, 2001 (dec.). L.Sc., U. Lille, 1932; MD, U. Paris, France, 1934, D. Sc., 1945; PhD, U. Montreal, 1942; DSc Acadia (hon.), McGill U., 1982, York U., 1985; DSc (hon.), Sherbrooke Univ., 1988. Asst. histology U. Lille and U. Paris, France, 1934-35; Rockefeller fellow anatomy Yale, 1935-37; charge biology div. Lab. Synthese Atom, Paris, 1937-40; research fellow U. Rochester, N.Y., 1940-41; mem. faculty McGill U., Montreal, Canada, 1941—2007, prof. anatomy, 1948—2007, chmn. dept., 1957-75. Author: L'Acide Ascorbique dans les Tissues et sa Detection, 1936, Radioautography as a Tool in the Study of Protein Synthesis, 1965; contbr. articles to profl. jours. Decorated companion Nat. Order Can., grand officer Order of Quebec; recipient Marie-Victorian Prize, Quebec, 1992, Duncan Graham award, Royal Coll. Physicians and Surgeons of Can., 1986, E-B Wilson Award, 1982, Issac Schour award, 1974; named to Can. Med. Hall of Fame, 1995; scholar Fogarty scholarship, NIH, 1975. Fellow: Prix. Scientifique du Que., Am. Acad. Arts and Scis., Can. Assn. Anatomists (J.C.B. Grant award 1979), Am. Assn. Anatomy (Centennial award 1979, Henry Grey award 1978), Royal Soc. Can. (McLaughlin Medal 1983), Royal Soc. London. Achievements include research in cell and tissue dynamics. Home: Montreal, Canada. Died Apr. 10, 2007.

**LEDERER, LUCY KEMMERER,** retired artist; b. Milton, Pa., Oct. 8, 1891; d. William Benjamin and Katherine Elizabeth (Krumrine) Kemmerer; m. Eugene Herman Lederer, June 29, 1918 (dec. Oct. 1960); 1 child, Eugene William. Student, Pratt Inst., 1912; student, Simmons Coll., 1913; BA, Pa. State U., 1914; postgrad., Arts Students League, NYC, 1943-45. Tchr. Bellefonte (Pa.) Sch. System, 1914-15; tchr. Lower Merion Sch. Dist., Wayne, Pa., 1916-18; artist State College, Pa., 1930-91. Real estate developer State Coll., 1920-91. Mem. AAUW, Art Students League N.Y. (life), DAR, Daus. Am. Colonists, Am. Legion Aux. Lutheran. Home: 1236 Penfield Rd State College PA 16801-6417

**LEDERIS, KAROLIS PAUL (KARL LEDERIS),** pharmacologist, educator, researcher; b. Noreikoniai, Lithuania, Aug. 1, 1920; arrived in Can., 1969; s. Paul Augustus and Franciska (Danisevicius) L.; m. Hildegard Gallistl, Feb. 28, 1952 (dec. Nov. 2000); children: Aldona Franciska, Edmund Paul. Diploma, Tchrs. Coll., Siauliai, Lithuania, 1939; BSc, U. Bristol, UK, 1958, PhD, 1961, DSc, 1968. From jr. lectr. to reader U. Bristol, 1961-69; prof. pharmacology and therapeutics U. Calgary, Alta., Canada, 1969-89, prof. emeritus Alta., from 1989. Vis. prof. univs. in Fed. Republic Germany, Austria, Chile, Argentina, Sri Lanka, Switzerland, Lithuania, France, USA, USSR, 1963-79, U. Bristol, 1979, U. Kyoto, Japan, 1980; career investigator, mem., chair grants com. Med. Rsch. Coun., Ottawa, Ont., Can., 1970-89, coun. mem., exec., 1983-90; mem. internat. com. Centres Excellence Networks, Ottawa, 1988-89. Author, editor: 5 books on hypothalamic hormones; editor in chief Jour. Exptl. and Clin. Pharmacology, 1977-89; contbr. approximately 350 book chpts. and articles to profl. jours.; patentee hormonal peptides. Recipient Upjohn award in pharmacology, 1990, various fellowships and scholarships in U.K., Fed. Republic of Germany, US. Fellow NAS, Royal Soc. Can.; mem. Western Pharmacol. Soc. (pres. 1982-83), Brit. Can. US Soc. Pharmacology Endocrinology and Biochemistry, Kiwanis, Lithuanian Club (London), Men's Can. Club, Cabot Yacht and Cruise Club (Bristol). Avocations: music, sailing, golf. Home: Victoria, Canada. Died Mar. 17, 2007.

**LEE, JACKSON FREDERICK,** former mayor; b. Fremont, Nebr., Apr. 8, 1920; s. Earl J. and Rebecca (Pierce) Lee; m. Virginia Ann White, Sept. 5, 1941; children: Jackson Frederick Jr., Tom, David, Virginia Ann Lee Statke. BSc, U. Nebr., BA, 1941. Sales mgr.-mgr. Sta. WILM, Wilmington, Del., 1946—60; owner, gen. mgr. Sta. WFAI Fayetteville, NC, 1960—71; v.p., acct. exec. Murchison & Bailey, Fayetteville, 1971—79. Chmn. NC Republican Party, Raleigh, 1977—81. Vice chmn. airport commn., Fayetteville, 1965—71; mayor, 1971—75; trustee Fayetteville State U., 1973—78. Capt. USAAF, 1943—46, col. USAF, ret. Mem.: N.C. Assn. Broadcasters (pres. 1969), Fayetteville Area C. of C. (pres. 1971), Executive (Fayetteville) (pres. 1966), Masons (32d degree). Republican. Died June 10, 2014.

**LEE, JINTAE,** computer science educator, researcher; b. Kangrim, Kangwondo, Korea, Dec. 12, 1957; s. Hag-Ui and Ok-Soon (Kim) Lee; m. Hyun-Sook Kim, Aug. 16, 1990; children: John, Sung-Un, Herald. BS, Seoul U., Republic of, 1981; MS, Korea Advanced Inst. Sci. & Tech., Seoul, 1983; DSci, U. Tokyo, 1993. Cert. computer engr. level 1. Sr. rschr. Korea Inst. Sci. & Tech., Seoul, 1983-89; visiting rschr. George Washington U., Washington, 1998-99; assoc. prof. U. Aizu, Aizu-Wakamatsu, Japan, from 1993. Inventor modeled painting brush; contbr. articles to profl. jours. Recipient Excellent Rschr. award Syss. Engring. Rsch. Inst., Seoul, 1989. Mem. IEEE Computer Soc., Info. Processing Soc. Japan, Korea Info. Sci. Soc. Avocations: music, tennis, swimming. Home: Aizu-Wakamatsu, Japan. Died Apr. 9, 2002.

**LEE, LYNDA MILLS,** librarian; b. Shreveport, La., Mar. 3, 1944; d. Donald Clarle and Eva Dell (Wooley) Mills; divorced; 1 child, Jennifer Lynn Netherland. BA, Northwestern La. State U., 1966; MLS, La. State U., 1968. Cert. libr., La. Libr. Westlake (La.) High sch., 1966-67; ref. libr. East Tex. State U., Comniere, Tex., 1968-70; tchr. Morehouse Parish, Bootrop, La., 1970-71; br. libr. Ocachita Parish Pub. Libr., Monroe, La., 1971-72; dir. Bossier-Red River Parish Pub. Libr., Benton, La., 1972-78, Calcasieu Parish Pub. Libr., Lake Charles, La., from 1978. Named Outstanding Young Women, Bossier Jaycees, 1975. Mem. AAUW, Bus. and Profl. Women, Family and Youth Counseling Bd. (pres. 1986-87), Children's Mus. Bd., La. Libr. Assn. (Mid-Career award 1979, coord. legisl. network 1975-78, 83-86, pres. 1978-79), Art. Humanities Counsel (adv. bd., pres. 1986-88), Quota Club Lake Charels (pres. 1978-79). Methodist. Home: Lake Charles, La. Died Nov. 17, 1997.

**LEE, RICHARD VAILLE,** internist, educator; b. Islip, NY, May 26, 1937; s. Louis Emerson and Erma Natalie (Little) L.; m. Susan Bradley, June 25, 1961; children: Matthew, Benjamin. BS, Yale U., 1960, MD cum laude, 1964. Diplomate Am. Bd. Internal Medicine, Am. Bd. Family Practice. Intern Grace-New Haven Hosp., 1964-65, asst. resident in internal medicine, 1965-66, 69-70; fellow in inflammatory disease Yale U., New Haven, 1970-71, asst. prof. medicine, 1971-74, assoc. prof. clin. medicine, 1974-76; practice medicine specializing in internal medicine New Haven, 1969-76, Buffalo, from 1976; family practice Poplar, Mont., 1966-68, Chester, Mont., 1968-69; prof. medicine SUNY, Buffalo, from 1976, prof. pediat., from 1985, adj. prof. anthropology, from 1989, prof. obstetrics, from 1992, adj. prof. social & preventive medicine, from 2010, chief divsn. gen. internal medicine, 1979-82, chief divsn. maternal and adolescent medicine, from 1982, chief divsn. geog. medicine, from 1991; dir. primary care ctr. Yale-New Haven Hosp., 1975-76, dir. med. clinics, 1971-75; chief med. svc. Buffalo VA Hosp., 1976-79; head dept. medicine Children's Hosp. Buffalo, 1979-96; fellow WHO Collaborating Ctr. for Health in Housing, from 1985, chief med. officer, from 1995; founding editor obstetric medicine, from 2011; hon. prof. Capital Med. U., Beijing, from 2012. Cons. internal medicine N.Y. Zool. Soc., from 1973; cons. physician Buffalo Zool. Soc., from 1980; aviation med. examiner, 1980—2001; med. dir. Ecology and Environment, Inc., Lancaster, NY; mem. N.Y. State Bd. for Medicine, from

1995; mem. com. Nat. Bd. Med. Examiners, from 1999; mem. N.Y. State Office for Profl. Med. Conduct, 2001—10; mem., bd. govs. Shaw Festival, Niagara Lake Ont., Canada, from 2010. Author: Outside Rounds, 2005; editor: When I Was a Boy in China, 2003; sr. editor: Current Obstetric Medicine, 1989—95; corr. editor Jour. Obstetrics and Gynecology, London, from 1989; mem. editl. bd.: Internat. Jour. Environ. Health, from 1994; cons. editor Am. Jour. Medicine, 1976—86, chair editl. bd. Obstetric Medicine, 2008—11; contbr. chapters to books on obstetrics and toxicology, articles to profl. jours. Served with USPHS, 1966-68. Recipient C.G. Barnes award, Internat. Soc. Obs. Medicine, from 2006. Master: ACP (sr. editor Med. Care of the Pregnant Patient 2000, contbg. editor Med. Care of the Pregnant Patient, 2d edit. 2008, Laureate award 2002); fellow: Royal Soc. Asian Affairs, Royal Geog. Soc., Explorers Club N.Y.C.; mem.: AMA, Am. Coll. Occupl. and Environ. Medicine, Internat. Soc. of Travel Medicine, Soc. Obstetric Medicine (pres. 1991—93, C. G. Barnes award for disting. svc. to obstetric medicine 2006), Infectious Disease Soc. Am., Am. Soc. Tropical Medicine and Hygiene, Gen. Internal Medicine, Am. Fedn. Clin. Rsch. Soc., N.Y. Acad. Sci., Yale China Assn. (trustee 1992—2001, sec. 1995—2001), Nat. Bd. Med. Examiners, Am. Soc. History of Medicine, Royal Soc. Medicine, Great Lakes Interurban Clin. Club, Alpha Omega Alpha. Achievements include editing and reprinting, with introduction and photographs, his grandfather's book When I Was a Boy In China, 2003. Home: Orchard Park, NY. Deceased.

**LEE, YOUNGSOOK,** botanist, educator; BS, Seoul Nat. U., South Korea, 1978, MS, 1980; PhD, U. Conn., Storrs, 1988. Postdoctoral fellow Harvard U., Mass., 1988—90; assoc. prof. dept. life sci. Pohang U. Sci. and Tech., Republic of Korea, 1990—2001, prof. lab. plant cell biology, from 2001. Contbr. articles to sci. jours. Deceased.

**LEECH, CHARLES RUSSELL, JR.,** lawyer; b. Coshocton, Ohio, July 29, 1930; s. Charles Russell and Edna (Henry) L.; m. Patricia Ann Tubaugh, June 20, 1953; children— Charles Russell III, Timothy David (dec.), Wendy Ann. AB cum laude, Kenyon Coll., 1952; JD, Ohio State U., 1955; MA, U. Toledo, 1969. Bar: Ohio 1955. Assoc. Fuller & Henry Ltd. and predecessors, Toledo, 1957-64, ptnr., 1964-97, counsel, 1997-99. Mng. editor: Ohio State Law Jour, 1955. Mem. exec. com. alumni council Kenyon Coll., 1967-72, trustee coll., 1974-80. Served with USNR, 1955-57. Fellow Ohio State Bar Found.; mem. ABA, Ohio Bar Assn., Kenyon Coll. Alumni Assn. Maumee Valley (past pres.), Beta Theta Pi, Phi Delta Phi. Republican. Home: Gambier, Ohio. Died May 17, 2013.

**LEECH, GEOFFREY NEIL,** English language educator; b. Gloucester, Eng., Jan. 16, 1936; s. Charles Richard and Dorothy Eileen (Foster) L.; m. Frances Anne Berman, July 29, 1961; children: Thomas, Camilla. BA, U. Coll. London, 1959, MA, 1963, PhD, 1968; PhD (hon.), Lund U., Sweden, 1987; DPhil (hon.), Lancaster U., Eng., 2002; D (hon.), Charles U., 2012. Asst. lectr. U. Coll. London, 1962-64, lectr., 1965-69; reader Lancaster (Eng.) U., 1969-74, prof., 1974-96, rsch. prof., 1997—2001, chmn. inst. English lang. edn., 1985-90, chair univ. ctr. corps. rsch. lang., 1995—2014, prof. emeritus, 2002—14. Hon. prof. Beijing Fgn. Studies U., 1994-2014; chair Internat. Computer Archive Modern and Medieval English Author: Semantics: The Study of Meaning, 1981, Principles of Pragmatics, 1983; co-author: Style in Fiction, 1981, A Comprehensive Grammar of the English Language, 1985; author, editor over 20 books. Harkness fellow MIT, 1964-65, British Acad. fellow, U. Coll. London fellow Mem. Acad. Europea, Norske Videnskaps Acad. Liberal Democrat. Anglican. Avocations: music, piano, organ. Home: Cumbria, England. Died Aug. 19, 2014.

**LEESER, MARIO RAFAEL,** business information services executive; b. Buenos Aires, Sept. 19, 1953; arrived in Germany, 1993; s. Fritz and Ellen (Plaut) L.; m. Ruth Yedid, 1980; children: Andrew, Alan. BA in Econs., German Lit., Middlebury Coll., Vt., 1975; MBA in Fin., Boston U., 1976. Bus. analyst Dun & Bradstreet Inc., Boston, 1976; Dunsfile mgr. Dun & Bradstreet Internat., NYC, 1977; ops. mgr. Dun & Bradstreet SACV, Mexico City, 1977-80, br. mgr. Monterrey, Mex., 1980-81; gen. mgr. Dun & Bradstreet SA, Lima, Peru, 1981-83; dir. ops. Latin Am. Dun & Bradstreet Internat., NYC, 1984-87; mng. dir. Austria and Ea. Europe Dun & Bradstreet Schimmelpfeng GmbH., Vienna, 1987-90; v.p., area mgr. Dun & Bradstreet Info. Svcs., Melbourne, Australia, 1990-93; dir. Dun & Bradstreet Australia Ltd., 1990-93, Dun & Bradstreet New Zealand Ltd., 1990-93; pres. A.C. Nielsen Holding GmbH, Vienna, 1988-90; v.p. Germany and Ctrl. Europe A.C. Nielsen Internat., 1993-95, v.p. info. sources Europe, 1995-96, sr. v.p. ops. Europe, Mid. East, and Africa, 1996-97, sr. v.p. and mng. dir., 1997-98, sr. v.p. Western Europe, 1998, group exec. Central Europe, 1998—2001, exec. v.p. Europe, 2001—03, COO Europe, from 2003. Dir. Riddell Pub. Ltd., 1991-93. Dir. Am. C. of C., Lima, 1983; mem. audit com. bd. dirs. Am. Internat. Sch., Vienna, 1989-90; bd. dirs. Frankfurt Internat. Sch., Germany, 1995-97. Avocations: squash, tennis. Died Sept. 2006.

**LEE-SMITH, HUGHIE,** artist, educator; b. Eustis, Fla., Sept. 20, 1915; s. Luther and Alice (Williams) Smith; m. Mabel Louise Everett, 1940 (div. 1953); 1 child, Christina; m. Helen Nebraska, 1965 (div. 1974); m. Patricia Thomas-Ferry, 1978. Student, Art Sch. of Detroit Soc. Arts and Crafts, 1934-35; grad., Cleve. Inst. Art, 1938; BS, Wayne State U., 1953; DFA (hon.), Md. Inst. Coll. Art, 1995. Instr. painting Grosse Pointe War Meml., Mich., 1956-66, Studio-on-the-Canal, Princeton, N.J., 1959-64; art tchr. Princeton Country Day Sch., 1964-65; artist-in-residence Howard U., 1969-71; instr. painting Art Students League, NYC, 1972-87, ret., 1987. Adj. prof. Trenton State Coll., 1972-73 One-man shows include Detroit Artists Market, Howard U. Gallery, Washington, Grand Central Art Galleries, N.Y.C., Janet Nessler Gallery, N.Y.C., U. Chgo., June Kelly Gallery, N.Y.C., Butler Inst. Am. Art, Youngstown, Ohio, Chgo. Cultural Ctr., Greenville (S.C.) Mus. Art, Ogunquit (Maine) Mus. Am. Art, Pensacola (Fla.) Mus., Appleton Mus., Ocala, Fla., others; exhibited group shows Cleve. Mus. Art, Detroit Inst. Arts, Butler Inst. Am. Art, Youngstown, Bklyn. Mus., Wadsworth Atheneum, Boston Mus., San Francisco Mus., Mus. Modern Art, Whitney Mus., Am. Acad, and Inst. Arts and Letters, N.Y.; represented in permanent collections Met. Mus., Phila. Mus., Detroit Inst. Arts, Parrish Mus., Southampton, L.I., N.J. State Mus., Standard Oil of Ohio, AT&T, Wadsworth Atheneum, U. Mich., Wayne State U., Schomburg Coll., N.Y.C., Howard U., Nat. Mus. Am Art, U.S. Navy Art Ctr., Chase Manhattan Bank, N.Y.C., Forbes Mag. Collection, N.Y.C., Kidder & Peabody Co., N.Y.C., Mus. Internat. Art, Sofia, Bulgaria, Century Assn., N.Y.C., Lagos (Nigeria) Mus. With USN, 1944-45. Recipient Thomas B. Clark prize NAD, 1959, prize Allied Artists Am., 1958, Emily Lowe award, 1957, Founders prize Detrout Inst. Arts, 1953, cert. of commendation USN, 1974, Art Achievement award Wayne State U., Key to the City of Hartford (Conn.) award, Ranger Fund purchase award NAD, 1977, Audubon Artist prizes, 1982, 83, 85, 86, Medal of Merit Lotos Club, 1996, Benjamin West Clinedinst Meml. medal Artists Fellowship Inc., 1996, Key to City of Eustis, Fla., 1998, others; named Mich. Painter of Yr. Detroit News, 1953. Mem. Artists Equity Assn. (bd. dirs.), Allied Artists Am., Princeton Art Assn., Mich. Acad. Sci., Arts and Letters, NAD (mem. coun., awards juries), Audubon Artists (pres. 1980-82, exhbn. coord.), Artists Fellowship (trustee, v.p. 1985-88), Century Assn., Lotos Club (N.Y.C.) Home: Albuquerque, N.Mex. Died 1999.

**LEGASPI, LEONARD ZAMORA,** retired archbishop; b. Meycauayan, Phillipines, Nov. 25, 1935; AB in Philosophy, U. Hong Kong, 1955; STL, Pontifical & Royal U. Santo Tomas, 1962; BS in Edn. Mgmt., Harvard Bus. Sch., 1971; PhD, U. Santo Tomas, 1975. Priest of Order of Friars Preachers Catholic Church, Philippines, 1960—77; auxiliary bishop Diocese of Manila, Philippines, 1977; titular bishop of Elephantaris in Mauretania Philippines, 1977—83; archbishop Diocese of Caceres, Philippines, 1983—2012, archbishop emeritus, 2012—14; pres. Catholic Bishop's Conf. Philippines, 1988—91. Roman Catholic. Died Aug. 8, 2014.

**LE GOFF, PIERRE YVES,** chemical engineering educator; b. Brest, France, Feb. 8, 1923; s. Joseph and Jeanne (Lariviere) Le G.; m. Jacqueline Gerard, Aug. 1, 1949; 1 child, Herve. Degree in chem.engring., U. Nancy, France, 1947, PhD, 1955. Asst. lectr. U. Nancy, France, 1947-54, lectr., 1954-57, sr. lectr., 1957-59; prof., chair Inst. Nat. Polytech. Lorraine, Nancy, France, 1959-93, prof. emeritus, from 1993. Dir. engring. dept. U. Nancy, 1964-80, dir. rsch. lab., 1980-96. Decorated comdr. de la Legion d'Honneur, comdr. des Palmes Academiques. Home: Nancy, France. Died Mar. 7, 2005.

**LEGUM, COLIN,** journalist; b. Kestell, South Africa, Jan. 2, 1919; s. Louis Samuel and Jane (Horwitz) L.; m. Eugenie Leon, May 5, 1941 (dec. 1958); 1 child, David Antony (dec. 1995); m. Margaret Jean Roberts, Aug. 10, 1960; children: Kate, Elizabeth, Josephine. Matriculation, Piet Retief, Kestell, South Africa; LLD (hon.), Rhodes U. South Africa, 2000; DLitt, PhD, U. South Africa, 2002. Polit. editor Sunday Express, Johannesburg, 1938-39; editor The Forward, The Mineworker, Johannesburg, 1939-45, Illustrated Labour Bulletin, Johannesburg, 1945-48; assoc. editor The Observer, London, 1951-87; editor Third World Reports, London, from 1987. Author (20 books) ballets; editor: Africa Contemporary Record, 1968—2002. City councillor Johannesburg City Coun., South Africa, 1943-48. Named Hon. Anciens Lectr. NATO, 1989; disting. vis. fellow U. Ind., Bloomington, 1998, 99. Mem. Africa Ednl. Trust, Diplomatic and Commonwealth Writers. Mem. British Labour Party. Avocations: gardening, photography, fishing. Home: Kalk Bay Cape, South Africa. Died June 8, 2003.

**LEHNE, PASCAL HORST,** chemistry educator, consultant; b. Hamburg, Germany, Apr. 17, 1915; s. Richard Wilhelm and Clarita (Voigt) L.; m. Julita Tapang Dawat, Aug. 4, 1972; 1 child, Rowena. Diploma in chemistry, U. Heidelberg, Germany, 1944. Asst. master Gewerbeschule Hansestadt Hamburg, 1956-65, sr. asst. master, 1966-80, ret., 1980, temporary appointed tutor, 1981-83; hon. coworker Mus. für Hamburgische Geschichte, Hamburg, from 1994. Vice dir. evening sch. English Inst., Heidelberg, 1950-52; subdir., tutor Inst. für Lernsysteme, Hamburg, 1980-86. Author: The Normal Gauge Electric Light Railway Altrahlstedt-Volksdorf-Wohldorf, 4 edits., 1954-86; co-author: Lead and Silver, 1966, 2nd edit., 1975, About the Mariana Islands, 1972; calculator of orbital elements of comet Paraskevopoulos (1941c) from pvt. observations; author numerous edits. Periodic Chart of Elements, 1938-52; contbr. articles to profl. jours. Mem. Gesellschaft Deutscher Chemiker, Bund für Deutsche Schrift, The Planetary Soc., Wöhler-Vereinigung für Anorg.Chemie. Avocations: preparing tagalog-german dictionary, compilation of comprehensive collections of elements and inorganic compounds, completion of a gear drive for presenting mean sidereal movements of the major planets. Home: Ammersbek, Germany. Died Jan. 26, 2002.

**LEHOTKA, GÁBOR,** music educator, composer; b. Vác, Hungary, July 20, 1938; s. Gábor Lehotka and Mária Halász. Diploma, Liszt Ferenc Acad. of Music, Budapest, 1965. Organ tchr. Béla Bartók Conservatorium of Budapest, 1969—85; prof. Liszt Ferenc Acad. of Music, Budapest, from 1985. Composer: Noël, 1981, Baroque sonata for trumpet and organ, 1988, Latin Mass, 1993, Sermon on the Mount, 2002, 1st Symphonies 1-4, 2002, 50 recordings. Jury mem. internat. organ contest, Leipzig, Germany, 1980, Linz, Austria, 1982, Budapest, Budapest, Hungary, 1999. Recipient Ferenc Liszt prize, Ministry of Culture, 1974, 'Artist of Merit of the People's Republic of Hungary', The Govt. of Hungary, 1978, Chevalier De L'ordre Des Arts Et Des Lettres, Min. of Culture of France, 1986. Mem.: Internat. Kodály Soc., Ferenc Liszt Soc. Seventh-Day Adventist. Home: Vác, Hungary. Died Dec. 29, 2009.

**LEHTO, SAKARI TAPANI,** lawyer, manufacturing executive, writer; b. Turku, Finland, Dec. 26, 1923; s. Reino R. and Hildi A. (Heinonen) Lehto; m. Karin Margareta Hilden; children: Maarit Roos, Merja Torikka, Marika Paajanen. BSc in Econs., Helsinki Sch. Econs. and Bus. Adminstrn., 1945, EconD (hon.), 1991; LLB, U. Helsinki, 1948; TechD (hon.), Helsinki U. Tech., 1981. Sec. Employers Confedn., Helsinki, 1949—52; legal counselor, bd. dirs. Oy United Paper Mills Ltd., Valkeakoski, Finland, 1952—64; pres. Oy United Internat., Valkeakoski, Finland, 1961—64; mng. dir. Fedn. Finnish Industries, Helsinki, 1964—71; pres., CEO Partek Corp., Helsinki, 1971—87, vice chmn., 1987—95. Chmn. Kaleva Ins. Corp., Helsinki, Tamfelt Corp., Tampere, Finland, Keskus-Sato Corp., Helsinki, Sampo Ins. Corp., Turku; mem. supervisory bd. Aspo Group, Helsinki; bd. dirs. Finnish Nat. Bd. Def., Finnish and fgn. cos. Author: Managing Change--Strategies and Thoughts, 1990, Experiences in the Finnish Industry, 1996, With Luck? And Now?--Challenges for Leaders, 2001; contbr. articles to profl. jours. Active Found. Innovations; min. fgn. trade Govt. of Finland, 1975—76. Capt. Finnish Army, 1941—44. Decorated comdr. 1st class Order of Liberty (Finland), Order of White Rose (Finland), Order of Pole Star (Sweden), comdr. Order of Lion (Finland); recipient title of min., Pres. of Finland, 1977. Mem.: Finnish Law Assn. Economists (chmn. 1984—89), Soc. Future Studies (hon.), Finnish Assn. Club Rome. Avocations: sailing, golf. Died June 30, 2006.

**LEIBBANDT, GEORGE,** mathematics educator; b. Berlin, Oct. 23, 1937; arrived in Can. s. Gottlieb and Elisabeth (Bukovski) L.; m. Martha Cecily Clark, Sept. 15, 1962; children: Martha, George, Sylvia. BSc, McMaster U., 1961; MSc, McGill U., 1964, PhD, 1967. Lectr. McGill U., Montreal, Can., 1965-66; asst. prof. U. Guelph, Can., 1966-72, assoc. prof., 1972-79, prof., from 1979. Bd. dirs. Perimeter Inst. for Theoretical Physics, Waterloo, Can., founding mem. 1999; cons. U. Western Ont., London, 1991; vis. prof., guest lectr. Tech. U. of Vienna, 1990-97; vis. prof. U. Cambridge, Eng., 1997, 82-83; sr. vis. rsch. scientist Queen Mary Coll. U. London, 1980-81; hon. rsch. assoc. Lyman Lab. of Physics Harvard U., Cambridge, 1977-78; acad. visitor Imperial Coll., London, 1970-71. Author: Noncovariant Gauges, 1994; co-editor: Combinatorics and Renormalization in Quantum Field Theory, 1973; contbr. articles to profl. jours.; refereed jours. Annals of Physics, N.Y., Can. Jour. of Physics, Classical and Quantum Gravity, European Physics Jour., others. Mem. Can. Assn. of Physists, Am. Phys. Soc. Avocations: ancient history and greek mythology, ballroom dancing, chess. Home: Guelph, Canada. Died Apr. 2001.

**LEIDEN, CARL,** political scientist, educator; b. Boone, Iowa, Feb. 6, 1922; s. Carl Eric and Christine Olivia (Bergstrom) L.; m. Mary Katherine Rood, Sept. 5, 1945; children: Lisa Ingrid, Derek Stefan. BS, Iowa State Coll., 1945; MPA, Wayne U., 1947; PhD, State U. Iowa, 1949. Instr. State U. Iowa, Iowa City, 1946-49; from asst. prof. to assoc. prof. Marshall Coll., Huntington, W.Va., 1949-59; assoc. prof. Am. U., Cairo, Egypt, 1959-61; from assoc. prof. to prof. polit. sci. U. Tex., Austin, 1961-87, prof. emeritus, from 1987. Fulbright lectr. Peshawar U., Pakistan, 1952-53; vis. assoc. prof. U. Calif., Berkeley, 1957; prof. Nat. War Coll., Washington, 1972-73. Author, co-author eight books on polit. sci. Volker Found. fellow, 1945-46; Fulbright Teaching grant, 1952-53, 66; Earhart Found. grant, 1970. Deceased.

**LEIGH-PEMBERTON, ROBIN See LORD KINGSDOWN**

**LEITE, JOÃO VERDI CARVALHO,** aerospace executive; b. Alfenas, Brazil, June 25, 1935; s. João Soares and Maria Conceição (Carvalho) L.; m. Sonia Regina Brasil- (dec.), July 17, 1965; 1 child, João Brasil Carvalho. Degree in aero. engring., Inst. Tech. Aero., São José Dos Campos, Brazil, 1958; DSc in Aerospace Rsch., Internat. U. Found., 1989. Registered aero. engr. Pres. dir. Avibras Aerospacial S/A, São José Dos Campos, 1974—2008. Chmn., CEO Tectran S/A São José Dos Campos, 1982-2008, Powertronics S/A, São José Dos Campos, 1983-2008, Avibras Found. for Edn. and Work, São José Dos Campos, 19832008; chmn., dir. Avibras Internat. Ltd., Jersey, Channel Islands, 1989-2008; chmn., dir. Avibras Divisao Aerea e Naval, Jacarei, SP, 1995-2008; adviser CEBEU (Brazil-US Enterprise Coun.), CEBRU (Brazil-UK Enterprise Coun.). Patentee in field. Recipient award, Federacao Assn. Comerciais Sao Paulo, 1994, Order Merit Aeronautics, Grau de Oficial, 1997, Comenda da Lagião do Merito do Engenheiro Militar, Grau de Alta Distincao, 2000, Engenharia Militar, Academia Brasileira, 2005, Ordem do Rio Branco, Grau de Oficial, 1980, Ordem do Ipiranga, Grau de Comendor, 1986, Medalha do Pacificador, 1982, Ordem do Merito Militar, Garu de Oficial, 1984, Ordem do Merito de Oficial, 1984, Ordem do Merito das Forcas Armadas, Grau de Comendador, 1986. Mem. Am. Assn. Advancement Sci., AIAA (sr.), Am. Def. Preparedness Assn., Am. Soc. for Metals, Exptl. Aircraft Assn., Seaplane Pilots Assn., Assn. of US Army, Am. Helicopter Soc., NY Acad. Scis., Rotary Club, Soc. Automotive Engrs. Brazil, Nat. Geog. Soc., Inst. de Engenharia. Avocations: flying, scuba diving, parachuting, yachting, motorbiking. Home: São Jose Campos, Brazil. Died Jan. 2008.

**LEMOINE, MICHEL JULES,** retired research scientist, educator; b. Neuilly, France, Mar. 7, 1937; s. Henri and Gabrielle (Besnard) L.; m. Armelle Marie Guidon, Aug. 25, 1960; children: Gwenola, Loeiz, Gael, Hervelina. Lic. de Lettres, Sorbonne U., Paris, 1958, diplome d'etudes superieures, 1959, PhD, 1981. Tchr. Foyer St-Georges, Meudon, France, 1960-62; bibliographe, 1962-84; ingénieur d'études Centre Nat. de la Recherche Scientifique, Paris, 1984-88, ingénieur de recherche, 1988-97; mem. com. Nat. de la Recherche Scientifique, Paris, 1978-83; ret., 1997. Bd. dir. U. Paris, 1978-83; instr. U. Catania, Italy, 1987, 92, 95, 97, 2000, Nat. U., Pusan, South Korea, 1995, U. Sarah Lawrence, Paris, 1981-97. Author: L'ile Morte, 1983, William of Saint-Thierry, de Natura Corporis et Animae, 1988, Théologie et platonisme au XIIe, Intorno a Chartres, 1998, Par le menu, 2002, Les Caissières, 2002, Théologie et Cosmologiè au XIIe, 2004; editor-in-chief Cahiers Universitaires Catholiques, 1986-93; contbr. articles to profl. jours. Mem. Conv. des Instns. Rèpublicaines, Paris, 1967-69. Recipient medaille du Centre Nat. de la Recherche Scientifique, 1998. Mem. Soc. Internat. pour L'ètude de la Philosophie Mèdievale, Assn. Internat. D'ètudes Patristiques, Soc. Nat. des Antiquaires de France, La Marmite (pres.) Roman Catholic. Avocations: water painting, poetry, choir. Home: Le Chesnay, France. Died Jan. 6, 2007.

**LENGYEL, JUDITH ANN,** biologist, educator; b. Rochester, NY, May 15, 1945; d. Bela A. and Helen Margaret (Wilmann) Lengyel; m. Frederick A. Eiserling. BA, UCLA, 1976, MA, 1968; PhD, U. Calif., Berkeley, 1972. Postdoc. fellow U. Calif., 1973, MIT, Cambridge, 1973—75; asst. prof. biology UCLA, 1976—81, assoc. prof., 1981—2004; mem. NSF Devel. Biology Panel, 1980—84; ad hoc reviewer NIH. Contbr. articles to profl. jours., chapters to books; reviewer devel. biology, biochemistry and genetics. Rsch. grantee, NIH, NSF. Mem.: AAAS, Genetics Soc. America, Am. Soc. Cell Biology, Soc. Devel. Biology (bd. dirs.). Died Sept. 25, 2004.

**LENKE, LEIF BERTIL,** criminologist; s. Claes Uno and Hertha Magnhild Lenke; m. Britt-Marie Wik; children: Charlotta Sofia, Malin Katarina. LLB, Stockholm U., 1969; PhD, Lund U., Sweden, 1989. Rschr. Coun. Europe, Strasbourg, France, 1972—74; expert Swedish Commn. Alcohol Policy, Stockholm, 1980—82; Swedish del. expert drug epidemiology group Pompidou Group Coun. Europe, Strasbourg, 1983—94; dir. criminology Stockholm U., 1992—93, prof. criminology, from 2000. Contbr. articles to profl. jours. Mem.: Kettil Bruun Soc. Social Study Alcohol (bd. mem. 1993—97). Home: Täby, Sweden. Died Sept. 15, 2008.

**LENNOX BUCHTHAL, MARGARET AGNES,** retired neurophysiologist; b. Denver, Dec. 28, 1913; d. William Gordon and Emma Stevenson (Buchtel) L.; m. Gerald Klatskin, 1941 (div. 1947); 1 child, Jane Herner; m. Fritz Buchthal, Aug. 19, 1957. BA, Vassar Coll., 1934; MD, Yale Sch. Medicine, 1939; D of Medicine, Copenhagen U., 1972. Intern pediatrics Strong Meml. Hosp., Rochester, N.Y., 1939-40; asst. resident pediatrics N.Y. Hosp., NYC, 1941-42; instr. Yale Sch. Medicine, New Haven, Conn., 1942-44, asst. prof. dept. psychiatry, 1945-51; asst. prof. U. Copenhagen, Inst. Neurophysiology, Denmark, 1957-72, assoc. prof., 1972-81; ret., 1981. Head clin. electroencephalography Yale U. Sch. of Medicine, 1942-51, head clinic epileptology, 1942-51; chief editor Epilesia Pub. by Elsevire, 1967-73. Contbr. articles to profl. jours. Republican. Methodist. Home: Santa Barbara, Calif. Died Aug. 24, 2001.

**LEONARD, HUGH (JOHN KEYES BYRNE),** playwright; b. Dublin, Nov. 9, 1926; s. Nicholas Keyes and Margaret (Doyle) Byrne; m. Paule Jacquet, 1955; 1 child. Student, Presentation Coll., Ireland, 1941-45. Civil servant, Dublin, 1945-59; TV script editor Granada TV, Manchester, Eng., 1961-63; freelance writer London, 1963-70; lit. editor Abbey Theatre, Dublin, 1976-77. Author: (plays) The Italian Road, 1954, The Big Birthday, 1956, A Leap in the Dark, 1957, Madigan's Lock, 1958, A Walk on the Water, 1960, The Passion of Peter McGinty, 1961, Stephen D, 1962, Dublin One, 1963, The Poker Session, 1963, The Family Way, 1964, The Saints Go Cycling In, 1965, Mick and Nick, 1966, The Quick, and the Dead, 1967, The Late Arrival of the Incoming Aircraft, 1968, The Au Pair Man, 1968, The Barracks, 1969, The Patrick Pearce Motel, 1971, Da, 1973 (Tony award for best play 1978, N.Y. Drama Critics' Circle award for best play 1978, Drama Desk award for outstanding new play 1978, Outer Critics Circle award for outstanding play 1978), Thieves, 1973, Summer, 1974, Irishmen, 1975, Time Was, 1976, Some of My Best Friends Are Husbands, 1976, Liam Liar, 1976, A Life, 1979 (Harvey award), Moving Days, 1981, Kill, 1982, Pizzazz, 1982, Good Behaviour, 1983, O'Neill, 1983, The Mask of Moriarty, 1985, Moving, 1991, Senna for Sonny, 1994, The Lily Lally Show, 1994; (autobiographies) Home Before Night, 1979, Out After Dark, 1987; (essays) Leonard's Last Book, 1978, A Peculiar People and Other Foibles, 1979, Rover and Other Cats, 1992; (novels) Parnell and the Englishwoman, 1990, The Off-Off-Shore Island, 1993; (screenplays) Great Catherine, 1968, Interlude, 1968, Whirligig, 1970, Percy, 1971, Our Miss Fred, 1972, Herself Surprised, 1977, Da, 1988, Widow's Peak, 1994; (teleplays) The Irish Boys, 1962, A King of Kingdom, 1963, The Second Wall, 1964, A Triple Irish, 1964, Realm of Error, 1964, My One True Love, 1964, The Late Arrival of the Incoming Aircraft, 1964, Second Childhood, 1964, Do You Play Requests?, 1964, The View From the Obelisk, 1965, I Loved You Last Summer, 1965, Great Big Blond, 1965, The Lodger, 1966, The Judge, 1966, Insurrection, 1966, The Retreat, 1966, Silent Song, 1966 (Italia prize Internat. Concourse for Radio and TV 1967, Merit award Writers Guild of Gt. Britain 1967), A Time of Wolves and Tigers, 1967, Love Life, 1967, Great Expectations (Dickens), 1967, Wuthering Heights (Bronte), 1967, No Such Thing as a Vampire, 1968, The Egg on the Face of the Tiger, 1968, The Corpse Can't Play, 1968, A Man and His Mother-in-Law, 1968, Assassin, 1968, Nicholas Nickleby (Dickens), 1968, A Study in Scarlet, 1968, The Hound of the Baskerville (Doyle), 1968, Hunt the Peacock, 1969, Talk of Angels, 1969, The Possessed (Dostoevsky), 1969, Dombey and Son (Dickens), 1969, P and O (Maugham), 1969, Jane (Maugham), 1970, A Sentimental Education (Flaubert), 1970, White Walls and Olive Green Carpets, 1971, The Removal Person, 1971, Pandora, 1971, The Virgins, 1972, The Ghost of Christmas Present, 1972, The Trugh Game, 1972, The Moonstone (Collins), The Sullen Sisters, 1972, The Watercress Girl (Bates), 1972, The Higgler, 1973, High Kampf, 1973, Milo O'Shea, 1973, Stone Cold Sober, 1973, The Bitter Pill, 1973, Another Fine Mess, 1973, Judgement Day, 1973, The Travelling Woman, 1973, The Hammer of God, 1974, The Actor and the Alibi, 1974, The Eye of Apollo, 1974, The Forbidden Garden, 1974, The Three Tools of Death, 1974, The Quick One, 1974, London Belongs to Me, 1977, The Last Campaign, 1978, The Ring and the Rose, 1978, Strumpet City, 1979, The Little World of Don Camillo, 1980, Kill, 1982, Good Behaviour, 1982, O'Neill, 1983, Beyond the Pale, 1984, The Irish RM, 1985, Troubles, 1987, Hunted Down, 1989, Parnell and the Englishwoman, 1991, The Celadon Cup, 1993; (TV series) Saki, 1962, Jezebel Ex-UK, 1963, The Hidden Truth, 1964, Undermine, 1964, Blackmail, 1965, Public Eye, 1965, The Liars, 1966, The Informer, 1966, Out of the Unknown, 1966-67, The Sinners, 1970-71, Me Mammy, 1970-71, Tales from the Lazy Acre, 1972, Father Brown, 1974. Died Feb. 12, 2009.

**LÉONTIEFF, ALEXANDRE,** former French Polynesian government official; b. Teahupoo, Tahiti, Oct. 20, 1948; s. Maxime Léontieff and Louise Teahu; m. Demecia Jurd, 1972; 2 children. Degree in Economics, U. Rennes, 1970. Mem. Territorial Assn. French Polynesia, from 1977; v.p. Govt. Polynesia, 1984-86, min. economy, of the sea and tourism, 1986-87, pres., 1987-91; dep. French Nat. Assn., 1986—93; head Caisse de Prévoyance Sociale (CPS), 2004—09. Died Mar. 2, 2009.

**LEOPOLD, MARTIJN GELLIUS,** child psychiatrist, adult and child psychoanalyst; b. Hengelo, OV, Holland, Nov. 20, 1933; s. Robert Louis Leopold and Celine Th. A. (Verstijnen) Deenik; m. Elisabeth van Braam, Oct. 10, 1969 (div. Aug. 1989); children: Jochem, Roelof Pieter, Bas; m. Marion Keyzer, Sept. 8, 1989. Grad., Vossius Gymnasium, Amsterdam, 1953; med. diploma, 1962. Cert. neuropsychiatry, child psychiatry. Pvt. practice child and adult psychiatry, Amsterdam, The Netherlands, from 1969; pvt. practice adult psychoanalyst, from 1977; pvt. practice child psychoanalyst, from 1997. Leading psychiatrist Child Guidance Clinic, Amstelveen, 1970-86; cons. psychiatrist Presch. Daycare Centre, Amsterdam, 1970-86, Psychotherapeutic Inst., Amsterdam, 1986-94; group analyst Trust F. Group Analysis, London, 1970-97. Capt. Med. Forces, 1962-64. Mem. Dutch Soc. Psychiatry, Kon. Ned. Maatschappy Tot Bevordering Der Geneeskunst, Landelyke Specialisten Vereniging, Amsterdamse Specialisten Vereniging (exec. com. 1990-94), Nederlandse Vereniging Voor Psychoanalyse, Soc. Dutch Psychiatrists (past pres., hon. mem.), Dutch Soc. Med. Specialists (exec. com. 1983-89), Dutch Psychiat. Assn. (hon.). Avocations: literature, philosophy, culture. Deceased.

**LEPONIEMI, ARVI KALEVI,** economist, educator; b. Jämijärvi, Finland, July 18, 1926; s. Oskari and Aleksandra (Myllykangas) L.; m. Hilkka Tuulikki Marikainen, Dec. 26, 1956; 2 children. MA, U. Turku, 1949; D of Social Scis., U. Helsinki, 1966. Scientist, sci. dir. Kyösti Haataja Found., Helsinki, 1961—68; prof., docent Helsinki Sch. Econs. and Bus. Adminstrn., 1966-91, pres., 1981-90, reg., 1991. Assoc. prof. U. Helsinki, 1968-73. Editor-in-chief Finnish Econ. Jour., 1990-94; editor books, monographs, and articles in profl. jours. Recipient Fulbright Rsch. award U. Pa., 1962-63. Mem. Finnish Acad. Sci. and Letters (awards 1977, 80), Finnish Soc. Econ. Rsch., Finnish Econ. Assn. (pres. 1974). Avocations: history, literature. Home: Helsinki, Finland. Died Apr. 1, 2002.

**LESACA, REYNALDO MENDOZA,** civil engineer, environmental engineer, sanitary engineer, mathematician, consultant; b. Lipa City, Batangas, The Philippines, Nov. 28, 1922; s. Jose and Rosario (Mendoza) L.; m. Florinda Benitez Jacob; children: Albert, Reynaldo Jr., Evelyn, Robert, Florinda, John, Karl, Bertrand. BS in Civil Engring. cum laude, U. Philippines, Manila, 1943, MS in Math., 1958; MS in Sanitary Engring., U. N.C., 1948; DEng, Johns Hopkins, 1955; MS in Biology, U. Rochester, 1961. Registered civil engr., sanitary engr., environ. planner The Philippines. Prof. pub. health U. Philippines, Manila, 1943-63; commr. Nat. Poll. Contr. Commn., Manila, 1968-76; regional dir., rep. UN environment program Bangkok, 1976-83; sr. advisor on environment Philippine Senate, Manila, 1987-91; pres. Technics, Evaluation, Simulation and Test Cons. Inc., Manila, 1994—95; free-lance environ. engring. cons. Manila, from 1994. Dir. TEST Conss., Inc., Manila, 1985-95; dir., stockholder Asian Inst. Strategic Studies, Manila, 1996—; corp. sec. Asian Inst. Strategic Studies Rsch. Found., Inc., Manila, 1998—; chair bd. sanitary engring. Profl. Regulation Commn., Manila, 1998-2002. Contbr. articles to profl. jours., chpts. to books. Dir. Haribon Found. for Nat. Resources Conservation, Manila, 1984-97, Nat. Integrated Protection Areas, Manila, 1994-97. Recipient Centenary award Sci. and Tech., Adriatico Centennial Commn., 1969, Cert. of Merit award Assn. Govt. Civil Engrs. of the Philippines, 1969, Disting. Alumni award Nat. Def. Coll. The Philippines, 1975, Achievement award Nat. Rsch. Coun. Philippines, 1989; Spl. fellow Woodrow Wilson Internat. Ctr. Scholars, Washington, 1972, East-West Ctr.'s Environment and Policy Inst., Hawaii, 1983; named Outstanding Sanitary Engr., Profl. Regulation Commn., Philippines, 1984. Fellow Philippines Assn. for the Advancement of Sci., Philippine Soc. Sanitary Engrs.; mem. Philippine Assn. Environ. Assessment Profls. (bd. dirs.), Mensa Philippines (chmn.), Toastmasters Internat., Phi Kappa Phi. Roman Catholic. Avocation: flying radio-controlled model planes and helicopters. Home: Quezon City, Philippines. Died Sept. 8, 2005.

**LESLIE, JOHN WILLIAM,** public relations and advertising executive; b. Indpls., Nov. 22, 1923; s. John Edward and Catherine (Harris) L.; m. Joan Williams, Dec. 26, 1970; 1 dau. by previous marriage, Catherine Alexandra. Student, U.S. Naval Acad., 1943-44, George Washington U., 1949, Indsl. Coll. Armed Forces, 1956. Dep. excise adminstr., Ind., 1946-47; pvt. pub. relations bus., 1947-49; dir. pub. relations Ind. Democratic State Central Com., 1948-49, Ind. Dept. Vets. Affairs, 1949; press officer Dept. Labor, 1949-51, acting asst. dir. info., 1951-52, asst. dir., 1952-56, dep. dir., 1956-59, dir., 1959—62; dep. asst. sec. Labor and Dir. Info., 1962—81; charter mem. US Sr. Exec. Svc., from 1979; sr. assoc. Kamber Group, Washington, 1981-84, counselor, 1984-88, exec. v.p., COO, 1988-96, vice chmn., sec., 1997-98, pub. rels. cons., from 1998, also bd. dirs. Mem., dir. pub. D.C. Com. Employment Physically Handicapped, 1952-53 Author numerous articles in field. Advt. cons. Pres.'s Com. on Youth Employment, 1964-80; U.S. del Internat. Graphic Design Coun., Japan, 1973; trustee Washington chpt. Leukemia Soc. Am., 1976-82; chmn. Pub. Printers Adv. Com. on Printing and Publs, 1977-79. Served with USN and USNR, 1941-46. Recipient commendation President's Com. Employment Physically Handicapped, 1954; Disting. Service award Dept. Labor, 1962; citation outstanding service Navy Dept., 1964; Presdl. citation, 1966; Merit award Internat. Labor Press Assn., 1969; Disting. Career Service award Dept. Labor, 1973; Communications award Ga. chpt. Pub. Relations Soc. Am., 1972; Sec. Labor's Recognition award, 1974; Communicator of Yr. award Nat. Assn. Govt. Communicators, 1981 Mem. Am. Assn. Polit. Cons., Am. League Lobbyists, Nat. Press Club, English Speaking Union, Univ. Club (Winter Park, Fla.), Stag Club of Winter Park. Episcopalian. Home: Charlottesville, Va. Died May 16, 2014.

**LESNIK-OBERSTEIN, MAX,** child psychiatrist, educator; b. Havana, Cuba, Mar. 3, 1932; s. Isak Lesnik and Chaya Oberstein; m. Margriet Bijlholt, Mar. 11, 1964 (dec. Sept. 1995); children: Karín, Sarit, Saskia, Maaike. AB, U. Chgo., 1951, BA, 1954, BSc, 1957; MD, U. Amsterdam, The Netherlands, 1969; diploma in psychiatry, U. Toronto, Can., 1972, diploma in child psychiatry, 1975. Traveling fellow Maudsley Hosp., London, 1972-73; lectr. U. Ottawa, Can., 1974-75; head adolescent child psychiatry divsn. Bloemendaal Hosp., The Netherlands, 1975-79; assoc. prof. Free U., Amsterdam, 1979-92; prof. child psychiatry Abenepi, Brazil, from 1984. Head emotional child abuse sect. ISPCAN, Amsterdam, 1981; lectr. numerous univs., 1981—. Assoc. editor: Child Abuse & Neglect, The Internat. Jour., 1986-92; contbr. numerous articles to profl. jours. Fellow Can. Psychiat. Assn.; mem. Royal Coll. Psychiatrists of Gt. Britain, Dutch Psychiat. Assn. Avocations: reading, music, nature, travel. Home: Vouzan, France. Deceased.

**LESNIKOWSKI, WOJCIECH GRZEGORZ,** architectural educator; b. Lublin, Poland, May 9, 1938; s. Roman and Irena Lesnikowski; m. Rebecca James, 1987. MA, Krakow Sch. Architecture & Urban Planning, 1961. Architect Harrison & Abramovitz; prof. architecture Yale U., 1969—72, Cornell U., 1972—78, U. Pa., 1975—79, U. Ill., 1981—88; Hatch prof. archtl. & urban design U. Kans., Lawrence, 1989—2014. Recipient Ordre des Arts et des Lettres, 1990, Krakow Laurel award, 2013. Died Apr. 17, 2014.

**LESSENBERRY, D. D.,** educator; b. Ky., Sept. 7, 1896; s. James David and Martha (Sanders) L.; m. Elona J. Spence, Aug. 28, 1926 (dec. June 1933); m. Bess McC. Dahlinger, Dec. 26, 1945 (dec. Jan. 1973). BS, Duquesne U., 1928; A.M., N.Y.U., 1934; LL.D., Westminister Coll., 1943. Tchr. Allegheny High Sch., Pitts., 1919-27; prin. Allegheny Eve. High Sch., 1923-29, Bus. High Sch., Pitts., 1929-30; dir. courses bus. edn. U. Pitts., 1930-55, prof. edn., 1930-62, prof. edn. emeritus, from 1962. Author: College Typewriting, coll. edit, 1930-42, 7th edit, (with S.J. Wanous and C. H. Duncan), 1964-65, 8th edit., 1969, 9th edit., 1976, 20th Century Typewriting, complete, (edit. 1-10), 1927-71, (with others) Century Typewriting 21, 2d edit, 1977. Recipient John Robert Gregg award, 1955 Mem. Nat. Bus. Tchrs. Fedn. (pres. 1935), Eastern Bus. Tchrs. Assn. (bd. dirs. 1930-35, pres. 1944), Nat. Bus. Edn. Assn., Tri-State Bus. Edn. Assn. (pres. 1942), Phi Delta Kappa, Kappa Phi Kappa, Delta Delta Lambda, Delta Pi Epsilon (pres. 1941-42), Phi Eta Sigma. Clubs: Duquesne (Pitts.). Home: Pittsburgh, Pa. Died Dec. 5, 1988.

**LESSING, DORIS MAY,** writer; b. Kermanshah, Persia, Oct. 22, 1919; d. Alfred Cook and Emily Maude (McVeagh) Tayler; m. Frank Charles Wisdom, 1939 (div. 1943); children: John(dec.), Jean; m. Gottfried Anton Nicholas Lessing, 1945 (dissolved 1949); 1 child, Peter (dec.). Educated in, Southern Rhodesia; DLitt (hon.), Princeton U., 1989, Durham U., 1990; D Fellow in Lit., Sch., Eng. American Studies (hon.), U. East Anglia, 1991; DLitt (hon.), Warwick U., 1994; LittD (hon.), Bard Coll., 1994, Harvard U., 1995, Open Univ., 1999, Univ. London, 1999. Author: (nonfiction) In Pursuit of the English, 1961, Particularly Cats, 1967, Going Home, 1968, Prisons We Choose to Live Inside, 1987, The Wind Blows Away Our Words...and Other Documents Relating to the Afghan Resistance, 1987, African Laughter: Four Visits to Zimbabwe, 1992, Particularly Cats and Rufus the Survivor, 1993, A Small Personal Voice, 1994, Under My Skin: Volume One of My Autobiography, to 1949, 1994 (James Tait Black Meml. prize, 1995, LA Book prize, 1995), Walking in the Shade: Volume Two of My Autobiography, 1949-62, 1997, The Old Age of El

Magnifico, 2000, On Cats, 2002, Time Bites, 2004, On Not Winning the Nobel Prize, 2008, (novels) The Grass is Singing, 1950, Retreat to Innocence, 1959, The Golden Notebook, 1962 (Prix Médicis, France, 1976), Children of Violence, 5 vols., 1964—69, Briefing For a Descent Into Hell, 1971, The Summer Before the Dark, 1973, The Memoirs of a Survivor, 1975, Shikasta, 1979, Marriages Between Zones Three, Four and Five, 1980, The Sirian Experiments, 1981, The Making of the Representative for Planet 8, 1982, The Sentimental Agents in the Volyen Empire, 1983, The Good Terrorist, 1985 (W.H. Smith Lit. award, 1986), The Fifth Child, 1988, Playing the Game, 1995, Love, Again, 1996, Mara and Dann, 1999, Ben, In The World, 2000, The Sweetest Dream, 2001, Love Child, 2003, The Story of General Dann and Mara's Daughter Griot and the Snow Dog, 2006, The Cleft, 2007, Alfred and Emily, 2008, (Children of Violence series) Martha Quest, 1952, A Proper Marriage, 1954, A Ripple from the Storm, 1958, Landlocked, 1965, The Four-Gated City, 1969, (under pseudonym Jane Somers) Diary of a Good Neighbour, 1983, and If the Old Could..., 1984, (short story collections) This Was the Old Chief's Country, 1952, Five Short Novels, 1953 (Somerset Maugham award, Soc. Authors, 1954), The Habit of Loving, 1957, A Man and Two Women, 1963, African Stories, 1965, The Black Madonna, 1966, Winter in July, 1966, The Story of a Non-Marrying Man, 1972, This Was the Old Chief's Country: Collected African Stories, Vol. 1, 1973, The Sun Between Their Feet: Collected African Stories, Vol. 2, 1973, The Temptation of Jack Orkney and Other Stories, 1978, To Room 19: Collected Stories, Vol. 1, 1978, Through the Tunnel, 1990, London Observed: Stories and Sketches, 1992, The Real Thing: Stories and Sketches, 1992, Spies I Have Known, 1995, The Pit, 1996, The Grandmothers, 2003, (plays) Each in His Own Wilderness, 1958, Play with a Tiger, 1973, The Singing Door, 1973, (poetry) Fourteen Poems, 1959, (Operas) (music by Philip Glass) The Making of the Representative for Planet 8, 1988, The Marriages Between Zones Three, Four and Five, 1997. Recipient Austrian State prize for European lit., 1981, Shakespeare prize, Germany, 1982, Grinzane Cavour award, Italy, 1989, Cataluna Internat. award, Spain, 1999, David Cohen British Literature prize, 2001, Prince of Asturias prize for Literature, Spain, 2001, S.T. Dupont Golden PEN award, 2002, Nobel Prize in Literature, Swedish Acad., 2007. Died Nov. 17, 2013.

**LESUR, DANIEL,** composer; b. Paris, Nov. 19, 1908; s. Robert and Alice (Thiboust) L.; m. Simone Lauer, Mar. 30, 1943; children: Christian, Beatrice (Mrs. J.P. Brichant). Student, Paris Conservatoire, 1919-29. Pianist, organist suppleant Basilica of Sainte-Clotilde, 1927-37; organist Benedictine Abbey, Paris, 1937-44; prof. counterpoint Schola Cantorum, 1935-57, prof. composition, 1957-64, dir., 1957-61, hon. dir., 1966—2002. Composer music for films; mus. adviser Radiodiffusion-Television Française, Paris, 1961-69, Administrateur Reunion des Theatres Lyriques Nationaux, 1971-73; insp. music Ministry Cultural Affairs, 1969-78, insp. gen. Mem. French commn., 1969-78, ins. gen. Mem. French commn. UNESCO, 1958-2002. Composer: Suite Francaise, 1935, Passacaille, 1937, Pastorale, 1938, Ricercare, 1939, Suite Pour Quatuor A Cordes, 1940, Suite Medievale, 1946, Sextuor, 1949, Andrea Del Sarto (symphonic poem) 1949, Ouverture for a Festival, 1951, Annonciation (oratorio), 1951, Song of Songs, 1953, Chamber Concerto for piano and orch., 1953; Cantique des Colonnes for voice and orch., 1954; Le Bal du Destin (ballet), 1954, Serenade, 1954; Elegie 2 guitars, 1956; Dance Symphony, 1956; Jubilee Mass, 1960; Fantasy for 2 pianos, 1962, Andrea del Sarto (opera), 1968, Symphonie, 1975; Ondine (opera) 1982, La Reine Morte, 1987 (opera); Dialogues dans La Nuit, Encore un Instant de Bonheur (cantate), Le Voyage D'automne, 1991, A La Lisiere Du Temps, 1991, Permis De Sejour, 1991, Stele, flute and orch., 1991, Dialogues Imaginaires, 1991; Fantasie Concertante for cello and orch., 1992, Vert Paradis, 1992, for voices and string quartet Quatre Nocturnes, 1993, La Nuit Reve, for two voices and orch., 1994, Lamento, 1995; contbr. articles to profl. jours. Decorated grand officier Legion of Honor, comdr. Nat. Order of Merit, comdr. Order Arts and Letters; recipient Grand prize Gen. Council Seine, 1964, Ville de Paris, Conseil Municipal, 1969; grand prize Soc. Authors and Composers, Prix Samuel-Rousseau, Academie des Beaux-Arts, Prix Internat. Maurice Ravel, 1994, Grand prix du Disque, Nouvelle Acad. du Disque, 1994. Mem. Acad. Charles Cros (prés d'honneur), Inst. France, Royal Acad. Belgium, Acad. Européenne Scis., des Arts et des Lettres. Home: Puteaux, France. Died July 2, 2002.

**LETSINGER, ROBERT LEWIS,** chemistry professor; Student, Ind. U., 1939-41; BS in Chemistry, MIT, 1943, PhD in Organic Chemistry, 1945; DSc (hon.), Acadia U., Can., 1993. Research assoc. MIT, 1945-46; research chemist Tenn. Eastman Corp., 1946; faculty Northwestern U., 1946—2014, prof. chemistry, 1959—86, chmn. dept., 1972-75, joint prof. biochemistry and molecular biology, 1974—91, Clare Hamilton Hall prof. chemistry, 1986—91, Clare Hamilton Hall prof. emeritus chemistry, 1991—2014; co-founder Nanosphere Inc., 2000—14; adj. prof. Ind. U., 2002—05. Med. and organic chemistry fellowship panel NIH, 1966-69, mem. physiol. chemistry review group, 1984, bio-organic and natural products chemistry study sect., 1985, chmn. spl. proposal rev. com., 1992; medicinal chem. A study sect., 1971-75; bd. on chem. scis. and tech. NRC, 1987-90, chmn. site visit NRC rsch. assocs., Frank J. Seiler rsch. lab, 1990; mem. steering com. Inst. Medicine Workshop; mem. AIDS project concept rev. panel, 1987; mem. program rev. divsn. biochem. and biophysics, FDA; mem. spl. rev. com. human genome program, 1992; mem. spl. emphasis panel for nat. coop. drug discovery groups for treatment of HIV infection. Bd. editors: Nucleic Acids Rsch., 1990—2002, Oligonucleotides, 2002—08. Recipient Rosenstiel medallion, 1985, NIH merit award, 1988, Arthur C. Cope scholar award, 1993, B.F. Goodrich Collegiate Inventors award, 1997, Humboldt prize, Germany, 1989; Guggenheim Fellow, 1956, JSPS fellow, Japan, 1978. Fellow American Acad. Arts & Sciences, Nat. Acad. Sciences, American Assn. Arts & Sciences, Royal Soc. Chemistry; mem. American Chem. Soc. (bd. editors 1969-72, adv. bd. for bioconjugate chemistry 1992-2014, editl. bd. oligonucleotides, 2004-14), Sigma Xi, Phi Lambda Upsilon (hon. mem.). Achievements include development of chemistry (eg. solid phase synthesis of DNA and utilization of phosphite intermediates) enabling the rapid and effecient synthesis of DNA that has facilited development of molecular biology; medical diagnostics, and the chemistry of self assembly systems. Avocations: golf, hiking. Home: Seattle, Wash. Died May 26, 2014.

**LEVEY, MICHAEL VINCENT,** art historian, author; b. London, June 8, 1927; s. O. L.H. and Gladys Mary (Milestone) Levey; m. Brigid Brophy, June 12, 1954; 1 child, Katharine Jane. Grad. in English Lang. & Lit. with honours, Exeter Coll., Oxford, 1950; DLitt (hon.), Manchester U. Asst. keeper Nat. Gallery, London, 1951—66, dep. keeper, 1966—68, keeper, 1968—70, dep. dir., 1970—73, dir., 1973—86. Slade prof., fine art Cambridge U., 1963—64, Oxford U., 1994—95; Wrightsman lectr. NY U., 1968; hon. fellow Exeter Coll., 1973. Author: National Gallery Catalogues, 1956, 1959, 1971, Painting in XVIIIth Century Venice, 1959, rev. edit., 1994, From Giotto to Cezanne, 1962, Durer, 1964, Later Italian Pictures in the Royal Collection, 1964, rev. edit., 1991, Rococo to Revolution, 1966, Early Renaissance, 1967 (Hawthornden prize, 1968), Concise History of Western Art, 1968, Painting at Court, 1971, The Life and Death of Mozart, 1971, Art and Architecture in 18th Century France, 1972, High Renaissance, 1975, The World of Ottoman Art, 1976, The Case of Walter Pater, 1978, (exhbn. catalogue) Sir Thomas Lawrence, 1979, (fiction) Tempting Fate, 1982, An Affair on the Appian Way, 1985, Giambattista Tiepolo, 1986 (Banister Fletcher prize, 1987), Men at Work, 1989, Painting and Sculpture in France 1700-1789, 1992, Florence: A Portrait, 1996; editor: Pater's Marius the Epicurean, 1985. Capt. King's Shropshire Light Inf., with Edn. Corps, 1945—48. Decorated Lt. Victorian Order, knight batchelor. Fellow: Royal Soc. Lit., Brit. Acad.; mem.: Ateneo Veneto (fgn. mem.). Home: Lincolnshire, England. Died Dec. 28, 2008.

**LEVINGSTON, JOHN COLVILLE BOWRING,** telecommunications executive; b. Rawalpindi, Punjab, Pakistan, Apr. 10, 1929; came to U.S. 1961; s. Thomas Clarke and Kathleen Patricia (Farley) L.; m. Elizabeth Ann Baumer, June 6, 1958 (div. Apr. 1968); m. Paula Angela Eriksen, Feb. 29, 1980 (div. Jan. 2000); children: Thomas Arthur, Alexandra Jane. Grad., Harrow Sch., Eng., Royal Mil. Acad., Sandhurst, Eng. Sales mgr. British-Am. Tobacco Co., East Africa, 1952-55, W.L. Mackenzie Co., Vancouver, B.C., Can., 1957-61; v.p. Precipitator Inc., Santa Fe Springs, Calif., 1973-78; cons. Calif. Inst. Tech., Pasadena, 1979; v.p. Kingmont Oil, Pine Knot, Ky., 1980; cons. Sta. KCET-TV, Hollywood, Calif., 1981; founder, chmn. Straightley Films, Hollywood, 1982-86; founder, chmn., chief exec. officer Interactive Telemedia, Sherman Oaks, Calif., 1986-89; chmn. Levingston & Assocs., Beverly Hills, Calif., from 1989; founder, CEO, Home Savings Trust Ltd., from 1994. Inventor Straightley automobile, 1969. Lt. Parachute Regt., 1950-52. Mem. NATAS, SAG, Internat. Platform Assn., Masons. Avocations: music, writing, racquetball, golf. Deceased.

**LEVINSON, MON,** artist; b. NYC, Jan. 6, 1926; BS, U. Pa., 1948. One man shows, 1961-2014, Fine Art Mus. L.I., 1981, Getler/Pall Gallery, N.Y.C., 1981, Andre Zarre Gallery, N.Y.C., 1989, Fridholm Fine Arts, Asheville, N.C., 1989, G.K. Harris Gallery, N.Y.C., 1997-98; exhibited in numerous group shows, 1960-2014, including Newark Mus., Whitney Mus. American Art, 1978, Albright Knox Art Gallery, 1980, Bklyn. Mus., 1987; represented in permanent collections Albright-Knox Gallery, Bklyn. Mus., Herbert F. Johnson Mus. Art, Malmo Art Mus., Newark Mus., Rose Art Mus., Smithsonian Instn., Whitney Mus., many others. Recipient CAPS award N.Y. State Coun. on Arts, award Cassandra Found.; grantee Nat. Endowment Arts. Home: New York, NY. Died Mar. 25, 2014.

**LEVIT, WILLIAM HAROLD,** lawyer; b. San Francisco, Jan. 11, 1908; s. Morris and Fannie (Jacobs) Levit; m. Barbara Kaiser, June 9, 1933 (dec. Aug. 1986); children: Jacqueline Weisberg, William H. Jr.; m. Marion Elizabeth Miller, May 11, 1987. BA, Stanford U., 1928, JD, 1930. Bar: Calif. 1930, US Dist. Ct. (no. and cen. dists.) Calif. 1930, US Ct. Appeals (9th cir.) 1930, US Supreme Ct. 1942. Ptnr. Long & Levit, San Francisco and LA, 1930—62; judge Superior Ct. Calif. LA County, 1962—76; instr. jud. adminstrn. U. Southern Calif. Law Ctr., 1968—71; mem. faculty Nat. Jud. Coll., 1965—68, 1973, Jud. Council Calif., 1969—71; co-founder, dean Calif. Jud. Coll., 1971; founding mem. governing bd. Calif. Ctr. Jud. Edn. and Rsch., 1973—76; of counsel LA, 1976—78, Stroock & Stroock & Lavan, LA, NYC, Washington, Miami, Fla., from 1978. Author: Pretrial Conference Manual, 1966, Coordination of Civil Actions, 1976, California Judicial Retirement Handbook, 4th edit., 1989; contbr. articles to legal and other profl. publs. Vice pres. Calif. Judges Assn., 1971—72. Served to lt. col. JAGC US Army, 1942—45. Decorated Bronze Star; recipient President's Cup, Calif. Judges Assn., 1983. Fellow: Am. Coll. Trial Lawyers; mem.: Inst. Jud. Adminstrn., Italian Bar (hon.). Deceased.

**LEVY, HAROLD P.,** public relations consultant; b. Trinidad, Colo., Mar. 8, 1907; s. Phan and Fannie (Akerman) Levy; m. Alice Klund Levy, Sept. 9, 1938. AB, U. Wash., 1929. Reporter Seattle Union Record and Seattle Post-Intelligencer, 1926—2029; reporter, editor Seattle Times, 1929—34; resident writer Henry St. Settlement, NYC, 1934—2029; dir. publicity Nat. Conf. Social Work, Columbus, Ohio, 1935—39; rsch. assoc. Russell Sage Found., NYC, 1939—45; nat. dir. pub. rels. Commn. Cmty. Interrelations, NYC, 1945—47; founder, pres. Harold P. Levy Pub. Rels., LA, 1947—87; faculty U. Calif. Ext., 1947—49. Bd. dirs. Pub. Health Nursing, 1949—52, Tb and Health Assn., LA County, 1958—64, Pasadena Symphony Orch., 1981—84; pres. Tb and Health Assn., 1962—63. Author: A Study in Public Rels., 1943, Building a Popular Movement, 1944, Public Relations Social Agys., 1956, There Were Days Like That, 1985; contbr. articles to profl. jours. Mem.: Sigma Delta Chi, Pub. Rels. Soc. Am., Athenaeum, Assocs. Calif. Inst. Tech. Died Aug. 15, 1989.

**LEVY, JACK I.,** lawyer, business executive; b. Brownsville, Pa., Aug. 22, 1910; s. Morris and Belle (Wise) L.; m. Hariet Mindich, June 11, 1943; children— Margaret J. (Mrs. Castro), James B. AB, U. Mich., 1931, JD, 1934. With law firm Sonnenschein, Carlin, Nath & Rosenthal, Chgo., 1935-59; v.p., dir. Gen. Am. Transp. Corp., Chgo., 1959-80; ret., 1980. Mem. Am., Ill., Chgo. bar assns. Home: Fort White, Fla. Died Oct. 1988.

**LEWIS, DANIEL EDWIN,** lawyer; b. Goshen, Ind., May 2, 1910; s. Daniel Arthur and Emma (Williams) Lewis; m. Annette Jean Fewell, July 28, 1934; children: Daniel E., Nancy Jean Haswell. AB, Hanover Coll., Ind., 1932; MS, Ind. U., 1939; JD, Valparaiso U., 1949. Bar: Ind. 1949. Tchr. Secondary Schs., Ind., 1932—43; dir. indsl. rels. Allis-Chalmers, LaPorte, Ind., 1943—55; ptnr. Newby, Lewis & Kaminski, LaPorte, from 1955, counsel. Author: (fiction) At the Crossroads, 1980, So It Comes to Arbitration, 1982. Chmn. LaPorte County ARC, 1948—49; pres. LaPorte Bd. Edn., 1952—55, United Fund, 1957—65, LaPorte YMCA, 1960—62, LaPorte County Human Rels. Bd., 1967—68, LaPorte County Family Svc., 1975—77; treas. Health Care Fedn., 1982; vice chmn. Pottawatomie County Boy Scouts America, 1963—69. Recipient Alumni Achievement award, Hanover Coll., 1965; named to Football Hall of Fame, LaPorte. Fellow: Ind. State Bar Found.; mem.: ABA, Soc. Profls. Dispute Resolution, LaPorte City and County Bar Assn., Ind. State Bar Assn., Masons, Elks (Elk of Yr. 1989), Kiwanis (Kiwanian of Yr. 1987). Presbyterian. Died Oct. 15, 1997.

**LEWIS, EMANUEL RAYMOND,** historian, psychologist, retired librarian; b. Oakland, Calif., Nov. 30, 1928; s. Jacob A. and Rose Lewis; m. Joan R. Wilson, Feb. 7, 1954; 1 son, Joseph J.; m. Eleanor M. Gamarsh, Aug. 24, 1967. BA, U. Calif., Berkeley, 1951, MA, 1953; PhD, U. Oreg., 1962. Asst. prof. psychology We. Oreg. U., 1961-62, Oreg. State U., 1962-67; project mgr. System Devel. Corp., Falls Church, Va., 1968-69; vis. postdoctoral research asso. in Am. history Smithsonian Instn., Washington, 1969-70; chief historian, dir. rsch. Contract Archeology, Alexandria, Va., 1971-73; libr. US House of Representatives, Washington, 1973-95, libr. emeritus, 1995. Author: Seacoast Fortifications of the United States, 1970, 2d edit. 1979, 3d edit. 1993; editor: The Educational Information Center, 1969. Served with M.I. U.S. Army, 1954-56. NIMH research fellow, 1960 Home: Washington, DC. Died May 14, 2014.

**LEWIS, GRAHAM THOMAS,** analytical inorganic chemist; b. Broken Hill, NSW, Australia, May 28, 1944; s. Lawrence Michael and Jessie (Ripper) L.; m. Susanne Brook, May 10, 1969; children: Melissa Jean, Simon Matthew, Katrina Jane. BS, U. NSW. Cadet metallurgist North Broken Hill Ltd., 1962-69, asst. chief chemist, 1970, chief assayer, 1970, chief analyst, 1971-76, chief chemist, 1976-85, supt. metall. lab., 1985-89; supt. analytical svcs. Pasminco Mining, Broken Hill, 1989-93. Mem. Broken Hill Lead Dust Monitoring Com., 1986-91. Fellow Australasian Inst. Mining and Metallurgy (past br. chmn., local com.); mem. Royal Australian Chem. Inst. (local committeeman 1978-93, br. chmn. 1991-93). Anglican. Home: Glen Osmond, Australia. Died Oct. 12, 2001.

**LEWIS, PETER BENJAMIN,** insurance company executive; b. Cleve., Nov. 11, 1933; s. Joseph M. and Helen (Rosenfeld) Lewis; m. Toby Devan, June 19, 1955 (div. 1980); children: Ivy, Jonathan, Adam; m. Janet Rosel, 2013. AB, Princeton U., NJ, 1955. Underwriting trainee Progressive Ins. Cos., 1955; exec. trainee Progressive Casualty Ins. Co., pres., CEO, 1965-94, Progressive Corp., Ohio, 1965-2000, chmn. bd., 2000—13. Bd. trustees Solomon R. Guggenheim Mus. Named one of The Top 200 Collectors, ARTnews Mag., 2004, The Forbes 400: Richest Americans, 2006—13. Democrat. Achievements include a contribution to Princeton University, which allowed the university to establish a science library and the Lewis-Sigler Institute for Integrative Genomics; one of the most significant benefactors in all of Princeton University's history in 2006, recent contribution will allow for the expansion of the creative & performing arts program. Avocation: collecting Contemporary art. Home: Avon Lake, Ohio. Died Nov. 23, 2013.

**LEWIS, SAMUEL WINFIELD,** retired federal agency administrator, diplomat; b. Houston, Oct. 1, 1930; s. Samuel Winfield and Sue Roselle (Hurley) L.; m. Sallie Kate Smoot, June 20, 1953; children: Pamela Gracelle, Richard Winfield. BA magna cum laude, Yale U., 1952; MA, Johns Hopkins U. Sch. Advanced Internat. Studies, 1954; PhD (hon.), Tel Aviv U., 1985, Hebrew U. Jerusalem, 1985, Weizman Inst. Sci., 1985; DHL (hon.), Hebrew Union Coll., 1986, Balt. Hebrew U., 1988; LLD (hon.), Salem-Teikyo U., 1991. Exec. asst. American Trucking Assn., Washington, 1953-54; fgn. svc. officer US Dept. State, Washington, 1954-85; consular officer US Embassy, Naples, Italy, 1954-55, consul Florence, Italy, 1955-59, officer-in-charge Italian affairs Washington, 1959-61; spl. asst. to under sec. US Dept. State, Washington, 1961; spl. asst. to spl. rep. of Pres. The White House, Washington, 1961-63; dep. asst. dir. Mission to Brazil US Agy. for Internat. Devel. (USAID), Rio de Janeiro, 1964-65; exec. officer US Embassy, Rio de

Janeiro, 1965-67; dep. dir. Office Brazil Affairs US Dept. State, Washington, 1967-68; sr. staff mem. for Latin American Affairs NSC, Washington, 1968-69; spl. asst. for policy planning Bur. Inter-American Affairs US Dept. State, Washington, 1969, spl. asst. to dir. gen. Fgn. Svc., 1970-71; dep. chief mission & counselor embassy US Embassy, Kabul, Afghanistan, 1971-74; dep. dir. policy planning US Dept. State, 1974-75, asst. sec. for internat. orgn. affairs Washington, 1975-77, US amb. to Israel Tel Aviv, 1977-85; lectr., diplomat-in-residence Johns Hopkins Fgn. Policy Inst., Washington, 1985-86; pres. US Inst. of Peace, Washington, 1987-93; dir. policy planning US Dept. State, Washington, 1993-94, cons., 1994-95. Sr. internat. fellow The Dayan Ctr., Tel Aviv U., 1986-87; chmn. bd. overseers Harry S. Truman Rsch. Inst. for Advancement of Peace, Hebrew U., 1986-91; guest scholar The Brookings Inst., Washington, 1987; mem. bd. advisors Washington Inst. Near East Policy, 1986-93, 98-2014, counselor, 1995-98; adv. com. Search for Common Ground in the Mid. East, Washington, 1994-2014, chmn., 2005-14; vis. prof. Hamilton Coll., spring 1995, fall 1997, spring 2008, adj. prof. Sch. Fgn. Svc., Georgetown U., 1996; sr. advisor Israel Policy Forum, 1998-2014; profl. lectr. Nitze Sch. Advanced Internat. Studies, Johns Hopkins U., 2006; lectr. in field. Author: Making Peace Among Arabs and Israelis, 1991; contbg. author: The Middle East: Ten Years After Camp David, 1988, Soviet-American Competition in the Middle East, 1988, Israel: The Peres Era, 1987, The United States States and Israel: Evolution of an Unwritten Alliance, 1999; contbr. articles to profl. jours., also NY Times, Washington Post. Bd. dirs. Inst. for Study Diplomacy, Georgetown U., 1994-2014; vice chmn. Ctr. Preventive Action, Coun. Fgn. Rels., 1994-97. Recipient William A. Jump award for Outstanding Service in Public Adminstrn., 1967, Meritorious Honor award US Dept. State, 1967, Meritorious Honor award US Agy. for Internat. Devel. (USAID), 1967, Pres.' Mgmt. Improvement cert., 1971, Distinguished Honor award Dept. State, 1977, 85, Disting. Alumnus award Johns Hopkins U., 1980, Wilbur J. Carr award US Dept. State, 1985; vis. fellow Princeton U., 1963-64. Mem. American Acad. Diplomacy (bd. dirs. 1995-2014, vice chmn. bd. dirs. 1995-99), Am. Fgn. Svc. Assn., US Interreligious Com. for Peace in the Middle East, UN Assn., Middle East Inst., Assn. Diplomatic Studies and Tng. (bd. dirs. 1995-2005, 2006—09), Ch. Mid. East Peace, Inst. World Affairs (bd. dirs. 1996-2005), Ch. Middle East Peace (advisor 2011-14), Ptnrs. for Dem. Change (bd. dirs. 2004-14), Cousteau Soc., Sierra Club, Phi Beta Kappa. Episcopalian. Died Mar. 10, 2014.

**LEWIS, SYDNEY,** retail company executive; b. Richmond, Va., Oct. 24, 1919; s. Julius Beryl and Dora (Lewis) L.; m. Frances Aaronson, Sept. 3, 1942; children: Sydney Jr., Andrew Marc, Susan (Mrs. Dixon Butler). BA, Washington and Lee U., 1940; postgrad. in law, Washington Lee U., 1940-42; postgrad. bus. adminstrn., Harvard, 1942-43; LLB, George Washington U., 1946; HHD (hon.), Va. Commonwealth U., 1983; degree in patron of arts (hon.), Va. Mus. Fine Arts. Bar: Va. 1942, D.C. 1947. V.p. New Standard Pub. Co. Inc., Richmond, 1947-58, pres., from 1958; also dir.; founding pres., chmn. Best Products Co. Inc., Richmond, from 1951, also dir. Pres. Richmond Jewish Community Council, 1953—, Va. Mus., 1986—; trustee Washington and Lee U., Lexington, Va., Va. Union Univ., Richmond; trustee Hirshorn Mus., Washington, 1976—, chmn., 1985, pres., 1985—; trustee Inst. Contemporary Art, Phila., 1975—, Sch. Visual Arts, Boston U., 1976—, Va. Environ. Endowment Fund, Va. Found. for Humanities and Public Policy, Hebrew Union Coll., Cin., Hirshorn Mus., 1985—, Bklyn. Acad. Music, N.Y., 1985—; mem. bd. assocs. U. Richmond.; trustee Va. Mus. Fine Arts, 1980—, pres., 1986—; trustee Council of Nat. Gallery Art, Washington, 1983; bd. dirs. Jobs for Va. Grads., Commonwealth of Va., 1985. Recipient Disting. Virginian award, 1972, nat. honoree award Beta Gamma Sigma, 1976, ann. award Federated Arts Council of Richmond, 1976, Jackson Davis award for disting. service to higher edn. in Va., 1978, Thomas Jefferson award for pub. service, 1978, Retailer of Yr. award Va. Retail Mchts. Assn., 1982, Medal of Honor Nat. DAR, 1983, Hon. Degree Dr. of Humanities, Va. Commonwealth U., 1983, Gov.'s awards Arts of Va., 1985, Disting. Retailers award Retail Mchts. Assn. Greater Richmond, 1985, Archtl. Medal for Va. Service award Va. Soc. AIA, 1986, Pres.'s Nat. Medal of Arts award, 1987, Skowhegan Gertrude Vanderbilt Whitney award, 1990, William P. Robinson Sr. Dem. award, 1989, Detocqueville Soc. Greater Richmon award, 1990, ABG Disting. Svc. award, 1991, Va. Cultural Laureate award, 1992, Bernard Glasser Meml. award Anti-Defamation League of B'nai B'rith; named to Richmond Bus. Hall Fame, 1989. Mem.: Lakeside Country. Home: Richmond, Va. Died Mar. 12, 1999.

**LIACOS, PAUL JULIAN,** retired judge; b. Peabody, Mass., Nov. 20, 1929; s. James A. and Pitsa K. (Karis) L.; m. Maureen G. McKean, Oct. 6, 1954; children: James P., Diana M., Mark C., Gregory A. AB magna cum laude, Boston U. Coll. Liberal Arts, 1950; LLB magna cum laude, Boston U., 1952; LLM, Harvard U., 1953; diploma, Air Command and Staff Sch., 1954; LLD, Suffolk U., 1984, New Eng. Sch. Law, 1985; LHD (hon.), Salem State Coll., 1988; LLD, Northeastern U., 1991, Boston U., 1996. Bar: Mass. 1952, U.S. Dist. Ct. Mass. 1954, U.S. Ct. Mil. Appeals 1955, U.S. Ct. Appeals (1st cir.) 1971, U.S. Supreme Ct. 1980. Ptnr. firm Liacos and Liacos, Peabody, Mass., 1952-76; prof. law Boston U., 1952-76, adj. prof. law, 1976-89; assoc. justice Mass. Supreme Jud. Ct., 1976-89, chief justice, 1989-96; Disting. lectr. on law U.S. Mil. Acad., West Point, N.Y., 1972; lectr. Suffolk U. Sch. Law, 1978-79; U.S. Constn. Bicentennial lectr. Boston Pub. Libr., 1987; cons. on staffing and pers. Atty. Gen. of Mass., 1974-75; lectr. on criminal evidence Boston Police Acad., 1963-64; reporter New Eng. Conf. on Def. of the Indigent, Harvard Law Sch., 1963; reader and cons. on legal manuscripts Little, Brown & Co., Boston, 1968-76; editl. cons. Warren, Gorham & Lamont, 1968-69; mem. State Ethics Commn., from 1998. Mem. steering com. Lawyers Com. for Civil Rights under Law, Boston, 1969-72; chmn. com. on discrimination in the cts. Conf. of Chief Justices, 1993-96. Author: Handbook of Massachusetts Evidence, 6th edit., 1994, supplement, 1998, 98; contbr. articles in field to legal jours.; book rev. editor Boston U. law Rev., 1952. Trustee Suffolk U., Boston, 1993-99; trustee, mem. exec. com. Chamberlayne Sch. and Jr. Coll., Boston, 1982-84; trustee Anatolia Coll., Salonika, Greece, 1980-99, exec. com., 1986-89; hon. trustee Deree-Pierce Colls., Athens, 1976-99; corp. mem. MIT, 1989-96 Named Man of Yr. Boston U. Law Sch., 1952, Man of Yr. Alpha Omega, 1977, Mem. Colleguum Disting. Alumni Boston U. Coll. Liberal Arts, 1974; recipient Disting. Pub. Svc. award Boston U. Alumni, 1980, Allied Profl. award Mass. Psychol. Assn., 1987, Man of Vision award Nat. Soc. to Prevent Blindness, 1988, State Bill of Rights award Nat. Assn. Criminal Def. Lawyers, 1988, Good Neighbor award Mishkan Tefila Brotherhood, 1990, Founders' award Lawyers Com. for Civil Rights Under the Law, Boston Bar Assn., 1993, citation of jud. excellence Boston Bar Assn., 1995, Ehrman award Mass. Crime and Justice Found., 1996, award Fed. Bar Assn., 1996, Mass. Jud. Conf. award, 1996, Social Law Libr. award, 1996. Mem. ABA (jud. cert. of appreciation 1994), ATLA (editor 1968-73, Outstanding State Appellate Judge 1982), Mass. Bar Assn. (criminal law com. 1964-66), Essex County Bar Assn., Peabody Bar Assn., Greater Lowell Bar Assn. (hon.), Harvard Law Sch. Assn., Mass. Supreme Jud. Ct. Hist. Soc. (chmn. 1996—), Boston U. Law Sch. Alumni Assn. (Silver Shingle award 1977), Phi Beta Kappa. Democrat. Mem. Greek Orthodox Ch. Home: Peabody, Mass. Died May 6, 1999.

**LIBA, PETER MICHAEL,** Canadian provincial government official, retired communications executive; b. Winnipeg, Man., Can., May 10, 1940; s. Theodore and Rose Liba; m. Shirley Ann Collett, May 4, 1963; children: Jennifer Lacombe, Jeffrey, Christopher. LLD (hon.), U. Manitoba, 2001, Brandon U., 2004. Reporter, news editor The Daily Graphic, The Neepawa Press, Portage la Prairie, Man., 1957-59; reporter The Winnipeg Tribune, 1959-67, city editor, 1967-68; ind. comm. cons. Winnipeg, 1968-73; v.p. pub. affairs CanWest Broadcasting Ltd., Winnipeg, 1974-75, exec. v.p., 1979-97; asst. gen. mgr. Sta. CKND-TV, Winnipeg, 1975-79, mgr., 1980-87, gen. mgr., 1987-92; pres., CEO CKND TV Inc./SaskWest TV Inc., Winnipeg, 1988-94; exec. v.p. CanWest Global Comm. Corp., Winnipeg, 1993—99; lt. gov. Province of Man., Canada, 1999—2004; regional chmn. Can. Forces Liaison Coun., 2004—06, nat. vice chmn., from 2006. Bd. dirs. Global Comm. Ltd., Toronto, CanWest Broadcasting Ltd., Winnipeg, CanWest TV, Inc., Winnipeg, CanWest Prodns., Ltd., Winnipeg, CanWest Properties Ltd., Winnipeg, CanWest Maritime TV, Inc., Halifax, TV 3 Network, New Zealand, Network Ten, Australia; pres. Peli Ventures, Inc., 1975—; global advisor, dir. Global Coll., U. Winnipeg, 2005—; dir. Winnipeg Harvest Foodbank, CanWest Mediaworks; bd. chair, trustee Canwest Mediaworks Fund. Trustee Transcona-Springfield Sch. divsn., Winnipeg, Winnipeg, Canada, 1964—67; founding chmn. Variety Club Telethon, Manitoba, Canada; chmn. Winnipeg Conv. Ctr/; bd. dirs. Conv. Ctr. Corp., Winnipeg, 1976—86, chmn. bd. dirs., 1981—84; bd. dirs. Atomic Energy of Can., Ltd., Ottawa, Ont., 1981—86, St. Boniface Gen. Hosp., Winnipeg, 1987—99. Named to Can. Broadcasters Hall of Fame, 1998, Spl. Gold Ribbon award 1999. Mem. Broadcasters Assn. Man. (pres. 1981-82), Western Assn. Broadcasters (pres. 1984-85, Broadcaster of Yr. award 1991, Broadcaster of Decade award 1994), Can. Assn. Broadcasters (chmn. bd. 1990-92, Spl. Gold Ribbon award 1999, named to Can. Broadcasters Hall of Fame, 1998), Variety Club Man. (chief barker 1984-85). Home: Winnipeg, Canada. Died June 21, 2007.

**LIBRETTO, ELLEN VIRGINIA,** writer; b. NYC, Feb. 7, 1947; d. George Émile and Virginia Dorothea (MacPherson) Stauffer; m. Adam Conrad, Nov. 12, 2000. BA, CUNY, 1968, MLS, 1970. Libr. N.Y. Pub. Libr., NYC, 1968—78; libr. cons. Queens (N.Y.) Borough Pub. Libr., 1978—97, ret., 1997; mktg. mgr. Random House, NYC. Cons. to pub. librs., pub., schs. Author: High/Low Handbook, 2d edit., 1985, High/Low Handbook Encouraging Literacy in the 1990s, 3d edit., 1990, High/Low Handbook, 4th rev. edit., 2002, New Directions for Young Adult Services, 1983, The General Slocum Steamboat Fire of 1904, 2004; contbr. articles to periodicals; appeared on C-SPAN. Recipient Cmty. Svc. award Black Spectrum Theatre, 1995. Mem. ALA (bd. dirs. 1979-82, chair Hi/Lo com. 1976-80), Young Adult Libr. Svcs. Assn. (bd. dirs. 1979-82), N.Y. Libr. Assn., Authors Guild, N.Y. Libr. Club (pres., bd. dirs. 1986-91). Episcopalian. Avocations: tennis, weaving, hiking. Home: Mastic Beach, NY. Died May 4, 2013.

**LICHANG, ZHANG,** Chinese government official; b. Nanpi, Hebei, China, July 1939; Grad., Beijing Econ. Correspondence U., 1968. Dep. sec. Communist youth league com. Tianjin Steel Tube Mill, China, 1960—66, dep. dir., 1966—68, workshop dir., constrn. sect. chief, 1968—72, dir., dep. sec. party com., 1972—80; mem. standing com., party com., dep. dir. gen. Tianjin Mcpl. Metallurgical Industry Bur., 1980—85; dir. gen. Tianjin Mcpl. Econ. Commn., 1983—86; vice mayor Tianjin, 1986—93; mayor, 1997—98; sec. indsl. working com. Tianjin Mcpl. Com. Communist Party China, 1986—89, dep. sec., 1989—97, sec., 1997—2008; chmn. standing com. Tianjin Mcpl. People's Congress, 2002—08; mem. polit. bur. Ctrl. Com. Communist Party China, 2002—08. Mem. Communist Party China, 1966—2008. Died Jan. 10, 2008.

**LIEBENBERG, ALGERNON CHARLES,** civil engineer; b. Bredasdorp, We. Cape, S. Africa, Dec. 13, 1926; s. Louis Wilhelm and Johanna Martha (Loxton) L.; m. Francina Salomina Jurgens, Oct. 6, 1951; children: Wilhelm, Franciscus, Deon, Louis, Annette. BS Engring., U. Cape Town, 1948, PhD, 1965, DSc in Engring. (hon.), 1995. Chartered profl. engr. S. Africa, U.K. Asst. design engr. A F Bisschop Cons. Engrs., Cape Town, 1949-50; rsch. asst. civil engring. dept. U. Cape Town, 1951-52; sr. ptnr. A C Liebenberg Cons. Engr., Cape Town, 1951-54, Liebenberg & Stander, Cape Town, 1954-93, cons., 1993-2001; ret., 2001. Chmn. local and regional bds. of PERM Bldg. Soc., Cape Town, 1970-92; mem. Civil Engring. Adv. Coun., Bldg. Industries Adv. Coun., Sci. Adv. Coun., 1988-90, Bd. Nuclear Accelerator Ctr., Faure, 1991-94. Author: Concrete Bridges: Design and Construction, 1992; co-author: Handbook of Structural Concrete, 1983, Bridge Aesthetics Around the World, 1991; contbr. articles to profl. jours. Recipient Order for Meritorious Svc. (Gold) Chancery of Orders, State Pres. of South Africa, Fedn. Internat. de la Précontrainte medal, 1997. Fellow Acad. Engrs. of South Africa (founder, pres. 1991), Royal Acad. Engring. U.K. (fgn. mem.), South Africa Inst. Civil Engrs. (hon., pres. 1976, Gold medal 1993); mem. ASCE (life), South African Assn. Cons. Engrs. (hon., pres. 1969-70), Assn. Sci. and Tech. Soc. of South Africa (Gold medal 1983), South African Inst. Archs. (hon.). Achievements include identification and analysis of arch action in concrete slabs; devel. of a stress-strain function (non-linear) for concrete, analytical procedure to determine interaction between shear walls and frames in tall bldgs., risk analysis of bridges subjected to flooding, suspended by cables method of constructing large concrete arch bridges; identified planar force in stairs; responsibility for design of several large span concrete bridges and tall buildings in South Africa. Home: Western Cape, South Africa. Died Oct. 31, 2003.

**LIEHR, JOACHIM GEORG,** pharmacology educator, cancer researcher; b. Namslau, Silesia, Germany, June 20, 1942; came to U.S., 1965; s. Georg and Anna Maria (Skupin) L.; m. Katherine M. Meakin, Dec. 17, 1988; children: Christopher Joachim, Patrick Reinhard. Diploma, U. Mûnster, Germany, 1965; PhD, U. Del., 1968. Postdoctoral fellow U. Calif., Berkeley, 1968-69; rsch. asst. Tech. U. Munich, Germany, 1970-72; vis. asst. prof. Baylor U., Houston, 1972-74; spectroscopist Ciba-Geigy Ltd., Basle, Switzerland, 1974-76; asst. prof. biochemistry Med. Sch. U. Tex., Houston, 1976-83, asst. prof. pharmacology Med. Sch., 1983-85; assoc. prof. Med. Sch. U. Tex., Galveston, from 1985, prof., from 1989. Mem. chem. pathology study group NIH, Nat. Cancer Inst., Washington, 1986-90 Contbr. articles to sci. jours. Achievements include research in synthesis of estrogens with decreased carcinogenic activity, mechanism and prevention of estrogen-induced carcinogenesis. Home: Houston, Tex. Deceased.

**LIENERT, JAMES PAUL,** missionary priest; b. Lawrence, Nebr., May 24, 1925; arrived in Mexico, 1967; s. John Paul Lienert and Josephine Elizabeth Kohmetscher. M in Latin, St. Louis U., 1959. Ordained priest Roman Cath. Ch., 1954 at Kenrick Sem., St. Louis. Prof. Holy Family Sem., St. Louis, 1955-61, 64-67; rector St. Thomas Aquinas Sem., Farmington, Mo., 1961-64; pastor Nuestra Señora del Refugio, La Esmeralda, Coahuila, Mexico, from 1967. Com. mem. TV Re-Transmitter, La Esmeralda, 1984—. Roman Catholic. Avocations: construction, studying science, geology and biology. Died Jan. 4, 2010.

**LIFLAND, BURTON RAYMOND,** federal judge; b. Bklyn., Sept. 30, 1929; m. Elaine Lifland; children: Howard, Craig. BA, Syracuse U., 1951; LLB, Fordham Law Sch., 1954. Bar: N.Y. Pvt. practice, NYC; chief judge bankruptcy appellate US Ct. Appeals (2d cir.), NYC, 1980—2014; chief judge US Bankruptcy Ct. (southern dist.) N.Y., NYC, 1998—2000. Adj. faculty Nat. Jud. Coll.; lectr. Practicing Law Inst., others; condr. seminars, retreats; mem. faculty N.Y. Inst. Credit; mem. jud. conf. subcom. Bankruptcy Case Mgmt. on Bankruptcy; U.S. del. to UN Commn. on Internat. Trade Law. Contbg. author: Chapter 11 Theory and Practice: A Guide to Reorganization; contg. editor: Norton Bankruptcy Law and Practice. Fellow American Coll. Bankruptcy. Died Jan. 12, 2014.

**LIGOCKI, GORDON MICHAEL,** artist, educator; b. Hammond, Ind., Sept. 7, 1943; s. Michael and Regina (Hlodnicki) L.; m. Rita K. Herdaliska, Jan. 25, 1968 (div. June 1980); 1 child, Ian Gabriel; m. Linda Lee Heinsen, Oct. 30, 1994. BFA, Ohio Wesleyan U., 1965; MA in Drawing, U. Iowa, 1967; MFA in Sculpture, U. Ill., 1968; postgrad., Gov.'s State U., 1987-92. Writer Arts Ind., Indpls., 1987-91; writer, art critic Hammond (Ind.) Times, 1985-93; instr. life drawing Art Barn, Valparaiso, Ind., from 1989; assoc. prof. Purdue U., Hammond, 1992-97; gallery dir., adj. prof. Ind. U. N.W., Gary, 1992—2001; assoc. prof. Valparaiso U., 1990—2001; asst. prof. Ancilla Coll., from 2003; prof. art & sociology, spirituality Lindenwood Retreat, Donaldson. Panelist Ind. Arts Commn., Indpls., 1989; cons. on drawing Collegiate Press, Alta Loma, Calif., 1995; curator individual shows Midwest Mus. of Am. Art, Elkhart, Ind., 1991, No. Ind. Art Assn., Munster, Ind., Gary Comty. Mental Health, Hammond Pub. Libr. One-person shows include R.H. Love Gallery, Chgo., 1992, Herr Chambliss Gallery, Hot Springs, Ark., 1992, Uncle Freddies Gallery, Highland, Ind., 2003-06, The Mechanic and the Handyman, Brauer Mus., 2011, Valparaiso University, 2012, Nakeslor Gallery, Mich., 2012, Gordon Mgocki & Robert study Lakeside Gallery, Mich. Ind.; contbr. articles to newspapers and profl. publs. Named Friend of the Arts in Edn., Ind. Art Edn. Assn., 1991. Mem.: Internat. Soc. of Visual Sociology. Avocation: gardening. Home: Winamac, Ind. Died Jan. 13, 2014.

**LIN, WILLIAM BING-TSANG,** accountant; b. Changhwa, Taiwan, Republic of China, Dec. 4, 1941; s. Shui-Tsai and Pei (Wu) L.; m. Shui-Lien Yen, Nov. 23, 1967; children: Kai-cheng, Kai Min. BBA, Nat. Taiwan U., 1966; M of Accountancy, U. Mo., 1971; postgrad., Asian Inst. of Mgmt., 1972. CPA, Taiwan. Clk. Internat. Comml. Bank of China, Taipei, 1960-68; audit mgr. Arthur Andersen, Taipei, 1968-70, 71-74; vice chmn. Deloitte & Touche, Taipei, from 1975. Lectr. of auditing Nat. Taiwan U., 1968—; asst. prof. acctg. Soochow U., Taipei, 1968—; sub.-com. mem. Econ. Reform Com. Exec. Yuan, Taipei, 1985. Exec. editor Internal Auditor, 1988-96. Recipient Alumni Achievement award Asian Inst. of Mgmt. Alumni Assn., 1993. Mem. Internal Auditors Assn. of Republic of China (chmn. 1988-92), Nat. Fedn. of CPAs Assn. (chmn. ethics com. 1991-94), Acctg. R&D Found. (vice chmn. auditing stds. com. 1985—). Home: Taipei, Taiwan. Died Jan. 11, 2003.

**LIN, YANG-KANG,** Chinese government official; b. Nantou County, Taiwan Province, China, June 10, 1927; s. Lin Chih-Chang and Lin Chen Ruan; m. Chen Ho, 1945; 4 children. Student, Nat. Taiwan U. Chmn. Yunlin County Hdqs., Kuomintang, 1964-67; magistrate Nantou County, 1967-72; commr. Dept. Reconstrn. Taiwan Provincial Govt., 1972-76; mayor City of Taipei, 1976-78; gov. Govt. of Taiwan Province, 1978-81; min. of interior Govt. of China, 1981-84; vice premier Exec. Yuan, 1984-87; premier Judicial Yuan, 1987-94. Avocations: hiking, reading, studying, music, films. Died Apr. 13, 2013.

**LINDEN, DAN PETER,** electrical engineer; b. Stockholm, Feb. 27, 1951; s. Hans Lennart and Gertrud Ingrid (Cederberg) L.; m. Charlotta Margareta Bergstrom, June 21, 1975 (div. 1981); children: Jonas, Karolina; m. Sylvia Margareta Bergman; children: Felicia Linden-Bergman, Filippa Linden-Bergman. MS, Royal Inst. of Tech., Stockholm, 1977. Med. engr. St. Erik Hosp., Stockholm, 1977-78; rsch. and devel. engr. Siemens Elema AB, Stockholm, from 1978. Achievements include patents within respiratory care, equipments and methods. Home: Stockholm, Sweden. Died Mar. 4, 2008.

**LINDSAY, DALE RICHARD,** research administrator; b. Bunker Hill, Kans., Aug. 9, 1913; s. Charles Edwin and Iva (Missimer) L.; m. Sybil Anne McCoy, June 6, 1937; children: Martha Lou Lindsay Cover, Judith Anne Lindsay Clapp, Patricia Dale. AB, U. Kans., 1937, MA, 1938; PhD, Iowa State Coll., 1943. Entomologist Dept. Agr., summers 1937-39; teaching fellow, instr., research asso. Iowa State Coll., 1938-43; commd. officer USPHS, 1943—2002, scientist dir., 1955; assigned malaria control in war areas, 1943-45; entomologist charge operations Communicable Disease Center Activies, Pharr, Tex., 1945-48; chief Thomasville (Ga.) field sta., 1948-53; chief program evaluation sect., div. research grants NIH, 1953-55, asst. chief div., 1955-60, chief div., 1960-63; dep. to gen. dir. Mass. Gen. Hosp., Boston, 1963-65; spl. asst. to chancellor health scis. U. Calif. at Davis, 1965-67, asst. chancellor research and health scis., 1968-69; asso. commr. sci. FDA, 1969-71; asso. dir. med. and allied health edn. Duke U., 1971-75; asst. dir. for sci. coordination Nat. Center for Toxicol. Research, Jefferson, Ark., 1975-76; adj. prof. medicine U. Ark. Med. Sch., 1975-76; asso. dept. family and community medicine U. Ariz., 1977-82. Agrl. bd. Nat. Acad. Sci.-NRC, 1970-73; mem. exec. com., public trustee Nutrition Found., 1972-76, Environ. and Agrl. Found., 1974-79; chmn. sci. adv. bd. Nat. Center for Toxicol. Research, 1972-74. Fellow AAAS, Am. Public Health Assn.; mem. Entomol. Soc. Am. (gov. bd. 1958-62), Commd. Officer Assn. USPHS (treas. nat. exec. com. 1959-61), Sigma Xi, Phi Kappa Phi, Gamma Sigma Delta. Home: Davis, Calif. Died Nov. 3, 2002.

**LINDSAY, HELEN MILLS,** psychotherapist; b. Cleve., June 02; d. Don Parmenter Mills and Grace Elidia Stroup; m. Harry Anderson Lindsay, July 21, 1991. BA, Case Western Ress. U., 1932; MS of Social Sci., Boston U., 1947. Lic. clin. social worker. Sr. sen. Calif. Sr. Legislature, from 1985; pres. Aux. Laguna Hills Adult Day Health Care, from 1993. Mem. Leisure World Dem. Club (pres. 1984-85, Leisure Worlder of Month 1996). Avocations: playing piano, gardening. Deceased.

**LINDSTROM, WENDELL DON,** mathematician, educator; b. Kiron, Iowa, Feb. 7, 1927; s. Bert E. and Alice C. (Larson) L.; m. Miriam Bratt, Dec. 16, 1950; children: Astrid J., Greta S. BA, U. Iowa, 1949, PhD, 1953; DSc (hon.), Kenyon Coll., 1988. Asst. prof. Iowa State U., Ames, 1953-58; from assoc. prof. to prof. Kenyon Coll., Gambier, Ohio, 1958-88, prof. emeritus, from 1988, chmn. dept. math., 1967-74, 81-84. Vis. scholar U. Oreg., Eugene, 1966; vis. prof. Robert Coll., Istanbul, Turkey, 1968-69. Co-author: A Primer of Discrete Mathematics, 1987. With USNR, 1945-46. NSF fellow U. Calif., Berkeley, 1962-63, U. Iowa fellow, 1952-53. Mem. Am. Math. Soc., Math. Assn. Am., Phi Beta Kappa. Died Dec. 9, 1999.

**LINGS, MARTIN,** author, lecturer, museum curator; b. Burnage, Lancashire, Eng., Jan. 24, 1909; s. George Herbert and Gladys Mary (Greenhalgh) L.; m. Lesley Smalley. BA in English, Oxford U., Eng., 1932, MA, 1937; BA in Arabic, London U., 1954, PhD in Sufism, 1959. Sec. Anglo-Polish Soc., Gdynia, Poland, 1934-35; lectr. in Anglo-Saxon U. Vitautas the Gt., Kaunas, Lithuania, 1935-39; lectr. in Shakespeare U. Fuad I., Cairo, 1941-52; asst. keeper Brit. Mus., London, 1955-70, keeper of Oriental manuscripts and printed books, 1970-73, Brit. Libr., London, 1973-74. Cons. World of Islam Festival, London, 1974-76; mem. The Arts of Islam exhbn. com. Arts Coun. Gt. Britain, London, 1974-76; lectr. Royal Coll. Art, Prince of Wales Inst. Arch., Temenos Acad., C.S. Lewis Soc. Author: Collected Poems, 1987, 2d edit., 2000, The Eleventh Hour, 1987, 2d edit., 2000, Ancient Beliefs and Modern Superstitions, 1991, Symbol and Archetype, 1991, Muhammad: His Life Based on the Earliest Sources, 4th edit., 1991, The Book of Certainty (the Sufi Doctrine of Faith Vision and Gnosis), 3d edit., 1992, What is Sufism, 4th edit., 1993, A Sufi Saint of the Twentieth Century: Shaykh Ahmad al-Alawi, 3d edit., 1993, The Sacred Art of Shakespeare (To Take Upon Us the Mystery of Things, 4th edit., 1998, Summits of Qur'an Calligraphy and Illumination, 2000. Fellow Royal Asiatic Soc. (mem. coun. 1970-74); mem. Brit. Museum Soc. Avocations: gardening, music, walking. Home: Kent, England. Died May 12, 2005.

**LINK, PHOEBE FORREST,** educator, author, social worker, poet; b. Palmerton, Pa., Feb. 20, 1926; d. John Nevins and Phoebe Eleanor (Lewis) Forrest; m. Robert H. Link, July 13, 1962; children: David Forrest, Anne Harris. BA in Psychology, Pa. State U., State Coll., 1947, MS in Child Devel. and Family Relationships, 1952; postgrad., U. Rochester, NY, 1957—59, Harvard U., 1958. Dir. teen age program YWCA, Lansing, Mich., 1947—50, Rochester, NY, 1952—56; rsch. asst. Pa. State U., State College, 1950—52; tchr. Rochester, 1956—60; demonstration tchr. William Antheil Sch., Trenton, NJ, 1960—63; mem. faculty Trenton State Coll., 1960—63; tchr. State College Area Schs., 1971—93. Lectr. Am. Home Econs. Assn. Conf.; cons. family studies, leader continuing edn. workshops Pa. State U., 1977, others; mem. staff dean women Harvard U., Cambridge, Mass., 1958; dir. Children's Program for Pa. Dist. Attys.; featured author TV series The Writing Life; reader-editor WPSX-TV. Author: Small? Tall? Not At All, 1973, 1st edit., 1973, 2nd edit., 2009, Passionate Realist, 1994; staff writer: Horizon, 1985—87, author, creator: Heartthrob series, 1987; contbr. articles to profl. jours. Trustee Schlow Pub. Libr., State College, 1980—83; founder, 1st chmn. poetry com. Ctrl. Pa. Festival Arts; featured spkr. 50th class reunion Pa. State U.; mentor Women's Leadership Initiative, Pa. State U., 2004; dir. youth choir Univ. Bapt. Ch.; vis. deacon spiritual ministry team State College Presbyn. Ch., 2002; mem. aux. com. Centre Vols. in Medicine, 2004. Recipient Excellence in Edn. award with highest distinction, Pa. State U., 1993, merit award, William Antheil Sch., 1958. Mem.: NEA, AAUW (Simmons grantee 1984), State College Area Edn. Assn. (scholarship com.), Peterson Soc., Mortar Bd. Alumni (founder, 1st pres., pres.), Pa. State U. Coll. Human Devel. Alumni (bd. dirs.), Tau Phi Sigma, Omicron Nu Alumni, Phi Delta Kappa. Died Aug. 2, 2013.

**LINOSA, SALVATORE MOSÉ,** military officer; b. Catania, Italy, Jan. 4, 1927; s. Michele Linosa and Maria Fonseca; m. Aurelia Valdambrini; children: Maria Egle, Danilo. Degree, Mil. Sch., 1953, Polytechnic Application Artillery, 1956. Commd. lt. Italian Army, 1954, advanced through grades to col., 1967, stationed at Redstone Arsenal Huntsville, Ala., 1960—63, chief calibration svcs. NATO Chateauroux, France, 1967—73, dep. dir. NATO/NAMSA Brussels, 1973—76, Luxembourg, 1973—76, chief support br., Hawk Sys. Mgmt., 1976—93; ret., 1993; pres. Logistics Experts NATO/Hawk, Paris, 1977—79; with European Def. Agy., Luxembourg, from 2005. Author: Ecole des Arts Culinaires de l'Ordre du Lys de la Gastronomie Européenne Culinary Books, 1983. Decorated knight Mil. Order of Italian Rep., commdr. Grace Souverein Order Saint John Jerusalem; recipient Gold medal, Ministry Def., 1981. Mem.: Cordons Bleus de France (pres. European group commdr.), Italian Cultural Soc. (pres. Soc. Dante Alighieri, Luxembourg com.), Ordre dy Lys de la Gastronomie Européenne (pres.). Avocations: tennis, electronic devices. Died Dec. 17, 2009.

**LINTACKER, MARCEL ALPHONSE SIDNEY,** finance company executive, consultant; b. St. Niklaas, Flanders, Belgium, Apr. 28, 1926; s. Joseph Ferdinand L. and Leonie Rose Foubert; m. Maria Magdalena Gyselinck, Aug. 17, 1946 (dec. Aug. 1995); 1 child, Huguette. Indsl. Engr. A1, Tech. Inst., Antwerp, Belgium, 1946. With rail ways, Belgium, 1946-53; prodn. mgr. PRB, Belgium, 1953-56, EXSA, Peru, 1956-63; owner, mgr. Belgian Mfg. Co., Peru, 1964-71; owner, gen. mgr. SIPOPSA, Peru, 1971-90, Globimpex, Peru, from 1991; owner, pres. IFIRCO, Panama and Peru, from 1996. Bd. dirs. PAIX, Peru; bd. dirs., cons. ACG-Holdings, Peru; cons. Profl. Status, Peru, 1986—; mandate ARVIA, France, 1996—; advisor fgn. trade Belgian Embassy, Peru; chmn., CEO Flanders Mining Corp., Peru, 1998. Hon. Belgian consul, Iquitos, Peru, 1971-88; dean Consular Corps, Iquitos, 1972-85. Decorated 6 Highest Gold Medals WWII Def. Ministry of Belgium, 1946-55, Officer in the Crown Order King of Belgium, 1993. Mem. Internat. Soc. Financiers USA (cert. internat. financier), Oxford Club, Lions (zone chmn. 1964—, Gold Key 1985). Roman Catholic. Avocations: fishing, hunting, recreational activities. Home: Lima, Peru. Died Sept. 10, 2005.

**LIPETZ, LEO E.,** biophysicist, researcher; b. Lincoln, Nebr., Aug. 10, 1921; s. Elijah Y. and Ruth D. (Leavitt) L.; m. Dorothea Ogulnick, July 4, 1947; children: Philip David, Timothy Joseph, Robert Eugene. BEE, Cornell U., 1942; PhD in Biophysics, U. Calif., Berkeley, 1953. Jr. engr. U.S. Signal Corps, Balt., 1942-43; mem. tech. staff Bell Telephone Labs., NYC, 1943-46; from instr. to prof. Ohio State U., Columbus, 1954-88, prof. emeritus, from 1989. Mem. com. on vision NRC, Washington, 1962-69, mem. biophys. scis. tng. com. NIH, Bethesda, Md., 1968-70; chmn. dept. biophysics Ohio State U., Columbus, 1965-76. Co-author: The Relation of Physiological and Psychological Intensity, 1971, Some Neuronal Circuits of the Turtle Retina, 1985, The Anatomical Basis for Color Vision in the Vertebrate Retina, 1990. Treas. Columbus Art League, 1989—. NIH sr. fellow, 1962-63, Japan Soc. for Promotion of Sci. sr. rsch. fellow, 1981. Mem. Biophys. Soc. (founder 1958, chmn. 17th annual meeting 1973, dir. placement svc. 1975—), Soc. for Neurosci. (chartered), Assn. for Rsch. in Vision and Ophthalmology. Achievements include research in mechanisms of the x-ray and radion phosphenes, in the tandem retinal horizontal cells neuronal circuit for vertebrate color vision. Home: Columbus, Ohio. Died Oct. 11, 1991.

**LIPKIN-SHAHAK, AMNON,** former Israeli government official, retired military officer; b. Tel Aviv, Mar. 18, 1944; m. Tali Lipkin-Shahak; 5 children. BA in Gen. History, Tel Aviv U.; grad., Israel Def. Force Command & State Coll., Nat. Def. Coll., Israel. With Israel Def. Force, 1962—98, apptd. to Ctrl. Command, 1983—86, head intelligence br., 1986—91, dep. chief of gen. staff, 1991—95, chief of gen. staff, 1995—98; mem. Knesset, 1999—2001; min. tourism Govt. of Israel, 1999—2000, min. tourism, min. transp. Jerusalem, 2000—01. Paratroop comdr. Six Day War, 1967; dep. paratroop brigade comdr. Yom Kippur War, 1973. Decorated 2 Medals of Valor. Center Party. Jewish. Died Dec. 19, 2012.

**LISHNEVSKII, ERIC NIKOLAEVICH,** geologist, researcher; b. Moscow, Mar. 24, 1932; s. Nicolay Semenovich Lishnevskii and Anna Dmitrievna Kruglova; m. Natalia Sidorovna Chukanova, Nov. 7, 1979 (div. 1994); children: Anton, Ekaterina. MSc, Gubkin State Acad. Oil & Gas, Moscow, 1955; candidate sci., All Union Rsch. Inst. for Gas, Moscow, 1964. Engr. All Union Inst. for Geophysics, Moscow, 1955-59, sr. geologist, 1960-63, jr. rschr., 1964-67, sr. rschr., 1968-69, Inst. Mineralogy, Geochemistry of Rare Elements, Moscow, 1970-91, Geol. Inst. Russian Acad. Sci., Moscow, 1992-99; sr. rschr., expert forecaster Inst. Geology Ore Deposits, Petrograohy, Mineralogy and Geochemistry Russian Acad. Sci., from 2000. Contbr. articles to profl. jours. Recipient Govtl. medal Veteran of Labor, 1989; grantee Russian Found. for Basic Rsch., 1994-95, 96-98. Avocations: politology, history, tourism before 1992. Home: Moscow, Russia. Deceased.

**LITTLE, MALCOLM See MALCOLM X**

**LITTLETON, HARVEY KLINE,** artist; b. Corning, NY, June 14, 1922; s. Jesse Talbot and Bessie (Cook) Littleton; m. Bess Toyo Tamura, Sept. 6, 1947; children: Carol Louise Littleton Shay, John Christopher, Kathryn Tamara(dec.). Student, U. Mich., 1939-42, B in Design, 1947; MFA, Cranbrook Acad. Art, 1951; DFA (hon.), Phila. U. Arts, 1982, RISD, 1996, U. Wis., 2000; Docorate (hon.), N.C. State U., Raleigh, 2004. Instr. ceramics Toledo Mus. Art, 1949-51; prof. art U. Wis., Madison, 1951-77, chmn. dept., 1964-67, 69-71, prof. emeritus, 1977—2013; CEO Littleton Studios, Spruce Pine, NC, 1981—2013. Author: Glass Blowing - A Search for Form, 1971; exhibitions include Lee Nordness Galleries, NYC, 1969—70, Maison de Culture, Liege, Belgium, 1974, J & L Lobmeyr, Vienna, 1974, Brooks Meml. Art Gallery, Memphis, 1975, Contemporary Art Glass Gallery, NYC, 1977—79, Habatat Gallery, Detroit, 1980—81, Heller Gallery, NYC, 1980—85, Glasmuseum Ebeltoft, Sweden, 1989, Royal Copenhagen Gallery, 1989, Finnish Glasmuseum, Riihimaki, Finland, 1989, Kunsthaus am Mus., Cologne, Germany, 1990, Immenhausen, Germany, 1990, Glasmuseum, Frauenau, Germany, 1992, Yokohama Mus. Art, Japan, 1995, retrospective exhbn., High Mus. Art, Atlanta, 1984, Renwick Gallery, Mus. Arts & Design, Iowa State U., Milw. Art Mus., Portland Mus. Art, Maine, Mint Mus. Craft & Design, Charlotte, NC, 1999—2000, Ark. Art Ctr. Decorative Arts Mus., Little Rock, St. John's Mus. Art, Wilmington, NC, Hunter Mus. Art, Chattanooga, Chazen Mus. Art, Madison, Represented in permanent collections Victoria and Albert Mus., London, mus., Germany, Holland, Switzerland, Belgium, Austria, Czechoslovakia, Met. Mus. Art, NYC, Mus. Modern Art, Mus. Arts & Design, LA County Mus. Art, Corning Mus. Glass, Toledo Mus. Art, Detroit Art Inst., Milw. Art Ctr., Smithsonian Instn., Washington, High Mus. Art, Atlanta, Chrysler Mus., Norfolk, Va., U. Mich., U. Ill., Ohio State U., Phila. Mus. Art, The White House, Washington, numerous other pub. and pvt. collections. Bd. dirs. Penland Sch., NC, pres. bd. dirs. NC, 1986—88. With Signal Corps US Army, 1942—45, ETO. Recipient diploma of honor, Glass Mus., Frauenau, Fine Arts award, Gov. NC, 1987, Master of Medium award, James Renwick Alliance, 1997, Disting. Alumnus award, U. Mich. Sch. Art, Wis. Visual Art Lifetime Achievement award, 2004, honor for contbn. and leadership, Studio Glass Movement Nat. Am. Glass Club, 2005; named Living Treasure, State of NC; grantee, Louis Comfort Tiffany Found., 1970—71, Corning Glass Works, 1974, Nat. Endowment Arts, 1978—79; Rsch. grantee, U. Wis., 1954, 1957, 1962, 1973, 1975, Toledo Mus. Art, 1962. Fellow: American Crafts Coun. (trustee 1957, 1961—64, trustee emeritus 1964—2013, gold medal 1983), Wis. Acad. Arts & Sciences, Corning Mus. Glass (Rakow award for Excellence in Art of Glass); mem.: Nat. Assn. Schools Art & Designs, American Ceramic Soc. (hon.), Glass Art Soc. (hon. Lifetime Achievement award 1993), Nat. Coun. Edn. Ceramic Arts (hon. Disting. Svc. in Visual Arts citation 1996, Urbanglass award for Lifetime Achievement in Glass 1998). Home: Spruce Pine, NC. Died Dec. 13, 2013.

**LIVINGSTON, DEAN BENNETTE,** retired newspaper publisher; b. North, SC, Jan. 9, 1933; s. Alexander Hamilton and Madge (Rogers) L.; m. Grace Dukes, Dec. 22, 1955; children: Donna, Dean Jr. BA, U. S.C., 1955. Sports editor The Times and Democrat, Orangeburg, S.C., 1954-55, mng. editor, 1959-62, publisher, 1962—99. Author: Yesteryears, 2006. 1st lt., USAF, 1956-59. Mem. S.C. Press Assn. (pres. 1969-70), S.C. Press Assn. Found. (pres. 1981-84), Orangeburg C. of C. (pres. 1968-69). Home: Orangeburg, SC. Died May 20, 2014.

**LIZT, SARA ENID VANEFSKY,** lawyer, educator; b. USSR, Mar. 10, 1913; came to U.S., 1921; d. Max and Yocheved (Koval) Vanefsky; widowed. LLB, CUNY, Bklyn., 1941, LLM, 1962. Bar: N.Y. 1946, U.S. Dist. Ct. (so. and ea. dists.) N.Y. 1946. Pvt. practice Bklyn., from 1946. Prof. CUNY, Bklyn., 1966-80. Deceased.

**LOCKHART-MURE, DAVID See RIGHT HON. LORD RENTON**

**LOCKWOOD, DANIEL RALPH,** retired academic administrator, religious studies educator; b. Portland, Oreg., Sept. 29, 1948; s. Milton Cutts and Esther (Williams) L.; m. Janet Yuko Iguchi, Dec. 30, 1972; 1 child, Elise Nicole. AB cum laude, Westmont Coll., 1970; ThM with high honor, Dallas Theol. Sem., 1976, ThD, 1982. Ordained to ministry Cen. Bible Ch., 1980. Instr. in Christian Edn. Dallas Theol. Sem., 1977-79; interim pastor Lewisville (Tex.) Congl. Ch., 1978-79; assoc. pastor adult edn. Mountain Park Ch., Lake Oswego, Oreg., 1988-91; prof. theology Multnomah Sch. of Bible, Portland, 1979—2013, v.p., 1990—97, pres., 1997—2013; dean grad. sch. Multnomah Grad. Sch. Ministry, Portland, 1990—97. Elder Mountain Park Ch. Mem. Evang. Theol. Soc. (vice chmn. N.W. regional chpt. 1986-87, chmn. 1987-88), Portland Soc. Magicians (v.p. 1983-84). Home: Portland, Oreg. Died July 9, 2014.

**LODER, JAMES EDWIN,** philosophy educator; Mary D. Synnott Chair of the Philosophy of Christian Edn. Princeton Theol. Sem., NJ, 1982—2001. Died Nov. 9, 2001.

**LOEWENSTEIN-WERTHEIM-FREUDENBERG ZU, PRINCE RUPERT LOUIS FERDINAND,** financial consultant; b. Palma, Majorca, Aug. 24, 1933; s. Prince Leopold and Countess Bianca H-M Fischler von Treuberg; m. Josephine Lowry-Corry, July 18, 1957; children: Rev. Rudolf, Rev. Konrad, Maria Theodora; m. Manfredi della Gherardesca, Sept. 26, 1998. MA, Magdalen Coll., Oxford, 1953. With Bache & Co., London, 1953—62, Leopold Joseph & Sons, Mcht. Bankers, Ltd., London, 1963—81, jt. mng. dir., 1966—81; ind. financial cons. London, 1981—2014; mgr. Rolling Stones, 1968—2007. Decorated bailiff grand cross of honor and devotion Sovereign Mil. Order of Malta, bailiff grand cross of justice Constantine Order of St. George. Mem.: Regency Club (N.Y.C.), Brook Club, Beefsteak Club (London), Pratt's Club, Portland Club, Whites Club, Boodles Club, Bucks Club. Conservative. Roman Catholic. Died May 20, 2014.

**LOGVINOV, SERGUEI,** nuclear engineer, researcher; b. KErch, Crimea, Jan. 30, 1935; s. Aleksey Logvinov and Zinaida Logvinova; m. Valentina Logvinova, Nov. 23, 1962; 2 children. Degree in mech. engring., Moscow Power Inst., 1959. Engr. OKB Gidropress, Moscow, 1959—62, head exptl. group, 1962—64, head exptl. lab., 1964—74, head dept. thermal hydraulics, 1974—96, leading specialist, from 1996. Author: Devoted to Steam Generators of Horizontal Type, 2001, Devoted to VVER-type Reactors, 2004. Recipient Russian Govt. award, 1995. Mem.: Nuclear Soc. Russia. Home: Podolsk, Russia. Died Oct. 4, 2004.

**LOMHOLT, NIELS FINSEN,** retired pharmacologist; b. Copenhagen, Mar. 16, 1932; s. Svend and Gudrun (Finsen) Lomholt; m. Bodil Elizabeth Parkes, June 29, 1955 (div. Nov. 1978); children: Margrethe Lomholt Kemp, Thorkild Finsen; m. Hanne Dorthe Graabek Jensen, Nov. 25, 1978 (dec. Apr. 1993); 1 child, Trine; m. Hanne Flinker, Mar. 15, 1997. MD, U. Copenhagen, 1961. With dept. anesthesiology U. Copenhagen, 1963—65, asst. prof. dept. pharmacology, 1968—99, sr. scientist, 2000—10. Scholar Dept. Anesthesiology scholar, U. Copenhagen, 1965—68. Achievements include patents for in field. Home: Horsholm, Denmark. Died Aug. 23, 2013.

**LOMINADZE, JUMBER GEORGE,** physicist; b. Tbilisi, Georgia, Sept. 20, 1930; s. George Sergo Lominadze and Ketevan Polievkt Kalandadze; m. Lia Vasiliy Tsabashvili, Apr. 2, 1954; 1 child, George Jumber. MS, Moscow State U., 1955. Sci. sec. Inst. Physics Georgian Acad. Sci., Tbilisi, 1958—74; rsch. scientist All-Union Rsch. Inst. Theoretical Physics, Cheliabinsk, Russia, 1956—58; dep. academician sec. Georgian Acad. Sci., Tbilisi, 1974—82; dir. Abastumani Astrophys. Obs., Tbilisi, 1991—2000; chair Georgian Space Agy., Tbilisi, 2003—06; head Space Rsch. Ctr. Inst. Geophysics, Tbilisi, 2006—14; head dept. math. & physics Georgian Nat. Acad. Sci., Tbilisi, 1982—2014. Chmn. Ctrl. State Election Com., Tbilisi, 1997—2003. Actor: (movie) Candle on the Jesus Grave (Golden Knight, Moscow Film Festival, 2008). Mem.: Internat. Astronomy Union, American Phys. Soc. Achievements include development of plasma astrophysics. Home: Tbilisi, Georgia. Died Jan. 20, 2014.

**LONG, ISAAC ADELBERT,** retired banker; b. Herndon, Va., Aug. 8, 1899; s. Isaac T. and Ada White L.; m. Lydia Ann Kimbrough; children: Lydia Ann, Ada White, Claxton Allen (dec.). Student, U. Va., Am. Inst. Banking; Grad., Am. Inst. Banking. With Royal Bank Can., 1920-22, Peoples Nat. Bank, Leesburg, Va., 1923-27; v.p. Mercantile Trust Co., St. Louis, 1927-53; chmn. emeritus S.W. Bank of St. Louis. Bd. dirs. Investment Bankers Assn. of Am.; faculty Sch. of Banking, U. Wis. Past pres. St. Louis Bd. Police Commrs., 1953-57, 68-69, Mary Inst. Bd. Trustees, Cen. Inst. for Deaf, St. Louis Mcpl. Bond Club, St. Louis Corp. Fiduciaries Assn., Noonday Club/St. Louis, Racquet Club/St. Louis; past chmn. St. Louis Housing Authority, St. Louis Land Clearance Authority, Citizens Sch. Improvement Com., others. Named Ky. Col., Ark. Traveler, col. on staff of Gov. Donnelly, State of Mo., 1955-57. Mem. Jefferson Nat. Expansion Meml. Assn. (chmn. emeritus, trustee), Mo. Acad. of Squires, others. Home: Saint Louis, Mo. Died Nov. 15, 1993.

**LONGENECKER, MARTHA W.,** retired museum director; b. May 18, 1920; BA in Art, UCLA; MFA, Claremont Grad. Sch.; studied with Millard Sheets, Shoji Hamada, Tatsuzo Shimaoka. Owner ceramics studio, Claremont, Calif.; prof. art San Diego State U., 1955—90; founder, dir. Mingei Internat. Mus., San Diego, 1978—2005. Coord. editing, design and prodn. of exhbn. documentary publs.; condr. tours. Contbr. chpts. to books; developer videotapes; exhibited at Dalzell Hatfield Galleries. San Diego State U. Found. grantee, 1967, Calif. State U. Rsch. grantee, 1978; recipient Disting. Alumna award Claremont Grad. Sch., 1980, Essence of Life award ElderHelp of San Diego, 1993, Living Legacy award Women's Internat. Ctr., 1994, Women of Distinction award Soroptimist Internat. of La Jolla, 1994, Headliner of Yr. Art, San Diego Press Club, 1998, Disting. Svc. medal, San Diego State U., 1998, Reischauer Internat. Edn. award, Japan Soc. San Diego and Tijuana, 1999, San Diego Women Who Mean Bus. award, Foley Vardner Attys. at Law, San Diego Bus. Jour., 2000, Gold Rays with Rosette, Order of Rising Sun, Emperor of Japan, 2003, Golden Hanger Spl. award, Fashion Careers of Calif. Coll., 2004; named to The San Diego Women's Hall of Fame, 2011 Died Oct. 29, 2013.

**LONIE, ALEXANDER ALASDAIR,** business educator; b. Glasgow, Scotland, July 3, 1940; s. Robert Paterson and Janet Mein (Caldow) L.; m. Rosemary Little, July 8, 1965; 4 children. MA, U. Glasgow, 1962. Temp. asst. lectr. econs. U. St. Andrews, Dundee, Scotland, 1966-67; lectr. econs. U. Dundee, 1967-82, lectr. accountancy and bus. fin., 1982-92, sr. lectr., from 1992, dep. head dept., 1994-97, acting head dept., 1995-96, head dept., from 1997. Cons. Scottish Equitable Life Assurance, Edinburgh, 1992. Co-author: (with Miller) Microeconomic Effects of Monetary Policy, 1978; contbr. articles to profl. jours. Policy convenor Social Dem. Party, Dundee, Angus, Scotland, 1982-88, vice chmn., Angus, 1986-87. Fellow Royal Soc. Arts; mem. Brit. Acctg. Assn., Internat. Trade and Fin. Assn. Avocations: reading, travel, weight training, watching sports. Home: Dundee, Scotland. Died Feb. 10, 1999.

**LOPEZ-GUEVARA, CARLOS ALFREDO,** lawyer; b. Pocri, Panama, Jan. 7, 1929; s. Santiago Lopez Montenegro and Erundina (Guevara) Lopez; m. Rosa Elena Navarro, Dec. 23, 1954; children: Carlos Alfredo (dec.), Juan Alexis, Pedro Antonio, Alina Del Carmen, Santiago Emilio, Nina Emilia. Degree in law and polit. sci., Panama U., 1954; M of Comparative Law, NYU, 1961; ML, Harvard U., 1957, SJD, 1964. Ptnr. Fábrega, López & Pedreschi, Panama, Panama, 1958-88; prof. law U. Panama, 1964-68; sr. ptnr. Fábrega, López and Barsallo, Panama, 1988-93, Lopez, Lopez and Assoc., Panama, from 1994. Min. fgn. affairs coun. Rep. of Panama, 1968-69, fgn. rels. coun., 2005; spl. amb. for Panama Canal treaty negotiations Govt. Panama, 1971-78, amb. to U.S.A., Can., 1978-80; v.p. Omar Torrijos Found., 2005 Author: A Canal Without A Canal Zone. Pres. Labor Party, Panama, 1990-94, Panama-Israel Cultural Inst., 1979-92; bd. dirs. Omar Torrijos Found. Recipient Commendatore award Rep. of Italy, 1975, Harold Weil medal NYU, 1984. Fellow Panama Execs. Orgn., Panama Maritime Law Commn., Rotary. Avocations: ping pong/table tennis, swimming, theater, opera, classical music. Died Mar. 2, 2008.

**LOPUSZANSKI, JAN TADEUSZ,** retired physicist, educator; b. Lwów, Poland, Oct. 21, 1923; s. Wladyslaw Jakób and Janina Maria (Kuzmicz) L.; m. Halina Emilia Pidek, July 14, 1956 (div. 1968); 1 child, Maciej; Barbara Zaslonka, Apr. 14, 1969. MA, U. Wroclaw, Poland, 1950; PhD, Jagellonian U., Cracow, Poland, 1955. From asst. to assoc. prof. U. Wroclaw, 1947-68, full prof., 1968-95; retired, 1995. Vice dean math., physics, chemistry faculty U. Wroclaw, 1957-58, dean, 1962-64; vis. prof. U. Utrecht, 1958, NYU, 1960-61, Inst. Advanced Study, Princeton, 1964-65, SUNY, Stony Brook, 1970-71, U. Göttingen, 1984, 91-92; dir. Inst. Theoretical Physics, U. Wroclaw, 1970-84. Author: An Introduction to the Conventional Quantum Field Theory, 1976, Rachunek Spinorow, 1985, An Introduction to Symmetry and Supersymmetry in Quantum Field Theory, 1991, The Inverse Variational Problem in Classical Mechanics, 1999; co-author Fizyka Statystyczna, 1969; mem. editl. bd. Reports on Mathematical Physics, Progress in Physics; contbr. over 100 articles to profl. jours. Decorated Chevalier Cross Order Polonia Restituta, Officer Cross Order Polonia Restituta. Mem. Polish Acad. Scis. (permanent), Polish Acad. Arts and Scis. in Crakow (corr.), Polish Phys. Soc., Assn. of Mems. of Inst. for Advanced Study Princeton, Internat. Assn. Mathematical Physics, Internat. Union Pure and Applied Physics. Roman Catholic. Home: Wroclaw, Poland. Died Dec. 4, 2006.

**LORD, JERE JOHNS,** retired physics professor; b. Portland, Oreg., Jan. 3, 1922; s. Percy Samuel and Hazel Marie (Worstel) L.; m. Miriam E. Hart, Dec. 30, 1947; children—David, Roger, Douglas. Physicist U. Calif. Radiation Lab., Berkeley, 1942-46; research asso. U. Chgo., 1950-52; asst. prof. physics U. Wash., Seattle, 1952-57, assoc. prof., 1957-62, prof., 1962-92, prof. emeritus, from 1992. Fellow AAAS, Am. Phys. Soc.; mem. Am. Assn. Physics Tchrs. Deceased.

**LOSKARN, RYAN (JESSE RYAN LOSKARN),** former legislative staff member; b. Baltimore, Apr. 17, 1978; s. Chuck and Laura Loskarn. BA in History & Polit. Sci., Tulane U., New Orleans, 2000. Legislative asst. to Rep. Wally Herger US House of Representatives, Washington, 2000—01, comm. dir. to Rep. Marsha Blackburn, 2003—07; dep. press sec. US House Rules Com., 2001—03; dir. comm. US Senate Republican Conf., 2007—09, staff dir., 2009—13; chief of staff to Senator Lamar Alexander US Senate, Washington, 2011—13. Named one of The Fabulous 50, Roll Call, 2009. Mem.: Kappa Sigma. Republican. Died Jan. 23, 2014.

**LOTMAN, HERBERT,** retired food products executive; b. Phila., Oct. 9, 1933; s. Samuel Meyer and Gertrude Lotman; m. Karen Levin, Apr. 6, 1957; children: Shelly Hope, Jeffrey Mark. Pres., chmn. bd. Keystone Foods Corp., Bryn Mawr, Pa., 1951, pres., 1960, chmn., CEO, 1960—2014. Bd. dirs. Nat. Juvenile Diabetes Found. Served US Army, 1952—54. Mem.: Young Pres. Orgn. Home: Haverford, Pa. Died May 8, 2014.

**LOUGHEED, ALAN LESLIE,** economics educator; b. Nanango, Queensland, Australia, Apr. 13, 1927; s. Leslie Francis and Lucy Ada (Wells) L.; m. Jill Carmel Blackmore; children: Brett Robert, Damon Leslie, Kirstin Carmel. BA, U. Queensland, Brisbane, 1955, B Comm., 1960, B Econ., 1965, PhD, 1974. Tchr. Queensland H.S., Australia, 1947-64; lectr. in econs. U. Queensland, Brisbane, 1964-68, sr. lectr., 1968-83, assoc. prof., 1983-92, hon. rsch. fellow, from 1992. Vis. rsch. fellow U. Kent, Canterbury, Eng., 1971, 76, 83; vis. lectr. U. New Eng., Armidale, 1980, 81; vis. scholar U. Kent, Canterbury, 1988; vis. rsch. fellow U. Glasgow, Scotland, 1996. Co-author: Australian Banking, 1966, The Growth of the International Economy, 1820-1960, 1971, 4th edit. 1999, Towards New Policies for Foreign Aid and Development, 1979, Technological Diffusion and Industrialization Before 1914, 1982, others; author: The Brisbane Stock Exchange 1884-1984, 1984, Australia in the World Economy in the Twentieth Century, 1988, Cyanide and Gold, 2000, others. Vice-chancellors rep. Secondary Sch. Studies, Brisbane, 1975-87 Recipient Univ. medal for Outstanding Achievement, U. Queensland, 1965; vis. fellow grantee U. Glasgow, 1996; recipient Archibald scholarship, 1962. Mem. Australian Econ. Soc. (v.p. Brisbane br. 1973, 74, 76, pres. 1975, treas. 1967-70). Avocations: tennis, walking, surfing, golf. Home: Sunshine Coast, Australia. Died Sept. 27, 2002.

**LOUIS-DREYFUS, ROBERT,** advertising executive; b. June 14, 1946; s. Jean and Jeanne (Depierre) L.; m. Margharita Louis-Dreyfuss; 3 children MBA, Harvard U. Chmn. IMS Internat., 1982—89; CEO Saatchi & Saatchi plc, London, 1989—93; chmn. mgmt. bd. Adidas AG, 1993—2001; chmn. Neuf Telecom, 2001—06; chmn., CEO Louis-Dreyfuss Group, 2006—09. Bd. dirs. Neuf Cegetel. Named one of The Top 25 Managers, BusinessWeek, 1997. Died July 4, 2009.

**LOUNDON, DAVID AVRUM,** engineering executive; b. Pueblo, Colo., Aug. 31, 1922; arrived in France, 1953; s. Judah and Charlotte (Sonnenschein) Fine; m. Sabine Körner. Student, Trinidad Jr. Coll., Colo., 1941; BS in Aero. Engring., U. Wash., 1942; AA in Dramatic Arts, U. Calif., San Jose, 1947. Registered profl. engr. Calif., Oreg., Wash. Pvt. practice engring., including constrn. of 8,800 houses, France. Lt. (j.g.) USNR, 1942-46. Mem. ASME, French Soc. Mech. Engrs., Soc. Am. Mil. Engrs. (past. pres.). Died Oct. 24, 1999.

**LOURDUSAMY, DURAISAMY SIMON CARDINAL,** cardinal; b. Kalleri, Pondicherry, India, Feb. 5, 1924; Attended, Loyola Coll., Madras, India; Doctorate in Canon Law, Pontifical Urbaniana U., Rome, 1956. Ordained priest of Pondicherry, 1951, dir. various ecclesiastical organizations, sec. and diocesan to archbishop; appointed Titular Bishop of Sozusa in Libya, 1962, ordained, 1962; auxiliary bishop of Bangalore, India, 1962—64, coadjutor archbishop, 1964—68, archbishop, 1968—71; appointed Titular Archbishop of Filippi, 1964; official Congregation for the Evangelization of Peoples, 1971—73, adjunct sec., 1971—73, sec., 1973—85; elevated to cardinal, 1985; prefect Congregation for the Oriental Churches, 1985—91, prefect emeritus, 1991—2014; cardinal-deacon of Santa Maria delle Grazie alle Fornaci fuori Porta Cavalleggeri (Saint Mary of Grace alle Fornaci fuori Porta Cavalleggeri), 1985—96, cardinal-priest, 1996—2014. Choir master, Cathedral in Pondicherry, 1956-1962; pres. Nat. Liturgical Commn. for India; creator Nat. Liturgical and Catechetical Centre of Bangalore; mem. Bishops' Catechetics Commission; delegate to the first ordinary assembly of the Synod of Bishops, 1967; representative of the Bishops of India, Pan-Asiatic Catechetical-Liturgical Conference of Manila, 1967, v.p. liturgy section, pres.; pres. Pontifical Missionary Work, 1973; vice-grand chancellor Pontifical Urbaniana U., 1973; dir. Catholic Doctors' Guild, Catholic Medical Students' Guild, Newman Associations, Catholic University Students Union and of other ecclesiastical organizations Editor of weekly catholic magazine, Sava Viaby. Roman Catholic. Avocation: piano. Died June 2, 2014.

**LOVE, ERIC RUSSELL,** retired mathematics educator, researcher; b. London, Mar. 31, 1912; arrived in Australia, 1922; s. Robert Russell and Lilla May Reeves (Scott) L.; m. Elvie Cadle, Aug. 20, 1938; children: Antony Russell, Solway Elvie Nutting, Bernard Robert William. BA with honours, U. Melbourne, Australia, 1933, DSc, 1992; BA with honours, Cambridge U., Eng., 1935, PhD, 1938, ScD, 1978. Chartered mathematician Inst. Math. and Its Applications, Eng. Asst. lectr. U. London Queen Mary Coll., 1938-39, Durham (Eng.) U., 1939-40; math. cons. Munitions Supply Labs., Melbourne, 1942-43, Aero. Lab., CSIR, Melbourne, 1943-45; sr. lectr. math. U. Melbourne, 1940-41, 45-48, assoc. prof., 1948-52, prof., 1953-77, emeritus and hon. prof., from 1978. Referee math. jours.; speaker over 20 math. confs., Europe, U.S., Japan.; rschr. in math. analysis. Referee Jour. Math. Analysis and Applications, 1980-91, assoc. editor, 1991-96; contbr. over 90 articles to math. jours. Mem. Cambridge Scientists' Anti-War Group, 1935-38. Home: Melbourne, Australia. Died Aug. 7, 2001.

**LOVE, RONALD JACKSON,** secondary school educator; b. Nortonville, Ky., Aug. 6, 1943; s. Herbert Jackson and Myrtle Louise (Stone) L.; m. Janeice Lynette Evans. BS, Murray State U., 1966, MA, 1969. Tchr., basketball coach Kearsley Community Schs., Flint, Mich., 1966-80, Savannah (Ga.) High Sch., from 1988. Coach Ga. Coll. All-Star Basketball Game, 1986; mem. selection com. Atlanta Tip-Off Club Allstate Basketball Team, 1986; mem. adv. bd. Converse Nationwide Satellite Basketball Clinic, 1988.

Named Hon. Ky. Col., 1979, 85; named Coach of Yr., WTOC-TV, 1985, Savannah News Press, 1986. Mem. Nat. Fedn. Interscholastic Coaches Assn., Ga. Athletic Coaches Assn. (Region 3 Class AAAA Coach of Yr. 1985, 86, 87), Savannah Sports Hall of Fame Assn. Avocation: golf. Home: Savannah, Ga. Died Apr. 8, 1996.

**LOVERIDGE, SIR JOHN,** former member of parliament; b. Bowden, Cheshire, England, Sept. 9, 1925; s. Claude Warren and Emilie Warren (Malone) L.; m. Jean Marguerite Chivers, Dec. 6, 1954; children: Amanda, Michael, Emma, Steven, Robert. MA, St. John's Coll., Cambridge, Eng. Prin. of coll., London, 1954-92; justice of the peace West Ctrl. Divsn., 1963—2007, South Westminster, London, 1964-78; mem. British Parliament, 1970-83. Author: God Save the Queen, 1981, Hunter of the Moon, 1983, Hunter of the Sun, 1984; co-author: Moving Forward, 1982. Pres. Hampstead and Highgate Conservative Assn., 1986-91, Upminster Conservative Assn., Greater London Area Conservatives, 1993-96, v.p. 1984-93, 96—; liveryman Worshipful Co. Girdlers. Fellow Royal Astron. Soc., Royal Agrl. Soc.; mem. Royal Inst. Internat. Affairs, Dinosaurs Club (chmn.). Avocations: painting, poetry, historic houses, shooting. Home: London, England. Died Nov. 13, 2007.

**LOWE, MARY JOHNSON,** federal judge; b. NYC, June 10, 1924; m. Ivan A. Michael, Nov. 4, 1961; children: Edward H. Lowe, Leslie H. Lowe, Bess J. Michael. BA, Hunter Coll., 1952; LLB, Bklyn. Law Sch., 1954; LLM, Columbia U., 1955; LLD, CUNY, 1990. Bar: N.Y. 1955. Pvt. practice law, NYC, 1955-71; judge NYC Criminal Ct., 1971-72; acting justice NY State Supreme Ct., 1972-74; judge Bronx County Supreme Ct., 1975—76; justice NY State Supreme Ct., 1977—78; judge US Dist. Ct. (so. dist.) N.Y., 1978-91, sr. judge, 1991—99. Recipient award for outstanding service to criminal justice system Bronx County Criminal Cts. Bar Assn., 1974, award for work on narcotics cases Asst. Dist. Attys., 1974 Mem. Women in Criminal Justice, Harlem Lawyers Assn., Bronx Criminal Lawyers Assn., N.Y. County Lawyers Assn., Bronx County Bar Assn., N.Y. State Bar Assn. (award for outstanding jud. contbn. to criminal justice Sect. Criminal Justice 1978), NAACP, Nat. Urban League, Nat. Council Negro Women, NOW. Died Feb. 27, 1999.

**LOWE, WILLIAM CLELAND (BILL LOWE),** retired business products and systems company executive; b. Easton, Pa., Jan. 15, 1941; m. Cristina Lowe; children: Michelle, Gabriela, Daniela, Julie, James. BS in Physics, Lafayette Coll., 1962. With IBM Corp., Armonk, NY, 1962-88, dir. devel. mfg. ops. gen. systems div., 1975-77, dir. strategic devel., then adminstrv. asst. to div. pres., 1977-78, system mgr. entry level systems, then lab. dir. gen. systems div., 1978-81, v.p. info. system div., gen. mgr. Rochester, NY, 1981-82, v.p. system devel., system products div., 1982-83, asst. group exec. info. systems and communications group, 1983-85, pres. entry systems div., 1985-86, v.p., pres. entry systems div., 1986-88; exec. v.p. devel. mfg. Xerox Corp., Stamford, Conn., 1988-91; chmn., CEO Gulfstream Delaware Corp., Savannah, Ga., 1991—93. Died Oct. 19, 2013.

**LOWERY, LEONA FAITH,** retired secondary school and college educator; b. Killbuck, Ohio, Mar. 19, 1921; d. Frederick William and Sybil Anna (Middaugh) Duncan; m. Robert Charles Lowery, June 10, 1942 (dec.); 1 child, James Keith. BS, Ohio No. U., 1942; MA, Vanderbilt U., 1958, EdS, 1970. Cert. social sci., speech, drama, English and Latin tchr., Ohio. Tchr. Middle Point H.S., Ohio, 1943-45, Beaver H.S., Pa., 1952-56, Huntsville (Ala.) H.S., 1956-67, 68-70, Prince George County (Md.) Schs., 1967-68, Long Branch (N.J.) H.S., 1970-71, Marlboro (N.J.) H.S., 1971-87, Brookdale Coll. Br., Guayaquil, Ecuador, 1987-88, Mississippi Gulf Coast Coll., 1989-94; civil svc. Panama Canal Zone, 1945-46, Ohio State U., 1947-48. Contbr. articles to profl. jours. Pres. Ala. Classroom Tchrs., 1965-66. Recipient Minuteman Debating award Newark Acad., 1979; named Profl. Tchr. of Yr., Huntsville, Ala., 1970. Mem. DAR (state chmn. vet.-patients 1995—), Daus. Am. Colonists (parliamentarian 1995—), Ocean Springs Geneal. Soc. (pres. 1975-76), Friends of Libr. (pres. 1995—), Colonial Dames Am., Colonial Dames of 17th Century (2d v.p. 1995—), Alpha Delta Kappa (recording sec., Miss. chaplain 1991-92, pres. N.J. chpt. 1983-85, chaplain Zeta chpt. 1996—, internat. v.p. 1985-87, Honored Mem. of Yr. 1988, Pres.'s award Miss. chpt. 1995). Democrat. Presbyterian. Avocations: reading, travel, genealogical research, handicrafts, volunteer work. Home: Brandon, Miss. Died July 18, 2008.

**LOWRY, DOUGLAS A.,** retired dean, composer, conductor; s. Mildred Lowry; m. Marcia J Rhoads, Dec. 28, 1971; children: Jennifer A, Melanie J, Timothy J. MusB, U. Ariz., 1974; MusM, U. Southern Calif., 1978; DMus (hon.), U. Rochester Eastman Sch. Music, 2013. Assoc. dean U. Southern Calif. Thornton Sch. Music, L.A., 1992—2000; Thomas James Kelly prof. music, dean U. Cin. Conservatory Music, Cin., 2000—07; dean U. Rochester Eastman Sch. Music, 2007—11, Joan & Martin Messinger Dean, 2011—13, 2013. Composer: (songs) Christen the Voyage. Bd. dirs. Cin. (Ohio) Symphony Orch., 2000. Recipient Article of the Yr. award, American Music Tchr., 2004. Home: Rochester, NY. Died Oct. 2, 2013.

**LOWRY, JOHN CHRISTOPHER,** maxillofacial surgeon; b. Timperley, Eng., June 6, 1942; s. Arnold Leslie and Betty (Hornby) L.; m. Valerie Joyce Smethurst, July 6, 1968; children: Michelle Victoria, Jonathan Karl. BDS, U. Manchester Dental Sch., 1963; M.B.Ch.B, U. Manchester Med. Sch., 1970; honoris causa, GR Popa U. Iasi, Romania, 2004. Cert. MHSM, 1993, Edinburgh, 1999; registered Gen. Med. Coun., Gen. Dental Coun. House surgeon U. Dental Hosp., Manchester, 1963; sr. house officer Manchester Royal Infirmary, Manchester, 1964; registrar plastic & maxillofacial Bradford/Wakefield, Yorkshire, 1965; house surgeon, house physician to professorial units U. Hosp., South Manchester, 1971; sr. house officer Surg. Units Plastic/Orthopaedic Withington Hosp., Manchester; sr. registrar Manchester Royal Infirmary, North/South Manchester, 1972-76; cons. surgeon Royal Bolton Hosp. and East Lancashire Maxillofacial Svc., England, from 1976; hon. prof. U. Bucharest, Romania, 2007. Examiner U. Manchester Cell & Structural Biology, 1976—, Royal Coll. Surgeons of Edinburgh (Scotland), 1993—, Intercollegiate Assessment Bd., 1995-2000; referee Brit. Jour. Oral and Maxillo Facial Surgery, 1976—; Jour. Cranio-Maxillo Facial Surgery, 1992—; hon. cons. Def. Med. Svc., 2004.; vis. prof. U. Cen. Lancashire, 2004—. Fellow Leverhulme Travelling Brit. Assn. Oral and Maxillofacial Surgeons, Royal Coll. Surgeons, Eng., 1974-75; named Comdr. Brit. Empire, 2003. Fellow Am. Assn. Oral and Maxillofacial Surgeons (hon.), Brit. Assn. Oral & Maxillofacial Surgeons (pres. 2001, Down Surgical medal 2004, Colver Gold medal 2006), Royal Coll. Surgeons Eng. (examiner 2001—, dean faculty 2001-04), Manchester Med. Soc. (pres. 2004—), Internat. Assn. Oral and Maxillofacial Surgeons (exec. com. 2003—), Royal Coll. Anaesthetists; mem. European Assn. Cranio-Maxillofacial Surgery (sec.-gen. 1998—, exec. com.), Faculty Royal Coll. Surgeons, Eng. (bd. dirs. 1993—, specialist adv. com. 1994—), Hungarian Assn. Oral and Maxillofacial Surgeons (hon.), Acad. Med. Royal Colls, New Zealand Assoc. Oral and Maxillofacial Surgeons (Meritorious award, 2007), Romanian Assoc. OMFS (award Excellence, 2008, Croation Assoc. Plastic and Maxillofacial Surgery (hon. 2006), Assoc. Plastic Reconstructive and Maxillofacial Surgery (hon. 2006), Brit. Acad. Cosmetic Practice (chmn. 2008-). Avocations: athletics, motor sports, music, writing. Home: Bolton, England. Died Sept. 29, 2008.

**LUCENTE, GREGORY L.,** humanities educator; b. Evanston, Ill., Apr. 10, 1948; s. Martin M. and Verle (Straus) L.; m. Gloria Lauri-Lucente. BA, Yale U., 1970. With Johns Hopkins U., Balt., 1979-88; prof. Dept. Romance Langs. U. Mich., Ann Arbor, from 1988. Died June 26, 1997.

**LUCEY, PATRICK JOSEPH,** former Governor of Wisconsin; b. LaCrosse, Wis., Mar. 21, 1918; s. Gregory Charles and Ella Young (McNamara) Lucey; m. Jean Vlasis, 1951 (dec. 2011); children: Paul, Laurie, David. BA, U. Wis., Madison, 1946. Mem. Wis. State Assembly, 1949—50; exec. dir. Democratic Party Wis., 1951—62, state chmn., 1957—63; lt. gov. State of Wis., 1965—66, gov., 1971—77; US amb. to Mex. US Dept. State, Mexico City, 1977—79; dep. campaign mgr. Edward Kennedy for Pres., 1980. Del. Democratic Nat. Conv., 1968, 1976; ind. candidate for Vice Pres. US Presdl. Election, 1980; instr. Harvard U., 1983, Marquette U., 1984; sr. v.p. Cassidy & Associates, 1990—95. From pvt. to capt. US Army, 1941—45. Democrat. Roman Catholic. Died May 10, 2014.

**LUCKNER, HERMAN RICHARD, III,** interior designer; b. Newark, Ohio, Mar. 14, 1933; s. Herman Richard and Helen (Friednour) L. BS, U. Cin., 1957. Cert. interior designer and appraiser. Interior designer Greiwe Inc., Cin., 1957-64; owner, internat. designer Designers Loft Interiors, Cin., from 1964; owner Designer Accents, Cin., from 1991. Mem. bd. adv. Ohio Valley Organ Procurement Ctr., Cin., 1987—, U. Cin. Fine Arts Collection and Hist. Southwest Ohio, 1987-97; bd. dirs. Cin. Club Travelers, 1997-2000. Mem.: Appraisers Assn. Am., Am. Soc. Interior Designers, Met. Club. Republican. Avocation: needlepoint. Died Oct. 19, 2013.

**LUCKSTEAD, EUGENE FREDDIE, SR.,** medical educator, consultant; b. Wyoming, Iowa, Nov. 20, 1938; s. Freddie William and Velda Edwina Luckstead; m. Margaret Ann Dandl, June 24, 1961; children: Eugene Freddie, Ann Marie Gosdin, Erik Louis. BA in Liberal Arts, U. Iowa, Iowa City, 1960; MD, U. Iowa, Coll. Medicine, 1963. Tchr Med. Sch., Kans., Okla., Va., Iowa; exec. med. dir. King's Daughters Children's Hosp., Norfolk, Va., 1996—2000; prof. pediat., cardiology Tex. Tech U. Health Scis. Ctr., Amarillo, from 2000. Med. dir. Cook Children's Med. Ctr., Ft. Worth, 1988—96. Served with USN, 1963—68, Calif. Fellow: Am. Acad. Pediat. (Young Investigator of Yr., sect. cardiology 1970, Thomas Shaffer award, sports medicine 2004). Home: Amarillo, Tex. Died Dec. 17, 2013.

**LUETSCHWAGER, LONNIE ROGENA THEDE,** elementary school educator; b. Black Creek, Wis., Aug. 28, 1936; d. Lonson Roger and Esther (Freeman) Thede; m. Frederick G. Luetschwager, Aug. 1, 1959; children: Lynn Warner, Frederick II, Benjamin. 7 yr. lic., Outagamie Tchrs. Coll., 1956; BA, U. Wis., Oshkosh, 1962, MA in Reading, 1983. Cert. tchr., reading specialist, Wis. Tchr. Pleasant Dale Sch., Appleton, Wis., 1956-62; 1st grade tchr. Shiocton (Wis.) Sch. Dist., 1962-83, reading specialist, from 1983. Com. mem. Edn. for Employment, Outagamie County, Wis., 1987—, Competency Based Test, Wis., 1988—. Co-author: Shadows on the Wolf, 1987. Recipient Excellence in Edn. award Hillshire Farm, 1988; named Outstanding Historian Outagamie County, 1988. Fellow Internat. Reading Assn.; mem. ASCE, Mid East Reading Assn., Wis. Reading Assn. Lutheran. Avocations: sewing, making quilts. Died Oct. 15, 1997.

**LUFT, CECILE E.,** music educator; b. Brooklyn, NY, May 14, 1925; d. Jacob and Sophie Burrows; m. Morris Luft; children: Tamara, Leslie Noymer. Diploma in piano, Juilliard School of Music, NYC, 1946; MA, C.W. Post U., Brookville, NY, 1985—87. Choir dir. Temple Beth El, Bellmore, NY, 1953—56; music dir. Reform Jewish Congregation, Westbury, NY, 1960—68; music tchr. Pvt. Lessons, Merrick, NY, 1950—2001; music dir. Camp Rosemont & Roselake, Honesdale, Pa., 1967—68. Choir dir. Evangelical Covenant Ch., Floral Park, NY, 1986—2001. Mem.: Assn. Piano Tchrs. Long Island Inc. Avocations: travel, swimming. Died Nov. 1, 2005.

**LUISADA, ALDO A.,** cardiologist, educator; b. Florence, Italy, June 26, 1901; came to U.S., 1939, naturalized, 1944; s. Ezio and Elisa (Rignano) L.; m. Anna Passigli, Apr. 12, 1931; 1 child, Claude G. MD cum laude, Royal U., Florence, 1924. Assoc. Royal U. Padua (Italy) Med. Sch., 1927-30; faculty Royal U. Naples (Italy) Med. Sch., 1931-35; prof. medicine Royal U. Sassari, Italy, 1935-36, U. Ferrara, Italy, 1936-38; faculty Tufts Coll. Sch. Medicine, 1943-49, Chgo. Med. Sch., 1949-71, prof. medicine, 1960-71, prof., dir. div. cardiovascular research, 1961-71, also prof. physiology, 1969-71, disting. prof. physiology and medicine, from 1972; attending cardiologist Mt. Sinai Hosp., Chgo., 1960-71; chmn. dept. cardiology Oak Forest Hosp., 1971-83; disting. mem. hon. staff Michael Reese Hosp., Chgo., from 1985. Cons. medicine Hines (Ill.) VA Hosp., 1955-65, Cook County Hosp., 1968-72; prof. health care U. Ill. Sch. Pub. Health, 1972-76 Author: Hypotension, 1929, Constrictive Pericarditis, 1936, Cardiologia, 1938, Heart, 1949, (with C.K. Liu) Cardiac Pressures and Pulses, 1956, Intracardiac Phenomena, 1958, (with L.M. Rosa) Therapy of Cardiovascular Emergencies, 1960, (with A. Jacono) Attualità Cardiologiche, 1956, From Auscultation to Phonocardiography, 1965, (with S.J. Slodki) Differential Diagnosis of Cardiovascular Diseases, 1965, (with G. Sainani) Primer of Cardiac Diagnosis, 1968, Pulmonary Edema, 1970, Sounds of Normal Heart, 1972, Sounds of Diseased Heart, 1973, (with P.K. Bhat and G. Perez) An Atlas of Non Invasive Techniques, 1976, (with F. Portaluppi) The Heart Sounds, 1982; also numerous articles; editor-in-chief: Cardiology, 5 vols, 1958-61. Recipient Morris Parker award for research Chgo. Med. Sch., 1953 Fellow AMA (Gold medal for exhibit 1954), AAAS, ACP, Am. Heart Assn., Am. Coll. Cardiology, Am. Coll. Chest Physicians, Inst. Medicine Chgo., Am. Physiol. Soc., Am. Coll. Angiology; mem. Sigma Xi, Alpha Omega Alpha; hon. mem. cardiol. socs. of Argentina, Brazil, Chile, Peru, Uruguay, India, Piedmont Soc. Cardiac Surgery, Greek Heart Assn., Japan Coll. Angiology, Philippine Heart Assn., Rome Acad. Medicine, Turin (Italy) Acad. Medicine. Research on normal function of arteries and bronchi; pulmonary edema, mechanism and its treatment by defoaming method; auscultation; phonocardiography; heart failure, stress tests, heart in anesthesia. Home: Chicago, Ill. Died Nov. 20, 1987.

**LUKANOV, ANDREY KARLOV,** former Prime Minister of Bulgaria; b. USSR, Sept. 26, 1938; s. Karlo Lukanov. Grad. with honors, Moscow State Inst. Internat. Rels. Head internat. orgns. dept. Fgn. Trade Ministry, Sofia, Bulgaria, 1966-72, dep. min., 1972-73, lst dep. min., 1973-76; mem. Nat. Asssembly, Sofia, from 1976; dep. chmn. Coun. Mins., Sofia, 1976-86, 1st dep. chmn., 1986-87; mem. Bulgarian Communist Party, Sofia, from 1965, full mem. Cen. Com., from 1977; min. fgn. econ. rels. Govt. of Bulgaria, Sofia, 1987-89, prime min., 1990. Chmn. UN Coun. on Trade and Devel., 1974-75; permanent rep. of Bulgaria to Coun. for Mut. and Econ. Aid, 1976, chmn. exec. com., 1980; chmn. Bulgarian-Swedish Commn. on Econ., Indsl. and Tech. Cooperation, 1975, Bulgarian-Romanian Commn., 1977-85, Bulgarian-German Dem. Republic Commn., 1978-82, Bulgarian-Hungarian Comm., 1978-82, Bulgarian-Czechoslovakian Com., 1984, Bulgarian-Soviet Commn., 1984, Bulgarian-Nicaraguan Commn., 1984, Bulgarian-French Com., 1984, numerous others. Assassinated Oct. 2, 1996.

**LUKMAN, RILWANU,** former Nigerian government official; b. Zaria, Kaduna, Nigeria, Aug. 26, 1938; s. Qadi and Ramatu Lukman; m. Amina Abdullahi, Dec. 1965; children: Ramatu, Ahmed, Salihu. Gen. cert. of edn., Nigerian Coll. Art/Sci./Tech., Zaria, 1958; BSc in Engring./Mining, Imperial Coll. Sci. & Tech., London, 1962; postgrad. cert., U. Mining & Metallurgy, Leoben, Austria, 1968; postgrad., McGill U., Can., 1977-78; PhD in Chem. Engring. (hon.), U. Bologna, Italy, 1988; DSc (hon.), U. Maiduguri, Nigeria, 1989, Ahmadu Bello U., Zaria, 1991; PhD (hon.), Moore House Coll., Atlanta, 1992. Registered profl. engr. Asst. mining engr. AB Statsgruvor, Sweden, 1962-64; inspector, sr. inspector of mines Mines divsn. Ministry of Mines and Power, Jos, Nigeria, 1964-67, acting asst. chief inspector of mines, 1968-70; gen. mgr. Cement Co. No. Nigeria, Sokoto, 1970-74; gen. mgr., CEO Nigerian Mining Corp., Jos, 1974-84; min. of mines, power, and steel Govt. Nigeria, Nigeria, 1984-85, min. of petroleum resources, 1986-89, 2009—10, minister fgn. affairs Nigeria, 1989-90, presdl. adviser on petroleum and energy, 1999—2003, strategic adviser on energy, 2007—08; pres. Orgn. Petroleum Exporting Countries (OPEC), Vienna, 1986-89, 2002, sec. gen., 1995-2000; chmn., bd. dirs. Nat. Electric Power Authority, Lagos, Nigeria, 1993-94. Fellow Imperial Coll. London, 1987; decorated Knight of the British Empire, British Monarch, London, 1989, Officer of the Legion d'Honneur of France, Govt. of France, Paris, 1990, Order of the Liberator 1st Class, Govt. of Venezuela, Caracas, 1990; proclamation of Dr. Rilwanu Lukman Day, Gov. of Ga., 1989. Fellow: Nigerian Metall. Soc., Nigerian Mining and Geoscience Soc. (past. pres.), Inst. Mining and Metallurgy, London; mem.: Chartered Engring. Inst. Avocations: reading, walking. Died July 21, 2014.

**LUMBARD, ELIOT HOWLAND,** retired lawyer; b. Fairhaven, Mass., May 6, 1925; s. Ralph E. and Constance Y. Lumbard; m. Jean Ashmore, June 21, 1947 (div.); m. Kirsten Dehner, June 28, 1981 (div.); children: Susan, John, Ann, Joshua Abel, Marah Abel. BS in Marine Transp., US Mcht. Marine Acad., 1945; BS in Economics, U. Pa. Wharton Sch. Finance & Commerce, 1949; LLB, Columbia U. Law Sch., NYC, 1952; DSc (hon.), US Mcht. Marine Acad., 2005. Bar: NY 1953, US Supreme Ct. 1959, Pa.

1983, cadet-midshipman, 1944. Assoc. Breed, Abbott and Morgan, NYC, 1952-53; asst. US atty. (southern dist.) NY US Dept. Justice, NYC, 1953-56; assoc. Chadbourne, Parke, Whiteside & Wolff, NYC, 1956-58; ptnr. Townsend & Lewis, NYC, 1961-70, Spear and Hill, NYC, 1970-75, Lumbard and Phelan, P.C., NYC, 1977-82, Saul, Ewing, Remick & Saul, NYC, 1982-84; pvt. practice law NYC, 1984-86; ptnr. Haight, Gardner, Poor & Havens, NYC, 1986-88; pvt. practice law NYC, 1988-92. Chief counsel NY State Commn. Investigation, 1958-61; spl. asst. counsel for law enforcement to Gov. NY, 1961-67; organizer NY State Identification and Intelligence Sys., 1963-67; chair Oyster Bay Conf. on Organized Crime, 1962-67; criminal justice cons. to Gov. Fla. and other states, 1967; chief criminal justice cons. to NJ Legislature, 1968-69; chmn. com. on organized crime NYC Criminal Justice Coordinating Coun., 1971-74; organizer first schs. of Criminal Justice at SUNY Albany and Rutgers, 1965, Newark; mem. departmental disciplinary com. First Dept., NY Supreme Ct., 1982-88; trustee bankruptcy Universal Money Order Co., Inc., 1977-82, Meritum Corp., 1982-88, Ira Haupt & Co., 1964-73; spl. master in admiralty Hellenic Lines Ltd., 1984-86; chmn. Palisades Life Ins. Co. (former Equity Funding subs. 1974-75); bd. dir. RMC Industries Corp.; chair Am. Maritime History Project, Inc., Kings Point, NY, 1996—; lectr. trial practice NYU Law Sch., 1963-65; mem. vis. com. Sch. Criminal Justice, SUNY-Albany, 1968-75; adj. prof. law and criminal justice John Jay Coll. Criminal Justice, CUNY, 1975-85; arbitrator Am. Arbitration Assn. and NY Civil Ct.-Small Claims Part, NY County; mem. Vol. Master Program US Dist. Ct. (southern dist.) NY Bd. dirs. Citizens Crime Commn. NYC, Inc., Big Brothers Movement, Citizens Union; trustee Trinity Sch., 1964-78, NYC Police Found., Inc., 1971-92, chmn., 1971-74, emeritus. Lt. j.g. USNR, 1943-52, founder & chair NY Att's Police Found., 1971- Lt. USNR. Recipient 1st Disting. Svc. award SUNY, Albany, 1985, US Merchant Marine Acad. Mem. Assn. Bar City NY, NY County Lawyers Assn., ABA, NY State Bar Assn., Maritime Law Assn., Down Town Assn. Club. Republican. Home: Nashua, NH. Died Nov. 6, 2013.

**LUMUMBA, CHOKWE,** Mayor, Jackson, Mississippi; b. Detroit, Aug. 2, 1947; s. Lucien and Priscilla Taliaferro; m. Nubia Lumumba (dec. 2003); children: Kambon Mutope, Rukia Kai, Chokwe Antar. BS in Polit. Sci., Kalamazoo Coll., Mich., 1969; JD cum laude, Wayne Stste U., Detroit, 1975. Bar: Mich., Miss. Mem. Defenders Office of City of Detroit, 1976—77; founding mem. Ashford, Cannon, Edison, Jarrett, Lumumba, Ottison, and Shakoor, Detroit, 1977—91; sr. ptnr. Lumumba, Freelon and Associates, Jackson, Miss., 1991—2014; councilman, Ward 2 Jackson City Coun., 2009—13; mayor City of Jackson, 2013—14. Mem. SW Miss. Legal Services, 1990. Dir., coach, youth mentor Jackson Panthers Basketball Orgn.; organizer Miss. Disaster Relief Coalition, Gulf Coast Survivors Assembly; mem. Word and Worship Christian Ch.; bd. dirs. Wayne County Legal Services, Detroit, People's Hurricane Relief Fund; co-founder, mem. Malcolm X Grassroots Movement. Mem.: NAACP, Magnolia Bar Assn., Nat. Conf. Black Lawyers, Miss. Bar Assn., Miss. Freedom Dem. Party. Democrat. Died Feb. 25, 2014.

**LUND, FREDRIK,** physician; b. Sodertälje, Sweden, Mar. 10, 1916; s. David and Gunhild L.; m. Gunvor Henriks; children: Gunilla, Agneta, Staffan. Cert. physician, Karolinska Inst., Stockholm, 1943; Grad., 1951. Asst. physician Med. Clin. Södersjukhuset, Stockholm, 1943-45; in charge vascular lab.pt. Caridovascular Clinic Södersjukhuset, Stockholm, 1951-56; researcher Clin. Rsch. Ctr. Södersjukhuset, Stockholm, from 1991; resident Stockholms Sjukhem, 1946-51; with pharmacology dept. Karolinska Inst., Stockholm, 1949-51; head physician Geriatric Sjukhus, Enskede, Stockholm, 1957-82; pvt. practice cardiovascular diseases Stockholm, 1957-97. Cons. in clin. physiology Lund (Sweden) U., 1982-83, clin. physiology dept. Karolinska Hosp., Stockholm, 1983-90, clin. physiology dept. Sodersjukhuset, Stockholm, 1984-90. Fellow Internat. Coll. Angiology (sci. coun.); mem. Swedish Soc. Med. Angiology (hon.), Internat. Com. on Standardization Angiological Methods. Achievements include research in geriatrics and angiology; invention of diagnostics and methods in vascular disease: principles of analysis and evaluation of digital pulse wave form to reveal vasospasm and early structural changes in arterial narrowing and elasticity loss; studies of the course of disease and effect of vasoactive drugs and changes in lifestyle; overview of evaluation of nutritional blood perfusion of the skin and microvascular permeability by a new technique of rapid sequence or video fluorescein imaging; introduction of the transcutaneous route of drug administration (nitroglycerin for systemic and local use); treatment of advanced peripheral arterial disease with e.g. thrombolysis, and oral longterm anticoagulation; in addition to initial intravenous hydroxyethylrutosides for prevention of amputation in end pont ischemia. Home: Stockholm, Sweden. Deceased.

**LUNDGREN, LEONARD, III,** retired secondary school educator; b. San Francisco, June 22, 1933; s. Leonard II and Betty (Bosold) L.; m. Jane Gates, June 12, 1976. AA, City Coll. San Francisco, 1952; AB, San Francisco State U., 1954, MA, 1958, postgrad., 1958—71. Cert. tchr., Calif. Phys. edn. tchr., athletic coach Pelton Jr. H.S., San Francisco, 1958-59; social studies tchr., dept. chair, phys. edn. tchr., athletic coach Luther Burbank Jr. H.S., San Francisco, 1959-78; history, govt. econs., geography tchr. George Washington H.S., San Francisco, 1978-93. Water safety instr. ARC, San Francisco, 1946-61; mem. Calif. Quality Teaching Ctr. Conf. Bd., 1965-67. Author: Guide for Films and Filmstrips, 1966, Teacher's Handbook for Social Studies, 1966, Guide for Minority Studies, 1968. V.p. Lakeside Property Owners Assn., San Francisco, 1986—88, legis. advocate, 1988—95; v.p. West of Twin Peaks Coun., San Francisco, 1986—87; pub. affairs polit. econ. cons. Calif. Fulbright scholar, Greece, 1963; recipient Svc. Pin, ARC, 1961. Mem.: AARP (cmty. coord. San Francisco 1986—87, rep. 2001—04), PTA (sch. v.p. 1980—81), NEA (life; del. 1970, 1972—76), San Francisco Classroom Tchrs. Assn. (pres. 1972—73, Gavel award 1973), Calif. Coun. Social Studies (v.p. San Francisco chpt. 1969—70), Nat. Coun. Social Studies, Calif. Tchrs. Assn. (state coun. rep. 1963—74), Calif. Assn. Health, Phys. Edn., Recreation and Dance (life; treas. San Francisco chpt. 1959—60), Calif. Ret. Tchrs. Assn. (life; legis. chmn. San Francisco divsn. 1995—99, 1st v.p. 1997—99, pres. 1999—2000, legis. co-chmn. 2001—04, Recognition award 2000), World Affairs Coun. No. Calif., San Francisco State U. Alumni Assn. (life; treas. 1959), Nat. Geog. Soc. (life), Fryers Club San Francisco, Commonwealth Club of Calif., Phi Delta Kappa (life; pres. chpt. 1965—66). Avocations: travel, swimming, gardening. *A career in education for me is my life from learning to teaching over and over again. History, government, geography and economics are my major subjects. World travel gives me the chance to see the places I studied and taught.* Deceased.

**LÜNING, FREDRIK N.,** transportation executive; b. Stockholm, Aug. 7, 1936; s. Nils Gustav Adolf and Anna Maria (Wolke) L. Master Mariner, Stockholm Acad. Navigation, 1960; 2d engring. cert., Härnösand Acad. Navigation, 1968; MBA, Stockholm Sch. Econs., 1973. Cert. competency as master mariner, Nat. Swedish Adminstrn. Shipping and Navigation. Apprentice, mcht. navy officer Swedish Mcht. Navy, Stockholm, 1952-60; cadet, officer Royal Swedish Navy, Stockholm, 1960-64; merchant navy officer Johnson Line, Stockholm, 1964-70, marine supt. Yokohama, Japan, 1973-75, area rep. Mid. East Khorramshahr, Iran, 1975-77; gen. mgr. Gulf Agy. Co. Ltd., Khorramshahr, 1978-81, Lagos, Nigeria, 1981, Abu Dhabi, United Arab Emirates, 1981-83; mng. dir. Algosaibi Shipping Agy. Group/Gulf Agy. Co., Dammam, Saudi Arabia, 1983-93; dir. Lüning Shipping Inc., Berkeley Heights, NJ, from 1993; mng. dir. Gulf Agy. Co. Pte. Ltd., Singapore, 1994-95; gen. mgr. Al-Hamd Internat. Container Terminal (Pvt.) Ltd., Karachi, Pakistan, 2001—03. Consul of Sweden Swedish Fgn. Ministry, United Arab Emirates, 1981-84. Author: The Gulf War As I Experienced It, 1994. Lt. comdr. Royal Swedish Navy Res. Recipient medal of merit Swedish Ministry Fgn. Affairs, Riyadh, Saudi Arabi, 1991. Mem. Royal Inst. Navigation (London), Nautical Inst. London, Inst. Marine Engrs. (consociate), Royal Nat. Lifeboat Instn. (gov. life 1990), Royal Swedish Motorboat Club (life), Swedish Tall/Deep Sea Sailing Ship Assn., Swedish Shipping and Navy League (life), Swedish Assn. Economists, Swedish Assn. for Saving of Lives at Sea (life), Royal Swedish Navy Officers Club, Royal Swedish Res. Officers Assn., Swedish Royal Navy Old Comrades Assn. (life), Stockholm Anti-Aircraft Artillery Assn. (life), Royal Swedish Cavalry Forces Old Comrades Assn. (life), Assn. for Preservation of The Royal Horse Guards (life). Avocations: travel, history, politics. Deceased.

**LURIE, ROBERT,** diversified financial services and chemical manufacturing company executive; Pres., dir. Gt. Am. Mgmt. & Investment Inc., Chgo. Died 1990.

**LUSINCHI, JAIME,** former president of Venezuela, pediatrician; b. Clarines, Venezuela, May 27, 1924; m. Blanca Lusinchi. MD, Ctrl. U., Caracas, Venezuela, 1947. Founder Venezuela Democratic Party, 1941, parliamentary leader, 1967—80, sec.-gen., 1980—83, party leader, 1980; dep. Venezuela House of Deputies, 1958—84, senator, from 1989; pres. Govt. of Venezuela, Caracas, Venezuela, 1984—88. Mem.: American Acad. Pediatricians. Died May 21, 2014.

**LUTTMAN, HORACE CHARLES,** retired aeronautical engineer; b. Banbury, Oxford, Eng., May 30, 1908; arrived in Can., 1947; s. Walter Charles and Ruth Mary (Wilkinson) L.; M. Jean I. M. Morrison, Oct. 6, 1934 (dec. 1987); children: 1 child, Rachel Mary. BA in Mech. Scis., Cambridge U., 1930, MA in Mech. Scis., 1947. Apprentice Armstrong Whitworth Aircraft, Coventry, Eng., 1930-33; chief ground engr. London, Scottish & Provincial Airways, London, 1934; examiner Vickers Aircraft Ltd. Aero. Inspection Directorate British Air Ministry, Weybridge, Eng., 1935-36, asst. insp. Fairey Aviation Ltd. Stockport, Eng., 1936-38, insp. N. Am. Aviation, Inc. Inglewood, Calif., 1938-40; insp. in charge ea. group British Air Commn., NYC, Washington, 1940-41, asst. chief insp. aircraft Washington, 1941-45; prin. prodn. officer standardization Ministry of Supply (Air), London, 1946-47; patents officer A.V. Roe Can., Ltd., Malton, Ontario, 1947-52, contracts adminstr., 1952-54; sec., treas. Canadian Aero. Inst., Ottawa, 1954-62, Canadian Aero. and Space Inst., Ottawa, 1962-73. Editor Canadian Aero. Jour., 1955-62, Canadian Aeronautics and Space Jour., 1962-73, Canadian Aeronautics and Space Inst. Transactions, 1968-73. Recipient Canada Centennial Medal, Canadian Govt., 1967. Named by the Canadian Aeronautics and Space Inst. Charles Luttman Scholarship, 1996. Fellow AIAA (assoc.), Canadian Aeronautics and Space Inst., Royal Aero. Soc.; mem. Sigma Gamma Tau. Achievements include initiating. in 1947, standardization of single high tensile bolt in place of two types (high and low tensile) then standard in British aero. mfg.; founder (with others) Canadian Aero. Inst.; holds 2 or 3 aircraft related patents. Home: Sevenoaks, England. Died Apr. 17, 2001.

**LUZI, MARIO,** poet, playwright; b. Castello, Italy, Oct. 20, 1914; m. Elena Monazi, 1942; 1 child. Student, U. Florence, 1930-36; PhD (hon.), Queen's U., Belfast, 1987. Tchr., various cities, 1938-55; prof. French U. Florence, Italy, from 1955. Author: (verse) La barca, 1935, Avvento notturno, 1940, Un brindisi, 1946, Quaderno gotico, 1947, Primizie del deserto, 1952, Onore del vero, 1957, Il giusto della vita, 1960, Nel magma, 1963, Dal fondo delle campagne, 1965, Su fondamenti invisibili, 1971, Poesie, 1974, In the Dark Body of Metamorphosis and Other Poems, 1975, Al fuoco della controversia, 1978, Semiserie, 1979, Tutte le poesie: Il giusto della vita, 1934-57, Nell'opera del mondo, 1957-78, 2 vols., 1979, Reportage: un poemetto; seguito dal, Taccuino di viaggio in Cina, 1980, Per il battesimo dei nostri frammenti, 1985, L'alta, la cupa fiamma, 1990, Frasi e incisi di un canto salutare, 1991, Spazio, stelle, voce: il colore della poesia, 1992, (plays) Ipazia, 1973, Libro di Ipazia, 1979, Rosales, 1983, Hystrio, 1987, Corale della città di Palermo per S. Rosalia, 1989, Il Purgatorio; La notte lava la mente; Drammaturgia di un'ascensione, 1990, (other works) L'opium chrétien, 1938, Un'illusione platonica e altri saggi, 1941, Biografia a Ebe, 1942, L'inferno e il limbo, 1949, Studio su Mallarmé, 1952, Aspetti della generazione napoleonica ed altri saggi di letteratura francese, 1956, Lo stile di constant, 1962, Trame, 1963, Tutto in questione, 1965, Poesia e romanzo, 1973, Vicissitudine e forma, 1974, Discorso naturale, 1980, Il silenzio, la voce, 1984, Cronache dell'altro mondo, 1989, Scritti, 1989, De quibis, 1991, Non sono sazi della loro vita, 1992; translator: Vita e letteratura (Charles du Bos), 1943, Poesia e prose (Samuel Coleridge), 1949, Andromaca (Jean Racine), 1960, Cantico delle colonne (Paul Valéry), 1960, La Fonte (Jorge Guillén), 1961, Riccardo II (William Shakespeare), 1966, La cordigliera delle Ande, 1983; editor: L'idea simbolista, 1959, (with Tommaso Landolfi) Anthologie de la poésie lyrique française, 1950; editor, translator: Francamente, 1980. Recipient Carducci prize, 1953, Marzotto prize, 1957, Etna-Taormina prize, 1964, Fiuggi prize, 1971, Viareggio prize, 1978, Mondello award, 1985, Librex Guggenheim, 1986. Died Feb. 28, 2005.

**LWIN, U.,** government official; b. Dec. 10, 1912; married; 4 children. Former officer Burma Army; amb. to Fed. Republic of Germany, 1966-71; amb. to Netherlands, 1969-71; permanent rep. to UN, 1971-72; min. for Planning and Fin., 1972-75; min. for Information, 1975-77; dep. prime min. of Burma, 1974-77; pres., 1988; former gen. sec. Nat. League of Democaracy, Yangon, Myanmar. Died Apr. 10, 2004.

**LYALL, GAVIN TUDOR,** author, journalist; b. Birmingham, U.K., Sept. 5, 1932; s. Joseph Tudor and Agnes Ann (Hodgkiss) L.; m. Katharine Elizabeth Whitehorn, Apr. 1, 1958; children: Bernard James, Jake Christopher. BA, Pembroke Coll., Cambridge, 1956, MA, 1987. Journalist Picture Post, London, 1956-57, Sunday Graphic, London, 1957-58; prodn. asst. BBC TV, London, 1958-59; journalist, aviation editor Sunday Times, London, 1959-63. Author: The Wrong Side of the Sky, 1961, The Most Dangerous Game, 1964 (Crime Writers' Assn. Silver Dagger award 1964), Midnight Plus Ong, 1965 (Crime Writers' Assn. Gold Dagger award 1965), Shooting Script, 1966, Venus With Pistol, 1969, Blame the Dead, 1978, Judas Country, 1975, The Secret Servant, 1980, The Conduct of Major Maxim, 1982, The Crocus List, 1986, Uncle Target, 1988, Spy's Honour, 1995, others; editor: Freedom's Battle: The War in the Air, 1968. Mem. Air Transport Users Com., London, 1979-94, Air Travel Trust Com., London, 1982—. Flying officer, Royal Air Force, 1952-53, U.K. Mem. Royal Air Force Club, Detection Club, Crime Writers' Assn. (chmn.). Avocations: model making, model photography, painting. Home: London, England. Died Jan. 18, 2003.

**LYMPANY, DAME MOURA,** concert pianist; b. Saltash, Cornwall, Eng., Aug. 18, 1916; d. John and Beatrice Johnstone; m. Colin Defries, 1944 (div. 1950); m. Bennet Korn, 1951 (div. 1961); 1 child. 1st performance, Harrogate, England, 1929. Recording, Decca, HMV, EMI, Olympia, Erato. Decorated Comdr. Order of Crown Belgium, Comdr. Order Brit. Empire, Dame Comdr. Brit. Empire; recipient 2d prize, Ysaye Internat. Piano Competition, 1938, Cultural medal, Rep. Portugal, Charles Heidseick prize, Royal Philharm. Soc.; named Chevalier des Arts et Lettres, French Govt., 1992; fellowship, Royal Acad. Music. Died Mar. 28, 2005.

**LYTTELTON, HUMPHREY RICHARD ADEANE,** musician, band-leader, writer; b. Eton, Bucks, Eng., May 23, 1921; s. George William Lyttelton; m. Patricia Mary Braithwaite, 1948 (dissolved 1952); 1 child; m. Elizabeth Jill Richardson, 1952; 3 children. Degree, Eton Coll.; DLitt (hon.), Warwick, 1987, Loughborough U. Tech., 1988; DMus (hon.), U. Durham, 1989; postgrad., U. Keele. Free-lance journalist; with Camberwell Art Sch., 1947—48; leader Humphrey Lyttelton's Band, 1948—2008; cartoonist Daily Mail, 1949—53; founder Calligraph Records, 1984. Performer numerous recs. & TV appearances, Compere BBC Jazz Programes, The Best of Jazz; author: I Play as I Please, 1954, Second Chorus, 1958, Take it from the Top, 1975, The Best of Jazz: Basin Street to Harlem, 1978, Humphrey Lyttelton's Jazz and Big Band Quiz, 1979, The Best of Jazz II, 1983, Why No Beethoven, 1984, Melody Maker, 1954—60, Reynolds News, 1955—62, Sunday Citizen, 1962—67, Harper's & Queen's, 1968—76, Punch. Pres. Soc. Italic Handwriting. With Grenadier Guards, 1941—46. Home: Hertfordshire, England. Died Apr. 25, 2008.

**MA, YUANXI,** Chinese and English language educator, literature educator, translator; b. Shanghai, Feb. 18, 1933; arrived in US, 1985, naturalized, 1999; d. Shu Yuan and Jingxing Ma; children: Xiaodan, Jia. BA, Beijing Fgn. Studies U., China, 1953, MA, 1956, SUNY, Buffalo, 1988, PhD, 1992. Cert. hospitality educator Am. Translators Assn., translator. Assoc. prof. Beijing Fgn. Studies U., 1953-82; assoc. prof., vice-chair English dept. Inst. Internat. Rels., Beijing, 1982-85; assoc. dir. Sch. Chinese Studies, China Inst., NYC, 1989-95; dir. translation Baker & McKenzie Law Firm, Chgo., 1995—2004; dir., intensive English program Les Roches Jinjiang Hotel Mgmt. Coll., 2004—07; dir., project devel. Aston Ednl. Group, 2007—12. Adj. prof.

NYU, 1990-95, The New Sch. for Social Rsch., 1991; interpreter, translator Conf. Internat. Coop. Alliance, Washington, 1985, interpreter, Am.-Chinese Friendship Group traveling in China, 1975; head of lang. Les Roches Jin Jiang Internat. Hotel Mgmt. Coll., Shanghai, China, 2004-2007; dir. project devel. Aston Ednl. Group, Beijing and Shanghai 2007-11; dir., Aston Internat. Acad. Austin, Tex., 2011-2012; tutor, legal translation, U. Chgo. Graham Sch. 2003-. Author: College English, 1983, English, I-V, 1978, 79, TV English, I-III, 1980, English Textbooks, I, II, 1962; translator of lit. and legal works; editor-in-chief of translation collections, articles to books; contbr. to profl. jours. and textbooks; numerous presentations in field. Mem. U.S.-China Friendship Assn., Internat. Fedn. Translators, Nat. Assn. Women's Studies, Translation Assn. China, Am. Translators Assn. (accredited English and Chinese translator). Home: Chicago, Ill. Died May 17, 2013.

**MAAZEL, LORIN VARENCOVE,** conductor, composer, violinist; b. Neuilly-sur-Seine, France, Mar. 6, 1930; s. Lincoln and Marie (Barnet) Maazel; m. Miriam Sandbank (div.); m. Israela Margalit (div.); m. Dietlinde Turban, 1986; 3 children; 4 children from previous marriage. Studies with Vladimir Bakaleinikoff; student, U. Pitts., Mus. D. (hon.), 1968; HHD, Beaver Coll., 1973. Violinist Fine Arts Quartet Pitts., 1946—50; condr. Deutsche Oper Berlin, 1965—71, Berlin Radio Symphony Orch., 1965—75; music dir. Cleve. Orch., 1972—82; gen. mgr., chief condr. Vienna State Opera, 1982—84; music cons. Pitts. Symphony Orch., 1984—88, music dir., 1988—96; chief condr. Bavarian Radio Symphony Orch., Munich, 1993—2002; music dir. NY Philharm., 2002—09, Palau de les Arts Reina Sofia, Valencia, Spain, 2006—11. Debut as condr., 1938; European debut, 1953; festivals include Bayreuth, Salzburg, Edinburgh; tours include South America, Australia, USSR, Japan, Korea, People's Republic China; albums include Holst: Planets, 2006. Decorated Comdr.'s Cross of Merit, Fed. Republic Germany, Legion of Honor, France, Knight Grand Cross, Italy, Comdr. of Lion, Finland; named a Goodwill Amb., UN. Achievements include 500 opera and concert performances with 150 orchestras; raising millions of dollars for benefit of UNESCO, World Wide Fund for Nature, Red Cross, and UN High Commisioner for Refugees. Avocations: tennis, swimming, collecting American paintings and Oriental art. Died July 13, 2014.

**MABIN, ANN MARIE,** artist management executive, consultant; b. Memphis, Apr. 22; d. Jim and Pearline White; m. Robert Mabin (div. 1989); children: Camille, Diane. AA, Wayne State C.C., 1974, BS, 1977; postgrad., UCLA, 1979-81. Artist rels. Motown Records, Detroit, 1968-79; pres. artist mgmt. Mary Jane Prodn., L.A., NYC, 1979-91, Klasact Entertainment, LA, from 1991. Tour cons. Mary Jane Girls, L.A., 1982-87. Author (poem) Smile, 1989 (Golden Poet award 1990); coord. (record album) Street Songs, 1981 (Am. Music award 1982), Mary Jane Girls, 1983 (Am. Music award 1984), Super Freak, 1981 (Grammy award 1991). Vol. Dem. Conv., Detroit, 1975. Mem. Prestigious Women Assn., Starlight Found. (vol.), Braille Inst. for Blind (vol.). Baptist. Avocations: gourmet cooking, nature walks, music, writing. Home: Los Angeles, Calif. Died Jan. 27, 2001.

**MACAFEE, ALASTAIR LOWRY,** retired orthopedist; b. Jan. 11, 1935; MB, BChir, BAO, Queens U., Belfast, Northern Ireland, 1959; MD, 1963. House officer Nat. Health Svc., Northern Ireland, 1959—60; tutor Dept. Pathology, Belfast, 1960—63; surgeon, 1963—73; cons., trauma opthop. surgery Ulster Hosp., 1973—95. Past pres. Irish Orthop. Assn., Medico Legal Soc., Northern Ireland. Contbr. articles to profl. sci. jours. Fellow: RCS, Brit. Orthop. Assn. (sr.); mem.: Brit. Med. Assn., Ulster Med. Soc. Home: Donaghadee, Northern Ireland. Died 2010.

**MACAULEY, WARD,** dean, retired career officer; b. Richmond Hill, NY, Dec. 30, 1923; s. James Oliver and Jocelyn (Ward) M.; m. Sallie Wells (dec. Oct. 5, 1987); children: Ward Henson, Wesley Adams; m. Lydia Sargent, July 23, 1988. BS in Acctg., San Diego State Y., 1969, MS in Acctg., 1974. Commd. 2d. lt. U.S. Army, 1942, advanced through grades to col., 1969, retired, 1974; prof. acctg. Mesa Coll., San Diego, 1974-79, assoc. dean, 1979-81, dean sch. bus., 1988-90, San Diego City Coll., 1982-87. Pres. Darwell Co., San Diego, 1967-74; forensic auditor U.S. Atty., So. Calif., 1980-82. Decorated Air medal with 3 bronze oak leaf clusters, D.F.C. Mem. Dist. Flying Cross Soc. (treas. 1996-2000). Republican. Episcopalian. Home: La Jolla, Calif. Deceased.

**MACCANICO, ANTONIO,** Italian government official; b. Avellino, Italy, Aug. 4, 1924; m. Maria Ciuci; 1 child. JD, U. Pisa. Mem. parliamentary profl. staff, 1947; head legis. office Ministry State Enterprise, 1962-63; head comm. dept. Chamber of Deputies, 1964, drafter minutes, 1969, dep. sec.-gen., 1972; pres. ad hoc com. direct election European Parliament, Brussels, 1975, sec.-gen., 1976, Presidency of Italian Republic, 1978-87; chmn. Mediobanca, 1987-88; min. regional affairs and instl. reforms Govt. of Italy, Rome, 1988-91, min. post & telecom., 1996-99, min. instutional reform, 2000—01; senator Italian Republican Party, 1992—2013. Contbr. articles to profl. jours. Decorated Knight Grand Cross Order Merit Italian Republic. Mem. Circolo Montecitorio, Circolo Tevere Remo. Avocations: tennis, swimming, sailing. Died Apr. 23, 2013.

**MACCORMICK, SIR NEIL (DONALD NEIL MACCORMICK),** law educator, writer, broadcaster; b. Glasgow, Scotland, May 27, 1941; s. John MacDonald and Margaret Isobel (Miller) MacC.; m. Caroline Rona Barr, Nov. 6, 1965 (div. 1992); children: Janet, Morag, Sheena; m. Flora Margaret Milne, June 12, 1992. MA, U. Glasgow, 1963; BA, Balliol Coll. Oxford U., Eng., 1965, MA, 1969; LLD (hon.), U. Edinburg, 1982, U. Uppsala, Sweden, 1986,

U. The Saarland, Germany, 1994, Queen's U., Kingston, Ont., Can., 1995. Barrister, Inner Temple, 1971. Lectr. jurisprudence U. St. Andrews, Scotland, 1965-67; fellow, tutor in jurisprudence Balliol Coll., 1967-72; lectr. law Oxford U., 1968-72; Regius prof. pub. law U. Edinburgh, 1972—2008, dean faculty of law, 1973-76, 85-88, provost law & social sciences, 1993-97, Leverhulme rsch. prof., 1997—99, 2004—08. Mem. Econ. and Social Rsch. Coun., U.K., 1995-2008, Convention on the Future of Europe, 2002-03 Author: Legal Reasoning and Legal Theory, 1978, Legal Right and Social Democracy, 1982, Rhetoric and The Rule of Law, 2005, Institutions of Law, 2007; co-author: (with O. Weinberger) An Institutional Theory of Law, 1986. Named Scottish Euro MP of the Yr., 2001, Scottish Euro MP of the Year, 2002, 2003; named a Knight Comdr. of the Most Excellent Order of the British Empire, Her Majesty Queen Elizabeth II, 2001. Fellow Brit. Acad., Royal Soc. Edinburgh; mem. Finnish Acad. Scis. (fgn.); mem. Academia Europaea. Mem. Scottish Nat. Party. Avocations: hill walking, sailing, bagpipes. Home: Edinburgh, Scotland. Died Apr. 5, 2009.

**MACDONALD, DAVID MOFFAT,** surgeon; b. Glasgow, Scotland, May 5, 1912; s. Kenneth Macdonald and Jean Moffat; m. Dorothy Thomson, Mar. 11, 1961; children: Roderick, Caroline. LDS, U. Glasgow, 1935. Fellow: Royal Soc. Medicine Glasgow, Internat. Assn. Oral Surgeons; mem.: Royal So. Yacht Club (yachtmaster). Mem. Church Of England. Home: Lymington, England. Died Feb. 29, 2004.

**MACDOUGALL, SIR DONALD (SIR GEORGE DONALD ALASTAIR MACDOUGALL),** economist; b. Glasgow, Scotland, Oct. 26, 1912; s. Daniel Douglas and Beatrice Amy (Miller) MacD.; m. Bridget Christabel Bartrum, 1937 (dissolved 1977); children: John Douglas, Mary Jean; m. Laura Margaret Hall, 1977 (dec. 1995). MA, Oxford U., 1938; LLD (hon.), U. Strathclyde, 1968; LittD (hon.), U. Leeds, 1971; DSc (hon.), U. Aston, 1979. Asst. lectr., then lectr. econs. U. Leeds, 1936-39; with statis. br. Office First Lord Admiralty, 1939-40, Office Prime Min., 1940-45; ofcl. fellow Wadham Coll. Oxford U., 1945-50, domestic bursar, 1946-48, hon. fellow, from 1964, faculty fellow Nuffield Coll., 1947-50, professorial fellow, 1950-52, ofcl. fellow, 1952-64, first bursar, 1958-64, hon. fellow, from 1967, U. Nuffield reader internat. econ., 1950-52; hon. fellow Balliol Coll., Oxford U., 1992—2004. Econ. dir. Orgn. European Econ. Cooperation, Paris, 1948-49; chief adv. statis. br. Office Prime Min., 1951-53; vis. prof. Australian Nat. U., Canberra, 1959, MIT Ctr. Internat. STudies, New Delhi, 1961; econ. dir. Nat. Econ. Devel. Office, 1962-64; mem. Turnover Tax Com., 1963-64; dir. gen. Dept. Econ. Affairs, 1964-68; head govt. econ. svc., chief econ. adv. Treasury, 1969-73; chief econ. adv. Confedn. Brit. Industry, 1973-84. Author: The World Dollar Problem, 1957, The Dollar Problem: A Reappraisal, 1960, Studies in Political Economy, 2 vols., 1975, Don and Mandarin: Memoirs of an Economist, 1987; co-author: Measures for International Economic Stability, 1951, The Fiscal System of Venezuela, 1959; chmn. EEC Report of Study Group on Role of Public Finance in European Integration, 1977; contbr. articles to profl. publs. Decorated Knight, Officer Order Brit. Empire, commdr.; scholar George Webb Medley Jr., 1934, George Webb Medley Sr., 1935. Fellow Brit. Acad.; mem. Coun. Royal Econ. Soc. (pres. 1972-74), Nat. Inst. Econ. and Social Rsch. (chmn. exec. com. 1974-87), Soc. Strategic and Long-Range Planning (pres. 1977-85), Soc. Bus. Eocnomists (v.p. 1978—), Reform Club (London). Home: London, England. Died Mar. 22, 2004.

**MACE, DEAN TOLLE,** educator; b. Neosho, Mo., May 21, 1922; s. Rector Tolle and Beatrice B. (Dunkeson) M.; m. Mary Ann Fitz-Hugh, June 24, 1950; children: Thomas Fitz-Hugh, Sarah Tolle. BA, Washington U., St. Louis, 1948; MA, Columbia, 1949, PhD, 1952. Instr. English Washington U., 1950-52; faculty Vassar Coll., Poughkeepsie, N.Y., 1952-87, prof. English, 1966-87, prof. emeritus, 1987, chmn. dept., 1968-79. Vis. reader English U. York, Eng., 1966-67; vis. sr. fellow Bedford Coll., U. London, 1981-82 Contbr. articles to profl. jours. Served with inf. AUS, 1942-45. Vassar Coll. faculty fellow for research, 1959 Mem. Modern Lang. Assn., AAUP. Home: Poughkeepsie, NY. Died Sept. 1999.

**MACFARLANE, ROBERT BRUCE,** retired lawyer; b. Portsmouth, Eng., Jan. 29, 1896; s. Charles and Caroline (Capsey) Macfarlane; m. Rebecca Williams Fitzhugh, May 1, 1934; children: Mary Parke, Robert Bruce. JD, U. Richmond, 1934. Bar: Va. 1932. Engring. cons. Macfarlane & Sadler, Richmond, Va., 1938—60; pvt. practice law Richmond, 1960—80. Examiner US Patent Office, Richmond, 1943—45. Mem. zoning appeals City Richmond, 1950—62, mem. planning commn., 1954—62. Mem.: Richmond Bar Assn., Va. Bar Assn., Masons club. Home: Kill Devil Hills, NC. Deceased.

**MACIEL, JOHN IGNATIUS,** lawyer; s. Joseph Cornelius and Joyce Philomena Maciel. BSc, LLB, Monash U., Melbourne, Australia, 1985. Lawyer Cores, Victoria, Australia, 1985—86; assoc. Baker & McKenzie, Sydney, Australia, 1987; sr. lawyer Freebills, Melbourne, 1988—97; ptnr. Piper Alderman, Melbourne, from 1997. Died Feb. 13, 2008.

**MACK, JULIA COOPER,** retired judge; b. Fayetteville, NC, July 17, 1920; d. Dallas L. and Emily (McKay) Perry; m. Jerry S. Cooper, July 30, 1943 (div.); 1 dau., Cheryl; m. Clifford S. Mack, Nov. 21, 1957 (dec. 1971) BS, Hampton Inst., 1940; LLB, Howard U., 1951; JD (hon.), U. DC, 1999. Bar: DC 1952. Legal cons. OPS, Washington, 1952-53; atty.-advisor Office Gen. Counsel Gen. Services Adminstrn. (GSA), Washington, 1953-54; trial appellate atty. criminal

divsn. US Dept. Justice, Washington, 1954-68; civil rights atty. Office Gen. Counsel, EEOC, Washington, 1968—73, dep. gen. counsel, 1973—75; assoc. judge DC Ct. Appeals, Washington, 1975-89, sr. judge, 1989—2001. Mem. ABA, Fed. Bar Assn., Nat. Bar Assns., Nat. Assn. Women Judges. Home: Washington, DC. Died Jan. 17, 2014.

**MACKAY, GRAHAM (ERNEST ARTHUR GRAHAM MACKAY),** retired brewing company executive; b. Johannesburg, July 26, 1949; s. James and Mary Mackay; 6 children. BSc. Various mgmt. positions South African Breweries Ltd., 1978—97, group mng. dir., 1997—99, chief exec., 1999—2002, SABMiller, London, 2002—13. Bd. dirs. Reckitt Benckiser Group plc, Philip Morris Internat. Inc., from 2008. Died Dec. 18, 2013.

**MAC KENZIE, NORMAN HUGH,** retired English educator, writer; b. Salisbury, Rhodesia, Mar. 8, 1915; s. Thomas Hugh and Ruth Blanche (Huskisson) MacK.; m. Rita Mavis Hofmann, Aug. 14, 1948; children: Catherine, Ronald. BA, Rhodes U., South Africa, 1934, MA, 1935, Diploma in Edn., 1936; PhD (Union scholar), U. London, 1940; DLitt (hon.), St. Joseph's U., Phila., 1989. Lectr. in English Rhodes U., South Africa, 1937, U. Hong Kong, 1940-41, U. Melbourne, Australia, 1946-48; sr. lectr.-in-charge U. Natal, Durban, 1949-55; prof., head English dept. U. Coll., Rhodesia, 1955-65, dean Faculty Arts and Edn., 1957-60, 63-64; prof., head English dept. Laurentian U., Ont., Can., 1965-66; prof. English Queen's U., Kingston, Ont., 1966-80, emeritus prof., from 1980, dir. grad. studies in English, 1967-73, chmn. council grad. studies, 1971-73, chmn. editorial bd. Yeats Studies, 1972-74. Exec. Central Africa Drama League, 1959-65; exec. com. Can. Assn. Irish Studies, 1968-73 Author: South African Travel Literature in the 17th Century, 1955, The Outlook for English in Central Africa, 1960, Hopkins, 1968, A Reader's Guide to G.M. Hopkins, 1981; editor: (with W.H. Gardner) The Poems of Gerard Manley Hopkins, 1967, rev. edit., 1970; Poems by Hopkins, 1974, U. Natal Gazette, 1954-55; The Early Poetic Manuscripts and Notebooks of Gerard Manley Hopkins in Facsimile, 1989, The Poetical Works of Gerard Manley Hopkins, 1990, rev. 1992, The Later Poetic Manuscripts of G.M. Hopkins in Facsimile, 1991; contbr.: chpts. to Testing the English Proficiency of Foreign Students, 1961, English Studies Today-Third Series, 1963, Sphere History of English Literature, Vol. VI, 1970, rev. edit., 1987, Readings of the Wreck of the Deutschland, 1976, Festschrift for E.R. Seary, 1975, British and American Literature 1880-1920, 1976, Myth and Reality in Irish Literature, 1977, Muses and Reason, 1994, Dispersal and Renewal: Hong Kong University during the War Years, 1998 (autobiography) Hopkins Variations, 2002; contbr. articles to profl. jours. Served with Hong Kong Vol. Def. Corps, 1940-45; prisoner of war, China and Japan 1941-45. Brit. Council scholar, 1954; Killam sr. fellow, 1979-81; Martin D'Arcy lectr. Oxford U., 1988-89. Fellow Royal Soc. Can.; mem. English Assn. Rhodesia (pres. 1957-65), So. Rhodesia Drama Assn. (vice chmn. 1957-65), Hopkins Soc. (pres. 1972-75), Yeats Soc. (life), MLA (life), Internat. Hopkins Assn. (bd. scholars 1979—), Queen's U. Saturday Club (sec. 1977-97). Home: Kingston, Canada. Died 2003.

**MACKLEN, ERIC DOUGLAS,** engineer, researcher; b. Swindon, England, July 5, 1929; s. Douglas James and Elizabeth (Hollingdale) Macklen; m. Pamela Mary Tye, July 24, 1954; children: Karen, Alison. BSc, Brighton Tech. Coll., Eng., 1952; MSc, No. Poly., London, 1955, PhD, 1959. Solid state chemist, rschr. Std. Telecom. Lab., Harlow, Essex, England, 1952—61, dept. head solid state, 1961—68; chief engr. thermistor divsn. Std. Tel. and Cables, Taunton, Somerset, England, 1968—85; mng. dir. Peak Components now Peak Products, Taunton, Somerset, England, from 1985. Author: Thermistors, 1979; contbr. articles to profl. jours. Achievements include research in gas solubility, microphone carbons, ferrites, thermistor materials, thermal decomposition of oxalates, carbon products; patents in field. Died Mar. 1, 2004.

**MACMILLAN, C(HARLES) J(AMES) B(ARR),** education educator; b. Auburn, NY, Apr. 30, 1935; s. John Walker and Margaret Ethel (Barr) Macmillan; m. Joan T. Reinberg, June 15, 1958; children: Ann Tyler, Tyler Lash. BA, Cornell U., 1957, PhD, 1965; MA, Colgate U., 1960. Acting asst. prof. UCLA, 1962—64; asst. prof. Temple U., Phila., 1964—68, assoc. prof., 1968—70; assoc. prof. philosophy edn. Fla. State U., Tallahassee, 1970—84, prof., from 1984. Bd. dirs. Betton Hills Neighborhood Assn., 1973, pres., 1987, Coun. Neighborhood Assns., Tallahassee, 1990—92. Editor: (book) Psychological Concepts and Education, 1967; contbr. to profl. lit.; co-author A Logical Theory of Teaching. Mem.: Am. Ednl. Rsch. Assn., Philosophy Edn. Soc. (sec., treas. 1980—82, pres. 1983—84), Southeast Philosophy Edn. Soc. (pres. 1973), Fla. Philos. Assn., Sturgeon Lake Sailing (Ontario). Home: Tallahassee, Fla. Died Feb. 11, 1998.

**MACQUARRIE, JOHN,** theologian; b. Renfrew, Scotland, June 27, 1919; s. John and Robina (McInnes) M.; m. Jenny Fallow Welsh, Jan. 17, 1949; children: John Michael, Catherine Elizabeth, Alan Denis. MA, U. Glasgow, 1940, PhD, 1954, D.Litt., 1964; D.D., U. Oxford, Eng., 1981; S.T.D. (hon.), U. of South, Tenn., 1967, Gen. Theol. Sem., NYC, 1968; D.D. (hon.), U. Glasgow, 1969, U. Dayton, 1995. Ordained priest, 1965. Lectr. U. Glasgow, Scotland, 1953-62; prof. systematic theology Union Theol. Sem., NYC, 1962-70; Lady Margaret prof. div. U. Oxford, Eng., 1970-84; pres. Inst. Religion and Theology of Gt. Britain and Ireland, 1982-85. Author: Principles of Christian Theology, 1966, Existentialism, 1972, In Search of Humanity, 1982, In Search of Diety, 1984, Jesus Christ in Modern Thought, 1990, A Guide to the Sacraments. 1997. Capt. Brit. Army, 1945-48. Territorial Decoration, Brit. Army, 1962. Mem. Brit. Acad. Died May 28, 2007.

**MAC RAE, HERBERT FARQUHAR,** retired college president; b. Middle River, NS, Can., Mar. 30, 1926; s. Murdoch John and Jessie MacLennon; m. Mary Ruth Finlayson, Sept. 24, 1955; children— Roderick John, Elizabeth Anne, Christy Margaret, Mary Jean. Diploma NS, Agrl. Coll., 1952; BSc, McGill U., 1954, MSc, 1956, PhD, 1960, DSc (hon.), 1987; LLD (hon.), Dalhousie U., 2000. Chemist, food and drug directorate Dept. Nat. Health and Welfare, Ottawa, Ont., 1960-61; mem. faulty Macdonald Coll. McGill U., 1961-72, assoc. prof. animal sci. Macdonald Coll., 1967-70, prof. animal sci. dept. Macdonald Coll., 1970-72; prin. N.S. Agrl. Coll., Truro, 1972-89, ret., 1989. Named to Can. Agrl. Hall of Fame, 1994. Fellow: Agrl. Inst. Can.; mem.: Can. Soc. Animal Sci., Rotary Internat. (Four Aves. of Svc. citation 2002), Order of Can. Died June 24, 2002.

**MADDOX, IRIS CAROLYN CLARK,** secondary school educator; b. Wardell, Mo., Apr. 20, 1936; d. Newman Walter and Mary Elizabeth (Edney) Clark; m. James P. Maddox, June 4, 1954; children: James Steven, Sandra Jean. BS cum laude, Prairie View A&M U., 1983, MEd in Indsl. Edn., 1984, MEd in Counseling., 1990. Cert. counselor and tchr., Tex. Tchr. Spring Branch Ind. Sch. Dist., Houston, 1982—97. Sec. Bus. Office Svcs. Adv. Com., Houston, 1991-92. Mem. Am. Vocat. Assn., Tex. Assn. Continuing Adult Edn., Nat. Assn. Classroom Educators in Bus. Edn., Chi Sigma Iota. Avocations: gardening, collecting antiques and coins. Home: Houston, Tex. Died June 27, 1997.

**MADDOX, SIR JOHN ROYDEN,** retired journal editor; b. Penllergaer, Swansea, Wales, Nov. 27, 1925; s. Arthur John Maddox and Mary Elizabeth Davies; m. Nancy Fanning, Mar. 12, 1949 (dec. 1960); 2 children; m. Brenda Power Murphy, Nov. 11, 1960; 2 children. BA in Chemistry, Oxford U., Eng., 1947, MA, 1952; D Univ. (hon.), U. Surrey, 1982; DLitt (hon.), U. East Anglia, 1992; DSc, U. Liverpool, Eng., 1992; DSc (hon.), Nottingham Trent U., 1994; DLitt, U. Glamorgan, Wales, 1997. Lectr. theoretical physics U. Manchester, Eng., 1949-55; sci. editor Manchester Guardian, 1955-64; asst. dir., coord. Nuffield sci. tchg. project Nuffield Found., London, 1964-66, dir., 1975-80; chmn. Maddox Editl. Ltd., London, 1973-75; editor Nature, London, 1966-73, 80-95, editor emeritus, from 1995. Mem. Royal Commn. on Environ. Pollution, 1976-81, Genetic Manipulation Adv. Group, 1977-82; chmn. European Union Conf. on Growth Promoters, 1985. Author: Revolution in Biology, 1963, The Doomsday Syndrome, 1972, Beyond the Energy Crisis: A Global Perspective, 1974, What Remains to Be Discovered: Mapping the Secrets of the Universe, the Origins of Life, and the Future of the Human Race, 1998 Chmn. Queen Elizabeth Coll., U. London, 1980-85; mem. Erwood Cmty. Coun., 1987-2009, chmn., 1999-2009. Named a Knight Comdr. of the Most Excellent Order of the British Empire, Her Majesty Queen Elizabeth II; Recipient cultural award Eduard Rhein Found., Germany, 1997. Fellow Am. Acad. Arts and Scis. (hon. fgn.), Royal Soc.; mem. Am. Inst. Physics. Mem. Liberal Democratic Party. Died Apr. 12, 2009.

**MAEROFF, GENE I. (EUGENE IRVING MAEROFF),** academic administrator, journalist; b. Cleve., Jan. 8, 1939; s. Harry B. and Charlotte (Szabo) Maeroff; m. Joyce Maeroff; children from previous marriage: Janine Amanda, Adam Jonathan, Rachel Judith. BS, Ohio U., 1961; MS, Boston U., 1962. Tchg. fellow Boston U., 1961-62; news bur. dir. R.I. Coll., 1962-64; religion editor Akron (Ohio) Beacon Jour., 1964-65; with Cleve. Plain Dealer, 1965-71, assoc. editor, 1969-71; edn. writer The NY Times, NYC, 1971-86; sr. fellow Carnegie Found. Advancement Tchg., Princeton, NJ, 1986-97; dir. Hechinger Inst. Columbia U. Teachers Coll., NYC, 1997—2014. Mem. Edison Bd. Edn., NJ, 2008—14, pres., 2010—13. Author: (book) Don't Blame the Kids, 1981, School and College, 1983, The Empowerment of Teachers, 1988, The School-Smart Parent, 1989, Sources of Inspiration, 1992, Team Building for School Change, 1993, Altered Destinies, 1998, Imaging Education, 1998, The Learning Connection, 2001, A Classroom of One: How Online Learning Is Changing Our Schools and Colleges, 2003, Building Blocks, 2006, School Boards in America: A Flawed Exercise in Democracy, 2010, The School-Smart Parent, 2012, Reforming a School System, Reviving a City: The Promise of Say Yes to Education in Syracuse, 2013; author: (with others) The New York Times Guide to Suburban Public Schools, 1976, Scholarship Assessed, 1997; co-author: The Human Encounter: Readings in Education, 1976, Human Dynamics in Psychology and Education, 1977, Social Problems, 1978, Education Reform in the 90's, 1992, Teachers as Leaders, 1994; contbr. articles to mags. Trustee Guild-Times Scholarship Fund, Ed Bang Journalism Scholarship Found.; mem. adv. bd. Nat. Ctr. Postsecondary Governance, Inst. Ednl. Mgmt., Harvard U., Ednl. Resources Info. Ctr., U.S. Dept. Edn. Recipient Writing award, Press Club Cleve., A.P. Soc. Ohio, Edn. Writers Assn., AAUP, Internat. Reading Assn. Mem.: Blue Key, Phi Sigma Delta, Kappa Tau Alpha, Omicron Delta Kappa. Died July 25, 2014.

**MAFFEI, PAOLO,** astronomer; b. Arezzo, Italy, Jan. 2, 1926; s. Mario and Angela (Cimarelli) M.; m. Maria Assunta Morganti, Jan. 25, 1956; children: Marta, Marina. Grad. in math., Florence U., 1952; Libera Docenza in Gen. Astronomy, U. Rome, 1967. Asst. prof. astronomy U. Bologna, Italy, 1955-59; astronomer Asiago Astrophys. Obs., 1959-63; asst. prof. astrophysics U. Rome, 1963-76; prof. astronomy U. Catania, 1976-80; prof. astrophysics U. Perugia, Italy, 1980—99, prof. emeritus, 2002—09. Dir. Catania Astrophys. Obs., 1976-80. Author: Al di la della Luna, 1973, I mostri del Cielo, 1976, L'Universo nel tempo, 1982, La Cometa di Halley, 1984, Giuseppe Settele, il suo Diario e la questione galileiana, 1987; contbr. articles to profl. jours. Mem. Am. Astron. Soc., Astron. Soc. Pacific, Brit. Astron. Assn., Internat. Astron. Union, Royal Astron. Soc., Royal Astron. Soc. Can., Soc. Astronomica Italiana, Soc. Astronomique de France, Soc. Belge d'Astronomie de Metereologie et de Physique du Globe. Achievements include research on comets, variable stars and astronomy history; discovery of two infrared galaxies named Maffei I and Maffei II; proposer and for many years principal investigator for the Italian Robotic Anctartic Infrared Telescope. Home: Perugia, Italy. Died Mar. 1, 2009.

**MAGASANIK, BORIS,** retired microbiology educator; b. Kharkoff, U.S.S.R., Dec. 19, 1919; arrived in US, 1938; s. Naum and Charlotte (Schreiber) M.; m. Adele Magasanik (dec. 1991); m. Helen Donis-Keller; 1 stepchild, Christine BS, CCNY, 1941; PhD, Columbia U., 1948; MS (hon.), Harvard U., 1958. Tech. asst. Mt. Sinai Hosp., NYC, 1939-41; rsch. asst. Columbia U., NYC, 1948-49; Ernst fellow Harvard U. Med. Sch., Boston, 1949-51, assoc. to assoc. prof., 1951-59; prof. microbiology MIT, Cambridge, 1960-77, prof. emeritus, 1977—2014, Jacques Monod prof., 1977, head dept. biology, 1966—77. Tutor in biochem. sciences Harvard U., 1951. Contbr. over 250 sci. articles and revs. to profl. publications With M.C., U.S. Army, 1942-45, ETO. Guggenheim fellow, 1959; Markle scholar in Med. Sciences, 1951-56; recipient SelmanA. Waksman Award in Microbiology Nat. Acad. Sciences, 1994, Lifetime Achievement award Abbott-ASM, 2000. Mem. NAS, American Acad. Arts & Sciences, American Soc. Microbiology(Abbott-ASM Lifetime Achievement award, 2000), American Soc. Biol. Chemists. Home: Cambridge, Mass. Died Dec. 25, 2013.

**MAGEE, JOHN FRANCIS,** research and development company executive; b. Bangor, Maine, Dec. 3, 1926; s. John Henry and Marie (Frawley) M.; m. Dorothy Elma Hundley, Nov. 19, 1949 (dec. May 31, 2009); children: Catherine Anne, John Hundley, Andrew Stephen. AB, Bowdoin Coll., 1947; MS, U. Maine, 1952; MBA, Harvard U., 1948; LLD, Bowdoin Coll., 1996. With Arthur D. Little, Inc., Cambridge, Mass., 1950-98, v.p., 1961-72, pres., 1972-86, chief exec. officer, 1974-88, chmn., 1986-98, also dir., 1968-98. Author: Physical Distribution Systems, 1967, Industrial Logistics: Analysis and Management of Physical Supply and Distribution Systems, 1968, (with D. M. Boodman) Production Planning and Inventory Control, 1968; (with W. Capacino and W. Rosenfield) Modern Logistics Management, 1985. Former sec., trustee Emerson Hosp.; emeritus trustee Thompson Island Outward Bound Edn. Ctr., chair, 1995—2000; emeritus trustee Bowdoin Coll.; hon. trustee Woods Hole Oceanographic Instn.; chmn. trustees Bowdoin Coll., 1990—94; overseer emeritus Mus. Sci., Boston; overseer Isabella Stuart Gardner Mus.; former gov. New England Aquarium. Officer USN, 1944—46. Recipient Disting. Leadership award, MIT, 1977. Fellow: Inst. for Ops. Rsch. and Mgmt. Sci., Phi Beta Kappa (life); mem.: Am. Soc. Metals (disting. life mem.), Inst. Mgmt. Scis. (pres. 1971—72), Ops. Rsch. Soc. Am. (pres. 1966—67, Kimball medal 1978), Comml. Club (pres. 1992—94), Somerset Club (Boston), The Country Club (Brookline, Mass.), Concord (Mass.) Country Club (gov. 1971—74), Phi Kappa Psi. Avocation: painting. Home: Concord, Mass. Died May 6, 2014.

**MAGGIOLINI, ALESSANDRO,** retired bishop; b. Bareggio, Milan, Italy, July 15, 1931; s. Severino and Ernesta (Cattaneo) M. Student, Venegono (Italy) Sem., 1947-55; degree in theology, Theol. U., Milan, 1959. Ordained priest Roman Cath. Ch., 1955. Tchr. philosophy, 1959-67; prof. Cath. U., Milan, 1967-82; bishop See in Carpi-Modena, Italy, 1983-89, Diocese of Como, Italy, 1989—2006. Religious speaker on radio and TV, Como, Milan; journalist Osservatore Romano, The Vatican, Avvenire, Milan, Nouvelle Revue Teologique, L'Informazione, Milan, 1993-2006; asst. Fedn. Cath. Union; students asst. Cath. Lawyers, 1968-78; episcopal vicar for univs. in Milan, 1978-83, dir. of the rev. of the Italian Clergy. Co-author: Cathecism of the Catholic Church, 1992. Died Nov. 11, 2008.

**MAGNUSON, ROGER JAMES,** lawyer; b. St. Paul, Jan. 25, 1945; s. Roy Gustaf and Ruth Lily (Edlund) M.; m. Elizabeth Cunningham Shaw, Sept. 11, 1982; children: James Roger, Peter Cunningham, Mary Kerstin, Sarah Ruth, Elizabeth Camilla, Anna Clara, John Edlund, Britta Kristina. BA, Stanford U., 1967; JD, Harvard U., 1971; BCL, Oxford U., 1972. Bar: Minn. 1973, U.S. Dist. Ct. Minn. 1973, U.S Ct. Appeals (4th, 8th, 9th, 10th, 11th cirs.) 1974, U.S. Supreme Ct. 1978. Chief pub. defender Hennepin County Pub. Defender's Office, Mpls., 1973; ptnr., trial group Dorsey & Whitney, Mpls., 1972—2013, and head, nat. strategic litig. group. Dean Oak Brook Coll. of Law and Govt. Policy, 1995-2013; chancellor Magdalen Coll., 1999-2013. Author: Shareholder Litigation, 1981, Are Gay Rights Right, The White-Collar Crime Explosion, 1992, Informed Answers to Gay Rights Questions, 1994, Internat. Judicial Asst. in Civil Matters, 1999, Barracuda Bait, 2007, Advising Minn. Corps., 2011; contbr. articles to profl. jours. Elder, Straitgate Ch., Mpls., 1980—2013. adv. mem., Minn. Corp. & Other Bus., 2011. Fellow, Ctr. of Internat. Legal Studies, Litig. Counsel America; mem. Christian Legal Soc., The Am. Soc. Writers of Legal Subjects, Mpls. Club, White Bear Yacht Club. Republican. Home: Saint Paul, Minn. Died Nov. 30, 2013.

**MAGRINI, UGO ENRICO,** engineering educator; b. Milan, Feb. 18, 1929; s. Umberto and Armanda (Calosso) M.; m. Elena Iandelli, July 27, 1961; children: Anna, Umberto, Alessandra. Laurea Indsl. engring., U. Genoa, Italy, 1955, PhD in Applied Physics, 1964. Registered profl. engr., Italy. Asst. prof. engring. U. Genoa, 1957-60, assoc. prof., 1960-67, prof. thermo engring., from 1967, dir. Inst. Tech. Physics, 1973-83. Pres. Normalisation Com., Milan, 1974-90, Nat. Inst. Refrigeration, Padua, Italy, 1975-81. Contbr. articles to sci. publs. Mem. Accademia Ligure di Scienze e Lettere, Rotary (sr. mem.). Avocations: sailing, agriculture. Home: Genoa, Italy. Died Jan. 2006.

**MAGUIRE, RAYMER F., JR.,** lawyer; b. Orlando, Fla., Oct. 20, 1921; s. Raymer F. Sr. and Ruth (McCullough) M.; m. Sara Corry, Aug. 13, 1951; children: Craig Corry, Raymer F. III, Sara Maguire LeMone, Edmund Corry. BA, U. Fla., 1943, JD, 1948. Bar: Fla. 1948, U.S. Dist. Ct. (so. dist.) 1948, U.S. Supreme Ct. 1969. Assoc. Maguire, Voorhis & Wells, P.A., Orlando, 1948-53, mem., from 1953. Bd. dirs. Sun Bank, N.A.; bd. dirs. and trustee various corps. and trusts. Elder First Presbyn. Ch., 1961—; mem., chmn. community coll. coun. State of Fla., 1976-79, mem. community coll. coordinating bd., 1979-83, vice chmn. 1979-81, chmn. 1981-82; trustee Valencia Community Coll., 1967-86, chmn. 1967-72; bd. dirs. Orange County Hist. Soc., 1982—, pres., 1987-88; chmn. bd. Cen. Fla. chpt. Am. Heart Assn., 1966-67; bd. dirs. Valencia Community Coll. Found., pres., 1974-75; chmn. citizens com. Orange County Sch. Bd. Referendum, 1964. Named in honor of Raymer F. Maguire Jr. Learning Resource Ctr., Valencia Community Coll., 1977. Mem. ABA, Fla. Bar Assn. U. Fla. Alumni Assn. (bd. dirs. 1954—, pres. 1959-60, Disting. Alumnus award 1975), Kiwanis (pres. 1962), U. Fla. Found. Republican. Deceased.

**MAHAMA, ALIU ALHAJ,** former Ghanaian government official; b. Yendi, Northern Region, Ghana, Mar. 3, 1946; Attended, U. Sci. and Tech. V.p. Republic of Ghana, Greater Accra, 2001—09. Died Nov. 14, 2012.

**MAHUTA, ROBERT TE KOTAHI,** university director; b. Te Kuiti, Waikato, New Zealand, Apr. 26, 1939; s. Koroki and Te Atairangikaahu (Herangi) M.; m. Eliza Irimana Edmonds, 1964; children: Tukaroto Koroki, Nanaia Cybele, Tipa Te Atawhai Serena. MA, U. Auckland, New Zealand, 1973; postgrad., Wolfson Coll., Oxford, Eng., 1976-78. Univ. lectr. U. Auckland and Waikato, New Zealand, 1970; dir. Ctr. for Maaori Studies and Rsch., New Zealand, from 1972. Prin. negotiator Waikato Raupatu Claim, New Zealand; chmn. Maaori Devel. Corp., New Zealand; commr. Treaty of Waitangi Fisheries Commn., New Zealand. Named 1st Knight Companion, New Zealand Order of Merit, 1996. Avocations: reading, fishing. Home: Huntly, New Zealand. Died Jan. 31, 2001.

**MAILLART, ROBERT,** structural engineer; b. 1872; Prin. works include Schwandbach Bridge, 1933. Died 1940.

**MAKAREVICH, IVAN FOMICH,** pharmacist, chemist, educator; b. Orsha, Belarus, Feb. 17, 1936; s. Foma Makarevich and Fedosya Marchenko; m. Alla Vladimirovna Strelchenko; 1 child, Sergey Ivanovich. D. in Chem. Sci., Highest Attestational Com., Moscow, 1976. Cert. pharmaceutist Moscow Med. Inst., 1959. Scientist, mgr. phytochemical lab. Chemical-Pharm. Rsch. Inst., Kharkov, Kharkov Region, Ukraine, 1958—2003; chair prof. chemistry Nat. Pharm. U., Kharkov, from 2003. Author: (book) Cardiotonic Steroids; contbr. over 300 sci. paper to profl. publs. Mem.: Sci. Engring Acad. Achievements include discovery of new physico-chemical phenomenon; 67 patents and certificates on inventions. Home: Kharkov, Ukraine. Deceased.

**MALABANAN, ERNESTO HERELLA,** internist; b. Lemery, Batangas, Philippines, Aug. 8, 1919; s. Lazaro Mendoza and Emilia Atienza (Herella) M.; m. Simplicia de Guzman Diego, Sept. 29, 1957; children: Maria Susan, Sheila Rosalia, Ernesto, Emmanuel, Edgar, Edwin. AA, U. Philippines, 1938, MD, 1943. Diplomate and fellow Philippines Coll. Chest Physicians. Intern Philippine Gen. Hosp., Manila, 1942-43; pvt. practice medicine Batangas City, 1946-54; resident in medicine Goldwater Meml. Hosp., NYC, 1954-55; resident in cardio-pulmonary svc. Bellevue Hosp., NYC, 1955-56; resident in pulmonary svc. Cleve. City Hosp., 1956-57; pvt. practice specializing in internal medicine Batangas City, from 1957. Cons. St. Patrick Hosp., Batangas City, 1966—, Philippine Heart Ctr., Quezon City, 1975— Mem. Police Adv. Coun. and Peace and Order Coun., Batangas City, 1975—, Adv. Coun., Batangas City Mayor, 1986—. 1st lt. Philippine Army, 1944-46. Named Most Outstanding Physician, Philippine Med. Assn., 1966, Frederick Stevens Award Masons, 1972, Grand Lodge of Philippines award, 1990-91, Gov.'s Achievement award, Lions, 1970, 73, Most Outstanding Physician of Batangas Med. Soc., Phila. Med. Assn., 2004, others. Fellow Philippine Coll. Cardiology, Internat. Coll. Angiology, Am. Coll. Chest Physicians (chpt. pres. 1979-81), Philippine Acad. Family Physicians, Fedn. Pvt. Med. Practitioners (pres. 1963-65), Batangas Med. Soc. (pres. 1965-67), Philippine Heart Assn. (chpt. pres. 1979-81), Phillippine Med. Assn. (emeritus; Most Disting. Physician 2004), Phillippine Coll. Cardiology (life), Lions (pres. 1967-69), Knights of Rizal (comdr. 1986—), Masons (33 deg., named one of top ten outstanding masons in medicine, Abad Santos medal 2001). Roman Catholic. Avocations: sports, basketball, baseball, swimming. Home: Batangas, Philippines. Died Aug. 23, 2006.

**MALCOLM X, (MALCOLM LITTLE, AL HAJJ MALIK SHABAZZ),** civil rights leader; b. Omaha, May 19, 1925; s. Earl and Louise Langdon (Norton) Little; m. Betty Jean Sanders, Jan. 14, 1958; children: Attilah, Qubilah, Ilyasah, Gumilah, Malaak, Malikah. Student, pub. schs., Lansing, Mich. Waiter Small's Paradise nightclub, Harlem; shoe shiner Lindy Hop Nightclub; paroled from prison sentence, 1952; minister Nation of Islam, Temple Number 11, 1953; converted to orthodox Islam, 1964; founder Muslim Mosque Inc., 1964; co-founder with A. Peter Bailey

& others Orgn. Afro-Am. Unity, 1964; travelled to Africa 4 times, 1959—64; Made hadji to Mecca, 1964. Co-author (with Alex Haley): The Autobiography of Malcolm X, 1972. Died Feb. 21, 1965.

**MALERBA, LUIGI,** author; b. Berceto, Parma, Italy, Nov. 11, 1927; s. Pietro and Maria Olari; m. Anna Lapenna, 1962; 2 children. Student, Liceo Classico Romagnosi di Parma, Faculty Law, U. Parma. Dir. rev. Sequenze, 1948-51. Advt. mgr. rev. Discoteca, 1956-60, editor, 1960-65. Author: La scoperta dell'alfabeto, 1963, Ai poeti non si spara, 1966 (Internat. TV Festival of Monte Carlo Golden Nymph award, 1966), Il Serpente (premio Selezione Campiello), 1966, Salto mortale, 1968 (Premio Sila, French prix Mèdicis for best non-French novel), Il Protagonista, 1973, Le rose imperiali, 1974, Mozziconi, 1975, Storiette, 1977, Le parole abbandonate, 1977, Pinocchio con gli stivali, 1977, Il pataffio, 1978, C'era una volta la città di Luni, 1978, La storia e la gloria, 1979, Dopo il pescecane, 1979, Le galline pensierose, 1980, Diario di un sognatore, 1981, Storiette tascabili, 1984, Cina Cina, 1985, Il pianeta azzurro, 1986 (Premio Mondello, 1987), Testa d'argento, 1988, Il Fuoco greco, 1990, Le Pietre Volanti, 1992, Premio Viareggio, 1992, Premio Selezione Campiello, 1992, Il viaggiatore sedentario, 1993, Le maschere, 1995, Che vergogna scrivere, 1996, Itaca per sempre, 1997, Interviste impossibili, 1997, Avventure, 1997, La superficie di Eliane, 1999, Citta' e Dintorni, 2001, Il Circolo di Granada, 2002, La composizione del sogno, 2002, Ti saluto filosofia, 2003, Le Lettere di Ottavia, 2004, Fantasmi romani, 2006; author: (narrator, on-film commentator) New North, 1989, Sea of Slaughter, 1990; co-author (with Tonino Guerra, illus. by Adriano Zannino): Storie dell'Anno Mille, 1969—71. Died May 8, 2008.

**MALMAN, MYLES HENRY,** lawyer; b. NYC, Feb. 27, 1947; s. Louis M. and Pearl (Wolff) M.; m. Jill A. Saperstein, Aug. 9, 1997; children: Parker, Mallory BA, Fairleigh Dickinson U., 1967; JD, N.Y. Law Sch., 1974. Bar: N.Y. 1975, US Dist. Ct. (southern & eastern districts) N.Y. 1975, Fla. 1988, Pa. 1993, US Dist. Ct. (eastern dist.) Pa. 1993, US Ct. Appeals (3d cir.) 1993, US Dist. Ct. (southern dist.) Fla. 1993, US Ct. Appeals (3d cir.) 1993, US Ct. Appeals (11th cir.) 1994, US Dist. Ct. (middle dist.) Fla. 1995, US Ct. Appeals (2d cir.) 1995. Asst. dist. atty., sr. trial atty. NY County, NYC, 1974-84; spl. counsel to US atty. (southern dist.) Fla., US Dept. Justice, Miami, 1984-89, dep. 1st asst. U.S. atty., 1989-92; ptnr. Hornsby & Whiserand, Miami, 1988-89, Kohn Nast & Graf, P.C., Miami, 1992-94, Lehtinen O'Donnell Malman Vargas & Reiner, Miami, 1995-96; pvt. practice North Miami, Fla., 1996—2014. Testified before Congress re FBI and Drug Enforcement Agy. merger, Washington, 1993. Served in U.S. Army, 1967-69, Vietnam. Named to The Pinnacle Soc., Fairleigh Dickinson U., 2010. Avocation: bicycling. Home: Hollywood, Fla. Died Apr. 20, 2014.

**MALONE, GAYLE,** lawyer, consultant; b. Trenton, Tenn., Sept. 3, 1916; s. Robert Duvall and Sadie Lou (Ingran) Malone; m. Mary Beasley, June 22, 1944; children: Gayle Jr., Cecilia, Robert, Patrick, Christopher. Attended, George Washington U., 1935—36; LLB, Catholic U. America, 1940, JD, 1967; postgrad., U. Miss., 1953—54. Bar: Tenn. 1940, US Supreme Ct. 1957, US Ct. Appeals (6th cir.) 1966. Atty. US Army, Southeast US, 1943—46; sole practice Trenton, 1946—67; legislature State of Tenn., 1967—71; judge 9th Chancery Divsn. Tenn., 1971—73; ptnr. Malone, Holmes & Gossum, Trenton, from 1973. Cons. Brown Shoe Co., St. Louis, 1954—67, Gibson County, Trenton, from 1960, Citizens State Bank, Trenton, from 1965. Bd. dirs. West Tenn. Coun. Boy Scouts America, 1970. Staff sgt. US Army, 1940—42, World War II. Recipient Human Relations award, NAACP, 1970, Commitment and Svc. to Edn. award, Trenton Sch. Dist., 1975, 1976; named Hon. Citizen, Gibson County, 1978. Mem.: Tenn. Bar Assn., Tenn. Trial Lawyers Assn., Assn. Trial Lawyers America, Am. Judicature Assn. Democrat. Baptist. Home: Trenton, Tenn. Died 1986.

**MALONE, LAURENCE ADAMS,** economist, consultant; b. Cleve., Dec. 4, 1911; s. Cornelius Fitzgerald and Grace Adams (True) M.; m. Ethel Whatley, Jan. 2, 1962 (dec. 1987); m. Nettie Allen, July 24, 1987. LLB, Chgo. U., 1962; PhD, Columbia Pacific U., 1967. Contracting officer USN Sea Systems Command, Washington, 1941-79; economist Direct Answer Publishing Inc, Chagrin Falls, Ohio. Author: An Evolving World, 1972, Restoration, 1972, Our Debt Money Systems, 1985, How to Stop Foreclosure, 1982; patentee in field. Decorated Order of St. John, Knights of Malta. Roman Catholic. Avocations: research, writing, poetry. Home: Chagrin Falls, Ohio. Died Nov. 18, 1996.

**MALONE, NANCY,** actress; b. Queens Village, NY, Mar. 19, 1935; d. James and Bridget (Sheilds) M. Freelance actress, dir., producer, writer. Performer (TV series) The First Hundred Years, Naked City, The Long, Hot Summer (Best Performance by an Actress award); Broadway debut in Time Out For Ginger, other stage performances include Major Barbara, The Makropoulis Secret, A Touch of the Poet, The Trial of the Catonsville Nine; touring performances include The Chalk Garden, The Seven Yr. Itch, A Place For Dolly; actress (films) The Violators, I Cast No Shadow, An Affair of the Skin, Intimacy, The Trial of the Cantonsville Nine, The Man Who Loved Cat Dancing, Capricorn One; producer (TV series) including Bionic Woman, 1978, Husbands, Wives and Lovers, 1978, The Great Pretender, 1984, (special) Bob Hope: The First 90 Years, 1993 (Emmy award, Outstanding Variety, Musical or Comedy Special, 1993), Womanspeak, 1983; dir. (TV series) Dynasty, 1984-87, Hotel, 1984-87, Colbys, 1985, Cagney and Lacey, 1987, Star Trek Voyager, 1997, Burning Zone, 1997, Fame l.A. 1997-98, Rosie O'Niel (Emmy nomination), Sisters (Emmy nomination), Melrose Place, 1992-99, Beverly Hills, 1990-2000, Picket Fences, Judging Amy, 1999-, Resurrection Blvd., 2000-02; producer, dir. (film) There Were Times Dear, 1986 (John Muir Trustees award, Cine Golden Eagle, Blue Ribbon); founder Nancy Malone Prodns., 1975, Lilac Prodns., 1979. Fellow Leaky Found.; mem. American Film Inst. (mem. founder), Women in Film (trustee, Chrystal award, Founders award 1996). Home: Toluca Lake, Calif. Died May 8, 1024.

**MAN, CHU HUY,** Vietnamese army officer and politician; b. 1913; Mem. Central Com., Lao Dong Party; maj.-gen. Viet-Nam People's Army; former polit. comdr. Western Highlands; mem. Politbureau of Communist Party of Viet-Nam, from 1976; vice chmn. State Council, 1982-87. Decorated Gold Star Order Vietnam Govt., Ho Chi Minh Order, others. Died July 1, 2006.

**MAN, RAY (EMMANUEL RADNITZKY),** photographer, painter, filmmaker, sculptor; b. Phila., Aug. 27, 1890; arrived in Paris, 1921, arrived in Calif., 1940; Student, Nat. Acad. Design, 1908, Ferrer Sch. Graphic designer, typographer; profl. fashion and portrait photographer Paris, 1921. Co-founder (with Marcel Duchamp and Francis Picabia) DADA Group, N.Y.C., 1917; co-organizer (with Katherine S. Dreier and Marcel Duchamp) Soc. Anonyme, Mus. Modern Art, 1920; pub. 1 issue of N.Y. DADA with Marcel Duchamp; mem. DADA and Surrealist groups, Paris, 1934-39; developed rayograph technique in photography, 1921. One-man exhbns. include Galerie Vanleer, Paris, 1929, Galerie Vignon, Paris, 1932, Curt Valentine Gallery, N.Y.C., 1936, Librairie Six, Paris, 1939, London Gallery, 1939, Julien Levy Galleries, N.Y.C., 1945, Copley Gallery, Hollywood, 1948, Frank Perls Gallery, 1941, Paul Kantor Gallery, 1953, Galerie Furstenberg, Paris, 1954, Galleria Schwarz, Milan, Italy, 1964, Princeton, 1963, Cordier & Elkstrom, Inc., 1963, Galerie Rive Droite, Paris, 1959; group exhbns. include Soc. Anonyme, 1920, Bklyn. Mus., 1926, Springfield (Mass.) Mus. Fine Arts, 1929, Mus. Modern Art, 1936, Whitney Mus., 1946, Yale, 1948; represented in permanent collection Mus. Modern Art; created abstract and surrealist films Le Retour de la Raison, 1923, Emak Bakia, 1926, L'Etoile de Mer, 1928, Les Mysteres due Chateau de Des, 1929. Died Nov. 18, 1976.

**MANDABA, JEAN-LUC,** former Prime Minister of Central African Republic; Min. of health Govt. of Ctrl. African Republic, Bangu, 1981, imprisoned for polit. opinions, case dismissed, 1982, prime min., 1993—95; vice chair Mouvement de Libération du Peuple Centrafricain. Died Oct. 22, 2000.

**MANDELA, NELSON ROLIHLAHLA (ROLIHLAHLA DALIBHUNGA MANDELA),** advocate, former president of South Africa; b. Transkei, South Africa, July 18, 1918; m. Evelyn Ntoko, 1944 (div. 1958); children: Madiba(dec.), Makgatho(dec.), Makaziwe; m. Winnie Madikizela-Mandela, 1958 (div. 1996); children: Zeni, Zindzi; m. Graça Machel, 1998. Attended, Univ. Coll. Ft. Hare, South Africa, U. Witwatersrand, Johannesburg; LLD (hon.), Nat. U. Lesotho, 1979, CCNY, 1983; DLitt (hon.), Calcutta U., 1986; LLB (hon.), U. South Africa, 1989. Pvt. practice atty. Mandela and Tambo, Johannesburg, 1952; pres. Republic of South Africa, 1994-99; founder Nelson Mandela Children's Fund, 1995; sec. gen. Non-Aligned Movement, 1998—99; founder Nelson Mandela Found., The Mandela-Rhodes Found. Nat. organizer African Nat. Congress (ANC), pres., 1991—97; on trial for treason 1956-61 (acquitted 1961); arrested, sentenced to five years' imprisonment Nov. 1962; on trial for further charges with fellow ANC leaders 1963; sentenced to life imprisonment June 1964, released Feb. 1990. Author: No Easy Walk to Freedom, 1965, I Am Prepared to Die, 1979, The Struggle Is My Life, 1986, The Long Walk to Freedom, 1994, Nelson Mandela in His Own Words, 2004, Conversations with Myself, 2010. Founder, hon. mem. The Elders, 2007—13. Recipient Jawaharlal Nehru award, India, 1979, Bruno Kreisky prize for Human Rights, 1981, Simon Bolivar Internat. prize, UNESCO, 1983, Third World Found. prize, 1986, Sakharov prize, European Parliament, 1988, Gaddafi Internat. prize for human rights, 1989, Nobel Peace Prize, Norwegian Nobel Com., 1993, Tun Abdul Razak award, 1994, Anne Frank medal, 1994, Presdl. Medal of Freedom, The White House, 2000; named an Hon. Citizen, Rome, 1983; named one of The 100 Most Influential People in the World, TIME mag., 2004, 2005. Died Dec. 5, 2013.

**MANGUM, GARTH LEROY,** retired economist; b. Delta, Utah, July 23, 1926; s. James L. and Golda (Elder) M.; m. Marion Poll, Nov. 20, 1953; children: Stephen, David, Mary, Elizabeth. BS, Brigham Young U., 1956; MPA, Harvard U., 1958, PhD, 1960; JD, U. Utah, 1989. Instr. econs. Harvard U., 1960; asso. prof. econs. Brigham Young U., 1960-63; sr. staff analyst Presdl. R.R. Commn., 1961; research dir., subcom. employment and manpower U.S. Senate, 1963-64; exec. dir. President's Com. Manpower, 1964-65; exec. sec. Nat. Com. Tech., Automation and Econ. Progress, 1965-66; research prof. econs. George Washington U., 1967-71; co-dir. George Washington U. (Center Manpower Policy Studies), 1967-69; Max McGraw prof. econs. and mgmt. U. Utah, Salt Lake City, 1969-97, prof. emeritus, from 1997, dir. Inst. Human Resource Mgmt., 1969-90. Adj. prof. edn. leadership Brigham Young U., 2003—; lectr. U. Tel Aviv, Israel, 1969, 84, Am. Seminar at Salzburg, 1975, U. South Africa, 1977, Monash U., Australia, 1984; spl. mediator Fed. Mediation and Conciliation Svc., 1962-63; mem. Adv. Coun. Vocat. Edn., 1966-67; vice chmn. Nat. Manpower Policy Task Force, 1966-69, chmn., 1969-71; mem. Nat. Coun. on Employment Policy, 1976—, chmn., 1979-81, sec.- treas., 1990-2002; chmn. Nat. Inst. Career Edn., 1976-81; cons. internat. agencies, fed., state and local govts., bus. firms, govts. of, Saudi Arabia, Kuwait, Jordan, Oman, Yemen, Bahrain, United Arab Emirates, Indonesia, Yugoslavia, Romania, Uganda, Nigeria, Israel, South Africa, Russia, Brazil, Argentina, Chile, Uruguay, Mexico, Philippines, Taiwan, Republic of Korea, China, others; cons. AID, ILO, World Bank; also arbitrator; v.p. Retired Faculty Assn., U. SC, 2006-. Author: The Operating Engineers: Economic History of a Trade Union, 1964, MDTA, Foundation of Federal Manpower Policy, 1968, The Emergence of Manpower Policy, 1969, Federal Work and Training Program in the 1960's, 1969, Economic Opportunity in the Ghetto, 1970, Human Resources and Labor Markets, 1971, Career Education: What It Is and How To Do It, 1972, A Decade of Manpower Development and Training, 1973, Career Education and the Elementary School Teacher, 1973, Career Education in the Middle/Junior High School, 1973, Manpower Planning for Local Labor Markets, 1974, Career Education for the Academic Classroom, 1975, Employability, Employment and Income, 1976, Career Education in the High School, 1976, Your Child's Career, 1977, The Lingering Crisis of Youth Unemployment, 1978, Coming of Age in the Ghetto, 1978, Job Market Futurity, 1979, The Coal Industry and its Industrial Relations, 1985, Capital and Labor in American Copper, 1992, Labor Struggle in The Post Office, 1992, The Mormons War on Poverty, 1993, Union Resilience in Troubled Times, 1994, Portable Pension Plans for Casual Labor Markets, 1995, Transnational Industrial Marriages, 1996, The Rise, Fall and Replacement of Industry-Wide Bargaining in the Basic Steel Industry, 1996, Programs in Aid of the Poor, 8th edit., 2003, On Being Poor in Utah, 1997, The Public Employment Svc. In a One Stop World, 1998, Poverty Ain't What It Used To Be, 1999, Confronting The Youth Demographic Challenge, 2000, The Persistance of Poverty in the United States, 2003, Struggling at the Golden Door: International Refugees in Utah, 2007; also articles, monographs.; editor: The Manpower Revolution: Its Policy Consequences, 1965, Automation and Economic Progress, 1966, Metropolitan Impact of Manpower Programs, 1973, The T in CETA, 1981, Of Heart and Mind: Social Policy Essays in Honor of Sar A. Levitan, 1996, Utah's Poor: Solutions for Today's Economy, 2005. With USAAF, 1944-45. Mem. Ch. of Jesus Christ of Latter-day Saints (missionary 1950-53, bishop 1971-78, other positions). Home: Bountiful, Utah. Died June 7, 2014.

**MANI, JEAN-CLAUDE,** science administrator; b. Nimes, Gard, France, July 13, 1939; s. Leon Roger and Jeanne (Ortega) M.; m. Marie-France Lise Kuntz, July 10, 1941 (div. 1987); children: Jean-Christophe, Veronique, Frederique. Lic. Actual Maitrise, U. Montpellier, France, 1960, PhD, 1964; Ingenieur, Ecole Nat. Superieure de Chimi, 1961. Cert. engr., immunoanalysis expert. Charge de rescherche 2 CNRS, Montpellier, 1961-66, charge de rescherche 1, 1966-72, dir. 2, 1972-92; dir. 1. Postdoctoral fellow NATO U. Calif., Riverside, 1966-67, Karolinska Inst., Stockholm, 1969. Author: Photochimie et Reactions Moleculaires, 1969, Photochemistry and Molecular Reactions and Differentiation, 1988. Officer French Navy, 1964-66. NATO fellow, Riverside, Calif., 1966-67, Fulbright fellow, 1966-67; recipient award French-Swedish Rsch. Assn., Stockholm, 1969. Mem. French Soc. Immunology, comite Nat. de la Recherdo (pres. section 22 pharmacology). Home: Montpellier, France. Died Apr. 30, 2001.

**MANNING, MARGUERITE,** university dean, clergywoman; b. Phoenix; d. Walter Jerald and Elizabeth (Smith) Manning. AB, Scarritt Coll., 1942; MA, Boston U., 1943; MDiv, Union Theol. Sem., 1957; MA, Columbia Tchrs. Coll., 1966, EdD, 1975. Ordained to ministry Congregationalist Ch.; dir. student activities U. Tenn., 1943—46; ednl. asst. Riverside Ch., NYC, 1947—55; parish worker East Harlem Protestant Parish, 1955—57; min. East Congl. Ch. and Waits River Meth. Ch., Vt., 1958—61; tchr. English and phys. edn. Baghdad HS, Iraq, 1961—62; adminstrv. asst., dept. guidance and student pers. adminstrn. Columbia Tchrs. Coll., 1962—66; rsch. assoc. Bank St. Coll. Edn., NYC, 1966—68; with Bur. Rsch., NYC Bd. Edn., 1968—69; sec. pers. United Bd. Christian Higher Edn. Asia, 1969—71; dean student affairs Rutgers U., Newark, from 1971. Active Red Feather Dr.; social worker ARC, Camp Shanks, NY World War II; moderator Grafton-Orange Assn. Congl. Chs.; mem. min's. assn. Vt. Congl. Conf., 1958; pres. Women of Grace Ch., Newark; bd. dirs. YWCA. Mem.: NEA, Bus. and Profl. Women's Club, Am. Assn. U. Adminstrs., Am. Assn. Higher Edn., Am. Pers. and Guidance Assn., Am. Assn. Ednl. Rsch., Nat. Assn. Women Deans and Counselors, Phi Delta Kappa, Kappa Delta Pi, Pi Lambda Theta (pres. Alpha Epsilon chpt. 1966—68, treas. 1969—72, chmn. nat. nominating com. 1966—67). Home: Newark, NJ. Died Dec. 14, 1998.

**MANO, YUKIO,** medical educator, physician; b. Nagoya, Aichi-ken, Japan, Aug. 26, 1943; s. Yutaka and Takeko Ml m. Kiyoko Takeuchi; children: Tomoo, Yukiko. MD, Nagoya U., Japan, 1968, PhD, 1979. Intern Nagoya Univ. Hosp., 1968-69; resident Nagoya 1st Red Cross Hosp., 1969-71, Nagoya U., 1972, cons., 1976-78; resident NYU, 1972-74; resident, asst. instr. Baylor Coll. Medicine, 1974-75; rsch. fellow U. Md., 1975-76; chief of rsch. Nat. Inst. Nervous, Mental and Muscular Disorder, Tokyo, 1978-80; assoc. prof. Nara Med. U., Kashihara, Japan, 1981-95; prof., chmn. dept. rehabilitative medicine Hokkaido U., Sapporo, Japan, from 1995. Editor: Jour. Neurol. Therapeutics, 1995—' mem. editl. bd. Jour. Electromyography and Kinesiology, 1990—. Mem. Japanese Soc. Rehabilitative Medicine (mem. coun. 1997—), Japanese Soc. Electrophysiology and Kinesiology (pres. 1997—), Japanese Soc. Neurol. Therapy (mem. coun. 1997—), Japanese Soc. Clin. Environ. Medicine (1994—). Home: Aichi-ken, Japan. Deceased.

**MANTEL, DIRK GUSTAV,** retired chemical engineer; b. Bandung, Java, Indonesia, Nov. 22, 1923; s. Peter Gustav and Justine (Willems) M.; m. Vera Edna Shaw, June 6, 1932; children: Jennifer, Peter, Leigh, Andrew. Grad., Lyceum, Hilversum, The Netherlands, 1943; MIChemE, Inst.

Chem. Engrs., UK, 1955. Chartered engr. Chem. engr. African Explosives and Chem. Industries, South Africa, 1952-60; tech. dir. White's S.A. Portland Cement Co., South Africa, 1960-72, Salisbury Portland Cement Co., Rhodesia, 1965-72; group tech. mgr. Pretoria (South Africa) Portland Cement Co., 1973-92; ret., 1992. Cons. in cement tech., 1992—. Contbr. articles to profl. jours.; patentee in treating steels/slag as raw material prodn. portland cement, treating phosphogypsum to remove water soluble and insoluble P205. Mem. Inst. Chem. Engring., N.Y. Acad. Scis. Methodist. Deceased.

**MANTOOTH, MARGARET LARAH,** retired educator; b. Springer, Okla., Mar. 17, 1909; d. Robert Oliver and Nora Belle (Hobson) Beam; m. Laurence Mantooth, Oct. 26, 1929. BS, U. Sci. and Arts of Okla., 1959. Cert. tchr., Okla. Tchr. Okla. Edn., Sulphur, 1930-33, Purcell, 1942-44; buyer, bookkeeper Purcell, 1938-48; acct. U.S. Govt., Beaumont, Calif., 1944-45. Adult tchr. 1st Bapt. Ch.; pres. Bapt. Women of Bapt. Ch., 1990-92; mem. cemetery bd. City of Purcell, 1990-92; coord. style shows Purcell C. of C., 1977-85. Recipient Svc. award Okla. Gardens, 1985, ARC Svc. award for Cols. Mcpl. Hosp., 1977, award for Best Red, White and Blue Flower Bed Okla. State Gardens, 1977; named to Waynes High Sch. Hall of Fame, 1993. Mem. Gladiolus Garden Club (charter), Univ. Sci. and Arts Alumni (bd. dirs. 1990-92), AARP (asst. state dir. 1977-79). Democrat. Avocations: growing african violets, walking, reading, needle point, travel. Home: Purcell, Okla. Died Feb. 29, 1996.

**MARA, JOHN LAWRENCE,** retired veterinarian, consultant; b. Whitesboro, NY, May 17, 1924; s. William Edward and Olive Pearl (Brakefield) M.; m. Kathleen Keefe, 1946 (div. 1958); children: William, Michael, Daniel, Patrick; m. Patricia Louise Paulk, 1970 (div. 1994); children: Jennifer Lee, Kennon. DVM, Cornell U., 1951. Diplomate Am. Coll. Vet. Nutrition. Intern N.Y. State Coll. Vet. Medicine, Cornell U., Ithaca, 1951-52; assoc. veterinarian L.W. Goodman Animal Hosp., Manhasset, NY, 1952-55; owner, pres. Mara Animal Hosp., Huntington, NY, 1955-79; profl. rep. Hills Pet Products, Topeka, 1979-80, mgr. profl. rels., 1980-81, dir. profl. affairs, 1981-88, dir. vet. affairs, 1988-94, sr. fellow profl. and acad. affairs, 1994-97, sr. fellow global vet. bus. devel., 1997-2000; ret., 2000. V.p. Huntington United Fund; chmn. Huntington Taxpayers Party, 1968-78, Ch. in the Garden, Garden City, N.Y., 1975-77, trustee, 1975-77; trustee, v.p. vet. divsn. Morris Animal Found.; bd. dirs. Topeka Symphony; mem. dean's coun. Kans. State U. Coll. Vet. Medicine. Sgt. U.S. Army, 1943-45, ETO. Recipient Disting. Svc. award We. Vet. Conf., 1988; named hon. alumnus Coll. Vet. Medicine, Wash. State U.; Jack L. Deans scholarship named in his honor Sch. Vet. Medicine U. Pa. Mem. AVMA (Pres.'s award, Jack L. Mara vet. technician program), L.I. Vet. Medicine Assn., N.Y. State Vet. Medicine Assn. (Outstanding Svc. award 2001), Am. Animal Hosp. Assn. (disting. life, Outstanding Svc. award 1996-97), Kans. Vet. Medicine Assn., Am. Coll. Vet. Nutrition (hon. diplomate), Greater Topeka Area C. of C. (legis. com.). Republican. Baptist. Avocations: gardening, swimming, reading. Died 2003.

**MARAVEL, PATRICIA,** academic administrator; b. Bklyn., Sept. 29, 1949; d. James Peter and Lillian (Xanthos) M.; children: Jessica Maravel-Piccolo, Alex Maravel-Piccolo. BA in Sociology, SUNY, Stony Brook, 1971, postgrad., 1972-77, Hofstra U., 1977, St. Rose's Coll., 1977. Cert. secondary tchr., N.Y. Tchr. A. Fantis Sch., Bklyn., 1971-72, Commack (N.Y.) Pub. Schs., 1972-78; dir. adminstrn. L.I. Assn. for AIDS Care, Inc., Huntington Station, N.Y., 1986-89; exec. dir. Resurrection House, Inc., Wheatley Heights, N.Y., 1989-92; dir. ops. People with AIDS Coalition, Lindenhurst, N.Y., 1992-93; acad. adminstr. SUNY, Stony Brook, from 1993, ast. for spl. projects Dean's Office, Sch. Health Tech. and Mgmt., Health Scis. Ctr., from 2000. Cons. L.I. Assn. for AIDS Care, Huntington Station, 1989, hotline counselor and coord., 1985-86. Facilitator support group Village Parenting Ctr., Huntington, 1981-84, treas.; hotline counselor The Place, Northport, N.Y., 1982; mem. com. on health, hunger and homelessness Suffolk Community Coun., 1989-92; mem. women and AIDS subcom. Suffolk County Dept. Health, 1990-92. Mem. NOW. Democrat. Deceased.

**MARCHESI, GIAN FRANCO,** psychiatry educator; b. Perugia, Umbria, Italy, Mar. 11, 1940; s. Mario and Pina (De Notaris) M; m. Maria Ida Catagna, Jan. 20, 1973; 1 child, Piergiorgio. MA, U. Perugia, 1958, MD, 1964; PhD in Neuro-Psychiatry, Ancona U., Italy, 1975. Asst. prof. U. Perugia, 1971-73; vis. prof. U. Glasgow (Scotland), 1974; assoc. prof. U. Ancona, 1975-79, prof., from 1981, counselor Univ. Office Data Processing, 1978-82; vis. prof. SUNY, NYC, 1980, Nat. Acad. Scis., Prague, Czechoslovakia, 1982; dir. Inst. Psychiatry, Ancona, from 1984. Dir. Clin. Neurophysiology Specialization, Ancona, 1984-87, Psychiatry Specialization Sch., Ancona, 1984—, Psychiat. Rehab. Specialization, Ancona, 1989—, Psychiat. Social Worker Specialization, Ancona, 1990—. Author, co-editor: Manual of Neurology, 1979, Principles of Neurology and Psychiatry, 1985; author, editor: Manual of Psychiatry, 1992; contbr. articles to profl. jours. Counselor Adminstrv. Univ. Coun., Ancona, 1979-82, Region Office Univ. Student Svcs., Ancona, 1980-88; pres. Assn. Against Psychol. Suffering, Ancona, 1986—. Grantee Ministry Edn., Rome, 1971-88, NRC, Rome, 1978-86, Dept. Health, Marche Region, Ancona, 1980—, Ministry of Univs., Rome, 1989—. Mem. AAAS, Am. Med. Electroencephalographic Assn., Am. Acad. Neurology, World Fedn. Soc. Biol. Psychiatry, Collegium Internat. Neuro-Psychopharmacologicum, Am. Acad. Clin. Neurophysiology, World Fedn. Sleep Rsch. Socs. Home: Ancona, Italy. Died 1998.

**MARCHISANO, FRANCESCO CARDINAL,** cardinal, archbishop; b. Racconigi, Italy, June 25, 1929; Licentiate in Sacred Scripture, ThD. Ordained priest of Turin, Italy, 1952; undersecretary Congregation for Catholic Edn., Rome, 1969—88; appointed Titular Bishop of Populonia, 1988, ordained, 1989, apppointed Titular Archbishop, 1994; sec. Pontifical Commn. for the Conservation of the Artistic and Historical Patrimony of the Church (now known as Pontifical Commn. for the Cultural Heritage of the Church), 1988—91, pres., 1993—2003, pres. emeritus, 2003—14; pres. Pontifical Commn. for Sacred Archaeology, 1991—2004, pres. emeritus, 2004—14; raised to dignity of archbishop, 1994; pres. Fabric of Saint Peter, 2002—05, pres. emeritus, 2005—14; archpriest Patriarchal Vatican Basilica (Saint Peter Basilica), Rome, 2002—06, archpriest emeritus, 2006—14; vicar gen. His Holiness for Vatican City State, 2002—05, vicar gen. emeritus, from 2005; elevated to cardinal, 2003; cardinal-deacon of Santa Lucia del Gonfalone (Saint Lucy of Gonfalone), 2003—14; pres. Labor Office of the Apostolic See, Rome, 2005—09, pres. emeritus, 2009—14. Mem. Roman Pontifical Acad. of Archaeology; pres. Artistic-Cultural Commission of the Great Jubilee of the Year 2000, Permanent Commn. for the Custody of the Historical and Artistic Monuments of the Holy See, 2003—09. Roman Catholic. Died July 27, 2014.

**MARCOUX, CARL HENRY,** former insurance company executive, writer, historian; b. San Francisco, Jan. 6, 1927; s. Henry Roderick and Margaret (Carlin) M.; m. Ana Virginia Penate-Melara, Nov. 11, 1967; children: Eric Henry, Grant Reynold. BA, Stanford U., 1950; MBA, Golden Gate U., San Francisco, 1958; MA in Latin Am. History, U. Calif., Irvine, 1988; PhD in Latin Am. History, U. Calif., Riverside, 1994. Gen. mgr. Nat. Union Ins. Co., Pitts., 1953-68; exec. v.p. Transam. Ins. Co., 1968-85. Author: (novels) Sailing West, 2001, A Few Years At Sea, 2009. Served with U.S. Mcht. Marine, 1944-46; USAF, 1951-53. Mem. Stanford Alumni Assn. Home: Newport Beach, Calif. Died Nov. 20, 2013.

**MARCUS, DOROTHY MANN,** social worker, speech pathologist; b. Chgo., Sept. 3, 1926; d. Sigmund Mann and Sarah (Newman) Maslansky; m. Irwin M. Marcus, Jun 29, 1948; children: Randall, Sherry Marcus Wise, Melinda Marcus Jacobson. BS, Northwestern U., 1947; MSW, Tulane U., 1977. Lic. social worker, La. Social worker Irwin M. Marcus MD & Assocs., New Orleans, 1978-80; pvt. practice New Orleans, from 1981. Contbr. articles to profl. jours. Pres., bd. dirs. women's aux. Touro Inf. Bd. of Mgrs., New Orleans, 1973-75. Fellow Internat. Conf. for Advancement of Clin. Social Work (bd. dirs. 1980—, pres.-elect 1991); mem. NASW, Am. Bd. Examiners in Clin. Social Work, La. Soc. Clin. Social Work. Avocations: golf, travel, gardening. Died Oct. 13, 1992.

**MARGARIAN, ANDRANIK,** Prime Minister of Armenia; b. Yerevan, Armenia, June 12, 1951; married, 1973; 3 children. Grad., Yerevan Polytech Inst, 1972. With Yerevan Sect. Gas Industry All-Union Rsch. Inst., Inst. Power Engring., Computing Ctr. Trade Min., State Office Spl. Programs, 1972—90; chmn. Rep. Party, 1992; dep. Nat. Assembly, 1995—99, leader Unity Alliance, dep., 1999—2000; prime min. Govt. of Armenia, 2000—07. Mem.: Rep. Party of Armenia. Died Mar. 25, 2007.

**MARÍN, JESÚS,** pharmacologist; b. Molina de Segura, Murcia, Spain, Mar. 27, 1944; s. José and Mercedes (López) M.; m. Esperanza Serrano, Aug. 3, 1974; children: María Esperanza, Margarita Irene, Jesús Miguel. Chemist, U. Murcia, 1971; pharmacist, Complutense U., 1975, MD, 1984, PhD in Pharmacy, 1979; PhD in Chemistry, Autonomous U., 1975, PhD in Medicine, 1985. Rsch. asst. dept. pharmacology Autonomous U., Madrid, 1971-75, asst. prof. pharmacology, 1976-88, prof. pharmacology, 1989—2000. Sec. of faculty Autonomous U., 1987-99, dean, 1999-2000. Contbr. articles to profl. jours. Fellow Ministry of Edn. and Sci., 1975. Mem. Serotonin Club, Spanish Soc. of Pharmacology, Spanish Soc. of Neurosci., Spanish Soc. Gerontology. Avocations: fishing, cars, football. Home: Madrid, Spain. Died June 9, 2000.

**MARINHO, ROBERTO,** communication executive; b. Rio de Janeiro, Dec. 3, 1904; s. Irineu Marinho Coelho de Barros and Francisca (Pisani) Barros; m. Stella Goulart (div. 1971); children: Roberto Irineu, Paulo Roberto (dec.), Joao Roberto, Jose Roberto; m. Ruth Albuquerque (div. 1991); m. Lily Monique de Carvalho. D honoris causa, Fed. U. Brasília, Brazil, Fed. U. State Rio Grande do Norte, Gama Filho U., Rio de Janeiro, Fed. U. State of Ceará, Brazil, U. Uberlândia, Minas Gerais, Brazil. Pres. O Globo newspaper, Rio de Janeiro, from 1925, Globo Radio System, Rio de Janeiro, from 1944; pres., gen. dir. Globo TV Network, Rio de Janeiro, from 1965. Brazilian del. to UN, 1952; pres. Roberto Marinho Found.; chancellor Nat. Merit Order, pres. Merit Book Permanent Commn., 1960-67, 86—. Decorated govts. of Argentina, Austria, Belgium, Chile, Republic of China, France, Iran, Italy, Lebanon, Mex., Peru. Poland, Portugal, Spain, Vatican City, Venezuela; recipient Maria Moors Cabot citation medal Columbia U., 1957, gold medal, 1965, Emmy internat. prize Coun. Nat. Acad. Arts and Scis., 1983; named Man of Yr., Brazilian Am. C. of C., 1980, Midem Orgn., 1992. Mem. Inst. Cooperación Ibero Am., Brazilian Acad. Letters. Avocations: horsemanship, classical music, paintings, sculptures, skin diving. Home: Rio de Janeiro, Brazil. Died Aug. 6, 2003.

**MARINSKY, HARRY,** artist; b. London, May 8, 1909; s. Isaac and Debora (Divorkin) M. Student, R.I. Sch. of Design, Providence, 1927; grad., Pratt Inst. Art, Bklyn., 1928-29. Art editor Am. Home Country Life, NYC, 1935-39. One-man shows include One War One Peace Grand Central Palace, N.Y.C., 1946, Adelphia U., Garden City, N.Y., 1965, Interiors Anna-Maria, Stephen Kellen Archives of Parsons Sch. Design, 1972, Hammer Galleries, N.Y.C., 1981, 84, 94, La Galerie Shayne, Montreal, 1984, Montclair (N.J.) Art Mus., 1988; group exhbns. include Whitney Mus., N.Y.C., 1956, Internat. Sculpture Exhbn., Pietrasanta, Italy, 1993, Naples, Italy, 1990; represented in permanent collections Vets. Meml. Pk., Norwalk, Conn., The Great Bird Smell & Touch Garden, Stamford (Conn.) Mus., York U., Ont., Can., Commedia Dell Arte Group, Englewood, Colo., Rivotorto Assisi, Italy, Mus. Outdoor Art, Englewood, Hunt Botanical Libr., Pa., Westmoreland Mus., Greenburg, Pa., Alice in Wonderland Park, Englewood, One War One Peace Hist. Mus. The Resistance, St. Anna, Stazzema, Toscany, Italy, St. Francis Commn. Inaugurated Pietrasanta, Italy, Ctr. for Arts and Scis., East Charleston, W.Va., Brookgreen Gardens; illustrator Mexico in Your Pocket, 1937, Isabelle Elizabeth, 1946, Puffy Goes to Sea, 1946, Woman's Day Book of Houseplants, 1963. Recipient Award of Distinctive Merit, Art Dirs. Club, N.Y.C., 1945, Henry Hering Meml. Medal award, Nat. Sculpture Soc., N.Y.C., 1988, Merit of Honor award Pietrasanta and Versilia in the world, 2002, Merit of Honor award sculpture from Firenze, Tuscany, 2003. Fellow Nat. Sculpture Soc. Home: Pietrasanta, Italy. Died Feb. 21, 2008.

**MARKS, DAVID HENRY,** lawyer; b. Indpls., Feb. 5, 1947; s. Robert Henry and Sophia (Gerson) Marks; m. Claudia Ellen Blank, Apr. 8, 1978. BA, Yale U., 1968, JD, 1971. Bar: Ind. 1971, Ill. 1971, NY 1974, U.S. Dist. Ct. (so. dist.) Ind. 1971, U.S. Dist. Ct. (no. dist.) Ill. 1971, U.S. Dist. Ct. (so. dist.) NY 1974, U.S. Ct. Appeals (7th cir.) 1972, U.S. Ct. Appeals (2d cir.) 1974, U.S. Supreme Ct. 1976. Law clk. to judge U.S. Ct. Appeals (7th cir.), Chgo., 1971—73; assoc. Lord, Day & Lord, NYC, 1973—79, ptnr., 1979—86, Coudert Bros., NYC, from 1986. Editl. adv. bd.: European Competition Law Rev. Mem.: ABA, N.Y.C. Bar Assn., Am. Law Inst., Phi Beta Kappa. Died Dec. 4, 1992.

**MARKWELL, NOEL,** psychology professor; b. Covington, Ky., May 24, 1933; s. Quentin Roosevelt and Lelia Rose (Workman) M. AB, Lafayette Coll., 1955; MS, Purdue U., 1958, PhD, 1959. Lic. psychologist, Md. Psychologist Warley Hosp., Brentwood, Essex, Eng., 1960-61, D.C. Gen. Hosp., 1962-66, Law Sch. Georgetown U., Washington, 1967-72; cons. Gen. Acctg. Office, Washington, 1980-81; pvt. practice clin. psychology Md., 1972-1990; prof. Union Inst. Grad. Sch., Cin., from 1980. Pres., bd. dirs. Inst. for Victims of Trauma, Washington, 1987—; cons.-sr. reviewer, Nat. Register of Health Svc. Providers in Psychology, Washington, 1975—. Dissertation Rsch. grant U.S. Office of Edn., Purdue U., 1958-59; Am.-Scandinavian Found. scholar U. Stockholm, 1959-60. Mem. Internat. Soc. of Polit. Psychology (founder, treas. 1986-96); mem. APA, World Fedn. for Mental Health. Deceased.

**MARLAND, ALKIS JOSEPH,** leasing company executive, computer scientist, educator, financial planner; b. Athens, Mar. 8, 1943; arrived in U.S., 1961, naturalized, 1974; s. Basil and Maria (Pervanides) Mouradoglou; m. Anita Louise Malone, Dec. 19, 1970 (dec. Mar. 27, 2003); children: Andrea Weber, Alyssa. BS, Southwestern U., 1963; MA, U. Tex., Austin, 1967; MS in Engring. Adminstrn., So. Meth. U., 1971. CLU; cert. data processing, enrolled agt., fund specialist, ChFC, CFP, accredited tax advisor, accredited tax preparer. With Sun Co., Richardson, Tex., 1968-71, Phila., 1971-76; mgr. planning and acquisitions Sun Info. Svcs. subs. Sun Co., Dallas, 1976-78; v.p. Helios Capital Corp. subs. Sun Co., Radnor, Pa., 1978-83; pres. ALKAN Leasing Corp., Wayne, Pa., from 1983, also bd. dirs. Prof. dept. computer scis. and bus. adminstrn. Ea. Coll., St. Davids, Pa., 1985—87; prof. math. Villanova (Pa.) U., 1987—89. Contr. Christian Counseling and Ednl. Found., 2003—05; bd. dirs. Radnor Twp. Sch. Dist., 1987—91, Delaware County Intermediate Unit, 1988—91. Mem.: IEEE, Assn. Investment Mgmt. and Rsch., Phila. Union League, World Affairs Coun. Phila., Fgn. Policy Rsch. Inst., Phila. Fin. Assn. (mem. award 1988, sec. 1989—92, bd. dirs. 1989—92), Fin. Planning Assn. (treas. 2000—01, bd. dirs. Phila. Tri-State Area 2000—04, pres.-elect 2002, pres. 2003, chmn. 2004), Fin. Analysts Phila., Nat. Assn. Pub. Accts., Nat. Assn. Tax Practitioners, Nat. Assn. Enrolled Agts., Inst. Cert. Fin. Planners (bd. dirs. Phila. Tri-State Area 1993—99, v.p. membership 1994—95, treas. 1995—99), Am. Assn. Equipment Lessors, Fin. Svc. Profls., Data Processing Mgmt. Assn., Assn. Computing Machinery, Main Line C. of C., Wayne Club, Rotary Club (pres. 1989—90, asst. gov. 1990—92, 1993—94, treas. dist. 7450 2002—07, dist. 7450 gov. elect 2008—09, gov. 2009—10), Masons. Republican. Died Mar. 6, 2012.

**MARLEAU, DIANE,** former Canadian government official; b. Kirkland Lake, Ont., Can., June 21, 1943; d. Jean-Paul and Yvonne (Desjardins) LeBel; m. Paul C. Marleau, Aug. 3, 1963; children: Brigitte, Donald, Stéphane. Student, U. Ottawa, Ont., 1960-63; BA in Econs., Laurentian U., Sudbury, Ont., 1976. With Donald Jean Acctg. Services, Sudbury, 1971-75; receiver mgr. Thorne Riddell, Sudbury, 1975-76; treas. Northern Regional Residential Treatment Program for Women, Sudbury, 1976-80, Com. for the Industry and Labour Adjustment Program, Sudbury, 1983; mem. transition team Ont. Premier's Office, Toronto, 1985; firm adminstr. Collins Barrow-Maheu Noiseux, Sudbury, 1985-88; M.P. from Sudbury House of Commons, Ottawa, 1988—2008; min. of nat. health & welfare Govt. of Canada, 1993-96, min. of public works, 1996-97, min. for internat. cooperation, 1997-99, min. for La Francophonie, 1997—99. Councilor Regional Municipality of Sudbury, 1980-85, chair finance com., 1981; alderman City of Sudbury, 1980-85; mem. Northern Devel. Coun., Sudbury, 1986-88; vice chair Nat. Liberal Standing Com. on Policy, 1989; chair Ont. Liberal Caucus, 1990; apptd. nat. exec. Liberal Party Can., 1990, assoc. critic Govt. Ops., 1990, Dep. Opposition Whip, 1991, assoc. critic finance, 1992; vice chair standing com. finance, 1992.

Chmn. fund-raising Canadian Cancer Soc., Sudbury, 1987-88; co-chmn. Laurentian Hosp. Cancer Care Services fund-raising campaign, Sudbury, 1988; chair bd. govs. Cambrian Coll., 1987-88, bd. govs., 1983-88; mem. Sudbury and Dist. Health Unit Bd., 1981-82; mem. finance com., bd. dirs. Laurentian Hosp., 1981-85; chair Can. Games for the Physically Disabled, 1983; apptd. Ont. Adv. Coun. Women's Issues, 1984. Recipient Paul Harris award, 1996, Bernadine Yackman award Bus & Profl. Women's Club Greater Sudbury, 2009 Mem. Sudbury Bus. & Profl. Women Club. Liberal Party Can. Avocations: playing piano, gardening, cooking. Home: Sudbury, Canada. Died Jan. 30, 2013.

**MARMO, FRANCESCO,** embryologist, medical consultant; b. San Rufo, Italy, Feb. 14, 1934; s. Orazio Marmo and Rosa Santoro; m. Isabella Bianconi, Sept. 2, 1967; children: Fabrizio, Valerio, Francesca-Rosa, Silvia. MD summa cum laude, U. Naples, Italy, 1959. Diplomate Bd. Otorhinolaryngology. Asst. prof. gen. biology U. Naples, 1960—62, asst. prof. genetics, 1963—71, prof. anatomy, 1968—76, asst. prof. gen. biology, 1969—80, 1971—78, asst. prof. histology and embryology, 1978—80, prof. histology and embryology, from 1980. Contbr. Histology, 1981, articles to profl. publs. Mem.: Pontaniana Acad. Naples, NY Acad. Sci., Unione Zoologica Italiana, Italian Soc. Otorhinolaryngology, Gruppo Embriologico Italiano. Achievements include discovery of carbonic anhydrase role on otolith morphogenesis. Home: Rome, Italy. Died Mar. 8, 2013.

**MAROWITZ, CHARLES,** retired theater director; b. NYC, Jan. 26, 1934; s. Harry Yudel Marowitz and Tillie Rosencrantz; m. Jane Windsor. Grad. high sch., NYC. Freelance dir. theaters in Oslo, Bochum and Wiesbaden, Fed. Republic German, Bergen, Norway, Rome; assoc. dir. London Traverse Theater, London, 1965-67; co-dir. Royal Shakespeare Co. Exptl. Group, London, 1966; artistic dir. Open Space Theater, London, 1967-80; assoc. dir. Los Angeles Theater Ctr., Los Angeles, 1984—89; artistic dir. Malibu Stage Co., 1990—2002. Corr. The Guardian, London, 1982—, Plays Internat. mag., London, 1982—. Author: Confessions of a Counterfeit Critic, 1978, Marowitz Shakespeare, 1986, Act of Being, 1986, Prospero's Staff, 1987, Potboilers, 1987, Sherlock's last Case, 1987. Served to cpl. U.S. Army, 1952-54. Recipient Order of Purple Sash award Denmark Senate 1965, Whitbread award Whitbread Trust, London, 1967. Mem. Writers Guild America, Dramatists Guild. Home: Malibu, Calif. Died May 2, 2014.

**MARSELLA, SAMUEL ANTHONY,** lawyer; b. White Plains, NY, Nov. 22, 1931; s. Anthony and Maria (Panfilo) M.; m. Carol Joan Levitre, June 22, 1957; children: Karen, Kevin, James, Mary. BA, Villanova U., 1953; LLB, Boston U., 1956. Bar: Mass. 1956, U.S. Ct. Mil. Appeals 1959, U.S. Supreme Ct. 1959, U.S. Dist. Ct. Mass. 1960, U.S. Ct. Appeals (1st cir.) 1979. City prosecuter City of Springfield (Mass.), 1962-64; sr. ptnr. Doherty, Wallace, Pillsbury & Murphy, P.C., Springfield, from 1964. Chmn. Springfield Bd. Police Commrs., 1980-84; mem. Mass. Gov.'s Jud. Conduct Commn., 1982-85, Mass. Gov.'s Jud. Nominating Coun., 1987-90. Mem. ABA, Mass. Bar Assn., Am. Acad. Hosp. Attys. Deceased.

**MARSH, STANLEY, III,** artist; b. Amarillo, Tex., Jan. 31, 1938; m. Gwendolyn O'Brien; 5 children. BA in Economics, U. Pa., MA in American Civilization. Owner Sta. KVII, Amarillo, Tex., 1967—2002, Cadillac Ranch. Art collector; farmer, rancher. Died June 17, 2014.

**MARSHALL, ENID ANN,** law educator; b. Boyndie, Scotland, July 10, 1932; d. John and Lizzie (Gilchrist) M. MA with 1st class honors, U. St. Andrews, Scotland, 1955, LLB with distinction, 1958, PhD, 1966. Law apprentice Pagan & Osborne, Cupar, Scotland, 1956-59; lectr. law Dundee Coll. Tech., 1959-72; lectr. bus. law U. Stirling, Scotland, 1972-74, sr. lectr. bus. law, 1974-77, reader in bus. law, 1977-94, reader in Scots law rsch., 1994-99. External examiner U. Scotland, 1973-79, Colls. in Scotland, 1974-83; moderator Scotvec, Scotland, 1972-90; external lectr. Coll. Estate Mgmt., Reading, Eng., 1989-94. Author: General Principles of Scots Law, 7 edits., 1971-99, Scots Mercantile Law, 3 edits., 1983-97, Scottish Cases on Contract, 2 edits., 1978-93, Oliver and Marshall's Company Law, 10th to 12th edits., 1987-94, Gill on Arbitration, 3d and 4th edits., 1984-2001; editor Scottish Law Gazette, 1983-2001. Chmn. Social Security Appeal Tribunals, Stirling & Falkirk, Scotland. Fellow Royal Soc. Arts; mem. Chartered Inst. Arbitrators (assoc.), Royal Instn. Chartered Surveyors (hon. assoc.), Law Soc. Scotland (solicitor). Home: Stirling, Scotland. Died July 11, 2008.

**MARSHALL, STANLEY (J. STANLEY MARSHALL),** retired academic administrator; b. Cheswick, Pa., Jan. 27, 1923; s. Walter W. and Mildred (Crawford) M.; m. Ruth Cratty, June 10, 1944 (div. 1966); children: David, Sue, John; m. Shirley Ann Slade, Sept. 10, 1966; children: Kimberly, James Andrew. BS, Slippery Rock State Tchrs. Coll., Pa., 1947; MS, Syracuse U., 1950, PhD, 1956; D of Pub. Svc. (hon.), U. Fla., 1998. Tchr. sci. Mynderse Acad., Seneca Falls, N.Y., 1947-52; asst. prof. sci. State U. N.Y. Coll. Edn., Cortland, 1953-55, asso. prof., 1956-57, prof., 1957-58; instr. Syracuse U., 1955-56; prof., head dept. sci. edn. Fla. State U., Tallahassee, 1958; asso. dean Fla. State U. (Sch. Edn.), 1965-67; dean Fla. State U. (Coll. Edn.), 1967-69, pres., 1969-76, Sonitrol of Tallahassee, Inc., 1978-87, COMSAFE Inc., 1981-84, James Madison Inst. for Public Policy Studies, 1987-90, chmn. bd. dirs., 1990-98. Pres. Southern Scholarship and Research Found., 1968-69 Author: (with E. Burkman) Current Trends in Science Education, 1966, (with I. Podendorf and C. Swartz) The Basic Science Program, 1965, Tumultuous Sixties: Campus Unrest and Student Life at a Southern University, 2006; Editor: Jour. of Research in Sci. Teaching, 1962-66; Mem. editorial bd.: Science World, 1962-65; Contbr. articles to profl. jours. Mem. U.S. Navy Sec.'s adv. bd. edn. and tng. U.S. Army adv. panel ROTC, 1975-79; bd. regents Nat. Libr. Medicine, 1970-75; bd. dirs. Tallahassee Meml. Regional Med. Ctr., 1980-86; mem. Citizens Commn. on the Fla. Cabinet, 1995-96; mem. Fla. Constn. Revision Commn., 1997-98; trustee Bethune Cookman Coll., 1993-2004, chmn. 2001-05; bd. trustees Fla. State U., 2001-05 Fellow AAAS; mem. American Inst. Physics, Nat. Sci. Tchrs. Assn., Fla. Acad. Sciences, Fla. Assn. Sci. Tchrs., Southern Assn. State Univs. and Land-Grant Colls (pres. 1971-72), Nat. Assn. Research Sci. Teaching, NEA, Fla. Edn. Assn., Sigma Xi, Phi Delta Kappa, Kappa Delta Pi. Home: Tallahassee, Fla. Died June 8, 2014.

**MARTENS, WILFRIED,** former prime minister of Belgium; b. Sleidinge, Belgium, Apr. 19, 1936; m. Lieve Verschroeven, Nov. 13, 1998 (div.); children: Chris, Ann, Feich, Sophie, Fimdi; m. Miet Smet, Sept. 27, 2008; children: Kris, Anne, Sarah, Sophie, Simon. D.Laws, Cath. U. Louvain, 1960, Lic. Notary Sci., 1960; B of Thomistic Philosophy, K U. Louvain, 1960; B, Harvard U., 1968; PhD (hon.), Panteion U. Social & Polit. Scis., 2010, U. Social & Polit. Scis., 2010. Barrister, Ct. of Appeal Gent. Pres. Union Flemish Students, 1958—59; adv. to Prime Minister Govt. of Belgium, 1965-68, prime min., 1979—81, 1981—92; pres. European's People's Party, 1990—2003, Christian Dem. Internat., 2000—01. Chargé de mission to Office Minister Cmty. Affairs, 1968-72; mem. exec. com. Flemish Nat. Movement; pres. juniors Christian Social Party, 1967, pres. party, 1972; mem. Chamber Deputies from Gent-Eeklo Dist., 1974-91; senator Brussel-Halle-Vilvoorde, 1991-94; pres. European Union Christian Democrats, 1993-96; chmn. EPP group European Parliament, 1994-99 Contbr. articles to profl. publs. Recipient Robert Schuman medal, 1987, Kaal Theatre award, 1993, Robert Schuman medal, 1995, Charles V Price award, EU Spain, 1998, Grand Croix de l'Ordre de Leopold II award, Belgium, 2000, BeNeLux Europa prize, 2008, Graben Leopold Kunschak Preis award, 2010. Democrat. Roman Catholic. Died Oct. 9, 2013.

**MARTIN, CHRISTOPHER JOHN,** medical educator, surgeon; b. Sydney, June 10, 1948; s. Hans Lorenz and Nora Helen (Fyldes) Martin; m. Margaret Dimity Pallis, Jan. 5, 1980; children: Jonathan, James, Isabella. BSc with 1st honors, U. Sydney, 1971, MSc, 1972, M.B.B.S. with honors, 1974. Sr. lectr. surgery U. Melbourne, Victoria, Australia, 1982—85, assoc. prof. surgery, 1985—97; prof. surgery U. Sydney, from 1993; surgeon St. Vincent's Hosp., Melbourne, 1982—92; surgeon, head dept. Nepean Hosp., Sydney, from 1993. Vis. scientist Med. Coll. Wis., Milw., 1988; examiner in surgery Royal Australasian Coll. Surgeons, 1995—2004. Co-author (and co-editor): Clinical Gastroenterology: A Practical Problem-Based Approach, 1996. Recipient Univ. medal, U. Sydney, 1971, Peter Bancroft prize, 1972; grantee, NHMRC grantee, 1986—96, from 2006. Fellow: Royal Australian Coll. Surgeons; mem.: Internat. Soc. for Diseases of Oesophagus, Surg. Rsch. Soc. Australasia (pres. 1994—95). Avocations: sailing, skiing. Home: Sydney, Australia. Deceased.

**MARTIN, FRANCES LEE,** nursing educator; b. Filbert, Pa., Sept. 17; d. Mack and Nellie (Allen0 Marshall; 1 child, Tanya. Diploma in nursing, Fordham Hosp., 1951; BSN, Hunter Coll., 1957, MSN, 1964; MS in Edn., Bklyn. Coll., 1974. Instr. nursing Cumberland Hosp., Bklyn., 1959-61; substitute tchr. Sara Hale Vocat. HS, Bklyn., 1963-64; instr. Meth. Sch. Nursing, Bklyn., 1964-70; asst. prof., then assoc. prof. Coll. S.I., NY, from 1970; instr. Coney Island Hosp., Bklyn., 1989. Mem. adv. bd. CRTS South Beach Psychiat. Ctr., S.I., NY, 1981—; mem. adv. bd. NY Urban League, S.I., 1988—, vice chairperson, 1990—; clin. cons. Regents Coll., Mineola, NY, 1988—; presenter in field. Author: Nurse Test Medical-Surgical Nursing, 1992; contbg. author: Nursing Decision, 1982; contbr. articles to profl. publs. Vol. tutor First Ctrl. Bapt. Ch., SI, NY, 2005. Mem. ANA (cert.), AAUP, NAACP, Assoc. Degree Orgn. Nursing Edn., Nat. League Nursing, NY Urban League, Sigma Theta Tau. Democrat. Avocations: theater, tennis, reading, sewing. Home: Miami Shores, Fla. Died Apr. 28, 2014.

**MARTIN, JACK,** physician; b. Northport, Ala., Aug. 11, 1927; s. Marvin Oscar and Glenavis (Rice) M.; m. Ann Inman, Apr. 7, 1957; children: Sarah, Richard, Charles Randall, Robert. BS, U. Ala., 1949; MD, Vanderbilt U., 1953. Intern Charity Hosp., New Orleans, 1953-54; resident in adult and child psychiatry Cin. Gen. Hosp., 1954-58; dir. child psychiatry U. Tex. Health Scis. Ctr., Dallas, 1958-67, clin. prof. child psychiatry, from 1967; med. dir. Shady Brook Rsch. Ctr., Richardson, Tex., 1963-81; physician pvt. practice, Dallas, from 1981. With USNR, 1945-47. Independent. Episcopalian. Avocations: bridge, golf. Home: Dallas, Tex. Died Sept. 7, 2013.

**MARTIN, LEONARDO S.J.,** retired urologist, surgeon; b. Macati, Rizal, The Philippines, Nov. 26, 1926; came to U.S., 1953; s. Nemesio Martin and Felicidad San Juan; m. Helen Mary Dougherty, May 24, 1958; children: Leonard, John and David (twins), Mark, Regina Mary Martin Dawson, Daniel. AA, U. The Philippines, 1947; MD, U. Santo Tomas, Manila, The Philippines, 1952. Diplomate Am. Bd. Urology; cert. physician and surgeon, Calif. Resident in urology Phila. Gen. Hosp., 1954-57; fellow in urology Mass. Gen. Hosp., Boston, 1957-59; urologist Manila Specialists Med. Ctr., 1959-63; instr. urology U. Santo Tomas, 1959-63; assoc. cancer urologist Roswell Pk. Meml. Hosp., Buffalo, 1963-65; urologist Sunnyvale (Calif.) Med. Ctr., 1965-94; mem. clin. tchg. staff Stanford (Calif.) Med. Ctr., 1965-94; cons. urology Los Altos, from 1994. Commr., med. expert Calif. Med. Bd. Licensure, Sacramento, 1987-2000. Contbr. articles to profl. jours. Bd. dirs. Flint Cultural Ctr., Cupertino, Calif., 1970-80; past adv. bd. Santa Clara County unit Boys and Girls Club Am. Named one of 10 Outstanding Young Men, Jaycees, The Philippines, 1960, Disting. Men of Medicine, U. The Philippines Coll. Medicine, 1960. Fellow ACS (cert. merit 1964); mem. AMA (cert. Inc. merit 1964), Am. Urol. Assn. (AUA, Inc. cert. merit 1964), Am. Assn. Clin. Urologists, Philippine-Am. Urol. Soc. (founding pres. 1972), U. Santo Tomas Med. Alumni Assn. in Am. (pres. 1996-97, Most Outstanding Alumnus of Yr. 2000, Most Outstanding Golden Jubilarian of Yr., 2002). Republican. Roman Catholic. Avocations: painting, piano, tennis, golf. Deceased.

**MARTIN, ROBERT RICHARD,** emeritus college president, retired state senator; b. McKinney, Ky., Dec. 27, 1910; s. Henry Franklin and Annie Frances (Peek) M.; m. Anne French Hoge, May 31, 1952. AB, Eastern Ky. U., 1934; MA, U. Ky., 1940; EdD, Columbia U., 1951. Tchr., prin. pub. schs., Mason and Lee counties, Ky., 1935-48; with Ky. Dept. Edn., 1948-59, beginning as auditor, successively dir. finance, head bur. adminstrn. and finance, 1948-55, supt. pub. instrn., 1955-59; commr. finance Commonwealth Ky., 1959-60; pres. Eastern Ky. U., Richmond, 1960-76, pres. emeritus, from 1976; mem. Ky. Senate, 1977-86; chmn. health and welfare com.; assisted devel. found. program for financing of edn. in Ky. Bd. dirs. Bank One; chmn. health and welfare com.; assisted devel. found. program for financing edn. in Ky. Bd. dirs. Pattie A. Clay Hosp., Telford Community Center, Ky. Diabetes Assn.; mem. Ky. Cancer Commn.; bd. dirs. Jud. Form Retirement; hon. chmn. United Way Madison County, 1978—; trustee, elder Presbyn. ch. Tech. sgt. USAAF, 1942-46; meteorologist. Recipient Outstanding Alumnus award Eastern Ky. State Coll., 1956; named Kentuckian of Yr. Ky. Press Assn., 1964; recipient Service award Joint Alumni Council Ky., 1970, Civilian Service award Dept. Army, 1971; Danforth Found. grantee, 1971. Mem. NEA, Am. Assn. Sch. Adminstrs., English-Speaking Union, Civil War Roundtable (bd. dirs.), Ky. Hist. Soc. (pres. 1974—), Ky. Edn. Assn., Am. Assn. State Colls. and Univs. (pres. 1971-72), Phi Delta Kappa, Kappa Delta Pi. Lodges: Masons (Shriners), Rotary, Filson. Democrat. Presbyterian. Home: Richmond, Ky. Died Nov. 29, 1997.

**MARTIN, WALTER PATRICK,** retired physician; b. LA, Nov. 3, 1912; s. George M. and Viola (Rimill) M.; children by previous marriage: Judith Martin Fisher, Kathlyn Martin Gausephol, Timothy Martin, James Martin; m. Margaret Ann Byrnes, Sept. 1, 1966; children: Mark DiPiazza, Greg DiPiazza, Walter Patrick II; adopted children: Paul Wegner, Mary Wegner (Mrs. Bryan McGee). BS, UCLA, 1933; MD, St. Louis U., 1937. Intern Los Angeles County Hosp., 1937-38, resident internal medicine, 1938-40; chmn. attending staff Harbour Gen. Hosp., Torrance, Calif., 1950-90; chief staff St. Mary's Hosp., Long Beach, Calif., 1970-90; clin. prof. UCLA Sch. Medicine, 1960-82, clin. prof. emeritus, 1982-90, pres. Harbour Collegium, 1977-78. Chmn. bd. dirs. Harriman Jones Clinic, Long Beach, 1976-79; trustee Audio Digest, 1974-78. Served to maj. M.C., AUS, 1941-45. Recipient Disting. Service and Leadership award Harbor Gen. Hosp., 1969; named hon. clin. prof. internal medicine for meritorious services UCLA, 1977; Rockefeller fellow, 1940-41; Walter P. Martin Research Ctr. named in his honor Harbor-UCLA Med. Ctr., 1987. Fellow ACP (regional bd. govs. 1973-77, Laureate award 1990), Am. Coll. Cardiology; mem. L.A. Acad. Medicine (bd. govs., pres. 1975-76), Calif. Med. Assn. (chmmn. continuing med. edn. 1975, sci. bd. 1975, adv. panel on internal medicine 1981, mem. sci. bd. 1976-81). Home: Bonsall, Calif. Died Mar. 6, 1997.

**MARTÍN MUNICIO, ANGEL,** science academy executive; b. Haro, La Rioja, Spain, Nov. 30, 1923; m. Pilar de Montaud; 1 child. Degree in chemistry, U. Salamanca; degree in pharmacy, U. de Santiago de Compostela/Corunna; D in Chemistry, Complutense U., Madrid, D in Pharmacy; postgrad., U. London, Cambridge U., Eng., Newcastle U. Asst. prof. organic chemistry Complutense U., Madrid, dep. rector rsch., 1983-88, prof. emeritus, 1988—2002; sci. collaborator, rschr., head biochemistry sect. CSIC, prof. biochemistry, dir. dept. biochemistry and molecular biology; pres. Royal Acad. de Ciencias Exactas, Fisicas y Naturals, Madrid. Contbr. articles to profl. jours. Recipient Gold medal La Rioja Autonomous Cmty., Cross, Order of Alfonso X el Sabio, Grand Cross, Order of Mil. Merit. Mem. OECD (Spanish rep.), UNESCO (nat. com.), Spanish Royal Soc. Physics and Chemistry (v.p., Rsch. Merit medal), European Molecular Biology Orgn. (Spanish rep., v.p. conf.), Spanish Royal Acad. Avocations: gardening, literary reading. Home: Madrid, Spain. Died Nov. 23, 2002.

**MARTINO, EVA ELLENA,** artist; b. Overbrook, Pa., Oct. 15, 1929; d. Michael and Florence (Ricca) Marinelli; m. Giovanni Martino, May 28, 1946; children: Nina, Babette. Student, La France Art Inst., Phila., 1943—46, Pa. Acad. Fine Arts, 1943—45; Diploma di Maestro d'Arte (hon.), Centro Artistico e Culturale Internazionale, Nopoli, Italy, 1984. Painter various exhibitions, from 1953. Lectr. in field. Exhibitions include Nat. Acad. Design, N.Y.C., Pa. Acad. Fine Arts(fellowship), Allied Artists of Am., N.Y.C., Butler Inst. Am. Art, Ohio, Reading (Pa.) Mus., Audubon Artists, N.Y.C., Mus. of the Great Plains, Okla., Edinboro (Pa.) State Tchrs. Coll., Italian Cultural Ctr., Ill., Acad. Artists, Mass, Civic Ctr. Mus., Salon des Amis Gallery, Malvern, Pa., 2001, Atlantic City Art Ctr., N.J., Centro Cultural, San Miguel de Allende, Mex., 2002, 2003-05, Butler Inst. Am. Art, Ohio, Woodmere Art Mus., Phila., 2004-05, Phila. Paintings by the AMrtino Family-Eva, Bahetta & Giuuonni Montino, 3 Martino's, Widener U. Art Gallery, Chester, 2008; represented in permanent collections Butler Inst. of Am. Art (Juror's Choice award 1994), Ohio, Mohawk Valley Community Coll., Utica, N.Y., New Music West, Calif., Meridian Bank, Reading, Pa., Milford (Conn.) Fine Arts Coun. Recipient Bronze medal Da Vinci Art Alliance, 1953, 1st pl. award Plymouth Meeting Art Show, 1969, 2d pl. Perkiomenville Art League, 2d pl. award Norristown

ArtLeague, 2d pl. award Gertrude Fogelson Art award, 2d pl. Merit award Internat. Miniature Soc. of Fla., 1980, Third Nat. Bank award Springfield Art League, 1982, 1st pl. award, Perkiomen Valley Art Ctr., 1983, Recommended for Purchase award, Lawton Jr. Service League, 1983, 85, The Framing Mill award Berks Art Alliance, 1983, 3d pl. award William Penn Meml. Mus., 1984, Antonelli Inst. of Art and Photography award, 1984, La Grande Targa del Sindaco di Napoli Centro Artistico e Culturale Interazionale, 1984, Merit award Berks Art Alliance, 1984, Meridian Bancorp Purchase award, 1985, Purchase award Community Arts Council, 1986, Ruth Eingorn Meml. award Cheltenham Art Ctr., 1987, Purchase award Milford Fine Arts Coun., 1987, 91, 1st Pl. award Washington & Jefferson Coll., Pa., 1991, Equitable Life Assurance Soc., 1991, Renee McNeely award Phillips Mill Art Assn., Pa., 1991, Jack & Sue Onofrio award, Kans., 1991, Honorable Mention award San Bernardino County (Calif.) Mus., 1991, Paul Mazza award Cheltenham Ctr. of Art, 1995, Pilyna Sitarchuk award, 1996, Painting award Cheltenham Art Ctr., 1997, Painting award Philips Mill Art Assn., 1997, Founders award Cheltenham Art Ctr., 1999, Peddlers Village award Bianco Art Found., 1999, H.V. Howley award, P.A. Acad. Fine Arts, Phila., 2001, Gold medal of Honor, Anderson Arts, NYC, 2002, C. Gibson Granger award, 2003, Mary Butler Meml. Fund Purchase award, PAFA, 2006, Buttler Fund Purchace award, 2006. Fellow: Pa. Acad. Fine Arts (Granger award 1998, Hawley award 2001); mem.: Allied Artists America (NYC) (Charles J. Romans Meml. award), Audubon Artists Inc. (NYC) (Gold medal of Honor 2002). Died Apr. 30, 2012.

**MARTLAND, T(HOMAS) R(ODOLPHE),** philosophy educator; b. Port Chester, NY, May 29, 1926; s. Thomas Rodolphe and Anne Elizabeth (Newbury) M.; m. Agatha Murphy, Apr. 3, 1952; children: David Allen, Luke Thomas. BS magna cum laude, Fordham U., 1951; MA, Columbia U., 1955, PhD, 1959. Asst. prof. Lafayette Coll., Easton, Pa., 1959-65; assoc. prof. So. Ill. U., Carbondale, 1965-66; assoc. prof. philosophy U. Albany, N.Y., 1966-84, prof. N.Y., 1984-97, rsch. prof. N.Y., from 1997, dir. religious studies program N.Y., 1980-87, dir. philosophy grad studies program N.Y., 1988-91. Disting. Jeannette K. Watson vis. prof. of religion, Syracuse U., 1987; dir. Master of Arts in Liberal Studies Program, 1995-97. Author: Religion as Art: An Interpretation, 1982; The Metaphysics of William James and John Dewey, 1969; mem. editl. bd. Jour. Comparative Lit. and Aesthetics, 1982-91; guest editor Annals of Scholarship, 1982; contbr. articles to profl. jours., essays to profl. publs. Served to lt. (s.g.) USN, 1944-47, 51-53. Faculty Exch. Guest scholar, 1976-77, rsch. fellow, 1967, 68, 71, 87; Jones Fund award Lafayette Coll., 1962-63, Signum Laudis award for excellence in tchg. and rsch., 1986. Mem. Am. Philos. Assn., Am. Soc. Aesthetics (steering com. 1985-88), Internat. Assn. Philosophy and Lit. (exec. com. 1976-81). Deceased.

**MARTY, RENÉ PIERRE,** obstetrician, gynecologist; b. Paris, Apr. 9, 1929; s. Rémy and Simone Renée (Grousseaud) M.; m. Genoveva Elisa Dotremont, Apr. 9, 1955; children: Audrey, Sabine. 2 baccalauréats, U. Paris. Cert. Gynecologist & Obstetrician, Faculté de médecine de Paris, 1978. Attaché in gynecology U. Hosp., Avicenne-Paris, 1977-88, attaché en Premier, 1988-90, attaché cons., from 1990, Jean Verdier-Paris, from 1995. Vis. prof. Cleveland Clin. Edn. Found., 1994; vis. surgeon Mayo Clin. Med. Sch., 1969; head Fibrohysteroscopic Unit Diagnostic & Operative with Laser Surgery, Hosp Avicenne-Paris, 1987, Hosp. Jean Verdier-Paris, 1995. Author: (book) Hysteroscopy, Principles & Practice, 1984, Hysteroscopy Update, 1991, Office Hysteroscopy, 1996. Internat. spkr. in field. Mem. Internat. Soc. Gynecol. Endoscopy (bd. dirs. 2001—), European Soc. Gynecol. Endoscopy, Am. Assn. Gynecologic Laparoscopists (internat. advisor), Am. Fertility Soc., Soc. Argentina Cirugia Laparoscopica (hon.), French Club Gynecologique D' Endoscopie Flexible (founding mem., bd. dirs.), 1991. Home: Neuilly-sur-Seine, France. Died May 2005.

**MARX, CHICO (LEONARD MARX),** actor; b. NYC, Mar. 22, 1887; s. Minnie Marx. Actor; musician. Apppeared in vaudeville and in films with the Marx Brothers; appeared in films including: Humorisk, 1920, The Cocoanuts, 1929, Animal Crackers, 1930, The House That Shadows Built, 1931, Monkey Business, 1931, Hollywood on Parade No. 5, 1932, Horse Feathers, 1932, Duck Soup, 1933, Hollywood on Parade No. 9, 1933, A Night at the Opera, 1935, A Day at the Races, 1937, Room Service, 1938, At the Circus, 1939, Go West, 1940, The Big Store, 1941, Screen Snapshot No. 110, 1943, A Night in Casablanca, 1946, Love Happy, 1949, The Story of Mankind, 1957. Died Oct. 11, 1961.

**MARX, HARPO (ADOLPH MARX),** actor; b. Nov. 23, 1888; m. Susan Fleming, Sept. 28, 1936; 4 adopted children: Bill, Alex, Jimmy, and Minnie. Actor, New York. Appeared in vaudeville and in films with the Marz Brothers; films include The Cocoanuts, 1929, Animal Crackers, 1930, Monkey Business, 1931, Horsefeathers, 1932, Duck Soup, 1933, A Night at the Opera, 1935, A Day at the Races, 1937, Room Service, 1938, At the Circus, 1939, Go West, 1940, Love Happy, 1949. Died Sept. 28, 1964.

**MASALIYEV, ABSAMAT,** Kyrgyz government official; b. Kyrgyzstan, USSR, 1933; Grad., Mining Inst., Moscow. Engr. Kyrgyzugol Trust, 1956-61; former mem. Communist Party of USSR; instr. Oblast com., dep. chmn. Oblast com. for People's Control Kyrgyz Communist Party, 1961-68, dep. dept. head Cen. Com., 1st sec. Tash-Kumyr City Com., 1968-71, mem. Cen. Com., 1971—90; head dept. industry & transport Cen. Com. Kyrgyz Communist Party, 1971-73; chmn. exec. com. Frunze City Sov. of People's Deps., 1973-74; mem. Bur. Cen. Com. Kyrgyz Communist Party, sec., 1974-79; dep. to Supreme Soviet Kyrgyz Soviet Socialist Republic; 1st sec. Issyk-Kul Oblast com. Kyrgyz Communist Party, first sec., 1985—90; mem. Parliament Kyrgyzstan, 2000—04. Died July 31, 2004.

**MASCHLER, MICHAEL BAHIR,** retired mathematician; b. Jerusalem, July 22, 1927; s. Oscar and Bertha Bahir Maschler; m. Hanna Steiner; children: Yael Maschler Inbar, Amir Bahir Maschler, Gideon Bahir Maschler, Dorit Bahir Maschler(dec.). Degree in math., Hebrew U., Jerusalem, 1968. Tchr., rschr. Hebrew U., from 1955, prof. math., from 1972, prof. emeritus, from 1995. Vis. prof. Princeton U., 1961—63, CUNY, 1966—67, Stanford U., 1972, Rice U., 1972, Cornell U., 1984, UCLA, 1985, U. BC, 1989, Northwestern U., 1990, UCLA, 1990, U. Va., Charlottesville, 2000—04. Author rsch. papers, books in field. Edn. The State of Israel and other organizations, Israel, 2000. Officer Israel Defence Army, 1948—49, Israel. Recipient Lanchester prize, 1995; named Hon. Prof., U. Qingdao, China, 2002. Achievements include research in game theory and its applications. Avocations: photography, travel. Home: Jerusalem, Israel. Died July 20, 2008.

**MASLOFF, SOPHIE,** former mayor; b. Pitts., Dec. 23, 1917; d. Louis and Jennie Friedman; m. Jack Masloff, 1939 (dec. 1991); 1 child, Linda. Grad. high sch., Pitts. Chief investigator Ct. of Common Pleas, Allegheny County, Pa., 1940—76; city councilman City of Pitts., 1976-88, coun. pres., 1988, mayor, 1988—94. Alternate del. Democratic Nat. Conv., 1968, del., 1978, 92; pres. Allegheny League of Municipalities, 1992, Pa. League of Cities. Mem. Allegheny County Democratic Women's Guild, Pa. Fedn. Democratic Women, Lodges: B'nai B'rith, Hadassah. Democrat. Jewish. Died Aug. 17, 2014.

**MASON, JOHN WAYNE,** psychoneuroendocrinologist, retired medical educator; b. Chgo., Feb. 9, 1924; s. John Ralph and Frances Elsie (Swedman) Mason; m. Joyce Ann Towne; children: John Mark, Victoria Joyce, Peter Brooke. AB, Ind. U., Bloomington, 1944; MD, Ind. U., Indpls., 1947; MA (hon.), Yale U., New Haven, 1977. Diplomate in pathol. anatomy Am. Bd. Pathology. Surg. intern NY Hosp.-Cornell Med. Ctr., NYC, 1947—48, resident in pathology, 1948—50; chief dept. neuroendocrinology Walter Reed Army Inst. Rsch., Washington, 1953—74; prof. emeritus psychiatry Yale U. Sch. Medicine, New Haven, from 1977. Cons. and dir. psychoendocrine lab. Adult Psychiatry br. NIMH, Bethesda, Md., 1960—65; sci. advisor, neuropsychiatry br. Walter Reed Army Inst. of Rsch., Washington, 1974—77; dir. psychoendocrine lab. Nat. Ctr. for PTSD, VA Med. Ctr., West Haven, Conn., 1977—2000; lectr. and invited lectr. in field. Contbr. more than 170 sci. rsch. publs. to profl. jours., 24 chpts. to books, also revs. in field; author: (monograph) Organization of Psychoendocrine Mechanisms, 1968 (Med. Lit. Citation Classic award). Website builder finishing-of-our-faith.com; faculty sponsor, Campus Crusade for Christ ministry Yale U., 1983; Bible tchr. Trinity Evang. Free Ch., Woodbridge, Conn., 1978—2009. Served to maj. M.C. US Army, 1948—53. Recipient Rsch. Scientist Career award, NIMH, 1981-1991, medal, Pavlovian Soc., 1985, Meritorius Civilian Svc. award, Dept. of Army, 1960, Sustained Superior Performance Civil Svc. awards, 1960, 1966, 1969, Lifetime Achievement award, 21st Century Traumatology Conf., Georgetown U. Med. Ctr. Founds., 1996; grantee, NIMH, 1989-2000. Mem.: Assn. Psychosomatic Medicine (editl. bd. mem. 1963—91), Internat. Soc. Psychoneuroendocrinology (Lifetime Achievement award 2005), Endocrine Soc., Am. Psychosomatic Soc. (pres. 1969—70, Pres.'s award 2000), Alpha Omega Alpha, Phi Beta Kappa. Achievements include long term systematic basic and clinical research on the importance of psychosocial influences upon a wide range of endocrine systems in relation to stress and stress-related clinical disorders; major pioneering contributions to the development of the field of psychoneuroendocrinology and to exploring its far-reaching clinical implications for psychiatry and medicine; development of psychoendocrine strategies using concurrent hormonal and psychological measurements providing new leverage for the interdisciplinary study of; intrapsychic processes including emotional states, psychological defenses and coping styles; established that psychosocial and physical stress stimuli produce broadly organized multihormonal patterns of change involving many interdependent endocrine systems; received national and international recognition as a leader providing landmark experimental and conceptual contributions in the fields of psychoendocrinology and stress research; development of an unusual profile of thyroid hormonal alterations in PTSD patients, which provides compelling leads concerning the pathogenesis and possible treatment of this disorder. Home: Silver Spring, Md. Died Mar. 4, 0214.

**MASON, ROBIN,** education educator; d. John Beresford Anderson and Rosalind Cecilia Young; children: Quentin John, Lydia Eleanor. BA, U. Toronto, 1967; PhD, Open U., Milton, Keynes, Eng., 1990. Prof. ednl. tech. Open U., from 1990. Co-author (with Frank Rennie): (educational text) Elearning: The Key Concepts, 2006. Died June 15, 2009.

**MASSIGNON, DANIEL,** educator; b. Paris, Apr. 9, 1919; s. Louis and Marcelle Dansaert-Testelin Massignon; m. Nicole Deney, Apr. 24, 1970; 1 child, Berengere. DSc, U. Paris, 1955. With Nat. Ctr. Sci. Rsch., Paris, 1945—56; dep. head phys. chemistry Commissariat l'Energie Atomique, Paris, 1956—70, head chem. physics dept., from 1969. Asst. prof. statis. mechanics U. Paris, 1956—75; mem. nat. com. Nat. Ctr. Sci. Rsch., Paris, 1966—75. Author: Mecanique Statistique des Fluides, 1957, Cours de Mecanique Statistique, 1961, Uranium Enrichment by Gaseous Diffusion, 1979; contbr. Russian transl. Recipient officer Legion Honor, Prix La Caze, French Acad. Sci., 1976, Prix Doistau-Blutel, 1980. Mem.: Internat. Union Pure & Applied Chemistry, Am. Inst. Chem. Engrs., European Phys. Soc., Am. Phys. Soc., French Chem. Soc., French Phys. Soc. Roman Catholic. Achievements include patents in field. Died Dec. 25, 2000.

**MASTERS, EDWARD EUGENE,** association executive, former foreign service officer; b. Columbus, Ohio, June 21, 1924; s. George Henry and Ethel Verena (Shaw) M.; m. Allene Mary Roche, Apr. 2, 1956; children: Julie Allene, Edward Ralston. Student, Denison U., 1942—43; BA with distinction, George Washington U., 1948; MA, Fletcher Sch. Law and Diplomacy, 1949; grad., Nat. War Coll., 1964. Joined U.S. Fgn. Svc., 1950; intelligence rsch. analyst Near East Dept. State, 1949-50; resident officer Heidelberg, Germany, 1950-52; polit. officer embassy Karachi, Pakistan, 1952-54; Hindustani lang. and area tng. U. Pa., 1954-55; consul, polit. officer Madras, India, 1955-58; intelligence rsch. specialist South Asia Dept. State, 1958-60, chief Indonesia-Malaya br. Office Rsch. Asia, 1960-61, officer-in-charge Thailand affairs Bur. Far Eastern Affairs, 1961-63; counselor for polit. affairs Am. embassy, Djakarta, 1964-68; country dir. for Indonesia Dept. State, 1968-70; dir. Office East Asian Regional Affairs, 1970-71; minister Am. embassy, Bangkok, 1971-75; amb. to Bangladesh, 1976—77; amb. to Indonesia, 1977—81; adj. prof. diplomacy Fletcher Sch. Law and Diplomacy, 1981-82; sr. v.p. Natomas Co., 1982-84; pres. Nat. Planning Assn., 1985—92, Edward Masters & Assocs., Washington, 1992—2009; founder US Indonesia Soc., 1994, pres., 1994—2000, chmn., 2000—09, co-chair emeritus, from 2009. Adj. prof. Sch. Advanced Internat. Studies, 2000—02. With US Army, 1943—46. Mem. Am. Fgn. Svc. Assn., Cosmos Club, Phi Beta Kappa, Omicron Delta Kappa, Pi Gamma Mu, Delta Phi Epsilon. Home: Washington, DC. Died Mar. 22, 2014.

**MATHER, MERRILIE,** literature educator; b. Melrose, Mass., Mar. 28, 1921; d. Thomas Ray and Ruth Evelyn (Hutchins) Mather. AB, Boston U., 1942, MA, 1943, PhD, 1950. Teaching fellow Sargent Coll., Boston U., 1943—44; children's room Dorchester Br., Boston Pub. Library, 1946—47; instr. Morningside Coll., Sioux City, Iowa, 1947—51; prof. English and children's lit. Eastern Ill. U., Charleston, from 1951. Mem.: Delta Kappa Gamma, Phi Beta Kappa. Unitarian Universalist. Deceased.

**MATHEWS, HARLAN,** former United States Senator from Tennessee; b. Walker County, Ala., Jan. 17, 1927; s. John William and Lillian (Young) Mathews; m. Patsy Jones; children: Stanley, Lester, Richard. BA, Jacksonville State U., 1949; MA in Public Adminstrn., Vanderbilt U., 1962; JD, Nashville Sch. Law, 1962. Mem. planning staff to Gov. Gordon Browning State of Tenn., Nashville, 1950—54, mem. budget staff to Gov. Frank Clement, 1954—61, commr. finance & adminstrn., 1961—71; sr. v.p. Amcon Internat., Inc., Memphis, 1971—73; legal asst. to Comptr. William Snodgrass State of Tenn., Nashville, 1973—74, state treas., 1975—87, dep. gov., sec. state, 1987—93; US Senator from Tenn., 1993—94. Served in USN, 1944—46. Scholar Vanderbilt U. Democrat. Protestant. Died May 9, 2014.

**MATHIAS, CORINNE FLORENCE,** consulting company executive; b. Buffalo, June 10, 1926; d. Sidney and Florence (Vincent) O'Neill; m. Richard Charles Mathias, Sept. 6, 1947 (dec. Apr. 20, 1972); children: Richard Charles, Micheal William, Corinne Mary, Marc Francis. AA, Citrus Coll., 1979. Dir. Universal Product Code and Direct Store Set-UP, El Monte, Calif., Vons Grocery Co., El Monte, Calif., 1958—78; pres. Direct Delivery Data, Glendora, Calif., owner, from 1978. Author clerk's manual. Fellow: Bus. and Profl. Women, So. Calif. Grocers Assn., Women in Mgmt. scholar, Redlands Community Music Assn.(Calif.), Com. Against Govt. Waste(Washington), LA Art Mus. Democrat. Roman Catholic. Avocations: bridge, tennis, travel, photography. Deceased.

**MATHIEU, ROBERT P.,** state official; b. Providence, June 6, 1926; s. Peter N. and Ida (Racine) M.; m. Jane Frances Corley, Aug. 25, 1951; children— Jane Frances, Robert Phillip, Patricia Anne, Peter Francis, Susan Marie. AB, Providence Coll., 1950, postgrad., 1950-51, Boston U., 1951; MS, Northwestern U., 1953. Adminstrv. asst. R.I. Hosp., Providence, 1950-51, Michael Reese Hosp., Chgo., 1951-52; adminstrv. resident Worcester (Mass.) City Hosp., 1952-53; asst. adminstr. Meml. Hosp., Pawtucket, 1953-58; assoc. adminstr., coordinator med., nursing and profl. relations and edn., 1958-61; adminstr. Dr. U.E. Zambarano Meml. Hosp., Wallum Lake, R.I., 1961-78, Charles V. Chapin Hosp., Providence, 1966-69; asst. dir. div. hosps. Dept. Mental Health, Retardation and Hosps., 1970-78; dir. policy and programs State of R.I., 1978-86; cons. hosp. health care Pub. Health Adminstrn., Providence, R.I., from 1986. Prof. hosp. and nursing home adminstrn. U. R.I.; Cons. Nat. Commn. Nursing Services, 1955—; cons. to dir. health City of Pawtucket, 1955—; mem. Gov.'s Adv. Commn. Vocational Rehab., 1967—; tech. adv. com. Health Facilities Planning Council, 1968—; chmn. extended care facilities study commn. USPHS, 1968— Author: Hospital and Nursing Home Management, 1971. Bd. dirs. Foster Grandparent Program Office Equal Opportunity, 1967-69. Served with USNR, 1944-46. Fellow Am. Coll. Hosp. Adminstrs., Am. Pub. Health Assn.; mem. Am. Hosp. Assn., Hosp. Assn. R.I. (trustee 1970-78), New Eng. Hosp. Assembly, New Eng. Pub. Health Assn. Home: Narragansett, RI. Died Apr. 24, 1989.

**MATHUR, NAVNENDRA,** medical educator; b. Alwar, Rajasthan, India, Sept. 28, 1951; s. Babu Prasad and Rajesh Kumari Mathur; m. Sushma Saraf; children: Divita, Asmita. MS in Orthop., SMS Med. Coll., Jaipur, Rajasthan, 1980; DNB in Phys. Medicine & Rehab., Nat. Bd. Exam., New Delhi, 1985. Med. officer E.S.I. Hosp., Jaipur, 1981—90; orthop. specialist King Fahd Hosp., Jedha, Saudi Arabia,

1990—95; asst. prof. SMS Med. Coll. & Hosp., 1995—99, assoc. prof., 1999—2004, prof. head, from 2004. Contbr. scientific papers to rsch. publs. Mem.: Indian Assn. Phys. Medicine & Rehab., Indian Orthop. Assn. (J & J fellowship 1986, A.O. fellowship, Nottingham, Eng. 1992). Home: Jaipur, India. Died July 3, 2009.

**MATINYAN, LEVON ARSHALUYS,** physiologist, educator; b. Tbilisi, Georgia, Sept. 11, 1923; s. Arshaluys Mkrtich and Satenik Bagrat Matinyan; m. Seda Mkrtich Isahakyan, July 20, 1949; children: Mariam Levon, Anahit Levon. Magister (hon.), Tbilisi State Med. U., Georgia, 1946; PhD in Biological Scis., Acad. Scis. Armenia, 1970; Candidate, Orbeli Inst. Physiology, 1952. Cert. Professor Acad. of Sciences of Armenia, 1984. Sr. lab. asst. Orbeli Inst. of Physiology, Yerevan, Armenia, 1947—48, jr. sci. worker, 1948—59, sr. sci. worker, 1959—71, dep. dir., 1985—94, chief lab. neuroendocrine interrelations, 1971—2005. Author: (book) Enzyme therapy in organic lesions of Spinal Cord, Comp. physiological features of compensatory adaptation during lesions of Spinal Cord, Essays of Physiologist. Recipient The 20th Century award for Achievments, IBC, Eng., 2001, Gold medal of Lomonosov, Internat. Acad. of Ecology & Life Protection Sci., 2003. Mem.: Internat. Acad. Ecology of N.Y. Acad., Internat. Med. Soc. of Paraplegia (assoc.), Physiol. Soc. of Armenia, Europe (assoc.). Achievements include research in Regeneration of injured Spinal Cord. Home: Yerevan, Armenia. Died Apr. 22, 2009.

**MATTHIESSEN, PETER,** author; b. NYC, May 22, 1927; s. Erard A. and Elizabeth (Carey) Matthiessen; m. Patricia Southgate, Feb. 8, 1951 (div.); m. Deborah Love, May 8, 1963 (dec. Jan. 1972); children: Lucas, Sara, Rue, Alexander; m. Maria Eckhart, Nov. 28, 1980. BA, Yale U., New Haven, 1950; degree (hon.), Yale U., 2007. Co-founder The Paris Review, 1953. Author: (fiction) Race Rock, 1954, Partisans, 1955, Raditzer, 1961, At Play in the Fields of the Lord, 1965, Far Tortuga, 1975, On the River Styx and Other Stories, 1989, Killing Mister Watson, 1990, Lost Man's River, 1997, Bone By Bone, 1999, Shadow Country, 2008 (Nat. Book award for fiction, 2008), In Paradise, 2014, (non-fiction) Wildlife in America, 1959, The Cloud Forest: A Chronicle of the South American Wilderness, 1961, Under the Mountain Wall: A Chronicle of Two Seasons in the Stone Age, 1962, The Shorebirds of North America, 1967, Oomingmak, 1967, Sal Si Puedes: Cesar Chavez and the New American Revolution, 1969, Blue Meridian. The Search for the Great White Shark, 1971, The Tree Where Man was Born, 1972, The Snow Leopard, 1978 (Nat. Book award, 1980), Sand Rivers, 1981, In the Spirit of Crazy Horse, 1983, Indian Country, 1984, Nine-headed Dragon River: Zen Journals 1969-1982, 1986, Men's Lives: The Surfmen and Bayen of the South Fork, 1986, African Silences, 1991, Baikal: Sacred Sea of Siberia, 1992, East of Lo Monthang: In the Land of Mustang, 1995, The Peter Matthiessen Reader: Nonfiction, 1959-1961, 2000, Tigers in the Snow, 2000, The Birds of Heaven: Travels With Cranes, 2001, End of the Earth: Voyages to Antarctica, 2003. Trustee NY Zool. Soc., 1965—78. Named Offl. State Author of NY, NY State Writers Inst., 1995—97. Mem.: AAAL, AAAS. Home: Sagaponack, NY. Died Apr. 5, 2014.

**MATTMAN, LIDA HOLMES,** microbiologist, educator; b. Denver, July 31, 1912; d. Eureka Spurgeon and Lillie Edith (Henry) Holmes; children: Sandra, Paul. BA, U. Kans., 1933, MA, 1934; PhD, Yale U., 1940. Head clin. labs. UN Relief and Rehab., 1944; sr. bacteriologist dept. pub. health Commonwealth of Mass., Boston, 1947-48; instr. Wayne State U., Detroit, 1949-85; instr. immunology Oakland U., Rochester, Mich., 1986; rsch. investigator, emeritus prof. Wayne State U., Detroit, from 1986; prof. Howard Hughes Inst. Immunology, 1992, 94. Cons. immunology U.S. Dept. Justice, Detroit, NSF. Author: Cell Wall Deficient Forms, 1975, Cell Wall Deficient Forms, Stealth Pathogens, 1992; contbr. chpts. to books and numerous articles to profl. jours. Grantee, AMA, Am. Thoracic Soc., Damon Runyon Soc., Mich. Cancer Soc., Mich. Heart Assn., Detroit Tuberculosis Soc., Wayne County Tuberculosis Soc., USPHS, Wayne State U.; Yale U. scholar, U. Pa. rsch. fellow. Mem. Am. Soc. Microbiology (pres. Mich. br.), Mich. Acad. Scis. (chmn. med. div.). Avocation: gardening. Home: Essexville, Mich. Died Aug. 6, 2008.

**MATUSIK, JANUSZ,** pathologist; b. Strzelce Wielkie, Poland, Feb. 25, 1941; s. Ignacy and Helena Matusik; m. Alicja Swiatek, Mar. 20, 1965; 1 child, Piotr. MD, Med. Acad., Cracow, Poland, 1964. Cons. Med. Acad., Cracow, 1966—79, Södra Älvsborg sjukhus, Borås, Sweden, from 1985. Home: Borås, Sweden. Died 2003.

**MAUD, SIR HUMPHREY JOHN HAMILTON,** diplomat, international civil servant; b. Oxford, Eng., Apr. 17, 1934; s. Lord and Lady Redcliffe-Maud; m. Maria Eugenia Gazitua, 1963; children: Andrew, David, Stephen. Instr. classics U. Minn., 1958-59; fgn. svc. entrant London, 1959; 3d sec. British Embassy, Madrid, 1961-63, 2d Havana, 1963-65; mem. cabinet office FCO, London, 1966-69, head financial rels. dept., 1975-79, asst. under sec. of state for econ. affairs, 1985-88; sec. British Embassy, Paris, 1970-74, min. Madrid, 1979-82, amb. to Luxembourg Luxembourg, 1982-85; high commr. Brit. High Commn., Nicosia, 1988-90; amb. to Argentina British Embassy, Buenos Aires, 1990-93; commonwealth dep. sec.-gen. econ. & social London, 1993—99. Co-author: (book) A Marshall Plan for the 90s, 1988. Lt. Coldstream Guards, 1953-55. Decorated Companion of the Order of St. Michael and St. George, 1982, Knight Comdr., 1993. Avocations: music (cellist), golf, tennis, ornithology. Home: London, England. Died Nov. 10, 2013.

**MAULDEN, WESLEY M.,** aerospace company executive; b. Spokane, Wash., June 23, 1925; s. Robert W. and Willena (Morrison) M.; children: Penny, Gregory, Dean, David. BA, U. Puget Sound, 1951; S.M., MIT, 1961. With Boeing Co., Seattle, from 1951, asst. mgr. SST div., asst. mgr. group program comml. airplane group, v.p., asst. gen. mgr., exec. v.p., sr. v.p. Lectr. econs. U. Puget Sound, Tacoma, 1950-51 Served with AUS, 1943-46. Mem. Mu Sigma Delta Home: Seattle, Wash. Died May 16, 1989.

**MAUNG MAUNG KHA,** former prime minister of Burma; b. Nov. 2, 1917; Formerly mng. dir. Heavy Industry Corp.; minister of labour Socialist Republic of the Union of Burma, 1973—74; min.of industry, 1973—75; min. of mines, 1975—77; prime min., 1977—88. Mem. cen. exec. com. Burma Socialist Programme Party; mem. State Coun., 1977—88. Died Apr. 30, 1995.

**MAURER, ARMAND AUGUSTINE,** priest, former philosophy educator; b. Rochester, NY, Jan. 21, 1915; arrived in Can., 1957; s. Armand Augustine and Louise (Ribson) M. BA, U. Toronto, Ont., Can., 1938, MA, 1943, PhD, 1947; MSL., Pontifical Inst. Mediaeval Studies, Toronto, 1945. Joined Congregation Priests of St. Basil, Roman Cath. Ch., 1940; ordained priest, 1945; lectr. in philosophy St. Michael's Coll., U. Toronto, 1946-55, asst. prof. philosophy, 1955-58, assoc. prof., 1948-62, prof., from 1962. Asst. prof. philosophy Pontifical Inst. Mediaeval Studies, 1949-53, prof., 1953-84; ret., 1984 Author: Medieval Philosophy, 1962, 2d rev. edit., 1982, (with others) Recent Philosophy: Hegel to the Present, 1966, St. Thomas and Historicity, 1979, About Beauty, 1983; editor: Siger of Brabant. Quaestiones in Metaphysicam, 1983, Being and Knowing. Studies in Thomas Aquinas and Later Medieval Philosophers, 1990; contbr. numerous articles to philos. Jours. Guggenheim fellow, 1954-55 Mem. Royal Soc. Can., Am. Cath. Philos. Assn. (pres. 1979), Metaphys. Soc., Soc. Internat. pour l'Étude de la Philosophie Médiévale. Died Mar. 22, 2008.

**MAURI, GIUSEPPE,** retired secondary school physics educator; b. Monza, Italy, Jan. 1, 1943; s. Angelo and Natalina (Capra) M. Diploma, Lycée, Monza, 1962; DS, U. Milan, Italy, 1968. Sr. H.S. tchr., Carate, Italy, 1970-71, 77-84, Monza, 1971-73, Desio, Italy, 1985-92. Adv. to dir. general and deputy dir. general IBC. With Italian Def. Svc., 1969-70. Recipient Testimonial of Achievement and Distinction, IBC, Decree of Merit, Cert. of Distinction; named Internat. Educator of Yr., Internat. Bio. Ctr. Cambridge. Home: Monza Milan, Italy. Died Jan. 28, 2005.

**MAXWELL, ALLEN,** former state legislator; b. Warren, Ark., Apr. 19, 1943; s. Allen and Ruby Maxwell; m. Dana Maxwell, Oct. 12, 1961; children: Paige, Al. Attended, U. Ark., Monticello. With Southwestern Bell, 1958—91; staff mem. to Rep. Jay Dickey US House of Representatives; mem. Dist. 10 Ark. House of Reps., 2004—10; mayor City of Monticello, 2011—14. Democrat. Baptist. Died Mar. 10, 2014.

**MAXWELL, ANNA CAROLINE,** nursing administrator; b. Bristol, NY, Mar. 14, 1851; Diploma, Boston Hosp. Training Sch., 1880. Nursing supt., Montreal, Boston, NYC, 1829-1921; instr., adminstr. Presbyn. Hosp., NYC. Recipient medal French govt. Mem. Am. Soc. of Supts. Training Sch. for Nurses, Nat. League for Nursing, Nurses' Associated Alumnae of U.S. and Can., Internat. Coun. of Nurses, ARC Nursing Svc. Achievements include participation in founding of Am. Jour. of Nursing and Isabel Hampton Robb Scholarship. Died 1929.

**MAXWELL, HAMISH WALTER HYSLOP,** retired diversified consumer products company executive; b. Liverpool, Eng., Aug. 24, 1926; s. Alexander and Doris (Gailbraith) Maxwell; m. Georgene Mathewson (dec. 2013); children: Graham, Robin. BA, Cambridge U., Eng., 1949. With Thomas Cook Sons & Co., 1949-54, Philip Morris, Inc., 1954-85, salesman Richmond, Va., 1954-69, v.p., 1969-76, sr. v.p., 1976-78, exec. v.p., 1978-83, pres., COO, 1983-84, chmn., CEO, 1984-85; with Philip Morris Internat., 1961-83, advt. dir., 1961-63, v.p. mktg., 1963-65, regional v.p., Asia/Pacific region, 1965-73, exec. v.p. Canadian & Asia/Pacific regions, 1973-75, exec. v.p. Can./Asia & Europe/Middle East/Asia regions, 1975-78, pres., CEO, 1978-85; chmn., CEO Philip Morris Companies, Inc., 1985-91, chmn. exec. com., 1991—95; chmn. WPP plc, London, 1996—2001. Bd. dirs. Philip Morris Companies, Inc., 1985—91, Bankers Trust Corp., 1984—99, News Corp., 1992—97. Served with RAF, 1944-47. Died Apr. 19, 2014.

**MAYER, ERNEST,** aeronautical engineer, researcher; b. Arad, Romania, June 4, 1916; s. Henry and Adele (Popper) Mayer; m. Elizabeth Weiss, Feb. 6, 1943; children: Vivian F., Virginia A. BS, CCNY, 1939; MA, Columbia U., 1941; PhD, Poly. Inst. Bklyn., 1952. Instr. physics CCNY, 1939—43; instr. aerospace sys. mgmt. U. Southern Calif., LA, 1969—74; rsch. engr. Westinghouse Labs., Pitts., 1943—46; rsch. devel. engr. Kellogg Co., Jersey City, 1946—52; staff scientist Arde Assns., Newark, 1952—57; tech. specialist Rocketdyne Co., Canoga Park, Calif., 1957—60; assoc. dir. Scis. Nat. Engring Sci. Co., Pasadena, Calif., 1960—68; sr. scientist Hughes Aircraft Co., El Segundo, Calif., 1974—99. Cons. in field. Contbr. articles to profl. jours. Mem.: AIAA, Combustion Inst., Am. Rocket Soc., Phi Beta Kappa, Sigma Xi. Died Apr. 6, 1999.

**MAYER, WILLIAM DIXON,** pathologist, educator; b. Beaver Falls, Pa., Oct. 5, 1928; s. Emil Leroy and Elizabeth (Townsend) M.; m. Donna S. Dashiell; children: Elizabeth Ann, David Dixon, William Dixon, Kathy Dashiell AB, Colgate U., 1951; MD with honor, U. Rochester, 1957; D.Sc. (hon.), U. Osteopathic Medicine and Health Scis., 1988. Intern, then resident pathology Strong Meml. Hosp., Rochester, N.Y., 1957-61; instr., mem. faculty U. Mo. Sch. Medicine, 1961-76, dir. Univ. Med. Center, 1967-74; dean U. Mo. Sch. Medicine (Sch. Medicine), 1967-74, prof. pathology, 1967-76; asst. chief med. dir. for acad. affairs VA, Washington, 1976-79; pres. Med. Coll. Hampton Roads, Norfolk, Va., 1979-87. Assoc. dir. div. regional med. programs NIH, 1966-67; mem. exec. com. Nat. Bd. Med. Examiners, 1969-81, treas., 1975-79, vice-chmn., 1979-81, hon. mem., 1981—, fin. com., 1987-93; bd. regent Nat. Libr. of Medicine, 1980-84, chmn., 1982-84. Bd. dirs., 1st v.p. Future of Hampton Rds., 1983—; bd. dirs. Greater Norfolk Corp., 1987-91—, exec. v.p., 1989-90; founding mem. bd. dirs. Town Point Club, 1983-91. With USMC, 1946-48. Markle scholar acad. medicine, 1962-67 Fellow Coll. Am. Pathologists; mem. AMA, Assn. Am. Med. Colls. (Disting. Service mem.), C. of C. (bd. dirs. 1986-91), Sigma Xi, Alpha Omega Alpha. Episcopalian. Deceased.

**MAYFIELD, CURTIS LEE,** musician; b. Chgo., June 3, 1942; s. Kenneth and Marion (Washington) M.; children—Tracy, Curtis, Todd, Sharon, Tymphani, Kirk. Co-pres. Curtom Records Inc. Performer with group Impressions, 1958-70, People Get Ready: The Curtis Mayfield Story, 1996; solo albums include Curtis, 1970, Curtis Live, Roots, 1971, Back to the World, 1973, Sweet Exorcist, 1974, America Today, 1975, Never Say You Can't Survive, 1977, Do It, We Came in Peace with a Message of Love, 1985, Give, Get, Take and Have, 1992, The Heart of Chicago Soul: the Songs of Curtis Mayfield, 1997; composer, arranger, performer soundtrack; also actor film Super Fly, 1972; now rec. artist, producer, songwriter film. Recipient: Nat. Acad. of Recording Arts & Sciences Lifetime Achievement Award, 1994. Home: Chicago, Ill. Died Dec. 26, 1999.

**MAYHEW, ELZA EDITH,** sculptor; b. Victoria, BC, Can. d. George Mayhew and Alice (Bowden) Lovitt; m. Alan Mayhew (dec.); children: Anne, Garth. BA in French, Latin with honors, U. BC, 1936; studied with Jan Zach, Victoria, 1955—58; MFA in Sculpture with honors, U. Oreg., 1963. Artist one woman shows Point Gallery, Victoria, 1960, 1962, Art Gallery Greater Victoria, 1961, 1964, 1971, Fine Arts Gallery, 1961, Lucien Campbell Plaza, U. Oreg., 1963, Ker Gallery, 1964, Venice Biennale, Can. Pavilion, 1964, Dorothy Cameron Gallery, Toronto, 1965, Backroom Gallery, Victoria, 1978, Burnaby Art Gallery, 1979, Equinox Gallery, Vancouver, 1980, Albert White Gallery, Toronto, 1980; exhibitor group shows Can. Religious Art Today, Willowdale, Ont., 1966, Centennial Sculpture Exhbn. Queen Elizabeth Plaza, Vancouver, 1967, Retrospective Show Art Gallery Greater Victoria, 1971, Spectrum Can., Sculpture Can., 1978, RCA Show Olympic Games, 1976, Wallach Gallery, Dirs. Choice Show, 1981; prin. works Coast Spirit, U. Victoria, U. Concordia, Brock U., St. Catharine, Column of Sea Confederation Ctr., Charlottetown; artist mural Bank of Can. Bldg., Vancouver, Zong I. Author. Recipient Sir Otto Beit medal, Royal Soc. Brit. Sculptors, 1962, Purchase award, Centennial Sculpture Exhbn., BC, 1967. Mem.: Internat. Sculpture Ctr. (bd. dirs. 1968—79), Art Gallery Greater Victoria (acquisitions com. from 1983), Royal Can. Acad. Home: Victoria, Canada. Deceased.

**MAYNARD, ELLIOTT E. (SPIKE MAYNARD),** former state supreme court justice; b. Williamson, W.Va., Dec. 8, 1942; BS in Psychology, Fla. Southern Coll., 1967; JD, W.Va. U., 1974. Atty. priv. practice, Williamson, W.Va., 1974—81; prosecuting atty. Mingo County, 1976—81; judge W.Va. Cir. Ct. 30th Jud. Cir., 1982-97; justice W.Va. Supreme Ct. Appeals, Charleston, 1997—2008, chief justice, 2000, 2004. Mng. dir. Tug Valley Chamber of Commerce, 1968-70; active Boy Scouts America; dist. chmn. Mingo-Pike Dist., Chief Cornstalk Dist.; bd. dirs. Buckskin Coun. With USAF, 1961—66. Recipient Silver Beaver award Boy Scouts America Mem.: ABA, W.Va. Bar Assn., American Judicature Soc., American Judge's Assn. Republican. Died May 1, 2014.

**MAYNE, LUCILLE STRINGER,** finance educator; b. Wash DC, June 6, 1924; d. Henry Edmond and Hattie Benham (Benson) Stringer; children: Pat A., Christine Gail, Barbara Marie. BS, U. Md., College Park, 1946; MBA, Ohio State U., Columbus, 1949; PhD, Northwestern U., Evanston, Ill., 1966. Instr. fin. Utica Coll., 1949-50; lectr. fin. Roosevelt U., 1961-64, Pa. State U., 1965-66, asst. prof., 1966-69, assoc. prof., 1969-70; assoc. prof. banking and fin. Case Western Res. U., 1971-76, prof., 1976-94, prof. emerita, 1994—2012, grad. dean Sch. Grad. Studies, 1980-84. Sr. economist, cons. FDIC, 1977-78; cons. Nat. Commn. Electronic Fund Transfer Sys., 1976; rsch. cons. Am. Bankers Assn., 1975, Fed. Res. Bank of Cleve., 1968-70, 73; cons. Pres.'s Commn. Fin. Structure and Regulation, 1971, staff economist, 1970-71; analytical statistician Air Materiel Command, Dayton, Ohio, 1950-52; asst. to promotion mgr. NBC, Washington, 1946-48; expert witness cases involving fin. instns. Assoc. editor: Jour. Money, Credit and Banking, 1980-83, Bus. Econs., 1980-85; contbr. articles to profl. jours. Vol. Cleve. Soc. for Blind, 1979-2004, Benjamin Rose Inst., 1995-2005; bd. dirs. Women's Cmty. Found., 1994-96. Grad. scholar, Ohio State U., 1949, doctoral fellow, Northwestern U., 1963—65. Mem. policyholders nominating com. Tchrs. Ins. and Annuity Assn./Coll. Retirement Equities Fund, 1982-84, chair com., 1984; LWV (bd. dirs. Shaker Heights chpt. 1999-2012), Midwest Fin. Assn. (pres. 1991-92, bd. dirs. 1975-79, officer 1988-93), Phi Kappa Phi, Beta Gamma Sigma. Home: Shaker Heights, Ohio. Died Nov. 26, 2012; Ohio.

**MAYO, LOUIS ALLEN,** policy management counseling company executive; b. Durham, NC, Nov. 27, 1928; s. Louis Allen and Amy Earl (Overton) M.; m. Emma Jean Minshew, Oct. 31, 1953 (div.); children: Louis Allen III, Robert Lawrence, Carolyn Jean; m. Myrna Ann Smith, Feb. 16, 1980 (div.). Student, Calif. State Poly. Coll., 1948—50; BA in Criminology, Calif. State Coll., Fresno, 1952; MA in

Pub. Adminstrn., Am. U., 1960, PhD in Pub. Adminstrn., 1983; postgrad., U. So. Calif., 1960—62. Spl. agt. U.S. Secret Svc., Treasury Dept., LA, 1956-58, 60-63, White House, Washington, 1958-60, 63-66; program mgr. law enforcement Office Law Enforcement Assistance, Justice Dept., 1967-68; acting chief Rsch. Ctr., rsch. program mgr. Nat. Inst. Law Enforcement and Criminal Justice, 1968-74; alternate assoc. mem. Fed. Coun. on Sci. and Tech., White House, 1973-74; dir. tng. and testing divsn. Nat. Inst. Justice, 1975—87; pres. Mayo, Mayo & Assocs., Alexandria, Va., from 1987. Lectr. criminology Armed Forces Inst. Tech., 1954-55; professorial lectr. Am. U., 1974-82; adj. prof. August Vollmer U., 1990-95. 2d lt. to 1st lt. USAF, 1952-56. Mem. Police Assn. Coll. Edn. (exec. dir., founder), Internat. Assn. Chiefs of Police, ASPA (nat. chmn. sect. on criminal justice adminstrn. 1975-76), Acad. Criminal Justice Scis., Police Exec. Rsch. Forum, Soc. Police Futurists Internat., Pi Sigma Alpha. Methodist. Died May 11, 2013.

**MAZOWIECKI, TADEUSZ,** former prime minister of Poland; b. Plock, Poland, Apr. 18, 1927; widowed, 1970; 3 sons Grad. in law, U. Warsaw, Poland; D (hon.), U. Genua and Cath. U. Louvain, 1991. Editor-in-chief Wroclawski Tygodnik Katolicki, until 1954; co-organizer, now dep. pres. Warsaw Club Cath. Intelligentsia, 1956; co-founder, editor-in-chief Wiez monthly, 1958-81; MP, ZNAK parliamentary group Polish Parliament, Warsaw, 1961-72, MP, Poznan constituency, 1991—97, MP, Krakow constituency, 1997—2001; chief advisor Solidarity Trade Union, 1980-89; prime min. Republic of Poland, Warsaw, 1989-90; pres. Democratic Union, 1991—94; spl. rapporteur to the former Yugoslavia UN, 1992—95; pres. Freedom Union, 1994—95; co-founder Democratic Party, Poland, 2005—06; spl. advisor Office of Pres., Poland, 2010—13. Editor-in-chief: Tygodnik Solidarnosc, 1980-81, 88-89. Roman Catholic. Died Oct. 28, 2013.

**MAZUREK, RAYMOND,** electronics executive, electrical engineer; b. NYC, Dec. 17, 1935; s. Edward and Olga (Pisk) Mazurek; m. Nina K. Mazurek, June 7, 1958; children: Larissa, Elaine, Peter. BEE, CCNY, 1957; MEE, Pratt Inst., 1961. Chief engr. Trak Electronics Inc., Wilton, Conn., 1961—65; dir. rsch. Tele-Dynamics divsn. AMBAC, Phila., 1965—75; gen. mgr. Satellite Comm. divsn. Cober Electronics, Stamford, Conn., 1975—77; dir. engring. T-Bar Inc., Wilton, 1977—79, asst. v.p. engring., 1979—82, v.p. tech. mktg., from 1982. Mem.: IEEE, Countermeasures Soc., Assn. Old Crows. Home: West Redding, Conn. Died Aug. 18, 1998.

**MAZURSKY, PAUL,** screenwriter, theatrical director and producer; b. Bklyn., Apr. 25, 1930; s. David and Jean (Gerson) M.; m. Betsy Purdy, Mar. 12, 1953; children: Meg, Jill. BA, Bklyn. Coll., 1951. Film critic Vanity Fair, 2011—14. Night club comedian, 1954-60; co-writer: (films) I Love You, Alice B. Toklas, 1968; actor: (films) Deathwatch, Miami Rhapsody, 1995, (voice) The Majestic, 2001, Do it for Uncle Manny, 2002; (TV series) Once & Again, 1999-2001; writer, dir.: (films) Bob & Carol & Ted & Alice, 1969, Alex in Wonderland, 1970, Blume in Love, 1972, Harry & Tonto, 1973, Next Stop, Greenwich Village, 1976, An Unmarried Woman, 1978, Willie & Phil, 1980, Tempest, 1982, Moscow on the Hudson, 1984; writer, prodr., dir.: (films) Down and Out in Beverly Hills, 1986, Moon Over Parador, 1988; co-scriptwriter, prodr., dir. (films): Enemies, A Love Story, 1989, Scenes From a Mall, 1990, The Pickle, 1992, Faithful, 1995, Winchell, 1998, Coast to Coast, 2003; author: (autobiography) Show Me the Magic, 1999 Recipient Screen Laurel award, Writers Guild America, 2014. Died June 30, 2014.

**MAZZOLA, JOHN WILLIAM,** retired performing company executive, consultant; b. Bayonne, NJ, Jan. 20, 1928; s. Roy Stephen and Eleanor Burton (Davis) M.; m. Sylvia Drulie, Mar. 7, 1959; children: Alison, Amy (dec. 2011) AB, Tufts U., 1949; LLD, Fordham U., 1952. Bar: N.Y. 1956. Mem. firm Milbank, Tweed, Hadley & McCloy, NYC, 1952-64; sec., exec. v.p. Lincoln Center for Performing Arts, NYC, 1964-68, gen. mgr., CEO, 1968—70, mng. dir., CEO, 1970-77, pres., CEO, 1977-84; exec. v.p. Embassy Pictures, 1984—86. Cons. performing arts ctrs. in U.S. and abroad, also motion pictures, non-profit orgns. Bd. dirs. various charitable orgns.; mem. adv. bd. Santa Fe Symphony. With Air Force USN, 1945—46, with CIC US Army, 1953—55. Decorated cavaliere ufficiale Ordine al Merito della Repubblica Italiana; Officer Ordre des Arts et des Lettres France; Benjamin Franklin fellow Royal Soc. Arts. Mem. Watch Hill Yacht Club, Misquamicut Club (R.I.). Episcopalian. Home: New York, NY. Died July 24, 2014.

**MBAYE, KEBA,** judge; b. Kaolack, Senegal, Aug. 5, 1924; s. Abdoul and Coura Mbaye; m. Mariette Diarra, Mar. 27, 1951; children: Aminata, Fatou, Abdoul, Ndeye Coura, Cheikh Tidiane, Ibrahima, Mame Aissatou, Maguette. Diploma in Civil Law, U. Paris, 1957; LLD (hon.), Emory U., 1992. Lic.: U. Dakar (in Law) 1964. Dep. pub. prosecutor, St. Louis, Senegal; dir., cabinet Minister of Justice Fedn. Madi; presiding justice to 1st hon. pres. Supreme Ct. of Senegal; former v.p. Internat. Ct. of Justice, The Hague, Netherlands; mem. Internat. Lumpic Com., 1973—2002, exec. bd. mem., 1984—88, v.p., 1988—92, exec. bd. mem., 1993—98, chmn., ethics commn., 1999—2007. Contbr. chapters to books & articles to publs. Died Jan. 11, 2007.

**MC ALLISTER, GERALD NICHOLAS,** retired bishop, minister; b. San Antonio, Feb. 23, 1923; s. Walter Williams and Leonora Elizabeth (Alexander) McA.; m. Helen Earle Black, Oct. 2, 1953; children: Michael Lee, David Alexander, Stephen Williams, Elizabeth. Student, U. Tex., 1939-42, Va. Theol. Sem., 1948-51, DD (hon.), 1977. Ordained to ministry Episcopal Ch. as deacon, 1953, as priest, 1954. Rancher, 1946-48; deacon, priest Ch. of Epiphany, Raymondville, Ch. of Incarnation, Corpus Christi, St. Francis Ch., Victoria, Tex., 1951-63; 1st canon Diocese of West Tex., 1963-70; rector St. David's Ch., San Antonio, 1970-76; consecreated Episcopal bishop of Okla., Oklahoma City, 1977-89, ret., 1989; bishop-in-residence Episcopal Theol. Sem., Austin, Tex., 1990-93. Trustee Episcopal Theol. Sem. of S.W., 1961-2000, adv. bd., 1974—; mem. Case Commn. Bd. for Theol. Edn., 1981-82; pres. Tex. Council Chs., 1966-68, Okla. Conf. Chs., 1980-83; bd. dirs. Presiding Bishop's Fund for World Relief, 1972-77; chmn. Nat. and World Mission Program Group, 1973-76; mem. Structure of Ch. Standing Commn., 1979, mem. standing com. on Stewardship/Devel., 1979-85; founder Chaplaincy Program, Bexar County Jail, 1968; mem. governing bd. nat. council Ch. of Christ, 1982-85; chmn. standing commn. on stewardship Episcopal Ch., 1983-85; v.p., trustee The Episc., Episc. Theol. Sem. of Southwest, 1987-93, chmn. bd. trustees, 1993-97. Author: What We Learned from What You Said, 1973, This Fragile Earth Our Island Home, 1980. Bd. dirs. Econ. Opportunity Devel. Corp., San Antonio, 1968-69; mem. exec. com. United Way, 1968-70, vice-chmn., 1970. With U.S. Mcht. Marines, 1942; to 1st lt. USAAF, 1942-45. Recipient Agudas Achim Brotherhood award, 1968. Mem.: Alumni Coun. Va. Theol. Sem. Episcopalian. Home: San Antonio, Tex. Died June 10, 2014.

**MCCARGAR, ELEANOR BARKER,** artist; b. Presque Isle, Maine, Aug. 30, 1913; d. Roy and Lucy Ellen (Hayward) Barker; m. John Albert McCargar, Feb. 18, 1947; children: Margaret, Lucy, Mary. Cert. elem. sch. tchg., Aroostook State Normal Sch., Presque Isle, 1933; student, Acadia U., 1935-36; B of Sociology, Colby Coll., 1937; summer student, Harvard U., 1939; and, Cambridge Sch. Art, 1939; studied portrait painting with Kenneth Washburn, Thomas Leighton, Maria von Ridelstein, Jean Henry, 1957-67. Ltd. svc. credential in fine and applied arts and related techs. Calif. C.C. Tchr. sci. and geography Limestone (Maine) Jr. H.S., 1937-41; ins. claim adjuster Liberty Mut. Ins. Co., Boston, 1941-42, Portland, Maine, 1943; ARC hosp. worker 20th Gen. Hosp., Ledo, Assam, India, 1944-45; portrait painter Burlingame and Apple Valley, Calif., from 1958. Commns. include more than 800 portraits in 10 states and 4 fgn. countries. Recipient M. Grumbacher Inc. Merit award for outstanding contbn. to arts, 1977; named Univ. of Maine Disting. Alumnus in Arts, 1981. Avocations: canoeing, camping, travel, studying. Died Feb. 28, 2002.

**MCCARTHY, IAN ELLERY,** physics educator, researcher; b. Adelaide, Australia, June 19, 1930; s. James Crimeen Ellery and Gwendolen Helen (Ure) McC.; m. Janet Lesley Furze, Jan. 7, 1956; children: Catherine, Helen, James, Jane, Patrick. PhD, U. Adelaide, 1955. Postdoctoral fellow Jesus Coll., Cambridge (Eng.) U., 1955-57; rsch. assoc. U. Minn., Mpls., 1957-59, UCLA, 1959-60; lectr. U. Adelaide, 1960-63; assoc. prof. U. Calif., Davis, 1963-65; prof. physics U. Oreg., Eugene, 1965-68, Flinders U. South Australia, Adelaide, 1968-96, emeritus prof. physics, from 1997, assoc. dir. Spl. Rsch. Ctr. Electronic Structure Materials, 1988—92, dir., 1992—96. Author: Introduction to Nuclear Theory, 1968, Nuclear Reactions, 1969, (with E. Weigold) Electron-atom Collisions, 1995, Electron Momentum Spectroscopy, 1999. Fellow Am. Phys. Soc., Australian Acad. Sci. Roman Catholic. Avocations: music, golf. Home: Erindale, Australia. Died Apr. 23, 2005.

**MCCARTHY, MARIANNE,** government agency administrator; BA, UCLA; MA in Edn., U. No. Colo.; PhD in Psychology, UCLA. Prin. Woodview Calabasas Sch., Erikson H.S.; dir. edn. program NASA, from 1996. Vol. tchrs. asst. UCLA Neuropsychiat. Inst. Deceased.

**MCCLOSKEY, JOHN EDWARD,** apparel executive; b. NYC, Jan. 14, 1921; s. John Edward and Martha Gertrude (Williams) McCloskey; m. Dorothy Elizabeth Carley, Nov. 11, 1942; children: Kathleen Elizabeth, Kevin John. At, Pratt Inst., 1942. Buyer Bullock's, LA, 1946—52; pres. Patty Woodward, Inc., 1952—84; dir. Calif. Fashion Creators, 1955—84. To 1st lt. CBI USAAF, 1942—46. Mem.: Am. Arbitration Assn. (arbitrator from 1975), Annandale Golf Club (Pasedena). Republican. Roman Catholic. Home: San Marino, Calif. Died June 22, 1995.

**MCCOLLISTER, JOHN YETTER,** former United States Representative from Nebraska, manufacturing executive; b. Iowa City, June 10, 1921; s. John M. and Ruth (Yetter) McCollister; m. Nanette Stokes, Aug. 22, 1943; children: John Stokes, Stephen J., Bruce C. BS in Commerce, U. Iowa, 1943. Sales rep. IBM Corp., Moline, Ill., 1946-50, Waterloo, Iowa, 1950-51, spl. rep. Chgo., 1951-53; sales mgr. United Petroleum Corp., Omaha, 1953-61; pres. McCollister & Co., Omaha, 1961-70, chmn. bd. Council Bluffs, Iowa, 1977—79; mem. US Congress from 2d Nebr. Dist., Washington, 1971-77. Pres. Mid-Am. Council Boy Scout America, Omaha, 1963-66, chmn. Region 8, 1968-70; chmn. 2d Congressional Dist. Rep., Omaha, 1960-64; commr. Douglas County, Nebr., 1965-71; del. Republican Nat. Conv., 1968; pres. Nebr. Soc. in Washington, 1974; sr. pres. Nebr. Republican Founders Day, 1968. Lt. USNR, 1943-46, PTO. Mem. Kiwanis (pres. Omaha chpt. 1961). Mem. United Ch. Christ. Home: Omaha, Nebr. Died Nov. 1, 2013.

**MCCORMACK, MIKE,** former professional sports team executive, retired professional football player; b. Chgo., June 21, 1930; m. Ann Helsby, 1956; children: Michael, Tim, Molly, Colleen. Offensive tackle NY Yankees, 1951, Dallas Texans (formerly NY Yanks), 1952, Cleveland Browns, 1954—62; asst. coach Washington Redskins, 1965—72; head coach Phila. Eagles, 1973—75; asst. coach Cin. Bengals, 1976—79; head coach Baltimore Colts, 1980—81; interim head coach Seattle Seahawks, 1982, dir. football ops, 1982—83, pres., gen. mgr., 1983—89, Carolina Panthers, Charlotte, NC, 1993—97. Served in US Army, 1952—54. Named to The Pro Football Hall of Fame, 1984, The NFL Pro Bowl Team, 1951, 1956—57, 1960—62. Achievements include being a member of two NFL championship teams with the Cleveland Browns, 1954, 1955. Died Nov. 15, 2013.

**MCCORMACK, WILLIAM JEROME,** retired bishop; b. NYC, Nov. 24, 1924; Attended, Christ the King Sem., St. Bonaventure U. Ordained priest Archdiocese of New York, 1959; ordained bishop, 1987; aux. bishop Archdiocese of New York, 1986—2001, aux. bishop emeritus, 2001—13. Nat. dir. Soc. for Propagation Faith, 1980. Roman Catholic. Died Nov. 23, 2013.

**MCCORMICK, KATHERINE DEXTER,** civil rights advocate; b. 1875; B in Biology, MIT, 1904. V.p., treas. Nat. Am. Woman's Suffrage Assn. Provided funds for rsch. that led to discovery and devel. of oral hormone contraceptive. Mem. LWV (co-founder, 1st v.p.). Died 1967.

**MCCOY, DOROTHY ELOISE,** writer, educator; b. Houston, Sept. 4, 1916; d. Robert Major and Evie Letha (Grimes) Morgan; m. Roy McCoy, May 22, 1942; children: Roy Jr., Robert Nicholas (dec.). BA, Rice U., 1938; MA, Tex. A&I U., 1968; postgrad., Ind. U., 1971, U. Calif., Berkeley, 1972, U. Calif., Santa Cruz, 1977. Cert. secondary tchr. BA Corpus Christi (Tex.) Independent Schs., 1958-84, MA, 1985; freelance writer Corpus Christi, from 1987; co-owner United Iron and Machine Works, Corpus Christi, 1946-82. Freelance lectr.; master tchr. Nat. Coun. Tchrs. English, 1971, Nat. Humanities Faculty, Concord Mass., 1977-78; mem. steering com. Edn. Summit, Corpus Christi, 1990-91, mem. summit update, 1991. Author: A Teacher Talks Back, 1990, Let's Restructure the Schools, 1992; contbr. articles and columns to profl. jours. Sr. advisor to U.S. Congress, Washington, 1982-85; trustee Corpus Christi Librs., 1987-90; mem. Corpus Christi Mus.; mem. Friends Corpus Christi Librs., chmn. publicity com., 1988; participant Walk to Emmaus Group, 1990, UPDATE, U. Tex., 1978-92; cons. Libr. Bd. Democracy competition Am. 2000; sec. adminstrv. bd. First United Meth. Ch., 1992-93. Recipient Teacher of Yr. Paul Caplan Humanitarian award, 1981, Advanced Senior Option Program award, 1968. Mem. AAUW, LWV, Phi Beta Kappa. Avocations: gardening, writing. Home: Montgomery, Tex. Died May 7, 2008.

**MCCRUM, MICHAEL WILLIAM,** academic administrator, educator; b. Gosport, Hampshire, Eng., May 23, 1924; s. Cecil Robert and Ivy Hilda Constance (Nicholson) McCrum; m. Christine Mary Kathleen fforde, Sept. 6, 1952; 4 children. Student, Corpus Christi Coll., Cambridge, 1946-48, MA, 1950; DEd (hon.), U. Victoria, 1989. Asst. master Rugby Sch., Warwickshire, 1948-50; tutor Corpus Christi Coll., 1950-62, master, 1980-94; head master Tonbridge Sch., Kent, 1962-70, Eton Coll., Berkshire, 1970-80; vice-chancellor Cambridge U., 1987-89; chmn. Cathedrals Fabric Commn. for Eng., 1991-99; gov. King's Sch., Canterbury, 1980-94, Sherborne Sch., 1980-94, United World Coll. Atlantic, 1981-94, Rugby Sch., 1982-94. Joint author Select Documents of the Principates of the Flavian Emperors A.D. 68-96, 1961, Thomas Arnold Head Master, 1989, The Man Jesus, 2000. Sub-lt. RNVR, 1943-45. Named comdr. Order de Isabel la Cátolica, 1988, CBE, 1996. Mem. Clubs: Athenaeum, United Oxford and Cambridge, East India and Pub. Schs., Hawks. Died Feb. 16, 2005.

**MCCUE, EDMUND BRADLEY,** retired mathematics professor; b. Worcester, Mass., Mar. 8, 1929; s. Felix Frederick and Frances (Bradley) McC. AB, Union Coll., 1950; MS, U. Mich., 1951; PhD, Carnegie-Mellon U., 1960. Asst. prof. Ohio U., Athens, 1958-63; prof. Inter-American Statistics Tng. Ctr. (CIENES), Santiago, Chile, 1963-64; assoc. prof. American U., Washington, 1964-87, prof. emeritus, 1987—2013. Mem. Inst. Math. Statistics, American Statistics Assn., Math. Assn. America Home: Washington, DC. Died Nov. 6, 2013.

**MC CULLOCH, FRANK W.,** lawyer, government official, educator, arbitrator; b. Evanston, Ill., Sept. 30, 1905; s. Frank H. and Catharine (Waugh) McC.; m. Edith F. Leverton, 1937; children: William Holt, Frank H. AB, Williams Coll., 1926; LLB, Harvard U., 1929; LLD, Olivet Coll., 1945, Chgo. Theol. Sem., 1961; LL.D., Williams Coll., 1971. Bar: Ill. Practiced, Chgo., 1930-35; indsl. relations sec. Council Social Action Congregational-Christian Ch., 1935-46; exec. dir. Chgo. br. Union for Democratic Action, 1942-46; vis. prof. Pacific Sch. Religion, 1939-40, Chgo. Theol. Sem., 1943-45, McCormick Theol. Sem., 1945; dir. labor edn. div. Roosevelt U., Chgo., 1946-49; asst. to Sen. Paul Douglas, 1949-61; chmn. NLRB, 1961-70; vis. prof. law U. N.C., 1971; prof. law U. Va., Charlottesville, 1971-76; also mem. Center Advanced Studies, U. Va., 1971-74, scholar in residence, from 1976. Vis prof. N.Y. State Sch. Indsl. and Labor Relations, Cornell U., 1976; cons. Task Force on Labor Relations, Pres.'s Reorgn. Project, 1977. Author: (with Tim Bornstein) The National Labor Relations Board, 1974. Contbr. articles to legal jours. Mem. panel Regional War Labor Bd., World War II; mem. Adminstrv. Conf. U.S., 1968-70; adv. com. on fed. hearing examiners Civil Service Commn., 1962-70; Am. team Anglo-Am. adminstrv. Law Exchange, 1969; mem. roster arbitrators Fed. Mediation and Conciliation Service, 1970-88; pub. rev. bd. UAW, 1971-88, Com. on Pub. Employee Rights, Va., 1972-76, Ill. Employee Labor Relations Council, 1973-82; mem. com. experts on application of convs. and recommendations ILO, Geneva, Switzerland, 1974-85; bd. dirs. Migrant Legal Action Program, Washington, 1973-85; mem. Indsl. Devel. Authority Albemarle County, Va., 1977-87. Mem. ABA, Fed. Bar Assn., Ill. Bar Assn., Chgo. Bar Assn., Am. Arbitration Assn. (panel arbitrators), Phi Beta Kappa. Home: Charlottesville, Va. Died July 9, 1996.

**MCCULLOH, JUDITH MARIE,** editor; b. Spring Valley, Ill., Aug. 16, 1935; d. Henry A. and Edna Mae (Traub) Binkele; m. Leon Royce McCulloh, Aug. 26, 1961. BA, Ohio Wesleyan U., 1956; MA, Ohio State U., 1957; PhD, Ind. U., 1970. Asst. to dir. Archives of Traditional Music, Bloomington, Ind., 1964-65; asst. editor U. Ill. Press, Champaign, 1972-77, assoc. editor, 1977-82, sr. editor, 1982-85, exec. editor, 1985—2007, dir. devel., 1992—2003, asst. dir., 1997—2007. Advisor John Edwards Meml. Forum, LA, 1973—2014. Mem. Editorial Bd. American Music, 1980-89, 2007-14, Jour. American Folklore, Washington, 1986-90; co-editor Stars of Country Music, 1975; editor (LP) Green Fields of Ill., 1963, (LP) Hell-Bound Train, 1964, Ethnic Recordings in America, 1982; gen. editor Music in American Life series, 1972-2007. Trustee Am. Folklife Ctr., Libr. of Congress, Washington, 1986—2004, chair, 1990—92, 1996—98, trustee emerita, from 2004. Fulbright grantee, 1958-59; NDEA grantee, 1961, 62-63; grantee Nat. Endowment for the Humanities, 1978; recipient Disting. Achievement citation Ohio Wesleyan U. Alumni Assn., Disting. Svc. award Soc. for American Music, Lifetime Achievement award Belmont U. Curb Music Industry, Disting. Achievement award Internat. Bluegrass Music Assn. Fellow: American Folklore Soc. (exec. bd. 1974—79, pres. 1986—87, exec. bd. 2001—03); mem.: American Musicological Soc. (mem. coun. 2005—07), American Anthropol. Assn., Soc. Ethnomusicology (hon.; treas. 1982—86, coun. 1976—79, 1983—86, 1990—93), Soc. American Music (1st v.p. 1989—93). Democrat. Home: Urbana, Ill. Died July 13, 2014.

**MCCUNE, JOHN R.,** state senator; b. May 27, 1926; AB, Princeton U.; MA, Notre Dame U. Mem. Okla. Senate, from 1969. Republican. Died Aug. 12, 1993.

**MCCURN, NEAL PETERS,** federal judge; b. Syracuse, NY, Apr. 6, 1926; AB, Syracuse U., 1950, LLB, 1952, JD, 1960. Bar: N.Y. 1952. Ptnr. Mackenzie Smith Lewis Mitchell & Hughes, Syracuse, 1957-79; judge US Dist. Ct. (northern dist.) NY, 1979-88, chief judge, 1988-93, sr. judge, 1993—2014. Del. N.Y. State Constl. Conv., 1976; mem. 2d Cir. Jud. Council, 1987-93. Pres. Syracuse Common Coun., 1970-78. Served in USNR, 1944—46. Mem. ABA, N.Y. State Bar Assn. (chmn. state constn. com.), Onondaga County Bar Assn. (past pres.), American Coll. Trial Lawyers, American Judicature Soc. (bd. dirs. 1980-84). Died Sept. 7, 2014.

**MCDERMID, ALICE MARGUERITE CONNELL (MRS. RALPH MANEWAL MCDERMID),** civic and political worker, lecturer; b. Sterling, Ill., May 25, 1910; d. William Hayes and Margaret (Durr) Connell; m. Ralph Manewal McDermid, Nov. 28, 1931; children: Ralph Manewal, Jane Dillon (Mrs. Anders Wiberg), Michael Metcalf, John Fairbanks. AB, U. Ill., 1931. Bd. dirs. Scarsdale (N.Y.) Woman's Exchange, 1953-60; mem. social service bd. N.Y. Infirmary, 1960-76, vice chmn., 1964-76; trustees team United Hosp. Fund, 1965-75; case policy bd. Spence-Chapin Adoption Service, from 1960; fund raising Greer Sch., 1958-73, Vis. Nurses Assn., 1960-64; co-chmn. UN Program, Westchester County; founder Jane Todd Meml. Scholarship, 1966; mem. adv. council Morse Gallery of Art, Winter Park, Fla., from 1974. Sec. exec. com. Morse Gallery Art Assocs., 1977-78, v.p., 1978-80, pres., 1980-82; bd. dirs. Council Arts and Scis. Central Fla., 1975-86, v.p., 1976-78; bd. dirs. Charles Hosmer Morse Found., 1980-82. Sec., Young Republicans Ill., 1930-31; bd. dirs. Scarsdale (N.Y.) Women's Rep. Club, 1961-67, pres., 1965-67, legis. chmn., 1981—; del. Washington Conf. Nat. Fed. Rep. Women, 1965-72; mem. council Fedn. Women's Rep. Clubs N.Y. State, 1967-76; Rep. dist. leader, 1967-75; del. Rep. Jud. Conv., 1969-71; vice chmn. Rep. Town Com., 1969-75, mem. Rep. Presidents Club, Scarsdale; mem. N.Y. State Rep. Com., 1970-72; N.Y. Rep. committee woman 90th Assembly Dist., 1970-72. Recipient Rep. Woman of Yr. award, Scarsdale, 1974, other awards. Mem. Women's Rep. Federated Club of Winter Park (pres. 1978-80), Lock Haven Art Center, Friends of Winter Park Library, Winter Park Hist. Soc., English Speaking Union U.S., Town Club Winter Park, Morse Mus. Am. Art, Morse Mus. Art Assocs., Friends of Cornell Fine Arts, Lock Haven Arts Soc., Alpha Xi Delta. Clubs: Scarsdale Women's, Ladies Harvard, Women's Nat. Rep. (N.Y.C.); Women's of Winter Park (dir. 1977-79), Racquet (Winter Park). Episcopalian. Died. Home: Winter Park, Fla. Deceased.

**MCDONALD, ANDREW JOSEPH,** bishop emeritus; b. Savannah, Ga., Oct. 24, 1923; s. James Bernard and Theresa (McGrael) McDonald. AB, St. Mary's Sem., Balt., 1945, STL, 1948; JCB, Cath. U. America, 1949; JCD, Lateran U., Rome, 1951. Ordained priest Diocese of Savannah, Ga., 1948, chancellor, 1952-68, vicar gen. Ga., from 1968, vice oficialis Ga., 1952-57, oficialis Ga., 1956-72; curate Port Wentworth, Ga., 1952-57; pastor Blessed Sacrament Ch., Savannah, 1963-72; bishop Diocese of Little Rock, 1972-2000, bishop emeritus, 2000—14; with St Joseph's Home Elderly. Named Papal Chamberlain, Roman Cath. Ch., 1956, Domestic Prelate, 1959. Roman Catholic. Home: Palatine, Ill. Died Apr. 1, 2014.

**MCDOUGAL, BRUCE WILLIAM,** finance company executive; b. Duluth, Minn., Oct. 15, 1941; s. William Donald McDougal and Margurite (Ancliff) Iliff; m. Nancy Jean Carpenter, Jan. 24, 1964; children: Brendon, Ryan. BSBA, Calif. State U., Chico, 1963. CPA Calif. Acct. Price Waterhouse, Sacramento, 1963—66, audit mgr. Cin., 1969—73; exec. v.p. Genway Corp., Chgo., 1973—86, pres., from 1986. Bd. dirs. Warren Capital Corp., Novato, Calif., v.p. and treas., from 1983. Mem.: AICPA, Fin. Execs. Inst., Chgo. Athletic Club. Republican. Home: Chico, Calif. Died Mar. 29, 1997.

**MCEACHERN, ALLAN,** academic administrator, retired judge; b. Vancouver, BC, Can., May 20, 1926; s. John A. and Blanche L. (Roadhouse) McE.; m. Gloria, July 17, 1953 (dec. Sept. 1997); children: Jean Williams, Joanne Evans; m. Mary Victoria Newbury. BA, U. B.C., Vancouver, 1949, LLB, 1950, LLM (hon.), 1990. Assoc., sr. ptnr., barrister, solicitor Messrs. Russell & DuMoulin, Vancouver, 1950-78; chief justice Supreme Ct. B.C., Vancouver, 1979-88, Ct. Appeals B.C., Vancouver, 1988—2001; assoc. counsel Faskin Martineau, Vancouver, 2001—08; chancellor U. B.C., 2002—08. Douglas McK. Brown vis. prof. U.B.C., 2001—02, Peter Wall Disting. Fellow, 2001—02. Pres. Kats Rugby Club, Vancouver, 1953-64, B.C. Lions Football Club, Vancouver, 1967, 68, 69, We. Football Conf., 1964, Can. Football League, 1967-68, commr. 1967-68. Mem. Can. Bar Assn. (bd. dirs.), Can. Jud. Coun. (vice chair 1996-2001), Vancouver Bar Assn. (bd. dirs.), Legal Aid Soc. (pres. 1977-78), Law Soc. B.C. (bencher 1971-79). Avocations: sailing, gardening, walking. Home: Vancouver, Canada. Died Jan. 10, 2008.

**MCFARLAND, LEE CRAIG,** energy company executive; b. Long Beach, Calif., Aug. 16, 1920; s. John and Edna (Fehrm) McFarland; m. Ruth Smails, June 22, 1943; children: John, Stuart, Andrew, William. BS in Petroleum Engring., U. Calif., Berkeley, 1942. Registered petroleum engr., Calif. Petroleum. Engr. Tidewater Assoc., Santa Fe Springs, Calif., 1945—46; petroleum engr. and geologist Universal Consol., LA, 1946—64; area mgr. Gulf Oil, 1964—66; cons. Occidental Petroleum, 1966—70; pres. and chmn. McFarland Energy, Inc., Santa Fe Springs, from 1970. To lt. USN, 1942—45, PTO. Mem.: AIME, Ind. Petroleum Assn. Am., Am. Assn. Petroleum Geologists, Calif. Ind. Producers Assn. (pres.), Calif. Club (L.A.), Petroleum Club. Republican. Died 1994.

**MCGAUGHEY, ALBERT WAYNE,** retired mathematics educator; b. Russellville, Ind., July 16, 1914; s. Walter Lee and Belvia Jane (Harbison) McG.; m. Margie V. Silverthorn, July 11, 1940; children: Stanley W., Dennis M., Lynn D. McGaughey Kearney, Donna J. McGaughey Defenbaugh. AB in Liberal Arts, Wabash Coll., 1935; MS in Physics, State U. Iowa, 1937; PhD in Math., U. Cin., 1940. Instr. math. Purdue U., West Lafayette, Ind., 1940-41; asst. prof. U.S. Naval Acad., Annapolis, Md., 1941-46; prof., chmn. dept. Westminster Coll., New Wilmington, Pa., 1946-48, Bradley U., Peoria, Ill., 1948-79, dir. NSF Summer Inst., 1961-66; ret., 1979. Part-time prof. Eureka (Ill.) Coll., 1954-81; tchr.-trainer Indian high sch. math. tchrs. AID Summer Inst., Burdwan U., 1967; assoc. dir. secondary edn. dept. NSF, Washington, 1968-69. Mem. Ctrl. Ill. Agy. on Aging, 1970—, also past coun. chmn. and dept. chmn.; bd. dirs., vol., treas., com. chmn. Common Place, 1970—. Mem. Phi Beta Kappa, Sigma Psi, Math Assoc. America (sec. treas. Ill. sect.). Republican. Mem. Christian Ch. (Disciples Of Christ). Avocation: volunteering. Died Oct. 16, 2001.

**MCGEE, RODNEY WILLIAM,** civil engineer; b. Hobart, Tasmania, Australia, Dec. 12, 1954; m. Margaret Jessica McAllister, Feb. 11, 1978; children: Heather, Andrew. B Engring. with honors, U. Tasmania, Hobart, 1976; B Social Sci., Charles Sturt U., Bathurst, 1997; A diploma in emergency mgmt., U. Tasmania, Hobart, 1995; grad. diploma bus., Tasmanian State Inst. Tech., Launceston, 1989. Chartered profl. engr. Engr. Pub. Works Dept., Launceston, 1977-78, Dept. Main Rds., Hobart, 1978-90; asset mgmt. engr. bridges Dept. Transport, Hobart, 1990-97; mgr. asset strategies Dept. Infrastructure, Energy, Resources, Hobart, from 1997. Contbr. articles to profl. jours. Recipient Emergency Svcs. medal Australian Govt., 2000. Fellow Instn. Engrs. Australia; mem. Concrete Inst. Australian, Commn. 5. Achievements include research in concrete durability, especially chloride ingress. Home: Blackmans Bay, Australia. Died Jan. 31, 2002.

**MC GINNISS, JOE,** writer; b. NYC, Dec. 9, 1942; s. Joseph Aloysius and Mary (Leonard) McG.; m. Christine Cook, Sept. 25, 1965 (div.); children: Christine, Suzanne, Joe; m. Nancy Doherty, Nov. 20, 1976; children: Matthew, James. BS, Holy Cross Coll., 1964. Reporter Port Chester (N.Y.) Daily Item, 1964, Worcester (Mass.) Telegram, 1965, Phila. Bull., 1966, Phila. Inquirer, 1967-68. Author: The Selling of the President, 1968, The Dream Team, 1972, Heroes, 1976, Going to Extremes, 1980, Fatal Vision, 1983, Blind Faith, 1989, Cruel Doubt, 1991, The Last Brother: The Rise and Fall of Teddy Kennedy, 1993, The Miracle of Castel di Sangro, 1999, The Big House, 2004, Never Enough, 2007, The Rogue: Searching for the Real Sarah Palin, 2011 Died Mar. 10, 2014.

**MCGOVERN, JAMES,** author; BA in Journalism and Polit. Sci., U. Minn., postgrad. Radio talk show host "Let's Talk Turkey" WDGY, Mpls., 1950; news dir., TV news anchor, newscaster, reporter WDGY, KGTV, KSTP, KMSP-TV, WISN-CBS, SUN Newspapers; local news feed corres. NBC, CBS, ABC; instr. journalism Lakewood Jr. Coll., 1967-68. Polit. advisor, speechwriter, nat. presdl. campaign advance man.; former speechwriter, news, pub. rels., mktg., video prodr. and orgnl. cons. various Minn. businesses and CEO's, including 3M, Honeywell, Control Data, others; trumpeter and leader Jim McGovern Swing Band. Writer, prodr., narrator PURSUIT series of tv documentarie; author 3 dramatic plays, 2 novels; contbr. articles to profl. jours. Mem. Twin Cities Musicians Union (local 30-73); hon. mem. Chinese (Nationalist) Air Force. With USAF. Decorated DFC with one oak leaf cluster, Air Medal with 2 oak leaf clusters; winner Nat. Headliners award for best pub.affairs documentary in U.S., 1963; recipient Award of Merit, Minn. Coll. Radio Network for outstanding leadership in radio news reporting through the "Behind the Parade" radio series on KSTP, 1960. Mem. ASCAP (assoc.), Am. Soc. Composers, Artists and Pubs., DFC Soc. (charter), 14th AAF Flying Tigers, Hump Pilots Assn., U. Minn. Alumni Assn., Irish Nat. Caucus (charter). Died June 27, 2002.

**MCGOVERN, PATRICK JOSEPH, JR.,** communications executive; b. Aug. 11, 1937; m. Lore Harp; 4 children. BA in biophysics, M.I.T., 1959. Founder Internat. Data Corp., Framingham, Mass., 1964, chmn., 1976—2014; founder IDG Comm. Inc., 1987, CEO, 1999. Trustee McGovern Inst. for Brain Rsch., 2000-14 Recipient James Smithsonian Bicentennial Medal, Smithsonian Inst., Entrepreneurial Leadership Award, MIT Enterprise Forum of Cambridge, Inc., The Bus. Pub. of the Year award Delaney Report, The Communicator of the Year award N.Y. Chpt. Bus. Profl. Advertisers Assn., The Entrepreneur of the Year award Ernst & Young, Lifetime Achievement award, American Soc. Bus. Publ. Editors, 2004, Top Innovator in Bus. Publishing Award, BtoB Media Bus. mag., 2004, Lifetime Achievement award, Mag. Publishers of America., 2005, Robert J. Krakoff Lifetime Achievement award American Bus. Media, 2008; Named one of The 25 Entrepreneurs We Love, Inc. mag., 2004, The 50 Most Generous Philanthropists, Fortune Mag., 2005, Forbes 400: Richest Americans, 1999-2013, World's Richest People, 2001-14. Fellow: American Acad. Arts & Sciences. Achievements include providing a $350 mil. endowment to M.I.T. Died Mar. 19, 2014.

**MCGOVERN, THOMAS AQUINAS,** retired utility executive; b. NYC, Mar. 2, 1933; s. Thomas Aquinas and Helen Frances (Carroll) McG.; m. Miriam Anne Howley, July 16, 1955; children: Cecilia, Louise, Pamela. BS in History, Coll. of the Holy Cross, 1954; MA in Econs., L.I. U., 1965. Dep. asst. Consol. Edison Co. of N.Y., NYC, 1958-61, supts. asst., 1961-66, asst. supt., 1967-68, supt., 1968-69, staff dir., 1969-70, asst. to exec. v.p., 1970-72, exec. dir., 1972-82, asst. v.p., 1982-89, v.p., 1989-95; sr. assoc. John Hall Co., Danbury, Conn., from 1995. Mem. Edison Elec. Inst. Sec. Commn., Washington, 1976-90, Mailers' Tech. Adv. Com., Washington, 1990-91; vice-chmn. Nat. Postal Coun., Washington, 1982—; pres. D.C.K. Mgmt. Corp., N.Y.C., 1982-94; mem. Real Estate Bd. N.Y., N.Y.C., 1988-94. Mem. N.Y.C. (N.Y.) Health and Hosps. Security Adv. Com., 1985; pres. Westchester County Police Meml., White Plains, N.Y., 1987—. With U.S. Army, 1954-56. Recipient Svcs. to Nation and FBI award FBI, N.Y.C., 1984, Svc. to Law Enforcement Community award N.Y. State Chiefs of Police, Albany, N.Y., 1989, Appreciation for Svc. award N.Y. State Fedn. of Police, Briarcliff Manor, N.Y., 1989, Svc. to Orgns. award FBI Marine Corps Assn., Cresskill, N.J., 1989, Svc. to Orgns. award N.Y.C. Honor Legion, Richmond Hill, N.Y. Mem. KC, VFW, Am. Legion, Assn. of U.S. Army, U.S. Naval Inst., FBI Marine Corps Assn., Friendly Sons of St. Patrick, VFW, Holy Cross Varsity Club (dir.), Pi Gamma Mu. Roman Catholic. Avocations: U.S. military history, postcard collecting, toy soldier collecting, Royal Doulton china collecting. Deceased.

**MCGRATH, JAMES EDWARD,** chemistry professor; b. Easton, NY, July 11, 1934; s. Thomas Augustine and Marguerite Monica (Hiland) McG.; m. Marlene Mary Potter, May 9, 1959; children: Colleen McGrath Kraft, Patricia McGrath Hoover, Matthew, Barbara, Elizabeth McGrath Throckmorton, Joseph. BS in Chemistry, St. Bernadine of Siena Coll., 1956; MS in Chemistry, U. Akron, 1964, PhD in Polymer Sci., 1967. Rsch. chemist rsch. divsn. Rayonier, Inc., Whippany, N.J., 1956-59, Goodyear Tire & Rubber Co., Akron, Ohio, 1959-65; mem. staff Inst. Polymer Sci., U. Akron, 1965-67; sr. rsch. chemist Union Carbide Corp., Bound Brook, N.J., 1967-69, project scientist, 1969-72, rsch. scientist, 1972-74, rsch. scientist, group leader, 1974-75; asst. prof. chemistry Va. Poly. Inst. and State U., Blacksburg, 1975-76, assoc. prof. chemistry, 1976-79, prof. chemistry, 1980-87, dir. Materials Inst., 1987-89 and from 96, prof. dept. chem., co-dir. polymer materials and interface lab., 1979—2014, Ethyl prof. polymer chemistry, 1986—2014, dir. Ctr. for Polymer Adhesives and Composites, 1989—2000, Univ. disting. prof., 1996—2014. Adj. prof. materials sci. & engring. Gwangju Inst. Sci. & Technology, 1995—2014; adj. prof. chemical engring. Va. Commonwealth U., 1996—2014. Author, editor: Polyimides: Materials, Chemistry and Characterization, 1989; co-author (with Noshay): Block Copolymers: Overview and Critical Survey, 1977; mem. editl. bd. Jour. Polymer Sci., Polymer, High Performance Polymeric Polymers; adv. bd. Jour. Polymer Sci., Advances in Polymeric Sci. Capt. U.S. Army, 1957. Recipient H.F. Mark award Polymer divsn. American Chem. Soc., 1996, Outstanding Alumni award U. Akron, 1997, Award in Applied Polymer Sci. American Chem. Soc., 2002, Paul J. Flory Polymer Edn. award, 2004, Polymer Chemistry award, 2007,'08, George S. Whitby award for Disting. Teaching & Rsch., 2009, Charles G. Overberger Internat. prize for Excellence in Polymer Rsch., 2013; named Va. Scientist of Yr., 1997; named to The Soc. Plastic Engineers Plastics Hall of Fame, 1997. Mem. NAS (mem. nat. materials bd. 1992-95), NAE, Soc. Plastics Engrs. (Internat. Rsch. award 1987, Outstanding Achievement award 1992); fellow American Chemical Soc. Republican. Roman Catholic. Avocations: music, tennis, travel. Home: Blacksburg, Va. Died May 17, 2014.

**MCGRUDER, JAMES PATRICK,** lawyer; b. LA, Mar. 11, 1926; s. James S. and Margaret T. (McHugh) McG.; m. Patricia M. Harrison, June 28, 1952; children: Eileen, Coleen, Mark. JD, Denver U., 1953. Bar: Colo. 1954. Asst. city atty. City of Denver, 1954-61; asst. U.S. atty. U.S. Dept. Justice, Denver, 1961-64; regional counsel Prudential Ins. Co., LA, Denver, 1964-75, div. counsel LA, from 1975. With USMC, 1943-46. Mem. Calif. Bar Assn., Colo. Bar Assn., Am. Land Title Assn. (assoc.). Democrat. Deceased.

**MC ILWAIN, BILL (WILLIAM FRANKLIN MC ILWAIN),** newspaper editor, writer; b. Lancaster, SC, Dec. 15, 1925; s. William Franklin and Docia (Higgins) McI.; m. Anne Dalton, Nov. 28, 1952 (div. 1973); children: Dalton, Nancy, William Franklin III; m. K. L. Brelsford, June 5, 1978 (div. 1983). BA, Wake Forest Coll., 1949; postgrad., Harvard, 1957-58. Various positions with Wilmington (N.C.) Star, 1943, Charlotte (N.C.) Observer, 1945, Jacksonville (Fla.) Jour., 1945, Winston-Salem (N.C.) Jour.-Sentinel, 1949-52, Richmond (Va.) Times-Dispatch, 1952-54; chief copy editor Newsday, Garden City, N.Y., 1954-57, day news editor, 1957-60, city editor, 1960-64, mng. editor, 1964-66, editor, 1967-70; writer-in-residence Wake Forest U., 1970-71; dorm leader Alcoholic Rehab. Ctr., Butner, N.C., 1971; dep. mng. editor Toronto Star, 1971-73; mng. editor The Record, Hackensack, N.J., 1973-77; editor Boston Herald Am., 1977-79; dep. editor Washington Star, 1979-81, exec. mng. editor, 1981; editor Ark. Gazette, 1981-82; founding editor N.Y. Newsday, 1982-84; exec. editor Sarasota (Fla.) Herald-Tribune, 1984-90; sr. editor N.Y. Times Regional Newspaper Group, 1991-92; chmn. Bill Mc Ilwain, Inc., 1993—2014. Author: The Glass Rooster, 1960, (with Walter Friedenberg) Legends of Baptist Hollow, 1949; collaborator: (with Newsday staff) Naked Came The Stranger, 1969, A Farewell to Alcohol, 1973, Dancing Naked with the Rolling Stones, 2007; contbr. articles to popular mags. including Reader's Digest, Harper's, Esquire, Atlantic Monthly; editor N.C. Writer's Workshop. Mem. Pres. Johnson's Commn. on Civil Rights; adv. bd. Pulitzer Prize, 1982; served in USMC, 1944. Named to The N.C. Journalism Hall of Fame, 2004. Mem. American Soc. Newspaper Editors, Soc. Nieman Fellows. *As Fats Waller said, "One never knows, do one?".* Died Aug. 8, 2014.

**MCKAY, ALEXANDER GORDON,** classics educator; b. Toronto, Dec. 24, 1924; s. Alexander Lynn and Marjory Maude Redfern (Nicoll) McKay; m. Helen Jean Zulauf, Dec. 24, 1964; stepchildren: Julie Anne Stephanie Brott, Danae Helen Fraser. BA, U. Toronto, 1946; MA, Yale U., 1947, Princeton U., 1948, PhD, 1950; LLD (hon.), U. Man., 1986, Brock U., 1990, Queen's U., 1991; DLitt (hon.), McMaster U., 1992, U. Waterloo, 1993. Mem. faculty classics Wells Coll., 1949-50, U. Pa., 1950-51, U. Man., 1951-52, 55-57, Mt. Allison U., 1952-53, Waterloo Coll., 1953-55; mem. faculty McMaster U., 1957-90, prof., chmn. dept. classics, 1962-68, 76-79, dean humanities, 1968-73, mem. univ. senate, 1968-73, 85-87, prof. emeritus, from 1990; Disting. vis. prof. classics U. Colo., 1978; prof. in charge Intercollegiate Center for Classical Studies, Rome, 1975; vis. mem. Inst. Advanced Study, Princeton, 1979, 81. Vis. scholar U. Tex., Austin, 1987, Hardt, Vandoevres, Geneva, 1988; vis. fellow Trinity Coll., Cambridge, 1988; adj. prof. humanities York U., 1990—96; Disting. vis. lectr. Concordia U., Montreal, 1992—93, prof. emeritus, from 2001; vis. scholar Rockefeller Study and Conf. Ctr., Bellagio (Como), Italy, 1993. Author: Naples and Campania: Texts and Illustrations, 1962, Roman Lyric Poetry: Catullus and Horace, 2d edit., 1974, Vergil's Italy, 1970, Cumae and the Phlegraean Fields, 1972, Naples and Coastal Campania, 1972, Houses, Villas and Palaces in the Roman World, 1975, reprint, 1998, Roman Satire, 1976, Vitruvius, Architect and Engineer, 1978, 2d edit., 1985, Römische Häuser, Villen und Paläste, 1980, Roma Antiqua: Latium and Etruria, 1986; co-author: Selections from Vergil, Aeneid I, IV and VI (Dido and Aeneas), 1988, Festschrift, The Two Worlds of the Poet: New Perspectives on Vergil, 1992, Tragedy, Love, and Change: Roman Poetic Themes and Variations, 1994, Arma Virumque: Heroes at War (Aeneid 10 and 12), 2 vols., 1998, Classics at McMaster (1890-2000), 2000, A Song of War: Readings from Vergil's Aeneid, 2003. Pres., bd. govs. Hamilton Philharm. Orch., 1967-69, Hamilton Chamber Music Soc., 1965-67, Hamilton br. Archtl. Conservancy Ont., 1965-67, Hamilton and Region Arts Coun., 1971-72; bd. dirs. Can. Fedn. Humanities, 1980-82; v.p., dir. Internat. Acad. Union, 1978-90; v.p. U. Bristol Inst. Greece, Rome and Classical Tradition, 1997—; trustee Hamilton Found., 1972-75; bd. govs. Art Gallery Hamilton; bd. govs., dir. Boris Brott Summer Music Festival, 1989-2000 (pres. 2001), Montreal Chamber Music Festival, 1997—; presdl. bd. trustees McMaster U. Art Gallery, 1985-91; pres. Sir Ernest MacMillan String Ensemble, 1988-90, pres. Nat. Acad. Orch., 2001--; mem. adv. bd. Inst. for Classical Tradition, Boston U., 1987-88; v.p., dir. Bach-Elgar Choral Soc., Hamilton, 1992-95. Decorated knight comdr. Order St. John of Jerusalem; officer Order of Can.; recipient Silver Jubilee medal Queen Elizabeth II, 1977, 125th Anniversary medal Can. Confedn., Golden Jubilee medal Queen Elizabeth II, 2002; Woodrow Wilson fellow, 1947-48, Can. Coun. fellow, 1973-74, Killam rsch. fellow, 1979-80, fellow Vanier Coll., York U., 1991—, vis. scholar, 1996—. Fellow Royal Soc. Can. (hon. editor 1970-83, pres. 1984-87, past pres. 1987-89, Centennial medal 1982); mem. Vergilian Soc. (pres. 1972-74, Hon. Pres. for Life 1988—, chmn. Villa Vergiliana mgmt. com. 1993—), Classical Assn. Mid. West and South (pres. 1972-73, award of merit com. 1989-91), Classical Assn. Can. (v.p. 1970-72, 76-78, pres. 1978-80), Ont. Classical Assn. (hon. pres. 1994—), Master Print and Drawing Soc. (Toronto) (v.p. 1998-2001, pres. 2001-05), Yale Club (N.Y.C.), Tamahaac Club (Ancaster), Arts and Letters Club (Toronto), X Club (Toronto), Univ. Club (McMaster). Home: Hamilton, Canada. Died Aug. 31, 2007.

**MC KEE, KINNAIRD ROWE,** retired military officer; b. Louisville, Ky., Aug. 14, 1929; s. James H. and Kathleen (Sutton) McK.; m. Betty Ann Harris, June 23, 1953; children: James Henry III, Anne Arnold. BS, U.S. Naval Acad., 1951; grad., Nuclear Power Tng., 1958. Commd. ensign U.S. Navy, 1951, advanced through grades to adm., 1982; served in Pacific fleet destroyer Marshall, Korean War; served in div. naval reactors AEC, 1964-66; comdg. officer nuclear attack submarine DACE, 1966-69; asst. to dir. program planning USN, Washington, 1969-70; exec. dir. Chief Naval Ops. Exec. Panel, 1970-73; comdr. U.S. and NATO submarine forces, 1973-75; supt. US Naval Acad., Annapolis, 1975-78; comdr. US Third Fleet, 1978-79; dir. naval warfare USN, Washington, 1979-82, dir. naval nuclear propulsion, 1982-88, ret. Mem. U.S. Naval Inst. Died Dec. 30, 2013.

**MC KINLEY, JOHN KEY,** retired oil industry executive; b. Tuscaloosa, Ala., Mar. 24, 1920; s. Virgil Parks and Mary Emma (Key) McK.; m. Helen Grace Heare, July 19, 1946 (dec. Jan. 11, 2002); children: John Key Jr., Mark Charles. BS in Chem. Engring, U. Ala., 1940, MS in Organic Chemistry, 1941; Grad., Advanced Mgmt. Program, Harvard U., 1962; LL.D. (hon.), U. Ala., 1972, Troy State U., 1974. Registered profl. engr., Tex. With Texaco Inc., 1941-86, asst. dir. research Beacon, NY, 1957-59, asst. to v.p., 1959-60, mgr. comml. devel., 1960, gen. mgr. petrochem. dept. NYC, 1960-67, v.p. petrochem. dept., v.p. in charge supply and distbn., 1967-71, sr. v.p. worldwide refining, petrochems., also supply and distbn., 1971, pres., 1971-80, pres., COO, chmn. exec. com., 1980, chmn., pres., CEO, 1980-83, chmn., CEO, 1983-86. Bd. dirs. emeritus Federated Dept. Stores, Inc. Patentee for chem. processing. Hon. bd. dirs. Met. Opera Assocs.; nat. chmn. Met. Opera Centennial Fund, 1980; bd. dirs. The Americas Soc.; mem. Bus. Coun. Maj. AUS, 1941-45, ETO. Decorated Bronze Star; recipient George Washington Honor medal Freedoms Found., 1972; Andrew Wellington Cordier fellow Columbia U.; named to The Ala. Bus. Hall of Fame, 1982, Ala. Acad. Honor, 1983, State of Ala. Engring. Hall of Fame, 1992. Fellow American Inst. Chem. Engrs.; mem. American Petroleum Inst. (hon. dir.), Wee Burn Country Club, Brook Club, Augusta Nat. Golf Club, Blind Brook Country Club, North River Yacht, Sigma Xi, Tau Beta Pi, Gamma Sigma Epsilon, Kappa Sigma. Home: Buffalo, Wyo. Died June 12, 2014.

**MCKINNEY-LUDD, SARAH LYDELLE,** middle school education, librarian; b. Feb. 29, 1948; BA, U. Md., 1973; MA, Cen. Mich. U., 1975; MA in Legal Studies, Antioch Sch. Law, Washington, 1982; postgrad., Sch. Edn. George Washington U., from 1989; PhD in Christian Edn., Family Bible Coll. and Seminary. Cert. advanced profl. tchr. grades 5 through 12, Md., cert. adminstr. Tchr. of learning disabled Azores (Portugal) Elem. Sch., 1974-76; tchr. English Spaulding Jr. High Sch., Forestville, Md., 1976-82, Prince George's Cmty. Coll., 1982-84, Benjamin Tasker Sch., Bowie, Md., 1982-85, Crossland Night Sch., Temple Hills, Md., 1984-85, Thomas Pullen Mid. Sch., Landover, Md., 1985-87, Kettering (Md.) Mid. Sch., 1985-88, Kenmoor Mid. Sch., Landover, 1988-91; tchr. English, libr. Drew Freeman Mid. Sch.(formerly Francis Scott Key Mid. Sch.), District Heights, Md., from 1991. Chair multicultural com., chair sch. based mgmt. Francis Scott Key Mid. Sch., 1992—; reader Jarvis Grants, U.S. Dept. Edn., 1990—; acad. coord. Prince George's County Steel Band-Positive Vibrations. Contbr. articles to various publs. Mem. Md. State Tchr.'s Legis. Com., 1987-90; chairperson Profl. Rights and Responsibility, 1978-81; active Prince George's Com. on Acad. Achievement, Prince George's Com. Women's Fair Steering Com., Md. State Hosp. Bd., Prince George's County affiliate United Black Fund, area speakers bur.; programs chairperson, sec. Project Safe Sts.-2000, 1989; pres. Bowie Therapeutic Nursery; judge ACT-SO NAACP, Washington, 1989—; mem. exec. bd. Prince George's County chpt., 1984-89; active polit. campaigns; bd. dirs. Landover Ednl. Athletic Recreational Non-Profit Found. of Washington Redskins. Recipient Dorothy Wyod award for women's rights, 1998, Agnes Meyer Outstanding Educator award Wash. Post, 2000. Mem. Md. State Tchrs. Assn. (editor Women's Caucus, Dorothy Lloyd award for Women's Rights 1998), Sigma Gamma Rho (Community Activist award 1992), Delta Kappa Gamma. Deceased.

**MCKINZIE, BEVERLY OMA,** artist; b. Denver, Oct. 27, 1927; d. Allen Worley and Shereal (Vaagen) Chapalis; m. Raymond Clem McKinzie; children: Jeanne, Teresa, Scott, Mark. Statistician Denver Post, 1945-47; payroll clk. Firth Carpet, Firthcliffe, N.Y., 1948-49; proofreader Cornwall (N.Y.) Press, 1949-50; electronic tech. USN, Great Lakes, Ill., 1950-51; bookkeeper Foodmaker, San Diego, 1968-70; salesperson Liberty House, San Jose, 1971. Embroidered The Birth Project, 1982-83. With USN, 1950-51. Recipient award for excellence No. Calif. Handweavers, 1992. Mem. Peninsula Stitchery Guild, Fiber Artisans, Handweaver's Guild Am. Avocation: collecting dolls. Deceased.

**MCLAREN, ANNE,** research scientist; d. Henry and Christabel (McNaughten) McLaren; m. Donald Michie, Oct. 6, 1952 (div. 1959); children: Susan Fiona, Jonathan Mark, Caroline Ruth. MA, U. Oxford, 1949, PhD, 1952. Rsch. fellow Univ. Coll., London, 1952—55, Royal Veterinary Coll., London, 1955—59; staff agrl. rsch. coun. U. Edinburgh, 1959—74; dir. mammalian devel. unit Med. Rsch. Coun., 1974—92; fgn. sec. Royal Soc., 1991—96; Fullerian prof. physiology Royal Inst., 1991—99; disting. group leader Wellcome Trust Cancer Rsch., Cambridge, England, 1992—2007. Author: Mammalian Chimaeras, 1976, Germ Cells and Soma: A New Look at an Old Problem, 1980. Recipient Japan prize, 2002; named a Dame Comdr. of the British Empire, 1993. Mem.: Assn. for Women in Sci. and Engring. (pres. 1993—94). Died July 7, 2007.

**MCLEAN, EDWARD BURNS,** corporate financial executive; b. Winchester, Mass., Nov. 13, 1937; s. Vadm Ephraim (Rankin) and Janet (Burns) McLean; m. Paula Sparre, May 21, 1966; children: J. Lachlan, Mark S. BA with honors, U. Va., 1958; post grad., Yale U., 1959—60, NYU, 1961—64. With Proctor & Gamble, 1958—59; v.p. Chase Manhattan Bank, NYC, 1961—71; dir. gen. adjunto Liga Financiera, Madrid, 1971—72; mng. dir. Chase Manhattan Ltd., London, 1972—74; CFO The Commodore Corp., Syracuse, Ind., 1983—86, GoodMark Foods Inc., Raleigh, NC, from 1987. V.p. and trustee Episcopal Charities Chgo., 1976—82; bd. dir. Mid-Am. Chpt. Blood Svcs. ARC, Chgo., 1978—82, Cathedral Shelter Chgo, 1974—77, WCPE-FM, Wake Forest, NC, from 1991. To capt. USAR, 1965—69. Woodrow Wilson fellow, 1960. Mem.: Fin. Execs. Inst., Univ. Club (Chgo.), Rotary (bd. dir. North Raleigh chpt. from 1992), Omicron Delta Kappa, Phi Delta Kappa. Republican. Episcopalian. Home: Raleigh, NC. Died Oct. 14, 1992.

**MCMANUS, LOUISE,** nurse, advocate; b. 1896; Creator Inst. for Nursing Rsch., Tchrs. Coll. Columbia U. Developer Patient Bill of Rights. Recipient numerous awards, including Florence Nightingale Internat. Red Cross Soc. citation and medal, Mary Adelaide Nutting award for leadership. Died 1993.

**MC MILLEN, THOMAS ROBERTS,** lawyer, arbitrator, mediator, retired judge; b. Decatur, Ill., June 8, 1916; s. Rolla C. and Ruth (Roberts) Mc M.; m. Anne Ford, Aug. 16, 1946; children: Margot F., Patricia R., Anne C. Scheyer. AB, Princeton U., 1938; LLB, Harvard U., 1941. Bar: Ill. 1941, U.S. Supreme Ct. 1948. Mem. firm Bell, Boyd, Lloyd, Haddad & Burns, Chgo., 1946-66; judge Cook County Cir. Ct., Cook County, Ill., 1966-71, U.S. Dist. Ct. (7th Cir.) Ill., Chgo., 1971-85; pvt. practice Chgo., from 1985; ret. Mem. arbitration panels Fed. Med. and Conciliation Svc., Chgo. Bd. Options Exch., Ill. State Bd. Edn., Judicate. Maj. CIC, AUS, 1941-45. Decorated Bronze Star medal, European Battle Stars (4), Croix de Guerre. Mem. Chgo. Bar Assn. (mem. bd. mgrs. 1964-66), 7th Cir. Bar Assn., Counter Intelligence Corps Assn., Chgo. Farmers (bd. dirs. 1989), Assn. Am. Rhodes Scholars, Indian Hill Country Club, Univ. Club Chgo., Phi Beta Kappa. Died Sept. 17, 2002.

**MCMINN, J. B.,** retired philosophy educator, composer; b. Pt. Neches, Tex., Nov. 12, 1922; s. Joe Byron and Mary Thelma (Odom) McMinn; m. Dorothy Louise Smith, Aug. 31, 1944 (div. May 15, 1969); children: Jan Branton, Robert Errol. BA in English and Religious Studies, La. Coll., 1943; ThM in Hellenistic Greek, So. Sem., 1946, PhD in Hellenistic Greek, 1951; postgrad., La. State U., 1948; MA in Classical Greek and Philosophy, Tulane U., 1960, postgrad., 1968, U. Athens, 1970, postdoctoral in Modern Greek, 1979. Asst. prof. English La. Coll., 1948—51; tchg. asst. in classics Newcomb Coll., 1951—52, Tulane U., 1952—54, asst. prof. classics, 1953—58; from asst. prof. philosophy to prof. philosophy U. Ala., 1960—87. Vis. prof. philosophy Miles Coll., 1990; vis. assoc. prof. philosophy and classics Tulane U., 1960, 1961; spkr., lectr., presenter in field. Contbr. spirit song for Million Dollar Band, U. Ala. Fight On to Victory, 1987, poetry to anthologies;, composer piano and vocal pieces; author: (book of poetry and songs) Une Petite Ménagerie, 1997, (plays) Waiting for Gotdough, 1995, (book) Mythtaken: Le Mot de L' Énigme, 2002; contbr. articles to profl. jours. Rep. commr., New Orleans, 1956—60; mem. So. Soc. Christian Leadership Conf., New Orleans, 1954—60. Cadet officer USNR, 1941—42. Recipient Merit award, U. Ala. Band Assn., 1991, VIP award, Internat. Soc. Poets, 1996, Fulbright Adj. Lectr. award., 1972, West Germany Lectr. award, 1973, Merit award, Internat. Poet., 1996. Mem.: ASCAP, Poetry Soc. Am., Acad. Am. Poets, Nat. Acad. Popular Music-Songwriters Hall of Fame, Internat. Soc. Poets (life), Eta Sigma Phi. Home: Odessa, Tex. Died Apr. 24, 2014.

**MCNAIR, JOHN WILLIAM, JR.,** civil engineer; b. Asheville, NC, June 17, 1926; s. John William and Annie (Woody) McN.; m. June Clemens Kratz; childrn: Jeffry, Marsha, Cathy. BS in Forestry, Pa. State U., 1950; BSCE, Va. Poly Inst. State U., 1955; postgrad., U. Va., 1957—2004. Registered profl. engr., Va., Md., W.Va., Pa., NY, Ky. Forester U.S. Forest Svc., Flagstaff, Ariz., 1950, U.S. Gypsum Co., Altavista, Va., 1951; mem. engring. faculty U. Va., Charlottesville, 1955—58; prin. John McNair & Assocs., Waynesboro, Va., from 1958; owner Brucheum Group, Waynesboro, from 1983; chmn., CEO Info. Systems Support, Inc., Waynesboro, 1998—2007. With Va. Bd. Architects, Profl. Engrs. and Land Surveyors, 1969-79, v.p., 1977-78, pres., 1978-79. Author numerous engring. and land mgmt. study reports. Mem. Waynesboro City Coun., 1968-72, vice mayor, 1970-72; chmn. Waynesboro Indsl. Devel. Authority, 1984-2000. Capt. AUS, 1944-46, 51-53, France, Okinawa. Recipient Disting. Svc. cert. Va. Soc. Profl. Engrs., 1971. Fellow ASCE; mem. Am. Acad. Environ. Engrs. (bd. cert. environ. engr.), Rotary, Rappahannock River Yacht Club (founding mem.). Republican. Presbyterian. Home: Waynesboro, Va. Died June 18, 2014.

**MCNAMARA, JOHN J.,** special education educator; b. Rochelle, Ill., Dec. 6, 1909; s. John and Grace (Campbell) McNamara; m. Hazel D. Dionne, Aug. 11, 1936; children: John, Denise, Carole, Michael, Terrence, Kevin. Tchr. St. Albans Acad., Sycamore, Ill., 1932—34; faculty St. Viator Coll., Kankakee, Ill., 1934—37; asso. prof. U. Detroit, 1937—43; head tng. div. Republic Aviation Corp., 1943—45; pres. M & M Candy, Hackettstown, NJ, 1945—59; dir. M & M Mars (now Mars Inc.), McLean, Va., 1952—62; chmn. bd. Uncle Ben's Rice, Houston, 1959—62; corp. mktg. adv. Warner Lambert Pharm. Co., Morris Plains, NJ, 1966—67; prof. No. Ill. U., DeKalb, 1970—78; prof. dept. mktg. Calif. State Coll., Bakersfield, 1978—80; Calcot-Kennedy disting. prof., from 1980. Contbr. articles to profl. jours. Recipient Chick Evans award and svc. award, Northern Ill. U., 1971; named NIU Football Hall of Fame. Mem.: Am. Assn. Advt. Agys., Stockdale Country, Phi Delta Kappa, Sigma Xi. Home: Carlisle, Mass. Died Apr. 27, 1989.

**MC NAMARA, JOSEPH DONALD,** researcher, retired police chief; b. NYC, Dec. 16, 1934; s. Michael and Eleanor (Shepherd) McN.; divorced; children: Donald, Laura, Karen. BS, John Jay Coll. Sch. Criminal Justice, 1968; fellow, Harvard Law Sch., 1970; DPA (Littauer fellow) (hon.), Harvard U., 1973. Served to dep. insp. NYC Police Dept., 1956-73; police chief Kansas City, Mo., 1973-76, San Jose, Calif., 1976-91; rsch. fellow Hoover Instn., Stanford U., 1991—2014. Adj. instr. Northeastern U., 1972, John Jay Coll., 1973, Rockhurst Coll., 1975-76, San Jose State U., 1980; cons. U.S. Civil Rights Commn., 1978; lectr., appearances on nat. TV; apptd. nat. advisory bd. U.S. Bur. Justice Stats., 1980, US Drug Control Policy Office, 1993; commentator Public Broadcasting Radio. Author: (non-fiction) Safe and Sane, 1984, (novel) The First Directive Crown, 1985, Fatal Command, 1987, The Blue Mirage, 1990, Code 211 Blue, 1996; contbr. articles to profl. publs. Bd. dirs. Drug Policy Found., Washington; active NCCJ. Served in US Army, 1958-60. Named one of The 200 Young American Leaders Time mag., 1975; recipient disting. alumni award John Jay Coll., 1979, Pres.'s award Western Soc. Criminology1979, Morrison Gitchoff award Western Soc. Criminology, 1992, H.B. Spear award Drug Policy Found., 1992; Kansas City police named Best in Country by Nat. Newspaper Enterprises, 1974, San Jose Police Dept., Nat. Model U.S. Civil Rights Commn., 1980; named Law Enforcement Officer of Yr., Calif. Trial Lawyers Assn., 1991. Mem. Internat. Assn. Chiefs of Police, Calif. Police Chiefs Assn., Calif. Peace Officers Assn., Major Cities Police Chiefs Assn., Police Exec. Research Forum (dir.) Home: Menlo Park, Calif. *In our country, social mobility is possible for people from even the most humble backgrounds. Despite problems, our nation has provided more liberty and dignity for the common individual than any other civilization in history. Continuation of our free society depends upon how successful we are in teaching each new generation an appreciation of our precious freedoms and the patience to achieve progress within our democratic process.* Died Sept. 19, 2014.

**MCNAUGHTON, WILLIAM FRANK,** translator, educator; b. Westboro, Mo., May 21, 1933; s. Frank McNaughton and Ruth Ellen (Flanders) Francis; m. Margaret Orminski, Apr. 4, 1956 (div. 1971); children: John Ferenc, Dorothy Ellen; m. Li Ying, Apr. 8, 1990; 1 child, Andrea. Student, U. Mo., 1951-53; studied poetry and translation with, Ezra Pound, 1953-56; student, Georgetown U., 1953-54; BA, Bklyn. Coll., 1961; PhD, Yale U., 1965. Asst. prof. Oberlin (Ohio) Coll., 1965-70; lectr. Exptl. Coll., Oberlin, 1970-71; vis. lectr. Bowling Green (Ohio) State U., 1972-74, Denison U., Granville, Ohio, 1972-78; prof. Program for Afloat Coll. Edn. (PACE) USN, Norfolk, Va., 1978-84; vis. prof. King Saud U., Abha, Saudi Arabia, 1984-85; sr. lectr. English, translation City Poly. Hong Kong, 1986-89, prin. lectr. translation, 1989-94; univ. sr. lectr. City U., Hong Kong, 1994-95, assoc. prof., 1995-98; retired, 1998. Guest lectr., U. degli Studii, Venice, Italy, 1975; coord. Tri-Coll. Chinese program, Gt. Lakes Colls. Assn., Ann Arbor, 1965-68; cons., Asian Lit. program, Asia Soc., N.Y.C., 1967-80, Nat. Translation Ctr., Austin, Tex., 1965-68, Ballantine Books, N.Y.C., 1985, Princeton U. Press, 1965; presenter papers at lit. confs. Author: Reading and Writing Chinese, 1979, rev. edit., 1999, Simplified Character Edit., 2005, Pound's Usura and the Islamic Concept of Riba, 1996; co-translator: Poem Without a Hero and Selected Poems of Anna Akhmatova, 1989, As Though Dreaming: The Tz'u...of Li Ch'ing-chao, 1977, A Gold Orchid: The Love Poems of Tzu Yeh, 1972; editor, translator: Light from the East, 1978, The Confucian Vision, 1974, The Book of Songs, 1971, The Taoist Vision, 1971, Guerilla War, 1971; contbr. articles to profl. publs., translations to various lit. mags.; editor-in-chief: City Univ. Bull., 1995-98; mem. editl. bd. City Univ. Press, 1996-98. Woodrow Wilson Found. fellow, 1961-62; modern fgn. lang. fellow, NDEA, 1962-65; grantee, Nat. Translation Ctr., Austin, 1967, Gt. Lakes Colls. Assn., Ann Arbor, 1965, 67-68, Asia Soc., N.Y.C., 1971-72, 74; Fulbright fellow, 1968-69. Avocations: sailing, music, venetian culture and history. Died Mar. 18, 2008.

**MCREYNOLDS, ROSALEE,** librarian; b. Fukuoka, Japan, Sept. 17, 1950; arrived in U.S., 1952; d. Donald Samuel McReynolds and Lois June Schaefer; m. Eric Christopher Sands, May 29, 1982. BA in English, U. Colo., 1972; MLS, Simmons Coll., 1977; M in Liberal Arts, Boston U., 1980. Head serials Main Libr. Loyola U., New Orleans, 1980—98, libr. spl. collections, from 1998. Contbr. articles to profl. jours. Founder Carrollton, Riverbend Neighborhood Assn., New Orleans, 1990. Recipient Preservation Hero award, Preservation Resource Ctr., 1998, Justin Winsor award, Libr. History Roundtable, 1987. Deceased.

**MEAD, THOMAS FRANCIS,** journalist, author; b. Sydney, May 4, 1918; s. Robert George and Lillian Margaret (Ryan) Mead; m. Vaila Margaret Pender, Apr. 5, 1947; children: Elizabeth Vaila, Richard Thomas, Warwick Robert, David. Degree, Marcellin Coll., 1935. Sub-editor Courier-Mail, Brisbane, 1947—49; chief editl. staff Daily Telegraph, Sydney, 1955—60; mng. editor Suburban Publs., Sydney, 1960—65, editl. dir., 1978—82; chmn., dirs. Manly Daily, Sydney, 1974—82; mng. dir. Newspaper & Media Svcs., Sydney, from 1982. Editl. cons. Eastern Suburbs Newspapers, Sydney, 1983—88. Author: Man is Never Free, 1946, Killers of Eden, 1961, A Newspaper Style Guide, 1981, North Head Goes South, 1987, Manly Ferries of Sydney Harbour, 1988, The Fatal Lights, 1993, Empire of Straw, 1994, Breaking the News, 1999. Mem. NSW Parliament Seat of Hurstville, 1965—76, NSW State Exec. Liberal Party of Australia, 1978—83; govt. rep. City of Sydney Eisteddfod, 1966—76; bd. govs. NSW State Conservatorium Music, Sydney, 1966—78. Recipient Order of Australia medal, Australian Govt., 1994. Mem.: Sydney Journalists, Commonwealth Parliamentary Assn., Australian Nat. Com. Commonwealth Press Union, Australian Suburban Newspapers Assn. (nat. pres. 1978—79). Roman Catholic. Died Jan. 22, 2004.

**MEADERS, PAUL LE SOURD,** lawyer; b. Amarillo, Tex., Feb. 1, 1930; s. Irene (Pumroy) Lorna; m. Rockefeller Patricia, Mar. 21, 1953 (dec.); m. W. Dickely Jane, Apr. 2, 1966; children: P. Phyllis, Paul Le Sourd III. BA, U. Va., 1952; LLB, U. Tex., 1957; LLM, NYU, 1961. Bar: Tex. 1956, NY 1959. Atty. office chief counsel IRS, 1957—59; asst. US Atty. So. Dist, NY, 1951—61; assoc. Breed Abbott & Morgan, NYC, 1961—63; ptnr. Morris & McVeigh, NYC, 1967—77, McKenzie, Meaders & Ives, NYC, 1977—90, Meaders, Duckworth & Moore, from 1990. Reid & Priest, NYC, 1963—67. 1st lt. US Army, 1952—54. Mem.: ABA (with estate tax com. tax sect.), U. Va. Alumni Assn. (pres. NYC chpt. 1982—84), Internat. Bar Assn., Tex. Bar Assn., NY State Bar Assn., Friendly Sons St. Patrick (life), Vets. Corps Arty. (life), Carlton Club, London, Bronxville Field Club, Pilgrims US Club, Ch. Club. Episcopalian. Home: Bronxville, NY. Deceased.

**MEAGHER, GEORGE VINCENT,** mechanical engineer; b. Halifax, NS, Can., Apr. 23, 1919; s. John Nicholas and Blanche Margaret (Seals) M.; m. Evelyn Margaret Hamm, June 2, 1945; children: Maureen, Lindsey, Lise, Shelagh. BSc, Dalhousie U., Halifax, 1940; B of Engring., McGill U., 1942. Engring. and mgmt. positions in industry, 1942—56; with Dilworth, Secord, Meagher & Assocs. Ltd., Toronto, Canada, 1957—92, chmn., 1985—96; chmn., CEO Champlain Power Products, Ltd., 1970—80; vice chmn. Tata-DSMA, Bombay, 1970—93; pres., CEO DSMA Internat., Inc., 1980—88; dir. State Bank India, Can. Ltd., Toronto, 1984—94; founding dir., past chmn. Can.-India Bus. Coun.; pres. George V. Meagher Inc., Tatacan, Ltd., from 1985. Fellow: Engring. Inst. Can.; mem.: Profl. Engrs. Ont. Home: Toronto, Canada. Died Nov. 26, 2007.

**MEANS, GORDON PAUL,** political science educator; b. Spokane, Wash., May 9, 1927; s. Paul Banwell and Nathalie (Toms) M.; m. Ingunn Norderval, June 11, 1956 (div. Aug. 1985); children: Kristin Louise, Norval Paul, Erik Banwell, Kaia Elizabeth; m. Laurel Braswell, Oct. 10, 1987. Student, Grinnell Coll., 1947-48; BA in Polit. Sci., Reed Coll., 1950; MA, U. Wash., 1952, PhD, 1960. Asst. prof. Willamette U., Salem, Oreg., 1958-60, Gustavus Adolphus Coll., St. Peter, Minn., 1960-65, U. Iowa, Iowa City, 1965-66; assoc. prof. U. Wash., Seattle, 1966-67, McMaster U., Hamilton, Ont., Can., 1967-73, prof., from 1973. Smith-Mundt vis. prof. U. Malaya, Kuala Lumpur, Malaysia, 1962-63; assoc. polit. scientist U. Calif., Berkeley, 1968-69; vis. prof. U. Sumatera Utara, Medan, Indonesia, 1973-74, Inst. Advanced Studies, U. Malaya, Kuala Lumpur, 1982-83; vis. fellow Inst. Southeast Asian Studies, Singapore, 1988-89. Author: MAlaysian Politics, 1970, 2d edit., 1976, Malaysian Politics: The Second Generation, 1991; editor: Development and Underdevelopment in Southeast Asia, 1977, The Past in Southeast Asia's Present, 1978; co-editor: (with Nathalie Meansand Paul Means) Sengoi-English, English-Sengoi Dictionary, 1986. With USN, 1945-46. With USN, 1945-46. Recipient Ford Found. Rsch. award, Malaya, 1954-55, Smith-Mundt, U.S. Govt., Malaya, 1962-63. Ford Found. award Indonesia, 1974-75, Soc. Sco. and Human Rsch. Coun. of Can. award, Indonesia, 1974-75, Socia. Sci. and Humanities Rsch. Coun. Can. award, Malaysia, 1987. Mem. Can. Coun. for SE Asian Studies (v.p. 1971-74, pres. 1976-77), Can. Soc. for Asian Studies, Assn. for Asian Studies, Can. Polit. Sci. Assn., Royal Asiatic Soc., Am. Polit. Sci. Assn. Methodist. Avocations: photography, tennis, skiing. Home: Dundas, Canada. Died Aug. 12, 2010.

**MEANS, ROSALINE,** finance company executive, finance educator; b. Manila; came to U.S., 1952; d. Cheng Peng and Lu Chong (Siy) Limtiuco; m. Cyril Chestnut Means, Jr., Nov. 8, 1958 (dec. Oct., 1992); children: Elizabeth Rose Thayer Means, Annette Thayer Means, Cyril III. AA in Pre-law, U. Santo Tomas, Manila, The Philippines, 1949; BS in Comm. Edn., U. East, Manila, 1951; MA in Edn., U. Iowa, 1953; postgrad., CUNY, 1956-58. Tchr. Chinese Rep. Sch., Manila, 1947-52; corp. dir. and officer various cos. and corps., 1950-70; edn. specialist U. Hosp. Sch., Iowa City, 1952-53; lectr. SUNY Urban Ctr., Bklyn., 1967-73; adj. lectr. cmty. coll. CUNY, 1969-72, various positions, 1973-84; adj. prof. L.I. U., Bklyn., 1978; lectr. Ednl. Opportunity Ctr., Bklyn., 1973-95. Author: First Steps in Conversation, 1954; stage performances include Two for the Seesaw, The Defender, Stage Door. Mem. Legis Adv. Com. N.Y. State Senate, 11th. Dist., 1990; treas. PSC/CUNY. Recipient Cmty. Leaders and Noteworthy Ams. award, 1975-76, formal recognition Bus. and Profl. Women of Cape Ann, 1996; named Goddess of Arts-Beauty Queen, 1954, Miss Fashion Model of Yr., 1954; finalist Mrs. N.Y. Am. Beauty Pageant, 1990. Mem. Liedenkranz of City of N.Y. (music libr. and treas.). Avocations: classical music, fishing, boating. Deceased.

**MEDVED, DAVID B.,** optical communications company executive; b. Phila., Feb. 21, 1926; s. Harry and Sarah (Rossman) Medved; m. Renate Rose Hirsch, Oct. 25, 1947; m. Yael Amishav Medved, Sept. 12, 1990; children: Michael, Jonathan, Ben, Harry. BA in Chemistry, U. Pa., 1949; MS in Physics, 1951, PhD, 1955. Rsch. engr., group leader Convair div. Gen. Dynamics Co., San Diego, 1954—63; lectr., assoc. prof. solid state electronics UCLA, 1961—65; chief scientist Electro-Optical Sys., Pasadena, Calif., 1963—69; pres., tech. dir. MERET, Inc., Santa Monica, 1969—90; founder, mng. dir. Optical Link Techs., from 1990. Lectr. San Diego State U., 1961—63. Contbr. articles to various publs. Mem.: IEEE, Sierra (LA). Achievements include patents for on microwave antennas. Home: Jerusalem, Israel. Died Mar. 11, 2009.

**MEEKS, WILLIAM HERMAN, III,** lawyer; b. Ft. Lauderdale, Fla., Dec. 30, 1939; s. Walter Herman Jr. and Elise Walker (McGuire) M.; m. Patricia Ann Rayburn, July 30, 1965; 1 son, William Herman IV; m. 2d, Miriam Andrea Bedsole, Dec. 28, 1971; 1 child, Julie Marie. AB, Princeton U., 1961; LLB, U. Fla., 1964; LLM in Tax, NYU, 1965. Bar: Fla 1964, US Dist. Ct. (so. dist.) Fla. 1965, US Tax Ct. 1966, US Ct. Appeals (11th cir.) 1981, US Supreme Ct. 1985. Ptnr. McCune, Hiaasen, Crum, Ferris & Gardner, Ft. Lauderdale, 1964-89, Fleming, O'Bryan & Fleming, Ft. Lauderdale, 1990-95, Dobbins, Meeks, Raleigh & Dover, Ft. Lauderdale, from 1995. Dir. Attys. Title Svcs., Inc., 1978-79, Attys. Title Svcs. of Broward County, Inc., 1971—, chmn., 1976-77; mem. Attys. Real Estate Coun. Broward County. Mem. ABA, Fla. Bar Assn., Broward County Bar Assn., Attys. Title Ins. Fund, Ft. Lauderdale Hist. Soc., Ft. Lauderdale Mus., Kiwanis, Lauderdale Yacht Club, Tower Club (Ft. Lauderdale), Phi Delta Phi. Democrat. Presbyterian. Home: Fort Lauderdale, Fla. Died Jan. 30, 2014.

**MEIER, MARIANNE MARLYN,** hospital chaplain; b. Milw., Jan. 19, 1939; f. Helmuth Diederich and Gertrude Rose (Elschner) M.; m. Wayne V. Dittrich, Feb. 8, 1964 (div. June 1980); children: Victor W. Dittrich, Elizabeth Dittrich Acharya, Wayne W. H. Dittrich. BS, Washington U., St. Louis, 1965; MA, U. Mich., 1976, EdD, 1986; MDiv, Wesley Theol. Sem., 1995. Pub. rels. adminstrv. asst. Concordia Sem., St. Louis, 1959—62; English tchr. N.E. Sr. H.S., Kansas City, Mo., 1965—69; fashion merchandising tchr. Baker Coll., Flint, Mich., 1976—79, Cleary Coll., Ypsilanti, Mich., 1980—83; acad. advisor, mem. faculty Coll. Lifelong Learning Concordia Coll., Ann Arbor, Mich., 1988—91; 1st resident chaplain William Beaumont Hosp., Royal Oak, Mich., 1992—93; student asst. min. Good Shepherd United Meth. Ch., Silver Spring, Md., 1993—95; assoc. min. pastoral care and visitation First United Meth. Ch., Birmingham, Mich., 1995—97, Immanuel United Meth. Ch., Eastpoint, Mich., 1995—97; pastor Grace United Meth. Ch., Britton, Mich., 1997—98; chaplain William Beaumont Hosp., Royal Oak, Mich., from 1998. Lectr. in ednl. founds. and philosophy Oakland U., Rochester, Mich., 1998—99. Author: Understanding the School Prayer Issue and the Related Character Education and Charter School Movements, 2002. V.p. bd. dirs. Chandler Park Acad., Detroit, 1996-99; parent vol. Ann Arbor Schs. Open Classroom Program, 1980-86; pres., v.p., program chair, chaplain Lapeer County (Mich.) Gen. Hosp. Aux., 1972-76; bd. dirs. Lapeer County Day Care Ctr., 1974. Mem.: S.E. Mich. Healthcare Chaplains Assn., Mich. Acad. Sci., Arts and Letters. Avocations: reading, writing, travel. Home: Bloomfield Hills, Mich. Died Aug. 20, 2002.

**MEILKE, PETER A.,** lawyer, accountant; b. Seattle, Oct. 23, 1946; s. Arthur J. and Helen J. (Damon) M.; m. Charlene M. Hamrah, Jan. 9, 1982. BA, Whitworth Coll., 1968; JD, U. Mich., 1975; LLM in Taxation, NYU, 1980. Bar: N.Y. 1977, U.S. Dist. Ct. (so. and ea. dists.) N.Y. 1977, U.S. Tax Ct. 1977. Tax supr. Coopers & Lybrand, NYC, 1975-79; assoc. Haight, Gardner, Poor & Havens, NYC, 1979-82; assoc. gen. counsel Skandia Am. Group, NYC, 1982-84; sole practice NYC, 1984-89; ptnr. Meilke & Holladay, NYC, from 1989. Adj. asst. prof. econ. Hunter Coll. CUNY, N.Y.C., 1985—; treas., dir. Regional EMS Council N.Y.C., Inc., 1979—. Mem. ABA, N.Y. State Bar Assn. Home: New York, NY. Died Feb. 1, 1999.

**MELADY, THOMAS PATRICK,** academic administrator, ambassador, author, public policy expert, educator; b. Norwich, Conn., Mar. 4, 1927; m. Margaret Judith Badum; children: Christina, Monica. BA, Duquesne U., 1950; MA, Cath. U. Am., 1952, PhD, 1954. Faculty mem. Fordham and St. John's Universities; founder Inst. African Affairs Duquesne U., 1957; cons. to founds., govt. corps., 1959-67; hon. doctorates from 28 univs. Africa Service Inst.; prof. Afro-Asian affairs, chmn. dept. Asian studies and NonWestern civilization Seton Hall U., South Orange, N.J., 1967-69, regent, 1987-90; prof. Afro-Asian affairs, dir. Office of Internat. Studies, 1973-74; exec. v.p., prof. politics St. Joseph's U., Phila., 1974-76; pres. Sacred Heart U., Fairfield, Conn., 1976-86, prof. polit. sci., 1976-86, pres. emeritus, 1986—2014; asst. sec. for postsecondary edn. US Dept. Edn., Washington, 1981-82; US amb. to Burundi US Dept. State, Bujumbura, 1969-72, US amb. to Uganda Kampala, 1972-73; sr. adviser to U.S. del. to 25 UN Gen. Assembly, 1970; chmn. Conn. Conf. Ind. Colleges, 1979-81; pres., CEO Conn. Public Expenditures Coun., 1986-89; US amb. to The Holy See US Dept. State, Vatican City, 1989-93, 94-95; exec. dir. Cath. Network of Vol. Svc., 1993-94; v.p. Capital Formation Counselors, 1993—2014. Disting. vis. prof. George Washington U. and St. John's U., 1993—94; vis. prof. Rome Grad. Ctr., 1998—99, Pontifical Gregorian U., 2001; chmn. nat. com. Cath. Campaign for America, 1994—99; counsel to govts. and bus.; prof., sr. diplomat in residence Inst. of World Politics, 2001—14. Author: Ambassadors Story: The United States and The Vatican in World Affairs, 1994, (memoirs) Faith Family Friends, 2003, and 16 other books. Knighted by Pope Paul VI, 1968 and by Pope John Paul II, 1983, 91; honored by 6 countries; recipient Native Son award, Grand Cross, Order of Malta, 1993. Mem.: Soc. of The Cincinnati, The Sacred Mil. Constantinian Order of St. George, Order of Malta. Home: Washington, DC. Died Jan. 6, 2014.

**MELIA, KEVIN CHRISTOPHER,** retired manufacturing executive; b. Ashford; s. Richard and Mary (Doyle) Melia; m. Ann Marie Lally; 4 children. Various positions Digital Equipment Corp., 1973—89; exec. v.p. ops. Sun Microsystems, Inc., 1993—94; CEO Manufacturers' Services Ltd., Concord, Mass., 1994—2002; non-exec. chmn. Iona Technologies PLC, 2003—08, A.Net, 2003—07, Vette Corp., 2009—12. Bd. dirs. Greatbatch, Inc., 2007—14, Analogic Corp., 2009—14. Died June 17, 2014.

**MELLERS, WILFRID HOWARD,** musician, educator; b. Leamington, Warwickshire, Eng., Apr. 26, 1914; s. Percival Wilfrid and Hilda Maria (Lawrence) M.; m. Vera Hobbs, 1939 (div. 1948); m. Peggy Pauline Lewis, 1950 (div. 1976); children: Judith, Olivia, Caroline, Sarah; m. Robin Stephanie Hildyard. BA, Cambridge U., Eng., 1936, MA, 1939; DMus, Birmingham U., 1960; DPhil, City U., London, 1982. Tutor in English Downing Coll., U. Cambridge, 1945-48; tutor in music extra mural dept. Birmingham (Eng.) U., 1948-60; Disting. Andrew Mellon prof. music U. Pitts., 1960-63; prof. music, head dept. music U. York, Eng., 1964-81, Wilfrid Mellers emeritus prof., 1981—2008; fellow Guildhall Sch. Music, Eng., 1982. Advisor sundry pubs.; mem. music festival coms. Author: Francois Couperin and the French Classical Tradition, 1950, 2d. edit., 1987, Music in a New Found Land, 1964, 2d revised edit., 1988, Bach and the Dance of God, 1980, Beethoven and the Voice of God, 1983, Angels of the Night: Popular Female Singers of Our Time, 1986, The Masks of Orpheus, 1987, Le Jardin Retrouve: The Music of Frederic Mompou, 1988, Vaughan Williams and the Vision of Albion, 1989, Percy Grainger, 1992, Francis Poulenc, 1993, Between Old Worlds and New, 1997, Singing in the Wilderness: Music and Ecology in the Twentieth Century, 2000, Celestial Music?: Some Masterpieces of European Religious Music, 2002 Named to Order of Brit. Empire, 1984. Died May 16, 2008.

**MELTON, BUCKNER FRANKLIN,** lawyer, former mayor; b. Arlington, Ga., Oct. 24, 1923; s. Henry Martin and Mary (Layman) M.; m. Tommie Jean Beck, Oct. 24, 1954; children: Mary Leigh, Buckner Franklin. Student, Norman Coll., 1941-42; AB, Mercer U., 1949; LL.B., Walter F. George Sch. Law, 1949. Bar: Ga. 1948. Pvt. practice law, Macon, Ga., 1949-51, 53-64; sr. mem. Melton, McKenna & House, Macon, 1964-75; mayor City of Macon, Ga., 1975-80; chmn. bd. dirs. Filmworks U.S.A., Inc., Atlanta, 1975-80. Lectr. Inst. Continuing Edn. (Legal) in Ga., 1971; bd. dirs. Forest Services, Inc., Macon, YKK Industries (U.S.A.), Inc., Macon; city atty., Macon, 1959-63; atty. Middle Ga. Coliseum Authority, 1963-75, Macon Bibb County Indsl. Authority, 1964-75 Contbr. articles in field to profl. jours. Mem. Ga. Bd. Industry and Trade, 1978-83; bd. visitors Ga. Coll.; exec. com. Forward Macon; bd. govs. Mercer Med. Sch. Served with USN, 1942-46, 51-52. Recipient Lawyer of Year award Macon Bar Assn., 1972; Algernon Sydney Sullivan award Mercer U., 1975 Mem. ABA, Macon Bar Assn. (pres. 1961), State Bar Ga., Greater Macon Chamber of Commerce (pres. 1971) Clubs: Macon Civic (pres. 1961), Idle Hour Golf & Country (pres. 1970), Elks. Democrat. Baptist. Home: Macon, Ga. Died Mar. 5, 2014.

**MENDEL, LOUISE A.,** interior design company executive; b. New Orleans, Nov. 3, 1896; d. Jacob and Stella (Bloom) Abraham; m. Walter Scott Mendel, Aug. 2, 1916; children: Louise Stella, Charles. With Strassel Co., Louisville, from 1929, pres., 1946—79, chmn. bd. dirs., from 1979. Mem.: Nat. Antique and Art Dealers Assn. America Inc., Am. Soc. Interior Decorators. Republican. Died July 1992.

**MENDOZA, LEANDRO RAMOS,** Philippine government official; b. San Juan, Batangas, Philippines, Mar. 17, 1946; m. Soledad Latorre; 6 children. BSc., Philippine Mil. Acad.; MA in Pub. Mgmt., U. Philippines, Cebu City. Platoon leader 2nd Spl. Forces; commdg. officer 3rd METROCOM Patrol Co., 1970—72; chief Spl. Ops., MPIS, 1972—74; dep. comdr. Investigations and Intel Unit, METROCOM, 1974—75; commdg. officer Investigation Unit, METROCOM, 1975—79; dep. comdr. South Sector PC METROCOM, 1979—80; provincial comdr. PS Cebu, 1980—84; sector comdr. Eastern Sector, PCM, 1985—86; provincial comdr. Rizal, 1985—86, Bulacan, 1985—89, Pangasinan, 1989—90; chief of staff Regional Command 4, 1990—91; TF Comdr. Mina de Oro Task Force, 1991; chief directorial staff ARMM, 1991—92; dep dir. Directorate for Intelligence, 1992—93; regional dir. Regional Command 4, 1994—95, Nat. Capital Region Ctr. (NCRC), 1995—96; chief directorial staff, 1995—96; dep. chief PNP for Adminstr., 1997—98; vice-chmn PSMBFI, from 1997; exec. dir. Philippine Ctr. on Transnational Crime, 1999—2001; acting chief Philippine Nat. Police, 2001, chief, 2002; sec. Philippine Dept. Transp. & Comm., 2002—10; exec. sec. Govt. of Philippines, 2010. Decorated PNP Distinguished Service medal (3) Philippine Army, Distinguished Conduct Star, Distinguished Service medal (5), Spl. service medal; recipient Plaque of Merit and Letters of Commendation, Distinguished Personalities and Socio-Civic Orgns.; scholar U. Philippines. Mem.: Philippine Mil. Acad. Alumni Assoc., Inc. (PMAAAI) (pres. 1998—99), Assoc. of Chief of Police of the Philippines Inc. (ACCPI). Died Oct. 7, 2013.

**MENNELLA, VINCENT ALFRED,** automotive manufacturing and airplane company executive; b. Teaneck, NJ, Oct. 7, 1922; s. Francis Anthony and Henrietta Vernard (Dickson) M.; m. Madeleine Olson, Aug. 18, 1945; children: Bruce, Cynthia, Mark, Scott, Chris. BA in Acctg., U. Wash., 1948. Various sales and bus. mgmt. positions Ford divsn. Ford Motor Co., 1949-55; founder, pres. Southgate Ford, Seattle, 1955-80; pres. Flightcraft, Inc., Seattle, 1973-86; chmn. bd. Stanley Garage Door Co., Seattle, 1981-86, Zman Magnetics, Seattle, from 1990. Past chmn. March of Dimes. Capt. USNR, 1942-45. Mem. Rainier Golf Club, Seattle Tennis Club, Rotary (past pres. Seattle). Republican. Roman Catholic. Home: Seattle, Wash. Died 2001.

**MENSINGER, PEGGY BOOTHE,** retired mayor; b. Modesto, Calif., Feb. 18, 1923; d. Dyas Power and Margaret (Stewart) Boothe; m. John Logan Mensinger, May 25, 1952; children: John B., Stewart I., Susan B. AB in Polit. Sci, Stanford U., 1944. Reporter San Francisco Red Cross Chpt. News Bur., 1944; acting mgr. Boothe Fruit Co., Modesto, Calif., 1945; asst. dir. Stanford (Calif.) Alumni Assn., 1947; exec. sec. pub. exercises com. Stanford U., 1949-51; mem. Modesto City Council, 1973-79, mayor, 1979-87; ret., 1987. Mem. adv. bd. Agrl. Issues Ctr. U. Calif., 1988-94. Bd. dirs. Nat. coun. Girl Scouts U.S.A., 1978-87, Calif. Planning and Conservation League, 1980—; adv. bd. U. Calif. Agricultural Issues Ctr., 1988-94; Friends Outside Nat. Bd., 1991-93; chmn. Citizens Com. for Internat. Students, 1965-70; pres. Modesto PTA Coun., 1967-69, Modesto chpt. Am. Field Svc., 1969-70, Stanislaus County Hist. Soc., 1970-71; mem. state bd. Common Cause, 1973-75; chmn. Modesto City Cultural Commn., 1968-73; del. White House Conf. on Families, L.A., 1980; chmn. Stanislaus Area Assn. Govts., 1976-77; chmn. air quality subcom. U.S. Conf. Mayors, 1985-87. Recipient Woman of Yr. award VFW Aux., 1980, Man of Yr. award Am. Legion, 1987, State of Calif. Legislature Women of Yr. Mem. Nat. League Am. Pen Women (assoc.), Stanford Assocs. (pres. 1985-87), Soroptimist (hon., Women Achievement award 1980), Phi Beta Kappa, Gamma Phi Beta. Unitarian Universalist. Died 2002.

**MERCER, RICHARD JOSEPH,** retired advertising executive, freelance writer; b. Elizabeth, NJ, Mar. 29, 1924; s. George Washington and Margaret Elizabeth (Walsh) M.; m. Muriel Davis, June 24, 1945 (dec. Mar. 1999); children: Richard George, Karen, James Davis, Lesley Ann; m. Joan Youmans Cozens, Apr. 2, 2001. L.B. in Journalism, Rutgers U., 1949. Announcer, copywriter, news reporter Sta. WCTC, New Brunswick, N.J., 1946-49; asso. creative dir., then v.p., dir. BBDO, Inc., NYC, 1949-76; sr. v.p., creative exec. SSC&B, Inc., NYC, 1977-83, exec. v.p. creative, 1983-85; sr. v.p., assoc. creative dir. McCann-Erickson, Inc., NYC, 1985-87. Lectr. Rutgers U. Sch. Bus., New Brunswick, NJ, 1988-89; spkr. in field. Chmn. Roselle (N.J.) Police Raise Referendum Com., 1958; promotion chmn. Cranford (N.J.) United Fund, 1960; publicity dir. Friends of Mendham (N.J.) Libr., 1974-75; bd. dirs. Friends of Nantucket Atheneum, 1991-2000, pres., 1996-98; trustee Atheneum, 1993-98; mem. Nantucket Airport Commn., 1999-2002. With A.C. USNR, 1943-45. Decorated Air medal.; Recipient 10 Clio awards, 2 Effie awards, also Silver Key award Advt. Writers Assn. N.Y.C. Mem. NATAS, Air Force Assn. (life), Nat. Assn. Scholars, Col. Henry Rutgers Soc., Am. Fedn. Musicians, Broadcasters Found. Roman Catholic. Died Dec. 20, 2006.

**MERCIER, PAUL,** retired Canadian government official; b. Brussels, July 26, 1924; widowed; children: Cécile, Pascal. Degree in math., Belgium. Travelling rep. Colocoton Co., Belgian Congo, 1947-54; exec., univ. ofcl. Ruanda-Urundi Univ., Elisabethville, Belgian Congo, 1957-60; exec. Internat. Inst., Lubumbashi, Zaire, 1961-63; tchr. secondary sch. Athenée, Ciney, Belgium, 1963-64; prof. math. Coll. d'enseignement gén. et profl. Lionel-Groulx, St. Thérese, Que., Can., 1964-89; mayor City of Blainville, Que., 1977-93; mem. parliament Can. House of Commons, Blainville-Deux Montagnes, 1993-97, Terrebonne-Blainville, 1997—2000. With Belgian Army, 1944-45. Mem. Assn. Intermunucipal Transport Bds. (founder, former pres.). Died Aug. 7, 2013.

**MERDINGER, CHARLES JOHN,** civil engineer, military officer, academic administrator; b. Chgo., Apr. 20, 1918; s. Walter F. and Catherine (Phelan) M.; m. Mary McKelleget, Oct. 21, 1944; children: Anne, Joan, Susan, Jane. Student, Marquette U., 1935-37; BS, U.S. Naval Acad., 1941; BCE, Rensselaer Poly. Inst., 1945, MCE, 1946; DPhil (Rhodes scholar), Brasenose Coll., Oxford U., Eng., 1949; LHD (hon.), Sierra Nev. Coll., 1987; DLitt (hon.), U. Nev., Reno, 1994. Registered profl. engr., Wis. PFC Wis. Nat. Guard, 1935—37; commd. ensign USN, 1941, advanced through grades to capt. Civil Engr. Corps, 1959; served aboard USS Nevada, USS Alabama Atlantic and Pacific, 1941-44; design, constrn. pub. works Panama, 1946—47, Washington, Bremerton, Adak, Miramar, 1949—56; comdg. officer, dir. U.S. Naval Civil Engring. Lab., Port Hueneme, Calif., 1956-59; pub. works officer U.S. Fleet activities, Yokosuka, Japan, 1959-62; head English, history and govt. dept. U.S. Naval Acad., Annapolis, Md., 1962-65; asst. comdr. ops. & maintenance Naval Facilities Engring. Command, Navy Dept., 1965-67; pub. works officer Seabees (NSA), DaNang, Vietnam, 1967-68; comdg. officer Western div. Naval Facilities Engring. Command, San Bruno, Calif., 1968-70; 21st pres. Washington Coll., Chestertown, Md., 1970-73; v.p. Aspen Inst. Humanistic Studies, Colo., 1973-74; dep. dir. Scripps Instn. Oceanography, La Jolla, Calif., 1974-80; dir. Avco, from 1978. Author: Civil Engineering Through the Ages, 1963; contbr.: articles to Ency. Britannica; others. Mem. Md., Calif., Oreg. and Nev. Selection Coms. for Rhodes Scholars, sec. Nev. Com., 1982-89; exec. vol. Boy Scouts Am.; sec., mem. exec. com. Md. Ind. Coll. and Univ. Assn., 1971-72; mem. So. Regional Edn. Bd, 1971-73, Nat. Com. History and Heritage of Am. Civil Engring., 1965-72; Alumni trustee U.S. Naval Acad., 1971-74; mem. coun. Rensselear Poly. Inst., 1972—; trustee Found. for Ocean Rsch., 1976-80, Desert Rsch. Inst. Found., Nev., 1983-92, U. Nev. Reno Found., 1986-93; chmn. bd. trustees Sierra Nev. Coll., 1980-87, chmn. bd. emeritus, 1987; commr. N.W. Assn. Commn. on Colls., 1988-93. Decorated Legion of Merit with combat V; named All-Am. in lacrosse, 1945, Papal Knight Grand Cross Equestrian Order of Holy Sepulchre of Jerusalem, 1992; inducted into Rensselaer Athletic Hall of Fame, 1983; recipient Disting. Eagle Scout award, 1984. Fellow ASCE (Nat. History and Heritage award 1972), Explorers Club, Soc. Am. Mil. Engrs. (Toulmin medal 1952, 57, 61); mem. NSPE, Am. Soc. Engring. Edn., Brasenose Soc., Pearl Harbor Survivors Assn., Nat. Eagle Scout Assn. (regent), Phalanx, Sigma Xi, Tau Beta Pi, Chi Epsilon. Clubs: Vincent's, Oxford. Roman Catholic. Home: Incline Village, Nev. Died Dec. 13, 2013.

**MERRILL, WILLIAM DICKEY,** architect; b. Honolulu, Mar. 21, 1909; s. Arthur Merton and Grace (Dickey) M.; m. Evelyn Gregory Selfridge, Oct. 23, 1936 (dec. Mar. 1997); children: Elizabeth, Thomas Selfridge. BA, U. Calif., Berkeley, 1930; MArch, Harvard U., 1932; PhD, Edinburgh U., 1974. Staff achitect Am. Schs. Oriental Rsch., Jerusalem, 1933-35; assoc. C.W. Dickey, architect, Honolulu, 1936-42; ptnr. Merrill, Simms and Roehrig, architects, Honolulu, 1942-60; pres. Merrill, Roehrig, Onodera and Kinder, Inc., Honolulu, 1960-65; cons. architect Honolulu, 1965-81. Mem. affiliate grad. faculty U. Hawaii, 1971. Prin. works include Neill Blaisdell Concert Hall, campus Mid-Pacific Inst., campus Kamehameha Elem. Sch., class rm. bldg. Kamehameha Girls Sch., Foremost Dairies, TH-3 Hawaii Housing Authority, other comml., indsl., ednl. and mil. structures, hosps. in Hawaii. Mem. com. mgmt. Armed Svcs. YMCA, 1952-69; bd. dirs. Hawaiian Humane Soc., 1954-65, Hawaiian Mission Children's Soc., 1945-64. Fellow AIA (past pres. Hawaii, mem. emeritus). Home: Carmel, Calif. Deceased.

**MERRITT, AGNES SOMMER,** retired educator; b. NYC, Mar. 13, 1899; d. Max and Meta (Bleier) Sommer; m. Lester Michael Merritt, Feb. 23 1920 (dec. 1958); 1 child, Croft Sommer. BA cum laude, Hunter Coll., 1920; MSc, Ohio State U., 1922. Tchr. Wallace Sch. for Girls, Columbus, Ohio, 1922-32, Columbus Pub. Schs., 1932-65. State chmn. Women's State Com. for Pub. Welfare, Health and Edn., 1941-47; trustee Columbus Citizenship com., 1975—; mem. pub. affairs com. YWCA, 1970, mem. Friends of YWCA Group, 1982—; founder Ohio Am. Legion Auxiliary Buckeye Girls' State, 1947, dean of govt., 1947-68, bd. dirs., 1968-79; mem. Ohio's Status of Women Com., 1961-63; founder Franklin County Children's Soc.; mem. legis. com. Columbus Edn. Assn.; mem., parliamentarian Ohio Rep. Women's Fedn.; pres. Columbus Women's Rep. Club, 1968-70; mem. women's div. Ohio Bur. Employment Svcs., 1976-84. Recipient Freedom Found. Tchrs. award, 1961, Ohio House of Reps. Commendations, 1960, 79, 83, State of Ohio Digests Citations and Plaques, 1960-70, Good Neighbor award, 1985, 86, Columbus Mayor's award Vol. Svcs., 1979, Woman of Yr. award. Columbus Women's Rep. Club of Ohio, 1986; nominated to Ohio State Woman's Hall of Fame, 1978, Nat. Register of Prominent Women, 1960; named to Hunter Coll. Alumnae Hall of Fame, 1974. Mem. Ohio Fedn. of Bus. and Profl. Women (pres. Columbus chpt. 1959, state pres., nat. legis. chmn. 1960, Woman of the Yr. 1973, state parliamentarian), AAUW (pres. Columbus chpt. 1967-68, parliamentarian 1984—, Br. Woman of the Month 1964, Woman of the Yr. 1966, 87), Res. Officers Assn. Ladies Club (state parliamentarian 1975—), Am. Inst. Parliamentarians (cert.), Am. Legion Aux. (state pres. 1932-34, nat. area chmn. 1935, nat. conv. resolutions chmn., pres. Franklin County Coun. 1968, state parliamentarian 1967—), Nat. and County Retired Tchrs. Assn., Delta Kappa Gamma (pres. Beta Lambda chpt. 1964-66, cert. and state parliamentarian), Phi Beta Kappa, Pi Mu Epsilon. Home: Columbus, Ohio. Deceased.

**MERRY, FRIEDA ANNETTA,** educator; b. Dayton, Ohio, July 20, 1897; d. Charles Albert and Caroline Agnes (Schaefer) Merry; m. Ralph Vickers Merry, June 1, 1929 (dec. 1972). BA, Ohio State U., 1921, PhD, 1927; MA, U. Mich., 1923; postgrad., U. Wash., 1923—24. Rsch. asst. U. Mich., Ann Arbor, 1921—23; psychol. examiner Pub. Schs., Seattle, 1923—24; asst. prof. psychology Whittenberg Coll., Springfield, Ohio, 1924—26; dir. dept. spl. studies Am. Found. Blind, NYC, 1927—32, Perkins Inst. Blind, Watertown, Mass., 1927—32; prof. psychology, dean women Alfred Holbrook Coll., Lebanon, Ohio, 1933—34; prof. psychology Morris Harvey Coll., Charleston, W.Va., 1934—62; prof. emeritus, from 1962; cons. in field. Mem. editorial bd. W.Va. Single Curriculum. Chmn. W.Va. Com. Human Growth and Devel.; mem. quality fund U. Charleston, 1981. Author (with Ralph V. Merry): (book) From Infancy to Adolescence, 1940; author: The First Two Decades of Life, 1950; contbr. articles to profl. jours. and publs. Fellow: Internat. Council Psychologists, Am. Psychol. Assn. (emeritus); mem.: AAUP (emeritus), AAAS (life), W.Va. Psychol. Assn. (life; co-founder, Disting. Psychologist 1983), Nat. Congl. Club. Lutheran. Avocations: reading, travel, genealogy. Home: Charleston, W.Va. Deceased.

**MERTÉ, HANNS-JÜRGEN,** ophthalmologist; b. Jena, Thüringen, Germany, Aug. 17, 1921; s. Willy Walter and Antonie Isabella Philomena M.; m. Gertrud Maria Elisabeth Richter, July 21, 1956; children: Birgit, Nicole, Ralph-Laurent, Egmont. MD, Friedr-Schiller U., 1945. Specialist in ophthalmology. Asst. U. Hosp. of Internal Medicine, Friedr.-Schiller U., Jena, 1945; univ. asst. eye hosp. Ludwig Maxim. U., Munich, 1945-48, head of policlinic, 1948-63; chief eye depts. of hosps. City of Munich, 1963-67; dir. of eye infirmary, prof. ordinarius, chair ophthalmology Tech. U. of Munich, 1967-90, prof. ordinarius emeritus, from 1990. Senator Ludwig-Maximillian U., Munich, 1952-53; examiner on med. examination State of Bayern, Munich, 1950-90; curator Bavarian Acad. of Occupl. Medicine, 1974-90; Bavarian state expert on affairs of blind and visual handicapped persons, others, 1962—. Editor, author: Pathogenesis of Glaucomas, 1978, Metipranolol-Pharmacology of Beta-Blocking Agents and Use of Metipranolol in Ophthalmology, 1983-84; editor, co-editor, author many books; contbr. articles to profl. jours. Pres. scientific dept. eye and sight German Green Cross, 1976-90; mem., councillor Kuratorium Gutes Sehen, Cologne, 1976-90; mem. Internat. Glaucoma Congress, 1977—, v.p. 1989. Asst. Friedrich-Wilhelms-Akademie, 1941-45. Recipient Johann-Heinrich August Duncker gold medal Kuratorium Gutes Sehen, 1987, Sir Stewart Duke Elder Glaucoma award Internat. Glaucoma Congress, 1989, Martti Liesma medal Ergophthalmol. Soc. of Finland, 1984, Ernst von Bergmann Plakettes, 1981, Bundes-Ärzte-Kammer Physicians Fed. Republic Germany. Mem. Societas Ergophthalmologica Internationalis (founding pres. 1966-78, hon. life pres. 1978), Academia Ophthalmologica Internationalis. Achievements include research on Glaucomas, and in cornea immunology; developments of methods, and implements of eye examinations, and inventions of eye operation instruments; guidelines for methods of diagnosis, treatments and care of glaucomas. Home: Munich, Germany. Died Apr. 13, 2003.

**MERTENS, JOSEF WILHELM,** aerospace engineer; b. Aachen, Rheinland, Germany, Aug. 6, 1946; s. Joseph Peter and Maria (Schrouff) M.; m. Barbara Kuesters, Aug. 28, 1970 (div. Jan. 1994); children: Yvonne, Birgit, Stephan, Monika; m. Astrid Gumbrecht, Mar. 13, 2000. Diplomate aerospace, U. Tech., Aachen, 1972, PhD in Aerospace Engring., 1983. Asst. Lehrstuhl fuer Mechanik, U. Tech., Aachen, 1972-84; with theoretical aerodyn. Transport und Verkehrsflugzeuge Messerschmitt-Boelkow-Blohm GmbH, Bremen, Germany, 1984-86; coord. aerodyn. for high speed aircraft and reentry vehicles dept. EF1 Deutsche Airbus GmbH, Bremen, 1987-2000; prof. fluid dynamics Aachen U. Applied Scis., from 2000. Mem. steering com. Minister for Rsch. and Tech. Study on High Speed Transport, Bonn, Germany, Munich, 1986-87, Brite-Euram: Supersonic Flow, Brussels, 1987-92, Eurosup, EC, Brussels, 1996-98; tech. mem. Supersonic Comml. Transport Internat. Study Group Sonic Boom, 1990—96; mem. BMFT Group Hypersonics, Bonn, 1989—94; head German tech. programme on Cruise Drag Reduction, 1994—98; bilateral study on supersonic transport Boeing DASA, 1992—94; trilateral study on Supersonic Transport, AS BAe DASA, responsible for DASA Aerodynamics, 1994—96; subject group leader aerodynamics Adaptive Wing project DB, DLR, DASA, 1997—2000; head German tech. programme Megaflug, 1999—2000; chmn. Airbus Area coord. Group Aerodynamics, 1999—2000; expert for aerodynamics and MDO in FP5 and FP6 EC, Brussels, 2001—08; lectr. U. Aachen, Bremen, Internat. Ctr. Mech. Scis. confs., Udine, Italy, Von Karman Inst., Brussels, from 1980. Author, co-author publs., from 1983. Recipient Wilhelm Borchers medal, U. Tech., 1984. Mem.: AIAA (sr.), Orgn. Sci. et Technique Internat. de Vol à Voile, Deutsche Gesellschaft fuer Luft-und Raumfahrt. Roman Catholic. Home: Aachen, Germany. Died Aug. 27, 2008.

**MERTENS, THOMAS ROBERT,** biology professor; b. Fort Wayne, Ind., May 22, 1930; s. Herbert F. and Hulda (Burg) M.; m. Beatrice Janet Abair, Apr. 1, 1953; children: Julia Ann, David Gerhard BS, Ball State U., 1952; MS, Purdue U., 1954, PhD, 1956. Research assoc. dept. genetics U. Wis.-Madison, 1956-57; asst. prof. biology Ball State U., Muncie, Ind., 1957-62, assoc. prof., 1962-66, prof., 1966-93, dir. doctoral programs in biology, 1974-93, George and Frances Ball disting. prof. biology edn., 1988-93, prof. emeritus, from 1993. Author: (with A. M. Winchester) Human Genetics, 1983 (with R.L. Hammersmith) Genetics Laboratory Investigations, 13th edit., 2007 (co-recipient William Holmes McGuffey Longevity award Text and Acad. Authors Assn. 1998); contbr. numerous articles to profl. jours. Co-recipient Gustav Ohaus award for innovative coll. sci. tchg. NSTA, 1986, recipient Disting. Svc. to Sci. Edn. citation, 1987; fellow NSF, 1963-64, Ind. Acad. Scis., 1969. Fellow AAAS; mem. Nat. Assn. Biology Tchrs. (pres. 1985, hon. mem. 1988), Am. Genetic Assn., Genetics Soc. Am. Episcopalian. Home: Muncie, Ind. Died Jan. 3, 2014.

**MESSERLE, HUGO KARL,** electrical engineer, consultant; b. Haifa, Palestine, Oct. 25, 1925; arrived in Australia, 1942; s. Theophil and Anna (Blaich) M.; m. Renate Ursula Meyer, June 6, 1955; children: Karin, Barbara. BEE, U. Melbourne, Australia, 1950, M Engring. Sci., 1951; PhD, U. Sydney, Australia, 1958; DSc, U. Melbourne, Australia, 1968. Lectr. in elec. engring. U. Sydney, Australia, 1952-55, sr. lectr., 1955-59, reader, 1959-66, prof. elec. engring., 1966-90, head of sch., 1972-83, 87-90, emeritus prof., from 1991. Vis. prof. Cornell U., Ithaca, N.Y., 1964-65; guest prof., U. Stuttgart, 1972; dir. Elec. Engring. Found., U. Sydney, 1980-83, 87-90; mem. Internat. Liaison Group on Magneto-Hydrodynamic Elec. Power Generation (ILG-MHD), 1962—, chmn., 1982-90, founder, mem. bd. ILG-Engring. Edn., 1989—, chmn., 1989-93, chmn. Internat. Conf. on Engring. Edn., Sydney, 1989, chmn. internat. confs., Cambridge, Mass., 1980, Moscow, 1983, Tsukuba, 1986, Beijing, 1990, Whitefish, U.S., 1993; founder, chmn. Australian Computer Rsch. Bd., 1968-70. Author: Dynamic Circuit Theory, 1964; Energy Conversion Statistics, 1969, Magneto-Hydro-Dynamic Electrical Power Generation, 1995; contbg. author: MacMillan Encyclopedia of Energy, 1999; contbr. numerous articles to profl. jours. Sec. com. on edn. for ministry NSW Synod, Uniting Ch. of Australia, 1991-94. Fullbright fellow Cornell U., Ithaca, N.Y., 1958-59; recipient medal Australasian Assn. of Engring. Edn., 1994, Centenary medal, 2003. Fellow IEEE (life, centenary medal, 1984), Australian Acad. Tech. Scis. (coun. mem. 1995—, chmn. comm. sustainable devel., 1992—), Inst. Elec. Engrs. (U.K.), Instn. of Engrs. (Australia, many coms.). Avocation: music. Died Sept. 16, 2004.

**MESSINGER, SHELDON L(EOPOLD),** law educator; b. Chgo., Aug. 26, 1925; s. Leopold J. and Cornelia (Eichel) M.; m. Mildred Handler, June 30, 1947; children— Adam J., Eli B. PhD in Sociology, UCLA, 1969. Assoc. rsch. sociologist Ctr. Study Law and Soc. U. Calif., Berkeley, 1961-69, rsch. sociologist, 1969-70, prof. criminology, 1970-77, prof. law jurisprudence and social policy program, 1977-88, Elizabeth J. Boalt prof. law, 1988-91, prof. law emeritus, from 1991, prof. grad. sch., 1995-97, vice chmn., 1961-69, acting dean criminology, 1970-71, dean criminology, 1971-75, chmn. program, 1983-87. Author, co-author numerous books, articles. Mem. Coun. U. Calif. Emeriti Assns. (chair-elect 1999-2000, chair 2000-01). Home: Berkeley, Calif. Died Mar. 6, 1977.

**MESSNER, ZBIGNIEW,** former prime minister of Poland, politician, economist; b. Stryj, Poland, Mar. 13, 1929; married; 2 children. Grad., Higher Sch. of Econs., Katowice, 1951; M. Econs., Higher Sch. Econs., Cracow, 1952, Dr. Econs., 1961, Dr. Habilitatis, 1969. Dep. prime min. Govt. of Poland, Warsaw, 1983—85, prime min., 1985—88. Mem. ctrl. com. Polish United Workers' Party, 1981—88. Author: numerous publs. in field. Decorated Comdrs. Cross of Polonia Restituta, First Class Banner of Labour; recipient Prizes of Ministry of Sci., Higher Edn. and Tech., Nat. Edn. Commn. medal, 1973, Award Meritorious Tchr. of People's Poland, 1974; named Hon. Miner of Polish People's Republic, 1983. Mem.: Polish Acct. Standards Com., Acctg. Inst. Economics U., Polish Exam. Com. for Candidates for Cert. Auditors, Polish Acctg. Assn., Accts. Assn. in Poland (chmn. sci. coun. 1992—2003), Polish Econ. Soc. (v.p. main bd. 1971—81). Communist. Home: Konstancin-Jeziorna, Poland. Died Jan. 10, 2014.

**MEYER, DIETER SHIPLEY,** retired pathologist; b. Hamburg, Germany, Dec. 8, 1933; s. Hans Carl Friedrich and Hildegard Hertha Meyer; m. Ursula Rollmann, Feb. 4, 1966; children: Carsten, Hilke, Anja. Dr.med., U. Tübingen, Germany, 1958. Sr. pathologist U. Tubingen, 1969-75; head pathology Hosp. Ludwigsburg, Germany, 1976-80; head dept. pathology & toxicology Boehringer Pharms., Ingelheim, Germany, 1981-93; ret., 1994. Prof. pathology U. Tübingen, 1974. Author: The Juxtaglomerular Apparatus in the Human Kidney, 1972; co-author: The Kidney-Structure and Function, 1984, Modern Drug Research, 1989; contbr. articles to profl. jours. Mem. German Soc. Pathology, Internat. Acad. Pathology, Soc. Toxicological Pathologists. Home: Gau-Algesheim, Germany. Died Mar. 14, 2007.

**MEYER, NORMAN J.,** physicist; b. Wilkes-Barre, Pa., Aug. 5, 1930; s. Nathan and Helen (Goldstein) Meyer; m. Shirley Nast Meyer, Aug. 23, 1953 (dec.); children: Lee Ann, Jack, Neal, Joanne. BS, Pa. State U., 1951, MS, 1953; PhD, UCLA, 1959. Rsch. engr. Lockheed Co., Burbank, Calif., 1956—57; rsch. physicist Ford Aerospace, Newport Beach, 1959—61; dir. rsch. Ling-Temco-Vought, Anaheim, Calif., 1962—70; pres., founder Ocean and Atmospheric Sci.-Western, Santa Ana, Calif., 1970—72; dir. rsch. Wyle Labs., El Segundo, 1973—84; v.p., dir. Hearing Conservation Svcs., Inc., Commerce, Calif., 1967—70; clin. prof. cmty. environ. medicine U. Calif., Irvine, from 1979; mem. com. on hearing Nat. Acad. Scis./NRC. Contbr. articles to various publs. inventor momentum transducer for impacting particles. Bd. dirs. Fairview State Hosp., Costa Mesa, Calif., 1963—68; mem. Orange County Fair Bd., 1963—67. Mem.: Acoustical Soc. America, Masons. Democrat. Jewish. Home: Manhattan Beach, Calif. Died Aug. 1990.

**MICHIE, DONALD,** research scientist; b. Rangoon, Burma, Nov. 11, 1923; s. James Kilgour and Marjorie Crain (Pfeiffer) M.; m. Zena Marguerite Davis; 1 son, Christopher; m. Anne McLaren, 1952 (div. 1959); children: Susan Fiona, Jonathan Mark, Caroline Ruth; m. Jean Elizabeth Hayes, Mar. 1, 1971. MA, Oxford U., 1949, PhD, 1953, DSc, 1971. Rsch. assoc. U. London, 1952-58; sr. lectr., reader dept. surg. sci. U. Edinburgh, Scotland, 1958-64, dir. exptl. programming unit, 1965, chmn. dept. machine intelligence rsch. unit, 1974-84, prof. emeritus, 1985—2007. Prof. computer sci. U. Strathclyde, U.K., 1985-90; exec. dir. Turing Inst., 1983-84, chief scientist, 1985-90; tech. dir. Intelligent Terminals Ltd., 1984-87; hon. mem. Josef Stefan Inst., Slovenia, 1995-2007. Author: On Machine Intelligence, 1974, 2d edit., 1986, Machine Intelligence and Related Topics, 1982; co-author: An Introduction to Molecular Biology, 1974, The Creative Computer, 1984; editor-in-chief: Machine Intelligence Series, 1967—. Recipient Pioneer award Internat. Embryo Transfer Soc., 1988, Achievement award Inst. Elec. Engring., 1995, Feigenbaum award The World Congress on Expert Sys. Fellow Zool. Soc., Royal Soc. Edinburgh, Brit. Computer Soc. Died July 7, 2007.

**MICKUM, GEORGE BRENT, III,** lawyer; b. Washington, Jan. 13, 1928; s. George Brent and Anna May (Love) Mickum; m. Lora Mattare, June 27, 1953; children: George Brent, Luke Anthony, Ann Elizabeth, Paul Christopher, Joseph Benedict, Mark Andrew. BS, Georgetown U., 1949, LLB, 1952. Bar: (US Dist. Ct.) 1952, US Ct. Appeals (D.C. cir.) 1952, US Supreme Ct. 1960, (US Ct. Appeals (4th cir.)) 1967, (US Ct. Appeals (2d cir.)) 1975, (US Ct. Appeals (9th cir.)) 1977, (US Ct. Appeals (5th and 7th cirs.)) 1981. Law clk. U.S. Ct. Appeals DC, Washington, 1952—53; law clk. assoc. justice Stanley F. Reed, US Supreme Ct., 1953—54; pvt. practice, from 1954; mem. Steptoe & Johnson Chartered, Chevy Chase, Md.; dir. Gen. Bus. Svcs. Inc., Rockville, Md. Served to sgt. US Army, 1944—46. Mem.: ABA (sect. litigation), Columbia Country (Chevy Chase), Internat. (Washington), Bar Assn. DC, DC Bar. Democrat. Roman Catholic. Died Feb. 1985.

**MIDDLETON, STANLEY,** writer; b. Bulwell, Nottingham, Eng., Aug. 1, 1919; s. Thomas and Elizabeth Ann (Burdett) M.; m. Margaret Shirley Welch, Dec. 22, 1951; children: Penelope Jane, Sarah Ursula Judith. BA, London U., 1940; MEd, Nottingham U., 1952, MA (hon.), 1975; M.Univ. (hon.), Open U., 1995; DLitt (hon.), De Montfort U., 1998. Cert. tchr., Eng. Head English dept. High Pavement Coll., Nottingham, 1958-81; Judith E. Wilson vis. fellow Emmanuel Coll., Cambridge, England, 1982-83. Author: A Short Answer, 1958, Harris's Requiem, 1960, A Serious Woman, 1961, The Just Exchange, 1962, Two's Company, 1963, Him They Compelled, 1964, Terms of Reference, 1966, The Golden Evening, 1968, Wages of Virtue, 1969, Apple of the Eye, 1970, Brazen Prison, 1971, Cold Gradations, 1972, A Man Made of Smoke, 1973, Holiday, 1974, Distractions, 1975, Still Waters, 1976, Ends and Means, 1977, Two Brothers, 1978, In a Strange Land, 1979, The Other Side, 1980, Blind Understanding, 1982, Entry into Jerusalem, 1983, The Daysman, 1984, Valley of Decision, 1985, An After-Dinner's Sleep, 1986, After a Fashion, 1987, Recovery, 1988, Vacant Places, 1989, Changes and Chances, 1990, Beginning to End, 1991, A Place to Stand, 1992, Married Past Redemption, 1993, Catalysts, 1994, Toward the Sea, 1995, Live and Learn, 1996, Brief Hours, 1997, Against the Dark, 1998, Necessary Engs, 1999, Small Change, 2000. With Royal Artillery and AEC, 1940-46. Recipient Booker prize for fiction, 1974. Avocations: music, walking, water-color painting. Home: Sherwood Nottingham, England. Died July 25, 2009.

**MIHAILEANU, ANDREI CALIN,** energy researcher; b. Arad, Romania, Mar. 5, 1923; s. Gheorghe M. and Cleopatra (Bestelei) Pascu; m. Ileana Dana Demetrescu, July 15, 1948 (div. 1954); 1 child, Serban Alexandru; m. Simona Niculescu, Jan. 12, 1957; 1 stepson, Dan Georgescu. Diploma Electromech. Engring., Polytech. Inst., Bucharest, Romania, 1945, D in Elec. Engring., 1972. Profl. elect. engr., energetics. Power plant engr. Concordia-Electrica, Câmpina, Romania, 1945-47; chief engr. Regional Electricity Utility, Bucharest, 1947-52; dep. dir. Tech. Div., Ministry of Elec. Energy/Electrotech. Industry, Bucharest, 1952-58, sr. rsch. officer IRME, 1958-64; gen. mgr. Elec. Energy Dept. Ministry of Mines and Elec. Energy, Bucharest, 1964-65; researcher and dir. Elec. Energy and Co-Generation Rsch. Inst., Bucharest, 1967-74; rsearcher and gen. mgr. Cen. Energy Rsch. Inst., Bucharest, 1974-84, researcher and sci. sec., 1984-87; cons., sr. rsch. officer Energy Rsch. and Modernising Inst.-ICEMENERG, Bucharest, Romania, 1974—87, 1990—94; adviser to gen. mgr. IRMEB S.A., from 1994. Assoc. prof. Polytech. U., Bucharest, 1950-70, 94—; registered cons. PHARE / TACIS, 1996—. Author six books, three inventions and over 150 scientific papers in field, 1946—; editor: Energetica, 1953-87, ENERG, 1996-98. Recipient Traian Vuia prize Romanian Acad., 1979, Scientific Merit 1st Class Order, State Council, Bucharest, 1974. Mem. UN Econ. Commn. for Europe-Geneva (vice-chmn. Electric Power Com. 1956-58), Internat. Coun. on Large High Voltage Electric Systems, CIGRE (chmn. Romanian nat. com. 1976-98, hon. life chmn. 2000, expert 1998—, hon. life mem. 1998), World Energy Coun. (conservation commn., vice chmn. Romanian nat. com. 1991-2001, hon. life mem. 2001), Romanian Energy Policies Assn. (founding 1995—). Roman Catholic. Home: Bucharest, Romania. Died Nov. 2006.

**MIHALAS, DIMITRI,** retired astrophysicist, educator; b. LA, Mar. 20, 1939; s. Emmanuel Demetrious and Jean (Christo) M.; children: Michael, Alexandra. BA with highest honors, UCLA, 1959; MS, Calif. Inst. Tech., 1960, PhD, 1963. Asst. prof. astrophys. scis. Princeton U., 1964-67; asst. prof. physics U. Colo., 1967-68; asso. prof. astronomy and astrophysics U. Chgo., 1968-70, prof., 1970-71; adj. prof. astrogeophysics, also physics and astrophysics U. Colo., 1972-80; sr. scientist High Altitude Obs., Nat. Center Atmospheric Research, Boulder, Colo., 1971-79, 82-85; astronomer Sacramento Peak Obs., Sunspot, N.Mex., 1979-82; mem. staff Los Alamos (N.Mex.) Nat. Lab., 1998—2004, fellow, 2004—12; G.C. McVittie prof. astronomy U. Ill., 1985-98, g. c. prof. astronomy emeritus, 1998—2013; ret. Cons. Los Alamos Nat. Lab, 1981-98; vis. prof. dept. astrophysics Oxford (Eng.) U., 1977-78; sr. vis. fellow dept. physics and astronomy Univ. Coll., London, 1978; mem. astronomy adv. panel NSF, 1972-75 Author: Galactic Astronomy, 1969, 2d edit, 1981, Stellar Atmospheres, 1970, 2d edit., 1978, Theorie des Atmospheres Stellaires, 1971, Foundations of Radiation Hydrodynamics, 1984, Computational Methods for Astrophysical Fluid Flow, 1998; assoc. editor Astrophys. Jour, 1970-79, Jour. Computational Physics, 1981-87, Jour. Quantitative Spectroscopy, 1984-94; mem. editorial bd. Solar Physics, 1981-89. NSF fellow, 1959-62; Van Maanen fellow, 1962-63; Eugene Higgins vis. fellow, 1963-64; Alfred P. Sloan Found. Research fellow, 1969-71; Alexander von Humboldt Stiftung sr. U.S. scientist awardee, 1984. Mem. U.S. Nat. Acad. Sci., Internat. Astron. Union (pres. commn. 36 1976-79), Am. Astron. Soc. (pub. bd. 1995-99, mem. coun. 2000—03, Helen B. Warner prize 1974), Astron. Soc. Pacific (dir. 1975-77) Home: Santa Fe, N.Mex. Died Nov. 21, 2013.

**MIKHALKOV, SERGEY VLADIMIROVICH,** poet, playwright; b. Moscow, Mar. 13, 1913; children: Nikita, Andrej Kouchalouski. Author: (with El-Registan) Soviet Anthem, 1943; publs. include: Dyadya Styopa, 1936, Collected Works (poems, stories, plays), From Carriage to Space Ship, 1975, Jolly Hares, 1969; film script: Frontline Friends, 1941; plays: Tom Kenti, 1938, Red Neckerchief, 1947, Ilya Golovin, Y khochu domoi, 1949, Lobsters, 1952, Zaika-Zaznaika, 1955, Basni Mikhalkova, 1957, Sombrero, 1958, A Monument to Oneself, 1958, Dikari, 1959, Green Grasshopper, 1964, In the Museum of Lenin, 1968, Fables, 1970, Disobedience Day, 1971, Selected Works, 1973, Bibliographical Index, 1975, Selected Works, 3 vols., 1992. Mem. Communist Party, 1950-91. Recipient 4 Orders of Lenin, Hero Socialist Labour, 1973, Red Banner, Red Banner of Labour, Red Star, Lenin prize, 1970, Mem. Union Writers (1st sec. Moscow br., 1965-70, chmn. union of Russian Fedn., 1970-90). Died Aug. 27, 2009.

**MILLER, BECKY LYNN,** small business owner; b. Waseca, Minn., Nov. 23, 1958; d. Wallace John and Helen Marlene (Strauss) Abraham; m. Franklin Lee Miller, June 9, 1978; children: Joshua Lee, Justin Lynn, Ashley Lynn. Grad. h.s., Janesville, Minn. Belt reader Brown Printing Co., Waseca, 1977-78; clk. E.F. Johnson Co., Waseca, 1978-81; exec. sec. Donahue Real Estate, Waseca, 1982-84, Design Homes Minn., Waseca, 1984-85, Norwest Bank,

Mankato, Minn., 1985-88; daycare provider, Janesville, Minn., 1989-90, 92-93; pest control insp. Orkin Pest Control, St. Paul, 1990-91; owner, mgr. Miller's Carriage House Florals, Janesville, from 1978. Danceline coach Waseca H.S., 1979-81; office mgr. Matchmaker Home, Mankato, Minn., 1993-95. Campaign worker state rep. candidates, Mankato, 1989; weather spotter Waseca County CF, 1978—; founder, exec. dir. A Caring Sharing Christmas, 1985—; exec. dir., exec. prodr., bus. mgr. Miss Waseca County Scholarship Pageant, 1981-84; exec. dir., exec. prodr., bus. mgr. Miss Mankato Scholarship Program, 1987, 91-92, cert. judge, 1982—; yearbook editor People Assisting Learning, Janesville Elem. Sch., 1988—; mem. Am. Legion Aux., jr. activity leader, 1988—, mem. exec. bd., 1992-93, 1st dist. jr. activities chmn. Recipient Good Neighbor award Sta. KOWO, Waseca, 1990, 91, Good People/Jefferson award Sta. KEYC-TV, Mankato, 1992. Mem. U.S. Women of Today (pub. rels. dir. 1994-95, personal enrichment dir. 1995-96, U.S. Presdl. medallion and award of excellence 1994-95), Janesville Jaycee Women/Women of Today (pres. 1983-84, 92-93, 93-94, bd. dirs., Outstanding Mem. of Yr. award 1983, 88, Outstanding Dist. Pres. award, Minn. Presdl. medallions 1982, 84, 85, 86, 88, U.S. Outstanding Spkr. award 1982, Nat. Outstanding Program Mgr. award 1985). Avocations: music, dance, crafts, photography. Home: Janesville, Minn. Died Mar. 2, 1999.

**MILLER, CLARA BURR,** education educator; b. Higganum, Conn., July 19, 1912; d. Eugene Orlando and Mabel (Clark) Burr; m. James Golden Miller, Sept. 19, 1942; children: Clara Elizabeth, Eugenia Manelle. BA, Mt. Holyoke Coll., 1933; MA, Columbia U., 1942. Cert. tchr., Conn., N.Y., Pa., Ariz. Tchr. Suffield (Conn.) Jr. High Sch., 1934-36, Rockville (Conn.) High Sch., 1936-41, Buckeley High Sch., Hartford, Conn., 1941-42, Pitts. Schs., 1952-55, Winchester-Thurston Sch., Pitts., 1955-58, Vail-Deane Sch., Elizabeth, N.J., 1959-69, Kingman (Ariz.) High Sch., 1971-76; mem. res. faculty Mohave C.C., Kingman, 1978-94. Pres. bd. edn., clk. Mohave Union H.S. Dist. 30, 1983-91, bd. dirs.; bd. dirs. Mohave Mental Health Clinic, v.p. bd. dirs., 1988, pres. bd. dirs., 1989-90. Author: Trails, Rails and Tales, 1981; (with others) Short Stories, 1984; editor Metamorphosis, 1999—. Sec. Good Samaritan Assn., Inc., Kingman, 1979—95; pres. Ch. Women United, 1972—74, Presbyn. Women, 1987; elected elder session Kingman Presbyn. Ch., 1983—95; mem. Mohave County Cmty. Action Bd., Western Ariz. Coun. Govts.; coord. League Friendship Indians and Other Americans, 1981—95; co-chmn. Women Making History Com., 1981—95; elected head Montview Manor social activities, 1996—98, bd. mgrs., 1998—2001; elected deacon Montview Blvd. Presbyn. Ch., from 1997; Bd. dirs. No. Ariz. Comprehensive Guidance Ctr., Flagstaff, 1985—90, Kingman Aid to Abused People. Recipient Nat. Community Svc. award Mohave County Ret. Tchrs. Assn., 1987, Leta Glancy/Cecil Lockhart-Smith award No. Ariz. Comprehensive Guidance Ctr., 1990; named one of Women Making History Kingman Multi-Club Com., 1985. Mem. NEA, AAUW (pres. 1979-81), Ariz. Edn. Assn., Ariz. Sch. Bds. Assn., Soc. Profl. Journalists, Mohave County Ret. Tchrs. Assn. (v.p. 1991-93, pres. 1993-95), Footprinters, Colonial Dames of the 17th Century, Sigma Delta Chi. Democrat. Avocations: travel, painting, writing, reading, church activities. Deceased.

**MILLER, JACK (JOHN PETER MILLER),** journalist; b. Aug. 3, 1928; s. Wesley and Margaret (Baker) M.; m. Helen DeMars, July 30, 1949 (dec.); children: Candice-(dec.), Gregory(dec.). Student, Welland and Toronto. From sports page editor to front page editor Welland Evening Tribune, 1949—53; with Hamilton (Ont.) Spectator, 1953—71, radio and TV columnist, 1955—71; with Toronto Daily Star, 1971—91, radio and TV columnist, 1971—78, comm. editor, 1979—85, sci. columnist, 1982—85, sci. writer, 1985—89, sci. editor, 1989—91, sci. corr., 1991—95; prof. journalism Niagara Coll., 1996—99. Frequent TV and radio appearances. Contbr. stories to mags. Mem.: Can. Sci. Writers Assn. (2 writing awards 1985, writing award 1987, 2 writing awards 1988, writing award 1989). Deceased.

**MILLER, JOSEPH BAYARD,** lawyer; b. Highland, La., Feb. 25, 1920; s. Harrison Coleman and Jeannette (Donaldson) M.; m. Gloria Berthelot, Dec. 31, 1950; children: Joseph Bayard Jr., Melinda May. BA in Arts and Scis., Tulane U., 1939, LLB, 1941. Bar: La. 1941, U.S. Dist. ct. (ea. dist.) La. 1941, U.S. Ct. Appeals (5th cir.) 1941, U.S. Supreme Ct. 1969. Assoc. Milling, Godchaux, Saal & Milling, New Orleans, 1941-47; ptnr. Milling, Benson, Woodward, Hillyer, Pierson & Miller, New Orleans, from 1948. Bd. dirs. Continental Land & Fur Co., Inc., New Orleans. Maj. USAAF, 1942-46, PTO. Mem. New Orleans Country Club, City Energy Club. Episcopalian. Avocations: hunting, fishing, horses. Home: New Orleans, La. Died Nov. 4, 2001.

**MILLER, JUDSON FREDERICK,** retired military officer; b. Tulsa, Dec. 5, 1924; s. Herbert Frederick and Martha (Davidson) M.; m. June Hirakis, Aug. 4, 1967; children by previous marriage: Kathleen, Shelley, Douglas, Judson Frederick. BS, U. Md., 1961; postgrad., Army War Coll., 1961-62; MA, George Washington U., 1962; JD, U. Puget Sound, 1980. Bar: Wash. 1981. Commd. 2d lt. U.S. Army, 1943, advanced through grades to maj. gen., 1975; platoon leader, co. comdr. 4th Cav. Group, Europe, 1944-46, 82d Airborne Div., 1947-50; with 187th Airborne RCT and Hdqrs. 8th Army, 1950-52; instr. Armored Sch., 1953-56; bn. comdr. 14th Armored Cav., 1958-60; with Hdqrs. U.S. Strike Command, 1963-65; brigade comdr., chief of staff 4th Inf. Div., Vietnam, 1966-67; mem. gen. staff Dept. Army, 1967-68; dep. comdg. gen. Ft. Ord, Cal., 1968-69; asst. chief of staff Hdqrs. Allied Forces Central Europe, 1969-71; asst. comdr. 3d Inf. Div., Germany, 1971-73; chief of staff I Corps Group, Korea, 1973-75; dep. comdg. gen. VII Corps, Germany, 1975-77; ret., 1977. Decorated Silver Star, Legion of Merit, Bronze Star with V device and oak leaf cluster, Joint Service Commendation medal, Air medal with 8 oak leaf clusters, Purple Heart, Vietnamese Gallantry Cross with palm; named to Okla. Mil. Acad. Hall of Fame, 1988. Mem. ABA, Assn. U.S. Army. Clubs: Tacoma Country, Lakewood Racquet. Home: Tacoma, Wash. Died Aug. 31, 2010.

**MILLER, LARRY (LAWRENCE G. MILLER),** state legislator; b. Bridgeport, Conn., Apr. 19, 1936; m. Mildred Miller; children: John, Leslie, Andrea. BS in Bus Adminstrn., U. Bridgeport. Pres. Milo Oil, Stratford, Conn.; mem. Dist. 22 Conn. House of Reps., 1991—2014. Mem. Stratford Town Coun., 1977—85, Planning & Zoning Commn., 1985—89, chair, 1989—93. Vol. United Way, Stratford Red Cross; past chair bd. mgr.'s Bridgeport Young Men's Christian Assn. Mem.: Stratford C. of C. (past bd. dirs.), Stratford Young Men's Christian Assn., Catholic Sokols, Knights of Columbus. Republican. Died June 1, 2014.

**MILLER, MURIEL AGNES,** education educator, consultant; b. St. Paul, Minn., 1916; d. Edward William and Mayme Blanche (Vandelac) Oestreich; m. Carl Stinson Miller, Aug. 19, 1944; children: Suzanne Marie Rechtzigel, Dennis William. BS, St. Catherine's Coll., 1937; postgrad., U. Minn., 1960. Registered parliamentarian. High sch. tchr. Minn. Edn. Assn. high schs., Murray, Monroe, St. Paul, 1937—47; pres. Minn. State Assn. Parliamentarian, 1973—75, 1977—79; profl. vol. AAUW, Interclub Coun., Minn. Federalists, Minn. U., Libr. St. Paul, Bus. & Profl. Women, parliamentarian, pres. St. Paul, St. Paul Branch AAUW; pres. Friends Pub. Libr., St. Paul; dir. St. Paul YWCA, Twin Cities Opera Guild, Minn. Opera; served as nat. parliamentarian White House Conf. Families, Minn., Am. Assn. Hosp. Adminstrs, Am. Assn. Social Workers, Nat. Bus. & Profl. Women; state parliamentarian LPNs, Minn., Minn. Dental Assts. Assn., Minn. LWV, AAUW, Minn., Minn. Nurses Assn., Minn. Soil & Water Conservation Dists; v.p., chmn. coms. Minn. State Assn. Parliamentarian, in charge two state seminars & two convs.; charter pres. St. Paul Unit Parliamentarians; instr. parliamentary procedure St. Thomas Coll, St. Catherine's Coll., St. Paul Sch. System Adult Edn.; parliamentary procedure judge Office Edn. Assn. Contbr. articles. Recipient Bus. & Svc. award, Office Edn. Assn., 1979. Fellow: AAUW; mem.: Minn. Assn. Parliamentarians (pres. 1960), Assn. Parliamentarians (pres. St. Paul unit), Nat. Assn. Parliamentarians (dist. V bd. dirs.), St. Paul's Womans Club (pres.), St. Paul City Club (pres.). Republican. Unitarian Universalist. Avocations: travel, theater. Deceased.

**MILLER, ROSS HAYS,** retired neurosurgeon; b. Ada, Okla., Jan. 30, 1923; s. Harry and Helen (Rice) M.; m. Catherine Railey, May 2, 1943; children— Terry Hays, Helen Stacy. BS, East Central State Coll., Ada, 1943; MD, U. Okla., 1946; MS in Neurosurgery, U. Minn., 1952. Diplomate: Am. Bd. Neurol. Surgery (chmn. exam. com. 1978-84). Intern St. Luke's Hosp., Cleve., 1946-47; fellow in neurosurgery Mayo Clinic, Rochester, Minn., 1950-54; instr. in neurosurgery Mayo Med. Sch., 1954-63, asst. prof. neurosurgery, 1963-73, asso. prof., 1973-75, prof., chmn. dept. neurosurgery, from 1975, now ret. Vis. prof. neurol. surgery Med. Coll. Ga., Augusta Contbr. articles to profl. jours. Trustee East Central State U. Found. Served as capt., M.C. U.S. Army, 1947-49, Korea. Named to Okla. Hall of Fame, 1977, Athletic Hall of Fame, East Central U. Okla., 1977; recipient Disting. Alumnus award East Central U. Okla., 1974, Mayo Found. Disting. Alumnus award, 1992. Mem. AMA, ACS, Am. Assn. Neurol. Surgeons (chmn. com. profl. practice 1976-79, dir. 1976-79, v.p. 1979, rep. to Council Med. Splty. Socs. 1980-84), Congress Neurol. Surgeons (exec. com. 1963-65), Minn. Soc. Neurol. Scis., Neurosurg. Soc. Am. (v.p. 1975), Soc. Neurol. Surgeons (v.p. 1983), Sigma Xi. Home: Greeneville, Tenn. Died May 10, 2014.

**MILLER, WILLIAM DYKSTRA,** forestry educator; b. Portland, Oreg., Sept. 26, 1897; s. George William Henry and Marie (Dykstra) M.; m. Catherine Ritchey, June 7, 1928; children: William Ritchey, Alden Dykstra. BA, Reed Coll., 1923; M in Forestry, Yale U., 1930, PhD, 1932. Rsch. asst. No. Rocky Mountain Forest Expt. Sta., Priest River, Idaho, summer 1930; forestry instr. U. Idaho, Moscow, 1932-33, 34-35; technician Southwestern Forest and Range Expt. Sta., Flagstaff and Tucson, Ariz., 1933-34; asst. prof. forestry N.C. State Coll., Raleigh, 1935-36, assoc. prof. forestry, 1936-62, prof. forestry, 1962-63, prof. emeritus, 1963—. Field asst. Yale U. Demonstration and Rsch. Forest, Keene, N.H., summers 1929, 31; translator in five langs. for Tree Improvement Coop. N.C. State U., Raleigh, 1989—, abstractor, 1965-80. Author: (with others) Bulletin on Virginia Pine, 1953; Compiler History of Hofmann Forest, 1969, Annotated Bibliography of Southern Hardwoods, 1968; contbr. articles to profl. jours. With U.S. Army, 1917-19. Fellow AAAS; mem. Soc. Am. Foresters (Golden mem.), Sigma Xi. Democrat. Presbyterian. Avocations: music, hiking. Home: PO Box 27886 Raleigh NC 27611-7886

**MILLER DAVIS, MARY-AGNES,** social worker; b. Montgomery, Ala., Jan. 21; d. George Joseph and Mollie (Ingersoll) M.; m. Edward Davis, Sept. 20, 1941. BA, Wayne State U., 1944; MSW, U. Mich., 1970. Lic. social worker, Mich. Social caseworker Cath. Family Ctr., Detroit, 1946-48; foster homes worker Juvenile Ct., Detroit, 1953-57; youth svc. bur. League of Cath. Women, Detroit, 1957-59; mayor's cmty. action for youth com. worker City of Detroit, 1963; instr. urban sociology Madonna Coll., Livonia, Mich., 1968; pers. cons. Edward Davis Motor Sales, Detroit, 1963-70; exec. cons. Edward Davis Assocs., Inc., Detroit, from 1975. Founder Co-Ette Club, Inc., Detroit, 1941—, Met. Detroit Teen Conf. Coalition, Detroit, 1983—; program chair Wayne State U.-Merrill Palmer Inst., Detroit, 1976—, founder Met. Detroit Teen Conf. Editor Girl Friends, Inc. Mag., 1960-62; contbr. articles to profl. jours. Life mem. NAACP, League of Cath. Women, ARC; charter mem. Meadowbrook Summer Music Festival, com. of Oakland (Mich.) U.; adv. bd. Women for the Detroit Symphony Orch.; mem./patron Founder's Soc. the Detroit Inst. of Arts; bd. dirs., other offices ARC, Detroit, 1974—; active The Detroit Hist. Soc., Heart of Gold Coun., Women for United Found. (named to Heart of Gold coun. 1968), Friends of the Detroit Libr., Mich. Opera Theatre; mem. nat. hon. com./nat. vol. week United Cmty. Svc. and Nat. Vol. Ctr., Washington, 1990—; former bd. dirs. United Community Svcs. Women's Com., Campfire Girls, LWV, Neighborhool Svcs. Orgn., Cath. Interracial Coun. and others; founder Met. Detroit Teen Conf. Coalitions Merrill Palmer Inst. Wayne State U. Recipient Nat. Cmty. Leadership award Nat. Coun. Women of U.S., Inc., 1984, Am. Human Resources award Am. Bicentennial Rsch. Inst., 1976, Heart of Gold award United Way, 1968, Nat. Leadership award United Negro Coll. Fund, 1963, Recognition award Westin Hotel, 1991, Top Ladies of Distinction award, 1994, Civic award Am. Assn. Bus. Women, 1998, Youth Leadership award Merrill Palmer Inst. of Wayne State U., 1999, Cmty. Leadership award, 1999, Civic/Social Vol. Leadership award Automobile Industry and Edward Davis Found./Edn. and Scholarships for Youth, 2001; named one of Mich. Outstanding Women City of Detroit, 1976, Michiganer of the Yr., Detroit News Newspaper, 2001; Heart of Gold 25th Anniversary honoree United Way Southeastern Mich., 1992; Vassar Summer Seminar scholar NCCJ, 1953, Notre Dame Summer Seminar scholar, 1960; named one of Most Outstanding Women of Decade, Nordstrom's Dept. Store, 1996. Mem. NASW, ARC (bd. dirs. 1973—, life), Nat. Conf. of Social Work, The Cons. Club of Detroit (adv. bd. edn. com.), Detroit Econ. Club (adv. com.). Home: Detroit, Mich. Died Apr. 18, 2001.

**MILLIGAN, FREDERICK JAMES,** lawyer; b. Upper Sandusky, Ohio, Nov. 14, 1906; s. William G. and Grace (Kuenzli) Milligan; m. Virginia Stone, June 30, 1934; children: Frederick James, David Timothy. BA, Ohio State U., 1928; LLB, Franklin U., 1933; JD, Capital U., 1966. Asst. nat. sec. Phi Delta Theta, 1928; asst. dean men Ohio State U., 1929—33; asst. atty. gen. State Ohio, 1933—36; pvt. practice Columbus, Ohio, from 1937; exec. sec. Adminstrv. La. Commn. Ohio, 1940—42, Gov. Ohio, 1947; dir. commerce State Ohio, 1948; sec. Louis Bromfield Malabar Farm Found., 1958—60; pres. Central Ohio council Boy Scouts Am.; trustee Columbus Town Meeting; asst. dir. Pres.'s Commn. on Inter-govt. Rels., 1953; pres. Ohio Information Com., Inc., 1966—83; chmn. Blendon Twp. Bicentennial Commn., 1974—77. Mem. athletic council Ohio State U., 1958—64; trustee Blendon Twp., 1971—78. Served from 1st lt. to maj. USAAF, 1942—45. Decorated Legion Merit; recipient Silver Beaver award, Boy Scouts Am., 1949, Ann. History award, Franklin County Hist. Soc., 1957, Citizenship award, D.A.R., 1958, Distinguished Svc. citation, Ohioana Library Assn., 1970. Mem.: Amvets (state comdr. 1949), Ohio State U. alumni assn. (trustee 1952—55), Franklin County Hist. Soc (pres. 1954—56), Ohio Hist. Soc. (trustee 1952—77, pres. 1963—65), Columbus bar assns., Ohio, Am., Columbus Jr. C. of C. (life; pres. 1934), League Young Republican Clubs of Ohio (pres. 1941—42), Ohio State U. Faculty Club, Univ. Club (trustee 1956—58), Am. Legion, S.A.R. Died 1997.

**MILLNS, ANTHONY THOMAS COWLING,** retired financial and maritime consultant; b. Brentwood, Essex, Eng., Oct. 7, 1935; s. Cecil Thomas and Lissie Muriel (Simons) M.; m. Elizabeth Ann Way, Aug. 20, 1959 (div. Oct. 1963); children: Tina, Richard; m. Pamela Ann Donne, Apr. 9, 1966; children: Philip, Geoffrey. Grad. in nav., U. Southampton, 1952. Cert. master on fgn. going S.S. Navigating officer Alfred Holt & Co., Liverpool, Eng., 1953-56, Union Castle Mail S.S. Co. Ltd., London, 1956-65; area mgr. Esso Petroleum Co. Ltd., London, 1965-90; sr. adviser Hill Samuel, London, 1965-93; fin. cons. DGR Hunt Ind. Fin. Svcs., Bishop's Waltham, Eng., 1993-99; prin. A.T.C. Millns Ind. Fin. Consultancy, 1999-2001; ret., 2001. Presenter Nat. Conf. on Preventing Collisions at Sea, 1996. Contbr. articles to profl. jours., including Jour. Nav. Pres. Henleaze Neighbourhood Soc., Bristol, Eng., 1986-88. Named freeman City of London, 1968. Fellow Royal Inst. Nav.; mem. Personal Finance Soc. (cert.). Avocations: sailing, swimming, walking. Home: Bristol, England. Died Nov. 10, 2005.

**MILLS, JANET IONE,** music educator, writer, researcher; b. Stockport, Cheshire, United Kingdom, May 11, 1954; d. John Bernard and Winifred Ione Mills. BA, U. York, UK, 1975; PhD, U. Oxford, UK, 1983. Music head Holy Family Sch., Keighley, West Yorkshire, England, 1976—79, Brighouse Girls' Grammar Sch., Brighouse, West Yorkshire, England, 1979—81; sr. lectr. Westminster Coll., Oxford, England, 1983—88; lectr., music chair U. Exeter, Exeter, England, 1988—90; her majesty's insp. schools HM Govt./Ofsted, London, 1990—2000; specialist music adv. Ofsted, London, 1995—2000; rsch. fellow Royal Coll. Music, London, from 2000. Editl. bd. Brit. Jour. Music Edn., from 2002. Author: (book) Music in the School, Music in the Primary School; editor: The Arts Inspected: Good Teaching in Art, Dance, Drama and Music; contbr. over 40 articles to profl. jours. Recipient Nat. Tchg. Fellow, Higher Edn. Acad., 2004. Mem.: Brit. Ednl. Rsch. Assn., Internat. Soc. Music Edn., Soc. for Edn., Music and Psychology Rsch. (SEMPRE). Home: Oxford, England. Died Dec. 24, 2007.

**MILNE, MARION CARSON,** retired state legislator; b. NYC, Jan. 2, 1935; m. Donald G. Milne; three children. BA in Political Sci., Goddard Coll., 1975. Mem. Vt. House of

Reps., Montpelier, 1995—2001. Del. White House Small Bus. Conf., 1980, 86; pres. Milne Travel American Express, 1975-2014 Trustee Calef Meml. Libr. Named Woman of Yr. Ctrl. Vt. Bus. & Profl. Club, 1987. Mem. Soc. Travel Agents, Ctrl. Vt. Chamber of Commerce (past pres.). Republican. Died Aug. 11, 2014.

**MILONGO, ANDRÉ,** former Prime Minister of the Republic of Congo; b. 1935; Prime min., chief of armed forces, min. mines and energy Govt. of Republic of Congo, Brazzaville, 1991—92, pres. Nat. Assembly, 1992—97. Died July 23, 2007.

**MINGO, JAMES WILLIAM EDGAR,** lawyer; b. Halifax, NS, Can., Nov. 25, 1926; s. Edgar Willard and Lila Theresa (McManus) M.; m. Edith Peppard Hawkins, July 6, 1953; children: Sarah M. (Mrs. J.P. Camus), James A., Johanna E., Nancy S. (Mrs. S.J. Overgaard-Thomsen), Charles H. BA, Dalhousie U., Halifax, 1947, LL.B., 1949; LL.M., Columbia U., 1950; LL.D. (hon.), St. Mary's U., 1981; LL.D. (hon), Dalhousie U., 1998. Bar: N.S. 1950, Queen's counsel 1966, mem. Order of Can., 2004. Ptnr. Stewart, McKelvey, Stirling & Scales (and predecessors), Halifax, from 1958, assoc., 1950-57, chmn. exec. com., 1979-92. Pres., dir. Canning Investment Corp. Ltd., Halifax; Minas Basin Pulp & Power Co. Ltd., Hantsport, N.S., Minas Basin Holdings Ltd., Hantsport, The Great Ea. Corp. Ltd., Charlottetown, P.E.I. and Halifax, Oxford Frozen Foods Ltd., Oxford, N.S.; trustee Forum for Young Canadians. Mem. Halifax-Dartmouth Port Commn., 1955-83, chmn., 1960-83; chmn. Halifax Grammar Sch., 1971-73; mem. Halifax Port Authority, 1972-84; chmn. nat. treasury com. Liberal Party Can., 1976-85; dir. N.S. Legal Aid, 1977-80; mem. Med. Rsch. Coun. Working Group on Human Experimentation, 1977-78. Mem. Can. Bar Assn. (exec. com. 1973-76, spl. com. on legal ethics 1969-75, 84-87), N.S. Barristers Soc. (pres. 1975-76), Halifax club, Saraguay club, Royal N.S. Yacht Squadron club, Ashburn club. Died 2006.

**MINKOWSKI, ALEXANDRE,** neonatology educator, retired; b. Paris, Dec. 5, 1915; s. Eugeniusz and Franciszka (Brockmann) M.; m. Marcelle Thiedot, 1942 (div. 1943); 1 child, Marianne; m. Mary-Ann Wade, Apr. 2, 1950; children: Anoine, Nicolas, Marc, Laurent. MD, U. René Descartes, Paris, 1944. Rockefeller fellow Harvard U., Cambridge, Mass., 1946-47; chief of staff Faculté Cochin, Paris, 1962; prof. pediatrics U. René Descartes, 1966-80, prof. emeritus, 1980, ret., 1980. Dir. Ctr. for Rsch. in Biology of the Foetus and the Newborn INSERM, 1962-80. Author: Le Mandarin aux Pieds nus: Entretiens avec Jean Lacouture, 1975, Pour un Nouveau-né Sans Risque, 1983, Ce que je Crois Grasset, 1997. Former Mem. UNICEF; counsellor Conseil Regional D'Ile de France; sci. counselor Partage Avec les Enfants du Monde, Paris. With French Army, 1939-45. Recipient Prix Monthion Acad. Scis., 1965, Prix de la Maternité European Perinatal Soc., 1987, Nils Rosen von Rosenstein Medal, U. Uppsala, 1999. Fellow Royal Col. Physicians, Royal Coll Pediatrics and Child Health (London); mem. Am. Pediat. Soc. (hon.), Neonatal Soc. U.K. Avocations: music, sports, skiing, mountain climbing, tennis. Home: Paris, France. Died May 8, 2004.

**MINTZ, HARRY,** artist, educator; b. Warsaw, Sept. 27, 1909; s. Zysman and Rachel Sari (Milgram) M.; m. Rosabelle Truglio, Sept. 1, 1958; children: William Zysman, Sari Rachel. M.F.A., Warsaw Acad. Fine Arts, 1927. Tchr. art Evanston Art Ctr., 1940-70, North Shore Art League, 1950-59; prof. emeritus Art Inst. Chgo. Vis. prof. Washington U., St. Louis, 1954-55; faculty Art Inst. Chgo., 1955-70, now emeritus prof. advanced painting. One man shows, Art Inst. Chgo., Heller Gallery, N.Y.C., Feingarten Galleries, Chgo. and Beverly Hills, Calif., 1961, Ruth Volid Gallery, Chgo., 1986, Galleria del Arte, Guadalajara, Mex., 1987, others; exhibited local, nat., internat. shows, Art Inst. Chgo., 1932—, also N.Y. World's Fair, 1940, Whitney Mus. Am. Art, N.Y.C., Pa. Acad. Fine Arts, Carnegie Internat., Pitts., Venice Biennale, Italy, Palace Legion of Honor, San Francisco, Mus. Modern Art, N.Y.C., Old Town Art Fair, 1953-93, 94, WFMT Art Exhbt., 1989, others; represented in permanent collections, Art Inst. Chgo., Whitney Mus., Warsaw Acad. Fine Arts, Mus. Art Tel-Aviv, Mus. Modern Art Rio de Janeiro, Evansville (Ind.) Mus., Notre Dame U., Northwestern U., Columbus U. (Ohio), others. Recipient awards Art Inst. Chgo., 1937, 39, 45, 46, 49, 52, 54, 55, 61, Palace Legion of Honor Nat. Exhbn. San Francisco, 1946, Palace Legion of Honor Nat. Exhbn. U. Chgo., 1953, Palace Legion of Honor Nat. Exhbn. Union League Exhibit, Chgo., 1959, Palace Legion of Honor Nat. Exhbn. Old Orchard, Chgo., 1958-73, Palace Legion of Honor Nat. Exhbn. Sarasota (Fla.) Nat. Exhibit, 1959, others. Mem. Renaissance Soc., Chgo. Soc. Artists, Inc. Home: Chicago, Ill. Died Sept. 15, 2002.

**MIRZA, MAHMUD,** bookseller, consultant; b. Lahore, Punjab, Pakistan, Nov. 15, 1927; s. Mohammed Noor and Fatima (Ghulam) M.; m. Sultana Tasawar, Nov. 11, 1962; children: Shahid Mahmood, Qasim Mahmood, Asia Bano, Tariq Mahmood, Aamina. Engr., Punjab Coll. Engring. and Tech., 1949. With Workshop Instrn. Punjab Coll. Engring. and Tech. (named change to U. Engring. & Tech.), Lahore, Pakistan, 1950-51; tech. dir. Pak Pubs., Inc., Karachi, Pakistan, 1968-81; mng. ptnr. Mirza Book Agy., Lahore, until 1988, proprietor, from 1988; book cons., 1994. Leader 1st Pakistani Booksellers Inward Mission, U.K., 1985; Asia rep. to UNESCO at Internat. Booksellers Fedn. Gen. Assembly, Padua, Italy, 1986, Madrid, Spain, 1992, Amsterdam, Holland, 1995; mem. internat. adv. bd. Logos, London, 1990-95; Pakistani rep. to Internat. Pub. Assn. Congress, New Delhi, India, 1992; active Internat. Com. for Protection of Intellectual Property Rights, 1984—; speaker in field; organizer 1st Internat. Seminar on copyright, piracy & reprinting in Pakistan, 1984; book cons., 1994—; Pakistani rep. pub. workshop on reprinting and copyrights U.S. Info. Agy., 1996. Contbr. articles to profl. jours. Mem. ALA, Pakistan Assn. Advancement of Sci. (life), Pakistan Libr. Assn. (life), Pakistan Assn. Sci. and Sci. Profession (life), Horticulture Soc. Pakistan (life), Pakistan Inst. Mgmt. (assoc. life), Bangladesh Libr. Assn. (life), Internat. Bookseller Fedn. (assoc.), Lahore Chamber and Industry (mem. coms.), Pakistan Pubs. and Booksellers Assn., Pakistan Am. Alumni Assn., Nat. Assn. Coll. Stores, Afro-Asia Book Coun. Muslim. Avocations: reading, writing, listening to fgn. radio stas., collecting books, watching games. Home: Lahore, Pakistan. Died Sept. 28, 2003.

**MISKIN, RAYMOND JOHN,** retired mechanical engineer; b. Ipswich, Suffolk, Eng., July 4, 1928; s. Sidney George and Hilda (Holdsworth) M.; m. Betty Tavener, July 14, 1951 (div. Nov. 1981); children: Gerald, Karen; m. Brenda Elizabeth, June 3, 1991. Cert. in mech. engring., Southall Tech. Coll., Middlesex, Eng., 1951. Chartered mech. engr., Eng. Apprentice Fairey Aviation Co. Ltd., Hayes, Middlesex, 1945-49, devel. engr., 1949-54, sect. leader devel. engr., 1956-59, dep. chief inspector, 1959-63; dep. chief technician Self Priming Punp Co. Ltd., Slough, Bucks, Eng., 1954-56; quality mgr. Graviner (Colinbrook, Eng.) Ltd., 1963-69; sec., CEO Inst. Quality Assurance, London, 1969-73; dep. sec. Inst. Prodn. Engrs., London, 1973-76, sec., CEO, 1976-87; cons. Royal Acad. Engring., London, 1987-89; CEO Cadlas Ltd., Chesterfield, Derbyshire, Eng., 1989-93; cons. quality assurance Sheffield, Eng., from 1993. Vice chmn. Nat. Coun. for Quality and Reliability, London, 1973-75, chmn., 1975-77. Recipient Internat. Indsl. Tech. Mgmt. award San Fernado Valley Engrs.' Coun., 1978, Internat. Contbns. award L.A. Coun. Engrs. and Scientists, First Shuttle Flight Achievement award, 1982, Internat. Interprofl. Achievement award NSPE, 1983, Outstanding Tech. Transfer award Calif. Coun. Indsl. and Bus. Assns., 1984, Internat. Tech. Comms. award Calif. Engring. Found., 1985, Gold medal Hungarian Soc. Mech. Engrs., 1985, Disting. Econs. Devel. Programs award Soc. Mech. Engrs., 1992. Fellow Instn. Mech. Engrs., Inst. Elec. Engrs., Inst. Quality Assurance, Indian Instn. Prodn. Engrs. (hon.), Soc. Mfg. Engrs.; mem. Royal Aero. Soc. Mem. Ch. of England. Avocations: golf, photography, model making. Home: Mosborough, England. Died Apr. 9, 2006.

**MITCHELL, BARBARA J.,** elementary school educator; b. Ann Arbor, Mich., July 20, 1936; d. Lee W. and Fannie Vandecar; m. Robert Means Mitchell (dec.), Aug. 8, 1958; children: Robert J., David M., Gary L. (dec.). BS, Ea. Mich. U., 1957, MA in Reading, 1962. Tchr. 2nd grade Van Buren pub. schs., Belleville, Mich. Named Woman of the Yr., 1973. Mem.: Bus. and Profl. Women (past pres.), Interlochen Music Camp. Deceased.

**MITCHELL, ROBERT LEE, III,** corporate financial executive; b. Smyrna, Tenn., July 31, 1957; s. Robert Lee Jr. and Mary Helen (Lee) M. BA, U. Nebr., 1978; postgrad., U. St. Thomas, U. Minn. Div. sales mgr. J.L. Brandeis, Omaha, 1978-80; asst. mgr. Postal Thrift, Omaha, 1980-82; br. mgr. Security Pacific Fin. Svcs., Council Bluffs, Iowa, 1982-84, internal auditor Omaha, 1984-91, br. mgr., 1991-94, sr. employee dev. spec., 1994-95, v.p. Bank America Chesapeake, Va., Atlanta, 1995—97; dist. mgr. Avco Fin. Svcs., Kansas City, 1998—99; bank mgr. Comml. Fed. Bank, 1999-2001; dist. mgr. First Horizon Money Ctr., Mpls., 2001—02; indirect lending mgr. Affinity Plus Fed. Credit Union, St. Paul, 2002—03; bus. svcs. mgr. Hiway Fed. Credit Union, St. Paul, 2003—05; v.p., comml. banker Highland Bank, St. Paul, from 2005. Decorated Nat. Def. medal. Mem. U.S. Naval Res. Avocations: travel, hiking, golf, photography, genealogy. Died Aug. 1, 2008.

**MITCHELL, ROSS GALBRAITH,** pediatrics educator; b. Nov. 18, 1920; s. Richard Galbraith and Ishobel Mark (Ross) M.; m. June Phylis Butcher, Sept. 16, 1950; children: Andrew, Lindsay, Alison, Christine. B in Medicine and Surgery, U. Edinburgh, Scotland, 1944, MD, 1954. House physician Hosp. for Sick Children, London, 1949-50; pediatric registrar Royal Hosp. for Sick Children, Edinburgh, 1950-51; Rockefeller fellow Mayo Clinic, Rochester, Minn., 1952-53; lectr. in child health U. St. Andrews, Scotland, 1952-55; cons. pediatrician Dundee (Scotland) Royal Inf., 1955-63; prof. child health U. Aberdeen, Scotland, 1963-72, U. Dundee, 1973-85, prof. emeritus, from 1985. Mem. Gen. Med. Coun., U.K., 1983-86; dean faculty of medicine U. Dundee, 1978-81; chmn. editorial bd. Mac Keith Press, London, 1980-95. Author: Disease in Infancy and Childhood, 1973; editor: Child Health in the Community, 1977; contbr. chpts. in books and profl. jours. Surgeon lt. Royal Navy, 1944-47. Decorated Burma Star (U.K.), 1945. Fellow Royal Coll. Physicians, Royal Coll. Paediatrics and Child Health; mem. Assn. Physicians Gt. Britain, Am. Acad. Cerebral Palsy and Devel. Medicine (fgn. corr.), Internat. Cerebral Palsy Soc. (hon.). Mem. Ch. of Scotland. Home: Dundee, Scotland. Died 2006.

**MITGANG, HERBERT,** writer, journalist; b. NYC, Jan. 20, 1920; s. Benjamin and Florence (Altman) M.; m. Shirley Kravchick, May 13, 1945; children: Esther (dec. 2007), Lee, Laura. LLB, St. John's Law Sch., 1942. Bar: N.Y. 1942. Sports stringer Bklyn. Eagle, 1938-39; screen writer Universal-Internat. Pictures, 1945; copy editor, reviewer N.Y. Times, NYC, 1945-54; supervising editor Sunday Times drama sect., 1955-62; editorial writer, mem. editorial bd. N.Y. Times, 1963-64, 67-76, deputy editor Op-Ed page, 1970-76, publishing, cultural corr., book critic, 1976-94; asst. to pres., exec. editor CBS News, 1964-67. Instr. English evening divsn. CCNY, 1948-49; vis. lectr. English, guest fellow Silliman Coll., Yale U., 1975-76; lit. advisor White House Libr, 1977-81. Writer, prodr.: (film documentaries) Henry Moore: Man of Form (award Ohio U. 1966), D-Day Plus 20 Years, Sandburg's Prairie Years, Degas' Racing World (Duke Ellington score), Ben-Gurion on the Bible, Anthony Eden on Vietnam; author: Lincoln As They Saw Him, 1956, The Return, 1959, The Man Who Rode the Tiger: The Life and Times of Judge Samuel Seabury, 1963 (Pulitzer Prize finalist in biography, Silver Gavel award ABA), Working for the Reader, 1970, Get These Men Out of the Hot Sun, 1972, The Fiery Trial: A Life of Lincoln, 1974, The Montauk Fault, 1981, Kings in the Counting House, 1983, Dangerous Dossiers: The Secret War Against America's Greatest Authors, 1988, Words Still Count With Me: A Chronicle of Literary Conversations, 1995, Once Upon a Time in New York: Jimmy Walker, Franklin Roosevelt, and the Last Great Battle of the Jazz Age, 2000, Newsmen in Khaki: Tales of a World War II Soldier Correspondent, 2004; editor: Washington, D.C., in Lincoln's Time, 1958, Civilians Under Arms: Stars and Stripes, Civil War to Korea, 1996, The Letters of Carl Sandburg, 1968, America at Random, 1969, Spectator of America, 1971, Selected Writings of Abraham Lincoln, 1992; (plays) Mister Lincoln, 1980, Adlai, Alone, 2005; contbr. to the New Yorker, Art News, American Heritage, The Progressive, The Nation, Chicago Tribune, Newsday, New York Times, Washington Post. Mem. exec. bd. Newspaper Guild of N.Y., CIO, 1948-49; bd. dirs. Theatre for a New Audience, N.Y., 1998-2013; Served with counter-intelligence sect. 5th wing USAAF, 1942-43, MTO; Army corr., mng. editor Stars and Stripes, Oran-Casablanca and Sicily edits. 1943-45. Decorated six battle stars, Knight Order of Merit (Italy); recipient Human Rights award Newspaper Guild of N.Y., 1958, Broadcast Preceptor award San Francisco State Coll., 1970, N.Y. State Bar Assn. Media award, 1976, Lincoln award Civil War Roundtable of N.Y., 1981, George Polk Career award Long Island U., 1993, 25 Yr. News Achievement award Soc. of Silurians, 1993, Lit. Lions award N.Y. Public Libr. Fellow Soc. American Historians; mem. Authors League (pres. fund 1976-97, pres. emeritus 1998-2013), Dramatists Guild, Authors Guild (pres. 1971-75), Internat. P.E.N. (U.S. del. London) Clubs: Century Assn. (N.Y.C.). Jewish. Died Nov. 21, 2013.

**MIWA, HIROHIDE,** electronics executive; b. Himeji, Hyogo-Ken, Japan, Jan. 12, 1924; s. Yuzoh and Kiyo (Abe) M.; m. Miyoko Koike, Apr. 24, 1949; children: Hiroaki, Keiko Ishida, Kenichiro. B of Physical Engring., Tokyo Imperial U., 1946; PhD, Tokyo U., 1959. Cert. radiation protection supr. Vice mgr. Kobekogyo Atomic Energy Divsn., Kobe, Japan, 1956-66; vice pres. Kobekogyo Lab., Kobe, Japan, 1966-69; gen. mgr. Fujitsu Ltd., Tokyo, 1969-78; dir. Fujitsu Labs., Tokyo, 1978-86; exec. dir. Crown Corp., Tokyo, 1986-88; pres. Cosmos R&D Co., Ltd., Tokyo, 1989-95, Miwa Sci. Lab., Kawasaki, 1995—2007, Miwa Sci. Co., Kawasaki, 2002—07. Chmn. DGPS com., Japan GPS Coun., Tokyo, 1993—; vice chmn. Electronic Application Club, Tokyo, 1970—; dir. Matsushita Graphic Sci. Sys., Inc., Tokyo, 1973-81; exec. dir. Inst. Hosp. Sys. Devel., Tokyo, 1977-80. Author: Applied Radiation Gauging, 1961 (Ohkohchi Meml. prize 1968); inventor 100 products in field; patentee in field. Recipient Invention prize Japan Inst. Invention and Innovation, Tokyo, 1952, 69, Chmn. prize C. of C., Hyogo, Japan, 1954, Best Paper of Yr. award Japan Soc. Med. Electronics, 1986. Mem. IEEE (sr. life mem., U.S.), Japan Radioisotope Assn. Buddhist. Achievements include succeeded world's first local subcutaneous fat reduction after 5 years research on ultrasound lipolysis with 6 universities. Avocations: haiku, calligraphy, swimming, world fruits collective cultivation, archaeology. Home: Kawasaki, Japan. Deceased.

**MOCKARY, PETER ERNEST,** clinical laboratory scientist, researcher, medical writer; b. Zghorta, Lebanon, Jan. 6, 1931; came to U.S., 1953; s. Ernest Peter and Evelyn (Kaddo) M.; m. Yvette Fadlallah, Aug. 27, 1955; children: Ernest, Evelyn, Paula, Vincent, Marguerite. BA in Philosophy, Coll. des Freres, Tripoli, Lebanon, 1948; MB, Am. U. Beirut, 1950, postgrad., 1950-52. Cert. clin. lab. scientist, Calif.; cert. clin. lab. scientist Nat. Certification Agy. Chief hematology unit VA Wadsworth Med. Ctr., West Los Angeles, Calif., 1956-81; CEO Phoenicia Trading Co., 1981-88; dir. Coagulation Lab. Orthopaedic Hosp., LA, 1988-97. Lab. supr. Westside Hosp., L.A., 1964-79; lectr. hematology UCLA, West Los Angeles, 1970-78. Pres. World Lebanese Cultural Union, L.A., 1978-79. With U.S. Army, 1954-56. Recipient outstanding performance award lab. svc. VA Wadsworth Med. Ctr., 1972-76. Republican. Roman Catholic. Avocations: billiards, reading, classical music. Deceased.

**MOCKER, DONALD WILBUR,** retired dean; b. St. Louis, Oct. 18, 1935; s. Wilbur H. and Bernice (Dexheimer) M.; m. Carole L. Stites, Oct. 28, 1961; children: Jeffrey S., Amy L. BS, Mo. Valley Coll., 1963; MS, U. Mo., 1968; EdD, SUNY, Albany, 1974. Life tchg. cert., Mo. Admissions counselor Mo. Valley Coll., Marshall, 1961-63; program coord. U. Mo., St. Louis, 1963-69, Kansas City, 1969-74, asst. prof., 1974-77, assoc. prof., 1977-81, prof., 1981-89, dean, 1989-94; interim provost, vice chancellor U. Wis., Oshkosh, 2000—01, dean Coll. Edn. & Human Svc., 1994—99. Mem. advisory bd. Fox Valley Tech. Coll., Oshkosh, 1994-97, Oshkosh Ednl. Found., 1996-97. Author: Teaching Adults to Read, 1986; co-author: Urban Education: Bibliography, 1978; co-editor Jour. of Life Long Learning, 1983-86. Mem. Bd. Edn., Kansas City, 1977-78; alderman City of Raymore, Mo., 1982-84, mayor, 1984-85; mem. advisoy bd. Fox Valley (Wis.) Diabetes Assn., 1997; served in US Army, 1958-63. Recipient Outstanding Achievement award Mo. Assn. for Adult Edn., 1974, Edn. award Urban League, Kansas City, 1992, Outstanding Alumnus award Mo. Valley Coll., Marshall, 1994. Mem. ASCD, American Assn. Adult and Continuing Edn., Phi Delta Kappa (Kappan of the Yr. award Zeta Delta chpt. 1990). Avocations: biking, bird watching, fishing. Home: Overland Park, Kans. Died Aug. 24, 2014.

**MOFFITT, JOHN FRANCIS,** art history educator, writer; b. San Francisco, Feb. 25, 1940; BFA, Calif. Coll. Arts and Crafts, 1962; MA in Art History, Calif State U., San Francisco, 1963; PhD, U. Madrid, 1966. Asst. prof. art and art history East Carolina U., Greenville, N.C., 1966-68, Sonoma (Calif.) State Coll., 1968-69; from asst. prof. to prof. history of art N.Mex. State U., Las Cruces, 1969-96, prof. art history emeritus, from 1996. Author: Spanish Painting, 1973, Occultism in Avant-Garde Art: The Case of Joseph Beuys, 1988, Velázquez, práctica e idea: Estudios dispersos, 1991, Art Forgery: The Case of the Lady of Elche, 1995, Spanish edit., 1996, The Arts in Spain, 1999, Spanish edit., 1999; co-author: O Brave New People: The European Invention of the American Indian, 1996. Home: Las Cruces, N.Mex. Died June 1, 2008.

**MOHOROVIC, JESSE ROPER,** retired energy company executive; b. Apr. 1, 1943; s. Joseph Peter and Desanka (Petrovic) M.; m. Joan Marie Vroman, Apr. 15, 1967; children: Caroline, Joseph. AB in English, Fordham U., 1963. V.p. Ruder & Finn, Inc., NYC, 1971-72; dir. investor relations SCA Services, Inc. Boston, 1972-74; v.p., dir. pub. relations Ingalls Assocs., Boston, 1974-79; v.p. corp. and indsl. relations Eastern Gas and Fuel Assocs., Boston, 1979-89, also sec. retirement com.; v.p. mktg. communication Sea-Land Svc., Inc., Edison, 1989—2003. Vice chmn. Candidates Better Govt., Boston, 1982-84. Served to lt. USN, 1966-70. Mem. Nat. Investor Relations Inst., Public Relations Soc. America (chmn. sr. adv. com. Boston chpt. 1986). Clubs: Advt. of Boston, Bay of Boston, Scituate Harbor Yacht (chmn. tennis com. 1987). Roman Catholic. Avocations: tennis, gardening, sport fishing. Home: Scituate, Mass. Died Aug. 6, 2005.

**MOISEYEV, IGOR ALEKSANDROVICH,** choreographer; b. Kiev, Russia, Jan. 21, 1906; s. Alersandr Michajlovich and Anna Aleksandrovna (Gren) M.; m. Tamara Akekseevna Seifort, 1940; 1 child, Olga Igorevna; m. Irina Alekseevna Chagadaeva. Student, Bolshoi Theater Ballet Sch., Moscow, Univ. of Art. Soloist Bolshoi Theater, Moscow, 1924-37; artistic dir. State Acad. Ensemble of Folk Dance, Moscow, 1937—54. Recipient Lenin prize, 1967, State prize 1942, 47, 52, 81, 95; named Honored Artist of USSR, 1953, Hero of the Socialist Labour, 1976. Avocations: chess, books. Home: Moscow, Russia. Died Nov. 2, 2007.

**MOKRZYNSKI, JERZY BOGUSLAW,** architect; b. Rzeszów, Poland, Sept. 22, 1909; s. Joseph and Helen (Tabaczkowska) M.; m. Mary Potczynska-Armotowicz, Apr. 6, 1945; 1 child, Teres. Degree in (architecture), Polytechnic Sch., Warsaw, 1935. Diplomate in architecture. Pvt. practice architecture, 1936-39; with Architectonic State Office, 1945-80. Author: Tourist Facilities, 1962, 72, Vacation Houses, 1977, Architecture of the Leisure Time, 1988; prin. works include Free U., Lódz, Poland, Bank of Investment, Poznan, Poland, Recreation Center, Romanowo, Poland, Philharmonic Hall and Music Sch., Rzeszów, Poland, Labour Party Bldg., Warsaw, Hotel and Mus. Biatowieza, Poland, Railway Stn., Katowice, Poland, Puppet Theatre, Bialystok, Acad. Boarding House, Warsaw, Habitable Forest Quarter Anin.,Warsaw., Music and Fine Arts Sch., Lublin, Poland, Conf. Ctr., Warsaw, Tourist Hotel, Lowicz, Poland, Mus. Tatra Nat. Pk., Zakopane, Poland, Hotel Seamen's Home, Szczecin, Poland, Mus. Comtemporay Art, Skopje, Yugoslavia, Polish Pavillions, New Delhi and Thesaloniki, Greece. Recipient Golden Badge Rebuilding Warsaw award, 1957, Officer's Cross of Polonia Restituta, 1957, Order Banner of Labour, 1969, Golden Medal Ministry of Bldg., 1973, 83, State Art awards grade III, 1951, grade II, 1955, grade I, 1974, Hon. Badge Activist of Culture, 1978. Mem. Polish Assn. Architects (v.p. 1952-56, hon. distinctions), Assn. Authors. Zaiks (sec. architects, hon. distinctions 1968). Roman Catholic. Avocations: nature, travel. Home: Warsaw, Poland. Died June 4, 1997.

**MOLINIE, PHILIPPE GERMAIN ANDRE,** chemist, researcher; b. Paris, Jan. 24, 1946; s. Philippe Albert and Suzanne Cecile (Helbert) M.; m. Chantal Odette Jonquet, July 21, 1971; children: Roland and Viviane (twins). Engr. in Chemistry, Nat. Inst. Applied Scis., Lyon, France, 1970; PhD in Solid State Chemistry, U. Nantes, France, 1977. Attaché de recherche Solid Chemistry Lab. CNRS, Nantes, 1975-79, head of rsch. Mixed Unit of rsch., 1980-91, dir. rsch. Material Inst., from 1991, mgr. rsch. group, 1989-95 and from 2000, chief magnetic measurement dept., from 1980; team dir. physics and chemistry low dimensional solids rsch. groups, 1999—2007; assoc. rschr. Cornell U., Ithaca, NY, 1978. Contbr. articles to profl. jours.; patentee in field. Mem. Neutronic French Soc., Mecanosynthesis French Soc., ACS. Avocation: sailing. Home: Saint-Herblain, France. Died Apr. 26, 2008.

**MOLNAR, GABOR,** mechanical engineer; b. Belisce, Croatia, June 9, 1942; s. Josip and Paulina (Timaric) M.; m. Dusanka Jerosimic, Feb. 16, 1980; 1 child, Zoltan. Diploma in engring., U. Zagreb, 1973. Designer Tehnomehanika factory, Marija Bistrica, Croatia, 1980-84, Koncar Generators, Zagreb, Croatia, 1984-90. Home: Velika Gorica, Croatia. Died Jan. 30, 2001.

**MONDALE, JOAN ADAMS,** wife of the former Vice President of the United States; b. Eugene, Oreg., Aug. 8, 1930; d. John Maxwell and Eleanor Jane (Hall) Adams; m. Walter Frederick Mondale, Dec. 27, 1955; children: Theodore, Eleanor Jane (dec. Sept. 17, 2011), William Hall. BA, Macalester Coll., 1952. Asst. slide librarian Boston Mus. Fine Arts, 1952-53; asst. in edn. Mpls. Inst. of Arts, 1953-57; weekly tour guide Nat. Gallery of Art, Washington, 1965-74; hostess Washington Whirl-A-Round, 1975-76; Second Lady of the US, 1977—81. Author: Politics in Art, 1972, Letters from Japan, 1998. Bd. govs. Women's Nat. Democratic Club; hon. chmn. Fed. Coun. on Arts and Humanities, 1978-80; bd. dirs. Associated Coun. of Arts, 1973-75, Reading Is Fundamental, American Craft Coun., NYC, 1981-88, J.F.K. Ctr. Performing Arts, 1981-90, Walker Art Ctr., Mpls., 1987-93, 97-03, Minn. Orch., Mpls., 1988-93, 97-2003, St. Paul Chamber Orch., 1988-90, Northern Clay Ctr., 1988-93, St. Paul, 1988-93, Nancy Hauser Dance Co., Mpls., 1989-93, Minn. Landmarks, 1991-93; trustee Macalester Coll., 1986-2008; chair Hiawatha Light Rail Transit Pub. Art and Design com., 2000-04; active Walker Art Ctr., 2003-07 Mem.: Phi Beta Kappa Epsilon. Democrat. Presbyterian. Home: Minneapolis, Minn. Died Feb. 3, 2014.

**MONGA, SITA,** secondary school educator; b. Ferozepore, Punjab, India, Dec. 20, 1936; came to U.S., 1956; d. Mohanlal Arora and Raj Rani Chabbra; m. Balraj Monga, July 23, 1961. Teaching diploma, St. Xavier's Coll., Bombay, 1956; BA, Mankato State Coll., 1959; MA, Columbia U., 1965-66. Cert. tchr. With UN, NYC, 1960-64; tchr. Bd. Edn., NYC, from 1966. Avocation: computers. Home: Forest Hills, NY. Died May 16, 2008.

**MONORY, RENÉ CLAUDE ARISTIDE,** French legislator; b. Loudun, France, June 6, 1923; s. Aristide and Marguerite (Devergne) M.; m. Suzanne Cottet, 1945; 1 child. Attended, Ecole primaire supérieure de Thouars. Chair agrl. machinery and oil cos.; pres. Mayor's Assn. Vienne; councillor Canton of Loudun, from 1961; mcpl. judge Sen. for Vienne, 1968-77, 81-86; rapporteur Sen. Finance Com., 1976-77; min. ind. and trade, 1977-78; min. economy, 1978-81; min. edn., 1986-88; chair interim com. of bd. of govs. IMF, 1981; pres. Assn. de l'union républicaine des présidents de conseils généraux, 1983-86, Conseil géneral Poiton-Charentes, 1985; sen. Vienne, 1995; pres. French Senate, 1992—98; founder-pres. The Futuroscope, from 1987. Author: Combat pour le bon sens, 1983, les Clefs du Futur, 1995. Died Apr. 11, 2009.

**MONTAZERI, HOSSEIN ALI,** religious leader; b. Najafabad, Iran, 1922; Incarcerated, 1974—78; ayatollah of Tehran Qom, Iran; Friday prayer leader; dep. to Ayatollah Khomeini Iran. Died Dec. 20, 2009.

**MONTEITH, STAN (STANLEY KIMBALL MONTEITH),** radio talk show host, orthopedic surgeon; b. Oakland, Calif., Feb. 17, 1929; s. Clayton and Blanche (Hart) M.; m. Barbara Elizabeth Johnston, Mar. 1974; children: David, Dorothy DeKock, David Culp. BS, U. Calif., Berkeley, 1949; MD, U. Calif., San Francisco, 1952. Diplomate American Bd. Orthopedic Surgery. Intern San Francisco Gen. Hosp., 1952-53; resident physician Santa Cruz (Calif.) County Hosp., 1955-56; orthopedic trainee U. Calif., 1956-59; sr. resident orthopedic surgery Alameda (Calif.) County Hosp., 1959-60; pvt. practice orthopedic surgery Santa Cruz, 1960—74; prin. surgeon orthopedic dept. U. Free Orange State, Bloemfontein, South Africa, 1974-77; host Radio Liberty. Author: AIDS: The Unnecessary Epidemic-America Under Seige, 1991, Brotherhood of Darkness, 2000, Hidden Agenda: The Fluoride Decption, 2004 Co-chmn. health & human svcs. com. Calif. State Republican Ctrl. Co., 1992. 1st lt., M.C., U.S. Army, 1953-55. Mem. American Acad. Orthopedic Surgeons, Leroy C. Abbot Orthopedic Soc., Western Orthopedic Soc. Christian. Avocation: historical research. Died Sept. 29, 2014.

**MONTES, GREGORIO SANTIAGO,** medical educator, researcher; b. Buenos Aires, Apr. 1, 1952; arrived in Brazil, 1978; s. Roberto Mario Montes and Martha Sara Welch. Degree in vet. surgery, U. La Plata, Buenos Aires, 1974, PhD, 1975. Assoc. prof. U. La Plata, 1976, head prof., 1985-86, U. Lomas Zamora, Buenos Aires, 1977-78; assoc. prof. U. São Paulo, Brazil, from 1988. Vis. prof. U. São Paulo, 1979-84. Contbr. articles to profl. jours. Recipient Rsch. award Argentine Sci. Soc., 1977. Mem. Brazilian Soc. Cell Biology (pres. 1988-94), Brazilian Acad. Scis. Roman Catholic. Avocation: literature. Home: São Paulo, Brazil. Died Oct. 2002.

**MONTGOMERY, ELIZABETH FLANAGAN (MRS. STEWART MAGRUDER MONTGOMERY),** church and civic worker; b. Cary, Miss., July 25, 1898; d. Robert Edward Lee and Annie May (Purdy) Flanagan; m. Stewart Magruder Montgomery, Jan. 5, 1935. Grad., Northwestern Sch. Speech, 1918; AB, Miss. State Coll. Women, 1924; student, Peabody Coll., U. Cal., Columbia. Instr. elem. grades, HS, English and dramatics, Cary, 1924—51. Dir. Indian work, spkr. internat. conv.; state pres. Miss. Women's Cabinet, 1954—55, mem. pub. rels. com., from 1961, recreation chmn.; mem. adv. coun. Miss. Children's Code Commn.; mem. edn. com. Miss. Assn. Mental Health, from 1958, dir., exec. com., nominating com., 1963—66, dir., from 1966, sec., from 1973; county campaign chmn. ARC, 1962; del. Nat. Mental Health Conv., 1963; chmn. Miss. Mental Health Conv., 1964; county commr. Fifth Region Mental Health Ctr., from 1967; dir. State Mental Health Bd.; sec. Miss. Mental Health Assn., 1971—73. Trustee King's Daus. Home, Natchez, Miss., 1948—52, pres. gov.'s bd., from 1956, gov.'s bd. trustees, from 1965; state pres. Women's Orgn., 1952—55; mem. Gov.'s Ladies Staff, Miss., 1960—64, Sharkey County Mental Health Commn., from 1967; sec. Miss. Mental Health, from 1969; pres. IV province Episcopal Ch., 1957—60. Recipient Woman Achievement award, Rolling Fork Bus. and Profl. Women, 1965, Cmty. Leader award, Hist. Preservation America, 1979—80; named Outstanding Civic leader America, 1967. Mem.: Am. Royal Descent, Soc. Magna Charta Dames, Daus. Confederacy, Dames Ct. Honor, Colonial Dames XVII Century, Order of Wash., Daus. Am. Colonists, Internat. Platform Assn., Daus. of 1812, Miss. King's Daus. and Sons (historian from 1969, parliamentarian, state pres. 1955—56), Delta Debutante Club (patron from 1961), Highland Club (pres. aux. 1963—64), Zeta Phi Eta. Episcopalian. Deceased.

**MONTGOMERY, Mrs. STEWART MAGRUDER See MONTGOMERY, ELIZABETH**

**MOODY, GAYLE ANN LAWSON,** English language educator; b. Junction City, Kans., Oct. 21, 1951; d. Ellis Lawrence and Carolyn Marie (Beaven) L.; m. Craig Loring, Nov. 15, 1969; 1 child, Charlotte. BA, S.W. Mo. State U., 1983, MA, 1985; PhD, Baylor Univ., 1993. English instr. U. Md., Heidelberg, Germany, 1985-86, El Paso (Tex.) C.C., 1987, Cen. Tex. Coll., Killeen, 1989-91; asst. prof. English Jarvis Christian Coll., Hawkins, Tex., from 1991. Adv. com. Baylor Univ., 1989-90; adviser Jarvis Christian Coll., 1991-93, mem. lyceum com., self-study editing com., 1991-92, scholarship com., sec. libr. com., 1992-93, chair curriculum com., faculty devel. com. 1992-93. With U.S. Army, 1975-81. Mem. MLA, Nat. Coun. for Tchrs. of English, Coll. Composition and Comms., South Cen. MLA. Avocations: quilting, writing. Home: Pickton, Tex. Died June 7, 1996.

**MOODY, ROBERT ELBRIDGE,** historian; b. Rushville, NY, Apr. 20, 1897; s. Edward Lincoln Moody and Alice Stearns; m. Edith Johncox, Oct. 19, 1921 (dec. Oct. 1962); children: Priscilla Saxby, Jante Merriman, Edward Lewis; m. Oneta Hayes Hawkins, May 28, 1966. AB, Cornell U., 1918. Tchr., history & English Rushville HS, NY, 1928—39; tchr., history Middlesex Valley Ctrl., Rushville, 1939—62; civil svc. commr., Ont. county Canandaigua, 1942—63; town supr. Gorham, NY, 1966—70; town historian, from 1971. Author: (plays) Hiawatha, 1956, Dekanawida, 1957, Outline of Rushville's History, 1976, America's First Rushville, 1991; editor: Town of Gorham Scrapbook, 1976. Deceased.

**MOORE, MARGARET CARRINGTON,** medical educator; b. McKinney, Tex., Oct. 9, 1896; d. John Moses and Margaret (Carrington) M. BS, U. Chgo., 1921; MS, Tulane U., 1931; post grad., U. Colo., 1929, U. N.C., 1941; PhD (hon.), La. State U. Med. Ctr., 1985. Research chemist, editorial writer AMA, Chgo., 1921-25; asst. state chemist La. State Bd. Health, 1926-35, cons. nutrition, 1935-64; abstractor Biol. Abstracts, 1932-64; research asst. dept. chemistry Tulane U. Sch. Medicine, New Orleans, 1933-36, lectr., asst. prof., 1949-69; lectr. La. State U., Baton Rouge, 1945-64, La. State U. Sch. Medicine, New Orleans, 1954-64, vis. assoc. prof., 1969-90; ret., 1990, 1990. Author: What Shall I Eat and Why, 1938, 5th rev. edit., 1955, Dietary-Atherosclerosis Studies on Deceased Persons, 1967, rev. edit., 1981; (software program) DAta Base: Extended Table of Nutrient Values, 1974, 3d rev. edit., 1986, 4th rev. edit., 1988. Pres. French Quarter Residents Assn., New Orleans, 1979—. Recipient First Pioneer award Nutrient Date Base Conf., 1985; named La. Woman of Yr. The Progressive Farmer, 1958; Royal Soc. for Health fellow. Fellow Am. Inst. Chemists (faculty exchange with China med. schs.), Am. Pub. Health Assn.; mem. La. Dietetic Assn. (hon.), Am. Chemists Soc., N.Y. Acad. Scis. Democrat. Presbyterian. Home: Turnersville, NJ. Deceased.

**MOORE, THOMAS HOLMES,** retired school administrator; b. Grafton, NH, June 14, 1920; s. Thomas R. and Lillian Alice (Thompson) M.; m. Norma Jean Smith, Sept. 9, 1944; children: Thomas, Andrew, Jamyn, Robinson, Elibet. Grad., New Hampton Sch., 1938; AB, Middlebury Coll., 1946; postgrad., Breadloaf Sch. English, 1948; PhD (hon.), Franklin Pierce Coll., 1977. With New Hampton Sch., NH, 1946—92, instr. English, head dept., registrar NH, 1946-53, dir. admissions summer session NH, 1949-53, exec. headmaster NH, 1954-59, headmaster NH, 1959-72, 90-92, pres. NH, 1972-90; headmaster emeritus, from 1992; trustee, from 2009. Chmn. bd. Bristol Bank, 1982-83, 85—92; dir. Concord Group Ins. Co., 1992-; pres. NH Ednl. Broadcasting Coun., 1963-68, treas., 1964—, sec., 1970—; mem., chmn. commn. ind. schs. New Eng. Assn. Schs. and Colls., 1970-71, mem. exec. com., 1972—, interim exec. dir., 1973, treas., 1974, v.p., 1975, pres., 1976; chmn. NH Non-Pub. Sch. Adv. Coun.; mem. NH Libr. Commn.; chmn.-elect dist. 1 Coun. Advancement and Support of Edn. Bd. dirs. N.H. Music Festival (pres. 1966, 88), Laconia Hosp., Gordon-Nash Library; pres. No. New Eng. Found. Served to lt. (s.g.), AC USNR, 1941-45. Decorated Air medal, Peitee medal; recipient: Granite State award. Mem. Ind. Schs. Assn. No. New Eng. (pres. 1966), N.H. Library Trustees Assn. (chmn. legislative com.), Bristol C. of C. (dir. 1958) Home: New Hampton, NH. Died Aug. 18, 2013.

**MORA, FRANCISCO,** artist, printmaker; b. Uruapan, Mexico, May 7, 1922; s. Jose Maria and Clotilde (Perez) Mora; m. Elizabeth Catlett Mora, Oct. 31, 1946; children: Francisco, Juan, David. Student, Escuela de Pintura y Escultura La Esmeralda, 1941-46. Tchr. drawing Sch. Pub. Edn. Mexico, 1949-54; art adviser Mexican Acad. Edn., 1956—2002. Mem.: Mex. Acad. Edn. (founder), Salon de la Plastica Mexicana (founder). Died 2002.

**MORAHAN, DANIEL MICHAEL,** management consultant, economist; b. Washington, Aug. 15, 1940; s. John Joseph and Eileen Alice (McKeown) M. AA, George Washington U., 1963, BBA, 1965. Libr. technician and asst. D.C. Pub. Libr., Washington, 1969-62; reference info. cataloger U.S. Libr. Congress, Washington, 1962-65; occupational analyst USES, Washington, 1965-66; manpower analyst Dept. Labor, Washington, 1966-67; economist Bur. Labor Stats., NYC, 1967-68; classification specialist Office U.S. Army Chief Staff, Arlington, Va., 1968-73; economist Office U.S.Army Chief Staff, Arlington, Va., 1973-74; regulation writer Office U.S. Army Adj. Gen., Washington, 1972-73; comml. and govt. counsellor M.E.T.R.A. Enterprise, Hyattsville, Md., from 1974. Pub. policy researcher

Am. Enterprise Inst., Washington, 1977-81. Sgt.-at-arms, rec. sec. Prince Georges Rep. Club, Largo, Md., 1976-81; fellow Nat. Rep. Com., 1978. Mem. NAFE (male mem.), Assn. Trial Lawyers Am. (assoc.), Armed Forces Mgmt. Assn., Am. Security Coun. (Va. advisor 1974-88), Am. Inst. Mgmt. (exec. coun. 1969-80), Res. Officers Assn. U.S., Aerospace Edn. Found. (charter), Air Force Assn., Mil. Dist. Washington Officers Club. Democrat. Roman Catholic. Avocations: singing, concerts, collecting music. Deceased.

**MORDEK, HUBERT KLAUS WOLFGANG,** humanities educator; b. Namslau, Silesia, Fed. Republic Germany, May 8, 1939; s. Alfons and Maria (Kulessa) M. PhD, U. Tübingen, 1969, Habilitation, 1975. Scholar German Hist. Inst., Paris and Rome, 1966-69, collaborator Rome, 1971-74; asst. U. Tübingen, 1969-70, lectr. and prof., 1975-78; prof. medieval history U. Freiburg, Fed. Republic Germany, from 1978. Bd. dirs. Hist. Inst. U., Freiburg, dean Faculty of Philosophy IV, 1980-81, vice-dean, 1981-82; vis. prof. Univs. Basel and Shandong, China, 1982, 86. Author: Kirchenrecht und Reform im Frankenreich, 1975, Bibliotheca Capitularium Regum Francorum Manuscripta, 1995, Studien zur fränkischen Herrschergesetzgebung, 2000; co-editor: (series) Quellen und Forschungen zum Recht im MA, from 1982; editor: (series) Freiburger Beiträge zur ma. lichen Geschichte, from 1990, Festschrift for the 60th Birthday: Quellen, Kritik, Interpretation, from 1999, Festschrift for the 65th Birthday: Scientia veritatis, from 2004. Recipient acad. scholarship Stiftung Volkswagenwerk, 1983-84, Dt. Forschungsgemeinschaft, 1990-91; fellow U. Berkeley, 1991, Princeton Inst. for Advanced Study,94-95. Roman Catholic. Avocations: manuscripts, books, music, sports, travel. Home: Freiburg, Germany. Died Mar. 17, 2006.

**MOREHOUSE, DAVID FRANK,** geologist; b. Charles City, Iowa, Dec. 8, 1943; s. Neal Francis and Florence E. (Schwendener) M. BS in Gen. Scis., State U. Iowa, 1967; MS in Geology, Iowa State U., 1970; postgrad., Pa. State U., 1970-74. Staff geologist Nat. Gas Survey and Planning and Spl. Projects Div., FPC, Washington, 1974-78; dir. Info. Processing and Interpretation and Analysis Divs. Oil and Gas Info. System, Energy Info. Adminstrn., Washington, 1978-80, sr. supervisory geologist, 1980-95, sr. petroleum geologist, 1996—2011; cons., from 2011. Advisor petroleum data sys. U. Okla., Norman, 1975-86; Energy Info. Adminstrn. rep. Am. Gas Assn. Com. on Natural Gas Res., Washington, 1991-95, Potential Gas Com., Boulder, Colo., 1991—2011; Dept. of Energy rep. Fed. Geog. Data Com. Coordination Group, 1997-2011, Homeland Security Working Group, 2001-10; Nat. Critical Infrastructure Task Force Energy Group, 1998—2002, Dept. Energy Lab. Energy R & D Working Group, 2004-, Potential Gas Com., Boulder, Colo., 2011- V.p. Iowa Jr. Acad. Sci., 1961. Recipient awards for outstanding performance Fed. Govt., Washington, 1974-2008. Fellow Nat. Speleological Soc.; mem. AAAS, AIME, AGI, Am. Geophys. Union, Internat. Assn. Math. Geology, Potential Gas Com. Congregationalist. Achievements include first evidence that sulfuric acid can be important to speleogenesis; exercising the prin. responsibility for design and establishment of fed. govts. domestic oil and gas reserves estimation and analysis program. Home: Arlington, Va. Died Mar. 11, 2014.

**MORGAN, JOHN DAVID,** middle school educator; b. Wilmington, Del., June 7, 1937; s. Eberlin Starr and Elizabeth M. (McKelvie) M. BS, West Chester U., 1960, MEd, 1966. Tchr. Chichester Jr. High Sch., Boothwyn, Pa., 1960-71, Beverly Hills Jr. High Sch., Upper Darby, Pa., 1971-80, Beverly Hills Mid. Sch., Upper Darby, 1980-92; sec. membership First Presbyn.Ch., West Chester, Pa., from 1997. Vol. AARP, Meals on Wheals, 1992-, Habitat for Humanity of Chester County, 1999-. Presbyterian. Avocations: collectibles, stamps, travel. Deceased.

**MORGAN, THOMAS BRUCE,** author, editor, public affairs executive; b. Springfield, Ill., July 24, 1926; s. David Edward and Mabel Ariel (Wolfe) M.; m. Joan T. Zuckerman, Oct. 3, 1950 (div. 1972); children: Katherine Tarlow, Nicholas David; m. Mary Clark Rockefeller, May 4, 1974 (div. 1988); stepchildren: Geoffrey, Michael, Sabrina Strawbridge; m. Hadassah Teitz Brooks, Aug. 19, 1990 (dec. 2012); stepchildren: Shoshana Goldhill, Benjamin Brooks. BA, Carleton Coll., 1949. Assoc. editor Esquire Mag., NYC, 1949-53; sr. editor Look Mag., NYC, 1953-58; freelance writer NYC, 1958-69; press sec. to Mayor John V. Lindsay NYC, 1969-73; sr. editor New York Mag., 1974-75; editor The Village Voice, NYC, 1975-76; publisher Politicks mag., NYC, 1976-79; novelist, freelance writer, 1979-89; pres. WNYC Comm. Group, NYC, 1990-94; pres., CEO UN Assn. of U.S.A., NYC, 1994-95; freelance writer, 1996—2014. Press sec. Stevenson for Pres., 1960, McCarthy for Pres., 1968. Author: Friends and Fellow Students, 1956, Self-Creations, 1965, (novel) This Blessed Shore, 1966, Among the Anti-Americans, 1967, (novel) Snyder's Walk, 1987; screenwriter documentary feature film Albert Schweitzer, 1957 (Acad. award); contbr. numerous articles to nat. mags. Trustee Carleton Coll., Northfield, Minn., 1975-79 Mem. PEN, Authors Guild, Century Assn. Democrat. Jewish. Home: Bethlehem, Pa. Died June 17, 2014.

**MORGENROTH, EARL EUGENE,** entrepreneur; b. Sidney, Mont., May 7, 1936; s. Frank and Leona (Ellison) M.; children: Dolores Roxanna, David Jonathan, Denise Christine BS, U. Mont., Missoula, 1961. From salesman to gen. mgr. Sta. KGVO-AM Radio, Missoula, Mont., 1958-65; sales mgr. Stas. KGVO-TV, KTVM-TV and KCFW-TV, Missoula, Butte, Kalispell, Mont., 1965-66, gen. mgr., 1966-68, Sta. KCOY-TV, Santa Maria, Calif., 1968-69; v.p., gen. mgr. Western Broadcasting Co., Missoula, 1966-69, gen. mgr., pres., 1969-81, numerous cos. in Mont., Calif., Idaho, PR, Ga., 1966-84; pres., chmn. Western Broadcasting Co., Missoula, 1981-84, Western Comm., Inc., Reno, 1984-90; prin. Western Investments, Reno, 1984—2010. Chmn. Western Fin., Morgenroth Music Ctrs. Inc., Mont. Band Instruments, Inc., E&B Music Inc., 2007, Times Square, Inc., Rio Plumas Ranches, LLC, 2008; mem. pres. adv. coun. U. Mont., from 1991. Mem. Mont. Bank Bd., Helena; commencement spkr. U. Mont., 1988, mem. pres.' adv. coun., 1992—, mem. biol. scis. adv. coun., 2001—; bd. dirs. U. Mont. Found., 1985-95. With. US Army, 1954-57. Named Boss of Yr. Santa Maria Valley J.C.s, 1968, Alumnus of the Yr., U. Mont. Bus. Sch., 1998. Mem. U. Mont. Century Club (pres.), Missoula C. of C. (pres.), Rocky Mountain Broadcasters Assn. (pres.), Craighead Wildlife-Wildlands Inst. (bd. dirs. 1991-97), Boone and Crockett Club (pres. 2001-02), Grizzly Riders Internat. (bd. dirs., v.p. 1991—, pres. 2008-11), Bldg. A Scholastic Heritage (bd. dirs. 1987-97), Mont. Mus. Arts & Culture (bd. mem. 2001-11), Wildlife Biology U. Mont. (bd. mem. 2000-). Independent. Methodist. Home: Missoula, Mont. Died Mar. 14, 2013.

**MORGENSTERN, SHELDON JON,** symphony orchestra conductor; b. Cleve., July 1, 1938; s. Irwin Arthur and Harriet Sue Morgenstern; m. Patricia Lou Bradshaw; 1 child, Sali Sharpe Hagan. MusB, Northwestern U., 1961; MusM, New Eng. Conservatory, 1966; DMA (hon.), Greensboro Coll., NC, 1986. Mem. conducting staff New Eng. Conservatory, 1965-66; music dir. Greensboro Symphony Orch., 1967-74; prin. guest condr. Betica Philharm., Seville, Spain, 1978-82, Polish Radio Orch., Warsaw, from 1990. Music advisor Miss. Symphony Orch., 1985-86; bd. mem. Istanbul Internat. Festival, Turkey, 1975—, Company for Televised Theatre; mus. cons. U.S. Dept. Interior for Wolf Trap Farm Park, 1972; mem. adv. bd. Avery Fisher Award, 1978—; music dir. Ea. Music Festival, Greensboro, 1962-98, music dir. emeritus, 1998—; artistic adv. Arts Sans Frontieres, 2005-; adv. coun. mem. Kent/Blossom Music Festival, 2006-. Author: No Vivaldi in the Garage, 2001. Mem. adv. bd. Blossom Cleve. Orch. Festival, from 2006. Recipient O'Henry award City of Greensboro, 1980, Long Leaf Pine award State N.C., 1989, Nat. Alumni award Northwestern U., 1990. Home: Collonges, France. Died Dec. 17, 2007.

**MORIGUTI, SIGEITI,** retired statistician, educator, researcher; b. Utinomi, Japan, Sept. 11, 1916; s. Kise (Miyosi) M.; m. Sumi Otani, Apr. 8, 1943; children: Kimi Matutani, Miti Iwatubo. Kogakusi, Tokyo Imperial U., 1938; DEng, U. Tokyo, 1954. Lectr. Tokyo Imperial U., 1938-44; assoc. prof. U. Tokyo, 1944-56, prof., 1956-77, U. Electro-Comms., Tokyo, 1977-82, Tokyo Denki U., 1982-87. Vis. prof. Columbia U., N.Y.C., 1960-61; pres. Internat. Statis. Inst., The Netherlands, 1985-87, Statis. Coun. Govt. Japan, Tokyo, 1978-86. Author: Elementary Mechanics, 1950, Jis Fortran, 1972 and others. Capt. Japanese Army. Recipient Deming prize Deming Prize Com., Tokyo, 1955, Order of Rising Sun Gold and Silver Stars, Japanese Govt., 1990. Mem. Ops. Rsch. Soc. Japan (pres. 1974-76). Home: Tokyo, Japan. Died Oct. 2, 2002.

**MORITZ, ALOIS KLAUS,** research scientist; Head dept. Spranger Labs., Ingolstadt, Germany, from 1987. Died 2008.

**MORLEY, SHERIDAN ROBERT,** film critic, author, journalist, broadcaster; b. Ascot, Eng., Dec. 5, 1941; s. Robert and Joan (Buckmaster) M.; m. Margaret Gudejko, July 18, 1965 (div. 1990); children: Hugo, Alexis, Juliet; m. Ruth Leon, June 7, 1995. MA in Modern Langs. with honors, Oxford U., Eng., 1963; postgrad., U. Hawaii, 1963-64. Newscaster, reporter, scriptwriter ITN, London, 1964-67; interviewer Late Night Line Up BBC-TV, London, 1967-73, presenter Film Night, 1972; dep. features editor, asst. editor The Times, London, 1973-75, arts diarist, TV critic, 1989-90; arts editor and drama critic Punch, London, 1975-88; London drama critic Internat. Herald Tribune, from 1979, Spectator, from 1992; film critic Sunday Express, London, 1992-94, Arts Diarist Punch, from 1997. Mem. drama panel Brit. Coun., 1982-89; presenter Kaleidoscope, Meridian; radio and TV broadcasts on performing arts, Arts Programme, Sheridan Morley Meets..., BBC Radio 2 Arts Programme, 1990-2006; host Theatreland, 1995-96. Author: A Talent to Amuse: the Life of Noel Coward, 1969, Oscar Wilde, 1976, Sybil Thorndike, 1977, Marlene Dietrich, 1977, Gladys Cooper, 1979, (with Cole Lesley and Graham Payn) Noel Coward and his Friends, 1979, The Stephen Sondheim Songbook, 1979, Gertrude Lawrence, 1981, Tales from the Hollywood Raj, 1983, Shooting Stars, 1983, The Theatregoers' Quiz Book, 1983, Katharine Hepburn, 1984, The Other Side of the Moon, 1985, Ingrid Bergman, 1985, The Great Stage Stars, 1986, Spread a Little Happiness, 1986, Out in the Midday Sun, 1988, Elizabeth Taylor, 1988, Odd Man Out: the life of James Mason, 1989, Our Theatres in the Eighties, 1990, Robert My Father, 1993, Audrey Hepburn, 1993, Ginger Rogers, 1995, (with Ruth Leon) Gene Kelly, 1996, Marilyn Monroe, 1996, Hey Mr. Producer: The Musicals of Sir Cameron Mackintosh, 1998, If Love Were All; editor: (with Graham Payn) The Noel Coward Diaries, 1982, Bull's Eyes, 1985; editor Hutchinson Theatre Annuals, 1969-73, Studio Vista Film Studies, Punch at the Theatre, 1980, Methuen Book of Theatrical Short Stories, 1992, Methuen Book of Movie Stories, 1993, Rank Outsider, The Life of Dirk Bogarde, 1996, (with Ruth Leon) Gene Kelly, 1997, Marilyn Monroe, 1998, Hey Mr. Producer!, 1999, Chronicle of Theater, 1999, Beyond the Rainbow*Judy Garland, 1999, Private Lives, 1999, Companion to Noel Coward, 1999, John G: The Authorized Biography, 2000; dir. Song at Twilight, 1999; Noel and Gertie (writer and dir.), 1997,98, contbr. numerous articles to various mags. and jours. Named BP Journalist of Yr., 1989. Mem. Garrick Club. Avocations: talking, swimming, eating. Home: London, England. Died Feb. 16, 2007.

**MORRICE, NORMAN ALEXANDER,** retired ballet company director; b. Agua Dulce, Mex., Sept. 10, 1931; s. Norman and Helen (Vickers) Morrice. Attending, Rambert Sch. Ballet. Ballet Rambert as dancer, 1952; prin. dancer, 1958; asst. dir., 1966—70; dir., 1970—74, Royal Ballet Co., London, 1977—86, Royal Ballet Choreographic Group, Choreographic Studies Royal Ballet Sch.; choreographer ballets; choreographer with Two Brothers, 1958; 2nd ballet Hazana (Premiere, Sadler's Wells Theatre), London, 1958; ballet Hazard Bath Festival, England, 1967; free-lance choreographer, 1974—77. Choreographer (ballets) 1-2-3, Them and Us, Pastorale Variee, Ladies, Spindrift, Numerous Others. Recipient Elizabeth II Coronation award. Died Jan. 11, 2008.

**MORRIS, JOHN WOODLAND, II,** retired engineering consultant, military officer; b. Princess Anne, Md., Sept. 10, 1921; s. John Earl and Allice (Cropper) M.; m. Geraldine Moore King, May 12, 1947; children: Susan K., John Woodland III. BS, U.S. Mil. Acad., 1943; MS, U. Iowa, 1948; postgrad., Army War Coll., 1961—62, U. Pitts., 1966. Commd. 2d lt. U.S. Army, 1943, advanced through grades to lt. gen., 1976; dep. dist. engr. Savannah, Ga., 1952-54; resident engr. Goose Bay, Labrador, 1955-57; staff officer Office Chief Engrs., 1957-60; comdg. officer 8th Engr. Bn., Korea, 1960-61; dist. engr. Tulsa, 1962-65; dep. comdt. U.S. Mil. Acad., 1965-67; dep. chief legis. liaison Office Sec. Army, Washington, 1967-69; comdg. gen. 18th Engr. Brigade, Vietnam, 1969-70; div. engr. Missouri River Div., Omaha, 1970-72; dir. civil works Office C.E., Washington, 1972-75; dep. chief engr. U.S. Army, 1975-76, chief engr., 1976-80; ret., 1980; exec. dir. Royal Volker Stevin, 1980-84; pres. J.W. Morris Ltd., 1981—2010; ret., 2006; prof. U. Md., 1983-86; chmn. bd., CEO PRC Engring., 1986-88. Engr. advisor, cons. Zorc, Rissetto, Weaver & Rosen, 1988-92; engr. advisor Seltzer & Rosen, 1992-98; bd. dirs. Air Water Tech., Morganti Constrn. Co., Search Techs. Inc., Thaco Rsch. Inc., Dutra Corp.; mem. adv. bd. AMEC Ltd., cons. Coear d' Alene Mines, 1998-2010 Mem. Indian Nations coun. Boy Scouts Am., 1962-65; chmn. Water Resources Congress, 1988-90; trustee U.S. Mil. Acad. Assn. Grads, 1986—98; advisor dean engring. and math. U. Vt., 1990-96. Decorated Legion of Merit with three oak leaf clusters, Army D.S.M., Def. D.S.M.; recipient Merit award Am. Cons. Engrs. Council; Palladium medal Audubon Soc.; Excellence award, Constrn. Industry Inst., 1997. Fellow ASCE (Disting. Constructor award 2000, Opal award, 2010); mem. AIA (hon.), Internat. Navigation Congress (v.p.), U.S. Soc. Mil. Engrs. (pres.), Nat. Acad. Engrs. (Founders award 1996), U.S. Com. on Large Dams (named Eng News Record Constrn. Man of Yr. 1977, Navigation Hall of Fame 1990, Golden Beaver award for engring. 1995, Golden Eagle award, 1998, Acad. of Dist. Eng. U. Iowa, 1998, Dist. Grad. of U.S. Mil. Acad., 1998). Episcopalian. Died 2013.

**MORRIS, LOUISE B.,** interior designer; b. Hubbard, Ariz., Aug. 21, 1925; d. William Franklin and Mary Anne (Adams) Butler; m. Gilbert Lavoy Morris, June 3, 1943; children: David, Joanne, Karen Morris Grissom, Donald, Gena Morris Raban, Irene, Dwayne. Prin. Morris Draperies and Interiors, Yuma, Ariz., from 1961. Lectr. in field. Contbr. articles to profl. jours. Rep. precinct committeeman Yuma County, from 1961; mem. relief soc. Ch. Jesus Christ Latter-day Saint, past. primary sec., past pres., past. Sunday sch. and primary tchr. Mem.: Internat. Drapery Assn. (area bd. dirs.), Am. Soc. Interior Designers (assoc.). Republican. Home: Yuma, Ariz. Died Oct. 4, 1991.

**MORRIS, ROBERT,** education educator; b. Akron, Ohio, Nov. 21, 1910; s. Joseph and Katherine (Spielberger) Schmaltz; m. Sara Goldman, Dec. 20, 1940. AB, U. Akron, 1931; MSc, Western Res. U., 1935; DSW, Columbia U. Sch. Social Work, 1959; D of Humane Letters (hon.), Brandeis U., 1984. Prin. welfare officer UNRRA, 1945; regional dir. social services VA, Chgo., 1946-48; social planning cons. Council Jewish Fedns. and Welfare Funds, NYC, 1948-58; prof. social planning Brandeis U., Waltham, Mass., 1959-68, Kirstein prof. social planning, 1968-83, Kirstein prof. social planning emeritus, 1983—2005. Cardinal Medeiros lectr. U. Mass., Boston, 1983—, lectr. Harvard U. Sch. Pub Health, 1974-88; prof. Inst. Health Professions, Mass. Gen. Hosp., 1980-83, U. Md. cons. adj. prof., 1999—; mem. adv. com. Aging Rsch., U.S. Dept. Health, Edn. and Welfare, 1971, Helen Keller Internat. Found. on the Overseas Blind, 1971-74; mem. spl. med. adv. group VA, Washington, 1969-71; cons. on Geriatric Rsch., Nat. VA, 1974-78, U.S. Office of Human Devel. Svcs., 1978-79; v.p. Vis. Nurses Assn., Boston, 1979-92; mem. Fed. Adv. Coun. on Aging Rsch., Mass. State Health Coord. Coun., 1984-85; vice chmn. Mass. Health Data Consortium, 1979-89; chmn. Internat. Rev. Com. Brookdale Inst. for Gerontology and Adult Human Devel., Israel, 1982-83, cons., 1984-85; chmn. Am. Found. for the Blind Com. on Geriatric Blindness, 1969-74; adv. com. Md. Dept. Health and Mental Health, 1993-95; pub. policy com. Nat. Coun. on the Aging, 1993-95, Ctr. for Health Planning, Program and Devel., U. Md. Baltimore County, 2000-03. Author: Feasible Planning for Social Change, 1966, Urban Planning and Social Policy, 1968, Centrally Planned Change, 1964, Trends and Issues in Jewish Social Welfare in the U.S., 1966, Encyclopedia Social Work and Social Welfare, 1971, Toward a Caring Society, 1974, Centrally Planned Change: A Re-Examination of Theories and Concepts, 1974, Social Policy of the American Welfare State, 1979, 2d edit., 1985, Allocating Resources for the Aged and Disabled, 1981, Rethinking Social Welfare: Why Care for the Stranger, 1986, Retirement Reconsidered, 1988, Economic Roles for the Elderly, 1987, 88, Testing the Limits of Social Welfare; International Perspectives on Policy Changes in Nine Countries, 1988, International Perspectives on State and Family Support for the Elderly, 1993, The National Government and Social Welfare, 1997, Personal Assistance: The Future of Home Care, 1998, Welfare Reform 1996-2000: Is There a Safety Net, 1999, Social Work at the Millenum, 2000; editor Jour. of Social Work, 1960-72, Jour. Aging and Social Policy, 1983—. Cons. NIMH, 1964-70; chmn. adv. bd. Mass. Dept. Welfare, 1968-69; profl. adv. com. Easter Seal Soc., 1971-80; mem. Mass. Gov.'s Commn. on Nursing Homes, 1962-67, on Aging, 1962-67, on Hosp. Costs, 1967, Mass. Soc. Prevention Blindness, 1971-75; organizer Odyssey Forum on Federal Social Policy, 1995—. With AUS, 1943-44. Fulbright award, Italy, 1965-66, 68, Ford Found. fellow U.K., 1969-70; recipient rsch. awards Ford Found., 1960-65, Treuhaft Found., 1964, 72, Max and Anna Levinson Fund, 1970, 72, U.S. Pub. Health Svcs., 1957, 59, 65, NSF, 1975-78, W.K. Kellog Found., 1997, Retirement Rsch. Found., 1998, Louis Lowy award Mass. Gerontology Soc., 1994. Fellow AAAS, APHA, Gerontol. Soc. Am. (Kent award 1988, Maxwell Pollack award 1992, pres. 1966-67), Mass. Pub. Health Assn. (Lemuel Shattuck medal 1976), Ctr. for Applied Gerontology (Heritage award 1987), Commonwealth of Mass. and Assn. for Gerontology in Higher Edn. (Spl. Recognition award 1987), Columbia U. Sch. Social Wor (centennial award for leadership in edn.). Died 2005.

**MORRISON, CLARENCE CLAPP,** retired economics professor; b. Greensboro, NC, June 19, 1932; s. Clarence Nickolson and Ava Clapp Morrison; m. Geraldine Whitesides Morrison, Sept. 11, 1955; children: Robert Hall, Frederick Clapp. BS, Davidson Coll., NC, 1954; MA, U. NC, Chapel Hill, 1956, PhD, 1964. Instr. Norfolk Coll. of William & Mary, Va., 1959—60; asst. prof. U. Va., Charlottesville, 1964—67; assoc. prof. U. Ga., Athens, 1967—70; prof. Ind. U., Bloomington, 1970—96, prof. emeritus, from 1996. Vis. prof. U. NC, Chapel Hill, 1976. Bd. editors Atlantic Econ. Jour., St. Louis, from 1977; contbr. articles to profl. jours. Unit leader United Way Ind. U. Dept. Econs., 1995—2005. Lt. j.g. USN, 1956—59. Recipient A.K. Pfifer award in econs., Davidson Coll., 1953—54; tchg. fellow, U. NC, 1955—56, Wachovia fellow, 1962—63. Mem.: So. Econ. Assn., Am. Econ. Assn., Internat. Atlantic Econ. Soc. (v.p. 1979—80, pres. 1995—96). Presbyterian. Avocations: travel, genealogy. Home: Bloomington, Ind. Died Aug. 6, 2008.

**MORRISON, LUCILE PHILLIPS,** psychologist, writer; b. LA, Sept. 8, 1896; d. Lee A. and Catherine (Coffin) Phillips; m. Wayland Augustus Morrison, Dec. 27, 1917; children: Wayland Lee, Richard Holt, Lee Allen, Keith Norman; 1 adopted child, Patricia Lee. BA, Vassar Coll., 1918; MA in Psychology, George Pepperdine Coll., 1958; LittD (hon.), Calif. Sch. Profl. Psychology, 1978. Cert. psychologist Calif., lic. Calif.; marriage, family and child counselor Calif. Intern Am. Inst. Family Rels., LA, 1952—53, asso. counselor, 1954—55, counselor, 1955—64, v.p. bd. dirs., 1964. Dir. Children's Hosp., LA, 1921—44; pres. (founding mem.) Duarte Cmty. Svc. Coun., Calif., 1946—48, v.p., 1948—50, health chmn., 1951—54; dir., mem. Duarte Cmty. Ctr. Bd., Calif., 1949—57. Author: Mystery Gate, 1928, The Attic Child, 1929, Blue Bandits, 1930, The Lost Queen of Egypt, 1938 (Nat. Pen Women's award for fiction, 1938); co-author: Taylor-Johnson Temperament Analysis, 1967; editor: Doll Dreams (4 vols.), 1927—32, The World of Books (for Scripps Coll.), 1934; contbr. articles to profl. jours. Trustee mem. coms. Scripps Coll., 1930—72; chmn. ednl. policy com., 1965—70; trustee emeritus, from 1972; constituent mem. bd. fellows Claremont U. Ctr., Calif., 1967—70; mem. adv. bd. Inst. Antiquity and Christianity, Claremont Grad. Sch., from 1968; mem. The Founders, Music Ctr. Performing Arts, LA; v.p., dir. mem. staff Psychol. Guidance Ctr., Anaheim, Calif., 1960—63; trustee Westminster Gardens Presbyn. Ch., 1953—66, hon. life trustee, from 1966; bd. dirs. Calif. Sch. Profl. Psychology, 1973—79, exec. coun., 1973, acad. commn., 1974—78. Recipient Ellen Browning Scripps Assocs. award, 1976; named Woman of Yr., Marlborough Sch. LA, 1979. Mem.: AAUW, Calif. State Marriage Counselors Assn., Am. Assn. Marriage Counselors, Western Psychol. Assns., Acad. Psychologists in Marital Counseling, Hist. Soc. Southern Calif., Child Study Assn. America, NY Acad. Scis., So. Calif. Symphony Assn., Women's University Club (LA), Psi Chi, Delta Kappa Gamma, Phi Beta Kappa. Home: Peoria, Ariz. Died 1991.

**MORRISON, ROGER BARRON,** geologist; b. Madison, Wis., Mar. 26, 1914; s. Frank Barron and Elsie Rhea (Bullard) M.; m. Harriet Louise Williams, Apr. 7, 1941 (dec. Feb. 1991); children: John Christopher, Peter Hallock and Craig Brewster (twins). BA, Cornell U., 1933, MS, 1934; postgrad., U. Calif., Berkeley, 1934—35, Stanford U., 1935—38; PhD, U. Nev., 1964. Registered profl. geologist, Wyo. Geologist U.S. Geol. Survey, 1939-76; vis. adj. prof. dept. geoscis. U. Ariz., 1976-81, Mackay Sch. Mines, U. Nev., Reno, 1984-86; cons. geologist; pres. Morrison and Assocs., Morrison Cons. Corp., from 1978. Prin. investigator 2 Landsat-1 and 2 Skylab earth resources investigation projects NASA, 1972-75. Author 3 books; co-author 1 book; co-editor 2 books; editor Quaternary Nonglacial Geology, Conterminous U.S., Geol. Soc. Am. Centennial Series, vol. K-2, 1991; mem. editl. bd. Catena, 1973-88; contbr. over 250 articles to profl. jours. Fellow Geol. Soc. Am.; mem. AAAS, Internat. Union Quaternary Rsch. (mem. Holocene and paleopedology commns., chmn. work group on pedostratigraphy), Am. Soc. Photogrammetry and Remote Sensing, Internat. Soil Sci. Soc., Am. Quaternary Assn. Achievements include research in on Quaternary geology and geomorphology, hydrogeology, environmental geology, neotectonics, remote sensing of Earth resources, paleoclimatology, pedostratigraphy; technology for converting waste wood, garbage, municipal solid waste, natural gas, landfill gas, etc. to mixed-alcohol motor fuel; development of of forest and range land and a new town in western Paraguay; research in nuclear waste issues at Yucca Mtn., Nev. Died 2006.

**MORRISS, FRANK,** writer, educator; b. Pasadena, Calif., Mar. 28, 1923; s. B. Gerard Morriss and Regina Spann; m. Mary Rita Moynihan, Feb. 11, 1950 (dec. Oct. 23, 1996); children: Patricia, Mary Ellen Hill, Regina Sister M. John, OSF(dec.), Gerard. BS in Philosophy magna cum laude, Regis Coll., Denver, 1943; JD, Georgetown U., 1948. Editor Register Newspapers, Denver, 1949—61, 1963—67; assoc. editor Vt. Cath. Tribune, Burlington, 1961—63; contbg. editor The Wanderer, St. Paul, 1967—2007; educator Colorado Cath. Acad., Wheat Ridge, Colo., from 1973. Bd. dirs. Wanderer Forum Found., St. Paul, from 1969; policy expert Heritage Found., from 1995. Author: Saints In Verse, Two Chapels, The Divine Epic, The Catholic as Citizen, The Conservative Imperative, Boy of Philadelphia, Alfred of Wessex, The Adventures of Broken Hand, Submarine Pioneer, (lectrs. on CD) Saints Speak to Modern World, Francis Thompson: A Reflection on the Poetic Vocation. Founder Colo. Cath. Acad., Wheat Ridge, 1970—2002. Sgt. US Army, 1943—45, PTO. Recipient Frederic Ozanam award, Soc. Cath. Social Scientists, 2003. Mem.: Fellowship of Cath. Scholars, VFW. Republican. Roman Catholic. Home: Wheat Ridge, Colo. Died Jan. 25, 2014.

**MORROW, RICHARD MARTIN,** retired oil company executive; b. Wheeling, W.Va., Feb. 27, 1926; B.M.E., Ohio State U., 1948. With Amoco Corp., 1948-91; v.p. Amoco Prodn. Co., 1964-66; exec. v.p. Amoco Internat. Oil Co., 1966-70, Amoco Chem. Corp., 1970-74, pres., 1974-78, Amoco Corp., 1978-83, chmn. chief exec. officer, 1983-91; ret., 1991. Trustee U. Chgo. and Rush U. Med. Ctr. Died 2013.

**MORSE, EMILY BOMBERGER (SWOPE),** elementary school educator; b. Tulpehocken Twp., Pa., May 10, 1899; d. Daniel and Mary Jane (Baumberger/Bomberger) Swope; m. Wilbert Morse, Aug. 22, 1923; children: Winifred Morse McLachlan, Mary Ellen Morse Branin. Tchr.'s cert., Keystone State Normal Sch., Kutztown, Pa., 1919; BS in Elem. Edn., Newark State Tchr.'s Coll., 1958. Tchr. elem. sch., Northampton, Pa., 1919-23, Verona, N.J., 1951-64; tchr. Miss Beards Pvt. Sch. for Girls, Orange, N.J., 1966-68. Author (all with Winifred McLachlan): The Swope Family Book of Remembrance, 1972, The Baumberger/Bomberger Family Book of Remembrance, 1982, The Morse Family Book of Remembrance, 1978. Chairperson Needlers, United Hosps. Med. Ctr., Newark. Mem. AARP, AAUW, DAR, Ladies Aux. of VFW, Jost Schwab and Jakob Schwob Family Assn. (founder, award for Swope reunion for 21 yrs. 1989). Avocations: genealogy, writing, reading, knitting afghans. Died Sept. 7, 1997.

**MORSE, WILLIAM FRANCIS,** clergyman; b. Western Springs, Ill., Aug. 25, 1899; s. Francis William and Phoebe A. (Kelsey) M. m. Mary Quintila Shirley, Feb. 22, 1929; children: William George, Patricia Anne Student, Eugene Bible U., 1920-23, Linfield Coll., 1940-41. ordained to ministry Christian Ch., 1935. Farmer, Harrisburg, Oreg., 1923-26; retail salesman Chase Gardens, Harrisburg, Eugene, 1927; mgr. Sunnyside Greenhouses, Portland, Oreg., 1928, owner, operator florist bus. Newberg, Oreg., 1928-40; mgr. relief work east end Yamhill County, Newberg, Oreg., 1932-33; founder Mt. Top ch., Newberg, Oreg., 1932-40; pastor Ch. of Christ, Amity, Oreg., 1940-44, 48-50, Seaside (Oreg.) Christian Ch., 1944-48; organizer Wi-Ne-Ma Christian Camp, Inc., Cloverdale, Oreg., 1944, pres., 1944-69, gen. mgr., 1950-67, trustee, 1944-70; pastor Wi-Ne-Ma Christian Ch., 1951-70, researcher, genealogist, 1970—. Author: (autobiography) Beyond What We Ask or Think, 1986 Mem. Newburg Park Commn., 1933-40, Sch. Bd., 1936-40; trustee Turner Meml. Home, 1946-80, trustee emeritus, 1980—; chmn. bd. trustees Oretown Cemetery Assn., 1970-78, trustee, 1979—; chmn. Area Agy. on Aging, Dist. 1, Tillamook-Clatsop County, Oreg., 1976-79, mem. exec. bd., 1976-82; bd. dirs. Am. Indian Evangelism Assn., 1977-86. With U.S. Army, World War I. Mem. Nestucca Fellowship (pres. 1966-67), Oretown Grange Vets. World War I. Home and Office: 25620 Chinook St Cloverdale OR 97112-9600

**MORTENSEN, DALE THOMAS,** economics professor; b. Enterprise, Oreg., Feb. 2, 1939; s. Thomas Peter and Verna Bernice Mortensen; m. Beverly Patton, July 13, 1963; children: Karl, Lia Osborne, Julie Glanville. BA, Willamette U., 1961; PhD, Carnegie-Mellon U., 1967; DSc (hon.), Willamette U., 2011. Asst. prof. economics Northwestern U., Evanston, Ill., 1965—71; assoc. prof. Northwestern U, Evanston, Ill., 1971—75; chmn. dept. economics Northwestern U., Evanston, Ill., 1979—82, prof., 1975—2014, Ida C. Cook prof. economics, 1985—2014. Fellow Inst. for Advanced Study, Hebrew U., Jerusalem, 1979; vis. Morgenstern prof. economics NYU, N.Y.C., 1985; vis. economist Cen. Inst. Math.-Econ., Moscow, 1989, Australian Nat. U., Canberra, 1996, vis. researcher Centre for Labor Market & Social Rsch., 1998, rsch. fellow Inst. for Study of Labor (IZA), 2001-14, rsch assoc., Nat. Bur. Econ. Rsch., 2005-14, Niels Bohr vis. prof. economics U. Aarhus, 2006-10 Contbr. articles to profl. jours.; author: Wage Dispersion: Why Are Similar Workers Paid Differently?, 2005 Recipient Alexander Henderson award, 1965, IZA prize in Labor Economics, 2005, Soc. Labor Economics Mincer prize, 2007; co-recipient Nobel Prize in Economics, Royal Swedish Acad. Sciences, 2010. Fellow Econometric Soc., American Acad. Arts & Sciences Home: Evanston, Ill. Died Jan. 9, 2014.

**MORTIER, GERARD,** opera company director; b. Ghent, Belgium, Nov. 25, 1943; D (hon.), U. Antwerp, Belgium. Adminstr. asst. Flanders Festival, 1968—72; artistic planner Duetsche Oper am Rhein, Düsseldorf, 1972—73; asst. adminstr. Oper der Stadt Frankfurt am Main, 1973—77; dir. artistic prodn. Hamburg Staatsoper, 1977—79; tech. program cons. Théâtre Nat. de 'Opéra de Paris, 1979—81; gen. dir. Théâtre Royal de la Monnaie, Brussels, 1981—91, Salzburger Festspiele, Austria, 1990—2001; founding dir. Ruhr Triennial Arts Festival, Germany, 2001—04; gen. dir. Opéra National de Paris, 2004—09; gen. mgr., artistic dir. NYC Opera, 2007—08; artistic dir. Teatro Real, Madrid, 2009—13. Decorated Comdr. des Arts et des Lettres, France; recipient Nat. Medal of Honor, Belgium, Germany. Mem.: Acad. Arts Berlin. Died Mar. 9, 2014.

**MORTLAND, DONALD FRANK,** retired English professor; b. Searsport, Maine, Jan. 20, 1927; s. Ralph Irving and Annie Rolfe (Buck) M.; m. Jacqueline Alice Currier, Aug. 23, 1956; children: Deborah, Pamela. AB, Bowdoin Coll., 1950; AM, Yale U., 1953; D of New Eng. Lit. (hon.), Unity Coll., 1980. English tchr. Potter Acad., Sebago, Maine, 1950-52, Pemetic High Sch., Southwest Harbor, Maine, 1953-56, South Portland (Maine) High Sch., 1956-57, Searsport High Sch., 1957-59, New Hampton (N.H.) Sch., 1959-66; prof. English Unity Coll., Maine, 1966—96. Editor: Sea Stories, 1987; contbr. article, story to profl. publs. Speaker Unity Union Ch., 1990. Staff sgt. U.S. Army, 1945-46. Mem. Phi Beta Kappa. Republican. Methodist. Avocation: local history and architecture. Home: Milton, Mass. Died Feb. 27, 2014.

**MORTON, SIR ALASTAIR,** business executive; b. Jan. 11, 1938; s. Harry Newton Morton and Elizabeth Martino; m. Sara Bridget Stephens, 1964; 2 children. BA, Witwatersrand U., South Africa; MA, Oxford U., Eng.; postgrad., MIT, 1964; LLD (hon.), U. Bath, Eng., 1990, U. Kent, 1992; D (hon.), U. Brunel, Eng., 1992; DSc (hon.), U. Warwick, Eng., 1994, U. Cranfield, 1996. With Anglo Am. Corp. of South Africa, London and Cen. Africa, 1959-63, Internat. Fin. Corp., Washington, 1964-67, Indsl. Reorgn. Corp., London, 1967-70; dir., chmn. Draymont Securities, London, 1970-76; mng. dir. Brit. Nat. Oil Corp., London, 1976-80; CEO Guinness Peat Group, London, 1982-87, chmn., 1987; co-chmn. The Eurotunnel Group, London, 1987-96, hon. chmn., 1997—2004; former chmn. bd. Brit. Railways and Shadow Strategic Rail Authority. Chmn. Kent TEC, 1990-95, Chancellor's Pvt. Fin. Panel, 1993-95, Chartered Inst. Transport, 1992-94. Mem. coun. Royal Inst. Internat. Affairs, 1990-96; chmn. Nat. Youth Orch. of Great Britain, 1994—. Named Knight, 1991, Comdr. de la Légion d'Honneur, France, 1994; gold medalist Instn. of Civil Engrs., 1994. Mem. Univ. Club (N.Y.C.), Itchenor Sailing Club, Country Club (Johannesburg, South Africa). Avocations: sailing, walking, touring. Home: London, England. Died Sept. 1, 2004.

**MORTON, BRUCE ALEXANDER,** retired news correspondent; b. Norwalk, Conn., Oct. 28, 1930; s. Alexander X. and Jeanette Mae (Cook) M.; divorced; children: Sarah J., Alexander J. AB, Harvard U., 1952. Corr. ABC News, London, 1962-64, CBS News, Washington, 1964-93; nat. corr. CNN, Washington, 1993—2006; ret., 2006. Contbr. The Picture Man, 1993; author: (memoirs) The Place to Be, 2008 Served in US Army, 1952-55. Recipient Emmy awards (6) TV Acad., Peabody award U. Ga., Polk award Overseas Press Club. Mem. Soc. Profl. Journalists. Avocations: reading, tennis. Home: Washington, DC. Died Sept. 5, 2014.

**MORTON, WOOLRIDGE BROWN, JR.,** lawyer; b. NYC, Nov. 11, 1914; s. W. Brown and Lucie Crommelin (Taylor) Morton; m. Louisa Lay, June 10, 1935; children: Lisa Morton Chute, W. Brown III, Lucie Morton Garrett; 1 child, Marion H. Morton Carroll. BS, U. Va., 1936; LLB, 1938. Bar: Va. 1938, NY 1940, DC 1951. Assoc. Pennie, Davis, Marvin & Edmonds, and Successor Firms, NYC & Wash., 1938—50, ptnr., 1950—64, McLean, Morton & Boustead, NYC & Wash., 1964—70, Morton, Bernard, Brown, Roberts & Sutherland, Wash., 1970—77, Morton and Roberts, 1978Wash., 1977; pvt. practice King George, Va., 1980—81, Warsaw, Va., from 1981. Lectr. U. Va., Charlottesville, 1959—82. Maj. US Army, 1941—46. Decorated Croix de Guerre France. Mem.: ABA (house dels. 1965—79), Am. Intellectual Property Law Assn. (pres. 1964—65), DC Bar Assn., Va. Bar Assn. Episcopalian. Deceased.

**MOSCA, AUGUST,** artist; b. Naples, Italy, Aug. 19, 1905; U.S. citizen; Student, Yale Sch. Fine Arts, Pratt, Inst., Art Student's League, Grand Cen. Art Sch. Painter, printmaker Libr. Congress, Washington, Bklyn. Mus., N.Y. Pub. Libr., Grey Coll., NYU, Fordham U. Instr. art and drawing Pratt Inst., Bklyn., 1955, Tuxedo Park Sch., N.Y., 1968-72, others. Commns. include Portrait of Heywood Brown, Newspaper Guild of N.Y., 1955 & Newspaper Guild of Am., Washington, 1957; exhbns. in Bklyn. Mus. Watercolor Internat. Ann., 1959, Mus. Modern Art, N.Y., 1961, Butler Inst. Am. Art, Youngstown, Ohio, 1962, Impressionists and Post-Impressionists, Grand Cen. Art Galleries, N.Y., 1988, A Fifty-Year Retrospective, Grand Cen. Art Galleries, N.Y., 1990, Silverpoint Etcetera: Contemporary Metalpoint Drawings, ACA Galleries, N.Y., Newark Mus., N.J., others; group exhbns. ACA Gallery, 29, Italian-Am. Artists, Hunter Col., 1994, Daniel Lewitt Gallery, N.Y., 1995-96, Millenium Gallery, Easthampton, N.Y., and others; 32 works in the S.I. Hist. Soc. Recipient Calif. Palace of the Legion of Honor Silver medal, 1945, Audubon Artists Pres.'s award, 1976, Barney Paisner Purchase Award, Soc. Am. Graphic Artists, 1976; Soc. Am. Graphic Artists Purchase award 1977, cert. of merit Audubon Artists, 1984; Award of Merit, 1984; Jane Peterson Award, Soc. of Painters and Sculptures, 1984; celebrated "Gus Mosca Day", Shelter Island, N.Y., 1996. Achievements include work in the permanent collections of the Libr. of Congr., Grey Mus. at N.Y.U., the Brooklyn Mus., Butler Inst. of Am. Art, Roy Nerberger Mus., N.Y. Pub. Libr., Shelter Island Hist. Soc. Died 2003.

**MOSELY, JACK MEREDITH,** thoracic surgeon; b. Hodge, La., July 20, 1917; s. Charles Hodge and Lucille (Hays) M.; m. Kathryn L. Stephenson, Apr. 30, 1954 (div. May 1972); children: Kathryn S. Mosely-Bennett, Jack

Meredith Jr.; m. Elberta Pate, Sept. 23, 1995. BS, La. State U., Baton Rouge, 1939; MD, La. State U., New Orleans, 1943. Diplomate Am. Bd. Surgery, Am. Bd. Thoracic Surgery. Intern Univ. Hosp., Mpls., 1943-48, resident in surgery, head resident, instr. Syracuse, N.Y., 1946-48, 49-50; fellow in surgery Lahey Clinic, Boston, 1948-49; resident in thoracic surgery Herman Kiefer Hosp., Detroit, 1952-53; instr. thoracic surgery Tulane U. Med. Sch., New Orleans, 1953; pvt. practice thoracic surgery, New Orleans, 1953, Santa Barbara, Calif., from 1953. Chmn. health sect. Welfare Planing Coun., Santa Barbara, 1955-57; mem. Atty. Gen.'s Vol. Adv. Coun., State of Calif., 1974-75; chmn. dept. thoracic and cardiovascular surgery Cottage Hosp., Santa Barbara, 1995—. Pres. bd. dirs. Wood Glen Hall, Santa Barbara, 1971-73. Capt. M.C., U.S. Army, 1944-46. Fellow ACS, Am. Thoracic Soc., Pan Am. Med. Assn., Southeastern surg. Congress; mem. Valley Club of Montecito. Avocations: golf, travel, reading, gardening. Home: Santa Barbara, Calif. Died July 24, 1999.

**MOSER, JÜRGEN KURT,** mathematician, educator; b. Konigsberg, Germany, July 4, 1928; s. Kurt E. and Ilse I. (Strehlke) M.; m. Gertrude Courant, Sept. 10, 1955; children: Nina Moser-Rathbun, Lucy Moser Jauslin. Dr.rer.nat., U. Göttingen, Germany, 1952; Dr. honoris causa, U. P. and M. Curie, Paris, 1990; Dr.rer.nat. h.c., Ruhr U., Bochum, Germany, 1990. Asst. prof. NYU, 1956-57, prof., 1960-80, dir. Courant Inst., 1967-70; asst. prof. MIT, Cambridge, Mass., 1957-58, assoc. prof., 1958-60; prof. math. ETH, Zürich, Switzerland, 1980-95, dir. rsch. inst., 1984-95. Co-author: Lectures on Celestial Mechanics, 1971; author: Stable and Random Motions, 1973, Integrable Hamiltonian System, 1981; contbr. articles to profl. jours. Recipient G.D. Birkhoff prize Am. Math. Soc. and SIAM, 1968, Craig Watson medal Nat. Acad. Sci., U.S.A., 1969, L.E.J. Brouwer medal, Groningen, Holland, 1984, Cantor medal German Math. Soc., 1992, Wolf prize, Israel, 1994/95. Mem. Nat. Acad. Scis., Internat. Math. Union (pres. 1983-86), Am. Assn. Arts and Sci., Finnish Acad. Sci. and Letters, Acad. Wiss. and Literatur, Royal Swedish Acad. Sci. (fgn. mem.), Deutsche Acad. Leopoldina (senate 1992), Russian Acad. Scis. (fgn. mem.); recipient Wolf Prize in Mathematics, 1994. Mem. French Acad. Scis. (fgn.), Moscow Math. Soc. (hon.), Nat. Acad. Scis. of Ukraine (fgn.). Died Dec. 17, 1999.

**MOSER, LIDA,** photographer, writer; b. Aug. 17, 1920; Represented in permanent collections Nat. Portrait Gallery, Washington, London, Libr. of Congress, Washington, NY Hist. Soc., Can. Ctr. for Architecture, Montreal, Nat. Archives of both Ottawa and Quebec, Scottish Nat. Portrait Gallery, Toledo Mus. of Art, J.P. Morgan & Co., Hallmark Fine Art Collection, exhibitions include Fraser Gallery, Washington, D.C., 2005; author: Fun in Photography, 1974, Grants in Photography, 1979, Amphoto Guide to Special Effects, 1980, Photography Contests, 1981, Quebec a l'ete 1950, 1982, Career Photography, 1983; columnist: NY Sunday Times. Home: Rockville, Md. Died Aug. 11, 2014.

**MOSEROVA, JAROSLAVA,** Czech senator; b. Prague, Czech Republic, Jan. 17, 1930; s. Jaroslav and Anna M.; m. Milan David, 1963; 1 child, Tomas. MD, Charles U., Prague, Czech Republic, 1955, DS. House surgeon Duchcov, Czech Republic, 1955-60; house surgeon, dir. rsch. Med. Sch., Charles U., Czech Republic, 1960-90; nat. coun. deputy Czech Republic, 1990-91; amb. to Australia, 1991-93; gen. sec. Nat. UNESCO Commn., Czech Republic, from 1993; v.p. senate Prague, Czech Republic, 1996-98; senator The Senate, Valdstejnske nam, Czech Republic, 1998—2006; pres. GC UNESCO, Czech Republic, 1999—2001, 2003—06. Mem. exec. bd. UNESCO, pres. Czech commn. Contbr. articles to profl. jours. Decorated officer Order of Merit (France); recipient Polish Med. Acad. award, 1982, Charles Un Med. Sch. award, 1994, Gold medal UNESCO, 2004 Mem. Artists Union, PEN Inernat., Rotary. Avocations: writing, translating novels. Home: Prague, Czech Republic. Died Mar. 23, 2006.

**MOSES, CARL E.,** former state legislator; b. Santa Cruz, Calif., July 16, 1929; m. Laresa Moses; children: Lewis, Arline. Student, U. Wash. Owner, operator Carl's Coml. Co., 1966—77; pres. Aleut Corp., 1975—80, Carl's Inc., 1977—2014; mem. Alaska House of Reps., 1964—72, Alaska House of Reps., 1993—2007. Mem. King Cove City Coun., 1963—64, Alaska Rural Housing Bd., 1966, ADF&G Bd., 1973. With US Army. Mem.: Unalaska Chamber of Commerce (bd. dirs.), American Legion. Democrat. Avocations: hunting, fishing. Died Apr. 30, 2014.

**MOSHIER, MARY BALUK,** lawyer; b. Pitts., Aug. 20, 1905; d. Andrew and Johanna (Hlebasko) Baluk; m. Ross Warren Moshier; children: Thomas, Stephen. BA, U. Ark., 1929; postgrad., U. Chgo., 1945-46; JD, No. Ky. U., 1962. Bar: U.S. Patent Office 1944, Ohio 1962. Tchr. Gary (Ind.) Pub. Schs., 1930-35; tech. libr. Monsanto Co., Dayton, Ohio, 1936-41, patent chemist, 1942-45, agt., atty., 1949-66; patent adviser U.S. Office of Naval Rsch., San Francisco, 1948-49; patents cons., patent lawyer, pvt. practice, from 1969. Co-author: Anydrous Aluminum Chloride in Organic Chemistry, 1941. Mem. AAAS, AAUW, NOW, Lawyers Club of Sun City, Nat. Assn. Ret. Fed. Employees, Phi Alpha Delta Legal Frat. Internat. Democrat. Episcopalian. Avocations: reading, bridge, chess, gardening. Deceased.

**MOSLEY, CHARLES GORDON,** writer; b. London, Sept. 14, 1948; s. George Gordon and Christine Daisy Ord (Dowland) M; m. Alice Jean Hyde, Mar. 17, 1981 (div. Aug. 1990); m. Lesley Vere Lake, Jan. 18, 2003 (dec. 2013) Student, Eton, Eng., 1963-67; BA, King's Coll., Cambridge, Eng., 1970, MA, 1973. Dep. editor Adam Internat. Rev., London, 1970-71; libr. Ency. Britannica, London, 1971-74, dep. London editor, 1983-85, London editor, 1985-86; mem. info. rsch. dept. Fgn. and Commonwealth Office, London, 1974-77; database cons., Rome, 1977-79; editor Debrett's Peerage Ltd., London, 1979-83, editor-in-chief, 2004—06; writer, journalist London and Ireland, 1987-93; editor-in-chief Burke's Peerage and Baronetage, 1993—2004. Author/editor: Debrett's Handbook, 1982; author: Lichfield in Retrospect, 1988, American Presidential Families, 1993, Debrett's Guide to Entertaining, 1994, Debrett's Guide to Bereavement, 1995, Blood Royal: From the Time Alexander the Great to Queen Elizabeth II, 2002, The Art of Oratory, 2007, Charles Dickens: A Celebration of His Life and Work, 2011, The Daffodil Library, 2013; contbr. articles to newspapers and mags. Vice-chmn. Families for Defence, London, 1984-87. Mem. Reform Club London, Kildare Street and Univ. Club, Dublin. Avocations: reading, music, wine, walking dachshund dog. Died Nov. 5, 2013.

**MOURAVIEFF-APOSTOL, ANDREW,** association executive; b. Cannes, France, Feb. 7, 1913; s. Wladimir and Nadine (Tereschenko) M.-A.; m. Mary C. Hall-Caine, Nov. 10, 1938; m. 2d, Ellen Marion Rothschild, Nov. 12, 1956; children: Michael, Nicholas, Christopher A. BS, Geneva U., 1935; Dr (hon.), Tumen U. Paris and Berlin corr. London Daily Telegraph, 1936-40; columnist Evening Standard, London, 1940-48; resettlement officer UN High Commn. for Refugees, Geneva, 1949-67; hon. pres. Internat. Fedn. Social Workers. Dir. info. P.C./UNESCO, London, 1946-48; UN advisor to Govt. Peru, 1951-52. Decorated Bailiff Grand Cross Order of St. John of Jerusalem; Grand Cross Order of St. Saba; Order Homayun (Iran); Order of Merit (Chile). Mem. Russian Acad. of Learning, Royal Soc. St. George (life gov.), Naval and Military Club (London) Mem. Anglican Church. Home: Geneva, Switzerland. Died Aug. 13, 2001.

**MOWAT, FARLEY MCGILL,** writer; b. Belleville, Ont., Can., May 12, 1921; s. Angus McGill and Helen (Thomson) M.; m. Frances Elizabeth Thornhill, Dec. 21, 1947 (div.); children: Robert Alexander, David Peter; m. Claire Angel Wheeler, 1965. BA, U. Toronto, 1949, LLD, 1973; DLitt (hon.), Laurentian U., 1970; LLD, U. Lethbridge, Alta., 1973, U. P.E.I., 1979; DLitt, U. Victoria, B.C., 1982, Lakehead U., Thunder Bay, Ont., 1986; LHD (hon.), McMaster U., Hamilton, Ont., 1994; LLD (hon.), Queen's Univ., Kingston, Ont., 1995; DLitt (hon.), U. Coll. of Cape Breton, Sydney, Nova Scotia, 1996. Arctic exploration, sci. work, 1947-48. Author: People of the Deer, 1952, The Regiment, 1955, Lost in the Barrens, 1956, The Dog Who Wouldn't Be, 1957, Coppermine Journey, 1958, The Grey Seas Under, 1958, The Desperate People, 1959, Ordeal By Ice, 1960, Owls in the Family, 1961, The Serpent's Coil, 1961, The Black Joke, 1962, Never Cry Wolf, 1963, Westviking, 1965, The Curse of the Viking Grave, 1966, Canada North, 1967, The Polar Passion, 1967 (with John de Visser) This Rock Within the Sea, 1968, The Boat Who Wouldn't Float, 1969, The Siberians, 1971, A Whale for the Killing, 1972, Tundra, 1973, (with David Blackwood) Wake of the Great Sealers, 1973, The Snow Walker, 1975, Canada North Now, 1976, And No Birds Sang, 1979, The World of Farley Mowat, 1980, Sea of Slaughter, 1984, My Discovery of America, 1985, Woman in the Mist, 1987, The New Founde Land, 1989, Rescue the Earth, 1990, My Father's Son, 1992, Born Naked, 1993, Aftermath, 1995, The Farfarers, 1998, Walking on the Land, 2000; author documentary script The New North (Gemini award 1989); (films) Sea of Slaughter (Conservation Film of Yr. award 1990, ACE award finalist 1990, award of Excellence Atlantic Film Festival 1990). Served to capt. inf. Canadian Army, 1939-45. Recipient Pres. Medal Univ. Western Ont., 1952, Anisfield Wolfe award, 1954, Gov. Gen.'s medal, 1957, Book of Yr. Medal Can. Library Assn., 1958, Hans Christian Anderson Internat. award, 1958, 65, Can. Women's Clubs award, 1958, Boys Clubs American award, 1962, Nat. Assn. Ind. Schs. award, 1963, Can. Centennial medal, 1967, Stephen Leacock medal for Humor, 1970, Leacock Medal for Humour, 1970, Vicky Metcalf award, 1970, Mark Twain award, 1971, Book of Yr. award, 1976, Curran award, 1977, Queen Elizabeth II Jubilee medal, 1978, Knight of Mark Twain, 1980, Can. Author's award, 1981, 85, Can. Author of Year award, 1988, Can. Book of Yr. award, 1988, Torgi Can. Talking Book of Yr. award, 1989, Can. Achievers award Toshiba Can., 1990, Take Back the Nation award Coun. Cans., 1991, Authors award, Author of Yr. Found. for Advancement of Can. Letters, 1993, Nat. prize for Fgn. Lit. books Beiyue Lit. and Art Pub. House, Taiyuan, China, 1999; decorated officer Order of Can., 1981, L'Etoile de la Mer, 1972. Died May 6, 2014.

**MOWERY, HAROLD F., JR.,** retired state legislator; b. Chambersburg, Pa., Jan. 4, 1930; m. Phyillis Shearer. BA in Economics & Psychology, Dickinson Coll., 1954. Mem. Dist. 87 Pa. House of Reps., Harrisburg, 1977-90; mem. Dist. 31 Pa. State Senate, Harrisburg, 1993—2004. Republican. Died Mar. 3, 2014.

**MOYER, KENNETH EVAN,** psychologist, educator; b. Chippewa Falls, Wis., Nov. 19, 1919; s. John Evan and Margaret (Lashway) M.; m. Doris Virginia Johnson, May 29, 1943; children: Robert Stephen, Cathy Lita. AB with honors, Park Coll., 1943; MA, Washington U., St. Louis, 1948, PhD, 1951. Mem. faculty Carnegie-Mellon U., Pitts., 1949—2006, prof. psychology, 1961—2006. Cons. on higher edn. Gov. Norway, 1954; mem. research adv. com. Pa. Commonwealth Mental Health Found. Author: The Physiology of Hostility, 1971, You and Your Child: A Primer for Parents, 1974, The Psychobiology of Aggression, 1976, Physiology of Aggression and Implications for Control, 1976, A Reader's Guide to Aggressive Behavior, 1977, Neuroanatomy, 1980, Bibliography of Aggressive Behavior: A Reader's Guide to the Literature, Vol. II, Violence and Aggression, 1987. Recipient Carnegie Found. award for excellence in teaching, 1954 Fellow AAAS, Am. Psychol. Assn.; mem. Psychonomic Soc., So. Soc. Philosophy and Psychology, Pitts. Psychol. Assn. (past dir.), Sigma Xi, Theta Kappa Theta. Achievements include research, publs. endocrinology emotion, startle response avoidance behavior, physiology aggression; demonstrated young children have capacity for prolonged attention spans if proper toys are used, that adrenal glands are not essential for effects electroconvulsive shock on behavior; devel. physiol. theory aggressive behavior. Died 2006.

**MOYERS, ERNEST EVERETT S.,** retired computer research scientist; b. Gadsden, Ala., Sept. 4, 1933; s. Ernest Everett S. Moyers and Lena Mae (Goode) Grigsby; m. Mary Violet Roden, Oct. 25, 1952; children: Mary N., Ernest E.S. III, Nora E., Karl H., Barton V., Troy W. BS, Midwestern U., 1954; MS, U. Miss., 1957; postgrad., Rice U.; PhD, Pacific Western U., 1969. Mathematician various cos., 1963-76; rsch. scientist other def. contractors, Huntsville, Ala., 1976-82; missile scientist Delta Rsch., Inc., Huntsville, from 1982, v.p., 1989-95; nat. missile def. testbed scientist Aegis Rsch., Inc., Huntsville, 1997-2000. Dir. Evangel Christian Sch., Huntsville, 1977-80; assoc. prof. computer sci. Ala. A&M U., 1999-2008. Designer anti-tank missile system, 1985; contbr. articles to tech. publs. Pastor Grace Bapt. Ch., Huntsville, 1977-79, Parkview Bapt. Ch., Ardmore, Ala., 1984-89; dir. Missions Skyline Bapt. Ch., Madison, Ala. Lawrence Livermore Nat. Lab. Summer Rsch. fellow, 2001, NASA IV&V Software Rsch. fellow, 2002, USN Surface Warfare Ctr., 2003. Mem. IEEE, Math. Assn. Am., Soc. Computer Simulation (chmn. 1983-94), Soc. for Indsl. and Applied Math., Am. Math. Soc., Toastmasters (founder High Noon club). Republican. Home: Madison, Ala. Died Aug. 1, 2012.

**MPELKAS, CHRISTOS CHARLES,** plant physiologist, consultant; b. Lynn, Mass., Apr. 16, 1920; s. Charles and Katherine (Thomas) M.; m. Angela Vlahakis, June 8, 1947; children: Charles, John, William, Katherine. AS, Essex A&T Inst., Mass., 1942; BS, U. Mass., 1949; MS, U. Conn., 1950. Rsch. product mgr. Star Supermarkets, Newtonville, Mass., 1950-52; rsch. technician Mass. Agrl. Expt. Sta., Waltham, 1952-53; head vegetable crops dept. Essex A&T Inst., Hathorne, Mass., 1953-61; with Sylvania Lighting Products, Danvers, Mass., 1916-71, sr. applications engr., 1971-77; resource devel. specialist U. Mass., Amherst, 1971-77; plant physiologist, mgr. Hort. Lighting Tech. divsn. GTE Sylvania, 1977, ret., 1977. Now cons. photobiol. and hort. applications, head Controlled Environ. Techs. Co., Lynn, Mass.; with Lynn Conservations Svc., 1974—; tech. adv. Essex Agrl. & Tech. Inst., Danvers; bd. dirs. Cmty. Credit Union, Lynn. Served with USAF, 1943-46. Mem. AAAS (biol. scis. sect.), Am. Soc. Agrl. Engrs., Am. Inst. Biol. Scis., Am. Soc. Plant Physiologists, Am. Soc. Photogiologists, Am. Soc. Hort. Sci., Bot. Soc. Am., Illuminating Engring. Soc., Nat. Elec. Mfrs. Assn. (photobiology com.), Assn. U.S. Army, Nahant Lions Club, Masons, Shriners. Greek Orthodox. Died Jan. 6, 2001.

**MPHAHLELE, ES'KIA,** writer; b. Marabastad Township, Pretoria, South Africa, Dec. 17, 1919; s. Moses and Eva M.; m. Rebecca Mochadibane, 1945; children: Anthony, Teresa Kefilwe (dec.), Motswiri, Chabi Robert, Puso. Student, Adams Tchrs. Tng. Coll., 1939-40; BA with honors, U. South Africa, 1949, MA, 1956; PhD, U. Denver, 1968. Tchr. English and Afrikaans Orlando High Sch., Johannesburg, South Africa, 1945-52; lectr. English Lit. U. Ibadan, Nigeria, 1957-61; dir. African programs Internat. Assn. Cultural Freedom, Paris, 1961-63; dir. Chemchemi Creative Ctr., Nairobi, Kenya, 1963-65; lectr. U. Coll., Nairobi, 1965-66; sr. lectr. English U. Zambia, Lusaka, 1968-70; prof. English U. Pa., Phila., 1974-77; sr. resident rsch. fellow U. Witwatersrand, Johannesburg, from 1978, prof. African Lit., 1983-87. Sec. for inst. for the blind, 1941-45; tchg. fellow U. Denver, 1966-68; assoc. prof. English, 1970-74; edn. officer No. Transvaal. Author: Man Must Live and Other Stories, 1947, The Living and the Dead and Other Stories, 1961, The African Image, 1962, The Role of Education and Culture in Developing African Countries, 1965, A Guide to Creative Writing, 1966, In Corner B and Other Stories, 1967, The Wanderers, 1971 (African Arts Mag. prize 1972), Voices in the Whirlwind and Other Essays, 1972, Father Come Home, 1984, Let's Talk Writing: Prose, 1985, Let's Talk Writing: Poetry, 1985, (autobiography) Down Second Avenue, 1959, (under name Es'kia Mphahlele) Chirundu, 1981, The Unbroken Song: Selected Writings of Es'kia Mphahlele, 1981, Afrika My Music: An Autobiography, 1957-83, 1984, Bury Me at the Marketplace: Selected Letters of Es'kia Mphahlele, 1984; fiction editor Drum Mag., 1955-57; editor Black Orpheus, 1960-66; mem. editorial staff Presence Africaine, 1961-63, Jour. Ne African Lit. and the Arts; editor: (with Ellis Ayitey Komey) Modern African Stories, 1964; editor, contbr.: African Writing Today, 1967; contbr. to numerous anthologies. Died Oct. 27, 2008.

**MROZ, JOHN EDWIN,** political scientist; b. Lowell, Mass., May 1, 1948; s. Edwin T. and Margaret Mary (Little) Mroz; m. Karen Linehan, June 17, 1972; children: Jonathan E. R., Jessica, Jeffrey. BA in Soviet and East European studies, U. Notre Dame, 1970; MA, Northeastern U., 1972; MALD, Tufts U., 1974. Exec. sec. UN Assn. Greater Boston, 1971—73; exec. v.p., dir. Middle East Studies, Internat. Peace Acad., Inc., NYC, 1976—81; pres. Inst. East West Studies, NYC, 1981—2014; cons. US Govt. intermediary in Middle East, US Dept. State, 1981—82, Fgn. Svc. Inst., Dept. State, 1977—81. Tchg. fellow NSF, 1971—72. Author: Beyond Security: Private Perceptions Among Arabs and Israelis, 1980; contbr. articles to profl. jours. Decorated Officer's Cross of Order of Merit Germany. Mem.: Internat. Inst. Strategic Studies, Coun. Fgn. Rels. Republican. Avocation: travel. Home: New York, NY. Died Aug. 15, 2014.

**MUDGE, MICHAEL RICHARD,** mathematical consultant; b. Twyford, Hampshire, Eng., Nov. 5, 1936; s. William Robert and Edith Jane (Bond) M.; m. Sheila Gladys Akers (div.); 1 child, Sarah Katherine Spurgeon; m. Valerie Dawn Scourfield Jenkins, Apr. 20, 1991. BSc in Math. and Physics with honors, U. Birmingham, Eng., 1967. Chartered engr.; chartered mathematician. Theoretical neutron physicist English Electric Co., Leicester, 1957-61; lectr. U. Aston, Birmingham, 1961-84; math. cons. Carmarthen, Wales, from 1984. Author Numbers Count column Personal Computer World, more than 150 months. Fellow Brit. Computer Soc., Inst. Math. and Its Applications; mem. Mathematical Assn. (mem. coun. 1997—). Achievements include research in the boundaries of numerical methods and number theory including Monte-Carlo techniques. Avocation: gardening. Died Sept. 21, 2002.

**MUELLER-SUUR, HEMMO,** pathologist; b. Koenigsberg, Germany, Nov. 11, 1911; s. Karl and Helene (Suur) Mueller; m. Giesela Zelle, Apr. 11, 1939; children: Niels, Almuth, Ingrid, Roland. Asst. physician Allenstein, 1939-44; head physician Goettingen, 1945-69; prof. psychopathology, 1969-77. Author books; contbr. articles to profl. jours. Home: Goettingen 37085, Germany. Died May 3, 2001.

**MUETH, JANE ELLEN,** secondary school educator; b. Bellville, Ill., Feb. 19, 1946; d. Charles John and Marjorie Jane (Hempen) M. BA, So. Ill. U., Edwardsville, 1969, MA, 1976. Cert. secondary tchr. in speech and theater. Tchr. speech, drama, film Dist. 201 West Pub. Schs., Belleville, 1970—95. Facilitator Transformational Fantasy, Belleville, 1987—. Reader for blind Our Lady of Snows Ch., Belleville, 1980-84; founder Comet Prodns., Belleville, 1982, sec.-treas., 1982-84. Mem. Internat. Listening Assn., Nat. Coun. on Self Esteem, Internat. Platform Assn., Assn. for Supervision and Curriculum Devel. Avocations: designing greeting cards, writing children's stories, seminar presentations on communication. Died Nov. 1, 1995.

**MULCAHY, GABRIEL M.,** pathologist; b. Jersey City, Feb. 16, 1929; s. Joseph Alphonsus and Anna Elizabeth Mulcahy; m. Vesna Maria Mulcahy, May 24, 1958; children: Mary, Michael, Robert, Richard, Thomas, John, Gabriel Jr. AB, St. Peter's Coll., Jersey City, 1950; MD, Georgetown U., 1954. Diplomate Nat. Bd. Med. Examiners, Am. Bd. Pathology. Intern St. Michaels Hosp., Newark, 1954-55; med. officer U.S. Pub. Health Svc., Crownpoint, N.Mex., 1955-57, resident in pathology Seattle, 1957-59, Staten Island, NY, 1959-61, chief pathology svc. Detroit, 1961-62; with pathology faculty Creighton U., Omaha, 1962-69; dir. pathology Jersey City Med. Ctr., 1969-78; mem. pathology faculty Univ. Medicine and Dentistry N.J., Newark, 1978-2001; chief lab. med. Univ. Hosp., Newark, 1978-2001. Mem. editl bd.: Annals of Clin. and Lab. Sci., from 2000; contbr. articles to profl. jours. Mem. adv. bd. St. Ann's Home for the Aged, Jersey City, 1973-89, sec., 1973-83; pres. bd. edn. St. Paul's Parish Sch., Jersey City, 1973-78. Mem. AAAS, Am. Soc. Human Genetics, Am. Assn. Blood Banks, Assn. Clin. Scientists (sci. coun. 1999—), Coll. Am. Pathologists, Soc. Med. Decision Making. Roman Catholic. Avocations: history, philosophy, philology, photography. Home: Jersey City, NJ. Died May 10, 2014.

**MULHERN, PATRICK J.,** lawyer, banker; b. NYC, Mar. 17, 1928; s. John J. and Beatrice (Gilholly) Mulhern; m. Joan F. Cassidy, June 14, 1952; children: John, Eileen, Barbara. BS, Fordham U, 1952, JD, 1955. Bar: NY 1955. Atty. US Dist. Ct. (so. dist.), NY Assoc. counsel Sherman & Sterling, 1955—66; v.p. cashier's adminstrn. Citibank NA, NYC, 1966—79; sr. v.p. Office of Gen. Counsel, 1979—80, sr. v.p., gen. counsel, 1980. USAR, 1946—47. Mem.: Fed. Bar Assn., ABA, Am. Soc. Corp. Sec., Assn. Bar City of NY, Unqua Corinthian Yacht, NYC Univ., KC Kiwanis. Died Nov. 1991.

**MULLE, GEORGE ERNEST,** petroleum geologist; b. Collingswood, NJ, Dec. 21, 1919; s. George Melvi and Eleanor Matilda (Clevenger) M.; m. Molly Elizabeth Jones, Nov. 17, 1950; children: Alan Russell, David George, William Ernest. Student, Rutgers U., 1942—44; AB in Earth Scis., U. Pa., 1948. Geologist Tide Water Oil Co., Houston and Corpus Christi, 1948—51; dist. geologist La Gloria Oil & Gas Co., Corpus Christi, Tex., 1952—60; ptnr. Santa Rosa Gas Co., 1960—62; pvt. practice Corpus Christi, 1962—73, 1975—80, 1983—99. V.p. Corpus Christi Mgmt. Co., 1973—75; sec.-treas. Villas Harbor Oaks Owners Assn., 1985—88; v.p., 1992—96. Author: (book) spec.; editor: AAPG Symposium Natural Gases N.America, 1968. With USN, 1944—46. Mem.: Soc. Ind. Profl. Earth Scientists, Corpus Christi Geol. Soc. Republican. Baptist. Avocation: photography. Home: Rockport, Tex. Died June 19, 1999.

**MULLEN, ANDREW JUDSON,** physician; b. Selma, Ala., June 23, 1923; s. Andrew J. and Helen (Johnson) Mullen; children: J. Thomas, Debbie, Gail, Andrea, Shawn, Connie, Beth. AB, Vanderbilt U., 1948; MD, Jefferson Med. Coll., 1952. Diplomate Am. Bd. Psychiatry and Neurology. Intern US Marine Hosp., Galveston, Tex., 1952—53; resident Tex. Med. Ctr., Houston, 1954—57; chief neurology and psychiatry svc. VA Hosp., Jackson, Miss., 1957; dir. Mobile Mental Health Ctr., Ala., 1957—58; pvt. practice Shreveport, La., from 1958; chief female svc. Confederate Meml. Med. Ctr., 1959—63, bd. dirs., chmn. pub. rels. com., 1964—72; med. dir. Shreveport Child Guidance Ctr., 1961—64; mem. med. adv. bd. Humana Corp.; cons. psychiatry and neurology Barksdale AFB, VA Hosp.; chief staff Brentwood Neuro-Psychiat. Hosp., Shreveport, 1970—73; clin. prof. psychiatry La. State U. Sch. Medicine, from 1975. Dep. coroner, cons., Caddo Parish, La., 1964; chmn. mental health com. Community Council, from 1964; chmn. bd. dirs. Brentwood Hosp., Shreveport, 1982—84; chief med. staff, 1985—86; bd. dirs. Humana, Brentwood hosps., from 1986; psychiat. dir. Charter Outreach Program, Shreveport, from 1987; chief of staff, med. dir. Charter Forest Hosp, from 1988, Caddo Oaks Hosp., from 1993; charter Forest Hosp., 1988—94. With RCAF, 1941—42, sgt. US Army, 1942—45. Decorated Purple Heart with oak leaf cluster, Bronze Star. Fellow: Am. Coll. Psychiatrists, So. psychiat. assns.; mem.: AMA, Flying Physicians Assn., Am. Soc. Psychol Analytical Physicians, Shreveport Med. Soc. (dir. 1971—72), So. Med. Assn., Nu Sigma Nu, Alpha Tau Omega. Episcopalian. Home: Little Rock, Ark. Died 1997.

**MULLENAX, CHARLES HOWARD,** veterinarian, researcher; b. Sterling, Colo., Feb. 5, 1932; s. Guy William and Evelyn Irene (Simpson) M.; m. Phyllis Jean Brown, June 11, 1954 (div. 1972); children: Mark David, Craig Collins, Jean Gail, Nancy Alba; m. Lidia Hincapie, Nov. 7, 1974. BS, Colo. State U., 1953, DVM, 1956; MS, Cornell U., 1961; diploma de honor, Ctrl. U., Quito, Ecuador, 1966. Cert. in epidemiology Ctrs. for Disease Control, USPHS. Owner Mt. Pks. Vet. Hosp., Evergreen, Colo., 1956-59; teaching and rsch. asst. Cornell U., Ithaca, N.Y., 1959-61; rsch. veterinarian Nat. Animal Disease Ctr., Agrl. Rsch. Svc., USDA, Ames, Iowa, 1961-64; Fulbright prof., dir. of clinics Ctrl. Univ., Quito, 1964-66; pathologist, tng. leader Rockefeller Found., Internat. Ctr. for Tropical Agriculture, Bogotá and Cali, Colombia, 1966-71; project dir., cons. World Bank, Washington, 1971-74; prof., rschr. Tech. U. Llanos, Villavicencio, Colombia, 1974-84; mem. acad. staff Univ. Calif. and Univ. Mo., 1985-87; rsch. assoc. Rural Devel. Inst., Univ. Wis., River Falls, from 1988. Cons. Bahamas Livestock Co., Eleuthera, 1956-57, U.S. Agy. Internat. Devel., Washington, 1985-87; ofcl. rep. Colombian Ministry Agr., Bogotá, 1972-73, Livestock Prodrs. Assn. of Meta, Villavicencio, 1982-83. Contbr. more than 50 articles to sci. jours. Lay min. Presbyn. Bd. Nat. Missions, Lapwai, Idaho, 1955; pres. grad. student bd. Cornell U., 1960-61; pres. sch. bd. Am. Sch., Quito, 1965. Recipient Medal of Merit, Colombian Vet. Pharm. Inst. and Livestock Prodrs. Assn. of Meta, Bogotá, 1985. Mem. Soc. Tropical Vet. Medicine, N.Y. Acad. Scis., Internat. Soc. for Ecosys. Health. Achievements include first discovery and reporting of cosmic, solar, and terrestrial electromagnetic interactions at the planetary boundary layer and their effect on the biosphere; these interactions override the traditionally employed local climatic and geog. variables and produce globally synchronous annual and longer-term, cyclic variations in marine and terrestrial soil chemistry, plant growth, and animal health and productivity. Home: Beldenville, Wis. Died Oct. 26, 1999.

**MULLER, GERT HEINZ,** mathematics educator; b. Troppau, Czechoslovakia, May 29, 1923; PhD in Philosophy, U. Graz, Austria, 1947; PhD in Math., U. Heidelberg, Fed. Republic Germany, 1962. Tutor, sci. asst. Astron. Inst., U. Graz, 1945-48; sci. asst. Math. Inst. Fed. Inst. Tech., Zurich, Switzerland, 1949-60; docent U. Heidelberg, 1963-65, assoc. prof., 1965-73; leader Logic Group Heidelberg Acad. Scis., 1969-89; prof. math. U. Heidelberg, 1973-90, prof. emeritus, from 1990. Guest prof. Math. Inst. U. Bonn, Fed. Republic Germany, 1964-65, Math. Inst. U. Leeds, 1966-67, Math. Inst. Hebrew U., Jerusalem, 1975, Math. Inst. U. Tromso, Norway, 1976, Math. Inst. U. Marseille-Luminy, France, 1979, Sophia U., Tokyo, 1979-80, Phil. Inst. Nat. U. Canberra, Australia, 1984, Math. Inst. U. Sydney, Australia, 1984, Doshisha U., Kyoto, Japan, 1985, Math. Inst. Prague, Czechoslovakia, 1986, Math. Inst. U. Nanjing, People's Republic China, 1987, Math. Inst. Normal U. Beijing, 1987, Ctr. Computer Sci. Acad. Sci. USSR, 1988, 90, Inst. Computer Sci. Academia Sinica, Beijing, 1990; dir. Math. Inst. Heidelberg, 1972-74; dean faculty math. U. Heidelberg, 1977-79, 88-89; v.p. div. logic, methodology and philosophy of sci. IUPHS, 1979-83. Editor in chief Studium Generale, 1967-71; cons. editor Jour. Symbolic Logic, 1958-84, Zeitschrift fur Mahematische Logik und Grundlagen der Mathematik, 1972-92. Grantee Inst. Henri Poincare, Sorbonne, Paris, 1951-52, Math. Inst. U. Heidelberg, 1960-63. Mem. Internat. Soc. Study Time (pres. 1976-79), German Soc. Math. Logic and Founds. Math. (pres. 1976-80), Am. Math. Soc., Assn. Symbolic Logic, Deutsche Math. Vereinigung, Acad. Internat. Phil. des Scis. (Brussels)(v.p. 1996-99), Math. Inst. Univ. Nanjing, Math. Inst. Normal Univ. Beijing. Home: Heidelberg, Germany. Died Mar. 9, 2006.

**MULONDO, LARRY YAWE,** management consultant, educator, researcher; b. Kampala, Buganda, Uganda, Jan. 18, 1943; s. James Kidza and Ida Joan (Nakaketo) Mukasa; m. Jane Frances Nandaula, Jan. 5, 1967; children: Florence, Richard, Georgina, Carol, Eddie. BS in Econs., U. Hull, Eng., 1963; postgrad. diploma mgmt., Glasgow U., Scotland, 1967; MA in Devel. Econs., Inst. for Econ. Devel. Studies, Naples, Italy, 1986. Cert. export promotion, indsl. project planning. Sec. Uganda Govt., Kampala, 1963-64, East African Community, Nairobi, Kenya, 1964-65; corp. exec. Uganda Devel. Corp., Kampala, 1967, head div., 1970-73, asst. mgr., 1974-75; gen. mgr. several cos. Kampala, 1976-84; mktg. mgr. Gava Property Agy., Kampala, 1984-85; prin. cons. M&M Consultancy, Kampala, from 1987. Part-time lectr. various instns., Kampala, 1974—; bd. dirs. numerous cos., 1969—. Author study manuals in econs. and bus. adminstrn.; mem. editorial bds.; mem. jour. adv. bds. Chmn. Internat. Confederation of Christian Family Movement, Uganda; adv. several ch. bodies and couns. Mem. Brit. Inst. Mgmt., Uganda Econ. Assn., East African Econ. Assn. Avocations: gardening, social work, reading, writing, travel. Home: Kampala, Uganda. Died 2006.

**MUNDY, CARL EPTING, JR.,** retired military officer; b. Atlanta, July 16, 1935; s. Carl. Epting Sr. and Anne Louise (Dunn) M.; m. Linda Stringfield Sloan, Nov. 28, 1957 (dec. 2013); children: Elizabeth Anne, Carl Epting III, Timothy Sloan BS, Auburn U., 1957; MS, Naval War Coll., 1977. 2d lt. USMC, 1957, advanced through grades to gen., 1991, comdt. Washington, 1991-95; pres., CEO The United Service Organizations, Inc. (USO), 1996—2000. Bd. dirs. Schering-Plough Corp., 1995—2009, Gen. Dynamics Corp., 1998—2009. Decorated Legion of Merit, Bronze Star, Purple Heart, Navy Commendation medal. Mem. Phi Kappa Tau. Home: Washington, DC. Died Apr. 2, 2014.

**MUNGER, PAUL R.,** retired engineering educator; b. Hannibal, Mo., Jan. 14, 1932; s. Paul O and Anne M.; m. Frieda Anna Mette, Nov. 26, 1954; children: Amelia Ann Munger Fortmeyer, Paul David, Mark James, Martha Jane Munger Cox. BSCE, Mo. Sch. Mines and Metallurgy, 1958, MSCE, 1961; PhD in Engring. Sci., U. Ark., 1972. Registered profl. engr., Mo., Ill., Ark. Instr. civil engring Mo. Sch. Mines and Metallurgy, Rolla, 1958-61, asst. prof., 1961-65; assoc. prof. U. Mo., Rolla, 1965-73, prof., 1973-99; dir. Inst. River Studies, U. Mo., Rolla, 1976-93; exec. dir. Internat. Inst. River and Lake Systems, U. Mo., Rolla, 1984-93, interim chmn. civil engring. dept., 1998-99, prof. emeritus civil engring., 2000—14. Mem. NSPE, Mo. Soc. Profl. Engineers, American Soc. Engring. Edn., ASCE, Nat. Coun. Engring. Examiners (pres. 1983-84), Mo. Bd. Architects, Profl. Engr. and Land Surveyors (chmn. 1978-84, 95-2002). Home: Rolla, Mo. Died Apr. 19, 2014.

**MUNNEKE, GARY ARTHUR,** law educator, consultant; b. Cedar Rapids, Iowa, Dec. 29, 1947; s. Leslie Earl and Margaret Frances (Fortsch) M.; children: Richard Arthur, Matthew Frederick. BA in Psychology, U. Tex., 1970, JD, 1973. Bar: Tex. 1973, Pa. 1987. Asst. dean, dir. placement U. Tex., Austin, 1978-80; asst. prof., asst. dean Widener U. Law Sch., Wilmington, 1980-84, assoc. prof., 1984-87; pres. Legal Info. Sys., 1987-92; prof. law Pace U. Sch. Law, 1988—2012. Contbr. articles to profl. journals Fellow American Bar Found., Coll. Law Practice Mgmt.; mem. ABA (chmn. standing com. on profl. utilization and career devel. 1981-85, articles editor Legal Econs. mag. 1984-86, chmn. law practice mgmt. sect. public bd. 1992-95, chmn. law practice mgmt. sect. 1998-99, house of dels. 2000-09, bd. govs. 2006-09), State Bar Tex. Home: North East, Md. Died Nov. 22, 2012.

**MURATA, ITARU,** international relations educator; b. Tokyo, Nov. 22, 1928; s. Tangue and Hatsuko (Hama) M. Student, Tokyo U. Fgn. Studies, 1945-48. Officer-in-charge of liaison with Supreme Cmdr. Allied Force Ministry Fgn. Affairs, Tokyo, 1948-54, politico-mil. officer-in-charge U.S.-Japan security treaty, 1955-58, asst. to dep. chief of protocol, 1964-65, asst. dir. nat. security affairs divsn. N.Am. affairs bur., 1966-69, dep. dir. 2d internat. econ. affairs divsn., 1971-72, dep. dir. nat. security affairs divsn., 1980-89; rschr. Ministry of Fgn. Affairs, Tokyo, from 1992. Attache politico-mil. arrairs Embassy of Japan, Washington, 1959-64, 2d sec., Caracas, Venazuela, 1969-71, 1st consul-gen., Kansas City, Mo., 1979-80, sr. consul, dir. politico-mil. affairs, N.Y.C., 1990-92; prof. internat. rels., polit. sci. Yamamura Women's Coll. Active Mus. Modern Art, Solomon R. Guggenheim Mus., Phillips Meml. Gallery, Corcoran Gallery Art. Mem. Japan Soc., Asia Soc., Japan-Am. Soc. Kansas City (hon.), Japan-Am. Soc. St. Louis (hon.), U.S. Strategic Inst., Rsch. Inst. for Peace and Security, Japan Inst. Internat. Affairs, Japan Acad. Internat. Polit. Sci., Japan Ground Warfare Acad., Acad. Polit. Sci. N.Y.C. Buddhist. Home: Tokyo, Japan. Died Oct. 22, 2003.

**MURATORI, GIUSEPPE PAOLO,** engineering executive; b. Turin, Piemont, Italy, Mar. 6, 1934; s. Mario and Maria (Bongiovanni) M.; m. Violetta Goffi, July 15, 1971. Degree in engring., U. Turin, 1958. Cert. signal intelligence engr. Mgr. Inst. Ricerche Communicazioni Sociali, Turin, 1965-67, chief exec., 1968-98. Intelligence head master World Intelligence Forum, Geneva Inst. Intelligence Rsch., 1997, speaker at conferences including World Econ. Forum. Author: Signal Intellignece, 1970, Ency. of the Espionnage, 1993; journalist Informatore, 1959-62, editor, 1963—, editor newspaper, 1975. With Italian Army, ret. Mem. HTI (prize 1958), World Intelligence Found. (hon. pres.) Avocations: tennis, swimming, riding. Home: Torino, Italy. Died May 6, 2002.

**MURCH, ANNA VALENTINA,** artist, educator; b. Dunbarton, Scotland, Dec. 7, 1948; arrived in US, 1976, naturalized, 1977; d. Norman Robbins and Valentina (Gordikova) Murch. BA, Leicester Poly. Eng., 1971; MA, Royal Coll. Art, London, 1973; grad. diploma, Archtl. Assn., London, 1974. Vis. lectr. Salisbury Coll. Art, Wiltshire, England, 1974, Epson Coll. Art, Surrey, England, 1974—75; architecture dept. lectr. Calif. Poly. Inst. San Luis, Obispo, 1983, vis. artist, 1983—85; art dept. lectr. U. Calif.-Berkeley, 1984—86, Coll. San Mateo, 1986; vis. artist East Carolina U., 1987; vis. lectr. San Francisco Art Inst., 1987—89; vis. artist Mills Coll., 1991—92, prof. art, 1992—2008, prof. studio art, 2012—13, Joan Danforth chair, 2012—13. One-man shows include, 1981, Kaiser Ctr. Sculpture Gallery, Oakland, 1981, Mills Coll., 1982, Ctr. Contemporary Arts, Santa Fe, 1985, Khiva Gallery, 1986, San Francisco Mus. Modern Art, 1986, Fesno Arts Ctr. & Mus., 1989, Mincher Wilcox Gallery, 1989, Commissions, If Wishes Were Fishes We Would All Cast Nets (suspended light sculpture Ferrucci Jr HS), Puyallup, Wash. State Arts Commission, 1987, Chaotic Chains, Exploratorium, San Francisco, 1989, Railway Suite, outside waiting room, Calif. Train Station, Santa Clara, Calif. Arts Council, 1990, Arroyo Suite, Century City, LA, 2003, Waterscores, Performing Arts Ctr. Plaza, Miami, 2006. Mem.: Orgn. Women Architects & Design Profs., San Francisco Art Inst. (artists & exhbns. com. mem.). Home: San Francisco, Calif. Died Mar. 26, 2014.

**MURPHY, KATHRYN MARGUERITE,** archivist; b. Brockton, Mass. d. Thomas Francis and Helena (Fortier) M. AB in History, George Washington U., 1935, MA, 1939; MLS, Cath. U., 1950; postgrad., Am. U., 1961. With Nat.

Archives and Records Svc., Washington, 1940-89, ret., supervisory archivist Ctrl. Rsch. br., 1958-62, archivist, from 1962. Mem. fed. women's com. Nat. Archives, 1974, rep. to fed. women's com. GSA, 1975; docent, 1989—; lectr. colls., socs. in U.S., 1950—; lectr. Am. ethnic history, 1978-79; free lance author and lectr. in field. Contbr. articles on Am. ethnic history to profl. publs. Founder, pres. Nat. Archives lodge Am. Fedn. Govt. Employees, 1965—, del. conv., 1976, 78, 80, recipient award for outstanding achievement in archives, 1980. Recipient commendation Okla. Civil War Centennial Commn., 1965; named hon. citizen Oklahoma City, Mayor, 1963. Mem. ALA, Soc. Am. Archivists (joint com. hosp. librs. 1965-70), Nat. League Am. Pen Women (corr. sec. Washington 1975-78, pres. chpt. 1978-80), Bus. and Profl. Womens' Club Washington, Phi Alpha Theta (hon.). Deceased.

**MURPHY, ROSEMARY,** actress; b. Munich, Jan. 13, 1927; came to U.S., 1939; d. Robert D. and Mildred (Taylor) M. Student, Paris, France and Kansas City, Mo. Broadway appearances include Look Homeward Angel, 1958, Night of the Iguana, World premier at Spoleto (Italy) Festival of Two Worlds, 1959, Period of Adjustment, 1961, King Lear, 1963, Any Wednesday, 1964-66, Delicate Balance, 1966, Weekend, 1968, Butterflies are Free, 1970, Lady Macbeth, Stratford, Conn., 1973, Ladies of the Alamo, 1977, John Gabriel Borkman, 1980, Learned Ladies, 1982, Coastal Disturbances, 1987, The Devil's Disciple, 1988, A Delicate Balance, 1996, Waiting in the Wings, 1999; (films) To Kill a Mockingbird, 1962, Any Wednesday, 1966, Ben, 1972, Walking Tall, 1972, You'll Like My Mother, 1972, Forty Carats, 1973, Julia, 1976, September, 1987, For the Boys, 1991, And The Band Played On, 1993, The Tuskegee Airmen, 1995, Message in a Bottle, 1998, Dust, 2001, The Savages, 2006, Synecdoche New York, 2007; TV appearances: Eleanor and Franklin, 1975 (Emmy award for Best Supporting Actress, 1976), George Washington, 1983 (Tony award nominations 1961, 64, 67, award Motion Picture Arts Club 1966), A Woman Named Jackie, 1991, E-Z Streets, 1996, The Unicorn's Secret, 1998, Frasier, 1997, 99. Recipient Variety Poll award, 1961, 67. Died July 5, 2014.

**MURPHY, THOMAS FRANCIS,** retired federal judge; b. NYC, Dec. 3, 1905; s. Thomas Michael and Susan Anne (White) M.; m. Katherine F. Hotaling, June 28, 1957. AB, Georgetown U., 1927; LL.B., Fordham, 1930; LL.D., St. Joseph's Coll., 1950. Bar: N.Y. bar 1930. Asst. U.S. atty. So. Dist., N.Y., 1942-50; police commr. NYC, 1950-51; U.S. dist. judge, 1951-95. Decorated knight Equestrian Order of Holy Sepulchre of Jerusalem. Mem. Friendly Sons St. Patrick. Clubs: Sharon Country. Died 1995.

**MURRAY, ALLEN EDWARD,** deceased oil company executive; b. NYC, Mar. 5, 1929; s. Allen and Carla (Jones) M.; m. Patricia Ryan, July 28, 1951; children: Allen, Marilyn, Ellen, Eileen, Allison. BS in Bus. Adminstrn, NYU, 1956. Trainee Pub. Nat. Bank & Trust Co., NYC, 1948-49; acct. Gulf Oil Corp., 1949-52; various fin. positions Socony-Vacuum Overseas Supply Co. (Mobil), 1952-56; with Mobil Oil Corp. (subs. Mobil Corp.), 1956-94, v.p. planning N.Am. div., 1968-69, v.p. planning, supply and transp. N.Am. div., 1969-74, exec. v.p. N.Am. div., 1974, pres. U.S. mktg. and refining div., exec. v.p., 1975-82, pres. worldwide mktg. and refining, 1979-82, corp. pres., 1983-84, COO, 1984-86, CEO, COO, chmn. exec. com., 1986—2002, chmn. bd., 1986—2002, also dir., 1976—2002; pres., chief operating officer Mobil Corp., NYC, 1984-86, chmn., pres., chief exec. officer, 1986—2002, dir., 1977—2002, Met. Life Ins. Co., 3M Co., Morgan Stanley Dean Witter & Co., St. Francis Hosp. Found. Trustee NYU. Served with USNR, 1946-48. Mem. Am. Petroleum Inst. (hon. dir.), Coun. Fgn. Rels., Bus. Coun. Clubs: Huntington Country. Died Aug. 11, 2002.

**MUSANTE, TONY (ANTHONY PETER MUSANTE JR.),** actor; s. Anthony Peter and Natalie Anne (Salerno) M.; m. Jane Ashley Sparkes, June 2, 1962. BA (Baker scholar), Oberlin Coll., 1958; postgrad., Northwestern U., 1957; student, HB Studios, NYC, 1961-65. Appearances include: (off Broadway prodns.) Borak, 1960, Zoo Story, Night of the Dunce, The Collection, Match-Play, Kiss Mama, L'Histoire du Soldat, A Gun Play, Falling Man, Cassatt, Grand Magic, The Big Knife, The Taming of the Shrew, Two Brothers, The Archbishop's Ceiling, Souvenir, A Streetcar Named Desire, Double Play, Dancing in the End Zone, Snow Orchid, Wait until Dark, Widows, Anthony Rose, Mount Allegro, Frankie and Johnny in the Clair de Lune, Breaking Legs, The Flip Side, Love Letters, The Sisters, Italian Funerals and Other Festive Occasions (Broadway prodns.) PS Your Cat is Dead, 1975 (N.Y. Drama Desk nomination), Memory of Two Mondays, 27 Wagons Full of Cotton, The Lady from Dubuque; films: Once a Thief, 1964, The Incident (Best Actor award Mar del Plata Internat. Film Festival), 1967, The Detective, 1968, The Mercenary, 1968, One Night at Dinner, 1969, Bird with the Crystal Plumage, 1970, Anonymous Venetian, 1970, Grissom Gang, 1971, The Last Run, 1971, Pisciotta Case, 1972, Goodbye and Amen, 1977, Break-Up, 1978, Collector's Item, 1985, The Repenter, 1985, Devil's Hill, Appointment in Trieste, 1987, Nocturne, The Pope of Greenwich Village, 1984, The Deep End of the Ocean, The Yards, Life As It Comes, Love's Promise, We Own The Night, 2007; (TV appearances) Ride with Terror, 1963, star series Toma, 1973-74 (Photoplay Gold medal award 1974), scriptwriter several episodes; Oz, 100 Centre Street; also starred in TV miniseries and movies: Pompeii, Traffic, Exiled, The Seventh Scroll, Deep Family Secrets, A Kiss In the Dark, High Ice, Breaking Up is Hard to Do, The Baron, Legend of the Black Hand, The Story of Esther, My Husband is Missing, Nowhere to Hide, The Quality of Mercy, Court Martial of Lt. William Calley, Night Heat, Rearview Mirror, Nutcracker: Money, Madness and Murder, Acapulco HEAT, Nothing Sacred, American Playhouse: Weekend, Last Waltz on a Tightrope; daytime TV (guest star): Loving, ABC, 1993, As The World Turns, CBS, 2000. Mem. SAG, AFTRA, ATAS, Actors Equity Assn., Writers Guild America West, Acad. Motion Picture Arts & Sciences Died Nov. 26, 2013.

**MUSTO, RAY (RAPHAEL JOHN MUSTO),** former state legislator; b. Pittston Township, Pa., Mar. 30, 1929; s. James Musto and Rose Frushon M.; m. Frances Panzetta, 1953; children: James M., Raphael Jr., Michael, Frances Ann. BS in Acctg., Kings Coll., 1971, HHD (hon.); LHD (hon.), Wilkes U. Mem. Dist. 118 Pa. House of Reps, 1971—80; mem. US Congress from 11th Pa. Dist., Washington, 1980—81; mem. Dist. 14 Pa. State Senate, 1983—2010, Democratic caucus sec., 1997—2004. Corporal US Army, 1951—53. Mem.: Kings Coll. Alumni Assn., Pittston Township Lions Club (charter mem.), Greater Pittston Chamber of Commerce (dir.), KofC, Pittston Township Vol Fire Co. (life). Democrat. Roman Catholic. Died Apr. 24, 2014.

**MUTA, SHOHEI,** archivist, researcher; b. Fukuoka-shi, Japan, Nov. 23, 1953; m. Hiromi Fukuzawa; children: Takuhiro, Naohiro. BA, Waseda U., Tokyo, 1977; MA, U. London, 1981. Sr. program officer Japan Ctr. Internat. Exch., Tokyo, 1996—2002; sr. rschr. Japan Ctr. Asian Hist. Records, from 2002; archival specialist Nat. Archives Japan, from 2005. Rschr. Libr. Congress, Washington, 1994—95. Fulbright Scholarship, 1994. Achievements include design of basic concept for Library of Congress Japan Documentation Center; digital archive system for Japan Center for Asian Historical Records. Deceased.

**MYATT, SANDRA D.,** real estate broker; b. Fort Wayne, Ind., May 26, 1943; d. Gaylord Murrey and Marjorie Jean (Anderson) Van Der Veer; m. Jack Lytton Dillard, Feb. 22, 1961 (div. 1965); m. Benjamin F. Myatt, Jan. 1, 1981; 1 child, Randolph William Dillard. Grad, Fla. Atlantic U., 1974, Realtors Inst. Tenn., 1984. Real estate broker Rose Martin Inc., Realtors, Dickson, Tenn., from 1981. Mem.: Nat. Rifle Assn., Nashville Bd. Realtors, Dickson County Bd. Realtors (sec. 1984, chmn. grievance com. 1986, Million Dollar Sales Club 1982—85, chair long range planing com. 1987, profl. standards com.), Tenn. Assn. Realtors, Nat. Assn. Realtors, Ladies Aux. VFW, Women of the Moose. Republican. Avocations: sports, fishing. Home: Dickson, Tenn. Died Apr. 14, 1991.

**MYERS, DONALD LEE,** controller; b. Feb. 28, 1945; m. Margie Bryant, 2007. BS in Bus. Adminstrn., Shepherd Coll., 1968; MBA in Finance, American U., Washington. Asst. v.p. finance, asst. treas. American U., Washington, 1975-80, treas., 1980-82, v.p. finance, treas., 1982—2014. Bd. cons. Riggs Nat. Bank; treas., bd. mem. Washington Rsch. Libr. Consortium. Mem. DC Chamber of Commerce, Econ. Club of Washington, Greater Washington Bd. of Trade, Nat. Eastern & Southern Associations of Coll. & Univ. Bus. Officers, Soc. of Coll. & Univ. Planners, Consortium of Univ. Treas. Home: Bethesda, Md. Died Jan. 6, 2014.

**MYERS, HOWARD,** aerospace scientist, systems analyst; b. NYC, Jan. 27, 1928; s. Howard G. and Sally (Kline) M.; m. Lois Marie Lowe, July 19, 1948 (dec. Apr. 1969); children: Susanna, William, Sally Joy. PhB, U. Chgo., 1948, BS, 1950, MS, 1958. Scientist Hughes Rsch. Labs., Culver City, Calif., 1953-57; tech. specialist Douglas Aircraft Co., Santa Monica, Calif., 1957-61; program mgr. Aerospace Corp., El Segundo, Calif., 1961-66; mem. tech. staff TRW Inc., Redondo Beach, Calif., 1966-69; sr. tech. specialist McDonnell Douglas, St. Louis, 1969-80; sr. systems engr. GE, 1980-92; pres. CPRL, Boardman, Ohio, from 1968. Leader, scientist supporters NASA's Project Galileo, 1972-78. Contbr. articles to profl. jours.; patentee elastometer. Prin. collaborator Nobel prize for chemistry, 1983. Mem. AAAS, Am. Chem. Soc., Am. Geophys. Union, Math. Assn. Am., N.Y. Acad. Sci., Sigma Xi. Democrat. Died Sept. 13, 2000.

**MYERS, LEGH RICHMOND,** sculptor; b. Ventnor, NJ, Nov. 11, 1916; s. Legh Richmond and Emma (Hautman) Myers; m. Laura Marie Wilson Kitchel, Apr. 4, 1942 (div. 1954); children: Legh Richmond Jr., Laura Marie Myers Hudspeth; m. Gloria Glenn Fitzsimmons, Aug. 26, 1962. Student, Pa. State U., 1936, Lehigh U, 1939, J. Wallace Kelly, Phila., 1954. Artist Madison Gallery, NYC, 1961, Ruth White Gallery, NYC, 1965, Chapman Sculpture Gallery, NYC, 1969, Alonzo Gallery, NYC, 1976, Cumberland County Libr., Bridgeton, NJ, 1979, Key Gallery, Bridgeton, 1963, Sculpture House, Bridgeton, 1966, Audubon Artists, 1960—84, Knickerbocker Artists Assn., 1957—81, Sculpture Ctr., NYC, 1959—60. Lt. USNR, 1942—46. Recipient Audubon Artists medal, 1970, Margaret Hirsch Levine Meml. prize, Audubon Artists at NAD, 1972. Mem.: Artists Equity, Knickerbocker Artists, Audubon Artists, Mem. Am. Sculptors Guild (sec., dir.). Republican. Episcopalian. Home: Linwood, NJ. Deceased.

**MYERS, WALTER DEAN,** children's and young adult book author; b. Martinsburg, W.Va., Aug. 12, 1937; s. Herbert Julius and Florence Dean; m. Constance Brendel, June 19, 1973; 1 child, Christopher;children from previous marriage: Karen, Michael Dean. BA, Empire State Coll., SUNY, 1984. Employment supr. NY State Dept. Labor, Bklyn., 1966—70; sr. trade book editor Bobbs-Merrill Co., Inc., NYC, 1970-77. Author: (children's/young adult lit.) Where Does the Day Go?, 1969 (Coun. Interracial Books for Children award, 1968), The Dragon Takes a Wife, 1972, The Dancers, 1972 (Children's Book of Yr., Child Study Assn. America, 1972), Fly, Jimmy, Fly!, 1974, Fast Sam, Cool Clyde, and Stuff, 1975, Brainstorm, 1977, Mojo and the Russians, 1977, Victory for Jamie, 1977, It Ain't All for Nothin', 1978, The Young Landlords, 1979 (Coretta Scott King award, ALA, 1980), The Black Pearl and the Ghost; or, One Mystery after Another, 1980, The Golden Serpent, 1980, Hoops, 1981, The Legend of Tarik, 1981 (Nat. Coun. Social Studies/Children's Book Coun. Notable Children's Trade Book, 1982), Won't Know Till I Get There, 1982 (Parents' Choice Found. award, 1982), The Nicholas Factor, 1983, Tales of a Dead King, 1983 (Authors award, NJ Inst. Tech., 1983), Mr. Monkey and the Gotcha Bird, 1984, Motown and Didi: A Love Story, 1984 (Coretta Scott King award, ALA, 1985), The Outside Shot, 1984 (Parents' Choice Found. award, 1984), Adventure in Granada, 1985 (Children's Book of Yr., Child Study Assn. America, 1987), The Hidden Shrine, 1985, Duel in the Desert, 1986, Ambush in the Amazon, 1986, Sweet Illusions, 1986, Crystal, 1987 (Parents' Choice Found. award, 1987), Scorpions, 1988, Me, Mop, and the Moondance Kid, 1988, Fallen Angels, 1988 (Parents' Choice Found. award, 1988, Authors award, NJ Inst. Tech., 1988, Coretta Scott King award, ALA, 1989, Children's Book award, SC Assn. Sch. Librarians, 1991), The Mouse Rap, 1990 (Parents' Choice Found. award, 1990), Now is Your Time! The African-American Struggle for Freedom, 1991 (Coretta Scott King award, ALA, 1992), Somewhere in the Darkness, 1992, Mop, Moondance, and the Nagasaki Knights, 1992, The Righteous Revenge of Artemis Bonner, 1992 (Parents' Choice Found. award, 1992), The Prince, 1993, The Party, 1993, Sort of Sisters, 1993, Young Martin's Promise, 1993, A Place Called Heartbreak: A Story of Vietnam, 1993, The Glory Field, 1994, Darnell Rock Reporting, 1994, The Story of the Three Kingdoms, 1995, The Shadow of the Red Moon, 1995, The Dragon Takes a Wife, 1995, Smiffy Blue: Ace Crime Detective: Case of the Missing Ruby and Other Stories, 1996, How Mr. Monkey Saw the Whole World, 1996, One More River to Cross: An African American Photograph Album, 1996, Toussaint L'overtoure: The Fight for Haiti's Freedom, 1996, Harlem: A Poem, 1997, Amistad; A Long Road to Freedom, 1997, Angel to Angel, 1998, Slam!, 1998 (Coretta Scott King award, ALA, 1997), At Her Majesty's Request, 1999, Monster, 1999 (Michael L. Printz award, ALA, 2000, NY Times Notable Book), The Journal of Joshua Loper: A Black Cowboy, Chisholm Trail, 1871, 1999, Malcolm X: A Fire Burning Brightly, 2000, The Blues of Flats Brown, 2000, 145th Street: Short Stories, 2000, The Greatest: The Life of Muhammad Ali, 2000, Three Swords for Granada, 2002, The Journal of Biddy Owens: The Negro Leagues, 1948, 2001, Patrol: An American Soldier in Vietnam, 2002, Handbook for Boys: A Novel, 2002, A Time to Love: Stories from the Old Testament, 2003, Blues Journey, 2003, The Dream Bearer, 2003, The Beast, 2003, Shooter, 2004, I've Seen the Promised Land; Martin Luther King, 2004, Constellation, 2004, Antarctica, 2004, Here In Harlem: Poems in Many Voices, 2004, Autobiography of My Dead Brother, 2005, The Hellfighters: When Pride Met Courage, 2006, Jazz, 2006, Street Love, 2006, Harlem Summer, 2007, What They Found, 2007, Game, 2008, Sunrise Over Fallujah, 2008, Ida B. Wells, Let the Truth Be Told, 2008, Amiri & Odette, 2009, Dope Sick, 2009, Lockdown, 2010, Sunrise Over Fallujah, 2010, Kick, 2011, The Cruisers, 2011, We Were Heroes: The Journal of Scott Pendleton Collins, World War II Soldier, 2011, The Cruisers Checkmate, 2012, The Cruisers Book 3: A Star Is Born, 2012, Darius & Twig, 2013, Invasion, 2013, (nonfiction) The World of Work: A Guide to Choosing a Career, 1975, Social Welfare, 1976, Malcolm X: By Any Means Necessary, 1993, Bad Boy: A Memoir, 2001, (photographs accompanied by poems) Brown Angels: An Album of Pictures and Verse, 1993, Glorious Angels: An Album of Pictures and Verse, 1995, (novels) On a Clear Day, 2014. Svc. with US Army, 1954—57. Recipient Jeremiah Ludington award, Ednl. Paperback Assn., 1993, Margaret A. Edwards award, Young Adult Libr. Services Assn., 1994. Mem.: PEN, Harlem Writers Guild. Died July 2, 2014.

**MYSLOBODSKY, MICHAEL S.,** psychology educator; b. Vilna, Poland, Jan. 2, 1937; Israel; s. Simon and Paula (Glick) Myslobodsky; m. Alexandra Parmet Myslobodsky, Oct. 6, 1960. MD summa cum laude, Charkow Med. Sch., USSR, 1960; PhD, Moscow Inst. Higher Nervous Activity, 1965, DSc, 1971. Resident Neuropsychiatry Hosp. USSR, 1960—62; jr. rsch. asst. to sr. rschr. Inst. Higher Nervous Activity and Neurophysiology, Moscow, 1962—73; assoc. prof. dept. psychology Tel-Aviv U., Ramat Aviv, Israel, 1974—78, prof., dir. psychobiology rsch. unit, from 1978. Vis. scientist NIMH, Bethesda, Md., 1985—87; editl. bd. mem. Internat. Jour. Psychophysiology, from 1983. Co-author: Seizure Acitivity, 1970; author: Hypersynchronous Activity of the Brain, 1973, Petit Mal Epilepsy, 1976; editor: Hemisyndromes, 1983; co-editor (with A. Mirsky): Elements of Petit Mal Epilepsy, 1988; contbr. articles to profl. jours. Mem.: Acad. Rodinensis Pro Remediatione, Soc. Neuroscis. US (fgn. mem.), Psychobiol. Soc. Israel, Israel Med. Assn. Home: Tel Aviv, Israel. Died May 28, 2010.

**NAALSUND, JON IVAR,** labor union administrator; b. Oslo, Aug. 11, 1942; s. Ole Bernhard and Bodhild N.; m. Liv Eivor Johansen, March 29, 1973; 1 child, Hege. Grad. H.S., Trondheim, Norway, 1960. Economic advisor Metal Workers Union, Oslo, 1974-79; asst. gen. sec. European Trade Union Confederation, Brussels, 1979-82; head indsl. policy dept. Metal Workers Union, Oslo, 1982-88; state sec. Ministry of Industry, Oslo, 1988-89, Ministry of Fgn. Affairs, Oslo, 1990-93; internat. sec. Norwegian Confederation of Trade Unions, Oslo, from 1994. Vice chmn. Norwegian Fgn. Policy Inst., Oslo, 2000—; bd. dirs. Statkraft SF, Oslo, 1996—, Europaprogrammet, Oslo, 1994—. Home: Oslo, Norway. Died Jan. 4, 2003.

**NAGEL, STEVEN RAY,** retired astronaut; b. Canton, Ill., Oct. 27, 1946; s. Ivan R. and Helene Nagel; m. Linda Maxine Godwin; children: Whitney, Lauren. BS in Aeronautical & Astronautical Engring., U. Ill., 1969; MS in Mech. Engring., Calif. State U., Fresno, 1978. Commd. 2d lt. USAF, 1969; advanced through grades to col.; ret. USAF,

1995, NASA, 1995; pilot F-100 jets 68th Tactical Air Force Squadron, England AFB, La., 1970—71; instr. Laotian Air Force, Utorn RTAFB, Thailand, 1971—72; student test pilot sch. Edwards AFB, Calif., 1975—76; instr. pilot USAF, England AFB, 1976—79; astronaut NASA, 1979—95; dep. dir. ops/ devel., safety, reliability, and quality assurance office Johnson Space Ctr., Houston, 1995; rsch. pilot Aircraft Ops. Divsn., 1996; lectr. Dept. Mech. Engring. U. Mo., Columbia, 2011—14. Decorated Disting. Flying Cross and Air medal with 7 Oak Leaf Clusters USAF; recipient 4 NASA Space Flight medals, Flight Achievement award, AAS, 1992, Outstanding Alumni award, U. Ill., 1992, Disting. Alumni award, Calif. State U. (Fresno), 1994, Lincoln Laureate, State of Ill., 1994. Mem.: Order of Daladiens (life), Phi Eta Sigma (hon.), Sigma Tau (hon.), Sigma Gamma Tau (hon.), Tau Beta Pi (hon.), Alpha Delta Phi (life). Achievements include 4 space missions, 773 hours spent in space contributing to knowledge of that environment. Avocations: flying, music. Died Aug. 21, 2014.

**NAGY, IVAN,** retired ballet company artistic director; b. Debrecen, Hungary, Apr. 28, 1943; m. Marilyn Burr; children: Aniko, Tatjana Dancer Budapest (Hungary) State Opera Ballet, 1960, N.Y.C. Ballet, 1968; guest artist, dancer Nat. Ballet, Washington, 1965-68; premier danseur, also tchr. American Ballet Theatre, NYC, 1968—78; artistic dir. Ballet de Santiago, Chile, 1981-86, Cin. Ballet, 1986—89, English Nat. Ballet, London, 1990—93. Guest dir., restager works for Australian Ballet, Hong Kong Ballet, P.R. Ballet de San Juan; former tchr. Darvash Ballet Sch., N.Y.C.; former assoc. prof. dance SUNY, Purchase. Recipient bronze medal Varna Dance Competition, Bulgaria, 1965. Died Feb. 22, 2014.

**NAPOLITAN, JOSEPH,** political consultant; b. Springfield, Mass., Mar. 6, 1929; s. Pasquale and Lucy (Anzalotti) N.; m. Mary T. Nelen, Oct. 13, 1952; children: Christine, Joseph Jr., Luke, Martha. BA, Am. Internat. Coll., Springfield, Mass., 1952, DHL (hon.), 1971; LLD (hon.), Our Lady of the Elms Coll., Chicopee, Mass., 1994. Reporter Springfield Union, 1946-56; pres. Joseph Napolitan Associates, Inc., Springfield, 1956—2013. Advisor to nine fgn. heads of state. Author: The Election Game and How to Win It, 1952, 100 Things I've Learned in 30 Years as a Political Consultant, 1986. Campaign staff Pres. John F. Kennedy, Pres. Lyndon B. Johnson, V.P. Hubert H. Humphrey. Named one of The 100 Most Influential Public Relations People of the Century, PR Week, 1999; Pew Found. honoree, 2000. Mem. Internat. Found. for Election Sys., Internat. Assn. Polit. Cons. (pres., dir.), American Assn. Polit. Cons. (Hall of Fame 1991). Democrat. Home: Springfield, Mass. Died Dec. 2, 2013.

**NARASAKI, HISATAKE,** chemist, educator; b. Fukuoka, Kyushu, Japan, Nov. 13, 1933; s. Kumeo and Tsutae Narasaki; m. Satoko Masuzawa, Nov. 1965; children: Junichi, Masako. BS, Kyushu U., 1956; MS, U. Tokyo, 1962, PhD, 1965. Lectr. Saitama U., Urawa, Japan, 1965—67, asst. prof., 1967—87, prof. analytical chemistry, 1988—99, prof. emeritus, from 1999; cons. Saitama-ken Environ. Analysis and Rsch. Assn., from 1999. Vis. rsch assoc. N.E. London Polytech., 1975-76. Author: Talanta: The Use of Approximation Formulae in Calculations of Acid-Base Equilibria, 1980, Analytical Chemistry: Automated Hydride Generation Atomic Absorption Spectrometry, 1985. Mem.: Japan Soc. Analytical Chemistry. Achievements include research in determining hydride forming elements by hydride generation inductively coupled plasma atomic emission spectrometry and by inductively coupled plasma high-resolution mass spectrometry; determination of pesticides by GC/MS and LC/MS. Home: Saitama, Japan. Died Nov. 6, 2007.

**NARUTO, MICHIO,** electronics executive; b. Shizuoka, Japan, Mar. 19, 1935; BA in Law, Tokyo U., 1958. Joined corp. planning dept. Fujitsu Ltd., 1962, bd. dirs., 1985, corp. sr. v.p., 1988, corp. exec. v.p., 1994, chmn., 1996—2002, vice chmn., 1998—2000, special rep., 2000—04, advisor, 2004—05, from 2004. Chmn. Toyota Info Technology Ctr. Co., Ltd., 2001—09; advisor to pres. Nat. Inst. for Rsch. Advancement, from 2004; bd. dirs. Axcelis, from 2005. Decorated Commander of the British Empire; recipient award from Minister of Economy, Trade and Industry in Japan, 1997, award from Minister of Pub. Mgmt., Home Affairs, Posts and Telecommunications in Japan, 2004. Mem.: Global Info. Infrastructure Commn. Died July 14, 2009.

**NARVASA, ANDRES,** retired judge; b. Nov. 30, 1928; m. Janina Yuseco; children: Andres Jr., Raymundo, Gregorio, Socorro. Bachelor of Laws magna cum laude, U. Santo Tomas, 1951; LLD (hon.), Pamantasan ng Lungsod ng Maynila, 1992, U. Santo Tomas, 1992, Angeles U. Found., 1993. Prof. law U. Santo Tomas, 1952—67, dean Faculty of Civil Law, 1967—73, vice rector student affairs, 1969—72; assoc. justice Supreme Ct. of The Philippines, Manila, 1986—91, chief justice, 1991—98. Chmn. Preparatory Commn. for Constitutional Reform, 1999—2000. Recipient Award of Distinction, U. Santo Tomas, 1972, Papal award Pro Ecclesia et Pontifice, 1977, Award for Outstanding Achievement in Legal Edn., U. Santo Tomas, 1981, Award for Meritorious Svc., 1981, Placque of Merit as Most OUustanding Alumnus, U. Santo Tomas Alumni Found., Inc., 1984, Human Rights award, Concerned Women of the Philippines, 1984, Ninoy Aquino Movement for Freedom, Justice, Peace & Democracy of the United States of America, 1985, Knight Grand Cross of Rizal, 1992. Avocation: golf. Died Oct. 31, 2013.

**NASH, LEONARD KOLLENDER,** retired chemistry professor; b. NYC, Oct. 27, 1918; s. Adolph and Carol (Kollender) N.; m. Ava Byer, Mar. 3, 1945; children: Vivian C., David B. BS, Harvard, 1939, MA, 1941, PhD, 1944. Rsch. asst. Harvard U., Cambridge, Mass., 1943-44, instr., 1946-48, asst. prof., 1948-53, assoc. prof., 1953-59, prof. chemistry, 1959-86, chmn. dept., 1971-74; rsch. assoc. Columbia, 1944-45; instr. U. Ill., 1945-46; ret. Staff Manhattan Project, 1944-45 Author: Elements of Chemical Thermodynamics, 1962, The Nature of the Natural Sciences, 1963, Stoichiometry, 1966, Elements of Statistical Thermodynamics, 1968, ChemThermo, 1972. Recipient Mfg. Chemists' award, 1966; James Flack Norris award, 1975 Home: Chestnut Hill, Mass. Died Nov. 9, 2013.

**NASOETION, ANDI HAKIM,** statistics, educator; b. Jakarta, Indonesia, Mar. 30, 1932; s. Anwar and Siti Marjam (Loebis) N.; m. Amini Soekadi, Jan. 27, 1942; children: Marlina Dumasari, Andini Nauli, Nizwar Hidayat. Degree in agr., U. Indonesia, Bogor, 1958; PhD in Statistics, N.C. State U., 1964. Acad. sec. Acad. of Agr., Ciawi-Bogor, 1958-65; dean Faculty of Agr. Inst. Pertanian Bogor, 1966-69, dean Grad. Sch., 1970-78, rector, 1978-87, dean Faculty of Math. and Sci., 1991-95, prof. statistics, from 1971. Chair Indonesian Young Scientists Contests, Jakarta, 1972—; leader Indonesian Math. Olympiad Team, 1990—. Author, editor 15 books. Scoutmaster Pandu Rakyat Indonesia, Bogor, 1950-60. Recipient medal for disting. svc. Min. of Edn., Jakarta, 1972, 1st class medal for disting. svc. Pres. of the Republic, 1994. Mem. Biometrics Soc. (nat. sec. group Indonesia 1970-90), Internat. Statis. Inst. (The Hague), Am. Statis. Assn., Inst. Math. Statistics. Muslim. Avocations: photography, biking. Home: Bogor, Indonesia. Died 2002.

**NASS, CLIFFORD IVER,** communications educator, magician; b. Teaneck, NJ, Apr. 3, 1958; s. Jules and Florence Nass. BA in Math. cum laude, Princeton U., 1981, MA in Sociology, 1985, PhD in Sociology, 1986. Researcher IBM Rsch. Ctr., Yorktown Heights, NY, 1983—88; software systems engr. Intel Corp., 1986—87; asst. prof. dept. communication Stanford U., 1986—93, assoc. prof. dept. communication, 1993—2000, prof. dept. communication, 2000—06, Thomas More Storke Prof. Communications, from 2006, prof. computer sci. by courtesy, prof. sociology by courtesy, prof. of edn. sch. by courtesy, prof. communication, affiliated faculty, sci., technology, and soc. by courtesy, affiliated faculty symbolic systems (cognitive sci. by courtesy). Profl. magician, 1997—2013; founder, dir. Communications between Humans and Interactive Media Lab (CHIMe), 2003—13; co-dir., Kozmetsky Global Collaboratory and Auto-X Stanford U., 2003—13; rsch. has been applied to several media products and services including Microsoft, Toyota, Nissan, BMW, Philips, Sony, Time-Warner, Hewlett-Packard, Charles Schwab, and Fidelity; spkr. in the field; co-principal investigator in the field; statistical cons., from 1986; social interface cons. involved in the design and develop. of several products and services for domestic and internat. clients, from 1993. Co-author (with Byron Reeves): The Media Equation: How People Treat Computers, Television, and New Media Like Real People and Places, 1996 (Internat. Communication Assn. Fellows Book award nominee, 2007, Choice Outstanding Academic Book of 1997); co-author: (with Scott Brave) Wired for Speech: How Voice Activates and Advances the Human-Computer Relationship, 2005 (Internat. Communication Assn. Outstanding Book award, 2007); co-author: (with Corina Yen) The Man Who Lied to his Laptop: What Machines Teach Us About Human Relationships, 2010, author of several papers on psychology of technology and statistical methodology; referee for several publications; contbr. chapters to books; assoc. editor Communication Concepts Series, mem. of several editl. bds. Recipient Best paper award, Interaction, 2000, Most Cited Paper award, Internat. Journal of Human -Computer Studies, 2005—07, 2008. Mem.: Internal. Brotherhood of Magicians, Soc. of American Magicians. Achievements include patents in field. Died Nov. 2, 2013.

**NATCHEFF, NATCHO DONKOFF,** physiologist; b. Sofia, Bulgaria, May 2, 1922; s. Josifoff Donko Natcheff and Tina Diankova (Kovatcheva) Natcheva; m. Milka Todorva Angelova, Mar. 5, 1950; 1 child, Doriana. MD, Univ. Med. Faculty, 1947; PhD, Med. Faculty Med. Acad., 1961. Asst. prof. Dept. Physiology, Med. Faculty, Sofia, Bulgaria, 1947-61, assoc. prof., 1961-69, prof., from 1969, head dept. physiology, med. faculty, 1965-81, head of sect., 1965-88, cons. prof., from 1988. Dep. dir. Medico-Biol. Inst., Sofia, 1975-77, dep. rector Higher Med. Inst., Sofia, 1981-86; mem. exec. com. Bulgarian Soc. Physiology, 1965-72. Editor/author Kidney and Body Fluids, 1968 (award, 1969), Hypothalamus, 1990, Physiology Regulation of the Basic Life Processes, 1987, Physiology for Medical Students, 1985 (award, 1986), 2000. Grant State Dept., 1966. Mem. Hungarian Soc. of Physiology (hon. mem.), German Soc. of Nephrology, Union of Scientific Med. Socs. of Bulgaria (hon. pres.), Exec. Com. Internat. Organ. Med. Sci., Bulgarian League Hypertension, Bulgarian Nat. Acad. Medicine (hon.). Orthodox. Avocation: amateur photography. Home: Sofia, Bulgaria. Deceased.

**NATHAN, PHIL OVE,** physicist, educator; b. Copenhagen, Jan. 12, 1926; s. Frits and Amelie (Friedmann) N.; m. Marianne Wandall, Apr. 1956; children: Marietta, Camilla. MS, Tech. U. of Copenhagen, 1952; DSc, U. Copenhagen, 1964. Full prof. The Niels Bohr Inst. U. Copenhagen, 1970, inst. dir., 1971-75, 80-82; pres., rector The U. Copenhagen, 1982-93; prof. physics The Niels Bohr Inst., Copenhagen, 1994-96; chmn. The Danish UNESCO Commn., 1996-99. Editor: Taenk Ogvaelg, 1980, The Challenge of Nuclear Armanments, 1986, The Challenge of An Open World, 1989, Rescue 43-Xenophobia and Exile, 1993, (autobiography) My Own Ways, 1998, (with Henrik Smith) The Harmonic Enthusiasm, 1999, The Poor Einstein, 2000. Recipient E.E.C. Gad prize, 1969, Rosenkjaer prize Danish State Broadcasting System, 1974, Oersted medal, 1999; Niels Bohr grantee, 1969, Joergen Vedel Petersen grantee, 1987. Mem. Royal Danish Acad. Scis. and Letters, Danish Acad. Tech. Scis. Avocations: gardening, mathematics, theater. Home: Hellerup, Denmark. Deceased.

**NAULT, FERNAND,** choreographer; b. Montreal, Dec. 27, 1921; Leading character dancer, ballet master Am. Ballet Theatre, NYC, 1944-65; dir. ABT's Sch. of Classical Ballet, NYC, 1960-64; co-artistic dir., resident choreographer Les Grands Ballets Canadiens, 1965-73, resident choreographer, 1973-90, artistic advisor, 1987-90, choreographer emeritus, from 1990; adv. dir. L'Ecle Supérieure de Danse du Québec, 1973-90; guest choreographer Colorado Ballet, 1978-81, artistic dir., 1981-82. Choreographer works, Am. Ballet Theatre, Joffrey Ballet Co., Harkness Co., Colo. Concert Ballet Co., Md. Ballet Co., Atlanta Ballet, Ballet Fedn. Phillipines; works choreographed include Claytonia, 1960, The Lonely Ones, 1960, Iskushenye, 1960, Giosco, 1961, Latin American Symphoniette, 1961, Cyclic, 1962, Roundabout, 1962, The Sleeping Beauty, 1963, Carmina Burana, 1966, Pas d'Eté, 1966, La Lettre, 1966, Hip and Straight, 1970, Tommy, 1970, Coppelia, 1971, Cantique des cantiques, 1974, Liberté Temperée, 1976, La Scouine, 1977. Other choreographed works include Aurki, Ceremonie, Casse-Noisette/The Nutcracker, Chants de douleur chants d'allégresse/Songs of Joy and Sorrow, Gehenne, Incohérence, L'Oiseau de feu, La fille mal gardée, Les sept péchés capitaux/The Seven Deadly Sins, Les sylphides, Miribilia, Mobiles, Paquita (Pas de deux), Pas d'époque, Pas rompu, Quintan, Quintessence, Symphonie de psaumes, Ti-Jean, Try, Ready, Go, Visages. Recipient Silver medal for choreography 7th Internat. Ballet Competition Varna, Bulgaria, 1976; Order of Canada, 1977, Prix Denise-Pelletier, Quebec, 1985, Chevalier de l'ordre national du Quebec, 1990. Died Dec. 26, 2006.

**NAUMANN ZU KÖNIGSBRÜCK, CLAS MICHAEL,** museum director, zoology educator; b. Dresden, Sachsen, Germany, June 26, 1939; s. Eberhard Bruno and Freda Irene (Hannemann) Naumann zu Königsbrück; m. Storai Nawabi, Dec. 17, 1974; children: Alexander Eberhard, Roxana Jamila. Dr.rer.nat., U. Bonn, Germany, 1970; Dr.rer.nat.habil., U. Munich, 1977. Tchr. U. Kabul, Afghanistan, 1970-72; sci. asst. U. Bonn, 1973-74, U. Munich, 1975-77; prof. U. Bielefeld, Germany, 1977-89, U. Bonn, Germany, 1989—2004; dir. Zoologisches Forschungsinstitut und Museum Alexander Koenig, Bonn, 1989—2004. Mem. presidium Arbeitsgem., Afghanistan, 1985, Germany, 1985; cons. referee Deutsche Forschungsgemeinschaft, Germany, 1992—99; mem. sci. adv. bd. WWF Germany, 1992—95; mem. German Nat. Com. for Unesco Program-Man and Biosphere, 1992—95; vice chmn. UNESCO program, Diversitas Deutschland, from 1997; coord. Biodiversity Transect Analysis Africa/East, 2000—04; chmn. Kabul com. U. Bonn, 2000—04; pres. German-Afghan U. Soc., 2002—04; chmn. Global Biodiversity Info. Facility, Germany-Verte-brata, 2002—04. Author: Die Kirghisen des Afghanischen Pamir, 1977; co-author: The Western Palaearctic Zygaeidae, 1999; editor (editor-in-chief): Zoologischer Anzeiger, from 1994, Entomologische Zeitschrift, from 1999; editor: (mng. editor) Handbook of Palaearctic Macrolepidoptera, from 1988. Fellow Rotary; mem. Russian Entomol. Soc. (hon.), Societas Europaea Lepidopterologica (hon.), 2000. Avocations: travel, books, entomology, photography, music. Home: Wachtberg, Germany. Died Feb. 15, 2004.

**NAUNIN, DIETRICH HANS,** electrical engineering educator; b. Münster, Germany, Nov. 2, 1937; s. Helmut and Gisela (Güldner) N.; m. Mirja Helena Turtola, July 20, 1968; children: Martti, Marja. Diploma in engring., Tech. U., Aachen, Fed. Republic Germany, 1963; D. in Engring., Tech. U., Berlin, 1968, Habilitation, 1971. Rsch. asst. Tech. U., Berlin, 1963-68, Allgemeine Elektrizitats Gesellschaft, Berlin, 1968-70, Deutsche Forschungsgemeinschaft, 1970-72; prof. Tech. U., Berlin, from 1972; vis. prof. MIT, Cambridge, Mass., 1973-74, 79; dir. Inst. Electronics, Tech. U., Berlin, 1984-99; head elec. engring. dept. Tech. U. Berlin, 2000—02. Chmn. Internat. Electric Vehicle Symposium, Berlin. Mem. German Electric Vehicle Assn. (pres. 1987, 2001), Verband Deutscher Elektrotechniker. Died Dec. 17, 2006.

**NAYLOR, JAMES CHARLES,** psychologist, educator; b. Chgo., Feb. 8, 1932; s. Joseph Sewell and Berniece (Berg) N.; m. Georgia Lou Mason, Feb. 14, 1953; children— Mary Denise, Diana Darice, Shari Dalice. BS, Purdue U., 1957, MS, 1958, PhD, 1960. Asst. prof. Ohio State U., 1960-63, asso. prof., 1963-67, prof. vice chmn. dept. psychology, 1967-68; prof. Purdue U., Lafayette, Ind., 1968-86, head dept. psychol. scis., 1968-79; prof., chmn. dept. psychology Ohio State U., Columbus, 1986-98, prof. emeritus, from 1999. Fulbright rsch. scholar, Umea, Sweden, 1976; Disting. scholar, vis. scientist Flinders U., South Australia, 1982-83, UNESCO ednl. cons. to Hangzhou U., Peoples Republic of China, 1984; chmn. Coun. Grad. Depts. Psychology, 1993-94; lead reviewer Psychology Program Rev., State U. Sys. Fla., 1996. Author: Industrial Psychology, 1968, A Theory of Behavior in Organizations, 1980; founder, editor: Organizational Behavior and Human Decision Processes; mem. editorial bd.: Prof. Psychology; Contbr. articles to profl. jours. Served with USN, 1950-54. Fellow AAAS, Am. Psychol. Soc., Am. Psychol. Assn.; mem. Psychonomic Soc., Psychometric Soc., Internat. Assn. Applied Psychology, Soc. Organizational Behavior (founder), Midwestern Psychol. Assn. (coun. 1994-97), Phi Beta Kappa, Sigma Xi. Home: Columbus, Ohio. Died July 12, 2013.

**NDAYISENGA, THE MOST REV. SAMUEL,** retired bishop; b. Buhiga, Kakuzi, Burundi, 1935; m. Joy Ciza Ndayisenga, 1956. Student, Anglican Ch., Ngozi, Burundi, 1963-65, Bishop Barnham Theol. Coll., Buye, Burundi, 1963—65, Trinity Coll., Bristol, Eng., 1966—68. Ordained deacon 1970, priested 1971. Consecrated bishop Diocese of Buye, 1979—2005; enthroned Archbishop of Burundi Anglican Ch. of Burundi, 1998—2005; Bishop of Buye; ret. Died Apr. 26, 2008.

**NEALIS, JAMES GARRY THOMAS, III,** pediatric neurologist, educator, author; b. NYC, Mar. 7, 1945; s. James and Catherine N.; m. Arlene Dee Kramer, Feb. 6, 1981; children: Peyton Colleen, Douglas Andrew, Gregory Haynes, James Garry Thomas IV, Patrick Ryan. BA, Fordham U., 1966; MD, U. Miami, 1971. Diplomate Am. Bd. Psychiatry and Neurology, Am. Bd. Electroencephalography. Intern in pediatrics Babies Hosp., Columbia Presbyn. Med. Ctr., Columbia U. Sch. Medicine, NYC, 1971—72, resident, 1972—73; resident neurology Boston U. Sch. Medicine, 1973—76, Harvard U. Sch. Medicine, Boston, 1975—76, instr. pediatric neurology, 1976—78; chief resident Boston City Hosp., 1975—76; asst. neurophysiology Boston Children's Hosp., 1976—78; founder Neuro-Ednl. Evaluation Clinic, 1977—78; asst. prof. clin. neurology U. Fla., Jacksonville; chief pediatric neurology Jacksonville Children's Hosp., from 1979; lectr. U. N. Fla.; clin. instr. neurology cons. Naval Regional Med. Ctr., Jacksonville, from 1979. Adviser Pres.'s Com. Med. Ethics, Washington, 1980; sec. Fla. Neurol. Inst., 1985; lectr. in field; host radio talk show. Author: Physical Disabilities and Health Impairments; contbr. chapters to books, articles to med. jours. Founder, bd. dirs. Northeast Fla. League Against Reye's Syndrome; bd. dirs. Speech and Hearing Clinic; trustee Epilepsy Found.; active Jacksonville Police Coun., from 1981; founder Jacksonville Alzheimer's Ctr.; profl. adviser Parents Action Against Drugs and Substance Abuse, from 1983; with To Your Health, WJXT, 1983, The Brain, WJXT, 1985, Drugs and Your Brain, 1986, Alzheimers Disease, 1984, The 700 Club, CBN, 1985. Named Outstanding Young Man of Yr., Bold City Jr. C of C, 1980. Mem.: Jacksonville C of C, Coun. Exceptional Children, Fla. Med. Assn., Fla. Soc. Neurology, Child Neurology Soc. (mem. nat. com. med. ethics 1984—85, adv. 1985—86, nat. adv. pediatric brain death 1985, practice com.), Duval County Med. Soc. (trustee), Am. Epilepsy Soc., Jacksonville Assn. Children Learning Disabilities (bd. advisers), Am. Med. Electroencephalographic Assn. (pres. 1984), Eastern Assn. EEG, Am. Acad. Neurology. Home: Jacksonville, Fla. Died May 5, 2011.

**NEEDHAM, HAL,** film director, writer, stuntman; b. Memphis, Mar. 6, 1931; s. Howard and Edith May (Robinson) N.; m. Dani Crayne, June 28, 1981 (div.); children: Debra Jean, Daniel Albert, David Allyn; m. Ellyn Wynne Williams, 1996 Student pub. schs. Founder Stunts Unltd., Los Angeles, 1956, stuntman, 1956-68, dir. and stunt coordinator second unit, 1968-76, dir., writer, 1976—99. Dir., writer: (films) Smokey and The Bandit, 1977, Hooper, 1978, The Villain, 1979, Smokey and The Bandit, II, 1980, The Cannonball Run, 1981, Mega Force, 1982, Stroker Ace, 1983, Cannonball Run Part 2, 1984, Rad, 1986, Body Slam, 1987, (TV films) Bandit: Beauty and the Bandit, 1994, Bandit Bandit, 1994, Bandit Goes Country, 1994; dir., writer, exec. prodr.: (films) Bandit, 1993; dir. pilot TV series Stunts Unltd.; dir. TV films, Hard Time: Hostage Hotel, 1999; movie of the week Death Car on the Freeway, B.L. Stryker, 1989; stuntman in over 95 films Served in 82nd Airborne Divsn. US Army, 1951—54. Recipient Scientific & Engring. award, Acad. Motion Pictures Arts & Sciences, 1986, Governors award, 2012. Mem. Screen Actors Guild, Dirs. Guild America, Writers Guild America, AFTRA. Owner Budweiser Rocket Car (fastest car in the world) displayed at Smithsonian Inst.; introducted the air ram, air bag, car cannon turnover, nitrogen ratchet, jerk-off ratchet, rocket power, and Shotmaker Camera Car to film. *I feel that if I can become successful with less than ten years of education, anyone in this country is capable of the same goals with positive thinking and total dedication.* Died Oct. 25, 2013.

**NEEL, JOHN DODD,** cemetery executive; b. McKeesport, Pa., Aug. 7, 1923; s. Harry Campbell and Anna (Dodd) N.; m. Daisy Jean Wyatt, Feb. 11, 1948 (dec.); children: Harry C., John Dodd II, W. Wyatt (dec.), Jeffrey J BA, Pa. State U., 1946. From salesman to pres. Jefferson Meml. Park, Pitts., 1946-88, chmn. bd. dirs., from 1988; chmn. Jefferson Meml. Funeral Home. Former mem., and chmn Zoning Hearing Bd., Pleasant Hills, Pa., from 1970. Mem. emeritus adv. bd. Pa. State U., Greater Allegheny; former mem. Pa. State Real Estate Commn. 1st lt. USAAF, 1943-45 Decorated Air medal with 4 clusters, D.F.C., Joseph A. Dougan Hall of Valor, Soldiers & Sailors Meml. Hall & Mus.; recipient George Washington cert. Freedom Found., 1974 Mem. Pa. Cemetery Cremation Funeral Assn. (pres. 1963-65), Internat. Cemetery Cremation and Funeral Assn. (pres. 1973-74), West Jefferson Hills C. of C. (pres. 1984), VFW, Am. Legion 57th Bomb Wing Assn., South Hills Country Club, OX-5CLUB, Kiwanis (pres. 1959), Masons, Shriner, Tau Kappa Epsilon, Delta Sigma Pi. Presbyterian. Died July 3, 2013.

**NEILL, RICHARD ROBERT,** retired publishing executive; b. NYC, June 20, 1925; s. Robert Irving and Mildred Mary (Hall) N.; m. Patricia Mae Robinson, Dec. 27, 1952; 1 son, Robert Kenneth. AB summa cum laude, Princeton U., 1948; MA, N.Y. U., 1953. With Prentice-Hall, Inc., NYC and Englewood Cliffs, NJ, 1948-85, bus. books editor, 1950—53, advt. mgr., 1953-58, v.p. advt., 1958-62; pres. Executive Reports Corporation, 1962-85, ret., 1985. Regional chmn. Princeton Alumni Giving, Yonkers, N.Y., 1960-63, Tarrytown-Irvington, N.Y., 1977-80 Pres. Tarrytown (N.Y.) Jr. High Sch. PTA, 1971-72; bd. dirs. Martling Owners, Tarrytown, 1980-84, 89-93. Lt. (j.g.) USNR, 1943-46, PTO. Mem. USN Meml. Found., Princeton Terrace Club (bd. govs. 1986-92), Phi Beta Kappa. Republican. Mem. Reform Ch. Home: Sleepy Hollow, NY. *A thought acquired from one of my first bosses: "Everything happens for the best - or can be made to do so." This has been a lifelong help during times of difficulty.* Died Mar. 7, 2014.

**NEISSER, ERIC ROBERT,** law educator; b. NYC, Oct. 17, 1947; s. Gerard Ernst and Rose (Gelernter) N.; m. Joan Ruth Lehrich, June 26, 1969; children: Michelle Elaine, Yvette Suzanne. BA, U. Chgo., 1967; JD, Yale U., 1972. Bar: Mass. 1973, N.Y. 1976, N.J. 1984; U.S. Supreme Ct. 1978. Law clk. to chief judge U.S. 1st Cir. Ct., Portland, Maine, 1972-73; appellate counsel Mass. Defenders Comm., Boston, 1973-74; staff atty. Legal Aid Soc./Prisoners' Rights Project, NYC, 1974-76; asst. dir. Prisoners' Legal Svcs., NYC, 1976-78; dir. U.S. Ct. Appeals (9th cir.) Office of Staff Attys., San Francisco, 1980-82; legal dir. ACLU of N.J., Newark, 1986-89; prof. of law Rutgers U. Law Sch., Newark, 1978-99, assoc. dean, 1997-98, acting dean, 1998-99; dean Franklin Pearce Law Ctr., Concord, N.H., from 1999. Cons. in field, Newark, 1990—; vis. prof. Stanford U., Calif., 1982-83; dir. Inst. of Internat. Comparative Law, Dublin, 1991, Oxford, Eng., 1997. Author: (book) Recapturing the Spirit: Essays on the Bill of Rights, 1991 (Nat. Archives honor 1992); contbr. articles to profl. jours.; editor: Notes and Comments, Yale Law Rev., 1971-72. Named Top Lawyer, 1st Amend. Law, N.J. Monthly Mag., 1997; Sr. Fulbright scholar, 1996. Mem. ABA, N.J. State Bar Assn. (co-chmn. ind. rights 1988-90), Phi Beta Kappa. Avocation: racquetball. Home: Somerville, Mass. Died Nov. 8, 1999.

**NELSON, CHRISTINE A.,** occupational therapist; b. Hartford, Conn., Apr. 30, 1937; BS in Occupational Therapy, Va. Commonwealth U., 1959; MS in Child Devel., U. Wis., 1963; cert. in Neurodevelopmental Treatment, Dr. Karel and Mrs. Berta Bobath, Madison, Wis., 1963; PhD in Human Devel., U. Md., 1973. Evaluator of blind and physically handicapped children Sunland Tng. Ctr., Gainesville, Fla., 1960-62; creator occupational therapy program, in-service staff instr. Cen. Wis. Colony, Madison, 1962-65; dept. dir. Easter Seal Community Agy., Balt., 1965-67; cons. Children's Guild, Balt., 1967-76; pvt. practice specializing in therapy for neurologically impaired children, Balt., 1967-77; devel. cons. Maternal-Infant Health Care Project div. Balt. City Health Dept., 1969-74; coordinator cert. courses in Neurodevel. Treatment, from 1975; clin. practitioner, clin. coordinator Centro de Aprendizaje de Cuernavaca, Mexico, from 1977. Contbr. articles to profl jours. Fellow Am. Occupational Therapists Assn.; mem. Alpha Delta Kappa. Died Apr. 6, 2008.

**NELSON, FORD R., JR.,** lawyer; b. Miami Beach, Fla., 1942; AB, U. Mo., 1964, JD, 1967. Bar: Mo. 1967, federal cts Mo., Supreme ct. Kans. and Eighth cir. ct Appeals. Ptnr. Armstrong, Teasdale, Schlafly & Davis, Kansas City, Armstrong Teasdale LLP, Kansas City. Kans. City C. of C., Downtown Coun., Citizens Assn., Friends Zoo, Inc. Kans. City, Mo., Downtown Rotary Club 13 (bd mem. and Officer) Listed Best Lawyers Am. (2007) Real Estate Law, recognized as a 2005-2006 Mo./Kans. Super Lawyer. Mem. ABA (mem. real property, probate and trust law sects., mem. bus. law sect.), The Mo. Bar (mem. property law com.), Kansas City Met. Bar Assn. Died Nov. 14, 2012.

**NELSON, WALTER HENRY,** communications consultant, author; b. Munich, Mar. 23, 1928; parents Am. citizens; m. Rose Marie Carson, Mar. 4, 1950; children: Roger Stuart, Gregory Eugene, Victoria Eugenie; 2d marriage to Rita L. Christoffersen, June 30, 1962; 1 child, Samantha Christine. Student, NYU, 1944, Norwich U., 1944-46, Columbia U., 1949-50. News editor, info. analyst Radio Free Europe, NYC, Munich, 1950-53; dir. mag. info. Am. Heritage Found., NYC, 1953-55; mag. pub. dir., editor quar. Am. Petroleum Inst., 1955-57; dir. pub. rels. Reach, McClinton & Co., Inc., NYC, 1957-59; v.p., gen. mgr. Candygram, Inc., Chgo., 1959-60; asst. to pres. Stevens Candy Kitchens, Inc., Chgo., 1960-61; assoc. in pub. rels. Fred Rosen Assocs., Inc., 1961-62; ptnr. Prittie and Nelson Internat. Pub. Rels., London, 1975-81; chmn. Nelson Assocs. Ltd., London, 1981-93; freelance author and comms. cons., from 1993. Pub. rels. dir. William H. Rentschler for U.S. Senator, 1959-60. Author: Small Wonder: The Amazing Story of the Volkswagen Beetle, 1965, rev., 1998, German edit., 1966, Br. edit., 1967, rev., 1971, Dutch edit., 1968, Spanish edit., 1974, revised edit., 1998, The Great Discount Delusion, 1965, The Berliners: Their City and Their Saga, 1969, Br. edit., 1969, The Soldier Kings: The House of Hohenzollern, 1970, Br. and Italian edits., 1971, German edit., 1972, 98, Ernest Hemingway, 1971, Germany Rearmed, 1972, The Londoners: Life in A Civilized City, 1974, Br. edit., 1975, Japanese edit., 1976, 77, (with Terence Prittie) Economic War Against the Jews, 1977, Br. Edit., 1978, the Siege of Buckingham Palace, 1980, The Minstrel Code, 1979, Spanish edit., 1982, Gautama Buddha: His life and his Teaching, U.K. edit., 1998, Buddha: Life & Teaching, U.S. edit., 2000; contbr. articles to popular mags., newspapers. Served in U.S. Army, 1946-49. Deceased.

**NESBITT, MARTIN LUTHER, JR.,** state legislator; b. Asheville, NC, Sept. 25, 1946; s. Mary Cordell Nesbitt; m. Deane Sellers; 2 children. BA, U. NC, Chapel Hill, 1970; JD, U. NC, 1973. Atty., from 1973; mem. Dist. 51 NC House of Reps., 1979—2002; mem. Dist. 49 NC State Senate, NC, 2004—14, minority leader, 2011—14. Democrat. Died Mar. 6, 2014.

**NEUGEBAUER, GERRY (GERHARDT OTTO NEUGEBAUER),** retired astrophysicist; b. Göttingen, Germany, Sept. 3, 1932; came to U.S., 1939; s. Otto E. and Grete (Brück) N.; m. Marcia MacDonald, Aug. 26, 1956; children: Carol, Lee. BS, Cornell U., 1954; PhD, Calif. Inst. Tech., 1960. Asst. prof. physics Calif. Inst. Tech., 1962—65, assoc. prof. Pasadena, 1965—70, prof., 1970—2002, Howard Hughes Prof. Physics, 1985—2002, chmn. divsn. physics, math and astronomy, 1988-93, Robert Andrews Millikan prof. physics, 1996—98, Robert Andrews Millikan prof. physics emeritus, 1998—2014; mem. staff Hale Observatory, 1970-80; acting dir. Palomar Observatory, 1980-81, dir., 1981—94. Served with AUS, 1961-63. Recipient Except. Sci. Achievement medal NASA, 1972, 1984, Richtmyer Lectr. award, 1985, Space Sci. award American Inst. Aeronaut and Astronaut, 1985, Rumford Premium American Acad. Arts & Sci., 1986, Henry Norris Russell Lectureship American Astron. Soc., 1996, Catherine Wolfe Bruce Gold medal, Astronomical Soc. Pacific, 2010 Fellow American Acad. Arts & Sciences; mem. NAS, American Philos. Soc., American Astron. Soc., Royal Astron. Soc. (Herschel medal, 1998), Internat. Astron. Union. Died Sept. 26, 2014.

**NEUHAUS, PHILIP ROSS,** investment banker; b. Houston, Dec. 25, 1919; s. Hugo Victor and Kate Padgitt (Rice) N.; m. Elizabeth Lacey Thompson, Oct. 31, 1942 (div. 1967); children: Philip Ross (dec.), Lacey Neuhaus Dorn, Elizabeth Neuhaus Armstrong, Joan Neuhaus Schaan; m. Barbara R. Haden, Aug. 14, 1968(dec. Feb 14, 2008); 5 stepchildren. Grad., St. Mark's Sch., Southborough, Mass., 1938; BA, Yale, 1942. Cert. Bd. Tex. Children Hosp. Houston, 2012. With Nat. City Bank of Cleve., 1946-47, McDonald & Co., Cleve., 1947; with Neuhaus & Co., 1947; chmn. Underwood, Neuhaus & Co., Inc., Houston, 1948-89; hon. chmn. Lovett Underwood Neuhaus & Webb, Houston, 1989-92; sr. v.p. Kemper Securities Inc., Houston, 1992-95, Everen Securities, Inc., Houston, 1995-99, Wells Fargo Advisors (formerly Wachovia Securities Inc.), Houston, from 1999. Chmn. bd. Voss-Woodway, Inc., 1994-2007. Mem. adv. bd. Tex. Children's Hosp., 1973-; assoc. Rice U.; advisory bd. Salvation Army, Houston, 1969-91. Served to capt., cav. AUS, 1942-45. Recipient Most Outstanding award. Mem. Securities Industry Assn. Am. (bd. govs., chmn. Tex. dist. 1973, exec. com. 1975), Houston Soc. Financial Analysts (pres. 1959), Stock and Bond Club Houston (past pres.), Nat. Fedn. Financial Analysts (v.p. 1963, dir.) Clubs: Bayou, Houston Country, Houston, Eagle Lake Rod and Gun. Home: Houston, Tex. Died Apr. 23, 2013.

**NEUMANN, BERNHARD HERMANN,** mathematician; b. Berlin-Charlottenburg, Germany, Oct. 15, 1909; s. Richard and Else (Aronstein) N.; m. Hanna von Caemmerer, Dec. 22, 1938 (dec. Nov. 1971); children: Irene Brown, Peter, Barbara Cullingworth, Walter, Daniel; m. Dorothea Zeim, Dec. 24, 1973. Student, U. Freiburg, Germany, 1928-29; Dr.phil., U. Berlin, 1932; PhD, Cambridge U., Eng., 1935; DSc, U. Manchester, Eng., 1954; DSc (hon.), U. Newcastle, Australia, 1974, Monash U., 1982, U. Western Australia, 1995, U. Hull, Eng., 1995, Australian Nat. U., 2001; D.Math. (hon.), U. Waterloo, 1986; Dr.rer.nat. (hon.), Humboldt U., Berlin, 1992. Lectr. Univ. Coll., Hull, 1946-48; faculty U. Manchester, 1948-61; prof., head dept. math. Inst. Advanced Studies, Australian Nat. U., Canberra, 1962-74, hon. univ. fellow, from 1975. Hon. rsch. fellow divsn. Math. and Info. Sci., Commonwealth Sci. and Indsl. Rsch. Orgn., Canberra, (hon. fellow, 2000—), 1978-99. Editor Houston Jour. Math., 1974—; editor, pub. IMU Canberra Circular, 1972-99, other editorships; contbr. numerous articles to math. jours. Served with Brit. Armed Forces, 1940-45. Decorated Companion Order of Australia, 1994; recipient prize Wiskundig Genootschap, Amsterdam, The Netherlands, 1949, Adams prize U. Cambridge, 1952-53. Fellow Royal Soc., Australian Acad. Sci. (v.p. 1969-71, Matthew Flinders lectr. 1984), Inst. Combinatorics and Its Applications (hon.), Australian Math. Soc. (hon., v.p. several terms, pres. 1964-66, hon. mem. 1981—, editor bull. 1969-79, hon. editor 1979—); mem. London Math. Soc. (v.p. 1959-61, editor proc. 1959-61), many other profl. orgns., also chess and musical clubs and socs. Avocations: classical music (cello), chess, bicycling, camping. Deceased.

**NEUWIRTH, ROBERT SAMUEL,** obstetrician, gynecologist, educator; b. NYC, July 11, 1933; s. Abraham Alexander and Phyllis Neuwirth; children from previous marriage: Susan, Jessica, Laura, Michael, Alexander. BS in Chemistry, Yale U., 1955, MD, 1958. Intern Presbyn. Hosp., NYC, 1958-59, resident, 1959-64; asst. prof. ob-gyn. Columbia U., NYC, 1964-68, assoc. prof., 1968-71, prof., 1972-2001, Babcock prof., 1977-2001, Babcock prof. emeritus, 2001—13. Dir. ob-gyn. Bronx Lebanon Hosp., NYC, 1967-72, Woman's Hosp., NYC, St. Luke's Hosp. Ctr., 1974-2013, St. Luke's Roosevelt Hosp., 1981-91; prof. Albert Einstein Coll. Medicine, 1971-72; cons. WHO, NIH, AID, FDA; interim dir. St. Luke's Roosevelt Hosp., 1998-2000. Author: Hysteroscopy, 1975; contbr. articles to profl. jours. Mem.: ACOG, Assn. Vol. Sterilization, American Assn. Professionals Ob-Gyn., NY Obstet. Soc., Soc. Gynecol. Investigation, American Gynecol. & Obstet. Soc. Died Dec. 17, 2013.

**NEVINS, JOHN JOSEPH,** bishop emeritus; b. New Rochelle, NY, Jan. 19, 1932; Student, Iona Coll., NYC, Cath. U. Washington; MA, Tulane U., 1969. Ordained priest Archdiocese of Miami, Fla., 1959; ordained bishop, 1979; aux. bishop Archdiocese of Miami, 1979—84; first bishop Diocese of Venice, 1984—2007, bishop emeritus, 2007—14. Roman Catholic. Died Aug. 26, 2014.

**NEWCOMB, HELENE E.,** retired research scientist; b. NYC; d. Otto Wilhelm Post and Hella (Drexler) Walburga; m. Frederick J Newcomb, Aug. 15, 1953; children: J Mark, Paula Marie. Author: (books of poetry) Echoes in the Wind, 2002, On the Wings of Thought, 2002, (best poems and poets) Internat. Libr. Poetry, 2003. Mil. case worker ARC Mountain Valley Chpt., Provo, Utah, from 1978; Telecare ARC Mountain Valley Chpt., from 1980. With US Army, 1951—53. Recipient Vol. of Yr. award, ARC, 1981, Roberta Drissler Disting. Svc. award, 1986, Mil. Social Svc. Caseworker award, Clara Barton award, 1999, Portrait of Character award, Farm Bur. Mut. Ins. Co., Editors Choice awards, 2000, Merit Silver award Bowl, Internat. Soc. of Poets, 2002, Editors Choice awards, 2003, Silver cup, Internat. Soc. Poets, 2003, Silver Bowl and Medalian award, 2004, Editors Choice award, 2006, Pres.'s Vol. Svc. award, 2007, Vol. Svc. award, Utah Lt. Gov. Gary R. Herbert, 2008. Mem. Lds Ch. Avocations: stamp collecting/philately, crocheting. Home: Santaquin, Utah. Died Sept. 24, 2013.

**NEWCOMBE, HOWARD BORDEN,** biologist, consultant; b. Kentville, NS, Can., Sept. 19, 1914; s. Edward Borden and Mabel Elsie (Outerbridge) N.; m. Beryl Honor Callaway, Feb. 14, 1942; children— Kenneth Donald, Charles Philip, Richard William B.Sc., Acadia U., Wolfville, NS, 1935; Assoc., Imperial Coll. Tropical Agr., Trinidad, 1938; PhD, McGill U., Montreal, P.Q., Can., 1939; D.Sc. (hon.), McGill U., 1966, Acadia U., 1970. Sci. officer Brit. Ministry of Supply, London, 1940-41; rsch. assoc. Carnegie Instn. Washington, 1946-47; rsch. sci. Atomic Energy of Can. Ltd., Chalk River, 1947-79, head biology br., 1949-70, head population rsch. br., 1970-79. Vis. prof. genetics Ind. U., Bloomington, 1963; mem. Internat. Commn. on Radiol. Protection, 1965-77, chmn. com. on biol. effects, 1965-72 Contbr. articles to profl. jours. Served to lt. Brit. Royal Naval Vol. Res., 1941-46 Fellow Royal Soc. Can.; mem. Genetics Soc. Am. (sec. 1956-58), Am. Soc. Human Genetics (pres. 1965), Genetics Soc. Can. (pres. 1964-65) Home: Deep River, Canada. Died Feb. 14, 2005.

**NEWHALL, DAVID SOWLE,** history educator; b. Burlington, Vt., July 26, 1929; s. Chester Albert and Nella Perry (Tillotson) N.; m. Edna Irene Newton, Mar. 25, 1952; children: Rebecca, John Newton, Jesslyn, Melissa, David Chester. BA, U. Vt., 1951; postgrad., Boston U., 1953—55; AM, Harvard U., 1956, PhD, 1963. Instr., asst. prof. U. Vt., Burlington, 1959-66; asst. prof., assoc. prof. history Centre Coll., Danville, Ky., 1966, prof., 1970, chmn. divsn. social studies, 1968—74, 1981—85, disting. prof. humanities Danville, Ky., 1987, Pottinger disting. prof. history, 1994-95; Pottinger disting. prof. history emeritus, from 1995. Mem. adv. com. Danville High Sch., 1980-81; cons. dept. history Berea (Ky.) Coll., 1983, 2001; rep. Ky. Coun. on Internat. Edn., Lexington, 1984-85. Author: Clemenceau: A Life at War, 1991; contbr. to Historical Dictionary of the Third French Republic, 1988, Kentucky Ency., 1992, Historic World Leaders, 1994, Women in World History: A Biographical Encyclopedia, 1999-2002, Ency. of Appalachia, 2003-. Elder Presbyn. Ch., U.S.A., Danville, 1969—; officer Danville H.S. Band Parents Assn., 1968-82; bd. dirs. Project Opportunity, Lee and Breathitt Counties, Ky., 1968-74; mem. Citizens Com. on Coal-Hauling Traffic, Boyle County, Ky., 1982—; mem. adv. bd. Ky. Elderhostel, 1996—. With U.S. Army, 1951-53, Korea. Recipient Acorn award Ky. Advocates for Higher Edn., 1994; Nat. Meth. scholar Boston U., 1953-55. Mem. Soc. for French Hist. Studies, Nat. Coun. for History Edn., Phi Beta Kappa (officer Centre Coll. 1971-95, 2005—), Omicron Delta Kappa, Phi Alpha Theta. Avocations: singing, railroading. Deceased.

**NEWLIN, LYMAN WILBUR,** bookseller, consultant; b. Buda, Ill., May 26, 1910; s. Fred Matheny and Maude Lillian (Potter) N.; m. Evy Ottonia Magnusson, 1966; children: Fred M. II, Erik B.M. Student, Coll. Emporia, Kans., 1928-30, U. Chgo., 1930-32. Buyer, bus. mgr. Follett Book Co., Chgo., 1934-44; mgr. Minn. Book Store and Macalester Coll. Book Store, Mpls. and St. Paul, 1944-48; co-owner Broadwater Lodge, Hackensack, Minn., 1948-65; founder, owner Broadwater Books, Lewiston, NY, from 1948; buyer, dept. mgr. Kroch's & Brentano's Book Store, Chgo., 1951-65; regional mgr. Richard Abel and Co., Portland, Oreg. and Zion, Ill., 1966-69, asst. to pres., 1969-75; founder, prin. counselor Lyman W. Newlin Book Trade Counsellors, Lewiston, NY, from 1975; mdse. mgr. Coutts Library Services, Inc., Lewiston, 1976-90; pub. rels. advisor The Charleston (Coll. Libr.) Conf., from 1985; pub. liaison Book News, Inc., Portland, from 1989; v.p. Zenaida Pub., Amherst, Mass., from 2004. Program coord. Acad. of Scholarly Pub. seminar Coll. of Charleston, 1995—; cons. Rutgers U. Press, New Brunswick, N.J., 1975-81; panelist and lectr. to acad. librs. and schs., booksellers. Pub. Rev. Index Quar. Guide to Profl. Revs., 1941-43; co-editor: Scholarly Publishing, Books, Journals, Publishers and Libraries in the Twentieth Century, 2002; pub. rels. advisor, contbr. Bi-Monthly Publ. Against the Grain, 1985—; contbr. articles to profl. jours. Founder, 1st pres. Boy River Chain of Lakes Improvement Assn., Cass County, Minn., 1961-65, Concerned Parents Orgn., Freehold, 1976-79; trustee, v.p., sec., chmn. new libr. bldg. com. Lewiston Pub. Libr., 1985-98, pres. bd. trustees, 1998-2002; committeeman Niagara County Dem. Party, 1987—, sec., 1988-90; mem. coun. Luth. Ch. Messiah, Lewiston, 1982-93, deacon, 1992-97; mem. Town of Lewiston Sr. Citizens Adv. Bd., 1992—; mem., com. person Zion Luth. Ch., Niagara Falls, N.Y., 1995—. Named Dem. of Yr., Town of Lewiston, 2003. Mem. ALA, Assn. Book Travelers (50 Yr. award 1984), Am. Booksellers Assn. (50 yr. bronze plaque 1998), Soc. Scholarly Pub. (program com. 1985), Am. Assn. Pubs. (emeritus), Pi Kappa Delta. Lutheran. Democrat. Avocations: amateur ornithology, American folk music, New Orleans jazz, collecting books. *If the Golden Rule is truly one's rule in living, no other rule is needed.* Died Sept. 20, 2005.

**NEWMAN, REBECCA KAY,** retired principal; b. Saginaw, Mich., 1946; m. Anthony Paul; 1 child, Dominique. BA, Mich. State U., 1968; MEd, U. Kans., 1975, EdD, 1978. Cert. spl. edn. grades K-12 Md., secondary prin. and supr. Md., supt. Md., elem. edn. K-8 Mich., spl. edn. K-12 Mich., English 9-12 Mich., social studies 7-9 Mich. Head tchr. adolescent unit Lafayette Clinic, Detroit, 1968—70; asst. prin., tchr. Island View Adolescent Ctr., Detroit, 1970—71; head tchr. children's unit Lafayette Clinic, Detroit, 1971—73; ednl. dir. Mid-Continent Psychiat. Hosp., Olathe, Kans., 1973—75; program mgr. Severe Personal Adjustment Program, Kansas City, Kans., 1975—78; asst. prin. Rock Terrace H.S. Montgomery County Public Schools, 1978—80, prin. Regional Inst. for Children & Adolescents, 1980—86, prin. Mark Twain Mid.-Sr. H.S., 1986—90, supr. secondary instrn. Area 3, 1990—91, acting asst. prin. Wootton H.S., 1991—92, prin. Paint Branch H.S., 1992—95, prin. Wootton H.S., 1995—2003. Mem. Corporate Partnerships Task Force, Montgomery County, 1996; participant prin.'s view Montgomery County Public Schools Public TV, 1989; mem. adv. bd. multidisciplinary master's degree tng. program for tchrs. of the behaviorally disordered/emotionally disturbed U. Md., College Park, 1985—86; pres. Montgomery County Assn. Administrators & Principals, 2003—11. Mem. editl. bd.: Focus on Autistic Behavior, 1990—91. Mem.: Montgomery County Assn. Adminstrv. and Supr. Pers. (mem. negotiations team 1993—96). Died Nov. 5, 2013.

**NEWMAN, RONALD CHARLES,** physicist, researcher; b. London, Dec. 10, 1931; s. Charles Henry and Margaret Victoria May (Cooper) N.; m. Jill Laura Weeks, Apr. 7, 1956; children: Susan Laura Newman Lee, Vivienne Heather Newman Cadman. BSc, Imperial Coll., London, 1952, DIC, 1954, PhD, 1955; postgrad., Chelsea Poly., 1952-53. Rsch. scientist AEI Rsch. Lab., Aldermaston Court, UK, 1955-63, sr. rsch. scientist, 1963-64; lectr. Reading U., England, 1964-69, reader in physics, 1969-75, prof. physics, 1975-89; assoc. dir. IRC Semicondr. Materials Lab. Imperial Coll., 1989-99, emeritus prof., sr. rsch. fellow, from 1999; prof. London U., 1989-99. Vis. prof. Reading U., 1989—, U. Manchester in Sci. and Tech., 2000—; cons., lectr. in field; vice chmn. Fachbeirat, Max-Planck Inst., Halle, 1995-98. Author: Infrared Studies of Crystal Defects, 1973; contbr. numerous articles, revs. to profl. publs.; mem. editl. bd. Jour. Physics C Solid State Physics, 1975-77. Fellow Royal Soc. Avocations: music, photography, foreign travel. Home: Reading, England. Died July 30, 2014.

**NEWMAN, RUTH TANTLINGER,** artist; b. Hooker, Okla., May 28, 1910; d. Walter Warren and Jean Louise (Hayward) Tantlinger; m. John Vincent Newman; children: Peter Vincent, Michael John. Student, Pomona Coll; BFA, UCLA, 1932; postgrad., Instituto Allende, U. Guanajuato, Mex. Art tchr. Santa Ana (Calif.) Schs., 1933-34, Santa Ana Adult Edn., 1934-40; watercolor tchr. Ventura (Calif.) Recreation Ctr., 1941-50; pvt. tchr. watercolor Calif., 1950-85. One-woman shows include Ventura County Mus. History and Art, 1993, Santa Barbara Art Assn., Ojai Art Ctr., Ventura Art Club, Oxnard (Calif.) Art Club, Art Club of Westlake Village, Thousand Oaks (Calif.) Art Club, others; commd. to paint 12 Calif. Missions, 1958, watercolors at San Juan Bautista Retreat House, Calif., oils at Ch. of San Bernardino, Mallorca, Spain; book featuring reproductions of selected works, Ruth Newman: A Lifetime of Art, introduced at her solo show in Ventura Mus., 1993. Mem. Westlake Village Art Guild, Thousand Oaks Art Club, Buena Ventura Art Club (charter). Deceased.

**NEY, EDWARD NOONAN,** former ambassador, retired advertising executive; b. St. Paul, May 26, 1925; s. John Joseph and Marie (Noonan) N.; m. Suzanne Hayes, 1950 (div. 1974); children: Nicholas, Hilary, Michelle; m. Patricia Murray Wood, May 1, 2010. BA (Lord Jeffrey Amherst scholar 1942), Amherst Coll., 1947. With Young & Rubicam, Inc., NYC, 1951-86, chmn., pres. CEO, 1970-86; chmn. Paine Webber/Young & Rubicam Ventures, NYC, 1987-89; vice-chmn. Paine Webber, Inc., NYC, 1987-89; US amb. to Canada US Dept. State, Ottawa, Ont., 1989-92; chmn. bd. advisors Burson-Marsteller, NYC, 1992-98; chmn. emeritus Young & Rubicam Advt., NYC, 1999—2014. Mem. Coun. on Fgn. Rels.; mem. advisory bd. Ctr. for Strategic & Internat. Studies (CSIS). Life Trustee Amherst Coll., from 1979; Trustee Bush Presidential Libr. Found., James A. Baker III Inst. for Public Policy, Rice U., Museum of TV/Radio (MTR), from 1982. Republican. Died Jan. 8, 2014.

**NG, TAI-KEE,** philosophy educator; b. Guangzhou, Guangdong, China, Jan. 6, 1920; s. Yung-Shuan and Chao-Mei (Sheu) N.; m. Chao-Heng Wong, Sept. 1, 1951 (div. Nov. 1954); m. An-Gel He, July 15, 1956; 1 child. BSc in Physics, Nat. Sun Yet-Sen U., Pinshih, China, 1942. Instr., assoc. prof. of math. and philosophy Nat. Sun Yet-Sun U., Pinshih, Guangzhou, 1942-49; prof., proxy pres. Guangzhou Fine Art Jr. Coll., 1948-49; assoc. prof., prof., master tutor of math. and philosophy South China Normal Coll. and U., Guangzhou, from 1950; prof., v.p. Ling-Hai Sr. Citizen U., Guangzhou, from 1984. Originator, dir. Nat. Philosophy Rsch. Com. China, Chengjian, Pinshih, Guangzhou, 1939-49. Author: A Treatise on the Development of Knowledge, 1947, Abstracts of 8th International Congress of Logic, Methodology and Philosophy of Science, 1987, Information Technology and Society, 1989, Structures in Mathematical Theories, 1990. Mem. Psychonomic Soc. U.S.A. (assoc.). Avocation: individual and group consciousness in mathematics and wave mechanics. Home: Guangzhou, China. Died 1999.

**NGEI, PAUL,** politician; b. Machakos, Kenya, 1923; BSc in Econs., Makarere Coll., Kampala, Uganda. Founder Wasya wa Mukamba newspaper and Uhuru wa Mwafrika, 1950; dep. gen. sec. Kenya African Union, 1951-52; pres. Kenya African Farmers' and Traders' Union, 1961; founder African People's Party, 1962; chair Maize Mktg. Bd., 1963-64; minister co-operatives and mktg. Kenya Govt., 1964-65, minister housing and social services, 1965-66, minister for housing, 1966-74, minister local govt., 1974-75, M.P. for Kagunda, 1976, minister of co-operative devel., 1976-79, minister of works, 1979-82, minister of livestock devel., 1982-83, minister of lands and settlement, 1983-84, minister of environment and nat. resources, 1984-85, minister of water devel., 1985, min. of culture and social svcs., 1988-89, former min. for manpower devel. Mng. dir. Akamba Carving and Indsl. Co. Died Aug. 15, 2004.

**NICHOLLS, RALPH WILLIAM,** physicist, researcher; b. Richmond, Surrey, Eng., May 3, 1926; s. William James and Evelyn Mabel (Jones) Nicholls; m. Doris Margaret McEwen, June 28, 1952. BSc, Imperial Coll., U. London, 1945, PhD, 1951, DSc in Spectroscopy, 1961. Cert. profl. physicist, chartered physicist. Sr. demonstrator in astrophysics Imperial Coll., U. London, 1945-48; instr. physics U. Western Ont. (Can.), London, 1948-50, lectr. physics, 1950-52, asst. prof. physics, 1952-56, assoc. prof., 1956-58, prof., 1958-63, sr. prof., 1963-65; prof. York U., Toronto, from 1965, Disting. Rsch. prof. physics, 1983-96, Disting. Rsch. prof. physics emeritus, 1996—2008, chmn. dept. physics, 1965-69; dir. Centre for Rsch. in Earth and Space Sci., 1965-92, dir. emeritus, 1996—2008; dir. atmospheric physics lab. Inst. for Space and Terrestrial Sci., 1987-94. Vis scientist Nat. Bur. Stds., 1959; vis. prof. Stanford U., 1964, 1968, 1973, 1990. Author (with B. H. Armstrong): (book) Emission, Absorption and Transfer of Radiation in Heated Atmospheres, 1972; editor: Can. Jour. Physics, 1986—92; editor: (assoc. editor) JQSRT Jour., 1960—2008; contbr. Decorated officer Order of Can.; Walter Gordon rsch. fellow, York U., 1982—83. Fellow: U.K. Inst. Physics, Can. Aero. and Space Inst., Am. Phys. Soc., Optical Soc. Am., Royal Soc. Can. Home: Thornhill, Canada. Died Jan. 25, 2008.

**NICHOLS, LAURIE I.,** nurse; d. Halsey T. Jr. and Jean Lois Nichols; 1 child, Andrew. AAS in Nursing, Ocean County Coll., 1979; BA in Applied Arts and Scis., Georgian Ct. U., 2006. RN NJ. Nurse ICN St. Peters U. Hosp., New Brunswick, NJ. Home: Brick, NJ. Died Aug. 3, 2008.

**NICHOLSON, THEODORE H.,** retired school system administrator; b. Chgo., July 27, 1929; children: Craig, Kimberlee, Kimberlee, Rhonda, Katrina, Alexandra. BS, Loyola U., Chgo., 1951; MS, No. Ill. U., 1955; postgrad., Rockford Coll., 1955; PhD, U. Wis. Madison, 1967. Tchr. Morris Kennedy Sch., Winnebago County, Ill., 1951—53, Rockford (Ill.) Public Schs., 1953—55, evening sch., 1955—59; prin. Marsh Schs., Dist. 58, Winnebago County, 1959—65, supt., 1959—66, Dearborn Twp. Sch. Dist. 8, Dearborn Heights, Mich., 1967—68, Wilmington (Ohio) City Sch., 1968—72; supr. schs. Wausau, Wis., 1972—90; assoc. prof. edn. leadership U. No., Colo., 1990—93. Vis. prof. Central State U., Wilberforce, Ohio, 1969—70; assoc. Univ. Wis. Madison, 1993—94, teaching asst., rsch. asst.; lectr. U. Wis., 1976, assoc. prof., assocs., 1993—94, lectr.; cons. Univ. Council Ednl. Adminstrn.; mem. coordinating com. Partnership Schs.; v.p. NC Data Processing Ctr., 1974—81; active Cen. Wausau Progress, 1973—82; mem. Pvt. Industry Coun.; bd. dirs. Wausau Performing Art Found., 1986—91, Wausau Area Community Found., 1988—91. Contbr. articles in field to profl. publs. Served USN, 1943—46. Recipient Citizenship award, City Rockford, 1960, 1964, Recognition award, State Wis. Dept. Pub. Instr., 1989, Wausau Bd. Edn., 1989, Community Leader award, Sta. WXCO, Wausau, 1974. Mem.: Phi Delta Kappa, C. of C. (bd. dirs., edn com., Businessman's Roundtable), Am. Assn. Supervision and Curriculum Devel., Wis. Assn. Sch. Dist. Adminstrs. (state bd. dirs., Adminstr. Yr. award spl. edn. dept. 1986, Recognition award 1989), Am. Assn. Sch. Adminstrs. Home: Wausau, Wis. Died Feb. 28, 1998.

**NIEFELD, JAYE SUTTER,** advertising executive; b. Mpls., May 27, 1924; s. Julius and Sophia (Rosenfeld) N.; m. Piri Elizabeth Von Zabrana-Szilagy, July 5, 1947; 1 child, Peter Wendell. Cert., London U., 1945; BA, U. Minn., 1948; BS, Georgetown U., 1949; PhD, U. Vienna, 1951. Project dir. Bur. Social Sci. Research, Washington, 1952-54; research dir. McCann-Erickson, Inc., NYC, 1954-57; v.p., dir. mktg. Keyes, Madden & Jones, Chgo., 1957-60; pres., dir. Niefeld, Paley & Kuhn, Inc., Chgo., 1961-71; exec. v.p. Bozell, Inc., Chgo., 1971-89; pres. The Georgetown Group, Inc., from 1991. Cons. U.S. Dept. State, Commerce, HEW, also others; lectr. Columbia U., Northwestern U., U. Chgo., 1989-94; chmn. Ctr. Advanced Comm. Rsch.; owner Glencoe Angus Farms, Glencoe Arabians; comm. adv. com. Arabian Horse Registry Am.; ptnr. Sunny Valley Farm, Talcott-Fromkin Freehold Assocs., Neptune Realty, J&J Enterprises; bd. dirs. Mktg. Decisions, Inc., E. Morris Comms., Inc. Author: The Making of an Advertising Campaign, 1989; (with others) Marketing's Role in Scientific Management, 1957, Advertising and Marketing to Young People, 1965, The Ultimate Overseas Business Guide for Growing Companies, 1990; contbr. articles to profl. jours. Mem. adv. bd. Glencoe Family Svc.; bd. dirs. Big Bros. Met. Chgo.; exec. v.p. City of Hope; mem. Theodore Thomas Soc. Chgo. Symphony Orch., Overture Soc. Lyric Opera Chgo. Capt. AUS, 1942-46. Decorated Bronze Star. Mem. Am. Assn. Pub. Opinion Rsch., Am. Film Inst., Am. Mktg. Assn., Am. Sociol. Assn., Smithsonian Instn., Internat. Arabian Horse Assn., Arabian Horse Registry (comm. com.), The Caxton Club, Chgo. Horticultural Soc. (governing bd.), Chgo. Coun. on Fgn. Rels. Died Sept. 27, 2005.

**NIELSEN, ERIK HERSHOLT,** former Canadian government official; b. Regina, Sask., Can., Feb. 24, 1924; s. I. and Mabel Elizabeth (Davies) N.; m. Pamela June Louth, May 3, 1945 (dec. 1969); children— Lee Scott, Erik Rolf, Roxanne; m. 2d, Shelley Coxford, Apr. 4, 1983 LL.B., Dalhousie U., 1950. Bar: Ont. 1950. Mem. House of Commons, Ottawa, Ont., Can., 1957-87, minister pub. works, 1979, opposition house leader, 1981, leader ofcl. opposition, 1983, opposition house leader, dep. nat. leader Progressive Conservative Party, 1983-84, dep. leader ofcl. opposition, 1984, dep. prime min., 1984—87, min. nat. def., 1985-86; chmn. Nat. Transp. Agy., 1987—92. Pres. Her

Majesty's Can. Privy Council, 1984-85. Mem. Canadian Bar Assn., N.S. Barrister Soc., Whitehorse C. of C. (hon.), Yukon Chamber Mines. Progressive Conservative. Anglican Died Sept. 4, 2008.

**NIEMCZYK, JULIAN MARTIN,** former ambassador; b. Fort Sill, Okla., Aug. 26, 1920; m. Margaret McCann. Student, Cameron State Coll., 1937-39, Okla. U., 1939-40, Am. U., 1949-50; BA, U. Phillipines, 1955. Enlisted USAAF, 1940, advanced through grades to col.; assignments with OSS, Burma and China, WWII; served in U.S. Embassies, Manila, Warsaw, Poland and Prague, Czechoslovakia, Prague during Warsaw Pact invasion; served 4 yr. tour duty Nat. Security Agy.; later dir. Ea. European office Internat. Security Affairs, Office Strategic Def., Pentagon, Washington; ret. USAAF, 1971; dir. heritage groups div. Republican Nat. Com., Washington, 1973-80; dir. nationalities div. Reagan-Bush Campaign Com., 1980; chief exec. officer People to People Internat., 1983-86; US amb. to Czechoslovakia US Dept. State, Prague, 1986-89. Presdl. appointee bd. visitors U.S. Air Force Acad., 1983-86. Decorated Bronze Star, Legion of Merit, Def. Commendation medal, Achievement Honor award US Dept. State, 1968, Legion of Honor award Armed Forces Phillipines; named to Field Arty. Hall of Fame Ft. Sill, Okla. Died Sept. 16, 2009.

**NIGRO, LOUIS JOHN, JR.,** former ambassador; b. Brooklyn, NY, May 19, 1947; m. Tarja Nigro. BA in History, U. Va., 1969; MA in History, Vanderbilt U., 1972; PhD in Modern European Hist., Vanderbilt U., Washington, 1973. Fulbright-Hays rsch. fellow, Italy; instr. modern European hist. Stanford U., Calif.; officer Calif. Army Nat. Guard; joined Fgn. Svc. US Dept. State, 1980; counselor for polit. affairs US Embassy, Port-auPrince, Haiti, 1992—94, dep. chief of mission, 1994—97, Conakry, Guinea, 1997—2000; dep. dir. Office Canadian Affairs US Dept. State, Washington, 2000—01, dep. US Interests Section Havana, Cuba, 2001—04, US amb. to Chad Ndjamena, 2007—10. Prof. internat. rels. US Army War Coll., 2004—06; diplomat in residence U. Houston, 2006—07. Author: The New Diplomacy in Italy: American Propaganda and U.S.-Italian Relations, 1917-1919, 1999. Recipient Superior Honor award, US Dept. State. Died Jan. 1, 2013.

**NIINI, HEIKKI ILMARI,** geologist, educator; b. Helsinki, Feb. 4, 1937; s. Eino M. and Aune (Kyöstilä) N.; m. Sirkka Pylvänäinen, 1961; children: Suvi, Ilkka, Yrjö. MS, U. Helsinki, 1961, PhD, 1968. Asst. Helsinki U. Tech., 1961-65, prof. econ. geology, head lab. engring. geology/geophysics, 1982-2000; geologist Nat. Bd. Pub. Rds. and Waterworks, Helsinki, 1965-69; sr. fellow Acad. Finland, Helsinki, 1969-75, prin. rsch. scientist, 1975-77; project leader Geol. Survey Finland, Espoo, 1977-81. Cons. IAEA, 1978-82; project evaluator, chmn. Finnish Ministry for Fgn. Affairs, Nairobi, Kenya, 1987; project evaluator Nordic Coun. Mins., Copenhagen, 1991-95; sect. head Rt. Selection of 120-km Bedrock Tunnel, Päijänne-Helsinki for Water Supply, 1965-69; chmn. local organizing com. of internat. conf. IAEA/OECD Underground Disposal of Radioactive Wastes, 1979. Co-editor: Earth and Rock Construction, (Finnish) 1976, Methods of Computation of Quantitative Changes in the Hydrological Regime (UNESCO Casebook), 1980, Large Rock Caverns, I, II, 1986, Fennoscandian 3rd Workshop on Hardrock Hydrogeology, 2005, Environmental Geology (Finnish), 2007; contbr. articles to profl. jours. Recipient Fountain Pen award Suomen Kuvalehti, 1955. Mem. Engring.-Geol. Soc. Finland (hon. mem., chmn. 1972-73, 79-81), Internat. Assn. Engring. Geology (exec. com. 1972-78), Geol. Soc. Finland (pres. 1990). Home: Helsinki, Finland. Died May 31, 2008.

**NIKAIDO, HUKUKANE,** economics researcher, educator; b. Tokyo, June 28, 1923; s. Michinosuke and Yone (Kanesaka) N.; m. Chisato Tange, Oct. 29, 1957; children: Masako, Kazuko. BS, U. Tokyo, 1949, DSc, 1961. Asst., assoc. prof. Tokyo Coll. Sci., 1950-57; assoc. prof. to prof. Osaka U., Toyonaka, Japan, 1957-69; prof. Hitotsubashi U., Tokyo, 1969-83, prof. emeritus, from 1998; prof. U. Tsukuba, Japan, 1983-87, Tokyo Internat. U., Kawagoe, Japan, 1987-97, prof. emeritus, from 1997. Author: Convex Structures and Economic Theory, 1968, Monopolistic Competition and Effective Demand, 1975, Prices, Cycles and Growth, 1996. Anti-aircraft artillery Japanese Army, 1945. Fellow Econometric Soc.; mem. Japan Econs. Assn. (pres. 1978-79). Home: Tokorozawa, Japan. Died Aug. 21, 2001.

**NILSSON, MARTIN (JOHN),** organic chemistry educator; b. Stockholm, Dec. 21, 1929; s. John A. and Marta K. (Andersson) N.; m. Ann-Catrine Teger, Aug. 7, 1954; children: Thomas M., Annika E. MSc in Chem. Engring., Royal Inst. Tech., Stockholm, 1954, licentiate of tech., 1957, D. Tech., 1961; PhD (hon.), Åbo Akademi (Finland), 1988. Asst. prof. Royal Inst. Tech., Stockholm, Sweden, 1961, assoc. prof., 1965-69, prof., 1969-72; prof. organic chemistry Chalmers U. Tech., Göteborg, Sweden, 1972-94, prof. emeritus, 1994—2001. Contbr. articles to profl. jours. Recipient Arrhenius award Swedish Chem. Soc., 1968. Mem. Royal Swedish Acad. Engring. Scis. (chmn. sec. chem. engring. 1996-98, Royal Soc. Arts and Scis. in Gothenburg. Home: Mölndal, Sweden. Died June 27, 2001.

**NIR, YEHUDA,** psychiatrist, educator; b. Stanislawow, Poland, Mar. 31, 1930; came to U.S., 1959; s. Samuel and Sidia (Hager) Grunfeld; m. Eva Roos, June 3, 1957; children: Daniel, Aaron; m. Bonnie Maslin, Nov. 4, 1973; children: David, Sarah. MD, Hebrew U., Jerusalem, 1958. Internship Hadassah Hosp., Jerusalem, 1958-59; residency in psychiatry Phila. Psychiat. Ctr., Phila., 1959-61, Mt. Sinai Hosp., NYC, 1961-62; fellow in child psychiatry Jewish Bd. of Guardians, NYC, 1962-64; Asst. prof. psychiatry Mt. Sinai Med. Sch., NYC, 1973-79, NYU, NYC, 1975—2014; Assoc. prof. psychiatry Cornell U. Med. Coll., NYC, 1979—2014; chief child psychiatry Meml. Sloan Kettering Cancer Ctr., 1979—86. Author: Loving Men for the Right Reasons, 1983, Not Quite Paradise, 1987, Lost Childhood: The Complete Memoir, 1989. Bd. dirs. American Gathering of Jewish Holocaust Survivors. Mem. American Psychiat. Assn. (human rights com. 1988). Jewish. Avocations: opera, art. Home: New York, NY. Died July 19, 2014.

**NISHIKAWA, MASAO,** historian, educator; b. Tokyo, July 15, 1933; s. Masami and Kiyoko Nishikawa; m. Junko Monna Nishikawa, Aug. 3, 1960; 1 child, Masashi. BA, U. Tokyo, 1956, MA, 1958. Asst. U. Tokyo, 1962—66, prof., 1968—94, prof. emeritus; prof. Tokyo Woman's Christian U., 1966—68, Senshu U., Tokyo, 1994—2004. V.p. Japanese Nat. Com. of the Cish, 1981—85; pres. Hist. Sci. Soc. Japan, 1989—93; hon. com. mem. Internat. Conf. Labour Historians, Vienna, from 1992. Author: Der Erste Weltkrieg und die Sozialisten, 1999. Recipient Viktor Adler prize, Bundesministerium fur Forschung, 1985. Avocation: calligraphy. Home: Musashino-shi Tokyo, Japan. Died Jan. 28, 2008.

**NISHIMOTO, IKUO,** physician, educator, pharmacologist, department chairman; b. Wakayama, Japan, Jan. 28, 1956; s. Yukio and Ruriko Nishimoto. BD, U. Tokyo, 1976, MD, 1980, PhD, 1997. Instr. U. Tokyo, 1984—85, asst. prof., 1985—92; assoc. prof. Harvard Med. Sch., Boston, 1992—96; prof., chair Keio U. Sch. Medicine, Tokyo, from 1996. Contbr. articles to profl. jours. Recipient award, Tokyo Med. Assn., 1996; postdoctoral fellow, Stanford U. Sch. Medicine, 1989—90. Mem.: Am. Soc. Biochemistry and Molecular Biology, Soc. for Neurosci., Japanese Pharmacol. Soc. (adv. bd.). Died Oct. 17, 2003.

**NIZAMI, WAJIH AHMAD,** parasitologist; b. Meerut, India, Aug. 22, 1950; s. Khaliq and Razia N.; m. Rahat Faridi, Jan. 18, 1981; children: Moin, Amin. BSc, Aligarh Muslim U., 1970, MSc, 1972, MPhil, 1974, PhD, 1976. From lectr. to prof. Aligarh Muslim U., India, from 1979. Royal Soc. fellow Br. Univs., England, 1984; Br. Coun. fellow Queens U., Belfast, Ireland, 1990-91; mgr. Ahmadi Sch. for Blind, Aligarh, 1991-94. Fellow Helminthological Soc. India, Soc. Bioscis. of India, Zool. Soc. India. Avocations: reading autobiographies, mysticism, machine repair, gardening. Home: Aligarh, India. Deceased.

**NKALA, ENOS MZOMBI,** retired Zimbabwean government official; b. Filabusi, Zimbabwe, Aug. 23, 1932; Widowed; 3 children. Student, Eden Sch., Mzinyati, Zimbabwe; degree in law and commerce, dip. in accountancy, bus. mgmt. and pub. adminstrn. With Bantu Missor, Salisbury, Zimbabwe, 1952-55; in ins., 1956; active Youth League; caretaker sec.-gen. Nat. Dem. Party, Zimbabwe, then dep. sec.-gen., 1960; founding mem. Zimbabwe African Nat. Union, 1963, treas.-gen. Gwelo, 1964; min. home affairs Govt. of Zimbabwe, 1985-87, min. def., 1988-1989. Died Aug. 21, 2013.

**NKOMO, JOHN LANDA,** Zimbabwean government official; b. Aug. 22, 1934; m. Georginah Nkomo, 1963; 6 children. Sch. tchr., 1957-64; mem. ctrl. com. ZAPU, 1975-89; dep. min. of industry Govt. of Zimbabwe, 1981-82, min. of state Office of Prime Min., 1982-84, min. of labor manpower planning & social welfare, v.p., 2009—13; spkr. Zimbabwean Parliament, 2005—08. Pres. Internat. Labor Conf.; chmn. African Regional Labor Ctr.; mem. pub. accounts com., 1980-81; chmn. Com. of Estimates of Expenditure, 1985-87. Recipient Zimbabwe Gold Liberation medal, Zimbabwe Silver Liberation medal. Mem. Southern Rhodesia Tchrs. Assn. (exec. mem.), Highlanders Football Club, Bulawayo Club, Matebeleland Turf Club (hon. life pres.), Lions Club. Zimbabwe African Nat. Union (Zanu-Pf). Died Jan. 17, 2013.

**NOBEL, JOEL J.,** biomedical researcher; b. Phila., Dec. 8, 1934; s. Bernard D. and Golda R. (Nobel) Judovich; m. Bonnie Sue Goldberg, June 19, 1960 (div.); children: Erika, Joshua; m. Loretta Schwartz, Oct. 28, 1979 (div.); 1 child, Adam; m. Qingging Lu, Aug. 28, 2010. AB in English, Haverford Coll., 1956; MA in Internat. Rels., U. Pa., 1958; MD, Thomas Jefferson Med. Coll., Phila., 1963. Intern Presbyn. Hosp., Phila., 1963-64; resident in surgery Pa. Hosp., Phila., 1964-65; resident in neurosurgery U. Pa. Hosp., 1965-66; practice medicine specializing in biomed. engring. rsch. and healthcare tech. assessment, hosp. planning and mgmt., Phila., from 1968; dir. research Emergency Care Research Inst., Plymouth Meeting, Pa., 1968-71, dir., pres., 1971—2001; bd. dirs. Consumers Union, 1976—79, 1980—2005, Conflict Interest Com., from 2008; pres. Plymouth Inst., from 1979; founder, pres. emeritus ECRI, 2001—14; founder, pres. ECRI Bhd, Malaysia, 2001—14; CEO The Nobel Group, 2002—14, chmn. Arab Health award, 2004—14; mng. dir. IMD, 2006—10. Chmn. tech. policy com., exec. bd., chmn. strategic planning com. Consumers Union; cons. in field. Publisher Health Devices, 1971-2001, Health Devices Alerts, 1977-2001; contbr. articles to profl. jours. With submarine force USN, 1966—68. Smith, Kline & French fgn. fellow, 1962; grantee US Dept. Health, Edn. & Welfare (HEW), 1968-72; grantee American Heart Assn., 1965-66 Mem. AMA, APHA, Assn. Advancement Med. Instrumentation, Critical Care Med. Soc., Pa. Med. Assn., Navy League, US Naval Inst., Brit. Officers Club Phila. Home: Gladwyne, Pa. Died Aug. 20, 2014.

**NOGUCHI, HIROSHI,** structural engineering educator; b. Tokyo, Aug. 9, 1946; s. Kou and Kimie (Ohtake) N.; m. Yoriko Ito, Jan. 8, 1982; children: Mariko, Eriko. B in Engring., U. Tokyo, 1970, M in Engring., 1972, DEng, 1976. Registered architect 1st class. Rsch. assoc. U. Tokyo, 1976-77; asst. prof. Chiba (Japan) U., 1977-79, assoc. prof., 1979-90, prof., from 1991, councilor, vice dean, from 2002. Vis. rschr. U. Toronto, 1984-85, U. Tex., 1997-98. Author: (with others) Shear Analysis of Reinforced Concrete Structures, 1983, Finite Element Analysis of Reinforced Concrete Structures, 1986, Shear Resistance Mechanisms of Beam-Column Joints Under Reversed Cyclic Loading, 1987, Guidelines for Application of FEM to RC Design, 1989, Development of Mixed Structures in Japan, 1990, Experimental Studies on Shear Performances of RC Interior Column-Beam Joints with High-Strength Materials, 1992, Finite Element Analysis of Reinforced Concrete Structures II, 1993, Analytical Study on the Shear Performance of Beam-Column Connections in Hybrid Structures with RC Column and S Beams, 1995, Nonlinear Finite Element Analysis on Shear and Bond of RC Interior Beam-Column Joints with Ultra High-Strength Materials, 1995, Analytical Study on the Shear Performance of Steel Beam-R/C Column Connections in Hybrid Structures, 1996, Analysis of Beam-Column Joints in Hybrid Structures, 1997, Shear Strength of Beam-Column Joints with High-Strength Concrete, 1998, FEM Analysis for Structural Performance Design of Concrete Structures, 1999, Research on RC/SRC Column Systems, 2000, FEM Analysis of Hybrid Structural Frames with R/C Columns and Steel Beams, 2000. Design of Moder Highrise RC structures, 2002; author: State-of-the-Art of Theoretical Studies in Membrane Shear Behavior in Japan, 1991, Recent Developments of Researches and Applications of RCFEM in Japan, 1991, Finite Element Analysis of Shear Behavior of RC Members with High Strength Materials, 1993, Shear Resisting Mechanisms of Reinforced Concrete Members Based on FEM Analysis, 1994, Concrete Model Code for Asia, 1996, Toward a High-quality FEM Analysis of RC Members Subjected to Reversed Cyclic Sheet, 2003. Mem. ASCE, Archtl. Inst. Japan (Meritorious Paper award 1997), Japan Concrete Inst. (Meritorious Paper award 1985), Tokyo Soc. Architects, Am. Concrete Inst., Internat. Assn. Bridges and Structural Engring. Avocations: swimming, skiing, classical music. Deceased.

**NOIRET, PHILIPPE,** actor; b. Lille, France, Oct. 1, 1930; s. Pierre and Lucy (Heirman) N.; m. Monique Chaumette, 1962; 1 child, Frederique. Pbt. tng. for the stage. Worked as nightclub entertainer. Film appearances include Zazie dans le metro, 1960, Le Crime ne paie pas, 1963, Therese Desqueyroux, 1963, Monsieur, 1964, Lady L, 1964, Woman Times Seven, 1967, The Night of the Generals, 1967, The Assassination Bur., 1969, Topaz, 1970, Most Gentle Confessions, 1971, Le Serpent, 1973, L'Horlager de Saint Paul, 1974, Le Jeu avec le feu, 1974, Monsieur Albert, 1976, Who Is Killing the Great Chefs of Europe?, 1978, Two Pieces of Bread, 1979, La Grande Carnaval, 1983, Masques, 1986, The Gold-Rimmed Glasses, 1987, Cinema Paradiso, 1990, The Palermo Connection, 1991, Especially on Sunday, 1993, Il Postino, 1994; appeared on TV; stage appearances include Lorenzaccio, N.Y.C., 1958, Marie Tudor, N.Y.C., 1958, Le Cid, N.Y.C., 1958, also in Richard III, Oedipus, Don Juan, The Odd Couple. Recipient Best Actor award Venice Film Festival, 1963, Etoile de Cristal for best actor, 1969, Cesar award for best actor, 1976, 90, Rio de Janeiro Film Festival award for best actor, 1984, European Film award for actor of yr., 1989, David award for best fgn. actor, 1990, Brit. Acad. Film and TV award for best actor, 1990. Mem. SAG. Died Nov. 23, 2006.

**NOLAN, MARILYN ANN,** health facility administrator; b. Brighton, Mass., July 17, 1935; d. Anthony Henry and Anne Claire Nikiel; m. George F. Nolan (dec.); 2 children. BA, Trinity Coll., Washington, 1957; MSS in Social Wk., Boston U., 1959. Cert. hyponotherapist Am. Inst. Hypnotherapy; lic. ind. clin. social worker, clin. soc. bd. cert., bd. cert. NASW. Med. social worker Peter Bent Brigham Hosp., Boston, 1959—60; geriatric and psychiat. social worker Modesto State Hosp., Calif., 1960—63; psychiat. social worker, geriatric med. substance abuse therapist, visual impairment svc. coord. VA Med. Ctr., Bedford, Mass., 1966—87, psychiat. social worker, substance abuse therapist, 1989—91, visual impairment svc. team coord. Long Beach, Calif., 1987—89, St. Petersburg, Fla., 1991—2004; pvt. practice guided imagery, visualization and stress mgmt. Largo, Fla., Wareham, Mass., from 2004. Chmn. disabled people's program Bay Pines VA Med. Ctr., St. Petersburg, 1991—94; field work instr. Boston Coll., 1972—86, Boston U., 1972—86. Recipient Outstanding Contbn. award, Am. Legion, 1990, Tampa Bay Fed. Equal Employment Opportunity, 1993, Blinded Vets. Assn., 2002. Mem.: NASW (bd. cert. diplomate), Acad. Cert. Social Workers. Roman Catholic. Avocations: reading, piano, accordion. Died Oct. 14, 2013.

**NOLL, CHUCK,** retired professional football coach; b. Cleve., Jan. 5, 1932; s. William & Katherine (Steigerwald) N.; m. Marianne Noll; 1 son, Chris. BA, U. Dayton, 1953. Guard, linebacker Cleve. Browns, 1953-59; defensive line coach San Diego Chargers, 1960—61, defensive coord., defensive backfield, 1962—65, Balt. Colts, 1966-68; head coach Pitts. Steelers, 1969-91. Named American Football Conf. Coach of Yr., UPI, 1972, Coach of Yr. Maxwell Football Club, 1989; named to The Pro Football Hall of Fame, 1993, The Pitts. Pro Football Hall of Fame, 2011 Achievements include coaching the Pittsburgh Steelers to 4 Super Bowl championships 1974-75, 78-79. Died June 13, 2014.

**NOLLER, RUTH BRENDEL,** retired education educator, consultant, researcher; b. Buffalo, Oct. 6, 1922; d. John Michael and Ellen (Bement) Brendel; m. David Conrad Noller, June 7, 1947; children: David Carl, Paul John. BA, U. Buffalo, 1942, EdM, 1944, EdD, 1952. Inst. math. U. Buffalo, 1942-52; professorial lectr. math. SUNY, Buffalo, 1957-71, rsch. asst. in creativity, lectr., 1964-69; assoc. prof. creative studies State U. Coll. Buffalo, 1969-78, prof., 1978-82, disting. svc. prof. emeritus, from 1982. Alex F. Osborn vis. prof. State U. Coll., Buffalo, 1992-93; cons. in field. Author 12 books; contbr. articles to profl. jours. Lt.

(j.g.) WAVES, USNR, 1944-46. Mem. AAUW (edn. chmn. 1985-93, endowment honoree edn. found. program 1988), United U. Professions, Creative Edn. Found. (colleague, disting. leader exceptional svc. award 1988, svc. and commitment award 1987), N.Y. Tchrs., Sch. Vols. of Sarasota County, Delta Kappa Gamma. Democrat. Episcopalian. Avocations: travel, bell collecting, gardening, photography. Home: Sarasota, Fla. Died June 3, 2008.

**NOONAN, MICHAEL JOSEPH,** retired Irish legislator; b. Bruff, County Limerick, Ireland, Sept. 4, 1935; s. John and Hannah (Slattery) N.; m. Helen Sheehan, Nov. 28, 1961; children: Marie Noonan Madden, Ann Noonan Edmiston, John, Catherine Noonan Justice, Carmel, Patrick. Student, Salesian Coll., Pallaskenry, County Limerick, 1960. MP, Limerick West constituency Dail Eireann, Dublin, 1969—97; opposition spokesman on agr. Fianna Fail Party, Dublin, 1983-87; min. def. Govt. of Ireland, Dublin, 1987-89; min. State of Marine Ireland, Dublin, 1989-92; ret., 1997. Roman Catholic. Avocation: sports. Died Sept. 17, 2013.

**NORDBERG, ERIK MAGNUS,** physician, researcher; b. Harnosand, Sweden, Feb. 2, 1935; arrived in Kenya, 1996; s. John and Gunnel Maria (Huss) N. MD, U. Gothenburg, 1965, BA in Sociology, 1971; MPH, Nordic Sch. Pub. Health, Gothenburg, 1987; PhD in health care rsch., Karolinska Inst., Stockholm, 1995. Provincial med. officer Ministry of Health, Nakamte, Ethiopia, 1971-74; dep. head med. svcs. Min. Health, Addis Ababa, Ethiopia, 1974-75; dep. provincial med. officer Harnosand, Stockholm, 1975-78; med. dir. African Med. and Rsch. Found., Nairobi, Kenya, 1978-82, 96-99; dep. provincial med. officer Stockholm, 1982-85; rschr. dept. internat. health care rsch. Karolinska Inst., 1985-96. Cons. in internat. health Swedish Internat. Devel. Agy., 1983-95. Author: Environmental Hygiene in Developing Countries, 1979; editor: Society, Environment and Health in Low Income Countries, 1990; contbr. articles to profl. jours. Avocations: sports, science fiction. Home: Stockholm, Sweden. Died Jan. 2002.

**NORDEN, KARL ELIS,** management consultant; b. Stockholm, Feb. 27, 1921; s. Daniel Henrik and Ella Amanda (Larsson) N.; m. Beatrice Buff; children: Jan-Henrik, Gunilla, Carl-Magnus, Astrid Lethin (div). BEE, Royal Inst. Tech., Stockholm, 1954. Devel. engr. Swedish Radio AB, 1940-44; chief radar devel dept. Royal Swedish Air Bd., 1944-54; founder, pres. Elenik Automation AB, Stockholm, 1955-64, Norden Automation Systems AG, Zurich, Switzerland, 1964-79, NAS Austria, Vienna, 1966-79, NAS Holland, Woudenberg, 1968-79. Mgmt. cons. to airlines, and specialized on yield improvement in iron, steel and chem. industry, specialist in motion weighing, computer controlled material handling; pres. Norden Consulting Internat. Ltd., Sargans, Switzerland, 1987—, Inst. Yield Tech., Ltd., Sargans, Switzerland, 1999—; course dir. modern electronic weighing Ctr. Profl. Advancement, East Brunswick, N.J.; tchr. Royal Swedish Air Force High Sch., 1955-64; chmn. bd. dirs. Inst. Yield Tech. Ltd., Sargans, Switzerland, 1999—. Author: The Inventors Book, 1963, Pulp and Paper, 1968, Aufbereitungstechn, 1972, Electronic Weighing in Industrial Processes, 1984, Electronic Weighing, 1992, Handbook of Electronic Weighing, 1998; patentee in field. Mem. Swedish Inst. Tech., Swedish Assn. Elec. Engrs., Assn. Instrument Tech., Verein Deutscher Eisen-Hüttenleute, Inst. Materials London (affiliate). Died Apr. 26, 2004.

**NORGAARD, CARL AAGE,** law educator; b. Svenstrup, Denmark, Sept. 15, 1924; m. Hedvig Hauberg, Mar. 17, 1951; 1 child, Helene Hauberg Lehrmann. CandJur, U. Aarhus, Denmark, 1954, DrJur, 1962; postgrad., U. Cambridge, Eng., 1954-55, Inst. Internat. Studies, Geneva, 1959-60; DrJur (hon.), U. Lund, Sweden, 1994. Asst. U. Aarhus, 1955-58, lectr., 1958-64, prof. law, 1964-91; mem. European Commn. of Human Rights, Strasbourg, France, 1973-95, v.p., 1976—81, pres., 1981—95. Mem., chmn. various Danish law preparing coms.; ind. jurist with regard to release of polit. prisoners in Namibia, UN, 1989-90; cons. South African Ministry of Justice, 1994-96. Author: The Position of the Individual in International Law, 1962; Administrative Law Procedure, 1972, 5th edit. (with J. Garde and K. Revsbech), 2001; co-author: Administration and Citizens, 1973, 2d edit., 1984; contbr. articles to profl. jours. Served to lt. Danish Army, 1945-47. Decorated Danish Grand Cross; German Grand Order of Merit with star and sash; recipient French Prix de la Tolerance, 1998. Home: Galten, Denmark. Died June 16, 2009.

**NORI, ANDREW HANAIPEO,** retired Solomon Islands government official, lawyer; b. 1952; m. Marie Jacinta, 1979; 1 child. LLB, U. Papua New Guinea, 1979. Bar: High Ct. Solomon Islands. Sr. legal officer Govt. of Solomon Islands, 1980-81, govt. min., 1985-88, min. finance, 1993—94; pvt. law practice, 1982—2013. Died July 9, 2013.

**NORTHFIELD, TIMOTHY CLIVE,** gastroenterologist, consultant; b. London, Feb. 16, 1935; s. Douglas William (Claridge) and Marjorie Northfield; m. Rosemary Norton; children: Jane, John. MA, MD Radley Coll., 1964; MA in Local and Regional History, Radley Coll., 2000, DSc, 2003. Registrar gastroenterology unit Central Middlesex Hosp., London; travelling fellow gastroenterology unit Mayo Clinic, Rochester, Minn.; sr. registrar Guys Hosp., London. Prof. medicine and gastroenterology St. Georges Hosp. Med. Sch., London, 1990—2003. Contbr. articles to profl. jours. 2d lt. German mil., 1953—55. Recipient Hopkins prize, British Soc. Gastroenterology, 1987. Fellow: Royal Coll. Physicians; mem.: Royal Soc. Medicine (chmn. 1988). Mem. Ch. Eng. Home: Surrey, England. Died May 2, 2008.

**NOTLEY, THELMA A.,** retired librarian, educator; b. Ogbomosho, Nigeria, Feb. 7, 1928; came to U.S., 1931; d. John Spurgeon and Della (Black) Richardson; m. Loren Spencer Notley, June 16, 1946 (dec.); children: Dan, Kathleen, R. Steven, Laura. BS in Lang. Arts, Okla. State U., Stillwater, 1961; MS in LS, Okla. U., 1972. Tchr. English, Helena (Okla.) Pub. Schs., 1962-64, Skiatook (Okla.) Pub. Schs., 1964-66, Tulsa Pub. Schs., 1966-67, sch. libr., 1967-86; tchr. ESL Dongbi U. Fin. and Edn., Dalian, China, 1988-90; tchr. English, libr. Anglican Internat. Sch., Jerusalem, Israel, 1994-96. Author: China Bound, 1999; contbr. articles to profl. jours. Republican. Episcopalian. Avocations: writing, quilting, travel. Died Nov. 24, 2006.

**NOVAK, JONATHAN BLANDING,** utilities executive; b. Pitts., Aug. 11, 1944; s. John and Violet Emelia (Dicey) Novak; m. Betty Jane DeMoss, July 2, 1966; children: Kimberly Layne, Christopher Taylor, Tiffany Beth. BA in Sociology and Psychology, Eckerd Coll., 1968; MBA, Brenau Coll., 1984. Tech. cons., group leader computer and teleprocessing services Sears Roebuck & Co., Atlanta, 1968—81; ops. support mgr., mgmt. info. sys. Ga. Power Co., Atlanta, 1981—83; mgmt. info. sys. dir. devel. mgr., 1983—85; info. services mgr. product rsch., 1985—86; sr. tchg. assoc. Inst. Sys. Sci., Nat. U. Singapore, Kent Ridge, from 1986. Adj. faculty Brenau Coll., Atlanta, 1984; instr. Am. Mgmt. Assn., Oglethorpe U., Atlanta, 1985, Edison Electric Inst. Computer Com.; mem. office automation Singapore Nat. Computer Bd., from 1986. Contbr. articles to profl. jours. Adult sunday sch. tchr. Highlands Presbyn. Ch., 1970—71, 1981—85; founding vice chmn. Stone Mountain Civic Assn., 1972; pres. Redan Hills Civic Assn., 1976; coord. Dekalb (Ga.) Police Target Hardening Opportunity Reduction, 1980—86, Atlanta Private Industry Coun., 1982; asst. emergency flight ops. officer CAP, 1985. Mem.: CAP, Aircraft Owners and Pilots Assn., Am. Mgmt. Assn., Edison Electric Inst., Soc. for Info. Mgmt., Mensa, Singapore Computer Soc. Died Jan. 13, 2010.

**NOVAKOVICH, NADA,** lawyer; b. Feb. 24, 1924; d. Peter and Ljuba (Matyasevich) Novakovich; m. Luke Aluevich Novakovich, 1961 (dec. 1971). LLB, George Washington U., 1950. Bar: Nev. 1950, US Dist. Ct. Nev. 1950, US Dist. Ct. DC 1950. Pvt. practice, Reno, from 1950; mem. Gov.'s Adv. Com. Status of Women, 1959. Mem. Gov.'s Fulbright Scholarship Com. Author: And His Name Was Luke, 1976. Dem. candidate US House of Reps., 1956. Mem.: ABA, Reno C. of C. (dir. 1973—76), DC Bar Assn., Washoe County Bar Assn. (sec. 1951—56), Nev. Bar Assn., Soroptimists Club (Reno), Phi Delta Delta. Serbian Orthodox. Home: Reno, Nev. Died Oct. 1998.

**NOVOGRODSKY, ABRAHAM,** medical research director; b. Jerusalem, Apr. 14, 1932; MD, Hebrew U., Jerusalem, 1959; PhD, Weizmann, Rehovot, 1974. Dir. Rogoff Med. Rsch. Inst., Beilinson Med. Ctr., Petah-Tikva, Israel, from 1979. Died July 30, 2008.

**NOWACKI, JÓZEF,** law educator; b. Lodz, Poland, July 21, 1923; s. Józef and Helena (Kurowska) N.; m. Zofia Nogacka, Nov. 13, 1948; 1 child, Thomas. LLM, U. Lodz, 1952, JD, 1959, D Habilitatus, 1964. From asst. prof. to prof. U. Lodz, 1952-74; prof. Silesian U., Katowice, Poland, 1974—2005, dean faculty law, 1981. Author: Analogia Legis, 1966, Legal Praesumption, 1976, Rule of Law, 1977, Two Studies on Rule of Law, 1980, Legal Prescription and Legal Norm, 1988, Public Law-Private Law, 1992, Rule of Law-Two Problems, 1995; author: (with Z. Tobor) Introduction to Jurisprudence, 2000. Mem. Soc. Scientiarum Lodziensis, Internat. Vereinigung Rechts & Social Philosophie. Home: Katowice, Poland. Died Aug. 14, 2005.

**NOWACZEK, FRANK HUXLEY,** venture capital executive; b. Bklyn., July 6, 1930; s. Frank Huxley and Louise (Blake) N.; m. Alice Elaine Novak, May 21, 1955; children: Richard Alan, Elaine. Student, St. Lawrence U., 1948-50; BS in Hotel Adminstrn., Cornell U., 1952; postgrad. in polit. sci. and pub. rels., George Washington U., 1954-58, Am. U., 1954-57. Spl. agt. spl. ops. br. security divsn. Def. Dept., Nat. Security Agy., 1954-59; asst. to pres., dir. Nat. Cable TV Assn., Washington, 1959-64; asst. to pres. TeleSystems Corp., Glenside, Pa., 1964-66; v.p., part-owner Newport Cablevision, Vt., 1966-68; v.p. Blackburn & Co., Inc., Washington, 1968-76; v.p. Mid Atlantic region Warner Amex Cable Comms., NYC, 1976-80; sr. v.p. eastern divsn. Ft. Washington, Pa., 1980-82; sr. v.p. nat. divsn. Columbus, Ohio, 1982-83; owner Cable Media Co., Washington, Ohio, 1983-86; pres. Newcable TV Corp., 1985-86; COO Bachow & Elkin, Inc., Phila., 1986-92; ops. dir. Communications Industries Bachow & Assocs., Bala Cynwyd, Pa.; sr. advisor Bachow Investment Ptnrs., 1992-95; mng. dir. Bachow and Assocs., Inc., from 1995. V.p. Digital Access, Inc., 1999—; bd. advisors Columbus Investment Interest Group; spkr. various orgns. Served with CIC, U.S. Army, 1952-54. Mem. IEEE, Pub. Rels. Soc. Am., Soc. Relay Engrs. (Gt. Britain), Cable TV Adminstrn. and Mktg. Assn., Nat. Cable TV Pioneers Assn., Nat. Acad. Cable Programmers, Soc. Cable Telecom. Engrs., Pa. Cable TV Assn. (pres., dir.), Pa. Calbe TV Pioneers Assn. (Founders award), Phila. Cable TV Club (founder), Cornell Soc. Hotelman (life), Am. Mgmt. Assn., Nat. Cable TV Assn. (sec. tech. stds. com. 1961 chmn. membership com. 1965-66), World Futurist Soc., Soc. Telecomm. Engrs., Ohio Hist. Soc., Cornell U. Alumni Club, Phi Delta Theta. Republican. Roman Catholic. Home: Columbus, Ohio. Died 2001.

**NOWAK, JAN ZDZISLAW,** writer, consultant; b. Warsaw, May 15, 1913; came to U.S., 1977; s. Waclaw Adam and Elisabeth (Piotrowski) Jezioranski; m. Jadwiga Zaleski, Sept. 7, 1944. MS, U. Poznan, Poland, 1936; Doctorate honoris causa, U. Poznan, U. Wroclaw, 1999, U. Cracow, 2000. Sr. researcher U. Poznan, 1937-39; emissary Polish resistance movement, 1941-45; editor BBC, London, 1947-51; dir. Polish Service Radio Free Europe, Munich, Fed. Republic of Germany, 1951-76; v.p., nat. dir. Polish Am. Congress, Washington, 1979-96. Cons. Nat. Security Coun., 1979-92. Author: Courier from Warsaw, 1982, War on Airways, 1985, Poland From Afar, 1988; contbr. articles to mags. Served to maj. Polish Army, 1939-45. Decorated Virtuti Militari; decorated Cross of Valour, King's medal for Courage, Order of White Eagle, Poland, gt. ribbon Polonia Restituta, Comdrs. Cross of Merit with star (Poland), Order of Grand Duke Gedyminas (Lithuania), Presdl. Medal of Freedom, 1996. Roman Catholic. Home: Warsaw, Poland. Died Jan. 20, 2005.

**NOWAK, KURT LUDWIG,** church historian; b. Leipzig, Germany, Oct. 28, 1942; s. Ludwig Franz and Alice Wilhelmine (Pempel) N.; m. Gisela Margot Groetzsch, Jan. 30, 1937; 1 child, Clemens. Diploma, U. Leipzig, Germany, 1969, D of Theology, 1971, DPhil, 1984. Asst. U. Leipzig, Germany, 1971-83, lectr., 1983-87, prof., 1987-92, from 1992. Author: Euthanasie und Sterilisation im Dritten Reich, 3d edit., 1984, Protestantismus und Demokratie, 2d edit., 1988, Schleiermacher und die Fruehromantik, 1986, Geschichte des Christentums, 1995, Das Christentum. Geschichte-Glaube-Ethik, 1997, Vernünftiges Christentum? Zur Erforschung der Aufklärung, 1999, Friedrich Schleiermacher.Leben, Werk und Wirkung, 2001. Mem. German-French Soc. (exec.), Schleiermacher Soc., Luther Soc., Comité Franco-Allemand, Saxon Acad. Scis. (sec.). Home: Leipzig, Germany. Died Dec. 31, 2001.

**NTLOLA, PETER MAKHWENKWE,** retired translator; b. Phillipstown, Cape, South Africa, July 7, 1908; s. Fanteni and Sarah Notsitsa (Bonani) N.; m. Constance Nomalanga Siningwa, July 7, 1949 (dec. Mar. 1976). Pub. serials on Man's Footprints on the Moon in state-sponsored monthly, 1963-76; columnist to 3 African monthly periodicals; specialist cons. on all spiritual matters and problems generally. Journalist, editor, reporter, proofreader, photographer, layout artist 5 books translated from English, 1966-86. Served as sgt. in World War II. Died Feb. 8, 2002.

**NULAND, SHERWIN,** surgeon, writer; b. NYC, Dec. 8, 1930; s. Meyer and Violet (Lutsky) N.; m. Sarah Peterson, May 29, 1977; children: Victoria Jane, Andrew Meyer, William Peterson, Amelia Rose. BA, NYU, 1951; MD, Yale U., 1955. Surgeon Yale-New Haven Hosp. (Conn.), 1962—92; clin. prof. surgery Yale Sch. Medicine, New Haven, 1962—91. Author: The Origins of Anesthesia, 1983, Doctors: The Biography of Medicine, 1988, Medicine: The Art of Healing, 1991, How We Die: Reflections on Life's Final Chapter, 1994 (Nat. Book award for non-fiction, 1994, Pulitzer prize finalist, 1995), The Wisdom of the Body: How We Live, 1997, The Mysteries Within: A Surgeon Reflects on Medical Myths, 2000, Leonardo da Vinci, 2000, Lost in America, 2003, The Doctors' Plague, 2003, Maimonides, 2005, The Art of Aging, 2007, The Uncertain Art: Thoughts on a Life in Medicine, 2008; contbg. editor The New Republic, mem. editl. bd. Perspectives in Biology and Medicine. V.p. Conn. Hospice, New Haven, 1978-80; bd. dirs. Hastings Ctr. Hastings Ctr. fellow. Fellow AAAS, ACS; mem. New Eng. Surg. Soc., Associates of Yale Med. Sch. Libr. (chmn. 1982-94), Yale-China Assn. (chmn. med. 1988-93), History of Medicine and Allied Scis. (chmn. bd. jour. 1979-2002). Democrat. Jewish. Avocation: tennis. Home: Hamden, Conn. Died Mar. 4, 2014.

**NUMOTO, KATSUAKI,** literature educator; b. Okayama, Japan, 1943; m. Misako Numoto, Mar. 1972. B in pedagogy, Hiroshima U., Japan, 1966; MLitt, Hiroshima U., 1968, DLitt, 1983. Asst. prof. Shinnsyu U., Matsumoto, Nagano, Japan, 1972—87, Hiroshima U., Higashi-hiroshima, 1987—89, prof., 1989—2007, Yasuda Women's U., Hiroshima, Japan, 2007—13; ret. Lectr. Osaka U., 1991, Yamaguchi U., 1992, Kyusyu U., Hukoka, 1994, Nagoya U., 1995, Tokyo U., 1996, Broad-Cast U., 1998—2007; profl. lectr. Chinese Lang. Soc. Japan, Waseda U., Tokyo, 2003, Inst. Ea. Culture, Tokyo, 2005. Author: A Study of Sino-Japanese in the Heian and Kamakura Periods (Dr.Kinndaichi Kyosuke Meml. Prize, 1981), The History of Sino-Japanese, A Historical Study on the Japanese Pronunciation of Chinese Characters (Shinnmura Izuru Prize, 1999). Splty. mem. The Cultural Coun., Ministry of Edn., Culture, Sports, Sci. and Tech., Tokyo, Japan, 1998—2003, The Cultual Property Coun., Agy. Cultural Affairs, Tokyo, Japan, 2001—10. Recipient Japan Acad. prize, 2002. Fellow: Soc. Diacritical Lang. (assoc.; pres. 2009—12). Achievements include research in old scriptures of Ninnaji-Temple; old Documents of Kozanji-Temple; cultural property of Ishiyamadera-Temple. Home: Kurashiki, Japan. Died Mar. 11, 2014.

**NUNUPAROV, SERGEY MARTINOVICH,** marine engineer; b. Tbilisi, Georgia, Nov. 25, 1928; s. Martin Sergeevich Nunuparov and Maria Pavlovna Pavlova; m. Nelli Nunuparova, Oct. 7, 1952; children: Martin Sergeevich, Sergey Sergeevich. Degree in Naval Arch., Odessa Nat. Marine Engrs. U., Ukraine, 1952; DSc, Nat. Maritime Acad., Odessa, 1974, Prof., 1992; Academician, Transport Acad., Odessa, 1993. Mech. engr. Caspian SS Co., Baku, Azerbaijan, 1952—57; head tech. dept. Black Sea shipping Co., Odessa, 1957—64; head of marine environ. protection USSR Ministry Merchant Marine, Moscow, 1964—2000; dir. R&D develop. inst. Merchant Marine Ukraine, Odessa, 1991—2000; co-chmn. working group USA-USSR Coop. Program Protection of Marine Environ. Shipping Pollution, 1985—90; sci. advisor R&D inst. Ukrainian Maritime Adminstrn., Odessa, from 2000. Author: (book) Preventing Pollution of the Sea From Ships, Preventing Pollution of the Sea by Oil, Cargo and Special Systems of an Oil Tanker; contbr. articles to profl. jours. Mem. City Hall, Odessa, Ukraine, 1970—91. Recipient Gold Medal for sci. achievements, USSR Coun. Mins., Order the Badge of Honour, Ministry Transport; named Hon. worker of the Mcht.

Marine of USSR and Ukraine. Achievements include patents for field of protection of the marine environment. Avocations: yachting, swimming. Home: Odessa, Ukraine. Deceased.

**NURBAKHSH, MOHSEN,** bank executive; b. Tehran, May 18, 1948; Mem. Majlis; dep. min. of fin. & econ. affairs Govt. of Iran, min. of econ. affairs and fin., 1989—93, v.p., 1993—94; gov. Bank-e Markazi Jomhouri-ye Islami ye Iran, Tehran, 1994—2003. Died Mar. 23, 2003.

**NUSBAUM, MURRAY L.,** obstetrician, gynecologist; b. Utica, NY, Feb. 22, 1922; s. Morris and Anna Gertrude Nusbaum; m. Bridgetta A. Nusbaum, July 31, 1949; children: Devra L., Korrine P. AB, Antioch Coll., 1946; MD, Case We. Res. U., 1947. Diplomate Am. Bd. Ob-Gyn. Rotating intern No. Permanente Hosp., Vancouver, Wash., 1947—48; resident in ob-gyn. and pathologoy Dr.'s Hosp., Cleve., 1948—50; surg. resident Woman's Hosp., Detroit, 1950, 1953; sr. resident in ob-gyn. Florence Crittenden Hosp., Detroit, 1953—54; clin. asst. prof. SUNY, Syracuse, 1974—80, assoc. prof., 1980—83, prof., 1983—94; pvt. practice Utica, 1954—94; ret., 1994. Med. dir. Ferre Inst., Utica, 1975—, Planned Parenthood of Mohawk Valley, Utica, 1966-83; hon. staff Faxton Hosp., utica, St. Elizabeth Hosp., Utica, St. Luke's Meml. Hosp. Ctr., Utica; cons. Masonic Home, Utica; mem. adj. staff State Univ. Hosp., Syracuse. Contbr. articles to profl. jours. Bd. dirs. Utica Coll. of Syracuse U., 1972-81, mem. emeritus, 1982—; bd. dirs. Temple Emanuel, Utica, Family Svcs. of Greater Utica, 1962-64; past pres., bd. dirs. Jewish Social Svcs., Utica. With USN, 1942-45, 50-52. Fellow Am. Coll. Ob-Gyn (life, med. advisor, exec. com. local dist. 1988—, grievance com. 1996—, internat. affairs com., nominations com., Pres.'s Cmty. Svc. award 1995, Outstanding Dist. Svc. award 1988); mem. AMA, Med. Soc. N.Y. (com. on state legislation 1988—), Am. Acad. Medicine and Sci. (bd. dirs.), Am. Soc. Reproductive Medicine (life), Ctrl. N.Y. Acad. Medicine (past pres., Scroll award 1984, 97), Ctrl. N.Y. Assn. Gynecologists and Obstetricians (past pres.), Fertility Soc. Upstate N.Y., Am. Assn. Gynecol. Laparoscopists, Soc. Reproductive Surgeons, Fallopius Internat. Soc. Avocations: skiing, gardening. Home: Utica, NY. Died Dec. 19, 2013.

**NYHART, ELDON HOWARD,** employee benefits consultant, lawyer; b. Lafayette, Ind., Jan. 17, 1927; s. Howard E. and Mabel (Keller) N.; m. Frieda Erni, Apr. 12, 1971; children: Maria, Malott, Sallie, Eldon Jr. AB cum laude, Princeton U., 1948; JD, Ind. U., 1952. Exec. v.p. The Nyhart Co., Inc., Indpls., 1953-55, pres., chief exec. officer, 1955-60, chief exec. officer, 1960-91, chmn. bd. dirs., 1991-96, chmn. emeritus, from 1996. Lectr. Purdue U., Lafayette; tchr. Ind. U. Grad. Sch. Bus., Bloomington, dir. Midwest Pension Conf. Contbr. articles to profl. jour. Life trustee Indpls. Mus. Art, bd. govs., 1990—; bd. dirs. Ind. Swiss Found., pres. 1991—, Ind. State Symphony Soc., 1990—, Eiteljorg Mus., 1990, Contemporary Art Soc., 1991—, Friends of Herron Gallery, 1990—; del. White House Conf. on Aging. Mem. ABA, Internat. Bar Assn., Ind. Bar Assn., Assn. Pvt. Pension and Welfare Plans, trustee 1987-91, Am. Judicature Soc., Am. Pension Conf., Woodstock Club, Univ. Club (Indpls.), Princeton Club (N.Y.). Episcopalian. Home: Indianapolis, Ind. Deceased.

**OBERG, MURIEL CURNIN,** community health nurse, health facility manager; b. Bridgeport, Conn., July 12, 1925; d. James P. and Lillian (Bannister) Curnin; m. Leonard E. Oberg, Nov. 9, 1946; 1 child, Douglas P. Diploma in Nursing, St. Vincent's Med. Ctr., Bridgeport, 1946; BSN, U. Bridgeport, 1963, MS, 1972; postgrad., Fairfield U., 1991. RN, Conn.; cert. in nursing adminstrn.; cert. profl. educator. Inservice edn. supr. Bridgeport Hosp., 1963-65, health careers counselor Sch. of Nursing, 1966-69; health careers counselor Quinnipiac Coll., 1970-71; asst. dir. maternal and child health Vis. Nurse Assn., New Haven, 1972-81; dir. pub. health nursing Dept. Health City of New Haven, New Haven, from 1981. Recipient USPH traineeship, 1962. Mem. ANA, Conn. Nurses Assn. Home: Fairfield, Conn. Died 1998.

**OBERHUBER, KONRAD JOHANNES,** art museum curator, educator; b. Linz/Donau, Austria, Mar. 31, 1935; PhD, U. Vienna, Austria, 1959, Dozent, 1971. Asst. U. Vienna; delegated as research fellow to Austrian Inst. in Rome, 1959-61; asst., then curator Albertina, Vienna, 1961-71; research curator Nat. Gallery Art, Washington, 1971-74; guest lectr. Fogg Art Mus., Harvard U., Cambridge, Mass., spring 1974, curator of drawings, prof. fine arts, 1974-85, Ian Woodner curator of drawings, prof. fine arts, 1985-87; dir. Graphische Sammlung Albertina, Vienna, from 1987; T.A.O. prof. U. Vienna, 1991. Italian Ministry of Culture scholar, Rome, winter 1958; asst. prof. Smith Coll., 1964-65; Kress fellow Harvard Center for Renaissance Studies, Florence, Italy, 1965-66; guest prof. Cambridge (Eng.) U., 1968 Author: Raphael, Die Zeichnungen, 1983, Poussin, The Early Years in Rome, 1988; contbr. articles to profl. jours. Fellow Inst. Advanced Study Princeton, N.J., 1974-75; Nat. Endowment Humanities grantee, 1979-80; Gerda Henkel Stiftung grantee, 1983-84 Died Sept. 12, 2007.

**OBERMAN, SHELDON ARNOLD,** writer, educator; b. Winnipeg, Man., Can., May 20, 1949; s. Allan and Dorothy Oberman; m. Lee Anne Block, Sept. 8, 1973 (div. Mar. 9, 1990); children: Adam, Mira; m. Lisa Ann Dveris, Sept. 2, 1990; 1 child: Jesse. BA in English, U. Winnipeg, 1972; BA in English with honors, U. Jerusalem, Israel, 1973; teaching cert., U. Man., 1974. Tchr. W. C. Millar Collegiate, Altona, Man., Can., 1975-76, Joseph Wolinsky Collegiate, Winnipeg, Man., Can., 1976-95. Author: The Folk Festival Book, 1983, Lion in the Lake: A French English Alphabet Book, 1988, Julie Gerond and the Polka Dot Pony, 1988, TV Sal and the Game Show From Outer Space, 1993, This Business With Elijah, 1993, The Always Prayer Shawl, 1994, The White Stone in the Castle Wall, 1995, By the Hannukah Light, 1997, The Shaman's Nephew: A Life in the Far North, 1999, The Wisdom Bird: A Tale of Solomon and Sheba, 2000; co-editor: A Mirror of a People: The Canadian Jewish Experience in Poetry and Prose, 1985 (Sydney Taylor honor 2000, McNalley Robinson Book award 2001), Island of the Minotaur: Greek Myths of Crete, 2003. Recipient Parents Choice Silver Honour, 1999, Norma Fleck award for children's non fiction, 1999, Parents Coun. Outstanding Book, 1999, Nat. Jewish Book award Jewish Book Coun., 1995, Sydney Taylor award, 1995, Best Book of the Yr. A Child's Mag., 1994, Pick of the List award Am. Bookseller, 1994, Can. Author Short Story award Canadian Author's Assn., 1987, Bliss Carmen Poetry prize Banff Sch. of Fine Arts, 1980; various writer and film maker grants. Avocations: public address, acting, collage sculptor, canoing. Home: Winnipeg, Canada. Died Mar. 26, 2004.

**OBERSTAR, JAMES LOUIS (JIM OBERSTAR),** former United States Representative from Minnesota; b. Chisholm, Minn., Sept. 10, 1934; s. Louis and Mary (Grillo) O.; m. Jo Garlick, Oct. 12, 1963 (dec. July 1991); children: Thomas Edward, Katherine Noelle, Anne-Therese, Monica Rose; m. Jean Kurth, Nov. 1993; stepchildren: Corinne Quinlan Kurth, Charles Burke Kurth, Jr. BA summa cum laude, St. Thomas Coll., 1956; postgrad. in French, Laval U., Que., Can.; MS in Govt. (scholar), Coll. Europe, Bruges, Belgium, 1957; postgrad. in govt, Georgetown U. Adminstrv. asst. to Rep. John A. Blatnik US House of Representatives, 1963-74; adminstr. US House Public Works Com., 1971-74; mem. US Congress from 8th Minn. Dist., 1975—2011; chmn. US House Subcommittee on Aviation, 1989—95; ranking minority mem. US House Transp. & Infrastructure Com., 2005—07, chmn., 2007—11; sr. adv. National Strategies, LLC (NSI), Washington, 2011—14. Vis. scholar U. Minn. Hubert H. Humphrey Sch. Public Affairs, 2011—14, chair advisory bd. Ctr. for Excellence in Rural Safety, 2011—14. Trustee The John F. Kennedy Ctr. for the Performing Arts, 1995—2014; bd. mem. Mineta I.I. STPS Inst., San Jose State U. Mem.: American Polit. Sci. Assn. Dfl. Roman Catholic. Home: Potomac, Md. Died May 3, 2014.

**OBOTE, MILTON (APOLLO MILTON OBOTE),** former President of Republic of Uganda; b. Lango, Uganda, Dec. 28, 1925; s. Stanley Obote; m. Miria Kalulu, Nov. 9, 1963. Ed, Mwiri Coll., Busoga, 1947, Makerere U., Kampala, 1950. Laborer; clk.; salesman; trade union organizer Kenya, 1950—55; founder Kenya African U., mem., Uganda Nat. Congress, 1952—60, Uganda Legis. Coun., 1957; founder Uganda People's Congress, mem., 1960; leader opposition, 1961—62; prime minister, 1962—66; min. def. & fgn. affairs, 1963—65; pres., 1966—71, 1980—85; min. fgn. affairs, 1980—85; min. fin. exile Tanzania, 1971—80, 1985—2005. Died Oct. 10, 2005.

**O'BRIEN, CONOR CRUISE,** writer; b. Dublin, Nov. 3, 1917; s. Francis Cruise and Katherine (Sheehy) O'Brien; m. Christine H. Foster O'Brien, 1939 (div. 1962); children: Donal, Fidelma; m. Maire MacEntee O'Brien, 1962; adopted children: Margaret, Patrick. BA, Trinity Coll., Dublin, 1940, BA, 1941, PhD, 1953; DLitt, U. Bradford, 1971, U. Ghana, 1974, U. Edinburgh, 1976, U. Nice, 1978, Coleraine U., 1981, U. Liverpool, 1987. With Irish Civil Svc., 1942, Dept. Finance Govt. of Ireland, 1942—44; staff mem. Dept. External Affairs Govt. of Ireland, 1944—61; head Info. and Cultural Sect.; mng. dir. Irish News Agy., 1948—55, counsellor Paris, 1955—56; del., head UN Irish Sect., 1955—61, asst. sec. gen. dept., 1960; rep. Sec. Gen. UN, Katanga, Democratic Republic of Congo, 1961, Shaba, Zaire; vice chancellor U. Ghana, 1962—65; regents prof., holder Albert Schweitzer chair in humanities NYU, 1965—69; mem. Dail Eireann, Dublin, 1969—77; min. Posts and Telegraphs, 1973—77; vis. fellow Nuffield Coll., 1973; pro-chancellor U. Dublin, senator, 1977—79; editor-in-chief The Observer, London, 1978—81; cons. edn., 1981—2008. Author: Maria Cross, 1952, Parnell and His Party: 1880-90, 1957, To Katanga and Back: A UN Case, 1962, Conflicting Concepts of the United Nations, 1964, Writers and Politics, 1965; author: (with Northrop Frye and Stuart Hampshire) The Morality of Scolarship, 1967; author: The United Nations: Sacred Drama, 1967, Conor Cruise O'Brien Introduces Ireland, 1969, Camus, 1970; author: (with Maire Cruise O'Brien) A Concise History of Ireland, 1972; author: The Suspecting Glance, 1972, States of Ireland, 1972, Herod Reflections on Political Violence, 1978, Religion and Politics, 1984, The Siege: The Saga of Israel and Zionism, 1987, God Land, 1988, Passion and Cunning: Essays on Nationalism, Terrorism and Revolution, 1988, The Great Melody: A Thematic Biography of Edmund Burke, 1992, Conor: An Anthology, 1994, Ancestral Voices, 1994, On the Eve of the Millennium, 1994, The Long Affair: Thomas Jefferson and the French Revolution, 1785-1800, 1996, (plays) Murderous Angels, 1968, King Herod Explains, 1969; editor: The Shaping of Modern Ireland, 1960, Power and Consciousness, 1969, Edmund Burke's Reflections on the Revolution in France, 1969. Recipient Valiant for Truth Media award, 1979; fellow, St. Catherine's Coll., Oxford, 1978—81. Mem.: Royal Irish Acad. Died Dec. 18, 2008.

**O'BRIEN, ELMER JOHN,** librarian, educator; b. Kemmerer, Wyo., Apr. 8, 1932; s. Ernest and Emily Catherine (Reinhart) O'B.; m. Betty Alice Peterson, July 2, 1966. AB, Birmingham So. Coll., 1954; Th.M., Iliff Sch. Theology, 1957; MA, U. Denver, 1961. Ordained to ministry Methodist Ch., 1957; pastor Meth. Ch., Pagosa Springs, Colo., 1957—60; circulation-reference librarian Boston U. Sch. Theology, 1961—65; asst. librarian Garrett-Evang. Theol. Sem., Evanston, Ill., 1965—69; librarian, prof. United Theol. Sem., Dayton, Ohio, 1969—96, prof. emeritus, from 1996; abstractor Am. Bibliog. Center, 1969—73; dir. Ctr. for Evang. United Brethren Heritage, 1979—96; acting libr. Iliff Sch. Theology, 2000—01. Chmn. div. exec. com. Dayton-Miami Valley Libr. Consortium, 1983-84; rsch. assoc. Am. Antiquarian Soc., 1990. Author: Bibliography of Festschriften in Religion Published Since 1960, 1972, Religion Index Two: Festschriften, 1960-69; contbg. author: Communication and Change in American Religious History, 1993, Essays in Celebration of the First Fifty Years, 1996; pub. Meth. Revs. Index, 1818-1985, 1989-91, The Wilderness, the Nation, and the Electronic Era: American Christianity and Religious Communication 1620-2000; contbr. articles to profl. jours. & bibliograpgy Recipient theol. and scholarship award Assn. Theol. Schs. in U.S. and Can., 1990-91; Libr. Staff Devel. grant Assn. Theol. Schs. in U.S. and Can., 1976-77, Rsch. grant United Meth. Ch. Bd. Higher Edn. and Ministry, 1984-85 Mem. ALA, Acad. Libr. Assn. Ohio, Am. Theol. Libr. Assn. (head bur. personnel and placement 1969-73, dir. 1973-76, v.p. 1977-78, pres. 1978-79), Am. Antiquarian Soc. (rsch. assoc. 1990), Delta Sigma Phi, Omicron Delta Kappa, Eta Sigma Phi, Kappa Phi Kappa. Clubs: Torch Internat. (v.p. Dayton club 1981-82, pres. 1982-83). Home: Boulder, Colo. Died May 2, 2014.

**O'BRIEN, GRACE WILHELMINA EHLIG,** retired educational administrator, genealogical consultant, psychologist, writer; b. LA, Aug. 27, 1922; d. Max Carl and Janette (Rentchler) Ehlig; m. Louis J. O'Brien, Nov. 8, 1947; children: Carol Jean, Lawrence John, Perry Lewis. AA, Pasadena City Coll., 1942; BA, UCLA, 1944, postgrad., 1946, Riverside City Coll., 1946, Calif. State U., LA, 1957—66, postgrad., 1970—78, MA in Guidance, 1964. Tchr. Perris Union HS, Calif., 1944—46; tchr. counselor, psychometrist, psychologist LA City Schs., 1946—66; cons. counselor, sch. psychologist Elem. Secondary Edn. Act, Edn. & Guidance program, 1966—68; head counselor, asst. prin. Garden Gate Opportunity Sch., 1968—73; vice prin. Markham Jr. HS, 1973, Belvedere Jr. HS, 1974; asst. prin. Garfield HS, 1974—75, Mt. Vernon Jr. HS, 1975—76, Gage Jr. HS, 1976—77; prin. Garden Gate HS, 1977—80, Johnson HS, 1980—84; LDS libr. & tchr., 1984—2005; geneal. cons., from 1984. Den mother chmn. Cub Scouts, 1964—66. Recipient Spl. Svc. award, Boy Scouts, 1964. Mem.: AAUW, DAR (treas. from 2008, regent, bd. dirs. San Marino Chpt., Dist. X Dir.), Calif. Assn. Sch. Adminstrs., Associated Adminstrn. LA, UCLA Alumni Assn., Calif. Tchrs. Assn. (ret. mem.), Phrateres, Chi Delta Phi, Pi Lambda Theta, Phi Delta Kappa, Daus. Am. Colonists (bd. dirs. from 1994, treas. 1995—2007). Presbyterian. Home: Pasadena, Calif. Died July 24, 2013.

**O'BRIEN, VINCENT (MICHAEL O'BRIEN),** horse trainer, owner, breeder; b. Apr. 9, 1917; s. Daniel P. and Kathleen (Toomey) O'B.; m. Jacqueline Wittenoom, 1951; 5 children. Grad., Mungret Coll., Ireland; LLD (hon.), Nat. U. Ireland, 1983; DSc (hon.), U. Ulster, 1995. Champion trainer Nat. Hunt, Gt. Britain, 1952-53; champion trainer Flat, 1966, 67; winner of all major English and Irish hurdle & steeplechases; winner 3 consecutive Grand Nats., 4 Gold Cups and 3 Champion Hurdles; trained flat racing winners of 44 Classics including 6 Epsom Derbys, 6 Irish Derbys and 1 French Derby; also 3 Prix de l'Arc de Triomphe, Breeders Cup Mile and Washington Internat.; trainer of Nijinsky. Named trainer of century both for flat and nat. hunt racing in Gt. Britain and Ireland, 1999. Avocation: golf. Died June 1, 2009.

**OBZINA, JAROMÍR,** Czechoslovak government official, educator; b. Brodek, May 28, 1929; s. Frantisek and Zofie (Obzinova) Obzina; m. Svetla Obzinova; 2 children. PhD, CPSU Higher Edn. Coll., Moscow. Sec. Chrudim Dist. Com. CP of Czechoslovakia; 1st. sec. Policka & Pardubice Dist. Com.; instr. Pardubice Regional Com.; with Main Polit. Bd. Czechoslvok People's Army, 1953—56; comdr. Antonin Zapotocky Mil. Acad. Polit. Dept., 1956—64; head, divsn. sci. CP Ctrl. Com. Dept. Edn. & Sci., 1965—68; dep. comdr. Czechoslovak People's Army Inst. Sci. Affairs, 1968—69; head divsn. sci. & dept. head Dept. Edn. & Sci., 1969—73; mem. House of the People of Fed. Nat. Assembly, 1973, CP Ctrl. Com., from 1973; min., interior, 1973—83; chmn. State Commn. Sci., Tech., & Investments, 1983—88; dep. prime min., 1983—90. Died Jan. 29, 2003.

**OCHS, ROBERT DAVID,** history educator; b. Bloomington, Ill., Mar. 27, 1915; s. Herman Solomon and Fannie Leah (Livingston) O. AB, Ill. Wesleyan U., 1936; MA, U. Ill., 1937, PhD, 1939; MA, Oxford U., Eng., 1964. Research dir. Anti-Defamation League, 1939-41; mem. faculty U. S.C., from 1946, prof. history, 1957-76, disting. prof. emeritus, from 1976, chmn. dept., 1960-74; acting dean U. S.C. (Coll. Arts and Sci.), 1970-71; asso. editor U. S.C. Press, 1950-53; vis. prof. Merton Coll., Oxford U., 1964. Mem. S.C. Archives Commn., 1960-74 U.S. cons.: History of The 20th Century, 1967. Bd. dirs. Columbia Music Festival Assn., 1957-64, 77-85, v.p., 1961-62, pres., 1962-63; dir. Columbia Lyric Opera, Columbia Mus. Art, 1966-69, 74-77, McKissick Mus., 1991-96. Maj. AUS, 1941-46; lt. col. Mem. Am. Hist. Assn., So. Hist. Assn. (exec. council 1973-76), S.C. Hist. Assn. (editor 1947-55, pres. 1956-57), Am. Studies Assn., Orgn. Am. Historians, Southeastern Am. Studies Assn. (pres. 1960-61), Omicron Delta Kappa. Deceased.

**OCHSENBEIN, PETER ENGELBERT,** library administrator, educator; b. Solothurn, Switzerland, July 15, 1940; s. Engelbert Paul and Agnes (Schwaller) O.; m. Rosmarie Rehmann, Mar. 8, 1968. PhD, U. Basel, Switzerland, 1969, PD PhD, 1987, prof. PhD, 1990. Asst. U. Basel, 1968-74; rsch. asst. Schweiz. Nationalfonds, Bern, 1975-81; dir. Abbey Libr., St. Gallen, Switzerland, 1981-2000. Author:

Studies About Anticlaudian of Alanus ab Insulis, 1974, The Great Prayer of Swiss Citizen, 1989, Pray with Picture and Word, 1996. Avocation: music. Home: Saint Gallen, Switzerland. Died Mar. 13, 2003.

**OCKELS, WUBBO JOHANNES,** retired astronaut; b. Almelo, The Netherlands, Mar. 28, 1946; s. Johan Hendrik Maarten and Annemarie Elisabeth (Ritter) O.; m. Johanna Swaving, Mar. 7, 1969; children: Geanneke, Martin. HBS-B, U. Groningen, 1965, grad. in physic and math. cum laude, 1973, PhD, 1978. Exptl. physicist Nuclear Physics Accelerator Lab., Groningen, 1973-78; scientist, astronaut European Space Agy., Cologne, 1979-80; astronaut candidate Johnson Space Ctr., Houston, 1980-82; back-up crew Marshall Space Flight Ctr., Huntsville, Ala., 1982-83; D-1 Spacelab flight crew German Aerospace Agy., Cologne, 1984-86; prof. Faculty of Air and Space Tech Tech. U. Delft, 1992—2014; head Educational Projects Outreach Activities European Space Agy., 1999—2003. Presenter popula sci. TV show, The Netherlands, 1987— Inventor astronaut sleeping restraint, 1987, variable pressure glove for space, 1988, absorptive tether, 1986. Recipient Verdienst Kreuz 1st Klasse, Fed. Republic of Germany, 1986, title Officer of Oranje, Nassau, Queen of Holland, 1985, Public Svc. award NASA, 1984, Space Flight award, 1985, Wubbo Ockels prize, Town of Groningen, Netherlands, 1985. Mem. American Phys. Soc., Assn. Space Explorers (mem. exec. com. 1990), Mensa. Home: Aerdenhout, Netherlands. Died May 18, 2014.

**ODA, JUN,** hotel company executive; b. Kobe, Japan, Aug. 9, 1938; s. Hidesaburoh and Teruno (Miaki) O.; m. Yoshiko Isaji, Feb. 6, 1966; children: Megumi, Hiroshi. LLB, Kwansei Gakuin U., Kobe, 1961. Dir. planning and devel. Miyako Hotel, Tokyo, 1979-83, dir. sales, 1983-90, exec. mgr., food & beverage dept., 1990-94, exec. mng. dir. sales and mktg., 1994-98; exec. gen. mgr. Hotel Maiko Villa, Kobe, 1999—2003; mng. dir. YJ Hotel Mgmt. Assn., from 2003. Mem. Skål Internat. Avocations: tennis, golf, reading. Home: Ibaraki-ken, Japan. Died Feb. 20, 2002.

**ODOM, BOB (ROBERT FULTON ODOM JR.),** retired state official; b. Haynesville, La., July 14, 1935; s. Robert Fulton Sr. and Mary Matthews Odom; m. Mildred Randolph, 1968; children: Robert Fulton III, Ashley Lynn. BS in Animal Sci., Southeastern U. Chief Pesticides Applicators La. Dept. Agriculture, Baton Rouge, 1964—74, dir. tech. services, 1974—76; commr. La. Dept. Agriculture & Forestry, Baton Rouge, 1980—2008. Co. commander USMC, Okinawa, Japan, retired as Lt. Col. US Marine Corps Reserve USMC. Mem. Nat. Assn. State Dept. Agriculture (v.p.), So. United Trade Assn. (exec. com), Southern Assn. State Dept. Agriculture (bd. dirs.), East Baton Rouge Parish Farm Bur., La. Farm Bur. Fedn., World Trade Ctr. New Orleans and La. Environmental Health Assn. Democrat. Southern Baptist. Avocations: fishing, hunting, woodworking. Home: Zachary, La. Died May 17, 2014.

**OEHLER, DIETRICH,** law educator; b. Görlitz, Fed. Republic Germany, Oct. 4, 1915; s. Hans and Helene (Miser) O.; m. Margot, Aug. 20, 1948 (dec. 1975); children: Bodo, Verena, Gesine; m. Emmy-Margarete Dehne, Sept. 16, 1976. JD, U. Halle, Fed. Republic Germany, 1939; Habilitation, U. Münster, Fed. Republic Germany, 1949. Ordentlicher prof. law Free U., Berlin, 1951-57, dean of faculty, 1957-61; ordentlicher prof. law U. Cologne (Fed. Republic Germany), 1961-68, dean of faculty, 1967-69. Dir. Kriminal-Wissenschaftliches Inst., U. Colognes, 1967-85, dir. Rundfunkrechtiches Inst., 1968-97. Author many publs. on criminal law and European Market law. Festschift für D. Oehler named in his honor, 1985. Mem. Japan Soc. Criminal Law (hon.), Japan Soc. Fed. Law (hon.), Futer-Am. Rsch. Inst. Montreal. Lutheran. Home: Cologne, Germany. Died Dec. 27, 2005.

**OGDEN, LOUANN MARIE,** dietitian, consultant; b. Enid, Okla., Dec. 16, 1952; d. Raymond Michael Schiltz and Donna Mae Stuever; m. Wendell Edwin Ogden, Jan. 5, 1979; 1 child, Gregory Jacob Jeremiah. BS in Home Econs., Okla. State U., 1974, MS, 1977. Registered dietitian; lic. dietitian, Tex. Dietetic intern Ind. U. Med. Ctr., Indpls., 1974; therapeutic dietitian-clin. svcs. and trayline ops. Bapt. Med. Ctr. Okla., Oklahoma City, 1975-76; grad. teaching asst. lower and upper level food preparation Okla. State U., Stillwater, 1976-77, teaching assoc. lower and upper level food preparation, 1977; chief clin. dietitian adminstrv. and clin. coordination Borgess Hosp., Kalamazoo, 1978; dietary cons. nutrition program Iowa Commn. on Aging, Des Moines, 1979-80; asst. food svc. dir., adminstrv. dietitian Timberlawn Psych. Hosp., Dallas, 1980-92; rep. group one purchasing program, mem. student tng. program Zale Lipshy U. Hosp., Dallas, 1992-93, food svc. cons., from 1993. Mem. Am. Dietetic Assn., Am. Soc. Hosp. Food Svc. Adminstrn. (nat. nominating com. 1990-91, Disting. Health Care Food Svc. Adminstr. 1992, North ctrl. Tex. chpt.: corr. sec. 1985-86, comms. chair 1986-87, rec. sec. 1987-89, pres.-elect 1989-90, pres. 1990-91, nominating com. chair, health care food svc. week com. chair 1991-92, Outstanding Mem. award 1992), Tex. Dietetic Assn., Dallas Dietetic Assn. Democrat. Roman Catholic. Avocations: photography, travel. Died May 23, 2001.

**OGDEN, VALERIA MUNSON,** management consultant, retired state legislator; b. Okanogan, Wash., Feb. 9, 1924; d. Ivan Bodwell and Pearle (Wilson) Munson; m. Daniel Miller Ogden Jr., Dec. 28, 1946; children: Janeth Lee Ogden Martin, Patricia Jo Ogden Hunter, Daniel Munson Ogden. BA magna cum laude, Wash. State U., 1946. Exec. dir. Potomac Coun. Camp Fire, Washington, 1964-68, Ft. Collins (Colo.) United Way, 1969-73, Designing Tomorrow Today, Ft. Collins, 1973-74, Poudre Valley Community Edn. Assn., Ft. Collins, 1977-78; pres. Valeria M. Ogden, Inc., Kensington, Md., 1978-81; nat. field cons. Camp Fire, Inc., Kansas City, Mo., 1980-81; exec. dir. Nat. Capital Area YWCA, Washington, 1981-84, Clark County YWCA, Vancouver, Wash., 1985-89; pvt. practice mgmt. cons. Vancouver, from 1989; mem. Wash. House of Reps., 1991—2003, spkr. pro tempore, 1999—2002. Mem. adj. faculty public adminstrn. program Lewis & Clark Coll., Portland (Oreg.) State U., 1979-94; mem. Pvt. Industry Coun., Vancouver, 1986-95; mem. regional Svcs. Network Bd. Mental Health, 1993-03. Author: Camp Fire Membership, 1980. Mem. Wash. State Coun. Vol. Action, Olympia, 1986—90; trustee Wash. State Sch. for Deaf, from 2011; county vice-chair Larimer County Dems., Ft. Collins, 1974—75; spkr. pro tem Wash. Ho. of Reps., 1999—2002; rep. Gov. Chris Gregoire S.W. Wash., 2005; bd. mem. Unitarian Universalist Ch. Dem., from 2012; mem. precinct com. Clark County Dems., Vancouver, 1986—88; treas. Mortar Bd. Nat. Found., Vancouver, 1987—96; bd. dirs. Clark County Coun. for Homeless, Vancouver, 1989—2004, chmn., 1994; bd. dirs. Wash. Wild Life and Recreation Coalition, 1995—2002, Human Svcs. Coun., 1996—2002, Wash. State Hist. Soc., 1996—2006, State Legis. Leaders Found., 2001—02, Columbia Springs Environ. Edn. Ctr. Found., 2003—06, Clark County Skill Ctr. Found., 2003—06; emeritus mem.; mem. S.W. Wash. Child Care Consortium, from 2003; chair arts and tourism com. Nat. Conf. State Legis., 1996—97; chair Affordable Cmty. Environments, 1998—2009, Wash. State Interagy. Com. for Outdoor Recreation, 2003—09, Wash. State Historic Preservation Fund, 2003—06, S.W. Wash. Ctr. for the Arts, 2003; pres. Nat. Order of Women Legislators, 1999—2001; mem. exec. com. Nat. Conf. State Legis., 2000—02; mem. adv. bd. Wash. State U., Vancouver, from 2002. Named Citizen of Yr. Ft. Collins Bd. of Realtors, 1975, State Legislator of Yr., Wash. State Labor Coun., 2000, Citizen of Yr., Vancouver, Wash., 2002, First Citizen, Clark County, 2006; recipient Gulick award Camp Fire Inc., 1956, Alumna Achievement award Wash. State U. Alumni Assn., 1988; named YWCA Woman of Achievement, 1991, 100 Most Powerful Women, Clark County, 2007, Caring Heart award, 2009, Unitarian Jerry king award, 2011, Wash. Wildlife & Recreation Coalition Joan Thomas award, 2011, Wash. State U. Vancouver Cmty. Svc. award, 2013. Mem. AAUW, Internat. Assn. Vol. Adminstrs. (pres. Boulder 1989-90), Nat. Assn. YWCA Exec. Dirs. (nat. bd. nominating com. 1988-90), Sci. and Soc. Assn. (bd. dirs. 1993-97), Women in Action, Philanthropic and Ednl. Orgn., Soroptimists, Phi Beta Kappa. Democrat. Avocations: hiking, travel. Home: Vancouver, Wash. Died Mar. 9, 2014.

**OGI, AKIRA,** professional baseball coach; b. Nakama, Fukuoka, Japan, Apr. 29, 1935; Second baseman Nishitetsu Lions, 1954—67; mgr. Kintetsu Buffaloes, 1988—92, Orix Blue Wave, from 1994. Achievements include winning Japanese Baseball Pacific League Penant as Mgr. of Kintetsu Buffaloes, 1989. Died Dec. 15, 2005.

**OGINO, HIROSHI,** general manager; b. Tokyo, Aug. 16, 1942; m. Tsuneko. BS, Sci. U., Tokyo, 1967; MS in Indsl. Chemistry, Tokyo U. Agriculture and Tech., 1969; PhD in Indsl. Chemistry, Tokyo Met. U., 1976. Lectr. Sagami Inst. Tech., Fujisawa, Japan, 1978-79; rsch. assoc. U. Ariz., Tucson, 1979-83; sr. rschr. Taiyo Toyo Sanso Co., Ltd., Kawasaki, Japan, 1984-91, gen. mgr., from 1991. Author: Advanced Technology '87, 1987, Encylopedia of Analytical Sciences, 1995. Mem. Am. Chem. Soc., Japan Chem. Soc., Japan Soc. Analytical Chemistry, Medico-Legal Soc. Japan. Home: Tokyo, Japan. Died 1999.

**OGLE, ROBBIN SUE,** criminal justice educator; b. North Kansas City, Mo., Aug. 28, 1960; d. Robert Lee and Carol Sue (Gray) O. BS, Ctrl. Mo. State U., 1982; MS, U. Mo., 1990; PhD, Pa. State U., 1995. State probation and parole officer Mo. Dept. Corrections, Kansas City, 1982-92; collector J.C. Penney Co., Mission, Kans., 1990-92; instr. U. Mo., Kansas City, 1990-92; grad. lectr. Pa. State U., University Park, 1992-95; prof. criminal justice dept. U. Nebr., Omaha, from 1995. Author: Battered Women Who Kill: A New Framework, 2002, The Wienie Dog Adventure Series: The Great Ham Heist, 2005; contbr. articles to profl. jours. Athletic scholar Ctrl. Mo. State U., Warrensburg, 1978-82. Mem. AAUW, ACLU, NOW, Am. Soc. Criminology, Acad. Criminal Justice Scis., Am. Correctional Assn., Phi Kappa Phi. Avocations: reading, watching basketball, walking dog. Home: Omaha, Nebr. Died July 9, 2012.

**O'GORMAN, NED (EDWARD CHARLES O'GORMAN),** poet; b. Sept. 26, 1929; married; 1 child, Ricardo Diego. AB, St. Michael's Coll., L.H.D., 1983; A.M., Columbia U. Tchr. Bklyn. Coll.; New Sch. Social Research, Manhattan Coll.; American studies specialist State Dept., Chile, Argentina and Brazil, 1966; headmaster, founder Children's Storefront Pre-Sch. & Elementary Sch. Author: (poetry)The Night of the Hammer, 1961, Adam Before His Mirror, 1963, The Buzzard and the Peacock, 1965, The Harvesters' Vase, 1968, The Flag the Hawk Flies, 1972; (nonfiction) The Storefront: A Community of Children on Madison Avenue and 129th Street, 1970, The Wilderness and the Laurel Tree: A Guide for Parents and Teachers on the Observation of Children, 1972, The Children Are Dying, 1978, Terrible Steel, Perfected Crystal: Anthology of Spiritual Readings, 1981, How To Put Out a Fire, 1984The Other Side of Loneliness, 2006; (children's book) The Blue Butterfly, 1971; Sr. editor: Jubilee mag, 1962-65; editor: Prophetic Voices: Ideas and Words on Revolution, 1969, Seabury Press. Guggenheim fellow, 1956, 62; Ford Found. study fellow, 1972; Rockefeller Found. Centre for Study fellow Bellagio, Italy, 1977; recipient Rothko Chapel Truth and Freedom award, 1981 Mem.: Metropolitan Opera. Died Mar. 7, 2014.

**OGURO, HARUO,** aeronautics educator; b. Tokyo, Mar. 21, 1926; s. Sojiro and Yasu Oguro; m. Kumiko Oguro Okada; children: Caroline June, Stephenie Mae, Mark Akio. BS in Physics, U. Tokyo, 1948, DSc in Physics, 1962; MS in Aeronautics, Calif. Inst. of Tech., Pasadena, 1957, doctoral studies, 1957-60. Rsch. assoc. Inst. Space and Aeronautics Sci., U. Tokyo, 1948-56; teaching asst., rsch. asst. Calif. Inst. Tech. Aeronautics, Pasadena, 1956-60; asst. prof. Dept. of Mech. Engring., U. N.C., Raleigh, 1960-62; assoc. prof. Dept of Aerospace Engring., U. Cin., 1962-72; sr. scientist Aerospace Rsch. Lab., WPAFB, Dayton, Ohio, 1962-64; prin. investigator Two Phase Flow, NASA NGR, Cleve., 1964-69; vis. prof. Inst. of Plasma Physics, Nagoya (Japan) U., 1973-75; prof. Dept. of Aeronautics and Astronautics Tokai U., Hiratsuka, Japan, 1972-96; prof. emeritus Tokai (Japan) U., from 1996; dept. head Dept. of Aeronautics and Astronautics Tokai U., Hiratsuka, Japan, 1979-84. Mem. AIAA, AAAS, N.Y. Acad. Scis., Japan Soc. Fluid Mech., Inst. Aeronautics and Astronautics, Japan Astron. Soc. (pres.). Home: Setagaya, Japan. Died Nov. 15, 2002.

**OI, WALTER YASUO,** economics professor; b. L.A., July 1, 1929; s. Matsunosuke and Toshiko (Kawada) Oi; m. Marjorie Louise Robbins; children: Jessica Sumiye, Eleanor Haruko. BS, UCLA, 1952, MA in Economics, 1954; PhD in Economics, U. Chgo., 1961. Instr. economics Iowa State Coll., Ames, 1957-58; rsch. economics Northwestern U., Evanston, 1958-62; from assoc. prof. to prof. U. Wash., Seattle, 1962-67; prof. grad. sch. mgmt. U. Rochester, NY, 1967-75, prof. economics, 1975—2013, chmn. dept. economics, 1976-82, 83-84, Elmer B. Milliman prof. economics, 1978—2013. Economist Inst. Def. Analyses, Arlington, Va., 1966; dir. econ. analysis sect. Mil. Manpower Policy Study, U.S. Dept. Def., Washington, 1964-65; staff economist President's Commission on All-Volunteer Force, Washington, 1969-70. Adult co-chmn. Task Force on Draft and Nat. Svc. White House Conf. on Youth, 1970-71; vice chmn. President's Com. on Employment of People with Disabilities, 1983-89; chmn. N.Y. State Advisory Com. to U.S. Commn. on Civil Rights, 1988-2013 Emma and Carol Disting. Vis. scholar Hoover Inst., Stanford U., 1970-71; Ctr. for Advanced Study in Behavioral Scis. fellow, Stanford, 1988; recipient Sec. Def. Medal for Outstanding Public Svc., 1999. Fellow Econometrics Soc., American Acad. Arts & Sciences, American Econs. Assn. (disting.); mem. Western Econs. Assn. Internat. (pres. 1991-92). Republican. Home: Pittsford, NY. Died Dec. 24, 2013.

**OKADA, SHUICHI,** physician, researcher; b. Yokosuka, Kanagawa, Japan, Aug. 26, 1957; s. Masao and Katako Okada; m. Mariko Kato, Jan. 24, 1988; 1 child, Akihiro. MD, Chiba U., Japan, 1982, PhD, 1991. Resident Chiba U., 1982-83; head Chiba Cancer Ctr., 1988-90, Nat. Cancer Ctr. Hosp., Tokyo, from 1990. Author: Liver Cancer, 1998, Viral Hepatitis, 1998. Home: Edogama-ku, Tokyo, Japan. Died Oct. 2, 2002.

**O'KEEFE, RAYMOND PETER,** lawyer, educator; b. NYC, Jan. 16, 1928; s. William Bernard and Catherine Irene (Smith) O'Keefe; m. Stephanie Ann Fitzpatrick, June 19, 1954; children: Raymond, William, Ann, Kevin, Mary, James, John. AB cum laude, St. Michael's Coll., 1950; JD, Fordham U., 1953. Bar: N.Y. 1954, Fla. 1976, U.S. Dist. Ct. (so. dist.): N.Y. 1955, U.S. Ct. Claims: 1960, U.S. Ct. Appeals (2d cir.): 1963, U.S. Supreme Ct.: 1971. Assoc. Thayer & Gilbert, NYC, 1953—55; prof. law Fordham U. Sch. Law, NYC, 1955—63; sr. assoc. Carter, Ledyard & Milburn, NYC, 1963—68; ptnr. Ide & Haigney, NYC, 1968—74; sr. ptnr. McCarthy, Fingar, Donovan, Drazen & Smith, White Plains, NY, from 1974. Adj. prof. Pace U. Sch. Law, White Plains, from 1979, Fordham U. Sch. Law, from 1983; lectr. N.Y. Med. Coll., Valhalla, NY, from 1979; prof. St. Thomas of Villanova Miami Sch. Law, from 1984; vis. prof. Thomas M. Cooley Sch. Law, Lansing, 1991, Fordham U. Sch. Law, 1992; justice State of N.Y. Justice Ct., 1978—81. Trustee Am. Irish Hist. Soc.; chmn. bd. Westchester Halfway House, 1974—78; bd. dirs. Westchester Youth Shelter, 1980. With USN, 1945—48. Recipient Alumni award, St. Michael's Coll., 1961, Humanitarian award, Fordham Law Sch., 1999. Mem.: ABA (commn. on youth, drugs and alcoholism 1984), Assn. of Bar of City of N.Y., N.Y. State Trial Lawyers Assn., Assn. Trial Lawyers Am., Fla. Bar Assn., N.Y. State Bar Assn. (chmn. spl. com. on lawyer alcoholism and drug abuse from 1979), Surf Club, Harbor View Club, Larchmont Shore Club. Deceased.

**OKINAGA, SHOICHI,** academic administrator, obstetrician, gynecologist; b. Tokyo, June 29, 1933; s. Shobei and Kin (Ino) O.; m. Yoko Ishida, May 5, 1968; children: Shohachi, Yoshihito. MD, Tokyo U., 1958, PhD in Med. Scis., 1963; Dr. Law (hon.), Kyung Hee U., Seoul, Korea, 1993, Salem-Teikyo U., W.Va., 1990. Fellow Teikyo U. Found., Tokyo, from 1954, bd. trustees, from 1958; prin. Teikyo U. Sr. HS, 1961-71, Teikyo Dai-go Sr. High Sch., Tokyo, from 1963; pres. Teikyo Women's Jr. Coll., 1965-71 and from 92, Teikyo U., from 1966, head spl. sch. for kindergarten tchrs. and nurses, 1967-84, prof. medicine, from 1971, founder, chancellor, from 2002; pvt. practice ob/gyn., from 1971. Pres. Teikyo Univ. Hosp., 1971-82; prin. Teikyo Sr. Nursing Sch., 1972-84, Teikyo U. Sr. High Sch., 1986; pres. Teikyo U. Ichihara Hosp., Chiba, 1986-88, Teikyo Jr. Coll., 1992—; prin. Nishiki Kindergarten, Tokyo, 1992—; mng. dir. Teikyo U. Internat. Ctr. (Hong Kong) Ltd., 1992—; chmn. bd. dirs. Teikyo SDN BHD, Kuala Lumpur, Malaysia; chmn. Teikyo Post U., Waterbury, Conn., 1991—, Teikyo Found. (UK) Ltd., London, 1991—, Teikyo U. Durham (U.K.) Ltd., 1992—, Teikyo Found., Berlin, 1993—; Okinaga vis. prof. Harvard U., 1993. Author: Hitasura no Michi, 1984; contbr. numerous articles to profl. jours. Bd. trustees Sozan Acad. Found., Tokyo, 1972-85, chmn. bd. trustees, 1978-81; chmn. bd. trustees Nishi-Tokyo Acad. Found., Tokyo, 1975-84; bd. trustees Okinaga Acad. Found., Tokyo, 1981-2002; chmn. bd. trustees Teikyo U. Found., Tokyo, 1981—, Teikyo Acad. Tech. & Sci. Found., 1986—; chmn. Teikyo Found., Inc., Fla., 1989—, Teikyo Sch. U.K., London, 1989-92; chmn. Okinaga Found., Des Moines, 1990-96, Salem Teikyo U. W. Va., 1990—, Teikyo Loretto Hts. U., Denver, 1990-95, Teikyo Westmar U., LeMars, Iowa, 1990-95. Hon. citizen State of W.Va., 1990; Wadham Coll., Oxford U. found. fellow, 1991; hon. fellow St. Edmund's Coll., Cambridge U., 1991, Dept. East Asian Studies, Durham U., 1993. Mem. Japan Obstetrics and Gynecology Inst. (senator 1971-90), Japan Contraception Inst. (senator 1973-90), Inst. for Stds. of Japanese Univs. and Colls. (senator 1978-90), Fund for Promotion and Devel. of Med. Edn. (bd. dirs. 1979-85), Japan Inst. for Study of Hormones (senator 1980-84), Assn. Japanese Pvt. Univs. and Colls. (bd. dirs. 1981-88, mng. dir. bd. 1988—), Assn. Japanese Pvt. Univs. and Colls. Medicine (mng. bd. dirs. 1981-87), Assn. Japanese Pvt. Jr. Colls. (dir. 1984-88), Judo Fedn. Tokyo (chmn. 1987—). Home: Tokyo, Japan. Died Sept. 2008.

**OKOSO, YOSHINORI,** food company executive; b. Takamatsu, Kagawa, Japan, Feb. 2, 1915; s. Atsushi and Nobu (Uehara) O.; m. Hisae Itasaka, May 3, 1946. Founder, since pres. Nippon Meat Packers, Osaka, Japan, from 1951. Mgr. Japan Processed Meats Orgn., Tokyo, Japan Ham and Sausage Industry Union, Tokyo, Japan Hamburger Orgn., Tokyo. Recipient Blue Ribbon medal Japanese Gov., 1973, Imperial medal, 1988. Died Apr. 27, 2005.

**OKRENT, DAVID,** engineering educator; b. Passaic, NJ, Apr. 19, 1922; s. Abram and Gussie (Pearlman) O.; m. Rita Gilda Holtzman, Feb. 1, 1948 (dec. June 2005); children: Neil, Nina, Jocelyne. ME, Stevens Inst. Tech., 1943; MA, Harvard, 1948, PhD in Physics, 1951. Mech. engr. NACA, Cleve., 1943-46; sr. physicist Argonne (Ill.) Nat. Lab., 1951-71; regents lectr. UCLA, 1968, prof. engring., 1971-91, prof. emeritus, rsch. prof., from 1991. Vis. prof. U. Wash., Seattle, 1963, U. Ariz., Tucson, 1970-71; Isaac Taylor chair Technion, 1977-78 Author: Fast Reactor Cross Sections, 1960, Computing Methods in Reactor Physics, 1968, Reactivity Coefficients in Large Fast Power Reactors, 1970, Nuclear Reactor Safety, 1981; contbr. articles to profl. jours. Mem. adv. com. on reactor safeguards AEC, 1963-87, also chmn., 1966; sci. sec. to sec. gen. of Geneva Conf., 1958; mem. U.S. del. to all Geneva Atoms for Peace Confs. Guggenheim fellow, 1961-62, 77-78; recipient Disting. Appointment award Argonne Univs. Assn., 1970, Disting. Service award U.S. Nuclear Regulatory Commn., 1985. Fellow Soc. for Risk Analysis, Am. Phys. Soc., Am. Nuclear Soc. (Tommy Thompson award 1980, Glenn Seaborg medal 1987, George C. Lawrence Pioneering award 2007), Nat. Acad. Engring. Died Dec. 14, 2012.

**OKUDA, KUNIO,** medical educator; b. Tokyo, May 21, 1921; s. Kinmatsu and Hatsue (Hashida) O.; m. Hinae Katsumata, May 30, 1947; children: Hiroaki, Keiko. MD, Manchuria Med. Coll., 1944; DSc, Chiba Med. Coll., Japan, 1951; PhD, Fukuoka U., 1983. With med. staff Chiba (Japan) Nat. Hosp., 1945-51; asst. prof. Yamaguchi Med. Coll., Ube, Japan, 1951-53, assoc. prof., 1953-63; asst. prof. Johns Hopkins Sch. Medicine, Balt., 1958-60; prof. medicine Kurume U. Sch. Medicine, Japan, 1963-71, Chiba U. Sch. Medicine, 1971-87, emeritus prof., from 1987. Past pres. Japanese Soc. Hepatology, Tokyo, 1977-78; v.p. Orgn. de Gastro-Enterologie, 1982-86, hon. pres., 1986—. Contbr. articles to profl. jours. Recipient Spl. award, Japanese Med. Assn., 1967, Abbott award, Japanese Nuclear Medicine Soc., Publ. and Translation Cultural award, Japanese Publ. Soc., 1977, Disting. Svc. award, Am. Assn. for Study of Liver Diseases, 1990, Bockus medal, Orgn. de Gastro-Enterologie, 1998. Mem. Japan Vitamin Soc. (pres. 1987-91, Spl. award 1963), Orgn. Mondiale de Gastro-Enterologie (hon. pres. 1986—), Internat. Assn. Study of Liver (past pres. 1978-80), Asian Pacific Assn. Study of Liver (past pres. 1980-82, hon. pres. 1990—), Am. Gastroenterological Assn., Soc. Scholars Johns Hopkins U. Lodges: Rotary. Avocations: violin, music, stamp collecting/philately. Home: Chiba, Japan. Died Feb. 2, 2003.

**OLA, SIS RAM,** Indian government official; b. Rajasthan, India, July 30, 1927; s. Choudhary Mangla Ram. Mem. Rajasthan Legis. Assembly, 1957—90, 1993—96; various positions including min. of rural devel., forest and environ., public health Rajasthan Govt., 1980—90; mem. Pradesh Congress Com., 1960—95, All India Congress Com., from 1972, Lok Sabha (Indian Parliament), from 1996, mem. petitions com., mem. of parliament local area devel. scheme com., food, civil supplies and public distribution com., 1999—2004; min. chemicals & fertilizers Indian Govt., 1996—97, min. water resources, 1997—98, min. labour & employment, 2004, 2013, min. mines, 2004—09. Mem. Rajasthan Mines and Minerals Adv. Bd., Bd. of Tourism, Rajasthan Desert Devel. Commn.; adv. bd. Territorial Army Adv. Com. Died Dec. 15, 2013.

**OLEJNICEK, JIRI,** entomologist, researcher; b. Brno, Czechoslovakia, Aug. 5, 1946; s. Vilem and Libuse (Mahelkova) O.; m. Anna Ondrejkova; children: Jiri, Jana, Lukas. MS, J.E. Purkyne U., Brno, Czech Republic, 1969, RNDr, 1975; PhD, Czech Acad. Scis., Prague, 1980. Rschr. Inst. of Parasitology, Acad. Sci. Czech Republic, Prague, 1970-80; sr. scientist Inst. of Parasitology, Ceske Budejovice, Czech Republic, from 1980. Thesis supr. South Bohemian U. Ceske Budejovice, 1982—; cons. Pharmallerga C. Budejovice, 1992—. Co-author: Key to identification of Czechoslovak Fauna, 1977, Check-list of Czechoslovak Insects Dolichopodidae, 1987; editor procs.; author some 100 sci. papers. Recipient prize for best sci. paper Czech Lit. Found. Prague, 1987. Mem. Soc. for Vector Ecology, Czech Soc. Entomology, Czech Soc. Zoology, Czech Soc. Parasitology, Am. Mosquito Control Assn. Christian. Home: České Budějovice, Czech Republic. Died Nov. 7, 2005.

**OLIEVENSTEIN, CLAUDE SAMI,** anthropologist, physician; b. Berlin, June 11, 1933; s. Maurice and Leni (Gold) O. Dir. Marmottan Hosp., Paris. Died Dec. 14, 2008.

**OLINS, WALLY,** marketing executive; b. London, Dec. 19, 1930; m. Mara Renate Olga Laura Steinert (div.); 3 children; m. Dornie Watts; 1 child. MA in History, St.Peter's Coll., Oxford, 1954. Trainee Ogilvy, 1954—57, ceo Mumbai, 1957—62; chmn. Wolff Olins Ltd, 1965—2000, Saffron Brand Consultants Ltd, 2001—14. Vis. lectr. design mgmt. London Bus. Sch., 1984—89; vis. prof., mgmt. sch. Imperial Coll., London, 1987—91; vis. prof. Lancaster U., 1991—2002, Copenhagen Bus. Sch., 1993—2005; vis. fellow Said Bus. Sch., Oxford, 2002—09. Author: Corporate Identity, 1989, On Brand, 2003, Brand Handbook, 2008, Corporate Personality, 1978, Brand New, 2014. Recipient Designers prize, Prince Philip Found., 1999, Comdr. Brit. Empire, Her Majesty Queen Elizabeth II, 1999, Bicentenary medal, Royal Soc. Arts, 2000, President's award, Design & Art Dirs. Soc., 2003, Hon. Prof. award, UPC, Lima, Peru; Hon. fellow, St. Peter's Coll., Oxford. Mem.: Brit. Coun. Arts Adv. Group, Acad. Urbanism, Soc. Chartered Designers. Avocations: reading, movies, walking. Died Apr. 14, 2014.

**OLIVA, L. JAY (LAWRENCE JAY OLIVA),** retired academic administrator, history professor; b. Walden, NY, Sept. 23, 1933; s. Lawrence Joseph and Catherine (Mooney) Oliva; m. Mary Ellen Nolan, June 3, 1961; children: Lawrence Jay, Edward Nolan. BA in English, Manhattan Coll., 1955; MA, Syracuse U., 1957, PhD in Russian History, 1960; postgrad., U. Paris, 1959; DHL (hon.), Manhattan Coll., 1987; LLD (hon.), St. Thomas Aquinas Coll., 1988; DHL (hon.), Hebrew Union Coll., 1992; DLitt (hon.), Univ. Coll., Dublin, 1993; PhD (hon.), Tel Aviv U., 1994. Prof. history NYU, 1969—2002, assoc. dean, 1969—70, vice dean, 1970—71, dean faculty, 1971—72, dep. vice chancellor, 1970—75, v.p. acad. planning and services, 1975—77, v.p. acad. affairs, 1977—80, provost, exec. v.p. acad. affairs, 1980—83, chancellor, exec. v.p., 1983—91, pres., 1991—2002, pres. emeritus, 2002—14. Author: Misalliance: A Study of French Policy in Russia during the Seven Years' War, 1964, Russia in the Era of Peter the Great, 1969; editor: Russia and the West from Peter to Khruschev, 1965, Peter the Great, 1970, Catherine the Great, 1971; contbr. articles to profl. jours. Trustee Inst. Internat. Edn.; active Onassis Found., UN Assn. of N.Y. Advisory Coun., NYC Partnership, Assn. for Better N.Y., American Mus. Immigration; adv. bd. U. Athletic Assn.; bd. dirs. Chatham House, Royal Inst. Internat. Affairs, American Bd. Directors Coun. for U.S. and Italy Nat. Collegiate Athletic Assn., N.Y. State Commn. on Nat. and Cmty. Svc. Recipient Medal of Sorbonne, U. Paris, 1992, Man. in Edn. award, Italian Welfare League, medal of honor, Ellis Island; fellow Fribourg fellow, 1959. Mem.: Irish-American Cultural Inst., Assn. Colleges & Universities of State of N.Y, American Coun. Edn., Soc. Fellows NYU, Phi Gamma Delta, Phi Beta Kappa. Home: New York, NY. Died Apr. 17, 2014.

**OLLERENSHAW, KATHLEEN,** research mathematician; b. Manchester, Eng., Oct. 1, 1912; d. Charles and Mary (Stops) Timpson; m. Robert Ollerenshaw, Sept. 6, 1939 (dec. Oct. 1986); children: Charles, Florence (dec.). BA with honors, Oxford U., Eng., 1934, MA, PhD, Oxford U., Eng., 1946; DSc (hon.), Salford U., Eng., 1975, CNAA, 1976, Lancaster U., 1992; LLD (hon), Manchester U., 1976. Rsch. asst. Shirley Inst., Manchester, 1935-41; lectr. Oxford U., Manchester U., 1942-54; dep. pres. U. Manchester Inst. Sci. and Tech., 1976-86; pres. Ins. Math. & it's Applications, Manchester, 1978—79; dep. pro-chancellor U. Salford, 1980-89. Pres. St. Leonards Sch., Fife, Scotland, 1981-2003 Contbr. articles to profl. jours. Councillor City Coun., Eng., 1954-81; Lord Mayor City of Manchester, 1975-76, Freeman, 1984. Named Dame Commander, Order of British Empire, 1971, Dame of Grace, Order of St. John of Jerusalem, 1984, Dep. Lt., County of Greater Manchester. Fellow City Guilds of London Inst., Manchester Poly., U. Manchester Inst. Sci. and Tech., Coll. of Preceptors, Inst. Math. Applications (hon.); mem. Royal No. Coll. Music Conservative. Anglican. Avocations: astronomy, computer studies, music, walking, reading. Died Aug. 10, 2014.

**OLLERTON, JACQUELINE,** librarian, information science professional; b. Barnsley, Eng., May 29, 1945; d. Jack and Kathleen Ollerton; m. Owen Luder, May 10, 1989. Associateship, Loughborough, Eng., 1964-66. Sr. asst. Wandsworth Borough Coun., London, 1966-68; libr. Farmer & Park Architects and Engrs., London, 1968-72; sr. info. officer Poly. of Ctrl. London, 1972-73; head architects ctr. constructional, engring. & surveying svc. Greater London Coun., 1973-80, head tech. info. svcs., 1983-85; mgr. info. and libr. svc. Instn. Mech. Engrs., London, 1985-2000; dir. Comm. in Constrn. Ltd., Westminster, England, from 2000. Author: (bibliography) Building Control and Related Issues-Research Document Guide No. 21, 1981; co-author: (with Nabeed Hamdi) (bibliography) PSSHAK Primary System Support Housing Assembly Kit, 1975. Recipient Libr. Assn./TC Farries pub. rels. and publicity awards, performance award, Spl. award for spl. libr., 1990, Commendation for Prints, 1994. Mem. Inst. Info. Scientists, Inst. Mgmt., Fedn. Constrn. Documentation Ctrs. (sec. 1982-2000). Avocations: art, architecture, poetry, football, swimming. Home: London, England. Died Jan. 21, 2008.

**OLSCHKI, ALESSANDRO,** book publishing executive; b. Florence, Italy, Feb. 12, 1925; s. Aldo Manuzio and Rita (Roster) Olschki; m. Gigliola Serroni, Mar. 26, 1949 (dec. 1985); children: Daniele, Costanza; m. Lydia Boretti, Nov. 20, 1985. Student, Coll. Alla Querce, Florence. Asst. head Leo S. Olschki Publs., Florence, Italy, 1945—63, head, from 1963. Author: Underwater Spearfishing, 1962, 2d. edit., 1965, Visto Si Stampi, 1995, Centotredici Anni, 1999, Marcella, 2002, Scritti subacquei, 2005. Recipient Italian Underwater Spearfishing Champion, 1956, World Champion Underwater Spearfishing, 1957, 1960. Mem.: Underwater Tech. and Sci. Rsch. Group (pres. from 1966), Acad. Underwater Scis., Hist. Diving Soc. (hon.). Home: Florence, Italy. Deceased.

**OLSEN, ARILD KARL,** surgeon, consultant; b. Framnes, Gildeskaal, Norway, Jan. 31, 1938; s. Henry Nelson and Halda Julie Olsen; m. Baerbel Regina Grossmann, Feb. 8, 1941; children: Gabriele, Arne, Ralf. MD, Kiel U., 1965. Med. officer, Flatanger, Norway, 1966-70, Namdal Hosp., Namsos, Norway, 1970-73, Ctrl. Hosp., Stavanger, Norway, 1973-80; cons. surgeon Aker U. Hosp., Oslo, 1981-84, Ctrl. Hosp., Stavanger, 1984-86, sr. cons. surgeon, from 1986. Capt. Norwegian Army Med. Corps, 1968. Mem. Internat. Gastro-Surg. Club, Internat. Hepato-Pancreato-Biliary Assn., Collegium Internat. Chirurgiae Digestive. Avocations: hunting, fishing. Home: Stavanger, Norway. Died Sept. 17, 2005.

**OLSEN, HANS PETER,** lawyer; b. Detroit, May 21, 1938; s. Hans Peter and Paula M. (Olsen) O.; m. Elizabeth Ann Gayton, Sept. 14, 1968; children: Hans Peter, Heidi Susanne, Stephanie Elizabeth BA, Mich. State U., 1961; JD, Georgetown U., 1965; LLM, NYU, 1966. Bar: Mich. 1967, Pa. 1969, R.I. 1974. Law clk. Monaghan, McCrone, Campbell & Crawmer, Detroit, 1964, U.S. Ct. of Claims, Fed. Appellate Ct., Washington, 1966—68; assoc. Pepper, Hamilton & Scheetz, Phila., 1968—72; ptnr. Hinckley, Allen, & Snyder, Providence, 1974—2008; prin. Sansiveri, Kimball & McNamee, LLP, 2009—10. Adv. planning com. U. R.I. Fed. Taxation Inst.; continuing legal edn. adv. bd., tax symposium adv. bd. Bryant Coll.; mem. Gov.'s State Task Force, R.I. Pub. Expenditure Coun.; cons. Bur. Nat. Affairs; liaison Bar Assn. and North Atlantic region IRS; tax adminstrs. adv. com. R.I.; lectr. tax insts. and other profl. groups N.Y., L.A., Phila., Boston, R.I.; advisor R.I. Econ. Policy com. Contbr. articles to profl. jours. Fellow Am. Bar Found.; mem. ABA (sect. taxation, exempt orgns. com., subcom. healthcare, corp.-shareholders rels. com., partnerships com.), R.I. Bar Assn. (sect. taxation, sec.-treas. 1977-80, liaison with CPAs, specialization com., mem. various coms.), Providence C. of C., R.I. C. of C. (chmn. com. on bus. taxes and public spending, mem., past chmn. legis. action council), Mich. State Bar, Pa. State Bar, RI Bar Assn. Home: Providence, RI. Died Oct. 28, 2011.

**OLSEN, MONTE,** retired state legislator; b. Cheyenne, Wyo., Aug. 6, 1956; m. Lisa Glenn Olsen; children: Reed, Dane. Sec., chmn., vice chmn. Albany County Tourism Bd., 1989—92; mem. Dist. 22 Wyo. House of Reps., Wyo., 2002—08. Mem.: Profl. Ski Instrs. America, Wyo. Travel Industry Coalition (bd. dir. 1989—92), Ski Wyo. Inc. (pres. 1989—91), Laramie Area C. of C. (bd. dir. 1989—92). Republican. Died Apr. 8, 2014.

**OLSON, ARTHUR VICTOR,** social sciences educator; b. Lawrence, Mass., June 6, 1929; s. Arthur V. and Mary Agatha (Callahan) Olson; m. Aila Kaarina Uusitalo; children: Robert, Virginia, Randolph. BS, Mass. State Coll., 1952; MS, U. Mass., 1954; EdD, Boston U., 1957. Assoc. prof. U. Maine, Orono, 1957—63; dir. instrn. Macomb County, Mich., 1963—64; prof. U. Ga., Athens, 1964—68, Ga. State U., Atlanta, 1969—77; prof., chmn. dept. cmty. & social founds. U. Victoria, BC, Canada, from 1977. Author: Teaching Reading in Secondary School, 1970, Accountability, 1972; contbr. articles to profl. jours. Warren Rsch. fellowship. Mem.: Can. Soc. Study of Edn., Internat. Reading Assn. Died Mar. 23, 2008.

**OLSON, BARRY GAY,** advertising executive, creative director; b. Glendale, Calif., July 3, 1933; s. Gay Frank and Dorothy Barry (Guay) O. Student, U. So. Calif., 1952-54, UCLA, 1953, Coll. of San Mateo, Calif., 1954. In prodn. Neiman-Marcus, Dallas, 1956; prodn. mgr. Grant Advt., San Francisco, 1957-60; copywriter D'Arcy, MacManus, Masius, San Francisco, 1960-62, Norman, Craig & Kummel, NYC, 1965-67, W. B. Doner, Balt., 1967-68, Ted Bates, LA, 1969; creative dir., v.p. McCann-Erickson, Melbourne, Australia, 1963-65, J. Walter Thompson, Detroit, 1972-75, Vickers & Benson, Montreal, Can., 1976-77, Meldrum & Fewsmith, Cleve., 1971-72, 77-79, Stockton West Burkhart, Cin., 1981-82; creative dir. Hitchcock Fleming, Akron, Ohio, 1982-83, Muller Jordan Weiss, St. Louis, 1984-85; creative dir., v.p., shareholder Innis-Maggiore-Olson, Canton, Ohio, 1985-91; exec. v.p., creative dir., ptnr. Olson and Gibbons, Cleve., 1991-98, also bd. dirs.; exec. v.p., creative dir. Watt/Fleishman-Hillard Advt. Ltd., Cleve., from 1998. Instr. creative advt. part-time Dynamic Graphics Edn. Found., Peoria, Ill., 1989. Contbr. to textbooks: American Corporate Identity 11 and 12, and to Contemporary Advertising. Trustee Big Bros., San Francisco, 1962, Palace Theater Assn., Canton, 1987, N.E. Ohio chpt. March of Dimes Birth Defects Found., 1991-93, Cleve. Signstage Theater, 1996—, Boy Scouts Am. Greater Cleve. Coun., 1999—; trustee, v.p. Cleve. Soc. Communicating Arts, 1971; mem. Mus. Modern Art, N.Y.C., 1980-95, Cleve. Mus. Art, 1996—. With USAF, 1954-55. Recipient Spl. Jury Gold award Atlanta Film Festival, 1975, Advertising Club of N.Y., Andy, 1975, Clio, 1976, One Show, Gold, 1976, Silver and Bronze Lions Cannes Film Festival, 1977, Ace award B/PAA of N.Y.C., 1989, Best of Show awards Columbus Advt. Club, 1981, Canton Advt. Club, 1988, 89, 90, Mktg. Mag. Silver award, Toronto, Can., 1976, Spl. Merit award Inst. Outdoor Advt., N.Y., 1986, Silver Microphone radio awards, Nat. Winners, 1987, 90, 96; 86 Gold Addy awards Akron Advt. Club, Canton Club, Cleve. Advt. Assn., Columbus Advt. Club, 1981, 85, 86, 87, 88, 90, 95, 5th Dist. Addy awards, 1995, 96, Gold Plaque award Chgo. Internat. Film Festival, 1992, Bronze Telly award, 1995, 96, Silver Telly award, 1996, 4 Gold Tower awards BMA

Cleve., 1994, 96; voted one of top 100 creative people in Am. Ad Daily mag., 1971. Mem. Cleve. Advt. Assn., Cleve. Athletic Club, Hermit Club, Cleve. Play House Club. Deceased.

**OLSON, WALTER GILBERT,** lawyer; b. Stanton, Nebr., Feb. 2, 1924; s. O.E. Olson and Mabel A. Asplin; m. Gloria Helen Bennett, June 26, 1949; children: Clifford Warner, Karen Rae Olson. BS, U. Calif., Berkeley, 1947, JD, 1949. Bar: Calif. 1950, U.S. Dist. Ct. (no. dist.) Calif. 1950, U.S. Tax Ct. 1950, U.S. Ct. Appeals (9th cir.) 1950. Assoc. Orrick, Herrington and Sutcliffe (formerly Orrick, Dahlquist, Herrington and Sutcliffe), San Francisco, 1949-54, ptnr., 1954-88. Bd. dirs. Alltel Corp., Little Rock, 1988-94; mem. Commn. to Revise Calif. Corp. Securities Law, 1967-69, Securities Regulatory Reform Panel, 1978-80; mem. corp. security adv. com. Calif. Commr. of Corps, 1975-88. Editor-in-chief Calif. Law Review, 1948-49. Bd. dirs. Internat. Ho., Berkeley, 1981-86. With U.S. Army, 1943-46, ETO. Fellow Am. Bar Found.; mem. ABA (trust divsn. nat. conf. of lawyers and reps. of Am. Bankers Assn.), Calif. Bar Assn. (chmn. corps com. 1975-76, exec. com. bus. law sect. 1977-78), San Francisco Bar Assn., U. Calif. Alumni Assn., Boalt Hall Alumni Assn. (bd. dirs. 1982-90, sec. 1985, v.p. 1987, pres. 1988), Order of Coif, Menlo Country Club (Woodside, Calif.), Pacific-Union Club. Home: Portola Valley, Calif. Died Oct. 10, 2012.

**OLSSON, ROLF GUNNAR,** medical educator; b. Göteborg, Sweden, Mar. 24, 1936; s. Olof Bruno and Signe Maria (Larsson) O.; m. Barbro Marianne Grenthe, May 11, 1962; children: Lars-Erland, David, Kristina. Candidate in Medicine, U. Göteborg, 1958, MD, 1964, PhD, 1966. Asst. reader dept. anatomy U. Göteborg, 1957-66, asst. reader dept. geriatric, 1966-68, clin. reader, cons. internal medicine, 1972-96, prof. medicine, from 1996; house officer Sahlgrenska Hosp., 1968-72. Mem. Swedish Adverse Drug Reaction Adv. Com., 1986—. Author: Internal Medicine for Nurses, 1985, 86, 88, 91, 96, Practical Hepatology, 1991, 99; contbr. articles to profl. jours. Recipient Pedagogic award Ednl. Bd. Med. Faculty, 1990, Pedagogic Cup Med. Students Assn., 1994. Mem. European Assn. Study of Liver, N.Y. Acad. Scis., Swedish Internal Medicine Liver Club (chmn. 1984—). Home: Göteborg, Sweden. Died Feb. 27, 2008.

**O'MALLEY, PATRICK PEARSE,** neurologist, psychiatrist; b. Newtown Hamilton, Ireland, Apr. 22, 1918; s. Patrick and Susan (McKee) O'M.; m. Mary Hickey, Sept. 16, 1947; children: Kieran Darragh, Donal Lysaght, Conor Plunket. MB, BChir, BAO, Queen's U., Belfast, No. Ireland, 1941; Diploma in Psychol. Medicine, Royal Coll. Physicians, Dublin, Ireland, 1942; Diploma in Pub. Health, Univ. Coll., Dublin, 1943, MRCP, 1945. Med. officer St. Patrick's Hosp., Dublin, 1941-44; clin. asst. Bristol (Eng.) Mental Hosp., 1944-45; clin. clk. Nat. Hosp. for Nervous Diseases, London, 1945-46; rsch. asst. in neuropathology Maudsley Hosp., London, 1945-46; dir. setting up Neuro-Psychiat. Clinic, Mater Hosp., Belfast, 1946-81; clin. tchr. Queen's U., Belfast, 1946-81; cons. neurologist and psychiatrist Ulster Ind. Clinic, 1981-92, ret., 1992. Mem. Mental Health Appeals Tribunal, Northern Ireland, 1960-71; co-founder Threshold Literary mag., 1957. Author: Clinical Neuro-Psychiatry, 2000, reprinted with Appendix, 2003; contbr. articles to profl. jours. Co-founder lyric Players Theatre, Belfast, 1951; found. trustee Lyric Cultural Charitable Trust, 1960; founder Granuaile Trust of O'Malley Clan, Dublin, 1986. Fellow Royal Coll. Physicians (Ireland), Royal Coll. Psychiatrists (London); mem. Brit. Med. Assn., Irish Med. Assn. Home: Dublin, Ireland. Deceased.

**ÖPIK, ILMAR,** power engineering educator, thermal physicist; b. Tallinn, Estonia, June 17, 1917; s. Paul and Ella (Pani) Ö.; m. Elsa Aarma, June 4, 1946 (div. 1978); 1 child, Andres; m. Lia Raud, May 6, 1978. DiplEngr, Tech. U., Tallinn, 1940, PhD, 1953; DSc, Power Engring. Inst., Moscow, 1963. Constructor Franz Krull Ltd., Tallinn, 1937-41; engr. Teploelektroproekt, Sverdlovsk, Russia, 1942-44, oil shale industry, Tallinn, 1944-48; tchr., lab. head Tech. U., Tallinn, 1944-68; divsn. head Estonian Acad. Sci., Tallinn, 1968-77, v.p., 1977-87, emeritus, from 1987. Prof. Tech. U., Tallinn, 1968-77; advisor Ministry Econ. Affairs, Tallinn, 1990-2000; bd. dirs. RAS Kiviter, Kohtla-Jarve, 1992-97. Decorated Arms of Estonian Order; recipient Medal of Merit, Tech. U., 1967, Paul Kogerman medal, Acad. Sci. and Tech. U., 1991. Mem. Estonian Naturalists Soc. (K.E. v. Baer medal 1984), Estonian Acad. Sci. (v.p., medal, 1987), Finnish Acad. Tech. (fgn. mem., medal of Merit 1992). Lutheran. Avocation: bridge. Home: Tallinn, Estonia. Died July 29, 2001.

**OPPENHEIM, IRWIN,** retired chemistry professor; b. Boston, June 30, 1929; s. James L. and Rose (Rosenberg) O.; m. Bernice Buresh, May 18, 1974; 1 child, Joshua Buresh. AB summa cum laude, Harvard U., 1949; postgrad., Calif. Inst. Tech., 1949-51; PhD in Physical Chemistry, Yale U., 1956. Physicist Nat. Bur. Standards, Washington, 1953-60; chief theoretical physics Gen. Dynamics/Convair, San Diego, 1960-61; assoc. prof. chemistry MIT, Cambridge, 1961-65, prof., 1965—96, prof. emeritus, 1996—2014. Lectr. physics U. Md., 1953-60; vis. assoc. prof. physics U. Leiden, 1955-56, Lorentz prof., 1983; vis. prof. Weizmann Inst. Sci., 1958-59, U. Calif., San Diego, 1966-67; Van der Waals prof. U. Amsterdam, 1966-67. Author: (with J.G. Kirkwood) Chemical Thermodynamics, 1961; editor: Phys. Rev. E, 1992-2001. Recipient John Henry Hildebrand award, American Chemical Soc., 1998. Fellow American Phys. Soc., American Acad. Arts & Sciences, Washington Acad. Sci.; mem. Phi Beta Kappa, Sigma Xi. Achievements include research in quantum statis. mechanics, statis. mechanics of transport processes, thermodynamics. Home: Cambridge, Mass. Died June 3, 2014.

**ORDMAN, JEANNETTE,** performing company executive; b. Germiston, Republic of South Africa, Nov. 8, 1935; arrived in Israel, 1965; Grad., Damelin Coll., Johannesburg, Republic of South Africa, 1951; A.R.A.D. Solo Seal, Royal Acad. Dance London, Johannesburg. Prin. dancer Johannesburg Festival Ballet, 1957-60; soloist, lead dancer London TV Ballet, 1960-66; dir. rehearsals Batsheva Dance Co., Tel Aviv, 1966; artistic dir. Bat-Dor Studios Dance, Tel Aviv, 1967—2007, Beer Sheva, Israel, 1975—2007, Bat-Dor Dance Co., Tel Aviv, 1968—2007. Introduced Royal Acad. Dance London syllabus and Pilates system tng., Israel; mem. Jury Internat. Ballet Competition, Jackson, Miss., 1982, vice chmn., 1986, 1990; chmn. profl. adv. com. Israel Dance Medicine Ctr., 1985. Recipient 1st prize Guild Loyal Women Bursary, 1948, Ceccheti award Acad. Medicea, Florence, Italy, 1984, Am. Yafe Am. Ehad award, 1988, The Pres.'s award Royal Acad. of Dancing, London, 1998, numerous others; hand and foot imprinted Civic Theatre, Johannesburg, South Africa, 1976. Avocations: reading, music, dogs. Home: Tel Aviv, Israel. Died Feb. 7, 2007.

**ORDWAY, FREDERICK IRA, III,** science educator, consultant, researcher, writer; b. NYC, Apr. 4, 1927; s. Frederick Ira and Frances Antoinette (Wright) O.; m. Maria Victoria Arenas, Apr. 13, 1950 (dec. Feb 15, 2012); children: Frederick Ira IV, Albert James, Aliette Marisol. SB, Harvard U., Cambridge, Mass., 1949; postgrad., U. Alger, 1950, U. Paris, France, 1950-51, 53-54, U. Barcelona, Spain, 1953, U. Innsbruck, Austria, 1954, Air U., 1952-63, Alexander Hamilton Bus. Inst., 1952-58, Indsl. Coll. Armed Forces, 1953-63; DSc (hon.), U. Ala., Huntsville, 1992. Midshipman USNR, 1945; with Mene Grande Oil Co., San Tome, Venezuela, 1949-50, Orinoco Mining Co., Cerro Bolivar, Venezuela, 1950; capt. USAFR, 1951—78; with engring. divsn. Reaction Motors, Inc., Lake Denmark, NJ, 1951-53; with guided missiles divsn. Republic Aviation Corp., 1954-55; pres. Gen. Astronautics Rsch. Corp., Huntsville, Ala., 1955-59, 65-66; v.p. Nat. R & D Corp., Atlanta, 1957-59; asst. to dir. Saturn Systems Office, Army Ballistic Missile Agy., Huntsville, 1959-60; chief space info. systems br. George C. Marshall Space Flight Ctr. NASA, 1960-64; prof. sci. and tech. applications Sch. Grad. Studies and Rsch., U. Ala. Rsch. Inst., 1967-73; cons. Sci. and Tech. Policy Office, NSF, 1974-75; cons. ops. analysis divsn. Gen. Rsch. Corp., 1974-75; asst. to adminstr. ERDA, 1975-77, US Dept. Energy, 1977-94, policy/internat. affairs dir. spl. projects office, also participant internat. energy devel. program Office of Asst. Sec. Internat. Affairs, 1978-79; also participant internat. energy devel. program Latin America Australia New Zealand, 1970—80. Cons. to industry, Ency. Britannica, American Coll. Dictionary of English Lang., M.G.M. film 2001: A Space Odyssey, 1965-66, Paramount Picture Corp., The Adventurers, 1968-69; internat. lectr. space flight and energy programs. Author: (with C.C. Adams) Space Flight, 1958, (with Ronald C. Wakeford) International Missile and Spacecraft Guide, 1960, Annotated Bibliography of Space Science and Technology, 1962, (with J.P. Gardner, M.R. Sharpe, Jr.) Basic Astronautics: An Introduction to Space Science, Engineering and Medicine, 1962, (with Adams, Wernher von Braun) Careers in Astronautics and Rocketry, 1962, (with Gardner, Sharpe, R.C. Wakeford) Applied Astronautics: An Introduction to Space Flight, 1963, (with Wakeford) Conquering the Sun's Empire, 1963, Life in Other Solar Systems, 1965, (with Roger A. MacGowan) Intelligence in the Universe, 1966, (with W. von Braun) History of Rocketry and Space Travel, 1966, 1969, 1975, L'Histoire Mondiale de l'Astronautique, 1968, 70, (with W. von Braun) Rockets' Red Glare, 1976, (with C.C. Adams, M.R. Sharpe) Dividends from Space, 1972, Pictorial Guide to Planet Earth, 1975, (with W. von Braun) New Worlds: Discoveries From Our Solar System, 1979, (with M.R. Sharpe) The Rocket Team, 1979, paperback edit., 1982, 2nd edit., 2003, 3rd edit. 2007, (with F.C. Durant and R.C. Seamans) Between Sputnik and the Shuttle, 1981, (with E.M. Emme) Science Fiction and Space Futures, 1982, (with von Braun, Dave Dooling) Space Travel: A History, 1985, (with Ernst Stuhlinger) Wernher von Braun: Aufbrach in den Weltraum, 1992, Wernher von Braun: Crusader for Space (2 vols.), 1994, rev. 1996, single vol. edit., 1996, (with Randy Liebermann) Blueprint for Space, 1992, Visions of Spaceflight, (with Adam K. Johnson), 2001: The Lost Science, 2012, (with Fred Clarke) Arthur C . Clarke: A Life Remembered, 2013, (with Robert Godwin) 2001: The Heritage and Legacy of the Space Odyssey, 2014; editor: Advances in Space Science and Technology, vols. I-XII, 2 supplements, 1959-72, (with R.M.L. Baker, N.W. Makemson) Introduction to Astrodynamics, 1960, (with others) From Peenemünde to Outer Space, 1962, Astronautical Engineering and Science, 1963; mem. editl. bd.: IX Internat. Astronautical Congress procs., 2 vols, 1959, Xth Congress procs., 2 vols, 1960; guest editor: Acta Astronautica, 1985, 94, History of Rocketry and Astronautics, Vol. IX, 1989, Digital book Mars: Target for Tomorrow Microsoft Network & Internet, 1996; Co-developer of biographical film He Conquered Space, 1996, History of Astronautics Video, 1996, inter-active CD Rom, 1997, rev., 2001, interactive CD ROM and video versions) Mars: Past, Present, Future, 1998; contbr. articles to profl. jours., chpts. to books; organizer Blueprint for Space exhbn., 1991-95, US Space and Rocket Ctr., IBM Gallery of Sci. and Art, NASA Vis. Ctr., Houston, Spaceport USA, Cape Canaveral, Fla., Nat. Air and Space Mus., Washington, Va. Air and Space Ctr., Hampton Shaping The Vision exhibit, Art Inst. Chgo., 2001, Bruce Mus. Art and Scis., Greenwich, Conn., 2001, Mus. Flight, Seattle, 2002, others. Co-recipient diploma of honor French Commn. d'Histoire, Arts et Letters, Paris, 1969, citation Arthur C. Clarke Found., 2005; recipient Arthur C. Clarke Lifetime Achievement award, 2013; recommended for contbns. to US Space and Rocket Ctr., Ala. Space Sci. Exhibit, US Space Walk of Fame Found., many commendations. Fellow: AIAA (internat. activities com. 1980—89, 2003 Centennial of Flight Ctr. 1998, Hermann Oberth award 1977, K.E. Tsiolkowski award 1988), AAAS, Brit. Interplanetary Soc. (guest editor 1992—96); mem.: Internat. Förderkreis für Raumfahrt (Hermann Oberth Gold medal 1996), US Space and Rocket Ctr. (co-chmn. Explorer I satellite Americas anniversery celebration 2008, Legacy award 2008), Acta Astronautica (guest editor 1994, 1997), Eurasian Acad. Scis., Nat. Space Soc. (bd. dirs. 1986—95, publs. com. 1987—88, nominating com. 1990—92, Space Pioneer award 2012), Am. Astron. Soc. (Emme award 1994, Nat. Space Club award 1997), Internat. Acad. Astronautics (Luigi Napolitano Lit. award 1992), Arthur C. Clarke Found. (bd. dirs. 2000—11), Washington Golf and Country Club, Harvard Club NY, Cosmos Club (bd. mgmt. 1986—91, v.p. 1988—90, award 2001). Achievements include donation of spaceflight, lunar & planetary astronomy & rocketry collection to the Centre Library & Archives of the US Space & Rocket Centre in Huntsville; Alabama consisting of 200 lots and other donations transferred from 1978 through 2011; energy research & development collection & some spaceflight material to the M. Louis Salmon Library of the University of Alabama in Huntsville; space fiction collection to the Harvard College Library, Cambridge, Massachusetts & family material to the Dyer Library & Saco Museum, Saco, Maine. Died July 1, 2014.

**ORECHIO, FRANK ANTHONY,** publishing executive; b. Somerville, NJ, June 12, 1917; s. Pasquale and Rose (Cocchiola) Orechio; m. Edith Johnson, July 5, 1953. Student, United Radio-TV Inst.; student in Bus. Adminstrn., Rutgers U., 1938. Pub. Orechio Publs. Inc., Nutley, Nutley Sun, Belleville Times, Bloomfield Life, Orechio Broadcasting Co., Glen Ridge Voice; self-employed acct. Nutley, NJ, 1945—51; pres. OK Electronic Corp., Nutley, 1951—58, Durlin Co., Newark, 1986—90; project coord. North Jersey Wanaque South Water Project; chmn. North Jersey Dist. Water Supply Commn., 1966—82. Del. Rep. Nat. Conv., 1972; Essex County campaign mgr., com. re-election pres. Nixon; pres. Parker Highland East Condominium Assn.; mem. Passaic Valley Sewerage Authority, NJ Racing Commn., 1992; chmn. NJ Young Reps., 1947—49, Essex County Bd. Elections, 1955—59; campaign dir., US senator Clifford P. Case, 1954. With US Army, 1941—43. Mem.: Aberdeen C. of C. (Fla.), Upper Montclair C. of C. (NJ), Belleville C. of C. (past chmn. bd.), Nutley C. of C. (past pres.), Le Club (NYC), Boca Raton Resort & Club, Nat. Press Club. Deceased.

**ORIE, NICOLAAS G.M.,** pulmonologist, retired medical educator; children: Sybrand, Gan, Affons, Cato, Nico, Jos, Marrsen. MD, U. Utrecht, 1939. Resident internal medicine St. Joseph Hosp., Eindhoven, Netherlands, 1940—42; with Sanatorium Berg en Bosch, Bilthoven, Netherlands, 1942; pvt. practice Coevorden, Netherlands, 1943—44; physician TB Dispensary Locum Tenens, Zwolle, Netherlands, 1944—45; lectr. U. Hosp., Groningen, Netherlands, 1951—55, prof., 1945—79, dean med. faculty, 1969—73, ret., 1979. Head Dept. Pulmonary Diseases Academic Hosp., Groningen, 1951—69; vis. prof. in field; mem. various coms. Netherland Health Coun.; chmn. med. coun. The Netherlands Asthma Fund, 1963—78; mem. asthma com. T.N.O., Netherlands; mem. com. Bronchitis and Emphysema EGKS. Author: Practical Advices for People with Asthma and Bronchitis, 1980, Cara en de therapie in de huisarspraktijk, 1982; mem. editl. bd.: Lung, Revue Francaise des Maladies Respiratoires, Medicina Toracica, Netherlands Jour. Medicine, Scandinavian Jour. Respiratory Diseases; contbr. over 600 articles to profl. jours. Recipient Thymfund medal, 1953, Swieringa medal, 1988, prize, Asthma Found., 1990. Mem.: Inst. Tisiologia and Pneumologia, Thoracic Pathology Soc. France, French Allergy Soc., French Soc. Respiratory Patholoy, Royal Soc. Medicine, Dutch Soc. Allergy, Dutch Soc. Lung Disease and TB (corr.; pres.), Deutsche Gesellschaft Pneumonologie (hon.), Gesellschaft Lungen und Almungsforschung (hon.), Soc. Europaea Pneumologica (hon.), Coll. Medicos Tisiologos (hon.). Roman Catholic. Died July 5, 2006.

**ORLANDO, CARL,** medical research and development executive; b. Palermo, Italy, Sept. 26, 1915; came to U.S., 1928; s. Peter and Maria (Bongiorno) O.; m. Ann Bovè, May 29, 1943; children: Ann Marie, Francine, Patricia, Charleen, Joan. BS, Columbia U., 1941; postgrad., Rochester U., 1943. Chief photo optics U.S. Army Elec. Commd., Ft. Monmouth, N.J., 1945-75; cons. pvt. practice, New Shrewsbury, N.J., 1975-79; v.p. rsch. & devel. Analytical R&D Inc., Eatontown, N.J., 1979-88; cons. rsch. & devel. Engring. Devel. Co., Tinton Falls, N.J., 1986-88; pres., rsch. & devel. dir. Sens-O-Tech Indsutries Inc., Eatontown, N.J., 1988-99. Chmn. bd. dirs. Sens-O-Tech Industries, 1988-92. Contbr. articles to profl. jours. Bd. dirs. Monmouth Regional High Sch., Tinton Falls, 1974; com. mem. Tinton Falls Environ. Unit, 1984; chmn. Entertainment Activities St. Dorothaas Ch., Eatontown, 1983. With USN, 1945. Recipient Monetary Suggestion award Signal Corp. Engring. Lab., 1948. Mem. Soc. Photographic Scientist & Engrs. (sr. mem.), Soc. Imaging Sci. & Tech., N.Y. Acad. Scis., Elks, Battle Ground Country Club. Republican. Roman Catholic. Achievements include over 20 patents in various fields including non-invasive heart and breathing alarm monitors, moving target indicator, photographic reproduction in 0.2 second, one step photographic technic, image stabilization system, perk-type automatic drip coffee maker, military tactical image interpretation facility, production and reconstruction of holograms, device for intensifying photoelectrostatic images, bandwidth compression of photographic images, Natinol photographic high speed shutter. Died Sept. 29, 1999.

**ORLEBEKE, WILLIAM RONALD,** retired lawyer, writer; b. El Paso, Tex., Jan. 5, 1934; s. William Ronald and Frances Claire (Cook) O.; children: Michelle, Julene, David; m. Susan K. Nash, 2000. BA, Willamette U., Salem, Oreg., 1956, JD, 1966; MA, U. Kans., Lawrence, 1957. Bar:

Calif. 1966, US Dist. Ct. (no. dist.) Calif. 1967, US Ct. Appeals (9th cir.) 1967, US Ct. Appeals (7th cir.) 1989, US Dist. Ct. (no. dist.) Ill. 1989, US Dist. Ct. (cen. dist.) Calif. 1989. Mem. staff Travelers Ins. Co., Sacramento, 1957-61; br. claim mgr. NY Life Ins. Co., 1961-62; branch claim mgr. Transamerica Ins. Co., San Francisco, 1962-63; spl. investigator Oregon State Police, 1963—65; assoc. Eliassen & Postel, San Francisco, 1966-69; ptnr. Coll, Levy & Orlebeke, Concord, Calif., 1969-77, Orlebeke & Hutchings, Concord, Calif., 1977-89; prin. Law Offices W. Ronald Orlebeke, 1989-98; hearing officer Contra Costa County, Calif., 1981-98; arbitrator Contra Costa County Superior Ct., 1977-98, US Dist. Ct. No. Calif., 1978-98, Mt. Diablo Mcpl. Ct., 1987-89; ret., 1998. Judge pro tem Mt. Diablo Mcpl. Ct., 1973-75; criminology prof. Pioneer-Pacific Coll., 2002-03; instr. Am. history & modern European history Salem Ctr., 2009-. Author: Orlebeke Family in Europe and America, 1570-1990, 1988, Don't Tell Me I Can't, 2003, (novels) Code Jeremiah, 2004, Lightning, 2004. Alumni bd. dir. Willamette U., 1978-81, trustee, 1980-81 scholar chmn. Concord Elks, 1977-79; del. Joint US/China Internat. Trade Law Conf., Beijing, 1987. With USMCR, 1952-59. Sr. scholar Willamette U., 1955-56; Woodrow Wilson fellow Kans. U., 1956-57, US Bur. Nat. Affairs fellow, 1966, others. Mem. SAR, Sons of Union Vets. Civil War, First Marine Divsn. Assn., Order Ea. Star (worthy patron 1980), Masons (life; sec. Capitol Masonic Ctr., 2001-04, corp. sec. Oreg. Masonic Low Twelve Club, Inc 2005-07, spl. trustee Oreg. chpt. 2006-07), Elks, Rotary (charter pres. Clayton Valley/Concord Sunrise club 1987-88, chmn. dist. 5160 Calif. membership devel. 1989-90, dist. gov. liaison dist. 5160 1990-92, dist. Rotarian of Yr. 1989-90, Paul Harris fellow 1988, 1992 dist. conf. chmn. benefactor 1990, Merit award 1990), Shriners, Salem Shrine Club (v.p. 2006-07, pres. 2008, trustee 2009-, treas. 2011-13). Republican. Home: Keizer, Oreg. Died June 11, 2014.

**ORR, ESTON WYCLIFFE, SR., (WYC ORR),** lawyer; b. Tifton, Ga., Oct. 28, 1946; s. John H. and Emogene (Gaskins) Orr; m. Lyn Harden, Aug. 12, 1967; children: Cristine E., Eston W. BS with honors, Auburn U., 1968; JD, U. Tenn. Law Sch., 1970. Bar: Ga. 1971, US Dist. Ct. (mid. dist.) Ga. 1972, US Ct. Appeals, 5th cir. 1972, 11th cir. 1981, US Dist. Ct. (no. dist.) Ga. 1974. Tax acct. Arthur Andersen & Co., Atlanta, 1970—71; assoc. Greer, Sartain & Carey, Gainesville, Ga., 1974—75; ptnr. Greer, Deal, Birch, Orr & Jarrard, Gainesville, 1976—77, Deal, Birch, Orr & Jarrard, Gainesville, 1977—79, Simpson & Orr, Tifton, Ga., 1979—80; pvt. practice Gainesville, 1981—2014; mem. Ga. House of Reps., 1989—93. Adj. prof. Brenau Coll., Gainesville, 1976. Contbr. articles to profl. jours. Pres., bd. dirs. Lanier Ednl. Found.; T-Ball coach Hall County Boys Club; bd. dirs. Ga. Indigent Def. Coun., The Arts Coun., Vol. Gainesville, Jr. Achievement Northeast Ga., Chestatee Regional Libr., 1977—79; past pres. Hall County unit Am. Cancer Soc., chmn. bd. dirs., from 1982. Served to capt. JAGC US Army, 1971—74. Decorated Army Commendation medal; recipient Wall St. Jour. Fin. award, 1967, Delta Sigma Pi Outstanding Bus. Grad. award, Auburn U., 1968. Mem.: ABA, Gainesville-Hall County Chamber of Commerce (bd. dirs.), State Bar Ga. (chmn. arbitration and mediation com.), Rotary Club, Phi Eta Sigma, Phi Kappa Phi, Order Coif. Democrat. Methodist. Died May 28, 2014.

**ORRELL, JOHN OVERTON,** literature and language professor; b. Maidstone, Kent, Eng., Dec. 31, 1934; arrived in Can., 1958; s. William Ramsden and Mabel (Hallam) Orrell; m. Wendy Phillips Orrell, June 23, 1956; children: Katherine, David. MA, Oxford U., Eng., 1968, U. Toronto, Can., 1959, PhD, 1964. Asst. prof. U. Alta, Edmonton, Canada, 1961—68, assoc. prof., 1968—74, prof., 1974—2003. Former adviser World Shakespeare Globe Ctr., London. Author: Fallen Empires, 1982, The Quest for Shakespeare's Globe, 1983, The Theatres of Inigo Jone and John Webb, 1985; contbr. articles to profl. jours.; editor: Studies of Major Works in English, 1968. With RAF, 1953—55. Grants, 1959. Fellow: Royal Soc. Can.; mem.: Shakespeare Assn. America. Home:, Canada. Died Sept. 16, 2003.

**ORTENBERG, ARTHUR,** retired apparel executive; b. Newark, Aug. 13, 1926; m. Muriel Kotchever (div.); children: Neil, Nancy m. Liz Claiborne, July 5, 1957 (dec. June 26, 2007); 1 stepchild, Alexander Pres. Fashion, Inc., 1971-76; co-founder, company sec. Liz Claiborne, Inc., NYC, 1976—90. Author: Liz Claiborne: The Legend, the Woman, 2009. Jewish. Died Feb. 3, 2014.

**ORTLUND, ANNE (ELIZABETH ANNE ORTLUND),** writer, musician; b. Wichita, Kans., Dec. 3, 1923; d. Joseph Burton and Mary Elizabeth (Weible) Sweet; m. Raymond Carl Ortlund, Apr. 27, 1946; children: Sherrill Anne, Margot Jeanne, Raymond Carl, Nels Robert. Student, Am. U., 1941—43; AA, Am. Guild Organists, 1944; MusB, U. Redlands, Calif., 1945. Organist Old-Fashioned Revival Hour and Joyful Sound, Radio World-Wide, 1960—75; composer hymns, anthems NYC, 1963—77. Composer: Macedonia, 1966, 250 hymns; author: Up with Worship, 1975, Disciplines of the Beautiful Woman, 1977, The Gentle Ways of the Beautiful Woman, 1998, How Great Our Joy, 2001, Up With Worship, rev. and updated, 2001, A Fresh Start for Your Friendships, 2001; author: (with Raymond Carl Ortlund) The Best Half of Life, 1976, Discipling One Another, 1979, Children Are Wet Cement, 1981 (Christie award Christian Booksellers Assn., 1982), Joanna: A Story of Renewal, 1982, Building a Great Marriage, 1984; author: (with Raymond C. Ortlund) Staying Power, 1986, Disciplines of the Heart, 1987, Renewal, 1989, Confident in Christ, Disciplines of the Home, 1990, Fix Your Eyes on Jesus, 1991, My Sacrifice His Fire, 1993, In His Presence, 1995, Lord, Make My Life a Miracle, rev. and updated, 2002. Recipient SESAC award, Gospel Musicians, 1978, award, Commd. Conservative Congl. Christian Conf., 2008; named Profl. Woman of Yr., Pasadena Bus. and Profl. Women, 1975. Home: Whittier, Calif. Died Nov. 4, 2013.

**ORTOLI, FRANCOIS-XAVIER,** economist; b. Feb. 16, 1925; Student, Ecole Nationale; degree (hon.), Oxford U., Athens U. Insp. fins. French Govt., 1948-51, tech. advisor to the Office of Minister of Econ. Affairs and Info., 1951-53, tech. advisor to the Office of Minister of Fins., 1954-55, asst. dir. to Sec. of State for Econ. Affairs, 1955-57; sec.-gen. Franco-Italian Com. of EEC, 1955-57; head comml. politics service Sec. of State for Econ. Affairs, 1957-58; dir.-gen. Internal Market Div. of the EEC, 1958-61; sec.-gen. Inter-Ministerial Com. for Questions of European Econ. Cooperation, Paris, 1961-62; dir. Cabinet of Prime Minister France, 1962-66; Commr.-Gen. of the Plan, 1966-67; Minister of Works France, 1967-68; Minister of Edn., 1968; Minister of Fin., 1968-69; Minister of Indsl. and Scientific Devel., 1969-72; pres. Com. of European Communities, 1973-76; v.p. for Econ. and Monetary Affairs Govt. of France, 1977-84; pres., exec. dir. TOTAL Co. Française Des Petroles, from 1984. Bd. dirs. Philips NV; adv. dir. Unilever Corp.; pres. Coll. of Europe. Decorated Légion d'Honneur, Croix de Guerre, Médaille Militaire, Médaille de la Résistance, numerous others. Home: Paris, France. Died Nov. 30, 2007.

**OSAKI, HUMIO,** retired parasitology educator, physician; b. Hirosaki, Japan, June 4, 1916; s. Bunhitiro and Taka (Takahara) S.; m. Omori Toyoko, Dec. 3, 1961; children: Masami, Yoko. MD, Okayama Med. Sch., Japan, 1942; D Med. Sci., Osaka U., Japan, 1960. Physician Nagata Health Ins. Clinic, Kobe, Hyogo, Japan, 1947-55; rsch. assoc. Duke U., Durham, N.C., 1956-58; asst. prof. Osaka U. Dental Sch., 1959-61; assoc. prof. Okayama U. Med. Sch., 1961-66; prof. U. Tokushima (Japan) Sch. Medicine, 1966-81; v.p. Kochi Med. Sch., Nankoku, Kochi, Japan, 1982-86; hon. dir. Yagi Hosp., Mihara, Hyogo, from 1987; dir. juridical person Awaji-shima Fukushikai, Mihara, from 1987; prof. emeritus U. Tokushima, Japan, 1984, Kochi Med. Sch., Japan, 1986. Capt. med. dept. Japanese Army, 1942-46. Fellow Royal Soc. Tropical Medicine and Hygiene (London); mem. Japanese Soc. Parasitology (hon., Koizumi-Syo award 1970), Japanese Soc. Tropical Medicine (hon.), Japanese Soc. Clin. Parasitology (hon.), Japan Soc. Protozoology (hon.), Japanese-German Assn. Protozoan Diseases (v.p.), Soc. Protozoologists (emeritus), Mt. Desert Island Biol. Lab. (life), Friendship and Exch. Soc. (hon.), Sigma Xi (life). Buddhist. Home: Kobe, Japan. Died Apr. 8, 2005.

**OSBORN, ERIC FRANCIS,** educator; b. Melbourne, Victoria, Australia, Dec. 9, 1922; s. William Francis and Hilda Pearl (Gamlen) O.; m. Lorna Grace Grierson, Dec. 20, 1946; children: Robert Stanley, Eric Peter. MA, U. Melbourne, Australia, 1948; PhD, U. Cambridge, Eng., 1954, BD, 1971, DD, 1977; DD (honorary), Coll. of Divinity, Melbourne, 1987. Prof. New Testament and Early Ch. History Queen's Coll., U. Melbourne, Melbourne, Australia, 1958-87; hon. prof. La Trobe U., Melbourne, from 1989; professorial fellow U. Melbourne, from 1998. Author: The Philosophy of Clement of Alexandria, 1957, Justin Martyr, 1973, Ethical Patterns in Early Christian Thought, 1976, The Beginning of Christian Philosophy, 1981, The Emergence of Christian Theology, 1993, Tertullian, First Theologian of the West, 1997, Irenaeus of Lyons, 2001, Clement of Alexandria, 2005. Served with Australian Army, 1941-44. Recipient fellow Queen's Coll., Melbourne, 1987, Acad. of Humanities, 1971. Died May 2007.

**OSBORNE, MARY D.,** state agency administrator; b. Ohio, Apr. 27, 1875; Grad., Akron City Hosp. Sch. Nursing, 1902. Supr. nurses for voluntary agy., NYC, 1912; supr. Divsn. Maternal and Child Health Miss. State Bd. Health, 1921, supr. pub. health nurses; ret., 1946. Author: Manual for Midwives, 1922. Active ARC. Died 1946.

**OSSIP, JEROME J.,** food service executive, consultant; b. NYC, Mar. 15, 1920; s. Harry A. and Fannie Ossip; m. Audrey A. Herman, May 30, 1949; children: Dale Ava, Brad Henry, Michael Ian. BS, U. Ill., 1940; MBA, NYU, 1949. Pres. Bards Sys., Inc., NYC, 1950—73, Churchills Enterprises, Inc., NYC, 1953—58, Cambridge Inns, Inc., Paramus, NJ, 1960—72, Greentree Restaurants, Inc., NYC, 1974—83; chmn. Guardian Food Svc. Corp., NYC, 1974—86, Ossip Cons., Inc., NYC, from 1986. Editor: 509th Composite Group, 1946. Past pres. Nat. Dem. Club. Capt USAF, 1943—46. Mem.: Nat. Restaurant Assn., NY Restaurant Assn., NY Vis. Conv. Bur., Braeburn Country Club, Delaire Golf Club, Sixty East Club. Died Nov. 15, 1989.

**OSTROVOY, DMYTRIY YURIYEVICH,** research scientist; b. Kyiv, Ukraine, Dec. 4, 1958; s. Yuriy Dmytriyevich and Gulzifa Ramazanovna (Bedretdinova) O. Diploma in Mech. Engring., Kyiv Poly. Inst., 1982; degree in Sci., Nat. Acad. Scis. Ukraine, Kyiv, 1993, postgrad., 1991—93; degree (hon.), Highest Cert. Commn. Ukraine, Ukraine, 2000. Engr. Design Bur., Inst. Problems of Srength Nat. Acad. Scis. Ukraine, Kyiv, 1984-87, jr. rsch. fellow Inst. Problems of Strength, 1987-92, rsch. fellow, sr. rsch. fellow Inst. Problems of Strength, from 1993; sr. rschr. Korean Inst. Sci. and Tech., Seoul, 1995-96. Sec. tech. com. for standardization State Com. Ukraine Tech. Regulation and Consumer Policy, Kyiv, 1997—. Contbr. articles to profl. jours. Recipient Soros Humanitarian Found. award Am. Phys. Soc., 1993; grantee Internat. Sci. Found, 1994, State fund for fundamental Rsch. of Ukraine, 2001. Avocations: stamp collecting/philately, literature. Home: Kyiv, Ukraine. Died Jan. 20, 2006.

**O'TOOLE, PETER,** actor; b. County Galway, Ireland, Aug. 2, 1932; s. Patrick Joseph and Constance (Ferguson) O'T.; m. Sian Phillips, 1959 (div. 1979); children: Kate, Pat; m. Karen Brown, 1983 (div.); 1 child, Lorcan. Student, Royal Acad. Dramatic Arts. Actor Bristol Old Vic Co., 1955-58; London stage debut in Major Barbara, 1956; other stage appearances include Present Laughter, The Apple Cart, 1986, Pygmalion, 1987, Jeffrey Bervard is Unwell, 1989; films include Kidnapped, 1960, The Day They Robbed the Bank of England, 1960, Savage Innocents, 1961, Lawrence of Arabia, 1962, Becket, 1964, Lord Jim, 1965, What's New, Pussycat?, 1965, How to Steal a Million, 1966, The Bible... in the Beginning, 1966, The Night of the Generals, 1967, Great Catherine, 1968, The Lion in Winter, 1968, Goodbye Mr. Chips, 1969, Murphy's War, 1971, Under Milk Wood, 1971, Brotherly Love, The Ruling Class, 1972, Man of LaMancha, 1972, Rosebud, 1975, Man Friday, 1975, Foxtrot, 1976, Coup d'Etat, 1977, Zulu Dawn, 1978, Power Play, 1978, Caligula, 1979, The Stuntman, 1980, The Antagonists, 1981, My Favorite Year, 1982, Supergirl, 1984, Creator, 1985, Club Paradise, 1985, The Last Emperor, 1987, High Spirits, 1988, On a Moonlit Night, 1989, Helena, Wings of Fame, 1990, The Nutcracker Prince (voice), 1990, The Rainbow Thief, 1990, King Ralph, 1991, Rebecca's Daughters, 1992, The Seventh Coin, 1993, Fairy Tale: A True Story, 1997, Phantoms, 1997, Illumination, 1997, The Manner, 1999, Molokai: the Story of Father Damien, 1999, Global Heresy, 2002, The Final Curtain, 2002, Bright Young Things, 2003, Troy, 2004, Ratatouille (voice), 2007, Stardust, 2007, Dean Spanley, 2008; (TV films) Rogue Male, 1976, Strumpet City, 1979, Svengali, 1982, Man and Superman, 1982, Pygmalion, 1983, Kim, 1983, The Dark Angel, 1987, Crossing to Freedom, 1990, Civvies, 1992, Heavy Weather, 1995, Gulliver's Travels, 1996; TV series Heavy Weather, 1995, Coming Home, 1998, Joan of Arc, 1999, The John Thaw Story, 2002, Hitler: The Rise of Evil, 2003, Imperium: Augustus, 2003; Troy, 2004, One Night with the King, 2005; (TV series) The Tudors, 2008-, Iron Road, 2009; TV mini-series Masada, 1981, Heaven & Hell: North and South, Book III, 1994, Heim Kehr, 1998; acted, dir., prodr. Jeffrey Bernard Is Unwell, 1997; Author: Loitering with Intent (autobiography), 1993. Decorated Comdr. des Arts et des Lettres, 1988, Laurence Olivier Theatre award, 2000, Honorary Academy award, 2003. Died Dec. 14, 2013.

**OTREMBA, MARY ELLEN,** former state legislator; b. Bertha, Minn., Sept. 26, 1950; m. Ken Otemba (dec. Sept. 4, 1997); 4 children. BA in Home & Cmty. Svc., Coll. St. Benedict; MA in Child & Family Studies, St. Cloud St. U., Minn. Nutritionist Todd County Dept. Public Health, 1984—89; tchr. Freshwater Educational Dist., 1986—89, Eagle Valley High Sch., 1989—94; mem. Dist. 11B Minn. House of Reps., 1999—2011, asst. minority leader, 2001—04. Dfl. Roman Catholic. Home: Long Prairie, Minn. Died July 16, 2014.

**OTTINGER, GUY EMEREL,** accountant; b. Lakeland, Fla., Mar. 24, 1921; s. Isaac and Hattie Irene (Neas) O.; m. Vivian Hampton, Aug. 12, 1947; children: David J., Lois I. Ottinger Gonzalez. BSBA, U. Fla., 1942. CPA, Fla. With various acctg. firms, Lakeland, Fla., 1946-58; pvt. practice pub. acctg. Lakeland, Fla., from 1959. Mem. Salvation Army, 1967—, past adv. chmn.chmn. bd. and treas. Capt. U.S. Army, 1942-52, col. USAR, ret. 1975. Mem. AICPAs, Fla. Soc. CPAs, Lakeland Area C. of C., Kiwanis Club of Lakeland. Republican. Lutheran. Avocation: lapidarist. Home: Lakeland, Fla. Died Dec. 6, 1999.

**OVERMAN, DENNIS ORTON,** anatomist, educator; b. Union City, Ind., Oct. 16, 1943; s. E. Orton and Marjorie J. (Mills) O.; m. Sue A. Sappenfield, June 4, 1966; children: Andrew D., Michael M., Amy S. BA, Bowling Green State U., 1965; MS, U. Mich., 1967, PhD, 1970. Tchr. Community Sch., Tehran, Iran, 1967-68; rsch. assoc. U. Colo., Boulder, 1970-71; from instr. to assoc. prof. anatomy W.Va. U., Morgantown, 1971-76, prof., from 1999, clin. prof. orthodontics, from 1985. Vis. lectr. U. B.C., Vancouver, Can., 1979; vis. rschr. U. Turku, Finland, 1993, 96. Author: (book chpt.) Bioethics and the Beginning of Life, 1990; editor: English transl. of Japanese textbook; mem. abstract com. Cleft Palate Jour., 1976—; contbr. articles to profl. jours. Mem. Soc. for Devel. Biology, Teratology Soc., Toastmasters Internat., Rotary Internat. Democrat. Mem. Mennonite Ch. Avocations: woodcarving, pottery. Died Jan. 3, 2000.

**OVERSETH, OLIVER ENOCH,** physicist, researcher; b. NYC, May 11, 1928; s. Oliver Enoch and Ione (Johnson) O.; m. Anneke deBruyn, Aug. 28, 1954 (divorced); children— Alison, Tenley. BS, U. Chgo., 1953; PhD, Brown U., 1958. Instr. physics Princeton, 1957-60; mem. faculty U. Mich., Ann Arbor, from 1961, prof. physics, from 1968; assoc. physicist Cern, Geneva, from 1983. Died July 17, 2008.

**OWEN, EARL,** microsurgeon, surgical research center director; b. Sydney, 1934; married; 4 children. Grad., Sydney U. Postgrad. study, England, Great Ormond St Hosp. for Sick Children, London; med. dir. Microsearch Found. Australia (includes the Inst. of Medicine of both the Univ. and Internat. Coll. Surgeons and Sydney Microsurgery Centre (relocated in 1997), Lane Cove, Sydney; assoc. prof. Macquarie U., Sydney. Mem.: Internat. Coll. Surgeons (World pres. 1996). Achievements include Best known as the father of microsurgery and vasectomy reversal; designed micro instruments. microscopes and new operations to save congenitally abnormal babies from dying at birth in the 1960's; set-up in one of Sydney's Major University Hospitals the world's first microsurgery reconstruction center in 1970; first surgeon to sew back a child's finger in 1970; first to perform micro-reversal of a vasectomy in 1971; first successful micro-reversal of a women's tubal sterilisation in

1972; led the first hand transplant team in Lyon France, September, 1998; co-leader of the team that performed the world's first double hand transplantation in Lyon, France, January, 2000; taught and lectured about microsurgery to thousands of surgeons throughout the world; developed a laser/solder fusion technique makes clips or tiny stitches of microsurgery obsolete; invented the special pen-holder grip instruments that makes extremely delicate work possible; designed an ergonomic operating chair. Avocation: music. Died June 3, 2014.

**OWEN, WILLIAM FREDERICK,** engineering and management consultant; b. Pontiac, Mich., July 27, 1947; s. Webster Jennings and Elizabeth (Hayes) W.; m. Delores T. Owen, Mar. 30, 1974 (div. Dec. 1978); m. Janice L. Pierce, July 29, 1983. BS, Mich. Tech. U., 1972; MS, U. Mich., 1973; PhD, Stanford U., 1978. Research engr. Neptune Microfloc, Corvallis, Oreg., 1973-75, process applications engr., 1975-76, Dr. Perry McCarty, Stanford, Calif., 1976-78; sr. engr. Culp/Wesner/Culp, Cameron Park, Calif., 1978-82; pres. Owen Engring. and Mgmt. Cos., Denver, 1982—98. Author: Energy in Wastewater Treatment, 1982, Turbo Mainenance Manager. Del. People-to-People, People's Republic China, 1986. Served with USN, 1965-68. Recipient Local Govt. Innovations award Denver Regional Council Govt., 1983, Boettcher Innovations award Denver Regional Council Govt., 1984, Energy Innovations award Colo. Council Energy Ofcls., 1983. Mem.: Pinehurst Country (Denver). Avocations: tennis, golf, downhill skiing. Died 1998.

**OWENS, MAJOR ROBERT ODELL,** former United States Representative from New York; b. Memphis, June 28, 1936; s. Ezekiel & Edna Owens; m. Ethel Werfel, 1956 (div.); children: Christopher, Geoffrey, Millard; m. Maria Cuprill; stepchildren: Carlos, Cecilia BA with high honors in Math., Morehouse Coll., Atlanta, 1956; MLS, Atlanta U., 1957; grad. student, Columbia U. V.p. Metropolitan Coun. Housing, 1964; chair Bklyn. Congress of Racial Equality, 1964—66; cmty. coord. Bklyn. Public Libr., 1964—66; exec. dir. Brownsville Cmty. Coun., 1966—68; commr. NYC Cmty. Devel. Agy., 1968—73; dir. cmty. media libr. prog. Columbia U., 1973—75; mem. Dist. 17 NY State Senate, 1974—82; mem. US Congress from 12th NY Dist., 1983—93, US Congress from 11th NY Dist., 1993—2007; sr. fellow DuBois- Bunche Ctr. Medgar Evers Coll., Bklyn, NY, 2007—13. Mem. Internat. Commn. on Ways of Implementing Social Policy to Ensure Maximum Pub. Participation and Social Justice for Minorities, The Hague, Netherlands, 1972; keynote speaker White House Conf. on Libraries, 1979. Public author and lectr. on libr. sci. Chmn. Democratic Ops. Com. Major R. Owens Day named in his honor, City Bklyn., 1971; named one of The Most Influential Black Americans, Ebony mag., 2006. Mem.: ALA, NAACP. Democrat. Baptist. Home: Brooklyn, NY. Died Oct. 21, 2013.

**OXNER, GEORGE DEWEY, JR.,** lawyer; b. Greenville, SC, Dec. 31, 1933; s. George Dewey and Frances (Ruckman) O.; m. Louise Earle, Sept. 16, 1960(dec. July 7, 2013); children: Frances, Dewey, Earle. BA, Washington & Lee U., 1956; LLB, U. S.C., 1959. Bar: S.C. 1959, U.S. Dist. Ct. S.C. 1959, U.S. Ct. Appeals (4th cir.) 1959. From assoc. to mng. ptnr. Haynsworth, Marion, McKay & Guerard, Greenville, 1959-98, ptnr., from 1998. Co-chair Chief Justice's Commn. on the Profession. Fellow Am. Coll. Trial Lawyers (state chair 1994), SC Def. Trial Attys. Assn. (pres. 1976), SC Bar Assn. (sec. 1997-98, treas. 1998—), Assn. (sec. 1997-98, treas. 1998-99, pres. elect, 1999-00, pres. 2000-01), Am. Bd. Trial Advs. (pres. 1990-91, pres. SC, 1990-91) Home: Greenville, SC. Died July 7, 2013.

**OZANICH, RUTH SHULTZ,** artist, poet, retired elementary school educator; b. Calif., Feb. 12, 1915; d. Charles Andrew Shultz and Martha Viola Boring; m. Anton M. Ozanich, Nov. 1931; children: Antom M., Saralen Elaine, Marc Charles Dee. BEd, Fresno State U., Calif., 1956. Life cert. tchr. credential, Calif. Tchr. Beardsley Elem. Sch., Oildale, Calif., 1954-65, Sierra Vista Elem. Sch., Arvin, Calif., 1965-70; ret., 1970. Exhibited in group shows Bakersfield Art Assn. Gallery, Cunningham Gallery, Bakersfield, Kern County Fair, Calif. (numerous blue ribbons); contbr. poetry to anthologies. Elder Paiute Coun., Lake Isabella Calif.; treas. Mexican Am. Srs. Mem. Internat. Poetry Hall of Fame (life), Calif. Tchrs. Assn., Kern River Valley Poets and Writers Club (founder, past pres.), Bakersfield Art Assn. (founder, past treas.), Ladies Moose. Avocations: arts and crafts, reading, poetry, writing. Home: Kent, Ohio. Died Feb. 23, 2008.

**PABST, ALFRED MARK,** lawyer; b. Albia, Iowa, Mar. 8, 1908; s. Mark Dell and Myrtle Dora (Hilliard) Pabst; m. Mary Aileen Jenkins, June 28, 1932; children: Janis Aileen Pabst Boenker, Mark Dell, John Alfred. LLB, U. Iowa, 1930. Bar: Iowa 1930. Pvt. practice, Albia, 1930—72; ptnr. Pabst & Pabst, Albia, Iowa, from 1972. Fellow: Am. Bar Found.; mem.: ABA, 8th Jud. Dist. Iowa Bar Assn. (pres. 1942), Iowa Bar Assn. (gov. 1964—68, pres. 1971, advisor to bd. govs. from 1972, Merit award 1981). Home: Albia, Iowa. Died June 1, 1989.

**PACE, O(LE) B(LY), JR.,** lawyer; b. Wellington, Ill., Mar. 10, 1915; s. Ole Bly and Ruth A. (Parrish) P.; m. Loey Ann Patterson, Aug. 22, 1937; children: Ole B. III, Steven P., Ann. BS, Ill. Wesleyan U., 1936; LLB, U. Ill., 1939. Bar: Ill. 1939. Asst. state's atty. Marshall County, Ill., 1946-48, 64-68, state's atty. Ill., 1948-64; asst. atty. gen. State of Ill., Springfield, 1968-72; sr. ptnr. Pace and Paolucci, Lacon, Ill., 1966-74, Pace and McCuskey, Lacon, 1977-81, Pace, McCuskey & Galley, Lacon, 1981—93. Bd. dirs. First Nat. Bank Lacon. Adv. bd. St. Francis of Assisi and St. Joseph Nursing Home, Lacon, 1962-93, also pres.; trustee Ill. Wesleyan U., 1962-86. Served to lt. USNR, 1942-45. Mem. Am. Legion (comdr. 1946-47), Phi Delta Phi. Lodges: Masons, Rotary (local pres. 1957-58). Republican. Methodist. Died Jan. 9, 1993.

**PAEK, NAM SUN,** North Korean government official; b. Kilchu, North Hamgyong Province, North Korea, Mar. 13, 1929; Grad., Kim Sung-Il U. Dep. dir. Workers Party Internat. Dept., 1968—74; vice chair Com. for Cultural Relations with Foreign Countries, 1972; adv. mem. Red Cross Ctr. Com., 1972—74; amb. Poland, 1974—79; dep. dir. Workers' Party Propaganda Dept., 1979; sec. gen. Com. for Peaceful Reunification of the Fatherland; pres. Sci. encyclopedia gen. publ., 1988; 9-11 period rep. The Supreme People's Assembly (SPA), 1990; bur. chief Standardized Com. Clerk, 1991; polit. sectional chmn., 1992—93; mem. The Supreme People's Assembly (SPA), from 1993; min. fgn. affairs Govt. of N. Korea, Pyongyang, 1998—2007. Died Jan. 3, 2007.

**PAIGE, RICHARD E.,** inventor; b. NYC, Dec. 30, 1904; s. Louis and Florence (Elias) Paige; m. Evelyn Kitz, Apr. 26, 1931. Student, Voltaire Sch. Music, Grand Central Sch. Art. Salesman Reproduction Products, Bklyn., 1929—31; idea man, constrn. expert Display Finishing Co., LI, NY, 1931, v.p., 1936—40; founder Richard E. Paige Co., NYC, 1940, Paige Tng. Aids, 1944, Paige Lab., 1946, Paige Co., 1948, Paige Co. Internat; with Hallmark Cards, Inc., 1960—70. Chmn. bd. Paper Products Devel. Corp., from 1964; rschr. steel foil Bethlehem Steel Co., 1964—65; tech. cons. Procter & Gamble Co., Ivorydale Tech. Ctr., 1970; lectr. in field. Author: Complete Guide to Making Money with Your Ideas and Inventions, The Science of Creating Ideas for Industry, Little Inventions that made Big Money, 1982, Lines to Remember, SIMPLICITY The Key to Successful Inventions, 1986; contbr. articles to propular mags.; musician: Radio Sta. WHN, Band of a Thousand Melodies; composer: in field; exhibitions include Pratt Inst. Recipient Bronze Plaque, Advertising Club of Greater Providence C. of C., 1956, Top Design award, Design Mag.; named to Packaging Hall of Fame, 1975. Mem.: Point of Purchase Advt. Inst., Inventors Workshop Internat. (hon.; guest lectr.), Advertising Club (NYC). Achievements include patents in field; invention of instructional sighting device; development of can carriers, corrugated floor display stands. Home: New York, NY. Died Aug. 15, 1988.

**PAINTER, TERENCE JOHN,** retired biochemist, researcher; b. Dartford, Kent, Eng., Aug. 10, 1933; arrived in Norway, 1967; s. Arthur Harold and Florence (Jones) P. BS, Bristol U., Eng., 1954; MA, Queens Coll., Kingston, Can., 1956, PhD, 1957; D in Tech., Norwegian U. Sci. and Tech., 1981. Hibbert meml. fellow McGill U., Montreal, 1957-58; asst. rsch. officer Nat Rsch. Coun., Halifax, 1958-60; rsch. stipendiate Lister Inst., London, 1960-65; lectr. Royal Free Hosp. Med. Sch., London, 1965-67; rsch. fellow Swiss Fed. Inst. Tech., Zürich, 1967-68; prof. Norwegian Inst. Tech., Trondheim, 1968-2000, prof. emeritus, from 2000. Referee Royal Soc. Chemistry, London, 1960-67, Acta Chemica Scandinavica, Stockholm, 1968—, Can. Jour. Chemistry, Ottawa, 1968—, Elsevier Sci. Pub., Amsterdam, 1970-93; cons. Internat. Found. for Sci., Stockholm, 1987—, NSF, Washington, 1985—, UNIDO, Vienna, 1986, UNFAO, Rome, 1960-68; plenary lectr. Internat. Carbohydrate Orgn., Vancouver, Can., 1982, UNIDO, Trieste, Italy, 1986. Author: The Polysaccharides, 1983; contbr. articles to profl. jours. including Jour. of the Chem. Soc., Acta Chemica Scandinavica, among others. Recipient Outstanding Rsch. award Norwegian Rsch. Coun., 1992. Mem. Royal Norwegian Soc. for Scis. and Letters, Norwegian Chem. Soc., Norwegian Biochem. Soc. Mem. Conservative Party. Roman Catholic. Avocations: music, palaeontology, archaeology. Deceased.

**PAISLEY, IAN RICHARD KYLE,** Northern Ireland political leader, clergyman; b. Armagh, Northern Ireland, Apr. 6, 1926; s. James Kyle and Isabella Paisley; m. Eileen Emily Cassells, Oct. 13, 1956; children: Sharon, Rhonda, Cherith, Kyle, Ian. Student, South Wales Bible Coll., Ref. Presbyn. Theol. Coll., Belfast, Northen Ireland; DD (hon.), Bob Jones U., Greenville, SC, 1966. Ordained to ministry 1946. Co-founder, leader Democratic Unionist Party, 1951—2008; co-founder Free Presbyn. Ch., 1951; founder Ulster Democratic Unionist Party, 1971; first min. Northern Ireland Assembly, 2007—08. Min. Martyrs' Meml. Free Presbyn. Ch.; moderator Free Presbyn. Ch. of Ulster, 1951—2007; mem. Northern Ireland Parliament, 1970—2010, leader of opposition, 1972; mem. Westminster Parliament, North Antrim, 1970—2010, Northern Ireland Assembly, 1973—74, 1982—86, 1998—2003, European Parliament, Northern Ireland, 1979—2004; founder, pres. Whitefield Coll. of the Bible, 1981; mem. Northern Ireland Forum for Polit. Dialogue, 1996—98. Author: History of the 1859 Revival, 1959, Christian Foundations, 1960, Ravenhill Pulpit, Vol. I, 1966, Vol. II, 1967, Exposition of the Epistle to the Romans, 1968, Billy Graham and the Church of Rome, 1970, The Massacre of Saint Bartholomew, 1972, Paisley, The Man and His Message, 1976, America's Debt to Ulster, 1976, The Life of Dr. James Kidd, 1982, Those Flaming Tenants, 1983, Be Sure, 1987, Jonathan Edwards: Theologian of Revival, 1987, What a Friend We Have in Jesus, 1994, Understanding Events in Northern Ireland: An Introduction for Americans, 1995; editor: Revivalist, Protestant Telegraph, Protestant Blueprint; contbr. article to profl. jours. Patron Margaret Newton Meml. Protestant Victims Fund. Fellow Royal Geog. Soc.; mem. Internat. Cultural Soc. Korea. Democratic Unionist Party. Free Presbyterian. Avocation: reading. Died Sept. 12, 2014.

**PAKARINEN, TERTTU,** professor emeritus; b. Mänty-harju, Finland, July 22, 1946; MSc, U. Tech., Otaniemi, 1974; Dr.Tech., Tampere U. Tech., Finland, 1985. Rsch. asst. Tampere U., Finland, 1974—76, lectr., 1977—78; planner; prof. Sch. Arch., 1997—2011; prof. emeritus, faculty built environ. Tampere U. Tech., 2010. Home: Tampere, Finland. Deceased.

**PALKOVITZ, HERBERT,** lawyer; b. McKeesport, Pa., Dec. 1, 1942; BA, Washington & Jefferson Coll., 1964; JD, Cleve. U., 1968. Bar: Ohio 1969, U.S. Dist. Ct. (no. dist.) Ohio 1970, U.S. Supreme Ct. 1972, U.S. Ct. Appeals (6th cir.) 1982. Pvt. practice, Cleve., from 1969. Mem. alt. dispute com. Ohio Supreme Ct., Columbus. Chmn. mediation adv. bd. Jewish Family Svc. Assn., Cleve. Fellow Internat. Acad. Matrimonial Lawyers, Am. Acad. Matrimonial Lawyers (pres. Ohio chpt., bd. govs. 1990—); mem. ABA, Cleve. Bar Assn. (chair family law sect.), Cuyahoga County Bar Assn. (chair family law sect.). Home: Cleveland, Ohio. Died Apr. 5, 2008.

**PALMER, GEORGE E.,** lawyer; b. Washington, Ind., Feb. 3, 1908; s. Milford N. and Katherine (Sanford) P.; m. Ruth Isabel Hamersly, July 7, 1935; children— Julia Palmer Gzella, Steven Sanford, Katherine Ann. AB, U. Mich., 1930, JD, 1932; LL.M., Columbia U., NYC, 1940. Bar: Ind. bar 1932. Practiced in, Indpls., 1932-39; asst., then asso. prof. law U. Kans., Lawrence, 1940-46; atty. and asso. gen. counsel OPA, 1942-45; atty. Dept. Justice, 1945; mem. faculty U. Mich. Law Sch., from 1946, prof. law, 1951-78, prof. emeritus, from 1978. Vis. prof. Stanford U., U. Chgo., UCLA, U. Tex., U. Calif. Hastings Coll. Law, U. Fla.; lectr. Ohio Law Forum, 1961 Author: (with J.P. Dawson) Cases on Restitution, 2d edit, 1969, Mistake and Unjust Enrichment, 1962, Cases on Trusts and Succession, 2d edit, 1968, Law of Restitution, 1978. Mem. Order of Coif. Democrat. Home: Naperville, Ill. Died 1994.

**PALMER, MICHAEL STEPHEN,** writer, medical association administrator; b. Springfield, Mass., Oct. 9, 1942; s. Milton and May Palmer; children: Matthew, Daniel, Luke. BS, Wesleyan U., Middletown, Conn., 1964; MD, Case Western Res. U., Cleve., 1968. Diplomate American Bd. Internal Medicine. Intern internal medicine Boston City Hosp., 1968—69, resident, 1971—72; resident internal medicine Mass. Gen. Hosp., 1972—73; assoc. dir. physician health svcs. Mass. Med. Soc., 1982—2013. Clin. instr. medicine Tufts U., Medford, Mass. Author: (novels) The Sisterhood, 1982, Side Effects, 1985, Flashback, 1988, Extreme Measures, 1991, Natural Causes, 1994, Silent Treatment, 1995, Critical Judgment, 1996, Miracle Cure, 1998, The Patient, 2000, Fatal, 2002, The Society, 2004, The Fifth Vial, 2007, The First Patient, 2008, The Second Opinion, 2009, The Last Surgeon, 2010, A Heartbeat Away, 2011, Oath of Office, 2012, Political Suicide, 2013, Resistant, 2014. Died Oct. 30, 2013.

**PANGELINAN, VICENTE CABRERA (BEN PANGELINAN),** territorial legislator; b. Saipan, Aug. 24, 1962; Attended, Acad. Our Lady of Guam; BA, Georgetown U. Staff asst. to Rep. Antonio B. WonPat US House of Reps.; senator Guam Legislature, Barrigada Dist., 2007—14. V.p. Fifth Wheel, Inc., Graphic Ctr., Inc. Henry Toll Fellow, 1997, Pacific America Found Fellow, 1998. Democrat. Died July 8, 2014.

**PANKHURST, EMMELINE,** civil rights advocate; b. Manchester, Eng., July 14, 1858; m. Richard Pankhurst, 1879. Founder Women's Social and Polit. Union, 1903. Advocate, spkr. on women's suffrage. Imprisoned 12 times for suffrage activities in 1912 under Cat & Mouse Act in England. Died June 14, 1928.

**PANNENBERG, WOLFHART,** systematic theology educator; b. Stettin, Poland, Oct. 2, 1928; s. Kurt Bernhard Siegfried and Irmgard Pannenberg; m. Hilke Sabine Schütte, May 3, 1954. ThD, Heidelberg U., Germany, 1953; DD (hon.), U. Glasgow, Scotland, 1972, U. Manchester, UK, 1977, Trinity Coll. Dublin, 1979, U. St. Andrews, Scotland, 1993, U. Cambridge, 1997, U. Commillas, Madrid, 1999. Privatdozent U. Heidelberg, 1955-58; prof. systematic theology U. Wuppertal (Fed. Republic Germany), 1958-61, U. Mainz (Fed. Republic Germany), 1961-67; prof. systematic theology, head ecumenical inst. U. Munich, 1967-94. Mem. Bavarian Acad. Sciences, Brit. Acad. Avocations: history, music, philosophy. Home: Gräfelfing, Germany. Died Sept. 5, 2014.

**PAPADIAS, BASIL C.,** education educator; b. Volos, Thessaly, Greece, Sept. 18, 1932; s. Constantinos B. and Pelagia C. (Kalozakis) P.; m. Vassiliki B. Klotsas, July 10, 1965; children: Constantinos, Alexandros. Mech.-Elec. Engr., Nat. Tech. U., Athens, 1956, D Engring., 1969; MEE, Rensselaer Polytechnic Inst., 1972, D Engring., 1975. Elec. engr. Pub. Power Corp., Athens, 1959-68, head rsch. sect., 1968-71, tech. cons., from 1976; rschr. RPI, Troy, 1971-73, head of system studies Athens, 1973-76; prof. elec. engring. dep. Nat. Tech. U., Athens, from 1976. Author: (text books) Transmission Lines of Electric Energy, 1985, Analysis of Electric Energy Systems, Vol. I and II, 1985, Transient Phenomena in Electric Power Systems, 1997; author/coauthor articles in profl. jours. and publs. Fellow IEEE; mem. Nat. Acad. Scis. of N.Y., Tech. Chamber of Greece. Avocations: country hiking, classical music, cinema. Home: Athens, Greece. Died Apr. 4, 2002.

**PARDO, DON (DOMINICK GEORGE PARDO),** retired broadcasting announcer; b. Westfield, Mass., Feb. 22, 1918; s. Dominik J. and Waleria (Romaniak) P.; m. Catherine A. Lyons, Aug. 22, 1939 (dec. July 8, 1995); children: Paula Kay, Dona Marie, Michael D., David J., Katherine A. Student, Emerson Coll., 1942. Announcer Sta. WJAR, 1942-44. Actor, 20th Century Players, Sta. WJAR, Providence, 1938-40; announcer radio and TV, NBC, N.Y.C., 1944—2004; announcer: (radio shows) Pepper Young's Family, The Doctors, The Magnificent Montague, 1950-51,;

(TV shows) The Colgate Comedy Hour, 1951, Ford 50th Anniversary Show, 1953 (Sylvania TV award), Fred Allen's Judge for Yourself, Martha Raye Shows, 1953-58, Arthur Murray Party, Four Star Revue, Colgate Comedy Hour, Kate Smith Hour, Show of Shows, Caesar's Hour, Jonathan Winters Show; TV game shows Winner Take All, 1950, Price is Right, 1956-63, Jeopardy, 1964-75, Saturday Night Live, 1975-81, 1983-2014; actor: (films) Radio Days, 1987, Honeymoon in Vegas, 1992, Stay Tuned, 1992 Named to The RI Radio Hall of Fame, 2009, The Acad. Television Arts & Sciences Hall of Fame, 2010. Died Aug. 18, 2014.

**PAREDES, JAMES ANTHONY,** anthropologist; b. NYC, Sept. 29, 1939; s. Antonio Paredes Piñeiro and Mildred Olene (Brown) P.; m. Anna Hamilton, Nov. 25, 1959 (div. 1984); children: J. Anthony Jr., Anna Teresa P. Lesinski, Sara Caroline P. Campbell; m. Elizabeth Dixon Purdum, Aug. 10, 1985 (div. 1994): 1 stepchild, David Joseph Plante; m. Alleen Dimitroff Deutsch, July 24, 2003. BA, Oglethorpe U., 1961; MA, U. N.Mex., 1964, PhD, 1969. Rsch. coord. Upper Miss. Mental Health Ctr., Bemidji, Minn., 1964-67; asst. prof., acting dir. Am. Ind. Studies Bemidji State Coll., 1967-68; community devel. specialist U. Minn. Agrl. Extension Svc., Bemidji, 1967-68; asst. prof. dept. anthropology Fla. State U., Tallahassee, 1969-74, assoc. prof., 1974-78, prof., 1979-99, emeritus prof., from 1999, chmn. dept., 1974-77, 84-90; chief ethnography and Indian affairs S.E. regional office Nat. Park Service, Atlanta, 1999—2006. Adj. prof. dept. anthropology U. Fla., Gainesville, 1979-2004; cons. Nat. Marine Fisheries Svc., Galveston, Tex., 1987-88, Bur. Indian Affairs, Washington, 1985, 92, Fed. Recognition Panel, Assn. on Am. Indian Affairs, N.Y.C., 1987-88. Author: Indios de los Estados Unidos Anglosajones, 1992; editor: Anishinabe: Six Studies of Modern Chippewa, 1980, Indians of the Southeastern United States in the Late 20th Century, 1992; co-editor: Classics of Practicing Anthropology: 1978-1998, 2000; co-editor: Anthropologists and Indians in the New South, 2001, Red Eagle's Children: Weatherford vs. Weatherford et al., 2012; founding series editor: Contemporary American Indian Studies, U. Ala. Press.; author or co-author numerous articles, chpts. in books, revs. Mem. Sci. and Statis. Com., Gulf of Mex. Fishery Mgmt. Coun., Tampa, Fla., 1978-88. Recipient svc. award Poarch Creek Indians, 1990, Woodrow Wilson Found. fellow U. N.Mex., 1961-62; Nat. Inst. Mental Health predoctoral fellow U. N.Mex., 1968-69; Rockefeller Ctr. for Study of So. Culture and Religion fellow, Fla. State U., 1978. Fellow: Soc. for Applied Anthropology (assoc. editor 1983—88, pres. 1993—95), Am. Anthrop. Assn. (exec. bd. 2004—07); mem.: Assn. Sr. Anthropologists (pres. 2008—10), Fla. Acad. Scis. (sect. chair 1984—85), So. Anthrop. Soc. (pres. 1988—89), Sigma Xi (Fla. State U. chpt. pres. 1977—78). Democrat. Avocation: walking. Home: Atlanta, Ga. Died Aug. 24, 2013.

**PARENT, GILBERT,** retired Canadian legislator; b. Mattawa, Ont., Can., July 25, 1935; children: Michèle Hundertmark, Monique Finley, Madeleine Thomas, Thérèse Perruzza. BSc, St. Joseph's Coll., LLD (hon.), 1995; MA, Niagara U.; MEd, U. N.Y.; LLD (hon.), Niagara U., 1995, Brock U., 1996. Mem. Ho. of Commons, Ottawa, 1974—84, 1988—2000, Speaker, 1994—2001; parliamentary sec. to min. veterans affairs Govt. of Can., Ottawa, Ont., Canada, 1977-79, parliamentary sec. to min. labour, 1979-81, parliamentary sec. to min. fitness & amateur sports, 1981-83. Appted. Critic for Youth, 1989, Labour, 1992; assoc. critic CIDA, 1989, Industry, 1992. Mem. Parliament for Niagara Ctr. (formerly the Riding of Welland - St. Catharines - Thorold). Mem. Can.-U.S. Parliamentary Assn. (vice-chair). Died Mar. 3, 2009.

**PARK, BARBARA LYNNE,** writer; b. Mt. Holly, NJ, Apr. 27, 1947; d. Doris and Brooke Tidswell; m. Richard A. Park, 1969; children: Steven, David. Attended, Rider Coll., 1965—67; BS in History & Political Sci., U. Ala., 1969. Author: (children's books) Don't Make Me Smile, 1981, Operation: Dump the Chump, 1982 (Tennessee Children's Choice Book award, 1986), Skinnybones, 1982, Beanpole, 1983, Buddies, 1985 (Parents' Choice award, 1985), Kid in the Red Jacket, 1987 (Library of Congress Book of the Yr., 1987), Almost Starring Skinnybones, 1988, Mother Got Married: and Other Disasters, 1989, Rosie Swanson, 1991, Junie B. Jones and the Stupid Smelly Bus, 1992, Junie B. Jones and Her Big Fat Mouth, 1993, Junie B. Jones and a Little Monkey Business, 1993, Junie B. Jones and Some Sneaky Peeky Spying, 1994, Mick Harte Was Here, 1995, Junie B. Jones and the Yucky Blucky Fruitcake, 1995, B. Jones Loves Handsome Warren, 1996, Junie B. Jones and that Meanie Jim's Birthday, 1996, Junie B. Jones Loves Handsome Warren, 1996, Junie B. Jones has a Monster Under Her Bed, 1997, Junie B. Jones is Not a Crook, 1997, Junie B. Jones is a Party Animal, 1997, Junie B. Jones is a Beauty Shop Guy, 1998, Psst! It's Me...the Bogeyman, 1998;: Junie B. Jones Smells Something Fishy, 1998, Junie B. Jones is Almost a Flower Girl, 1999, Junie B. Jones and the Mushy Gushy Valentine, 1999, Junie B. Jones has a Peep in her Pocket, 2000, Junie B. Jones is Captain Field Day, 2001, Junie B. Jones is a Graduation Girl, 2001, Junie B. Jones: First Grader (at Last!), 2001, Junie B., First Grader: Boss of Lunch, 2002, Junie B., First Grader: Toothless Wonder, 2002, Top Secret, Personal Beeswax: A Journal by Junie B., 2003, Junie B., First Grader: Cheater Pants, 2003, Junie B., First Grader: One-Man Band, 2003, Junie B., 1st Grader: Shipwrecked, 2004, Junie B., First Grader: Boo...and I MEAN it!, 2004, Junie B., First Grader: Jingle Bells, Batman Smells! (P.S. so does May), 2005, Junie B., First Grader: Aloha-ha-ha!, 2006, Junie B., First Grader: Dumb Bunny, 2007, Junie B., First Grader: Turkeys We Have Loved and Eaten (And Other Thankful Stuff), 2012. Recipient Young Hoosier award, 1985, Milner award, 1986. Died Nov. 15, 2013.

**PARKER, CAMILLE KILLIAN,** physician, surgeon; b. Columbus, Ohio, June 28, 1918; d. John Vincent and Myrtle (Kagy) Hill; m. E.W. Killian, Apr. 25, 1943 (dec.); children— Paul Wesley, Clyde Bernard; m. Francis W. Parker, Dec. 7, 1958 Student, U. Chgo., 1942-43; BS, U. Ill., 1945; MD, 1946; postgrad. in ophthalmology, Northwestern U., 1947-48. Diplomate Am. Bd. Ophthalmology. Intern Wesley Meml. Hosp., Chgo., 1946-47; resident in ophthalmology Ill. Eye and Ear Infirmary, Chgo., 1949-51; practice medicine specializing in med. and surg. ophthalmology Logansport, Ind., from 1951; sec. staff Meml. Hosp., Logansport, 1959; pres. med. staff St. Joseph Hosp., Logansport, 1965. Pres., Logansport Council for Pub. Schs., 1961,62; mem. Lake Maxinkuckee Mgmt. Com., Culver, Ind., 1981—; chmn. social concern Meth. Ch., 1963-65, ofcl. bd., 1961-65 Recipient Service award Culver Mil. Acad., 1969 Fellow Am. Acad. Ophthalmology and Otolaryngology; mem. AMA (physicians recognition award 1971, 75, 79, 82, 85, 88, 93, 94, 97), Soc. Eye Surgeons (charter), Logansport C. of C., Cass County Med. Soc. (pres. 1971), Ind. State Med. Assn., Ind. Acad. Ophthalmology and Otolaryngology (pres. 1979-80). Clubs: Altrusa (v.p. 1967-69), Culver Mothers (pres. 1968-69). Republican. Deceased.

**PARKER, CLEA EDWARD,** retired academic administrator; b. Talisheek, La., Apr. 2, 1927; s. William A. and Lutritia (Davis) P.; m. Peggy Ann Faciane, June 21, 1953; children: Brian, Stephen, Karen, Robin. BA, Southeastern La. U., 1948; M.Ed., La. State U., 1952, Ed.D., 1965. Coach, tchr. Rugby Acad., New Orleans, 1948-50; tchr., prin., supr. instr., dir. curriculum and instrn. St. Tammany Parish Sch. Bd., 1950-67; prof. edn., head dept. student teaching Nicholls State Coll., Thibodaux, La., 1967-68; acting pres. Southeastern La. U., Hammond, 1968, pres., 1968-80, pres. emeritus, 1980—86. Liaison La. State Dept. Edn., Higher Edn. and Bds. for Edn. in La., 1986; vis. lectr. La. State U. at NC, 1965-69; past pres. St. Tammany Parish Tchrs. Assn., La. Assn. Supervision and Curriculum Devel.; past pres. elementary dept. La. Tchrs. Assn.; chmn. Pres.'s Coun. La. Bd. Edn., 1972-73; v.p. Conf. La. Colls. and Univs., 1973-74, pres., 1974-75; pres. elect Gulf South Conf., 1974-75, pres., 1975-76; mem. Steering Com. on Curriculum Devel. and Revision for Career Edn. for State La., 1973; mem. adv. council for State Plan for Career Edn., 1973 Mem. planning com. Governor's Conf. on Aging, 1976; v.p. chpt. 15 La. Good Samaritans, 1987-88; bd. dirs. Assn. for Retarded Citizens, pres.-elect, 1981; mem. Zemurray Park Recreation Commn., Hammond, 1992-95; chmn. bd. dirs. Lallie Kemp Meml. Hosp., 1993-94; bd. dirs. Lallie Kemp Med. Ctr., 1994—, chmn., 1994-95. With USCGR, 1945, 93-94. Named Hon. State Farmer La., 1970, Disting. Alumnus of Yr., Southeastern La. U. Alumni Assn., 1977, 91, 92; inductee La. Spl. Olympics Hall of Fame, 1998. Mem. American Assn. State Colleges & Universities (com. on nat. svc. 1972-73, task force on aging 1975-76, 78-79, com. agr. renewable resources and rural devel. 1979-80, Svc. to Edn. award 1980), Hammond C. of C., La. Assn. for Sch. Execs., Ozone Ramblers Camping Club (pres. 1988), KC (lectr. 1982, 85, 90-91, chancellor 1983-84, dep. grand knight 1995-96), Rotary (bd. dirs. Hammond, internat. svc. dir. 1972), Phi Delta Kappa, Kappa Delta Pi. Home: Hammond, La. Died Apr. 15, 2014.

**PARKER, HAROLD TALBOT,** history educator; b. Cin., Dec. 26, 1907; s. Samuel Chester and Lucile (Jones) P.; m. Louise Salley, July 9, 1980. PhB, U. Chgo., 1928, PhD, 1934; postgrad., Cornell U., 1929-30. Mem. faculty Duke U., Durham, N.C., 1939—, assoc. prof., 1950-57, prof. history, 1957-77, emeritus, from 1977; adj. prof. U. Ala., Huntsville, 1978-81; faculty U. N.C., Chapel Hill, 1984. Author: The Cult of Antiquity and the French Revolutionaries, 1937, Three Napoleonic Battles, 1944, 83, (with Marvin Brown) Major Themes in Modern European History, 3 vols., 1974, Bureau of Commerce in 1781, 1979, An Administrative Bureau During the Old Regime, 1993, History of St. Philip's Episcopal Church (Durham, N.C.) 1978-1994, 1997, Sermons From St. Philips, 1912-1994, 2000; editor: (with Richard Herr) Ideas in History, 1965, Problems in European History, 1979, (with Georg Iggers) International Handbook of Historical Studies, 1979, Theory and Social History, 1980, (with L.S. Parker) Proc. Consortium of Revolutionary Europe, 1981, 84, 85, 86; assoc. editor Historical Dictionary of Napoleonic France, 1985; regional editor, contbg. author: Great Historians of the Modern Age, 1991; contbr. articles to profl. jours. With USAAF, 1942-45. Recipient Disting. Svc. award Consortium on Revolutionary Europe, 1993, Disting Svc. award So. Hist. Assn. European History Sect., 1993. Mem. Soc. for French Hist. Studies (pres. 1957, Disting. Svc. award 1989), AAUP (pres. Duke U. chpt. 1960), Phi Beta Kappa (pres. Duke chpt. 1961) Episcopalian. Home: West Columbia, SC. Deceased.

**PARKER, JOHN VICTOR,** federal judge; b. Baton Rouge, Oct. 14, 1928; m. Mary Elizabeth Fridge, Sept. 3, 1949 (dec. 2010); children: John Michael, Robert Fridge, Linda Anne. BA, La. State U., 1949, JD, 1952. Bar: La. 1952. Atty. Parker & Parker, Baton Rouge, 1954-66; asst. parish atty. City of Baton Rouge, Parish of East Baton Rouge, 1956-66; atty. Sanders, Downing, Kean & Cazedessus, Baton Rouge, 1966-79; chief judge US Dist. Ct. (middle dist.) La., Baton Rouge, 1979—98, sr. judge, 1998—2014. Vis. lectr. law La. State U. Law Sch. With JAG US Army, 1952—54. Mem.: ABA, Baton Rouge Bar Assn. (past pres.), La. State Bar Assn. (past mem. bd. govs.), American Arbitration Assn., American Judicature Soc., Baton Rouge Country Club, Kiwanis (past pres.), Masons (32 degree), Order of Coif, Phi Delta Phi. Democrat. Methodist. Died July 14, 2014.

**PARKER, WARREN ANDREW,** public health dentist, consultant; b. Swedesboro, NJ, May 31, 1932; s. Warren Henry and Mary Jane (Morrison) P.; m. Eileen Frances Grabosky, Oct. 12, 1957; children: Denise, Warren A., Gail Lamb, Stephen. DDS, U. Md., Balt., 1958; MPH, U. Calif., Berkeley, 1966. Diplomate Am. Bd. Dental Pub. Health. Pvt. practice dentistry, Swedesboro, 1958-60; resident in dental pub. health USPHS, San Francisco, 1967; asst. chief div. preventive dentistry Inst. Dental Rsch., Walter Reed Army Med. Ctr., Washington, 1967-74; chief health care studies divsn. Acad. Health Scis./U.S. Army, San Antonio, 1974-78, chief dental studies office, 1978-81; assoc. prof. grad. sch. Baylor U., Waco, Tex., 1978-92; prof. dept. cmty. health Baylor Coll. Dentistry, Dallas, 1981-88, prof., chmn. dept. cmty. health, 1988-92; dental pub. health cons. in pvt. practice, San Antonio, from 1992. Cons. Agy. for Children and Families, Dept. HHS, Dallas, 1984—; cons. divsn. dental health Tex. Dept. Health, Austin, 1987-92; cons. Inst. for Family Studies, Tex. Tech. U., Lubbock, 1992—; mem. adv. com. Dental Health Programs, Inc., Dallas, 1989-92. Contbr. articles to profl. jours. Mem. exec. com. St. Vincent DePaul Soc., Lancaster, Tex., 1990-95; mem. com. Vis. Nurses Assn., Dallas, 1988-95; rep. Tex. Cancer Coun., Austin, 1989-90; vol. Habitat for Humanity. Col. U.S. Army, 1959-81. Decorated Legion of Merit; recipient Cert., Tex. Agy. on Aging, 1987. Fellow APHA, Am. Coll. Dentists, Tex. Pub. Health Assn. (chair oral health 1990-91, exec. dir. 1992—); mem. ADA, Am. Assn. Pub. Health Dentistry, Delta Omega. Avocations: fishing, gardening. Died Oct. 15, 2001.

**PARLAMIS, MICHAEL FRANK,** civil engineer, construction executive; b. Bklyn., May 29, 1940; s. Frank Michael and Phyllis (Burnago) P.; m. Marguerite Koskinas, Aug. 21, 1966; children: Franklin, Christine, Alexander. BSCE, MIT, 1962, BS in Indsl. Mgmt., 1962; MSCE, Stanford U., 1963. Registered profl. engr., NY. Engr. Port Authority of NY and NJ, 1963—64; asst. to chief engr. George A. Fuller Co., NYC, 1964-67; pres. Frank Parlamis Inc., Bklyn., from 1968, Parlamis Bros. Inc., Bklyn., from 1968, Hermes Constrn. Corp., Bklyn., from 1968; ptnr. City Path LLC, City Jam LLC, 128 MAC LLC, 128 MAPP LLC, 29 Prime Numbers, LLC, Prime Chicken LLC, New Rome Religous Supplies Inc. Author: CPM/PERT As Basis for Management Information Systems in Building Construction, 1966, Regulation of Building Construction in the City of New York, 1967, Greece and the Panama Canal, 1988. Chmn. expansion program Greek Orthodox Cathedral St. John the Theologian, Tenafly, NJ, 1978—; mem. Leadership 100 of Greek Orthodox Ch.; Archon of Ecomenical Patriarchate, Greek Orthodox Ch., regional commdr. State of NJ; mem. ednl. coun. MIT, William Barton Rogers Soc.; trustee Frank Parlamis Sr. Citizens Ctr., Jamaica, NY, Space Camp Turkey, Izmir; founder Michael F. Parlamis endowed fellowships, MIT, St. John the Theologian Peace Meml. Gymnasium; exec. dir. St. John the Theologian World Peace Inst.; founding trustee New Euclidean U. 250 Charitable Trust. Recipient Ellis Island medal of honor, 2002, Gold Key award for best engineered restaurant in USA, Internat. Hotel, Motel an Restaurant Show, 1992. Mem. Am. Hellenic Progressive Assn., Bklyn. Tech. Rsch. Found. (life), Tau Beta Pi, Chi Epsilon, Am. Turkish Soc. Republican. Avocations: engineering and religious history, peace advocacy, ecumenical religious activities. Home: Tenafly, NJ. Died Oct. 6, 2013.

**PARROT, KENT KANE,** producer, writer; b. LA, June 4, 1911; s. Kent Kane and Mary (Alsop) P.; m. Deirdre Barbara Elland Lumley-Savile, Oct. 21, 1948; children: Jonathan Kent, Richard Halifax, Barbara Elland. BS, U.S. Mil. Acad., 1935; postgrad., Air War Coll., 1955-56; MA in Internat. Affairs, George Washington U., 1967, M of Philosophy, 1975, PhD, 1978. Commd. 2d lt. U.S. Army, 1935; advanced through grades to col. USAF, 1955, ret., 1965; fgn. svc. res. officer Arms Control and Disarmament Agy., 1965-70; owner, producer Markane Co., Inc., Chevy Chase, Md., from 1960. Producer radio mus. The Catch Colt, 1986—; contbr. articles to profl. jours. Mem. com. on Russia and the Republics Commn. on Peace Episcopal Diocese of Washington, 1984—. Mem. ASCAP, Am. Fgn. Svc. Assn., Internat. Soc. Polit. Psychology, Fedn. Am. Scientists, Ctr. for Def. Info. (adv. coun. 1987—), Chevy Chase Club, Met. Club of Washington. Democrat. Avocations: swimming, golf, ice skating, aerobics. Died Apr. 28, 1995.

**PARSONS, HENRY MCILVAINE,** psychologist; b. Lenox, Mass., Aug. 31, 1911; s. Herbert and Elsie Worthington (Clews) P.; m. Renee Oakman, 1938 (div. 1945); 1 son, Jack; m. Marina Svetlova, 1949 (div. 1957); m. Marjorie Thorson, 1957. BA, Yale U., 1933; MA, Columbia U., 1947; PhD, U. Calif., Los Angeles, 1963. Reporter N.Y. Herald Tribune, 1935-42; organizer N.Y. Newspaper Guild, 1942; asst., then lectr. psychology Columbia U., 1947-52; research asso. N.Y. U., 1951-52; supr. Electronics Research Labs., Columbia U., 1952-58; mem. human factors staff Douglas Aircraft Co., Long Beach and Santa Monica, Calif., 1956-58; sr. human factors scientist, br. head System Devel. Corp., Santa Monica and Falls Church, Va., 1958-68; self-employed cons., 1968-69; 70-73; v.p. research Riverside Research Inst., NYC, 1969-70; exec. dir. Inst. Behavioral Research Inc., Silver Spring, Md., 1974-79; pres. Exptl. Coll. of Inst. Behavioral Research, Silver Spring, 1974-80; mgr. human factors projects Human Resources Research Orgn., Alexandria, Va., 1980-83; sr. staff scientist Essex Corp., Alexandria, Va., 1983-90; mgr. Ctr. for Human Factors Rsch. Human Resources Rsch. Orgn., Alexandria, from 1990; adj. prof. Lehigh U., 1983-84. Author: Man-Machine System Experiments, 1972; also chpts. in books, articles in jours. Served with USNR, 1942-45. Fellow AAAS, APA (pres. divsn. 21 1975-76, Franklin V. Taylor award 1992), Human Factors and Ergonomics Soc. (pres. 1968-69, Pres.'s Disting. Svc. award 1993), Washington

Acad. Scis., Am. Psychol. Soc.; mem. N.Y. Acad. Scis., Ergonomics Soc., Sigma Xi. Clubs: Century (N.Y.C.); Cosmos (Washington). Deceased.

**PARSONS, SARA ELIZABETH,** hospital administrator, nurse, writer; b. Northboro, Mass., Apr. 24, 1864; Student, Boston City Hosp. Tng. Sch.; grad. Boston Tng. Sch., Mass. Gen. Hosp., 1893; cert. course in hosp. econs., Tchrs. Coll., Columbia U.; course in hosp. adminstr., Mass. Gen. Hosp. Various positions, including head nurse, supr., supt.; supt. nurses Adams Nervine Hosp., Mass.; supt. Mass. Gen. Hosp., 1910-1920; chief nurse Base Hosp. #6, France, 1917-1919; ret., 1926. Established nurse tng. sch., R.I., 1896. Author: (books) Nursing Problems and Obligations, 1916, History of the Massachusetts General Hospital Training School for Nurses, 1922; contbr. numerous articles to nursing jour. Vol. nurse Bay State hosp. ship. Mem. Mass. Nurses Assn. (pres.). Died Oct. 25, 1949.

**PARTANEN, CARL RICHARD,** biology professor; b. Portland, Oreg., Nov. 23, 1921; s. Emil and Ellen (Engstrom) P.; m. Jane Nelson, June 24, 1961; children: Karen, Kirsten, Richard (dec.) Student, Multnomah Jr. Coll., 1946-48; BA, Lewis and Clark Coll., 1950; MA, Harvard, 1951, PhD, 1954. Am. Cancer Soc. postdoctoral research fellow Columbia, 1954-55, Harvard, 1955-57; research asso. Childrens Cancer Research Found., Boston, 1957-61; asso. prof. biology U. Pitts., 1961-64, prof. biology, 1964-86, chmn. biology, 1964-70, prof. emeritus, from 1987; Research fellow U. Edinburgh, Scotland, 1971-72, U. Nottingham, Eng., 1978-79. Contbr. articles to profl. jours. Served with AUS, 1942-45, ETO. Recipient Distinguished Achievement award Lewis and Clark Coll., 1968 Mem. AAAS, Bot. Soc. Am., Soc. for Devel. Biology, Soc. for In Vitro Biology. Home: Pittsburgh, Pa. Died Feb. 4, 2014.

**PARTSCH, KARL JOSEF H.,** legal educator; b. Freiburg, Germany, June 24, 1914; s. Josef and Ilse E. (Roesler) P.; m. Juliane Bernhardt; 1 child, Susanna. D, U. Freiburg, 1937; assessor, Cologne Ct. Appeals, 1948. Legal adviser bank and machine factory, Berlin, Cologne and Ulm, Germany, 1938-41; constl. analyst Deutscher Städtetag, Cologne, 1948-50; asst. legal adviser Auswärtiges Amt, Bonn, Fed. Republic Germany, 1950-54; consul Fed. Republic Germany Naples, Italy, 1955-57; prof. law U. Kiel, Fed. Republic Germany, 1957-60, U. Mainz, Fed. Republic Germany, 1960-66, U. Bonn, 1966-79, prof. emeritus, from 1979. Lectr. law U. Bonn, 1953-57, rector, 1968-69; mem., reporter com. on elimination racial discrimination UN, 1970—; mem. com. on human rights UNESCO, Paris, 1981—. Author: Europ Menschenrechte, 1966, Zoologische Station Neapel, 1980; co-author: Victims of Armed Conflicts, 1982; contbr. articles to profl. jours. Bd. dirs. German Civil Liberties Union, Cologne, 1949-54. Recipient Gt. Cross Merit, Pres. Fed. Republic Germany, 1984, Peace medal Sec. Gen. UN, 1984. Mem. Deutsche Staatsrechtslehrer, Gesellschaft Für Völkerrecht, Am. Soc. Internat. Law, German Assn. UN. Avocation: Italian history and culture. Home: Ingelheim am Rhein, Germany. Died Dec. 30, 1996.

**PARULIS, CHERYL,** English, drama and speech educator; b. Charlotte, NC, Apr. 11, 1944; d. Francis August and Evelyn Louise (Scott) Bogacki; m. Albert William Parulis, June 25, 1966 (Apr. 1984); children: Albert William Jr., Christa Suzanne. M in Sports Adminstrn., Mercyhurse Coll., Erie, Pa., 1962-63; student, Indiana U. Pa., 1963-64, U. Que. at Trois Riviers, Can., 1987; BA in English Lit., Clarion U. Pa., 1987, MA in English Lit., 1989; BEd, permanent cert. in English edn., St. Thomas U., Miami, Fla., 1995. Permanet cert. English tchr., Fla. Substitute tchr. Brigantine (N.J.) Pub. Sch. Sys., 1970-72, Dubois (Pa.) Area Sch. Sys., 1982-84, Clarion Intermediate Unit 6, 1984-86; residential aide Pathways, Inc., Clarion, 1987-88; asst. Writing Ctr., Clarion U. Pa., 1987-88, grad. asst., English and computer tutor, 1988-89; tchr. English, St. Jospeh Sch., Miami Beach, Fla., 1991-93, Msgr. Edward Pace H.S., Miami, 1993-98; adj. prof. composition, speech, Am. lit. and drama St. Thomas U., from 1994; adj. prof. English and lit. Internat. Fine Arts Coll., Miami, from 1998. Partitipant Fla. Thespian Festival, 1997, 98; presenter in field; cheerleading coach, Miami, 1995-98. Hospice vol., Miami, 1993-94; vol. Miami Beach Dem. Com., 1994—, Habitat for Humanity, Miami, 1998-99. Recipient Msgr. Edward Pace Golden Apple award of excellence, 1994, 97. Mem. Nat. Coun. Tchrs. English, Dade County Tchrs. Assn., Sigma Tau Delta (life). Roman Catholic. Avocations: theater, film, decorating, stage directing, dance. Died Feb. 13, 2006.

**PASCO SEMINARIO, ROBERTO ABEL,** biomedical engineer; b. Callao, Peru, Nov. 29, 1942; s. José Abel Pasco Villarreal and Rosa Ricardina Seminario Verano; married; children: Carla, Fabiola, Fiorela, Cintia. B in Electro-Mech. Engring., Nat. U. Engring., 1966. Registered profl. engr. With NASA Satellite Tracking Sta. Minitrack, Ancón, Peru, 1962—64; asst. prof. Nat.U. Engring., 1964; asst. dept. electronics Indsl. Sounded Radio, Peru, 1964—65; engr. operator Minitrack Nr-6, Peru, 1966; rsch. asst. IGP Radiates Observatory Jicamarca, Peru, 1967; engr. office of R&D Ministry of Navy of Peru, Peru, 1968; adv. Nat. Inst. Neoplasics Illness, Peru, 1969—70; from asst. prof. to assoc. prof. San Marcos Mayor Nat. U., Faculty of Human Medicine, Peru, 1976—88; assoc. prof. San Marcos Mayor Nat. U., 1988—89; tech. mgr. Signature A & G Pasco S.R.L., Peru, 1990—98; adv., cons. Bioelectronics S.R.L., Peru, from 1998. Jury and contr. of admission in found. Nat. U. Callao, 1967; pres. Com. of Pan-Am. Journey of Biomedical Engring. 12th Conv., Lima, Peru, 1972—73; presenter in field; cons. in field; lectr. in field. Contbr. articles to profl. jours. Recipient Rolex award, APIB, Switzerland, 1998; scholar, Nat. Commn., Buenos Aires, Argentina, 1973. Mem.: IEEE, Peruvian Assn. Biomedical Engring. (founder, pres.), World Fedn. Orgs. Engring., Pan-Am. Union of Assns. of Engring., Coll. Engrs. Peru, Soc. Engrs. Peru (assoc.). Avocations: soccer, reading, mentoring. Home: Lima, Peru. Died May 2, 2008.

**PASTOR, ROBERT ALLEN,** political science professor, retired federal official; b. Newark, Apr. 10, 1947; s. Norman and Ruth (Kagan) P.; m. Magaret Pastor, June 16, 1979; children: Tiffin Margaret, Robert Kiplin. Student, Birmingham U., Eng., 1967-68; BA, Lafayette Coll., 1969; MPA, Harvard U., 1974, PhD, 1977. Vol. Peace Corps., 1970-72; exec. dir. Linowitz Commn. on U.S./LA Rels., 1975-77; dir. office Latin American & Caribbean affairs NSC, Washington, 1977-81; sr. adviser on Latin America Hon. Walter Mondale, Washington, 1981-84; faculty rsch. assoc. U. Md., College Park, 1982-85; Fulbright prof. El Colegio de Mexico, 1985-86; prof. polit. sci. Emory U., Atlanta, 1985—2014, dir. Latin American & Caribbean program Carter Ctr., 1985—2014; v.p. internat. affairs American U., 2002—07; cons. US Dept. Def., 1995. Author: Congress and the Politics of U.S. Foreign Economic Policy, 1980, Limits to Friendship: The U.S. and Mexico, 1988 (Hubert Herring award 1989), Condemned to Repetition: The U.S. And Nicaragua, 1988, Democracy in the Americas: Stopping the Pendulum, 1989, Whirlpool: U.S. Foreign Policy Toward Latin America and the Caribbean, 1992, Integration with Mexico: Options for U.S. Policy, 1993; bd. editors Jour. Inter-American Studies and World Affairs, Studies on Comparative Internat. Devel., Hemisphere; appeared in: (documentaries) Water on the Table, 2010 Home: Washington, DC. Died Jan. 8, 2014.

**PATAKI, NÁNDOR,** engineer; b. Salgótarján, Hungary, Jan. 8, 1930; s. Nándor and Irma Mária (Kozalik) P.; m. Elisabeth Pálovits, June 25, 1971. Civil engr., Tech. U. Budapest, 1952, dr. hydraulic engring., 1968; golden diploma, Budapest Tech. U. Cert. engr. Tech. mgr. Enterprise for Mineral & Water Prospecting & Drilling, Várpalota, Hungary, 1952-54; chief of dept. Geol. Authority, Budapest, 1954-57; chief engr. Enterprise for Water Prospecting and Drilling, Budapest, 1957-70; chief of expedition, gen. mgr. Transing and Export Co. for Hydraulic Engring. Products, 1970-76; gen. mgr. Water Prospecting and Drilling Co., 1976-80; asst. prof. Tech. U. of Miskolc, from 1980. Asst. prof. UNESCO, Budapest, 1970—; expert in hydrogeology, 1990—; scientific and mktg. expert 16 countries; lectr. in field. Author 6 books; editl. bd. Köolaj és Földgáz; contbr. articles to profl. jours. Recipient Dionyza Stura Commemorative medal Tchécoslovaquie, 1978, Zsigmondy W. Commemorative medal Hungarian Mining and Metallurgical Soc., 1988, Medal Internat. Thermal Affair, 1990, Medal Pro Facultate Rerum Metalicarum, Miskolc U., 1995. Mem. Hungarian Hydrol. Soc. (hon., sect. of hydrogeology, Bogdánfy Ö Commemorative medal 1987, Dr. Schafarzik Ferenc Commemorative medal 1998, Pro Aqua medal 2001), Hungarian Mining and Metallurgical Soc. (dep. pres. oil, gas and water sect. 1975—, chmn. water well dept. oil, gas and water sect.). Avocations: gardening, swimming, archeology. Home: Budapest, Hungary. Died July 17, 2004.

**PATERSON, BASIL ALEXANDER,** lawyer; b. NYC, Apr. 27, 1926; s. Leonard J. and Evangeline (Rondon) P.; m. Portia Hairston, 1953; children: Daniel, David. BS, St. John's Coll., 1948; JD, St. John's U., 1951. Bar: N.Y. 1952. Ptnr. Paterson, Michael, Dinkins and Jones, NYC, 1956—77, Meyer, Suozzi, English & Klein, P.C., Garden City, NY, from 1983; mem. Dist. 31 NY State Senate, 1965, mem. Dist. 27, 1967—70; dep. mayor for labor rels. NYC, 1978; sec. of state State of NY, Albany, 1979—83. Pres. Inst. Mediation and Conflict Resolution, 1971-77; chmn. 2d Jud. Screening Com., 1985-95; assoc. chmn. N.Y. State Sentencing Guidelines Com.; commr. Port Authority N.Y. and N.J., 1989-95 Bd. dirs. St. Benedict's Day Nursery, 1999-2014; vice chmn. Democratic Nat. Com., 1972-78, mem., 1972-78; chmn. Nat. Grid Found., 2003 Recipient Eagleton Inst. Politics award, Disting. Svc. award Guardians Assn. N.Y. Police Dept., City Club N.Y. award, Black Expo award, Excellence medal St. John's U., Kibbe award CUNY, Citizens Union Civic leadership award, ABA, Lawyers & Problem Solve award. Roman Catholic. Died Apr. 16, 2014.

**PATINKIN, SHELDON ARTHUR,** artistic director, theater and music educator; b. Chgo., Aug. 27, 1935; s. Sam and Eva (Brezinsky) Patinkin. BA in English Lit., U. Chgo., MA in English Lit., 1956. Prodn. mgr., mus. dir. Playwrights Theater Club, Chgo., 1953-55; instr. English Wilson Jr. Coll., Chgo., 1956-60; gen. mgr. The Second City, Chgo., 1960-62, artistic dir., 1962-68; instr. improvisation, acting Am. Acad. Dramatic Arts, NYC, 1971-72; artistic dir. ETC Theater Co., NYC, 1972-74, The Second City in Toronto, Ont., Can., 1974-76; writer, assoc. producer The Second City TV, Toronto, 1976-78; writer The Second City Film and TV Devel., Chgo., 1978-80; chmn. dept. theater/music Columbia Coll., Chgo., from 2014, artistic dir. The New Mus. Project, 1986—2014; artistic dir. The Nat. Jewish Theater, Skokie, Ill., 1987—2014. Artistic dir. Getz Theater; instr. acting, improvisation, comedy Steppenwolf Theater; mem. theater panel Ill. Arts Coun. Asst. dir. (1st Chgo. prodn.) The Caucasion Chalk CIrcle, 1953; screenwriter: (with others) Loving, The Magician of Lublin, Player Piano, My Bodyguard; scriptwriter: (TV shows) Second City TV, The David Steinberg Show; dir. stage prodns.: (Chgo., N.Y.C. and Toronto) Death of a Salesman, Woyzeck, Arms and the Man, The Price, Twelfth Night, Waiting for Lefty, 1979, I'd Rather Be Right, The Madwoman of Chaillot, Sexual Perversity in Chicago, The Women, Member of the Wedding, Taming of the Shrew, The Caretaker, The Sea Gull, Candide, Waiting for Godot, The Caucasion Chalk Circle, Art, Ruth and Trudy, The Dybbuk, After the Fall, Uncle Vanya, 2001; dir. opera prodns. including The Barber of Seville, Tristan and Isolde, Tosca, Madame Butterfly, Amahl and the Night Visitors, The Masked Ball, The Telephone, Carmen, The Magic Flute, Hansel and Gretel; other stage credits include Bernstein's Candide, Let's Step Out: An Evening of Weill, Porter, Berlin and Ellington, Puttin' On the Ritz: An Evening of Irving Berlin Songs; author: Second City: Backstage at the World's Greatest Comedy Theater, 2000, No Legs, No Jokes, No Chance: A History of the American Musical Theater, 2008 Bd. dirs. League of Chgo. Theaters. Recipient Twenty-Fifth Anniversary award Urban Getaways, 1986; grantee Paul and Gabriella Rosenbaum Found., 1986, 87. Died Sept. 21, 2014.

**PATTERSON, DAVID,** academic administrator, educator, scholar, retired; b. Liverpool, Eng., June 10, 1922; s. Louis and Sarah (Marshak Davis) P.; m. Josephine Lovestone, Nov. 19, 1950; children: Deborah, Louise, Daniel, Benjamin. BA, U. Manchester, UK, 1949, MA, 1954, U. Oxford, 1956; PhD, U. Manchester, 1962; D of Hebrew Letters (hon.), Balt. Hebrew U., 1988; DHL (hon.), Hebrew Union Coll., 1989. Lectr. U. Manchester, 1953-56, U. Oxford, 1956-89; fellow St. Cross Coll., Oxford, 1965-89; prof. Cornell U., 1966-71; founding pres. Oxford Ctr. for Hebrew and Jewish Studies, 1972-92; prof. Mt. Holyoke Coll., 1987-88; emeritus pres., hon. fellow Oxford Ctr. for Hebrew and Jewish Studies, from 1993. Vis. prof. Northwestern U., 1983, 85, 93, Sydney (Australia) U., 1993, Smith Coll., 1994, 95, Hampshire Coll., 1996; hon. fellow Ctr. for Jewish Studies, U. Manchester, 1998—. Author: Abraham Mapu, 1964, The Hebrew Novel in Czarist Russia, 1964, 1999, A Phoenix in Fetters, 1988; editor: Tradition and Trauma, 1994; translator: The King of Flesh and Blood, 1957, Out of the Depths (Brenner), 1992, Random Harvest (Bialik) with E. Spicehandler, 1999. Chmn. adult edn. com. B'nai B'rith, Gt. Britain, 1969-73; coun. mem. World Union Hebrew Studies, Jerusalem, 1979—; mem. bd. regents Internat. Ctr. for Tchg. Jewish Civilisation, Jerusalem, 1982-92; mem. senate Hochschule für Jüdische Studien, Heidelberg, Germany, 1992-99. Recipient Brotherhood award Nat. Conf. Christians and Jews, 1979, Stiller prize for literature Balt. Hebrew U., 1988, Webber prize for translation Oxford Ctr. for Hebrew and Jewish Studies, 1989, Remembering for the Future award, 2000. Mem. Brit. Assn. for Jewish Studies (pres. 1984), United Oxford and Cambridge Club London, European Assn. for Jewish Studies, Lotos Club N.Y. Jewish. Avocations: music, reading, walking. Home: Oxford, England. Died Dec. 2005.

**PATTERSON, JOHN C.,** psychiatrist, educator; b. Freehold, NJ, Dec. 1, 1918; s. William Corlies and Iris Cora (Harvey) P.; m. Inez Decker, Aug. 7, 1948; children: Marie Harvey, Laura Jane, Mary Iris, John William. BS, Rutgers U., 1938; MD, Jefferson Med. Coll., 1942. Diplomate: Am. Bd. Neurology and Psychiatry. Intern Fitkin Hosp., Neptune, N.J., 1942-43; resident VA Hosp., Phila., 1946-48; practice medicine, specializing in psychiatry Phila., 1948-59, Independence, Iowa, 1960-62, Augusta, Maine, 1963-71; staff mem., chief psychiatrist VA Mental Hygiene Clinic, Phila., 1949-59; staff psychiatrist Jefferson Med. Coll., 1949-59; mem. psychiat. vis. staff Phila. Gen. Hosp., 1950-59; dir. out-patient services Mental Health Inst., Independence, 1959-62; supt. Augusta State Hosp., 1963-71; dir. Freehold (N.J.) Psychiat. Clinic, 1972-80; attending in psychiatry Monmouth Med. Center, Long Branch, N.J., from 1972. Clin. asso. prof. psychiatry Rutgers Med. Sch., 1973— Served to maj., M.C. AUS, 1943-46. Fellow Am. Psychiat. Assn. (life); mem. N.J. Psychiat. Assn. (past pres.), AMA. Clubs: Rotary. Died Sept. 12, 1989.

**PATTERSON, PAUL H.,** biology educator, neuroscientist; b. Chgo., Oct. 22, 1943; s. Paul H. and Marjorie (Hall) P. BA, Grinnell Coll., 1965; PhD, Johns Hopkins U., 1970. Postdoctoral fellow, dept. neurobiology Harvard Med. Sch., Boston, 1970-73, asst. prof. neurobiology, 1973-78, assoc. prof., 1978-83; prof., biology Calif. Inst. Technology, Pasadena, 1983—2005, Anne P. & Benjamin F. prof. biological sciences, 2005—14, Anne P. & Benjamin F. prof. biological sciences emeritus, 2014. Cons. AMGEN, Thousand Oaks, Calif. Author: Readings in Developmental Neurobiology, 1982; assoc. editor: Ann. Rev. Physiology, 1982-83, Jour. Neurosci., 1980-85, Neuron Recipient Research Career Devel. award NIH, Bethesda, Md., 1974, W. Alden Spencer award Columbia Coll. Physicians and Surgeons, N.Y.C., 1984, McKnight Found. Neurosci. award, Mpls., 1982, 85, 88; Rita Allen Found. scholar, 1979; Jacob Javits Neurosci. Investigator award NIH, 1988; Burton L. Baker lectr. U. Mich., 1989. Fellow AAAS, mem. Soc. for Neurosci., Soc. Developmental Biology, American Soc. Cell Biology. Died June 25, 2014.

**PATTY, CHARLES EDGAR, JR.,** physicist, researcher; b. Anniston, Ala., Aug. 29, 1946; s. Charles Edgar and Velma Doris (Roper) P.; m. Stephanie Ruth Carter, May 8, 1971; children: Charles Edgar III, Kira Dawne. BS, Jacksonville State U., 1969; MS, U. Ala., 1977, PhD, 1983. Rsch./tchg. asst. U. Ala., Huntsville, 1974-79; dir. Redstone Arsenal (Ala.) Br. Columbia Coll. Extended Studies Divsn., 1979-82; electronics engr. U.S. Army Missile Lab., Redstone Arsenal, 1982-84; sr. systems analyst Teledyne Brown Engring., Huntsville, 1984-2000, Teledyne Solutions, Inc., Huntsville, from 2000. Mem. adj. faculty Columbia Coll., Redstone Arsenal, 1978—. Author: Introduction to Experimental Physics, 1975, Experiment and Knowledge, 1986. Block capt. Neighborhood Watch., 1982-83; chmn., founding mem. Coun.Sci. Students, U. Ala., Huntsville, 1976; chmn. bd. Bingham Mountain Landowners Assn., 1984-85. Served as officer with USAF (SAC), 1969-74. Mem.: Sigma Pi Sigma, Sigma Xi. Baptist. Home: Huntsville, Ala. Died Feb. 1, 2001.

**PAUL, TERRY (TERRANCE DAVID PAUL),** information technology executive, lawyer; b. Streator, Ill., Sept. 23, 1946; s. Willard and Marguerite (Voelker) Paul; m. Judith Paul; children: Bliss, Alyssa, Mia, Alexander. BS in Economics, U. Ill.; JD, U. Ill. Coll. Law; MBA, Bradley U. With Caterpillar Tractor Co., Peoria, Ill.; CEO Best Power

Technology, 1980—94; co-founder Renaissance Learning, Inc., from 1986, vice chmn., 1996—2001, co-chmn., 2001—02, 2003—06, CEO, 2002—03, 2006—10, pres., 2006, chmn., 2010—11. Died Sept. 5, 2014.

**PAULUS, ELEANOR BOCK,** professional speaker, author; b. NYC, Mar. 12, 1933; d. Charles William Bock and Borghild (Nelson) Garrick; m. Chester William Paulus Jr., Sept. 6, 1952; children: Chester W. III, Karl Derrick, Diane Paulus Henricks. Student, Smith Coll., 1952-53. Owner, founder Khan-Du Chinese Shar-Pei, Somerset, N.J., from 1980; dir. Pet Net, Santa Fe, N.Mex., from 1992; co-owner, CFO Am. Dream TV Prodns., Washington, from 1993; co-owner, exec. prodr. Capitol Ideas, 1995-2001, Pierre Salinger's Round Table, 1997; pets and animals columnist www.goodnewsbroadcast.com, from 2000. Lectr., cons. on Chinese Shar-Pei and canine health, 1980—; internat. con., lectr. on pet care and health. Author: Health Care Handbook for Cats, Dogs and Birds, The Proper Care of Chinese Shar-Pei; contbr. articles to mags. and jours. including Dog Fancy, chpts. to books, including The World of the Chinese Shar-Pei; creator, prodr. World of Dogs, 1996—. Dir. bd. trustees Rutgers Prep. Sch., Somerset, 1970-76, v.p. bd. trustees, 1976-81, pres. PTA, 1966-76; chmn. Raritan River Festival, New Brunswick, N.J., 1980-91. Named Woman of Yr., City of New Brunswick, 1982. Mem. Dog Writers Am. Assn., Dog Fanciers N.Y.C., Bonzai Clubs Internat., Koi Internat. N.Y., Raritan Valley Country Club, Chinese Shar-Pei Club of Am. (v.p. 1982-86, bd. dirs. east sect. 1980-82, Humanitarian award 1986). Avocations: travel, dog related activities, gardening. Died 2004.

**PAUPERIO, ARTHUR MACHADO,** lawyer; b. Rio de Janeiro, July 15, 1914; s. Arthur and Júlia Machado P.; m. Maria José de Castro, Dec. 8, 1938; children: Celso, Helder, Heraldo. BS, Coll. São Bento, Rio de Janeiro, 1932; Tchr., Inst. Cath. Est. Sup., Rio de Janeiro, 1936; Lawyer, Fac. Nat. Dir., Rio de Janeiro, 1937; Psychologist, Psicol. da UB, Rio de Janeiro, 1944. Prof. Fac. Dir., Rio de Janeiro, 1951-84; mem. Svc. Jurid da Uniao, Rio de Janeiro, 1953-82; prof. Fac. de Dir. da. Pucrj, Rio de Janeiro, 1945-53, Fac. de C.J. do, Rio de Janeiro, 1951-60, Fac. Brasil.de C. Jur., Rio de Janeiro, 1953-60, Un.Int.de E.S. Prodeo, Rio de Janeiro, 1965-68; coord. Curs.Pos-G.F.D. UFRJ, Rio de Janeiro, 1974-84; vice-dir. Direito UFRJ, Rio de Janeiro, 1971-74; dir. Fac.De Direito UFRJ, Rio de Janeiro, 1974-78; cons. juridico Min.do. Trabalho, I.C., Rio de Janeiro, 1960. Author: (books) Teoria Geral do Estado, 1953, 8th edit. 1983, O Conceito Polêmico de SobeRania, 1949, 3rd edit. 1997, O Direito Politico de Resis, 1962, 3rd edit. 1997, Introducão ao Estudo do Direito, 1969, 11th edit. 1996. Mem. Com. Nat. Moral Civismo, Rio De Janeiro, 1973. Recipient awards pres. Senado, 1976, Ordem do Merito Judiciario, 1984, others. Mem. Efetivo Inst. Adv. Brasil, Titular AC.Bras.L.Jurid (sec. gen.), Titular Assn. Int. D.Const. Roman Catholic. Home: Rio de Janeiro, Brazil. Died Sept. 22, 2005.

**PAURUS, NORMAN WILBERT,** computer company executive, electronics executive; b. Sebeka, Minn., June 2, 1933; s. William and Hilda (Holappa) Paurus; m. Irja Fannie Salmela, June 18, 1955; children: Curtis F., Karen V. BS, U. Minn., 1959, BEE, 1960. From elec. design engr. to v.p. Control Data Corp., Mpls., 1960—84; pres. Anderson Cornelius Co., Mpls., from 1984. Councilman City of Medicine Lake, Minn., 1956—67, City of Orono, Minn., 1973—80; chmn. Lake Minnetonka Conservation Dist., Minn., 1978. With USN, 1952—55. Recipient Dynamo award, U. Minn., 1959. Mem.: Soc. Advancement Mgmt. (pres. 1959), Eta Kappa Nu. Lutheran. Home: Wayzata, Minn. Died Jan. 2, 1997.

**PAYNE-GAPOSCHKIN, CECILIA HELENA,** astronomer; b. Wendover, Eng., May 10, 1900; came to U.S., 1923, naturalized, 1931; d. Edward John and Emma Leonora Helena (Pertz) Payne; m. Sergei Illarionowitsch Gaposchkin, March 6, 1934; children: Edward Michael, Katherine Leonora, Peter John Arthur. AB, Newnham Coll., Cambridge, Eng., 1923; PhD, Radcliffe Coll., 1925; DSc, Wilson Coll., 1942, Cambridge U., 1950, Smith Coll., 1951, Western Coll. for Women, 1953. With Harvard Observatory, Cambridge, Mass., from 1923; Phillips astronomer Harvard U., from 1938, prof. astronomy, from 1956. Author: (with Sergei I. Gaposchkin) Variable Stars, 1938, Stars in the Making, 1952, Introduction to Astronomy, 1953, Galactic Novae, 1957, Stars and Clusters, 1979; contbr. articles to profl. jours. Mem. AAAS, Am. Astron. Soc., Royal Astron. Soc., Am. Philos. Soc., Phi Beta Kappa, Sigma Xi (pres. Radcliffe chpt. 1945-47). Home: Lexington, Mass. Died Oct. 1979.

**PAZ ESTENSSORO, VICTOR,** Bolivian politician; b. Tarija, Bolivia, Oct. 2, 1907; s. Domingo Paz Rojas and Carla Estenssoro de Paz; m. Carmela Cerruto Calderón, 1936; children: Miría, Ramiro; m. Teresa Cortéz Velasco; children: Patricia, Moira, Silvia. Grad., Faculty of Law, Universidad Mayor de San Andrés, La Paz, Bolivia. Founder, leader Nat. Revolutionary Movement in Bolivia, from 1942, nat. dep., 1938-39, 40-43, nat. senator, 1944-46. Sec. Nat. Office of Fin. Stats., La Paz, fin. ofcl. Permament Fiscal Commn., La Paz, 1930-32, comptroller Gen. of Republic, La Paz, 1932; atty. Credit Union of the Workers, La Paz, 1936, undersec. Ministry of Fin., La Paz, 1936-37, minister of econs., La Paz, 1942, minister of fin., La Paz, 1944-46, pres. Republic of Bolivia, 1952-56, 60-64, 85-89; ambassador of Netherlands to U.K., Amsterdam, 1956-59; pres. Banco Minero de Bolivia, La Paz, 1939; corr. Revista de Económica Continental de México, Buenos Aires, 1947; project dir. Compania Fabril Financiera de Buenos Aires, 1948-49; functionary Fábrica de Hilados de Lana Lanasur, Montevideo, Uruguay, 1950-51; prof. history of econ. process Universidad de San Andrés, La Paz, 1939-46; prof. introduction to planning and theories of econ. devel. Universidad Nacional de Ingeniería, Lima, Peru, 1966-70; prof. comtemporary history of S.Am., UCLA, 1977, U. N.Mex., Albuquerque, 1978; sole practice law, 1938-46. Contbr. articles to profl. jours. Recipient numerous awards and decorations from Peru, Colombia, Ecuador, Yugoslavia, Panamá, Guatemala, France, Brazil, Venezuela, Federal Republic of Germany, Uruguay, Egypt, Malta, Argentina, Eng. Home: La Paz, Bolivia. Died June 7, 2001.

**PEARL, CHAIM,** rabbi, author; b. Liverpool, Lancashire, Eng., Nov. 25, 1919; came to U.S., 1964; s. Alexander and Rebecca (Epstein) P.; m. Anita Newman, Nov. 16, 1941; children: David, Jonathan, Simon, Judith. BA, U. London, 1947, PhD, 1956; MA, U. Birmingham, Eng., 1952; DD (hon.), Jewish Theol. Sem. Am., 1981. Ordained rabbi, 1964. Asst. min. Birmingham Hebrew Congregation, 1945-49, chief min., 1949-60; min. The New West End Synagogue, London, 1960-64; rabbi Conservative Synagogue Riverdale, NYC, 1964-80, ret., 1980. Lectr. Buber Inst., Hebrew U., Jerusalem, 1991, also various Jewish religious instns., Jerusalem. Author: The Guide to Jewish Knowledge, 1956, The Medieval Jewish Mind, 1974, Rashi, 1988, Sefer Ha-Aggadah, 1988, others; assoc. editor The Jewish Bible Quar. Home: Jerusalem, Israel. Died Dec. 18, 1995.

**PEARLMUTTER, FLORENCE NICHOLS,** psychologist, therapist; b. Bklyn., Mar. 17, 1914; d. William and Marie Elizabeth (Rugamer) Griebe; m. Wilbur Francis Nichols, Aug. 17, 1940 (dec. 1967); 1 child, Roger F.; m. F. Bernard Pearlmutter, June 27, 1969. BS, NYU, 1934, postgrad., 1965-75; MS, Yeshiva U., 1960. Psychologist P.P.P. Counseling Ctr., Northport, N.Y., 1967-69; hypnotherapist Robert E. Peck, M.D., Syosset, N.Y., 1969-75; therapist Arthur J. Gross, M.D., Hicksville, N.Y., from 1975. Rsch. asst. and prof. rsch. in field. Mem. NEA, AAUW, Nassau County Psychol. Assn., N.Y. State Psychol. Assn. (assoc.), Nat. Women's Hall of Fame, Kappa Delta Pi. Avocations: cooking, phototgraphy, travel, fishing. Home: Huntington, NY. Died Nov. 26, 2001.

**PEARLSON, JORDAN,** rabbi; b. Somerville, Mass., Sept. 2, 1924; s. Jacob and Freda (Spivak) P.; m. Geraldine S. Goldstein, Jan. 19, 1958 (div. 1989); children: Joshua Seth, Nessa Yocheved, Abigail Sara. BA in Econs. with honors, Northeastern U., 1948, JD, 1950; B Hebrew Letters, Hebrew Union Coll., 1954, M Hebrew Letters, 1958; DD (hon.), Union Coll., 1981. Ordained rabbi, 1956. Mem. faculty grad. program for Jewish religious educators Hebrew Union Coll., Cin., 1955-56; chmn. nat. religious adv. com. CBC, 1974-75; nat. chmn. joint pub. rels. com. Can. Jewish Congress, 1974, mem. nat. exec. com., from 1974, mem. nat. bd. Can.-Israel com., from 1974; rabbi Temple Sinai Congregation, Toronto, Ont., Can. Mem. exec. com. bd. govs. Hebrew Union Coll.; Can. sr. del. Internat. Commn. on Interreligious Consultation, Geneva, 1973, London, 1975; founding mem. Nat. Christian-Jewish Consultation of Can. Jewish Congress, Can. Coun. Chs., Can. Conf. Cath. Bishops, Toronto Top Level Clerical Interreligious Luncheon Group; mem. Can. Jewish Congress, Anglican Ch. Consultation; participant internat. exploratory meetings with evangs. and fundamentalists, L.A., Houston; participant World Co. Chs. Gen. Assembly; commentator CBC TV religious programs. Columnist editor Toronto Star; corr. editor Christian-Jewish Rels.; contbr. articles to various publs. Nat. pres., bd. govs. Friends Ben Gurion U., Can. Coun. Christians and Jews, Juvenile Diabetes Rsch. Found., Crusade against Leukemia, Dysautonomia Found. Can., Found. against Addictive Gambling; chaplain Variety Club, Toronto. Recipient Scroll of Honour Toronto, Nat. Humanitarian award Can. Coun. Christians and Jews, 1990; named hon. citizen Municipality of Met. Toronto; Samuel Abrams fellow Hebrew Union Coll., Cin., 1951; scholar-in-residence N.Y. Sch. of Hebrew Union Coll., Jewish Inst. Religion, 1981; Rabbi Jordan Pearlson outreach program named in his honor Ben Gurion U., Negev, Israel. Mem. Cen. Conf. Am. Rabbis (fin. sec. 1976-79), Toronto Bd. Rabbis (past pres.), Hebrew Union Coll. Rabbinic Alumni Assn. (pres. 1976-77). Home: Willowdale, Canada. Died Feb. 19, 2008.

**PEARLSTEIN, STEPHANIE LILIENTHAL,** social worker, consultant, therapist; b. NYC, May 6, 1915; d. Jacob and Rose (Adlerstein) Lilienthal; m. Benjamin Jacob Pearlstein, May 30, 1946; 1 child, Arne J. BA, Hunter Coll., CUNY, 1940; MSS, Smith Coll., 1942. Lic. clin. social worker. Social worker Jewish Bd. of Guardians, NYC, 1942-45; asst. field dir. overseas hosp. svc. Army Gen. Hosp.-ARC, France, 1945-46; psychiat. social worker VA Brentwood (Calif.) Psychiat. Hosp., 1946; social worker, student supr. Jewish Family Svc., L.A. and Santa Monica, Calif., 1946-48; mental health cons. L.A. County Dept. of Mental Health, 1965-68; social worker Harbor Gen. Hosp., Torrance, Calif., 1968-69, supr. psychiat. social svc., 1969-77; oncology svc. social worker Daniel Freeman Hosp., Inglewood, Calif., 1977-78; ind. after care cons. LA, 1978-87; ret. Community cons. head start and elem. schs., L.A., 1968-69. Mem. Nat. Assn. Social Workers, Acad. Cert. Social Workers, Plato Soc. Avocations: current events, gardening, sewing, reading, concerts and theater. Died May 1, 1993.

**PEASE, ELLA LOUISE,** elementary school educator; b. Kokomo, Ind., May 31, 1928; d. James E. and Carrie Alice (Ringer) Earnest; m. Harold Edwin Pease, Aug. 10, 1985; children: Charles Miller, James Miller, Ricky Ensley, Wanda Cisna. BS, Ball State U., 1956, MA, 1959; postgrad., Ind. U., Ft. Wayne. Tchr. 1st grade Union Twp. (Ind.) Pub. Schs., 1953-56, Wells City (Ind.) Pub. Schs., Forest Park Sch., Ft. Wayne, Ind., 1956-93. Docent Ft. Wayne Art Mus. Mem. NEA-Ret., Ret. Ind. Tchrs. Assn., Ft. Wayne Ret. Tchrs. Assn. Methodist. Deceased.

**PEASE, STEPHEN L.,** nursing management administrator; b. Worcester, Mass., Sept. 5, 1953; BSN, Regents Coll., Albany, NY, 1985; MSN, Anna Maria Coll., Paxton, Mass., 1993. Nursing supr. Univ. Commons, Worcester, from 1993; adminstr. mgr. U. Mass. Med. Ctr., Worcester. Mem. ANA, Mass. Nurses Assn. Died Aug. 21, 2001.

**PEATMAN, JOHN GRAY,** statistician, psychologist; b. Centerville, Iowa, Mar. 16, 1904; s. Clarence Albert and Oriel (Gray) Peatman; m. Lillie Burling Peatman, 1927; children: Alice Peatman Dettmers, John, William; m. Madeline Martin Peatman, 1948 (dec. 1984); 1 child, Mary Peatman Fitzpatrick. Attended, U. Colo., 1923—25; AB, Columbia U., 1927, MA, 1928, PhD, 1931. Pres., dir. Office Rsch. NY, 1941—58; vis. prof. stats. Columbia U., 1948; ednl. cons. US Air Force, 1949—50; cons., chmn. arbitration panels ASCAP, 1954—56; bd. dirs. Silvermine, Conn. Cmty. Assn., 1962—63; pres., dir. Res. Cons., Inc., Norwalk, Conn., from 1950; mem. faculty CCNY, 1929—70, prof. psychology, 1946—70, chmn. dept., 1953—62, assoc. dean, 1943—53, emeritus prof., from 1970. Author: Descriptive and Sampling Statistics, 1947, Introduction to Applied Statistics, 1963; contbr. articles in field to profl. lit. Fellow: AAUP, Psychonomic Soc., NY State Psychol. Assn. (pres. 1949—50), Am. Psychol. Assn. (chmn. policy and planning bd. 1949—50, past chmn. various coms.); mem.: U. Club, Sigma Xi (pres. CCNY chpt. 1961—62), Phi Beta Kappa. Died Mar. 9, 1997.

**PECK, ELLIE ENRIQUEZ,** retired state administrator; b. Sacramento, Oct. 21, 1932; d. Rafael Enriquez and Eloisa Garcia Rivera; m. Raymond Charles Peck, Sept. 5, 1959(dec. July 30, 2013); children: Reginaldo, Enrico, Francisca Guerrero, Teresa, Linda, Margaret, Raymond Charles, Christina. Student polit. sci., Sacramento State U., 1974. Tng. svcs. coord. Calif. Divsn. Hwys., Sacramento, 1963-67, tech. and mgmt. cons., 1968-78; expert examiner Calif. Pers. Bd., Sacramento, 1976-78; tng. cons. Calif. Pers. Devel. Ctr., Sacramento, 1978; spl. cons. Calif. Commn. on Fair Employment and Housing, Sacramento, 1978; cmty. svcs. rep. U.S. Bur. of Census, No. Calif. counties, 1978-80; project dir. Golden State Sr. Discount Program, 1980-83; dir. spl. programs Calif. Lt. Gov., 1983-90; ret., 1990; pvt. cons. Sacramento, from 1990. Project dir. SSI/QMB Outreach Project, 1993-94; cons., project dir. nat. sr. health issues summit Congress Calif. Srs. Edn. and Rsch. Fund, 1995; project dir. various post-White House Conf. on Aging seminars and roundtables, 1995-97; coord. Calif. Sr. Legis., 1995-97, 2000-05; exec. dir. SMART Coalition Calif., 1997-2004. Mem. editl. adv. bd. Latino Jour. Mag., 1996—2002. Campaign workshop dir. Chicano/Latino Youth Leadership Conf., from 1982; chmn. ethnic minority task force sacramento, sierra Am. Diabetes Assn., 1988—90; steering com. Calif. Self-Esteem Minority Task Force, 1990—93; v.p. Comision Femenil Nacional, Inc., 1987—90; del. Dem. Nat. Conv., 1976, White House Conf. Aging, 1995; mem. exec. bd. Calif. Dem. Ctrl. Com., 1977—95, mem., 1997—2001; bd. dirs. Sacramento/Sierra Am. Diabetes Assn., 1989—90; trustee Stanford Settlement Inc., Sacramento, 1975—79; bd. dirs. Sacramento Emergency Housing Ctr., 1974—77, Sacramento Cmty. Svcs. Planning Coun., 1987—90, Calif. Advs. for Nursing Home Reform, 1990—96, v.p., 1994—96; bd. dirs. Calif. Human Devel. Corp., 1995—2003. Recipient Outstanding Cmty. Svc. award, Comunicaciones Unidos de Norte Atzian, 1975, 1977, Vol. Svc. award, Calif. Human Devel. Corp., 1998, Outstanding Svc. award, Chicano/Hispanic Dem. Caucus, 1979, Vol. Svc. award, Calif. Human Devel. Corp., 1981, Outstanding Advocate award, Calif. Sr. Legis., 1988—89, Meritorious Svc. to Hispanic Cmty. award, Comite Patriotico, 1989, Cert. Recognition, Sacramento County Human Rights Commn., 1991, Tish Sommers award, Older Women's League/Joint Resolution Calif. Legislature, 1993, Latino Eagle award in govt., 1994, Mentor Yr. award, Latina Leadership Network, 2002, Outstanding Vol. Svs. Throughout Yrs. award, Calif. Sr. Legislature, 2003, Outstanding Vol. award, CLYLP, 2005; named Outstanding Advocate on Aging Issues, Calif. State Senate, 1998, Dem. Yr., Sacramento County Dem. Com., 1987. Mem. Hispanic C. of C., Older Women's League, Nat. Coun. Silver Haired Legislators, Nat. Coun. La Raza, Congress Calif. (sr.), Folson Dem. Club. Died July 30, 2013.

**PECK, GARNET EDWARD,** pharmacist, educator; b. Windsor, Ont., Can., Feb. 4, 1930; s. William Crozier and Dorothy (Marentette) P.; m. Mary Ellen Hoffman, Aug. 24, 1957; children: Monique Elizabeth, Denise Anne, Philip Warren, John Edward. BS in Pharmacy with Distinction, Ohio No. U., 1957; MS in Indsl. Pharmacy, Purdue U., 1959, PhD, 1962. Sr. scientist Mead Johnson Research Center, 1962-65, group leader, 1965-67; assoc. prof. indsl. and phys. pharmacy Purdue U., West Lafayette, 1967—73, prof., 1973—2003, dir. indsl. pharmacy lab., from 1975, assoc. dept. head, 1989-96, prof. emeritus, from 2003. Cons. in field. Contbr. articles to profl. jours. Mem. West Lafayette Mayor's Advisory Com. on Community Devel., 1973-; mem. West Lafayette Citizen's Safety Com., 1974-81; mem. West Lafayette Park Bd., 1981-2010, pres., 1983-96. Served with U.S. Army, 1951-53. Recipient Lederle Faculty award Purdue U., 1976 Fellow APHA, AAAS, Am. Inst. Chem., Am. Assn. Pharm. Scientists; mem. Am. Chem. Soc., Acad. Rsch. and Sci. (Sidney Riegelman award 1994), Am. Assn. Colls. Pharmacy, Cath. Acad. Sci. (founding mem.), KC, Knight of Holy Sepulchre, Sigma Xi, Rho Chi, Phi Lambda Upsilon, Phi Kappa Phi, Phi Sigma Lambda, Phi Lambda Sigma. Roman Catholic. Home: West Lafayette, Ind. Died Sept. 16, 2014.

**PECZENIK, ALEKSANDER,** law educator; b. Krakow, Poland, Nov. 16, 1937; s. Karol and Zofia Peczenik; m. Irena Nowak, Jan. 1, 1993; 1 child, Karol Nowak. ML, Jagiellonian U., Krakow, 1960, LLD, 1963, Dr. habil. Law, 1966; postgrad., Stockholm U., 1970—75; PhD, Lund U.,

Sweden, 1983, LLD (hon.), 1987. Assoc. prof. Silesian U., Katowice, Poland, 1966—69, Stockholm U., Stockholm, 1970—75; prof. jurisprudence Lund U., from 1978. Mem.: Internat. Assn. Philosophy Law (pres. from 2003). Home: Lund, Sweden. Died Sept. 2005.

**PEDERSEN, WESLEY NIELS MUNKHOLM,** public relations and public affairs counselor; b. South Sioux City, Nebr., July 10, 1922; s. Peder Westergaard and Marie Gertrude (Sorensen) P.; m. Angeline Kathryn Vavra, Oct. 17, 1948; 1 son, Eric Wesley. Student, Tri-State Coll., Sioux City, Iowa, 1940-41; BA summa cum laude, Upper Iowa U., Fayette; postgrad. in Russian, George Washington U., 1958—59. Editor, writer Sioux City Jour., 1941-50; corr. N.Y. Times, Life, Time, Fortune, 1948-50; editor US Dept. State, 1950—52, fgn. svc. officer Hong Kong, 1960-63; fgn. affairs columnist, roving corr., counselor summit meetings and fgn. ministers conferences US Info. Agy. (USIA), 1952—60, chief, worldwide spl. publications & graphics programs, 1963-69; chief Office Spl. Projects, Washington, 1969-78, Office Spl. Projects, Internat. Comm. Agy., 1978-79; v.p. Fraser Associates, Washington, 1979-80; dir. comm. & public rels. Public Affairs Coun., Washington, 1980—2006; prin. Wes Pedersen Communications, 2006—13. Lectr. creative comm. Upper Iowa U., 1975; chmn., Europe, Ambassadorial Internat. Affairs Seminar, Fgn. Svc. Inst., 1975; lectr. internat. public rels. Pub. Rels. Inst., American U., 1976; lectr. bus. and mgmt. divsn. NYU, 1976-78; cons. pub. rels., editl. and design; del. founding sessions 1st Amendment Congress, Phila. and Williamsburg, Va., 1980, exec. com., 1980; columnist O'Dwyer Pub. Relations Newsletter, 2008-13, O'Dwyer's Magazine, 2008-13. Columnist: (as Paul L. Ford) The World Today, 1952-60; (as Benjamin E. West) Behind the Curtain, 1952-60; White House Report, 1966-69 (as Wesley Pedersen), Washington Report-Pub. Rels. Jour., 1980-85; author: Mr. President: Lyndon B. Johnson, 1964, Legacy of a President: The Memorable Words of John F. Kennedy, 1964, Journey to the Pacific, 1965, decision '68', How Am. Elect Their Pres., Mr. President: Richard M. Nixon, 1969, Pres. Nixon in Europe, 1969, American Heroes of Asian Wars, 1969; co-author: Effective Government Public Affairs, 1981; editor: The Imam's Story, 1961, Escape at Midnight and Other Stories (Pearl S. Buck), 1962, Exodus From China (Harry Redl), 1962, Macao, 1962, The Dividing Line (Arturo Gonzalez), 1962, China's Men of Letters (K.E. Priestley), 1963, Children of China (Pearl S. Buck and Margaret Wylie), 1963, Destination the Moon (William Howard), 1964, Man on the Moon, 1964, Nine From Little Rock, 1964, We Shall Overcome, 1964, To the Moon and Beyond, 1965, Bounty From the Land, 1965, Workers Paradise Lost (Eugene Lyons), 1967, The Americans and the Arts (Howard Taubman), 1969, The Dance in America (Agnes de Mille), 1969, Getting the Most From Grassroots Public Affairs Programs, 1980, Computer Applications in Public Affairs, 1984, Cost-Effective Management for Today's Public Affairs, 1984, Making Community Relations Pay Off: Tools and Strategies, 1988, Winning at the Grassroots: How to Succeed in the Legislative Arena by Mobilizing Employees and Other Allies, 1989, Leveraging State Government Relations, 1990, Managing the Business-Employee PAC, 1992, Adding Value to the Public Affairs Function, 1994, Winning at the Grassroots (with Tony Kramer), 2000, Managing the Corporate Political Action Committee, 2001; Pub. Affairs Rev. Mag., 1980-86, 2000-05, Impact newsletter Columnist O'Dwyer Pub. Rels. Newsletter, 2008-; on nat. and internat. pub. affairs, 1980-2006; contbr. to The Commissar, 1972, Informing the People: A Public Affairs Handbook, 1981, The Practice of Public Relations, 1984, 2d edit., 2003, Legislative Careers: Why and How We Should Study Them, 1999, Encyclopedia of Public Relations, 2004, Corporate Public Affairs: Interacting with Interest Groups, Media, and Government, 2006, Implausible Deniabilities, 2007; mem. editl. bd. Pub. Rels. Quar., 1975-2013, Washington editor, Pub. Rels. Quar., 1998—2008, Fgn. Svc. Jour., 1975-81; mem. editl. adv. bd. Pub. Rels. News, 1991-98, contbg. editor Pub. Affairs News Mag., London, 2004-13; author scripts Uncle Walter's Doghouse radio show, 1938; contbr. articles to profl. jours. Founding chmn. bd. dirs. Nat. Inst. for Govt. Pub. Info. Rsch., American U., 1977-80. Served with Air Corps, US Army, 1943-46. Recipient 3 awards A.P. Mng. Editors Assn., Iowa, 1948-49, Meritorious Svc. award USIA, 1963, Superior Svc. award USIA, 1964, Presdl. commendation, 1964, 70, 1st prize Fed. Editors Assn., 1970, 74-75, Agy. Dir.'s citation USIA, 1965, 74, 78, Soc. Tech. Comm., 1974-76, Gold award Internat. Newsletter Conf., 1982, Silver award, 1985, Eddi award for design excellence Editor's Workshop, 1983, Gold Circle award Am. Soc. Assn. Execs., 1983-89, 97-2000, Ten Cool award American Soc. Assn. Execs., 2001, Editors' Forum award, 1988-90, 94-96, Assn. Trends award, 1989-2005, Lifetime Great Assn. Communicator award, Assn. Trends, 1999, Best of Century Comm. award, Assn. Trends, 2001, spl. citation Assn. Trends, 2001, 07, PR Week 2008, Silver award 2004, 05, Gold award, 2004, Excellence award, 2006, Grand prize Internat. Ann. Report Conf., 1989, Gold award 1997, Comm. Concepts awards, 1989-2006, Grand Comm. Concepts awards, 1992, 95, 2000, 02, 04-06, MerComm awards, 1990-2000, Nat. Media Conf. award, 1989-90, Internat. Acad. Comm. Arts & Sciences award, 1994-98, 2000, Grand prize, 1995, awards Printing and Graphic Assn., 1987, 91, 96-97, 2000, Excell award Soc. of Nat. Assn. Publishers, 2000, Judges' award 2000; named Most Outstanding Info. Officer in Exec. Br. Govt. Info. Orgn., 1975, Ky. Col. and Adm. Nebr. Navy, 1984. Mem. DAV, American Fgn. Svc. Assn., American Legion, Internat. Assn. Bus. Communicators (Communicator of Yr. Washington chpt. 1978, various awards 1973, 76-78, 84, 90, 94-2004, Winners' Circle awards dist. III 1996-2003), Nat. Assn. Govt. Communicators (pres. 1978-79, Communicator of Yr. 1977, Disting. Svc. award 1978), Pub. Rels. Soc. America (mem. Counselor's Acad. 1980—, chmn. 1st Amendment task force 1980-81, hall of fame steering com. mem., 2008-2009, co-recipient Thoth award 1980-81, 94, twin Thoth awards 1995-97, 2003, Thoth awards 1998-2003, Bronze Anvil award 2000, named to Hall of Fame 2005), Am. Soc. Profl. Communicators (Colonial award 2002, Masters award 2004), World Affairs Coun., Soc. Profl. Journalists, The Acad. Polit. Sci. Episcopalian. *Keenness of mind and an abundance of luck, it is said, are the key ingredients of personal success. The truth be told, however, I've performed only one act of brilliance in my lifetime: the selection of my parents. But I've had an enormous amount of good fortune, a fact manifestly clear to anyone who has ever met my wife, my son and my granddaughters. They, thank goodness, chose me.* Died Dec. 4, 2013.

**PEEBLES, CHRISTOPHER SPALDING,** anthropologist, educator, academic administrator; b. Clearwater, Fla., May 26, 1939; s. Frederick Thomas and Corinne deGarmendia (Stephens) P.; m. Laura Ann Wisen, Oct. 6, 1993. AB, U. Chgo., 1963; PhD, U. Calif., Santa Barbara, 1974. Asst. prof. U. Windsor, Ont., Canada, 1970-74; asst. curator U. Mich., Ann Arbor, 1974-81; prof. prehistory U. Amsterdam, Netherlands, 1981-82; prof. Ind. U., Bloomington, from 1983, dean acad. computing, assoc. v.p., 1992—2005, dean emeritus, assoc. v.p. emeritus. Author: Excavations at Moundville, 1974, Representations in Archaeology, 1992. With USAF, 1956-60. Mem. Cosmos Club. Avocation: flying. Home: Bloomington, Ind. Died Apr. 16, 2012.

**PELLETIER, JEAN,** former mayor; b. Chicoutimi, Que., Can., Feb. 21, 1935; s. Burroughs and Marie (Desautels) P.; m. Hélène Bhérer, June 3, 1961; children: Jean, Marie. Student, Laval U., Quebec. Journalist Sta. CFCM-TV, Quebec, 1957; corr. Radio Can., Québec, 1958-59; press sec. Premier's Office, 1959—60; exec. sec. Commn. des monuments historiques Qué., 1960-62; stock broker Levesque & Beaubien, 1964-70; v.p. Dumont Express, Québec, 1970-73, L'Action Sociale Ltée, Québec, 1973-77; mcpl. councillor City of Quebec, 1976-77, mayor, 1977-89; chief of staff Leader of the Opposition, 1991-93; chief of staff to prime min. Govt. of Can., 1993—2001; chmn VIA Rail, 2001—04. Mem. exec. com. Quebec Urban Community; pres. Expert Group on Old Age People Policies, 1990-91. Past pres. Assn. des scouts du Can., 1969-72; pres. Carnaval de Quebec, 1973; ex-dir. gen. Centraide, 1973-77; v.p. Festival d'art dramatique du Can., 1961-65; mem. Quebec-Ont. Task Force on the Rapid Train Project for Quebec-Windsor Corridor; officer of Ordre de la Pleiade of the Internat. Assembly of French Parliamentarians. Decorated Order of Can., 1985, Officer, 2003; Legion of Honor (France), 1987, Comdr, 1998; Officer del l'Ordre national du Quebec, 1990 Mem. Fedn. Can. Municipalities (past pres.), Union Municipalities Québec (past pres.); Assn. Mayors French-Speaking Capitals of the World (v.p.) Roman Catholic. Home: Quebec, Canada. Died Jan. 10, 2009.

**PELLICONE, WILLIAM,** artist, sculptor, architect, writer; b. Phila., Apr. 12, 1915; s. Emilio and Amelia (Practico) P.; m. Marle Guzzette, July 1964 (div. 1992); m. Ilka Bartel, Aug. 5, 1992. Student, Temple U., Pa. Acad. Fine Arts. Lectr. art Phila. Parkway Mus., Queens Settlement, N.Y., U. Iowa, Iowa City, Delaware Sch. Sys., Converse Coll., S.C., Ednl. Alliance, N.Y. One-man shows include Allen Stone Gallery, N.Y., Beryl Lush Gallery, Phila., Trylon Gallery, Southampton, N.Y., Capricorn Gallery, Bethesda, Md., Opus 127 Gallery, Soho, N.Y.C., Harpers Coll., Binghamton, N.Y., Phoenix Gallery, N.Y., Creighton Univ., Nebr., Gallery East, East Hampton, N.Y., Frederick Spratt Gallery, San Jose, Calif., Cheltenham (Pa.) Gallery, Goodman Gallery, South Hampton, N.Y., Woodmere (Pa.) Mus., Frederick Spratt Gallery, San Jose; group shows include Allan Stone Gallery, N.Y., Egan Gallery, N.Y., Alan Gallery, N.Y., Betty Parsons Gallery, N.Y., Tanager Gallery, N.Y., Phoenix Gallery, N.Y., M & L Gallery of Fine Art, N.Y., Arsenal Gallery, N.Y., Camino Gallery, N.Y., Trylon Gallery, N.Y., March Gallery, N.Y., Capricorn Gallery, Bethesda, Md., Brata Gallery, N.Y., Art Alliance, Phila., Landmark Gallery, N.Y., Tenth St. Days, N.Y., Profile Gallery, N.Y., Noho Gallery, N.Y., Gallery East, East Hampton, N.Y., Marie Pellicone Gallery, N.Y., Parish Mus., Southampton, N.Y., Elaine Benson Gallery, Bridgehampton, N.Y., Belanthi Gallery, A Retrospective, Bklyn., Lombardi Gallery, Retrospective, Austin, Tex., 1997; represented in permanent collections, including Met. Mus. Art, N.Y.C., Boston Mus., Smithsonian Inst., Washington, Am. Broadcasting Collection, Iowa Mus., Iowa City, Bayonne (N.J.) Mus., Martin-Rathburn Gallery, San Antonio. With Merchant Marines, 1943-45, France. Grantee Barnes Found., Temple U., Pa. Acad. Fine Arts, Greek Govt., others; exhibited first in Pa. Acad. Fine Arts, Phila. Republican. Avocations: musician, sailing, carpentry, writing. Deceased.

**PELTOLA, PENTTI JOHANNES,** clinical pharmacology educator; b. Oct. 30, 1918; Clinical pharmacology educator; b. Ilmajoki, Finland, Oct. 30, 1918; s. Viljo T. and Kaisa M. (Latikka) P.; m. Ziricli Freja Nikkinen, Apr. 22, 1951 (dec. 1970); children— Outi Inkeri, Riitta Sinikka; m. Leena Liisa Wallenius, June 16, 1973. M.A., U. Helsinki, 1945. Specialist in internal med., 1948, in pharmacology, 1952, reader in internal medicine, 1962, specialist clin. pharmacol., 1966. Asst. dept. pharmacology Kivela Hosp., Helsinki, 1945-51, asst. dept. internal medicine, 1945-56, chief physician, 1957-71; prof. clin. pharmacology U. Helsinki, 1971— . Co-author numerous med. books. Mem. editorial bd. Internat. Jour. Clin. Pharmacology, 1967—, Jour. Internat. Med. Research, 1973— . Contbr. articles to profl. jours.; head adminstrn. Vets. Hosp., Kauniala, 1953—; mem. council Prosthesis Found., 1953—, Kaskisaari Rehab. Ctr., 1958— . Served to capt. M.C., Finnish Armed Forces, 1938-44. Mem. Finnish Pharm. Soc. (sec. 1949-58), Finnish Rheumatol. Assn. (sec. 1953-67), Scandinavian Clin. Pharmacologists (chmn. Finnish sect. 1975—), Internat. Soc. Internal Medicine, Royal Soc. Medicine (Eng.), European Thyroid Assn. (founding mem.), European Soc. Clin. Investigation (founding mem.), N.Y. Acad. Scis. Lutheran. Deceased.

**PENCE, JEAN VIRGINIA (JEAN PENCE),** retired real estate broker; d. William Roscoe and Sophie Cottrell; m. Robert Albert Pence, June 14, 1947; children: Marjorie Pence Tuinstra, Robert J. Grad., Realtors Inst., Ill. Assn. Realtors. Cert. in real estate Central YMCA Coll., 1976. Sales assoc. William Knight Co., Realtors, LaGrange, Ill., 1962—70, sales mgr., 1970—76; pres. Pence & Co., Realtors, LaGrange, 1976—86; freelance writer Sun City Center, Fla., from 1999. Chmn. LaGrange Go-Getters Com. Channel 11 WTTG, Chgo., 1973—74. Author: (genealogy) The Cottrell Adventure With the Wright Connection, (novel) The Apprentice Angel, short stories; contbr. articles to profl. publs. Sec. bd. deacons St. Andrew Presbyn. Ch., Sun City Center, 2003—05. Recipient award, Freelance Writer Report Contests, Cross TIME Sci. Fiction Anthology, Spl. award, Abilene Writes Group, Top Ten award, By Line Mag. Short Fiction Contest. Mem.: DAR (vice regent Clearwater chpt. 1984—86), Women's Coun. Realtors (pres. West suburban chpt. 1979—81), DuPage Bd. Realtors, LaGrange Bd. Realtors (sec.-treas. 1973—75, dir. multiple listing service 1978, chmn. profl. standards com. 1985—86), Nat. Assn. Realtors, Coterie (pres. 1982—83), LaGrange Park Woman's (sec. 1967—68), Pierre Chastain Family Assn. (press chmn. 1998—2001). Home: Sun City Center, Fla. Died Sept. 18, 2013.

**PENDSE, ARVIND KASHINATH,** surgeon; b. Mumbai, India, Feb. 11, 1938; s. Kashinath Narayan and Leelawati Kashinath (Joshi) P.; m. Vinaya Arvind Hegde,Nov. 30, 1963; children: Anjali, Narayan. MB BChir, SMS Med. Coll., Jaipur, India, 1960, MS in Gen. Surgery, 1963. Cert. surgeon Raj Med. Coun. Resident surgeon SMS Med. Coll., Jaipur, 1960-63; CAS, tutor surgeon Govt. Rajasthan, Jaipur, 1965-66, from asst. prof. surgery to assoc. prof. surgery, 1966-84, prof. surgery, 1984-94, sr. prof. surgery, from 1994. Head dept. surgery RNT Med. Coll., Udaipur, India, 1994-96. Author: (book) Bed-Side Clinics in Surgery, 1990; editor: (books) Multidimensional Approach to Urolithiasis, 1988, Emerging Concepts in Urolithiasis, 1988, Free Radicals in Health and Disease, 1999. Mng. trustee Dr. Singh Trust, Udaipur, 1995—; life mem. Red Cross Soc. Recipient Dist. award Family Welfare Collector, 1983-84; named Expert All India Radio, 1977. Fellow Internat. Coll. Surgeons (Best Paper 1988), Assn. Surg. India, Indian med. Assn. (life), Udaipur (life), Urolithiasis Soc. Ind. (life). Avocations: photography, reading. Home: Udaipur, India. Died Apr. 8, 2005.

**PENNINGTON, DOROTHY CAROLYN,** financial planner; b. Imogene, SD, Dec. 24, 1921; d. Ruben Allan and Ida Millie (Obst) Haggart; m. Charles J. Pennington, May 31, 1947 (dec. Oct. 1955); m. James E. Shreffler. Student, Black Hills Tchrs. Coll., 1939-41; BBA, Golden Gate U., 1965, MBA, 1968. Cert. fin. planner. Adminstrv. asst. Crowley Enterprises, San Francisco, 1955-70; registered rep. Putnam Fin. Svcs., San Rafael, Calif., 1968-73, Waddell & Reed, Kansas City, Mo., 1973-74, Pace Securities Inc., San Francisco, 1974-76, Ind. Fin. Planners, Parsippany, N.J., 1976-80, Judy & Robinson Securities, Menlo Park, Calif., 1980-87; br. mgr. Planned Investments, Inc., Murphys, Calif., 1987-95; ret., 1995. V.p. Faith Luth. Ch., Murphys, 1988-90, pres., 1990-92; auditor Republican Women, Calaveras County, Calif., 1989-92; mem. AAUW, Calaveras County, 1987-92. Avocations: reading, sewing, computers. Home: Murphys, Calif. Died Dec. 22, 1999.

**PEPOL, ANNA TERESA,** librarian; b. Matyszolika, Poland, Nov. 1, 1945; d. Albin and Janina Jackowska Wnukowski; m. Jerry Pepol, Apr. 28, 1973; children: Magdalena, Marek, Stefan. MS, U. Poland. Libr. acquisitions dept. Olsztyn, Poland, 1972-76, libr. serials dept., 1976-83, head dept., 1983-90; with Brit. Coun., Warsaw, 1984-90; with info. dept. Olsztyn, 1990-93, system mgr., from 1993, dep. libr., 1998—2002. Contbr. articles to profl. jours. Roman Catholic. Avocations: classical music, terroist. Home: Olsztyn, Poland. Died Dec. 8, 2002.

**PEPPER, CURTIS BILL,** writer; b. Huntington, W.Va., Aug. 30, 1920; s. Curtis Gordon and Edwina Neihl (Sheppard) P.; m. Beverly Stoll, Oct. 11, 1949; children: Jorie Graham, John Randolph. Student, U. Ill., 1937-39, U. Florence, Italy, 1947-49. Free-lance writer, TV, films, 1949-55. Reporter UP, Rome, 1955-57, CBS, 1957-58; bur. chief Newsweek, Rome, 1958-68; free-lance writer, author, N.Y.C., 1968-2014 Author: The Pope's Back Yard, 1966; An Artist and the Pope (Book of Month Club), 1968; (with Christiaan Barnard) One Life (Lit. Guild), 1969; Marco (Book of Month Club alt.), 1977; Kidnapped! 17 Days of Terror, 1978; We the Victors, 1984, Leonardo, 2012, Happiness: Fragments of Happiness in the Lives of the Famous and Others Among Us, 2014 Served to major U.S. Army, 1943-47, ETO. Decorated bronze star, Knight of New Europe. Mem. Authors Guild, Century Assn., Overseas Press Club, City Athletic Club (N.Y.C.). Avocations: tennis, swimming. Home: Kermit, W.Va. Died Apr. 4, 2014.

**PERKIN, HAROLD JAMES,** retired social historian, educator; b. Nov. 11, 1926; s. Robert James and Hilda May (Dillon) P.; m. Joan Griffiths, July 3, 1948; children: Deborah Jane, Julian Robert. BA with 1st class distinction, Cambridge U., 1948, MA, 1952. From asst. lectr. to lectr. social history Manchester U., 1951-65; sr. lectr. Lancaster U., 1965-67, prof. social history, 1967-84, dir. ctr. social history, 1975-84, vis. prof., 1984-97, prof. emeritus, 1997—2004; prof. history Northwestern U., Evanston, Ill., 1985-97, prof. higher edn., 1987-97, prof. emeritus, 1997—2004. Vis. fellow Princeton U., 1979-80; fellow Nat. Humanities Ctr., N.C., 1982-83; hon. prof. U. Wales,

Cardiff, 1997—. Author: The Origins of Modern English Society, 1780-1880, 1969, new edit., 2002, Key Profession: The History of the Association of University Teachers, 1969, New Universities in the U.K., 1969, The Age of the Railway, 1970, The Age of the Automobile, 1976, The Structured Crowd, 1980, Professionalism, Property and English Society since 1880, 1981, The Rise of Professional Society: England since 1880, 1989, new edit., 2002, Higher Education and English Society, Japanese transl., 1993, The Third Revolution: Professional Elites in the Modern World, 1996, The Making of a Social Historian, 2002. With RAF, 1948-50. Recipient Gold medal Nat. Inst. Ednl. Rsch., Tokyo, 1982; maj. scholar Cambridge U., 1945-48; John S. Guggenheim fellow, 1989-90. Fellow Royal Hist. Soc.; mem. Social History Soc. U.K. (life v.p., founder 1976), Econ. History Soc., History of Edn. Soc., Assn. Univ. Tchrs. (pres. 1970-71). Home: London, England. Died Oct. 16, 2004.

**PERL, MARTIN LEWIS,** physicist, educator, chemical engineer; b. NYC, June 24, 1927; children: Jed, Anne, Matthew, Joseph. B in Chem. Engring., Poly. Inst. Bklyn., 1948; PhD, Columbia U., 1955; ScD (hon.), U. Chgo., 1990; D (hon.), U. Belgrade, 2009. Chem. engr. Gen. Electric Co., 1948—50; asst. prof. physics U. Mich., 1955—58, assoc. prof., 1958—63; prof. Stanford U., 1963—2004, prof. emeritus, 2004—14. Author: High Energy Hadron Physics, 1975, Reflections on Experimental Science, 1996; contbr. articles on high energy physics and on relation of sci. to soc. to profl. jours. Served in US Mcht. Marine, 1944—45 US Army, 1946—47. Recipient Wolf prize in Physics, Wolf Found., Israel, 1982, Nobel Prize in Physics, Royal Swedish Acad. Sciences, 1995. Fellow: American Phys. Soc.; mem.: NAS, American Acad. Arts & Sciences. Home: Palo Alto, Calif. Died Sept. 30, 2014.

**PERLIN, BERNARD,** artist; b. Richmond, Va., Nov. 21, 1918; Student, New Sch. of Design, 1936—37, Art Students League, 1936—37. Illustrator Life Mag., Fortune Mag.; instr. Wooster Cmty. Art Ctr., Danbury, Conn., 1967—69. Represented in permanent collections US Post Off., Tate Gallery, London, Nat. Collection Fine Art, Smithsonian Inst., Mus. Modern Art & Whitney Mus. Am. Art, NYC, Va. Mus. Fine Art. Recipient Nat. Inst. Arts & Letters award, 1964; grantee Koscuiszko Found. award, Poland, Fulbright Fellow, 1950, John Simon Guggenheim Fellow, 1954—55, 1959. Mem.: NAD (assoc. 1957—94, academician from 1994). Home: Ridgefield, Conn. Died Jan. 14, 2014.

**PERNY, GUY CHARLES-MARIE,** retired physicist, educator; b. Sarreguemines, Moselle, France, June 7, 1923; s. Charles-Marie and Florentina (Sandrino da Pino) P.; m. Marilène Paulus, Aug. 2,1949; children: Chantal, Geneviève, Michel. Cert. higher diploma, École Nat. d'Ingénieurs, Strasbourg, 1947; PhD in Phys. Scis., U. Strasbourg, France, 1957. Asst. prof. edn., 1948-52; rsch. fellow Ctr. Nat. Recherche Sci., 1952-57; prof. physics École Nat. Supérieure de Chimie, Mulhouse, France, 1957-59; assoc. prof. Faculty of Scis., Strasbourg, 1959-63, prof., 1964-77, U. de Haute-Alsace, 1977-85. Dir. Ctr. Nat. Conservatory of Arts and Crafts, Mulhouse-Colmar, 1959-61; dir., founder U. Inst. Tech., Mulhouse-Colmar, 1967-71, Physics-Chemistry Lab. of Thin Films, Mulhouse, 1957; co-founder Spectroscopy and Optics Lab. for Solid State, U. Strasbourg, 1952-57. Author: Aspects du Haut Moyen Age Alsacien, 1995, Sur la prééminence des Alsaciens, 1997, Nouvelles Recherches sur la Fondation de l'Ordre des Hospitaliers de Saint Jean de Jérusalem, 1999, Nos Ancêtres les Alsaciens, 2000, La Belle Strasbourgeoise, 2001, La Famille des Andlauer, 2002, Centenaire de la naissance d'Alfred Kastler, Nobel Prize for Physics, 1966, 2003, Adalric Duc d' Alsace, 2004, Waldrade de Marlenheim, 2005; contbr. numerous sci. articles to profl. publs. Coll. Pres. Pierre Pflimlin, France, 1945-48; collaborator Liberation Com. With French Resistance, 1940-45. Recipient Medal of Honor, City of Colmar, 1993, Hungarian Acad. Scis., 1995, City of Rosheim, 2000, City of Soultz, 2005 Dipl. Honor, City of Pino Lago Maggiore, 2005, also several mil. and civil medals; named Citizen of Honor, City of Andlau, 1994. Mem. AAAS, French Soc. Physics, Divsn. Atomic and Molecular Physics (mem. bur. 1984-93), Hist. Soc. France, N.Y. Acad. Scis. (emeritus), Acad. Stanislas, Nat. Acad Metz., Acad. Alsace (chancellor 1984-87), Louis de Broglie Found. Achievements include discovery of new concept Ef in physics, chemistry, medicine and economy, 1988-91. Home: Strasbourg, France. Died May 9, 2006.

**PERRAULT, RAYMOND JOSEPH,** retired Canadian legislator; b. Vancouver, BC, Can., Feb. 6, 1926; s. Ernest Alphone and Florence (Riebel) P.; m. Barbara Joan Walker, Aug. 10, 1963; children: Yvonne Marie, Mark Raymond, Robert Ernest Albert. BA, U. B.C., 1947. Mem. B.C. Legislature, 1960-68; mem. Can. Ho. of Commons, 1968—72; parliamentary sec. Minister of Labor, 1970, Manpower and Immigration, 1971; mem Canadian Senate, 1973—2001, leader of govt., 1974-79, 1980-82, leader of opposition, 1979-80; min. state (fitness & amateur sport) Govt. of Can., 1982—83. Can. sessional del. and spokesman of Spl. com., UN, N.Y.C., 1969; mem. 1st Can. govt. delegation to Peoples Republic China, 1971; Can. rep. and govt. spokesman Internat. Labour Orgn., Geneva, Switzerland, 1972; mem. Can. Parliamentary delegation to USSR, 1975; leader Can. delegation UN Water Conf., 1977; Leader Liberal Party, B.C., 1959; mem. standing senate com. on banking, trade and commerce, standing senate com. on transp. and comm., mem. spl. joint com. reviewing Can. fgn. policy, mem. spl. senate com. on euthanasia and assisted suicide; bd. dirs. Citizens Trust. Bd. dirs. N.W. Sports; hon. chmn. Vancouver Baseball Canadians. Mem. Vancouver Club. Roman Catholic. Died Nov. 24, 2008.

**PERRY, CHARLES EDWARD,** university administrator; b. Holden, W.Va., July 25, 1937; m. Betty Laird, Sept. 17, 1960; children: Thomas Edward, Lynnette Eleanor. BA with honors in Polit. Sci., Bowling Green State U., 1958, BS in English and History, 1959, MA, 1964, LHD (hon.), 1970; cert. in philosophy, U. Mich., 1972; LL.D. (hon.), Bethune-Cookman Coll., 1969. Tchr. East Detroit pub. schs., 1959; admissions counselor Bowling Green State U., 1959-61, dir. admissions, 1961-64, dir. devel., 1964-67, asst. to pres., 1965-67; spl. asst. to gov. Fla., 1967-68; vice chancellor State Univ. System Fla., 1968-69; pres. Fla. Internat. U., Miami, 1969-75; pres., pub. Family Weekly mag., NYC, 1975-76; corp. officer communications, pub. group Charter Co., Jacksonville, Fla., 1975-76; pres., chief exec. officer Golden Bear Internat./ Jack Nicklaus Cos., North Palm Beach, Fla., 1976-85; chmn., chief exec. officer Worldvest, Inc., Columbus, Ohio, 1985-87; pres., CEO The Friedkin Cos., Houston, 1987-90; chmn., CEO Western Trading & Mgmt., Houston, 1990-93; dean grad. sch. mgmt. U. Dallas, from 1993. Bd. dirs. B.C. Golf, Ltd, Guardian Savs. Inc., Perry Investments Inc., Worldvest Asia Ltd., Biomed. Waste Systems Inc., Heartland Group, Applied Conversation Techs. Inc. Former bd. dirs. Orange Bowl, Palm Beach-Martin County Med. Ctr., Community TV Found. South Fla., Am. Revolution Bicentennial Commn., Fla. Internat. U. Found., Mus. Sci. Greater Miami, United Cerebral Palsy Miami, Third Century U.S.A., Houston Ballet Found., Houston Symphony; bd. visitors Longwood Coll., Fla. Commn. Quality Edn., Fla., Fla. Edn. Council, Edn. Commn. of the States, So. Region Edn. Bd. Recipient Silver Anvil award Pub. Relations Soc. Am., 1964; Spl. Appreciation award for outstanding contbns. to Fla., 1968; Certificate of Merit award Edinboro State Coll., 1972; Diamond Jubilee Celebration award City of Miami, 1971; Outstand Young Man of Am., U.S. Jaycees, 1971; Man of Year award Phi Delta Kappa, 1972; Medal of Honor Acción Pro Darien Soc., Colombia, 1973; Disting. Service award Marshall U., 1973; Distinguished Alumnus award Bowling Green State U., 1975; Centennial Alumnus award Nat. Assn. State Univs. and Land Grant Colls. Mem. Am. Assn. State Colls. and Univs., Am. Assn. Higher Edn., World Bus. Coun., Young Pres.' Orgn., Fla. C. of C. (dir.), Nat. Golf Found., U.S. Golf Assn., Fla. Hist. Soc., Pi Sigma Alpha, Alpha Kappa Delta, Phi Delta Kappa., Sigma Nu Clubs: Old Port Cove Yacht; Lost Tree (North Palm Beach); Muirfield Village Golf (Dublin, Ohio); The Golf, Columbus (Columbus, Ohio); Buffalo Creek Golf Club (Rockwall, Tex.); Loxahatchee Golf (Jupiter, Fla.); La Cima Club (Las Colinas, Tex.); Chandler's Landing Yacht Club (Rockwall). Died 1999.

**PERRY, FRANCIS STEPHEN,** retired physician, researcher; b. Meriden, Coventry, Eng., Jan. 10, 1926; s. Thomas Hattam and Clare (O'Brien) P.; m. Elizabeth Lena Moody-Stuart, Feb. 2, 1952; children: Timothy, Mark, Matthew, Clare. BA, Cambridge U., Eng., 1947, MB, BChir, 1951. Diplomate Royal Coll. Obstetricians and Gynecologists. Intern St. Thomas's Hosp., London, 1951-52; gen. med. practice Nat. Health Svc., Albrighton, Eng., 1956-86; ret., 1986. Contbr. articles on power frequency electromagnetic fields and health to Health Physics, Pub. Health. Squadron leader RAF, 1952-56. Mem. Liberal Democrat Party. Achievements include suggesting the use of acrylic lens implants following cataract removal and design of hobcart for use by paraplegic children. Home: Wolverhampton, England. Died Apr. 12, 2001.

**PERRY, GEORGE WILLIAMSON,** lawyer; b. Cleve., Dec. 4, 1926; s. George William and Melda Patricia (Arther-Holt) P. BA in Econs., Yale U., 1949; JD, U. Va., 1953. Bar: Ohio 1953, DC 1958, US Supreme Ct. 1958, US Ct. Appeals (DC cir.) 1959. Atty. US Dept. Justice, Washington, 1954—56; assoc. Roberts and McInnis, Washington, 1957-59; atty. assoc. counsel Com. on Interstate Fgn. Commerce, US Ho. Reps., Washington, 1960—65; atty., advisor ICC, Washington, 1965-68; assoc. dir. devel. Yale U., New Haven, 1968-70; trust officer The No. Trust Co., Chgo., 1970-71; dir. tax rsch. Pan Am. World Airways, NYC, 1973-75; hearing officer Indsl. Commn. Ohio, Cleve., 1978-81; sole practice Cleve., from 1981. With US Army, 1945-46. Mem. Soc. Cin. in State of Conn., Ancient and Hon. Artillery Co. (mem. Boston-hereditary), Phi Delta Phi, Chi Delta Theta. Home: Cleveland, Ohio. Died Aug. 8, 2013.

**PERRY, LOUIS BARNES,** retired insurance company executive; b. L.A., Mar. 4, 1918; s. Louis Henry and Julia (Stoddard) P.; m. Genevieve Patterson, Feb. 8, 1942; children: Robert Barnes, Barbara Ann, Donna Lou. BA, UCLA, 1938, MA, 1940, PhD, 1950; fellow in econs., Yale U., 1941; LL.D., Pacific U., 1964; L.H.D., Whitman Coll., 1967, Linfield Coll., 1981; D.C.S., Willamette U., 1977. Teaching asst. UCLA, 1940-41, research teaching asst., 1946-47; faculty Pomona Coll., 1947-59, asst. to pres., 1955-57, prof. economics, 1957-59; pres. Whitman Coll., Walla Walla, Wash., 1959-67; v.p., treas. Standard Ins. Co., Portland, Oreg., 1967-68, exec. v.p., 1968-71, pres., 1972-83, chmn., 1983-85. Investment counselor, broker Wagenseller & Durst, L.A., 1951-59; rsch. coord. Southern Calif. Rsch. Coun., 1952-54; cons. Carnegie Survey Bus. Edn., 1957-58. Author: (with others) Our Needy Aged, 1954, A History of the Los Angeles Labor Movement, 1963; Contbr. (with others) articles to profl. jours. Mem. Oreg. Bd. Higher Edn., 1975-87, pres., 1975-80. Served to maj. AUS, World War II; lt. col. Res. Mem. American Coll. Life Underwriters (trustee 1972-81), Rotary, Phi Beta Kappa, Beta Gamma Sigma, Phi Delta Kappa, Pi Gamma Mu, Alpha Gamma Omega, Artus. Methodist. Home: Walla Walla, Wash. *In looking back over the years, an unspoken and oftentime subliminal guiding principle has been to reach beyond one's realistic grasp. This concept coupled with an interest in treating others as one would like to be treated has made it possible to react to new challenges. Successfully meeting the latter has provided a varied career in a number of different fields of activity.* Died Sept. 28, 2013.

**PERRY, THOMAS OLIVER,** retired forestry educator, consultant; b. Cleve., May 31, 1925; s. Emmanuel von Betzen and Gertrude Irene (Green) P.; m. Hazel Eaton, Sept. 10, 1949; children: Susan, Beth, Crag, Thomas II, Karen. BS, Harvard U., 1949, MA in Genetics and Physiology, 1950, PhD in Genetics, Physiology of Trees, 1952. From asst. to assoc. prof. forestry U. Fla., Gainesville, 1952-59; sr. postdoctoral fellow NSF, Calif. Inst. Tech., Pasadena, 1959-60; prof. Forestry and Landscape Architecture N.C. State U., Raleigh, 1960-87, prof. emeritus, 1988. Owner, mgr. Natural Systems Assocs., 1974—; cons. Ctrl. Park Commn., Nat. Capital Park Svc.; lectr. at nat. meetings tree care specialists. Contbr. over 130 articles to profl. jours. and other publs. Mem. City of Raleigh Planning Commn., 1974, 75, Greenway Commn., 1976-82; cons. Nature Conservancy on land use history, forestry and natural resource mgmt., mem. stewardship com. With U.S. Army, 1943-44. Recipient Conservator award N.C. Nature Conservancy, Nat. award for Urban Forestry, Nat. Tree Trust, US Forest Svc., Assn. So. Foresters, 1996, Citizens award N.C. Assn. Landscape Archs.; named Doctor Arboreum Superbum, Wake County, Raleigh Trees programs. Mem. AAAS, Soc. Am. Foresters (past chmn., tree physiology com., past mem. tree improvement Com.), Internat. Soc. Arboriculture (mem. editl. bd. Jour. Arborculture), Met. Forest Tree Improvement Alliance (past pres.), Mcpl. Arborists Assn. Died July 28, 2008.

**PERRY, WILLIAM SHELBERN,** lawyer; b. Abilene, Tex., Jan. 26, 1936; s. Litt Shelbern and Emma Jane (Swanger) Perry; m. Deborah Lynn McCoy, Feb. 11, 1978; 1 child, Lindsay Kate; children: William Shelbern, Michael M. BS in Commerce, Tex. Christian U., 1958; LLB, Baylor U., 1963; JD, 1969. Bar: Tex. 1963. Assoc. David L. Hooper, Abilene, 1963—64; ptnr. Hooper and Perry, Abilene, 1964—69, Hooper, Perry and Bradshaw, Abilene, 1969—71; pvt. practice William S. Perry PC, Abilene, from 1979. Dir., v.p. Abilene Community Theater; dir. Abilene Met. Ballet Co. Dir., crusade vice chmn., chmn. Abilene chpt. Am. Cancer Soc., 1968—69; mem. Abilene Fine Arts Mus., Abilene Philharmonic Assn. With US Army, 1954—61, NG. Recipient Svc. awards, Am. Cancer Soc., Abilene, Abilene Planning and Zoning Commn. Mem.: Abilene C. of C., Abilene Bar Assn. (sec. 1965), State Bar Tex. (sec., chmn. grievance com. dist. 15D), Key City Kiwanis (v.p. 1965—69), Abilene Country, Fairway Oak Golf and Racquet, Phi Delta Thera, Phi Alpha Delta. Democrat. Mem. Christian Ch. (Disciples Of Christ). Home: Abilene, Tex. Died 1989.

**PERSICO, JOSEPH EDWARD,** historian; b. Gloversville, NY, July 19, 1930; s. Thomas Louis and Blanche (Perrone) P.; m. Sylvia La Vista, May 23, 1959; children: Vanya, Andrea. BA in English & Political Sci., SUNY-Albany, 1952, PhD (hon.), 1996; postgrad., Columbia U., 1955. Writer on staff of Gov. State of NY, Albany, 1955-59; commd. fgn. service officer US Info. Agy., 1959, served in Buenos Aires, Rio de Janeiro, 1959-62; speechwriter to commr. Dept. Health State of NY, Albany, 1963-66, chief speechwriter for Gov. Nelson Rockefeller, 1966-74; speechwriter for Vice Pres. Nelson Rockefeller The White House, Washington, 1975-77. Commr. Am. Battle Monuments Commn. Author: My Enemy My Brother: Men and Days of Gettysburg, 1977, Piercing the Reich: The Penetration of Nazi Germany by American Secret Agents During World War II, 1979, The Imperial Rockefeller: A Biography of Nelson A. Rockefeller, 1982, Edward R. Murrow: An American Original, 1988, Casey: William J. Casey, From the OSS to the CIA, 1990, Nuremberg: Infamy on Trial, 1994, Roosevelt's Secret War: FDR and World War II Espionage, 2001, Eleventh Month, Eleventh Day, Eleventh Hour: Armistice Day, 1918, 2004, Franklin and Lucy: President Roosevelt, Mrs. Rutherfurd, and the Other Remarkable Women in His Life, 2008, Roosevelt's Centurions: FDR and the Commanders He Led to Victory in World War II, 2013; co-author (with Colin Powell): Colin Powell: My American Journey, 1995; author: (novels) The Spiderweb, 1979. Served to lt. (j.g.) USN, 1952-55. Recipient Disting. Alumnus award SUNY-Albany, 1982 Mem.: Coun. Fgn. Rels., Authors Guild, Inc. Home: Guilderland, NY. Died Aug. 30, 2014.

**PESEK, JAMES ROBERT,** management consultant; b. Chgo., May 30, 1941; s. James F. and Elizabeth A. (Ord) P.; children: Becky, Shelly. BS in Mech. Engring. with honors, U. Ill., 1964; MBA, U. Nebr., 1966. Cert. mgmt. cons. Adminstrv. svcs. mgr. Cummins Engine Co., Columbus, Ind., 1966-68; cons. divsn. Arthur Andersen & Co., Milw., 1968-72; mgr. distbn. divsn. ADG, Indpls., 1972-74; mgr. Mgmt. Adv. Svcs. Wolf & Co., Chgo., 1974-79; pres. Ind. Mgt. Svcs., Hinsdale, Ill., from 1979. Cons., spkr., tchr. Mem. Am. Prodn. and Inventory Control Soc., Inst. Mgmt. Cons., Am. Arbitration Assn. Home: Milltown, Ind. Died Dec. 30, 1997.

**PETER, RICHARD ECTOR,** zoology educator, dean; b. Medicine Hat, Alta., Can., Mar. 7, 1943; s. Arthur E. and Josephine (Wrobleski) P.; m. Leona L. Booth, Dec. 27, 1965; children: Jason E., Matthew T.B. BSc with honors, U. Atla., 1965; PhD, U. Wash., 1969. Postdoctoral fellow U. Bristol, Eng., 1969-70; asst. prof. U. Alta., Edmonton, 1971-74, assoc. prof., 1974-79, prof., from 1979, chmn. dept. zoology, 1983—92, dean of sci., 1992—2002; v.p. Alta. Rsch. Coun., 2002—04; CEO, Inst. for Food and Agrl. Scis. Alta., 2005; dir. Bamfield Marine Scis. Ctr., 2006—07. Contbr. over 300 papers to sci. publs. Recipient Outstanding Leadership in Alberta Sci. award Alberta Sci. and Tech. Leadership Awards Found., 1998, Excellence in Mentoring award U. Alberta, 2002; named Disting. Biologist, Can. Coun. Univ. Biology Chairmen. Fellow AAAS, Royal Soc. Can.; mem. Can. Soc. Zoology (pres. 1991-92), Endocrine Soc., Internat. Soc. Neuroendocrinology, Can. Coun. of Univ. Biology Chmn. (pres. 1986-87), Internat. Fedn. Comparative Endocrinol. Socs. (pres. 1989-93, Pickford medal 1985), Canadian Conf. of Deans of Sci., 1995-96 (pres.), Western Can. Univs. Marine Scis. Soc. (pres. 2001-02). Died Mar. 8, 2007.

**PETER, ROLAND,** biologist, educator; b. Vienna, Mar. 13, 1940; s. Franz and Maria (Haberhauer) P.; m. Hedwig Kocko, Mar. 25, 1972. PhD, U. Vienna, 1971. Asst. prof. dept. genetics and gen. biology U. Salzburg, Austria, 1972—81, assoc. prof., 1982—2001, prof. cell biology and genetics, from 2001. Mem. editl. bd. Jour. Applied Biomedicine; mem. sci. com. Cells confs., Czech Republic; mem. adv. com. Internat. Symposium in Flatworm Biology, Innsbruck, Austria, 2006. Contbr. articles to profl. jours. Mem.: Deutsche Gesellschaft fur Zellbiologie, Deutsche Zoologische Gesellschaft, Freshwater Biol. Assn. U.K., N.Y. Acad. Scis. Home: Salzburg, Austria. Deceased.

**PETERICH, FRANK-NORBERT,** biomedical engineer; b. Hamburg, Germany, June 21, 1955; s. Johannes and Hannelore (Kanese) P.; m. Gabriele Dirszus, Jan. 29, 1988; 1 child: Erik. Diploma in Engring./Biomed. Engr., Fachhochschule Giessen, Germany, 1982. Cert. biomed. engr. Svc. engr. Oxford Med., Germany, 1982-83, svc. supr., 1983-84, svc. mgr., 1984, svc. mgr. Europe, 1984-86, mktg. mgr. Europe, 1986-87; sales/mktg. mgr. cardiology Nihon Kohden, Germany, 1988; market specialist and cardiology ultrasound GE Med./Cen. Europe, 1989-90; gen. mgr. Synergy Med., Germany, 1990-94; pres. Foxmed gmbH Innovative Med. Techniques, Germany, from 1994. Speciality includes support of multicenter studies in internal medicine. Patentee Microprocessor Controller of Spark and Wire Erosion, 1981. Sgt. Germany Army, 1974-78. Avocations: motorsports, jogging, skiing. Home: Idstein, Germany. Died Aug. 23, 2003.

**PETERMANN, JÜRGEN,** chemical engineering educator; b. Niederstriegis, Germany, Feb. 14, 1942; Diploma in physics, Göttingen U., 1968, PhD in Solid State Physics, 1970. Rsch. assoc. Bochum U., 1970-72, Gothenburg (Sweden) Tech. U., 1972-74, Saarbrücken (Germany) U., 1974-76; vis. scientist U. Del., 1976; prof. Tech. U. of Hamburg-Harburg, 1982-93, Dortnumd (Germany) U., from 1993, chmn. materials sci., from 1993. Vis. prof. Guangzhou Inst. of Chemistry, China, 1993. Contbr. articles to profl. jours. Mem. German Phys. Soc., German Soc. for Materials Sci. Died 2001.

**PETERS, FRANCES ELIZABETH,** librarian; b. Phila., Nov. 25, 1915; d. Alexander and Sarah Mower (Scott) P. BSEd, U. Pa., 1936, MA in Latin, 1938; BSLS, Drexel Inst. Tech., 1940; MLS, Drexel U., 1966. Br. libr. Free Libr. Phila., 1951-52, 57-62, asst. in office of work with adults, 1953-57, asst. in art dept., 1945-48, asst. extension div., 1941-45; libr. Holiday mag. Curtis Pub. Co., Phila., 1948-51; asst. libr. Pedagogical Libr., Sch. Dist. Phila., 1962-63; libr. Cheltenham High Sch., Wyncote, Pa., 1963-66, Community Coll., Temple U., Phila., 1966-67; head libr. Pa. Coll. Podiatric Medicine, Phila., 1968-82, libr., from 1982. Mem. Salvation Army Aux. Mem. AAUW, DAR, Nat. Soc. Daus. 1812, Classical Assn. Atlantic States, Phila. Classical Assn., Hist. Soc. Pa., Cruiser Olympia Assn., Pa. Classical Assn., Pi Lambda Theta, Eta Sigma Phi, Beta Phi Mu, Phi Delta Gamma, Phi Kappa Phi. Republican. Baptist. Home: Philadelphia, Pa. Died Feb. 7, 2008.

**PETERS, ROBERT LOUIS,** retired English educator, poet, critic, actor; b. Wis., Oct. 20, 1924; m. Jean Powell, 1950 (div. 1971); children: Robert Louis II, Meredith Jean, Richard (dec.), Jefferson; life ptnr. Paul Trachtenberg. BA, U. Wis., Madison, 1948, MA, 1949, PhD, 1952. Teaching asst. U. Wis., Madison, 1950-52; instr. English U. Idaho, 1952-53, Boston U., 1953-55; asst. prof. English Ohio Wesleyan U., 1955-58; assoc. prof. English Wayne State U., 1958-63; prof. English U. Calif., Riverside, 1963-68, Irvine, 1968-92, prof. English emeritus, 1993—2014. Mem. exec. bd. Ren Hen Press Publs., 1999-2014 Author: Songs for a Son, 1960, The Sow's Head and Other Poems, 1961, Poems: Selected and New, Crunching Gravel: On Growing Up in the Thirties, 1993, Nell: A Sister's Story, 1995, For You Lili Marlene: A Memoir of WWII, 1995, Feather: A Child's Death and Life, 1997, (fiction and play) Snapshots for A Serial Killer, 1991, Zapped, 1993; contbg. editor: American Book Review, 1976-2014, Contact II, 1977-92, Poetry Australia, 1989-2014; co-editor The Letters of John Addington Symonds, 3 vols., 1959-62. Recipient Hilberry Pub. prize, 1965, Borestone Mountain award, 1967, poetry Soc. Am. Hawker de Castagnola prize, 1984, Larry P. Fine Criticism award, 1985; named Outstanding Alumnus U. Wis., 1999; nominee Pulitzer prize, 1993, Pushcart award, 1993; American Coun. Learned Socs. grantee, 1963, Nat. Endowment for Arts grantee, 1974; Guggenheim fellow, 1966-67, NEA fellow, 1992. Mem. Pen N.Y., Pen L.A., Authors Guild, American Soc. Aesthetics (trustee 1965-68). Avocations: Scrabble, gardening, reading, cooking, weightlifting. Home: Huntington Beach, Calif. Died June 13, 2014.

**PETERSON, ARTHUR FERDINAND,** sales executive; b. Brainerd, Minn., Apr. 17, 1899; s. Toger and Pauline (Gulbrandsen) Peterson; m. Delma Drusella Coovert, Jan. 31, 1920 (dec. Dec. 1977); 1 child, Vivian Rozmund; m. Muriel Frances Herting, June 17, 1920. PhG, Valparaiso U., 1919; postgrad., Pharmacist G.H. Sohrbeck Co., Moline, Ill., 1920—21; PhC, Valparaiso U., 1920; attending, Alexander Hamilton Inst., 1925—26; BS, U. Minn., 1927. Salesman E.R. Squibb & Sons, Chgo., 1922—24; chemist Nat. Lead Battery Co., St. Paul, 1925; profl. svc. rep. William S. Merrell Co., Mpls., 1926; instr. chemistry U. Minn., Mpls., 1927—29; profl. svc. rep. supr. E.R. Squibb & Sons, Chgo., 1929—38; mgr. profl. svc. mgr. domestic sales div. Schering Corp., Bloomfield, NJ, 1939—46; sales mgr. biologics div. Heyden Chem. Corp., NYC, 1947—48; dir. mktg., mem. mgmt. com. Geigy Pharms., NYC, Ardsley, NY, 1949—64; pvt. practice Elmhurst, Ill., from 1965. Founder Delma Coovert Meml. Endowed Scholarship, Valaparaiso U., Delma Coovert Peterson Meml. Author: (book) Pharmaceutical Selling, Detailing and Sales Training, 1949—59; contbr. articles to profl. jours. Served US Army, 1918. Recipient Faculty award, Valparaiso U., 1988, Valparaiso U. Alumni Profl. Achievement award, 1988. Mem.: AMA (affiliate), Stockholders Am. Inc., Am. Legion, Am. Inst. History Pharmacy, Midwest Pharm. Advt. Council, Am. Assn. Individual Investors, Am. Pharm. Assn., Shriners, Founders (Valparaiso), Masons (32 degree), Phi Delta Chi, Tau Kappa Epsilon. Republican. Presbyterian. Avocation: writing. Deceased.

**PETERSON, CHASE NEBEKER,** retired academic administrator; b. Logan, Utah, Dec. 27, 1929; s. E.G. and Phebe (Nebeker) P.; m. Grethe Ballif, 1956; children: Erika Elizabeth, Stuart Ballif, Edward Chase. AB, Harvard U., 1952, MD, 1956. Diplomate: American Bd. Internal Medicine. Asst. prof. medicine U. Utah Med. Sch., 1965-67; assoc. Salt Lake Clinic; dean admissions & financial aid to students Harvard U., 1967-72, v.p. univ., 1972-78; v.p. health sciences U. Utah, Salt Lake City, 1978-83, prof. medicine, 1983—91, pres., 1983-91, clin. prof. medicine, 1991—2014. Recipient Harvard Alumni Assn. medal, 2006. Mem. Nat. Assn. State Universities & Land-Grant Colleges (chmn. 1988-89, chair U.S. Ofc. Tech. Assessment adv. bd. 1990-92). Lds Church. Home: Salt Lake City, Utah. Died Sept. 14, 2014.

**PETERSON, LEROY,** retired secondary education educator; b. Fairfield, Ala., Feb. 15, 1930; s. Leroy and Ludie Pearl (Henderson) P.; m. Theresa Petite, Apr. 6, 1968 (div. Oct. 1984); children: Leroy III, Monica Teresa; m. Ruby Willodine Hopkins, July 21, 1985 (div. Mar. 1996). Cert. in piano, Bavarian State Acad., Wuerzburg, Fed. Republic Germany, 1954; BS in Music Edn., Miami U., Oxford, Ohio, 1957. Life credential music tchr., Calif. Tchr. music Cleve. Pub. Schs., 1957-62, L.A. Unified Schs., 1963-94; retired, 1994. Song composer. With U.S. Army, 1952-54. Mem. Alpha Phi Alpha, Phi Mu Alpha Sinfonia. Republican. Avocations: amateur concert pianist, composing, photography. Deceased.

**PETERSON, MICHAEL J.,** state legislator; b. Sept. 18, 1941; m. Robin Peterson. JD, U. Mo. Kans. City Sch. Law, 1971. Mem. Dist. 33 Kans. House of Reps., 1979—90, mem. Dist. 37, 2005—14. Democrat. Died Feb. 18, 2014.

**PETERSON, ROBERT JOHN,** surgical products company executive; b. Sayre, Pa., Dec. 15, 1930; arrived in Brazil, 1957; s. Harold Francis and Grace Alice (Enwright) Peterson; m. Lilia Dalva Gomes Peterson, Apr. 26, 1958; children: John, Suzanne, Steven, Lilianne, Lucianne. AB, U. Notre Dame, 1952; MA, Duke U., 1953. Trainee Becton Dickinson Co., Rutherford, New Zealand, 1953—56; plant mgr. B-D Brazil, Juiz de Fora, 1958—75, dir., from 1975. Served with US Army, 1953—55. Named Hon. Citizen, Juiz de Fora, 1983. Mem.: Radio (Juiz de Fora), Dom Pedro. Roman Catholic. Avocation: amateur radio. Home:, Brazil. Died Aug. 18, 2009.

**PETILLON, LEE RITCHEY,** lawyer; b. Gary, Ind., May 6, 1929; s. Charles Ernest and Blanche Lurene (Mackay) Petillon; m. Mary Anne Keeton, Feb. 20, 1960; children: Andrew G., Joseph R. BBA, U. Minn., 1952; LLB, U. Calif., Berkeley, 1959. Bar: Calif. 1960, U.S. Dist. Ct. (so. dist.) Calif. 1960. V.p. Creative Investment Capital, Inc., LA, 1969—70; corp. counsel Harvest Industries, LA, Calif., 1970—71; v.p., gen. counsel, dir. Tech. Svcs. Corp., Santa Monica, Calif., 1971—78; ptnr. Petillon & Davidoff, LA, 1978—92, Gipson Hoffman & Pancione, 1992—93; pvt. practice Torrance, Calif., 1993—94; ptnr. Petillon & Hansen, Torrance, 1994—2003, Petillon & Hiraide LLP, Torrance, 2004—06, Petillon, Hiraide, Loomis & Katz LLP, Torrance, from 2006, Petillon Hiraide & Loomis LLP, from 2008. Co-author: R&D Partnerships, 2d edit., 1985, Representing Start-Up Companies, 1992, 19th edit., 2012; contbr. chapters to books. Chmn. Neighborhood Justice Ctr. Com., 1983-85, Middle Income Co., 1983085; active Calif. Senate Commn. on Corp. Governance, State Bar Calif. Task Force on Alternative Dispute Resolution, 1984-85; chmn. South Bay Sci. Found., Inc.; vice-chmn. Calif. Capital Access Forum, Inc.; dir., legal counsel ACE-Net.org, Inc. Recipient Cert. of Appreciation L.A. City Demonstration Agy., 1975, United Indian Devel. Assn., 1981, City of L.A. for Outstanding Vol. Svcs., 1984, Outstanding Vol. award Torrance C. of C., 2000, Small Bus. Adv. of Yr. award Torrance C. of C., 2001, Marvin Greene award Los Angeles County Bar Assn., 2005; named Small Bus. Adv. of Yr. Calif. C. of C., 2001. Mem.: ABA (venture capital and pvt. equity com.), Los Angeles County Bar Assn. (trustee 1984—85, alt. dispute resolution sect. 1992—94, bus. and corp. law sect. from 2000, chmn. law tech. sect., Griffin Bell Vol. Svc. award 1993), Los Angeles County Bar Found. (bd. dirs.), Calif. State Bar Assn. (pres., Pro Bono Svcs. award 1983). Avocations: backpacking, reading, music, painting. Home: Palos Verdes Estates, Calif. Died 2013.

**PETRENKO, VITALIY,** nuclear scientist; b. Dnepropetrovsk, Ukraine, Sept. 12, 1934; married. Sr. sci. rschr. Inst. Nuc. physics, Tashkent, Uzbekistan, 1974—98, leading sci. rschr., from 1998. Recipient Dustlik Order award, Uzbekistan Govt. Deceased.

**PETROV, LYUDMIL KIRILOV,** historian, educator; b. Varna, Bulgaria, July 12, 1947; s. Kiril Ivanov Petrov and Ivanka (Nikolova) Petrova; m. Valentina Dmitrievna Nikola; 1 child, Kiril Lyudmilov. M, U. St. Kliment Ohridsky, 1973; PhD in History, U. Sofia, Bulgaria. Sci. rschr., reader Inst. Mil. Hist., Sofia, Bulgaria, 1975—92; dir. Nat. Ctr. Mil. Hist. Ministry Def., Sofia, from 1992. Sci. rschr. Ctrl. Dept. Archives Bulgarian Govt., Sofia, from 1996; assoc. prof. Varna Free U., Varna, Bulgaria, from 2000, U. Nat. and Worlds Econs., Sofia, from 1996; councillor Coun. for Granting Acad. Ranks and Sci. Degs., Sofia, from 1997. Author: Problems of Military Politics of Bulgaria, 1991, Military Economics of Bulgaria 1919-1945, 1999, Bulgaria and Turkey 1931-1941, 2001. Lt. col. Bulgarian Armed Forces, 1993. Mem.: Internat. Commn. Mil. History, Bulgarian Hist. Assn. Avocations: coin collecting/numismatics, scuba diving, bibliophile, speleology. Home: Sofia, Bulgaria. Died Sept. 22, 2003.

**PETROVIC, ALEXANDRE GABRIEL,** physician, physiology educator, medical research director; b. Belgrade, Yugoslavia, July 10, 1925; naturalized French citizen; s. Gabriel M. and Maria S. (Miskovic) P.; m. Suzanne Durry, Feb. 25, 1956; 1 child, Nicole Gasson. MD, Strasbourg Med. Sch., 1954, DSc, 1961; postgrad., McGill U. Med. Sch., 1961-62. Assoc. staff physician, asst. prof. Northwestern U. Med. Sch., Chgo., 1965-68; prof. U. Montreal Med. Sch., 1970-71; dir. rsch. Nat. Inst. Health and Med. Rsch., Strasbourg, 1968-94; prof. human physiology U. Louis Pasteur Med. Sch., Strasbourg, 1976-90. Lectr. in biomed. rsch., methodology, 1989-96, also mem. sci. coun.; vis. rsch. scientist Ctr. for Human Growth and Devel., U. Mich., Ann Arbor, 1976-78; vis. prof. La. State U. Med. Ctr., New Orleans, 1979-97; van der Klaauw prof. U. Leiden, Netherlands, 1985; prof. U. Cattolica del Sacro Cuore, Rome, Italy, 1992-96; prof. honoris causa U. Camilo Castelo Branco, São Paulo, Brazil, 1989—; charge of French med. missions to USSR, 1969, Yugoslavia, 1969, 74, 76, 78, 81, Argentina, Peru, Brazil and Chile, 1974, U.S., 1977, 78, 82, Cuba, 1986. Recipient prize Vlès, Strasbourg Med. Sch., 1954, prize Laborde, Biol. Soc., 1961, E. Sheldon Friel award European Orthodontic Soc., 1976, Calvin Case award for orthodontic rsch., 1984, Disting. Sci. Craniofacial Biology Rsch. award Internat. Assn. Dental Rsch., 1994, Medalha de Merito Sociedade de Ortodontia, Brazil, 1998. Mem. Acad. of ALSACE, Soc. Cryobiology (charter), Acad. Medicine (Belgrade, hon. mem.), Academia Ibero-Latino-Am. de Disfunction Craneomandibular (hon. mem.), Club Internat. de Morphologie Faciale, Assn. des Physiologistes, European Tissue Culture Soc., Greek Orthodontic Soc. (hon.), Italian Orthodontic Soc. (hon.), Colegio de Esjecialistas en Ortodoncia y Ortofellia Maxilar de Celaya (hon.), others. Achievements include contbg. author various books and sci. papers on a cybernetic theory of the mechanisms of craniofacial bone growth, on cytopathogenesis of craniostenosis and on philosophy of biomed. research; discovered feasibility of orthopedically stimulating the growth of the mandible; described new ways in orthodontic decision making; pioneer research studies on treatment of otospongiosis by sodium fluoride and disphosphonates, on theory of auto-immune origin of otospongiosis; new classification of bone tumors; discovered possibility of prefecondatory hereditary male contribution by penetration of spermatozoary DNA into intraovarian ovocytes. Home: Strasbourg, France. Died Nov. 22, 2003.

**PETROVSKY, GURY TIM,** chemist; b. Leningrad, Russia, Aug. 5, 1931; s. Timofej Tim Petrovsky and Maria Petrovna Timofeeva; m. Marina Lazarevna Balon, Feb. 18, 1966; children: Igor, Olga. Degree in chemistry, Tech. Inst., Russia, 1955; PhD, Tech. Inst., Prague, Chech Republic, 1959; DSc, State Optical Inst., Russia, 1968. Scientist State Optical Inst., St. Petersburg, Russia, 1959-64, head lab., 1964-49, gen. dir., 1994—2002; dir. Inst. Optical Materials, Russia, 1969-94, hon. dir., from 2002. Prof. Tech. Inst., St. Petersburg, 1966-76; hon. prof. Inst. Precise Optics, 1980—. Contbr. over 650 articles to profl. jours. Recipient State prize USSR, 1969, 82, Russian Fedn., 1998, Badge of Honor, 1976, Badge of Friendship, 1985. Mem. SPJE, Acad. Sci. Russia (academician), Optical Soc. (pres.). Avocation: reading. Home: Saint Petersburg, Russia. Died Sept. 29, 2005.

**PETSCHEK, THOMAS H.,** banker; b. Jan. 19, 1932; s. Charles and Josefa (May) Petschek; m. Joyce S. Sherman, 1955 (div. 1973); children: Robert C., Nicholas L., Carla J.; m. Marie Luise Eglau, Apr. 16, 1981. BA, Harvard U., 1953. V.p. Mfrs. Hanover Trust, NY, 1956—71; asst. mng. dir. Mfrs. Hanover, Ltd., London, 1971—72; exec. dir. S.G. Warburg & Co., Ltd., 1972—81; gen. mgr. DG Bank, London, from 1981. Mayor Village of Saltaire, NY, 1967—68. Home: London, England. Died Dec. 6, 2009.

**PEYSER, PETER A.,** former United States Representative from New York; b. Cedarhurst, NY, Sept. 7, 1921; s. Percy A. and Rubye (Hoeflich) P.; m. Marguerite Richards, Dec. 23, 1949; children: Penny, Carolyn, Peter, James, Tommy. BA in Classical Greek, Colgate U., 1943. Mgr. Mut. N.Y. Ins. Co., NYC, 1956-70; mem. US Congress from 25th NY Dist., 1971—73, US Congress from 23rd NY Dist., 1973—77, 1979—83; mayor City of Irvington, NY, 1963-70; nat. dir., sr. v.p. investment mgmt. Taft-Hartley Pension Funds, 1989—95; sr. v.p. Gabelli Asset Mgmt. Co., 1995—2014. Served in US Army, 1943-46. Decorated Bronze Star; Belgian Fourragere. Democrat. Episcopalian. Home: Irvington, NY. Died Oct. 9, 2014.

**PHADKE, RATNA SURESH,** physicist; b. Bombay, Oct. 28, 1939; d. Trimbak Jagannath and Usha Trimbak (Limaye) Gondhalekar; m. Suresh Phadke, May 13, 1964; children: Nitin, Aparna. BS, Inst. Sci., 1959, PhD, 1967; MS, Presidency Coll., 1961. Prof., head RKT Coll., Ulhasnagar, India, 1972-80; fellow Tata Inst. Fundamental Rsch., Bombay, 1980-94, reader, 1994-95, assoc. prof., from 1995. Mem. molecular electronics program Dept. Sci. and Tech., New Delhi, 1987-92; scientific sec. Internat. Conf. Molecular Electronics and Biocomputing, Goa, India, 1994; v.p. Nat. Forum on Molecular Electronics, 1995—. Patentee in field; editor spl. issue Material Sci. and Engring., 1996. Mem. Internat. Soc. for MEBC (gov. bd. 1994-96, 96-97), Internat. Soc. for Molecular Electronics and Biocomputing (chmn. nomination com. 1992-93), Indian Biophys. Soc., Internat. Women Sci. Assn., Women Grad. Union. Named Most Honored Citizen Kalyan Mcpl. Corp., 1985. Avocations: yoga, gardening, music, photography. Home: Bombay, India. Died 2001.

**PHELPS, DOROTHY FRINK,** civic worker; b. Macon, Ga., June 15, 1906; d. James Richard and Alma (Hall) Frink; m. John Grady Phelps, Feb. 18, 1929 (dec. Oct. 1981); children: Judith Ann Phelps Austin (dec.), John Richard Phelps. Cert. in bus. law, commerce, Fla. State Coll. Women, Tallahassee. Sec. Dir. Pub. Health and Welfare, Miami, 1925-39; ret., 1939. Editor Ch. News Notes, 1st United Meth. Ch., former offices held include chmn. Christian edn.; pres. Silver Bluff Elem. PTA, 1948; v.p. Shennandoah Jr. H.S. PTA; mem. exec. bd., pres. Miami Sr. H.S. PTA; vol. mentor program Milam Elem. Sch., Hialeah, Fla. Recipient award for 76 years serving in Christian edn., 1st United Meth. Ch., 1996. Mem. DAR, Miami Women's Panhellenic Assn. (pres. 1930-31), Miami Woman's Club, Delta Delta Delta Mother's Club, Delta Zeta. Democrat. Died Mar. 2001.

**PHELPS, FLORA L(OUISE) LEWIS,** editor, anthropologist, photographer; b. San Francisco, July 28, 1917; d. George Chase and Louise (Manning) Lewis; m. C(lement) Russell Phelps, Jan. 15, 1944; children: Andrew Russell, Carol Lewis, Gail Phelps Smith. Student, U. Mich.; AB cum laude, Bryn Mawr Coll., 1938; AM, Columbia U., 1954. Acting dean Cape Cod Inst. Music, East Brewster, Mass., summer 1940; assoc. social sci. analyst U.S. Govt., 1942-44; co-adj. staff instr. anthropology Univ. Coll., Rutgers U., 1954-55; mem. editorial bd. Américas mag. OAS, Washington, 1960-82; mng. editor, 1974-82; contbg. editor, 1982-89. N.J. vice chmn. Ams. Dem. Action, 1950; mem. Dem. County Com. N.J., 1948-49. Author articles in fields of anthropology, art, architecture, edn., travel; contbr. Latin Am. newspapers. Mem. AAAS, Am. Anthrop. Assn., Archaeological Inst. Am., Latin Am. Studies Assn., Soc. for Am. Archaeology, Soc. Woman Geographers. Home: Annville, Pa. Died Oct. 4, 1999.

**PHILLIPS, ERIC MILES,** monk; b. Sheffield, Yorkshire, Eng., Mar. 22, 1910; s. Miles H. and Edna (Sinnock) Phillips; children: Eric, John. Student, Inst. Britanique, Paris, 1927—28, Ealing Priory, 1928—29, Downside Abbey, 1929, Caldey Abbey, 1934. Ordained priest Roman Cath. Ch., professed as Monk. Monk Downside Abbey, Somerset, England, 1929—34; curate Cambridge, England, 1936—45; priest St. Gregory's Ch., Northampton, England, 1936—77; monk Downside Abbey, Somerset, England, from 1977. Named Hon. Canon, Northampton, 1973. Roman Catholic. Deceased.

**PHILLIPS, MARION GRUMMAN,** civic volunteer, writer; b. NYC, Feb. 11, 1922; d. Leroy Randle and Rose Marion (Werther) Grumman; m. Ellis Laurimore Phillips, Jr., June 13, 1942; children: Valerie Rose (Mrs. Adrian Parsegian), Elise Marion (Mrs. Edward E. Watts III), Ellis Laurimore III, Kathryn Noel Phillips, Cynthia Louise (Mrs. Charles Prosser). Student, Mt. Holyoke Coll., 1940-42; BA, Adelphi U., 1981. Civic vol. Mary C. Wheeler Sch., 1964-68, Historic Ithaca, Inc., 1972-76, Ellis L. Phillips Found., 1960-91. Bd. dirs. North Shore Jr. League, 1960-61, 64-65, 68-69, Family Svc. Assn. Nassau County, 1963-69, Homemaker Svc. Assn. Nassau County, 1959, 61. Author: (light verse) A Foot in the Door, 1965, The Whale-Going, Going, Gone, 1977, Doctors Make Me Sick (So I Cured Myself of Arthritis), 1979; editor: (with Valerie Phillips Parsegian) Richard and Rhoda, Letters from the Civil War, 1982, Wooden Shoes the story of my Grandfather's Grandfather (F.M. Sisson), 1990, Irish Eyes, family hist. of McTarsneys and Sissons, 1990, The Log Chapel, A History of the Congregational Community Church, Rockwood, Maine, 1999; editor Jr. League Shore Lines, 1960-61, The Werthers in America-Four Generations and their Descendants, 1987; A B-Tour of Britain, 1986; contbr. articles on fund raising to mags. Mem. New Eng. Hist. Geneal. Soc., N.Y. Geneal. Biographical Soc., Hannah Adams Womens Club, PEO Sisterhood, Medfield Garden Club. Congregationalist. Home: Dedham, Mass. Died May 14, 2013.

**PHILLIPS NARIGON, FRANCES MARIE,** state agency administrator, educator; b. St. Joseph, Mo., Oct. 1, 1934; d. Francis Michael Horan and Katherine Jane Pardee Martin; m. Philip K. Phillips, July 26, 1952 (div. 1978); children: Douglas Leland, Cynthia K. Phillips Ayala, John Patrick; m. Joseph Edward Narigon, June 23, 1990. BA, Iowa State U., 1982, MS, 1990. Farmer, Webster City, Iowa, 1969; coord. urban youth programs Webster County Ext., Ft. Dodge, Iowa, 1973-78; head food svc. tech. Trinity Regional Hosp., Ft. Dodge, Iowa, 1978-80; exec. dir. Ames/Iowa State U. YWCA, 1982-84; program coord. rural concern Iowa Coop. Ext./Iowa State U., 1985-89; spl. resources coord. Iowa Comprehensive Human Svcs., Des Moines, 1989-90; supr. resident counselors House of Mercy, Mercy Med. Ctr., Des Moines, 1990; adj. instr. Des Moines Area Community Coll., Ankeny, 1992-94; program planner Iowa Dept. Agr. and Land Stewardship, Des Moines, 1991-94. Commr. Iowa Emergency Response Commn., Des Moines, 1991-94; mem. coord. com. Iowa Ctr. for Agrl. Safety and Health, Iowa City, 1991-94; adv. commn. offices of Rural Health, Iowa Dept. Health, Des Moines, 1992--94; adv. com. Great Plains Staff Tng. and Devel. for Rural Mental Health, U. Nebr., Lincoln, 1989; mem. conf. planning com. The Forgotten Half: Pathways to Success, Iowa Dept. Edn., Des Moines, 1989; bd. dirs. Iowa Coun. on Family Rels., 1985-87, Black Cultural Ctr., Ames, 1982-83; others; vol. Carnegie Pub. Libr., Eureka Springs, Ark.; mem. Holday Island Arts Assn., Eureka Springs, Holiday Island Community Ch., Holiday Island Fire Aux., Holiday Island Neighborhood Watch. Mem. Indianola Golf and Country Club. Democrat. United Ch. of Christ. Avocations: painting, golf, camping, reading, swimming. Home: Holiday Island, Ark. Died Apr. 3, 1999.

**PHIPPS, DARLEEN MARIE,** artist; b. Baraboo, Wis., June 13, 1929; d. Rudolph Frederick and Marie Amelia Rehbein; m. Robert Maurice Phipps, Aug. 23, 1952; children: David Marshall, Robert Maurice II, Christina Marie. High sch. grad., Baraboo, Wis.; student, Cuyahoga Valley Art Ctr., 1959. Instr. Which Craft?, Creve Cour Mo., Downriver YMCA, Wyandotte, Mich., Roselawn Gallery, Pittsford, N.Y., Valley Manor, Rochester, N.Y. One-woman shows include Norfolk Gallery, Four Seasons Gallery, St. Louis, Hilton Gallery, Century Club, 1570 Valley Manor Gallery, AAUW Art Forum, Seven Artist's Gallery, Rochester, Chautauqua Art Assn. Galleries; juried exhibits at Scarab Club Silver Medal Show, Detroit, Dreams and Fantasies Show, Cuyhago Falls, Ohio (juror's award 1986), Small Painting Exhibit, Ky. Highlands Mus., Ashland (purchase award 1987), Internat. Dogwood Festival, Atlanta Still Live Now, Bald Eagle, others. Recipient Grumbacher award Beaux Arts, St. Louis, Best of Show award DuPage Art League, Wheaton, Ill., 1978, Penfield Art Assn., 1990, juror's award 48th Finger Lakes Exhbn. at Meml. Art Gallery, Rochester, N.Y., 1989, Philip Isenberg award at Salmagundi Club, N.Y., 1992. Mem. Penfield Art Assn., Rochester Art Club, Salmagundi Club. Republican. Presbyterian. Avocations: crafts of all kinds, gardening. Home: Mayfield, Ky. Died 1999.

**PICARD, PAULINE,** former Canadian government official; b. St. Gabriel de Kamouraska, Que., Can., Apr. 27, 1947; Grad., U. Que., Three Rivers, Can. Dir. Com. on NON of Drummond, Charlottetown, 1992; dep. Canadian Parliament, 1993, mem., 1993—2008; v.p. Permanent Com. on Health, 1993; treas. of the exec. coun. Que. Party of Drummond; prin. spkr. Matters of Health, 1994-97. Adminstrv. treas. Ho. of Women, 1987-89; dir., treas. of the adminstrv. coun. Indsl. Adminstrn. Club, 1990; com. mem. Drummondville Folklore Festival and 175th Anniversary, 1990-92. Died June 29, 2009.

**PICKERT, ROBERT WALTER,** accountant; b. Aurora, Ill., Sept. 4, 1936; s. Conrad Bonifas and Margaret Catherine (Brummel) P.; m. Tonda Ruth Sloane, Sept. 14, 1963 (div. Nov. 1966); children: Kelly, Christopher, Katherine, Mary Ellen, Scott; m. Patricia Ann Petersen, Aug. 16, 1986. BS in Bus. Adminstrn., U. Montana, 1964. CPA, Wis. Supr. Ernst and Young, CPAs, Chgo., 1964-68, Milw., 1968-73; v.p. fin., ops. Republic Bank, Milw., 1973-76; prin. Robert W. Pickert, CPA, Minocqua, Wis., from 1976. Bd. dirs., treas. Howard Young Med. Ctr., Inc., Woodruff, Wis., Howard Young Health Care, Inc., Woodruff, 1985-95; pres. PIC-WEL, Inc., Minocqua, 1991—; chmn. bd. dirs. Howard Young Health Care, Inc., 1995—. Fellow AICPA, Wis. Inst. CPAs; mem. Rotary (treas. 1978-83). Republican. Roman Catholic. Avocations: travel, fishing, hiking. Deceased.

**PIENAAR, LOUIS ALEXANDER,** retired South African government official; b. Stellenbosch, Republic of South Africa, June 23, 1926; s. Jaocbus Alexander and Eleanora Angelique (Stiglingh) P.; m. Isabel Maud van Niekerk, Dec. 11, 1954; children: Jacobus Francois, Isabel Maud, Willie Van Niekerk. BA in Law, U. Stellenbosch, 1945; LLB, U. South Africa, Pretoria, 1952. Mcpl. employee Municipalities of Brakpan, Vereniging and George, Republic of South Africa, 1946-52; atty. at law Bellville, Republic of South Africa, 1954-75; M.P. Govt. of South Africa, Bellville, 1970-75, amb. to France Paris, 1975-79, mem. Pres.'s Council Cape Town, 1981-85, adminstr. gen. S.W. Africa territory Windhoek, Namibia, 1985-90, chmn. Pub. Appeals Bd. Pretoria, 1990-91, min. nat. edn. & environment Cape Town, 1991-92, min. home affairs & environ., 1992-93, M.P. Maitland, 1991-94. Advocate Cape Town Bar, 1979-85. Mem. provincial council Cape of Good Hope, Cape Town, 1966-70. Decorated Grand Officer Nat. Order of Merit (France), Order of Meritorious Svcs. Gold Class (South Africa). Mem. Nat. party. Mem. Dutch Reformed Ch. Avocations: hiking, golf. Home: Bellville, South Africa. Died Nov. 5, 2012.

**PIENE, OTTO,** artist, educator; b. Laasphe, Westphalia, Germany, Apr. 18, 1928; s. Otto and Anne (Niemeyer) P.; children: Annette, Herbert, Claudia, Chloe. Student, Acad. Fine Arts, Munich, Germany, 1949-50, Acad. Fine Arts, Dusseldorf, Germany, 1950-52; Staatsexamen in Philosophy, U. Cologne, Germany, 1957; DFA, U. Md., Balt., 1995. Co-founder Group Zero, Dusseldorf, Germany, 1957; vis. prof. U. Pa. Grad. Sch. Art, Phila., 1964; prof. environ. art MIT Sch. Architecture & Planning, Cambridge, Mass., 1972-93, dir. Ctr. for Advanced Visual Studies, 1974-94; dir. emeritus Ctr. for Advanced Visual Studies MIT, 1994—2014. Dir. Sky Art Conf. MIT, 1981, 82, 83, 86; vis. artist, guest prof. numerous univs.; prin. artist, designer numerous archtl. and environ. art commns. and pub. celebrations. Author: (with Heinz Mack) Zero 1, 2, 3, 1958, 61, More Sky, 1973, Sky Art Conf. Proc., 1981, 82, 83, Feuerbilder und Texte, 1988; one man exhbns. include, Howard Wise Gallery, N.Y.C., 1965, 69, 70, Galerie Heseler, Munich, 1971, 72, 75, 77, 78, 79, 83, 86, MIT, 1975, 93, Galerie Schoeller, Düsseldorf, Fed. Republic Germany, 1977, 79, 83, 87, 91, 95, Fitchburg (Mass.) Art Mus., 1977, Galerie Watari, Tokyo, 1983, Pat Hearn Gallery, N.Y.C., 1985, Gallery 360, Tokyo, 1991, 92, Galèrie d'Art International, Paris, 1993, Städt Kunstmuseum, Düsseldorf, 1996; numerous group exhbns. U.S. and abroad including, Guggenheim Mus., NYC, 1964, 66, 84, Albright-Knox Gallery Buffalo, 1968, Nat. Mus. Modern Art, Tokyo, 1969, Tate Gallery, London, 1974, Smithsonian Instn., Washington, 1978, Royal Acad. Art, London, 1985, National Gallery, Berlin, 1986, Statsgalerie, Stuttgart, 1986, Berlinische Galerie, Berlin, 1988-89, 91-92, MIT, 1994, Haus der Kunst, Munich, 1995, Bundeskunsthalle, Bonn, 1995, others; also represented in numerous permanent collections (recipient award Internat. Exhibition Graphic Art, Ljubljana, Yugoslavia 1967, 69, prize 8th Internat. Biennial Prints Nat. Mus. Modern Art, Tokyo, Japan 1972, Kohler-Maxwell prize 1987). Recipient Sculpture prize, AAAL, 1996, Leonardo Da Vinci World Award of Arts, World Cultural Coun., 2003. Mem. Deutscher Kunstlerbund. Home: Groton, Mass. Died July 17, 2014.

**PIEPER, MICHAEL JOSEPH,** television producer, actor, talk show host; b. Detroit, July 12, 1958; s. Frank John Pieper and Marie Yolanda Dansereau; m. Barbara Marie Michalik (div. Feb. 1990); children: Melanie Lynn, Heather Irene. Student, Marygrove Coll., 1976—78, Specs Howard Sch. Broadcast Arts, 1988. Ordained min. Universal Life Ch., 2000. Owner, prodr. Quixote Video, Lake City, Fla., from 1981. Actor (TV series) T-bone Playhouse, 1981—82, actor, co-prodr. comedy soap opera, Daze of Our Wives, 1982—85; performer: (TV series) game show, Out-patient Bonanza, 1984—85; actor: (radio series) Proceed With Caution, 1985—86; (TV films) Streetlevel, 1983, The Banana Republic, 1983; actor, co-prodr. (TV films) Bartolo's Cafe, 1984, The Paper, 1992, host, co-prodr. (talk show) Forum, 1983—85, host Detroit Metro Magazine, 1985; actor: (music video) Man Boobs, 2008; songwriter Feathersong, 1996; songwriter: Legacy, 2006. Mem.: Internat. Platform Assn. (life). Avocations: singing, painting, photography, metaphysics. Died June 16, 2014.

**PIERAS, JAIME, JR.,** federal judge; b. San Juan, May 19, 1924; s. Jaime Pieras and Ines Lopez-Cepero; m. Elsie Castaner, June 6, 1953; 1 child, Jaime Pieras Castaner AB in Economics, Catholic U. America, 1945; JD, Georgetown U., 1948. Bar: P.R. Pvt. practice, San Juan, 1949-82; judge US Dist. Ct. PR, San Juan, 1982—93, sr. judge, 1993—2011. Mem. Com. on the Bicentennial of the Constitution, Judicial Conf. U.S.; mem. Puerto Rico Commn. on the Bicentennial of the U.S. Constituion. Contbr. article to Cath. U. Law Rev., 1986. Chmn. fin. Statehood Republican Party, San Juan, 1963-64; Rep. nat. committeeman for P.R., San Juan 1967-80. 2nd Lt. U.S. Army (Mediterranean) 1946-47, MTO; Res., 1949. Mem. ABA (exec. bd., Nat. Conf. Fed. Trial Judges), P.R. Bar Assn., D.C. Bar Assn. Lodges: Rotary. Died June 11, 2011.

**PIERPONT, ROSS Z.,** retired surgeon; b. Woodlawn, Md., Sept. 7, 1917; s. Edwin Lowell and Ethel Celeste (Zimmerman) P.; m. Grace Schmidt, Feb. 5, 1942; 1 child, Christine Pierpont von Klencke. BS in Pharmacy, U. Md., 1937, MD, 1940. Diplomate Am. Bd. Surgery. Intern Md. Gen. Hosp., Balt., 1940-41; resident in surgery Balt. City Hosps., 1941-44, U. Iowa, Iowa City, 1944-45; asst. clin. prof. emeritus U. Md.; pres., CEO Pierpont Sys. Cons. Internat. Pres. PSCI Internat. Healthcare; cons. pres. Gempro Internat. Mfg. of Healthcare Supplements; with Pierpont Health Ctr. Author: Indicted, 1982, Towson & The Tax Cap, 1991, Health Care System for USA "Its Not the Health Care it's the Health Care System Stupid", 1999, (autobiography) Never Never Ever Give Up, 2001. Bd. dirs. Pres. Club Heritage Found., Washington, 1995; mem. Empower Am., Washington, 1996; Rep. nominee U.S. Senate (Md.), 1998; chmn. adv. bd. Rep. Nat. Com.; active Rep. Senatorial Inner Cir.; candidate for Gov. of Md., 2002. Recipient Ronald Reagan Gold medal, U.S Congress, 2005. Fellow ACS; mem. AMA, Soc. Am. Gastrointestinal and Endoscopic Surgeons, Kiwanis Internat. Republican. Methodist. Deceased.

**PIKE, OTIS GREY,** former United States Representative from New York; b. Riverhead, NY, Aug. 31, 1921; m. Doris Orth, 1946 (dec. 1996); children: Lois, Douglas, Robert-(dec.); m. Barbe Bonjour, 2002. AB, Princeton U., 1946; LLB, Columia U. Law School, 1948. Pres. South Oaks Hosp., Amityville, NY; justice of the peace Town of Riverhead, NY, 1954—60, mem. town bd., 1954—60; mem. US Congress from 1st NY Dist., 1961—79; chmn. US House Select Com. on Intelligence, 1975—76; columnist Newhouse Newspapers, 1979—99. Served in USMC, 1942—46. Democrat. Died Jan. 20, 2014.

**PILLINGER, COLIN TREVOR,** planetary sciences educator; b. Bristol, Eng., May 9, 1943; s. Alfred and Florence (Honour) Pillinger; m. Judith Mary Hay; children: Shusanah Jane, Nicolas Joseph. BSc in Chemistry, U. Wales, Swansea, 1965, PhD in Mass Spectrometry, 1968; DSc (hon.), U. Bristol, 1984. From rsch. asst. to assoc. U. Bristol, 1968-76; from rsch. assoc. to sr. assoc. U. Cambridge, 1976-84; from sr. fellow to prof. Open U., Milton Keynes, England, 1984—2014, Gresham prof. astronomy, 1996-2000, Gresham fellow, 2000—14. Advisor Sci. & Engring. Rsch. Coun., 1976-94, Royal Soc., 1993-2014, Particle Physics and Astronomy Rsch. Coun., 1994-2014, Natural Environment Rsch. Coun., European Space Agy.; prin. investigator European Spacy Agy. Rosetta Mission; lead scientist Beagle 2 project for European Space Agy. Mars Express mission Contbr. more than 1000 refereed papers, conf. proceedings, abstracts reports, sci. jours. and three books; author: (autobiography) My Life on Mars: The Beagle 2 Diaries, 2010. Recipient Aston medal, British Mass Spectrometry Soc., 2003, award, CBE, 2003, A.C. Clarke award, 2004, Space Achievement medal, Brit. Interplanetary Soc., 2005, Reginald Mitchell Meml. medal, 2006, Michael Farraday prize, 2011; named Pillinger asteroid 15614 in his honor; fellow, U. Coll., Swansea, 2003. Fellow Royal Soc. (com. mem.), Royal Astron. Soc. (coun.), Meteoritical Soc., Royal Geographical Soc., Internat. Astron. Union, Univ. Coll. Swansea. Achievements include development of high sensitivity isotope mass spectrometers and their application to primitive meteorites (discovery of interstellar grains); research in Martian meteorites (trapped and atmospheric weathering components); lunar samples (solar wind species); terrestrial samples. Avocations: farming, animals, football. Home: Cambs, England. Died May 7, 2014.

**PIMENTEL-GOMES, FREDERICO,** retired engineering educator, editor; b. Piracicaba, Brazil, Dec. 19, 1921; s. Raymundo and Sylvia Souza (Gomes) P.; m. Mary Lee Fonseca de Bem, Nov. 8, 1941; children: Marli de Bem Gomes, Valquíria de Bem Gomes, Vangri de Bem Gomes. Dr. Agronomy, U. São Paulo, Brazil, 1948, Agronomy Engr., 1943. Asst. prof. U. São Paulo, 1944-58, prof., 1958-59, Cathedratic prof., from 1959; dir. Escola de Engenharia de Piracicaba, 1970-73, Revista de agricultura, Piracicaba, from 1968, editor, from 1988. Vis. scholar N.C. State U., 1952-53; vis. prof. U. Buenos Aires, 1983, U. La Plata, Argentina, 1983, 96; sci. cons. Pesquisa Agropecuária Brasileira Jour., 1966—; cons. Instituto de Pesquisas e Estudos Florestais, Piracicaba, 1990-95. Author: Curso de Estatística Experimental, 14th edit. 2000, Iniciacão à Estatística, 6th edit., 1978, A Estatística Moderna na Pesquisa Agropecuária, 3d edit., 1987; co-author: Experimentos de Adubacão: Planejamento e Análise Estatística, 1987, Análise Matemática, 2d edit., 1980, Adubos e Adubacoes, 2000, (with C.H. Garcia) Establitica Aplicada a Experimentos Agronômicos e Florestais: exporiçao com exemplos e orientaçoẽs para uso de aplicativos, 2002; contbr. numerous articles to profl. jours. Recipient Medal of Bicentenary of Piracicaba, Municipality of Piracicaba, 1967, Medal Prudente de Morais, Hist. and Geog. Inst. of Piracicaba, State of São Paulo, 1995. Home: Piracicaba, Brazil. Died Nov. 24, 2004.

**PINCHER, CHAPMAN (HARRY CHAPMAN PINCHER),** investigative writer, novelist, journalist; b. Ambala, India, Mar. 29, 1914; s. Richard Chapman Pincher and Helen Foster; m. Constance Sylvia Wolstenholme; children: Patricia, Michael. BS with honors, London U., 1936; grad., Mil. Coll. Sci., Shrivenham, UK, 1943; LittD (hon.), Newcastle U., Newcastle-upon-Tyne, UK, 1979. Staff dept. biology Liverpool (Eng.) Inst., 1936-46; def., sci. and med. editor Daily Express, London, 1946-79, asst. editor, freelance writer. Author: Breeding of Farm Animals, 1946, A Study of Fishes, 1947, Into the Atomic Age, 1947, Spotlight on Animals, 1950, Evolution, 1950, (with Bernard Wicksteed) It's Fun Finding Out, 1950, Sleep, and How to Get More of It, 1954, Sex in Our Time, 1973, Inside Story, 1978, Their Trade is Treachery, 1981, Too Secret Too Long, 1984, The Secret Offensive, 1985, Traitors-the-Labyrinths of Treason, 1987, A Web of Deception, 1987, The Truth About Dirty Tricks, 1991, One Dog and Her Man, 1991, (autobiography) Pastoral Symphony, 1993, A Box of Chocolates, 1993, Life's a Bitch!, 1996, Tight Lines!, 1997, Treachery, Betrayals, Blunders and Cover-ups: Six Decades of Espionage Against America and Great Britain, 2009, Chapman Pincher: Dangerous to Know, 2014; author: (novels) Not with a Bang, 1965, The Giantkiller, 1967, The Penthouse Conspirators, 1970, The Skeleton at the Villa Wolkonsky, 1975, The Eye of the Tornado, 1976, The Four Horses, 1978, Dirty Tricks, 1980, The Private World of St. John Terrapin, 1982, Contamination, 1989; contbr. numerous articles to sci., agrl. and sporting jours.; rschr. in genetics. Served to capt. Royal Armored Corps, 1940-46. Recipient Journalist of Yr. award Granada TV, 1964, Reporter of Decade award Granad TV, 1964. Fellow King's Coll. London. Avocations: fishing, shooting. Died Aug. 5, 2014.

**PINCUS, ED (EDWARD RALPH PINCUS),** filmmaker; b. Bklyn., July 6, 1938; s. Jules and Anne (Schehr) P.; m. Jane Abigail Kates, June 22, 1960; children: Sami, Ben. AB in Philosophy, Brown U., 1960; MA in Philosophy, Harvard U., 1967. Pres. Cambridgeport Film Corp., Roxbury, Vt., from 1965; assoc. prof. MIT, Cambridge, Mass., 1967-80. Vis. lectr. Harvard U., Cambridge, 1981-83. Dir., prodr.: (documentaries) Panola, 1965, Black Natchez, 1965, One Step Away, 1967, The Way We See It, 1969, Life and Other Anxieties, 1977, Diaries, 1981; author: Guide to Filmmaking, 1968, The Filmmaker's Handbook, 1984, The Axe in the Attic, 2007 Selectman Town of Roxbury, Vt., 1979-80. Fellow Guggenheim Found., 1977, NEA, 1976, 79, 81. Avocations: gardening, bonsai, Aikido. Died Nov. 5, 2013.

**PINKERTON, IVOR LENNOX,** civil engineer, consultant; b. Crookwell, NSW, Australia, Oct. 12, 1915; s. Harry Willoughby and Lillian Esther P.; m. Mary Elizabeth Jackson, Dec. 31, 1941; children: John David, Robin Lennox, Marianne Elizabeth James, Margaret Ann. BSc, U. Sydney, Australia, 1935, BE, 1937. Registered profl. engr. Civil engr. ARC Cons. Engrs., Sydney, 1938-39, Commonwealth Dept. of Works, Sydney, 1940-46, Water Resources Commn., Sydney, 1946-49; chief designing engr. Snowy Mountains Authority, Cooma, NSW, Australia, 1949-72, Snowy Mountains Engring. Corp., Cooma, 1972-76; internat. cons. Canberra, Australia, from 1976. Named Commdr. of Most Noble Order of the Crown of Thailand, 1980, Mem. Order of Australia, Gov.-Gen. of Australia, 1990. Fellow ASCE (Rickey medal 1963, responsible for design of snowy mountains scheme nominated one of the seven greatest engring. achievements of the 20th century), Instn. of Engrs. Australia (medal). Home: Canberra, Australia. Died Apr. 12, 2001.

**PINKERTON, JAMES SAUNDERS,** travel company executive, consultant; b. Naracoorte, Australia, July 21, 1940; s. Thomas Peter and Ruth Constance (Saunders) P. Cert., Scotch Coll., Adelaide, Australia, 1955; tourism diploma, Fgn. U., Perugia, Italy, 1976; advanced fares diploma, Lufthansa Sch., Germany, 1982. Stockman Dalgety & Co., Naracoorte, Australia, 1957-60; real estate clk. Saunders & Co., Adelaide, Australia, 1960-63; traveling edn., 1963-64; travel cons. TAA, Adelaide, Australia, 1964-68; co. dir. Travel Assocs., Sydney, Australia, 1972-88; exec., mgr. Wentworth Travel, Sydney, Australia, 1988-97. Mem. Panam Travel Agt. Adv. Bd., Sydney, Australia, 1982-85, Australian Inst. Internat. Affairs, Sydney, Australia, 1975-82. Com. Young Liberals, Naracoorte, 1958-60. Fellow Australian Inst. Travel & Tourism; mem. Sydney Swans Football Club. Mem. Ch. Eng. Achievements include opening Vietnam to Australian tourists in 1977; organization of first tour group to Vietnam after war ended. Home: Sydney, Australia. Deceased.

**PIPPARD, ALFRED BRIAN,** retired physicist; b. Sept. 7, 1920; s. A. J. S. and F. L. O. (Tucker) Pippard; m. Charlotte Frances Dyer, 1955; 3 children. Degree, Cambridge U., Eng. Sci. officer Radar Rsch. & Devel. Establishment, 1941—45; demonstrator, physics Cambridge U., 1946, lectr., 1950, reader, 1959—60, Plummer prof., physics, 1960—71, pres., Clare hall, 1966—73, Cavendish prof., 1971—82. Author: Elements of Classical Thermodynamics, 1957, Dynamics of Conduction Electrons, 1962, Forces and Particles, 1972, Physics of Vibration, 1978, 1983, Response and Stability, 1985, Magnetoresistance, 1989; contbr. articles to profl. jours. Decorated Created knight; recipient Holweck medal, 1961, Dannie-Heineman prize, U. Gottingen, 1969, Guthrie medal, 1970. Fellow: Royal Soc. (Hughes medal 1959). Home: Cambridge, England. Died Sept. 21, 2008.

**PIRELLI, LEOPOLDO,** retired manufacturing executive; b. Varese, Italy, Aug. 27, 1925; s. Alberto and Ludovica (Zambeletti) P.; children: Cecilia, Alberto. Degree in mech. engring., Milan Poly., 1950. Chmn., ptnr. Pirelli & C.A.p.A., Milan, 1957-99; dep. chmn. Soc. Internat. Pirelli, Basel, Switzerland, 1979-99; pres. (hon.) Pirelli & C.A. apa., Milan, 1999—2007. Chmn. Pirelli S.p.A., Milan, 1965-96. Mem. Confindustria (exec. coun. 1957-82, dep. chmn. 1974-80, bd. dirs. 1974-82). Died Jan. 23, 2007.

**PIRRO, VINCENZO,** history and philosophy educator; b. S. Severo, Foggia, Italy, Nov. 13, 1938; s. Umberto and Francesca (Molino) P.; m. Michelinz Anna Bisceglia, Oct. 19, 1965; children: Alessandra, Danilo Sergio. s. Umberto and Francesca (Molino) P.; m. Michelina Anna Bisceglia, Oct. 19, 1965; children: Alessandra, Danilo Sergio. Diploma, Liceo Classico, S. Severo, 1959; laurea, Filosofia U., Rome, 1963. Cert. tchr. sr. H.S. Tchr. philosophy State Sch., Terni, Italy, 1964-83, tchr. philosophy and history, from 1993; philosophy asst. U. Perugia, Italy, 1974-81; rschr. ednl. studies Pub. Edn. Ministry, Perugia, 1983-93, dir. course of adjournament for tchrs. Umbria, Italy, 1983-95. Promoter Congress of Studies, 1982-95; tchr. Univ. of Third Age, Terni, 1983-95; pres. Inst. for History of Italian Risorgimento, Dist. of Terni, 1980—. Author: Filosofia e Politica in Benedetto Croce, 1967, Terni Nell'Età Rivoluzionaria E Napoleonica, 1984, Terni e la Sua Provincia Durante la Republica Sociale, 1990; editor: L'Altro Mediterraneo, 1991, Giuseppe Petroni, 1990, Epistemologia e Didattica Della Storia, 1991, Gli Arabi e Noi, 1995. Hon. judge Dept. Ministry of Justice, Perugia, 1988-95; pres. Hist. Studies, Terni, 1989. Home: Terni, Italy. Died 2009.

**PISANKO, HENRY JONATHAN,** command and control communications company executive; b. Trenton, NJ, Mar. 14, 1925; s. Isadore Stephen and Victoria (Gula) P.; m. Sophia Emily Zudnak, May 29, 1949 (dec. 1998); children: Barbara, Henry Jonathan, Jr., Michael. B in Naval Sci., U. Notre Dame, 1945, BA, 1947; cert. in Japanese, U. Colo. and Okla. State U., 1945; postgrad. Woodrow Wilson Sch., Princeton U., Columbia U., 1948-50. Constrn. reporter ea. div. F.W. Dodge div. McGraw-Hill, NYC and Phila., 1950-52; internat. affairs analyst Dept. Def., Washington, 1953-59, ops. officer Pacific Rim, Japan and Hong Kong, 1960-63; sr. intelligence officer Internat. Security Affairs, Dept. Def., Washington, 1964-70; overseas adminstr. diplomatic telecommunications Dept. State, Asia, Africa, 1971-73; spl. advisor Def. Intelligence Coll., Washington, 1974-75; ctr. dep. chief, adminstrn. dir. Intelligence Community, Washington, 1976-82; exec. officer USA-EIGO Svcs. Co., Rockville, Md., 1983-87, Princeton, N.J., 1983-87, now bd. dirs.; pres. P.K. Co. Ltd., Bethesda, from 1987, chmn. bd. dirs. emeritus Hong Kong; assoc. Dawson Sci. Corp., Hong Kong, from 1996. Bd. dirs. Asia Mgmt. Internat., Princeton; assoc. Bi-Lingual U.S.A. Corp., Bethesda, Md., 1984, Mgmt. Logistics Internat., Arlington, Va., 1983-86; hon. dir. Pacific Rim Enterprises, Hong Kong, 1996. Editor, translator: Yoshio Kodama, 1952; author: (monographs) Items of Inquiry Far East, 1983, Japanese Technology-Ancient Culture, 1985, August, 1994 (pamphlet) Fiber Optics Across the Pacific, 1989; editor (handbook) Japanese-English Proprietary Business Lexicon for Command Control Communications Intelligence, 1990-93; author, producer handbook: Telecommunications Operations for Pacific Rim Enterprises, 1996. Sponsor, contbr. Pisanko-Kikan, 1982, Hotel Okura, Japan, 1983, Bungei Shunju, Japan, 1988. Lt. J.G., USN, 1942-46. Trenton Times scholar, 1942; recipient Moe Berg award Pub. Security Investigation Agy.-Japan, Tokyo, 1961, Order of Cariboe, Philippines, 1960-63, Telecommunications award Thai Gen. Staff, Bangkok, 1972, Shimoda Diplomatic award, Japan. Mem. Asian Rsch. Svc., Bus. Devel. Africa, Internat. Inst. Japan, Bus. Execs. for Internat. Security, Internat. Platform Assn., Info. Processing Soc. Japan, Naval Res. Officers Tng. Corps, Unit Alumni Club, Boulder (Colo.) Boys-Japanese Club, Shek-O Club (Hong Kong). Avocations: rare book collecting, cryptology, desert safaris. Home: Chicago, Ill. *"I seek no other man's shoes. If I've misdirected my priorities, and I'm confident this is not so, I've had a fair time in lost country. There are no regrets."Moe Berg Pr #23.* Died Dec. 4, 1999.

**PITCHER, WALLACE SPENCER,** retired science educator; b. Acton, Eng., Mar. 3, 1919; s. Harry George and Bertha Irene (Harris) Pitcher; m. Stella Ann Scott, Aug. 23, 1947; children: Margaret, John, Robert, Elizabeth. BSc, Chelsea Coll., London, 1947; PhD, Imperial Coll., London, 1951; DSc, U. London, 1964; DSc (hon.), U. Dublin, Ireland, 1983; Dr (hon.), Paris-Sud, 1993. Lectr. Imperial Coll., London, 1947—54; reader King's Coll., London, 1954—62; chmn., prof. U. Liverpool, England, 1962—81, Leverhulme fellow emeritus, 1981—83, hon. rsch. fellow, from 1983. Author, editor Controls of Metamorphism, 1965, Magmatism at a Plate Edge: The Peruvian Andes, 1985; author (with A.R. Berget): Geology of Donegal: Granite Magmas, 1972; author: Nature & Origin of Granite, 1993, 2d edit., 1997, A Master Class Guide to the Donegal Granites, 2003. Chmn. rsch. grants Natural Environ. Rsch. Coun., London, 1978—81. Sgt. Royal Army M.C., 1939—44. Recipient Silver medal, Geol. Soc. Liverpool, 1962. Fellow: Geol. Soc. London (pres. 1977—78, hon. sec. 1970—75, Lyell Fund award 1956, Bigsby medal 1963, Murchison medal 1979, Aberconway medal 1983), Geol. Soc. Am. (hon.), Royal Soc. Edinburgh (hon.); mem.: Royal Irish Acad. (hon.), Soc. Geol. Peru (hon.). Achievements include research in on the nature, origin and emplacement of granites. Avocation: genealogy. Deceased.

**PITRONE, JEAN MADDERN,** writer, educator; b. Ishpeming, Mich., Dec. 20, 1920; d. William Courtney and Gladys Mae (Beer) Maddern; m. Anthony Pitrone, Oct. 26, 1940; children: Joseph, Jill, Anthony Jr., Joyce, John, Janet, Julie, Jane, Cheryl. Grad. high sch., Ishpeming. Short story instr. Writer's Digest Sch., Cin., 1971-89. Author: Trailblazer, 1969, Tangled Web: Legacy of Auto Pioneer John F. Dodge, 1989 (Book of Distinction award Soc. Automotive Historians 1990), Hudson's: Hub of America's Heartland, 1991, F.W. Woolworth and the American Five and Dime-A Social History, 2003, others. Mem. Detroit Women Writers (pres. 1981-83). Republican. Roman Catholic. Avocations: music, piano, organ. Home: Trenton, Mich. Died Mar. 12, 2008.

**PITSEOLAK, See ASHOONA, PITSEOLAK**

**PLACE, ULLIN THOMAS,** philosopher; b. Northallerton, Eng., Oct. 24, 1924; s. Thomas and Dorothy Foster (Abraham) P.; m. Anna Nanette Wessel, July 1949 (div. 1962); children: Thomas Wessel, Frances Dorothy; m. Norah Peggy Townsend, Oct. 24, 1964. BA, Oxford U., 1949, MA, 1950, diploma in anthropology, 1950; DLitt, U. Adelaide, 1972. Chartered psychologist. Lectr. in psychology U. Adelaide, 1951-54; clin. psychologist Ctrl. Hosp., Warwick, Eng., 1960-63; sr. clin. psychologist Hollymoor Hosp., Birmingham, Eng., 1963-66; lectr. in psychology U. Aston, Birmingham, 1967; lectr. in clin. psychology U. Leeds, Eng., 1968-69, sr. lectr. in philosophy, 1970-82. Author: Dispositions: A Debate, 1996. Fellow British Psychol. Soc.; mem. Assn. for Behavior Analysis, Assn. for the Scientific Study of Consciousness. Liberal Democrat. Avocations: sheep farming, wild edible fungi, english place names, archaeology, model railways. Home: Thirsk, England. Died Jan. 2, 2000.

**PLONKA, ANDRZEJ,** physical chemistry educator; b. Lodz, Poland, Nov. 3, 1936; s. Stanislaw and Eugenia P.; m. Ewa Krystyna Wilczynska, May 30, 1970; 1 child, Wojciech. MSc in Dipl. Engring., Tech. U., Lodz, 1959, PhD, 1964, DSc, 1969. Head radioisotope lab. Mil. Acad. of Medicine, Lodz, 1960-64; head of esr lab. Tech. U. of Lodz, from 1970, prof. chemistry, from 1983; rsch. scientist Wayne State U., Detroit, 1975-76; rsch. scientist for strahlenchemie Max-Planck-Inst., Mülheim, Germany, 1980; vis. prof. U. Houston, 1983-84. Nat. rep. Commn. on Radiochemistry and Nuclear Techniques, IUPAC, 1991—. Contbr. 180 articles to profl. jours.; author 5 scientific monographs. Mem. Internat. Assn. for Radiation Rsch. (councillor 1983-87), Miller Trust for Radiation Chemistry (com. mem. 1993—). Achievements include research on ESR studies on structure and reactivity of radiation and photo-produced intermediates in condensed media; development of dispersive kinetics. Home: Lodz, Poland. Died Sept. 5, 2001.

**PLOWCHA, CHARLENE SNYDER,** education and home economics educator; b. Indiana, Pa., Nov. 19, 1946; d. Gordon and Blanche (Burba) Snyder; m. Paul G. Plowcha, Oct. 12, 1968; 1 child, P. Adam Plowcha II. BS, Indiana U. Pa., 1968, MEd, 1977; EdD, Pa. State U., 1987. Cert. home economist. Tchr. home econs. Brockton (Mass.) Sr. High Sch., 1970-74; assoc. prof. edn. Mansfield (Pa.) U., from 1978, asst. to v.p. student affairs, 1988-90, chair dept. home econs., 1989-91, athletic mentor, 1993-94. Chpt. 5 field support adv. com. mem. Higher Edn. Rep., 1992—; chmn., developer tng. package: Processes for Generating Transitional Outcomes for Pa. Implementation of Chpt. 5 Curriculum Regulations, 1994. Editor (newsletter) Interface, 1986-87. Chair So. Tioga Home Econs. Adv. Bd., Mansfield, 1987-90; com. mem., counselor Boy Scouts Am. Troop 106, Mansfield, 1987—. Recipient Univ. Liaison for Outcome Based Edn. award Tioga Sch. Dist./Mansfield U., 1992-94; Urban Edn. fellow State System Higher Edn., Harrisburg, Pa., 1988-90; Bur. Vocat. Edn./Pa. State U. grantee, 1988-89. Mem. ASCD, Pa. Assn. for Supervision and Curriculum Devel., Am. Vocat. Assn., Assn. of Consumer and Family Scis., Pa. Home Econs. Assn. (ctrl. area v.p. 1988-89), Phi Delta Kappa, Kappa Omicron Nu (advisor 1986-92). Avocations: reading, sewing, spectator sports. Home: Mansfield, Pa. Died May 1998.

**PLUNKET, DOLORES,** art educator, archaeology educator; b. Chgo., Sept. 2, 1916; d. John Nagoda and Evangeline Kompare; m. John T. Plunket, July 15, 1944; children: Lucy Silver, Robert, John T. Jr., Patricia. BS, U. Ill., 1937; MA in Pre-Colombian Art, Nat. U. Mexico, Mexico City, 1975. V.p. Mexican-N.Am. Cultural Inst., Mexico City, 1985-88; dir. lecture series Selby Libr., Sarasota, Fla., 1992-96; lectr. in field. Co-author: (with A.R. L'huillier) Vision del Mundo Maya, 1978; editor Gardening in the Federal District, 1986;

contbr. articles to profl. jours. V.p. Friends Selby Libr., 1992-95; pres. Mexico City Garden Club, 1985; bd. dirs. Am. Soc. Mexico, 1986-88. Died Nov. 15, 2005.

**POE, TERRY LYNN,** music educator; b. Asheboro, NC, Mar. 30, 1952; s. George McLamb and Christine Teague Poe. B in music edn., Wake Forest U., 1970—74. Assoc. dir. Raleigh Boychoir, Raleigh, NC, 1974—94; chapel organist St. Mary's Coll., Raleigh, 1979—84; church organist Trinity U. Meth. Ch., Raleigh, NC, from 1976; choral music tchr. Wake County Pub. Schools, 1974—2008. Mentor coord. Carroll Mid. Sch., Raleigh, NC, 1995—2008, fine arts chmn., 1979—2008, beta club coun. chmn., 1994—2008. Mem. Wake County Exec. PTA Coun., 1988—89, Boy Scouts Am., 1965—70. Recipient Secondary Tchr. of Yr., Wake Cty. Pub. Sch., 1988. Mem.: Am. Guild Organists, Nat. Edn. Assn. Democrat. Baptist. Avocation: flying. Home: Star, NC. Died Nov. 12, 2013.

**POE, WILLIAM FREDERICK (BILL POE),** insurance company executive, retired mayor; b. Tampa, Fla., July 22, 1931; s. Fred Holland and Zula Blanche (Willoughby) P.; m. Elizabeth Ann Blackburn, June 21, 1954; children: William, Keren, Janice, Marilyn, Charles. Student, Duke U., 1950; BS in Bus., U. Fla., 1953. Founder, pres. Poe & Associates, Tampa, 1956-74, chmn., 1979-87, chmn. bd., 1987-93; mayor City of Tampa, 1974-79. Mem. Hillsborough County Port Authority, 1961, chmn., 1963; pres. chpt. ARC, United Way of Greater Tampa. Served with USAF, 1955-56. Mem. Tampa Assn. Ins. Agents, Chief Executives Orgn. Clubs: Yacht. Democrat. Baptist. Home: Tampa, Fla. Died May 1, 2014.

**POGUE, WILLIAM REID,** retired astronaut, aerospace scientist, consultant; b. Okemah, Okla., Jan. 23, 1930; s. Alex W. and Margaret (McDow) P.; m. Tina Joyce Pogue; children from previous marriage: William Richard, Layna Sue, Thomas Reid. BS in Secondary Edn., Okla. Bapt. U., 1951, D.Sc. (hon.), 1974; MS in Math., Okla. State U., 1960. Commd. 2d lt. USAF, 1952, advanced through grades to col., 1973; combat fighter pilot Korea, 1953; gunnery instr. Luke AFB, Ariz., 1954; mem. acrobatic team USAF Thunderbirds, Luke AFB and Nellis AFB, Nev., 1955-57; asst. prof. math. USAF Acad., 1960-63; exchange test pilot Brit. Royal Aircraft Establishment, Ministry Aviation, Farnborough, Eng., 1964-65; instr. USAF Aerospace Research Pilots Sch., Edwards AFB, Calif., 1965-66; astronaut NASA Manned Spacecraft Center, Houston, 1966-75; pilot 3d manned visit to Skylab space sta.; ret. Author: How Do You Go to the Bathroom in Space?, 1991, Space Trivia, 1993, But for the Grace of God: An Autobiography of an Aviator and Astronaut, 2011; co-author (with Ben Bova): (novels) The Trikon Deception, 1992. Decorated Air medal with oak leaf cluster, D.S.M.; named to Five Civilized Tribes Hall of Fame, Choctaw descent; recipient Distinguished Service medal NASA, Collier trophy Nat. Aero. Assn.; Robert H. Goddard medal Nat. Space Club; Gen. Thomas D. White USAF Space Trophy Nat. Geog. Soc.; Halley Astronautics award, 1975; de la Vaalx medal Fedn. Aeronautique Internat., 1974; V.M. Komarov diploma, 1974; inducted into Okla. Aviation and Space Hall of Fame, 1980, U.S. Astronaut Hall of Fame, 1997. Fellow Acad. Arts & Sciences of Okla. State U., American Astron. Soc.; mem. Soc. Exptl. Test Pilots, Explorers Club, Sigma Xi, Pi Mu Epsilon. Baptist (deacon). Home: Cocoa Beach, Fla. Died Mar. 3, 2014.

**POLIDORI, GINO H.,** former state legislator; b. Dearborn, Mich. m. Betty Polidori; children: Gino Jr., Laura, Rita. City councilman, Dearborn, Mich.; firefighter & fire chief, 1974—96; mem. Dist. 15 Mich. House of Reps., 2005—10. Mem.: Mich. State Fire Chiefs Assn. (pres. 1987—88). Democrat. Died Jan. 26, 2014.

**POLITE, EDMONIA ALLEN,** consultant; b. Washington, June 22, 1922; d. Thomas Samuel and Narcissus Bertha (Porter) Allen-Sylvester; m. George Frederick Polite, Jan. 5, 1947; 1 child, Frederick Gartrell. BA, Roosevelt U., 1958; MEd, Loyola U., Chgo., 1966; PhD in Adminstrn. and Supervision, Purdue U., 1973; DDiv, Ea. U., Tampa, Fla., 1971; DEd in Psychology, Ea. U., 1972. Dir. Media Ctr., Chgo., 1958-69, 73-81; instr. media scis. Purdue U., West Lafayette, Ind., 1969-73; pres. Cons. Inc., Chgo., Orlando, Fla., from 1974; dir. Community Tutoring Ctr., Chgo., 1974-80, EAP Enterprises, from 1984. Dir. workshop U. Cen. Fla., 1987; cons. Lake Region Conf., Detroit, 1966, Librarians, Inc., Chgo., 1970-71. Author: In Passing, 1970, People Who Help Us, 1982. Founder South End Parents Council, Chgo., 1960, Humanitarian Profls., Chgo., 1974, Orlando, 1983—; bd. dirs. Salem House, Chgo., 1980—. Recipient Outstanding Service award Lions Club, Chgo., 1975, Outstanding Educator award Fla. Agrl. and Mech. U. Alumni Assn. Mem. Nat. Assn. Club Women (dir. archives 1980-84), Ill. Audio Visual Assn., Phi Delta Kappa. Club: Successful Progressors (Orlando) (pres. 1983-95). Avocations: writing, community service, counseling. Deceased.

**POLLACK, WILLIAM,** immunologist; b. London, Feb. 26, 1926; s. David and Rose Pollack; m. Alison Calder (dec. 2006); children: Malcolm, David. BSc in Chemistry & Physics, London U., 1948; MSc in Physiology & Biochemistry, St. George's Hosp. & Med. Sch., London, 1950; PhD in Immunology & Immunochemistry, Rutgers U. Gen. pathology St. George's Hosp. Med. Sch., London, 1948—54; dir. blood bank, dir. clin. labs. Royal Columbian Hosp., New Westminister, B.C., Canada, 1954—56; v.p., dir. rsch., bd. mem. Ortho Diagnostics Sys. Inc, Raritan, NJ, 1956—81; v.p. R&D, exec. com. Purdue Frederick Co., Norfolk, Conn., 1981—85; chmn. CEO Atopix Pharm. Corp., Carlsbad, Calif., from 1994. Immunology standards com. WHO, Geneva. Contbr. articles. Lt. Royal Navy, 1943—46. Recipient Lasker award for Clinical Medical Rsch., Albert & Mary Lasker Found., 1980, John Scott award, Phila. Bd. Dirs. City Trusts, 1976. Fellow: Royal Coll. Pathology; mem.: AAAS, Am. Assn. Immunologists, Am. Assn. Blood Banks (Karl Landsteiner award 1969), NY Acad. Medicine. Achievements include first to discovered prevention for Rhesus Disease of the Newborn; Eight Patents, including RhoGam and the first In Vitro Pregnancy Test. Avocation: piano. Died Nov. 3, 2013.

**POLLEY, WILLIAM ALPHONSE,** retired power systems engineer; b. Milw., Dec. 1, 1942; s. William O. and Florence V. P.; m. Connie A. Pippert, Aug. 28, 1965; children: Christopher, Karen, Craig, Carl. BSME, Marquette U., 1966. Engr. co-op Allis Chalmers, Milw., 1962-66; sales engr. Westinghouse, Duluth, Minn., 1966-79, applications engr. Appleton, Wis., 1979-88, systems engr., 1988-89; power systems engr. Kimberly-Clark, Neenah, Wis., 1989-2001, energy mgmt. cons., 2001. Chmn. St. Michael's Parish Coun., Duluth, 1977-79; scoutmaster Boy Scouts Am., Appleton, 1989-92, scout commr., 19925; exec. couple Nat. Marriage Encounter, Appleton, 1985-87. Mem. IEEE, Instrument Soc. of Am., Assn. Energy Engrs., Internat. Maint. Inst. Avocations: computers, gardening, travel. Home: Neenah, Wis. Died Mar. 7, 2008.

**PONCET, DOMINIQUE MATTEO,** lawyer, educator; b. Geneva, Aug. 31, 1929; s. Jean Francis and Giuseppina Poncet; m. Eliane Uldry, July 12, 1967; children: Isabelle, Philippe. Licentiate of Laws, U. Geneva, 1951, Doctor of Laws, 1967. With Lord Nathan Oppenheimer's Chambers, London, 1954; lawyer Geneva, from 1953; sr. ptnr. Poncet Turrettini Amaudruz Neyroud & Assocs., Geneva, from 1953; prof. criminal procedure U. Geneva, 1967-97. Dir. various cos.;mem. expert commn. to draft New Swiss Criminal Code; alternate mem. Geneva State Ct. Cassation; pres. Fiat Auto Suisse. Author: L'information contradictoire dans le système de la procédure pénale genevoise, 1967, Droit à l'assistance de l'avocat, 1970, L'extradition et le droit d'asile, 1976, La protection de l'accusé par la Convention Européenne des droits de l'homme, 1977, Le nouveau code de procédure pénale annoté, 1978, Extradition: The European Model, 1986, Le statut du dirigeant d'entreprise en Suisse, 1989, La surveillance des banques étrangères, 1993, Systeme accusatoire: Etats Unis, 1994; La responsabilité pénale des personnes morales, 2000. Decorated comdr. Order of Merit (Italy). Mem. Swiss Fedn. Lawyers, Geneva Law Soc., Swiss Soc. Jurists, Swiss Soc. Criminal Law, Rotary Club. Mem. Conservative Party. Avocations: golf, skiing, conjuring. Home: Vandoeuvres, Switzerland. Died June 16, 2004.

**PONTIUS, JAMES WILSON,** foundation administrator; b. Orrville, Ohio, Aug. 29, 1916; s. Howard Taggart and Nova Clementine (Mead) P.; m. Kathryn Jane Sharp, Mar. 12, 1938; children: Howard Garrett, Janne Pettibone, Carolyn Jean, Jon Brewster. BA, Miami U., Oxford, Ohio, 1937. Fin. and taxes GE, Schenectady, N.Y., 1937-47, traveling auditor, 1947-50, cons. electronic data sys., 1953-62, project mgr. internal automation dept. Waynesboro, Va., 1962-64, mgr. advanced info. systems Schenectady, N.Y., 1964-78; retired, 1978; mgr. treasury svcs. GE Supply Corp., Bridgeport, Conn., 1950-53; pres. William Gundry Broughton Charitable Pvt. Found., Inc., Glenville, N.Y., from 1992. Mem. adv. com. use of computers in bus. activities U.S. Dept. Def., Washington, 1955-56. Mem. Niskayuna (N.Y.) Sch. Bd., 1965-70, 71-72, 85-86; sec., treas., pres. Schenectady (N.Y.) Rotary Club Found., 1977-80; bd. dirs. Niskayuna (N.Y.) Cmty. Found., 2000—. Republican. Reformed. Avocations: bridge, golf, amateur radio, personal computers, pool. Home: Schenectady, NY. Died Sept. 10, 2001.

**POP, VICTOR V.,** zoologist, researcher; b. Targu Mures, Romania, Apr. 14, 1946; s. Victor and Rozalia Pop; m. Adriana Ileana b. Tudorica, Aug. 21, 1976; 1 child, Pop Adriana Antonia. BSc in Biology (hon.), Babes-Bolyai U., Cluj-Napoca, Romania, 1959, PhD in Biology, 1976. Sci. rschr. Inst. Biol. Rsch., Cluj-Napoca, Romania, 1960—2008, soil zoologist, from 1961, sci. sec., 1990—2000. Contbr. scientific papers to profl. jours. Recipient Ion Ionescu de la Brad award, Romanian Acad. Scis. Soil Sci., 1964. Mem.: Internat. Orgn. Oligochaeta Taxonomists. Achievements include research in taxonomy and ecology of earthworms; soil biology and evolution. Home: Cluj-Napoca, Romania. Died 2004.

**POPE, MARVIN HOYLE,** language educator, writer; b. Durham, NC, June 23, 1916; s. Charles Edgar and Bessie Cleveland Sorrell Pope; m. Helen Thompson, Sept. 4, 1948 (dec. Feb. 1979); m. Ingrid Brostrom Bloomquist, Mar. 9, 1985. AB, Duke U., 1938, AM, 1939; PhD, Yale U., 1949. Instr. dept. religion Duke U., Durham, 1947-49; asst. prof. Hebrew Yale U., New Haven, 1949-55, assoc. prof., 1955-64, prof. Semitic langs. and lit., 1964-86, prof. emeritus, sr. rsch. scholar, from 1986. Haskell lectr. Oberlin Coll., 1971, vis. lectr. Cath. U. Lublin, Poland, 1977, Fulbright lectr. U. Aleppo, Syria, 1980; Wickenden lectrs. Miami U., Oxford, Ohio, 1982; Fulbright Rsch. scholar Inst. Ugaritforschung U. Muenster, Germany, 1986, 90; Hooker disting. vis. prof. McMaster U., Hamilton, Ont. Can., 1986; dir. Hebrew Union Coll. Bibl. and Archeol. Sch., Jerusalem, 1966-67; trustee Albright Inst. Archeol. Rsch., Jerusalem; fellow Pierson Coll. Yale U. Author: El in the Ugaritic Texts, 1955; The Book of Job, 1973, Song of Songs, 1977 (Nat. Religious Book award 1978), Syrien Die Mythologie der Ugariter und Phoenizier, 1962, Collected Essays, 1994; contbr. articles to scholarly jours. and dictionaries. Mem. Revised Standard Version Bible com. Nat. Coun. Chs., 1960—; mem. First Ch. Round Hill. With USAF, 1941-45, PTO. Nat. Endowment for Humanities Rsch. grantee, 1980—. Mem. Am. Oriental Soc., Am. Schs. Oriental Rsch., Soc. Bibl. Lit., Am. Soc. Study Religions, Columbia U. Seminar for Study of Hebrew Bible, Yale Club, Oriental Club New Haven, Mory's Club, Lakeview Club (Austin, Tex.), Phi Beta Kappa. Home: Greenwich, Conn. Died June 15, 1997.

**POPOVIC, KREŠIMIR M(ARIJAN),** chemical engineer; b. Zagreb, Croatia, Feb. 11, 1940; s. Marijan and Mejra Antonija (Nežic) P.; m. Silvija Šimat, July 1, 1967; children: Hrvoje, Maja. BSc, U. Zagreb, 1963, MSc, 1971, DSc in Chem. Engring., 1974. Rsch. engr. Assn. of Cement Producers, Zagreb, 1965-72, head tech., rsch. divsn., 1972-79; tchg. asst. U. Zagreb, 1966-68, asst. prof. material sci., Faculty of Civil Engring., 1975-82, assoc. prof. material sci. and cement materials, 1982-91; head cement materials divsn. Civil Engring. Inst. of Croatia, Zagreb, from 1991, v.p. sci. coun., from 1993, sci. advisor, from 1992. Cons. chem. engring. Editor: Role of Croatian Cement Industry in the System of Waste Management, 1998; editor Civil Engring. abstracts, 1985-90; patentee in field. Fellow U. Zagreb Almae Matris Alumni Assn.; mem. Croatian Soc. chem. Engrs. (founder, pres. 1987—), Croatian Acad. for Tech. Scis. (assoc. 1994—). Avocations: tennis, singing. Home: Zagreb, Croatia. Died Apr. 2003.

**POPOVKIN, VLADIMIR ALEKSANDROVICH,** former aerospace agency executive; b. Dushanbe, Tajikistan, Sept. 25, 1957; 2 children. Grad., Leningrad Mil.-Space Acad., 1979; grad. with excellent marks, Mil. Acad. Strategic Rocket Forces, 1986. Engr., launch comdr. Launch Pad 1 Baikonur Cosmodrome, 1979; joined Directorate of Space Sys. Russian Ministry of Def., 1986, gen. staff, 1991—2001; chief of staff Russian Space Forces, comdr. space forces, 2004; chief armaments Russian Ministry of Def., 2008—09, first dep. min. def., 2009—11; gen. dir. Russian Fed. Space Agency, 2011—13. Decorated Medal of Order for Disting. Svc. to the Homeland 4th Class Govt. of Russia; recipient Sci. and Tech. award, 2005. Mem.: K.E. Tsiolkovsky Russian Space Acad., Russian Arty. Missile Sci. Acad. (corr.). Died June 18, 2014.

**POPP, BERNARD FERDINAND,** bishop emeritus; b. Nada, Tex., Dec. 6, 1917; s. Ferdinand and Anna Staff Popp. Attended, St. John's Sem., San Antonio. Ordained priest Archdiocese of San Antonio, 1943, sec. to archbishop Robert E. Lucey, 1945—68; rector San Fernando Cathedral; ordained bishop, 1983; aux. bishop Archdiocese of San Antonio, 1983—93, aux. bishop emeritus, 1993—2014. Roman Catholic. Home: San Antonio, Tex. Died June 27, 2014.

**PORTER, ELIZABETH KERR,** dean, nursing educator; b. Pitts., 1894; Diploma, Western Pa. Hosp. Sch. Nursing, 1930; BS, Columbia U., 1935; MS, U. Pa., 1936, EdD, 1946, doctorate (hon.). Prof. Sch. Nursing U. Pa.; faculty Francis Payne Bolton Sch. Nursing Case Western Res. U., Cleve., 1949, prof., dir. grad. program in nursing, dean, 1953. Bd. dirs. Nat. Health Coun. Recipient Pa. Ambassadorial award, 1954, Florence Nightingale medal Internat. Red Cross. Mem. ANA (pres., formed Nat. Student Nurses' Coun., Shirley Titus award), Ohio Nurses Assn. (pres. 1958-60), Am. Nurses Found. (v.p.). Died 1989.

**PORTER, JOSHUA ROY,** priest, theology studies educator; b. Godley, Cheshire, Eng., May 7, 1921; s. Joshua and Bessie Evelyn Porter. MA, U. Oxford, Eng., 1945. Fellow, chaplain Oriel Coll., Oxford, 1949—62; prof. theology, dept. head U. Exeter, Exeter, England, 1962—86, prof. emeritus, 1986. Canon of wightring and exceit Chichester (Eng.) Cathedral, 1965—2001, canon emeritus, 2001; pres. Soc. for Old Testament Study, London, 1979—83; chmn. Gen. Synod Ch. of Eng., London, 1984—86. Author: Synodical Government in the Church of England, 1990, Illustrated Guide to the Bible, 1995, Jesus Christ, 1999, The First and Second Prayer Books of Edward VI, 1999, The Lost Bible, 2001, The New Illustrated Companion to the Bible, 2003, Supernatural Enemies, 2003, La Bible Oubliée, 2004. Kennicott Hebrew fellow, U. Oxford, 1955, Sr. Denyer and Johnson scholar, 1958. Fellow: Ancient Monuments Soc.; mem.: Anglican Assn. (pres. 1986), Prayer Book Soc. (vice chmn. 1980), Folklore Soc. (pres. 1979), King's Head Theatre, Friends Royal Acad., Victorian Soc. Independent. Avocations: theater, opera, collecting books, travel. Home: London, England. Died Dec. 31, 2006.

**POTTER, BARBARA ANN,** music educator; b. Freeport, Ill., Sept. 16, 1941; d. Nelson Thomas and Hazel Althea (Park) P. BA, Culver-Stockton Coll., 1965; MA, Goddard Coll., 1980. Cert. music tchr., Conn., Mo. Tchr. LeMo Pub. Sch. Dist., Lewistown, Mo., 1965-66, Henry County Regional Ind. Sch. Dist., Windsor, Mo., 1966-69; tchr. music Bristol (Conn.) Pub. Schs., from 1969. Instr. classroom tchrs. courses for use of music in classroom; trainer tchrs. for edn. project Wesleyan U., project participant music in the classroom, Conn. State Dept. Edn. Author: Do It My Way: The Child's Way of Learning, 1977; Mem. editorial bd. The Orff Echo, 1987—. Mem. Am. Orff-Schulwerk Assn. Conf. (clinician nat. confs. Phoenix 1979, Chgo. 1987, Atlanta 1989, region V rep. for bd. of trustees 1983-87, pres. Conn. chpt. 1978-80). Avocations: performing, kite flying, cooking, sewing. Deceased.

**POTTER, JOHN MCEWEN,** retired neurosurgeon and medical educator; b. London, Feb. 28, 1920; s. Alistair Richardson Potter and Mairi Chalmers Dick; m. Kathleen Gerrard, Apr. 21, 1943; children: James Gerrard, Andrew John, Simon Stephen. BA, MB, BChir., U. Cambridge, 1943, MA, 1945; MA, BM, BCh, U. Oxford, 1963, DM, 1964. Lectr. St. Bartholomew's Hosp., London, 1948-50, jr. chief asst. surg. professorial unit, 1950-51; grad. asst. to Nuffield prof. surgery U. Oxford, Eng., 1951-56, dir. postgrad. med. edn., 1972-87; cons. neurosurgeon Manchester (Eng.) Royal Infirmary, 1956-61, Radcliffe Infirmary, Oxford, 1961-87; fellow, professorial fellow, sub-warden

Wadham Coll., Oxford, 1969-87, emeritus fellow and dean of degrees. V.p. Fourth Internat. Congress Neurol. Surgery; vis. prof. UCLA, 1967; examiner in medicine Univs. Oxford and Cambridge, 1970-74; bd. govs. United Oxford Hosps., 1973; mem. Gen. Med. Coun., London, 1973-89; lectr. Cairns Trust, Adelaide, Australia, 1974; mem. Oxfordshire Health Authority, 1982-89, hebdomadal coun. U. Oxford, 1983-89, Med. Appeals Tribunal, London, 1987-90. Author: The Practical Management of Head Injuries, 1961, 4th edit., 1984; contbr. articles to profl. jours., chpts. to books. Capt. Royal Army Med. Corps, 1944-47. E.G. Fearnsides scholar U. Cambridge, 1954-56. Fellow Royal Coll. Surgeons (Hunterian Professor 1955); mem. Am. Assn. Neurol. Surgeons (lifetime inactive), Royal Soc. of Medicine (pres. sect. neurology 1975-76), Soc. Brit. Neurol. Surgeons (sr., formerly hon. sec. and archivist), Deutsche Gesellschaft Fur Neurochirurgie (corr.), Sociedad Luso-Espanhola De Neurocirurgia (corr.), Egyptian Soc. Neurol. Surgeons (hon.). Mem. Ch. Eng. Avocation: fishing. Home: Oxford, England. Died Feb. 6, 2002.

**POULSEN, EMIL,** toxicological advisor; b. Ebeltoft, Denmark, July 12, 1921; s. Niels Carl Waldemar Poulsen and Johanne Cecilie Carstensen; m. Ellen Elisabeth Kibaek, Feb. 24, 1945; children: Per, Jorgen, Hanne. DVM, Royal Vet. & Agrl. U., Copenhagen, 1943, D of Medicine Veterinariae, 1957. Asst. in veterinary practice, Kolind, Denmark, 1943-44; asst. prof. Royal Vet. & Agrl. U., Copenhagen, 1944-48, 51-64; vet. supr. Pub. Health, Copenhagen, 1948-51; assoc. prof. Dept. State Vet. Medicine, Copenhagen, 1964-68; dir. Nat. Food Agy. Inst. Toxicology, Copenhagen, 1968-86; chief advisor toxicology Ministry of Health and Ministry of Environ., Copenhagen, 1986-91, toxicol. advisor, from 1991. Mem. EU Scientific Com. for Food, 1974-95, pres., 1980-86. Fellow Acad. Toxicology; mem. Toxicology Forum (bd. dirs. 1979-98, George Scott Meml. award 2001), Internat. Life Scis. Inst. Europe (bd. dirs. 1989-95). Home: Humlebaek, Denmark. Died July 26, 2006.

**POURIER, MIGUEL A.,** former prime minister of the Netherlands Antilles; b. Bonaire, Netherlands Antilles, Sept. 29, 1938; Degree in Fiscal Law, U. Tilburg, The Netherlands. Min. gen. affairs Netherlands Antilles, Willemstad, Curaçao, from 1994; head dept. excise & import duties, dir. taxes Inspectorate of Taxes, 1962-73; min. devel. cooperation Netherlands Antilles, Willemstad, Curaçao, 1973-78, min. finance, 1978, min. econ. affairs, 1978, prime min., 1978—79, 1999—2002; dir., gen. dir. ABN Bank Trust, N. Antilles, Aruba, 1980-91; adviser to govt, fin. cons., 1991-94. Mem., Partido Antía Restrukturá. Died Mar. 23, 2013.

**POUTSMA, JACOB ALBERTUS,** physician, psychologist, hypnotherapist; b. Pontianak, Borneo, Indonesia, Mar. 5, 1922; arrived in Australaia, 1945; s. Izaak Hendrik Johan and Frieda Wilhelmina (Vorstman) P.; m. Marie Lois Gibson, Jan. 13, 1951; children: Anna Marie, Nicholas, Louisa, Anthony Gibson. MB, BS, U. Melbourne, Australia, 1952, BSc, 1967. Resident med. officer Prince Henry Pub. Hosp., Melbourne, 1953-54, Sunbury (Australia) Mental Hosp., 1954-55, Royal Park Psychiat. Hosp., Melbourne, 1955-57; pvt. practice Yarraville-West Footscray, VIC, Australia, 1957-79, Brunswick Heads, NSW, Australia, 1979-88, Mullumbimby, NSW, Australia, 1979—99. Vis. med. officer Mullumbimby and Dist. Hosp. Health Svcs., 1980—99. Sgt. Netherlands East Indies Fleet-Air Arm, 1942-45 (POW in Ujung Pandang, Sulawesi). Mem. Australian Soc. Hypnosis, Internat. Soc. Hypnosis, Doctors for Disaster Preparedness, N.Y. Acad. Scis. Avocations: cosmology, nuclear energy, futurology. Died Aug. 4, 2002.

**POWER, SIR NOEL PLUNKETT,** retired judge; b. Dec. 4, 1929; s. John Joseph and Hilda Power; m. Irma Maroya; 3 children. Student, Downlands Coll., 1948-50; BA, LLB, U. Queensland. Magistrate, Hong Kong, 1965-76; pres. Lands Tribunal, Hong Kong, 1976-79; judge High Court Hong Kong, 1979-87; judge of appeal, 1987-93; v.p. Ct. of Appeal, Hong Kong, 1993—99. Non-permanent mem. Ct. of Final Appeal, 1997—2009. Editor Lands Tribunal Law Reports, 1976-79. Named a Knight Comdr. of the Most Excellent Order of the British Empire (KBE), Her Majesty Queen Elizabeth II, 1999. Mem. Hong Kong Club, Queensland Club (Brisbane, Australia). Avocations: travel, cooking, reading. Died Nov. 19, 2009.

**POYNOR, KENNETH J.,** realtor; b. Chelsea, Okla., July 3, 1916; s. James Madison and Nova K. (Aldridge) Poynor; m. Dorothy O. Smith, May 24, 1937. B, Okla. State U., 1937. With US Dept. Agr., Stillwater, Okla., 1938—43, tchr. vocat. agr. Noble, Okla., 1943—44, Altus, Okla., 1944—45; owner, operator Ken Poynor Agy., real estate & ins. Norman, Okla., 1951; owner, operator farms & ranches. Mem Okla. Ho. Reps., 1958—62. Named, Norman Realtor of Year, 1969. Mem.: C. of C., Norman Bd. Realtors (pres. 1960—71), Okla. Realtors (state chmn. legis. com. 1965—73, agrl. rsch. and edn. com. 1965—73), Okla. State U. Alumni Assn. (life), Kiwanis Club, Shriners Club, Masons Club. Home: Norman, Okla. Died Sept. 1992.

**POZZI, GIOVANNI PAOLO,** humanities educator; b. Locarno, Ticino, Switzerland, June 20, 1923; s. Ettore and Maria (Patocchi) P. Doctorship, U. Fribourg, Switzerland, 1952, Univ. Tchg. Qualification, 1955; Dr. honoris causa, U. Bologna, Italy, 1991, U. Geneva, Switzerland, 1991. Asst. Università Cattolica S.C., Milan, Italy, 1954-55, prof. Tchg. Faculty, 1958, U. Fribourg, Switzerland, from 1955, full prof., from 1967, dean Faculty of Letters, 1968-69. Directorship Collana "Biblioteca di Scrittori italiani", Milan, Fondazione Bembo, 1992—, Collana "Medioevo e Umanesimo", Padova, Antenore, 1969—. Author: Saggio sullo stile dell'oratoria sacra nel Seicento, Rome, 1954, Sull'orlo del visibile parlare, Milan, Adelphi, 1993, Alternatim, Milan, Adelphi, 1996 (Premio Viareggio 1996), La parola dipinta, Milan, Adelphi, 1991, 96, Grammatica e retorica dei santi, Milan, Vita e Pensiero, 1997, Ad uso di...applicato alla libreria dei Cappuccini di Lugano, Roma, 1996, Chiara d'Assisi, Lettere ad Agnese: La Visione dello specchio, 1999, Inventario dell'ex voto dipinto nel Ticino, Bellinzona, 1999, Tacet, Milan, 2001; editor: Scrittrici mistiche italiane, 1988, Angela da Foligno, Il libro dell'esperienza, 1992, Maria Maddalena de'Pazzi, Le parole dell'estasi, 1984, 95; co-editor: F. Colonna, Hypnerotomachia Poliphili, 1964. Recipient Premio Angelini, 1994, Premio Viareggio, 1996, Premio Società Alighieri Amedeo Maiuri, 1997. Mem. Accademia della Crusca, Accademia dell'Arcadia. Franciscan Order of Capuchin's friars. Home: Lugano, Switzerland. Died July 20, 2002.

**PRAMMER, BARBARA,** Austrian government official; b. Ottnang, Austria, Jan. 11, 1954; 2 children. With Occupational Tng. & Rehab. Ctr., 1986-89, Upper Austrian Employment Svc., 1989-91; deputy spkr. Upper Austrian State Parliament, 1991-95; min. Fed. Ministry Women's Issues & Consumer Protection, Vienna, 1997—2000; v.p. The Nat. Coun. of Austria, 2004—06, pres., 2006—14. Social Democratic Party. Died Aug. 2, 2014.

**PREDIERI, ALBERTO,** lawyer, educator; b. Turin, Italy, Mar. 7, 1921; s. Alessandro and Anna Maria (Serpieri) P.; m. Francesca Rousseau Colzi dal Vivo, July 3, 1993. Law degree, U. Bologna, Italy, 1943. Tchr. constnl. law U. Siena, Italy, 1958-64; prof. pub. law U. Florence, Italy, 1966-69, full prof. pub. law, 1969-89, U. Rome, from 1989; liquidating commr. EFIM in Compulsory Adminstrv. Liquidation, Rome, from 1992. Dep. vice chmn. Cassa di Risparmio S.p.A., Florence, 1980-94. Author: Pianificazione e Costituzione, 1963, Urbanistica, Tutela del Paesaggio, Espropriazione, 1969, Abusivismo Edilizio, Condono e Nuove Sanzioni, 1985, Il Legislatore Recalcitrante, 1987, Il Nuovo Assetto Dei Mercati Finanziari e Creditizi Nel Quadro Della Concorrenza Comunitaria, 1992, Il Potere Della Banca Centrale: Isola o Modello?, 1996, La Certa Osmosi-Gli Incerti Paradigmi, Istituzioni e Mercato Nello Stato Prefederativo, 1996; editor rev. Il Doritto dell'Unione Europea, 1996, L'erompere delle autoritè amministrative indipendenti, 1997, Carl Schmitt, un nazista senza coraggio, 1998, Ernest Junger e Carl Schmitt, 1998. Lt. Italian Army, 1940-45. Recipient medal for mil. valour, 1943. Avocation: collecting antique books and napoleonic memorabilia. Home: Fiesole Florence, Italy. Died Aug. 16, 2001.

**PREHN, OLE,** dean; b. Thisted, Denmark, Jan. 31, 1952; s. Peter and Harriet Prehn; m. Jytte Smedegaard, June 26, 1948. Cand.phil., U. Aarhus, 1977. Head rsch. sec. Aalborg U., Denmark, sr. assoc. prof., 1984—90, head dept., 1985—87, elected dean, 1990—2005, exec. dean, 2005—08. Sec. gen. Internat. Assn. Media and Communication Rsch., Paris, from 2000; chmn. bd. Danish Acad. Digital Interactive Entertainment. Named to Danish Royal Knight's Cross of Order of Dannebrog, Queen of Denmark, 2004. Mem.: Internat. Assn. Media and Comm. Rsch., Deans Academic European Network, Danish Assn. Media Rsch. (pres. 1983—86). Achievements include research in mass media rsch. Home: Nibe, Denmark. Died Nov. 2008.

**PRENGLE, HERMAN WILLIAM, JR.,** chemical engineer, educator; b. Pa., Nov. 6, 1919; s. Herman William and Irene (Smith) P.; m. Ruth Hamilton, Dec. 6, 1941; children: Pixie Bernice Irene, Karl William, Scott Hamilton. BS, Carnegie-Mellon U., 1941, MS, 1947, DSc, 1949. Registered profl. engr., Tex. Rsch. engr. Linde Air Products Co., Tonwanda, N.Y., 1941; sr. engr. Shell Oil Co., Houston, 1949-53; assoc. prof. U. Houston, 1953-59, prof., 1959-97, prof. emeritus, from 1997, chmn. chem. engring. dept., 1958-61, assoc. dean Cullen Coll. Engring., 1981-85, dir. MChE program chem. engring. dept., 1985-97. Vis. scholar chemistry dept. Cambridge (Eng.) U., 1971-72, Corpus Christi Coll., 1988, Darwin Coll., 1990; cons. chem. and petroleum industries U.S. Govt., 1958—; panel mem. peer rev. of rsch. U.S. EPA, Washington, 1975-97. Contbr. articles to profl. jours. Chmn. Charter Commn., Friendswood, Tex., 1970-71; mem. Nat. Rep. Com., Washington, 1980—; mem. Rep. Presdl. Task Force, Washington, 1983—; mem. U.S. Com. Battle Normandy Mus., Caen, France, 1988—. Lt. col. U.S. Army, 1941-46, ETO. Decorated Bronze Star with oak leaf cluster; recipient Kittinger Tchg. award U. Houston Cullen Coll. Engring., 1971, award of Merit, Pollution Engring. Mag., Chgo., 1976, Tchg. Excellence award Haliburton Found., 1989, 92, 94, 96. Fellow Am. Inst. Chemists; mem. AIChE, Am. Chem. Soc., Royal Chem. Soc. (London), Army-Navy Club, Brotherhood of St. Andrew, Sigma Xi, Tau Beta Pi, Phi Kappa Phi. Episcopalian. Achievements include 3 patents (with others) for ozone-UV advanced oxidation prodess for water borne toxic compounds; invention (with other) of ammonium hydrogen sulfate (AHS) and duplex AHS solar energy storage process; invention (with others) of infrared radiometry spectroscopy method (IRSM) for remote sensing of temperatures, gradients and pollutant concentrations from stationary emission sources; invention (with others) of the hydrogen peroxide-VisUV process (HP/VisUV) for treatment of hazardous water borne substances and gaseous emissions; invention and patent (with others) for improved apparatus for fractional distillation of multi-component hydrocarbon mixtures. Deceased.

**PRESTAGE, JEWEL LIMAR,** political scientist, educational consultant; b. Hutton, La., Aug. 12, 1931; d. Brudis L. and Sallie Bell (Johnson) Limar; m. James J. Prestage, Aug. 12, 1953; children— Terri, James, Eric, Karen, Jay. BA, So. U., Baton Rouge, 1951; MA, U. Iowa, 1952, PhD, 1954; LHD (hon.), U. D.C., 1994, Loyola U., Chgo., 1999; LLD (hon.), Spelman Coll., 1999. Assoc. prof. polit. sci. Prairie View (Tex.) Coll., 1954-55, 56; assoc. prof. polit. sci. So. U., 1956-57, 58-62, prof., from 1962, chairperson dept., 1965-83, dean pub. policy and urban affairs, 1983-89, dist. prof. emeritus, dean emeritus pub. policy, from 1989; prof. polit. sci. Prairie View U., 1989-90; dean Benjamin Banneker Honors Coll., Prairie View (Tex.) Coll., 1990-98, prof. political sci., from 1998, disting. prof. Prairie View, 2000—02. Chmn. La. adv. com. to U.S. Commn. on Civil Rights, 1975-85; mem., chmn. nat. adv. coun. on women's ednl. programs U.S. Dept. Edn., 1980-82; dist. vis. prof. U. Iowa, 1987-88. Author: (with M. Githens) A Portrait of Marginality: Political Behavior of the American Woman, 1976; contbr. articles to profl. jours. Rockefeller fellow, 1951-52; NSF fellow, 1964; Ford Found. postdoctoral fellow, 1969-70; Hon. Thurgood Marshal Scholarship Fund, 2005. Mem. NAACP, Am. Polit. Sci. Assn. (v.p. 1974-75, Frank Goodnow award 1998), So. Polit. Sci. Assn. (pres. 1975-76, Manning Dauer award 1998), Nat. Conf. Black Polit. Scientists (pres. 1976-77), Nat. Assn. African Am. Honors Programs (pres. 1993-94), Am. Soc. for Pub. Adminstrn. (pres. La. chpt. 1988-89, nat. exec. coun. 1989-90), Policy Studies Orgn. (exec. coun. 2000), Links Inc., Alpha Kappa Alpha, Congl. Black Caucus Found. (chair faculty adv. coun., 2003-04) Home: Houston, Tex. *Commitments which guide my life are: (1) maximum development of personal potential through pursuit of excellence in all endeavors; (2) fair play, respect, compassion and quest of community in relations with fellow human beings; (3) utilization of personal talents in the interest of removing impediments to the good life "for all persons"; (4) pursuit of truth as the pervasive concern in academia; and (5) transmission of the above as priority goals to all with whom I have contact.* Deceased.

**PRICE, RAY (NOBLE RAY PRICE),** musician, vocalist; b. Perryville, Tex., Jan. 12, 1926; m. Janie M. Price; 1 child, Clifton Ray. Student, N. Tex. Agrl. Coll., Arlington, 1946-49. Owner Ray Price Enterprises, Ray Price Booking Agy., Ray Price Promotion Co., Ray Price Music Public Co., Janie Price Music Public Co., Ray Price Internat. Fan Club, Golden Cross Farm, Ray Price Racing Stables. Rec. artist Bullet Records, 1949—50, Columbia Records, 1950—74, 1977—2013, ABC/DOT Records, 1975—77, Myrrh Religious Records, 1974—2013, Monument Records, 1978—79, radio appearances WSM, Nashville, 1950—63, Grand Ole Opry, Nashville, 1952—63, Red Foley's Ozark Jubilee U.S.A., 1960—63, appearances (TV series) Marty Robbins Show, Johnny Carson Show, Merv Griffin Show, Dean Martin Comedy Hour, Pop Goes to Country, others, songs recorded Crazy Arms (Gold Guitar award, Gold record, Billboard award, Cash Box award), Under Your Spell Again, Heartaches By The Number (Gold Guitar award, Gold record, Billboard award, Music Reporter Hit award), Release Me (Gold Guitar award, Gold record), Burning Memories, A Thing Called Sadness, A Way To Survive, Touch My Heart (Billboard award), Danny Boy (Gold Guitar award, Gold record, ASCAP Chart Buster award), I'm Still Not Over You, Sweetheart of the Year (Gold Guitar award), She Wears My Ring, For the Good Times (Grammy award, Gold Guitar award, Gold record, Billboard awards), I Won't Mention It Again (Gold Guitar award, Gold record), (with Willie Nelson) Lost Highway, 2007 (Grammy award, Country Collaboration with Vocals, 2008), others, albums For The Good Times (Platinum album, Gold album), I Won't Mention It Again (Album of Year, 1972), Faith, San Antonio Rose, Night Life, Love Life, Burning Memories, The Other Woman, Another Bridge to Burn, Touch My Heart, Talk to Your Heart, You're the Best Thing That Ever Happened To Me, Welcome To My World, Like Old Times Again, Say I Do, Rainbows and Tears, Hank N Me, Ray Price and the Cherokee Boys Reunited, This Time Lord, Precious Memories, How Great Thou Art, Born to Love Me, Feet, There's Always Me, Happens to be the Best, Priceless, 1986, Lay Me Down. Recipient numerous awards, Outstanding Profl. Achievement award, U. Tex. at Arlington Alumni Assn., 1972, Spl. citation, State of Tex., 1971, Dallastar award, Press Club of Dallas, 1972; named Number One Country and Western Singer, 8 times; named to Walk Way of Stars, Country Music Hall of Fame, 1971, Country Music Hall of Fame, 1996. *Each time I move an audience to laugh when I laugh, cry when I cry and be moved by my innermost emotions which I project through my songs, I leave the stage totally contented with the feeling of having removed each person from the ordinary into a world of ecstasy.* Died Dec. 16, 2013.

**PRIESTMAN, BRIAN,** retired conductor; b. Birmingham, England, Feb. 10, 1927; Came to the U.S., 1962; s. Miles and Margaret Ellen (Messer) P.; m. Mary-Ford McClave, Mar. 2, 1972; 1 child, Catherine Kelly. BMus., Birmingham U., 1950, MA, 1952; DFA (hon.), Regis Coll., 1973; DHL (hon.), U. Colo., 1974. Music dir. Royal Shakespeare Co., 1960-64, Edmonton Symphony, 1964-68; prin. conductor Balt. Symphony, 1968-70; music dir. Denver Symphony, 1970-78, Fla. Philharmonic, 1978-80; dean Sch. Music U. Cape Town, 1980-86; prin. conductor Malmö (Sweden) Symphony, 1988-90; artist-in-residence U. Kans., 1992—2002. Music dir. Nat. Youth Orch. Canada, 1967—69. Avocations: cooking, travel. Died Apr. 18, 2014.

**PRINCE, GEORGE EDWARD,** retired pediatrician; b. Erwin, NC, Nov. 25, 1921; s. Hugh Williamson and Helen Herman (Hood) P.; m. Millie Elizabeth Mann, Nov. 26, 1944; children: Helen Elizabeth, Millie Mann, Susan Hood, Mary Lois. MD, Duke U., 1944. Diplomate Am. Bd. Pediatrics, Am. Bd. Med. Examiners. Intern Boston Children's Hosp. Harvard Svc., Boston, 1944-45; resident pediatrics Children's Hosp., Louisville, 1945-47; instr. pediatrics U. Louisville, 1947; founder Gastonia (N.C.) Children's Clinic, 1947, pediatrician, 1947-86; pub. health physician Gaston County Health Dept., Gastonia, N.C., 1986-98, med. dir., 1995-98, ret., 1998. Chmn. bd. dirs. Carolina State Bank; bd. dirs. So. Nat. Bank, Gastonia, 1979-95, Hospice, Gastonia, 1987-92; organizer, dir. AIDS Adv. Coun., Gaston County, N.C., 1988-94; coord. N.C.

chpt. Pediatric Rsch. in Office Setting, 1986-92. Contbr. articles to profl. jours. Mem. Gaston County Human Rels. Com., Gastonia, 1966; mem. Sch. Health Adv. Coun., Gaston County, 1980-97. Maj. USAF, 1955-57. Recipient Balthis Heart Assn. award, Gaston County, 1981, 1998, Good Amb. award, Health Dept., 1986, Family Adv. award, Commn. on the Family, Gaston County, 1995, commendation, City of Gastonia, 2001, Gaston County Bd. Commrs., 2001. Fellow Am. Acad. Pediatrics (pres. N.C. chpt. 1984-86); mem. AMA, N.C. Pediatric Soc. (hon., pres. 1970), N.C. Med. Soc., Gaston County Med. Soc. (pres. 1966), Rotary (pres. 1984), County Club (bd. dirs. 1975-76). Democrat. Methodist. Avocations: golf, skiing, sailing, bridge. Died Nov. 27, 2013.

**PRITCHARD, DAVID RALPH,** special education educator; b. Detroit, Oct. 19, 1937; s. David Davies and Mary Francis (Townsend) P.; m. Eleanor Suzanne Braman, Aug. 17, 1958; children: Debra Leigh, Daniel Ray, David Arthur, Denise Sue. BA, Mich. State U., 1959, MA, 1965, EdS, 1973; EdD, Wayne State U., 1988. Speech therapist Barry County Schs., Hastings, Mich., 1959-62, East Detroit (Mich.) Pub. Schs., 1962-68, tchr. cons., 1968-73; audiologist Detroit Speech and Hearing Ctr., 1968-69; curriculum resource cons. Macomb Intermediate Sch. Dist., Mt. Clemens, Mich., from 1973. Vis. lectr. Eastern Mich. U., Ypsilanti, 1988—; coord. Materials Ctr., Macomb Intermediate Schs., Mt. Clemens, Mich., 1973—; mem. State Tech. Adv. Com., Lansing, 1989. Contbr.: Adaptive Devices for the Handicapped, 1984, Reading and Writing Quar., 1992. Mem. Mich. Spl. Edn. Curriculum Resource Consortium (chairperson 1983-85), Mich. Coalition Orgns. to promote use of Tech. in Spl. Edn. (chairperson 1988-89), Mich. Coun. Exceptional Children (film festival co-chairperson 1988—, pres. chpt. 304, 1992-93). Avocations: music, camping, photography. Home: Warren, Mich. Died Oct. 14, 1995.

**PROSSER, C. LADD,** physiology educator, researcher; b. Avon, NY, May 12, 1907; s. Clifford James and Izora May (Ladd) P.; m. Hazel Blanchard, Aug. 25, 1934; children—Jane Ellen, Nancy Ladd, Loring Blanchard AB, U. Rochester, 1929; PhD, Johns Hopkins U., 1932; degree (hon.), Clark U., 1975. Asst. prof. physiology Clark U., Worcester, Mass., 1934-39; asst. prof physiology U. Ill., Urbana, 1939-47, assoc. prof. physiology, 1947-52, prof. physiology, 1952-74, prof. emeritus, from 1975. Asst. sect. chief Metallurgy Lab. U. Chgo., 1943-46; vis prof. U. Hawaii, U. Wash., U. Mass., Ariz. State U. Author: Adaptational Biology, 1986; author, editor: Comparative Animal Physiology, 1st edit., 1951, 4th edit. 1991; contbr. numerous articles to profl. jours. Guggenheim fellow, 1963-64; Fulbright fellow, 1971-72 Fellow Am. Acad. Arts and Scis.; mem. Nat. Acad. Scis., Soc. Gen. Physiologists (pres. 1958-59), AAAS (v.p. 1960), Am. Soc. Zoologists (pres. 1961), Am. Physiol. Soc. (pres. 1969-70), Bavarian Acad. Sci. Unitarian Universalist. Avocations: music; gardening. Home: Urbana, Ill. Deceased.

**PROST, EDMUND KAZIMIERZ,** food hygiene educator; b. Janów Lubelski, Poland, Apr. 9, 1921; s. Edmund and Kazimiera Julia (Rylska) P.; m. Maria Salomea Waligórska, Apr. 26, 1943; 1 child, Marek Edmund. DVM, U. M. Curie-Skłodowska, Lublin, 1949, PhD, 1950; Dr. honoris causa, Humboldt U., Berlin, 1990, U. Lublin, 1999. Asst. prof. U. M. Curie-Sklodowska, Lublin, 1948-57; assoc. prof Agrl. U., Lublin, 1957-64, prof. food hygiene, 1964—2008. Author: Meat Hygiene, 1975, 2nd edit., 1985, Polish Sanitary and Veterinary Regulations, 16th edit., 2001, Outstanding Polish Veterinarians in XX Century, 2005, Food Animals and Meat-evaluation and Hygiene, 2006; editor-in-chief Vet. Medicine, 1963—2008; contbr. articles to profl. jours. Mem. Polish Soc. Vet. Scis. (pres. 1964-98), World Vet. Assn. (v.p. 1993-98), World Assn. Vet. Food Hygienists (v.p. 1981-89), Lublin Sci. Soc. (pres. 1990—2008), Polish Soc. Vet. Scis. (hon.), Hungarian Vet Sci. Soc. (hon.), German Vet. Assn. (hon.), World Vet. Assn. (hon.). Avocation: belles-lettres. Home: Lublin, Poland. Died Jan. 20, 2008.

**PROVIS, DOROTHY L(OUISE),** retired artist, sculptor; b. Chgo., Apr. 26, 1926; d. George Kenneth Smith and Ann Hart (Day) Smith Guest; m. William H. Provis Sr., July 28, 1945; children: Timothy A., William H. Jr. Student, Sch. Art Inst., Chgo., 1953-56, U. Wis.-Milw., 1967-68, 69-70. Sculptor, Port Washington, Wis., 1963-97; ret., 1997. Pres. bd. dirs. West Bend Gallery of Fine Arts, Wis., 1984-86, bd. dirs., 1987-89; speaker, presenter in field. Co-curated exhbn. West Bend Gallery of Fine Arts, 1992. Author, lobbyist Wis. Consignment Bill, Madison, 1979; presenter Art of Bead Making Charles Allis Art Mus., Milw., 1991, Fimo, polymer clay jewelry techniques Moraine Valley C.C., Palos Hills, Ill., 1992; panelist Women's Caucus for Art Conf., Phila., 1983, Coalition Women's Art Orgn. at Coll. Art Assn. Conf., Seattle, 1993; mem. adv. bd. Percent for Art Pro., 1985-87; mem. adv. bd. Wis. Arts Bd., salary assistance program, 1991; pres. workshop Milw. Art Mus., 1990; conf. panelist Coll. Art Assn., N.Y.C., 1990. Wis. Arts Bd. Designer-Craftsmen grantee, NEA, 1981. Mem. Coalition of Women's Art Orgns. (del. to continuing com. Nat. Women's Conf. 1979, panelist conf. 1981, v.p. for membership/nominations, 1981-83, pres. 1983-85, nat. pres. 1985-87, 89-91, 91-93, 93-95, 95-97, v.p. communications 1987-89, editor CWAO newsletter 1985-97, rep. CWAO at Am. Coun. for Arts Advocacy Day, Washington, 1993, panelist Southeastern Coll. Art Conf. 1995), Wis. Painters and Sculptors (life mem., pres. 1982-84, editor newsletter 1982-85), Wis. Women in Arts (legis. liaison 1978-80), Nat. Women's Studies Assn. (conf. presenter 1988), Artists for Ednl. Action (corr. 1979-85), Wis. Designer Crafts Coun. (membership chair 1991-93, editor newsletter 1993-95), Women's Caucus for Art (panelist 1981, 83, 86, 87, conf. com. panelist 1987, presenter 1989), Chgo. Artists Coalition. Home: Port Washington, Wis. Died June 5, 2002.

**PRPIC-MAJIC, DANICA,** retired chemist; b. Komušina, Bosnia-Herzegovina, Mar. 14, 1929; d. Josip and Marija Prpic; m. Mirko Veljko Majic, Dec. 20, 1954. B Chem. Engring., U. Zagreb, Croatia, 1954, PhD, 1965; postgrad., Ministry of Health, Zagreb, 1960-64. Med. chemist Gen. Hosp., Split, Croatia, 1955-59; head clin. toxicol. lab. Inst. Med. Rsch. and Occupl. Health, Zagreb, 1959-96, rsch. asst., 1959-65, asst. prof., 1965-74, assoc. prof., 1974-83, prof., 1983-2000, head clin. toxicol. lab., 1959-96. Spl. cons. State Dept. Pub. Health, Berkeley, 1969-71. Contbr. over 100 articles to profl. jours; author 6 books, including: Pathology of Work, Assessment of Invalidity and Residual Working Capacity in Subjects with Previous Occupational Diseases, Assessment of Human Exposure to Lead and Cadmium through Biological Monitoring. Decorated Order of Merit with Golden Wreath (Yugoslavia); Order of Croatian Danica with image Rugjer Boškovic (Croatia). Mem. Croatian Toxicol. Soc. (mem. presidency 1991-2000), Soc. European Socs. Toxicology (del.), Croatian Soc. Chem. Engrs. and Technologists, Soc. Graduated Engrs. and Friends of Chem. Tech. Study Zagreb. Avocations: music, painting, art. Home: Zagreb, Croatia. Died 2005.

**PRUDDEN, JOHN FLETCHER,** surgeon; b. Fostoria, Ohio, Feb. 4, 1920; s. Meryl Ashley and Sallie Wells (Gibson) Prudden; m. Ruth Carla Williamson, Jan. 22, 1955; children: Peter, Pamela, Elaine, John Fletcher, Sarah Milford, James Nelson. BS cum laude, Harvard U., 1942; MD, 1945; SCD, Columbia Coll. Physicians and Surgeons, 1950. Intern Bellevue Hosp., NYC, 1945—46; resident Roosevelt Hosp., NYC, 1947—49, Peter Bent Brigham Hosp., Boston, 1950—51, Pondville Cancer Hosp., Walpole, Mass., 1951—52; instr. Columbia Coll. Physicians and Surgeons, 1954—62, asst. prof., 1962—67, assoc. prof., surgery, 1967—76; cons., surgery Harlem Hosp., NYC, 1964—76, NY. Rehab. Hosp., Haverstraw, 1967—81; attending surgeon Delafield Hosp., NYC, 1966—76, Nyack Hosp., NY, 1976—84, Drs. Hosp., NYC, from 1976, Roosevelt Hosp., NYC, 1977—81; assoc. attending surgeon Presbyn. Hosp., NYC, 1967—76; dir. Barinco Inc., Blooming Grove, NY, 1978—82; chmn., sci. dir., chief exec. officer Lescarden Inc., NYC, from 1981. Contbr. articles to profl. jours. Trustee Nyack Hosp., NY, 1974—80. Capt. US Army, 1952—54. Mem.: AAUP, AMA, AAAS, ACS, Whipple Soc., Pan Pacific Surg. Assn., NY County Med. Socs., NY State, Am. Chem. Soc., Am. Geriat. Assn., NY Acad. Scis., Soc. Alimentary Tract Surgery, Harvey Soc., Soc. Exptl. Biology and Medicine, NY Surg. Soc., Hay Harbor Club, U. Club (NYC), Fishers Island Country Club, Mid-Ocean Club (Bermuda). Achievements include patents in field. Home: Nyack, NY. Died Sept. 12, 1998.

**PRZYLUSKI, JAN,** chemical technology educator, researcher; b. Poznan, Poland, Oct. 20, 1930; s. Bronisław and Jadwiga (Arkuszewska) P.; m. Elżbieta Wacława Rolinska, Feb. 9, 1964; children: Jakub, Katarzyna, Jan. MSc, Warsaw U. Tech., Poland, 1954, D Habilitation, 1968; DSc, Tech. U. Mendeleev, Moscow, 1961. Engring. diplomate. 0dir. inst. Tech. U. Warsaw, 1974-81; asst. High Econ. Sch., Szczecin, Poland, 1950-51; chief technologist Food Industry Machine Plant, Warsaw, 1954-57; instr. chem. tech. Tech. U. Warsaw, 1952-57, assoc. prof., 1961-74, prof., head dept., 1981-98. Cons. design office PEWA, Warsaw, 1976-89; dir. sci. bd. Inst. Nuclear Chemistry, Warsaw, 1987-91. Author: Conducting Polymers—Electrochemistry, 1991; contbr. over 100 articles to sci. jours.; 60 patents in material engring. Cons. Polish Ministry Edn., Warsaw, 1984-91. Col. chem. br. Polish Army Res. Recipient diploma Salon Inst. New Tech. Inventions, 1974, Master of Techniques awrd Polish Tech. Assn., 1977 Mem. IEEE (sr.), N.Y. Acad. Scis., Asiac Solid State Ionics Assn. (hon.), EAST (coord. for Poland 1989). Avocation: skiing. Home: Warsaw, Poland. Died July 23, 1998.

**PUCCIO, ANDREA,** retired marine engineer; b. Genova, Italy, Mar. 9, 1927; arrived in US, 1947; s. Vittorio Puccio and Rosa Ferrari; m. Rosa Zerega Puccio; children: Vittorio, Paolo, Antonella, Barbara. Degree in Marine Engring., Nautical Inst., Genova, Italy, 1946. Lic. chief engr. Italian Ministry of Merchant Marine, 1950, cert. super chief engr. Italian Ministry of Merchant Marine, 1972. V.p., rep. Home Lines Inc. Cruise Co., NYC; mng. passenger vessels dept. Am. Bureau Shipping, Paramus, NJ, 1990—91. Owner's rep. Constrn. M/V Atlantic, France, 1980, Constrn. M/V Homeric, Germany, 1985. Mem.: Soc. Naval Arch. and Marine Engrs. Home: Genoa, Italy. Died 2008.

**PUCKETT, ALLEN EMERSON,** retired aeronautical engineer; b. Springfield, Ohio, July 25, 1919; s. Roswell C. and Catherine C. (Morrill) Puckett; m. Betty J. Howlett; children: Allen W., Nancy L., Susan E.; m. Marilyn I. McFarland; children: Margaret A., James R. BS, Harvard U., 1939, MS, 1941; PhD, Calif. Inst. Tech., 1949. Lectr. aeronautics, chief wind tunnel sect. Jet Propulsion Lab., Calif. Inst. Tech., 1945—49; with Hughes Aircraft Co., Culver City, Calif., 1949—87, exec. v.p., 1965—77, pres., 1977—78, chmn., CEO, 1978—87, chmn. emeritus, 1987—2014. Tech. cons. U.S. Army Ordnance, Aberdeen Proving Ground, Md., 1945—60; mem. sci. adv. com. Ballistic Rsch. Labs., 1958—65; chmn. rsch. adv. com. control, guidance and navigation NASA, 1959—64; vice-chmn. Def. Sci. Bd., 1962—66; mem. Army Sci. Adv. Panel, 1965—69, NASA tech. and rsch. adv. com., 1968—72, space program adv. coun., 1974—78; Wilbur and Orville Meml. lectr. Royal Aero. Soc., 1981. Author (with Hans W. Liepmann): Introduction to Aerodynamics of a Compressible Fluid, 1947; editor (with Simon Ramo): Guided Missile Engineering, 1959; contbr. tech. papers on high-speed aerodynamics. Fellow: AIAA (pres. 1972); mem.: AAAS, NAE, NAS, Aerospace Industries Assn. (chmn. 1979), L.A. World Affairs Coun. (pres.), Phi Beta Kappa, Sigma Xi. Died Mar. 31, 2014.

**PULIDO, MIGUEL LAZARO,** marketing professional; b. Havana, Cuba, Dec. 17, 1934; s. Jose Fabriciano and Maria Dolores (Perez) P.; m. Janie Ham, Nov. 28, 1980; 1 child, Michael James. AE, Sugar Techs., Havana U., 1956; MS, La. State U., 1961, PhD, 1965; completed Exec. Program, U. Va., 1986. Agrl. engr. Agrl. and Indsl. Bank Cuba, Havana, 1956-58, mgr. agrl. and eastern devel. div., 1958-59; agrl. engr. Productora Superfosfatos, Havana, 1959-60; asst. mgr. Tech. Svcs. div. Velsicol Chem. Co., Chgo., 1965-67; v.p. internat. mktg. Buckman Labs., Memphis, from 1985. Editor Jour. Fitopatologia, 1969-74; contbr. articles to profl. jours. Fellow Pan Am. U., 1960-62. Mem. AAAS, Am. Phytopathol. Soc., Weed Sci. Soc., Plant Growth Regulator Soc., Biol. Soc., Internat. Sugarcane Techs. Soc., Tech. Assn. Pulp and Paper Industry. Republican. Home: Eads, Tenn. Died 1994.

**PUNGOR, ERNÖ,** chemist, educator; b. Vasszécsény, Hungary, Oct. 30, 1923; s. Jozsef and Franciska (Faller) P.; m. Elisabeth Lang, Oct. 26, 1950; children: Ernó, Andras, Katalin; m. Tünde Horváth, Sept. 8, 1984. Diploma of chemistry, Pazmany Peter U., Budapest, 1948; Dr.h.c., Tech. U. Vienna, 1983; Consejo cultural mondial diploma, Heidelberg, 1987; doctorate (hon.), Tech. U. Bratislava, 1988, U. Bucharest, 1993, Tech. U. Budapest, 1993, Lomonosov U., Moscow, 1999, U. Miskolc, 1999, U. Veszprém, 1999, Babes-Bolyai U., 2000. Asst. prof. Inst. Inorganic and Analytic Chemistry, Eotvos Lorand U., Budapest, 1948-51, reader, 1951-53, assoc. prof., 1953-62; prof. Inst. Analytical Chemistry, U. of Chem. Industry, Veszprém, 1962-70, Inst. for Gen. and Analytical Chemistry, Tech. U. Budapest, 1970-90; dir. Bay Zoltán Inst. Applied Rsch., 1994—2001; prof. emeritus Budapest U. Tech. & Econ., from 1993. Minister without portfolio, pres. Hungarian Nat. Comm. Technol. Devel., 1990-94; mem. nat. environ. com. Com. for Nat. Tech. Devel. of Hungary; redwood lectr. English Soc. for Analytic Chemistry, 1979; hon. prof. Agrl. U. Lima, 1973, Shanghai Tchrs. U., 1987, Árpád Acad., 1989; mem. sci. adv. bd. Orgn. Prohibition Chem. Weapons, 1998—; mem. sci. adv. bd. Hungarian Govt., 1999-2002. Author: Oscillometry and Conductometry, 1965, Flame Photometry Theory, 1962, Ion Selective Electrodes, 1973, 5th edit., 1989, Lab Manual, 1974, Coulometric Analysis, 1979, Medizinische und Biologische Bedeutund der Thiocyante, 1982, Modern Trend in Analytical Chemistry, 1984, Bio-electroanalysis I, 1987, A Practical Guide to Instrumental Analysis, 1994, For the Development of Hungary, 1996, My Years, My Researches, 1998, The Theory of Ion Selective Electrodes, 1998, (with K. Toth) Indicator Electrode, 1973, (with E. Lindner, K. Toth) CRC Book series: Dynamic Characters of Ion Selective Electrodes, 1988, Profession and Creed/For the Development of Hungary, 1998; mem. editl. bd. Acta Chimica Hungarica, 1967—, Periodica Polytech., 1972, Mikrochimica Acta, 1964; gen. editor Magyar Kémiai Folyóirat Kémiai Közlemények, 1970-2002, Talanta, 1968, Analyst, 1970, Analitica Chimica Acta, 1966, Analytical Letters, 1967, Bull. des Soc. Chimiques Belges, 1974, Bunseki Kagaku, 1981; mem. adv. bd. Analytical Chemistry, 1985-88; contbr. over 500 articles to profl. jours., chpts. to books. Recipient Talanta Gold medal, 1986, gold medal, Tech. U. Vienna Inst. for Analytical and Microchemistry, 1988, medal, R7. Mem. Internat. Union Pure and Applied Chemistry (titular mem. electroanalytical commn. 1979-87, dep. chmn. electroanalytical commn. 1985-87, pres. nat. Adhering Orgn. 1985—), European Sci. Acad., Fedn. European Chem. Socs. (chmn. working group of European analysts 1981-87), Hungarian Chem. Soc. (head analytical group), Hungarian Acad. Sci. (head analytical divsn., gold medal 1988), Indian Acad. Scis. (hon.), Czechoslovakian Acad. Scis. (hon. mem. chemistry divsn.), Austrian Analytical and Microanalytical Soc. (hon.), Finnish Chem. Soc. Tech. (hon.), Finnish Tech. Soc. (hon.), Chem. Soc. Finland (hon.), Austrian Analytical and Microanalytical Soc. (hon.), Japanese Analytical Chem. Soc. (hon.), Royal Soc. Chemistry (hon.), Acad. Sci. India (hon.), Egyptian Pharm. Soc. (hon.). Died 2009.

**PUNNING, JAAN-MATI,** environmental scientist; b. Tartu, Estonia, Mar. 13, 1940; s. Karl and Marta (Madison) P.; m. Karin Raba, Sept. 10, 1963; children: Marika, Herod. Diploma in physics and chemistry, Tartu U., Estonia, 1963; degree in geology, Estonian Acad. Sci., Tallinn, 1968; D in Geography, Inst. Geography, Moscow, 1981. Engr. Geol. Survey, Tallinn, 1963-72; head lab. Inst. Geology, Tallinn, 1972-87; dep. dir. Inst. Electrophysics, Tallinn, 1987-92; prof. Tartu U., 1989-92, Tallinn Pedagogical U., 1993—2009; dir. Inst. Ecology, Tallinn, 1992—2006. Cons. Ministry of Environment, Tallinn. Editor: Human Impact on Environment, 1993; guest editor Radiocarbon, 1993; contbr. articles to profl. jours.; inventor in field. Decorated 4th class Order of the White Star; recipient K.E. Baer medal Estonian Acad. Scis., 1990, N. Vavilov medal All-Union Coun. Scis., Russia, 1988, Sci. award Republic of Estonia, 1995, Acad. Sci. Estonia medal, 1998, Tallinn Pedagogical U. medal, 2002, IV kl White Star medal, 2001. Mem.: Eurosci., Ea. European Assn. 14C Lab. (steering com. 1992—2002), Estonian Geog. Soc. (hon.; pres. 1985—2009). Avocations: literature, art, tourism, sports. Home: Tallinn, Estonia. Died Nov. 21, 2009.

**PUNT, LEONARD CORNELIS,** educational services company executive; b. Kisangani, Republic of the Congo, Nov. 16, 1940; arrived in US, 1954, naturalized, 1960; s. Harry Marius and Clara VandeGevel Punt; m. Sarah Elizabeth Walton, Dec. 18, 1966; children: John, Amy, Brian. BA, Wheaton Coll., Ill., 1964; MEd, Loyola U., Chgo., 1981. Owner, dir. Reading Tree Inc., Downers Grove, Ill., 1976—2007; v.p. Am. Bus. Comm., Downers Grove, from 1978; owner, pres. Learning Sys., Inc., Westmont, Ill., from

2007. Contbr. articles to profl. jours.:; author: Dyslexia: Definition and Solutions, 2005. Conservative. Presbyterian. Avocations: photography, travel, golf. Died Feb. 12, 2013.

**PURSCELL, HELEN DUNCAN,** sociologist, educator; b. Cottonwood County, Minn., Jan. 8, 1926; d. Arthur Albert Frenzen and Pearl Blanche Pope; m. Boyd Alvah Duncan (dec.); children: Bruce Howard(dec.), Stuart Lachlan(dec.), Scott Boyd; m. Keith William Purscell, June 17, 1994. BA, Mankato State U., 1963, postgrad., 1981—84; MA, U. Iowa, 1967; postgrad., U. Minn., 1969—73. Cert. sex educator Am. Assn. Sex Educators, Counselors and Therapists. Elem. sch. tchr., Redwood County, Minn., 1944—45, Cottonwood County, 1945—46; English tutor Parsons Coll., Fairfield, Iowa, 1964—65; asst. instr. Minn. State U., 1965—66, instr., 1966—68, asst. prof., 1968—90, assoc. prof., 1990—94; ret. Home: Mankato, Minn. Died Aug. 14, 2014.

**PUTMAN, CHARLES EDGAR,** medical educator, clinician, academic administrator, radiologist; b. Cleburne, Tex., July 22, 1941; s. Edna P.; m. Mary Clark, June 19, 1966; children: Camille Clark, Shannon Bandy, Charles Garrett. BA, U. Tex.-Austin, 1963; MD, U. Tex. Med. Br., Galveston, 1967. Diplomate: Am. Bd. Internal Medicine, Am. Bd. Radiology. Intern U. Iowa City, Iowa Ctiy, 1967-68; resident U. Tex. Med. Br., Galveston, 1968-71, U. Calif., San Francisco, 1971-73; asst. prof. radiology Yale U., New Haven, 1973-75, assoc. prof. radiology and internal medicine, 1976-77, clin. dir. diagnostic radiation, 1976-77; prof. radiology, chmn. dept. radiology Duke U. Med. Ctr., Durham, NC, 1977-85, James B. Duke prof. of medicine and radiology, 1983—99, sr. v.p. rsch. admin. and policy, 1982—99, vice chancellor for health affairs, vice provost, 1985-86, vice provost Sch. Med., Research, Devel., 1986-89. Author: Intensive Care Radiology Imaging of the Critically Ill, 1982, 3d edit. 1991Pulmonary Diagnosis Imaging and Other Techniques, 1982. Mem. Fleischner Soc., Assn. Univ. Radiologists (pres.-elect 1983), Soc. Chairmen Acad. Radiology Depts. (pres. 1983), Am. Coll. Radiology. Died May 11, 1999.

**PYM, BARON FRANCIS LESLIE,** retired British legislator; b. Abergavenny, Wales, Feb. 13, 1922; s. Leslie Ruthven and Iris Rosalind (Orde) Pym; m. Valerie Fortune Daglish, 1949; 4 children. Attending, Cambridge U., Eng. Chmn. English-Speaking Union of Commonwealth; mem. Liverpool U. Coun., England, 1949—53, Herefordshire County Coun., England, 1958—61; M.P. Cambridgeshire, 1961—83, Cambridgeshire SE, 1983—87; opposition dep. chief whip Cambridgeshire SE, 1967—70; govt. chief whip & parliamentary sec. to treasury, 1970—73; sec., state for northern Ireland, 1973—74; opposition spokesman, agr., 1974—76; opposition spokesman, fgn. commonwealth affairs House of Commons Affairs & Devolution, 1976—79; sec., state for def., 1979—81; lord pres. of coun. & leader House of Commons, 1981—82; chancellor Duchy Lancaster & Paymaster Gen., 1981; sec., state fgn. & commonwealth affairs, 1982—83; pres. Atlantic Treaty Assn., 1985—88. Author: The Politics of Consent, 1984. With 9th Queen's Royal Lancers, 1942—46, North Africa, Italy. Decorated Mil. Cross. Fellow: Magdalene Coll. (hon.). Home: Sandy, England. Died Mar. 7, 2008.

**QIAN, XUESEN (HSUCH-SEN CHIEN),** aerospace engineer; b. Shanghai, Dec. 1910; m. Jiang Ying, 1947; 2 children. Grad., Shanghai Jiao Tong U., 1934; M, MIT; PhD in Aerospace and Mathematics, Calif. Inst. Tech., 1939. Dir. rocket sect. US Nat. Def. Sci. Advisory Bd., 1945—49; prof. MIT, 1946—49, Calf. Inst. Tech., 1949—55; dir. China Inst of Mechanics, 1956; pres. Dynamics Soc., 1956—63; mem. Dept. for Math., Physics, and Chem., Acad. of Sciences, from 1957; pres. Dynamics Soc., 1957—82; vice-chmn. Sci. and Tech. Commn. for Nat. Defense, from 1978; vice-min. Commn. for Sci., Tech., and Industry for Nat. Defence, 1982—87, sr. adv., 1987—2009; chmn. China Assn. for Sci. and Tech., 1986—91, hon. chmn., 1991—2009. Mem. 9th Chinese Communist Party Ctrl. Com., 1969—73, 10th Chinese Communist Party Ctrl. Com., 1973—77, 11th Chinese Communist Party Ctrl. Com., 1977—82, 12th Chinese Communist Party Ctrl. Com., 1982—85; vice.-chmn. Nat. Com. 6th Chinese People's Polit. Consultative Con., 1986—88, Nat. Com. 7th Chinese People's Polit. Consultative Con., 1988—93, Nat. Com. 8th Chinese People's Polit. Consultative Con., 1993—98; sr. fellow Chinese Acad. of Sciences, from 1998, Chinese Acad. of Engring, 1998—2009; hon. pres. Astronautics Soc., 1980—2009; Hon. Pres. Soc. of Syestems Engring, 1980—2009. Author of various research papers. Recipient Meritorious Svc. Medal (for devel. of China's 1st atomic bomb, hydrogen bomb, and satellite), Chinese Communist Party Ctrl. Com., State Coun. and Ctrl. Mil. Command, 1999. Died Oct. 31, 2009.

**QUADRI, SANTO BARTOLOMEO,** retired archbishop; b. Ossanesga, Bergamo, Italy, Dec. 2, 1919; Ordained priest Roman Cath. Ch. 1943; consecrated bishop 1964. Elected titular see, Villanova, 1964-73; bishop Terni-Nerni, 1973-83; archbishop Modena-Nonantola, 1983—96. Former cons. Sacred Congregation for the Clergy. Died Oct. 17, 2008.

**QUANTRELLE, GLEN RICHARD,** marketing professional; b. Hamilton, Victoria, Australia, Jan. 30, 1930; s. Glen Stuart and Nell Irene Quantrelle; m. Dorothy Darch, Mar. 3, 1951; children: Elizabeth Anne, Wendy Joy, Robert Glen, Amanda Jane. Grad. h.s., Victoria, 1945. Pres., life gov. Burwood Boys Home (now Child and Family Care Network), Victoria, 1984—; dir. Found. for Homeless Youth, 1995; active numerous cmty. svc. orgns., 1973-74; past bd. chmn. Ch. of Christ. Named Citizen of Yr., 1973-74. Mem. Rotary Internat., Nunawading Rotary (pres. 1978-80, Paul Harris fellow 1980). Avocations: football, tennis, ping pong/table tennis, cricket, gardening. Home: Melbourne, Australia. Died May 4, 2001.

**QUARLES, PEGGY DELORES,** professor; b. Dalton, Ga., July 14, 1947; d. Henry Lemuel and Mae Bradford (Hester) Q. BA, Trevecca Nazarene Coll., 1969; MEd, U. Ga., 1981; EdS, West Ga. Coll., 1987; EdD, Univ. Sarasota, 2001. English tchr. Darlington County Schs., Lamar, SC, 1969—78, Murray County Schs., Chatsworth, Ga., 1978—2004; assoc. prof. grad. sch. coll. edn. Lincoln Meml. U., Harrogate, Tenn., from 2004. Mem. Shakespeare Inst., NEH, Washington, 1985, Writing Inst., Boulder, Colo., 1988, Italian Renaissance Inst., Del., Ohio and Florence, Italy, 1990, Women in Renaissance Inst., Richmond, Va., 1992; participant Armonk Inst. to Germany, 1998. ARC, from 1987; mem. Dalton Little Theater, from 1980; bd. dirs. Friends of Libr., 1989—92; mem. NW Ga. Humane Soc. Named Teacher of Yr., Murray County Bd. of Edn., 1989, Murray County Schs., 2001—02. Mem. NEA, Nat. Coun. Tchrs. English, Ga. Coun. Tchrs. English (H.S. English Tchr. of Yr. 1994-95), Carpet Capital Running Club (pres. 1980-82, v.p. 1993-94), Lesche Lit. Club (v.p. 2001—). Avocations: running, travel, cooking, reading, theater. Home: Dalton, Ga. Died Mar. 1, 2014.

**QUICK, LESLIE CHARLES, III,** brokerage house executive; b. Bklyn., Mar. 15, 1953; s. Leslie C. Jr. and Regina A. (Clarkson) Q.; m. Eileen Manning, July 7, 1979; children: L. Christopher, Ryan F., Kelsey M., Maura G. BBA in Fin., St. Bonaventure U., 1975; postgrad., Stanford U., 1987. Prin., pres. Quick & Reilly Group, NYC, from 1975. Trustee St. Bonaventure U., N.Y., 1985—; bd. dirs. Mt. Iraneus-Franciscan Mountain Retreat, St. Bonaventure, N.Y., 1981—, Ireland/U.S. Coun. for Commerce and Industry, Inc., 1991—, St. Vincents Hosp., N.Y.C., 1992—. Mem. Securities Industry Assn. (bd. dirs. 1993), Nat. Assn. Securities Dealers (com. dist. 10 1989-91), Nat. Acad. Design (bd. advisors 1992—), Downtown Athletic Club, Plainfield Country Club (Edison, N.J.). Roman Catholic. Avocations: golf, family activities. Deceased.

**QUILLIAN, WILLIAM FLETCHER, JR.,** retired banker, former college president; b. Nashville, Apr. 13, 1913; s. William Fletcher and Nonie (Acree) Q.; m. Margaret Hannah Weigle, June 15, 1940; children— William Fletcher III, Anne Acree, Katherine, Robert. AB, Emory U., 1935, Litt.D. (hon.), 1959; B.D., Yale, 1938, PhD, 1943; postgrad., U. Edinburgh, 1938-39, U. Basel, 1939; Day fellow from, Yale, 1938-39; Rosenwald fellow, 1940-41; LL.D., Ohio Wesleyan U., 1952, Hampden-Sydney Coll., 1978, Randolph-Macon Coll., 1967; D.H.L., Randolph-Macon Woman's Coll., 1978. Ordained to ministry Meth. Ch., 1942. Student asst. Stamford (Conn.) Presbyn Ch., 1936-38; del. Gen. Com. of World Student Christian Fedn., Bievres, France, 1938; discussion leader World Conf. Christian Youth, Amsterdam, Holland, 1939; pastor Clarendon (Vt.) Community Ch., summer 1940; asst. prof. philosophy Gettysburg Coll., 1941-43, prof., 1943-45; prof. philosophy Ohio Wesleyan U., 1945-52; pres. Randolph Macon Woman's Coll., 1952-78, pres. emeritus, 1978—2014; sr. v.p. Central Fidelity Bank, 1978-88; exec. dir. Greater Lynchburg (Va.) Community Trust, 1988-97. Tchr. Garrett Biblical Inst., summer 1951. Author: The Moral Theory of Evolutionary Naturalism, 1945, Evolution and Moral Theory in America, Evolutionary Thought in America, 1950; Contbr. articles to philos. and religious jours. Pres. bd. dirs. United Way Cen. Va., campaign chmn., 1987; bd. dirs. Alpha Tau Omega Found., Lynchburg Gen. Hosp.; hon. life trustee Va. Found. Ind. Colls., pres., 1958-61. Mem. Assn. Va. Colls. (past pres.), Southern U. Conf. (pres. 1967-68), Southern Assn. Colleges for Women (pres. 1956), Nat. Assn. United Methodist Colls. and Univs. (pres. 1973), American Philos. Assn., Soc. for Values in Higher Edn. (mem. central com. 1945-48, chmn. 1947-48), Nat. Assn. Bibl. Instrs., AAUP, Greater Lynchburg Chamber of Commerce (dir. pres. 1979-80), Phi Beta Kappa., Omicron Delta Kappa, Alpha Tau Omega (dir. found.) Died Mar. 4, 2014.

**QUINN, ALEXANDER JAMES,** bishop; b. Cleve., Apr. 8, 1932; Attended, St. Charles Coll., Catonsville, Md., St. Mary Sem., Cleve., Lateran Sem., Rome, Cleve. State U. Ordained priest Diocese of Cleve., 1958; ordained bishop, 1983; aux. bishop Diocese of Cleve., 1983—2008, vicar western region, aux. bishop emeritus, 2008—13. Roman Catholic. Home: Westlake, Ohio. Died Oct. 18, 2013.

**QUINN, FRANCIS XAVIER,** arbitrator, mediator, writer, law educator; b. Dunmore, Pa., June 9, 1932; s. Frank T. and Alice B. (Maher) Q.; m. Marlene Stoker Quinn. BA, Fordham U., NYC, 1956, MA, 1958; STM, Woodstock Coll., Md., 1964; MS in Indsl. Rels., Loyola U., Chgo., 1966; PhD in Indsl. Rels., Calif. Western U., LA, 1976. Assoc. dir. Inst. Indsl. Rels. St. Joseph's Coll., Phila., 1966-68; Manpower fellow Temple U., Phila., 1969-74, asst. to dean Sch. Bus. Adminstrn., 1972-78; v.p. Nat. Acad. Arbitrators, 1999—2000. Arbitrator Fed. Mediation and Conciliation Svc., Nat. Mediation Bd., Am. Arbitration Assn., Nat. Assn. Railroad Referees; pres. apptd. to presdl. Emergency Bd. 186, 1975, to Fgn. Svc. Grievance Bd., 1976, 78, 80. Author: The Ethical Aftermath of Automation, 1963, Ethics and Advertising, 1965, Population Ethics, 1968, The Evolving Role of Women in the World of Work, 1969, Developing Community Responsibility, 1970, Understanding the Railroad Labor Act, 2009; editor: The Ethical Aftermath Series; contbr. articles to profl. jours. Chmn. Tulsa City-County Mayor's Task Force to Combat Homelessness, 1991-92; mem. exec. bd. Tulsa Met. Ministries, 1990-92, Labor-Religion Coun. Okla., 1990-98; pres. pastoral coun. Ft. Worth Holy Family Roman Cath. Ch., 2000-03, formation adv. bd., 2002-05. Named Tchr. of Yr. Freedom Found., 1969; recipient Human Rels. award City of Phila., 1970; inducted into Hall of Fame, Internat. Police Assn., 2000. Fellow Coll. Labor Employment Lawyers; mem. Am. Arbitration Assn. (arbitrator), Nat. Assn. Railroad Refs. (pres. 2000-04) Democrat. Home: Fort Worth, Tex. Died Oct. 10, 2012.

**QUINN, ROBERT HENRY,** former state attorney general; b. Boston, Jan. 30, 1928; s. Michael Joseph and Katherine Elizabeth (Burke) Q.; m. Claudina C. Pyne, July 18, 1959; children: Andrea Bernardo, Michael, Elaina Aikens, Stephanie. AB, Boston Coll., 1952; LLB, Harvard U., 1955; DDL (hon.), Anna Maria Coll., 1972; LLD (hon.), N.E. Sch. of Law, 1973, U. Mass., 1992; LLD (hon.), Curry Coll., 1996. Bar: Mass. 1955, U.S. Dist. Ct. Mass. 1956, U.S. Supreme Ct. 1970. Clk. Mass. Superior Jud. Ct., Boston, 1955-56; mem. Mass. House of Reps., Boston, 1957—69, spkr., 1967-69; atty. gen. State of Mass., Boston, 1969-75; bd. trustees, chmn. U. Mass., Boston, 1981-86. Mem. Comm. Public Counsel Services, Boston, 1978-97. Democrat. Roman Catholic. Avocations: reading, boating. Home: Milton, Mass. Died Jan. 12, 2014.

**QUOIREZ, FRANÇOISE See SAGAN, FRANÇOISE**

**QUOYESER, CLEMENT LOUIS,** corporate executive; b. Norristown, Pa., Mar. 29, 1899; s. Louis Clement and Jane Theresa (Bradley) Q.; m. Rosie Marie Brown, June 6, 1932; children: Patricia Anne, Clement Bradley, Thomas Brown (dec.), Camille James. Grad. high sch., Norristown, Pa. Printer John Hartenstine Printers, Norristown, 1914-19; sales corr. Clarke & Courts, Inc., Galveston, Tex., 1919-22, regional sales mgr. La., 1922-78; chmn. Quoyeser, Inc., Lafayette, La., 1978-92. Home: Lafayette, La. Deceased.

**RAABE, JOACHIM CARL,** fluid mechanical engineer; b. Berlin, July 10, 1920; s. Oswald Carl and Maria Josefine (Harzer) R.; m. Berta Louise Gruber, July 31, 1949; children: Heidemarie, Thomas, Michael. B of Engring., U. Tech., Dresden, Germany, 1940; M of Engring., U. Tech., Munich, 1949, PhD, 1953. Engring. trainee Henschel & Son Locomotive, Kassel, Germany, 1938-39; rsch. asst. Lab. Hydraulic Machinery, Munich, 1949-55, chief engr., 1956-57; asst. prof. U. Tech., Munich, 1955-56, prof., 1962-88, prof. emeritus, 1988, dir. chair, lab., 1962-88; chief designer Sulzer Escher Wyss, Ravensburg, Germany, 1957-62. Vis. prof. Indian Inst. Tech., Madras, 1975, Sch. Engring. U. São Paulo, 1975, Laval U., Quebec, 1978, Huazong Inst. Tech., Wuhan, China, 1982, Dongfang Works, Deyang, China, 1997. Author: Hydro Power, 1985, (in German) Hydraulic Machinery and Equipment, 2nd edit., 1989, Strength of Runner Crown of a Francis Turbine, 2000, Strength of a Spiral Case, 2000; contbr. over 700 articles to profl. jours. Lt. German Navy, 1940-45; prisoner of war, France. Recipient Golden Sport medal German State, 1967. Mem. German Soc. Engrs. (chmn. bd. 1970, Bronze medal 1970, Gold medal 1987), Internat. Assn. Hydraulic Rsch. (mem. editl. bd.), Internat. Hydraulic Book Co. (hon.). Achievements include strength calculation of important parts of hydroturbines and Kaplanturbines with respect to efficiency and susceptibility to cavitation; Laser Doppler measurements of unsteady flow in pipes and turbine runner. Home: Pullach, Germany. Died Oct. 4, 2002.

**RACAMIER, HENRY,** metal products executive; b. Pont-de-Roide, Doubs, France, June 25, 1912; s. Paul and Elisabeth (Mettetal) R.; m. Odile Vuitton, Apr. 27, 1943; two children. Lic. en Droit, Faculté Droit, Paris, 1934; diploma, Ecole Hautes Etudes Commles., Paris, 1934. CPA, Paris. Dep. comml. mgr. Peugeot Steel Co., Paris, 1936-41; head of group Assn. Alloy Steel Producers, Paris, 1941-46; chmn., CEO Stinox, Paris, 1946-77; pres., CEO Louis Vuitton, Paris, 1977-90; gen. dir. Vuitton Investment Gestion, Paris, from 1977; pres. strategic bd., gen. dir. LVMH, Paris, 1987-89; pres., CEO Orcofi, Paris, 1990-93. Pres. Assn. Orcofi for Opera, Music and Arts, Paris, 1990—; mem. chmn.'s coun. Met. Mus. Art, N.Y.C., 1990—; mem. com., bd. dirs., pres. Assn. pour le Rayonnement de l'Opéra de Paris, 1995-99; bd. dirs. N.Y. Internat. Festival of the Arts, N.Y.C., 1990—, Festival d'Automne a Paris, UCAD. Named Chevalier of the Legion d'Honneur, Officer de l'Ordre Nat. du Mérite, comdr. l'Ordre Arts et Lettres. Mem. Cercle Interallié, Cercle du Bois de Boulogne, Yacht Club de France. Avocations: opera, music, yachting. Home: Paris, France. Died Mar. 29, 2003.

**RACE, GEORGE JUSTICE,** pathology educator; b. Everman, Tex., Mar. 2, 1926; s. Claude Ernest and Lila Eunice (Bunch) R.; m. Annette Isabelle Rinker, Dec. 21, 1946; children: George William Daryl, Jonathan Clark, Mark Christopher, Jennifer Anne (dec.), Elizabeth Margaret Rinker. MD, U. Tex., Southwestern Med. Sch., 1947; MS in Pub. Health, U. N.C., 1953; PhD in Ultrastructural Anatomy and Microbiology, Baylor U., 1969. Intern Duke Hosp., 1947-48, asst. resident pathology, 1951-53; intern Boston City Hosp., 1948-49; asst. pathologist Peter Bent Brigham Hosp., Boston, 1953-54; pathologist St. Anthony's Hosp., St. Petersburg, Fla., 1954-55; staff pathologist Children's Med. Center, Dallas, 1955-59; dir. labs. Baylor U. Med. Center, Dallas, 1959-86, chief dept. pathology, 1959-86, vice chmn. exec. com. med. bd., 1970-72; cons. pathologist VA Hosp., Dallas, 1955-71; adj. prof. anthropology and biology So. Meth. U., Dallas, 1969; instr. pathology Duke, 1951-53, Harvard Med. Sch., 1953-54; asst. prof. pathology U. Tex. Southwestern Med. Sch., 1955-58, clin. assoc. prof., 1958-64, clin. prof., 1964-72, prof., 1973-94, prof. emeritus, from 1994, dir. Cancer Center, 1973-76, assoc. dean for continuing edn., 1973-94, emeritus assoc. dean, from 1994. Pathologist-in-chief Baylor U. Med. Ctr., 1959-86, prof. biomed. studies Baylor Grad. sch., 1989-94; chmn. Baylor Rsch. Found., 1986-89; prof. microbiology Baylor Coll. Dentistry, 1962-68, prof. pathology, 1964-68, prof., chmn. dept. pathology 1969-73, dean A. Webb Roberts Continuing Edn., 1973-94; spl. advisor on human and animal diseases to gov. State of Tex., 1979-83. Editor: Laboratory Medicine (4 vols.), 1973, 10th edit., 1983; Contbr. articles to profl. jours., chpts. to textbooks. Pres., Tex. div. Am. Cancer Soc., 1970; chmn. Gov.'s Task Force on Higher Edn., 1981. Served with AUS, 1944-46; flight surgeon USAF, 1948-51, Korea; col. Civil Air Patrol, 1922. Decorated Air medal. Fellow AAAS, Coll. Am. Pathologists, Am. Soc. Clin. Pathologists; mem. AMA (chmn. multiple discipline research forum 1969), Am. Assn. Pathologists, Internat. Acad. Pathology, Am. Assn. Med. Colls., Explorers Club (dir., v.p. 1993-2000), Sigma Xi, Alpha Omega Alpha. Home: Dallas, Tex. Died Dec. 17, 2013.

**RADEMAKERS, FONS (ALPHONSE MARIE RADEMAKERS),** film director; b. Roosendaal, Brabant, The Netherlands, Sept. 5, 1920; s. Alfred Alouis and Amelia Catherina M. (Kuypers) R.; m. Lili Veenman, May 24, 1960; children: Alphonse Alouis, Alfred Adriaan Michael. Student, Acad. Dramatic Arts, Amsterdam, The Netherlands, 1941. Dir. (films) Village on the River, 1959, That Joyous Eve..., 1960, Max Havelaar, 1976, The Assault, 1986. Recipient Acad. award nomination, 1959, Silver Bear Berlin Festival, 1960, Golden Ibis Teheran Festival, 1976, Golden Globe award Hollywood Fgn. Press Assn., 1986, Oscar, 1986. Home: Amsterdam, Netherlands. Died Feb. 22, 2007.

**RADMACHER, CAMILLE J.,** librarian; b. Monmouth, Ill., Apr. 14, 1917; d. Harry M. and Esther (Greenleaf) Radmacher. Student, Monmouth Coll., 1935—37. With adult dept. Warren County Libr., Monmouth, 1937—48, head county libr., from 1948; exec. dir. Western Ill. Libr. Sys., 1965—82, Nat. Library Week State Ill., 1959. Mem. Monmouth Coll. Cmty. Concert Lecture Bd., 1967—72; mem. adv. com. Ill. State Libr., 1962—72. Mem.: DAR, Womens Nat. Book Assn., Ill. Libr. Assn. (Ill. Librarian Citation award 1967), Altrusa (treas. 1968—69, dir. 1978—80), Order Eastern Star. Methodist. Died Mar. 30, 1989.

**RADZIKOWSKI, WLADYSLAW,** econometrician, researcher; b. Lodz, Poland, Feb. 5, 1929; s. Bronislaw and Stanislawa (Bajer) R.; m. Danuta Eleonora Kielkiewicz Radzikowski, Sept. 27, 1947; children: Pawel, Maciej. M in Econ., Main Sch. Planning & Stat., Warsaw, Poland, 1955; PhD in Math. Programming, 1964; degree in Econometrics, Econ. Acad., Wroclaw, Poland, 1969. Head of dept. Inst. Organ. in Machine-Build. Industry, Warsaw, Poland, 1955-66; deputy dir. rsch. Inst. Industry Econ. and Organ., Warsaw, Poland, 1966-68; head dir. Inst. Organ. in Machine-Build. Industry, Warsaw, Poland, 1968-71; deputy dir. rsch. R&D Ctr. of Informatics, Warsaw, Poland, 1971-73; head of chair Warsaw U., Warsaw, Poland, from 1974; prof. in ordinary Nicolai-Copernicus U., Torun, Poland, from 1990. Vis. prof. Fordham U., 1976, 78, 79, Fachhochschule fuer Wirtschaft, 1982, U. Detroit, 1984; supv. tchr. U. Milano, 1991, U. Amsterdam, 1992; v.p. Sci. Soc. for Orgn. and Mgmt., Warsaw, Poland, 1977—; chmn. Sci. Bd., 1981-89. Author: Project Management, 1979, Informatics Systems in Organization and Management, 1981, Development of the School of Management, 1987, Operations Research in Management, 1985, 94, 97. Mem. Polish Acad. Scis. (mem. com. orgn. and mgmt.), Polish Soc. for Ops. and Sys. Rsch., Polish Econ. Soc. (vice chmn. Warsaw divsn. 1971-72, chmn. 1997—), German Soc. for Ops. Rsch., Gesellschaft der Hochschullehrer für Betriebs-Wirtschaft, Inst. for Ops. Rsch. and Mgmt. Scis., Internat. Input-Output Assn. Roman Catholic. Avocations: stamp collecting/philately, canoeing. Home: Warsaw, Poland. Died 2004.

**RAGLAND, NAN HOWARD,** minister; b. Memphis; d. Terry James Howard and Clara Mae Bright; m. Joe M. Ragland. BSN, Miss. Coll. Pres. Nan Ragland Ministries. Avocations: prayer, walking, working out. Home: Jackson, Miss. Deceased.

**RAHMAN, MUHAMMAD HABIBUR,** former prime minister of Bangladesh; b. Dec. 3, 1928; Lectr. history Dhaka U., 1952; dean faculty of law Rajshahi U., 1961, reader in history, 1962—64; justice Bangladeshi Supreme Ct., 1995; prime minister Govt. of Bangladesh, Dhaka, 1996. Died Jan. 11, 2014.

**RAHMAN, ZILLUR (MOHAMMED ZILLUR RAHMAN),** President of Bangladesh; b. Mar. 9, 1929; s. Muhammad Meher Ali; m. Ivy Rahman (dec. Aug. 21, 2004); 3 children. LLB, Dhaka U., Bangladesh, 1954, MA in History with honors, 1954. V.p. Student Union Zazlul Huq Hall, Dhaka U., 1953; vice chmn. election steering com. United Front Election, Mymenshing dist., 1954; pres. East Pakistan Awami Sechchhasebak League; founding pres. Kishorgonj Awami League, 1956; gen. sec. Dhaka Dist. Bar Assn.; MP Pakistan Nat. Assembly, 1970—71; gen. sec. Awami League, Bangladesh, 1972—75, 1992, 1997, presidium mem., 1981, acting pres., 2007; mem. Bangladesh Constituent Assembly, 1972; MP Bangladesh Jatiya Sangsad (Parliament), Bangladesh, from 1973, dep. leader, 1996—2001; incarcerated, 1975—79, 1986; min. local govt., rural devel. & cooperatives Govt. of Bangladesh, 1996—2001; pres. People's Republic of Bangladesh, 2009—13. Died Mar. 20, 2013.

**RAJA, RAJENDRAN,** physicist; b. Guruvayur, Kerala, India, July 14, 1948; arrived in US, 1974; s. P.K. Sreeveerarayan and Chandramathi Raja; m. Selitha Barbara Freundorfer, 1976; 1 child, Anjali. BA with honors, Cambridge U., Eng., 1970, MA with honors, 1974, PhD, 1974. Rsch. assoc. Fermilab, Batavia, Ill., 1975—78, assoc. scientist, 1978—83, scientist I, 1983—88, scientist II, from 1988. Monte Carlo convenor DO Expt., 1986—97, top quark physics convenor, 1990—94; head DO Software Support Group, 1986—93, DO Electron ID Group, 1989—94; head emittance exch./ring coolers group Muon Collider/Neutrino Factory Collaboration, 2001—03; spokesman Mipp Expt. Fermilab, Batavia, from 2001; fellow Trinity Coll. Cambridge U., 1973; bd. dirs. Indo Am. Ctr., Chgo., from 2008. Contbr. over 300 articles to profl. jours. Pres. Cambridge U. India Soc., 1969—70. Mem.: AAAS, Planetary Soc., Am. Phys. Soc. Achievements include discovery of top quark. Home: Naperville, Ill. Died Feb. 15, 2014.

**RAKOTOMAHANINA, ETIENNE MARIE,** lawyer, editor; b. Antananarivo, Madagascar, Jan. 28, 1952; s. Charles and Henriette Ravoahangiarisoa; m. Delia Ramalalaharisoa, Jan. 20, 1973; children: Rainandriamampandry Oswald Graham, Andrianiaina Franklin James, Ravanomboahangy Rachel Jane Collins, Lalaharisoa Mary Huguette, David Alden Einsten, Ruth Valentina, Andriana Volamenaharisoa, Andrianamarotia Sandra, Brunel MacGyver Heriniaina. BA in Law and Comm., U. Madagascar, 1974; cert. High Jurisconsult in Litigious Affairs and Pub. Rels. Tng., SINTP Ankorondrano, Antananarivo, Madagascar, 1983; postdoctoral, Faith and Devel. Inst., 1989. Founder of the bar Comorian State, 1975-76; counsel of govt., 1975-78; journalist Apec-Inter, from 1975; jurisconsult High Ct., Stuttgart, Germany, 1987; high bus. cons. svcs. Cabinet Mitantana, Madagascar, from 1996. Contbr. articles to profl. jours. Mayor's counsel Bemasoandro, 1983-89; mem. C.L.S., Anosimasina, 1992-96. Maj. gen. Anti-Gang, 1975-76. Recipient Chevalier Nat. Order Madagascar winner. Mem. Internat. Christian Media Coun. (corr.), Internat. Comm. Tng. Inst., Amade Monaco. Avocations: philatelist, geography, photography, graphology. Home: Antananarivo, Madagascar. Died June 1, 2005.

**RAMADAN, TAHA YASIN,** former Iraqi government official; b. Mosul, 1938; Grad., mil. coll. Mem. regional coun. Arab Ba'ath Socialist Party; pres. Office of Arab Affairs, 1969; mem. Revolutionary Command Coun., 1970; pres. Spl. Ct., 1970; min. of industry Govt. of Iraq, 1970-72, min. of economy, 1971; pres. High Coun. of Resistance, 1972; mem. regional command Socialist Arab Ba'ath Party, 1974; min. of labor and housing Govt. of Iraq, 1976-77; mem. nat. command Arab Ba'ath Socialist Party, 1977; dep. prime min. Govt. of Iraq, 1979—91; v.p., mem. Revolutionary Command Coun.; comdr. People's Army; v.p. Govt. of Iraq, Baghdad, 1991—2003. With Iraqi Army. Mem. Arab Ba'ath Socialist Party. *Sentenced to death by an Iraqi Tribunal for crimes against humanity on Feb. 12, 2007.* Died Mar. 20, 2007.

**RAMANNA, RAJA,** physicist; b. Bangalore, Karnataka, India, Jan. 28, 1925; s. Bindig Ivavile and Rukhivi R.; m. Malathi Ramanna; children: Nina, Shyah, Nirupa BS with honors, Madras Christian Coll., India, 1945; PhD, U. London, 1948; DSc (hon.), several univs.; lic., Royal Sch. Music, London. Prof. Tala Inst. Fundamental Research, Bombay, 1948-72; dir. Bhabha Atomic Research Ctr., Bombay, 1972-83; sec., advisor Govt. India, New Delhi, 1983-87, chmn., 1983-87; council chmn. Indian Inst. Sci., Bangalore, from 1987. Author many books in field; contbr. articles to profl. jours. Recipient Bhalnajar award, Padma Vibushau award Govt. India. Fellow Indian Acad. Scis.; Internat. Atomic Energy Agy. (chmn. sci. adv. com. 1983-87). Clubs: Bangalore. Hindu. Avocation: european music. Home: Bangalore, India. Died Sept. 24, 2004.

**RAMIS, HAROLD ALLEN,** film director, screenwriter, actor; b. Chgo., Nov. 21, 1944; s. Nathan and Ruth (Cokee) R.; m. Anne Jean Plotkin, July 2, 1987 (div.) 1984; 1 child, Violet; m. Erica Mann May 7, 1989; children: Julian, Daniel. BA, Washington U., St. Louis, 1966, ArtsD (hon.), 1993. Assoc. editor Playboy mag., 1968-70; actor, writer Second City, Chgo., 1970-73, Nat. Lampoon Radio Hour, Lampoon Show, 1974-75; actor, head writer SCTV, 1977-78; producer, head writer Rodney Dangerfield Show, ABC-TV, 1982. Co-screenwriter (with Douglas Kenny & Chris Miller) National Lampoon's Animal House, 1978, (with Janice Allen, Len Blum and Dan Goldberg) Meatballs, 1979, (with Douglas Kenny, Brian Doyle-Murray) Caddyshack, 1980; (with Len Blum and Dan Goldberg) Stripes, 1981, (with Dan Aykroyd) Ghostbusters, 1984, Ghostbusters II, 1989; (with Brian Doyle-Murray) Club Paradise, 1986; co-screenwriter (with Peter Torokvei) Armed and Dangerous, 1986; writer (with Dan Akroyd) Rover Dangerfield, 1991; dir. Stuart Saves His Family, 1995, The Ice Harvest, 2005; dir., prodr. Multiplicity, 1996, Bedazzled, 2000; dir., writer: Caddyshack, 1980, National Lampoon's Vacation, 1983, Club Paradise, 1986, Analyze This, 1999, Analyze That, 2002; writer, dir. prodr. Groundhog Day, 1993, Year One, 2009; exec. prodr. The First $20 Million is Always the Hardest, 2002; exec. prodr., co-screenwriter: (with Rodney Dangerfield) Back to School, 1986; actor: (films) Stripes, 1981, Baby Boom, 1987, Stealing Home, 1988, As Good As It Gets, 1997, High Fidelity, 2000, Orange County, 2002, I'm With Lucy, 2002, The Last Kiss, 2006, Knocked Up, 2007, Walk Hard: The Dewey Cox Story, 2007 Mem. AFTRA, SAG, Writers Guild America, Directors Guild America Died Feb. 24, 2014.

**RAMOVS, PRIMOZ,** composer; b. Ljubljana, Slovenia, Mar. 20, 1921; s. Franc and Alba (Zalar) R.; m. Stefanija Schubert, Jan. 17, 1955; children: Klemen, Polona, Ales. Diploma, Acad. Music, 1941; MusD (hon.), Marquis Guiseppe Scicluna Internat. U. Found., Malta, 1988. Libr. Slovene Acad. Scis. and Arts, Ljubijana, 1945-52, libr.-in-chief, 1952-87; prof. Conservatory in Ljubljana, 1948-52, 55-64. Composer 6 symphonies, musiques funèbres, Profils, Symphonic Portrait, Polyptych, Organofonia, 33 concertos for various instruments, symphonie chamber and instrumental music (over 450 opuses). With Naval Inf., 1947. Decorated Order of Work with Golden Wreath, Order of Sainsts Cyrille and Method, Eques Comendator Ordinis Sancti Gregorii Magni; recipient awards Philharm. Soc., 1944, Festival, 1958, Fund of Preseren, 1962, Yugoslav Radio, 1967, 69, 70, 76, diploma Cop, 1971, Internat. Cultural Diploma Honor, 1988, Slovene Philharm., 1978, Chevalier Comdr., 1989, World Decoration of Excellence, 1989. Mem. Soc. Slovene Composers Ljubljana (v.p. 1967-71), Soc. Slovene Librs. Ljubljana, Slovene Acad. Scis. and Arts (Preseren's prize 1983, medal of honor 1986), Slovene Alpine Soc., Slovene Lit. Soc., Croatian Acad. Scis. and Arts, European Acad. Scis. and Arts, World U. (doctoral mem.), Slovene Philharm. (hon.). Roman Catholic. Home: Ljubljana, Slovenia. Died Jan. 10, 1999.

**RAMSAY, DONALD ALLAN,** physical chemist; b. London, July 11, 1922; s. Norman and Thirza Elizabeth (Beckley) Ramsay; m. Nancy Brayshaw, June 8, 1946 (dec. July 25, 1998); children: Shirley Margaret, Wendy Kathleen, Catharine Jean, Linda Mary; m. Marjorie Craven Findlay, Apr. 13, 2000. BA, Cambridge U., Eng., 1943, MA, PhD, Cambridge U., Eng., 1947, ScD, 1976; D honoris causa, U. Reims, France, 1969; Filosofie hedersdoktor, U. Stockholm, Sweden, 1982. With divsn. chemistry Nat. Rsch. Coun. Can., Ottawa, 1947-49, with divsn. physics, 1949-75; with Herzberg Inst. Astrophysics, 1975-87, sr. research officer, 1961-68, prin. research officer, 1968-87, guest worker, 1987—2001, Steacie Inst. Molecular Scis., rschr. emeritus, from 2002. Vis. prof. U. Minn., 1964, U. Orsay, 1966, U. Stockholm, 1967, 1971, 1974, U. Calif., Irvine, 1970, U. Sao Paulo, 1972, 1978, U. Bologna (Italy), 1973, U. We. Australia, 1976, Australian Nat. U., 1976, East China Normal U., Shanghai, 1987, Tex. Christian U., 1988, U. Wuppertal, Germany, 1988, U. Canterbury, Christchurch, New Zealand, 1991, 1996, U. Ulm, Germany, 1992, Germany, 1996, Germany, 1997. Editor: (with J. Hinze) Selected Works of Robert S. Mulliken, 1975; contbr. articles to profl. jours. Recipient commemorative medal for 125th anniversary Confederation Can., 1992, Alexander von Humboldt Rsch. award, 1993-95; decorated Queen Elizabeth Silver Jubilee medal. Fellow: Chem. Inst. Can. (Chem. Inst. Can. medal 1992), Am. Phys. Soc., Royal Soc. London, Royal Soc. Can. (life; treas. 1976—79, 1988—91, Centennial medal 1982); mem.: Order of Can. Mem. United Ch. of Canada (organist 1954-97). Club: Leander (Henley-on-Thames, Eng.). Achievements include research in molecular spectra and molecular structure. Home: Ottawa, Canada. Died Oct. 25, 2007.

**RAMSAY, JACK (JOHN T. RAMSAY),** retired professional basketball coach; b. Phila., Feb. 21, 1925; m. Jean Ramsay (dec. 2010); children: Chris, John, Sharon, Carolyn, Susan BA, St. Joseph's Coll., 1949; MS, U. Pa., 1952, EdD, 1963. Head coach St. Joseph's Coll., Phila., 1955-66, Phila. 76ers, 1968-72, Buffalo Braves, 1972-76, Portland Trail Blazers, Oreg., 1976-86, Ind. Pacers, Indpls., 1986-88; commentator, basketball analyst Miami Heat, 1992—2002. Co-author (with John Strawn): The Coach's Art, 1978. Named to The Naismith Meml. Basketball Hall of Fame, 1992. Roman Catholic. Achievements include coaching the Portland Trail Blazers to an NBA Championship, 1977. Died Apr. 28, 2014.

**RANALD, RALPH ARTHUR,** former government official, educator; b. NYC, Nov. 25, 1930; s. Josef A. and Pearl R.; m. Margaret Florence Loftus, Feb. 26, 1955; 1 dau., Caroline. AB, UCLA, 1952, MA, 1954; AM, Princeton U., 1958; postgrad., Harvard U., 1961—62, postgrad., 1976—77, postgrad., 1999—2000; grad., Exec. Program Nat. and Internat. Security, 1978; PhD, Princeton U., 1962; JD, Fordham U., 1997. Bar: N.Y., U.S. Supreme Ct. 2000. Tchg. asst. UCLA, 1952—54; fellow, rsch. asst. Princeton U., NJ, 1956—59; asst. prof. Fordham U. Grad. Sch., NYC, 1959—65; asst. dean acad. affairs, prof. Coll. Arts and Scis. NYU, 1965—69; prof. CUNY, from 1969; spl. policy asst. HEW, Washington, 1968—69, Office of Mgmt. and Budget, 1976—77; sr. cons. U.S. Dept. Def., 1969—70, 1977—78; mem. staffs Dept. Def. and Army Gen. Staff U.S. Govt. Long Com., 1989, U.S. Dept. Def., 1995—96. Vis. prof. and cons. univs. including U. So. Calif., summers 1968-74, Calif. State U., UCLA, summers 1985, 98; vis. scholar Harvard Law Sch., 1999—2003. Author: Management Development in Government, 1979, George Orwell, 1965; contbr. reports, articles to publs. in law, govt. and edn. Treas. N.Y. State Com. for Pub. Higher Edn., 1975-78, mem. com., 1970—. 1st lt. U.S. Army, 1953-56, to col., 1977-78, res., 1978—. Recipient U.S. Legion of Merit, 1983; sr. fellow Am. Soc. Pub. Adminstrn. (selection com. for fellows, 1970-74); mem. Res. Officers Assn. U.S. (life), Harvard U. Law Sch. Assn., Assn. of Princeton U. Grad. Alumni, U.S. Army War Coll. Alumni Assn., John F. Kennedy Sch. of Govt. Alumni Assn., Princeton Club of N.Y., Army and Navy Club, Phi Beta Kappa. Deceased.

**RAND, MICHAEL JOHN,** pharmacologist; b. Frekenham, England, Aug. 19, 1927; arrived in Australia, 1941; s. Jackson Allan and Dora E. (White) R.; m. Ilse Marie Kupcs. BS, U. Melbourne, 1949, MS, 1953; PhD, U. Sydney, 1957. Demonstrator dept. physiology U. Mebourne (Australia), 1950-52; demonstrator dept. pharmacology U. Oxford (England), 1957-58; lectr. dept. pharmacology U. London, 1960-61; prof. dept. pharmacology U. Melbourne, 1965-92, prof. emeritus, from 1993. Adj. prof. Royal Melbourne Inst. Tech., 1993—. Author: Textbook of Pharmacology, 1980, others; contbr. articles to profl. jours. Commr., mem. Nat. Food Authority, Canberra, Australia, 1991-96; chmn., mem. Joint FAO/WHO Expert Com. Food Authority, Geneva & Rome, Italy, 1969-92. Rsch. fellow U. Sydney, 1953-56, U. Oxford, 1958-59, U. London, 1960-61, sr. rsch. fellow U. Sydney, 1959-60. Mem. Australasian Soc. Clin. and Exptl. Pharmacology (pres. 1974, 87), Australian Physiol. and Pharmacology Soc. (pres. 1989-91), Brit. Pharmacology Soc. (hon.), Chinese Pharmacology Soc. (hon.), Japanese Pharmacology Soc. (hon.), Pakistan Pharmacology Soc. (hon.). Deceased.

**RANIS, GUSTAV,** economist, educator; b. Darmstadt, Germany, Oct. 24, 1929; s. Max and Bettina (Goldschmidt) R.; m. Ray Lee Finkelstein, June 15, 1958; children: Michael Bruce, Alan Jonathan, Bettina Suzanne. BA summa cum laude, Brandeis U., 1952, hon. degree, 1982; MA, Yale U., 1953, PhD, 1956. Dir. Pakistan Inst. of Development Economics, 1958—61; asst. adminstr. for program & policy US Agy. for Internat. Devel. (USAID), 1965-67; dir. Econ. Growth Ctr. Yale U., New Haven, 1967-75, prof. economics, 1964—81, Frank Altschul prof. internat. economics, 1981—2005, Frank Altschul prof. emeritus internat. economics, 2005—13, dir. Ctr. Internat. & Area Studies, 1996—2004. Ford Found. vis. prof. U. De Los Andes, Bogota, Colombia, 1976-77; Ford Found. vis. prof. Colegio de Mex., 1971-72; fellow Inst. for Advanced Study, Berlin, 1993-94; cons. World Bank, AID, Ford Found., ILO, FAO, Inter-Am. Devel. Bank. Author: (with John Fei) Development of the Labor Surplus Economy: Theory and Policy, 1964;(with Fei and Shirley Kuo) Growth with Equity: The Taiwan Case, 1979; (with Keijiro Otsuka and Gary Saxonhouse) Comparative Technology Choice in Development, 1988; (with F. Stewart and E. Angeles-Reyes) Linkages in Developing Economies: A Philippine Study, 1990; (with S.A. Mahmood) Political Economy of Development Policy Change, 1992; (with John C. H. Fei) Growth and Development from an Evolutionary Perspective, 1997, Globalization and the Nation State, 2006, Globalization and Self-Determination: In the Nation-State Under Siege?, 2006; editor: Taiwan: From Developing to Mature Economy, 1992, En Route to Modern Economic Growth: Latin America in the 1990s, 1994, Japan and the U.S. in the Developing World, 1997,; co-editor: The State of Development Economics, 1988, Science and Technology: Lessons for Development Policy, 1990; mem. editl. bd. Jour. Internat. Devel., 1995-2013, Oxford Devel. Studies, 1996-2013, Internat. Econ. Jour., 2005-13. Trustee Brandeis U., 1967-93, chmn. acad. affairs com., 1986-93. Social Sci. Rsch. Coun. fellow, Japan, 1955-56, Carnegie scholar, 2004-06. Mem. American Econ. Assn., Coun. Fgn. Rels., Overseas Develop. Coun. (mem. adv. com.); fellow. Human Devel. & Capability Assn. Home: Woodbridge, Conn. Died Oct. 15, 2013.

**RANKIN, ROBERT ALEXANDER,** mathematics educator; b. Garlieston, Wigtownshire, Scotland, Oct. 27, 1915; s. Oliver Shaw and Olivia Theresa (Shaw) Rankin; m. Mary Ferrier Llewellyn, July 25, 1942; children: Susan Mary Llewellyn, Charles Richard Shaw, Fenella Kathleen Clare, Olivia Roberta Mary. BA, U. Cambridge, Eng., 1937, PhD, 1940, MA, 1941, ScD, 1959. Fellow Clare Coll. U. Cambridge, 1939-51, asst. lectr., then lectr., 1945-51; prof. math. Birmingham U., Eng., 1951-54, Glasgow U., Scotland, 1954-82, prof. emeritus math., from 1982. Clk. of senate Glasgow U., 1971-78, dean of faculties, 1985-88; chmn. Scottish Math. Council, 1967-73. Author: Mathematical Analysis, 1963, The Modular Group, 1969, Modular Forms and Functions, 1977; contbr. articles to profl. jours. Chmn. Clyde Estuary Amenity Council, 1969-81. Recipient Keith prize Royal Soc. Edinburgh, 1964, Sr. Whitehead prize London Math. Soc., 1987; Royal Scottish Acad. Music and Drama fellow, 1982. Fellow Royal Soc. Edinburgh (mem. council 1957-63); mem. London Math. Soc. (v.p. 1966-68), Edinburgh Math. Soc. (pres. 1957-58, 78-79), Math. Assn., Am. Math. Soc., Am. Math. Assn., Scottish Gaelic Texts Soc. (v.p.), Gaelic Soc. Glasgow (hon. pres.). Avocations: music, hill walking, gaelic studies. Died Jan. 27, 2001.

**RASKOB, ABRAHAM I.,** physician, anesthesiologist, educator; b. Bklyn., Jan. 26, 1913; s. Benjamin and Fannie (Goodman) R.; m. Edith Lakin, June 8, 1940; children: Gerald Victor, Barbara Ann Raskob Godlewicz, Michael Gordon. BS, CCNY, 1935; postgrad., St. Mungo's Med. Sch., 1936-39; MD, Middlesex U. Med. Sch., 1943. Chief anesthesia dept. Caledonian Hosp., Bklyn., 1950-53; attending anesthesiologist Kings County Med. Ctr., Bklyn., 1952-65 and from 1979, U. Hosp., Bklyn., from 1982; from clin. asst. prof. to clin. prof. Downstate Med. Sch., Bklyn., from 1979; asst. med. dir. U. Hosp., Bklyn., from 1988, dir. risk mgmt., from 1989. Cons. Bklyn. State Hosp., 1953-62, malpractice panel Kings County Court, Bklyn., 1960-81; chmn. bylaws com. U. Hosp., 1984—, Kings County Hosp., 1982-89; chmn. risk mgmt. com. U. Hosp., 1989—. Trustee Bnai Israel Midwood Synagogue, 1955—. Fellow N.Y. Acad. Medicine, Am. Coll. Anesthesiologists; mem. Am. Soc. Anesthesiologists (del. 1983-85). Jewish. Home: Morganville, NJ. Died July 7, 1991.

**RASMUSSEN, KJELD LEISGAARD,** gynecologist, obstetrician, consultant; b. Skovsborg, Denmark, Apr. 2, 1957; s. Svend Rasmussen and Ella Jensen; m. Kirsten Overgaard Jensen. MD, U. Aarhus, Denmark, 1984. Resident various hosps., Denmark, 1984—91, sr. resident, 1991—96; cons. hosp., Herning, Denmark, from 1996. Lectr. U. Aarhus, Denmark, 1997, censor ob-gyn., Aarhus, Odense, Copenhagen, 2002; censor obstet. Sch. Midwifery, Aalborg, Copenhagen, Denmark, 1998. Contbr. articles to profl. jours. Mem.: Danish Soc. Ob-Gyn. Avocations: sports, history, archaeology, public debate. Home: Kjellerup, Denmark. Died Mar. 26, 2007.

**RATNER, GERALD,** lawyer; b. Chgo., Dec. 17, 1913; s. Peter I. and Sarah (Soreson) R.; m. Eunice Payton, June 18, 1948. PhB, U. Chgo., 1935, JD cum laude, 1937. Bar: Ill. 1937. Since practiced in, Chgo.; sr. ptnr. Gould & Ratner and predecessor firm, 1949—2014. Donor, Gerald Ratner Athletics Ctr., Disting. Svc. Professorship Law Sch., Ratner Law Sch., JE Ratner Meml. Scholarships Bus. Sch., Eunice Payton Ratner Gallery Smart Art Mus. With U. Chgo., Ratner Law Scholars Fund Law Sch., Eunice Payton Ratner Gallery Smart Art Mus. Capt. US Army, 1942—46. Gerald Ratner Athletics Ctr. named in his honor, U. Chgo.; recipient Disting. Svc. medal, 2005, Disting. Service Professorship of Law, 2007, U. Chgo., Alumni Svc. medal, 2009. Mem. ABA, Ill. Bar Assn., Chgo. Bar Assn., Order of Coif, Phi Beta Kappa. Home: Chicago, Ill. Died June 20, 2014.

**RATZLAFF, DAVID EDWARD,** minister; b. Kansas City, Mo., Mar. 12, 1938; s. John Henry and Amy May (Cathcart) R.; m. Shiela Paige Hickerson, June 9, 1958; children: Perry Dean, Kevin Lee, Kalista Kay. BA in Ministry, Nebr. Christian Coll., 1961; MDiv, Memphis Theol. Sem., 1991; DMin, Lake Charles Bible Coll., 1996. Ordained to ministry Christian Ch., 1962. Min. Christian Ch., Neligh, Nebr., 1959-67; owner, mgr. Kordsman Evangelistic Assn., Hiawatha, Kans., 1967-75; sr. min. Christian Ctr., Hiawatha, Kans., 1970-72; salesman Saladmaster Co., Springfield, Mo., 1975-76; ops. coord. Blackwood Bros. Quartet, Memphis, 1976-79, 85; mgr. sales and svc. Elliot Impression Products, Memphis, 1980-85; elder, tchr. Lindewood Christion Ch., 1985—2003; min. Bethany Christian Ch., Eads, Tenn., 1986-95; owner Soma Co., 1993-96; sales cons., fleet mgr., dealership coord. Midway Ford, Collierville, Tenn., 1996-99; customer rels. mgr. Landers Ford, 1999—2001; assoc. pastor Macon Christian Ch., Collierville, Tenn., 1997-99; courtesy delivery dealer trade mgr. Hutton Chevrolet, from 2001; sr. cons. pastor Morning Star Bible Ch., Nashville, 2003—05, Kirk's Christian, 2005—09, Sumerville Christian Ch., from 2011. Program chair exec. commn. on ministry com. Christian Chs. (Disciples of Christ), Tenn., 1988—95, ch. cons., 1996; western area moderator, mem. gen. and exec. bds. Region of Christian Ch. of Tenn., 1991—93; small bus. founder, 1993; mem. pastoral adv. bd. Genesis Crisis Ctr., Memphis, 1994; cons. WYLT-FM Radio, Collierville, 1997—2001, WUVLL-AM Radio, Mobile, Ala., 1997—2001. Author: At the Table, 2006; coauthor: (songbook) Kordsman Presents, 1966; recorded and produced 6 long play albums, 1966-74. Bd. dirs. Memphis Family Link, 1985-86; mem. United Cerebral Palsy, 1983-86; asst. police chief City of Neligh, 1962-67, coord., 1965-67. Mem. Nat. Arts and Recording Artists, Collierville Ministerial Assn., Christian Ch. Ministers Memphis. Republican. Mem. Disciples Christ. Avocations: fishing, weightlifting, basketball, coaching baseball and softball. Home: Memphis, Tenn. Died Feb. 23, 2013.

**RAWLINSON, JOSEPH ELI,** foundation administrator, lawyer; b. Delta, Utah, May 9, 1915; s. Eli Wilford and Dora Pearl (Day) Rawlinson; m. Elaine Millicent Andersen, June 2, 1947; children: James, Jolene, Nancy, Rex, Anina, Cheryl, Mark, Lisa, David. BS, U. Utah, 1936; JD, Loyola U., 1958. CPA Calif.; bar: Calif. 1959. Agt. IRS, Wichita, Kans., 1938—52; acct. Serene Koster, Barbour, Calif., 1952—62; pvt. practice Calif., 1959; pres., CEO Fritz B. Burns Found., Burbank, Calif., from 1980. Recipient Silver medal, Am. Inst. Accts., 1942. Died Sept. 30, 2011.

**RAY, RICHARD BELMONT,** congressman; b. Crawford County, GA, Feb. 2, 1927; m. Barbara Elizabeth Giles, 1947; children: Susan, Charles, Alan. Farmer, 1946-50; founder, operator Ray Services Inc., 1950-62; mgr. Southeastern region Getz Inc., 1962-72; adminstrv. asst. to Senator Sam Nunn of Ga., 1972-82; mem. 98th-102nd Congresses from 3d Dist. Ga., from 1983; mayor Perry, Ga., 1964-70. Mem. Perry City Council, 1962-64; pres. Ga. Mcpl. Assn., 1969-70; bd. stewards Perry 1st United Meth. Ch. Democrat. Died May 29, 1999.

**RAYMOND, LLOYD WILSON,** retired machinery company executive, consultant; b. Middleboro, Mass., Jan. 4, 1922; s. Millard Edgar and Ethel (Morrison) R.; m. Joyce Elaine Cox, Nov. 10, 1972. Student, N.Y.U., 1952; ThB, Christian Bible Coll., Rocky Mount, NC, 1995, ThM, 1996, PhD in Religion, 1998; D Min., S.W. Bible Coll. and Sem., Sulphur, La., 1997; MBA, M. Photography, Internat. U., 1999. Clk. Pub. Housing Adminstrn., Washington, 1941-42, adminstrv. asst. devel. dept. Washington and NYC, 1946-55; machinery data mgr., warehouse mgr. Nat. Machinery Exch., Inc., Newark, 1955-76, office mgr., machinery data mgr., sales exec. Pico Rivera, Calif., 1976-2000; ret., 2000. Ind. machinery cons. Author: Titanic-What Went Wrong; composer (opera) Rag Doll, 1999; designer computerized info. mgmt. and quote generating sys., 1991, registered trademark Infodex. Founder, dir. Living Pictures Programs, 1965-95. Mem. Soc. Profl. Journalists, Investigative Reporters and Editors. Avocations: writing, woodworking, photography. Died Aug. 31, 2001.

**REANEY, JAMES CRERAR,** poet, playwright; b. South Easthope, Ont., Can., Sept. 1, 1926; s. James Nesbit and Elizabeth Henrietta (Crerar) R.; m. Colleen Thibaudeau, Dec. 29, 1951; children: James Stewart, Susan Alice. BA, U. Toronto, 1948, MA, 1949, PhD, 1957; DLitt, Carleton U., 1975. Asst. prof. English U. Man., Canada, 1949-60; prof. English U. Western Ont., London, Canada, 1960—2008. Author: (poetry) The Red Heart, 1949 (Gov. General's award for Poetry, 1949), A Suit of Nettles, 1958 (Gov. General's award for Poetry, 1958),Twelve Letters to a Small Town, 1962 (Gov. General's award for Poetry, 1962), The Dance of Death at London, 1963, Poems, 1972, Performance Poems, 1990, Souwesto home, 2005; (plays) The Killdeer and Other Plays, 1960 (Massey award 1960), Colours in the Dark, 1969, Masks of Childhood, 1972, Listen to the Wind, 1972, Apple Butter and Other Plays for Children, 1973, Sticks and Stones: The Donnellys Part I, 1973, The Donnellys Part II, 1974, The St. Nicholas Hotel, 1975 (Floyd S. Chalmers award for Best Canadian play, 1975), 14 Barrels from Sea to Sea, 1975, Handcuffs: The Donnellys Part III, 1977, The Dismissal, 1978, Wacousta, 1980, King Whistle, 1982, I the Parade, 1983, The House by the Churchyard, 1985, Alice Through the Looking-Glass, 1994, Zamorna: The Story of Branwell Bronte, 1999; (children's books) The Boy with an R on his Hand, 1963, Take the Big Picture, 1986, Box Social & Other Stories, 1996, The Donnelly!, 2000, The Donnelly Documents: An Ontario Vendetta, 2004; (opera libretti) Night Blooming Cereus, 1959, The Shivaree, Serinette, Taptoo, 1999, Scripts, 2004; editor, pub.: Alphabet, 1960-70; contbr. articles to profl. jours. Decorated Order of Can. Fellow Royal Soc. Can.; mem. Playwrights Union Can., League Can. Poets. Mem. New Democratic Party. Home: London, Canada. Died June 11, 2008.

**REBHAN, HERMAN,** retired labor union administrator; b. Poland, Oct. 2, 1920; s. William and Frieda (Weinberger) R.; m. Dorothy Dishman, Oct. 26, 1941 (dec. 2000); children: James Bertram, Gail Susan. Student, U. Chgo.; student (Ford Found. scholar 1954-55). With Chrysler Corp., Chgo., 1941-45; electro-motive divsn. Gen. Motors Corp., LaGrange, Ill., 1945-56; rep. UAW, 1956-61, 62-66, adminstrv. asst. to pres., 1969-70, dir. internat. affairs dept. Washington, 1971-74; adminstrv. asst. Ill. Dept. Labor, 1961-62; coordinator Internat. Metalworkers Fedn., Geneva, 1966-69, gen. sec., 1974—89; mem. exec. com. Internat. Confedn. Free Trade Unions. U.S. del. metal trades com. ILO; vice-chmn. bd. Ford Motor Co. Ger. Author: Trade Unions and the World, 1980. Mem. UAW. Democrat. Home: Geneva, Switzerland. Died Dec. 16, 2006.

**RECTOR, MARGARET HAYDEN,** freelance/self-employed writer; b. Azusa, Calif., May 23, 1916; d. Floyd Smith and Anna Martha (Miller) Hayden; m. Robert Wayman Rector, Aug. 25, 1940; children: Cleone Rector Grabowski Black, Robin Rector Krupp, Bruce Hayden. AA, Citrus Jr. Coll., 1936; BA, Pomona Coll., 1938; postgrad., Stanford U., 1938-40, Columbia U., 1942-46, St. John's Coll., Annapolis, Md., 1946-56, U. So. Calif., 1959-65, UCLA, 1959-66. Mem. advt. staff Curt Wagner, Redondo Beach, Calif., 1957-67; writer Am. Home Mag., NYC, 1942-46, House Beautiful Mag., NYC, 1942-46; author children's books Grossmont Press, San Diego, 1974-76. Invited lectr. Crystal Cruises, 1997. Author: Norton and Gus, 1976; Alva, That Vanderbilt-Belmont Woman, 1992; editor: History of Citrus, 1994; playwright, screenwriter. Dem. organizer, Annapolis, Md., 1946-56; mem. UCLA affiliates; bd. dirs. Friends of Rsch. Libr. Mem. AAUW (life), PEN, Women in Film, Women in Theatre, UCLA Faculty Wives Writers Group, Surfwriters Palos Verdes Peninsula, First Stage, The Audrey Skirball-Kenis Theatre, Dramatists Guild, Authors Guild, Womens Internat. Ctr. in San Diego, Pomona Coll. Alumni, Stanford U. Alumni. Avocations: performing arts on stage, for tv, and at comedy clubs. Died Nov. 9, 2002.

**REDFIELD, JEAN M.,** electric power company executive; With McKinsey & Co., Inc.; mgr. corp. stratety Detroit Edison Co., 1994-97; pres. Detroit Edison Co. Am., from 1997. Deceased.

**REDHEAD, PAUL AVELING,** physicist; b. Brighton, Eng., May 25, 1924; m. Doris Packman, 1948; children: Janet, Patricia. BA with honors in Physics, Cambridge U., Eng., 1944, MA, 1948, PhD, 1969. Sci. officer dept. naval ordnance Brit. Admiralty, 1944-45, svcs. electronics rsch. lab., 1945-47; rsch. officer NRC Can., Ottawa, Ont., 1947-69, dir. planning group, 1970-72, dir.-gen. planning, 1972-73, dir. div. physics, 1973-86, chmn. com. of lab. dirs., 1981-86, sec. sci. and tech. policy com., 1986-89, researcher emeritus, from 1989. Author: Physical Basis of Ultrahigh Vacuum, 1968, 2d edit., 1993; editor: Jour. Vacuum Scis. and Tech., 1969-74; contbr. numerous articles to profl. jours.; patentee in field. Fellow IEEE, Royal Soc. Can., Am. Phys. Soc., Am. Vacuum Soc. (past pres., Medard W. Welch award 1975); mem. Can. Assn. Physicists (medal for achievement in physics 1989). Home: Ottawa, Canada. Died July 9, 2005.

**REED, BARRY C., JR.,** lawyer; b. Oct. 9, 1958; BS, Holy Cross Coll., Worcester, Mass., 1980; JD, Suffolk U., 1983. Bar: Mass., U.S. Dist. Ct. Mass. Atty. Reed, O'Reilly & Brett, Boston, from 1983. Deceased.

**REED, H. OWEN (HERBERT OWEN REED),** retired music educator; b. Odessa, Mo., 1910; m. Esther M. Reed (dec.); children: Sara Jo Ferrar, Carol Ann Wetters; m. Mary L. Arwood, 1982. Student, U. Mo., 1929—33; MusB in Music Composition, La. State U., 1934, MusM in Music Composition, 1936, BA in French, 1937; PhD in Music Composition, U. Rochester, 1939. Educator Mich. State U., 1939—76, chmn. theory and composition, 1939—67, acting head, Sch. Music, 1957—58, chmn. music composition, Sch. Music, 1967—76, prof. emeritus, 1976—2014; ret., 1976. Physics educator Army Spec. Tng. Program, 1943—44; guest prof. Mont. State U., 1950, Gettysburg Coll., Pa., 1969, U. Pacific, Stockton, Calif., 1983; founding mem. Geriatric Six Plus One Jazz Ensemble. Asst. conductor, arranger: The La. Kings Brass Ensemble, second trumpet: Lansing Symphony Orchestra, band leader: The Missourians Jazz Ensemble; composer: (orchestral works) Evangeline, 1938, Symphony No. 1, 1939, Overture, 1940, Symphonic Dance, 1942, Concerto for Cello and Orchestra, 1949, Overture for Strings, 1961, La Fiesta Mexicana, 1964, The Turning Mind, 1968, Ut Re Mi, 1979;: Christmas Eve, 2001, Song of Acapulco, 2001, (winds and percussion) Spiritual, 1947, Missouri Shindig, 1951, Theme and Variations, 1954, Renascence, 1958;: Che-Ba-Kun-Ah, 1959, The Touch of the Earth, 1971, For the Unfortunate, 1972, Ut Re Mi, 1980, The Awakening of the Ents, 1985; composer: (for marching band) La Fiesta Mexicana, 1986; composer: Of Loth Lorien, 1987, The Heart of the Morn, 1987, Frolicking Winds, 2006, Overture 1940 (arranged by William Berz), The Song of Acapulco, 2001, (chamber work) Piano Sonata, 1934, String Quartet, 1937, The Passing of John Blackfeather, 1945, Scherzo for Clarinet & Piano, 1947, Three Nationalities, 1947, Dusk, 1947, Wondrous Love, 1948, Mountain Meditation, 1948, Nocturne, 1953, Symphonic Dance, 1954, Christmas Eve, 1954, The Song of Acapulco, 1954, El Muchacho, 1962, El Son De La Negra, 1975, Give the Fiddler a Dram, 1976, Fanfare for Remembrance, 1986,

Make a Joyful Noise, 2005, (choral works) Two Tongue Twisters, 1950, Close Beside the Winding Cedar, 1957, Ripley Ferry, 1958, Proud Chieftains, 1958, A Tabernacle for the Sun, 1963, Lord God of Sea, 1963, Rejoice! Rejoice!, 1977, Make a Joyful Noise, 2004, (stage works) The Masque of Red Death, 1936, Michigan Dream, 1955, Earth Trapped, 1960; author: A Workbook in the Fundamentals of Music, 1947, Basic Music, 1954, Basic Music Workbook, 1954, Composition Analysis Chart, 2004; co-author (with Paul Harder): Basic Contrapuntal Technique, 1964; co-author: (with Greg Steinke) rev. edit., 2003; co-author: (with Joel T. Leach) Scoring for Percussion and the Instruments of the Percussion Section, 1969, rev. edit., 1979; co-author: (with Robert G. Sidnell) The Materials of Music Composition, 1978; co-author: (with Joel Leach, Deanna Hudgins) Scoring for Percussion: and the Instruments of the Percussion Family, 2010. Recipient Composers Press Symphonic award for Concerto for Cello and Orchestra, 1949, Disting. $1000 award, Mich. State U., 1962, Recognition and Honors for Scholarly Contbns. and Publ. of La Fiesta Mexicana, 1999, Award for Psalm of Praise, Basic Contrapuntal Techniques, Belwin Mills Pub., 2004, Libr. Public award for sound recording of Awakening of the Ents, La Fiesta Mexicana, For the Unfortunate, and Missouri Shindig, 2005, Citation for Disting. Contbns. in Arts, George Romney and Greater Mich. Found., 1963, Neil A. Kjos Meml. award for For The Unfortunate, 1975, various ann. awards, ASCAP, from 1978, Award of Merit, Youth Arts Festival, 1978, Hon. Mention for Rejoice! Rejoice!, Brown U. Choral Composition Competition, 1978, Nat. Arts Assoc. award, Sigma Alpha Iota, 1983, First Place award for Butterfly Girl and Mirage Boy, Bklyn. Coll. Chamber Opera Competition, 1985, Edwin Franco Goldman Meml. Citation for conspicuous svc. in interest of bands and band music in America, American Bandmasters Assn., 1994, Owen the Midwest medal, Midwest Clinic, 2012; fellow for Creative Work in Musical Composition, Guggenheim, 1948—49; Resident Fellowship, Huntington Hartford Found., Pacific Palisades, Calif., 1960, Helene Wurlitzer Found., Taos, N.Mex, 1967. Mem.: Nat. Assn. Composers (mem. nat. coun.), American Music Ctr., ASCAP, Music Teachers Nat. Assn. (chmn. theory composition section), Mich. Sch. Band & Orchestra Assn. (hon.), Phi Mu Alpha Sinfonia (Orpheus award, Gamma Epsilon chpt. 1976). Home: Athens, Ga. Died Jan. 6, 2014.

**REED, HELEN TARASOV,** translator, interpreter, econoist; b. Toronto, Ont., Can., Nov. 23, 1915; arrived in US, 1916, naturalized, 1927; d. Peter P. Reed and Claudia M. (Yurevich) Tarasov Reed; m. Haldee Lee Reed, Feb. 18, 1946 (dec. 1978); children: Claudette Reed Upton Keeley, Ronald Peter, Andrew Douglas. BA, Western Res. U., 1936; credit in Ecole. libr., Sci. Po. Paris, 1934—35; MA, Fletcher Sch. Law & Diplomacy, 1937; postgrad., New Sch. Social Rsch., 1939. Cert. contract interpreter Russian-English, US State Dept., 1984. Economist US Govt., Washington, 1939—45, Berlin, 1945—46; instr. U. NC, Asheville, 1945—46; coord. fgn. lang. Asheville Country Day Sch., 1959—73. Pvt. practice as sci. translator, Asheville, from 1952; instr. in adv. English South China Inst. Tech., Guangzhou, China, 1984—85, Nanjng Inst. Posts & Telecom., 1985—86, Gansu Province Inst. Membrane Sci. & Tech., 1986; held workshops in fgn. lang. tchg. Independent Schs. Assn.; evening course U. NC in Russian; spl. courses YWCA in parliamentary law, procedure; parliamentarian N.C. convs. LWV; mem., sec. Western Carolina Devel. Assn. Forestry commn., 1980—84; mem. energy task force AAUW, Washington, 1977—79. Recipient All-State Environ. Svc. award, NC Sierra Club, 1983, French Broad River award, Land of Sky, 1982. Mem.: AAUW (past pres., treas.), Am. Soc. Interpreters, Am. Translators' Assn., Am. Forestry Assn., Am. Econ. Assn., Am. Enka, Unitarian-Universalist, Carolina Mountain Club, League of Women Voters, Sierra Club. Home: Asheville, NC. Died Jan. 28, 1993.

**REED, LOU (LEWIS ALLAN REED),** singer, songwriter; b. Bklyn., Mar. 2, 1942; s. Sidney Joseph and Toby (Futterman) R.; m. Bettye Kronstadt, 1973 (div.); m. Sylvia Morales, Feb. 14, 1980 (div. 1994); m. Laurie Anderson, April 12, 2008 BA in Literature, Syracuse U., 1964. Songwriter Pickwick Records, NYC, 1965; founding mem., singer The Velvet Underground, 1966—70; solo artist, 1972—2013. Singer: (albums with The Velvet Underground) The Velvet Underground and Nico, 1967, White Light White Heat, 1968, The Velvet Underground, 1969, Loaded, 1970, Live at Max's Kansas City, 1972, 1969: The Velvet Underground Live, 1974, VU, 1985, Another View, 1986, Velvet Underground Live MCM XCIII, 1993, The Best of Lou Reed and the Velvet Underground, 1995, Peel Slowly and See, 1995, Fully Loaded, 1997, Bootleg Series Volume 1: The Quine Tapes, 2001; (solo albums) Lou Reed, 1972, Transformer, 1972, Berlin, 1973, Rock 'N' Roll Animal, 1974, Sally Can't Dance, 1974, Metal Machine Music, 1975, Lou Reed Live, 1975, Coney Island Baby, 1976, Rock and Roll Heart, 1976, Street Hassle, 1978, Live, Take No Prisoners, 1978, The Bells, 1979, Growing Up in Public, 1980, The Blue Mask, 1982, Legendary Hearts, 1983, New Sensations, 1984, Live in Italy, 1984, Mistrial, 1986, New York, 1989, Songs for Drella, 1990, Magic and Loss, 1992, Between Thought and Expression: The Lou Reed Anthology, 1992, Different Times: Lou Reed In The 70's, 1996, Set The Twilight Reeling, 1996, Perfect Night: Live in London, 1998, Ecstasy, 2000, American Poet, 2001, The Raven, 2003, Animal Serenade, 2004, Le Bataclan '72, 2004, Lou Reed's Inner Spaces, 2007, Hudson River Wind Meditations, 2007, Berlin: Live at St. Ann's Warehouse, 2008; (albums with John Zone & Laurie Anderson) The Stone: Issue Three, 2008, The Essential Lou Reed, 2011; (albums with Metal Machine Tro) The Creation of the Universe, 2008; (albums with Metallica) Lulu, 2011; touring with Andy Warhol's The Exploding Plastic Inevitable; exhibited series of photographs Photographic Resource Ctr., 1997, Soho Triad Gallery, 1998, Le Printemps de Cahors, France, 1999, Closure, 1998; author: Between Thought and Expression, 1991, Pass Thru Fire, 2000 Decorated Chevalier Comdr. Arts & Letters (France); recipient Best New Poet award Coun. on Small Lit. Magazines, 1977, Heroes award N.Y. chpt. NARAS, 1997, Grammy award for Best long Form Music Video, 1998; inducted into The Rock & Roll Hall of Fame (as mem. of The Velvet Underground), 1996 Mem. Musician's Union Local 802, Screen Actors Guild Jewish. Died Oct. 27, 2013.

**REES, THOMAS DEE,** plastic surgeon, educator; b. Nephi, Utah, Feb. 2, 1927; s. Don M. and Norma (Anderson) R.; m. Natalie Bowes, Mar. 25, 1949 (dec. 2012); children: Thomas, David (dec. 1990), Elizabeth. BA, U. Utah, 1946, MD, 1948. Diplomate: American Bd. Plastic Surgery (dir. 1979-84, vice chmn. 1983-84). Intern, then asst. resident in surgery Genesee Hosp., Rochester, N.Y., 1948-51; resident N.Y. Hosp.-Cornell U. Med. Center, 1948-50, 52-53; research fellow neurosurgery Yale U. Med. Center, 1951; resident in plastic surgery VA Hosp., Bronx, N.Y., 1953-55; mem. staff N.Y. U.-Bellevue Med. Center, Univ. Hosp.; chmn. dept. plastic surgery Manhattan Eye, Ear and Throat Hosp. Attending Doctors Hosp., VA Hosp.; cons. Southampton (N.Y.) Hosp.; clin. prof. surgery NYU Med. Sch.; internat. chmn. African Med. and Research Found. Author: Cosmetic Facial Surgery, 1972, Cancer of the Skin, 1976; Aesthetic Plastic Surgery, Vols. I and II, 1980, Daktari: A Surgeon's Adventures with the Flying Doctors of East Africa, 2002; also articles. Served to lt. comdr. 1945, 57-58. Recipient Disting. Service award Young Men's Bd. Trade, N.Y.C., 1961, Gates award for Global Health, 2005; Disting. Service award and Young Man of Year award N.Y. State Jaycees, 1961; grantee USPHS, 1964; NIH, 1965-69 Fellow ACS; mem. American Assn. Plastic Surgeons, AMA, Med. Soc. County N.Y., American Soc. Plastic and Reconstructive Surgeins, American Soc. Cleft Palate Rehab., Soc. Rehab. Facially Disabled, Pan-Pacific Surg. Assn., Pan-Am. Med. Assn., American Soc. Aesthetic Plastic Surgery, N.Y. Acad. Medicine, N.Y. Med. Soc., N.Y. Regional Soc. Plastic Surgery, Northeastern Soc. Plastic Surgeons, Internat. Confedn. Plastic Surgeons. Clubs: N.Y. Athletic. Mem. Lds Ch. Home: Santa Fe, N.Mex. Died Nov. 14, 2013.

**REESE, CARL-GEORG ØRSKOV,** textiles executive; b. Copenhagen, Sept. 26, 1927; s. Edwin and Nina R. Reese; m. Margot Jensen Reese, Sept. 30, 1950; 1 child, Susanne Vibeke Birgitte Reese Jakob. Acct. Handelshojskolen, Copenhagen, 1953—59, Christiansen & Engelbrechtsen, Copenhagen, 1946—67; mng. dir. Dansk Presenning A/S, Copenhagen, from 1967, dir., Dependable Protect (T-H) Ltd., London, from 1973, Otto Sandgreen Holding A/S, Copenhagen, from 1974. Bd. dirs. Otto Sandgreen Found., Copenhagen, from 1974. Home: Copenhagen, Denmark. Deceased.

**REGAL, EVAN CHARLES,** lawyer; b. Port Jefferson, NY, Feb. 27, 1948; s. Evan C. and Agnes (Holly) Regal; m. Mary E. Murphy, Oct. 11, 1975; children: Thomas E., Christopher A., Ellen M. AB, Syracuse U., 1970; JD, Albany Law Sch., Union U., 1974; grad., NY State Bankers Assn. Estate Adminstrn. Sch., 1975, NY State Bankers Assn. Trust Adminstrn. Sch., 1976; student, Northwestern U. Nat. Grad. Trust Sch., 1978—79. Bar: NY 1975, US Dist. Ct. (northern dist.), NY 1975, US Tax Ct. 1981. Trust officer State Bank Albany, NY, 1974—80; assoc. and predecessor firm Tate Bishko & Regal, Albany, 1980—84, ptnr., 1984—87; prin. Hinman Straub Pigors & Manning, P.C., 1987—99. Mem. bd. editors Adminstrn. NY Estates. Mem.: Estate Planning Coun. Northeastern NY, Albany County Bar Assn., NY State Bar Assn. (com. continuing legal edn. trusts and estates sect. 1982—93, exec. com. trusts & estates sect. 1988—92, com. surrogate's ct. trusts and estates sect. from 1993), Rotary (Albany) (bd. dirs.). Roman Catholic. Home: Delmar, NY. Died Jan. 7, 1999.

**REGAN, JOHN BERNARD (JACK REGAN),** community relations executive, state senator, state legislator; b. Chgo., Feb. 2, 1934; s. Andrew J. and Frances (O'Born) R.; m. Rosemary E. Seger, Aug. 17, 1980. BA, So. Ill. U., 1960. V.p. Collins Bros., Las Vegas, Nev., 1971-76; pres. Terra, Inc., Las Vegas, 1973-80; owner Jack's Place, Las Vegas, 1980-98; govt. and mil. affairs liaison C.C. So. Nev., North Las Vegas, 1984-95. Dist. dir. Nat. Coun. for Community Rels., 1984-86; nat. treas. Nat. Coun. Mktg. and Pub. Rels., 1986-88; state dir. Internat. Coun. of Shopping Ctrs., Nev., 1976. State assemblyman Nev. State Legis., Carson City, 1988-90, 92-93, state senator 1994-98; past chmn. Am. Legis. Exch. Coun., 1990-93; trade, travel and tourism com. mem. Nat. Conf. of State Legis., 1990-98, com. on devel. disabilties, mem. exec. com., 1996-98, mem. exec. com., co-vice chair arts, tourism and econ. devel.; mem. fin. com. Coun. State Govt.; active Las Vegas Habitat for Humanity. With USN, 1951-55. Recipient Lion of Yr. award Las Vegas Lions Club, 1978, Paragon award Nat. Coun. for Cmty. Rels., 1985, Legislator of Yr. award Am. Legis. Exch. Coun., 1996. Mem. Thunderbird Chpt. Air Force Assn. (pres. 1989-90, named hon. Thunderbird, Nighthawk, stealth fighter), North Las Vegas C. of C. (v.p. 1986). Democrat. Jewish. Avocations: reading, community service, coin collecting/numismatics. Home: Las Vegas, Nev. Died Jan. 21, 1999.

**REICHAW, MEIR,** mathematician, educator; b. Grodek Jagiellonski, Poland, Dec. 20, 1923; arrived in Israel, 1957; s. Joseph and Klara (Podhoretz) Reichbach; m. Halina Sawicka Reichaw, Nov. 26, 1955. MSc in Math., U. Wrocław, 1950, PhD in Math., 1956. Dep. asst., asst. Polytechnic of Wrocław, 1948-51, sr. asst., adj., 1951-57; from lectr. to sr. lectr. Technion-Israel Inst. Tech., Haifa, Israel, 1957-63, assoc. prof., 1963-69, prof., 1969-92, prof. emeritus, from 1992. Contbr. articles to profl. jours. Fellow Fulbright Found., 1963, NSF, 1970. Mem. Israel Math. Union, Am. Math. Soc. Avocations: physics, history of the world. Home: Haifa, Israel. Died Feb. 25, 2000.

**REICHMANN, PAUL,** real estate corporation executive; b. Vienna, Sept. 27, 1930; s. Samuel and Renee Reichmann; m. Lea Feldman. Exec. v.p. to pres. Olympia & York, Toronto, 1964. Bd. dirs. Abitibi-Price Inc., Toronto, Gulf Can. Corp., Toronto, GW Utilities Ltd., Toronto, Trizec Corp., Calgary Jewish. Died Oct. 25, 2013.

**REID, BILL (WILLIAM EARL REID),** Canadian provincial official; b. Nelson, BC, Can., Aug. 13, 1934; s. William Earl and Dolly (Renwick) R.; m. Marion Joan Meehan, June 21, 1957; children: Cathy Darlene, Laurie Joan, Gail Patricia, Sheila Marie. Alderman, Delta, B.C., 1973-78; charter mem. Urban Transit Authority, 1978-79; chmn. bd. Metro Transit Authority, 1980-85; mem. B.C. Legis., 1983—86, chief govt. whip, 1985-86, min. tourism, recreation & culture, 1986-88, min. tourism, provincial sec., 1988—91. Candidate Progressive Conservative election, 1972. Recipient Queen Diamond Jubilee award, 2012. Mem.: Kinsmen, Rotary. Anglican. Died May 29, 2013.

**REIFERS, RICHARD FRANCIS,** retired packaging and machinery company executive; b. Lafayette, Ind., Jan. 12, 1919; s. John Stevenson ALexander and Ann (Schaack) R.; m. Elizabeth Diane Goulet, April 21, 1951; children: Meriane, Beth, Mark, Collette, John. BA Inst. Design, Ill. Inst. Tech., 1949. Designer W.C. Ritchie & Co., Chgo., 1949-51; designer, tech. dir. Gen. Package Corp., Chgo., 1951-57; dir. packaging devel. Diamond Internat. Corp., NYC, 1957-62, corporate v.p., 1962-84. Cons. research and devel. in packaging field Holder numerous U.S. and fgn. patents. Served to maj. USAAF, 1941-46. Mem.: Country of New Canaan. Home: New Canaan, Conn. *It was fundamental for me to believe I could succeed. It required inexhaustable drive and patience to take whatever time and effort required to achieve the most perfect solution possible. To do this I had to communicate clearly, inspire others, instill mutual respect and trust in order to work well with others. This created the synergy necessary for productive achievement.* Died Feb. 22, 2014.

**REILEY, MAME CARRIGAN (MARY ANNE REILEY),** political strategist; b. Newport News, Va., Dec. 24, 1952; d. Bernard Campbell and Joan (Carrigan) R. BA in Liberal Arts, Sacred Heart Coll., 1974; cert., Cornell U., 1977. Asst. mgr. Watergate Hotel, Washington, 1975-83; real estate agt. Watergate Mgmt., Washington, 1980-84; dir. mktg., producer spl. events Courtesy Associates, Washington, 1983-90; campaign mgr. Jim Moran for Congress, Alexandria, Va., 1990—91; chief of staff to Rep. James Moran US House of Reps., 1991—96; gen. mgr. Washington Inc./Production Group Internat., 1996—2001; pres. The Reiley Group, 2001—14. Guest lectr. American U., Washington, 1987; bd. dirs. Rte One Corridor Housing. Mem. finance com. Democratic Nat. Com., Washington, 1983 Mem. Washington Performing Arts Soc. (chmn. public relations com. 1985-89) Democrat. Avocations: swimming, tennis. Home: Alexandria, Va. Died June 2, 2014.

**REIMERS, JØRGEN,** surgeon; b. Copenhagen, Feb. 6, 1931; s. Frithjof and Pylle (Albeck) R.; m. Vibeke Irving, Apr. 6, 1955; children: Martin, Jesper, Carsten. MD, U. Copenhagen, 1959. Cons. Rigshospitalet, Copenhagen, 1969-81, chief orthopedic surgeon, 1981-99; cons. Ebberødgård, 1969-81, Vangedehuse, 1969-94, Geelsgård Boarding Sch., 1981-91, Faroe Islands, 1986-2000. Co-author: Nordic Textbook of Paediatry, 1973, Basisbook of Medicine and Surgery, 1979, The Diplegic Child, 1992. Lt. Med. Corps Danish armed forces, 1962-92. Recipient Cerebral Palsy prize of hon., 1995. Mem. European Pediatric Orthopedic Soc. (pres. 1991-93). Home: Lyngby, Denmark. Deceased.

**REINL, HARRY CHARLES,** economist, researcher; b. Muttersdorf, Suden, Germany, Nov. 13, 1932; arrived in U.S., 1946; s. Carl and Angela (Plass) Reinl. BS, Fordham U., 1953; MA, George Washington U., 1968; cert. in career English, USDA, Washington, 1966; HHD, London Inst. Applied Rsch., 1992; PhD, Brownell U., 1993. Head market rsch. Timex Mfg., Waterbury, Conn., 1955-58; jr. observer Sperry-Rand Corp., NYC, 1958-62; labor economist manpower adminstrn. US Dept. Labor, Washington, 1962-68; labor economist Office Pers. Mgmt. US Civil Svc. Commn., Washington, from 1968. Mgr. NY br. Willmark Svc., NYC, 1971; prof. rsch. Haute Ecole Rsch. Alliance Universelle pour la Paix par la Connaissance, Paris, 1992; rsch. bd. advs. Am. Biog. Inst., Raleigh, NC, 1991; mem. adv. coun. Internat. Biog. Ctr., Cambridge, England, 1992. Author (on microfilm): The Story of My Life, 1984. Founding mem. Nat. Campaign Tolerance, Montgomery, Ala., 2004; with Willmental health testing VA Med. Ctr., Washington, from 1989; charter mem. Nat. D-Day Mus., New Orleans, from 2004; mem. Diesen Ranch, Santa Barbara, Calif., from 2005; founder Colonial Williamsburg, Va.; mem. Found. for Nat. Archives, Washington, 2005; founder Martin Luther King Jr. Nat. Meml., Washington, 2005; life mem. Rep. Nat. Com., Washington, from 1979; mem. Rep. Nat. Senatorial Com., Washington, 1990, adv. mem., 2006; founding mem. Wold Peace and Diplomacy Forum, Cambridge, 2003; host NYC com. Rep. Nat. Conv., 2004; team mem. Bush-Cheney 2004; inner cir. co-chair inaugural festivities Rep. Nat. Party, 2005; mem. George Bush Presdl. Libr. Found., Tex. A&M U., College Station. Decorated Knight Templar Bur. Internat.; recipient John Edgar Hoover Meml. award, Police Assn., 1983, HIR citation of Leadership, Rep. Nat. Conv., 1996, medal of Freedom, Rep. Nat. Senatorial Inner Cir., 1999, Order of Merit, Nat. Rep. Congl. Com., 2006; fellow, AA, from 1988. Mem.: World War II Soc., London Diplomatic Acad., Academic Coun., NY Acad. Scis., George

Mason U. Mercatus Ctr. (contbr.), Family Immigration History Ctr. Ellis Island, Collegiate Network, Inc. (hon. sponsor), Pres.'s Club, Fordham Univ. Club Washington. Mem. Lds Ch. Deceased.

**REIS, JEAN STEVENSON,** administrative secretary; b. Wilburton, Okla., Nov. 30, 1914; d. Robert Emory and Ada (Ross) Stevenson; m. George William Reis, June 24, 1939 (dec. 1980). BA, U. Tex., El Paso, 1934; MA, So. Meth. U., 1935; postgrad., U. Chgo., 1937—38, U. Wash., 1948—49. Tchr. El Paso H.S., 1935—39; safety engr., trainer Safety and Security Divsn., Office of Chief Ordnance, Chgo., 1942—45; tchr. Lovenberg Jr. H.S., Galveston, Tex., 1946; parish sec. Trinity Parish Episcopal Ch., Seattle, 1950—65; adminstrv. sec., asst. Office Resident Bishop, United Meth. Ch., Seattle, 1965—94; ret., 1994. Observer Africa U. installation, Mutare, Zimbabwe, 1994; com. on legislation for 1996 gen. conf. Hist. Soc. of United Meth. Ch. Recipient Bishop's award, 1980. Mem. AAUW, Beta Beta Beta. Deceased.

**RELMAN, ARNOLD SEYMOUR,** physician, editor, educator; b. NYC, June 17, 1923; s. Simon and Rose (Mallach) Relman; m. Harriet Morse Vitkin, June 26, 1953; children: David Arnold, John Peter, Margaret Rose. AB, Cornell U., 1943; MD, Columbia U., 1946; LLD (hon.), U. Pa.; ScD (hon.), Med. Coll. Wis., Union U., Med. Coll. Ohio, CUNY; DMSc (hon.), Brown U.; DLH (hon.), SUNY; LittD (hon.), Temple U. Diplomate American Bd. Internal Medicine. House officer New Haven Hosp., Yale, 1946—49; NRC fellow Evans Meml., Mass. Meml. hosps., 1949—50; practice medicine, specializing in internal medicine Boston, 1950—68, Phila., 1968—77; asst. prof., prof. medicine Boston U. Sch. Medicine, 1950—68; dir. Boston U. Med. Services, Boston City Hosp., 1967—68; prof. medicine, chmn. dept. medicine U. Pa.; chief med. services Hosp. of U. Pa., 1968—77; editor New Eng. Jour. Medicine, Boston, 1977—91, editor emeritus, from 1991; sr. physician Brigham and Women's Hosp., Boston, from 1977; prof. medicine and social medicine Harvard Med. Sch., 1977—93, prof. medicine and social medicine emeritus, 1993—95, prof. emeritus, 1995—2014. Cons. NIH, USPHS; mem. bd. registration in medicine Commonwealth of Mass., 1995—2001. Author: A Second Opinion, 2007; editor: Jour. Clin. Investigation, 1962—67; editor: (with F.J. Ingelfinger and M. Finland) Controversy in Internal Medicine, Vol. 1, 1966, Controversy in Internal Medicine, Vol. 2, 1974; contbr. articles to profl. jours. Trustee Columbia U., 1990—96; bd. dirs. Hastings Ctr., 1981—83. Recipient Columbia Alumni Gold medal, 1980, Disting. Svc. award, American Coll. Cardiology, 1987, McGovern award, Cosmos Club Washington, 1991, John Peters award, American Soc. Nephrology, 1992, George Polk award in Journalism, 2003. Master: ACP (John Phillips medal 1985); fellow: American Acad. Arts & Sciences; mem.: AMA, American Fedn. Clin. Rsch. (past pres.), American Soc. Clin. Investigation (past pres.), Inst. of Medicine of NAS (coun. 1979—82), Mass. Med. Soc., American Physiol. Soc., Assn. American Physicians (coun., pres. 1983—84, Kober medal 1993), Alpha Omega Alpha, Phi Beta Kappa (senator 1991—98). Home: Cambridge, Mass. Died June 17, 2014.

**REMMERT, HERMANN HEINRICH,** zoologist, ecologist, educator; b. Hanover, Germany, Mar. 29, 1931; s. Hugo and Agnes (Meyer) R.; m. Lisa Mull, July 20, 1959; 1 child, Soenke. D in Natural Scis., U. Kiel, 1953, Dr. habil., 1963. Asst. prof. Univ. Kiel, Germany, 1962-68; prof. Univ. Erlangen, Germany, 1968-76, Fachbereich Biologie Univ., Marburg, Germany, from 1976. Mem. founding com. Univ. Bayreuth, 1973-80, Univ. Passau, 1975-85; mem. Humboldt Found., Bonn, 1976-86. Author: (textbooks) Ecology (various fgn. lang. edits.), 1978, 5th German edit., 1992, Arctic Animal Ecology, 1980, Naturschutz, 1989, 2d edit., 1991, The Mosaic Cycle Concept of Ecosystems, 1991. Mem. Polish Acad. Scis. (elected mem.). Home: Niederweimar, Germany. Deceased.

**RENOFF, PAUL VERNON,** retired electrical manufacturers representative; b. Balt., July 17, 1911; s. John Henry and Mary E. (Snyder) R.; m. Margaret Hamilton Houghton, June 18, 1937; children: Ronald Hamilton, Lois Ellen Brockett, Cynthia Houghton Taler. BEE, Johns Hopkins U., 1932. Registered profl. engr., Md. Engr. H.R. Houghton, 1933—36; ptnr. Houghton & Renoff, 1936—45, Paul V. Renoff Co., 1945—66; pres. Renoff Assocs., Inc., 1966—73. Former dir. Edwin L. Wiegand Co., Skan-A-Matic Corp., United Co.; past pres. Roland Ct. Maintenance Corp. Past pres. Arundel Beach Improvement Assn.; mem. Magothy River Assn.; former dir. Roland Park Civic League. Mem.: EIII, Md. Acad. Sci., Md. Hist. Soc., U.S. Power Squadron, Chartwell Golf & Country Club (Severna Park, Md.), Johns Hopkins Club, Engrs. Club. Democrat. Episcopalian. Home: Baltimore, Md. Died Sept. 19, 1987.

**RENTON, RIGHT HON. LORD (DAVID LOCKHART-MURE),** retired lawyer; b. Dartford, Kent, Eng., Aug. 12, 1908; s. Maurice Waugh and Eszma Olivia (Borman) R.; m. Claire Cicely Duncan, July 17, 1947 (dec. Apr. 24, 1986); children: Caroline, Clare, Davina. MA BCL, Oxford U., Eng., 1930-33. Barrister-at-law, 1933—; Queen's Counsel, 1954. Practicing barrister, 1933-39, 45-55, 62-70; M.P. for Huntingdon Eng., 1945-79; Parliamentary sec. Ministry of Power, 1955-58; under sec. of state Home Office, 1958-61; minister of state, 1961-62; life peer, from 1979; dep. speaker House of Lords, London, 1982-88. Vice chmn. Coun. of Legal Edn., Eng. and Wales, 1973-77; mem. Bar Coun., Eng. and Wales, 1938-39, 68-79; treas. Lincoln's Inn, 1979. Mem. Royal Commn. on Constn., 1972-74; chmn. Royal Soc. for Mentally Handicapped Children, 1978-82; apptd. Privy Coun., 1962; pres. All Party Arts and Heritage Group; chmn. Com. on Preparation of Legis., 1973-75. Decorated Knight Brit. Empire, Territorial Efficiency Decoration; hon. fellow Univ. Coll., Oxford, 1990—. Conservative. Anglican. Avocations: gardening, travel, charities. Home: Huntingdon, England. Died May 24, 2007.

**RESHTIA, SAYED QASSEM,** writer, diplomat; b. Kabul, Afghanistan, Mar. 21, 1913; s. Sayed Habib and Zainab (Azimi) R.; m. Noorjahan Ziaee, May 17, 1930 (dec. Sept. 1946); children: Sayed Ehsanullah, Leila Enayat-Seraj; m. Golalai Seraj, Dec. 19, 1971. Student, Kabul U., 1935-39, 54-56; Cultural Doctorate (hon.), World U. Round Table, 1986. Editor Kabul Almanch and Kabul Mag., 1936-38; v.p. publs. div. Afghan Acad., 1938, dir.-gen. publs., press dept., 1940-44, pres., 1948; planning bd. liaison officer UN Tech. Coop. Mission, Afghanistan, 1950; pres. econ. planning bd., 1950-51; head govt. co-op. orgn., 1951-54; Minister of Info., 1956-60, 1963-64; Minister of Fin., 1964-65; vice-chmn. Com. to Draft Constitution, 1964. Ambassador to Czechoslovakia, Poland, and Hungary, 1960-62, to United Arab Republic, Lebanon, Sudan, and Greece, 1962-63, to Japan, 1970-73. Author: Afgthanistan in the 19th Century, 1947, Jawani Afghan, 1949, Jamaluddin Afghani, 1977, The Second Anglo-Afghan War, 1978, The Price of Liberty, The Tragedy of Afghanistan, 1984, Between Two Giants (A Political History of Modern Afghanistan), 1986, also several novels. Died Mar. 26, 1998.

**RESNICK, ROBERT,** physicist, researcher; b. Balt., Jan. 11, 1923; s. Abraham and Anna (Dubin) R.; m. Mildred Saltzman, Oct. 14, 1945; children— Trudy, Abby, Regina. AB, Johns Hopkins U., 1943, PhD (Pres.'s Fund scholar 1946-49), 1949. Physicist NACA, Cleve., 1944-46; asst. prof., assoc. prof. physics U. Pitts., 1949-56; assoc. prof., prof. physics Rensselaer Poly. Inst., Troy, NY, 1956-93, prof. emeritus, 1993—2014, chmn. interdisciplinary sci. curriculum Troy, NY, 1973-88, Edward P. Hamilton Disting. prof. sci., 1975-93; hon. research fellow Harvard U., 1964-65; Fulbright prof. Peru, 1971. Hon. vis. prof. Peoples Republic of China, 1981, 85; mem. Commn. on Coll. Physics, 1960-68; commencement speaker Rensselaer Poly. Inst., 1993; mem. U.S. adv. bd. Quantum Joint USSR/USA sci. mag., 1989-93. Author: A Manual for Laboratory Physics, 1954, (with D. Halliday) Physics, 1960, 3d edit., 1978, 4th edit., 1991, 5th edit., 2000, (with Halliday and Krane) extended version, 1986, 2d edit. extended version, 1991, 3rd edit., 2000, 5th edit., 2003, (with Halliday and Krane) Introduction to Special Relativity, 1968, (with R. Eisberg) Notes on Quantum Theory, 1968, Notes on Modern Physics, 1969, Quantum Physics of Atoms, Molecules, Solids, Nuclei and Particles, 1974, 2d edit., 1985, (with D. Halliday) Fundamentals of Physics, 1970, 5th edit., 1996, extended version, 1988, 2d edit., 1993, 3rd edit., 1996, 4th edit., 1999, (with J. Walker and D. Halliday) 7th edit., 2004, (with others) Student Study Guide for Physics, 1970, 6th edit., 2001, Basic Concepts in Relativity and Early Quantum Theory, 1972, 2d edit., 1985, Basic Concepts in Relativity, 1991; author: (with others) Sourcebook for Programmable Calculators, 1978, (with E. Derringh) Solutions to Physics Problems, 1980, 5th edit., 1996, (with K. Brownstein) Tests for Physics, 1987, (with J. Walker and D. Halliday) CD Physics, 1993, 3rd edit., 2000; books translated into numerous fgn. langs; So You Want to Write a Textbook, 1999 (video); mem. adv. bd., project staff: Physical Science for Non-Scientists, 1964-68, pub., 1968; co-dir.: Project Physics Demonstration Experiments, 1962-70; pub. project, 1970, Workshop on Apparatus for College Physics, 1964-65, 66, Videotapes in Physics Instruction, 1975-78; dir. Physics Demonstration and Laboratory Apparatus Workshop, 1960-61; adv. editor: John Wiley & Sons, Inc., 1967-89, Macmillan Pubs., 1990-94. Recipient Disting. Svc. citation American Assn. Physics Tchrs., 1967, Hans Christian Oersted medal, 1974, Disting. Alumnae award Johns Hopkins U., 2005; named to Hall of Fame, Balt. City Coll., 1989, Rensselaer Poly. Inst., 2003; Robert Resnick Ctr. for Physics established at Rensselaer Poly. Inst., 1993, Robert Resnick Ann. Sci. Lectr. series endowed, 1993. Fellow AAAS, American Phys. Soc.; mem. AAUP, American Assn. Physics Tchrs. (v.p. 1986, pres.-elect 1987, pres. 1988), American Soc. Engring. Edn., American Inst. Physics (governing bd. 1987-90, mem. coun. Ctr. for History of Physics), Philosophic Soc. South Fla. (exec. bd. 1997-2000), Textbook Author Assn. (coun. 1990-93), Phi Beta Kappa, Sigma Xi. Achievements include rsch. publications in aerodynamics, nuclear physics, atomic physics, upper atmosphere physics, history of physics, physics edn. Home: Pittsburgh, Pa. Died Jan. 29, 2014.

**RESOR, HELEN LANSDOWNE,** advertising executive; b. Grayson, Ky., Feb. 20, 1886; d. George and Helen (Bayleff) Lansdowne; m. Stanley Resor, 1917 (dec.). Grad. h.s. With World Mfg. Co.; bill auditor Procter and Collier, Cin.; advt. writer Comml. Tribune newspaper, St. Rwys. Advt. Co., 1906; advt. writer N.Y. hdqs. Procter & Collier; copywriter J. Walter Thompson, Cin., 1908, writer NYC, 1911, v.p., then dir.; ret., 1961. Presdl. invitee to campaign for conservation of food, 1917-18; advt. campaigner for YMCA and ARC; former pres. Travelers Aid Soc.; supporter Radcliffe Coll., Planned Parenthood Assn., Babies Ward of N.Y. Postgrad. Hosp.; active feminist movement. Inductee Advt. Hall of Fame, 1967. Died Jan. 2, 1964.

**RESTOUT, DENISE,** musician; b. Paris, Nov. 24, 1915; arrived in US, 1941; d. Fernand Emile Jules and Juliette Louise François Restout. Grad., Nat. Conservatoire de Musique, Paris, 1930. Asst., sec. to Wanda Landowska Ecole de Musique Ancienne, St. Leu-La Foret, France, 1935-41, Lakeville, Conn., 1941-59; dir. Landowska Ctr., Lakeville, from 1959. Mem jury, hon patron Int Bach Competitions, 1969—81; lectr in field. Author: (book) Landowska on Music, 1965; contbr. articles, concert revs to mags; musician (soloist): Chamber Orchestra, 1939; musician: (accompanying harpsicordist) Landowska concert, 1943; musician: (solo harpsicordist) Bach Suites, others; musician: (recorded) Bach Suites (REBI); musician: (solo recorded accompanying harpsicord) Bach ETE with Landowska CCD; musician: recitals; appeared various radio and TV programs: Voice of America, 1950, Radio-Geneve, 1952, CBS Radio, 1960, 1985, Conn Pub Radio, 1985, Radio France, 1990, Video TV, 1999; appeared in documentary film: Visionary; co-prodr.: (several CDs for Pearl and others). Organist St Mary's Ch, Lakeville, 1971—97. Recipient Amicus Poloniae, Poland Mag, 1973, St. Joseph medal, Archdiocese of Hartford, 2002, Pietrzak's prize, Civitas Christiana U., Warsaw, 2003, Cardinal Glemp Gold medal, Polish Ch. Mem.: French and Am Musicological Assn., Am. Guild Organists, French Guild Organists, Am. Fedn. Musicians (Woman of the Yr 1996). Republican. Roman Catholic. Avocations: reading, photography. Deceased.

**REUBEN, DON,** lawyer; s. Michael B. and Sally (Colucci) R.; m. Evelyn Long, Aug. 27, 1948 (div.); children: Hope Reuben Boland, Michael Barrett, Timothy Don, Jeffrey Long, Howard Ellis; m. Jeannette Hurley Haywood, Dec. 13, 1971; stepchildren: Harris Hurley Haywood, Edward Gregory Haywood. BS, Northwestern U., 1949, JD, 1952. Bar: Ill. 1952, Calif. 1996, U.S. Supreme Ct. 1957. With firm Kirkland & Ellis, Chgo., 1952-78, sr. ptnr., Reuben & Proctor, Chgo., 1978-86, Isham, Lincoln & Beale, Chgo., 1986-88; sr. counsel Winston & Strawn, Chgo., 1988-94; of counsel Altheimer & Gray, Chgo., 1994—2003. Spl. asst. atty. gen. State of Ill., 1963—64, 1969, 1984; gen. counsel Tribune Co., 1965—88, Chgo. Bears Football Club, 1965—88, Cath. Archdiocese of Chgo., 1975—88; counsel spl. session Ill. Ho. of Reps., 1964, for Ill. treas. for congl., state legis. and jud. reapportionment, 1963; spl. fed. ct. master, 1968—70; mem. citizens adv. bd. to sheriff County of Cook, 1962—66, jury instrn. com., 1963—73; past mem. pub. rules com. Ill. Supreme Ct., 1963—73; past mem. pub. rels. com. Nat. Conf. State Trial Judges; com. study caseflow mgmt. in law divsn. Cook County Cir. Ct., 1979—88; adv. implementation com. U.S. Dist. Ct. No. Dist. Ill., 1981—82; mem. Chgo. Better Sch. Com., 1968—69, Chgo. Crime Commn., 1970—80; supervisory panel Fed. Defender Program, 1971—78; sec. gen. counsel, chair audit com. Palm Springs Air Mus., from 1998. Bd. dirs. Lincoln Pk. Zool. Soc., 1972—84; trustee Northwestern U., from 1977; mem. vis. com. U. Chgo. Law Sch., 1976—79; bd. dirs. Blood Bank of the Desert, 1999—2004, vice-chmn., 2003—04; chmn. gen. plan adv. com. City of Rancho Mirage, 1994—96; dir., sec. Friends of the Animal Campos, from 2004. Recipient Northwestern U. Law Sch. Alumni Merit award, 2002. Fellow: Am. Bar Found., Internat. Acad. Trial Lawyers; mem.: ABA (standing com. on fed. judiciary 1973—79, standing com. on jud. selection, tenure and compensation 1982—85), ADR Sys. America, Calif. Bar Assn., Am. Arbitration Assn. (nat. panel arbitrators 1998—2008), Am. Coll. Trial Lawyers (Rule 23 com. 1975—82, judiciary com. 1987—91), Am. Law Inst., Chgo. Bar Assn. (chmn. subcom. propriety and regulation of contingent fees com. devel. 1966—69, subcom. on media liaison 1980—82, com. on profl. info. 1980—82), Ill. Bar Assn., Casino Club, Tamarisk Country Club (hon.), Chgo. Club, Order of Coif, Beta Gamma Sigma, Beta Alpha Psi, Phi Eta Sigma. Roman Catholic. Avocation: pedigree dogs. Died Feb. 3, 2014.

**REUTER, GEORGE SYLVESTER, JR.,** educator, minister; b. Holden, Mo., Feb. 9, 1920; s. G.S. and Laura Ethelyn (Angle) R.; m. Helen Hyde, Aug. 18, 1956; children: Don L., M. Allan, K.L. BEd, Cen. Mo. State U., 1941, MEd, 1949; EdD, U. Mo., 1952; PhD (hon.), Golden State U., 1984. Cert. edn. supt., Mo., Ill., Wis., Idaho, Ariz., Ark.; ordained So. Bapt. minister. Prof., dir. U. Ark., Monticello, 1952-57; acad. dean, dir. Minot (N.D.) State U., 1957-58; res. dir. Am. Fedn. Tchrs., Chgo., 1958-65; prof. So. Ill. U., Edwardsville, 1965-66; pres. Sioux Empire Coll., Hawarden, Iowa, 1966-70; supt. schs. New Madrid Co., Howardsville, Mo., 1970-75; visiting prof. So. Ill. U., Carbondale, Ill., 1975-78; pres. Internat. Accrediting Commn., Holden, Mo., 1978-88, Internat. Assocs. for Christians, from 1989. Hon. chancellor Trinity Coll., Aba, Nigeria; provost Internat. Acad. Edn., Hawaii; vis. prof. Pusan (Korea) Union Theol. Sem., fall 1992; cons. Am. Social Hygiene Assn., Washington, 1953-58, Ark. Expt. in Tchr. Edn., Little Rock, 1952-57, Pakistani Ministry Edn., Karachi, 1980-81, Mo. Bapts. on Aging, Jefferson City, 1968-74. Co-author: One Blood, 1954, rev. edit., 1988, Democracy and Quality Education, 1955, rev. edit., 1987. Dem. committeeman, South Holden, 1986—; chmn. Deacons, First Bapt. Ch., 1984-88. Mem. Am. Assn. Sch. Adminstrs., Kiwanis (pres. Lilbourn chpt. 1967-69), Rotary (pres. New Madrid chpt. 1970), Phi Delta Kappa (Man of Yr. award N.W. chpt. 1974). Baptist. Avocation: traveling around the world. Died Apr. 16, 2001.

**REUTHE, MARJORIE SNYDER,** retired orthodonitst; b. Canadian, Tex., Apr. 16, 1914; d. Edward Henry and Nona Agnes (Alexander) Snyder; m. John Julius Reuthe, July 29, 1939; children: John Edward, Susan Kay Reuthe Gatten. Student, Park Coll., 1931-33; DDS, Baylor U., 1937; MS in Orthodontics, Northwestern U., 1939. Pvt. practice, South Bend, Ind., 1939-83; ret., 1983. Contbr. articles to profl. jours. Bd. dirs. St. Joe County Scholarship Found., South Bend; trustee First Presbyn. Ch., 1983-86. Fellow Am. Coll. Dentists, Internat. Coll. Dentists; mem. AAUW, ADA, Am. Assn. Orthodontists, Ind. State Assn. Orthodontists (past sec.-treas.), Angle Assn. Orthodontists (past pres. Mid-West comp.), St. Joe County Dental Assn., Ind. State Dental Soc. (Disting. Svc. award 1988), DAR (chaplain, sec., regent 1987-89), South Bend Altrusa Club (charter), Internat. Svc. Club, Omicron Kappa Upsilon. Avocations: lake activities, swimming, reading, sewing. Home: Mishawaka, Ind. Died May 27, 2008.

**REYES, FELICIANA AQUINO,** retired academic administrator; b. Talavera, Nueva Ecija, Philippines, June 9, 1927; d. Victorino delos Ama and Antonia de Jesus Aquino; m. Roman Domingo Reyes, Apr. 23, 1955; children: Roman Victor Aquino Reyes Jr., Rainerio Vicente Aquino Reyes, Roberto Virgilio Aquino Reyes, Ricardo Val Aquino Reyes, Ronald Vidal Aquino Reyes, Regina Vivian Aquino Reyes. BEd, Centro Escolar U., Manila, 1950, PhD in Edn., 1962; MA in English, Bryn Mawr Coll., Pa., 1953. HS tchr. Centro Escolar U., 1950—51, instr., 1953—65, grad. sch. prof., 1965—92, dean, coll. arts and scis., 1965—92, asst. v.p. student affairs, 1983—92; v.p. academic affairs Manila Ctrl. U., Caloocan City, Philippines, 1992—2004; ret., 2004. Editor: The Beige Register, Newsletter, Inner Wheel Club, 1970—74; co-author (with Lourdes Ceballos, Alfredo Sanchez): (textbooks) Cooperatives: A Direction Towards Progress, 1975; co-author: (with Luz C. Bucu) Integrating Values in the Communication Arts, Vol. 1 - 4, 1995; co-author: (with Luz C. Bucu, Emiterio Tiburcio, et. al) Educational Psychology, 1995; co-author: (with Luz C. Bucu, Rosalinda San Mateo) College Teaching in the Philippines, 1995; author: Can We Perfect the Individual, 2008. Pres. Fedn. Accrediting Agencies Philippines, Manila, 2003—05. Recipient Centennial Outstanding Alumna, Centro Escolar U., 2008. Mem.: Casa Romana Learning Ctr., Inc. (bd. chmn. 2010), Philippine Assn. Colls. and U. Commn. Accreditation (chmn. emeritus 2005). Home: Metro Manila San Juan City, Philippines. Died 2013.

**REYNOLDS, ALBERT MARTIN,** former Prime Minister of Ireland; b. Rooskey, Co. Roscommon, Ireland, Nov. 3, 1932; m. Kathleen Coen, 1962; children: Philip, Miriam, Emer, Leonie, Abbie, Cathy, Andrea Educated, Summerhill Coll., Sligo. Min. posts & telegraphs & for transport Republic of Ireland, Dublin, 1979-81, min. transp., 1980—81, min. industry & energy, 1982, Opposition spokesperson for industry and employment, 1983-85, Opposition spokesperson for energy, 1985-87, min. industry & commerce, 1987-88, min. finance, 1988-92, prime min., 1992-94; dir. Jefferson Smurfit Group, Dublin, from 1996. Leader Fianna Fáil, 1992-94; bd. dirs. AON McDonagh Boland Ltd., P.L.C. Mem. Oireachtas Joint Com. on Comml. State-Sponsored bodies, 1983-87; pres. Longford Chamber of Commerce, 1974-78. Fianna Fáil. Catholic. Home: Dublin, Ireland. Died Aug. 21, 2014.

**RHINEHART, SHELBY A.,** state legislator; b. White County, Tenn., May 5, 1927; married; 1 child. MS in Pharmacy, Samford U. Mem. Tenn. State Legis., 1958—62, 1979—2002. Democrat. Baptist. Died Sept. 19, 2002.

**RICARD, JACQUES LOUIS,** microbiologist; b. Neuilly, Seine, France, May 23, 1926; arrived in Sweden, 1968; s. Joseph Honoré and Suzanne (Chalon) R.; m. Odette Cadart, 1948 (div. 1970); children: Suzanne, Michele; m. Suoma Kanerva Leinonen, June 19, 1971; 1 child, Thomas. Diploma, Institut Agricole, Fribourg, Switzerland, 1945; AB with honors, U. Calif., Davis, 1955, MA, 1961; PhD, Oreg. State U., 1966. Cert. secondary tchr., Calif. Bacteriologist Campbell Soup Co., Sacramento, 1948-60; rsch. asst. U. Calif., Davis, 1960-61; instr. Sacramento City Coll., 1961-63; rsch. asst. Oreg. State U., Corvallis, 1963-66, asst. prof., 1966-68; vis. scientist Skogshögskolan, Stockholm, 1968-69; mgr. IC Lab., Incentive AB, Stockholm, 1969-72; pres. BINAB Bio-Innovation AB, Ålgarås, Sweden, 1972-98, tech. adviser, 1998—2008. With French infantry, 1944-45. Roman Catholic. Achievements include patents for biofungicides. Avocation: aquaculture. Home: Mariestad, Sweden. Died Jan. 22, 2014.

**RICH, ANDREA LOUISE,** retired academic administrator; b. San Diego, July 20, 1943; d. Leo and Ida Beck; m. John Rich, 1966 (div. 1985); children: Anthony, Robert. BA, UCLA, 1965, MA, 1966, PhD, 1968. Asst. prof., comm. studies, asst. dir., Office Learning Resources UCLA, LA, 1976, acting dir., media ctr., 1977, dir., office of instructional devel., 1978—80, asst. vice chancellor, office of instructional devel., 1980—86, asst. exec. vice chancellor, 1986—87, vice chancellor, acad. adminstrn., 1987—91, exec. vice chancellor, 1991—95; pres., CEO Los Angeles County Mus. Art, 1995—2006, Wallis Annenberg dir., 2003—06. Bd. dirs. Mattel, Inc., 1998—2014, Douglas Emmett, Inc., 2007—13. Trustee Save the Children Fedn., 2009—13. Died July 28, 2014.

**RICHARDS, (A)LBERT DEWEY,** retired physician, medical educator, writer; b. industry, Maine, Mar. 4, 1927; s. Albert Dodge and Nellie (Booker) Richards; m. Loretta Maychild, Sept. 7, 1992; stepchildren: Andrea Tilden, Julie Tilden, Sarah Warner, Robin Tilden; m. Emily Ricker Gamage (dec. June 7, 1989); children: Susan Finch, Michael, Donna Cotton, Catherine Hill, John, Daniel. BS with honors, U. Maine, Orono, 1956; MD, Tufts U. Sch. Medicine, Boston, 1960. Cert. Am Bd. Family Practice, 1985. Intern Maine Med. Ctr., Portland, 1960, 1961; rsch. assoc. Dartmouth Med. Sch., Hanover, NH, 1973—75; asst. prof. Tufts U. Sch. Medicine, Boston, 1975—78, assoc. prof., 1978—80; prof. Ea. Va. Med. Sch., Norfolk, 1980—85, chmn. dept. family medicine, 1980—85; ret. Pres. No. Cumberland Meml. Hosp., Bridgton, Maine, 1974; residency dir. EMMC Family Practice, Bangor, Maine, 1975—80; chief FP svc. Ea. Maine Med. Ctr., Bangor, 1975—80; residency assistance program cons. Am Acad. Family Practice, Kansas City, Mo., 1977—84; exec. com Norfolk Gen. Hosp., 1975—80; founder and pres. Mednow Urgent Care Ctrs., Orono, 1985—95, Hartland, Maine, 1985—95, Ellsworth, Maine, 1985—95, Saco, Maine, 1985—95, Salsbury, Maine, 1985—95. Author: (books) Solutions, 2002, Wide Swath, 2003, Detective's Apprentice, 2003, Live Lively Longer, 2004, Just My Luck, 2005. Cpl. 82nd airborne divsn. US Army, 1946—48, Ft. Bragg, NC. Fellow: Am. Acad. Family Practice. Home: Bridgton, Maine. Died Aug. 10, 2008.

**RICHARDS, LINDA,** nurse, educator; b. 1841; Diploma, New Eng. Hosp. Women/Children. Supt. Boston Tng. Sch. Established nursing schs., Japan; established and headed numerous tng. schs., also spl. instns. for people with mental illness. Mem. Am. Soc. Supts. Tng. Schs. (first pres.). Died 1930.

**RICHARDSON, ESTHER HARBAGE COLE,** art museum administrator; b. Phila., Nov. 11, 1894; d. John Albert and Elizabeth MacIntosh (Young) Harbage; m. Dr. Russell Richardson., Apr. 18, 1940 (dec.); children— Jane (Mrs. Paul A. McShane), Basil Smith Cole, Jr. Student, U. Wyo. Dir. bur. mdse. information Gimbels, Phila., 1935-43; dir. Clubwomen's Centre, Phila., 1943-47; cons. customer relations, 1947-50. Scientific sec. divsn. of chemistry Bulgarian Acad. of Scis., Sofia, 1972—82, vice sec. gen., 1989—91; cons. scientist Verila Chem. Works, Sofia, 1995—97. Clinic relations com., bd. dirs. Cerebral Palsy Assn., Phila. and vicinity.; Trustee Phila. Mus. Art, 1952-88, hon. trustee, 1988—. Mem. Fashion Group Inc. of N.Y. (Phila. regional dir. 1946-48, permanent chmn. costume wing Phila. Mus. Art), Phila. Peale. Episcopalian. Home: Philadelphia, Pa. Deceased.

**RICHARDSON, EVERETT VERN,** hydraulic engineer, educator, administrator, consultant; b. Scottsbluff, Nebr., Jan. 5, 1924; s. Thomas Otis and Jean Marie (Everett) R.; m. Billie Ann Kleckner, June 23, 1948; children: Gail Lee, Thomas Everett, Jerry Ray. BS, Colo. State U., 1949, MS, 1960, PhD, 1965. Registered profl. engr., Colo. From hydraulic engr. to project chief US Geol. Survey, Wyo., 1949—52, Iowa, 1952—56, rsch. hydraulic engr., 1956—63, project chief Ft. Collins, Colo., 1963—68; adminstr. Engring. Rsch. Ctr. Colo. State U., Ft. Collins, 1968—88, dir. Egypt water use project, 1977-84, prof. in charge of hydraulic program, 1982-88, dir. hydraulic lab. Engring. Rsch. Ctr., 1982-88, prof. emeritus, from 1988, dir. Egypt irrigation improvement project, 1985-90; dir. Egypt Water Rsch. Ctr. Project, Ft. Collins, 1988-89; sr. assoc. Ayers Assocs. Inc. (formerly Resource Cons./Engr., Inc.), Ft. Collins, from 1989. Dir. Consortium for Internat. Devel., Tucson, 1972-87; developer stream stability and scour at hwy. bridges course for State Dept. Transps. for NHI, FHWA; investigator for NTSB 1987 I-90 bridge failure, NY, 1997, railroad bridge failure, Ariz., CALTRAN 1995 I-5 bridge failure; chmn. peer rev. panel Turnefairbanks Rsch. Ctr. Hydraulics Lab., 2004; cons. in field; lectr. in field. Sr. author Highways in the River Environment: Hydraulic and Environmental Considerations, FHWA, 1975, 1990, Evaluating Scour at Bridge, FHWA, 1991, 1993, 1995, 2001, FHWA Hydr. Design Series No. 6: River Engineering for Highway Encroachments, 2001, Civil Engring. Handbook, 1995; co-author: Engring. Handbook, 1995, 2003; contbr. Handbook of Fluid Dynamics and Fluid Machinery, 1996, Water Resources-Environmental Planning, Management and Development, 1996, more than 200 articles to profl. jours. Mem. Ft. Collins Water Bd., 1969-84; mem. NY State Bridge Safety Assurance Task Force, 1988-91. Decorated Bronze Star, Purple Heart, Combat Infantry Badge; named hon. diplomate Am. Acad. Water Resources Engring. 2005; U.S. Govt. fellow MIT, 1962-63. Fellow: ASCE (chair task com., bridge scour rsch. 1990—96, editor Compendium of Stream Stability and Scour Papers 1991—98, vice chair 1997—2002, J.S. Stevens award 1961, hydraulics divsn. task com. excellence award 1993, Hans Albert Einstein award 1996); mem.: Am. Acad. Water Resource Engrs. (hon. diplomate 2005), Internat. Congress for Irrigation and Drainage, Sigma Xi, Sigma Tau, Chi Epsilon. Home: Fort Collins, Colo. Died 2013.

**RICHARDSON, H. SMITH, JR.,** manufacturing executive; b. 1920; Pres. Richardson-Vicks, Inc., 1958—62, chmn., dir. Wilton, Conn. Chmn. Smith Richardson Found. Died 1999.

**RICHARDSON, IAN WILLIAM,** actor; b. Edinburgh, Apr. 7, 1934; s. John and Margaret R.; m. Maroussia Frank, Feb. 2, 1961; children: Jeremy, Miles. Diploma in Acting and Teaching, Royal Scottish Acad. Music and Drama, D in Drama, 1999; D (hon.), Stirling U., 2006. Actor Royal Shakespeare Co., Stratford on Avon and London, 1960-75, Shaw Festival Theatre, Niagara, Ont., Can., 1977. Appeared in plays including My Fair Lady, Broadway, 1976-77, The Miser, 1995, The Magistrate, 1997-98, The Seven Ages of Man, 1999, The Hollow Crown, 2002-04, The Creeper, 2005; films and TV plays include Tinker, Tailor, Soldier, Spy, Private Shulz, The Sign of Four, The Hound of the Baskervilles, Phantom of the Opera, 1990, The Gravy Train, 1990, House of Cards, 1991, The Gravy Train Goes East, 1991, To Play the King, 1993, Foreign Affairs Remember, Savage Play, 1994, The Final Cut, 1995; films include Brazil, Whoops!, Apocalypse, The Fourth Protocol, Cry Freedom, The Fifth Province, 1996, Dark City, 1998, From Hell, 2000, Remake, 2005; TV programs includes Star Quality, Porterhouse Blue, The Winslow Boy, 1989, An Ungentlemanly Act, 1992, Catherine the Great (miniseries), 1994, Gormenghast, 1999, (miniseries) Magician's House, 1999, Murder Rooms, 1999, Murder Rooms II, 2000, Strange, BBC TV, 2001, 03, (ITV) Miss Marple, 2004, Bleak House, 2005, Booze Cruise2-BBC, (films) Joyeux Noël, 2005, Greyfriars Bobby, 2005, Desaccord Parfair, 2006; author prefaces to Shakespearean works. Recipient CBE award, 1989, BAFTA award, 1991, award Royal TV Soc., 1991. Fellow Royal Scottish Acad. Music and Drama; mem. SAG, Brit. Actors Equity, Actors Equity. Home: London, England. Died Feb. 9, 2007.

**RICKARDS, RICHARD BARRIE,** palaeontologist, educator, curator; b. Leeds, Eng., June 12, 1938; s. Robert and Eva (Sudborough) Rickards; m. Christine Townsley (div. 1991); 1 child, Jeremy. BSc, Hull U., Eng., 1960, PhD, 1963, DSc, 1990; ScD, Cambridge U., Eng., 1977. Chartered geologist. Curator Univ. Coll. London, 1963-64; rsch. asst. U. Cambridge, 1964-67; sr. scientific officer Brit. Mus. Natural History, London, 1967; lectr. in geology Trinity Coll., Dublin, 1967-69; univ. lectr., curator Sedgwick Mu. U. Cambridge, 1969-90, univ. reader, curator, 1990-2000, prof. paleontology and biostratigraphy, 2000—05, prof. emeritus, from 2005. Professorial fellow and ofcl. lectr. Emmanuel Coll., U. Cambridge, 1978-2004, life fellow, 2004-, cur. mus., 1994-99, admissions tutor in scis., 1983-87; univ. proctor U. Cambridge, 1983-85. Author: (with R. Webb) Fishing for Big Pike, 1971, Big Pike, 3d edit., 1986, Perch, 1974, (with R. Webb) Fishing for Big Tench, 1976, 2d edit., 1986, Pike, 1976, (with K. Whitehead) Plugs and Plug Fishing, 1976, Spinners, Spoons and Wobbled Baits, 1977, A Textbook of Spinning, 1987, (with N. Fickling) Zander, 1979, 3d edit., 1990, (with K. Whitehead) Fishing Tackle, 1981, (with K. Whitehead) A Fishery of Your Own, 1984, Angling: Fundamental Principles, 1986, (with M. Gay) A Technical Manual of Pike Fishing, 1986, (with M. Gay) Pike, 1989, (with M. Bannister) The Ten Greatest Pike Anglers, 1991, Success with Pike, 1992, Success with the Lure, 1993, Fishers on the Green Roads, 2003, (with M. Bannister), The Great Modern Piles Anglers, 2006, The Great Modern Pike Anglers, 2007; Richard Walker: Biography of An Angling Legend, 2007, (with Tim Baily) Nile Perch: The Ultimate Guide, 2008; co-author: Encyclopaedia of Fishing, 1991; editor: River Piking, 1987, Best of Pikelines, 1988; contbr. over 700 articles on angling to newspapers and mags.; author: Graptolites: Writing in the Rocks, 1991; editor: (with D.C. Palmer) H.B. Whittington, Trilobites, 1992; contbr. over 250 scientific articles and monographs, mostly on fossils and evolution, to profl. jours. Fellow Geol. Soc. U.K. (coun. 1960—, Murchison Fundaward 1982, Lyell medal 1997); mem. Palaeontol. Assn. (coun. 1987-95), Yorkshire Geol. Soc. (John Phillips medal 1988). Avocations: marathon running, angling, fisheries management, environment agency work, writing. Home: Swaffham Bulbeck, England. Died Nov. 5, 2009.

**RICKETTS, WALTER PAXTON,** state health official, physical education educator; b. Greensburg, Kans., Mar. 29, 1926; s. Joe Glen and Cora Luella (Dent) Ricketts; m. Elliott Winifred Douglas, Aug. 28, 1949; children: Paxton Douglas, Marla Sue, Dent Kerry. BA, U. Nebr., 1950; MA, U. Wyo., 1963. Tchr. phys. edn., coach Jr. and Sr. HS, Torrington, Wyo., 1950—64; tchr. phys. edn. Elem. Sch., Torrington, 1964—68; head dept. phys. edn. Eastern Wyo. Coll., Torrington, 1968—71; con. Wyo. State Dept. Edn., Cheyenne, 1971—86; dir. Wyo. State Health, Phys. Edn., Recreation and Dance, Cheyenne, 1971—86. Cons. presenter in field. Contbr. articles to state publs. Explorer leader Wyo.-Nebr. Coun. Boy Scouts Am, 1952—60, council mem., 1955—58; mgr.-lifeguard swimming pool Torrington; dir. Jaycees Summer Youth Recreation programs, 1950—59; golf pro Goshen County Golf Course, 1965—71; cons. Wyo. and Rocky Mountain Area Nat. Golf Found., 1974—85. Served with USN, 1944—46, served with USN, 1951—52, Korea. Recipient Outstanding Svc. award, Am. Alliance Wyo. Health, Phys. Edn., Recreation and Dance, 1983. Mem.: AAHPERD(Wyo.) (pres. 1969—70, Honor award 1974), AAHPERD(Ctrl. Dist) (life; pres. 1980—81, Appreciation Svc. cert. 1980), NEA (life), Nat. Intramural Assn., Nat. Intramural Assn., Wyo. State Employees Assn., Wyo. Assn. Suprs. and Curriculum Dirs., Nat. Soc. State Dirs. Health, Phys. Edn., Recreation and Dance (sec., treas 1982—83), Order Eastern Star, Shriners, Masons, Phi Delta Kappa. Republican. Congregationalist. Home: Cheyenne, Wyo. Died May 6, 1996.

**RICKEY, JUNE EVELYN MILLION,** retired educator; b. Joliet, Ill., Oct. 15, 1923; d. Lawrence Ernest and Ethel Alden (Ringler) Million; m. Paul Rickey, June 29, 1944; children: William, Mary Ann, John, James. BS in Edn., Ill. State U., 1946; MA in Journalism, Adams State Coll., 1970. Cert. tchr., Colo. Tchr. English Ottawa (Ill.) Twp. High Sch., 1946-47, Alamosa (Colo.) High Sch., 1953-55, 59-77, Evans Jr. High Sch., Alamosa, 1956-59; tchr. drama McAllen (Tex.) High Sch., 1955-56. Publicity chmn. Women's Citizenship Club, Alamosa, 1978, Am. Cancer Soc., bd. dirs., 1986—; editorial staff San Luis Valley Hist. Soc., Alamosa, 1985—, Ethnic heritage Project, 1977-78; trustee Creede (Colo.) Repertory Theatre, 1987, sec.-treas., 1987-90. Wall St. Jour. grantee, 1964. Mem. AAUW (sec. 1983-87), Adams State Coll. Alumni Assn. (bd. dirs.), PEO Sisterhood, DAR. Democrat. Roman Catholic. Avocations: sw history, collecting indian jewelry. Deceased.

**RICOEUR, PAUL,** philosopher, literary critic; b. Valence, France, Feb. 27, 1913; s. Jules and Florentine (Favre) R.; m. Simone Lejas, Aug. 14, 1935; children: Jean-Paul, Marc, Noëlle, Olivier (dec.), Etienne. Grad., U. Rennes, France, 1932, U. Sorbonne, Paris, 1935, LittD, 1950; PhD (hon.), U. Basel, Switzerland, 1964, U. Montreal, 1968, U. Chgo., 1969, U. Nijmegen, 1970, Ohio State U., 1970, DePaul U., 1973, U. Zurich, Switzerland, 1973, Boston Coll., 1975. H.s. tchr., Saint-Brieuc, France, 1933-34, Colmar, France, 1935-36, Lorient, France, 1937-39; attaché de recherche Ctr. Nat. de la Recherche Sci., 1945-48; prof. philosophy U. Strasbourg, France, 1948-57, U. Paris, Sorbonne, France, 1957-67, U. Paris-X, Nantone, 1967-81. Vis. prof. Yale U., New Haven, 1964, U. Montréal, 1965, U. Louvain, 1970; John Nuveen prof. of Philosophy, U. Chgo., 1971. Writings include: Karl Jaspers et la philosophie de l'existence, 1947, Gabriel Marcel et Karl Jaspers: Philosophie du mystere et philosophie du paradoxe, 1948, Philosophie de la volonté, 3 vols., 1950-60, Histoire et vérité, 1955, Etre: Essence et substance chez Platon et Aristotle, 1960, Husserl: An Analysis of His Phenomenology, 1968, De l'Interprétation: Essai sur Freud, 1967, (with others) Pourquoi la philosophie?, 1968, Le Conflit des interprétations: Essais d'hermeneutique, 1969, (with Alistair MacIntyre) The Religious Significance of Atheism, 1969, Les Incidences theologiques des recherches actuelles concernant le langage, 1969, (with Leon Dion and Edward Sheffield)

L'Enseignement superieur: Bilans et prospective, 1971, Political and Social Essays, 1974, La Métaphore vive, 1975, (with others) Les Cultures et le temps: Etudes preparees pour L'UNESCO, 1975, (with Emmanuel Levinas and Xavier Tilliette) Jean Wahl et Gabriel Marcel, 1976, (with others) La Revelation, 1977, La Sémantique de l'action, 1977, The Philosophy of Paul Ricoeur: An Anthology of His Work, 1978, Main Treads in Philosophy, 1978, The Contribution of French Historiography to the Theory of History, 1980, Essays on Biblical Interpretation, 1980, Hermeneutics and the Human Sciences: Essays on Language, Action and Interpretation, 1981, Temps et récit, 1983, La Configuration du temps dans le récit de fiction, 1984, Le temps raconté, 1986, Du texte à l'action, 1986, Soi-même comme un autre, 1990, Lectures I, 1991, Lecture II, 1992, Lectures III, 1993; editor: Historie de la philosophie allemande, 3d edit., 1954, L'Homme et sa raison, 1956. Served French Army, 1936-37, 39-45, prisoner of war, 1940-45. Decorated Croix de Guerre with palme; recipient Prix Cavailles, 1951, Prix Hegel République fédérale d'Allemagne, 1985, Prix Karl-Jaspers de l'université de Heidelberg, 1990, Prix Leopold Lucas de l'université de Tubingen, 1989, Grand prix de philosophie de l'Académie française, 1991. Home: Châtenay-Malabry, France. Died May 20, 2005.

**RIEDEL, BERNARD EDWARD,** retired pharmaceutical sciences educator; b. Provost, Alta., Can., Sept. 25, 1919; s. Martin and Naomi E. (Klingaman) R.; m. Julia C. McClurg, Mar. 5, 1944 (dec. Mar. 1992); children: Gail Lynne, Dwain Edward, Barry Robert; m. Della Williams, Sept. 2, 2000. BS in Pharmacy, U. Alta., Edmonton, 1943, MS in Pharmacology, 1949, DSc (hon.), 1990; PhD in Biochemistry, U. Western Ont., 1953. Lectr., asst. prof. Faculty of Pharmacy U. Alta., Edmonton, 1946-49, asst. prof. then assoc. prof., 1953-58, prof., 1959-67, exec. asst. to v.p., 1961-67; dean, prof. Faculty Pharm. Scis. U. B.C., Vancouver, Canada, 1967-84, coord. Health Scis. Centre, 1977-84. Mem. sci. adv. com. Health Rsch. Found. of B.C., 1991-95. Contbr. numerous articles on pharmacology to profl. jours. Elder Ryerson United Ch.; mem. exec. bd. Boy Scouts Can., Edmonton Region, Alta.; mem. Cancer Control Agy. of B.C., trustee 1979-86, v.p., 1984, pres. 1985-86; bd. dirs. B.C. Lung Assn., 1988-2000, v.p., 1989, pres., 1990-91; chmn., bd. dirs. B.C. Organ Transplant Soc., 1986-89, hon. bd. dirs., 2000. Wing comdr. RCAF, 1943-46, 49-67. Decorated mem. Order of Can.; recipient Gold medal in Pharmacy, 1943; Centennial medal, 1967, 75th Anniversary medal U. B.C., 1990; Can Forces decoration, 1965; Commemorative medal for 125th Anniversary of the Confedn. of Can., 1992, Spl. Svcs. award Assn. Faculties of Pharmacy of Can., 2001, Queen Elizabeth II Golden Jubilee medal, 2002. Mem. Alta. Pharm. Assn. (hon. life), Can. Pharm. Assn. (hon. life), Assn. of Faculties of Pharmacy of Can. (hon. life, chmn. 1959, 69, Spl. Svc. award 2001), Can. Biochem. Soc., Pharmacol. Soc. Can., Can. Assn. of Univ. Tchrs., Can. Soc. Hosp. Pharmacists, B.C. Coll. Pharmacists (hon. life), U. B.C. Profs. Emeriti Divsn. Alumni Assn. (pres. 1993-95). Home: Vancouver, Canada. Deceased.

**RIETVELD, PIET,** economist; b. Berkel en Rodenrijs, Netherlands, Dec. 15, 1952; s. Aart Rietveld and Trijntje Van der Voort; m. Marjoke Van Wingerden, Oct. 11, 1950. PhD, Vrije Universiteit, Amsterdam, 1980. Economics U., 1980. Assoc. prof. Free U., Amsterdam, 1985—90, prof., 1990—2013. Chmn. NECTAR, Amsterdam, Netherlands, 2001—05. Recipient Hendrik Muller prize, KNAW, 1999. Fellow: Tinbergen Inst. (life). Died Nov. 1, 2013.

**RIGANTI DI SERRES, MARIO,** reliability engineer; b. Turin, Italy, Jan. 2, 1930; s. Enrico and Angelina (Gruppi) Riganti. Projector Fiat Auto, Turin, 1948-65, Fiat Rsch., Turin, 1965-70, Fiat Nuclear, Turin, 1965-85; coord. modern and particle physics Ancient's U., Turin, from 1995. Adviser Assn. Ex-Allievi Fiat, Turin, 1957; magister emeritus in sci. Pro Deo U. of N.J., 1997-99; mem. h.c. nuclear physic Acad. Europeau U. Moscow. Contbr. articles to profl. jours. Judge Corte Assise d'Appello, Turin, 1971. Mem. Ancients Group Fiat, Soc. Italian Orgn. Internat., Ctr. Internat. Study Sturziani. Roman Catholic. Avocations: study of astrophysics and relativity, finance, economic policy. Deceased.

**RIGAUT, JEAN PAUL,** medical and biomathematical researcher; b. Paris, Apr. 3, 1944; s. Pierre and Jeannette Boraly; m. Françoise Petitguillaume, 1966 (div. 1976); 1 child, Benoît; m. Lise Barreau, 1976 (div. 1985); 1 child, Aloys; m. Angela Downs, Aug. 22, 1992. MD, U. Paris, 1970; diploma in Enzymology, U. Paris 7, 1972; PhD, U. Paris 13, 1978, DSc, 1984. Externe Hosp. Paris, 1963-68; med. cons. Hosp. Robert Ballenger, Aulnay, France, 1970-88, Hosp. St. Denis, France, 1972-80, neonatologist, 1972-85; lectr. U. Paris 7, 1980-85; chargé rsch. Nat. Inst. Health and Medicine, Paris, 1985—87; dir. rsch. Nat. Inst. Health and Med. Rsch., Paris, from 1987. Expert rsch. cons. European Union, Luxembourg, 1983-88, WHO-Europe, Copenhagen, 1984-87; with Internat. Com. Epidemiology of Nickel, 1988-90; dir. Image Analysis in Cell Pathology Lab. Hosp. St. Louis, U. Paris VII, 1995—. Co-editor: Quantitative Image Analysis in Cancer Cytology and Histology, 1986; joint creator (with P. Kueny) computer assisted art; mem. referees and editl. coms. internat. scis. jours., including Jour. Microscopy, Cytometry, others; contbr. 110 articles to sci. jours., 25 chpts. to books. Fellow Royal Microscopical Soc.; mem. Internat. Soc. for Stereology, Internat. Soc. for Analytical Cytology, European Soc. for Analytical Cellular Pathology (hon.), Assn. Française de Cytométrie (hon.). Avocations: music, oboe, genealogy, northumbrian small pipes. Home: Triel-sur-Seine, France. Died Apr. 24, 2005.

**RIGHTS, EDITH MARIE ANDERSON,** retired librarian; b. Kearney, Nebr., Sept. 27, 1927; d. Frans Leander and Ruth Mary (Gitchel) Anderson; m. Robert Matthew Rights, Aug. 21, 1949; children: David Leander, Bruce Theodore, John Christian. BA, Bethany Coll., 1950; MA, Montclair State Coll., 1962; MS in Libr. Sci., Columbia U., 1983. Acting libr. Bethany Coll. Libr., Lindsborg, Kans., 1948; part-time staff Montclair (N.J.) State Coll., 1950-52; part-time staff mem. Upsala Coll., East Orange, N.J., 1966-68; libr. Montclair Art Mus., 1968—97, Soc. African Missions, 1997—2002. Seminar panelist grad. sch. Rutgers U., New Brunswick, 1980; libr. cons. Parrish Art Mus., Southampton, 1983. Curator, author (exhbn. and catalog) Ex Libris: Selected Bookplates of Arthur Nelson Macdonald, 1986, The Bookplate Work of David McNeely Stauffer, 1990, (book) The Bookplates of A.N. Macdonald, 1986, The Modern Pictorial Bookplate in the United States, 1990, Bookplates from the Permanent Collection, Kaleidiscopic Views, 1993, Charles Dexter Allen, 2000, Women Bookplate Artists, 2002-05, Bookplate for Matthew Taylor Melluni, 2003; editor: The Gitchel Letter, 1995—. Co-chairperson Art in Sussex County (N.J.), 1980-82; chairperson Art Librs. Soc. N.J., 1970-72, 80-82. Recipient 1st prize 4th Annual Exbn., Sumi-e Soc. N. Am., N.Y.C., 1966. Mem. AAUW, Art Librs. Soc. N.Am., Am. Soc. Bookplate Collectors and Designers, Bookplate Soc. London. Republican. Lutheran. Avocations: reading, music, genealogy, oragami, sumi-e. Home: Montclair, NJ. Died Sept. 20, 2013.

**RIMEL, IRA WESLEY,** writer, US Navy supply officer, real estate specialist, real estate appraiser, real estate broker; b. Wibaux, Mont., Jan. 10, 1921; s. Ira Dice and Hazel Barbara (Webber) Rimel; m. Mary Mackinlay Weir, Dec. 13, 1943 (div.); children: Patricia, Valerie, Linda, David, Glenn. Basic sci./engring, Mont. Sch. Mines, 1943—44; BA in mgmt./acctg., U. Wash., 1943—47; Navy supply, acctg. grad., Harvard Grad. Sch. Bus., 1945—46; nat. security, econ., Indust. Coll. Armed Forces, 1965. Tech. writer Military Manuals Co., Renton, Wash., 1952—55; indsl. agent No. Pacific Railway, Seattle, 1955—58; right of way agent/supr. Mont. Hwy. Dept., Helena, 1958—65; right of way agent Lane County, Eugene, Oreg., 1965—86; columnist Fishing & Hunting News, Seattle, 1992—95; freelance writer, from 1956; pres. Republic of Korea; supply officer Korea Liaison Office; rep. USN, Republic of Korea; supply officer USS Burlington; mem. North Korea Wonsan Harbor. Ensign, reserve, supply, disbursing, acctg. officer U.S. Navy Naval Prison, Norfolk, Va., 1946; LTJG supply officer liaison U.S. Navy, Republic of Korea, 1950—51. Author: (short stories) Dynamic Tension, 1990 (First Prize, 1990), Lucky Man, 2002 (Best of Show/Class, 2002), Winter Travel, 2002 (First Prize, 2002). Adj., publicity officer/comdr. Disabled Am. Vet., Renton, Wash., 1952—58, Wash. publicity officer Seattle, 1953—58; lifetime mem. VFW, Marcola, Oreg., 1960—2013. Lt. jr. grade USN, 1942—46, WWII, Korea, lt. jr. grade USN, 1950—51, WWII, Japan, selected for V-12 Coll. Prog. USN, supply officer USN. Recipient corr., Mont. Sports Outdoors, Missoula, 1959, Author "Lady Gets Her Buck", 1959, Korean Svc. medal, Korean War Svc. medal, Appreciation award; named rep. to Rep. Korea, Yokosuka, Japan, Celebration of Commissioning Frigates to Korea, U.S. Navy, 1950; named to ND Directory Writers, from 2004. Mem.: Am. Legion (life), DAV (life). Avocations: hunting, fishing, boating, horseback riding, gardening. Home: Saint Marie, Mont. Died July 13, 2014.

**RING, HANS,** metal working company executive; b. Stockholm, May 19, 1927; s. Albert Herman and Anna Louise (Diem) R.; m. Ruth Viola (Pettersson), Mar. 27, 1954; children: Kristina, Elisabet, Helena. Diploma in engring., Stockholm Tech. Inst., Stockholm, 1945. Flight engine test engr. ABA/SILA (name changed to SAS), Stockholm, 1945—47; engr. Royal Swedish Air Force Hdqr., Sweden, 1949—51; mgr. motor works BMW MC Sweden, Stockholm, 1951—54; prin. Hans Ring Motor and Sport, Borås, Sweden, 1954—60; sales rep. various companies, Borås, Sweden, 1960—65; propr. Hans Ring and Co. AB, Borås, Sweden, 1965—80, cons. Anderstorp, Sweden, 1980—97. Patentee of mounting arrangement. Capt. Royal Swedish Air Defence Res., 1947-78. Avocations: photography, motorcycling. Home: Fristad, Sweden. Died Oct. 19, 2004.

**RISKA, ERIK BERNHARD,** medical educator; b. Oct. 12, 1924; MD, U. Helsinki, Finland, 1956; specialist in gen. surgery, 1963, specialist in orthop. surgery, 1963. Registration Nat. Med. Bd., 1951. Registrar surg. dept. U. Ctrl. Hosp., Helsinki, 1952, 55, 57; registrar Orthopaedics Hosp. of the Invalid Found., Helsinki, 1958-62, sr. registrar, asst. head, 1963-65; sr. surgeon surg. dept. Koskela Hosp., Helsinki, 1966-68; sr. surgeon, asst. head dept. orthopaedics & traumatology U. Ctrl. Hosp., Helsinki, 1969-77, assoc. prof. clin. surgery dept. orthopaedics & traumatology, 1978-88, ret., 1988; head Dextra Med. Ctr., Helsinki, 1964-86, prof., head, from 1987. Sec. meeting Nordic Orthopaedic Assn., Helsinki, 1964; guest spkr. in field. Corr. editor Injury (The Brit. Jour. Accident Surgery), 1973—, Orthopaedics, 1989—, Jour. Orthopaedic Rheumatology, 1989—, Orthopaedic Internat., 1992—; mem. editl. bd. Acta Orthopaedica Scandinavica, 1979-86, chmn. editl. bd., 1979-86; contbr. numerous articles to profl. jours. Mil. svc., 1944-45. Recipient award Nordic Orthopaedic Assn., 1964. Fellow Internat. Coll. Surgeons (bd. mem. 1965-70, v.p. Finnish sect. 1979-80, pres. Finnish sect. 1981-85); mem. Brit. Orthopaedic Traveling Assn. (corr. mem.), Österreichische Gesellschaft für Unfallchirurgie (corr. mem.), Am. Orthopaedic Assn. (corr. mem.), Finnish Orthopaedic Assn. (hon. mem., bd. mem. 1964-70), Finska Läkaresällskapet, Finnish Med. Assn., Finnish Surg. Assn., Finnish Orthopaedic Assn., Scandinavian Surg. Assn., Scandinavian Orthpaedic Assn., European Hip Soc. (pres. 1995-97, pres. 2nd Domestic Meeting 1996), many others. Home: Helsinki, Finland. Died Mar. 2005.

**RISSER, PAUL GILLAN,** retired academic administrator, botanist; b. Blackwell, Okla., Sept. 14, 1939; s. Paul Crane and Jean (McCluskey) R.; children: David, Mark, Stephen, Scott, Amy, Sarah BA, Grinnell Coll., 1961; MS in Botany, U. Wis., 1965, PhD in Botany and Soils, 1967. From asst. prof. to prof. botany U. Okla., 1967-81, asst. dir. biol. sta., chmn. dept. botany and microbiology, 1977-81, prof., chmn. rsch. cabinet, 2006—14, exec. dir. Econ. Devel. Generating Excellence, 2008—14; dir. Okla. Biol. Survey, 1971-77; chief Ill. Natural History Survey, 1981-86; program dir., ecosystem studies NSF; provost and v.p. acad. affairs U. N.Mex., 1989-92; pres. Miami U., Oxford, Ohio, 1993—96, Oreg. State U., 1996—2002; chancellor Okla. Sys. Higher Edn., 2003—06; acting dir. Nat. Mus. Nat. History, Washington, 2007—08; exec. dir. Econ. Devel. Generating Excellence (EDGE), Okla., 2008—12. Author: (with Kathy Cornelison) Man and the Biosphere, 1979, (with others) The True Prairie Ecosystem, 1981; contbr. numerous articles to profl. jours., chapter to books, sci. papers. Trustee Pioneer Multi-County Library Bd. Mem. American Acad. Arts & Scis., Ecol. Soc. America (pres.), Brit. Ecol. Soc., Soc. Range Mgmt., Southwestern Assn. Naturalists (pres.), American Inst. Biol. Sci. (pres.), Torrey Bot. Club, Nat. Rsch. Coun. (chair bd. Environ. Sci. and Toxicology), Inst. Ecol. Scis. (chair bd.); fellow American Acad. Advancement Sci. Presbyterian. Died July 10, 2014.

**RITTER, BRUCE,** priest, former religious charity organization administrator; b. Trenton, NJ, Feb. 25, 1927; s. Louis Charles and Julia Agnes (Morrissey) R. S.T.D., Seraphicum Pontifical U. of St. Bonaventure, Rome, 1958; L.H.D. (hon.), Niagara U., 1979, Lemoyne Coll., 1980, Fairfield U., 1981, Iona Coll., Amherst Coll., St. Francis Coll., 1982, Fordham U., 1983, Bellarmine Coll., 1984, Drew U., St. Peter's Coll., Pace U., U. Medicine and Dentistry, NJ, 1985; H.H.D. (hon.), Stonehill Coll., St. Francis Coll., Loretto, Pa., 1981, Franciscan Community; D.Ministry honoris causa, Immaculate Conception Sem., 1981; D.Pub. Service (hon.), Villanova U., 1981; LL.D., Chestnut Hill Coll., 1981; D.Humanitarian Services (hon.), Duquesne U., Providence Coll., 1982; D.Sc. (hon.), Boston Coll., 1983, Quincy Coll., 1985. Joined Order Minor Conventuals (Franciscan); ordained priest Roman Catholic Ch., 1956. Prof. theology Manhattan Coll., NYC, 1963-68; founder, pres. Covenant House, NYC, 1972-90. Author: Covenant House: Lifeline to the Street, 1987, Sometimes God has a Kid's Face, 1988. Commr. Atty. Gen.'s Commn. on Pornography, Dept. Justice, 1985; mem. adv. com. N.Y. State Clergy; bd. dirs. Americares Found., New Canaan, Conn. Served with USN, 1945-46 Recipient numerous awards including Elizabeth Ann Seton medal Coll. Mt. St. Vincent, 1978, Elliot Black award Am. Ethical Union of Boston, 1978, Golden Doughnut award Salvation Army, 1979, Franciscan Internat. award, 1979, Robert E. Gallagher award Cath. Charities Family and Children's Services, 1980, Kewetanda award Camp Fire Council Greater N.Y., 1981, Msgr. Lester Quinn Community and Humanity award, 1981, youth activity award N.J. State council K.C., 1982, Dr. Luke Mulligan Met. award Carmelite Scholarship Dinner, 1982, Pub. Service medal N.Y. State Bar Assn., 1982, St. Francis award St. Francis Boys' Homes, Inc., 1984, Jefferson Cup Exec. Forum, 1984, Cardinal Gibbons award Cath. U. Am., 1984 Life mem. Nat. Chaplain's Assn. (Legion of Honor award 1980) Died Oct. 7, 1999.

**RIVERA-REYES, GLADYS M. (GLADYS DALTON),** retired stenographer, court reporter; b. Carthage, Ill., Dec. 7, 1909; d. Carl Olaf and Anna Mathilda Sundstrom; m. Henry Gerry Dalton, Oct. 15, 1937 (dec.); 1 child, Denny Carlanne Dalton Fritsche; m. Ramon Luis Rivera-Reyes, July 1, 1969 (dec.). Student, Kans. U., 1928—29; BS, tchr.'s cert., Northwestern U., 1931. Head cashier Chgo. World's Fair, 1933—34; entertainer, pianist, accordianist, singer, actress Chgo. Fedn. Musicians, 1934—37; civilian gen. ct. martial reporter USAF, 1944—46; stenotype conv. reporter, 1949—89; entertainer Denver Musicians Assn., 1952—61, 1989. Contbr. poetry to anthologies. Mem.: Nat. Ct. Reporters Assn. (life), Denver Musicians Assn. (life), Chgo. Fedn. Musicians (life). Avocations: poetry, painting, singing, piano. Deceased.

**RIVERS, JOAN (JOAN ALEXANDRA MOLINSKY),** comedienne; b. NYC, June 8, 1937; d. Meyer C. and Beatrice (Grushman) Molinsky; m. Edgar Rosenberg, July 15, 1965 (dec. Aug. 14, 1987); 1 child, Melissa. BA, Barnard Coll., 1958. Fashion coordinator Bond Clothing Store; founder Joan Rivers Classics Collection, 1990, Joan Rivers Worldwide Enterprises, 1996. Mem. From Second City, 1961-62; TV debut Tonight Show, 1965; Las Vegas debut, 1969; nat. syndicated columnist Chgo. Tribune, 1973-76; creator: CBS TV series Husbands and Wives, 1976-77; host: Emmy Awards, 1983; guest hostess: Tonight Show, 1983-86; hostess The Late Show Starring Joan Rivers, 1986-87, Hollywood Squares, 1987, (morning talk show) Joan Rivers (Daytime Emmy award 1990), 1989-93, Can We Shop? Home Shopping Network, 1994, (radio) The Joan Rivers Show, 1997-2002, (TV series) E! Pre-awards Show, 1995-2004, red carpet events, TV Guide Channel, 2005-07, Fashion Police, 2011-14; originator, screenwriter TV movie The Girl Most Likely To, 1973, How to Murder A Millionaire, 1990, Jackie Collins' Lady Boss, 1992, Tears and Laughter: The Joan and Melissa Rivers Story, 1994; cable TV spl. Joan Rivers and Friends Salute Heidi Abromowitz, 1985; (films) The Swimmer, 1968, Uncle Sam, The Muppets Take Manhattan, 1984, The Smurfs, 2011; co-author, dir.: (films) Rabbit Test, 1978, Spaceballs (voice only), 1987, Serial Mom, 1994 Goosed, 1998, L'Intern, 2000, Shrek 2, 2004; actress: theatre prodn. Broadway Bound, 1988, Sally Marr...and her escorts, 1994; featured in (documentaries) Joan Rivers: A Piece of Work, 2010; recs. include: comedy album What Becomes a Semi-Legend Most, 1983; author: Having a Baby Can be a Scream, 1974, The Life and Hard Times of Heidi Abromowitz, 1984, (autobiography with Richard Meryman) Enter Talking, 1986, (with Richard Meryman), Still Talking, 1991, Jewelry, 1995, Bouncing Back: I've Survived Everything...and I Mean Everything...and You Can Too!, 1997, From Mother to Daughter: Thoughts and Advice on Life, Love and Marriage, 1998, Don't Count the Candle, Just Keep the Fire Lit, 1999, Men Are Stupid...And They Like Big Boobs: A Woman's Guide to Beauty Through Plastic Surgery, 2008, Murder at the Academy Awards: A Red Carpet Murder Mystery, 2009, I Hate Everyone...Starting With Me, 2012, Diary of a Mad Diva, 2014; debuted on Broadway (play) Broadway Bound, 1988; creator: (seminar) You Deserve To Be Happy, 1995; columnist (magazines) She Says/She Says, McCall's mag. (with daughter Melissa), 1999-2000, Star Mag. Fashion column (with daughter Melissa), 2002-03; actress (guest appearances) Suddenly Susan, 1998-99, Spaceballs: The Animated Series, 2008-09, Louie, 2011; actress: (reality TV series) Joan & Melissa: Joan Knows Best?, 2011-14 Nat. chmn. Cystic Fibrosis, from 1982; benefit performer for AIDS, 1984; hon. chair Night of A Thousand Gowns, Imperial Court of NY, 2009; vol. God's Love We Deliver, bd. dirs., 1994—2014. Recipient CLIO awards for comms., 1976, 1982, Jimmy award for best comedian, 1987, 1991, Accessories Coun. award of Excellence, 1997, Rebekah Kohut award for Svc. in Cmty., 2004, winner Celebrity Apprentice, 2009; named Hadassah Woman of Yr., 1983, Harvard Hasty Pudding Soc. Woman of Yr., 1984. Mem. Phi Beta Kappa. Jewish. Died Sept. 4, 2014.

**RIX, DONALD MELVIN,** food products executive; b. Bluffton, Ind., June 12, 1930; s. Lewis Wilbur and Ova Pauline (Collins) R.; m. Donna B. Cox, Aug. 1, 1956 (dec. May 1975); children: Carol, Tamara, Donald M.; m. Lenora A. Mace, Feb. 4, 1977. Meat mgr. Marsh Super Markets Inc., Indpls., 1950—59, meat supr., 1959—62, meat buyer Yorktown, Ind., 1962—70, meat merchandiser, 1970—79, dir. merchandising, 1979—82, v.p. merchandising, 1982—97. Mem.: Ind. Beef Cattle Assn. (bd. dirs.), Ind. Pork Prodrs. Assn. (bd. dirs.), Nat. Pork Prodrs. Assn. (advisor). Republican. Methodist. Home: Muncie, Ind. Died Feb. 7, 1997.

**RIZZO, LAWRENCE LOUIS,** data processing executive; b. Bridgeton, NJ, Apr. 16, 1950; s. Santo and Catherine (Campregher) R.; m. Kay Lovonne Linderman, Aug. 23, 1969; children: Kelly Louise, Santo James. Registered bus. programmer. Computer operator Gen. Data Processing Co., Bridgeton, 1969; asst. data processing mgr. M.C. Schrank Co., Bridgeton, 1969—72; data processing mgr. Bridgeton Dyeing & Finishing Co., 1972—73; database adminstr. Wheaton Glass Co., Millville, N.J., 1973—79; pres. CLM Assocs., Bridgeton, 1975—81, Rizzo Data Systems Corp., Bridgeton, 1981—97. Mem.: Assn. Computer Programmers and Analysts, Rotary Club. Roman Catholic. Died Sept. 23, 1997.

**ROBAK, JENNIE,** retired state legislator; b. Surprise, Nebr., May 4, 1932; m. Cleo F. Robak; children: Karen, Kim, Frank, Kurt, Tony, Andrea. With Fed. Emergency Mgmt. Agy., Kansas City, Mo.; owner, operator RKR Foods, Inc.; mem. Dist. 22 Nebr. State Senate, Lincoln, 1989—2003. Trustee Jr. Achievement Columbus; bd. dirs. Platte County Red Cross; den mother Boy Scouts American Col. Nebr. Army N.G. Recipient Breaking Rule of Thumb award Nebr. Domestic Violence and Sexual Assault Coalition, 1989, Communicaiton and Leadership award Toastmasters Internat., 1992; named Woman of Distinction Soroptomist Internat. Colubmus, 1990. Mem. VFW Aux., Nat. Orgn. Vol. Leaders, Cath. Daus., Mrs. Jaycees, Kiwanis, Eagles Aux. Democrat. Died Jan. 3, 2014.

**ROBBINS, VERNON EARL,** lawyer, accountant; b. Balt., Md., Aug. 16, 1921; s. Alexander Goldborough and Anne Jeanette (Bubb) Robbins; m. Ruth Adele Holland, Oct. 21, 1941; m. Alice Sherman Meredith, Feb. 17, 1961; 1 child, Sharon R. Fick; 1 stepchild, Susan V. Henry. ABA, Md. Sch. Acctg., 1941; JD, U. Balt., 1952. Bar: Md. 1952. Internal revenue agt. IRS, Balt., 1945—52; ptnr. Robbins, Adam & Co., C.P.A. firm, Cambridge, Md., from 1952; pvt. practice law Cambridge, from 1952; bd. dirs. Bank Eastern Shore. Served with US Maritime Svc., 1941—45. Named Boss of Yr., Tidewater chpt. Nat. Secs. Assn., 1978. Mem.: AICPAs, ABA, Dorchester Art Ctr., Dorchester County Hist. Soc., Navy League, Am. Judicature Soc., Am. Assn. Atty. CPAs, Md. Assn. CPAs, Md. bar Assn., Cambridge Yacht club, Shriners lodge, Masons lodge, Elks lodge. Democrat. Methodist. Died Dec. 31, 1999.

**ROBERTS, PRISCILLA WARREN,** artist; b. Montclair, NJ, June 13, 1916; d. Charles Asaph and Florence (Berry) R. Student, Art Students League, 1937-39, Nat. Acad., 1939-43. Represented in permanent collections Met. Mus., Cin. Art Mus., Canton (Ohio) Art Inst., Westmoreland County Mus. Art, Pa., IBM, Dallas Mus., Walker Art Ctr., Mpls., Butler Inst., Youngstown, Ohio, Nat. Mus. Am. Art, Washington, Nat. Mus. Women in the Arts, Washington. Recipient Proctor prize, 1947, popular prize Corcoran Biennial, 1947, prize Westmoreland County Mus., 3d prize Carnegie Internat., Pitts., 1950, Nat. Mus. Women in Arts, Washington, Snite Mus., U. Notre Dame, Ind. Mem. Nat. Acad. Design (Hallgarten prize 1945), Allied Artists Am. (Zabriskie prize 1944, 46), Catherine Lorillard Wolfe Assn. (hon.). Deceased.

**ROBERTS, TOMMY ED,** retired state legislator; b. Hartselle, Ala., Oct. 19, 1940; s. Luther E. Roberts & Katherine Hewlett; m. Pat Hogan; children: Andy, Stacey Wade. Student, Jacksonville State Coll., U. Okla., Econs. Devel. Inst. Pres., CEO Morgan County Econ. Development Assn., 1980—2001; mem. Ala. House of Reps., Montgomery, 1974—78, Ala. State Senate, Montgomery, 1994—2006. Served in USAR. Mem. American Econ. Devel. Coun., Ala. Econ. Developers Assn., Southern Econ. Devel. Coun., Rotary. Democrat. Methodist. Avocations: hunting, fishing, golf. Died Mar. 1, 2014.

**ROBERTSON, ABEL L., JR.,** pathologist; b. St. Andrews, Argentina, July 21, 1926; came to U.S., 1952, naturalized, 1957; s. Abel Alfred Lazzarini and Margaret Theresa G. (Anderson) R.; m. Irene Kirmayr Mauch, Dec. 26, 1958; children: Margaret Anne, Abel Martin, Andrew Duncan, Malcolm Alexander. BS, Coll. D.F. Sarmiento, Buenos Aires, Argentina, 1946; MD suma cum laude, U. Buenos Aires, 1951; PhD, Cornell U., 1959. Fellow tissue culture div. Inst. Histology and Embryology, Sch. Medicine Inst. Histology and Embryology, 1947-49; surg. intern Hosp. Ramos Mejia, Buenos Aires, 1948-50; fellow in tissue culture research Ministry of Health, Buenos Aires, 1950-51; resident Hosp. Nacional de Clinicas, Buenos Aires, 1950-51; head blood vessel bank and organ transplants Research Ctr. Ministry of Health, Buenos Aires, 1951-53; fellow dept. surgery and pathology Sch. Medicine Cornell U., NYC, 1953-55; asst. vis. surgery U. Hosp. N.Y., NYC, 1955-60; asst. prof. research surgery Postgrad. Med. Sch. NYU, NYC, 1955-56; asst. vis. surgeon Bellevue Hosp., NYC, 1955-60; assoc. prof. research surgery NYU, 1956-60, assoc. prof. pathology Sch. Medicine and Postgrad Med. Sch., 1960-63; staff mem. div. research Cleve. Clinic Found., 1963-73, prof. research, 1972-73; assoc. clin. prof. pathology Case Western Res. U. Sch. Medicine, Cleve., 1968-72, prof. pathology, 1973-82, dir. interdisciplinary cardiovascular research, 1975-82; exec. head dept. pathology Coll. Medicine, U. Ill., Chgo., 1982-88; prof. pathology Coll. Medicine U. Ill., 1982-93, prof. emeritus, from 1993; vis. prof. emeritus cardiovascular med. Core Analysis Lab., Stanford U. Coll. Medicine, from 1995, cardiac pathologist, from 2000. Rsch. fellow N.Y. Soc. Cardiovasc. Surgery, 1957-58; mem. rsch. study subcom. of heart com. N.E. Ohio Regional Med. Program, 1969—. Mem. internat. editl. bd. Atherosclerosis, Jour. Exptl. and Molecular Pathology, 1964—, Lab. Investigation, 1989—, Acta Pathologica Japonica, 1991—; contbr. articles to profl. jours. Recipient Rsch. Devel. award NIH, 1961-63, Disting. Alumnus award Grad. Sch. Med. Sci. Cornell U., 2003. Fellow AAAS, Am. Heart Assn., Am. Coll. Cardiology, Am. Coll. Clin. Pharmacology, Am. Heart Assn. (established investigator 1956-61, nominating com. coun. on arteriosclerosis 1972), Royal Microscopical Soc., Royal Soc. Promotion Health (Gt. Britain), Am. Geriat. Soc., N.Y. Acad. Scis., Cleve. Med. Library Assn.; mem. AMA, AAUP, Am. Soc. for Investigative Pathology, Am. Inst. Biol. Scis., Am. Judicature Soc., Am. Soc. Cell Biology, Am. Soc. Pathologists, Am. Soc. Nephrology, Assn. Am. Physicians and Surgeons, Assn. Computing Machinery, Electron Microscopy Soc. Am., Assn. Pathology Chmn., Internat. Acad. Pathology, Soc. Cardiovasc. Pathology, Internat. Cardiovasc. Soc., Internat. Soc. Cardiology (sci. council on arteriosclerosis and ischemic heart disease), Internat. Fed. on Genetic Engring. and Biotechnology, Internat. Soc. for Heart Rsch., Internat. Soc. Nephrology, Internat. Soc. Stereology, Pan Am. Med. Assn. (life, councillor in angiology 1966), Ill. Registry Anatomical Pathology (treas. 1985-87), Chgo. Pathology Soc., Reticuloendothelial Soc. Leucocyte Biology, Soc. Cryobiology, Tissue Culture Assn., Ohio Soc. Pathologists, Electron Microscopy Soc. Northeastern Ohio (pres., trustee 11966-68), Heart Assn. Northeastern Ohio, N.Y. Soc. Cardiovasc. Surgery, N.Y. Soc. Electron Microscopists, Cuyahoga County Med. Soc., Cleve. Soc. Pathologists, The Oxygen Soc., Sigma Xi. Home: Half Moon Bay, Calif. Died Sept. 14, 2013.

**ROBINS, DANIEL J.,** retired lawyer; b. NYC, May 6, 1924; s. Elias and Ida Zaluda (Robins) Robins; m. Lucille Simon Robins, Mar. 17, 1949; children: Lynne, Kenneth. BA, NYU, 1946; LLB, Columbia U., 1948. Bar: NY 1949. Mem. Gold & Nickorson, NYC, 1949—50, Rosston, Hort & Brussel, NYC, 1950; atty. FTC, NYC, 1951—52; sr. v.p. gen. counsel Mut. Am. Life Ins. Co., NYC, 1952—86. Served US Army, 1942—45. Mem.: Life Ins. Coun. NY (legis. com. from 1977), Am. Coun. Life Ins. (subcom. NY legis.), Assn. Life Ins. Counsel, Assn. Bar City NY. Republican. Died 1991.

**ROBINSON, ARTHUR NAPOLEON RAYMOND (A.N.R. ROBINSON),** former president of Trinidad and Tobago; b. Calder Hall, Trinidad and Tobago, Dec. 16, 1926; s. James A. and Isabella R.; married; 2 children. Student, Castara Meth. Sch., 1931-38, Bishop's High Sch., 1938-45; LLB, London U., 1949; degree (hon.), St. John's Coll., UK, 1955. Acting 2d class clk. Magistracy, Tobago, Trinidad, 1946, St. George West, Trinidad, 1946; 2d class clk. Social Services Dept., 1947; registrar Gen. Dept., 1951; with Sir Courtenay Hannays, barrister, Port of Spain, Scarborough, Trinidad and Tobago, 1955; treas. Peoples Nat. Movement, Trinidad, 1956-1959; mem. Fed. Parliament Trinidad, 1958-61; 1st minister of fin. Trinidad and Tobago, 1961-67; dep. polit. leader People's Nat. Movement, Trinidad and Tobago, 1966, minister of external affairs, 1967-70; mem. of opposition Parliament, Trinidad and Tobago, 1971-85; chmn. Tobago House of Assembly, Trinidad and Tobago, 1980-86; polit. leader Nat. Alliance for Reconstruction, Trinidad and Tobago, 1985-97; prime minister Govt. of Trinidad & Tobago, Port of Spain, Trinidad and Tobago, 1986-91, min. economy, 1986-88, pres., 1997—2003. Cons. to UN on Internat. criminal law and human rights. Author: The Mechanics of Independence, 1971, Carribean Man, 1986; contbr. articles to profl. jours. and article on Trinidad and Tobago to Encyclopedia Brittanica, 1971 edit. Died Apr. 9, 2014.

**ROBINSON, CHARLES WESLEY,** boat design company executive; b. Long Beach, Calif., Sept. 7, 1919; s. Franklin Willard and Anna Hope (Gould) R.; m. Tamara Lindovna, Mar. 8, 1957; children: Heather Lynne, Lisa Anne, Wendy Paige. BA in Econs. cum laude, U. Calif., Berkeley, 1941; MBA, Stanford U., 1947. Asst. mgr. mfg. Golden State Dairy Products Co., San Francisco, 1947-49; assoc. McKinsey & Co. Mgmt. Cons., 1950—51; v.p., then pres. Marcona Corp., San Francisco, 1952-74; undersec. of state for econ. affairs Dept. State, Washington, 1974-75; dep. sec. of state, 1976-77; sr. mng. ptnr. Kuhn Loeb & Co., NYC, 1977-78; vice chmn. Blyth Eastman Dillon & Co., NYC, 1978-79; chmn. Energy Transition Corp., Santa Fe and Washington, 1979-82; pres. Robinson & Assocs., Inc., Santa Fe, from 1982. Pres. Merged Memebership Co., San Diego, 1992—, M Ship Co., San Diego, 1998, Builder of the Stiletto-Naval Mil. Craft; dir. emeritus NIKE, Inc. Patentee slurry transport and both sail and power boat designs, boat engr. Brookings Instn., Washington, 1977—; mem. Pres.'s Cir. NAS. Lt. USN, 1941-46. Recipient Disting. Honor award Dept. State, 1977, Lifetime Achievement award, N.Mex., 2007, N.Mex. Living Treas. award. Independent. Methodist. Died May 20, 2012.

**ROBINSON, EFFIE,** social worker, educator; b. Healdsburg, Calif., Jan. 7, 1920; d. Jessie C. Robinson and Elzora Emily Harper Robinson. AB, San Francisco State U., 1943; MSW, U. Calif., Berkeley, 1945. From case worker to acting dir. San Francisco Family Svc. Agy., San Francisco, 1945—63, dir. sr. program, 1964—87; ret., 1987. Devel. sr. housing San Francisco Housing Authority; chmn. edn. com. UN Assn. of San Francisco, from 1994, bd. dirs.; devel. U.N. Program Tchr. Tng. Co-author (with David Christenson): Social Activity and Housing Environment of the Elderly, 1975. Life mem. NAACP; founder San Francisco Housing Authority Program Centuries 2002, San Francisco, 1972; founding mem. Internat. Mus. of Women, 2002. Recipient Wave award, Lifeprint, 2000, Koshland award, San Francisco Found., 1974; named in Ladies Home Jour. Mag., 1975. Mem.: AAUW, Calif. Women's Agenda, Am. Women Internat. Understanding, AKA. Democrat. Protestant. Avocations: ballet, opera, symphony, book club. Deceased.

**ROBINSON, EVELYN EDNA,** secondary school educator; b. St. John, Maine, Feb. 23, 1911; d. Registe Jalbert and Olive Michaud; m. Carl Robinson, July 19, 1939; children: Robert, James. BA in Math., U. Maine, 1934; MS, U. N.H., 1963; MEd, Hillyer Coll. U., 1960. Tchr. English and math. Ft. Kent (Maine) H.S., 1934; tchr. English and math., coach girls basketball Madewaska (Maine) H.S., 1935-55; tchr. math. Stamford (Conn.) H.S., 1955-56; tchr. math and English, Bristol (Conn.) H.S., 1956-63; prof. math. Worcester (Mass.) State Coll., 1963-77, chmn. dept., 1970-77. Coord. cmty. bus. Worcester State Coll., 1970-77, class advisor, 1968-72, salary equity bd., 1971-73. Vol. libr. Madawaska Pub. Libr., 1936-55; lector Christ the King, Worcester, 1974-2000. Mem. Delta Kappa Gamma. Republican. Roman Catholic. Avocations: decorating, flower arrangements, ceramics, tailoring. Home: Spencer, Mass. Died Mar. 29, 2008.

**ROBINSON, FRANK MALCOLM,** writer, editor; b. Chgo., Aug. 9, 1926; s. Raymond and Leona (White) R. BS in Physics, Beloit Coll., 1950; MS in Journalism, Northwestern U., 1955. Asst. editor Family Weeklysupplement, Chgo., 1955-56, Sci. Digest mag., Chgo., 1956-59; editor Rogue mag., Evanston, Ill., 1959-65; mng. editor Cavalier, LA, 1966-67; editor Censorship Today, LA, 1968-69; staff writer Playboy mag., Chgo., 1969-72; writer San Francisco, 1972—2014. Author: The Power, 1956 (filmed 1968), The Dark Beyond the Stars, 1991, Waiting..., 1997; co-author: The Glass Inferno, 1974 (filmed as The Towering Inferno 1974), The Prometheus Crisis, 1975, The Nightmare Factor, 1978, The Gold Crew, 1980 (filmed as TV movie The Fifth Missile), The Great Divide, 1982, Blow-Out, 1987, Death of a Marionette, 1995, Waiting, 1999; co-editor: The Truth About Vietnam, 1966, Sex, American Style, 1971. Served with USN, 1944-46, 50-52. Mem. Phi Beta Kappa, Pi Kappa Alpha (pres. 1949-50). Democrat. Avocations: collecting books, pulp mags. Died June 30, 2014.

**ROBINSON, HELENE M.,** retired music educator; b. Eugene, Oreg., May 30, 1912; d. Kirkman K. and Emily A. Robinson. BA in Music, U. Oreg., 1935; MusM, Northwestern U., Evanston, Ill., 1945. Piano tchr. No. Ariz. U., Flagstaff, 1952—60, Calif. State U., Fullerton, 1960—61, U. Calif., Santa Barbara, 1961—62, Ariz. State U., Tempe, 1963—77. Author: Basic Piano for Adults, vol. I and II, 1964, Intermediate Piano for Adults, vols. I and II, 1970; author: (with others) Teaching Piano in Classroom and Studio; contbr. articles to profl. jours. Mem.: Music Tchrs. Nat. Assn. (spkr. convs. 1974—76), Phi Beta. Avocation: piano. Deceased.

**ROBINSON, J. MACK,** philanthropist, retired communications executive; b. Atlanta, May 7, 1923; m. Harriet J. Holloway, 1960. Attended, Ga. Evening Coll., 1941. Chmn. Gulf Capital Corp; founder Dixie Finance Co., 1948; owner, chmn. Atlantic American Corp., Atlanta, 1974—95. Served in US Army, 1941—45. Died Feb. 7, 2014.

**ROBINSON, WILLIAM JAMES, SR.,** lay worker; b. Erie, Pa., Aug. 17, 1896; s. William James and Margaret Fraser (Sweatman) R.; children: Nancy Robinson Weaver, William J. BA, Yale U., 1918; JD, Harvard U., 1923. Ordained elder Presbyn. Ch., 1946. Elder Presbyn. Ch., Lake Erie, Pa., from 1946. 1st lt. U.S. Army, 1917-19. Mem. Hemlock Nat. (life), Rotary (life), Masons (life). Home: Tucson, Ariz. *Love is the dominant force, so it will ultimately prevail over evil.* Died Nov. 3, 1996.

**ROBLEK, BRANKO,** science educator; b. Slovenia, Yugoslavia, Jan. 9, 1934; s. Viktor and Marija (Kern) Roblek. Diploma in Physics, U. FNT, Ljubljana, Slovenia, 1959; diploma in Math., 1962. Tchr. Primary Sch., Zg. Gorje, Slovenia, 1960—62, Secondary Sch., Skofja Loka,

1962—69, 1973—81; prof., math., 1964; insp., cons. Inst. Edn., Ljubljana, 1969—73, mem., physics edn. faculty, from 1981; cons. Soc. Computer Sci., Ljubljana, 1973—81; tchr. math., physics and computer sci. Edn. Ctr., Skofja Loka, 1981—92. Co-author (with others): AAAIII Zbirka vaj, 1969, Racunalnistvo ZN, 1980. Chmn. Syndicate Civilizing Worker, Skofja Loka, 1966; mem. The Planetary Soc., Pasadena. Fellow: Soc. Math.; mem.: Physicists and Astronomers of R Slovenia. Died Nov. 26, 2000.

**ROCK, PETER ALFRED,** chemistry educator, researcher, consultant, dean; b. New Haven, Sept. 29, 1939; s. Alfred Milton and Mabel (Neider) R.; m. M. Elaine Rousseau, Dec. 5, 1959; children: Michael, Deborah, Lisa. AB summa cum laude, Boston U., 1961; PhD in Chemistry, U. Calif., Berkeley, 1964. Prof. chemistry U. Calif., Davis, from 1964, chmn. dept., 1980—85, dean divsn. math. and phys. scis., from 1995. Cons. World Book Ency., N.Y.C., 1985—, Dorland Med. Dictionary, Phila., 1978-82; expert witness in the energy field and product liability for numerous law firms, Calif., 1979—. Author: Chemical Thermodynamics, 1983, General Chemistry, 1986, 1991, Descriptive Chemistry, 1986; editor: Isotopes and Chemical Principles, 1975, Special Topics in Electrochemistry, 1977; contbr. World Book Ency., 1990, Ency. of Geochemistry, 1994, McGraw-Hill Ency. of Sci. and Tech., 1999, Ency. of Geochemistry, 1998, over 60 rsch. papers to profl. jours. Named to Collegium Disting. Alumni, Boston U., 1974; Chemistry Achievement award Chem. Mfrs. Assn., 1961. Mem.: Phi Beta Kappa, Sigma Xi. Avocation: writing. Deceased.

**ROCKEFELLER, RICHARD GILDER,** medical association administrator; b. NYC, Jan. 20, 1949; s. David and Margaret (McGrath) Rockefeller; married; 2 children. MD, Harvard U., 1979, EdM. Diplomate Am. Bd. Family Practice. Intern Highland Hosp.-U. Rochester, 1979—80, resident family practice, 1980—82; founder, pres. Health Commons Inst., Portland, Maine, 1992—2014; clin. instr. family medicine Maine Med. Ctr.-Mercy Hosp. Family Practice Residency Program. Chmn. US advisory bd. Doctors Without Borders, 1989—2010. Bd. dirs. Rockefeller U.; bd. trustees Rockefeller Family Fund, Rockefeller Bros. Fund; bd. dirs. Maine Summer Dramatic Inst. Home: Falmouth, Maine. Died June 13, 2014.

**RODGERS, JUDY,** chef; b. Oct. 28, 1956; Grad., Stanford U., 1978. Lunch chef Chez Panisse; chef Union Hotel, Benicia, Calif.; exec. chef, owner Zuni Café, San Francisco, 1987—2013. Author: The Zuni Café Cookbook, 2002 (KitchenAid Cookbook of Yr. award, James Beard Found., 2003), Inside the California Food Revolution: Thirty Years That Changed Our Culinary Consciousness, 2013. Recipient S.Pellegrino Outstanding Restaurant award, James Beard Found., 2003; named Best Chef: Calif., 2000, Outstanding Chef, 2004. Died Dec. 2, 2013.

**RODGERS, MARY (MRS. HENRY GUETTEL),** composer; b. NYC, Jan. 11, 1931; d. Richard and Dorothy (Feiner) Rodgers; m. Julian B. Beaty Jr. (div. 1957); children: Richard, Linda Mackay, Constance Peck; m. Henry Guettel, Oct. 14, 1961; children: Adam Guettel, Alexander Guettel. Student, Wellesley Coll., 1948—51. Composer: (music, lyrics) Some of My Best Friends Are Children, 1952, Davy Jones' Locker, 1957, (book and lyrics) Three to Make Music, 1957, (Broadway shows) Once Upon a Mattress, 1959, Hot Spot, 1963, Mad Show, New Theatre, 1966—67, Pinocchio for Bil Baird Marionettes, 1974, (Mary Martin's children's spl.) Easter, NBC-TV, 1957; asst. to prodr. Philharmonic Young People's Concerts, CBS-TV, 1957—70, contbg. composer, editor Free to Be You and Me; author: The Rotten Book, 1969, Freaky Friday, 1972; author: (with Dorothy Rodgers) A Word to the Wives, 1970; author: A Billion for Boris, 1974, Summer Switch, 1982, (screenplay) Freaky Friday; author: (with Dorothy Rodgers) (monthly column) Two Minds, McCall's mag., 1971—78. Trustee Phillips Exeter Acad.; bd. dirs. Symphony Space. Mem.: ASCAP, Writers Guild, Authors Guild, Authors League (coun.), Dramatists Guild Found. (bd. dirs.), Dramatists Guild (coun.), American Guild Authors & Composers, Cosmopolitan Club. Died June 26, 2014.

**RODMAN, JANE E.,** editor; b. Washington County, Ind., June 7, 1921; d. Glenn O. and Pearl E. (Bartlett) Rodman. AB, Evansville Coll., 1942; MA, Ind. U., 1946. History tchr. Huntingburg HS, Ind., 1942—44, Evansville Coll., Ind., 1946—47; editl. asst., rschr. to prof. Ind. U., Bloomington, 1947—53; sec., editl. asst. Ind. U. Press, Bloomington, 1953—55, asst. editor, 1955—69, assoc. editor, 1969—77, editor, from 1977. Editor: The Pictorial History of Indiana, 1980; contbr. articles to profl. jours. Mem.: Women in Comm., Ind. Hist. Soc., Hist. Landmarks Found. Ind., Hoosier Heritage Mus. Soc., Bloomington Restorations, University Club (Bloomington), Women's Faculty Club. Republican. Mem. Christian Ch. (Disciples Of Christ). Home: Evansville, Ind. Died Oct. 1991.

**ROE, ROBERT A. (BOB ROE),** former United States Representative from New Jersey; b. Wayne, NJ, Feb. 28, 1924; s. Robert A. and Lillian (Thornton) R. Student, Oreg. State U., Wash. State U. Committeeman, Wayne Township, 1955—56; mayor, 1956-61; commr. conservation & econ. devel. State of NJ, Trenton, 1963-69; mem. US Congress from 8th N.J. Dist., 1969—93, US House Sci., Space & Technology Com., 1987—91; chmn. US House Public Works & Transp. Com., 1991—93. Mem. Passaic County Bd. Chosen Freeholders, 1959-63, dir., 1962-63 Mem. exec. bd. Altaha council Boy Scouts America, mem. nat. council; trustee Chilton Meml. Hosp.; mem. pres.'s adv. bd. Tombrock Coll., West Paterson, N.J.; mem. community adv. council William Paterson Coll. N.J. Served with AUS, World War II, ETO. Named Man of Year N.J. Jr. Chamber of Commerce, 1959, Water Conservationist of Yr. N.J. State Fedn. Sportsmen's Clubs, 1966, Ann. Golden Medal award Garden Clubs N.J., 1969, State of Israel Bonds Scroll of honor, 1971, D.A.V. citation, 1971, citations Nat. Small Bus. Assn., 1972, citations President's Com. Employment Handicapped, 1972, Nat. Humanitarian award Joint Handicapped Council Nat. Soc. Handicapped, 1972, Disting. Service award Nat. Council Urban Econ. Devel., 1975, numerous leadership and service awards. Hon. fellow American Acad. Med. Adminstrs.; mem. Wayne Chamber of Commerce (past pres.), VFW, American Legion. Clubs: Optimist, Elk. Democrat. Roman Catholic. Died July 15, 2014.

**ROELKER, NANCY LYMAN,** history professor; b. Warwick, RI, June 15, 1915; d. William Greene and Anna R. (Koues) Roelker. AB, Radcliffe Coll., 1936; PhD, Harvard U., 1953. Tchr. history Winsor Sch., Boston, 1941—63; from asst. prof. history to prof. Tufts U., 1963—71; prof. European history Boston U., 1971—80; vis. prof. Brown U., from 1980. Author: The Paris of Henry of Navarre, 1958; Editor, translator In Search of France, 1963, From Wilson to Roosevelt: American Foreign Policy 1913-1945, 1963, Queen of Navarre, Jeanne d'Albret, 1528-1572, 1968; contbr. articles to profl. jours. Recipient Disting. Achievement medal, Radcliffe Coll., 1970, Metcalf prize, Boston U., 1974, Gold medal, City of Paris, 1985; John Simon Guggenheim fellow, 1965—66. Mem.: Am. Hist. Assn. (v.p. rsch. divsn. 1975—78, US del. to Internat. Congress Hist. Scis. 1982—85, chmn. internat. activities com. 1982—85), Soc. French Hist. Studies (pres. 1977—78), Am. Acad. Arts and Sci., Am. Soc. Reformation Rsch. Home: East Greenwich, RI. Died Nov. 27, 1993.

**ROGAWAY, BETTY JANE,** retired school system administrator, social worker; b. San Francisco, Sept. 8, 1921; d. Irvine and Dorothy (Nathan) Hyman; m. Roderick Matthew Rogaway, Jan. 16, 1945 (dec. Aug. 1964); children: Stephen, Kathryn Rogaway Farrell. BA, U. Calif., Berkeley, 1942; MA, Calif. State U., San Jose, 1968. Lic. social worker, Calif. Social worker Travelers Aid, 1943, ARC, 1943-45, Child Welfare Svcs. Sutter County, Calif., 1945; juvenile welfare officer Palo Alto (Calif.) Police Dept., 1945-49; tchr., cons., coord. Palo Alto Unified Sch. Dist., 1958-82, ret., 1982. Cons. HeadStart, San Francisco, 1966, Calif. State Dept. of Edn., Sacramento, 1982. Co-author: Palo Alto: A Centennial History, 1993. Mem. City of Palo Alto Task Force on Child Care, 1973; mem. County Task Force on Reasonable Efforts for Child Abuse Protection, San Jose, 1988-90; mem., pres. Palo Alto Hist. Assn., 1989-92; v.p. Calif. Child Devel. Adminstrs. Assn., Sacramento, 1981-82; pres., mem. Children's Shelter Assn. of Santa Clara County, San Jose, 1983—. Avocations: reading, gardening, bird watching. Home: Palo Alto, Calif. Died Jan. 15, 2002.

**ROGERS, BENJAMIN F.,** publisher; b. Bklyn., Jan. 9, 1930; s. Anthony Joseph and Dorothy Agnes (Banfill) R.; m. Jule Marie McCarthy, May 8, 1954; children— Stephen, Brian, Douglas, Gregg, Claire BA, Fordham U., 1952. Sales rep. Parke, Davis & Co., NYC, 1954-68; sales rep. Romaine Pierson Pubs., Port Washington, N.Y., 1968-75, nat. sales mgr., 1975-80; pub., pres. Dominus Pub. Co., Inc., Williston Park, N.Y., from 1980. Served to 1st lt. U.S. Army, 1952-54 Mem. Assn. Ind. Clin. Pubs. (bd. dirs. 1985—), Pharm. Advt. Council. Roman Catholic. Avocations: jogging; piano; gardening; tennis. Home: Huntington, NY. Died Aug. 25, 1989.

**ROGERS, CRAWFORD R.,** publishing executive; b. Southard, Okla., Oct. 3, 1923; s. Phillip O. and Letha Louise (Downing) R.; div.; children: Michael M., Cherin Rae, Scott S. Attended, Carroll Coll., Golden Gate Coll. CLU. Engaged in ins. bus., 1946—47, 1955—84; with Fireman's Fund Am. Life Ins. Co., 1967—84; home office life and health claims analyst San Rafael, Calif., 1980—84; founder Crawford R. Rogers & Co. pubs. Rogers Claim Manuals, Life and Accidental Death and Dismemberment and Long Term Disability, 1984—96. Exec. sec. Burlingame Improvement Club Coun., Calif., 1953—57. With USAAF, 1943—45. Decorated Air medal. Mem.: Am. Soc. CLUs, Life Underwriters Assn. Republican. Methodist. Home: Las Vegas, Nev. Died Jan. 8, 1996.

**ROGERS, RUTH FRANCES,** retired microbiologist; b. Chgo., Nov. 5, 1925; d. Frank Joseph and Ruth Elizabeth (Abbott) Kucera; m. James Alvin Rogers, June 17, 1950; children: Kenneth James, David Wayne. BS, U. Ill., 1948. Microbiologist No. Rsch. Ctr., Nat. Ctr. for Agrl. Utilization Rsch., Peoria, Ill., 1963—85; ret., 1985. Contbr. articles to profl. jours. Recipient Sustained Superior Performance award USDA, 1984. Methodist. Home: Peoria, Ill. Died Oct. 4, 2013.

**ROLAND, CHARLES GORDON,** physician, medical educator, historian; b. Winnipeg, Man., Can., Jan. 25, 1933; s. John Sanford and Leona (McLaughlin) R.; m. Marjorie Ethel Kyles, 1953 (div. 1973); children: John Kenneth, Christopher Franklin, David Charles, Kathleen Siobhan; m. Connie Rankin, 1979; step-children: Gregory Irvine, Christopher Irvine, Randi Irvine. Student, U. Toronto, Ont., Can., 1952—54; MD, BSc, U. Man., 1958, DSc (hon.), 1997. Intern St. Boniface Hosp., Man., 1958—59; pvt. practice medicine specializing in family medicine Tillsonburg, Ont., 1959—60, Grimsby, Ont., 1960—64; sr. editor Jour. Am. Med. Assn., Chgo., 1964—69; head sect. publs. Mayo Clinic, 1969—70, chmn. dept. biomed. communications, 1970—77; prof. history medicine, prof. biomed. comm., coord. family practice track, chmn. adminstrv. com. dept. family medicine Mayo Med. Sch., 1971—77; mem. admissions, edn. and curriculum coordinators coms., hon. mem. med. staff West Lincoln Meml. Hosp., Grimsby; mem. grants com. Hannah Inst. History of Medicine, Toronto, 1974—77, 1987—91, mem. publs. com., 1991—95; Jason A. Hannah prof. history of medicine McMaster U., Hamilton, Ont., Canada, 1977—99, Hannah prof. emeritus, from 1999, assoc. mem. dept. history, 1978—96, chmn. archives com. Faculty of Health Scis., 1983—98; chmn. spl. grants com. Hannah Inst. for History of Medicine, 1981—85; Sid W. Richardson vis. prof. Inst. Med. Humanities U. Tex. Med. Br., Galveston, 1984. Devel. adv. com. Assoc. Med. Svcs., 1999-2003; inaugural Osler-McGovern lectr. Green Coll., Oxford U., Eng., 2001. Author: (with L.S. King) Scientific Writing, 1968, (with J.P. McGovern) William Osler, The Continuing Education, 1969, Good Scientific Writing, 1971, William Osler's The Master Word in Medicine: A Study in Rhetoric, 1972, (with L.S. Baker) You and Leukemia: A Day at a Time, 1976, (with P. Potter) An Annotated Bibliography of Canadian Medical Periodicals, 1826-1975, 1979, Clarence Meredith Hincks 1885-1964: Mental Health Crusader, 1990, Courage Under Siege: Starvation, Disease and Death in the Warsaw Ghetto, 1992, Harold Nathan Segall: Pioneer Canadian Cardiologist, 1995, Long Night's Journey Into Day: Prisoners of War in the Far East, 1941-45, 2001; editor: (E.P. Scarlett) In Sickness and In Health, 1972; co-editor: An Annotated Checklist of Osleriana, 1976, vol. 2, 2000, Sir William Osler 1849-1919: A Selection for Medical Students, 1982, Health Disease and Medicine: Essays in Canadian History, 1984, Sir William Osler 1849-1919: petite anthologie à l'intention des étudiants in médecine, 1987, Bibliography of Secondary Sources in Canadian Medical History, 1985, 2nd edition, 2000, (with J. Bernier) The Collected Essays of Sir William Osler (3 vols.), 1985, (with Henry Friedlander and Benno Muller-Hill) Medical Science without Compassion: Past and Present, 1992; editor, author introduction: Medical Topography of Upper Canada, 1985; (with Richard Golden) Sir William Osler: An Annotated Bibiography with Illustrations, 1987; co-editor: The Persisting Osler, 1984, The Persisting Osler II, 1994, The Persisting Osler III, 2001, Notable Surgeon, Fine Citizen: The Life of Archibald Edward Malloch, 1844-1919, 2008; editor-in-chief Can. Bulletin of Med. History, 1987-90; mem. editl. adv. bd. Can. Family Physician, 1964-72, Chest, 1966-95, Med. Comm., 1971-75, Postgrad. Med. Jour., London, 1967-72; exec. editor Mayo Clinic Procs., 1969-77, Bioscis. Comm., 1975-80, Ont. Med. Rev., 1979-84, HSTC Jour., 1980-87, Can. Bull. Med. History, 1983-90, Med. History (London), 1982-87, Jour. History of Medicine and Allied Scis., 1991-94, 96—. Mem. bd. curators Osler Libr., McGill U., Montreal, 1981—. Recipient Jason A. Hannah medal Royal Soc. Can., 1994. Fellow AAAS (coun. 1969-74), Am. Med. Writers Assn. (pres. 1969-70, Harold Swanberg award, 1975); mem. Can. Med. Assn., Am. Assn. History Medicine (sec.-treas. 1976-80, publs. com. 1979-85, 2002—, Garrison lectr. com. 2005—07), Acad. Medicine Toronto (Grogan lecture com. 1978-83, chmn. sect. med. history 1979-80, mus. com. 1983-84), Am. Mil. Inst., Internat. Inst. Prisoners of War, Soc. Internat. d'Histoire de la Medicine (internat. del. for Can. 1983-86), Can. Soc. for History Medicine (v.p. 1982-87, pres. 1993-95), Soc. Med. History Chgo. (sec.-treas. 1966-69), Can. Ctr. for Studies in Hist. Horticulture (exec. com. 1982-89), Coun. Biology Editors, Med. Hist. Club Toronto (pres. 1977-78), Ont. Hist. Soc., Can. Hist. Assn., Bibliog. Soc. Can., Am. Osler Soc. (sec.-treas. 1975-85, v.p. 1985-86, pres. 1986-87, historian, 1999-, Lifetime Achievement award, 2006), Japan Osler Soc. (hon.), Royal Soc. Medicine (London), Royal Can. Mil. Inst., Champlain Soc. (Toronto), History of Second World War (Can. com.), Soc. Army Hist. Rsch., Univ. Club (Rochester); Osler Club (London), Alpine Club Can., Lit. Club (Chgo.), Sigma Xi. Home: Burlington, Canada. Died June 9, 2009.

**ROLIN, JEAN GASTON,** lawyer, financial consultant; b. Nancy, Lorraine, France, Mar. 21, 1937; s. Roger Abel and Marie-Louise (Emilie) Thietry) R.; m. Marie-Louise Lucie Hamant, July 1, 1961 (div. Mar. 1972); 1 child, Jean-Christophe. Gen. Math. Degree, Sci. Faculty, Paris, 1959; Degree in Law, Faculty of Law, Paris, 1963, JD, 1964. Bar: France. Atty. Fiduciaire de France, Paris, 1965-75; pvt. practice Rolin Enterprise, Paris, from 1976. Fin./fiscal cons. Rolin Enterprise, Evry, France, 1976—. Contbr. articles to profl. jours. Hon. mem. Union of Police Retirees, Paris, 1992. Named Hon. Lawyer, Bar of Essonne, Paris-Evry, 1995. Mem. Am. Express Travel Club, L'Esprit Diners Club of France. Roman Catholic. Avocation: long-distance swimming. Home: Ris-Orangis, France. Deceased.

**ROMANO, PAUL EDWARD,** ophthalmologist, educator; b. Bronx, NY, Oct. 30, 1934; s. Paul Salvatore and Mary Elizabeth (Simms) R.; m. Judith Ann Robinson, Oct. 18, 1969. AB, Cornell U., 1955, MD, 1959; MS with distinction in Ophthalmology, Georgetown U., 1967. Diplomate Am. Bd. Ophthalmology. Intern in surgery Albany Med. Ctr. Hosp., N.Y., 1959-60, resident in gen. surgery N.Y., 1960-61; resident in ophthalmology Georgetown U. Hosp., Washington, 1964-67; fellow in ophthalmology Armed Forces Inst. Pathology, Washington, 1967, Wilmer Ophthal. Inst., Johns Hopkins Hosp., Balt., 1967-69; dir. ophthalmology Children's Meml. Hosp., Chgo., 1970-80; asst. prof. Northwestern U. Med. Sch., Chgo., 1969-73, assoc. prof., 1973-80; prof. ophthalmology U. Fla. Coll. Medicine, Gainesville, 1980-89; cons. VA Med. Ctr., Gainesville, 1980-90, Naval Regional Med. Ctr., Jacksonville, Fla., 1981-89. Sci. pub. owner Binocular Vision and Strabology Quarterly. Founding editor, pub. Binocular Vision and Strabismus Quar. Jour., 1985—; contbr. over 400 articles to profl. jours. Capt. U.S. Army, 1961-64. Fellowship Heed Found., 1968, NIH, 1968-69. Fellow Am. Acad. Ophthalmology, Am. Acad. Pediatrics; mem. Internat. Assn. Ocular Surgeons (charter), Internat. Strabismus Assn., Am. Assn. for Pediatric Ophthalmology (charter), Assn. for Rsch. in Vision and Ophthalmology, European Strabismus Assn., Von Noorden Fellows Assn., Soc. Heed Fellows, Wilmer Residents' Assn. Died June 16, 2014.

**ROMANOV, GRIGORIY VASILYEVICH,** Russian government official; b. Feb. 7, 1923; Degree, Leningrad Shipbldg. Inst. Designer, sect. head, constrn. bur. Ministry Shipbldg. Industry USSR, 1946—54; ofcl. mem. Communist Party, 1954—61; sec. Leningrad City Com., 1961—62, Communist Party Soviet Union, 1961—62, Leningrad Regional Com., 1962—70, 1st sec., 1970—83; dep. USSR Supreme Soviet, 1966—85. Mem. Ctrl. Com. Communist Party Soviet Union, 1966—89; candidate Politburo, 1973—76, mem., 1976—85; mem. presidium, 1970—85. Decorated Order Lenin. Died June 3, 2008.

**ROMBERGER, JOHN ALBERT,** biologist, historian, archivist; b. Klingerstown, Pa., Dec. 25, 1925; s. Ralph T. and Carrie (Bahner) Romberger; m. Margery Janet Davis, June 17, 1951; children: Ann I., Daniel D. Student, Hershey Jr. Coll., 1947—49; BA, Swarthmore Coll., 1951; MS, Pa. State U., 1954; PhD, U. Mich., 1957; postdoctoral, Calif. Inst. Th., 1957—60. Plant physiologist Forest Physiology Lab., U.S. Forest Svc., USDA, Beltsville, Md., 1961—82; vis. scientist Swedish U. Agrl. Scis., Alnarp, 1983, Inst. Agrl. Scis., Zamosc, Poland, 1985, Agrl. U., Warsaw, 1988. Editor: Internat. Rev. Forestry Rsch., 1963—70, Beltsville Symposia in Agrl. Rsch., 1976—78; contbr. articles to profl. jours.; author: Meristems, Growth and Development in Woody Plants, 1963, 1978; co-author (with Z. Hejnowicz and J.F. Hill): Plant Structure: Function and Development, 1993; co-author: Plant Structure: Function and Development, reprint edit., 2004, Finding Our Roots in Bavaria, 2003, 2007. With US Army, 1945—46. Recipient Poland U.S. Interacad. Exchange Program fellowship, U. Silesia, Katowice, 1981, 1983. Fellow: AAAS; mem.: Botanical Soc. Am., Hist. Soc. Pa., Sigma Xi. Lutheran. Home: Elizabethville, Pa. Died Jan. 2, 2014.

**ROMENSKI, KATHRYN B.,** physical therapy administrator; b. Pawtucket, RI, Aug. 13, 1948; BS in Phys. Therapy, Boston U., 1970. Staff phys. therapist Allied Svcs. Handicapped, Scranton, Pa., 1970—71, asst. chief phys. therapist, 1971—74, chief phys. therapist, 1974—77, dir. patient svcs., 1977—79, dir. phys. therapy, from 1979; mem. Allied Svcs. Fed. Credit Union, from 1970, treas., 1974—75, pres., 1984—86; mem. profl. adv. bd. Allied Svcs. Home Health Div., from 1985, Civic Ballet Co., from 1985. Mem.: Nat. Assn. Mgmt., Nat. Assn. Female Execs., Nat Rehab. Adminstrs. Assn., Am. Acad. Orthotics & Prosthetics, Am. Mgmt. Assn., Pa. Phys. Therapy Assn. (mem. nominating com. 1977—78, state conv. com. 1979, chair nominating com. from 1986), Am. Phys. Therapy Assn. (house dels. 1973, 1986). Home: Clarks Summit, Pa. Died Aug. 3, 1990.

**ROMERO, JOAQUIM JOSÉ BARBOSA,** engineering educator; b. Lisbon, Portugal, Jan. 11, 1928; s. Joaquim Gonçalves and Adosinda Encarnação (Barbosa) R.; m. Magda Otília Ricardo Cabrita, July 27, 1953; children: Joaquim Filipe, Manuel José, Fernando Carlos, Luís Miguel. Lic., Inst. Superior Ténico, Lisbon, Portugal, 1951; MSc, U. Birmingham, UK, 1961, PhD, 1967; agregado, U. Lourenco Marques, Moçambique, Portugal, 1972. Steering com. U. Minho, Braga, Portugal, 1974-81, dep. vice chancellor, 1978-81, dean Sch. Engring., 1984-89; dir. Inst. Indsl. Tech. INETI, Lisbon, 1981-84; mgr. subprogram higher edn. PRODEP, Lisbon, 1990-94; pres. Poly. Viana Castelo Sch. Tech. and Mgmt., Portugal, 1991-97; pres. sci. coun. Sch. Tech. and Mgmt. Poly. Viana Castelo, Portugal, 1991—2003. Cons. Lab. Normal Pharm., Lisbon, 1952-65, Portuguese Atomic Authority, Lisbon, 1956-65; advisor to dir. Nat. Inst. for Indsl. Rsch., Lisbon, 1965; dir. Prodn. Orfina (Fine Chems.), Lisbon, 1965-67; head Ctr. Engring. and Sys. of Prodn. and Ctr. of Rsch. in Energy and Prodn. Tech., U. Minho, 1994-98; coord. external evaluation com. degree programmes Portuguese Univs. Indsl. Engring., 1998-2000; mem. external evaluation com. degree programs Portuguese Polytechnic Chem. Engring., 2002-03. Contbr. scientific papers to profl. jours. Recipient Merit Gold medal Cath. U., 1994, Great Cross Portuguese Pub. Edn. Order, 1998, Silver medal U. Minho, 1999. Fellow Ordem dos Engenheiros; mem. IEEE, Soc. Portuguesa de Química, Inst. Chem. Engrs., Portuguese Acad. Engring. (founding mem.). Avocations: literature, music. Home: Braga, Portugal. Died Mar. 22, 2005.

**ROMMEL, MANFRED,** bank executive, mayor, municipal official; b. Stuttgart, Germany, Dec. 24, 1928; s. Erwin and Lucie Maria (Mollin) R.; m. Liselotte Daiber, 1954; 1 foster child. Degree in Law & Political Sci., U. Tübingen, Germany, 1952. Various positions Ministry of Interior, Baden-Württemberg Ministry of State, 1965-70; sr. civil servant, 1971; sec. of state Baden-Württemberg Ministry Finance, 1972; Lord Mayor City of Stuttgart, 1974—96; v.p., then pres. German Mcpl. Authorities; chmn. Baden-Württemberg Mcpl. Authorities; chmn. bd. dirs. Landesgirokasse Bank, Stuttgart. Author: Abschied vom Schlaraffenland-Gedanken über Politik und Kultur, 1981, Wir Verwirrten Deutschen-Betrachtungen am Rande der Großen Politik, 1986, Manfred Rommels Gesammelte Sprüche, 1989. Decorated Fed. Grand Cross of Merit, Grand Officer's Cross Order of Oranien-Nassau; Grand Officer's Cross of Merit (Italy); decorated for Disting. Civilian Svc.; named hon. citizen Cairo, 1979, knight Legion of Honor, Republic of France, 1985, Guardian of Jerusalem, 1987, comdr. Most Excellent Order of Brit. Empire, 1990; recipient Award for Svcs. to Internat. Rels., 1990. Mem. Assn. Local Authority Orgns. (pres.), Freiherr vom Stein Soc. (pres.), Zweckverband Bodensee Wasserversorgung (chmn.), others. Avocations: literature, painting, natural sciences. Died Nov. 7, 2013.

**ROMNEY, CARL F.,** seismologist; b. Salt Lake City, June 5, 1924; m. Barbara Doughty; children: Carolyn Ann, Kim. BS in Meteorology, Calif. Inst. Tech., 1945; PhD, U. Calif., Berkeley, 1956. Seismologist U.S. Dept. Air Force, 1955-58; asst. tech. dir. Air Force Tech. Applications Center, 1958-73; dep. dir. Nuclear Monitoring Research Office, Def. Advanced Research Projects Agy., 1973-75, dir., 1975-79; dep. dir. Def. Advanced Research Projects Agy., 1979-83; dir. Ctr. Seismic Studies, 1983-91; v.p. Sci. Applications Internat. Corp., 1987—2001. Tech. adviser U.S. reps. in negotiations Test Ban Treaty; mem. U.S. del. Geneva Conf. Experts, 1958, Conf. on Discontinuance Nuclear Weapons Tests, 1959, 60; negotiations on threshold Test Ban Treaty, Moscow, 1974; mem. U.S. del. Peaceful Nuclear Explosions Treaty, Moscow, 1974-75 Contbr. articles to tech. jours. Recipient Exceptional Civilian Service awards Air Force, 1959, Exceptional Civilian Service awards Dept. Def., 1964, 79; Pres.'s award for Distinguished Fed. Civilian Service, for outstanding contbns. to devel. of control system for underground nuclear tests, 1967; Presdl. Rank of Meritorious Exec., 1980; inducted in Hall of Honor, Air Intelligence Agy., 1996. Achievements include research on earthquake mechanism, seismic noise; generation, propagation, detection seismic waves from underground explosions. Home: Warrenton, Va. Died July 15, 2014.

**RONA, PETER ARNOLD,** oceanographer, researcher, educator; b. Trenton, NJ, Aug. 17, 1934; s. Gustav G. and Elizabeth Rona; m. Donna Cook, Aug. l6, l974 (dec. 2013); 1 child, Jessica. AB in Geology, Brown U., 1956; MS in Geology, Yale U., 1957, PhD in Marine Geology & Geophysics, 1967. Exploration geologist Standard Oil Co., N.J., 1957-59; rsch. assocs. Hudson Labs, Columbia U., Dobbs Ferry, NY, 1960-69; sr. rsch. geophysicist NOAA, Miami, Fla., 1969-94; prof. marine geology and geophysics, dept. geol. scis. Inst. Marine and Coastal Scis., Rutgers U., New Brunswick, NJ, 1994—2014, dir. grad. cert. in engring. geophysics, 2000—14. Cons. on seafloor resources UN, N.Y.C., 1970-2014, Internat. Seabed Authority, Jamaica, 1995-2014; trustee, advisor Internat. Oceanographic Found., Miami, 1981-95; cruise lectr. Royal Caribbean Line, 1991; Geraldine R. Dodge lectr. Liberty Sci. Ctr., 1999, Hudson adv. bd., 2003-14. Author: The Central North Atlantic Atlas, l980; editor: Seafloor Spreading Centers, l98l, Hydrothermal Processes at Seafloor Spreading Centers, l983; assoc. sci. dir.: Imax Film Volcanoes of the Deep Sea, 1999-2003, reviewer editor, Diversity of Hyprothermal Systems how Spreading Ocean ridges; contbr. over 250 articles to profl. jours. Trustee Mus. Sci., Miami, l974-2014, also past chmn.; officer Dade County Cultural Affairs Coun., Miami, l979-84. Recipient Shepard medal Soc. Econ. Paleontologists & Mineralogists, l986, Gold medal US Dept. Commerce, l987, Outstanding Sci. paper award NOAA, l989, Hans Pettersson Bronze medal of the Royal Swedish Acad. Sciences, 1999, Sci. Lit. award, NJ Assn. for Biomedical Rsch., 2005. Fellow Geol. Soc. America (assoc. editor 1975-82), AAAS, Soc. Econ. Geologists, Explorers Club, American Geophys. Union (assoc. editor 1988-92), Acoustical Soc. America; mem. American Assn. Petroleum Geologists, Sigma Xi. Died Feb. 20, 2014.

**RONDEAU, CLEMENT ROBERT,** petroleum geologist; b. Ironwood, Mich., July 6, 1928; BS, Tulane U., 1955. Geol. supr. Texaco, Inc., New Orleans, 1955-63; area mgr. Pubco Petroleum Corp., New Orleans, 1963-69; cons. petroleum geologist Harahan, La., from 1969; owner Natural Gas Exploration Co., Harahan, from 1977. Mem. AAAS, Am. Assn. Petroleum Geologists, Soc. Exploration Geophysicists, New Orleans Geol. Soc., N.Y. Acad. Sci., The Explorers Club, Phi Beta Kappa, Sigma Gamma Epsilon. Democrat. Roman Catholic. Died June 15, 2013.

**ROONEY, MICKEY (JOE YULE JR.),** actor; b. Bklyn., Sept. 23, 1920; s. Joe and Nell W. (Carter) Yule; m. Ava Gardner, Jan. 10, 1942 (div. May 21, 1943); m. Betty Jane Rase, Sept. 30, 1944 (div. June 3, 1949); children: Mickey Jr., Timothy (dec. 2006); m. Martha Vickers, June 3, 1949 (div. Sept. 25, 1952); m. Elaine Mahnken, Nov. 18, 1952 (div. May 18, 1958); m. Barbara Thomason, Dec. 1, 1958 (dec. Jan. 21, 1966); children: Kerry, Kyle, Kelly Ann, Kimmy Sue; m. Margie Lang, Sept. 10, 1966 (div. Dec. 14, 1967); m. Carolyn Hockett, May 27, 1969 (div. Jan. 24, 1975); 1 adopted child, Jimmy, 1 child, Jonell; m. Jan Chamberlin, July 28, 1978 (separated June 30, 2012); stepchildren: Chris Aber, Mark Aber. Student, Pacific Mil. Acad. Actor: (films) Judge Hardy's Children, Hold That Kiss, Lord Jeff, Love Finds Andy Hardy, Boys Town, Stablemates, Out West With the Hardys, Huckleberry Finn, Andy Hardy Gets Spring Fever, Babes in Arms, Young Tom Edison, Judge Hardy and Son, Andy Hardy Meets Debutante,Midsummer Nights Dream, 1937, Words and Music, 1946, Rachels, 1973, To Hong Kong with Love, 1975, Oddessy of the Pacific, 1979. Strike Up the Band, Andy Hardy's Private Secretary, Men of Boystown, Life Begins for Andy Hardy, Babes on Broadway, A Yank at Eton, The Human Comedy, Andy Hardy's Blonde Trouble, Girl Crazy, Thousands Cheer, National Velvet, Ziegfeld Follies, The Strip, Sound Off, Off Limits, All Ashore, Light Case of Larceny, Drive A Crooked Road, Bridges at Toko-Ri, The Bold and Brave, Eddie, Private Lives of Adam and Eve, Comedian, The Grabbers, St. Joseph Plays the Horses, Breakfast at Tiffany's, Somebody's Waiting, Requiem For A Heavyweight, Richard, Pulp, It's a Mad, Mad, Mad, Mad World, Everything's Ducky, The Secret Invasion, The Extraordinary Seaman, The Comic, The Cockeyed Cowboys of Calico County, Skidoo, B.J. Presents, That's Entertainment, The Domino Principle, Pete's Dragon, The Magic of Lassie, The Black Stallion, 1979, Arabian Adventure, Erik the Viking, My Heroes Have Always Been Cowboys, 1991, (voice) Little Nimo: Adventures in Slumberland, 1992, Long Road Home, 1996, Kings of the Court, 1997, Animals, 1997, Babe: Pig in the City, 1998, The Face on the Barroom Floor, 1998, Babe: Pig in the City, 1998;Internet Love, 1998, The First of May, 1999, (voice) Lady and the Tramp II: Scamps Adventure, 2001, Topa Topa Bluffs, 2002, Driving Me Crazy, 2012, Voices From Beyond, 2012, The Woods, 2012; (TV movies) Pinocchio, 1957, Leave 'Em Laughing, 1981, Bill, 1981 (Emmy, Golden Globe), Senior Trip!, 1981, Bill on His Own, 1983, Little Spies (Acad. Hon. award 1982), It Came upon the Midnight Clear, 1984, Bluegrass, 1988, Legend of Wolf Mountain, 1992, That's Entertainment! III, 1994, Revente of the Red Baron, 1994, Radio Star-die AFN-Story, 1994, The Legend of O.B. Taggart, 1995; appeared on stage in Sugar Babies, 1979, The Will Rogers Follies, 1993; appeared in TV series A Year at the Top, The Mickey Rooney Show; author: I.E. An Autobiography, 1965, Life Is Too Short, 1991, The Search for Sonny Skies: A Novel, 1994, Brother's Destiny, 1995, Michael Kael in Katango, 1997, Boys Will be Boys, 1997, Sinbad: The Battle of the Dark Knights, 1998, The First of May, 1998 Served in US Army. Recipient Spl. Acad. Award, 1940, Tony award for Best Actor in Musical, 1980; named one of The Top 10 Money-Making Stars, Herald-Fame Poll, 1938-43 Home: Alhambra, Calif. Died Apr. 6, 2014.

**ROOT, DORIS,** artist; b. Ann Arbor, Mich., June 28, 1924; d. George O. and Hazel (Smith) Smiley; m. Leonard Hays, Oct. 22, 2000. Student, Art Inst. of Chgo., 1943-45, N.Y. Sch. Design, 1976-77, Calif. Art Inst., 1984-85. Creative dir. All May Co.'s, LA, 1962-63; advt. sales pro. dir. Seibu, LA, 1963-64; v.p. Walgers & Assoc., LA, 1964-70; owner, designer At The Root of Things, LA, 1970-73; adv. sales pro. dir. Hs. of Nine, LA, 1973-74; asst. designer MGM Grand, Reno, Nev., 1974-76; designer, office mgr. Von Hausen Studio, LA, 1976-82; ABC libr. ABC/Cap Cities, LA, 1982-89; portrait artist (also known as Dorian), AKA Dorian, art studio, LA, 1982-2000. One-man shows include Cookeville, Tenn., 1989, Beverly Hills, Calif., 1991; artist in residence, Cookeville, 1989-90. Home: Los Angeles, Calif. *"I'm one of the luckiest women alive. I love fun and found a little of it the best space to create in my career and for my personal life. People feel free to try things in a fun place to work. And I must admit, I'm still having fun painting portraits!"*. Died May 11, 2001.

**ROSAND, DAVID,** art historian, educator; b. Bklyn., Sept. 6, 1938; s. Johan Herbert and Frieda (Grotenstein) R.; m. Ellen Fineman, June 18, 1961; children: Jonathan, Eric. AB in Art History, Columbia Coll., 1959; MA, Columbia U., 1962, PhD, 1965. Instr. art history Columbia U., NYC, 1964-67, asst. prof., 1967-69, assoc. prof., 1969-73, prof., 1973-95, chmn. Soc. of Fellows in the Humanities, 1979-83, Meyer Schapiro prof. art history, 1995—2010, prof. emeritus, 2010—14. Co-author (with Michelangelo Muraro): Titian and the Venetian Woodcut, 1976, Titian, 1978; co-author: (with others) Places of Delight: The Pastoral Landscape, 1988; author: Painting in Cinquecento Venice: Titian, Veronese Tintoretto, 1982, rev. edit., 1997, The Meaning of the Mark: Leonardo and Titian, 1988, Painting in Sixteenth-Century Venice, rev. edit., 1997, Robert Motherwell on Paper, 1997, Myths of Venice: The Figuration of a State, 2001, Drawing Acts: Studies in Graphic Expression and Representation, 2002, The Invention of Painting in America, 2004, Edward Korean: The Capricions Line, 2010; editor: Titian: His World and His Legacy, 1982, Interpretazioni Veneziane, 1984; co-editor (with Robert W. Hanning): Castiglione: The Ideal and the Real in Renaissance Culture, 1983. Mem. bd. advisors CASVA Nat. Gallery Art., 1990-94. Fulbright Commn. fellow, 1962-63; NEH fellow, 1971-72, 85-86, 91-92; John S. Guggenheim Meml. Found. fellow, 1974-75; recipient Great Teacher award Soc. Columbia Graduates, 1997 Mem.: Dedalus Found. (bd. dirs.), American Acad. Arts & Sciences, Renaissance Soc. America (mem. exec. bd. 1981—2014, Paul Oskar Kristeller award for Lifetime Achievement 2007, John Jay Profl. Achievement award 2010), Coll. Art Assn. America, Istituto Veneto di Scienze, Lettere ed Arti (fgn.), Ateneo Veneto (fgn.), Save Venice, Inc. (bd. dirs. 1998—2014). Home: New York, NY. Died Aug. 8, 2014.

**ROSE, MARY ETTA,** retired educator; b. Indpls., Oct. 3, 1917; d. Robert and Florence Etta (Brooking) Taylor; divorced, 1972. BS, Ball State U., 1937; MS, Butler u., 1947; DHL, Martin U., Indpls., 1995. Tchr. music Indpls. Pub. Schs., 1943-88. Choir dir., organist Bethel African Methodist Episcopal Ch., Indpls., 1942-64; organist, choir dir. Witherspoon Presbyn. Ch., Indpls., 1978—. Martin Luther King Human Rights award Indpls. Edn. Assn., 1987. Mem. NAACP (life), AAUW, Internat. Soc. Music Educators, Ind. Ret. Tchrs. Assn., Nat. Coun. Negro Women, Ctr. for Black Music Rsch./Columbia Coll., Phi Delta Kappa (sec. 1992-94). Avocations: listening to, performing and teaching about music. Home: Indianapolis, Ind. Died Mar. 27, 2008.

**ROSE, ROBERT ARTHUR,** lawyer; b. Indpls., Sept. 17, 1931; Arthur E. Rose and Sara (Rothbard) Rose Nides; m. Phyllis Mann Rose, June 13, 1954; children: Arthur R. Rose, Amy C. Rose, Anthony J. Rose. BA, U. Mich., 1953; LLB, Columbia U., 1956. Bar:Ind. 1956, U.S. Dist. Ct. (so. dist.) Ind. 1956, U.S. Ct. Appeals (7th cir.) 1957. Assoc. Bamberger & Feibleman, Indpls., 1956-59; ptnr. Klineman, Rose, Indpls., 1959-64, Klineman, Rose & Wolf, Indpls., 1964-79, Klineman, Rose, Wolf and Wallack, Indpls., 1979-95, Dann Pecar Newman & Kleiman, Indpls., from 1995. Mem. ABA, Ind. Bar Assn., Indpls. Bar Assn. Avocations: golf, swimming, travel, reading. Home: Indianapolis, Ind. Died July 14, 2001.

**ROSEN, STANLEY HOWARD,** retired humanities educator; b. Warren, Ohio, July 29, 1929; s. Nathan A. and Celia (Narotsky) R.; m. Francoise Harlepp, Sept. 5, 1955; children: Nicholas David, Paul Mark, Valerie. BA, U. Chgo., 1949, PhD, 1955; postgrad., Am. Sch. Classical Studies, Athens, Greece, 1955-56; D honoris causa, New U. Lisbon, 1997. Mem. faculty Pa. State U., 1956-94, prof. philosophy, 1966-94; Fulbright research prof. U. Paris, 1960-61; research fellow Humanities Research Inst., U. Wis., 1963-64; Inst. Arts and Humanities research sr. fellow Pa. State U., 1972—94, Evan Pugh prof. philosophy,

1985-94; Bowne Parker Bowne prof. philosophy Boston U., 1994—2008, univ. prof., 2000—08. Vis. prof. U. Calif., San Diego, 1978, U. Nice, 1981, Scuola Superiore Pisa, 1989; vis. lectr. U. Barcelona, Spain, 1992; Priestly lectr. U. Toronto, 1997; Cardinal Mercier lectr. Louvain U., 1998; Gilson lectr. Institut Catholique, Paris, 2003. Author: Plato's Symposium, 1968, Nihilism, 1969, G.W.F. Hegel, 1974, The Limits of Analysis, 1980, Plato's Sophist: The Drama of Original and Image, 1983, Hermeneutics as Politics, 1987, The Quarrel Between Philosophy and Poetry, 1988, The Ancients and the Moderns, 1989, The Question of Being, 1993, Plato's Statesman: The Web of Politics, 1995, The Mask of Enlightenment, 1995, Metaphysics in Ordinary Language, 1999; editor: The Examined Life: A Treasury of Western Philosophy, 2000, The Elusiveness of the Ordinary, 2002, La Production Platonicienne, 2005, Plato's Republic: A Study, 2005, Essays in Philosophy: Modern, 2013, Essyas in Phiosophy: Ancient, 2013, The Idea of Hegel's Science of Logic, 2013 Rsch. grantee American Philos. Soc., 1961, Earhart Found., 1971, 73, 81, 2000. Mem. Metaphys. Soc. America (pres. 1990-91). Home: Philadelphia, Pa. Died May 4, 2014.

**ROSENBERG, PETER DAVID,** lawyer, educator; b. NYC, Aug. 2, 1942; s. Frederick and Martha (Grossman) R. BA, NYU, 1962; B in Chem. Engring., 1963; JD, N.Y. Law Sch., 1968; LLM, George Washington U., 1971. Bar: N.Y. 1970, U.S. Ct. Appeals (2nd cir.) 1970, U.S. Dist. Ct. (no. and we. dists.) N.Y. 1979, U.S. Ct. Appeals (D.C. cir.) 1982, U.S. Ct. Internat. Trade, 1982, U.S. Ct. Mil. Appeals 1982, U.S. Ct. Appeals (fed. cir.) 1983; registered U.S. Patent and Trademark Office, Canadian Patent Office. Primary examiner U.S. Patent and Trademark Office, Washington, 1968-95; of counsel Harris Beach LLP, Syracuse, N.Y., from 1995. Adj. prof. law Syracuse U. Coll. Law. Recipient Silver Medal award U.S. Dept. Commerce, 1981. Author: Patent Law Fundamentals, 1975, 2nd edit., 1980, rev., 2001, Patent Law Basics, 1992, rev., 2001; asst. editor: Jour. Patent and Trademark Office Soc., 1968-95; contbr. articles to profl. jours. Mem. ABA (antiturst and intellectual property sects.). Home: Pierrepont Manor, NY. Died Sept. 2001.

**ROSENBERG, SEYMOUR,** psychologist, educator; b. Newark, Sept. 7, 1926; s. Morris and Celia (Weiss) R.; children: Harold Stanley, Michael Seth. BS, The Citadel, 1948; MA, Ind. U., 1951, PhD, 1952. Rsch. psychologist USAF, San Antonio, 1952-58, U. Kans., Lawrence, 1958-59, Bell Tel. Labs., Murray Hill, NJ, 1959-65; vis. prof. psychology Columbia U., NYC, 1965-66; prof. psychology Rutgers U., New Brunswick, NJ, 1966—2000, chmn. dept. psychology, 1981-83, 94-95, prof. emeritus psychology, from 2001. Adj. prof. Rutgers U. Med. Sch., 1974—2000; vis. scholar U. Leuven, Belgium, 1983, Belgium, 1992, Univ. de Provence, France, 1990; panel mem. NSF, 1970—72. Cons. editor Jours. Personality Social Psychology, 1968-69; assoc. editor, 1970-73; contbr. articles to profl. jours. With USN, 1945—46. Grantee, NSF, 1965—90, NIMH, 1966—68; Rsch. scientist grantee, 1968—73, Social Sci. Rsch. Coun. fellow, 1973—74. Fellow APA; mem. Soc. Exptl. Social Psychology, Psychometric Soc., Classification Soc., NY Acad. Sci., Ea. Psychol. Assn. Home: Bowling Green, Ohio. Deceased.

**ROSENTHAL, NAN,** curator, educator, author; b. NYC, Aug. 27, 1937; d. Alan Herman and Lenore (Fry) R.; m. Otto Piene (div.); m. Henry Benning Cortesi, Sept. 5, 1990. BA, Sarah Lawrence Coll., 1959; MA in Art History, Harvard U., 1970, PhD, 1976. Asst. prof. art history U. Calif., Santa Cruz, 1971-77, assoc. prof., 1977-84, prof., 1985-86, chair dept. art history, 1976-80; curator 20th-century art Nat. Gallery Art, Washington, 1985-92; sr. cons. dept. modern art Met. Mus. of Art, NYC, 1993—2008; Lila Acheson Wallace vis. prof. fine arts NYU Inst. Fine Arts, NYC, 1996, 2000. Vis. prof. art history Fordham U., Lincoln Ctr., 1981, 1985; vis. scholar N.Y. Inst. for Humanities, NYU, 1982—83; vis. lectr. visual arts Princeton U., 1985, 1988, 1992; adj. prof. art history Columbia U., 2002. Author: Painting: From 1950 to the Present, 1976, George Rickey, 1977, Terry Winters: Printed Works, 2001; also exhbn. catalogues, catalogue essays and articles; art editor Show, 1963-64; assoc. editor, then editor at large and contbg. editor Art in America, 1964-70. Radcliffe Inst. fellow, 1968-69, scholar, 1970-71; travelling fellow Harvard U., 1973-74, rsch. fellow U. Calif., 1978, Ailsa Mellon Bruce curatorial fellow Nat. Gallery of Art, 1988-89; rsch. and travel grantee U. Calif., Santa Cruz, 1974, 77-80, 82-85. Home: New York, NY. Died Apr. 27, 2014.

**ROSS, GEORGE E.,** clergyman; b. Kansas City, Mo., Nov. 20, 1933; s. Walter W. and Eugenia C. (Moeckel) R.; m. Joan M. Ruda, June 4, 1960 (div. 1981); children: Mary E., Joan M. BA, Ohio Wesleyan, 1955; M Div, Episcopal Theol. Sch., 1958. Ordained to priest Episcopal Ch., 1958. Asst. rector St. Stephen's Ch., Cals, Ohio, 1958-60; rector St. Peter's Ch., Delaware, Ohio, 1960-63; archdeacon Diocese of Idaho, Boise, 1963-65; dean St. Michael's Cathedral, Boise, 1965-72; rector St. Paul's Ch., Akron, Ohio, from 1972. Trustee Wesleyan U., Delaware, Ohio, Trinity Sem., Ambridge, Pa. Chaplain Akron Bluecoats, 1973—; trustee Habitat for Humanity, 1986—; pres. Akron Assn. Chs., Akron Intrfaith Council. Mem. Akron City, Rotary. Episcopalian. Home: Akron, Ohio. Died June 9, 1991.

**ROSS, ZOLA HELEN,** writer; b. Dayton, Iowa, May 9, 1912; d. Sherman Andrew and Bertha Ellen (Iles) Girdey; m. Frank William Ross, May 28, 1934. BA, MacMurray Coll., 1930. Writing tchr. Lake Washington Vocat.-Tech. Inst., Kirkland, Wash., from 1957; founder Pacific Northwest Writers Conf., 1956, trustee and program chmn., pres., 1962, advisor, from 1964. Author 26 adult novels (hists. and mysteries, some under pseudonym Helen Arre Bert Iles), 11 juvenile novels (with Lucile McDonald). Recipient Book of Yr. award, State Wash., 1948, Theta Sigma Phi award, 1948, Woman Achievement and Spl. award, Women Comm., 1982, Lit. and Tchg. award, Wash. State U., 1983. Mem.: Women Comm., Free Lancers, Nat. League Am. Penwomen, Soc. Children's Book Writers, Mystery Writers America, Western Writers America. Methodist. Home: Kenmore, Wash. Died Nov. 14, 1989.

**ROSSI, ALDO,** architect; b. Milan, May 3, 1931; Student, Sch. Somaschi Fathers, Como, Italy, 1940-42, Collegio Alessandro Voltas, Lecco, Italy, 1943-46; studies with Ernesto N. Rogers and Giuseppe Samona, Poly. Milan, 1949-59, diploma in architecture, 1959. Worked in studio of Ignazio Gardella and Marco Zanuso, Milan, 1956-57; pvt. practice Milan, from 1959; working with Gianni Braghiera, Milan, from 1971. Teaching asst. to Ludovico Quaroni, Scuola Urbanistics, Arezzo, Italy, 1963; vis. instr. Poly. Milan, 1965—, prof. archtl. composition, 1970-71, mem. coun., 1971—; prof. planning Eidgenössiche Technische Hochschule, Zürich, 1972-75; prof. archtl. composition U. Venice, Italy, 1975—; Mellon prof. Cornell U., Ithaca, N.Y.; vis. prof. Cooper Union, N.Y.C., 1976; prof. planning, Yale U. New Haven, 1980. Dir. archtl. sect. XV Triennale, Milan, 1973, Biennale, Venice, 1983, Internat. Seminar on Architecture, Santiago de Compostela, Spain, 1976; exhbns. include Triennale, Milan, 1960, Centro Arte Viva, Trieste, Italy, 1967, 1972-73), Italian Architecture of the Sixties (toured Italy and Iran), 1972-73, Eidenössische Technische Hochschule, Zürich, 1973, U. Stuttgart, 1974, Palau de la Virrenia, Barcelona, Spain (toured Spain), 1975, Inst. for Architecture and Urban Studies, N.Y.C., 1976, Galleria Solferino, Milan, 1976, Architecture I, Leo Castelli Gallery, N.Y.C., 1977, Cooper Union, 1977, I nodi della rappresentazione, Pinacoteca Comunale, Ravenna, Italy, 1978, Galleria Pan, Rome, 1979, Galleria Antonia Jannone, Milan, 1979, Galleria Cesare Manzo, Pescara, Italy, 1979, Inst. for Architecture and Urban Studies, 1979, Max Protetch Gallery, N.Y.C., 1979, Hayden Gallery, MIT, Cambridge, 1980, Il Teatro del Mondo, Galleria Antonia Jannone, 1980, Cooperativa Libraria di Architettura, Naples, 1980, Walker Art Ctr., Mpls., 1980 (traveled to Chgo., Ft. Worth, Houston, Purchase, N.Y., 1980-81), Teatro e spazio scenico at the Biennale, Venice, 1980, Galleria Antonia Jannone, 1981, Galleria Nazionale d'Arte Moderna, Rome, 1981, Aldo Rossi: architecture—Projects and Drawings, Inst. Contemporary Arts, London, 1983, Aldo Rossi, Jamileh Weber Galerie, Zürich, 1983, Blue Studio Architecture Gallery, Dublin, Ireland, 1983, Palazzina dei Giardini, Modena, Italy, Rocca Paolina, Perugia, Italy, 1983, Art Gallery of Ont., Toronto, Can., 1985, Munich, 1985; prin. works include (with V. Magistretti and G.U. Polesello) Peugeot Bldg., Buenos Aires, 1961, (with Luca Meda and G.U. Polesello) Monument to the Resistance, Cuneo, Italy, 1962, (with Luca Meda) Monumental Fountain, City Hall, Milan, 1962, (with V. Gavazzeni and G. Grassi), Sch., Villa Reale Pk., Monza, Italy, 1962, (with G.U. Polesello and Luca Meda) City Hall, Turin, Italy, 1962, Paganini Theatre and Piazza della Pilotta, Parma, Italy, 1964, (with M. Fortis and M. Scolari), City Hall, Scandicci, Italy, 1968, (with G. Braghieri) Town Hall, Muggio, Italy, 1972, (with G. Braghieri, B. Reichlin, F. Reinhart) Castle Restoration and Bridge, Bellinzona, Italy, 1974, (with C. Aymonino, others) City Ctr. Plan, Florence, Italy, 1978, Floating Theatre (Teatro del Mondo), Venice Italy, 1979, (with G. Braghieri and S. Getzel), Symbolic Monument, Melbourne, Australia, 1979, Tower for New Civic Ctr., Pesaro, Italy, 1979, (with M. Adjimia and G. Getonzi), New Palace of Congress, Milan, 1982; author: (with Carlo Aymonino, Concorso per la ricostruzione del Teatro Paganini di Parma, 1966, L'Architettura della citta, 1966, Scritti scelti sull'architettura e la citta, (edited by Rosaldo Banicalzi), 1975, (with Maria Teresa Balboni) Ugo Carrega, 1976, (with Carlo Aymonino, others) un progetto per Firenze, 1978, (with others) Costruzioni del territorio e spazio urban nel Cantone Ticino, 1979, Aldo Rossi Exhbn. Catalogue, 1980, A Scientific Autobiography, 1981, (with others) Teatro del Mondo, 1982, Il Libro Azzurro: i mei progetti, 1971; contbr. articles to profl. jours.; editor Continuita, Milan, 1955-64; mem. editorial bd. Il Contemporaneo, Milan, 1959. Recipient (with Gianni Braghieri) 1st prize Mcpl. Cemetery Competition, Modena, 1971, Pritzker prize for architecture, 1990. Died Sept. 4, 1997.

**ROSSITER, ALEXANDER, JR.,** publishing executive, author; b. Elmira, NY, Mar. 2, 1936; s. Alexander H. and Eleanor (Howell) R.; m. Sylvia Lee Vanlandingham, June 11, 1960; children: Alexander H. III, Jill Rossiter Kerns. BA, Rutgers U., 1958; postgrad., Emory U., 1959. With UPI, 1959-92; newsman Atlanta, 1959-61, Richmond, Va., 1961-63; bur. mgr. Cape Canaveral, Fla., 1963-73; sci. editor Washington, 1973-87; exec. editor, 1987-88; exec. editor, sr. v.p., 1988-91; editor, exec. v.p., 1991-92; asst. v.p., dir. news svc. Duke U., Durham, NC, 1992—2001, dir. com. Pratt Sch. Engrs., 2001—02, assoc. dean pub. affairs, 2003—08. Mem. nat. adv. bd. Knight Ctr. for Specialized Journalism, Colleg Pk., Md., 1988-92; mem. adv. bd. Med. Journalism Program, U. N.C., Chapel Hill, 2000-04. Recipient Grady-Stack medal Am. Chem. Soc., 1987, other journalism awards. Mem. Nat. Assn. Sci. Writers, NC Press Assn. *Enthusiasm is the key to success. Take on your education, your family responsibilities and your work with enthusiasm and good things will result.* Died Sept. 23, 2013.

**ROSZKOWSKI, STANLEY JULIAN,** retired federal judge; b. Boonville, NY, Jan. 27, 1923; s. Joseph and Anna (Christkowski) R.; m. Catherine Mary Claeys, June 19, 1948; children: Mark, Gregory, Dan, John. BS, U. Ill., 1949, JD, 1954. Bar: Ill. 1954. Sales mgr. Warren Petroleum Co., Rockford, Ill., 1954; ptnr. Roszkowski, Paddock, McGreevy & Johnson, Rockford, 1955-77; judge US Dist. Ct. (western dist.) Ill., Rockford, Ill., 1977—91, sr. judge, 1991—98; pres. First State Bank, Rockford, 1963-75. Chmn. Fire and Police Commn., Rockford, 1967-74, commr., 1974—77; chmn. Paul Simon Com., 1972; active Adlai Stevenson III campaign, 1968-71, Winnebago County Citizens for John F. Kennedy, 1962, Winnebago County Democratic Central Com., 1962-64; bd. dirs. Sch. of Hope; mem. Ill. Capital Devel. Bd.; With USAAF, 1943-45. Decorated Air medal with 2 oak leaf clusters.; recipient Pulaski Nat. Heritage award Polish Am. Congress, Chgo., 1982 Mem. ABA, Ill. Bar Assn., Fla. Bar Assn., Winnebago County Bar Assn., American Coll. Trial Lawyers, American Judicature Soc., Assn. Trial Lawyers America, Ill. Trial Lawyers Assns., American Arbitration Assn. (arbitrator), Fed. Judges Assn. Democrat. Home: Rockford, Ill. Died July 7, 2014.

**ROTH, WILLIAM MATSON,** retired shipping company executive; b. San Francisco, Sept. 3, 1916; s. William Philip and Lurline Berenice (Matson) R.; m. Joan Osborn, Apr. 13, 1946; children: Jessica, Margaret, Anna. AB in English & History, Yale U., 1939. With Barber Oil Corp., 1947, Honolulu Oil Corp., 1948-50; chmn. bd. Pacific Nat. Life Assurance Co., 1960-63; v.p. finance Matson Navigation Co., San Francisco, 1952-61; dep. spl. rep. for trade negotiations The White House, 1963-66, spl. rep. for trade negotiations with rank of ambassador, 1967-69. Hon. trustee Com. for Econ. Devel. Mem.: Pacific Union, Bohemian, Century. Died May 29, 2014.

**ROTH, WILLIAM STANLEY,** hospital foundation executive; b. NYC, Jan. 12, 1929; s. Sam Irving and Louise Caroline (Martin) Roth; m. Hazel Adcock, May 6, 1963; children: R. Charles, W. Stanley Roth'. AA, Asheville-Biltmore Jr. Coll., NC, 1948; BS, U. NC, Chapel Hill, 1950. Dep. regional exec. Nat. coun. Boy Scouts Am., 1953-65; exec. v.p. Am. Humanics Found., 1965-67; dir. devel. Bethany Med. Ctr., Kansas City, Kans., 1967-74; exec. v.p. Geisinger Med. Ctr. Found., Danville, Pa., 1974-78; found. pres. Bapt. Med Ctrs., Birmingham, Ala., from 1978. Sec. Western Med. Systems, Cherokee County Homes, Cullman Sr. Housing, Dekalb Sr. Housing, Limestone Sr. Housing, Oxford Sr. Housing. Editor: Torch and Trefoil, 1960—61. Mem.-at-large Nat. coun. Boy Scouts Am., 1972-86; chmn. NAHD Ednl. Fund, 1980-82; ruling elder John Knox Kirk, Kansas City, Mo., Grove Presbyn. Ch., Danville, Pa. Recipient Silver award United Meth. Ch., 1970, Mid-West Health Congress, 1971; Seymour award for outstanding hosp. devel. officer, 1983, 70 Yr. Vet. award Boy Scouts Am., 2011. Fellow Assn. for Healthcare Philanthropy (life; nat. pres. 1975-76); mem. Nat. Soc. Fund Raising Execs. (pres. Ala. chpt. 1980-82, nat. dir. 1980-84, mem. ethics bd. 1993-98, advanced cert fund raising exec., Outstanding Fund Raising Exec., Ala. chpt. 1983), Mid-Am. Hosp. Devel. Assn. (pres. 1973-74), Mid-West Health Congress (devel. chmn. 1972-74), Am. Soc. for Healthcare Mktg. and Pub. Rels., Ala. Soc. for Sleep Disorders, Ala. Heart Inst., Ala. Assn. Healthcare Philanthropy (pres. 1991-93, chmn. bd. 1993-94), Ala. Planned Giving Coun. (bd. dirs. 1991-2000, pres. 1994-95), Alpha Phi Omega (nat. pres. 1958-62, dir. 1950—, Nat. Disting. Scv. award 1962), Delta Upsilon (pres. NC Alumni 1963-65), Rotary (pres. club 1976-77), Relay House, Summit Club, Green Valley Club (bd. govs.), Elks, Order of the Arrow (Nat. Disting. Svc. award 1952), Order of Holy Grail, Order of Golden Fleece. Home: Vestavia, Ala. Died Oct. 13, 2013.

**ROTHMEIER, STEVEN GEORGE,** investment company executive, retired air transportation executive; b. Mankato, Minn., Oct. 4, 1946; s. Edwin George and Alice Joan (Johnson) R. BBA, U. Notre Dame, 1968; MBA, U. Chgo., 1972. Corporate finance analyst Northwest Airlines, Inc., St. Paul, 1973, mgr. econ. analysis, 1973-78, dir. econ. planning, 1978, v.p. finance, treas., 1978-82, exec. v.p., treas., 1982-83, exec. v.p. finance & adminstrn., treas., 1983, pres., COO, 1984, pres., CEO, 1985-86, chmn., CEO, 1986-89; pres. IAI Capital Group, Mpls., 1989-93; chmn., CEO Great North Capital, St. Paul, 1993—2014. Bd. dirs. Northwest Airlines Inc., 1986-89, Lenox Group, 1992-204, Precision Castparts Corp., 1994-2013, Waste Mgmt., Inc., 1997-2012, Meritor Inc., 2004-11 Chmn. U. Chgo. Lumen Christi Inst., 1999—2009. Served in US Army, Vietnam. Decorated Bronze Star. Mem. Mpls. Club, Chgo. Club. Republican. Roman Catholic. Home: Saint Paul, Minn. *Success is not an accident; it is a habit. Success is the result of desire, dedication, sacrifice, mental toughness, hard work— and prayer. And you are not successful until you can share your success with others.* Died May 14, 2014.

**ROUDANE, CHARLES,** metal and plastic products company executive; b. LA, July 16, 1927; s. Rudolph and Irene (Warner) R.; m. Orient Fox, Aug. 20, 1948; children: Mark, Matthew. BSME, Tulane U., 1950. Gen. mgr. Master divsn. Koehring Co., Chgo., 1955-67; gen. sales mgr. Wilton Corp., Schiller Park, 1967—70; dir. mktg. Flexonics divsn. UOP Inc., Bartlett, 1970—73, v.p., gen. mgr. divsn., 1973—83; pres., CEO, Resistoflex Co. divsn. Crane Co., Marion, NC, 1983—93; chmn., CEO, ASMCorp., Chgo., 1993—2004. Bd. dirs. Ctr. Indsl. Mktg. Planning, Inc., PowRhouse Products, Inc. With AUS, 1945-46. Mem. ASME, Am. Mgmt. Assn. (past trustee, chmn. mktg. coun., mem. internat. coun., elected to Inaugural Wall of Fame 1978), Chgo. Pres. Assn., Newcomen Soc. Gt. Britain. Republican. Presbyterian. Deceased.

**ROUSE, ROSCOE, JR.,** retired librarian, educator; b. Valdosta, Ga., Nov. 26, 1919; s. Roscoe and Minnie Estelle (Corbett) R.; m. Charlie Lou Miller, June 23, 1945 (dec. Nov. 06, 2013); children: Charles Richard, Robin Rouse Wells. BA, U. Okla., 1948, MA in Libr. Sci., 1952; student (Grolier Soc. scholar), Rutgers U., 1956; AMLS, U. Mich., 1958, PhD, 1962. Bookkeeper C & S Nat. Bank, Valdosta, Ga., 1937-41; draftsman R.K. Rouse Co. (heating engrs.), Greenville, SC, 1941-42; asst. librarian Northeastern State Coll., Tahlequah, Okla., 1948-49, acting librarian, instr. library sci., 1949-51; circulation librarian Baylor U., 1952-53, acting univ. librarian, 1953-54, univ. librarian, prof.,

1954-63, chmn. dept. library sci., 1956-63; dir. libraries State U. NY at Stony Brook, LI, 1963-67; dean libr. svcs., prof. Okla. State U., Stillwater, 1967-87, univ. libr. historian, 1987-92, chmn. dept. libr. edn., 1967-74; ret., 1987. Grolier Soc. scholar, Rutgers U., 1956; vis. prof. U. Okla. Sch. Library Sci., summer 1962, N. Tex. State U., summer 1965; acad. library cons.; pub. dir. Seretean Wellness Ctr., Okla. State U., 2002—07; mem. AIA-Am. Library Assn. Library Bldg. Awards Jury, 1976; bd. dirs. Fellowship Christian Libr. and Info. Specialists; in retirement, volunteers writing and photography for local newspaper. Author: A History of the Baylor University Library, 1845-1919, 1962; editor: Okla. Librarian, 1951-52; co-author: Organization Charts of Selected Libraries, 1973; A History of the Okla. State U. Library, 1992; contbr. articles, book revs., chpts. to publs. in field. Bd. dirs. Okla. Dept. Librs., 1989-92, chmn., 1990-92. 1st lt. USAAF, 1942-45. Sgt. USAF, 1942—45. Decorated Air medal with 4 oak leaf clusters; recipient citation Okla. State Senate, 1987, Rotary Outstanding Achievement award, 1996; named in 150 Prominent Individuals in Baylor's History. Mem. ALA (life, mem. coun. 1971-72, 76-80, 83-84, 84-88, chmn. libr. orgn. and mgmt. sect. 1973-75, planning and budget assembly 1978-79, coun. com. on coms. 1979-80, bldgs. and equipment sect. exec. bd. 1979-80, chmn. bldgs. for coll. and univ. librs. com. 1983-85, chmn. nominating com. libr. history roundtable 1993-94), AARP, (sec. local chpt. 1998-2000), Okla. Libr. Assn. (life, pres. 1971-72, ALA coun. rep. 1976-80, 83-84, OLA Disting. Svc. award 1979, Spl. Merit award 1987), S.W. Libr. Assn. (chmn. coll. and univ. div. 1958-60, chmn. scholarship com. 1968-70), Internat. Fedn. Libr. Assns. (standing com. on libr. bldgs. and equipment 1976-88), Assn. Coll. and Rsch. Librs. (chmn. univ. librs. sect. 1969-70, mem. exec. bd. and rep. to ALA Coun., 1971-72), U. Mich. Sch. Libr. Sci. Alumni Soc. (pres. 1979-80, Alumni Recognition award 1988), mem. Alumni Found. Com., 1992-94, Payne County Ret. Educators Assn. (v.p., pres. elect 1991-92, pres. 1992-93), Okla. State U. Emeriti Assn. (pres. 2000-01), Okla. Hist. Soc. (com. on Okla. Higher Edn. mus. 1985—, pub. dir. 2002—), Stillwater Rotary Club (pres. 1980-81, Rotarian of Yr. 1999, editor Rotary Weekly bulletin, various coms., pub. dir. 1998—), Beta Phi Mu, Archons of Colophon. Baptist (chmn. bd. deacons 1973). Home: Oklahoma City, Okla. *It is sometimes a hidden influence in our lives which drives us toward a set goal. We ourselves may not recognize the real source of that urge to fulfill a dream. Only after many years was I able to look back and discern the factors in my youth that pushed me toward my goal of attaining a good education. They grew out of the influence that the Great Depression had on my early life. Because of that experience the preparation for a career became my first goal in life, yet the ways and means for achieving it were virtually nonexistent. It was to be, however, and I was fortunate to realize that goal. It causes me to think now that perhaps the degree of determination and endurance one possesses is paced more by adverse condition than by times of comfort and ease.* Died June 21, 2014.

**ROUX, AMBROISE MARIE CASIMIR,** business executive; b. Piscop, France, June 26, 1921; s. Andre and Cecile (Marchilhacy) R.; m. Françoise Marion, June 17, 1946; children: Christian, Véronique. Student, Coll. Stanislas, Paris, Ecole Polytechnique, 1940, Ecole des Ponts & Chaussées, 1944, Ecole Supérieure d'Electricité, 1945. Engr. Dept. Civil Engring., France, 1944-51; exec. dir. Office Sec. States for Industry and Commerce, 1952-55; sr. v.p. Compagnie Générale d'Electricité, Paris, 1955-63, pres., 1963-69, chmn. bd., 1970-82, hon. chmn., from 1982; dir. Compagnie Générale d'Electricité (Alcatel-Alsthom), Paris, from 1986; also hon. chmn. Pétrofigaz, Afnor; chmn. AGREF, 1976-82, Association Française des entreprises Privées, from 1983, Compagnie Industrielle des Télécommunications (CIT-Alcatel), 1966-82, hon. chmn., from 1982; chmn. Compagnie Electro-Financière, 1969-82, hon. chmn., from 1982; vice chmn. Sté. des Plantations des Terres Rouges; dir. Barclays Bank, 1983-85, vice chmn., 1985-91; chmn. Conseil Surveillance, from 1991. Vice chmn. Compagnie Generale des Eaux, 1992—; bd. dirs. Cie. Financiére Paribas, 1972-82, 86-90, mem. Conseil Surveillance, 1990—; bd. dirs. CEP-Communication, Schneider, 1991—, Mines Kali Ste Thérèse, 1986—; dir. Sté du Louvre; mem. Conseil de Surveillance Printemps, 1991-92; chmn. Counseil de Surveillance, 1992—, Pinault-Printemps-Redoute; hon. dir. La Radiotechnique, 1993—; dir. FNAC, 1994—, Sté d'investissemente IENA, 1994—. Author: La Science et les Pouvoirs Psychiques de l'Homme. Decorated grand officer Légion d'Honneur, comdr. Mérite Comml., comdr. Instrn. Publique. Mem. the N.Y. Acad. of Scis., mem. Fedn. French Industries (vice chmn. 1966-75, 1st vice chmn. 1975-82, hon. 1st vice chmn. 1982—) Home: Paris, France. Died Apr. 1999.

**ROUX, MILDRED ANNA,** retired secondary school educator; b. New Castle, Pa., June 1, 1914; d. Louis Henri and Frances Amanda (Gillespie) R. BA, Westminster Coll., 1936, MS in Edn., 1951. Tchr. Farrell (Pa.) Sch. Dist., 1939-55; tchr. Latin, English New Castle (Pa.) Sch. Dist., 1956-76; ret., 1976. Chmn. sr. H.S. fgn. lang. dept. New Castle Sch. Dist., 1968-76, faculty sponsor sch. fgn. lang. newspapers, 1960-76, Jr. Classical League, 1958-76. Mem. Lawrence County Hist. Soc., Am. Classical League, 1958-76. Mem. AAUW (chmn. publicity, chmn. program com. Lawrence County chpt. 1992-96), Am. Assn. Ret. Persons, Nat. Ret. Tchrs. Assn., Pa. Assn. Sch. Retirees (chmn. cmty. participation com. Lawrence County br. 1976-81, telephone com. Lawrence County br. 1990-98), Coll. Club New Castle (chmn. sunshine com. 1989-91, mem. social com. 1991-92), Woman's Club New Castle (chmn. pub. affairs com. 1988-90, internat. affairs com. 1990-92, program com. 1990-92, telephone com. 1992-99). Republican. Roman Catholic. Avocations: singing, reading, civic interests. Deceased.

**ROWE, ANDREW JOHN BERNARD,** retired British legislator; b. London, Sept. 11, 1935; s. John Douglas R. and Mary Katherine (Storr) Luther; m. Alison Isobel Boyd Wolfe Murray, Apr. 9, 1960 (div.); 1 child, Nicholas; m. Sheila Leslie Finkle, Nov. 5, 1983; children: Nicholas, Kathryn, Louise. MA, Oxford U., Eng., 1959. Prin. Scottish Office, Edinburgh, 1962-67; asst. master Eton (Eng.) Coll., 1959-74; lectr. Edinburgh (Scotland) U., 1967-74; dir. cmty. affairs Consecutive Ctrl. Office, London, 1975-79; self employed London, 1979-83; M.P., 1983—2001. Trustee Nat. Soc. for Prevention of Cruelty to Children, London Author: Democracy Renamed, 1972; contbr. numerous articles to profl. jours. Trustee Cmty. Svc. Vols., London, 1984-97; dir. Small Bus. Bur., London, 1976-83; pres. North Downs Rail Concern, Kent, Eng.; Lt. Royal Naval Vol. Res., 1954-56. Mem. Kent County Engring. Club (former pres.). Conservative. Anglican. Avocations: golf, fishing, reading, writing. Home: Kent, England. Died Nov. 21, 2008.

**ROWE, HERBERT JOSEPH,** retired business, government trade association executive; b. Granite City, Ill., Mar. 25, 1924; s. Herbert Bernard and Maude (Klein) R.; m. Ann Muter, Dec. 2, 1950; children: Douglas H., Stephen F., James D., Edith L., Allen; 1st Lt, USMC, 1942-1946, 1950-1952 Student, U. Tex., 1942—43, Purdue U., 1943—44; BS in Mktg., U. Ill., 1948; LittD (hon.), London Inst. for Applied Rsch., 1975. With Edward Valves, Inc. (subs. Rockwell Mfg. Co.), 1948—50, Muter Co., Chgo., 1952—71, v.p., 1957—64, pres., 1964—71, treas., 1964—67, chmn. bd., 1965—71, also dir., 1957—71; pres., treas., dir. Wescoil Co., 1964—66, Tri-Axial Corp., 1966—67; v.p., treas. Gen. Magnetic Corp., 1965—67, chmn. bd., dir., 1967—70, Pemcor, Inc., Westchester, Ill., 1971—75; assoc. adminstr. external affairs NASA, 1975—78; sr. v.p. Electronic Industries Assn., 1978—89; chmn. Famro Corp., 1989—90; pres. Internat. Electronics Fedn., 1989—90. Sec.-treas. Englewood Elec. Supply Wis., Inc., 1972-75, Rahr's Inc., 1972-75; pres. Enclave of Naples, Inc., 1992-94, treas., 1994-96; pres. Rowe Corp., 1994-97; treas. Quality wholesale Foods of S.W. Fla., 1994-96. Pres. Pokagon Trails coun. Boy Scouts Am., 1964-66, pres. Calumet coun., 1966-68, region 7 exec. com., 1966-72, vice chmn., 1971-72, bd. dirs. East Ctrl. region, 1972-75, nat. program com., 1970-78, 90-94, nat. Cub Scout com., 1970-80, chmn., 1990-94, S.E. regional exec. com., 1975-78, So. regional exec. bd., 1993—, bd. dirs. Nat. Capital Area coun., 1978-90, adv. bd., 1990-94, exec. bd. S.W. Fla. coun., 1992—, nat. exec. com., exec. bd., 1990-95, nat. adv. bd., 1995—; membership chmn. Nat. Eagle Scouts Assn., 1976-80; corp. campaign chmn. Chgo. Met. Crusade Mercy, 1964-68; chmn. Bd. Edn. Caucus, Flossmoor, Ill., 1962; bd. dirs. Flossmoor United Party, 1963-68; mem. U. Ill. Found., 1967—; adv. com. U. Ill. Coll. Commerce and Bus. Adminstrn., 1968-78, 97-2002; bd. dirs. Electronic Industries Found., 1974-94; adv. bd. Air and Space Mus., Smithsonian Inst., 1975-78; active Moorings Presbyn. Ch., Naples, Fla. With USMCR, 1942-46, 1st lt. 50-52; mem. Ernest Thompson Seton Inst., 1910 Soc. Boy Scouts Am. 1st lt. USMC, 1942—46, 1st lt. USMC, 1950—52. Recipient Silver Beaver award Boy Scouts Am., 1966, Silver Antelope award, 1969, Silver Buffalo award, 1994; NASA team award Bicentennial Expo on Sci. and Tech., Exceptional Svc. medal, 1978, Baden-Powell fellow World Scout Found., 1992. Mem. AIAA, AAAS, Electronic Industries Assn. (hon., bd. dirs. 1967-69, bd. govs. 1969-75, exec. com. parts divsn. 1966-75, vice chmn. parts divsn. 1970-74, chmn. 74-75, bd. dirs. consumer electronics divsn. 1972-75, chmn. world trade com. 1968-70, vice-chmn. 1970-73, chmn. membership and scope com. 1972-74, Disting. Svc. award 1989), Am. Loudspeaker Mfrs. Assn. (v.p., dir. 1967-68, pres., bd. dirs. 1968-70), Am. Inst. Archeology, Assn. Electronic Mfrs. (bd. dirs. 1970-73), Nat. Space Club, Nat. Space Inst., Am. Acad. Polit. Social Sci., Am. Soc. Assn. Execs. (vice chmn. internat. sect. 1986-87, chmn. 1987-88), US Naval Inst., Field Mus. Natural History, European Soc. Assn. Execs., Greater Washington Soc. Assn. Execs., Naples Coun. World Affairs (bd. dirs. 2003-05), Explorers Club, Chgo. Art Inst., Am. Legion, Chaine des Rôtisseurs, L'Ordre Mondial, Internat. Wine and Food Soc. (pres. Naples br. 2001-07), English-Speaking Union (pres. Naples chpt. 1996—2007, chmn. 2007-, nat. dir. 1997—2012, chmn. fin.com. 2007-2008, regional vice chmn. 2000-03, Audit Com., 2003-06, Fin. Com., 2007-, Conservancy, S.W. Fla., Forum Club S.W. Fla. (bd. dirs. 2000-03), Naples Press Club (bd. dirs. 1998-2000), Royal Poinciana Golf Club, Naples Yacht Club, Circumnavigators Club, Traveler's Century Club, Beta Gamma Sigma, Alpha Phi Omega, Sigma Chi (dir. Kappa Kappa corp. 1954-75, sec. 1971-73, pres. 1973-75, Charles J. Kiler award 1975, Grand Consul's citation 1976, Significant SIG award 2006), Res. Officers Assn., Marine Corps. League. Home: Naples, Fla. Died Dec. 2, 2013.

**ROWLEY, JANET DAVISON,** physician; b. NYC, Apr. 5, 1925; d. Hurford Henry and Ethel Mary (Ballantyne) Davison; m. Donald A. Rowley, Dec. 18, 1948; children: Donald, David, Robert, Roger. PhB, U. Chgo., 1944, BS, 1946, MD, 1948; DSc (hon.), U. Ariz., 1989, U. Pa., 1989, Knox Coll., 1991, U. So. Calif., 1992, St. Louis U., 1997, St. Xavier U., 1999, Oxford U., Eng., 2000, Lund U., Sweden, 2003, Dartmouth U., 2004; degree (hon.), U. Calif, San Francisco, 2008; DSc, Lake Forest Coll, Harvard, 2011. Diplomate Am. Bd. Med. Genetics. Rsch. asst. U. Chgo., 1949—50; intern Marine Hosp., USPHS, Chgo., 1950—51; attending physician Infant Welfare and Prenatal Clinics Dept. Public Health, Montgomery County, Md., 1953—54; rsch. fellow Levinson Found., Cook County Hosp., Chgo., 1955—61; clin. instr. neurology U. Ill., Chgo., 1957—61; USPHS spl. trainee Radiobiology Lab. The Churchill Hosp., Oxford, England, 1961—62; rsch. assoc. dept. medicine and Argonne Cancer Rsch. Hosp. U. Chgo., 1962—69, assoc. prof. dept. medicine, 1969—77, prof. dept. medicine and Franklin McLean Meml. Rsch. Inst., 1977—84, Blum-Riese Disting. Svc. prof., dept. medicine and dept. molecular genetics and cell biology, from 1984, Blum-Riese Disting. Svc. prof. dept. human genetics, from 1997, interim dep. dean for sci. biol. sciences divsn., 2001—02. Bd. sci. counsellors Nat. Inst. Dental Rsch., NIH, 1972—76, chmn., 1974—76; mem. Nat. Cancer Adv. Bd., Nat. Cancer Inst., 1979—84, Nat. Adv. Coun. for Human Genome Rsch. Inst., 1999—2004; adv. com. Frederick Cancer Rsch. Facility, 1983—84; bd. sci. counsellors Nat. Human Genome Rsch. Inst., NIH, 1994—99, chmn., 1994—97; adv. bd. Howard Hughes Med. Inst., 1989—94, MD Anderson Cancer Ctr., 1998—2005; vis. com. dept. applied biol. scis. MIT Corp., 1983—86; bd. sci. cons. Meml. Sloan-Kettering Cancer Ctr., 1988—90; adv. com. Ency. Britannica U. Chgo., 1988—96; Presdl. Symposium American Soc. Pediatric Hematology/Oncology, 1995; chmn. sci. adv. com. Translational Genomics Rsch. Inst., Phoenix., 2004—13; med. adv. bd. Calif. Inst. Regenerative Medicine, 2005—13; mem. sci. adv. coun. Children's Hosp., Boston, 2005—13. Co founder co editor: Genes, Chromosomes and Cancer, mem. editl. bd.: Oncology Rsch., Cancer Genetics and Cytogenetics, Leukemia Rsch., Internat. Jour. Hematology, Genomics, Leukemia; past mem. editl. bd. Internat. Jour. Cancer, Blood, Cancer Rsch., Hematol. Oncology, Leukemia Rsch.; contbr. chapters to books, articles to profl. jours. Adv. com. for career awards in biomedical sciences Burroughs Wellcome Fund, 1994—98; selection panel for Clin. Sci. award Doris Duke Charitable Found., 2000—02, 2006; mem. Pres.'s Advisory Coun. on Bioethics, 2001—09; mem. med. rsch. material command leukemia program U.S. Army, 2002—04; mem. selection com. Rosalind Franklin young investigator award, 2004, Rosalind Franklin Young Investigator award, 2007—13, 2009; nat. adv. com. McDonnell Found. Program for Molecular Medicine in Cancer Rsch., 1988—98; mem. advisory bd. Leukemia Soc. American, 1979—84; selection com. scholar award in biomed. sci. Lucille P. Markey Charitable Trust, 1984—87; trustee Adler Planetarium, Chgo., from 1978; med. adv. bd. G&P Charitable Found., 1999—2013. Recipient Esther Langer award, Ann Langer Cancer Rsch. Found., 1983, First Kuwait Cancer prize, 1984, A. Cressy Morrison award in Natural Sciences, NY Acad. Sciences, 1985, Past State Pres. award, Tex. Fedn. Bus. & Profl. Women's Clubs, 1986, Karnofsky award and lecture, American Soc. Clin. Oncology, 1987, Antoine Lacassagne Lique prize, Nat. Francaise Contre le Cancer prize, 1987, Katherine Berkan Judd award, Meml. Sloan-Kettering Cancer Ctr., 1989, Steven C. Beering award, U. Ind. Med. Sch, 1992, Robert de Villiers award, Leukemia Lymphoma Soc., 1993, Return of the Child award., 2005, Kaplan Family prize for cancer rsch. excellence, Oncology Soc. Dayton, 1995, Cotlove award and lecture, Acad. Clin. Lab. Physicians and Scientists, 1995, Nilsson-Ehle lecture, Mendelian Soc. and Royal Physiographic Soc., 1995, Gairdner Found. Internat. award, 1996, Medal of Honor, Basic Sci. American Cancer Soc., 1996, Nat. Medal of Sci., The White House, 1998, Lasker-DeBakey Clin. Med. Rsch. award, Lasker Found., 1998, Woman Extraordinaire award, Internat. Women's Associates, 1999, Golden Plate award, American Acad. Achievement, 1999, Women Achieving Excellence award, YWCA of Met. Chgo., 2000, Philip Levine award, American Soc. Clin. Pathology, 2001, Emile M Chamot award, State Microscopy Soc. Ill., 2001, Mendel medal, Villanova U., 2003, Benjamin Franklin medal, American Philos. Soc., 2003, Dist. Alumni Award, U. Chgo., 2003, Norman McLean Mentorship award, 2006, Medal, Lake Forest Coll., Harvard, 2008, Award for Excellence, Assn. Molecular Pathology, 2007, Disting. Scientist award, American Assn. Cancer Inst., 2009, Peter & Patricia Gruber Found. Genetics Prize, 2009, Presdl. Medal of Freedom, The White House, 2009, Hope Funds for Cancer Rsch. award, 2012; co-recipient King Faisal Internat. prize in medicine, 1988, Charles Mott prize, GM Cancer Rsch. Found., 1989, Pearl Meister Greengard prize, Rockefeller U., 2010, Japan prize, 2012; named Chicagoan of Yr., Chgo. mag., 1998. Fellow: AAAS (nominating com. 1998); mem.: NAS (chmn. sect. 41 1995—99, mem. com. 2004, Jessie Stevenson Kovalenko medal 2010), Chgo. Network (lectr. 2003—13), Inst. Medicine (coun. 1988—90), Cancer Rsch. (G.H.A. Clowes Meml. award 1989, Charlotte Friend award 2003, Dorothy P. Landon award 2005), American Soc. Hematology (lectr. Millenium Symposium 1999, Presdl. Symposium 1982, Dameshek prize 1982, Ham-Wasserman award 1995, Henry M. Stratton medal 2003, Marion Spencer Fay Lifetime Achievement award 2006, Ernest Beutler award 2010), Genetical Soc., American Soc. Human Genetics (pres.-elect 1992, pres. 1993, Allen award and lectr. 1991, Disting. Sci. lectr. 2003), American Philos. Soc., American Acad. Arts & Sciences (nominating com. 1998), Phi Beta Kappa (hon.), Sigma Xi (William Proctor prize for sci. achievement 1989), Alpha Omega Alpha (hon.). Episcopalian. Home: Chicago, Ill. Died Dec. 17, 2013.

**ROWLEY, WILLIAM RICHARD CHARLTON,** experimental physicist, consultant; b. Bath, Somerset, Eng., Mar. 11, 1935; s. Francis Bernard and Isabella (Matthews) R.; m. Cynthia Diana Garland; children: Alexandra Kate, Patrick Anderson Charlton. BS, Durham U., Eng., 1956, PhD, 1959. Chartered physicist. Sci. officer Nat. Phys. Lab., U.K., 1959-63, sr. sci. officer, 1963-68, prin. sci. officer, 1968-75, sr. prin. sci. officer, 1975-95, cons., from 1995. Rapporteur Consultative Com. for Definition of Metre, 1973=93. Author: (chpt.) A Guide to the Laser, 1967; contbr. over 90 articles to profl. jours.; patentee in field. Fellow Inst. Physics. Achievements include development of first frequency stabilized laser; frequency stabilized He-Ne lasers; techniques of interferometric length measurement. Home: Twickenham, England. Died Feb. 2007.

**ROY, BIMALENDU NARAYAN,** ceramic engineering educator; b. Calcutta, India; s. Sachindra Nath and Prativa (Dhar) R.; m. Manju Gupta, Sept. 17, 1979; 1 child, Niladri. BSc, Calcutta U., 1961, BA, 1963, LLB, 1966; postgrad.

diploma, Leeds U., Eng., 1968; PhD, London U., 1972. Lectr. U. Sains Malaysia, Penang, 1973-76; sci. officer Cen. Glass and Ceramic Rsch. Inst., Calcutta, 1977-78; sr. lectr. U. Sci. and Tech., Kumasi, Ghana, 1978-80; vis. prof. Mont. State U., 1981-82, Ariz. State U., 1983-84; sr. rsch. fellow U. Northumbria, Newcastle, Eng., 1984-85; chief rsch. officer U. Essex, Eng., 1986-89; sr. lectr. Sheffield (Eng.) Hallam U., 1990-92, U. Brunei Darussalam, Brunei, 1993-97; lectr. and sr. rch. fellow Brunel U., Eng., 1997-99; vice-rector acad. affairs and rsch. Poly. of Namibia, 2001—02; vis. prof. PNG U. Tech., Papua, Papua New Guinea, from 2002. Freelance abstractor Derwent Pub., London, 1969-71, PRM Sci. and Tech. Agy., London, 1972-73, Inst. Metals, London, 1985-88; vis. scientist Cavendish Lab., Cambridge U., 1994, Dept. Engring., 1995; adj. faculty Fairfax U., La., 1988—; fellow Inst. Physics, U.K. Author: Crystal Growth from Melts: Applications to Growth of Groups 1 and 2 Metals, 1991, Principles of Modern Thermodynamics, 1995, Fundamentals of Classical and Statistical Thermodynamics, 2002; contbr. articles to profl. jours. Gen. sec. community orgn., London, 1985-86, v.p., 1988-92; gov., chmn. curriculum com. Stockwell Pk. Sch., London, 1998-2001. Rsch. grantee Lady Mountbatten Trust, Eng., Sidney Perry Found., Eng., Curzon Wylie Found., Eng., 1969-71, Ministry Edn., Malaysia, 1974, U. Sci. and Tech. Ghana, 1979, Royal Soc., London, 1991, U. Brunei Darussalam, Brunei, 1994, 1995; recipient First Literary prize Belur Sch., India, 1951, 52, 53, 54, Rotary Internat., India, 1955, Nehru Birth Day Celebration Com., India, 1955, Ctrl. Calcutta Coll., 1960, 61, Second prize Bally Cultural and Lit. Soc., India, 1961, Youth Festival Com., India, 1964. Fellow: Inst. Physics; mem.: Royal Soc. Chemistry. Avocations: writing, travel, photography, scouting, games. Deceased.

**ROY, NARENDRA NARAYAN,** chemistry educator, researcher; b. Sakarpura, Bihar, India, Apr. 7, 1934; s. Ramanuj and Bhagyavati (Singh) R.; m. Ratna Prabha, May 8, 1955; children: Atish Kumar, Satish Kumar, Tanuja Roy Chaudhary, Rashmi Roy Dixit. BSc with honors, Patna Coll, India, 1954, MSc, 1956; PhD, U. Wash., 1970. Lectr. Patna U., 1956-60, Regional Inst. Tech., Jamshedpur, India, 1960-82; tchg. asst. dept. chemistry U. Wash., Seattle, 1966-70, tchg. assoc. dept. chemistry, 1970; reader in phys. chemistry Tribhuwan U., Kathmandu, Nepal, 1973-76; asst. prof., reader Regional Inst. Tech., Jamshedpur, 1982-85, prof., head dept. chemistry, 1987-92, 94, prin. investigator Univ. Grants Commn. rsch. project, from 1994; postdoctoral fellow dept. chemistry U. Ga., Athens, 1985. Contbr. articles and numerous rsch. papers to nat. and internat. jours. in field. Vol. CARE, Bihar, India, 1967. Fellow Indian Assn. Environ. Mgmt. (life); mem. Indian Sci. Congress Assn. Avocations: gardening, reading political magazines, social and charitable work. Home: Jamshedpur, India. Died Dec. 9, 2005.

**ROY, WILLIAM ROBERT (BILL ROY),** obstetrician, former United States Representative from Kansas; b. Bloomington, Ill., Feb. 23, 1926; s. Elmer Javan and Edna Blanche (Foley) R.; m. Jane Twining Osterhoudt, Sept. 7, 1947 (dec. Oct. 18, 2010); children: Robin Jo, Randall Jay, Richelle Jane, William Robert, Renee Jan, Rise Javan. BS, Ill. Wesleyan U., 1946; MD, Northwestern U. Medical Sch., 1949; JD with honors, Washburn U. Law Sch., 1970. Pvt. practice medicine, 1955-70, 79-89; mem. US Congress from 2d Kans. Dist., 1971-75; exec. dir. Kans. Med. Edn. Found., 1976-94; newspaper columnist The Topeka Capital-Journal, 1989—2014. Delegate Democratic Nat. Convention, 1976, 1984; Democratic candidate for US Senate, 1974, 78. Served in. Mem. Inst. Medicine of Nat. Acad. Sciences Democrat. Methodist. Home: Topeka, Kans. Died May 26, 2014.

**ROZENBERG-GUGGENHEIM, ISABELLE,** physician, researcher, writer; b. Szczecin, Poland, Jan. 30, 1949; d. Menasze Rozenberg and Anna Perlmutter; m. Hans Josef Guggenheim, Oct. 30, 1998; m. Pierre Berkman, May 12, 1977 (div. June 18, 1980). BA in chemistry and biology, Faculty of Sci., Paris, 1968; MD, Faculty of Medicine, Paris, 1979; Endocrinology, 3rd cycle, Faculty of Sci., Paris, 1979. Cert. Pediats. France, 1979, Endocrinology, Diabetes Nutrition France, 1979, Endocrinology France, 1979, Internal Medicine France, 1984, Endocrinology Metabolic Diseases France, 1986. Intern Marseilles U. Hosps., France, 1974—78; sci. asst. prof. Paris U. Hosps., 1981, clin. asst. prof. Paris- Creteil, 1981—84, hosp. practitioner, head, 1988—89; clin. practice Paris, from 1984. Clin. cons. Roussel Pharm., Paris, 1984—85. Co-author: (book) Les Endocrines et le Milieu, 1975, INSERM - CNAM Publications, 1983, Lessons from Animal Diabetes, 1984; author: (med. daily newspaper) Le Quotidien du Medecin, 1984—96, (med. ency.) Encyclopedie Medico- chirurgicale, 1985—92. Vol. physician Paris Refugee Med. Ctr. under care of Paris Mayor, 1981—83. Mem.: Am. Diabetes Assn., European Fedn. of Internal Medicine, French Soc. of Internal Medicine, Endocrine Soc., Internat. Sci. Writer Assn. Avocations: antiques, piano, perfume design, mountain trekking, travel. Home: London, England. Died May 27, 2006.

**RUANE, J. MICHAEL,** state legislator; Mem. City Council, Mass., 1970—75, Mass. Ho. of Reps., from 1975. Died June 25, 2006.

**RUBIN, BARRY MITCHEL,** foreign policy analyst, writer; b. Washington, Jan. 28, 1950; s. David and Helen Victoria (Segal) R.; m. Judith Colp; children: Gabriella, Daniel. BA, Richmond Coll., 1972; MA, Rutgers U., 1974; PhD, Georgetown U., 1978. Sr. fellow CSIS, Washington, 1978-85, Washington Inst. Near East Policy, Washington, 1988-91; congl. fellow Coun. Fgn. Rels., Washington, 1985-86; fellow Johns Hopkins SAIS, Washington, 1986-93, prof., 1986-93; sr. fellow U. Haifa Jewish-Arab Ctr., from 1993; sr. resident scholar BESA Ctr., 1996-99, dep. dir., 1999; dir. Global Rsch. in Internat. Affairs (GLORIA) Ctr. Adj. prof. Johns Hopkins SAIS, Washington, 1986-93, dir. SAIS project polit. study terrorism; mem. fgn. policy staff US Senate, 1985-86; prof. Hebrew U., 1994-95. Author: Paved with Good Intentions, 1980, The Arab States and the Palestine Conflict, 1982, Secrets of State, 1985, Modern Dictators, 1987, Istanbul Intrigues, 1989, Islamic Fundamentalists in Egyptian Politics, 1991, Cauldron of Turmoil, 1992, Resolution Until Victory?: The Politics of the PLO, 1994, Assimilation and its Discontents, 1995, Essays on the Middle East's New Era, 1997, From Revolution to State—Building the Transformation of Palestinian Politics, 1999, The Long War for Freedom: The Arab Struggle for Democracy in the Middle East, 2006, The Truth About Syria, 2008; co-author: (with Judith Colp Rubin) Hating America: A History, 2004; editor: (with others) The Human Rights Reader, 1979, The Israel-Arab Reader, 1984, 95, 2001, Central American Crisis Reader, 1987, The Politics of Terrorism, 3 vols., Iraq's Road to War, 1994, Turkey and the World, 2001; contbr. articles to profl. jours. including Middle East Review International Affairs, Turkish Studies Jour., among others. Internat. affairs fellow Coun. on Fgn. Rels., 1984-85, Fulbright fellow, 1990-91; grantee US Inst. of Peace, 1989-91, Davis Inst., 1994; Harry Guggenheim fellow, 1990. Mem. Assn. Israel Studies (v.p. 1984-89). Died Feb. 3, 2014.

**RUBIN, LILLIAN BRESLOW,** sociologist; b. Phila., Jan. 13, 1924; d. Sol and Rae (Vinin) Breslow; m. Seymour Katz, Mar. 6, 1943 (div. Oct. 1961); m. Henry M. Rubin, Mar. 4, 1962 (dec. 2011); 1 child, Marci R. BA, U. Calif., Berkeley, 1967, MA, 1968, PhD in Sociology, 1971; LHD, SUNY, Albany, 1992. Rsch. sociologist Inst. for Study of Social Change U. Calif., Berkeley, 1971—2014; alumni prof. interpretive sociology Queens Coll., CUNY, 1988-94. Author: Worlds of Pain: Life in the Working Class Family, 1976, Women of a Certain Age: The Mid-Life Search for Self, 1979, Intimate Strangers: Men and Women Together, 1983, Just Friends: The Role of Friendship in Our Lives, 1985, Families on the Fault Line, 1994, The Transcendent Child: Tales of Triumph Over the Past, 1996 Recipient Woodrow Wilson Honorable Mention, 1968. Mem. American Sociol. Assn., Calif. Assn. Family Therapists, Nat. Coun. on Family Rels., American Orthopsychiat. Assn., Phi Beta Kappa. Democrat. Jewish. Home: San Francisco, Calif. Died June 17, 2014.

**RUBIN, LOUIS DECIMUS, JR.,** retired language educator, writer, publishing executive; b. Charleston, SC, Nov. 19, 1923; s. Louis Decimus and Janet (Weinstein) R.; m. Eva M. Redfield, June 2, 1951; children: Robert Alden, William Louis. Student, Coll. of Charleston, 1940-42, LittD (hon.), 1989; AB, U. Richmond, 1946, LittD (hon.), 1972; MA, Johns Hopkins U., 1949, PhD, 1954; LittD (hon.), Clemson U., 1986, U. of the South, 1991, U. N.C. at Asheville, 1993, U. N.C., Chapel Hill, 1995. Instr. Johns Hopkins U.; editor Hopkins Rev., 1950-54; fellow criticism Sewanee Rev., 1953-54; exec. sec. American Studies Assn., asst. prof. American civilization U. Pa., 1954-56; assoc. editor Richmond (Va.) News Leader, 1956-57; assoc. prof. English Hollins Coll., 1957-60, prof., chmn. dept., 1960-67; prof. English U. N.C., 1967-73, Univ. Disting. prof., 1973-89, prof. emeritus, 1989—2013. Editor Hollins Critic, 1963-68; vis. prof. history La. State U., 1957; Fulbright lectr. U. Aix-Marseille, 1960; lectr. Breadloaf Writer's Conf., 1961; vis. prof. U. N.C., 1965, Harvard U., 1969; lectr. Aerican. studies seminars Kyoto (Japan) U., 1979; founder, pub., editl. dir. Algonquin Books Chapel Hill, 1982-91. Author: Thomas Wolfe: The Weather of His Youth, 1955, No Place on Earth, 1959, The Golden Weather, 1961, The Faraway Country, 1963, The Teller in the Tale, 1967, The Curious Death of the Novel, 1967, George W. Cable, 1969, The Writer in the South, 1972, William Elliott Shoots A Bear, 1975, Virginia: A History, 1977, The Wary Fugitives, 1978, Surfaces of a Diamond, 1981, A Gallery of Southerners, 1982, The Even-Tempered Angler, 1983, The Edge of the Swamp, 1989, The Algonquin Literary Quiz Book, 1990, The Mockingbird in the Gum Tree: A Literary Gallimaufry, 1991, Small Craft Advisory, 1991, The Heat of the Sun, 1995, Babe Ruth's Ghost, 1996, Seaports of the South, 1998, A Memory of Trains, 2000, An Honorable Estate: My Time in the Working Press, 2001, My Father's People: A Family of Southern Jews, 2002, Where The Southern Cross the Yellow Dog: On Writers and Writing, 2005, The Summer The Archduke Died, 2008, Uptown/Downtown in Old Charleston, 2010; editor: Southern Renascence: Literature of the Modern South, 1953, The Lasting, South, 1957, Teach the Freeman: R.B. Hayes and the Slater Fund for Negro Education, 1959, The Idea of an American Novel, 1961, South: Modern Southern Literature in Its Cultural Setting, 1961, Bibliographical Guide to the Study of Southern Literature, 1969, The Comic Imagination in American Literature, 1973, The Literary South, 1978, The American South, 1980, The History of Southern Literature, 1985, An Apple for My Teacher: Twelve Authors Tell About Teachers Who Made the Difference, 1987, A Writer's Companion, 1995, The Quotable Baseball Fanatic, 2000; co-editor: Southern Lit. Jour., 1968-89; contbr. articles to periodicals. Served with AUS, 1943-46. Guggenheim fellow, 1958-59, fellow American Coun. Learned Societies, 1964, Fulbright fellow, Oliver Max Gardner award, Mayflower award, Disting. Virginian award, NC award for Lit., 1992, R. Hunt Parker Meml. award for Lifetime Contributions to NC Lit. Heritage, Academy award in Lit., American Acad. of Arts & Letters, 2004, Ivan Sandrof Lifetime Achievement award, Nat. Book Critics Cir., 2005, John Tyler Caldwell award for the Humanities, 2005, Authors Guild award, 2008. Fellow Southern Writers (chancellor 1991-93); mem. Soc. Study Southern Lit. (pres. 1975-76), Phi Beta Kappa. Died Nov. 16, 2013.

**RUBIN, STANLEY CREAMER,** television producer, film producer; b. NYC, Oct. 8, 1917; s. Michael Isaac and Anne (Creamer) R.; m. Elizabeth Margaret von Gerkan (actress Kathleen Hughes), July 25, 1954; children: John, Chris (dec.), Angela, Michael. Student, UCLA, 1933-37, BA, 2006. Writer Universal Studios, Universal City, Calif., 1940-42, Columbia Pictures, Los Angeles, 1946-47; writer, producer NBC-TV, Burbank, Calif., 1948-49; theatrical film producer various studios, 1949-55, Rastar Prodns., Columbia Pictures, 1988-91; TV producer CBS-TV, Los Angeles, 1956-59, Universal Studios, Universal City, 1960-63, 20th Century-Fox, Los Angeles, 1967-71, MGM Studios, Culver City, Calif., 1972-77; pres. TBA Productions, Los Angeles, 1978—2014. Producer: (films) The Narrow Margin, 1950, My Pal Gus, 1950, Destination Gobi, 1951, River of No Return, 1952, Promise Her Anything, 1966, The President's Analyst, 1967, Revenge, 1989; co-producer White Hunter, Black Heart, 1990; TV prodns. include G.E. Theatre, 1959-63, Ghost and Mrs. Muir, 1968-69, Bracken's World, 1969-71; writer, producer: (TV films) The Diamond Necklace, 1948 (Emmy award 1949); producer: (TV films) Babe, 1975 (Hollywood Fgn. Press Golden Globe award, Christopher medal), And Your Name is Jonah, 1978 (Christopher medal 1979), The Story of Satchel Paige, 1980 (Image award 1981); exec. producer TV prodn. Escape from Iran: The Canadian Caper, 1981. Producer spl. programming Democratic Nat. Conv., San Francisco, 1984, Columbia Pictures and Rastar Prodns., 1988-91. 1st lt. USAAF, 1942-46. Mem. Writers Guild America (dir. 1941-42), Producers Guild America (bd. dirs. 1968-74, pres. 1974-79, v.p. 1987-94, bd. dirs. 1994-2000), Acad. Motion Picture Arts & Sciences, Acad. TV Arts & Sciences (bd. govs. 1971, 73), Phi Beta Kappa. *I'm still too young to sum up my life, but here's a thought in progress: Stay curious.* Died Mar. 2, 2014.

**RUBY, KARINE,** professional snowboarder; b. Bonneville, France, Jan. 4, 1978; Degree in commerce, IUT, Annecy, France. Snowboarder French Nat. Team, 1989—2006. Recipient Gold medal women's snowboard giant slalom Olympic Games, Nagano, Japan, 1998; Silver medal women's snowboard giant slalom, Olympic Games, Salt Lake City, 2002 Achievements include being the most decorated female snowboarder in the world with 2 Olympic medals, 6 world championship titles & 67 snowboard World Cup victories. Avocation: mountain climbing. Died May 29, 2009.

**RUDEL, JULIUS,** conductor; b. Vienna, Mar. 6, 1921; came to US, 1938, naturalized, 1944; s. Jakob and Josephine (Sonnenblum) R.; m. Rita Gillis, June 24, 1942 (dec. May 1984); children: Joan, Madeleine, Anthony Jason. Student, Acad. Music, Vienna; diploma in conducting, Mannes Coll. Music, 1942; diploma hon. doctorates, U. Vt., 1961, U. Mich., 1971; doctorates hon. causa, Pace Coll., Manhattan Coll., 1994, Mannes Coll. Music, 1994, Manhattanville Coll., 1994, Manhattan Sch. Music, 1996. With NYC Opera, 1943-79, 2004, debut, 1944, gen. dir., 1957-79, 3rd St. Music Sch. Settlement, 1945-52, mus. dir. Chautauqua Opera Assn., 1958-59, Caramoor Festival, Katonah, NY, 1964-76, Cin. May Festival, 1971-72, Kennedy Ctr. Performing Arts, 1971-75; music advisor Wolf Trap Farm Pk., 1971, Phila. Opera, 1978-81; condr. Spoleto (Italy) Festival, 1962-63; music dir. Buffalo Philarm. Orch., 1979-85, debut as condr. Met. Opera, 1978, San Franciso Opera, 1979, Vienna State Opera, 1976, Royal Opera, Covent Garden, 1984, Rome Opera, 1987, Opera de la Bastille, 1992, Teatro Colon, Buenos Aires, 1992, Royal Danish Opera, Copenhagen, 1993, LA Opera, 1995; condr. Am. premiere of Braunfels's Die Vogel at Spoleto Festival USA, 2005; condr. Cosi fan Tatte, NYC Opera, 2006; dir. prodn.: Kiss Me Kate, Vienna Volksoper Opera, 1956; prin. guest condr. Palm Beach Opera, 2003; guest condr. Chgo. Symphony, Phila. Orch., NY Philharm., Boston Symphony, Detroit Symphony, Israel Philharm., Paris Opera, Munich Opera, Hamburg State Opera, Vienna State Opera, other symphonic, operatic orgns. in US and Europe; co-author: (with Rebecca Paller) First and Lasting Impressions: Julius Radel Looks Back on a Life in Music, 2013 Decorated Croix du Chevalier in arts and letters, France; recipient gold medal, Nat. Arts Club, 1958, citation, Nat. Assn. American Composers and Conductors, 1958, citation, Nat. Fedn. Music Clubs, 1959, Ditson award, Columbia, 1959, Page One award in music, Newspaper Guild, 1959, hon. insignia for arts and sci., Govt. of Austria, 1961, Handel medallion for music, City of NY, 1965, citation, Nat. Assn. Negro Musicians, 1965, citation, Nat. Opera Assn., 1971, Comdr.'s Cross, German Order Merit, 1967, hon. lt., Israeli Army, 1969, Julius Rudel award for young condrs., Pan American/Pan African award for humanism, 1981, Peabody award, 1985, Disting. Achievement award, Kurt Weill Found., 2000, Opera News award, 2008, Opera Index award & Nat. Endowment for the Arts Opera honor, 2009. Died June 26, 2014.

**RUDZKI, EUGENIUSZ MACIEJ,** chemical engineer, consultant; b. Warsaw, Feb. 24, 1914; came to U.S., 1955. s. Aleksander and Wanda (Łukaszewicz) R.; m. Fiorina Maria Di Vito, Feb. 23, 1952; children: Robert Alexander, Marcella Wanda Rudzki Meddick. Diploma with honors, Warsaw Poly. Inst., Poland, 1937; Chem. Engr., Polish U. Coll., London, 1951. Project devel. and field engr. Chance Bros. Ltd., Eng., 1951-54; head instr. chem. engring. dept. U. Toronto, Can., 1954-55; rsch. engr. T.C. Wheaton Co., N.J., 1955-56, Bethlehem (Pa.) Steel Corp., 1956-61, supr. rsch. dept., 1961-82, ret., 1982. Cons. Am. Flame Rsch. com., 1982—. Patentee in field, U.S., Eng., Can., Belgium; contbr. articles to profl. jours. Active The Polish Inst. Arts and Scis., N.Y.C., 1975, The Kosciuszko Found., N.Y.C., 1977; polit. prisoner Gulag Abis forced labor camp, Peczora, USSR, 1940-41. Maj. 2d Polish Army Corp. Gen. Anders, 1942-46. Decorated the Virtuti Militari Order, The Cross of Valor with Bar, The Silver Order of Merit with Swords. Fellow

Inst. Energy London, Coun. Engring. Insts. London (chartered engr.); mem. AIME, AIChE, Combustion Inst., Polish Vets. WWII, Assn. Vets. of 2nd Polish Army Corp. Roman Catholic. Avocations: gardening, reading, travel. Died Jan. 12, 2001.

**RUESCH, HANS,** author; b. Naples, Italy, May 17, 1913; s. Arnold and Ginevra Ruesch; m. Marialuisa De La Feld, 1949 (separated); children: Hans Jun, Peter, Vivian. Author: Top of the World, 1950, The Racer, 1953, South of the Heart: A Novel of Modern Arabia, 1957, Back to the Top of the World, 1973, Slaughter of the Innocent, 1978, Naked Empress, 1982. Founder CIVIS publ. house, Klosters, Switzerland. Home: Klosters, Switzerland. Died Aug. 27, 2007.

**RUFFNER, FREDERICK GALE, JR.,** retired publishing executive; b. Akron, Ohio, Aug. 6, 1926; s. Frederick G. and Olive Mae (Taylor) R.; m. Mary Ann Evans, Oct. 8, 1954 (dec. 2010); children: Frederic G. III, Peter Evans. BBA, Ohio State U., 1950. Advt. mgr. Jim Robbins Co., Royal Oak, Mich., 1950-52; research mgr. Gen. Detroit Corp., 1953-54; pres. Gale Research Co., Detroit, 1954-87. Editor: Ency. of Assns, 1956-68, Code Names Dictionary, 1963, Acronyms and Initialisms Dictionary, 1965, Allusions Dictionary, 1985; publisher Gold Coast Mag.; patentee in field. Bd. dirs. Friends of Detroit Public Libr., pres., 1975-76; mem. exec. bd. Detroit coun. Boy Scouts America, v.p., 1976-82; pres. Coun. for Fla. Libraries; trustee Bon Secours Hosp., Grosse Pointe, Mich., 1980-81; v.p. Etruscan Found., Florence, Italy; pres. Mich. Ctr. for the Book, 1990, Literary Landmarks Assn., Gold Coast Jazz Soc., Ft. Lauderdale; bd. dirs., v.p. Ohio State U. Found., Bonnet House, Ft. Lauderdale, 1992; 1st lt. AUS, 1944-46. Decorated Bronze Star, Combat Inf. award; recipient Centennial award Ohio State U., 1970, Benjamin Creativity award Assn. American Publications, 1985, Career medal Ohioana Libr. Assn., 1988, Lifetime Achievement award American Libr. Trustees Assn., 1992; named to The Entrepreneurs Hall of Fame, Nova U. Mem. American Antiquarian Soc., ALA (hon. life), American Mgmt. Assn., American Assn. Mus., Detroit Hist. Soc., American Hist. Print Collectors Soc., Bibliog. Soc. American, Sierra Club, Pres. Assn., Audubon Soc., American Name Soc., Early American Industries Assn., Nat. Press Club (Washington), Ephemera Soc., Johnny Appleseed Soc., Navy League, Newcomen Soc., Cen. Bus. Dist. Assn. Detroit (vice-chmn. 1985-87), Jazz Forum (Grosse Pointe Farms, Mich.), Nat. Trust Hist. Preservation, Fairfield Heritage Soc., Archives American Art, Pvt. Libraries Assn., Friends Ft. Lauderdale Pub. Libr. (pres. 1974-78), Phileas Soc., Ohio State U. Club (pres. Detroit club 1958, nat. chmn. Ohio State U. campaign, 1985-88), Masons, Shriners, Book Club, Detroit Athletic Club, Econ. Club, Prismatic Club (pres. 1990), Fontenada Soc. (pres. 1990-91), Detroit Club, Country Club Detroit, Ocean Reef Club, Grosse Pointe Yacht Club, Coral Ridge Yacht Club, Lauderdale Yacht Club, Princeton Club, Salmagundi Club, Grolier Club, Century Assn., Marco Polo Club, Faculty Club Ohio State U., Old Club, Commonwealth Club (San Francisco), Gross Pointe Club, Wawetonong Club, Tau Kappa Epsilon. Republican. Presbyterian. Home: Grosse Pointe, Mich. Died Aug. 12, 2014.

**RUGGERI, ANDREA PIETRO,** auditor; b. Messina, Italy, Sept. 2, 1943; s. Giuseppe and Teresa (Ciraolo) R.; m. Jennifer Anne Lusby, Apr. 22,1 976; children: Alexandra Teresa, Edward Giuseppe. Bus. adminstrn. degree, U. Messina, Italy, 1968. Cert. auditor. Lectr. SDA Bocconi U., Milan, Italy, 1968, U. Florence, Genoa, Bologna and, Cagliari, LUISS, U. Pisa; auditor Deloitte, Milan, Italy, 1969-76, mgr., 1976-80, ptnr.-in-charge Florence, Italy, 1980-94. Mem. exec. com. DRT, Milan; resp. multinats. Deloitte & Touche, Italy, mng. ptnr., chmn. mgmt. com., mem. D&T European bd., 1994. Mem. Ugolino Golf Club-Chianti, Rotary. Roman Catholic. Home: Florence, Italy. Died Oct. 22, 2007.

**RUIZ-JARABO COLOMER, DÁMASO,** judge; b. 1949; Judge Consejo Gen. del Poder Judicial; prof. law; head Pvt. Officeof Pres. of Consejo Gen. del Poder Judicial; ad hoc judge European Ct. of Human Rights; judge Tribunal Supremo, from 1996; advocate gen. Ct. of Justice of European Cmtys., Luxembourg, 1995—2009. Died Nov. 11, 2009.

**RUSH, RICHARD HENRY,** finance company executive, educator, writer; b. NYC, Mar. 6, 1915; s. Henry Frederick and Bessie (Vreeland) R.; m. Julia Ann Halloran, Aug. 15, 1956; 1 dau., Sallie Haywood. BA summa cum laude, Dartmouth Coll., 1937, MCS, 1938; MBA with highest distinction, Harvard U., 1941, DCS (Littauer fellow), 1942. Chief economist, chmn. planning com. All Am. Aviation (U.S. Air), 1943—45; dir. aviation U.S. Bur. Fgn. and Domestic Commerce, 1945—46; dir. aircraft divsn. Nat. Security Resources Bd., 1948—51; Washington rep. to J. Paul Getty, 1951—52; ptnr. Rush & Halloran, 1953—58; pres., chmn. bd. N.Am. Acceptance Corp., Atlanta, Washington, 1956—59; owner Richard H. Rush Enterprises, Greenwich, Conn., Washington, 1953—73; prof., chmn. dept. finance and investments Sch. Bus. Adminstrn., Am. U., Washington, 1967—70, Sch. Bus. Adminstrn. Am. U., Washington, 1977—79. Author: Art as an Investment, 1961, A Strategy of Investing for Higher Return, 1962, The Techniques of Becoming Wealthy, 1963, Antiques as an Investment, 1968, The Wrecking Operation: Phase One, 1972, Investments You Can Live With and Enjoy, 1976, Techniques of Becoming Wealthy, 1977, Automobiles as an Investment, 1982, Selling Collectibles, 1982, Collecting Classic Cars for Profit and Capital Gain, 1984, Collector Cars: Classics for the New Century, 2001; contbr. over 700 articles to newspapers, mags. and profl. jours.; editor series of books on starting businesses for U.S. Dept. Commerce; contbg. editor Wall St. Transcript, 1971-97, Art/Antiques Investment Report, 1972-97. Trustee, exec. com. Finch Coll., 1968-72. Recipient Pres.'s med., CCNY, 1997. Mem. AAUP, Am. Mktg. Assn. (chmn. nat. com.), Am. Econ. Assn., Am. Statis. Assn., Internat. Platform Assn., Harvard Club N.Y.C., Royal Palm Yacht Club (Ft. Myers), Phi Beta Kappa, Phi Kappa Phi, Omicron Delta Kappa. Episcopalian. Achievements include Richard H. Rush Library at Edison State college, Fort Myers, Florida is named after him. Died May 4, 2011.

**RUSKIN, IRA,** former state legislator; b. NYC, Nov. 12, 1943; m. Cheryl Ruskin. BA in History, U. Calif., Berkeley, 1968; MA in Comm., Stanford U., 1983. City councilman, Redwood City, Calif., 1995—2004; mayor Redwood, Calif., 1999—2001; mem. Dist. 21 Calif. State Assembly, 2004—10. Democrat. Jewish. Died July 3, 2014.

**RUSKIN, JOSEPH RICHARD,** actor, director; b. Haverhill, Mass., Apr. 14, 1924; s. Ely and Betty Edith (Chaimson) Schlafman; m. Patricia Herd, 1959 (div. 1976); m. Barbara Greene; 1 child, Alicia Ruskin Bucklan. Grad., Carnegie Inst. Tech., 1949. Founder Rochester Arena Theatre, NY, 1949-52. Actor: NY stage plays, 1949—52; (plays) Theater Group, UCLA, Mark Taper Forum, 1959, You Can't Take It With You, 2012, The Crucible, 2013; (films) Fall of Legs Diamond, 1959, Magnificent Seven, 1960, Escape from Zahrein, 1963, Robin and the Seven Hoods, 1965, Prizzi's Honor, 1985, Longshot, 1987, Indecent Proposal, 1992, Spider-Man, 1994, (voice) Star Trek: Insurrection, 1998, King Cobra, 1999, The Scorpion King, 2002, The Streetsweeper, 2002, IceMaker, 2003, Smokin' Aces, 2006; (TV series) Untouchables, Land of the Giants, The Twilight Zone, Mission Impossible, Charlie's Angels, Knight Rider, Spider-Man, Star Trek, Alias; dir.: (plays) Houston Alley, 1965—69. With USNR, 1943—46. Mem.: SAG, AFTRA, Actors Equity Assn. (mem. nat. coun.). Home: Los Angeles, Calif. Died Dec. 27, 2013.

**RUSLIM, MICHAEL DHARMAWAN,** financial services executive; b. Bandung, Java, Indonesia, Nov. 29, 1953; s. Budiman and Nietje (Tejasuryani) R.; m. Trisni Puspitaningtyas Soedjalmo, June 6, 1992; children: Gisela Deamanda Prasadhistika, Mayongga Gilang Pragiwaksana. BS in Engring., U. Calif., Berkeley, 1976; MBA, U. Wis., 1978. Merchant banking head Citibank, N.A., Jakarta, 1978-83; exec. dir. Astra Internat., Indonesia, 1983—2005, chief exec. officer, pres. dir., from 2005. Home: Kuningan/Jakarta, Indonesia. Deceased.

**RUSSELL, DAVID EMERSON,** mechanical engineer, consultant, writer; b. Jacksonville, Fla., Dec. 20, 1922; s. David Herbert and Wilhelmina Russell. BMech Engring., U. Fla., 1948; postgrad., Oxford U., Eng. Registered profl. engr., Fla., Ga. Mech. engr. United Fruit Co., NYC, 1948-50; civilian mech. engr. U.S. Army C.E., Jacksonville, 1950-54; mech. engr. Aramco, Saudi Arabia, 1954-55; v.p. Beiswenger Hoch and Assocs., Inc., Jacksonville, Fla., 1955-57; owner, operator David E. Russell and Assocs., Cons. Engrs., Jacksonville, 1957-98; cons. engr., from 1998. Author: The Old Arabia and the New Arabia-An American Engineer in Saudi Arabia 1954 and Again in 1982, 2004; contbr. articles pub. to profl. jours. Chmn. Jacksonville Water Quality Control Bd., 1969-73; bd. dirs. Jacksonville Hist. Soc., 1981-82; mem. Jacksonville Bicentennial Commn., 1973-79. 2d lt. AUS, 1943-46, PTO. Recipient Outstanding Svs. award City of Jacksonville, 1974. Mem. ASME (chmn. N.E. Fla. 1967-68), NSPE, ASHRAE, Fla. Engring. Soc., Univ. Club (Jacksonville), Jacksonville Humane Soc. (life). Episcopalian. Achievements include 5 patents including the ability to detect the arrival of important mail at a remote location. Avocations: world travel, boating, classical music. Deceased.

**RUSSELL, FRANK ELI,** retired newspaper publishing executive; b. Kokomo, Ind., Dec. 6, 1920; s. Frank E. and Maude (Wiggins) R.; children: Linda Carole Russell Atkins, Richard Lee, Frank E. III, Rita Jane Russell Eagle, Julie Beth Russell; m. Nancy M. Shover, Oct. 5, 1991 AB, Evansville Coll., 1942; JD, Ind. U., 1951; LLD (hon.), U. Evansville, 1985; HHD (hon.), Franklin Coll., 1989. Bar: Ind. 1951; CPA, Ind. Ptnr. George S. Olive & Co., Indpls., 1947—53; exec. v.p. Spickelmier Industries, Inc., Indpls., 1953—59; bus. mgr. Indpls. Star & News, 1959—77; v.p., gen. mgr. Ctrl. Newspapers, Inc., Indpls., 1977—79, pres., 1979—95, chmn., bd. dirs., 1996—98; ret., 1998; also bd. dirs. Ctrl. Newsprint; pres. Bradley Paper Co., also bd. dirs. Past chmn. adv. bd. Met. Indpls. TV Assn., Inc.; trustee retirement trust Ctrl. Newspapers, Inc.; chmn. retirement com. Hoosier State Press. Bd. dirs. Ariz. Cmty. Found., 1992-96, Eiteljorg Mus., 1994—; trustee, chmn. bd. Nina Mason Pulliam Charitable Trust, 1997— Recipient Disting. Alumni award Ind. U. Sch. Law, 1989, Life Trustee award U. Evansville, 1991, Ralph D. Casey award, 1997 Mem. ABA, AICPA, Ind. Bar. Assn., Indpls. Bar Assn. (past bd. dirs., past treas.), Ind. Assn. CPA (past dir.), Tax Execs. Inst. (past pres.), Ind. Assn. Credit Mgmt. (dir., v.p.), Inst. Newspaper Controllers and Fin. Officers (dir., past pres.), Ind. Acad. Ind. Assn. Colls., Midwest Pension Conf. (Ind. chpt.), Newspaper Advt. Bur. (bd. dirs.), Salvation Army (life, award 1989), Columbia Club, Meridian Hills Country Club, Masons, Shriners, Order of Coif, Phi Delta Phi, Sigma Alpha Epsilon Methodist. Home: Indianapolis, Ind. Died 2013.

**RUTTER, DOLORES ELIZABETH,** elementary school educator; b. E. St. Louis, Ill., Feb. 14, 1924; d. Okie Horace and Effie (Loyd) Gilliland; m. Robert Barron Rutter, Jan. 2, 1950; children: Pamela, Jeanne. BS in Edn., Washington U., 1949; Tchg. Certs., So. Ill. U., 1943; postgrad. in arts, U. Ill., Champaign, 1957-58. Cert. elem. tchr., Ill. Tchr. first grade Centerville (Ill.) Pub. Sch., 1944-45; tchr. first through third grades E. St. Louis Pub. Schs., 1945-50, tchr. first grade, 1952-60; model Patricia Stevens, Inc., St. Louis, 1949; tchr. first grade Belleville (Ill.) Pub. Sch., 1960-64. Tchr. Sunday Sch. Signal Hill Meth. Ch., Belleville, 1957-62, mem. commn. on edn., 1962-64; bd. dirs. Mental Health Orgn. of St. Clair County, E. St. Louis, 1958-64, sec., 1958-64, chmn. spl. com. emotionally disturbed children, 1961-64. Recipient scholarship County Supt. of Schs., St. Clair, 1941. Mem. AAUW, Decatur Geneal. Soc., DAR, Questers, Alpha Gamma Delta. Avocations: antiques, genealogy, painting. Home: Normal, Ill. Died Jan. 5, 1999.

**RYAN, PATRICIA,** retired editor; b. Unionville, Pa., June 18, 1938; d. James Ryan; m. Ray Cave; stepchildren: John, Catherine. BS in History, Columbia U. With Sports Illustrated Mag., 1960—78, sr. editor, 1970—78, People Mag., 1978—80, asst. mng. editor, 1980—81, exec. editor, 1981—82, mng. editor, 1982—87; editor Life mag., 1987—89. Died Dec. 27, 2013.

**RYANS, REGINALD VERNON,** music education educator, special education educator; b. Easton, Md., Oct. 12, 1955; s. Alfred Sr. and Alfreda Elizabeth (Thomas) R. AA, Chesapeake Coll., 1975; BS, Morgan State U., 1980; postgrad., Liberty U., Faith Biblical Theol. Inst.; MA, Coll. Notre Dame of Md., 2002. Cert. tchr., Md. Tchr. music Balt. City Pub. Schs., 1980-82; minister of music Faith Unity Fellowship Ch., Millington, Md., 1987-92; tchr. spl. edn. inclusion Balt. City Pub. Sch. Sys., 1997-99; spl. edn. tchr. Anne Arundel County Pub. Sch. Sys., from 1999. Guest musician various chs., Queen Anne's County, Md., 1970—; European tour to Switzerland, Belgium, France, Germany, The Whosoever Will Choir of Balt., Md., 1995. Mng. editor (news publ.) In Touch, 1992. Mem. NAACP. Recipient Svc. award St. James Male Chorus, 1990, Cert. of Appreciation Faith Unity Fellowship Ministries, 1992; ordained elder Faith Unity Ministries, 1992; scholar Raskob Found., 1975, Md. State Senate. Avocations: photography, travel. Deceased.

**RYBAK, BORIS,** physiologist, consultant; b. Paris, Jan. 22, 1923; s. Isaac and Pessy (Givatovski) R.; m. Paulette, Sept. 19, 1945 (div. 1987); 1 child, Léonard (dec. 1997). Lic., Sci. Faculty, Rennes, 1942; DSc, Sorbonne, Paris, 1954. Charge of mission Liberation's Ministry of Edn., Paris, 1944; rschr. CNRS Pasteur Inst., Paris, 1945-50; chief asst. Fac. Sc. Nancy, Bordeaux, 1952-57; assoc. prof. Fac. Sc. Caen, 1958-63, prof., 1964, Sorbonne, U. Paris, 1977-91, prof. emeritus, from 1991. Invited lectr. Am. Heart Assn., 1962; lectr. IRCAM, Paris, 1978-80; vis. prof. SUNY, Bklyn., 1970; vis. rsch. prof. Johnson Found., Phila., 1967; vis. rsch. prof. Inst. Muscle Rsch., Woods Hole, 1971; dir. NATO-Advanced Study Inst. Advanced Technobiology, Paris, 1978; dir. 2 collections Gauthier-Villars, Paris, 1961-71; head Biophysics Ctr. Documentation, CNRS, Paris, 1972; hon. expert on med. physics Appeal Ct. Paris. Author: Anachroniques, 1962, Principles of Zoophysiology, 1962, English edit., 1968, Psyche, Soma, Germen (biological basis of ethics), 1968, Vers un nouvel entendement, 1973, Biologie de l'oxygène, 1974, L'identité humaine, 1990; mem. editl. bd. Life Sci., Jour. Internat. Cycle Rsch., Biosci. Com.; contbr. numerous articles to profl. jours. Served with Refractory STO, 1943-44. Recipient prix Decouverte, 1957; Franco-Italian Stazione Zoologica CNRS fellow, Napoli, 1950, Wenner Gren Inst. fellow, Stockholm, 1952. Mem. Royal Soc. Scis. Liege, Journees Nat. Métrologie Mesures Bio-Medicine (pres.), Internat. Inst. Human Rights (exec. mem. 1977), Sci. Coun. Assn. René Cassin (pres.). Achievements include electron microscopy detection of oligo-phage, 1948; mechanisms of crown-gall immunity; molecular physiology of fertilization; development of open heart technique; discovery of mechanical and biochemical processes triggering heart automatism; introduction of minimum interference physiology and medicine; invention of topoelectronic, of dactylophone, of millisecond time-response spirometer promoting isochrone aero-acoustic; catheterizable physico-chemical sensors (including absolute photometer) and remote transmission from the patient resting or moving; discovery of high resolution morphological specificity of air flow while speaking; conception of chaotic order; discovery of the lingual code of speech realization (specific morphology for each linguistic sound of longitudinal dorsal channel of the tongue); creation of robotic surgery; invention of radiosurgery and telemedicine; creation of topological logic; creation of projective geometry on uneven varieties; creation of general non-standard geometry, of the informational motor (in auto-adjunct processes), of uranometric time generation algorithm; invention of Transcorporeal telephony. Avocations: piano, poetry. Deceased.

**RYDELL, AMNELL ROY,** artist, landscape architect; b. Mpls., Sept. 17, 1915; s. John S. and Josephine Henrietta (King) R.; m. Frances Cooksey, Jan. 24, 1942 (dec. May 1998). BFA, U. So. Calif., 1937; postgrad., Atelier 17, Paris, 1938, U. Calif., Berkeley, 1939-40, U. Calif., Santa Cruz, 1988. Instr. engring. Douglas Aircraft, El Segundo, Calif., 1940-46; ind. artist, designer San Francisco, 1946-48, Santa Cruz, from 1948; ind. landscape architect, 1958-91. Author, cons.: Low Maintenance Gardening, 1974; restoration design Sesnon House Garden Cabrillo Coll., 1995-98; one-man shows include S.C. Mus. Art and History, 2000, Eloise Pickard Smith Gallery U. Calif., Santa Cruz, 2000. Pres. Santa Cruz Hist. Soc., 1978-79, Rural Bonny Doon Assn., 1955-56, Santa Cruz Orgn. for Progress and Euthenics, 1977-78; mem. vision bd. City of Santa Cruz, 1991-92; mem. task force Ctr. for Art and History, 1986-94; bd. dirs. Santa Cruz Hist. Trust, 1978-94, Art Mus. Santa Cruz County, 1982-94; donor advisor Roy and Frances Rydell Visual Arts Fund, Greater Santa Cruz County Cmty. Found.; archivist pers. hist. archives, spl. collections Libr. U. Calif., Santa Cruz; mem. steering com. Pub. Art City of Santa Cruz, 1997-98; mem. Joint Cultural Coun. & Santa Cruz Cmty. Found., 1998, Art Gang Cultural Coun. Santa Cruz County, 1998. Recipient Eloise Pickard Smith award

County of Santa Cruz Arts Commn., 1997, Cert. of Appreciation, Bd. S.C. Mus. Art and History, 1999; exhbn. garden in his honor S.C. Mus. Art and History, 2000. Mem. Am. Soc. Landscape Architects (emeritus), William James Assn. (vice chair bd. 1979-95, chair 1995-96), Art Forum (chair 1983-90), Art League (Disting. Artist 1996), Friends of Sesnon Gallery U. Calif., Santa Cruz. Avocation: gardening. Home: Aptos, Calif. Died Oct. 26, 2000.

**RYDHOLM, RALPH WILLIAMS,** retired advertising executive; b. Chgo., June 1, 1937; s. Thor Gabriel and Vivian Constance (Williams) R.; m. Jo Anne Beechler, Oct. 5, 1963; children: Kristin, Erik, Julia. BA, Northwestern U., Evanston, Ill., 1958, postgrad. in bus. adminstrn, 1958-59; postgrad. Advanced Mgmt. Program, Harvard U., Cambridge, Mass., 1982. Acct. trainee, copywriter Young & Rubicam Advt., Chgo., 1960-63; copywriter Post-Keyes-Gardner Advt., Chgo., 1963, E. H. Weiss Advt., Chgo., 1963-65; copy group head BBDO Advt., Chgo., 1965-66; with J. Walter Thompson Advt., Chgo., 1966-86, creative dir., v.p., 1969-76, exec. creative dir., 1976-86, sr. v.p., 1972-80, exec. v.p., 1980-86; exec. v.p., chief creative officer, dir. Ted Bates Worldwide, NYC, 1986-87; mng. ptnr., chmn. mgmt. com., chief creative officer, chmn., CEO, EURO RSCG Tatham Advt., Chgo., 1987-98; pres. R2 Cons., from 1999; spl. counsel J. Walter Thompson, 1999-2000. Bd. dirs., ops. com., chmn. creative com., vice chmn., 1996, chmn., 1997-98; American Assn. Advt. Agys. guest spkr. Ad Age Workshop, 1969, 77, 86, Adweek Seminar, 1993, CLIO awards, 1995; keynote spkr. Stephen B. Kelly Awards, 1993, CEBA Awards, 1997; chmn. CEBA Awards, 1997. Staff sgt. USAFR, 1959—65. Recipient Clio awards, Internat. Broadcast award, Lion awards, Cannes Film Festival, Addy awards; named one of The Top 100 Creative Ad People Ad Daily, 1972, Advt. Exec. of Yr. Adweek, 1991, Best Man in Advt. McCalls and Adweek, 1992; named to The Creative Leader Hall of Fame, Wall St. Jour., 1994, chmns. award Exec. Svc. Corps. Mem.: ASCAP, Chgo. Advt. Fedn., Am. Advt. Fedn. (Silver medal lifetime svc. 1997), Lincoln Park Zoo, Art Inst. Chgo., Friends of Chgo. River, Openlands, Chgo. Com. Coun. on Global Affairs, Hon. Order Ky. Cols., Friends of the Pks., Fernwood, Lost Dunes Club (Mich.), Chikaming Country Club (Mich.), Execs. Club Chgo., Harvard Club Chgo., Econ. Club Chgo. (bd. dirs. 1996—98), Saddle and Cycle Club, Northwestern Club Chgo., Harvard Club NYC, Carlton Club, Dunes Club (Mich.), Phi Delta Theta. Home: Chicago, Ill. Died May 24, 2014.

**RYOO, ZAEYOUNG,** research scientist; b. Republic of Korea, Aug. 26, 1964; PhD, Dohoku U., 1993. Deceased.

**SAAD, SAMIR FAHMY,** pharmacology educator, neuropharmacology research; b. Cairo, May 30, 1940; s. Gergis Fahmy and Etimad Ibrahim (Shalaby) S.; m. Taghreed Tadros Fam, Aug. 4, 1966; children: Ehab, Bassem, Baher S.F. BPharm, Cairo U., 1960, MPharm, 1964, PhD in Pharmacology, 1967. Demonstrator dept. pharmacology Cairo U., 1961-66, lectr. dept. pharmacology, 1967-72, asst. prof., 1973-77, prof., from 1978, dir. dept. pharmacology, from 1993. Cons. dept. pharmacology Faculty of Medicine, Baghdad, Iraq, 1978-82; cons. Permanent Com. of Egyptian Pharmacopoeia, Ministry of Health, Cairo, 1990—; cons. Com. for Promotion to Professorships Degrees of Pharmacology, Supreme Coun. Univs., 1983-95. Editor, author: Fundamentals of Toxicology, 1974, Biological Assays and Screening in Pharmacology and Toxicology, 1974; contbr. numerous articles to profl. jours. Mem. Egyptian Pharmacol. Soc., Egyptian Physiol. Soc., Egyptian Syndicate of Pharmacists, N.Y. Acad. Scis. Christian. Avocations: photography, museums, reading, beach vacations. Home: Dokki, Egypt. Deceased.

**SABATER-PI, JORDI,** anthropologist and psychologist, educator; b. Barcelona, Aug. 2, 1924; s. Narcis Sabater Bros and Elena Pi Ferrer; m. Nuria Coca Estalella, June 18, 1950; children: Oriol, Francesc. Lic. Anthropology and Psychology, Barcelona U., Spain, 1970, PhD, 1975; D Hon. Causa, U. Autónoma Madrid, 1993; D. Hon. Causa, U. Autónoma Barcelona, 1996. Prof. anthropology, psychology Barcelona U., chmn. ethology dept. Author: 10 books on Ecology and Primatology; exposition of African drawings, Barcelona Mus. Sci., 1992-95, expostion of bot. drawings, Barcelona U., 1997; contbr. 160 articles to sci. publs. Recipient Fundació Catalana, per ala Recerca, Barcelona, 1991, Gold Medal of Sci. City of Barcelona, 1996, Gold Medal, Barcelona Faculty of Medicine, 1997, Gold medal of Sant Jordi, Catalonia Govt., 2000. Achievements include contributions to the knowledge of cultural behavior of chimpanzees in the wild, including gorillas feeding and nesting in the wild, giant frog (Conraua goliath) behavior in the wild in W. Africa, Colobus behavior and Mangabey behavior bonobo ecology and behavior in Congo in the wild, biology and culture in Primatology; pioneer work in study of lowland gorillas in the wild in West Africa. Home: Barcelona, Spain. Died Aug. 5, 2009.

**SABIN, JACK CHARLES,** engineering and construction firm executive; b. Phoenix, June 29, 1921; s. Jack Byron and Rena (Lewis) Sabin; m. Frances Jane McIntyre, Mar. 27, 1950; children: Karen Lee, Robert William, Dorothy Ann, Tracy Ellen. BS, U. Ariz., 1943; BS in Chem. Engring., U. Minn., 1947. Registered profl. engr., Calif., Alaska, lic. gen. engring. contractor, Ariz., Calif. With Std. Oil Co., Calif., 1947—66, sr. engr., from 1966. Pres., dir. Indsl. Control & Engring., Inc., Redondo Beach, Calif., from 1966; owner, mgr. Jack C. Sabin, Engr.-Contractor, Redondo Beach, from 1968; dir. Alaska Pacific Petroleum, Inc., from 1968, Marlex Petroleum, Inc., from 1970; staff engr. Pacific Molasses Co., San Francisco, 1975—77; project mgr. E & L Assocs., Long Beach, Calif., 1977—79. Served US Army, 1942—46, capt. Chem. Corps, Res., 1949—56. Mem.: Calif. Tax Reduction Com., Conservative Caucus, Ind. Liquid Terminals Assn., Nat. Soc. Profl. Engrs., Town Hall Calif., Elks Club, Phi Lambda Upsilon, Tau Beta Pi, Phi Sigma Kappa. Republican. Deceased.

**SACHS, LEO,** geneticist, educator; b. Leipzig, Germany, Oct. 14, 1924; s. Elijah and Louise (Lichtblau) Sachs; m. Pnina Salkind; 4 children. BSc, U. Wales, Bangor, 1948; PhD, Trinity Coll., Cambridge U., 1951; DHC (hon.), Bordeaux U., 1985; MD (hon.), Lund U., 1997. Rsch. scientist John Innes Inst., 1951-52; mem. sci. staff Weizmann Inst. Sci., Rehovot, Israel, 1952—2013, prof., chmn. genetics dept., 1962—2013, Otto Meyerhof prof. molecular biology, 1968—2013. Contbr. articles to profl. jours. Recipient Israel prize for Natural Sci., 1972, Rothschild prize in Biol. Sciences, 1977, Wolf Found. prize in Medicine, Israel, 1980, Sloan prize, GM Cancer Rsch. Found., 1989, Warren Alpert prize, Harvard Med. Sch., 1997, Emet prize in Life Sciences, 2002. Fellow: Royal Soc.; mem.: NAS (fgn. assoc.), Israeli Acad. Sci. & Humanities, Internat. Cytokine Soc. (hon. life). Died Dec. 12, 2013.

**SADIE, STANLEY (JOHN),** writer, editor; b. London, Oct. 30, 1930; s. David and Deborah (Simons) Sadie; m. Adèle Bloom, Dec. 10, 1953 (dec. May 1978); children: Graham Robert, Ursula Joan, Stephen Peter; m. Julie Anne McCornack, July 18, 1978; children: Celia Kathryn, Matthew David. BA in Music, Cambridge U., Eng., 1953; PhD, Gonville and Caius Coll., Cambridge U., 1958; LittD (hon.), Leicester U., Eng., 1982. Music critic The Times, London, 1964-81; critic Gramophone, London, from 1965. Vis. fellow Sidney Sussex Coll., Cambridge, 1993. Author: (books) Handel, 1962, 1966, 1972; co-author: Opera Guide, 3d edit., 1984, Stanley Sadie's Music Guide, 1986; author: Mozart Symphonies, 1987; editor: New Grove Dictionary Music and Musicians, 20 vols., 1980, 2001, New Grove Dictionary of Musical Instruments, 3 vols., 1984; editor: (joint) New Grove Dictionary of American Music, 4 vols., 1986; editor: Norton/Grove Concise Encyclopedia of Music, 2d edit., 1993, History of Opera, 1989, New Grove Dictionary of Opera, 4 vols., 1992, New Grove Book of Operas, 1997, Man and Music/Music in Society, 8 vols. (series), 1989—93; co-editor: Music Printing and Publishing, 1989, Performance Practice, 2 vols., 1990; editor: Master Musicians, from 1976; author: Mozart, 1966, New Grove Mozart, 1982; editor: Musical Times, 1967—87, (books) Wolfgang Amadè Mozart: Essays on his Life and his Music, 1996. Chmn. Handel House Trust, 1994-96, pres., 1996-2005 Decorated comdr. Order Brit. Empire. Fellow: Gonville and Caius Coll., Royal Coll. Music (hon.); mem.: Critics' Circle, Internat. Musicol. Soc. (pres. 1992—97), Royal Acad. Music (hon.), Am. Musicol. Soc. (corr.; fgn.), Royal Mus. Assn. (pres. 1989—94). Home: Somerset, England. Died Mar. 21, 2005.

**SAENGER, HANNS HERMANN,** retired administrator; b. Berlin, Aug. 16, 1919; s. Curt and Irma (Eisenhardt) S.; m. Fritzi Weil, Nov. 5, 1959 (dec. June 1974); 1 child, Ingrid. BS, Janson De Sailly, Paris, 1935. CEO Greatermans Ltd., South Africa, 1945-67, Consol. Light, Johannesburg, South Africa, 1969-75, Gresham Ltd., Johannesburg, 1975-86. Chmn. South African Jewish Trust, 1980-99; treas. South African Jewish Bd. Deps., 1972-99, hon. life pres., 1998; vice chair South African Friends of Hebrew U., 1986-99; past pres. United Hebrew Congregation Johannesburg; past chmn. Sunfield Home for Mentally Handicapped Children; mem. South African Com. for Tertiary Jewish Studies, Jewish Affairs Editl. Bd.; hon. life pres. Our Parents Home. Served in armed forces, World War II. Recipient Cert. of Honor United Hebrew Congregation, 1998; named Internat. Man of Yr., Cambridge, 1991-92; hon. fellow Hebrew U., 1996. Mem. Lansdowne Club. Democrat. Jewish. Home: Sandton, South Africa. Died Nov. 22, 2001.

**SAFON, DAVID MICHAEL,** lawyer; b. Boston, Sept. 6, 1962; s. Kenneth Norman and Barbara Safon; m. Lisa Eileen Spector, Aug. 28, 1988; children: Jennifer, Keith, Noah. BA in Econs. with honors, Coll. William and Mary, 1984; JD cum laude, Cornell U., 1987. Bar: N.Y. 1988, U.S. Dist. Ct. (so. and ea. dists.) N.Y. 1988. Assoc. Proskauer, Rose, Goetz & Mendelsohn, NYC, 1987-89, Benetar, Bernstein, Schair & Stein, NYC, 1989-96, ptnr., from 1997. Contbg. editor: (supplements) Age Discrimination, Employment Discrimination. Mem. ABA (com. on fed. labor stds. legis.), N.Y. State Bar Assn. (labor and employment law sect., com. on labor rels.), Assn. of Bar of City of N.Y., Phi Beta Kappa. Deceased.

**SAFRA, MOISE Y.,** bank executive; b. Aleppo, Syria, Apr. 27, 1935; s. Jacob Safra; m. Chella Cohen; children: Jacob, Edmond, Ezra. Co-owner Safra Group; pres. Safra Bank Brazil. Vice-chmn. bd. dirs. Banque Safra, Luxembourg. Contbr. Jewish Endowment Arts and Humanities, Hazon Yeshaya Soup Kitchens. Named one of World's Richest People, Forbes Mag., 2000—04. Jewish. Bank holdings span the Caribbean, New York and Europe and include Safra Bank NY, Banque Safra Luxembourg and First Internat. Bank Israel. Died June 15, 2014.

**SAGAN, FRANÇOISE (FRANÇOISE QUOIREZ),** writer; b. Cajarc, France, June 21, 1935; d. Pierre and Marie (Laubaud) Quoirez; m. Guy Schoeller, 1958 (div. 1960); m. Robert James Westhoff, 1962 (div. 1963); 1 child, Denis. Student, Convent des Oiseaux and Convent due Sacre Coeur, Paris. Author: (fiction) Bonjour Tristesse, 1954 (Prix des Critiques 1954), Un Certain Sourire, 1956 (pub. as A Certain Smile, 1956), Dans un mois, dans un an, 1957 (pub. as Those Without Shadows, 1957), Aimez-vous Brahms, 1959, Les Merveilleux Nuages, 1961 (pub. as Wonderful Clouds, 1961), La Chamade, 1965, Le garde du coeur, 1968 (pub. as The Heart-Keeper, 1968), Un Peu de soleil dans l'eau froide, 1969 (pub. as A Few Hours of Sunlight, 1971, Sunlight on Cold Water, 1971), Des Bleus à l'âme, 1972 (pub. as Scars on the Soul, 1974), Un Profil perdu, 1974(pub. as Lost Profile, 1976), Des yeux de soie, 1976 (pub. as Silken Eyes, 1977), Le Lit défait, 1977 (pub. as The Unmade Bed, 1978), Le Chien Couchant, 1980 (pub. as Salad Days, 1984), Musiques de scènes, 1981 (pub. as Incidental Music, 1983), La Femme fardée, 1981 (pub. as The Painted Lady, 1983), Un Orage immobile, 1983 (pub. as The Still Storm, 1986), De Guerre lasse, 1985 (pub. as A Reluctant Hero, 1987, Engagements of the Heart, 1988), La Maison de Raquel Vega: Fiction d'après le tableau de Fernando Botero, 1985, Un Sang d'aquarelle, 1987 (pub. as Painting in Blood, 1988), La Laisse, 1989 (pub. as The Leash, 1991), Les Faux-Fuyants, 1991, Evasion, 1993; (ballet) Le Rendez-vous manqué, 1958; (plays) Château en Suède, 1960, Les Violons parfois, 1961, La robe mauve de valentine, 1963, Bonheur, impair et passe, 1964, Le Cheval évanoui: L'Écharde, 1966, Un Piano dans l'herbe, 1970, Il fait beau jour et nuit, 1978, L'Excès contraire, 1987; (screenplays) Landru, 1963, Le Sang doré des Borgia, 1977, Encore un Hiver, 1979; (other writings) Toxique, 1964, Mirror of Venus, 1966, Il est des parfums, 1973, Résponses, 1954-1974, 1974 (pub. as Réponses: The Autobiography of Françoise Sagan, 1979, Night Bird: Conversations with Françoise Sagan, 1980), Brigitte Bardot, 1975, Avec Mon Meilleur Souvenir, 1984 (pub. as With Fondest Regards, 1985), Sarah Bernhardt: Le Rire incassable, 1987 (pub. as Dear Sarah Bernhardt, 1987), La Sentinelle de Paris, 1988, Au marbre: chroniques retrouvées 1952-1962, 1988, The Eiffel Tower, 1989; editor: Sand & Musset: lettres d'amour, 1985; dir.: (film) Les Fougeres bleues, 1976. Recipient Prix de Monaco, 1985. Home: Hanfleur, France. Died Sept. 24, 2004.

**SAGIE-WEBER, ABRAHAM,** psychologist, researcher; b. Jerusalem, Sept. 9, 1947; s. Arye and Pnina (Frenkel) Weber; s. Raaya Neuberger, Nov. 19, 1972; children: Inbal, Navit, Yoash, Shachar, Zohar. BA, Hebrew U., Jerusalem, 1972, MA, 1977; PhD, Bar-Ilan U., Ramat-Gan, Israel, 1987. Project leader Yael Software House, Ramat-Gan, 1982-84, IBS, Tel-Aviv, 1984-87; computer ctr. mgr. Aman Engrs., Tel-Aviv, 1986-87; gen.mgr. Yaad, Jerusalem, 1987-98; lectr. Sch. Bus., Bar-Ilan U., Ramat-Gan, 1988-95, dep. dir., 1995-97, dir., from 1999, assoc. prof., from 1999. Cons. Israel Assn. Cmty. Ctrs., Jerusalem, 1994—, Israel Nat. Res. Authority, Jerusalem, 1988-92, Israel Postal Svcs., Tel-Aviv, 1988-92. Author: (with Meni Koslowsky) Participation and Empowerment in Organizations, 2000; guest editor Jour. Orgnl. Behavior, 1996; contbr. articles to profl. jours. Capt., Israeli Def. Forces, 1965-68. Recipient prize Israeli System Analyst Assn., 1990; Japan Soc. for Promotion Rsch. grantee, 1996; Govt. of Can. grantee, 1996. Mem. Acad. of Mgmt., Israeli Psychol. Assn., Internat. Soc. for Study of Work and Orgnl. Values (sec.-treas. 1996-2000, chair sci. com. 2000—). Jewish. Home: Beit Horon, Israel. Died Mar. 2003.

**SAHAGIAN, ARTHUR H.,** painter, educator; b. Cleve., Oct. 16, 1924; s. Vartavar and Rose Sahagian; m. Laima Sahagian, Oct. 15, 1980; children: Arthur, Sandra. BS, Western Res. U., Cleve., 1947; postgrad., Cleve. Sch. Art, 1947; MA, Northwestern U., Chgo., 1972. Supr. art Garfield Hts. Bd. Edn., Cleve.; merchant dealer A&S Utilities, Chgo.; unit mgr. Mutual Omaha, Chgo.; gen. agt., pres. Agy. A&S, Chgo.; tchr. art Chgo. Bd. Edn., Chgo., Smith Ctr., Skokie, Ill., 1985—98, Highland Park, Ill., 2000—01; artist, owner Arthurian Gallery, Skokie, Ill.; artist, pub. Nat. Art Found., Skokie; art supr. Garfield Heights Bd. Edn., Cleve., 1947—50. Exhibitions include Watts in Calie, DuSable Mus., Chgo., Ill., 1980, exhibitions include (oil portrait) Nancy Reagan, Say No Found., Ventura, Calif., 1987, Chgo. Transit Authority, Ill., 1988, Gerald Ford, Calif., 1989, exhibitions include (Presdl. showing) Herbert Hoover Mus., Iowa, 1988, Represented in permanent collections Lindon Baines Hohnson Mus., Houston, Mo. Mus. Art, Jackson, 6 Square, Clown Hall Fame Mus., Delavan, Wis., 1998, Lillies Won't Do, Mus. Human Rights, Memphis, 2006. Tchr. Skokie Pk. Dist.; bd. dirs. Skokie Art Guild; dir. Nat. Arts Found., Skokie. Recipient 1st Place, Renata Gallery, 1987, Prism Art Gallery, 1993, Spl. Recognition, Skokie Art Show, 1990—93. Mem.: Skokie Fine Arts Com. (bd. mem. 1992—96), Armenian Artist, Programes Skokie Artists Guild, Nat. Art Found. (bd. mem. 1985), Ret. Tchrs. Assn., Masons. Presbyterian. Died Feb. 18, 2008.

**SAHL, RICHARD JOACHIM,** architect; b. Leipzig, Germany, Jan. 11, 1919; s. Max Walter and Olga Berta (Bröse) S.; m. Anna Gassen, 1944; children: Richard, Hanns-Jochen; m. Wiltrud Anna Diehl; 1 child, Ricarda. Grad., Staatsbauschule, Leipzig, 1940, Bauhochschule, Weimar, W.Ger., 1945, Landesverwaltungsschule, Finsterbergen, 1947. Lic. architect, W.Ger. Staff dist. bd. works Landkreis Rural Dist., Weimar, 1945-51; chief architect German Bauakademie, Berlin, 1951-53; gov. body German Krankenhausinsitut, Dusseldorf, W.Ger., 1953-96; ret., 1996. Expert adv. panel WHO, Geneva, 1983-96. Contbr. articles to profl. jours. Fellow AIA (hon.); mem. Internat. Union Arch. (sec. pub. health 1970—), Bund German Architekten (bd. dirs.), Verband der Krankenhausdirektoren Deutschlands, Architektenkammer, Bund German Architekten (cert.). Lutheran. Home: Ratingen, Germany. Died Jan. 15, 2003.

**SAINE, BETTY BOSTON,** elementary school educator; b. Newton, NC, Dec. 1, 1932; d. Glenn and Carrie Queen Boston; m. Thomas Paul Saine, Aug. 3, 1968; 1 child, Carrie Ann. BA, Lenoir Rhyne Coll., 1956. Tchr. grade 4 High Point (N.C.) City Schs., 1956-59, Charlotte City Schs./Charlotte-Mecklenburg Schs., 1959-66; art tchr. grades 1-8 Newton-Conover City Schs., 1966-67; tchr. grade 4 Charlotte-Mecklenburg Schs., 1967-68; tchr. grade 6 Lincolnton (N.C.) City Schs., 1968-70; tchr. grades 5 and 6 Lincolnton City Schs./Lincoln County Schs., 1972-90; ret. Historian, publicity chair beautification com. Sunflower

Garden Club, Lincolnton, 1976-87. Mem. Alpha Delta Kappa (various offices and coms.). Meth. Avocations: painting, creative embroidery, horticulture, calligraphy, children's books. Died Dec. 12, 2002.

**ST. CLAIR, KENNETH HILE,** retired academic administrator; b. Brighton, Colo., June 1, 1927; s. John William and Lida (Dennhardt) St. Clair; m. Ida Belle North, Oct. 24, 1948; children: Linda Sue St. Clair Nier, Jeffrey Lynn. BS, U. Ill.-Urbana, 1956, MS, 1963. Instr. Gem City Coll., Quincy, Ill., 1952—55; acct. Gray, Hunter, Stenn & Co., 1957—59; asst. prof. Cedarville Coll., Ohio, 1959—63, bus. mgr., 1963—82, v.p. bus., 1982—92. Treas. Village of Cedarville, 1962—78; councilman, 1978—81. With USNR, 1945—46, with USNR, 1950—52. Mem.: Assn. Bus. Adminstrators Christian Colleges (v.p. 1974—75, pres. 1976—77), Ohio Soc. C.P.A.s, American Inst. C.P.A.s, Nat. Assn. Coll. & U. Bus. Officers. Republican. Baptist. Avocation: auto restoration. Home: Cedarville, Ohio. Died Oct. 3, 2013.

**ST GERMAIN, FERNAND JOSEPH,** former United States Representative from Rhode Island; b. Blackstone, Mass., Jan. 9, 1928; s. Andrew Joseph and Pearl (Talaby) St Germain; m. Rachel O'Neill, Aug. 20, 1953 (dec. 1998); children: Laurene, Lisette. PhB in Social Sci, Providence Coll., 1948, LLD, 1965; LLB, Boston U. Law Sch., 1955; JSD (hon.), Suffolk U., 1976; DCL (hon.), Our Lady of Providence Sem., 1968; DBA (hon.), Bryant Coll., 1981; D in Pub. Svc. (hon.), Roger Williams Coll., 1981; LLB, Brown U., 1985. Bar: R.I. 1956, Fed. 1957, U.S. Supreme Ct. 1983. Mem. RI House of Reps., 1952-60, US Congress from 1st RI Dist., 1961-1989; chmn. US House Banking, Finance & Urban Affairs Com., 1981—89. Served in US Army, 1949-52. Recipient Silver Shingle award for Disting. Public Service Boston U. Sch. Law Alumni Assn., 1981, Alumni award for Disting. Public Service Boston U. Sch. Law, 1982 Mem. ABA, R.I., Bar Assn. Fed. Bar Assn., Our Lady of Providence Sem., Providence Coll., Boston U. Law Sch., American Legion. Democrat. Home: Saint Petersburg, Fla. Died Aug. 16, 2014.

**ST. GOAR, HERBERT,** retired food corporation executive; b. Hamburg, Germany, Apr. 7, 1916; came to U.S., 1938, naturalized, 1943; s. Otto and Thekla St.G.; m. Maria Karsch, Sept. 3, 1954; children: Edward, Elisabeth. Student schs., Hamburg, Germany; LL.B., Chattanooga Coll. Law, 1943. With Internat. Harvester Co., Hamburg, Germany, 1936-38; with Dixie Saving Stores, Inc., Chattanooga, 1938—, pres., 1969-98, chief exec. officer, 1969-98, pres. emeritus, 1998-99; ret., 1999. Author: Autobiography: Taking Stock of My Life, 2000. Bd. dirs. Chattanooga Opera Assn., Jr. C. of C., 1945-54; mem. Hamilton County Juvenile Ct. Commn. Served with Intelligence Sect., U.S. Army, World War II. Decorated Bronze Star, Legion of Merit.; Named Disting. Citizen Chattanooga, 1979 Mem. Southeastern Food Coop. Assn. (past pres.), Tenn. Wholesale Grocers Assn. (bd. dirs. 1988-91), Retailer-Owned Food Distrbrs. Assn. (bd. dirs. 1988-98), NGA Retailer-Owned Exec. Coun., Asparagus Club. Deceased.

**SAISSELIN, REMY GILBERT,** fine arts educator; b. Moutier, Bern, Switzerland, Aug. 17, 1925; came to U.S., 1938, naturalized, 1944; s. Paul A. and Jeanne (Nydegger) S.; m. Nicole M. Fischer, May 31, 1955; children: Anne, Juliet, Peter. BA, Queens Coll., 1951; MA, U. Wis., Madison, 1952, MA in French, 1953, PhD, 1957. Asst. prof. French Western Res. U., Cleve., 1956-59; asst. curator publs. Cleve. Mus. Art, 1959-65; prof. French lit. U. Rochester, N.Y., 1965-70, prof. fine arts N.Y., 1970-87; prof. humanities Hobart & William Smith Coll., 1987-90. Asst. editor: Jour. Aesthetics and Art Criticism, 1959-62; author: Taste in Eighteenth Century France, 1965, Rule of Reason and Ruses of the Heart, 1970, Literary Enterprise in XVIII Century France, 1979, The Bourgeois and the Bibelot, 1984, The Enlightenment Against the Baroque, 1992; exhbns. landscapes, still lifes, and abstractions in France, 1997. Served with U.S. Army, 1944-46. Guggenheim fellow, 1972-73 Mem. Phi Beta Kappa. Home: Saint Ceols, France. Died Aug. 19, 2009.

**SAKRY, CLIFF R.,** writer, publicist, film writer, speaker, trainer, consultant; b. St. Cloud, Minn., Aug. 27, 1914; s. Paul Edward and Monica Sophy (Thomalla) Sakry; m. Donna Cecilia Barthelemy, Oct. 11, 1946; children: Michelle Marie, Donna Lynnelle, Clifford Mark, Brian John. Student, St. Cloud State U., 1932—38, U. Minn., 1942—43, Harvard U., 1944, St. John's U., 1947, Stanford U., 1951. Pub. rels. dir. Coll. St. Benedict; co-founder & exec. sec. Midwest Conservation Alliance, 1933—34; reporter & proof reader St. Cloud Daily Times, Minn., 1935—37, columnist, spl. features writer, regional and farm editor, pub. rels. dir. Minn., 1946—51; spl. features writer & editor AP, 1937—38, regional news corr., 1938—41; news writer, editor, announcer Sta. KNSI, 1938—41, sta. mgr., pub. relations dir., commentator, 1946—51; co-founder, organizer & exec. dir. Minn. Conservation Fedn., 1952—55; radio-TV dir. Olmstead and Foley Advt., Mpls., 1954; founder Minn. Youth Firearms Safety Tng. Program, 1954—55; creative dir., sales, script writer, film dir. & musical coord. Promotional Films Inc., 1955—66; dir. Benedicta Arts Ctr., 1966—71; programming mktg. rsch. sales & program coord. Pers. Dynamics Inc., Mpls., 1971—76; free-lance writer, from 1975; cons., incentive tng. & mktg. Ctrl. Minn. Group Health Plan, from 1975, bd. dirs., from 1986. Author (editor): Boondocks Baseball, 1980; author: History of Farming in Stearns County, 1988; editor (founder): Minn. Out-of-Doors, 1953—55; author (composer, producer): (stage musical) Minnesota, 1949—51, 1958, 1976, 1983; author: (dir.) over 80 documentary films; author: (poem) The Titan Lake Encounter, 1986; author: (co-prodr.) Kimball Centennial Stage Pageant, 1986, composer (lyricist) songs tributing ctrl. Minn.; contbr. numerous articles to newspapers and mags.; plays, Bohemian Girl, 1937, Treasure, 1939, Pirates of Penzance, 1940, opera, Mikado, 1940, Student Prince, 1941; host TV talk show Lifespan, from 1987. Founder, 2 scholarships St. Cloud State U.; co-founder & organizer St. Cloud Blood Donors Guild, 1939—41; del. convs., 1954—55, 1958; TV panelist Sportsmen's Round Table and Minn. Outdoors, 1958—63; co-founder, 1st pres. St. Cloud Cmty. Arts Coun., 1970—71; sr. adv. Whitney Sr. Ctr., St. Cloud, from 1981, mem., adv. bd., 1981—88; vol. Ret. Srs. Vol. Program, from 1984, mem., adv. bd., 1984; mem. St. Cloud's Human Rights Commn., from 1983, Stearns County Hist. Soc.; active mem. Nat. Wildlife Fedn. Served to lt. (j.g.) USNR, 1941—46, ETO. Recipient Disting. Svc. award, St. Cloud Jaycees, 1950, Robert G. Green Disting. Svc. award, Mpls. Jaycees, 1953, Alumni Svc. award, St. Cloud State U., 1983, 50th Anniversary Minn. Conservation Fedn. Founders award, 1986, World Poetry Golden Poet award, 1987—88; named Congl. intern, 1983, Govs. Citation Sr. of Yr., Stearns County, 1986. Mem.: Minn. Film Prodrs. Assn. (co-founder, pres. 1966), Kiwanis Lodge (Golden K pres. 1983—84, Sr. Yr. Citation award 1986). Roman Catholic. Avocations: music, literature, poetry, golf, politics. Died Dec. 20, 1988.

**SALADINO, JOSEPH CHARLES,** lawyer; b. South Beloit, Ill., Mar. 4, 1920; s. Agostino and Josephine (DiGiovanni) Saladino; m. Lois Marie Guidotti, Aug. 25, 1951; children: Jo-Ann, LeAnn, Mark J. BS, U. Ill., 1947; JD, 1950. Bar: Ill. 1950. Pvt. practice, South Beloit, from 1950; ptnr. Saladino & Saladino. Capt. US Army, 1942—46. Decorated Bronze Star. Mem.: ABA, Winnebago County Bar Assn., Ill. Bar Assn. Republican. Roman Catholic. Home: South Beloit, Ill. Died July 25, 1993.

**SALEH, JOHN,** lawyer; b. O'Donnell, Tex., June 29, 1928; s. Nahum and Arslie S. BBA, U. Tex., 1950, JD with honors, 1952; cert. U.S. Army Judge Advocate Sch., U. Va., 1953. Bar: Tex. 1952, US Ct. Mil. Appeals, 1953, US Tax Ct. 1954, US Dist. Ct. (no. dist.) Tex. 1956, US Ct. Appeals (5th cir.) 1960, US Supreme Ct. 1961, DC 1982. Pvt. practice, Lamesa, Tex., from 1954. Tchg. instr. legal rsch. writing U. Tex. Sch. Law, 1950-52 Mem. editl. bd. Tex. Law Rev., 1951-52. Mem. ABA, ATLA, Tex. Law Rev. Assn. (life), Tex. Bar Assn. (spl. com. to study rev. code criminal procedure 1969-71), DC Bar Assn., Tex. Trial Lawyers Assn., Tex. Bar Found., Order of the Coif, The Million Dollar Advocates Forum, Phi Delta Phi. Died May 14, 2013.

**SALISBURY, TAMARA PAULA,** retired foundation administrator; b. NYC, Dec. 14, 1927; d. Paul Terrance and Nadine (Korolkova) Voloshin; m. Franklin Cary Salisbury, Jan. 22, 1955 (dec. 1997); children: Franklin Jr., John, Elizabeth, Elaine, Claire. BA, Coll. Notre Dame, 1948; postgrad., American U., George Washington U. Chemist departments pathology & chemotherapy NIH Cancer Inst., Bethesda, Md., 1946-52; asst. to chief of chemistry Office of Naval Rsch., Bethesda, 1953-55; v.p., COO Nat. Found. for Cancer Rsch., Bethesda, 1973—2003. Mem. Assn. Internat. Cancer Rsch., 1995. Decorated d'Officier De L'Ordre De Leopold II; outstanding contbns. award Internat. Soc. Quantum Biology, 1983, Award of Appreciation Beth Israel Hosp., Harvard Med. Sch., Brigham & Women's Hosp., 1993. Mem. AAAS, American Chem. Soc., N.Y. Acad. Sciences, Inst. Phys. & Chem. Biology (fgn.), Krebforschung Internat., Nat. Liberal Club. Home: Washington, DC. Died Nov. 12, 2013.

**SALOP, ARNOLD,** retired internist; b. Oct. 19, 1923; s. Alexander and Anna (Lefrak) S.; m. Maryellen Kolt, June 27, 1979; children: Andrea, Holly, Evan Arnold. AB, Oberlin Coll., 1943; MB, Northwestern U., 1949, MD, 1950. Intern, resident in internal medicine Beth Israel Hosp., 1949-52; resident in internal medicine Goldwater Meml. Hosp., 1950-51, Kingsbridge VA Hosp., 1952-53; pvt. practice medicine specializing in cardiology and internal medicine Ossining, N.Y., 1957-90; ret. Pres. med. staff affairs, sr. attending Phelps Meml. Hosp., North Tarrytown, N.Y, 1988-90; sr. v.p., med. dir. Phelps Meml. Hosp, North Tarrytown, 1991—. Served with AUS, 1943-45; 1st lt. USAF, 1953-54. Fellow ACP, Am. Coll. Cardiology; mem. Am. Heart Assn., Am. Geriat. Assn., Am. Rheumatism Assn., Alpha Omega Alpha. Deceased.

**SALTIN, BENGT,** physiologist; b. Stockholm, June 3, 1935; s. Sven Hilmer and Margaretha (Johansson) S.; m. Ann-Sofi Elin Colling, Jan. 23, 1963; children: Ola, Åsa, Anna. MD, PhD, Karolinska Inst., Stockholm, 1964; degree (hon.), U. Paris, 1992, U. Athens, Greece, 1994, Aristotles U., Thesaloniki, Greece, 1997, U. Guelph, Can., 1998, U. Oslo, 1998, U. Tartu, 1999, U. Jyväskylä, 2000, U. Loughborough, 2003; degree, Concordia U., Montreal, Can., 2005, Mid Sweden U., 2006, Birmingham, 2007, York U., Toronto, Can., 2011. Asst. prof. Karolinska Inst., 1964-68, assoc. prof., 1968-73, prof., 1990-94, U. Copenhagen, 1973-90, prof., dir., 1994—2003, sr. rschr., 2004—14. First pres. European Coll. Sport Scis., Germany Author, editor: Muscle Metabolism During Exercise, 1971, The Racing Camel, 1994; editor: Biochemistry of Exercise, 1985, Skeletal Muscle Metabolism in Exercise and Diabetes, 1998. Chmn. S.W. Orienteering Fedn., Stockholm, 1970-76; pres. Internat. Orienteering Fedn., U.K., 1982-88. Recipient citation award American Coll. Sports Medicine, 1976, honor award, 1990; inauguration lecture A.D. Adolph, American Physiol. Soc., 1994, Novo Nordisk award, 1999, August Krogh prize, 2001, rsch. prize Danish Heart Assn., 2002, Joc Olympic prize, 2002, Prosana award, 2005, award, danish Rheumatology Assn., 2006, Nutrim award, Netherlands, 2008, Biochemistry Exercise award, Canada, 2009. Mem. Danish Acad. Sci. Home: Fårevejle, Denmark. Died Sept. 12, 2014.

**SALTSMAN, DONALD L.,** former state legislator; b. Peoria, Ill., Dec. 15, 1933; m. Eva Saltsman, 1956; 4 children. Student, Ill. Ctrl. Coll., U. Ill. Mem. Dist. 92 Ill. House of Reps., 1981-97. Formerly firefighter. Democrat. Died July 3, 2014.

**SAMFORD, YETTA GLENN, JR.,** lawyer, director; b. Opelika, Ala., June 8, 1923; s. Yetta Glenn and Mary Elizabeth (Denson) S.; m. Mary Austill, Sept. 6, 1949; children: Mary Austill Lott, Katherine Park Alford, Yetta Glenn III (dec.). BS, Auburn U., Ala., 1947; LLB, U. Ala., Tuscaloosa, 1949, LLD (hon.), 1995; DHL (hon.), U. Mobile, Ala., 2001. Bar: Ala. 1949, U.S. Dist. Ct. (mid. dist.) Ala. 1950, U.S. Ct. Appeals (5th cir.) 1961, U.S. Ct. Appeals (11th cir.) 1981. Pvt. practice, Opelika, Ala.; ptnr. Samford & Denson LLP and Predessors, from 1949. Mem. Ala. Senate from Lee and Russell counties, 1958-62; mem. bd. edn.Opelika City, 1963-75, pres. 1966-74; mem. State of Ala. Bd. of Corrections, 1969-75; mem. adv. bd. State Docks, 1987-2000. Trustee U. Mobile, 1963-92, life trustee, 1992—, trustee U. Ala., 1972-93, trustee emeritus, 1993— Mem. Ala. Law Inst. (exec. com.), Ala. Acad. Honor (exec. com. mem.), Masons, Phi Delta Phi, Omicron Delta Kappa, Alpha Tau Omega. Republican. Baptist. Home: Opelika, Ala. Died Dec. 28, 2013.

**SAMPSON, ANTHONY TERRELL SEWARD,** author; b. Billingham, Durham, Eng., Aug. 3, 1926; s. Michael Treviskey and Phyllis Marion (Seward) S.; m. Sally Virginia Sampson, May 31, 1965; children: Katharine, Paul. Degree in English, Oxford U., Eng., 1950. Editor Drum Mag., Johannesburg, South Africa, 1951-55; mem. editl. staff Observer newspaper, London, 1955-74; editl. adviser Brandt Commn., 1979-83. Author: Drum: A Venture into the New Africa, 1955, The Treason Cage, 1958, Commonsense About Africa, 1960, Anatomy of Britain, 1962, Anatomy of Britain Today, 1965, Macmillan: A Study in Ambiguity, 1967, The New Europeans, 1968, The New Anatomy of Britain, 1971, The Sovereign State of ITT, 1973, The Seven Sisters, 1975, The Arms Bazaar, 1977, The Money Lenders, 1981, The Changing Anatomy of Britain, 1982, Empires of the Sky, 1984, (with Sally Sampson) The Oxford Book of Ages, 1985; editor: The Sampson Letter, 1984-86, Black and Gold, 1987, The Midas Touch, 1989, Essential Anatomy of Britain, 1992, Company Man, 1995, The Scholar Gypsy, 1997, Mandela: The Authorized Biography, 1999, Who Runs this Place?, 2004. Trustee Scott Trust, 1993-96. Fellow Royal Soc. Literature; mem. Soc. Authors (chmn. 1992-94), Beefsteak Club (London), Groucho Club. Home: Wilts, England. Died Dec. 18, 2004.

**SAMSON, GORDON EDGAR,** educator, consultant; b. Waterville, Que., Can., Oct. 25, 1923; came to U.S., 1952; s. Edgar John Knox and Ethel May (Holyon) S. BSc, Bishop's U., 1942, MEd, 1948; PhD, U. Chgo., 1955. Cert. tchr. h.s., 1943. Tchr., prin. various sch. sys., Que., 1943-52; rsch. asst. U. Chgo., 1952-54; exec. asst. Ednl. Policies Commn., NEA, Washington, 1954-57; chmn. dept. edn. Fenn Coll., Cleve., 1957-65; assoc. prof. Cleve. State U., 1965-85, acting dean, 1965-67, prof. emeritus, 1985—2001. Vis. scholar Brock U., St. Catharines, Ont., summer 1986, 87, external examiner, 1988. Contbr. articles to profl. jours. Mem. NEA (life), Am. Ednl. Rsch. Assn., Nat. Soc. for Study of Edn., Phi Delta Kappa. Avocations: genealogy, reading. Died Dec. 14, 2001.

**SAMUELS, GORDON JACOB,** retired judge; b. Aug. 12, 1923; m. Jacqueline Kott, Apr. 4, 1957; 2 children. Student, Oxford U., Eng.; DSc, U. New South Wales, 1994. Bar: Inner Temple, 1948, NSW, 1952. Challis lectr. in pleading U. Sydney, Australia, 1964-70; judge Supreme Ct. of NSW, 1972-92, judge Ct. Appeals, 1974-94; mem. coun. U. NSW, 1969—94, chancellor, 1976—94; gov. New South Wales, 1996—2001. Chmn. Australia Legal Edn. Coun., 1981-85, N.S.W. Law Reform Commn., 1993-96, Migrant Employment And Qualifications Bd.; pres. Security Tribunal, 1980-90. Served to capt. Royal Devon Yeomanry, 1942-46. Recipient Centenary medal, 2003; named a Companion of the Order of Australia, 1987, Comdr. of the Royal Victorian Order, 2000. Mem. Australian Club. Died Dec. 9, 2007.

**SAMUELS, HANNA,** artist; b. Buffalo, Apr. 26, 1908; d. Emil and Rachel (Span) S. Student, Art Inst. Buffalo, 1937-54. Sr. clk. in charge of catalog Buffalo State Coll., 1966-73, vol. cons. on art. Represented in permanent collections at Erie County Hist. Soc., Vincent Price Collection, Judaic Mus., Temple Beth Zion, Buffalo, Butler Libr., Buffalo State Coll., Cox Conv. Hall, Pentecostal Temple Ch., Buffalo, Burchfield-Penney Art Ctr., Buffalo; exhibited in group shows Smithsonian Instn., Kenan Ctr., Lockport, N.Y.; exhbns. of sculpture include Burchfield-Penney Art Ctr., Buffalo, Albright-Knox Art Gallery, Memphis, Jr. League, Smithsonian Instn., Washington, Castellani Art Mus., Smithsonian Assocs. Nat. Mem. The Libr. of Congress. Vol. USO, Buffalo, 1942-45. Mem. Patteran Artists (rec. sec.), Castellani Art Mus. Niagara U., Libr. Congress (nat.), Smithsonian Inst. (assoc.). Democrat. Avocations: painting, music. Deceased.

**SANABRIA, SHERRY ZVARES,** artist; b. Washington; d. Simon and Belle (Herzfeld) Zvares; m. Phillip Kasten, Aug. 31, 1958 (div. Dec. 1985); childrn: Jessica L., Alex S.; m. Robert Sanabria, Jan. 24, 1986. BA, George Washington U., 1959; MFA, Am. U., 1974. Lectr. in field. One-woman shows include Phillips Collection, Washington, 1980, Baumgartner Galleries, Washington, 1981, 83, 86, 88, Genest Gallery, Lambertville, N.J., 1987, KPMG Peat Marwick, Washington, 1989, David Adamson Gallery, Washington, 1989, 91, 93, 95, Ellis Island Immigration Mus., N.Y.C., 1991-92, Marymount U., McLean, Va., 1992, Dorothy McRae Gallery, Atlanta, 1994, George Washington U., Ashton, Va., 1997, Washington Hebrew Congregation, 1998, Ea. Loudoun Libr. Sys., 2000, Am. Inst. of Architects,

Washington, 2002; AIA, Balt., 2004; Rentz Gallery, Richmond, Va. 2004, Washington County Mus. Fine Arts, Hagerstown, Md., 2005, The Athenaeum, Alexandria, Va., 2007, Northern VA CC, Hoorn-Ashby Gallery, NYC, 2008, George Washington U., Va., 2009, Art Sq., Va., 2010, Rust Libr., Va., 2012, Cosmos Club, Washington, 2013, Willyer Art Space, Washington, 2013; exhibited in group shows, including Washington Women's Arts Ctr., 1977, So. Alleghenies Mus., Loretto, Pa., 1978, Arts Gallery, Balt., 1980, 81, Corcoran Gallery Art, Washington, 1980, Frostburg (Md.) State Coll., 1981, Art Barn, Washington, 1982, Am. Acad. Arts and Letters, N.Y.C., 1983, Williams Coll. Mus. Art, Williamstown, Mass., 1984, Cornell U., Ithaca, N.Y., 1985, Fed. Reserve Sys., Washington, 1985, 89, Washington County Mus. Fine Arts, Hagerstown, Md., 1986, Vanderbilt U., 1989, Gallery 10 ltd., Washington, 1991, Watkins Gallery, Am. U., Washington, 1992, U. Richmond, Va., 1992, Emerson Gallery, McLean, Va., 1993, U. Del., 1994, B'nai B'rith Kluznick Mus., Washington, 1996, Gallery Henoch, N.Y.C., 1999, Md. Art Place, Balt., 2000, Nat. Gallery of Bermuda, 2003, Katzen Gallery, Washington, 2007, Osuna Gallery, 2008, Conrad Wide Gallery, Ariz., 2009, Washington Hebrew Congregation, 2012; represented in permanent collections Phillips Collection, Washington, Philip Morris USA, Washington, Associated Gen. Contractors Am., Washington, Artery Orgn., Md., First Nat. Bank Boston, Charles E. Smith Co., Va., Loudoun Med. Ctr., Va., McGraw Hill Pubs., N.Y., N.Y., Benchmark Capitol, Calif., Am. Univ., Washington, US Vice Pres.'Residence Found., Washington, others Mem. Women's Caucus for Arts, Loudoun Arts Coun. Home: Leesburg, Va. Died Mar. 3, 2014.

**SANBORN, THEODORE S.,** insurance and real estate company executive; b. St. Paul, Jan. 31, 1921; s. Bruce W. and Conradine (Schurmeier) S.; m. Dorothy Louise Cammack, Jan. 14, 1949; children: Bruce C., David S., Margaret A., Conradine W.; m. Jean Campbell Brooks, Mar. 3, 1989 Student, U. Minn., 1940-43. Agt. Minn. Mut. Life Ins. Co., St. Paul, 1945-46; agy. supr. Modern Life Ins. Co., 1946-48, v.p., 1948, exec. v.p., 1949-50; pres. North Cen. Life Ins. Co., St. Paul, 1950-64, chmn., chief exec. officer, 1964-87, chmn., 1987-90; founder, chmn., chief exec. officer The Fin. Life Cos., St. Paul, from 1960; pres. White Bird Realty, Inc., Naples, Fla., 1984-89. Bd. dirs. Am. Nat. Bank. Past trustee Hamline U., Breck Sch., House of Hope Ch. Served to 1st lt. USAAF, 1943-45. Mem. Nat. Consumers Credit Ins. Assn. (past pres.), Chief Execs. Orgn., Minn. Execs. Orgn. (past pres.) Presbyterian. (trustee). Home: Naples, Fla. Died Nov. 9, 1990.

**SANDBLOM, PHILIP JOHN,** retired medical educator, writer; b. Chgo., Oct. 29, 1903; arrived in Sweden, 1909; s. John Nicolaus and Ellen Therese (Chinlund) S.; m. Grace Susan Schaefer, Mar. 28, 1932; children: John, Susanna, Catherine, Carl-Louis, Gustav. MD, Karolinska Inst., Stockholm, 1930, PhD, 1944; MSc, Northwestern U., Chgo., 1934; MD (hon.), U. Glasgow, Scotland, 1965, U. Paris, 1967, U. Cordoba, Argentina, 1967; PhD (hon.), U. Lund, Sweden, 1968; MD (hon.), U. Lausanne, Switzerland, 1974; degree (hon.), Ehrenbürger Christian Albrecht Univ., Kiel, Germany. Resident Lasarettet, Örebro, Sweden, 1932-37, Serafimer Lasarettet, Stockholm, 1937-40; assoc. prof. Karolinska Inst., Stockholm, 1940-45; chmn. dept. pediat. surgery Crown Princess Louse's Children's Hosp., Stockholm, 1945-50; prof., chmn. dept. surgery U. Lund, Sweden, 1950-70. Guest prof. surgery U. Calif., San Diego, 1971-72, U. Lausanne, Switzerland, 1973-80, U. Taipei, Taiwan, 1981-82; rector, pres. U. Lund, 1958-68. Author: Function of the Human Gall Bladder, 1932, Tensile Strength of Healing Wounds, 1949, The Difference in Men, 1969, Hemobilia, 1972, Creativity and Disease, 1982, 12th edit., 1999. Pres. Svensk Kirurgisk Förening, Stockholm, 1957-58, 69-70, Internat. Soc. Surgery, 1965-67; bd. dirs. Swedish Art Soc., 1943-70. Recipient Bronze medal (sailing) Olympic Games, 1928. Fellow ACS (hon.), Royal Coll. Surgeons (Eng.) (hon.), Royal Coll Surgeons (Edinburgh) (hon.), Royal Coll. Surgeons (Ireland) (hon.); mem. Am. Surg. Assn. (hon.), So. Surg. Assn. (hon.), Internat. Surg. Assn. (hon.), Surg. Assn. Sweden (hon.), Surg. Assn. Switzerland (hon.), Surg. Assn. Denmark (hon.), Surg. Assn. Gt. Britain (hon.), Surg. Assn. France (hon.), Surg. Assn. Italy (hon.), Surg. Assn.Germany (corr.), Surg. Assn. Norway (corr.), Surg. Assn. Finland (corr.). Avocations: sailing, skiing, art collecting. Died Feb. 21, 2001.

**SANDERS, JOHN R.,** professional football team manager; b. San Antonio, July 26, 1922; s. Ira William and Johnnie Laurie (Manning) S.; m. Margaret Jean Werner, July 6, 1946; 2 children. BA, Occidental Coll., 1949. Head football coach North Hollywood (Calif.) High Sch., 1952-58; dir. athletics, football coach U.S. Grant High Sch., Van Nuys, Calif., 1959-63; dir. player personnel Los Angeles Rams, 1964-75, asst. gen. mgr., 1967-75; asst. to pres. San Diego Chargers, 1975, gen. mgr., from 1976. Served with USN, 1943-46. Named NFL Exec. of Yr., 1979. Republican. Baptist. Died Oct. 26, 1990.

**SANDS, MATTHEW LINZEE,** physicist, researcher; b. Oxford, Mass., Oct. 20, 1919; m. Freya Sands, 1978; children: Michael, Richard, Michelle. BA, Clark U., 1940; MA, Rice U., 1941; PhD, MIT, 1948. Physicist U.S. Naval Ordnance Lab., 1941-43, Los Alamos Sci. Lab., 1943-46; research asso., then asst. prof. physics Mass. Inst. Tech., 1946-50; sr. research fellow, asso. prof., prof. physics Calif. Inst. Tech., 1950-63; prof., dep. dir. Linear Accelerator Center, Stanford, 1963-69; prof. physics U. Calif.-Santa Cruz, 1969-85, prof. emeritus, from 1985, fellow Kresge Coll.; vice chancellor for sci., 1969-72; pres. Sands-Kidner Assocs., Inc., 1986-90. Vis. prof. U. Paris-Sud, spring 1976; mem. Commn. Coll. Physics, 1960-66, chmn., 1964-66; cons. Office Sci. and Tech., ACDA, Inst. Def. Analyses, 1962-67; mem. Pugwash Conf. Sci. and World Affairs, 1960-63; cons. on accelerator physics, 1975-93. Author: (with W.C. Elmore) Electronics-Experimental Techniques, 1948, (with R.P. Feynman and R.B. Leighton) The Feynman Lectures on Physics, 3 vols, 1965, (with others) Physical Science Today, 1973; mem. editl. bd.: Il Nuovo Cimento, 1972-85; contbr. articles to profl. jours. Fulbright scholar Italy, 1952-53. Fellow Am. Phys. Soc. (Robert R. Wilson prize 1998); mem. Am. Assn. Physics Tchrs. (Disting. Service award 1972), Fedn. Am. Scientists, AAAS. Achievements include research in electronic instrumentation for nuclear physics; electron storage rings; science and public affairs; science education; high-energy physics; accelerators; cosmic rays. Home: Santa Cruz, Calif. Died Sept. 13, 2014.

**SANDY, CATHERINE ELLEN,** librarian; b. Italy, 1908; d. Felice Antonio and Guglielma Elena (Santaniello) Sandy. Student, Rosary Coll., 1933—34, U. Florence, Italy, 1951; BS, Columbia U., 1953. Libr. Port Wash. Pub. Libr., NY, 1926—73, bd. dirs., Art Adv. Coun.; trustee, charter mem. Cow Neck Peninsula Hist. Soc. Contbr. articles to profl. jours. Recipient Alumni medal Columbia, 1970. Mem.: Gen. Studies Alumni Assn. Columbia, UN Assn., Am., NY, NC Libr. Assns. Roman Catholic. Deceased.

**SANGER, FREDERICK,** biochemist; b. Rendcomb, Gloucestershire, Eng., Aug. 13, 1918; s. Frederick and Cicely Sanger; m. Margaret Joan Howe, 1940; children: Robin, Peter Frederick, Sally Joan. BA, St. John's Coll., U. Cambridge, 1940, PhD, 1943; DSc (hon.), Leicester U., 1968, Oxford U., 1970, Strasbourg U., 1970. Beit meml. med. rsch. fellow U. Cambridge, 1944-51, rsch. scientist, dept. biochemistry, 1944-61, rsch. scientist, divsn. head Med. Rsch. Coun. Lab. Molecular Biology, 1962-83. Contbr. articles to profl. jours. Decorated Comdr., Order of Brit. Empire, Order Companions of Honour; recipient Corday-Morgan medal and prize, Chem. Soc., 1951, Nobel Prize in Chemistry, Royal Swedish Acad. Sciences, 1958, 1980, William Bate Hardy prize, Cambridge Philos. Soc., 1976, Copley Medal, Royal Soc., 1977, Louisa Gross Horwitz prize, Columbia U., 1979, Albert Lasker Basic Medical Rsch. award, Lasker Found., 1979. Fellow: Royal Soc., Royal Coll. Pathologists (hon.); mem.: Acad. Sci. Brazil, American Acad. Arts & Sciences (fgn.), Japanese Biochemical Soc. (hon.), American Soc. Biol. Chemists (hon.), Argentine Chem. Soc. (corr.), Acad. Sci. Argentina. Achievements include discovery of the complete amino acid sequence of the two polypeptide chains of insulin; development of several methods to sequence the nucleic acids DNA and RNA including methods reading DNA using special bases called chain terminators, the use of very thin gel systems and the adaptation of efficient cloning methods to produce both DNA strands and the whole-genome shotgun. Home: Cambridge, England. Died Nov. 19, 2013.

**SANGSTER, ROBERT EDMUND,** horse breeder, owner; b. Liverpool, Eng., May 23, 1936; s. Vernon Sangster. Student, Repton Coll. Chmn. Vernon Orgn., 1980—88, Sangster Group, from 1988; race horse owners The Minstrel, Alleged, Jaazeiro, Detroit, Beldale Ball, Kings Lake, Our Paddy Boy, Golden Fleece, Assert, Lomond, Caerleon; El Gran Senor, Sadler's Wells, Gildoran, Law Society, Committed, Marooned, Marauding, Midnight Fever, Bluebird, Prince of Birds, Lady Liberty, Handsome Sailor, Rodrigo de Triano, Riverina Charm, Kostroma, Royal Heroine; leading winning race-horse owner, 1977—78, 1982—84; leading owner Royal Ascot, 1977, 1979, 1984, 1987, Australia, 1986—87. Died Apr. 7, 2004.

**SANKS, ROBERT LELAND,** environmental engineer, retired educator; b. Pomona, Calif., Feb. 19, 1916; s. John B. and Nellie G. (Church) Sanks; m. Mary Louise Clement, May 16, 1946 (dec. Oct. 1994); children: Margaret Russell, John Clement; m. Edith Millen Harrington, Dec. 2, 1999 (dec. Aug. 14, 2010); m. Carol Jane Asleson Sanks, Mar. 23, 2012. AA, Fullerton Jr. Coll., Calif., 1936; BS, U. Calif., Berkeley, 1940; MS, Iowa State Coll., Ames, 1949; PhD, U. Calif., Berkeley, 1965. Draftsman City of La Habra Calif., 1940; asst. engr. Alex Morrison cons. engr., Fullerton, Calif., 1941; jr. engr. US Army Engrs., LA, 1941-42; asst. rsch. engr. dept. civil engring. U. Calif.-Berkeley, 1942-45; structural engr. The Austin Co., Oakland, Calif., 1945-46; instr. dept. civil engring. U. Utah, Salt Lake City, 1946-49, asst. prof., 1949-55, assoc. prof., 1955-58; structural engr. The Lang Co., Salt Lake City, 1950; instrument man Patti McDonald Co., Anchorage, 1951; checker Western Steel Co., Salt Lake City, 1952; structural engr. Moran, Proctor, Meuser and Rutledge, NYC, 1953, F.C. Torkelson Co., Salt Lake City, 1955; soils engr. R.L. Sloane & Assocs., Salt Lake City, 1956; prof., chmn. dept. civil engring. Gonzaga U., Spokane, Wash., 1958-61; ret. profl. engr. Mont., 1966—2010; prof. dept. civil engring. Mont. State U., Bozeman, 1966-82, prof. emeritus, from 1982; vis. prof. U. Tex.-Austin, 1974-75; part-time sr. engr. Christian, Spring, Sielbach & Assoc., Billings, Mont., 1974-82. Cons. engr., 1945-2010; lectr. at pumping sta. design workshops, 1988—2009; assoc. specialist San. Engring. Research Lab., 1963-65, research engr., 1966. Author: Statically Indeterminate Structural Analysis, 1961; co-author: (with Takashi Asano) Land Treatment and Disposal of Municipal and Industrial Wastewaters, 1976, Water Treatment Plant Design for the Practicing Engineer, 1978; editor-in-chief: Pumping Station Design, 1989 (award Excellence profl. & scholarly pub. div. Assn. Am. Pubs. 1989), 2d edit., 1998, co-editor 3d edit., 2006; contbr. articles on civil engring. to profl. publs. Mem. Wall of Fame, Fullerton H.S., 1987, Hall of Fame, Mont. Profl. Engrs., 2005; NSF fellow, 1961-63 Mem. ASCE (life, chmn. local qualifications com. intermountain sect. 1950-56, pres. intermountain sect. 1957-58), Am. Water Works Assn. (pres. Mont. sect. 1981-82, George Warren Fuller award), Mont. Water Environ. Fedn., Assn. Environ. Engring. Profs., Rotary, Sigma Xi, Chi Epsilon. Home: Bozeman, Mont. Died Sept. 18, 2012.

**SAN-SEGUNDO, MARIA J.,** economics professor; b. Medina del Campo, Spain, Mar. 25, 1958; BA in Economics, U. Basque Country, Bilbao, Spain, 1980; MA in Economics, Princeton U., NJ, 1982, PhD in Economics, 1985. Assoc. prof. U. Basque Country, 1985—89, U. Carlos III, Madrid, 1989, vice-rector student affairs, 2000—04; advisor sec. state univs. and rsch. Ministry Edn. and Sci., Madrid, 1994—96; min. edn. and sci. Spanish Govt., Madrid, 2004—06, amb. to Unesco París, from 2006, min. edn. and sci.; mem. Nat. Coun. Univs., Madrid, 2000—04. Chair-person World Heritage com. World Heritage Com., Paris, from 2008. Contbr. scientific papers to profl. jours. Advisor com. to support the socialist candidate Mr. Zapatero, Madrid, 2004. Deceased.

**SANTAVIRTA, SEPPO S.,** orthopaedic surgeon, educator; b. Helsinki, Finland, Dec. 5, 1945; m. Nina Sandelin; children: Torsten and Robin. MD, U. Zürich, Switzerland, 1972; PhD, Helsinki U., 1979. Intern, resident, fellow in orthopaedics Univ. Ctrl. Hosp., Helsinki, 1972-81; asst. prof. Helsinki U., 1983-96, prof., chmn. dept orthopaedics, from 1996. Died 2005.

**SANTOS, ROBERT DAVID,** health and fitness educator, consultant; b. Chalan, Pago, Guam, Jan. 1, 1952; s. Joaquin L. G. and Carmen I. (Pinaula) S.; m. Elaine Marie Pudwill, Sept. 1, 1975; children: Zane, Deylene, Makao, Shane. AAS in Gen. Studies, Pierce County C.C., Wash., 1973; EdB in Physical Edn., Ctrl. Wash. U., 1975; MPE, U. Oreg., 1979; PhD in Higher Edn. Adminstrn. and Adult Edn., U. North Tex., 1990; ABD in Adminstrn. in Kinesiology, Tex. Woman's U. Cert. tchr. Physical edn. tchr. George Washington H.S., Guam, 1975-76, John F. Kennedy H.S., Guam, 1978-80; math, physical edn., health tchr. Battle Mt. H.S., Battle Mt., Nev., 1981-82; math. tchr. E.C. Best Jr. H.S., Fallon, Nev., 1982-83; rsch. cons. Sitterly Mgmt. and Cons. Firm, Ft. Worth, Tex., 1986-87; health tchr. S. Sanchez H.S., Guam, 1989-91; dir., mem. gov.'s cabinet Guam Health Planning and Devel. Agy., 1991-93; lectr. divsn. health, physical edn. and athletics Western Oreg. State Coll., Monmouth, from 1993; instr. dept. physical edn. and health Linn-Benton C.C., Albany, Oreg., from 1994; pvt. personal fitness instr., 1992-95. Dir. fundraiser Sports Medicine Design by Guam--A Wholistic Approach, 1992; dir. 1st Ann. Gov.'s Health Task Forces' Forum, 1992; rsch. dir. Gov.'s 21st Century Health Work Force Survey, 1991-93; wellness cons. Clark Hatch Health and Fitness Ctr., 1992-93; fitness cons. Gold's Gym, 1992-93; coaches' lectr., cons. athletic injuries Oreg. H.S., 1977-79; student teaching asst. supr. U. Nev.-Reno, 1981; wellness instr. U. North Tex., 1986-90, adj. prof. kinesiol. studies, 1986-90 Co-author: (with John Eddy) Circle of Excellence: Basketball, 1986; contbr. articles to profl. jours. Clinic dir. Albany Boys and Girls Club, 1993; mem. fellowship com. WHO; hon. amb.-at-large Gov. Joe Ada, Guam, 1991. Recipient Coat of Arms, Mayor of Rutherford, Eng., 1991. Mem. AAHPERD, Internat. Coun. for Health, Phys. Edn., Recreation, Sport and Dance (dir. philosophy edn. and sport commn.), Am. Assn. for Wellness Edn., Counseling & Rsch., Oreg. Athletic Trainer's Soc., Nat. Athletic Trainers Assn. (cert.). Roman Catholic. Deceased.

**SAQEB, GHULAM NABI,** education educator; b. Gujranwala, Punjab, Pakistan, Apr. 1, 1931; arrived in Eng., 1959; s. Noor Hussain and Rabia Begum Lakhanpal; m. Rashida Begum, Mar. 18, 1948 (div. Feb. 1958); children: Shahnaz Kausar, Farrukh Zaheer; m. Rehana Nasreen Malik, July 14, 1967; children: Iram, Nauman Pasha, Rehan Pasha, Salmaan Pasha. BA, U. Punjab, Lahore, Pakistan, 1952, EdB, 1954; acad. diploma in edn., U. London, 1960, MPhil, 1964, PhD, 1974. Sr. tchr. D.B. H.S., Gujranwala, 1954—58, Inner London Edn., 1960—66; English tchr. Ministry Edn., Makkah, Saudi Arabia, 1966—70; asst. prof. King Abdulaziz U., Makkah, 1974—84, assoc. prof. Jeddah, Saudi Arabia, 1984—92; prof. edn. Internat. Islamic U., Kuala Lumpur, Malaysia, 1997—2002, vis. prof., guest writer, from 2002. Vis. lectr. U. London, 1984—92; ednl. cons. Iqra Trust, London, 1992—94, Islamic Schs. Trust, London, 1994—96. Author: On Modernization of Muslim Education; assoc. editor: Islamic Edn. Quarterly, from 1997; contbr. articles to profl. jours. Gov. Nat. Muslim Edn. Coun./Union Muslim Orgns., London, from 1985; mem. standing adv. coun. on religious edn. London Borough Westminster, 1992—96. Mem.: Internat. Hearing Soc., Comparative and Internat. Edn. Soc., Comparative Edn. Soc. India (life). Muslim. Avocations: reading, writing, travel. Home: London, England. Died May 2008.

**SARSFIELD, GEORGE P.,** lawyer; b. Vancouver, B.C., Can., Jan. 14, 1913; (parents Am. citizens); s. John M. and Margaret (LaValle) Sarsfield; m. Margeret Davis Sarsfield, May 23, 1942. BA; JD, U. Mont., 1950. Blk., laborer, miner, 1930—41; admitted to Mont. bar., 1950; with Butte. Past pres. Butte YMCA. Repub. Nominee Congress, Mont., 1960. Chmn. exec. bd. Mont. Coll. Mineral Sci. and Tech., 1968—71; chmn. bd. trustees U. Mont. Devel. Fund, 1967—70; adv. bd. Salvation Army, from 1952. Capt. US Army, 1941—46. Recipient Disting. Service award, U. Mont., 1971, Pantzer award, 1975, Former Mont. open golf champion award; named Mont. amateur golf champion. Mem.: ABA (past v.p.), US Golf Assn. (mem. sectional affairs com. from 1968), Mont. State Golf Assn. (past pres.), U. Mont. Alumni Assn. (pres. 1964, chmn. bd. 1964—66), Am. Trial Lawyers Assn., Mont. Bar Assn., Butte Country (past pres.), Rotary (past local pres., dist. gov. 1963—64, chmn. internat. constn. and by-laws com. 1969—70, internat. dir. 1973—75, internat. 1st v.p. 1974—75, chmn. exec. com. internat. bd. dirs. 1974—75), Phi Delta Theta, Alpha Kappa Psi, Phi Delta Phi. Died Dec. 1993.

**SARTOR, DANIEL RYAN, JR.,** lawyer; b. Vicksburg, Miss., June 2, 1932; s. Daniel Ryan and Lucy Leigh (Hubbs) S.; m. Olive Guthrie Moss, Oct. 12, 1957; children— Clara

M., Daniel Ryan, Walter M. BA, Tulane U., 1952, LL.B., 1955. Bar: La. 1955. Instr. Tulane U., New Orleans, 1955-56, asst. prof., 1956-57; ptnr. Snellings, Breard, Sartor, Inabnett & Trascher, Monroe, La., 1957—2001, of coun., from 2002. Contbr. articles to profl. jours. Fellow Am. Coll. Trust and Estate Counsel, Am. Bar Found., La. Bar Found.; mem. La. State Law Inst. (mem. coun. 1969—, sec. civil law sect. 1969-97, sr. officer 1997—), La. State Bar Assn. (chmn. sect. on trust estate, probate and immovable property 1973-74, bd. govs. 1974-75), Lotus Club, Bayou DeSiard Country Club. Democrat. Methodist. Home: Monroe, La. Died 2012.

**SAUNDERS, ADAH WILSON,** physical education educator; b. Balt. d. William Llewellyn and Irene Bertha (Dorkins) Wilson; 1 child, Leigh Robert. BS, Hampton U., 1967; MS, Columbia U. Tchrs. Coll., 1971. Instr. phys. edn. Hunter Coll., CUNY, NYC, 1967-68, Bronx C.C., CUNY, NYC, 1968-69; tchr. phys. edn. N.Y.C. Bd. Edn., from 1971, dean students, 1993-96. Coach N.Y. Jr. Tennis League; dir. summer camps N.Y.C. Dept. of Human Resources, 1969-72. Inventor: (bd. game) The Presidency; patentee: Rollice Shoe, 1991. Tchr. Leonardo Da Vinci Sch., N.Y.C. Bd. Edn., Corona, N.Y. Grantee N.Y.C. Bd. Edn., The Early Morning Health Club, 1985. Mem. United Fedn. Tchrs., Am. Fedn. Tchrs., Queens C. of C. Home: Flushing, NY. Died May 14, 1999.

**SAUNDERS, NINA ALEXANDER,** interior designer; b. Lemberg, Poland, Jan. 1, 1934; arrived in US, 1951, naturalized, 1955; d. Leopold and Ann (Erbsen) Alexander; m. Roger Alfred Saunders, Oct. 4, 1953; children: Gary L., Jeffrey G., Todd R., Tedd R. Attended, CCNY, 1951—52, NYU, 1952—53. Ptnr. J & N Interior Design, Brookline and Chestnut Hill, Mass., 1971—79; pres. Interior Design Assocs. Boston, from 1979; jr. League showhouse invitee Newton, 1975, Milton, 1976, Bklyn., 1977; dir. Hotels Tradition, Boston, 1980. Judge nat. lodging-hosp. design awards, 1983; bd. dirs. women's div. Combined Jewish Philanthropies, Boston, from 1985, Friends of Pub. Garden, Boston, from 1985; trustee New Eng. Aquarium, Boston, from 1981, Met. Opera Boston, from 1982; mem. exec. bd. Mus. Fine Arts Ladies Com., Boston, from 1982; honored by proclamation Nina A. Saunders day mayor, Boston, 1981. Mem.: Longwood Cricket Club (Chestnut Hill), Badminton and Tennis Club (Boston), Algonquin Club, Belmont Country (Mass.). Avocations: tennis, skiing, painting, travel. Home: Boston, Mass. Died Nov. 3, 1991.

**SAUTER, FRANZ FABIAN,** consulting and structural engineer; b. San Jose, Costa Rica, Feb. 7, 1933; s. Federico and Hilda (Fabian) S.; m. Maria Angeles Ortiz, June 30, 1957; children: Arnold, Hans Peter, Krista Maria, Manfred, Helmuth. BS in Civil Engring., U. Costa Rica, 1956; MS in Earthquake Engring., Internat. Inst. Seismology and Earthquake Engring., Tokyo, 1964. Structural engr. Leonhardt & Andrä, Stuttgard, Germany, 1957—58; chief engr., then dir. in charge engring. and sales Productos de Concreto S.A., San Jose, 1958—63; pres., prin. ptnr. Franz Sauter & Asociados S.A., Cons. Engrs., San Jose, from 1965; prof. civil engring. U. Costa Rica, 1965—70. Mem. seismic code com. Colegio Federado de Ingenieros y Arquitectos de Costa Rica; bd. dirs. World Seismic Safety Initiative, 1994-98; former bd. dirs. in main indsl. corps., Costa Rica; pres. Asociacion Centroamericana del Cemento y Concreto, 1967-72, Institucion Cultural Germano-Costarricense, San Jose, 1969-73. Co-author: Study of Earthquake Insurance, 1978; author: Introduction to Seismology, 1989, In Search of the Middle Ages, 2000; contbr. articles to profl. jours. Decorated Bundesverdienstkreuz 1st class (Germany); named Disting. Engr. of Yr., Colegio Ingenieros Civiles, Costa Rica, 2001; grantee, UNESCO, 1963—64. Mem. ASCE, Asociacion Centroamericana Cemento y Concreto (hon.), Colegio Federado de Ingenieros y Arquitectos de Costa Rica, Earthquake Engring. Rsch. Inst., Am. Concrete Inst., Prestressed Concrete Inst., Costa Rican Assn. Structural and Seismic Engring. (hon. pres.). Achievements include research in earthquake insurance and damage assessment, earthquake hazard and vulnerability, earthquake-resistant design for construction projects. Died Oct. 6, 2003.

**SAUVÉ, GEORGES,** surgeon; b. Paris, Sept. 10, 1925; s. Louis de Gonzague andMarie (Bourdon) S.; m. Monique Lemaigre, June 11, 1955; children: Frédérique, Jacques-Phillipe, Diane, Claire, Marie-Amelie, Bérengère. MD, U. Paris, 1956. Intern Hosp. de Paris, 1952-57, chief of surgery, 1975-62; practice surgery, Laval, France, from 1962. Author: Les fils de Saint Come, 1987, De Louis XV à Poincaré, 1989, Le Collège Stanislas, 1994. Mem. Internat. Coll. Surgeons, Lauréat Acad. Médecine, Acad. Maine, Acad. Généalogie. Roman Catholic. Avocations: music, art, literature. Home: La Templerie, France. Died Dec. 8, 2007.

**SAVELIEVA, ELENA IGOREVNA,** chemist; b. St. Petersburg, Russia; d. I.V. Volf and V.V. Sibirskaya; m. Dmitriy D. Saveliev; 1 child, Alexey. Grad., Inst. Tech., St. Petersburg, 1983; D in Chemistry, State U., St. Petersburg, 1997. Engr. Inst. Hydrolyses, St. Petersburg, 1983-86; investigator Mil. Medicine Acad., St. Petersburg, 1986-87, Hygiene Profl. Pathology Inst., St. Petersburg, from 1987. Contbr. articles to profl. jours. Home: St Petersburg, Russia. Deceased.

**SAWICKI, JANUSZ LUDWIK,** electronic engineering educator; b. Poznań, Poland, May 25, 1936; s. Stefan and Wanda (Danecka) S.; m. Maria Odroń, July 26, 1973; children: Michael, Christoph. MSc, Poznań U. Tech., 1958; DSc, Slask U. Tech., Gliwice, Poland, 1965, Warsaw U. Tech., Poland, 1973. Asst. Poznań U. Tech., 1958-65, ast. prof., 1965-74, assoc. prof., 1974-95, prof. electronic engring. and digital signal processing, from 1995. Co-translator: Examples in Control Theory, 1973 (Min. of Edn. award 1974); contbr. articles to profl. jours.; patentee in field. Recipient Golden Cross of Merit, State Coun., 1980, Chevalier Cross of Polonia Restituta, 1989. Mem. IEEE, Polish Soc. Elec. Engrs. Roman Catholic. Avocations: swimming, backpacking, foreign languages. Home: Poznan, Poland. Died Nov. 25, 2007.

**SAWYER, JOHN WESLEY,** retired mathematics and computer science educator, consultant; b. Nov. 2, 1917; s. Joseph Edmond and Inez Avent Sawyer; m. Edna Matthews, Aug. 31, 1939 (dec. Jan. 31, 2002); 1 child, John Wesley Jr. BA, Wake Forest Coll., 1938, MA, 1941, U. Mo., 1948, PhD, 1951. Instr. math. U. Mo., Columbia, 1946—51; assoc. prof. math. Ga. State U., Atlanta, 1951—53, U. Richmond, Va., 1953—56; prof. computer sci. Wake Forest U., Winston-Salem, NC, 1956—88, emeritus prof. computer sci., from 1988. In-house cons. R. J. Reynolds Tobacco Co., Winston-Salem, 1958—86. Contbr. (book) Operations Research Tools for Systems Engineering, articles to profl. jours. Music dir. Wake Forest Bapt. Ch., Winston-Salem, 1964—89; bd. dirs. Salemtowne Retirement Cmty., Winston-Salem, 1999—2004; pres. (4 terms) Atlantic Coast Conf., Greensboro, NC, 1964—86; v.p. NCAA, Kansas City, Mo., 1980—84. Named Tar Heel of Week, Raleigh (N.C.) News & Observer, 1977; grantee NSF, 1960. Fellow: AAAS (life); mem.: Math. Assn. Am., Ops. Rsch. Soc. Am. Achievements include development of computer simulations for business and manufacturing operations; creation and development of computer science department at Wake Forest University. Died July 13, 2013.

**SAWYERR, HARRY,** former Ghanaian government official; b. Abokobi, Accra, Ghana, Apr. 15, 1926; married; 4 children. Student in estate mgmt., U. London, 1953; A cert., Royal Inst. Chartered Surveyor, Eng., 1953, Inst. Chartered Arbitrators, 1953. Learner valuer Lands Dept., London, 1950-53, district valuer, 1955-58; probationer London Country Coun. Valuation Dept., London, 1953-55; pvt. practice surveyor, valuer, estate agent, devel. cons., 1958-62; valuer Kumasi City Coun., 1962-63; chief lands officer Nigeria, 1963-67; pvt. practice devel. cons., 1962-88; chief Nii Djan We, Ga Traditonal Area, 1970-72; mem. Parliament, Osu Klottey, 1970-72; min. edn. & culture Govt. of Ghana, Accra, 1993—97. Mem. Ghana Instn. Surveyors (pres. 1970-72). Died Nov. 8, 2013.

**SAX, JOSEPH LAWRENCE,** lawyer, educator; b. Chgo., Feb. 3, 1936; s. Benjamin Harry and Mary (Silverman) S.; m. Eleanor Charlotte Gettes, June 17, 1958 (dec. 2013); children: Katherine Elaine Dennett, Valerie Beth Sax, Amber Sax Rosen. AB, Harvard U., 1957; JD, U. Chgo., 1959; LLD (hon.), Ill. Inst. Tech., 1992; LLD (hon.), Columbia U., 2009. Bar: D.C. 1960, Mich., 1966, US Supreme Ct. 1969, US Ct. Appeals (Fed. cir.), 2008. Atty. US Dept. Justice, Washington, 1959-60; pvt. practice law Washington, 1960-62; prof. U. Colo., 1962-65, U. Mich., Ann Arbor, 1966-86; dep. asst. sec., counselor US Dept. Interior, Washington, 1994-96; prof. U. Calif. Law Sch., Berkeley, 1986—2014. Fellow Ctr. Advanced Study in Behavioral Sciences, 1977-78, Order of the Coif Disting. Visitor, 2004. Author: Waters and Water Rights, 1967, Water Law, Planning and Policy, 1968, Defending the Environment, 1971, Mountains Without Handrails, 1980, Legal Control of Water Resources, 4th edit., 2006, Playing Darts with a Rembrandt: Public and Private Rights to Cultural Treasures, 1999. Recipient Blue Planet prize, Asahi Glass Found., 2007. Fellow: AAAS. Home: San Francisco, Calif. Died Mar. 9, 2014.

**SAYEED, AKRAM (ABULFATAH),** retired physician; b. Jessore, Bangladesh, Nov. 23, 1935; s. Mokhles and Noor Jehan (Muncie) Ahmed; m. To Hosne-Ara Ali, Oct. 11, 1959; children: Dina Jesmin, Rana Ahmed, Reza Abu. MB BS, U. Dhaka, Bangladesh, 1958. House officer, 1958-59; rotating intern, 1960-61; sr. house officer, 1961-63; gen. practice Leicester, England, 1964—2003. Mem. Cmty. Rels. Commn., U.K., 1968-77; hon. advisor Ministry of Health, Govt. of Bangladesh, 1990—; mem. Gen. Optical Coun., 1994-98, Gen. Med. Coun., 1999-2003. Author: Letters from Leicester, 2004; co-author: Care of Asian Patients in the NHS, 1990; editl. bd. ODA News Rev., 1976-96, Asian Who's Who; contbr. weekly column to Bangladesh Today, 2003-04, Bangladesh Obs. Active DoH Working Groups on Ethnic Minority Health, BBC-TV and Radio Adv. Svcs. on Asian Programmes, 1972-79, Home Sec. Adv. Coun. on Race and Cmty. Rels., 1983-88. Decorated officer Brit. Empire. Fellow Royal Coll. Gen. Practitioners, Royal Coll. Physicians, Coll. Physicians and Surgeons Bangladesh, Overseas Doctors Assn. (gen. sec. 1975-77, v.p. 1977-86, vice chmn. 1986-90, chmn. 1993-96), Royal Soc. Health, Bangladeshi Coll. Gen. Practitioners; mem. Royal Coll. Gen. Practitioners (mem. inner city task force 1991-97, Brit. Med. Assn. (pres. 1993-94, immediate past pres. 1994-95, mem. gen. med. svcs. com. 1989-95, mem. agenda com. 1991-96), Gen. Med. Coun., Med. Jour. Assn. U.K., Bangla Acad. Muslim. Avocation: stamp collecting/philately. Died Jan. 18, 2008.

**SAYLES, LETORY BRUNO,** retired priest, monk; b. New Orleans, La., Apr. 24, 1918; s. George Rene and Evangeline (Letory) Sayles. BA, Zavier U. of La., 1939; MA, U. of Minn., Mpls., 1959. Vows to become Benedictine monk 1944, ordained Roman Cath. priest, 1948. Benedictine monk St. John's Abbey, Collegeville, Minn., from 1944; music instr. St. John's U., Collegeville, 1947—57; Roman Cath. priest St. John's Abbey, Collegeville, 1948—2002; faculty instr. St. Augustine's Coll., Nassau, Bahamas, West Indies, 1957—70; co-pastor St. Anselm's Ch., NYC, 1970—71, part-time asst., 1971—75; chaplain Convent of St. Benedict's, St. Joseph, Minn., 1980—86. Dir. Gregorian chant choir St. John's U., Collegeville, 1947—57; cons. Gregorian chant parish chs. in various locations, Collegeville, 1948—50; dir. Lucayan Chorale, Nassau, 1964—70. Mem.: Nat. Assn. Tchrs. of Singing (life; founding mem., emeritus mem.), Nassau Music Soc. Democrat. Roman Catholic. Deceased.

**SAYRE, PHILIP RUSSELL,** engineer; b. Springfield, Mass., Nov. 28, 1932; s. Clifford Morrill and Eleanor (Crowell) Sayre; m. Harriet S. Welles, July 17, 1954; children: Debra, Lisa, Daniel, Ann. BS in Chemical Engring., MIT, 1954, MS in Mgmt., 1973; postgrad., Harvard U., 1973, Dept. Def. U., 1977. Tech. mgr. Gen. Tire Co., Akron, Ohio, 1958—67; div. mgr. Emeloid Guilford Div., Conn., 1967—72; pres. Sprague Textron, Bridgeport, Conn., 1973—82; pres. chief exec. officer Balzers AG., Hudson, NH, 1982—83; exec. v.p. George Schmitt & Co., Branford, Conn., from 1984; bd. dirs. Goodwill Industries, Bridgeport, 1977—80; chmn. United Way Fairfield County, Bridgeport, 1980—81. Served to lt. col. USAF, 1955—58. Alfred P. Sloan fellow, MIT, 1972. Mem.: NE Gas Assn. (bd. dirs. 1980—81), Res. Officers Assn., Am. Assn. Cost Engrs., Am. Gas Assn. (esec. com. 1977—80), Am. Chem. Soc., Am. Inst. Chem. Engrs., Sayre Mgmt. Scis., MIT New Haven (v.p.), Sachem's Head Yacht (Guilford). Achievements include patents in field. Avocations: flying, sailing. Deceased.

**SBORDONE, ROBERT JOSEPH,** neuropsychologist, educator; b. Boston, Mass., May 6, 1940; s. Saverio and Phylliss (Dellaria) Vella; m. Melinda Welles Sbordone, June 30, 1972 (div. 1977). AB, U. Southern Calif., 1967; MA, Calif. State U., LA, 1969; PhD, UCLA, 1976, postgrad., 1977. Diplomate Am. Bd. Profl. Neuropsychology, Am. Bd. Clin. Neuropsychology, cert. in neuropsychology, clin. psychology; psychologist Calif. Mem. staff psychology UCLA, 1977—78; pvt. practice psychology LA, 1978—80; asst. prof. psychology U. Calif., Irvine, 1980—82, asst. clin. prof., 1983—2014; pres. Robert Sbordone Inc., Calif., 1982—2014. Editl. bd. mem. Internat. Jour. Clin. Neuropsychology; edit. adv. bd. mem. Jour. Head Trauma Rehabilitation; goodwill amb. to Mid. East, 1963. Contbr. articles to profl. jours., chapters to books; author: Client from the Future, 2013. Served in USAF, 1962—66. Named to The Mass. Track Assn. Athletic Hall of Fame, 2009; NIMH grantee, 1973—77. Fellow: Nat. Acad. Neuropsychology; mem.: NY Acad. Sciences, Internat. Soc. Rsch. in Aggression, Nat. Head Injury Found., Internat. Neuropsychol. Soc., American Psychol. Assn. Achievements include research in neuropsychological assessment of brain injured; development of computer software for assessment and rehabilitation of brain injured patients. Home: Laguna Beach, Calif. Died Aug. 3, 2014.

**SCAIFE, RICHARD MELLON,** publishing executive, philanthropist; b. Pitts., July 3, 1932; s. Alan and Sarah Mellon Scaife; m. Frances L. Gilmore (div.); children: Jennie, David; m. Margaret Battle, June 1, 1991 (div. 2005). BA in English, U. Pitts., 1957. Owner, pub. Tribune-Review Publishing Co. Trustee, The Heritage Found., 1985-2014; Chmn., trustee Sarah Scaife Found., Inc.; donor, chmn., trustee Carthage Found., Allegheny Found. Named one of The Forbes 400: Richest Americans, 2006—14, The 25 Most Influential Republicans, Newsmax Mag., 2008. Republican. Died July 4, 2014.

**SCALES, JOHN TRACEY,** biomedical engineering clinician, medical consultant; b. Colchester, Eng., July 2, 1920; s. Walter Laurence and Ethel Margaret (Tracey) S.; m. Cecilia May Sparrow, May 22, 1945 (dec. 1992); children: Sally Anne Cecilia, Helen Rebecca. Student, Kings Coll., London, 1938-43. Casualty officer, resident anesthetist Charing Cross Hosp., 1944; house surgeon Royal Nat. Orthop. Hosp., London and Stanmore, Eng., 1944-45, house surgeon to sr. registrar, 1947-57, from lectr. to reader, 1952-74; prof. biomed. engring. Inst. Orthop., U. London, 1974-87, prof. emeritus, 1987—2004; hon. dir. rsch. RAFT Inst. Plastic Surgery, Mt. Vernon Hosp., Northwood, Middlesex, Eng., 1988-93, hon. dir. pressure sore prevention, 1994-97. Hon. cons. Mt. Vernon Hosp., Northwood, 1968-97, Royal Orthop. Hosp., Birmingham, 1978-87, Royal Nat. Orthop. Hosp., London, 1958-2004; vis. prof. Cranfield U., 1997-98. Contbr. over 175 articles to profl. jours. and books. Capt. Royal Army Med. Corps, 1945-47. Decorated officer Order Brit. Empire; recipient T.H. Green prize in surgery, 1943, award for contbns. to applied rsch. in biomaterials Clemson U., 1974, A.A. Griffith Silver medal Inst. Materials, 1980; named to Hon. Order Ky. Cols., 1986; elected Freeman, City of London, 1995. Fellow Biol. Engring. Soc. (hon.), Inst. Physics and Engring. in Medicine (hon.), Royal Coll. Surgeons Eng. (James Berrie prize 1973), Royal Soc. Medicine (S.G. Brown award 1974), Brit. Med. Assn., Brit. Orthopaedic Assn. (sr. companion), Brit. Assn. Plastic Surgeons (hon.). Achievements include development of Development of individual major bone and joint prosthieses. Stanmore standard total hip & knee prostheses. Also, airstrip dressings and low air loss mattresses. Avocation: china. Home: Pangbourne, England. Died Jan. 30, 2004.

**SCARNE, JOHN,** game company executive; b. Steubenville, Ohio, Mar. 4, 1903; s. Fiorangelo and Maria (Tamburro) S.; m. Steffi Kearney, 1956; 1 son, John Teeko. Student pub. schs., Guttenberg, NJ. Pres. John Scarne Games, Inc., North Bergen, NJ, from 1950. Gaming cons. Hilton Hotels Internat. Magician stage, screen and television; Author: Scarne on Dice, 1945, Scarne on Cards, 1950, Scarne on Card Tricks, 1950, Scarne on Magic Tricks, 1952, Scarne's New Complete Guide to Gambling, 1962, The Odds Against Me, 1967, Scarne's Encyclopedia of Games, 1973, The Mafia Conspiracy, 1976, Scarne's Guide to Casino Gambling; Scarne's Guide to Modern Poker; Contbr. to: World Book Ency, 1970, Ency. Brit, 1975. Cons. to U.S.

Armed Forces, 1941-45. Named Man of Year for Police Chiefs of U.S., 1960 Achievements include creating the board games Teeko, Scarney, plus dice, card and solitaire games. Died July 1985.

**SCHACHTER-SHALOMI, ZALMAN,** rabbi; b. Zhovka, Poland, Aug. 28, 1924; s. Shlomo and Hayyah (Gittel) Schachter; m. Even Ilsen; 11 children. MA in Psychology of Religion, Boston U., 1956; studied Near Eastern and Judaic Studies Dept., Univ. Manitoba, in Winnipeg; PhD in Theology, Hebrew Union Coll.-Jewish Inst. Religion. Co-founder Havurah Congregation; founder B'nai Or Congregation, Boston; World Wisdom Chair Prof., prof. emeritus Naropa Inst., Boulder, Colo.; prof. Jewish mysticism & the psychology of religion Temple U., 1975—95, prof. emeritus Phila., 1995—2014; founder ALEPH Ordination Program, ALEPH: Alliance Jewish Renewal. Author: Fragments of a Future Scroll, 1975, Spiritual Intimacy: A Study of Counseling in Hasidism, 1991; co-author (with Daniel Gropman): The First Step, 1983; co-author: (with Ronald Miller) From Age-ing to Sage-ing, 1995; co-author: (with Joel Siegel) Jewish with Feeling: A Guide to Meaningful Jewish Practice, 2005; co-author: (with Daniel Siegel) Credo with a Modern Kabbalist, 2005, Integral Halachah: Transcending and Including, 2007; co-author: (with Yair Hillel Goelman) Ahron's Heart: The Prayers, Teachings, and Letters of Ahrele Roth, a Hasidic Reformer, 2009; co-author: (with Netanel Miles-Yepez) A Heart Afire: Stories and Teachings of the Early Hasidic Masters, 2009; co-author: (with Sara Davidson) The December Project: An Extraordinary Rabbi and a Skeptical Seeker Confront Life's Greatest Mystery, 2014; author: Gate to the Heart, 1993, Paradigm Shift, 1993, Wrapped in a Holy Flame, 2003. Named one of The Top 50 Rabbis in America, Newsweek Mag., 2007. Jewish Renewal. Died July 3, 2014.

**SCHAFER, EVA CADY,** elementary school educator, musician; b. Seattle, May 7, 1918; d. Osman Horace and Hazel Bradley (Carpenter) Cady, m. Tillman Howard Schafer, June 7, 1942; children: Lyle, Steven, Martin, Gretchen, Hollace, Walter. BA in Zoology, UCLA, 1941, MA in Zoology, 1942. Tchr. San Diego Pub. Sch., 1941-49, Natural History Mus., San Diego, 1960; environ. coord. title 3 Mass. Audubon, Lincoln, 1967; sci. tchr. Concord (Mass.) Pub. Schs., 1969-82; tchr. adult edn. Concord and Bedford (Mass.) Pub. Schs., 1975-80. Played viola La Jolla Symphony, 1960-67; naturalist San Diego Mus. Natural History in orthitheology; played violin Sudbury Sayoyards Gilbert and Sullivan musicals, 1968; mem. Concord Music Club (pres., sec., treas., 1970; mem. Bedford Conservation Commn., Mass., 1998. Columnist Concord Pub. Schs. Bull., 1975-81; violist San Diego Symphony, 1956-68; prin. violist Concord (Mass.) Symphony, 1969-84; prin. 2nd violinist Waltham (Mass.) Philharmonic, 1984—. Co-dir. revolutionary music Concord (Mass.) Mus., 1981—; mem. Merrimack River Watershed Coun., Middlesex County, Mass., 1995—; camp dir. San Diego Girl Scouts USA, 1960-69. Recipient Arts Lottery award in music State of Mass., 1986, 87, 91. Mem. N.E. Antiquities Rsch. Assn., Bedford (Mass.) Garden Club (v.p. 1995-98, pres. 1998—), Sigma Alpha Iota. Avocations: music, gardening, organizing and leading nature walks, hiking. Home: Bedford, Mass. Died Oct. 4, 2001.

**SCHARFENBERG, JOACHIM,** theology and psychoanalysis educator; b. Erfurt, Germany, May 10, 1927; Grad. in theology, U. Jena, 1951; grad. in psychology, U. Kiel, 1953, ThD, 1953; grad., Psychoanalytical Inst., Berlin, 1961. Pastor, Berlin, 1954-58; counsellor, psychotherapist, 1958-68; lectr. U. Tübingen (Fed. Republic Germany), 1968-71; prof. practical theology and psychoanalysis U. Kiel (Fed. Republic Germany), from 1971. Author several books. Home: Bredenbek, Germany. Died 1996.

**SCHARFF, CONSTANCE KRAMER,** artist; b. Bklyn. d. Charles and Rebecca (Blankfort) Kramer; m. Harry Scharff (dec.); 1 child, Matthew. Studied painting and printmaking with Adja Younkers, Louis Shanker, Bklyn. Exhibited in group shows at Libr. of Congress, Bklyn. Mus., Silvermine Guild, Einstein Coll. Medicine, Greenville Mus., Lenox Libr., maj. N.Y. galleries; represented in permanent collections Bkln. Mus., Smithsonian Archives, Butler Inst., Phila. Mus. Art, Norfolk Mus., Ga. Mus. Art, Columbia U., N.Y. Pub. Libr., Inst. Jamaica. Mem. Soc. Am. Graphic Artists, Nat. Assn. Painters in Consein Acrylic (rec. sec. 1977-89, Elsie Ject Key award 1988), Artists Equity, Audubon Artists (Medal of Honor. Avocation: gardening. Died Nov. 9, 1998.

**SCHECHTMAN, SAUL,** conductor; b. Winchester, Conn., Sept. 4, 1924; s. Isidore Schechtman and Clara Goodman; m. Carolyn Raney, July 31, 1952; children: Carol, Julia. BA, Bklyn. Coll., 1947; post grad., Juilliard Sch. of Music, NYC, 1949. Music dir. Bronx Symphony Orch., NYC, 1953—56; conductor, music dir. Omnibus Program (CBS), NYC, 1954—57; music dir. Bergen Philharmonic, Teaneck, NJ, 1956—60, Carnival (Broadway show), NYC, 1961—63, Hello Dolly, NYC, 1966—70, Orch. Piccola, Balt., 1976—80; kapellmeister Theatre Oberhausen, Oberhausen, Germany, 1981—84. Composer: Auntie Mame, 1956, Diaspora variations, 1989, German Radio Orchs., 1990—94; dir.: (plays) Kiss Me Kate, 1958, How To Succeed in Business, 1963—64, My Fair Lady, 1960. Pvt. 1st class US Army, 1943—46, Europe. Fellowship in orch. conducting, Juilliard Sch. of Music, 1949—51. Mem.: Am. Soc. Composers, Authors and Publishers. Avocation: tennis. Home: Pownal, Maine. Died Feb. 6, 2013.

**SCHEELE, NICK (NICHOLAS V. SCHEELE),** retired automotive executive; b. Essex, England, Jan. 3, 1944; married; 3 children. With Ford British and European Ops., 1978; pres. Ford of Mex., 1988; chmn., CEO Jaguar Cars Ltd., 1992—99; chmn. Ford of Europe, 2000—01; group v.p. Ford North America, 2001—02; pres., COO Ford Motor Co., 2001—04; chmn. Key Safety Systems Inc., 2007—14, Stackpole Internat. Inc., 2013—14. Bd. dirs. Fod Motor Co., 2001—04; non-exec. dir. British-American Tobacco plc, 2005—13; chancellor U. Warwick, 2002—08. Active Save the Children, St. Basil's Appeal for Homeless Children; mem. advisory. bd. British American Chamber of Commerce; chmn. Foresight 2020. Decorated knight British Queen, Order of St. Michael and St. George. Master: Nat. Soc. for the Prevention Cruelty to Children (life); mem.: Soc. Motor Manufacturers & Traders (exec. com.). Avocations: reading, music. Died July 18, 2014.

**SCHEIMER, LOUIS,** film and television producer; b. Pitts., Oct. 19, 1928; s. Sam and Lena (Kessler) S.; m. Jay Wucher, Dec. 29, 1953 (dec. 2009); children: Lane, Erika; m. Maryanne Wucher BFA, Carnegie Inst. Tech., 1952. With various animation studios, 1955-62; founder, pres. Filmation Studios, Woodland Hills, Calif., 1962-89; pres. Lou Scheimer Productions, Woodland Hills, Calif., 1989—2013. Producer: (animated TV programs) Archie, 1968, Fat Albert, 1972 (Wilbur award, Scott Newman Drug Abuse Prevention award 1985), Star Trek, 1973 (Emmy award 1974), Isis, 1975, Tarzan, 1976, Space Academy, 1977, He-Man and Masters of the Universe, 1983, She-Ra Princess of Power, 1985, Ghostbusters, 1986, BraveStarr, 1987, Arch Angels, 1995 (feature film) Pinocchio and the Emperor of the Night, 1987, Happily Ever After, 1989. Recipient Christopher award, 1972, Emmy award, 1979. Mem. Nat. Acad. TV Art & Sciences, Motion Picture Acad. Jewish. Died Oct. 17, 2013.

**SCHELL, JONATHAN EDWARD,** writer; b. NYC, Aug. 21, 1943; s. Orville H. and Marjorie Bertha S.; m. Elspeth Fraser; children: Matthew, Thomas, Phoebe Staff writer New Yorker Mag., NYC, from 1967. Author: The Village of Ben Suc, 1967, The Military Half: An Account of Destruction in Quang Ngai and Quang Tin, 1968, The Time of Illusion, 1975, The Fate of the Earth, 1982, The Abolition, 1984, The Gift of Time: The Case for Abolishing Nuclear Weapons Now, 1998, The Unfinished Twentieth Century, 2001, The Unconquerable World, 2003, The Seventh Decade: The New Shape of Nuclear Danger, 2007 Died Mar. 25, 2014.

**SCHELL, MAXIMILIAN,** actor, director; b. Vienna, Dec. 8, 1930; s. Hermann Ferdinand and Margarethe (Noé von Nordberg) Schell; m. Natalya Andreychenko, 1985 (div. 2005); 1 child, Nastassja; m. Iva Mihanovic, 2013. Student, Humanistisches Gymnasium, Basel, Switzerland, Freies Gymnasium, Zürich, Switzerland, also univs., Zürich, Basel and Munich. Various appearances on stage in Switzerland and Germany, 1952-55; other stage appearances include Resurection Blues, 2006; German film debut in Children, Mothers and a General, 1955; Am. film debut in Young Lions, 1958; on Broadway stage in Interlock, 1958; (films) Judgment at Nuremberg, 1961 (Acad. award for Best Actor, 1961), Five Finger Exercise, 1961, Reluctant Saint, 1962, Condemned of Altona, 1962, Topkapi, 1963, Return from the Ashes, 1965, The Deadly Affair, 1966, Counterpoint, 1967, The Castle, 1968, Simon Bolivar, 1969, First Love, 1970, Pope Joan, 1971, Paulina 1880, 1972, The Man in the Glass Booth, 1974, The Odessa File, 1974, Assassination in Sarajewo, 1975, Cross of Iron, 1976, A Bridge Too Far, 1977, Julia, 1976, The Black Hole, 1979, Players, 1978, Avalanche Express, 1978, The Chosen, 1980, Les Iles, 1981, Man Under Suspicion, 1983, The Assisi Underground, 1984, The Rosegarden, 1989, The Freshman, 1989, Labyrinth, 1990, A Far Off Place, 1993, Little Odessa, 1995, Left Luggage, 1997, The Eighteenth Angel, 1997, Telling Lies in America, 1997, Deep Impact, 1998, Vampires, 1998, Wer Liebt, dem Wachsen Flügel, 1999, I Love You, Baby, 2000, Just Messing About, 2000, Festival in Cannes, 2001, The Brothers Bloom, 2008, Flores negras, 2009, Darkness, 2009; (various stage appearances) Hamlet, Prince of Homburg, Mannerhouse, Don Carlos, Durell's Sappho, A Patriot for Me, London, 1965, Broadway, 1969, Old Times Vienna, 1972, Everyman, Salzburg Festival, 1978-82, Poor Murderer, Berlin, 1982, Der Seidene Schuh, Salzburg Festival, 1985; prodr., dir.: (films) The Pedestrian, 1973, End of the Game, 1975, Tales from the Vienna Woods, 1978; prodr.: (films) Ansichten eines Clowns, 1975; dir., writer: (documentaries) Marlene, 1984, My Sister Maria, 2002; dir., co-author screenplay, actor in film First Love, 1969, Marlene, 1983; stage dir. plays include All For the Best, Vienna, 1966, Hamlet, Munich, 1968, Pygmalion, Dusseldorf, 1970; (opera) La Traviata, 1975, Tales from the Vienna Woods, London, 1977, The Undiscovered Country, Salzburg Festival, 1979, 80, Opera Cornet, Deutsche Opera, Berlin, 1985, Glaube Liebe Hoffnung, Moscow, 1989, Der Rosenkavalier, 2005; (TV films) Heidi, 1968, The Diary of Anne Frank, 1980, Phantom of the Opera, 1983, miniseries Peter the Great, 1984-85, Young Catherine, 1990, Wiseguy, 1990, Miss Rose White, 1991, Stalin, 1992 (Cable Ace award, Best Supporting actor), Abraham, 1994, The Thorn Birds: The Missing Years, 1996, Joan of Arc (miniseries), 1999, The Song of the Lark, 2001, Coast to Coast, 2003, The Return of the Dancing Master, 2004, Die Liebe eines Priesters, 2005, Die Alpenklinik, 2006, The Shell Seekers, 2006, House of the Sleeping Beauties, 2006, Die Rosenkönigin Die, 2007. Cpl. Swiss Army, 1948—49. Recipient NY Critics Circle award, 1961, 78, 86, Acad. award, 1961, Golden Globe award, 1962, 74, Silver Shell award, 1970, 75, German Fed. award, 1971, 79, 80, 84, Chgo. Film Critics award, 1973, Golden Cup award, Germany, 1974, Gold Hugo award, 1979, Nat. Soc. Film Critics award, 1986. Home: Zurich, Switzerland. Died Feb. 1, 2014.

**SCHELL, PAUL E.S.,** former mayor; b. Fort Dodge, Iowa, Oct. 8, 1937; m. Pam Schell. BA, U. Iowa, 1960; JD, Columbia U., 1963. Pvt. practice, 1963-74; dir. dept. cmty. devel. City of Seattle, 1974-77, mayor, 1998—2001; pres., founder Cornerstone Columbia Devel. Co., 1979-87; commr. Port of Seattle, 1989-99, pres. commn., 1995-99; dean U. Wash. Sch. Architecture & Urban Planning, 1992-95; strategic adv. & bus. developer NBBJ Architectural Firm, Seattle, 2001—14. Past bd. dirs. Intiman Theatre, A Contemporary Theater; past pres. Allied Arts; founder, active Cascadia Project; bd. dirs. Trade Devel. Alliance; mem. Friends of the Pike Place Market; sr. adv. & bd. mem. Columbia Hospitality, Seattle. Democrat. Died July 27, 2014.

**SCHERER, OLGA,** narratology scholar; b. Cracow, Poland, Jan. 6, 1927; arrived in France, 1957; d. Wiktor and Eleonora Scherer; m. Alfred Virski Scherer, Nov. 19, 1947 (div. 1955). BA, Hunter Coll., NYC, 1945; MA, Columbia U., 1945, PhD, 1952. Instr. lit. Bard Coll., Annandale-on-Hudson, NY, 1946—48; rsch. assoc. lit. Yale U., New Haven, 1953—57; vis. asst. prof. Ind. U., Bloomington, 1959—60; rsch. assoc. Ctr. Nat. de la Recherche Scientifique, Paris, 1961—65; lectr. lit. Am. Coll., Paris, 1968—70; prof. narratology U. Paris, from 1969. Author: (book) The Modern Polish Short Story, 1955, novels,; contbr. articles to profl. jours. Exec. bd. mem. Fund. Continuity Polish Ind. Lit., Paris, from 1982. Fellow, ACLS, 1948—52, Guggenheim Found., 1957—58. Mem.: Internat. Assn. Comparative Lit., French Assn. Slavonic Lit., French Assn. Profs. US Lit., French Assn. Profs. English. Home: Paris, France. Deceased.

**SCHERER, VICTOR RICHARD,** physicist, computer scientist, musician, consultant; b. Poland, Feb. 7, 1940; came to U.S., 1941; s. Emanuel and Florence B. Scherer; m. Gail R. Dobrofsky, Aug. 11, 1963; children: Helena Cecile, Markus David. BS magna cum laude, CCNY, 1960; MA, Columbia U., 1962; PhD, U. Wis., 1974. Health physics asst. Columbia U., NYC, 1961-63; rsch asst. physics. dep. U. Wis., Madison, 1967-74; project assoc., project mgr. Inst. for Environ. Studies, World Climate-Food Rsch. Group, 1974-78; specialist computer sys. U. Wis. Acad. Computing Ctr., 1978—2008; coord., sr. cons. Divsn. Info. Tech. U. Wis., Madison; concert pianist; tchr.; promoter contemporary composers. Researcher in particle physics, agroclimatology, soil-yield relationships and computer graphics; cons. on computer sys., electronic mail, geographic analysis, help desk and supercomputing applications. Fellow AEC, 1960-61. Mem. AAAS, Am. Phys. Soc., Am. Meteorol. Soc., Am. Soc. Agronomy, Assn. Computing Machinery, Nat. Computer Graphics Assn., Phi Beta Kappa, Sigma Xi. Home: Madison, Wis. Died Aug. 2012.

**SCHEUERMAN, ELEANOR JOYCE MILLER,** medical association administrator; b. Jersey City, July 7, 1937; d. Lawrence Houseman and Bridie E.J. (Moran) M.; m. William Henry Scheuerman, Jr., Sept. 5, 1969; 1 child, Sheila Brigid. BS in Nursing, Seton Hall, 1959; MA in Pub. Health, N.Y.U., 1964. RN, N.J., Mass. Pvt. duty nurse Jersey City Med. Ctr., 1959-60; pub. health nurse Pub. Health Nursing Svc. of Jersey City, 1959-63, 66; health educator Acad. St. Aloysius, Jersey City, 1962-64; instr. sch. nursing Seton Hall Univ., South Orange, N.J., 1964-67; dir. Pub. Health Nursing Agy., Washington, N.J., 1967-93; head nurse Soldiers Home, Holyoke, Mass., 1994-95; charge nurse Anchorage Nursing Home, Shelburne, Mass., from 1996. Head nurse Hunterdon Devel. Ctr., Clinton, N.J., 1989-93; bd. dirs. Warren County Office on Aging, 1974-93, Legal Svc. of Warren County, 1976-77; med. and health staff chief Warren County Civil Def. and Disaster Control, 1979; info. and referral svc. area com. Warren County Human Svcs., 1985-91, adv. coun., 1983-91, chair protective svcs. com., 1984-91. Chair suprs.' workshop com. Home Health Assembly of N.J., 1974-75; adv. coun. for practical nursing Warren County Vocat. Tech. Sch., 1986-93; vol. Right to Read Program, Franklin Med. Ctr., Cmty. Meals Blessed Sacrament Parish. Mem. Nat. League for Nursing (bd. dirs. 1977-78), APHA, Am. Sch. Health Assn. (fellow 1965), Am. Nursing Assn. (pub. health sect., membership chair 1960, v.p. dist. 2 1962), N.J. State Nurses Assn. (membership chair 1965), Sigma Theta Tau. Home: Townshend, Vt. Died Aug. 11, 2001.

**SCHEUNEMANN, DIETRICH F.G.,** language educator; b. Schlawe, Germany, Sept. 16, 1939; s. Franz and Edith Scheunemann; m. Sieglinde Kunisch, Apr. 13, 1995. MA, U. Heidelberg, 1973; Dr. phil., U. Heidelberg, Germany, 1977. Mem. faculty U. Heidelberg, 1973—77, Free U., Berlin, 1977—85; reader U. Sussex, 1985—90; prof. German U. Edinburgh, 1990—2004. Dir. Grad. Sch. Asian and Modern European Languages, U. Edinburgh, 1995—2004. Author: (book) Romankrise, 1978; editor: Regelkram und Grenzgange, 1988, Orality, Literacy, and Modern Media, 1996, (with P. Goetsch) Text und Ton im Film, 1997, European Avant-Garde: New Perspectives, 2000, Expressionist Film-New Perspectives, 2003; contbr. articles to profl. jours. Fellow: Inst. Contemporary Scotland. Died June 9, 2005.

**SCHEY, JOHN ANTHONY,** metallurgical engineering educator; b. Sopron, Hungary, Dec. 19, 1922; came to U.S., 1962; s. Mihaly and Hedvig Terez (Topfl) S.; m. Margit Maria Sule, Sept. 13, 1926; 1 child, John Francis. Diplome metall. engring., Tech. U., Sopron, 1946; PhD in Tech. Scis., Acad. Scis., Budapest, Hungary, 1953; D of Engring. (hon.), U. Stuttgart, 1987, U. Heavy Industry, Miskolc, Hungary, 1989. Cert. mfg. engr. Chief technologist Iron and Metal Works, Csepel, Hungary, 1947-51; reader Tech. U., Miskolc, Hungary, 1951-56; dept. head Brit. Aluminium Co. Research Labs., 1957-62; metall. advisor Ill. Inst. Tech. Research Inst., Chgo., 1962-68; prof. U. Ill., Chgo., 1968-74, U. Waterloo, Ont., Can., 1974-88, disting. prof. emeritus, 1988. Resource person Niagara Inst., Ontario, 1980; course dir. Forging Industry Assn., Cleve., 1978; cons. to various corps. in U.S. and Can. Author: Tribology in Metalworking, 1983, Introduction to Manufacturing Processes, 3d edit., 2000; patentee in field. Recipient W.H.A. Robertson award Inst. Metals, 1966. Fellow Am. Soc.

Metals, Soc. Mfg. Engrs. (Gold Medal award 1974); mem. Nat. Acad. Engring., fgn. mem. Hungarian Acad. Scis. Avocations: music, history, impact of technology on soc. Home: Waterloo, Canada. Died Apr. 23, 2010.

**SCHIELE, PAUL ELLSWORTH, JR.,** retired academic administrator, writer; b. Phila., Nov. 20, 1924; s. Paul Ellsworth Sr. and Maud (Barclay) S.; m. Sarah Irene Knauss, Aug. 20, 1946; children: Patricia Schiele Sommers, Sandra Schiele Kicklighter, Deborah Schiele Hartigan. AT, Temple U., Phila., 1949; BA, LaVerne U., 1955; MA, Claremont Grad. U., Calif., 1961; PhD, U.S. Internat. U., San Diego, 1970. Cert. sec. tchr., Calif. 1961. Tchr. sci. and math. Lincoln High Sch., Phila., 1956-57, Ontario (Calif.) Sch. Dist., 1957-65; math. and sci. cons. Hacienda La Puente U. Sch. Dist., Calif., 1965-75; asst. prof. Calif. State U., Fullerton, 1975-83; pres., owner Creative Learning Environments and Resources, Glendora, Calif., from 1983, cons. sci. curriculum, from 1985. Dir. title III project ESEA, 1974-75, cons. for project, 1975-77; cons. in field. Author: (student workbook) Beyond the Earth, 1969, Primary Science, 1972, 2d edit., 1976, (novel) Under Cover of Night, 1995, Chasing the Wild Geese, 1996, Deceptive Appearances, 1997; editor: A Living World, 1974, 2d edit., 1986; writer 9 sound filmstrips, model units for sci. and math. activity books, 10 sci. activities for L.A. Outdoor Edn. Program, 1980; editor 21 sci. and math. activity books, 1975-76; writer, co-dir. (TV) Marine Biology Series, 1970-71; contbr. munerous articles to profl. mags., 1960-85; writer and designer of 2 sci. ednl. games; designer in field. Apptd. adv. com. Sci. and Humanities Symposium Calif. Mus. Sci. and Industry, 1974; mem. State Sci. Permit Com., Tide Pools of Calif. Coast, 1974-75; mem. Friends of Libr., Friends Libr. Found. Mem. Internat. Platform Assn., Internat. Soc. Photographers, Glendora Hist. Soc., ABI Rsch. Assn. (bd. govs.), Calif. Elem. Edn. Assn. (hon.), Nat. PTA (hon.), Calif. Inter-Sci. Coun. (pres., chmn. 1971, 72), Elem Sch. Scis. Assn. (past pres., bd. dirs.), Paddlewheel Steamboating Soc. of Am., Phi Delta Kappa (chartered). Republican. Lutheran. Avocations: travel, etchings, art collecting, fencing. Deceased.

**SCHIFFER, JOHN C.,** state legislator; b. Chadron, Nebr., Aug. 17, 1945; m. Nancy Schiffer; children: Ben, Wynne. BA, Colo. Coll., 1967. Rancher The Hat Ranch, 1971—87, 48 Ranch, 1987—2014; mem. Johnson Co. Sch. Bd., 1978—87, Johnson Co. Agricultural Stabilization and Conservatio Svc. Bd., Wyoming Environ. Quality Coun.; dir. Inst. Environ. & Natural Resources, 1997—2014; mem. Dist. 22 Wyo. State Senate, 1993—2014, v.p., 2003—04, majority floor leader, 2005—06, pres., 2007—08. Mem. North Fork Water Users, Wyo. Environmental Quality Control, Ruckleshous Inst. for Environment, 1996—2004; mem., dir. Wyo. Chpt. of the Nature Conservancy, 1998—2004. Served USN, 1967—70. Wyoming & Nat Stockgrowers; North Fork Water Users. Republican. Episcopal. Died June 19, 2014.

**SCHIFFRIN, ANDRE,** publisher; b. Paris, June 12, 1935; came to U.S., 1941; s. Jacques and Simone (Heymann) S.; m. Maria Elena de la Iglesia, June 14, 1961; children: Anya, Natalia BA summa cum laude, Yale U., 1957; MA with 1st class honors, Cambridge U., Eng., 1959. With New Am. Library, 1959-63; with Pantheon Books, Inc., NYC, 1962-90, editor, then editor in chief, mng. dir., 1969-90; pub. Schocken Books subs. Pantheon Books Inc., 1987-90; pres. Fund for Ind. Pub., NYC, 1990—2013; dir., editor in chief The New Press, NYC, 1992—2013. Vis. fellow Davenport Coll., 1977-79; vis. lectr. Yale U., 1977, 79; bd. dirs. The New Press, N.Y.C. Author: Edition sans Editeurs, 1999, The Business of Books: How International Conglomerates Took Over Publishing and Changed the Way We Read, 2000, A Political Education: Growing Up in Paris and New York, 2007, Words and Money, 2010; columnist Chronicle Higher Edn.; contbr. articles to profl. jours., including N.Y. Times Book Rev., Nation, New Republic. Bd. dirs. N.Y. Coun. for Humanities, mem. exec. com., 1979-80; bd. dirs. N.Y. Civil Liberties Union; mem. Freedom to Publish Com. Assn. American Publications, 1976-78; mem. U.S. cultural del. to Peoples Republic China, 1983, 87 Mellon fellow Clare Coll., 1957, hon. scholar, 1959; hon. fellow Trumbull Coll.; Fulbright travel grantee, 1958-59. Fellow N.Y. Inst. for the Humanities. Died Dec. 1, 2013.

**SCHIMEL, JOHN L.,** psychiatrist; b. East Orange, NJ, Oct. 24, 1916; s. David and Sadie (Freedman) S.; m. Phyllis Lessler; children: David, Joshua, Elizabeth. BS, St. Peter's Coll., Jersey City, 1938; MD, Georgetown U., 1943. Cert. Am. Bd. Psychiatry and Neurology. Rotating intern Flower-Fifth Ave Hosp, 1946; resident Bellevue Psychiatric Hosp., NYC, 1947-49; assoc. dir. William Alanson White Psychoanalytic Ctr., NYC, from 1949; clin. prof. psychiatry N.Y.U., from 1979. Author books. Mem. Am. Acad. Psychoanalysis, N.Y. Soc. Adolescent Psychiatry, Am. Soc. for Adolescent Psychiatry. Home: New York, NY. Died Dec. 15, 1991.

**SCHIMKE, ROBERT TOD,** retired biochemist; b. Spokane, Wash., Oct. 25, 1932; s. Tolbert Daniel and Marion (Evans) S.; m. Faith Fagan, July 5, 1952 (dec. 1958); children: Steven R., Caroline E.; m. Ruth Buddington, Feb. 6, 1959; children: Cynthia E., Allison R.; m. Mary Content, June 16, 1973 (dec. 1975); m. Hope Raymond, June 25, 1977 (div. Apr. 1992); m. Pat Jones, Apr. 11, 1992. AB, Stanford U., 1954, MD, 1958. Intern, asst. resident medicine Mass. Gen. Hosp., Boston, 1958-60; commd. officer Lab. Biochemical Pharmacology sect. on pharmacology Nat. Insts. Arthritis and Metabolic Diseases, 1960-63, med. officer internal medicine research, 1963-65, chief sect. biochem. regulation, 1965-66; assoc. prof. pharmacology and biology dept. pharmacology Stanford U., 1966-69, prof., 1969-73, chmn. dept., 1970-73, prof. biology, 1973—95, chmn. dept. biol. sci., 1978-82, American Cancer Soc. research prof. biology, 1983—95, dir. med. scientist tng. program, 1969-75. Mem. molecular biol. study sect. NIH, 1970-74, nat. adv. council on aging, 1978-81; mem. adv. panel on nucleic acid and protein synthesis American Cancer Soc., 1971-75, Nat. Acad. Scis., 1976, American Acad. Arts & Sciences, 1977, Inst. Medicine, Nat. Acad. Sciences, 1983. Mem. editorial bd.: Jour. Biol. Chemistry, 1968-72; asso. editor, 1975-81; editorial bd.: Molecular Pharmacology, 1969-72; exec. editor: Archives Biochem. Biophysics, 1973-75. Named Outstanding Young Scientist of Yr., Md. Acad. Sci., 1964; recipient Chas. Pfizer award American Chem. Soc., 1969, Boris Pregal award N.Y. Acad. Sciences, 1974, W.C. Rose award in Biochemistry American Nutrition Found., 1983, Sloan prize Gen. Motors Cancer Rsch. Found., 1985, Lila Gruber Meml. Cancer Rsch. award American Acad. Dermatology, 1988, Wallace E. Sterling prize Stanford. U. Sch. Medicine, 2009 Mem. American Soc. Biochemistry Molecular Biology (pres. 1988-89), Phi Beta Kappa, Alpha Omega Alpha. Home: Palo Alto, Calif. Died Sept. 6, 2014.

**SCHINDLER, SEPP ROLF,** psychologist; b. Vienna, Dec. 14, 1922; s. Josef Schindler and Josefine Augesky; m. Elfriede Onder, Aug. 28, 1964; 3 children. PhD, U. Vienna, 1949; Univ. Doz., U. Salzburg, Austria, 1969. Cert. clin. psychologist, public officer. Tchr. prison adminstr., Vienna, 1949—56; psychologist Vienna, 1957—60; dir. probation svc., 1960—73; prof. U. Salzburg, 1973—87, head of psychology dept., 1985—87. Recipient Gold medal, Fed. Republic of Austria, 1983. Died 2012.

**SCHINDLMAYR, THOMAS,** advocate; b. Munich, July 10, 1969; s. Wulf-Eike and Edith Schindlmayr; m. Julia Baldock. BA, Sch. Oriental and African Studies, London, 1992; MSc, London Sch. Econs., 1993; ASB, Internat. Corr. Sch., Scranton, Pa., 1996; PhD, Australian Nat. U., Canberra, 1999, M in Internat. Law, 2001. Rschr. Australian Nat. U., 2001—03; assoc. population affairs officer UN, NYC, 2003—04, social affairs officer, 2004—07. Cons., Canberra, 2000—03. Contbr. articles to profl. jours., columns in newspapers. Achievements include raising awareness of the new Convention on the Rights of Persons with Disabilities. Home: New York, NY. Died Apr. 26, 2008.

**SCHIRO, JAMES JOSEPH,** retired insurance company executive; b. Bklyn., Jan. 2, 1946; m. Tomasina Schiro; children: Justine, James Jr. BS, St. John's U., 1967, D (hon.) of Comml. Sciences, 1995; MBA, Dartmouth Coll. Tuck Sch. Exec. Program. CPA. Joined Price Waterhouse, 1967, chmn., CEO, 1995—98; CEO PricewaterhouseCoopers, NYC, 1998—2001; COO Zurich Financial Services Group, 2002, CEO, 2002—09; sr. adv. CVC Capital Partners Ltd., 2012—14. Bd. govs. World Econ. Forum; bd. dirs. PepsiCo, Inc., 2003-14, Goldman Sachs Group Inc., 2009-14, REVA Medical Inc., 2010-14; mem. supervisory bd. Royal Philips Electronics, 2005-14 Trustee American Friends Lucerne Festival, Inst. Advanced Study, Princeton, St. John's U; mem. bd. advisors Tsinghua Sch. Economics, Beijing. Recipient Ellis Island Medal of Honor, 1994, St. John's U. Alumni Pietas medal, 1992, Avenue of the Americas Assn.'s Gold Key award, 1992, Nat. Human Relations award American Jewish Com., 1997 Republican. Died Aug. 13, 2014.

**SCHLESINGER, JAMES RODNEY,** economist, former United States Secretary of Defense; b. NYC, Feb. 15, 1929; s. Julius and Rhea (Rogen) S.; m. Rachel Line Mellinger, June 19, 1954 (dec. Oct. 10, 1995); children: Cora K., Charles L., Ann R., William F., Emily, Thomas S., Clara, James Rodney. AB summa cum laude, Harvard U., 1950, AM, 1952, PhD, 1956; LLD (hon.), The Citadel, 1975, U. SC, 1976, Ind. U. Pa., 1976, NYU, 1976, Ohio State U., 1977; DHL (hon.), Wittenburg U., 1977, Occidental Coll., U. Toledo, U. NC, Asheville, Hampden-Sydney Coll., Northern Va. Cmty. Coll. Asst. prof. economics U. Va., 1955—58, assoc. prof., 1958—63; sr. staff mem. RAND Corp., Santa Monica, Calif., 1963-67, dir. strategic studies, 1967-69; cons. Bur. of Budget, 1965—69, asst. dir., 1969—70, acting dep. dir., 1969-70; asst. dir. Office Mgmt. & Budget, Exec. Office of the Pres., 1970-71; chmn. Atomic Energy Commn., 1971-73; dir. CIA, 1973; sec. US Dept. Def., 1973-75; vis. scholar Johns Hopkins Sch. Advanced Internat. Studies, 1976-77; spl. adv. to Pres. on energy The White House, 1977; sec. US Dept. Energy, 1977-79; counselor Georgetown U. Ctr. for Strategic & Internat. Studies, 1979—2014; sr. adv. Lehman Brothers Holdings, Inc. Acad. cons. Navel War Coll., 1957; cons. bd. govs. Fed. Reserve Bd., 1962—63; bd. trustees MITRE Corp., 1985; mem. US Commn. on Nat. Security/21st Century (Hart/Rudman Commn.), 1998—2001, Panel to Assess the Reliability, Safety, & Security of the U.S. Nuclear Stockpile, 1999—2003, Homeland Security Adv. Coun., 2002, Arms Control & Nonproliferation Advisory Bd., 2006; chmn. Ind. Panel Investigation of Abuses at Abu Ghraib Prison, 2004; co-chmn. Def. Sci. Bd., 2006; chmn. Task Force on Nuclear Weapons Mgmt., US Dept. Def., 2008—09. Author: The Political Economy of National Security, 1960, America at Century's End, 1989; co-author: Issues in Defense Economics, 1967. Recipient Disting. Intelligence Svc. Medal, 1975, Disting. Svc. Medal, Dept. Army, 1976, Disting. Pub. Svc. Medal, Dept. Navy, 1976, Exceptional Civilian Svc. Medal, Dept. Air Force, 1976, Nat. Security Medal, 1979, Nat. Meritorious Citation, Navy League, Disting. Svc. Award, Mil. Order of World Wars, James Doolittle Award, William Oliver Baker Award; grantee Frederick Sheldon prize fellow, Harvard U., 1950—51. Fellow: Nat. Acad. Public Adminstrn.; mem.: American Acad. Diplomacy, Phi Beta Kappa. Republican. Presbyterian. Died Mar. 27, 2014.

**SCHMITZ, ROGER ANTHONY,** chemical engineer, educator, academic administrator; b. Carlyle, Ill., Oct. 22, 1934; m. Ruth Mary Kuhl, Aug. 31, 1957; children: Jan, Joy, Joni. BSChemE, U. Ill., 1959; PhD in Chem. Engring., U. Minn., 1962. Prof. chem. engring. U. Ill., Urbana, 1962-79; Keating-Crawford prof. chem. engring. U. Notre Dame, Ind., 1979—2005, prof. emeritus, 2005—13, chmn. dept. chem. engring. Ind., 1979-81, dean engring. Ind., 1981-87, v.p., assoc. provost Ind., 1987-95. Cons. Amoco Chemicals, Naperville, Ill., 1966—77; vis. prof. Calif. Inst. Tech., LA, 1968—69. Contbr. articles to profl. jours. With US Army, 1953—55. Fellow, Guggenheim Found., 1968. Mem.: AIChE (A.P. Colburn award 1970, R.H. Wilhelm award 1981), American Soc. Engring. Edn. (George Westinghouse award 1977), Nat. Acad. Engring. Roman Catholic. Home: South Bend, Ind. Died Oct. 11, 2013.

**SCHMITZ, WOLFGANG KLEMENS,** retired bank executive; b. Vienna, May 28, 1923; s. Hans and Maria (Habel) Schmitz; children: Johanna, Dorothea Pfersmann, Theres Holzinger, Veronika, Stefan. Dr.jur., U. Vienna, 1949. Pvt. practice, 1949—50; with Austrian Fed. Econ. Chamber, 1950—64; sec. econ. policy dept. Austrian nat. com. Internat. C. of C., 1950—64; chmn. Beirat fur Wirtschafts-und Sozialfragen, 1963—64, head econ. policy dept., 1964; min. fin. Govt. of Austria, 1964—68; pres. Austrian Nat. Bank, Vienna, 1968—73; gov. World Bank, Austria, 1964—68, IMF, 1968—73; cons., lectr. in field. Author: International Investment, Growth and Crisis-A Plea for Freedom of Movement for International Private Investment Capital, 1975, Die antizyklische Konjunkturpolitik-eine Illusion, Grenzen der Machtbarkeit durch Globalsteuerung, 1976, Die Gesetzesflut-Folge und Ausdruck der Uberforderung des Staates, Gutachten fu r den Siebenten Osterreichischen Juristentag, 1979, Die Wahrung-eine offene Flanke staatlicher Verfassungsordnung, ihre Schliessung-ein Beitrag zur Festigung der freiheitlichen Demokratie, 1983; contbr. articles to profl. jours. Mem.: Johannes Messner-Gesellschaft, List Gorres Gesellschaft, Ludwig Erhard-Stiftung, Verein fur Socialpolitik. Roman Catholic. Home: Vienna, Austria. Died Nov. 16, 2008.

**SCHNARE, PAUL STEWART,** computer scientist, mathematician; b. Berlin, NH, Oct. 16, 1936; s. Herbert Stewart and Roma (Dahl) S.; m. Dorothy Hopkins, Jan. 11, 1960; children: Sigmund, Col, Kurt (dec.). BA, U. N.H., 1960, MS, 1961; PhD, Tulane U., 1967. Instr. U. New Orleans, 1961-66; asst. prof. U. Fla., Gainesville, 1967-74, Colby Coll., Waterville, Maine, 1974-75, Fordham U., Bronx, N.Y., 1975-76, Univ. Petroleum and Minerals, Dhahran, Saudi Arabia, 1976-80; assoc. prof. computer sci. Ea. Ky. U., Richmond, 1980—99. Cons. Ea. Cons. Assocs., Durham, N.H., 1961; NSF sci. faculty fellow Tulane U., New Orleans, 1966-67. Contbr. articles to Am. Math. Monthly, Fundamenta Mathematicae, Gen. Topology, other publs. Mem. Am. Assn Adv. Sci., London Math Soc., Math Assn. Am. (life mem.). Home: Berea, Ky. Died Feb. 1999.

**SCHNEIDER, GÜNTER,** zoologist, educator, retired; b. Berlin, May 13, 1918; s. Berthold and Frieda S.; m. Renate Löhr, Mar. 28, 1953; children: Marianne, Andrea, Iris. D in Natural Scis., Göttingen, Würzburg, Fed. Republic Germany, 1953; habil., U. Würzburg, 1961. Sci. asst. Zoolog. Inst. U. Wüzburg, Fed. Republic Germany, 1953-61, asst. prof., 1961-66; prof. Zoolog. Inst. U. Düsseldorf, Fed. Republic Germany, 1966-83, prof. emeritus, from 1983. Dean Faculty of Scis., U. Düsseldorf, 1968-69. Mem. Deutsche Zoologische Gesellschaft, Verband Deutscher Biologen. Home: Düsseldorf, Germany. Died Apr. 2, 2000.

**SCHNEIDER, MARIE LUISE,** gynecologist; b. St. Wendel, Saarland, Germany, Dec. 6, 1940; d. Andreas and Hilde Schneider. MD, U. Saarland, Homburg, 1964. Intern St. Michael's Hosp., Völklingen Saar, 1965-67, resident in gynaecology Völklingen, 1967-69; resident in gynecology St. Johannes Hosp., Duisburg, 1969-71, sr. physician dept. gynecology, 1969-71; physician Inst. for Clin. Cytology, Tech. U. Munich, 1971-73; vice chmn. gynecologic dept. Ludwigshafen/Rh Cmty. Hosp., 1974-80; sr. physician U. Erlangen, 1980-86, Free U., Berlin, 1986-89; head dept. gynecology Cmty. Hosp., Aurich, 1989-93; pvt. practice ob-gyn. Trier, 1993—2002; ret., 2003. Dir. gynecologic cytologic lab. Cmty. Hosp., Ludwigshafen, 1974-80, U. Erlangen, 1980-86, Free U. Berlin, 1986-89. Author: Atlas der gynäkologischen Differentialzytologie, 1976, 2d edit., 1981, Different Diagnostic Atlas Gynecologic Cytology, 1995, Untersuchung zur Effektivität eines gezielten zytologischen Fruherkennungsprogrammes beim Endometriumkarzinom, 1985. Fellow Internat. Acad. Cytology. Avocations: literature, classical music, arts, travel. Died Mar. 30, 2009.

**SCHNEIDER, MARY LOUISE,** retired elementary school educator; b. Waterville, Wash., Oct. 17, 1918; d. John Steve and Alice Ray (Jones) S. BA in Edn., Holy Names Coll., 1940. Cert. elem. tchr. Wash., 1940. Tchr. Mud Springs/Douglas County, Mansfield, Wash., 1941-42; elem. tchr. Mansfield Sch. dist., Douglas County, Wash., 1942-43, Waterville (Wash.) Sch. Dist., Douglas County, Wash., 1943-49, Lewis and Clark Elem. Sch., Wenatchee, Wash., 1949-60; spl. reading tchr. H.B. Ellison Jr. High, Wenatchee, 1960-62, Orchard Jr. High, Wenatchee, 1962-67; lang. arts tchr. Pioneer Jr. High, Wenatchee, 1967-77; retired, 1977. Author lang. arts learning packages for students, 1967; co-author: Name on the Schoolhouse, 1989. Vol. Am. Heart Assn., Wenatchee, 1975-90, Am. Cancer Soc., Wenatchee, 1975-88. Recipient Cert. of Recognition, Wash. State Ct. Cath. Daus. of the Ams., 1970, 72, 74. Mem.: AAUW (treas. 1973—75), PEO (pres. CP chpt. 1980—82, pres. 1988—90), Chelan-Douglas County Sch. Retirees Assn. (com. chmn. 1989—90), Cath. Daus. of the Ams. (local ct. pres. 1958—60, state pres. 1984—86, nat. evangelization chmn. 1986—88, author Wash. State Ct. of Cath. Daus. 1988, local ct. pres. 1999—2001), Delta Kappa Gamma (pres. Zeta chpt. 1966—68). Avocation: sewing. Home: Spokane Valley, Wash. Died Jan. 18, 2013.

**SCHNETZLER, MATTHIAS JOHANNES,** research scientist; b. Basel, Switzerland, Feb. 19, 1973; s. Bruno Johannes Schnetzler and Maya Schnetzler-Schaub. DSc, Swiss Fed. Inst. Tech., Zurich, 2005. Rsch. asst. Swiss Fed. Inst. Tech., Zurich, 2000—05, sr. rsch. assoc., from 2005. Pres. Assn. of Sci. Staff at the Swiss Fed. Inst. Tech. Dept. of Indsl. Mgmt., Zurich, Switzerland, 2002—05. Contbr. articles to profl. jours. Recipient Matura award, Sandoz (now Novartis), 1995. Mem.: ETH Zurich Alumni. Died 2007.

**SCHOLZ, UWE,** ballet director, choreographer, stage director; b. Jugenheim, Germany, Dec. 31, 1958; s. Erwin and Elsbeth (Buchler) S. Student, Wurttembergischen Staatstheatr, 1973-76, Sch. Am. Ballet, 1976, John-Cranko Ballet Acad., 1976-79. Dancer Stuttgart Ballet, 1979-80, choreographer, 1976-82, resident choreographer, 1982-85; ballet dir., chief choreographer Operahouse Zurich, 1985-91, Leipzig (Germany) Opera, from 1991; choreographer Frankfurt Opera, 1980-84, Teatro Comunale, Florence, 1984, Royal Ballet, Stockholm, 1984. Hon. prof. choreography Felix Mendelssohn Coll., Leipzig. Stage dir. Testimonium Festival, Jerusalem and Tel Aviv, Israel, 1983, La Scala, Milan, 1986, Vienna Stateopera, Monte Carlo, 1984, Ballet de Zaragoza, 1990, 93, Vienna State Opera, 1994, Ballet B.C. (Can.), 1993, Nederlands Dance Theatre, 1986, Teatro Mcpl. Santiago de Chile, 1988, German Opera, Linden Opera, Berlin, 1990, Bavarian State Ballet, Munich, 1991, Aterballetto, Reggio Emilia, Italy, 1993, Les Ballets de Monte-Carlo, 1993, Teatro Alla Scala, Milan, 1995, Semper Opera, Dresden, 1995, Stuttgart Ballet, 1990, 91, 96, Ankara State Ballet, 1997. Decorated cross Order of Merit (Germany); recipient Omaggio Alla Danza Dance award, Bavarian Theater awrd, 1998, German Dance award, 1999. Avocations: music, literature. Died Nov. 21, 2004.

**SCHOOLEY, DOLORES HARTER,** entertainment administrator; b. Nora Springs, Iowa, May 2, 1905; d. Amil A. and Elizabeth (Sefert) Zemke; m. Leslie J. Harter, June 5, 1934 (dec. 1963); m. Charles Earl Schooley, Apr. 1, 1966. BE, U. Colo., BA, 1927; MA, Northwestern U., 1931. Tchr. HS Consol. Schs., Johnstown, Colo., 1927—28, Byers, Colo., 1928—29, Clayton, Mo., 1931—34; theatrical makeup artist, 1937—86; instr. Theatrical Makeup Dramatic Clubs, NJ; tchr. HS Consol. Schs., Johnstown, Colo., 1927—28, Byers, Colo., 1928—29, Clayton, Mo., 1931—34, theatrical makeup artist, 1937—86; instr. theatrical makeup dramatic clubs N.J. Theatre League; lectr., demonstrator theatrical makeup, dramatic and women's clubs, HS NJ and NY area, 1937—53; nat. officer, entertainer, dir. internat. entertainment project for mil. posts Phi Beta Nat. Profl. Fraternity Creative & Performing Arts, 1951—61; cons. radio broadcast series Sta. WNYC, NY, 1962—65; dir. cmty. rels. Wingspread Summer Theatre, Colon, Mich., 1955; co-chmn. Valley Shore Community Concerts, Conn., 1958—61, artist mgr., from 1959; founder, pres. Berkshire Hills Music and Dance Assn., Conn., 1970—78; mem. Music Mountain Corp., Falls Village, Conn., 1975—81; trustee Sharon (Conn.) Creative Arts Found., 1970—73; hon. trustee Bar Harbor Maine Festival, 1968—80; founder, pres. Wingspread Found., Conn., from 1977; mem. adv. bd. Cmty. Found. Henderson County, NC, 1990—93; trustee Brevard (N.C.) Music Ctr., 1990—93. Mem.: Hendersonville Country Club (NC), Sharon Country Club, Sharon Rep. Women's Club, Sharon Women's Club (Conn), Rehearsal Club, Montclair Dramatic Club (NJ), Montclair Women's Club (NJ) (dir.plays, chmn. drama dept.), Phi Beta, Alpha Omicron Pi. Congregationalist. Died 1992.

**SCHOONOVER, FRANK E.,** small business owner, retired; b. Kankakee, Ill., May 2, 1959; s. William Harold and Ruth Agnes (Thompson) S. BA, Eureka Coll., 1982. Receptionist Eureka (Ill.) Coll, 1980-81; salesman Walt's Camera Shop, Effingham, Ill., 1981-82; photographer Burgess Studio, Cisne, Ill., 1983-85; studio proprietor The Focal Point, Louisville, Ill., 1986-90. Mem. Fine Arts, County of Effingham. Mem. Internat. Platform Assn. Avocations: creative photography, dance, entertaining, fishing, swimming. Home: Alton, Ill. Died Sept. 9, 1991.

**SCHOUTEN, CEES,** plastic company executive; b. Alkmaar, North Holland, Netherlands, May 20, 1927; arrived in Belgium, 1974; s. Johannes Adrianes and Petronella (Bakker) Schouten; m. Afra Catharina Leering, Apr. 23, 1954; children: Ellen, Inge, Joppe. Diploma in Civil Engring., HTS, Amsterdam, 1952. Registered prof. engr. Netherlands. Engr., Saudi Arabia, 1953—56, Netherlands, 1953—56; chief engr. Du Pont Co., Netherlands, 1956—62; mng. dir. DYMO, Netherlands, 1962—70; v.p. Borg-Warner Co., Netherlands, 1973—78, Belgium, 1973—78; chief exec. officer Nederland B.V., from 1978, NV Gent, dir.; exec. Exec. European-Enterprises, France, 1970—73. Served with Dutch Army, 1948—50. Roman Catholic. Home: Saint Genesius-Rode, Belgium. Deceased.

**SCHREIBER, AVERY LAWRENCE,** actor; b. Chgo., Apr. 9, 1935; s. George and Minnie (Shear) S.; m. Rochelle Isaacs, Dec. 16, 1962; children: Jenny, Benjamin Joshua. Cert., The Goodman Theatre Sch., Chgo., 1960. Actor, from 1960. Appeared in numerous Broadway and theater prodns. including Metamorphosis (Los Angeles Critics Circle award 1971), Dreyfus in Rehearsal, 1974, Ovids Metamorphoses, 1971, Can-Can, 1981, Welcome to the Club, 1981; films include The Monitors, Deadhead Miles, Don't Drink the Water, Jimmy the Kid, The Last Remake of Beau Geste, Airport 79--Concorde, Galaxina, Silent Scream, Caveman, The Hunk, Saturday the 14th Srikes Back; TV films include Flatbed Annie and Sweetiepie, Escape, More Wild, Wild West Revisted, Second Chance, Outlaws; TV series include My Mother the Car, 1965-66, Our Place, summer 1967, Globetrotters Popcorn Machine, Ben Vereen's Comin' At Ya, Burns & Schreiber Comedy Hour; TV appearances include Love American Style, The Doris Day Show, The Ghost and Mrs. Muir, That Girl, Chico and the Man, The Ascent of Mount Fuji, The Muppets, Fantasy Island, Love Boat, Down to Earth, Rocky Road, New Love American Style, Shadow Chasers, What a Country, Twilight Zone, The Wizard, Days of Our Lives, Wake, Rattle & Roll; commls. include Doritos (Clio award 1977); numerous cartoon voices including The Smurfs. Hon. spokesman Angels of the World Fund, Fla., 1990. With USAR, 1951-53. Mem. AFTRA, Screen Actors Guild, Actors Equity Assn., AGVA, Writers Guild Am. (award 1973), Soc. Stage Dirs. and Choreographers. Democrat. Jewish. Avocations: macrame, songwriting. Died Jan. 7, 2002.

**SCHREIBER, BARBARA LOUISE,** civic worker; b. Canton, Ohio, Apr. 10, 1915; d. Ralph Mitchell and Lela May (Hower) Fawcett; m. Robert Edward Schreiber, June 17, 1938 (dec. Oct. 1974); children: Ralph F., Barbara Binkley, Susan Spring, Linda Parkos. BA, Conn. Coll., New London, 1937; student, Kent State U., 1937-38. Cert. tchr., Ohio. Mem. Bd. Edn., Canton City Schs., 1964-96, pres., 1967, 70, 75, 78, 80, 86, 89, 91, 94; trustee Ohio Sch. Bds. Assn., Westerville, 1967-96, mem. policies and legislation, 1975-96, mem., past pres. N.E. region exec. com., 1966-96; cons. to bd. dirs. Nat. PTA, Chgo., 1982-83; bd. dirs. Nat. Sch. Bds. Assn., Alexandria, Va., 1978-84; mem. Large City Schs. Commn., Ohio, 1967-96, pres., 1974, 90; mem. bd. advisors, treas. Philomatheon Soc. of the Blind, Canton, 1957—; chmn. pers. Gt. Trail coun. Girl Scouts U.S., Ohio, 1982—, pres., 1976-82; life mem. Ohio PTA; bd. dirs. Malone Coll., 1986-92, sec. bd.; mem. women's adv. coun. Malone Coll., 1966—, pres., 1967; chmn. lay adv. com. dept. edn. Walsh Coll., 1983-93; sec. adv. com. Walsh U., 1980-90; mem. women's com. Walsh U., 1968—; mem. Canton Recreation Bd., 1976-96, pres., 1986, 93. Recipient Appreciation award Greater Canton C. of C., 1981, Recognition award Phi Delta Kappa, 1978, Ohio Oaktree award Ohio PTA; named in her honor Barbara F. Schreiber Elem. Sch. Mem. Jr. League of Canton (pres. 1954-56, Woman of Yr. 1968), Coll. Club of Canton (pres. 1961-63), Rotary (Paul Harris fellow), Delta Kappa Gamma (hon.), Kappa Delta Pi. Republican. Presbyterian (elder, Sunday sch. tchr.). Died May 24, 2002.

**SCHRIER, MORRIS M.,** consultant; b. NYC, Dec. 22, 1909; s. Frank and Sophie (Nesati) Schrier; m. Margie Rocamora, Nov. 11, 1939 (dec. Jan. 1975); children: Carol R. (Schrier) Katowitz, Daniel R. BS, NYU, 1931; JD, Columbia U, 1934. V.p., sec., gen. counsel MCA Inc., NYC, 1959—79, legal cons., from 1979. Mem.: Assn. Bar City NY, Rockefeller Inst., ABA, United Cerebral Palsy, Nat. Cancer Adv. Bd (Bd. dir.), Nat. Cancer Inst., Friars NYC, Harmonie. Jewish. Died Aug. 18, 1992.

**SCHRODER, WIL,** retired state supreme court justice; b. Ft. Mitchell, Ky., 1946; m. Susan Wahlbrink; children: Stephanie, Lydia, Wil. BA, JD, U. Ky.; LLM, U. Mo. Bar: Ky. 1970, Mo. 1972. Atty. Kansas City Legal Aid Soc., 1971; corp. atty. St. Paul Ins. Co., 1971—72; asst. law prof. Chase Law Sch., Ky., 1972—75; pvt. practice Covington, Ky., 1975—83; trial ct. judge Kenton County Dist. Ct., Ky., 1983—91; judge Ky. Ct. Appeals, 1991—2006; justice for 6th Supreme Ct. dist Ky. Supreme Ct., 2007—13. Hearing officer Ky. Personnel Bd., 1981—83. Died Oct. 26, 2013.

**SCHULTZ, NORBERT J.,** retired music educator; b. Gardner, Ill., Apr. 25, 1937; s. Lewis H. and Vera Schultz; m. Janet A. Schultz, Aug. 19, 1979; children: Sonia, Shelly Luppen 1 stepchild, John Bracamontes. BS in Music Edn., Ill. State U., 1959. Band, vocal and gen. music tchr., grade and H.S. Kempton and Cabrey (Ill.) Schs., 1959—61; vocal tchr. Piper City (Ill.) Grade and H.S., 1961—63; band and vocal dir. Taft Grade Sch., Lockport, Ill., 1963—67; band dir. Lyons (Ill.) Sch. Dist., 1967—70, Edwardsville (Ill.) elem, jr. high and H.S., 1970—85; gen. music tchr. Shenandoah and Woodward Elem. Schs., St. Louis, 1986—99; beginning and intermediate band dir. St. Paul's Luth. Sch., Troy, Ill., 1999—2001; ret., 2001; painist & choir dir. Scott Air Force Base Chapel. Profl. entertainer, band dir. Musical dir. chapel Charles Melvin Price Support Ctr. Army Facility, Granite City, Ill., 1995—2000; deacon Holy Cross Luth. Ch., Collinsville, Ill., 1988—96, elder, 1999, St. Paul's Luth. Ch., Troy, from 2002. Recipient numerous 1st pl. band awards at state competitions; named team mem. in citizen ambassador program elementary edn. del. to Vietnam, Eisenhower award, U. Toledo, 1994. Mem.: Music Tchrs. Nat. Assn., Ill. State Music Tchrs. Assn. Republican. Lutheran. Avocations: fishing, travel, private teaching. Home: Edwardsville, Ill. Died Feb. 9, 2014.

**SCHUSTER, BERNARD,** lawyer; b. Bialyston, Poland, May 17, 1928; arrived in US, 1947, naturalized, 1953; s. Jacob and Sarah (Maretzki) Schuster; m. Jane M. Moress, July 3, 1952; children: Deborah, James, Miriam. BA, U. Rochester, 1952; JD, Harvard U., 1955. Bar: NY 1957. Law clk. US Ct. Appeals, NYC, 1955—57; ptnr. Claus, Curry, Schustre & Schwartzman, Rochester, NY. Tchr., lectr. in field. Active mem. various cmty. ogns. Mem.: Monroe Bar Assn., NY State Bar Assn. Democrat. Jewish. Home: Rochester, NY. Died 2003.

**SCHUSTER, BERTRAM,** recruiter, management consultant, publisher; b. NYC, Jan. 7, 1940; s. Harry and Lillian (Grossfield) S.; m. Zohara Teena Glassman, Mar. 16, 1980. BA, CUNY, 1986; postgrad., U. Pa. Sales dir. Franklin Mint, Franklin Center, Pa., 1971-74; nat. dir. AMR Internat., NYC, 1974-77; pub., COO Vital Mag., Chgo., 1977-79; v.p. Morgan Stanley Dean Witter, Chgo., 1980-86; mng. dir. Robbins Trading Co., Chgo., 1986-91; pub., COO Futures Mag., Cedar Falls, Iowa, 1992-94; mgmt. cons. George S. May Internat., Inc., Park Ridge, Ill., 1994-96; pub., CEO Traveler Pub. Corp., Chgo., from 1996; ptnr. DHR Internat., Chgo., from 1998. Author: The Insider's Edge, 1985; contbr. articles to profl. publs. Bd. dirs. Winston Tower 1 Condominiums, pres., 1997-99. With U.S. Army, 1963-69. Mem. Managed Futures Trade Assn. (founding bd. dirs. 1985-88). Avocations: reading, music, race car driving, photography, swimming. Deceased.

**SCHWAB, VICTOR OPPER,** advertising executive; b. Hoboken, NJ, Mar. 13, 1898; s. Albert James and Letitia (Irvine) S.; m. Vilma Noble, Feb. 11, 1946; 1 child, Gretchen Vicky. Student, Columbia U., 1917-18. Copy chief Ruthrauff & Ryan, Chgo., 1921-22; promotion mgr. Thompson Barlow Co., London, 1924, F.E. Compton & Co., Chgo., 1926-27; pres. Schwab, Beatty & Porter, Inc., from 1928. Lectr. advt. Columbia U., N.Y.U. Author: How to Write a Good Advertisement, 1942; textbook mail order advt. Internat. Corr. Schs., 1949; contbr. articles to profl. jours. Mem. Am. Assn. Advt. Agys. (dir. 1954-56, chmn. bd. govs. N.Y. coun. 1938), Advt. Coun. (dir. 1955-57), Am. Mktg. Assn. Home: New York, NY. Deceased.

**SCHWARTZ, LEON,** retired foreign language educator; b. Boston, Aug. 22, 1922; s. Charles and Celia (Emer) S.; m. Jeanne Gurtat, Mar. 31, 1949; children: Eric Alan, Claire Marie. Student, Providence Coll., 1939-41; BA, UCLA, 1948; certificat de phonetique, U. Paris, 1949; MA, U. So. Cal., 1950, PhD, 1962. Tchr. English, French, Spanish and Latin Redlands Jr. HS, Calif., 1951—54; tchr. Spanish and French Redlands HS, 1954—59; prof. French Calif. State U., LA, 1959—87, chmn. dept. fgn. langs. and lit., 1970—73, prof. emeritus, 1987—2013; instr. Osher Learning Inst., 2006. Author: Diderot and the Jews, 1981, Poems That Sing by French Masters, 2008, A Scion of the Times: Leon Schwartz Memoirs, & Family Annals, 2009, Limericks Converbs And Utter Folly, 2010, Loose Goose: Limericks, Converbs, and Other Rib-Ticklers, 2011, Nude Dude: LImericks, 'Converbs' and Other Brainstorms, 2013; co-author: Mortier-Tresson, Dictionnaire de Diderot, 1999; contbr. (documentary film) On Eagles' Wings: The American Air Force in World War II, 2005; editor: Gonzalez and Clark Translation of Fernando del Paso Noticias del Imperio, 2009. Served as 2d lt. USAAF, 1942-45. Decorated Air medal with 5 oak leaf clusters; recipient Outstanding Prof. award Calif. State U. LA, 1976. Mem. Calif. State U. LA Emeriti Assn. (pres. 1998-2000), Phi Beta Kappa, Phi Kappa Phi, Pi Delta Phi, Sigma Delta Pi, Alpha Mu Gamma. Home: Silver Spring, Md. Died Aug. 22.

**SCHWARZ, ROSE OBERMAN,** artist; b. Jan. 24, 1910; d. William and Florence Oberman; m. Sidney Schwarz, July 31, 1929 (dec. Mar. 1984); children: Lillian, Elaine. Student, South Fla. Art Inst., 1977—99. Ins. salesperson. Exhibitions include Bacardi Gallery, Miami, Fla., 1979, Miami Beach City Hall, Fla., 1981—82, Viscaya, 1981, Met. Mus., Coral Gables, Fla., 1985, Bay Harbor Gallery, Fla., from 1985. Recipient Rex Art award, Hollywood Cultural Ctr., 1981, hon. mention, Pioneer Mus., 1982, Best in Show award, Hollywood Art Guild, 1983, hon. mention, Pioneer Mus., 1983, Best in show, Hollywood Cultural Ctr., 1984, Best in Show, 1985. Avocations: dress making, piano. Died Dec. 30, 2002.

**SCHWEBEL, MILTON,** psychologist, educator; b. Troy, NY, May 11, 1914; s. Frank and Sarah (Oxenhandler) S.; m. Bernice Lois Davison, Sept. 3, 1939; children: Andrew I., Robert S. AB, Union Coll., 1934; MA, SUNY, Albany, 1936; PhD, Columbia U., NYC, 1949; Cert. in Psychotherapy, Postgrad. Ctr. Mental Health, NYC, 1958; LHD, LHD, Saybrook U., 2010. Lic. psychologist, NY, NJ; diplomate American Bd. Examiners Profl. Psychology. Asst. prof. psychology Mohawk Champlain Coll., 1946-49; asst. to prof. edn., dept. chmn., assoc. dean NYU, 1949-67; dean, prof. Grad. Sch. Edn., Rutgers U., New Brunswick, NJ, 1967-77; dean emeritus Grad. Sch. Applied & Profl. Psychology, 1977—2013, prof., 1977-85, prof. emeritus, 1985—2013. Vis. prof. U. Southern Calif., U. Hawaii; postdoctoral fellow Postgrad. Ctr. Mental Health, NYC, 1954-58, lectr. psychology, 1958-90; cons. NIMH, US, state & city depts. edn., UNESCO, ednl. ministries in Europe, Asia, univs. and pub. schs., UNESCO; pvt. cons. psychologist and psychotherapist, 1953-2013; disting. cons. & faculty Saybrook Grad. Sch. & Rsch. Ctr., 1999-2013, adj. rsch. faculty Inst. Transactional Psychology, 2005-13. Author: A Guide to a Happier Family, 1989, Personal Adjustment and Growth, 1990, Student Teachers Handbook, 3d edit., 1996, Interests of Pharmacists, 1951, Health Counseling, 1953, Who Can Be Educated?, 1968, Remaking America's Three School System: Now Separate and Unequal, 2003; editor: Mental Health Implications of Life in the Nuclear Age, 1986, Facilitating Cognitive Development, 1986, Promoting Cognitive Growth Over the Life Span, 1990, Behavioral Science and Human Survival, 1965, The Impact of Ideology on the I.Q. Controversy, 1975; editor Peace & Conflict: Jour. Peace Psychology, 1993-2000 (vol. 9, no. 4. named Pioneer in Peace Psychology: Milton Schwebel); co-editor Bull. Peace Psychology, 1991-94; mem. editl. bd. American Jour. Orthopsychiatry, Readings in Mental Health, Jour. Contemporary Psychotherapy, Jour. Counseling Psychology, Jour. Social Issues, others. Mem. sci. adv. bd. Internat. Ctr. for Enhancement of Learning Potential, 1988-2013; trustee Edn. Law Ctr., 1973-81, Nat. Com. Employment Youth, Nat. Child Labor Com., 1967-75, Union Exptl. Colleges & Universities, 1976-78; pres. Nat. Orgn. for Migrant Children, 1980-85; pres. Inst. of Arts & Humanities, 1984-95. Served with AUS, 1943-46, ETO. Recipient Disting. Leader in Edn. award, Grad. Sch. Edn. Rutgers U., 2006; Met. Applied Rsch. Coun. fellow, 1970—71. Fellow APA, American Psychol. Soc., American Orthopsychiatry Assn., Soc. Psychol. Study Social Issues, Jean Piaget Soc. (trustee), American Ednl. Rsch. Assn., NY Acad. Scis., Psychologists for Social Responsibility (pres.), Sigma Xi. Died Oct. 3, 2013.

**SCOON, PAUL,** former governor general of Grenada; b. Gouyave, Grenada, July 4, 1935; m. Esmai Monica Lumsden, 1970 (dec.); 3 stepchildren. Student, Inst. Edn., Leeds U., Eng.; BA, M.Ed., Toronto U., Ont., Can. Tchr. Grenada Boys' Secondary Sch., 1953-67. Chief edn. officer, Grenada, 1967-68, permanent sec., 1969, sec. to cabinet, 1970-72; dep. dir. Commonwealth Found., 1973-78; gov. Centre for Internat. Briefing, Farnham Castle, 1973-78; gov. gen. of Grenada, 1978-92 Created Knight. Mem. Civil Svc. Assn. Grenada (v.p. 1968), Assn. Masters and Mistresses of Grenada (co-founder, past pres.), Rotary Internat. (Paul Harris fellow). Died Sept. 2, 2013.

**SCOTT, H(ERBERT) ANDREW,** retired chemical engineer; b. Marion, Va., Mar. 29, 1924; s. Charles Wassum and Carolyn Enyde (Snider) S.; widowed; children: Mark Andrew, Paul Ethan; m. Helen R. LaFollette, July 21, 1984. BSChemE, Va. Tech. Inst. and State U., 1944, MSChemE, 1947. Registered profl. engr., Tenn. Chem. engr. Tenn. Eastman Co., Kingsport, 1947-55, asst. to works mgr., 1955-60, supt. glycol dept., 1960-64, supt. polymers dept., 1964-67; plant mgr. Holston Def. Corp., Kingsport, 1967-70, dir. systems devel., 1970-73, dir. engring. dvsn., 1974-87. Vis. prof. U. Alaska, Fairbanks, 1988-89; mem. standards com. Eastman Kodak Co., Rochester, N.Y., 1982-87. Mem. mayor's adv. com. City of Kingsport, 1971-76; chmn. Kingsport Park Commn., 1976-80. Sgt. AUS, 1944-46. Named Engr. of yr., Tenn. Soc. Profl. Engrs., 1984. Fellow AIChE (mem. Inst. Chem. Process Safety 1984-87, vocat. guidance com. 1960-64, chmn. local sect. 1956); mem. Am. Soc. Engring. Edn., Am. Soc. Engring. Mgmt., Kiwanis. Republican. Presbyterian. Achievements include patent in process for manufacture of acetic anhydride, implement pioneering quality management for knowledge workers, design for manufacturing chemicals from coal. *Being born of honest, ambitious and loving religious parents in a small town in the mountains of the USA was a great start. Work was a virtue, wages in a depression a life-saver! Successfully practicing chemical engineering in one of America's great companies complete the image.* Deceased.

**SCOTT, IAN JAMES,** accountant; b. Glasgow, Scotland, Feb. 10, 1930; s. Wilfrid Henry and Violet Margaret Handasyde (Mackay) S.; m. Aileen Rennie Wright, June 14, 1961; children: Charles Roderick, Carolyn Louise, Hermione Lorna, Lorne Hamilton Mackay. Chartered Acct., Inst. Chartered Accts Scotland, Glasgow, 1958. Ptnr. R.A. Clement & Co., Glasgow, 1960-74, Ian J. Scott & Co., Helensburgh, Scotland, 1974-95; cons. Hammond & Co., Helensburgh, 1995—2002. Dir. A.W.D. Shipping, Glasgow; dep. chmn. T.S.B. Scotland, Edinburgh, 1986. Collector of the House Trades House of Glasgow, 1995-96; deacon Incorporation of Gardeners, Glasgow, 1993-94; deacon convener Trades of Glasgow, 1997-98; freeman City of London, 1995; mem. Worshipful Co. of Gun-makers, London, 1995, Insolvency Practitioners Assn., 1970. Recipient Silk Cut Nautical award for svcs. to nat. yachting, 1986, Corinthian award for svcs. to nat. yachting, 1993. Mem.: Royal Yacht Assn. (judge 1990—2001), Partick Curling Club (pres. 2000), Sandyford Burns Club (pres. 2001), Clyde Corinthian Yacht Club (hon. commodore). Conservative. Mem. Ch. of Scotland. Avocations: sailing, curling, shooting. Home: Rhu Arqyll & Bute, Scotland. Died July 14, 2006.

**SCOTT, WILLODENE ALEXANDER,** retired library administrator; b. Ethridge, Tenn., Sept. 4, 1922; d. Jesse Cary and Maud (Goff) Alexander; m. Ray Donald Scott, Nov. 27, 1959; 1 child, Pamela Dean. BA, George Peabody Coll. Tchrs., 1946, BS in Lib. Sci., 1947, MA, 1949, EdS, 1972, PhD, 1986. Libr. Sylvan Park Elem. Sch., Nashville, 1947—51, Waverly Belmont Jr. HS, Nashville, 1951—54, Howard HS, Nashville, 1954—62, Peabody Demonstration Sch., Nashville, 1962—63, McCann Elem. Sch., Nashville, 1963—66; supr. instrnl. materials, libr. divsn. Metro Nashville-Davidson County Schs., Nashville, 1966—73, dir. instrnl. materials, libr. svcs., 1973—87; dir. librs. Watkins Inst., Nashville, 1987—88; ret.; lectr. Peabody Coll. Libr. Sch., Nashville, 1950—66, 1971—72, 1976, U. Tenn., Nashville Ctr., 1970; Tenn. rep. White House Conf., 1970. Pub. Experiencing Lit. With Children, Elementary English, 1967, Instrnl. Materials Ctr.,Tenn. Libr., 1969; Chmn. nat. alumni fund-raising George Peabody Coll. Tchrs., 1975—76, nat. alumni pres., 1977—78, trustee, 1976—78; bd. dirs. Friends Music, 1977—79; mem. vis. com. bd. trustees Vanderbilt U., 1979—85. Recipient Disting. Alumni award, Peabody Libr. Sch., 1987, Tenn. Libr. Assn. Honor award, 1986. Mem.: DAR (organizing treas. Buffalo River chpt. 1967—69), AAUW, ALA, NEA (life), Embroidery Guild America (vol. libr. Cheekwood chpt.), Woman's Nat. Book Assn. (charter mem.), Met. Nashville Ret. Tchrs. Assn., Tenn. Edn. Assn. (libr. sect. pres. 1954), Tenn. Libr. Assn. (membership chmn. 1955, 1964, treas. 1977—78, Honor award 1986), Southeastern Libr. Assn. (scholarship com. 1968—70), Nashville Libr. Club (pres. 1952—53), Delta Kappa Gamma (v.p. 1984—86). Baptist. Home: Nashville, Tenn. Died 2011.

**SCRUGGS, CHARLES G.,** editor; b. McGregor, Tex., Nov. 4, 1923; s. John Fleming and Adeline (Hering) S.; m. Miriam June Wigley, July 5, 1947; children— John Mark, Miriam Jan BS, Tex. A&M U., 1947. Assoc. editor Progressive Farmer, Dallas, 1947-61, editor, from 1962, v.p., from 1964, exec. editor, 1972, editorial dir., from 1973, editor-in-chief, 1982-87; editorial chmn. So. Progress Pubs., 1987-89. Pres. Torado Land and Cattle Co., pres. Tex. Comml. Agr. Council 1953-54; chmn. bd. Sunlean Foods, Inc., 1989—. Author: The Peaceful Atom and the Deadly Fly, 1975, American Agricultural Capitalism Founding gen. chmn. Chancellors' Century Coun., Tex. A&M U. System, 1987-90; Mem. Gov.'s Com. for Agr., 1950, Tex. Animal Health Council, 1955-61; chmn. So. Brucellosis Com., 1956; pres. Tex. Rural Safety Com., 1957-59; chmn. Nat. Brucellosis Com., 1958-59, 71-72; del. World Food Congress, 1963; pub. mem. U.S. del. 17th Biennial Conf. of FAO, UN, Rome, 1973; chmn. Joint Senate-House Interim Com. Natural Fibers, Tex. Legislature, 1971; mem. coordinating bd. Tex. Coll. and Univ. System, 1965-69; bd. regents Tex. Tech U., 1971-78; founding pres. S.W. Animal Health Research Found. 1961-63, trustee, 1961— . Served to lt. col. U.S. Army; Res., ret. Recipient Christian Svc. Mass Media award, 1995, Abilene Christian U., Southwestern Cattle Raisers award, 1962, Am. Seed Trade Assn. award, 1963, award of honor Am. Agrl. Editors Assn., 1964, Reuben Brigham award Am. Assn. Agrl. Coll. Editors, 1965, Disting. Svc. award Tex. Farm Bur., 1966, Journalistic Achievement award Nat. Plant Food Assn., 1967, Nat. award for agrl. excellence Nat. Agri-Mktg. Assn., 1983, Agrl. Vision award Nat. Forum for Agr., 1994; named Disting. Alumnus Tex. A&M U., 1982. Mem. Am. Agrl. Editors Assn. (pres. 1963), Am. Soc. Mag. Editors, Tex. Assn. Future Farmers Am. (pres. 1940-41), Dallas Agrl. Club (pres. 1951), Nat. Livestock Confedn. Mexico (hon.), The Austin Club, Headliners Club, Alpha Zeta, Sigma Delta Chi Died July 24, 2001.

**SCULTHORPE, PETER,** artist, printmaker; b. Hamilton, Ont., Can., July 23, 1948; came to U.S., 1964; s. Albert George Sculthorpe and Elsie Jane Miller. Jurist Parkersburg Art Ctr., W.Va., 1993. One man shows include William Penn Meml. Mus., Harrisburg, 1978, Gallery Madison 90, N.Y.C., 1978, Judy Goffman Fine Arts, N.Y.C., 1982, Somerville/Manning Gallery, Wilmington, 1984, 86, 88, 90, 92, 94, 96, 98, Charles and Emma Frye Art Mus., Seattle, 1987, Sporting Gallery, Middleburg, Va., 1991, 93, Cudahy Gallery, N.Y.C., 1991, Chester County Art Assn., Pa., 1993, Parkersburg (W.Va.) Art Ctr., 1993; exhibited in group shows at Am. Watercolor Soc., N.Y.C., Nat. Acad. Design., N.Y.C., American Artists Profl. League, Phila. Sketch Club, Springfield (Mo.) Art Mus., 1986, 91, Del. Art Mus., Wilmington, 1987, Berman Art Mus., Collegville, Pa., 1991, Parkersburg (W.Va.) Art Ctr., 1992, New Orleans Art Assn., 1993, Ottawa Gallery, Sylvania, Ohio, 1993, Woodmere Art Mus., Phila., 1993, Saper Gallery, East Lansing, Mich., 1993, Carnegie Mus. Art., Pitts., 1993., Nat. Art League., N.Y., 1993, Butler Inst., Youngstown, Ohio, 1993, Salmagundi Exhibition, N.Y., 1993, Phila. Sketch Club., 1993., Pa. Acad. Fine Arts., Phila., 1993, Neville Mus., Green Bay, Wis., 1993, Audobon Soc., N.Y.C., 1994.; represented in permanent collections MBNA, Wilmington, Butler Inst., Bristol-Myers-Squibb Gallery, Princeton, N.J., Charles and Emma Frya Art Mus., Dunnegan Gallery Art, Bolivar, Mo., Parkersburg Art Ctr., Am. Embassy, Copenhagen, Denmark., Springfield Art Mus., Del. Art Mus., Brandywine River Mus., Chadds Ford, Pa., DuPont Co., Tokyo, William Penn Meml. Art Mus., Forbes Bldg., N.Y.C., Nabisco Hdqrs. Gallery, East Hanover, N.J., U.S. Fidelity & Guarantee, Balt.; author: (autobiography) Sun Music: Journeys and Reflections From a Composer's life, 1999 Recipient Artistic Excellence award American Artists Profl. League, 1984, Silver medal Phila. Sketch Club., 1986, Albert Woofler Nat. Realism award, 1991, Merit award La. Watercolor Soc., First Prize Oil Painting award Nat Art League, 1993; fellow Earthwatch, 1992. Mem. Watercolor U.S.A. Hon. Soc. Died Aug. 8, 2014.

**SCULTHORPE, PETER JOSHUA,** composer, educator; b. Launceston, Tasmania, Apr. 29, 1929; s. Joshua and Edna (Moorhouse) Sculthorpe. Ed., U. Melbourne, Wadham Coll., Oxford U.; D.Litt. (hon.), Tasmania; D.Mus. (hon.), U. Melbourne; LittD (hon.), U. Sussex. Lectr. to sr. lectr. in music U. Sydney, from 1963, prof. musical composition, 1991—2014. Vis. prof. music U. Sussex, 1971—72; mem. Australian Broadcasting Commn., Birmingham Chamber Music Soc., Australian Elizabethan Theatre Trust, Australian Ballet, Musica Viva Australia, Australian Chamber Orchestra. Composer: The Loneliness of Bunjil, 1954, Sonatina, 1954, Irkanda I, 1955, Irkanda II, 1959, Irkanda III, 1960, Irkanda IV, 1961, Ulterior Motifs, 1957—59, Sonata for Viola and Percussion, 1960, Theme and Journey's End, 1962, Sonata for Piano, 1963, The Fifth Continent, 1963, String Quartet No. 6, 1965, South by five, 1965, Sun Music I, 1965, Sun Music for Voices and Percussion, 1966, Sun Music III, 1967, Sun Music IV, 1967, Sun Music Ballet, 1968, Sun Music II, 1969, String Quartet No. 8, 1969, Morning Song for the Christ Child, 1966, Tabuh Tabuhan, 1968, Autumn Song, 1968, Sea Chante, 1968, Love 200 for pop group and orch., 1970, The Stars Turn, 1970, Music for Japan, 1970, Rain, 1970, Dream, 1970, Night Pieces, 1971, Landscape, 1971, How The Stars Were Made, 1971, Ketjak, 1972, Koto Music I, 1971, Rites of Passage, 1972—73, The Song of Tailitnama, 1974; author: Sun Music: Journeys and Reflections from a Composer's Life, 1999. Decorated Order Brit. Empire; recipient Composers' award, Australian Coun., 1975—78, Australian film award, 1980; Vis. fellow, Yale U., 1965—67. Died Aug. 8, 2014.

**SEALEY, RAPHAEL,** history professor; b. Middlesbrough, Yorkshire, Eng., Aug. 14, 1927; came to U.S., 1963; s. Bertram Izod and Florence Gladys (Heath) S.; m. Dagmar Schoelermann, Dec. 19, 1972 (div. Oct. 1977); 1 child, Dorte Freyja. BA, Oxford U., Eng., 1947, MA, 1951. Lectr. U. Coll. North Wales, Bangor, 1954—58, U. London, 1958—63; prof. State U. NY, Buffalo, 1963—67, U. Calif., Berkeley, 1967—2000. Author: Essays in Greek Politics, 1967, A History of the Greek City States, 1976, The Athenian Republic, 1987, Women and Law in Classical Greece, 1990, Demosthenes and His Time, 1993, The Justice of the Greeks, 1994. Sgt. British Army, 1947—49. Mem.: Am. Philological Assn. Avocation: literature. Home: Berkeley, Calif. Died Nov. 29, 2013.

**SEAMAN, CATHERINE HAWES COLEMAN,** retired anthropology educator; b. Nelson County, Va., Aug. 28, 1923; d. William Irby and Bertha Davis (Hughes) Coleman; m. John Anthony Seaman, Jan. 19, 1946; children: Catherine Fisher, Gwendolyn Whipp, John Anthony, Andrew. BS, U. Va., 1965, MA, 1967, PhD, 1969. Instr. U. Va., Charlottesville, 1966, Sweet Briar (Va.) Coll., Va., 1967-69, asst. prof. anthropology, 1969-74, assoc. prof., 1974-80, prof., 1980—93, prof. emeritus, 1993—2013. Assoc. prof. part-time U. Va., various dates, 1970's; dir. Title I, Sweet Briar Coll., 1970's. Author: Research Method, 3d edit., 1988, Lees of York County, Va., 1987; author, editor: Letters from Virginia, 1988, History of Lovingston, 1990; contbr. articles to profl. jours. Trustee Nelson County Sch. Bd., 1955-87; bd. dirs. Friends of Kiskiake, Richmond, Jefferson-Madison Reg. Library, Charlottesville, Va. Bapt. Hosp., Lynchburg, 1970's; bd. dirs., pres. Nelson County Hist. Soc.; 2nd lt. U.S. Army, 1946-47. Carnegie-Mellon Found. grantee, Eli Lilly grantee, NIMH grantee; Catherine Seaman scholar, 1987. Mem. Va. Social Sci. Assn. (pres. 1987-88), Anthropol. Med. Assn., American Ethnological Soc., American Anthropol. Assn., Jamestowne Soc. Avocations: oral history, gardening, remodeling old houses. Home: Faber, Va. Died Dec. 23, 2013.

**SEAMAN, DARYL KENNETH,** oil industry executive, professional sports team executive; b. Rouleau, Sask., Can., Apr. 28, 1922; BSME, U. Sask., 1948, LLD (hon.), 1982, U. Calgary, 1993. Cert. mech. engr. CEO Bow Valley Industries Ltd., Calgary, Alta., Canada, 1962-70, 85-91, chmn., CEO, 1970-82; chmn. Box Valley Industries Ltd., Calgary, Alta., Canada, 1982-85; pres. Bow Valley Industries Ltd., Calgary, Alta., Canada, 1985-87, chmn., 1991-92. Bd. dirs. Far West Mining Ltd., Pure Techs. Ltd., Bow Valley Energy Ltd.; co-owner Calgary Flames Hockey Club; chmn., pres. Dox Investments, Inc.; hon. regent Athol Murray Coll. of Notre Dame, 2001—09. Mem. Royal Commn. Econ. Union and Devel. Prospects for Can., 1982-85; active numerous coms. for fundraising U. Sask.; Served with RCAF, 1941-45, North Africa, Italy. Can. Oilmen's Hall of Fame, 1997, Calgary Bus. Hall of Fame, 2004. Mem. Assn. Profl. Engrs., Geologists and Geophysicists (hon. life, Frank Spragins award, 1985, McGill Mgmt. Achievement award, 1979), Order of Canada, 1993, Ranchmen's Club, RAF Club, Earl Grey Golf Club, Calgary Petroleum Club, Calgary Golf and Country Club, U. Calgary Chancellor's Club. Progressive Conservative. Mem. United Ch. Can. Achievements include being inducted into the Hockey Hall of Fame, 2010. Avocations: ranching, golf, hunting. Died Jan. 11, 2009.

**SEARLE, RODNEY NEWELL,** state legislator, farmer, insurance agent; b. Camden, NJ, July 17, 1920; s. William Albert and Ruby Marie (Barrus) S.; m. Janette Elizabeth Christie, May 17, 1941 (dec.); children: R. Newell Jr., Linda Jennison Grant, Alan John; m. Ruth Anne Bartlett, May 6, 2001. BA, Mankato State U., 1960; DHL, Winona State U., 2001. Prodn. coordinator Johnson & Johnson, New Brunswick, NJ, 1940-47; farmer Waseca, Minn., 1947—2014; spl. agt. John Hancock Mut. Ins. Co., Waseca, Minn., 1961-84; mem. Minn. House of Reps., St. Paul, 1957-80, speaker, 1979. Bd. pres. Minn. Legis. Soc., 1996—2008. Author: Minnesota Standoff-The Politics of Deadlock, 1990. Lay reader St. John's Episcopal Ch., 1952-2013; chmn. Upper Mississippi River Basin Commn., 1981-82; pres. Minn. State U. Bd., 1981-92; chmn. Minn. Higher Edn. Bd., 1991-92; bd. dirs. Minn. Wellsprings, 1984-90; emeritus mem. adv. bd. Hubert H. Humphrey Inst.; emeritus mem. coun. Minn. Hist. Soc.; bd. dirs. Minn. Agrl. Interpretive Ctr., 1983-02; mem. Waseca County Hist. Bd., 1995-2013; capt. Minn. Wing of the Civil Air Patrol. Named Minn. State Tree Farmer of Yr., 1978 Mem. American Tree Farm Sys., Nat. Conf. State Legislators, Minn. Forestry Assn. (bd. dirs. 1991-01), Masons, Rotary (pres. club 1968). Independent. Home: Waseca, Minn. Died Jan. 5, 2014.

**SEEGER, PETE,** folk singer, songwriter; b. NYC, May 3, 1919; s. Charles Louis and Constance de Clyver (Edson) Seeger; m. Toshi-Aline Ohta, July 20, 1943; children: Daniel Adams, Mika Salter, Tinya. Student, Harvard U., 1936-38. Co-founding mem. The Weavers, 1948—59. Singer: (albums) American Industrial Ballads, 1957, Dangerous Songs, 1966, Abiyoyo, 1967, World of Pete Seeger, 1973, Essential, 1978, Greatest Hits, 1987, Traditional Christmas Carols, 1989, Children's Concert at Town Hall, 1990, Folk Music of the World, 1991, Pete Seeger's Family Concert, 1992, Singalong-Live at Sanders Theatre, 1992, Darling Corey/Goofing Off Suit, Live at Newport, Waist Deep in the Big Muddy, 1993, Clearwater Classics, Link in the Chain, 1996, Pete, 1996 (Grammy award for Best Traditional Folk Album, 2006), American Favorite Ballads, 1997, Birds, Beasts, Bugs & Fishes, For Kids & Just Plain Folks, God Bless the Grass, If I Had a Hammer-Songs of Hope & Struggle, 1998, Headlines & Footnotes, 1999, American Folk Game & Activity, Stories & Songs for Little Children, 2000, Song and Play Time, 2001, Brothers and Sisters, 2006, At 89, 2008 (Grammy award for Best Traditional Folk Album, 2009), Pete Seeger at Bard College, 2009, Tomorrow's Children, 2010, A More Perfect Union, 2012, Pete Remembers Woody, 2012, The Storm King-Stories, Narratives, Poems, 2013; co-author (with Paul DuBois Jacobs): (children's book) The Deaf Musicians, 2006 (Schneider Family Book award); co-author: (with Rob & Sam Rosenthal) Pete Seeger: His Life in His Own Words, 2012. Served in US Army, 1942—45. Recipient Nat. Medal of the Arts, The White House, 1994, Kennedy Center Honor, John F. Kennedy Ctr. for the Performing Arts, 1994; named to The Rock & Roll Hall of Fame, 1996. Subject of book: How Can I Keep from Singing: Pete Seeger, by David King Dunaway, 1981. Died Jan. 27, 2014.

**SEGINER, ARNAN,** aerospace engineer, educator, researcher; b. Poprad, Czech Republic, Apr. 13, 1936; arrived in Israel, 1937; s. David Bernard and Borka Barbara (Korach) S.; m. Ora Targan, Oct. 15, 1959; children: Osnat, Vered. BSc in Aerospace Engring., Technion, Haifa, Israel, 1960; MSc in Aerospace Engring., Technion, 1963, DSc in Aerospace Engring., 1968. Postdoctoral rsch. assoc. Nat.

Rsch. Coun., U.S., 1968-70; sr. lectr. Technion, Haifa, 1970-75, assoc. prof., 1975-85, prof., from 1985. Sr. rsch. assoc. NASA/NRC, Moffett Field, Calif., 1975-77, 82-83; dir. continuing edn. Technion, 1986-90, v.p. rsch., 1990-95; chmn. Dimotech Ltd., Haifa, 1990-98; dir. S. Neaman Inst. Advanced Studies in Sci. and Tech., Haifa, 1996-99; Israeli rep. Joint Rsch. Ctr., European Union, Brussels, 1996—. Contbr. articles to profl. jours. Mem. Rothschild Prize Com., Israel, 1994—; bd. dirs. German-Israel Bi-Nat. Sci. Found., Jerusalem, 1996—. Lt. col. Israel Def. Forces., 1954-56 (reserves 1956-86). Recipient Outstanding Student award Ministry of Edn., Israel, 1957-60. Fellow AIAA (assoc.); mem. IEEE/Aerospace Engring. Scis. (Internat. Congress Instrumentation Aerospace Simulation Facilities panel), Supersonic Tunnel Assn., Nat. Coun. for R & D. Home: Haifa, Israel. Died Jan. 13, 2002.

**SEIDLER, GRZEGORZ LEOPOLD,** language educator; b. Stanislawow, Poland, Sept. 18, 1913; s. Teodor and Eugenia (Dawidowicz) S.; m. Alina Jadwiga Bogusz, Mar. 1, 1969. MA, Jagiellonian U., 1935, PhD, 1938; PhD (hon.), Maria Curie Sklodowska U., Lublin, Poland, 1970, Acad. Econs., Cracow, Poland, 1975, Lock Haven U., 1990. Lectr. Jagiellonian U., Cracow, 1945-50; prof. Marie Curie Sklodowska U., 1951-83. Dir. Polish Cultural Inst., London, 1969-71; vis. prof. U. Kiel, 1980-81; vis. fellow Clare Hall Cambridge U., 1981-82. Author: The Emergence of the Eastern World, 1968, Przedmarksowska Mysl Polityczna, 1974, Rechtssystem und Gesellschaft, 1985, O Istocie I Akceptacji Wladzy Panstwowej, 1995, Rozwazania, 2002. Mem. Polish Parliament, Warsaw, 1985-89. Decorated comdr.'s cross with star Order of Polonia Restituta, grand cross Order of Polonia Restituta. Mem. Am. Soc. 18th Century Studies, Rotary Club Lublin, United Oxford and Cambridge Univ. Club. Avocations: walking, studying european intellectual traditions. Home: Lublin, Poland. Died Dec. 28, 2004.

**SEIGENTHALER, JOHN LAWRENCE, JR.,** retired newspaper executive; b. Nashville, July 27, 1927; s. John Lawrence and Mary (Brew) Seigenthaler; m. Dolores Watson, Jan. 3, 1955; 1 child, John Jr. LLD (hon.), Colby Coll. Staff corr. Nashville Tennessean, 1949-60, editor, 1962-72, pub., 1973-82, pres., 1979-82, chmn., 1982-92; editorial dir. USA Today, 1982-92, ret., 1992. Chmn. freedom forum First Amendment Ctr., Vanderbilt U., Nashville, 1992—2014; adminstrv. asst. to atty. gen. Robert Kennedy US Dept. Justice, 1961; dir. Tennessean Newspapers, Inc., 1963—79, 1978—83. Author: A Search for Justice, 1971, The Year of the Scandal Called Watergate, 1974, James K. Polk: 1845-49, 2004. Mem. U.S. Adv. Commn. Info., 1962—64, Pres.'s Jud. Nominating Commn., 1978—79, Nat. Commn. Electoral Reform, 2001—02. Recipient Elijah Parish Lovejoy award, Colby Coll., 1996; Nieman fellow, Harvard U. Mem.: American Soc. Newspaper Editors (bd. dirs., pres. 1988—89), Sigma Delta Chi. Democrat. Roman Catholic. Home: Nashville, Tenn. Died July 11, 2014.

**SEILACHER, DOLF (ADOLF SEILACHER),** paleontologist; b. Stuttgart, Germany, Feb. 24, 1925; came to U.S., 1987; s. Adolf and Frida (Pfitzer) S.; m. Edith Drexler, July 20, 1957; children: Ulrike, Peter. PhD, U. Tübingen (Germany), 1951. Asst. prof. Tübingen U., 1951-57; docent Frankfurt (Germany) U., 1957-59; lectr. Baghdad (Iraq) U., 1959-61; prof. Göttingen (Germany) U., 1961-64, Tübingen U., 1964-90; adj. prof. geology & geophysics Yale U., New Haven, 1987—2014. Mem. adv. bd. Senckenberg Mus., Frankfurt, Naturkunde Mus., Berlin. Editor Neues Jahr Geol. Paleontol., Stuttgart With German Navy, 1943-45. Recipient Crafoord prize in Geosciences, Royal Swedish Acad. Sciences, Stockholm, 1992. Fellow AAAS; mem. Acad. Sciences Heidelberg, Geol. Soc. London (hon.), Royal Phys. Soc. Lund (hon.), Paleontological Assn. (Lapworth medal, 2006). Avocation: ballroom dancing. Home: Tübingen, Germany. Died Apr. 26, 2014.

**SEKIMOTO, MAYAKO,** English literature educator; b. Tokyo, Jan. 15, 1930; d. Kanzo and Misao (Tusumura) Mori; m. Tadahiro Sekimoto, Apr. 16, 1956; children: Masakazu, Sumito, Misako. Student, Tusda Coll., Tokyo, 1950; BA, Waseda U., Tokyo, 1953; MA, Tokyo U., 1956. Lectr. Seijo U., Tokyo, 1959-65, assoc. prof., 1965-74, prof. English lit., 1974-2000, prof. emeritus, from 2000. Author: The Duchess of Malfi: Study of J. Webster, 1965; contbr. articles to lit. publs. Mem. English Lit. Soc. Japan, Malone Soc. Avocations: travel, reading books, playing and listening to music, attending plays. Home: Tokyo, Japan. Died Feb. 12, 2007.

**SELDES, MARIAN,** actress; b. NYC, Aug. 23, 1928; d. Gilbert and Alice (Hall) S.; m. Julian Claman, Nov. 3, 1953 (div.); 1 child, Katharine; m. Garson Kanin, June 19, 1990 (dec. Mar. 1999). Grad., The Dalton Sch., NYC, 1945, Neighborhood Playhouse, 1947; DHL, Emerson Coll., 1979; DFA (hon.), Juilliard Sch., 2003. Faculty drama and dance divsn. Juilliard Sch. Lincoln Ctr., NYC, 1969-91; adj. faculty drama dept. Fordham U., 2003, 2005. Appeared with Cambridge (Mass.) Summer Theatre, 1945, Boston Summer Theatre, 1946, St. Michael's Playhouse, Winooski, Vt., 1947-48, Bermudiana Theatre, Hamilton, Bermuda, 1951, Elitch Gardens Theatre, Denver, 1953, The Cretan Woman, Lysistrata, 1955 (actress/artist-in residence Stanford U.), The Flowering Peach, L.A., 1956, Witness for the Prosecution, The Players' Ring, L.A., 1957; Broadway appearances include Medea, 1947, Crime and Punishment, 1948, That Lady, 1949, Tower Beyond Tragedy, 1950, The High Ground, 1951, Come of Age, 1952, Ondine, 1954, The Chalk Garden, 1955, The Wall, 1960, A Gift of Time, 1962, The Milk Train Doesn't Stop Here Any More, 1964, Tiny Alice, 1965, A Delicate Balance, 1967 (Tony award for best supporting actress), Before You Go, 1968, Father's Day, 1971 (Drama Desk award, Tony nomination), Mendicants of Evening (Martha Graham Co.), 1973, Equus, 1974-77, The Merchant, 1977, Deathtrap, 1978 (Tony nomination), Ivanov (Drama Desk nomination), 1997, Ring Round the Moon, 1999 (Tony nomination), 45 Seconds from Broadway, 2001 Dinner At Eight, 2003 (Tony nomination), Deuce, 2007; off-Broadway appearances include Diff'rent, 1961, The Ginger Man, 1963 (Obie award), All Women Are One, 1964, Juana LaLoca, 1965, Three Sisters, 1969, Am. Shakespeare Festival, Stratford, Conn., Mercy Street at Am. Place Theater, N.Y.C., 1969, Isadora Duncan, 1976 (Obie award), Other People, Berkshire Theatre Festival, 1969, The Celebration, Hedgerow Theater, Pa., 1971, Richard III, N.Y. Shakespeare Festival, 1983, Remember Me, Lakewood Theatre, Skowhegan, Maine, Painting Churches, 1983, 84 (Outer Critics Circle award 1984), Gertrude Stein and a Companion, White Barn Theatre, Westport, Conn., 1985, Lucille Lortel Theatre, N.Y.C., 1986, Richard II, N.Y. Shakespeare Festival, 1987, The Milk Train Doesn't Stop Here Anymore, WPA Theatre, N.Y.C., 1987, Happy Ending, Bristol (Pa.) Riverside Theatre, 1988, Annie 2 John F. Kennedy Ctr., Washington, 1989-90, Goodspeed Opera House, Chester, Conn., 1990, A Bright Room Called Day, N.Y. Shakespeare Festival, 1991, Three Tall Women, River Arts, Woodstock, N.Y., 1994, Another Time, Am. Jewish Theatre, 1993, Breaking the Code, Berkshire Theatre Festival, 1993, Three Tall Women, Vineyard Theatre, N.Y.C., 1994, Promenade Theatre, 1994-95, nat. tour, 1995-96, Boys From Syracuse, City Ctr., N.Y.C., 1997, Dead End: Williamstown, 1997, Dear Liar, Irish Repertory Theater, 1999, The Matchmaker: Williamstown, 1998, Tongue of a Bird, Mark Taper Forum, 1998, Sail Away, Carnegie Hall, 1999, Mad About The Boy, Carnegie Hall, 1999, The Torch-Bearers, 2000, Ancestral Voices, 2000, The Skin of our Teeth, 2000, Williamstown, The Play About the Baby, Alley Theatre, Houston, 2000, The Butterfly Collection, Playwrights Horizons, NY, 2000, The Play About the Baby, Century Ctr. Theatre, Helen, NY Shakespeare Festival, 2001, Play Yourself, N.Y. Theater Workshop, 2002, Beckett/Albee, Century Ctr. Theatre, N.Y.C., 2003, The Royal Family Ahmanson Theatre, L.A., 2004, Dedication or the Stuff of Dreams, Primary Stages, 2005; nat. tour Three Tall Women, 1995-96, La Fille du Regiment, Met. Opera, 2008; The Torch Bearers Williamstown, 2009, film appearances include The True Story of Jesse James, 1957, The Light in the Forest, 1958, The Greatest Story Ever Told, 1965, Gertrude Stein and a Companion, 1988, In a Pig's Eye, 1988, The Gun in Betty Lou's Handbag, 1992, Tom and Huck, 1995, Digging to China, 1997, Home Alone 3, 1997, Affliction, 1997, Celebrity, 1998, The Haunting, 1999, Town and Country, 1999, Duets, 1999, Hollywood Ending, 2002, Mona Lisa Smile, 2003, (documentary) Golden Age of Broadway, 2005, (narrator documentary) Ballet Russes, 2005, August Rush, 2006, The Visitor, 2007, (voice) The Toe Tactic, 2008, Home, 2008, Suburban Girl, 2008, Miriam, 2008, Leatherheads, 2008, The Extra Man, 2010; (TV) Good and Evil, 1991, Murphy Brown, 1992, Truman, 1995, Cosby, 1996, 98, Trinity, Sex and the City, 1998, Remember WENN, 1999, The Others, 2000, If These Walls Could Talk 2, 2000, Nero Wolfe, 2001 (A&E), The Education of Max Bickford, 2002, American Masters PBS "Juilliard Documentary, 2003", Plainsong Hallmark Hall of Fame, 2004, (narrator) Tracking the Lion in Winter, 2004, Frasier, 2004, The Book of Daniel, 2005, In From the Night, 2006, Big Day, 2006, Law and Order SVU, 2006; also appearedon radio CBSMystery Theater, 1976-81, Theatre Guild on The Air; author: The Bright Lights, 1978, Time Together, 1981; appeared in soap operas One Life to Live, Guiding Light, 1998. Bd. dirs. Neighborhood Playhouse, The Acting Co., Nat. Repertory Theatre; bd. trustees Broadway Cares/Equity Fights Aids. Winner Ovation award Theater L.A. for Three Tall Women, 1996, Conn. Critics award for Three Tall Women, 1996, Theatre Hall of Fame, 1996, Players Hall of Fame, 2008; recipient Madge Kennedy/Sidney Kingsley award Dramatists Guild Fund, 2000, Obie award for sustained achievement, Lucille Lortel award for Sustained Achievement, 2003, Edwin Booth award, Players Club, 2003, Lifetime Mem. award Theatre Libr. Assn., 2003, Breukelein Inst. Gaudium award, 2003, Julliard Sch. medal svc. to arts, 2005, Drama League award sustained achievement, 2006, Dutch Treat Gold medal award, 2006, Rebekah Koht award Nat. Coun. Jewish Women, 2006, Lifetime Achievement Tony award, 2010. Mem. Players Club, Women's City Club, Century Assn. Home: New York, NY. Died Oct. 6, 2014.

**SELIGMAN, RAPHAEL DAVID,** lawyer; b. Dublin, Nov. 29, 1919; s. Ephraim and Esther (Wigoder) S.; m. Lorna Duke, Aug. 19, 1962; children: Arthur, Helene, Edgar. BA (with honors), Trinity Coll., U. Dublin, 1939, LLB (with honors), 1940, MA, 1960. Admitted solicitor Supreme Ct. of Ireland 1942; bar: Bahamas 1967, Turks ans Caicos Islands 1966, Grays Inn London, 1996, Lincolns Inn London, 1997. Practiced in Dublin, 1942-57; internat. legal cons. Nassau, Bahamas, 1957-67; stipendiary magistrate, circuit justice, 1962-67; of counsel firm Seligman, Maynard & Co., Nassau, 1971-86, Graham, Thompson & Co., 1986-96, Harry B. Sands, Lobosky, and Co., from 1996; apptd. Queen's Counsel, 1996. Hon. consul gen. of Israel in Bahamas, 1974—, Turks and Caicos Islands, 1985—. Contbr. articles to legal jours. Fellow: Inst. Dirs. (London); mem.: Internat. Bahamas Bar Assn., Kildare St. and Univ. Club (Dublin), Naval and Mil. Club (London), Royal Nassau Sailing Club, Lyford Cay Club (Bahamas), Masons (33 deg., Supreme Coun. of Israel, past dist. grand master Bahamas and Turks, Grand Lodge of Eng., mem. Mahi Shrine Miami, past provincial Grand Master of Bermuda, Grand Lodge of Ireland). Home: Nassau, The Bahamas. Died Dec. 26, 2007.

**SELLARS, CHRISTOPHER MICHAEL,** metallurgist, educator; b. Rotherham, Yorkshire, Eng., Aug. 4, 1935; s. Frank and Olive Margaret (Storey) Sellars; m. Mavis Dorothy Lemmon, Mar. 19, 1960; children: Neil Robert, Ian Anthony, Helen Barbara. B in Metallurgy, U. Sheffield, 1956, PhD, 1959, D of Metallurgy, 1982; C Mech D (hon.), U. Navarra, 1989. Tube Investments rsch. fellow U. Sheffield, England, 1959—60; metall. engr. rschr. Carnegie Inst. Tech., Pitts., 1960—62; lectr. Metallurgy U. Sheffield, 1963—74, reader, prof., 1974—88, prof. iron and steel technol., 1988—2001, prof. emeritus, from 2001. Rschr. sect. leader Broken Hill Pty Co Ltd, Clayton, Victoria, Australia, 1969—70; head Dept. Engring. Materials U. Sheffield, 1991—95, dep. dean Faculty Engring., 1993—96, dean Faculty Engring., 1996—99. Co-author: Metall. Textbook, 1989, 2003; contbr. articles to profl. jours. Recipient Charles Hatchett award, Inst. Materials U.K., 1992, Thomas medal, 1996; Fulbright scholar, 1960—62. Fellow: Nat. Acad. Engring. India, Royal Acad. Engring., Inst. Materials, Minerals and Mining U.K.; mem.: Sheffield Metall. and Engring. Assn., Materials Rsch. Soc. India (hon.), Wine Soc., Abbeydale Golf Club. Achievements include patents in field. Avocations: golf, gardening, reading. Home: Sheffield, England. Died Nov. 15, 2012.

**SELTSER, RAYMOND,** epidemiologist, educator, preventive medicine physician; b. Boston, Dec. 17, 1923; s. Israel and Hannah (Littman) S.; m. Charlotte Frances Gale, Nov. 16, 1946; children: Barry Jay, Andrew David. MD, Boston U., 1947; MPH, Johns Hopkins U., 1957. Diplomate American Bd. Preventive Medicine (trustee, sec.-treas. 1974-77), American Bd. Med. Specialties (mem. exec. com. 1976-77). Asst. chief med. info. and intelligence br. U.S. Dept. Army, 1953-56; epidemiologist divsn. internal health USPHS, 1956-57; from asst. prof. to prof. epidemiology Johns Hopkins U. Sch. Hygiene & Public Health, Balt., 1957-81, assoc. dean, 1967-77, dep. dir. Oncology Ctr., 1977-81; dean U. Pitts. Grad. Sch. Public Health, 1981-87, prof. epidemiology, 1981-88, emeritus dean, emeritus prof. epidemiology, 1988—2014; assoc. dir. USPHS Centers for Disease Control, Rockville, Md., 1988-90; assoc. dir. Ctr. for Gen. Health Svcs. Extramural Rsch. Agy. for Health Care Policy and Rsch., Rockville, 1990-95, sr. advisor spl. population rsch. Ctr. Primary Care Rsch., 1995-98; med. and healthcare advisor Dept. Va Office Inspector Gen. Office Health Care Inspections, Chevy Chase, Md., 1997—2000. Cons. NIMH, 1958-70, also various govtl. health agys., 1958-79; expert cons. Pres.'s Commn. on Three Mile Island, 1979-80; mem. Three Mile Island Adv. Panel Health, Nat. Cancer Inst. Cancer Control Grant Rev. Com., Pa. Dept. Health Preventive Health Service Block Grant Adv. Task Force, Gov.'s VietNam Herbicide Info. Commn. Pa.; chmn. Toxic/Health Effects Adv. Com., 1985-87. Trustee, exec. com., chmn. profl. adv. com. Harmarville Rehab. Ctr., Pitts., 1982-87; bd. dirs. Health Edn. Ctr., Media Info. Svc.; chmn. USPHS Task Force on Improving Med. Criteria for SSA Disability Determination, 1988-92. Capt. AUS, 1951-53, Korea Decorated Bronze Star; recipient Centennial Alumni citation Boston U. Sch. Medicine, 1973; elected to Johns Hopkins Soc. of Scholars, 1986. Fellow AAAS, APHA (mem. governing coun. 1975-77, chmn. EPI sect. coun. 1979-80), Pa. Public Health Assn. (bd. dirs. 1985-88, pres.-elect 1986-88), American Coll. Preventive Medicine, American Heart Assn.; mem. American Epidemiol. Assn., Internat. Epidemiol. Assn., American Soc. Preventive Oncology, American Cancer Soc. (bd. dirs. Pa. divsn. 1985-87, exec. com. 1986-87), Assn. Schs. Public Health (sec. 1969-71, exec. com., chmn. edn. com. 1983-87), Soc. Med. Cons. Armed Forces, Soc. Epidemiologic Rsch., Nat. Coun. Radiation Protection and Measurements (consociate), Johns Hopkins Alumni Coun. (exec. com. 1994-97), Sigma Xi, Delta Omega. Died Feb. 16, 2014.

**SELUB, CLARICE,** pyschotherapy consultant; b. Bklyn. d. Julius and Sophie (Cohn) S. MSW, U. Pa., 1951. Lic. clin. social worker. Casework supr./intake supr., cons. Bklyn. Bur. Community Svc., 1951-78; psychotherapy cons., group therapist family and individual counseling Bridgehampton, N.Y., from 1971. Vol. Pianofest, Southampton, N.Y., 1990—, Migrant Farm Workers Lunch Prog., Bridgehampton, 1990—; mem. Group for South Fork, Bridgehampton, 1985—; vol. Friends of the Hampton Libr., 1985—. Mem. NASW. Avocations: painting, piano, volunter work. Deceased.

**SEMPLE, GOLDIE (MARIGOLD ANN KENNEDY),** actress; b. Vancouver, BC, Can., Dec. 11, 1952; d. Archibald Livingstone and Mary Calvert (Plewes) S.; m. Lorne Thomas Kennedy, Apr. 1, 1976. Student, U. B.C., 1970-73, Brighton U., Eng., 1975-77. With resident acting co. Manitoba (Can.) Theatre Centre, 1980-84; mem. Shaw Festival Co., 1981-85; actress Stratford, Ont. Appeared in plays including MacBeth, The Winters Tale, Titus Andronicus, Love for Love, Cat on a Hot Tin Roof, The Comedy of Errors, The Relapse, Richard III, Taming of the Shrew, The Three Musketeers, Othello, The Boys from Syracuse, Blithe Spirit, The Man Who Came to Dinner, Doc, Heartbreak House, Cavalcade, Candida, Camille; actress, asst. dir. Troilus and Cressida; worked with Arts Club Theatre, Bastion Theatre, City Stage, Belfry Theatre, Royal Alexandra Theatre, Stratford Shakespearian Festival, 1980, 86-91. Mem. Can. Actors Equity, Assn. Can. TV and Radio Artists. Avocation: dressage riding. Home: Toronto, Canada. Died Dec. 9, 2009.

**SEMPLE, LORENZO ELLIOTT, JR.,** screenwriter; b. New Rochelle, NY, Mar. 27, 1923; m. Joyce Miller, 1963; 3 children. Screenwriter: (films) Fathom, 1967, Pretty Poison, 1968, (with Larry Cohen) Daddy's Gone A-Hunting, 1969; The Sporting Club, 1970, The Marriage of a Young Stockbroker, 1971, (with Dalton Trumbo) Papillon, 1973; Super Cops, 1974, (with David Giler) The Parallax View, 1974, (with Tracy Keenan Wynn and Walter Hill) The Drowning Pool, 1975, (with David Rayfiel) Three Days of the Condor, 1975; King Kong, 1976, Hurricane, 1979, Flash Gordon, 1980, Never Say Never Again, 1983, Sheena, 1984, (TV series) Batman, 1966, (TV movie) Rearview Mirror, 1984. Mem. Writers Guild America Died Mar. 28, 2014.

**SENGUPTA, BARUN,** publishing executive, editor-in-chief; b. Kolkata, India, Jan. 23, 1934; With Ananda Bazar Patrika, Kolkata, 1960—84; founder, pres. Bartaman Pvt. Ltd., Kolkata; founder, editor, pub. Bartaman Patrika, Kolkata, 1984—2008; pub. Saptahik Bartaman, Sukhi Grihokon. Died June 19, 2008.

**SEN-GUPTA, NANDA DULAL,** retired atomic science researcher; b. Rangpur, India, Apr. 30, 1918; s. Shyam Lal and Amiya Bala (Das-Gupta) S-G.; m. Latika Sen-Gupta; June 4, 1958. BSc in Physics with honors, U. Rangpur, India, 1938; MSc in Physics, Calcutta U., India, 1940. Rsch. scholar Calcutta U., 1941-45, rsch. assoc., 1945-47; prof. physics Ruia Coll., 1949-62; vis. mem. Tata Inst. Fundamental Rsch., Bombay, 1962-64, emeritus scientist, from 1978; sci. officer Bhabha Atomic Rsch. Ctr., 1964-78. Contbr. over 100 articles to profl. jours; reviewer jours. in field. Mem. Calcutta Math. Soc. (life, past pres.), Indian Assn. for Cultivation of Sci., Indian Sci. Congress, Sci. Soc. of Bengal, Internat. Assn. Math & Physics (founder), Am. Math. Soc. Home: Vashi, India. Died Apr. 1, 2003.

**SENNETT, MACK,** producer, director; b. Danville, Quebec, Can., 1880; Founder Keystone Studio, later Triangle Film Corp., 1912; prin. Mack Sennett Comedies, 1917-23. Prodr., dir. more than 1000 silent films and several dozen sound films including: Tillie's Punctured Romance, 1914, Mickey, 1919, Young Oldfield, At First Sight, Long Live the King, Stone Goods, Ten Minute Egg, Rent Jumpers, A Lucky Leap, His Wooden Wedding, Be Your Age, Gussle the Golfer, Gussle's Day of Rest, Gussle Tied to Trouble, Gussle's Backward Way, Ambrose, Ambrose's Lofty Perch, Ambrose's Fury, Willful Ambrose, Those Bitter Sweets, many others. Died 1960.

**SESSLER, ANDREW MARIENHOFF,** physicist; b. Bklyn., Dec. 11, 1928; s. David and Mary (Baron) S.; m. Gladys Lerner, Sept. 23, 1951 (div. Dec. 1994); children: Daniel Ira, Jonathan Lawrence, Ruth. BA in Math. cum laude, Harvard U., 1949; MA in Theoretical Physics, Columbia U., 1951, PhD in Theoretical Physics, 1953. NSF fellow Cornell U., Ithaca, NY, 1953—54; asst. prof. Ohio State U., Columbus, 1954, assoc. prof., 1960; on leave Midwestern Unversities Rsch., 1955—56; vis. physicist Lawrence Radiation Lab., 1959—60; vis. physicist, summer Niels Bohr Inst., Copenhagen, 1961; rschr. theoretical physics U. Calif. Lawrence Berkeley Lab., Berkeley, 1961—73, rschr. energy & environment, 1971—73, dir., 1973—80, sr. scientist plasma physics, 1980—94, Disting. sr. staff scientist, 1994—2001, Disting. vis. scientist, 2001—02, Disting. scientist, 2002—14, dir. emeritus, 2002—14. U.S. advisor Panjab U. Physics Inst., Chandigarh, India; mem. U.S.-India Coop. Program for Improvement Sci. Edn. in India, 1966, high energy physics adv. panel to U.S. AEC, 1969-72, adv. com. Lawrence Hall Sci., 1974-78; chmn. Stanford Synchrotron Radiation Project Sci. Policy Bd., 1974-77, EPRI Advanced Fuels Adv. Com., 1978-81, BNL External Advisory Com. on Isabelle, 1980-82; mem. sci. pol. bd. Stanford Synchrotron Radiation Lab., 1991-92; L.J. Haworth dist. scientist Brookhaven Nat. Lab., 1991-92; spokesperson Neutrino Factory and Muon Collider Collaboration, 1999-2002, assoc. spokesperson 2002-14. Mem. editl. bd. Nuc. Instruments and Methods, 1969—2000, correspondent Comments on Modern Physics, 1969—71; contbr. articles to profl. jours.; co-author: The Development of Colliders, 1995, Engines of Discovery: A Century of Particle Accelerators, 2007, Innovation was not Enough, 2010. Mem. Superconducting Super Collider Sci. Policy Com., 1991—93; co-leader nuc. review Jsinghua U. Recipient E.O. Lawrence award US Atomic Energy Commn., 1970, US Particle Accelerator Sch. prize, 1988, Dwight Nicholson Medal for Humanitarian Svc. American Physical Soc., 1994, Robert R. Wilson prize 1997, Enriico Fermi award Italian Physical Soc., 2013; fellow Japan Soc. for Promotion Sci. at KEK, 1985. Fellow AAAS (nominating com. 1984-87), American Phys. Soc. (chmn. com. internat. freedom scientist 1982, study of directed energy weapons panel 1985-87, chmn. panel pub. affairs 1988, chmn. divsn. physics of beams 1990, chmn. com. applications of physics 1993, councilor for divsn. physics of beams 1994-97, pres.-elect 1997, pres. 1998, past pres. 1999, vice-chmn. forum on physics and soc. 2001, chmn.-elect 2002, chmn. 2003), N.Y. Acad. Sci.; mem. NAS (bd. on radiation effects rsch. 2002-05, nuclear radiation studies bd., 2005-08, Plasmasci. Com., 2010-14), NAS Naval Studies Bd., IEEE (sr.), Fedn. American Scientists Coun. (vice chmn. 1987-88, chmn. 1988-92), Assoc. Univ. Inc. (bd. dirs. 1991-98), Sigma Xi. Avocations: exercise, flute, walking. Home: Oakland, Calif. Died Apr. 18, 2014.

**SETLIFF, DEBORAH ANN WINSTON,** former legislative staff member; b. 1962; m. Jonathan Setliff, 2001. Reporter News Herald, Ohio; reporter, columnist Cleve. Plain Dealer, 1990—95; press sec., comm. dir. to Rep. Steven C. LaTourette US House of Reps., Washington, 1995—2012. Republican. Died Feb. 5, 2014.

**SEYBERT, RITA M.,** nursing administrator, nursing educator; b. Freeland, Pa., June 27, 1930; d. Ralph J. and Madeline (Grego) Pecora; m. Robert J. Seybert, Oct. 26, 1951; 1 child, Beverly. Grad., Hazleton State Gen. Hosp., Hazleton, Pa., 1951; BSEd, Bloomsburg U., 1965; MEd, Pa. State U., 1980. Indsl. nurse Milco Industries, Inc., Bloomsburg, The Magee Carpet Co., Bloomsburg; asst. dir. nursing practical nursing program Danville (Pa.) Area Sch. Dist., asst. dir., nursing practical nursing instr. Recipient Woman of Yr. award Bloomsburg Bus. and Profl. Women's Club. Mem. Nat. League for Nursing (accreditation visitor), ANA (trea. Pa. dist. 27), Pa. Assn. Coords. of Practical Nursing (sec.), Susquehanna Valley Div. of Cen. Pa. Lung and Health Assn. (adv. bd.). Home: Bloomsburg, Pa. Died July 15, 1990.

**SHA, REIN See SIR SHAW, RUN RUN**

**SHABEN, LAWRENCE,** government official; b. Mar. 20, 1935; s. Albert Mohammed and Lila (Kazeil) Shaben; m. Alma Amina Saddy, July 8, 1960; children: Linda, Carol, Larry, James, Joan. Student, U. Alta., 1954—55. Real estate agt. Lawrence Agys., Alta., 1962—66; dept. mgr. Sears Can. Ltd., Alta., 1966—67, retail mcht., 1967—78. Pvt. cons. Shaben World Enterprise Inc.; pres. Lawrence Devel. Ltd., High Prairie, Alta., Shaben Stores Ltd., High Prairie Housing Assn.; min. Econ. Devel. and Trade, Alta. Mem. High Prairie Town Coun., 1969—74, High Prairie Recreation Bd., 1969—74; pres. Lesser Slave Lake Progressive Conservative Assn., 1969—74; v.p. Peace Tourist Assn., 1970—72, bd. dirs.; pres. High Prairie Minor Hockey Assn., 1973—74; mem. legis. assembly Lesser Slave Lake dist. Govt. Alta., Edmonton, 1975—89, min. utilities, 1979—82, min. housing, 1982—89. Mem.: Lodges: Kiwanis, Northgate, Alta. (bd. dirs. 1965—66), Lions, Elks, Optimists (sec. local club 1967—71). Muslim. Home: High Prairie, Canada. Died Sept. 7, 2008.

**SHAH, JASHWANT CHIMANLAL,** solicitor; b. Malwan, India, June 20, 1932; s. Chimanlal and Vimala S.; m. Jyotsna Chimanlal; children: Deepika, Paresh, Kalpana, Kavita. BSc, Jai Hind Coll., Bombay, India, 1955; LLB, Law Coll. Bombay, 1961. Asst. Amin Desai, Bombay, 1961-63; ptnr. Rustomji & yinwala, Bombay, 1963-66; sr. ptnr. Shah & Sanghavi, Bombay, from 1966. Avocations: golf, music, reading, travel, drama. Home: Bombay, India. Died May 9, 2008.

**SHALTIEL, SHMUEL,** biochemist, researcher, educator; b. Thessaloniki, Greece, Jan. 12, 1935; s. Sabetay and Renée (Bourla) S.; m. Sarah Mass, May 10, 1956 (dec. July 1997); children: Orna, Ruth. MSc, Hebrew U., Jerusalem, 1960; PhD, Weizmann Inst., Rehovot, Israel, 1964. Rsch. assoc. U. Wash., Seattle, 1964-66; mem. faculty Weizmann Inst. Sci., 1964—2002, prof., 1975—2002, head chem. immunology dept., 1992-95, founder, head biol. reg. dept., 1995-2000. Dep. pres., acting pres. Weizmann Inst., 1985-88, bd. govs., 1988-2002, dean Feinberg Grad. Sch., Rehovot, 1978-84, chmn. sci. coun., 1976-77; mem. planning and budgeting com. Israeli Coun. for Higher Edn., Jerusalem, 1992-98; vis. prof. U. Calif., Berkeley, 1972-73, ETH, Zurich, Switzerland, 1992; Fogarty scholar-in-residence NIH, Bethesda, Md., 1981-83, 99. Co-author: New Horizons in Science, 1974; editor: Metabolic Interconversion of Enzymes, 1976; co-editor: Current Topics in Cellular Regulation: Modulation by Covalent Modification, 1985; author: The Biochemical Revolution in Medicine, 2001; inventor hydrophobic chromatography; co-editor sci. column Haaretz Daily, Israel, 1963-78; mem. adv. bd. European Jour. Biochemistry, 1974-80; mem. editl. bd. Analytical Chemistry, U.S., 1980-90, Archives of Biochemistry and Biophysics, 1995-1999; editor FEBS letters, 1989-2001. Chmn. bd. dirs. U.S.-Israel Ednl. Found., 1975-78; mem. Nat. Coun. for Higher Edn., Jerusalem, 1978-81; mem. sci. adv. panel Novartis (Ciba) Found., London, 1990-2001. With Israel Def. Forces, 1958-60. Fulbright grantee U.S.-Israel Edn. Found., 1964; Brainin fellow Weizmann Inst. Sci., 1968; recipient Landau prize in natural scis. Mifal Hapayis, 1980, Biochem. analysis prize German Soc. Clin. Chemistry, 1978, Weizmann prize in the exact scis. Tel Aviv Municipality, 1984, biology prize Rothschild Found., 1994. Mem. Israel Biochem. Soc. (Shlomo Hestrin prize 1971), Am. Biochem. Soc., Spanish Biochem. Soc., Israel Immunol. Soc., German Soc. Clin. Chemistry, European Molecular Biol. Orgn., Am. Soc. Biochem. and Molecular Biology (hon.). Home: Rehovot, Israel. Died Apr. 4, 2002.

**SHANE, RITA,** opera singer, educator; b. Bronx, Aug. 15, 1936; d. Julius J. and Rebekah (Milner) S.; m. Daniel F. Tritter, June 22, 1958 (div.); 1 child, Michael Shane. BA, Barnard Coll., 1958; postgrad., Santa Fe Opera Apprentice Program, 1962-63, Hunter Opera Assn., 1962-64; pvt. study with, Beverly Peck Johnson. Adj. prof. voice Manhattan Sch. Music, 1993-95. Prof. voice Eastman Sch. Music Rochester U., 1989—2014, Hamamatsu, Japan, 2000—02; judge Richard Tucker Music Found., Met. Opera Regional Auditions, Licia Albanese Puccini Found. Performer with numerous opera cos., including profl. debut, Chattanooga Opera, 1964, Met. Opera, San Diego Opera, Santa Fe Opera, Teatro alla Scala, Milan, Italy, Bavarian State Opera, Netherlands Nat. Opera, Geneva Opera, Vienna State Opera, Phila., New Orleans, Balt. Opera, Opera du Rhin, Strasbourg, Scottish Opera, Teatro Reggio, Turin, Opera Metropolitana, Caracas, Portland Opera, Minn. Opera, also others; world premiere Miss Havisham's Fire, Argento; American premieres include Reimann-Lear, Schat-Houdini, Henze-Elegy for Young Lovers; participant festivals, including Mozart Festival, Lincoln Center, N.Y.C., Munich Festival, Aspen Festival, Handel Soc., Vienna Festival, Salzburg Festival, Munich Festival, Perugia Festival, Festival Canada, Glyndebourne Festival, performed with orchs. including Santa Cecilia, Rome, Austrian Radio, London Philharmn., Louisville, Cin., Cleve., Phila., RAI, Naples, Denver, Milw., Israel Philharm., rec. artist, RCA, Columbia, Louisville, Turnabout, Myto labels, also radio and TV. Recipient Martha Baird Rockefeller award, William Matheus Sullivan award. Mem. American Guild Mus. Artists, Screen Actors Guild, Nat. Assn. Teachers Singing. Died Oct. 9, 2014.

**SHANER, BRONWYN MARIAN,** elementary school educator; b. Buffalo, Aug. 12, 1937; d. Warren Eugene and Myfanwy Rosetta (Murray) Boone; m. Byrns William Long, Mar. 4, 1961 (dec. Sept. 1983); 1 child, Karen Anne Long Clark; m. Richard Leroy Shaner, Mar. 30, 1991. BS in Edn., SUNY, Buffalo, 1960, MS in Edn., 1989. Cert. tchr., N.Y. Tchr. art Brittonkill Ctrl., Troy, N.Y., 1960-61; tchr. spl. and elem. edn. Buffalo Pub. Schs., 1961-66, tchr. elem., 1990—2001; ret., 1999. Dir. advt. Cayuga Mfg. Corp., Blasdell, N.Y., 1981-83. Actress, costume designer, stage hand East Aurora Children's Theater, 1971-74. Bd. dirs. LWV, Kenmore, East Aurora and Clarence, N.Y., 1967-90; bd. deacons 1st Presbyn. Ch., Clarence, 1991-93. Mem. DAR, NEA. Republican. Avocations: reading, cooking, sailing. Home: Clarence, NY. Died Aug. 10, 2001.

**SHANTHI, GOVINDASWAMY,** electronics engineer, educator; b. Coimbatore, Tamil Nadu, India, Oct. 28, 1966; d. Rengaswami Govindaswami and Lakshmaiah Dhanabagyam; m. Murugesh Rengaswami, Sept. 9, 1994; 1 child, Murugesh Arjhun. B Engring, Bharathiar U., 1988; M Engring., Govt. Coll. Tech., Coimbatore, 1992. Lectr. Kumaraguru Coll. Tech., Coimbatore, 1992—98, Amrita Inst. Tech. and Sci., Coimbatore, 1999—2001, PSG Coll. of Tech., Coimbatore, from 2001. Contbr. articles to profl. jours. Mem.: Inst. Electronic and Telecomm. Engrs. (assoc.), Assn. Computing Machinery (life), Inst. Engrs. (life). Achievements include research in Development of Novel Scheduling algorithms for Packet Switches for the next generartion Internet. Home: Coimbatore, India. Died Oct. 27, 2006.

**SHAPIRO, JACK,** public relations executive; b. Salinas, Dec. 6, 1924; s. Morris and Rebecca (Kuperman) Shapiro; m. Loretta Lowell, Oct. 11, 1946 (dec.); m. Jeannette Pearson, June 4, 1955; children: Karen Lynn Shepherd, David Douglas, Victor Morris. Student, Hartnell Coll., 1946—47, LA City Coll., 1948—49. Dir. Sta. KFI-TV, LA, 1949—50; v.p. Inter-Mountain Network, Salt Lake City, 1956—59; mgr. LA office Forjoe Co., 1960—62; founder, pres. Shapiro Advt. and Pub. Rels., Salt Lake City, 1963; semi-ret. Mem. Days of '47 Parade Com., 1965—67; mem. adv. bd. Salvation Army, Salt Lake City Police Dept. hon. Cols.; mem. steering com. Taxpayers for Accountable Govt.; mem. exec. com. Utah Rep. Com., 1971—73, Ctr. Com., 1971—73; chmn. Recreation Vehicle Adv. Coun., 1973—83; lectr. Brigham Young U., 1979, U. Utah, 1981; chmn. 1st Ann. Intermountain Pub. Rels. Seminar, 1980; importer, distbr. Myford High Precision Metal Turning Lathes, 1986. Served with US Army, 1943—45, PTO, Korea, served with US Army, 1950—51, PTO, Korea. Mem.: Masons, Shriners (editor Minaret 1977—85), Utah Westerners Club, Holladay Gun Club, Utah Assn. Advt. Agys. (pres. local chpt. 1976—77), World Media Conf., Pub. Rels. Soc. America (pres. local chpt. 1979). Died Feb. 17, 1998.

**SHARIF-EMAMI, JAFAR,** former Prime Minister of Iran; b. Tehran, Iran, Sept. 8, 1910; s. Haji Mohammad Hossein and Banu (Kobra) Sharif-E.; m. Eshrat Moazzami, Nov. 16, 1946; children: Shirin, Simin, Ali. Student, Reichsbahn Zentralschule, Brandenburg, Germany, Statens Tekniskaskolan, Boras, Sweden; Dr.H.C., Seoul U., 1978; diploma in computer programming, Internat. Corr. Sch., 1990. Joined Iranian State Rys., 1931, tech. dep. gen. dir., 1942-46; chmn., mng. dir. Ind. Irrigation Corp., 1946-50, gen. dir., 1950-51; undersec. to Minister Roads and Communications, 1950-51, minister roads and communications, 1951; mem. Senate of Iran from Tehran, 1955-57, 63—, pres. senate house, 1963-78; pres. 3d Constituent Assembly, 1967; min. industries & mines Govt. of Iran, 1957-60, prime min. Tehran, 1960—61, 1978; dep. custodian Pahlavi Found., 1962-78; pres. chamber of industries and mines, 1962-67; chmn. bd. Indsl. and Mining Devel. Bank, 1963-78. Mem. high council Plan Orgn., 1951-52, mng. dir., chmn. high council, 1953-54; pres. 22d Internat. Conf. Red Cross, 1973; bd. dirs. Royal Orgn. Social Services, 1962-78; trustee Pahlavi U., Shiraz, 1962-78, Nat. U., Tehran, 1962-78, Aria Mehr Tech. U., 1965-78, Queen Pahlavi's Found., 1966-78; bd. founders Soc. Preservation Nat. Monuments, 1966-78. Decorated 1st grade Order Taj, Iran; decorated 3d and 1st grade Order Homayoon, Iran, 1st grade Order Social Services, Iran, 1st grade Order Land Reform, Iran, 1st grade Order Labour, Iran, 1st grade Order Cooperative, Iran, 1st grade Order Coronation, Iran, 1st grade Order 25th Shahrivar, Iran, 1st grade Order of Celebration 2500th Anniversary Founding of Persian Empire by Cyrus the Great, Iran, chevalier de Grand Croix Italy, das Gross-Kreuz Verdienstorden Germany, grand officer Legion of Honor, France, grand cross Legion of Honor, France, Stora Korset av Kingl. Nordstjarneoden Sweden, grand cross Order de la Courone, Belgium, grand cordon Order Leopold, Belgium, Das Grosse Golden Ehrenzelchen am Bande Austria, Order St. Michael and St. George U.K., Order Sacred Treasure 1st grade Japan, Order of Rising Sun 1st grade Japan, Tudor Vladimirescu 1st grade Romania, knight grand cross Most Exalted Order of White Elephant 1st grade, Thailand, Alesteghlal 1st grade Tunisia, Den Kgl. Norske St. Olavs Orden 1st grade Norway, Order of Danbrok 1st grade Denmark, Order Al-Arsh 1st grade Morocco, Order Jugoslovenske Zvenzde Za Lentom Yugoslavia, Krzyz Wielki Order Odrodzenia Polski Poland, Di-Peliharakan Allah Panckuan Necara Malaysia, grand condon Order Menelik Second, Ethiopia, Order of Banner of Hungarian Peoples Republic 1st grade, Ghaede Azam Pakistan, 1st grade Veshahol Malek Abdol-Aziz Saudi Arabia, Order Nile 1st grade Egypt, Grand Croix Ordre du Merite Senegal, Esteghlal Qatar Fellow ASCE; mem. Red Lion and Sun (dir 1963, dep. chmn. 1966-78), Internat. Bankers Assn. (pres. 1975), Iranian Engrs. Assn. (pres. 1966-78) Died June 16, 1998.

**SHARIFY, NASSER,** librarian, educator, writer; b. Tehran, Iran, Sept. 23, 1925; came to U.S., 1953, naturalized, 1972; s. Ebrahim and Eshrat (Saghafy) S.; m. Homayoun Taslimy, June 14, 1950 (div. 1978); children: Sharareh, Shahab. Licencie es Lettres, U. Tehran, 1947; MS, Columbia U., 1954, Dr. L.S., 1958. Editorial staff Teheran jours. Rah-e Now, Jahan-e Now, Saba, Jonb va Jush, 1943-51; translator, announcer All India Radio, 1948-49; librarian, dep. dir. Library of Parliament Iran, Tehran, 1949-53; cataloger Library of Congress, 1954-55; program asst. libraries devel.

sect. UNESCO, Paris, 1959-61; acting chief servicing sect. Dept. Edn., 1962-63; dir. gen. Ministry Edn., Tehran, 1961-62; asst. prof. library and info. scis. and internat. edn. U. Pitts., 1963-66; founder, dir. Internat. Library Info. Center, 1964-66; vis. lectr. SUNY Albany Sch. Library Sci., summer, 1966; dir. internat. librarianship and documentation, internat studies and world affairs SUNY, Oyster Bay, 1966-68; dean, prof. grad. sch. library and info sci. Pratt Inst., Bklyn., 1968-87, chmn. inst. research council, 1971-89, disting. prof., dean emeritus sch. computer, info. and library scis., from 1987; pres. B.E.L.T., Inc., internat. planning cons., from 1981. Dir. Grad. Library Tng. Program, UNESCO Mission, Nat. Tchrs. Coll., Tehran, 1960; Iran's Ofcl. del. to UNESCO Conf. Ednl. Pubs., Geneva, 1961, SE Asia Edn. Secs. Conf., Murree, Pakistan, 1961, Internation Conf., on Cataloging Prins., Paris, 1961, CENTO Libr. Devel. Conf., Ankara, Turkey, 1962; chmn. standing com. for preparation reading materials for new literates UNESCO, Tehran, 1961-62; mem. U.S. AID Mission, Turkey, Iran, Pakistan, 1966; dir. Conf. on Internat. Responsibility Coll. and Univ. Librarians, Oyster Bay, 1967; U.S. del. 33d Conf. and Internat. Congress on Documentation, Tokyo, 1967; ALA del. UN Conf. on Non-Govtl. Orgn., 1969; cons. U.S. AID, Conf. on Book Devel., 1967; mem. adv. bd. Ency. Libr. and Info. Scis., 1969—; chmn. Pre-Am. Library Assn. Conf. Inst. on Internat. Libr. Manpower, Edn. and Placement in N.Am., Detroit, 1970; mem. Am. del. Internat. Fedn. Libr. Assn. Conf., Liverpool, Eng., 1971, Budapest, 1972, Grenoble, France, 1973, Washington, 1974, Brussels, 1977, Montreal, 1982, Chgo., 1985, Barcelona, 1992; organzier USAID sponsored Global Info. Village Conf., Rabat, Morocco, Bklyn., N.Y., 1997, spkr., 1997; bldg. cons. Learning Resources Center, Nat. Tchrs. Coll., Iran, 1972-73, cons. campus planning, 1972-73; UNESCO cons. missions to plan and evaluate Nat. Sch. Info. Sci., Morocco, 1973-74, 79-81, 89, 96-; cons. U.S. Info. Agy., Morocco, 1991, 92, 95; chmn. Conf. on Orgn. and Control of Info for Islamic Research, 1982; chmn. bd. cons. to Nat. U. Iran, 1974-75, Pahlavi Nat. Library of Iran, 1975-77; speaker Symposium Internat. sur l' information Economique, Casablanca, Morocco, 1990; inaugural speaker Ctr. Documentation et D'Information Multimedia, Rabat, Morocco, 1995. Author: cataloging of Persian works Including Rules for Transliteration Entry and Description, 1959, Book Production, Importation and Distribution in Iran, Pakistan and Turkey, 1966; Beyond the National Frontiers: The International Dimension of Changing Library Education for a Changing World, 1973; The Pahlavi National Library of the Future, 17 vols., 1976, other books; contbr. to Ency. of Library and Info. Sci., 1969, ALA World Ency. Library and Info. Services, 1980, 86, library jours., 1973—, Bookmark, 1972, Library Education in the Middle East, 1991, Remembering Rangathan: A Sentimental Reflection, 1992; contbr. poetry to various jours. and anthologies, 1947-51, 67, 91-93 lyrics to Iranian motion pictures and recs., 1948-52; works on display at Archieves of Hoover Inst. on War Revolution and Peace, Stanford U.; Contbr. to: film script for motion picture Morad, 1951-52. Trustee Bklyn. Public Library, 1970-82; pres. Maurice F. Tauber Found., 1981—. Recipient Taj (crown) medal and citation for disting. svc. Mohammad Reza Shah Pahlavi, Shah of Iran, 1978, Kaula Gold medal and citation for disting. svc. to internat. librarianship, 1985; named for Annual Nasser Sharify Lecture Series, Sch. of Computer Info. and Libr. Scis., Pratt Inst., 1988—; writings by and about Nasser Sharify are preserved at Archives of Hoover Instn. on wars, revolutions and peace., Stanford U., Stanford, Calif. Mem. ALA (chmn. com. equivalencies and reciprocity 1966-71, mem. UNESCO panel, mem. nominating com. 1970-71, chmn. Pakistan, Iran, Turkey, Morocco, and Middle East Resource panels, internat. libr. edn. com. 1973—, mem. com. internat. libr. schs. div. libr. edn. 1968-72, coord. country resources panels, internat. libr. edn. com. libr. edn. div. 1973-78, Citiation extraordinary and exemplary svc. internat. librarianship 1999, John Ames Humphry OCLC Forest Press award 2004), NY Libr. Assn. (dir. library edn. sect. 1969-72), Pub. Libr. Assn. (task force on internat. relations 1981-86), Am. Assn. Libr. Schs. (chmn. govtl. relations com., 1984-88), Am. Soc. Info. Sci., Spl. Libr. Assn., Internat. Fedn. Libr. Assns. (adv. group libr. edn. 1971-73, v.p. libr. schs. sect. 1973-77). Home: Westbury, NY. *If I am asked to wash a car, I try to make it spotless. If I am to write a book, I try to make it faultless. But it seems that I always find spots on the shining surface of the car, and faults in many well-written pages of the book. This gives me another reason to live for another day.* Died Aug. 23, 2013.

**SHARIR, DAVID,** secondary education educator, playwright, director; b. Jerusalem, May 14, 1940; s. Jacob Sharir and Batia Chaana; m. Dorit Weissberg, May 30, 1966; children: Jacob, Gili. BA, Tel-Aviv U., 1968; MA, Manchester U., 1970. Tchr. Telma Yalin H.S., Tel-Aviv, 1970-80; tchr., lectr. Tel Aviv U., 1972-86; supr. Ministry of Edn., Tel Aviv, 1980-86; tchr acting studio Tel Aviv; tchr. lit. and drama Ostrovsi in Raanana H.S., Tel Aviv, from 1992. Sgt. Israeli Army, 1960-61. Internat. Theatre Inst. scholar, 1967. Avocations: reading, writing. Home: Tel Aviv, Israel. Died Dec. 2001.

**SHARMA, CHANDRA SHEKHAR,** editor, mathematics professor; b. Kishanganj, India, June 17, 1933; arrived in Eng., 1960; s. Mahendra Prasad Sinha and Chandradhana (Devi) S.; m. Margaret Anthea Grubb, Sept. 21, 1974. BSc (hons.), Sci. Coll., Patna, India, 1953; MSc, Patna Univ., 1955, MSc math., 1960; D Phil, Wadham Coll., Oxford U., Eng., 1963. Lectr. in chem. Patna Univ., 1955-60; lectr. in math. Birkbeck Coll., London, 1962-69, reader in math., 1970-79, prof. math., 1979-98. Reviewer Math. Reviews, Ann Arbor, Zentralblatt für Math., Berlin. Author: Mathematical Foundations of Non Relatinstic Quantum Theory, 1992, Mathematical Foundations of The Special Theory of Relativity, 1993, Mathematical Foundations of Elementary Mechanics, 1994, Mathematical Foundations of Electrodynamics, 1995, Mathematical Foundations of the General Theory of Relativity, 1996, Complex Analysis in Relativity, 2000; editor, pub.: Jour. Natural Geometry, 1992-2003. Recipient Imam Gold medal Patna Univ., 1953, McPherson Gold medal, 1953, Univ. Gold medal, 1955. Fellow Royal Astromonical Soc.; mem. London Math. Soc., Am. Math. Soc. Achievements include research in role of math. in modelling, particularly under uncertainty; work on math. found. of Einstein's theory of relativity. Avocations: hill walking, photography. Deceased.

**SHARMAN, BILL (WILLIAM WALTON SHARMAN),** retired professional basketball coach; b. Abilene, Tex., May 25, 1926; m. Joyce Sharman; children from previous marriage: Jerry, Nancy, Janice, Tom. Student, U. So. Calif. Guard Washington Capitols, 1950-51, Boston Celtics, 1951-61; coach LA/Utah Stars, 1968-71; head coach L.A. Lakers, 1971-76, gen. mgr., 1976-82, pres., 1982-88; spl. cons. LA Lakers, from 1991. Author: Sharman on Basketball Shooting, 1965; co-author: (with John Wooden & Bob Selzer) The Wooden-Sharman Method: A Guide to Winning Basketball, 1975 Named to All Star 1st Team, NBA, 1956-59, 2nd Team, 1953, 55 (game MVP), 60, All League Team, 7 times, named Coach of Yr., 1972, One of Top Players in NBA History, league 50th anniversary, 1997, league leader free-throw percentage, 7 times; named to Basketball Hall of Fame, 1976, Naismith Basketball Hall of Fame (as player), 2004, (as coach), 2004; named All-American, 1950; inductee U. Southern Calif. Hall of Fame, 1994; Porterville H.S. gymnasium renamed in his honor, 1997; recipient John Wooden All-Time All-American award, 2003. Died Oct. 25, 2013.

**SHARON, ARIEL,** former Prime Minister of Israel; b. Kfar Malal, nr. Tel Aviv, Israel, Feb. 27, 1928; s. Samuel Scheinerman & Vera Schneirov; m. Maraglith Zimmerman (dec. 1962), 1 child, Gur (dec. 1967); m. Lilly Zimmerman (dec. 2000), children: Omri, Gilead. Student, Hebrew U., 1952-53; LLB in Law, Hebrew U., Jerusalem, 1962; student, Staff Coll., Camberley, UK, 1957-58, Tel Aviv U., 1966. Mem. Knesset, 1973—74, 1977—2006; adv. on security affairs to Prime Min. Yitzhak Rabin Govt. Israel, 1975—76, min. agr., 1977—81, min. def., 1981—83, min. without portfolio, 1983—84, min. industry & commerce, 1984—90, min. constrn. & housing, 1990—92, min. infrastructure, 1996—99, min. fgn. affairs, 1998—99, prime min., 2001—06, min. immigrant absorption, 2001—06. Instr. Jewish Police units, 1947; platoon comdr. Alexandroni Brigade, Israeli Def. Forces; regimental intelligence officer, 1948; co-comdr., 1949; comdr. Brigade Reconnaissance unit, 1949-50; intelligence officer Cen. Command and Northern Command, 1951-52; founder, head spl. 101 unit, 1953-57; tng. comdr. Gen. Staff, 1958; comdr. Inf. Sch., 1958-69; comdr. Armoured Brigade, 1962; head staff Northern Command, 1964; head Brigade Group during Six-Day War, 1967; resigned from Israeli Army, 1973; recalled as comdr. cen. sect. of Sinai Front during Yom Kippur War, 1973; founder Shlomzion Party, 1977, merged with Herut Party faction of Likud bloc, 1977, founder, mem. Likud Party 1973-2005, chmn. 1999-2005; chmn. Likud Cen. Com.; mem., fgn. affairs & def. com., Knesset, 1992-96; founder, Kadima Party, 2005 Author: (with David Chanoff) Warrior: The Autobiography of Ariel Sharon, 1989. Named one of The 100 Most Influential People in the World, TIME mag., 2005. Died Jan. 11, 2014.

**SHARP, RICHARD L. (RICK SHARP),** retired retail company executive; b. Washington, Apr. 12, 1947; m. Sherry Sharp; 2 children. Student, U. Va., 1965-66, Coll. of William and Mary, 1968-70. Programmer Group Health Inc., Washington, 1970-75; founder, pres. Applied Systems Corp., Washington, 1975-81; with Circuit City Stores, Inc., Richmond, Va., 1982—2002, exec. v.p., 1982-84, pres., 1984-86, pres., CEO, 1986-94, chmn., pres., CEO, 1994-97, chmn., CEO, 1997-2000, chmn., 1997—2002, CarMax Inc., Glen Allen, Va., 2002—07, Flextronics Internat. Ltd., 2003—07. Bd. dirs. Flextronics Internat. Ltd., 1993-2008, CarMax Inc., 2002-12, CROCS, 2005-11, Rock Creek Pharmaceuticals, Inc., 2011 With USAF, 1967-70. Named to The Consumer Electronics Hall of Fame, 2008. Home: Henrico, Va. Died June 24, 2014.

**SHARPS, JOHN GEOFFREY,** retired psychologist, author; b. Weaverham, Northwich, Eng., July 29, 1936; s. John Richard and Nellie (Street) S.; m. Heather Acheson, Aug. 19, 1966; children: Rosalind Helen May, Paul George John. MA in English (hons.), U. Edinburgh, Scotland, 1958; MEd in Psychology, Queen's U. Belfast, Northern Ireland, 1963; MLitt in English, U. Oxford, Eng., 1964; BTh (hons.), U. Hull, Eng., 1992. Chartered psychologist, chartered ednl. psychologist. Part-time lectr. Mid-Cheshire Ctrl. Coll. Further Edn., Hartford, Cheshire, Eng., 1963-64; lectr. North Riding Coll. Edn., Scarborough, Eng., 1964-71, sr. lectr., 1971-87. Part time tchr. Scarborough Sixth Form Coll., 2003. Author: Mrs. Gaskell's Observation and Invention: A Study of Her Non-Biographic Works, 1970. Fellow: Royal Econ. Soc., Royal Geog. Soc., Royal Soc. Arts, Brit. Psychol. Soc. (assoc.). Mem. Liberal Democrat Party. Anglican. Avocations: reading, television, films, theater, book collecting. Home: Scarborough, England. Died Jan. 6, 2006.

**SHAW, DENIS MARTIN,** university dean, former geology educator; b. St. Annes, Eng., Aug. 20, 1923; emigrated to Can., 1948; s. Norman Wade and Alice Jane Sylvia (Shackleton) S.; m. Pauline Mitchell, Apr. 6, 1946 (div. 1975); children— Geoffrey, Gillian, Peter; m. Susan L. Evans, Apr. 9, 1976. BA, Emmanuel Coll., Cambridge, Eng., 1943, MA, 1948; PhD, U. Chgo., 1951. Lectr. McMaster U., Hamilton, Ont., Can., 1949-51, asst. prof., 1951-55, asso. prof., 1955-60, prof. geology, 1960-89, prof. emeritus, from 1989, chmn. dept., 1953-59, 62-66, dean grad. studies, 1978-84. Assoc. prof. Ecole nationale supérieure de géologie appliquée, U. Nancy, France, 1959-60; invited prof. Inst. de Minéralogie, U. Genève, 1966-67 Exec. editor: Geochimica et Cosmochimica Acta, 1970-88; asso. editor: Handbook of Geochemistry, 1966—; Author: Masson Et Cie, 1964. Served with RAF, 1943-46. Fellow Royal Soc. Can. (W.G. Miller medal 1981); mem. Geol. Assn. Can., Geochem. Soc., Mineral. Assn. Can. (pres. 1964, Past Pres.' medal 1985), Am. Geophys. Union, AAAS, Geol. Soc. of Am. Deceased.

**SHAW, ELIZABETH ORR,** retired lawyer; b. Monona, Iowa, Oct. 2, 1923; d. Harold Topliff and Hazel (Kean) Orr; m. Donald Hardy Shaw, Aug. 16, 1946; children: Elizabeth Ann, Andrew Hardy, Anthony Orr. AB, Drake U., 1945; postgrad., U. Minn., 1945—46; JD, U. Iowa, 1948. Bar: Ill. 1949, Iowa 1956. Assoc. Lord Bissell & Brook, Chgo., 1949-52; pvt. practice Arlington Heights, Ill., 1952-56; ptnr. Wood & Shaw, Davenport, Iowa, 1968-72; mem. Iowa House of Reps., Des Moines, 1967—73, Iowa State Senate, Des Moines, 1973—79; county atty. Scott County, Davenport, 1977-78; atty. Deere & Co., Moline, Ill., 1979-89; pvt. practice Davenport, 1990-98; ret., 1999. Mem. Scott County Bar Assn. (com. chmn. 1970-72), Iowa State Bar Assn. (chmn. family law com. 1970-76), Order of Coif, Phi Beta Kappa, Kappa Kappa Gamma, PEO. Republican. Mem. United Ch. of Christ. Home: Columbia, Md. Died July 23, 2014.

**SHAW, HAROLD (FRANCIS HAROLD SHAW),** retired performing arts association administrator; b. Hebron, NY, June 11, 1923; s. Robert and Leslie Shaw. Student, Ithaca Coll., 1942, Columbia, 1944, N.Y. U. Extension, 1948. Former assoc. Hurok Concerts, Inc., NYC; chmn., owner Shaw Concerts, Inc., NYC, 1969-99; ret., 1999; performing arts dir. Seattle World's Fair, 1961-62. Former concert mgr. Nathan Milstein, Vladimir Horowitz, Dame Janet Baker, Jessye Norman, Helen Donath, Jacqueline duPre, Wolfgang Holzmair, Jard van Nes, Mitsuko Uchida, Garrick Ohlsson, Shura Cherkassky, Horacio Gutiérrez, Julian Bream, John Williams, Elmar Oliveira, Kyoko Takezawa, Robert Shaw, Andrew Davis, and over 100 artists and attractions; exec. dir. President's Shakespeare Ann. Com., 1964. Dir. exec. staff, mem. performing arts com. Cultural Commn., N.Y.C., 1966; nat. chmn. Performing Arts Energy Commn., 1974; chmn. bd. trustees American Shakespeare Theatre, Strafford, Conn., 1974. With USAAF, 1942-43. Mem.: American Summer Stock Managers Assn. (co-founder), Actors Equity Assn., Assn. Coll., Univ. & Cmty. Arts Adminstrators, American Symphony Orch. League, Internat. Performing Arts Adminstrs., Athletic Club, Phi Mu Alpha Sinfonia. Died Jan. 28, 2014.

**SHAW, MARK HOWARD,** lawyer, business owner, entrepreneur; b. Albuquerque, Aug. 26, 1944; s. Brad Oliver and Barbara Rae (Mencke) S.; m. Ann Marie Brookreson, June 29, 1968 (div. 1976); adopted children: Daniel Paul, Kathleen Ann, Brian Andrew; m. Roslyn Jane Ashton, Oct. 9, 1976; children: Rebecca Rae, Amanda Leith. BA, U. N.Mex., 1967, JD, 1969. Bar, N.Mex. 1969. Law clk. to presiding justice N.Mex. Supreme Ct., Santa Fe, 1969-70; ptnr. Gallagher & Ruud, Albuquerque, 1970-74, Schmidt & Shaw, Albuquerque, 1974-75; sr. mem. Shaw, Thompson & Sullivan P.A., Albuquerque, 1975-82; chief exec. officer United Ch. Religious Sci. and Sci. Mind Publs., LA, 1982-91; bus. owner, entrepreneur Santa Fe, N.Mex., 1991-94; mem. Coppler & Mannick, P.C., Santa Fe, N.Mex., 1994-98; pvt. practice Santa Fe, Albuquerque, from 1998. Trustee 1st Ch. Religious Sci., Albuquerque, 1974-77, pres. 1977; trustee Sandia Ch. Religious Sci., Albuquerque, 1980-82, pres. 1981-82; trustee United Ch. Religious Sci., Los Angeles, 1981-82, chmn. 1982; trustee Long Beach (Calif.) Ch. Religious Sci., 1983-86, chmn. 1983-86; chmn. Bernalillo County Bd. Ethics, Albuquerque, 1979-82, trustee Santa Fe Rape Crisis Ctr., 1997-2000, pres., 1999-2000. Served as sgt. USMCR, 1961-69. Mem. N.Mex. Bar Assn. Avocations: sailing, fly fishing. Died Nov. 30, 2002.

**SHAW, SIR RUN RUN (REIN SHA),** broadcast executive; b. Ningbo, Shanghai, China, Oct. 4, 1907; s. Yuh Hsuen Shaw; m. Mona Fong; m. Lily Shaw (dec. 1987); children: Vee Ming, Harold, Violet, Dorothy. DCL (hon.), Oxford U., 1992. With Unique Films Prodns., Singapore; co-founder Shaw Bros. Pvt. Ltd. (now Shaw & Shaw Pvt. Ltd.), Singapore, 1930; founder Shaw Studios, Kowloon, Hong Kong, 1961; co-founder Shaw Bros. (Hong Kong) Ltd., Hong Kong, 1971, chmn.; co-founder TV Broadcast Ltd., Kowloon, Hong Kong, 1973, chmn., 1980—2014. Founding mem. Fedn. Motion Picture Prodrs. in Asia Pacific (originally SE Asian Film Prodrs. Fedn.), Manila, 1953. Prodr.: (films) Empress Yang Kwei-fei, 1955, Bujang lapok, 1957, Pendekar bujang lapok, 1959, The Kingdom & the Beauty, 1958, Rear Entrance, 1959, Seniman bujang lapok, 1961, Love Parade, 1963, Sons of the Good Earth, 1964, The Dancing Millionairess, 1964, Lady General Hua Mu Lan, 1964, Lovers' Rock, 1964, The Grand Substitution, 1965, Hong ling lei, 1965, Monkey Goes West, 1966, Hong Kong Nocturne, 1966, Big Drunk Hero, 1966, The Cave of the Silken Web, 1967, Killer Darts, 1968, Hong Kong Rhapsody, 1968, Guess Who Killed My 12 Lovers, 1969, The Singing Thief, 1969, The 12 Gold Medallions, 1970, Whose Baby is in the Classroom?, 1970, Young Lovers, 1970, Thirteen Warlords, 1970, The Singing Killer, 1970, King Eagle, 1971, The Venus Tear Diamond, 1971, Fist Attack, 1971, Fingers of Doom, 1972, Bruce Lee & I, 1972, Seven Blows of the Dragon, 1972, Five Fingers of Death, 1972, Young People, 1972, Sacred Knives of Vengeance, 1972, Flower in the Rain, 1972, The Iron Bodyguard, 1973, Bamboo House of Dolls, 1974, Blood Money, 1974, Scandal, 1974, Blood Brothers, 1974, A Man Called Stoner, 1974, Bruce Lee: His Last Days, His Last Nights, 1975, Cleopatra Jones & the Casino of Gold, 1975, The Oily Maniac, 1976, The Mighty Peking Man, 1977, Brave Archer, 1977, Dreams of Eroticism, 1977, Shaolin Handlock, 1978, Shaolin Master Killer, 1978, Five Deadly Venoms, 1978, Invincible Shaolin, 1978, The Shadow Boxing, 1979, Dirty Ho, 1979, Mad Monkey, 1979, The Kings of Kung Fu, 1979, The Magnificent Ruffians, 1979, Meteor, 1979, Flag of Iron, 1980, A Deadly Secret, 1980, Clan of the White Lotus, 1980, 3 Evil Masters, 1980, Elders, 1981, Seeding of a Ghost, 1983, Twinkle Twinkle Little Star, 1983, Magnificent Pole Fighters, 1983; exec. prodr.: Trail of the Broken Blade, 1967, Man from Interpol, 1967, Death Valley, 1968, The Shadow Whip, 1971, New One-Armed Swordsman, 1971, The Anonymous Heroes, 1971, The Legend of the 7 Golden Vampires, 1974, Seven Blows of the Dragon II, 1975, The Killer Snakes, 1975, Revenge of the Zombies, 1976, Cannonball!, 1976, Chinatown Kid, 1977, Five Superfighters, 1978, Two Champions of Shaolin, 1978, Master Killer II, 1980, Heaven & Hell, 1980, Challenge of the Gamesters, 1981, Notorious Eight, 1981, Behind the Yellow Line, 1984, Master Killer III, 1985, My Name Ain't Suzie, 1985; assoc. prodr. (films) Blade Runner, 1982; prodr.: (films) Love Eterne, 1963. Co-founder Shaw Found., Singapore, 1957, Hong Kong, 1973; chmn. Hong Kong Red Cross; founder Hong Kong Red Cross Blood Transfusion Ctr., 1984, Sir Run Run Shaw Scholarship Program Grad. Studies, Shaw Prize, 2002. Recipient Montblanc de la Culture award, France, 1993, Grand Bauhinia Medal, 1998, BAFTA Spl. Award for Outstanding Contribution to Cinema, 2013; named a Comdr. of the Order of the British Empire, Her Majesty Queen Elizabeth II, 1974, Knight Comdr. of the Order of the British Empire, 1977. Died Jan. 7, 2013.

**SHAW, TEX RONNIE,** lawyer; b. Lubbock, Tex., Sept. 13, 1946; s. Clyde Bailey and Lucille Tennie (Luna) S.; m. Patricia Jean Lumsden, July 16, 1966; children: Jennifer Diane, Jonathan Porter. BS, East Tex. State U., 1973; JD, Tex. Tech U., 1981. Bar: U.S. Dist. Ct. (no. dist.) Tex. 1982, U.S. Dist. Ct. (ea. dist.) Tex. 1983; cert. in personal injury and in civil trial by Tex. Bd. Legal Specialization. Sole practice, Sulpher Springs, Tex., 1981-82; assoc. Windle Turley, P.C., Dallas, 1982-84; ptnr. Stark & Shaw, Gainesville, Tex., 1984-85, Sullivant, Woodlock, Underwood, Meurer, Shaw & Zielinski, Gainesville, from 1985. V.p. Camp Fire Girls, Gainesville, 1985, bd. dirs., 1986—; leader Boy Scouts Am., Gainesville, 1986—. Mem. Tex. Bar Assn., Assn. Trial Lawyers Am., Tex. Trial Lawyers Assn., Dallas Trial Lawyers Assn., Cooke County Bar Assn. Democrat. Mem. Assemly of God Ch. Lodge: Masons. Avocations: reading, fishing, boating. Deceased.

**SHEDD, ARTHUR B.,** retired school system administrator; b. Sherbrooke, Que., Can., Sept. 19, 1920; s. Burton D. and Jennie Ellis Shedd; m. Patricia Truman Thompson, Nov. 25, 1943; children: Candace Vancko, Wendy Rivera, Arthur Jr. EdB, Keene Tchrs. Coll., NH, 1943; MA, Columbia U., NYC, 1947, EdD, 1950. Cert. adminstr. NH, NY, tchr. NH. Tchr. Bergenfield HS, NJ, 1946—48; dir. NH secondary sch. svcs. NH Dept. Edn., Concord, 1949—51; HS prin. Scotia-Glenville Sch. Dist., NY, 1951—54; prin. Bedford Ctr. Dist., Mt. Kisco, 1954—61; supt. schs. Clarence Ctrl. Schs., 1961—63, North Shore Schs., Sea Cliff, NY, 1963—69, Cortland City Schs., NY, 1969—80; adj. prof. edn. SUNY, Cortland, 1984—2005; ret., 2005. Mem. commr.'s adv. bd. NY State Dept. Edn., Albany, 1961—64; pres. Syracuse Sch. Study Coun. Syracuse U., 1972—74. Pres. CAPCO Opportunities for Cortland, 1969—72; bd. dirs. Cortland Boy Scouts, 1972—76; pres. bd. dirs. YMCA, 1976—78. Lt. j.g. USNR, 1943—46. Mem.: Am. Assn. Sch. Adminstrs. (licentiate). Avocations: fly fishing, skiing. Home: Plantsville, Conn. Died Nov. 3, 2011.

**SHEEHAN, JUDITH EMANUEL,** school system administrator; b. NYC, Aug. 12, 1945; d. Meyer M. and Selma R. Emanuel; m. Daniel F. Sheehan, Apr. 3, 1966; children: Kimberly, Nicole. BA in Polit. Sci., U. Md., 1967. Asst. dir. intergovtl. rels. Prince George's County, Md., 1976-77; legis. policies and procedures officer Prince George's County Pub. Schs., 1977-92, spl. asst. to supt. on legis. policies and procedures, 1992-94, spl. asst. to supt. for bus. and cmty. outreach, 1994-97, chief divisional adminstr. outreach and comm., from 1997. Bd. dirs. Prince George's Ednl. Found., exec. dir., 1997-98; bd. dirs. Prince George's Arts Coun., pres. 1998-99; adv. Frederick County Bd. Edn., 1990. Bd. dirs. Md. Govt. Rels. Assns., 1991-92, Prince George's County Pvt. Industry Coun. Workforce Investment Bd., 1993-99, Boca Grande Condominium Owners Assn., 1999. Recipient Oustanding Pub. Svc. award C and P Telephone Co., 1982, legis. award for outstanding svc. and contributions to cmty. and state, 1980, Outstanding Svc. award Prince George's County C. of C., 1995, Above and Beyond award Jr. Achievement Nat. Capital area, 1995-96, Key to City of Louisville, 1964, cert. of appreciation Selective Svc. Sys., 1986, cert. of recognition Nat. Sch. Bds. Assn., 1982, cert. of appreciation, Prince George's County Coun., 1992, Assn. Sch. Bus. Ofcls., 1993, cert. of appreciation and commendation Md. Govt. Rels. Assn., 1992. Home: Upper Marlboro, Md. Died Mar. 4, 2002.

**SHEEN, ALBERT AUGUSTUS,** judge; b. St. Croix, July 11, 1942; m. Jada Finch Sheen; children: Albert, Nicole. BA, Lincoln U, 1965; JD, Howard U., 1968. Bar: VI. Mem. VI Legis., 1972—74; judge US Bankruptcy Ct., VI, 1982—84; US magistrate St. Croix, from 1984. Home: Saint Croix, . Died Jan. 13, 1993.

**SHEETS, DOLORES SANTOS,** minister; b. NYC, Feb. 4, 1937; d. August A. and Carmella (Roland) Santos; m. William Ralph Massey, May 30, 1957 (dec. 1968); children: Ronald Wynn, Russell Warren, Randall Walter; m. Elton Craig Sheets, Mar. 6, 1974. BS, Iowa State U., 1982; MDiv, Meth. Theol. Sch., 1986. Ordained to ministry, United Meth. Ch., 1988. Interim pastor Quad-City Hispanic Ministry, Rock Island, Ill., 1986; pastor Clarence (Iowa) United Meth. Ch., 1986-88, Hansell (Iowa)-West Fork United Meth. Ch., 1988-90, St. Mark's United Meth. Ch., Camanche, Iowa, from 1990. Mem. bd. of ordained ministry United Meth. Ch., 1988—; del. World Meth. Conf., Singapore, 1991. Mem. Kiwanis. Home: Britt, Iowa. Died Aug. 1996.

**SHEKHAR, CHANDRA,** former Prime Minister of India; b. Ballia, Uttar Pradesh, India, July 1, 1927; m. Dooja Devi; children: Pankaj, Neeraj. MS in Polit. Sci., Allahabad U., India. Sec. Dist. Socialist Party, Ballia. Joint sec. Uttar Pradesh State Socialist Party; gen. sec. Uttar Pradesh State Socialist Party, 1955; gen. sec. Congress Parliamentary Party, 1967-77; elected Lok Sabha seat, 1977; former pres. Janata Party; prime min., Govt. of India, 1990-91. Author: Meri Jail Diary; Dynamics of Social Change; editor weekly Young Indian. Died July 8, 2007.

**SHEPHERD, LEMUEL CORNICK, JR.,** retired military officer; b. Norfolk, Va., Feb. 10, 1896; s. Lemuel Cornick and Emma Lucretia (Cartwright) S.; m. Virginia Tunstall Driver, Dec. 30, 1922; children: Lemuel Cornick III, Wilson Elliott Driver, Virginia Cartwright. BS, Va. Mil. Inst., 1917; grad., Marine Corps Schs., 1930, Naval War Coll., 1937. Commd. 2d lt. USMC, 1917, advanced through grades to gen., 1952, ret., 1956; chmn. Inter-Am. Def. Bd., Washington, 1956—. Mil. career includes svc. with 5th Marines, AEF, France, 1917-19 participating in battles of Aisne, St. Mihiel and Meuse-Argonne and in defensive sectors Toulon-Troyons and Chateau-Thierry; with Army of Occupation in Germany until 1919; aide to comdt. Marine Corps, jr. aide at White House, 1920-22; U.S. ships Idaho and Nevada, 1922-25; 4th Marines, China, 1927-29; garde d'Haiti, 1930-34; comdr. 2d Bn., 5th Marines, 1st Marine Brigade, Fleet Marine Force, 1937-39; on staff, asst. comdt. Marine Corps schs., 1939-42; regtl. comdr. 9th Marines, 3rd Marine Divsn., 1942-43; participated in landing Cape Gloucester, New Britain, Dec., 1943; commdg. gen. 1st Prov. Marine Brigade, April, 1944; participated in landing, seizure Guam; commdg. gen. 6th Marine Divsn., Sept., 1944-Dec., 1945; participated in Okinawa campaign, April-June, 1945; received surrender Japanese forces, Tsing-tao, China, Oct., 1945; asst. comdt. and chief of staff USMC, 1946-48; cmdt. USMC schs., 1948-50; commdg. gen. Fleet Marine Force, Pacific, 1950-51; participated in Inchon landing and Communist China Aggression, Korea, 1950; comdt. USMC, 1952-56. Decorated Navy Cross, D.S.C., D.S.M. with two gold stars, Silver Star with two oak leaf clusters, Legion of Merit with combat V and oak leaf cluster, Bronze Star with combat V, Purple Heart with two oak leaf clusters and gold star, Presdl. Unit Citation with three bronze stars, Navy Unit Commendation with bronze star, Victory medal (WWI) with four bronze stars, Victory medal (WWII), Navy Occupation Svc. medal with Asia clasp, China Svc. medal, Korean Svc. medal with three bronze stars, UN Svc. medal, Croix de Guerre (France) with gilt star, Fourragere (France), Medaille pour la Braveure Militaire (Montenegrin), Order of Honor and Merit (Haiti), Disting. Svc. medal (Haiti), Order of the Cloud and Banner 2d grade (China), Order of the Mil. Merit Taiguk (Korea) with gold star, numerous other fgn. decorations. Office: 2600 16th St NW Washington DC 20441-0001

**SHERAK, THOMAS MITCHELL (TOM SHERAK),** former motion picture association executive; b. Bklyn., June 22, 1945; s. Myer and Freida (Rosenthal) S.; m. Madeleine Frankfurter, Nov. 22, 1967; children: Barbra, Melissa, William. AA in Mktg., N.Y. Community Coll., Bklyn., 1965. Salesman Paramount Pictures, NYC, Washington, St. Louis, 1970-74; booker film R/C Theatres, Balt., 1974-77; dist. film buyer Gen. Cinema, Cherry Hill, NJ, 1977-78, v.p. film NYC, 1978-82, v.p. head film buyer Cherry Hill, NJ, 1982-83; pres. domestic distbn. & mktg. 20th Century-Fox Pictures, Beverly Hills, Calif., 1983-85, pres. domestic distbn., 1985—2000; pres. Revolution Studios, Santa Monica, Calif., 2000—07. Vis. asst. prof. UCLA Sch. Theatre Film & Television. Mem. Southern Calif. Multiple Sclerosis Soc., Fulfillment Fund So. California, Southern California Variety, The Children's Soc. Served in US Army, 1967—69. Recipient Lifetime Achievement award, Variety mag., 2007. Mem.: Motion Picture & Television Fund, Acad. Motion Picture Arts & Sciences (bd. govs. 2003—12, treas. 2008—09, pres. 2009—12). Democrat. Home: Calabasas, Calif. Died Jan. 28, 2014.

**SHERIDAN, JOHN PATRICK, JR.,** hospital administrator, retired state official; b. Boston, Sept. 7, 1942; s. John Patrick and Rita Theresa (Brown) S.; m. Joyce Carol Sheridan, Aug. 26, 1967 (dec. Sept. 28, 2014); children: Matthew, Mark, Daniel, Timothy. BS, St. Peter's Coll., 1964; JD, Rutgers U., 1967. Bar: N.J. 1968, US Dist. Ct. NJ 1968, US Ct. Appeals (3d Cir.) 1971. Jud. clk. N.J. Superior Ct., Hackensack, 1967-68; dep. atty. gen. State of N.J., Trenton, 1970-72, 73-74, asst. counsel to Gov. William T. Cahill, 1972-73; minority counsel NJ State Senate, Trenton, 1974-82; ptnr. Cahill, McCarthy & Hicks, Princeton, N.J., 1974-82; commr. NJ Dept. Transp., Trenton, 1982-85; chmn. NJ Transit Corp., Trenton, 1982-85; ptnr. Riker, Danzig, Scherer, Hyland & Perretti, Morristown, NJ, 1985—2005; gen. counsel NJ Turnpike Authority; co-chair Gov. Christine Whitman's Transition Team, 1995; sr. exec. v.p. Cooper U. Health System, 2005—07, sr. exec. v.p., chief adminstrv. officer, 2007, pres., 2007—08, pres., CEO, 2008—14. Trustee Carrier Found., Belle Mead, N.J.; bd. dirs. N.J. Alliance for Action, Edison, N.J. Spl. Olympics, Piscataway. Co-counsel to Apportionment Commn., NJ, 1981, Gov. Tom Kean's Re-election Com., NJ, 1985, NJ Congressional Redistricting Commn., 1992; campaign mgr. Bob Dole Presdl. Campaign, NJ, 1987-88; chmn. Gov. Christine Whitman's Transition Team, 1995 Served in US Army, 1968—70. Recipient Disting. Svc. award NJ Soc. for Environ. & Econ. Devel., 1987, Charles A. Lindbergh Transp. award Gov. of N.J., 1986, Silver Gull award Monmouth-Ocean Devel. Coun., 1985. Mem. ABA, NJ Bar Assn. Republican. Roman Catholic. Home: Skillman, NJ. Died Sept. 28, 2014.

**SHERRATT, ANDREW GEORGE,** archaeologist; b. Oldham, Lancanshire, Eng., May 8, 1946; s. Kenneth and Dorothy Sherratt; m. E. Susan Dobson; children: Alistair, Matthew, Clare. BA, Peterhouse Coll., U. Cambridge, Eng., 1968, MA, 1972, PhD, 1976; MA, Merton Coll., U. Oxford, Eng., 1973; DPhil, Merton Coll., U. Oxford, 1986. Dir. Atlas Program, Brit.-Hungarian Field Project, 1979—82; asst. keeper Ashmolean Mus., U. Oxford, reader in archaeology, 1997—2002, prof., 2002—05. Editor: Cambridge Ency. of Archaeology, 1980; contbr. articles on prehistoric archaeology to profl. jours. Grantee, Brit. Acad., Leverhulme Trust, Nat. Geog. Soc., Sci. Rsch. Coun. Fellow: Cambridge Philos. Soc, Soc. Antiquaries; mem.: New Directions in Archaeology, Past and Present (editl. bd. mem.). Home: Oxfordshire, England. Died Feb. 24, 2006.

**SHERWOOD, MIDGE,** writer; b. Ironton, Ohio; d. Roy and Addie (Brace) Winters; m. Jack E. Sherwood, Jan. 19, 1946; children: Margaret Sherwood Simms, Melanie. BJ, U. Mo., 1938. Women's editor Ironton Daily Tribune, 1933—38; city editor Ironton Daily News, 1938—40; asst. mgr. west coast news bur. TWA, LA, 1940—42; pub. rels. dir. Western Air Lines, 1942—45; aviation columnist, corr. Skyways, Southern Flight, 1945—48; owner, operator Midge Winters Agy., 1945—48, conducted bond campaign to establish LA Airport; assoc. editor Matrix Mag., Women in Comm., 1950—55; book reviewer LA Times, 1963, Western Hist. Quarterly; pvt. practice, from 1958; columnist Pasadena Star-News, Calif., 1987; pub. rels. dir. LAX Bond Issue, 1945. Author: And How it Grew, 1965, San Marino Ranch to City, 1977, Days of Vintage, Years of Vision, Vol. 1, 1982, Vol. II, 1987, Fremont: Eagle of the West, 2002, Days of Vintage, Years of Vision, Vol. III, 2006, Western Journal Collection (1990-1995), Western Journal Collection (1995-2000), (plays) Peace at Last; contbr. columns in newspapers. Chmn. Hertrich Meml., 1967; mem. Soc. Fellows of Huntington Libr., 1967; founder, archivist San Marino Hist. Soc.; chmn. Ann. Fremont's Day, 2005; founder Western Jour. Recipient Commendation award, Gov. Pete Wilson, Calif., 1996, awards, Conf. Calif. Hist. Socs., 1987, 1000 Women of Excellent Achievement award, 2009, Decree of Excellence award, 2009; named Outstanding Citizen of San Marino, 1988; named one of Top 100 Writers of 2007, Internat. Biog. Ctr.; Paul Harris fellowship, Rotary. Mem.: Westerners Internat. (bd. dirs. 2002), Live Poet's Soc. Huntington Libr. (founder), Huntington Westerners (founder), Phi Mu. Home: San Marino, Calif. Died Jan. 31, 2014.

**SHEVARDNADZE, EDUARD AMVROSIYEVICH,** former President of Georgia; b. Mamati Lanchkhutsky Raion, Georgia, Jan. 25, 1928; s. Ambrosi Shevardnadze & Sophie Pateishvili S.; m. Nanuli Tsagareishvili, 1950 (dec. Oct. 20, 2004); children: Manana, Paata. Grad., Republican Party Sch. of Cen. Com., Communist Party of Georgia, 1951, Kutaisi Pedagogical Inst., 1959; Degree in Polit. Sci. & Diplomacy (hon.), U. Trieste, 1991, Harvard U. Joined Communist Party Soviet Union, 1948, Komsomol work, 1948-61; 2d sec. Cen. Com. Georgian Komsomol, 1956-57; 1st sec. Central Com. Georgian Komsomol, 1957-61; party work, 1961-91; mem. Cen. Com. Georgian Communist Party, 1961-91; 1st sec. Mtskheti Raion Com., 1961-63, Pervomaisky Raion Com., Tbilisi City, Communist Party of Georgia, 1963-64; 1st dep. minister for Protection of Public Order, 1961-65; minister (renamed Ministry of Internal Affairs 1968), 1965-72; 1st sec. Tbilisi City Com. of Central Com., Communist Party of Georgia, 1972; 1st sec. Central Com. Georgian Communist Party, 1972-85; min. fgn. affairs USSR, 1985-90, 91; mem. Central Com. of Communist Party Soviet Union, 1976-91; candidate mem. Politburo, 1978-85, dep. to USSR Supreme Soviet, 1978-91; mem. Presdl. Coun., 1990-91; chmn. State Coun. Republic of Georgia, Tbilisi, 1992-93, Pres. of Parliament, head of state, 1992-95, pres., 1995—2003. Author: My Choice, 1991, The Future Belongs to Freedom, 1991, The Great Silk Road, 1999, Thoughts about the Past and the Future, 2006. Decorated Order of Lenin (5), Order of Red Banner of Labour, Hero of Socialist Labour, (2), others. Died July 7, 2014.

**SHIFFER, JAMES DAVID,** retired utilities executive; b. San Diego, Mar. 24, 1938; s. Kenneth Frederick and Thelma Lucille (Good) S.; m. Margaret Edith Rightmyer, Sept. 5, 1959 (div. July 1986); children: James II, Elizabeth, Russell; m. Esther Zamora, Sept. 13, 1986; stepchildren: Bryan Boots, Jeremy Hellier, Marisol Loughead. BS in Chem. Engring., Stanford U., 1960, MS in Chem. Engring., 1962. Registered profl. engr., Calif. Nuc. engr. Pacific Gas & Electric Co., Humboldt Bay Power Plant, Eureka, Calif., 1961-71; tech. mgr. Pacific Gas & Electric. Co., Diablo Canyon Power Plant, Avila Beach, Calif., 1971-80; mgr. nuc. ops. Pacific Gas & Electric Co., San Francisco, 1980-84, v.p. nuc. power generation, 1984-90, sr. v.p., gen. mgr. nuc. power generation bus. unit, 1990-91; exec. v.p. Pacific Gas & Electric, San Francisco, 1991-97; ret., 1997; pres., CEO PG&E Enterprises, San Francisco, 1994-95, also bd. dirs. Bd. dirs. Math., Engring., Sci. Achievement, 1992-2002. Mem. AIChE, Am. Nuc. Soc., Commonwealth Club of Calif. (bd. govs. 1992-97). Republican. Episcopalian. Avocations: golf, music, painting. Home: Alamo, Calif. Died Mar. 20, 2014.

**SHINE, MARY TONISSEN,** retired advertising executive; b. Jacksonville, Fla., Apr. 16, 1926; d. Otto John and Anna Ruth (Simms) T.; m. James Munnerlyn Shine, Mar.12, 1955; children: James Munnerlyn Jr., Wallace Tonissen. Student, Salem Coll., 1944-45, Greenleaf Bus. Coll., 1945-46. Sec. Morris Plan Bank, Jacksonville, 1945-46, Riverside

Bank, Jacksonville, 1947; loan and discount teller Northwestern Bank, Hendersonville, N.C., 1947-48; sec. trust dept. Fla. Nat. Bank, Jacksonville, 1948-50; office mgr., sales asst. Harry E. Cummings Radio/TV Rep., Jacksonville, 1950-62; traffic and billing clk. Sta. WJAX, Jacksonville, 1963-64; media dir. William Cook Advt., Inc., Jacksonville, 1966-90. Bd. dirs. Meth. Regional Hosp. System, Jacksonville, 1986-92, Morning Star Sch., Jacksonville, 1985-92; com. mem. Communications Com., Drug and Substance Abuse Com., Episcopal Diocese Fla., Jacksonville, 1984-88. Recipient Jack Philipps Gold medal 4th Dist. Am. Advt. Fedn., 1984. Mem. Jacksonville Advt. Fedn. (bd. dirs. 1972-81, treas. 1973-74, v.p. 1974-76, pres. 1976-77, 77-78, Silver medal 1988, life). Democrat. Avocations: painting, playing piano and organ. Died Apr. 15, 2002.

**SHINN, GEORGE LATIMER,** investment banker, consultant, finance educator; b. Newark, Ohio, Mar. 12, 1923; s. Leon Powell and Bertha Florence (Latimer) S.; m. Clara LeBaron Sampson, May 21, 1949 (dec. 2010); children: Deborah, Amy, Martha, Sarah, Andrew. AB, Amherst Coll., 1948; LLD (hon.), Denison U., 1975, Amherst Coll., 1982; MA, Drew U., 1990, PhD, 1992. Trainee Merrill Lynch, Pierce, Fenner & Beane, 1948-49; various exec. positions, 1949-75; pres. Merrill Lynch & Co., Inc., 1973-75; chmn. bd., CEO 1st Boston Corp., 1975-83; investment banking cons., 1983—2002. Adj. prof. history Drew U., Madison, N.J., 1992—2002; mem. exec. com. President's Pvt. Sector Survey on Cost Control, 1982-84; exec.-in-residence Columbia U. Grad. Sch. Bus., 1983-85; bd. govs. Am. Stock Exch., 1970-74; bd. dirs., trustee Colonial Group Mut. Funds, 1983-98; bd. dirs. Kelso & Co., 1992—, N.Y. Stock Exch., 1975-83, vice chmn., 1979-83; bd. dirs. N.Y. Times Co., 1978-99, Phelps, Dodge Corp., 1983-95, N.Y. Life Ins. Co., 1983-94, Lehigh Press, 1983-91, Superior Oil Co., 1984-87, Congoleum Corp. Gen. chmn. United Hosp. Fund, N.Y.C., 1973-74; trustee Kent Pl. Sch., Summit, N.J., 1966-73, Carnegie Found. for Advancement Teaching, 1976-85, Pingry Sch., 1977-79, Lucille P. Markey Charitable Trust, 1985-97, Rockefeller Family Office Trust, 1989-97, N.J. Coun. for the Humanities, 1994-2000, Arts Coun. Morris Area, 1978-91, Philharmonic Symphony Soc. N.Y., 1983-91, Nat. Humanities Ctr., 1988-94; trustee emeritus Amherst Coll., 1968-82, chmn. bd. trustees, 1973-80; bd. dirs. Rsch. Corp., 1975-86. Capt. USMCR, 1942-52. Fellow American Acad. Arts & Sciences, N.Y. Acad. Medicine, River Club, Century Assn. Home: Scarborough, Maine. Died Dec. 16, 2013.

**SHINTO, HISASHI,** Japanese telecommunications company executive; b. Fukuoka, Japan, July 2, 1910; s. Yasuhide and Michiyo Shinto; m. Michiko Kushiro Shinto, 1936; 4 children. BS, Kyushu Imperial U., 1934, PhD, 1958. With Harima Shipbuilding & Engring. Co., Ltd., 1934, Nat. Bulk Carriers Corp., Kure Yard, 1951; mng. dir. Ishikawajima-Harima Heavy Industries Ltd., div. mgr. shipbuilding div., 1960, exec. v.p., 1964, pres., 1972—79, counsellor, 1979—80; pres. Shipbuilders Assn. Japan, 1977—79; mng. dir. Japan Ship Exporters Assn., 1979—80; counsellor Transp. Technics, Ministry Transp., 1979—83; pres., commr., mem. coun. mgmt. com. Nippon Telegraph and Telephone Pub. Corp., 1981—85; pres., chief exec. officer Nippon Telegraph & Telephone Corp., from 1985, chmn., from 1988; dir. Tokyo Shibaura Electric Co. Ltd., Toshiba, from 1966. Recipient Blue Ribbon award, Legion d' Honner. Avocations: golf, photography. Died Jan. 26, 2003.

**SHIRLEY-QUIRK, JOHN,** singer, educator; b. Liverpool, Eng., Aug. 28, 1931; arrived in US, 1990, naturalized, 2002; s. Joseph Stanley and Amelia (Griffiths) S.-Q.; m. Patricia May Hastie, July 1955 (dec. Feb. 1981); children: Kate, Peter; m. Sara Van Horn Watkins, Dec. 29, 1981 (dec. Dec. 1997); children: Benjamin, Emily (dec. 2001), Julia; m. Teresa May Perez, Mar. 2009. BSc, Liverpool U., 1953, MusD (hon.), 1977; D Univ., Brunel U., 1981. Asst. lectr. Acton Tech. Coll., London, 1956-60; vicar choral St. Paul's Cathedral, London, 1960-61; profl. singer, 1960—2014; joint artistic dir. Aldeburgh Festival, 1981-84. Mem. voice faculty Peabody Conservatory, Balt., 1991-2012; vis. artist Carnegie-Mellon U., Pitts., 1994-98; vis. lectr., Bath Spa U. (England) 2013-14. Numerous recs. and 1st performances, especially works of Benjamin Britten. Mem. ct. Brunel U., 1977-81. Flying officer RAF, 1952-55. Decorated comdr. Order of Brit. Empire. Mem. Royal Acad. Music (hon.), Royal Philharmonic Soc. Home: Wiltshire, England. Died Apr. 7, 2014.

**SHIVAS, MARK,** television producer; b. London, Apr. 24, 1938; s. James Dallas and Winifred Alice (Bristow) S. MA in Law, Oxford U., Eng., 1960. Asst. editor Movie mag., 1962—64; freelance journalist London, 1960-63; rschr., performer, prodr. Granada TV, Manchester, England, 1964-69; prodr. BBC, London, 1969-79; creative dir. Southern Pictures, 1979—81; freelance prodr. London, 1979-88; head drama and tv BBC, London, 1988-93, head films, 1993-97; ind. prodr. Perpetual Motion Pictures, London, 1997—2008. Coun. mem. BSAC, BAFTA, Prodr.: (TV episodes) Cinema, 1964, The Six Wives of Henry the Eighth, 1970, Casanova, 1971, The Edwardians, 1972-73, Play for Today, 1973-75, Black and Blue, 1973, Centre Play, 1975, BBC2 Play of the Week, 1977-79, Telford's Change, 1979, Jim Henson's The Storyteller, 1987 (Emmy award for Outstanding Children's Program, 1987), Telling Tales, 2000, Cambridge Spies, 2003; (TV movies) The Tragedy of King Richard II, 1970, Danton, 1970, Casanova, 1971, Joy, 1972, Poet Game, 1972, To Encourage the Others, 1972, Secrets, 1973, Soap Opera in Stockwell, 1973, Glorios Miles, 1973, The Evacuees, 1974, The Glittering Prizes', 1975, Abide with Me, 1976, Rogue Male, 1976, The Three Hostages, 1977, Hallelujah Anyhow, 1990, Heading Home, 1991, The Lost Language of Cranes, 1991, Maria Child, 1992, Memento Mori, 1992, Great Moments in Aviation, 1993, The Cormorant, 1993, Femme Fatale, 1993, Genghis Cohn, 1993, Clothes in the Wardrobe, 1993, The Long Roads, 1993, The Snapper, 1993, All Things Bright and Beautiful, 1994, Midnight Movie, 1994; (TV mini-series) The Glittering Prizes, 1976, Fathers and Families, 1977, Winston Churchill: The Wilderness Years, 1981, The Borgias, 1981, The Price, 1985, Talking Heads 2, 1998;; exec. prodr. (films) Richard's Things, 1980, Bad Blood, 1981, Moonlighting, 1982, A Private Function, 1984, The Witches, 1990 Truly, Madly, Deeply, 1990, The Grass Arena, 1991, Enchanted April, 1992, The Railway Station Man, 1992, The Trial, 1993, The Hawk, 1993, Century, 1993, A Man of No Importance, 1994, Captives, 1994, Priest, 1994, An Awfully Big Adventure, 1995, Two Deaths, 1995, Small Faces, 1996, The Van, 1996,Jude, 1996, The Designated Mourner, 1997, Regeneration, 1997, I Went Down, 1997, Painted Angels, 1998, The Revengers' Comedies, 1998, Hideous Kinky, 1998, The Claim, 2000, I Capture the Castle, 2003 Recipient Prodn. award Brit. Acad. Film and TV Arts, London, 1970, Emmy awards, N.Y., 1975, L.A., 1986. Fellow Royal TV Soc.; mem. BAFTA (coun. mem.), AMPAS L.A. (prodr.), Atelier Cinematographique Europeen (bd. mem.). Avocations: gardening, bicycling, swimming. Died Oct. 11, 2008.

**SHOENIGHT, PAULINE ALOISE SOUERS (ALOISE TRACY),** writer; b. Bridgeport, Ill., Nov. 20, 1914; m. James Richard Tracy, Sept. 18, 1946; m. Hurley F. Shoenight, June 25, 1976. BEd, Eastern Ill. U., 1937. Mem. hon. bd. advs. Am. Biog. Inst.; active mem. Nat. Arbor Day Found. Author: His Handiwork, 1954, Memory is a Poet, 1964, The Silken Web, 1965, A Merry Heart, 1966, In Two or Three Tomorrows, 1968, All Flesh Is Grass, 1971, Beyond The Edge, 1973. Mem.: Friends Foley Libr., Friends U. Mo. Librs., Acad. Am. Poets, Ala. State Poetry Soc., Ill. Poetry Soc., PEO Sisterhood, Nat. Ret. Tchrs. Assn., Baldwin Heritage Mus. Assn. (life; charter mem.), Am. Poets Fellowship Soc. (life), Eastern Ill. Alumni Assn. (life), Bible-A-Month Club, Pleasure Island Sr. Citizens Club (charter mem.). Republican. Died Aug. 18, 1996.

**SHOGAN, ROBERT MERTON,** retired news correspondent, writer; b. NYC, Sept. 12, 1930; s. Albert and Millie (Jacobs) S.; m. Ellen Shrewsbury, May 26, 1959 (dec. 2006); children: Cynthia Diane, Amelia Ford. BA in Journalism, Syracuse U., 1951; postgrad., U. Mich. Inst. Pub. Adminstrn., 1951, Columbia U., 1952. Reporter Detroit Free Press, 1956-59; telegraph editor Miami (Fla.) News, 1959-61; asst. editor The Wall St. Jour., NYC, 1961-65; evaluation officer Peace Corps, Washington, 1965-66; corr. Newsweek, Washington, 1966-73; nation polit. corr. L.A. Times, Washington, 1973-99. Profl.-in-residence Annenberg Sch. Communication, U. Pa., 1993; adj. prof. Johns Hopkins U., Ctr. for Study of American Govt., Washington, 1999—2010. Author: Question of Judgement, 1972, Promises to Keep, 1977, None of the Above, 1982, The Riddle of Power: Presidential Leadership from Truman to Bush, 1991, Hard Bargain: How FDR Twisted Churchill's Arm, Evaded the Law, and Changed the Role of the American Presidency, 1995, Fate of the Union, 1998, The Double-Edged Sword: How Character Makes and Ruins Presidents, from Washington to Clinton, 1998, Bad News: Where the Press Goes Wrong in the Making of the President, 2001, War Without End: Cultural Conflict and the Struggle for America's Political Future, 2002, The Battle of Blair Mountain, 2004, Backlash, 2006, No Sense of Decency, 2009, Prelude to Catastrophe: FDR's Jews and the Menace of Nazism, 2010, Harry Truman and the Struggle for Racial Justice, 2013; co-author: (with Tom Craig) The Detroit Race Riot: A Study in Violence, 1964. Served with U.S. Army, 1952-54. Recipient 1st prize Feature Writing, Mich. AP, 1959, Disting. Reporting Pub. Affairs award American Polit. Sci. Assn., 1969, Scribes Book award, 1972; rsch. grantee Harry S Truman Presdl. Libr., 1989, Lyndon B. Johnson Presdl. Libr., 1989, Gerald R. Ford Presdl. Libr., 1989; McCormick fellow Hoover Presdl. Libr., 1993; fellow Media Studies Ctr., 1998. Mem. Phi Beta Kappa Home: Chevy Chase, Md. Died Oct. 30, 2013.

**SHOKEIR, MOHAMED HASSAN KAMEL,** medical geneticist, educator; b. Mansoura, Egypt, July 2, 1938; emigrated to Can., 1969, naturalized, 1974; s. Hassan Sayed and Lolia Nora (Kira) S.; m. Donna Jean Nugent, Feb. 27, 1968; children: Marc Omar, Vanessa May. MB, BChir, Cairo U., 1960, D in Surgery, 1963, D in Surgery in Orthop., 1964; MS, U. Mich., 1965, PhD, 1969. Intern Cairo U. Hosps., 1960-61, resident, 1961-64; Fulbright rsch. scholar dept. human genetics U. Mich., 1964-69; asst. prof. pediat. U. Sask., Saskatoon, Can., 1969-71, assoc. prof., 1971-73, prof., from 1977, dir. divsn. med. genetics, 1975-97, head dept. pediat., 1979-96, Saskatoon Dist. Health Bd., 1993-96. Head sect. clin. genetics U. Man., Winnipeg, Can., 1973-75; mem. staffs Univ. Hosp., Saskatoon City Hosp., St. Paul's Hosp.; cons. Winnipeg Health Scis. Ctr., Regina Gen. Hosp. Contbr. articles to profl publs. Mem. Acad. Freedom and Tenure Com., Ottawa, Ont., Can., 1980-90, Queen Elizabeth II scientist, 1969-75. Med. Rsch. Coun. grantee, 1970-79; Can. Coll. Med. Geneticists Found. fellow, 1975— Fellow Can. Coll. Med. Geneticists, Can. Soc. Clin. Investigation (councillor 1974-76), Can. Med. Assn. (chmn., mem. adv. com. 1987-96); mem. APHA, Assn. Med. Sch. Pediat. Dept. Chairmen, Assn. Can. Univ. Dept. Chairmen, Am. Pediat. Soc., Soc. Pediat. Rsch., N.Y. Acad. Scis., Am. Geriat. Soc., Am. Fedn. Clin. Rsch., Mid-Western Soc. Pediat. Rsch., Western Pediat. Soc., Am. Soc. Human Genetics, Genetics Soc. Am., Genetics Soc. Can., Am. Genetic Assn. Home: Saskatoon, Canada. *Never tried to imagine what the future will bring, found the present and its implications enough to occupy me. The overriding passions in my life have been the love of man and the pity for his suffering. I have come to accept the futility of eliminating bias, even prejudice— mine or others'; my hope now is to recognize it and shield one's actions from it. What the world needs is more tolerance. Always found praise a bit embarrassing, confusing and altogether inhibiting— the most lavish for the least deserved accomplishment. Always thought the world is, at best, approximate. I now realize that in life one cannot have all bases covered.* Deceased.

**SHOMAN, ABDUL MAJEED ABDUL HAMEED,** banker; b. Jerusalem, June 15, 1912; s. Abdul Hameed Ahmad and Zahwa Shoman; m. Naila Ahmad Hilmi, 1946; children: Mohammad Abdul Hameed, Ahmad. BSc in Econs., NYU, 1934, MA in Econs., 1936. Asst. mgr. Arab Bank Ltd., Jerusalem, 1936-46, mgr., 1946-49, dep. chmn. Amman, Jordan, 1949-74; chmn., gen. mgr. Arab Bank Pub. Ltd. Co., Amman, 1974—2005. Chmn. Ubae Arab German Bank, Luxembourgh, Fed. Republic Germany, Jordan Petroleum Refinery Co., Amman, Comml. Bldg. Co., Beirut, Arab Bank (Austria) Vienna, Arab Investment Co., London. Mem. Upper House of Parliament, Heshemite Kingdom Jordan, 1984-86. Decorated Al-Nahda King Hussein Bin Talal; recipient 1st and 2d Independence award King Hussein Bin Talal. Muslim. Avocations: walking, reading. Home: Amman, Jordan. Died July 5, 2005.

**SHORT, EARL DEGREY, JR.,** psychiatrist, consultant; b. Talladega, Ala., Jan. 11, 1933; s. Earl DeGray and Adeline Eugenia (McWilliams) Short; m. Martha Burt Rossiter, Oct. 12, 1963; children: Earl D III, Philip A., Catherine E., William R. BS, The Citadel, 1956; MD, Med. U. S.C., Charleston, 1959. Commd. 2d lt. USAR, 1956; entered active duty U.S. Army, 1961, advanced through grades to col., 1976; bn. surgeon 4th Armored Bn., 8th Inf. div., Germany, 1961-62; resident psychiatry Walter Reed Army Med. Ctr., Washington, 1962-65; chief dept. psychiatry U.S. Army Hosp. and Mental Hygiene Consultation Svc., Ft. Polk, La., 1965-68, U.S. Walson Army Hosp. and Mental Hygiene Consultation Svc., Ft. Dix, N.J., 1968-70; student Command and Gen. Staff Coll., Ft. Leavenworth, Kans., 1970-71; divsn. surgeon, comdr. 2d Med. Bn., 2d Inf. divsn., Korea, 1971-72; chief psychiatry svc. Brooke Army Med. Ctr., Ft. Sam Houston, Tex., 1972-80; ret. U.S. Army, 1980; psychiatrist Mecklenburg County Mental Health Ctr., Charlotte, N.C., 1980-86; ret. Mecklenburg County, 1993; psychiatrist Behavioral Health Ctr.-Carolinas Med. Ctr.-Randolph, Charlotte, N.C., from 1986; pvt. practice Carolinas Med. Group, Psychiat. and Psychol. Assocs., from 1992. Psychiat. cons. Mecklenburg County, Charlotte, 1987—, Amethyst, Charlotte, 1993-95, Emergency Med. Svcs. Assocs., 1996-99, Murray Adolescent Tng. Acad., 1996—. Founder Philip Alexander Short Meml. Scholarship Fund, Wingate (N.C.) U., 1988, Short Endowment Fund, Wingate U., 1991, Philip Alexander Short Meml. Fund, Elon Homes for Children, Elon Coll., N.C., 1989. Decorated Meritorious Svc. medal with 1 oak leaf cluster, U.S. Army, 1972, 80, Army Commendation medal with 1 oak leaf cluster, U.S. Army, 1968, 70; recipient All Am. award The Citadel, 1956, and named Disting. Mil. Grad., 1956. Mem. AMA, Am. Psychiat. Assn., N.C. Med. Soc., N.C. Psychiat. Assn., Charlotte Psychiat. Soc., Assn. Mil. Surgeons, Mecklenburg County Med. Soc., Ret. Officers Assn., Am. Legion, VFW, Sons Am. Revolution, Nat. Assn. for Uniformed Svcs. Republican. Presbyterian. Avocations: genealogy, composing piano music, restoring ancestral homes, collecting stamps, books and coins. Died Sept. 10, 2001.

**SHORT, KEITH CHRISTOPHER,** academic administrator; b. Swawsea, Wales, Dec. 10, 1940; s. Clifford Garfield Short and Ruby Belle Poole; m. Irene Veronica Coad, July 23, 1968; 1 child, Jonathan Mark Adrian. BS with honors, Swawsea U., 1963, PhD, 1968, MEd, 1979. Rsch. demonstrator Swawsea U., 1966—68; Cabot Rsch. fellow Harvard U., Cambridge, Mass., 1968—70; Sci. Rsch. Coun. Rsch. fellow Nottingham (U.K.) U., 1970—71; lectr. Coventry (U.K.) Poly., 1971—72; rsch. biologist U. Calif., Irvine, 1972; lectr. U. Coll. Dublin, Ireland, 1972—73, North East London Poly., 1973, sr. lectr., 1974; vis. asst. prof. Harvard U., 1975; head plant scis. North East London Poly., 1976, dep. head dept. biology, 1977; Boots prof. life scis. Trent Poly., 1982, dean sci., 1985, asst. dir., 1986; gov. Wimbledon (U.K.) Sch. Art, 1990—93; dept. vice chancellor Nottingham Trent U., 1992; gov. Trent Coll., Nottingham, 1993—98, People's Coll., Nottingham, 1995—2000, Nottingham Trent U., 1993—2002. Contbr. over 85 articles to profl. jours. Named chartered biologist, Inst. Biology, London, 1984; fellow, 1984. Mem.: Reform Club. Mem. Ch. Eng. Avocations: swimming, theater. Home: Nottingham, England. Died July 2002.

**SHRESTHA, MARICH MAN SINGH,** former Prime Minister of Nepal; b. Jan. 1, 1942; Prime min., min. def. Govt. of Nepal, Kathmandu, Nepal, 1986-90. Died Aug. 15, 2013.

**SHUKLA, VIDYA CHARAN,** former Indian government official; b. Raipur, Madhya Pradesh, India, Aug. 2, 1929; Min. external affairs Govt. of India, 1990—91. Died June 11, 2013.

**SHULTIS, ROBERT LYNN,** retired finance educator, professional society administrator, consultant, corporate financial executive; b. Kingston, NY, June 30, 1924; s. Albert H. and Dorothy Elizabeth (Jenkins) S.; m. Bernice Elizabeth Johnson, Jan. 20, 1946; 1 son, Robert Lee. BS, Columbia Univ. Sch. Bus., 1949, postgrad., 1949-51. Staff acct. Price Waterhouse, NYC, 1949-52; credit mgr., controller Organon, Inc., West Orange, NJ, 1952-68; v.p., treas., chief fin. officer Arwood Corp., Rockleigh, NJ, 1968-72; v.p., controller Technicon, Tarrytown, NY, 1972-80; exec. dir. Inst. of Mgmt. Accts., Montvale, NJ, 1980-86; faculty, exec. dir. Ctr. for Exec. Devel. Coll. William & Mary, Williamsburg, Va., 1987-91. Instr. Rutgers U., 1964-74, Fairleigh Dickinson U., 1967-68; mem. Fin. Acctg. Standards Adv. Coun., 1981-86; lectr., seminar leader, cons. on controllership, activity-based costing, cost mgmt., cost sys. design Boston U., U. Calif., Berkeley, U. Minn., Michigan

State U., So. Meth. U., Baldwin Wallace Coll., George Mason U., James Madison U., U. N.C., Colo. State U., others, 1990—. Editor: Management Accountants' Handbook, and supplements, 1991-94; contbr. articles to profl. jours. Bd. advs. U. Fla. Sch. Accountancy, James Madison U. Sch. Accountancy; fin. and budget com. Kingsmill Cmty. Svcs. Assn.; interpreter Historic Jamestowne Island, 1997-07; Citizens Budget Advisory Com., Williamsburg, James City, With USAF, 1943-45 Decorated Presdl. Unit Citation, ETO Ribbon, eight battle stars. Mem. AAUP, Am. Legion, Fin. Execs. Internat., Inst. Mgmt. Accts., Assn. for Preservation of Va. Antiquities, Kingsmill Club, Beta Alpha Psi (adv. forum). Home: Williamsburg, Va. Died Mar. 31, 2014.

**SHVALB, VIL,** researcher; b. Odessa, Ukraine, Aug. 4, 1924; arrived in Israel, 1974; s. Michael Baitalsky and Eve Shvalb; m. Nina Guildenblat, Jan. 27, 1960. MSc, U. Moscow, 1952; PhD, Inst. Comm. Acad. Sci. USSR, Moscow, 1966. Rschr. Inst. for Comm. Problems, Acad. Sci. USSR, Moscow, 1959-70; head lab. Ctrl. Statis. Bd., Moscow, 1970-74; sr. rschr. Telecom. Corp., Tel Aviv, 1979-89; freelance rschr. Netanya, Israel, from 1989. Contbr. articles to books and jours. Soldier Russian Army, 1942-45, WWII. Mem. IEEE (affiliate), N.Y. Acad. Scis. Home: Nahariya, Israel. Died Oct. 4, 2006.

**SIDEMAN, SAMUEL,** chemical and biomedical engineer; b. Haifa, Israel, Feb. 6, 1929; s. Gad Yechiel and Ester Riesel S.; m. Naomi Rubin, Dec. 16, 1955; children: Gil, Annat, Adi. BS, Technion IIT, Haifa, 1953, DSc, 1960; MChemE, Polytechnic Inst. of Bklyn., 1955. Instr. Technion-IIT, Haifa, 1957, lectr., 1958, sr. lectr., 1963, assoc. prof., 1966, prof., 1969, chmn. dept. chem. engring., 1974-76, head Heart System Rsch. Ctr., 1983-95, chmn. dept. biomed. engring., 1980-85, 1987-88, 90-94. Dir. Julius Silver Inst. of Med. & Biomed. Engring., Technion, 1980-85, 87-88, 90-94; vis. prof. bioengring. N.J. Med. and Dental U., 1985—; disting vis. profl. elec. engring., biomed. engring., Rutgers U., Piscataway, N.J., 1985-87, 88, 96, 97; pres. Assembly of Internat. Heat Transfer Conf., 1990-94; exec. com. Internat. Ctr. of Heat and Mass Transfer, Ankara, Turkey, 1986-98, v.p., 1998; bd. dirs. Malibu Corp., Home Ctr. Ltd., Tel Aviv; chair numerous internat. confs. Co-editor: Problems in Chemical Engineering, 1957, Progress in Heat and Mass Transfer, 1972, Hemoperfusion: Kidney and Liver Supports and Detoxification, Parts I and II, 1980, Simulation and Imaging of the Cardiac System, 1985, Simulation and Control of the Cardiac System, Parts I, II and III, 1987, Activation, Metabolism and Perfusion of the Heart, 1987, Analysis and Simulation of the Cardiac System, 1989, Interactive Phenomena in the Cardiac System, 1993, Imaging in Transport Processes, 1993, Molecular and Subcellular Cardiology, 1995, Analytical and Quantitative Cardiology, 1997, others; patentee in field. Bd. dirs. Reali High Sch., Haifa, 1984-95. Maj. Israeli mil., 1948-88. Fellow Hebrew Technion, N.Y., 1953-55, Am. NSF, 1964-65; recipient Arnon award Israel Assn. of Engrs. and Architects, Israel, 1968, Landau award Israel Rsch. Awards Dirs., Israel, 1976, award for Most Original Rsch., Israel Cardiology Soc., 1990, Henry Gutwirth Rsch. award, 1992, Acad. Excellence award Technion, 1994, others. Fellow AIChE (citation 1965), N.Y. Acad. Sci., Coll. Circulation, Am. Heart Assn., Israel Inst. Chem. Engrs. (hon.), Internat. Ctr. Heat Mass Transfer (hon.), Sci. Acad. of Sci. Republic of Belarus (hon. dr.); mem. L'Academie Francophone d'Ingenieurs (founding mem. 1993, Samuel Sideman medal in cardiovasc. scis. named in his honor 1997). Home: Haifa, Israel. Died Feb. 12, 2008.

**SIEBERT, HORST,** economics professor, institute administrator; b. Neuwied, Germany, Mar. 20, 1938; s. Fritz and Anna (Heini) S.; m. Christa Causemann, Apr. 29, 1965. MA in Econs., U. Cologne, Fed. Republic Germany, 1963; PhD, U. Muenster, Fed. Republic Germany, 1965, habilitation, 1969. Asst. prof. Tex. A&M U., 1967-68; prof. economics U. Mannheim, Germany, 1969-84, U. Konstanz, 1984-89; prof. theoretical economics U. Kiel, 1989—2003; pres. Kiel Inst. World Econs., 1989—2003. Mem. Coun. Econ. Advisors, Germany, 1990-2003. Author: Economics of the Environment, 1987, 5th revised edit., 1998, Aussenwirtschaft, 7th edit., 2000, The New Economic Landscape in Europe, 1991, Geht den Deutschen die Arbeit aus?, 1995, Weltwirtschaft, 1997, The World Economy, 1999, 2d edit., 2002. Mem. Am. Econ. Assn., European Econ. Assn., Verein Fuer Socialpolitik. Died June 2, 2009.

**SIECK, HAROLD F.,** state legislator; b. Pleasant Dale, Nebr., Feb. 29, 1916; m. Elise Meinberg, Feb. 8, 1942; children: Thomas, Barbara, Roger, Gerald, Annette. Mem. Nebr. Legislature, from 1978. Bd. dirs. Seward County Rural Power Dist., Nebr., Lower Platte S. NRD. Precinct committeeman Dem. Party. Lutheran. Home: Pleasant Dale, Nebr. Died Mar. 1988.

**SIEGEL, ROBERT HAROLD,** English literature educator, writer; b. Aug. 18, 1939; married; 3 children. Student, Denison U., 1957-59; BA in English, Wheaton Coll., 1961; MA, Johns Hopkins U., 1962; PhD in English, Harvard U., 1968. Instr. Dartmouth Coll., 1967-68, asst. prof., 1968-75; vis. lectr. Princeton (N.J.) U., 1975-76; poet-in-residence, McManes vis. prof. Wheaton (Ill.) Coll., 1976; asst. prof. U. Wis., Milw., 1976-79, assoc. prof. English, 1979-83, prof., 1983—99, prof. emeritus, from 1999. Poet on faculty Summer Writers' Inst., Wheaton Coll., 1980, Wesleyan U., 1982, 83, New Eng. Young Writers Conf., 2002-2010; vis. prof. J. W. v. Goethe U., Frankfurt, Fed. Republic Germany, 1985; Nick Barker writer in residence, Covenant Coll., 2008; lectr., reader various univs. Author: (fiction) Alpha Centauri, 1980, Whalesong, 1981, The Kingdom of Wundle, 1982, White Whale, 1991, The Ice at the End of the World, 1994; (poetry) The Beasts and the Elders, 1973, In A Pig's Eye, 1980, The Waters Under the Earth, 2005, A Pentecost of Finches: New and Selected Poems, 2006, Within this Tree of Bones, 2013; contbr. poems to Atlantic Monthly, Sewanee Rev., other jours. Recipient Margaret O'Loughlin Foley award Am. mag., 1970, award Cliff Dwellers' Arts Found., 1974, Chgo. Poetry prize Soc. Midland Authors, 1974, Poetry prize Prairie Schooner, 1977, Jacob Glatstein Meml. prize Poetry mag., 1977, award Ingram Merrill Found., 1979, Gold medallion ECPA, 1981, Book of Yr. award Campus Life mag., 1981, 1st Pl. prize for juvenile fiction Coun. for Wis. Writers, 1981, 1st Pl. prize poetry Soc. Midland Authors, 1981, Matson award Friends of Lit., 1982, Golden Archer award Sch. Libr. Sci., U. Wis., Oshkosh, 1986, 1st prize Milton Ctr. Poetry Contest, 1994, EPA 1st place in poetry, 2003; Dartmouth Coll. faculty fellow, 1971; Gilman fellow Johns Hopkins U., 1961-62; tchg. fellow Harvard U., 1965-67, Yaddo Artists' Colony, 1974, 75, Transatlantic Rev. fellow Bread Loaf Writers Conf., 1974, Nat. Endowment for Arts, 1980; grantee U. Wis., 1978, 84, 88-89, 96-97, 99. Home: South Berwick, Maine. Died Dec. 20, 2012.

**SIEGLER, RICHARD LOUIS,** pediatric nephrologist, educator; b. Vallejo, Calif., May 5, 1939; s. Alfred Charles and Loyola Ann (Wolf) S.; m. Karen Koenig, June 25, 1963; children: Mark, Matthew, Amy. BA in Life Sci., Calif. State U., Sacramento, 1961; MD, Creighton U., 1965. Diplomate Am. Bd. Pediats., Am. Bd. Pediat. Nephrology. Intern in mixed medicine-pediatrics Creighton Meml. - St. Joseph's Hosp., Omaha, 1965-66, resident in pediatrics, 1966-67, U. Utah Med. Ctr., 1969-71; fellowship in nephrology Dept. Medicine, U. Utah Med. Ctr., 1971-72; asst. prof. U. Utah Sch. Medicine, Salt Lake City, 1972—78, chief pediat. nephrology dept. pediats., 1972—2001, assoc. prof., 1978—90, acting chmn. dept. pediats., 1982-83, vice chair clin. affairs, 1983-87, prof., 1990—2005, prof. emeritus, from 2005; prof. affilate, sch. medicine San Carlos U., Guatemala, from 2008. Mem. exec. com. Primary Children's Med. Ctr., Salt Lake City, 1982-83; dir. pediat. renal disease program U. Utah Health Scis. Ctr., Salt Lake City, 1982-86; bd. dirs. Sacramental Children's Home, 2008-11. Contbr. articles to profl. jours., book chpts. Bd. trustees Utah Children, Salt Lake City, 1989-90. Capt. U.S. Army, 1967-68, Viet Nam. Decorated Bronze Star; recipient Rsch. awards Southern Ariz. Found., 1990-91, Svc. to Children award Am. Acad. Pediat., Utah Chpt., 2006, Named Disting. Visitor, Mayor Guatemala City, 2012; Thrasher Rsch. Fund grantee, 1978-79, 82-85, RO1 grantee NIH, 1996-2001, R21 co-grantee NIH, 2006-08. Fellow Am. Acad. Pediats. (mem. exec. com. Utah chpt. 1986-90, pres. Utah chpt. 1988-90, chair legis. com. 1990-92); mem. Am. Soc. Nephrology, Am. Soc. Pediat. Nephrology. Achievements include being credited with the initial description of a new inherited disorder known as the "Siegler-Brewer-Syndrome"; being honored by the president of Guatemala at the opening cerymony of the Richard L. Siegler Pediatric Hemodialysis Center (the first such facility in the country). Avocations: bicycling, violin, photography. Home: Davis, Calif. Died Mar. 2014.

**SIGMUND, PAUL EUGENE,** political science professor; b. Phila., Jan. 14, 1929; s. Paul Eugene and Marie (Ramsey) S.; m. Barbara Rowena Boggs, Jan. 25, 1964 (dec. 1990); children— Paul Eugene, David, Stephen. AB, Georgetown U., 1950; AB Fulbright scholar, U. Durham, Eng., 1950-51; MA, Harvard, 1954, PhD, 1959; postgrad., U. Paris, France, U. Heidelberg, U. Cologne, Germany, 1955-56. Teaching fellow Harvard U., 1953-55, 58-59, instr., 1959-63; assoc. prof. politics Princeton U., 1963-70, prof. politics, 1970—2014. Author: Nicholas of Cusa and Medieval Polit. Thought, 1963; author: (with Reinhold Niebuhr) The Democratic Experience, 1969; author: Natural Law in Political Thought, 1971, 2d edit., 1981, The Overthrow of Allende and the Politics of Chile, 1977, Multinationals in Latin America.: The Politics of Nationalization, 1980, Liberation Theology at the Crossroads: Democracy or Revolution?, 1990, paperback, 1992, The U.S. and Democracy in Chile, 1993, The Ideologies of the Developing Nations, 1963; editor, 1967, 2d edit., 1972, Models of Polit. Change in Latin America, 1970; co-editor (with Pedro Aspe): The Polit. Economy of Income Distbr. in Mex., 1983; editor: Poder, Sociedad y Estado en USA, 1985, Evangelization and Religious Freedom in Latin Am., 1999, The Selected Political Writings of John Locke, 2005; translator: The Mil. and the State in Latin Am. (A. Roquié), 1987, St. Thomas Aquinas, On Politics and Ethics, 1988, Nicholas Cusa, The Cath. Concordance, 1991, 2d edit., 1995; assoc. editor: World Politics. Served to 1st lt. USAF, 1956-57. Mem. American Polit. Sci. Assn., Latin American Studies Assn., Phi Beta Kappa. Catholic. Home: Princeton, NJ. Died Apr. 27, 2014.

**SIGORSKY, VITALY PETROVICH,** engineer, researcher, educator, engineer, researcher, educator; b. Village Bubnova Slobidka, Cherkasy, Ukraine, Nov. 19, 1922; s. Petro Ivanovich and Marija Tryfonivna (Lysenko) S. Degree in elec. engring., Lviv Politech. Inst., 1949, PhD, 1952; D in Tech., Kyiv Politech. Inst., 1959. Dep. dir., head dept. Machinery and Automation Inst., Lviv, 1953-59, Auomation and Electrometrical Inst., Novosibirsk, 1959-62; head dept. Math. Inst., Novosibirsk, 1962-64; head chair Novosibirsk U., 1962-64; head chair, prof. Nat. Tech. U. Ukraine, Kyiv, from 1964. Author: Two-Port Theory, 1955, Method of Network Analysis with Multiple Components, 1958, Electronic Network Analysis, 1960, 5th edit., 1966, Mathematics for Engineers, 1975, 2d edit., 1977; contbr. more than 300 articles to profl. jours. Mem. Internat. Acad. Computer Scis. and Sys., Ukraine Acad. Engring. Scis., Internat. Acad. Info. Avocations: arts, travel, photography. Home: Kiev, Ukraine. Died Aug. 13, 2007.

**SIKHARULIDZE, DAVID,** physicist, researcher; b. Makharadze, Georgia, Apr. 4, 1947; arrived in England, 2000, permanent resident, 2004; s. German and Polina Sikharulidze; m. Tatiana Girol, Nov. 2, 1950; 1 child, Irakli. MSc, Tbilisi State U., Georgia, 1970, PhD, 1980; DSc, Georgian Tech. U., Tbilisi, 1995. Jr. rsch. scientist Inst. Cybernetics Georgian Acad. Sci., Tbilisi, 1970—73, sr. engr., 1973—78, group leader, 1978—80, sr. rsch. scientist, 1980—86, head lab., 1986—2000; rsch. scientist Hewlett-Packard Labs., Bristol, England, 2000—06, sr. rsch. scientist, from 2006. Vis. privat dozent Tech. U., Berlin, 1994—97; vis. sr. rsch. scientist physics dept. U. Calabria, Cosenza, Italy, 1997—2000. Co-author: Image Transdurces Based on MIS-Electrooptical Material Structure, 1986, Liquid Crystals with Helical Structure and Their Applications in Displays, 1988; contbr. articles to profl. jours. Recipient Silver medal, Nat. Achievements USSR, 1987, State prize in Sci., Republic of Georgia, 1989. Mem.: Soc. Info. Display. Achievements include patents in field; invention of silicon based metal-insulator-semiconductor-electroptical material type optical image converters; discovery of electrophoretic effect in liquid crystals; invention of electrophoretic effect based liquid crystal displays; development of metal-insulator-semiconductor-liquid crystal type optical image converter; liquid crystals with induced spiral structure and their application in display systems. Home: Bristol, England. Deceased.

**SILBERBERG, REIN,** nuclear astrophysicist, researcher; b. Tallinn, Estonia, Jan. 15, 1932; came to U.S., 1950; s. Jüri and Elisabeth (Linkvest) S.; m. Ene Liis Rammul, Aug. 28, 1965; children: Hugo Valter, Ingrid Kaja. MA, U. Calif., Berkeley, 1956, PhD, 1960. Postdoctoral rsch. Naval Rsch. Lab., Washington, 1960-62, rsch. physicist, 1962-81, head cosmic ray sect., 1981-85, dep. br. head cosmic and gamma ray, 1985-90. Co-dir., editor, lectr. Internat. Sch. Cosmic Ray Astrophysics, Erice, Italy, 1978-96; cons. Univs. Space Rsch. Assn., Washington, 1990-95; cons. in nuclear astrophysics Roanoke Coll., 1995—. Author: (with others) Albert Einstein 100-Year Memorial Volume, 1979; co-editor: Currents in High Energy Astrophysics, 1993, Cosmic Rays and the Interstellar Medium, 1991, Particle Astrophysics and Cosmology, 1995, Toward the New Millennium in Astrophysics, Problems and Prospects, 1997; contbr. chpts. to Ann. Revs. of Nuclear Sci., articles to Astrophys. Jour., Phys. Revs., and Radiation Rsch. Recipient Meritorious Civil Svc. award U.S. Govt., 1980, Handicapped Employee of Yr. award U.S. Govt., 1985. Fellow Am. Phys. Soc., Am. Astron. Soc., Am. Geophys. Union, Radiation Rsch. Soc., Internat. Astron. Union; mem. AAAS, N.Y. Acad. Scis., Cosmos Club. Achievements include development of Silberberg-Tsao cross section equations; derivation and explanation of cosmic ray source composition; pioneering development of theoretical high-energy neutrino astronomy, gamma-ray astrophysics; energy deposition by nuclear interactions; formulation of radiation protection requirements for lunar base and for manned Mars mission; calculation of single event upsets on shielded spacecraft; evaluation of models of cosmic-ray origin. Home: Silver Spring, Md. Died Aug. 31, 2001.

**SILVER, HORACE WARD MARTIN TAVARES,** composer, pianist; b. Norwalk, Conn., Sept. 2, 1928; s. John and Gertrude (Edmounds) S.; 1 son, Gregory Student pub. schs., Norwalk. Leader, Horace Silver Quintet, 1955—2014; Composer: Senor Blues, 1956, Doodlin', 1956, The Preacher, 1956, Nica's Dream, 1956, Lonely Woman, 1956, Home Cookin', 1956, Enchantment, 1956, Cookin' at the Continental, 1957, Moon Rays, 1957, Soulville, 1957, Sister Sadie, 1959, Come on Home, 1959, Peace, 1959, Finger Poppin, 1959, Blowin' the Blues Away, 1959, Strollin', 1960, Filthy McNasty, 1961, The Tokyo Blues, 1962, Silver's Serenade, 1963, Song For My Father, 1965, 89, Que Pasa, 1965; albums include Six Pieces of Silver, 1956, 86, Horace Silver and the Jazz Messengers, 1985, Serenade to a Soul Sister, 1986, The Best of Horace Silver, 1988, Volume 2, 1989, Horace Silver Trio, 1989, Song for my Father, 1989, The Cape Verdean Blues, 1989, Doin the Thing, 1989, Silver's Blues, 1989, Horace-Scope, 1990, It's Got To Be Funky, 1993, Pencil Packin' Papa, 1994, Hard Bop Grandpop, 1996, Re-Entry, 1996. Recipient Budweiser Mus. Excellence award, 1958, Silver Record award Blue Note Records, 1959, Citizen Call Entertainment award, 1960, President's Merit award, 2005; named a Jazz Master, NEA, 2005 Mem. A.S.C.A.P., American Fedn. Musicians. Died June 18, 2014.

**SILVERMAN, HUGH J.,** philosophy educator; b. Boston, Aug. 17, 1945; s. Leslie and Eleanore (Riffin) S.; m. L. Theresa Watkins, June 22, 1968 (div. Apr. 1983); children: Claire Christine, H. Christopher; m. Gertrude Postl, Sept. 1, 1987. BA, Lehigh U., 1966, MA, 1967; postgrad., U. Paris, 1968, 71-72; PhD, Stanford U., 1973. Lectr. Stanford U., Calif., 1973-74; asst. prof. SUNY, Stony Brook, 1974-79, assoc. prof., 1979-83, prof. philosophy and comparative lit., from 1983, affiliated faculty mem. dept. European langs., lits. and cultures, 2004, dept. art, from 2005. Vis. sr. lectr. U. Warwick, Coventry, Eng., 1980, U. Nice, France, 1980, 81; vis. prof. Duquesne U., Pitts., 1978, 2000, NYU, 1978-80, 85-86, U. Leeds, Eng., 1988, U. Torino, Italy, 1989, U. Vienna, Austria, 1993, 94, 97, 2000, U. Nice, France, 1994, U. Helsinki, Finland, 1997, 99, U. Sydney, Australia, 1998, U. Milan, U. Rome II, 2001, U. Trondheim, Norway, 2002, Ul Klagenfurt, Austrlia, 2003, 05; co-dir. Internat. Philos. Seminar, Alto Adige, Italy, 1991—; Fulbright Disting. chair humanities U. Vienna, 2000-01. Author: Inscriptions: Between Phenomenology and Structuralism, 1987, Textualities: Between Hermeneutics and Deconstruction, 1994 (German translation 1997), Inscriptions: After Phenomenology and Structuralism, 1997; editor: Piaget, Philosophy and the Human Sciences, 1980, 97 (Spanish translation 1989), Philosophy and Non-Philosophy since Merleau-Ponty, 1988, 97, Derrida and Deconstruction, 1989, (Korean translation 1999), Postmodernism - Philosophy and the Arts, 1990 (Korean translation 1990), Gadamer and Hermeneutics, 1991, Writing the Politics of Difference, 1991, Questioning Foundations: Truth/Subjectivity/Culture, 1993, Cultural Semiosis: Training the Signifier, 1997, Philosophy and Desire, 2000, Lyotard: Philosophy, Politics and the Sublime, 2002; co-editor: Jean-Paul Sartre: Contemporary Approaches to His Philosophy, 1980, Continental Philosophy in America, 1983, Hermeneutics and Deconstruction, 1985, Descriptions, 1985, Critical and Dialectical Phenomenology, 1987, Horizons of Continental Philosophy, 1987, Postmodernism and Continental Philosophy, 1988, The Textual Sublime: Deconstruction and its Differences, 1990, Merleau-Ponty: Texts and Dialogues: On Philosophy, Politics and Culture, 1992, 96, Textualität der Philosophie-Philosophie und Literatur, 1994, Derrida und Die Politiken der Freundschaft, 2003, co-editor; series editor: Routledge Continental Philosophy series, 1986—; co-editor: Humanities Press Humanity Books Contemporary Studies in Philosophy and the Human Sciences series, 1989—, assoc. editor, 1979-89; editor: Humanities Press Humanity Books Series in Philosophy and Literary Theory, 1989—, SUNY Press Contemporary Studies in Philosophy and Literature, 1988-96, Northwestern U. Press Series in Philosophy, Literature, and Culture, 1996-2001; Bull. for Rsch. in Humanities, 1983-84, Continuum Books Textures: Philosophy/Literature/Culture Series, 2001—; mem. editorial bd. Rsch. in Phenomenology, 1981—, Rev. of Existential Psychology and Psychiatry, 1979—, Symploké, 2000-, Chiasmi: Intz Merleau-Ponty Studies, 2001-; translator: Consciousness and the Acquisition of Language, 1973; contbr. numerous articles to profl. jours., and chpts. in books. Fulbright-French Govt. and Alliance Francaise fellow, Paris, 1971-72; faculty rsch. fellow SUNY-Stony Brook, 1977, 78, 81; rsch. fellow Am. Coun. Learned Socs., 1981-82; Experienced Faculty Travel fellowship SUNY, 1985, 88, 93, 99; Fulbright travel grant, Netherlands and Germany, 2001; recipient MLA travel grant (Brazil), 1993, N.Y. Coun. for Humanities grant, 1976-77, SUNY Chancellor's award for excellence in teaching, 1977, medal U. Helsinki, 1997. Mem. Soc. Phenomenology and Existential Philosophy (exec. co-dir. 1980-86), Internat. Assn. Philosophy and Lit. (exec. com. 1976—, exec. sec. 1979-87, exec. dir. 1987—), Brit. Soc. Phenomenology (exec. com. 1980-95), Merleau-Ponty Circle (chmn. publs. com. 1978-2001), Heidegger Conf., Am. Soc. Aesthetics, Am. Philos. Assn. (program adv. com. 1986-89, 2003-, lectures publs. and rsch. com. 1991-94). Home: Port Jefferson, NY. Died May 8, 2013.

**SIM, PENG CHOON,** manufacturing executive; b. Singapore, Dec. 20, 1932; s. Ban Chye and Lian Keow (Koh) S.; m. Alice Chong Swee Kheng, Nov. 21, 1958; children: Rita, Koon Weng, Grace, Su-San. Sr. Cambridge cert., Anglo Chinese Sch., Ipoh, 1951. Storekeeper Barlow & Co., Ltd., Kuala Lumpur, Malaysia, 1952; med. rep. Allen & Hanburys, Ltd., Singapore, 1953-56; mng. dir. H. Rogers & Co., Ltd., Kuala Lumpur, 1957-63; chmn., mng. dir. Polychem (M) Sdn. Bhd., Kuala Lumpur, from 1967, N.P. King Pte., Ltd., Singapore, from 1970, N.P. King (HK) Ltd., Hong Kong, from 1970. Bd. dirs. SKF Bearing Industries Sdn. Bhd., Malaysia; vice chmn. Kwan Inn Teng Found., Petaling. Dir. Selangor Tung Shin Hosp., Kuala Lumpur, 1981—, Cabot (Malaysia) Sdn. Bhd. Port Dickson, Selangor, 1988—; dir. Pacific Asia Carbon Black Divsn. (Cabot), Kuala Lumpur, Selangor, 1997-98, Cabot Specialty Chems., Inc., Cons., Asia Pacific Region, 1999—. Recipient Panglima Jasa Negara. Home: Kuala Lumpur, Malaysia. Died June 2008.

**SIMMONS, HAROLD CLARK,** metal products executive; b. Golden, Tex., May 13, 1931; m. Annette Caldwel Fleck, 1980; 2 stepchildren; 4 children from previous marriage. BA phi beta kappa, MA phi beta kappa, U. Tex. Chmn., CEO Amalgamated Sugar Corp., Ogden, Utah; investigator US Civil Service, 1952—55; book examiner Fed. Deposit Ins. Corp., 1955—56; loan officer Republican Nat. Bank, 1956—61; pres., CEO Contran Corp.; chmn. Nat. City Lines, Dallas; chmn., CEO Kronos Worldwide, Inc.; chmn. Valhi, Inc., Dallas, NL Industries, Inc., 1987, CEO, 2003—13; vice chmn. Titanium Metals Corp., 2004—05, CEO, 2005—06, chmn., 2006. Founder Harold C. Simmons Comprehensive Cancer Ctr., 1988; founder, chmn. Simmons Found., 1988. Named one of The Forbes 400: Richest Americans, 1999—2013, The World's Richest People, Forbes mag., 2001—13. Republican. Baptist. Died Dec. 28, 2013.

**SIMMONS, JOHN FRANKLIN,** writer; b. Detroit, Oct. 5, 1945; s. John Edward Simmons and Valeria Octavia (Spiller) Gibson; M. Debra Maxine Powell, Oct., 1962 (div. Jan. 1964); 1 child, Tracey Aileen; m. Laura Alice Jones, Jan. 8, 1965 (div. Oct. 1979); children: John Marque, Carla Valeria; m. Lynda Marie Watkins, Dec. 2, 1979 (div. Sept. 1991); children: Lisa Marie, Joshua Franklin. Student, U. Detroit, 1968-70, U. Hawaii, 1971. Child care worker Wayne County Child Devel. Ctr., Plymouth, Mich., 1967-68, Detroit Psychiat. Inst., 1968-70. Author numerous poems including Journey, 1982, Love of My Life, 1983, Note to a Graceful Lady, 1987, Titles and Atributes of God, 1988, Lotion, 1990, Older Lady, 1990, Greatest General, 1990, Abraham Lincoln, 1990, Love of My Youth, 1990, Worm, 1990. Active Rep. Presdl. Commn. Task Force, 1986, Nat. Rep. Senatorial Inner Circle Inaguration, Washington, 1989, Presdl. Round Table, Washington, 1989; co-founder Battle Normandy Mus., Caen, France, Am. Air Force Mus., Duxford, Eng., Nat. Law Enforcement Meml. Bldg., Washington, Police Hall of Fame, Miami, Fla., U.S. Naval Meml. Bldg., Washington. With U.S. Army, 1964-67. Mem. U.S. Naval Inst., Am. Assn. Advancement Sci., Am. Fedn. of Police, N.Y. Acad. Scis., Internat. Assn. Chiefs of Police (life), Internat. Platform Assn., Order of Michael the Archangel (knight chevalier 1989), Venerable Order of St. Francis of Assisi (Humanitarian award 1989). Mem. Jewish Christian Ch. Avocations: books, music, collecting art, nature, travel. Deceased.

**SIMMONS, PAUL ALLEN,** retired federal judge; b. Monongahela, Pa., Aug. 31, 1921; s. Perry C. and Lilly D. (Allen) S.; m. Gwendolyn O. Gladden, Sept. 2, 1950; children: Paul A., Gwendolyn Dale, Anne Marie. BA, U. Pitts., 1946; JD, Harvard U., 1949. Mem. faculty, prof. law SC State Coll. Law, 1949-52; prof. law NC Central U., 1952-56; pvt. practice law Monongahela, 1956-73; judge Ct. of Common Pleas, Washington County, Pa., 1973-78, US Dist. Ct. (western dist.) Pa., Pitts., 1978—90, sr. judge, 1990—2014. Mem. Pa. Human Relations Commn., 1963-68; mem. Pa. Minor Jud. Edn. Bd., 1970-86, Washington County Redevel. Authority, 1970-73. Mem. Pa. Bar Assn., N.C. Bar Assn., American Bar Assn., Washington County Bar Assn., Pa. Bar Assn., American Judicature Soc., NAACP. Democrat. Mem. African Meth. Episcopal Ch. Clubs: Masons, Elks. Home: Monongahela, Pa. Died Oct. 9, 2014.

**SIMMONS, S. DALLAS,** retired academic administrator; b. Ahoskie, NC, Jan. 28, 1940; s. Yvonne Martin; m. Mary A. Simmons, Feb. 10, 1963; children: S. Dallas Jr., Kristie Lynn. BS, N.C. Cen. U., 1962, MS, 1967; PhD, Duke U., 1977. Asst. prof. bus. adminstrn. N.C. Cen. U., Durham, 1967-71, asst. to chancellor, 1971-77, vice chancellor for univ. relations, 1977-81; pres. St. Paul's Coll., Lawrenceville, Va., 1981-85, Va. Union Univ., Richmond, 1985—99. Faculty cons. IBM, Research Triangle Park, N.C., 1968-71; cons. for edn. devel. officers Nat. Lab. for Higher Edn., Durham, 1972-73; staff asst. to Pres., White House Advance Office, Washington, 1975-76; univ. fed. liaison officer Moton Coll. Service Bur., Washington, 1972-80; mem. competency testing commn. N.C. Bd. Edn., 1977-81; bd. dirs., mem. loan com., mem. planning com. Pace American Bank, Lawrenceville, 1984-85. Bd. dirs. N.C. Mus. Life & Sci., Durham, 1972-75, Volunteer Services Bur, Inc., Durham, 1972-77, Va. Poly. Inst. and State U., 1982-83; mem. Durham Civic/Conv. Ctr. Commn., 1972-73, U.S./Zululand Ednl. Found., 1985; trustee, mem. exec. and pers. com. N.C. Cen. U., 1983-85; active various coms. United Negro Coll. Fund; mem. exec. bd. John B. McLendon Found., Inc., 1985. Named one of The Outstanding Young Men America, 1972, Citizen of Yr. Omega Psi Phi, 1983-84, Bus. Assoc. of Yr. American Bus. Women's Assn., 1984. Mem. Assn. Episc. Colleges (pres.-elect), Cen. Intercollegiate Athletic Assn., Nat. Assn. for Equal Opportunity in Higher Edn. (bd. dirs., chmn. leadership awards com. 1984-85), American Mgmt. Assn., Data Processing Mgmt. Assn. (cen. Carolina chpt.), American Assn. Sch. Adminstrators, American Assn. Univ. Adminstrators, Kappa Alpha Psi (Kappa of Month Dec. 1981), Sigma Pi Phi (alpha beta boulé). African Methodist Episcopalian. Club: Downtown. Lodges: Masons (32 degree), Shriners, Kiwanis, Optimists. Home: Richmond, Va. Died July 5, 2014.

**SIMON, SIMONE,** actress; b. Marseille, France, Apr. 23, 1911; d. Henri Louis Firmin and Erma Maria Domenica Giorcelli. Actress: (theater) Balthazar, 1931, Le Roi Pausole, 1931, Oh Mon Bel Inconnu, 1933, Le Bonheur Mesdames, 1934, Toi c'est Moi, 1934, Three After Three, 1939-40, Les Jours Heureux, 1942, Le Square du Pérou, 1947, Au Petit Bonheur, 1948, Les Cavaleurs, 1966, La Court-Paille, 1967; (films) On Opère sans Douleur, 1931, Le Chanteur Inconnu, 1931, Durand Contre Durand, 1931, La Petite Chocolatière, 1931, Un Fils d'Amérique, 1932, Le Roi des Palaces, 1932, Prenez Garde á la Peinture, 1932, Pour Vivre Heureux, 1932, L'Etoile de Valence, 1933, Tire au Flanc, 1933, Lac-aux-dames, 1933, Les Yeux Noirs, 1935, Les Beaux Jours, 1935, Girls Dormitary, 1936, Seventh Heaven, 1936, Ladies in Love, 1937, Love and Hisses, 1937, Josette, 1938, La Bête Humaine, 1938, Cavalcade d'Amour, 1939, All That Money Can Buy, 1941, Cat People, 1942, The Curse of the Cat People, 1943, Mademoiselle Fifi, 1944, Johnny Does Not Live Here Anymore, 1944, Petrus, 1946, Femmes sans Nom, 1949, La Ronde, 1950, Le Plaisir, 1951, Les Trois Voleurs, 1953, Double Destin, 1954, The Extra Day, 1955, La Femme en Bleu, 1972. Recipient Medaille de Vermeil Ville de Paris, 1984, Officier des Arts et des Lettres, 1985, Chevalier de la Legion d'Honneur, 1986. Roman Catholic. Avocations: painting, piano, crossword, puzzles. Home: Paris, France. Died Feb. 22, 2005.

**SIMPSON, FREDERICK JAMES,** retired science administrator; b. Regina, Sask., Can., June 8, 1922; s. Ralph James and Lillian Mary (Anderson) S.; m. Margaret Christine Simpson, May 28, 1947 (dec. Apr. 2003); children: Christine Louise, Steven James, Leslie Coleen, Ralph Edwin, David Glen. B.Sc., U. Alta., Can., 1944, M.Sc. in Agr., 1946; PhD in Bacteriology, U. Wis., 1952. With Nat. Research Council Can., 1946-84; asst. dir. Atlantic Research Lab., Halifax, N.S., 1970-73, dir., 1973-84; sci. cons., 1985-90. Vis. scientist U. Ill., Urbana, 1955-56, vis. prof., 1964; mem. exec. council Atlantic Provinces Interuniv. Com. on Scis., 1976-79, chmn., 1981-84; pres. Fed. Inst. Mgmt., Halifax, 1981-82 Contbr. numerous articles to profl. jours. Treas. Lunburg Condominium Corp. No. 1, 1998-2008. Decorated Queen's Silver Anniversary medal. Fellow Royal Soc. of Arts (London); mem. Can. Soc. Microbiologists (hon., sec.-treas. 1969-70, v.p. 1971-72, pres. 1972-73), Nova Scotian Inst. Sci. (v.p. 1975-76, pres. 1977-78), Internat. Phycological Soc., Aquaculture Assn. Can., Sigma Xi. Mem. United Ch. of Canada. Died Dec. 21, 2013.

**SINAISKY, NICHOLAS ALEKSEEVICH,** mechanical engineer, researcher, consultant; b. Volgograd, Russia, Aug. 10, 1924; came to U.S., 1992; s. Aleksey Ivanovich and Klavdja Stepanovna (Krasukova) S.; m. Elizaveta Agapovna Kargina, Mar. 16, 1962 (div. Nov. 1984); children: Natalia, Nadezda, Julia; m. Valentina Alekseevna Pilgasova Pokrovskaya, Jan. 16., 1985. BME, Tomsk Poly. U., Russia, 1958; MME, USSR Acad. of Sci., Moscow, 1968; PhD in ME, USSR Acad. of Sci., Novosibirsk, Russia, 1980. Sr. designer combustion Siberian Sci. Rsch. Inst. for Aviation, Novosibirsk, Russia, 1958-60; lead engr. Inst. Theoretical and Applied Physics Siberian Dept. of USSR Acad. Sci., Novosibirsk, Russia, 1960-62, sci. worker Inst. for Physics and Chem., 1962-68, sr. rsch. assoc. Inst. for Solid Matter, 1968-74; adj. prof., sr. rsc. assoc. Inst. for Constn. & Clinker, Novosibirsk-Krasnoyarsk, 1974-85; top mgr. in environ. protection Sci. Rsch. Inst. for Energy & Cavitator Enterprise, Baku, Azerbaijan, 1985-92; prin. rschr., cons. Cavitator LLC, Portsmouth, NH, from 1992. Patentee low temperature plasma and cavitation; contbr. numerous articles to Russian and Am. profl. jours. Polit. prisoner, north camps USSR, 1947-50, Kazakhstan, 1950-54. Recipient Vet. of Labour medal Presidium of the Supreme Ct. of the USSR, 1983, Golden medal and diploma 26th Salon Int. of Inventions, Geneva, Switzerland, 1998, Inventors laureate, Russia, 2000; named laureate in ecology Georgia Energo USSR, Tbilisi, 1990, 500 Leaders of Influence Presdl. Seal of Honor, 2001, Outstanding Scientists of 20th and 21st Century, Companion of Honor, Internat. Order of Merit, 2000, Am. medal of honor Imminent Scientists of Today, 2002, World Lifetime Achievement award, 2002; named to Contemporary Hall of Fame, 2002. Mem.: Assn. Victims Unlawful Polit. Repressions, Libr. Russian Acad. Scis. (hon.). Achievements include work in ballistic missile reentry radiation analysis, demonstrating short wave excitomic decay photoeffect in wide-gap insulators; atomization with atoms/molecules excitation/radiation through plural cumulative shock in spray used by means of cavitator to reduce boiler fouling, NOx/CO/SO2carbon emission and improve fossil fuel saving, including oil, coal-water slurries and orimulsion, coal-water slurries; leader in heavy cavitation assisted oil/orimulsion burning for power generation by North American, European, and Russian electric utilities. Died Dec. 13, 2002.

**SINDEN, SIR DONALD ALFRED,** actor, writer; b. Plymouth, Eng., Oct. 9, 1923; s. Alfred Edward and Mabel Agnes (Fuller) S.; m. Diana Mahony, May 3, 1948; children: Jeremy, Marc. First appeared on stage in 1942; actor: (plays) There's a Girl in My Soup, 1966, The Relapse, 1967, Twelfth Night, 1969, London Assurance, 1970, An Enemy of the People, 1975, King Lear, 1976, Much Ado About Nothing, 1976, Othello, 1979, Present Laughter, 1980, Uncle Vanya, 1982, School for Scandal, 1983, The Scarlet Pimpernel, 1985, Major Barbara, 1988, Oscar Wilde, 1990, She Stoops to Conquer, 1992, Hamlet, 1994, That Good Night, 1996, Ariadne Auf Naxos, 1997, Quartet, 1999; The Cruel Sea, 1953, Mogambo, 1953, Doctor in the House; (TV series) Two's Company, 1975-79, Never the Twain, 1981-91 Decorated Knight Comdr. of the Most Excellent Order of the British Empire, Her Majesty Queen Elizabeth II, 1997 Mem. Leicestershire Edn. Arts Com., London Acad. Music and Dramatic Arts, Fedn. Playgoers Socs. (pres.), Royal Theatrical Fund (pres.), London Appreciation Soc. (v.p.), Garrick Club (trustee), Beefsteak Club, MCC. Avocations: theatrical history, london, architecture, ecclesiology. Home: Kent, England. Died Sept. 11, 2014.

**SINDHUNATHA, KRISTOFORUS,** legal and business affairs consulting company executive; b. Jakarta, Indonesia, Mar. 20, 1933; s. Hok Lan Ong and Eugenia Lie; m. Hudiani Sutikna, Sept. 7, 1958; children: Marya Priyanti, Martina Dharmesti, Paulus Widya. Bandung, chr. Lyceum, Petrus Canisius Coll. Jakarta, Indonesia, 1953; LLM, U. Indonesia, Jakarta, 1961. Maj. Indonesian Navy, 1961-70; pres., dir. PT Indulexco, Jakarta, 1975-93, chmn., from 1993. Acting gen. sec. Maritime Def. Command, Min. Def., Jakarta, 1968-70; commr. PT Citra Tubindo, Jakarta, 1990—, Kabil Indonusa Estate, Batam, Indonesia, 1994-97., Chmn. Bakom-PKB, Jakarta, 1977-96; mem. Indonesia Red Cross Com., Jakarta, 1987-94; mem. Peoples Consultative Assembly Indonesia, Jakarta, 1982-92. Recipient Chevalier Ordre Nat. Merit, France, 1982, Mahaputera Pratama Rep. Indonesia award, 1998. Mem. Trisakti Found. (founder, chmn., bd. dirs. 1966—), LDD Found. Archbisdom Jakarta (chmn. 1975-97), Retired Mil. Officers Orgn., Lions Club. Roman Catholic. Avocations: tennis, reading. Home: Jakarta, Indonesia. Died Aug. 16, 2005.

**SINGER, GEORGE MILTON,** clinical psychologist; b. Phila., Oct. 13, 1924; s. Benjamin and Bessie (Podlisker) S.; m. Carol Ann Horton, June 15, 1977; children: Elizabeth Carol, Susan Theresa, Sonnet Marie-Anne. BA, Temple U., 1950, AM, 1952, PhD, 1958. Grad. asst. exptl. psychology lab. Temple U., Phila., 1950-51, grad. asst. psychol. clinic, 1951-53, lectr., 1953-54; chief psychologist Phila. State Hosp., 1953-56; dir. psychol. services Pennhurst State Hosp., Spring City, Pa., 1958-61; clin. psychologist Kern County Mental Health Dept., Bakersfield, Calif., 1961-68; project dir., coordinator Kernview Community Mental Health Ctr., Bakersfield, 1968-70; pvt. practice clin. psychology Bakersfield, 1953—2001; ret., 2001. Mem. med. staff Kern View Mental Health Ctr. and Hosp., Bakersfield, Calif., 1988-92; mem. med. staff Meml. Ctr. for Behavioral Health, Bakersfield, 1992-97; affiliated med. staff Hoag Meml. Hosp., Newport Beach, Calif., 1972-73; cons. psychologist Pioneer Cmty. Hosp., 1976-83. Cons. editor Dictionary of Psychology, Corsini, 1999. Mem. Kern County Mental Health Adv. Bd., 1976-83, adv. bd. Patton State Hosp., 1979-85; bd. dirs. Orange County Child Guidance Clinic, 1973-74. Served with USAAF, 1943-46, ETO, MTO. Recipient Service award Psi Chi, 1952, Cert. of Achievement Southeast Pa. Mental Health Assn., 1956. Mem. AAAS, APA, Calif. Psychol. Assn., Am. Soc. Clin. Hypnosis, Kern County Soc. Clin. Psychologists (pres. 1993-94), Kern County Psychol. Assn. (pres. 1968-69), Internat. Soc. Hypnosis, Rotary of Spring City (pres. 1960-61). Deceased.

**SINGER, SIR HANS WOLFGANG,** educator; b. Elberfeld, Rhineland, Germany, Nov. 29, 1910; s. Heinrich and Antonia (Spier) S.; m. Ilse Lina Plaut(dec. 2001); 1 child,

Stephen. Diploma in polit. sci., Bonn U., 1931; PhD, Cambridge U., 1936; degree (hon.), Univ. Nacional del Litoral, Santa Fe, Argentina, 1989, U. Sussex, Eng., 1990, U. Glasgow, Scotland, 1993, U. Lisbon, Portugal, 1994. Researcher Pilgrim Trust, London, 1936-38; asst. lectr. Manchester (Eng.) U., 1938-44; economist Ministry of Town and Country Planning, London, 1945-46; lectr. Glasgow (Scotland) U., 1946-47; dir. UN Secretariat, NYC, 1947-69; fellow Inst. Devel. Studies at U. Sussex, Brighton, England, 1969—2006. Author: Men Without Work, 1938, Strategy of Economic Development, 1959, Food Aid, 1988. Recipient Frances Wood Meml. prize Royal Statistical Soc., 1939; hon. fellow Inst. Social Studies, The Hague, The Netherlands, 1975. Mem. Soc. for Internat. Devel. (pres. U.K. and N.Y. brs. 1968-70), Devel. Studies Assn. (pres.). Mem. Labour Party. Home: Brighton, England. Died Feb. 26, 2006.

**SINGER, JOSEF,** aerospace engineer, educator; b. Vienna, Aug. 24, 1923; arrived in Israel, 1933; s. Zvi and Etel (Isler) S.; m. Shoshana, June 29, 1954; children: Gideon, Tamar, Uri. BSc Mech. Engring. (1st class hon.), Univ. London, 1948, DIC Aero. Engring., 1949; MAero. Engring., Poly Inst. Bklyn., 1953, DAero. Engring., 1957; DSc (hon.), Poly. Inst., NYC, 1983; D honoris causa, Univ. d'Aix, Marseilles, 1986; D Engring. honoris causa, U. Glasgow, 1993. Engring. officer Israel Air Force, 1949-55, head test and devel. sect., 1953-55; from sr. lectr. to prof. Technion IIT Aeronautical Engring., Haifa, Israel, 1955-91, prof. emeritus, 1991—2009, head dept., 1958-60, 65-67; pres. Technion IIT, Haifa, Israel, 1982-86. Vis. assoc. prof. aeronautics, Stanford (Calif.) U., 1963-64; vis. prof. aeronautics Calif. Inst. Tech., Pasadena, 1968-69, U. London, 1988, 91, RWTH Aachen, Germany, U. Calif., 1990-91; sr. v.p. engring. Israel Aircraft Industries, 1971-73, chmn. rsch. and devel. com., 1979-82, 86-87, chmn. bd. dirs., 1986-87; cons. in field; rschr. in field. Editor Congress ICAS Proceedings, 1974, 78, 80, Babcock Meml. Volume, 1989, Congress IUTAM Proceedings, 1993; mem. editl. adv. bd., reviewer various sci. jours.; contbr. articles to profl. jours. Mem. Israel Coun. Higher Edn., 1975-81. RAF Major Israel Air Force, 1949-55. Recipient Wilhelm Exner medal, Austria, 1994, Israel prize in Engring. Rsch., 2000; scholar Sherman Fairchild Distingi scholar, Calif., Inst. Tech., 1987—88, 1989; Vinton Hayes sr. fellow, Harvard U., 1976—77. Fellow: City and Guilds London Inst., Inst. Mech. Engring, RAeS, AIAA; mem.: ISAA (hon.), Soc. Exptl. Stress Analysis, Israel Soc. Aeronautics and Astronautics (founding mem., past pres.), Deutsche Gesellschaft Luft & Raumfahrt (hon. Ludwig-Prandtl-Ring 1994), Academie Nat. de l'Air et d'Espace (fgn. assoc.), Internat. Acad. Astronautics, U.S. Nat. Acad. Engring. (fgn. assoc.), Internat. Coun. Aero. Scis. (pres. 1982—86, internat. program. com., chmn. 1978—82, exec. com. from 1974, Maurice Roy medal 1990). Home: Haifa, Israel. Died Nov. 12, 2009.

**SINGH, VISHWANATH PRATAP,** former Prime Minister of India; b. Allahabad, India, June 25, 1931; s. Ram Gopal; m. Sita Kumari, June 25, 1955; children: Ajeya, Abhay Student, Allahabad U., Poona U.; BA, BS, LLB. Mem. Uttar Pradesh Legis. Assembly, Vidhan Sabha, India, 1969-71, 80-82; whip Congress Legis. Party, 1970-71; mem. Lok Sabha, 1971-77, 84, 88-89 and from 89; dep. min., then min. state Union Coun.; chief min. of Uttar Pradesh, 1980-82; min. commerce & supply Govt. of India, 1983-84, min. fin. New Delhi, 1985-87, min. def., 1987, prime min., 1989—90. Mem. Rajya Sabha, 1983-88; pres. Uttar Pradesh Congress Com., 1984; founder, leader Jan Morcha Party; mem. All India Congress Com., 1969-71. Died Nov. 27, 2008.

**SINGLETON, DONALD EDWARD,** retired journalist; b. Morristown, NJ, Nov. 8, 1936; s. Edward Leslie and Charlotte (Angerbauer) S.; m. Maureen Ann McNiff, Aug. 8, 1959 (div. 1977); children: Nancy Ann, Mark Aram, Jill Susan. Student, Fairleigh Dickinson U., 1955-58. Reporter Dover (N.J.) Advance, 1959-61, Morristown Daily Record, 1961-63, Newark Eve. News, 1963-64; feature reporter-writer NY Daily News, 1964—2007; ret., 2007. Organizer Com. to Save Church Sq. Park, Hoboken, N.J.; vice chmn. Hoboken Environment Com.; mem. due process com. ACLU., Mem. bd. edn., City of Hoboken, 1974-77. Recipient Pub. Service award N.Y. Council Civic Affairs, 1967; President's Distinguished Service award N.Y.C. Council, 1969; Newspaper award merit Women's Press Club N.Y.C., 1970, 79; citation VFW, 1970; Heywood Broun Meml. award American Newspaper Guild, 1970; Silver medal for pub. service journalism N.Y. chpt. Pub. Relations Soc. America, 1970; certificate merit American Bar Assn., 1971; Page One award Newspaper Guild N.Y., 1970; Feature award Newspaper Reporters Assn. N.Y., 1972; Consistent Excellence award Uniformed Firefighters Assn., 1991. Mem. American Newspaper Guild. Clubs: Press (N.Y.C.). Home: Jersey City, NJ. *In reporting, I try very hard to avoid gathering facts in such a way as to fulfill a preconception. I also attempt to force myself to review constantly my opinions about my subjects, and to keep my mind as open as possible. In writing, I try to ask myself the following questions regularly: "Is this what I really believe? Or am I simply writing this way because I believe that this is what some other person or group would like me to write?" Unless I can answer the first question in the affirmative, and the second in the negative, I am not satisfied with a particular story.* Died Mar. 2, 2014.

**SINNAPILLAY, JOHN CHELLIAH,** trade association executive; b. Kuala Lumpur, Malaysia, Apr. 26, 1935; m. P. Chandramani, June 16, 1962; children: Jane Manning, Janet Vasanthi, Raj Kumar, Rajesh Kumar. Diploma, Royal Soc. Health, London. Pub. health inspector, Petaling Jaya, Malaysia, 1956-60; jr. asst. commr. for labour Ministry of Labour, Kuala Lumpur, 1960-64, indsl. rels. officer Johore, 1964-67, asst. dir. for labour Pahang, 1967-71, asst. dir. indsl. rels. Kuala Lumpur, 1971-73; indsl. rels. officer The Malayan Agrl. Prodrs. Assn., Kuala Lumpur, 1973-76, sec., 1976-78, asst. dir., 1978-80, dir., from 1980. Mem. bd. Employees Provident Fund; mem. Nat. Labour adv. Coun., South Indian Labour Fund Bd., Indsl. Ct. Employers' Panel; mem. Nat. Inst. Occupl. Safety and Health, mem. Nat. Council for Occpl. Safety and Health. Hon. treas. Diocesan Coun., Evang. Luth. Ch. in Malaysia and Singapore, 1990-95; chmn. PTA La Salle's Secondary Sch., 1995. Mem. Malaysian Inst. of Pers. Mgmt. (hon. sec. 1981), Sentosa Lodge (past sr. warden 1990, almoner 1993-94, worshipful master 1994-95), Joseph Eu Lodge (sec. 1996—). Home: Kuala Lumpur, Malaysia. Died 1996.

**SINOWATZ, FRED,** former chancellor of Austria; b. Neufeld, Leitha, Feb. 5, 1929; 2 children. Dr. phil., U. Vienna, 1953. Entered svc. Burgenland Govt., 1953. Mem.: Provincial party sec. Austrian Socialist Party (SPO) Burgenland (chmn. SPO 1983—88), Nat. Austria (mem. nat. coun. 1971—83, fed. minister edn. and arts Austria 1971—83, vice chancellor 1981—83, fed. chancellor 1983—86), landesrat (councillor provincial govt. 1966—71), Burgenland Landtag (provincial assembly) (pres. 1964). Died Aug. 11, 2008.

**SIPOS, ALBIN PAUL,** civil engineer, educator, architect; b. Werschetz, Temes, Hungary, Mar. 1, 1918; arrived in Fed. Rep. of Germany, 1965; s. Paul and Anna (Werdonitsch) S.; Ilona Katalin Galiba, Oct. 12, 1973. Diploma in engring., Tech. U., Budapest, 1945. Chief engr. Industry Norm Office, Budapest, 1947-50; structural engr. planning prefabricated houses State Planning Office, Budapest, 1950-56; patent judge Patent Office, Budapest, 1956-59; rsch. arch. Hungarian Sci. Inst. for Structural Engring., Budapest, 1959-65; rsch. engr. Inst. for Arch. with Plastics, Darmstadt, 1965-69; prof. Tech. Acad., Darmstadt, 1969-87. Author: Proportions Coordination in Architecture, 1952, Plastics Curtain Wall, 1962; constrn. reinforced plastic domes, 1964; contbr. articles to profl. jours. Mem. Arch. and Engr. Assn. (sec. Darmstadt chpt. 1969-79), N.Y. Acad. Scis. Calvinist. Avocation: damaged buildings consultant. Home: Seeheim-Jugenheim, Germany. Died Dec. 19, 2005.

**SIRI, JEAN BRANDENBURG,** advocate; b. Lakota, ND, Mar. 11, 1920; d. Tunis Orville and Edith Marion (Molloy) Brandenburg; m. William E. Siri, Dec. 3, 1947; children: Lynn, Ann. BS, Jamestown Coll., 1942; postgrad., U. Calif., San Francisco, 1944, U. Calif., Berkeley, 1945—46. Biologist, Donner Lab. U. Calif., Berkeley, 1945—52; mem. State Solid Waste & Resource Recovery Adv. Coun., Sacramento, 1973—75; dir., chmn. Stege Sanitary Dist., El Cerrito, Calif., 1975—79; elected bd. dirs. ward 1 East Bay Regional Park, from 1993, pres., 1998. Coun. mem. El Cerrito City Coun., 1980—85, 1987—91, mayor, 1982—83, 1988—89. Mem. Save San Francisco Bay Assocs., Contra Costa Hazardous Waste Task Force, 1985—86, County Environ. Health Coordinating Coun., 1985—88, County Hazardous Materials Commn., 1986—92, County Pub. and Environ. Health Adv. Bd., 1987—99; founder, chmn. West County Toxics Coalition, 1986—2000; alternate solid waste West Contra Costa Joint Powers Authority, 1988—89; bd. mem. Fresh Start, from 2004. Recipient Clean Air award, Lung Assn. Santa Clara, 1976, Sol Feinstone Environ. award, U. Syracuse, 1977, Get Tough on Toxics Environ. award, 1986, Spl. award, Homeless and Hungry, Vols. of Am., 1987; named to El Cerrito Wall of Fame, 1995, Women's Hall of Fame, Contra Costa County, 2001. Mem.: NAACP, LWV, West Contra Costa Transp. Joint Powers Authority, West Contra Costa Conservation League (pres.), Calif. State Local Emergency Planning Com. (rep. 1990—92), Gray Panthers, Native Plant Soc., Audubon Soc., League of Conservation Voters (dir. 1978—79), Sierra Club (city rep. to county homeless adv. com. 1988—93, Scope Environ. award 1986). Democrat. Deceased.

**SIROTKOVIC, JAKOV IVO,** economist, educator; b. Rab, Croatia, Yugoslavia, Nov. 7, 1922; s. Ivo and Lucija (Canki) S.; m. Ecija Ljubetic; 1 child, Maja. Grad. in Econs., Faculty of Econs., Zagreb, Yugoslavia, 1948, PhD, 1951. Pres. Rep. Com. for Planning, Zagreb, 1947-51; dir. Inst. of Econs., Zagreb, 1952-55; assoc. prof. Faculty of Econs., Belgrade, 1956-60, Zagreb, 1950-56, 61-64, prof., 1964-91. Rector U. Zagreb, 1966-68; editor-in-chief Yugoslav Encyclopedic Inst., Zagreb, 1984-91. Author: Expanded Reproduction and Methods of Analysis, 1956, The Planning System in Yugoslavia, 1961, The Theory of Development and Foundations of Yugoslavian Economics, 1964; Yugoslavia's Economic System and Economic Policy, 1983, Economic Development Yugoslavia, 1990. Mem. fed. parliament Govt. of Yugoslavia, Belgrade, 1968-70, v.p. fed. exec. coun., 1970-74; pres. exec. coun. Socialist Republic of Croatia, 1974-78. Recipient AVNOJ award Yugoslav Fed. Assembley, 1982. Mem. Yugoslav Acad. Scis. and Arts (pres. 1978-91, head Econs. Inst. 1980—). Home: Zagreb, Yugoslavia. Died Nov. 1, 2002.

**SISSON, CHARLES HUBERT,** poet; b. Bristol, England, Apr. 22, 1914; s. Richard Percy and Ellen Minnie (Worlock) S.; m. Nora Gilbertson (dec. 2003), Aug. 19, 1937; children: Janet Louth, Hilary Cook. BA in Philosophy and Eng. Lit. with honors, U. Bristol, England, 1934; postgrad., U. Berlin, 1934-35, U. Sorbonne, Paris, 1935-36; DLitt (hon.), U. Bristol, 1980. Asst. prin. Dept. Employment, Ministry Labour, London, 1936—42, prin., 1945—53, asst. sec., 1953—62, under sec., 1962—68, asst. under sec. state, 1968—71; dir., Occupation, Safety & Health Dept. Employment, London, 1971—73. Author essays, poems, collected poems; An Asiatic Romance, 1953, Versions and Perversions of Heine, 1955, Poems, The Spirit of British Administration and Some European Comparisons, 1959, Twenty-One Poems, 1960, The London Zoo: Poems, 1961, Numbers, Art and Action, Christopher Homm, 1965, Catullus (translated), 1966, The Disincarnation: or, How the Flesh Became Word and Dwelt Among Us, 1967, Essays, 1967, Metamorphoses: Poems, 1968, Roman Poems, 1968, English Poetry 1900-1950: An Assessment, 1971, The Case of Walter Bagehot, 1972, In the Trojan Ditch: Collected Poems and Selected Translations, 1974, The Corridor (translated), The Poetic Art by Horace (translated), 1975, Lucretius (translated), 1976, Anchises, 1976, Selected Poems of Swift (ed.), 1977, Hardy's Jude the Obscure (ed.), The Avoidance of Literature, 1978, Selected Contes, by La Fontaine (translated), 1979, The Divine Comedy of Dante (translated), 1980, Phillip Mairet's Autobiographical and Other Papers (ed.), Selected Poems, 1981, Anglican Essays, 1983, Collected Poems 1943-1983, 1984, The Aeneid of Virgil (translated), 1986, Racine's Britannicus, Phaedra, Athaliah, God Bless Karl Marx, 1987, On the Look-out: A Partial Autobiography, 1989, In Two Minds: Guesses at other writers, 1990, Antidotes, 1991, English Perspectives, 1991, Is There a Church of England, What and Who, 1994, Selected Poems, 1995, Collected Translations, 1996, Collected Poems, 1998. Served with Brit. Army, 1942-45, India. Fellow Royal Soc. Lit. Anglican. Home: Somerset, England. Died Sept. 5, 2003.

**SIVE, DAVID,** lawyer; b. Bklyn., Sept. 22, 1922; s. Abraham Leon and Rebecca (Schwartz) S.; m. Mary Robinson, July 23, 1948; children: Rebecca, Helen, Alfred, Walter, Theodore. AB in Political Sci., Bklyn. Coll., 1943; LLB, Columbia Law Sch., 1948. Bar: N.Y. 1948, U.S. Supreme Ct. 1964. Ptnr. Sive, Paget & Riesel, and predecessors, NYC, 1957—2014; prof. Pace U. Law Sch., White Plains, NY, 1995—2014. Adj. prof. law Columbia Law Sch.; short term sr. Fulbright scholar, 1994. Author: (with Reed Rowley) Rowley on Partnerships, 1959; contbr. articles to law revs. Democratic candidate for N.Y. State Supreme Ct., 1965; Democratic candidate for Congress, 1958; trustee Natural Resources Def. Coun., Inc., 1969-93; served in US Army, 1943-45. Decorated Purple Heart and oak leaf cluster. Mem. ABA, N.Y. State (Root/Stimson award for Public Service 1977) bar assns., Assn. of Bar of City of N.Y. (mem. exec. com. 1972-76, chmn. environ. law com. 1971-75), American Law Inst., Sierra Club (chmn. Atlantic chpt. 1968-69, nat. dir. 1968-69) Home: Margaretville, NY. Died Mar. 12, 2014.

**SKELTON, DARRELL JEAN,** lawyer; b. Pratt, Kans., May 4, 1924; s. Roy Daniel and Cora Bell (Pennington) Skelton; m. Lucille Evelyn McMerney; children: Michael D., Darrilyn J. Skelton Girard, Mark Roy, Kathleen Louise Skelton Kuenning, Martha Skelton Langin; children: 1 Louise Skelton, Mary Skelton Perrella. Student, U. Florence, Italy, 1945; BSBA, U. Denver, 1950, JD, 1952. Bar: Colo. 1952, US Dist. Ct. Colo 1953, US Ct. Appeals (10th cir.) 1954, US Supreme Ct. 1957. Mem. Colo. House Reps., 1964—65; ptnr. Tilly & Skelton, Oviatt & O'Dell, Wheat Ridge, Colo., from 1966; pres. Colo. Horsemen's Coun. Instr. Westernaires youth horse mounted drill team, Jefferson County, Colo., from 1958; chmn. Colo. Recreational Trails Com., 1971—75, Jefferson County Open Space Advisement Com., 1973—9177; capt. Jafferson County Sheriff's Mounted Posse. Mem.: ABA, Denver Bar Assn., 1st Jud. Dist. Bar Assn., Colo. Bar Assn., Kiwanis Club (pres. East Denver, lt. gov. divsn. 3). Republican. Roman Catholic. Died June 3, 1987.

**SKELTON, IKE (ISAAC NEWTON SKELTON IV),** lawyer, former United States Representative from Missouri; b. Lexington, Mo., Dec. 20, 1931; s. Isaac Newton and Carolyn (Boone) Skelton; m. Susan B. Anding, June 22, 1961 (dec. Aug. 23, 2005); children: Ike, Jim, Page. AA, Wentworth Mil. Acad., 1951; student, U. Edinburgh, Scotland, 1953; AB in Hist., U. Mo., Columbia, 1953, LLB, 1956. Bar: Mo. 1956. Pvt. law practice, Lexington, Mo.; prosecuting atty. Lafayette County, Mo., 1957-60; spl. asst. atty. gen. State of Mo., 1961-63; mem. Dist. 28 Mo. State Senate, 1971—76; mem. US Congress from 4th Mo. Dist., Washington, 1977—2011; ranking mem. US House Armed Services Com., Washington, 1998—2007, chmn., 2007—11; ptnr. Husch Blackwell LLP, Washington, 2011—13. Vice chmn. bd. trustees Harry S. Truman Scholarship Found. Recipient W. Stuart Symington award, Air Force Assn., 1994, Henry M. Jackson Disting. Svc. award, Jewish Inst. Nat. Security Affairs, 1999, Hon. Commandant award, Indsl. Coll. Armed Forces, 2005, Mil. Order of Iron Mike award, Marine Corps League; named Minuteman of Yr., Res. Officers Assn. US, 1995. Mem.: Sigma Chi, Mo. Bar Assn., Nat. Eagle Scout Assn., Shriners Club, Elks Club, Masons Lodge, Phi Beta Kappa. Democrat. Home: Mc Lean, Va. Died Oct. 28, 2013.

**SKINNER, CORNELIA BENNETT,** librarian; b. El Paso, Aug. 26, 1928; d. John Thomas and Lucille (Pierson) Bennett; m. John Shaw Skinner, Aug. 20, 1946 (dec. Jan. 1978); children: John Shaw, Mary Jacobina, Walter William, Nelson Pierson. BS, Sul Ross State U., 1966, MA, 1971. Reading tchr. Centennial Sch., Alpine, Tex., 1966-69; tchr. classroom 5th grade Alpine Elem., 1969-71; tchr. English grades 6, 7, 8 Alpine Jr. High, 1971-81; tchr. classroom grades 1, 2 Our Lady of Peace Sch., Alpine, 1982-83; libr. elem. schs. Pecos (Tex.) Ind. Schs., 1983-88; libr. supr. 1st-12th grades Franco Jr. High, Presidio, Tex., from 1988; libr. sci. tchr. Presidio Elem., from 1988; libr. media ctr. Presidio High Sch., from 1988; libr. bookmobile Candelaria Elem., Presidio, from 1988. Beekeeper, Marathon, Tex., 1953-63; camp asst. AFTOSA Eradication Patrol, Hot Springs, Tex., support personnel Bur. Animal Industry Big Bend Nat. Park, Tex., 1948-51; corr. area newspapers, 1950-54; libr. media specialist Rotan (Tex.) Ind. Sch. Dist., 1993-95. Cub scout leader Boy Scouts Am., Alpine, 1961-63; girl scout leader Girl Scouts U.S., Alpine, 1959-60; mem. adv. bd. Redford (Tex.) Devel. Assn. Dairy Goat Coop., 1992-93. Mem. Tex. State Tchrs.' Assn. (v.p. and prees. Alpine dist. 1972-91), Nat. Trust for Hist. Preservation, Native Plant Soc. Tex., Chihuahuan Desert Rsch. Inst., Presidio Valley Woman's Club Federated Internat. (v.p. 1988-92, pres. 1992-94), Am. Legion Aux. (v.p. 1960, pres. Alpine unit 79 1961). Democrat. Roman Catholic. Avocations: gardening, camping, building, reading, travel. Home: Alpine, Tex. Deceased.

**SKINNER, ORIN ENSIGN,** retired artist, foundation executive; b. Sweden Valley, Pa., Nov. 5, 1892; s. Enos Eton and Catherine Ines (Dunbar) S.; m. Frances Van Arsdale, 1916 (dec. 1979); 1 child, Charles Van Arsdale (dec.); m. Marilyn B. Justice, 1993. Student, Rochester Athenaeum and Mechanics Inst., 1912-16. Craftsman, artist, sec. Charles J. Connick Studio, Boston, 1920-86, pres., 1945-86, The Charles J. Connick Stained Glass Found., Ltd., Newtonville, Mass., from 1985. Lectr. on stained glass throughout U.S., 1926—, Columbia U., N.Y.C., 1949. Contbr. articles on stained glass to profl. publs. Fellow Stained Glass Assn. Am. (pres. 1948-50, editor Quar. 1933-48), Soc. Arts and Crafts (master craftsman), Tuesday Club. Avocations: photography, fishing, canoeing. Home: Newton, Mass. Deceased.

**SKOK, VLADIMIR IVANOVICH,** neurophysiologist, researcher; b. Kiev, Ukraine, June 4, 1932; came to the U.S., 1959; s. Ivan Maximovich and Elena Ivanovna; m. Irina Nikolaevna Alexeeva, Nov. 5, 1955; 1 child, Marina Vladimirovna. PhD in Biol. Scis., Ukrainian Acad. Scis., 1969. Head lab. Bogomoletz Inst. Physiology, Kiev, 1971—2005. V.p. Ukrainian Acad. Sci. Co-editor-in-chief Neurophysiology, 1992-2005; author: Physiology of Autonomic Gahglia, 1973 (Sechenov prize 1973); co-author: Neuronal Nicotinic Acetylcholine Receptors, 1989, Natural Activity of Autonomic Ganglia, 1989, Neuro-Muscular Physiology, 1986. Mem. Ukranian Acad. Sci., Russian Acad. Sci., Ukranian Pedagogic Acad. Sci., Polish Acad. Sci. Home: Kiev, Ukraine. Died Dec. 20, 2003.

**SKOLL, PEARL A.,** retired special education educator, retired mathematics educator; b. NYC, Apr. 15, 1927; d. Samuel and Lillian Ruth Adler; m. Ralph Lewis Skoll (dec. 1959); children: Jeffrey A., Steve, Lyle. BA, Hunter Coll., 1950; MA in Adminstrn./Supervision, Calif. State U., Northridge, 1974. Math. tchr. various schs., L.A. and NYC, 1954-71; program coord. The Mobilecomputer Math Lab L.A. Unified Sch. Dist., LA, 1971-77, leader tchr. tng., 1967-83, mainstream tchr., 1977-83, spl. edn. vocat. assessment counselor, 1983-86; retired, 1986. Mem. task force State Dept. of Edn., Sacramento, Calif., 1976; instr. Calif. State U., Northridge, 1975-76, Pepperdine U., Malibu, Calif., 1975-76. Author (book) Coping with the Calculator, 1975; editor (book) The Calculator Book, 1975; contbr. articles to profl. jours. Reader tapes for literacy program U. Nev., Las Vegas, 1986-87; hon. mem. adv. coun. IBC, Cambridge, Eng. 3d Internat. Congress of Math. Edn. grantee U.S. Office of Edn., 1976, Internat. Biog. Ctr. (Cambridge, Eng.) 20th Century award for Meritorious Achievement, 1994, IB Citation of Meritorious Achievement in Math. Svcs., various miscellaneous honors from IBC, 1995; named Woman of Yr., Am. Biog. Inst., 1994. Mem. Calif. Math. Coun., Nat. Coun. of Tchrs. of Math., Calif. State U. Alumni Assn. Democrat. Jewish. Avocations: volunteer work, cooking, baking, jigsaw & crossword puzzles, gardening. Deceased.

**SLAGA, SZCZEPAN WITOLD,** philosophy educator; b. Łukowica, Poland, Dec. 26, 1934; s. John and Kunegunda (Dziedzic) S. M in Philosophy, Cath. U. of Lublin, 1961, PhD, 1965. Ordained priest Roman Cath. Ch., 1957. Asst. prof. philosophy Acad. of Cath. Theology, Warsaw, 1965-76, assoc. prof., 1977-82, prof. of philosophy of nature, from 1982. Holder of the chair of philosophy of nature Acad. of Cath. Theology, 1981—; assoc. dean faculty of philosophy, 1984-90; lectr. of philosophy Seminary of Dioecesan in Łódź, 1965—. Author: Current Poblems of Philosophy of Science, 1980, 2d edit., 1992, Search for Truth, 1987, Philosophy of Nature for Students, 1992; co-editor: Problems of the Philosophy of Science and the Philosophy of Nature, vol. 14; editor-in-chief Studia Philosphiae Christianae. Recipient Award Ministry of Edn., 1977, 80, Gold Cross Polonia Restituta, Pres. of Poland, 1990. Mem. Polish Acad. of Sci. (biol. com. 1984—), Scientific Soc. of Cath. U. of Lublin. Avocation: collector ancient clocks. Home: Lodz, Poland. Died Dec. 16, 1995.

**SLAP, CHARLES S.,** clergyman; b. NYC, Oct. 6, 1933; s. Leonard and Elizabeth (Goodman) S.; m. Jacquelyn Anne Becker, June 14, 1970 (div. 1983); children: Andrew, Derek. BA, NYU, 1954; JD, Columbia U., 1959; postgrad., Harvard Div. Sch., 1965-66; DMin, Meadville Theol. Sch., Chgo., 1969. Bar: N.Y., D.C. Staff atty. office chief counsel U.S. Customs Svc., Dept. Treasury, Washington and NYC, 1961-65; minister Unitarian Fellowship of Greater Lafayette, West Lafayette, Ind., 1969-71, Unitarian Ch. of Davis, Calif., 1971-76, First Unitarian Ch., Springfield, Mass., 1976-84, First Unitarian Soc., Schenectady, from 1985. Trustee Unitarian Universalist Assn., Boston, 1981-84, mem. Gen. Asys. Planning Com., 1982-84, chmn. Melcher Book Awd. Com., 1988—. Contbr. articles to profl. jours. Bd. dirs. Law, Order and Justice Ctr., Schenectady, 1988-89. 1st lt. U.S. Army, 1954-56. Mem. Unitarian Universalist Ministers Assn. (bd. dirs. 1979-81), English Speaking Union U.S. (pres. Albany area br. 1989-90), Torch Club (sec. Schenectady 1989-90), Harvard Club, Harvard Faculty Club, Masons. Home: Niskayuna, NY. Died Nov. 1992.

**SLATER, SHIRLEY,** travel writer; b. Lynchburg, Va., Jan. 30, 1935; d. Alexander Breckenridge and Janet Marie Bell Withers; m. Clem C. Slater, Jr., Sept. 8, 1955 (div. 1976); children: John Withers, Christopher; m. Harry Basch, Aug. 24, 1988. BA Theatre Arts/Journalism, U. Ga., 1956. Travel columnist LA Times, 1983—2002; TV travel commentator various, 1985—2002; guidebook author Fielding Worldwide, Redondo Beach, Calif., 1995—2002. Actress Am. Cons. Theatre, San Francisco, 1968-74, LA Music Ctr., 1974-75, Alley Theatre, Houston, 1976. Author: (guidebooks) Fielding's Worldwide Cruises, 1996-98, Freewheelin' USA, 1995, European Cruises, Alaska Cruises, 1997, Frommer's Exploring America by RV, 2000, MacMillan Travel, N.Y.C., 1999-2002. Recipient Pederson award Am. Soc. Travel Agts., 1990. Died Aug. 23, 2002.

**SLATTERY, JOHN PATRICK,** news correspondent; b. Springfield, Mo., Sept. 28, 1950; m. Suzy Slattery; children: Kathleen, Meghan, Patrick. AB in Econs., Xavier U. Reporter, Chapaign-Urbana, Ill.; reporter, weekend anchor Sta. WCAU-TV, Phila.; gen. assignment corr. Sta. WABC-TV, NYC, Sta. WCBS-TV, NYC, 1984—2014. Died Sept. 24, 2014.

**SLAUGHTER, D. FRENCH, JR.,** congressman; b. Culpeper, Va., May 20, 1925; s. Daniel French and Caroline (Strother) S.; m. Kathleen Wilson Rowe (dec.); children: D. French III, Kathleen Slaughter Frey BA, U. Va., 1949, LL.B., 1953. Bar: Va. 1953. Pvt. practice law, Culpeper, Va., 1953-84; mem. Ho. of Dels., Gen. Assembly Va., 1958-78, 99th-101st Congresses from 7th Va. dist., Washington, 1985-91. Bd. mgrs. U. Va. Alumni Assn., Charlottesville, 1962-71, pres., 1969-70; bd. visitors U. Va., Charlottesville, 1978-82, rector, 1980-82; mem. local adv. bd. Germanna Community Coll., Locust Grove, Va., 1979-84. Served to cpl. U.S. Army, 1943-47 Mem. Va. Bar Assn. (exec. com. 1971-74), Raven Soc., Omicron Delta Kappa, Delta Psi, Am. Legion, DAV, VFW, Farm Bur., Culpeper County C. of C. Republican. Episcopalian. Died Oct. 2, 1998.

**SLAUGHTER, FREEMAN CLUFF,** retired dentist; b. Estes, Miss., Dec. 30, 1926; s. William Cluff and Vay (Fox) S.; m. Genevieve Anne Parks, July 30, 1948; children: Mary Anne, Thomas Freeman, James Hugh. Student, Wake Forest U., 1944, Emory U., 1946-47; DDS, Emory U. Sch. of Dentistry, 1951. Lic. real estate broker. Practice gen. dentistry, Kannapolis, N.C., 1951-89; ret. Mem. N.C. State Bd. Dental Examiners, 1966-75, pres., 1968-69, sec.-treas., 1971-74; chief dental staff Cabarrus Meml. Hosp. (now Carolinas Med. Ctr. NE), Concord, N.C., 1965-66, 75; mem. N.C. Adv. Com. for Edn. Dental Aux. Pers.-N.C. State Bd. Edn., 1967-70; advisor dental asst. program Rowan Cabarrus C.C., 1974-76; Duke Med. Ctr. Davison Century Club. Trustee N.C. Symphony Soc., 1962-68, pres. Kannapolis chpt., 1961; mem. Cabarrus County Bd. Health, 1977-83, chmn., 1981-83, acting health dir., 1981; vice chmn. Kannapolis Charter Commn., 1983-84; mem. City Coun. Kannapolis, 1984-85; Mayor protem, Kannapolis, 1984-85; past active Boy Scouts Am., Eagle scout with silver palm. QM2C asst. navigator on USS Xenia AKA 51, co-navigator on USS Gen. George O. Squier AP 130 with USN, 1944-46, WW II, ETO, MTO. Recipient Kannapolis Citizen of Yr. award, 1982. Fellow Am. Coll. Dentists (life); mem. ADA (life), Am. Legion, Kannapolis Jr. C. of C. (v.p. 1952), Toastmasters Internat. (pres. Kannapolis chpt. 1963-64), Am. Assn. Dental Examiners (Dentist Citizen of Yr. 1975, v.p. 1977-79, Recognition plaque, 1980), So. Conf. Dental Deans and Examiners (v.p. 1969), N.C. Dental Soc. (resolution of commendation 1975), N.C. Dental Soc. Anesthesiology (pres. 1964), Southeastern Acad. Prosthodontics, So. Acad. Oral Surgery, Am. Soc. Dentistry for Children (pres. N.C. unit 1957), Internat. Assn. Dental Rsch., Cabarrus County Dental Soc. (pres. 1953-54, 63-64, 69), N.C. Assn. Professions (dir. 1976-80), Kannapolis Music Club (pres. 1962-63), Emory U. Corpus Cordis Aureum (Emory U. disting. alumnus award 2006), Masons, Shriners, Rotary (dir. 1977-80), Omicron Kappa Upsilon, Alpha Epsilon Upsilon. Home: Kannapolis, NC. Died Dec. 23, 2013.

**SLYM, KARL,** automotive executive; b. Derby, England, Feb. 9, 1962; Grad. in production engring., Derby Univ., England, 1984; MS, Stanford Univ., 2002. Gen. assembly mgr. Toyota UK; mfg. adv. & gen. assembly mgr. Opel Eisenach plant General Motors Co., 1995—97, dir. mfg. Opel Polska plant Gliwice, Poland, 1997—99, asst. plant mgr. Oshawa plant Ontario, Canada, 1999—2001, plant mgr. Oshawa plants 1 & 2, 2001—02, v.p. quality GM Asia Pacific & GM Daewoo, 2006—07; pres. CAMI Automotive (GM & Suzuki Motor joint venture), 2002—06; pres., mng. dir. GM India, 2007—11; mng. dir. Tata Motors, 2012—14. Sloan Fellow. Died Jan. 25, 2014.

**SMALLMAN, BEVERLEY N.,** retired biology professor; b. Port Perry, Ont., Can., Dec. 11, 1913; s. Richard Benjamin and Ethel May (Doubt) S.; m. Hazel Mayne, Dec. 11, 1937 (dec. 1962); 1 child, Sylvia Gail; m. Florence Hazel Cook, July 27, 1965 BA, Queens U., Kingston, Ont., 1936; MSc, Western U. Ont., Can., 1938; PhD, U. Edinburgh, Scotland, 1941; LLD (hon.), Trent U., Can., 1982. Mem. staff Stored Grain Insect Investigations Bd. of Grain Commnrs., Winnipeg, 1941-45; officer-in-charge Stored Products Lab., Agrl. Can., Winnipeg, 1945-50; head entomol. sect. rsch. inst. Agrl. Can., London, 1950-57, chief entomol., rsch. dir. entomology, plant pathology Ottawa, 1957-63; prof., head dept. biology Queens U., Kingston, Ont., 1963-73, prof. biology, 1973-78, prof. emeritus biology, 1979—2005. Vis. scientist Nat. Inst. Med. Rsch., London, Eng., 1954-56, CSIRO Labs., Brisbane, Australia, 1970-71, 76; apiary insp. Province of Ont., 1981-91; cons., lectr. in field. Prin. author: Agricultural Science in Canada, 1970, Queen's Biology, 1992; co-author: Good Bye Bugs, 1983. Contbr. articles to profl. jours. Fellow Royal Soc. Can.; mem. Entomol. Soc. Can., Zool. Soc. Can., Entomol. Soc. Man. (founding pres. 1945), Entomol. Soc. Ont. Avocation: reading. Home: Kingston, Canada. Died May 4, 2005.

**SMITH, ADAM** **See GOODMAN, GEORGE**

**SMITH, ANTHONY JOHN FRANCIS,** writer; b. Taplow, Bucks, Eng., Mar. 30, 1926; s. Hubert John Forster and Diana (Watkin) S.; m. Barbara Dorothy Newman, Sept. 1, 1956 (div. Aug. 1983); children: Adam, Polly, Laura; m. Margaret Ann Holloway, Apr. 6, 1984; 1 child, Quintin; 1 stepchild, Zena. BA in Zoology, Balliol Coll., Oxford, Eng., 1951; MA, Oxford U., 1951. Reporter Manchester Guardian, U.K., 1953; mgr. Drum, Africa, 1954-55; sci. corrs. Daily Telegraph, U.K., 1957-63; freelance writer, 1964—2014. Author numerous books including: Swaps, 1992, Best Friends, 1990, Which Animal Are You?, 1988, The Free Life, 1995, Explorers of the Amazon, 1990, The Great Rift, 1988, Smith & Son, 1984, The Mind, 1984, A Sideways Look, 1983, A Persian Quarter Century, 1979, Wilderness, 1978, Animals on View, 1977, The Human Pedigree, 1975, Good Beach Guide, 1973, Beside the Seaside, 1972, Mato Grosso, 1971, The Dangerous Sort, 1970, The Seasons, 1970, The Body, 1968, Jambo: African Balloon Safari, 1963, others. Coun. mem. Royal Geographical Soc., Fauna Preservation Soc., Zool. Soc. of London. Mem. Royal Air Force, 1944-48. Recipient Glaxo award for Sci. Writers, 1977, Cherry Kearton medal, Royal Geograph. Soc., 1978, Montgolfier diploma, Fedn. Aeronautique Internat., Paris, 1975. Mem. Brit. Balloon and Airship Club (founder 1965), Explorers Club. Avocation: lighter-than-air flying. Home: London, England. Died July 7, 2014.

**SMITH, ARTHUR,** radio and television producer, composer; b. Clinton, SC, Apr. 1, 1921; s. Clayton Seymour and Viola (Fields) S.; m. Dorothy Byars, Apr. 12, 1941; children: Arthur Reginald, Constance (Mrs. Wiley Brown), Robert Clayton. Grad. high sch. Rec. artist RCA Victor, 1936-38; band leader, composer Sta. WSPA, Spartanburg, S.C., 1938-41, Sta. WBT, Charlotte, N.C., 1941-43; band leader, composer, producer CBS Radio, WBT, WBTV, Charlotte, 1945-70; producer WSOC-TV Cox Broadcasting Co., Charlotte. Pres. Clay Music Corp., Charlotte, 1960-76; owner Arthur Smith Studios, Charlotte; v.p. CMH Records, L.A.; founder Arthur Smith King Mackerel Tournament, Myrtle Beach, S.C., 1976, Arthur Smith Kingfish, Dolphin, Wahoo Tournament of the Palm Beaches (Fla.), 1983, Queen City Records, 1997. Prin.: The Arthur Smith Show, 1971-76; composer: numerous compositions, including Guitar Boogie, 1946; also rec. artist: more than 100 albums for MGM, DOT, Monument and Starday, numerous compositions, including Dueling Banjos, 1973 (BMI Song of Year 1973); composer: (with Clay Smith) sound track of film Death Driver, 1975, Dark Sunday, 1976; musical score for Living Legend and Lady Grey-Superstar, 1979; co-host with Clay Smith of syndicated radio show "The Arthur Smith Sportsman Journal". Bd. dirs. Charlotte Sch. of Arts, American Heart Assn., Marine Sci. Coun.; trustee, dir. Gardner Webb Coll.; trustrr Boys Home N.C.; founder, chmn. Arthur Smith Bluefish Tournament of N.Y.; chmn. Alzheimer's Assn. Served with USN, 1943-45. Named Bapt. Layman of Yr. Southeastern Sem. Louisville, 1969; named to The N.C. Broadcasters Hall of Fame, 1990; recipient Religion Emphasis award American Legion, 1971, S.C. Tourism award State of S.C., 1979, Cine Golden Eagle award for film The Hawk and John McNeely, 1980, Lung Assn. award, 1993. Mem. American Fedn. Musicians (dir. local 342, pres. local 342 1943-76), AFTRA, Salt Water Anglers Tournament Soc. (founder, chmn. bd.), U.S. Sportsfishing Assn. (chmn. 1985). Clubs: Masons, Shriners, Kiwanis, Charlotte City, Red Fez. Democrat. Home: Charlotte, NC. *To me, success is not a destination - it's a journey. Integrity is not a business principle - it's a matter of right or wrong. Whatever I shall achieve in this world I owe to complete trust in, and commitment to God through Christ, a loving and understanding wife and family and loyal associates.* Died Apr. 3, 2014.

**SMITH, AXEL,** retired theology and social ethics educator; b. Grimstad, Norway, Mar. 19, 1924; s. Nils Jörgen and Solveig (Tangevald) S.; m. Liv Helena Bö, July 12, 1952; children: Gunvor, Solveig, Anders, Liv Helene. Candidate in theology, Norwegian Luth. Sch. Theology, Oslo, 1950; M Religious Edn., Princeton Theol. Sem., 1952; degree in gen. edn., intermediate subj., U. Oslo, 1954. Tchr. Primary Sch., Holla, Norway, 1952-54; lectr. Coll. Edn., Volda, Norway, 1954-61, Bergen, Norway, 1961-68; rsch. scholar State Rsch. Bd., Oslo, 1968-71; lectr. Norwegian Luth. Sch. Theology, 1971-85, prof. theology and social ethics, 1985-90, prof. emeritus, from 1990. Author: Anton Fridrichsens kristendomsforstaaelse, 1976, Rett fordeling, 1982; editor: På skaperens jord, 1984, Praekener i Aarene 1772-1821, 1997; contbr. articles to profl. jours. Home: Stavanger, Norway. Died July 25, 2002.

**SMITH, BARBARA ANN,** nursing educator; b. Salem, Ohio, Aug. 20, 1948; d. Charles Francis and Helen Elizabeth (Lederle) Smith. BSN, Case Western Res. U., 1975, MSN, 1978; PhD, Ohio State U., 1986. Staff nurse St. Elizabeth Hosp., Youngstown, Ohio, 1969-70; supr. Salem (Ohio) Hosp., 1970-78; instr. Ind. U., Indpls., 1978-81; coordinator Marion County Health Dept., Indpls., 1979-81; sr. rsch. assoc. NAS, Washington, 1981-83; NIH fellow Ohio State U., Columbus, 1983-86, asst. prof., from 1986. Cons. Salem Hosp., 1987—, Richland Hosp., Mansfield, Ohio, 1988—. Contbr. articles to profl. jours. Mem. Am. Heart Assn., Am. Coll. Sports Medicine, Am. Pub. Health Assn., Ohio Cardiac Rehab. Assn., Am. Nurses Assn., Ohio Nurses Assn., Potomac Appalachian Trail Club. Avocations: hiking, bicycling. Home: Alabaster, Ala. Died July 2, 2008.

**SMITH, BETTY MURNAN,** educator; b. Indpls., Sept. 11, 1921; d. Carl J. and Helene Alice Murnan (Stephens) Smith; m. Richard Norman Smith, Oct. 21, 1951; children: Allegra Louise Smith Jrolf, Timothy, Michael. BA with cum laude in English, Butler U., 1944; MA in English, State U. Iowa, 1950. Tchr. Kingsford HS, Mich., 1944—46, Bosse HS, Evansville, Ind., 1946—48; instr. english Ely Jr. Coll., Minn., 1950—51, U. Wis., Waukesha County, 1966—70, acting instr. Milw., 1961—66; asst. prof., 1970—81; assoc. prof., from 1981; assoc. prof. emerita, sr. lectr., from 1992; senator U. Wis. Ctr. Sys., 1980—81; lectr. field. co-prin. Hdqrs. Freedom Sch. Mil. Sch. Boycott, 1963; bd. dirs. Waukesha Symphony Orch., 1969—72, Waukesha Civic Theatre, 1973—74; sec. Waukesha Equal Opportunity Commn., 1970—73. Contbr. poetry to mags. Mem. Com. Women's Issues Forum, 1979—80. Recipient Outstanding Achievement award, Cmty. Svcs., U. Wis., Waukesha, 1979. Mem.: Midwest MLA, MLA, AAUP (pres. chpt. 1969—70), Assn. U. Wis. Faculties, Am. Fedn. Tchrs. (treas. Milw. chpt. 1962—66), Nat., Wis. Coun. Tchrs. English, Sigma Tau Delta, Kappa Delta Pi. Presbyn. Deceased.

**SMITH, CHARLES PHILIP,** retired state official; b. Chgo., June 18, 1926; s. William Arthur and Lillian Christine (Christensen) S.; m. Bernadette C. Carroll, Aug. 23, 1947; children: Charles Philip, II, Stephen, Megan, Haley. BS in History & Sociology, Milton Coll., 1950. Field rep. Guardian Life Ins. Co., Coll. Life Ins. Co., 1958-67; prodn. supr. Olin Corp., Baraboo, Wis., 1967-71; treas. State of Wis., Madison, 1971-90. Pres. Madison Rivers and Lakes Commn., 1965-71; vice chmn. Dane County (Wis.) Democrats., 1969-70; McGovern del. Nat. Democratic Conv., 1972, Kennedy del., 1980; Hart del., 1984; bd. dirs. Big Brothers of Dane County, pres., 1981; bd. dirs. Madison Opportunity Center, treas., 1980-81; bd. dirs. Wis. Spl. Olympics., sec., 1980-82. Served with USMC, 1944-45. Decorated Purple Heart, Presdl. Unit Citation. Mem. Nat. Assn. State Treasurers (regional v.p., sec.-treas.), Nat. Assn. Unclaimed Property Adminstrs. (treas.). Democrat. Roman Catholic. Home: Madison, Wis. Died July 12, 2014.

**SMITH, DEE GLEN,** holding company executive; b. Sept. 30, 1925; Chmn., pres., CEO, dir. Smith's Mgmt. Corp., Salt Lake City. Died June 30, 1984.

**SMITH, DONALD HEADINGS,** surgeon; b. Williamsport, Pa., Aug. 15, 1939; s. J. Stanley and Eleanor D. (Mussina) S.; married Oct. 7, 1961; children: Gregory, Jeffrey, Eric. AB in Biology, Lehigh U., 1961; MD, Jefferson Med. Coll., 1965. Diplomate Am. Bd. Surgery. Intern Lankenau Hosp., Phila., 1965-66, resident in surgery, 1966-70; staff Easton (Pa.) Hosp.; clin. asst. prof. surgery Hahnemann Med. Coll. Pres. Northampton County Med. Soc., 1979, Easton Hosp. Med. Staff, 1982-83; exec. dir. Valley Health Svcs., Easton, 1995-96; spkr. in field. Contbr. articles to profl. jours. Past bd. dirs. C. of C., Rotary, United Way. Fellow ACS; mem. AMA, Am. Soc. Gen. Surgery (pres. 1995), Pa. Med. Soc. (pres. 1999-00). Deceased.

**SMITH, DUNBAR WALLACE,** retired physician, clergyman; b. Dunbar, Nebr., Oct. 17, 1910; s. Clarence Dunbar and Marie Christine (Eden) S.; m. Kathryn Avis Johnson, May 2, 1935; children: Dunbar Wesley, John Wallace. BSc, La Sierra Coll., Riverside, Calif., 1949; MD, Loma Linda U., 1950; DTM and Hygiene, Sch. of Tropical Med. London U., 1951; MPH, Columbia U., 1967. Diplomate Nat. Bd. Med. Examiners. Pastor 7th-day Adventist Chs., San Diego, Omaha, N.Y., India, Ceylon, 1935-44; med. dir. 7th-Day Adventist Mission Hosps., India, 1951-056; adminstr. Battle Creek (Mich.) Sanitarium, 1957-62; med. dir. Bates Meml. Hosp., Yonkers, N.Y., 1962-67; dep. commr. health Nassau County, N.Y., 1967-69; dir. dept. health for Africa, 7th-day Adventist Ch., 1969-76, dir. dept. health for Far East, Singapore, 1976-80; adj. asst. prof. internat. health Loma Linda (Calif.) U., 1980-90; v.p. Emerald Health and Edn. Found., Health Ministry Found., Loma Linda, 1986-2000. Author: Report of CME (now Loma Linda U. Sch. Medicine) Rsch. to Date, 1946, (textbook) Home Health Aide, 1960, Autobiography of Dunbar W. Smith, 1994, American Family, 1997, (booklet) The Cold Turkey Way to Stop Smoking, 1967, The Smiths and Their Kinship with over 500 Doctors of Medicine and Dentistry, 1997; contbg. author: The Dunbar Pedigree, 1996; contbr. numerous articles to various publs. V.p. Emerald Health and Edn. Found., 1991—. Recipient Honored Alumnus award Loma Linda U. Sch. Medicine, 1975, Golden award La Sierra U. Alumni Soc., 1992. Fellow AMA, SAR, Adventist Internat. Med. Soc. (leprosy edn. rsch. found.), Am. Coll. Nutrition, Royal Soc. Tropical Medicine, Royal Soc. Health, Internat. Med. Assn. (bd. dirs. 1987—); mem. N.Y. Acad. Scis. Republican. Avocations: photography, travel. Deceased.

**SMITH, DUNCAN MCLAURIN, JR.,** lawyer; b. Mobile, Ala., July 24, 1926; s. Duncan McLaurin and Louise J. (Davies) Smith; m. Sallie Coco, June 25, 1955; children: Duncan McLaurin III, Sherrill L., Allison L., Ashley C., Stuart M. Student, N.E. Jr. Coll. La. State U., 1943—44, US Mil. Acad., 1945—46; BS in Petroleum Engring., La. State U., 1949, JD, 1953. Bar: La. 1953, Tex. 1957, La. (US Dist. Ct. (we. dist.)) 1953, La. (US Dist. Ct. (ea. dist.)), US Ct. Appeals (5th cir.) 1963, La. (US Dist. Ct. (mid. dist.)) 1964, US Supreme Ct. 1970, US Ct. Appeals (11th cir.) 1981; registered registered profl. engr. La., cert. Tex. Drilling and prodn. engr. California Co., 1949—52; assoc. Hargrove, Guyton, VanHook & Hargrove, Shreveport, La., 1953—56; div. atty. Tidewater Oil Co., Houston, 1956—58; pvt. practice Lafayette, La., from 1958; adj. prof. petroleum engring. U. Southwestern, La., from 1973; mem. adv. bd. Salvation Army, Lafayette; pres. Lafayette Natural History Mus. and Planetarium; trustee La. Moral and Civic Found., 1976—79. Served USNR, 1944—45, with US Army, 1945—46. Mem.: ABA, Am. Legion, Lafayette Geol. Soc., 15th Jud. Dist Bar Assn., Lafayette Bar Assn., Soc. Petroleum Engrs., Am. Assn. Petroleum Geologists, State Bar Tex., La. State Bar Assn., Shriners, Petroleum Club Lafayette, Masons, Phi Delta Phi, Kappa Sigma. Democrat. Methodist. Home: Lafayette, La. Died May 26, 1992.

**SMITH, EMORY CLARK,** lawyer, financial advisor; b. Denton, Tex., Nov. 2, 1910; s. James Willis and Julia (Miller) S.; 1 child, Cynthia Smith O'Brien. BA, U. North Tex., 1929; MA, U. Tex., 1933; JD, So. Meth. U., 1937; SJD, George Washington U., 1954. Bar: Tex. 1937, Okla. 1937, U.S. Supreme Ct. 1954, U.S. Ct. Mil. Appeals 1955, U.S. Ct. Claims 1956, U.S. Ct. Customs and Patent Appeals 1956. Pvt. practice, Oklahoma City, 1937-42; commd. USN, 1942-72, advanced through grades to capt., chief U.S. pros. atty., staff Gen. Douglas MacArthur, 1946—48; chief counsel USN Oceanographic Office U.S. Civil Svc., Washington, 1972-73; cons. antitrust atty. Foster Assocs., Washington, 1973-84; pvt. practice Washington, 1994; ret., 1995. Adj. prof. internat. law Am. U., Washington, 1977-84; energy cons. Foster Assocs., 1973-84; fin. advisor Friday Music Found., Washington, 1988-94; lectr. in field. Author: Law of the Sea, 1954; contbr. articles to profl. jours. Vestryman St. Alban's Ch., Washington, 1957-59, St. Paul's Within the Walls, Rome, 1967-68. Named Disting. Alumnus U. North Tex., 1972. Fellow N.Y. Explorers Club, Fed. Bar Assn., Inter-Am. Bar Assn. (natural resources com. chmn. 1973-76), Masons. Republican. Episcopalian. Avocation: farming. Deceased.

**SMITH, GEORGIA FLOYD,** molecular biologist, educator; b. Atlanta, Ga., Jan. 17, 1949; d. Acey LeRoy and Annette Herald; m. Randall Allen Smith, Aug. 12, 1978; children: Kendall Allen, Jessica Leanne. BA, U. Claif. Santa Barbara, 1972; MPH, U. Mich., 1974; PhD, U. Calif. Riverside, 1979. Post-doctoral fellow Yale U., New Haven, Conn., 1979-82, post-doctoral assoc., 1983-85; asst. prof. Az. State U., Tempe, 1985-91, assoc. prof., from 1991. Panel adhoc review com., NSF, 1996. Recipient Rsch. Career Devel. award, NIH, 1989, First award, NIH, 1988; grantee Az. Disease Control Rsch. Commn., 1985, Am. Cancer Soc., 1988. Mem. Am. Chem. Soc., Internat. Soc. Interfeon and Cytokine Rsch., Am. Assn. Advancement Sci., Am. Soc. Biochemistry and Molecular Biology, Internat. Cytokine Soc., Sigma Xi. Meth. Methodist. Avocations: skiing, swimming, hiking, birding. Home: Tempe, Ariz. Deceased.

**SMITH, GREGORY WHITE,** writer; b. Ithaca, NY, Oct. 4, 1951; s. William R. and Kathryn (White) S. BA, Colby Coll., 1973; JD, Harvard Law Sch., 1977; MEd, Harvard U., 1980. Bar: Mass., 1980. Fellow Thomas J. Watson, 1973-74; co-founder, editor Woodward/White, Inc. (publishers of Best Lawyers in America, Best Doctors in America, Best Dentists in America), 1981—2014. Author: (with Steven Naifeh) Moving Up in Style: The Successful Man's Guide to Impeccable Taste, 1980, Gene Davis, 1981, How to Make Love to a Woman, 1982, What Every Client Needs to Know About Using a Lawyer, 1982, The Bargain Hunter's Guide to Art Collecting, 1982, Why Can't Men Open Up?: Overcoming Men's Fear of Intimacy, 1984, The Mormon Murders: A True Story of Greed, Forgery, Deceit, and Death, 1988, Jackson Pollock: An American Saga, 1989 (Pulitzer Prize for biography 1991), Final Justice: The True Story of the Richest Man Ever Tried for Murder, 1993, A Stranger in the Family: A True Story of Murder, Madness, and Unconditional Love, 1995, On a Street Called Easy, In a Cottage Called Joye: A Restoration Comedy, 1996, Making Miracles Happen, 1997; editor: (with Naifeh) The Best Lawyers in America series, The Best Doctors in America series, The Best Dentists in America series. Chmn. Aiken Historic Preservation Commn. Died Apr. 10, 2014.

**SMITH, GROVER CLEVELAND, JR.,** language educator; b. Atlanta, Sept. 6, 1923; s. Grover C. and Lillian Julia (McDaniel) S.; m. Phyllis Jean Snyder, June 19, 1948 (div. 1965); children: Alice Elizabeth, Charles Grover; m. Dulcie Barbara Soper, Dec. 29, 1965; children: Stephen Kenneth, Julia Margaret. BA with honors, Columbia U., 1944, MA, 1945, PhD, 1950. Instr. English Rutgers U., 1946-48, Yale U., 1948-52, Duke U., 1952-55, asst. prof., 1955-61, assoc. prof., 1961-66, prof., 1966-93, prof. emeritus, from 1993. Mem. summer faculty CUNY, 1946, 47, 48, Columbia U., 1963, 64, NYU, 1963, Wake Forest U., 1966, vis. lectr., 1963, 64; instr. coll. entrance exam bd. Summer Inst. Commn. on English, 1962. Author: The Poems of T.S. Eliot 1909-1928: A Study in Symbols and Sources, 1950, T.S. Eliot's Poetry and Plays: A Study in Sources and Meaning, 1956 (Poetry Chapbook award) rev. edit., 1974, Archibald MacLeish, 1971, Ford Madox Ford, 1972, The Waste Land, 1983, T.S. Eliot and the Use of Memory, 1996; editor: Josiah Royce's Seminar, 1913-1914: As Recorded in the Notebooks of Harry T. Costello, 1963, Letters of Aldous Huxley, 1969. Mem. Christian Gauss Award com., 1973-75; mem. com. of sponsors Sir Julian Huxley Tribute, NY Soc. for Ethical Culture, 1975. With U.S. Army, 1943. Alexander M. Proudfit fellow Columbia U., 1945-46; Guggenheim fellow, 1958; Am. Philos. Soc. grantee, 1965; Am. Learned Socs. grantee, 1965; NEH grantee, 1979, fellow, 1980. Mem. T.S. Eliot Soc. (hon., 2000-, Eliot Meml. Lectr. 1986, bd. dirs. 1986-94, 96-99, v.p. 1986-88, editor News and Notes, 1987-88, 90-91, pres. 1989-91, supr. elections 1992-94, sec. 1996-99), Am. Lit. Assn. (rep. to coun.of Am. Author Socs. 1990-91), Nat. Assn. Scholars. Home: Durham, NC. Died June 10, 2014.

**SMITH, HUGH HALL,** retired lawyer; b. Apr. 4, 1909; s. Hugh Young and Ida (Hall) Smith; m. Gertrude Mellom, July 4, 1942. AB, Syracuse U., 1932; JD, Harvard U., 1936. Bar: N.Y. 1937, U.S. Dist. Ct. (no. dist.) N.Y. 1944. City judge City Ct., Gloversville, NY, 1950—55; ptnr. Maider & Smith, Gloversville, 1955—84. Mem.: N.Y. State Bar Assn., Fulton County Bar Assn. Roman Catholic. Home: Gloversville, NY. Deceased.

**SMITH, JAMES MICHAEL,** urologist, consultant; b. Kells, Ireland, May 21, 1940; s. Matthew John Smith and Mary Anne Duffy; m. Patricia Anne Webster; children: Clare, Hannah, James, Rebecca, Nicholas. B Medicine and Surgery, U. Coll., Dublin, 1964. Sr. registrar Gen. Surgery, Cambridge, England, 1970—73; sr. registrar urology Dublin, 1973—78; cons. urologist Temple St. Hosp., Dublin, from 1978, Mater Hosp., Dublin, from 1978; lectr. in surgery U. Coll., from 1978. Bd. dirs. Mater Hosp.; hon. sec. Med. Bd., Dublin. Contbr. articles to med. jours. Fellow: Royal Coll. Surgeons London, Royal Coll. Surgeons Dublin (Millin lectr. 1978); mem.: Brit. Assn. Urol. Surgeons, Am. Urol. Assn., U. Coll. Dublin Med. Soc. (pres. 1994), Irish Soc. Urology (pres. 1996), Dublin Hosp. Sailing Soc. (capt. 1989, pres. 1996), Dublin Giol. Club, Headfort Golf Club (capt. 1978, pres. 2001). Avocations: travel, golf, gardening. Home: Ashbourne, Ireland. Died Feb. 9, 2008.

**SMITH, JOSEPHINE CARROLL,** retired school system administrator; b. Washington, 1884; d. Dennis and Alice (Morgan) Carroll; m. William H. Smith, June 14, 1918 (dec. Feb. 1963). AB, Howard U., 1930; MA, Columbia U., 1937. Tchr. pub. schs., Washington, 1916-30, prin., 1930-31, adminstrv. prin., 1931-41, demonstration sch. prin., 1941-46, 46-55, divisional dir. div. 10, dir. elem. edn. in charge adminstrn., from 1955, ret., 1955-63; ret. V.p. Northwest Boundary Civic Assn., 1961—; mem. program com. Girl Scouts D.C. Mem. LWV D.C., Nat., D.C. edn. assns., D.C. Coun. Adminstrv. Women, Am. Assn. Sch. Adminstrs., Washington Planning and Housing Assn., Zeta Phi Beta (regional dir.). Baptist. Home: Silver Spring, Md. Died 1997.

**SMITH, KEITH LARUE,** research company executive; b. Salida, Colo., Dec. 15, 1917; s. Leroy Holt and Verna Lea (Tunnell) S.; m. Evelyn May De Bruler, Aug. 29, 1943; 1 child, Eric Douglas. AB in Math., Ind. U., 1946; postgrad., DePauw U., 1946-47; MA in Internat. Affairs, Harvard U., 1955; MPA, Calif. State U., Fullerton, 1979. Mil. intelligence rsch. specialist Dept. of Army, Washington, 1951-60; staff engr. Librascope divsn. Gen. Precision, Inc., Glendale, Calif., 1960-61; sr. ops. rsch. analyst Space divsn. N.Am. Rockwell Corp., Downey, Calif., 1961-71; dir. rsch. Am. Rsch. Corp., Paramount, Calif., 1972-80; cons. model bldg. and gaming techniques, from 1960; mgmt. cons., from 1970; CEO K.L. Smith and Assocs., from 1988. Instr. math. and polit. sci. DePauw U., 1946-47; instr. math. and sci. Verbum Dei High Sch., 1974-85. Adult leader Boy Scouts Am., Long Beach, Calif., 1961-75; treas. UN Coun., Harvard U., 1947-49, Young Dem. Club, Arlington, Mass., 1949-50. Served to capt. USAAF, 1941-46, ETO. Recipient scholarship award Inst. World Affairs, 1947, Outstanding Efficiency award Dept. Army, 1960, Apollo 8 and Apollo 11 medallions NASA, 1969-70. Mem. Am. Mus. Natural History, Nat. Geog. Soc., Harvard Alumni Assn., Masons, Pi Sigma Alpha. Achievements include research on military operations and war game model building, research management techniques. Home: Santa Ana, Calif. Died Aug. 2, 2001.

**SMITH, KENNEDY,** chemicals executive; b. Pitts., July 12, 1922; s. R. Templeton and Eliza (Kennedy) S.; m. Mary Elizabeth Rutter, Feb. 7, 1945; children: Kennedy, Edward Caldwell, Frederick A., Mary E. Smith Podles, Mark T., Ann Templeton Seabright. AB, Harvard U., 1943, LLB, 1948. Bar: Pa. 1949. Asst. sec. Ben Venue Labs. Inc., Pitts., 1948—67, asst. to pres., 1967—68, pres., 1968—87, chmn. bd., CEO, 1988—90, chmn. emeritus, from 1990; dist. justice Pa. Dist. Ct., Pitts., 1971—77. With USNR, 1943—46. Home: Pittsburgh, Pa. Died Jan. 3, 1996.

**SMITH, MARGARET CHASE,** senator; b. Skowhegan, Maine, Dec. 14, 1897; d. George Emery Chase and Carrie Murray; m. Clyde Harold Smith, May 14, 1930 (dec. 1940). Attended, Colby Coll.; recipient of 95 hon. degrees. Tchr. Pitts Sch., Skowhegan, Maine, 1916—17; telephone operator Maine Telephone and Telegraph Company, 1918; with Independent Reporter, Skowhegan, Maine, 1919—27; office mgr. Cummings Woolen Mill, Skowhegan, Maine, 1928; mem. Maine Rep. State Com., 1930—36; sec. Congressman Clyde Smith, 1937—40; with Ho. of Reps., Maine 2nd dist., 1940—49; senator Maine, 1949—73; vis. prof. Woodrow Wilson Nat. Fellowship Found., 1973—76; dedicates Margaret Chase Smith Libr., Northwood U., Maine, 1982. Chair Spl. Com. on Rates of Compensation, 83rd Congress; ranking Rep. mem. Armed Svcs. Com., 90th-92nd Congresses, Aero. and Space Scis. Com., 88th-91st Congresses; chair Senate Rep. Conf., 1967—72. Writer: syndicated nat. newspaper column Washington and You, 1949—54. Founder Skowhegan Bus. and Profl. Women's Club, 1922; pres. Maine Fedn., Bus. and Profl. Women, 1923. Lt. col. USAFR, 1950—58. Recipient Medal of Americanism, VFW, 1954, Disting. Svc. award, Nat. Fedn. Bus. and Profl. Women, 1955, Minutemen award, Reserve Officers Assn., 1964, Pathfinders award, Women of the Rep. Party, 1984, Presdl. Medal of Freedom, 1989, Elizabeth Blackwell award, Hobart and William Smith Coll., 1991, Margaret Chase Smith Am. Democracy award, Nat. Assn. Secretaries of State, 1992, Carrie Chapman Catt award, League of Women Voters, 1992, Am. Spirit award, USAF; named Woman of Yr. in Politics, AP, 1948—50, 1957; named one of Ten Most Influential Women in the World, UPI, 1967, Outstanding Women in Govt., US Jaycee Women, 1984; named to Nat. Women's Hall of Fame, Seneca Falls, NY, 1973, Maine Women's Hall of Fame, 1990. Fellow: Am. Acad. Arts and Scis.; mem.: Sigma Kappa. Republican. Achievements include delivering the famous "Declaration of Conscience" speech on June 1, 1950 and Second "Declaration of Conscience" speech in 1970; first woman to be elected to both the US House and the Senate, and the first woman from Maine to serve in either; misses first vote in Congress in 13 years after hip surgery. At that time, held record for consecutive roll-call votes with 2,941 in 1968; first woman to be placed in nomination for the presidency at a major party convention in 1964; longest serving female senator in US history. Died May 29, 1995.

**SMITH, MARY ASKEW BACKER,** librarian, retired; b. Cin., Jan. 26, 1897; d. Matthew Jackson and Martha Goldsborough (Henry) Askew; m. John William Backer, Sept. 11, 1920 (dec. Feb. 1948); children: Mary Elizabeth Backer Hubbard, John Matthew; m. Russell Evans Smith, Aug. 9, 1969 (dec.). BA, U. Cin., 1918; libr. cert., U. Wis., 1919; MA, John Hopkins U., 1953. Profl. asst. N.Y. Pub. Libr., NYC, 1919-20; br. libr. Enoch Pratt Free Libr., Balt., 1943-64; instr. Catonsville (Md.) Community Coll., 1967-68. Author: (booklet) The College Club-A History of the Baltimore Branch of the American Association of University Women, 1981; contbr. articles to profl. jours. Pres. AAUW Balt. br., 1964-66, Legis. Clearing House of Md., Balt., 1981-82. Mem. Md. Libr. Assn. Republican. Methodist. Avocations: reading, music. Deceased.

**SMITH, MICHAEL K.,** former state legislator; b. Canton, Ill., May 23, 1966; s. Betty Smith; m. Donna Shaw. BA in Polit. Sci., Bradley U., 1988. Legislative asst. to Rep. Thomas J. Homer Ill. House of Reps., Ill., 1986—92; field coord. Dukakis/Bentsen Presdl. Campaign, 1988; mem. Dist. 91 Ill. House of Reps., 1995—2010. Religion class instr. St. Mary's Cath. Ch. Mem.: III Dem. Country Chairman's Assn. (v.p. from 1992), America Heart Assn., Canton Area C. of C (former pres.). Democrat. Catholic. Died Aug. 8, 2014.

**SMITH, PATRICK D.,** writer; b. Mendenhall, Miss., Oct. 8, 1927; s. John D. and Nora (Eubanks) S.; m. Iris Doty, Aug. 1, 1948; children: Jane L., Patrick D. BA, U. Miss., 1947, MS in English, 1959. Dir. public info. U. Miss., Oxford, to 1966; dir. coll. relations Brevard Chamber of Commerce, Cocoa, Fla., 1966-88. Lectr. in field. Author: The River is Home, The Beginning, Forever Island, 1973, Angel City, 1978, Allapattah, A Land Remembered, 1984 (Tebeau prize for Most Outstanding Fla. Hist. Novel); contbr. articles to profl. jours. Recipient Coun. for Fla. Libraries, 1986, Author award, 1987, Outstanding Fla. Author award Fla. Space Coast Writers Conf., Gannett, Fla. Today, 1987, 90, 92, Best Writer award, Toastmasters Internat., 1987, Communication Achievement award, Fla. Audubon Soc., 1987, Environ. Writers award, Medal of Honor Nat. Soc. DAR, 1988, Order of the South award Southern Acad. Letters, Arts & Sciences, 1995, Amb. of the Arts award Fla. US Dept. State, 1996, Fla. Cracker Heritage award, 1997, Fla. Cracker Trail Assn., 1997, Fay Schweim award Fla. Historical Soc., 2002; named to The Fla. Artists Hall of Fame, 1999 Died Jan. 26, 2014.

**SMITH, PHILIP MEEK,** science administrator, consultant; b. Springfield, Ohio, May 18, 1932; s. Clarence Mitchell S. and Lois Ellen (Meek) Dudley. BS, Ohio State U., 1954, MA, 1955; DSc (hon.), NC State U., 1986. Mem. staff U.S. Nat. Com. for Internat. Geophys. Yr., NAS, 1957-58; program dir. NSF, 1958-63, dir. ops. U.S. Antarctic Rsch. program, 1964-69, dep. head divsn. polar programs, 1970-73, exec. asst. to dir. and sci. advisor to pres., 1974-76; chief gen. sci. br. Office Mgmt. and Budget Exec. Office of Pres., 1973-74; assoc. dir. Office Sci. and Tech. Policy, Exec. Office of Pres., 1976-81; exec. officer NRC-NAS, Washington, 1981-94; ptnr. McGeary and Smith, Washington, 1995—2004; chmn. external adv. com. Nat. Computational Sci. Alliance, 1997—2001, mem., 2002—03; prin. Smith Sci. Policy and Mgmt., Santa Fe, from 2004. Bd. dirs. Aurora Flight Scis. Corp.; adv. cons. bd. U. Ala. Geophys. Inst., 1994—98; adv. bd. Sci.'s Next Wave, 1998—2002; advisor Com. for Econ. Devel., 1997; com. on sci., tech. and health aspects fgn. policy agenda US NRC, 1998—2000, com. on sci. and tech. counter terrorism, 2001—02, mem. com. sci. bases Colo. River Basin water mgmr., 2005—07, mem. com. sci. basis decision making internat. sustainable devel. orgns., 2002—05; chair com. orgn. & strategy Sci. Com. Antarctic Rsch., 1999—2000; co-chair adv. bd. Calif. Inst. Telecom. & Info. Tech., 2000—11, mem., from 2012, US Nat. Com. Internat. Polar Yr., 2003—05; history of geophysics com. Am. Geophys. Union, 2004—11; bd. dirs. found. Los Alamos Nat. Lab., 2006—07; chair Review Group Sci. Com. Antarctic Rsch., 2008—09; mem. Grand Canyon Hist. Soc., from 2012. Author: (with others) The Frozen Future, a Prophetic Report from Antarctica, 1973; contbr. articles to profl. jours. Bd. dirs. Washington Project for Arts, 1983-84, Washington Sculptors Group, 1983-84; mem., bd. mem. Grand Canyon River Heritage Mus. Coalition, 2009-2010, dir. 2011-13; mem. Namingha Inst. Gov. Com. Mus. Northern Ariz., 2013-. 1st lt. U.S. Army, 1955-57. Recipient Alumni Disctinction award, Springfield Ohio Pub. Sch., 2007, Mercier Svc. award, Ohio State U., 2007. Fellow AAAS, Antarctican Soc.; mem. Cosmos Club (Washington), SCAR (hon.), Am. Alpine Club (Golden, Colo.), Sigma Xi, Grand Canyon River Guides. Home: Santa Fe, N.Mex. Deceased.

**SMITH, RAYMOND KERMIT,** former educational administrator; b. Hahnville, La., July 6, 1915; married. BA, Xavier U., 1946; MA in Adminstrn. and Supervision, 1951; postgrad. in reading, No. Mich. U., 1962. Tchr.-prin. St. Charles Parish Schs., Luling, La., 1937—42; supr. instrn., 1942—79; asst. supt. instrn., 1979—81; ret., 1981. Evening, weekend instr. reading Loyola U., New Orleans, 1968—75; pres. United Givers Fund St. Charles Parish, 1971—72; v.p. Bayou-River Health Planning Coun., 1974—77; pres., from 1977. Contbr. articles to profl. jours. Lector, commentator, eucharistic min. Holy Rosary Ch., Hahnville. Recipient Outstanding Svc. award, United Way St. Charles Parish, 1993. Mem.: NEA, West St. Charles Rotary, KC, Famous G Social New Orleans. Deceased.

**SMITH, RICHARD EMERSON (DICK SMITH),** make-up artist; b. Larchmont, NY, June 26, 1922; s. Richard Roy and Coral (Brown) S.; m. Jocelyn De Rosa, Jan. 10, 1949; children: Douglas Todd, David Emerson. BA, Yale U., 1944. Pioneer dir. first TV make-up dept. NBC-TV, NYC, 1945-59; make-up dir. David Susskind Prodns., NYC, 1959-61; freelance make-up artist, cons., 1961—2014. Lectr. Yoyogi Animation Sch., Tokyo, 1992-2014, Polytek Devel. seminar, 1996; key spkr. Internat. Make-up and Effects Trade Show, 1997-99; featured make-up expert in Movie Magic tv documentaries, Monster Effects, 1994, Aging Effects, 1995; lectr. on spl. make-up effects Douglas Edn. Ctr., Monessen, Pa., 2004-14 Credits include Requiem for a Heavyweight, 1962, The World of Henry Orient, 1963, Mark Twain, Tonight!, 1967 (Emmy award 1967), Midnight Cowboy, 1968, Little Big Man, 1969, The Godfather, 1971, The Exorcist, 1973, The Godfather, Part II, 1974, The Sunshine Boys, 1975, Taxi Driver, 1975, Altered States, 1979, Scanners, 1980, Ghost Story, 1981, The Hunger, 1982, Amadeus, 1983 (U.S. Acad. award 1984, Brit. Acad. award 1985), Starman, 1984, Poltergeist III, 1987, Everybody's All-American, 1988, Sweet Home (Japanese film), 1988, Dad, 1989, Death Becomes Her, 1991, Forever Young, 1992; author: The Advanced Professional Make-Up Course, 1985, The Basic 3-D Make-up Course, 2002; permanent exhbn. of make-up work from Little Big Man, The Exorcist, Amadeus, others, at N.Y. Mus. of the Moving Image, 1992-2014; columnist Makeup Artist Mag., 1997-2014 Honored on his 50th ann. in make-up by American Film Inst., Visionary Cinema, Cinefex mag., 1995, 60 Yrs. Achievement in Makeup, Internat. Make-Up Artists Trade Show, 2005. Died July 31, 2014.

**SMITH, SIR ROLAND,** retired academic administrator; b. Oct. 1, 1928; s. Joshua and Hannah Smith; m. Joan Shaw, 1954. BA, U. Birmingham, Eng.; MSc, U. Manchester, PhD in Econs. Lectr. econs. U. Liverpool, 1960, dir. Bus. Sch., 1963; prof. mktg. U. Manchester, 1966-88, hon. vis. prof., 1988—2003, chancellor, 1996—2002, prof. emeritus mgmt. sci., 1988—2003; non-exec. chmn. Sr. Engring. Ltd., 1973-92; chmn. Temple Bar Investment Trust Ltd., 1980—99, House of Fraser, 1981-86, Readicut Internat., 1984-96, Hepworth plc, 1986-97, Brit. Aerospace, 1987-91, P & P plc, 1988—97, Manchester United Plc, 1991—2002. Dir., cons. various pub. cos. Flying officer RAF, 1953. Avocation: walking. Died Nov. 20, 2003.

**SMITH, ROWLAND JAMES,** educational administrator; b. Johannesburg, Aug. 19, 1938; s. John James and Gladys Spencer (Coldrey) S.; m. Catherine Anne Lane, Sept. 22, 1962; children: Russell Claude, Belinda Claire. BA, U. Natal, 1959, PhD, 1967; MA, Oxford U., Eng., 1967. Lectr. English U. Witwatersrand, Johannesburg, 1963-67; asst. prof. Dalhousie U., Halifax, N.S., Canada, 1967-70, assoc. prof. English, 1970-77, prof., 1977-88, McCulloch prof., 1988-94, chmn. English dept., 1977-83, 85-86, dir. Centre for African Studies, 1976-77, asst. dean arts and scis., 1972-74, dean arts and social scis., 1988-93, provost Coll. Arts and Scis., 1988-89, 90-91, 92-93; vis. prof., rsch. assoc. Multidisciplinary Ctr. Can. Studies, U. Rouen, 1994; prof. Wilfrid Laurier U., Waterloo, 1994—2004, v.p. acad., 1994—2004; prof. English U. Calgary, from 2004, dean humanities, from 2004. Author: Lyric and Polemic: The Literary Personality of Roy Campbell, 1972; editor: Exile and Tradition: Studies in African and Caribbean Literature, 1976, Critical Essays on Nadine Gordimer, 1990, Postcolonizing the Commonwealth: Essays in Literature and Culture, 2000. Bd. govs. Halifax Grammar Sch., 1972-74, Neptune Theatre Found., 1977-78; selection com. IODE Meml. Scholarships for N.S., 1969-71, Rhodes Scholarships N.S., 1972-74; edn. com. Victoria Gen. Hosp., 1986-90; dir. publicity and promotion N.S. Rugby Football Union, 1987-89; chair liaison com. edn. dept. N.S. U., 1990-93; book prize jury Can. Fedn. for Humanities, 1990, regional judge (Can. and the Caribbean) Commonwealth Writers Prize, 1991; chair com. on employment and ednl. equity Coun. Ont. Univs., 1996-99, chair working group on post-diploma degrees, 1999-2001; bd. dirs. Opera Ontario, 2001-04; active Coll. Univ. Consortium Coun., 2000-02; chmn. Ontario Coun. Acad. V.P., 2002-04. Recipient Transvaal Rhodes scholar, 1960; vis. fellow Dalhousie U., 1965-66, vis. scholar Ctr. Canadian Studies U. Western Sydney, Macarthur, New South Wales, 1996; Can. Council leave fellow, 1974-75, research grantee, 1977; grantee Social Scis. and Humanities Research Council of Can., 1978, internat. grantee, 1985, grantee Cultural Personalities Exchange program Assn. Canadian Studies in Australia and New Zealand, 1996, grantee Cultural Personalities Exch. Program, Assn. in Can. Studies in German Speaking Countries, 1997. Mem. Assn. Can. Univ. Tchrs. English (sec.-treas. 1968-70, profl. concern com. 1979-81), Can. Assn. for Commonwealth Lit. and Lang. Studies (exec. mem. 1989-92, pres. 1995-99), Can. Assn. Chmn. English (v.p. 1981-82, pres. 1982-83, exec. mem.-at-large 1985-86), Can. Fedn. Humanities (aid to scholarly publs. com. 1979-85, bd. dirs. 1992-94), MLA (div. chmn. 1984, mem.), Social Scis. and Humanities Rsch. Coun., Can. (chair rsch. grants adjudication com. 1994-96), Can. Rsch. Chairs Program (Coll. Reviewers 2000—), Internat. Coun. for Can. Studies (Can. scholarship and fellowship selection com. 2003-07), Can. Fedn. for the Humanities and Social Scis. (aid to scholarly publs. com. 2004—), Dept. Fgn. Affairs and Internat. Trade (Internat. Scholarships Programs Selection com. 2003-07), Can. Network for Japanese Studies, Prince Takamodo Japan Can. Meml. Fund (mgmt. com. 2007-). Home: Calgary, Canada. Died Oct. 20, 2008.

**SMITH, STEVE,** state legislator; b. Hennepin County, Minn., Nov. 29, 1949; m. Cindi Smith; 1 child, Ryan. BA in Polit. Sci., U. Minn.; JD, Okla. City U. Sch. Law. Coun. mem., Mound, 1984—86; councilman Town of Mound, 1984—86, mayor, 1987—90; atty. Smith-Fisher Attorneys; mem. Dist. 33A Minn. House of Reps., 1991—2013, dep. minority leader. Mem.: Hennepin County Bar Assn., Minn. County Bar Assn. Republican. Home: Mound, Minn. Died Apr. 7, 2014.

**SMITH, W. JAMES,** health facility administrator; b. Shenandoah, Iowa, Mar. 26, 1942; s. Willis C. and Lois M. (Hurst) S.; m. Sharon E. Hogue, May 4, 1940; children: Sharon Wendy, W. James II, Stacey E. BA in Psychology, Nat. Coll. Kansas City, 1960; MA in Psychology, Gerontology, John F. Kennedy U., 1969. Lic. nursing home adminstr., Fla., Iowa, Nebr., Calif. Pres. Retirement Svcs., Oakland, Calif., 1966-77; adminstr. Good Samaritan Soc., Sioux Falls, S.D., 1977-80; pres. Good Shepherd Ctrs., Palm Harbor, Fla., 1980-84; program coord. Hospice of Fla. Suncoast, Inc., Largo, Fla., 1984-91; founder, pres., CEO, Alzheimer's Ctrs., Inc., Palm Harbor, Fla., from 1991; pres., founder The House of Friends, Inc., from 1997, Fundación La Casa de Amigos, Guatemala, from 1997. Deceased.

**SMITH, WILLIE TESREAU, JR.,** retired judge; b. Sumter, SC, Jan. 17, 1920; s. Willie T. and Mary (Moore) Smith; m. Anna Marie Clark, June 9, 1955; 1 child, willie Tesreau III. Student, Benedict Coll., 1937—40; AB, Johnson C. Smith U., 1947; LLB, SC State Coll., 1554; JD, SC State Coll., 1976. Bar: SC 1954. Pvt. practice, Greenville, 1954; past exec. dir. Legal Svcs. Agy. Greenville County, Inc.; state family ct. judge 13th Jud. Circuit SC, 1977—91; ret., 1991. Past mem. adv. bd. Greenville Tech. Edn. Ctr. Adult Edn. Program and Para-Legal Program; mem. adv. bd. Greenville Tech. Coll. Found. Bd.; mem., past bd. visitorsc Presbyn. Coll., Clinton, SC; past bd. dirs. Greenville Urban League; past trustee Greenville County Sch. Dist.; past v.p. Peace Ctr. Performing Arts.; represented Bell South African Am. History Calendar. With US Army, 1942—45, with USAF, 1949—52. Mem.: NAACP, Phillis Wheatley Assn. (dir.), Greater Greenville C. of C. (past dir.), Am. Legion, Nat. Coun. Juvenile and Family Ct. Judges, Southeastern Lawyers Assn., Greenville County bar assns., SC County bar assns., Am., Nat. (jud. coun.), Rotary, Masons, Shriners, Delta Beta Boule, Omega Psi Phi, Sigma Pi Phi. Presbyterian (past chmn. bd. trustees Fairfield-McClelland Presbytery, past moderator Foothills Presbytery). Deceased.

**SMITHERS, SIR PETER,** British government official; b. Moor Allerton, Yorkshire, England, Dec. 9, 1913; s. H. Otway and Ethel M. M. (Berry) S.; m. Dojean Sayman, June 6, 1943; children: Sarah, Amelia. MA, Magdalen Coll., Oxford, Eng., 1937; DPhil, Oxford, 1954; DJur, U. Zurich, 1970. Barrister Inner Temple, Lincoln's Inn, Eng., 1936-40; asst. naval attache British Embassy, Washington, 1940-46; acting naval attache Mexico, Cen. Am., Panama, 1942-46; mem. of parliament Eng., 1950-64; parliamentary under sec. of state Fgn. Office, 1962-64; del. UN Gen. Assembly, 1960-62; sec. gen. Coun. of Europe, Strasbourg, 1964-69; sr. fellow UN Inst. for Tng. and Rsch., NYC, 1970-77. Author: Adventures of a Gardener, 1995, Life of Joseph Addison, 1966; over 20 one-man shows for photography, U.S., France. Lt. comdr., 1940-64. Decorated Naval Vol. Res. medal for disting. svc.; recipient 8 gold medals for photography, Schulthess prize for best plant collections in Switzerland, 2001; named Hon. Swiss Citizen, 1995. Mem. Carlton Club (London), Everglades Club (Palm Beach, Fla.), Bath and Tennis Club (Palm Beach). Avocations: gardening, photography. Home: Vico Morcote, Switzerland. Died June 8, 2006.

**SMOLAREK, WALDEMAR,** artist, printmaker; b. Warsaw, Sept. 5, 1937; Came to Canada, 1971; Student, Warsaw Sch. Art, 1952-55, Warsaw Acad. Fine Arts, 1955-57. Instr. form and color composition Warsaw Sch. Art, 1957-60. Instr. continuing edn. U. B.C., 1972. One-man shows include Warsaw, Poland, 1958-65, Artist Coop. Gallery, San Francisco, 1959, Kunsterhaus Wien, Vienna, Austria, 1961, Selected Artist Gallery, N.Y.C., 1962, Miami (Fla.) Mus. Modern Art, 1962, Gallerie Classigua, Stockholm, 1967, Gallery Herder, Stockholm, 1969, Presentation House, North Vancouver, B.C., Can., 1976, Langton Gallery, London, 1977, Kilakyushu (Japan) City Mus. Art, 1982, Galeria Fernando Vijande, Madrid, 1982, Gallery Silvia Menzel, Berlin, 1984, Galeria Daniel Templon, Paris, 1985, Harrison Galleries, Vancouver, B.C., Can., 1986, Osaka Found. of Culture, Japan, 1991, Montserrat Gallery, N.Y.C., 1992, Warsaw Mus. History, 1998, Gallery Forma and Colour, Warsaw, 1998; represented in permanent collections Miami Mus. Modern Art, Mus. Modern Art, Stockholm, Nat. Mus., Warsaw. Home: Vancouver, Canada. Deceased.

**SMYTH, DACRE HENRY DEUDRAETH,** retired naval officer; b. London, May 5, 1923; s. Nevill Maskelyne and Evelyn Olwen (Williams) S.; m. Jennifer Haggard, Jan. 11, 1952; children: Benita, Bronwen, Belinda, Bambi, Osmond. Commd. naval officer Royal Australian Navy, 1940-78; commanding officer HMA Ships, Latrobe, 1947-48, Hawkesbury, 1953-54, Supply, 1968-70, Cerberus, 1971-72; capt. Royal Australian Naval Coll., Jervis Bay, 1964-65; commodore Australian Naval Rep., London, 1966-68, Naval Officer in-charge, Victoria, 1971-78, ret., 1978. Dir. The Age Newspaper, Melbourne, 1982-93; trustee Shrine of Remembrance, Melbourne, 1978-2000, Overseas Students Assistance Fund, Melbourne, 1979-2007, Polly Woodside Maritime Mus., 1990-2000. Author, artist The Bridges of the Yarra, 1979, The Lighthouses of Victoria, 1980, Historic Ships of Australia, 1982, Old Riverboats of the Murray, 1982, Views of Victoria, 1984, The Bridges of Kananook Creek, 1986, Waterfalls of Victoria, 1988, Gallipoli Pilgrimage, 1990, Immigrant Ships to Australia, 1992, Pictures in my Life, 1994, Images of Melbourne, 1998, Australia from the Air, 2001, Australia from the Sea, 2003, The Marquesas Islands, 2005; over 27 one-man shows. Gov. Corps. of Commrs., Melbourne, 1989-2000; pres. Naval and Mil. Club, Melbourne, 1984; councillor Scout Assn. of Australia, Melbourne, 1978-83, Australian Maritime Trust, 1978-2003; patron N Class Destroyer Assn., 1971-2004. Named Officer of the Order of Australia, 1977, Order of Merit of France, 1994, Internat. Order of Merit, 1991, Legion of Honour of France, 2004. Fellow Australian Inst. of Co.

Dirs.; mem. Melbourne Club and Naval and Mil. Club, Victorian com. for the ANZAC Awards(chmn.). Avocations: painting, writing, designing and crafting stained glass windows. Home: Toorak, Australia. Deceased.

**SMYTH, JOSEPH PATRICK,** retired military officer, physician; b. Norwalk, Conn., Mar. 2, 1933; s. Patrick and Helen (Heffernan) Smyth; m. Ursula Marie Kirwin, Feb. 22, 1961; children: Donna, Jennifer, Joseph. BA, Fairfield U., 1960; MD, Creighton U., 1964. Diplomate Am. Bd. Med. Examiners. Commd. ensign USN, 1963, advanced through grades to rear adm., 1988; intern Phila. Naval Hosp., 1964-65, internal medicine resident, 1965-68, staff physician, 1968-69; internist, chief of medicine U.S. Naval Hosp., DaNang, Vietnam, 1969-70, Orlando, Fla., 1970-76, chief of medicine, exec. officer Yokosuka, Japan, 1976-80, exec. officer Oakland, Calif., 1980-82, comdg. officer, 1984-86, Okinawa, Japan, 1982—84, Naval Med. Command European Region, London, 1986-90; dep. dir. for med. readiness The Joint Staff, Pentagon, Washington, 1990-92; retired US Navy, 1992; med. dir. Volusia County (Fla.) Dept. of Corrections, 1994—2005. Instr. medicine Jefferson Med. Coll., 1966—69; preceptor USN Physician Asst. Program, Orlando, 1971—76; instr. mgmt. course Navy Med. Dept., Washington, 1986; med. coord. entire Gulf War buildup to Joint Chief Staff chmn. Gen. Colin Powell Operation Desert Shield/Storm, Saudi Arabia, 1990—91; med. dir. Volusia County Dept. Corrections, Fla., 1994—2005. Physician Orange County Fla. Alcohol Ctr., Orlando, 1974—76. Decorated Def. Superior Svc. medal, Legion of Merit, Meritorious Svc. medals with 2 oak leaf clusters, Navy Commendation medal with combat V. Mem.: AMA, Orange County Med. Soc., Am. Acad. Physician Execs., Fla. Med. Assn., Am. Acad. Med. Adminstrs. (Levandowski award 1991), Assn. Mil. Surgeons U.S. Republican. Roman Catholic. Home: Longwood, Fla. Died May 12, 2013.

**SNGUON, CHEM,** Cambodian government official; Sec. gen. Cambodia-Laos Friendship Assn., 1979; dep. sec. gen. ctrl. com. Kampuchean Nat. United Front for Nat. Salvation, 1980, dep. sec. gen. nat. coun., 1981-86; min. state and justice Govt. of Cambodia, Phnom-Penh, from 1992. Active Cambodian People's Party. Died 1999.

**SNIDER, DELBERT ARTHUR,** economics educator; b. Fayetteville, Ohio, Jan. 11, 1914; s. Chris Charles and Florence (Berger) S.; m. Helen Nancy Kuller, Sept. 4, 1939; children: Suzanne, Chris. AB, U. Cin., 1936, MA, 1937; student, Geneva Sch. Internat. Studies, summer 1936; PhD, U. Chgo., 1951. Economist Treasury Dept., 1940-43, 45-47; mem. faculty Miami U., Oxford, Ohio, 1947-48, 49-84, prof. econs., 1953-84, prof. emeritus, from 1984, chmn. dept., 1963-66; U.S. mem. Greek Currency Commn., Athens, 1948-49; cons. Fed. Res. Bd., 1965. Author: Introduction to International Economics, 7th edit, 1979, Economics: Principles and Issues, 1962, Economic Myth and Reality, 1965, International Monetary Relations, 1966, Economic Essentials, 1972. Served to lt. (j.g.) USNR, 1943-45. Mem. Am., Econ. Assn., Midwest Econ. Assn. (pres. 1971-72), Ohio Assn. Polit. Scientists and Economist, AAUP. Home: Oxford, Ohio. Died Nov. 21, 1988.

**SNIJDER, ADRIANUS GERARDUS,** priest; b. Amersfoort, Utrecht, The Netherlands, May 2, 1926; s. Jacob and Margaretha Cornelia (Rood) Snijder. Degree in Philosophy and Theology, Bergeijk U., 1952; Dr. French Lang. and Lit., U. Utrecht, The Netherlands, 1964. Ordained Assumption Father, Roman Cath. Ch. Tchr. Gymnasium, Boxtel, Netherlands, 1952—62; pastor Jacob-Roelands Lyceum, Boxtel, 1962—86, Molenweide, Boxtel, from 1972. Author: The Depths of Our Heart, 1992, To the Land of the Future, 1994, Learn by the Lite, In the Mirror of the Scripture, 1998, 2000. Roman Catholic. Home: Boxtel, Netherlands. Died May 7, 2002.

**SNOW, CLYDE COLLINS,** anthropologist; b. Ft. Worth, Tex., Jan. 8, 1928; s. Wister & Sarah Isobell (Collins) S.; m. Jerry Whistler, 1970; 5 children. BS, Eastern NMex. U., 1950; MS in Zoology, Tex. Tech. Coll., 1955; PhD in Anthropology, U. Ariz., 1967. Diplomate American Bd. Forensic Anthropology. Rsch. asst. anatomy Med. Sch. S.C., 1960-61, rsch. anthropologist, 1961-65; chief application biology sect. Civil Aeromed. Inst. Fed. Aviation Agy., 1965-69, chief phys. anthropology rsch., 1969-79; forensic anthrop. cons., 1979—2014. From adj. instr. to adj. asst. prof. anthropology U. Okla., 1962-80; trustee Forensic Sci. Found., 1973-79; forensic anthrop. cons. Okla. State Med. Examiner, 1978-2014; cons. US House Select Com. on Assasinations, 1978-79; pres. Forensic Sci. Edn., Inc., 1982-86. Mem. American Acad. Forensic Sci. (v.p. 1978-79), American Anthrop. Assn., American Assn. Phys. Anthropology, American Soc. Forensic Odontology, Soc. Study Human Biology, Sigma Xi. Achievements include research in forensic anthropology, study of human skeletal remains to establish personal identification and cause of death. Died May 16, 2014.

**SOBIN, GUSTAF PETER,** poet; b. Boston, Nov. 15, 1935; arrived in France, 1962; s. Newton Harrison and Rena (Pearl) S.; m. Susanna Estelle Bott Sobin, Mar. 2, 1968; children: Esther Renee, Gabriel Olivier. BA, Brown U., Providence, RI, 1958. Prof. creative writing Sarah Lawrence Coll., Lacoste, France, 1974-80, Cleve. Inst. Art, Lacoste, France, 1981-96, Bard Coll., Lacoste, France, 1997-98. Author: The Earth as Air, 1984, Voyaging Portraits, 1988, Breaths' Burials, 1995, Venus Blue, 1991, The Fly-Truffler, 1999, Luminous Debris (Reflecting on Vestige in Provence & Languedoc), 1999. Home: Goult, France. Died July 7, 2005.

**SOBOLEV, VICTOR VENIAMINOVICH,** physicist, researcher; b. Odessa, Ukraine, USSR, Oct. 2, 1946; m. Natlaia Tatikyan; 1 child, Alice. MSc, U. Novosibirsk, USSR, 1968; PhD in Physics, Siberian Br. Acad. Sci., Novosibirsk, 1973; DSc, Rsch. Ctr. Machine Bldg., Moscow, 1991. Chartered Engr., Engring. Coun. London. Jr. rschr. Inst. Nuclear Physics, Novosibirsk, 1968-69; postgrad. computer ctr. Siberian Br. Acad. Sci., Novosibirsk, 1969-72, rschr. computer ctr., 1972-75, head rsch. group computer ctr., 1975-76, head rsch. lab. dept. physics tech. problems metallurgy, 1988-92; head rsch. lab. Electrosteel Ctr., Krasnoyarsk, USSR, 1976-88; vis. prof., head rsch. group U. Barcelona, Spain, 1992-99; head rsch. group INASMET, San Sebastian, Spain, 1999—2002, gen. coordinator stategic programme, from 2002. Author 5 books; contbr. more than 300 articles to profl. jours. Fellow Inst. Materials London; mem. Am. Soc. Metallurgy. Achievements include 21 patents on methods and installations of continuous casting of steel, on methods of continuous casting of alumunum alloys, on utilization of metallurgical slags (granulation and use of their heat), on non-ferrous metallurgy (copper-nickel matte, lead, bismuth), development of models of thermal spraying and formation of solidified structure. Home: Barcelona, Spain. Died Mar. 18, 2005.

**SOLHAUG, JAN HELGE,** surgeon; b. Oslo, Mar. 24, 1938; s. Helge and Margit (Nygaard) S.; m. Anna Cecilie Helland-Hansen, Dec. 29, 1962; children: Dag, Rune, Tone, Trine. Med. cand., U. Groningen, The Netherlands, 1962; cand. med., U. Gothenburg, Sweden, 1966, U. Oslo, 1970; PhD, U. Bergen, Norway, 1979. Chief surgeon Torsby Hosp., Sweden, 1956-85, Elverum Hosp., Norway, 1985-89, Diakonhjemmets Hosp., Norway, from 1989. Resident Hosp. Karlstad, Sweden, 1966-71, Haukeland Hosp., Norway, 1971-76; dir. Elverum Hosp., 1986-87; sec. gen. United European Gastroenterology Week, Oslo, 1994. Author: Prostheses and Abdominal Wall, 1994, Tratamento Cirurgico Da Obesidade Morbida, 1994; mem. editl. bd. Current Surgery, 1980; contbr. over 100 articles to profl. jours. Mem. Assn. des Socs. Nat. European et Mediterraneennes di Gastroenterologie (v.p. 1995-98), Scandinavian Clinics for Ulcer Rsch. (bd. dirs. 1982—). Avocations: classic music, paintings. Home: Oslo, Norway. Deceased.

**SOLINSKY, LEONARD P.,** accountant; b. Pitts., May 1, 1935; s. Joseph Antohony and Amalia H. (Hajduk) S.; m. Margaret M. Petrancosta, May 30, 1959; children: Joseph A., Philip L., Keith R., Devin E., James B., Marianne M. Student, Duquesne U., 1962-63. Pvt. practice acctg., life ins. sales Solinsky & Assocs., Pitts., 1964-72, Tucson, from 1972. V.p. St. Vincent De Paul Soc., Tucson; pres. St. Francis De Sales Conf., Polio Epic, Tucson. Mem. Nat. Soc. Pub. Accts., Nat. Assn. Tax Practitioners. Lodges: Elks. Avocations: camping, bowling, ch. activities. Home: Tucson, Ariz. Died Apr. 16, 1989.

**SOLODUKHOV, VYACHESLAV VASILIEVICH,** engineering educator, research scientist; b. Kuibyshev (now Samara), Russia, Apr. 17, 1939; s. Vasiliy Dmitrievich Solodukhov and Olga Ivanovna Solodukhova; m. Nina Trofimovna Solodukhova, Nov. 16, 1963; 1 child, Irene Vyacheslavovna Borodulina. PhD, Moscow Power Engring. inst., 1964. Engr., sr. rsch. engr., prin. expert, assoc. prof. Moscow Power Engring. Inst., from 1964, assoc. prof., from 1964. Contbr. scientific papers. Trade union Moscow Power Engring. Inst., 1973—85. Grantee, Russian Fund Fundamental Investigations, 1999—2002. Achievements include patents for Line of Ultra High Frequency Broadcasting. Home: Moscow, Russia. Died Oct. 15, 2007.

**SOLOMENTSEV, MIKHAIL SERGEYEVICH,** Russian government official; b. Nov. 7, 1913; Grad., Leningrad Poly. Inst., 1940. Engr., workshop foreman, chief engr., factory dir. Lipetsk and Chelyabinsk regions, 1940—54; sec. Chal-yabinsk Regional Com. of Communist Party Soviet Union, 1954—57, 2d sec., 1954—57; chmn. Chelyabinsk Nat. Econ. Coun., 1957—59; 1st sec. Karaganda Regional Com. Communist Party of Kazakhstan, 1959—62; 2d sec. Central Com, 1962—64; 1st sec. Rostov Dist. Com. of CPSU, 1964—66; sec. CPSU Central Com., 1966—67; head dept. heavy industry, 1967—71; chmn. Coun. of Ministers of R.S.F.S.R., 1971—83, mem., 1983—88; chmn. CP Control Com., 1983—88, Ctrl. Auditing Com., 1984—86; mem. Ctrl. Com. of CPSU, 1961—89; cand. mem. Politburo, 1971—89. Decorated Order of Lenin; recipient Sixty Years of Armed Forces of USSR medal. Died Feb. 15, 2008.

**SOLOMON, ELINOR HARRIS,** electronic money consultant, writer; b. Boston, Feb. 26, 1923; d. Ralph and Linna Harris; m. Richard A. Solomon, Mar. 30, 1957 (dec. 2005); children: Joan S. Griffin, Robert H., Thomas H. AB, Mt. Holyoke Coll., 1944; MA, Radcliffe U., 1945; PhD, Harvard U., 1948. Jr. economist Fed. Res. Bank Boston, 1945-48; economist Fed. Res. Bd. Govs., Washington, 1949-56; internat. economist US Dept. State, Washington, 1957-58; profl. lectr. American U., Washington, 1964-66; sr. economist antitrust divsn. US Dept. Justice, Washington, 1966-82; prof. economics George Washington U., Washington, 1982—94. Econ. cons., Washington, 1982—2013; expert witness antitrust, finabcial networks, electronic funds transfer cases, Washington, 1988—2013. Author: Virtual Money, 1997; author, editor: Electronic Funds Transfers and Payments, 1987, Electronic Money Flows, 1991; contbr. articles on economics, banking and law to profl. jours. Mem. American Econs. Assn., Nat. Economists Club (bd. govs. 1997-98), The Cosmos Club (chmn. program com. 2004-06, bd. mgmt. 2006—09, mem. admission com. 2009-12, mem. libr. com., 2012-). Home: Chevy Chase, Md. Died Oct. 31, 2013.

**SOLOMON, HANNAH GREENBAUM,** cultural organization administrator; b. 1858; Organizer nationwide Jewish Women's Congress as part of 1890's World Fair, which later became Nat. Coun. Jewish Women; first pres. Nat. Coun. Jewish Women; co-creator Coun. Women of U.S.; activist with Susan B. Anthony and Jane Addams; established penny lunch stas. in pub. schs.; chairperson of all Chgo. ward leaders. Died 1942.

**SOLOMON, SAMUEL,** biochemistry educator, administrator; b. Brest Litovsk, Poland, Dec. 5, 1925; s. Nathan and Rachel (Greenberg) S.; m. Sheila R. Horn, Aug. 11, 1953 (div. 1974); children: David Horn, Peter Horn, Jonathan Simon; m. Augusta M. Vineberg, July 12, 1974. BS with honors, McGill U., 1947, MS, 1951, PhD in Biochemistry, 1953. Rsch. asst. Columbia U., 1953-55, assoc. in biochemistry, 1958-59, asst. prof., 1959-60; assoc. prof. biochemistry and exptl. medicine McGill U., 1960-66, prof., 1967-95, prof. emeritus, from 1995, prof. ob-gyn., 1976-95; dir. endocrine lab. Royal Victoria Hosp., Montreal, Que., 1965-95, dir. research inst., 1982-85; affilate dept. pharmacology U. Sherbrooke, from 1995. Mem. endocrinology and metabolism grants com. Med. Rsch. Coun. Can., 1967-71, regional dir. for Que., 1993-95; vis. prof. endocrinology U. Vt., 1964; cons. in field; Joseph Price orator, 1982, Am. OB-GYN Soc.; mem. steering com. Pharm. Mfg. Assn. Med. Rsch. Coun. Can. Partnership, 1993—; Med. Rsch. Coun. Can. dir. for McGill U., 1993-95. Co-editor: Chemical and Biological Aspects of Steroid Conugation, 1970; mem. editl. bd. Endocrinology, 1962; assoc. editor Can. Jour. Biochemistry, 1967-71, Jour. Med. Primatology, 1971; contbr. articles to profl. jours. Mem. bd. govs. McGill U., 1975-78; mem. steering com. European Study Group on Steroid Hormones, 1974-99, chmn. steering com., 1983-99, chmn. program com., 1990-91; mem. Dubin Commn. on Inquiry Drugs in Athletes, 1988-90. Decorated officer Order of Can. 1997; recipient McLaughlin medal Royal Soc. Can., 1989, Michel Sarrazin prize, 1997. Fellow Chem. Inst. Can., Am. Ob-Gyn. Soc. (hon.), Perinatal Rsch. Soc. Am. (pres. 1976), Soc. Gynecol. Investigation (program chmn. 1980), Endocrine Soc. (publ. com. 1986-89). Home: Montreal, Canada. Died Dec. 13, 2008.

**SOLOMONOFF, RAY J.,** physicist, researcher; b. Cleve., July 25, 1926; s. Julius and Sarah Solomonoff; m. Grace Solomonoff. PhD, U. Chgo., 1948, MS in Physics, 1951. Physicist Avion Instrument Corp., Paramus, N.J., 1951-54, Tech. Rsch. Group, NYC, 1954-57; prin. scientist Zator Co., Cambridge, Mass., 1958-72; mem. rsch. staff MIT Artificial Intelligence Lab., Cambridge, 1973-74; prin. scientist Oxbridge Rsch., Cambridge, 1975—90; vis. researcher U. des Saarlandes, Saarbrücken, Germany, 1991-92; vis. prof. Dalle Molle Inst. for Artificial Intelligence, Lugano, Switzerland, 2001. Participant Founding Symposium on Artificial Intelligence, Dartmouth, N.H., 1956; referee NSF, Washington, 1984-90; vis. researcher U. Saarlandes, Saarbrücken, Fed. Republic Germany, 1990-91. Referee Annals of Math. and Artificial Intelligence, 1989-90, Machine Learning, 1990; contbr. articles to profl. jours. With USN, 1944-46. Rsch. on Inductive Inference grantee Air Force Office Sci. Rsch., 1958-68. Mem. AAAS, IEEE, Assn. for Computing Machinery. Achievements include discovery of algorithmic (program-length) complexity and probability; invention of probablistic languages; application of algorithmic probability to artificial intelligence and machine learning; first use of formal languages and of training sequences for mechanized induction. Home: Saarbrücken, Germany. Died Dec. 7, 2009.

**SOLOW, ROBERT A.,** physician; b. Newark, Sept. 11, 1925; m. Marilyn Anes, Dec. 25, 1949; children: Lawrence Jay, Lee Howard, Bruce Alan, Brian Keith, Margaret Ann. AA, Princeton U., 1944; MD, N.Y. Med. Coll., 1948. Diplomate Am. Bd. Psychiatry and Neurology. Intern Jersey City Med. Ctr., 1948-49; resident in psychiatry Winter VA Hosp., Topeka, Kans., 1949-52; fellow Menninger Found. Sch. Psychiatry, Topeka, Kans., 1949-52; staff psychiatrist Topeka State Hosp., 1952; attending staff psychiatrist Mt. Sinai Hosp., Los Angeles, 1956-59; child psychiatrist Reiss Davis Child Study Ctr., 1955-70; vis. staff psychiatrist U. Calif. Hosp. and Clinics, Los Angeles, 1958-86, UCLA Neuropsychiat. Inst., from 1958. Mem. courtesy staff Westwood Hosp., L.A., 1960-77; mem. teaching staff Menninger Found. Sch. Psychiatry, 1958-62; asst. clin. prof. psychiatry, UCLA Sch. Medicine, 1962-69, assoc. clin. prof. 1969-78, clin. prof., 1978—; med. examiner State of Calif.; ind. med. examiner State of Calif. Dept. Indsl. Med.; med. adv. com. Muscular Dystrophy Assn. Am., 1955-80. Co-author: The Joys and Sorrows of Parenthood, 1973, Speaking Out for Psychiatry, 1987; mem. editorial bd. Adolescent Psychiatry, 1969-76; mem. editorial rev. bd. Am. Jour. Psychiatry, Am. Jour. Hosp. and Community Psychiatry. Chmn. exec. com. Boy Scouts Am., L.A. chpt., 1968-74. Capt. M.C., USAF, 1952-54. Recipient Silver Bruin award Boy Scouts Am., 1969, Hon. Svc. award Calif. Congress Parents and Tchrs., 1970, Resolution, City of L.A., 1977. Fellow Am. Psychiat. Assn. (life), Am. Soc. for Adolescent Psychiatry (life), So. Calif. Psychiat. Soc. (life, past. pres.), So. Calif. Soc. for Adolescent Psychiatry (life), Am. Coll. Psychiatrists, Am. Assn. Social Psychiatry, World Assn. for Social Psychiatry; mem. Internat. Assn. for Adolescent Psychiatry (exec. bd.), Group for Advancement of Psychiatry (editorial bd.), Calif. Med. Assn. (past chmn. sect. on psychiatry), So. Calif. Soc. Child Psychiatry (past pres.), Physicians for Social Responsibility, Calif. Soc. Indsl. Medicine and Surgery. Clubs: Mountaingate Country. Home: Los Angeles, Calif. Died July 1993.

**SORBER, CHARLES ARTHUR,** retired academic administrator; b. Kingston, Pa., Sept. 12, 1939; s. Merritt Walter and Marjory (Roachford) S.; m. Linda Ellen Babcock, Feb. 20, 1972; children: Kimberly Ann, Kingsley Charles. BS in Sanitary Engring., Pa. State U., 1961, MS in Sanitary

Engring., 1966; PhD, U. Tex., 1971. Sanitary engr. US Army, 1961-65; chief gen. engring. br. US Army Environ Hygiene Agy., Edgewood Arsenal, Md., 1966-69; comdr. US Army Med. Environ. Rsch. Unit, Edgewood Arsenal, Md., 1971-73; dir. environ. quality divsn. US Army Med. Bioengring. R&D Lab., Frederick, Md., 1973-75; asst. dean coll. scis. and math. U. Tex., San Antonio, 1976-77, acting dir. divsn. earth & phys. scis., 1977-80, dir. Ctr. Applied Rsch. & Tech., 1976-80, assoc. dean Coll. Engring. Austin, 1980-86, L.B. (Preach) Meaders prof., 1985; dean sch. engring. U. Pitts., 1986-93; pres. U. Tex.-Permian Basin, Odessa, 1993-2001; prof. U. Tex., Austin, from 2001; interim vice chancellor for spl. engring. programs U. Tex. Sys., 2002—03; interim pres. U. Tex., Arlington, 2003—04, spl. engring. advisor; pres. U. Tex.-Permian Basin; interim pres. U. Tex.-Pan Am., 2009. Bd. dirs., adv. coun., cons. various cos. and agys. Author, co-author more than 140 papers, book chpts., reports on land application of wastewater and sludges, water and wastewater reuse, water and wastewater disinfection and higher edn. Recipient Disting. Alumnus award Wilkes Coll., 1987, Disting. Grad. award Coll. of Engring., U. Tex., Austin, 1994, Outstanding Engring. Alumnus award Pa. State U., 1994; John A. Focht teach fellow U. Tex.-Austin, 1982. Fellow: ASCE; mem.: NSPE, Coun. Pub. Univ. Presidents & Chancellors (exec. com. Tex. 1994—95, sec.-treas. 1999—2001), American Water Works Assn., American Soc. Engring. Edn., Water Environ. Fedn. (com. chmn. 1983—85, 1986—89, bd. control 1988—94, v.p. 1990—91, pres.-elect 1991—92, pres. 1992—93, com. chmn. 1993—96, Svc. award 1985, 1989, 1990, 1996), American Acad. Environ. Engineers (trustee 1994—97, Gordon Maskew Fair award 1993), The U. Tex. Club. Home: Austin, Tex. Died Oct. 18, 2013.

**SORENSEN, PABLO OVE,** banker; b. Buenos Aires, Apr. 4, 1920; s. Harold and Kathrine (Mortensen) S.; m. Olga Ester Galvan, June 29, 1974; children: Julieta Laura, Maria Noel, Diego Gonzalo, Juan Pablo. Lic. Economy, U. Buenos Aires, 1959; postgrad., Am. U., Washington, 1963, MIT, Cambridge, Mass., 1969. Econ. research asst. Argentine Central Bank, Buenos Aires, 1942-46; fgn. exchange broker Fgn. Exchange Mkt., Buenos Aires, 1948-62; econ. researcher UN, Latin Am. Econ. Commn., Chile, 1950, Interam. Devel. Bank, Washington, 1963; fin. mgr. Gurmendi S.A. Metalurgic Industry, Buenos Aires, 1964-66; dep fin. dir. Fiat-Concord S.A., Buenos Aires, 1966; undersec. fin. Ministry of Economy, Buenos Aires, 1967-69; bd. govs. Banco del Buen Ayre, Buenos Aires, 1979-2001; ptnr. Di Baja & Sorensen, 1991-2001. Roman Catholic. Home: Olivos, Argentina. Deceased.

**SORIANO, JOVENTINO,** botany educator, researcher; b. Alcalaa, Pangasinan, Philippines, Feb. 8, 1920; s. Lamberto Aquino and Jacinta Dumlao (Duque) S.; m. Beatriz Tejada Aglibut, Aug. 14, 1944; children: Joy, Jerry, Joji, James, Jennifer, Janice, Jason. PhD, U. Chgo., 1957. Chair dept. botany U. Philippines, Quezon City, 1968-74, prof. botany, 1971-86, rsch. dir. Quezon City, 1971-80; professorial chair, 1974-76; acting dean grad. sch. U. Philippines, 1976-80; academician Nat. Acad. Sci. and Tech. Philippines, from 1980. Rsch. coord. Nat. Sci. Devel. Bd.-U. Philippines Integrated Rsch. Program, 1973-80; lectr. Internat. Atomic Energy Agy., 1978-86. Contbr. articles to profl. jours. 1st lt. U.S. Army, 1941-46. Travel grantee Royal Soc. London, 1984. Mem. AAAS, Am. Nuclear Soc. (emeritus, life), Pacific Sci. Assn. (life), Indian Soc. Genetics and Plant Breeding (life). Avocations: hiking, aerobics, gardening, coin collecting/numismatics, stamp collecting/philately. Home: Antipolo City, Philippines. Died Jan. 9, 2004.

**SORSCHER, MARVIN LOEB,** religious studies educator, rabbi; b. Bklyn., Apr. 29, 1924; s. Abraham and Miriam (Cohen) S.; m. Sylvia London, Feb. 7, 1954; children: Esther S. Rister, Abraham M., Sroya S. BA, Yeshiva Coll., 1946; MA, Hunter Coll., 1950; MHL, Yeshiva U., 1950, MS, 1958, DHL, 1968. Cert. sch. adminstr. and supr., N.Y.; cert. guidance counselor, N.Y. Pres. Yeshiva Haichel Ha Torah, Bklyn., from 1969; guidance counselor John D. Wells Jr. H.S., Bklyn., 1970-74, Franklin D. Roosevelt H.S., Bklyn., 1975-89; chmn. fgn. lang. dept. Washington Irving Evening H.S., Bklyn., 1973-80; rabbi Beth Aaron Synagogue, Bklyn., from 1990; chmn. Hebrew regents testing com. N.Y. State Edn. Dept., from 1976; instr. Yeshiva Tores Emes H.S., Bklyn., from 1997. Mem. edn. adv. bd. Yeshiva Gedolah Acad., Bklyn., 1990—; exam. scorer (in Hebrew and Yiddish) oral and written tchr. cert. lics. Nat. Evaluations Systems, N.Y.; translator Hebrew and Yiddish langs. N.Y.C. Bd. Edn., Bd. of Hearing-Visually Impaired Bur., 1997—. Author: Havah Nasocheach, Part I, 1969, Part 2, 1972; Manual of Tape Scripts, 1970, Lashon V'Dibbur, 1971, The Laws of Shabbos Erev Pesach, 1974, Blessings and Prayers for the Sabbath Holidays and Special Occasions, 1974, Hakshaiv Va Anai, 1976, I Can Learn Hebrew, 1986. Recipient 1st prize (trip to Israel) Torah Quiz Contest, Jewish Press, 1989. Mem. Am. Assn. Tchrs. Hebrew (pres. 1970—), Assn. Orthodox Jewish Tchrs. (life mem.; former v.p., mem. exec. bd. 1972—). Home: Brooklyn, NY. Died Apr. 26, 1999.

**SOTTSASS, ETTORE, JR.,** architect, interior and industrial designer; b. Innsbruck, Austria, Sept. 14, 1917; (parents Italian citizens); m. Fernanda Pivano, 1949 (div.). Dip.Arch., Politenico, Turin, Italy, 1939; PhD (hon.), Rhode Island Sch. Design, 1993, Royal Coll. Art, London, 1996. Free-lance writer, 1937-40; free-lance architect, designer Milan, 1945—2007; worked in studio of designer George Nelson NYC, 1956; design cons. Olivetti Co., Turin, 1958—80; founder, mem. Global Tools group, Milan, 1975; with Studio Alchymia design group, Milan, 1979; prin. Sottsass Associati, Milan, 1980—2007; founder Memphis design group, Milan, 1981. Exhibited in group shows Milan Triennale, 1954, Mus. Modern Art, N.Y.C., 1972, Internat. Design Zentrum, West Berlin, 1976, Ctr. de Creation Industrielle, Paris, 1976, Cooper-Hewitt Mus., N.Y.C., 1976, UCLA, 1979, La Jolla (Calif.) Mus. Art, Phila. Mus. Art, Venice Biennale, 1991, 96, A Masieri Found., Venice, 1992, Deichtorhallen Mus., Ambourg, 1993, Centre Georges Pompidou, Paris, 1994, Centro per l'Arte Contemporanea L. Pecci, Prato, 1999, Glasgow Sch. Art, Glasgow, 1999, Niitsu Art Forum, Nigeria, 1999, Living Design Ctr. Ozone, Tokyo, 1999, Mus. Modern Art, Gifu, 2000, Suntory Mus., Osaka, 2000, Marugame Mus. Contemporary Art, Japan, 2000, L.A. County Mus. Art, 2006; represented in permanent collections Phila. Mus. Art, Mus. Modern Art, N.Y.C.; prin. archtl. works include INA-CASA housing devels., Romentino, Arborea, Carmagnola and Meina, Italy, 1950-54, Galleria de Naviglio, Milan, Galleria del Cavallino, Venice, Italy, 1956, Galleria Il Quadrante, Florence, Italy, Galleria Sperone, Turin, others; author: Europe e America, 1946, Arte Astratta e Concreta, 1948, Ceramiche dell'tenebre, 1963, Miljo for en Ny Planet, 1969, De l'Objet Fini a la Fin de l'Objet, 1977, Esercizio Formale, 1979, Esercizio Formale II, 1980, Memphis Milano 1986: The Firm, 1986; (with others) Alcantara, 1983, Sottsass Associati, 1988; contbr. articles to profl. jours. Recipient Compasso d'Oro award, 1959; IF Award Design Kopfe Industrie Forum Design Hannover. Died Dec. 31, 2007.

**SOULER, BENJAMIN KERWIN,** retired research chemist, pharmacist, consultant; b. Woonsocket, RI, Aug. 8, 1917; s. Harry Nelson and Elizabeth (Kerwin) Souler; m. Cornelia Carruthers, Mar. 26, 2005; m. Priscilla Jepson, Feb. 7, 1942 (dec. Sept. 20, 1999); children: Mary Elizabeth Hardwich, Priscilla Ann Henry. BS, U. RI, Kingston, 1939; MS, U. So. Calif., LA, 1941. Rsch. chemist United Rexall Drug Co., Boston, 1941—46; lab. dir. Am. Home Foods Co., Boston, 1946—47, Elkhart, Ind., 1946—47; sr. rsch. scientist Bristol-Myers Squibb Co., Syracuse, NY, 1947—72; pharmacist cons. various pharmacies Cape Cod, Mass., 1972—86, Orleans Convalescent and Retirement Ctr., Mass., 1986—86; ret. Spkr. in fielf. Candidate US congress NY State Conservative Party, Onadaga County, NY. Pvt. 243rd regiment coastal arty. RI N.G., 1935—38, Woonsocket, pvt. coastal gun crew RI N.G., 1935—38, Ft. Henry G. Wright, Fishers Island, NY, pharmacist's mate USN, 1943—44, lt. comm. cryptographic officer USN, 1944—46, lt. officer courier USN, 1944—46, Philippine Liberation Campaign, lt. tng. officer USN, 1952—53. Mem.: DAV, Sampson WWII Sailors, Am. Legion, Bristol Employee's Assn. (pres. 1962), Syracuse Lions Club (pres. 1954). Achievements include patents for war gas (lewisite) decontaminant; highly stable ointment base. Avocations: history, botany, stamp collecting/philately. Home: Prescott, Ariz. Died Apr. 23, 2014.

**SOUTH, FRANK EDWIN,** physiologist, educator; b. Norfolk, Nebr., Sept. 20, 1924; s. Frank Edwin and Gladys (Brinkman) S.; m. Berna Deane Phyllis Casebolt, June 23, 1946; children: Frank Edwin, Robert Christopher. AB, U. Calif., Berkeley, 1949, PhD, 1952. Asst. prof. physiology U. P.R. Sch. Medicine, 1953-54, U. Ill. Coll. Medicine, 1954-61; assoc. prof. Colo. State U., 1961-62, prof., 1962-65, U. Mo., 1965-76; prof., dir. Sch. Life and Health Scis., U. Del., Newark, 1976-82; prof. emeritus U. Del., Newark, 1989, Sch. Life and Health Scis., U. Del., Newark, from 1989. Mem. governing bd., dir. Hibernation Info. Exchange, 1959— Mem. editorial bd. Cryobiology, 1989; contbr. numerous articles on physiology of hibernation, temperature regulation, renal function, marine mammals, artificial atmospheres, and sleep to profl. jours. Bd. dirs. Del. Lung Assn., 1976-82, Del. Cancer Network, 1977-82; mem. research com. Del. Heart Assn., 1977-82; mem. N.E. regional research com. Am. Heart Assn.; mem. med. adv. bd. A.I. DuPont Inst., Wilmington, Del., 1978-83. Served with AUS, 1943-45. Decorated Purple Heart with oak leaf cluster, Bronze Star with oak leaf cluster, Pres. unit citation, Croix de Guerre (unit); NIH career devel. awardee, 1961-65; recipient European African Mid East campaign medal with bronze spear head and silver star, World War II victory medal, Army of Occupation medal with Germany clasp, combat med. badge. Fellow AAAS, Sigma Xi; mem. Am. Physiol. Soc.; Clubs: Ranger Bns. Assn. World War II (pres. 2005-06, 2008-), Haven Yacht Club. Episcopalian. Home: Newark, Del. Died 2013.

**SOUTHWOOD, THOMAS RICHARD EDMUND,** zoologist, educator; b. Gravesend, Kent, Eng., June 20, 1931; s. Edmund William and Ada Mary (Regg) S.; m. Alison Langley Harden, Sept. 10, 1955; children: Richard Mark, Charles William. BSc 1st class, U. London, 1952, PhD, 1955, DSc, 1963, U. Oxford, 1987; DSc (hon.), Griffith U., Australia, 1983; Fil.Doc., U. Lund, Sweden, 1986; ScD (hon.), U. East Anglia, 1987; DSc (hon.), McGill U., Montreal, Que., 1988, U. Warwick, 1989, U. Durham, 1994, U. Sussex, 1994, U. Victoria, B.C., Can., 1994; LLD (hon.), U. London, 1991, Brookes U., Oxford, 1993, U. Bristol, 1994. Rsch. asst., lectr. Imperial Coll. U. London, 1955-64, reader in insect ecology, 1964-67, prof. zoology and applied entomology, 1967-79; Linacre prof. zoology U. Oxford, 1979-93, vice chancellor, 1989-93, pro-vice chancellor, 1987-89, prof., 1993—98. Apptd. fellow Merton Coll., 1979-2005, Eton Coll., 1993-01, hon. fellow Kellogg Coll., 2000-2005, Mansfield Coll., 2000-2005, Harris Manchester Coll., 2004; dir. Glaxo-Wellcome p.l.c., 1992-99; vis. prof. Collegio de Postgraduados, Escuela Nacional de Agricultura, Chapingo, Mex., 1964, N.C. State U., 1970-71, Fla. State U., 1971, U. Dar-es-Salaam, Tanzania, 1972-73, U. Tex., Austin, 1977, Rhodes U., South Africa, 1979; vis. assoc. prof. dept. entomology U. Calif., Berkeley, 1964-65; Spencer lectr. U. B.C., 1978; vis. disting. prof. ecology U. Wyo., 1984, Colo. State U., 1984; A.D. White prof.-at-large Cornell U., 1985-91; cons. WHO, FAO, 1966-74; del. Oxford U. Press, 1980-94; adv. coun. biology dept. Princeton U., 1982-86; pres. Coimbra Group of European Univs., 1992-93; chmn., head environ. scis. and policy dept., mem. senate Ctrl. European U., Budapest Coll., 1991-95. Author: Land and Water Bugs of the British Isles, 1959, Life of the Wayside & Woodland, 1963, Ecological Methods, 1966, 2d edit. 1978, 3d edit., 2000, The Story of Life, 2003; co-author (with D. Strong and J.H. Lawton): Insects on Plants, 1984; editor: Insect Abundance, 1968; co-editor: Insects and Plant Surfaces, 1986, Radiation and Health: The Biological Effects of Low-Level Exposure to Ionizing Radiation, 1987, The Treatment and Handling of Wastes, 1992; editl. bd. Entomologists Mo. Mag., Entomologist's Gazette, Brit. Jour. Entomology and Natural History, Biol. Jour. of Linnean Soc., Polish Jour. Environ. Scis., Cimbebasia; contbr. articles to profl. jours. Chmn. trustees Brit. Mus. Natural History, London, 1980-83; dep. lt. Oxfordshire, 1993-2005; mem. coun. Royal Holloway and Bedford Colls., London U., 1983-85; mem. Hebdomadal coun. Oxford U., 1981-94; chmn. Royal Commn. on Environ. Pollution, 1981-86, Nat. Radiol. Protection Bd., 1985-94; trustee Rhodes, 1986-2005, chmn., 1999—; trustee Lawes, 1987-2005, chmn., 1991-2005; trustee East Malling, 1987-99, Lloyds Tricentennial Trust, 1992-94, Habitat Trust, 1991—, Rank Prize Fund, 1993-2005, World Resources Found., 1995-2000; gov. Glasshouse Crops Rsch. Inst., 1969-81; mem. Agrl. Rsch. Coun. Adv. Com./Rsch. Grands Bd., 1970-83, JCO Arable & Forage Crops Bd., 1972-79; mem. tropical medicine panel Welcome Trust, 1977-79; co-chmn. U.K. Roundtable on Sustainable Devel., 1994-97, chmn., 1997-99; chmn. Inter-Agy. Com. on Global Environ. Change, 1997-2000, many others. Decorated Knight Bachelor, 1984; Order of Merit (Italy), Ordem de merito II (Portugal); recipient Forbes medal Imperial Coll., 1952, Huxley medal, 1962, Sci. medal Zool. Soc., 1969, Gold medal in zoology Linnean Soc., 1988, Marie Theresa medal Pavia U., 1997. Fellow Inst. Biology, Royal Soc., Royal Coll. Physicians London (hon.), Royal Coll. Radiologists (hon.); mem. Am. Acad. Arts and Scis. (hon. fgn.), Norwegian Acad. Sci. and Letters (hon. fgn.), U.S. Nat. Acad. Scis. (fgn. assoc.), Academia Europaea, Pontifical Acad. Scis., Royal Netherlands Acad. Arts and Scis. (fgn.), Hungarian Acad. Sci. (hon.), Royal Soc. London (v.p. 1982-84), Acad. Med. Scis., Royal Entomol. Soc. (pres. 1983-85), Brit. Ecol. Soc. (pres. 1976-78), Linnean Soc. London (v.p. 1982-84), Zool. Soc. London (coun. 1984, v.p. 1985-88), Ecol. Soc. Am. (hon.), Am. Soc. Naturalists, Japanese Soc. Population Ecology, Australian Ecol. Soc., Brit. Naturalists Assn. (hon. v.p. 1984-2005), Game Conservancy (hon. life, v.p. 1985—), Earthwatch (Europe) (chmn. sci. panel 1990-98), European Environ. Rsch. Orgn., Field Studies Coun. (exec. com. 1957-61, 65-68, hon. treas. 1961-64, hon. v.p. 1992—), Club of Earth. Home: Oxford, England. Died Oct. 26, 2005.

**SOWADA, ALPHONS AUGUSTUS,** bishop emeritus; b. Avon, Minn., June 23, 1933; s. Alphonse B. and Monica (Pierskalla) Sowada. Student, Onamia Sem., Minn., 1947-53; grad., Crosier House of Studies, Ft. Wayne, Ind., 1959; MA, Cath. U. Am., 1961. Ordained priest Canons Regular of the Holy Cross, 1958; arrived in Irian Jaya to work among Asmat, 1961; selected as mission superior, 1966; ordained bishop, 1969; bishop Diocese of Agats-Asmat, Indonesia, 1969—2001, bishop emeritus, 2001—14. Mem. exec. com. Indonesian Conf. of Bishops Contbr. to: Nat. Geog. Yearbook, 1968, other publications Mem. Order of Alhambra, Crosier Order, Kappa Delta Gamma. Roman Catholic. Died Jan. 11, 2014.

**SOWELL, LAVEN,** retired music educator; b. Wewoka, Okla., Jan. 9, 1933; s. Vestal Laven and Viola Jane Sowell. MusB, U. Okla., 1955; MA, Columbia U., 1964; postgrad., Manhattan Sch. Music, 1956—57, Conservatoire de Musique de Fontainebleu, France, 1966; studied with Clark Snell, Martial Singher, Joseph Benton, John Brownlee, Samuel Margolis, Nadia Boulanger, studied choral conducting with Harry Robert Wilson. Choral condr. Edison H.S., Tulsa, 1961—70; chorus master Tulsa Opera, 1962—94, chorus master emeritus, from 1994; dir. music 1st Presbyn. Ch., Tulsa, 1969—85; prof. music U. Tulsa, 1970—91. Vocal adjudicator various mus. orgns.; tchr. pvt. voice lessons. Co-author: Tulsa Opera Chronicles, 1992; author: My Music Notebook, 2000, With Affection, 2006. Bd. dirs. Tulsa Opera. Recipient Gov.'s Arts award, State of Okla., 1991. Mem.: Tulsa Accredited Music Teacher's Assn., Okla. Music Teacher's Assn. Democrat. Presbyterian. Avocations: travel, reading, opera. Home: Tulsa, Okla. Died Nov. 2, 2013.

**SOWELL, R. DOUGLAS,** medical association administrator, podiatrist; m. Linda Sowell; 1 child, Jennifer. BS in Psychology, U. Okla., 1971; DPM, Ill. Coll. Pediat. Medicine, 1978. Diplomate Am. Bd. Podiatric Surgery. Resident Thorek Hosp. and Med. Ctr.; podiatrist St. Anthony Hosp., Hillcrest Hosp. and Med. Ctr., Edmond Regional Med. Ctr., Deaconess and Bapt. Hosps., Oklahoma City. Fellow: Am. Coll. Podiatric Med. Rev., Am. Coll. Podiatric Physicians, Am. Coll. Foot and Ankle Surgeons; mem.: Am. Podiatric Med. Assn. (trustee, pres.). Deceased.

**SPAETH, NICHOLAS JOHN,** lawyer, former state attorney general; b. Mahnomen, Minn., Jan. 27, 1950; m. Cindy Spaeth; children: Gawain Kevin, Carl Wilson, William James, Elizabeth Bedont. AB, Stanford U., 1972, JD, 1977; BA, Oxford U., Eng., 1974. Bar: Minn. 1979, US Dist. Ct. Dist. Minn. 1979, US Ct. Appeals 8th cir. 1979, ND 1980, US Dist. Ct. Dist. ND 1980, US Supreme Ct. 1984, Calif. 1999, US Dist. Ct. Calif. 1999, Mo. 2005. Law clk. US Ct. Appeals (8th Cir.), Fargo, ND, 1977-78; law clk. to Justice Byron White US Supreme Ct., Washington, 1978-79; pvt. law practice, 1979-84; atty. gen. State of ND, Bismarck, 1985—93; ptnr. Dorsey & Whitney, LLP, Fargo, ND, 1993-99, Oppenheimer Wolff & Donnelly, Mpls., 1999, Cooley Godward, Palo Alto, Calif., 1999—2000; sr v.p., gen. counsel, sec. GE Employers Reinsurance Corp., Overland Park, Kans., 2000—03; sr v.p., gen. counsel & sec. Intuit, Inc., Mountain View, Calif., 2003—04; sr. v.p., law & pub. policy, chief legal officer H&R Block, Inc., Kansas

City, Mo., 2004—07; ptnr. Kirkpatrick & Lockhart Preston Gates Ellis LLP, 2007; exec. v.p., gen. counsel, chief risk officer Fed. Home Loan Bank of Des Moines, 2007—09. Adj. prof. law U. Minn., 1980-83. Rhodes scholar, 1972-74. Democrat. Roman Catholic. Died Mar. 16, 2014.

**SPAIN, JAMES WILLIAM,** political scientist, writer; b. Chgo., July 22, 1926; s. Patrick Joseph and Mary Ellen (Forristal) S.; m. Edith Burke James, Feb. 21, 1951; children: Patrick, Sikandra, Stephen, William. MA, U. Chgo., 1949; PhD, Columbia U., 1959. Cons. sec. army, 1949—50; with U.S. Fgn. Svc., 1951—53; rschr., lectr. Columbia, 1955—62; mem. policy planning coun. State Dept., 1963—64; dir. Office Rsch. and Analysis for Near East and South Asia, 1964—66; country dir. Pakistan and Afghanistan, 1966—69; charge d'affaires Am. Embassy, Rawapindi, 1969; consul gen. Istanbul, Turkey, 1970-72; minister Am. embassy, Ankara, 1972-74; diplomat-in-residence, vis. prof. history and govt. Fla. State U., Tallahassee, 1974-75; amb. to Tanzania Dar es Salaam, 1975-79; amb., dep. permanent rep. UN, NYC, 1979; amb. to Turkey, Ankara, 1980-81; amb. to Sri Lanka, Colombo, 1985-89; fgn. affairs fellow Carnegie Endowment for Internat. Peace and Rand Corp., Washington, 1982-84; guest resident investor Colombo, Sri Lanka, from 1991. Chmn. Lanka Infrastructure Ltd.; bd. dirs. Hawk Mountain Fed. Express, Ltd.; adj. prof. polit. sci. Am. U., Washington, 1965-67. Author: The Way of the Pathans, 1962, The Pathan Borderland, 1963, American Diplomacy in Turkey, 1984, Pathans of the Latter Day, 1995, Innocents of the Latter Day, 1997, In Those Days: A Diplomat Remembers, 1998, Holding Out in the Eternal City, 2000, The Emperor's Medallion, 2000, The Devils' Mountain, 2000, Digging the Desert, 2000, The Tribsmen's Treasure, 2000, The Monks; Secret, 2000, The Islands' Quota, 2000, Holy Ireland, 2001, Out Beyond, 2002, Innocents, 2002, To Boil a Stew, 2002. Trustee Joseph Frazer Meml. Hosp. With U.S. Army, 1946-47. Fellow Ford Found., 1953-55; recipient Presdl. Exec. award, 1983, Wilbur I. Carr award for Disting. Diplomacy, 1989. Mem. Coun. Fgn. Rels., Washington Inst. Fgn. Affairs, Assn. Diplomatic Studies and Tng., Cosmos Club. Home: Colombo, Sri Lanka. Died Jan. 2, 2008.

**SPALLONE, JEANNE FIELD,** retired state judge; b. NYC, Jan. 18, 1928; d. Charles William and Flora (Kopp) Field; m. Daniel Francis Spallone, June 4, 1950; children: Janne Field Spallone, Niel Francis Spallone, James Field Spallone. BS, U. Conn., 1950. News and feature writer, reporter Middletown (Conn.) Press, 1952-53, 59-65; adminstrv. asst. to amb. Hon. Chester Bowles, Essex, Conn., 1953-56; mem. Conn. State Legislature, Hartford, 1959-61; columnist op-ed Middletown Press, 1993-96; judge of probate State of Conn., Dept. Judiciary, Dist. of Deep River, Hartford, 1979-95. Contbr. articles to jours., books, newspapers. Trustee, historian Deep River Hist. Soc., 1976-94; chmn. bd. dirs. Winthrop Cemetery Assn., 1978—. Mem. Conn. Order Women Legislators, Soroptimists (pres. local chpt. 1982-84), Block Island (R.I.) club (pres. 1982-84). Democrat. Avocations: family history, travel. Died Aug. 5, 2008.

**SPANGLER, MARY SCHUHSLER,** retired academic administrator; b. NYC, 1942; d. Alfred A. and Mary (Lentz) Schuhsler; m. Clifford Eugene Spangler (dec.); 1 child, Clifford Eugene. BA, Chestnut Hill Coll., 1964; MA in English, UCLA, DEdn, 1994. Prof. English L.A. Valley Coll., assoc. dean admissions, dean student services, v.p. acad. affairs, pres., 1997—2003; chancellor Oakland Cmty. Coll., Mich., 2003—07, Houston Cmty. Coll., 2007—13. Co-author four textbooks; contbr. articles to profl. jours. Named one of The 50 Most Influential Women in Houston, Houston Woman mag., 2009. Mem. Hollywood Chamber of Commerce (bd. dirs.), American Assn. for Higher Edn., Nat. Coun. for Rsch. & Planning, Assn. for Rsch. on Nonprofit Organizations & Vol. Action, Assn. of Calif. Cmty. Coll. Adminstrs., Pi Lambda Theta. Died June 14, 2014.

**SPEAKES, LARRY MELVIN,** public relations executive, former White House press secretary; b. Cleveland, Miss., Sept. 13, 1939; s. Harry Earl and Ethlyn Frances (Fincher) Speakes; m. Aleta Merkel, Oct. 5, 2001; children from previous marriage: Sondra LaNell, Barry Scott, Jeremy Stephen. Student, U. Miss., 1957-61; Litt. D. (hon.), Ind. Central U., 1982, BA in Journalism, 2001. News editor Oxford Eagle, Miss., 1961-62, Bolivar Comml., Cleveland, 1962-63, mng. editor, 1965-66; dep. dir. Bolivar County Civil Def., 1963-65; gen. mgr. Progress Publications, Leland, Miss., 1966-68; editor Leland Progress, Hollandale Herald, Bolivar County Democrat, Sunflower County News; press sec. to Senator J.O. Eastland US Senate, 1968-74; staff asst. The White House, 1974, press asst. to spl. counsel to Pres., 1974, asst. to press sec., 1974-76, asst. press sec., 1976-77, press sec., 1977; v.p. Hill & Knowlton, Inc., Washington, 1977-81; asst. to Pres., prin. dep. press sec. The White House, Washington, 1981-87; sr. v.p. Merrill Lynch & Co., Inc., NYC, 1987-88; v.p. comm. Northern Telecom Ltd., Washington and Toronto, 1991-93; sr. v.p. corporate rels. US Postal Svc., Washington, 1994-98, sr. advisor to postmaster gen., 1998—2008, mgr. of advt., 2001—08. Corporate comm. cons., lectr. on press & politics, 1988-91. Author: (with Robert Pack) Speaking Out: The Reagan Presidency From Inside the White House, 1989; contbr. Crisis Repsponse: Inside Stories on Managing Image Under Siege, 1993 Recipient Presdl. Citizens medal, 1987, Gen. Excellence award Miss. Press Assn., 1988, Disting. Journalism Alumni award U. Miss., 1981, Hall of Fame, 1985, Silver Em. Miss. Scholastic Press Assn., 1988, Spl. Achievement award Nat. Assn. Govt. Communicators, 1983, Silver Anvil award Pub. Rels. Soc. America, 1988, NY Addy Gold TV comml. award; named to The Top 100 PR Profls. of Century, PR Week mag., 1999, Pub. Rels. Hall of Fame, D.C. chpt. PRSA, 1999. Mem. Arthur Page Soc. (trustee), Pub. Rels. Seminar, Sigma Delta Chi, Kappa Sigma (Man of Yr. 1982), Lambda Sigma, Omicron Delta Kappa. Methodist. Home: Bethesda, Md. Died Jan. 10, 2014.

**SPEARS, WARREN,** choreographer, artistic director; b. Detroit, May 2, 1954; s. Walter and Theresa Wilma (Davis) S. Student, Juilliard Sch., NYC, 1971-74. Solo dancer Alvin Ailey Am. Dance Theater, NYC, 1974-78; co. dir. The Spears Collection, NYC, 1978-81; artistic dir., resident choreographer New Danish Dance Theatre, Copenhagen, Denmark, from 1987. Freelance dancer various N.Y. cos. and European TV, films and theater, 1978-80; asst. prof. dance NYU, Purchase, 1979-80; prof. dance Copenhagen U., 1989-91; choreographer Jutland Opera Co., Denmark, 1991; mem. Danish Theatre Coun., 2001-02. Choreographer of over 20 ballets for the New Danish Dance Theatre and for numerous dance cos. including Alvin Ailey Repertory Ensemble, Royal Danish Ballet, Dayton Contemporary Dance Co., Kaleidoscope Dance Co.(Ind.), Impulse Dance Co. (Boston), Djazzex Dance Co. (Holland), also choreography for theatre and mus. in Denmark, France and U.S.A. Recipient Copenhagens Dance award, 1991, Queen Margetha award, 1994, Order of Dannebrog, 2003; grantee Danash Art Found., 2001-03. Avocations: doll collecting, music, painting. Died Jan. 8, 2005.

**SPENCE, ROBERT LEROY,** publishing executive; b. Carlisle, Pa., Sept. 13, 1931; s. Leroy Oliver and Esther Helen (Lau) S.; m. Barbara Amelia Hunter, Sept. 1, 1954 (div. Sept. 1978); children— Robert Roy, Bonnie Leigh; m. 2d, Maryanne Elizabeth Yacono, Jan. 10, 1979 BA, Dickinson Coll., 1953; postgrad, Temple U., 1955-57, Rutgers U., 1956, 59-60, U. Pa., 1960. Cert. tchr., N.J. Chmn. dept. math. Haddon Heights High Sch., NJ, 1954-62; sr. editor Silver Burdett Co., Morristown, NJ, 1962-64; editor-in-chief Harcourt Brace Jovanovich, Inc., NYC, 1964-81; v.p., pub. Harper & Row Publishers, Inc., NYC, 1981-85, Scribner Ednl. Pubs. div. Macmillan, Inc., NYC, 1985; pres. R&M Spence, Inc., Sparta, NJ, from 1985. Author textbook series: Growth in Mathematics, 1978, Excel in Mathematics, 1989-90, Mathematics Plus: Multicultural Projects, 1993; editor: Financial Planning for The Baby Boomer Client, 2000, 2d edit., 2004, Money Forever, 2002. Mem. Assn. Am. Pubs. (mem. exec. com. 1981-84), Nat. Council Tchrs. Math., Internat. Reading Assn., Am. Numismatic Assn. Avocations: rare coin collecting, coin newsletter author and publisher, artist, writer. Died Oct. 5, 2012.

**SPENCER, ANTHONY JAMES MERRILL,** retired mathematician; b. Birmingham, England, Aug. 23, 1929; s. James Lawrence and Gladys (Merrill) S.; m. Margaret Bosker, Jan. 1, 1955; children: John Myles Anthony, Timothy James, Richard Nicholas. BA, Cambridge U., 1952, MA, 1955, ScD, 1980; PhD, U. Birmingham, 1955. Rsch. assoc. Brown U., Providence, R.I., 1955-57; sr. scientific officer U.S. Atomic Energy Authority, Aldermaston, England, 1957-60; lectr. U. Nottingham, England, 1960-63, reader, 1963-65, prof., 1965-94, emeritus prof. theoretical mechanics, from 1994. Vis. prof. Brown U., Providence, 1966, 71, Lehigh U., Bethlehem, Pa., 1978, U. Queensland, Brisbane, Australia, 1982; cons. Marmara Inst., Istanbul, Turkey, 1975; mem., acting chmn. math. com. Sci. and Engring. Rsch. Coun., London, 1978-81; mem. math. scis. subcom. Univ. Grants Com., London, 1982-87. Author: Deformations of Fibre-Reinforced Materials, 1972, Continuum Mechanics, 1980; author, editor: Engineering Mathematics, Vols. 1 and 2, 1977; contbr. articles to profl. jours. Active phys. scis. com. Coun. for Nat. Acad. Awards, London, 1989-91. Lance cpl. Brit. Army, 1948-49. Erkine fellow, 1995, Leverhulme emeritus fellow, 1995-97. Fellow: Royal Soc.; mem.: Am. Acad. Arts & Sciences (hon. fgn.), Internat. Soc. Interaction of Math. and Mechanics (hon.), Brit. Soc. Rheology (hon.), London Math. Soc. Home: Nottingham, England. Died Jan. 26, 2008.

**SPERELAKIS, NICHOLAS, SR.,** retired physiology and biophysics educator, researcher; b. Joliet, Ill., Mar. 3, 1930; s. James and Aristea (Kayaidakis) S.; m. Dolores Martinis, Jan. 28, 1960; children: Nicholas Jr., Mark (dec.), Christine, Sophia, Thomas, Anthony. BS in Chemistry, U. Ill., 1951, MS in Physiology, 1955, PhD in Physiology, 1957. Cert. in electronics, radio and radar US Navy & Marine Corps Electronics Sch., 1952. Tchg. asst. U. Ill., Urbana, 1954-57; instr. Case Western Res. U., Cleve., 1957-59, asst. prof., 1959-66, assoc. prof., 1966; prof. U. Va., Charlottesville, 1966-83; Joseph Eichberg prof. physiology Coll. Medicine U. Cin., 1983-96, chmn. dept., 1983-93, Eichberg prof. emeritus, from 1996. Cons. NPS Pharm., Inc., Salt Lake City, 1988-95, Carter Wallace, Inc. Cranbury, N.J., 1988-91; vis. prof. U. St. Andrews, Scotland, 1972-73, U. San Luis Potosi, Mex., 1986, U. Athens, Greece, 1994; Rosenblueth prof. Centro de Investigacion y Avanzades, Mex., 1972; mem. sci. adv. com. several internat. meetings, editl. bds. numerous sci. jours. Co-editor: Handbook of Physiology: Heart, 1979; editor: Physiology and Pathophysiology of the Heart, 1984, 2d edit., 1988, 3rd edit., 1994, 4th edit., 2000, Calcium Antagonists: Mechanisms of Action on Cardiac Muscle and Vascular Smooth Muscle, 1984, Cell Interactions and Gap Junctions, vols. I and II, 1989, Frontiers in Smooth Muscle Research, 1990, Ion Channels in Vascular Smooth Muscle and Endothelial Cells, 1991, Essentials of Physiology, 1993, 2d edit., 1996, Cell Physiology Source Book, 1995 (Outstanding Acad. Book, Choice Am. Libr. Assn. 1996, 98), 3d edit., 2001, 4th edit., 2011, Electrogenesis of Biopotentials, 1995; assoc. editor Circulation Rsch., 1970-75, 75-80, Molecular Cellular Cardiology; regional editor Current Drug Targets, 2000-02; contbr. more than 500 articles to profl. jours. Lectr. Project Hope, Peru, 1962. Sgt. USMC, 1951—53, Korean War, with USMCR, 1953—59. Recipient Disting. Alumnus award Rockdale (Ill.) Pub. Schs., 1958, Rsch. Excellence award Am. Heart Assn. Ohio, 1995, Visionary award Am. Heart Assn., S.W. Ohio, 1996; U. Cin. Grad. fellow, 1989; NIH grantee, 1959-99. Mem. IEEE, Engring. in Medicine and Biology, Am. Physiol. Soc. (chair steering com. sect. 1981-82), Biophys. Soc. (coun. 1990-93), Am. Soc. Pharmacology and Exptl. Therapeutics, Internat. Soc. Heart Rsch. (coun. 1980-89, 92-98), Am. Hellenic Ednl. Progressive Assn. (pres. Charlottesville chpt. 1980-82), Ohio Physiol. Soc. (pres. 1990-91), Phi Kappa Phi. Independent. Greek Orthodox. Avocations: stamp collecting/philately, coin collecting/numismatics. Home: Cincinnati, Ohio. Died May 21, 2013.

**SPERLING, JOHN GLEN,** educational services company executive; b. Willow Springs, Mo., Jan. 9, 1921; s. Leon Birchfield and Lena (McNama) S.; m. Virginia Vandergrift, June 1951 (div. 1965); 1 child, Peter Vandegrift. BA, Reed Coll., 1948; MA, U. Calif., 1952; PhD, U. Cambridge, Eng., 1955. Mem. faculty Northern Ill. U.; instr. U. Md., 1955-57; asst. prof. Ohio State U., Columbus, 1957—61; prof. humanities San Jose (Calif.) State U., 1961—73, dir., Right to Read Project, dir., NSF Cooperative Coll.-Sch. Sci. Prog in Econ.; pres. Inst. Profl. Devel., San Jose, 1972-76; founder, pres. U. Phoenix, 1976-80; founder, dir. Apollo Group, Inc., Phoenix, 1973—2014, pres., 1973—98, CEO, 1973—2001, chmn., 1973—2004, acting exec. chmn., 2006—08, exec. chmn., 2008—14. Author: The South Sea Company, 1964, Great Depressions: 1837, 1893, and 1929, 1966, Against All Odds, 1989, Rebel With a Cause: The Entreprenur Who Created the University of Phoenix and the For-Profit Revolution in Higher Education 2000, The Great Divide: Retro vs. Metro America, 2004; co-author: (with Peter Dixon) War Finance 1698-1714, (with Suzanne Helburn) Economic Concepts and Institutions, 1974, Industry Performance, 1974, National Economic Policies, 1974, Social and Economic Priorities, 1974, Communist Economics, 1974, Third World Economics, 1974, (with Robert Tucker) For Profit Higher Education: Developing a World Class Workforce, 1997; contbr. articles to profl. jours. including Hist. Jour., Econ. History Rev., Bull. NASSP, Rule Mag., among others. Cons. Combating Juvenile Delinquency, Sunnyvale, Calif., 1972-75. Recipient Ehrman Studentship, Kings Coll., Cambridge U., 1953-55, Acad. Freedom award Calif. Fedn. Teachers, L.A., 1988; named one of The Forbes 400: Richest Americans, 2006-14 Mem. Arizona Club. Democrat. Founder the U. Phoenix, which has established itself as a leading provider of higher education programs for working adults by focusing on servicing the needs of the working adult; Primary investor in Genetic Savings and Clone, Inc., "Missyplicity Project" (cloned dog) and "Operation CC" (cloned cat that was created was called CopyCat), made first sale: a cloned male kitten, for $50,000 in December, 2004; latest quest: to research, develop, and sell the new science of longevity; opponent of drug prohibition and is actively financing initiatives to legalize medical marijuana in the US. Home: Phoenix, Ariz. Died Aug. 22, 2014.

**SPERRY, ARMSTRONG WELLS,** writer, illustrator; b. Nov. 7, 1897; Illustrator: Carnack, the Life-Bringer: The Story of a Dawn Man, Told by Himself, 1928, Tarzan and the Lost Empire, 1929, Magic Portholes, 1932, Carmen, Silent partner, 1935, Mistress Jennifer & Master Jeremiah: A Story of the Building of Old Ironsides, 1937, New World Builders: Thrilling Days with Lewis and Clark, 1937, Shuttered Windows, 1938, Hell on Ice: The Saga of the "Jeannette", 1938, Brothers of the Frontier, 1938, through the Lands of the Bible, 1938, Klondike Gold, 1938, The Story of Mankind, 1938 (Newbery medal 1922), Island of the Red God, 1939, Boat Builder: The Story of Robert Fulton, 1940, Teri Taro from Bora Bora, 1940, Courage over the Andes, 1940, Two Children of Brazil, 1940, Faraway Ports, 1940, House Afire!, 1941, Nicholas Arnold, Toolmaker, 1941, Winabojo, Master of Life, 1941, Tall Timber, 1941, Runaway, 1941, Ocean Outposts, 1942, Night Boat, 1942, Dogie Bay, 1943, Clipper Ship Men, 1944, Mystery at Thunderbolt House, 1944, Story Parade Star Book, Jungle River, 1945, Sky Highways: Geography from the Air, 1945, The Jinx Ship, 1946, Zebulon Pike, 1950, The Story of Hiawatha, 1951, Prince Henry, 1951, Johann Gutenberg, 1951, Secret of the Congo, 1955; author, illustrator: One Day with Manu, 1933, One Day with Jambi in Sumatra, 1934, One Day with Tuktu, an Eskimo Boy, 1935, All Sail Set: A romance of the "Flying Cloud", 1935 (Newbery honor), The Codfish Musket, 1936 (Newbery honor), Little Eagle, a Navaho Boy, 1938, Call It Courage, 1940 (Newbery medal 1941), Bamboo, the Grass Tree, 1942, Coconut, the Wonder Tree, 1942, The Boy Who Was Afraid, 1942. Died Apr. 26, 1976.

**SPICER, BRIAN MILTON,** physics educator; b. Melbourne, Victoria, Australia, Oct. 7, 1928; s. William Milton Ashford and Mavis Pearl (Rees) S.; m. Lesley Patricia Parry, Feb. 21, 1958; children: Carol Mavis, David Brian, Trevor Leslie. BS, U. Melbourne, 1950, MS, 1952, PhD, 1956, DS, 1965. Lectr. physics U. Melbourne, Parkville, Victoria, Australia, 1956-57, sr. lectr., 1957-61, reader in physics, 1961-62, assoc. dir. nuclear rsch., 1962-65, prof. physics, 1965-88, prof. emeritus, from 1988. Vis. scientist Ind. U. Cyclotron Facility, 1971-79, Triumf Lab., Vancouver, Can., 1981-93; chmn., head Sch. Physics U. Melbourne, 1972-77; mem. Australian Ionizing Radiation Adv. Coun., 1973-87; cons. Nat. Office Overseas Skills Recognition, Canberra, Australia, 1985-96, chmn. gen. acad. panel, 1994-96; mem. edit. adv. com. Australian Jour. of Physics, 1977-82. Author: (with D.E. Caro & J.A. McDonell) Modern Physics, 1961; contbr. articles to profl. jours. Deacon North Balwyn Bapt. Ch., Melbourne, 1967-90, 95-98; v.p. Bapt. Union Victoria, 1978-79, pres., 1979-80. Sr. Fgn. Scientist fellow NSF, 1971; Dixson & Prof. Kernot Rsch. scholar U. Melbourne, 1952; recipient David Syme prize for rsch., 1960. Fellow Inst. Physics (London)(chmn. Victorian divsn. 1962), Australian Inst. Physics (hon., chmn. Victorian br. 1962-63, chmn. nuc. and particle physics group 1973-74), Am. Phys. Soc., Australian Inst. Nuc. Sci. and Engring. (hon.). Home: Melbourne, Australia. Died Aug. 19, 2004.

**SPIES, HOWARD A.,** lawyer; b. Hays, Kans, Mar. 31, 1936; s. Adolph A. and Margaret R. (Coltrane) Spies; m. Carolyn C. Hain, Aug. 13, 1960; children: Christine, Howard, Cathleen, Karen. BS, Fort Hays State Coll., 1958; JD, Washburn U. Topeka, 1961. Bar: Kans. 1961, US Dist. Ct. Kans. 1961, (US Dist. Ct. Kans.) 1961, (US Ct. Appeals (10th cir.)) 1964, US Supreme Ct. 1971, US Tax Ct. 1971. With Alcoholic Beverage Control, Atty. Gen.'s Office, State of Kans., 1961—63; ptnr. Schroeder, Heeney, Groff, Spies & Hiebert, Topeka, 1963—77; pvt. practice Kans., 1977—80, Ohio, 1977—80; v.p., gen. counsel Cardinal Industries, Columbus, Ohio, from 1980. Served with US Army, 1955—57. Mem.: ABA, Worthington Hills (Ohio) Country, Phi Alpha Delta. Republican. Roman Catholic. Deceased.

**SPILLER, ROBERT ERNEST,** educator, literary historian; b. Phila., Nov. 13, 1896; s. William G. and Helen Constance (Newbold) S.; m. Mary Scott, June 17, 1922 (dec. Mar. 1971); children: William Scott, Constance Newbold (Mrs. Thomas J. Johnston), Mary Miles; m. Anna Moss Wright, Mar. 15, 1975. BA, U. Pa., 1917, Harrison fellow, 1919-20, MA, 1921, PhD, 1924; Guggenheim fellow for foreign study, 1928-29; Litt.D. (hon.), Thiel Coll., 1964, Coll. Wooster, 1968; Dr. phil. h.c., Christian Albrechts U., Kiel, Germany, 1965; Dr. Humane Letters (hon.), U. Pa., 1967. Instr. English U. Pa., 1920-21; with Swarthmore Coll., 1921-45, prof., English, 1934-45; chmn. Swarthmore Coll. (Humanities Div.), 1935-41, Swarthmore Coll. (Curriculum Com.), 1942-45; prof. English, summers Duke U., 1927, Harvard U., 1930, Columbia U., 1931, 1937, U. So. Calif., 1933, U. Mich., 1936, Bread Loaf Sch. of Eng., 1948, U. Minn., 195l, U. Colo., 1956; vis. prof. U. Oslo, 1950, New Sch. for Social Research, 1943-44, U. London (King's and Bedford Colls.), 1958-59, U. N.C., 1968, U. So. Fla., 1969; prof. English U. Pa., 1945-61, Felix E. Schelling prof. English, 1961-67, Schelling prof. emeritus, from 1967, chmn. dept. Am. civilization, 1947-49, 51-53, 55-57. Adv. editor to Am. Literature, 1928-31 and 1940-55, editor, 1932-40; Chmn. editorial bd. Am. Quar., 1951-70 Author: The American in Eng. During The First Half Century of Independence, 1926, Fenimore Cooper, Critic of His Times, 1931, 63, The Roots of National Culture; anthology, 1933, 48; The Cycle of American Literature, 1955, 1956, 67; (with others) anthology Eight American Authors, 1956; The Early Lectures of Ralph Waldo Emerson, 1959, Vol. II, 1964, vol. III, 1971, The Third Dimension: Studies in Literary History, 1965, The Oblique Light, 1968, The Mirror of American Life, 1971, The Philobiblon Club of Philadelphia: The First Eighty Years, 1973, Milestones in American Literary History, 1977, Late Harvest, 1981; editor: Fenimore Cooper, Gleanings in Europe, France, 1928, 70, England, 1930, 70, Switzerland, 1980, A Descriptive Bibliography of James Fenimore Cooper, (with P.C. Blackburn), 1934, James Fenimore Cooper, Representative Selections, 1936, Satanstoe, (with J.D. Coppock), 1937, Esther, by Henry Adams, 1938, Five Essays on Man and Nature, (by R.W. Emerson), 1955, American Perspectives, 1961, Social Control in a Free Society, 1960, A Time of Harvest, 1961; chmn. editorial bd.: Literary History of The United States, 1948, 4th edit., 1974, Tahiti, by Henry Adams, 1946, The American Literary Revolution: 1783-1837, 1967, The Van Wyck Brooks-Lewis Mumford Letters, 1921-63, 1970, The Collected Writings of R.W. Emerson Vol. 1, (with A.R. Ferguson) Nature, Addresses and Lectures, 1971, 79; assoc. editor: Etudes Anglaises, France, Jahrbuch für Amerikastudien, Germany; Contbr. to mags. Bd. dirs. American-Scandinavian Found., chmn. com. fellowships, 1966-70; bd. dirs. Swarthmore (Pa.) Pub. Library, 1953-56, pres., 1955, 56; hon. cons. Am. cultural history Library of Congress, 1967-69; chmn. Am. studies adv. com. Am. Council Learned Socs., 1960-66. Served with AEF, World War I. Fellow N.Y. State Hist. Assn. (hon.); mem. Hist. Soc. Pa., Am. Studies Assn. (pres. 1955), Modern Lang. Assn. Am. (chmn. Am. lit. group 1930, 31, 1st v.p. 1957), Phi Beta Kappa. Clubs: Philobiblon (Phila.) (pres. 1964-68), Franklin Inn (Phila.) (pres. 1961-64). Deceased.

**SPIRO, IRVING J.,** aerospace company executive; b. Chgo., Sept. 20, 1913; BS, Ill. Inst. Tech., 1936; MS, postgrad., UCLA, 1963. Chief engr. Borman Engring., Inc., North Hollywood, Calif., 1950—56; chief mech. optics engr. Aerophysics Corp., Santa Barbara, Calif., 1956—58; sect. head Space Tech. Labs., El Segundo, Calif., 1958—60; mgr. The Aerospace Corp., El Segundo, from 1960. Editor: SPIE Proceedings, 1976—86, Optical Engring., 1977, 1984; assoc. editor, from 1978. Recipient Gov.'s award, SPIE, 1981. Fellow: Internat. Soc. Optical Engring. (chpt. pres. 1968—70, gov. 1968—71, 1981—86), SPIE, Optical Soc. America; mem.: Tau Beta Pi, Sigma Xi. Home: Sherman Oaks, Calif. Died Feb. 21, 1991.

**SPIRO, ROBERT HARRY, JR.,** foundation and business executive, educator; b. Asheville, Dec. 5, 1920; s. Robert Harry and Eoline Peterson (Shaw) S.; m. Juanita T. Henderson, June 25, 2006; children by previous marriage: Robert Timothy, Elizabeth Susan, James Monroe. BS, Wheaton Coll., Ill., 1941; postgrad. Navy Supply Sch., Harvard U., 1943; postgrad., U. N.C., 1945-46; PhD, U. Edinburgh, Scotland, 1950; student, Union Theol. Sem., summers 1951-53; postdoctoral, Duke U., summer 1956; ScD (hon.), Fla. Inst. Tech. Assoc. prof. King Coll., Bristol, Tenn., 1946-50; prof. history Miss. Coll., 1950-57; pres. Blue Ridge Assembly, Black Mountain, NC, 1957-60; dean Coll. Liberal Arts Mercer U., prof. history, 1960-64; pres. Jacksonville U., Fla., 1964-79; under sec. Dept. Army, US Dept Def., 1980-81; cons. to bus., 1981-84, 86-99; nat. exec. dir. Res. Officers Assn. U.S., 1984-86; chmn. RHS Imprinted Products Inc., 1988-99; bd. managers Voyager Variable Annuity of Fla., 1972-79. V.p. Am. Security Coun. Found., 1991—99, chmn., 2002—06, emeritus chmn., from 2006; pres. Nat. Security Caucus Found., 1997—2002; past pres. Fla. Assn. Colls. and Univs.; mem., past chmn. Ind. Colls. and Univs., 1964—79, chmn, 1967; sec.-treas. Assn. Urban Univs., 1968—76; past mem. Fla.-Columbia Ptnrs.; gen. chmn. Jacksonville Sesquicentennial Commn., 1970—72; mem. N.C. Tricentennial Commn., 1959—65; past mem. adv. coun. Robert A. Taft Inst. Govt., Inst. Internat. Edn. Editor (with D.F. Winkler and J.C. Reilly Jr.) Destroyer Squadron Two From Leyte Gulf Through Okinawa, 2002; contbr. articles to profl. publications & encyclopedias Trustee Southwestern Bapt. Theol. Sem., 1968—78; chmn. bd. Bapt. Coll. and Sem., Washington, 1989—2001. Ensign to lt. USNR, 1941—45, ret. rear adm. USNR, 1978. Decorated Palmes Academique (France); recipient Disting. Civilian Svc. award, Dept. of Army, 1981, Disting. Alumnus award, Navy Supply Corps Sch., 2000, Disting. Svc. award, Mil. Order Carabao, 2005; named U. Benefactor, U. Edinburgh, 2006. Mem. Navy League U.S. (former pres. Jacksonville coun.), Naval Res. Assn. (nat. adv. coun.), Res. Officers Assn. U.S. Naval Inst., Clan Munro Assn., American Legion, Kiwanis (pres. Clinton, Miss. 1956-57; pres. Georgetown, D.C. Club 1991-92), Phi Delta Kappa, Alpha Kappa Psi, Phi Alpha Theta, Phi Kappa Phi. Home: Charlotte, NC. *Esse Quam Videre "To Be Rather than to Seem" is an eloquent apothegm I learned in high school Latin classes. For me it has been a demanding goal for daily living, a worthy aspiration for each task in life and a challenging vision of what I wish and ought to be.* Died Oct. 1, 2013.

**SPITZ, SAMUEL H.,** physician; b. Nashville, Oct. 2, 1911; s. Joseph and Forence (Levy) Spitz; m. Sherie K. Spitz, Aug. 30, 1951; children: Katherine, Joe. BA, Vanderbilt U., 1931, MD, 1935. Diplomate Am. Bd. Internal Medicine. Intern L.I. Hosp., Bronx, NY, 1935—36, resident in pathology, 1936—37, clin. prof., 1942—50; in internal medicine King's County Hosp., 1937—38; Eli Lilly fellow, 1938—41; clin. prof. Downstate Med. Ctr. SUNY, Bklyn., 1950—70; practice medicine specializing in internal medicine L.I. Coll. Hosp., 1946—71, Swedish Hosp., Bklyn., 1946—71, Corrales, N.Mex.; asst. physician U. N.Mex. Sch. Medicine, Albuquerque, 1971—81; med. dir. Family Health Clinic, Albuquerque, 1971—76. Bd. dirs. Albuquerque Mus., from 1970; mem. Corrales Watershed Bd. Contbr. articles to profl. jours. Served to lt. col. US Army, 1940—46. Decorated Bronze Star. Fellow: ACP. Died July 31, 1990.

**SPLITTSTOESSER, DON FREDERICK,** microbiologist, educator; b. Norwalk, Wis., Aug. 17, 1927; s. Frederick Albert and Martha (Rosenwald) S.; m. Clara Mae Quinnell, Mar. 19, 1959. BS, U. Wis., 1951, MS, 1952, PhD, 1956. Mem. faculty Cornell U.; prof. microbiology N.Y. State Agrl. Expt. Sta., Geneva, chmn. dept. food sci. and tech., 1982-89; chmn. food protection com. NRC, 1981-85. Editor: Food Microbiology: Public Health and Spoilage Aspects, 1976, Compendium of Methods for the Microbiological Examination of Foods, 3d edit., 1992; contbr. articles to profl. jours. Bd. dirs., treas. Family Counseling Svc., Geneva, 1960-63; chmn. Geneva Zoning Bd. Appeals, 1972-83. 1st lt. U.S. Army, 1956-58. Fellow Inst. Food Technologists (chmn. N.Y. sect. 1970); mem. Am. Soc. Microbiology (pres. N.Y. br. 1966), Am. Soc. Enology and Viticulture (chmn. ea. sect. 1979), Torch Club (pres. 1970), Geneva Country Club. Democrat. Unitarian Universalist. Avocations: sinemaking, golf. Home: Geneva, NY. Deceased.

**SPOELDERS, MARC HUBERT PAUL,** education educator; b. Antwerp, Belgium, Mar. 14, 1947; m. Anne-Marie Cotton; children: Seth, Sara, Simon. Tchg. Cert. in Lower Secondary Edn., Pius X Tchr. Tng. Coll., Antwerp, 1966, lic. in psychol. and ednl. scis., 1970; PhD, U. Ghent, Belgium, 1975. Rschr. Belgian Sci. Rsch. Fund, 1970-80; asst. prof. U. Ghent, 1981-91, prof., from 1991. Editor-in-chief Scientia Paedagogica Experimentalis jour., 1988—. Mem. Internat. Assn. Applied Linguistics (sec. gen. 1987-93, pres. 1993-96). Home: Laarne, Belgium. Deceased.

**SPORN, MICHAEL VICTOR,** producer, director; b. NYC, Apr. 23, 1946; s. Mario and Amy (Young) Rosco.; m. Heidi Stallings BFA, N.Y. Inst. Tech., 1967. Asst. dir. Hubley Studio, NYC, 1972-76; supr., coord. R. Williams Animation, NYC, 1976-77; asst. dir. R.O. Blechman Productions, NYC, 1977-79; founder, owner, dir. Michael Sporn Animation Inc., NYC, 1980—2014. Prodr., dir.: Doctor DeSoto, 1984, The Amazing Bone, 1985, Lyle Lyle Crocodile, 1987, Abel's Island, 1988, Red Shoes, 1989, Mike Mulligan and His Steamshovel, 1990, The Marzipan Pig, 1990, Ira Sleeps Over, 1992, Whitewash, 1995, Goodnight Moon and Other Stories, 1999, Happy to Be Nappy and Other Tales, 2006, I Can Be President, 2011; dir.: The Man Who Walked Between the Towers, 2005 (American Libr. Assn. Carnegie Medal, 2006), 30 other animated films. Served in USN. Recipient Ace awards Acad. Cable Arts, 1990-92. Mem. ASIFA East, Acad. Motion Picture Arts & Sciences Died Jan. 19, 2014.

**SPRAGUE, GEORGE FREDERICK,** geneticist, educator; b. Crete, Nebr., Sept. 3, 1902; s. Elmer Ellsworth and Lucy Kent (Manville) S. BS, U. Nebr., 1924, MS, 1926, D.Sc., 1958; PhD, Cornell U., 1930. With Dept. Agr., 1924-72, leader corn and sorghum investigations, 1958-72; mem. faculty U. Ill., Urbana, 1973-86, prof. emeritus, 1986-93. Editor: Corn and Corn Improvement, 3d edit, 1989; contbr. articles to profl. jours. Recipient Superior Svc. award USDA, 1960, Disting. Svc. award, 1970, Wolf prize in agr., Wolf Found., 1978, Nat. Coun. Plant Breeders award, DeKalb Career award; inducted into USDA-Agrl. Rsch. Svc. Sci. Hall of Fame. Fellow AAAS, Washington Acad. Scis., Am. Soc. Agronomy (pres. 1960, Crops Rsch. award 1957); mem. NAS, Crops Sci. Soc. (pres. 1951), Am. Genetics Assn., Genetics Soc. Am., Am. Soc. Plant Physiologists, Am. Naturalists, Biometrics Soc. Died Nov. 24, 1998.

**SPRUCE, FREDERICK,** chemical engineer, consultant; b. Crowton, Cheshire, England, Jan. 12, 1918; s. Fred and Hannah Spruce; m. Edna Ouitrain, July 11, 1940; children: Gillian Mary, Judith Ann. AMIET, Coll. Advanced Tech. Manchester, 1939; DIP, U. London, 1944; AMCT, U. Manchester, 1947. Sr. rsch. scientist ICI Mond divsn., Northwich/Runcom, 1934—77; tchr., rschr. U. Manchester, 1977—87; proposer designs to indsl. engrs. including ICI, BP and Esso, 1986—90; developer biolog. fluidised bed treatment for water and wastewater, 2000—02. Careers advisor U. Manchester, 1975—86; cons. county edn. dept., Cheshire, from 1987; cons. sr. engrs. for new chem. processes, from 1990; cons. indsl. health and safety, from 1980. Author (patentee): Development of Polythene, 1950—60, Electrolytic Cells for Industry, 1972—75, Bed Filtration for the Eradication of Mirco-organisms, 1992—2004. SNCO RAF, 1939—46, Middle East. Grantee fuel cell devel., 1990—93, deep bed filter for the eradication of micro-organisms, from 2001. Mem.: Soc. Ops. Engrs., Brit. Inst. Mgmt., Inst. Plant Engring. Methodist. Achievements include invention of electrode system for the most energy-efficient diaphragm/membrane cell at present in operation in the world. Avocations: tennis, football, organic fruit-growing. Home: Barnton, Northwich, Cheshire, England. Died May 2005.

**SPRUGEL, GEORGE, JR.,** retired ecologist; b. Boston, Sept. 26, 1919; s. George and Frances Emily (Strong) S.; m. Catharine Bertha Cornwell, Oct. 27, 1945; 1 son, Douglas George. BS, Iowa State U., 1946, MS, 1947, PhD, 1950. Instr., then asst. prof. zoology and entomology Iowa State U., 1946-54; asst. head biology br. Office Naval Research, 1951-53; spl. asst. to asst. dir., div. biology and medicine NSF, 1953-54, program dir. environ. biology, 1954-64; chief scientist Nat. Park Service, 1964-66; chief Ill. Natural History Survey, 1966-80, chief emeritus, from 1980. Cons. in field; mem. adv. com. environ. biology NSF, 1965; dir. program conservation of ecosystems U.S. Internat. Biol. Program, 1969-72; mem. study group on role lunar receiving lab. NASA, 1969-70, mem. life scis. com., 1972-78; mem. ecology adv. com. Bur. Reclamation, 1972-74; mem. Gov. of Ill. Sci. Adv. Com., 1967-80, Ill. Environ. Quality Council, 1970-73; mem. environ. studies bd. com. to devel. protocol for toxic substances Nat. Acad. Scis.-Nat. Acad. Engring., 1972-73; mem. NRC, 1968-72 Served as officer USNR, 1940-45, 51-53. Fellow AAAS (council 1961-73, v.p., chmn. sect. biol. scis. 1971); mem. Am. Inst. Biol. Scis. (mem.-at-large gov. bd. 1969-72, exec. com. 1972-75, pres. 1974), Ecol. Soc. Am. (council 1961-78, v.p. 1968), Am. Soc. Zoologists (sec. 1970-72, chmn. div. ecology 1971), Sci. Research Soc. Am., Sigma Xi. Home: Seattle, Wash. Died Oct. 10, 1999.

**STAFFORD, JOHN ROGERS,** retired pharmaceutical executive; b. Harrisburg, Pa., Oct. 24, 1937; s. Paul Henry and Gladys Lee (Sharp) S.; m. Inge Paul, Aug. 22, 1959 (dec. 2012); children: Carolyn, Jennifer, Christina, Charlotte. AB, Dickinson Coll., 1959; LLB with distinction, George Washington U., 1962, Degree (hon.), 1994. Bar: D.C. 1962. Assoc. Steptoe & Johnson LLP, Washington, 1962-66; gen. atty. Hoffman-LaRoche, Nutley, NJ, 1966-67, group atty., 1967-70; gen. counsel American Home Products Corp., NYC, 1970-74, v.p., 1972-77, sr. v.p., 1977-80, exec. v.p. Madison, NJ, 1980-81, pres., from 1981; chmn., CEO Wyeth, 1986—2001, chmn., 2001—02. Bd. dirs. American Home Products Corp., 1980—2001, JP Morgan Chase & Co., 1982—2005, NYNEX Corp., 1989—97, Honeywell Internat. Inc., 1993—2010, Verizon Comm. Inc., 1997—2011. Bd. dirs. Christopher Reeve Paralysis Found. Recipient John Bell Larner 1st Scholar award George Washington U. Law Sch., 1962, Outstanding Achievement Alumnus award, 1981 Mem.: NAM (bd. dirs.), ABA, DC Bar Assn., Baltusrol Club, Essex Fells (NJ) Country Club. Died Apr. 18, 2014.

**STAKHIEV, YURY MIKHAILOVICH,** mechanical engineer; b. Konotop, USSR, Feb. 19, 1934; s. Mikhail Konstantinovich Stakhiev and Nina Nikolaevna Stakhieva; m. Nelly Alekseevna Bekrjeva, 1961 (div. Dec. 1963). Cand. of Sci., Leningrad Forest Engring. Acad., Archangelsk, USSR, 1966, DSc, 2002. Chief mechanic Sawmill, Engels, Russia, 1956—60; sr. sci. Central Scientific Rsch. Inst. Mech. Processing Wood, Archangelsk, 1962—64, head lab., from 1964, mem. experts coun., from 1964, mem. sci. coun., from 1964, chmn. sect. wood cutting and tools br. coord. coun., 1965—90, mem. editl. bd. sci. procs., from 1964. Mem. sci. and tech. coun. Ministry Forest Industry Russian Fedn., 1970—90; mem. sci. com. internat. conf. U. Zvolen Slovak Republic, 2000, 2002. Contbr. articles to mags. and newspapers. Coun. mem. Soc. Knowledge, Archangelsk, Russia, 1975—80, House of Scientists, Archangelsk, Russia, 1995—2000; mem. analytical and experts coun. Adminstrn. Archangelsk oblast, Archangelsk, Russia, from 1995. Recipient medal, Exhbn. Nat. Econ. Achievement, 1965, 1974, 1977, 1979, 1981, 1990, medal For Valiant Labour, 1970, Order People Friendship, 1981, prize, Lomonosov's Fund, 1994. Mem.: Acad. Natural Sci. (corr.). Achievements include research in disk problems; patents in field. Avocation: chess. Home: Archangelsk, Russia. Died Mar. 29, 2004.

**STALLINGS, (CHARLES) NORMAN,** lawyer; b. Tampa, Fla., Apr. 3, 1914; s. Otto Pyromus and Minnie Henderson (Mitchell) S.; m. Mary Phillips Powell, Feb. 6, 1943 (dec. 1999); children: Charles Norman, Jean Katherine (dec.), Mary Anne. AB, U. Fla., 1935; JD, Harvard U., 1938, LL.M., 1940. Bar: Mo. 1939, Fla. 1940, D.C. 1941, Ga. 1946. Asso. firm Ryland, Stinson, Mag & Thomson, Kansas

City, Mo., 1938-39, Sutherland, Tuttle & Brennan, Washington, 1940-41, Atlanta, 1946-49; mem. firm Shackleford, Farrior, Stallings & Evans, Tampa, Fla., 1949-84, of counsel, 1984—2002, Gray & Robinson, from 2003. Vice chmn. Hillsborough County (Fla.) Aviation Authority, 1955-61. Served to lt. col. U.S. Army, 1941-46, ETO. Decorated Bronze Star; Croix de Guerre avec Palma, Belgium. Fellow Am. Coll. Trial Lawyers; mem. ABA, Hillsborough County Bar Assn. (past pres.), Fla. Bar (past gov.), Univ. Club (past pres.), Tampa Yacht and Country Club (past gov.), Ye Mystic Krewe of Gasparilla (past capt. and king), Phi Delta Phi, Kappa Alpha. Republican. Episcopalian. Home: Tampa, Fla. Died Mar. 23, 2010.

**STAMBERGER, EDWIN HENRY,** farmer, civic leader; b. Mendota, Ill., Feb. 16, 1916; s. Edwin Nicolaus and Emilie Anna Marie (Yost) S.; m. Mabel Edith Gordon, Oct. 6, 1937; 1 child, Larry Allan. Farmer seed corn, livestock, machinery devel., Mendota, from 1939; bd. dirs. Mendota Coop. & Supply Co., 1949-67, pres., 1958-67. Mem. coun. Mendota Luth. Ch., 1958-64, chmn., 1964, treas. N.W. conf., 1966-68, trustee Bible camp; mem. Mendota Watershed and Flood Ctrl. Com., 1966-73, 77-79, started flood control City of Mendota, Ill., rev. and comment com. subregion and region Ill. Ctr. Comprehensive Health Planning Agy., 1974-76; asst. in devel. Mendota Hosp., Mendota Lake; chmn. bldg. com. Mendota Luth. Home, 1972-73; bd. dirs. LaSalle County Mental Health Bd., 1969-74, U. Ill. County Extension, 1963-67, chmn., 1966-67; bd. dirs. Soil and Water Dist., 1968-73, vice chmn., 1971-73. Recipient Future Farmers Am. award, Honor award R.R. Mus., 1998; Disting. Svc. medal Railroad Mus. Mem. Am. Soc. Agrl. Engrs., Ill. Coun. Watersheds, Smithsonian Inst., Mental Health Assn., People-to-People Internat., Internat. Platform Assn., Mendota C. of C. (Honor award 1974), Mendota Sportsman's Club, Loyal Order of Moose, Odd Fellows, Lions (bd. dirs. Mendota chpt. 1965-67, Honor award 1981, Legacy of Lions 1998). Died June 18, 2002.

**STAMM, STEPHEN JEFFREY,** labor union administrator; b. Bklyn., Jan. 21, 1948; s. Raymond and Mildred Stamm; m. Michell Ann Smith (div. Dec. 1995); children: Michael, Rachel, Brian. BA, San Jose State U., Calif., 1975. Labor organizer UFCW #28, 1977-81, union rep., 1981-82; v.p. United Food and Comml. Workers' Union local 428 AFL-CIO, San Jose, 1983-92, sec.-treas., from 1992. Mem. faculty San Jose State Coll., 1990—; treas. South Bay labor coun., San JOse, 1991—. Chmn. Santa Clara County Dem. Ctrl. Com., San Jose, 1990-92. With U.S. Army, 1967-70, Vietnam. Home: San Jose, Calif. Died 2001.

**STANBERRY, D(OSI) ELAINE,** English literature educator, writer; b. Elk Park, NC; m. Earl Stanberry; 1 child, Anita St. Lawrence. Student in Bus. Edn., Steed Coll. Tech., 1956; BS in Bus. and English, East Tenn. State U., 1961, MA in Shakespearean Lit., 1962; PhD, Tex. A&M U., 1975; postgrad., North Tex. State U., U. South Fla., NYU, Duke U., U. N.C. Prof. Manatee Jr. Coll., Bradenton, Fla., 1964-67; Disting. prof. English Dickinson State U., ND, 1967-81; retired, 1981. Author: Poetic Heartstrings, Mountain Echoes, Love's Perplexing Obsession Experienced by Heinrich Heine and Percy Bysshe Shelley, Poetry from the Ancients to Moderns: A Critical Anthology, Finley Forest, Chapel Hill's Tree-lined Tuck, (plays) The Big Toe, The Funeral Factory; contbr. articles, poetry to jours., mags. Recipient Editor's Choice award Nat. Libr. Poetry, 1988, 95, Distinguished Professor of English Award, Dickinson State U., 1981; included in Best Poems of 1995. Mem. Acad. Am. Poets, N.C. Writers Network, N.C. Poetry Soc. (Carl Sandburg Poetry award 1988), Poetic Page, Writers Jour., Poets and Writers, Friday-Noon Poets, Delta Kappa Gamma. Deceased.

**STANGOS, NICOLAS,** publishing executive; b. Athens, Greece, Nov. 21, 1936; arrived in U.K., 1965; s. Constantine and Natalia (Syvrides) S. BA with honors, Denison U., 1958; postgrad., Harvard U., 1958-60; Fulbright scholar, Wesleyan U., Middletown, Conn., 1955-56. Edn. dir. Sch. Ekistics Doxiadis Assocs., Athens, 1962-65; press attaché Greek Embassy, London, 1965-67; sr. commissioning editor Penguin Books Ltd., London, 1967-74; editl. dir. Thames and Hudson Ltd., London, from 1974. Mem. cons. bd. Inst. Contemporary Arts, London, 1967-72, Arts Coun. Gt. Britain, 1976-81. Author: Selected Poems, 1975, The Familiar Surrounding of Words, 1981; editor: John Berger Sel Essays, 1972, Concepts of Modern Art, 1974, Hockney by Hockney, 1976, David Hockney: That's the Way I See It, 1993; translator numerous books. Mem. Cranium Club, Groucho Club. Avocation: music. Home: London, England. Died Apr. 16, 2004.

**STAPLETON, PATRICK J.,** former state senator; b. Jan. 7, 1924; s. Patrick J. and Bertha (Stadtmiller) S.; m. Madeline Fiedler; children: Patrick J. III. BA, Pa. State U., 1950. Pa. state senator Dist. 41, 1970—2001; chmn. minority policy com. Pa. State Senate, 1983—2001. Mem. K.C., VFW, Am. Legion. Died Mar. 10, 2001.

**STARK, HERBERT H.,** physician; b. Walnut, Kans., Aug. 3, 1922; s. Alvah C. and Letha Lee (Schroyer) S.; m. Dorothy Newman, Dec. 27, 1949; children— William C., Robert N., Thomas M., John B. Student, U. Chgo., 1943-47, DePaul U., 1946; MD, Loyola U., Chgo., 1951. Diplomate: Am. Bd. Orthopedic Surgery. Intern St. Francis Hosp., Evanston, Ill., 1951-52, resident in surgery, 1952-53, resident in orthopedic surgery, 1954, Northwestern U., 1954; practice ltd. to surgery of hand LA, from 1958; mem. staff Calif. Hosp., Orthopedic Hosp., L.A. County Gen. Hosp./U. So. Calif. Med. Ctr., Hosp. Good Samaritan; hand cons. Long Beach VA Hosp.; clin. prof. surgery (U. So. Calif.); chief hand clinic L.A. Orthopedic Hosp., from 1962; prof., chmn. div. orthopaedic surgery Drew-King Med. Ctr., LA, 1985-89. Mem. Calif. Med. Adv. Bd. to Indsl. Accident Commn., 1973-79 Pres. Little League South Pasadena; bd. dirs. South Pasadena-San Marino YMCA, 1963—; fin. chmn. South Pasadena Tournament Roses Com. Served with USN, 1955-57. Mem. Los Angeles County Med. Soc., AMA, Am. Acad. Orthopedic Surgeons, Western Orthopedic Assn., Calif. Soc. Plastic Surgeons, Am. Soc. Plastic and Reconstructive Surgeons, Am. Soc. Surgery of Hand, Am. Orthopedic Assn., Internat. Soc. Orthopedic Surgery and Traumatology, Wilson Interburban Club, Twentieth Century Orthopedic Assn., Calif. Med. Assn. Clubs: Los Angeles; Annandale Golf (Pasadena). Home: Saint Augustine, Fla. Died Sept. 1990.

**STARNES, JAMES WRIGHT,** lawyer; b. East St. Louis, Ill., Apr. 3, 1933; s. James Adron and Nell (Short) S.; m. Helen Woods Mitchell, Mar. 29, 1958 (div. 1978); children: James Wright, Mitchell A., William B. II; m. Kathleen Israel, Jan. 26, 1985. Student, St. Louis U., 1951-53; LLB, Washington U., St. Louis, 1957. Bar: Mo. 1957, Ill. 1957, Fla. 1992. Assoc. Stinson, Mag & Fizzell, Kansas City, Mo., 1957-60, ptnr., 1960-90, Mid-Continent Properties Co., 1959-90, Fairview Investment Co., Kansas City, 1971-76, Monticello Land Co., 1973-99; of counsel Yates, Mauck, Bohrer, Elliff, Croessmann & Wieland, P.C., Springfield, Mo., from 1995. Sec. Packaging Products Corp., Mission, Kans., 1972-89; chmn., treas. Galerie of Naples (Fla.), Inc., 1990-92. Adv. bd. Washington U. Law Quar., 1957-90. Bd. dirs. Mo. Assn. Mental Health, 1968-69, Kansas City Assn. Mental Health, 1966-78, pres., 1969-70; bd. dirs. Heed, 1965-73, 78-82, pres., 1966-67, fin. chmn., 1967-68; bd. dirs. Kansas City Halfway House Found., exec. com., 1966-69, pres., 1966; bd. dirs. Joan Davis Sch. for Spl. Edn., 1972-88, v.p., 1972-73, 79-80, pres., 1980-82; bd. dirs. Sherwood Ctr. for Exceptional Child, 1977-79, v.p., 1978-79. With AUS, 1957. Mem. ABA, Mo. Bar, Fla. Bar, Springfield Bar Assn., Kansas City Bar Assn., Washington U. Law Alumni Assn. (bd. govs. 1990-92). Presbyterian (deacon). Home: Springfield, Mo. Deceased.

**STARR, ILA MAE,** elementary school educator; b. La Grande, Oreg., Dec. 27, 1917; d. Samuel Fulmer Andrew and Ida Luella Perry; m. James Marion Starr, Mar. 2, 1940; children: Jacqueline Ann Starr Brandon, James Steven Starr. BA, U. Wash., 1939; BS, Eastern Oreg. Coll., LaGrande, Oreg., 1960, Tchr. Cert. Oreg., 1940. Cert. Wash. 1962, Calif. 1974. Mus. tchr. La Grande (Oreg.) Pub. Schs., 1939-40; girl scout exec. Girl Scouts of Am., Grand Coulee, Wash., 1940-41; Elem. Sch. Tchr. Centralia (Wash.) Pub. Schs., 1954; elem. sch. tchr. Wenatchee (Wash.) Pub. Schs., 1956-64, Lancaster (Calif.) Pub. Schs., 1964-68, Marysville (Calif.) Pub. Schs., 1968-79. Pvt. mus. tchr., Seattle, Grand Coulee and Wenatchee, Wash., 1940—. Bd. dirs. Community Concert Assn., Yuba City, Calif., 1986-88; inspiration chmn. Republican Women, Yuba City, 1986-88. Recipient Hon. Pub. Sch. Award, Masonic Lodge 437, Lancaster, 1966; Nominee for Tchr. of Yr., Marysville Pub. Schs., 1978. Mem. Am. Assn. U. Women (program v.p. 1976; Grant Honoree 1977), PTA (hon. life mem. 1965), The Seminar Club (program chmn.), Innerwheel Club (pres. 1985-86). Mem. Lds Ch. Avocations: music, singing. Deceased.

**STASSEN, GLEN HAROLD,** religious studies educator; b. St. Paul, Feb. 28, 1936; s. Harold Edward and Esther (Glewwe) S.; m. Dorothy Jean Lively, Aug. 31, 1957; children: Michael, William, David. BA in Physics, U. Va., 1957; BD, Union Theol. Seminary, 1963; PhD, Duke U., 1967. Nuclear physics rsch. Naval Rsch. Lab., Melpar Rsch. Lab., Washington, 1956-57; pastor New Salem Baptist Ch., Deatsville, Ky., 1957-59; assoc. minister 2d Baptist Ch. Germantown, Phila., 1959-60; instr. dept. religion Duke U., Durham, N.C., 1963-64; asst. prof., chmn. dept. religion Ky. So. Coll., Louisville, 1964-69; vis. scholar Harvard U., Cambridge, Mass., 1969-72; assoc. prof. philosophy & religion Berea Coll., Louisville, 1972-76; assoc. prof. Christian ethics Southern Baptist Theol. Sem., Louisville, 1976-83, prof. Christian ethics, 1983—2014. Strategy com. Nuclear Weapons Freeze Campaign, 1982-84, co-chair, 1983-84; exec. com., bd. dirs. Louisville Area Coun. on Peacemaking, co-chair arms race and internat. conflict com.; peacemaking study group Nat. Coun. chs. Apostolic Faith Commn.; bd. dirs. Peace Action. Author: Journey into Peacemaking, 1983, 87, Just Peacemaking: Transforming Initiatives for Justice and Peace, 1992, Living the Sermon on the Mount:A Practical Hope for Grace and Deliverance, 2006, A Thicker Jesus: Incarnational Discipleship in a Secular Age, 2012; co-author: (with John Howard Yoder & Diane Yeager), Authentic Transformation: A New Vision of Christ and Culture, 1994, (with David Gushee) Kingdom Ethics: Following Jesus in Contemporary Context, 2003; editor: Capital Punishment: A Reader, 1998, Just Peacemaking: Ten Practices for Abolishing War, 1998, Peace Action: Past, Preent and Future, 2007, Just Peacekeeping: The New Paradigm for the Ethics of Peace and Mind, 2008, The War of the Lamb: The Ethics of Nonviolence and Peacemaking, 2009 Bd. advisors Clergy and Laity Concerned, Witness for Peace; bd. dirs. Baptist Peace Fellowship North America, Jefferson Townhouse Corp., Abbey of Gethsemane Ctr. for Ethics. Harvard Ctr. for Internat. Rsch. fellow, 1971-72, NEH fellow, 1969-70, American Assn. Theol. Studies fellow, 1981-82; recipient Peace & Justice award Peace and Justice Commn. Catholic Archdiocese Louisville, 1983, Long Run Baptist Assn. Louisville, 1991, Denton & Janice Lotz Human Rights award Baptism World Alliance, 2013 Mem. American Acad. Religion (chair religious social ethics 1977-82) Democrat. Baptist. Avocations: tennis, running, reading. Home: New York, NY. Died Apr. 25, 2014.

**STATON, MICK (DAVID MICHAEL STATON),** former United States Representative from West Virginia; b. Parkersburg, W.Va., Feb. 11, 1940; s. Ernest Rutherford and Delta Rachael (Gumm) S.; m. Lynn May Spencer, Mar. 20, 1965; children: Cynthia Lynn, David Michael Jr. Diploma, Parkersburg (W. Va.) High Sch., 1958; student, Concord Coll., Athens, W.Va., 1961-63. Salesman Norhwestern Mut. Life, Parkersburg, W.Va., 1964-67, Burroughs Corp., Parkersburg, Wilmington, Del., 1967-72; v.p. Kanawha Valley Bank (now One Valley Bank), Charleston, W.Va., 1972-80; mem. US Congress from 3rd W.Va. Dist., Washington, 1981-83; pres. Mick Staton Associates, Washington, 1983-91; exec. US Chamber of Commerce, Washington, 1984-90; exec. v.p. Delchamps Associates, Washington, 1990-92; chmn. Berkeley County Republican Party, 2007—12. Contbr. Perspectives (Washington Close Up textbook) 1987, Human Events and Citizen's Voice. Explorer Post Adv., Jaycees; coach Kanawha Valley Midget Football League 1979-80; del. 1980 Republican Nat. Conv.; served in W.Va. N.G., 1957-65, USAR. Recipient Guardian of Small Bus. award Nat. Fedn. Ind. Bus., Watchbog of the Treasury Golden Bulldog award 1981-82, American Security Coun. Leadership award 1982, American Conservative Union Conservative Conscience of the Congress award 1981, Fraternal Order of Police Appreciation award 1981. Mem. NRA, W.Va. U. Alumni Assn., Concord Coll. Alumni Assn., W.Va. Soc. of Washington, D.C. (pres. 1994-95). Republican. Methodist. Avocations: hunting, fishing, backpacking, camping, whitewater rafting, weightlifting. Home: Inwood, W.Va. Died Apr. 14, 2014.

**STAVIG, ALF RUSTEN,** lawyer; b. Rosholt, SD, Oct. 26, 1917; s. Edwin Lars and Lydia Agnethe (Rusten) Stavig; m. Dorothy Emily Glorvick, July 5, 1944; children: Susan J. Searle, Barbara Stavig Doane. BA, Concordia Coll., 1939; LLB, Harvard U., 1946. Bar: SD 1947, Calif. 1949. Spl. agt. FBI, 1941—45; spl. agt. charge Compliance Enforcement div. War Assets Adminstrn. and GSA, Denver, Salt Lake City, San Francisco, 1946—49; pvt. practice Sacramento, from 1950. Govt. appeal agt. SSS, 1950—55; mem. state bldg. standards com., State of Calif., 1969—81. Author: (books) The Employers Right of Free Speech, 1946. Recipient merit award, Republican Assocs. Sacramento, 1962. Mem.: ABA, SD Bar Assn., Calif. Bar Assn., Harvard Sacramento (founding pres.), Rotary, Book Calif. Republican. Lutheran. Home: Sacramento, Calif. Died Jan. 23, 1993.

**STECK, BRIAN JASON,** brokerage house executive; b. Montreal, Que., Can., Dec. 26, 1946; s. Edward and Lottie (Potofsky) S.; married; 1 child, Stephen Mitchell. B in Commerce, Sir George Williams U., 1968; MBA, U. Pa., 1969. Cert. fin. analyst. Research analyst Nesbitt Thomson, Inc., Montreal, 1969-72, assoc. mem. corp. fin., 1972-73, dir., v.p. research and instl. sales, 1974-77; pres., chief operating officer Nesbitt Thomson Deacon Inc., Toronto, Ont., Can., 1978-86, pres., chief exec. officer, 1986, chmn., chief exec. officer, bd. dirs., from 1990; pres., chief exec. officer Fahnstock and Co. Inc., Toronto, 1985-87, Nesbitt Thomson Deacon Ltee, Toronto, 1987, chmn., chief exec. officer, bd. dirs., from 1990, Nesbitt Thomson Inc., Toronto, from 1990, Nesbitt Thomson Securities Ltd., Toronto, from 1990; vice chair Bank of Montreal. Bd. dirs. Can. Post Corp.; chmn. N. N.Y. Gen. Hosp. Bd. dirs. North York Gen. Hosp. Fellow Can. Securities Inst.; mem. Investment Dealers Assn. Can. (chmn. 1990-91), Toronto Soc. Fin. Analysts, Fin. Rsch. Inst., Oakdale Golf and Country Club, Cambridge Club, St. Andrews Golf Club. Avocations: golf, reading. Home: Stouffville, Canada. Died Nov. 6, 2009.

**STEELE, DWIGHT CLEVELAND,** lawyer; b. Alameda, Calif., Jan. 23, 1914; s. Isaac Celveland Steele and Mirah Dinsmore Jackson; m. Alberta Evelyn Hill, Oct. 19, 1940; children: Diane Smith, Marilyn Steele. AB, U. Calif., Berkeley, 1935, LLB, JSD, 1939. Bar: Calif. 1939. V.p., mgr. Distributors Assn. of San Francisco, 1941-46; pres. Hawaii Employers Coun., Honolulu, 1946-59; pres., gen. counsel Lumber and Mill Employers Assn., Oakland, Calif., 1961-76, League to Save Lake Tahoe, 1976-78 and from 89; chmn. citizens adv. com. Bay Conservation and Devel. Co., San Francisco, from 1997; chmn. Citizens for Eastshore State Park, Calif., from 1986; v.p. Save San Francisco Bay Assn., Berkeley, 1988-91. Dir. Spirit of Stockholm Found., Nairobi, Kenya, 1975-89, Planning and Conversation Found., Sacramento, 1975-91, Eugene O'Neill Found., Walnut Creek, Calif., 1976-81, Tahoe Baikal Inst., 1991—; chmn. Heart Fund Drive, Hawaii, 1959; advisor Legis. Land Use Task Force, Sacramento, 1975-77. Mem. ABA, Hawaii Bar Assn. Democrat. Avocations: skiing, travel. Home: Tahoe City, Calif. Deceased.

**STEELE, JAMES HARLAN,** retired veterinarian; b. Chgo., Apr. 3, 1913; s. James Hahn and Lydia (Nordquist) S.; m. Aina Oberg, 1941 (dec. 1969); children: James Harlan, David, Michael; m. 1970 Maria-Brigitte Meyer. DVM, Mich. State Coll., 1941; MPH, Harvard U., 1942. With US Public Health Svc. (USPHS), 1943-71; advancing through grades to asst. surgeon gen. for vet. affairs and chief vet. officer; chief vet. pub. health activities Communicable Disease Center, Atlanta, 1947-71; prof. environ. health U. Tex. Sch. Public Health, Houston, 1971-83, prof. emeritus, 1983—2013. Cons. WHO, 1950-2005, Pan-Am. Health Orgn., 1945-2013, FAO, UN, 1960. Author: (with J. Arthur Myer) Bovine Tuberculosis Control in Man and Animals, 1969, 95, (with Charles Thoen), Mycobacterium Bovis Infections, revised edit., 2005, (with James Steele) Hendrik Stafseth and Public Health Veterinarians Ole Stalheim, 2005; editor-in-chief CRC Zoonoses Handbooks, 1979-84, cons. editor, 1994, 8 vols. transl. into Russian and Farsi, Bacterial & Viral Zoonoses, 2 vols. rev. by Beran; mem. editl. cons. bd. APHA Control Communicable Disease, 1960-2000, Merck Vet. Manual, 1955-2005; contbr. articles to profl. jours. and sects. to books on food hygiene, pasteurization, and irradiation. Recipient Carlos Finlay medal Cuba Acad. Sci., 1952, Mich. State U. Centennial award, 1955, Mich. State U. Alumni award, 1958, USPHS Order of Merit, 1963, Karl F. Meyer Gold Head Cane award, 1966, Mich. State U. Coll. Vet. Medicine award,

1972, hon. mem. Epidemic Intelligence Svc., 1975, James Law lectr. Cornell U., 1983, Centennial award U. Pa., 1984, American Vet. Med. Assn. Internat. Vet. award, 1984, Public Svc. award, 1993; Disting. Svc. award American Vet. History Soc., 1995, James H. Steele award Ctr. for Disease Control, 1998, Disting. Alumni award Mich. State U., 2001, Calvin Schwabe Lifetime Achievement award, 2005, James McCallam award Mil. Surgeons, 2005, Surgeon General's Medallion USPHS, 2005, Abraham Horowitz award, Pan American Edn. Health Org., Wash., 2006; named James H. Steele ann. lectr. in his honor U. Tex. Health Sci. Ctr., 1993, James H. Steele Epidemiology Professorship in his honor, 1996, James Steele Ann. Conf. Diseases Nature, Tex. Health Dept., Austin, 2007, Recognized Oldest Living Alumni award, Harvard Sch. Pub. Health, 2012, Lifetime Achievement award, American Vet. Epidemiology Soc., & Hartz Mountain Corp, 2012, Pan American Health Assoc., 2012, Knight of Golden Cir., Army Navy Club, 2012, OIE Meritorious award, Internat. Office Epizootics World Animal Health Orgn., 2012. Fellow APHA (emeritus, 1984; Bronfman award 1971, Centennial award 1972), American Coll. Epidemiology (founding fellow, Life Time Merit award, 2009); mem. American Soc. Tropical Medicine (emeritus), American Coll. Vet. Preventive Medicine (founder, hon. diploma 1983, Pres.'s award 1994), Nat. Acad. Health Practioners, American Vet. Epidemiology Soc. (pres. 1968-88), World Vet. Assn. (hon.), Philippines Vet. Med. Assn. (hon.), Peru Vet. Med. Assn. (hon.), Hellenic Vet. Soc. (Athens Greece, hon. diploma, 1977), U.S. Animal Health Assn. (life), U.S.-Mex. Public Health Assn. (hon., life, Border award 2003), Mil. Surgeons Assn. (hon. life), Infectious Disease Soc. America (emeritus), XXI World Vet. Congress, Athens (hon. Moscow, hon. diploma 1979), German Health Svc. (hon. diploma, 1988, Order of Merit 1993), Harvard U. Alumni Assn. (Alumni award 1998), Alpha Psi. Episcopalian. Home: Houston, Tex. *I have believed throughout my career that I share my knowledge and expertise with my fellow man, be he American or citizen of the world. Those of us who are more fortunate to be endowed with intellectual advantages have an even greater responsibility to share.* Died Nov. 10, 2013.

**STEEN, REIULF,** former Norwegian government official; b. Saetre, Hurum, Norway, Aug. 26, 1933; s. Nils and Astrid Steen. Factory worker, 1951; journalist Fremtiden, 1955; sec. Labor Party Jr. Orgn. (AUF), 1958, chmn., 1961-64; sec. parliamentary group Labor Party, 1964, vice chmn., 1966-75, chmn., 1975-81; min. communications, Govt. of Norway, Oslo, 1971-72, min. commerce & trade, 1979—81, amb. to Chile Santiago, 1992—96. Dep. mem. Storting, 1961-65 Norwegian Labour Party. Avocations: literature, politics. Home: Oslo, Norway. Died June 5, 2014.

**STEERS, NEWTON IVAN, JR.,** former congressman; b. Glen Ridge, NJ, Jan. 13, 1917; s. Newton Ivan and Claire L. (Herder) S.; m. Nina Auchincloss, June 20, 1958 (div. 1976); m. Gabriele Irwin, Dec. 29, 1978; children: Newton Ivan III, Hugh A., Burr G. Grad., Hotchkiss Sch., 1935; AB in Econs., Yale U., 1939, JD, 1948; certificate advanced meteorology, MIT, 1943. Asst. in plant mgmt. E.I. duPont de Nemours Co., Inc., Parlin, N.J., 1939-40, asst. supt. tech. tests Seaford, Del., 1940-41; asst. works mgr. Gen. Aniline & Film Corp., 1948-51; asst. to br. chief AEC, 1951, div. dir., 1952, asst. gen. mgr., 1953, commr., 1953; pres., dir. Atomics, Physics & Sci. Fund, Inc., Washington, 1953-65; ins. commr. State of Md., 1967-70; mem. Md. Senate, 1971-76, 95th Congress from Md. Chmn. Md. Republican Com., 1964-66 Capt. USAF Res. Died Feb. 11, 1993.

**STEFANSSON, BALDUR ROSMUND,** retired plant scientist, educator; BSA, U. Manitoba, 1950, MSc, 1952, PhD, 1966, ScD (hon.), 1997, U. Iceland, 2000. Rsch. assoc. Dept. Plant Sci., U. Manitoba, 1952-66, assoc. prof., 1966-74, prof., 1974-86, prof., sr. scholar, from 1986, prof. emeritus, from 1987; prof. emeritus Faculty of Agrl. and Food Scis. U. Man., Winnipeg, Can. Contbr. articles to profl. jours. Recipient Royal Bank award, 1975, Queen's Jubilee medal, 1977, Grindley medal, 1978, H.R. MacMillan Laureate in Agr., 1980, Agronomy Merit award, 1980, CSP Foods Canola award, 1981, Man. Inst. Agrologists Disting. Agrologist award, 1981, Can. Barley and Oilseed Conf. award, 1982, GCIRC Internat. Award for Rsch. in Rapeseed, 1987, McANSH award, 1989, Commemmorative Medal for the 125th Anniversary of the Confedn. of Can., 1992, Wolf prize in agr., Wolf Found., Israel, 1998, Order of the Buffalo Hunt, 1998, Order of Man., 2000, Icelandic Order of the Falcon, 2000. Fellow Agrl. Inst. of Can.; mem. Am. Contract Bridge League, Swedish Seed Assn., Manitoba Inst. of Agrologists (hon. life), Can. Seed Growers Assn. (hon. life, Manitoba stock seed distbn. com. Manitoba br.), others. Achievements include pioneering research in breeding rapeseed leading to the development of canola oil. Home: Winnipeg, Canada. Died Jan. 3, 2002.

**STEGEMAN, CHARLES,** fine arts educator, lecturer, consultant; b. Ede, Netherlands, June 5, 1924; s. Leendert Gerrit and Christina Anna S.; m. Françoise André, Dec. 9, 1950 (div. July 1981); children: Charles François, Marc Alexandre, Daniel John; m. Marie-Thérèse Zenner, Nov. 9, 1984 Diploma in painting, Akademie van Beeldende Kunst, The Hague, Netherlands, 1945-46, Académie Royale des Beaux-Arts, Brussels, 1946-49, National Hoger Instituut van Schoone Kunsten, Antwerp, Belgium, 1949-50. Instr. U. BC, Vancouver, 1953—62; tchr. summer sch. Banff Ctr. Sch. Fine Arts U. Calgary, Alta., 1953—75; artist-in-residence Art Inst. Chgo., 1962-69, assoc. prof., 1966—69; tchr. North Shore Art League, Winnetka, Ill., 1963-69; adj. faculty mem. Roosevelt U., Chgo., 1965-67; prof. fine arts, dept. founder Haverford Coll., Pa., 1969—2000, emeritus prof. fine arts, from 2000, vis. prof. gen. programs, 2002—05. Humanitites fellow Med. Coll. Pa., Phila., 1981—88, adj. faculty mem. humanities, 1982—85, adj. faculty mem. dept. radiology, 1985—90; adj. faculty mem. New Sch. Music, 1982—85, Sch. Medicine U. Pa., 1986—98. Author: Les Cryptes de la Cathédrale de Chartres, 1993; contbr. articles to profl. works; Represented in permanent collections Nat. Gallery Can., Ottawa, Ont., Ont. Mus. Art, Toronto, Phila. Mus. Art, Vancouver Art Gallery, BC, Can., Art Gallery Gtr. BC, Vancouver, U. Alta., Edmonton, Banff Ctr. Arts, Kresge Collection, Detroit, Sears Collection, Chgo., Vincent Price Collection, LA, Nat. Collection Belgian Govt., Brussels, Lewison Collection, Vancouver, Draeseke Collection, San Francisco, Estenne Collection, Brussels, Bayens Collection, Balin Collection, Phila., Chehi Collection, Wilmington, Del., pvt. collections, US, Eng., France, Belgium, Holland, Germany, Can. Australia, New Zealand and Israel, exhibitions include Ars et Amicita, Amsterdam, 1946, 44th Ann. Exhbn. of NW Artists, Seattle Art Mus., 1958 (Winnipeg Ann. award for Most Popular Painting, 1958), Old Orchard Art Festival, 1965—69, Portrait of a Civilization, Comfort Gallery, Haverford Coll., 1973, Provident Nat. Bank Gallery, Phila., 1986, The Vigil of Spring, Cantor Fitzgerald Gallery, Haverford Coll., 1997, Zomerexpositie, Galerie Blom, Dordrecht, The Netherlands, 2003, and numerous others. Mem. Assn. Villard de Honnecourt for the Interdisciplanary Study of Medieval Tech., Sci. and Art (co-founder, pres. 1984-90, mem. bd. dirs. 1984-92, 94—), Sociètè archèologique d'Eure-et-Loir, Coll. of Physicians (exec. com. sect. arts-medicine 1995—). Died Oct. 3, 2013.

**STEIN, RALPH MICHAEL,** law educator, lawyer, arbitrator, mediator, consultant; b. Far Rockaway, NY, July 14, 1943; s. Siegfried and Ruth (Spier) Stein; m. Susan Heineman Stein, Feb. 23, 1969 (div. Aug. 1982); m. Marla B. Rubin Stein, Oct. 31, 1982; 1 child, Theodore Alan Rubin. BA, New Sch. Social Rsch., 1971; JD, Hofstra U., 1974. Assoc. Skadden, Arps, Slate, Meagher & Flom, NYC, 1974—75; vis. prof. law Syracuse U., NY, 1975—76; prof. law Pace U. Sch. Law, White Plains, NY, 1976—2013; spl. counsel med. malpractice legislation to Lt. Gov. State of NY, Albany, 1982—85; chief hearing officer Greenburgh Police Dept., NY, 1982—92. Co-author: Comparative Negligence, 1984; prodr.(moderator): (TV series) You and the Law, 1971—74; contbr. articles to profl. law jours. Investigator US Senate Subcom. Constl. Rights, Washington, 1970—71; mem. legal com. Anti-Defamation League, Westchester, NY, Westchester Chpt. ACLU. Served to capt. US Army, 1965—68. Grantee, Pace U., 1979, 1981—83, 1985, 1987—88, 1991—93. Mem.: American Civil Liberties Union, Navy League US, Civil War Roundtable NY, American Soc. Law & Medicine, American Soc. Legal History, Soc. American Law Professors. Democrat. Avocations: reading, cooking, travel, classical music, opera. Home: Cortlandt Mnr, NY. Died Oct. 16, 2012.

**STEINER, JOHN MICHAEL,** sociologist, educator; b. Prague, Czech Republic, Aug. 3, 1925; arrived in US, 1953; s. Kurt John and Ilse (Ornstein) Steiner; 1 child, Ingmar Michael Augustus. BA, U. Melbourne, 1952; MA, U. Mo., 1955; PhD, U. Freiburg, 1968. Liaison officer United Relief and Rehab. Adminstrn. Mission, Prague, 1946—48; immigration officer Dept. Immigration, Canberra, Melbourne, Australia, 1949—52; indsl. therapist Hosp. No. 1, Fulton, Mo., 1955—56; lectr. speech U. Calif., Berkeley, 1956—59; rsch. social psychologist USAF, Wright-Patterson AFB, Ohio, 1959—61; rsch. assoc. Inst. World Civilization, Freiburg, Germany, 1963—64; vis. asst. prof. Dept. Criminology, 1964—65; prof. sociology Sonoma State U., Rohnert Park, Calif., 1968—92, sr. scholar in residence, from 1993, prof. emeritus, from 1992. Founding dir. Sonoma State Holocaust and Genocide Studies Ctr., 1984—92. Author: (book) Power Politics and Social Change in National Socialist Germany, 1975; author: (with Joel E. Dimsdale) Survivors, Victims, and Perpetrators Essays on the Nazi Holocaust, 1980; author: (with Craig, Haney, Curtis Banks and Philip Zimbardo) Das Stanford Gefängnis Experiment, 1984; contbr. articles to profl. jours., books, chpts. to books on polit. crime; performer: (numerous appearances on TV) Hitler Man and Myth, from 2002. Co-founder, v.p. Ams. Dem. Action, Berkeley, 1960. Recipient Disting. cross Svc. and Valor, Czech Republic, 1948, cert. recognition, Calif. State Assembly, 1994, Order of Merit, Pres. Germany, 2002; fellow, Fulbright Found., 1974—75, 1981—82; Alexander von Humboldt rsch. fellow, U. Freiburg, 1964—67, 1990. Mem.: Fulbright Assn., Czechoslovak Acad. Arts and Scis., Acad. Criminal Justice Scis., Alexander von Humboldt Assn., Am. Sociol. Assn., Alpha Pi Zeta. Democrat. Achievements include research in authoritarian personality based on SS (Nazi) perpetrators; role margin as the site of moral and social intelligence; case of Germany and national socialism; Hitler's exemptions from the Nuremberg Racial Laws. Avocations: art, antiques, swimming, photography. Home: Novato, Calif. Died May 6, 2014.

**STEINER, ROBERT L.,** economist; b. Charlevoix, Mich., Aug. 12, 1923; s. Albert and Therese Steiner; children: Carl, Therese; m. Joan Friedlander, June 25, 1949 (div. 1959); children: Robert Cockburn, Lorraine. BA magna cum laude, Dartmouth Coll., Hanover, 1947; MA in Econ., Columbia U., NYC, 1948. V.p. to pres. Kenner Products Co., Cin., 1948—72; adj. prof. mktg. Coll. Bus. Adminstrn., U. Cin., 1974—78; staff econ. FTC Robert L. Steiner Consulting, Cin., 1973—2006; sr. rsch. fellow Am. Antitrust Inst., DC, from 2004. Dir., chair mktg. com. Toy Manufacturers America, NYC, 1966—67; dir. Clopay Corp., Cin., 1976—86, Wcet TV, Cin., 1975—78. Contbr. articles to profl. jours. Dir. Am. Coun. Judaism, Ponte Vedra, Fla., 2001—09; dir., pres. Robert Krohn Livingston Meml. Camp, Cin., 1950—70; dir., v.p. legislative action Charter Com., Cin., 1952—72; commr. Ohio Commn. Local Govt. Svc., Columbus, 1973—74. 1st lt. Navigator Army Air Force, 1942—45. Decorated Air medals 8th Air Force. Mem.: U. Club Cin., Am. Mktg. Assn., Am. Economic Assn., Phi Beta Kappa. Avocations: fly fishing, tennis, squash, reading. Died Oct. 26, 2013.

**STEINFELD, JESSE LEONARD,** retired academic administrator, former Surgeon General of the United States; b. W. Aliquippa, Pa., Jan. 6, 1927; s. Jack and Lena Helen (Klein) S.; m. Mildred Stokes, July 12, 1953; children: Mary Beth, Katherine Jody, Frances Susan. BS, U. Pitts., 1945; MD, Western Res. U., 1949; LL.D. (hon.), Gannon Coll., 1972. Sr. investigator Nat. Cancer Inst., Bethesda, Md., 1952-58, dep. dir., 1968-69, cons., 1961-68, 74—; acting chief medicine City of Hope Med. Center, Duarte, Calif., 1958-59; asst. prof. medicine U. Southern Calif., Los Angeles, 1959-62, assoc. prof., 1962-66, prof., 1967-68; surgeon gen. US Dept. Health & Human Services (HHS), Washington, 1969-73; dir. Comprehensive Cancer Center Mayo Clinic, Rochester, Minn., 1973-74; prof. medicine U. Calif., Irvine, 1974-76; dean Sch. Medicine, Med. Coll. Va., Richmond, 1976-83; pres. Med. Coll. Ga., Augusta, 1983-87. Cons., chmn. ad hoc com. on research and smoking American Cancer Soc. Contbr. articles on cancer chemotherapy, metabolic changes in cancer patients, and smoking and pub. health to med. jours. Chmn. YMCA Phys. Fitness and Health Nat. Policy Bd. Served with USPHS, 1952-58, 69-73. Fellow A.C.P., Royal Soc. Health (hon.); mem. American Soc. Clin. Oncology (pres. 1970), American Assn. Cancer Research, Soc. Nuclear Medicine, American Soc. Hematology. Home: Pomona, Calif. Died Aug. 5, 2014.

**STEINFELD, RAY, JR.,** food products executive; b. Portland, Oreg., Nov. 21, 1946; s. Ray and June Catherine (Cox) S.; children: Erik, Blair. Student, Wheaton Coll., 1964-66, Drew U., 1967; BS in Polit. Sci., Lewis and Clark Coll., 1968. Sales rep. Continental Can Co., LA, 1969-72; co-chmn. bd., CEO, Steinfeld's Products Co., Portland, Oreg., from 1972. Chmn. Oreg. Mus. Sci. in Industry, 1992-94. Treas., bd. dirs. Portland Recycling Team, 1973—; pres. exec. bd. Stop Oreg. Litter and Vandalism, 1973-92, pres., 1976; chmn., exec. com. Oreg. Landmark of Quality, 1985-87, Oreg. Ballet Theatre, 1994—, bd. dirs., 1995—, v.p. devel., 1997—, pres., 1998—; pres. exec. com. William Temple House, 1985-91; vestry mem. Trinity Episcopal Ch., 1987-90; chmn. Oregn. Strategic Plan Agrl. Dept., 1988, World Trade Week, Portland, 1989; mem. Gov. Robert's Task Force, Salem, Oreg., 1991-92; bd. dirs. Oreg. Enterprise Forum, 1992-96, chmn., 1995; bd. dirs. Portland Advocates for Student Arts, 1999—. Mem. Pickle Packers Internat. (mem. mdse. com.), Portland C. of C. (bd. dirs. 1995-99). Democrat. Episcopalian. Avocations: tennis, golf, bridge. Home: Portland, Oreg. Deceased.

**STEN, HARRISWELL WARMPHAIGN,** education educator; b. Barato Village, Meghalaya, India, Nov. 1, 1938; s. Lamarre Harriswell and Mon Sten; m. Salemfort Konglah; children: Tranquillity, Shibboleth, Zenith. BA, Gauhati U., India, 1967; MA in English, North Eastern Hill U., India, 1975, PhD in Khasi Lit., 1982. Lectr. Sankardev Coll., India, 1975-82; reader North Eastern Hill U., India, 1982-92, prof., from 1992; dir. North Eastern Hill Univ. Publ., India, 1993-94. Mem. acad. coun. Univ. Bd. Postgrad. Studies, 1978—, chmn. bd. 1987-89, mem. ct., 1992—; mem. Indian Sch. Bd., 1982—, Shillong Club Ltd., 1982 Author (book) A History of Khasi Language (in Khasi); (text) An Introduction to Literary Rsch., 1994; editor Rsch. Jour., Khasi Studies, 1987-95. Citation and honors Bangia Sahitya Parisad. Skillong, 1989. Citation and honors by Assam Journalist Assn., 1996. Mem. Sahitya Acad., State Acad. for Lit., Fine arts and Performing Arts. Hill People Union. Presbyterian. Avocations: writing, journalism, gardening, joking, reading. Home: Shillong, India. Died Sept. 7, 1997.

**STEPANEK, JOSEPH EDWARD,** real estate developer, consultant; b. Ellinwood, Kans., Oct. 29, 1917; s. Joseph August and Leona Mae (Wilson) S.; m. Antoinette Farnham, June 10, 1942; children: Joseph F., James B., Antoinette L., Debra L. BSChemE, U. Colo., 1939; DEng in Chem. Engring., Yale U., 1942. Registered profl. engr., Colo. Engr. Stearns-Roger Mfg., Denver, 1939-45; from asst. to assoc. prof. U. Colo., Boulder, 1945-47; from cons. to dir. UN, various countries, 1947-73; cons. internat. indsl devel., U.S.-China bus. relations Boulder, from 1973. Bd. dirs. 12 corps., 1973—. Author 3 books on indsl. devel.; contbr. 50 articles to profl. jours. Exec. dir. Boulder Tomorrow, 1965-67. Recipient Yale Engring. award Yale Engring. Assn., 1957, Norlin award U. Colo. 1978, Annual award India League of Am., 1982. Mem. AAAS. Democrat. Unitarian Universalist. Avocation: ranching. Home: Boulder, Colo. Died Jan. 31, 2008.

**STEPHENS, JAMES W.,** utility company executive; b. Pleasant Green, Mo., Mar. 8, 1920; s. James Wilbur and Mary Elizabeth (Parrish) Stephens; m. Sarah Maxine Dump, May 10, 1942; children: James Michael, John Robert. BSEE, U. Mo., Rolla, 1947; degree in elec. engring., U. Mo., 1957, D (hon.) of Engring., 1971. With Mo. Pub. Svc. Co., 1940—42, 1947—85, asst. to pres. Kansas City, 1960—64, v.p. cmty. svcs., 1964—76, sr. v.p., 1976—85. Dir. Boatman's Baytown Bank, Mo. Pres. Met. Jr. Coll. Bd. of Kansas City, 1966—69; chmn. bd. trustees 4-H Found., 1966—67; pres. U. Mo. Alumni Alliance, 1968—70. With USNR, 1942—45. Mem.: NSPE, Soc. Indsl. Realtors, So. Indsl. Devel. Coun., Am. Econ. Devel. Coun. (pres. 1972), Mo. Soc. Profl. Engrs., Greater Kansas City C. of C. (pres. 1970—71), Associated Industries Mo. (chmn. bd. dirs. 1980—82), Masons. Democrat. Methodist. Died Jan. 30, 1989.

**STERN, JOHN PETER,** electronics executive, educator; b. NYC, Nov. 8, 1954; s. Walter and Marion (Tyson) S.; m. Sakumi Murakami, Mar. 17, 1982; children: George, Ken. AB summa cum laude, Princeton U., 1976; JD, Harvard U.,

1979. Bar: Calif. 1980, N.Y. 1984, D.C. 1985; lic. real estate broker, Calif. With Graham & James, LA, 1981-84; exec. dir. U.S. Electronics Industry Office, Tokyo, 1984-88; v.p. Asian ops. Am. Electronics Assn., Tokyo, 1988-95; v.p. Am. Express Fin., Tokyo, 1995-2000; pres., CEO Red Tag Japan, Inc., Tokyo, 2000—02; prof. Nihon U. Law Sch., Tokyo, from 2003; bd. dirs. The Global Emerging Tech. Inst., Ltd., from 2003. Speaker Deming Quality Control Awards Ceremonies, 1988; bd. dirs. Telecommunication Tech. Com.; mem. Japan Indsl. Standards Optoelectronic Tech. Com., Tokyo, 1987—, Telecomm. Tech. Study Coun. Standards Policy Working Group, 1990-96; mem. Japanese Ministry of Posts and Telecomm. Future Broadcast Satellite Procurement Study Group, 1990-91; testified before U.S. Senate, 1989; mem. Japan Indsl. Standards Info. Tech. Div. Coun., Tokyo, 1991—; advisor Walter F. Mondale, U.S. Amb. to Japan, 1993-96; legal com. Securities Investor Protection Fund, 2000. Author: The Japanese Interpretation of the "Law of Nations", 1854-1874, 1979; editor: Yearbook of Japanese Data Transmission and Telecommunications, 1994; contbr. monthly column to newspaper, 1988; co-author: Interfirm Production Supply Systems, 1989, The Business Guide to Japan, 1996, The Bureaucrats' Super-Power, 1996, Japan's Technical Standards: Implications for Global Trade and Competitiveness, 1997, Unlocking the Bureaucrat's Kingdom: Deregulation and the Japanese Economy, 1998, An Introduction to American Law, 2005. Lectr., U.S. Info. Svc., Japan, 1985—; mem. Bilateral Working Group on Symmetrical Access, Washington, 1988; trustee, Princeton in Asia, 1980-85. Telecom Day award Japanese Ministry Posts and Telecomm., 1992. Mem. State Bar Calif., State Bar NY, Bar of DC, Am. Arbitration Assn. (internat. arbitration panel 1983—), Chartered Inst. Arbitrators (East Asia br.), Tokyo Am. Club, Fgn. Corr., Am. Electronics Assoc. Japan Coun. (exec. com. 1999-2000). Home: Tokyo, Japan. Died 2011.

**STERN, KURT,** pathologist, educator; b. Vienna, Apr. 3, 1909; arrived in Israel, 1969; s. Leopold and Elsa (Heller) S.; m. Florence Shirley Sherman, May 28, 1939 (dec. May 1989); children: Elsa Libby, Josef Judah, David Michael. MD, U. Vienna, 1933. Cert. Am. Bd. Pathology. Resident physician State Inst. Study Malignant Disease, Buffalo, N.Y., 1943-45; asst. pathologist Mt. Sinai Hosp., Chgo., 1945-60; assoc. prof. pathology Chgo. Med. Sch., 1949-60; prof. pathology U. Ill. Sch. Medicine, Chgo., 1960-69; prof. life scis. Bar-Ilan U., Ramat-Gan, Israel, 1969-80; rsch. prof. Hebrew U., Hadassah Med. Sch., Jerusalem, from 1980. Assoc. dir. rsch. Mt. Sinai Med. Rsch. Found., Chgo., 1946-60; dir. Blood Ctr., Mt. Sinai Hosp., Chgo., 1950-60. Co-author: Die Wege and Ergebnisse Chemisher Krebs Forschung, 1936, Biochemistry of Malignant Tumors, 1943; contbr. articles to profl. jours. and chpts. to books. Recipient Disting. Svc. award Am. Soc. Clin. Pathologists, 1968, Disting. Svc. award Am. Assn. Blood Banks, 1968, John Elliott Meml. award, 1972, award Internat. Soc. Blood Transfusions, 1999. Fellow AAAS, Am. Soc. Clin. Pathologists, N.Y. Acad. Sci. Home: Jerusalem, Israel. Deceased.

**STERRETT, SAMUEL BLACK,** lawyer, former judge; b. Washington, Dec. 17, 1922; s. Henry Hatch Dent and Helen (Black) S.; m. Jeane McBride, Aug. 27, 1949; children: Samuel Black, Robin Dent, Douglas McBride. Student, St. Albans Sch., 1933-41; grad., US Mcht. Marine Acad., 1945, BS, 2004; BA, Amherst Coll., 1947; LLB, U. Va., 1950; LLM in Taxation, NYU, 1959. Bar: D.C. 1951, Va. 1950. Atty. Alvord & Alvord, Washington, 1950-56; trial atty. Office Regional Counsel, Internal Revenue Service, NYC, 1956-60; ptnr. Sullivan, Shea & Kenney, Washington, 1960-68; municipal cons. to office vice pres. U.S., 1965-68; judge U.S. Tax Ct., 1968-88, chief judge, 1985-88; ptnr. Myerson, Kuhn & Sterrett, Washington, 1988-89; of counsel Vinson & Elkins, Washington, 1990—2002; pvt. practice Washington, 2002—11, Chevy Chase, Md., 2007—09. Bd. mgrs. Chevy Chase Village, 1970-74, chmn., 1972-74; 1st v.p. bd. trustees, exec. com. Washington Hosp. Ctr., 1969-79, chmn. bd. trustees, 1979-84, trustee, 1999-2007; chmn. bd. trustees Washington Healthcare Corp., 1982-87; chmn. bd. trustees Medlantic Healthcare Group, 1987-89; mem. audit com. Medstar Health, 1990-2006; trustee Prostestant Episcopal Cathedral Found., 1973-81, 99-2007, fin. com., 1998-2007, chmn., 1999-2006; governing bd. St. Albans Sch., 1977-81; trustee Louise Home, 1979-89. Wwith AUS, 1943, with U.S. Mcht. Marine, 1943-46. Fellow Am. Bar Found. (life); mem. ABA, D.C. Bar Assn., Am. Coll. Tax Counsel, Soc. of the Cincinnati, Coun. for Future, Am. Inns. of Ct., Chevy Chase Club (bd. govs. 1979-84, pres. 1984), Met. Club, Lawyers Club, Alibi Club, Alfalfa Club, Ch. of N.Y. Club, Beta Theta Pi. Episcopalian. Died Sept. 8, 2013.

**STEVENS, ANNIE BICKETT PARKER,** retired architect; b. Marshville, NC, Dec. 25, 1921; d. Benjiman Carl and Rosa Mae (Blakeney) Parker; m. Jack Elmer Stevens, Mar. 31, 1945 (dec.); children: Susan, Barbara, Martha. Student, U. N.C., Greensboro, 1938—40, Syracuse U., 1940—42; BArch, Columbia U., 1945; postgrad., U. N.C., 1971—75. Archtl. draftsman J.N. Pease & Co., Charlotte, NC, 1942, draftsman, 1944, So. Mapping and Engr., Greensboro, NC, 1943, Charles and Edward Stotz, Pitts., 1945—51; ptnr. Jack E. Stevens Builder, Pitts., 1951—68, Chapel Hill, NC, 1969—74, Charlotte, 1975—77, Pinehurst, NC, 1978—82; pvt. practice Parker Stevens Builder, Pinehurst, 1983—84, Anne P. Stevens Builder, Surf City, NC, 1984—2001; ret., 2001. Avocations: art, painting. Deceased.

**STEVENS, EARL PATRICK,** minister; b. Vicksburg, Miss., Nov. 21, 1925; s. Elton Alva and Mary Elizabeth (Keathley) S.; m. Vonda Jean Tuttle, Aug. 7, 1949; children: Teresa Darlene, Deborah Lalene, Earl P. II, David Paul. BA, Abilene Christian U., 1949; BRE, Coll. of the Bible, 1966; MA, MRE, Nat. Christian U., 1968, ThM, PhD, ThD, Nat. Christian U., 1969; DD (hon.), Ohio Christian Coll., 1968. Ordained to ministry Ch. of Christ, 1943; cert. neuropsychiat. technician. Minister Ch. of Christ, Olden, Tex., 1946-49, Barrackville, W.Va., 1949-62, Parkersburg, W.Va., 1962-66, St. Mary's, W.Va., 1966-77, Shinnston, W.Va., 1977-90, Fairmont, W.Va., 1990-96, Mt. Nebo, W.Va., 1990-96, Pleasant Valley, W.Va., from 1996. Instr. Ohio Valley Coll., Parkersburg, 1964-66; prof. Nat. Christian U., Ft. Worth, 1968-78. Author: The Glory of Christ, 1963, Doctrinal Study of I Timothy, 1987, 100 Years Preaching, 1995, Doctrines of Scripture Preservation, 1997, 26 other books. Served with USN, 1944-46. Named to Eagle Scout, Boy Scouts Am., 1942; recipient Golden Record award Word Records, 1968, Colin Anderson award Colin Anderson Ctr., 1968. Mem. So. Assn. Marriage Counselors, Am. Numismatic Assn. Democrat. Avocations: writing, stamps, hunting and fishing, golf, bowling. *Every life has value; the strong must protect the weak; men belong together; friendship is a two-way street; everyone must mould his heart, shape his life and enrich his mind. These are living guidelines for my life and all others, too. Neglect any or all and we are the poorer for it.* Died Feb. 19, 2011.

**STEVENS, GERALD M.,** lawyer; b. Detroit; married; 3 children. BS in Forestry, Mich. State U., 1951; JD, U. Detroit, 1957. Sr. atty. legal div. Bd. Wayne County Rd. Commrs., 1955—61; assoc. Langs, Molyneaux & Armstrong, Detroit, 1961—65; pvt. practice Owosso, Mich., from 1965; pros. atty. County Shiawassee, Mich., 1968—72. Speaker ednl. numerous sch. groups; tchr. law John Wesley Coll., Lansing Community Coll. Trustee Nardin Pk. Meth. Ch., atty.; v.p. bd. trustees First United Meth. Ch., Owosso; vice chmn. Mich. Aviation Edn. Found.; bd. dirs. YMCA, Cmty. Concert, Inc., Shiawassee County unit Am. Cancer Soc.; pres. Owosso Day Care Ctr., Lung Assn. Genesee Valley; chmn. Edn. Subcom. Mich. Aeronautics Commn.; chair emeritus Mich. State Bar Aviation Law Sect., State Bar Mich. Sr. Lawyers Sect. Served to 1st. lt. US Army, 1951—53. Mem.: ABA, Owosso-Corunna C. of C., Genesee County Bar Assn., Aircraft Owners and Pilots Assn. (approved atty. prepaid legal plan), Lawyers Pilots Bar Assn. (Mich. rep.), Mich. Trial Lawyers Assn., Assn. Trial Lawyers Am., Shiawassee County Bar Assn., Detroit Bar Assn., State Bar Mich., Kiwanis club, Masons club. Deceased.

**STEVENS, LYDIA HASTINGS,** community volunteer; b. Highland Park, Ill., Aug. 2, 1918; d. Rolland T.R. and Ruth Shotwell (Beebe) Hastings; m. George Cooke Stevens, Nov. 2, 1940; children: Lydia Stevens Gustin, Priscilla Stevens Goldfarb, Frederick S., Elizabeth Stevens MacLeod, George H., Ruth Stevens Stellard. BA, Vassar Coll., 1939. Mem. Dist. 151 Conn. House of Reps., Greenwich, 1988-92. Cons. Nat. Exec. Svc. Corps, N.Y.C., 1985. Pres. Greenwich YWCA, 1971-74, Greenwich Housing Coalition, 1982-86; v.p. planning Greenwich United Way, 1973-76; sr. warden Greenwich Christ Episcopal Ch., 1981-86; chmn. rev. commn. Episcopal Diocese of Conn., 1985-87; bd. dirs. Greenwich Libr., 1985-93; chmn. Greenwich Commn. Aging, 1986-88; pres., bd. dirs. Greenwich Broadcasting Corp., 1977-79; bd. dirs. Fairfield County Cmty. Found., 1992, United Way of Greenwich, Save the Sound, 1996-2014, League Conservation Voters Conn., 1999. Recipient Golden Rule award J.C. Penney, 1987, President's award Greenwich YWCA, 1992, Brava award, 1994, Conn. Assn. for Human Svc. Dirs. award, 1992, Spirit Greenrid award YWCA; named Layperson of Yr., Coun. Chs. and Synagogues, 1995. Republican. Episcopalian. Avocations: sailing, organic gardening. Home: Guilford, Conn. Died Feb. 25, 2014.

**STEVENS, NETTIE,** biologist; b. 1861; Student, Stanford U.; PhD, Bryn Mawr Coll., 1903. Tchr. Author rsch. paper that demonstrated that chromosomes known as "X" and "Y" were responsible for determining the sex of individuals. Died 1912.

**STEVENSON, NOEL C.,** lawyer, writer; b. Sacramento, Dec. 24, 1907; s. Ernest E. and Emma (Walker) Stevenson; m. Mary Elizabeth Galton, Oct. 15, 1965. JD, Pacific Coast U., 1943. Bar: Calif. 44, US Supreme Ct. 51. Dist. atty., Sutter County, Calif., 1951—55; sole practice Laguna Hills, Calif., from 1956. Author: How To Build a More Lucrative Law Practice, 1967, Successful Cross Examination Strategy, 1971, Genealogical Evidence, 1979; contbr. articles to profl. jours. Fellow: Am. Soc. Genealogists; mem.: Supreme Ct. Hist. Soc., Am. Name Soc., State Bar Calif. Died Dec. 24, 1991.

**STEVENSON, ROBERT EDWIN,** accountant, consultant; b. Iowa City, Jan. 5, 1917; s. Russell A. and Edna Lorraine (Kampenga) Stevenson; m. Pauline Louise McCracken, Sept. 1, 1939 (dec. Oct. 31, 1980); children: Jean Stevenson Simpson, Robert Harold; m. Lois Boynton Cruea, Feb. 18, 1981. BBA, U. Minn., 1939; MBA, NYU, 1954; grad. in Exec. Devel. Program, Stanford U., 1958. With Mut. Implement and Hardware Co., Owatonna, Minn., 1939—43, Aero Divsn. Mpls. Honeywell Regulator Co., 1943—44, Exxon Corp. and Affiliated Cos., 1944—77; sr. tax acct. Esso Std. Oil Co., Baton Rouge, 1944—48; head divsn. departmental adminstrn. Std. Oil Co., NYC, 1948—59; asst. contr. carter divsn. Humble Oil & Refining Co., Tulsa, 1960—64, acctg. rsch. coord. Houston, 1964—72, Exxon Corp., NYC, 1972—77; fin. and acctg. cons. New Canaan, Conn., from 1977. Advisor acctg. Prins. Bd., 1964—71. Contbr. articles to profl. jours. Mem.: Nat. Assn. Accts., Am. Petroleum Inst. (appreciation cert. 1967), Fin. Execs. Inst., Am. Acctg. Assn. (nat. v.p. 1970—71), Masons, Beta Alpha Psi (nat. adv. bd. 1975—81). Republican. Presbyterian. Died Mar. 6, 1999.

**STEVENSON, WILLIAM HENRI,** author; b. London, June 1, 1924; s. William and Alida (Deleporte) S.; m. Glenys Rowe, July 28, 1945; children: Andrew, Jacqueline, Kevin, Sally. Student, Royal Navy Coll., 1942. Fgn. corr. Toronto (Ont., Can.) Star, 1948-58; Toronto Globe & Mail, 1958-63; Ind. TV News, London, Eng., 1964-66; CBC, 1966-77; ind. writer, broadcaster, from 1977. Author: Travels In and Around Red China, 1957, Rebels in Indonesia, 1964, Chronicles of the Israeli Air Force, 1971, A Man Called Intrepid, 1976, Ninety Minutes at Entebbe, 1976, The Ghosts of Africa, 1981, Kiss the Boys Goodbye: How the United States Betrayed Its Own POWS in Vietnam, 1990, Past to Present: A Reporter's Story of War, Spies, People and Politics, 2012; producer: TV documentaries; movie screenplays include The Bushbabies, 1970. Served as aviator Royal Navy, 1942-45. Mem. Assn. Naval Aviation U.S.A., Authors Guild, Royal Overseas League (London). Mem. Progressive Conservative Party Can. Mem. Church of England. Clubs: Royal Bermuda Yacht, Royal Hong Kong Yacht. Home: Warwick, Bermuda. Died Nov. 26, 2013.

**STEVENSSON, KJELL-INGE,** music educator; b. Kila., Säffle, Sweden, Aug. 31, 1950; s. Karl-Erik and Elvy Stevensson; m. Margareta Eva Sjöberg; children: Baltzar, Magda, Sebastian. Diploma in Clarinet, Kungl.Musikhögskolan i Stockholm, 1972; diploma, Vlaamse Muziekkonservatorium Antwerp, Belgium, 1973. Solo clarinetist Swedish Radio Symphony Orch., Stockholm, from 1971; tchr. to prof. Kungl. Musikhögskolan, 1978. Home: Sigtuna, Sweden. Deceased.

**STEWARD, LESTER HOWARD,** psychiatrist, academic administrator, educator; b. Burt, Iowa, Nov. 6, 1930; s. Walter and Helen Steward; m. Patricia Byrness Roach, June 17, 1953; children: Donald Howard, Thomas Eugene, Susan Elaine, Joan Marsha. BS, Ariz. State U., 1958, MA in Sci. Edn., 1969; postgrad., Escuela Nat. U., Mex., 1971-80; PhD in Psychology, Calif. Coast U., 1974; MD, Western U. Hahnemann Coll., 1980. Rschr. drug abuse and alcoholism Western Australia U., Perth, Australia, 1970-71; intern in psychiatry Helix Hosp., San Diego, Calif., 1971-72; rschr. drug addiction North Mountain Behavioral Inst., Phoenix, 1975-77; exec. v.p., CEO James Tyler Kent Coll., 1977-80; pres., CEO Western U. Sch. Medicine, 1980-86; instr. psychology USN Westpac, Subic Bay, Philippines, 1988-91. Pvt. practice preventive medicine Tecate, Baja California, Mexico, 1971-88; instr. Modern Hypnosis Instrn. Ctr., 1974—, Maricopa Tech. Community Coll., Phoenix, 1975-77; mem. Nt. Ctr. Homeopathy, Washington, Menninger Found., Wichita, Kans. Contbr. numerous papers to profl. confs. Leader Creighton Sch. dist. Boy Scouts Am., Phoenix, 1954-58. Fellow Am. Acad. Med. Adminstrs., Am. Assn. Clinic Physicians and Surgeons, Internat. Coll. Physicians and Surgeons, Am. Coll. Homeopathic Physicians, Am. Counc. Sex Therapy; mem. numerous orgns. including Nat. Psychol. Assn., Am. Psychotherapy Assn., Royal Soc. Physicians, World Med. Assn., Am. Acad. Preventive Medicine, Am. Bd. Examiners in Psychotherapy, Am. Bd. Examiners in Homeopathy, Western Homeopathic Med. Soc. (exec. dir.), Ariz. Profl. Soc. Hypnosis (founder 1974). Home: Phoenix, Ariz. Died Sept. 28, 2001.

**STEWART, ALICE MARY,** epidemiologist, researcher; b. Sheffield, Yorkshire, Eng., Oct. 4, 1906; d. Albert Ernest and Lucy (Wellburn) Nash; m. Ludovick Drumin Stewart, June 17, 1933 (div. 1952); children: Anne Katarine, Hugh Drumin. MA, Cambridge U., 1930, MD, 1933. Intern Royal Free Hosp., London, 1933, non-resident med. registrar, 1935—39; intern Childrens Hosp., Manchester, England, 1934; physician EGA Hosp., London, 1939—42, Radcliffe Infirmary, Oxford, England, 1942—45; reader in social medicine Oxford U., 1945—74; sr. research fellow Birmingham U., England, from 1974. Cons. Nat. Coun. Occupl. Health, 1968—74; epidemiologist Bur. Radiol. Health, Rockville, Md., 1970, Pitts. Sch. Pub. Health, 1975—76, Portland State U., 1984—85. Contbr. articles to profl. jours. Fellow: RCP (London). Home: Charlbury, England. Died June 23, 2002.

**STEWART, JACK CARLTON,** retired chemical engineer, consultant; b. Waynesfield, Ohio, Dec. 8, 1922; s. Charles Scott and Helen Gail (Baker) S.; m. Mildred Irene Loyer, June 30, 1946 (dec. July 1975); children: Joe, Gregg. BMechE, Santa Clara U., 1943; BChemE, Ohio State U., 1948. Rubber compounder Goodyear Tire and Rubber Co., St. Marys, Ohio, 1948-54; from process engr. to process supt. Vistron Corp., Lima, Ohio, 1954-74; process supt. Agrico Chem. Co., Blytheville, Ark., 1974-76, tech. supt., 1976-80, process designer Tulsa, 1980-81, Italy, Eng., Trinidad, 1981-85; engring. mgr. The Lemm Corp., Memphis, 1986-96; ret. Cordova, Tenn., 1996. Cons. in field. Sgt. U.S. Army, 1943-46, ETO. Mem. AIChE (program com. ammonia symposium 1975-80). Republican. Methodist. Avocations: golf, bowling. Died 2007.

**STEWART, LAUREL JEAN,** home economics educator; b. Pikeville, Ky., Mar. 15, 1938; d. Robert Lee and Wilmadiea Alice (McGuire) Shepherd; m. Henry G. Stewart, Sept. 14, 1957; 1 child, Alice. BS, Berea Coll., 1966; MS, Eastern Ky. U., 1976. Cert. vocat. home econ., kindergarten tchr., Ky. Home econ. tchr. Wolfe County High Sch., Campton, Ky., 1966-69; presch. tchr. Berea (Ky.) Coll., 1971-72; home econ. tchr. Berea Community Sch., from 1972, chair home econ. dept., from 1977, chair vocat. edn., from 1978. Named Woman of Yr., Berea C. of C., 1990. Mem. Am. Vocat. Assn., Ky. Vocat. Assn., Ky. Vocat. Home Econ. Tchrs. (regional pres. 1977), Berea Bus. and Profl. Women's Club (past pres., v.p., sec.). Democrat. Baptist. Died 1995.

**STIBBE, AUSTIN JULE,** retired accountant; b. St. Paul, Mar. 29, 1930; s. Austin Julius and Agnes Dorothea (Delaney) S.; m. Mary Elizabeth King, May 29, 1952; children: Anne Marie, Craig Jule, David King, Karen Lee. BSB in Acctg., U. Minn., 1952. CPA, Minn., Wis. Tax acct. Ernst & Ernst, Mpls., 1955-60; corp. tax mgr. EcoLab, Inc.,

St. Paul, 1960-65; audit mgr. Coopers & Lybrand, Mpls., 1965-74; v.p. Wilkerson, Guthmann & Johnson, Ltd., St. Paul, 1974-93, of counsel, 1993—2006; ret., 2006. Exec. officer Twin Cities Squadron, U.S. Naval Sea Cadet Corps, Mpls., 1974-80; bd. dirs., treas., mem. Twin Cities coun. Navy League, 1970—, pres., 1979-81, treas., 1975-79, 81-91; mem. adv. coun. to dept. acctg. U. Minn., Mpls., 1983-86; bd. dirs., chmn. audit com. St. Paul Area Coun. Chs., 1985-87; mem. adv. bd. Headwaters Soc., 1987-88; mem. fin. reporting com. United Way St. Paul Area, 1981-93, mem. audit com., 1991-93; dist. commr. staff Indianhead coun. Boy Scouts Am., 1962-65. Lt. USN, 1952-55. Mem. Minn. Soc. CPAs (life), U.S. Naval Inst. (life), Belle Taine Lake Assn. (dir. 1995-2001, treas. 1996-2001), Hubbard County COLA Print Com., 1995-98, Friends of Heritage, 1996—, Hubbard County Works of Improvement (steering com. 2001), VFW (life), Am. Legion, Heritage Campus (bd. mem., 2007-). Presbyterian. Avocations: music, boating, history. Home: Nevis, Minn. Died July 24, 2013.

**STICKNEY, DOROTHY HAYES,** actress, writer; b. Dickinson, ND, June 21, 1896; d. Victor Hugo and Margaret (Hayes) S. PhD (hon.), Dickinson State U. Ind. actress Chicago, The Front Page, Another Language, Life With Father, A Lovely Light. Author: Openings and Closings. Named to N.D. Hall of Fame. Mem.: Cosmopolitan. Died June 2, 1998.

**STIDHAM, MELVIN ROBERT,** lawyer; b. Detroit, Sept. 5, 1925; s. Melvin Robert and Jean J. (Klein) Stidham; m. Barbara Louise Durrett, June 5, 1952; children: Dabney L., Stidham Mueller, Stacy L. Stidham Peronto, Allison D. Stidham Suarez, Shelley K. BS in Mech. Engring., Ill. Inst. Tech., 1945; JD, Southern Meth. U., 1952. Bar: Tex. 1952, Calif. 1960, US Patent Office 1954, US Supreme Ct. 1966. Assoc. Baker-Botts, Houston, 1954—57; ptnr. Arnold & Stidham, Houston, 1957—59, Gregg & Stidham, San Francisco, 1959—68; patent atty. Walworth Co., San Francisco, 1968—71; prin. Melvin R. Stidham, P.C., San Rafael, Calif., from 1971. Trustee Dixie Sch. Dist., San Rafael, 1963—71. Served with USN, 1943—46. Mem.: Marin Country (Novato, Calif.) club. Republican. Deceased.

**STINSON, RICHARD FLOYD,** retired horticulturist, educator; b. Cleve., Feb. 4, 1921; s. Floyd Earl and Helen M. (Schiemann) S.; m. Lois D. Stinson; children: Leigh, Laurie, Glenn, Paul, Cathy. BS, Ohio State U., 1943, MS, 1947, PhD, 1952. Instr. floriculture SUNY, Alfred, 1947-48; asst. prof. floriculture U. Conn., Storrs, 1948-55; asst. prof. horticulture Mich. State U., East Lansing, 1955-59, assoc. prof. horticulture, 1959-67; assoc. prof. agrl. edn. and horticulture Pa. State U., University Park, 1967-73, prof., 1973-89, sr. faculty mem., 1979-89, prof. emeritus, from 1990. Cons. in field. Contbr. articles to profl. jours. Lt. (j.g.) USNR, 1943-46. Mem. N.Am. Assn. Colls. and Tchrs. Agr. (E.B. Knight Jour. award 1992), Sigma Xi, Alpha Tau Alpha, Gamma Sigma Delta, Phi Delta Kappa. Deceased.

**STOCK, RICHARD JOHN,** retired cardiologist; b. Newark, Feb. 19, 1923; s. Archie Frank and Marie (Lergenmiller) S.; m. Eleanor Marguerite Schwarz, Sept. 1, 1945; children: Hilary Ann, Alan Constable; m. Martha Rusk Sutphen, Nov. 27, 2007. BS, Yale U., 1944; MD, Columbia U., 1947. Diplomate Am. Bd. Internal Medicine. Intern Presbyn. Hosp., NYC, 1947-48, resident in internal medicine, 1948-49, trainee Nat. Heart Inst., 1949-50; asst. physician in cardiology Columbia U. Hosp., NYC, 1949-50, asst. physician in medicine, 1951-61, asst. attending physician, 1961-64, assoc. attending physician, from 1981, attending physician; vis. fellow Nat. Heart Inst. Coll. Physicians and Surgeons Columbia U., NYC, 1949-50, asst. in medicine, 1951-56, instr. medicine, 1956-61, assoc. in medicine, 1961-64, asst. clin. prof., 1964-71, assoc. clin. prof., 1971-81, clin. prof., 1981-97, clin. prof. emeritus, spl. lectr., from 1997. Clin. prof. emeritus, spl. lectr. Coll. Physicians and Surgeons Columbia U., N.Y.C., 1997—. Author: Columbia Presbyterian Therapeutic Talks, 1963, 2nd edit., 1964; contbr. articles to profl. jours. Bd. dirs. N.Y. Heart Assn., 1979-85, mem. dir.'s coun., 1985—. Recipient Conspicuous Svc. medal Columbia U. Alumni Fedn., 1976; 2 Richard J. Stock Professorships in dept. of medicine Columbia U., endowed, 1986. Fellow Am. Coll. Cardiology; mem. P & S Alumni Assn. (mem. admissions com. 1973-79, 81—, treas. 1973-81, mem. exec. com. 1973—, chmn. Alumni Day 1971-75, pres.-elect 1981-83, pres. 1983-85, chmn. capital campaign 1985—, Silver medal 1975, Gold medal 2004). Avocations: sculpture, music, skiing, tennis. Home: New York, NY. Died Nov. 7, 2013.

**STOCKER, THOMAS EDWIN,** lawyer; b. Canton, Ohio, Oct. 12, 1953; s. Homer Eugene and Doris Verna (Schweitzer) S.; m. Patricia Ann Popko, Mar. 7, 1981; 1 child, Joshua Adam. BA, Grove City Coll., 1976; JD, U. Akron, 1979. Bar: Ohio 1979, U.S. Dist. Ct. (no. dist.) Ohio 1980. Law clk. to presiding justice U.S. Bankruptcy Ct., Canton, 1979-81; sole practice Canton, from 1981. Tchr. Career Studies Inst., Canton, 1984—. Mem. Canton City Council representing 10th ward. Mem. ABA, Ohio Bar Assn., Stark County Bar Assn. (chmn. young lawyers com. 1982-84, bankruptcy com. 1984-86), Plain Twp. Jaycees (pres. 1981-82). Home: Phoenix, Ariz. Died Mar. 1, 1989.

**STOCKHAUSEN, KARLHEINZ,** composer; b. Mödrath, Germany, Aug. 22, 1928; m. Doris Andreae, 1951; children: Suja, Christel, Markus, Majella; m. Mary Bauermeister, 1967; children: Julika, Simon. Student, Musikhochschule, Cologne, Germany, 1947—51; student acoustical scis., U. Bonn, 1954—56; studied with Werner Meyer-Eppler, Olivier Messiaen; PhD (hon.), Free U., 1996, Queen's U., 2004. Composer, condr. first pub. score for electronic music; dir. Electronic Studio, Cologne; condr., tchr., editor rev. of serial music; performance own works, U.S., Can., 1958; with Westdeutscher Rundfunk Electronic Music Studio, Cologne, 1953-98, artistic dir., 1963-77; guest prof. U. Pa., 1964, U. Calif., Davis, 1966-67; prof. Musikhochschule, Cologne, 1971-77. Composer: Kreuzspiel for six players, 1951; Spiel for orch., 1952; Eleven Piano Pieces, 1952-56; Punkte for orch., 1952; Kontrapunkte for ten instruments, 1952-53; Gruppen for 3 orchs., 1955-57; Zeitmasze, 1955-56; Gesang der Jünglinge, 1956; Zyklus, Refrain, Carré for 4 choirs and 4 orchs., 1959; Kontakte for electronic sounds, piano and percussion, 1959-60; Momente for 4 choirs, 13 instruments, solo-soprano, 1962-2007; also numerous works for solo instruments; Originale, mus. theatre, 1961; Plus-Minus, 1963; Mixture for orch. and electronic modulators, 1964; Mikrophonie I, 1964, Telemusik, 1966, Hymnen, 1967, Stimmung, 1968, Mantra, 1970 (Edison prize, Holland, 1996), Trans, 1971, Inori, 1974, Cadenzas, 1978, Light The 7 Days of the Week, 1977-2003, Invisible Choirs, 1979, Donnerstag aus Licht, 1981, Samstag aus Licht, 1984, Montag aus Licht, 1988, Dienstag aus Licht, 1993, Freitag aus Licht, 1996, Mittwoch aus Licht, 1998, Sonntag aus Licht, 2003, Klang The 24 Hours of the Day, 2004; composer over 350 compositions; over 100 recs. of works; author: Towards a Cosmic Music, 1989, Texte zur Musik (10 vols.); subject of numerous books and articles. Foremost exponent of electronic music. Recipient German Critics award, 1964, Italian award for Orchestral Works, 1968, Grand Prix du Disque, 1968, 69, 71, Edison prize, 1974, German Record prize, 1983, Ernst von Siemens Music prize, 1986, Bach award, City of Hamburg, 1995, Picasso medal UNESCO, 1992, Order of Merit Nordrhein-Westfalen, 1992, German Music Publishers Soc. award 1992, 94, 97, 2000, 01, 03, Cologne Culture prize, 1996, Polar Music prize 2001. Fellow Royal Irish Acad. Music (hon.); mem. Royal Swedish Acad., Acad. Arts Berlin, Philharmonic Acad. Rome, Am. Acad. and Inst. Arts and Letters, European Acad. Sci., Arts and Letters, Royal Acad. Music (hon.), Am. Acad. Arts and Scis. (hon.), Nat. Acad. St. Cecelia (hon.), German Soc. for Electro-Acoustic Music (hon.), Royal Acad. Scis., Letters, and Arts (assoc.), Free Acad. Arts, Acad. Royale. Died Dec. 5, 2007.

**STOCKHOLM, CARL GEORGE,** corporation executive, civic worker; b. Withee, Wis., Mar. 4, 1897; s. John Wissing and Albertina E. (Turnell) Stockholm; m. Marguerite A. Penfield, Aug. 11, 1934; children: Raymond Carl, Jon Robert, Gail Ann, Nancy Jane. Degree, Ill. Inst. Tech. Pres. Carl Stockholm Inc.; owner & mgr., farms Dane County, Wis., Lake County, Ill.; owner & mgr., orange groves; former treas. Chgo. Med. Ctr. Commn.; dir., exec. com. Chgo. Chpt. ARC; vis. com., numerous dignitaries; co-chmn. U-505; dir. & past pres. Garfield Bus. Men's Assn.; past pres. Mdse. Mart Retailers Assn.; owner & mgr. Carl Stockholm Cleaners, Chgo., 1927—74; mem. Chgo. Charter Jubilee Com., Citizens Adv. Com. U. Ill., 1956—82, Mayor's Adv. Com. City of Chgo., 1956—96. Western rep. Nat. Cycling Assn.; mem., bicycle racing divsn. Am. Olympic Team, 1920; mem. Olympic Cycling Com., 1936; trustee U. Chgo. Cancer Rsch. Found., 1956—82. With inf. US Army, World War I, with AEF, lt. to comdr. USNR, 1942—45. Recipient plaques and awards, Disting. Pub. Svc. medal, USN, 1954, 1957, Rehab. award, Ill. Am. Legion, 1967, Chgo. Bd. Health award, 1970. Mem.: DAV, Ill. C. of C., Golden Gem Growers Inc., Am. Legion (Ill. state chmn., naval affairs 1948—58), Def. Orientation Conf. Assn., Navy League US (nat. pres. 1955—57, nat. adv. coun., exec. com. 1954—84, Robert M. Thompson Nat. award 1964), Am. Mil. Chaplains Assn. (hon.), Mil. Order World Wars, Chgo. Farmers Club, US Auto Club, Army-Navy Club (Washington), Olympians Club, Oak Pk. Country Club, Shriners Club, Masons Club, Mchts. & Mfrs. Club (past gov.). Home: Oak Park, Ill. Deceased.

**STOKES, DONALD GRESHAM,** retired automotive executive; b. London, Mar. 22, 1914; s. Harry Potts and Marie Elizabeth (Yates) S.; m. Laura Elizabeth Courteney Lamb, May 25, 1939 (dec. Apr. 1995); 1 child, Michael Donald; m. Patricia Pascall, 2000 Grad. mech. engring., Harris Inst. Tech., Preston, Eng., 1933; LL.D., U. Lancaster, 1967; PhD in Tech, U. Loughborough, 1968; D.Sci., U. Southampton, 1969, U. Salford, 1971. Student apprentice Leyland Motors Ltd., London, 1930, export mgr., 1946-49, gen. sales and service mgr., 1949-53, dir., 1963-67; mng. dir., dep. chmn. Brit. Leyland Motor Corp. Ltd., 1967, chmn., mng. dir., 1968-73, chmn., chief exec., 1973-75; pres. Brit. Leyland Ltd., 1975-79; chmn. Brit. Arabian Adv. Co. Ltd., 1977-85; pres. Jack Barclay Ltd., 1980-90; Dutton-Forshaw Motor Group Ltd., 1980-90. V.p. Empresa Nacional de Autocamiones S.A., Spain, 1965-73; chmn. Reliant Group, 1990-94, Two Counties Radio Ltd., 1990-94. Dep. lt. for County Palatine of Lancashire; v.p. Inst. Sci. and Tech., U. Manchester, 1968-72, pres., 1972-75. Lt. col. R.E.M.E., 1939-45. Created knight, 1965, baron (life peer), 1969; decorated Territorial Decoration; officier de l'ordre de la Couronne Belgium; comdr. de l'Ordre de Leopold II. Fellow Inst. Mech. Engrs. (coun., v.p. 1971, pres. 1972), Inst. Road Transport Engrs., Inst. Civil Engrs., Royal Acad. Engring.; mem. Nat. Econ. Devel. Com. (chmn. electronics com. 1966-68), Soc. Motor Mfrs. and Traders (coun., pres. 1961-62), Worshipful Company Carmen. Home: Poole, England. Died July 21, 2008.

**STOL, MIROSLAV BOHUSLAV,** biomaterials researcher; b. Heralec, East Bohemia, Czechoslovakia, Oct. 19, 1938; s. Josef and Josefa (Stejdirova) S.; m. Blanda Prochazkova, Apr. 28, 1964; children: Kristina, Jan. MSc, Inst. Chem. Tech., Prague, Czechoslovakia, 1966. Engineering diplomate. Technician FATRA, Napajedla, Czechoslovakia, 1953-64, IMC CSAV, Prague, 1964-66, rschr., 1966-81, Rheumatol. Inst., Prague, 1981-95; cons. Prague, from 1995; rschr. Inst. Thermomechanics, Czech Acad. Scis., from 1999. Cons. Ministry of Health, Prague, 1985-96. Author and co-author 64 inventions (Golden medal Czech Ministry of Health 1989); contbr. articles to profl. jours. Grantee IGA Ministry Health, Prague, 1992. Mem. Rheumatology Soc., Clin. Biochemistry Soc., Czech Med. Soc., N.Y. Acad. Scis. Roman Catholic. Avocations: pets, nature's turistic, historical literature. Deceased.

**STOLARCZYK, JULIAN SEWER,** medical educator; b. Warsaw, Jan. 8, 1929; s. Edmund Jozef and Maria (Sobotkowska) S.; m. Ewa Maria Smigielska, Oct. 1, 1960; 1 child, Luke. MD, Med. Sch. Gdansk, 1952, MS, 1956. Diplomate in Internal Medicine, Pathology. Asst. dept. pathology Med. Sch. Gdansk, 1952-56, asst. prof., 1956-63, assoc. prof. dept. pathology, 1965-78, prof. pathology, chief dept. pathophysiology, 1978-2000, prof. emeritus, from 2000. Rsch. fellow Northwestern U., Chgo., 1963-64, 1969, vis. prof., 1974. Contbr. articles to profl. jours. Lt. Mil. Field Hosp., Poland. Recipient Nat. III Med. award Ministry of Health, Poland, 1976, 79. Mem. Soc. Polish Physicians (pres. 1986—). Roman Catholic. Home: Gdansk, Poland. Died Sept. 17, 2007.

**STONE, MINNIE STRANGE,** retired automotive service company executive; b. Palatka, Fla., Mar. 10, 1919; d. James Arrious and Pansy (Thomas) Strange; m. Fred Albion Stone, Nov. 30, 1939; children: Fred Albion, James Thomas, Thomas Demere. Student, Massey Bus. Coll., 1938-39. Sec., bookkeeper Sears, Roebuck & Co., Jacksonville, Fla., 1939-41; fin. sec. U.S. Army, Macon, Ga., 1941, Atlanta, 1942; sec., bookkeeper Raleigh (N.C.) Spring & Brake Svc., Inc. (now Stone Heavy Duty), 1953-84, sec.-treas. corp., 1960-84, dir., sec. Vol. Wake County Mental Health, 1970-80; pres. YWCA, Wake County, 1973-76, bd. dirs., 1966-76; bd. dirs. Urban Ministry Ctr. Raleigh, 1983-89, mem. adv. bd., 1989-94; former mem. subcom. Gov. Coun. Older Adult Fitness; trustee Bapt. Children's Homes, N.C., 1994—. Mem. N.C. Mus. History Assocs., N.C. Art Soc., Monthly Investors Club, Coley Forest Garden Club. Republican. Baptist. Home: Raleigh, NC. Died Apr. 15, 2001.

**STOTLER, ALICEMARIE HUBER,** federal judge; b. Alhambra, Calif., May 29, 1942; d. James R. and Loretta M. Huber; m. James Allen Stotler, Sept. 11, 1971. BA, U. Southern Calif., 1964, JD, 1967. Bar: Calif. 1967, US Dist. Ct. (northern dist.) Calif. 1967, US Dist. Ct. (ctrl. dist.) Calif. 1973, US Supreme Ct. 1976; cert. criminal law specialist. Dep. Orange County Dist. Attorneys Office, 1967-73; mem. Stotler & Stotler, Santa Ana, Calif., 1973-76, 83-84; judge Orange County Mcpl. Ct., 1976-78, Orange County Superior Ct., 1978-83, US Dist. Ct. (ctrl. dist.) Calif., LA, 1984—2005, chief judge, 2005—09, sr. judge, 2009—14. Assoc. dean Calif. Trial Judges Coll., 1982; lectr., panelist, numerous orgns.; standing com. on rules of practice and procedure U.S. Jud. Conf., 1991-98, chair, 1993-98; chair 9th cir. Public Info. and Cmty. Outreach, 2000-04; mem. exec. com. 9th Cir. Jud. Conf., 1989-93, Fed. State Jud. Coun., 1989-98, jury com., 1990-92, planning com. for Nat. Conf. on Fed.-State Jud. Relationships, Orlando, 1991-92, planning com. for Western Regional Conf. on State-Fed. Jud. Relationships, Stevens, Wash., 1992-93; chair dist. ct. symposium and jury utilization Ctrl. Dist. Calif., 1985, chair atty. liaison, 1989-90, chair U.S. Constn. Bicentennial com., 1986-91, chair magistrate judge com., 1992-93; mem. State Adv. Group on Juvenile Justice and Delinquency Prevention, 1983-84, Bd. Legal Specializations Criminal Law Adv. Commn., 1983-84, victim/witness adv. com. Office Criminal Justice Planning, 1980-83, U. Southern Calif. Bd. Councilors, 1993-2001; active team in tng. Leukemia Soc. America, 1993, 95, 97, 2000; legion lex bd. dirs. U. Southern Calif. Sch. Law Support Group, 1981-83. Winner Hale Moot Ct. Competition, State of Calif., 1967; named Judge of Yr., Orange County Trial Lawyers Assn., 1978, Most Outstanding Judge Orange County Bus. Litig. Sect., 1990. Mem. ABA (nat. conf. fed. trial judges com. on legis. affairs 1990-91), American Law Inst., American Judicature Soc., Fed. Judges Assn. (bd. dirs. 1989-92), Nat. Assn. Women Judges, U.S. Supreme Ct. Hist. Soc., Ninth Cir. Dist. Judges Assn., Calif. Supreme Ct. Hist. Soc., Orange County Bar Assn. (mem. numerous coms., Franklin G. West award 1984), Calif. Judges Assn. (mem. com. on jud. coll. 1978-80, com. on civil law and procedure 1980-82, Dean's coll. curriculum commn. 1981), Calif. Judges Found. Died June 9, 2014.

**STOUT, RANDALL PAUL,** architect; b. Knoxville, Tenn., May 6, 1958; m. Joelle Stout; children: Colton, Logan, Grace. BArch (with hons.), U. Tenn., 1981; MArch, Rice U., 1989. Registered Calif., Tex., Tenn. With Frank O. Gehry & Assocs., sr. assoc., then lead; with Skidmore Owings & Merrill, Houston; intern FKP, Inc., Houston; with solar design group TVA; pres. Randall Stout Architects, LA, 1993—2014; assoc. prof. architecture U. Nev., Las Vegas. Adj. prof., lectr. U. Tex., Austin, 2001; adj. prof. UCLA, 2001, recruitment com., 2002, admissions rev. com., 2002. Recipient Design award, TAAST, 1981, Cmty. Svc. award, Houston Proud, 1985, Graphic Design award, Tex. Soc. Arch., 1988, Progressive Arch. award, 1993, Innovation in Tech. award, SOLTEC Germany, 1998; fellow Pittman fellow, Rice U., 1988; scholar Gen. Shale scholar, 1980. Fellow: AIA (environment com. from 1997, Henry Adams medal 1981, Honor award 1992, 1995, 1998, 2000, Merit award 1998, Design citation 2000). Died July 11, 2014.

**STOWERS, JAMES EVANS, JR., (JIM STOWERS),** investment company executive; b. Kansas City, Mo., Jan. 10, 1924; s. James Evans Sr. and Laura (Smith) S.; m. Virginia Ann Glasscock, Feb. 4, 1954; children: Pamela (dec. 2010), Kathleen, James Evans III, Linda. AB, U. Mo., 1946, BS in Medicine, 1947. Chmn. bd. American Century Investment Mgmt. Inc. (formerly Twentieth Century Mutual Funds). Author: Why Waste Your Money on Life Insurance, 1967, Principles of Financial Consulting, 1971, Yes, You Can...Achieve Financial Independence, 1992; co-author: (with Jack Jonathan) The Best is Yet to Be: A Story of Innovation, Generosity & Success, 2007 Co-founder, chmn.

Stowers Inst. for Med. Rsch., Kansas City, 1987; Capt. USAAF, 1943-45; USAFR, 1945-57. Mem. Kansas City Chamber of Commerce, Sigma Chi Republican. Home: Kansas City, Mo. Died Mar. 17, 2014.

**STOYAN, HORTENSIA RODRÍGUEZ-SÁNCHEZ,** library administrator; b. Yabucoa, P.R., June 9, 1917; d. Antonio and Juana (Sanchez) R.; m. Hector Aponte (dec.); children: Gloria, Jose. BA, U. P.R., Rio Piedras, 1943; MA, State Tchrs. Coll., 1946; MS, Columbia U., 1955. Cert. pub. librarian. Tchr. elem. and jr. H.S. Town of Juncos (P.R.) Dept. Edn., 1941-44; pub. libr. Bklyn. Pub. Library, Bklyn., 1954-58; head libr. John A. Howe Library, Albany, N.Y., 1958-65; asst. dir. Farmingdale (N.Y.) Pub. Library, 1967-77, ret., 1977. Author: History of Yabucoa, 1993; contbr. articles Cana Guarapo y Melao, 1995-98. Bd. dirs. Mentally Ill Assn., 1984-98. Mem. AAUW (bd. dirs. 1996, pres. Queens N.Y. br. 1999-2001). Avocation: poetry. Died Oct. 10, 2004.

**STRAIT, GEORGE A.,** law educator, law library administrator, lawyer; b. Providence, Nov. 20, 1914; s. George Albert and Myra Elizabeth (Esser) Strait; m. Benita Lessin Strait, Sept. 30, 1976; 1 child, George A. BA, Howard U.; JD, Suffolk U.; postgrad. in Libr. Sci., La. State U. Bar: Mass., US Ct. Appeals (1st cir.), US Supreme Ct. Libr. asst. Social Law Libr., Boston; law libr., instr. Southern U., Baton Rouge; law libr. Worcester County Law Libr., Worcester, Mass.; asst. libr. Harvard U. Law Sch. Libr., 1958—67, assoc. libr., 1969—70, 1971—72, 1974—76, acting libr., 1970—73; law libr., assoc. prof. law Northeastern U., 1967—69; law libr., prof. law Antioch Sch. Law Libr., 1972—74; dir. Law Libr.; prof. U. Iowa, from 1976; cons. Iowa Bar Assn.; mem. Iowa State Arts Coun., Iowa Hist. Records Adv. Bd. Selectman, Natick, Mass.; mem. city coun., Iowa City, from 1983. Served to capt. US Army, World War II. Recipient award, Northeastern U. Sch. Law, 1978; named 1 of 75 Outstanding Grads., Suffolk U. Law Sch., 1980; grantee Internat. Law Librs. Travel grantee, Rome, 1972;, Budapest, Hungary, 1977, fellow, Suffolk U. Alumni, 1973. Mem.: NAACP (life), Boston Bar Assn., Am. Assn. Law Schs., Am. Assn. Law Librs. Died Nov. 6, 1989.

**STRAND, THERESA,** educational consultant; b. NYC, Jan. 11, 1921; d. Louis and Anna Siegel; m. Peter Strand, June 17, 1944; 1 child, Robert Dennis. BA in Liberal Arts, CCNY Bklyn. Coll., 1942; MA in Fine Arts and Art Edn., Columbia U. Tchrs. Coll., NYC, 1946; PhD in Ednl. Evaluation and Rsch., Wayne State U., Detroit, 1975. Sr. profl. assoc. Ednl. Testing Svc., Evanston, Ill., Princeton, NJ, 1969—92; CEO Strand Consulting Svcs., Glenview, Ill., from 1992. Educator, evaluator, trainer, rschr., author, editor, cons. in field. Founding mem., mem. steering com. Assn. for Devel. Guidance of Adults, Wayne State U., Detroit, 1967—69; historian, archivist, coun. mem. Midwest Ednl. Rsch. Assn., Ill., 1994—2000. Mem.: Nat. Mus. Women in Arts, Wash., DC, Mus. Contemporary Art, Chgo., Block Mus. Art, Northwestern U., Evanston, Nat. Coun. Measurement in Edn., Am. Ednl. Rsch. Assn. Avocations: visual arts, theater, documentary films, computers. Died Jan. 3, 2013.

**STRANG, MIKE (MICHAEL LATHROP STRANG),** former United States Representative from Colorado; b. Bucks County, Pa., June 17, 1929; s. Stephen Barton and Ellen (Lathrop) S.; m. Kathleen Sherry, Nov. 26, 1960; children: Michael Lathrop, Fitzhugh Scott, Laurie and Bridget (twins) AB in History, Princeton U., 1956; Graduate Studies, U. Geneva, 1956—57. Investment banker, 1957—85; mem. US Congress from 1st Colo. Dist., Washington, 1985—87. Served to 2d lt. U.S. Army, 1950-53 2nd Lt. US Army, 1950—53. Republican. Episcopalian. Home: Indio, Calif. Died Jan. 12, 2014.

**STRATTON, DOROTHY E.,** painter, printmaker; b. Worchester, Mass., Dec. 21, 1908; d. Robert Alexander and Edith Amy Stratton; m. William Asbury King, Oct. 22, 1947 (dec. 1989); m. Michael Hicks-Beach, May 25, 1928 (dec. 1994); 1 child, Heather Hicks-Beach. Studied drawing and painting, Pratt Inst., Bklyn., 1942, Bklyn. Mus. Sch., 1943, Acad. Grande Chaumiere, Andre Lhote, Paris, 1947—48; studied with Rico Lebrun, UCLA, 1956—57; studied printmaking, U. Calif., San Diego, 1966—67. Profl. artist; adminstr. art asst. LA Mcpl. Art Commn. Gallery, 1952—61; contbr. Arts In Embassies Program, 1965—80; registrar La Jolla Mus. Sch., Calif., 1965—69. Tchr. printmaking U. Calif., San Diego, 1966—67. Represented in permanent collections Georgetown U. Fine Print Collections, Corcoran Mus. Art, Washington, DC, Nat. Mus. Women in Arts, Smithsonian Instn., Acadia U., Nova Scotia, Can., U. San Diego, Pushkin Mus. Fine Art, Moscow, Long Beach Mus. Art, Calif., LA Mcpl. Art Commn., and others, one-woman shows include Pasadena Art Mus., 1959, La Jolla Mus. Contemporary Art, Calif., 1962, Jefferson Gallery, La Jolla, 1963, Maison of Culture, Tunis, Tunisia, 1965, Athenaeum, La Jolla, 1966, 1978, Roberts Gallery, Santa Monica, Calif., 1969, U. San Diego Founders' Gallery Retrospectives, 1980, 1994, Spectrum Gallery, San Diego, 1982, San Diego Print Club Gallery, 1984—85, Washington Printmakers Gallery, Washington, DC, 1985, 1988, Marymount U., Arlington, Va., 1990, Acadia U., Nova Scotia, 1991, Washington Printmakers Gallery, Washington, DC, 1992, exhibited in group shows at Calif. Soc. Printmakers Nat. Traveling Exhibits, 1972—90, Pratt Graphics Ctr., NY, 1980—83, Washington Printmakers Gallery, 1983—94, Brighton Press Gallery, San Diego, 1986, Corcoran Gallery Art, Washington, DC, 2000, Barbican Internat. Exch. Printmakers, Great Britain, Pushkin Mus. Fine Art, Moscow, Calif. Soc. Printmakers, Internat. Graphic Arts Found., Darien, Conn., San Diego Mus. Artist's Guild, St. Michael's Printmakers Assn., St. John's, Newfoundland, Washington Print Club, Washington, DC. Recipient numerous awards, honors, achievements. Mem.: Artists Equity Assn. (life), Washington Printmakers Gallery (life; founding mem.). Died 2007.

**STRAUSS, ROBERT SCHWARZ,** lawyer, retired ambassador; b. Lockhart, Tex., Oct. 19, 1918; s. Charles H. & Edith Violet (Schwarz) S.; m. Helen Jacobs, 1941 (dec. 2006); children: Robert A., Richard C., Susan. LL.B., U. Tex., 1941. Bar: Tex. 1941, DD 1971. Spl. agt. FBI, 1941-45; founding ptnr. Akin Gump Strauss Hauer & Feld LLP, Dallas, 1945-77 and from 81, sr. exec. ptnr. Washington and Dallas; chmn. AG Global Solutions (joint venture between Akin Gump and First Internat. Resources, Inc.); treas. Democratic Nat. Com., 1970-72, chmn., 1973—76, Jimmy Carter's Presdl. Campaign, 1976, Pres. Jimmy Carter's Re-Election Campaign, 1980; spl. rep. for trade negotiations Exec. Office of the Pres., 1977-79; President's personal rep. for Middle East negotiations The White House, 1979-81; US amb. to Russia US Dept. State, Moscow, 1991—92. Bd. dirs. Archer-Daniels-Midland Co., Decatur, Ill., Gulf Stream Corp., Savannah, Ga., Gen. Instruments, NYC; lectr. in field. Contbr. articles to profl. jours. Recipient The Presdl. Medal of Freedom, The White House, 1981; Lifetime Achievement award The American Lawyer mag, 2004. Mem. ABA, Dallas Bar Assn., DC Bar Assn. Democrat. Jewish. Died Mar. 19, 2014.

**STRECKER, FRANCES IRENE BROWN,** volunteer; b. Denver, Aug. 28, 1897; d. Edward Newton and Frances Evelyn (Hittson) Brown; m. George O. Strecker, Oct. 21, 2022 (dec. May 1962); children: Muriel Frances, Roger William. Student, Colo. Woman's Coll., 1917. Pres. women's aux. Highland Pk. Hosp., Ill., 1956—60, Northwestern U. Settlement, 1960—64; pres. Glencoe Sr. Aux. Infant Welfare Soc. Chgo., 1968—71; corr. sec. Eng. Women HEW, 1978—80, chaplain, 1980—82. Mem.: DAR (north shore regent 1946—48, 1953—54, chaplain Stamford chpt. 1975—77, libr. 1984—86, chmn. manuals 1979—85), Colo. Hist. Soc., Conn. Daus. Am. Colonists (v.p. 1976—78, 1982—84, pres. 1978—80, libr. 1984—86), Stamford Hist. Soc., Conn. Hist. Soc., Conn. Soc. Genealogists (pres. 1975—77), Nat. Soc. Daus. Founders and Patriots America, Ill. Soc. Daus. Colonial Wars (rec. sec. 1968—71, chaplain 1974—77, corr. sec. Conn. 1977—80), Greenwich New Eng. Women (libr. from 1982), Women's Descs. Ancient and Hon. Arty. County, Colonial Dames America (pres. chpt. 1965—71), New Eng. Women Club (chaplain 1984—86), Denver Athletic Club, Stamford Woman's Club. Republican. Died Sept. 7, 1996.

**STREET, LAIROLD MAURICE,** lawyer; b. Akron, Ohio, Apr. 2, 1951; s. Alonzo James and Ruby Vivian (Christian) S.; m. Kathryn Ferger, Aug. 5, 1978; children: Chipalo Nathan, Jalika Christine. AB, Oberlin Coll., 1974; MA, John Hopkins U., 1977; JD, Ind. U., 1982. Bar: Ind. 1982, D.C. 1989, Ohio 1989. Internat. economist Overseas Devel. Coun., Washington, 1974-77; internat. economist US Dept. Commerce, Washington, 1977-78; atty. Internat. Trade Commn., Washington, 1981-83, EEOC, Washington, 1983—95. Contbr. articles to U. Md. Internat. Law Jour., 1981, NYU Internat. Law Jour., 1987, Howard U. Law Jour., 1988. Bd. trustees Akron (Ohio) Urban League, 1973-75; mentor D.C. Schools, Washington, 1987-89. Recipient Danforth award Danforth Found., 1979-81. Mem. ABA (mentor 1989, several coms.), Internat. Bar Assn., American Soc. Internat. Law, Fgn. Law Soc., Nat. Bar Assn., Ind. Bar Assn., Ind. Bar Assn., Ohio Bar Assn., D.C. Bar Assn. Died Dec. 17, 2013.

**STREZH, PETR EVGENYEVICH,** physicist, researcher; b. Moscow, Apr. 8, 1937; s. Evgeniy Grigoryevich Strezh and Elena Petrovna Artemkina. Diploma in physics, Moscow State U., 1961, degree in phys. and math. scis., 1968. Engr. Ctrl. Sci. Rsch. Inst. Mech. Engring., Kaliningrad, Russia, 1961-64; rsch. asst. Russian Peoples' Friendship U., Moscow, 1968, sr. lectr., 1969, asst. prof., from 1970. Sr. rschr. Contractual Works, Moscow, 1979-83; supr. studies for postgrad. students, Moscow, 1975-82. Author: Electrical Oscillations and Waves, 1997; contbr. articles to profl. publs. Dep. Dist. Soviet, Moscow, 1973-79. Recipient Honor of Higher Sch., Ministry of Higher and Secondary Spl. Edn., 1987, Vet. of Labor award, 1990. Avocations: piano, painting, collecting books. Home: Moscow, Russia. Died July 26, 2003.

**STRIDER, MARJORIE VIRGINIA,** artist, educator; b. Guthrie, Okla. d. Clifford R. and Marjorie E. (Schley) S. BFA, Kansas City Art Inst., 1962. Faculty Sch. Visual Arts, NYC, 1970-2001; artist-in-residence City U. Grad. Ctr. Mall, NYC, 1976, Fabric Workshop, Phila., 1978, Grassi Palace, Venice, Italy, 1978. One-woman shows include Pace Gallery, N.Y.C., 1963-64, Nancy Hoffman Gallery, N.Y.C., 1973-74, Weather Spoon Mus., U.N.C., Chapel Hill, 1974, City U. Grad. Center Mall, 1976, Clocktower, N.Y.C., 1976, Sculpture Center, N.Y.C., 1983, Steinbaum Gallery, N.Y.C., 1983, 84, Andre Zarre Gallery, 1993, 95, Outdoor Installation, N.Y.C., 1997, Selby Gallery, Ringling Sch. of Art, Sarasota, Fla., 1998, Neuberger Mus., Purchase, N.Y., 1999, Andre Zarre Gallery, 2008; exhibited in group shows at Sculpture Center, N.Y.C., 1981, Drawing Biennale, Lisbon, Portugal, 1981, Newark Mus., 1984, William Rockhill Nelson Mus., Kansas City, 1985, Danforth Mus., Framingham, Mass., 1987, Delahoyd Gallery, N.Y.C., 1992; represented in permanent collections Guggenheim Mus., N.Y.C., U. Colo., Boulder, Albright-Knox Mus., Buffalo, Des Moines Art Center, Storm King (N.Y.) Art Center, Larry Aldrich Mus., Ridgefield, Conn., City U. Grad. Center, N.Y.C., Hirschhorn Mus. and Sculpture Garden, Washington, Santa Fe (N. Mex.) Mus. of Art, also pvt. collections. Grantee Nat. Endowment for Arts, 1973, 80, Longview Found., 1974, Pollock-Krasner Found., 1990, 2009, Florsheim Art Fund, 1998, 2000; Va. Ctr. for Creative Arts fellow, 1974, 92, Millay Colony for Arts fellow, 1992, Yaddo Colony, 1996-97 Home: Saugerties, NY. Died Aug. 27, 2014.

**STRITCH, ELAINE,** singer, actress; b. Detroit, Feb. 2, 1925; d. George Joseph and Mildred (Jobe) S.; m. John M. Bay, Feb. 2, 1973 (dec. 1973). Student drama workshop, New Sch. for Social Research; studies in singing with Burt Knapp, Drama Workshop, from 1948. Appeared in Broadway prodns. Loco, 1946, Three Indelicate Ladies, 1947, Yes M'Lord, 1949, Pal Joey, 1962, On Your Toes, Bus Stop, 1955, Sail Away, 1961, Who's Afraid of Virginia Woolf?, 1962, 65, Wonderful Town, 1967, Private Lives, 1968, Company, 1970, 1993, also London prodn., 1972, Love Letters, 1990, Show Boat, 1994, A Delicate Balance, 1996 (Drama Desk award for Outstanding Featured Actress, 1996), Elaine Stritch At Liberty, 2002 (Outstanding Book of a Musical & Outstanding Solo Performance, Drama Desk Awards, 2002); off-Broadway prodns. include At Home at the Carlyle, 2005, 2006, Endgame, 2008; appeared in Follies in Concert, NYC, 1982; (films) The Scarlet Hour, 1956, Three Violent People, 1956, A Farewell to Arms, 1957, The Perfect Furlough, 1958, Who Killed Teddy Bear?, 1965, Pigeons, 1971, The Spiral Staircase, 1975, Providence, 1977, September, 1988, Cocoon II: The Return, 1988, Cadillac Man, 1990, Out to Sea, 1997, Screwed, 2000, Small Time Crooks, 2000, Autumn in New York, 2000, Monster-in-Law, 2005, Romance & Cigarettes, 2005, ParaNorman (voice), 2012; (TV series) My Sister Eileen, 1960-61, The Trials of O'Brien, 1965-66, (British) Two's Company, 1975-76, The Ellen Burstyn Show, 1987, Stranded, 1986, Life's a B*tch, 2003, 30 Rock, 2007-12; (TV films) Chance of a Lifetime, 1991, An Unexpected Life, 1998, Paradise, 2004; (TV miniseries) An Inconvenient Woman, 1991, Elaine Stritch: At Liberty, 2002 (Emmy award Outstanding Individual Performance in a Variety or Music Program, 2004, Drama Desk award, outstanding solo performance, Drama Desk award, Outstanding Book of a Musical, Tony award for Best Solo Musical Performance HBO 1991); author: Am I Blue?: Living With Diabetes and, Dammit, Having Fun, 1984. Recipient Nightlife award, outstanding cabaret female vocalist in a major engagement, 2006, Creative Arts Primetime Emmy for Outstanding Guest Actress in Comedy Series, Acad. TV Arts and Scis., 2007. Died July 17, 2014.

**STRUCK, PETER,** former German government official; b. Goettingen, Germany, Jan. 24, 1943; married; 3 children. Grad. in Law, 1971. Personal advisor to pres. U. Hamburg, 1971—72; town councillor and dep. dir. City of Uelzen, 1978—83; mem. Bundestag (German parliament), 1980—2009; atty. Dist. Ct. Uelzen and Regional Ct. Leuneburg, 1983—2012; min. def. Govt. of Germany, 2002—05. Social Democratic Party. Died Dec. 19, 2012.

**STRYKER, DANIEL RAY,** adult education educator; b. Ruslip, Eng., July 15, 1957; came to U.S., 1959; s. Theodore Ray and Nina Margaret (Bryant) S. BS, Sam Houston State, 1980; MEd, U. Houston, 1988; EdD, Sam Houston State, 1996, MA in History, 2002. Pulmonary functions technician St. Joseph Hosp., Houston, 1981; rschr. U. Tex. Med. Br., Houston, 1981-82; taxpayer svc. rep. IRS, Houston, 1982-85; substitute tchr. Conroe (Tex.) Schs., 1986-88, 91-95; tchr. Aldine Schs., Houston, 1988-90; instr. U. Houston, 1995—96, Western Carolina U., Cullowhee, 1997-98; instr. dept. history and geography Houston C.C., from 1998; instr. dept. history N. Harris Coll., Houston, from 1998, adj. prof., 2008. Author: A Cognitive Approach to Teaching History, 1994, Twilight in the City, 1996, Nowhere in the Shadow, 1996, Mirror of Dreams, 1996. Precinct judge Klein Schs., Houston, 1992-96. Athletic scholar, Sam Houston State, Huntsville, 1976. Avocations: reading, writing, camping, mountain climbing. Home: Houston, Tex. Died Nov. 13, 2013.

**STUART, ROBERT DOUGLAS, JR.,** former ambassador, retired food products executive; b. Hubbard Woods, Ill., Apr. 26, 1916; s. Robert Douglas and Harriet (McClure) S.; m. Barbara McMath Edwards, May 21, 1938 (dec. 1993); children: Robert Douglas III, James McClure, Marian Stuart Pillsbury, Alexander Douglas; m. Lillian Lovenskiold, 1995 BA, Princeton U., 1937; JD, Yale Law Sch., 1946. Bar: Ill. 1946. With Quaker Oats Co., Chgo., 1947-84, CEO, 1966-81, chmn., 1981-84; US amb. to Norway US Dept. State, Oslo, 1984-89. Mem. Republican Nat. Com., 1964-72; bd. dirs. William Benton Found., Chgo., 1980-84, Chgo. Urban League, 1963-84, Atlantic Coun. of U.S., Washington Ctr. for Internships & Acad. Seminars, John G. Shedd Aquarium, Ctr. for Media and Public Affairs; trustee Princeton U., 1972-82; mem. Nat. Commn. on Public Svc.; mem. Base Closure & Realignment Commn., 1991, 1993; vice chmn. Ill. Commn. on Future of Public Svc., 1991; chmn. midwest regional advisory bd. Inst. Internat. Edn.; Served to maj. U.S. Army, 1942-45, ETO. Mem. Bus. Coun., Coun. American Ambassadors (pres.), Washington Inst. Fgn. Affairs. Clubs: Chgo., Commercial, Conway Farms Golf, Old Elm, Onwentsia; Shore Acres; River, Links (N.Y.C.); Bohemian, Birnam Wood Golf (Calif.), Valley Club of Montecito; Metropolitan (Washington). Lodges: Rotary. Republican. Presbyterian. Avocations: skiing, tennis, golf, fishing, other sports. Home: Lake Forest, Ill. Died May 8, 2014.

**STUNKARD, ALBERT JAMES,** psychiatrist, educator; b. NYC, Feb. 7, 1922; s. Horace Wesley and Frances (Klank) Stunkard. BS, Yale U., 1943; MD, Columbia U., 1945; MD (hon.), U. Edinburgh, 1992, La. State U., 2006. Intern in medicine Mass. Gen. Hosp., Boston, 1945—46; resident physician psychiatry Johns Hopkins Hosp., 1948—51, rsch. fellow psychiatry, 1951—52; 1rsch. fellow medicine Columbia U. Svc., Goldwater Meml. Hosp., NYC, 1952—53; Commonwealth rsch. fellow, then asst. prof. medicine

Cornell U. Med. Coll., 1953—57; mem. faculty U. Pa., 1957—73, 1976—97, prof. psychiatry, 1962—73, 1976—97, Kenneth Appel prof. psychiatry, 1968—73, chmn. dept., 1962—73, prof. emeritus, 1997—2014; prof. psychiatry Stanford U. Medical Sch., 1973—76. Contbr. 500 articles on psychol., physiol., sociol., therapeutic and genetic aspects of obesity to profl. jours. Capt. M.C. AUS, 1946—48. Recipient Disting. Svc. award, Am. Psychiat. Assn., 1994, Goldberger award, AMA, 1990, Willendorf award, Internat. Assn. Study of Obesity, 1998, Sarnat award mental health, NAS Inst. Medicine, 2004, Disting. Achievement medal medicine, Columbia U. Coll. Physicians and Surgeons, 2005; fellow, Ctr. Advanced Study in Behavioral Scis., 1971—72. Mem.: Soc. Behavioral Medicine (past pres.), Assn. Rsch. Nervous and Mental Diseases (past pres.), American Psychosomatic Soc. (past pres.), Acad. Behavioral Medicine Rsch. (past pres.), American Assn. Chmn. Dept. Psychiatry (past pres.), Inst. Medicine of NAS. Achievements include contributions to the behavioral, pharmacological, community and surgical treatment of obesity and to understanding of sociological, physiological, psychological and genetic aspects of the disorder; contributions also to nosology and treatment of the eating disorders. Died July 12, 2014.

**STURANOVIC, ZELJKO,** former prime minister of the Republic of Montenegro; b. Niksic, Montenegro, Jan. 31, 1960; married; 2 children. Grad. in Law, Podgorica, Montenegro, 1983. Sr. officer, head legal dept. Niksic Steel Factory; rep. House of Citizens Parliament of Montenegro, 1993, head Democratic Party Socialists Caucus; min. justice Govt. of Montenegro, 2001—06, prime min., 2006—08. Died June 30, 2014.

**STUTTERHEIM, NIKO,** engineering consultant, company director; b. Bethal, Transvaal, South Africa, Nov. 2, 1915; s. Nicolaas Anton and Elizabeth Catherina (Van Nouhuijs) S.; m. Mary Elizabeth Connell, Feb. 7, 1942; children: Jan Anton, Catherine Mary, Konrad, Adrian Henk, Philip Oswald. BSc in Engring., U. Witwatersrand, Johannesburg, South Africa, 1937, DSc in Engring., 1961, LLD (hon.), 1989; DSc (hon.), U. Cape Town, South Africa, 1979. Chartered engr., South Africa. Chem. engr. Pretoria (South Africa) Portland Cement, 1938-43; rsch. engr. U. Witwatersrand, 1943-45; sr. rsch. officer CSIR, South Africa, 1946-55, dir. NBRI, 1955-59, v.p., 1959-67, dep. pres., 1967-70; mng. dir. Noristan Holdings, South Africa, 1970-77; chmn. or dir. 26 cos., —, from 1977. Dep. chmn. Atomic Energy Corp., South Africa, 1981-85; bd. dirs. Dekra Cert. Svcs., South Africa, Elcon Systemtechnik (Pty.) Ltd., South Africa; pres. Assoc. Sci. and Tech. Socs. South Africa, 1977-78. Contbr. over 60 articles on chem. and civil engring. to profl. jours. Sec. CCTA Inter-African Housing Commn., Africa South of Sahara, 1955-60. Decorated Order for Meritorious Svc. (South Africa). Fellow South African Inst. Chem. Engrs. (hon.); mem. South African Inst. Civil Engrs. (hon. life), South African Acad. Sci. and Tech. (Havenga prize 1971, M.T. Steyn medal 1986), Wits Club. Avocations: travel, reading, computers, woodworking. Died Nov. 2005.

**STÜWE, HEIN PETER,** physicist, researcher; b. Königsberg, Ostpreussen, Germany, Sept. 14, 1930; s. Kurt and Gertraude (Werner) S.; m. Ursula Biermann, Jan. 10, 1957; children: Kurt, Barbara, Klaus. Dr.rer.nat., U. Göttingen (Germany), 1955; dozent habil., RWTH Aachen, 1961; DHC (hon.), Miskolc U., Hungary, 1985. Rsch. assoc. U. Ill., Urbana, 1956-58; rsch. asst. RWTH Aachen, 1958-62, asst. prof., 1962-66; prof. Tech. U. Braunschw (Germany), 1967-71, Montanuniv Leoben, Austria, 1971—96. Vis. prof., U. Sao Paulo, Brazil, 2000; rsch. vis. Kinsei Ken, Tokyo, 1966-67; vis. prof. Indian Inst. of Tech., Madras, 1970; guest prof. Univ. Politecnica, Madrid, 1986; dir. Inst. for Solid State Physics Österreichische Akademie der Wissenschaften, Leoben, Austria, 1971-1996, dir. Inst. Metal Physics; rector, vice rector Montanuniversität, Leoben, 1978-84. Fellow ASM Internat.; mem. Austrian Acad. Scis. (corres.). Avocation: go-game. Home: Leoben, Austria. Died Sept. 19, 2005.

**SUÁREZ GONZÁLEZ, ADOLFO (DUKE OF SUÁREZ),** former Prime Minister of Spain; b. Cebreros, Avila, Spain, Sept. 25, 1932; s. Hipolito Suarez Guerra and Herminia Gonzalez Prado; m. Amparo Illana Elortegui, July 15, 1961 (May 17, 2001); children: Maria Amparo (March 7, 2004), Adolfo, Laura, Sonsoles, Javier. Baccalaureat, San Juan de la Cruz Coll.; Dr. of Law cum laude, U. Madrid, 1958. Pvt. sec. to Nat. Del. for the Spanish Provinces, 1958-61. Chief of cabinet of Vice Sec. of Nat. Movement. 1961-64; program dir. Spain's TV network, 1965-68; civil gov. Province of Segovia, Spain, 1968-69; dir.-gen. of Spanish Broadcasting TV System, 1969-73; family rep. to Spanish Parliament from Province of Avila, 1967-77; pres. of Democratic Union of Spanish People, 1975; prime minister of Spain and pres. Council of Ministries, 1976-81; leader Unión Centro Democrático, 1977-81, leader Centro Democrático y Social, pres., 1982-91; pres. Internat. Liberals, 1988-91. Recipient numerous decorations. Mem. Madrid Bar Assn., Inst. of Polit. Studies, Spanish Trial Law Inst. Died Mar. 23, 2014.

**SULLIVAN, COLLEEN ANNE,** anesthesiologist, educator; b. Lucknow, India, Feb. 11, 1937; arrived in U.S., 1961; d. Douglas George and Nancy Irene (MacLeod) Sullivan; m. Alexander Walter Gotta, July 17, 1965; 1 child, Nancy Colleen Gotta. MB, ChB, U. St. Andrews, Scotland, 1961. Diplomate Am. Bd. Anesthesiology, Am. Coll. Anesthesiologists. Rotating intern Nassau Hosp. (now Winthrop U. Hosp.), Mineola, N.Y., 1961-62; clin. instr. Cornell U., NYC, 1962-64; resident in anesthesiology N.Y. Hosp./Cornell U., 1962-64; fellow in anesthesiology Meml. Sloan-Kettering Cancer Ctr., NYC, 1964-67, asst. prof. Cornell U. Med. Coll., 1978-79; assoc. dir. anesthesia St. Mary's Hosp.-Cath. Med. Ctr., Bklyn., 1968-78; clin. assoc. prof. SUNY, Bklyn., 1979-90, clin. dir. anesthesia, 1990-93, clin. prof. anesthesiology, 1990-97. Clin. dir. anesthesia Kings County Hosp., Bklyn., 1983—90, med. dir. ambulatory surg. unit, 1993—97. Contbr. chapters to books, articles to profl. jours. Mem.: N.Y. State Soc. Anesthesiologists (mem. ho. of dels. 1983—97, asst. editor Sphere 1990—95, mem. com. sci. program 1990—97), Woman's Club Great Neck (bd. dirs. 2005). Republican. Roman Catholic. Avocations: reading, cooking. Home: Great Neck, NY. Died May 26, 2013.

**SULLIVAN, MARTIN EDWARD,** museum director; b. Troy, NY, Feb. 9, 1944; s. John Francis and Helen Edna (Lynch) S.; m. Katherine Mary Hostetter, May 9, 1981; children: Abigail, Bethany. BA in History, Siena Coll., 1965; MA in History, U. Notre Dame, 1970, PhD in History, 1974. Exec. dir. Ind. Commn. for Humanities, Indpls., 1972-75; dir. pub. programs NEH, Washington, 1976-81; pres. Inst. on Man and Sci., Rensselaerville, NY, 1981-83; dir. NY State Mus., State Edn. Dept., Albany, 1983-90, Heard Mus., Phoenix, 1990-99, Historic St. Mary City, Md., 1999—2008, Smithsonian Nat. Portrait Gallery, Washington, 2008—12. Trustee American Indian Ritual Object Repatriation Found., N.Y.C., 1992-98; chmn. US Govt. Cultural Property Advisory Com., 1995-2003. Author: Museums, Adults and the Humanities, 1981, Inventing the Southwest: The Fred Harvey Company and Native American Art, 1996; contbr. articles to profl. jours. Trustee American Fedn. Arts, 1994-98; mem. Native American Repatriation Act Adv. Com., 1992-2005. With U.S. Army, 1966-68. Mem. American Assn. Mus. (v.p. 1990-93, mem. accreditation commn. 1997—2012; named to Centennial Honor Roll, 2006). Democrat. Home: Saint Marys City, Md. Died Feb. 25, 2014.

**SULTANBAWA, M. U. S.,** science academy executive; B. Sc. (chemistry), M. Sc., U. of Ceylon; PhD, Imperial Coll. London. Founder, gen. secretary Chemistry Soc. of Ceylon; worked with Profs. E A Braude and L N Owen; rsch. fellow Industrial Rsch. Lasboratory by D.H. Balfour; prof. of chemistry U. of Ceylon; pres. Nat. Acad. Scis., Colombo, Sri Lanka. Vidya Jothi by HE the President of Sri lanka, Fellow of the Indian Nat. Acad., Guinness award for Scientific Achievement 1978, Presidential award. Died May 7, 1999.

**SULTANGAZIN, UMIRZAK MAKHMUTOVICH,** science foundation director; b. KazakhSSR, USSR, Oct. 4, 1936; s. Sultungazy Makhmutov and Nurila (Temirbaeva) Makhmutova; m. Raikhan Ganievna Meirmanova, Mar. 14, 1958; children: Zhanat, Almas. Student, Kazakh State U., Almaty, USSR, 1953-58; PhD in Physics and Mathematics, USSR Acad Scis., Novosibirsk, USSR, 1966, DSc in Mathematical Physics, 1972. Asst. prof. Kazakh State U., Almaty, USSR, 1958-60, assoc. prof., 1960-64, prof. mathematics, 1972-78; chair, prof. numerical math. Inst. Math. and Mechanics, 1978-88; v.p. Acad. Scis., Almaty, USSR, 1986-88, pres., 1988-94; v.p., 1st dep. min. Ministry of Sci., Acad. Scis. Republic of Kazakstan, from 1996. Vis. prof. Karlov U., Czechoslovakia, 1972, Kyoto U., Japan, 1994-95, 1999-2000. Author: (monograph) Mehtod of Spherical Harmonics in Kinetic Transport Theory, 1979, (monograph) Mathematical Problems of Kinetic Transport Theory, 1986, Discrete Nonlinear Models of Boltzmann Equation, 1987. Mem. Parliament of Kazakh SSR, Almaty, USSR, 1987-89, Parliament USSR, Moscow, 1989-91, ctrl. com. Communist Party USSR, Moscow, 1989-91. Recipient State Pirze of USSR in Sci. and Tech. Com. on State Prizes, 1987 prize of Acad. of Scis. Czechoslovakia, 1988. Mem. NAS Kazakhstan (v.p. 2002-03), Math. Com. Republic of Kazakhstan (chmn. 1994-2005), Fedn. Cosmonautics Kazakhstan (chmn.), Internat. Inst. Applied Syss. Analysis Coun. (Austria), Internat. Union Radio Sci. (Belgium) (corr. 1994-2005). Avocations: history, mountain tourism. Home: Almaty, Kazakhstan. Died May 23, 2005.

**SUMMERFIELD, ARTHUR,** psychologist; b. Wilmslow, Cheshire, Eng., Mar. 31, 1923; s. Arthur and Dora Gertrude (Perman Smith) S.; m. Aline Torday, June 21, 1946 (div. 1974); children: Arthur Quentin, Anne Penelope; m. Angela Barbara Steer, Feb. 9, 1974. BSc Tech., U. Manchester, Eng., 1947; BSc with 1st class honors, U. London, 1949. Prof. psychology U. London, 1961-88; head dept. psychology Birkbeck Coll., London, 1961-88; chmn. LearnIT, Thirsk, 1990—2001. Vis. prof. U. Calif., Irvine, 1968. Editor: (with Hannah Steinberg) David Katz's Animals and Men, 1951; sci. editor jour. Brit. Med. Bull., 1964, 71, (with D.M. Warburton) 81, British Jour. Psychology, 1964-67. Lt. Royal Navy, 1943-46. Fellow Brit. Psychol. Soc. (hon. life; pres. 1963-64), Inst. Dirs.; mem. APA (internat. com. 1977-79), Internat. Union Psychol. Sci. (pres. 1976-80), Internat. Social Sci. Coun. (pres. 1977-81), Assn. for Advancement Sci. (pres. psychology sect. 1976-77), Athenaeum. Mem. Ch. Eng. Home: North Yorkshire, England. Died Sept. 10, 2005.

**SUMSION, JOHN WALBRIDGE,** information scientist; b. Gloucester, Eng., Aug. 16, 1928; s. Herbert Whitton and Alice Hartley (Garlichs) S.; m. Annette Dorothea Wilson (div. 1979); children: Bridget, Christopher, Michael, Kate; m. Hazel Mary Jones, 1979. BA in Modern History, Cambridge U., Eng., 1952, MA, 1981; MA in Econs., Yale U., 1953. Prodn. mgr. K Shoemakers, Kendal, Eng., 1954-62, dir., 1962-81; registrar Pub. Lending Right, Eng., 1981-91; dir. libr. and info. stats. unit Loughborough (Eng.) U., 1991-96, sr. fellow dept. info. scis., from 1996. Mem. Copyright Tribunal, Eng., 1990-93; non-exec. dir. TeleOrdering Ltd., Alton, Eng., 1992-94;mem. Libr. & Info. Svcs. Coun., Eng., 1992-95. Author: PLR in Practice, 1st edit., 1988, 2d edit., 1991; joint author: Perspectives of Public Library Use, 1995, Library Performance Indicators and Library Management tools, 1995; contbr. articles to profl. jours. Decorated Order Brit. Empire. Fellow Libr. Assn.; mem. Internat. Fedn. Libr. Assns. (hon. chmn. stats. sect. 1995-99). Liberal Democrat. Anglican. Avocations: singing, flute, walking. Home: Leicestershire, England. Died Feb. 21, 2003.

**SUN, JI WU,** energy economist, educator; b. Shanghai, Mar. 6, 1948; arrived in Finland, 1990; s. XinFu Sun and Xue AnMao; children: Jian, Jin, Maria. MSc, Elec. Power Rsch. Inst. China, Beijing, 1984; licentiate, Turku Sch. Econs., Finland, 1993, D, 1996. From lectr. to asst. prof. XinJiang Industry U., 1971-78; sr. fellow State Statis. Bur. China, Beijing, 1984-86, Youth Polit. Inst., Beijing, 1986-89, Turku Sch. Econs., from 1990. Contbr. articles to profl. jours. Avocation: reading. Home: Turku, Finland. Died Aug. 2006.

**SURACI, CHARLES XAVIER, JR.,** retired federal agency administrator, air transportation executive, consultant; b. Washington, Feb. 10, 1933; s. Charles Xavier and June Celcia (Hunter) Suraci; m. Florence Patricia De Mino, May 23, 1970. Grad., Widener U. (formerly Pa. Mil. Coll.), Chester, 1955, Nat. Acad. Broadcasting Sch., Washington, 1959; student, Columbia Union Coll., 1962-63, 72, Catholic U., 1969; grad. extension course, CAP Staff Coll., 1974; BA, Calif. Christian Coll., 1977, HHD (hon.), 1977; grad., USAF Inspectors Gen. Sch., Eglin AFB, Fla., 1982; also grad. numerous other govt. schs. and courses. Served with USAF, 1953-57; enlisted CAP, 1957, commd. 1st lt., 1961; advanced through ranks to Col. CAP USAF Aux, 1974; co-founder Wheaton-Silver Spring Cadet Squadron; comdr. Nat. Capital Wing, 1973-76; dep. chief of staff cadet activities Middle East region, 1977-79, dir. cadet tng., 1979-82, insp. gen., from 1982. With Henry Diamond Lab. U.S. Army, Adelphi, Md., from 1963, materials publs. asst. Harry Diamond Lab., 1963—68, later asst. to motor transp. officer, now supply specialist, logistics sect.; bd. dirs. Centro Tepeyac Crisis Pregnancy Ctr., Silver Springs, Md. Mem. youth com. YMCA, Silver Spring, 1962—69, mem. bd. mgmt., from 1967; bd. dirs. Am. Youth Com.; mem. Commn. on Children and Youth Bd., Montgomery County, Md., Montgomery County Juvenile Ct. Com., 1978—86; co-chmn. Right to Life com. KC-Rosensteel Coun.; bd. dirs. Pregnancy Aid Ctr., College Park, Md.; choir mem. Blessed Sacrament Cath. Ch., Washington. Recipient Leader and Svc. award, YMCA Silver Spring, 1968, 1969, CAP Meritorious Svc. award, Dept. Def., 1969, 1977, Cert. of Commendation, Pres. Richard Nixon, 1970, CAP Exceptional Svc. award, Congressman Lester Wolff of N.Y., 1972, award, Montgomery County C. of C., 1973, Commendation, Gov. of Tenn., 1975, Letter of Commendation, Washington Mayor Walter Washington, 1977, Outstanding Patriotic Civilian Svc. award, Dept. Def., 1977, Md. Vol. Cmty. honor award, Montgomery County, 1981, Vol. Activist award, 1984, George Washington honor medal, Valley Forge Freedom Found., 1995, Patrick Henry medal for Patriotic Achievement, Mil. Order of World Wars, 1995, Honor, Md. Ho. Dels., 1974, D.C. Govt., 1977, numerous AF and CAP ribbons and medals, Dept. of Army Spl. Act or Svc. award, Dept. of Army Superior Performance award, 1987, Cmty. Svc. award, Wheaton-Kensington News, Bethesda Chevy Chase Current, Montgomery County Press Assn., 1990, Outstanding Support Aviation Career Day Tuskegee Airmen and Commdg. Gen. of D.C., Air Nat. Guard, 1992, Spl. award for tng. over 1000 youth cadets in CAP in 31 yrs., State of Md., 1986, Plaque Name Displayed at U.S. Army-Harry Diamond Lab., Pro-Life award, KC-Rosensteel Coun., 1992, 1999—2002, Frank G. Brewer Meml. Aerospace award-CAP Mid. East Region HQ, 1984, 1991, 1992, CAP-USAF Aux. Meritorious Svc. award, Mid. East Region HQ, 1993, Cert. Appreciation Aerospace Edn. of Md., Air Force Assn., 1993—95, Exceptional Svc. award, USAF Aux., 1994—95, Sr. Officer of Yr. Mid East Region, USAF Aux.-CAP, 1998, Colonel Robinson Lifetime Leadership award, Nat. Capital Wing, 2001, Leadership award, Cen. East Region Air Force Assn., 2001, numerous others, 50th Yr. award, Blessed Sacrament Ch., 2007, Outstanding award, Air Force Assn. Chpt. Pres., 2011; named Air Man of Month, USAF, 1956, Grand Marshall Meml. Day Parade, Rockville, Md., 1971, Man of Yr. State of Md., Air Force Assn., 1993, Outstanding Mender, Thomas W. Anthony Chpt., AFA, 2009—11; nominee Pres.'s Vol. Action award, Pres. of U.S., 1988, 1991. Mem.: Md. Pvt. Industry Coun. (bd. dirs. Opportunity Skyway program), Md. Press. Assn. Montgomery County, Nat. Officers Assn., Mil. Order of World Wars (jr. vice comdr. Bethesda chpt. from 1996, Outstanding staff officer of the yr. 2005), Tuskegee Airmen Inc., Fed. Ret. Employees Assn., Army Aviation Assn., Navy League, Nat. Aerospace Assn., Air Force Assn. (v.p. aerospace edn. Thomas W. Anthony chpt. from 1996, pres. Thomas W. Anthony chpt. from 1998, bd. dirs., nat. liaison officer to Civil Air Patrol-Aux. USAF 2004, Medal of Merit 1990, Exceptional Svc. award 1991, Disting. Svc. as Inspector Gen. 1991, Exceptional Svc. award 1994, Commd. Officer of Yr. 1995, Spl. Cert. Appreciation 1996, Mem. Distinction award Thomas W. Anthony chpt. 2000—02, Cen. East Region Chpt. Pres. of Yr. for State of Md. 2002, named Outstanding Mem. 2004, Outstanding Pres. of the Thomas W. Anthony chpt. 2004, Thomas W. Anthony Chptr. pres. of the Yr. 2005, Pres. of Yr. Thomas Anthony chpt. 2006, pres. of Yr. Thomas W. Anthony Chpt., Ctrl. East Recon 2008, named Outstanding Pres. in Thomas W. Anthony chpt. 2011), Alumni Assn. Widener U., Andrews AFB Officers Club, KC (chmn. Pro-Life Father Rosensteel coun., Outstanding Leadership Pro-Life activities 1990—91, Outstanding Svc. award 1993—94, Honored Guest of Yr. 1996—97, Outstanding Cmty. award 2003, 2004, Achievement award of the Yr. 2005, Pro-Life award 2010, Pro-Life Plaque, Rosensteel Coun., Silver Spring 2011), Chester Lodge. Democrat. Achievements include 2 plaques in his name displayed at Columbia Union Coll., Takoma Park, Md., Widener U. (formerly Pa. Mil. Coll.), Chester. Died Nov. 23, 2011.

**SURER, PATRICK,** surgeon; b. Nantes, France, Sept. 9, 1938; s. Gaetan Surer and Marie-Andree Baugier; m. Jacqueline Gouray; 6 children. MD, Nantes U., France, 1970. Orthopedic qualification 1974. Clinic mgr. Nantes Hosp., 1970—73; orthopedic surgeon pvt. clinic, Chateaubriant, France, 1973—2000. Surg. cons. Ceraver Osteal SA, Surfix Techs. SA. Inventor, patentee principle of fixation for medical device in orthopedics, 1988. Lt. French Army. Mem.: SOO, SOFOOT. Roman Catholic. Avocations: boating, skiing, tennis. Home: Nantes, France. Died Aug. 2002.

**SURMATIS, JOSEPH D.,** retired chemist; b. Dickson City, Pa., Mar. 22, 1913; s. George and Constance (Mickulski) Surmatis; m. Geraldine Duff, Feb. 12, 1945; 1 child, Anthony. BS, Penn. State U., 1936, MS, 1937, PhD, 1942. Instr. chemistry Penn. State U., State Coll., Pa., 1940—42; cons., rsch. G.J. Esslen, Inc., Boston, 1942—44; sr. tech. fellow Hoffman-La Roche, Nutley, NJ, 1945—78; ret., 1978. Chmn. Internat. Symposium Carotinoid Chemistry, New Mex. State U., 1969, Internat. Symposium Cartenoid Chemistry, Cluj, Romania, 1972. Contbr. scientific papers over 20; referee (Jour. of Organic Chemistry), 1978. Fellow: Am. Assn. Advancement of Sci., Am. Inst. of Chemists; mem.: NY Acad. of Sci. Achievements include patents in field of indsl. synthesis including vitamins E, A, biotin, myxin and beta-carotene (over 100). Deceased.

**SUSA, CONRAD,** composer; b. Springdale, Pa., Apr. 26, 1935; BA cum laude, Carnegie Mellon U., 1957; studied composition with, Nikolai Lopatnikoff; MS, Juilliard Sch. Music., 1961. Composer-in-residence for city schs., Nashville, field dir. dept. edn., Lincoln Center, N.Y.C., staff pianist, Pitts. Symphony Orch.; composer-in-residence Old Globe Theatre, San Diego, from 1959; music dir. Am. Shakespeare Theatre Festival, 1969-71; field dir. Lincoln Center, 1967-71; engaged in theatre composition: works include Transformations (on texts of Anne Sexton's book), 1973, Eulogy (for string orch.), Love-in (ballet after Handel), Pastorale (string orch.), Serenade for a Christmas Night (chamber music), The Birds (Belloc text), A Lullaby Carol, 2 Marian Carols; 3 mystical carols, 2 rock carols (Peterson text); Black River (text by Richard Street and composer); opera, 1975, engaged in theatre conducting, 1975 (Gretchaninoff Composition prize, George Gershwin Meml. scholar). Recipient Benjamin award (2), Marion Fresche award; Ford Found. fellow; Nat Endowment Arts grantee, 1974-83 Died Nov. 21, 2013.

**SUSSER, MERVYN WILFRED,** epidemiologist, educator; b. Johannesburg, Sept. 26, 1921; came to U.S., 1965; s. Solomon and Ida Rose (Son) S.; m. Zena Athene Stein, Mar. 28, 1949; children: Ida, Ezra, Ruth. MB, BChir, U. Witwatersrand, Union of South Africa, 1950; diploma pub. health, London Conjoint Bd., 1960; DMS (hon.), U. Witwatersrand, 1993. Med. officer, then supt. Alexandra Health Centre and Univ. Clinic, Johannesburg, 1952-55; successively lectr., sr. lectr., reader, head dept. social and preventive medicine Manchester (Eng.) U., 1957-65; prof., chmn. divsn. epidemiology Columbia U. Sch. Public Health, NYC, 1966-78, Gertrude H. Sergievsky prof. epidemiology, dir. Sergievsky Ctr., 1977-91, Sergievsky prof. emeritus, spl. lectr., 1992—2014. Hon. prof. Nat. Sch. Public Health, Madrid; cons. WHO, 1962, 66-72, 79, 90, NIH, NAS. Author: (with W. Watson) Sociology in Medicine, 1962, 2d edit., 1971, (with W. Watson and K. Hopper), 3d edit., 1985, Community Psychiatry: Epidemiologic and Social Themes, 1968, Causal Thinking in the Health Sciences: Concepts and Strategies of Epidemiology, 1973, (with others) Famine and Human Development: Studies of the Dutch Hungerwinter 1944-45, 1975, (with D. Rush and Z. Stein) Diet in Pregnancy: A Randomized Controlled Trial of Nutritional Supplements, 1980, Epidemiology, Health and Society: Selected Essays, 1987, (with Jennie Kline and Zena Stein) Conception to Birth: Epidemiology of Prenatal Development, 1989; editor American Jour. Pub. Health, 1992-98; festschrift in his honor. Pres. Com. Health in Southern Africa, 1984-94. With South African Defence Force, 1940-45. Recipient Disting. Svc. award, Coll. Physicians & Surgeons, Columbia U., 1994, Jubilee medal, U. Witwatersrand, South Africa, Abraham Lilienfeld award, 1999; named Gaylord Anderson lectr., U. Minn. Sch. Public Health, 2007; Belding scholar, Assn. Aid Crippled Children, 1965—66, Guggenheim fellow, 1972. Fellow: APHA (Rema Lapouse lectr. 2005, John Snow award 1994, Maternal and Child Health Epidemiology Lifetime Achievement award 2005), N.Y. Acad. Medicine, American Epidemiol. Soc., Royal Coll. Physicians (Edinburgh), Faculty of Public Health Medicine of Royal Coll. Physicians U.K. (hon.), American Coll. Epidemiology (hon.); mem.: Physicians for Human Rights, Inst. Medicine (sr.), Soc. Pediat. Epidemiol. Rsch., Soc. Social Medicine U.K. (hon.), Soc. Epidemiol. Rsch., World Psychiat. Assn., Internat. Epidemiol. Assn. Home: Hastings On Hudson, NY. Died Aug. 14, 2014.

**SUSSMAN, DEBORAH EVELYN,** interior designer, small business owner; b. NYC, May 26, 1931; d. Irving and Ruth (Golomb) S.; m. Paul Prejza, June 28, 1972. Student, Bard Coll., 1948-50, DHL (hon.), 1998; student, Inst. Design, Chgo., 1950-53, Black Mountain Coll., 1950, Hochschule für Gestaltung Ulm, Germany, 1957-58. Art dir. Office of Charles and Ray Eames, Venice, Calif., 1953-57, 61-67; graphic designer Galeries Lafayette, Paris, 1959-60; prin. Deborah Sussman and Co., Santa Monica, Calif., 1968-80; founder, pres. Sussman-Prejza and Co., Inc., Santa Monica, Calif., 1980-90, Culver City, Calif., 1990—2014. Spkr., lectr. UCLA Sch. Arch., Archtl. League N.Y.C., Smithsonian Inst., Stanford Conf. on Design, Am. Inst. Graphic Arts Nat. Conf. at MIT, Design Mgmt. Inst. Conf., Mass.; spl. guest Internat. Design Conf., Aspen, Colo.; Fulbright lectr., India, 1976; spkr. NEA Adv. Coun., 1985, Internat. Coun. Shopping Ctrs., 1986, USIA Design in Am. seminar, Budapest, Hungary, 1988. One-woman shows include Visual Arts Mus. Sch. Visual Arts, N.Y.C., 1995; participant exhbn., Moscow, 1989, Walker Art Ctr., Mpls., 1989; mem. editl. adv. bd. Arts and Arch. Mag., 1981-85, Calif. Mag., Arch. Calif. Fulbright grantee Hochschule für Gestaltung Ulm, 1957-58; recipient award AIA Nat. Inst. Honors, 1985, 88, American Inst. Graphic Arts, Calif. Coun. AIA, Comms. Arts Soc., LA County Bd. Suprs., Vesta award Women's Bldg. LA, Golden Arrow award Soc. Environ. Graphic Designers, 2006. Fellow Soc. Environ. Graphic Design; mem. AIA (hon., Medal for XXIII Olympiad 2004), Am. Inst. Graphic Arts (bd. dirs. 1982-85, founder LA chpt., chmn. 1983-84, Legacy medal 2004), Am. Ctr. Design (hon.), LA Art Dirs. Club (bd. dirs., award), Alliance Graphique Internat., Archs., Designers, and Planners Social Responsibility, Calif. Women in Environ. Design (adv. d.), Trusteeship (affiliate Internat. Women's Forum, chmn.'s cir. Town Hall). Democrat. Jewish. Avocation: photography. Died Aug. 19, 2014.

**SUSSMAN, WENDY RODRIGUEZ,** artist, educator; b. NYC, June 3, 1949; BA, Empire State Coll., 1978; MFA, Bklyn. Coll., 1980. Lectr. Touro Coll., NYC, 1985-86, Pratt Inst., Bklyn., 1987-89; asst. prof. U. Calif., Berkeley, 1989-96, assoc. prof., 1996—2001. One-woman shows include Bowery Gallery, N.Y.C., 1982, 87, John Bergruen Gallery, San Francisco, 1992, D.P. Fong Gallery, San Jose, Calif., 1994, Platt Gallery U. Judaism, L.A., 1995, Jan Baum Gallery, L.A., 1996, The Jewish Mus., San Francisco, 1996; group shows include Bowery Gallery, 1980-88, Munson-Williams-Proctor Inst. Mus. Art, 1982, Reading (Pa.) Pub. Mus. and Art Gallery, 1983, Queens Mus., N.Y.C., 1983, Colby Coll. Mus. Art, Waterville, Maine, 1983, Butler Inst. Am. Art, Youngstown, Ohio, 1983, Bklyn. Coll., 1983, Am. Acad. Inst. Arts and Letters, N.Y.C., 1984, Am. Acad. in Rome, 1987, John Berggruen Gallery, San Francisco, 1992, San Francisco Arts Commn. Gallery, 1992, 94, D.P. Fong Gallery, 1994, Boulder Mus. Art, 1995, Gallery Paule Anglin, San Francisco, 1996, 98, Jan Baum Gallery, L.A., 1996, U. Calif. San Diego Art Gallery, 1997. Rome Prize fellow in painting Am. Acad. in Rome, 1986-87, Visual Arts fellow NEA, 1989, Guggenheim fellow, 1998; Pollock-Krasner grantee Pollock-Krasner Found., 1988; recipient Max and Sophie Adler award Jewish Mus., Judah Magners Mus., 1996. Died Mar. 29, 2001.

**SUTHERLAND, DIANA WESTLAKE,** visual artist; b. Martins Ferry, Ohio, Apr. 15, 1931; d. Melvin Jones and Dorothy Virginia (Pickens) Westlake; m. James Frederick Sutherland, Aug. 2, 1951; children: Laurie Giudice, Jan Hundley, Eve Curtis. Student, Carnegie Mellon U., Pitts., 1949-51. Sec. Minn. Region 2 Arts Coun., Bemidji, 1981-82. Recipient 24 awards including Revington Arthur Found. award Stamford (Conn.) Mus., 1996, Purchase award Sunrise Art Mus, Charleston, W.Va., 1975, Butler Inst. Am. Art, Youngstown, Ohio, 1973, Huntington (W.Va.) Mus. Art, 1972. Avocations: piano, organ, harpsichord, recorders. Died Sept. 8, 2002.

**SUTHERLAND, HAMILTON D'ARCY,** retired thoracic surgeon; b. Adelaide, SA, Australia, Dec. 12, 1913; s. Alan D'Arcy and Elsie Letitia Sutherland; m. Rosemary Gail Graetz, 1980; children: Andrew, Elizabeth, Peter. MBBS, U. Adelaide, Australia, 1937, MS, 1944. Ho. surgeon Royal Adelaide Hosp., Australia, 1938, surg. registrar, 1940, sr. surg. registrar, 1946—47, cardio-thoracic surgeon, 1951—77; cardiac surgeon Adelaide Children's Hosp., 1950—77, Royal Melbourne Children's Hosp., 1977—80; ret., 1980. Pres. Cardiac Soc. Australia and New Zealand, 1975. Surg. lt. comdr. Royal Australian Navy, 1940—45. Named commdr. Brit. Empire, 1980. Fellow: ACS (hon.), Royal Coll. Surgeons England, Royal Australasian Coll. Surgeons Melbourne (pres. 1978—79). Anglican. Avocation: bridge. Home: Beaumont, Australia. Died July 19, 2008.

**SUTTER, WILLIAM PAUL,** lawyer; b. Chgo., Jan. 15, 1924; s. Harry Blair and Elsie (Paul) S.; m. Helen Yvonne Stebbins (Winkie), Nov. 13, 1954; children: William Paul, Helen Blair Sutter. AB, Yale U., 1947; JD, U. Mich., 1950. Bar: Ill. 1950, Fla. 1977, U.S. Supreme Ct. 1981. Assoc. Hopkins & Sutter (and predecessors), Chgo., 1950-57, ptnr., 1957-89, of counsel, 1989—2001. Mem. Ill. Supreme Ct. Atty. Registration Commn., 1975-81 Contbr. articles on estate planning and taxation to profl. jours. Chmn. Winnetka Caucus Com., 1966-67; pres., trustee Lucille P. Markey Charitable Trust, 1983-98; precinct capt. New Trier Twp. (Ill.) Rep. party, 1960-68; asst. area chmn. New Trier Rep. Orgn., 1968-72; trustee Gads Hill Center, pres., 1962-70, chmn., 1971-80; trustee Northwestern Meml. Hosp., 1983-98, life trustee, 1998—; bd. dirs. Chgo. Hort. Soc., 1982-2005, life dir., 2005—; mem. dean's coun. Sch. Medicine, Yale U., 1991-97; bd. visitors Waisman Ctr., U. Wis., 1996-2002; corr. sec. Yale U. Class of 1945, 1990—2009. Served to 1st lt. AUS, 1943-46 Fellow Am. Bar Found., Am. Coll. Trust and Estate Counsel (bd. regents 1977-83, exec. com. 1981-83); mem. ABA (ho. dels. 1972-81, chmn. com. on income estates and trusts, taxation sect. 1973-75), Ill. Bar Assn. (bd. govs. 1964-75, pres. 1973-74), Chgo. Bar Assn. (chmn. probate practice com. 1963-64), Am. Law Inst., Internat. Acad. Estate and Trust Law, Am. Judicature Soc., Ill. LAWPAC (pres. 1977-83), Order of Coif, Phi Beta Kappa, Phi Delta Phi, Chi Psi, Indian Hill Club, Gulf Stream Golf Club, Country Club Fla., Ocean Club (Fla.) (bd. govs. 1993-99, sec. 1993-97, pres. 1997-99), Lawyers Club Chgo. Episcopalian. Home: Village Of Golf, Fla. Died Aug. 16, 2013.

**SUVAR, STIPE,** Yugoslav government official; b. Zagvozd, Croatia, Yugoslavia, Feb. 17, 1936; D in Law, Zagreb U., Croatia, 1958. Sec. Ideological-Polit. Commn., Croatian Communist Youth Cen. Com., 1959-61; head social dept. Agrarian Inst., 1961-65, dir., 1965-68; lectr., assoc. prof., prof. philosophy Zagreb U.; min. edn. and culture State of Croatia, 1974-82; former mem. Presidium Croatian League Communists Cen. Com.; dep. Nat. Assembly Croatia, from 1982; one of 3 Croatian reps. in Presidium, Yugoslav Community Party Cen. Com., 1986; pres. League Communists Yugoslavia, 1988-90; former mem. presidency Govt. of Yugoslavia, Belgrade, former v.p., 1990. Author several books on sociology and politics; editor-in-chief Studentski list, 1956-60, Nase teme (Our Topic), 1968-72; former chief and responsible editor Socijalizm. Died June 22, 2004.

**SUZUKI, ZENKO,** former prime minister of Japan; b. Yamada, Honshu, Japan, Jan. 11, 1911; m. Sachi Suzuki, 1939; children: Shun'ichi, Motoko, Kazue, Chikako. Degree in Edn., Fishery Tng. Inst., Ministry of Agr. & Forestry. Mem. Japanese Ho. Reps., from 1947, Socialist Party, 1947—49, Liberal Party, 1949—55; former mem. Liberal Dem. Party, chmn. exec. council, 1968—82, pres., 1982, minister posts and telecom., 1960; minister health & welfare, 1965—67; minister agr. & forestry, 1976—77; prime minister Japan, 1980—82. Died July 19, 2004.

**SWAIN, MARILYN J.,** nursing administrator, educator; b. Elgin, Ill., June 19, 1930; d. Leslie Hayes and Vivian Grace (Eddy) S.; div.; children: Mary Leslie Naker, Vicki Lynn Edwards. Diploma, Ill. Masonic Med. Ctr., Chgo., 1951; student, Lying-In Hosp., Chgo. Cert. rehab. nurse, intravenous therapist. In-svc. dir. Holy Family Hosp., Des Plaines, Ill.; DON Brookwood Nursing Home, Des Plaines; nurse State of Ill., Elgin. Vol. Sherman Hosp. Material Mgmt./Dialysis Unit Nat. Kidney Found., Elgin; vol., instr. ARC; active Girl Scouts Am. Mem. ANA. Died Apr. 21, 1991.

**SWAMINATHAN, JAGDISH,** artist; b. June 21, 1928; m. Bhavani Swaminathan, 1955; 2 children. Student, Delhi Poly., Acad. Fine Arts, Warsaw. Freedom fighter, trade unionist, journalist, writer children's books; mem. Delhi State-Com. Congress Socialist Party and Edn.; mem. weekly orgn. Mazdoor Awaz; sr. art tchr. Cambridge Sch., New Delhi; founder-mem. Group 1890; avant-garde group India artists. One-man shows include, New Delhi, 1962—66, Bombay, 1966, exhibited in group shows, Warsaw, 1961, Saigon, 1963, Tokyo Biennale, 1965, Seven Indian Painters, London, 1967; contbr. articles to profl. jours. Fellow Jawaharlal Nehru rsch. fellowship. Mem.: Delhi Slipi Chakra, Internat. Assn. Arts. Died Apr. 25, 1994.

**SWANSON, DONALD F.,** economics and business administration educator; b. Galesburg, Ill., June 9, 1928; s. Otto B. and Mary L. (Keegan) S.; m. Shirley Sheets, June 21, 1985; children: Donald E., David F., Marcia K., Douglas G. BA, Knox Coll., 1950; MA, U. Fla., 1956, PhD, 1960. Assoc. prof. econs. U. S.C., Columbia, 1959-62, 65-69; prof. econs. and bus. adminstrn. Ind. U. S.E., New Albany, from 1969. Author: The Orgins of Hamilton's Fiscal Policies, 1963; contbr. articles to profl. jours. Cpl. U.S. Army, 1950-52. Mem. Phi Beta Kappa. Home: New Albany, Ind. Died Aug. 1992.

**SWARZ, SAHL,** sculptor; b. NYC, May 4, 1912; s. Samuel and Ida (Fass) S.; m. Naoco Kumasaka, May 1978. Student, Clay Club, NYC, 1928-34, Art Students League, 1930-31. Assoc. dir. Clay Club (now Sculpture Center), 1938-54; creative sculpture Italy, 1951-63; residence Am. Acad., Rome, 1955-57; lectr. sculpture Columbia U., NYC, 1966-68, asst. prof., 1969-78. Vis. assoc. prof. Brandies U., 1964; instr. Pratt Inst., Bklyn., 1964; instr. New Sch. for Social Rsch., 1965, 66; vis. lectr. art U. Wis., 1966; trustee Mus. Contemporary Sculpture, Tokyo; lectr. art dept. Nippon U., Tokyo, 1997. Author, illustrator: Blueprint for the Future of American Sculpture, 1943, also monograph.; one man exhbn. Sculpture Ctr., 1954, 57, 60, 62, 66, 71, 74, 78, Art Alliance, Phila., 1958, Fairweather-Hardin Gallery, Chgo., 1963, Brandeis U., Waltham, Mass., 1964, (retrospective exhbn.) Fair Lawn (NJ) Pub. Library, 1977, Saikaya Gallery, Fujisawa, Japan, 1983, Mus. Contemporary Sculpture, Tokyo, 1985, Shonan Gallery, Fujisawa, Japan, 1985, 90, 93, 2001 (retrospective exhbn., 2004) Toni de Rossi Gallery, Verona, Italy, 1983, 87, 91, Takashimaya Gallery, Yokohama, Japan, 1984, Atagoyama Gallery, Tokyo, 1988, 91, 94, 99, 1st exhibition of painting Toni de Rossi Gallery, Verona, Italy, 1992, 96, Move Gallery Chigasaki, Japan, 1993; group shows include Fairmont Park Internat., Phila., 1948, Whitney Mus. Am. Art, 1948, 58, 60, 62, 64, Pa. Acad., 1948, 52, 54, 57, 60, 62, 66, Bklyn Mus., 1935, Detroit Inst. Fine Arts, 1957, San Francisco Mus., 1955, U. Ill., 1960, 62, others; represented in permanent collections Norfolk (Va.) Mus., Whitney Mus. Am. Art, Ball State Tchr. Coll., Williams Coll. Mus., Ford Found., Mpl. Inst. Fine Arts, Va. Mus. Fine Arts, Richmond, Newark Mus., NJ State Mus. at Trenton, Vatican Mus. Collection Modern Religious Art, Rose Art Mus., Brandeis U., Stamford (Conn.) Mus., Columbia U., Tokyo Mus. Contemporary Sculpture, others; bronze group The Guardian at Brookgreen (SC), Gardens Mus.; terra cotta wall sculpture, Linden, (NJ), Post Office, sculptural designs, Fed. Courthouse, Statesville, NC; equestrian monument Gen. Bidwell, Buffalo; fountain commn., Spruce Run State Park, NJ; mall sculpture, Pittsfield, Mass.; monument to Demeter in stainless steel, Fujisawa, Japan; subject of biography: Fifty Years of Sculpture by Sahl Swarz. Chmn. sculpture panel N.J. Coun. on Arts. With AUS, 1941-45. Grantee Am. Acad. Arts and Letters, 1955; Guggenheim fellow, 1955, 58 *The essence of creativity is in the searching after the form. Search leads to revelation, understanding, knowledge. Realization of one's ignorance is the first step to the attainment of wisdom. A wise man makes a work of art out of life itself.* Died Oct. 24, 2004.

**SWEET, WILLIAM BECK,** holding company executive; b. Enid, Okla., Jan. 26, 1909; arrived in Brazil, 1942; s. Ross Atwood and Alta Bell (Beck) S.; m. Astri Annmari

Sjöstedt, Jan. 2, 1943 (div. 1976); children: Eric, Astri, Carl; m. Maria Mellin, 1977. BBA, U. Wash., 1930; MBA, Harvard Bus. Sch., 1932. Asst. to pres. RFC Mortgage Co., Washington, 1932-35; with Losuma Corp., NYC, 1935-38; with mkt. rsch. dept. U.S. Steel Corp., Pitts., 1938-41; pres., organizer Liquid Carbonic of Brasil, Argenting, Uruguay, Spain, 1945-66; organizer, owner various cos., from 1966; founder Rosalta Ltd., Rio de Janeiro, from 1970. Grad. Army Indsl. Coll.; chmn. army steel com. of combined joint chiefs of staff U.S. Army, 1940—42, 1942—45; mem. Brazil U.S. Mil. Commn., Rio de Janeiro. Lt. col. U.S. Army, 1941-45. Mem. U.S. C. of C. Brasil, Rio de Janeiro (permanent dir. 1952—, pres. 1952), Rio de Janeiro Country Club, Am. Club, Harvard Club Brazil, Harvard Club N.Y.C. Avocations: photography, travel, fishing. Home: Rio de Janeiro, Brazil. Died Jan. 7, 2009.

**SWEETING, ANTHONY EDWARD,** retired history professor; b. Newport, Gwent, United Kingdom, Apr. 20, 1938; s. Richard Edward and Hilda Annie (Horner) Sweeting; m. Sansan Teh-chih Ching, July 23, 1975; children: Juliette Nicholson, Jonathan Anthony, Janine Tanya Gibbs, Justinian Caradoc Renald Ching, Jacinta Louise Rhiannon Read. BA, Oxford U., Eng., 1959, MA, 1964; postgrad. cert. edn. with distinction, London U., 1962; PhD, U. Hong Kong, 1989. Asst. master Croesyceiliog Grammar Sch., Cwmbran, Gwent, England, 1962—64; govt. edn. office M.P. Shah Ctrl. HS, Thika, Central Province, Kenya, 1964—66, Thika HS, Kenya, 1966—69; lectr. dept. edn. U. Hong Kong, Spl. Adminstrv. Region, 1969—79, sr. lectr. dept. curriculum studies, 1979—91, prof. dept. curriculum studies, 1991—98, hon. rsch. fellow Ctr. Asian Studies, from 1998, hon. prof. history dept., from 1998. Founding pres., exec. com. mem. Hong Kong History Soc., 1971—81; chmn. history co-ordinating com. Hong Kong Examinations Authority, 1981—91, chmn. history moderation com., 1982—2000; exec. com. mem. Comparative Edn. Rsch. Coun., Hong Kong, 1998—2005. Author: Education in Hong Kong, Pre-1841 to 1941: Fact and Opinion, 1990, A Phoenix Transformed: the Reconstruction of Education in Postwar Hong Kong, 1993, Education in Hong Kong, 1941 to 2001: Visions and Revisions, 2004; co-editor (with Paul Morris): Education and Development in East Asia, 1995; actor: (radio play) Dragon Island, 1996, (play for voices) Under Milk Wood, 1997; composer (and singer): (popular song) Are You the One?; contributing poet (poems) Poetry Reading, Hong Kong Arts Festival, 1977; contbr. chapters to books, articles to profl. jours. Coord., vice-chmn. Edn. Action Group, 1973—75; hon. adviser Hong Kong History Mus., 1995—2001, Coun. Early Childhood Edn. and Svcs., Hong Kong, from 1990; exec. com. mem. Educators' Social Action Coun., Hong Kong, 1973—75. Scholar Meyricke Exhbn. in Modern History, Jesus Coll., Oxford U., 1956—59; Levehulme scholar in econs., London Sch. Econs., U. London, 1956, State scholar, Govt. UK, 1956—59, Rsch. grantee, Edn. and Manpower Br., Hong Kong Govt. Secretariat, 1991—95, Conf. and Rsch. Grants Com., U. Hong Kong, 1996—98. Mem.: Rsch. in Comparative and Internat. Edn. (mem. editl. bd. from 2005), Comparative Edn. Rsch. Coun. (assoc. editor from 2002). Achievements include research in education policy making in Hong Kong, 1955-1991; effects of the medium of instruction on the achievement of form 2 students in Hong Kong secondary schools; virtual architecture of time travel: pilot study of two buildings significant in the history of education in Hong Kong; production of curriculum materials for the teaching of local history in Hong Kong; effects of the medium of instruction on the learning of history at secondary forms 1 - 3 levels; effects of the medium of instruction on the achievement of form 2 students in Hong Kong secondary schools. Avocations: music, literature, art, computers, sports. Home: Hong Kong, Hong Kong. Died July 2008.

**SWINEFORD, EDWIN JOSEPH,** adult education educator; b. Thomasville, Colo., Mar. 15, 1911; s. Jay Howard and Nellie Marshall Swineford; m. Starene McCanless, June 14, 1938 (dec. July 1961); m. Evangeline Kelly, Aug. 2, 1969; children: Kriss Ray, Douglas William. AB, Fresno State Coll., 1936; MA, U. Calif., Berkeley, 1939; EdD, U. Va., 1954. Faculty mem. U. Va., Coll. William and Mary, Lynchburg Coll., U. Calif., Santa Barbara; prof. emeritus Calif. State U., Fresno. Self-pub. Kilroy Was There Press. Author: Wits of War, 1988, Ridiculous History of World War II, 1994, Hitler and National Socialism, 1996. Sgt. U.S. Army, 1943-46, ETO. Home: Fresno, Calif. Died 2001.

**SWING, M(ARIE) JOAN,** elementary school educator; b. Lansing, Mich., Nov. 24, 1930; d. Michael John and Marie Pauline (Nemeth) Hynes; m. Herbert Ralston Swing, Jr., June 7, 1952; children: Sandra Lynne, Michael Daniel. BA in Elem. Edn., Wittenburg U., 1966; MA in Reading, U. Md., 1970; EdD in Reading, U. No. Colo., 1978. Cert. B-type teaching, reading K-12, D-type adminstrv. Tchr. Elem. Schs., Ohio, Md., 1962—71, Air Acad. Jr. High Sch., Colo. Springs, Colo., 1971—74; reading coord. Air Acad. Sch. Dist., Colo. Springs, from 1974; chpt. I coord.; cons.; lectr. lang. arts K-12. Author: The Family that Reads Together Succeeds Together, 1981; co-author: Grooving with Reading Games, 1976, What Do I Do Next Teacher?, 1978. Mem.: Internat. Reading Assn., Delta Kappa Gamma, Phi Delta Kappa. Republican. Mem. Christian Ch. Home: Colorado Springs, Colo. Died Mar. 31, 1994.

**SWOPE, WILLIAM RICHARDS,** retail executive; b. Washington, Oct. 17, 1920; s. King and Mary Margaret (Richards) S.; m. Bobbie Wylie Stringfellow, June 17, 1944 (div. Sept. 1993); children: Robert Cromwell, William Richards Jr.; m. Dorothy S. Taylor, Feb. 3, 1994. AB, U. Ky., 1941; LLB, Harvard U., 1947. Bar: Ky. 1947. V.p., sales mgr. Stringfellow Lumber Co., Inc., Birmingham, Ala., 1951—58; pres., owner Swope Co., Inc., Birmingham, 1958—98. Bd. deacons Ind. Presbyn. Ch., Birmingham, 1953—56, 1961—64, 1971—74. Maj. US Army, 1942—45. Mem.: Lincoln's Inn Soc., Nat. Fedn. Ind. Bus., N.Am. Wholesale Lubmer Assn., ABA, Idle Hour Country Club (Lexington), Lions (pres. 1957—58), The Club, Birmingham Country Club, Ph Delta Theta, SAR, First Families Va., Ams. Royal Descent, Order of the Crown. Republican. Presbyterian. Died Aug. 25, 1998.

**SYKES, ALFRED GEOFFREY,** chemist, educator; b. Huddersfield, Jan. 12, 1934; s. Alfred H. and Edith A. Wortley S.; m. Elizabeth Blakey; 3 children. PhD, U. Manchester, 1958, DSc, 1973; DSc (hon.), Free State U., South Africa, 2003. Postdoctoral fellow Princeton U., NJ, 1958—59, U. Adelaide, 1959—60; lectr. U. Leeds, England, 1961—70, reader, 1970—80; prof. inorganic chemistry U. Newcastle-upon-Tyne, 1980—99, prof. emeritus, from 1999. Panel mem. SERC Inorganic Chem., 1980-83, EPSRC/BBSRC com., writing panels; vis. prof. Argonne Nat. Labs., 1968, Heidelberg U., 1975, Northwestern U., 1978, U. Berne, 1981, U. Sydney, 1984, U. Kuwait, 1989, U. Adelaide, 1992, U. Melbourne, 1992, Meml. U. Nfld., 1995, U. West Indies, 1997, U. Lausanne, 1998, U. South Africa, 1999, U. La Laguna, Spain, 2000, City U. Hong Kong, 2001, 2002, Danish Tech. U., 2002. Author: Kinetics of Inorganic Reactions, 1964; editor: Advanced Inorganic Chemistry, Vols. 32-53; contbr. over 470 articles to chemistry jours. Recipient Tilden medal Royal Soc. Chem., 1984; fellow Japan Soc. Phys. Sci., 1984 Fellow Royal Soc. Avocations: travel, classical music, sports, birdwatching. Home: Newcastle upon Tyne, England. Died July 10, 2007.

**SYMON, KEITH RANDOLPH,** physics professor, consultant; b. Ft. Wayne, Ind., Mar. 25, 1920; s. James Jefferson Keith Symon and Claribel Crego; m. Mary Louise Reinhardt, July 3, 1943; children: Judith Elizabeth, Keith Joseph, James Randolph, Rowena Louise. BSc, Harvard Coll., 1942; MA, Harvard U., 1943, PhD, 1948. Scientist Naval Rsch. Lab., Washington, 1943—46; instr. to assoc. prof. Wayne State U., Detroit, 1947—55; asst. prof. to prof. U. Wis., Madison, 1955—89, prof. emeritus, from 1989. Tech. dir. Midwestern Universities Rsch. Assn., Madison, Wis., 1956—67; acting dir. acad. computing ctr. U. Wis., 1982—83, acting dir. synchrotron radiation ctr., 1983—85. Author: (books) Mechanics, 1953, 1960, 1971; contbr. Handbook of Accelerator Physics and Engring., 1999, articles Ency. Brittannica, 1965, to profl. jours.; author: Innovation Was Not Enough A History of the Midwestern Universities Research Association (MURA), 2010. Scoutmaster Boy Scouts, Madison, Wis.; mem. bd. Friends of the Libr., Spring Green, Wis., 1993—2002, Spring Green Lit. Festival, 1997—2005, pres., 2000—01. With USNR, 1944—51. Recipient Particle Accelerator Sci. and Tech. award, IEEE, 2003, Robert R. Wilson prize, Am. Physical Soc., 2005; fellow Ford Found., Geneva, 1962—63. Fellow: Am. Phys. Soc. (R.R. Wilson prize 2005), Am. Assn. Advancement of Sci.; mem.: Am. Assn. of Physics Tchrs. Achievements include invention of fixed field alternating gradient accelerators, distbn. pushing method numerical simulation of plasmas. Avocations: skiing, whitewater canoeing, wilderness camping. Home: Spring Green, Wis. Died Dec. 16, 2013.

**SYMONETTE, LYS,** foundation executive, musician, writer; b. Mainz, Germany, Dec. 21, 1920; came to U.S., 1936; d. Max Weinschenk and Gertrude (Metzger) Honheisser; m. Randolph Symonette, Sept. 1, 1949; 1 child, Victor. Student, Curtis Inst., Phila., 1937-39. Piano accompanist to internat. singers, from 1940. Musical asst. to Kurt Weill and L. Lenya, 1945-81; tchr. Curtis Inst., Phila., 1976—; musical exec., v.p. Kurt Weill Found., N.Y.C., 1981—. Translator operas from English to German and German to English, 1945—; co-editor Speak Low, Family Letters, 1996. Mem. Am. Fedn. Musicians, Alumni Assn. Curtis Inst. Music. Deceased.

**SYMONS, MARTYN CHRISTIAN,** chemistry educator; b. Suffolk, Eng., Nov. 12, 1925; s. Stephen White and Marjorie (Lebraseur) S.; m. Janice Olive O'Connor, Jan. 12, 1970 (dec. 1995); children: Rebecca, Richard; ptnr. Irene White, 1998. BS, Battersea Poly., London, 1946, PhD, 1953, DSc, 1960. Lectr. Battersea Poly., 1948-53, Southampton (Eng.) U., 1953-60; prof. phys. chemistry Leicester (Eng.) U., 1960-88, rsch. prof. chemistry, 1988-93; vis. rsch. prof. chemistry DeMontfort U., from 1993, Nottingham Trent U., from 1997; vis. prof. biol. chemistry U. Greenwich, from 1997. Cancer Rsch. Campaign sr. fellow, Leicester, 1988-93; vis. prof. biol. chemistry U. Essex, 1997—, chemistry St. Bartholomew Med. Sch., London, 1997—. Author: Structure of Inorganic Radicals, 1967, Chemical Aspects of Electron Spin Resonance Spectroscopy, 1978, Techniques in Free Radical Research, 1991, Iron and Free Radicals: Chemistry, Biology and Medicine. Fellow Royal Soc., Royal Soc. of Chemistry (Brucker lectr. 1986, R.A. Robinson lectr. 1987), Am. Chem. Soc., Royal Soc. Arts. Avocations: watercolor painting, piano. Died Jan. 28, 2002.

**SYNAK, BRUNON,** sociologist, researcher, educator; b. Podjazy, Gdansk, Poland, Oct. 23, 1943; s. Ambrozy and Helena (Kotlowska) S.; m. Jadwiga Pior, Aug. 1, 1968; 1 child, Xymena. MA, U. Gdansk, 1969, Habil, 1983; PhD, U. Warsaw, 1973. Asst. prof. U. Gdansk, 1973-82, assoc. prof., 1982-90, prof., 1990—2013, v.p., 1984-85, 90-96, dep. dir. Inst. Philosophy and Sociology, 1985-89. Mem. exec. com. Kashubian Inst. Author: Migration and Adaptation of the Elderly to New Environment, 1982, Early Retirement, 1987; co-author: Voluntary Sector in a Changing Society. A Polish-American Dialogue, 1996; editor: Ethnic Identities of European Minorities, Theories and Case Studies, 1995; co-editor: Post-Communist Poland, 1994. Mem. adv. bd. Pres. of Poland, 1993-95; chmn. sci. commn. Com. for Celebration of 1000th Anniversary of Gdansk Decorated Silver Cross, Pres. of Poland, 1987, Golden Cross, 1992; Medal of Edn. Ministry of Edn., 1995. Mem. Polish Assn. Gerontology (v.p. 1985-89), Polish Acad. Scis., Internat. Sociol. Assn., Internat. Assn. Gerontology, Kashubian Folk Unv. Coun. Roman Catholic. Avocations: skiing, swimming, theater. Home: Gdańsk, Poland. Died Dec. 18, 2013.

**SYTKO, VLADIMIR,** physicist, educator, researcher; b. Grodno, Belarus, Oct. 11, 1951; s. Vladimir Alexander and Alexandra Ivan (Rudenya) S.; m. Olga Yakov Yunakova, June 16, 1990; m. Natalia Vladimir Chashchina, July 6, 1974 (div. Jan. 1988); 1 child, Andrew. DS in physics, Gomel (Belarus) State U., 1974. Rschr. Belarus State U., Minsk, 1974-77, Gomel State U., 1977-87, prof., from 1987, chief metrologist, from 1997, mem. sci. degree coun., from 1995. Mem. Belarus Metrological Acad., Minsk, 1994-97, academician, 1998—. Author: Theoretical Metrology, 1997, Photonics of Hexavalent Uranium Compounds, 2000; contbr. articles to profl. jours; patentee in field. Recipient Testimonial award World Exhbn. of Achievements of Young Inventors, 1985. Mem. Belarussian Engring. Acad. Minsk (corr. mem.). Russian Orthodox. Avocations: fishing, travel. Home: Gomel, Belarus. Died Apr. 20, 2006.

**SZABO, MAGDA (MRS. TIBOR SZOBOTKA),** author; b. Debrecen, Hungary, Oct. 5, 1917; d. Alexis and Lenke (Jablonczay) Szabo; m. Tibor Szobotka, June 5, 1948. D. Phil. in Latin Philology, Debrecen U. Author numerous novels, short stories, dramas, others, trans. into 33 langs.; novels include: Fresko, 1958, The Fawn, 1959, Island-Blue, 1959, Night of the Pig-Killing, 1960, Pilate, 1963, The Danaid, 1964, Genesis I, 22, 1967, Kathlin-Street, 1969, Lala the Fairy, 1965, Old Well, 1970, Old-Fashioned Story, 1977, The Battle, 1982, The Onlookers, 1974, The Door, 1987, Noises, 1957, Outside of the Circle, 1985, Meranian Boy, 1981, The Battle, 1981, King Bella, 1983, On the Heights of Age, 1987, The Wednesday of the Cats, 1989, The Moment, 1990, (essays) The Apathy of the Semigods, 1992, The Logic of the Butterflies, 1996. Recipient József Attila prize, 1959, 72, Kossuth prize, 1978, Getzs Corp. prize, 1992, Prix Femina award, 2003 Mem. Acad. Europienne (Beaux arts sect.), Acad. Scéchenyi of Lit. and Arts in Hungary, Internat. Pen Club. Home: Budapest, Hungary. Died Nov. 19, 2007.

**SZABOLCS, ISTVAN,** soil science educator; b. Turkeve, Hungary, Feb. 23, 1924; s. Arpad Szabolcs and Iren Lowinger; m. Katalin Darab, 1995. PhD, U. Debrecen, Hungary, 1948; CS, Acad. of Agr., Moscow, 1953; DS, Hungarian Acad. Sci., Budapest, 1959. Dep. dir. Rsch. Inst. of Irrigation and Amelioration, Szarvas, Hungary, 1953-54, Rsch. Inst. for Soil Sci. and Agr. Chemistry/RISSAC of HAS, Budapest, 1954-59; dir. RISSAC, Budapest, 1959-80, sr. soil sci. profl., from 1980. Chmn. Subcommn. on Salt Affected Soils of ISSS, Budapest, 1964-82; dep. sec. gen. Internat. Soc. of Soil Sci., Budapest, 1974-90. Editor-in-chief: Internat. Scientific Ctr. of Fertilizers, Agrokemia es Talajtan, Budapest, 1961—; author: (book) Salt Affected Soils in Europe, 1974, others; contbr. articles to profl. jours. Recipient Tessedik Gold medal Hungarian Agronomy Soc., 1978, award of Hungarian Union of Scientific and Technol. Socs., 1979, Treitz medal Hungarian Soil Sci. Soc. Mem. Internat. Soc. of Soil Sci. (hon.). Home: Budapest, Hungary. Died 1997.

**SZAJNA, JOZEF,** painter, stage designer, theater director; b. Rzeszow, Poland, Mar. 13, 1922; s. Julian and Karolina S.; m. Bozena Sieroslawska, July 19, 1953; 1 child, Lukasz. Diploma graphics, Acad. Fine Arts, Cracow, Poland, 1952, diploma stage designing, 1953. Mem. faculty Acad. Fine Arts, Cracow, 1954-65, prof. scene-designing Warsaw, Poland, from 1972. Mgr., supr., dir., stage designer Nowa Huta (Poland) Theatre, 1955-66; stage dir. Teatr Stary, Cracow, 1966-70; mgr., theatre dir., designer Studio Teatr Galeria, Warsaw. Scenographer: Princess of Turandot, 1956, Akropolis, 1962, Macbeth, 1970; dir. plays: The Empty Field, 1965, The Bath House, 1968; author's performances: Faust, 1971, Replika I, 1971, Witkacy, 1972, Replika II, 1972, Replika III, 1973, Gulgutiera, 1973, Dante, 1974, Cervantes, 1976, Majakowski, 1978, The Death on the Pear-Tree, 1978, Dante Alive, 1981, Dante Contemporary, 1985, Replika VII, 1986, Dante, 1992, Earth, 1993, Trace, 1993, Trace II, 1993, vida Y Muerte Del Poeta Cervantes, 1993, The Rest's, 1995, Deballage, 1997; numerous one-man and group exhbns. include Venice XXXV Biennial, 1970, Prague Quadrennial (gold medal), 1971, Warsaw (1st prize and gold medal), 1972, Munich (Silver medal), 1974, São Paulo Bienniale, 1979, 89, Berlin, 1980, 88, Moscow, 1987, Paris, 1987, Venice Biennale, 1990, Warsaw, Poznan, 1992, Gdansnk, 1992, Internat. Triennale, Majdanek, 1994, Auschwitz, Frankfurt A/M, Düsseldorf, Bochum, Warsaw, Weimar-Buchenwald, 1995, Opole, Weimar-Buchenwald, Kalisz, 1996, Rzeszow, Warszawa, Graz, Oronsko, 1997, Szajina Galéria, Rieszow, 1997, Szczecin-Zamek, 1998, Wroclaw Nat. Mus., 1998, Osaka Nat. Mus., 1998, Polish Kultur Inst., Budapest, 1999, Polish Kultur Inst., Rome, 2000, Milan Mus. Permanente, 2000; prin. works include European Art Banner Italian Accademia d'Europa, Statue of Victory, Centro Studi E Richerche Delle Nazioni in Salsmaggiore, 1984, numerous others. Held prisoner concentration camps, Oswiecim and Buchenwald. Decorated knight and comdr. Cross of Order of Polonia Restituta, also comdr. Cross with star of Polonia Restituta, Big Cross of Polonia Restituta; recipient Polish Reviewers award, 1957; Nowa Huta Artistic award, 1959; Minister of Culture and Arts (Poland) award, 1962, 71, 79; City of Cracow award, 1971; Gold medal Accademia Italia delle Arti e del Lavoro, 1981, Order Banner of Labour 1st Class, 1985, Medal Meritorious for Nat. Culture, 1986; Gold Centaur award Accademia Italia delle Arti del Lavoro, 1981, Oscar d'Italia '85 Accademia Italia, Artistic award Warsaw, 1986, Gold Mask award Bielsko Biala, 1994, Alfred Jurzykowski Found. award, 1995, Replika VI award Internat. Que. Theatre

Festival, 1986, Internat. award Golden Lion, 2000. Mem. Internat. Assn. Soc. Européene de Culture, Art-AIAP (UNESCO) (hon. counsellor 1979 for Leonardo da Vinci world award - Mex.), Internat. Coun. Auschwitz-Birkenau. Home: Warsaw, Poland. Died June 24, 2008.

**SZEEMANN, HARALD ETIENNE,** curator; b. Bern, Switzerland, June 11, 1933; s. Etienne E. and Julia E. (Kambly) S.; m. Françoise Paule Bonnefoy, 1958 (div. 1976); children: Jérôme Patrice, Valérie Claude; m. Ingeborg Lüscher, June 30, 1992; 1 child, Una Alia. Dr.Phil., U. Bern, 1960. Dir. Kunsthalle, Bern, 1961-69, Documenta, Kassel, Germany, 1970-72, Mus. of Obsessions; freelance curator Kunsthaus, Zürich, Switzerland. Author: (with Jean-Christophe Ammann) Von Hodler zur Anti-Form, 1970, Bachelor Machines, 1975, Monte Verità, 1978 (prize 1978), Museum der Obsessionen, 1981, Der Hang zum Gesamtkunstwerk, 1983, Individuelle Mythologien, 1985, Visionäre Schweiz, 1991, Zeitlos auf Zeit, 1994; translator: Voglio fare subito un libro (Mario Merz) 1985, Texte, Interviews 1970-1989 (Richard Serra) 1990. Recipient Literary prize State of Bern, 1970, Premio Lago Maggiore award, 1978, Art Cologne prize, 1989. Home: Tegna, Switzerland. Died Feb. 18, 2005.

**SZENTIVANYI, BÉLA ANDREW,** civil engineer; b. Budapest, Hungary, June 19, 1948; s. Béla Szentivany and Helen Wanda Doroghy. MSCE, Tech. U. Budapest, 1971, postgrad. in engring. math., 1972—74; Dr.Sci.Tech., Tech. U. Gdansk, Poland, 1991; PhD, Hungary, 1992. Asst. prof. civil engring. mechanics Tech. U. Budapest, 1971—78, prof. mechanics, 1988—93; rsch. fellow in applied mechanics Hungarian Acad. Scis., Budapest, Hungary, 1978—93, sr. rsch. assoc. in tech. mechanics, from 1993. Vis. asst. prof. Tech. U. Cracow, Poland, 1975; expert Ministry of Bldg. Affairs, Budapest, 1988—98. Mem. Hungarian Trade Union Workers in Highest Edns., 1971—96. Mem.: AAAS, Scandinvavian Simulation Soc., Assn. SIMULA Users, Computer Sci. Soc. Roman Catholic. Avocations: travel, languages, reading, swimming. Home: Budapest, Hungary. Deceased.

**SZOKA, EDMUND CASIMIR CARDINAL,** cardinal, archbishop emeritus; b. Grand Rapids, Mich., Sept. 14, 1927; s. Casimir and Mary (Wolgat) Szoka. BA, Sacred Heart Sem., 1950; JCB, Pontifical Lateran U., 1958, JCL, 1959. Ordained priest of Marquette, Mich., 1954, matrimonial tribunal, defender of bond, 1960—71, asst. chancellor, 1962—69, chancellor Mich., 1970—71; asst. pastor Saint Francis Parish, Manistique, Mich., 1954—55; sec. to Bishop Noa Marquette, 1955—57, 1959—62; chaplain Saint Mary's Hosp., Marquette, 1955—62, Air base of Sawiyer, 1956; parish priest Saint Pius X Church, Ishpeming, Mich., 1962—63, Saint Christopher Church, Marquette, 1963—71; honorary prelate of His Holiness, 1963; bishop of Gaylord, Mich., 1971—81, ordained Mich., 1971; archbishop of Detroit, 1981—90, archbishop emeritus, from 1990; elevated to cardinal, 1988; cardinal-priest of Santi Andrea e Gregorio al Monte Celio (Saints Andrew and Gregory at Monte Celio), 1988—2014; pres. Prefecture of Economic Affairs of the Holy See, Rome, 1990—97, Pontifical Commn. for Vatican City State, 1997—2006, pres. emeritus, 2006—14; pres. Governatorate of Vatican City State, 2001—06, pres. emeritus, 2006—14. Secretary-treasurer Episcopal Conference of Mich., Lansing, 1972—77, pres. bd. dirs.; pres. Nat. Conf. Cath. Bishops, 1972—77, treas., adminstrv. bd. and adminstrv. com., budget and financial com., 1981—84; pres. administration coun. Provincial Sem. of Saint John, Plymouth, 1981, Provincial Sem. of Saints Cyril and Methodius, Orchard Lake, 1981; mem. exec. com. Catholic U., pres. com. for university relations; administrator Nat. Sanctuary of the Immaculate Conception; mem. Congregation for Clergy, Congregation for Evangelization of Peoples, Congregation for Bishops, Congregation for Causes of Saints, Congregation for Insts. Consecrated Life and Socs. Apostolic Life. Trustee Nat. Shrine of the Immaculate Conception, Washington, 1981—90; chmn. bd. trustees Cath. Telecommunications Network America, 1984—90; trustee, exec. com., chmn. com. for university rels. Cath. U. America, 1981—90. Roman Catholic. Died Aug. 21, 2014.

**SZOKOLAY, SANDOR,** composer; b. Kunagota, Hungary, Mar. 30, 1931; s. Balint and Erzsebet (Holecska) Szokolay; m. Sari Szesztay, 1952; m. Maja Weltler, 1970; 5 children. Student, Budapest Music Acad.; student with Szabo and Farkas, 1950—57. Mem. faculty Budapest Acad. Music, 1966—2013; musical adv. Hungarian TV. Composer: (Operas) Blood Wedding, 1963, Hamlet, 1968, Samson, 1973, Ecce Homo, 1987, Deploration, requiem in memory of Poulenc, 1964, zene hatalma (The Power of Music), 1969, Musza Dag, 1969, (ballets) Az iszonyat balladaja (the Ballad of Horror), Tetemrehivas (Ordeal of the Bier), (oratorios) A tuz marciusa (March Fire), Ister pokoljarasa (Ishtar's Descent to Hell), songs, chamber music & choral works; concertos for violin, piano & trumpet. Recipient Erkel prize, 1960, 1965, Kossuth prize, 1966, Golden Star prize, Paris Internat. Dance Festival, 1967, Merited Artist award, 1976, Honoured Artist award, 1986, Bartok-Pasztory Prize, 1987. Mem.: Hungarian Kodaly Soc. (chmn.). Died Dec. 8, 2013.

**SZOVERFFY, JOSEPH,** educator, medieval scholar; b. June 19, 1920; MA, State Coll. HS Tchrs., Budapest, 1944; PhD, U. Fribourg, 1950. Prof. fgn. lang. Glenstall Coll., Iceland, 1950—52; archivist Irish Folklore Commn., Dublin, 1952—57; spl. prof. classics and medieval Latin U., Ottawa, 1957—58, asst. prof., 1958—59; asst. prof. to assoc. prof. German Philology U. Alta., 1959—62; assoc. prof. mediaeval German Lit. Yale U., 1962—65; prof. German, Medieval Lit. Boston Coll., 1965—70, acting chmn. German studies, dir. grad. studies, 1968—70; prof. comparative lit. SUNY, Albany, 1970—77, chmn. dept., 1972—75; vis. prof. Byzantine studies Dumbarton Oaks Ctr. Byzantine Studies, Washington, 1977—78; prof. medieval lit. Sch. Hist. Studies, Inst. Advanced Study, 1978—79; Richard Merton vis. prof. Inst. Medieval Studies Freie U., Berlin, from 1980. Hon. rsch. assoc. Harvard Ukrainian Rsch. Inst., Harvard U., from 1975; with Inst. Advanced Studies, Berlin, 1983—84; vis. prof. Medieval Studies U., Vienna, 1984—85, 1987—88. Author: Der hl Christophorus und sein Kult, 1942, Irisches Erzahlgut im Abendland, 1957, Annalen der lateinischen Hymnendichtung I-II, 1964—65, Weltliche Dichtungen des lateinischen Mittelaters, 1970, Peter Abelard's Hymnarius Paraclitensis Vol I-II, 1979—80, Germanistische Abhandlugen, 1977, A Guide to Byzantine Hymnography, Vol I-II, 1979—80, Repertorium Novum Hymnorum Medii Aevi, Vol I-IV, 1982, Religious Lyrics of the Middle Ages, 1983, A Concise History of the Medieval Latin Hymnody, 1985, Typology of Latin Hymns, 1988, Turnhout Across the Centuries...Harvard Lectures, 1988, Secular Latin Lyrics, Vol. I-IV, 1992—95, Memoirs, 1996. Mem.: MLA, West Berlin Acad., Conn. Acad., Am. Comparative Lit. Assn., Mediaeval Acad. America. Died June 28, 2001.

**TABACHUK, EMELIA,** banker; b. Passaic, NJ, Aug. 3, 1926; d. Michael and Fannie (Stefanyk) T. Student, Drake Bus. Coll., 1956, N.Y. Inst. Credit, 1978-80. With Marine Midland Bank, NYC, from 1946, adminstrv. asst., 1975-76, ops. asst., 1976-78, comml. banking officer, from 1978, asst. v.p., 1982-85, retired, 1985. Mem. Nat. Assn. Bank Women, Nat. Assn. Female Execs., Am. Soc. Profl. and Exec. Women. Home: Clifton, NJ. Deceased.

**TABACK, SIMMS,** illustrator; b. East Bronx, NY, Feb. 13, 1932; m. Gail Taback; children: Jason, Lisa 1 stepchild, Emily. Grad., Cooper Union. Graphic designer Columbia Records; freelance advt. artist Eastern Airlines; graphic designer The NY Times; tchr. Sch. Visual Arts Syracuse U. Illustrator (children's books) Spacy Riddles, Snakey Riddles, Buggy Riddles, Fishy Riddles (Katy Hall and Ilsa Eisenberg) (Katy Hall), I Know an Old Lady Who Swallowed a Fly, 1998 (Caldecott Honor award medal, 1998), Joseph Had a Little Overcoat, 2000 (Caldecott Honor award medal, 2000); author: Postcards from Camp, 2010. Served in US Army. Died Dec. 25, 2011.

**TAFFE, RICHARD,** educational association administrator; b. Sydney, Nov. 13, 1960; s. Cecil Richard Taffe and Lesley Anthea Bower. PhD, U. Sydney, 2001. Courses dir. Charles Sturt U., Thurgoona, NSW, Australia, from 2010. Deceased.

**TAHER, TARMIZI,** retired Indonesian government official; b. Padang, Indonesia, Oct. 7, 1936; Grad. in medicine, Airlanagga U., Surabaya, Indonesia, 1964; postgrad., Sch. Command Staff, 1976. Commd. officer Indonesian Navy, med. officer, 1964-79; div. head Navy Ctr. for Mental Guidance, 1979, chief dept., 1980-84; lectr. Sch. Mil. Staff Command, 1984-87; sec. gen. Ministry Religious Affairs, Jakarta, min. religious affairs, 1993—98; amb. to Norway & Iceland Ministry Fgn. Affairs, 1998—2002; pres. Az-zahra Islamic U., Jakarta, 2004—08; chmn. Dewan Masjid Indonesia, 2006—11. Died Feb. 12, 2013.

**TAILOR, MAHESHCHANDRA CHETANLAL,** chemical engineer; b. Surat, Gujarat, India, June 27, 1944; s. Chetanlal Ishwarlal and Bhiki (Chetanlal) Bhagat; m. Jayagauri Maheschandra Magan, Nov. 22, 1965; children: Sheema, Deepan. BSChE, U. Bombay, 1971. Chem. engr. Kotak Chemicals Pvt. Ltd., Surat, India, 1971—73, Vuji-Chem. Industry, Vadodara, India, 1976—77; supr. New India Chem. Industries, Surat, 1977—78; quality contr. United Refineries, Bulawayo, Zimbabwe, 1978—79; asst. process mgr. Hippo Valley Estate Ltd., Chiredzi, Zimbabwe, 1979—82; sr. process engr. Zimbabwe Phosphate Industries Ltd., Harare, 1982—91; asst. oil plant mgr. Nat. Foods Ltd., Harare, 1991—2000; mgr. Superfoam, Harare, 2001—02; adminstrn. mgr. House of Tiles, Harare, 2002—03; adminstr. Superfoam, Harare, from 2003. Fellow: Zimbabwe Instn. Engrs.; mem.: Zimbabwe Sci. Assn., Lions. Hindu. Avocations: reading, meditation. Home: Harare, Zimbabwe. Deceased.

**TAIT, SYLVIA AGNES SOPHIA,** retired endocrinologist; b. Tumen, Siberia, Russia, Jan. 8, 1917; arrived in Eng., 1920, U.S., 1958; d. James William and Ludmila (Zaharof) Wardropper; m. Anthony James Simpson, Apr. 6, 1940 (dec. Oct. 1941); m. James Francis Tait, Sept. 1, 1956. BSc in Zoology with honors, Univ. Coll., London, 1939; DSc (hon.), Hull U., 1979. Rsch. asst. anatomy dept. Oxford (Eng.) U., 1941-44; biol. rsch. asst. Courtauld Inst. Biochemistry Middlesex Hosp. Med. Sch., London U., 1944-55, mem. MRC external sci. staff biochemistry dept., 1955-58, joint head dept. med. physics MRC biophys.-endocrinology, 1970-82; sr. scientist Worcester Found. for Exptl. Biology, Shrewsbury, Mass., 1958-70; ret. Mem.-at-large Howard Florey Inst. Exptl. Physiology and Medicine, Melbourne, Victoria, Australia, 1973—. Contbr. over 200 sci. papers to profl. jours. Recipient Tadeus Reichstein award Internat. Soc. for Endocrinology, 1976, Ciba award Am. Heart Assn. for Hypertention, 1977, Sir Henry Dale medal Soc. for Endocrinology, 1979, Douglas Wright medallion U. Melbourne, 1989. Avocations: bird watching in new forest, gardening, cooking. Home: Brockenhurst, England. Died Feb. 28, 2003.

**TAKAGI, SHIGEO,** administrator; b. Hashimashi, Japan, Aug. 12, 1923; s. Koitsu and Chieno (Noda) T.; m. Tamiko Morinaga, May 3, 1952; children: Koichiro, Kenjiro. Grad., Nihon U. Med. Faculty, 1947; MD, Nihon U. Sch. Medicine, 1950; D of Medicine, Tokyo U., 1955. Resident Tokyo U., 1948-52; dir. dept. ob-gyn. Gumma Chuo Hosp., Tokyo, 1952-59, Tokyo Kotsukyoku Hosp., 1959-63; assoc. prof. Nihon U. Sch. Medicine, Tokyo, 1963-72, prof., chmn., 1972-89, rsch. prof., 1989-90, prof. emeritus, 1991; chmn. bd. dirs. Higashi Jujo Hosp., Tokyo, from 1992. Author: Synthesis and Metabolism with Emphasis on Materni-Fetal Interrelations, 1971, The Climacteric Disroders, 1980; editor: Data Book of Obstetrics, 1985, The Mechanisms of Labor Pains and Thier Regulation, 1988, The Placenta: Basic Physiology and Clinical Aspects, 1992. Eli Lilly Internat. fellow, 1968. Mem. Japan Soc. Ob-Gyn. (pres. 1979), Japan Fertility Soc. (pres. 1984), Japan Nidation Soc. (pres. 1984), Japan Soc. Electron Microscopy, Japan Soc. Nutrition, Japan Soc. Endocrinology, Japan Soc. Neonatolog, Japan Soc. Inherited Disorders, Japan Soc. Microscopy, Japan Soc. Maternal Fetal Welfare, Am. Fertility Soc., Internat. Soc. Microscopy, Soc. for Study Reporduction, Endocrine Soc., Soc. Advancement Contraception (Japan dir., Japan chmn. 1988). Home: Asaka, Japan. Died Dec. 6, 2001.

**TAKAHASHI, MICHIAKI,** virologist; b. Osaka, Japan, Feb. 17, 1928; s. Shoji and Masako Takahashi; m. Hiroko Ohya Takahashi, Nov. 15, 1958; children: Teruyuki, Rie. MD, Osaka U., 1954; D in Med. Scis., 1959. Rsch. assoc. dept. virology Rsch. Inst. Microbial Diseases, Osaka U., 1959—63; assoc. prof. virology, 1963—78; prof., head dept. virology, 1978—2013. Rockefeller found. postdoc. fellow div. exptl. biology Baylor Coll. Medicine, Houston, 1963—64; postdoc. fellow Fels Research Inst., Temple U. Sch. Medicine, 1964—65. Recipient Kojima Saburo Meml. Cultural award, Kojima Saburo Meml. Soc., 1975, Asahi award, Asahi Newspaper Co., 1985. Mem.: Japanese Assn. Infectious Diseases (councilor), Japanese Cancer Assn. (councilor), Soc. Japanese Virologists (dir.). Achievements include development of live chickenpox vaccine. Home: Osaka 565, Japan. Died Dec. 16, 2013.

**TAKAHASHI, YOSHINDO,** retired transport company executive; b. Tokyo, Apr. 21, 1931; s. Yoshio and Antonina Nikolaiuna (Razmowa) T.; m. Noriko Masago, Oct. 7, 1955; children: Hiroshi, Kaoru, Yukie. BS, Aoyama Gakuin U., Tokyo, 1955. Mgr. Hino Motors Ltd., Tokyo, 1961-77, mgr. overseas ops.; mng. dir. Hino Motors Hellas S.A., Athens, 1963-68; comptroller Thai Hino Motor Sales Ltd., Bangkok, 1970-71; mng. dir. Okamoto Freighters Ltd., Tokyo, 1977-94, ret., 1994. Home: Tokyo, Japan. Deceased.

**TAKASHIMA, SHOJI,** retired sociologist, retired dean; b. Osaka, Japan, Dec. 13, 1931; m. Keiko Ibuki, Mar. 20, 1964; 1 child, Masato. BA, Kobe U., Japan, 1955; MA, Kyoto U., Japan, 1957, LittD, 1964. Asst. prof. Kyoto U., 1960-64; assoc. prof. Aichi U. Edn., Kariya, Japan, 1964-73, prof., 1973-79, Kyoto Prefectual U., 1979-83, dean faculty of arts and scis., 1981-83; prof. Ryukoku U., Kyoto, 1983-98, dean faculty sociology, 1993-95; prof., dean faculty social welfare Kogakkan U., Nabari, Japan, 1998—2002; ret., 2002. Counselor, mediator Nagoya (Japan) Family Ct., 1969—81, Kyoto Family Ct., 1981—2002. Editor: (book) Sociology: Theories, History and Problem, 1979, Contemporary Sociology at the Cross Roads, 1980; author: Foundations of Contemporary Sociology, 1981, The Family, Social Welfare and State in Sweden, 1997; co-author: Readings on Japanese Political Society, 1987. Avocations: travel, stamp collecting/philately. Home: Karamaguchi-dori, Kita-ku Kyoto, Japan. Died Dec. 2004.

**TAKEYAMA, YASUO,** economic strategist, international consultant; b. Tokyo, Feb. 1, 1923; s. Sadao and Chie (Hasegawa) T.; m. June Nakatani (dec. Sept. 1982); n. Janet Fay Nelson, Mar. 20, 1985. M in Econs., Tokyo U. Econs., 1946. Corr. Nihon Keizai Shimbun, Tokyo, from 1947, staff corr. NYC and Washington, 1952-55, chmn. bd. editorials Tokyo, 1968-83, editor-in-chief, 1970-80, mng. dir., 1975-83; chmn. Takeyama Assocs., Tokyo, from 1983; pres. Global Resources, Tokyo, from 1983. Mem. adv. bd. Ctr. for Strategic and Internat. Studies, Washington, 1980; advisor Ministry of Labor, Tokyo, 1970—. Author: The Structure of American Capitalism, 1958 (Japan Econs. Book prize 1958), Business Leadership, 1970, Japan: A Punching Bag of the World, 1972. Mem. Econ. Coun., Tokyo, 1956, Fgn. Capital Liberalization Coun., Tokyo, 1956—, Indsl. Restructuring Coun., Tokyo, 1956—, Price Stabilization Coun., Tokyo, 1956—, Overseas Econ. Coop. Coun., Tokyo, 1956—. Lt. Imperial Navy of Japan, 1943-45. Recipient Miles Vaughn prize UPI, Tokyo, 1972. Buddhist. Avocations: golf, reading, hot springs. Died Apr. 20, 2005.

**TAL, JOSEF,** composer; b. Pinne, Germany, Sept. 18, 1910; arrived in Israel, 1934. s. Julius and Ottilie (Bloch) Gruenthal; m. Rosie Loewenthal, 1933 (div. 1938); 1 child, Reuwen; m. Pola Pfeffer, Jan. 1940; 1 child, Etan. Student, Staate Acad. Music, Berlin; Dr. (hon.), Tel Aviv U., Acad. Music, Hamburg, 1996, Hebrew U., 1998. Dir. Israel Acad. Music, Jerusalem, 1948-52, Israel Centre Electronic Music, Jerusalem, 1961-81; head dept. musicology Hebrew U., Jerusalem, 1965-71; prof. musicology Hebrew U., 1970-84. Composer numerous operas and symphonies. Recipient Israel State prize, 1971, Arts prize City Berlin, 1975, Wolf prize in arts (music), 1982 Wolf Found., Israel, 1983; fellow for Rsch. in Electronic Music UNESCO, Paris and U.S., 1955-56, Inst. for Advanced Studies, Berlin, 1984. Mem. Acad. Arts Berlin, Am. Acad. Inst. Arts and Letters (hon.), Verdienstkreuz (1 Klasse), l'Ordre Artes et Lettres (comdr. 1985), Israel Sect. Internat. Music Coun. (pres. 1974-82). Avocations: theater, films. Home: Jerusalem, Israel. Died Aug. 25, 2008.

**TALMOR, SASCHA,** editor; b. Balti, Romania, Nov. 1, 1925; d. Gershon Starosta and Lily (Lewinson) Ronen; m. Ezra Talmor; children: Edna, Avital. BA with honors, London U., PhD in Aesthetics, 1959. Sr. lectr. in English lit. Haifa U.; editor History European Ideas, 1980-95, The European Legacy, from 1996. Mem. Kibbutz Nachshonim, 1945—; co-chair bi-yearly confs. Internat. Soc. Study of European Ideas. Author: Glanvill: The Uses and Abuses of

Scepticism, 1981, The Rhetoric of Criticism: From Hobbes to Coleridge, 1984, Living Novels: My Journey Through 20th Century Fiction, 2006; co-author: Encyclopedia of the Scientific Revolution, 2000; contbr. articles to profl. jours. Avocation: reading and reviewing novels. Home: DN Merkaz, Israel. Died 2005.

**TANIKAWA, HISASHI,** academic administrator; b. Tokyo, June 21, 1929; LLB, U. Tokyo, 1953, LLM, 1955, PhD in Law, 1958. Assoc. prof. Osaka City U., Japan, 1958—66; prof. Seikei U., Tokyo, 1966—98, emeritus prof., from 1998; mng. dir. Japan Energy Law Inst., Tokyo, 2001—11, pres., from 2011. Author: System and Characteristics of Maritime Private Law, 1958, Commentary on the Security Law on Compensation for Oil Pollution Damage, 1979. Recipient Medal with blue ribbon, Japan Govt., 1984, Gold and Silver Star, Order of Rising Sun, 2001. Mem.: Internat. Nuc. Law Assn. (hon. pres. from 1992), Internat. Maritime Cmty. (hon. v.p. from 2001). Budhism. Died June 9, 2014.

**TANJUNG, FEISAL,** retired Indonesian military officer; b. Sumatra, Indonesia, June 17, 1939; Commdr. in chief Indonesian Armed Forces; coordinating min. Ministry for Econs., Fin., and Industry; coordinating min. polit. affairs and security. Died Feb. 18, 2013.

**TANNER, ALTHEA CLAIRE,** artist; b. New Orleans, Aug. 2, 1918; d. Tabor Orme and Rose Janette (McTogue) Dodson; m. Warren Tanner, Mar. 1948 (div. 1955). Student, Augustine Bus. Sch., New Orleans, 1939. Sales person Sears, Roebuck & Co., New Orleans, 1939-41; layout Metairie (La.) Herald; furniture artist, lettering Barnett's, New Orleans, 1954-62; layout Metairie (La.) Herald, 1963; lettering artist Motion Picture Advt., New Orleans, 1964-72; typing, filing, lettering art T. Smith & Son Stevedoring Co., New Orleans, 1972-82. One-woman show Aerial Gallery, N.Y.C., 1992; exhibited in group shows at Winners Circle Gallery, Van Nuys, Calif., 1984, Arts Council of New Orleans, 1992; represented in permanent collection Old State Capitol, Baton Rouge, 1992. Contbr. donated art works WYES, channel 12, 1980-95, Arts for Aids, 1986-97, Contemporary Arts Ctr., 1992, Pops Found. 1995-96; active seminars Arts Coun. of New Orleans, 1992. Mem. Nat. Mus. of Women in the Arts, La. Women's Caucus for Art, La. Watercolor Soc., New Orleans Mus. Art, Contemporary Art Ctr. of New Orleans. Republican. Roman Catholic. Avocations: art work, crafts, poetry. Home: Metairie, La. Died Jan. 6, 2014.

**TANNER, IRA E., JR.,** lawyer; b. Denver, Mar. 25, 1921; s. Ira E. Tanner and Irena M. Seller; m. Patricia Prey, Sept. 17, 1960; children: David, Virginia, Brooke, Sule. AB, Colo. U., 1942. Bar: Colo. Of counsel Clanahan Tanner Downing & Knowlton, Denver. Mem. ABA, Denver Bar Assn. Died June 9, 2008.

**TANQUARY, OLIVER LEO,** minister; b. Springfield, Ill., Nov. 18, 1918; s. Lawrence Henry and Minnie (Potter) T.; m. Winifred Lillian Keen, June 24, 1939; children: Sylvia June, Lowell Emerson. BA, U. Pacific, 1933; MA, Boston U., 1940, STB, 1941; EdD, Fla. State Christian Coll., 1972; postgrad., Walden U., 1977-79. Ordained to ministry United Meth. Ch., 1941; cert. tchr., pub. sch. adminstr., Calif. Min. Hughes Meml. Meth. Ch., Edmonds, Wash., 1941-44; dir. guidance and rsch. County of Humboldt, Calif., 1948-52; min. Union Congl. Ch., Braintree, Mass., 1952-58, Paradise Hills Congl. Ch., San Diego, 1958-62; dir. guidance and counseling Paso Robles (Calif.) City Schs., 1962-68; dir. guidance and vocat. counseling County of Inyo, Calif., 1968-72; min. lst Congl. Ch., Big Timber, Mont., 1972-77, lst Meth. Ch., Big Pine, Calif., 1979-84, United Ch. of Christ, Quartz Hill, Calif., 1984-91. Chaplain Mayflower Gardens Retirement Cmty., Quartz Hill, 1986-91; dir. vocat. counseling YMCA, San Diego, 1958-61; del. So. Calif. Conf., United Ch. of Christ, Pasadena, Calif., 1984-91, moderator Kern Assn., Calif., 1990; pres. Big Timber Ministerial Assn., 1967. Author: Choosing My Vocation, 1968, Foundations to Fulfillment, 1991, Our Rewarding Responses, 1997, (booklets) At Home in the Universe, 1944, Providential Guidance, 1954; contbr. articles to denominational publs. Mem. Inter-County Libr. Bd. So. Calif., 1982, Inyo County Schs. Adv. Bd., 1982-83, Inyo County Grand Jury, 1983-84. lst lt., chaplain USAAF, 1944-48. Recipient svc. award Kiwanis Club, Paso Robles, Calif., 1965. Mem. Masons. Died Nov. 2001.

**TANSEY, ROBERT PAUL, SR.,** pharmacist, consultant; b. Newark, Apr. 27, 1914; s. William Austin and Charlotte E. (Endler) Tansey; m. Natalie C. McMahon, Feb. 22, 1941; children: Barbara, Carol, Robert, David. BS, Rutgers U., 1938; MS in Pharm., Organic Chemistry, 1950. Sect. head Schering Corp., Bloomfield, NJ, 1953—58; mgr. rsch. Strong Cobb Arner, Inc., Cleve, 1958—63; tech. dir. Vet. Labs., Inc., Kans., Lenexa, Kans., 1963—84, cons., from 1984. Mem.: Am. Pharm. Assn., Toastmasters Club, Kappa Psi, Rho Chi. Achievements include patents in field. Deceased.

**TARNOPOLSKII, YURI,** mechanical engineer, researcher; b. Sevastopol, The Crimea, USSR, Dec. 16, 1929; s. Matvej and Anna Tarnopolskii; m. Rita Kalnberzina; children: Alla, Yelena. Grad., Latvian State U., Riga, 1952, CadnTechScis, 1957; HabilDrTechScis, Moscow Inst Problems of Mechs., 1968. Sci. worker Latvian Acad. Scis., from 1954; head of lab. Inst. Polymer Mechanics, Riga, from 1963; prof. mechanics Riga Tech. U., from 1969. Co-author: Static Test Methods for Composites, 1985, Spatially Reinforced Composites, 1993; co-editor: Handbook of Composites, Vol. 2. Structures and Design, 1989, Composite Engineering Handbook, 1997, Lubin's Handbook of Composites II, 1998. Recipient Latvian State prize, 1965, USSR State prize, 1985, Canders prize Latvian Acad. of Sci., 1998; named Honoured Sci. Worker of Latvia, 1990. Mem. Latvian Acad. Scis., Inernat. Com. for Composite Materials, Nat. Com. on Theoretical and Applied Mechanics. Home: Riga, Latvia. Deceased.

**TAUSSKY, OLGA (MRS. JOHN TODD),** mathematics educator; b. Olomouc, Czechoslovakia, Aug. 30, 1906; came to U.S., 1934, naturalized, 1953; d. Julius David and Ida (Pollach) T.; m. John Todd, Sept. 29, 1938. PhD in Math., U. Vienna, 1930, Golden D diploma (hon.), 1980; MA (hon.), U. Cambridge, Eng., 1937; DSc (hon.), U. So. Calif., 1988. Fellow Girton Coll., Cambridge, Eng., 1934-40; asst. lectr. U. London, Eng., 1937-43; sci. officer Ministry Aircraft Prodn., London, 1943-46; mathematician Nat. Bur. Standards, Washington, 1947-57; research assoc. Calif. Inst. Tech., Pasadena, 1957-71, prof. math., 1971—95. Contbr. articles to profl. jours.; editor numerous books in field. Recipient Ford prize Math. Assn. Am., 1971; Fulbright prof. U. Vienna, 1965; decorated Gold Cross of Honor 1st Class (Austria). Fellow AAAS; mem. Am. Math. Soc. (council 1972-74, 83-85, v.p. 1986-88), Austrian Acad. Scis. (corr.), Bavarian Acad. Scis. (corr.). Home: Pasadena, Calif. Died Oct. 7, 1995.

**TAVENAS, FRANÇOIS,** civil engineer, educator; b. Bourg de Péage, Drôme, France, Sept. 12, 1942; arrived in Can., 1966; s. Adrien and Marie Thérèse (Bazin) T.; m. Gundula Schlichting, Apr. 27, 1963; children: Anne Catherine, Philippe, Sophie. BCE, Inst. Nat. Scis. Appliquées, Lyon, France, 1963; PhD, U. Grenoble, France, 1965. Registered profl. engr., Que. Engr. Piette & Assocs., Que., Can., 1966-70; asst. prof. civil engring. Laval U., Que., 1970-73, assoc. prof., 1973-79, prof., 1979—85, 1997—2002, dean, 1985-89; vice-prin. planning and resources McGill U., Montreal, Que., 1988-97; rector Laval U., 1997—2002, Luxembourg U., 2003—04. Cons. Golder & Assocs., Toronto, 1973-75, Terratech, Montreal, 1975-85, Soc. d'Energie de la Baie James, Montreal, 1980-84; mem. coun. Natural Scis. and Engring. Rsch. Coun. Can., 1989-95; bd. dirs. Groupe Pour l'avancement Technique et Indsl., Que.; pres. RISQ (Que. Internet), 1998—2002; v.p. Conf. Rectors and Prins. of Univs. in Que., 1997-99, pres., 1999-2001; chmn. bd. Québec Metro Hi Tech Park; bd. dirs. Assn. Univs. and Colls. of Can., 1998—2002; mem. Adv. Com. for On-Line Learning, Industry Can., 2000-2001. Author: (with others) Embankments On Soft Soils, 1985; contbr. articles to profl. jours. Recipient Chevalier of the French Legion of Honor, 1999, Grosses Bundergverdienstkreuz of the Fed. Republic of Germany, 2002 Mem. Can. Geotech. Soc. (v.p. 1982-85, pres.-elect 1990, pres. 1991-92), Internat. Soc. Soil Mechanics and Found. Engring., Assn. Can. Francaise pour L'Avancement des Scis. (pres. 1997-98). Avocations: tennis, travel, sailing. Home: Sillery, Canada. Died Feb. 13, 2004.

**TAYLOR, JAMES C.,** writer; b. Nashville, Oct. 17, 1924; s. James Custer Taylor and Winnie Olive Duncan. AB in Journalism and Psychology, U. Ky., 1941; postgrad., Vanderbilt U., 1941, Notre Dame U., Ind., 1942, Kans. U., 1942. Sports writer Topeka State Jour., Kans., 1950—52; reporter, editor Kansas City Star, Mo., 1953—57; sr. editor TV Guide Mag., 1957—82; fgn. corr. Internat. Am., various locations, 1982—2000; ret., 2000. Guest columnist CDL Report, World Intelligence Rev.; lectr. in field. Author: (book) Dubious Duty, 1976, Pearl Harbor II, 1978, Khadafy, Man or Myth, 1984. Referee H.S. football games, Ariz., 1980—2000. With French Foriegn Legion, Algeria, lt. comdr. USNR, 1941—61. Recipient Outstanding Book award, Mark Twain Soc., St. Louis, 1958, Del Oro award, Fria Ord, Stockholm, 1982; nominee Nobel Peace prize, 2008. Republican. Roman Catholic. Home: Lake Ozark, Mo. Deceased.

**TAYLOR, JOHN WILLIAM RANSOM,** writer, editor; b. Ely, Cambridgeshire, Eng., June 8, 1922; s. Victor Charles and Florence Hilda (Ransom) Taylor; m. Doris Alice Haddrick Taylor, Sept. 7, 1946; children: Susan Hilda Haddrick, Michael John Haddrick. DEng. (hon.), Kingston U., 1993. Design engr. Hawker Aircraft Ltd., Kingston Upon Thames, England, 1941—47; editl. publicity officer Fairey Aviation Group, London, 1947—55; air corr. Meccano Mag., Liverpool, England, 1943—72; editor Air BP, London, 1956—72; editor-in-chief, compiler Jane's All the World's Aircraft, London, 1959—89; editor emeritus, compiler CIS Sect., 1989—99. Joint editor Guinness Book Air Facts & Feats, London, 1974—84, History Aviation Partwork, New English Lib., London, 1972—73; contbg. editor Air Force Mag., Washington, 1971—97, Jane's Defence Weekly, London, 1984—87; corr. specialist Jane's Intelligence Rev., London, 1989—97. Author: (book) Spitfire, 1946; co-author (with D. Mondey): Spies in the Sky, 1972; co-author: (with K. Munson) History of Aviation, 1973; co-author: 2d edit., 1978, History of Aerial Warfare, 1974; co-author: (with R.A. Mason) Aircraft, Strategy and Operations of the Soviet Air Force, 1986; co-author: CFS-The Birthplace of Airpower, 1987; contbr. articles in field to profl. jours. Dist. commr. Boy Scouts Assn., Surbiton, Surrey, England, 1964—69, former v.p.; former warden Christ Ch., Surbiton Hill, 1976—80; pres. Chiltern Aviation Soc., Ruislip, Middlesex, England. Recipient C. P. Robertson Meml. Trophy, Air Pub. Relations Assn., Ministry of Defence, London, 1959, Lauren D. Lyman award, Aviation/Space Writer's Assn., 1990; named Cert. of Honor, Commn. of Bibliography, History& Arts, Aero Club de France, Paris, 1971, Freeman, Liveryman, Freedom City of London, Guild of Air Pilots & Air Navigators, London, 1983, Order of Merit, World Aerospace Edn. Orgn., 1981, Officer Order of Brit. Empire, 1991. Fellow: AIAA (assoc.), Royal Hist. Soc., Royal Aero. Soc.; mem.: Horse Rangers Assn. (gov. Hampton Ct. Palace), Academie Nationale de l'Air et de l'Espace France, Avro 504 (Manchester), City Livery (London), Royal Aero, RAF (life; hon. mem.). Mem. Ch. Of England. Died Dec. 12, 1999.

**TAYLOR, ROWAN SHAW,** music educator, composer, conductor; b. Ogden, Utah, June 1, 1927; s. Hugh Taylor and Lucille (Olsen) Gaenger; m. Dorothy Foulger, June 26, 1946 (div. 1953); children: Kathleen, Scott; m. Priscilla Pulliam, Aug. 29, 1957; children: Mark, Dianne, Paul, John (dec.), Eric, Brent, Charlotte. BA, Brigham Young U., 1952, MA, 1957. Tchr. San Juan Sch. Dist., Blanding, Utah, 1948-50; with C.F. Braun Engring. Firm, 1950-58; tchr. L.A. Unified Dist., 1958-64; from instr. to prof. L.A. C.C., Woodland Hills, Calif., from 1964. Condr., composer numerous symphonies and mus. works. With U.S. Army, 1955-56, Korea. Republican. Mem. Ch. Jesus Christ of LDS. Avocation: collecting cologne bottles. Deceased.

**TAYLOR, VESTA FISK,** real estate broker, educator; b. Ottawa County, Okla., July 15, 1917; d. Ira Sylvester and Judie Maude (Garman) Fisk; m. George E. Taylor, Aug. 17, 1957 (dec. Oct. 1963); stepchildren: Joyce, Jean, Luther. AA, Northea. Okla. A&M, 1936; BA, N.E. State U., Tahlequah, Okla., 1937; MA, Okla. State U., 1942. Life cert. Spanish, English, history, elem. Tchr. rural sch. grades 1-4, Ottawa County, Okla., 1931-33; tchr. rural sch. grades 1-8, 1933-38; tchr. H.S. Spanish, English Wyandotte, Okla., 1938-42; tchr. H.S. Spanish, English, math. Miami, Okla., 1942-57; tchr. H.S. Spanish Jacksonville, Ill., 1960-65; tchr. H.S. Spanish, English Miami, 1965-79; owner, broker First Lady Realty, Miami, from 1979; tchr. real estate for licensing N.E. Okla. Vocat.-Tech., Afton, 1980-94. Radio spellmaster weekly-county groups Coleman Theater Stage, 1954-57; radio program weekly 4-H, Miami, 1953-57; weekly radio program telling story of Pilot Club Internat., Jacksonville, Ill., 1960-61. Author: (poem) The Country School, 1994. Vol. sec. Ottawa County Seniors' Ctr., 1993—; mem. restoration com. Friends of Theater, 1993—; mem. Friends of the Libr., 1994—. Named Outstanding Coach Ottawa County 4-H Clubs, Miami, 1955, 67, Outstanding Alumnus All Yrs. H.S. Reunion, Wyandotte, Okla., 1992, Champion Speller N.E. Okla. Retirees, Oklahoma City, 1991. Mem. AAUW (pres. 1978-80, treas. 1994-98), Ottawa Coutny Ret. Educators (treas. 1990-95, corr. sec. 1995—), Miami Classroom Tchr. (v.p. 1973-77), Tri-state Travel Club (purser 1989-95), Kappa Kappa Iota (pres. 1988-92, treas. 1986-88). Democrat. Baptist. Avocations: gardening, reading, travel, volunteering. Died 2000.

**TEELE, ARTHUR EARLE, SR.,** educator, former university dean; b. Vaughan, NC, Nov. 11, 1910; s. George Washington and Cora (Williams) T.; m. Florazelle Swayze, Dec. 11, 1937; children: Synthia Florabeale, Arthur Earle. AB, N.C. Coll., 1934; A.M., Cornell U., 1941, PhD, 1953. Instr., chmn. dept. social studies Warren County Tng. Sch., Wise, N.C., 1934-39; ednl. therapist VA Hosp., Roanoke, Va., 1946-50; prof. edn., history, head dept. edn. St. Augustine's Coll., 1953-54; prof., chmn. dept. edn. Prairie View (Tex.) A. and M. Coll., 1954-57; prof., head dept. secondary edn. Fla. A. and M. U., Tallahassee, 1957-70, dir. prins., suprs. workshop, 1964-66, prof., dean grad. studies, 1970-76, prof. edn., 1976-78; cons. grad. programs U.S. Office Edn., 1978-81; field reader and evaluator, grad. and profl. programs U.S. Dept. Edn., Washington, 1977-87. Dir. Hardee County Curriculum Workshop, 1960, Hampton Jr. Coll. Workshop, 1962; mem. research council Coop. Coll. Projects (Land Grant TVA), 1963-64; cons. for grad. and profl. programs U.S. Dept. Edn., Washington, 1988. Contbr. to various publs. in field. Mem. United Fund steering com. Fla. A. and M. U., 1961-67; Bd. dirs. Leon County United Fund, 1962-69; pres. Coll. Terrace Community, 1963-68; mem. adv. bd. Salvation Army Corps, Tallahassee, 1984—; commr. 192d Gen. Assembly, United Presbyn. Ch. U.S.A., Detroit, 1980, Synod of the South, Tuscaloosa, Ala., 1985. Served with USAAF, 1943-45. Recipient Grant-in-Aid for research Cornell U., 1952; named Distinguished Alumnus N.C. Coll., 1960 Mem. N.E.A., Fla. Edn. Assn., Nat. Assn. Secondary Sch. Prins. (nat. adv. bd. 1971-75), Tallahassee Frontiers Internat. (pres. 1972), Nat. Black Alliance for Grad. Edn. (exec. bd., steering com. 1971-80, Disting. Prof. Emeritus 1983), Conf. So. Grad. Deans, Kappa Alpha Psi, Phi Delta Kappa, Kappa Delta Pi, Sigma Pi Phi. Died Aug. 2, 1999.

**TELEGA, JÓZEF JOACHIM,** mathematician, educator; b. Przyszowice, Katowice, Poland, Mar. 24, 1943; s. Jan and Zofia (Pyka) T.; m. Hanna Jadwiga Frackiewicz, Apr. 24, 1975; children: Agnieszka, Paweł Jan (dec.). MSc in Tech. Edn., Silesian U., Katowice, Poland, 1968, MSc in Math., 1970; PhD, Silesian U. Tech., Gliwice, Poland, 1972; habil., Polish Acad. Sci., Warsaw, Poland, 1991. From asst. to asst. prof. Silesian U. Tech., Gliwice, Poland, 1968-74; assoc. prof. Tech. Univ., Kielce-Radom, Poland, 1974-77; assoc. prof. Inst. Fundamental Tech. Rsch. Polish Acad. Sci., Warsaw, 1977-91, prof. Applied Mechanics, from 1992. Editor: Mathematical Problems of Plasticity, 1981; co-author: Plates, Laminates and Shells--Asymptotic Analysis and Homogenization, 2000; tech. editor: Applied Mechanics Revs., from 1992; assoc. editor Applied Mech. Rev., from 2002; editor: Polish Sci. Abstract on Mechanics, 1984—92, Inst. Fundamental Technol. Rsch. Reports, from 1991; editor: (guest) Jour. Theoretical Applied Mechanics, 1999, Engring. Transactions, 2001; editor:, 2003; mem. editl. bd.: Archives of Mechanics, from 1999, Mat. Stosowana (Applied Math.), 2000, Acta Bioengring. Biomechanics, from 1999, exec. editor: AMAS, Lecture Notes, IFTR, 2001, AMAS Conf. Proc., IFTR, from 2002, mem. internat. editl. bd.: Russian Jour. Biomechanics, 2000, mem. editl. com.: Applied Mechanics Libr., from 1999; contbr. over 300 articles to profl. jours. and book procs. Mem.: European Soc. Biomechanics, Polish Math. Soc., Polish Soc. Biomechanics, Polish Soc. Theoretical and Applied Mechanics, Am. Math. Soc., Internat. Soc. for Interaction of Math. and Mechanics. Roman Catholic. Avocations: classical music, foreign languages, bible studies, history/history of science, theology and philosophy. Home: Warsaw, Poland. Died Jan. 28, 2005.

**TELEGDI, VALENTINE LOUIS,** physicist, educator; b. Budapest, Hungary, Jan. 11, 1922; s. George and Ella (Csillag) T. MS in Chem. Engring., U. Lausanne, Switzerland, 1946; PhD, ETH, Zurich, Switzerland, 1950; Doctors (hon.), U. Louvain, Belgium, 1989, U. Budapest, Hungary, U. Chgo., 1991. Various prof. levels U. Chgo., 1951-72, Enrico Fermi disting. svc. prof., 1972-76; prof. ETH, Zurich, 1976-89; vis. prof. Calif. Inst. Tech., Pasadena, 1979-92; adj. prof. U. Calif. San Diego, La Jolla, 1996-98; faculty assoc. Calif. Inst. Tech., from 1999. Vis. prof. CERN, Geneva, Switzerland, 1976—, chmn. scientific policy com., 1978-83. Recipient Wolf prize in physics, Wolf Found., Israel, 1991, J.E. Lilienfeld prize of APS, 1995. Mem. Nat. Acad. Sci., Am. Acad. Arts and Scis., Accad. Dei Lincei, Accad. di Torino, Acad. Patavina, Accad. Europea, Hungarian Acad. Sci., Royal Swedish Acad. Sci., Russian Acad. Sci., French Acad. Sci. Avocations: jazz, gastronomy, travel. Home: Geneva, Switzerland. Died Apr. 2006.

**TELEMAN, OLLE ULF,** physicist, educator, researcher; b. Lund, Skane, Sweden, Aug. 15, 1957; s. Ulf Sven Helmer and Margareta Lillie (Blomgren) T.; m. Anita Britt-Louise Andersson, Oct. 20, 1984. M in Engring., Lund U., 1980, D in Engring., 1986. Tchg. asst. Lund U., 1980-86, rsch. asst., 1986-89, asst. prof., 1989-91; rsch. prof. Tech. Rsch. Ctr. Finland, Espoo, 1991-96; sci. dir. Ctr. for Sci. Computing (CSC), Espoo, 1997-98; vice pres. basic rsch. Swedish Pulp and Paper Rsch. Inst., Stockholm, from 1999. Fellow Finnish Acad. Tech.; mem. Chemists Soc. Finland (chmn. 1994-98), Assn. Chem. Socs. Finland (vice chmn. 1997-98). Avocations: literature, music, model railways, badminton. Home: Djursholm, Sweden. Died 2003.

**TEMPLE BLACK, SHIRLEY (MRS. CHARLES A. BLACK),** retired ambassador, retired actress; b. Santa Monica, Calif., Apr. 23, 1928; d. George Francis and Gertrude Temple; m. John Agar, Jr., Sept. 19, 1945 (div. Dec. 5, 1950); 1 child, Linda Susan Falaschi; m. Charles Alden Black, Dec. 16, 1950 (dec. Aug. 4, 2005); children: Charles Alden Jr., Lori Alden. Grad., Westlake Sch. Girls, 1945; D (hon.), Santa Clara Univ., Lehigh Univ. Rep. to 24th Gen. Assembly UN, NYC, 1969-70; US amb. to Ghana US Dept. State, Accra, 1974-76, US amb. to Czechoslovakia Prague, 1989-92; chief of protocol The White House, Washington, 1976-77. Mem. U.S. Delegation on African Refugee Problems, Geneva, 1981; mem. public adv. com. UN Conf. on Law of the Sea; dep. chmn. U.S. del. UN Conf. on Human Environment, Stockholm, 1970-72; spl. asst. to chmn. Pres.'s Coun. on Environ. Quality, 1972-74; del. treaty on environment USSR-USA Joint Commn., Moscow, 1972; mem. U.S. Commn. for UNESCO, 1973; hon. U.S. Fgn. Svc. officer. Actress: (films) Stand Up and Cheer, Little Miss Marker, Baby Take a Bow, Bright Eyes, Our Little Girl, The Little Colonel, Curly Top, The Littlest Rebel, Captain January, Poor Little Rich Girl, Dimples, Stowaway, Wee Willie Winkie, Heidi, Rebecca of Sunnybrook Farm, Little Miss Broadway, Just Around the Corner, The Little Princess, Susannah of the Mounties, The Blue Bird, Kathleen, Miss Annie Rooney, Since You Went Away, Kiss and Tell, 1945, That Hagen Girl, War Party, The Bachelor and the Bobby-Soxer, Honeymoon, 1947; narrator, actress: (TV series) Shirley Temple Storybook, NBC, 1958, Shirley Temple Show, NBC, 1960; author: Child Star: An Autobiography, 1988. Dir. Bank of Calif.; dir. Fireman's Fund Ins. Co., BANCAL Tri-State Corp., Walt Disney, Del Monte Corp.; Mem. Calif. Adv. Hosp. Council, 1969, San Francisco Health Facilities Planning Assn., 1965-69; Republican candidate for US House of Reps., 1967; bd. dirs. Nat. Wildlife Fedn., Nat. Multiple Sclerosis Soc., UN Assn. U.S.A.; bd. dirs. exec. com. Internat. Fedn. Multiple Sclerosis Socs. Appointed col. on staff of Gov. Ross of Idaho, 1935; commd. col. Hawaiian N.G.; hon. col. 108th Rgt. N.G. Ill.; dame Order Knights Malta, Paris, 1968; recipient Ceres medal FAO, Rome, 1975; Kennedy Center Honoree, John F. Kennnedy Ctr. for the Performing Arts, 1998, Nat. Bd. Review Career Achievement award, Screen Actors Guild Life Achievement award for Career Achievement & Humanitarian Accomplishment, 2005. Mem. World Affairs Coun. Northern Calif. (dir.), Coun. Fgn. Rels., Nat. Com. for U.S./China Rels. Clubs: Commonwealth of Calif. Republican. Home: Woodside, Calif. Died Feb. 10, 2014.

**TENOPYR, MARY LOUISE WELSH (MRS. JOSEPH TENOPYR),** psychologist; b. Youngstown, Ohio, Oct. 18, 1929; d. Roy Henry and Olive (Donegan) Welsh; m. Joseph Tenopyr, Oct. 30, 1955. AB, MA, Ohio U., 1951; PhD, U. So. Calif., 1966. Psychometrist Ohio U., Athens, 1951—52, also house mother Sigma Kappa; personnel technician to rsch. psychologist USAF, 1953—55, Dayton, Ohio, 1952—53, Hempstead, NY; indsl. rsch. analyst to mgr. employee evaluation N.Am. Rockwell Corp., El Segundo, Calif., 1956—70; assoc. prof. Calif. State Coll., LA, 1966—70; assoc. rsch. educationalist UCLA, 1970—71; program dir. U.S. CSC, 1971—72; dir. selection and testing AT&T, NYC, 1972—98. Lectr. U. So. Calif., LA, 1967—70; vice chmn. rsch. com. Tech. Adv. Com. on Testing, Fair Employment Practice Commn. Calif., 1966—70; adviser on testing Office Fed. Contract Compliance, U.S. Dept. Labor, Washington, 1967—73; mem. tech. adv. bd. ePredix, Inc., from 2000. Mem. editl. bd.: Jour. Applied Psychology, 1972—87, Jour. Vocat. Behavior, 1992—2000, cons. editor: Jour. Applied Psychology, from 2000, Jour. Personal Social Psychology, from 2002; contbr. chpts. to books, articles to profl. jours. Pres. ASPA Found., 1985—87; mem. Army Sci. Bd.; trustee NJ Psychol. Found., 1995—97, Am. Bd. Assessment Psychology. Mem.: NAS (coms. on ability testing, math. and sci. edn., panel on secondary edn.), APA (pres. divsn. evaluation, measurement and stats. 1994—95, bd. profl. affairs, edn. and tng. bd., mem. coun. reps., pres. divsn. indsl. orgnl. psychology, Outstanding Profl. Psychology award Divsn. Indsl. Orgn., Disting. Svc. award, Karl F. Heiser award), Am. Ednl. Rsch. Assn., NJ Psychol. Assn. (bd. trustees 1995—98), Met. NY Assn. Applied Psychology, Psychometric Soc., Nat. Coun. Measurement in Edn., Soc. Indsl. and Orgnl. Psychology (pres. 1979—80, Profl. Practices award 1984), Am. Soc. Pers. Adminstrn. (bd. dirs. 1984—87), Ea. Psychol. Assn., Am. Bd. Assessment Psychology (trustee from 1997), Kappa Phi, Alpha Lambda Delta, Psi Chi, Sigma Kappa, Sigma Xi. Deceased.

**TER BEEK, AURELUS LOUIS (RELUS TER BEEK),** former Dutch government official; b. Coevorden, The Netherlands, Jan. 18, 1944; married; 2 children. Student polit. and social scis., U. Amsterdam, Amsterdam. Chmn. Fedn. Labor party youth groups Dutch Labor Party, 1968-69; former internat. sec., mem. nat. exec. com.; rsch. asst. VARA Broadcasting Assn., 1970-71, also former mem. works coun.; elected to Lower House of States Gen., 1971; former chmn. Dem. Socialist Students Assn. (Politeia); former mem. Consultative Assembly, Coun. Europe; former mem. Assembly of Western European Union, North Atlantic Assembly; min. def. Govt. of The Netherlands, The Hague, 1989—94. Died Sept. 29, 2008.

**TESORO, GEORGE ALFRED,** retired lawyer; b. Rome, Feb. 6, 1904; s. Alfred and Anna (Russi) Tesoro; m. Gilda De Mauro, Mar. 18, 1934; children: Alfred W., Alexandra L., Tesoro Miller. JD, U. Rome, 1925; PhD in Polit. Sci, 1929, PhD in Taxation, 1930. Bar: DC 1948, US Supreme Ct. 1965. Corp. lawyer, Rome, 1927—48; instr. to lectr. taxation U. Rome, 1930—35; assoc. prof. pub. fin. and taxation U. Bari, Italy, 1935—38; news editor Sta. WOV, NYC, 1941—42; lectr. economics Lawrence Coll., 1942; vis. prof., lectr., adj. prof. economics Am. U., 1942—55; cons. Bd. Econ. Warfare, 1943; econ. analyst to chief sect. Fgn. Econ. Adminstrn. and Office Fgn. Liquidation Commn., 1944—46; economist to dep. econ. adv. div. econ. devel. Office Western European Affairs, Dept. State, 1946—55; sr. econ. officer to counselor US Mission, Geneva, 1956—65; counsel Cox, Langford & Brown, Washington, 1965—69, Coudert Bros., Washington, 1969—82, Dempsey and Bastianelli, Washington, 1982—83; ptnr. to counsel Bosco, Curry & Tesoro, 1984—89; chmn. emeritus Am. U. Rome, Republic of Korea, from 1985. Dir. Ferrero USA, Inc., Bencor Corp. Am., Inc.; founder to editor Italian Jour. Fiscal Law, 1937—38. Author: La Psicologia della Testimonianza, 1929, Le Penalita delle Imposte Dirette, 1930, Pricipii di Diritto Tributario, 1938. Recipient Comdr. Merito della Repubblica, 1971. Deceased.

**THACH, WILLIAM THOMAS, JR., (TOM THACH),** retired neurologist; b. Okla. City, Jan. 3, 1937; s. William Thomas and Mary Elizabeth T.; m. Emily Ransom Otis, June 30, 1963 (div. 1979); children: Sarah Brill, James Otis, William Thomas III. AB in Biology magna cum laude, Princeton U., 1959; MD cum laude, Harvard Medical Sch., 1964. Diplomate American Bd. Psychiatry & Neurology (in Neurology). Intern Mass. Gen. Hosp., Boston, 1964-65, asst. residency, 1965-66; staff assoc. physiology sect. lab. clin. sci. NIMH, Bethesda, Md., 1966-69; neurology resident, clin. and rsch. fellow Mass. Gen. Hosp., 1969-71; from asst. prof. neurology to assoc. prof. neurology Yale U. Sch. Medicine, New Haven, 1971-75; assoc. prof. neurobiology and neurology dept. anatomy and neurobiology Washington U. Sch. Medicine, St. Louis, 1975-80, prof. neurobiology and neurology dept. anatomy and neurobiology, 1980—2012, chief divsn. neurorehab. dept. neurology, 1992—2012. Acting dir. Irene Walter Johnson Rehab. Inst. Washington U. Sch. Medicine, 1989-91, dir., 1991-92; attending neurologist Barnes Hosp., med. dir. dept. rehab.; attending neurologist Jewish Hosp., St. Louis Regional Hosp.; bd. sci. counselors NINCDS, 1988-92; mem. NIH Study Sect. Neurology A, 1981-85. Assoc. editor Somatosenory and Motor Research; contbr. numerous articles to profl. jours. Fulbright grantee U. Melbourne, Australia, 1959-60; NIH grantee, 1971 Mem. Physiol. Soc., American Acad. Neurology, Soc. Neurosci., American Neurol. Assn., American Soc. Neurorehab., Phi Beta Kappa, Sigma Xi, Alpha Omega Alpha. Achievements include research on brain control of movement and motor learning, roles of the basal ganglia and the cerebellum in health and disease. Home: Saint Louis, Mo. Died July 1, 2014.

**THEISEN, BIANCA,** foreign language educator; b. Apr. 26, 1960; MA, Bonn U., Germany, 1987; PhD, Stanford U., 1992. Asst. prof. Johns Hopkins U., Balt., 1992-98, assoc. prof., 1998—2002, prof., from 2002. Deceased.

**THEISEN, HENRY WILLIAM,** lawyer; b. NYC, Feb. 21, 1939; s. Charles and Jennie J. (Callahan) T.; m. Kathleen Anne Brennan, Jan. 23, 1966 (div. Oct. 1992); children: Gordon H., Anne, Maureen R., William R.; m. Deborah S. Lynch, June 11, 1994. BBA, Manhattan Coll., 1961; JD, Fordham U., 1966. Bar: N.Y. 1967, U.S. Dist. Ct. (no. dist.) N.Y. 1968, U.S. Ct. Appeals (2d cir.) 1971, U.S. Supreme Ct. 1974. Acct. Patterson & Ridgway, CPAs, NYC, 1961-64; ptnr. Adams, Theisen & May, Ithaca, N.Y., from 1967; prosecutor City of Ithaca, 1969; estate tax atty. N.Y. State, Albany, 1976-90; county atty. Tompkins County, Ithaca, from 1994. Examining counsel Ticor Title Guaranty Co., Monroe Title Ins. Corp.; corp. sec., bd. dirs. Paleontol. Rsch. Instn., Ithaca; lectr. wills and trusts adult edn. program Bd. Coop. Ednl. Svcs., Tompkins County, N.Y., 1995-99. Author: (fin. and estate planning) Financial and Estate Planning Records, 1996. Pres. Ithaca Cmty. Music Sch., 1970; bd. reps. Tompkins County, Ithaca, 1976-81; bd. dirs. Tompkins Cmty. Hosp., 1980-83, Ctr. for Arts at Ithaca, Inc. (Hangar Theatre), 1989-92, Suicide Prevention Found. Tompkins County, 1996—; race dir. Finger Lakes Marathon, 1992-96; bd. dirs. Spl. Children's Ctr., 1969-74, pres., 1973-74; bd. dirs. Tompkins County SPCA, 1973-76, pres., 1976; chmn. task force orgn. Ithaca Pub. Edn. Initiative Inc., 1995-96; panel mem. Jud. Candidate Rating Panel, Binghamton, N.Y., 1993-94; candidate Supreme Ct. Justice, N.Y., 1992 Mem. Tompkins County Bar Assn. (pres. 1990), Tompkins County C. of C. (pres. 1993), Estate Planning Coun. Tompkins County (co-founder, pres. 1985), Ithaca Rotary Club. Democrat. Roman Catholic. Avocations: watercolor painting, long distance running. Home: Ithaca, NY. Deceased.

**THEODORE, HERBERT ROBINSON,** neurophysiologist; b. Bindraban, U.P., India, Apr. 6, 1933; s. Ramzy and Kathryn Theodore; m. Snehlata Sen, Dec. 21, 1963; children: Sanjay, Raj. BSc, Punjab U., Ludhiana, India, 1961; postgrad., U. Ill., Chgo., 1963-64, Wellington Poly., New Zealand, 1975. Sr. technician Hosp. for Nervous Diseases, London, 1972-74; chief technician Wellington Hosp., 1974-78, 79-85, tech. devel. officer, 1987-96; tech. officer Children's Hosp., Adelaide, Australia, 1978-79, King Khalid U., Riyadh, Saudi Arabia, 1985-87; cons. Wellington Neurophysiol. Svcs., 1990-97; dir. Neurotrek Sys., Ltd., Wellington, from 1997. Contbr. articles to profl. jours.; inventor in field. Mem. N.Z. Soc. Neurophysiology Tech. (founding mem.). Avocations: fishing, hiking, reading science fiction. Home: Otaki, New Zealand. Deceased.

**THEODORESCU, RADU AMZA SERBAN,** mathematician, educator; b. Bucharest, Romania, Apr. 12, 1933; emigrated to Can., 1968, naturalized, 1975; s. Dan and Ortensia Maria (Butoianu) T.; children: Dan, Paul, Anne; m. Marie-José Michiels. BSc, U. Bucharest, 1954, DSc, 1967; PhD, Acad. Romania, 1958. Asst. prof. Inst. Math. Acad., 1954-57, sr. asst. prof., 1957-60, assoc. prof., sci. sec., 1960-64; prof., head dept. Center Math. Statistics, 1964-68; prof. U. Bucharest, 1968-69, Laval U., Quebec, Canada, 1968—99, prof. emeritus, 1999—2007. Guest prof., lectr. univs. in Europe, N.Am., and Australia. Author: (with G. Ciucu) Processes with Complete Connections, 1960, (with S. Guiasu) Mathematical Information Theory, 1968, Uncertainty and Information, 1971, (with M. Iosifescu) Random Processes and Learning, 1969, (with W. Hengartner) Concentration Functions, 1973, 2d edit., 1980, Monte-Carlo Methods, 1978, (with E. Bertin and I. Cuculescu) Unimodality of Probability Measures, 1997; mem. editl. bd. Annales des Sciences Mathématiques du Québec, 1976-99, Optimization, 1970-2000, Statistics and Decisions, 1981-2003, Revstat, 2002—; contbr. articles to profl. jours. Mem. bd. European Orgn. Quality Control, 1966-69. Recipient prize Acad. Romania, 1960 Fellow Inst. Math. Stats., Am. Soc. Quality; mem. Statis. Soc. Can. (hon.), Statis. Soc. Romania (hon.), Am. Math. Soc., Internat. Statis. Inst. Home: Quebec City, Canada. Died Aug. 14, 2007.

**THIEL, PHILIP,** retired design educator; b. Bklyn., Dec. 20, 1920; s. Philip and Alma Theone (Meyer) T.; m. Midori Kono, 1955; children: Philip Kenji, Nancy Tamiko, Susan Akiko, Peter Akira (dec.) BSc, Webb Inst. Naval Architecture, 1943; MSc, U. Mich., 1948; BArch, MIT, Cambridge, 1952. Registered arch., Wash. Instr. naval architecture MIT, Cambridge, 1949—50; instr. architecture U. Calif., Berkeley, 1954—56, asst. prof., 1956—60; assoc. prof. U. Wash., Seattle, 1961—66, prof. visual design and experiential notation, 1966—91; guest prof. Tokyo Inst. Tech., 1976—78; vis. prof. Sapporo Sch. Arts, Japan, 1992—98. Lectr., US, Can., Japan, Norway, Denmark, Sweden, Eng., Austria, Switzerland, Peru, Bolivia, Korea; cons. FAO, Rome, 1952; co-founder Environment and Behavior, 1969; founder Ctr. for Exptl. Notation, Seattle, 1981 Author: Freehand Drawing, 1965, Visual Awareness and Design, 1981, People, Paths and Purposes, 1997; patentee in field Soc. Naval Architects and Marine Engrs. scholar, 1947; Rehmann scholar AIA, 1960; grantee NIMH, 1967, Nat. Endowment for Arts, 1969, Graham Found., 1995 Mem. Soc. Naval Archs. and Marine Engrs. (assoc.), Phi Beta Kappa, Sigma Xi Home: Seattle, Wash. Died May 10, 2014.

**THIGPEN, ALTON HILL,** transportation executive; b. Kinston, NC, Feb. 3, 1927; s. Kirby Alton and Alice (Hill) T.; m. Rebecca Ann Braswell, May 16, 1953; children: David Alton, Jennifer Ann, Steven Roy. BS in Indsl. Engring., N.C. State U., 1950. With Assoc. Transport, Inc., Burlington, NC, 1950-71, engr., 1950-57, asst. terminal mgr. Phila., 1957-58, terminal mgr. Knoxville, Tenn., 1959, regional mgr. Valley region, 1960-62, South region, 1962-68, v.p.,dir. So. divsn., 1968-71; v.p. R.S. Braswell Co. Inc., Kannapolis, NC, 1971-80, pres., from 1980, Hartford Motor Inn Inc., North Myrtle Beach, SC, from 1982, A.T. Developers, Inc., North Myrtle Beach, 1983-97. Pres. Cherokee 2 Inc., Shelby, N.C., 1986-95, bd. dirs.; bd. dirs. Wachovia Bank, Earl Ownsby Studios Inc., Shelby. Bd. regents Berkshire Christian Coll., Lenox, Mass., 1975—; mem. adv. bd. Salvation Army, chmn. adv. bd., 1997-99. Served with USNR, 1945-46. Mem. Motor Carriers Va. (pres. 1967-68), N.C. Motor Carriers Assn. (dir. 1968-), Masons (32d degree), Lions, Sigma Chi, Tau Beta Pi. Mem. Advent Christian Ch. Home: Kannapolis, NC. Died Apr. 25, 2012.

**THIRRING, WALTER EDUARD,** theoretical physics educator; b. Vienna, Apr. 29, 1927; s. Hans and Antonia (Krisch) T.; m. Helga Georgiades, Dec. 22, 1952; children: Klaus, Peter. PhD, U. Vienna, 1949. Scholar Dublin (Ireland) Inst. Adv. Studies, 1949-50; fellow Glascow (Scotland) U., 1950; asst. Max-Plack Inst., Göttingen, Germany, 1950-51; UNESCO fellow Fed. Inst. Tech., Zurich, Switzerland, 1951-52; asst. U. Bern, Switzerland, 1952-53, lectr., 1954-56, prof., 1958; mem. Princeton (N.J.) Inst. Tech., 1953-54; prof. U. Vienna, 1959—2014. Vis. prof. MIT, Cambridge, 1956-57, U. Wash., Seattle, 1957-58; mem. Directorate of Cern, Geneva, 1968-71. Author: Einführung in die Quantenelektrodynamik, 1955, Elementary Quantum Field Theory, 1962, Lehrbuch der Mathematischen Physik, 1977-80, Cosmic Impressions, 2007, The Joy of Discovery: Great Encounters Along the Way, 2010; contbr. articles to profl. jours. Recipient Erwin Schrödinger prize Austrian Acad. Sci., 1969, R. Eötvös medal Hungarian Phys. Soc., 1973, Max-Planck medal German Phys. Soc.,

1976, Henri Poincaré prize, Inst. Math. Phys., 2000. Mem.: NAS (fgn. assoc.), Acad. Scientiarum et Artium Europaea, Academia Europaea, Pontifical Acad. Scis., Acad. Naturforscher Leopoldina, Austrian Acad. Scis., Hungarian Acad. Scis. (hon.), Hungarian Eotvos Soc. (hon.). Avocations: music, sports. Home: Vienna, Austria. Died Aug. 19, 2014.

**THOMAS, ANN VAN WYNEN,** retired law educator; b. The Netherlands, May 27, 1919; arrived in U.S., 1921, naturalized, 1926; d. Cornelius and Cora Jacoba (Daansen) Van Wynen; m. A. J. Thomas, Jr., Sept. 10, 1948. AB with distinction, U. Rochester, NY, 1940; JD, U. Tex., 1943; degree, So. Meth. U., Dallas, 1952. US fgn. svc. officer, Johannesburg, London, The Hague, Netherlands, 1943-47; rsch. atty. Southwestern Legal Found. So. Meth. U. Sch. Law, Dallas, 1952-67, asst. prof. polit. sci., 1968-73, assoc. prof., 1973-76, prof., 1976-85, prof. emeritus, from 1985. Author: Communism versus International Law, 1953, Non-Intervention - The Law and Its Import in the Americas, 1956, OAS: The Organization of American States, 1962, International Legal Aspects of Civil War in Spain, 1936-1939, 1967, Legal Limitations on Chemical and Biological Weapons, 1970, The Concept of Aggression, 1972, An International Rule of Law - Problems and Prospects, 1974, Presidential War Making Power: Constitutional and International Law Aspects, 1981; author: (with A. J. Thomas, Jr.) International Treaties, 1950; author: What I did in World War 2, 2007. Chmn. time capsule com. Grayson County Commn. Tex. Sesquicentennial, 1986—88; co-chmn. Grayson County Commn. Bicentennail US Constn., 1988—93, Grayson County Commn. Millenium, from 1997; co-chmn. com. Grayson County Sesquicentennail, 1994—97. Recipient Am. medal, Nat. DAR, 1992. Mem.: Grayson County Bar Assn., Am. Soc. Internat. Law, Tex. Bar Assn. Home: Pottsboro, Tex. Deceased.

**THOMAS, JOAB LANGSTON,** retired academic administrator, biologist, educator; b. Holt, Ala., Feb. 14, 1933; s. Ralph Cage and Chamintney Elizabeth (Stovall) Thomas; m. Marly A. Dukes, Dec. 22, 1954; children: Catherine, David, Jennifer, Frances. AB, Harvard U., 1955, MA, 1957, PhD, 1959; DSc (hon.), U. Ala., 1981; LLD (hon.), Stillman Coll., 1987; LHD (hon.), Tri-State U., 1994; LHD (hon.), N.C. State U., 1998. Cytotaxonomist Arnold Aboretum, Harvard, 1959—61; prof. biology U. Ala., University, 1966—76, 1988—91, asst. dean Coll. Arts & Sciences, 1964—65, 1969, dean for student devel., 1969—74, v.p., 1974—76, dir. Herbarium, 1961—76, dir. Arboretum, 1964—69, pres. Tuscaloosa, 1981—88; chancellor N.C. State U., Raleigh, 1976—81; pres. Pa. State U., University Park, 1990—95, pres. emeritus, 1995—2014. Intern acad. adminstrn. American Coun. on Edn., 1971. Author: A Monographic Study of the Cyrillaceae, 1960, Wildflowers of Alabama and Adjoining States, 1973, The Rising South, 1976, Poisonous Plants and Venomous Animals of Alabama and Adjoining States, 1990. Bd. dirs. Internat. Potato Ctr., 1977—83, chmn., 1982—83; bd. dirs. Internat. Svc. for Nat. Agrl. Rsch., 1985—91. Recipient Ala. Acad. Honor, 1983, Palmer Mus. Art medal, Coll. President's award, All-American Football Found., 1997, Spl. Recognition award, Assn. for Continuing Higher Edn., 1998; named Citizen of Yr., City of Tuscaloosa, 1987. Mem.: Golden Key, Phi Kappa Phi, Omicron Delta Kappa (Laurel Crowned Circle award 2001), Sigma Xi, Phi Beta Kappa. Home: Tuscaloosa, Ala. Died Mar. 3, 2014.

**THOMPSON, ANTHONY,** retired corporate executive; b. St. Olaves, Eng., Apr. 26, 1932; came to U.S., 1958; s. Joseph and Elsie Caroline (Buck) T.; div. 1985; children: Suzanne Elizabeth, Bridget Caroline. DLC in Engring., Loughborough U., Eng., 1950. V.p. sales Jaguar Cars, Inc., NYC, 1958-68; v.p. Jaguar divsn. Brit. Leyland Motors, Leonia, N.J., 1968-69; pres. AMCO Industries, Chgo., 1969-73; exec. v.p. Frederick Weisman Assoc., LA, 1973-75; pres., CEO Rolls-Royce, Beverly Hills, Calif., 1975-85; exec. v.p. Carriage House Motor Cars, NYC, 1985-88; dir. internat. bus. MagneTek, Inc., LA, 1988-91, dir. European bus. London and Frankfurt, 1991-96, dir. govt. & utilities devel. Nashville, 1996-99, ret., 1999. Chmn. Brit. Olympic Assn., L.A., 1981-84; pres., chmn. Brit./Am. ChofComm., L.A., 1980-84; dir. Royal Oak Found., L.A., 1976-85, English Speaking Union, L.A., 1984-85. Capt. Royal Elect. & Mech. Engrs., 1953-55, Germany. Named Officer Most Excellent Order Brit. Empire Her Majesty The Queen, London, 1985, Freeman City London Lord Mayor London, 1982; elected Liveryman Worshipful Co. Coachmakers & Coachharness Makers, London, 1982. Mem. Soc. Automotive Engrs., Rolls-Royce Dealer Coun. (chmn., pres. 1976-79). Episcopalian. Avocations: classical music, broadcasting, steam trains, classic cars. Home: Nashville, Tenn. Died Mar. 2001.

**THOMPSON, BARRY B.,** retired academic administrator; b. Pecos, Tex., May 12, 1936; s. Tommy and Louise Thompson; m. Sandra Sue Davison, 1955; children: Karol, Kim, Scott, Bart. BA, Tarleton State U.; MA, Tex. Tech. U. Tchr., Andrews, Tex.; prof. U. Tex.-Edinburg, 1971—75; provost., v.p. for acad. affairs Tex. A&M U., Commerce, 1975—82; pres. Tarleton State U., Stephenville, Tex., 1982—90, pres. emeritus, 2001—14; pres. West Tex. State U., Canyon, 1991—94; chancellor Tex. A&M System, 1994—99, chancellor emeritus, 1999—2014. Methodist. Died Mar. 1, 2014.

**THOMPSON, DAVID BERNARD,** bishop emeritus; b. Phila., May 29, 1923; Ordained priest Archdiocese of Phila, 1950; ordained bishop, 1989; coadjutor bishop Diocese of Charleston, SC, 1989-90, bishop, 1990—99, bishop emeritus, 1999—2013. Pub. New Cath. Miscellany, Charleston, SC. Recipient Bishop John England award, Cath. Press Assn., 1997. Roman Catholic. Died Nov. 24, 2013.

**THOMPSON, LIBBIE MOODY (MRS. CLARK THOMPSON),** civic worker; b. Galveston, Tex., Nov. 22, 1897; d. William Lewis and Libbie Rice (Shearn) Moody; m. Clark W. Thompson, Nov. 16, 1918 (dec.); children: Clark W., Libbie(dec.). Student, Holton-Arms, Washington, 1915. Past dir. YWCA, ARC, Galveston; bd. dir. Nat. Eye Found., Meridian House Internat.; mem., nat. bd. Med. Coll. Pa.; mem., fine arts com. state dept. Washington; mem., chancellor's coun. U. Tex.; mem., pres.'s club U. Tex. Med. Br.; founding mem. Jr. Welfare. Mem.: UDC, LWV (past dir.), UN Assn., ARC Aux., Hubert H. Humphrey Leadership Fund, Com. Ireland (charter), Nat. Preservation Hist. Internat. Fund Monuments, Friends of Am. Philos. Soc., Pres.'s Assocs. Med. Coll. Pa., Fine Arts Soc. Tex. (dir.), Friends of LBJ Libr., Friends of Rosenberg Libr. (Galveston), Friends of Kennedy Ctr., Salvation Army Aux. Washington, Descs. Most Noble Order of Garter, Order of Washington, Huguenot Soc., Am. Legion Aux., Daus. Republic Tex., Colonial Dames America, Plantagenet Soc., Jr. League (hon.), Smithsonian Soc. of Assocs. (life; mem., James Smithson soc.), Soc. Sponsors USN (life), Galveston Arty. Club, Am. Newspaper Women's Club, Georgetown Club, 1925 F St. Club (Washington), Women's Nat. Dem. Club, Sulgrave Club, Magna Charta Dames. Home: Galveston, Tex. Deceased.

**THOMPSON, WILLIAM PAUL, JR.,** aerospace company executive; b. Elmira, NY, June 3, 1934; s. W. Paul and Helen Katharine (Bruce) T.; m. Sally W. Lessig, Aug. 1955 (div. Apr. 1977); children: Helen W., Bruce A., Leila E., Judith A.; m. Anne Stevenson, Dec. 11, 1977. BS in physics, Yale U., 1955; MS in Physics, Lehigh U., 1957, PhD in Physics, 1963. Research and teaching asst. Lehigh U., Bethlehem, Pa., 1955-61; instr. Moravian Coll., Bethlehem, 1957-58, Los Angeles Trade-Tech., 1967; mem. tech. staff labs Aerospace Corp, LA, 1961-68; head dept. reentry systems Aerospace Corp., San Bernardino, Calif., 1968-72, assoc. group dir. LA, 1972-79, dir. space tech., 1979-81, dir. aerophysics lab, 1981-89, prin. scientist devel. group, 1989-92, prin. dir. Strategic Planning Office, from 1993. Vis. com. Sch. Aerospace Engring. U. Okla., 1987—; adv. bd. minority engring. program UCLA, 1987—. Contbr. articles to profl. pubs., chpt. to books. Fellow AIAA (assoc., mem. laser tech. com. 1986-89, chmn. 1989-91); mem. Am. Phys. Soc., Sigma Xi. Republican. Episcopalian. Avocations: baritone soloist, light opera, sailplane flying. Home: Altadena, Calif. Died Oct. 1999.

**THOREN, LARS OLOF,** surgeon, educator; b. Gothenburg, Sweden, Nov. 18, 1921; s. Lars Einar and Anna Juliana (Thorn) T.; m. Ingrid Tyra; children: Birgitta, Gunnar, Karin, Gunilla. MD, U. Uppsala, Sweden, 1949, PhD, 1957. Chmn. dept. surgery Orebro (Sweden) Hosp., 1964; prof. surgery, chmn. dept. surgery U. Hosp. Uppsala, 1965-87, prof. emeritus, from 1988. Contbr. articles to profl. jours. Fellow Am. Coll. Surgeons (hon.); mem. Swedish Surg. Soc. (hon.), Swedish Soc. Med. Scis. (hon.), Finnish Surg. Soc. (hon.), Finnish Med. Soc. (hon.). Deceased.

**THORNER, RETA M.,** theatre administrator, realtor; b. Salem, Mass., May 11, 1924; d. Harris Francis and Beatrice (Crossman) Stevenson; m. Walter Thorner, Aug. 10, 1947 (dec.); children: Walter III, Wendy Thorner Shurtleff. AAB, Burdett Coll., 1942. Lic. realtor, Fla. Exec. dir. Venice (Ill.) Little Theatre, from 1977. Mem. Sarasota (Fla.) County Art. Rev. Com., 1988—. With USN, 1944-46. Recipient Best of Show award SARA-Photography Show, Sarasota, 1987. Mem. WAVES Nat., C. of C. Avocations: photography, golf, acting. Reta Thorner scholarship named in her honor. Died Feb. 24, 1991.

**THRING, MEREDITH WOOLDRIDGE,** physicist, engineer, educator; b. Melbourne, Victoria, Australia, Dec. 17, 1915; arrived in Eng., 1919; s. Walter Hugh and Dorothy (Wooldridge) T.; m. Alice Margaret Hooley, Dec. 14, 1940; children: Susan Margaret Thring Kalaugher, John Meredith, Robert Hugh. BA, Cambridge U., 1937, MA, 1941, ScD, 1964; Dr. (hon.), Open U., 1982. Head combustion lab. Brit. Coal Utilisation Rsch. Assn., London, 1937-46; head dept. physics Brit. Iron and Steel Rsch. Assn., London, 1946-53; prof., head fuel tech. and chem. engring. dept. Sheffield U., 1953-64; prof., head dept. mech. engring. Queen Mary Coll., London U., 1964-81, prof. emeritus, from 1981. Gen. supt. Internat. Flame Rsch. Found., Ijmuiden, Holland; convenor African Adv. Group, 1998—. Author: The Science of Flames and Furnaces, 1952, 62, Man, Machines and Tomorrow, 1972, How To Invent, 1977, The Engineer's Conscience, 1980, Robots and Telechirs, 1983, Quotations from G.I. Gurdjieff's Teaching, 1998. Recipient Robert Hadfield medal Iron and Steel Inst., 1949. Fellow Royal Acad. Engring. (founder fellow), Inst. Energy (sr. fellow, pres. 1962-63), Inst. Physics, Instn. Elec. Engrs., Inst. Chem. Engrs., Athenaeum (London). Mem. Ch. of England. Avocations: forestry, wood carving. Died Sept. 15, 2006.

**THROWER, RANDOLPH WILLIAM,** lawyer; b. Tampa, Fla., Sept. 5, 1913; s. Benjamin Key and Ora (Hammond) T.; m. Margaret Munroe, Feb. 2, 1939 (dec. 2009); children: Margaret MacCary, Patricia Barmeyer, Laura (Mrs. David T. Harris, Jr.), Randolph William, Mary (Mrs. George B. Wickham). Grad., Ga. Mil. Acad., 1930; BPh, Emory U., 1934, JD, 1936. Bar: Ga. bar 1935, D.C. bar 1953. Ptnr. Sutherland, Asbill & Brennan, Atlanta, Washington, 1947—69, 1971—2014; commr. IRS, US Dept. Treasury, 1969—71. Spl. agt. FBI, 1942-43; mem. Arthur Andersen & Co. Bd. of Rev., 1974-80, Nat. Council on Organized Crime, mem. exec. com., 1970-71 Past pres. Ga., Met. Atlanta mental health assns.; chmn. City of Atlanta Bd. Ethics 1981-93; past trustee Emory U., Clark Coll.; past chmn., trustee Wesleyan Coll.; bd. govs. Woodward Acad.; past chmn. bd. visitors Emory U. Served as capt. USMCR, 1944-45. Recipient Spl. Svc. award, Ct. Federal Claims, 1995, American Inns of Ct. Professionalism award for the 11th Cir., 2003. Mem. Atlanta Legal Aid Soc. (past pres.), Emory U. Alumni Assn. (past pres.), ABA (chmn. spl. com. on survey local needs 1971-78, past chmn. sect. taxation, mem. house of dels. 1964-66, 74-89), Ga. Bar Assn., Atlanta Bar Assn. (Leadership award, 1992), American Bar Found. (dir. 1980-88, pres. 1986-88, medal 1993), American Law Inst., Atlanta Lawyers Club (past pres.), U.S. Claims Ct. Bar Assn. (pres. 1987-88), Phi Delta Phi. Clubs: Commerce (Atlanta), Capital City (Atlanta), Piedmont Driving (Atlanta). Republican. Methodist. Home: Atlanta, Ga. Died Mar. 8, 2014.

**THULIN, LARS UNO,** banker; b. Uddevalla, Sweden, Mar. 25, 1939; came to Norway, 1939; s. Haakon Erling and Signe Ingeborg (Thulin) Hansen; m. Anne Skard, Oct. 7, 1977 (div.). MSc, Norwegian Inst. Tech., 1965, Dr. Ing., 1970. Lectr., scientist U. Trondheim, 1965-70, dep. dean univ. planning unit, 1970-74; mng. dir. Norwegian Agy. Devel. Aid, Trondheim, 1974-75; undersec. Ministry Rsch. and Edn., Oslo, 1975-76, Ministry Industry and Energy oslo, 1976-77; exec. v.p. Den Norske Creditbank, Oslo, from 1977; mng. dir. den Norske Creditbank Plc, London, from 1987. Exec. v.p., head internat. div. Den Norske Creditbank, Oslo, 1989; sec. gen. Royal Norwegian Ministry of Industry, Oslo, 1989—; pres., CEO STATKRAFT, 1992—. Home: Oslo, Norway. Died Mar. 14, 2002.

**THURLIMANN, BRUNO,** retired structural engineering educator; b. Gossau, Switzerland, Feb. 6, 1923; s. Josef and Alice (Braegger) Thurlimann; m. Susi Gimmel, 1953; children: Christoph, Peter, Elisabeth. Diploma in Civil Enging., Swiss Fed. Inst. Tech., 1946; PhD in Civil Enging., Lehigh U., Bethlehem, Pa., 1951; D in Civil Engring. (hon.), U. Stuttgart, Germany, 1983; D of Engring. (hon.), U. Glasgow, Scotland, 1997. Rsch. assoc. Brown U., Providence, 1951-52; rsch. prof. Fritz Engring. Lab., Lehigh U., 1952-60; prof. structural engring. Swiss Fed. Inst. Tech., Zurich, 1960-90, prof. emeritus, from 1990. Technical consult German Concrete Soc, others. Contbr. articles to sci publs. Recipient Julius Adams Stratton prize, Friends of Switzerland, Inc., Boston, 1989, Ostenfield Gold Medal, Technical Univ Denmark, 1991, Prix Albert Caquot, Assoc Francaise pour la Construction, 1993. Fellow: ASCE (hon. Research Prize 1961, Norman Medal 1963, Moisseiff Award 1964, Ernest E Howard Award 1986); mem.: Swiss Acad Eng. Scis., Swiss Engrs. and Architects Soc., Nat. Acad Eng., Internat. Assn. Bridge and Structural Engrs. (pres 1977—85, hon pres 1985, Int Award Merit 1997), Spanish Acad. Eng. (corr.), Serbian Acad. Scis. and Arts (corr.), Am. Concrete Inst. (hon. Alfred E Lindau Award 1996). Home: Egg, Switzerland. Died July 29, 2008.

**TIDBALL, M. ELIZABETH PETERS,** physiologist, educator; b. Anderson, Ind., Oct. 15, 1929; d. John Winton and Beatrice (Ryan) Peters; m. Charles S. Tidball, Oct. 25, 1952. BA, Mt. Holyoke Coll., 1951, LHD, 1976; MS, U. Wis., 1955, PhD, 1959; MTS summa cum laude, Wesley Theol. Sem., 1990; DSc (hon.), Wilson Coll., 1973, Trinity Coll., 1974, Cedar Crest Coll., 1977, U. of South, 1978, Goucher Coll., 1979, St. Mary-of-The-Woods Coll., 1986; LittD (hon.), Regis Coll., 1980, Coll. St. Catherine, 1980, Alverno Coll., 1989; HHD (hon.), St. Mary's Coll., 1977, Hood Coll., 1982; LLD (hon.), St. Joseph Coll., 1983; LHD (hon.), Skidmore Coll., 1984, Marymount Coll., 1985, Converse Coll., 1985, Mt. Vernon Coll., 1986. Tchg. asst. physiology dept. U. Wis., 1952—55, rsch. asst. physiology dept., 1958—59; rsch. asst. anatomy dept. U. Chgo., 1955-56, rsch. asst. physiology dept., 1956-58; USPHS postdoctoral fellow NIH, Bethesda, Md., 1959-61; staff pharmacologist Hazleton Labs., Falls Church, Va., 1961, cons., 1962; assoc. in physiology George Washington U. Med. Ctr., 1960-62, asst. rsch. prof. dept. pharmacology, 1962-64, assoc. rsch. prof. dept. physiology, 1964-70, rsch. prof., 1970-71, prof., 1971-94, prof. emeritus, 1994—2014; asst. dir. M of Theol. Studies program Wesley Theol Sem., 1993-94; Disting. rsch. scholar Hood Coll., Frederick, Md., 1994—2014, co-dir. Tidball Ctr. for Study of Ednl. Environments, 1994—2014. Lucie Stern Disting. vis. prof. natural scis. Mills Coll., 1980; scholar in residence Coll. Preachers, 1984, Salem Acad. and Coll., 1985, bd. visitors charter class, 1987-93, Wesley Theol. Sem., 1992; Disting. scholar in residence So. Meth. U., 1985; vis. trustee prof. Skidmore Coll., 1995; cons. FDA, 1966-67, assoc. sci. coord. sci. assocs. tng. programs, 1966-67; com. on NIH tng. programs and fellowships NAS, 1972-75; faculty summer confs. American Youth Found., 1967-78; founder, dir. Summer Seminars Women American Youth Found., 1987-95; cons. for instl. rsch. Wellesley Coll., 1974-75; exec. sec. com. on edn. and employment women in Sci. & Engring. Commn. on Human Resources, NRC/NAS, 1974-75, vice-chmn., 1977-82; cons., staff officer NRC/NAS, 1974-75; cons. Woodrow Wilson Nat. Fellowship Found., 1975-99, NSF, 1974-91; cons. Middle State Assn. Colls. & Schs., 1986-94, bd. mentor Assn. Governing Bds. Universities & Colleges, 1991-2000, Gale Fund for the Study of Trusteeship Advisory Comm., 1992-98; cons. Women's Coll. Coalition Rsch. Advisory Com., 1992-2000; Single Gender Schooling Working Group, US Dept. Edn., 1992-94, Women's Colls. Roundtable, 1998; rep. to DC Commn. on Status of Women, 1972-75; nat. panelist American Coun. on Edn., 1983-90; panel mem. Congressional Office Tech. Assessment, 1986-87; fellows selection com., fellows mentor Coll. Preachers, 1992-05. Lead author: Taking Women Seriously: Lessons and Legacies for Educating the Majority, American Council on Education Higher Education Series, 1999; columnist Trusteeship, 1993-95; mem. editl. bd. Jour. Higher Edn., 1979-84, cons. editor, 1984—; mem. editl. bd. Religion and Intellectual Life, 1983—; contbr. articles to profl. jours. Trustee Mt. Holyoke Coll., 1968-73, vice chmn., 1972-73, trustee fellow, 1988—2010; trustee Hood Coll., 1972-84, 86-92, exec. com., 1974-84, 89-92, trustee emerita, 1997-2014; overseer Sweet Briar Coll., 1978-85, dir. emerita, 2003-14; trustee Cathedral Choral Soc., 1976-

90, pres. bd. trustees, 1982-84, hon. trustee, 1991-2014; trustee Skidmore Coll., 1988—11, exec. com., 1993-2009, trustee emerita, 2011-14; trustee Bishop Claggett Ctr., 2003-14; governing bd. Cathedral Coll. of Preachers, 1979-85, chmn., 1983-85; governing bd. Protestant Episcopal Cathedral Found., 1983-85, exec. com., 1983-85; bd. vis. Salem Coll., 1986-93; ctr. assoc. Nat. Resource Ctr., Girls Club America, 1983-90; governing bd. Buckinham's Choice Residents' Assn., 1999-2002; cathedral vol. coun. Washington Nat. Cathedral, 2006-09. Recipient Alumnae medal Honor, Mt. Holyoke Coll., 1971, Outstanding Svc. award, Am. Youth Found., 1975, Valuable Contbns. Gen. Alumni Assn. award, George Washington U., 1982, 1987, Pres.'s medal, 1999, medal Outstanding Achievement, Chestnut Hill Coll., 1987, Lifetime Svc. and Scholarship award, Bd. Women's Coll. Coalition and Nation's Women's Coll. Presidents, 1998, Order of Merit, Cathedral Choral Soc., 2000, Kemball-Cook Trustee award, Skidmore Coll., 2008; named Outstanding Grad., The Penn Hall Sch., 1988; Shattuck fellow, 1955—56, Mary E. Woolley fellow, Mt. Holyoke Coll., 1958—59, postdoctoral fellow, USPHS, 1959—61. Mem. AAAS, American Physiol. Soc. (chmn. task force on women in physiology 1973-80, com. on coms. 1977-80, mem. emeritus 1994-2014), American Assn. Higher Edn., Mt. Holyoke Alumnae Assn. (dir. 1966-70, 76-77), Histamine Club, Sigma Delta Epsilon, Sigma Xi. Episcopalian. Home: Adamstown, Md. Died Feb. 3, 2014.

**TIMMS, GENE (EUGENE DALE TIMMS),** wholesale business owner, retired state legislator; b. Burns, Oreg., May 15, 1932; s. Morgan Oscar and Dorothy Vera (Payne) T.; m. Edna May Evans, Aug. 24, 1953; children: Tobi Eugene, Trina Maria. BA, Willamette U., 1954; grad. studies, U. Wash. Mem. Oreg. State Senate, Salem, 1982—2000, majority leader, 1992—93, asst. majority leader, 1995—97. Pres. Harney City Chamber of Commerce; bd. trustees Assoc. Oreg. Industries; chmn. Parks & Recreation Dist. Bd.; mem. Harney City Hosp. Bd. Mem. SBA, Jaycees (state v.p.), Elk Lodge, Masonic Lodge, Al Kader Harney City Shrine Club. Republican. Presbyterian. Avocations: fishing, hunting, reading, movies, sports. Home: Burns, Oreg. Died Apr. 21, 2014.

**TIN, WIN,** journalist; b. Pegu, Burma, Mar. 12, 1930; 1 child. BA in English Lit., Modern History & Political Sci., Rangoon U., 1953. Editor-in-chief Hanthawaddy; freelance journalist & translator, 1978—89; incarcerated Insein Prison, Insein, Myanmar, 1989—97, Yangon Gen. Hosp. prison ward, Yangon, 1997—2008. Vice-chmn. Myanmar Writers' Assn. Author: Human Rights Abuses in the Junta's Prisons, 1995, What's That? A Human Hell, 2010. Sec. exec. com. Nat. League for Democracy, Myanmar, 1988—89. Recipient Human Rights award, France, 1998, Golden Pen of Freedom, World Assn. Newspapers, 2000, 2001, Guillermo Cano World Press Freedom Prize, UNESCO, 2001. Died Apr. 21, 2014.

**TING, LAWRENCE SHAN-LI,** international development company executive; b. Kiang-su, China, Jan. 25, 1939; s. Wee Non and Hsiu Chin (Hsia) Ting; m. Sylvia Tsong-Ching Fei, May 29, 1966; children: Iris Kwang-I., Joyce Kwang-Yu, Albert Kwang-Chin, Arthur Kwang-Hung. BS, Chinese Mil. Acad., 1961. Commd. 2d lt. Chinese Army, 1957, advanced through grades to maj., 1971; ret., 1971; v.p., gen. mgr. Hwa-yi Chem. Indsl. Corp., 1971—73; v.p. China Gulf Plastics Corp., Taipei, Taiwan, 1973—76, exec. v.p., dir., 1976—83; vice chmn. Taiwan Indsl. Fastener Corp., 1983—2004; chmn. Alexander & Alexander (Taiwan) Ltd., 1984—97, Alexander & Alexander Ins. Agy. Ltd., 1984—97, Chin Cheng Investment Corp., 1988—2004, Cen. Trading & Devel. Corp., 1989—2004; dir. Cen. Investment Holding Co., Ltd., 1989—94. Vice chmn. Chinese Taipei Olympic Com., 1975—82. Decorated Medal of Honor Ho Chi Minh City, Vietnam; named to Order Chi-Hsueh, Order Hwa Hsia, Order Phys. Edn.; Republic of China Nat. Def. scholar, 1964—66, Paul Harris fellow, 1981. Mem.: Chinese Mil. Acad. Alumni Found. (chmn. 1989—2004), Taiwan Area Plastics Assn. (chmn. 1988—94), Chinese Inst. Engrs., Taipei Rotary Club. Achievements include patents for household appliances. Home: Taipei, Taiwan. Died Sept. 23, 2004.

**TINKER, MICHAEL HARRY,** physicist, research scientist; Prof. physics U. Reading, England. Recipient Bragg medal and prize, Inst. of Physics, 2002. Deceased.

**TISDALE, PHEBE ALDEN,** cryptographer; AB, Radcliffe/Harvard, 1932. Author: CAMEL-OT, 1998, Sparrowgrass Treasury of Religious Poetry, 2000, Connections, 2001. Mem. AAAS, N.Y. Acad. Scis. Deceased.

**TOADVIN-BESTER, JOSEPHINE VESELLA,** academic administrator, educator; b. Toledo, Oct. 22, 1926; d. Albert and Verona Mae (Haynes) Toadvin; m. Raymond Bester, June 18, 1948; children: Michael Bruce, Douglas Alan, Jeffrey Royce. BEd, U. Toledo, 1948, M in Elem. Curriculum, 1970, cert., 1972. Cert. elem. edn. tchr., Ohio. Tchr. Toledo Pub. Schs., 1948-82, cons. tchr., intern intervention program, 1982-85, with career ladder, 1987-88; supr. U. Toledo, from 1987, mem. undergrad. rev. bd. Planner Execellence in Action, Toledo, 1985—; tutor Friend's Ctr., Toledo, 1987—, Toledo Excel Program, 1989—; mem. student devel., honors and awards com. Siena Hghts. Coll.; mem. minorities com. Bishop's Edn. Coun. Mem. adv. bd. Office of Black Caths., Toledo, 1984—, Cen. City Ministries of Toledo, 1984—; trustee Elizabeth A. Zept Mental Health, Toledo, 1984—, Siena Hts. Coll., 1991—; mem. Bishops' Edn. Coun., 1989—; mem. child care adv. com. YMCA, 1990—; chair minorities com.; mentor Top Teen Am., Toledo Symphony League, 1999—; mem. Toledo Opera Guild, 1999—. Recipient Sister Thea Bowman medallion, 1994; Martha Holden Jennings Found. scholar, 1975-80; named Outstanding Educator N.W. Ohio, 1985. Mem. Toledo Fedn. Tchrs. (bd. dirs. 1980-87), Top Ladies of Distinction, Negro Bus. and Profl. Women (rec. sec. 1993), Phi Delta Kappa, Kappa Delta Pi, Delta Sigma Theta (sec. 1945), Pi Lambda Theta. Democrat. Avocation: volunteer tutor. Deceased.

**TOCKMAN, GERALD,** lawyer; b. St. Louis, Sept. 29, 1937; BA, Washington U., St. Louis, 1958; JD, Washington U., 1960. Bar: Mo., DC 1971, Calif. 1984, US Supreme Ct. 1976. Pvt. practice, St. Louis, from 1960. Contbr. articles to profl. jours. Mem.: ABA, Nat. Bd. Trial Adv. (cert/ trial adv.), Assn. Trial Lawyers Am., St. Louis Bar Assn., Ill. Bar Assn., Mo. Bar Assn. Died June 16, 1998.

**TODD, NORMA ROSS,** retired government official; b. Butler, Pa., Oct. 3, 1920; d. William Bryson and Doris Mae (Ferguson) Ross; m. Alden Frank Miller, Jr., Apr. 16, 1940 (dec. Feb. 1975); 1 child, Alden Frank III; m. Jack R. Todd, Dec. 23, 1977 (dec. Sept. 1990). Student, Pa. State U., Donora, 1944—46, Yale U., New Haven, Conn., 1954-57. Exec. mgr. Donora C. of C., Pa., 1950-57, pres. Pa., 1972; exec. mgr. Donora Cmty. Chest, 1950-57; office mgr. Donora Golden Jubilee, 1951; staff writer Donora Herald-American, 1957, city editor, 1957-70; assoc. editor Daily Herald, Donora and Monongahela, 1970-73; svc. rep. Pitts. Telesvc. Ctr., Social Security Adminstrn., HHS, 1977-83. Mem. Mayor's Adv. Coun., Donora, 1965-69, Citizens' Adv. Coun., Donora, 1965-69; mem. Donora Bd. Edn., 1954-60, pres., 1960; mem. Donora Borough Coun., 1970-72; bd. dirs. Mon Valley chpt. ARC, 1964-99, sec. bd., 1964-97, chmn. bd. dirs., 1997-99, mem. lifetime adv. bd., 2000; bd. dirs. Washington County Tourism Agy., 1970-90, sec., 1972-90; bd. dirs. Washington County History and Landmarks Found., 1971-80, 91-92, sec., 1975-80, 91-93, hon. life mem., 1996; bd. dirs. Mon Valley YMCA, 1960-66, Mon Valley coun. Camp Fire Girls, 1965-79, Mon Valley Drug and Alcoholism Coun., 1971-78; hon. life mem. Pa. Congress PTAs; bd. dirs. United Way Mon Valley, 1973-82, chmn. pub. rels., 1973-74; rep. nat. com. Eisenhower Commn., 2005; Platinum mem. Presdl. Task Force, 2004-06; commr. Rep. Sen. Inner Cir., 2005. Recipient Fine Arts Festival of Pa. Poetry first prize award Fedn. Women's Clubs, 1987, 1st and 2d pl. awards for photography Washington County Fine Arts Festival, County Fedn. Women's Clubs, 1990, Disting. Svc. award Donora Rotary Club, 1997, Millenium Peace award, India, 2001, Two World Poets awards J. Mark Press, 2002, U.S. Rep. Senatorial Medal of Freedom, 2003, 2006, Congl. Order Merit, 2003, Cert of Recognition U.S. Justice Found, 2004, cert. appreciation Ronald Reagan Presdl. Found., 2006; pub. in Best Poems of 1995 Nat. Libr. of Poetry, Best Poems of 1996, Best Poems of 1997, Outstanding Poets of 1998, Am. at the Millennium The Best Poets of the 20th Century, The Best Poems and Poets of 2001, The Best Poems and Poets of 2002, of 2003, 04, 05 and numerous anthologies in U.S., Italy, Great Britain and India. Mem. Svc. Corps Ret. Execs. (sec. 1998-2005), Pa. Soc. Newspaper Editors, Pitts. Press Club, Donora C. of C. (pres. 1971-72), DAR (regent Monongahela Valley chpt. 1974-77, treas. 1992-2001), Internat. Platform Assn. (finalist Acad. of Poets Competition, 2001), World Poetry Soc. Internat., Internat. Poets Acad., Famous Poet Soc., U.S. Poets, Metverse Muse (hon. life, India), Washington County Poetry Soc. (pres. 1967-69), Donora Hist. Soc. (curator 1990—), Family of Bruce Internat. Descs. of King Robert the Bruce of Scotland, Clan Ross Assn., Mt. Vernon Ladies Assn., Washington County Fedn. Women's Clubs (rec. sec. 1964-66, pub. rels chmn. 1990-92), Order Ea. Star (worthy matron 1966-67, treas. 1986-94, 98—2003, bd. dirs. Western Pa. Eastern Star Home 1997-98, adv. bd. Masonic Eastern Star Home-West 1998-2000), White Shrine of Jerusalem (high priestess 1973-74, treas. 1995-2001), Order of Amaranth (royal matron 1966, dist. dep. 3 times, grand rep. W.Va. 1979-80), Donora Forecast (pres. 1957-59), Donora Unidon (pres. 1965-66, 56-57). Avocation: genealogy. Home: Donora, Pa. Deceased.

**TODD, RICHARD ANDREW PALETHORPE,** actor, writer; b. Dublin, June 11, 1919; s. Andrew William and Marvill (Agar-Daly) Palethorpe-Todd; m. Catherine Grant-Bogle, Aug. 13, 1949 (div. 1970); children: Peter (dec.), Fiona; m. Virginia Anne Mailer, 1972 (div. 1992); children: Andrew, Seumas (dec. 1997) Student privately, Shrewsbury, England. Founder, mem. Dundee (Scotland) Repertory, 1938-39, 1947-49; stage appearances include An Ideal Husband, London, 1965, Dear Octopus, 1967, Equus, Australia, 1975, Nightfall, Republic of South Africa, 1979, This Happy Breed, 1980, The Business of Murder, London, 1981-88, Intent to Kill, 1990, The Woman in Black (Australia), 1991, Beyond Reasonable Doubt, 1992, Scrooge in a Christmas Carol, 1993, Brideshead Revisited, 1994-95, An Ideal Husband, 1996-97; founder, Triumph Theatre Co., 1970; (films) The Hasty Heart, 1949, Stage Fright, 1950, Lightning Strikes Twice, 1951, Robin Hood, 1952, The Sword and the Rose, 1953, Rob Roy: The Highland Rogue, 1954, The Dam Busters, 1955, A Man Called Peter, 1955, The Virgin Queen, 1955, D-Day: The Sixth of June, 1956, Saint Joan, 1957, Chase a Crooked Shadow, 1957, Never Let Go, 1961, The Longest Day, 1962, Operation Crossbow, 1965, The Last of the Long-Haired Boys, 1968, Asylum, 1972; Author: (autobiographies) Caught in the Act, 1986, In Camera, 1989 Commd. King's Own Yorkshire Light Inf., then capt. parachute regiment, 1940-46, ETO. Recipient Brit. Nat. Film Award, Picturegoer Award, Daily Express-Tribunal Award; decorated Order Brit. Empire (OBE), 1993. Mem. Masons, Army and Navy Club. Avocations: game shooting, gardening. Died Dec. 4, 2009.

**TODD, RUTH,** artist; b. Sanford, NC, Nov. 10, 1909; m. Judson Cornelius and Flora Thomas; m. Littleton Todd, May 19, 1934. Student, Anderson Coll., 1927-28, U. Miami, 1930-31, Colorado Springs Coll., 1954. One-woman shows Morris Gallery, N.Y.C., 1958, Bodley Gallery, N.Y.C., 1962, Internat. House, Denver, 1964, U. Colo., Boulder, 1968, Joseph Magnin Gallery, Denver, 1975, Merrill-Chase Galleries, Chgo., 1977, West End Gallery, Winston-Salem, N.C., 1979, also others; exhibited in numerous group shows, including Santa Fe Mus., Sweat Meml. Art Mus., Portland, Maine, Creative Galleries, N.Y.C., N.Y.C. Ctr. Gallery, N.C. State Mus. Art, Raleigh, Mulvane Art Ctr., Topeka, Denver Art Mus., U. N.Mex., Albuquerque, Colorado Springs (Colo.) Fine Arts Ctr., La Galléria Escondido, Taos, N.Mex.; represented in permanent collections Princeton U., NYU, also corp. and pvt. collections. Recipient awards for art including Soc. Four Arts Mus., Palm Beach, Fla., Nelson Adkins Gallery, Kansas City (Mo.) Mus., George Walter Vincent Smith Art Mus., Springfield, Mass., Joslyn Art Mus., Omaha, Okla. Fine Arts Ctr., Oklahoma City; 1st award Nat. Space Art Exhibit, 1969, 3d award, 1975. Episcopalian. Deceased.

**TODMAN, TERENCE ALPHONSO,** retired ambassador; b. St. Thomas, V.I., Mar. 13, 1926; s. Alphonso and Rachel (Callwood) T.; m. Doris T. Weston, July 26, 1952; children: Terence A., Patricia, Kathryn, Michael. BA, Poly. Inst., PR, 1951; MPA, Syracuse U., 1953; postgrad., American U., 1953-54; D (hon.), Colgate U., 1981; LLD (hon.), Syracuse U., 1986; D in Public Svc. (hon.), Morgan State U., 1986; LLD (hon.), Boston U., 1987. Asst. personnel officer Govt. of V.I., 1951; internat. relations officer US Dept. State, 1952-54, fgn. affairs officer, 1955; U.S. nominee UN intern program, 1955; adviser U.S. delegation UN Gen. Assembly, 1956-57; U.S. rep. UN trusteeship council petitions com. and com. rural econ. devel. UN, 1956-57; 2d sec., polit. officer US Embassy, Beirut, 1960-61, Tunis, 1961-63, counselor, dep. chief of mission Lome, Togo, 1965-68; dir. Office East African Affairs US Dept. State, 1968-69, US amb. to Chad N'Djamena, Chad, 1969-72, US ambassador to Guinea Conakry, 1972-74, US ambassador to Costa Rica San Jose, 1975-77, asst. sec. for Inter-American affairs Washington, 1977-78, US amb. to Spain Madrid, 1978-83, US amb. to Denmark Copenhagen, 1983-89, US amb. to Argentina Buenos Aires, 1989-93. Trustee Coll. of the Virgin Islands. Served to 1st lt. AUS, 1945-49. Recipient Superior Honor award US Dept. State, 1966, Medal of Honor, Govt. of V.I., Grand Cross of the highest order of Isabela la Catolica (Spain), Grand Cross of Order of Dannebrog (Denmark), Grand Cross of Order of San Martin (Argentina), Presdl. Svc. award, Nat. Public Svc. award, Presdl. Disting. Svc. award, 1985, Sec. of State Disting. Svc. award, 1993; attained rank of Career Ambassador, 1989. Mem. American Fgn. Svc. Assn., Coun. on Fgn. Rels., Nat. Acad. of Public Adminstrn. Died Aug. 13, 2014.

**TOKIOKA, MASAYUKI,** mortgage and finance company executive; b. Okayama, Japan, May 22, 1897; arrived in Hawaii, 1909; s. Tozo and Katsu (Baba) T.; m. Harue Fujiyoshi, Aug. 2, 1929; children: Mitsuko, Yukio, Makoto. AB, U. Hawaii, 1925; MBA, Harvard U., 1927; LLD, U. Hawaii, 1982. Cashier-treas. Internat. Trust Co., Honolulu, 1927—36; mgr. Coffee Plantation, Hamakua, Hawaii, 1928—30; sec. Kaneohe Land Co., 1935; propr. Newfair Dairy, 1928—46; sec.-treas. Hawaii League Bldg. & Loan Assns., 1940; pres., gen. mgr. Island Ins. Co., Ltd., 1940—69, chmn. bd., from 1969. Pres., gen. mgr. Nat. Mortgage & Fin. Co. Ltd., from 1936; chmn. bd. Internat. Savs. & Loan Assn., Ltd., Nat. Securities & Investment, Inc., Nat.-Braemar, Inc., 1960—69. Chmn. bd. Kuakini Hosp., 1960; trustee State of Hawaii Employees Retirement System; mem. Honolulu Japanese C. of C., pres., 1953—54. Recipient Merit award, City of San Francisco, commendation for devel. of Japanese Culture & Trade Ctr. in City-by-the-sea, Calif State Legis.; named to Third Order of the Rising Sun, Emperor of Japan, 1985. Mem.: Lions Club. Christian Ch. Home: Honolulu, Hawaii. Died Aug. 2, 1998.

**TOLLETT, GLENNA BELLE,** accountant, mobile home park operator; b. Graham, Ariz., Dec. 17, 1913; d. Charles Harry and Myrtle (Stapley) Spafford; m. John W. Tollett, Nov. 28, 1928; 1 child, Jackie J., 1 adopted child, Beverly Mae Malgren. Bus. cert., Lamson Coll. Office mgr, Hurley Meat Packing Co., Phoenix, 1938-42; co-owner, sec., treas. A.B.C. Enterprises, Inc., Seattle, from 1942; ptnr. Bella Investment Co., Seattle, from 1962, Four Square Investment Co., Seattle, from 1969, Warehouses Ltd., Seattle, from 1970, Tri State Partnership, Wash., Idaho, Tex., from 1972; pres. Halycon Mobile Home Park, Inc., Seattle, from 1979. Co-owner, operator Martha Lake Mobile Home Park, Lynwood, Wash., 1962-73. Mem. com. Wash. Planning and Community Affairs Agy., Olympia, 1981-82, Wash. Mfg. Housing Assn. Relations Com., Olympia, 1980-84; appointed by Gov. Wash. to Mobile Home and RV Adv. Bd., 1973-79. Named to RV/Mobile Home Hall of Fame, 1980. Mem. Wash. Mobile Park Owners Assn. (legisl. chmn., lobbyist 1976-85, cons. 1984, pres. 1978-79, exec. dir. 1976-84, This is Your Life award 1979), Wash. Soc. of Assn. Execs. (Exec. Dir. Service award 1983), Mobile Home Old Timers Assn., Mobile Home Owners of Am. (sec. 1972-76, Appreciation award 1976), Nat Fire Protection Assn. (com. 1979-86), Aurora Pkwy. North C. of C.)sec. 1976-80), Fremont C. of C. Republican. Mem. Lds Ch. Avocations: needlecrafts, gardening, fishing, swimming, trailering. Home: Seattle, Wash. Died May 31, 2001.

**TOMII, MASAHIDE,** civil engineer, consultant; b. London, Jan. 26, 1926; arrived in Japan, 1931; s. Shu and Hide (Nakamura) T.; m Akiko Tomii (Horii), May 25, 1957; children: Hiroko Yamasaki, Taeko Goto. B of Engring., U. Tokyo, 1948, D of Engring., 1959. Cert. AIJ. Asst. prof. Kyushu U., Fukuoka, Japan, 1955-62, prof., 1962-89, councilor, 1987-89, prof. emeritus, from 1989; v.p. Aoki Corp., Tokyo, 1989-91, prin. Tech. Rsch. Ctr., 1989-93, cons. advisor, 1991-96. Author: Proceedings of the Tom Paulay Symposium, 1993; contbr. articles to profl. jours. Recipient Decorated with the Order of the Sacred Treas. Gold Rays with Neck Ribbon, 2006. Mem. Archtl. Inst. Japan (life, trustee 1963-65, 67-69, 81-83, dir. representing Kyushu chpt. 1979-80, hon. mem. 2008, prize, 1971), Japan Concrete Inst. (hon., dir. 1973-75). Achievements include patent on transverse reinforcing method of reinforced concrete columns by bellows square steel tube. Home: Shibuya-ku Tokyo, Japan. Died Apr. 11, 2008.

**TOMLINSON, JOHN RACE GODFREY,** education educator; b. Manchester, Eng., Apr. 24, 1932; s. John Angell and Beatrice Elizabeth Race (Godfrey) T.; m. Audrey Mavis Barrett, Mar. 27, 1954; children: John, Susan, Janet, Graham. BA, Manchester U., 1953, MA, 1955; DLitt (hon.), U. Hull, 2002; DUniv. (hon.), Open U., 1999; EdD (hon.), UWE, 2000; DEd (hon.), U. Reading, 2000. Tchr. LEA, Stoke-on-Trent, Eng., 1958-60, adminstrv. officer Shropshire County, Eng., 1960-63, asst. edn. officer Local Edn. Authority Lancashire County, Eng., 1963-67, from dep. dir. to dir. edn. Local Edn. Authority Cheshire County, 1967-85; dir. Inst. Edn. U. Warwick, Warwickshire, 1985-97. Chmn. Schs. Curriculum Award com., Eng., 1982-98, Schs. Coun. for England and Wales, 1978-82, Royal Soc. Arts, Eng., 1989-91; chair Nat. Forum on Learners with Disabilities, 2001-2004. Editor Grenville Papers, 1963-65; co-editor Changing Government of Education, 1986, Teacher Appraisal, 1989. Served to flight lt. RAF, 1955-58. Decorated comdr. Order Brit. Empire. Fellow Brit. Inst. Mgmt., Coll. Preceptors, Royal Soc. Arts; mem. Royal No. Coll. Music, Army and Navy Club, Athenaeum. Home: Coventry, England. Died Aug. 6, 2005.

**TOMLINSON, KENNETH Y.,** former broadcast executive, former editor-in-chief; b. Mt. Airy, NC, Aug. 3, 1944; s. Young and Mattie (Wingate) Tomlinson; m. Rebecca Moore, Apr. 25, 1975; children: William Moore, Lucas Young. BA in History, Randolph Macon Coll., 1966. Reporter Richmond Times Dispatch, 1965—68; corr. Reader's Digest, Pleasantville, NY, 1968—81, editor, 1981—82, mng. editor, 1984—85, exec. editor, 1985—90, editor-in-chief, 1989—96; dir. Voice of America, 1982—84; bd. dirs. Corp. for Public Broadcasting, Washington, 2000—05, chmn., 2003—05. Mem. US Bd. for Internat. Broadcasting, 1986—94; pres., dir. Nat. Sporting Libr., 1999—2002. Co-author: History of American Prisoners of War in Vietnam, 1975. Chmn. Nat. Commn. Librs. and Info. Sci., 1986—87; active Nat. Commn. Vol. Svc., 1981—83. Republican. Episcopalian. Home: Middleburg, Va. Died May 1, 2014.

**TONNING, ANDREAS ANSGAR,** electrical engineering educator; b. Stryn, Norway, July 23, 1922; s. Rasmus and Thora Tonning; m. Signe Overwien, Nov. 13, 1965; 1 child, Cecilie. Degree in elec. engring., Norwegian Inst. Tech., Trondheim, 1948, D of Tech., 1958. Rsch. engr. Norwegian Def. Rsch., 1948-62; prof. elec. engring. Norwegian Inst. Tech., Trondheim, from 1962. Bd. dirs. numerous rsch. orgns. Contbr. papers to profl. jours. Mem. IEEE, Am. Phys. Soc., Norsk Ingeniorforening. Home: Trondheim, Norway. Died Mar. 9, 2002.

**TOOMING, HEINO ÜLO,** meteorologist, natural scientist, climatologist, ecologist, researcher; b. Mustvee, Tartumaa, Estonia, Oct. 22, 1930; s. Gustav and Amanda (Kadak) T.; m. Ilje Born, July 27, 1957 (div. 1971); children: Tõnis, Reet; m. Aili Maare Lauringson, June 7, 1976. Diploma in Geophysics, Tartu U., Estonia, 1954, Candidate Phys. Math., 1961, DSc in Biology, 1972. Sr. rsch. scientist in geophysics Diploma, 1967; prof. meteorology, agrometeorology, climatology Diploma, 1990. Fellow Inst. Physics & Astronomy Estonian Acad. Scis., Tartu, USSR, 1954-74; fellow Eston Agrometeorol. Lab. Main Geophys. Observatory, Leningrad, USSR, 1974-76; fellow Estonian Agrometeorol. Lab. Inst. Exptl. Meteorology, Obninsk, USSR, 1976-77, Inst. Agrl. Meteorology, Obninsk, USSR, 1977-91; chief rschr. Estonian Meteorol. and Hydrol. Inst., Tallinn, Estonia, 1991—99; prof. applied meteorology Estonian Nat. Def. and Pub. Svc. Acad., Tallinn, 1995—99; sr. rsch. assoc. Estonian Meteorol. and Hydrology Inst., Tallinn, 1999—2001; prof. applied meteorology Pub. Svc. Acad., from 1999. Mem. coun. ecology Acad. Scis., Moscow, 1971-76, yield programming Acad. Agrl. Scis., Moscow, 1974-91. Author: (with B.I. Guljaev) Methods of Measurements of Photosynthetically Active Radiation, 1967, Japanese edit., 1971, Solar Radiation and Yield Formation, 1977, Japanese edit., 1982, Ecological Principles of Maximum Crops Productivity, 1984; editor: Meteorology in Estonia in Johannes Letzmann's Times and Today, 1995, Weather and Men, 2001; mem. editl. bd. Agrometeorology of the Hydrometeorological Pub. House, Leningrad, 1974-91; contbr. articles to profl. jours. Mem. Estonian Geograph. Soc., Estonian Ecol. Coun., Russian Soc. Plant Physiology (hon. corr.), Estonian Naturalists Soc. (hon., chair sec. exact sci. 1963-68), European and African Region Internat. Assn. Wind Engring. (Estonian contact 1995-2001). Avocations: essayistics, chess, stamp collecting/philately, music, arts. Home: Tallinn, Estonia. Died Sept. 18, 2004.

**TORII, TETSUYA,** retired science educator; b. Takao, Taiwan, May 14, 1918; s. Nobuhei Torii and Masako Suzuki; m. Noriko; children: Tohru, Mari Tanaka, Nobuya. MS, Univ. Tokyo, 1943, DSc (hon.), 1956. Chem. lectr. Kanagawa U., Yokohama, Japan, 1952-55; assoc. prof. chem. Chiba U., Japan, 1955-62, prof. chem., 1962-63, Chiba Inst. Tech., 1963-90; exec. dir. The Japan Polar Rsch. Assn., Tokyo, 1964-94; pres. Japan Polar Rsch. Assn., Tokyo, from 1995. Dir. Japan Chem. Analysis Ctr., Chiba, 1980-90. Editor: pictorial book Antarctica 1970 (adapted to put into the time capsule); discoverer: new mineral in Antarctica antarcticite 1965. Officer Japanese Navy, 1943-45. Recipient Silver Cup, Prime Minister of Japan, 1962, citation Ministry of Edn., Sci. and Culture, 1977, prize Geochem. Rsch. Assn., 1977. Mem. Am. Geophys. Union, Geochem. Soc. Japan, Balneological Soc. Japan (pres. 1988, advisor 2005), Explorer Club (U.S.A.). Avocation: mountain climbing. Home: Tokyo, Japan. Died 2008.

**TORNOE, JAMES FREDRICK,** retail executive; b. Beckley, W.VA., June 9, 1935; s. Leo Ejnar and Clytie Ethel (Sneed) T.; m. Jacqueline Louise Smith, Sept. 9, 1959; children: Eric, Julie, Greg. BSBA, U. Fla., 1960, M.B.A/, 1962. Vice-pres. John A. Brown Co., Oklahoma City, 1971-73, sr. v.p., 1973-75, B. Dalton Bookseller, Mpls., 1975-78, Dayton's Dept. Stores, Mpls., 1978-80; pres. Miller and Rhoads Co., Richmond, Va., 1980-81; vice-chmn. J.L. Hudson Co., Detroit, 1981-84, Dayton Hudson Dept. Store, 1984-85. Bd. dirs. NCCJ, Detroit, 1983; bd. dirs. Citizens Research Council, 1981; mem. United Found., 1981; chmn. Opportunities Indsl. Ctrs., Oklahoma City, 1973. Served with USMC, 1953-56. Mem. Fin. Execs. Inst., Beta Gamma Sigma, Phi Kappa Tau (v.p. 1958-60) Home: Eden Prairie, Minn. Died Apr. 18, 1998.

**TORRE, GARY JEROME,** retired lawyer; b. Oakland, Calif., Oct. 14, 1919; s. Giove M. and Jessie (Garibotto) Torre; m. Carol Desaussiere Goodrich, Dec. 25, 1948; children: Michael Durham, Alicia Hayden, Nicholas Goodrich. BA, U. Calif., 1941, JD, 1948. Bar: Calif. Law clerk Justice William Douglas, Wash., DC, 1948—49; ptnr. Litlick, Geary, Wheat, Adams and Charles, San Francisco, 1949—81; ret., 1981. Lt. USAF, 1942—45. Mem.: Sierra Club (pres., dir. legal defense fund 1968—93). Democrat. Home: San Francisco, Calif. Died Jan. 19, 2013.

**TOSCANO, JACQUELINE SUEANN,** aerospace transportation administrator; b. Portland, Oreg., Aug. 26, 1945; d. Arthur Martin and Mary Kathrin (Brunkala) Miller; m. Robert Kenly, Mar. 5, 1982 (div. 1983); m. John J. Toscano, Dec. 15, 1990. Student, Wright Jr. Coll., Chgo., 1963-64, Lewis U., Lockport, Ill., 1968-69. Aircraft mechanic Continental Airlines, LA, 1964-77; plant electrician Procter and Gamble Co., Chgo., 1977-79, Wester Electric, Chgo., 1979; avionics mechanic Am. Airlines, Chgo., 1979-80, sr. instr. aircraft maintenance, 1980-82, sr. instr., tech. specialist Tulsa, 1982-84, supr. Chgo., from 1984. Sgt. U.S. Army, 1965-68. Mem. Am. Theatre Organ Soc., Chgo. Area Theatre Organ Enthusiasts, Chgo. Hort. Soc., Internat. Soc. of Cert. Electronic Technicians, Coachlite Skate Club. Democrat. Roman Catholic. Avocations: competitive artistic roller skating, theatre organs. Home: Palatine, Ill. Died Jan. 11, 2008.

**TOTSUKA, YOJI,** physics educator; b. Fuji, Japan, Mar. 6, 1942; s. Kazuo and Mitsuko (Ono) T.; m. Hiroko Miyata, Jan. 2, 1944; children: Hirofumi, Yumi. BS in Physics, U. Tokyo, 1965, MS, 1967, DSc, 1972. Rsch. assoc. U. Tokyo, 1972-79, asst. prof., 1979-87, prof. physics, 1987—2001, prof., Inst. for Cosmic Ray Rsch., 2001—03, Spl. U. prof. emeritus, 2003—08, dir., Kamioka Observatory, 1995—2002, dir., Inst. for Cosmic Ray Rsch., 1997—2001; dir.-gen. High Energy Accelerator Rsch. Orgn. (KEK), Ibaraki, Japan, 2003—06. Studied ultra-high-energy interactions in nuclear emulsions, 1965—66; studied muon bundles observed underground, 1967—72; guest scientist, particle physicist investigated electron-positron collisions in experiments like DASP DORIS Accelerator, 1972—76; studied e+e-collisions PETRA, DESY, 1977—80; searched for proton decay and study of supernova-solar-and atmospheric-neutrinos with Kamiokande-I,-II and -III, 1981—95; studied astrophysical neutrinos and search for proton decay with Super-Kamiokande, 1991; guest scientist, particle physicist investigated electron-positron collisions in experiments like JADE PETRA Accelerator, 1996—98; mem. Physics Rsch. Com. (PRC), 1996—98. Recipient Nishina Meml. prize Nishina Found., 1987, Asahi prize 1988, 1999, Rossi prize Am. Astronomical Soc., 1989, Inoue prize, 1990, Spl. prize, European Phys. Soc., 1995; co-recipient Benjamin Franklin medal in Physics, Franklin Inst., 2007. Mem. Japan Phys. Soc., Japan Astron. Soc., Am. Phys. Soc.(W.K.H. Panofsky prize in Exptl. Particle Physics, 2002). Home: Chiba, Jordan. Died July 10, 2008.

**TOUATI, CHARLES,** religious studies educator; b. Tlemcen, Algeria, Feb. 1, 1925; arrived in France, 1945; s. Haïm and Rose (Sultan) T.; m. Madeleine Meyer, Aug. 10, 1949 (dec. July 1993); children: Pierre-Yves, Joël, Laurent. Rabbi, Jewish Sem. of France, Paris, 1948; Dr. in History of Philosophy, Sorbonne, Paris, 1965, Dr d'Etat Lettres, 1971. Asst. prof. Ecole Pratique Hautes Etudes, Paris, 1967-72, full prof., 1972-94; prof. Jewish Sem. of France, Paris, 1950-88. Mem. Comite Nat. de Recherche Scientifique, Langues et Civilisations Orientales, 1971-75; dir. Revue des etudes Juives, Paris, 1981-97; dir. Collection de la Revue des Etudes Juives, Louvain, 1981—. Author: La Pensée de Gersonide, 1973, 2d edit., 1992, Prophètes, Talmudistes, Philosophes, 1990 (Couronné par Acad. des Scis. Morales et Politiques 1991), Juda Hallévi; Le Kuzari, 1994; contbr. articles to profl. jours. Decorated chevalier de la Légion d'Honneur. Mem. Mekisey Nirdamim Acad. Jerusalem, Acad. Jewish Philosophy (hon. fellow), Soc. des Etudes Juives (pres. 1970-72, v.p. 1972—), Assn. French Rabbis (hon. pres. 1999—). Avocations: reading, languages. Died 2006.

**TOWBIN, BELMONT,** bank executive; b. NYC, June 16, 1910; s. Harry and Minna (Berlin) Towbin; m. Phoebe Jacobs, Apr. 20, 1941. BA, Johns Hopkins U., 1931; MBA, Harvard U., 1933. With C.E. Unterberg, NYC, 1933—49; ptnr. Unterberg Towbin Co., 1949—77; ltd. ptnr. L.F. Rothschild Unterberg Towbin, from 1977. Dir. Cobe Labs., Inc., Denver, Gerber Sci. Inc., Hartford, Conn., Swedlow, Inc., Calif., Jeffrey Martin, Inc., NJ. Lt. comdr. USNR, 1942—46. Mem.: N.Y. Soc. Security Analysts, Woodstock Country Club, Bond Club N.Y., Harvard Bus. Sch. Club, Harvard Club. Home: New York, NY. Died Aug. 2, 1993.

**TOWNSEND, ANNA STOFFLET,** civic worker, retired educator; b. Vicksburg, Mich., Sept. 12, 1899; d. John Howard and Ada (Rosenberry) S.; m. Ray Winthrop Townsend, Dec. 20, 1931. BA in English summa cum laude, U. Wis., 1920; postgrad., U. Calif., 1932-40; MA in English, U. S.C., 1940. Tchr. Cen. High Sch., Tulsa, 1920-25, Woodrow Wilson High Sch., Long Beach, Calif., 1927-61, head English dept., 1931-61; ret., 1961. Sustaining mem. Nat. Com. GOP Congl. Com., 1960--. Mem. AAUW (pres. Long Beach br. 1937-38, Calif. div. coms. 1939-44, v.p. 1945-47, pres. Calif. 1950-52, nat. v.p. So. Pacific region 1955-63, bd. dirs., 1955-63, Anna S. Townsend Internat. Fellowships Endowment founded in her honor Calif. div. 1968—, organized Hawaii state div. 1962, alt. vol. del. to IFUW Triennial conf. Mexico City 1962), Nat. Support Pub. Schs., PEO (pres. 1965-67), Ebell Club, Phi Beta Kappa, Phi Kappa Phi, Delta Kappa Gamma, Alpha Xi Delta. Republican. Presbyterian. Avocations: reading, world travel, speaking to church and social groups. Home: Long Beach, Calif. Died Feb. 3, 1992.

**TOWNSEND, FRANK MARION,** pathology educator; b. Stamford, Tex., Oct. 29, 1914; s. Frank M. and Beatrice (House) T.; m. Gerda Eberlein, 1940 (dec. div. 1944); 1 son, Frank M.; m. Ann Graf, Aug. 25, 1951; 1 son, Robert N. Student, San Antonio Coll., 1931-32, U. Tex., 1932-34; MD, Tulane U., 1938. Diplomate: Am. Bd. Pathology. Intern Polyclinic Hosp., NYC, 1939-40; commd. 1st lt. M.C., U.S. Army, 1940, advanced through grades to lt. col., 1946; resident instr. pathology Washington U., 1945-47; trans. to USAF, 1949, advanced through grades to col., 1956; instr. pathology Coll. Medicine, U. Nebr., 1947-48; asso. pathologist Scott and White Clinic, Temple, Tex., 1948-49; asso. prof. pathology Med. Br. U. Tex., Galveston, 1949-59; flight surgeon USAF, 1950-65; dir. labs. USAF Hosp. (now Wilford Hall USAF Hosp.), Lackland AFB, Tex., 1950-54; cons. pathology Office of Surgeon Gen. Hdqrs. USAF, Washington, 1954-63, chief cons. group Office of Surgeon Gen. Hdqrs., 1954-55; dep. dir. Armed Forces Inst. Pathology, Washington, 1955-59, dir., 1959-63; vice comdr. aerospace med. divsn. Air Force Systems Command, 1963-65, ret., 1965; practice medicine specializing in pathology San Antonio, from 1965; dir. labs. San Antonio State Chest Hosp.; consulting pathologist Tex. Dept. Health hosps., 1965-72; clin. prof. pathology U. Tex. Med. Sch., San Antonio, 1969-72, prof., chmn. dept. pathology Health Sci. Ctr., 1972-86, emeritus chmn., prof., 1986—2001. Cons. U. Tex. Cancer Ctr.-M.D. Anderson Hosp., 1966-80, NASA, 1967-75; mem. adv. bd. cancer WHO, 1958-75; mem. Armed Forces Epidemiology Bd., 1983-91; bd. govs. Armed Forces Inst. Pathology, 1984-95. Mem. editorial bd. Tex. Med. Jour., 1978-86; contbr. articles to med. jours. Mem. adv. coun. Civil War Centennial Commn., 1960-65; bd. dirs. Alamo Area Sci. Fair, 1967-73. Decorated D.S.M., Legion of Merit; recipient Founders medal Assn. Mil. Surgeons, 1961, medal of honor DAR, 1997; recipient Comdr.'s award Armed Forces Epidemiol. Bd., 1990; F.M. Townsend Chair of Pathology endowed in his honor by faculty of Dept. Pathology, U. Tex. Health Sci. Ctr., 1987, The Annual Frank M. Townsend M.D. lectr. endowed in hist honor by faculty dept. pathology U. Tex. Health Sci. Ctr., San Antonio, 1999. Fellow ACP, Coll. Am. Pathologists (edn. advisor on accreditation, commr. lab. accreditation South Ctrl. States region 1971-84), Am. Soc. Clin. Pathologists (Ward Burdick award 1983), Aerospace Med. Assn. (H.G. Mosely award 1962); mem. AMA, AAAS, Tex. Med. Assn., Internat. Acad. Aviation and Space Medicine, Tex. Soc. Pathologists (Caldwell award 1971), Am. Assn. Pathologists, Internat. Acad. Pathology, Acad. Clin. Lab. Physicians and Scientists, Soc. Med. Cons. to Armed Forces, Torch Club. Home: Harwood, Tex. Died Oct. 31, 2001.

**TRACY, ALOISE** See SHOENIGHT, PAULINE ALOISE SOUERS

**TRAFICANT, JAMES ANTHONY, JR.,** former United States Representative from Massachusetts; b. Youngstown, Ohio, May 8, 1941; s. James Anthony & Agnes T. Traficant; m. Patricia Coppa; children: Robin, Elizabeth BS in Edn., U. Pitts., 1963, MS, 1973, Youngstown State U., 1976. Exec. dir. Mahoning County Drug Program, Ohio, 1971-81; sheriff Mahoning County, Ohio, 1981-85; mem. US Congress from 17th Ohio Dist., Washington, 1985—2002. Democrat. Died Sept. 27, 2014.

**TRAN, JACK NHUAN NGOC,** gas and oil reservoir engineer; b. Quang Binh, Vietnam, Sept. 21, 1933; came to U.S., 1975; s. Dieu Ngoc and Ly Thi (Nguyen) T.; m. Christine Quang Huynh; children: Quoc Dung, Ann Nga Huyen, Ephram Anh Dung, John Hung Dung. BS, U. San Francisco, 1977, MBA, 1978. With Republic of Vietnam Mil., 1952-67; cadet Rep. Vietnam Mil. Acad., Dalat, 1952-53; 1st lt., co. comdr. 1st Republic of Vietnam Bn., South Vietnam, 1953-54; editor-in-chief Republic of Vietnam Revs., Saigon, 1955-57; commandant Republic of Vietnam Aerial Photo Ctr., Saigon, 1958-61, Republic of Vietnam Mil. Intelligence Sch., Caymai and Saigon, 1962-67; mem. Republic of Vietnam Senate, 1967-73; v.p. The Meteco Corp., Saigon, Vietnam, 1971-72; pres., chmn. bd. Meteco-Vinaseco Co., Saigon, 1972-75; air photo analyst Std. Oil Co., San Francisco, 1975-79; gas and oil engr. Chevron Oil Co., San Francisco, from 1980; col. U.S. Intelligence, Calif., 1980-90. Author: Flower in the Battle Field, 1956, Geological Survey of the Kndu, CA, 1982, Beluga River Oil Development, 1984, The Military Life, 1992; editor-in-chief Chien-Si Quoc-Gia Mag. Recipient Hon. Key of the City, City of Omaha, Nebr., 1989, Hon. Citizen City of Fayetteville, N.C., 1969; Resolution of Recognition, Senate of State of Hawaii, 1969, Senate of State of Tex., 1969. Mem. The U. of San Francisco Alumni Assn., Rotary Internat. Roman Catholic. Avocations: swimming, music, reading, travel. Deceased.

**TRAORE, DIARRA,** former prime minister of Guinea; b. 1935; Career officer Guinean Armed Forces; prime min. Republic of Guinea, 1984—85; min. state nat edn. Govt. of Guinea, 1985. Died 1985.

**TRAORE, JEAN,** former Guinean government official; Advanced through grades to maj. Guinea Army; min. mines and geology Govt. of Guinea, Conakry, 1984, min. state for planning and natural resources, 1985-86, min. fgn. affairs, 1986—92. Died July 20, 1999.

**TRAPPE, PAUL,** sociologist; b. Trier, Germany, Dec. 12, 1931; s. Johannes and Ottilie (Kaess) T.; children: Luzius, Simon, Sonia. Student, U. Innsbruck, 1951-52, U. Paris, 1952, U. Freiburg, 1953, U. Frankfurt, 1953-55; PhD, U. Mainz, West Germany, 1959; habilitation, U. Bern, Switzerland, 1964. Asst. U. Mainz, 1959-61, U. Bern, 1961-63, docent, 1964-66, Freiburg, West Germany, 1965-66; prof., dir. Inst. Sociology, U. Kiel, West Germany, 1966-69; dir. Inst. Sociology, U. Basel, Switzerland, 1968—2002. Author books; contbr. numerous articles to profl. jours.; editor Social Strategies, 1975—. Recipient Triennial Jubilee prize Internat. Coop. Alliance, 1970, Festschrift in his honor P. Lang Pub., 2003. Mem. Soc. Advancement of Sci., N.Y. Acad. Scis., Internat. Sociol. Assn., Soc. Internat. Devel., Soc. Study of Internat. Problems (pres. 1967-81), Internat. Assn. Philosophy of Law and Social Philosophy (pres. 1979-83), Soc. Econ. Devel. (chairperson interdisciplinary rsch. unit 1994-2000), European Faculty Land Use and Devel. (pres. 1999—). Died Mar. 22, 2005.

**TRASK, JAMES STEPHEN,** artist, forester; b. Keene, NH, Dec. 26, 1941; s. Norman Owen and Vina (Soucy) T.; m. Florence G. Gadoury, Oct. 2, 1971 (div. Aug. 1995); children: Richard Lewis, John Adam, Samuel Phillip. BS in Forestry, U. N.H., 1964; MS in Forestry, Pa. State U., 1967. Asst. county forester U.N.H. Ext. Svc., Exeter, 1966; instr. forestry and biology Nichols Coll., Dudley, Mass., 1968-70; resource conservation svc. forestry Maine Forest Svc., Alfred, 1971-77, svc. forester, 1977-81; pvt. cons. forester, Sanford, Maine, 1981-93; artist, from 1993. Docent Wells Nat. Estuarian Res., 1995—. With U.S. Army, 1966-68, Vietnam. Named Vol. Extraordinaire, Wells Nat. Estuarian Res., 1998. Mem. Maie Women in Arts, Art Assn. Sanford and Springvale (2nd place award 1997, 99, Best of Show 2003), Keene Art Assn., Danforth Gallery, Sharon Art Ctr., Petersboro, N.H., The Vault, Springfield, Vt., Lions (pres. Sanford 1980-81, 2000-01). Democrat. Avocations: gardening, photography. Home: Sanford, Maine. Died July 19, 2008.

**TRAVELL, CLARK,** financial services consultant; b. NYC, Aug. 29, 1923; s. J. Willard and Edith (Talcott) T. Home: Wilton, Conn. Died May 9, 1999.

**TREADWAY, EVERETT A.,** labor union official; b. Maple Grove, Md., Oct. 25, 1930; s. Bruce Franklin and Dessie Amanda Treadway; m. Joan Treadway, 1955; 4 children. Mem. Internat. Union Elevator Constructors, Columbia, Md., from 1956, gen. sec.-treas., from 1974, now pres. Died Dec. 16, 1991.

**TREANOR, GERARD FRANCIS, JR.,** lawyer; b. Medford, Mass., July 1, 1943; AB, Holy Cross Coll., Worcester, Mass., 1965; JD, Cath. U., Washington, 1968. Bar: D.C. 1969. Law clk. to Hon. Edward M. Curran US Dist. Ct. DC, Washington, 1968-69; spl. counsel US House of Representatives, Washington, 1972-73; asst. US atty. US Dept. Justice, Washington, 1973-77; ptnr. Dolan & Treanor, Arlington, Va., 1977-86, Venable, Baetjer, Howard & Civiletti, Washington, 1986-92 and from 97, 1997—2010, Cacheris & Treanor, Washington, 1993-97. Lt. USNR, 1969-72, Australia. Fellow American Bar Found., American Coll. of Trial Lawyers. Home: Arlington, Va. Died Oct. 30, 2013.

**TRECKER, FRANCIS J.,** machinery company executive; b. Milw., Dec. 17, 1909; s. Emma (Pufahl) T.; m. Dorothy G. Knowles, July 1968. BS in Mech. and Adminstrv. Engring., Cornell U., 1935; postgrad., Marquette U., 1928-32. With Pratt & Whitney Aircraft Corp., Hartford, Conn.; with Pratt & Whitney Machine Tool Corp., Hartford, Conn.; cons. engr. Stevenson, Jordan & Harrison, Inc., NYC; various mfg. and sales dept. positions Kearney & Trecker Corp., Milw., asst. chief engr., pres., dir., 1947, chmn., from 1968, chief exec. officer, 1968-73; chmn., dir. Trecker Aircraft Corp., Milw.; vice chmn. Cross & Trecker Corp., Bloomfield Hills, Mich., from 1979. Pres., dir. Cleereman Machine Tool Corp., Racine, Wis.; v.p., dir. Milw. Community Devel. Corp.; dir. Gorton Machine Corp., Racine, Kearney & Trecker, Ltd., Eng. KTTK, Tokyo, Japan, 1968-73; cons. to Sec. of War of subcontracting and facilities procurement, 2 years; cons. to sec. air force, 1964-68, chmn. air force ad hoc com. vice chmn. Tools for Freedom; chief of engring. and subcontracting OPM and WPB, 1 year, also dep. dir. def. contract service WPB Trustee Ripon Coll., Council Tech. Advancement, Am. Heritage Found., Ducks Unltd. Fellow in perpetuity Met. Mus. Art, N.Y.C. Mem. Nat. Machine Tool Builders Assn. (dir. 1950-53, 59-62, pres. 1961-62), ASME, Am. Soc. Tool Engrs., Wis. C. of C. (chmn. aviation com.), Am. Arbitration Assn., Young Presidents Orgn. (dir. 1952-58), Chief Execs. Forum (pres. 1962-63), Shikar Safari, Air Power League (charter), Nat. Aero. Assn. (life). Clubs: Milwaukee Country, Milwaukee, University (Milw.); Paradise Valley Country (Scottsdale, Ariz.). Home: Paradise Vly, Ariz. Died Nov. 16, 1987.

**TRETCHIKOFF, VLADIMIR GRIGOREVICH,** artist; b. Russia, Dec. 13, 1913; s. Gregori Vasilevich and Anastasia Kizminishna (Razvalaeva) T.; m. Natalie M. Telpougoff, Jan. 8, 1935; 1 dau., Mimi Mercorio. Fifty one-man internat. exhbns. of painting, 1933-2006, including Shanghai, China, 1933, U.S. tours, San Francisco, San Jose, Calif., Los Angeles, 1952, Dallas, Milw., Chgo., 1953, Cleve., Seattle, 1954, Can. tours, toronto, Montreal, 1954, 65, Vancouver, Victoria, 1955-65, Winnipeg, 1965, London, 1962, Birmingham and Manchester, Eng., 1972, Edinburgh (Scotland) Internat. Festival, 1973, South African tours, 1948, 52, 59, 68, 76, 77-78; films include Green Lady, BBC, London, 1974-79, Man of Merit, 1978, Tretchikoff Unlimited, 1978, Day in the Life of an Artist, Eurovision Internat., 1980, Day in Life of Tretchikoff Eurovision, 1981; author: (autobiography) Pigeon's Luck, 1973; Portfolio Ten Commandments, 1979 (cast in Gold Medallions by S.A. Hist. Mint). Served with Brit. Ministry Info, Malaya, World War II. Recipient medal Gallery Sci. and Art, N.Y.C., 1939. Mem. South African Assn. Art. Clubs: Western Province Sports. Greek Orthodox. Died Aug. 26, 2006.

**TREVES, SAMUEL BLAIN,** geologist, educator; b. Detroit, Sept. 11, 1925; s. Samuel and Stella (Stork) T.; m. Jane Patricia Mitoray, Nov. 24, 1960; children: John Samuel, David Samuel. BS, Mich. Tech. U., 1951; postgrad., U. Otago, New Zealand, 1953-54; MS, U. Idaho, 1953; PhD, Ohio State U., 1959. Geologist Ford Motor Co., 1951, Idaho Bur. Mines and Geology, 1952, Otago Catchment Bd., 1953-54; mem. faculty U. Nebr., Lincoln, 1958—2004, prof. geology, 1966—2004, chmn. dept., 1964-70, 74-89, assoc. dean Coll. Arts and Scis., 1989-96, emeritus, 2004. Curator geology Nebr. State Mus., 1964—; participant expdns. to Antarctica and Greenland, 1960, 61, 63, 65, 70, annually 72-76. Rsch. and publs. on geology of igneous and metamorphic rocks of Idaho, New Zealand, Mich., Antarctica, Nebr., Can., Greenland with emphasis on origin of Precambrian granite complexes and basaltic volcanic rocks. Fulbright scholar U. Otago, New Zealand, 1953-54. Fellow Geol. Soc. Am.; mem. Am. Mineral Soc., Am. Geophys. Union, Sigma Xi, Tau Beta Pi, Sigma Gamma Epsilon. Home: Omaha, Nebr. Died June 10, 2013.

**TROEDSSON, INGEGERD,** retired Swedish government official; b. Vaxholm, Sweden, June 5, 1929; d. Emil Johan and Gerd (Wibom) Cederlof; m. Tryggve Bengt Johan, 1949. BA, Stockholm Univ., 1951; MA in Polit. Sci., Stockholm U., 1952. Mem. parliament, 1974—94; min. cabinet health care, 1976—78; first dep. spkr. Rikstag, 1979—91, spkr., 1991—94. Author: (book) Politics for the 70's-les, 1969, The Commanded Family, 1999, Release of the Family, 2001, History from Enkoping, 2006, The Battle of Gestilren 1210, 2009. Bd. dir. Moderata Samlingspartiet, 1966—76, 1978—91, 2d dep. chair, 1987—91. Home: Grillby, Sweden. Died Nov. 3, 2012.

**TROITSKI, YURI VLADIMIROVICH,** physicist, researcher; b. Semipalatinsk, USSR, July 10, 1928; s. Vladimir Mikhailovich and Zinaida Fedorovna (Lapshina) T.; m. Galina Stepanovna Rodyukova, June 22, 1955; children: Sergei, Dmitri. MSc, State U. Nizhni Novgorod, Russia, 1952; DSc, USSR Acad. Scis., Novosibirsk, 1972. Postgrad. rschr. USSR Acad. Scis., Novosibirsk, 1955-60, head lab. Inst. Semiconductor Physics, 1963—69, head lab. Inst. Automation and Electrometry, 1973—98; chief scientist Siberian divsn. Inst. Automation and Electrometry Russian Acad. Sci., from 1999; prof. USSR Acad. Scis., Novosibirsk, from 1990. Author: Single Frequency Gas Lasers, 1975, Mulitple Beam Reflection Interferometers, 1985; contbr. over 200 articles to sci. publs.in microwaves, optics, lasers, interferometers, thin films, gravitational wave detectors. Grantee Internat. Sci. Found., N.Y., 1993, Ministry of Sci. of Russian Fedn., Moscow, 1994-2001, Russian Found. for Basic Rsch., 2004—; named Hon. Scientist of the Russian Fedn., 2002. Mem. N.Y. Acad. Scis. Achievements include invention of 14 in field. Home: Novosibirsk, Russia. Died Jan. 28, 2005.

**TROLANDER, HARDY WILCOX,** engineering executive, consultant; b. Chgo., June 2, 1921; s. Elmer Wilcox and Freda Marie (Zobel) T.; m. Imogen Davenport, July 3, 1946 (dec.); children: Megan, Patricia. BS in Engring., Antioch Coll., 1947. Instr. Antioch Coll., Yellow Springs, Ohio, 1947-48; co-founder, CEO Yellow Springs Instrument Co., Inc., 1948-86. Dir., co-founder Cook Design Ctr., Dartmouth Coll., Hanover, N.H., 1975-88; bd. dirs. Dessinier Corp., Yellow Springs, Camax Tool Co., Arvada, Colo.; mem. evaluation panel Inst. Basic Stds., Nat. Bur. Stds., 1977-79. Contbr. articles to profl. jours.; patentee in field. Co-founder, trustee Yellow Springs Community Found., 1974-83; trustee Autioch Coll., 1968-74, chmn. bd., 1972-74; trustee Engring. and Sci. Found., Dayton, 1982-96, Engrs. Club Dayton Found., 1994-2005, Engring. and Sci. Hall of Fame, 1994-2002; mem. adv. bd. Coll. Engring. and Computer Sci. Wright State U., 1993-2005; bd. dirs. united Way Greater Dayton Area, 1984-92; small bus. innovative rsch. grant panels Nat. Sci. Found., 1988—. 1st lt. USAF, 1943-46. Named Outstanding Engr., Dayton Affiliate Socs., 1967, 89. Fellow Dayton Engrs. Club, Am. Inst. for Med. and Biol. Engring.; mem. ACLU, Nat. Acad. Engring., Am. Inst. Biol. Scis. (bioinstrumentation adv., coun. 1969-75), Internat. Orgn. of Legal Metrology (tech. advisor, sec. 1975-82), Amnesty Internat. Democrat. Achievements include co-development of melting point of gallium which has become recognized as a primary defining point of the International Temperature Scale. Home: Cedarville, Ohio. Died Oct. 11, 2013.

**TROSPER, ORVILLE WENDELL,** education educator; b. Corbin, Ky., Oct. 18, 1918; s. William E. and Zora B. Trosper. Student, Berea Coll., 1938-40; BA, U. Ky., 1942; postgrad., Cin. Conservatory, 1948, Marseille Conservatory, France, 1946, Nice Conservatory, 1946; M.Mus., VanderCook Coll. Music, 1953; MA, Columbia U., 1958, EdD, 1962; postgrad., Northwestern U., 1965-70, Cin. Conservatory, Marshall U., Marseille Conservatory, France, Nice Conservatory. Tchr. music Harlan County (Ky.) Schs., 1946-48; band dir., tchr. history Huntington (W.Va.)-Cabell County Schs., 1948-55; band dir., instrumental and gen. music tchr. Croton-on-Hudson (N.Y.) Sch., 1955-64; assoc. prof. music Berea Coll., 1964-66, VanderCook Coll. Music, Chgo., from 1966, chmn. dept. edn., 1967-74. Owner, pres. Trosper Ednl. Cons., Chgo., 1968-74; ret. agt. FBI. Author: The Principles and Practice of Producing Vibrato in Brass Instruments. Deacon, 1st Bapt. Ch., Ossining, N.Y., 1963-64. With USAAF, 1942-46, ETO. Mem. AAUP, NEA, VFW, MEA, Coll. Band Dirs. Assn., Masons (32 deg., 50 Yr. Membership 1998), Am. Legion, Shriners, Phi Mu Alpha, Kappa Delta Pi, Phi Delta Kappa, Alpha Sigma Phi. Deceased.

**TROTTER, CHARLIE,** chef, restaurateur; b. Wilmette, Sept. 8, 1959; s. Robert and Dona-Lee Trotter; m. Rochelle Smith, 2010; 1 child from previous marriage, Dylan. BS in Polit. Sci., U. Wis., 1982. Cook Sinclair's, Chgo.; owner, chef Charlie Trotter's, Chgo., 1987—2012, Trotter's To Go, Lincoln Park, Ill., 2000—12, "C", Los Cabos, Mexico, 2004—08, Restaurant Charlie, Las Vegas, 2008—10. Founder Charlie Trotter Culinary Edn. Found., from 1999. Co-author (with Paul Clarke): Lessons in Excellence, 1999; co-author: (with Paul Lawler) Lessons in Service, 2001; co-author: (with Roxanne Klein) Raw, 2003; co-author: (with others) Knife Skills in the Kitchen, 2008; author: Charlie Trotter's, 1994, Charlie Trotter's Vegetables, 1996, Charlie Trotter's Seafood, 1997, Gourmet Cooking for Dummies, 1997, Charlie Trotter's Desserts, 1998, The Kitchen Sessions with Charlie Trotter, 1999, Charlie Trotter Cooks at Home, 2000, Charlie Trotter's Meat and Game, 2001, Workin' More Kitchen Sessions with Charlie Trotter, 2004, Homecooking with Charlie Trotter, 2009; host: (TV series) Kitchen Sessions with Charlie Trotter, 1999 (Best National Cooking Show, James Beard Found., 2000); appeared in (films) My Best Friend's Wedding, 1997. Established Charlie Trotter Culinary Edn. Found.; chair American Cancer Soc. Vin Affair, Literacy Chgo. Book Auction; bd. mem., host of annual scholarship luncheon Ill. Restaurant Assn. Edn. Recipient Anti-Defamation League's Torch of Liberty award, Moreau award for Excellence in the Culinary Arts, Frederick Wildman & Sons, Frederick L. Dame award, Court of Master Sommeliers, Fine Dining Ivy award, Restaurants and Institutions, 1990, Grand award, Wine Spectator, from 1993, Outstanding Wine Service, James Beard Found., 1993, Outstanding Chef award, 1999, Best Food Photography, Desserts, 1999, Outstanding Restaurant, 2000, Outstanding Service, 2002, Best Food Photography, Meat & Game, 2003, Chgo.'s Rising Stars Mentor award, StarChefs.com, 2008, Silver Plate award, Internat. Food Manufacturers Assn., 2008, Gold Plate award, 2008, World Green Gastronomy award, The White Guide, Sweden, 2008; named Best Chef: Midwest, James Beard Found., 1992, The Best Restaurant in the World for Wine and Food, Wine Spectator, 1998, The Best Restaurant in the US, 2000, Humanitarian of the Yr., Internat. Assn. Culinary Professionals, 2004, America's Best Wine-Driven Restaurants, Wine Enthusiast, 2006, The #1 Best Place to Eat in America Now, Golf Connoisseur Mag., 2006, Most Sustainable Chef, Share Our Strength's Taste of the Nation, 2007, Humanitarian of the Yr., James Beard Found., 2012; named one of The 5 Heroes, America's Promise, The 50 Power Players, Nation's Restaurant News, 2000; named to The Fine Dining Hall of Fame, 1991, The Who's Who in Food & Beverage in America, James Beard Found., 1996. Achievements include being one of 5 heroes to be honored by America's Promise. Died Nov. 4, 2013.

**TROTTER, NANCY LOUISA,** life science educator; b. Monaca, Pa., July 26, 1934; d. Robert J. and Mary Lou (Braham) T. AB, Oberlin Coll., 1956; ScM, Brown U., 1958, PhD, 1960. Cert. electron microscopist. Instr. Columbia U., NYC, 1961-64, asst. prof., 1964-67; assoc. prof. Thomas Jefferson U., Phila., 1967-90, assoc. prof. emeritus anatomy, from 1990. Contbr. articles to profl. jours. Mem. Am. Assn. Anatomy. Republican. Presbyterian. Avocation: swimming. Home: New Castle, Pa. Died Apr. 6, 2008.

**TROYAN, RONALD J.,** real estate developer; b. San Francisco, July 9, 1930; s. Jack G. and Aileen I. (Reed) T.; m. Eileen I. Pope, June 15, 1953; children: Maryeileen, Kevin, John, Bernadette. BSc, Santa Clara U., 1952. Gen. ptnr. Capitola Knolls Investors Ltd., San Jose, 1972—83; v.p. cons. Robert Pope and Assocs., Palo Alto. Lt. USN, 1952—57. Named Investment Exchanger of Yr., San Jose Real Estate Bd., 1969. Mem.: San Jose Assn. Realtors, Nat. Assn. Realtors. Home: San Jose, Calif. Died Apr. 28, 1990.

**TROYANOVSKY, OLEG ALEXANDROVICH,** diplomat; b. Moscow, Nov. 24, 1919; s. Aleksandr Antonovich and Nina Nikolaevna (Pomorskaya) Troyanovsky; m. Tatyana Aleksandrovna Popova, Nov. 20, 1953; 1 child, Maria. Student, Inst. Philosophy Lit. & History, Moscow, 1938—41; grad., Inst. Fgn. Langs., Moscow, 1956. With Soviet Informbur., Moscow, 1942—44, USSR Embassy, London, 1944—47, Ministry Fgn. Affairs, Moscow, 1947—58, former counselor; asst. to chmn. Coun. Mins., Moscow, 1958—67; amb. to Japan Tokyo, 1967—76; permanent rep. of USSR to UN NYC, 1977—86; amb. to Beijing China, 1986—90. Former sr. v.p. UN Assn. of USSR. Decorated Order of Lenin, Order of October Revolution, Order of Red Banner of Labour,, Order of Badge of Merit. Died Dec. 21, 2003.

**TROYAT, HENRI TARASOFF,** writer; b. Nov. 1, 1911; s. Tarasoff Aslan and Abessolomoff (Lydie) T.; m. Marie a Marguerite Saintagne, Sept. 23, 1948 (dec.); 2 children. Student, Lycee Pasteur, France, U. Paris. Author: Faux-jour (Prix Populiste), 1935, L'araigne (Prix Goncourt), 1938, La neige en deuil (Grand prix litteraire de Monaco), 1952, Tant que la terredurera (three vols.), 1947-50, Les semailles et les moissons (five vols.), 1953-58, La lumiere des justes (five vols.), 1960-63, Les Eygletiere (three vols.), 1965-67, Les heritiers de l'avenir, 1968, Anne Predaille, 1973, Le Moscovite, 1974, La Derision, 1983, Aliocha, 1991, numerous others; (biographies) Dostoievsky, Pouchkine, Tolstoi, Gogol, Catherine la Grande, Pierre le Grand, Alexandre Ier, Ivan le Terrible, Tchekhov, Tourgueniev, Gorki, Flaubert, Maupassant, Zola, Rasputin, Nicolas I, Nicolas II, others. Decorated Legion d'honneur. Mem. Acad. Francaise. Died Mar. 4, 2007.

**TRUDEL, MARC J.,** botanist, educator; PhD, Cornell U. Prof. plant physiology and horticulture Laval U., 1969—2003, prof. emeritus, from 2005, former dean sch. agrl. and food scis., 1983-91, former dir. gen. continuing edn., 1992-97, v.p. devel., 1997—2003. Died Mar. 1, 2009.

**TRULL, ANDREW,** pharmacologist, researcher; b. London, Eng., Feb. 13, 1956; s. Kenneth and Jillian Trull; m. Rosemary Young, June 1, 1985; children: Thomas, Nicholas, Alice. BSc, Hull U., Yorkshire, 1977; PhD, London U., 1983. Post-grad. scientist Guy's Hosp., London, 1978—83; post-doctoral rsch. asst. Addenbrooke's Hosp., Cambridge, England, 1983—85, sr. clin. biochemist, 1985—91, prin. clin. biochemist, 1991—2000; head dept. clin. pharmacology Papworth Hosp., Cambridge, from 2000. Organizer chair European Meeting on Biomarkers of Organ Damage and Dysfunction, 2000. Contbr. articles to profl. jours. Sch. gov. Cheveley Primary Sch., Newmarket, Suffolk, England, 1994—98. Grantee, Indsl. and Charitable Sources, 1987—2002. Mem.: Assn. Clin. Biochemists. Deceased.

**TRUNZ, ERICH,** humanities educator; b. Königsberg, Germany, June 13, 1905; s. August and Helene (Fähser) T.; widowed 1983; 1 child: Hermann. PhD, U. Berlin, 1931; Habilitation, U. Freiburg, Germany, 1937. Prof. German U., Prague, 1940-45, U. Münster, Germany, 1950-57, U. Kiel, Germany, 1957-70. Author: J.M. Meyfart, 17th Century Theologian and Author, 1987, A Day in Goethe's Life, 1990, Thought and Poetry in Baroque Germany, 1992, Thought and Literature of the Age of Goethe, 1993; editor: Goethe's Works, Hamburg edit., 14 vols. 1948-60, 15th revised edit., 1993; contbr. articles to profl. jours. Home: Altenholz bei Kiel, Germany. Died Apr. 26, 2001.

**TSENG, CHENG KUI,** marine biologist; b. Xiamen, China, June 18, 1909; s. Bi Cong and Sui Qing (Lin) T.; m. N. Y. Ye June 15, 1931 (div. Sept. 1952); m. Yi Fan Zhang, May 15, 1954; children: Yun Peng, Zhen Li, William Yun Chi, Lillian S.L. Wang. BSc, Xiamen U., 1931; MSc, Lingnan U., 1934; DSc, U. Mich., 1942. Botany asst. and instr. Xiamen U., China, 1930-35; assoc. prof. Shandong U., Qingdao, China, 1935-38, Lingnan U., Guangzhou and Hong Kong, 1938-40; postdoctoral fellow U. Mich., 1942-43; rsch. assoc. Scripps Inst. Oceanography, La Jolla, Calif., 1943-46; prof. Shandong U., 1946-52; rsch. prof., asst. dir., dir., then dir. emeritus Inst. Oceanology, Qingdao, China, from 1950. Author: Common Seaweeds of China, 1983, Oceanology of China, 1994; editor: Manual of Laminaria Cultivation, 1962, Chinese Economic Seaweeds, 1962, Encyclopedia Sinicarum--Atmospheric, Oceanological and Hydrological Sciences, 1987; contbr. articles to profl. jours. Mem. AAAS, Chinese Soc. Oceanology & Limnology (pres. 1979-88, pres. emeritus), Internat. Seaweed Assn. (coun. mem. 1980-92), Internat. Phycological Soc. (pres. 1986-87), Chinese Soc. Botany, Chinese Oceanography Soc. (pres. emeritus), Chinese Phycological Soc. (hon. life, pres. 1979-91, pres. emeritus 1991—), World Aquaculture Soc., N.Y. Acad. Scis., Chinese Acad. Scis., 3d World Acad. Scis. Avocation: music. Died Jan. 20, 2005.

**TUDDENHAM, READ DUNCAN,** psychology educator; b. Salt Lake City, Sept. 4, 1915; s. John Charles and Helen A. (Underwood) T.; m. Eileen Whelan, May 30, 1943; children: William J., Helen. AB, U. Utah, 1935; PhD, U. Calif., Berkeley, 1941. Diplomate in clin. psychology: Am. Bd. Profl. Psychology. With dept. psychology U. Calif., Berkeley, from 1946, prof. psychology, from 1959. Cons. to U.S. Govt., VA, Dept. of Army, Calif. Dept. Mental Hygiene. Contbr. articles profl. jours. USPHS grantee to U. Geneva, 1961-62 Fellow AAAS, Am. Psychol. Assn.; mem. Western Psychol. Assn., Soc. Research in Child Devel., Phi Beta Kappa, Sigma Xi, Phi Kappa Phi. Deceased.

**TUELL, JACK MARVIN,** retired bishop; b. Tacoma, Nov. 14, 1923; s. Frank Harry and Anne Helen (Bertelson) T.; m. Marjorie Ida Beadles, June 17, 1946; children: Jacqueline, Cynthia, James. BS, U. Wash., 1947, JD, 1948; MDiv, Boston U., 1955; MA, U. Puget Sound, 1961, DHS, 1990; D.D., Pacific Sch. Religion, 1966; LLD, Alaska Pacific U., 1980. Bar: Wash. 1948; ordained to ministry Meth. Ch., 1955. Practice law with firm Holte & Tuell, Edmonds, Wash., 1948-50; pastor Grace Meth. Ch., Everett, Wash., 1950-52, South Tewksbury Meth. Ch., Tewksbury, Mass., 1952-55, Lakewood Meth. Ch., Tacoma, 1955-61; dist. supt. Puget Sound dist. Meth. Ch., Everett, 1961-67; pastor 1st United Meth. Ch., Vancouver, Wash., 1967-72; bishop United Meth. Ch., Portland, Oreg., 1972-80, Calif.-Pacific Conf., United Meth. Ch., LA, 1980-92, ret., 1992; interim sr. pastor First United Meth. Ch., Boise, Idaho, 1995; interim supt. Seattle Tacoma Dist., 2004—05. Mem. gen. conf. United Meth. Ch., 1964, 66, 68, 70, 72; pres. coun. of Bishops United Meth. Ch., 1989-90. Author: The Organization of the United Methodist Church, 1970, 11th edit. 2008, (autobiography) From Law to Grace, 2004. Pres. Tacoma U.S.O., 1959-61, Vancouver YMCA, 1968; v.p. Ft. Vancouver Seamens Cnt., 1969-72; vice chmn. Vancouver Human Rels. Commn., 1970-72; pres. Oreg. Coun. Alcohol Problems, 1972-76; trustee U. Puget Sound, 1961-73, Vancouver Meml. Hosp., 1967-72, Alaska Meth. U., Anchorage, 1972-80, Willamette U., Salem, Oreg., 1972-80, Willamette View Manor, Portland, 1972-80, Rogue Valley Manor, Medford, Oreg., 1972-76, Sch. Theology at Claremont, Calif., 1980-92, Methodist Hosp., Arcadia, Calif., 1983-92; pres. nat. div. bd. global ministries United Meth. Ch., 1972-76, pres. ecumenical and interreligious concerns div., 1976-80, Commn. on Christian Unity and intereligious concerns, 1980-84, Gen. Bd. of Pensions,1984-92, Calif. Coun. Alcohol Problems, 1985-88. Jacob Sleeper fellow, 1955. Methodist. Died Jan. 10, 2014.

**TURF, BARBARA ANN,** retired home-furnishings company executive; b. Feb. 28, 1943; Grad., U. Ill. Urbana-Champaign. Sales rep. Crate & Barrel/Euromarket Designs, Inc., Chgo., 1967, store mgr. Wilmette, Ill., 1968—72, asst. dir. store ops. & pers., 1972—75, dir. mdse. & mktg., exec. v.p. mdse. & mktg., 1993—96, pres., 1996—2008, pres., CEO, 2008—12; founder Turf Internat. Development Group, Skokie, Ill., 2012—14. Bd. dirs. Ann Taylor Stores Corp., 2004—06. Died July 12, 2014.

**TURING, ALAN MATHISON,** mathematician; b. London, June 23, 1912; s. Julius Mathison and Ethel Sara (Stoney) Turing. Student, Sherborne Sch., 1926; grad., King's Coll., Cambridge, Eng., 1934; postgrad., Princeton U., 1936-37. Mem. staff Cambridge U., 1947-48; prof. math. U. Manchester, Eng., 1948. Designer computer Nat. Phys. Lab., London, 1946. Author papers in field. Fellow King's Coll., 1935; recipient Smith's prize, 1936. Fellow Royal Soc. London; mem. Walton Athletic Club. Achievements include original detailed design and prospectus for computer; developed decoding methods; appplication of mathematical theory to biology forms; study of morphogenesis, the development of pattern and form in living organisms. Died June 7, 1954.

**TURK, JAMES CLINTON,** federal judge; b. Roanoke, Va., May 3, 1923; s. James Alexander and Geneva (Richardson) T.; m. Barbara Duncan, Aug. 21, 1954; children: Ramona Leah, James Clinton, Robert Malcolm Duncan, Mary Elizabeth, David Michael. AB, Roanoke Coll., 1949; LLB, Washington & Lee U., 1952. Bar: Va. 1952. Assoc. Dalton & Poff, Radford, Va., 1952-53; ptnr. Dalton, Poff & Turk, Radford, 1953-72; mem. Va State Senate, 1959-72; minority leader Va. State Senate, 1965—72; judge US Dist. Ct. (western dist.) Va., Roanoke, 1972—2002, chief judge, 1973—93, sr. judge, 2002—14. Dir. 1st & Mchts. Nat. Bank of Radford Trustee Radford Community Hosp.; Served with AUS, 1943-46. Mem.: Order of Coif, Omicron Delta Kappa, Phi Beta Kappa. Baptist (deacon). Home: Radford, Va. Died July 6, 2014.

**TURLEY, STANLEY F.,** retired state legislator; b. Snowflake, Ariz., Feb. 27, 1921; s. Fred A. and Wilma (Fillerup) T.; m. Cleo Fern Olson, 1944 (dec. 2004); children: Tauna Lee, Margo Yvonne, Jana, Fredrick C., Miriam K., Lisa, Leslie. Student, Brigham Young U. Mem. Ariz. House of Reps., 1964-72, speaker, 1967-72; mem. Ariz. State Senate, 1973—87, pres., 1983—87. Mem. Ariz. Bd. Exec. Clemency, 1989-98; bd. dirs. Ariz. Cotton Growers Served with USAF, 1944-46. Mem. Farm Bur., Ariz. Cattle Growers Assn. Lodges: Rotary. Republican. Mem. Lds Ch. Died Apr. 26, 2014.

**TURNBULL, ROBERT SCOTT,** retired manufacturing executive; b. North Dumfries, Ont., Can., Dec. 19, 1929; s. Leslie William and Marjorie Clara (Scott) T.; m. Dawna Rose Sinclair, Feb. 17, 1956 Sr. Matriculation, Galt U., Ont., 1950; M.T.C., U. Western Ont., 1975. Cert. mgmt. acct. Credit mgr Can. Gen. Tower, Cambridge, Ont., 1951-53, gen. acct., 1953-62, comptroller, 1962-68, v.p. mktg., 1968-78, v.p., gen. mgr., 1978-96, pres., 1996-99, dir., sr. officer; ret., 2001. Mem. Chem. Fabrics and Films Assn. (bd. dirs.), Soc. Plastics Industry (mem. Automotive Coun.), Japan Soc. (bd. dirs.), Soc. Mgmt. Accts. Home: Cambridge, Canada. Deceased.

**TWOMBLY, STEPHEN DOANE,** magazine publisher; b. Summit, NJ, July 26, 1953; s. Doane and Betty (Bowers) T.; m. Jean Sawyer. BA summa cum laude, Drew U., 1976. Dist. mgr. McGraw-Hill Publs. Co., NYC, 1978-83; dir. advt. IDG Communications, Peterborough, NH, 1983—84, pub. RUN, 1984—87, pub. AmigaWorld, 1985—88, v.p., 1988-89, exec. v.p., 1989—90, exec. v.p., pub. dir. PCResource, 1989—90; group pub. Consumer/Home Mag., Special Products, 1987-88; pub. dir. PC Resource, 1988—90; exec. v.p., pub. dir. PCResource Cahners Pubs. Co., Newton, Mass., 1990—97; nat. sales mgr. Datamation, 1990—92, assoc. pub., 1993—94; pub. Digital News & Rev., 1994—95, Reseller Mgmt., 1995—97; v.p. sales IDG Channel Svcs. Corp., Framingham, Mass., 1997—98; v.p., pub. New Age Jour. & Body & Soul, 1998—2001; pub. dir. Weider Pubs. Natural Health mag., 2001—03; group pub. Advanstar Comm. Sensors & Frontline Solutions, 2003—04; pub. CMO mag. Internat. Data Group, 2004—06; pub. Boston Globe Media Design New Eng., from 2006. Spkr. in field. Mem. Sigma Phi. Avocations: composing, painting, outdoor sports. Home: New London, NH. Died 2013.

**TYDLITÁT, DAVID,** veterinarian, consultant; b. Brno, South Moravia, Czech Republic, Sept. 21, 1974; s. Jan Tydlitát and Olga Tydlitátová; life ptnr. Lucie Brízová (div.); m. Natalija Stefanova, July 7, 2001 (div. Nov. 23, 2003). DVM, Vet. and Pharm. U., Brno, 1999, PhD, 2008. Vet. Radika ltd., Brno, 1999—2000; cons. swine diseases SEVARON ltd., Brno, from 2000. Swine health expert European Swine Adv. Group, Paris, from 2005. Mem.: Czech Pig Vet. Soc. Avocations: skiing, bicycling, travel, flying. Home: Brno, Czech Republic. Died Aug. 2009.

**TYLER, FRANK HILL,** medical educator; b. Villisca, Iowa, Jan. 5, 1916; s. Royal Frank and Fausta Alice (Hill) T.; m. Inez Betty Hannan, June 22, 1941 (dec.); children: Karen June, Royal Hannan, Frank Peter; m. Alida Woolley, Mar. 19, 1962. AB, Willamette U., 1938; MD, Johns Hopkins U., 1942. Diplomate Am. Bd. Internal Medicine. Mem. faculty U. Utah Coll. Medicine, Salt Lake City, from 1947, asst. prof., 1950-54, assoc. prof., 1954-59, prof. medicine, from 1959. Mem. USPHS gen. med. study sect. NIH, 1957-63, mem. research career program com., 1967-71, gen. clin. research ctr. com., 1971-75; mem. nat. adv. com. Arthritis/Metabolic Disease Council, 1963-67. Author: Harrison's Principles of Internal Medicine, Strauss and Welt—Diseases of the Kidney; contbr. articles to profl. jours. Served to lt. (j.g.) MC, USNR, 1944-46, PTO. Recipient Disting. Research award, U. Utah, 1978. Mem. ACP (Master 1981), Assn. Am. Physicians, Western Assn. Physicians (pres. 1963-64), Am. Fedn. Clin. Research, Am. Soc. Clin. Investigation, Western Soc. Clin. Investigation (pres. 1957-58), Am. Clin. and Climatol. Assn. Deceased.

**TYURKYAN, RAFFI ARMENAKOVICH,** mining executive; b. Poti, Georgia, Apr. 3, 1929; arrived in Ukraine, 1951; s. Armenak A. and Russana M. (Karapetyan) T.; m. Liana G. Aristakesyan, Sept. 1954; 1 child, Karine. Diploma in engring., Inst. Tech., Tbilisi, Georgia, 1951; cand. of sci., Mining Inst., Moscow, 1965, DSc, 1989. Exec. dir. mine bldg., Donetsk, 1953-55; dir. vertical mine tunnel bldg. Ukrainian Mining Arch. Trust Donetskshakhoprokhodka, 1955-76; gen. dir. Ukrainian Ministry Mining Bldg., 1976-87, Orthekhshakhtostrov Project Inst., Donetsk, from 1987; prof. Donetsk U. Tech., from 1991. Tech. supr. bldg. of underground sect. of hull Chernobil (Ukraine) Atomic Sta., 1986. Author: Technic and Technology of Building of Vertical Mines Tunnels, 1970, Building and Digging of Vertical Mines Shafts, 1982, Work of Miners in Chernobil for Liquidation of Accident in Chernobil Atomic Station, 1996; contbr. chpts. to books, articles to profl. jours.; 45 patents in field. Recipient Lenin Premium award Cabinet of Mins., Moscow, 1957, Order for Participation in liquidation of accident in Chernobil Atomic Sta., Supreme Coun., USSR, 1986, 2 Orders of Lenin medals, 15 others, 1955-85. Mem. Ukrainian Acad. Mining Sci., Ukrainian Acad. Mining Arch., N.Y. Acad. Scis. Avocations: philosophy, history, travel. Home: Donetsk, Ukraine. Died Jan. 1, 2004; Mushketov Cemetery Donetsk Ukraine.

**TZALLAS, NIOVE,** painter; b. Jannina, Greece, Jan. 26, 1938; d. George and Kaliroi (Papastergiou) Georgopoulos; m. Neocosmos Tzallas, Aug. 21, 1959. Student, Athens Sch. Beaux Arts, 1955-58, Atelier Andre Lhote, France, 1958-59, Cen. Sch. Arts and Crafts, Eng., 1959-61. One-woman shows at Paris, 1962, Rome, 1963, Gallery Royal Soc. Painters, London, 1964, Gallery du Damier, Paris, 1968, Gallery U. Paris, 1969, 72, Mus. de Havre, France, 1971, Galerie Vallombreuse, Biarritz, France, 1974, Gallery Mouffe, Paris, 1975, Gallery Bernheim-Jeune, Paris, 1982, BH Corner Gallery, London, 1985, 86, Everarts Galerie, Paris, 1988, 90, 93, Montserrat Gallery, N.Y., 1994, Galerie Art Present, Paris, 1996; exhibited in floating exhbns. aboard S.S. Pegassos, S.S. Semiramis, 1966, S.S. Olympia, 1967; exhibited in group shows at Salon des Independents, Grand Palais des Champs Elysees, 1973-98, Grand Prix Internat. de la Baie des Anges, Nice, France, Galerie Riviera, Nice, 1974, Galerie Blaise St. Maurice, Paris, 1974-77, Galerie l'Arthotèque, Monte Carlo, 1975, Salon Populiste, Paris, 1975, Maison de la Culture à Villeneuve-la Garenne, 1976-77, Ctr. Cultural de Mussidan, Dordogne, France, 1977, The Breakers Gallery, Palm Beach, Fla., 1976-78, Ctr. European Delobbe à Olloy Sur Viroin, Belgium, 1978, Galerie la Roue, Paris, 1978-79, Salon de l'Art Libre, Paris, 1978-79, Festival d'Art Graphique d'Osaka, Japan, 1983-84, Metropolis Galerie Internat. D'Art, Geneva, 1984, Mus. Luxembourg, Paris, L'Union des Femmes Peintres et Sculpteurs, 1981, 82, Galerie Hautefeuille, Paris, 1988-9, Galerie, Quincampoix, Paris, 1989, Espace Delpha, Paris, 1989, Espace Laser, Paris, 1989, Galerie Jules Salles, Nimes, France, 1993, Salon de Academie Culturelle Internat. des Artistes de France de la ville de Gimont, 1993, Salon Internat. d'Art Contemporain Home: Attica, Greece. Died Oct. 17, 2003.

**UBUKA, TOSHIHIKO,** biochemist, educator, academic administrator; b. Kagaminocho, Okayama, Japan, Jan. 31, 1934; s. Yoshio and Shigeko (Hashimoto) U.; m. Satoko Iwamiya, Oct. 18, 1960; children: Takayoshi, Hiromi, Atsue. MD, Okayama U., 1959, PhD, 1964. Rsch. assoc. Med. Coll. Cornell U., NYC, 1968—71; with Okayama U., Japan, 1964-73, asst. prof., 1973-80, assoc. prof. Med. Sch., 1980-81, prof. Med. Sch., 1981-99, dean Med. Sch., 1997-99, prof. emeritus, from 1999; prof., dean Kawasaki U. of Med. Welfare, 1999—2001, prof., v.p., 2001—05, prof., dean, v.p., 2005—07, prof., v.p., from 2007. Co-author: Methods in Enzymology, vol. 143, 1987; editor Acta Med. Okayama, 1980-99, Physiol. Chem. Phys. and Med. NMR, 1982—, Amino Acids, 1991—; chief editor Acta Med. Okayama, 1987-90. Fellow Japanese Biochem. Soc., Japanese Soc. Nutrition and Food Sci.; mem. AAAS, Am. Chem. Soc., NY Acad. Scis., Internat. Soc. Amino Acid Rsch., Soc. Study Inborn Errors Metabolism, The Protein Soc., The Japanese Soc. Amino Acid Scis. Achievements include research in sulfur biochemistry, sulfur nutrition, cysteine metabolism in mammals, protein modification with mixed disulfides; inborn errors of cysteine metabolism, analysis of sulfur compounds. Avocation: Kendo (Japanese fencing). Home: Okayama, Japan. Died Apr. 4, 2008.

**UCHIYAMA, SHOICHI,** mechanical engineer; b. Tokyo, Aug. 1, 1927; m. Teruko Shimizu Uchiyama, Nov. 12, 1962; children: Richard Junichi, Robert Hiroaki. BS, Chiba U., 1953; MS, UCLA, 1957, PhD, 1963. Asst. rsch. engr. UCLA, 1957-63; project engr. Aerospace Rsch. Assocs., Inc., W. Covina, Calif., 1963-65; mem. tech. staff N. Am. Rockwell, Downey, Calif., 1965-71; gen. mgr. NKK, Kawasaki, Japan, 1971-86; tech. counselor NKTEKS, Tokyo, 1986-93; tech. advisor Kawawa Internat. Patent Office, Tokyo, 1993-96. Coms. mem. High Temp. Com., Japan, 1973-77, Fluid Analysis Inst., 1975-78, ISES Com., Japan, 1975-80; rsch. lectr. Musashi Inst. Tech., Tokyo, 1987—2002, Toin U. Yokohama, Japan, 1990-95. Contbr. articles to profl. jours. Home: Togane, Japan. Died 2011.

**UDICK, ROBERT E.,** newspaper executive; b. Colorado Springs, Colo., May 27, 1922; s. Albert Earl and Edna (Young) U. Student, Colo. Coll. Staff corr. Rocky Mountain News, Denver, 1947-49, United Press, Denver and Santa Fe, 1950-51, war corr. Korea, 1951-53; later became mgr. Hong Kong and Manila burs.; then mgr. for Southeast Asia, hdqrs., Singapore; editor, pub. Bangkok World, until 1967; pub. Pacific Daily News, Agana, Guam, until 1985; cons. Gannett Co., Inc., from 1985. Mem. civilian adv. bd. 8th Air Force; mem. Navy League, Guam Stock Exchange. Bd. regents U. Guam. Served with Coast Arty., Inf., Signal Corps, World War II. Mem. Fgn. Corr. Assn. Thailand (pres.), Phi Delta Theta. Clubs: Rotary. *Given the opportunities and options actually available to you, you always do what you want to do most. 'Most' is the operative word. Anyone who acts or makes a decision and says, "I didn't want to do that" is trying to fool someone, perhaps, tragically, himself.* Died July 3, 1989.

**UDOVENKO, HENNADIY,** former Ukranian government official; Staff mem. UN, Geneva, 1965—71, dir. interpretation & meetings divsn. Dept. Conf. Services, 1977—80, v.p. econ. & social council, 1989—91; head pers. dept., internat. econ. organizations dept. Ukraininan SSR Ministry Fgn. Affairs, 1971—77; dep. min. fgn. affairs Ukrainian Soviet Socialist Republic, 1980—85, permanent rep. to the UN, 1985—92; dep. min. fgn. affairs Govt. of Ukraine, 1991—92, amb. to Poland, 1992—94, min. fgn. affairs Kiev, 1994—98; pres. UN Gen. Assembly, 1997—98. Chmn. People's Movement of Ukraine, 1999—2003. Died Feb. 12, 2013.

**ULEHLA, IVAN,** physicist, educator; b. Skalica, Czechoslovakia, Oct. 17, 1921; s. Miloslav and Anna Marie (Tilschova) Ulehla; m. Ludmilla Ulehla, Oct. 31, 1942 (div. 1966); children: Ivan, Josef, Katerina; m. Libuse Pouchla, Sept. 9, 1966; 1 child, Premysl. RNDr, Charles U., Prague, Czechoslovakia, 1949. Asst. Charles U., Prague, 1949-51, dir. Nu. Ctr., 1975-85, prof. physics, from 1967; asst. Komensky U., Bratislava, Czech Republic, 1951-54; sr. rschr. Inst. Nuc. Physics, Prague, 1954-60; asst. prof. Tech. U., Prague, 1960-63, prof., 1963-67. Vice-dir. Joint Inst. Nuc. Rsch., Dubna, Russia, 1964—67; sci. sec. Conf. Atomic Energy, Geneva, 1955, spl. asst., 1958. Author: books on nuc. physics, 1962, books on physics and philosophy, 1962, 1982. Decorated Order of Labor Czechoslovakia. Mem.: Czechoslovakian Union Math. and Physics, European Phys. Soc., Czechoslovakian Acad. Scis. (corr.; pres. 1981—87). Home: Prague, Czech Republic. Died Mar. 20, 2004.

**ULLO, CHRIS,** retired state legislator; b. New Orleans, Mar. 16, 1928; m. Joyce Ann Daigle, 1950. Grad., Tulane U. Retail bus. owner; mem. Dist. 84 La. House of Reps., Baton Rouge, 1972—78; mem. Dist. 8 La. State Senate, Baton Rouge, 1988—2007. Named Legislator of Yr., Alliance for Good Govt., 1986. Mem.: La. State Firemen's Assn., Lions Club (former pres., zone chmn.). Democrat. Catholic. Died Jan. 16, 2014.

**ULRICH, EDWIN ABEL,** retired oil company owner; b. Dec. 23, 1897; LHD (hon.), Wichita State U., 1988. Owner Dutchess Oil Corp., Poughkeepsie, N.Y., 1937-57. Charter mem., past pres., past dist. gov. Poughkeepsie-Arlington, N.Y. Rotary Club; charter mem. sr. bd. govs. Wichita State U. Name given to Wichita State U. Mus. Art, 1974. Mem. Fairmount Soc. (charter). Home: Hyde Park, NY. Deceased.

**ULRICH, JOHN AUGUST,** microbiology educator; b. St. Paul, May 15, 1915; s. Robert Ernst and Mary Agnes (Farrell) U.; m. Mary Margaret Nash, June 6, 1940 (dec. May 1985); children: Jean Anne, John Joseph, Robert Charles, Karl James, Mary Ellen, Lenore Alice; m. Mary Matkovich, July 19, 1986. BS, St. Thomas Coll., 1938; PhD, U. Minn., 1947. Instr. De La Salle High Sch., Mpls., 1938-41; rsch. asst. U. Minn., Mpls., 1941-45, 49, Hormel Inst., U. Minn., Austin, 1945-49; instr. Mayo Clinic, U. Minn., Rochester, 1949-55; asst. prof. Mayo Found., U. Minn., Rochester, 1955-66; assoc. prof. U. Minn., Mpls., 1966-69; prof. U. N.Mex., Albuquerque, 1969-82, prof. emeritus, from 1982. Chmn. Bacteriology & Mycology Study Sect., NIH, Washington, 1961-64, Communicable Diseases Study Sect., Atlanta, 1968-69; cons. VA Hosp., Albuquerque, 1970—, Sandia Labs., Albuquerque, 1971—, U.S. Hosp. Supply, 1978, Internat. Chem. Industries, U.S., 1979—, Minn. Mining and Mfg. Co., 1980—, Johnson and Johnson, 1981; mem. com. on surface sampling APHA, 1974; mem. FDA-Over the Counter Drugs Panel, 1975-77, FDA-Hosp. and Personal Use Device Panel, 1978-80; mem. internat. working group on air handling in hosps. and energy conservation U. Minn., 1978-79; rsch. chmn. in field; others. Chmn. Zumbro Valley exec. bd. Boy Scouts Am., Rochester, 1953-55; mem. Gamehaven exec. bd. Boy Scouts Am., Rochester, 1952-62, Dem. Com., Olmsted County, Minn., 1964-69. Recipient Silver Beaver award Boy Scouts Am., 1962, Bishop's award Winona Diocese, 1962, Katahli award U. N.Mex., 1980. Mem. Am. Soc. Microbiology (coun. mem. 1978-80), Am. Chem. Soc., Am. Bd. Med. Mycology, Am. Acad. Microbiology, Am. Acad. Dermatology (affiliate) Elks. Democrat. Roman Catholic. Achievements include discoveries in food preservation; survival of microorganisms at low temperatures; urinary amino acid excretions in variety of disease states; post-operative wound infections; bacterial skin populations; hospital epidemiology. Home: Manhattan Beach, Calif. Died Sept. 20, 2001.

**UMBRICHT, VICTOR HERMANN,** Swiss diplomat, association executive; b. Endingen, Switzerland, Oct. 25, 1915; s. Simon and Caroline (Meisel) Umbricht; m. Elisabeth Fresard; children: Christopher, Monique, Madeleine. Internat. Law, U. Bern, 1939, Student, U. Lausanne, U. Paris; D honoris causa, U. Basel, 1966; D, U. Zurich, 1987. Mem. Swiss Bar; with Swiss Diplomatic Svc., 1941; assigned to embassies Ankara, London, Washington, 1941—53; dep. dir. ops. Europe, Africa & Australia, World Bank, Washington, 1953—57; head ops. Swiss Treasury, Berne, 1957—60; pres. Ciba Corp., NYC, 1962—65, Monetary Coun. UN Mission Belgian Congo (now Zaire), 1960—61; sr. fin. adviser; chmn. FAO-Industry Coop. Program, 1966—70; mem. Mekong Adv. Bd., 1968—76; chief UN mission to Bangladesh, 1972—73; head UN mission to Pakistan, 1973—74; participant missions to Vietnam; mediator East African Cmty., Kenya, Tanzania, Uganda, 1978—86. Vice-chmn. Internat. Com. Red Cross, Geneva, 1970—86; chief of missions, Southeast Asia, India, Pakistan, Israel, Central America, 1971—77. Recipient Grotius medal, The Hague, 1984. Roman Catholic. Home: Basel, Switzerland. Died July 14, 1988.

**UNGERS, OSWALD MATHIAS,** architect, educator; b. Kaisersesch, Germany, July 12, 1926; arrived in U.S., 1969; s. Anton and Maria (Michels) U.; m. Liselotte Gabler, July 4, 1956; children: Simon (dec. 2006), Sibylle, Sophia. Diploma Tng., Tech. U., Karlsruhe, Germany, 1950; PhD (hon.), Tech. U., Berlin; Dr. (hon.), TU-Berlii, 1999, Univ. di Bologna, 2004. Archtl. practice, Cologne, Germany, 1950-62, Berlin, 1962-69, Itahaca, N.Y., from 1969; prof. architecture Tech. U. Berlin, 1963-73, dean faculty architecture, 1965-67; prof. architecture emeritus Cornell U., Ithaca, 1968—2007, chmn. dept., 1968-74. Vis. prof. Harvard U., 1972, 77, UCLA, 1973; prof. emeritus Kunstakademie Dusseldorf, 1986-90; organizer 1st and 2d Berlin Summer Acads. for Architecture. Author: (with wife) Megastructure in Habitation; also numerous articles on architecture to internat. mags., numerous chpts. in books; subject of O.M. Ungers 1951-90, 90-98, Bauten und Projekte; exhibited in biennale, Venice, Italy, 1976, also Berlin, London, N.Y.C., Vicenza, Italy, Dusseldorf, Cologne; prin. works include Mus. Architecture, Frankfurt, high rise bldg. and gallery, Frankfurt, Alfred-Wegener-Institut für Polarforschung, Bremerhaven, Badische Landesbibliôthek, Karlsruhe, Supreme Ct., Karlsruhe, family court Berlin-Kreuzberg, art mus. Hamburg, Bayerische Hypotheken-und Wechselbank Düsseldorf, thermae mus. Trier, German Embassy Residential Washington, Friedrichstadt-Passagen Berlin, new fair bldg., Berlin, Wallraf-Richartz-Mus. Koln, Pergamon Mus., Berlin. Recipient prizes in several urban design competitions, BDA prize Grosser, 1987, Prix Rhénan d'Architecture, 1989; decorated Comdrs. Cross of the Order of Merit of Fed. Republic Germany. Mem. AIA, Acad. di San Luca (Rome), BDA Berlin (hon.), Moscow Br. Internat. Acad. Architecture, Ehrenmitglied Hochschule fuer bildende Kunste Hamburg, Goethe-Plakette der Stadt Frankfurt/Main. Achievements include research on cast optimisation in large-scale housing, urban pattern devel. in N.Y. State, subsystems of cities. Designer large-scale pub. housing projects in Germany. Died Sept. 30, 2007.

**UPADHYAYA, DHARNI DHAR,** materials scientist, researcher; b. Almora, India, Mar. 4, 1946; s. Ganga Datt and Basanti Devi (Pathak) U.; m. Kala Tewari, Feb. 19, 1972; children: Sameer, Shailaja. BSc, Agra. U., Nainital, India, 1965; MSc in Physics, Agra U., Nainital, India, 1968; PhD in Physics, Kumaun U., Nainital, India, 1985. Sci. officer Bhabha Atomic Rsch. Ctr., Mumbai, India, from 1968. Rsch. scientist Max-Planck Inst. for Metals Rsch., Stuttgart, Germany, 1987-89. Mem. adv. bd. Asian Jour. Physics, 1997; contbr. articles to profl. jours. Mem. Powder Metallurgy Assn. India (mem. governing coun. 1990-95, award for best tech. paper 1991), Indian Ceramic Soc. (life, hon. sec. Bombay met. region chpt. 1995-96). Avocation: playing tennis. Home: Mumbai, India. Died 2004.

**UPWARD, CHRISTOPHER,** academic researcher, orthographer; b. London, Nov. 14, 1938; s. Edward Falaise and Hilda Maude (Percival) U.; m. Janet Hilary Hutcheon, July 30, 1963; children: Antony, Richard. BA, U. Cambridge, Eng., 1961; Cert. Edn., U. Bristol, Eng., 1962. Tchr. Bolton (Eng.) Sch., 1962-65; from lectr. to sr. lectr. Wolverhampton (Eng.) Poly., 1965-69, Aston U., Birmingham, Eng., 1970-95, rschr., from 1995. Translator Lawrence & Wishart, London, 1970-80. Author: Cut Spelling: A Handbook to the Simplification of Written English by Omission of Redundant Letters, 1992, 2d edit., 1996, (poetry) Apprehensions, 1982; translator: Karl Marx/Frederick Engels, Collected Works vol. 42, Letters 1864-68, 1987. Mem. Simplified Spelling Soc. (com. mem., editor-in-chief 1992). Avocations: languages, writing systems. Home: Birmingham, England. Died Apr. 8, 2002.

**URSACHE, VICTORIN (HIS EMINENCE THE MOST REVEREND ARCHBISHOP VICTORIN),** archbishop; b. Manastioara-Siret, Dist. of Suceava, Romania, 1912; Grad., State Lyceum of Siret; L.Th., U. Cernauti, Romania; postgrad., Bibl. Inst. Jerusalem. Ordained deacon Romanian Orthodox Ch., 1937, ordained priest, 1937. Consecrated bishop Romanian Orthodox Ch., 1966, elevated to archbishop, 1973; prof. religion Orthodox Lyceum of the Romanian Orthodox Metropolis of Cernautsi, 1936-37; prof. theology Seminary of Neamtzu Monastery, 1937-46, asst. dir. sem., 1937-40, dir. sem., superior of monastery, 1940-44; rep. Romanian Orthodox Ch. at Holy Places in, Jerusalem, 1946-56; bishop Romanian Orthodox Missionary Episcopate in Am., 1966-73; archbishop Romanian Orthodox Archdiocese in Am., from 1973. Mem. Holy Synod, Romanian Orthodox Ch. of Romania; bd. dirs. U.S. Conf., World Council Chs.; mem. central com.; mem. Standing Conf. Canonical Orthodox Bishops in, Ams. Editor: Locurile Sfinte. Died July 16, 2001.

**USKI, TORE KALEVI,** neurosurgeon, researcher; b. Kumla, Sweden, May 12, 1954; s. Toivo and Maire (Räsänen) U. Grad. in Medicine, Lund U., Sweden, 1975; MD, Lund U., 1979, PhD, 1984. House surgeon dept. neurosurgery Univ. Hosp., Lund, 1981-83, registrar, 1983-87, sr. registrar, 1987-89, sr. registrar, assoc. prof., 1989-94, cons., assoc. prof., from 1994, acting prof., chmn. acad. dept. neurosurgery, 1994-95. Rsch. scientist, acad. dept. neurosurgery, 1987-91. Contbr. articles, revs. to profl. jours. Fellow Swedish Soc. Medicine; mem. Soc. Cerebral Blood Flow and Metabolism (founding). Avocations: gliding, computers. Home: Lund, Sweden. Died Apr. 2003.

**VALASEK, JOSEPH,** retired physics educator, researcher; b. Cleve., Apr. 27, 1897; s. Josef and Frantska Maria (Pytlik) V.; m. Leila Elizabeth Munson, June 26, 1924 (dec. Oct. 1991); children: Frances Elizabeth, Marion Louise. BS, Case Inst. Tech., 1917; MA, U. Minn., 1920, PhD, 1921, DSc (hon.), 1983. Asst. physicist Nat. Bur. Standards, Washington, 1917-19; nat. rsch. fellow NAS, Mpls., 1921-22; teaching asst. U. Minn., Mpls., 1919-21, asst. prof. physics, 1922-28, assoc. prof., 1928-50, prof., 1950-65, prof. emeritus, from 1965. Author: Elements of Optics, 1927, Advanced Optics, 1949; rsch. on ferroelectricity. Avocations: photography, painting. Home: Minneapolis, Minn. Deceased.

**VALBUENA-BRIONES, ANGEL JULIAN,** retired language educator, author; b. Madrid, Jan. 11, 1928; naturalized, 1963; s. Angel Valbuena-Prat and Francisca Briones; m. Barbara Northrup Hobart, Nov. 9, 1957; children: Teresa, Vivian. Licenciado summa cum laude, Murcia U., Spain, 1949; PhD with honors, Madrid U., 1952. Prof. Ayudante Murcia U., 1949-51; lectr. Oxford (Eng.) U., 1953-55; prof. Ayudante Madrid U., 1955-56; vis. lectr. U. Wis., 1956-58; asst. prof. Yale U., 1958-60; Elias Ahuja prof. Spanish lit. U. Del., 1960-2000, Elias Ahuja prof. emeritus, from 1999. Lecture tour, S.Am., 1957; vis. prof. NYU, 1960, 61, U. Madrid, 1970-71, 1965, 77, U. Mex. at Aragon, 1979, Inst. Caro y Cuervo, Bogota, Colombia, 1980; mem. Fulbright-Hays nat. screening com., 1981-83, 89-90; mem. editl. com. for CD-ROM edit. Spanish Golden Age Theatre, Chadwyck-Healey/Spain, 1995-98; bd. dirs. publs. U. Barcelona, Spain, Bull. Comediantes, U. Calif., Riverside, Hispanic Jour., Pa., Juan de la Cuesta Edits., Del.; profl. cons. NEH. Author: Nueva Poesia de Puerto Rico, 1952, Extradinario Y Cathdratico Distinguido de la Literatura Espanola, Lienzos de la Escritura Sin Fonias del Recuerdo El Magisterio de Angel Valbuena Prat, 2012, Comedias de Capa y Espada de Calderon, 1954, Dramas de Honor de Calderon, 2 vols., 1956, Obras Completas de Calderon, vol. I, 1959, 3d reprinting, 1991, vol. II, 1956, 6th edit. 2 vols., 1988, Literatura Hispanoamericana, 1962, revised and enlarged, 1969, Perspectiva critica de los dramas de Calderon, 1965, Ideas y Palabras, 1968, El alcalde de Zalamea de Calderon, 1971, rev. 13th edit., 1995, Primera Parte de Comedias de Pedro Calderon de la Barca, Vol. 1, 1974, Vol. 2, 1981, La Dama Duende de Calderon, 1976, 8th printing, 1986, Calderon y la comedia nueva, 1977, La vida es sueno. Antes que todo es mi dama. Pedro Calderon de la Barca, 1988, El mayor monstruo del mundo. de Calderon, 1995; author (cd-rom) Teatro Espanol de Siglo de oro, 1998, Historia y Creación Literaria en Don Pedro Calderón de la Barca, 2002. Founder, pres. Valbuena Inst. Spanish Lit., Inc., 1986-99. Consejo Superior de Investigaciones Cientificas fellw, 1951, 70-71, Instituto de Cultura Hispánica fellow, 1951-52; recipient Excellence in Teaching award U. Del., 1988, Outstanding Scholar award U. Del. Coll. Arts and Sci., 1996. Mem. MLA, AAUP, Am. Assn. Tchrs. Spanish and Portuguese, Inst. Iberoam. Lit., Internat. Fedn. Modern Langs. and Lits., Assn. Lit. Scholars and Critics, Internat. Assn. Hispanists, Am. Comparative Lit. Assn., Assn. for Hispanic Classic Theatre, Old Bohemia Hist. Soc., Sigma Delta Pi (hon., Order of Don Quijote, 1999), Phi Kappa Phi. Home: Hockessin, Del. Died Feb. 5, 2014.

**VALDERRABANO, FERNANDO,** nephrologist; b. Madrid, Dec. 29, 1941; s. Jesus Valderrabano and Carmen Quintana; m. Isabel Vazquez, Dec. 27, 1965; children: Elena, Fernando, Miguel, Jaime, Antonio. Grad. in medicine, Complutense U., Madrid, 1965, PhD, 1979. Fellowship in nephrology Puerta de Hierro Hosp., Madrid, 1965-69; chief dept. of nephrology Hosp. Gregorio Maranon, Madrid, from 1969; assoc. prof. medicine Complutense U., 1970-82, prof. medicine, from 1982. Editor: Insuficiencia Renal Cronica, 1997, Nephrology, 2000; contbr. articles to profl. jours. Pres. 1st Iberoamerican Congress of Nephrology, 1992; chmn. European Symposium on Erythropoletin, Seville, Spain, 1994. Mem. Spanish Soc. of Nephrology (pres. 1987-93), Commn. for Advancement of Nephrology, European Renal Assn. (chmn. registry 1994-97, coun. mem. 1988-91, pres. 1999), Internat. Soc. of Nephrology, Am. Soc. of Nephrology, Portuguese Soc. of Nephrology (hon.), Argentina Soc. of Nephrology (hon.), Spanish Soc. of Nephrology (hon.). Achievements include research on end stage renal disease, anemia, renal replacement therapies, dialysis and transplantation. Home: Madrid, Spain. Died Sept. 2001.

**VALEGA, THOMAS MICHAEL,** retired health scientist, administrator; b. Linden, NJ, May 23, 1937; s. Paul and Anna (Bakalar) B.; m. Mary Margaret Orr, Aug. 30, 1958 (div. Dec., 1992); children: Margaret, Thomas, Vinson, Catherine; m. Heidi Hughes, Dec. 31, 1992. BS, Rutgers U., 1959, PhD in Chemistry, 1963. Chemist USDA, Beltsville, Md., 1963-67; grants assoc. NIH, Bethesda, Md., 1968; health science adminstr. NIAMD-NIH, Bethesda, 1969-72, NIDR-NIH, Bethesda, 1972-94; health sci. adminstr. EPA, 1972; ret., 1994; dir. Wabasha Area Chamber of Commerce, Minn., 1998-01; sci. dir. Nat. Eagle Ctr., Wabasha, 1998-99. Sec.-treas. Implantology Rsch. Group, IADR/AADR, Washington, 1985-91. Contbr. articles to profl. jours.; editor symposium proceedings, 1977. Fellow Soc. for Biomaterials (chmn. awards com. 1977, Spl. award 1984), American Bat Conservation Soc. (pres. 1992-96), Hawk Watch Internat. (dir. ABQ NMex. office 1997). Avocations: bird watching, chiroptera, classical music. Home: Warren, Minn. Died Jan. 28, 2014.

**VALLCORBA, JAUME (SANTIAGO VALLCORBA),** publisher, editor, educator; b. Tarragona, Spain, Nov. 21, 1949; s. Jaume and Teresa (Plana) Vallcorba. BA, Autonoma's U., Barcelona, Spain, 1974; PhD, U. Barcelona, 1983. Editor, pub. Quaderns Crema, Barcelona, 1979—2014. Author: Lectura De La Chanson De Roland, 1989, Noucentisme, Mediterraneisme: Classicisme, 1994, J.V. Foix, Investigador en Poesia, 2002; Artist: Alliance Manolo Hugue, 2007; editor: (14 books) Critical Edition of J.V. Foix's Poetry, 1983-97, Critical Edition of J.M. Junoy's Poetry, 1984; editor, pub. Acantilado, 1999. Mem. Plenari Del Milenari De Catalunya, Barcelona, 1988; senator Senat De Ciutadans, Barcelona, 1994, Barcelona 2004, 1997. Mem.: Reial Acad. Doctors. Home: Barcelona, Spain. Died Aug. 23, 2014.

**VAN ALLEN, KATRINA FRANCES (KATRINA FRANCES),** painter; b. Phoenix, Feb. 18, 1933; d. Benjamin Cecile Sherrill and Magdalen Mary (Thomas) Adams; m. Ray C. Bennett II, Dec. 31, 1950 (div. 1955); m. William Allen Van Allen, Mar. 15, 1963 (dec. Mar. 1971); m. Donovan Wyatt Jacobs, Apr. 22, 1972; children: Ray Crawford Bennett III, Sherri Lou Bennett Maraney. Student, Stanford U., 1950, 51, 52, Torrance C.C., 1962-63; MA, U. Tabriz, Iran, 1978; studied with Martin Lubner, Jerold, Burchman, John Leeper, LA; student, Otis Art Inst., Immaculate Heart Coll.; studied with the late Russa Graeme, 1968, 69, 70. Office mgr. H.P. Adams Constrn. Co., Yuma, Ariz., 1952-59; nurse Moss-Hathaway Med. Clin., Torrance, Calif., 1962-63; interviewer for various assns. NYC, 1964-70. Solo shows include: Zella 9 Gallery, London, 1972, Hambleton Gallery, Maiden Newton, Eng., 1974, Intercontinental Gallery, Teheran, Iran, 1976, USIA Gallery, Teheran, 1977, 78, Tabriz, 1977, Mashad, 1978, Esfahan, 1978, Shiraz, 1978, Coos Art Mus., Coos Bay, Oreg., 1993; exhibited in group shows at La Cienega Gallery, L.A., 1970, 79, 80, 81, 82, Design Ctr. Gallery, Tucson, 1985, Coos Art Mus., 1992-97, 98, 99, 2000, 01, 02, 03, Expressions West, 2000, 02; represented in permanent collections at Bankers Trust Bd. Room, London, Mfrs. Hanover Bank, London, U. Iowa Med. Sch., Iowa City, Bank of Am., Leonard E. Blakesley Internat. Law Offices, Marina del Rey, Calif., and numerous pvt. collections. Bd. dirs. Inst. for Cancer and Leukemia Rsch., 1966-67, 68. Recipient Five City Tour and Honorarium, Iran Am. Soc., 1977. Mem. Nat. Women in the Arts, L.A. Art Assn., Bay Area Art Assn., Lower Umpqa Flycasters, Coos Country Club. Avocations: fly-fishing, hiking, bridge, golf, the arts. Deceased.

**VAN CAMPEN, STEPHEN BERNARD,** executive recruiter, consultant; b. East Stroudsburg, Pa., Oct. 1, 1941; s. Bernard Allen and Marion (Van Whye) Van C.; m. Ellen Baars, July 22, 1989; children: Brendon, Regan, Meghan, Taylor, Hannah. BS in Sci. and Pre-Veterinary Med., Pa. State U., 1959-64; postgrad. in indsl. rels., George Washington U. Grad. Sch, 1965-68; law student, U. Balt., 1966-68. Lic. pvt. detective, pvt. investigator NJ, soria cert. NY State Police, cert. Homeland Security Worldwide Intelligence Svcs. With FDA, Balt., Washington, 1964-66; indsl. rels. officer Joseph E. Seagrams & Sons, Balt., NYC, San Francisco, 1966-72; worldwide dir. exec. staffing RCA/Hertz Corp., NYC, 1972-74; dir. internat. indsl. rels. Revlon Internat., NYC, 1974; pres., owner, cons. Gilbert & Van Campen Exec. Search, Internat. (subs.: J.B. Gilbert Assocs., Inc., Amtrade Assocs., Internat., GVC Fin. Svcs.), NYC, from 1974; past owner, pres. Lillagaard Hotel Corp., Ocean Grove, NJ, from 1992; owner N.J. Profl. Meeting Planners Group; chmn. No. Shore Region Convention and Vis. Bur., Encore Svcs., Hackettstown, NJ, from 1999; pres. spl. investigations and verifications divsn. Van Campen Assoc. Internat., from 2003; pres. Van Campen Security Svcs., from 2003; pvt. detective, pvt. investigaor NY. Appointed to NJ Gov.'s Commn. on Internat. Trade, 1992; Bush White House nominee to Nat. Parks Adv. Commn., Dept. Interior; chmn. internat. trade subcom. ad hoc NJ Assembly Small Bus. Adv. Coun.; bd. dirs. NJ SBDC, NJ Shore Region Tourism Coun.; named to Commerce and Econ. Devel. Transition Team for Gov.-elect Christine Todd Whitman; chmn. Econ. Devel. Task Force, Warren County, NJ, 1994; participant in meetings. with Pres. Castro 1st US-Cuba Bus. Summit, Havanna, 1998. Rep. fundraiser; active NJ Rep. Gov.'s Club, NJ State Fin. Com.; appointed to Congressman Zimmer's Warren County NJ Fed. Adv. Com., Warren County Econ. Adv. Coun., NJ Gov.'s appointee 1988— and chmn. fed. enacted Del. Water Gap Nat. Recreation Area citizens adv. com., Gov.-elect Christie Todd Whitman Transition Team-Commerce and Econ. Devel. and Tourism; elected to Warren County Rep. Com.; chmn. adv. bd. Warren Presdl. Correctional Facility; chmn. Calno Cemetery Assn.; chmn. Warner County Econ. Devel. Blue Ribbon Task Force; vice chmn. bd. trustees Warren County CC, 1983—, chmn. found. bd., presdl. search com. 2003, ops. com. 2003, ambassador NY Coun. Cmty. Colls.; exec. bd. Tri-County Washington coun. and George Washington coun. Boy Scouts Am.; bd. dirs. NJ Shore Regional Tourism Coun., NY dir. SBDC, NJ Juvenile Justice Adv. Bd.; mem. 1st NJ Trade Del. Soviet Union; mem. commerce and econ. devel. transition team Gov.-elect Christie Whitman, NJ, 1994; chmn. NJ assembly bus. retention Com. of Task Force for Bus. Rentention, Attraction, Expansion and Internat. Trade; chmn. NJ Gov.'s Conf. Travel and Tourism, Atlantic City, 1994; chmn. NJ No. Shore Region CUB Allaire Airport Conv. Ctr.; pres.-elect Warren County Econ. Partnership. Recipient Medal of Honor, Ellis Island, 1994, Disting. Citizen award Boy Scouts Am., 1992. Mem. ASTD, Am. Mgmt. Assns., Am. Coun. on Germany, US C. of C., Nat. Fgn. Trade Coun., World Trade Inst., US-USSR Trade and Econ. Coun., NY C. of C. and Industry, NJ C. of C., Commerce and Industry Assn. NJ, Am. C. of C.s and US Bus. Couns. Abroad, Soc. Human Resource Mgmt., Nat. Assn. Corp. and Profl. Recruiters, Employment Mgmt. Assn., NJ Hotel/Motel Assn. (bd. dirs., mem. exec. bd.), NJ Travel Industry Assn. (bd. dirs., v.p. exec. bd.), NY Pers. Mgmt. Assn., Soc. Plastics Engrs., Soc. Cosmetic Chemists, Small Bus. Adv. Coun., Ocean Grove C. of C. (vice chmn.). Republican. Methodist. Home: Hackettstown, NJ. Died June 7, 2013.

**VAN DER PLANK, DAVID,** historian; b. Cheltenham, Eng., Jan. 9, 1936; s. Arthur Lucas and Kathleen Nora (Hollingham) van der P.; m. Rosemarie Francis; children: Rebecca, Simon, Marie Rose, David. Assoc. Grocers Inst. Trainee Lipton Ltd., 1955-61; ptnr. Cornish Match Co., Cornwall, Eng., 1962-78; cons. Cornish Match Co. Ltd., London and Cornwall, 1978-88; owner David van der Plank Fine Labels, St. Ives and Cornwall, Eng., from 1978. Author: The Matchbox Label Collectors Handbook, 1972, The Index of British Trade Marks for Matches, 1979. Mem. The Brit. Matchbox Label and Booklet Soc. (past pres.). Died May 2, 1997.

**VAN DER PLOEG, RIENK RINDERT,** soil scientist, educator; b. Holwerd, Netherlands, Sept. 26, 1941; s. Rindert Rienks Van Der Ploeg and Antje Elzinga; m. Mechtilde Hermine Vrijling (div.); children: Welmoed, Eline, Philip; m. Maria Elisabeth Marquardt. BS, Groningen U., The Netherlands, 1962; MS, Utrecht State U., The Netherlands, 1967, Iowa State U., 1970, PhD, 1972; Habilitation, Georg-August U., Goettingen, Germany, 1979. Rsch. assoc. Iowa State U., Ames, 1968—72; rsch. soil scientist Georg-August U., 1972—81; prof. soil sci. Hohenheim U., Stuttgart, Germany, 1981—91, U. Hannover, Hannover, Germany, 1991—2005. Vis. prof. Iowa State U., 1989, Martin-Luther U., Halle/Saale, Germany, 1993—94. Contbr. more than 200 articles to profl. jours. Fellow: Soil Sci. Soc. Am. (Emil Truog award 1973), Am. Soc. Agronomy; mem.: Am. Geophys. Union. Mem. Lds Ch. Avocations: music, art, literature. Home: Wennigsen, Germany. Died Sept. 2005.

**VAN DER STOEL, MAX,** former Dutch government official; b. Voorschoten, Netherlands, Aug. 3, 1924; 5 children. Student, State U., Utrecht, Netherlands; LLD, U. Athens, 1977; LLD (hon.), Utrecht U., 1994, South East European U., 2005. With Wiardi Beckman Found.; rsch. bur. Labor Party, Partij van de Arbeid, 1953—58, internat. sec., 1958—65; mem. 1st Chamber of States Gen., 1960—63, 2nd Chamber of States Gen., 1963—65, 1967—73, 1978—81; state sec. Govt. of the Netherlands, 1965—66, min. fgn. affairs, 1973—77, 1981—82, amb. to the UN NYC, 1983—86; mem. Netherlands of Coun. State, 1986—93; high commr. on nat. minorities Org. for Security & Cooperation in Europe (OSCE), 1993—2001. Dutch Labor Party. Died Apr. 23, 2011.

**VAN DER WOUDE, FOKKE JOHANNES,** physician; b. Leeuwarden, The Netherlands, Sept. 30, 1953; m. H. Griesen, Jan. 14, 1978; children: Joanne, Diane. MD, State U. Groningen, 1977, PhD, 1984. Intern State Univ. Hosp. Groningen, 1975-77, resident, 1977-82; jr. staff mem. Renal Transplantation Unit, Groningen, 1982-85; postdoctoral fellow dept. pediatrics U. Minn., Mpls., 1985-87; head renal transplant unit, assoc. prof. medicine Univ. Hosp., Leiden, The Netherlands, 1987-95; prof., dir. V Med. Clinic U. Heidelberg, Germany, from 1995, full prof. Head V Med. Clin., Klinikum Mannheim, Germany; project leader European ANCA Study Group, EEC, Brussels, 1989-95. Contbr. articles to profl. jours. Postdoctoral fellow Dutch Kidney Found., 1985. Fellow Royal Soc. Medicine; mem. Dutch Soc. Nephrology, Dutch Soc. Immunology, Dutch. Soc. Transplantation, British Transplant Assn., Internat. Soc. for Nephrology, Am. Soc. Nephrology, Tranplantation Soc. Home: Hirschberg-Leutershausen, Germany. Died Dec. 4, 2006.

**VAN DER WYCK, HERMAN CONSTANTYN,** investment banker; b. The Hague, The Netherlands, Mar. 17, 1934; arrived in Eng., 1966; s. Hendrik Lodewyk and Berendina Johanna (van Welderen Baroness Rengers) van der W.; m. Edina Nathalie, Patrick Henri Louis, Edzard Lorillard, Alexander Lodewyk. MA in Polit. Sci., U. Geneva, 1959; MBA, Rotterdam U., 1968, U. Mich., 1968. With S.G. Warburg & Co., Ltd., 1969-73, dir., 1973-87; vice chmn. S.G. Warburg Group plc, London, 1987-95; vice chmn., mng. dir. UBS Warburg, 1995-99. Dir. Compagnie Internat. de Placements et Capitalization, Paris; mem. Amsterdam Inst. Finance Adv. Coun. Capt. Dutch Cavalry, ret. Mem. Inst. Econ. Affairs. Avocations: swimming, skiing, music. Deceased.

**VAN DORE, WADE (KIVEL),** poet, environmentalist; b. Detroit, Dec. 12, 1899; s. Peter Francis and Laura (Pennington) Van D.; m. Edrie Frances MacFarland, May 21, 1932; m. Erma Mae Jones, Oct. 11, 1946; 1 son, Peter Francis. Student, Bollitat Music Sch., 1917-19, Robert Frost, 1925-26. Housekeeper, hired man Robert Frost, 1929-43; freelance author, piano technician. Co-founder, v.p. Thoreau Fellowship, Inc. Poet-in-residence, Marlboro Coll., 1950; Author: (with Richard Eberhart) Declaration of Dependence (on nature), Far Lake, 1930, Robert Frost and Wade Van Dore: the Life of the Hired Man, 1987; contbr. poems, essays, articles to mags. Trustee Thoreau Lyceum. Mem. Wilderness Soc., Natural Resources of Maine Council, Poetry Soc. Am. (recipient Alice Fay di Castagnola award) *As an environmentalist, this is the thought that comes to me again and again: To focus attention on our national misuse of nature, America could not do better than proclaim a Declaration of Dependence on nature to supercede our 1776 Declaration of Independence from England. Along with this, Thoreau's Walden might be named our guidebook for attaining the ideal human-nature relationship.* Died Apr. 1989.

**VAN HOUWELINGEN, JAN,** former Dutch government official; b. Leerdam, Netherlands, Dec. 8, 1937; married; 4 children. Student in Chem. Engring., U. London, 1959—65. Mem. Provincial Coun. of Utrecht, 1969—73; state sec. for def., 1981—89; mayor Municipality of Haarlemmermeer, 1994—2003. Mem. Netherlands Reformed Ch. 2d lt. Royal Netherlands Army Res. Died Mar. 17, 2013.

**VAN NOORDWIJK, JACOBUS,** retired pharmacologist; b. Amsterdam, Jan. 3, 1920; s. Arie Johannes and Agatha Cornelia (Weber) van N.; m. Johanna Catharina Van Veen, Aug. 26, 1946; children: Arie Johannes, Meine, Maria Agatha. Lic. med. practice, U. Groningen, 1947; MSc in Biochemistry, U. Western Ont., London, Can., 1949; MD, U. Amsterdam, 1956. Registered pharmacologist, Netherlands. Chief asst. scientific civil svcs. U. Amsterdam, 1950-63; head unit biol. standards Nat. Inst. Public Health, Bilthoven, 1963-85, dir. div. of pharmacology, 1964-85; prof. pharmacology U. Utrecht, 1967-80; mem. drug lic. bd. Ministry of Public Health, Rijswijk, 1963-85; chmn. groups of experts European Pharmacopoeia, Strasbourg, 1984-97, ret., 1997. Mem. Netherlands delegation to European Pharmacopoeia, Strasbourg, 1984-96; chmn. com. LD50 Health Coun. of the Netherlands, The Hague, 1981-89. Author, editor (with others) Algemene Farmacotherapie, 1962-90. Chmn. Algemeen Humanistisch Trefpunt, Oegstgeest, 1982-91. Recipient Wallhäuser prize for reduction of animal use in quality control of pharms., Konzep, 1994, Kolff prize for contbn. to hemodialysis, Kolff Found., Kampen, 2003, Gold medal, Coun. Europe; named officer, Order of Orange Nassau, 1994. Mem. Koninklyke Nederlandse Maatschappy Bevordering Pharmacie (chmn. ECVAM Task Force on hormones 1995—), Med. Evaluation Testing Com. (chmn. 1995-2003). Home: Bosch en Duin, Netherlands. Died Oct. 27, 2008.

**VAN SCHOONEVELD, CORNELIS HENDRIK,** Slavic and linguistics educator; b. The Hague, The Netherlands, Jan. 19, 1921; s. Daniel and Antje (Steenstra) v.S.; m. Elizabeth Manby Starck, Nov. 21, 1951 (div. 1966); m. Dorothy Jean Abel, Jan. 2, 1967; children: Daniel, Eleanor Anne, Anne Laetitia. Doctorandus, Leiden U., The Netherlands, 1946; PhD, Columbia U., 1949. Prof. Baltic-Slavic langs. Leiden U., 1952-59; prof. Slavic langs. and lit. Stanford (Calif.) U., 1959-66, Ind. U., Bloomington, 1966-86, chmn. Slavic dept., 1973-80, ret., 1986. Vis. prof. Duke U., Durham, N.C., 1994. Author: A Semantic Analysis of the Old Russian Finite Preterite System, 1959, Semantic Transmutations, Vol. I, 1978, (with J.E. Buning) The Sentence Intonation of Contemporary Russian as a Linguistic Structure, 1960; editor: Internat. Jour. Slavic Linguistics and Poetics, The Roman Jakobson Series in Linguistics and Poetics. Rockefeller Found. scholar, 1946-49. Mem. Linguistic Assn. Am., Soc. Linguistica Europaea, Soc. Linguistique de Paris, Algemene Vereniging voor Taalwetenschap, Linguistic Cir. Prague (hon.). Home: Amancy, France. Died Mar. 18, 2003.

**VANSITTART, PETER,** novelist, lecturer, critic; b. Bedford, Eng., Aug. 27, 1920; s. Edward Morris and Mignon Therese V.; m. Jacqueline Goldsmith (div.) Student, Worcester Coll., Oxford U., 1940-41. Dir. Burgess Hill Sch., Hempstead, London, 1947—59. Author: I Am The World, 1942, Enemies, 1947, The Overseer, 1949, Broken Canes, 1951, A Verdict of Treason, 1953, A Little Madness, 1953, The Game and Ground, 1957, Orders of Chivalry, 1959, The Tournament, 1961, A Sort of Forgetting, 1961, Carolina, 1961, The Siege, 1962, Sources of Unrest, 1962, The Friends of God, 1963, The Lost Lands, 1964, The Dark Tower: Tales from the Past, 1965, The Shadow Land: More Stories from the Past, 1967, Green Knights, Black Angels: The Mosaic of History, 1967, The Storyteller, 1968, Pastimes of a Red Summer, 1969, Landlord, 1970, Vladivostock, 1972, Dictators, 1973, Worlds and Underworlds: Anglo-European History Through the Centuries, 1974, Quintet, 1976, Lancelot, 1978, Flakes of History, 1978, The Death of Robin Hood, 1981, Harry, 1981, Three, Six, Seven, 1983, The Ancient Mariner and the Old Sailor: Delights and Uses of Words, 1985, Paths from a White Horse: A Writer's Memoir, 1985, Aspects of Feeling, 1986, Happy and Glorious, 1988, Parsifal, 1988, Voices From the Revolution, 1989, The Wall, 1990, A Choice of Murder, 1992, London: A Literary Companion, 1992, A Safe Conduct, 1995, In the Fifties, 1995, In Memory of England: A Novelist's View of History, Survival Tactics: A Literary Life, 1999, Hermes in Paris, 2000, John Paul Jones, a rebellious spirit, 2003, Secret Protocols, 2006; editor: Voices from the Great War, 1981, Voices: 1870-1914, 1983, John Masefield's Letters from the Front, 1985, Happy and Glorious! An Anthology of Royalty, 1988, Voices of the Revolution, 1989, Kipps, 1993, Poems, 2005 Named an Officer of The Most Excellent Order of the British Empire, Her Majesty Queen Elizabeth II, 2008. Died Oct. 4, 2008.

**VAN VERSEVELD, HENK WILLEM,** microbiologist; b. Rotterdam, The Netherlands, July 27, 1949; s. W. J. and H. J. (Beens) Van V.; m. J. W. Stroer, Oct. 24, 1973; 5 children. Candidate Exam Biology and Chemistry, Vrije U., Amsterdam, 1970, D in Biology, 1973, PhD in Microbiology, 1979. Tchr. gen. biology Vrije U., 1973-79, univ. tchr., 1979-85, prin. univ. tchr., from 1985. Author: The Prokaryotes, 1992; editor: Microbial Growth on C-1 Compounds, 1987. Mem. Dutch Soc. Microbiology, Dutch Biotech. Soc., Soc. Gen. Microbiology. Home: Wilnis, Netherlands. Died July 2003.

**VARDANYAN, GEORGE G.,** electrical engineer, researcher; b. Erevan, Armenia, July 28, 1951; s. Gourgen Vardanyan and Hayastan Minassyan; m. Irina Tarakanova-Vardanyan, Oct. 9, 1976; children: Diana, Anna, Mariam. MSEE, Erevan Tech. U., 1973; post grad., Armenian Sci. Acad., 1988. Cert. translator English, Dutch, French, Russian, Ukrainian, Armenian Royal Court, 2001. Mgr. electronics Armenian Sci. Acad. Instn., Ashtarak, Armenia, 1974—93; electronics repair and installation technician Ukraine, 1993—97; test engr. Barco Projection Sys., Kuurne, Belgium, 2001—02; project engr. Waak, Kuurne, from 2005. Translator various sources. Translator; author: Armenian-Dutch Dictionary Book, 2003, Dutch-Armenian Dictionary Book, 2004, Dutch Conversation and Grammar Book for Armenians, 2006; contbr. articles to profl. jours. Sr. lt. Armenian Army, 1975—93. Achievements include patents in field; research in analysis and compensation methods of instrumental and technologic errors in shaft angle to code converters; development of method and system of any type shaft angle to code encoder's/converter's precision complete automated measurement and analysis; compensation method for any shaft angle to code encoder's/converter's errors, creating unlimited precision converters; analog encoding methods for code disks of shaft angle to code converters. Home: Wevelgem, Belgium. Deceased.

**VARJU, DEZSOE,** biologist, educator; b. Gasztony, Hungary, May 22, 1932; arrived in Germany, 1956; s. Johann and Anna (Hirschmann) V.; m. Heide Agner. Diploma Physics, U. Budapest, Hungary, 1956; PhD, U. Goettingen, Germany, 1958; univ. tchr., U. Tuebingen, Germany, 1967. Rsch. asst., rsch. assoc. Max Planck Inst., Tuebingen, 1958-59, 60-68; postdoctoral fellow Calif. Tech., Pasadena, 1959-60; prof. U. Tuebingen, 1968-97, prof. emeritus, from 1997. Author: Systems Theory, 1977, Mit den Ohren Sehen und den Beinen Hören, 1998; co-author: Polarized Light in Animal Vision, Polarization Patterns in Nature, 2004; editor: Localisation and Orientation in Biology and Engineering, 1984; co-editor: Biological Cybernetics Jour., 1993-2000; mem. adv. bd. Jour. Comp. Physiology. Avocations: gardening, skiing, tennis. Home: Tübingen, Germany. Died Aug. 17, 2013.

**VARLAMOV, VLADIMIR VALENTINOVICH,** mathematics educator; b. Moscow, June 30, 1957; s. Valentin Ivanovich and Elena Pavlovna (Angelopoulo) V.; m. Ludmila Vasilyevna Verba, Nov. 15, 1983. Candidate physics and math. scis., Moscow State U., 1983. Asst. prof. dept. math. Moscow Inst. Engring. Physics, 1983-88, assoc. prof. dept. math., from 1988. Contbr. articles to profl. jours. Mem. Moscow Math. Soc., Am. Math Soc. Orthodox. Avocations: running, swimming, bicycle riding, skiing, flute. Home: Moscow, Russia. Died June 15, 2010.

**VASCONCELLOS, JOHN BERNARD, JR.,** former state legislator; b. San Jose, Calif., May 11, 1932; s. John and Teresa (Jacobs) V. BS, Santa Clara U., 1954, LLB, 1959. Bar: Calif. 1960. Assoc. Ruffo & Chadwick, San Jose, 1959; travel sec. to Gov. Pat Brown State of Calif., Sacramento, 1960; mem. Dist. 24 Calif. State Assembly, Sacramento, 1966—74, mem. Dist. 23, 1974—92, mem. Dist. 22, 1992—96, chmn. ways and means com., 1980-96; mem. Dist. 13 Calif. State Senate, 1996—2004. Chmn. Assembly Dem. Econ. Prosperity Team, Sacramento, 1992—. Author: A Liberating Vision, 1979; developer program Toward a Healthier State. Founder Calif. Task Force to Promote Self Esteem and Personal and Social Responsibility, 1987; mem. Strategic Action Agenda--Toward a Calif./Japan Partnership, 1993. 1st lt. U.S. Army, 1954-56. Named Legislator of the Decade, Calif. C.C. Faculty Assn., 1980, Hi-Tech Legislator of Yr., Am. Electronics Assn., 1983, more than 100 other awards. Democrat. Avocations: racquetball, reading. Died May 24, 2014.

**VASILE, RADU,** former Prime Minister of Romania; b. Sibiu, Romania, Oct. 10, 1942; m. Mariuca Vasile; 3 children. Grad., U. Bucharest, 1967, PhD, 1977. Historian Village Mus., Bucharest, Romania, 1967-69; sci. rschr. History Inst. Nicolae Iorga Romanian Acad., 1969-72; asst. lectr. Acad. Econ. Studies, Bucharest, 1972, asst. prof., vice dean faculty trade, 1990, prof., from 1993; v.p. Romanian Senate, 1993—98; head Romanian del. Parliament Assembly Coun. Europe, 1996-98, v.p., 1997-98; mem. Christian Dem. Nat. Peasant Party, 1990-99, sec. gen., 1996-98; pres. Senate Parliament Group, 1996-98; prime minister Govt. of Romania, 1998-99, senator, 2000—04. Author: World Economy, Avenues and Stages of Modernization, 1987, Currency and Economy, 1994, Currency and Fiscal Policy, 1995, From the Iron Century to the Second World War, 1998, Between Recession and Equilibre, 1999, Equilibrium, 1999, Fabricius, 1999. Avocations: poetry, satirical literature, chess, football. Died July 3, 2013.

**VASILJEV, VALERY ALEXANDEROVICH,** metallurgical engineer, economist; b. Novo-Ukrainka, Ukraine, July 10, 1929; s. Alexander Pavlovich and Olga (Melnic) V.; m. Olga Vladimirovna Vasilejeva; 1 child, Alexander. Diploma in engring., Tech. Inst. Odessa, USSR, 1952; degree in econs., Moscow Inst. Mgmt., 1978; high scis. diploma, Inst. Mariupal, Ukraine, 1986; Dr., AESSE, 1995. Chief tech. office Igorsky Plant, St. Petersburg, Russia, 1952-54; main engr. Collective Farms, Kuragata, Dgambul, Kazakhstan, 1955-56; chief Br. metall. Plants of Ukraine, 1957-74; chief econ. dept./rsch. sector Ukrgipromez/Metall. Inst. Mariupol, Ukraine, 1975-86; sr. lectr. PriAzov, State Tech. U. Mariupol, from 1987. Mem. section sci. coun. Inst. Econ.-Law Rsch. NAS Ukraine, Mariupol, 1996-97; dir. Inst. Econ.-Social and Cultural Rsch., Mariupol, 1995—; pres.-chmn. Azov, Ukrainian Dept., Acad. Econ., Scis. and Entrepreneurship, 1999—; chmn. Civil Internat. Com., Tanais Reg., 2001-. Author: Law of Preservation of Labour., The Base of Management in Light of Law of Preservation of Labour, 2002, The Base of Organization of Production Example of Preservation of Labour, 2003, The Directory Founder, 2d edit., 1983, Methodological Priorities at Valuations Objective Expenditures of Labor in Market Economy, 1995, Methodological Fundamentals of Stabilization Socially of Economic Development, 2004, Fundamentals of Strategic Management in Light of Law of Preservation of Labor and Law of Non-destroy of Intelligently Spiritual Labor, 2004. Sponsor civil com. on restoration of Orthodox ch. in hist. ctr. of Mariupol, 1995. Recipient medal UFE, 1955, Labour-Vet. medal USSR, 1989, medal "Met. Gotey and Cafa, St. Ignatja", 1999, cert. Frederick P. Furth Found., 1990. Mem. Acad. Econ., Sci. and Entrepreneurship, Acad. Econ. Scis. Ukraine, N.Y. Acad. Scis., 1817 Heritage Soc. Home: Mariupol, Ukraine. Died Dec. 12, 2006.

**VAUGHAN, STUART,** director, actor, playwright; b. Terre Haute, Ind., Aug. 23, 1925; s. John Harwood and Pauletta Rosalie (Walker) V.; m. Gladys Regier, 1948, (div. 1960); m. Helen Quarrier, Aug. 22, 1960 (dec. Dec. 1963); m. Anne Thompson, Apr. 14, 1965. BA, Ind. State Coll., 1945; MA, Ind. U., 1946; studies with Harold Clurman, 1954-56. Dir.: (stage prodns.) I Knock at the Door, Kaufmann Auditorium, N.Y.C., 1956, Pictures in the Hallway, Playhouse Theatre, N.Y.C., 1957, As You Like It, Heckscher Theatre, 1958, The Beaux' Stratagem, Phoenix Theatre, 1959, Henry IV, Part I, Phoenix Theatre, 1960, Medea, Antioch Area Theatre, Yellow Springs, Ohio, 1962, Abe Lincoln in Illinois, Anderson Theatre, N.Y.C., 1963, Shadows of Heroes, Seattle Ctr. Playhouse, 1964, Assassination 1865, Goodman Theatre, Chgo., 1971, Ghost Dance, Trinity Square Repertory Theatre, Providence, 1973, A Country Scandal, CSC Repertory, Abbey Theatre, N.Y.C., 1975, others; producer: (stage prodns.) Long Day's Journey into Night, Seattle Ctr. Playhouse, 1966, Charley's Aunt, Repertory Theatre New Orleans, 1966, The War of the Roses, Delacorte Theatre, N.Y.C., 1969, others; actor: (Broadway debut) The Strong are Lonely, Broadhurst Theatre, 1953, (stage prodns.) The Clandestine Marriage, 1954, Thieves' Carnival, 1955, The Importance of Being Earnest, 1965, Measure for Measure, 1975, others; playwright Ghost Dance, 1973, The Royal Game, 1974; adaptor: (plays) Henry VI, Parts I, II, and II and Richard III as The War of the Roses, 1969, (with Anne Thompson) The Servant of Two Masters, 1975, Amoreuse, 1975; author: A Possible Theatre, 1969; co-editor: The Bantam Shakespeare, 1960. Recipient Vernon Rice award, 1958, Obie award Village Voice, 1958; grantee Rockefeller Found., 1947, Fulbright Found., 1949-50, Ford Found., 1961-62 Mem.: Players. Avocation: fencing. Died June 10, 2014.

**VAUX, DORA LOUISE,** retired sperm bank official, consultant; b. White Pine, Mont., Aug. 8, 1922; d. Martin Tinus and Edna Ruth (Pyatt) Palmlund; m. Robert Glenn Vaux, Oct. 25, 1941; children: Jacqueline, Cheryl, Richard, Jeanette. Grad. high sch., Bothell, Wash. Photographer Busco-Nestor Studios, San Diego, 1961-68; owner, mgr. Vaux Floors & Interiors, San Diego, 1968-82; cons., mgr. Repository for Germinal Choice, Escondido, Calif., 1983-91; adminstr. Found. for the Continuity of Mankind, Spokane, 1991-97. Republican. *Personal philosophy: It does not matter what our start in life has been, we can set goals and by our own hard work, achieve them. We must find our own answers to our problems and with this will come great pride and enjoyment.* Died 2000.

**VAZQUEZ, ALBERTO M.,** educator, former fgn. service officer; b. Yabucoa, P.R., Mar. 25, 1901; s. Modesto and Cristina (Rivera) V.; m. Hildegarde Wanous, Aug. 29, 1934; 1 son, Alberto Wanous. AB, U. Idaho, 1925, A.M., 1926; postgrad., U. Florence, Italy, 1933, U. Paris, 1934; PhD (Sterling fellow, Rockefeller grantee), Yale U., 1935. Instr. Romance langs. and lit. U. Idaho, 1925-31; instr. Romance langs. and lit. Dartmouth Coll., 1935-37, asst. prof., 1937-42; lectr. Spanish Am. lit. George Washington U., 1945-56; chief translator Dept. State, 1942-43; cons., research analyst OSS, 1943-44; sect. chief Office Internat. Information and Cultural Affairs, 1945-47, specialist Inter-Am. affairs, acting sect. chief div. research for Am. Republics, 1947-54, sect. chief div. research, 1954-56; fgn. service officer, 1956-61; 1st sec., consul, polit. officer Am. embassy, Mexico City, 1956-60; officer in charge Latin Am. area planning staff Bur. Ednl. and Cultural Affairs, 1960-61; vis. prof. Center Latin Am. Studies, Tulane U., New Orleans, 1962-77, prof. emeritus, from 1977. Vis. prof. Latin Am. culture Center for Latin Am. Studies, 1979-81, 81-82, acting chmn. dept. Spanish and Portuguese, 1973, prof. charge Tulane-Newcomb jr. year abroad, Paris, France, 1974-75; vis. prof. Spanish and Spanish-Am. lit. Pan Am. U., Edinburg, Tex., 1977-79; vis. lectr. Loyola U., New Orleans, 1979—; U.S. rep. OAS com. for cultural action, 1962-70, chmn. com., 1965-70; alt. U.S. mem. Inter Am. Indian Inst., 1957-59; directing council Inter-Am. Inst. Geography and History, 1959, Inter-Am. Inst. Geography and History (conf. on fin. and econ. control), Hot Springs, Va., 1942, UNESCO Assembly, Paris, 1946; del. 3d meeting Inter-Am. Cultural Council, San Juan, P.R., 1959, Inter-Am. Cultural Council (4th meeting), Washington, 1966, Inter-Am. Cultural Council (5th meeting), Maracay, Venezuela, 1968, Inter-Am. Cultural Council (6th meeting), Port of Spain, Trinidad and Tobago, 1969 Co-Author: Cartas de Don Diego de Mendoza, 1935, Spanish Grammar, 1940, Brief Spanish Course for Beginners, 1943; Editor Spanish publs. Decorated Order of Petion-Bolivar Haiti, Order Palmes Academiques France). Mem. Phi Beta Kappa. Home: Arlington, Va. Died May 30, 1991.

**VEIRA, STANFORD MAURICE,** accountant, religion writer, educator; b. NYC, June 9, 1915; s. Kenneth Stanley and Bridget Rosalind (Ryan) V.; m. Lillian Anne Elliott, July 20, 1946 (dec. 1950); m. Patricia Louise Hollyfield, Apr. 15, 1972. BA, Sir George Williams Univ., Montreal, Que., Can., 1951; diploma in secondary teaching, McGill U., Montreal, Que., Can., 1952. Tchr. high sch. Protestant Sch. Bd., Montreal, 1952-54; supr. encyclopedia sales Grolier Soc., Kansas City, Mo., 1955-60; tchr. high sch., bus. mgr. Daycroft Sch., Stamford, Conn., 1961-64; supr. purchasing dept. Bd. Edn., Stamford, 1965-68; owner, mgr. Cherry St. Apts., Stamford, 1969-74; sales supr. Liberty Nat. Life Ins., St. Petersburg, Fla., 1975-79; first reader, conductor of svcs. First Ch. of Christ Scientist, Seminole, Fla., 1980-83; acct., pub. rels. mgr. Bay Pines (Fla.) Builders, 1988-93. Dir. Christian Sci. Orgn., Sir George Williams Coll., Montreal, 1947-51; advt. rep. Christian Sci. Monitor, Stamford, Norwalk and Wilton, Conn., 1968-71; Christian sci. practitioner, 1994—. Author: (book) Awake Thou That Sleepest, 1989; contbr. articles to religious publs. Tennis coach Y.W.C.A., Kansas City, Mo., 1960; coord. Common Cause, St. Petersburg, 1977-79. With Royal Can. Navy, 1940-45, ETO. Christian Scientist. Avocations: bible study and writing, tennis, pool, swimming, flea-markets. Home: Saint Petersburg, Fla. Deceased.

**VEIT, PHILIPP F.,** language educator; b. Goddelau, Germany, Jan. 22, 1920; arrived in US, 1952, naturalized, 1958; s. Isaak and Bertha (Amram) V.; m. Johanna Loewy, June 15, 1947; children: Barbara S., Benjamin. BA, U. Toronto, 1947; MA, 1949, PhD, 1952. Mem. faculty U. Toronto, Ont., Canada, 1947—52, U. Pa., Phila., 1956—59, Marquette U., Milw., 1959—63, SUNY-Buffalo, from 1963; dir. summer sch., 1964—72; prof. dept. modern lang, from 1973; dir. elem. lang. instrn., from 1976. Contbr. articles to profl. jours. Avocation: photography. Died Sept. 1986.

**VERDAN, CLAUDE EDOUARD,** retired hand surgeon, educator; b. Sept. 21, 1909; s. Edouard and Adeline (Henrioud) V.; m. Sylva Malan, 1934 (dec. Sept. 1999); 2 children (1 dec.); m. Suzanne Leon-Forestier, Oct. 6, 2000. Degree in medicine, U. Lausanne, Switzerland, 1933. Specialist in surgery Foederatio Medicorum Helveticorum, 1946-80; chief surgeon, founder Clinique Chirurgicale et Permanence de Longeraie, Lausanne, Switzerland, 1946; prof. U. Lausanne, 1951-80; dean faculty medicine Swiss Acad., 1972-74, hon. prof., from 1979. Pres. Soc. Francaise de Chirurgie Plastique et Reconstructive, 1964; sec. gen., founder Groupe Suisse d'Etude de Chirurgie de la Main, 1966-72; pres. Commn. for War Surgery, Fed. Mil. Defence Dept., 1965-69; founder Mus. Human Hand, Lausanne, 1981; pres. numerous congresses and symposia. Author numerous books and articles on hand surgery; editor-in-chief Annales de Chirurgie de la Main, 1982-85. Hon. pres. Claude Verdan Found., 1990. Decorated Chevalier Legion d'Honneur, 1978, officer, 2001; recipient Gold medal, Prix Cesar Roux, 1933. Mem. Brit. Soc. Surgery of Hand (hon.), Belgian Soc. Forensic Traumatology (corr.), Italian Soc. Hand Surgery (corr.), French Acad. Surgery (assoc.), Am. Soc. Surgery of Hand (hon.), Swiss Soc. Medicine in Casualty (pres. 1961-66), Swiss Soc. Orthopedics (hon.), German-Speaking Assn. Hand Surgery, (hon.), Austrian Soc. Plastic Surgery (corr.), Spanish Soc. Hand Surgery (hon.), French Soc. Orthopedics and Traumatology (hon.), French Soc. Hand Surgery (pres. 1975-76, hon.), French Assn. Surgery (hon.), Swiss Soc. Surgery (hon.). Avocations: sculpting, collecting articles concerning the hand, art. Home: Cully, Switzerland. Died July 8, 2006.

**VERDI, NEJAT HASAN,** financial executive; b. Istanbul, Turkey, Feb. 14, 1913; s. Fazil Ibrahim and Fatma (Nigar) V.; m. Liselotte Annemarie Auer, Apr. 1, 1950; children: Aylin, Murat, Nilufer. M. Comml. Sci., Comml. Acad., Calw, Germany, 1933. Ptnr. Verdi Ticaret ve Sanayi A.S., Istabul, from 1927, chmn. bd., chmn. bd. subs., from 1950. Bd. dirs. Finans Bank A.S., Istanbul. Bd. dirs. Am. Hosp., Istanbul, 1967—81; chmn. Am. Hosp. and Nursing Sch. Com., 1967—81. Decorated 1st Class Cross of Merit Germany; named Hon. Ambassador of New Orleans, Istanbul, 1957. Mem.: Turkish-Am. Businessmen's Assn. (bd. dirs.), Middle East Assn., Moda Golf Club, Moda Yacht Club, Propeller Club N.Y. Home: Istanbul, Turkey. *In 1994, Mr. Nejat H. Verdi's son, Mr. Murat Verdi, and his two daughters, founded a company in Istanbul in the security sector with the Securicor Group of London, which is Europe's largest company in this sector. The name of the firm in istanbul is Securicor Verdi Security Services.* Died 1998.

**VERNON, LEE PERRY,** lawyer; b. Lane, Okla., Oct. 13, 1902; s. Charles Stuart and Nancy Catherine (Hutcheson) Vernon; m. Lois Juanita Ball, Apr. 17, 1930; children: Vernon, Terence Lee. BS, U. Okla., 1928, JD, 1930. Bar: Okla., US Dist. Ct. Okla. Claims atty. Tri-State Casualty Co., Oklahoma City, 1937—57, supt. claims, 1957—64; law clk. US. Dist. Ct. (we. dist.), Okla., 1964—68; asst. gen. counsel Okla. Dept. Human Svcs., 1968—83; pvt. practice. Oklahoma City, from 1983. Mem. Mayor's Com. on Employment, Oklahoma City, 1969. Mem.: U. Okla. Alumni Assn., Oklahoma County Bar Assn., Okla. State Bar Assn, Nat. Reciprocal and Family Support Assn. Democrat. Home: Edmond, Okla. Died 1996.

**VEST, CHARLES MARSTILLER,** former science association administrator, engineering educator, former academic administrator; b. Morgantown, W.Va., Sept. 9, 1941; s. Marvin Lewis and Winifred Louise (Buzzard) Vest; m. Rebecca Ann McCue, June 8, 1963; children: Ann Kemper, John Andrew. BS in Mech. Engring., W.Va. U., 1963; MS in Mech. Engring., U. Mich., 1964, PhD in Mech. Engring., 1967; D (hon.), Mich. Tech. U., 1992, W.Va. U., 1994, Ill. Inst. Tech., 1998, U. Notre Dame, 1998, Musashi Inst. Tech., 1999, NC State U., 2002, Colo. Sch. Mines, 2005, Harvard U., 2005, Ohio U., 2006; LLD (hon.), Cambridge U., Eng., 2006. Asst. prof. U. Mich., Ann Arbor, 1968—72, assoc. prof., 1972—77, prof. mech. engring., 1977—90, assoc. dean acad. affairs, Coll. Engring., 1981—86, dean Coll. Engring., 1986—89, provost, v.p. acad. affairs, 1989—90; pres. MIT, Cambridge, 1990—2004, prof. mech. engring., pres. emeritus, 2004—13. Vis. assoc. prof. Stanford U., Calif., 1974—75; chmn. Pres.'s Adv. Com. Redesign of Internat. Space Sta., 1993—94, US Dept. Energy Task Force Future of Sci. Programs, 2002—03; bd. dirs. E.I. du Pont de Nemours & Co., 1993—2007, IBM, 1994—2007; mem. Pres.'s Coun. Advisors on Sci. & Tech., 1994—2007; vice-chmn. Coun. Competitiveness, 1996—2004; co-founder Alliance Global Sustainability, 1997; panel mem. Commn. Intelligence Capabilities of US Regarding Weapons of Mass Destruction, 2004—05, Sec. of Edn. Commn. Future of Higher Edn., 2005—06; mem.

Rice-Chertoff Secure Borders & Open Doors Adv. Com., Sec. of State Adv. Com. Transformational Diplomacy. Author: Holographic Interferometry, 1979, Pursuing the Endless Frontier: Essays on MIT and the Role of Research Universities, 2005, American Research University from World War II to World Wide Web, 2007; assoc. editor Jour. Optical Soc. America, 1982—83; contbr. articles to profl. jours. Trustee Woods Hole Oceanographic Instn., Mass., 1991—2004, Univ. Corp. Advanced Internet Devel., 2002—04, WGBH Ednl. Found., Boston, 2002—04, New Eng. Aquarium, In-Q-Tel, Arlington, Va., Kavli Found., Ithaka Harbors. Recipient Excellence in Rsch. award, U. Mich., 1980, Engring. Alumni award, 2004, Centennial medal, Am. Soc. Engring. Edn., 1993, Nat. Leadership award, Phi Kappa Psi, 1999, Pres.'s award, Accrediation Bd. Engring. & Tech., 2002, Nat. Medal Tech., The White House, 2006, UCLA medal, 2008, Nat. Engring. award, 2010, Vannevar Bush award, Nat. Sci. Bd., 2011. Fellow: AAAS (Philip Hauge Abelson prize 2006), Royal Acad. Engring., American Philos. Soc., American Acad. Arts & Sciences, American Soc. Mech. Engring. (hon.), Optical Soc. America; mem.: NAE (councillor from 2005, pres. 2007—13, Arthur M. Bueche award 2000), Assn. Women in Sci., Chinese Acad. Engring., Academia Sinica (hon.), Assn. American Universities (past chmn.), Pi Tau Sigma, Tau Beta Pi, Sigma Xi. Presbyterian. Died Dec. 12, 2013.

**VETTORAZZI, GASTON,** toxicologist; b. Trent, Italy, Feb. 5, 1928; s. Rudolph and Mary (Dal Canale) Vettorazzi; m. Mary-Francis Armental Segade; children: Ariane, Lara. MD, U. Milan, 1954; MS, La. State U., 1970, PhD, 1972. Diplomate Acad. Toxicological Scis. Head, sci. dept. Am. Sch.; scientist, tropical medicine Ecuador, 1955—60; prof. & clin. chemist Sao Paulo U., Brazil, 1961—68; assoc. rschr., food toxicology La. State U., 1968—72; sr. toxicologist & exec. sec. JECFA & JMPR Internat. Program Chem. Safety WHO, Geneva, 1972—88; prof., exptl. toxicology U. Milan, Italy, from 1975; dir. Internat. Toxicology Info. Ctr., San Sebastian, Spain, from 1988, Vettorazzi Assocs., San Sebastian, from 1988. Vis. prof., dept. pathology U. Rio de Janeiro; cons., orgn. for MERCOSUL matters of food additives, food contaminents & pesticide safety. Contbr. articles to profl. publs.; mem., editl. bd. (sci. jours.). Recipient Internat. Soc. Regulatory Toxicology & Pharmacolgy award. Mem.: Am. Coll. Toxicology, Internat. Soc. Ecotoxicology & Environ. Safety, Inst. Food Tech., European Soc. Toxicology, NY Acad. Scis., Am. Soc. Toxicology, Nat. Acad. Medicine Buenos Aires (hon.), Gamma Sigma Delta, Phi Kappa Phi, Sigma Xi. Died Aug. 2002.

**VICTORIN, HIS EMINENCE THE MOST REVEREND ARCHBISHOP See URSACHE, VICTORIN**

**VIDALIS, ORESTIS EFTHIMIOS,** fiberglass company executive; b. Argos, Greece, Sept. 24, 1917; arrived in U.S., 1968; s. Efthimios John and Anthi Aristotelis (Kastritis) V.; m. Matina Vamvakaris, Jan. 15, 1950; 1 child: Efthimios O. BS, Greek Mil. Acad., 1937; postgrad., U.S. Army Command Gen. Staff Coll., 1952—53; MA in Polit. sci., Georgetown U., 1957. Served to lt. gen. Greek Army, 1937—67; mem. staff standing group NATO, Wash., 1954—57; sr. planner, corp. planning Owens-Corning Fiberglas Corp., Toledo, 1968—69, dir. orgn. procedures, 1969—73, dir. new bus. devel. internat., 1973—75, mng. dir. Middle East Regional Hdqrs. Athens, 1975—78, v.p. Middle East-Africa ops., 1978—87, chmn. Ctr. Polit. Rsch. and Info., from 1989. Decorated Hellenic medal of Valor (Greece) Order British Empire. Greex Orthodox. Home: Athens, Greece. Died Dec. 2001.

**VIGERSTAD, ALICE EMILY FROST,** retired educator; b. Bklyn., Sept. 6, 1907; d. Vincent Morse and Emily Alice (Randall) Frost; m. Josef Ewald Vigerstad, May 30, 1942; 1 child, Torgny Josef. AB cum laude, Radcliffe Coll., 1930; MA, Montclair State Coll., 1965. Cert. secondary sch. tchr., N.J. Substitute tchr. Essex County, N.J., 1930-31; clerk Mutual Benefit Life Ins. Co., Newark, N.J., 1931-35, Tchrs. Ins. Annuity Assn., NYC, 1935-36, 1st Boston Corp., NYC, 1936-43, Western Electric Co., NYC, 1943-48; substitute tchr. Essex County high schs., N.J., 1956-66; math. tchr. Seton Hall U., South Orange, N.J., 1966-69, Fairleigh Dickinson U., Madison, N.J., 1969-73; substitute tchr., home instr. Essex County high schs., N.J., 1973-89. Tutor East Orange, West Orange, South Orange, Maplewood, N.J., 1930—. Mem. Neighborhood Coalition, 1988—, campaign worker Elec. Bd. Edn., 1955—, West Orange High Sch. PTA. Recipient plaque for svc. to student athletes West Orange High Sch. Athletic Booster Club, 1979, plaque for 35-yr. PTA membership West Orange Bd. Edn., 1989. Mem. AAUW (life, treas. 1974-78), LWV (treas. 1983-87), N.J. Congress PTAs (life), Tryggve (sec. lodge # 88 1984-87), Ind. Order Vikings (sec. 1980-89), Order of Eastern Star (trustee N.J. chpt. 1978—). Republican. Mem. Swedenborgian Ch. Avocations: reading, music, sports, swimming, knitting. Home: Basking Ridge, NJ. Died 1983.

**VIGNELLI, MASSIMO,** architecture and design executive; b. Milan, Jan. 10, 1931; came to U.S., 1965; s. Ettore and Noemi (Guazzoni) V.; m. Lella Elena Valle, Sept. 15, 1957; children: Luca, Valentina. Student, Brera Sch. Art, Milan, 1948-50, Politecnico di Milano, 1950-53, U. Venice, 1953-57; DFA (hon.), Parsons Sch. Design, 1983, Pratt Inst., 1987, R.I. Sch. Design, 1988, Istituto Universitario di Architettura, Venice, 1994, Corcoran Sch. Art, 1994. Prin. Lella & Massimo Vignelli Office Design and Architecture, Milan, 1960-64; dir., sr. v.p. design Unimark Internat., Milan and NYC, 1965-71; co-founder, pres. Vignelli Associates, NYC, 1971—78; CEO Vignelli Designs, Inc., NYC, 1978—2014. Retrospective shows include: Parsons Sch. Design, N.Y.C., 1980, Padiglione d'Arte Moderna, Milan, 1980, Acad. of Art USSR, Moscow and Leningrad, 1989, Helsinki, 1989, London, 1990, Budapest, Barcelona, 1991, Copenhagen, Munich, 1992, Prague, Paris, 1992-93; represented in permanent collections Mus. Modern Art, N.Y.C., Cooper-Hewitt Mus., N.Y., Met. Mus. Art, N.Y., Bklyn. Mus., Die Neue Sammlung, Munich, Musée des Arts Décoratifs, Montreal, Tel Aviv Mus. Modern Art; designer: (dinnerware) Heller, 1964, (glass bakeware) 1975, (furniture), Sunar, 1979, Rosenthal, 1980, Knoll, 1985, Poltrona Frau, 1988, (tableware) Sasaki Crystal, 1985, (glassware) Steuben, 1993; interiors St. Peters Ch., Citicorp Ctr., N.Y.C., 1975, Inst. Fine Arts., Mpls., 1974; corp. image Knoll Internat., 1966, Lancia, 1978, Ciga Hotels, 1979, Solomon R. Guggenheim Mus., American Ctr. in Paris, 1994, COSMIT, Milan, 1994, Bayerische Ruck, Munich, Benetton Worldwide, graphics American Airlines, 1967, Bloomingdales, 1972, books for Rizzoli Internat.; author: Knoll Design, 1981 (American Inst. Graphic Arts award). Recipient Indsl. Arts medal AIA, 1973, Presdl. Design award, 1985, Gold medal for design Nat. Arts Club, 1991, Fellowship of Excellence Interior Product Designers, 1992, Lifetime Achievement award Bklyn. Mus., 1995, Hon. Royal Designer for Industry award Royal Soc. of Arts, 1996; named to Hall of Fame N.Y. Art Dirs. Club, 1982, Compasso d'Oro, 1964, Interior Design Hall of Fame, 1988. Mem. American Inst. Graphic Arts (pres. 1976-77 Gold medal 1983), Indsl. Designers Soc. America, Alliance Graphique Internationale (past pres.), Archtl. League N.Y. (v.p.) Home: New York, NY. Died May 27, 2014.

**VILCHES-O'BOURKE, OCTAVIO AUGUSTO,** accounting company executive; b. Havana, Cuba, Aug. 15, 1923; came to the U.S., 1962, naturalized, 1967; s. Bartolome and Isabel Susana (O'Bourke) Vilches; m. Alba Del Valle Junco, July 24, 1954; 1 son, Octavio Roberto. CPA, U. Havana, 1949, JD, 1951, PhD in Econ. Scis., 1953. Owner Octavio Vilches & Assocs., Havana, 1949-61; comptr. United RR of Cuba, 1950-53; cons. econ. affairs Cuban Dept. Labor, Havana, 1953; auditor Cuban Dept. Treasury, 1952-59; pres. Roble Furniture, Inc., San Juan, 1963-65; owner Hato Rey, PR, from 1963; pres. Mero Constrn. Corp., San Juan, 1973. Mem. Circulo Cubano P.R., Colegio Contadores Publicos en el Exilio, Colegio Abogados en el Exilio, Cuban Nat. Bar Assn., Nat. Soc. Pub. Accts., Am. Club (Miami, Fla.). Republican. Home: San Juan, PR. Died Oct. 24, 2013.

**VILLANUEVA, ARMANDO,** former prime minister of Peru; b. Lima, Nov. 25, 1915; m. Lucy Villanueva. Spkr. Chamber of Deputies Peruvian Congress, 1967—68, mem., 1963—68; senator Peruvian Senate, 1985—92, pres., 1986—87; prime minister Govt. of Peru, Lima, 1988-89, min. interior, 1989. Pres. Peruvian Aprista Party, 1979—85. Peruvian Aprista Party. Roman Catholic. Died Apr. 14, 2013.

**VINING, DANIEL RUTLEDGE,** economics educator; b. Birmingham, Ala., Aug. 12, 1908; s. George Joseph and Margaret Olivia Vining; m. Margaret McClanahan, June 17, 1936 (dec.); children: George Joseph III, Daniel Rutledge Jr. BBA, U. Tex., 1931, MA, 1935; PhD, U. Chgo., 1944. Prof. econs. Westminster Coll., Fulton, Mo., 1935-38; instr. econs. and stats. U. Ark., Fayetteville, 1938-40, asst. prof. econs. and stats., 1941-43, assoc. prof., 1944; prof. econs. U. Va., Charlottesville, from 1945. Statistician Fed. Res. Bank Atlanta, 1941; rsch. asst. Nat. Bur. Econ. Rsch., N.Y.C., 1948-49; vis. prof. Columbia U., N.Y.C., summer 1949, U. Calif. Berkeley, summer 1956, U. Minn., Mpls., summer 1956; chmn. Sch. Bus. Adminstrn., Charlottesville, 1952-54. Author: On Appraising the Performance of an Economic System, 1984; contbr. articles to profl. jours. Ford Found. Faculty Rsch. fellow, Charlottesville, 1956-57, So. Regional Sci. Assn. fellow, Atlanta, 1987. Mem. Am. Econ. Assn., Am. Stats. Assn., Regional Sci. Assn. Episcopalian. Avocation: farming. Home: New York, NY. Died Dec. 4, 1999.

**VIS, RONALD DIEDERIK,** physicist; b. Haarlem, The Netherlands, Mar. 4, 1945; s. Dirk and Georgina Kuthe V.; m. Renie Gaby de Ceuninck van Capelle, oct. 1, 1985; 1 child, Vincent. MS, U. Amsterdam, 1971; PhD, Free U., 1977. Chemist Lab. Nagel, Amsterdam, 1970-75, Free U., Amsterdam, 1975-77, asst. prof. of physics, from 1977. Bd. dirs. Dutch Vacuum Soc., Dutch Phys. Soc. Author: (book) The Proton Microprobe, 1985; editor publ. in field, 1990. Mem. cmty. coun. Breukelen, 1998—. Mem. Royal Dutch Chem. Soc. Avocation: internat. vet. tennis player. Home: Breukelen/Utrecht, Netherlands. Died May 9, 2001.

**VISSER, JOHANNES,** research scientist, biographer; b. Leeuwarden, The Netherlands, Nov. 27, 1936; s. Eeuwe and Marie (Van der Heul) V.; m. Johanna Catherina Elisabeth Van Kolmeschate; children: Katja, Derek. Degree in Chem. Engring., Technical U. Delft, The Netherlands, 1965; PhD, Coun. for Nat. Acad. Awards, London, 1973. Rsch. scientist Unilever Rsch., Vaardingen, The Netherlands, 1965-69, Port Sunlight, Eng., 1969-71, Vlaardingen, 1971-93, Netherlands Inst. for Dairy Rsch., Ede, 1993-96; invited scientist U. Minho, Braga, Portugal, 1997-2000, U. Porto, Portugal, from 2000. 1st dir. found. European Hygienic Equipment Design Group, 1997-98; organizer Symposium Protein Interactions, 201st annual meeting ACS, Atlanta, 1991. Editor: Protein Interactions, 1992, Simon Vestdijk, 1987; inventor in field; contbr. articles to profl. jours. Bd. dirs. Unilever Mgrs. Union, Rotterdam, 1977-91, chmn. Vestdijkkring, The Netherlands, 1998—; 1st lt. Dutch Signal Corps 1963-65. Recipient Friesian Press award Union of Friesian Journalists, Leeuwarden, The Netherlands, 1984, Author's award Unilever Rsch. Vlaardingen, 1992. Mem. Royal Dutch Chem. Soc., Genootschap voor Melkkunde, Canadian Assn. for Advancement of Netherlandic Studies. Achievements include research in reducing fouling in dairy industry by surface modification of stainless steel. Home: Maassluis, Netherlands. Died Aug. 22, 2001.

**VLADEM, STEVEN ALLEN,** writer, film producer, motivational speaker, entrepreneur; b. Chgo., July 24, 1949; s. Arthur and Elaine Edythe (Ascher) Vladem. BA with honors and distinction, U. Ill., Chgo., 1970; MEd in Math., Northeastern Ill. U., Chgo., 1973; MA in Ednl. Adminstrn./Supervision, Roosevelt U., Chgo., 1975; ScD, London Sch. Applied Rsch., 1993. Tchr. math. Chgo. Bd. Edn., 1971-81, statistician and evaluator dept. rsch. and evaluation, 1979; supr. program svcs. Dept. Planning, Chgo. City Hall, 1981; coord. alt. sch. without walls program Chgo. Met. HS, 1982-87, coord. computer assisted instrn., 1987-91; developer ednl. software Chgo., 1987-92; freelance computer cons., 1987-92; writer/lectr., from 1994; prodr. Image Lost Film, 2003—06. Lectr. in field; mktg. cons. Enoch Searle Prodns., 2001—09, Cosmic Films, 2001—06, Film Corp. Motion Picture Collaborative Afro Am. and Jewish Found., from 2006; motivational spkr. Profl. Spkrs. Bur. Internat., from 2001; spkr. Spkrs. Showcase, 2001, Hope Conf., Columbus, Ohio, 2009; distbr. ZIJA Internat., 2011, USANA, from 2011. Author: (poetry) The Jigsaw People, 1997; co-author: Second Sight, Inspiring Hope: Stories of Hopeful Living for More Success, 2009; exhibitions include Gallery Art, Internat. Congress Arts and Commn., Keble Coll., Oxford U., Eng., Internat. Platform Assn. Art Exhbn., 1995; prodr.: Image Lost Films, from 2003; exec. prodr.: (films) Gein, 2003; Viva La Causa, 2008; Royal Blue Book of Diploma and Science, 2010; 101 Industry Experts, 2011. Mem. Internat. Parliament Safety and Peace, Palermo, Italy, 1993—95; bd. dirs. Nat. Coalition Health Care Reform, from 1998; founder coun. London Diplomatic Acad., Internat. Diplomatic Acad., Albert Schweitzer Inst., Chgo. Coun. Fgn. Rels., Internat. Fellowship Christians and Jews, Northwestern U. Jewish Ctr.; sec.-gen. United Cultural Conv.; hon. amb. laureates Jr. Achievement and Chgo. Assn. Bus. and Industry, 1990; support group leader, outreach vol. Nat. Keratoconus Found., LA, from 1995; docent Tour of Old Town Old Town C. of C., Chgo., 1993; patron various arts orgns.; vol. Sight Savers Internat., Karin Or Ctr. Multi-Handicapped Blind Children, State of Ill. Transplant Program, 2003, Am. Transplant Assn., Cinema for Deaf Film Festival, 2003; charter mem. Compassion Cmty.; mem. Fetzer Inst.; judge Daniel Webster Acad. Poets Competition, 1998; nominator Col.'s Way Award. Recipient Congress Star of Distinction, Internat. Congress Arts and Comm./St. John's Coll., Cambridge U., 1992, medal of Merit, Republic of Peru, 1992, Albert Einstein medal, Holland, 1994, Alzheimers Rsch. award, Alzheimers Assn. Am., 2000, Touch for Global Inspiration award, 2000, Internat. Peace prize, 2002, Congl. medal of Excellence, 2002, Am. medal of Honor, 2002, Sci. & Peace medal, Albert Schweitzer Inst., Madrid, 2002, DaVinci Diamond award, 2008, TESLA award, 2011, Roll of Honor, Chgo. Film Prodrs. Assn.; named John W. Rogers Educator of the Yr., Jr. Achievement, Chgo., 1990; named to Wall of Tolerance, Civil Rights Meml. Ctr., 2003; finalist, U.S. Nat. Memory Championship, N.Y.C., 1997. Mem. IFP, NATAS, Ill. Prodn. Alliance, Internat. Platform Assn. (bd. govs. internet team, red carpet com., Gold Ribbon Most Popular Artist 1995), United Writers Assn. (life fellow), World Univ. Roundtable, Toastmasters Internat., Internat. Order of Merit (Cambridge, Eng.), Daniel Webster Acad. Poets (Cert. of Merit 1995), Chrysopoets, Order of Templars of Jerusalem (knight), Lofsensic Ursinius Order (knight comdr.), World Order of Sci. Edn. Culture. (knight-cavalier), Am. Order Excellence, Order of San Ciriaco (count), Internat. Diplomatic Acad. (Honorable Order of Ky. Cols., 2010), Niagara Found., Am. Legion (gold medal, sch. leadership award 1967), Rotary Club, Lions Club, Sierra Club, Dem. Nat. Com., Southern Poverty Law Ctr. (leadership coun.). Avocations: cinema, musical theatre, backgammon, architecture, world travel. Home: Northbrook, Ill. Died Sept. 2, 2012.

**VLADUTIU, ADRIAN O.,** physician, educator; b. Bucharest, Romania, Aug. 5, 1940; came to U.S., 1969, naturalized 1974; s. Octavian and Veturia (Chirescu) Vladutiu; m. Georgirene V. Dietrich; children: Christina Lynn, Catherine Joy. MD, Sch. Medicine, Bucharest, 1962; PhD in Immunopathology, Sch. Medicine, Jassy, Romania, 1968. Diplomate Am. Bd. Pathology. Asst. prof. physiopathology Sch. Medicine, Bucharest, 1968-71; assoc. prof. pathology SUNY Sch. Medicine, Buffalo, 1978-81, prof. pathology, 1981—2008, pathologist, 1974—2006; dir. clin. labs. Buffalo Gen. Hosp., 1982—2001, prof. microbiology, 1982—2008, prof. medicine, 1985—2008. Cons. Niagara Falls (N.Y.) Meml. Hosp., 1976—82, Tri-County Hosp., Gowanda, NY, 1991—93; acting head dept. pathology Buffalo Gen. Hosp, 1985—86; dir. lab. Deaconess Hosp. Buffalo, 1982—91, Columbus Meml., Buffalo, 1996—98. Author: Pleural Effusion, 1986; contbr. chapters to books, articles to profl. jours. Med. Rsch. Coun. Can. fellow, 1968, Buswell fellow, 1969; recipient rsch. prize Ministry Edn. Romania, 1965, rsch. award NIH, 1985. Fellow: ACP, Nat. Acad. Clin. Biochemistry, Coll. Am. Pathologists; mem.: Am. Soc. Investigative Pathology, Am. Assn. Immunologists. Achievements include first demonstration of the association of autoimmunity with major histocompability antigens; discovery of Buffalo thyroxine binding globulin gene. Home: Buffalo, NY. Died Jan. 9, 2014.

**VOGEL, WERNER PAUL,** retired machine company executive; b. Louisville, June 15, 1923; s. Werner George and Emma (Bartman) Vogel; m. Helen Louise Knapp, Oct. 2, 1954. B in Mech. Engring., U. Louisville, 1950. With Henry Vogt Machine Co., Louisville, 1942—86, asst. plant supt., 1957—60, plant supt., 1961—73, v.p., 1974—86; ret. Trustee City of Strathmoor, Ky., 1959—61; clk. City of Glenview Manor, Ky., 1967—73, trustee, 1974—75, treas., 1986—89; mem. adv. coun. Lindsey Wilson Coll., 1988—2003; bd. dirs. Louisville Protestant Altenheim, 1979—80, pres., 1985—90, ret. With USAAF, 1944—46. Mem.: ASME, Sigma Tau, Tau Beta Pi. Republican. Methodist. Home: Louisville, Ky. Died May 16, 2008.

**VOGNILD, LARRY LEE,** retired state legislator; b. Spokane, Jan. 21, 1932; s. James Howard and Helen Mildred (Pinkerton) Vognild; m. Dorothy L. Vognild; children: Valerie Ann, Margo Elaine. Mem. City of Everett Fire Dept., 1954—78, bn. chief Wash., 1976—78; mem. Dist. 38 Wash. State Senate, Olympia, 1978—94. With USN, 1951—54. Democrat. Lutheran. Home: Everett, Wash. Died Jan. 3, 2014.

**VOGRIN, JOSEPH EDWARD, III,** lawyer; BA magna cum laude, Duquesne U., Pitts, 1969, JD, 1972. Bar: Pa. 1972, U.S. Ct. Appeals (3rd cir.) 1972, US Supreme Ct. 1984. Dep. dist. atty. Dist. Atty's Office Allegheny County, Pitts., 1972—79; ptnr. Scott, Vogrin & Riester, Pitts., 1980—96, Vogrin & Riester, P.C., Pitts., 1996—2000, Meyer Darragh Buckler Bebenek & Eck, Pitts., 2000—07; of counsel Meyer Darragh, Pitts., from 2007. Solicitor Ohio Twp. San. Authority, Pitts., 1983—2007, Shaler Twp., Pitts., from 1986, Quaker Valley Coun. Govts., Pitts., 1987—2007, North Hills Coun. Govts., Pitts., from 1988, Boroughs Assn. Allegheny County, Pitts., 1991, 1994, 2003, Ross Twp. CSC, Pitts., 1993—2007, Borough Avalon, Pitts., 1992—2005, Twp. Res., Pitts., from 1998; co-counsel Allegheny County and Western Pa. Assn. Twp. Commrs., Pitts., 1997—2008. Mem.: Allegheny County Bar Assn. (chmn. assn. mcpl. and sch. solicitors Allegheny County 1998—99, Listed in Pa. Super Lawyers 2006—09). Home: Pittsburgh, Pa. Died 2013.

**VOGT, ROY SCHOPPAUL,** management consultant; b. Wilmington, NC, Apr. 9, 1919; s. Henry and Florence Johanna (Schoppaul) V.; m. Winifred Dorothy Sorg, June 23, 1951; children: Henry, Virginia. BA, Haverford Coll., 1941; attended exec. seminars, Grad. Sch. Bus. Harvard U., 1965, attended exec. seminars, 1969. Asst. to pres. Haverford Coll., Pa., 1944—45; mgr. adminstrn. dept. Smith, Kline & French Labs., 1945—51; purchasing mgr. Crawford Mfg. Co., Richmond, Va., 1951—55; adminstrv. officer Princeton U., 1955—71; treas., chief bus. officer Windham Coll., Putney, Vt., 1971—76; treas., sec. Fitz, Vogt & Assocs. Ltd., Brattleboro, Vt., 1977—87; tree farmer Vt. Officer Brattleboro Score chpt. SBA, 1978—99; chmn. ARC, Princeton, 1958, Cmty. Chest, 1957; bldg. com. Calvary Bapt. Ch., 1957—58; bd. mgrs. N.J. Bapt. Conv., 1957—60, mem. fin. com., 1957—60; mem. alumni coun. Haverford Coll., 1965, exec. com. alumni mem. corp., 1966. Mem.: Woodlot Owners Assn., Varsity Club Haverford, Founders Club Haverford Coll., Alpha Tau Omega, Phi Beta Kappa. Home: Brattleboro, Vt. Died May 25, 1999.

**VOJTKO, MARGARET MARY PAULA,** language educator; d. John Vojtko and Anna Labik. BA cum laude, U. Pitts., 1969, MA, 1970; ABD, Cath. U. America, Washington DC; Grad. Nurse, St Francis Med. Ctr. Sch. Nursing, Pitts., 1987. Cert. RN Commonwealth of Pa. Part-time instr. Carnegie-Mellon U. Translation Ctr., Pitts., 1975—78; lectr. in French Purdue U., Fort Wayne, Ind., 1978—81; part-time instr. CC Allegheny County, Pitts., 1991—94; adj. lectr. in French Duquesne U., Pitts., 1988—2013. Author booklets and articles. Pres. Homestead Historical Soc., Pa., 1982—2002; bd. mem. Turtle Creek Mental Retardation Agy., Braddock, Pa., 1982—90; rep. Cmty. Health Coun. South Hills Health Sys., Jefferson Boro, Pa., 1982—90. Recipient Disting. Grad., Vincentian HS Honors Hall, Pitts., 1998. Catholic. Avocations: choral singing, violin. Home: Homestead, Pa. Died Sept. 1, 2013.

**VOLKHOLZ, KLAUS LUDWIG,** electronics company executive; b. Berlin, Mar. 24, 1936; s. William Alfred and Gertrud Volkholz; m. Alida Lassooy; children: Detlev, Peter. MS in Engring., U. Mich., 1961, MA in Econs., 1963, PhD in Elec. Engring., 1964. Product mktg. mgr. Philips Electronics, Eindhoven, The Netherlands, 1964-72; mgmt. cons. Prognos, Basel, Switzerland, 1972-76; v.p. strategic planning Signetics, Sunnyvale, Calif., 1976-82; dir. Philips Comm., Nuremberg, Germany, 1982-86; sr. dir. corp. planning and strategy Philips Electronics, Eindhoven, from 1986. Dir. Navigation Techs., Sunnyvale, 1994—. Mem. IEEE, Strategic Mgmt. Soc., Phi Beta Kappa. Home: Heeze, Netherlands. Died Feb. 8, 2008.

**VOLOSOV, VADIM IVANOVICH,** physicist, researcher; b. Moscow, Sept. 5, 1932; s. Ivan Pavlovich and Anna Evgrafovna Volosok; m. Lyudmila Dmitrievna Glazunova, July 26, 1961 (dec. Feb. 26, 1994); children: Ol'ga, Aleksey; m. Ideya Timofeevna Firsova, Aug. 10, 1999. Degree in physics, Moscow State U., 1955. Jr. scientist Kurchatov Inst., Moscow, 1956—59; sr. scientist Budker Inst. Nuc. Physics, Novosibirsk, Russia, 1959—65, chief lab., 1965—99, leading scientist, from 1999. Achievements include research in properties of rotating plasma promising for nuclear fusion and technology. Home: Novosibirsk, Russia. Died Mar. 18, 2013.

**VON DER ESCH, HANS ULRIK,** lawyer; b. Nurnberg, Germany, Jan. 27, 1928; s. Hans Joachim and Kerstin Marianne (Sandstedt) von der E.; m. Marianne Hedvig Margaretha Celsing, Aug. 23, 1975; children: Ulric, Fredrik; 1 child by previous marriage: Alexandra Louise. MBA, U. Gothenburg, 1951; LLB, U. Stockholm, 1954. Bar: Sweden 1966. With Dist. Ct. Svc., Nykoping and Stockholm, 1954-57; pres.'s asst. counsel Bonniergroup, Stockholm, Hamburg, Geneva, NYC, 1957-63; pvt. practice Stockholm, 1963-66; ptnr. Advokatfirman Landahl, 1966—89, sr. ptnr., 1990—96, Landahl & Wistrand, Advokatbyrå, 1997—98, Advokat HU von der Esch AB, from 1999. Chmn., bd. dirs. Swedish and fgn. cos. With Swedish Army Cavalry, 1946-48; lt. col. res. Decorated Swedish Sign of Distinction, Finnish Golden Order of Merit, Norwegian Badge of Honor, Knight of the Order of St. John in Sweden. Mem. ABA (assoc.), Swedish Lawyers Assn. (divsn. dir. 1974-79, del. 1979-88, mem. disciplinary bd. 1984-88, 92-98), Swedish Army and Air Force Res. Officers League (pres. 1975-78), Swedish Parachute Assn. (pres. 1966-68), Royal Swedish Aero Club (bd. dirs. 1966-78, gen. counsel 1967-78, v.p. 1983-88), Internat. Bar Assn., Internat. Fiscal Assn., Nya Saellskapet Club. Lic. pvt. pilot for airplane, helicopter and glider; holder 5 world class records piston engine: Class C-1-c, speed record over recognized course: Sal, Rep. of Cape Verde to Funchal, Madeira 224.06 km/hr, Class C-1-c light aircraft 1750-3000 kgs, Funchal, Madeira to Lisbon 256.131 km/hour, Class C-1-c Paris to Stockholm, 248.67 km/hour, Class C-1-b light aircraft 500-1000 kgs, Stockholm to Rovaniemi, Finland, 126.31 km/hour and Class C-1-b Rovaniemi, Finland to Murmansk, U.S.S.R., 150.59 km/hour. Home: Stockholm, Sweden. Died Sept. 30, 2009.

**VON DER HEYDT, JAMES ARNOLD,** federal judge; b. Miles City, Mont., July 15, 1919; s. Harry Karl and Alice S. (Arnold) von der Heydt.; m. Verna E. Johnson, May 21, 1952. BA, Albion Coll., 1942; JD, Northwestern U., 1951. Bar: Alaska 1951. Dep. US marshal US Marshals Svc., Nome, Alaska, 1945—48; U.S. commr. US Dist. Ct. Alaska, Nome, 1951; US atty. Dist. Alaska US Dept. Justice, 1951—53; pvt. practice atty. Nome, Alaska, 1953—59; mem. Alaska House Reps., 1957—59; presiding judge Alaska Superior Ct., Juneau, Alaska, 1959—66; judge US Dist. Ct. Alaska, 1966—73, chief judge, 1973—84, sr. judge, 1984—2013. Author: Mother Sawtooth's Nome, 1990, Alaska, The Short and Long of It, 2000. Pres. Anchorage Fine Arts Mus. Assn. Recipient Disting. Alumni award Albion Coll., 1995, Professionalism & Ethics award Inn of Ct., 2005. Mem. Alaska Bar Assn. (bd. govs. 1955-59, pres. 1959-60), American Judicature Soc., Masons (32d degree), Shriners, Phi Delta Phi, Sigma Nu. Avocations: researching arctic bird life, creative writing, painting. Home: Anchorage, Alaska. Died Dec. 1, 2013.

**VON SINNER, WALTHER NICHOLAS,** radiologist; b. Lind, Austria, Apr. 28, 1930; s. Niko and Martina (Kobelmüller) S.; m. Barbro Wikander, Mar. 21, 1967; children: Niklas, Björn. MD, U. Zurich, 1955, MSc, 1960; MD, Karolinska Inst., Stockholm, 1966, PhD, 1978. Radiologist U. Gothenburg & Lund, Sweden, 1964-67; acting dept. head, chmn. thoracic clinics Karolinska Inst., Stockholm, 1974-77; prof. radiology U. Miami, 1977-83; cons. and head radiologist King Faisal Specialist Hosp. & Rsch. Ctr., Riyadh, Saudi Arabia, from 1985. Author, editor: Needle Biopsy and Transbronchial Biopsy, 1982; contbr. articles to profl. jours. Avocations: classical music, sailing, jogging, swimming, bicycling. Died Mar. 3, 2008.

**VON WRIGHT, GEORG HENRIK,** philosopher, writer; b. Helsinki, Finland, June 14, 1916; s. Tor von Wright and Ragni Elisabeth Alfthan; m. Baroness Maria Elisabeth von Troil, 1941; 2 children. Educated, U. Helsinki, Cambridge U.; D honoris causa, Helsinki U., Liverpool U., Lund U., U. Turku, Tampere U., Buenos Aires U., Salta U., Bologna U., St. Olaf Coll., Abo Acad., Tromso U., Stockholm U., Leipzig U., Innsbruck U. Lectr. in philosophy U. Helsinki, 1943-46, prof. philosophy, 1946-61. Prof. philosophy Cambridge U., 1948-51, Tarner lectr. Trinity Coll., 1969; hon. fellow Trinity Coll., Cambridge; vis. prof. Cornell U., 1954, 58, U. Calif., 1963, U. Pitts., 1966, U. Karlsruhe, 1975, U. Leipzig, 1994-95; Gifford lectr. U. St. Andrews, 1959-60; rsch. fellow Acad. Finland, 1961-86; Andrew D. White prof.-at-large Cornell U., 1965-77; chancellor at Abo Acad., 1968-77; Woodbridge lectr. Columbia U., 1972; Nellie Wallace lectr. U. Oxford, 1978. Author: The Logical Problem of Induction, 1941, A Treatise on Induction and Probability, 1951, An Essay in Modal Logic, 1951, Logical Studies, 1957, The Varieties of Goodness, 1963, Norm and Action, 1963, The Logic of Preference, 1963, An Essay in Deontic Logic, 1968, Explanation and Understanding, 1971, Causality and Determinism, 1974, Freedom and Determination, 1980, Wittgenstein, 1982, Philosophical Papers, I-III, 1983-84, Intellectual Autobiography, 1989, The Tree of Knowledge, 1993, Normen, Werte und Handlungen, 1994, Six Essays in Philosophical Logic, 1996, In the Shadow of Descartes, 1998. Recipient Wihuri Found. Internat. prize 1976, Alexander von Humboldt Found. rsch. award, 1986, Tage Danielsson Humanist award, 1998. Fellow Finnish Soc. Sci. (pres. 1966-67); mem. Philos. Soc. Finland (pres. 1962-73), Internat. Union History and Philosophy of Sci. (pres. 1963-65), Inst. Internat. de Philosophie Paris (pres. 1975-78), Royal Swedish Acad. Sci., Brit. Acad., Royal Danish Acad. Sci. Norwegian Acad. Sci. and Letters, European Acad. Arts, Scis. and Humanities, World Acad. Arts and Scis., Am. Acad. Arts and Scis. (hon. fgn. mem.). Deceased.

**VORONKOV, MIKHAIL GRIGORIEVICH,** chemist, consultant; b. Orel, Russia, Dec. 6, 1921; s. Grigori Vasilievich and Laisa Mikhailovna Voronkov; m. Lilia Iliinichna Makhnina; children: Viktor Mikhailovich, Valentina Mikhailovna. BS, Leningrad U., Russia, 1942, PhD, 1947; DSc in Chemistry, Acad. Scis. USSR, Moscow, 1961; PhD Honoris Causa, Gdansk Poly. Inst., Poland, 1975. Sr. scientist Leningrad U., 1944—54; prof., head lab. Inst. Silicate Chemistry Acad. Scis., Leningrad, 1954—61; prof., head lab. Inst. Organic Synthesis Latvian Acad. Scis., Riga, 1961—70; academician, dir. Inst. Organic Chemistry Siberian divsn. Acad. Scis. USSR, Irkutsk, 1970-94. Sci. advisor Mongolian Acad. Scis., Ulan-Bator, Industr. Corporn., Jilin, China, Kiev (Ukraine) Poly. Inst.; co-dir. Inst. Applied Chemistry, St. Petersburg, 1995-98. Contbr. more than 1500 rsch. articles to profl. jours. V.p. Presidium East Siberian Affiliation Siberian br. USSR Acad. Sci., 1973-77. lt. comdr. Leningrad Front, 1941-42. Mem. Acad. Sci. USSR, Russian Acad. Sci., Braunschweig Sci. Soc. Germany, Latvian Acad. Sci., Asian Pacific Countries Acad. Materials, Fla. Heterocyclic Compounds Ctr. Avocations: stamp and coin collecting, chemical humour. Home: Irkutsk, Russia. Died Feb. 11, 2014.

**VOTRUBA, LADISLAV,** water engineering educator, consultant; b. Radlice, Czech Republic, May 6, 1914; s. Jan and Marie (Šmejkal) V.; 1 child, Libor. Civil engr., Tech. U. Prague, Czech Republic, 1938, D in Tech., 1946, DSc, 1967. Cert. in hydraulic structures and water mgmt. Chief engr. Ctrl. Power Stas., Prague, 1941-45; asst. prof. engring. Tech. U. Prague, 1938-41, 45-57, prof. civil engring., 1957-87; cons. engr. Prague, 1987—2002. Former dean Faculty Civil Engring., Tech. U. Prague. Author: Temperature and Winter Regime in Water Cources, Reservoirs and Water Schemes, 1983, Analysis of Water Resource Systems, 1988, Water Management in Reservoirs, 1989, Reliability of Water Management Schemes, 1993, Water Management and Nature in Czech Republic, 1999, Education of Engineers to Creativity, 2000. Pres. Czechoslovak Nat. Com. on Large Dams, Prague, 1961-84, v.p. Internat. Commn. Large Dams, Paris, 1974-77; cons. Water Power and Dam Constrn., London, 1979—; mem. Com. on World Register of Dams, ICOLD, Paris, 1967-91; pres. Czech Tech. Found., 1991-95. Recipient Felber's Gold medal, Prague, 1974, J.A. Komensky's medal, Min. Schs., Prague, 1980, Fr. Křižík's Gold medal, Acad. Scis., Prague, 1984. Died Oct. 1, 2002.

**VOWLES, RICHARD BECKMAN,** literature educator; b. Fargo, ND, Oct. 5, 1917; s. Guy Richard and Ella (Beckman) V.; m. Ellen Noah Hudson, Aug. 1, 1942 (div. 1969); children: Elizabeth Ellen, Richard Hudson. BS, Davidson Coll., 1938; postgrad., U. N.C., 1938—39, U. Stockholm, 1939—40; MA, Yale U., 1942, PhD, 1950. Engr. Hercules Powder Co., Wilmington, Chattanooga, 1941—43; chemist Rohm & Haas, Knoxville, Tenn., 1943—44; econ. cons. War Dept., 1944; Am. vice consul Gothenburg, Sweden, 1945—46; asst. prof. English Southwestern U., Memphis, 1948—50, Queens U., NYC, 1950—51; asso. prof. English U. Fla., 1951—60; prof. Scandinavian and comparative lit. U. Wis., Madison, 1960—85, prof. emeritus, from 1985, chmn. comparative lit., 1962—63, 1964—67, 1971—72, chmn. Scandinavian studies, 1977—80. Am. specialist in Scandinavia Dept. State, 1963; vis. prof. NYU, 1964, U. Helsinki, Finland, 1968, Stockholm, 1969; lectr., Sydney, Australia, 1975, Paris, 1975; master ceremonies Santa Fe Scandinavian Film Festival, 1984 Editor: Eternal Smile, 1954, Dramatic Theory, 1956, Comparatists at Work, 1968; Adv. editor: Nordic Council Series, 1965-70, Herder Ency. of World Lit; contbr. articles to profl. jours. Am.-Scandinavian Found. fellow, Stockholm, 1939-40, Lassen fellow Am. Scandinavian Found., 1986, Fulbright fellow Copenhagen, 1955-56, Strindberg fellow Stockholm, 1973, Norwegian Govt. fellow, 1978; recipient Rsch. award Swedish govt., 1978. Mem. Modern Lang. Assn., Soc. Advancement Scandinavian Study (mem. exec. com.), Internat. Comparative Lit. Assn., Am. Comparative Lit. Assn. (adv. bd.), Strindberg Soc., Phi Beta Kappa. Home: Madison, Wis. Died Dec. 19, 2013.

**VROMAN, LEO,** author. artist, retired scientist; b. Gouda, Netherlands, Apr. 10, 1915; s. Sam Vroman and Anna Vromen; m. Georgine Marie Sanders, Sept. 10, 1947; children: Geraldine Griffin, Peggy Ann Gracy. PhD, Rijksuniversiteit, Utrecht, Netherlands, 1940. Cert. rsch. career scientist Vets. Adminstrn., 1980. Author Mt. Sinai Hosp., New York, Netherlands, 1947—2010. Contbr. articles; author: New York and Netherlands, frst was Gebchten Ouerido, 1947; Latest book Leo Vroman. Tekenaar. Pvt. 1st class Landstorm, 1941—46, Indonesia. Recipient award, U. Groningen Netherlands, 1948—49, 1961. Fellow: NY Assn. Scis. Achievements include discovery of vroman effect. Home: Fort Worth, Tex. Died Feb. 22, 2014.

**VUCELIC, DUSAN,** education educator; b. Belgrade, Yugoslavia; s. Rados and Vukosava (Tabakovic) V.; m. Vera Milakovic, Sept. 18, 1966; 1 child, Morana. BS, U. Belgrade, 1964, PhD in Phys. Chemistry, 1970. Scientific assoc. Begrade U., 1964-71, asst. prof., 1971-83, prof., from 1983; pres. bd. Holding Inst. Gen. and Phys. Chemistry, Belgrade, from 1990, ZEOLITE MIRA, Mira, Italy, from 1997. Scientific assoc. Stanford U., Calif., 1980-81; pres. IUPAB Commn. on Radiation and Environ. Biophysics, 1984-94. Contbr. more than 100 articles to profl. jours. and publs. Recipient Steinkopff prize German Colloid. Soc., Germany, 1993. Mem. N.Y. Acad. Scis., Yugoslav Biophys. Soc. (pres. 1986-96). Avocations: books, farming, tennis, skiing. Died 2000.

**VUONG, PHAT NGOC,** pathologist, cytologist, researcher; b. Hanoi, Vietnam, Feb. 2, 1945; s. Quynh Duy and Tan Thi (Nguyen) V.; m. Phuong Nguyen, 1969 (div. 1979); children: Tam Ngoc, Lan Ngoc; m. Sarra Houissa, Oct. 15, 1981; children: Anh Asma, Hien Hella. MD, U. Saigon, Vietnam, 1971, postgrad., 1973, U. Paris, 1977, 78, 82, PhD in Sci., 1992; DSc, U. Rouen, 1997. Titular intern Saigon Hosp., 1969-72, asst. prof. faculty medicine, 1972-73; affiliated pathologist Hosps. of Paris, 1975-82; dep. dir. Ctrl. Lab. St. Michel Hosp., Paris, 1981-83, chief dept. A.C.P., 1984-88, head unit A.C.P., from 1988; co-dir. Lab. Anatomical and Cytol. Pathology, Bièvres, France, from 1979. Ad hoc expert for legal testimony anatomical and cytol. pathology French Ministry for Justice Superior Ct., Versailles, Paris, 1986—; affiliated researcher Natural History Mus., Paris, 1985—, U. Rouen, 1997—. Contbr. articles, papers to profl. jours., books. Lt. MD South Vietnamese Army, 1973-74. Fellow Internat. Acad. Cytology; mem. AAAS, N.Y. Acad. Sics., European Soc. Pathology, Internat. Acad. Pathology, French Soc. Clin. Cytology, Anatomic Soc. Paris, French Soc. Lymphology, French Assn. Quality Assurance in Anatomic Pathology and Cytopathology., Coll. Med. Hosps. Paris. Home: Paris, France. Deceased.

**VYSUŠIL, JIŘÍ,** economics and management educator, consultant; b. Mělník, Czech Republic, Mar. 26, 1927; s. Josef and Marie (Trojanová) V.; m. Dagmar Červená, Aug.

17, 1950; 1 child, Dana. MA, Prague, Czech Republic, 1950, Econ. U., Prague, 1952, PhD in Econs., 1953. Economist Fedn. Horlogère, Switzerland, 1968-69; rschr. Lancaster (Eng.) U., 1969; asst. prof. econs. Czech Tech. U., 1953-65, assoc. prof., 1965-68, 70-91, head Inst., 1990-93, prof., 1991-97, prof. emeritus, from 1997. Cons., sci. rschr. Inst. Mgmt., Prague, 1965-76; mem. supervisory com. Tesla Holešovice, Prague, 1976-97, Beneš & Lát, Pruhonice, 1998—; mem. sci. coun. Econ. U., 1990-97, Czech Tech. U., 1990—; mem. accreditation com. Czech Govt. Author: Interindustry Balances, 1976, Information Systems, 1976, Quality of Information 1986 (Rector's prize), The Secret of Prosperity, 10 vols., 1993-98, Found. of Mgmt., 1996, Czech and American Accounting: A Comparison, 1997, Internal Enterprise Economics, 1998, Integration Methods in Controlling, 1999, Controlling in Six Steps, 2000, Concept of Computerized National Accounts and Interindustry Relations, 2000, others. Recipient Felber medal, 1977, Hasa medal, 1992. Mem. Acad. Club. Avocations: music, literature, recreational activities. Died Sept. 2, 2002.

**WACKER, JOHN M.,** music educator, director; s. A. Mainard and Sarah E. Wacker; m. Nancy E. Russell, Mar. 30, 1996; children: Brian R, Elizabeth I. MusB in Edn., U. Northern Colo., Greeley, 1983; MusM, Ind. U. of Pa., Ind., Pa., 1999; JD, U. Wyo., Laramie, 1994; DMA, U. North Tex., Denton, 2008. Dir. band Burns Jr. and Sr. HS, Wyo., 1983—85, Cheyenne Ctrl. HS, Wyo., 1985—90; music sales, clinician Yocum Music Co., Cheyenne, 1990—99; coord. instrumental music Laramie County C.C., Cheyenne, 1999—2001; tchg. fellow U. North Tex., Denton, 2001—04; prof. music., dir. bands Western State Coll. Colo., Gunnison, 2005—14. Pvt. practice music clinician, Gunnison, 1990—2014. Grantee, We. State Coll. Colo., 2006; fellow, U. North Tex., 2001—04. Mem.: Music Educators Nat. Conf., Internat. Trumpet Guild, Nat. Honor Soc., Phi Beta Mu, Kappa Kappa Psi. Home: Gunnison, Colo. Died May 11, 2014.

**WADENA, DARRELL EUGENE (CHIP WADENA),** indian tribe executive; b. White Earth, Minn., Nov. 23, 1938; s. John S. and Mary (Peabody) Wadena; m. Bonnie Londo, Apr. 7, 1959; children: Tony, Ann, Darrell Eugene, Shannon, Tracy, David. Heavy equipment operator W.E. Wylie Constrn. Co., Mpls. LA, 1962—63, Swingen Constrn., Grand Forks, ND, 1970—73; mng. dir. Minn. Chippewa Tribe Constrn. Co., Cass Lake, 1973—76. Pres. Minn. Chippewa Tribe; chmn. White Earth Band Chippewa Indians; mem. Internat. Union Operating Engrs. AFL-CIO, 1962—74. Served with US Army, 1956—59. Democrat. Roman Catholic. Died June 24, 2014.

**WADMAN, WILLIAM WOOD, III,** educational director, technical research executive, consulting company executive; b. Oakland, Calif., Nov. 13, 1936; s. William Wood and Lula Fay (Raisner) Wadman; m. Barbara Jean Wadman. MA, U. Calif., Irvine, 1978. Cert. program mgr. tng. Radiation safety specialist, accelerator health physicist U. Calif. Lawrence Berkeley Lab., 1957—68; campus radiation safety officer U. Calif., Irvine, 1968—79; dir. ops., radiation safety officer Radiation Sterilizers, Inc., Tustin, Calif., 1979—80; prin., pres. Wm. Wadman & Assocs. Inc., from 1980; mem. operational review team Princeton U. Rsch. Campus TOKOMAK Fusion Test Facility, 1993—94; technical project mgr. for upgrades projects Los Alamos Nat. Lab., 1994—96; mem. team No. 1, health physics appraisal program NRC, 1980. Trainer Mason & Hanger-Silas Mason Co., Los Alamos Nat. Lab.; instr. in medium energy cyclotron radiation safety UCLBL; with Amateur Radio Emergency Svc., Lake Oswego, from 2010; level 3 gen. FCC Lic. KFY JEJ. Contbr. articles to profl. jours. Active Cub Scouts; chief umpire Mission Viejo Little League, 1973. Served with USNR, 1955—63. Recipient Award, U. Calif. Alumni Assn., 1972, Outstanding Performance award, U. Calif., Irvine, 1973. Mem.: ASTM, Project Mgmt. Inst., Campus Radiation Safety Officers, Am. Public Health Assn., Am. Nuc. Soc., Health Physics Soc. Internat. Radiation Protection Assn. Achievements include research in radiation protection and environmental sciences. Avocations: sailing, Tae Kwon Do, woodworking, photography, amateur radio. Home: Lake Oswego, Oreg. *Personal philosophy: The continuous practice of patience, openmindedness, and open communication provide the essential ingredients for a full, satisfying personal and professional life. The timing of major decisions is not a matter of heart, but the culmination of the effective use of the practices above.* Died Feb. 22, 2014.

**WAGNER, BERNHARD RUPERT,** computer scientist; b. Munich, July 24, 1951; s. Richard L. and Therese (Kratzer) W.; m. Petra J. Hoermann, Dec. 4, 1976; children: Eva, Hubert, Barbara. MS, U. Pierre et Marie Curie, Paris, 1976; Dipl. Math., Ludwig-Maximilians U., Munich, 1978; PhD in Computer Sci., ETH, Zurich, Switzerland, 1986. Software engr. Siemens AG, Munich, 1978-82; rsch. asst. Swiss Fed. Inst. Tech., Zurich, 1983-86; asst. prof. Brigham Young U., Provo, Utah, 1986-87; computer scientist Ciba-Geigy AG, Basel, Switzerland, from 1987. Cons. Mettler AG, Greifensee, Switzerland, 1986; seminar developer Ciba-Geigy AG, Basel, 1987-90. Contbr. articles to profl. jours. Bd. dirs. Internationaler Bauorden, Worms, Germany, 1968—; mem. Freiburg-Madison Soc., Freiburg, 1989—. Mem. ACM, Spl. Interest Group for Operating Systems. Avocation: ski racing. Home: Freiburg, Germany. Died Oct. 5, 2001.

**WAGNER, CHARLES W.,** retired general merchandise company executive; b. Santa Fe, Apr. 30, 1919; s. M. and Flora M. W.; m. Harriett Marie Haninger, Feb. 1, 1939; children: Sandra Adamek, Charlene Devine, Roger, Craig. Student, Coll. Mines and Metallurgy, El Paso, Tex., 1937-39, Tex. A&M U., 1940-41. With Montgomery Ward, 1941-81; v.p., gen. mgr. Montgomery Ward (South Central region), Kansas City, 1969-75, dir. Chgo., 1970-81, sr. v.p., 1975-77, exec. v.p., 1977-81; chmn. Maxum Internat.; dir. Frank Paxton Co., Kansas City, Republic Ridglea Bank, Ft. Worth, Maxum Enterprises. Fin. adv. Ft. Worth Jr. League Mem. adv. bd. Boy Scouts Am.; mem. adv. bd. United Way. Mem. Am. Mgmt. Assn., Chgo. Assn. Commerce and Industry, Newcomen Soc. N.Am. Clubs: Chgo, Mid-Am, Internat; Fort Worth (Ft. Worth), Shady Oaks Country (Ft. Worth). Roman Catholic. Home: Fort Worth, Tex. Died Dec. 30, 1991.

**WAGNER, CLARENCE J.,** lawyer; b. St. Paul, July 9, 1905; s. George H. and Helen Marie (Jasper) W.; m. Hilaria Pontius, July 13, 1935 (dec. Feb. 1987); children— Thomas George (dec.), Mary Helen, Charles Joseph. Grad., St. Thomas Coll., 1928; LL.B., Minn. Coll. Law, 1932. Bar: Minn. bar 1932. Pvt. law practice, Mpls., 1932—; partner Wagner, Johnston, Falconer, Ltd.; formerly gen. counsel Credit and Fin. Mgmt. Assn.; formerly v.p. Murray's, Inc.; past sec. Kausel Foundry Co.; past treas. Service Ideas, Inc. Past pres. State Bank Mound.; past v.p. Mo Vu Devel. Co.; past treas. Northeast Plaza Inc.; past editor, pub. Robbinsdale Post-Post Pub. Co.; past dir. Kodiak, Inc.; Past pres. Lighthouse Point Fedn. Police Assos.; past pres. De La Salle Alumni Assn. Mem. Comml. Law League Am. (past nat. pres.), Minn. Bar Assn., Hennepin Co. Bar Assn. (past sec.), Sigma Delta Kappa. Clubs: K.C, Em Cee (past pres.), Deer Creek Golf, St. Croix Yacht, Deerfield Country (past pres.). Died Mar. 1, 1988.

**WAGNER, MICHAEL DUANE,** lawyer; b. Shiner, Tex., July 4, 1948; s. Martin Matthew and Mary Margaret (Prasek) W.; m. Patricia Ann Miller, July 1, 1972; children: Matthew Miller, Michael Patrick. BA, Tex. Christian U., 1970; JD, St. Mary's Sch. Law, San Antonio, 1973. Bar: Tex. 1973, U.S. Supreme Ct. 1977. Assoc. counsel United Svcs. Automobile Assn., San Antonio, 1973-78, asst. v.p., counsel, 1978-80; v.p., counsel United Scvs. Automobile Assn., San Antonio, 1980-98, sr. v.p., gen. counsel, 1999—2002. Counsel investment mgmt. co. United Services Automobile Assn., San Antonio, 1980—, pres., chmn. bd. dirs. fed. credit union, 1981-84. Counsel United San Antonio Found., 1982; rep. Target 90/Goals for San Antonio, 1985; chmn. bd. advisors Daus. Charity Svcs. San Antonio; trustee Boysville, 1988; bd. dirs. De Paul Family Ctr., San Antonio, 1985, Cancer Therapy and Rsch. Ctr., Friends of McNay, ARC, San Francisco, Archdiocese of San Antonio. Named one of Outstanding Young Men in Am., U.S. Jr. C. of C., 1984. Mem. ABA, Fed. Bar Assn., State Bar of Tex. (ethics and grievance com.) San Antonio Bar Assn., Phi Delta Theta, Phi Alpha Delta. Roman Catholic. Avocations: running, home renovation. Died Sept. 9, 2002.

**WAGNER, NORMAN ERNEST,** corporate education executive; b. Edenwold, Sask., Can., Mar. 29, 1935; s. Robert Eric and Gertrude Margaret (Brandt) W.; m. Catherine Hack, May 16, 1957; children: Marjorie Dianne, Richard Roger, Janet Marie. BA, MDiv, U. Sask., 1958; MA, U. Toronto, 1960, PhD in Near Eastern Studies, 1965; LLD, Wilfrid Laurier U., 1984. Asst. prof. Near Eastern studies Wilfrid Laurier U., Waterloo, Ont., 1962-65, assoc. prof., 1965-69, prof., 1970-78, dean grad. studies and rsch., 1974-78; pres. U. Calgary, Alta., Can., 1978-88; chmn. bd. Alta. Natural Gas Co., Ltd., 1988—93; pres. emeritus U. Calgary, Can., 1988-95; chmn. Knowledge at Work Ltd., from 1995; chmn., CEO Auxano Philatelic Svcs., Inc., from 2002. Bd. dirs., chmn. Terry Fox Humanitarian Award Program; pres. The Corp. Higher Edn. Forum, 1996-2000. Author: From Chaos to Wisdom: A Framework for Understanding, 1998, Emerging Saskatchewan: The Postal History of Assiniboia, 2002, (with others) The Moyer Site: A Prehistoric Village in Waterloo County, 1974. Mem. Adv. Coun. on Adjustment, OCO '88, Alta. Heritage Found. for Med. Rsch., Nat. Adv. Bd. Sci. and Tech., Internat. Trade Adv. Com. Decorated officer Order of Can. Mem. Can. Soc. Bibl. Studies. Lutheran. Home: Calgary, Canada. Died Dec. 10, 2004.

**WAITE, RALPH,** actor; b. White Plains, NY, June 22, 1929; s. Ralph H. and Esther (Mitchell) W.; m. Kerry Shear, 1972 (div. 1980); children: Kathleen, Suzanne, Liam; m. Linda East, 1982. BA, Bucknell U.; B.D., Yale U. Social worker, Westchester County, N.Y.; Presbyterian minister Garden City, N.Y.; publicity dir. and asst. religious books editor Harper & Row Pub. Co., NYC; founder Los Angeles Actors Theatre, 1975, artistic dir., from 1975. Stage appearances include Hogan's Goat, 1965, Watering Place, 1969, The Trial of Lee Harvey Oswald, 1967, Blues for Mr. Charlie, The Father, 1981, The Balcony, 1981, Buried Child, South Coast Repertory, Costa Mesa, Calif., 1986, All My Sons, Long Wharf Theatre, New Haven, Conn., 1986-87 season, Half Deserted Streets, off Broadway, 1988, Bunker Reveries, Roundabout Theatre, N.Y.C., 1987; (films) A Lovely Way to Die, 1968, Five Easy Pieces, 1970, Lawman, 1971, The Grissom Gang, 1971, The Sporting Club, 1971, The Stone Killer, 1973, On the Nickel, 1980, The Bodyguard, 1992, Cliffhanger, 1993, Sunshine State, 2002, Second Chance, 2002; voice (film) Homeward Bound II: Lost in San Francisco, 1996, Spirit, 2001; regular TV series The Waltons, 1972-80, The Mississippi, 1983; (TV movies) A Wedding on Waltons Mountain, 1982, Mother's Day on Waltons Mountain, 1982, A Day for Thanks on Waltons Mountain, A Season of Hope, 1995, A Walton Easter, 1997, The Secret Life of John Chapman, Red Alert, Ohms, Angel City, The Gentleman Bandit, A Good Sport, The President's Men, 2000; appeared in TV series Orleans, 1997, The Outer Limits, 1995, Chicken Soup for the Soul, 1999; (TV mini-series) Roots, 1977, The Third Twin, 1997. Democrat. Died Feb. 13, 2014.

**WALD, ROBERT LEWIS,** lawyer; b. Worcester, Mass., Sept. 9, 1926; s. Lewis and Freda Ann (Rosenfield) W.; m. Patricia Ann McGowan, June 22, 1952; children: Sarah Elizabeth, Douglas Robert, Johanna Margaret, Frederica Nora, Thomas Robert. AB, Harvard U., 1947; LLB, Yale U., 1951. Bar: Mass. 1951, D.C. 1959, U.S. Ct. Appeals (4th cir.) 1957, U.S. Supreme Ct. 1957, U.S. Ct. Appeals (D.C. cir.) 1959, U.S. Ct. Appeals (6th cir.) 1975. Clerk to Judge Irving R. Kaufman U.S. Dist. Ct. (so. dist.) N.Y., 1951-52; asst. to gen. counsel, chief div. export trade FTC, Washington, 1954—56; ptnr. Wald, Harkrader & Ross and predecessors, Washington, 1961—87, Nussbaum & Wald, Washington, 1989—96; sr. counsel Baach Robinson & Lewis, Washington, from 1996. Dir., trustee Washington Lawyers' Com. for Civil Rights, Urban Affairs and predecessor, from 1969, co-chmn., 1976—78; dir. Romanian-Am. Enterprise Fund, 1994—97, chmn., 1994—96; dir. Global Rights and predecessor, from 1991, Frederic B. Abramson Mem. Found., from 1998; hon. dir. Capital Area Immigrants' Rights Coalition, from 1999; dir. Internat. Sr. Lawyers Project, from 2001; bd. mgmt. trustees Internat. Assn. Women Judges, from 1997. Served to lt. USNR, 1944-46, 52-53. Mem. ABA, D.C. Bar Assn. Home: Washington, DC. Died Sept. 7, 2010.

**WALDEKRANZ, RUNE,** film educator emeritus; b. Södertälje, Sweden, Sept. 14, 1911; s. Einar August Valdemar and Olga Waldekranz; m. Brita Klein, Nov. 27, 1947; children: Cecilia Waldekranz Piselli, Jan. MA, Uppsala U., Sweden, 1937. Critic literature and film Svenska Dagbladet, 1939-42; film prodr. Sandrew Film, Sweden, 1942-64; head film sch. Swedish Film Inst., 1965-70, also bd. dirs.; prof. film research Stockholm U., 1970-78; pres. Swedish Film Acad., 1977-80. Author: The Growth of Film, 1941, The Birth of Film Drama, 1976, Film History, The First Hundred Years I-III, 1985-95, others. Recipient Prize for Hist. Rsch., Royal Swedish Acad., 1989, Golden Plaque of Svenska Vitterhets, Historie & Antikvitets Acad., King Carl XVI Gustaf, 1996. Died May 15, 2003.

**WALKER, MADAM C.J. (SARAH BREEDLOVE),** cosmetics company executive; b. Delta, La., Dec. 23, 1867; d. Owen and Minerva Breedlove; m. Moses McWilliam. Sales agt. Malone, Denver, 1905; founder personal products co. Madam C. J. Walker Mfg. Co., Denver and Indpls. First American woman to become a millionaire of her own efforts. Madam Walker Thither Ctr. named in her honor. Died 1919.

**WALKER, DAVID BRADSTREET,** retired political science educator; b. Salem, Mass., May 7, 1927; s. George Lincoln and Mildred (Bradstreet) W.; m. Jeanne Hallahan, Sept. 1955 (dec. 2011); children: Melissa J., Stephen B., Justin D. BA in Govt., Boston U., 1949, MA in Govt., 1950; PhD in Philosophy in Polit. Sci., Brown U., 1956. Instr. govt. Bowdoin Coll., Brunswick, Maine, 1956-57, asst. prof. govt., 1957-63; staff dir. US Senate Subcommittee on Intergovernmental Rels., Washington, 1963-66; asst. dir. for govt. structure & function Advisory Commn. on Intergovernmental Relations, Washington, 1966-84; prof. polit. sci. U. Conn., Storrs, 1984—2001. Dir. Inst. Public & Urban Affairs, U. Conn., Storrs, 1986-90; public & urban affairs keynote speaker ann. meetings of nat. orgns.; speaker at polit. sci. and govtl. orgns.; Fulbright prof. U. Göttingen, Germany, 1990-91. Author: Rufus Choate, An American Whig, 1957, Toward a Functioning Federalism, 1981, (with others) Managing Public Programs, 1989, (with others) The Great Society and its Legacy, 1986, The Rebirth of Federalism: Slouching Toward Washington, 1995; contbr. articles to profl. jours. Citizen mem. Conn. Advicory Commn. on Intergovt. Rels., Hartford, 1985-96, chmn., 1986-90. With U.S. Army, 1945-47. Recipient Disting. Citizen award Nat. Mcpl. League, 1986, Donald C. Stone award for Significant Contbn. to Intergovt. Mgmt. in Acad./Rsch. Areas Membership, Nat. Acad. Public Adminstrn., Bosworth Meml. award Conn. chpt. Mem. American Soc. Public Adminstrn., American Polit. Sci. Assn. (spl. achievement award 1995), Nat. Acad. Public Adminstrn. (bd. dirs.), Phi Alpha Alpha, Phi Beta Kappa. Democrat. Episcopalian. Avocations: swimming, gardening, white water rafting, fishing. Home: Washington, DC. Died Sept. 30, 2013.

**WALKER, JEWETT LYNIUS,** clergyman, church official; b. Beaumont, Tex., Apr. 7, 1930; s. Elijah Harvey and Ella Jane (Wilson) W.; m. Dorothy Mae Croom, Apr. 11, 1965; children: Cassandra Lynn, Jewett L., Kevin, Michelle, Ella, Betty Renne, Kent, Elijah H. BA, Calif. Western U., 1957; MA, Kingdom Bible Inst., 1960; B Religious Edn., St. Stephens Coll., 1966, DD, 1968; LLD, Union Bapt. Sem., 1971; postgrad., St. Paul Sch. Theology, 1979, Southwestern Bapt. Theol. Sem., 1985-86; grad., Nat. Planned Giving Inst., 1981, Philanthropy Tax Inst., 1982; DD, Clinton Jr. Coll., 1992; PhD, Mcpl. Govt., Concord, 2006. Ordained to ministry African Methodist Episcopal Zion Ch., 1957. Pastor Shiloh A.M.E. Zion Ch., Monrovia, Calif., 1961-64, Martin Temple A.M.E. Zion Ch., LA, 1964-65, 1st A.M.E. Zion Ch., Compton, Calif., 1965-66, Met. A.M.E. Zion Ch., LA, 1966-73, Logan Temple A.M.E. Zion Ch., San Diego, 1973-74, Rock Hill A.M.E. Zion Ch., Indian Trail, NC, 1974-79, Bennettsville A.M.E. Zion Ch., Norwood, NC, 1979-86, Price Meml. A.M.E. Zion Ch., Concord, NC, 1986-89, Mt. Zion A.M.E. Zion Ch., Hickory Grove, SC, 1989-91, NewHope AME Zion, Lancaster, SC, 1991—92, Mt. Zion A.M.E. Zion Ch., Lancaster, SC, 1992—2001, Mt. Moriah A.M.E. Zion Ch., Richburg, SC, 2001—03, New Hope A.M.E. Zion Ch., Lancaster, SC, 2003—06, North Corner A.M.E. Zion, Lancaster, from 2007. Sec.-treas. dept. home missions, brotherhood pensions and relief African Methodist Episcopal Zion Ch., Charlotte, N.C., 1974-92; mem. exec. bd. Prophetic Justice Unit Com. Nat. Coun. Chs., co-chairperson pers. com.; mem. World Meth. Coun., del. 14th World Conf Author: Is There a Man in the House, 1975, Lets Get Serious about Missions, 1991, Issues Facing the Ministry, 1991, The Denominational Dollar, 1992, also articles. Chmn. Minority Affairs Adv. Com., Mecklenburg County; trustee Clinton

Coll., dir. planned giving, 1992; trustee Rock Hill, Lomax-Hannon Coll., Greenville, Ala., Union Bapt. Theol. Sem., Birmingham, Ala.; bd. mgrs. McCrorey br. YMCA; pres. Am. Ch. Fin. Svc. Corp., Carolina Home Health Svc. Inc., Meth. Life Ins. Soc. Inc., bd. trustees State N.C. Coll. Found., Inc., 1987, del. Presbyn. Ptnrs. in Ecumenism Nat. Coun. Chs. Christ, 1986, pres., 1988—; pres. Walker Funeral Home Inc. (formerly The House of Irma Funeral Home), Concord, 1995, Am. Ch. Econ. Devel. Corp.; del. Presbyn. Ch. U.S. Gen. Assembly, 1985; mem. citizens parole accountability com. Mecklenburg County, Charlotte, 1993; mem. planned giving adv. bd. Livingston Coll., Salisbury, N.C.; pres. Jewett L. Walker & Assocs.; chmn. minority affairs adv. com. Mecklenburg County; com. mem. Charlotte Mecklenburg Citizen Parole Accountability Com., 1994, vice chmn., 1998; pres. Pardue St. Apts. Inc., Lancaster, S.C., 1997—, Am. Ch. Econ. Devel. Corp., 1999; elected to jud. coun. African Meth. Episcopal Zion Ch., 2000; mem. adv. bd. Mechanics and Farmers Bank, Charlotte, 2001 Fellow Nat. Assn. Ch. Bus. Adminstrs., Ch. Bus. Adminstrn., Presbyn. Ch. Bus. Adminstrn. Assn.; mem. NAACP (life), Nat. Soc. Fund Raising Execs., Am. Bible Soc. (state dir. vols., N.C. and S.C. dir. vol.), Nat. Spkrs. Bur., Christian Ministries Mgmt. Assn., Am. Soc. Assn. Execs., Funeral and Cremation Soc. South, Inc. (founding mem. 1998), Shriners, Masons (33 deg.), Prince Hall Affiliation. Republican. Home: Charlotte, NC. Died Apr. 12, 2012.

**WALKER, MOIRA KAYE,** sales executive; b. Riverside, Calif., Aug. 2, 1940; d. Frank Leroy and Arline Rufina (Roach) Porter; m. Timothy P. Walker, Aug. 30, 1958 (div. 1964); children: Brian A., Benjamin D., Blair K., Beth E. Student, Riverside City Coll., 1973. With Bank of Am., Riverside, 1965-68, Abitibi Corp., Cucamonga, Calif., 1968-70; with Lily div. Owens-Illinois, Riverside, 1970-73, salesperson Lily div. Houston, 1973-77; salesperson Kent H. Landsberg div. Sunclipse, Montebello, Calif., 1977-83, sales mgr., 1983-85, v.p., sales mgr. Riverside, from 1985. Mem. NAFE, Women in Paper (treas. 1978-84), Kent H. Landsberg President's Club (1st female to make club, 1994, 95, 96). Lutheran. Home: Long Beach, Calif. Died June 2001.

**WALKER, T-BONE (AARON THIBEAUX WALKER),** musician; b. Tex., May 26, 1910; s. Rance and Movelia W.; m. Vida Lee, 1934. Musician Ida Cox troupe, Dallas, from 1925, Columbia Records, Houston, from 1929, Rhumboogie Records, Chgo., from 1945, Comet Records, LA, from 1945, Imperial Records, Atlantic records, from 1955, Count Bassie band, 1960. Albums include Witchita Falls, Trinity River Blues, T-Bone Shuffle, Call it Stormy Monday (But Tuesday's Just as Bad), The Original American Blues Festival. Named to Blues Hall of Fame, 1980, Rock & Roll Hall of Fame, 1987; recipient Grammy award, 1972. Died Mar. 15, 1975.

**WALKER-SHIVERS, DAUPHINE,** humanities educator; b. Marion, Ark. d. Geoffrey and Myrtle Juanita Walker; m. James Shivers, Aug. 29, 1981 (dec. Apr. 1994). BA, Wayne State U., MA, 1967; PhD, U. Mich., 1980. Newspaper reporter Mich. Chronicle, Detroit, 1953-55; social worker Detroit Dept. Social Svcs., Detroit, 1955-56; tchr. Detroit Pub. Schs., 1956-60, U.S. Overseas Schs., France, 1960-64, Detroit Pub. Schs., 1964-70; prof. Wayne County C.C., Detroit, 1970-76 and from 81, dept. chair humanities, speech, philosophy, 1976-81. Pres., CEO Pub. Comm. & Concepts, Detroit, 1984-90. Editor: Detroit NAACP Reporter, 1984. Pres. Top Ladies of Distinction, Detroit, 1984-89, nat. historian, 1986-90; 1st v.p. Consortium Cmty. Orgns., 1995—; pub. local ch. newspapers, Detroit, 1983-88; mem. exec. bd. Fair Housing Ctr. Detroit, 1986—; fundraiser Detroit Inst. Arts, African Art Gallery, 1968-70. Named Top Solicitor Detroit NAACP, 1993, 93, 94; recipient Outstanding Svc. award Detroit NAACP, 1992, Sustained Superior Svc. award U.S. Overseas Schs., U.S. Army, France, 1964. Mem. AAUW, Met. Detroit Alliance Black Educators, Detroit Assn. Black Storytellers. Avocations: reading, interior decorating, travel, growing house plants. Deceased.

**WALLACH, ELI,** actor; b. Bklyn., Dec. 7, 1915; s. Abraham and Bertha (Schorr) W.; m. Anne Jackson, Mar. 5, 1948; children: Peter Douglas, Roberta Lee, Katherine Beatrice. AB, U. Tex., 1936; MS in Edn, CCNY, 1938; student, Neighborhood Playhouse Sch. of Theatre, 1940; doctorate (hon.), Emerson Coll., Boston, Sch. Visual Arts, 1991. Actor: Broadway plays include Antony and Cleopatra, 1948, Mr. Roberts, 1949-50, Rose Tatoo, 1950-52, Skydrift, 1951, Camino Real, 1953, Mademoiselle Colombe, 1953, Teahouse of the August Moon, 1954-55, London prodn., 1954, Major Barbara, 1956, Rhinoceros, 1961, Luv, 1964, Promenade All, 1972, Twice Around the Park, 1983, Opera Comique, Kennedy Ctr. Performing Arts, 1987, The Flowering Peach, Fla., 1987, Broadway, 1994, Cafe Crown, 1989; appeared off-Broadway prodn. Typists and the Tiger, 1962-63, London prodn., 1964, Saturday, Sunday, Monday, 1974, (with wife and 2 daus.) Diary of Anne Frank, 1977-78, Visiting Mr. Green, 1997; off-Broadway in Tennessee Williams Remembered, 1999; on tour Down the Garden Paths, 1998-99; appeared in: nat. tour co. Waltz of the Toreadors, 1973-74; (TV movies) Executioner's Song, 1982, Murder By Reason of Insanity, 1985, Monday Night Mayhem, 2000, Monday Night Mayhem, 2002; TV series Batman, 1966, Kojak, 1973, Highway to Heaven, 1984, Our Family Honor, 1985, L.A. Law, 1986, Law & Order, 1990; (TV miniseries) Christopher Columbus, 1985, The Education of Max Bickford, 2002; (films) Baby Doll, 1955, The Magnificent Seven, 1960, The Misfits, 1960, Rhinoceros, 1961, The Victors, 1962, Lord Jim, 1964, How To Steal a Million, The Good, the Bad and the Ugly, The Tiger Makes Out, Band of Gold, Zig-Zag, Cinderella Liberty, 1973, Crazy Joe, 1973, Movie, Movie, 1976, Sam's Son, 1985, Tough Guys, 1986, Rocket to the Moon, 1986, Nuts, 1987, The Impossible Spy, 1987, The Godfather Part III, 1990, The Two Jakes, 1990, Article 99, Mistress, 1991, Night and the City, 1991, Honey, Sweet Love, 1993, Two Much, 1995, The Associate, 1996, Keeping the Faith, 2000, Mystic River, 2003, King of the Corner, 2004, (voice) The Easter Egg Adventure, 2004, The Moon and the Son: An Imagined Conservation, 2005, A Taste of Jupiter, 2005, The Hoax, 2006, The Holiday, 2006, Mama's Boy, 2006, Wall Street: Money Never Sleeps, 2010, The Ghost WRiter, 2010; author: The Good, The Bad, And Me: In My Anecdotage, 2005, Tickling Leo, 2009, Nurse Jackie, 2009, The Ghost Roman Palanaly, 2009. Served to capt. Med. Adminstrn. Corps AUS, World War II, 1940-45 Recipient Donaldson, Theatre World, Variety, Antoinette Perry, Drama League awards, Brit. Film Acad. award, 1956, Disting. Alumnus award U. Tex., 1989, Career Achievement Award Nat. Bd. Review, 2006, Honorary Acad. award Acad. Motion Picture Arts & Sciences, 2006 Original mem. Actors Studio. Home: New York, NY. Died June 24, 2014.

**WALLACH, PHILIP C(HARLES),** financial, public relations consultant; b. NYC, Nov. 17, 1912; s. Edgar Smith and Rix Wallach; m. Magdalena Charlotta Falkenberg, Mar. 5, 1950. Student, NYU, 1930-33. Editor, writer Hearst Publs., NYC, 1933-42; editor Shell Oil Co., NYC, 1943-46; editor, dir. pub. relations W.R. Grace & Co., NYC, 1946-54; dir. pub. relations and advt. H.K. Porter & Co., NYC, 1954-58; pres. Wallach Assocs., Inc., NYC, 1958-85; officer and v.p. investor rels. Occidental Petroleum Co., LA, 1985-91; v.p. Occidental Internat. Corp., NYC, 1987-91, cons., 1991-92. Pres. St. Paul Guild, N.Y.C., 1959-68, bd. dirs., 1964-72; pres. Cath. Inst. Press, N.Y.C., 1959-75; co-founder Air Force Assn., Washington, 1946; nat. committeeman Rep. Party, N.Y., 1945-60; mem. Rep. Nat. Com., Greenwich, Conn., 1982-91; bd. dirs., mem. exec. com. U.S. Pakistan Econ. Coun. With USAF, 1942-43. Mem. Overseas Press Club. Home: Greenwich, Conn. Died Oct. 28, 1992.

**WALLER, H. EDWARD,** advertising executive; b. Lancaster, Pa., Nov. 12, 1928; s. H. Earl and Esther J. (Allen) W.; m. Barbara Jean Ritten, Dec. 13, 1934; children: John Allen, thomas Allworth. BS in Econs., U. Pa., 1954. Copywriter Cin. Milacron, 1954-61; account exec. David K. Burnap Advt., Inc., Dayton, Ohio, 1961-66; v.p. David K. Burnap Advt. Agy., Dayton, Ohio, 1966-83, exec. v.p., from 1983. Died Apr. 11, 2008.

**WALLIS, SUE,** state legislator; b. Oct. 9, 1957; m. Rod McQueary; 7 children. Writer, poet; team lead Rio Tinto Energy America; mem. Dist. 52 Wyo. House of Reps., 2007—14. Exec, dir. Recluse Cmty. Trust. Mem. Women in Govt., Partnership for America's Econ. Success-Invest in Kids Working Group; CPR-AED First Aid Instr. American Heart Assn.; EMT-Basic; Nat. Safety Coun. Defensive Driving Instr.; mem. Wyo. Humanities Coun. Bd., WyoAg Sustainable Agriculture Coalition, WyoLearn League for Edn. Accountability and Reform Network, Wyo. Early Childhood Partnership, KidsFIRST 24/7 Childcare Cooperative. Mem.: Wyo. Assn. for Public Charter Schools, SASSE Investment Club (pres.). Republican. Unitarian. Died Jan. 28, 2014.

**WALLOT, JEAN-PIERRE,** archivist, historian; b. Valleyfield, Que., Can., May 22, 1935; s. Albert and Adrienne (Thibodeau) W.; m. Denyse Caron; children: Normand, Robert, Sylvie. BA, Coll. Valleyfield, 1954; lic. es lettres, U. Montreal, 1957, MA in History, 1957, PhD in History, 1965; D (hon.), U. Rennes, France, 1987, U. Ottawa, Can., 1996. Reporter Le Progres de Valleyfield, 1954—61; from lectr. to prof. dept. history U. Montreal, 1961—65, dept. chmn., 1973—75, vice-dean studies faculty arts and scis., 1975—78, vice-dean rsch. Faculty Arts and Scis., 1979—82, academic v.p., 1982—85. Nat. archivist, Can., 1985-97; historian Nat. Mus. Man, Ottawa, Ont., 1966-69; assoc. prof. U. Toronto, 1969-71; prof. Concordia U., Montreal, Que., 1971-73; vis. prof. U. Ottawa, 1997—, dir. Ctr. Rsch. en Civilisation Canadienne-Francaise, 2000-07; dir. Etude Assn. Ecole Pratique des Hautes Etudes en Scis. Sociales, Paris, 1975, 79, 81, 83, 85, 87, 89, 94. Author: French and American Intrigues in Canada, 1965; author: (with John Hare) Imprints in Lower Canada, 1967; author: Confrontations, 1971; author: (with G. Paquet) Patronage and Power in Lower Canada, 1973, A Quebec that Changed, 1973; co-author (with Gilles Paquat): Un Québec Moderne, 1760—1840, 2007; editor (with R. Girard): Memoires de J.E. McComber, bourgeois de Montréal, 1981; editor: (with J. Goy) Evolution and Ruptures in the Rural World, 1986; editor: Identity Constructs and Social Practices, 2002, The Non-Existent Debate: The Pepin-Robarts Commission, 2003, Linguistic Governance, 2005. Pres. internat. adv. com. on Memory of the World UNESCO, 1993—99. Decorated officer Order Arts et Lettres, France; recipient Marie Tremaine medal, 1973, Tyrrell medal, 1982, Royal Soc. Centenary medal, 1994, Jacques Ducharme prize, 1997, Queen's Jubilee medal, 2002; Faculty of Arts and Scis. U. de Montreal Merit medal, 2004. Fellow Royal Soc. Can. (sect. pres. 1985-87, pres. 1997-99); mem. Am. Antiquarian Soc., Acad. des Lettres du Quebec, Inst. d'Histoire l'Amerique Francaise (pres. 1973-77), Can. Hist. Assn. (pres. 1982), Assn. Can.-Francaise l'Avancement Scis. (pres. 1981-83, emeritus mem.), Assn. Archivists Que., Assn. Can. Archivists, Internat. Coun. on Archives (v.p. 1988-92, pres. 1992-96, pres. emeritus). Roman Catholic. Home: Ottawa, Canada. Deceased.

**WALLS, DANIEL FRANK,** physics educator; b. Auckland, New Zealand, Sept. 13, 1942; s. James Reginald and Barbara Gertrude (Leddra) W.; m. Fari Khoy, Dec. 11, 1969 (div. 1986); children: Mark, Darian. BSc, U. Auckland, 1963, MSc, 1965; PhD, Harvard U., 1969. Postdoctoral fellow U. Stuttgart (Fed. Republic Germany), 1969-70, U. Auckland, 1970-71; sr. lectr. U. Waikato, Hamilton, New Zealand, 1972-76, reader, 1976-80, prof., 1980-87, U. Auckland, from 1987. Editor 7 books; contbr. numerous articles to profl. jours. Recipient Einstein prize Soc. on Lasers and Applications, 1990, Paul Dirac medal Inst. Physics U.K., 1995. Fellow Royal Soc. N.Z. (Hector medal), Royal Soc. London, Am. Inst. Physics, Optical Soc. Am., N.Z. Inst. Physics (pres. 1990-91). Anglican. Avocations: tennis, swimming, skiing, hiking. Home: Mission Ave, New Zealand. Died May 12, 1999.

**WALMSLEY, JULIAN KENNETH,** economist, consultant, software developer; b. Bangor, Northern Ireland, Nov. 21, 1948; s. Kenneth M. and Kathleen M. (Patterson) W.; m. Danena J. Wrightson-Hunt, Aug. 8, 1976. BA in Econs., Cambridge U., Eng., 1970. CFA. Economist Barclays Bank, London, 1970-77, econ. advisor, 1977-81, v.p. NYC, 1981-86; dir. Panmure Gordon Bankers, London, 1986-88; sr. investment officer Oil Ins., Hamilton, Bermuda, 1988-90; chief investment officer Mitsubishi Fin., London, 1990-91; mng. dir. Askeaton Assocs., Ltd., London, from 1991. Hon. fellow Isma Ctr., U. Reading, Eng., 1992—. Author: Dictionary of International Finance, 1979, Foreign Exchange and Money Markets Handbook, 1983, 3d edit., 2000, Global Investing, 1990, New Financial Instruments, 1986, 2d edit., 1998, The Repo Market in Euro: Making it Work, 1997, New Frontiers in Clearing and Settlement, 1999; editor newsletter The Euro Zone, 1997-99. Mem. Assn. for Investment Mgmt. and Rsch., Chartered Inst. Bankers U.K. Avocations: theater, art galleries. Home: Dorset, England. Died Feb. 20, 2002.

**WALSH, JOSEPH THOMAS,** retired state supreme court justice; b. Wilmington, Del., May 18, 1930; s. Joseph Patrick and Mary Agnes (Bolton) W.; m. Madeline Maria Lamb, Oct. 6, 1955; children: Kevin, Lois, Patrick, Daniel, Thomas, Nancy. BA, LaSalle Coll., 1952; LLB, Georgetown U., 1955. Bar: D.C. 1955, Del. 1955. Atty. Ho. of Reps., Dover, Del., 1961-62; chief counsel Pub. Svc. Commn., Dover, 1964-72; judge Del. Superior Ct., Wilmington, 1972-84; vice chancellor Ct. of Chancery, Wilmington, 1984-85; justice Del. Supreme Ct., Wilmington, 1985—2003. Adj. prof. Widener U. Sch. of Law, 2003—14. Capt. U.S. Army, 1955-58. Democrat. Roman Catholic. Home: Wilmington, Del. Died Aug. 15, 2014.

**WALSH, LAWRENCE EDWARD,** lawyer; b. Port Maitland, NS, Can., Jan. 8, 1912; came to U.S., 1914, naturalized, 1922; s. Cornelius Edward and Lila May (Sanders) W.; m. Mary Alma Porter, 1965 (dec. Dec. 22, 2012); children: Barbara Marie, Janet Maxine (Mrs. Alan Larson), Sara Porter, Dale Edward, Elizabeth Porter (Mrs. Peter LaColla). AB, Columbia U., 1932, LLB, 1935; LLD, Union U., 1959, St. John's U., 1975, Suffolk U., 1975, Waynesburg Coll., 1976, Vt. Law Sch., 1976. Bar: NY 1936, DC 1981, Okla. 1981, US Supreme Ct. 1951. Spl. asst. atty. gen. Drukman Investigation, 1936—38; dep. asst. dist. atty. NY County (Manhattan), 1938—41; assoc. Davis Polk Wardwell Sunderland & Kiendl, 1941—43; asst. counsel to Gov. State of NY, Albany, 1943—49, counsel to Gov., 1950—51; counsel Public Svc. Commn., 1951—53; gen. counsel, exec. dir. Waterfront Commn. of N.Y. Harbor, 1953—54; judge US Dist. Ct. (southern dist.) NY, 1954—57; dep. atty. gen. US Dept. Justice, 1957—60; ptnr. Davis, Polk & Wardwell LLP, 1961—81; counsel Crowe & Dunlevy LLP, Oklahoma City, 1981—2014. Ind. counsel Iran/Contra Investigation, 1986-93; chmn. N.Y. State Moreland Commn. Alcoholic Beverage Control Law, 1963-64; pres. Columbia Alumni Fedn., 1968-69; dep. head with rank of amb. U.S. del. meetings on Vietnam, Paris, 1969; counsel to N.Y. State Ct. on Judiciary, 1971-72; 2d cir. mem. US Cir. Judge Nominating Commn., 1978-80. Author: Firewall The Iran-Contra Conspiracy and Cover-Up, 1997, The Gift of Insecurity: A Lawyer's Life, 2003. Trustee emeritus Columbia U., Mut. Life Ins. Co., N.Y. Recipient Medal for Excellence Columbia U., 1959, Law Sch., Columbia U., 1980, John Jay award Columbia Coll., 1989. Fellow American Bar Found., American Coll. Trial Lawyers; mem. American Law Inst., ABA (pres. 1975-76), N.Y. State Bar Assn. (pres. 1966-67), Oklahoma County Bar Assn., Okla. State Bar Assn., Internat. Bar Assn., Assn. of Bar of City of N.Y., N.Y. County Lawyers Assn., Fed. Bar Coun., Law Soc. Eng. and Wales (hon.), Can. Bar Assn. (hon.), Mex. Bar Assn. (hon.), Century Assn., Oklahoma City Golf and Country Club, Beta Theta Pi. Presbyterian. Home: Oklahoma City, Okla. Died Mar. 19, 2014.

**WALSH, WILLIAM F.,** financial services professional; b. NYC, Dec. 7, 1914; s. Edward M. and Harriet (Lawlor) W.; m. Rosalie Elizabeth Borengasser, Apr. 10, 1950; children: William F. Jr., Charles, Rosemary, Gertrude. BS in Fgn. Svc., Georgetown U., 1946. Acct. Hong Kong and Shanghai Banking Corp., NYC, 1933-42; ops. officer Printing and Publishing div. War Prodn. Bd., Washington, 1942-45, IMF, Washington, 1947-69. Mem. KC. Democrat. Roman Catholic. Avocation: freelance writing. Home: Oxon Hill, Md. Died Feb. 1996.

**WALTERS, SIR ALAN ARTHUR,** economist; b. Leicester, Eng., June 17, 1926; m. Margaret Patricia Wilson, 1975. BSc in Econs., U. London, 1951; MA, Oxford U., 1981; DLit (hon.), U. Leicester, 1981; D in Social Sci. (hon.), U. Birmingham, 1984; PhD, Francisco Marroquin, Guatemala. Lectr. dept. econometrics and stats. U. Birmingham (Eng.), 1952-60, prof., 1961-68, head dept., 1961-68; Sir Ernest Cassel prof. econs. U. London, London Sch. Econs., 1968-75; prof. economics Johns Hopkins U., Balt., 1975-91; resident scholar Am. Enterprise Inst., Washington, 1983-84. Vis. prof. Northwestern U., 1959-60, U. Va., 1966-67, MIT, 1967-68, Monash U. (Australia), 1971; past cons. various ctrl. banks; mem. Commn. on London's Third Airport (Roskill), 1968-70; econ. adviser World Bank, 1976-80; chief econ adviser to Prime Minister, U.K., 1981-83, 89; dir. Am. Internat. Trading Group, Washington, 1991. Author:

(with R.W. Clower, G. Dalton and M. Harwitz) Growth Without Development, 1966; Integration in Freight Transport, 1968; The Economics of Road User Charges, 1968; An Introduction to Econometrics, 1968, 2d edit., 1969, Money in Bloom and Slump, 3d edit., 1971, Noise and Prices, 1975, (with P.R.G. Layard and McGraw Hill) Microeconomic Theory, 1978, (with E. Bennathan) Port Pricing and Investment in Developing Countries, 1979, Britqain's Economic Renaissance, 1986, Sterling in Danger, 1990, The Economics and Politics of Money, 1998; editor: Money and Banking, 1970; contbr. articles to profl. publs. Decorated knight; recipient Francis Boyer Lecture award, Am. Enterprise Inst., 1983; fellow (hon.) Cardiff U., 2001. Fellow Econometric Soc. Home: London, England. Died Jan. 3, 2009.

**WALTERS, JOHNNIE MCKEIVER,** lawyer; b. Hartsville, SC, Dec. 20, 1919; s. Tommie Ellis and Lizzie Lee (Grantham) W.; m. Donna Lucile Hall, Sept. 1, 1947; children: Donna Dianne Walters Gent, Lizbeth Kathern Walters Kukorowski, Hilton Horace, John Roy. AB, Furman U., 1942, LLD (hon.), 1973; LLB, U. Mich., 1948. Bar: Mich. 1948, N.Y. 1955, S.C. 1961, D.C. 1973. Atty. office chief counsel IRS, Washington, 1949-53; asst. mgr. tax div. law dept. Texaco, Inc., NYC, 1953-61; ptnr. firm Geer, Walters & Demo, Greenville, SC, 1961-69; asst. atty. gen. tax divsn. US Dept. Justice, Washington, 1969-71; commr. IRS, 1971-73; ptnr. firm Hunton & Williams, Washington, 1973-79, Leatherwood Walker Todd & Mann, P.C., Greenville, 1979-95; exec. v.p., gen. counsel Colonial Trust Co., Greenville, 1996—2005; ret., 2006. Bd. dirs. Textile Hall Corp., Greenville, Colonial Trust Co. Author: Our Journey, 2011. Mem. S.C. Coun. on Competitiveness, 1987—91, S.C. Ethics Commn., 2005—08. With USAF, 1942—45. Decorated Purple Heart. Fellow American Coll. Tax Counsel (founding regent), American Coll. Trust & Estate Counsel, American Bar Found., S.C. Bar Found. (bd. dirs. 1988-92); mem. ABA (taxation sect.), S.C. Bar (chmn. taxation sect. 1983-84), Rotary (pres. local club 1968-69, Frances Legion of Honor medal, 2012). Republican. Baptist. Home: Greenville, SC. Died June 24, 2014.

**WALTHER, HERBERT,** physicist, researcher; b. Ludwigshafen, Germany, Jan. 19, 1935; s. Philipp and Anna (Lorenz) W.; m. Margot Gröschel, July 27, 1962; children: Thomas, Ulrike. Diploma in physics, U. Heidelberg, 1960, PhD, 1962; PhD (hon.), Acad. Sinica, China, 1980; Hon. Dr. Degree of Lomonosov, U. Moscow, Russia, 1991, U. Hannover, Germany, 1994. Postdoctoral fellow U. Heidelberg, 1962-63; sci. asst. U. Hannover (Fed. Republic Germany), 1963-68, lectr., 1968-69; guest scientist lab. Aimé Cotton CNRS, Orsay, France, 1969; vis. fellow Joint Inst. for Lab. Astrophysics, U. Colo., 1970; prof. U. Bonn (Fed. Republic Germany), 1971; prof. physics U. Cologne (Fed. Republic Germany), 1971-75, U. Munich, 1975—2003, prof. emeritus, from 2003; dir. Max-Planck-Institut für Quantenoptik, Garching, Germany, 1981—2003, dir. emeritus, from 2003; v.p. Max-Planck-Soc., 1990-96. Mem. senate, coun. NSF, Fed. Republic Germany, 1978-84; mem. planning Max-Planck Soc., 1982-86; chmn. commn. atomic and molecular physics Internat. Union Pure and Applied Physics, 1984-87; Stanley H. Klosk lectr. NYU, 1985; Loeb lectr. Harvard U., 1990; Celsius lectr. Uppsala U., 1994; Hendrik de Waard lectr., Groningen, 1996; Regents lectr. U. Calif., Berkeley, 1997; James Franck Meml. lectr., Jerusalem, 1997, Hascoe lectr. U. Conn., 2004. Author: several books in field. Recipient Max Born prize Inst. of Physics, The German Phys. Soc., 1978, Einstein prize Indsl. and Univ. Rsch. Affiliates, 1988, Gauss medal Braunschweigische Wiss. Gesellschaft, 1989, Albert A. Michelson medal Franklin Inst., 1993, King Faisal Internat. Prize in Physics, Faisal Found., 1993, Alexander von Humboldt medal, 1997, Ernst Hellmut-Vits prize, Gesellschaft zur Förderung der Westfaelischen Wilhelms-Univ. zu Muenster, 1998, Alfried Krupp prize for sci., 2002, others. Fellow: Inst. Physics (London), Am. Phys. Soc., Optical Soc. Am. (pub. com. 1986, Charles Hard Townes award 1990, Frederic Ives medal/Jarus W. Quinn Endowment 2003); mem.: Convent for Tech. Scis. German Acads., Russian Acad. Scis. (fgn.), European Sci. Found. (exec. coun. 1998—2000), Heidelberg Acad. (corr.), Hungarian Acad. Scis. (hon.), Am. Acad. Arts and Scis. (hon.; fgn.), German Phys. Soc. (hon.; bd. dirs. 1979—82, Stern Gerlach medal 1998), Roland Eötvös Phys. Soc. (hon.), Romanian Acad. (hon.), Belarussian Phys. Soc. (hon.), Nordhein-Westfälische Acad. (corr.), Acad. Europaea, Acad. Naturfoscher Leopoldina (mem. senate from 1998), Bavarian Acad. Scis., European Phys. Soc. (divsn. chmn. 1985—89, chmn. quantum electronics divsn. 1987—89, Quantum Electronics prize 2000). Home: Munich, Germany. Died July 22, 2006.

**WALTNER, HARRY GEORGE, JR.,** personnel executive; b. Kans. City, Mo., Feb. 2, 1906; s. Harry George and Minnie Lee (Ruland) Waltner; m. Ruth Anna Laitner, June 28, 1927; children: Barbara Adams, Beverly Ruland, Lillian LeRoyce, Harry George III. Student, U. Mo., 1924, U. Kans. City, 1927. Bar: Mo. 1928. Assoc. Waltner & Waltner, 1928—32; asst. atty. gen. Mo., 1933—37; chief counsel, dir. Mo. Unemployment Compensation Com., 1937—44; social security specialist, ins. and social security dept. Standard Oil Co., NJ, 1945—50, asst. mgr., ins. and social security dept., 1950—55, social security adviser, 1955—58, Latin Am. adviser, 1958—63, Latin Am. benefit adviser, employee rels. dept., 1964—66; sr. employee benefits counselor Esso Inter-Am. Inc., 1966—71, cons., employee benefits and ins., 1971—72. Cons. NY Joint Legislative Com. Unemployment Ins., 1948, NY Joint Legislative Com. Labor and Indsl. Conditions, 1949; mem. Disability Benefits Adv. Coun.; chmn. NY Workmans Compensation Bd., 1949—60, Fed. Adv. Coun. Employment Security, 1954—58. Nominee, Am. Assembly Econ. Security, 1953; Paul Harris fellowship, Rotary Found. Rotary Internat. Mem.: NAM (employee, health and benefits com. 1950—55, chmn. 1955—59), Nat. Congl. Club, Rotarian, Am. Judicature Soc., Internat. Soc. Labor and Social Legis., Am. Pension Conf. (bd. govs. 1960—64), Pan-Am. Soc., U.S. C. of C (com. econ. security 1952—57), Kans. City Bar Assn., Mo. Bar Assn., Am. Bar Assn. (com. pensions and other compensation), Country Coral Gables Club, Delta Tau Delta, Phi Alpha Delta. Home: Miami, Fla. Died May 1991.

**WALTON, JEAN B.,** former college official; b. George School, Pa. d. George A. and Emily W. (Ingram) W. AB, Swarthmore Coll., 1935; A.M., Brown U., 1940; PhD, U. Pa., 1948. Tchr. math. Moorestown Friend's Sch., 1935-38; head dormitory Pembroke Coll., 1938-40; part-time instr. math., part-time asst. to deans Swarthmore Coll., 1940-42, asst. to deans, 1942-43, instr., 1943-45, acting dean women, summer 1945; instr. U. Pa., 1947-49; dean women Pomona Coll., Claremont, Calif., 1949-69, dean students, 1969-76, v.p. student affairs, 1976-79, emerita, from 1979; women's studies coordinator Claremont Colls., 1979-83; adj. prof. dept. edn. Claremont Grad. Sch., 1979-82. Lectr. Japan Women's U., Tokyo, 1955-56; cons. Danforth Found., 1962-63 Mem. Nat. Assn. Women Deans, Adminstrs. and Counselors (chmn. coll. sect. 1963-65, treas. 1967-69), Nat. Assn. Student Personnel Adminstrs. (Scott-Goodnight award 1974), Calif. Assn. Women Adminstrs. and Counselors (pres. 1957-59), Mortar Bd., Phi Beta Kappa., Soc. of Friends. Deceased.

**WANG, SING-WU,** retired librarian; b. China, Dec. 24, 1920; s. Zhi-tang and Zha Shi; m. May Wang, Nov. 20, 1947; children: Angela, Ruth, Kristina. BA, U. Zhejiang, China, 1944; MA, Australian Nat. U., 1969. Chief cataloguer, Chinese books Nat. Ctrl. Libr., Nanking, 1945—49; chief libr. Yang Ming Shan Inst. Libr., Taipei, Taiwan, 1949—55; exec. dir., bd. dirs. Libr. Assn. China, 1953—64, dir., libr. tng. sch. Taipei, 1956—58; dir. Taiwan Provincial Libr., Taipei, 1955—64; assoc. prof., prof. libr. sci., dept. social edn. Taiwan Normal U., Taipei, 1957—65; exch. libr. Cleve. Pub. Libr., 1959—60; with Sch. Libr. Sci., Western Res. U., Cleve., 1959—60; lectr., modern Chinese history Coll. Chinese Culture, Yang Ming Shan, Taiwan, 1963—64; sr. specialist libr. Orientalia Sect., Nat. Libr. Australia, Canberra, 1964—73, chief libr., 1973—85; lectr., Chinese classics, dept. Chinese Australian Nat. U., Canberra, 1966; vis. lectr., libr. sci. Beijing Normal U., 1985. Author: Introduction to the Classification of Books (in Chinese), 1955, On Library Services in Taiwan (in Chinese), 1963, The Organization of Chinese Emigration 1848-1888, 1978; Chinese translator Lincoln (Nathaniel Wright Stephenson), 1958; contbr. articles to profl. publs. Recipient Fgn. Libr. Program award, US Dept. State, 1959—60, medal, Order of Australia, 1986; fellow, The China Acad., Yang Ming Shan, 1968—2004. Mem.: ALA, East Asian Librs. Group Australia (newsletter editor 1980—82, chmn. 1982—85, vice chmn. 1985—86), Asian Studies Assn. Australia, Assn. Asian Studies, Libr. Assn. Australia. Baptist. Home: Fisher, Australia. Died Oct. 22, 2004.

**WAN-LIN, TSAI,** insurance executive; b. 1924; 3 children. Owner fruit and vegetable co., soy sauce factory, Taipei, Taiwan; co-founder Cathay Life Ins. Co., Taipei, 1962—2004, hon. chmn., 1979—2004. Died Sept. 27, 2004.

**WAPNER, SEYMOUR,** psychologist, educator, administrator; b. Bklyn., Nov. 20, 1917; s. Hyman and Rose S. (Liese) W.; m. Lorraine E. Gallant, June 4, 1946; children: Jeffrey Gallant, Amy Beth. AB, NYU, 1939; A.M., U. Mich., 1940, PhD, 1943. Instr., dir. U. Rochester Office Com. Selection and Tng. Aircraft Pilots, NRC, N.Y., 1943-46, 45-46; asst. prof. Bklyn. Coll., 1946-48, acting chmn. psychology dept., 1947-48; assoc. prof. dept. psychology Clark U., Worcester, Mass., 1948-56, prof., 1956-63, chmn. dept., 1960-86, G. Stanley Hall prof. genetic psychology, 1963-88, prof. emeritus, from 1988; chmn. exec. com. H. Werner Inst. Devel. Analysis, from 1957; mem. exec. bd. Council Grad. Depts. of Psychology, 1981-84; mem. U.S. Nat. Com. for Man and the Biosphere Directorate, 1975-86. Author: (with H.A. Witkin, et al), Personality Through Perception, 1954, (with H. Werner) Perceptual Development, 1957; editor: The Body Percept, 1965, (with W.A. Koelsch) Freud In Our Time, 1988, (with S.B. Cohen, B. Kaplan) Experiencing the Environment, 1976, (with B. Kaplan) Toward a Holistic Developmental Psychology, 1983, Perspectives in Psychological Theory, 1960, (with M. Bertini and L. Pizzamiglio) Field Dependence in Psychological Theory, Research and Application, 1986, (with L. Cirillo) Value Presuppositions in Theories of Human Development, 1986, (with L. Cirillo and B. Kaplan) Emotions in Ideal Human Development, 1989, (with J. Demick) Field Dependence-Independence, 1991, (with T. Yamamoto) Developmental Psychology of Life Transitions, 1992, Relations Between Psychology and Allied Fields, 1995, (with J. Demick, T. Yamamoto, T. Takahashi) Handbook of Japan-US Environment-behavior research: Towards a transactional approach, 1997, (with J. Demick, et. al.) Theoretical Perspectives in Environment-Behavior Research: Underlying Assumptions, Research Problems and Methodologies, 2000. Fellow APA, AAAS; mem. AAUP, Internat. Assn. Applied Psychology, Soc. Rsch. in Child Devel., Eastern Psychol. Assn. (dir. 1968-70, 71-74, 85-88, 93—, pres. 1979-80), New Eng. Psychol. Assn. (pres. 1979-80), Mass. Psychol. Assn., Phi Beta Kappa, Sigma Xi. Died 2003.

**WARDRUP, LEO C., JR.,** state legislator; b. Middlesboro, Ky., Sept. 5, 1936; s. Leo C. and Kathryn Callison Wardrup; m. Gloria Wirth Lowe, 1991; children: Ashley, Leo III, Suzannah(dec.), Christopher Lowe. BA, U. NC Chapel Hill; MA, George Washington U.; Grad., Naval War Coll. Chmn. Va. Beach Devel. Authority, 1990—91; mem. Dist. 83 Va. House of Delegates, Va., 1992—2007. Served in USN, 1958—86. Mem.: DAV, Fleet Res. Assn., Navy League, American Legion. Republican. Episcopal. Died July 2, 2014.

**WARE, ROBERT A.,** advertising executive, artist; b. Balt., Aug. 7, 1940; s. Robert and Chlorice (Smith) W.; m. Vivian Kelliebrew. BA, Md. Inst., 1976. Illustrator state employment agy. Sate of Md., Balt., 1971-73, illustrator mass transit adminstrn., 1973-74; pub. affairs specialist Dept. Human Resources, State of Md., Balt., 1974-76; public affairs specialist Dept. Edn., State of Md., Balt., 1976-80; owner Robert Ware Graphic Designers, Balt., 1980-81; public info. officer Dept. Transp., State of Md., Balt., 1981-83; dir. public info. Office on Aging, State of Md., Balt., 1983-85; mgr. advt. Balt.-Washington Internat. Airport, Balt., from 1985. Owner Art Pen Graphic Design Studios, Balt., 1985-86. Prin. works include portrait U.S. V.P. Spiro T. Agnew, 1967. Vol. art tchr. St. Francis Ctr., Balt., 1980-81; pub. info. officer Alcoholics Anonymous, Balt., 1982. Mem. Advt. and Profl. Club of Balt. Democrat. Episcopalian. Avocations: creative writing, painting, drawing, sculpting, swimming. Home: Baltimore, Md. Died Sept. 1992.

**WARE, WILLIS HOWARD,** computer scientist; b. Atlantic City, Aug. 31, 1920; s. Willis and Ethel (Rosswork) W.; m. Floy Hoffer, Oct. 10, 1943; children— Deborah Susanne Ware Pinson, David Willis, Alison Floy Ware Manoli. BSEE, U. Pa., 1941; MSEE, MIT, 1942; PhD in Elec. Engring, Princeton U., 1951. Research engr. Hazeltine Electronics Corp., Little Neck, NY, 1942-46; mem. research staff Inst. Advanced Study, Princeton U., NJ, 1946-51, North American Aviation, Downey, Calif., 1951-52; mem. corporate research staff, research engr. Rand Corp., Santa Monica, Calif., 1952—2013. Adj. prof. UCLA Extension Service, 1955-68; first chmn. American Fedn. Info. Processing Socs., 1961, 62; chmn. HEW sec.'s Advisory Com. on Automated Personal Data Systems, 1971-73; mem. Privacy Protection Study Commn., 1975-77, vice chmn., 1975-77; mem. numerous other adv. groups, spl. coms. for fed. govt., 1959—2013 Author: Digital Computer Technology and Design, vols. I and II, 1963. Recipient Computers Sciences Man of Yr. award Data Processing Mgmt. Assn., 1975, Exceptional Civilian Svc. medal USAF, 1979, Disting. Svc. award American Fedn. Info. Processing Societies, 1986, Nat. Computer Sys. Security award Nat. Computer Sys. Lab./Nat. Computer Security Ctr., 1989, Computer Pioneer award IEEE Computer Soc., 1993, Pioneer award Electronic Frontier Found., 1995, Kristain Beckman award Internat. Fedn. Info. Processing, 1999; named one of The Fed. 100 of 1994, Fed. Computer Week. Fellow IEEE (Centennial medal 1984), AAAS, Assn. for Computing Machinery; mem. NAE, AIAA, Sigma Xi, Eta Kappa Nu, Pi Mu Epsilon, Tau Beta Pi. Home: Santa Monica, Calif. Died Nov. 22, 2013.

**WARING, HEATON MANICE,** architect; b. Görlitz, Germany, Aug. 8, 1922; (parents Am. citizens); s. Heaton M. Waring, Sr. and Gertrude Charlotte Ernst; m. Irmgard Grabo, Aug. 10, 1955 (div. 1974); children: Susan, Brigit, William, Anne, Kathryn; m. Cynthia L. Turbak, Mar. 24, 1995. AA, U. San Francisco, 1943; BA, U. Calif., Berkeley, 1948; student, U. Zurich, Switzerland, 1948-49, U. Basel, 1949-50, U. Tübingen, Germany, 1950-51. Translator Spanish and German Office of Censorship, San Francisco, 1941; cartographer U.S. Geol. Survey, Sacramento, Calif., 1951-56; archtl. draftsman Harmon, Pray & Dietrich, Seattle, 1968-69; archtl. designer DeHart, Lands & Hall, Seattle, 1970; engring. archtl. coord. Skilling, Helle, Christiansen & Robertson, 1970-71; exec. dir. Kitsap Co. Housing Authority, Wash., 1972-74; archtl. assoc. John H. Rudolph, Bainbridge Island, Wash., 1974-77; pvt. practice Bainbridge Island, 1978-89. Archtl. draftsman Naramore, Bain, Brady & Johanson, Seattle, 1966-68. Chmn. Planning Commn., Bainbridge Island, 1970-72; Spanish-English interpreter Ometepe, Nicaragua, Bainbride Island, 1986. Sgt. U.S. Army, 1943-45, ETO. Recipient Good Conduct medal. Avocations: water color and oil painting, sculpture, translations (german-spanish). Home: Costa Rica, Costa Rica. Died Aug. 20, 2008.

**WARING, WALTER WEYLER,** literature and language professor; b. Sterling, Kans., May 13, 1917; s. Walter Wray and Bonnie Laura (Weyler) W.; m. Mary Esther Griffith, Feb. 8, 1946; children: Mary Laura, Helen Ruth, Elizabeth Anne, Claire Joyce. BA, Kans. Wesleyan U., 1939; MA, U. Colo., 1946; PhD, Cornell U., 1949. Tchr., English and chemistry Belleville (Kan.) High Sch., 1939-41; instr. U. Colo., Boulder, 1941-42, 46-47; mem. faculty Kalamazoo Coll., from 1949, prof. English, 1955-85, prof. emeritus, from 1985, chmn. dept., 1953-78, dir. humanities, 1978-83. Ednl. TV lectr.; vis. prof. Kenyon Coll., 1984-86, 90-91. Painter watercolors.; author: Thomas Carlyle, 1978, also articles. Served to 1st lt. AUS, World War II, PTO. Decorated Legion of Merit. Mem. Phi Beta Kappa. Deceased.

**WARNER, WILSON KEITH,** sociology educator; b. Heyburn, Idaho, Sept. 6, 1930; s. Wilson A. and Eva L. (Pratt) Warner; m. Vila Jenks Warner, Sept. 1, 1950; children: Karen, Janice, Randall, Neil. BS, Utah State U., 1958, MS, 1959; PhD, Cornell U., 1960. Asst. prof. rural sociology U. Wis., Madison, 1960—66, assoc. prof., 1966—69, prof., 1969—71; prof. sociology Brigham Young U., Provo, Utah, from 1971. Assoc. dir. U. Honors Program, 1978—79; vis. prof. Dept. Rural Sociology, 1984. Contbr. articles to profl. jours. Mem. steering com. cmty. progress program State of Utah, 1973. Served US Army, 1953—55. Named Outstanding Educator of America, 1972, 1974—75. Mem.: Arts and Letters, Utah Acad. Scis., Am. Sociol. Assn., Rural Sociol. Soc. (pres. 1973—74, Disting. Rural Sociologist award 1985), Sigma Xi. Home: Orem, Utah. Died 1996.

**WARNOCK, GEORGE FORRESTER,** gas industry executive; b. Flagstaff, Ariz., Jan. 16, 1932; s. Henderson Bennet and Helen (Schwartz) W.; m. Dorothy May Nicols, Aug. 21, 1955 (div. 1979); children: George, Pamela L., Vance, Robert; m. Diane Christine Coates, Apr. 22, 1983. BS in Mining Geology, U. Ariz., 1958, MS in Econ. Geology, 1963. Registered profl. geologist Ariz. Geologist Ariz. Exploration Unit Cerro de Pasco Corp., 1959—61; cons. Yukon Territory, Canada, 1961—62; tech. dir. Ore & Mining div., staff mining geologist W. R. Grace & Co., NYC, 1962—69; v.p. mining, dir. Goldfield Corp., NYC, 1969—70; v.p., dir. NRD Mining Ltd., B.C., 1970—75; cons., 1970—99; pres., dir. Todilto Exploration & Devel. Corp., Albuquerque, 1975—99, Coronado Resources Inc., Vancouver, B.C., 1984—99; dir. Southwest Nat. Bank, Albuquerque, 1981, Minerals Engring. Co., Denver. Lobbyest N.Mex. Mining Assn. before State Legis., Sante Fe, 1977—84. Sgt. USMC, 1951—54, Korea. Mem. Albuquerque Geol. Soc., Albuquerque Petroleum Club, AIME, Am. Assn. Petroleum Engrs., Am. Mining Congress, Ams. for Rational Energy Alternatives, Am. Inst. Profl. Geologists, Ariz. Geol. Soc., Assn. Profl. Engers. B.C., B.C. and Yukon Chamber of Mines, Can. Inst. Mining & Metallurgy, Engrs. Club Vancouver, Mining Club N.Y., Mining Club S.W., N.Mex. Geol. Soc., N.Mex. Mining Assn., Soc. Econ. Geologists. Republican. Died Apr. 7, 1999.

**WARREN, JACK HAMILTON,** retired diplomat, banker, trade policy advisor; b. Apr. 10, 1921; m. Hilary J. Titterington; children: Hilary Warren Nicolson, Martin, Jennifer Warren Part, Ian. Student, Queens U., Kingston, Ont., Can., 1938-41. Joined Dept. External Affairs, Canada, 1945; assigned London, 1948-51; fin. counsellor Washington, 1952—54; alt. Canadian dir. Internat. Monetary Fund; alternate dir. Internat. Bank Reconstruction Devel., Washington; fin. counsellor, del. OECD NATO, Paris, 1954—57; asst. dep. minister trade and commerce Ottawa, 1958-64; dep. minister, trade and commerce, 1964-68; dep minister industry, trade & commerce, 1968-71; high commr. to U.K., 1971-75; ambassador to U.S., 1975-77; Can. coord. Gatt multilateral trade negotiations, 1977-79; vice-chmn. Bank of Montreal, 1979-86; prin. trade policy advisor Govt. Que., 1986-94; N. American deputy chmn. Trilateral Comm. Served with Royal Canadian Navy, 1941-45; officer Order of Can., 1982. Recipient Pub. Svc. Outstanding Achievement award, 1976. Home: Ontario, Canada. Died Apr. 1, 2008.

**WARSOFF, STANLEY L.,** lawyer; b. NYC, Aug. 30, 1946; s. Louis A. and Sylvia (Pearl) W.; m. Ruth Peterson, Dec. 6, 1987. BA, CUNY, 1968; JD, St. John's U., 1972. Bar: N.Y. 1973, U.S. Dist. Ct. (ea. and so. dist.) N.Y. 1975, Fla. 1976, U.S. Supreme Ct. 1980. Atty. Home Life Ins. Co., NYC, 1972-75; counsel FDIC, NYC, 1975-80; assoc. Squadran, Ellenoff, Pleasant & Lehrer, NYC, 1981-82, Opton, Handler, Gottlieb & Feiler, NYC, 1982-84, Phillips, Nizer, Benjamin, Krim & Ballon, NYC, from 1984. Lectr. NYU Real Estate Inst., 1986—. Mem. St. John's U. Law Rev. Consumer counsel N.Y.C. Civil Ct. and Small Claims Ct., 1976-77. With USAR, 1968-71. Named St. Thomas More scholar St. John's U., 1970-71. Mem. ABA, N.Y. County Lawyers, N.Y. State Bar Assn. (mem. com. cooperatives and condominiums real property law sect.), Shakespeare Lodge, Masons. Home: New York, NY. Died Mar. 15, 1991.

**WASFI, SADIQ HASSAN,** chemistry professor; b. Basrah, Iraq, July 1, 1936; established residency in the U.S., 1978; s. Hassan Mohammed and Seniye (Omar) W.; m. Ellen Olivia Schwarz, Nov. 15, 1968; children: Yasmine, Dahlia, Ammar. BS in Chemistry Edn., Baghdad U., Iraq, 1961; MS in Analytical Chemistry, Georgetown U., 1966, PhD in Inorganic Chemistry, 1971. Lectr. chemistry Basrah U., 1971-77; rsch. assoc. U. Hawaii, Honolulu, 1975-76, Georgetown U., Washington, 1977-78; assoc. prof. Montgomery Coll., Takoma Park, Md., 1978-79; prof. chemistry Del. State U., Dover, 1979—2010; ret. Vis. assoc. prof. Georgetown U., 1980, 81; mng. editor Frontiers in Bio-Sci., 2003. Contbr. articles to profl. jours; patent in antimony oxometalate complexes having anti-viral activity, 1991. Mem. Am. Chem. Soc., Sigma Xi. Muslim. Home: Dover, Del. Died Sept. 11, 2012.

**WASHBURN, GLADYS HAASE,** retired church musician, educator, director; b. San Antonio, Feb. 19, 1919; d. Henry August and Rosa Sophie (Sundermeyer) Haase; m. Jost Brainard Washburn, Dec. 29, 1942 (dec.); children: Yvonne Rosalind, Henry Brainard, Diane Louise. Tchg. cert. in piano/organ, St. Louis Coll. Music, 1940. Cert. piano St. Louis Coll. Music, 1940. Ch. pianist Friedens Evang. Ch., 1932—38; organist, choir dir. St. Martin's Ch., High Ridge, Mo., 1939—40; choir dir. Bethany Evang. and Ref. Ch., San Antonio, 1940—42, organist, choir dir. New Orleans, 1952—55, St. Paul's Evang. and Ref. Ch., Corpus Christi, Tex., 1944—51, Bethlehem United Ch. of Christ, Buffalo, 1964—70, First Congl. United Ch. of Christ, Dwight, Ill., 1970—72, St. Michael's Episcopal Ch., Independence, Mo., 1985—92; dir. jr. choir Bethlehem Evang. and Ref. Ch., Buffalo, 1956—61; interim organist, choir dir. St. Paul's and St. Marks Ch., Buffalo, 1963, Village United Ch. of Christ, Blue Springs, Mo., 1992—93; interim organist chs. Greater Kansas City area, 1993—97; ret., 1997. Cons. chs. seeking organists, Buffalo, Blue Springs, Mo. Organ recitalist S.W. Conf. Nat. PTA Meeting, San Antonio, 1941, 1942; accompanist Harlandale Sch. Dist., San Antonio, 1941, 1942. Recipient Cert. in Ministry in Music, United Ch. Christ, 1992. Mem.: Am. Guild Organists. Republican. United Ch. Of Christ. Avocations: sewing, cooking, reading. Home: Blue Springs, Mo. Died Apr. 1, 2014.

**WATANABE, TERUO,** geologist, educator; b. Tokyo, Feb. 9, 1944; s. Mitsugu and Tsusoko (Okada) W.; m. Kinue Watanabe. DSc, Hokkaido U., Sapporo, Japan, 1975. Prof. geology Hokkaido U., from 1994. Home: Sapporo, Japan. Died May 9, 2002.

**WATERS, ETHEL,** actress, singer; b. Chester, Pa., Oct. 31, 1896; d. John Wesley Waters and Louisa Tar Anderson. Began as singer making first stage appearance at Lincoln Theater, Balt., about 1917; sang in nightclubs and Negro theaters; made first Broadway appearance at Daly's Theater in Africana, 1927; appeared in Blackbirds of 1930, Rhapsody in Black, 1931, As Thousands Cheer, 1933, At Home Abroad, 1935; made debut as dramatic star in Mamba's Daughters, Empire Theater, N.Y.C., 1939; starred in Cabin in the Sky, 1940-41; appeared in A Member of the Wedding (winner N.Y. Drama Critics award), radio artist, 1934—; also on TV; on radio programs for U.S.O. Camp Shows, Inc., 1942; concert at Carnegie Hall, 1938; featured singer Billy Graham Crusades; gained recognition for her singing of Dinah, Stormy Weather, Am I Blue, others; featured in motion picture On With the Show; also appeared in Tales of Manhattan, 1941, Cairo, Stage Door Canteen, 1943, Pinky, The Heart is a Rebel, 1956, The Sound and the Fury, 1958. Author: (with Charles Samuels) His Eye is on the Sparrow (autobiography), 1951, To Me It's Wonderful (autobiography), 1972. Coun. mem. Hollywood Victory com., 1942; mem. exec. coun. Actors Equity Assn., 1942-43; v.p. Negro Actors Guild Am., 1942-43. Hon. capt. Cal. State Militia and 7th Women's Ambulance Corps, 1942. Deceased.

**WATERS, RUDOLPH EARL,** retired academic administrator; b. Brookhaven, Miss., May 21, 1932; s. Leonard Douglas and Annie Mae (Thadison) W.; m. Kathleen Graham; children Rudolph E. Jr., Veronica. BSc, DePaul U., 1954; EdM, Boston U., 1958; PhD, Kans. State U., 1977. Registrar Utica (Miss.) Jr. Coll., 1954-55, dean of instrn., 1955-57; dean of students Alcorn State U., Lorman, Miss., 1957-58, dean of instrn., 1958-70, coord. of title III programs, 1967-75, v.p., 1970-93, exec. v.p., from 1993, interim pres., 1994-95. Mem. advisory com. Southern Growth Policies Bd. Alumni fellow Kans. State U., 1988. Mem.ASCD, American Assn. for Higher Edn., Nat. Soc. for the Study of Edn., American Assn. of Univ. Adminstrs., Phi Delta Kappa (chpt. pres. 1992), Delta Mu Delta, Sigma Pi Phi. Home: Lorman, Miss. Died Sept. 14, 2014.

**WATKIN, DAVID,** cinematographer; b. Margate, Eng., Mar. 23, 1925; Asst. cameraman Brit. Transport Films, 1950-55, cameraman, 1955-61; ind. filmmaker, 1961—2008. Cinematographer: (films) The Long Night Haul, 1956, The England of Elizabeth, 1957, Under Night Streets, 1958, Blue Pullman, 1960, The Six-Sided Triangle, 1963, Rhythmn 'n' Greens, 1963, The Knack...and How to Get It, 1964, Help!, 1965, Marat/Sade, 1966, Mademoiselle, 1966, How I Won the War, 1967, The Charge of the Light Brigade, 1968, The Bed Sitting Room, 1969, Catch 22, 1970, The Devils, 1971, The Boyfriend, 1971, The Homecoming, 1973, A Delicate Balance, 1973, The Three Musketeers, 1974, The Four Musketeers, 1976, Mahogany, 1975, To The Devil a Daughter, 1976, Robin and Marian, 1976, Joseph Andrews, 1977, Cuba, 1979, That Summer, 1979, Hanover Street, 1979, Endless Love, 1981, Cinderella, 1981, Chariots of Fire, 1981, Yentl, 1983, The Hotel New Hampshire, 1984, White Nights, 1985, Out of Africa, 1985, (Acad. award for Cinematography, 1986), Return of Oz, 1985, Sky Bandits, 1986, Moonstruck, 1987, The Good Mother, 1988, Masquerade, 1988, Last Rites, 1988, Journet to the Center of the Earth, 1989, Memphis Belle, 1990, Hamlet, 1990, The Object of Beauty, 1991, The Cabinet of Dr. Ramirez, 1991, Used People, 1992, This Boy's Life, 1993, Bopha!, 1993, Milk Money, 1993, Jane Eyre, 1994, Bogus, 1995, Night Falls on Manhatten, 1995, Through Roses, 1996, Critical Care, 1996, Obsession, 1997, Gloria, 1997, Tea with Mussolini, 1998, All Forgotten, 2000; (TV mini-series) Jesus of Nazareth, 1977; (TV movies) Murder on the Moon, 1989; author: Why Is There Only One Word for Thesaurus?, 1998, Was Clara Schumann a Fag Hag?, 2008 Home: Brighton, England. Died Feb. 19, 2008.

**WATKINS, JOHN CLETIS,** lawyer; b. Black Oak, Ark., Mar. 26, 1917; s. Joseph Cleveland and Sylvia Ann (Hamilton) Watkins; m. Arna Lana Shields, Sept. 11, 1924; 1 child, Mary lana. Attending, Ark. State U., 1939—40, attending, 1946—48; JD, U. Ark., 1952. Pvt. practice, West Memphis, Ark., 1951—54, Paragould, Ark., 1954—73; of counsel Joe Hollifield, Paragould; mcpl. judge City of Paragould, 1959—63. Author: (novels) With Another Mans Gold, 1986. Served to sgt. US Army, 1940—45. Mem.: DAV, VFW, Am. Legion, Ark. Bar Assn., Greene Clay Bar Assn. (pres. 1965), Masons. Died Jan. 23, 1993.

**WATSON, GEORGE A.,** pathologist; b. San Jose, Calif., Mar. 4, 1905; s. John Gilcrist and Jessie Anna (Rood) Watson; m. Evelyn Boelter Watson, June 1, 1931. BA, U. Calif., Berkeley, 1932; MD, U. Calif., 1940. Diplomate Am. Bd. Pathology, 1946. Intern San Francisco City and County Hosp., 1939—40; resident pathologist Highland Alameda County Hosp., Oakland, Calif., 1940—42, Fairmount Hosp., 1940—42; sr. resident Henry Ford Hosp., Detroit, 1942—43; assoc. pathologist Santa Clara County Hosp., 1944—45; pathologist Vallejo Cmty. Hosp., 1945—47, Hahnemann Hosp., San Francisco, 1945—66; sr. pathologist French Hosp., San Francisco, 1945—77; cons. pathologist Garden Hosp., San Francisco, 1959, Drs. Hosp., San Francisco, 1961, Polyclinic Hosp., 1965, Weimar Joint Sanitorium, 1948—62, Golden Gate Hosp., 1950, Laguna Honda Hosp., 1965. Fellow: Am. Geriatrics Soc., Coll. Am. Pathologists; mem.: AMA, Royal Soc. Medicine, Calif. Med. Assn., San Francisco Med. Soc., San Francisco Path. Soc., Calif. Soc. Pathologists, Soc. Nuclear Medicine, Am. Soc. Clin. Pathologists. Home: Belvedere Tiburon, Calif. Died Aug. 9, 1991.

**WAUGH, JOHN STEWART,** chemist, educator; b. Willimantic, Conn., Apr. 25, 1929; s. Albert E. and Edith (Stewart) W.; married Susan Walsh, 1983; children: Alice Collier, Frederick Pierce. AB, Dartmouth Coll., 1949; PhD, Calif. Inst. Tech., 1953; ScD (hon.), Dartmouth Coll., 1989. Rsch. fellow in physics Calif. Inst. Tech., 1952-53; instr. MIT, Cambridge, 1953—55, asst. prof. chemistry, 1955—58, assoc. prof., 1958—62, prof. Cambridge, 1962—96, Albert Amos Noyes prof. chemistry, 1973-88, inst. prof., 1989—96, prof. emeritus, 1996—2014. Vis. prof. U. Calif.-Berkeley, 1963-64, Max Planck Inst., Heidelberg, 1972; sr. fellow Alexander von Humboldt-Stiftung; vis. scientist Harvard U., 1976; mem. chemistry adv. panel NSF, 1966-69, vice chmn., 1968-69; mem. rev. com. Argonne Nat. Lab., 1970-74; mem. sci. and edn. adv. com. Lawrence Berkeley Lab., 1980-86; exchange visitor USSR Acad. Sciences, 1962, 75; mem. vis. com. Tufts U., 1966-69, Princeton, 1973-78; mem. fellowship com. Alfred P. Sloan Found., 1977-82; Joliot-Curie prof. École Supérieure de Physique et Chemie, Paris, 1985, 96; lectr. in field. Author: New NMR Methods in Solid State Physics, 1978; editor: Advances in Magnetic Resonance, 1965-87; assoc. editor: Jour. Chem. Physics, 1965-67, Spectrochimica Acta, 1964-78; mem. editl. bd. Chem. Revs., 1978-82, Jour. Magnetic Resonance, 1989-2014, Applied Magnetic Resonance, 1989-2014 Recipient Haseltine Chemistry prize, 1947, Irving Langmuir Chemical Physics award, 1976, Gold Pick Axe award, 1976, Pitts. award Spectroscopic Soc. Pitts., 1979, Wolf prize in Chemistry, Wolf Found., 1984, Pauling medal, 1985, Calif. Inst. Tech. Disting. Alumnus award, 1987, James R. Killian Jr. Faculty Achievement award, MIT, 1988, ISMAR prize, 1989, Richards medal, 1992, Evans award, 1994, Eastern Analytical Symposium award 1996, Russell Varian prize, 2006, Welch award, 2011; Sloan fellow, 1958-62, Guggenheim fellow, 1963-64, 72; Sherman Fairchild scholar Calif. Inst. Tech., 1989. Fellow: AAAS, American Phys. Soc. (chmn. divsn. chemistry and physics 1983—84), Sigma Xi; mem.: NAS, Slovenian Acad. Sci. and Arts (fgn. corr.), Nat. Magnetic Resonance Soc. India (hon.), Internat. Soc. Magnetic Resonance (coun. mem. 1989—95, exec. com. from 1996, v.p. from 1997, pres. 1999—2002), Phi Beta Kappa. Home: Lincoln, Mass. Died Aug. 22, 2014.

**WAUGH, MIKE (MICHAEL L. WAUGH),** state legislator; b. York, Pa, Dec. 17, 1955; s. William E. and Lucille L. Waugh; m. Wanda C. Waugh; 1 child, Joseph. Attended, Pa. State U., York. Twp. suprs. Shrewsbury Twp., Pa., 1989—92; vol. fire, rescue and emergency svcs. worker; asst. fire chief Shrewsbury Vol. Fire Co., 1981—93; mem. Dist. 93 Pa. House of Reps., 1993—98; mem. Dist. 28 Pa. State Senate, 1999—2014; mng. ptnr. Waugh Construction Co. V.p. York County Assn. of Townships of Second Class, 1992. Mem.: NFIB, Trades Advisor Com., York County Rep. Men's Club, York County Fire Police Assn., York County Farm Bureau, Hopewell Fish and Game Assn., York County Fire Chiefs and Firefighters Assn., York County Builders Assn., Shrewsbury Lodge No. 423 F. & A.M. Republican. Protestant. Died Oct. 8, 2014.

**WAYNE, DONALD,** editor; b. NYC, May 13, 1913; s. Benjamin and Rose (Frank) W.; m. Elaine Pailthorpe, Nov. 23, 1938 (dec. July 1972); children— Arthur, Christina, Victoria, Alistair; m. Helena Paula Malinowska Burke, June 29, 1974. BA, Cornell U., 1934. Editor Victory, Photo Review (overseas br. OWI), 1942-45; asst. mng. editor Parade mag., 1956-58, mag. editor, 1958-65; mng. dir. Roto Publs., Ltd., London, Eng.; editor-pub. Friday mag.; pub. Southeast Living mag.; editor The Am.; mng. dir. Am. Weekly Newspapers, Ltd.; pub. Historic London for Ams. Stage mgr. Broadway theatricals Ethan Frome, St. Helena, 1934-37; novelist, radio writer Broadway theatricals, 1937-40; screen writer, Selznick Studios, Hollywood, 1945-46, free lance writer nat. mags., 1945-56; Author: Fine Flowers in the Valley, 1937; screen Adaptation Thomas Wolfe's Look Homeward, Angel; film script: Arthur Kaestler's Scum of the Earth, 1983. Home: Cambridge, England. Deceased.

**WEAVER, E(LVIN) PAUL,** retired minister; b. Everett, Pa., Oct. 13, 1912; s. Mahlon J. and Fanny S. (Ritchey) W.; m. Zalma Faw, Aug. 6, 1936 (dec. 1966); children: Nelda Weaver Sollenberger, Bruce H.; m. Eleanor Snare Carter, June 21, 1968. AB, Elizabethtown Coll., Pa., 1937; BD, Bethany Theol. Sem., Chgo., 1945; postgrad., Kennedy Sch. Missions, Hartford, Conn., 1939. Ordained to ministry Ch. of the Brethren, 1933. Missionary Ch. of the Brethren, Nigeria, 1940-44, pastor Huntington County, Ind., 1945-51, Mexico (Ind.) Ch., 1951-59; dist. exec. Mid Dist. of Ind., North Manchester, Ind., 1959-71, Nappanee, Ind., 1971-80; pastor Union Ctr. Ch., SS Valley & Cherry Ln., Everett, Pa., 1980-88; ret., 1992. Pres. Ind. State Pastor Conf., Indpls., 1955; del. Nat. Coun. Chs., Detroit, Dallas; accredited visitor World Coun. Chs. Assemblies II, VI, VII, VIII; Ind. Christian Endeavor, 1948-78; rep. Ch. of Brethren at UN SSD III, 1988, non-govtl. orgns. Author: Journey Into Faith, 1994. Pa. advocacy and action team Pa. Coun. of Chs., 1987—; founder Do Something for Peace program, Nigeria, 1999. Recipient Ecumenical award Ind. Coun. Chs., 1975, Pa. Coun. Chs., 1988. *My life is dedicated to seeking to know and do God's will. I find many opportunities to work for Justice and Peace to Preserve all Creation.* Died Oct. 14, 2001.

**WEAVER, GERTRUDE SOPHIA,** retired educator; b. Phillipsburg, NJ, Aug. 12, 1916; d. Herbert Alexander and Gertrude Estelle (Paules) W. BA, Swarthmore Coll., 1938; student, U. Munich, 1936-37; MA, Columbia U., 1939. Cert. tchr., Pa. Tchr. Linden Hall, Lititz, Pa., 1939-40, Chester (Pa.) High Sch., 1940-47; instr. Swarthmore (Pa.) Ctr., Pa. State U., 1947-49, asst. prof. Swarthmore and Ogontz Ctrs., 1949-51; tchr., counselor Frankfurt (Germany) Am. High Sch., 1951-52, Munich Am. High Sch.,

1952-59; tchr. European history and German, Newark (Del.) Sr. High Sch., 1959-79; ret., 1979. Fgn. expert Qingdao (People's Republic China) Ocean U., spring 1983, 85, fall 1988. Program leader Fellowship House, Chester, 1945-46; discussion leader Amerika Haus, USIS, Munich, 1955-57; mem. nominating com. YWCA, Newark, 1980-82. Mem. NEA, ACLU, AAUW (bd. dirs., edn. rep. Newark 1980-83), LWV, Am. Assn. Tchrs. German (sec. Phila. chpt. 1948, treas. 1964-66). Del. Edn. Assn., Newark Schs. Edn. Assn., Common Cause, Nature Conservancy, Chinese-Am. Assn. Del., Friends Newark Free Libr. Democrat. Avocations: photography, travel, gardening. Home: Hockessin, Del. Died June 1998.

**WEAVER, WILLIAM H.,** broadcasting executive; b. Bklyn., Dec. 18, 1918; s. William A. and Minerva (Jones) W.; children: Michelle, Patrice, Karin, Brian. Grad. high sch. Announcer Radio Sta. KGFL, Roswell, N.Mex., Radio Sta. KBST, Big Spring, Tex.; then advt. mgr. Star Free Press, Ventura, Calif.; sales mgr. Radio Sta. KXOA, Sacramento; gen. mgr. Radio Star. KROY, Sacramento, Sta. KWIZ, Santa Ana, Calif.; now partner, gen. mgr. sta. KLOK, San Jose, Calif., KLOK-FM, San Francisco, KWIZ, and KARM-KFIG, Fresno, Calif. Served with USN, 1941-45. *My formula for success is to be frank and honest with everyone, make judgements based on logic rather than emotion and work harder than anyone else. Money should never become the primary motivation. Strive for personal excellence and to create value through new and better ideas ... money will come as a result.* Died Jan. 14, 1990.

**WEBB, ALAN JOHN,** management consultant, writer, journalist; b. Bristol, England, Feb. 7, 1946; s. Arthur and Florence Webb; m. Kathleen Mary Chubb, Mar. 27, 1971; 1 child, Julian. Grad. in Prodn. Engring. and Mgmt. with honors, Loughborough U., Eng., 1969. Contr. of machining (Concorde) Brit. Aircraft Corp., Filton Divsn., Bristol, Avon, England, 1972—74; mgmt. cons. WS Atkins Group, Epsom, Surrey, England, 1974—78; asst. project mgr., head of dept. Hunting Engring., Ampthill, Bedfordshire, England, 1978—86; sr. project mgr. Frazer Nash Def. Systems, Leatherhead, Surrey, England, 1986—90; project mgmt. cons. Alan Webb Mgmt. Consultancy, Horsham, West Sussex, England, from 1991. Mem. Brit. Stds. Instn., London, from 1993. Author: Managing Innovative Projects, 1999, Project Management for Successful Product Innovation, 2000 (Adopted by U. Shanghai and transl. into Chinese, 2004), The Project Manager's Guide to Handing Risk, 2003, Chinese edit., 2004, Using Earned Value - A project manager's guide, 2003, Chinese and Spanish edits., 2005; contbr. over 50 articles to profl. jours. Mem.: Instn. of Elec. Engrs. (Lord Hirst award 1997, Engring. Mgmt. Jour. award 1999), Assn. for Project Mgmt. (com. mem. 1999—2004). Achievements include development of original systems for managing complex supply situations on major weapons development programmes; computerized Earned Value management systems using a unique approach. Home: Horsham, England. Died Nov. 2005.

**WEBB, BERNICE LARSON,** writer, consultant, press owner, publisher, retired university professor; b. Ludell, Kans. d. Carl Godfred and Ida Genevieve (Tongish) Larson; m. Ralph Raymond Schear, Aug. 9, 1942 (div. July 1956, dec. Aug., 1981); children: William Carl Schear, Rebecca Rae Schear Gentry; m. Robert MacHardy Webb, July 14, 1961 (dec. June 1983). BA, U. Kans., 1956, MA, 1957, PhD, 1961; postgrad., U. Aberdeen, Scotland, 1959-60. Cert. counselor Nat. Multiple Sclerosis Soc., peer counselor for cancer, ARC. Asst. instr. English U. Kans., Lawrence, 1958-59, 60-61; asst. prof. U. Southwestern La., Lafayette, 1961-67, assoc. prof., 1967-80, prof., 1980-87; ret., 1987; former owner, publisher Spider Press. Vis. assoc. prof. S.S. Universe Campus/World Campus Afloat, 1972; coord. Poetry in the Schs., Lafayette Parish, La., 1974; dir. grad. seminars NDEA Inst. Intellectual and Cultural History, Lafayette, summer 1966; poetry cons. Acadiana Arts Coun., 1976-87, Lafayette Parish Schs., 1976-87; bd. dirs. Deep South Writers Conf., 1978-87; acting dir. English reading-writing lab. U. Southwestern La., summers 1977, 78, 79, former writing cons.; founder, coord. Webb's Writers. Author: The Basketball Man, 1973, transl. to Japanese, 1981, new edit., 1994, Beware of Ostriches, 1978, Poetry on the Stage, 1979, Lady Doctor on a Homestead, 1987, Two Peach Baskets, 1991 (with J. Allan) Born to Be a Loser, 1993, Spider Web, 1993, Mating Dance, 1996, From Acorn to Oakbourne, 1998; contbr. poetry and articles to various publs.; book reviewer Jour. Am. Culture, Jour. Popular Culture, 1980-87; actress Little Theater, La., 1969-83, off-off Broadway, 1980. Vol. Mayor's Commn. on the Needs of Women, City of Lafayette, 1976-86; vol. La. Talent Bank of Women, 1978-86; judge of writing contests for schs., clubs, profl. socs., La. and U.S.; newsletter editor Bayou Coun. Girl Scouts of Am., 1964-66; guest editor The New Laurel Rev., 1976. Mem. AAUW (bd. dirs. br. 1967-71, state editor 1967-71, grantee 1978-80, faculty rsch. grants U. Southwestern La. 1980-81, 85-86), Soc. for Values in Higher Edn. (Svc. award 1995), South Cen. Coll. English Assn. (pres. 1986-87), S.W. Br. Poetry (former pres.), La. State Poetry Soc. (Disting. Lifetime mem., pres. 1978-79, 81-82, editor 1970-90), South Cen. MLA, Coll. English Assn., Am. Folklore Soc., Conf. on Christianity and Lit., Nat. Fedn. State Poetry Socs., Inc. (Queen of Poetry 1993), Phi Beta Kappa (regional pres. 1976-77, 83-84). Democrat. Roman Catholic. Avocations: acting, travel, collecting oral history. Died Mar. 19, 1999.

**WEBER, LAVERN JOHN,** retired marine science administrator, educator; b. Isabel, SD, June 7, 1933; s. Jacob and Irene Rose (Bock) W.; m. Shirley Jean Carlson, June 19, 1959 (div. 1992); children: Timothy L., Peter J., Pamela C., Elizabeth T.; m. Patricia Rae Lewis, Oct. 17, 1992. AAS, Everett Jr. Coll., 1956; BA, Pacific Luth. U., 1958; MS, U. Wash., 1962, PhD, 1964. Instr. U. Wash., Seattle, 1964-67, asst. prof., 1967-69, acting state toxicologist, 1968-69; assoc. prof. Oreg. State U., Corvallis, 1969-75, prof., 1976—2002, asst. dean grad. sch., 1974-77, dir. Hatfield Marine Sci. Ctr. Newport, 1977—2002, supt. Coastal Oreg. Marine Exptl. Sta., 1989-98, assoc. dean Coll. Agrl. Sci., 1998—2002. Pres., trustee Newport Public Libr., 1991-92, Yaquina Bay Econ. Found., Newport, 1991-92; chmn. Oreg. Coast Aquarium, 1983-95. Recipient Pres. award Newport Rotary, 1984-85. Mem. South Slough Mgmt. Commn., American Soc. Pharm. and Exptl. Therapy, West Pharm. Soc., Soc. Toxicology, Soc. Exptl. Biol. Med. (n.w. divsn., pres. 1978, 82, 87), Pacific N.W. Assn. Toxicologists (chair 1985-86, coun. 1991-93), Nat. Assn. Marine Lab. (pres. elect 1998-99, 2000-02), Western Assn. Marine Lab. (pres. 1993). Avocations: woodworking, reading, walking, scuba diving, gardening. Home: South Beach, Oreg. Died May 5, 2014.

**WEDDING, CHARLES RANDOLPH,** architect; b. St. Petersburg, Fla., Nov. 16, 1934; s. Charles Reid and L. Marion (Whitaker) W.; m. Audrey Whitsel, Aug. 18, 1956 (div. Apr. 1979); children: Daryl L., Douglas R., Dorian B.; m. Vonnie Sue Hayes, June 22, 1984 (div. Dec. 1991); stepchildren: Stephanie W., Brian E.; m. June A. Free, Mar. 31, 1993; stepchildren: Gregory, Kristine. BArch, U. Fla., 1957. Registered arch., Fla., Ga., N.C., S.C., Del., Va., Tex., Ill., Ind., Kans., La., Mo., Okla., Tenn. Arch. in tng. Harvard & Jolly AIA, St. Petersburg, 1957-60; arch., prin., pres. Wedding & Assocs., St. Petersburg, from 1960. Mayor City of St. Petersburg, 1973-75; past chmn. Pinellas County Com. of 100, Bldg. Dept. Survey Team, City of St. Petersburg; trustee All Children's Hosp., 1968-70; sect. leader St. Petersburg United Fund, 1965-70; mem. city coun. Action Team for Pier Redevel., 1967-68; mem. exec. com. Goals for City of St. Petersburg, 1970-72; den leader Webelos, Boy Scouts Am., 1971-72; chmn., trustee Canterbury Sch. YMCA, 1968-72; mem. adv. com. Tomlinson Vocat. Sch., 1969-79; past trustee Mus. Fine Arts; past bd. dirs. Neighborly Ctr., Jr. Achievement Pinellas County; chair Downtown Partnership, 2001—, Mcpl. Pier Task Force, City of Petersburg, 2009-; chair Pinelles County Local PLanning Agy., 2010-. Served to 1st lt. U.S. Army, 1958-60. Fellow AIA (5 Silver Spike awards, Merit of Honor, Medal of Honor); mem. Am. Soc. Landscape Archs., St. Petersburg Assn. Archs. (past pres.), Fla. Assn. Archs. (8 Merit Design awards), St. Petersburg Yacht Club, Suncoasters Club. Republican. Episcopalian. Avocations: sailing, hunting, golf, tennis. Home: Saint Petersburg, Fla. Died Feb. 6, 2012.

**WEDZICHA, WALTER,** foreign language educator; b. Jezor, Poland, June 5, 1920; came to U.S., 1946; s. Wladyslaw and Maria (Kruczek) W.; m. Sabina Purzynska, Nov. 28, 1945; children: John M., Christine S. AB, U. Miami, 1965; MA, U. Pitts., 1966. Attaché Consulate Gen. of Poland, NYC, 1946-49; acct. Miami, 1950-65; asst. prof. German and Russian Clarkson U., Potsdam, N.Y., 1967-86, prof. emeritus, from 1986. Author: Song of the City, 1957, From Love of God and All Creation, 1992. Fellow NDEA, U. Pitts., 1965-66; grantee NEH, Ohio State U., 1977, NEH, U. Ill., 1978. Mem. MLA. Democrat. Avocations: photography, music, gardening. Deceased.

**WEEKES, SHIRLEY M.,** artist; b. Buffalo, May 9, 1917; d. Ray Roscoe and Loretta Marie (Ent) Thompson; m. Thomas Weekes Weekes, Mar. 27, 1942; children: Judith, Thomas. Grad., Detroit Art Acad., 1939. One-man shows include Frye Mus., Seattle, 1967, 1972, Haines Gallery, 1973, 1975, Challis Gallery, Laguna Beach, Calif., 1970, 1972, 1974, exhibited in group shows at Frye Mus., 1965—69, 1971—75, Seattle Art Mus., 1972, Represented in permanent collections Frye Mus., Laguna Beach Mus. Art. Mem.: San Diego Watercolor Soc. Home: Oceanside, Calif. Died May 1993.

**WEEKES, TREVOR C.,** astrophysicist; b. Dublin, May 21, 1940; came to U.S. 1966; s. Gerard and Florence (Murtagh) W.; m. Ann Katherine Owens, Sept. 30, 1964; children: Karina, Fiona, Lara. BSc, U. Coll. Dublin, 1962, PhD, 1966; DSc (hon.), Nat. U. Ireland, 1978; D (hon.), U. Chgo. Lectr. Univ. Coll. Dublin, 1964-66; postdoctoral fellow NRC, Cambridge, Mass., 1966-67; astrophysicist Smithsonian Astrophysics Observatory, 1967-92, sr. astrophysicist, 1992—2014; resident dir. Whipple Observatory, Amado, Ariz., 1969-76. Vis.prof. Royal Greenwich Obs., U.K., 1980-81; adj. prof. physics U. Ariz., 1995-2014 Assoc. editor astrophysics Phys. Rev. Letters, 1994-96. Recipient Bruno Rossi prize, American Astronomical Soc., 1997, Yodh prize, Internat. Union Pure & & Applied Physics, 2007. Mem. American Astron. Soc., American Phys. Soc., Royal Astron. Soc. Democrat. Roman Catholic. Home: Sahuarita, Ariz. Died May 26, 2014.

**WEGE, PETER MELVIN,** retired office furniture manufacturer executive; b. Grand Rapids, Mich., Feb. 19, 1920; s. Peter Martin and Sophia Louise Wege; children: Mary, Susan, Peter Martin II, Christopher Henry, Diana, Johanna, Jonathan. Attended, U. Mich., 1940—41, D (hon.), Aquinas Coll.; LLD (hon.), U. Mich., 2007. Joined Steelcase, Inc., 1946, vice chmn. Founder The Wege Found., 1967. Author: Economicology, 1998. Pres. The Wege Found.; pres. bd. dirs. Grand Rapids Art Mus. Found. Served in US Army Air Force, 1941—46. Recipient Conservation Achievement award, Nat. Wildlife Fedn., 2001, Russell G. Mawby award for Philanthropy, 2006, Paul G. Goebel Disting. Alumni in Athletics award, 2007, David Smith Humanitarian award, 2009. Died July 7, 2014.

**WEHLER, HANS-URLICH,** historian, educator; b. Freudenberg, Siegerland, Germany, Sept. 11, 1931; m. Renate Pfitsch, 1958; children: Markus, Fabian, Dominik. Ed., U. Bonn, Ohio U.; PhD, U. Cologne, Germany, 1960. Asst. prof. German history, Colgne, Germany, 1968—70; asst. prof. American history John F. Kennedy Inst. Free U., Berlin, 1970—71; profl., chmn. Dept. History U. Bielefeld, Germany, 1971—96, prof. emeritus, 1996—2014. Vis. prof. Harvard U., Mass., 1972, Mass., 1989, Princeton U., NJ, 1976, Stanford U., Calif., 1983—84, Calif., 2004, U. Bern, 1987—88, Yale U., Conn., 1997. Author: many books; contbr. articles to profl. journals. Mem.: American Hist. Assn. (hon.; fgn. mem.), American Acad. Arts & Sciences (hon.; fgn. mem. 2006). Died July 5, 2014.

**WEIDA, LEWIS DIXON,** marketing analyst, consultant; b. Moran, Ind., Apr. 23, 1924; s. Charles Ray and Luella Mildred (Dixon) Weida. Attended, Kenyon Coll., 1943, Purdue U., 1946; BS, Ind. U., 1948; MS, Columbia U., 1950. Mgr. statis. analysis unit Gen. Motors Acceptance Corp., NYC, 1949—55; asst. to exec. v.p. Am. Express Co., 1955—82. With USAAF, 1943—46, PTO. Mem.: Internat. Platform Assn., Masons. Democrat. Died 2006.

**WEIDENBAUM, MURRAY LEW,** economist, educator; b. Bronx, NY, Feb. 10, 1927; s. David and Rose (Warshaw) Weidenbaum; m. Phyllis Green, June 13, 1954; children: Susan, James, Laurie. BBA, CCNY, 1948; MA, Columbia U., 1949; MPA, Princeton U., 1954, PhD, 1958; LLD, Baruch Coll., 1981, U. Evansville, 1983, McKendree Coll., 1993. Fiscal economist Bur. Budget, Washington, 1949—57; corporate economist Boeing Co., Seattle, 1958—62; sr. economist Stanford Rsch. Inst., Palo Alto, Calif., 1962—63; faculty mem. Washington U., St. Louis, 1964—66, prof., chmn. dept. economics, 1966—69, Mallinckrodt prof., 1971—2014, dir. Ctr. for Study American Bus., 1974—81, Washingon U., St. Louis, 1982—95; chmn. Ctr. for Study American Bus. Washington U., St. Louis, 1995—2000; asst. sec. for econ. policy US Dept. Treasury, Washington, 1969—71; chmn. Coun. of Econ. Advisors Exec. Office of the Pres., Washington, 1981—82; hon. chmn. Weidenbaum Ctr. on the Economy, Govt. & Public Policy, St. Louis, 2001—14. Chmn. rsch. adv. com. St. Louis Regional Indsl. Devel. Corp., 1965—69; exec. sec. Pres.'s Com. on Econ. Impact of Def. & Disarmament, 1964; mem. US Financial Investment Advisory Panel, 1970—72; chmn. US Commn. to Rev. the Trade Deficit, 1999—2000. Author: Federal Budgeting, 1964, Modern Public Sector, 1969, Economics of Peacetime Defense, 1974, Economic Impact of the Vietnam War, 1967, Government-Mandated Price Increases, 1975, The Future of Business Regulation, 1980, Rendezvous With Reality: The American Economy After Reagan, 1988, Rendezvous With Reality: The American Economy After Reagan, paperback edit., 1990, Business, Government, and the Public, 1990, Small Wars, Big Defense, 1992, The Bamboo Network, 1996, Business and Government in the Global Marketplace, 2004, One-Armed Economist, 2004, Advising Reagan: Making Economic Policy, 1981-82, 2005, Competition of Ideas, 2008; mem. editl. bd.: Publius, 1971—2004, Jour. Econ. Issues, 1972—75, Challenge, 1974—81, from 1983, Business and the Contemporary World, 1997—2000. With US Army, 1945. Recipient Alexander Hamilton medal, US Dept. Treasury, 1971, Disting. Writer award, Georgetown U., Award for Disting. Tchg., Freedoms Found., 1980, Award for Best Book in Economics, Assn. American Publications, 1993; named Banbury fellow, Princeton U., 1952—54; named to The Free Market Hall of Fame, 1983. Fellow: Internat. Acad. Mgmt., American Acad. Arts & Sciences, Assn. for Pvt. Enterprise Edn. (Adam Smith award 1986), City Coll. Alumni Assn. (Townsend Harris medal 1969), Soc. Tech. Comm., Nat. Assn. Bus. Economists, Cosmos. Died Mar. 20, 2014.

**WEIGLE, MAURICE S.,** lawyer; b. Chgo., Dec. 2, 1912; s. Maurice and Grace M. (Stein) Weigle; m. Helen Rosenberg Weigle, June 22, 1937; children: Babs W. Maltenfort, Alice W. Kraus. PhB, U. Chgo., 1933, JD, 1935. Bar: Ill. 1935. Assoc. ptnr. Goldberg & Weigle, Chgo., 1936—74; ptnr. Jenner & Block, Chgo., from 1974. Served with USNR, 1945—46. Mem.: ABA, Chgo. Coun. Lawyers, Chgo. Bar Assn., Ill. Bar Assn., Birchwood (Highland Park, Ill.), Standard (Chgo.). Jewish. Died Aug. 27, 1989.

**WEIHERER, PATRICIA DEE,** retired librarian; b. West Reading, Pa., Sept. 17, 1933; d. Robert Peter and Marguerite (Sprout) Weiherer. BA, Albright Coll., Reading, Pa., 1955; MLS, Rutgers U., New Brunswick, NJ, 1961. English tchr. Manheim Ctrl., Pa., 1955—56; br. libr. Reading Pub. Libr., 1956—60, asst. ref. libr., 1961—95, ref. libr., from 1995. Democrat. United Ch. Of Christ. Avocations: piano, genealogy, needlepoint, reading. Home: Reading, Pa. Died Aug. 26, 2013.

**WEILL, ERNA,** sculptor; b. Jan. 1, 1904; Tchr. Schs., Mus., Community Ctrs. Prin. works include portraits Leonard Bernstein, Rudolph Serkin, Nathan Milstein, Andre Kostelanetz, La Guardia, F.D. Roosevelt, Prof. Martin Buber, Rabbi Leo Baeck, Prof. Linus Pauling, Dr. M.L. King, S.Y. Agnon, Golda Meir, Vladimir Horowitz, Prof. A. Heschel, Elie Wiesel, archtl. sculpture Teaneck Jewish Ctr., White Plains, Jewish Ctr., Temple Har-El, Jerusalem, La. Archtl. sculpture; one woman shows include Carleback Gallery, N.Y.C., Schoeneman Galleries, N.Y.C., Fairleigh Dickinson U., Bergen Community Mus., N.J.; exhibited in group shows at N.J. State Mus., Montclair Tchrs. Coll., Bklyn. Mus., Montclair Mus., Newark Mus., Mus. Natural History, N.Y.C., N.Y. Art Galleries, Jersey City Mus., N.Y. World's Fair, Jersey Pavillion, Lever House, N.Y., Jewish Mus., N.Y.C., Philharmoni Hall, N.Y.; represented in permanent collections Ga. State Mus., Athens, Birminham Mus., Jewish Mus., N.Y., House of Living Judaism, N.Y.C., Hyde Park Libr., Schomburg Collections, N.Y. Pub. Libr., Tel Aviv Mus., Israel, Israel Mus. Jerusalem, Hebrew U., Jerusalem, Fairleigh Dickinson U., Rutgers U., Ctr. for Study Dem. Insts., Atlanta Meml. Dr. M.L. King. Grantee

Meml. Found. Jewish Culture; recipient Artist award Craftsman of N.Y., Interchurch Ctr. Show award 1975, Best in Sculpture award. Home: Vestal, NY. Died Apr. 25, 1996.

**WEINBLATT, SEYMOUR SOLOMON,** lawyer; b. Bklyn., May 6, 1922; s. David and Lillian (Kantor) W.; m. Dorothy Robinovitz, Mar. 16, 1946 (div. May 1973); children: Jeffrey Howard, Jan Robin; m. Elizabeth Jean King Shelton, June 3, 1973; children: Eric H. Waser, Mark S. Waser (dec.). BA in Zoology, Ind. U., 1947; JD with honors, Rutgers U., 1950, postgrad., 1950-53. Bar: N.J. 1951, U.S. Dist. Ct. N.J. 1951, U.S. Supreme Ct. 1957, U.S. Ct. Appeals (3d cir.) 1975. Atty. City of Manville, N.J., 1962-64, atty. bd. edn. N.J., 1962-66; of counsel Joe E. Strauss, Flemington, N.J., from 1984. Mem. bd. edn. Twp. of Bethlehem, 1977-80, pres. bd. edn., 1979; mem. planning and zoning bd. Town of Juno Beach, Fla., 1998—, vice chmn. bd., 2001—. Mem. ABA, Hunterdon County (N.J.) Bar Assn., Am. Legion, Jewish War Vets. Jewish. Avocations: real estate, sports, journalism. Home: Juno Beach, Fla. Deceased.

**WEINER, MICHAEL S.,** labor union administrator, lawyer; b. Paterson, NJ, Dec. 21, 1961; s. Isaac Weiner and Regina Pomper; m. Diane Margolin; children: Margie, Grace, Sally. B in Polit. Economy, Williams Coll., Williamstown, Mass., 1983; JD, Harvard Law Sch., Mass., 1986. Law clk., Hon. H. Lee Sarokin US Dist Ct. NJ, Newark, 1986—88; union lawyer Maj. League Baseball Players Assn., NYC, 1988—2004, gen. counsel, 2004—09, exec. dir., gen. counsel, 2009—13, exec. dir., 2013. Named one of The 50 Most Influential People in Sports Bus., Street & Smith's SportsBus. Jour., 2009. Died Nov. 21, 2013.

**WEINERT, HENRY M.,** biomedical company executive; b. Nordhausen, Kassel, Fed. Republic Germany, May 31, 1940; s. Heinrich V. Nennenstiehl and Martha H. Weinert; m. Helen Koopmans, Feb. 14, 1966 (div. June 1982); children: Jason C., Brian T.; m. Kerri V. Keaton, Sept. 25, 1989. BA in Sci., Columbia Coll., 1962; MBA, Harvard Grad. Sch. Bus., 1970. Med. rsch. assoc. Columbia Univ., NYC, 1964-65; exec. v.p., founder Clin. Diagnostic Lab., New Haven, Conn., 1966-68; dir. planning, bus. devel. Lederle Labs./Am. Cyan., Pearl River, N.Y., 1970-73, mktg. dir., 1973-74; bus. devel. mgr. Corning (N.Y.) Glass Works, 1974-77; pres., founder Boston Biomed. Cons., Waltham, Mass., from 1977. Spl. ltd. ptnr. MedVenture Assocs., San Francisco, 1965—, Interwest Ptnrs., San Francisco, 1989; presenter, lectr. in field. Patentee laser fabrication of microsuture needles; contbr. articles to profl. jours. Pres. Svc. Soc., Columbia Coll., 1959; chmn. Student Union Com., Columbia Coll., 1961; treas. Class 1962, Columbia Coll., 1962-64; others. Recipient Alumni Achievement award Columbia Coll., 1962; grantee NIH, 1964-66. Mem. Biomed. Mktg. Assn. (bd. dirs. 1978-86, Recognition award 1986), Am. Assn. Clin. Chemistry, Van Slyke Soc. (bd. mem. 1991—). Lutheran. Avocations: reading science fiction and mystery novels, sailing, cars, landscaping. Deceased.

**WEINGARTEN, HERBERT N.,** lawyer; b. Detroit, Jan. 5, 1927; s. Harry and Pearl (Kandel) W.; m. Nancy Weisman, Aug. 14, 1953; children— Ann M. Weingarten Rock, James S. LL.B., U. Mich., 1951. Bar: Mich. 1951. Practice law, Detroit, from 1951; ptnr. Jacob & Weingarten, Troy, Mich., from 1957. Contbr. articles on bankruptcy, comml. law to legal publs. Served with USNR, 1945-46. Mem. Am. Bar Assn. (uniform comml. code com. 1963—, com. on comml. fin. services) Home: Birmingham, Mich. Died Apr. 18, 1991.

**WEINSTEIN, MORDECHAI MARCEL,** mathematician, researcher; b. Mogilev, Rumania, Sept. 6, 1942; s. Abraham Berl and Rebecca (Gaber) W.; m. Naomi Bardichef, Apr. 12, 1970; children: Semadar, Inbal, Amir. BS, Hebrew U., Jerusalem, 1967; MS, Weizman Inst., Rehovot, Israel, 1970; PhD, Imperial Coll. Sci. and Tech., London, 1975; postgrad., Univ. Coll., London, 1976-78. Rsch. asst. Weizman Inst., Rehovot, 1968-70; rsch. assoc. of J.T. Stuart Imperial Coll., 1975-76; rsch. assoc. of K. Stewartson Univ. Coll., 1976-78; assoc. sr. lectr. Tecnion, Haifa, Israel, 1983-84; sr. rschr. Rafael, Ministry of Def., Haifa, Israel, 1978-95. Vis. rsch. fellow City Univ., London, 1985-86, vis. sr. rsch. fellow, 1990-91; vis. prof. Tel Aviv U., 1993—. Contbr. articles to profl. jours. Recipient scholarship NASA, 1969-70, scholarship Sci. Rsch. Coun., London, 1975-76, 76-78, Vis. Sr. Rsch. Fellow award Sci. and Engring. Rsch. Coun., London, 1988, 89, 90, 93, 94. Mem. Am. Math. Soc., Israel Math. Soc., Planetary Soc., Israel Philatelic Soc. (com. 1987-92, award 1987, 89, 92), Imperial Coll. Alumni (Israel br. com. 1992-93). Avocations: history, stamp collecting/philately, reading, archeology. Home: Haifa, Israel. Died Nov. 18, 2000.

**WEINSTEIN, SIDNEY,** retired university program director; b. NYC, July 1, 1920; s. Jacob and Yetta W.; m. Celia Kahn, Mar. 6, 1943 (dec.); children: Risa, Jeri; m. Florence Landau, June 21, 1988. BA, Bklyn. Coll., 1951; MA, Columbia U., 1955; DPA, Indsl. Coll. Armed Forces, 1964. Contract adminstr. U.S. Corps Engrs., 1941-43; mgmt. analyst Dept. Army, NYC, 1946-55; dir. data processing procurement GSA, 1956-68, dep. asst. commr. automated data mgmt. services Washington, 1968-72, asst. commr. automated data and telecommunications, 1972-75; exec. dir. Assn. Computing Machinery, NYC, 1975-85; assoc. prof., dir. affiliates program Ctr. Research Info. Systems, Leonard N. Stern. Sch. Bus. NYU, 1985-99, ret., 1999. Cons. to chmn. U.S. CSC. Served with USAF, 1943-46. Recipient Exceptional service award, U.S. Govt., 1975. Mem. ABA (arbitrator 1989—), Coun. Engring. and Sci. Soc. Execs. (dir.), N.Y. Soc. Assn. Execs., Assn. Indsl. Coll. Armed Forces, Assn. Fed. Execs. Inst., Assn. Computing Machinery, Soc. Info. Mgmt. Home: New York, NY. Died Apr. 16, 2013.

**WEINSTOCK, ROBERT,** physics professor; b. Phila., Feb. 2, 1919; s. Morris and Lillian (Hirsch) W.; m. Elizabeth Winch Brownell, Apr. 22, 1950; children: Frank Morse, Robert B. Weinstock-Collins. AB, U. Pa., 1940; PhD, Stanford U., 1943. Instr. physics Stanford U., Calif., 1943—44, instr. math., 1946—50, acting asst. prof. math., 1950—54; rsch. assoc. radar countermeasures Radio Rsch. Lab. Harvard U., Cambridge, Mass., 1944—45; asst. prof. U. Notre Dame, Ind., 1954—58, assoc. prof. math., 1958—59; vis. assoc. prof. math. Oberlin Coll., Ohio, 1959—60, assoc. prof., 1960—66, prof. physics, 1966—83, emeritus prof., from 1983. Author: Calculus of Variations, 1952; contbr. numerous tech. articles to profl. jours. Fellow AAAS, Ohio Acad. Sci.; mem. ACLU, Am. Assn. Physics Tchrs., Am. Phys. Soc., History of Sci. Soc., Brit. Soc. for the History of Sci., Sigma Xi. Avocations: concert going, reading. Died 2006.

**WEINY, GEORGE AZEM,** physical education educator, consultant; b. Keokuk, Iowa, July 24, 1930; s. George Dunn and Emma Vivian (Kraushaar) W.; m. Jane Louise Eland, Sept. 29, 1956 (div. 1985); children: Tami L., Tomas A., Aaron A., Arden G.; m. Lori Arlene Rowe, Aug. 6, 1985; children: Austin George, Breck Philip. BA, Iowa Wesleyan Coll., 1957; MA, State U. Iowa, 1962; PhD, U. Beverly Hills, 1980. Phys. dir. YMCA, Keokuk, 1956-57; asst. dir. pub. relations Iowa Wesleyan Coll., Mt. Pleasant, Iowa, 1957-58; prin., tchr., coach Hillsboro (Iowa) High Sch., 1958-59; tchr., coach Burlington (Iowa) High Sch. and Jr. Coll., 1959-62, Pacific High Sch., San Bernardino, Calif., 1962-67; prof. phys. edn. Calif. State U., San Bernardino, from 1967. Ednl. cons. Belau Modekngei Sch., West Caroline Islands, 1984-85; swim meet dir. Nat. Collegiate Athletic Assn., 1982-84, 86-94; tng. dir. for ofcls. So. Calif. Aquatics Fedn., 1967-78; asst. swim coach Calif. State U., Chico, 1979, guest lectr. summer program water safety & mainstreaming spl. populations Calif. State U., San Bernardino, 1990-93; scuba tour guide Dive Maui Resort, Hawaii, 1982-83; salvage diver U.S. Trust Territories, 1973; coach YMCA swim team, San Bernardino, 1962-77, 84—. Editor: Swimming Rules and Case Studies, 1970-73; author: Snorkeling Fun for Everyone, 1982; contbr. articles to profl. jours. Mem. county water safety com. ARC, San Bernardino, 1968-80, 88-90, 91—; bd. dirs. YMCA, San Bernardino, 1970-77; mem. Bicentennial Commn., San Bernardino, 1975-76. Sgt. U.S. Army, 1953-55, Iowa N.G., 1955-58. Decorated Combat Infantryman's badge, Good Conduct medal, Nat. Def. Svc. medal, Korean Svc. medal, UN Svc. medal, Presdl. Unit citation; recipient Outstanding Svc. award So. Calif. Aquatics Fedn., 1978. Mem. ARC Water Safety (40-yr. Outstanding Svc. award 1990), Profl. Assn. Diving Instrs. (cert.), Nat. Assn. Underwater Instrs. (cert.), Am. Assn. Health Phys. Edn. Recreation and Dance, Coll. Swim Coaches Assn. Am. (25 Yr. Svc. award 1987), Nat. Fedn. Interscholastic Ofcls. Assn. (25 yr. award 1991), Am. Swim Coaches Assn. (cert.), Nat. Interscholastic Swim Coaches Assn. (25yr. Svc. award 1985), Sea Sons Dive Club (Rialto Calif., pres. 1982-83, sec. 1983-92, Diver of Yr. award 1983, 87, 91). Avocation: scuba diving. *Personal philosophy: Dare to be different. My own self at my very best all the time.* Deceased.

**WEIS, JOSEPH FRANCIS, JR.,** federal judge; b. Pitts., Mar. 12, 1923; s. Joseph Francis and Mary (Flaherty) Weis; m. Margaret Horne Weis, Dec. 27, 1958 (dec. 2012); children: Maureen, Joseph Francis, Christine. BA, Duquesne U., 1947; JD, U. Pitts., 1950; LLD (hon.), Dickinson Coll., 1989. Bar: Pa. 1950. Pvt. practice, Pitts., 1950—68; judge Ct. Common Pleas, Allegheny County, Pa., 1968—70, US Dist. Ct. (western dist.) Pa., Pa., 1970—73, US Ct. Appeals (3rd Cir.), Pitts., 1973—88, sr. judge, 1988—2014. Adj. prof. law U. Pitts., 1986—2014; chmn. Internat. Jud. Conf. the Joint Am.-Can. Appellate Judges Conf., Toronto, 1986, London, 1985; futurist subcom. bicentennial com. Ct. Common Pleas, Allegheny County, Pa., 1988; participant programs legal medicine, Rome, London; mem. Am.-Can. Legal Exch., 1987, US Jud. Conf., 1998—2004, com. on adminstrn. bankruptcy sys., subcommittee on jud. improvements, 1983—87, chmn. civil rules com., 1986—87, chmn. standing com. rules of practice and procedure, 1988. Contbr. articles to profl. jours. Active Mental Health and Mental Retardation Bd., Allegheny County, 1970—73, Leukemia Soc., 1970—73, Disabled American Vets., Cath. War Vets, Mil. Order of the World Wars; trustee Forbes Hosp. Sys., Pitts., 1969—74; bd. adminstrn. Cath. Diocese Pitts., 1971—83. Capt. US Army, 1943—48. Decorated Bronze Star, Purple Heart with oak leaf cluster, French War Cross with palm; recipient St. Thomas More award, 1971, Phillip Amram award, 1991, Edward J. Devitt Disting. Svc. to Justice award, 1993, History Makers award, 1997, Disting. Alumni award, U. Pitts., 2011. Fellow: American Bar Found., Internat. Acad. Trial Lawyers (hon.); mem.: ABA (chmn. appellate judges' conf. 1981—83), Inst. Jud. Adminstrn., American Judicature Soc., Acad. Trial Lawyers Allegheny County (past pres., Disting. Svc. award 1997, Jud. Leadership and Excellence award 2004), Allegheny Bar Assn. (past v.p.), Pa. Bar Assn., French Legion of Honor (knight), 4th Armored Divsn. Assn., American Legion, Knights of Malta, KC. Roman Catholic. Home: Pittsburgh, Pa. Died Mar. 19, 2014.

**WEISBERG, LEONARD R.,** retired engineering executive, researcher; b. NYC, Oct. 17, 1929; s. Emanuel E. and Esther (Raynes) W.; m. Frances Simon, Mar. 23, 1980; children: Glenna Weisberg Andersen, Orren Weisberg Falk, Frances Weisberg Brookner. BA magna cum laude, Clark U., 1950; MA, Columbia U., 1952. Rsch. asst. Watson Labs. IBM, NYC, 1953-55; with RCA Labs., Princeton, NJ, 1955-71, mem. tech. staff, 1955-66, head rsch. group, 1966-69, dir. semicondr. device rsch. lab., 1969-71; dir. materials rsch. lab. Itek Corp., Lexington, Mass., 1972-74, v.p., dir. ctrl. rsch. lab., 1974-75; dir. electronics tech U.S. Dept. Def., Washington, 1975-79; v.p. rsch. and engring. Honeywell Inc., Mpls., 1980-94, ret., 1994. Adv. group on electron devices US Dept. Def., 1981—99. Contbr. articles to profl. jours. Recipient award for initiating VHSIC program U.S. Dept. Def., 1979. Fellow IEEE; mem. Am. Phys. Soc., Sigma Xi. Died Mar. 23, 2014.

**WEISSMAN, ESTHER SWERDLOW,** lawyer; b. New Phila., Ohio, June 23, 1932; d. Robert and Sylvia (Heller) Swerdlow; children: Robert, Terri. Student, Temple U., 1949—51; LLB cum laude, Cleve. Marshall Law Sch., 1961. Bar: Ohio 1961, US Dist. Ct. (Northern Dist.) Ohio 1968, US Supreme Ct. 1965, US Ct. Appeals (6th cir.). Assoc. Day & Berkman, Cleve., 1962—63, Berger & Kirschenbaum, Cleve., 1963—77; legal asst. to clk. Cleve. Mcpl. Cts., 1977—79; sole practice Esther S. Weissman Co. L.P.A., Cleve., from 1978. Contbr. articles. Mem.: Am. Arbitration Assn., Ohio Acad. Trial Lawyers (chmn. workers compensation sect. 1971—78, pres. award 1976, svc. award 1977, 1979, 1982), Cleve. Bar Assn., Cuyahoga County Bar Assn. (chmn. civil liberties 1983—85), Ohio Bar Assn. Democrat. Deceased.

**WEIZSÄCKER, CARL FRIEDRICH VON,** philosophy educator; b. Kiel, Fed. Republic Germany, June 28, 1912; s. Ernst Freiherr and Marianne (von Graevenitz) von W.; m. Gundalena Wille, Mar. 31, 1937; children: Carl Christian, Ernst Ulrich, Heinrich, Elisabeth Raiser. Student, U. Leipzig, Göttingen, Germany, 1929-33; student, U. Copenhagen, 1929-33; PhD, U. Leipzig, 1933, Habilitation, 1936. Asst. inst. theoretical physics U. Leipzig, 1934-36; lectr. Kaiser-Wilhelm-Inst., Berlin, 1936-42; assoc. prof. U. Strasbourg (France), 1942-44; dept. head Max-Planck-Inst. for Physics, Göttingen, 1946-57; hon. prof. U. Göttingen, 1946-57; prof. philosophy U. Hamburg (Fed. Republic Germany), 1957-69; dir. Max-Planck-Inst. on Preconditions Human Life in Modern World, Starnberg, Fed. Republic Germany, 1970-80. Author: The History of Nature, 1951, The World View of Physics, 1952, The Relevance of Science, 1964, The Politics of Peril, 1978, The Unity of Nature, 1979, The Ambivalence of Progress, 1988, Die Atomkerne, 1937, Bedingungen des Friedens, 1963, Der ungesicherte Friede, 1969, Fragen zur Weltpolitik, 1975, Wege in der Gefahr, 1977, Der Garten des Menschlichen, 1978, Diagnosen zur Aktualität, 1979, Der bedrohte Friede, 1981, Wahrnehmung der Neuzeit, 1983, Aufbau der Physik, 1985, Die Zeit drängt, 1986, Bewusstseinswandel, 1988, Bedingungen der Freilieit, 1990, Der Mensch in seiner Geschichte, 1991. Recipient Max-Planck medal, 1957, 66, Goethe prize City of Frankfurt, 1958, Grand Cross of the Order of Merit with star, Fed. Republic Germany, 1959, Peace prize of order Pour le Mérite, 1961, Peace prize German book trade, 1983, Arnold Reymont prize for physics, 1965, Wilhelm Boelsche gold medal, 1965, Erasmus prize, 1969, Ernst Hellmut Vits prize, 1980, Heine prize City of Düsseldorf, 1983, Sigmund-Freud prize Deutschen Akademie für Sprache und Dichung, 1988, Theodor-Heuss-Preis, 1988, Templeton prize for Progress in Religion, 1989. Mem. Deutsche Akademie der Naturforscher Leopoldina (Halle, German Dem. Republic), Akademie der Wissenschaften (Göttingen), Joachim-Jungius-Gesellschaft der Wissenschaten (Hamburg), Bayerische Akademie der Wissenschaften (Munich), Deutsche Akademie für Sprach und Dichtung (Darmstadt), Osterreichische Akademie der Wissenschaften (Vienna), Sächsische Akademie der Wissenschaften zu Leipzig. Avocations: walking, chess. Home: Starnberg, Germany. Died Apr. 28, 2007.

**WELCH, BOB (ROBERT LYNN WELCH),** retired professional baseball player; b. Detroit, Nov. 3, 1956; m. Mary Ellen Welch; children: Dylan, Riley, Kelly. Student, Eastern Mich. U. Pitcher L.A. Dodgers, 1978-87, Oakland Athletics, 1988—94; pitching coach Ariz. Diamondbacks. Co-author (with George Vecsey): Five O'Clock Comes Early: A Cy Young Award-Winner Recounts His Greatest Victory, 1991. Recipient Cy Young award, 1990; named to The Sporting News All-Star team, 1990, Sporting News American League Pitcher of Yr., 1990. Died June 10, 2014.

**WELCH, JACK HAMILL,** retired internist; b. Columbus, Ohio, July 14, 1915; s. John Orr and Evelyn (Bigger) Welch; m. Mary Elaine Childs, Apr. 25, 1943 (div. 1976); children: David, Pamela, Michael; m. Alice Elizabeth Welch, May 6, 1978. BA, Ohio State U., 1936; MD, Duke U., 1940. Diplomate Am. Bd. Internal Medicine, Nat. Bd. Med. Examiners. From intern to resident Henry Ford Hosp., Detroit, 1940-42, 46-48; pvt. practice internal medicine Columbus, 1948-50, Hollywood, Calif., 1950-52, San Fernando Valley, 1952-83; ret., 1983. Instr. medicine White Meml. Hosp. Loma Linda Sch. Medicine, LA, 1954—56; moderator Nat. Issues Forum, 1985—91, participant, 1992—94; active supporter Calif. Proposition 186 Universal Health Care, Fresno, 1994. Author: Battalion Surgeon WWII, 1996. Mem. Visions of Cmty., 1984—94, chair, 1990—92; initiator Peace and Justice com. United Ch. of Christ, Fresno, 1990—97; co-founder, bd. dirs. Fresno Ctr. for Non Violence, from 1992, Black.White Dialogue Group, Fresno, from 1997. With M.C. US Army, 1942—45, ETO. Decorated Bronze Star; fellow, Ctrl. Calif. Inst., prog. pub. policy rsch. found., Fresno, 2003. Mem.: ACP, AMA, Fgn. Policy Assn., Physicians for Social Responsibility (ho. dels. 1987—88). Democrat. Avocations: singing, writing, walking, tv, golf. Died Feb. 10, 2008.

**WELLER, GEORGE ANTHONY,** foreign correspondent; b. Boston, July 13, 1907; s. George J. and Matilda (McAleer) W.; m. Katherine Deupree, 1932 (div. 1944); 1 dau., Ann; m. Charlotte Ebener, Jan. 23, 1948; 1 son, Anthony. Student, Roxbury Latin Sch., 1919-25; AB, Harvard U.,

1929; student, Max Reinhardt Sch., U. Vienna, 1930-31. Tchr. Evans Ranch Sch., Tucson, 1929-30; fgn. corr. N.Y. Times, Greece and Balkans, 1932-36; dir. Homeland Found., 1938-40; war corr. Chgo. Daily News, Balkans, Belgian Congo, Abyssinia, Singapore, Java, New Guinea, Solomons, 1940-72; roving corr. Mediterranean, Balkans, Middle East and periodically, Southeast Asia and U.N.; now fgn. corr. in Middle East and Mediterranean. Actor, Max Reinhardt Theater, Vienna, Austria, 1931; Author: Not to Eat, Not For Love, 1933, Clutch and Differential, 1936, Singapore is Silent, 1943, Bases Overseas, 1944, The Crack in The Column, 1949, The Paratroops, 1958, The Story of Submarines, 1960, plays Second Saint of Cyprus (winner internat. drama contest 1962), Walking Time, 1965; translator (pen-name Michael Wharf): Fontamara (Ignazio Silone), 1934; Lectr., contbr. fiction, articles to nat. mags. Recipient Pulitzer prize for journalism, 1943; George Polk Meml. award L.I.U., 1955; Navy Pub. Service pin and citation for ednl. services, 1968; Scarfoglio prize for journalism (Italy), 1984; Nieman fellow advanced study Harvard U., 1947-48 Fellow Explorers Club (N.Y.C.); mem. Dramatists Guild, Phi Beta Kappa (hon.) Clubs: Overseas Press (N.Y.C.); Stampa Estera (Rome) (pres. 1954-55, v.p. 1973-74). 1st war corr. to qualify as trained paratrooper in Pacific, 1943. Died Dec. 19, 2002.

**WELLINGTON, WILLIAM GEORGE,** entomologist, ecologist, educator; b. Vancouver, BC, Can., Aug. 16, 1920; s. George and Lilly (Rae) W.; m. Margret Ellen Reiss, Sept. 22, 1959; children: Katherine Jean, Stephen Ross. BA, U. B.C., 1941; MA, U. Toronto, 1945, PhD, 1947. Meteorol. officer Can. Meteorol. Svc., Toronto, 1942-45; rsch. entomologist Can. Dept. Agr., Sault Sainte Marie, Ont., 1946-51; head bioclimatology sect. Can. Dept. Forestry, Sault Sainte Marie, Ont., Victoria, B.C., 1951-67, prin. scientist Victoria, 1964-68; prof. ecology U. Toronto, Toronto, 1968-70; dir. Inst. Animal Resource Ecology, U. B.C., Vancouver, 1973—86, prof. plant sci. and resource ecology, 1970-86, hon. prof. dept. plant sci., from 1986, prof. emeritus, from 1986; Killam sr. rsch. fellow U. B.C., 1980-81. Inaugural lectr. C.E. Atwood Meml. Seminar Series, Dept. Zoology, U. Toronto, 1993; vis. prof. NC State U., 1972, 75, 81, San Diego State U., 1975, Laval U., 1981, U. Calgary, 1983, Simon Fraser U., 1987. Contbr. articles to profl. jours. Fellow Entomol. Soc. Can. (pres. 1976-78, Gold medal 1968), Royal Soc. Can., Explorers Club; mem. Am. Meteorol. Soc. (award 1969), Entomol. Soc. Am. (C. J. Woodworth award 1979), Japanese Soc. Population Ecology, Entomol. Soc. Ont., Am. Philatelic Soc. Club. Anglican. Home: Vancouver, Canada. Died Nov. 25, 2008.

**WELLS-BARNETT, IDA,** political activist, educator; b. 1862; Tchr. Part-owner Memphis Star newspaper. Contbr. articles to profl. publs. Mem. of del. to Pres. McKinley demanding govt. action in lynching case, S.C.; co-founder NAACP; active Negro Women's Club movement; active in women's suffrage and blocking sch. segregation. Died 1931.

**WELLS-MAXWELL, VIOLET,** writer, artist; b. Redkey, Ind., Aug. 3, 1927; d. James William Philebaum and Etta Catherine Hunt; m. Paul Eugene Wells, Sept. 5, 1947 (dec. May 1975); children: Carol Parrott, Randy Wells, Joy Wells; m. Rudolph Neff Maxwell, Sept. 22, 1990 (dec. Aug. 2002). BBA, Olivet Nazarene U., 1949. Sec. Olivet Nazarene U., Kankakee, Ill., 1947-49; receptionist Speech Clinic Ohio State U., 1950-54; art and music instr. Ea. Nazarene Coll., Boston, 1955-69; art tchr., 1960-99; receptionist Office for Fin. Aid to Students Mt. Vernon (Ohio) Nazarene Coll., 1970-73; realtor assoc. Gtr. Ohio Realty, Mt. Vernon, 1974-76; real estate assoc. Century 21 Dalbec, Willsboro, NY, 1976-82; nutrition supr. Shaklee Products, Mt. Vernon, Ohio, 1990—2002. Exhbns. include Dixie Days Street Fair, Mt. Vernon, 1997, Dan Emmett Festival, 1994-96, Mt. Vernon (Ohio) News, 1988, Lake Holm Ch. Gallery, Mt. Vernon, 1988, Heritage Hall Gallery, Mt. Vernon, 1996-98. Mem. ch. choir, Mt. Vernon, 1970-75; active Celebration of the Arts H.S., Mid. Sch., Mt. Vernon, 1992-99 Mem. Poetry Appreciation, Mt. Vernon Pub. Libr., Knox Valley Art League Avocations: Mark Twain, poetry, singing, restoring art work. Died Sept. 21, 2006.

**WELNA, CECILIA,** retired mathematics professor, dean; b. New Britain, Conn., July 15, 1927; d. Joseph and Sophie (Roman) Welna. BS, St. Joseph Coll., 1949; MA, U. Conn., 1952, PhD, 1960. Instr. Mt. St. Joseph Acad., 1949-50; asst. instr. U. Conn., 1950-55; instr. U. Mass., Amherst, 1955-56; prof., chmn. dept. math. and physics U. Hartford, 1956—82, dean Coll. Edn., Nursing and Health Professions, 1982—93, prof. math., from 1993. Mem.: Math. Assn. Am., Nat. Council Tchrs. Math., Assn. Tchrs. Math. Conn., Sigma Xi. Home: Berlin, Conn. Died Mar. 8, 2012.

**WELTMAN, HARRY,** retired professional sports team executive; b. 1933; m. Rosemary Weltman; children: Jeff, Mandy. Exec. v.p., gen. mgr. Cleve. Cavaliers, 1982-86; sr. v.p., gen. mgr. NJ Nets, Rutherford, 1987—90. Named to The Greater Cleve. Sports Hall of Fame, 2013. Died May 8, 2014.

**WEN, TIEN KUANG,** public property company executive; b. Meihsien, China, Feb. 11, 1924; m. Chong Chook Yew Wen, Dec. 24, 1946; children: Ming Kang, Sui Han, Chiu Chi, Hsia Min. BA, Fukien Christian U., China; MA, Columbia U., 1950, postgard; CD, World U. Roundtable, 1984; LLD, Marquis Found., 1988; DLitt. (hon.), Internat. U. Found., 1989; DSc, The Open Internat. U., 1994. Sec. Chinese C. of C., Chinese Mining Assn., 1952—55; chinese mgr. Banque de L'Indochine, Kuala Lumpur, 1958—71; dir. Nanyang U., 1962—74; chmn. Selangor Properties Bhd., Kuala Lumpur, from 1963, Chong Chook Yew Sdn. Bhd., TK Wen & Co. Sdn. Bhd., Bungsar Hill Holdings Sdn. Bhd., 20 other Cos.; mng. dir. Pusat Bandar Damansara Sdn. Bhd., Damansara Devel. Sdn. Bhd.; chmn. Malayan Public Library Assn., from 1957; others; CD World U. Conf., 1984; hon. chmn. bldg. com. Tung Shin Hosp., Justice of Peace, 1974. Decorated D.P.M.P. Sultan of Perak, P.S.M. King; recipient Cross of Merit, Albert Einstein Internat. Acad. Found., 1992; Brit. Coun. scholar, 1958. Mem.: Kwantung Assn. (gov. com.), Kayin Assn. (hon. chmn.), Table Tennis Assn. (hon. chmn.), Basketball Assn. (hon. chmn.). Home: Kuala Lumpur, Malaysia. Died Jan. 4, 2000.

**WERA, ANNE REGINA,** elementary and secondary educator; b. Winona, Minn., June 1, 1936; d. Bernard Stanislaus and Alvina Anne (Konter) W. BA, Viterbo Coll., 1958; MusM, U. Minn., 1960; D of Arts, Nat. Christian U., 1969, PhD in Adminstrn. K-12, 1974; MA in Edn. Adminstrn., Loras Coll., 1974. Cert. sch. supt., Wis., Ill., Iowa, Minn.; music educator, Iowa, Ill., Wis., Minn.; K-12 adminstr. Mid. sch. educator Logan Mid. Sch., LaCrosse, Wis., 1958-60; asst. to supr. music various schs., LaCrosse, 1960-64; acting head music U. Nev., Reno, 1965-66; asst. prof. U. Whitewater & River Falls, Wis., 1966-67; intern secondary adminstrn. Dubuque High Sch., Ind., 1973-74; regional supt. cons. Jo Davies County Sch. System, Galena, Ill., 1977-78; pers. head, asst. condr. Nat. Am. Youth Symphony & Chorus U.S.A., Duquaine U., Pitts., 1979-83; music specialist Dubuque Pub. Schs., Iowa, 1968-87; tchr., long term substitute, music cons. West Salem and LaCross Schs., La Crescent, Wis., 1986-90; K-12 prin. Lineville-Clio Consolidated Sch. Dist., Iowa. Masters' thesis reader Viterbo Coll., LaCrosse; tchr. praciticum; ednl. cons., 1986—. Ednl. cons. Preventive Edn., 1986-95. Mem. ASCD, IDEA, Am. Assn. Sch. Adminstrn., Nat. Assn. Secondary Sch. Principals, Wis. Sch. Music Assn., Phi Delta Kappa. Home: Onalaska, Wis. Died May 27, 1997.

**WERBA, GABRIEL,** public relations consultant; b. Paris, Feb. 28, 1930; came to U.S., 1941; s. Aron and Dina (Lewin) W.; m. Barrie Celia Sakolsky, June 1, 1952; children: Dean Steffen, Annmarie Alexandra Bragdon. BA in Journalism, U. Tex., 1948; postgrad., NYU Grad. Sch. Bus., 1948-49, NYU Sch. Law, 1961-62. Scriptwriter Paul Wendkos Prodns., NYC, 1949—53; exec. dir. Film Directions, NYC, 1953—59; account exec. Harold C. Meyers & Co., NYC, 1959-61; dir. pub. rels. and advt. Yardney Electric Corp., NYC, 1961-63, 57-59; sr. assoc. Shiefman & Assocs., Detroit, 1963-66; account exec. Merrill Lynch, Detroit, 1966-70; exec. v.p. Shiefman Werba & Assocs., Detroit, 1970-73; sr. v.p., exec. v.p., pres., chief oper. officer Anthony M. Franco, Inc., 1973-88; pres., chief exec. officer The Werba Group, Inc. and Gabriel Werba and Assocs., Inc., Detroit, 1988-94; prin. Durocher, Dixson, Werba, L.L.C., Detroit, 1994—2003; pres. Gabriel Werba & Assoc. LLC, Farmington Hills, Mich., 2004—05, Gabriel Werba & Assocs., Farmington Hills, from 2005. Contbr. articles to profl. jours. Bd. dirs. Oakland Citizens League, Detroit, 1970-93, Detroit Symphony Orch. Hall, Detroit Chamber Winds, 1985-91, The Common Ground Sanctuary, Mich., 1989-2007, vice chmn., Bloomfield Hills, 2000-06, governance com. chair, 2005-06, mem. strategic planning com., comm. com., bd. dirs. The Attic Theatre, Detroit, 1989-93, The Children's Ctr., Detroit; mem. strategic planning oversight com., chair strategic planning com., chmn. comm. com., bd. dirs., 1989-95, 1996-2002, 03-05, adv. bd., 1995-96, 2002-03; bd. dirs. NATAS, Detroit, 1993-98, The Jewish Cmty. Rels. Coun. Met. Detroit, 1989-95, 2004-2007, co-chair commn. com., 2006-2007, Margaret W. Montgomery Hosp., 1993-95, adv. bd. 1988-93; bd. dirs. Lawrence P. Doss Found., 2002—, 1st vice-chmn., 2002—09; Detroit Inst. Arts Commn. Com., 1986-92, exhibits com., 1990-2001. Named to PRSA-Detroit Hall of Fame, 2001. Mem. Nat. Investor Rels. Inst. (founding pres. Mich. chpt., past dir., pres. Detroit chpt., spkr., panelist 1969-89), Pub. Rels. Soc. Am. (bd. dirs. Detroit chpt. 1988-94, pres. 1992-93, past treas. Detroit Counselors' sect., PRSA, past co-chair nat. sect. coun., past nat. chmn. fin. sect., mem. nat. bd. ethics and profl. stds. 2003-06, chair nat. audit com. 2005-07, spkr., panelist), Fin. Analysts Soc. Detroit (past chmn. pub. info. com.), Am. Mensa (bd. dirs. 1975-95, 2003-05, nat. chmn. 1979-83), Internat. Mensa (bd. dirs. 1975-83, 85-95). Avocations: theater, art. Home: Farmington Hills, Mich. Died Nov. 7, 2012.

**WERNER, HELMUT,** business executive; b. Cologne, Germany, Sept. 2, 1936; m. Erika Werner; children: Jens, Britta. Diploma, U.Cologne, 1961. With Englebert & Co., GmbH, Aachen, Germany, 1961—67, sales mgr., 1969—70; gen. product mgr. Uniroyal Europe, Liege, Belgium, 1970—78, mng. dir., 1978—79; mem. exec. bd. Continental AG, Hannover, Germany, 1979—81, chmn., 1982—87; mem. exec. bd. Daimler Benz AG, Stuttgart; with Mercedes-Benz Aktiengesellschaft, Stuttgart, Germany. Died Feb. 6, 2004.

**WERREMEYER, GORDON DALE,** educational administrator; b. Holland, Ind., July 28, 1941; s. Roy William and Mary Norena (Hesson) W. B in Music Edn., U. Evansville, 1963; MS, Ind. State U., 1974, EdS in Edn. Adminstrn., 1977. Cert. sch. superintendent, principal. Tchr. E. Gibson Schs., Oakland City, Ind., 1963-68, Covington (Ind.) Community Sch., 1968-71; tchr., adminstr. Bloomfield (Ind.) Sch. Dist., 1971-84; adminstr. Whitko Community Schs., South Whitley, Ind., 1984-90; prin. Eminence (Ind.) Jr.-Sr. High Sch., from 1990. Mem. Bloomfield Library Bd., Ind., 1983-84. Mem. ASCD, Nat. Assn. Secondary Sch. Prins., Ind. Sch. Prins. Assn., Whitley-Huntington County Group Home, Ind. Secondary Sch. Adminstrs., Lions, Phi Mu Alpha, Phi Kappa Delta. Avocations: travel, antiques, reading, physical fitness, photography. Home: Oviedo, Fla. Died Sept. 1997.

**WERRING, HENRI TUXEN,** management educator; b. Kristiansund, Norway, Aug. 6, 1926; s. Sigurd and Germaine Amelie (Aubert) W.; m. Turid Andresen, Sept. 17, 1962 PhD in Philology, U. Oslo, Norway, 1954, practical pedagogics, 1954; mgmt. courses, 1972. Journalist Møre Dagblad/Morgenbladet, 1945-51; headmaster KA-Skolen, Oslo, 1959-65; pers. dir. Christiania Bank, Oslo, 1965-82; mng. dir. Norwegian Coll. Banking, Oslo, 1982-89, Norwegian Coll. Info. Tech., 1989-94; ednl. dir. Norwegian IT-Akademy, from 1999; dir. Inst. Polit. Knowledge, from 1999; with Werring Consulting, from 1999. Chmn. Orgn. for Tchrs. within Industry, Norwegian Inst. Pers. Adminstrn., Students of Mgmt., Com. for Pers. Mgmt. in Norwegian Banks; bd. dirs. Earth Charter Norway. Author: (books) Active Personnel Work, 1979, The Power of Talking Together, 1988, Personnel, The Scandinavian Way, 1996, Organization and Management, 1999; editor: (book) Ethics for Managers, 1987; contbr. numerous articles to newspapers and profl. mags. Chmn., polit. leader Liberal Party; mem. City Com., Oslo. Maj. Norwegian Air Force, 1955-59. Mem. Norwegian Assn. Writers, Ethics and Soc., Rotary (pres.). Liberal. Roman Catholic. Avocations: literature, football. Died Aug. 2003.

**WESLER, OSCAR,** retired mathematician, educator; b. Bklyn., July 12, 1921; s. Israel Edward and Sarah (Hartman) Wesler. BS, Coll. City N.Y., 1942; MS, N.Y. U., 1943; postgrad., Princeton U., 1943-46; PhD, Stanford U., 1955. Mem. faculty Stanford U., 1952-56, U. Mich., 1956-64; prof. stats. and math. N.C. State U., Raleigh, 1964—92, prof. emeritus, from 1992. Cons. Inst. Sci. and Tech., U. Mich., 1957—64, IBM, 1966; vis. prof. statis. Stanford U., 1962—63, 1973, 1974, 1978; vis. lectr. NSF, from 1963; vis. prof. statis. U. Calif., Berkeley, 1972—73. Author: Solutions to Problems in Theory of Games and Statistical Decisions, 1954; contbr. articles to profl. jours. Recipient Outstanding Tchr. award, N.C. State U., 1966. Mem.: Am. Math. Soc., Inst. Math. Stats., Sigma Xi, Phi Kappa Phi. Achievements include research in decision theory, probability, stochastic processes. Home: Palm Beach Gardens, Fla. Died Nov. 21, 2011.

**WESSENDORFF, ROBERT GARROW,** investor, retired banker; b. Houston, Jan. 14, 1927; s. Antone and Anne Elizabeth (Garrow) W.; m. Betty Shaw, June 24, 1950 (div. Oct. 1957); 1 child, Antone II; m. Patricia Ann Clendenin, Apr. 15, 1959; children: Suzanne Marie, Laura Garrow. BBA, U. Houston, 1951. Bookkeeper City Nat. Bank, Houston, 1950-51; various positions Bloomfield SS Co., Houston, 1951-52; with accounts payable dept. Transcontinental Gas Pipe Line, Houston, 1952-57; claims mgr. Bekins Van & Storage Co., Dallas, 1957-59; various positions, Dallas, 1959-62; note teller Preston State Bank, Dallas, 1962-66; v.p., owner White Rock Nat. Bank, Dallas, 1966-67, Comml. Nat. Bank, Dallas, 1967-69; sr. v.p., owner Commonwealth Nat. Bank, Dallas, 1969-85; pvt. investor, Dallas, from 1985. With USNR, 1944-45. Republican. Methodist. Home: Dallas, Tex. Died Aug. 16, 2008.

**WEST, CLARK DARWIN,** pediatric nephrologist, educator; b. Jamestown, NY, July 4, 1918; s. Clark Darwin and Frances Isabel (Blanchard) W.; m. Ruthann Asbury, Apr. 12, 1944 (div.); children: Charles Michael, John Clark, Lucy Frances; m. Dolores Lachenman, Mar. 1, 1986. AB, Coll. of Wooster, 1940; MD, U. Mich., 1943. Intern Univ. Hosp., Ann Arbor, Mich., 1943-44, resident in pediatrics, 1944-46; fellow in pediatrics Children's Hosp. Research Found., Cin., 1948-49, research asso., 1951-89, asso. dir., 1963-89, dir. div. immunology and nephrology, 1958-89; with cardiopulmonary lab. chest service Bellevue Hosp., NYC, 1949-51; attending pediatrician Children's Hosp., 1951-89; asst. prof. pediatrics U. Cin., 1951-55, asso. prof., 1955-62, prof., 1962-89. Mem. coms. NIH, 1965-69, 1972-73 Mem. editorial bd.: Jour. Pediatrics, 1960-79, Kidney Internat., 1977-89, Clin. Nephrology, 1989-96; contbr. articles to profl. jours. Served to capt. M.C., AUS, 1946-47. Decorated Army commendation medal; recipient recognition award Cin. Pediat. Soc., 1980, Mitchell Rubin award, 1986, Henry L. Barnett award, 1995, Daniel Drake medal, 1996, John P. Peters award, 1996; Founders award, 2008, Marvin and Emelie Snyder award, 2012. Mem. Soc. Pediatric Research (sec.-treas. 1958-62, pres. 1963-64), Am. Pediatric Soc., Am. Soc. Pediatric Nephrologists (pres. 1973-74, Founders award 2008), Am. Physiol. Soc., Am. Assn. Immunologists, Am. Soc. Nephrology, Internat. Pediatric Nephrology Assn., Sigma Xi, Alpha Omega Alpha. Achievements include research on immunopathogenesis and treatment of glomerulonephritides and in the complement system. Home: Harrison, Ohio. Died Jan. 11, 2014.

**WEST, JOHN OLIVER,** English educator; b. El Paso, Tex., Jan. 1, 1925; s. John Milton and Bertha Maxwell (Billingslea) W.; m. Lucy Lara Fischer, May 29, 1970; 1 dau. by previous marriage— Marianne; 1 son, John Martin. BA, Miss. Coll., 1948; MA, Tex. Tech. U., 1951; PhD, U. Tex. at Austin, 1964. Tchr. English and journalism Central High Sch., Jackson, Miss., 1948-50; teaching asst. English Tex. Tech. U., 1950-51, 54-55; tchr. history and journalism Gardiner High Sch., Laurel, Miss., 1951-52; asst. prof. English, journalism and pub. relations Miss. Coll., 1952-54; asst. prof. English W. Tex. State Coll., 1955-56; instr. English and journalism and pub. relations Odessa (Tex.) Coll., 1956-63; mem. faculty U. Tex. at El Paso, from 1963, prof. English, from 1966, head dept., 1965-71. Speaker in field. Author: Tom Lea: Artist in Two Mediums, 1967, Mexican-American Folklore, 1989, Cowboy Folk Humor, 1990; introduction Forty Years a Gambler on the Mississippi, 1967, Riders Across the Centuries (José Cisneros), 1984, also articles; editor Am. Folklore Newsletter, 1970-79; producer films on Hispanic folklore (foods, architecture, customs, and folk religion). County dir. Ector County (Tex.) chpt. Nat. Found., 1960-62. Served with USNR, 1942, 44-45. Mem. Tex. Folklore Soc. (councillor 1957-60, pres. 1968-69), Western Writers of Am. Home: El Paso, Tex. Died Mar. 14, 2010.

**WESTERMARK, TORBJORN ERIK GUNNAR,** chemical engineering educator; b. Solleftea, Sweden, Apr. 9, 1923; s. Gustaf E. and Mal (Samuelsson) W.; m. Ulla Hedquist, July 22, 1950; 1 child, Gunnar. MS in Chem. Engring., Royal Inst. Tech., Stockholm, 1945, D in Technology, 1961. Rsch. asst. Royal Inst. Tech., 1946-51, lectr. applied nuclear chemistry, 1952-62, prof. nuclear chemistry, 1962-88, prof. emeritus, from 1988. Contbr., co-contr. numerous articles to sci. publs., 1950— (Citation Classic award 1984 with A.G. Johnels). Bd. dirs. Swedish Coun. Mgmt. and Work Life Issues, Stockholm, 1986-89. Recipient Norblad-Ekstrand Gold medal Swedish Chem. Soc,. 1959, John Ericson Gold medal Assn. Swedish Engrs. in U.S.A., N.Y.C. and Stockholm, 1978, Rosenberg prize The Rosenberg Fund, Orebro, Sweden, 1987, (with A.G. Johnels) MIBIS prize Swedish Assn. for Water Hygiene, 1970, Environ. prize Assn. Swedish Chem. Engrs., 1991, grand prize Royal Inst. Tech., 1986. Fellow Royal Swedish Acad. Engring. Scis. (Gold medal 1989), Royal Acad. Scis. (Edlund award 1975, King Carl XVI Gustaf Gold medal 1989), Norwegian Acad. Natural Sci. (Oslo). Avocations: scandinavian floristics, ornithology. Home: Täby, Sweden. Died Oct. 2, 2001.

**WHELAN, ELIZABETH ANN MURPHY,** epidemiologist; b. NYC, Dec. 4, 1943; d. Joseph and Marion (Barrett) Murphy; m. Stephen T. Whelan, Apr. 3, 1971; 1 child, Christine B. BA, Conn. Coll., 1965; MPH, Yale U., 1967; MS, Harvard U., 1968, ScD, 1971. Coordinator County study Planned Parenthood, 1971-72; research assoc. Harvard Sch. Public Health, Boston, 1975-80; exec. dir. American Council Sci. & Health, NYC, 1980-92, pres., 1992—2014. Author: Sex and Sensibility: A New Look at Being a Woman, 1973, Making Sense Out of Sex: A New Look at Being a Man, 1974, Panic in the Pantry, 1975, 92, A Baby?...Maybe: A Guide to Making the Most Fateful Decision of Your Life, 1975, Boy or Girl?, 1976, The Pregnancy Experience, 1977, Preventing Cancer, 1978, The Nutrition Hoax, 1983, A Smoking Gun, 1984, Toxic Terror, 1984, 86, 93, Balanced Nutrition, 1988; contbr. articles to profl. jours. and consumer publs. Bd. dirs. Food and Drug Law Inst., Nat. Agrl. Legal Fund, Media Inst., N.Y. divsn. American Cancer Soc. Recipient Disting. Achievement medal Conn. Coll., 1979, award American Public Health Assn. Environ., 1992, Disting. Alumnus award Yale U., 1994-95, Ethics award American Inst. Chemists, 1996. Mem. APHA (Early Career award 1982, Homer Calver award 1992), Am. Inst. Nutrition, Am. Med. Writers Assn. (Walter Alvarez award 1986), U.S. Com. Vital Stats. Home: New York, NY. Died Sept. 11, 2014.

**WHELAN, FRANCIS C.,** federal judge; b. O'Neill, Nebr., Dec. 11, 1907; s. Edward H. and Susan (Quilty) W.; m. Patricia Brophy Lawo, Feb. 25, 1978. Student, San Diego State Coll., 1925-28; LL.B., U. Calif., 1932. Bar: Calif. 1932. Pvt. practice, San Diego, 1932-35, Los Angeles, 1948-61; asst. U.S. atty., 1935-39; spl. asst. Dept. Justice; also spl. asst. to U.S. atty. gen., 1939-48; U.S. atty. So. Dist. Calif., 1961-64; U.S. dist. judge Central Dist. Calif., from 1964; now sr. judge. Mem. ABA, Los Angeles County Bar Assn., Am. Judicature Soc. Clubs: K.C. Roman Catholic. Died Aug. 22, 1991.

**WHELAN, RAYMOND E.,** educator, researcher; b. Syracuse, NY, July 8, 1941; s. Maurice P. Whelan and Anne J. King; m. Chantal Le Sage, Dec. 30, 1979. MA in Eng., Pitts. State U., 1970; MA in French, U. Kans., 1977, PhD in French, 1985. Asst. vis. prof. Ind. Purdue U., Fort Wayne, Ind., 1985-86; asst. prof. Barton Coll., Wilson, N.C., 1986-90, assoc. prof., from 1990. Dir. academics U. Colo., Bordeaux, France, 1983-84, Academic Alliance, Wilson, N.C., 1987-93; bd. mem. Aid to Haitian Immigrants, Wilson, 1987-89. Editor Chimères, 1979-85. Mem. Crawford County Comprehensive Health Planning Commn., Pitts., Kans., 1968-75; gov. bd. Crawford County Mental Health Coun., Pitts., Kans., 1971-75. Burzle fellow U. Kans., Lawrence, 1983; scholar U. Kans., 1976, U. Clermont-Ferrand, France, 1977-78. Mem. AAUP, Am. Assn. Tchrs. French, Sigma Tau Delta, Pi Delta Phi. Avocations: tennis, boating, skiing, opera. Home: Wilson, NC. Deceased.

**WHINSTON, ARTHUR LEWIS,** lawyer; b. NYC, Feb. 5, 1925; s. Charles Nathaniel and Charlotte (Nalen) W.; m. Melicent Ames Kingsbury, Mar. 19, 1949; children: Ann Kingsbury, James Pierce, Melicent Ames, Louise Ellen, Patricia Kingsbury. B.C.E., Cornell U., 1945; MSE., Princeton U., 1947; JD, N.Y. U., 1957. Bar: N.Y. 1957, Oreg. 1964, U.S. Supreme Ct 1966, U.S. Patent Office 1958, U.S. Ct. Appeals (fed. cir.) 1959; registered profl. engr., N.Y., Oreg. Engr. Chas. N. & Selig Whinston, NYC, 1947-50; lectr. Coll. City N.Y., 1950-51; structures engr. Republic Aviation Corp., Farmingdale, NY, 1951-57; patent lawyer Arthur, Dry & Kalish, 1957-64, Klarquist Sparkman, LLP, from 1964; chmn. Oreg. Bar com. on patent, trademark and copyright law, 1968-69, 77-78, mem. com. unauthorized practice law, 1970-73, chmn., 1972-73, com. on profl. responsibility, 1973-75. Served as ensign, C.E.C., USNR, 1945-46. Recipient Fuertes medal Cornell U. Sch. Civil Engring., 1945 Mem. ABA, Oreg. Bar Assn., N.Y. Bar Assn., Multnomah County Bar Assn., Am. Intellectual Property Law Assn., N.Y. Intellectual Property Law Assn., Oreg. Patent Law Assn. (pres. 1977-78), Profl. Engrs. Oreg. (past state legis. chmn.), Sigma Xi, Chi Epsilon, Phi Kappa Phi. Clubs: Multnomah Athletic. Republican. Home: Portland, Oreg. Died Sept. 4, 2013.

**WHITACRE, JOHN,** apparel executive; b. Tacoma, 1953; s. Marshall and Hazel Whitacre; m. Genevieve Whitacre; children: Christopher, Stephanie. Student, U. Wash. With Nordstrom Inc., 1976—2000, v.p. Seattle, 1989, co-chmn., 1995-97, CEO, 1997-2000; consultant Harrods, 2001, mgr., 2001—02. Died Nov. 18, 2002.

**WHITCOMB, BENJAMIN BRADFORD, JR.,** neurosurgeon, educator; b. Ellsworth, Maine, Dec. 13, 1908; s. Benjamin Bradford and Katherine Evelyn (Laffin) W.; m. Margaret Pike, Aug. 1, 1936; children: Stuart Pike, Katherine (Mrs. Paul Joseph Dudzinski), Judith (Mrs. Horace Hunt), Benjamin Bradford III. AB, Bowdoin Coll., 1930; MD, C.M., McGill U., Montreal, Que., Can., 1935. Diplomate: Am. Bd. Neurol. Surgery (vice chmn. 1969-70). Intern Hartford (Conn.) Hosp., 1935-37, John A. Wentworth fellow, 1937-38, resident neurosurgery, 1941-42, neurosurgeon, from 1942, dir. dept. neurosurgery, 1968-75; asst. resident in surgery and neurosurgery New Haven Hosp., 1938-41; asst. clin. prof. neurosurgery Yale Med. Sch., 1949-65, asso. clin. prof., 1965-73, clin. prof., 1973-76; clin. prof. neurosurgery dept. surgery U. Conn. Med. Sch., from 1973. Contbg. author: Medical History of World War II; Author articles treatment for spinal disc pathology and various disorders of the brain. Served with AUS, 1943-46. Mem. Am. Acad. Neurol. Surgery (v.p. 1966-67, pres. 1973-74), A.C.S., A.M.A., Am. Assn. Neurol. Surgeons (v.p. 1971—), New Eng. Neurosurg. Soc. (pres. 1959-60), New Eng. Surg. Soc., Soc. Brit. Neurol. Surgeons (hon.), Scandanavian Neurosurg. Soc., Soc. Neurol. Surgeons (v.p. 1967-68) *To have a goal and pursue it with tenacity and patience controls ambition. To admire and commend the good work of others controls pride. To discipline oneself to work more insures growth. To hold each person in genuine affection insures cooperation. To hold honesty paramount controls men.* Deceased.

**WHITE, LEE CALVIN,** lawyer; b. Omaha, Sept. 1, 1923; s. Herman Henry and Ann Ruth (Ackerman) W.; m. Cecile R. Zorinsky, Nov. 19, 1989 (dec. Apr. 1996); children from previous marriage: Bruce D., Rosalyn A., Murray L., Sheldon R., Laura H., Lori J. BS in Elec. Engring., U. Nebr., 1948, LL.B., 1950. Bar: Nebr. 1950, D.C. 1958. Atty. legal div. TVA, 1950-54; legis. asst. to Senator John F. Kennedy US Senate, 1954-57; mem. Hoover Commn., 1954-55, asst. to Joseph P. Kennedy, 1954—55; counsel US Senate Small Bus. Com., 1957-58; adminstrv. asst. to Senator John S. Cooper US Senate, 1958-61; asst. spl. counsel to Pres. John F. Kennedy The White House, 1961-63, assoc. counsel to Pres. Lyndon Johnson, 1963-65, spl. counsel to Pres. Lyndon Johnson, 1965-66; chmn. Fed. Power Commn., 1966-69; of counsel Spiegel & McDiarmid LLP. Campaign mgr. R. Sargent Shriver (Democratic candidate v.p. U.S.), 1972; bd. dirs. Central Hudson Gas & Electric Corp., 1984-88 Author: Government for the People: Reflections of a White House Counsel to Presidents Kennedy and Johnson, 2008. Trustee Environmental Defense Fund, 1970—73; bd. govs. NY Mercantile Exchange, 1980—84, 1986—91. With USAR, 1943—46. Mem. D.C. Bar (gov. 1977-80) Democrat. Home: Washington, DC. Died Oct. 31, 2013.

**WHITE, MARSH WILLIAM,** physics educator, consultant; b. Claremont, NC, Apr. 22, 1896; s. William Franklin and Dora L. White; m. Stella Mae Steele, Sept. 14, 1917; children: Laurence Marsh, Kenneth Steele, Malcolm Arthur. AB in Physics, Park Coll., 1917; MS in Physics, Pa. State U., 1920, PhD, 1926; ScD (hon.), Park Coll., 1958. Asst. prof. physics Williams Coll., Williamstown, Mass., 1926-27; instr. Pa. State U., University Park, 1918-20, asst. prof., 1920-26, assoc. prof., 1926-42, prof., 1942-60, emeritus prof., from 1960. Expert cons. sci. manpower Office of Sci. R&D, War Dept., 1944-45; cons. R&D div. Asst. Chief of Staff, Dept. of Army, 1945-55; emeritus bd. dirs. Electronic Assoc., Inc., Long Branch, N.J., C-COR Electronics, Inc., State College, Pa., Centre Video Corp., State College. Author: (with K.V. Manning) Experimental College Physics, 1932, (with K.V. Manning and R.L. Weber) Practical Physics, 1943, College Physics, 1947, Physics for Science and Engineering, 1957, Basic Physics, 1958, (with others) Selective Experiments in Physics. Mem. Bd. Edn., State Coll., 1925-30. Fellow AAAS, Am. Phys. Soc.; mem. AAUP, ASEE, Am. Assn. Physics Tchrs. (v.p. 1945, pres. 1953, Citation for Outstanding Svc. 1952), Am. Inst. Physics (governing bd. 1947-50), Assn. Coll. Honor Socs. (coun., pres. 1950), Rotary Club (pres. 1956-57), Cosmos Club, Sigma Xi (exec. com. 1964-68), Pi Mu Epsilon, Sigma Pi Sigma (exec. sec. 1930-57, pres. 1957-58), Omicron Delta Kappa, Delta Chi (dir. scholarship, treas., sec., pres., pres. emeritus). Methodist. Home: State College, Pa. Deceased.

**WHITE, NORVAL CRAWFORD,** architect; b. NYC, June 12, 1926; s. William Crawford and Caroline Ruth (Taylor) W.; m. Joyce Leslie Lee, May 24, 1958 (div.); children: William Crawford, Thomas Taylor, Gordon Crawford, Alistair David; m. Camilla Cecilia Crowe, June 7, 1992. BS, Mass. Inst. Tech., 1949; student, Sch. Fine Arts, Fontainbleau, 1954; M.F.A., Princeton, 1955. Designer, assoc. Lathrop Douglass (Architect), 1955-59; prin. Norval C. White (Architect), NYC, 1959-62, 66-67; partner Rowan & White (Architects), NYC, 1962-66, Gruzen & Partners, NYC, 1967-70; prin. Norval C. White & Assos., NYC, 1970-74; ptnr. Levien, Deliso & White, 1974-80, Levien Deliso White Songer, 1980-86. Asst. prof. architecture Cooper Union, 1961-67; prof. architecture City Coll., CUNY, 1970-95, prof. emeritus, 1995-2009, chmn. dept. 1970-77. Author (with E. Willensky): AIA Guide to New York City, 1968, AIA Guide to New York City, 4th edit., 2000; author: The Architecture Book, 1976, New York: A Physical HIstory, 1987, The Guide to the Architecture of Paris, 1991; prin. works include Seiden House, Tenafly, N.J., 1960, Essex Terrace (housing), Bklyn., 1970, N.Y.C. Police Hdqrs., 1973, Brookhaven Parks (L.I.) Sanitary Landfill, 1971, Forsgate Indsl. Park, South Brunswick, N.J., 1978—86, Del Vista Condominiums, Miami, 1981, 61 Christopher Street, Greenwich Village, 1987, White House, Salisbury, Conn., 1998, Goodman House, Oyster Bay Cove, NY, 2003, White House, Mouchan, France, 2004. Trustee Bklyn. Inst. Arts and Scis., 1973-82, Bklyn. Pub. Libr., 1993-96; gov. Bklyn. Mus., 1973-82, adv. com., 1982-2006; mem. NYC Art Commn., 1975-86, sec., 1975-77, v.p., 1978-80. With USNR, 1944—46. Fellow AIA; mem. Soc. Archtl. Historians, N.Y. State Assn. Architects. Clubs: Century Assn. (N.Y.C.). Democrat. Died Dec. 26, 2009.

**WHITE, RHEA AMELIA,** library and information scientist; b. Utica, NY, May 6, 1931; d. John Raymond and Rhea Jane (Parry) White. BA, Pa. State U., 1953; MLS, Pratt Inst., Bklyn., 1965; postgrad., SUNY, Stony Brook, 1990—92; PhD (hon.), Inst. Transpersonal Psychology, 2006. Rsch. fellow Parapsychology Lab. Duke U., Durham, NC, 1954-58; editor Jour. Am. Soc. Psychical Rsch., NYC, 1959-62, 84-00, editor-in-chief, from 2001; libr. dept. psychiatry Maimonides Med. Ctr., Bklyn., 1965-67; dir. info. Am. Soc. Psychical Rsch., NYC, 1965-80; reference libr. East Meadow (N.Y.) Pub. Libr., 1965-95; founder, dir. Parapsychology Sources of Info. Ctr., Dix Hills, NY, 1981-90; editor Rsch. in Parapsychology, Metuchen, NJ, 1981-85, Theta, Durham, NC, 1981-86; founder, editor Parapsychology Abstracts Internat., Dix Hills, 1983-89, Exceptional Human Experience, Dix Hills, from 1990; founder, producer PsiLine Database, Dix Hills, from 1983; mng. editor Advances in Parapsychol. Rsch., NYC, 1977; founder, dir. Exceptional Human Experience Network, New Bern, 1990-94 and from 95; with Exceptional Human Experience News, 1994—2002. Rsch. fellow Menninger Found., Topeka, 1963-65; abstractor Psychol. Abstracts, Washington, 1967-91; cons. Scarecrow Press, Metuchen, NJ, 1980-85; referee Jour. Parapsychology, Durham, 1981-85; chmn., keynote spkr. conf. on women and parapsychology Parapsychology Found., Dublin, Ireland, 1991; keynote speaker Acad. Religion and Psychical Rsch. Conf., 1992; founder, editor EHE News, Dix Hills, 1994, New Bern, 1995—; instr. exceptional human experience course Portland (Oreg.) State U., 1999. Author: Parapsychology: Sources of Information, 1973, Surveys in Parapsychology, 1975, Parapsychology: New Sources of Information, 1990; (with M. Murphy) The Psychic Side of Sports, 1978; parapsychology book reviewer Libr. Jour., NYC, 1974-86, Reprint Bull., 1974-79, (with Michael Murphy) In the Zone, 1995; regional editor European Jour. Parapsychology, 1975-90; mem. editl. bd. Advances in Parapsychol. Rsch., 1980-85, Archaeus, 1985-93; contbr. over 100 articles to profl. jours. Recipient Hans Peter Luhn award Am. Soc. Info. Sci., N.Y.C. chpt., 1965. Mem.: Assn. Near-Death Studies, Acad. Religion and Psychical Rsch. (mem. bd. 1982—84, publs. com. 1982—97), Parapsychological Assn. (mem. coun. 1958, 1962—63, 1982—85, pres. 1984, dir. 1986, Lifetime Outstanding Rsch. award 1992, conf. spkr. 1993), Ctr. for Psychology and Social Change, Soc. for Anthropology of Consciousness, Internat. Assn. Religion and Parapsychology, Internat. Soc. for Study Subtle Energies and Energy Medicine, Found for Shamanic Studies, Penn State Alumni Assn. Coll. Liberal Arts. Avocations: hiking, gardening, animals, reading, listening to music. Deceased.

**WHITE, VIRGINIA JOYCELYN,** interior designer, consultant; b. Des Moines, Apr. 25, 1924; d. William Wood and Alwilda (Denning) White. Student, Art Inst. Chgo., 1941—43; BFA, Choinard Sch. Art, 1947; postgrad., Woodbury Coll. Design, 1947—48, UCLA, 1948—52, Southwestern U. Law, 1954—58. Designer Martin Young Furniture Mfg. Co., LA, 1947—52; owner, designer Va. White Interiors Co., LA, 1952—57, Studio City, 1966—80, Palm Desert, from 1980. Dir. design Gen. Fireproofing Co., LA, 1957—63, Barker Bros. Co., LA, 1963—66; instr. design Woman's Workshop, Northridge, Calif., 1973—79; cons., furniture mfrs. Contbr. articles to publs. Bd. dirs. Spastic Children's Fund, LA, 1952—56. Recipient Design award, Nat. Instn. Mag., 1958, McCall Mag., 1963. Mem.: Am. Soc. Interior Designers (cert. 1959), Calif. Fedn. Bus. & Profl. Women (charter pres. LA chpt. 1957—58), Ch. Religious Sci., Sigma Tau Psi (chpt. pres. 1945—46, nat. pres. 1952—54). Republican. Achievements include patents for furniture field. Home: Irvine, Calif. Died May 1994.

**WHITE, WILLIAM EARLE,** lawyer; b. Dinwiddie County, Va., Aug. 19, 1898; s. William Richard and Annie Eliza (Hone) White; m. Marian Louise Molloy, Apr. 24, 1924; children: Marion White Distanislao, William Earle Jr., Stephen Graham. BA, Richmond Coll., 1917; student, Law Sch. Am. Expeditionary Forces, Beaune, France, 1919, Harvard Law Sch., 1920. Bar: Va. 1920, US Ct. Appeals (4th cir.) 1940, US Supreme Ct 1941. Ptnr. Lassiter & White, 1922—54, White Hamilton Wyche & Shell, Petersburg, Va., from 1927; ret. dir. 1st & Mechants Nat. Bank, Commonwealth Natural Gas; chmn. Hosp. Authority City, Petersburg, Va. Cpl. USMC, 1917—19. Fellow: Am. Coll. Probate Counsel, Am. Bar Found., Am. Coll. Trial Lawyers; mem.: Va. State Bar (pres. 1963—64), Petersburg Bar Assn., Petersburg C of C, Am. Judicature Soc. Democrat. Died Jan. 1988.

**WHITING, GILLIAN MARY,** psychologist, researcher; b. Manchester, Lancashire, England, Feb. 26, 1933; d. Joseph Yates and Mary Ethelwynne Broxap; m. Donald Whiting. BA, U. South Africa, Pretoria, 1980, BA with honors, 1983; MA, U. Cape Town, South Africa, 1985; DPhil, U.Stellenbosch, South Africa, 1997. Cert. psychologist South Africa. Student advisor, lectr. U. Cape Town, Cape, 1985—90; pvt. practice psychologist Newlands, South Africa, from 1984. Psychologist, drug addiction counselor St Luke's Hospice, Kenilworth, South Africa, from 1990. Avocations: swimming, travel, sculpting, golf, gardening. Home: Newlands, South Africa. Died Dec. 31, 2006.

**WHITMAN, RUTH,** poet, educator, translator; b. NYC, May 28, 1922; d. Meyer David and Martha Harriet (Sherman) Bashein; m. Cedric Whitman, Oct. 13, 1941; children: Rachel Claudia, Leda Miriam; m. Firman Houghton, July 22, 1959; 1 child, David Will; m. Morton Sacks, Oct. 6, 1966. BA, Radcliffe Coll., 1944; MA, Harvard, 1947. Editor

Harvard U. Press, 1947-60; dir. poetry workshop Cambridge Ctr. Adult Edn., 1964-68; fellow poetry and translation Bunting Inst., Radcliffe Coll., 1968-70; instr. Radcliffe Seminars, 1969—99; faculty Harvard U., 1979-84; vis. poet Tufts U., 1972, 73; vis. poet in Israel, 1974, 77, 79, 81; poet-in-residence Hamden Sydney Coll., 1974, Trinity Coll., 1975, U. Denver, 1976, Holy Cross Coll., 1978, MIT, 1979, 1989, U. Mass., 1980, Centre Coll., Ky., 1980, 87, Ky. Arts Commn., 1981; founder, pres. Poets Who Teach, Inc., 1974—99. Dir. poetry writing program Mass. Council Arts, 1970-73; vis. prof. poetry MIT, 1989-92. Author: Selected Poems of Alain Bosquet, 1963, Anthology of Modern Yiddish Poetry, 1966, Blood and Milk Poems, 1963, Marriage Wig and other poems, 1968, Selected Poems of Jacob Glatstein, 1972, The Passion of Lizzie Borden: New and Selected Poems, 1973; editor: Poemmaking: Poets in Classrooms, 1975, Tamsen Donner: A Woman's Journey, 1977, Permanent Address: New Poems, 1973-80, 1980, Becoming a Poet: Source, Process and Practice, 1982, The Testing of Hanna Senesh, 1986, The Fiddle Rose, 1990, Laughing Gas: Poems New and Selected, 1963-90, 91, Hatshepsut, Speak to Me, 1992, An Anthology of Modern Yiddish Poetry, 3d edit., 1995. Recipient Alice Fay di Castagnola award, 1968, Kovner award, 1968, Chanin award, 1972, Guiness Internat. award, 1973; John Masefield award, 1976; grantee Nat. Found. Jewish Culture, 1968; Nat. Endowment Arts, 1974-75; Tananbaum Found. grantee, 1979, 80; R.I. Council grantee in lit., 1980; sr. Fulbright writer-in-residence fellow Hebrew U., Jerusalem, 1984-85. Mem. Authors League, P.E.N., Poetry Soc. Am., New Eng. Poetry Club, Phi Beta Kappa. Died Dec. 1, 1999.

**WHITMORE, TIMOTHY CHARLES,** botanist; b. Ruislip, Middlesex, England, June 6, 1935; s. Geoffrey and Ella Marguerite (Capon) W.; m. Wendy Ann Osborn, Sept. 16, 1961; children: Katherine, Thomas, Benjamin. MA, Cambridge U., 1960, PhD, 1961, DSc, 1977, Oxford U., 1978. Lectr. Southampton U., 1960-62, affl. lectr., vis. scholar, from 1989; govt. forest botanist British Solomon Islands, 1962-65; forest botanist Forest Rsch. Inst., Kepong, Malaysia, 1965-72; sr. rsch. officer Oxford U., 1974-89. Fellow St. John's Coll. Cambridge U., 1960-63; prin. rsch. fellow Natural History Mus., London, 1974-76 Author: Tropical Rain Forests of Far East, 1974, 85, Introduction to Tropical Rain Forests, 1991, 98, Palms of Malaya, 1972, 77, 98, Wallace's Line & Plate Techtonics, 1986. Mem. British Ecol. Soc. Achievements include research in understanding of tropical forest dynamics; sustainable utilization; biogeography and classification of tropical trees. Home: Cambridge, England. Died Feb. 14, 2002.

**WHITNEY, JANE,** foreign service officer; b. July 15, 1941; d. Robert F. and Mussette (Cary) W. BA, Beloit Coll., 1963; CD, U. Aix, Marseille, France, 1962. Joined Fgn. Svc., U.S. Dept. State, 1965; vice consul Saigon, Vietnam, 1966—68; career counselor, 1968—70; spl. asst. Office of Dir. Gen., 1970—72; consul Stuttgart, Germany, 1972—74, Ankara, Turkey, 1974—76; spl. asst. Office of Asst. Sec. for Consular Affairs, 1976—77; mem. Bd. Examiners Fgn. Svc., 1977—78, 1979—81; consul Munich, 1978—79, Buenos Aires, 1981—82; ethics officer Office of Legal Adviser, 1982—85; advisor Office of Asst. Sec. for Diplomatic Security, 1985—86; dep. prin. officer, consul Stuttgart, 1986—90; prin. officer, consul gen. Perth, Australia, 1990—91. Presbyterian. Recipient awards U.S. Dept. State, 1968, 70, 81, 85, 87, 90. Home: Lakewood, Wash. Died Nov. 12, 2013.

**WIENER, PHYLLIS,** artist; b. Iowa City, Iowa, Sept. 17, 1921; d. Charles Louis and Loretta A. (Tucker) Zager; m. Allen Downs, Dec. 26, 1939 (div. 1960); children: Gareth, Allison, Barbara Hodne, Amy; m. Daniel Norman Wiener, Dec. 9, 1971. Student, U. Iowa, Iowa City, 1940—41, U. Mo., Columbus, 1945, U. Minn., Mpls., 1951—52. Mem. panel of selection Minn. Artists Program Mpls. Art Inst., 1976-78; mem. adv. panel Minn. State Arts Bd., St. Paul, 1978-81; juror anniversary exhibition Minn. Artists Mpls. Art Inst., 1985. One-woman shows include Walker Art Ctr., Mpls., 1951, 1956, Mpls. Inst. Art, 1967, Nash Gallery U. Minn., Mpls., 1981, Tweed Mus. Art, Duluth, Minn., 1982, Pindar Gallery, N.Y.C., 1984, 1986, 1988, U. Wis. Gallery, La Crosse, 1993, Janet Wallace Fine Arts, Macalester Coll., St. Paul, 1993, Murphy Gallery at St. Catherine's Coll., 2001, Phipps Arts Ctr., Hudson, Wis., 2004, Howard Conn Art Ctr., Mpls., Minn., 2004, Grand Hand Gallery, St. Paul, Pvt. Art Gallery, 2007—08, exhibited in group shows at American Fedn. Arts, 1954—58, US Dept. State, European Embassies, 1962, Miller Art Mus., Sturgeon Bay, Wis., 2005, Minn. Mus. American Art, 2005—08, Minnetonka Art Ctr., Wayzata, Minn., 2005, Represented in permanent collections Mpls. Art Inst., Walker Art Ctr., Mpls., Frederick Weisman Art Mus, Mayo Clinic, Scottsdale, Ariz., Minn. State Hist. Soc., St. Paul, Total Petroleum Co., Denver, Northwestern Bell Telephone Co., Omaha, Mus. Kuopio, Finland, US Embassy, Papua New Guinea, Carlson Co., Mpls., St. Catherine's Coll., St. Paul, Mpls. Interdistrict Sch., Boynton Health Svcs. U. Minn., Mpls., Coll. Visual Arts, St. Paul. Recipient Individual Artist Project grant Minn. State Arts Bd., 1980. Home: Minneapolis, Minn. Died Jan. 1, 2013.

**WIGGLESWORTH, ERIC CLIFFORD,** public health specialist, researcher; b. Leeds, Yorkshire, England, May 21, 1926; arrived in Australia, 1964; s. Walter Henry Wigglesworth and Eleanor Maud Hooper; m. Leigh Carruthers Best, Dec. 22, 1962; children: Alison Mary, Sarah Dorothy Dods, Geoffrey John, Anne Phyllida. BS, U. Leeds, 1947; MS, 1972; D of Applied Sci., U. Melbourne, 1985; MD (hon.), U. Tasmania, Australia, 1998. Prin. safety officer 600 Group of Cos., London, 1952—62; dir. Injury Rsch. Project, Melbourne, Victoria, Australia, from 1971; exec. dir. Sir Robert Menzies Meml. Found., Melbourne, 1979—98. Editor 5 books; contbr. over 140 articles to profl. jours. Named Mem. Order Australia, Australian Govt., 2000. Fellow: Inst. Occupl. Safety and Health, Safety Inst. Australia (hon.; chmn. edn. com. 1971—83). Achievements include development of the first tertiary-level course in accidental injury prevention in Australia; research in prevention accidental injury. Home: Balwyn, Australia. Died Mar. 2009.

**WIGHTMAN, JOHN MARTIN,** securities trader, corporate financial executive; b. London, Jan. 27, 1944; s. John William and Nora (Martin) Wightman; m. Anne Leigh Paynter, Oct. 17, 1970; children: Antonia Leigh, Dominic Martin, Georgina Mary, Francesca Katherine, Gemma Theresa, Patrick John, Christiana Bernadette. Student, Oratory. Analyst David A. Bevan Simpson, London, 1968-70, de Zoete-Bevan (formerly David A. Bevan Simpson), London, 1970-83, corp. fin., 1983-86, ptnr., 1978-86, dir., 1986—96, Barclays de Zoete Wedd Securities Ltd., London, 1986—96; trustee, dir. Guildford No. 5 Project for Homeless, from 1996. Mem. Stock Exch., London, 1977—91, European Govt. Bus. Bus. Rels. Coun., 1992—96. Bd. dirs., chmn. bd. trustees Rydes Hill Prep. Sch., from 1996. Mem.: Fin.com (gift aid organizer), Guildford Conservative Assn. (mem. exec. com.), Shamley Green Conservative Assn. (chmn.), UK Investment Profls. (aff. assoc. investment mgmt. rsch. assoc.), Securities Investment Inst., Inst. Dirs., Franciscan Friary, Shamley Green Cricket Club, Guildford Rugby Club (v.p.). Conservative. Roman Catholic. Avocation: sports. Home: Shamley Green, England. Died July 11, 2005.

**WIKSTROM, MARILYN,** education educator; b. Defiance, Ohio, Mar. 1, 1935; d. Otho Webster and Orva Mildred (McCague) Mansfield; m. Gunnar Wikstrom Jr., May 16, 1959; children: Jeffrey Alan, Daryl Lyn, Milton Curtis, Byron Kent. BS in Edn., Defiance Coll., 1957; MS, No. State U., 1968; EdD, U. S.D., 1978. Prof. edn. Buena Vista Coll., Storm Lake, Iowa, from 1972. Adj. instr. Coll. of Idaho, Caldwell, 1985, 86; adj. instr. grad. program Drake U., 1983-90. Recipient Alumni Acad. Excellence citation Defiance Coll., 1988, Wythe award for teaching excellence Buena Vista Coll., 1991. Mem. Quint County Reading Coun. (bldg. rep.), Phi Delta Kappa (pres. 1986-87). Democrat. Avocations: poetry, walking. Home: Fridley, Minn. Died Sept. 1998.

**WILHELMI, ZDZISLAW LUDWIK,** nuclear physics professor, researcher; b. Lomza, Poland, Sept. 20, 1921; s. Mieczyslaw Antoni and Julia Walentyna (Moscicki) W.; m. Hanna Krystyna Szmit; children: Joanna, Dorota. MTech in Elec. Engring., Tech. U. Lódz, Poland, 1948; MS in Physics, Warsaw U., Poland, 1952; PhD in Physics Sci., Warsaw U., 1954. Asst. Tech. U., 1945-48, assoc. prof., chmn. tech. physics dept., 1953-54; head dept. nuclear physics Inst. Nuclear Rsch., Warsaw, Swierk, Poland, 1955-70; dir. div. nuclear safety and environ. protection Internat. Atomic Energy Agy., Vienna, Austria, 1970-73; asst. prof. Warsaw U., 1948-56, assoc. prof., 1956-61, prof., head dept. nuclear physics, 1961-91; chief coord. Cen. Program Basic. Rsch., Poland, 1986-91. Organizer, dir. Internat. Summer Sch. Nuclear Physics, Mikolajki, Poland, 1968-88. Contbr. articles to numerous sci. jours., also monographs and acad. textbooks. Mem. exec. com. European Phys. Soc., Geneva, 1975-78; mem., pres. exec. com. World Assn. Polish Home Army Soldiers, Warsaw, 1991-93. With Polish Anti-German Underground Army, 1939—45. Decorated Order of Polonia Restituta, Gold Cross of Merit with Crosses, Partsan Cross, Home Army Cross, BURZA Operational medal; recipient State Coun. Nuc. Engring. award, 1967, Order Polonia Restituta, Officer Cross award, 1991, Commander Cross, 2002. Fellow Am. Phys. Soc., Inst. Physics (UK); mem. Polish Physical Soc. (hon.; pres. 1974-81), Bulgarian Physical Soc. (hon. mem.), NY Acad. Scis. Avocations: poetry, sailing, photography. Home: Warsaw, Poland. Died Dec. 27, 2013.

**WILKES, CHARLES D.,** distribution and marketing companies executive, consultant; b. Paris, Apr. 14, 1920; s. Charles and Carmen (Priou-Perdonnet) D-W. Student, Breguet Coll., Paris, 1938—40; BS, Bur. des Temps Elementaires, Paris, 1947. Econ. commr., diplomat French African countries ECA-Mut. Security Agy., Am. Embassy, Paris, 1949—56; continental mgr. United Artists TV, NYC, 1956—63. Cons. Publicker, Phila., 1962—68; French European rep. Warner Bros. TV, LA, 1969—72; Europe, Mid East/Africa rep. N.T.A., 1972—80; exec. and dir. several world wide cos., from 1980. Econ. commr. Econ. Surveys, 1946—49. Lt. USN, 1941—46, PTO. Decorated Air medal, Legion of Honor (France). Mem.: Cercle Union Interalliee (Paris). Died June 18, 2008.

**WILKES, SIR MICHAEL JOHN,** retired military officer; b. June 11, 1940; s. Jack and Phyllis Wilkes; m. Ann Jacqueline Huelin, 1966; 2 children. Commd. Royal Army, 1960, comdr. spl. forces, 1964-67, battery commdr. Chestnut Troop, 1975-76, commdg. officer, 1977-79, mil. asst. to chief gen. staff, 1980-81; chief of staff 3rd Armored Divsn., 1982-83; dir. Spl. Air Svc. (SAS), 1986—88; gen. officer commdg. 3rd Armored Divsn., 1988-90; commdr. UK Field Army, 1990-93; adjutant gen. Royal Army, 1993-95; Lt. Gov. of New Jersey, 1995—2001. Bd. dirs. Heritage Oil plc, 2008—13, Blue Star Capital plc, 2008—13. Named Comdr. of the Order of the British Empire, 1988, Knight Comdr. of the Order of the Bath, 1991, Knight of the Venerable Order of Saint John, 1995; named an Officer of the Order of the British Empire (OBE), 1980. Mem. Naval and Mil. Club, Spl. Forces Club, Royal Thames Yacht Club. Avocations: golf, sailing, skiing, military history. Died Oct. 27, 2013.

**WILKEY, MALCOLM RICHARD,** retired ambassador, judge; b. Murfreesboro, Tenn., Dec. 6, 1918; s. Malcolm Newton and Elizabeth (Gilbert) W.; m. Emma Secul Depolo, Dec. 21, 1959. AB magna cum laude, Harvard U., 1940, LLB, 1948; LLD (hon.), Rose-Hulman Inst. Tech., 1984. Bar: Tex. 1948, NY 1963, US Supreme Ct. 1952, DC 1970. US atty. (so. dist.) Tex. US Dept. Justice, 1954-58, asst. atty. gen., 1958-61; ptnr. Butler Binion Rice & Cook, 1961-63; gen. counsel, sec. Kennecott Copper Corp., 1963-70; judge US Ct. Appeals (DC Cir.), 1970-85; US amb. to Uruguay US Dept. State, 1985-90. Ofcl. in charge fed. forces at Little Rock Sch. Crisis, Dept. Justice, 1958; mem. US-Chile Arbitration Commn., 1991-97; lectr. internat. constl. and adminstrv. law London Poly., 1979, 80; lectr. Tulane U. Law Summer Sch., Grenoble, France, 1981, 83, San Diego Law Summer Sch., Oxford, Eng., 1983, Brigham Young Law Sch., 1984, 93; vis. fellow Wolfson Coll., Cambridge U., 1985; chmn. Pres.'s Commn. on Revision Fed. Ethics Laws, 1989; spl. counsel to Atty. Gen. for inquiry into the House Banking Facility, 1992. Author: Is It Time For A Second Constitutional Convention, 1995, As the Twig is Bent, 2003. Del. Rep. Nat. Conv., 1960. Served from 2d lt. to lt. col. AUS, 1941-45. Named Am. mem., Fulbright Commn., from 2002; hon. fellow, Wolfson Coll., Cambridge. Fellow Am. Bar Found.; mem. Am. Law Inst. (adv. com. restatement fgn. rels. law of US), Jud. Conf. US (com. on standards for admission to fed. cts. 1976-79), Phi Beta Kappa, Delta Sigma Rho, Phi Delta Phi (hon.). Republican. Died Aug. 15, 2009.

**WILKINSON, ROBERT LEWIS,** trade association administrator; b. Colfax, Wash., Aug. 18, 1921; s. Ralph Lewis and Elizabeth (Stone) Wilkinson; m. Dorothy Pearl Lawrence, July 24, 1942; children: Robert Lewis, Bruce J. BA, Wash. State U., 1942. Mgr. Inland Empire chpt. Nat. Elec. Contractors Assn., Spokane, Wash., 1950—72, dir. labor svcs. Washington, 1972—73, dir. orgn., 1973—74, dir. svcs., 1974—86; pres. Assoc. Splty. Contractors, Inc., Washington, 1974—86. Author: Guide to Electrical Contracting Claims Management, vol. I, 1976, vol. III, 1980, Contract Documents, 1982, 1987. Chmn. Spokane Transit Commn., 1970—72; dist. pres. Reorganized Ch. of Jesus Christ of Latterday Saints, Spokane, 1962—72. Served to capt. US Army, 1942—44, ETO. Fellow: Acad. Elec. Contracting; mem.: Am. Soc. Assn. Execs. (Grand award for Mgmt. 1964), Am. Arbitration Assn. (mem. constrn. industry panel). Republican. Home: Ithaca, NY. Died Nov. 15, 1998.

**WILLIAMS, CHARLIE GUY,** school system administrator; b. Great Falls, SC, Mar. 22, 1928; s. Robert F. and Mabel (Robinson) W.; m. Edna Broome, March 10, 1951; children: Charlie Jr., Frank. BS in Sec. Edn., Newberry Coll., 1950; MEd in Sch. Administrn., U. S.C., 1954, PhD in Elem. Edn., 1966; LLD (hon.), Newberry Coll., 1982. Tchr., coach East Clarendon High Sch., Turbeville, S.C., 1952-53; prin. Turbeville Elem. Sch., 1953-55; tchr. Richland Sch. Dist. 1, Columbia, S.C., 1955-57, dir. instructional materials, 1962-64, coordinator fed. projects, 1964-66; prin. Logan and McCants Elem. Sch., Columbia, 1957-62; dir. research office S.C. Dept. Edn., Columbia, 1966-68, dep. supt. div. instrn., 1968-79, state supt. edn., 1979—98. Commr. Edn. Commn. of the States, Denver, 1979-98; bd. dirs. Coun. Chief State Sch. Officers, Washington, 1986-98, Agy. for Instl. Tech., Bloomington, Ind., 1984-98, Joint Coun. on Econ. Edn., N.Y.C., 1980-98; bd. dirs. Southeastern Edn. Improvement Lab., Research Triangle Park, N.C. Served with USN, 1945-46, 51-52, Korea. Mem. Am. Assn. Sch. Administrs., S.C. Assn. Sch. Adminstrs. Democrat. Baptist. Home: Columbia, SC. Died Sept. 7, 1998.

**WILLIAMS, CLIFFORD,** theatre director; b. Cardiff, Wales, U.K., Dec. 30, 1926; s. George Frederick and Florence Maud (Gapper) Williams Maycock; m. Josiane Eugenie Peset, Nov. 10, 1962; children: Anouk, Tara; m. Joanna Douglas, 1956 (div. 1959). Fellow Trinity Coll. Music, London, 1960—2005, Welsh Coll. Music and Drama, London, 1994—2005. Founder, dir., playwright Mime Theatre Co., London, 1950-53; dir. Marlowe Theatre, Canterbury, 1956, Queens Theatre, Hornchurch, 1957, Arts Theatre, London, 1957-60, Nat. Theatre of the Deaf Eng., London, 1979-80; assoc. dir. Royal Shakespeare Co., Stratford Upon Avon and London, 1963-05; dir. nat. theatres Gt. Britain, Yugoslavia, Spain, Mexico, Finland, Bulgaria, and in France, Denmark, Sweden, USSR, Canada, Japan, Ger., U.S., New Zealand, Australia. Broadway prodns. include The Comedy of Errors, Sleuth, Soldiers, Emperor Henry IV, As You Like It, Pack of Lies, Aren't We All, Breaking The Code, The Father; (film) Man and Superman; opera prodns. include Flying Dutchman, Savitri, Dido and Aeneas, Venus and Adonis, Bellman's Opera; musical prodns. include Our Man Crighton, Mardi Gras, Oh! Calcutta!, Carte Blanche (all in London); creator revues Matters Matrimonial, The Keys of the Kingdom, Saints and Sinners, and Adaptor Daphne du Maurier's, Rebecca, Albert Camus's The Fall, Rex Warner's The Wild Goose Chase, and Benjamin Disraelis Sybil; author children's plays including The Sleeping Princess, The Goose Girl, The Secret Kingdom; translator Ionesco Strindberg and Chekhov. Served to lt. Ordnance Corps. Brit. Army. Home: London, England. Died Aug. 20, 2005.

**WILLIAMS, SIR DENYS AMBROSE,** retired judge; b. Barbados, Oct. 12, 1929; s. George Cuthbert Williams and Violet Irene Williams Gilkes; m. Carmel Mary Coleman, 1954; 6 children. Student, Worcester Coll., Oxford U., Eng. Asst. legal draftsman, asst. to atty. gen. Govt. of Barbados, sr. parliamentary counsel, acting gov. gen., 1995—96; judge Barbadian Supreme Ct., 1967-86, chief justice, 1987—2001. Decorated Knight Comdr. Saint Michael and Saint George, Gold Crown of Merit. Avocations: horse-racing, tennis, gardening, walking. Home: Saint Michael, Barbados. Died Aug. 7, 2014.

**WILLIAMS, EDWARD F(OSTER), III,** retired environmental engineer; b. NYC, Jan. 3, 1935; s. E. Foster Jr. and Ida Frances (Richards) W.; m. Sue Carol Osenbaugh, June

5, 1960; children: Cecile Elizabeth, Alexander Harmon. BS in Engring., Auburn U., 1956; MA in History, U. Memphis, 1974. Registered profl. engr., Tenn. Engr. Buckeye Cellulose Corp. (subs. of Procter & Gamble), Memphis, 1957, process safety engr., 1960, resident constrn. engr. Perry, Fla., 1960-61, staff engr. Memphis, 1961-70; chief engr., v.p. Enviro-trol, Inc., Memphis, 1970-73; from v.p. to pres. Ramcon Environ. Corp., Memphis, 1973-80; pres. E.F. Williams & Assocs., Inc., Memphis, 1980-98; v.p. engring. Environ. Testing & Cons. of the Americas, Inc., 1998—2001, pres., 2001—06; ret., 2007. Chmn. bd. EFW Comml. Ventures, Inc., 1990—2011, Spiridon Press, Inc., 1998-99; bd. dirs. Mobile Process Tech. Inc., Memphis; v.p. Environ. Testing and Cons., Inc., Memphis, 1985-94; environ. coord. Shelby County, Tenn., 1995-96, bd. dirs., vice chmn., Pots A Lot Pottery LLC, New Orleans, LA, 2006-. Author: Fustest with the Mostest, 1968, Early Memphis and Its River Rivals, 1969, Great American Civil War Trivia Book, 1998; editor Environ. Control News for So. Industry, 1971-2001 Mem. N.B. Forrest Trail Com., from 1964, chmn., from 1975; mem. Shelby County Bd. Commrs., Memphis, 1978—94, chmn., 1987—88, 1990—92; mem. Shelby County Records Commn., 1978-, chmn., 1993-, Chickasaw Basin Authority, 1980-94, 98—, vice chmn., 1982-94; historian Shelby County, from 1994; environ. coord. Shelby County Mayor's staff, 1995—96; trustee Bolton Coll., from 1982, chmn., 1987—88, 1990—92; state chmn. Nat. Conf. Rep. County Ofcls., 1993—96; vice chmn. Shelby County Stormwater Steering Com., 1998—2002; vice-chmn. Memphis-Shelby local Emergency Planning Com., 1986—2003; vice chmn. Shelby County Courthouse Hist. Preservation Commn., 2000—08, Mid-South Commn. on Aging, 2003—13; bd. dirs. Better Bus. Bur., Memphis, 1995—2009; chmn. Shelby County Hist. Commn., 1997—98; bd. dirs. Southwest Tenn. C.C. Found., 2001—07; v.p. Memphis Belle War Meml. Found., 2000—05; adv. com. Boy Scouts of Am., Chickasaw Coun., 1980—2000; state rep. Tenn. Gen. Assembly, 1970—78; del. Rep. Nat. Conv., 1988, 1992, 1996, state exec. com., 1994—2002; vice chmn. Rep. Party of Shelby County, 2003—05; pres. Christ United Presbyn. Ch. Corp., 1995—98; trustee Faith Christian Acad., from 2009; bd. dirs. Shiloh Military Trail Inc., from 1962; mem. NB Forrest Camp 215 SCV, from 1963; comdr. NB Forest Camp 215 SCV, 1967—68. Lt. USAF, 1957—60, capt. res. USAF, 1961—71, wing comdr. staff, 1958, Chem., Biol., & Radiol. Warfare. Named Tenn. Water Conservationist of Yr., Tenn. Conservation League, 1973, Tenn. Legis. Conservationist of Yr., Nat. Wildlife Fedn., 1974, Memphis Outstanding Engr., Memphis Joint Engrs. Coun., 1980; recipient Shelby County Environ. Improvement award, 1983, Tenn. Lifetime Environ. Stewardship award Tenn. Dept. Environ. and Conservation, 1995, Herff Honor award U. Memphis Coll. Engring., 2006. Mem. NSPE, ASME, Am. Acad. Environ. Engrs. (diplomate), Environ. Assesment Assn., TSPE, Water Environ. Fedn., Am. Indsl. Hygiene Assn. (chpt. pres.), Am. Soc. Safety Engrs. (Outstanding Achievement award 1995-96), Air and Waste Mgmt. Assn., Engrs. Club Memphis (bd. dirs. 1979-80, 98-2002, pres. 2000-01), Tenn. Water and Wastewater Assn., Rotary, C. of C. (environ. coun. chmn. 1988-2000, chmn. emeritus 2000—), Tenn. Hist. Soc. (v.p. 1972), West Tenn. Hist. Soc. (pres. 1983-85), Am. Hist. Assn., Memphis Belle Meml. Assn. (bd. dirs. 2004-) Memphis-Shelby County Tenn. Bicentennial Commn. (chmn. 1994-96), Davies Manor Assn. (pres. 1999-2000, treas., 2011-), Miss. Hist. Soc., Tau Beta Pi, Omicron Delta Kappa, Pi Tau Sigma, Phi Kappa Phi. Republican. Presbyterian. Avocation: history. Home: Memphis, Tenn. *It has been my observation that history does not repeat itself, but human nature does. Knowledge of this principle can be put to use in politics, business, and other endeavors if one knows history.* Died Sept. 29, 2013.

**WILLIAMS, ELEANOR CLAFLIN (CLAFFY WILLIAMS),** artist; b. Brookline, Mass., Jan. 31, 1916; d. Thomas Mack and Alice Morton (Osborn) Claflin; m. Thomas Blake Williams, Jan. 26, 1940; children: Thomas B. Jr., Susan Williams Dickie, Eleanor Williams Wright, Sandra M. Williams Weiss. Student, Sweet Briar Coll. Art tchr.; lectr. on contemporary art. One woman shows include Pual Platt Libr., Cohasset, Mass., 1998, Cohasset Paul Pratt Meml. Libr., 1999; exhibited in various art shows including Copley Soc., Boston, 1974, 77, 98, 99, 2000, Chinese Cultural Inst., Boston, 1992, 98, 2000, South Shore Art Ctr., Cohasset, 1996, 97, 98, 2000, Modern Art D'unet, Tonniens, 1993, Chinese Cultural Inst., Boston, 1992, 96, Ariel Gallery, Soho, N.Y., 1990, Art Complex, Duxbury, Mass., 1982, 97; 3 paintings in book The Best in Acrylic Painting, 1996, Artexpo in N.Y.C. promoted by ARTREPS, 1998; 3 paintings in Creative Inspirations, 1997. Pres. bd. dirs. South Shore Art Ctr., Cohasset, Mass., 1985-87, mem. adv. bd., 1987—; dir. Prison Art Project, Boston, 1973-76; bd. dirs. Copley Soc., Boston, 1975-79. Recipient 1st prize for graphics North River Art Assn., Marshfield, Mass. Avocations: skiing, tennis, walking, reading, travel. Home: Cohasset, Mass. Died Apr. 19, 2008.

**WILLIAMS, EMORY,** retired retail executive; b. Falco, Ala., Oct. 26, 1911; s. William Emory and Nelle (Turner) W.; m. Janet Hatcher Allcorn, May 15, 1943; children: Nelle (Mrs. Gilbert Brown), Janet (Mrs. Edwin Harrison), Bliss (Mrs. Howell Browne), Carol (Mrs. James Schroeder), Emory III. AB, Emory U., 1932. With Sears, Roebuck & Co., 1933-75; pres. Sears, Roebuck (S.A.), Brazil, 1958-60, Homart Devel. Co., 1960-67, treas. parent co., 1962-64, v.p., treas., 1964-75; chmn., CEO Sears Bank & Trust Co., 1975-81. Chmn. bd. dirs., pres. Chgo. Milw. Corp., 1981-85; ptnr. Williams Realty Co.; chmn. Williams & Nichols Co., SureBlock Co., American Investors in China. Div. chmn. Chgo. Crusade of Mercy, 1962-64, gen. chmn., 1966, pres, 1976-78; chmn. Ill. Health Edn. Commn., 1968-70; pres. Adler Planetarium, 1972-75, Ravinia Festival Assn., 1972-78; pres. bd. dirs. Community Fund, 1970-73; trustee Emory U., Chgo. Community Trust, Northwestern Meml. Hosps., Kellstadt Found.; chmn. Chgo. Chamber Musicians. Lt. col. C.E., U.S. Army, World War II, CBI. Mem. Piedmont Driving Club (Atlanta); Chgo. Club, Old Elm Club (Chgo.), Commercial Club; Indian Hill Club (Winnetka, Ill.), Loblolly Club (Hobe Sound, Fla.), Seminole Golf Club (Juno Beach). Died Feb. 11, 2014.

**WILLIAMS, LAWRENCE ERNEST,** retired physicist; b. Youngstown, Ohio, Nov. 29, 1937; s. William Karapandza and Dorothy (Radulovich) Williams; m. Sonia Bell Bredmeyer; children: Erica, Beverley. BS in Physics, Carnegie-Mellon U., 1959; MS, U. Minn., 1962, PhD, 1965. Asst. prof. physics Western Ill. U., Macomb, 1968-70; asst. prof. radiology U. Minn., Mpls., 1973-78, NIH fellow, 1971-73, assoc. prof., 1978-80; imaging physicist City of Hope, Duarte, Calif., from 1980, prof., 2002—13; ret., 2013. Adj. assoc. prof. UCLA, 1982-92, adj. prof., 1992—2012; prof. Eurotech. Rsch. U., Palo Alto, Calif., 1983—; cons. Jet Propulsion Lab, Pasadena, Calif., 1981-84; mem. clin. oncology study sect. NIH, 2000-2003. Author: Radiopharmaceuticals, 2011; co-author: Biophysical Science, rev. 2d edit., 1979; editor Nuclear Medical Physics, 1987, assoc. editor, Med. Physics, 2005—; contbr. articles to med. jours.; patentee, inventor new method of abscess imaging; discoverer excited states in nuclear mass three system, mathematical model of tumor uptake of tracers; developer of a method to evaluate brake radiation doses; patentee, co-discoverer of tumor targeting by liposomes. Treas. United Meth. Ch., West Covina, Calif., 1982-83, mem. & supervisory com. Football Fed. Credit Union, Arcadia, Calif., 2012. Recipient Lifetime Svc. award Am. Bd. Radiology, 2010, Westinghouse Sci. Talent Search scholar, 1955, R.J. Wean scholar, 1957; NSF fellow U. Minn., 1961-62. Fellow Am. Coll. Angiology; mem. Soc. Nuclear Medicine (Gold medal exhibit 1983), Am. Assn. Physicists in Medicine, N.Y. Acad. Scis., Soc. for Computer Applications in Radiology, Sigma Xi. Methodist. Avocations: furniture refinishing, music, sketching. Home: Arcadia, Calif. Died July 17, 2014.

**WILLIAMS, LYNN RUSSELL,** retired labor union administrator; b. Springfield, Ont., Can., July 21, 1924; came to U.S., 1977; s. Waldemar and Emma Elizabeth (Fisher) W.; m. Audrey Hansuld, Sept. 12, 1946 (dec. 2000); children: Judith Williams Hocking, David, Barbara, Brian BA in Industrial Rels. & Economics, McMaster U., Hamilton, Ont., 1944, LLD (hon.), 1978; LittD (hon.), Brock U., St. Catherines, Ont., 1985. Organizer Can. Congress of Labour (now Can. Labour Congress), 1947-55; staff rep. United Steelworkers America, Toronto, 1956-57, area supr. Niagara Peninsula, 1958-62, asst. dir. Dist. 6 Toronto, 1963-73, dir. Dist. 6, 1973-77, internat. sec. Pitts., 1977-83, internat. pres., 1983—94. Mem. exec. council AFL-CIO, Washington, 1983, mem. exec. council Ind. Union Dept., 1983; mem. exec. com. Metalworkers Fedn., Geneva, 1983; dir. American Arbitration Assn., 1983; bd. dirs. African-American Labor Ctr., American Productivity Ctr., Citizen/Labor Energy Coalition, Com. for Nat. Health Ins., Work in American Inst.; trustee American Inst. for Free Labor Devel.; mem. exec. com. Can.-Am. Com.; mem. panel Econ. Policy Council; mem. adv. com. Labor Desk, USYC; trustee Labor Heritage Found.; v.p. Labor-Industry Coalition for Internat. Trade; mem. ad hoc com. Nat. Planning Assn.; mem. advisory bd. Niagara Inst.; visiting fellow, Inst of Politics. Vice pres. Americans for Democratic Action; bd. dirs. American Open U.; mem. steering group Council on Fgn. Relations; bd. dirs. Pitts. Symphony Soc., United Way of Allegheny County, World Affairs Council of Pitts.; bd. govs. United Way; mem. Aspen Inst., Econ. Policy Council of UN, USA; trustee Brother Brothers Found.; mem. Can.-American Commn.; Served with Canadian Navy, 1944-45 Avocations: running; jogging; reading; skiing. Died May 4, 2014.

**WILLIAMS, ROBIN,** actor, comedian; b. Chgo., July 21, 1951; s. Robert Fitzgerald and Laura McLaurin (Smith) W.; m. Valerie Velardi, June 4, 1978 (div. Dec. 6, 1988); 1 child, Zachary Pym; m. Marsha Garces, Apr. 30, 1989 (div. 2010); children: Zelda Rae, Cody Alan; m. Susan Schneider, Oct. 23, 2011. Attended, Claremont Men's Coll., 1969—73, Juilliard Sch., NYC, 1973—75. Started as stand-up comedian in San Francisco clubs, including Holy City Zoo, The Boardinghouse; actor: (TV series) Mork and Mindy, 1978-82, The Crazy Ones, 2013-14; (films) Popeye, 1980, The World According to Garp, 1982, The Survivors, 1983, Moscow on the Hudson, 1984, The Best of Times, 1986, Club Paradise, 1986, Seize the Day, 1986, Good Morning Vietnam, 1987 (Golden Globe award for Best Actor, 1988), The Adventures of Baron Munchausen, 1988, Dead Poets Society, 1989, Cadillac Man, 1990, Awakenings, 1990, Dead Again, 1991, The Fisher King, 1991, Dead Again, 1991, Hook, 1991, (voice only) Aladdin, 1992 (Spl. Achievement award Hollywood Fgn. Press, Nat. Bd. Rev. 1992), Toys, 1992, Nine Months, 1995, Jumanji, 1995, The BirdCage, 1996, Jack, 1996, The Secret Agent, 1996, Hamlet, 1996, Deconstructing Harry, 1997, Father's Day, 1997, Flubber, 1997, Good Will Hunting, 1997 (Acad. award for Best Actor in a Supporting Role, 1998, SAG award for Outstanding Performance by a Male Actor in a Supporting Role, 1998), What Dreams May Come, 1998, Patch Adams, 1998, Bicentennial Man, 1999, (voice) A.I.: Artificial Intelligence, 2001, One Hour Photo, 2002, Death to Smoochy, 2002, Insomnia, 2002, The Final Cut, 2004, The House of D, 2004, Noel, 2004, (voice) Robots, 2005, RV, 2006, The Night Listener, 2006, Man of the Year, 2006, (voice) Happy Feet, 2006, Night at the Museum, 2006, License to Wed, 2007, August Rush, 2007, World's Greatest Dad, 2009, Shrink, 2009, Night at the Museum: Battle of the Smithsonian, 2009, Old Dogs, 2009, (voice only) Happy Feet Two, 2011, The Big Wedding, 2013, The Face of Love, 2013, The Butler, 2013, The Angriest Man in Brooklyn, 2014, Merry Friggin' Christmas, 2014, Boulevard, 2014; (TV appearances) Laugh-In, 1977, Eight Is Enough, 1977, America 2-Night, 1978, Happy Days, 1978, '79, Out of the Blue, 1979, Homicide: Life on the Street, 1994, Friends, 1997, L.A. Doctors, 1999, Life with Bonnie, 2003, Law & Order: Special Victims Unit, 2008 (Favorite Scene-Stealing Guest Star, People's Choice Awards, 2009), (plays) Waiting for Godot, 1988, Bengal Tiger at the Baghdad Zoo, 2011; actor, exec. prodr.: (films) Mrs. Doubtfire, 1993 (Golden Globe award for Best Actor in a Musical or Comedy, 1994); actor, exec. prodr.: (films) Jakob the Liar, 1999; performer: (comedy albums) Reality, What a Concept, 1979 (Grammy award), Throbbing Python of Love, A Night at the Met (Grammy award); host Comic Relief, 1986; (comedy specials) ABC Presents a Royal Gala, 1988 (Emmy award, 1988), Carol, Carl, Whoopi & Robin, 1987 (Emmy award), Robin Williams: Live at the Met, 1986, Robin Williams Live, 1986, Comic Relief, 1986, Young Comedians All Star Reunion, 1988, Robin Williams: Live on Broadway, 2002 (Grammy award, 2003), Robin Williams: Weapons of Self Destruction, 2009; host, Shakespeare: The Animated Tales, 1993 (CableAce Award, Best Entertainment Host). Recipient Golden Apple award Hollywood Women's Press Club, ACE award, American Comedy award, 1987, 1988, Grammy award for Best Comedy Rec., 1987, Man of Yr. award Hasty Pudding Theatricals, 1989, People's Choice award Favorite Comedy Motion Picture Actor, 1994, ShoWest Conv. award Male Star of Yr., 1994, Cecil B. DeMille award, Hollywood Fgn. Press, 2005, Hollywood Career Achievement award Hollywood Awards, 2006, Favorite Funny Male Star, People's Choice Awards, 2007, 2008. Died Aug. 11, 2014.

**WILLIAMS, WALKER RICHARD, JR.,** social services administrator; b. Dayton, Ohio, July 11, 1928; s. Walker Richard Sr. and Addie Mary (Smith) W.; m. Eddora L. Saunders, Aug. 6, 1949 (dec. Sept. 1966); 1 child, Yvette R.; m. Emma Jean Griffin, Sept. 4, 1971; children: Timotny E., Walker R. III. Student, U. Dayton, 1946-48. Commd. 2d lt. U.S. Army, 1952; advanced through grades to capt. USAF, Wright Patterson AFB, Ohio, 1963, supply cataloger, supr., 1963, employee rels. specialist, pers. mgmt. specialist, 1966-71; EEO investigator and grievance examiner, chief EEO and affirmative action programs Army and Air N.G., Wright Patterson AFB, Ohio, 1971-88; retired USAR, 1988; program dir. Youth Svc. U.S.A.-Dayton, 1988-89; pvt. contractor Dayton, from 1989. Mem. Adjutant Gen. Ohio Minority Recruiting Adv. Com., 1988—; bd. dirs. Dayton Opportunities Industrialization Ctr., 1976—, Wright Patterson Domestic Action Programs, Inc., 1984—; pres. Jefferson Twp. Bd. Edn., 1980—; mem. Nat. Black Caucus of Black Sch. Bd. Mems., 1980—, Nat. Black Caucus Local Elected Officials, Gov.'s Com. to Preserve Statue of Liberty, 1987, Citywide Vocat. Ednl. Com., 1986—, adv. com. Dayton Bd. Edn., 1980—, Miami Valley Mil. Affairs Assn., Black Elected Democrats of Ohio. Recipient Air Force Civilian Svc. award, Dayton C. of C., Internat. Personnel Mgmt. Assn. Employee of the Yr., Blacks in Govt. Pres.'s award, Federally Employed Women's Supr. of the Yr. runner up, Hispanic Heritage Wk. Spl. award, NAACP Humanitarian award, Community Svc. award, Dayton Bd. Edn., James W. Cisco award, Vocat. Ednl. award Wilberforce U., Urban League Humanitarian award, Svc. to Youth award Girl Scouts U.S., Spl. award United Negro Coll. Fund, Beautillion Militaire Legacy award, Jack & Jill, 7 Air Force Logistics Command Significant Achievement awards, AG of Ohio award, Ohio State U. award, Black Studies Group award, Russell Lyle award Wright Patterson AFB Quarter Century Club, Student Intervention Program Radcliff Sch., Blacks in Glvt. Mediation award, others; a day named in his honor, Dayton, 1987, 88, Svc. award Jefferson Township Bd. Edn. Mem. Miami Valley Pers. Assn., Internat. Pers. Mgmt. Assn., Retired Officers Assn., Air Force Assn., NAACP, Urban League, Blacks in Govt., Dayton Intergovt. EEO Coun. (chmn., historian 1967—), Miami Valley Mil. Affairs Assn., Wright Patterson Quarter Century Club (past pres.). Democrat. Avocations: reading, photography. Home: Dayton, Ohio. Died May 23, 2008.

**WILLIAMSON, RICHARD SALISBURY,** lawyer, former ambassador; b. Evanston, Ill., May 9, 1949; s. Donald George Williamson and Marion (Salisbury) W.; m. Jane Thatcher, Aug. 25, 1973; children: Elizabeth Jean, Craig Salisbury, Richard Middleton. AB with honors, Princeton U., 1971; JD, U. Va. Law Sch., 1974. Bar: Ill., 1974, D.C., 1975. Legislative counsel, adminstrv. asst. to Rep. Philip M. Crane US House of Representatives, 1974-76; assoc. Winston & Strawn LLP, Washington, 1977-80, ptnr., 1980, Chgo., 2007—08; asst. to Pres. for intergovernmental affairs President's Task Force on Regulatory Relief, 1981-83; perm. rep. to UN US Dept. State, Vienna, 1983-85; sr. v.p., corporate & internat. relations Beatrice Companies, Inc., Chgo., 1985-86; ptnr. Mayer, Brown & Platt LLP, Chgo., 1986—2001; asst. sec. for internat. orgn. affairs US Dept. State, Washington, 1988-89, alt. rep. to UN for special polit. affairs, 2002—07, spl. envoy to Sudan, 2008—09; ptnr. Salisbury Strategies, LLC, Kenilworth, Ill.; sr. fellow for multilateral institutions Chgo. Coun. on Global Affairs, 2010—13; non-resident sr. fellow policy The Brookings Instn., 2010—13. Chief US Delegation to US-USSR Bilateral Negotiations on Nuclear Nonproliferation, 1983—84, US Delegation, Fourth Gen. Conf. UN Indsl. Org., 1984, US Delegation to Nuclear Nonproliferation Treaty, 1984; mem. Ill. Econ. Bd., 1987—88, Pres. Gen. Adv. Com. on Arms Control & Disarmament, US Arms Control & Disarmament Agy., 1987—93, Nat. Leadership Network, Inst. Contemporary Studies, 1989—2001; bd. advisors Ctr. for Security Policy, 1989—98; mem. UN Assn. USA, 1989—2001, Adminstrv. Conf. US, 1989—92, vice chmn., 1981—83; mem. Fed. Home Loan Bank Bd., Chgo., 1991—94; chmn. Ill. Sec. State Merit Commn., 1993—99, Ill. Regulatory Relief Task Force, 1994—98; co-chmn. Enterprise Works Worldwide, 1996—2001; mem. Gov.-Elect George Ryan's Transition Team, 1998, Panel on Eminent Persons on Strengthening the Effectiveness of the

Org. for Security & Cooperation in Europe, 2005, Coun. Fgn. Rels.; sr. adv. Nat. Bush for Pres. Campaign Com., 1987—88, Bush Adminstrn. Transition Team, 1988—89, US Delegation to UN Human Rights Commn., 1987, 1989; Roberta Buffet vis. prof. internat. rels. Northwestern U. Buffet Ctr., 2009—10; sr. dir. Albright Stonebridge Group, 2012—13. Editor: Trade & Economic Growth, 1993, United States Foreign Policy and the United Nations System, 1996; co-editor: (with Paul Laxalt) A Changing America: Conservatives View the 80's From the United States Senate, 1980; author: Reagan's Federalism: His Efforts to Decentralize Government, 1990, The United Nations: A Place of Promise and of Mischief, 1991, Disorder in the New World, 1997, Seeking Firm Footing: America in the World in the New Century, 2001, America's Mission in the World: Principals, Practices, and Predicaments Chmn. Ill. Republican Party, 1999-2002. Recipient Fgn. Affairs award for Public Svc., US Dept. State, 1986, Superior Honor award, 1989, 2004, Award of Merit, Boy Scouts America, 1996, Global Leadership award, Enterprise World Worldwide, 2001. Mem.: ABA, Washington DC Bar Assn., Ill. State Bar Assn. Republican. Died Dec. 8, 2013.

**WILLIS, EDGAR ERNEST,** retired communications educator; b. Calgary, Alta., Can., July 12, 1913; came to U.S., 1920, naturalized, 1931; s. Samuel Ernest and Ethel Annie (Fairbourn) W.; m. Zella Carine Nobles, Sept. 16, 1938 (dec. 2008); children: Richard, Franklin, Andrea, (Mrs. Richard Lee Weaver II). BA, Wayne State U., 1935, MA, 1936; PhD, U. Wis., 1940. Producer radio dept. Detroit public schools, 1935-43; asst. prof. speech Wayne State U., 1946; asso. prof. San Jose (Calif.) State Coll., 1946-51, prof., 1951-52; assoc. prof. U. Mich., Ann Arbor, 1952-57, prof., 1957—84, chmn. dept. speech communication and theatre, 1969-79, prof. emeritus, 1984—2014; news analyst WWJ-TV, Detroit, 1953-54; program asso. Nat. Ednl. TV, 1958-59; Fulbright lectr. in TV Gt. Britain, 1963-64. Cons. in TV Cyprus Broadcasting Corp., 1963 Author: Foundations in Broadcasting, 1951, A Radio Director's Manual, 1961, Writing Television and Radio Programs, 1967, (with others) Television and Radio, 1978, Writing Scripts for Television, Radio and Film, 1981, Television, Cable, and Radio, 1992; also articles. Bd. dirs. Family Service Assn., Ann Arbor, 1959-61. Served from ensign to lt. (j.g.) USNR, 1943-46, PTO. Mem. Speech Communication Assn. (adminstrv. council 1954-56, 67-69, chmn. radio-TV film div. 1957), Central States, Mich. speech assns., Phi Beta Kappa, Delta Sigma Rho. Baptist. Home: Perrysburg, Ohio. Died Jan. 25, 2014.

**WILLIS, GORDON HUGH,** cinematographer; b. Queens, NY, May 28, 1931; m. Helen Willis, 1955; 3 children Cinematographer: (films) End of the Road, 1970, Loving, 1970, The Landlord, 1970, The People Next Door, 1970, Little Murders, 1970, Klute, 1971, The Godfather, 1972, Up the Sandbox, 1972, Bad Company, 1972, The Paper Chase, 1973, The Godfather, Part II, 1974, The Parallax View, 1974, The Drowning Pool, 1975, All the President's Men, 1976, Sept 30, 1955, 1977, Annie Hall, 1977, Comes a Horseman, 1978, Interiors, 1978, Manhattan, 1979, Stardust Memories, 1980, Pennies from Heaven, 1981, A Midsummer Night's Sex Comedy, 1982, Zelig, 1983, Broadway Danny Rose, 1984, Purple Rose of Cairo, 1985, Perfect, 1985, The Money Pit, 1986, The Pick-Up Artist, 1987, Bright Lights, Big City, 1988, Presumed Innocent, 1990, The Godfather, Part III, 1990, Damages, 1992, Malice, 1992, The Devil's Own, 1997; (TV movies) The Lost Honor of Kathryn Beck, 1984; dir., cinematographer: (films) Windows, 1980. Served in USAF. Recipient Hon. Acad Award, Acad. Motion Picture Arts & Sciences, 2009. Mem.: American Soc. Cinematographers. Died May 18, 2014.

**WILSON, BOB (ROBERT C. WILSON),** former congressman; b. Calexico, Calif., Apr. 5, 1916; s. George Wellington and Olive (Richardson) W.; m. Shirley Haughey Sarrett, May 16, 1974; children by previous marriage: Frances (Mrs. James Wilson), Mary Ann (Mrs. Michael W. Chapple), Bryant. Student, San Diego State Coll., 1933-35. Mem. 83d-96th Congresses, dean Calif. del., 1979-80; chmn. Washington Industry Team, 1981. Chmn. Nat. Republican Congl. Com., 1961-73 Served with inf. AUS, World War II. Named Minute Man of 1976 Res. Officers Assn.; recipient James S. Forrestal award, 1979 Mem. San Diego Jr. C. of C. (past pres.), Navy League, Am. Legion, Fleet Res. Assn., SAR. Clubs: Elks, Rotary. Presbyterian. Died Aug. 12, 1999.

**WILSON, COLIN HENRY,** writer; b. Leicester, Eng., June 26, 1931; s. Arthur and Anetta Wilson; m. Joy Stewart; children: Sally, Damon, Rowan; 1 child from previous marriage, Roderick. Writer-in-residence Hollins (Va.) Coll., 1966—67; vis. prof. U. Wash., Seattle, 1967, Rutgers U., New Brunswick, NJ, 1974. Author: The Outsider, 1956, The Glass Cage, 1967, The Angry Years, 2007, Man Hunters, 2007, (novels) The Occult, 1971, The Black Room, 1971, The Space Vampires, 1975, Mysteries, 1978, others, (books) Access to Inner World, 1982, A Criminal History of Mankind, 1983, The Essential Colin Wilson, 1984, The Personality Surgeon, 1986, Spider World, 1987, The Misfits: A Study of Sexual Outsiders, 1988, Beyond the Occult: A Twenty-Year Investigation Into the Paranormal, 1988, Written in Blood, 1989; author: (with Donald Seaman) Modern Encyclopedia of Murder, 1983, The Serial Killers, 1989; author: (with Damon Wilson) Encyclopedia of Unsolved Mysteries, 1987, Crimes of Passion, 2006; author: others, (plays) Mozart's Journey to Prague, 1991, Spider World: The Magician, 1992, The Strange Life of P. D. Ouspensky, 1993, From Atlantis to The Sphinx, 1996, Atlas of Holy Places and Sacred Sites, 1996, Alien Dawn: An Investigation Into the Contact Experience, 1998, The Books in My Life, 1998, The Devil's Party, 2000, Spider World: The Magician, 2002, Spider World: Shadowland, 2003; author: (with Damon Wilson) Unsolved Mysteries Past and Present, 1993; author: (with Rand Fle'math) Atlantis Blueprint, 2000; author: (autobiography) Dreaming to Some Purpose, 2004, Atlantis and the Kingdom of the Neanderthals, 2006, The Angry Years, 2007, Super Consciousness, 2008. Mem.: Savage. Home: Saint Austell, England. Died Dec. 5, 2013.

**WILSON, GEORGE WHARTON,** newspaper editor; b. Phila., Feb. 22, 1923; s. Joshua Wharton and Eva (Frear) W.; m. Neva Jean Gossett, Nov. 18, 1950; children: Guy Richard, Lee Robert. BA, Western Md. Coll., 1947; postgrad., U. Pa., 1948. Reporter, city editor News-Chronicle, Shippensburg, Pa., 1945-46; asst. news dir. Sta. WILM-Radio, Wilmington, Del., 1947-48; sports editor Evening Chronicle, Uhrichsville, Ohio, 1948-49, editor, 1949-50, Daily Record, Morristown, N.J., 1950-54; chief editorial writer Standard-Times, New Bedford, Mass., 1954-59; editorial writer Phila. Inquirer, 1959-64, chief editorial writer, 1964-87. Author: Yesterday's Philadelphia, 1975, Stephen Girard: America's First Tycoon, 1995. Served with USAAF, 1942-45. Recipient George Washington honor medal Freedoms Found., 1961, 67, 72; Phila. Press Assn. award editorial writing, 1967, 68; award for editorial writing Pa. Press Assn., 1972, 79; award for editorial writing U.S. Indsl. Council, 1975, 77; Disting. Service award Sigma Delta Chi, 1977; Disting. Journalism award Citizens Com. on Public Edn. in Phila., 1978; Public Service award Phila. Convention and Visitors Bur., 1980; award for column writing N.J. Soc. Profl. Journalists, 1981; Elm award Fishtown Civic Assn., 1982 Mem. Am. Acad. Polit. and Social Sci., Franklin Inst., Acad. Natural Sci., Hist. Soc. Pa., Soc. Profl. Journalists, Phila. Mus. Art, Independence Seaport Mus., Phila. Writers Orgn., Phila. Zool. Soc., Pa. Soc., Friends of Independence Nat. Hist. Park, Huguenot Hist. Soc., Pa. Acad. Fine Arts, Pen and Pencil Club (Phila.), Elks, Am. Legion. Republican. Mem. United Ch. of Christ. Club: Pen and Pencil (Phila.). Home: Albrightsville, Pa. Died Apr. 28, 1999.

**WILSON, JOHN ANTHONY,** physicist; b. Halifax, Yorkshire, Eng., July 16, 1938; s. Harry and Ivy (Shaw) W.; m. Patricia Ann McNulty, Aug. 31, 1963; children: Daniel, Rebecca. BA, U. Cambridge, 1961, MA, 1964; PGCE, U. London, 1962; PhD, U. Cambridge, 1968, ScD, 1999. Jr. rsch. fellow Cavendish Lab., U. Cambridge, 1969-72; mem. rsch. staff Bell Telephone Labs., Murray Hill, N.J., 1972-79; Royal Soc. sr. rsch. fellow H.H. Wills Physics Lab., U. Bristol, 1979-86, George Wills sr. rsch. fellow, from 1986. Mem. rsch. com. Vb Inst. Laue-Langevin, Grenoble, France, 1989—. Asst. editor Jour. Physics, Inst. of Physics, 1982-86; contbr. articles to profl. jours. Mem. Inst. Physics U.K., European Phys. Soc., Am. Chem. Soc., Am. Phys. Soc. Mem. Ch. Eng. Achievements include research in solid state physics, metal-insular transition, charge density waves, and high temperature superconductivity. Home: Bristol, England. Died Oct. 7, 2013.

**WILSON, JOHN DAVID,** educational administrator, educator; b. Norristown, Pa., Dec. 27, 1946; s. John E. and Gail (Kane) W.; m. Patricia Borth, Mar. 10, 1984; children: Joshua M., Christopher I. AB, St. Joseph's U., 1968, MA, 1971. Cert. tchr., Pa. With Elwyn (Pa.), Inc., 1968-91, dir. ancillary svcs., 1986-89, dir. acad. affairs, 1989-91; dir. edn. Vanguard Sch., Paoli, Pa., from 1991. Vice chairperson Title IV ESEA adv. coun. Pa. Dept. Edn., 1979-80; bd. dirs. Trinity Coop. Day Care, Pa., 1981-83. Contbr. articles to profl. jours. V.p. Taxpayers for Quality Edn., Swarthmore, Pa., 1975-76; bd. dirs. Freedom Valley Disability Enablement, Inc., 1993—. Mem. Pa. Fedn. Coun. for Exceptional Children (pres. 1987-88), Pa. Mental Retardation (pres. Pa. chpt. 1988-89), Pioneers Divsn. (pres. Pa. chpt. 1993—), St. Joseph's U. Edn. Alumni (treas. 1993—). Avocation: travel. Home: Newtown Square, Pa. Died Oct. 13, 1998.

**WILSON, LOUISE,** fashion designer, consultant; b. Cambridge, England, Feb. 23, 1962; d. William and Pamela Elizabeth (Tebbs) Wilson; life ptnr. Thomas Kwamina Aggrey; 1 child, Timothy Wilson-Aggrey. MA Fashion, Ctrl. St. Martins Coll. of Art & Design, UK, 1984—86; BA Fashion (hon.), Preston Polythechnic, UK, 1980—84. Course dir., MA fashion course Ctrl. St. Martins Coll. of Art & Design, United Kingdom, England, 1992—2014; design dir. women's wear collection & licensing Donna Karan Internat., New York, 1997—99, cons. designer dir. women's collection, licensing, 1999—2002. Cons. Krizia, Italy, 1996, Ghost, London, 1999—2000, Hugo Boss Women's Wear, Milan, 2000. Recipient prof., U. of the Arts London, 2001. Christian. Avocations: travel, art, music, book collecting, fashion. Home: London, England. Died May 16, 2014.

**WILSON, SISTER MARY LAWRENCE,** former education educator; b. Toledo, June 6, 1907; d. Frank Dean and Margaret Agnes (Casey) W. Student, Mary Manse Coll., 1927-30; BS in Edn, DeSales Coll., 1936; MA, Fordham U., 1946, PhD, 1948. Elementary sch. tchr., 1927-41; elementary sch. supr. gen. edn., 1947-48; dean Mary Manse Coll., Toledo, 1949-64, pres., 1964-68, prof. edn., 1968-75. Curriculum dir. Toledo Diocesan Schs., 1971-77; prin. St. Angela Hall, 1977-79 Mem. Mayor's Dist. Council for Urban Renewal, Toledo.; Trustee Med. Coll. Ohio, Toledo, 1964-76, Med. Coll. of Ohio at Toledo Found., Inc. Recipient Stella Maris medal Mary Manse Coll., Mother Adelaide award Lourdes Coll., Outstanding Citizen award Med. Coll. Ohio, Golden Shamrock Outstanding Alumna award Cen. Cath. High Sch. Mem. Phi Kappa Phi. Clubs: Zonta Internat. Roman Catholic. Home: Toledo, Ohio. Died May 1993.

**WILSON, RALPH COOKERLY, JR.,** professional football team executive; b. Columbus, Ohio, Oct. 17, 1918; s. Ralph Cookerly and Edith (Cole) W.; children: Christy Cole, Linda Brown, Edith Denise. AB, U. Va., 1940; postgrad., U. Mich., 1940-41. Pres. Ralph C. Wilson Jr. Enterprises (privately owned family bus.); engaged in profl. football, roadbuilding Detroit, 1946—59; pres., owner Buffalo Bills Profl. Football Club, 1959—2014. Served in USNR, 1941-46. Decorated Commendation medal; named to Pro Football Hall of Fame, 2009. Mem. Ocean Club of Fla., Country Club of Detroit, Grosse Pointe (Mich.) Club, Buffalo Country Club, Shriners. Presbyterian. Home: Grosse Pointe Shores, Mich. Died Mar. 25, 2014.

**WILSON, ROBERT WARNE,** philanthropist; b. Detroit, Nov. 3, 1926; s. Clarence Warne Wilson and Margaret Ballantyne; m. Marillyn Buelow, Apr. 1957 (div. 1977). BA in Economics, magna cum laude, Amherst Coll., Mass., 1946; MA in Economics, U. Mich., 1947; postgrad., Mich. Law Sch., 1948-49. Trainee First Boston Corp., NYC, 1949-50, 52-53; securities analyst Nat. Bank of Detroit, 1953-58; securities analyst to v.p. Gen. American Inv., NYC, 1958-62; securities analyst A.G. Becker & Co., NYC, 1962-68; investor, 1968—86; philanthropist, 1987—2013. Bd. dirs. Bklyn. Mus., 1974-88, Bklyn. Botanic Garden, 1974-88, NYC Opera, 1977-98, chmn. 1981-93; adv. bd. Met. Opera, 1979-81; trustee Environtl. Def., 1986-2013, Lyric Opera of Chgo. Nat. Bd., 1995-01, Manhattan Inst., 1986-02, Whitney Mus. of American Art, 1978-2013, v.p., World Monuments Fund, 1990-2013 vice chmn., Deafness Rsch. Found., 1998-01. With US Army, 1951—52. Mem.: Phi Beta Kappa. Republican. Avocations: opera, museums, theater, movies, sightseeing. Home: New York, NY. Died Dec. 23, 2013.

**WILSON, THOMAS RUSSELL,** lawyer; b. Des Moines, Jan. 10, 1965; s. Russell Harry and Beverly Ann (Burchfield) W. BS, U. Iowa, 1986; JD cum laude, Harvard U., 1990. Bar: Calif. 1990. Fgn. lawyer Nauta Dutilh, Rotterdam, The Netherlands, 1990; fellow European Commn., Brussels, 1991; assoc. Morgan, Lewis & Bockius, LA, 1992-94; br. gen. counsel Valeo, S.A., Paris, 1994-97; assoc. Brobeck Phleger & Harrison, LLP, San Francisco, from 1997. Mem. State Bar of Calif. (intellectual property sect.), Bar Assn. San Francisco (sports and entertainment law sec.). Home: Oakland, Calif. Died Aug. 23, 2008.

**WILSON, WILLIAM JOSEPH,** chemist; b. Roxbrugh, NZ, Nov. 11, 1923; arrived in Can., 1959; s. William Joseph and Rhoda Ann (Weatherall) Wilson; m. Yvonne Jean Cougle Wilson, Jan. 20, 1958; children: Sarah Catherine, Lucy Ann. BS, U. Otago, Dunedin. NZ, 1947, MS, 1949. John Edmond rsch. fellow U. Otago, 1949—52; rsch. chemist N.Z. Dept. Sci. & Industry Research, Rotorua-Auckland, 1952—55; chemist Boliden Mining Co., Sweden, 1955—56; preservation chemist N.Z. Forest Rsch. Inst., Rotorua, 1956—59; rsch. chemist Fraser Cos., Ltd., Atholville, N.B., Can., 1959—66; sr. rsch. chemist Mac Millan Bloedel Rsch. Ltd., Vancouver, BC, 1966—69; chem. cons. Perth, Western Australia, 1969—70; exploration geologist Norseman Gold Mines, Western Australia, 1970—71; pres., dir. rsch. Atlantic Analytical Svcs. Ltd., Saint John, NB, from 1971. Pres. St. John Industry Parks, 1979; chmn. Small Bus. Com., St. John Bd. Trade. Fellow: NZ Inst. Chemistry; mem.: TAPPI, Can. Inst. Food Sci & Tech. (pres. NB chpt. 1979), Can. Mineral Analysts, Can. Inst. Mining & Metallurgy (bd. dirs. N.B. br. 1980—81), Assn. Exploration Geochemists, Can. Pulp & Paper Assn. (sr. mem. tech. sect., chmn. phys. and chem. standards com. from 1984), Am. Chem. Soc., Fortnightly (St. John) (pres. 1979). Achievements include patents in field. Home: Saint John, Canada. Died May 5, 2008.

**WING, LORNA,** psychiatrist, consultant, researcher; b. Gillingham, Kent, Eng., Oct. 7, 1928; d. Bernard and Gladys (Whittall) Tolchard; m. John Wing, May 15, 1950 (dec. April 18, 2010); 1 child, Susan (dec. 2009) MB BS, Univ. Coll., London, 1952; MD, U. London, 1965. Psychiat. registrar Netherne Hosp., Coulsdon, Eng., 1953-56; rsch. asst. Univ. Coll., 1958-64; mem. sci. staff Med. Rsch. Coun., London, 1964-90; hon. cons. Maudsley Hosp., London, 1972-90; hon. sr. lectr. Inst. Psychiatry, London, 1974-90; cons. psychiatrist Nat. Autistic Soc., 1990—2014. Author: The Autistic Spectrum, 1996; editor: Aspects of Autism-Biological Research, 1988; contbr. papers to profl. publications V.p. Nat. Autistic Soc., London; bd. dirs. Sussex (Eng.) Autistic Soc. Recipient award for work in field of mental retardation Internat. Assn. for Study of Mental deficiency, 1988; named to Order of the British Empire, Brit. Govt., 1995. Fellow Royal Coll. Psychiatrists. Avocations: gardening, reading, walking. Died June 6, 2014.

**WINKLER, NICHOLAS GARY,** lawyer; b. Sydney, June 24, 1948; BA, Sydney U., Australia, 1968, LLB, 1971, LLM, 1977. Law clk. Prudential Assurance Co., Sydney, Australia, 1969—71; solicitor State Bank of NSW, Sydney, Australia, 1971—82; chief solicitor Custom Credit Corp. Ltd., Sydney, Australia, 1982—87; prin. Nicholas Winkler & Turner, Sydney, Australia, 1984—94; sr. cons. Drake Mgmt. Cons., Sydney, Australia, 1994—96; dir. Nicholas Winkler Cons., Sydney, 1996—99; gen. counsel Tower Tech. Pty. Ltd., Lane Cove, Australia, 1999—2003; corp. counsel Caltex Australia Petroleum Pty Ltd., Sydney, from 2003. Contbr. articles to profl. jours. including Company Dir. and Law Soc. Jour. Patron, sponsor Pub. Info. Paper Series of Com. for Econ. Devel. of Australia, Sydney, 1993. Mem. Com. for Econ. Devel. of Australia (trustee 1990—, mem. internat. rels. com. 2000—), Law Soc. New South Wales, Australian Inst. of Co. Dir., Am. C. of C. in Australia, Am. Club Sydney, Cruising Yacht Club Australia. Home: Sydney, Australia. Died 2007.

**WINTER, JOHNNY (JOHN DAWSON WINTER III),** blues guitarist; b. Beaumont, Tex., Feb. 23, 1944; s. John Dawson II and Edwina (Holland) W. Singer, guitarist: (albums) The Progressive Blues Experiment, 1968, Johnny Winter, 1969, Second Winter, 1969, Johnny Winter-And, 1970, Live Johnny Winter And, 1971 (Gold Record award

1974), Still Alive and Well, 1973, Saints and Sinners, 1974, John Dawson Winter III, 1974, Captured Live!, 1976, Together with Edgar Winter, 1976, Nothin' But the Blues, 1977, White Hot and Blue, 1978, The Johnny Winter Story, 1980, Raisin' Cain, 1980, Guitar Slinger, 1984, Serious Business, 1985, 3rd Degree, 1986, The Winter of '88, 1988, Winter Scene, 1990, Let Me In, 1991, Hey Where's Your Brother, 1992, Scorchin' Blues, 1992, A Rock n' Roll Collection, 1994, Johnny Winter Live in New York City 1997, Live in NYC '97, 1998, I'm a Bluesman, 2004, The Johnny Winter Anthology, 2009, Roots, 2011, Essential Johnny Winter, 2013, True to the Blues: The Johnny Winter Story, 2014, Step Back, 2014; prodr.: (albums with Muddy Waters) Hard Again, 1977, I'm Ready, 1978, Muddy Mississippi Waters Live, 1979, King Bee, 1980. Mem. Broadcast Music Inc., Musicians Union. Died July 16, 2014.

**WIRAHADIKUSUMAH, UMAR,** former vice president of Indonesia, retired army officer; b. Sumedang, West Java, Oct. 10, 1924; Commd. officer Indonesian Army; ret.; platoon comdr. Tasakmalaya, 1942; mem. PETA, 1944; comdr. TKR, Cicalengka, West Java, 1945, Mil. Command of Greater City of Djakarta, 1958, Territory V/Java, 1960, Kostrad, 1966; chief, operational staff Gen. Divsn. Siliwangi, 1949; army chief of staff, 1969—73; chmn. Audit Bd., 1973—83; v.p. Indonesia, 1983—87. Participant, key role in defeating Islamic fundamentalist rebellions, West Java, 1945—49; rebellion Sumatra, 1956, Communist Coups, 1948, 1965. Decorated Indonesian medal, Fed. Rep. Germany, Netherlands, Yugoslavia, Republic of Korea, Belgium, Malaysia, US, Jordan. Died Mar. 22, 2003.

**WISE, HAROLD B.,** internist, educator; b. Hamilton, Ont., Can., Feb. 14, 1937; MD, U. Toronto, 1961. Physician Prince Albert Clin., Sask., Canada, 1962—63; resident Kaiser Found. Hosp., San Francisco, 1963—64, Montefiore Hosp. and Med. Ctr., Bronx, 1964—65; acting dir. ambulatory svc. and home care Morrisania City Hosp., 1965—66; dir. health ctr. Dr. Martin Luther King Jr. Health Ctr., 1966—71; assoc. prof. comty. health Albert Einstein Coll. Medicine, from 1970. Milbank Meml. Fund fellow; dir. internship and residency program social medicine Montefiore Hosp. and Med. Ctr., from 1969, dir. inst. health team devel., 1972; dir. Family Ctr. Health. Mem.: N.Y. Chiropractic Assn. (bd. mem. from 1972), Inst. Medicine-NAS. Died Aug. 15, 1998.

**WITHERS, ROBERT THOMAS,** exercise physiologist, educator; b. Birmingham, Eng., Aug. 26, 1938; arrived in Australia, 1974; s. Thomas and Ada (Ingram) W.; m. Pamela Sue Peridier, July 5, 1974. Cert. in edn., Alsager Coll. of Edn., Eng., 1961; diploma in phys. edn., St. Luke's Coll., Eng., 1962; MSc, Washington State U., 1967; PhD, U. Md., 1974. Emeritus prof. phys. edn. Flinders U., Bedford Park, Australia. Mem. Nat. Lab. Accreditation Com., Australian Sports Commn., 1990-96, chmn., 1997—, nat. sport sci. accreditation com., 1997—; adj. fellow Australian Inst. Sport. Assoc. editor Australian Jour. Sci. and Medicine in Sport, 1985—2006; mem. editl. bd. Internat. Jour. Sports Medicine, 1994—; contbr. over 100 articles to profl. jours. Fellow Australian Sports Medicine Fedn. (emeritus), Am. Coll. Sports Medicine (emeritus). Avocations: reading, weight-training, jogging, spectator sports. Home: Flagstaff Hill, Australia. Deceased.

**WITHERS, W. RUSSELL, JR.,** broadcast executive; b. Cape Girardeau, Mo., Dec. 10, 1936; s. Waldo Russell Sr. and Dorothy Ruth (Harrelson) W.; 1 child, Dana Ruth. BA, S.E. Mo. State U., 1958. Disc jockey Sta. KGMO Radio, Cape Girardeau, 1955-58; account exec. Sta. WGGH Radio, Marion, Ill., 1961-62; v.p. LIN Broadcasting Corp., Nashville, 1962-69; exec. v.p., dir. Laser Link Corp., Woodbury, NY, 1970-72; owner Withers Broadcasting of Hawaii, 1975-79, Withers Broadcasting of Minn., 1974-79, Withers Broadcasting Cos., Iowa, from 1981, Mood Music Ill., Mt. Vernon, from 1973, Mood Music, Inc., Cape Girardeau, from 1972, Royal Hawaiian Radio Co., Inc., others, WROY - WRUL, 2006, WYNG, 2007. Owner various radio and TV stas. including KREX-TV, Grand Junction, Colo., KREY-TV, Montrose, Colo., KREG-TV, Glenwood Springs, Colo., Page Ins. and Real Estate, Mt. Vernon, Ill.; chmn. bd., CEO Withers Beverage Corp., Mobile, Ala., 1973—79; chmn. adv. bd. Mut. Network; bd. dirs. Theatrevision, Inc., Turneffe Island Lodge, Ltd., Belize, Sta. WDTV, Clarksburg, W.Va., WMIX-AM-TV, Mt. Vernon, KGMO-KAPE, Cape Girardeau, KOKX AM-FM, Keokuk, Iowa, KTRC, Santa Fe, KRHW and KBXB, Sikeston, Mo., WKIB Anna, Cape Girardeau, WMOK, WREZ and WZZL, Paducah, Ky., WSDR-WSSQ, WZZL, Sterling Rock Falls, Ill., WILY, WRXX (FM), Centralia, Ill., WEBQ and WEBQ-FM, Harrisburg, Ill.; pres. Ill. Pub. Airports Assn.; co-chmn. TARPAC; chair NAB Radio Bd., 2007—08. Bd. dir., chmn. bd. Mt. Vernon Tourism and Conv. Bur.; chmn. Mt. Vernon Airport Authority; bd. regents Lincoln Acad.; past pres. IPAA; past chmn. Conv. & Visitors, Airport Authority; bd. dir. No. Colo. C.C., Libr. Am. Broadcasters, Radio Bd., AP. With U.S. Army, 1957-58. Recipient Alumni Achievement award, SEMO State U., 2007, Significant Signature award, Sigma Chi Fraternity, 2011; named Broadcaster of Yr., Ill., 2006, W.Va, 2007. Mem. Mt. Vernon C. of C. (bd. dir.), Nat. Assn. Broadcasters (bd. dir., exec. com.), Ill. Broadcasters Assn., Stadium Club, Mo. Athletic Club, Elks, Moose, AmVets, Masons, Shriners, Sigma Chi (Significant Sig award, 2011). Christian Scientist. Home: Mount Vernon, Ill. Died Jan. 2014.

**WITMEYER, JOHN JACOB, III,** lawyer; b. New Orleans, Dec. 18, 1946; s. John J. and Thais Audrey (Dolese) W. BS, Tulane U., 1968; JD with distinction, Duke U., 1971. Bar: NY. Assoc. Mudge Rose Guthrie & Alexander, NYC, 1971-76; ptnr. Ford Marrin Esposito & Witmeyer (now Ford, Marrin, Esposito, Witmeyer & Gleser LLP), NYC, from 1976. Bd. trustees Gregorian U. Found., from 1999; adv. coun. Paul Tulane Coll., Tulane U., 1998—2006, Sch. Liberal Arts Tulane U., from 2006, Newcomb-Tulane Coll., from 2011; bd. dirs. Tulane Assocs., Tulane U., 2001—10. Ret. col. US Army. Mem.: Order of the Holy Sepulchre (Knight Grand Cross). Home: New York, NY. Died July 31, 2013.

**WITTE, DEANN RENEE,** elementary school educator; b. Faulkton, SD, Oct. 20, 1964; d. Robert Arthur and Beth Irene (Bellack) W. BS in Elem. Edn., No. State U., 1987. 2d grade tchr. Crazy Horse Sch., Wanblee, S.D., 1989-90, White River (S.D.) Elem. Sch., from 1990. Advisor Johnson O'Mally Bd., White River, 1993—; asst. grant writer NSF, White River, 1993—. Active Dem. Ctrl. Com., Faulkton, 1981-82. Mem. Internat. Reading Assn., NEA, S.D. Edn. Assn., White River Edn. Assn. (officer 1990-99). Roman Catholic. Avocations: family activities, education for the future, reading, challenges. Died Apr. 5, 1999.

**WITTER, WENDELL WINSHIP,** financial executive, retired; b. Berkeley, Calif., Oct. 16, 1910; s. George Franklin Jr. and Mary Ann (Carter) W.; m. Florence Corder, Oct. 18, 1935 (div. Oct. 1973); 1 child, Wendelyn; m. Janet Hutchinson Alexander, Dec. 12, 1973 (dec. 1977); m. Evelyn Grinter Harkins Gooding, Mar. 26, 1978. BA, U. Calif., Berkeley, 1932; Diploma, Investment Bankers Inst., Wharton Bus. Sch., 1955. Salesman Dean Witter & Co., San Francisco, 1933-50, ptnr., 1950-68, exec. v.p., 1968-76; cons. Dean Witter, Reynolds, Inc., San Francisco, 1976-82, retired cons., 1982-99. Past Regent U. Calif., 1969-70; mem. Coordinating Coun. Higher Edn., Calif., 1970-71; trustee State Univs., Long Beach, Calif., 1971-79; past bd. dirs. San Francisco Symphony, ARC Golden Gate Chpt., Met. YMCA, Grace Cathedral, Better Bus. Bur. With AUS Res., 1941-46, Army Air Force, 1941-46, ret. lt. col. Mem. San Francisco Bond Club (pres. 1955), Assn. of Stock Exch. Firms (pres. 1962), Investment Bankers Assn. Am. (pres. 1965), U. Calif. Alumni Assn. (pres. 1969-70), Berkeley Fellows, Pacific Union Club, San Francisco Golf Club, Bohemian Club, Zeta Psi. Republican. Episcopalian. Avocations: golf, fishing. Home: San Francisco, Calif. Died Mar. 12, 2001.

**WOLFE, JOHN H.,** sales trainer, association executive; b. Honolulu, June 12, 1924; s. Fred R. and Dorothy Wolfe; m. Alice McCoy Wolfe; 1 child, Jann. BA, Dartmouth Coll., 1945. Pres. John Wolfe Inst., Houston, from 1964; pres., exec. dir. Sales-Mktg. Execs., Houston, from 1985. Author: Sell Like an Ace, Live Like a King, 1961, Miracle Platform Power, 1978, The Wrong Target, 1981, Drilling for Death, 1982. Recipient Hall of Fame award, Nat. Spkrs. Assn., 1977. Republican. Mem. Disciples Of Christ Ch. Avocation: flying. Home: Houston, Tex. Died Dec. 4, 1990.

**WOLFE, WILLIAM KEITH,** educational administrator; b. Potosi, Wis., Dec. 9, 1933; s. Vilas Dawson and Jessie May (Schramm) Wolfe; m. Kathleen Leola Grattan, Oct. 8, 1960; children: Gary, Gretchen, Aaron, Darwyn, Sean. BS, U. Wis. Platteville, 1961, MS, 1966. Tchr., Platteville, Potosi, Cassville, Wis., 1952—61; elem. prin. Platteville Pub. Schs., 1961—68, mid. sch. prin., 1968—69; comm. instr. Southwest Wis. Tech., Fennimore, 1969—89, divsn. chmn., gen. edn., 1980—86, NE Iowa CC, Peosta, from 1989. Author: Articulation of General Education and Occupational Competenties, 1974, Articulation of Adult Basic Education with Career Exploration, 1978; co-author: Vocat. Tech. Adult Education's Curriculum Guide for Career Development, 1977. With US Army, 1957—59. Recipient Outstanding Young Educator award, Platteville Jaycees, 1965. Mem.: NEA, Silas Shepherd Lodge Rsch., Blackhawk Schs. Edn. Assn. (sec. 1954—55), Platteville Edn. Assn. (pres. 1964—65), Upper Midwest Regional Edn. Lab. Assn., Wis. Assn. Vocat. Adult Edn. (bd. dirs. 1981—83, Tchg. Excellence award 1980), Am. Vocat. Assn., Phi Delta Kappa. Republican. Avocations: writing, acting, music, travel. Home: Potosi, Wis. Died Aug. 21, 1991.

**WOLFENSON, MARV (MARVIN EARLE WOLFENSON),** professional basketball team executive; b. Mpls., Aug. 13, 1926; m. Elayne Berman; children: Ellyn, Ernie, David. BA, U. Minn. Owner The N.W. Racquet, Swim & Health Club, Minn. Timberwolves, 1989—94. Served in US Army. Died Dec. 21, 2013.

**WOLFERT, RUTH,** Gestalt therapist; b. NYC, Nov. 10, 1933; d. Ira and Helen (Herschdorfer) W. BS summa cum laude, Columbia U., 1967, postgrad., 1966-68. Pvt. practice, NYC, from 1972; dir. Action Groups, NYC, 1974-76, Gestalt Groups, NYC, from 1976, Chrysalis Inst., NYC, from 1998. Mem. faculty coordinating bd. Women's Interart Ctr., N.Y.C., 1971-75, bd. dirs. 1981—; presenter Stockton (N.J.) State Coll., 1974-75; mem. faculty Inst. for Experiential Learning and Devel., 1988-92, Woodstock U., 1989-91, Gestalt Inst., Atlanta, 1989—' presenter in field. Author: The Broken Doll: A Survivor's Journey Into Life, 1996, The Spiritual Dimension of Gestalt Therapy, 1999, Self in Experience, Gestalt Therapy, Science and Buddhism: Moving Toward Synthesis, 2000; co-author: Adding Women's Voices: Feminism and Gestalt Therapy in Gestalt!, 1999, Gestalt Therapy in Action in Beyond Talk Therapy, 1999; contbg. author: (booklet) A Consumer's Guide to Non-Sexist Therapy, 1978; also articles. Bd. dirs. Women's Interart Ctr., 1981—. Mem. Assn. Humanist Psychology (bd. dirs. ea. regional network 1981-87, pres. 1985-87), N.Y. Inst. Gestalt Therapy (faculty 1980—, chair workshops program 1979-83, co-chair conf. 1983-85, brochure com. 1987-95, interim exec. com. 1988-90, conf. com. 1989-91, 96-97, v.p. 1993-95), Assn. Transpersonal Psychology (co-chair N.Y. discussion group 1991-92), Assn. Advancement Gestalt Therapy (bd. dirs. 1993—, co-chair Women's Issues in Gestalt Therapy interest group 1993—, conf. com. 1993-99). Deceased.

**WOLFMAN, BRUNETTA REID,** education educator; b. Clarksdale, Miss., Sept. 4, 1931; d. Willie Orlando and Belle Victoria (Allen) Reid Griffin; m. Burton Wolfman, Oct. 4, 1952; children: Andrea, Jeffrey. BA, U. Calif., Berkeley, 1957, MA, 1968, PhD, 1971; DHL (hon.), Boston U., 1983; DP (hon.), Northeastern U., 1983; DL (hon.), Regis Coll., 1984, Stonehill Coll., 1985; DHL, Suffolk U., 1985; DET (hon.), Wentworth Inst., 1987; AA (hon.), Roxbury Community Coll., 1988. Asst. dean faculty Dartmouth Coll., Hanover, N.H., 1972-74; asst. v.p. acad. affairs U. Mass., Boston, 1974-76; acad. dean Wheelock Coll., Boston, 1976-78; cons. Arthur D. Little, Cambridge, Mass., 1978; dir. policy planning Dept. Edn., Boston, 1978-82; pres. Roxbury C.C., Boston, 1983-88, ACE sr. assoc., 1988-94, NAWE sr. assoc., 1994-98; assoc. v.p. acad. affairs George Washington U., Washington, 1989-92, prof. edn., 1992-96, prof. edn. emeritus, from 1996. Mem. Accrediting Commn. on Edn. on Health Svcs. Administrn.; pres. bd. dirs. Literacy Vols. of Capitol Region; mem. comm. com. bd., pub. rels. com. LVA, Inc.; bd. dirs. Am. Coun. Edn., Harvard Cmty. Health Plan. Author: Roles, 1983; contbr. articles to profl. jours. Mem. bd. overseers Wellesley Coll., 1981, Boston Symphony Orch.; trustee Mus. Fine Arts, Boston; mem. Coun. on Edn. for Pub. Health; chair Provincetown bd. Coun. on Aging, 1999—2005; mem. Holocaust meml. com. NCCJ; bd. dirs. Boston-Fenway Program, 1977, Freedom House, Boston, 1983, Boston Pvt. Industry Coun., 1983; bd. dirs., co-chmn. NCCJ, Boston, 1983; bd. dirs. Elder Svcs. Cape Cod and the Islands, 2003, adv. coun. mem., 2009; mem. Cape Cod Outer Cape Interfaith Group on Holocaust, Genocide and Human Rights. Recipient Freedom award, NAACP No.Calif., 1971, Amelia Earhart award, Women's Edn. and Indsl. Union, Boston, 1983, Provincetown Sr. Citizen of Yr., 2004; named Wolfman Courtyard in their honor, Evergreen Ctr., 2000; scholar Nat. Assn. Women in Edn. Mem. AAUW, Am. Sociol. Assn. (mem. adv. group 2010), Assn. Black Women in Higher Edn., Greater Boston C. of C. (edn. com. 1982), Sierra Club, Mass. Audubon Soc., Cosmos Club (Washington), Provincetown Art Assn. (sec. bd. trustees, mus. sch. com., nominating com.), Alpha Kappa Alpha (Humanitarian award 1984), Phi Delta Kappa, Cape Cod Found. (bd. dir. 2008). Home: Provincetown, Mass. Died Nov. 15, 2013.

**WOLFORD, RONALD EUGENE,** computer operations professional; b. Steubenville, Ohio, May 2, 1953; s. James Everett and Patricia Louise (Smith) W.; m. Linda Marian Blenk, Aug. 24, 1974; children: Angela Patrece, Ross Albert. A in Gen. Bus., Washington Tech. Coll., 1974. Programmer Detail Mgmt. Corp., Marietta, Ohio, 1974-75, First Bank, Marietta, 1976-78, Forma Scientific, Marietta, 1978-81, Amfac Nurseries-Cole, Columbus, Ohio, 1981-82; programmer, analyst Whiting Mfg., Cin., 1982-84, Fries & Fries, Cin., 1985-88; sys. analyst Mike Albert Leasing, Inc., Cin., 1988-94, maintenance supr., 1994, ops. mgr., database adminstr., from 1994. Chmn., asst. coord. Blue Ash (Ohio) Youth Symphony Orch., 1993-95. Mem. Tri-State Midrange User Group. Democrat. Methodist. Avocations: reading, home computers, walking, tv and movies. Home: Cincinnati, Ohio. Deceased.

**WOLTERS, OLIVER WILLIAM,** history educator; b. Reading, Eng., June 8, 1915; came to U.S., 1964; s. Albert William and Gertrude (Lewis) W.; m. Euteen Khoo, Apr. 25, 1955; children: Pamela Gwyneth, Nigel Christopher. BA, Lincoln Coll., Oxford U., 1937; PhD, Sch. Oriental and African Studies, London, 1961. With Malayan Civil Service, 1938-57; lectr. Sch. Oriental and African Studies, London, 1957-63; prof. S.E. Asian history Cornell U., Ithaca, N.Y., 1964-74, Goldwin Smith prof. S.E. Asian history, 1974-85; ret., 1985. Author: Early Indonesian Commerce, 1967, The Fall of Srivijaya, 1970, History, Culture, and Region in Southeast Asian Perspectives, 1982, 2d edit., 1999, Two Essays on Dai-Viet in the Fourteenth Century, 1988; editor: (with others) Southeast Asian History, 1976; sr. editor: The Vietnam Forum, 1985-93. Trustee Breezewood Found., Md., 1964-84. Decorated Officer Order Brit. Empire, 1952; Guggenheim fellow, 1972-73; Bellagio fellow Rockefeller Found., 1982; recipient Disting. Scholarship award Assn. for Asian Studies, 1990. Episcopalian. Home: Ithaca, NY. Deceased.

**WOMACK, BOBBY (ROBERT DWAYNE WOMACK),** musician, songwriter; b. Cleve., Mar. 4, 1944; m. Barbara Campbell-Cooke, Mar. 1965 (div. Apr. 1971); 1 child, Vincent; m. Regina Banks; children: Truth(dec.), Bobby, Gina. Co-founding mem. of gospel group The Valentinos (formerly known as The Womack Brothers); solo artist, 1966—2014. Writer, singer: songs Looking for a Love, 1962, It's All Over Now, 1964, How I Miss You Baby, 1969, That's the Way I Feel About Cha, 1971, Woman's Gotta Have It, 1972, Harry Hippie, 1972, Nobody Wants You When You're Down and Out, 1973, Check It Out, 1975, Daylight, 1976, How Could You Break My Heart, 1979, Love Has Finally Come at Last, 1984, I Wish He Didn't Trust Me So Much, 1985, albums The Womack Live, 1967, Fly Me to the Moon, 1969, My Prescription, 1970, Communication, 1971, Understanding, 1972, Across 110th Street, 1972, The Facts of Life, 1973, Lookin' for a Love Again, 1974, I Don't Know What the World is Coming To, 1975, Safety Zone, 1975, I Can Understand It, 1975, BW Goes C&W, 1976, Home Is Where the Heart Is, 1976, Pieces, 1977, Roads of Life, 1979, The Poet, 1981, The Poet II, 1984, So Many Rivers, 1985, Someday We'll All Be Free, 1985, Womagic, 1986, Last Soul Man, 1987, Save the Children, 1989, I Still Love You, 1993, I Wanna Make Love to You, 1993, Soul Seduction Supreme, 1994, Resurrection, 1994, Back to My Roots, 1999, Traditions, 1999, Christmas Album, 2000; writer, singer (albums) The Bravest Man in the Universe, 2012; author: (memoirs) Midnight Mover, 2006. Recipient Pioneer award, Rhythm & Blues Found., 1996; named to Rock & Roll Hall of Fame, 2009. Died June 27, 2014.

**WONDERS, WILLIAM CLARE,** geography educator; b. Toronto, Apr. 22, 1924; s. George Clarence and Ann Mary (Bell) W.; m. Lillian Paradise Johnson, June 2, 1951; children: Karen Elizabeth, Jennifer Anne, Glen William. BA with honors, Victoria Coll., U. Toronto, 1946; MA, Syracuse U., 1948; PhD, U. Toronto, 1951; Fil. Dr. h.c., Uppsala U., 1981. Teaching asst. dept. geography Syracuse U., 1946-48; lectr. dept. geography U. Toronto, 1948-53; asst. prof. geography dept. polit. economy U. Alta., 1953-55, assoc. prof. geography, 1955-57, prof., head dept. geography, 1957-67, prof. dept. geography, 1967-87, Univ. prof., from 1983, prof. emeritus, 1987—2008, disting. emeritus prof., from 2009. Vis. prof. geography U. B.C., 1954, U. Okla., 1965-66, St. Mary's U., 1977, U. Victoria, 1989, J.F. Kennedy Inst., Free U. Berlin, 1990; guest prof. Inst. Geography, Uppsala (Sweden) U., 1962-63; rsch. fellow in Geography U. Aberdeen, Scotland, 1970-71, 78; vis. fellow in Can. Studies, U. Edinburgh, Scotland, 1987. Author: Looking at Maps, 1960, The Sawdust Fusiliers, 1991, Norden and Canada-A Geographer's Perspective, 1992, Alaska Highway Explorer, 1994; author: (with T. Drinkwater et al.) Junior Atlas of Alberta, 1979; contbr., editor: Canada's Changing North, 1971, rev. edit., 2003, The North, 1972, The Arctic Circle, 1976, Knowing the North, 1988, Geographica's Pocket World Reference, 2000, Frontiersmen & Settlers, 2002, Geordies, Yankees and Canucks, 2006; contbr. articles to jours. and encys., chapters to books. Active Nat. Adv. Com. on Geog. Rsch., 1965-69; chmn. Boreal Inst. No. Studies (Can. Circumpolar Inst.), 1960-62; mem. Can. Permanent Com. on Geog. Names, 1981-94, Alta. Hist. Sites Bd., 1978-83, vice-chmn., 1982-83; policy bd. Can. Plains Rsch. Centre, U. Regina (Sask.), 1975-86; adv. bd. Royal Tyrrell Mus. Paleontology, 1984-89; bd. dirs. Muttart Found., 1986-93, 95-98, v.p., 1991-93. Decorated Order of Can., Can. Forces Decoration; recipient Queen's Jubilee medal; NSF sr. fgn. scientist fellow, 1965-66; Can. Coun. leave fellow, 1969-70, 77-78; Nuffield Found. fellow, 1970-71. Fellow Arctic Inst. N.Am., Royal Soc. Can., Royal Can. Geog. Soc. (Massey medalist 1998); mem. Can. Assn. Geographers (past pres.), Can. Assn. Scottish Studies (councillor 1974-77), Scottish Soc. No. Studies, Champlain Soc. (councillor 1981-86), Sigma Xi, Gamma Theta Upsilon. Home: Victoria, Canada. Deceased.

**WONNELL, HAROLD EDWARD,** lawyer; b. Columbus, Ohio, July 2, 1923; s. Clarence Edward and Daisy (Van Fossen) W.; m. Nancy Kathleen Thomas, Aug. 20, 1940; children: Vikki Priest, Andre Jo Correale, Deirdre Jo Davis, Gabrielle A. Morton. BSBA, Ohio State U., 1949, LLB, 1951, JD, 1967. Spl. agt., field agt. in L.A. and Portland, on staff of J. Edgar Hoover, FBI, Washington, 1951-55; mem. pub. rels. and investigation Thoroughbred Racing Assn., Chgo., 1955-57; pvt. practice in law Columbus, Ohio; lawyer Wonnell & Wonnell Co., L.P.A., Columbus, from 1957. Spkr. Ohio No. U. Coll. of Law, 1961-69. Author: Ohio Traffic Law Handbook, 1969, 85. Judge Franklin County Common Pleas, Columbus, 1985-86; mem. past pres., dr. chmn. Charity Newsies, Columbus, 1962-97; past pres., bd. dirs. Big Bros./Big Sisters, Columbus, 1955-94; past chmn., bd. mgmt. Ctrl. YMCA, Columbus, 1961-73. With U.S. Marines, 1942-46. Recipient Svc. award Divsn. of Police, Lions Club. Fellow Ohio Sate Bar Found., Acad. of Law and Sci., Roscoe-Pound-Am. Trial Lawyers Found.; mem. ATLA, Ohio State Bar Assn. (chmn. various coms.), Columbus Bar Assn. (chmn. various coms.), Fed. Bar Assn., Soc. of Former Spl. Agts. of FBI (past pres. Columbus chpt.), Ohio Acad. Criminal Trial Lawyers. Democrat. Avocations: golf, reading, travel. Home: Columbus, Ohio. Died Mar. 9, 1999.

**WON PAT, ANTONIO BORJA,** congressman; b. Sumay, Guam, Dec. 10, 1908; s. Ignacio Won Pat and Maria Suriano Borja; m. Ana Salas Perez, 1932; children— Aveline (Mrs. Ploke), Marilyn A., Jacqueline, Ellen (Mrs. Chargualaf), Anthony B., Rosalind (Mrs. Wise), Judith T. (Mrs. Borja), Mark V. Ed. pub. schs.; LL.D., U. Guam. Tchr., Guam, 1928-33; elem. sch. prin., 1934-40; high sch. tchr., 1940-41; imports, wholesale and retail exec., 1945-54; real estate broker, ins. agt., 1954; pres., chmn. bd. Guam Comml. Corp., Inc., 1946-54; Wash. rep. Territory of Guam, 1965-72; mem. 93d to 98th Congress from Guam, 1973—85, armed service, interior, and insular affairs com. Assemblyman, Guam Assembly, 1936-41; mem. Guam Legislature, 1950-64, speaker, 1950-64; del. Democratic Nat. Conv., 1968, Mid-Term Conf., 1978 Recipient Community Leader Am. award, 1969, 71 Mem. Am. Acad. Polit. and Social Sci., Am. Soc. Pub. Adminstrn., Am. Judicature Soc., Internat. Platform Assn. Clubs: Nat. Press. Roman Catholic. Died May 1, 1987.

**WOOD, JEAN CAROL,** poet, lyricist; b. Oklahoma City, Apr. 6, 1940; d. Howard Melvin and Ethel Matillda (Carroll) Sage; m. Harold David Wood; children: Howard David, Troy Don, Kevin Dale, L'lana Cayé. Freelance writer, from 1976. Contbr. poems in collections; lyricist: songs As It Should Be, 2001—02, As It Should Be III, 2005, Glory, 2006; author: (poem) Rest On His Thumb, 2003, The Transport Of a Winged Being, Are You Ready for the Conflict, 2007, The Adventure (Best Poem, 2007), (book) Glory Land, 2006, (poems) Are You Ready For the Conflict, The Adventure, (song on CD) The Light of the World, Master Master, The Time Is Now, God's Gift of Love, 2010, Praise You Name Forever, Transport of a Winged Being, 2011. Recipient trophy, Internat. Soc. Poets, 2003. Mem.: Internat. Soc. Poets. Avocations: writing, gardening, reading. Home: Mustang, Okla. Deceased.

**WOOD, RAY LINCOLN,** publishing executive, editor-in-chief; b. Idutywa, Cape, South Africa, Dec. 18, 1932; s. Lincoln James Wood and Violet Wright; m. Barbara Fischer; children: Robin, Gregory, Janet, Andrea, Nicole. B in Commerce, U. Natal, Durban, South Africa, 1953; ICA, CAAP/U. Toronto, Can., 1967. Advt. mgr. Unilever, Durban, 1952-56; client svc. dir. Ronalds Reynolds, Toronto, 1963-68; mktg. dir. Food Corp., Johannesburg, 1968-82; chmn., creative dir. Lincoln Wood Benton & Bowles, Johannesburg, 1982-87; owner, chief cons. Growth Cons., Johannesburg, 1987-92; chmn., editor-in-chief Profl. Mgmt. Rev. Glboal, 1989—2002. Contbr. articles to profl. jours. Mem. Inst. Dirs., Bryanston Country Club (former chmn. tennis sect.). Avocations: wine, reading, food, tennis, theater. Home: Johannesburg, South Africa. Deceased.

**WOODHOUSE, DERRICK FERGUS,** ophthalmologist; b. Sutton, Surrey, U.K., May 29, 1927; s. Sydney Carver and Erica (Ferguson) W.; m. Jocelyn Laira Perry, Mar. 9, 1957; children: Karen Tace, Iain Kenrick, Gillian Erica. BM, BCh., Oxford U., Eng., 1951; DO, London Coll., 1956. Intern in medicine, surgery, ophthalmology St. Thomas Hosp., Plymouth, Exeter Hosps., London, 1952-53; registrar in ophthalmology Birmingham (Eng.) Eye. Hosp., 1958-60; sr. registrar in ophthalmology Bristol (Eng.) Eye Hosp., 1960-63; cons. eye surgeon Wolverhampton & Midland Counties Eye Infirmary, Eng., 1963-89; staff opthalmologist Liverpool Hosp., NSW, Australia, 1989-99, emeritus cons., from 1999. Lectr. ophthalmology U. Sydney, 1998—2002. Contbr. articles to profl. jours.; author: Ophthalmic Nursing, 1980. Mem. Wolverhampton Health Authority, 1970-77; treas. Ophthalmic Nursing Bd., 1970-84, chmn., 1984-88. With RAF, 1953-57. Recipient Gold medal, Nepal Med. Assn., 1989. Fellow Royal Coll. Surgeons, Royal Soc. Medicine, Royal Coll. Ophthalmologists, Royal Australian and New Zealand Coll. Opthalmologists; mem. Irish Coll. Ophthalmologists, N.Y. Acad. Scis. Mem. Soc. Of Friends. Deceased.

**WOODLAND, GORDON CARTER,** manufacturing executive; b. Aberdeen, Wash., Oct. 29, 1924; s. Earle Clement and Marian Alma (Carter) Woodland; m. Joanne Katherine Bouse, May 7, 1955; children: Michael Sean, Leslie Denise, Kristyn Ann, Kimberly Diane. Student, U. Oreg., 1942, Tex. A&M U., 1943, Princeton U., 1945, U. Willamette, 1945, U. Colo., 1946; AB, U. Wash., 1949; Cour Pratique, U. de Grenoble, France, 1950, Centre U. de Meditterraneen, 1950. Self employed in logging, Aberdeen, 1946—50; mgr. C. of C., Anacortes, Wash., 1951—54; mgr. sales and promotion Skagit Plastics, La Conner, Wash., 1955—60; west coast mgr. Traveler Boat divsn. Stanray Corp., Chgo., 1961—62, field sales mgr., 1962—63, gen. sales mgr., 1963—64, v.p. sales, 1964—66; gen. sales mgr. Pearson Yachts divsn. Grumman Allied Industries, Inc., Portsmouth, RI, 1966—74, asst. gen. mgr., dir. mktg., 1974—76, gen. mgr., 1976—85; yacht broker G.C. Woodland & Assoc., Inc., 1987—98. Cons. seminars Am. Mgmt. Assn.; spkr. seminars Sales Execs. Clubs NY, Chgo. Pres. Pheasant Hill Assn., Portsmouth, 1976; mem. local sch. bd. adv. com., 1971, Title I Reading Inst., Portsmouth Sch. Dist.; mem. Nat. Adv. Com. U.S. Trade Negotiations; campaign chmn. Wash. Gov. Arthur B. Langlie for U.S. Senate, 1956; mem. RI Gov.'s Adv. Com. Strategic Devel; bd. dirs. Seaport '76, 1976—98, Newport County Local Devel. Corp. With USN, 1941—45, lt. comdr. USNR, 1948—72, comrd. RI Naval Militia. Recipient cert. of appreciation, Am. Sail Tng. Assn., 1976, 1982, commendation, Sales Execs. Club NY, 1965, Plankower's cert., Seaport '76, 1978. Mem.: C. of C. Newport County (bd. dirs.), RI Assn. for Sail (bd. dirs.), RI Marine Trade Assn. (bd. dirs.), Boat Mfrs. Assn. (bd. dirs., chmn., sec.-treas.), Am. Sail Tng. Assn. (bd. dirs.), Nat. Marine Mfrs. Assn. (bd. dirs., sec., membership, shows coms.), Boating Industry Assn. (bd. dirs.), Nat. Assn. Engine and Boat Mfrs. Assn., U. Wash. Alumni Assn., Narragansett Bay Yachting Assn., Nat. Athletic Scholastic Soc., Naval Res. Assn., Barrington Yacht Club, RI Commodores Club, Twenty Hundred Club (commodore), Turtle Club, Sigma Nu. Republican. Roman Catholic. Home: West Palm Beach, Fla. Died Aug. 24, 1998.

**WOODS, ELSWORTH PETER,** educator, dean, retired; b. Estherville, Iowa, Aug. 4, 1912; s. Robert Elsworth and Elsie Elizabeth (Einsele) W.; m. Sylvia Curry, Aug. 19, 1936; children: Joan, Carmen, Elizabeth. BA, U. Iowa, 1936, MA, 1939, PhD, 1949. High sch. tchr. Sr. High Schs., Iowa and Ill., 1936-43; instr. Drake U., Des Moines, Iowa, 1946-47, dean liberal arts, 1955-72, prof. polit. sci., 1971-82; instr. U. Iowa, Iowa City, 1947-49; from asst. prof. to prof. Western Mich. U., Kalamazoo, 1949-55. Pres., charter mem. Golden K. Kiwanis, Des Moines. Carnegie Teaching fellow Harvard U., 1953-54, Fulbright Teaching fellow U. Papua, New Guinea, 1970. Mem. Torch Club (charter, pres. 1993-94). Presbyterian. Avocations: gardening, political activities, forums. Home: Des Moines, Iowa. Died 1998.

**WOODS, FRITZI GOULDSBY PIKES,** food products executive; b. Texarkana, 1960; m. Timothy Clyde Woods; 5 children. BS in Acctg., Stephen F. Austin State U., 1981. Auditor Arthur Andersen and Co.; v.p. finance & adminstrn. Greater Houston Conv. & Visitors Bur.; exec. dep. dir. for office adminstrn. Tex. Natural Resources Conservation Commn.; financial contr. semi conductor divsn. Motorola; v.p. internal audit The Dallas Morning News, 1997—98, sr. v.p. finance & adminstrn., 1998—2003; chmn., CEO PrimeSource FoodService Equipment, Inc., 2003—10; pres., CEO Women's Foodservice Forum (WFF), 2010—12. Bd. dirs. BUCA, Inc., 2005—08, Jamba Inc., 2011—13. Bd. dirs. Parkland Hosp. Found., United Way, Grace Fort Gouldsby Scholarship Found.; trustee SW Med. Found. Mem.: Internat. Women's Forum, Women Corp. Dirs., Young President's Orgn. Died Sept. 18, 2013.

**WOODWARD, VERN HARVEY,** retired engineering sales executive; b. Hawkeye, Iowa, Oct. 18, 1899; s. Willis Benton and Freda (Styier) W.; m. Florence Thompson, July 11, 1927 (dec. Jan. 1989). Student, U. Pitts., 1923, Carnegie Tech., 1929, Westinghouse Tech. Sch., 1924-28. Engr. Westinghouse Elec., East Pitts., 1922-31; engring. sales rep. Equitable Gas Co. (now Equitable Resources), Pitts., 1935-40, supr. architects, 1940-45, supr. architects and engr. svcs., 1945-64, mem. operating com., 1960-64. Auditor Chruchill Boro, 1957-69. Recipient 3 outstanding awards National Library of Poetry. Mem. Internat. Soc. Poets (disting.), Assn. Masonic Vets. Western Pa., Joshua Assn. Western Pa., KT, Masons (33 degree, supreme coun. 1968—), Red Cross of Constantine (U.S. Premier conclave 1965—). Republican. Presbyterian. Avocation: photography. Deceased.

**WOODWORTH, SEARCY J.,** radio station executive; b. Okla. City, Sept. 12, 1921; s. Lemuel Allen and LaVerne Ellen (Landes) Woodworth; m. Dorothy Mae Litchfield, 1951; children: Searcy F., Gary S., Ronald K., Gregory m. Ground radio operator Am. Airlines, Ft. Worth, 1942—44; flight radio operator Consolidated-Vultee Airlines, San Diego, 1944—45, Pan Am. Airways, San Francisco, 1945—48; chief engr. Sta. KVNC, Winslow, Ariz., 1954—56; owner, mgr. Sta. KVWM-AM-FM, Show Low, Ariz., from 1957. With USNR, 1945—48. Republican. Home: Show Low, Ariz. Died June 1988.

**WORDAL, BLAKE JORDAN,** county commissioner; b. Helena, Mont., Jan. 3, 1953; s. Edward J. and Delores E. W.; m. Patricia Moore, Aug. 7, 1976 (div. Feb. 1981). BA in Govt. and Internat. Rels., U. Notre Dame, 1975. Adminstrv. asst. to Gov. Tom Judge, Helena, 1975-80; exec. dir. Mont. Hardware and Implement Assn., Helena, 1981-85; city commr. City of Helena, 1984-90; staff asst. to pres. Mont. State Senate, Helena, 1985; exec. dir. Mont. Dem. Party, Helena, 1985-87; researcher Mont. State AFL-CIO, Helena, 1988-90; county commr. Lewis and Clark County, Helena, from 1990. Bd. dirs. Rocky Mountain Devel. Coun., 1986-89, A93—,areawide Planning Coun., 1984-86, Mont. Dem. Party, 1981-85. Chmn. Helena Citizens Coun., 1981-83; state coord. Mondale/Ferraro for Pres., Helena, 1984. Recipient Certs. of Appreciation Helena Human Rights Task Force, 1990, Helena Food Bank, 1989, Helena Indian Alliance, 1990. Episcopalian. Avocations: hunting, skiing, fishing, river rafting, reading. Home: Helena, Mont. Deceased.

**WORKMAN, NORMAN ALLAN,** accountant, management consultant; b. Boston, Apr. 20, 1918; s. William Horace and Estelle Emily (Hanlon) W.; m. Harriet Patricia Banfield, Aug. 1, 1946; children: Stephen, Mark, Brian, Patricia. Student, Coll. William and Mary, 1938-39; BS in Econs. magna cum laude, Bowdoin Coll., 1941. CPA, Oreg. Staff acct. Lybrand Ross Bros. & Montgomery, Boston, 1941-43, Whitfield Stratford & Co., Portland, Oreg., 1946-51; ptnr. Workman, Shephard & Co., CPAs, Portland, 1951-60; sole practitioner Portland, 1961-96; ret. Dir. Iron Fireman Mfg. Co., 1953—56, Electronic Specialty Co., 1956—65. Newsletter columnist Good Impressions, 1993-98. Chmn. bd. Sylvan Fire Bd., 1953-55, Sylvan Sch., Portland, 1956-57; pres. Doernbecher Children's Hosp. Found., Portland, 1963-85, Bowdoin Club Oreg., Portland, 1963—; trustee Oreg. Episcopal Schs., Portland, 1974-76. Lt. (j.g.) Supply Corps, USNR, 1944-46. Named Mr. Doernbecher, Doernbecher Children's Hosp. Found., 2002. Mem. AICPA, Inst. Mgmt. Accts. (pres. Portland chpt. 1954-55), Oreg. Soc. CPA's, Pacific Printing and Imaging Assn., Arlington Club, Multnomah Athletic Club, Phi Beta Kappa. Avocations: bird hunting, fishing, horticulture. Deceased.

**WORRELL, RICHARD VERNON,** orthopedic surgeon, dean; b. Bklyn., June 4, 1931; s. John Elmer and Elaine (Callender) Worrell; m. Audrey Frances Martiny, June 14, 1958; children: Philip Vernon, Amy Elizabeth. BA, NYU, 1952; MD, Meharry Med. Coll., 1958. Diplomate Am. Bd. Orthop. Surgery, Nat. Bd. Med. Examiners. Intern Meharry Med. Coll., Nashville, 1958—59; resident in gen. surgery Mercy-Douglass Hosp., Phila., 1960—61; resident in orthop. surgery State U. N.Y. Buffalo Sch. Medicine Affiliated Hosps., 1961—64; resident in orthop. pathology Temple U. Med. Ctr., Phila., 1966—67; pvt. practice orthop. surgery Phila., 1967—68; asst. prof. acting head divsn. orthop. surgery U. Conn. Sch. Medicine, 1968—70; attending orthop. surgeon E.J. Meyer Meml. Hosp., Buffalo, Millard Fillmore Hosp., Buffalo, VA Hosp., Buffalo, Buffalo State Hosp.; clin. instr. orthop. surgery SUNY, Buffalo, 1970—74; chief orthop. surgery VA Hosp., Newington, Conn., 1974—80; asst. prof. surgery (orthop.) U. Conn. Sch. Medicine, 1974—77, assoc. prof., 1977—83, asst. dean student affairs, 1980—83; prof. clin. surgery SUNY Downstate Med. Ctr., Bklyn., 1983—86; dir. orthop. surgery Brookdale Hosp. Med. Ctr., Bklyn., 1983—86; prof. orthop. U. N.Mex. Sch. Medicine, 1986—97, prof., vice chmn. dept. orthop., 1997—99, prof. emeritus, from 1999; dir. orthop. oncology U. N.Mex. Health Scis. Ctr., 1987—99; mem. med. staff U. N.Mex. Cancer Ctr., 1987—99; chief orthop. surgery VA Med. Ctr., Albuquerque, 1987—97. Cons. in orthop. surgery Newington (Conn.) Children's Hosp., 1968—70; mem. sickle cell disease adv. com. NIH, 1982—86. Bd. dirs. Big Bros. Greater Hartford. Served to capt. M.C. USAR, 1962—69. Fellow: ACS, Royal Soc. Medicine, London, Am. Acad. Orthop. Surgeons; mem.: AMA, N.Mex. Soc. Clin. Oncology, Internat. Soc. Orthop. Surgery and Traumatology, Orthop. Rsch. Soc., Internat. Fedn. Surg. Colls. (assoc.), Am. Soc. Clin. Oncology, Am. Soc. Clin. Pathologists, Am. Orthop. Assn., Alpha Omega Alpha. Home: Albuquerque, N.Mex. Died 2013.

**WORTLEY, GEORGE CORNELIUS,** lobbyist, former United States Representative from New York; b. Syracuse, NY, Dec. 8, 1926; s. George C. and Arlene (Hirsh) W.; m. Barbara Jane Hennessy, May 13, 1950 (dec. 2007); children: George C. IV, Ann Wortley Lavin, Elizabeth Wortley Ring. BS, Syracuse U., 1948. Newspaper publisher, pres. Manlius Publishing Corp., Fayetteville, NY, 1950-92; pres. Nat. Editorial Found., 1968-73; mem. US Congress from 32nd NY Dist., 1981—83, US Congress from 27th NY Dist., 1983—89; prin. Dierman, Wortley, Zola & Associates, Inc.

(DWZ), Washington, 1989—2014. Pres. American Newspapers Reps., 1966—68. Pres. Hiawatha coun. Boy Scouts America, 1972-75; mem. Nat. Commn. on Hist. Publications & Records, 1977-80, Fayetteville Sr. Citizen Housing Commn., 1977-80; mem. allocations com. United Way of Ctrl. N.Y., 1979-81; mem. public rels. com. St. Camillus Health Care Ctr., 1971-78; mem. fed. legis. com. American Lung Assn., 1974-77; bd. dirs. Crouse-Irving Meml. Hosp. Found., 1975-87, pres. 1979-81; bd. dirs. American Heart Assn., Upstate N.Y., 1960-80, chmn. public rels. com., 1970-74, chmn. legis. com. 1977, mem. fund raising adv. com., 1974-79; trustee Cazenovia Coll., 1981-94; bd. dirs. Onondaga Hist. Assn., 1980-90; dir. Global Leadership Inst., 1987-2001. Served with MMR, USNR, WWII. Recipient Silver Beaver award Boy Scouts America, 1973, Silver Antelope award, 1981 Mem. Nat. Newspaper Assn. (legis. com. 1976-80), Greater Syracuse Chamber of Commerce (dir. 1979-81), Upstate Coun. Indsl. Editors, LeMoyne Coll. Pres.'s Assocs., Syracuse U. Alumni Asn. (nat. treas. 1973-77), Former Members of U.S. Congress Assn., Navy League of U.S., Cosmos Club, Georgetown Club, Coral Ridge Yacht Club, Lions, KC, Kappa Sigma (pres. 1957-59). Republican. Roman Catholic. Home: Fort Lauderdale, Fla. Died Jan. 21, 2014.

**WRIGHT, BERNARD,** artist; b. Pitts., Feb. 23, 1938; s. Garfield and Emma (Jefferson) Wright; m. Corrine Westley, Mar. 7, 1964; 1 child, Jeffrey. Student, Otis Art Inst., LA, 1970, LA Trade Tech. Coll., 1973. Artist Traveling Art Show, Moscow, Baku, Leningrad, Alma Alta, Russia, European Capitals, 1966, LA City Hall Rotunda Gallery, 1967, Calif. Lutheran Coll., Thousand Oaks, 1967, Compton Calif. CC, 1967, 1989, Alley Gallery, Beverly Hills, 1968, Florenz Art Gallery, LA, 1969, San Diego Mus., 1969, Phillip E. Freed Gallery Fine Arts, Chgo., 1969, Playboy Club, Century City, Calif., 1971, Diplomat Hotel, Emerald Gallery, Hollywood Beach, Fla., 1971, Art West Gallery, LA, 1973, NJ State Mus., Trenton, Detroit Inst. Arts, Mich., 1974, U. Southern Calif., Calif. Mus. Sci. and Industry, 1974, City Art Mus., St. Louis, 1976, NYC Pub. Libr., 1977, Pitts. City Hall Rotunda, 1982, Mus. African Am. Art, LA, 1982, Main Bridge Art Gallery, LA City Hall, 1983, Howard U. Art Gallery, Washington, 1983, LA Pub. Libr., Baldwin Hills Br., 1984, Morgan State U., US Amada Ltd., Buena Park, Calif., 1985, LA Southwest Coll., 1986, Prairie View A&M U., Tex., 1987, Louis Newman Galleries, Beverly Hills, 1989, Mus. African & African Am. Art Antiquities, Buffalo, 1989, Griffon's Light Gallery, Denver, 1990, Sheraton Hotel, Akron/Cuyahoga Falls, Ohio, 1992, Hyatt Regency Hotel, Washington, 1992, U. Utah, Salt Lake City, 1993, many others; representer Pvt. and Pub. Collections including Howard U., Libr. Congress. Past pres. co-founder Wright's & Westley Prodns.; furniture and garment designers; with US Rep. Cardiss Collins, Ill., 1978; state senator Bill Greene, Calif., 1981, Mayor Richard S. Callguiri, Pitts., 1981, Mayor Coleman A. Young, Detroit, 1981, Mayor Tom Bradley, LA; bd. supr. Kenneth Hahn, LA, 1981. Active cmty. involvement Sta. KHJ-TV, 1982. Mem.: Art West Assn. (bd. dirs.). Home: Los Angeles, Calif. Died Feb. 7, 1999.

**WRIGHT, TOMMIE (THOMAS G. WRIGHT),** retired music educator, musician; b. Indianapolis, Ind. s. Benjamine Clinton and Bertha Alice (Denius) Wright; m. Rosalinda Gayoso; children: Jessica, Desirée, Nicole; children: Candy, Cindy. MusB magna cum laude, Butler Univ. & Arthur Jordan Conserv. (joint degree), Indpls., Ind., 1940; MusM, Ind. Univ., Bloomington, Ind., 1942; Mus D equal to doc., Columbia Univ., NYC, NY, 1946—49; grad., Arthur Jordan Conservatory of Music. Played in concerts throughout US, Ctrl. America, and Caribean. Performed soloist with major symphony orchestras in US. Prof. music Fla. State Univ., Tallahassee, 1949—2008. Headed the Internat. Dept. of Radio-TV at FSU for twelve years before it became the Sch. of Communications. With Co-Chmn. roy Flynn, I planned and administred the construction of WFSU-TV, educatonal TV station for the Univ. With USAF, 1942—46, 720th Flying Squadron, SE Tng. Command. Mem.: Monticello Opera House Bd. of Dir., Local 802, NYC, Am. Fed. of Musicians, Fla. State Music Tchr. Assoc., Music Tchr. Nat. Assoc., Artist List of the Baldwin Piano Co., Union Bd. Comm., FSU Faculty Senate, Arts and Sci. Faculty, Sch. of Music Faculty (at Fla. State Univ. 1949), No. 937, BPOE (Elks), Phi Delta Theta Alumni Club. Ch. Of Lds. I have taught piano, a course titled "An Introduction to Music Hist. and Appreciation", the Hist. and Appreciation courses continuously every yr. since 1949 and piano, Duo-Piano and Music Lit. courses. Home: Tallahassee, Fla. Died May 8, 2014.

**WRIGHT, WILLIAM GORDON,** foundation executive; b. Big Spring, Tex., Feb. 13, 1955; s. Emmett Gordon and Marilyn June (Ellis) W. BS in Adminstrv. Mgmt., Clemson U., 1978; JD, MBA, Western New England Col., 1981; LLM in Taxation, Boston U., 1982. Bar: Mass., D.C., N.J., U.S. Tax Ct., U.S. Ct. Appeals (1st cir.). Staff atty. Touche Ross & Co., Boston, 1982-84; atty. Womble, Carlyle, Sandridge & Rice, Winston-Salem, N.C., 1984-86; sr. atty. advisor U.S. Tax Ct., Washington, 1986-88; atty. Hannoch Weisman, Roseland, N.J., 1988-93, Proskauer Rose, LLP, NYC, 1993-96; chmn., exec. dir. Teresa G. Wright Promise Found., Randolph, N.J., from 1996. Co-founder, exec. com. mem. N.J. .08 Coalition, 1996—; delegate Lifesavers Hwy. Safety Conf., New Mexico, Fla., 1996, 97; alcohol/drug countermeasures rep. Morris County (N.J.) Hwy. Traffic Safety Com., 1996—. Contbr. chpts. to books, articles to profl. jours; spkr. in field. Minister, Fund-raising com. mem. St. Matthew's Ch., Randolph, N.J., 1994—; co-founder Family & Friends of Teresa Wright Orgn., Randolph, N.J., 1995-96. Recipient N.J. Equal Justice award N.J. Assn. of Crime Victim Advocates, 1996. Mem. D.C. Bar Assn., Mass. Bar Assn., N.J. Bar Assn., N.J. Assn. Crime Victim Advocates, Mothers Against Drunk Driving (pub. policy liason, state rep., youth com. co-chair). Roman Catholic. Avocations: running, racing, scuba diving, biking, music. Home: Orinda, Calif. Died 1997.

**WRONSKI, STANLEY PAUL,** education educator; b. Mpls., Apr. 8, 1919; s. John and Katherine (Kotvis) W.; m. Geraldine Breslin, May 27, 1943; children: Linda A., Mary Jo Tewinkel, Sandra J., John S., Paul S. BS in Edn., U. Minn., 1942, MA, 1947, PhD, 1950. Counselor Bur. Vet. Affairs U. Minn., Mpls., 1946-47, instr. Coll. Edn., 1948-49; tchr. Marshall High Sch., Mpls., 1947-48; asst. prof. Ctrl. Wash. Coll., Ellensburg, 1950-51; from asst. to assoc. prof. Boston U., 1951-57; from assoc. prof. to prof. Mich. State U., East Lansing, 1957-84, prof. emeritus, from 1984. Advisor Ministry of Edn., Bangkok, Thailand, 1964-66; pres. New Eng. Assn. Social Studies Tchrs., Boston, 1955-56, Mich. Coun. for Social Studies, 1960-61, Nat. Coun. for Social Studies, 1974. Co-author: Teaching Social Studies in High School, 1958, 73, Modern Economics, 1964, School and Society, 1964, Social Studies and Social Sciences, 1986; creator "The Sustainable Planet" interactive display at Impression 5 Mus., Lansing, Mich., 2000. Active U.S. Nat. Commn. for UNESCO, Washington, 1974-76, mil. adv. com. Ctr. for Def. Info., Washington, 1988—; pres. Greater Lansing UN Assn., 1986-88, 99-2000, chair Mich. UN at Fifty Planning Com., 1995. Comdr. USN, 1942-64. Recipient Internat. Educator award Pacific Rim Consortium, 1992, Glen Taggart award Mich. State U., 1995; named Outstanding Social Studies Educator, Social Studies Tchr. Jour., 1981. Mem. NEA (life), Nat. Peace Found. (charter), Univ. Club (charter). Avocations: golf, reading, volunteer work. Died Nov. 6, 2002.

**WUESTEFELD, NORMAN HENRY,** retired engineer executive; b. New Haven, Conn., June 17, 1930; s. Henry Albert and Helen Marie (Musch) W.; m. Paula Ida Urquhart, Dec. 19, 1953; children: Leslie Kim, Lance Urquhart, Dirck Henry, Kris Norman, Ashley Paige. BSBA in Indsl. Engring., U. Conn., 1957. From project dir. to sr. v.p. Wilbur Smith Assocs., Inc., New Haven, Conn., 1957-85, exec. v.p., 1985-99, chmn., 1999. Vice chair Newcomen Soc. U.S., Conn. com., 1989—. Bd. dirs. Achievement Found.; bd. dirs., past chmn. Jr. Achievement of So. Conn.; bd. govs., 2d v.p. Grad. Club, New Haven; bd. dirs. Gateway Cmty. Coll. Found.; bd. dirs., treas. Hunger Relief and Devel. Inc. Fellow Inst. Transp. Engrs. (life); mem. Internat. Soc. Macro Engring. (bd. dirs.), Am. Soc. Macro-Engring. (chmn., bd. dirs.), Conn. Engrs. Pvt. Practice (bd. dirs., past chair), Newcomen Soc. U.S. (vice chair Conn. com. 1989—), Internat. Bridge, Tunnel and Turnpike Assn. (hon. life). Avocations: sailing, gardening. Home: Clinton, Conn. Deceased.

**WULFF, ROGER LAVERN,** museum administrator; b. Olean, NY, Nov. 16, 1940; s. LaVern Theodore and Marjorie (Perkins) Wulff; m. Geraldine Schepker Wulff, July 3, 1971. AA, Montgomery Jr. Coll., Rockville, Md., 1968; BA, U. Md., 1970; postgrad., Pa. State U., 1971-73, The George Washington U., 1975-79. Cultural instn. value methodology specialist. Pres., chmn. bd. dirs. Mus. Svcs. Internat., Washington, from 1980. Founder Mus. Svcs. Internat., 1980—; speaker at various mus. confs.; mem. panel experts Tourism Sector Devel. Project, The Hashemite Kingdom of Jordan. Contbr. articles to profl. jours. Chmn. Internat. Com. on Mus. Security, 1986-92, editor, 1986—. With U.S. Army, 1959-62. Recipient Excellence in Leadership Svcs. award, Smithsonian Inst., Washington, 1989, Cert. Appreciation, African Am. Mus. Assn., Washington, 1988 Mem. U.S. Com. of the Internat. Coun. of Mus., Internat. Com. for Mus. Security, Internat. Coun. of Mus. (former chmn. internat. com. on mus. security), Internat. Com. on Exhbn. Exch., U.S./Internat. Coun. on Monuments and Sites (steering com.), Internat. Cultural Assistance Network, Am. Assn. Mus., Nat. Assn. Mus. Exhbn., Com. on Mil. Mus. in Am., Mus. Assn. Security Com., Com. on Mus. Evaluation and Rsch., Washington Mus. Collaborative. Avocation: gardening. Home: Cayo, Belize. Died July 12, 2003.

**WULLAERTS, LODE RENE ELISABETH,** finance executive; b. Louvain, Belgium, May 14, 1959; s. Marcel Wullaerts and Cecile Willemyns; m. Frieda Van Steenbergen, Feb. 14, 1983; 1 child, Isabelle. Licentiate in Law magna cum laude, U. Louvain, 1984, Licentiate in Philosophy magna cum laude, 1984, Licentiate in Econs. magna cum laude, 1985. Cert. tax cons., lawyer, fin. analyst. Mgmt. trainee G-Bank, Belgium, 1984-85, head fin. engring. Brussels, 1985-88; asst. gen. mgr. Bankers' Assn., Brussels, 1988-89; head of mergers and acquisitions Paribas, The Netherlands/Belgium, 1989-91; dir. corp. fin./investment banking Societé Générale, Paris and Brussels, 1991-94; exec. dir. corp. fin./investment banking Societé Générale Benelux, Paris/Brussels/Amsterdam, from 1995. Prof. Banking Sch., Brussels, 1988-93; spkr. numerous seminars and confs. in field of corp. fin., 1988—. Co-author: Merger Control in Europe, 1987; contbr. articles to profl. jours. and books. Fellow Philosophy Sch.; mem. Law Econ. Ancient Studies. Home: Kester, Belgium. Died June 12, 2001.

**WURZBURGER, STUARD A.,** labor relations consultant; b. NYC, Mar. 4, 1907; s. Walter and Norma (Shloss) W.; m. Eleanor Augusta Searle, May 23, 1941; children: Peggy Searle Foyle, Marie Searle Patrick. BA, Washington and Lee U., 1928. Mgmt. trainee Paul Block Newspapers, NYC, 1928-34; sales mgr. Hercules Cement Co., Phila., 1934-38; v.p., treas. So. Constrn. Co., NYC, 1938-42; labor rels. officer N.Y. Ordnance Dist., NYC, 1942-46; cons. Glen Ridge, N.J., 1946-71, NYC, from 1971. Adj. prof. Washington and Lee U., 1973-77. Pres. Glen Ridge Athletic Assn., 1958-60, del. Civic Conf. Com., 1956-68, chmn. Borough Recreation Com., 1966-67, bd. dir. Taxpayers Assn., 1959-66, Lexington Golf and Country, 1975-78. Recipient citation Chief of Ordnance, U.S. Army, 1945, N.Y. Ordnance Dist., 1945, Mayor and Coun., Glen Ridge, 1971. Mem. Am. Mgmt. Assn., Am. Ordnance Assn., Indsl. Rels. Rsch. Assn.; Washington and Lee U. Alumni Assn. (bd. dirs. 1953-57, N.Y. Alumni, 1935-71, 1928 Class Agt., 1973-78), The Circle. Avocation: fund raising washington and lee u. Died July 12, 1991.

**WURZEL, LEONARD,** retired candy manufacturing company executive; b. Phila., Feb. 4, 1918; s. Maurice L. and Dora (Goldberg) W.; m. Elaine Cohen, Aug. 18, 1949; children— Mark L., Lawrence J. BS, Washington and Jefferson Coll., 1939; MBA, Harvard, 1941. With US Army, 1941; pvt., 1943; 2nd lt.; 1st lt., 1945; capt., 1946; With Loft Candy Corp., Long Island City, NY, 1946-64, v.p., 1949-56, exec. v.p., 1956-57, pres., 1957-64, dir., 1949-64; chmn., dir. Calico Cottage Candies, Inc., 1964-94; ret., 1994; mayor Village of Sands Point, NY, 1989—2011. With Adj. Gen. Dept. European Head Qtrs., Eng. France & Germany. Decorated Bronze Star; award European-Am. Mid. Eastern medal with one battle star; Apptd. Chevalier French Legion of Honor Pres. France, 2013. Mem. Assn. Mfrs. Confectionery and Chocolate (bd. dirs., past pres., chmn.), Candy Chocolate and Confectionery Inst. (bd. dirs., treas.), Retail Confectioners Internat. (bd. dirs., past pres.) Home: Sands Point, NY. Died Nov. 16, 2013.

**WYCKOFF, ALEXANDER,** stage designer, educator; b. Leonia, NJ, Aug. 17, 1898; s. James Talmage and Wilhelmina (Ludwig) Wyckoff; 1 child, Peter Talmage. Student, Columbia Coll., 1916—17, Carnegie Inst. Tech., 1920. Designer H. Robert Law Studios, NYC, 1920—21, 1924—25; designer drama dept. Carnegie Inst. Tech., Pitts., 1921—24, instr., 1921—24; dir. Memphis Little Theatre, 1927—30; art dir. U. Mich., Ann Arbor, 1932—41; supr. design Phila. Mus. Sch., 1933—43; writer Leonia, NJ; illustrator, 1950—69, Tustin, Calif., 1971—88; art dir. pageant Rensselaer Poly. Inst., 1924, US Govt., Yorktown, Va., 1931, Joint City-Prodrs. Corp., Alexandria, Va., 1949; art dir. Cin. Art Theatre, 2025—26. Vol. advisor Performing Arts, Tustin HS, Calif., 1975—88. Co-author (with Edward Warwick and Henry Pitz): Early American Dress, 1964; editor: Arts of Design-Dunlap, 1965; author: 19th Century Dress, 1966—81, 1600 World Dress, 1982—83, Sketchbook of Aboriginal Dress, Western Hemisphere, Post-Glacial to 1866 A.D., 1987. Pres. Leonia players Guild, bd. dirs., 1920—53, Leonia Pub. Libr., 1962—69; hon. mem. Wyckoff House Found. With US Army, 1917—18. Mem.: Nat. Theatre Conf. (founding mem., bd. dirs.). Deceased.

**WYLAND, BEN F.,** minister; b. Harlan, Iowa, Mar. 16, 1882; s. Frank and Mary (Griffith) Wyland; m. Ada D. Beach, Jan. 14, 1909; children: Gordon B., Hugh C., Robert B., Molly G.; m. Mildred E. Oeschger, May 5, 1955. PhB, U. Iowa, 1905; BD, Yale, 1908, MDiv, 1971; LittD, Edward Waters Coll., 1954. Ordained to ministry Congl. Ch., 1908. Pastor, Worcester, Mass., 1918—26, Lincoln, Nebr., 1926—36, Bklyn., 1936—39; radio pastor Sta. KFAB, 1921—36, exchange pastor to Eng., 1933; in charge ch. rels. Herbert Hoover's Campaign, Food Small Democracies, 1940—41; exec. sec. United Chs. Greater St. Petersburg, Fla., 1948—56, Fla. Council Racial Cooperation, St. Petersburg, from 1956. Chmn. Com. To Preserve Negro Rights; founder Negro Girls Welfare Home, St. Petersburg, St. Petersburg Helping Hand Sr. Citizens; chmn. United Negro Coll. Fund. Recipient citation from Maj. Gen. Philip Hayes, 3d Service Command, B'nai B'rith Brotherhood award, St. Petersburg, 1954, Oscar, Community Chest dr., 1955, citation Met. Council, Inc., 1958, Bethune Cookman Coll., Edward Waters Coll., hon. citation Yale Div. Sch., 1982, Key to City of St. Petersburg, 1983. Mem.: Delta Sigma Phi, Food Commn. (chmn.), Americanization Com. (chmn.), Profl. Sr. Citizens of Eckerd Coll., Congl. Ministers (pres.), NYC Assn. Chs. (pres. bd. dirs.), Crime Prevention Soc. (dr.), Bklyn. Fedn. Chs. (dir.), Am. Com. Christian Refugees Bklyn. (exec. sec.), Am. Relief Assn. (dir.), Kiwanian, Mason (32 degree. K.T.), Alpha Chi Rho. Deceased.

**WYLER, MARJORIE GOLDWASSER,** producer; b. NYC, Sept. 23, 1915; d. Israel Edwin and Edith (Goldstein) Goldwasser; m. Wilfred Wyler, June 23, 1938; children: Ruth Wyler Messinger, Barbara Wyler Gold. BS, Bryn Mawr Coll., 1936, MA, 1937; postgrad., U. in Exile New Sch., NYC, 1937-38. With Jewish Theol. Sem., NYC, 1938-93, dir. dept. of pub. info., 1951-85, producer radio and TV, 1985-93. Cons. Jewish media programming; vice chair Odyssey TV network. Mem. Pub. Rels. Soc. Am. Democrat. Avocation: philanthropic activities. Died July 22, 2002.

**XING, QI YI,** retired research chemist, educator; b. Tianjin, Hebei, China, Nov. 24, 1911; m. Cun Rou Qian, Aug. 26, 1942; children: Zutong, Zujian. BS, Furen U., Beijing, 1933; PhD, U. Ill., 1936; postgrad., U. Munich, 1937. Assoc. rschr. Inst. Chemistry Academia Sinica, Shanghai, China, 1937-38, rschr. Kunming, China, 1938-42; prof. Mil. Med. U. Middle China, Tianchang, 1944-45, Peking U., Beijing, 1946-88, prof. emeritus, from 1988. Academician Acad. Scis., Beijing, 1980—; counselor Chem. Jour. Chinese Univs., Changchun, China, 1985—; group leader Nat. Natural Sci. Found. China, Beijing, 1986-91; chmn. spl. com. for edn. Chinese Chem. Soc., Beijing, 1986-90. Contbr. articles to profl. jours.; inventor in field of peptide chemistry and organic reactions. Mem. nat. com. Chinese People's Polit. Consultation Conf., Beijing, 1982-92; counselor China Internat. Culture Exch. Ctr., Beijing, 1985—. Recipient 1st class prize State Commn. Natural Scis., Beijing, 1982, Excellent Tchg. Material prize State Commn. of Edn., Beijing, 1988, Nat. Class prize for excellent tchg. Nat. Commn. Edn., Beijing, 1989. Home: Lanqiying Beijing, China. Died Nov. 4, 2002.

**YAACOBI, GAD,** former ambassador, former Israeli government official; b. Moshav Kfar Vitkin, Israel, Jan. 18, 1935; s. Alexander and Sara Y.; 3 children. Grad. in Econs.

and Polit. Sci., Tel Aviv U. Asst. to min. agr., head agrl. and settlement planning and devel. ctr. Govt. of Israel, 1960-66, dep. min. transport, 1971-74, min. transport, 1974-77, min. econs. and planning, 1984-88, min. comm., 1987-90, mem. Inner Cabinet, 1990, amb. to UN NYC, 1992-96; M.P. Knesset, 1969-92; chmn. Ports & Rlwys. Authority, Israel, 2000—04. Mem. Moshavim Movement, 1960-67; chair econ. coun. Histadrut, Labor Union, Rafi Faction; mem. parliamentary fin. com. Knesset, 1969-70, mem. parliamentary def. and fgn. affairs com., 1974; chmn. bd. dirs. Israel Elec. Corp., 1996; vis. prof. Inter-disciplinary Ctr., Herzlia, Israel. Author: (current politics) The Power of Quality, 1971, The Freedom to Choose, 1975, The Government, 1980, A Call for Change, 1983, Grace of Time, 1991, The New-York Diary, 1997, On the Razor's Edge, 1991, (poetry) A Place Nearby, 1998, Until the Day Will Come, 2005; contbr.; author: Grace of Time-An Autobiography, 2002. Mem. Israel Authors Assn. Avocations: theater, reading, writing. Home: Tel Aviv, Israel. Died Aug. 27, 2007.

**YAKOVLEV, ALEKSANDR NIKOLAYEVICH,** Russian government official; b. Dec. 2, 1923; Degree, Yaroslavl Pedagogical Inst., 1945. Mem. Communist Party Soviet Union, 1944-91, mem. Yaroslavl dist. com., 1946-53; head dept. sci. and culture Ctrl. Com. Communist Party Soviet Union, 1953-56, instr. dept. propoganda and agitation, 1962-64, head radio and TV broadcasting propoganda dept., 1964-65, 1st dep. head, acting head propoganda dept. Moscow, 1965-73, mem. cen. auditing com., 1971-76; amb. to Can., 1973-83; dir. Inst. for World Economy and Internat. Rels., 1983-85; head propoganda dept. Ctrl. Com. Communist Party Soviet Union, Moscow, 1985-86, sec. responsible for propoganda, 1986-87; mem. ctrl. com. Communist Party Soviet Union, 1986-91; candidate mem., then mem. Politburo Ctrl. Com. Communist Party Soviet Union, Moscow, 1987-89, head internat. policy com., 1988-91; mem. Presdl. Coun., 1990; chmn. Presdl. Commn. on Rehab. Polit. Prisoners, Moscow, from 1992, Russian Pub. TV Ltd., from 1995. Former pres. Democracy Found. Served with Soviet Army, 1941-43. Mem. Acad. Sci. (econ. dept. 1984). Home: Moscow, Russia. Died Oct. 18, 2005.

**YAMAGATA, HIDEO,** mathematician; b. Osaka, Japan, Sept. 13, 1930; s. Eizo and Takako Yamagata; m. Reiko Kusakabe, Oct. 22, 1960; children: Yasuko, Kiyoko. BA, Osaka U., 1953, MA, 1955; PhD, Kyoto U., Japan, 1981. Asst. Osaka U., Toyonaka, Japan, 1962—64; full-time lectr. U. Osaka Prefecture, Sakai, Japan, 1964—88, assoc. prof., 1988—94. Reviewer Zentralblatt für Mathematik, Berlin, from 1963, Math. Revs., Ann Arbor, Mich., from 1988; commuting editor Scientiae Mathematicae Japonicae, Sakai, Japan, from 2002. Co-author: Applied Mathematics, 1980; contbr. articles to profl. jours. Buddhist. Home: Ibaraki, Japan. Died Dec. 16, 2013.

**YANCEY, ANNE RICHARDSON,** civic worker; b. Brookline, Mass., Feb. 12, 1913; d. Otis Weld and Lucile (Johnston) Richardson; m. Charles Stephen Yancey, Apr. 9, 1942; children: Sherod Anne, Charles Stephen. BA, Vassar Coll., 1936. Rschr. & asst. sec. Mass. Investors Trust, Boston, 1937—40; rschr. Harvard Sch. Pub. Health, 1942—45; partner, co-adminstr. Fairlawn Nursing Home, 1963—73; pres. Dalmin Devel. Corp., Dallas, 1973—84; mem. Boston Jr. League, 1932—45, Dallas Jr. League, 1945—97. Pres. Dallas Vis. Nurse Assn., 1952—54; 1st v.p. Children's Bur., Dallas, 1945—47; bd. dirs. Dallas Planned Parenthood, 1956—58; exec. bd. Cmty. Coun. Greater Dallas, 1955—65; 1st v.p, 1959—61; chmn. family and children's div., 1957—59; mem. Linz Award Com., Dallas, 1961; bd. dirs. Dallas Civic Opera Guild, 1965—72, Nat. Conservancy, 1977—97; class fund chmn. Vassar Coll., Poughkeepsie, NY, 1977—81; lic. nursing home adminstr., Tex. Mem.: Am. Hort. Soc., Pan Am. Round Table, Nat. Soc. Colonial Dames Am., Nat. Assn. Jr. Leagues Am., Am. Coll. Nursing Home Adminstrs., Dallas Vassar, Harpswell Garden, Boston Vassar, Evergreen Garden, Garden Club Fedn. Maine, Dallas Garden, Dallas Women's. Episcopalian. Died Jan. 19, 1997.

**YANCEY, ASA G., SR.,** physician, educator; b. Atlanta, Aug. 19, 1916; s. Arthur H. and Daisy L. (Sherard) Yancey; m. Carolyn E. Dunbar, Dec. 28, 1944; children: Arthur H. II, Carolyn L., Caren L., Asa Greenwood Jr. BS, Morehouse Coll., Atlanta, 1937, ScD (hon.), 1991; MD, U. Mich., 1941; ScD (hon.), Howard U., Washington, DC, 1991. Diplomate Am. Bd. Surgery. Intern City Hosp., Cleve., 1941-42; resident Freedmen's Hosp., Washington, 1942-45, U.S. Marine Hosp., Boston, 1945; instr. surgery Meharry Med. Coll., 1946-48; chief surgery VA Hosp., Tuskegee, Ala., 1948-58; chief surgery of Hughes Spalding Pavilion, 1958-72; pvt. practice specializing in surgery Atlanta, 1958-86; from asst. prof. to assoc. prof. surgery Emory U., 1958—75, prof., 1975-86, prof. emeritus, from 1986, assoc. dean Sch. Medicine, 1972-89; med. dir. Grady Meml. Hosp., Atlanta, 1972-89, trustee, 1989—93; clin. prof. surgery Morehouse Sch. Medicine, from 1985; mem. staff Hughes Spalding Hosp., St. Joseph Hosp., Emory U. Hosp., 1986—88. Contbr. articles to profl. jours. Mem. Atlanta Bd. Edn., 1967—77, Fulton-De Kalb Hosp. Authority. 1st lt. M.C. US Army, 1942. Fellow: ACS, Am. Surg. Assn.; mem.: So. Surg. Assn., Inst. Medicine of NAS, Nat. Med. Assn. (1st v.p. 1988—89, trustee 1960—66, mem. editl. bd. jour. 1964—80). Baptist. Died Mar. 9, 2013.

**YANG, CHIN-PING,** chemist, engineering educator; b. Penghu Hsien, Taiwan, Republic of China, Dec. 25, 1931; s. Yee Yang and Chi Chao; m. Ye-ho Hwang, Oct. 10, 1961; children: Chung-Sheng, Chung-Chen, Chung-Cheng. BS in Chemistry, Taiwan Normal U., Taipei, Republic of China, 1956; M. Engring., Tokyo U., 1973; D. Engring., Tokyo Inst. Tech., 1986. Chmn., prof. chem. engring. dept. Tatung Inst. Tech., Taipei, 1970-89, prof. chem. engring. dept., from 1990. Chmn. grad. sch. chem. engring. Tatung Inst. Tech., Taipei, 1980-89; cons. Tatung Co., Taipei, 1963—. Contbr. articles to profl. jours.; patentee in field. Mem. Am. Chem. Soc., Japan Chem. Soc., Chinese Chem. Soc., Soc. Polymer Sci. Japan, Soc. Chinese Inst. Chem. Engrs. Home: Taipei, Taiwan. Deceased.

**YANKAUER, ALFRED,** pediatrician, preventive medicine physician, educator; b. NYC, Oct. 12, 1913; s. Alfred Sr. and Teresa (Loewy) Y.; m. Marian Wynn, May 22, 1948; children: Kenneth and Douglas (twins). BA, Dartmouth Coll., 1934; MD, Harvard U., 1938; MPH, Columbia U., 1947. Diplomate Am. Bd. Pediatrics, Am. Bd. Preventive Medicine and Pub. Health. Health officer N.Y.C. Dept. Health, 1947-50; asst. commr. of health Rochester (N.Y.) Health Bur., 1950-52; dir. maternal and child health bur. N.Y. State Dept. Health, Albany, 1952-61; WHO prof. child health Madras (India) Med. Sch., 1957-59; regional maternal and child health advisor Pan-Am. Health Orgn./WHO, Washington, 1961-66; sr. rsch. assoc. Sch. of Pub. Health Harvard U., Boston, 1966-73; prof. family and cmty. medicine and pediatrics Med. Sch. U. Mass., Worcester, from 1973. Asst. prof. health Cornell U. Med. Coll., N.Y.C., 1948-50; med. dir. pediatric nurse practitioner program Mass. Gen.Hosp./Northeastern U. Coll. of Nursing, Boston, 1972-79. Editor Am. Jour. Pub. Health, 1975-90; contbr. over 200 articles to profl. jours. Mem. health adv. com. Pub. Affairs Assn., N.Y.C., 1980-88; bd. dirs. Am. Social Health Commn., Research Triangle Park, N.C., 1984-90, chmn. rsch. adv. com., 1990—. Maj., M.C., U.S. Army, 1941-45, ETO. Fellow AAAS, Am. Acad. Pediatrics (Job Lewis Smith award 1979); mem. APHA (Excellence award 1990), Mass. Pub. Health Assn. (Lemuel Shattuck award 1987). Democrat. Home: Amherst, Mass. Deceased.

**YANO, KAZUNARI,** marine biologist; b. Tokyo, Apr. 16, 1956; s. Kazuhiro and Kinue (Shishikura) Y.; m. Kaori Baba; children: Toshikazu, Nobukazu, Nagisa, Hidekazu. BA in Fisheries, Tokai U., Shimizu, 1980, MA in Fisheries, 1982, PhD in Fisheries, 1986. Scientist Japan Marine Fisheries Resources Rsch. Ctr., Tokyo, 1987-92; sr. scientist Seikai Nat. Fisheries Rsch. Inst., Shimonoseki, 1992-95, chief sr. scientist Ishigaki Tropical Sta., from 1995. Contbr. articles to profl. jours. Home: Okinawa, Japan. Died Apr. 4, 2006.

**YAOTANG, LI See JIN, BA**

**YARNOLD, EDWARD JOHN,** theologian; b. Kingston-On-Thames, Surrey, England, Jan. 14, 1926; s. Edward Cabre Yarnold and Agnes Deakin. BA, Oxford U., Eng., 1954, MA, 1957, DDiv, 1974; STL, Heythrop Coll., Eng., 1961. Ordained Jesuit 1943, ordained priest 1960. Classics master St. Francis Xavier's Coll., Liverpool, England, 1954—57, St. Michael's Coll., Leeds, England, 1962—64; tutor-in-theology Campion Hall/Oxford U., England, from 1964, master, 1965—72. Author: (novels) (various, including) The Awe-Inspiring Rites of Initiation, 1994. Recipient Cross of the Order of St. Augustine of Canterbury, Archbishop of Canterbury, 1981. Roman Catholic. Home: Oxford, England. Died July 23, 2003.

**YAXLEY, JACK THOMAS,** secondary school educator; b. Detroit, June 30, 1943; s. Thomas William Yaxley and Evelyn Dora (Chandler) Dahlman. AS, Broward Community Coll., 1964; BS, Fla. Atlantic U., 1965, MEd, 1966, postgrad., 1968, 70-73, Brown U., 1969, Bowdoin Coll., 1972, B.C.C. Field Sch., Mex., 1979-80, Hope Coll., 1986, English for Speakers of Other Langs. Inst., 1991-92, Broward Schs. Macintosh Computer Tng. Inst., 1992. Cert. assoc. master tchr., tchr. English for speakers of other langs. Tchr. chemistry N.E. High Sch., Ft. Lauderdale, Fla., 1966-70; tchr. honors chemistry, chemistry, advanced placement chemistry South Plantation (Fla.) High Sch., from 1971, instr. gifted and honors earth/space sci., from 1990, sci. dept. head, from 1994. Chem. analyst Alfinco/Russell-Anaconda, Oakland Park, Fla., 1968-70; part-time instr. Fla. Atlantic U., 1970-71; cons. Broward Dist. Schs., Ft. Lauderdale, 1971-87, tchr. gifted summer camp, 1983-85; lab. instr. Broward C.C., 1982-83, lectr. chemistry, 1988-90; cons. textbooks Modern Chemistry, CBS/Holt-Rinehart, 1983, Holt. Phys. Sci., 1984, Modern Phys. Sci., 1984-85, Exploring Matter and Energy: Phys. Sci., 1990; presenter, editor workshop NSF, Broward Sch., 1986; presenter Dist. VIIa Leadership Tng. Inst. Phi Delta Kappa, 1991, 93; mem. bd. advisors, bd. dirs. com. Lake Emerald Svcs. Co., Inc.; panel mem. Home Testing Inst., Port Washington, N.Y.; instr. Sch. Tech. Inservice, 1995. Columnist Reflections of Lake Emerald, 1985-88. Mem., bd. dirs. Lake Emerald Owners Assn., 1983-93, chairperson activities com., 1985-88, security com., 1985-86, 89-92, handicapped facilities com., 1992, beautification com., 1993, v.p. bd. dirs., 1989-91, pres., 1991, v.p., 1992, mem. negotiations com., 1992-93, corp. sec., 1993, mem. budget and fin. com., 1994. Named Tchr. of Yr., Fla. Engring. Soc., 1985; recipient Tchr. of 3d Acad. Quarter award Fla. Power and Light, 1989, Outstanding Tchr. award Tandy Tech. Scholars, 1991-92, 92-93; fellow NSF, 1969, 72, 86. Mem. NEA (life, Broward faculty rep. 1987—), Fla. Assn. Sci. Tchrs. (life), Fla. Teaching Profession-NEA, Fla. Atlantic U. Alumni Assn. (bd. dirs. 1966-71), Fla. Atlantic U. Coll. Edn. Alumni Assn. (founding benefactor), Planetary Soc., Phi Delta Kappa (scholarship fund raising com. auction, treas. 1990-93, bd. dirs. 1990—, Victoria C.T. Reed Adopt a Scholar program com. 1991—, v.p. for programs 1993-94, mem. scholarship ball com. 1993, mem. juvenile diabetes project com. 1994-95, rsch. rep. 1994-95, Disting. Svc. award 1987, 88, 91, 93). Republican. Roman Catholic. Avocations: cultural anthropology, ethnographic research in mex. Home: Macomb, Mich. Died Mar. 22, 2000.

**YE, DU-ZHENG,** meteorologist; b. Anhui, China, Feb. 21, 1916; s. Chun-shi and Ren-lan (Chen) Yeh; m. Hui Feng Ye, June 24, 1953; children: Wei-jiang Yeh, Wei-ming Yeh, Wei-jian Yeh. B, Tsing-hua U., 1940; PhD, U. Chgo., 1948. Rsch. meteorologist Inst. Meteorology U. Chgo., 1946—50; chief, prof. Meteorology Lab. Inst. Geophysics, Chinese Acad. Scis., Peking, 1950—66; prof., dir. Inst. Atmospheric Physics, Chinese Acad. Scis., 1967—2013, v.p. acad., 1981; vice chmn. meteorol. sect. Commn. Sci. & Tech. China. Dep. to 3d Nat. People's Congress, China, 1964—68, 5th Nat. People's Congress, 1978—82, 6th Nat. People's Congress, 1983—87, 7th Nat. People's Congress, from 1988; officer joint sci. com. World Meteorol. Orgn.-Internat. Coun. Sci. Union, 1983—88. Author: Some Fundamental Problems of the General Circulation, 1957, The Blockings of Northern Hemisphere, 1963, The Problems of Adaptation in the Atmosphere, 1964, Meteorology of Tibetan Plateau, 1979; editor: Acta Meteorologica Sinica, 1956—64, Scientia Sinica, from 1984. Mem.: Finish Acad. Sci. & Letters, Chinese Acad. Sciences, Chinese Meteorol. Soc., Royal Meteorol. Soc. (hon.). Home: Beijing, China. Died Oct. 16, 2013.

**YEAGER, TWYNETTE,** antiques and gift shop owner, retired educator; b. Atmore, Ala., Feb. 18, 1924; d. Q.E. and Bettie (Webb) Wells; m. William B. Watson Sr. (div. 1960); children: William B. Jr., Byron W., Karen Watson Thomas; m. Thomas B. Yeager, Jr., 1972 (dec.). BA, Samford U., 1958; MA, U. Ala., Tuscaloosa, 1962, EdD, 1972. Edn. dir. First Bapt. Ch., Atmore, 1954-56; counselor Parrish H.S., Selma, Ala., 1958-60; dean of students Judson Coll., Marion, Ala., 1965-70; prof. edn., 1970-89; owner Twink's Antiques and Gifts, Marion, Ala., from 1995. Mem. Area Agy. on Aging, Silver Haired Legislator, Marion City Coun., 1992—2002, Siloam Bapt. Ch.; mem. steering com., bd. dirs. Perry County Project, Cooperative Bapt. Fellowship; bd. dirs., vice chair Marion Acad., 1992—2002; bd. dirs. Ala. Bapt. Hist. Commn., 1995—2002. Named Outstanding Alumnus Coll. Bus., Samford U., 1972. Mem.: Coalition of Marion Women Entrepreneurs (bd. dirs.), Nat. Fellowship Bapt. Educators, Ala. Hist. Soc., Perry County Assn. Elected Ofcls. (treas.), Delta Kappa Gamma (legis. chmn. 2002, past pres.). Republican. Avocations: music, reading, antiques. Home: Marion, Ill. Died Apr. 20, 2008.

**YEATMAN, HARRY CLAY,** biologist, educator; b. Ashwood, Tenn., June 22, 1916; s. Trezevant Player and Mary (Wharton) Y.; m. Jean Hansford Anderson, Nov. 24, 1949; children— Henry Clay, Jean Hansford. AB, U. NC, Chapel Hill, 1939, MA, 1942, PhD, 1953; student, Cornell U., Ithaca, NY, summer 1937. Asst. prof. biology U. of South, Sewanee, Tenn., 1950-54, asso. prof., 1954-60, prof., from 1960, Kenan prof., from 1980, chmn. dept., 1972-76, elderhostel tchr., 1987-88. Vis. prof. marine biology Va. Inst. Marine Sci., Gloucester Point, summer 1967; cons. Smithsonian Instn., Sci. Applications, Inc., La Jolla, Calif., Ctrs. for Disease Control, Atlanta, WHO, Ecol. Analysts, Inc., Balt., Duke Power Co., Charlotte, N.C., Helminthic Disease Branch. Contbr. articles to profl. jours. Served with AUS, 1942-46. Gen. Edn. Bd. fellow, 1941-42; Brown Found. fellow, 1984, State Naturalist award Tenn. Dept. Environ. & Concervation. Fellow AAAS; mem. Soc. Systematic Biology (charter), Soc. Limnology and Oceanography (charter), Soc. Ichthyology and Herpetology, Tenn. Acad. Sci., Am. Micros. Soc., Am. Ornithologists Union, Tenn. Ornithol. Soc., Tenn. Archeol. Soc., Nat. Speleological Soc., Blue Key, Phi Beta Kappa, Sigma Xi, Omicron Delta Kappa, Sigma Nu. Republican. Episcopalian. Home: Sewanee, Tenn. Died Nov. 20, 2013.

**YON HYONG-MUK,** Korean government official; b. 1925; Mem. Politburo party sec. Worker's Party, 1986, past vice premier, min. metals & machinery, 1985-86; premier Pyongyang, 1989—2005. Died Oct. 23, 2005.

**YOSHIDA, FUMITAKE,** chemical engineer, educator; b. Hanyu, Japan, Mar. 20, 1913; s. Jun and Toyo (Watanabe) Yoshida; m. Kazuko Yoshida (dec.); 2 children. B in Engring., Kyoto U., Japan, 1937, D in Engring., 1951; Dr-Ing (hon.), U. Dortmund, Germany, 1992. Chem. engr. Hitachi Ltd., Tokyo, 1937-45; lectr. Kyoto U., Japan, 1940—45, asst. prof., 1946-51, prof., 1951-76, prof. emeritus, from 1976. Vis. prof. U. Calif., Berkeley, 1963, U. Pa., Phila., 1970; guest prof. U. Dortmund, 1987; rsch. fellow Yale U., 1952, U. Wis., 1959. Editor: Chemical Engineering Science, 1987—96. Recipient Disting. Svc. citation, U. Wis., 1988. Mem.: NAE (fgn. assoc.), AIChE (hon.), Am. Chem. Soc. (hon.), Japanese Soc. Artificial Organs (hon.), Japanese Soc. Chem. Engrs. (hon.). Achievements include patents in field. Home: Kyoto, Japan. Died Sept. 5, 2007.

**YOSHII, HIROSHI,** retired historian; b. Osaka, Japan, Oct. 2, 1928; s. Masajiro and Tsune (Shimada) Y.; m. Hiroko Watanabe, Nov. 19, 1957; children: Midori, Seishi, Junshi. BA, U. Nagoya, Japan, 1952; PhD, U. Osaka, 1978. Prof. history Nagoya City U., 1964-94, prof. emeritus, from 1994; prof. Aichi Shukutoku U. Grad. Sch., Japan, 1995—2004; ret., 2004. Vis. prof. U. Bonn, Germany, 1976, 83, U. Marburg, Germany, 1990. Author: Diplomatic History of Showa Era, 1984, Kaiser William II's World Policy and the First World War, 1984, Japan-Germany-Italy Tripartite Pact and Japan-US Relations, 1987, International History, 1987, European History as Liberal Arts, 1989. With Imperial Japanese Naval Acad., 1945. Mem. Mil. History Soc. Japan (v.p. 1988-94). Home: Nagoya, Japan. Died May 26, 2008.

**YOSHIMURA, JUNZO,** architect, educator; b. Tokyo, Sept. 7, 1908; m. Takiko Ohmura, 1944; 1 child, Takako. Grad., Tokyo U. Arts, 1926. Registered 1st class arch., Japan. Mem. staff Antonin Raymond, Arch., Tokyo, Pa., 1931—41; pvt. practice Tokyo, from 1941; asst. prof. Tokyo U. Arts, 1944—62, prof., 1962—70, prof. emeritus, from 1970; pres. Junzo Yoshimura Arch., Tokyo, from 1970; arch. basic design Imperial Palace Japan, 1963, Aichi Prefectural U. Arts, 1970, Nara Nat. Mus., 1973, Japan House, NYC,

1971, Norwegian Embassy, Tokyo, 1978, Hotel Japan Shimoda, 1986, Mus. Modern Art, Ibaraki, 1988. Decorated 3rd Order Merit Japan; recipient medal, Parson Sch. Design, 1956, award, Japanese Acad. Art, 1975; named to Hall of Chamber Music, Yatsugatake, 1988, Sosei Country Club, Chiba, 1990, Kusatsu Ongaku no Mori Concert Hall, 1991. Mem.: AIA (hon.), Japan Archs. Assn., Archtl. Inst. Japan (Archtl. Inst. prize 1975), Japanese Acad. Art, Soc. Arqutectos Mexicanos (hon.). Home: Tokyo, Japan. Died 1997.

**YOUNG, BILL (CHARLES WILLIAM YOUNG),** United States Representative from Florida; b. Harmarville, Pa., Dec. 16, 1930; m. Beverly Angelo, 1985; children: Patrick, Billy 1 stepchild, Robbie; 3 children from previous marriage. Aide to Rep. William Cramer US House of Representatives, Washington, 1957—60; mem. Fla. State Senate, Tallahassee, 1961—70, minority leader, 1967—70; mem. US Congress from 8th Fla. Dist., 1971—73, 1983—93, US Congress from 6th Fla. Dist., 1973—83, US Congress from 10th Fla. Dist., 1993—2013, US Congress from 13th Fla. Dist., 2013; chmn. US House Appropriations Com., 1999—2005. Nat. committeeman Fla. Young Republicans, 1957—59, state chair, 1959—61; mem. Fla. Constn. Revision Commn., 1965—67. Served in Army Nat. Guard, 1948—57. Named Most Valuable Senator, Capitol Press Corps, 1969. Republican. Methodist. Died Oct. 18, 2013.

**YOUNG, DAVID NELSON,** media and communications consultant; b. Baton Rouge, Nov. 12, 1953; s. Nelson Joseph and Agnes (LeBlanc) Young; m. Michéle Marie-Therese Bedél, May 7, 1979; children: Jason, Jessica. Student, La. State U., 1972, U. SW La., 1975. News editor Gonzales Weekly, La., 1976—77. Organizer Soviet/Am. Culinary Exch., 1989, Soviet/Am. HS Basketball Excha., 1990; cons. in field. Host, Ascension Jour. TV Show. Bd. dirs. Ascension Cancer/Leukemia Soc., Gonzales, 1978—; organizer Societ/Am. High Sch. Basketball Exch.; nat. conmmitteeman La. Dem. Ctrl. Com., 1996-2000. Recipient Best-in-Depth Reporting award La. Newspaper Assn., 1984, Appreciation award USIA, 1988, Sovincentr Medal Honor, Moscow World Trade Ctr., 1988. Mem. East Ascension Genealogical Soc. (pres. 1980-81), East Ascension Sportsman League. Roman Catholic. Avocations: reading, computers, cooking. Deceased.

**YOUNG, HUGO JOHN,** journalist, writer; b. Sheffield, England, Oct. 13, 1938; s. Gerard Francis and Diana Graham Young; m. Lucy Waring, Dec. 22, 1990. MA, Jurisprudence, Balliol Coll., Oxford, 1961; DLitt (hon.), Sheffield U., 1993. Journalist, polit. editor, dep. editor Sunday Times, London, 1965—84; polit. columnist The Guardian, London, 1984—2003; chmn. Scott Trust, 1989—2003. Author: (novels) One of Us: a biography of Margaret Thatcher, 1989 (British Press awards, 1980, 83, 85), This Blessed Plot: Britain and Europe from Churchill to Blair, 1998. Home: London, England. Died Sept. 22, 2003.

**YOUNG, WAYLAND HILTON See LORD KENNET**

**YOUNGS, BETTIE BURRES,** writer, speaker; b. Belmond, Iowa, Feb. 24, 1948; d. Everett and Arlene Burres; 1 child, Jennifer Leigh. MS in Edn., Drake U., 1968, EdD, 1977; PhD, Walden U., 1975. Prof. San Diego State U., 1980-86; pres. Bettie Youngs and Assocs., Del Mar, Calif., from 1989. Author 14 books; radio and TV talk show guest. Mem. Calif. Assn. Sch. Adminstrs. (past pres.), Nat. Coun. for Self-Esteem. Deceased.

**YU, JOSEPH CHAN-WAH,** civil engineer; b. Hong Kong, Sept. 4, 1925; arrived in the United Kingdom, 1950; s. Kit Ting and Kim (Leung) Y.; m. Beryl Lilian House, Nov. 30, 1957; 1 child, Rosamund. BS in Engring., U. Hong Kong, 1950; diploma, Imperial Coll., 1951; PhD, U. London, 1954. Chartered civil and structural engr., United Kingdom, cons. engr., United Kingdom. Part-time engr. Sir Bruce White & Ptnrs., London, 1951-54, engr. in charge fluid mechanic dept., 1954-55; designing engr. Ove Arup & Ptnrs., London, 1955-56, design office chief, 1959-61; devel. engr. R&D labs. Portland Cement Assn., Chgo., 1956-58; sr. lectr., mgr. concrete rsch. labs. Imperial Coll. U. London, 1962-74; resident ptnr. Harris & Sutherland, Cons. Engr., Hong Kong, 1974-76; mng. ptnr. Harris & Sutherland, Far East Cons. Engr., London, 1976-79, exec. ptnr., 1980-90; cons. Harris & Sutherland Group, London, from 1990. Lectr. Northwestern U., Evanston, Ill., 1956-58; vis. prof. civil engring. King's Coll. London U., 1983-88; structural cons. Housing Devel. Bd. Govt. of Singapore, 1983—. Author: Limit Stte Design of Structural Concrete, 1973; contbr. articles to profl. jours. Fellow Royal Soc. Arts, Instn. Structural Engrs., Instn. Civil Engrs., ASCE. Achievements include development of concept of limit state design of concrete structures. Home: Powys, England. Died Dec. 12, 2001.

**YUDAIN, SIDNEY LAWRENCE,** editor, writer; b. New Canaan, Conn., May 6, 1923; s. Morris I. and Bertha (Jaffe) Yudain; m. Lael Marie Bairstow, Feb. 10, 1973; children: Rachel Jaffe, Raymond Lawrence. News editor Sta. WSTC, Stamford, Conn., 1941; reporter Norwalk Sentinel, Conn., 1942, mag. writer, motion picture corr., 1946—49; spl. asst. to Rep. Albert P. Morano US House of Representatives, Washington, 1950—58; founder, editor Roll Call, Congressional Newspaper, 1955—86. With US Army, 1943—46. Mem.: Nat. Republican Club, Nat. Democratic Club, Nat. Press Club, Sigma Delta Chi. Jewish. Home: Washington, DC. Died Oct. 20, 2013.

**YUE, ALFRED SHUI-CHOH,** metallurgical engineer, consultant; b. China, Nov. 12, 1920; s. Choy Noon-woo and Sze Man-hun (Tom) Yue; m. Virginia Chin-wen Tang, May 21, 1944; children: Mary, Raymond Yuan, John, Ling Tsao, David, Nancy Chang. BS in Geology, Chao-tung U., 1942; MS, Ill. Inst. Tech., 1950; PhD, Purdue U., 1956. Assoc. engr. Taiwan Aluminum Co., 1942-47; instr. Purdue U., 1952-56; research engr. Dow Chemical Co., Midland, Mich., 1956-62; sr. mem. Lockheed, Palo Alto Rsch. Lab., 1962-69; from prof. engring. and applied sci. to cons. UCLA, LA, 1969—95. Hon. prof. Xian Jiao-tong U., China, 1980. Sec.-gen. Chinese Culture Assn. U.S., 1967; bd. dirs. Chinese scholar to U.S. Recipient Outstanding Alumnus award, Nat. Chao Tung U., 2007. Fellow: AIAA (assoc.); mem.: AIME, Materials Rsch. Soc., American Soc. Metals, Sigma Xi, Phi Tau Phi (pres. 1978—82), Tau Beta Pia, Sigma Pi Sigma. Home: Cupertino, Calif. Died Feb. 4, 2014.

**YULE, JOE See ROONEY, MICKEY**

**ZABLUDOVSKY KRAWECKY, ABRAHAM,** architect; b. Mexico City, June 14, 1924; s. David Zabludovsky Rabinovitz and Raquel Krawecky; m. Alinka Kuperstoch, Dec. 5, 1953; children: Gina, Jaime, Moises. Grad. in architecture with honors, Escuela Nacional de Arquitectura, Mexico City, 1949. Practice architecture, Mexico City, from 1968; mem. faculty Composition Sch. Architecture, Mexico City, 1965-67; hon. examiner final exams. Sch. Architecture, Pratt Inst., NYC, 1980. Adv. dir.-gen. Mexico City Commn. Urban Devel. Prin. works include Centennial Civic Center May 5th, Puebla, Mexico, 1962, Wholesale Market of Mexico City, 1981, Tuxtla Gutierrez Theatre, Chiapas, Mex., 1981; apt. bldg. Parque-Polanco, Mexico City, 1981; central offices Multibanco Mercantil de Mex. S.N.C., 1981; subject of: Mexican Contemporary Architecture, 1969, Eight Housing Complexes, 1976, Ten Mexican Architects, 1977, Mexican Architecture: The Work of Abraham Zabludovsky and Teodoro González de León, 1978; work featured in: Archtl. Record, 1977, 81, Los Angeles Times, 1981, Anthony Krafft Editions, 1982, Revista Obras, 1983; Works published in books and mags. Mem. Soc. Architects Mex. (acad. mem. emeritus), Sch. Architects Mex., Soc. Architects Israel, Mexican Soc. Planning. Home: Mexico City DF 11020, Mexico. Died Apr. 9, 2003.

**ZABRISKIE, JOHN L.,** retired healthcare and agricultural products manufacturing company executive; b. Auburn, NY, June 8, 1939; s. John and Edith Virginia (Seldomridge) Zabriskie; m. Adelaide Zabriskie; children: Regina, Marie, Tina, Lance. BA, Dartmouth Coll., 1961; PhD in Organic Chemistry, U. Rochester, 1965. With Merck & Co., Inc., Whitehouse Station, NJ, 1965-93; chmn., CEO Upjohn Co., Kalamazoo, 1993-95; pres., CEO Pharmacia & Upjohn, Inc., Windsor, U.K., 1995-97, NEN Life Science Product Inc, Boston, 1997-99, chmn., 1999—2000, MacroChem Corp., 2001—08. Bd. dirs. Kellogg Co., 1995—2013, MacroChem Corp., 2000—08, Momenta Pharmaceuticals Inc., 2001—05, Array Biopharma, Inc., 2001—13, ARCA Biopharma Inc., 2005—13. Died Mar. 13, 2014.

**ZACHA, WILLIAM,** artist; b. Garland, Tex., Jan. 19, 1920; s. Martin Leopold and Ruth Bane Zacha; m. Jennie Malone, Aug. 28, 1954; 1 child, Lucia. BA, George Washington U., 1951. Secondary credential San Francisco State U., 1955; founder Mendocino Art Ctr., 1959, Bay Window Gallery, Mendocino, Calif., 1959. One-man shows include Schneiders, Rome, 1980, Kabutoya Gallery, Tokyo, 1981, 1985, Nagoya, 1985, Rogue Gallery, Medford, Oreg., 1982, Mendocino Art Ctr., 1984, Kanda Gallery, Tokyo, 1985, Plaze Gallery, Osaka, Japan, 1985, Artisan's, Mill Valley, Calif., 1986, Rogue Gallery, Medford, 1986, Calif. Mus. Art, Santa Rosa, 1986, Mendocino County Mus., Willits, Calif., 1986—87, permanent collections; author: (book) Tokaido Journey with 55 color plates of serigraphs of ancient Tokaido road in Japan; contbr. articles to profl. jours. Served USN, 1941—45. Mem.: Marine's Meml. (San Francisco). Democrat. Roman Catholic. Home: Mendocino, Calif. Died Mar. 18, 1998.

**ZACHARIASEN, FREDRIK,** physics educator; b. Chgo., June 14, 1931; s. William Houlder and Ragni (Durban-_Hansen) Z.; m. Nancy Walker, Jan. 27, 1957; children: Kerry, Judith. BS, U. Chgo., 1951; PhD, Calif. Inst. Tech., 1956. Instr. MIT, Cambridge, 1955-56; rsch. physicist U. Calif., Berkeley, 1956-57; asst. prof. physics Stanford U., Calif., 1957-60; prof. Calif. Inst. Tech., Pasadena, from 1960. Assoc. dir. Los Alamos Nat. Lab., 1982-83. Author: Structure of Nucleons, 1960, Hadron Physics, 1973, Sound Fluctuation, 1979. Sloan fellow, 1960-64, Guggenheim fellow, 1970; Green scholar Scripps Instn. Oceanography, 1997-98. Home: Pasadena, Calif. Died Dec. 9, 1999.

**ZACHMANN, MILO,** retired pediatric endocrinologist; b. Basel, Switzerland, June 9, 1936; s. Fritz and Marguerite (Bühler) Z.; m. Charlotte Schreiber, May 19, 1959; children: Claudia, Nicole, Sandra. MD, U. Basel, 1961. Cert. pediatrics, pediatric endocrinology. Asst. pediatric surgery U. Basel, 1962-63; resident Variety Children's Hosp., Miami, Fla., 1963-64; rsch. fellow Jackson Meml. Hosp., Miami, 1964-65; sr. lectr. U. Zurich, Switzerland, 1966-78, assoc. prof. dept. pediatrics, 1972-78, prof., from 1978. Bd. mem. Ares-Serono Pharm. Co.; hon. cons. U. Warsaw, 1987. Contbr. over 200 articles to profl. jours., chpts. to books. 1st lt. Med. Svc. Swiss Army. Mem. European Soc. Pediatric Endocrinology (sec. gen. 1972-78, Andrea Prader prize 1988), Swiss Pediatric Assn. (sec. gen., Fanconi award 1986), Swiss Endocrine Soc. (coun. mem.), Japanese Soc. Pediatric Endocrinology (hon.). Avocation: flying. Home: Zumikon, Switzerland. Died Aug. 28, 2002.

**ZACHRY, HENRY BARTELL,** construction company executive; b. Uvalde, Tex., Sept. 27, 1901; m. Marjorie Powell, Sept. 7, 1929 (dec. Apr., 1977); children: Mary Pat, Emma Leigh, Bartell, Suzanne, James. BS Civil Engring., U. Tex., 1922. Founder, chmn. bd. H.B. Zachry Co., San Antonio, from 1924; dir. Dallas Fed. Res. Bank Govs. S.W. Rsch. Inst., San Antonio, from 1947. Trustee Tex. A&M U. Rsch. Found., 1954-75; chmn. San Antonio Fair, Inc., 1967-68, CEO, 1968; mem. dist. bd. Alamo Heights Ind. Sch. Dist., 1948-57, chmn., 1952-53; bd. dirs. Tex. Bd. Spl. Schs. Hosps., 1950-52, Tex. A&M U., 1955-61, pres. bd. 1959-61; head Tex. Gov.'s Com. Edn. Beyond H.S., 1963-65; mem. coordinating bd. Tex. Colls. and Univs., 1965-71. Recipient Distinguished Alumnus award Tex. A&M U., 1964; named Engr. of Yr., Tex. Soc. Profl. Engrs., 1962. Mem. Assn. Gen. Contractors Am. (past pres.), San Antonio C. of C. (bd. dirs. 1975-80), Chi Epsilon (spl. honors). Died Sept. 5, 1984.

**ZACKS, GORDON BENJAMIN,** retired manufacturing executive; b. Terre Haute, Ind., Mar. 11, 1933; s. Aaron and Florence Melton (Spurgeon) Z.; m. Carol Sue Zacks (dec. 2012); children: Catherine E., Kimberly A. BA, Coll. Commerce, Ohio State U. With R.G. Barry Corp., Pickerington, Ohio, 1955—64, exec. v.p., 1964-65, pres., 1965—79, chmn. bd., 1979—92, chmn., CEO, 1992—2004. Nat. chmn. Bush for President Nat. Jewish Campaign Com., 1987—88; chmn. US & Fgn. Comml. Svc. Advisory Com., 1991—92. Mem. Nat. Republican Senatorial Com.(NRSC); hon. chmn. United Jewish Appeal; bd. dirs. numerous Jewish orgns., locally and nationally. Mem. Chief Exec. Officer Orgn., American Mgmt. Assn. Republican. Jewish. Home: Pickerington, Ohio. Died Feb. 1, 2014.

**ZADUNAISKY, PEDRO ELIAS,** mathematics professor; b. Rosario, Argentina, Dec. 10, 1917; s. Jacobo and Gitl Nitzkaner Zadunaisky; m. Rebeca Schor; children: Daniel, Gabriel. Degree in Civil Engring., Nat. U. Rosario, 1944, D (hon.), 2003. Rsch. asst. U. Inst. Math., Rosario, 1940—46; rsch. fellow U. Astron. Obs., La Plata, Argentina, 1946; prof. astronomy Nat. Tucuman U., Argentina, 1948—53; prof. Cel Mech Nat. Astron. Obs., La Plata, 1954—57; rsch. fellow IBM Watson Lab., Columbia U., NYC, 1957; staff mem. Princeton U., NJ, 1958; sr. astronomer Smithsonian Astrophysics Obs., Cambridge, Mass., 1958—61; assoc. rschr. Harvard Coll. Obs., Cambridge, 1958—61; prof. applied math U. Buenos Aires, 1961—84, prof. emeritus, 1984—2009, head math. dept., 1984—85. Prof. astronomy Nat. Com. for Space Rsch., San Miguel, Argentina, 1972—95; hon. prof. U. La Plata, 1988—2009. Author: A Guide to Astrodynamics, vol. 1, 1958, Introduction to Astrodynamics, vol. 3, 2003. Fellow, Guggenheim Meml. Found., 1957, 1978; sr. assoc., NAS, 1967—68. Mem.: Argentina Astron. Soc., Argentina Math. Union, Internat. Astron. Union. Achievements include minor planet named in his honor. Avocation: classical music. Home: Buenos Aires, Argentina. Died Oct. 7, 2009.

**ZAENTZ, SAUL,** film producer, former record company executive; b. Passaic, NJ, Feb. 28, 1921; m. Celia Mingus, 1960 (div.); m. Lynda Redfield (div.); children: Athena, Jonathan, Joshua, Dorian. Attended, Rutgers U. Owner Fantasy Records, 1975—2005. Founder Saul Zaentz Film Ctr., 1980. Producer: (films): One Flew Over the Cuckoo's Nest, 1975 (Acad. award for Best Picture, 1976), Three Warriors, 1977, Lord of the Rings, 1978, Amadeus, 1984 (Acad. award for Best Picture, 1985), The Unbearable Lightness of Being, 1988, At Play in the Fields of the Lord, 1991, The English Patient, 1996 (Academy Award for Best Picture, 1997), Goya's Ghosts, 2007; exec. producer: (films) The Mosquito Coast, 1986. Recipient Irving G. Thalberg Meml. award for Lifetime Achievement, 1997, Prodr. of Yr. Award, Nat. Bd. Review, 2005; fellow Acad. Fellowship, British Acad. Film Award (BAFTA), 2003. Died Jan. 3, 2014.

**ZAFFARONI, ALEJANDRO C.,** retired biochemist, biotechnology entrepreneur; b. Montevideo, Uruguay, Feb. 27, 1923; arrived in U.S., 44; s. Carlos and Luisa (Alfaro) Zaffaroni; m. Lyda Russomanno, July 5, 1946; children: Alejandro A., Elisa. B., U. Montevideo, 1943; PhD in Biochemistry, U. Rochester, 1949; Doctorate (hon.), U. Republic, Montevideo, 1983; M.Divinity, Cen. Bapt. Seminary, 1987. Dir. biochem. research Syntex S.A., Mexico City, 1951—54, v.p., dir. research, 1954—56; exec. v.p., dir. Syntex Corp., Palo Alto, Calif., 1956—68; pres. Syntex Labs. Inc., Palo Alto, Calif., 1962—68, Syntex Research, Palo Alto, Calif., 1962—68; founder ALZA Corp., Palo Alto, Calif., from 1968, CEO, 1968—97, founder, dir. emeritus, 1998—99, ret., 1999; founder, mem. policy bd. and exec. com. DNAX Research Inst. of Molecular and Cellular Biology, Inc. (acquired by Schering-Plough), Palo Alto, Calif., 1980—82, chmn., 1980—82; founder, chmn., chief exec. officer Affymax, N.V. (acquired by Glaxo plc), Palo Alto, 1988—95; founder Affymetrix, Inc., Santa Clara, Calif., 1991; co-founder Symyx Technologies, Inc., Santa Clara, Calif., 1994, Maxygen Inc., Redwood City, Calif., 1997, SurroMed, Inc., Mountain View, Calif., 1997; founder Alexza Pharm., 2000. Chmn. Internat. Psoriasis Research Found., Palo Alto; incorporator Neuroscis. Research Found. MIT, Brookline, Mass.; bd. govs. Weizmann Inst. Sci., Rehovot, Israel; mem. pharm. panel of com. on tech. and internat. econs. and trade issues Nat. Acad. Engring. Office of Fgn. Sec. and Assembly of Engring., Washington; hon. prof. biochemistry Nat. U. Mex., 1957, U. Montevideo, 1959; bd. dirs. Perlegen Sciences, from 2004; founding investor Genospectra; mng. ptnr. Technogen Associates, L.P. Contbr. numerous articles to profl. jours.; patentee in field. Recipient Barren medal, Barren Found., Chgo., 1974, President's award, Weizmann Inst. Sci., 1978, Chem. Pioneer award, American Inst. Chemists, Inc., 1979, Nat. Medal of Technology, The White House, 1995, Bower award for Bus. Leadership, Franklin Inst., 2005, Gregory Pincus award, Worcester Found., 2005, Biotechnology Heritage award, 2006. Fellow: American Pharm. Assn., American Acad. Arts & Sciences; mem.: AAAS, NAE, Christian Legal Soc., N.Y. Acad. Sciences, Internat. Soc. Research in Biology of Reproduction, Endocrine Soc., Biochem. Soc. Eng., Sociedad Mexicana de Nutricion y Endocrinologia, Soc. Exptl. Biology and Medicine, Internat. Soc. Study of Biol. Rhythms, Internat. Soc. Chronobiology, Internat.

Pharm. Fedn., Calif. Pharmacists Assn., Biomed. Engring. Soc., American Soc. Pharmacology & Exptl. Therapeutics, American Soc. Microbiology, American Soc. Biol. Chemists, Inc., American Inst. Chemists, Inc., American Found. Pharm. Edn., American Chem. Soc., Tau Kappa Epsilon (internat. pres. 1953—57). Died Mar. 1, 2014.

**ZAGAINOV, GERMAN IVANOVICH,** science educator; b. Kizon, Russia, July 31, 1935; s. Ivan Petrovich and Klovdia Alexeevna Zagainov; m. Tafyana Tzudyovna; 1 child, Irena Lushina; m. Olga Petzovna Zagainov, Jan. 1960 (div. 1999); children: Helena, Ivoia Pagoinev. Grad., Moscow Inst. Physics and Tech., 1959. Engr. ISAGI, Haeoveusi, 1959—67; chief devel. FSAAI, Zhuhovsrii, 1967—74; prof., cheif dept. MFTI, 1967—99; chief dept. TSAGI, 1974—89, dir., 1994—99; gen. dir. Assn. Network Rsch. Ctr., Moscow, 1994—99; dep. gen. designer Sekhoc Corp., 1999—2001; scientific sec. Sukha Civic, 2001—03; prof. Moscow Aviation Inst., 2002—03. Author: Control of Aircraft, 1991; contbr. articles to profl. jours. Mem.: Swedish Acad. Engring. Achievements include inventor in field. Avocation: skiing. Home: Moscow, Russia. Died Nov. 2007.

**ZAHN, LOUIS JENNINGS,** foreign language educator, administrator; b. Atlanta, Nov. 24, 1922; s. William Jennings and Rosina Marie (Hunerkopf) Z. AB, Emory U., 1947, MA, 1949; PhD, U. N.C., 1957. Instr. Armstrong Coll., Savannah, Ga., 1948-49, Emory U., Atlanta, 1950-57; asst. prof. Ga. Inst. Tech., Atlanta, 1957-60, assoc. prof., 1960-64, prof., from 1964. Head dept. modern langs., 1976-85, acad. adminstr. intensive courses English for fgn. students, 1958-85, dir. Lang. Inst., 1985-87, prof., dir. emeritus modern langs., 1988—; cons. 1987-95. Author: Vocabulario etimologico documentado del Libro de los exenplos por abc de Sanchez de Vercial, 1961, History of St. John's Lutheran Church, 1869-69, 69, Addendum, 1969-96, 1996, Teoria y ejercicios sobre la fonologia y la morfologia de la lengua espanola, 1974; Juan Ruiz, Libro de buen amor, Pat I, Stanzas 1-387, 1975, Part II, Stanzas 388-891 (student edits.), 1976. Vice pres. Circulo Hispanoamericano, Atlanta, 1958-60. Fellowship Emory U. 1947, U. N.C., 1949. Mem. Tchrs. English to Speakers of Other Langs., Nat. Assn. Fgn. Student Affairs, Am. Coun. Tchg. Fgn. Langs., Nat. Assn. Tchrs. Spanish and Portuguese (pres. Ga. chpt. 1958-62), Modern Lang. Assn. Am. (state coord. Spanish 1958-64), South Atlantic, Modern Lang. Assn., Phi Sigma Iota. Lutheran. Avocations: antiques, photography, travel. Home: Roswell, Ga. Died Feb. 13, 1999.

**ZAHORSKI, STEFAN,** physicist, researcher; b. Wilno, Poland, Mar. 22, 1933; s. Henryk and Zofia (Kowalewska) Z.; m. Renata Jadwiga Jakubowska, Feb. 11, 1961; 1 child, Izabela. MS, Tech. U., Warsaw, 1956, PhD, 1961; DSc, Polish Acad. Sci., Warsaw, 1966. Asst. Tech. U., Warsaw, 1954-61; rsch. assoc. Inst. Fundamental Tech. Rsch., Warsaw, 1961-67, asst. prof., 1967-72, prof., from 1972, head lab., from 1969. Author: Mechanics of Viscoelastic Fluid Flows, 1978, Mechanics of Viscoelastic Fluids, 1982. Recipient M.T. Huber award Polish Acad. Sci., Warsaw, 1969, Polish Acad. Sci. award Polish Acad. Sci., Warsaw, 1977. Mem. Gesellschaft für Angewandte Mathematik und Mechanik, Polish Soc. Mechanics. Avocations: history, long walks. Home: Warsaw, Poland. Died Sept. 26, 1999.

**ZAMBRANO, LORENZO HORMISDAS,** manufacturing executive; b. Monterrey, Mex., Mar. 27, 1944; BS in Mech. Engring., Tecnológico Monterrey, 1966; MBA, Stanford U., 1968. Founder CEMEX, 1968, CEO, 1985—95, chmn., CEO, 1995—2014. Chmn. bd. Monterrey Tech., 1997-12; former bd. dirs. Alfa, Femsa, Televisa, Grupo Fin. Banamex, Vitro; bd. dirs. IBM; former mem., internat. adv. bd. Allianz Cos., Citigroup. Bd. dirs., mem. adv. coun. Contemporary Art Mus. Monterrey (MARCO). Recipient Ernest C. Arbuckle award Stanford Grad. Bus. Sch. Alumni Assn., 1998, Woodrow Wilson award corp. citizenship, 2005, Gold medal disting. svc. The Ams. Soc., 2005, Excellence Leadership award Stanford Grad. Sch. Bus. Died May 12, 2014.

**ZANDER, DONALD VICTOR,** veterinarian, avian pathologist; b. Bellingham, Wash., Feb. 15, 1916; s. Almer Delaus and Rosa (Mezera) Z.; m. Verna Marie Mace, Aug. 17, 1945; children: Linda Jo, David Lee, Arnold Alan. BS, U. Calif., Bekeley, 1941; MS, Colo. State U., 1945, DVM, 1950; PhD, U. Calif., Davis, 1953. Asst. prof. Sch. Vet. Medicine, U. Calif., Davis, 1953-55; dir. health rsch. H&N Inc., Redmond, Wash., 1955-89. Contbr. articles to sci. jours. Com. chmn. Boy Scouts Am., Woodinville, wash., 1970-78. 1st lt. U.S. Army, 1945-47, ETO. Recipient Disting. Svc. award Redmond Kiwanis Club, 1968, Disting. award of Merit Boy Scouts Am., 1979, Disting. Svc. award Wash. Poultry Industry Assn., 1982, Cert. of Appreciation USDA, 1982. Mem. AVMA, Western Poultry Disease Conf. (past pres. 2 terms), Am. Assn. Avian Pathologists (pres. 1965, C.A. Bottorff award 1990), World Poultry Sci. Assn., World Vet. Poultry Assn. (Poultry Scientist of Yr. 1989). Methodist. Home: Woodinville, Wash. Died Dec. 29, 1999.

**ZANONI, UMBERTO,** banker, consultant; b. Verona, Italy, Oct. 28, 1937; s. Massimiliano and Giustina (Rivoldini) Z.; m. Luciana Signorati, Oct. 8, 1962; children: Andrea, Valeria, Michele. Degree in econs. and commerce, U. Padua, Italy, 1967. Acct. Cassa Risparmio Vr Vi Bl An, Verona, Italy, 1957-67, head br. office, 1967-68, sr. auditor, 1968-80, head cash dept., 1980-83, audit mgr., 1983-88, head audit dept., 1988-90, head revenues dept., 1990-96; pres. Verisparmio Gestri spa, Verona, 1996—2001. Cons. Centro Formazione Personale Casse Risparmio Italiane, Rome, 1976—, Società per l'Organizzazione e la Formazione Manageriale, Milan, 1978-79, Istituto Studi Bancari, Lucca, Italy, 1988-90, Istituto Superiore Direzione Aziendale, Rome, 1989-91; v.p. audit and control com. Internat. Savs. Banks Inst., Geneva, 1989—; bd. dirs. Consorzio Nat. Concessionari, Rome, 1990-95; lectr. nat. meetings, seminars and roundtables, Italy, 5th Internat. Auditing Conf., Amsterdam, The Netherlands, 1988, Internat. Seminar on Auditing in Banking, Paris, 1988; guest lectr. U. Pavia, 1985, U. Verona, 1988-91, Luiss Rome, 1990-91, SDA Bocconi Milan, 1989-91, U. Venice, 1990. Author: Internal Auditing in Italian Savings Banks, 1988; co-author: Principles in Internal Auditing in Banking, 1983; contbr. articles to profl. jours., chpt. to booK. Bd. dirs. Sindircasse, Rome, 1987-92, Federdirigenticredito, Rome, 1988-90, Confedn. Italian Dirigenti Azienda, Rome, 1988-92. Mem. Inst. Internal Auditors, Milan, (bd. govs. 1979-82, v.p. 1982-84, pres. 1984-86, chmn. bank auditing com. 1979-90), Ascotributi, Rome, (advisor 1990-97, bd. govs. 1996—), Istituto Per l'Automazione delle Casse di Risparmio Italiane, Rome,(advisor 1986-90, com. on computer crime), Italian Banking Assn., Rome, (mem. com. computer crime 1986). Home: Verona, Italy. Deceased.

**ZAPATA, CARMEN,** actress, producer; b. NYC, July 15, 1927; d. Julio and Ramona (Roca) Z.; m. Roy A. Friedman, July 1957 (div. 1963). Actress: (Broadway plays and touring cos.) Stop the World: I Want to Get Off, Oklahoma, Bloomer Girl, Carnival, 'Bye 'Bye Birdie, No Strings, Blood Wedding (Dramalogue award 1977), Fanlights (Dramalogue award 1979), others, (films) I Will!, I Will!, Pete and Tillie, A Home of Our Own; (TV shows) Flamingo Road, Marcus Welby, Hagen, Charlie's Angels, others, (PBS-TV bilingual children's show) Villa Alegre, 1974—; (TV series) Viva Valdez, 1976. Pres., producer Bilingual Found. of Arts, Los Angeles; Bd. dirs. Mexican Am. Opportunity Found., Monterey Park, Calif., Nat. Repertory Theatre Found., Los Angeles, L.A. Council Boy Scouts America, Performing Tree, Los Angeles, Am. Nat. Theatre & Acad. West; mem. Mayor's Com. on Arts, Los Angeles, Inter-Cultural Exchange Com., U. Southern Calif., Los Angeles-Mexico City Sister-City Affiliate Com.; chairperson Mexican-American Women's Conf., 1979. Recipient Nosotros award for Best Actress, 1971, El Angel award for Best Spanish Speaking Actress, 1973, Ruben Salazar award for communications Nat. Council of La Raza, 1980, Silver Achievement award Los Angeles YWCA, 1981, numerous others. Mem. Screen Actors Guild, Nat. Acad. TV Arts & Sciences, Actors Equity Assn., American Fedn. TV & Radio Artists, Calif. Theatre Council, Calif. Confedn. Arts, American Guild Variety Artists. Home: Van Nuys, Calif. Died Jan. 5, 2014.

**ZECKENDORF, WILLIAM, JR.,** retired real estate developer; b. NYC, Oct. 31, 1929; s. William Zeckendorf and Irma (Levy) Kolodin; m. Guri Lie, Feb. 4, 1956 (div. Aug. 1963); children: William Lie, Arthur William; m. Nancy King, Oct. 24, 1963. Student, U. Ariz., 1948-50; LHD (hon.), Long Island U., 1993. Pres. Webb & Knapp, Inc., NYC, 1950-65; chmn. bd. Gen. Property Corp., NYC, 1965-78; mng. gen. ptnr., developer Zeckendorf Co., NYC, 1981—92. Chmn. bd. Long Island U., Greenvale, N.Y., 1987-92, trustee, 1959-94; gov. Real Estate Bd. NY, 1986-89; bd. dirs. Santa Fe (N. Mex.) Chamber Music Festival, Coll. Santa Fe, 1997; served in U.S. Army, 1952-54. Recipient Lehman Coll. Leadership award, 1998. Mem. Confrerie des Chevaliers du Tastevin, Commanderie de Bordeaux Republican. Jewish. Home: New York, NY. Died Feb. 12, 2014.

**ZELLING, HOWARD EDGAR,** justice Supreme Court of South Australia; b. Adelaide, Australia, Aug. 14, 1916; s. Edgar Proctor and Florence May (Merritt) Z.; m. Sesca Ross Anderson, Jan. 21, 1950. LLB, U. Adelaide, 1938, LLB (hon.), 1941, D, 1983. Bar: South Australia 1938. Lectr. constl. law U. Adelaide, 1947-62, examiner, 1947-81, lectr. faculty econs., 1952-60; acting justice Supreme Ct. South Australia, Adelaide, 1969, justice, from 1969. Pres. Law Coun. of Australia, 1966-68; chmn. Law Reform Com. of South Australia, 1968-87. Contbr. articles to profl. jours. Procurator Presbyn. Ch. South Australia, 1945-69. Decorated comdr. Order Brit. Empire, officer Order of Australia. Mem. Adelaide Club, Grand Lodge South Australia (grand master 1972-76). Home: South Australia, Australia. Died Nov. 2001.

**ZEMANEK, HEINZ,** computer scientist; b. Vienna, Jan. 1, 1920; s. Ferdinand and Theresia (Renner) Z.; m. Maria Assumpta Lindebner, Aug. 12, 1950; children: Georg, Benedicta. Dipl. Ing., U. Tech. Vienna, 1944, Dr. techn., 1951; Dr. (hon.), U. Linz, Austria, 1982; Dr. Ing. (hon.), U. Erlangen, Fed. Republic Germany, 1986. Telecommunications researcher German Air Force, 1943-45; engaged in bus., 1945-47; mem. faculty U. Tech. Vienna, from 1947, prof. telecommunications & computer sci., from 1964. With IBM Corp., 1961-85, dir. IBM Lab., Vienna, 1961-75. Author: Information Theory, 1959, Calendar and Chronology, 1978, 4th edit., 1987, 5th edit., 1990; co-author: Computers, 1971; editor profl. jours. Internat. commnr. for Austria, Boy Scouts, 1949-53. Decorated Grosses Goldenes Ehrenzeichen Verdienste (Austria), 1974, Goldenes Ehrenzeichen Verdienste (Vienna), 1986; Heinz Zemanek Prize established in his honor Austrian Computer Soc., 1985; recipient Stefan medal Electro Tech. Soc. Austria, 1969; Prechtl medal U. Tech. Vienna, 1978; Computer Pioneer medal IEEE, 1986; Ov Plaquette German Mus., Munich, 1988; John Von Neuman medal Hungarian Computer Soc., 1989, Austrian Cross of Honour for Sci. & Art, 2005 Mem. West Berlin Acad. Arts, Austrian Computer Soc. (past pres.), Austrian Acad. Scis., Vienna Cath. Acad.; corr. mem. Spanish Acad. Scis.; hon. mem. Internat. Fedn. Info. Processing (pres. 1971-74), Computer Soc. Japan, Computer Soc. S. Africa, Russian Acad. Scis., Bavarian Acad. Sciences, hon. mem. Hungarian Acad. Sciences Designer 1st Austrian computer Mailuefterl, 1954-58. Home: Vienna, Austria. Died July 16, 2014.

**ZENGERLE, REMIGIUS,** engineering educator; s. Wilhelm and Katharina Zengerle; married. Dipl.-Ing., U. Stuttgart, 1974, PhD, 1979. Cert. prof., U. Kaiserslautern, 1996. Sci. collaborator Max-Planck Inst. Solid State Rsch., Stuttgart, 1976—79; sci. employee German Telecom, 1979—96; chair, prof. Tech. U. Kaiserslautern, from 1996. Achievements include first to photonic bandgaps, negative refraction and the superprism effect with visible light in 2-dimensional photonic crystals. Deceased.

**ZETZMAN, MARION RICE,** community medicine educator; b. Roscoe, Tex., May 10, 1939; s. Hugo Max and Ida (Rice) Z.; m. Sarah Pratt, Aug. 26, 1960; 1 child, Philip Marion. MPH, Tulane U., 1968; DrPH, U. Tex., Houston, 1972. Pub. health advisor USPHS, Houston, 1962-63; pub. health snaitarian Sweetwater (Tex.)-Nolan County Health Dept., 1964-65; health planner Tex. Dept. of Health, Austin, 1966-69; dir. health planning Office of the Gov., Tex., 1970-72, Tex. Dept. Human Svcs., Austin, 1973; prof. community medicine Southwestern Med. Sch. U. Tex., Dallas, 1974-96. Chmn. Tex. Statewide Health Coordinating Coun., Austin, 1984-91, Tex. Ctr. for Rural Health Initiatives, Austin, 1990—; cons. Tex. Med. Assn., Austin, 1977-96. Contbr. articles to jour. Med. Manpower, Rural Medicine, Pub. Health Issues. Cons. Office of the Gov. of Tex., Austin, 1984-88. WHO fellow, 1971. Fellow APHA (governing coun. 1975-77); mem. Am. Health Planning Assn. (treas. 1970-72), N.Y. Acad. Scis., Soc. Tchrs. Preventive Medicine. Home: Dallas, Tex. Died Nov. 7, 1996.

**ZHENG, XIULIN,** materials science and engineering educator; b. Nanjing, Jiangsu, China, Feb. 12, 1933; s. Yushu and Shujun (Liu) Z.; m. Yuxuan Xie, Aug. 4, 1962; children: Qingying, Qingxiong, Qinghao. BS, E. China Inst. Aeronautics, Nanjing, 1955. Tchg. asst. East-China Inst. Aeronautics, Nanjing, China, 1955-56, Northwestern Polytech. U., Xi'an, China, 1957-61, lectr. Xian, 1961-79, assoc. prof., 1979-85, prof., from 1985, PhD supr., from 1986. Vis. prof. Swiss Fed. Inst. Tech., Lausanne, 1980—82; mem. tech. rev. com. Internat. Conf. Fatigue, Fracture Mechanics, Corrosion Cracking and Filure Analysis, Salt Lake City, 1985; mem. China Nat. Com. for Unifying Natural Sci. and Tech. Terms, 1993—98; mem. acad. com. State Key Lab. for Materials and Strength of Xian Jiaotong U., from 1998. Author: (books) Quantitative Theory of Metal Fatigue, 1994, Mechanical Properties of Materials, 1990; co-author: Handbook of Fatigue Crack Propagation in Metallic Structures, 1994; translator: ECCS recommendations for fatigue design of steel structures; mem. editl. bd. Jour. of Materials for Mech. Engring., from 1998; contbr. over 250 articles in English and Chinese profl. jours. Dep. to Nat. People Congress of China, 1988-98. Named Excellent Tchr., People's Govt. of Shaanxi Province, China, 1985, Expert Making Outstanding Contbrns., Ministry Aero. and Astro. Industries of China, 1992. Avocations: reading, ping pong/table tennis, walking. Died Feb. 22, 2008.

**ZHIZNEVSKAYA, GENRIETTA YA,** research biochemist; b. Torzhok, Russia, Sept. 16, 1932; d. Yan Voldemar and Ksenia Alexandra (Yanushkovska) Peive; m. Alexander Fedor Zhiznevsky, Feb., 1955 (died Apr., 1977); children: Alexander, Evgeni. BS, Moscow State U., 1955; PhD, Botanical Inst., Leningrad, USSR, 1959; D in Biol. Scis., Inst. Plant Physiology, Moscow, 1970, prof., 1988. Jr. scientist Latvian Acad. Sci., Inst. Biology, Riga, 1958-61, sr. scientist, 1961-63, Inst. Plant Physiology, Moscow, 1963—77. Head lab., Inst. Plant Physiology, 1977-83, sr. scientist, 1983-99. Author: Copper, Molybdenum and Iron in Nitrogen Metabolism of Leguminous Plants, 1972; contbr. articles to scientific jours. Mem. European Assn. Grain Legumes (Paris), Botanic Soc. Scotland. Avocation: piano. Died Dec. 5, 2001.

**ZIEGLER, PETER ALFRED,** petroleum geologist; b. Winterthur, Switzerland, Nov. 2, 1928; s. Eugen and Adelheid Dorothea (Riggenbach) Z.; m. Yvonne Maria Bohrer, Oct. 22, 1960; children: Markus Peter, Christian Alfred. PhD, U. Zurich, 1955; Dr.h.c., Moscow State U., 1997, Tech. U., Delft, 2000. Field work Dead Sea area, wellsite geologist ISRAMCO, 1955; fieldwork Soc. des Pétroles de Madagascar, 1956; fieldwork in So. Algeria Compagnie d'Exploration Pétrolière, 1957; fieldparty supr. Shell Can. Ltd., Edmonton, 1958-63, tech. advisor foothills and offshore exploration divsn., 1964-66, subsurface geologist, and then exploration mgr. Calgary, 1967-70; region geologists No. Europe then acting exploration mgr. Shell Internat. Petroleum Mij., Den Haag, 1970-77, exploration cons., 1978—82, dep. head new ventures and exploration advice dept., 1982-84, sr. exploration cons., team leader global geology, 1984-88, ret., 1988; exploration cons. Petroleum Exploration Consultancy Svcs., 1988—2004; hon. lectr. U. Basel, 1990-96, prof. global geology, 1996—2008. Author: Geological Atlas of Western and Central Europe, 1982, 2d edit., 1990, Evolution of Arctic—North Atlantic and Western Tethys, 1988, Evolution of Laurussia, 1989; editor Geodynamics of Rifting, 1992, Structure and Prospects of Alpine Basins and Forelands, 1996, Peri Tethyan Rift/Wrench Basins and Passive Margins, 2001, The Transmed Atlas, 2004; bd. editors Marine and Petroleum Geology, 1985—2006, Tectonphysics, 1986—2008, Jour. of the Geol. Soc., 1988-97, Terra Naova, 1988-97, Basin Rsch., 1992-94, Geol. Quar., Warsaw, 1999—; contbr. numerous articles to profl. jours. 1st lt. Engr., 1949-55, Swiss Army. Recipient Fourmarier medal Geol. Soc. Belgium, 1986, William Smith medal Geol. Soc., 1988, Thomas Neville George medal Geol. Soc. of Glasgow, 1990, Robert H. Dott Sr. Meml. award Am. Assn. of Petroleum Geologists, 1990, Spl. Commendation award, 1995, Leopold von Buch medal Deutsche Geologische Gesellschaft, 1993, Pjotr Leonidovici Kaptsa medal Russian Acad. of Natural Scis., Stephan Müller medal European Geophys. Soc., 1998. Mem. Internat. Lithosphere Program Bur. (life), Royal Geol. and Mining Soc. of The Netherlands (Van

Waterschot van der Gracht medal 1987), Schweizerische Geologische Gesellschaft, Am. Assn. Petroleum Geologist (hon.), Royal Netherlands Acad. of Arts and Scis., Academia Europaea, European Union of Geoscientists (hon. mem.), Polish Geol. Soc. (hon. mem.), Polish Acad. Arts and Scis., Geol. Soc. (hon. mem., London), Polish Acad. Sci. (fgn. mem.), Russian Acad. Nat. Sci. (hon. mem.). Home: Binningen, Switzerland. Died 2013.

**ZIEL, WULFHILD ELISABETH,** Slavonicist, philosopher, researcher; b. Leipzig, Saxony, Germany, May 20, 1942; d. Henrik Emil and Irmgard Martha (Laussmann) Denert; m. Freddy Bernard Ziel; children: Lars-Gunnar, Corrie Barbara. Grad., Coll. Potsdam, Germany, 1968, ednl. diploma, 1969; Doctorate, U. Humboldt, Berlin, 1974. Tchr. Secondary Sch., Glesien, Germany, 1960-63, Rostock, Germany, 1963-65, ednl. diploma tchr. Berlin, 1968-77; Slavonical rschr. Inst. for History, Berlin, 1978-91, Devel. Program, Berlin, 1992-93, Devel. Program for Dresden and German Rsch. Cmty., Leipzig, Germany, 1994-97. Author: Der russische Volksbilderbogen in Bild und Text-ein kultur-u kunsthistor Intermedium, 1996-98, überarbeitete u erweiterte Auflagen, 1999, 3.fluflage, kyrillische Zitate; editor: Bibliographien zu V. Propp u N.J. Tolstoi, 1995, VCRW, 1995-98, Bibliographien zur ostslawisch-folkloristischen Volksdichtung, 1996. Mem. AJLA, LSP, SIEF. Avocations: geology, archeology, costumes, handcraft museum. Home: Berlin, Germany. Deceased.

**ZIMMER, DON (DONALD WILLIAM ZIMMER),** retired professional baseball coach, retired professional baseball player; b. Cin., Jan. 17, 1931; s. Harold Lesley and Lorraine Bertha (Ernst) Z.; m. Jean Carol Bauerle, Aug. 16, 1951; children: Thomas Jeffrey, Donna Jean. Student Pub. Schs., Cin. Profl. baseball player Dodger Farm Clubs, 1949-54, Bklyn. Dodgers, 1954-57, L.A. Dodgers, 1958-59, 1963, Chgo. Cubs, 1960-61, N.Y. Mets, 1962, Cin. Reds, 1962, Washington Senators, 1963-65, Toei Flyers, Tokyo, 1966; mgr. Cin. Reds Farm Clubs, Knoxville and Buffalo, 1967, Indpls., 1968, San Diego Padre Farm Clubs, Key West, Fla., 1969, Padre Farm Club, Salt Lake City, 1970; third base coach Montreal Expos, Que., Canada, 1971; mgr. San Diego Padres, 1972-73; third base coach Boston Red Sox, 1974-76, coach, 1992, mgr., 1976-80, Tex. Rangers, 1981-82; third base coach Chgo. Cubs, 1984, 85, 86, mgr., 1988-91; coach San Francisco Giants, 1987, Colo. Rockies, Denver, 1993-95, N.Y. Yankees, 1983, 1986, bench coach, 1996—2003; sr. baseball advisor Tampa Bay Rays, 2004—10. Mem. minor league All-Star Teams, Hornell, N.Y., 1950, Elmira, N.Y., 1951, Mobile, Ala., 1952, St. Paul, 1953; player World Series teams 1955, 56, 59; coach World Series teams 1975, 96, 98, 99, 2000, 01, 03; mem. adv. bd. Baseball Assistance Team. Co-author (with Bill Madden): Zim: A Baseball Life, 2001; author: The Zen of Zim: Baseballs, Beanballs and Bosses, 2004. Recipient Bill Stern award NBC, 1949; named St. Paul Rookie of Yr., 1953, All Star Team Player, 1961, All Star Coach, 1978, 81, 90, 97, 99, 2000, 01, 02, 03; named Nat. League Mgr. of Yr. 1989; named to The Boston Red Sox Hall of Fame, 2010. Mem. Profl. Baseball Players Assn. (life), Maj. League Baseball Players Alumni Assn., Old Time Ball Players Wis. Home: Seminole, Fla. Died May 4, 2014.

**ZIMMERMAN, JACOB W.,** state senator; b. Riverhead, NY, May 15, 1930; Degree, Villanova U. Chmn. Del. Agr. Stblzn. and Conservation Svc., 1961—64; mem. Del. Ho. Reps., 1965—71, minority leader, 1967—71; dem. candidate US Senate, 1970; mem. Del. Senate, from 1973; mem. coms. banking, edn., ins. and elections, cmty. affairs, edn., chmn. small bus. com. Mem.: Save Our Shores, Little Creek Vol. Fire Co., KC. Democrat. Roman Catholic. Home: Dover, Del. Died Oct. 9, 1996.

**ZIMMERMAN, RICHARD MORTON,** banker, lawyer; b. Hackensack, NJ, Aug. 31, 1940; s. Samuel Wallace and Shirley (Bloom) Zimmerman; children: Daniel Harris, Theodore Andrew. BS in Econs., U. Pa., 1963, JD, 1966. Bar: NY 1967. Trust mgr. First Nat. City Bank, NYC, 1966—68; asst. v.p., sr. trust officer Irving Trust Co., NYC, 1968—72; exec. v.p., group head Flagship N.B. of Miami, Fla., 1972—81; pres., CEO Sunset Comml. Bank, Miami, 1981—98, also bd. dirs. Bd. overseers U. Miami Med. Sch., 1982—98; bd. dirs. Mt. Sinai Med. Ctr., 1979—98, Jewish Home and Hosp. for Aged, Miami, 1977—98. Mem.: ABA, Am. Inst. Banking, NY Bar Assn., Grove Isle Club, Stds. Club. Republican. Jewish. Home: Miami, Fla. Died June 11, 1998.

**ZINOVYEV, NICKOLAY,** physicist; b. Sevastopol, Russia, Jan. 30, 1949; s. Nickolay Zinovyev and Lidiya Skosyreva; m. Tatyana Krymova, July 7, 2007; m. Natalia Kambarova, Feb. 11, 1972 (div. Nov. 23, 2006); 1 child, Maxim. MS in Radiophysics & Quantum Electronics, Poly. U., St.Petersburg, Leningrad, 1972; DSc in Philosophy, Ioffe Phys. Tech. Inst.USSR Acad.Sci., 1983; DSc in Physics & Math, Russian Acad.Sci., 1997. Cert. Sr. fellow in experimental physics USSR Acad. Sci., 1988. Rsch. asst. dept physics A. F. Ioffe Phys. Tech. Inst. USSR Acad. Sci., 1974—79, rsch. scientist dept physics, 1979—87, sr. rsch. scientist, 1987—97, leading rsch. scientist, from 1997; lectr. dept. physics Inst. Tech., 1989—91; sr. rsch. fellow Sch. Physics and Astronomy, U. Nottingham, England, 1991—99; vis. prof. Royal Soc. UK, 1991—92, Epsrc UK, 1993—99; sr. rsch. fellow Inst. Microwaves & Photonics, Sch. Electronic & Elec. Engring., U. Leeds, England, 2000—03; sr. fellow Nat. Phys. Lab., Teddington, England, 2003—05; assoc. sr. fellow Physics Dept., Durham U., Durham, England, 2006—08. Contbr. articles to profl. jours. Recipient Russian Innovations award, "Expert" Mag., Moscow, 2004. Mem.: Internat. Conferences Program Coms. Achievements include research in generation, electromagnetic radiation by moving real & virtual charges; Terahertz Electromagnetic transport, Wave Imaging & Spectroscopy. Home: Tyne & Wear, England. Died Aug. 1, 2009.

**ZIOLKOWSKI, RUTH,** foundation administrator; b. West Hartford, Conn., June 26, 1926; d. Frank Douglas and Lyda Catherine (Miller) Ross; m. Korczak Ziolkowski, Nov. 23, 1950; children: John, Dawn, Adam, Jadwiga, Casimir, Anne (dec. 2011), Mark, Joel, Monique, Marinka. Student, Hartford (Conn.) Jr. Coll.; DHL (hon.), S.D. Sch. Mines and Tech., 1991, U. S.D., 2002. Vol. asst. to Korczak Ziolkowski on Noah Webster statue, 1941; vol. asst. to Korczak Ziolkowski on Crazy Horse Meml., 1947; pres. Korczak's Heritage, Inc., Crazy Horse, 1968—2014; pres., CEO Crazy Horse Meml. Found., Crazy Horse, 1982—2014. Owner, asst. dairy farm, lumber mill. Recipient Reconciliation award S.D. Native American Day, 1990, Disting. Svc. award S.D. Newspaper Assn., 1991, Trailblazer award Old West Trail Found, 1992, Senate Commemoration No. 1 S.D. Legis., 1992, Spirit of Dakota award, 1993, We. American award Ctr. Western Studies Augustana Coll., S.D., 1996, Commemoration S.D. Legislature, 1997, Free Spirit award Freedom Forum, 1997, President's award Custer (S.D.) Chamber of Commerce, 1998, Spl. Achievement award Black Hills Badlands and Lakes Assn., 1998, Doane Robinson award S.D. Hist. Soc., 1999, numerous others; co-recipient with Family Outstanding Public Svc. award S.D. Sch. Mines and Tech., 1998, Commemoration S.D. Legis., 1998, Tom Didier Family Bus. award U. S.D. Sch. Bus., 1998; honoree among 10 South Dakotans The Journal, 1994, Acad. of Achievement award, Sales & Marketing Execs. Internat. Assn., 2004 Avocation: reading. Home: Crazy Horse, SD. Died May 21, 2014.

**ZIYANG, ZHAO,** former Chinese government official; b. Huaxian County, Henan Province, China, Oct. 17, 1919; m. Liang Boqi; 5 children. Joined Chinese Communist Party, 1938. Mem. standing com. South China Subbureau, Chinese Communist Party Cen. Com., 1950, sec. gen., 1952-54, dir. Rural Work Dept., 1953-55, 3d sec., 1954-55; mem. People's Council, Guangdong Province, 1955, dep. sec. Communist Party, 1955-56, sec., 1957-61, 73-74, 2nd sec., 1961-65, 1st sec., 1965, 74-75, vice chmn. Revolutionary Com., 1972-74, chmn. 1975; polit. commissar Guangdong mil. dist. People's Liberation Army, 1964; sec. Cen.-South bur. Chinese Communist Party Cen. Com., 1965-67; criticized and ousted from office in Cultural Revolution, 1967; vice chmn. Nei Monggol Revolutionary Com., 1971; sec. Chinese Communist Party Nei Monggol, 1971; chmn. Guangdong Revolutionary Com., 1972; mem. 10th Cen. Com., Chinese Communist Party, 1973, alt. mem. Politburo, 11th Cen. Com., 1977-79, mem., 1979, mem. Standing Com. of Politburo, 1980-89, mem. Politburo 12th Cen. Com., 1982, sec. gen. 1982; gen. sec. 12th Cen. Com., Chinese Communist Party, 1987-89, first vice chmn. mil. affairs commn., 1987-89; 1st sec. Communist Party, Sichuan Province, 1975-80; chmn. Sichuan Revolutionary Com., 1975-79; former exec. chmn. 5th Nat. Com., Chinese People's Polit. Consultative Conf., former vice chmn.; 1st polit. commissar Chengdu mil. dist. People's Liberation Army, 1976-80; vice premier then premier of State Council, 1980-87; former min. Commn. for Econ. Reconstrn. Died Jan. 17, 2005.

**ZOLOTOW, CHARLOTTE SHAPIRO,** retired author, editor; b. Norfolk, Va., June 26, 1915; d. Louis J. and Ella F. (Bernstein) Shapiro; m. Maurice Zolotow, Apr. 14, 1938 (div. 1969); children: Stephen, Ellen. Student, U. Wis., 1933-36. Editor children's book dept. Harper & Row, NYC, 1938-44, sr. editor, 1962-70; v.p., assoc. pub. Harper Jr. Books, 1976-81; editorial cons., editorial dir. Charlotte Zolotow Books, 1982-90; pub. emerita, advisor Harper Collins Children's Books, from 1991. Tchr. U. Colo. Writers Conf. on Children's Books, U. Ind. Writers Conf.; also lectr. children's books. Author: The Park Book, 1944, Big Brother, 1960, The Sky Was Blue, 1963, The Magic Words, 1952, Indian Indian, 1952, The Bunny Who Found Easter, 1998, new edit., 1999, In My Garden, 1960, But Not Billy, 1947, 2d edit, 1983, Not a Little Monkey, 1957, 2d edit., 1989, The Man With The Purple Eyes, 1961, Mr. Rabbit and the Lovely Present, 1962, The White Marble, 1963, A Rose, A Bridge and A Wild Black Horse, 1964, 2d edit., 1987, Someday, 1965, When I Have a Little Girl, 1965, If It Weren't for You, 1966, 2d edit., 1987, Big Sister, Little Sister, 1966, All That Sunlight, 1967, When I Have A Son, 1967, My Friend John, 1968, new edit., 1999, Summer Is, 1968, Some Things Go Together, 1969, The Hating Book, 1969, The New Friend, 1969, River Winding, 1970, 79, Lateef and His World, 1970, Yani and His World, 1970, You and Me, 1971, Wake Up and Goodnight, 1971, William's Doll, 1972, Hold My Hand, 1972, 2d edit., 1987, The Beautiful Christmas Tree, 1972, new edit., 1999, Janie, 1973, My Grandson Lew, 1974, The Summer Night, 1974, 3d edit. 1991, The Unfriendly Book, 1975, It's Not Fair, 1976, 2d edit., 1987, Someone New, 1978, Say It, 1980, If You Listen, 1980, 2d edit. 1987, The New Friend, 1981, One Step, Two ..., 1981, The Song, 1982, I Know a Lady, 1984, Timothy Too!, 1986, Everything Glistens, Everything Sings, 1987, I Like to be Little, 1987, The Poodle Who Barked at the Wind, 1987, The Quiet Mother and the Noisy Little Boy, 1988, Something's Going to Happen, 1988, This Quiet Lady, 1992, The Seashore Book, 1992, Snippets, 1992, The Moon was the Best, 1993, Peter and the Pigeons, 1993, The Old Dog, 1995, When the Wind Stops, 1995, Who is Ben, 1997, Wake Up and Goodnight, Some Things Go Together, new edits., 1998, Do You Know What I'll Do?, new edit., 2000, When I Have a Little Girl When I Have a Little Boy, 2000, The Three Funny Friends, 2003 Recipient Harper Gold award for Editorial Excellence, 1974, Kerlan award U. Minn., 1986, Corp. award for Children's Books Lit. Market Pl., 1990, Silver medallion U. Southern Miss., 1990, Tribute for Far Reaching Contbn. to Children's Lit., ALA, 1991, Otter award, 1997, Charlotte Zolotow award for Text of Disting. picture book U. Wis. named in her honor, 1998, Parent's Guide Children's Media Outstanding Achievement Poetry Books, 2002. Mem. PEN, Authors League. Home: Hastings On Hudson, NY. Died Nov. 19, 2013.

**ZUK, TOMASZ,** orthopedist; b. Sasiadowice, Poland, Nov. 12, 1921; s. Kazimierz and Wiktoria (Cymerman) Z.; m. Stanislawa Krawiec, June 29, 1946 (div. 1966); children: Jadwiga, Witold, Zbigniew; m. Barbara Borowska, Dec. 22, 1973; 1 child, Tomasz Grzegorz. Physician, Jagiellonian U., Krakow, Poland, 1948; MD, Med. Acad. Warsaw, 1957, docent med. sci., 1965, Prof. Orthopaedics, 1976. Resident Hosp. Myslowice, Szczecin, 1948-49; lectr. dept. orthopaedics Med. Acad. Warsaw, 1957-65, docent, 1965-66; head dept. orthopaedics and traumatology and chair Med. Acad. Szczecin, from 1966. Organizer, pres. Region Sect. of Crippled Rehab. Soc., Szczecin, 1966-82; cons. orthopaedics, traumatology Experts Supervisory Bd. of Province, Szczecin, 1965-82; organizer, cons. in field. Author: Fundamentals of Orthopaedics, 1972, 4th edit. 1983, Physician Propedeutic of Orthopedics, 1970, 2d edit. 1977, (for surgeons) Traumatology of Bones and Joints, 1983; contbr. over 140 articles to profl. jours. Maj. Polish Med. Corps, 1949-57. Recipient Gold Cross of Merit, State Coun. Warsaw, 1978, Polonia Restituta Order, 1980, Tchr. of Merits of Polish Republic, 1982, Medaille of Commr. of Nat. Edn., 1989, Guerilla Cross, Medaille of Victory and Freedom, 1982. Mem. Polish Orthopaedic, Traumatologic Soc. (organizer, pres. 1966-82), Szczecinian Sci. Soc. (surveyor), SICOT, SIROT, EULAR, ESSD. Christian-National Union. Roman Catholic. Avocation: decorative plants. Home: Szczecin, Poland. Died Nov. 22, 1993.

**ZUMINO, BRUNO,** physics educator, researcher; b. Rome, Apr. 28, 1923; came to U.S., 1951; naturalized, 1962; divorced. D in Math. Scis., U. Rome, 1945. From asst. prof. to prof. NYU, 1953-69; staff mem. European Orgn. for Nuclear Rsch. (CERN), Geneva, 1969-81; prof. physics U. Calif., Berkeley, 1981—94, Alfred C. & Mary Sprague Miller rsch. prof., 1989, prof. emeritus, 1994—2014. Loeb lectr. Harvard U., Cambridge, Mass., spring 1966; vis. prof. Columbia U., N.Y.C., fall 1978; disting. vis. prof. Enrico Fermi Inst., U. Chgo., spring 1983. Recipient Max Planck medal German Phys. Soc., 1989, Wigner medal Found. for Group Theory & Fundamental Physics, American Nuclear Soc., 1992, Humboldt Rsch. award, 1992, Giancarlo Wick Commemorative Gold medal, 1999; co-recipient Dirac medal Internat. Ctr. for Theoretical Physics, Trieste, Italy, 1987; Guggenheim Found. fellow, 1968-69, 87-88. Fellow American Phys. Soc. (co-recipient Heineman prize 1988), American Acad. Arts & Sciences; mem. NAS, Italian Phys. Soc. (Enrico Fermi prize, 2005) Died June 21, 2014.

**ZWERLING, DARRELL,** actor, optometrist; b. Pitts., 1929; OD, Northern Ill. Coll. Optometry, Chgo., 1949; student, H.B. Studio, NYC, 1963-64. Pvt. practice, Pitts., 1950-63; actor theater, films and TV NYC and Los Angeles, from 1963. Appeared in theater prodns. including Room Service New York Revival, 1970; (films) Chinatown, 1974, Doc Savage, Grease, 1978, ...And Justice for All, 1979 Ultimate Warrior; (TV series) Kojak Served in US Army, 1951-53. Home: West Hollywood, Calif. Died Sept. 16, 2014.

**ZWERNER, ALLAN J.,** retired retail executive; b. NYC, Aug. 4, 1944; s. Leon and Ruth (Morrison) Zwerner; m. Renee Rochelle Grosma, June 25, 1967; children: Brian Scott, Michelle Ellen. BBA in Mktg., Pace U., 1968. Trainee, buyer men's outerwear Gimbel's, NYC, 1970—73; buyer Donaldson's, Mpls., 1973—75, Burdine's, Miami, 1975—76, sr. v.p., 1982—89; mdse. mgr. Jordan Marsh Co., Boston, 1976—80, v.p., 1980—82; sr. product devel Macy's, 1996—99; pres. licensing Perry Ellis Internat., 1999—2002; pres. men's sportswear divsn. Tommy Hilfiger, 2002—06, pres. men's & women's, 2006—07. Jewish. Home: Miami, Fla. Died Oct. 27, 2012.